PROJECTIOLOGY

Waldo Vieira, M.D.

PROJECTIOLOGY

A Panorama of Experiences of the
Consciousness outside the Human Body

Translators:
Kevin de La Tour
Simone de La Tour

Rio de Janeiro, RJ – Brazil
International Institute of Projectiology and Conscientiology
2002

Printing History	English	1st Edition: 2002	4,500 copies
		Special Edition: 2002	500 copies
	Portuguese	1st Edition: 1986	5,000 copies
		2nd Edition: 1990	500 copies
		3rd Edition: 1992	5,000 copies
		4th Edition: 1999	4,500 copies
		Special Edition: 1999	500 copies
		5th Edition: 2002	1,500 copies
		Total	22,000 copies

The original pages of this edition were produced and revised using electronic desktop publishing and laser printing (text in Times New Roman; 3,699,871 characters; 623,826 words; 61,497 sentences and 25,832 paragraphs).

Revised by: Cristina Arakaki, Derrick Guy Phillips, Katia Arakaki, Leonardo Firmato and Luis Minero.

Bibliography: Cristiane Ferraro.

Electronic editing and typographic revision: Ernani Brito and Gisele Salles.

Photos and illustrations: Brasílio Wille, Fernando Alberto Santos and Francisco Mauro.

Printing and binding: OESP Gráfica S.A.

Card Catalog Information

V 657p   Vieira, Waldo, 1932-

Projectiology: A Panorama of Experiences of the Consciousness outside the Human Body / Waldo Vieira / Translated by: Kevin de La Tour and Simone de La Tour – 1st English Edition – Rio de Janeiro, Brazil: International Institute of Projectiology and Conscientiology, 2002.

1.248 pp; 27 cm

1. Projectiology   2. Conscientiology   I. Title

ISBN:85-86019-58-5   DDC 133

INTERNATIONAL INSTITUTE OF PROJECTIOLOGY AND CONSCIENTIOLOGY

Av. das Américas, 500, Bl. 2, Rm. 216/224, Barra da Tijuca
Rio de Janeiro, RJ 22640-100, Brazil
Phone: 55 21 3153-7575 Fax: 55 21 3153-7941
E-mail: iipc@iipc.org.br – Home page: www.iipc.org

TABLE OF CONTENTS

III – PHENOMENA OF PROJECTIOLOGY 121

INTRODUCTION

Information. This is a strictly technical work, the scope of which is to research a serious and specialized subject, as proposed and defined in the title and subtitle. Its objective is to share information with the scientific community and those interested in the topic.

Advice. The author, being practical in this technocentric era, recommends at the beginning of this book that those whose intention in consulting these pages is to pursue an objective other than the dispassionate and detailed study of its proposal – whether seeking a pastime, leisure, frivolity or *pleasure* – are best advised to abandon their efforts after this introductory topic. It will therefore not be worthwhile for them. It is better to stop reading, close the book, return it to the shelf and forget it, in order not to be disappointed, or waste time and consciential energy.

Experimentation. In spite of the *relatively small amount of structured knowledge* available on the projection of the consciousness from the human body, this book gathers the information that seems to be important for an understanding of the subject and individual, laboratory or group experimentation on the themes according to their complexity and ramifications, giving an overview as complete as circumstances allow.

Panorama. This work is an attempt to reveal an ample, integrative *comprehensive charting* of the proposed theme, or a panorama of contemporary projectiology and the secondary issues related to the main subject, which encompass an extensive field of investigation, as well as presenting hundreds of practical and useful procedures in the different stages of research and consciential projective exercises.

Sources. The massive amount of disparate, discordant and concordant data gathered here was obtained from 8 sources:

1. **Projections.** All types of spontaneous and provoked consciential projections experienced by the author since 1941 (at nine years of age) up until March 1985, totaling over 1,100 self-analyzed lucid projections.

Subsidies. This analysis was made as a theoretical and practical (theorical) researcher who is entirely independent, unencumbered and free, and has never been favored by official subsidies of any kind, whether municipal, state, national (federal) or international.

Accountability. Therefore, the author neither needs nor feels obligated to account for this work to any individuals or legal entities. This does not imply isolation in the research or a lack of technical updating *(small science)*. It does, however, imply freedom of personal expression which, according to his retrocognitions, has never occurred in his holobiography.

2. **Discussions.** The gathering of ideas and experiences in analyses and round-table discussions at fortnightly meetings with the specialized non-professional team of lucid projectors from the Center for Continuous Consciousness (disbanded) in the city of Rio de Janeiro, Brazil and monthly meetings with the general public in the cities of São Paulo, Brazil and Ribeirão Preto, Brazil, as well as other locations.

3. **Correspondence.** Personal correspondence, letters, dissertations, e-mails and reports received with essays, descriptions and responses to detailed questionnaires on lucid projection sent in by hundreds of lucid consciential projectors of all levels from around the world. All this material is currently kept on file at the International Institute of Projectiology and Conscientiology (IIPC).

4. **Intraphysical consciousnesses.** Personal interviews with both visited and visiting intraphysical lucid consciential projectors residing close to and distant from the work performed in Rio de Janeiro, Brazil.

5. **Extraphysical consciousnesses.** Direct extraphysical contact with ex-human-lucid-consciential-projectors, authors and readers of the subject – all currently members of extraphysical societies in the intermissive period – through direct evocation and, more intensively, indirect, *spontaneous evocation* achieved through *rapport* established from researching their works, reading new or, more frequently, used books that were written or merely read or thumbed through by them in their most recent human existences (lifetimes).

6. **Meetings.** Repeated personal meetings and parapsychic field research conducted in Brazil and abroad, especially in the United States of America and Europe, with directors, editors, researchers and members of institutions, laboratories, studios, bookstores, as well as private and public university and institutional libraries.

7. **Consultation.** Consultation of technical works, erudite works (papers), encyclopedias, dictionaries, anthologies, treatises, manuals, biographies, magazines (journals), dailies (newspapers), periodicals, bulletins, reports, expositions, dissertations, proceedings and documents in general. The respective authors of these works are from various countries, according to the collection listed in the International Bibliography of Projectiology at the end of this book.

8. **Additions.** Enhancements, revisions and additions made to the first edition of this book account for over 40% of its current volume.

CHSC. Approximately 92% of the titles of the international bibliography currently (2002) make up part of the collection of *artifacts of knowledge* in the holotheca at the Center for Higher Studies of the Consciousness (CHSC) in Iguassu Falls, Brazil. It now also includes 52,000 volumes or items on these specialized subjects which are available for bibliographic consultation and research by those interested in Brazil and abroad.

Objectives. This book is organized with 6 clear objectives in mind:

1. **Guide.** It serves as an introductory guide for the reader who is not familiar with the subject.

2. **Systematization.** It helps in systematically organizing technical findings in the experimental field, as well as providing guidance for those who are interested in producing lucid consciential projection for the first time without any greater preconceptions and neophobia.

3. **Responses.** It provides answers to questions, as far as currently possible, from those who have already experienced the state of the consciousness projected with lucidity and wish to develop in this area with correlated knowledge and efficient applications.

4. **Research.** It proposes new and as yet unanswered questions for subsequent study and theoretical and experimental research *(techniques)*. This can contribute to a desirable union among specialists who are thus far working independently and in isolation, performing their research unaware of the efforts of other researchers.

5. **Data.** It provides assistance and offers data and suggestions to studious individuals, teachers and academics of parapsychology universities, transpersonal psychology centers, institutions dedicated to lucid dream research, notably the centers of scientific investigation of the consciousness (conscientiology) and the current 22 offices of the IIPC, in spite of the inevitable inconvenience of this survey's intentionally excessive bulkiness. For example: this massive book does not lend itself to be read in bed.

6. *Bibliopoles.* It cooperates – through bibliographic information – with bibliophiles, librarians, publishers, book salespersons, printers, encyclopedists, cybernauts and I.T. adepts, and even international book merchants of all types and origins *(bibliopoles)*.

Amplification. Regarding this point, the reader is advised to consult the more current (1994) and expanded international bibliography of the book entitled "700 Conscientiology Experiments," composed of 5,116 titles, of editions originally published in 20 languages, from 37 different countries, where the books listed in this volume are also included.

Phenomenology. In this book, the author accepts the *hypothesis of the objective body* as being valid. Through the entire overview of projectiology, he endeavors to demonstrate that it is the most adequate hypothesis for explaining a greater series of consciential phenomena (phenomenology) which are currently considered to be parapsychic. This is, perhaps, the crucial point *(crux)* of this volume.

Hypothesis. Developing this research hypothesis, the coadjutant and confluent facts are presented that engender a convergence of evidence based not only upon observations and personal experiences, but also on the work of lucid projectors, researchers, projector-researchers and international authors in the West, with their research of the *external world* of the human being, the macrocosm, as well as those in the East, with their research into the *inner world,* the microcosm or micro-universe of the consciousness.

Model. As a corollary, it was possible to point out the immediate practical ramifications of such evidence as well as the consequent current short-term and future long-term effects produced by and upon the intraphysical consciousness. Finally, a factual theoretical model of the consciousness is presented.

Reader. Out of respect for the reader – who demands quality and equanimity, who should not be underestimated and is always alert to any *conscientiological slip* indicating a lack of balance, discernment, precision or sensibility – an endeavor was made to perform impartial, non-factional research or that which is far from being automatic.

Avoidances. The author avoided taking undue liberties with any religion, group, corporation, individual, language or *line of preconceptions,* endeavoring to encompass the entire range of this research without concealing facts and even confronting the more delicate issues while maintaining an independent position. For this, a broad exposition of the basic theme was made and different opinions, whether in agreement or otherwise, have been pointed out.

Conditions. The author also endeavored to act as efficiently as possible and to report faithfully, even selecting the sources cited. He was concerned at all times with the best way to examine relative truth and how to describe it clearly, separating the role of researcher from that of participant in a specific event or experiment.

Treatment. So-called *opinionated journalism* was avoided by seeking out as scientific a treatment of the theme as possible or, in other words, an approach devoid of preconceptions, with an open mind and without ingenuousness but, instead, employing all possible consciential acuity.

Coherence. The following are two coherent illustrations of the effort made to maintain an honest, impartial and fair standpoint:

1. **Distinction.** The clear distinction established between information, opinion and personal experience, according to the specific subject.

2. **Universalism.** The furnishing of the detailed International Bibliography of Projectiology that is thoroughly democratic and universalistic, enabling the reader to research the subject by him/herself and form his/her own opinion, irrespective of that of the author.

Improvement. This "do-it-yourself" book also suggests ideas, concepts and possibilities at the end of each topic regarding many fields of thought, allowing the reader to judge, develop, improve, and adapt them to his/her personal research problems and hypotheses.

Opinion. In this way, the reader is offered the possibility of arriving at his/her own opinion about the theme presented in each chapter.

Volume. Besides the dozens of suggested research hypotheses throughout the text, there are chapters which, by themselves, can be technically explored, developed and enlarged upon, resulting in an entire book with a specialized bibliography already available, as well as various other technical components on the subject in question, serving as a point of departure for further research.

Student. The main intention here is that the novice student of lucid projection (existential inverter, existential recycler) should have his/her thoughts clarified and personal life enriched by the information in this book.

Transmitter. As observed in the first topics of this introduction, the author – as a transmitter of information – has no intention of emotionally imposing upon, convincing or converting anyone. With the exception of concepts and research hypotheses, he has nothing to sell.

Rationality. On the other hand, while constantly endeavoring to vehemently defend rational scientific analysis, the author does not harbor the illusion that this text is always antiseptic or, in other words: politically, morally or socially neutral.

Pre-*serenissimus*. The author is human, a pre-*serenissimus* and is not a *Homo sapiens serenissimus*. He has sought in this text to eliminate the influence of subconscious elaborations from personal preconceptions (apriorisms), or dogmatically affirm anything (peremptoriness).

Intention. If this has occurred in any passage, as a result of imprecise terminology, it was clearly not the author's intention, as he was constantly striving to provide a *unified perspective*.

Values. An effort has been made to eliminate *non-scientific data* from scientific activity as far as possible.

Discussion. It is clear that projectiology constitutes an open theme for constructive discussion.

Proposal. The proposal of this book was elaborated over a period of 19 years (1966-1985) of specialized studies during which the author concentrated his efforts on rationalizing the phenomena of projectiology as far as possible. He has gathered as many definitions, equivalent expressions, hypotheses, theories, paradigms and existing classifications as possible through experiences, both personal and those of others, as well as through general reports and published works.

Ideas. The author once again suggests the plausibility of this compilation of ideas, reaffirming their basic premises now after more than 33 years (1966-1999) of full-time investigation, recognizing that they can be discussed and always fully admitting anyone's right not to accept them.

Complexity. Each intraphysical consciousness is extremely complex, having multiform individual experiences and unique evolutionary opportunities.

Balance. A highly concerted effort has been made to achieve a fair balance of *universal thought,* of consensus in relation to the themes through the study, comparison (confrontation of thosenes) and contrast of ideas.

Continuity. The gathering of knowledge is a continuous process.

Questions. New information begets new questions.

Discoveries. Today, in this era of acceleration of human history, new discoveries follow hard on the heels of others at such an unprecedented rate and with such a torrential volume, intensity and accumulation that it is beyond our ability to keep up with them.

Specialization. The *ocean of scientific information* that each specialist must have a command of is so vast that, besides the learning period being insufficient, an entire intraphysical life (lifetime) can be too short. One resource used here is the cosmogram.

Ignorance. This is why the more one knows, the higher one's level of ignorance, as questions arise faster than the amount of information processed and accumulated. With regard to this point, the number of questions will always be greater than the number of answers.

Truth. At his present level of *literate ignorance,* the author does not intend to give the final word, make definitive statements, or offer *final* truth, *absolute* truth, *total* truth and, much less, the truth about *everything*.

Search. The author merely submits himself to the purposes of science, which is not the act of *discovering* the truth but simply the obligation of *searching* for the truth, even though it be partial and temporary, and then disseminating it in the form of hypotheses in order to be analyzed, discussed and refuted.

Multidisciplinarity. Whenever possible, the problems of projectiology were examined from different standpoints, in a multidisciplinary (interdisciplinary, transdisciplinary) or universalistic manner. Aspects of lesser importance relative to the subject were also included, although a scientific approach was maintained through the strict observance of careful examination and ongoing research, in line with the language used on the eve of the twenty-first century.

Areas. The variety of fields that lucid projection touches on is astonishing.

Facts. An effort was made here to emphasize facts, observations and precise research, always intentionally isolating philosophical, theological or religious theories or placing them in a secondary position.

Database. After assembling an exhaustive, generalist and polyglot *database* on projectiology, an effort was made to interpret the data, rearrange and organize all the material into various categories – highlighting interrelationships, configurations, patterns and convergences of different perspectives – so as to clarify some of their implications which, if treated otherwise, would remain obscure.

Scope. The in-depth study of consciential projections in this book was undertaken with the aim of having as broad a scope as possible in order to clarify and help to structure data which would otherwise appear unrelated.

Self-Sufficiency. The purpose of gathering all the information in a single volume, including the International Bibliography of Projectiology, was to present the context of projectiology in a unified, massive, monobloc and self-sufficient text.

Priorities. The chapters were initially classified according to importance of subject such that the breakdown of details would reduce the complexity of the *structural model.*

Approach. The scientific approach here is based on the formal establishment of 14 aspects related to each parapsychic phenomenon in the projectiological field. Each aspect is analyzed by itself, in a separate *chapter-analysis:*

1. **Definition** (or definitions).
2. **Synonymy** (terminology, nomenclature).
3. **Description** (reports, scrupulous observations, case studies).
4. **Causes** (intraphysical somatic, extraphysical holosomatic).
5. **Effects** (consequences, derivations, results).
6. **Mechanisms** (physiology, paraphysiology).
7. **Characteristics** (particular specifications).
8. **Types** (categories, types).
9. **Rational classification** (systematization, codification, decoding).
10. **Enumerations** (enumerology lists).
11. **Correlations** (associations of ideas, panoramic vision of holomaturity).
12. **Comparisons** (confrontations, contrasts).
13. **Technical scales** (natural, logical, chronological, alphabetical or others).
14. **Specific bibliography** restricted to the International Bibliography of Projectiology (exhaustive).

Criterion. Using synthetic language eschewing oversimplification or overgeneralization, the expository criterion aims to clarify precisely the greater and lesser angles of the phenomena based on definitive norms defined by multiple technical processes in comparisons of similar characteristics, where possible.

Disparities. Disparities and discrepancies in conflicting themes were also pointed out. There is an inevitable overlapping of some subjects.

Remissive. The more exhaustive Remissive Index of Subjects permits rapid consultation of specific themes.

Text. The long and inquiring text, which is necessary for interfacing of the approaches, was kept uniform in order to facilitate its reading and, at the same time, to prevent subjects of lesser relevance being developed more than those with greater importance.

Sections. The text of this book is divided into 18 sections, or *mini-books,* which are entitled and numbered with *roman numerals,* and grouped into correlated themes.

Chapters. The sections divide the 525 chapters, treatises or booklets that define a specific subject and are entitled and numbered with *arabic numerals.* They are composed of thousands of limited topics, each one headed by a title-synthesis, like the ones on this page, in order to enrich computer databases.

Phases. The sections, chapters and topics develop coherently along the chronologically sequential stages of a hypothetical entire, lucid projection of the human consciousness.

Dictionary. The definitions and synonymies form a compilation of over 3,300 different terms and expressions that, by themselves, comprise a *small dictionary of projectiology* inserted into the text, beyond and independent from the various indexes and the Glossary of Projectiology.

Totals. The following are 3 examples of totals obtained through theoretical and practical, personal, laboratorial, group and bibliographical research:

1. **Relations.** Fifty-five chapter-analyses directly relate projectiology and lucid projection with fundamental topics for the human consciousness.

2. **Energies.** Forty-four chapters address consciential energetic manifestations.

3. **Techniques.** Sixty-six chapters exclusively address projective techniques.

Meaning. The compilation of over 300 working definitions – the first topic of all chapters that allow definitions – has the purpose of concisely expressing the precise meaning of the idea analyzed in the general context.

Didactic. It is common knowledge that there are never two perfect definitions for a single reality or thing. Nevertheless, all definitions which are not very similar in meaning among themselves were added for didactic purposes of consultation.

Standardization. The compilation of the more than 300 listed synonymies – the second item of the chapters with definitions – has the purpose of standardizing, as far as possible, equivalent concepts or *interchangeable terms* found in the extensive projectiological bibliography. They only differ in name and not in essence, and exist within the diverse schools of human thought regarding the material under analysis.

Terminology. These expressions, including technical terminology and ordinary words, many of which are considered unnecessary and undesirable, can have different shades of meaning and interpretation according to one's cultural background. Consequently, the most adequate, or universally more accepted terms were chosen in order to avoid entropy, confusion, misinformation or misunderstanding.

Thesaurus. The *Thesaurus of Projectiology* is already available for private use by the researchers of the International Institute of Projectiology and Conscientiology. It was specifically created in order to standardize the use of the most accurate terminology.

Summary. The synonymies also aim to better clarify the theme at hand and to expand its definition through derivations, meanings and new angles, besides offering a summary of the subject heretofore.

Patterns. The *extensive synonymy,* by itself, shows the initial patterns of the phenomenic occurrence. One of the synonymies alone includes 184 terms.

References. The total of more than 400 lists of projectiological bibliographical references on specific themes that end many chapters, interconnected with the general list inserted at the end of the book, only show the first author and the first page of the subject under analysis.

Citations. These exhaustive bibliographies list precise citations and add up to a total of 5,388 references.

Translations. One of the reasons for indicating the number of chapters in the bibliography is to provide a comparison between the originals and the translations, as well as between different translations.

Selectivity. Each specific bibliography, which is subordinated to the theme under analysis, is selective. In other words, it is exclusively restricted to the works that make up the International Bibliography of Projectiology.

Evidence. The *long projectiological bibliographies* highlight the popularity of certain themes, although serving, by themselves, as significant indicators of the convergence of experimental and observational evidence for dozens of parapsychic phenomena and the achievement of the broadest possible consensus on the subject through the similarity of testimonials supplied by the works listed (association of ideas, panoramic vision, *interconnection,* cosmogram technique).

Specific. The specific bibliographies, listed together with the projectiological bibliographies, at the end of certain chapters, refer exclusively to the theme of that chapter and are not related to other chapters, nor do they refer to the International Bibliography of Projectiology. These specific bibliographies, which raise the cultural level of this book, add up to a total of several dozen works.

Works. One of the specific bibliographical lists alone includes 118 works, or 6.18% of the total number of projectiological works originally cited.

Concentration. The intention here was to gather relevant information from clippings, written reports, books, magazines, journals, index cards, databases, diskettes, CD-ROMs, libraries, archives and other sources of knowledge. They provide a maximum concentration of data, ideas, facts and experiences assembled in a single *portable object,* in the smallest possible format or, in other words, this book. If this goal was not completely achieved and put into practice, at least the intention behind the effort required to generate it is placed on record at this juncture.

Confirmations. Some specific bibliographies include an *italicized* number indicating their position in the international bibliography, showing the best work on that subject according to current consensus, as well as the citations that are most frequently encountered at an international level.

Convergence. The bulk of chapters with a *reduced* projectiological bibliography are the result of the author's firsthand experiences and personal observations. They require ratification by experiences of other consciential projectors in order to reach a *convergence of evidence* through the universality of personal reports.

Flexibility. Various procedures have made the text adaptable to different purposes. The chapters can be viewed out of sequence and many can be entirely omitted without losing the technical panoramic vision. This flexibility with regard to the material was intentional.

Search. All chapters with reduced bibliographies, which may be considered by some readers as being excessively speculative or lacking in value, could have been excluded from this book. In case you are one of these readers, you should simply skip them.

Knowledge. The criterion adopted here is the principle that *circumspect technical speculation* is something that is always necessary in any field of investigation, and also within the scope of pure science. It is better to have such information than to ignore it.

Neophilia. It is far more intelligent to seek out leading-edge relative truth without respite rather than to remain indifferent – with arms crossed or withholding information, hypotheses and suggestions – to open-minded persons (neophiliacs). These chapters demand inquiry, impartial analysis and research, in the quest for rational support for the topics presented.

Pages. The International Bibliography of Projectiology was compiled only of works that *always* refer to the subject of "consciential experience outside the human body," even if only on one of its pages.

Themes. On the other hand, each book in the specific bibliography of each chapter, while *always* being an integral part of the International Bibliography of Projectiology, evidently *does not always* refer to the chapters or pages referred to in the international bibliography, as the themes can vary.

Dates. Dates of resoma and desoma (birth and death) of persons mentioned are *almost always* found only in the first citation so as to avoid repetition.

Program. The first outlines of this book were already being used over a decade ago as an "educational program" (curriculum) in the periodic projectiology meetings held in the cities of Rio de Janeiro, and São Paulo, Brazil. Thus, in order to maintain an educational orientation, enumerations of analytical aspects were made in a logical, chronological or alphabetical order whenever possible in order to provide a comprehensive view of each theme.

Topics. The chapters are composed of over 6,500 limited topics, each being headed by a brief title-synopsis.

Location. The division of the text into topics within each chapter, despite making prolonged reading arduous due to the fragmentation of the subjects, greatly facilitates the search for and location of a specific item, which is a highly important consideration in a massive book such as this.

Enumeration. More than 200 larger enumerations have numbered topics.

Redundancies. There are redundant topics and references including texts from other chapters. These have been included intentionally in order to improve the processing of ideas within this bulky volume.

Questionnaires. The author again extends his acknowledgement to those correspondents who have responded in writing to the questionnaires on lucid projection that were recently distributed.

Catalog. The data provided currently constitutes an invaluable catalog and contributes decisively towards the achievement of 4 objectives:

1. **Observation.** Establishment of convergent points of observation.

2. **Methodology.** Improvement of the methodology used in the production of lucid consciousness projection.

3. **Popularization.** Popularization, without superstitions or excesses, of technical projectiological practices or those at rational (theorical) levels.

4. **Science.** The consequent development of projectiology as a science, a specialized area within the ample world of conscientiology.

Affirmations. The enlightened reader will readily note that this book includes personal affirmations, observations resulting from exhaustive experimentation, transitory conclusions from laboratorial research, as well as prevailing speculative theories. They are gathered from various sources, never assembled before, in search of consistent, working hypotheses albeit still lacking conclusive or assertive proof that comprise reliable paradigms and more enduring theories.

Field. Summing up: this volume is indicative of the shifting sands, or minefield, of pioneering *frontline* research that is still very open to unexpected surprise and alteration.

Recommendation. It is recommended that theoretical researchers of any scientific background who are impatient and impetuously studious individuals produce lucid consciential projection by themselves – avoiding, whenever possible, the use of drugs, which adulterate the intraphysical and extraphysical perceptions of the consciousness – and investigate extraphysical issues firsthand, *in loco, de visu,* as eyewitnesses, or firsthand witnesses of the extraphysical events. They will consequently be able to reach firm conclusions and make statements on their own and without apriorisms, thereby helping everyone.

Participation. Participatory research seems to be indispensable to projectiology. At the moment, there is no ideal process for researching consciousness projection that does not rely on the participation and the consistent use of the *consciential paradigm.*

Independence. It must also be borne in mind that experience confirmed by independent evidence is far more valuable than any amount of illustrations taken from the pages of history, however authenticated that information may be.

Experience. One grain of experience is worth one bushel of theory.

Perfection. The reader will be forced to agree that, strictly speaking, just as there is no perfect human being, neither does the perfect author, writer, reader, nor much less the perfect work (in this case a book), without lapses, exist.

Paradox. This observation is highly pertinent in a book as bulky as this one which, above all, is paradoxically a *synthesis,* constructed by selection and condensation of the elements of the general database of projectiology that have been gathered up until now.

Revision. That is why, in spite of the overwhelming desire to succeed, it is not possible to construct a truly definitive, correct, accurate or perfect work, regardless of the efforts the author makes, as deficiencies, omissions and mistakes inevitably occur.

Reedition. It is imperative to insist upon revision, collection of new data, and the continued improvement of any serious intellectual work. This is the reason for this edition, which has been revised, updated and enlarged to assume an ever more didactic format.

Inventory. From an academic standpoint, it would be ideal to periodically revise and update this *inventory-book* in a process of constant development, where it would be continually updated, not only with regard to textual accuracy, but also notably with respect to the addition of new terms, techniques, experiments and other bibliographical entries.

Update. For this reason, the author intends, when possible, to revise, correct, update, establish new connections between themes and continually improve the text, particularly that involving theoretical studies, experimental techniques and bibliographies.

Quality. This will pursue the objective of eliminating any gaps, and rectifying any factual error, misinterpretation, imprecision and imperfection, in an attempt to arrange this book in the most objective manner possible and concisely in line with its information and didactics.

Ombudsman. It is hoped that an independent, uncommon, unusual, more interested and dispassionate reader of this book will appear – a type of ombudsman, a general auditor, a defender of the reader, a (volunteer) provider of justice, a monitor of the author's thoughts, a public attorney, a representative of the interests of the ordinary citizen, a bridge between reader and author, a critic who is attentive to everything published on these pages – noting each error in form or content, inaccuracy or false step (ethical or otherwise), representing other readers' complaints and observations.

Critiques. In light of the above and, in advance, the author would also like to thank the helpful reader, student and researcher of good will who is willing to contribute to this end through *heterocritiquing analyses,* contrathosenes, suggestions or information which will not be in vain but, quite to the contrary, will be warmly welcomed and studied with interest in order to be utilized in a future edition.

Form. It is common knowledge that no book is ever definitive.

Immaturity. While working on it, we are aware of the extent to which it is incomplete at the time of going to press.

Finalization. *This is the type of book that is never completed.*

Self-experiences. In spite of the didactic style of the text, which may be considered excessively normative by the more demanding reader, the most rational approach is to question all statements made in this technical work and prove everything possible by yourself through personal experiences or self-experiences. The content is what matters most in *confor.*

Repercussion. From the repercussion of the first edition of this book, in Portuguese, the 5,000 copies of which were distributed free of charge to interested intraphysical consciousnesses, libraries and specialized institutions in Brazil and abroad, it was possible to found the International Institute of Projectiology and Conscientiology (IIPC) – which replaced the Center for Continuous Consciousness (long-since disbanded) – in Ipanema, Rio de Janeiro, Brazil, where the author formally proposed the sciences of projectiology and conscientiology.

IIPC. After *1 decade of intense activities* already accomplished, the IIPC is active in *7 countries,* besides Brazil, with a total of *22 active offices* that promote studies, research and multiple, ample, educational activities. The IIPC has a mailing list of over 105,000 intraphysical consciousnesses.

Dedication. This didactic first edition in English, which is the translated version of the revised, updated and enlarged fourth edition in Portuguese, is dedicated to all veteran, new and anonymous volunteers with employment ties and/or consciential bonds with the Institute. Where possible, the topics in the current edition were listed or enumerated (enumerology), giving most chapters a form similar to a *technical booklet.* This was done in order to facilitate comprehension by younger students. The author hopes this work will prove of some benefit to all, and willingly accepts any other type of *help* or *self-thosene* that can assist in new research or future investigation in the fields of projectiology and conscientiology.

Waldo Vieira

PO Box 1.027
85851-000
Iguassu Falls – PR – Brazil
waldovieira@iipc.org.br

Rio de Janeiro, March 29, 2002.

I – Scientific Foundations of Conscientiology

01. ESSENTIAL CONCEPTS OF SCIENCE

Definitions. Science (Latin: *scire,* to know): organized set of knowledge related to a specific object, especially that obtained through observation, verification and experience relative to the facts and the method per se; system of rigorously demonstrated, constant, general propositions that are interconnected through subordinate relationships; knowledge that does not merely comprehend or register facts, but demonstrates them through their determinant or constituent causes.

Synonymy: organized set of knowledge; systematized knowledge.

Civilization. *Civilization* has existed on this planet for less than 100 centuries.

Infancy. Strictly speaking, science, as we know it, is a *human creation* of the last 4 centuries. It is therefore still in its infancy, as it has existed for only 4% of recorded human existence or terrestrial civilization.

Human. The person of science is, inevitably, a *human being* first and a scientist second. There are, for example, scientists who endeavor to *deify* science.

Geniuses. The greatest geniuses of science also become ill, can go insane, become senile, and even commit suicide. They are not immune from any defect or human weak trait.

Immaturity. From this arises the fact of a predominance of *immature* scientists who still maintain an incomplete science – one that is immature with regard to the consciousness – dominating the scientific "world".

Partiality. *Incomplete science* is that which restricts its research to the intraphysical dimension, being indefensibly partial or immature in the face of the holosomatic, multidimensional and multiexistential realities of the consciousness.

Limitations. As a *human undertaking,* equal to many others, scientific research, in its controlled observations, which are sometimes dry, monotonous, expensive and prolonged, depend upon availabilities and accidents. It is often limited by preconceptions, apriorities, stereotypes, conventions and prosaic *human realities.*

Theorice. There are researchers who are essentially practical, with anti-theoretical preconceptions (psychomyology or psychomotricity, the cerebellum, the predominance of endorphins, adrenaline and muscle fibers).

Neosynapses. There are theoretical researchers with anti-experimental preconceptions, lacking neosynapses (epistemology or the philosophy of science, a predominance of neurons and interneuronal networks).

Disciplines. Science establishes itself into numerous disciplines.

Categories. There are, among others, physical, chemical, biological, economic, historical, formal, factual, psychical and parapsychical sciences, generally speaking.

Opening. Distinct scientific disciplines, in turn, establish themselves into different schools of thought.

Oligarchies. Scientific schools, when incomplete, immature and oligarchic, are *humanly* similar to religious sects.

Scientificness. The level of scientificness varies from one science to another. The biologist, chemist and cosmologist see the same theory differently.

History. The history of science is not a linear one. It consistently shows 4 distinct results, upon which our accurate reflection is worthwhile:

1. Victories (intraphysical successes).
2. Progress (technological advances).
3. Failures (irrefutable defeats).
4. Mistakes (errors and omissions).

Experiments. The history of science includes useless experiments, data leading to errors, false theories, discrepancies, micro-hypotheses, controversy, counter-examples, disagreements, discontinuity or progress and setbacks.

Omniscience. The growth or progress of scientific knowledge is not an entirely logical, rational and continuous process. Not even this knowledge is omniscient.

Speculation. Many *speculative and dislocated theories* are capable of indicating the way toward new ideas, discoveries and inventions.

Hybridism. As beings who are naturally paradoxical, hybrid or two-sided, we are simultaneously two intraphysical realities:

1. **Thighs.** Cerebral-human-animals (biology; sexology; neurology), *evolving between the thighs* (belly-brain or abdominal sub-brain, sexochakra), when we still err more often than not.

2. **Ears.** Consciential-mental-animals (psychology; projectiology; conscientiology), *evolving between the ears* (brain, frontochakra, coronochakra), when we endeavor to make fewer errors.

Entanglement. Persons of science often become entangled with problems.

Chain. There are theories, for example, that explain 3 facts and contradict 2 facts having the same origin, order or nature, demanding another theory to explain these last facts, thereby forming a chain of events, experiments and an expenditure of time, health, consciential energy, finances, perseverance and a maximum of patience.

Considerations. From this, 2 facts arise which are also worthy of our consideration:

1. **Fragmentation.** There are more fragmentary theories than complete ones.
2. **Errors.** There are more erroneous theories than correct ones.

Career. The career scientist, logically, is careful to not expose his/her *bad work.*

Uncertainty. A *cloud of uncertainty* surrounds most scientific generalizations.

Necessity. Science originates from the need to know and understand.

Questioning. *Questioning* is the essence of science.

Questioning. Questioning is necessary for the continued elaboration of original ideas.

Conformity. The scientist does not seek conformity.

Questionnaire. The following 4 classic, irreplaceable questions need to be constantly used by the scientist:

1. **Who.** Who said this?
2. *Quid.* Why?
3. **Data.** What data is available?
4. **Proof.** Where is the proof?

Desacralization. Neither technical rules, nor formulated principles or even the facts are sacralized (sanctified or sacrosanct) in science.

Degeneration. Science can reach a level of complete degeneration.

Program. A vast scientific research program can degenerate and ruin its promoters, persons and institutions.

School. Even an entire scientific school can degenerate to *pseudoscience* or to shameless commercialism.

Evaluation. There are defined attitudes that cannot be violated in research, because they allow the researcher to separate science from non-science and critically evaluate speculations, suppositions, information, data, conjecture, experiences, concepts, hypotheses and findings.

Attitudes. The following 4 technical attitudes are considered to be basic elements indispensable for the achievement of all scientific knowledge:

1. **Empiricism.** The necessity for observing phenomena before arriving at any conclusion regarding them *(conditio sine qua non).*

2. **Probabilism.** Accept as true the probabilistic determinism that, on earth as in the universe, order and functional relationships exist ("scientific dogma").

3. **Parsimony.** Propose a complex or abstract scientific explanation only after all simpler explanations have been shown to be false or inadequate ("Occam's razor").

4. **Manipulation.** In the verification of two things that are assumed to be associated – either by a causal or merely accidental factor – the occurrence of one event must necessarily be altered or manipulated while observing what is occurring with the second.

Norms. Aside from the above-cited attitudes, 5 main norms are postulated in order to orient scientific activity:

1. **Knowledge.** The scientist must evaluate new knowledge critically and objectively.
2. **Disinterest.** The scientist must use the findings in a disinterested manner, from an economical-financial standpoint.
3. **Merit.** Scientific merit must be evaluated regardless of the scientist's social or personal qualities.
4. **Findings.** The findings are not the scientist's property, it being prohibited to keep them a secret.
5. **Neutrality.** Emotional neutrality with regard to the work is expected from the scientist.

Characteristics. Within science (which is still immature and insufficient), there are at least 18 characteristics of *scientific knowledge,* listed here in alphabetical order:

1. Accumulation.
2. Analysis (re-analysis).
3. Clarity.
4. Communicability.
5. Dependence upon methodical verification (exhaustibility).
6. Explicitness.
7. Factuality (reality).
8. Fallibility.
9. Generality.
10. Objectivity.
11. Openness.
12. Precision (in form and content).
13. Prediction (predictive science).
14. Rationality (logic, discernment, reason).
15. Systematization (coding, decoding, recoding).
16. Transcendence of the facts.
17. Utility (application, practicality, technology, technoscience).
18. Verifiability (reverifiability).

Cycle. Modern scientific method is based upon a sequence of 9 procedures, comprising the *cycle of investigation,* in the following natural or chronological order:

1. **Problem.** Discovery of the problem.
2. **Positioning.** Adequate positioning of the problem.
3. **Search.** Search for correlated knowledge.
4. **Solution.** Initial attempt at a solution.
5. **Hypotheses.** Hypotheses and speculation.
6. **Improvement.** Achievement of a better solution.
7. **Analysis.** Analysis of the consequences.
8. **Proof.** Proof of the solution.
9. **Improvement.** Improvement of the theory.

Steps. The scientific *corpus* is gradually composed through 6 steps:

1. **Fact.** The fact suggests the ideas.
2. **Conjecture.** Conjecture indicates experimentation.
3. **Experiment.** The experiment controls the hypothesis.

4. **Modifications.** The hypotheses and theories are gradually rejected, modified or confirmed.

5. **Law.** It is in this way that the goal of so-called *natural law* is arrived at.

6. **Model.** An advanced model (paradigm) is thereby established.

Contents. Data and hypotheses are the contents of science.

Methodolatry. *Methodolatry* is not allowed in science.

Attributes. Aside from the cold methodology within the scientific context, intuitive attributes, or trans-rational, parapsychic resources, are decisive in discoveries.

Concepts. There are two categories of concepts in science:

1. Concepts of postulation.

2. Concepts by intuition.

Accidentalism. The vigorous intellect does not underestimate the role played by accidentalism (*serendipitia,* serendipity) in scientific progress.

Evidence. The majority of scientific discoveries have been preceded by theories lacking the support of any solid evidence. This happens over the course of many exhaustive years of waiting and experimental research.

Reverification. Scientific work is performed on the basis of conjectures which, through successive verifications (reverification), undergo adjustments until they result in hypotheses or propositions. Finally, when verification is relatively complete, they arrive at consecrated theories.

Elimination. Science thus develops by way of hypotheses and consecrated theories which, in turn, eliminate and substitute each other.

Generations. Theories generate other hypotheses.

Derivations. Not all hypotheses are derived from theories.

Components. Among the components of science, 3 can be singled out:

1. **Objective.** The *objective* or concern in distinguishing the common characteristics or general laws which govern specific events.

2. **Function.** The *function* or improvement of the relationship of the consciousness with its existential dimension.

3. **Object.** The *object,* be it material, namely that which is to be researched; or formal, i.e. the special focus in the presence of diverse sciences having the same object.

Theory. A theory is a precise, detailed report of nature that is valid for one specific area.

Filling. All scientific theories serve to fill a gap.

Intolerance. Science is inherently *intolerant* in the sense that a new hypothesis excludes an older one if it is clearer, more adequate or far simpler.

Deduction. The *refined* scientific theory consists of a rigorous, logical deduction, based upon the defined postulates of that which should be observed under specific conditions.

Veracity. No theory is completely true. Not even the leading theory (dominant paradigm).

Useful. To the extent that a theory is, in practice, more useful and has different possibilities, the more rapidly and completely it will be reviewed and retested (refutation, verification of the theory).

Refutation. A theory is a working model and should be put to the test. Therefore, all possible means are used to *refute it* – make note – *not confirm it.*

Revisions. Hypotheses are always submitted to tests, rejected, improved and subjected to continual revisions.

Megarefutation. It is reasonable, therefore, that the dominant scientific paradigm also be refuted – *megarefutation* – when necessary, being changed or substituted by a better available alternative (leading theory).

Affirmation. In science, it is permissible to affirm *something* without knowing *everything.*

Totality. Some scientists are of the opinion that working toward total knowledge, researching global equations, in the complete description of the forces that govern the universe, or in the manner of a *unified field theory,* may be a fundamental mistake. In this case, it would be a waste of effort, time and consciential energy, a position lacking scientific significance.

Option. They think that the more practical, productive option is to endeavor to extract the maximum of that which is known and add new elements to this nucleus of knowledge, when possible.

Response. Nevertheless, there is no scientific response that is *strictly conclusive.*

Enunciations. Scientific enunciations are, in theory, the only ones which lead to safe, correct knowledge, because they are based on observational and experimental evidence and, as such, are based on facts, as far as possible.

Circumstance. There are no arguments against facts in this circumstance.

Method. The normal method of scientific thought is hypothetical-deductive-experimental.

Formulation. Theories need to be formulated as unambiguously as possible, so as to be completely open to refutation.

Risk. A genuinely scientific theory puts itself permanently at risk.

Refutability. Experimental refutability is the unanimously accepted *standard-measure* (consensual criterion) of the demarcation between science and non-science (myth).

Subjective. The method which demonstrates subjective reality by way of objective data has still not been discovered.

Denial. Nevertheless, there is no need to deny the subjectivity or inter-subjectivity between intraphysical consciousnesses – that of the evolutionary duo, for example.

Demonstration. Nor is there a method that demonstrates objective reality to someone.

Proof. Only the individual, on his/her own, decides to subjectively accept objective proofs. Thus, objectivity is based upon the subjective, and not the contrary.

Subjectivity. That which is subjective can come to know that which is subjective and objective. Nevertheless, that which is objective cannot come to know that which is subjective. It is currently known that, in any experiment, the observer takes part in the experiment which is being observed (holochakrology).

Machines. Strictly speaking, no science is completely objective. The data gathered by machines are only considered to be data from the moment that someone *subjectively* determines that they are important.

Interpretation. Even so, these data are meaningless as long as they have not been *subjectively interpreted.*

Technique. The scientist works based upon models acquired through education or technical literature.

Scientists. There are two categories of scientific minds (mentalsoma):

1. **Mathematical.** The *analytically-minded scientist* who has mathematical reasoning and uses equations or calculations.

2. **Imagistic.** The *pictographically-minded scientist* who has imagistic reasoning and uses diagrams or collections of reports.

Reliability. As reliable as they may be, human machines, apparatuses, artifacts, devices, inventions, instruments or equipment obviously do not think for themselves – not even the most evolved robots or microcomputers, including the computer that beats the world chess master.

Mega-strong-traits. There are two categories of scientist in regard to their mega-strong-traits or their overall qualification:

1. **Conventional.** The qualified, conventional scientist.

2. **Revolutionary.** The revolutionary, innovating, *paradigm creating* scientist.

Contemporaneity. The scientists of our time are equal, if not superior, to the competent scientists of the past; if not in their intellectual capacity, then at least in their methods, research, scope of concepts or the simple accumulation of information (stimuli).

Present. There are currently more scientists alive (intraphysical consciousnesses) than throughout the rest of human history. Immature science is still often reactionary, obscurantist and intolerant in regard to non-scientific knowledge.

Ineptitude. Ineptitude is not an attribute of uneducated, illiterate, robotized or ignorant persons. It is common in artistic, political, religious and scientific circles as well. Human nature never fails.

Perspectives. More than ever, the destructive possibilities, perverse aspects and terrifying perspectives of the high technology derived from science (technical-scientific sectors) become evident – and are cause for heated debate.

Technology. Technology (Greek: *téchne,* art or ability; *logos,* treatise) is not neutral and seeks efficiency. There are technologies which are stillborn.

Character. Science has a *universal* character, allows free access and its cogitations regarding original ideas are published.

Comparison. The following are 9 characteristics or a comparison of technology and science:

1. **Universe.** Technology is essentially local (economy, business).
2. **Development.** It seeks to develop a product (innovation).
3. **Access.** It does not offer free access, in the manner of science.
4. **Communication.** It is not published.
5. **Protection.** It is protected by patents (inventions, discoveries, improvements).
6. **Competition.** It develops through competition in the economy.
7. **Market.** It is acquired according to the quotation of the international market.
8. **Inducement.** It is induced by an economic or social demand.
9. **Spontaneity.** Technological research is rarely spontaneous which, on the other hand, often occurs with science (*serendipitia,* serendipity).

Confidence. In this particular reality, what gives inner peace to projectiologists or conscientiologists and confidence in what they do is that everything is under wise extraphysical controls that are more evolved than the human minds restricted by resoma (rebirth).

Discoveries. It is necessary to stimulate the discovery and improvement of the gifts of human intelligence.

Inventors. Over 90% of sages and inventors are of our time.

Intervals. The time gap between science and technology is closing in our anthropotechnocentric intraphysical society. The following illustrates the gap between 28 discoveries and their applications, notably in the physical sciences:

Electric motor:	65 years (1821-1886)	Teletype:	18 years (1931-1949)
Television:	63 years (1884-1947)	Stainless steel:	16 years (1904-1920)
Photography:	56 years (1782-1838)	Automatic transmission:	16 years (1930-1946)
Telephone:	56 years (1820-1876)	Transistor:	16 years (1940-1956)
Silicon:	38 years (1904-1942)	Frozen food:	15 years (1908-1923)
Helicopter:	37 years (1904-1941)	Photocopy:	15 years (1935-1950)
Radar:	35 years (1904-1939)	Nylon:	12 years (1927-1939)
Neon light:	33 years (1901-1934)	Nuclear reactor:	10 years (1932-1942)
Pacemaker:	32 years (1928-1960)	Ballpoint pen:	7 years (1938-1945)
Vacuum tube:	31 years (1884-1915)	Roll-on deodorant:	7 years (1948-1955)
Antibiotics:	30 years (1910-1940)	Atomic bomb:	6 years (1939-1945)
Radio:	24 years (1890-1914)	VCR:	6 years (1950-1956)
Instant coffee:	22 years (1934-1956)	LP record:	3 years (1945-1948)
X-ray tubes:	18 years (1895-1913)	Solar battery:	2 years (1953-1955)

Fig. 1: TIME GAP BETWEEN SCIENCE AND TECHNOLOGY

Potentialities. It is intelligent to wish that the potentialities of the knowledge and discoveries of science are always employed in favor of humanity.

Teaching. It is necessary to teach *what science* really *is,* in order for individuals to learn to use it.

Holomaturity. A day will come when mature science will be able to change humankind and renew its personal principles, which are still marked by ancestral immaturity.

Senselessness. In this way, it will be possible to avoid the senseless use of the potential of incomplete science in causes which are not in the interest of consciential evolution and universal well-being.

Objective. Scientists generally have the achievement of some accurate descriptions of their object of study as their primary objective. Their intention is to subsequently proceed to explanation, and/or prediction, and/or control. It is evident that not all scientists (or sciences) do all this.

Professionals. The following are 3 examples of scientific professionals:

1. **Astronomers.** Astronomers are adept at predicting their object of study, although they do not control it.

2. **Historians.** Historians are good at explaining, but do not predict.

3. **Physicists.** Physicists do not foresee if the 14:20 train will arrive 10 minutes late.

Source. A metaphysical enunciation frequently leads to a scientific enunciation or can even become one. An enunciation regarding *other realities* is always, potentially, a source of scientific progress. Above all, there has never been a science which has not had a specific *metaphysical measurement* in support of it.

Presuppositions. The entire human community needs an unverified set of metaphysical presuppositions to orient its research. This does not signify or imply that science is based upon metaphysics or supports itself upon affirmations of unverifiable absolute truth.

Logic. A considerable collection of restrictions to science can be raised, with unquestionable rationality and logic, when it is based upon the *ethics of the jungle.*

Institution. Nevertheless, being the most recent, aggressive and rigid human institution – although still not being the ideal way – science is the *least undesirable way* among the diverse forms of thought developed by humankind.

Hyperacuity. Science is the most noble of all works. It is the best of all the *arts* on the earth today for the consciousness to obtain a greater level of consciential expansion in the direction of evolutionary serenism (hyperacuity, holomaturity, serenology).

Rationalism. Rationalism, generated by consciential maturity, is the most important sphere in which humankind can proceed in a fertile manner with regard to its evolution.

Favor. If you, the reader, know of a theoretical and practical process (theorice), or a way toward the accessing of real (factual) knowledge capable of offering: freedom from secondary issues; the hastening of consciential discernment; the practical performance of the integral maturity of the personality; and the degree to which one truly experiences the universalistic sense in human existence; that is greater or more evolved than those supplied by the directives of science – when mature – will be doing the author a favor by informing him, as he is unaware of it.

Processes. In attempting to respond to the proposed question, you can present, for example, the following 4 arguments:

1. **Sense.** One says: *"Popular knowledge* exists (common sense, good sense, common knowledge or the *school of life*)." True, nevertheless, this is an inexact and unsystematic experiential selection based on moods and emotions.

2. **Philosophy.** Someone proposes, *"Philosophy* exists." True, but it is knowledge that can be neither confirmed or refuted, is merely a theoretical coadjutant, a *gray eminence* of science.

3. **Theology.** Another reader says, *"Religion exists."* True, but it is an imposed, infallible doctrine (theology) that absurdly dogmatizes and imposes impossible, unverifiable, absolute, definitive truths.

4. **Ideology.** Another affirms, "Turn to an *ideology* (straight-jacket). True, nevertheless, as historically (when not *hysterically*) conditioned thought, it does not embrace the necessary universalistic

overview of the proposed perspective, finally becoming narrow-minded, sectarian or parochial, opposed to pluralism, a provincial view; another *gray eminence* (worse) of science.

Strategies. Often, within civilization, the neutrality of incomplete science is still a myth. Even so, science has been a source of progress and authority in the determination of the basic strategies of life.

Unification. Science – as incomplete as it is – has turned the world into a single community some time ago. This cannot be said about any other way that humankind has taken, in the search for a world that is balanced and directed by order.

Movements. The nationalist and racial movements are the combative forces that most attempt to attract persons. Nevertheless, both negate precisely the universalistic principle of science.

Infantility. On the other hand, we always hope that religion will exercise its life-unifying function, being the most ample and integrative of all orientations of value. But this generally does not happen.

Religiosity. Invariably, religious sentiments are clearly more immature, reminiscent of infancy, being *ego-centralized constructions* in which a useful divinity is adopted in order to aid the immediate interests of the individual, like a Santa Claus or an excessively benevolent father.

Particularism. Religious sentiment can also be very particularistic. *My church is better than yours. God prefers my people.* In these cases, religion is utilitarian, being merely incidental in human existence.

Pride. Merely pandering to personal or group pride, religion often serves as a defense or escape mechanism. It neither embraces nor gives direction to life as a whole.

Prejudice. Racial prejudice is more common among those who attend church.

Self-comprehension. Religious practice supports exclusion, prejudice, hatred, holy wars and crusades that negate all of the simplest criteria of consciential maturity. In this way, the consciousness does not grow. There are no affectionate relationships with others. There is no emotional security, neither is there realistic perception, nor self-understanding, nor humor.

Divisiveness. It can be seen that the facts demonstrate that religion is frequently *a form of dividing* and not uniting intraphysical consciousnesses.

Subcourse. Strictly speaking, and with all due respect to the subject, religion is a kindergarten *subcourse,* with a low degree of consciential information, where the religious person (faithful, follower) is the student-consciousness, in the manner of these 3 examples:

1. **Subphylum.** The protochordate is an animal of a *subphylum.*
2. **Subclass.** The prototheria is a mammal of a *subclass.*
3. **Suborder.** The protomecoptera is an insect of a *suborder.*

Maturity. Why remain fossilized, repeating the same subcourse year after year? The maturity of the consciousness requires more evolution.

Protoknowledge. Religion is *fetal,* kindergarten, rudimentary *protoknowledge* for the intraphysical consciousness, as can be seen in the following 7 facts:

1. **Proto-history:** a *primitive,* initial history of the earliest historical periods.
2. **Protophony:** an orchestral introduction or a simple *opening* of a great work.
3. **Protocol:** a *note* that allows access to a megalibrary (holotheca).
4. **Proto-revolution:** the beginning of a revolution or a first, *initial,* primitive revolution.
5. **Protoxide:** an oxide that is *less* rich in oxygen.
6. **Proto-ore:** a *lower* grade ore, lacking economic value, that requires enriching.
7. **Protopathy:** a *primary* illness.

Class. Besides this *fetal* knowledge, there is other more developed, advanced and enriched knowledge. Why stop, dazzled by the light of the first class in the terrestrial school?

Subdiscourse. In religion, the *proto-understanding* of a subcourse – the religious one – holds the *student-consciousness* back, as can be observed with the following 6 facts:

1. **Protonaut:** that person who first navigated to certain parts (unknown).
2. **Proto-revolutionary:** the first revolutionary.

3. **Protopope:** the first pope.

4. **Protist** or protozoan: the single, one-celled (unicellular) organism.

5. **Protophyte:** the primitive plant, with an extremely simple organization, in need of improvement.

6. **Prototype:** the first, incipient type.

Consciousness. As can be seen, the consciousness deserves greater inner illumination. It cannot always continue being a *protoconsciousness* or a *subconsciousness.*

Cooperation. Based on the very universality of its supranational attributes, science offers its own favorable terrain – perhaps the firmest of all – upon which to create the cooperation of pure fraternity (megafraternity) among humankind.

Confinement. Literature and art can remain confined to a province, or even to a city. Science and technology cannot. That which they produce can be immediately understood and applied by all people. Secret science does not exist.

Citizens. Persons of science generally feel that they are *citizens of the world,* just as lucid consciential projectors feel they are *citizens of the cosmos.*

Education. Scientists – open disseminators – serve to educate the people with regard to science and its consequences.

Literate. In 1989 (the twentieth century), the population of England *officially* had an illiteracy rate of only 1%.

Literacy. Literacy is a condition that demands the *verification of quality.*

Illiteracy. In fact, in this same period (1989), 2/3 of Britons did not know that the earth takes 1 year to revolve around the sun. One third believed that *the sun revolves around the earth.*

Habits. It is imperative to teach people to formulate logical questions, change defective points of view and modify bad habits or mental laziness.

Colleagues. It is also imperative to educate colleagues (immature scientists) when they are narrow-minded (restricted mentality), shortsighted or consdentially myopic.

Dogmatism. Dogmatism is responsible for scientific anemia.

Recycling. Incessant consciential recycling (intraphysical recycling, existential recycling) affects all lucid beings.

Distinction. Religions are established upon and stagnated with simplistic thought, aiming to serve everyone, achieving understanding by the *populace.*

Popularization. Without any elitist intention, it is reasonable to suppose that it will always be very difficult for science to become entirely popular (popularization of rational knowledge).

Essential. Nevertheless, educational programs need to enable students with regard to certain essential facts of high quality, relevance or priority, relative to the individual's well-being and evolution.

Word. The distinction between science and pseudoscience is unmistakable. The written or typed word, regardless of its origin, is not self-corroborated. *Any paper will take ink;* the computer monitor also accepts everything.

Emphasis. Emphasis must be given to the *quality of the source* of information.

Question. It is necessary to observe whether each question helps the principles of science or exists in an isolated manner.

Rationality. Science emphasizes rationality and favors objectivity.

Occurrences. Thus, science endeavors to separate 4 occurrences or realities:

1. **Truth.** Truth from fiction (self-discernment).
2. **Reality.** Reality from imagery (imagination).
3. **Fabrication.** Fact from artificiality (fabrication).
4. **Accuracy.** Accuracy from logical errors (exactness).

Support. That is why science is the main support that humankind has against irrationality, obscurantism, mega-immaturities and all manner of *abdominal brainwashing.*

Prophylaxis. A prophylactic understanding of the persuasive techniques of rhetoric and eloquence relative to logical fallacies (deceitfulness, cunning, perfidy, cynicism), avoids errors in perspective.

Probability. Scientific laws are probable, at the highest possible level of conceiving probability.

Explanations. Scientific law is not simply a summary of the facts. It should go beyond the evidence to explain it. It interprets the results of observation.

Leading-edge. In science, there is never sufficient reason to believe that we have reached the truth. It is always advisable to work with vanguard or *leading-edge relative truth.*

Matrix. The scientist acknowledges that no theory can be taken as being definitive, final or absolute truth.

Remain. Scientific theories should always remain hypotheses.

Interminability. Nothing in the *interminable* edifice of science is permanently established. There is nothing in science that is inalterable, including the dominant paradigm (disciplinary matrix).

Attempt. Strictly speaking, all scientific discovery is, above all, considered to be an *attempt.* Nevertheless, science advances little by little, gradually increasing the minimal percentage of leading-edge relative truth.

World. In view of the ignorance of extraphysicology, the world of humankind (or intraphysicology) is invented more than discovered.

Rehearsal. The *rehearsal experiment* is an imaginary experiment used to clarify a theoretical idea.

Anticipation. Scientific reality, at times, surpasses even science fiction (imagery).

Power. The power of humans, through science, is equal to, and in some fields superior to, that of the *gods of ancient times* (mythology). The following are 8 technical endeavors, among others, in alphabetical order:

1. Artificial communication satellites.
2. Supersonic flight.
3. Television.
4. The achievements of computer science (multimedia).
5. The exploration of Mars (planet).
6. The exploration of the Moon (natural satellite).
7. The Hubble telescope.
8. The laser.

Accumulation. Science is the only aspect of human history that is truly cumulative. It progresses, accumulating units from among facts that are apparently separate and disparate.

Rework. In science, through bibliographic research, documentation, heuristics, analysis, the critiquing of important or valuable works and abstracts, one investigates thought which has been gradually accumulated over time – despite cycles, changes, recyclings, stages, errors and idiosyncrasies – and arrives at the large collection of reworked scientific results, connecting the scientific past and present.

Reading. The student who *reads just two hours* a day, at a speed of 350 words per minute, will, in 1 decade, read 1,800 books of 70,000 words each (whether they are printed works or eBooks).

Multimedia. It is worth reflecting upon this fact with regard to the theoretical enrichment of everyday life, which is even easier today through the use of the personal computer, multimedia and CD-ROMs.

Journal. Besides the invisible colleges of science, symposia, congresses, forums, encounters, seminars, conventions and fairs, the specialized technical magazine (journal) is the main product of scientific research. It is more useful from the point of view of technical updates because it presents more recent information (monthly, quarterly), as opposed to books, which present older information (yearly).

5. **Sacralization.** Imposition of static principles and sacralizations, without a right to question anything (anathema).

Advantages. We are aware of a greater number of advantages than disadvantages, in the scientific discoveries that we have up until now. On the other hand, scientific investigation has to be pure.

Limits. There should not be limits to scientific research.

Goal. What is scientifically done, or produced in a laboratory, should not always be realized with a predetermined goal.

Philosophy. Nevertheless, in light of the above, we can neither exclude philosophy as a useful coadjutant, nor ethics as a wise rule of behavior (cosmoethics) from science.

School. Every school has its specific policy.

Contention. Philosophy and ethics, as well as logic, are indispensable for restricting the excesses of human immaturity in the process of brutalization stemming from the abuses of applied science in technology (technicians, technological torture, technophobia/technolatry, technovictims/technodependents), and the actions of the public opinion agencies.

Biotechnology. The following are 19 examples, from 1997, of the so-called *monstrous threats* of biotechnology, *the great economic vector of the twenty-first century,* involving the 2 extremes of human life, the fetus/cradle and the elderly/grave:

1. Everyday and cutting-edge bioethics.
2. Artificial insemination.
3. Pre-embryos.
4. Rejected human embryos.
5. The Australian physician who had 10,000 children.
6. Human genome research.
7. Human abortion.
8. Euthanasia.
9. *Kidney-tranplant* tourism.
10. The human market or the marketing of human life.
11. The removal of organs from adopted children.
12. The exportation of children.
13. The genetically engineered rat.
14. The fly with 15 pairs of eyes.
15. The cloning of Dolly the sheep.
16. The cow Rose that produces human milk.
17. The cloning reproduction of the human being.
18. The bioethical question of arms.
19. The indiscriminate and careless use of nuclear energy.

Cosmoethics. Immature scientists avoid discussing *ends*. They only discuss *means*. Therein, the maturity of *cosmoethics,* which is still completely inexistent, should come into play.

Identity. Science, per se, does not have an identity. It has to be free and prospective.

Uses. The manner in which we use science is very important, as is its ethical utilization (cosmoethics).

Honesty. Scientific means should be perfectly honest. Let us observe what occurs in this world of modern bioethics. Ethics is not quantitative, but qualitative.

Technologism. For example, as military security measures (top secret), the ideologues (technocrats) of the technologistic (computerization of society) system, divide scientific projects into as many functional parts as possible, delivering their solution to separate groups.

Domestication. The scientist – usually a first-rate experimenter – *domesticated* in this manner, works in total ignorance of the *reason behind* his/her project.

Distortion. He/she is not aware of the true ideological determinants that govern his/her personal process (minicog), as a part of an entire structure or system (maximechanism), the primary proposal of which is the technologization of society. It is the distorted, *amoral,* model of scientific knowledge.

War. In war, evil is organized bureaucratically, through the interaction of science and technology, so that no one *beneath their superiors* can be held responsible for that which occurs.

Dilution. The *pointers of cosmoethical consciousnesses* become diluted.

Error. The cold application of Aristotelian and Newtonian concepts, tempered with Cartesianism, has drenched this planet with human blood, notably in the twentieth century.

Industry. Besides the *death industry,* which is maintained by political leaders and military technicians, the greatest error committed by the scientists of incomplete science, which is regulated by the still dominant Newtonian-Cartesian-mechanistic paradigm, is the myopic decision made by the majority of the professional community to continue to entirely ignore the extraphysical nature of the human consciousness.

Resistance. This is the absolute and absurd resistance to interdimensional or multidimensional relative truth. Scientific knowledge can be canonical, preconceived and pretentious.

Superficiality. Myopic researchers devote all of their attention exclusively to the physical, organic, peripheral or superficial areas of the personality, which are far more complex when addressed in a comprehensive manner. They thus feel vindicated.

Dermatology. Sheltered within *crippled-semiscience,* in the mutilation of knowledge and the explosion of fragmented knowledge, researchers with *temporal power* paralyze scientific research projects by establishing a lowest common denominator and committing their efforts to the *dermatology of the consciousness,* where they feel more secure and have greater economic and social support.

Dichotomy. Orthodox science (purism) and orthodox religion (fundamentalism) have both been institutionalized and frozen within a *mutually exclusive dichotomy.*

Sociopathy. This is a pathological, or a drastic sociopathy, because it maintains subcultures and selective blindness.

Protoknowledge. On the one hand, the author has therefore sought to eliminate all conditioning resulting from cultural development over decades, notably in regard to religion, a *protoknowledge* which is as outdated, in the phase of consciential maturity, as any other line of knowledge or *kindergarten-like course.*

Present-future. On the other hand, he guides himself through secularism, rationalism and empiricism, although based upon an integrative, greater, holosomatic, multidimensional, evolutionary universalism, endeavoring to see *today* and *tomorrow,* the here and now and *elsewhere,* the present-future.

Personal. The interdimensional, *transphysical* phenomena of projectiology surpass the current resources for the *physical* detection of universal occurrences that are utilized by conventional science. So far, they allow only the interested individual to directly access the processes and orientations developed here.

Empiricism. In summary: only *personal empiricism* is executed. They are still unable to offer traditional, direct, scientific replicability of consciential phenomena or, in other words, *public,* universal, easy or common *empiricism.*

Difference. When we compare knowledge gained through conventional, orthodox science with the knowledge gained through projectiology and conscientiology, we can identify the fundamental difference between one and the other.

Universal. *Traditional or conventional scientific knowledge* is contingent. Its propositions or hypotheses have their veracity or falsity perceived through non-participatory, *universal,* replicable experimentation. It is not obtained merely through reason, as occurs with philosophical knowledge.

Individual. The veracity or falsity of the propositions or hypotheses of *projectiological knowledge* are also currently based on experimentation, with the only difference being that it is a personal, *individual,* participative, non-universal and *non-public* (intraconsciential) experimentation.

Verifiability. Parapsychic knowledge allows only personal verifiability, the employment of reason and the mutual critiquing of experiences between experimenter projectors. This helps the exemplificative intraphysical consciousness.

Systematization. Despite the differences, similarities also occur. Traditional or conventional scientific knowledge, as well as projectiological knowledge, are *systematic*.

Connections. They stem from logically organized knowledge, forming systems of ideas or theories and not disperse, disconnected knowledge. The interested individual can bear out this fact with the projective techniques included in this book.

Fallibility. Both traditional scientific knowledge, as well as projectiological knowledge, constitute *fallible* knowledge, by virtue of the fact that they are not definitive, absolute or final. For this reason, they are *approximately exact.*

Propositions. New propositions and the development of conventional and projective techniques can reformulate the collection of existing theories.

Generality. Science cannot be limited in its research. Nevertheless, pure science always endeavors to be a *general science* and not an *individual science.*

Nomothetic. Science likes universals, not particulars. It deals only with broad, preferably universal (nomothetic) laws.

Idiography. Individuality cannot be studied correctly through existing conventional science (as will be seen in the next chapter), but by history, art or biography, the methods of which are not nomothetic or, in other words, involve the formation of general laws or seek out universal laws. They are, however, *idiographic,* namely, those which endeavor to study individual cases (reports, experiences, experiments).

Contradiction. This *scientific dogma* of universality is a contradiction because it places an arbitrary limitation upon the unlimited range of scientific investigation.

Evolution. Conventional scientists lack the priority module of *evolutionary intelligence.*

Problem. The consciousness is, nevertheless, a phenomenon, even when it is encountered only in individual forms. The *consciousness,* as an object, is an unwavering *trans-knowledge* that is before us.

Feelings. Conventional science, in an illogical and partial manner, does not take into account that which we really feel: the subjective experience (individual and collective). It describes the cosmos or a world of things that have no value, interacting as though humanity did not exist. It describes nature in a cold, incomplete and unsatisfactory manner.

Conscientiology. Individuality creates unique problems for conventional science. It may be the greatest relevant problem that conscientiology represents for the person of conventional science (participative consciousness).

Inconvenience. The *consciousness* is therefore a disturbance or an inconvenience for *incomplete science.*

Coherence. As the consciousness is a universal phenomenon, science – although remaining frozen in an exclusively nomothetic manner of thinking – has to study this nuisance in order to maintain its coherence. Nevertheless, *it cannot study it correctly,* except when it seeks the *individuality of standardization* (a paradox).

Alienation. This is the essential dilemma of incomplete or alienating science over the last 2 centuries, represented by the separation of subject and object. This began the logical exhaustion of the Newtonian-Cartesian-mechanistic paradigm, which is still in force.

Authority. From this point forward, the conventional scientist, who still possesses neither the authority nor the experience to *correctly* study the universal phenomenon of personality or the consciousness, also lacks the authority to *correctly* judge the research and findings of conscientiology or the personality, when considered in its *entirety* (holosomatic, multidimensional, pluri-existential, holobiographical). These are the facts.

Concessions. The individual who makes more concessions to intraphysical powers fairs better at that moment and in the world of superficial discoveries.

Conscientiality. The individual who seeks to transcend the common standard of scientific mediocrity, limiting personal concessions, is the only personality who will be able to attain the leading-edge relative truths of projectiology and obtain a better level of conscientiality in regard to personal intraconsciential and extraconsciential realities. This will allow the individual to overcome the dispensable self-mimicries that constantly attempt to monopolize that which we do in human life.

Events. Events directly related to human beings never repeat themselves the same way twice.

Individualities. There are no two similar or identical individualities.

Subjacency. Events can, however, have a subjacent determinism.

Replicability. This definitively makes the basic scientific determination of replicability of facts or laboratorial research inviable.

Partiality. This also eliminates material instruments or physical resources as being inadequate. It furthermore removes pure science and immature scientists from the scientific investigations of conscientiology – the science of the *whole* psychological individuality – and, consequently, from projectiology, both of which demand participative research (consciential energies, parapsychism) in order to reduce the current partial nature of incomplete science.

Individual. The idiographic or individual study of the personality or the consciousness, in an isolated manner, is extremely complex.

Isolation. In practice, it is extremely difficult to study an isolated individual, because *nobody exists alone* (a fundamental three-word megathosene).

Absurd. On the other hand, every time we measure, we are introducing a general or nomothetic law. If taken literally, the idiographic perspective is absurd. We can, however, accept it as an appeal to not neglect the individual in our search for general laws.

Foundation. The facts of projectiology definitively convince *only* the lucid projector through self-thosenization. Thus far, projectiology does not have a foundation capable of persuading non-practitioner or non-participant researchers.

Guiding myth. It is hoped that this possibility shall arise one day, with the development of refined technology applied to consciousness research. At this point, the mechanistic paradigm – the guiding myth of contemporary incomplete science – will have already been substituted by a new consciential paradigm defined by projectiology.

Ambiguities. This is the thought that progresses beyond the ingenuous logic of current human society, a less precise paradigm that is still contaminated with ambiguities that need to be eliminated.

Transition. Scientifically speaking, we are currently undergoing the crisis of transition, the pains of integration, the ethics of the interim, toward the primacy of a new paradigm.

Doubleness. There are even holistic researchers who think that we are currently living in a *post-paradigmatic period,* wherein 2 scientific paradigms – the depleted and the new – somehow peacefully coexist.

Challenge. Projectiology currently has little to offer the researcher who is a purist and a mechanist, in regard to the impersonalization of science and the inviolability of the principle of direct, systematic replicability, impeded from conducting experiments of a participative nature and, consequently, developing him/herself regarding the consciential aspect, whether it is due to temperament, mesological repressions, personal conditioning or an inability to tolerate crises of ambiguities.

Extraphysical melancholy. The author recommends the study (pattern-behavior *versus* exception-behavior) of post-desomatic parapsychoses and extraphysical melancholy to all colleagues, with a maximum of self-critique and heterocritique.

Instrumentation. The use of adequate, sophisticated instrumentation can one day substitute personal projectiological experiments in consciousness research. This instrumentation has not yet been invented. This is a challenge to our intelligence, which has remained undefeated since the nineteenth century.

Instrument. Today, in experimentology, the consciousness is the most efficient instrument of choice at hand in consciousness research. This, however, is not as bad, deficient or inefficient as it may seem to those less attentive individuals.

Adversaries. There are those – the adversaries of the consciential paradigm – who affirm that we should not research the consciousness by way of another consciousness, but instead, through the use of material apparatuses or physical instruments.

Questions. At this point, it is worth posing 4 rational questions and presenting their respective answers:

1. **Creation.** Who created these apparatuses and instruments? The creative human consciousness.
2. **Research.** Who performs research in all the areas of traditional and modern science? The human consciousness as researcher.
3. **Brain.** With which instrumentation, for example, does neurology research the human brain itself? Precisely with the brains of neurophysiologists or neuroscientists, researching the brains of human beings through the functioning of their own brains.
4. **Virus.** If the human consciousness cannot research itself and other consciousnesses, inevitably in a participative manner, who is it that these arguers and conventional science itself hope that will research it? The virus? This is *nonsense* or an absurdity.

Irrationality. As can be seen, this is an undoubtedly irrational argument. We can thereby rationally perceive how conventional science is indefensibly contradictory, omissive, immature and *mundane* (tropospheric).

Evasion. For 2 centuries, science has been irrationally and habitually concealing resources and constantly evading – a collective, group, lobbyist or corporatist defense mechanism – the direct, chakra-to-chakra, pore-to-pore research of the consciousness or the participative research of the researcher-object. We cannot dispute the facts.

Observation. The scientist is not merely a camera lens, recorder or computer. After all, direct observation is the best source of knowledge. This is so even when – or still when – this direct observation is multidimensional or is performed with the *para-eyes*.

Substitute. In regard to all this, there is one invariable reality: there is no substitute for personal experience.

Right hand. The reader knows that his/her right hand has 5 fingers and, furthermore, knows how to operate it to his/her benefit. No one needs to give this person lessons in this regard.

Techniques. Everything in our transitory life in this intraphysical dimension requires a technique. Even avoiding a sneeze.

Understanding. Nowadays, there are also logical, rational techniques for anyone who is interested in understanding him/herself in an integral or holosomatic manner.

Neosynapses. Fortunately or unfortunately, the fact is that conventional science, which remains myopic, does not possess these techniques. The interested individual endeavors to change paradigms and create neosynapses, devoid of neophobia.

Presuppositions. On the one hand, many of our propositions are still not science, being merely *scientific hopes,* in the sincere opinion of the mechanistic scientist, who is fearful of losing his/her professional security, being dependent on *financed survival* from conventional science, under the pressure of which he/she has been living (the author has been an independent researcher for the past 4 decades).

Semiscience. On the other hand, as with conventional, incomplete science, these projectiological propositions still constitute *handicapped-semiscience.*

Darkness. For this reason, the best way to facilitate the advent and the full implantation of matured science will be to understand how dense the darkness that we touch is – regarding conventional science, on the one hand, as well as regarding projectiology, on the other hand.

Provisional. Never forget, however, that the presuppositions of conventional natural science, with which we began, are provisional and subject to revision.

Debates. In scientific debates, a theory cannot be defended in an irrational manner, notably one which is old or antiquated.

Classification. Science requires classification.

Similarities. We are not able to obtain general knowledge unless we group phenomena on the basis of similarities (identities, affinities, interactions).

Enumerations. In this way arose the projective techniques, didactic enumerations, specialized terminology and the panorama of this book, which is quite rigid up to a certain point (all didactic *annotations* notwithstanding).

Losses. Through matured science, the individual who defends the theory of existential seriation will be able to prophylactically defend him/herself against the causes of repetitive existential lifetimes or unconscious self-mimicries.

Self-mimicries. Self-mimicries generate loss in energy, effort, mental time and evolutionary opportunities in the micro-universe of our consciousnesses.

Perspective. The great difference between conventional, mechanistic, physicalist science and conscientiology (a world of consciential and multidimensional research) is a matter of priority with regard to two perspectives:

1. **Scientist.** The conventional, materialist, four-dimensional or parochial scientist feels incompetent because he/she still *dies* in the transitory human body. This scientist would like to take shortcuts, living forever in an illusory matter, through the elixir of eternal youth.

2. *Serenissimus.* The *serenissimus,* having a multidimensional, holosomatic, maxi-universalistic perspective, feels incompetent because he/she still needs to *live* in the transitory human body. He/she would like to skip steps, living forever disconnected from matter, in his/her infinite self-evolutionary career.

Syntheses. The (universalistic and *interdimensional*) scientist, within the world of conscientiology research is, above all, as a first step, interested in attaining the most difficult of the last (but always relative) syntheses of the most essential (priority) analyses and investigations of the consciousness, or human personality, within the globalizing context of the physical universe.

Interest. This interest allows the individual to finally achieve, at a later stage, the context of the consciential universes that exist and can be reached by the ego that is restricted and immersed in the process of resoma.

Stages. These stages of more sophisticated – and the most important – investigation can only be achieved by the lucid consciousness through its intelligent performance, proceeding from the mentalsoma, controlling its holosoma, in order to control a truly more ample range of consciential dimensions, while in the mature human body.

Repetitions. The following are 13 factors, among many others, that predispose unnecessary repetitions in existential seriation or multiexistential experiences, presented here in alphabetical order:

1. Bad information, subinformation and disinformation.
2. Concealment of data.
3. Conditioned repressions.
4. Deeply rooted taboos.
5. Erudite charlatanism.
6. Exploitation of public credulity.
7. Fictional occultism.
8. Instinctive mysticism.
9. Irrational sacralizations.
10. Manipulation of vulnerable consciousnesses.
11. Popular beliefs.
12. Professional esoterism.
13. Subtle *abdominal brainwashing*.

Hopes. Faced with life's problems and the need to understand human nature and the structures of the consciousness, individuals tend to place excessive hope, or have *faith,* in conventional, mechanistic, incomplete science, as though it could solve *all* of humankind's problems.

Modes. To a considerable extent, many of these problems can be resolved in other ways of understanding reality, or other modes of cognition. For example: esthetic, religious forms or non-empirical suppositions.

Integration. The author nevertheless recommends, in all honesty – as always – the integration of conventional science with the simple consciential paradigm of projectiology.

Simplicity. All things being equal, we should prefer the simpler theory or that which resorts to fewer presuppositions and paradigms. This is a concept of conventional science itself: "Occam's razor."

Whims. At this point, it is valuable to understand our whims, in increasing order, which manifest in 3 ways:

1. **Biomemory.** The mind – in this case the intraphysical consciousness or the consciousness with its personal cerebral dictionary and biomemory – is *less* whimsical.

2. **Will.** The will is always *moderately* whimsical.

3. **Emotion.** The emotion is always *overly* whimsical.

Forms. As previously argued, the scientific form is a singular one, among many existing alternatives, for understanding our inner and external reality.

Mentalsoma. Science shows itself to be better, because it is founded on the bases of the *evolved* mental body or mentalsoma (the consciousness).

Discernment. This signifies: logic, rationality, discernment, refutation and vanguard, relative truth.

Priority. In summary: what is presently lacking in conventional science is the more refined discernment of priority. The majority of conventional scientists have still not discovered the existence of *evolutionary intelligence.*

Psychosoma. Other lines of knowledge and human inquiry, e.g., art, esthetics and religion, establish their bases in the *less evolved* emotional body or psychosoma.

Manipulation. This signifies systematic emotionality, dogmatism, perverse indoctrination, *abdominal brainwashing,* distorted truth (subinformation, disinformation) or disguised will (the quality of intention), in order to manipulate consciousnesses or social beings.

Anticosmoethical. This troublesome, anticosmoethical work has been efficiently performed throughout the twentieth century by opinion shapers, agitators, multifaceted demagogues, merchants of many origins and the shameless manipulators of robotized consciousnesses (existential robotization).

Religious person. The religious person, when based only in the emotional body and moved by sectarianism, repudiates, with violent suspicion, the consciential qualities coming from the mentalsoma. This individual combats open education, universalistic knowledge, the intellect and science.

Piety. This individual erroneously considers these things to be destroyers of instinctive sentiment, innate intuition, *natural piety* and innocent perspicacity. This does not, however, correspond to the reality of multidimensionality and applied cosmoethics.

Tranquility. Those who merely possess *natural good sense,* lacking the logical bases of scientific research, are afraid of expressing themselves and are anxious to demonstrate that their points of view are correct. They use all their passions and sophistic weapons to this end.

Decider. The rational decider, the pointer of the discerning consciousness, cannot be moved by emotions.

Serenity. Consciousness research only becomes established in the more serene researcher.

Whys. As previously affirmed, the main mechanistic model of conventional science is presently heading toward exhaustion. It alone cannot answer all of your (the reader's) questions and *whys* regarding the comprehension of your own complex personality. The simple intraphysical consciousness does not exist.

Self-control. For example, science still cannot explicate the following 3 aspects with reasonable explanations or techniques:

1. **Behavior.** Greater control of your personal behavior.
2. **Decisions.** Making of wiser choices in your daily life.
3. **Self-control.** The brilliant scientist's lack of emotional self-control.

Professionals. It should not be forgotten that we still encounter the following 7 categories, among others, of contradictory and embarrassing professionals with relative ease in this intraphysical society:

1. **Cardinal:** the cardinal who smokes (addicted to pipes and cigars).
2. **Dietician:** the obese dietician (addicted to food).
3. **Diplomat:** the monoglot chancellor.
4. **Journalist:** the illiterate journalist (the press).
5. **Nobelist:** the Nobel Prize winner found to be a pedophile.
6. **Lung specialist:** the lung specialist who is an inveterate smoker.
7. **Psychiatrist:** the onycophagic psychiatrist.

Participation. Therefore, if you are disillusioned with conventional science – which explains nothing about the *why,* but only about the *how* – you only stand to gain if, from this point on, you also begin your personal, participative research, in order to help improve this situation that disappoints you.

New. *Come over to science.* Help us to prove the new consciential paradigm, the emerging model, the most recent decoding or scientific systematization.

New perspective. This will signify 3 renovations or innovations:

1. **Life.** A new projectiological perspective on life.
2. **Science.** A recycling of science itself.
3. **History.** An alteration of the perspective of history.

Evidence. This is the clear objective of this book: to emphasize pieces of evidence, however small they may be, of this vanguard reality or this leading-edge relative truth, thereby presenting these ideas, which then no longer need to be reinvented in the near future, either in this human existence or in others.

Researcher. In the practical, daily life of the conscientiology (and the subdiscipline of projectiology) researcher, at least the 3 following scientific priorities, listed here in chronological order, are rationally *indispensable:*

1. **Self-organization.** Organize one's own intraconsciential, intraphysical and extraphysical life: personal discipline.

2. **Self-experimentation.** Accumulate the facts observed in the consciential dimensions: participative personal experimentation.

3. **Fixation.** Present the findings, independent of any other intercurrent factors or variables, placing the less impermanent scientific communications above the ephemeral intraphysical institutions: the fixating of leading-edge relative ideas into human life.

Self-relay. This formula, which is *simple* to present and *difficult* to execute, is a logical way for the consciousness to experience the meshing of healthy multiexistential self-relays, thereby becoming a *minicog* within a multidimensional, interconsciential, interpersonal, assistential *maximechanism.*

Fecundity. The theory defended here - in its first generation - for the integral analysis of the consciousness is stimulating and potentially fecund.

Developments. This theory at least presents a summarily influential structure in preparation for later technical developments.

Bibliography: Azevedo (63, p. 19), Grof (646, p. 1), Tart (1653, p. 153). The author's most recent work: *700 Conscientiology Experiments.*

03. ESSENTIAL CONCEPTS IN CONSCIENTIOLOGY

Definition. Conscientiology: the science that addresses the broad study of the consciousness, executed by the consciousnesses themselves through their consciential attributes, vehicles of manifestation and multidimensional consciential phenomena.

Synonymy: conscientiocentric megascience; *cosmonoetics;* egology; noetics; science of integral consciousness; *spirituality;* integral study of humans (intraphysical consciousness).

Subcourses. As affirmed in the 2 preceding chapters, religion is a kindergarten, infantile or protoknowledge consciential subcourse. Conventional, mechanistic science is yet another primary, immature consciential subcourse with regard to the multidimensionality of the consciousness.

Reinforcement. Philosophy and ideology, in turn, operate only as *gray eminences,* or secondary reinforcements, for the primary consciential evolutionary course of incomplete science.

Courses. Therefore, the study of conscientiology establishes itself as a more advanced course for the consciousness that has an integral approach, wherein the individual applies the better side of all positive knowledge that has been previously obtained throughout time (the periods of human history), in the consciential courses of religion, philosophy, ideology and incomplete science.

Sciences. The position of importance of conscientiology stands out *from all* sciences in light of its vital objectives for the consciousness itself. What is more important for us to study than our own essence? Due to its reach and scope, it transcends the studies of other advanced, correlated human sciences, such as parapsychology, psychology, psychotherapy, psychiatry and other branches or fields of knowledge.

Understanding. All science aims to broaden the understanding of the consciousness.

Anthropocentrism. The scope of human knowledge is essentially anthropocentric.

Relationships. This fact extends and generalizes the relationships of conscientiology to all sciences, without exception.

Projectiology. Of all the sciences, conscientiology's most direct, practical and evolutionary relationship is with its subdiscipline projectiology. This is due to the nature of its specialized study of the third consciential – projected – state, which projectiology researches and promotes.

Practicality. This book seeks to establish the foundations of projectiology, and not those of conscientiology, which, at first sight, might seem more logical. Nevertheless, in this case, it would only be so from a theoretical point of view.

Broadness. Besides the theoretical approach, the interest here is much broader regarding technical, suprascientific and *paratechnological* use for the intraphysical consciousness itself because it is based upon a multidimensional approach in relation to its evolutionary efforts.

Question. Within the scope of conscientiology, through a practical, experiential lens, the question remains: What better specialized study exists, in favor of the consciousness itself, than conscientiology, which has projectiology as one of its subdisciplines or areas of research?

Reflection. Reflect upon this and arrive at your own rational conclusion regarding the subject.

Goal. In this phase of consciential progress on the planet, projectiology, and the possibilities for the acceleration of evolutionary productivity that it offers, arise as the ideal and logical goal of technical investigation.

Inner. It is extremely difficult to obtain adequate data on the inner world (consciential micro-universe) of social beings or consciousnesses.

Subjectivity. Sometimes, important experimental studies can be better conducted, objectively speaking, when that which is occurring *inside* the subjects under analysis is unknown. This does not invalidate the attempt to know what *is* subjectively occurring inside the person under analysis, as well as the experimenter.

Nucleus. Obviously, any science of the consciousness – whether superficial or integral – should encounter a central or focal place for these inner or subjective facts.

Proposition. The term *conscientiology* was launched on page 15 of this book *Projectiology*, in its first edition, in 1986. There, the author categorically proposed conscientiology as a science.

Data. The science of conscientiology aims to engage itself in the study of consciousnesses in all their complexity, including subjective phenomena, whether in a partial or synthetic manner, and in a broad and analytical manner.

Methods. The author understands that there are convincing reasons for debating whether the data should be considered *scientific* while they have not satisfied the severe requirements of conventional scientific criteria. However, he disagrees that a field of study that is primarily interested in understanding human beings (and para-humans) refuses to deal with that which is superlatively human merely because it is difficult to develop conventional scientific methods for studying it, or because it would, in this way, violate expectations that are deeply rooted in any individuals, whoever they may be.

Study. Conscientiology places under scientific scrutiny all the characteristics and possibilities of the consciousness, which essentially include the inner attributes of the ego, its vehicles of manifestation and, finally, its existential, evolutionary and multidimensional consequences.

Attributes. To begin with, in any rational treatment of a subject, the primary mental capacities or the attributes of vast ingenuousness of the consciousness – but those classical, and thus far superficially known, attributes – stand out. The following, for example, are 11 attributes, among others, listed in alphabetical order, with regard to the diverse areas of conscientiology:

1. **Association.** The association of ideas or the most important overview (mentalsomatics).
2. **Attention.** Concentrated attention or concentration of attention (experimentology).
3. **Comparison.** Level of logical comparison.
4. **Comprehension.** Comprehension or understanding (thosenology).
5. **Imagination.** Imagination (paraprophylaxis, psychosomatics).
6. **Intelligence.** Intelligence or personal intelligences.
7. **Judgment.** Judgment or critical judgment, self-critique and heterocritique (conscientiometry).
8. **Memory.** Memory, holomemory or personal memories (mnemosomatics).
9. **Paraperceptibility.** Paraperceptibility or personal paraperceptions (paraperceptiology).
10. **Reason.** Reason (holomaturology).
11. **Reasoning.** Capacity for reasoning or elaboration of thought (mentalsomatics).

Holosoma. Next, we encounter the holosoma, or the 4 basic vehicles of manifestation of the consciousness:

1. **Soma.** The soma, physical perceptions and their potentialities, being the physical object most studied by humankind (somatics); most notably the brain *(mega-black-box)*, or the 2 cerebral hemispheres, the most relevant reality for us all.
2. **Holochakra.** The holochakra – consciential energy (CE) and its potentialities – a very obscure territory that challenges our investigation (holochakrology).
3. **Psychosoma.** The psychosoma, emotions and their potentialities, another area that is even more obscure (psychosomatics, paraneurology, parabrain).
4. **Mentalsoma.** The mentalsoma (the body of discernment), integral maturity and its potentialities, a merely incipient technical approach (mentalsomatics), because humankind has, for millennia, dedicated itself more to superficial literature (art and recreation) and the exaltation of its animal or infantile emotions, which maintain merely common good sense and the common social being (existential robotization of the unthinking human masses).

Rationality. The complexity of life and consciential manifestations require that the subtle facts involved with the consciousness be analyzed in the greatest possible detail in order to avoid confusion between occurrences and possible resulting errors in approach. The indispensable rationality presented here brings inarguably persuasive logic as its final compensation. Let us examine a practical example:

Holomemory. Let us now address a subtlety of holomemory or integral memory, in the micro-universe of the consciousness. For example, the extraphysical retrocognition of an intraphysical consciousness that occurred during a lucid projection which, in turn, took place during a prior resoma (a period of somatic, intraphysical, terrestrial rebirth).

Graphic. Each nuance of the facts needs to be evident and well-defined. Therefore, this *graphic analysis* is organized into 5 numbered blocks (1 to 5), with 3 variables (factors, conditions and phenomena) in each block (A, B and C), resulting in a total of 15 inseparable or interdependent analytical units (see figure 3).

A. FACTORS	B. CONDITIONS	C. PHENOMENA
1. General consciential factors: consciential attributes. They were not the consciential vehicles.	Essential consciential attribute: memory. It was not imagination or another attribute.	Essential mnemonic phenomenon: extraphysical retrocognition. It was not simulcognition or precognition.
2. General consciential state: an altered state of consciousness. It did not occur during the physical waking state.	Specific consciential condition: *transitory projective state.* It was not the intraphysical or extraphysical state.	Coadjutant projectiological phenomenon: human lucid projection (ALP). It was not para-human.
3. Factor that is most active in the consciousness: first consciential time (phase), present. It was not the consciential space.	Consciential evolutionary condition: current intraphysical state. It was not any desomatic or intermissive state.	New evolutionary phenomenon: *current intraphysical state.* The retrocognition did not occur in the past.
4. Factor most active in the consciousness: second consciential time (phase), past. It was not the consciential space.	Consciential evolutionary condition: prior intraphysical state. It was not any desomatic state.	Old evolutionary phenomena: *prior intraphysical state.* The earlier lucid projection did not occur in the current lifetime.
5. Pattern-consciential-phenomenon: recurring lucid projection. Beyond recall.	Pattern-consciential-condition: meshing of 3 lucid projective states (ALP, RLP and PLP).	Phenomena which are inset in the consciousness: recurring lucid projection (RLP) about lucid projection (PLP).

Fig. 3: GRAPHIC ANALYSIS OF AN EXTRAPHYSICAL RETROCOGNITION

Descriptive. Let us now summarize the facts in a *descriptive analysis,* from 5 different angles:

1. **Projectability.** An intraphysical consciousness, today, projects with lucidity (ALP or assisted lucid projection).

2. **Retrocognition.** During the lucid projection, the consciousness experiences an extraphysical retrocognition.

3. **Resoma.** The extraphysical retrocognition refers to a prior human existence of the projected intraphysical consciousness.

4. **Evocation.** The prior resoma (lifetime) which is recalled evokes a human lucid projection that was experienced in that period (RLP or retrocognitive lucid projection).

5. **Projection.** The lucid projection, which occurred in that previous human existence, refers precisely to the phenomenon of lucid projection (PLP or precognitive lucid projection).

Subtlety. The greatest subtlety lies precisely in the fact that 1 altered (xenophrenic) state of consciousness – the human lucid projection (no. 2C) – promoted interference in 3 evolutionary states of the same consciousness: the current intraphysical state (no. 3C); a transitory projective state (no. 2B); and a prior intraphysical state (no. 4C).

Multiplicity. Therefore, in this case, the same consciousness simultaneously analyzes the *omnifluent,* progressive, multiple vision in its internal consciential time, or 3 of its own lucid consciential projections that are encased in diverse periods and conditions.

Recollections. Chronologically, from the present to the past, 3 consecutive *recollections* also occurred:

1. **ALP.** The first, retrocognitive, current lucid projection (ALP or assisted lucid projection).

2. **RLP.** The second lucid projection (RLP or retrocognitive lucid projection) of the recalled previous human existence.

3. **PLP.** The third lucid projection inset in the other lucid projection (PLP or precognitive lucid projection), recalled in the previous intraphysical life.

Self-critique. In projective analyses, the use of self-critique is imperative.

Expectations. The contents of the extraphysical experiences can be shaped by the expectations of the projector.

Factors. In this process, 3 self-critiquing preponderant factors come into play:

1. **Bi-lucidity.** Firstly, the percentage of *extraphysical lucidity* and, secondly, the percentage of *physical lucidity.*

2. **Morphothosenes.** The knowledge of the extraphysical shapes of morphothosenes (thought-forms).

3. **Will.** The strength of the impulsion of the consciousness' will during the entire process.

Directions. But, that is not all. In any direction to which we direct the *pointer of our consciousness* in a rational search, within the consciential micro-universe, whether in the *infinity of the past,* the exploration of the present, or the *infinity of the future,* we will always encounter even more subtle and sophisticated occurrences.

Occurrences. Consciential occurrences tend to repeat themselves according to their own patterns, which are progressively encased, one inside the other, in an endless complex succession.

Processes. Still with regard to memory, other subtleties can be detected in different mnemonic processes. Examples: retrocognition of the lucid projection of our consciousness, when an extraphysical consciousness during an intermissive period; a common dream in which we dream about lucid projection; and many others.

Logic. The logic of commercial success, or shameless merchandizing (statistics, public opinion research, public opinion poll, *audience-mentality-index,* bestseller list), can neither impose the production of works in scientific institutions nor can it impose the production of works on conscientiological clarification tasks.

Truth. The rigid criterion that impels the clarification task is the *leading-edge relative truth* or polykarmality in the evolution of consciousnesses. This was the intention behind the production of this book.

Samples. The entire analysis was developed in this context without addressing the other consciential attributes, beyond memory and paraperceptibility, nor was a discrimination made of other manifestations of the vehicles of the consciousness, their actions and consequences in each circumstance.

Complexity. From the material presented above, we have only seen some samples of the complexity of the consciousness and, thereby, of conscientiology research, in its multiple areas or subdisciplines, in which projectiology is situated.

Bibliography: Vieira (1762, p. 15). The author's most recent works: *700 Conscientiology Experiments; 200 Conscientiology Theorices; Conscientiogram.*

04. SUBDISCIPLINES OF CONSCIENTIOLOGY

Integrality. In holomaturology, *conscientiology* is the science that studies the consciousness in an integral, holosomatic, multidimensional, multimillenary, multiexistential manner and, above all, according to its reactions in regard to immanent energies (IEs) and consciential energies (CEs), as well as in its multiple states of manifestation (thosenology).

Pulverization. It was not the intention to break up the world of conscientiology research into subdisciplines. However, in view of the broad scope of the relevant subjects that involve the intraphysical consciousness, the author could find no other educational resource than to confront this issue.

Criterion. The analysis of the synoptic table considered the *spatial presentation* of the subdisciplines into 6 logical orders as the criterion for their organization. In this case, each subdiscipline includes its successors in a logical subsequent order, each subdiscipline representing one area of delimited study within the subdiscipline of the previous logical order. For example: *holosomatics* proposes the study of the vehicles of manifestation of the consciousness: *soma, holochakra, psychosoma* and *mentalsoma.* Each of these vehicles is a very complex object of study, which makes the creation of the specific subdisciplines of each one very pertinent (see fig. 4).

Anatomy. According to the spatial criterion, the elaboration of the synoptic table is analogous to an anatomic study, through which we place each element (subdiscipline) accurately in relation to the others (parts) and the whole (conscientiology).

Evolution. Another argument that justifies this table is the *evolutionary criterion:* each subdiscipline is superior, from an evolutionary point of view, to the subdiscipline of the previous order. For example: *egokarmology, groupkarmology* and *polykarmology.* The evolutionary criterion does not allow its application in all cases. This is why the spatial presentation was the criterion most used in the elaboration of the synoptic table, as it is applicable in all cases.

Areas. The following are 70 areas (second version), or scientific subdisciplines, within the broad world of conscientiological research, and its main scientific subdisciplines:

1. **Androsomatics.** Androsomatics is the subdiscipline of conscientiology that studies the soma, specifically in regard to the male sex, or the *androsoma,* and its relationships to the human consciousness (intraphysical consciousness). It is a scientific subdiscipline of sexosomatics.

2. **Assistentiology.** Assistentiology is the subdiscipline of conscientiology that studies the techniques of interconsciential assistance, notably in reference to its effects for the consciousness when considered in an "integral," holosomatic and multimillenary manner, with holomaturity in view, a work of lucid solidarity between consciousnesses on the way to megafraternity. It is a scientific subdiscipline of coexistology.

3. **Coexistology.** Coexistology is the subdiscipline of conscientiology that studies consciential communicability, with respect to the dynamics of interrelationships that are established between consciousnesses or consciential principles that coexist in any dimension as well as their holokarmic and evolutionary consequences. It is a scientific subdiscipline of communicology.

4. **Communicology.** Communicology is the subdiscipline of conscientiology that studies all natures and forms of communicability of the consciousness, including interconsciential communication between consciential dimensions, taking lucid consciential projectability into account and addresses the "entire" consciousness. It is a scientific subdiscipline of experimentology.

5. **Conscientiocentrology.** Conscientiocentrology is the subdiscipline of conscientiology that studies social philosophy focusing its objectives on the consciousness and its evolution through the establishment and maintenance of the *conscientiocentric institution* within conscientiological intraphysical society, based on employment and consciential bonds of intraphysical consciousnesses, in the manner of a consciential cooperative. It is a scientific subdiscipline of parasociology.

Synoptic Table - 70 Subdisciplines of Conscientiology

1st Logical Order	2nd Logical Order	3rd Logical Order	4th Logical Order	5th Logical Order	6th Logical Order
thosenology	evolutiology	experimentology	parabiology	parabotany	
				parazoology	
			communicology	coexistiology	assistentiology
				projectiology	projectiography
					projectiocritique
					infocommunicology
			holoresomatics	cosmo-analysis	
				parapedagogy	
				intraphysicology	resomatics
					existential programology
					existential invertology
					existential recyclology
					desomatics
				extraphysicology	intermissiology
					parageography
				parasociology	conscientiocentrology
					paratechnology
			conscientiotherapy	parachronology	parahistory
				paratreatment	paraprophylaxis
					parasemiology
					paratherapeutics
					projectiotherapy
				parasurgery	para-anesthesia
					para-asepsis
					parahemostasis
					paracicatrization
		holosomatics: somatics	sexosomatics	androsomatics	
				gynosomatics	
			macrosomatics		cosmoconscientiology
		cosmoethics	conscientiometry	serenology	
				petifreeology	
		holomaturology	egokarmology		
		holokarmology	groupkarmology		
			polykarmology		
		holochakrology			
		psychosomatics	parageneses		
		mentalsomatics	paraneurology		
		para-anatomy	mnemosomatics		
		paraphysiology	paraphenomenology		
		parapathology	pararegeneration	paraperceptiology	
		homeostatics			

6. **Conscientiometry.** Conscientiometry is the subdiscipline of conscientiology that studies conscientiological (of the consciousness) measurements, through resources and methods that address the "entire" consciousness, capable of establishing the possible bases for the *mathematical analysis of the consciousness*. One example is the conscientiogram. It is a scientific subdiscipline of holomaturology.

7. **Conscientiotherapy.** Conscientiotherapy is the subdiscipline of conscientiology that studies the treatment, alleviation and remission of disturbances of the consciousness, through resources and techniques derived from addressing the "entire" consciousness, in its pathologies and parapathologies. It is a scientific subdiscipline of experimentology.

8. **Cosmo-analysis.** Cosmo-analysis is the subdiscipline of conscientiology that studies the practical application of the *cosmogram* or the technical data sheet for the evaluative determination of the realities of the universe, filtered by the multidimensional principles of conscientiology, through the maximal association of ideas (panoramic vision), stemming from the facts (phenomenology) that reach and involve the holothosene of the self- and heterocritiquing human personality. It is a scientific subdiscipline of communicology.

9. **Cosmoconscientiology.** Cosmoconscientiology is the subdiscipline of conscientiology that studies the expansion of the consciousness, or the phenomenon of cosmoconsciousness, in the mentalsoma. It is a scientific subdiscipline of paraperceptiology.

10. **Cosmoethics.** Cosmoethics is the subdiscipline of conscientiology that studies ethics or reflection upon multidimensional, cosmic morals, which define consciential holomaturity, situated beyond social, intraphysical morals or that which is presented under any human label, in the form of a maximum, moral and emotional discernment stemming from the intimacy of the micro-universe of each consciousness. It is a scientific subdiscipline of evolutiology.

11. **Desomatics.** Desomatics is the subdiscipline of conscientiology that studies the physical contexts of desoma (biological death), and the consciential, psychological, social, medicolegal and multidimensional contexts associated with the deactivation of the soma (human body), as well as the second and third desomas and their consequences. It is a scientific subdiscipline of intraphysicology.

12. **Egokarmology.** Egokarmology is the subdiscipline of conscientiology that studies the relationships or principles of cause and effect active in the evolution of the consciousness when centered exclusively on the ego itself. It is a scientific subdiscipline of holokarmology.

13. **Evolutiology.** Evolutiology is the subdiscipline of conscientiology that studies the evolution of the consciousness at a high-level, considered in an integral, holosomatic, multi-existential and multidimensional fashion, a subject matter specific to the evolutionary orienter or evolutiologist. It is a scientific subdiscipline of thosenology.

14. **Existential invertology.** Existential invertology is the subdiscipline of conscientiology that studies the philosophy, technique and practice of *existential* (human) *inversion*. It is a scientific subdiscipline of intraphysicology.

15. **Existential programology.** Existential programology is the subdiscipline of conscientiology that studies the *existential program* of intraphysical consciousnesses, in general, and its evolutionary consequences. It is a scientific subdiscipline of intraphysicology.

16. **Existential recyclology.** Existential recyclology is the subdiscipline of conscientiology that studies the philosophical, technical and practical aspects of existential recycling, within intraphysicality, which begins with intraconsciential recycling. It is a scientific subdiscipline of intraphysicology.

17. **Experimentology.** Experimentology is the subdiscipline of conscientiology that studies all forms and categories of evolutionary experiments of the consciousness. It is a scientific subdiscipline of evolutiology.

18. **Extraphysicology.** Extraphysicology is the subdiscipline of conscientiology that studies the relationships and experiences of the intraphysical consciousness in other dimensions beyond intraphysicality. It is a scientific subdiscipline of holoresomatics.

19. **Groupkarmology.** Groupkarmology is the subdiscipline of conscientiology that studies the relationships or principles of cause and effect active in the evolution of the consciousness when centered on the evolutionary group. It is a scientific subdiscipline of holokarmology.

20. **Gynosomatics**. Gynosomatics is the subdiscipline of conscientiology that studies the soma, specifically in regard to the female gender, or *gynosoma,* and its relationships with the human consciousness (intraphysical consciousness). It is a scientific subdiscipline of sexosomatics.

21. **Holochakrology.** Holochakrology is the subdiscipline of conscientiology that studies the quality of the manifestations of the human consciousness (intraphysical consciousness) deriving from the holochakra or energetic parabody. It is a scientific subdiscipline of holosomatics.

22. **Holokarmology.** Holokarmology is the subdiscipline of conscientiology that studies the holokarmic account of the consciousness in evolution encompassing egokarmality, groupkarmality and polykarmality. It is a scientific subdiscipline of evolutiology.

23. **Holomaturology.** Holomaturology is the subdiscipline of conscientiology that studies the holomaturity of the human consciousness – or integral, biological, psychological (mental) and multidimensional or holosomatic maturity – in all of its forms of manifestation and evolutionary consequences. It is a scientific subdiscipline of evolutiology.

24. **Holoresomatics**. Holoresomatics is the subdiscipline of conscientiology that studies existential seriality and evolutionary multiexistential cycles or successive intraphysical resomas, along with their implications for and repercussions upon the human consciousness, also relative to interplanetary transmigration. It is a scientific subdiscipline of experimentology.

25. **Holosomatics.** Holosomatics is the subdiscipline of conscientiology that studies the holosoma (the set of vehicles of manifestation), its functions and applications by the (intraphysical or extraphysical) consciousness. It is a scientific subdiscipline of thosenology.

26. **Homeostatics.** Homeostatics is the subdiscipline of conscientiology that studies the theorice of *holosomatic homeostasis* or the integrated, healthy, harmonic state of the holosoma, in order for the intraphysical consciousness to live better and with greater efficiency in the execution of his/her existential program. It is a scientific subdiscipline of holosomatics.

27. **Infocommunicology.** Infocommunicology is the subdiscipline of conscientiology that studies information technology applied the contexts of communication and the didactics of the consciousness, when considered as a "whole." It is a scientific subdiscipline of parapedagogy.

28. **Intermissiology.** Intermissiology is the subdiscipline of conscientiology that studies the *period of intermission* of the consciousness in evolution, situated between two of its personal lifetimes, within its multiexistential evolutionary cycle. It is a scientific subdiscipline of extraphysicology.

29. **Intraphysicology.** Intraphysicology is the subdiscipline of conscientiology that studies the relations and experiences of the intraphysical consciousness in this intraphysical or human dimension. It is a scientific subdiscipline of holoresomatics.

30. **Macrosomatics.** Macrosomatics is the subdiscipline of conscientiology that studies the macrosoma, the *extraordinary* soma suitable for the execution of a specific existential program. It is a scientific subdiscipline of somatics.

31. **Mentalsomatics.** Mentalsomatics is the subdiscipline of conscientiology that studies the mentalsoma (the parabody of discernment) and its evolutionary consequences for the consciousness. It is a scientific subdiscipline of holosomatics.

32. **Mnemosomatics.** Mnemosomatics is the subdiscipline of conscientiology that studies the soma specifically in relation to the intrasomatic memories, spanning from the cerebral memory or basic biomemory of the human being, up to the point of achieving holomemory. It is a scientific subdiscipline of mentalsomatics.

33. **Para-anatomy.** Para-anatomy is the subdiscipline of conscientiology that studies the anatomy that transcends intraphysicality, when considering the vehicles of manifestation of the consciousness other than the soma. It is a scientific subdiscipline of holosomatics.

34. **Para-anesthesia.** Para-anesthesia (para-anesthesiology) is the subdiscipline of conscientiology that studies the anesthesia that transcends the resources of intraphysicality, through parapsychism. It is a scientific subdiscipline of parasurgery (conscientiotherapy).

35. **Para-asepsis.** Para-asepsis is the subdiscipline of conscientiology that studies the asepsis that transcends the resources of intraphysicality, through parapsychism. It is a scientific subdiscipline of parasurgery (conscientiotherapy).

36. **Parabiology.** Parabiology is the subdiscipline of conscientiology that studies living beings, in their multidimensional and multivehicular relationships. It is a scientific subdiscipline of experimentology.

37. **Parabotany.** Parabotany is the subdiscipline of conscientiology that studies the manifestation of consciential principles in the primary condition of plants, or paraflora. It is a scientific subdiscipline of parabiology.

38. **Parachronology.** Parachronology is the subdiscipline of conscientiology that studies the chronology of manifestations of consciousnesses beyond intraphysicality, as well as the other consciential dimensions, holobiographies and multidimensionality. It is a scientific subdiscipline of holoresomatics.

39. **Paragenetics.** Paragenetics is the subdiscipline of conscientiology that studies compound and integral genetics, encompassing all of the consciousness' holosomatic inheritances from the retrosomas of previous lives – through the psychosoma and mentalsoma – up to the current human embryo as an intraphysical consciousness. It is a scientific subdiscipline of psychosomatics.

40. **Parageography.** Parageography is the subdiscipline of conscientiology that studies the description of the paratroposphere, including its parageographic accidents and extraphysical environments, as well as the relationships between this environment and the parapopulation (autochthonous and/or transient). It is a scientific subdiscipline of extraphysicology.

41. **Paracicatrization**. Paracicatrization is the subdiscipline of conscientiology that studies the healing which transcends the resources of intraphysicality, through parapsychism. It is a scientific subdiscipline of parasurgery.

42. **Parahemostasis.** Parahemostasis is the subdiscipline of conscientiology that studies the hemostasis that transcends the resources of intraphysicality, through parapsychism. It is a scientific subdiscipline of parasurgery (conscientiotherapy).

43. **Parahistory.** Parahistory is the subdiscipline of conscientiology that studies the history of the consciousness and the cosmos, beyond the autobiography of the intraphysical consciousness in the current human life, as well as human history, in a multidimensional manner through extraphysicology, retrocognitions and lucid consciential projectability. It is a scientific subdiscipline of parachronology.

44. **Paraneurology.** Paraneurology is the subdiscipline of conscientiology that studies the parabrain and its relationships with the physical brain, the nervous system and the other vehicles of the holosoma. It is a scientific subdiscipline of psychosomatics.

45. **Parapathology.** Parapathology is the subdiscipline of conscientiology that studies the pathology of the vehicles of manifestation of the consciousness or the holosoma (holochakra, psychosoma and mentalsoma), excluding the human body (soma). It is a scientific subdiscipline of holosomatics.

46. **Parapedagogy.** Parapedagogy is the subdiscipline of conscientiology that studies the philosophy of education and pedagogy beyond the resources of intraphysicality, through lucid multidimensionality, projectability of the human consciousness, and its consequences in human life. It is a scientific subdiscipline of communicology.

47. **Paraperceptiology.** Paraperceptiology is the subdiscipline of conscientiology that studies the paraperceptions of the consciousness, beyond the perceptions restricted to the human body (soma), its phenomena and evolutionary consequences. It is a scientific subdiscipline of paraphenomenology.

48. **Paraphenomenology.** Paraphenomenology is the subdiscipline of conscientiology that studies the parapsychic manifestations of the human consciousness, whether they are of a subjective (intraconsciential), ambivalent or objective (perceptible to the external environment) order, through the use of the holosoma and mobilization of consciential energies. It is a scientific subdiscipline of paraphysiology.

49. **Paraphysiology.** Paraphysiology is the subdiscipline of conscientiology that studies the functions of the vehicles of manifestation of the consciousness or holosoma (holochakra, psychosoma and mentalsoma), excluding the human body (soma). It is a scientific subdiscipline of holosomatics.

50. **Paraprophylaxis.** Paraprophylaxis is the subdiscipline of conscientiology that studies the prophylaxis that transcends the limits of intraphysicology in order to prevent the consciousness from errors and inconveniences in all dimensions wherein it manifests. It is a scientific subdiscipline of paratreatment (conscientiotherapy).

51. **Pararegeneration.** Pararegeneration is the subdiscipline of conscientiology that studies the anatomic and/or functional regeneration of the vehicles of manifestation of the consciousness (holosoma), beyond the human body, in which paracicatrization and paratransfiguration are included. It is a scientific subdiscipline of paraphysiology.

52. **Parasemiology.** Parasemiology is the subdiscipline of conscientiology that studies the investigation and identification – beyond intraphysicality – of para-symptomatology and the para-signs of disturbances and parapathologies of the consciousness, when considered as a "whole," (holosomatic, integral), through parapsychism and paraperceptiology. It is a scientific subdiscipline of paratreatment.

53. **Parasociology.** Parasociology is the subdiscipline of conscientiology that studies the philosophy, techniques and practices of conscientiological intraphysical society and extraphysical societies of extraphysical consciousnesses, as well as their consequences in human, extraphysical and projective life. It is a scientific subdiscipline of holoresomatics.

54. **Parasurgery.** Parasurgery is the subdiscipline of conscientiology that studies the surgery that transcends the resources of intraphysicality, through parapsychism (paraperceptiology). It is a scientific subdiscipline of conscientiotherapy.

55. **Paratechnology.** Paratechnology is the subdiscipline of conscientiology that studies the technology of the consciousness – when considered as a "whole" – and its consequences, applying all the specific methodology for the expansion of the intraphysical consciousness' self-knowledge, including projective techniques, in general. It is a scientific subdiscipline of extraphysicology.

56. **Paratherapeutics.** Paratherapeutics is the subdiscipline of conscientiology that studies the therapeutics or treatment of ill consciousnesses, as developed by conscientiotherapy. It is a scientific subdiscipline of paratreatment (conscientiotherapy).

57. **Paratreatment.** Paratreatment is the subdiscipline of conscientiology that studies the clinical practice or the care of sick patients beyond intraphysicality, through parapsychism. It is a scientific subdiscipline of conscientiotherapy.

58. **Parazoology.** Parazoology is the subdiscipline of conscientiology that studies the manifestation of the consciential principles which are in the condition of subhuman animals, or parafauna. It is a scientific subdiscipline of parabiology.

59. **Petifreeology.** Petifreeology is the subdiscipline of conscientiology that studies the petifree condition or the evolutionary, consciential quality of the awakened human being who no longer suffers from pathological interconsciential intrusions and all harmful evolutionary consequences of this uncomfortable condition. It is a scientific subdiscipline of conscientiometry (holomaturology).

60. **Polykarmology.** Polykarmology is the subdiscipline of conscientiology that studies the relationships or principles of cause and effect active in the evolution of the consciousness, when centered in the understanding and experience of cosmic maxifraternity, beyond egokarma and groupkarma. It is a scientific subdiscipline of holokarmology.

61. **Projectiocritique.** Projectiocritique is the subdiscipline of conscientiology that studies *projectiological critique* in general, which is extremely relevant within the consciential paradigm. It is a scientific subdiscipline of projectiology.

62. **Projectiography.** Projectiography is the subdiscipline of conscientiology that performs the technical study of projectiological accounts. It is a scientific subdiscipline of projectiology.

63. **Projectiology.** Projectiology is the subdiscipline of conscientiology that studies projections of the consciousness and their effects, including projections of consciential energies outside the

holosoma. This represents the subject and object of study of this book. It is a scientific subdiscipline of communicology (interdimensionality).

64. **Projectiotherapy.** Projectiotherapy is the subdiscipline of conscientiology that studies the prophylaxis and therapies derived from the research and techniques of projectiology. It is a scientific subdiscipline of paratreatment (conscientiotherapy).

65. **Psychosomatics.** Psychosomatics is the subdiscipline of conscientiology that studies the emotions of the consciousness stemming from the psychosoma, the parabody of desires. It is a scientific subdiscipline of holosomatics.

66. **Resomatics.** Resomatics is the subdiscipline of conscientiology that studies the somatic rebirth of the extraphysical consciousness which passes over to the temporary condition of being an intraphysical consciousness or, in other words, leaves extraphysicality for intraphysicality. It is a scientific subdiscipline of intraphysicology.

67. **Serenology.** Serenology is the subdiscipline of conscientiology that studies the *Homo sapiens serenissimus (serenissimus),* its personal traits, characteristics and evolutionary consequences. It is a scientific subdiscipline of conscientiometry (holomaturology).

68. **Sexosomatics.** Sexosomatics is the subdiscipline of conscientiology that studies the soma specifically in regard to its gender, or the *sexosoma,* and its relationships with the human consciousness, whether it is a man or woman. It is a scientific subdiscipline of somatics.

69. **Somatics.** Somatics is the subdiscipline of conscientiology that studies the soma (human body) within the holosoma, or in relation to the other vehicles of manifestation of the consciousness, in its multidimensional evolution. It is a scientific subdiscipline of holosomatics.

70. **Thosenology.** Thosenology is the subdiscipline of conscientiology that studies *thosenes* (*thoughts*, *sentiments* and *energies*), *thosenity* and the *thosenators* of the consciousness, its paraphysiology and parapathology. *Self-thosenity* is the mechanism of incessant expression of the consciousness in all of its manifestations, in any consciential dimension, thosenology consequently being the concept (theory) and substratum (practice) of the establishment of the science of *conscientiology,* an area not yet (2002) discovered by conventional sciences.

Course. According to mentalsomatics, a standard conscientiology course, within formal education, needs to include at least these 70 areas of study or disciplines and their most notable scientific subdisciplines.

Originality. Within these areas, there are 12 which are more original and more relevant in regard to their technical objectives and consequences. They are listed below, with their salient points for research:

1. **Conscientiocentrology:** the consciential bond in conscientiological intraphysical society.
2. **Conscientiotherapy:** the daily practice of *penta* (assistentiology).
3. **Cosmoethics:** evolutionary consciential incorruptibility.
4. **Existential invertology:** the performance of the *clarification task* by the evolutionary duo.
5. **Existential programology:** the self-aware conquest of *existential completism* and *existential moratorium.*
6. **Holomaturology:** the recuperation of *cons* or hyperacuity in human existence.
7. **Macrosomatics:** the intraphysical consciousness who has a *macrosoma*, being an active minicog in an assistential, interconsciential and multidimensional maximechanism.
8. **Paragenetics:** innate ideas and their consequences in intraphysical life.
9. **Petifreeology:** the lucid *consciential epicenter.*
10. **Projectiology:** the condition of multidimensional self-awareness (MS).
11. **Serenology:** *Homo sapiens serenissimus (serenissimus)* as an evolutionary model.
12. **Thosenology:** the personal or group *holothosene* and its fundamental *materthosene.*

Bibliography: Recent works by the author: *Evolutionary Duo Manual* (in Portuguese) and *200 Conscientiology Theorices* (in Portuguese).

05. ESSENTIAL CONCEPTS IN PROJECTIOLOGY

Definitions. Projectiology (Latin: *projectio,* projection; Greek: *logos,* treatise): the science that addresses the passage of the intraphysical, or extraphysical, consciousness to the projected state, as well as the conditions of the consciousness in this state; the human science that investigates the energetic projections of the consciousness using the energetic body and projections of the consciousness using the psychosoma and mentalsoma outward from the human body or, in other words, the actions of the consciousness operating outside the state of intraphysical cerebral restriction and the entire biological body.

Synonymy: discoincidentiology; holosomology; OBEology; projectionics; projectionism; projectionistics; projectionomy; projectiotronics; science of interdimensionality; study of extracorporeal phenomena; study of projections of the consciousness; systematized self-revelation; unfoldology.

Unity. According to existing didactic principles, the infancy of all science is characterized by focusing upon the search for relevant variables, singular data, unconnected classifications and hypotheses that subsequently establish relationships between these variables and explain the data.

Semi-empiricism. Here, the quest is precisely to overcome this initial, semi-empirical stage of science, which the author calls *projectiology,* a subdiscipline or area of conscientiology, giving it a logical unity.

Gaps. Although the phenomenon of lucid projection has been known for millennia, projectiology is a relatively new area of study that is still developing, because its systematic research is recent. There are thus a considerable number of gaps in its scientific field that will certainly be filled over time through the accumulation of investigations and judicious technical analysis.

Provisory. The data currently available on projectiology, albeit numerous, are provisory to the degree that they almost always represent tentative approaches to projective phenomena and their consequences.

Publications. A considerable number of scientific literary publications contain defects in structure, errors in statistical analysis and misleading interpretations.

Methods. Methods of experimentation and analysis are, nevertheless, constantly being improved.

Estimates. Quantitative estimates are gradually becoming more exact. However, this does not signify that previously developed work was not *scientific* or important for its time.

Evolution. The dynamic of science constantly changes and evolves.

Imagination. It only, erroneously, achieves the status of absolute truth in popular imagination.

Cycle. The *cycle of science* is the process of *selection* and comparison, which occurs on an ongoing basis in areas of research.

Truths. Thanks to the cycle of science, renovations and new leading-edge (vanguard) relative truths arise.

Research. On the other hand, what has been shown thus far, does not imply that existing individual studies and laboratory research on projectiology lack value or significance. Quite to the contrary, the continued analysis of these data – still valid – constitutes precisely the way which is currently adequate and ideal for achieving continuous progress.

Critique. With the critiquing of existing inconclusive data, there will doubtless arise new conditions and situations for which new research and data will be necessary, in a continuous process of inquiry and temporary solutions, as has occurred and will continue to occur in the evolution of any science.

Directions. At *best*, the experiments of today will determine new directions. At the very *worst*, they will prove to be fruitless.

Pseudoproblems. Nevertheless, many experiments will serve to remove *pseudoproblems,* the controversies of lesser value and the *methodological fallacies* that impede each stage of scientific advancement.

Results. In fact, there is no such thing as a negative or unsuccessful result in a scientific experiment. All data obtained offers information for the ready mind of the intraphysical consciousness, who respects the findings and does not allow the hypotheses to impede research and new investigations.

Security. In order for a science or a theory to be operational, it does not have to be attack-proof.

Medicine. Let us consider medicine, for example. It is based upon a vast body of concrete facts and sound theories. Nevertheless, it *cannot be applied* with mathematical certainty in many of its areas or subdisciplines.

Errors. Errors can be and are committed, even by the most experienced researchers and specialists in the medical field. There is and will always be a necessity for estimating possibilities, exercising critical judgment and applying intuitive perception, just as much in diagnostics as in therapeutics.

Reason. However, this fact does not constitute sufficient reason for abandoning medicine, returning to the days in which it was still not a science per se.

Hypotheses. Even though many hypotheses proposed by projectiology are still in a phase of research and experimentation, they possess the characteristics that scientific method requires, in terms of quality.

Manner. Projectiology is science, although it is not science in the same manner as physics, mathematics, or even biology.

Humanism. Projectiology is a human science, with its own scientific profile, characterized by a new, more evolved scientific model. As a human science, projectiology also needs to be complemented in the philosophical arena.

Complement. The comprehensive view of projectiology involves a treatment that is simultaneously scientific and philosophical, as both are complements of an organic and logical whole.

Singularity. Scientific projectiology cannot be reduced to experimental projectiology.

Experimentation. Science is not synonymous with experimentation. If some aspects of projectiology can be controlled experimentally, others do not fit within this type of model.

Scope. Projectiology is *also* science, but *not only* experimental science. It requires theories and methods that are adapted to the singularity of its scope – the human being – when considered in a broad, comprehensive, integral, holosomatic, multidimensional, multiexistential, holomnemonic manner.

Neoparadigm. Projectiology experiments are based upon the leading theory or the consciential neoparadigm.

Establishment. In spite of the aforementioned precedents, the author endeavors to clearly and rationally present and establish 9 objectives in this book:

1. Essential or theoretical concepts.
2. Postulates.
3. Parameters.
4. Objects of study.
5. Collimation of objectives.
6. Pragmatic, empirical and scientific applications.
7. Operational or pragmatic concepts.
8. Experiments.
9. The theoretical and scientific body, which defines the sphere of action of projectiology and differentiates it, making it distinct from other sciences.

Criteria. The author considers it unnecessary to explain scientific criteria and the epistemological validity of a given branch of human knowledge. This would be tiresome, as the average reader can easily evaluate them.

Naturalist. The characteristic aspect of the individual, subjective phenomenon of the human lucid projection experience, establishes the conditions for the existence of *subjective projectiology*. However, certain occurrences – such as physical bilocation – also speak in favor of a *naturalist* projectiology, or one of objective, ostensive, physically visible manifestations that stem from the consciousness, when projected.

Universalism. The truth and validity of knowledge has no boundaries. *Scientific* nationalism and *cultural* nationalism, in general, inevitably lead to stagnation.

Universal. Science is one thing only: it is either universal (international) or it is not science.

Limitations. Science in general, just as psychology or parapsychology in particular, and projectiology itself, are areas or branches of human knowledge that are entirely broad and universalistic. They cannot accept labels or limitations and should be developed without temporal human obligations, devoid of scientific or philosophical sectarianisms, or any kind of castrating ideologies.

Uncommitted. The dispassionate object of study and rational methodology of projectiology has no implicit or explicit commitment to any particular psychic, social, political, economic, philosophical or religious area.

Monopoly. In summary: projectiology should neither be monopolized by cults nor co-opted by competing or rival governments, whether from an ideological or military point of view.

Foundations. We present, in this book, the foundations of a science – projectiology. The attentive observer, based on the immaturity of every new science, may consider it inopportune or premature to ponder the *foundations* of projectiology.

Search. However, it is reasonable and fair to think about projectiological foundations, because other sciences, even those which are most *venerated*, continue to struggle in the search for their solid foundations, as can be seen with these two examples:

1. **Mathematics.** Mathematics, for example, is faced with its non-solid foundations, as it is still in search of a position regarding the irrational, abyssal inscrutability – which we cannot comprehend – of *whole natural numbers,* the fundamental parts upon which this science is essentially based.

2. **Physics.** Physics – hard science – dedicates itself to the area of the uncertainty principle, along with the probability theory (the *background* of the possible), the challenge of entropy and other worthy concepts, in order to overcome the immeasurability of the illimitable.

Presupposition. In physics, when applied to technology, the real experiment, e.g., a particle in a cyclotron, is a case of "more or less," of irrational, statistical presupposition. It does not adapt itself perfectly to calculated probability, therefore making it impossible to effect concrete, accurate and real predictions.

Senses. Many of the themes addressed and concepts cited here are treated more *descriptively* and not *explanatorily* due to the new and often unexplored globalizing nature of the perspectives themselves.

Bibliography: Recent work by the author: *700 Conscientiology Experiments* (in Portuguese).

---

06.   PROJECTIOLOGY   AND   TERMINOLOGY

Definition. Terminology: the set of terms characteristic of a science.

Synonymy: jargon; nomenclature; professional slang; technical language.

Organization. Until now, a consensus has not been achieved, at an international level, regarding the problem of composing and organizing international terminology, such as parapsychological terms.

Phenomena. The incongruity and multiplicity of existing names for the phenomena of projectiology show the uselessness and subsequent necessity for the use, creation or adoption of its own terms.

Discoveries. No one denies the need for new words, or acceptation of old distended words, in order to name new facts and new ideas. As with other sciences, projectiology needs its own words. How can the newness of its discoveries and conceptions be formulated without using new terms? The absence of preconceptions, even in terminology, is a condition for true discovery.

Precision. Science demands very precise language.

Language. Everyday language is not the ideal medium for parapsychic subtleties.

Sense. Any scientific discovery takes shape, not by molding to common sense, but by going beyond it or against it.

Senses. Ordinary language (colloquialism) does not have words for defining consciential structures and movements which do not exist according to common sense and are not restricted to the scope of the 5 basic senses of the human body (soma).

Polysemy. The same thing that happens with many other languages occurs with projectiological terminology: the inevitable incidence of polysemy and semantic overlap.

Barbarisms. The barbarisms and binomial expressions that exist within the scope of parapsychology – e.g., *psychometry* and *autoscopy* – sometimes require observations regarding their use, in order to avoid confusions regarding their meaning, especially when they refer to psychopathologies.

Systematization. It was necessary to invent new words having their own, general, systematic nomenclature in light of the reasons presented, for the sake of convenience, in order to avoid confusion, and to form a practical and functional vocabulary, in an effort to supply rationalization and organization for those occurrences that require it.

Neologisms. Therefore, a cast of coherent, inevitable neologisms, and their cognates, were proposed in a compilation of compound expressions, or umbrella terms, for phenomena which have no name or have no denomination within projectiology, such as the following 64: *adenoprojection; archeoprojection; audioprojection; bariprojection; biprojection; carbonoprojection; cephaloprojection; cephalosoma; chakroprojection; colorprojection; conscientiogram; conscientiologist; cosmoethics; cosmoprojection; deuterosoma; echocephalous; egokarma; electroprojection; epiprojection; groupkarma; gyroprojection; holochakra; holokarma; holosoma; hydroprojection; hypnoprojection; libidoprojection; megamaturity; musicoprojection; narcoprojection; nephoprojection; oligoprojection; omnicooperation; oneiroprojection; paraperceptibility; parapsychosphere; pedoprojection; pneumoprojection; podoprojection; polykarma; primoprojection; projectability; projectarium; projectiatry; projecting; projectiocritique; projectiography; projectiolatry; projectiologist; projectionalia; projectionate; projectionism; projectionomy; projectiophobia; projectiorrhea; projectiotherapy; projectiotoxin; psychomyology; self-hypnoprojection; stroboprojection; theorice; traumatoprojection; trithanatosis; verbaction; and others.*

Uninominality. As will be seen in the texts, the neologisms were not conceived arbitrarily. Preference was always given to the shortest possible uninominal expressions.

Problem. The problem is that there is not always a *less undesirable short expression.*

Encyclopedia. No encyclopedia can encompass the current world. More than half of the terms and concepts that the reader uses to speak about the present on an everyday basis, did not exist a century ago. These are of greater interest, because they direct your future. They are also the ones that the reader is frequently less familiar with.

Meanings. It will always be important to clearly differentiate expressions and the meanings of words, in order to avoid misunderstanding, subinformation and misinformation.

Tedium. Over time, terms bore people. We need to understand each other in order to comprehend the events around us.

Expressions. Words and expressions have a relative importance. As long as the necessary conventions, permitting an easy and accurate identification of the object named or the exact phenomenon under analysis are established, there is, in fact, no argument against the use of this or that nomenclature or terminology.

Glossary. This is why the *Glossary of Projectiology* was included at the end of this volume and the majority of chapters have their own synonymy in reference to their theme.

Fragmentation. Science is an engine that propels our intraphysical society. Nevertheless, it is being fragmented into more and more subdisciplines.

Codification. Each of these subdisciplines creates and uses its own coded language, obscure idiom or particular jargon.

Segregation. In ancient times, the precursors of science used Latin as a form of communication and, at the same time, as a way of distancing themselves from that which was popular. Today, specialized, scientific language *first* divides scientists into small *esoteric groups.* Closed off within the walls of university and research centers, researchers, professors and students work in premature and uninterrupted segregation. *Later,* the same *esoteric language* distances them from the public. These are the facts as they stand.

Myths. The *raison d'être* of science is to eliminate myths and mysteries. Unfortunately, however, we can conclude that science paradoxically creates its own myths and mysteries for the populace.

Divisiveness. In addition to the terminology of projectiology, and in order to minimize this great divisive problem of language, the technique of using the most universalistic (exhaustibility) definitions and copious synonymies, tending to establish a cohesion of ideas and efforts, with descriptive expressions, was used in this book. This aims to facilitate comprehension by the general reader.

Basis. We have named the phenomena and occurrences around us in a manner that is most adequate, according to our concepts, preconceptions and conditioning. Choose your favorite expressions. It will, however, be a measure of intelligence if one does not fail to understand the text and the experiments (basis, content, essence) because of the words.

Meanings. Words do not have meaning per se. Only concepts and experiences have significance. Here, background (content) does not deserve to be sacrificed in favor of form (frame), according to the intelligent premises of *confor* and *theorice.*

Symbol. Any word, however valid or appropriate it may be, is only a symbol of something that is behind it.

Word. Science does not have a word cult, nor does it perform *linguistic circumlocution.*

Fact. Words (linguistic symbols) rarely completely and accurately represent the fact or phenomenon to which they refer.

Content. Endless controversies regarding words *(word traps)* constitute a loss of resources, effort, time, attention and consciential energy.

Substance. It is essential that the priority questions of substance be studied.

Exoticism. Do not be surprised by the expressions. In the glossaries of technical terms, the interested individual will easily encounter expressions such as, "ageostrophic advection," "solstitial colure," or "hypergolic propergol" which, although exotic for the lay reader, are rational, coherent, precise and fluently employed in their fields, even in colloquial or everyday language.

Gongorism. The facts indicate that there is an inevitable international *technical Gongorism.*

Coherence. It is to be hoped that someone will appear in the near future and rename all parapsychic facts in a more adequate manner, establishing a coherent and even more concordant terminology.

Term. The author proposed the term *projeciologia* (projectiology) to name (or denominate) the science of consciential projection, on page 40 of the book *Projections of the Consciousness: A Diary of Out-of-Body Experiences,* published in São Paulo, Brazil, in 1981.

Translations. The following is the term *projeciologia* (Portuguese language) translated to 5 other languages:

1. **English:** *projectiology;*
2. **French:** *projectiologie;*
3. **German:** *projektiologie;*
4. **Spanish:** *proyecciología;*
5. **Italian:** *proiettologia.*

Certificate. The first edition of this book in Portuguese *(Projectiology: Panorama of Experiences of the Consciousness Outside the Human Body),* published in Rio de Janeiro, in 1986, constituted the birth certificate of this new science – *projectiology* – an area or subdiscipline of conscientiology.

Semantics. Semantics alters nothing in the structure of phenomena.

Conditioning. However, the conditioning and repression of the immature human being arises in all sectors of human existence.

Euphemisms. Researchers, even when *more advanced,* but *less* audacious, in the field of science, coin scientific euphemisms. They aim, with this attitude, to *sugarcoat* that which is non-orthodox (unorthodox, heterodox) or make it more acceptable or respectable.

Jargon. Thus, *fake technical jargon* is born. This is what generally happens nowadays in snobbish intraphysical societies or in the *dictionary of politically correct expressions.*

Glossed. The following, for example, are 13 *glossed* terms, or glossed expressions. They are *easier to swallow* for those who still prefer to maintain their narrow mindedness in regard to parapsychic phenomena:

1. **Autotelediplosia** – instead of physical bilocation.
2. **Biocommunication** – instead of telepathy or thought transmission.
3. **Dermo-optic vision** – instead of transposition of the sense of vision or extra-retinal vision.
4. **Ectestesia** – instead of exteriorization of sensitivity.
5. **Ectometaplasia** – instead of materialization of the extraphysical consciousness.
6. **Electrodermic points** – instead of acupuncture points.
7. **Electrophotography** – instead of *Kirlian photography.*
8. **Non-verbal communication** – instead of extrasensory perception.
9. **OBE** – instead of out-of-body experience.
10. **Parapsychology** – instead of metapsychics.
11. **Psychotronics** – instead of psychokinesis (parapsychology).
12. **Remote viewing** – instead of extracorporeal experience or departure of the consciousness from the human body with perceptions at a distance.
13. **Sophrology** – instead of mesmeric passes or animal magnetism.

Conscientiology. Projectiology remains definitively, structurally linked to the vast field of conscientiology (egology), namely to the center of sciences and the center of philosophies.

States. The study of conscientiology can be divided into 3 states:

1. **Extraphysicology.** The state of the extraphysical consciousness.
2. **Intraphysicology.** The state of the intraphysical consciousness.
3. **Projectiology.** The state of the projected consciousness (projective state).

Discoincidence. Projectiology presents a sufficiently broad field of research of manifestations if we include the exteriorization of energies, the *appendices* and exterior actions stemming from the consciousness. Nevertheless, all this occurs without the consciousness going along or, in other words: without it temporarily leaving its base in the cerebral hemispheres. Examples: the projection of the isolated holochakra (an energetic projection that some individuals confuse with projection of the mentalsoma); projections of the human aura; projection of the isolated *silver cord;* the common phenomenon of psychophony; and others.

Amplitude. In summary: only in regard to the occurrence of *discoincidentiology* is the world of projectiology research far more ample than it appears upon first analysis.

Autonomy. Those who wish to help make projectiology an entirely independent and autonomous science, with its own object and method, will need to use a *phenomenological perspective* (paraphenomenology) from this point forward.

Ordering. This will be done in the sense of updating, highlighting, delimiting, differentiating, describing and the systematic panoramic ordering – even greater than that which is indicated in this context – of the subjective (non-objectified) projectiological phenomena, as well as objective phenomena, per se.

Dispense. With the greatest of clarity, and under the permanent focus of scientific observation, projectiology presently assigns to a secondary status and will (in the near future) forever dispense with the submission of consciousnesses to religion, religionism or religiosity of any type, as practiced today, as well as parapsychism in any of its manifestations, when considered to be a vital, indispensable resource for consciential exchange (the interested individual can consider practicing penta, for example); besides many other aspects of nature and human life.

Number. Do not be surprised to find the circumstantiated presentation of a new scientific discipline in this book. The amount of sciences, which were far fewer at the beginning of the modern age, currently number approximately 2,000 and this figure grows moderately every year.

Approaches. This multiplication in the number of sciences implies the need to integrate them, uniting their research within interdisciplinary, transdisciplinary and multidisciplinary approaches.

Exchange. This is one of the objectives of this work: the exchange of information.

Rejection. New sciences should not be rejected based on the allegation that they contain many errors. An effort should be made to find grains of leading-edge relative truth among the chaff.

Culture. The singular cultural aspect inspired by projectiology places equal value on knowledge (consciential maturity), financial condition as a psychophysical anchor and the immortality of the nucleus of personal reality (personal evidence of survival of desoma), therefore attributing indispensable value to intellectuals, researchers and scholars in general.

Youths. This system of values has been strongly motivating more talented and ambitious youths or the new generations (group of existential inverters) to study this science.

Role. All this suggests that projectiology will occupy an important position in the set of human sciences and will eventually play a significant role in other sciences, as will be seen in the explicit arguments in various subsequent chapters.

Self-analysis. A profound study of the human consciousness (rational and circumscribed consciential self-analysis) can be efficaciously performed in 2 distinct ways or 2 senses:

1. **Qualification.** By the person in search of raw empiricism or by the researcher of modern science.

2. **Vision.** According to the development of an external, superficial, *centripetal* view, from outside inward; or in an internal, deep, *centrifugal* view, from inside outward.

Decompositions. In the first case, what occurs is the decomposable process of *humankind;* in the second case, the decomposable process of the *consciousness* is achieved.

Inner. Although, in both cases, all the data of the studies can be obtained by observing other personalities, each one of us has an inner life at hand that is open to our detailed inspection, the inspection of which is inalienable at no cost.

Categories. These self-analyses can fit within two basic categories: external and internal.

1. **External.** Rudimentary consciential self-analysis (decomposition of the human being-body) can be performed in a crescendo based upon 3 progressively more complex perspectives:

A. **Sociology.** Through sociology (including anthropology or somatics), or as an intelligent unit situated in various systems, such as the family and the state.

B. **Biology.** Through biology (including ancient natural history), or in its place among the known subhuman animals, in the natural order of physical or biophysical-chemical evolution.

C. **Physiology.** Through physiology (including human anatomy), or the functions of the chemical structure of its densest and most evident vehicle of manifestation, the human body (soma).

2. **Internal.** Sophisticated consciential self-analysis (decomposing of the consciousness-mind) can be performed in a crescendo based upon 3 progressively more complex approaches:

A. **Psychology.** Through psychology (including obscure psychoanalysis), or the way in which a personality presents itself.

B. **Parapsychology.** Through parapsychology (including the former science of metapsychics), or through its extrasensory manifestations (parapsychism) as individuality, beyond the 5 basic organic senses.

C. **Projectiology.** Through projectiology (including the condition of cosmoconsciousness), or through its integral self-awareness (animism, intraconscientiality) regarding meta-organisms and the latest, greatest *experimentum-crucis* with itself, arriving at the essence of the self, the final citadel of the intelligent principle, when the observer and the observed are the same object.

Holomaturity. Only at this point does the consciousness achieve true discernment regarding consciential maturity (holomaturity) and its consequences.

Position. This succinct, initial picture of the acquisition of *high priority knowledge,* or consciential self-analysis (conscientiogram) – *which is of supreme importance* – already allows the studious individual an initial, logical approach to the precise and unswervingly salient position of projectiology among the other sciences, as well as the extremely important role that this discipline will play in the existence of the human or social being from now on.

Forecast. Today, in 2002, thousands of persons – volunteers of the International Institute of Projectiology and Conscientiology (IIPC), the Center for Higher Studies of the Consciousness (CHSC), the International Academy of Conscientiology (IAC), the International Association for Evolution of the Consciousness (Aracê) and the International Campus of Conscientiology (ICC), active in 8 countries – can attest to this fact, which was forecast in 1985.

Polymathy. Let us be realistic: a culminant erudition or a plethora of encyclopedic knowledge (polymathy) of the entire human environment or all current philosophy, does little good without the individual becoming aware of the plenitude of consciential self-analysis (inner reform, self-overcoming).

Knowledge. The personal, direct knowledge obtained through projectiology, makes the following 11 occurrences dispensable, anachronistic, obsolete and outdated:

1. Theological faith.
2. Rationalized faith (self-corruption).
3. Revealed knowledge.
4. Theological knowledge.
5. The argument of authority *(magister dixit).*
6. Historical critiquing.
7. Acceptance of the explanations of others (belief).
8. Attitudes of faith.
9. Revealers of all types.
10. Incomplete ultra-specializations *(hemiplegic specialists).*
11. Non-universalist stagnated pseudosciences (factional, sectarian).

Path. Science is not the ideal way, but it is the *least undesirable.* It is also not the easiest, but it is the *most evolutionarily profitable* for the intraphysical consciousness.

Socialization. Projectiology does not have the slightest intention of emphasizing elitism in its procedures and research. We need to socialize our investigations as much as possible.

Square. However, the intraphysical projector, upon becoming self-aware on the face of the earth, is like the visitor who arrives at a *town square under siege,* where there is a *great* number of wounded persons and a *small* number of healthy persons and, albeit unwillingly and with great unease, is obliged to prioritize healthy persons.

Projectiologist. The *ideal projectiologist* is the individual who possesses a *refined* consciential tri-endowment or 4 professional strong traits in his/her human personality structure:

1. **Researcher.** The researcher with *spatial intelligence,* dedicated to the self- and hetero-investigation of intraphysical and extraphysical consciousnesses. He/she has a *mentalsomatic ego* (mentalsomatics), aiming at the realization of the existential maxiprogram, the clarification task and polykarmality.

2. **Sensitive.** The sensitive with *parapsychic intelligence,* dedicated to participative investigations of the multidimensionality of the consciousness. He/she possesses an *energetic ego* (holochakrology), aiming at conscientiotherapeutic self- and hetero-evaluations (consciential epicenter).

3. **Teacher.** The teacher with *communicative intelligence,* dedicated to conscientiological pedagogy and teaching. He/she possesses a *charismatic ego* (paragenetics), aiming to teach and publish books or produce consciential gestations.

4. **Philosopher.** The philosopher with *logical intelligence,* dedicated to studies, reading and debates. He/she possesses a *philosophical ego* (cosmoethics), aiming at the interdimensional experience or exemplification of cosmoethical principles.

Lines. Rationally speaking, the conscientiologist, in his/her consciential evolution – libertarian conscientiality – needs to respect the principles (and followers) of all lines of human knowledge while, at the same time, studying them deeply in order to be free of them, in this intraphysical life and in the next ones. The following 13 are examples: Cabalism, Christianity, Gnosis, Holistics, Orientalism, the Principles of Krishnamurti, the Principles of Pietro Ubaldi, Religious Syncretisms, Rosicrucianism, Spiritism, Theosophy, Umbandism, and Yoga. All were useful during a certain period for millions of intraphysical consciousnesses, but are now obsolete. Lucid projectability establishes a new level for consciential self-discernment. The execution of the advanced existential program requires *neophilia,* renovation, logical prioritizations within a personal universalistic holothosene without factiousness, and incessant *intraphysical recycling.*

Bibliography: Andrade (27, p. 146), Barros (86, p. 126), Bret (203, p. 21), Carvalho (253, p. 14), Franklin (548, p. 97), Green (632, p. 17), Paula (1208, p. 55), Vieira (1762, p. 40). The author's most recent works: *Conscientiology Redaction Manual; Miniglossary of Conscientiology; Conscientiogram.*

---

07. SCIENCES

Manners. Science can be performed in 2 manners:

1. **Orthodox.** First: orthodox, purely technological, mercantile or deep-rooted materialist (human body, soma). *Transitory* matter is the rudimentary representation of energy.

2. **Heterodox.** Second: universalistic, purely participative (heterodox or non-orthodox), evolutionary or deep-rooted consciential (mental body, mentalsoma, body of discernment).

Choice. For the scientific research of projectiology, in this context, the second, more advanced mode, was chosen.

Energy. The consciousness, when considered to be eternal, is more than mere energy.

Classification. In the generally accepted scheme of classification, sciences are divided into 4 categories:

1. Mathematical sciences.
2. Physical-chemical sciences.

3. Natural or biological sciences.

4. Moral and social sciences.

Social. The human moral and social sciences can be subdivided into 4 categories:

1. Logical.

2. Esthetical.

3. Moral.

4. Psychological.

Derivations. Parapsychology derives from psychology. Projectiology derives from parapsychology, or the earlier metapsychics.

Subdiscipline. Projectiology is currently (2002) more directly connected to and derived from conscientiology – the broadest world of sciences – as one of its dozens of areas or subdisciplines.

Principle. The fundamental principle of the scientific work is the rigid integrity of thought that accompanies the evidence of the facts wherever the evidence wishes to take this scientific work, within the limits of experimental error and the *honest mistake.*

Human. The human sciences, e.g., psychology, parapsychology, projectiology and conscientiology, fulfill all conditions required in order to be sciences.

Phenomena. The phenomena studied by human sciences are real and distinct from those addressed in experimental natural sciences.

Laws. The causes and laws discovered in the areas of human sciences express necessary relationships between facts and actions.

Conclusions. Its conclusions have an undeniable character of *approximations of certainty,* although of a different order from the approximations of certainty, which are characteristic of experimental natural sciences.

Observation. According to that which has been presented, experimental, natural science is generally based on careful observation. All scientific investigation must proceed from observed facts.

Inertia. In physical and biological sciences, the observed facts are, as a rule, *inert* facts. In this case, they are understood from the outside by an observer, who is neither disturbed by them, nor are they affected by the process of observation.

Microphysics. The uncertainty principle in microphysics tells us that the processes of observation disturb the field of that which is observed.

Mathematics. There are techniques in mathematics that keep the observer in a certain type of *relationship of exteriority* with that which is observed and, strictly speaking, even to his/her own techniques of observation.

Disturbance. However, in sciences of *personal interaction,* e.g., psychology, parapsychology, projectiology and conscientiology, the *self-psychic facts* develop in another manner. Not only is the reciprocal disturbance between the observer and the observed inevitable in all cases, but it is the reciprocal disturbance itself – and not the disturbed or disturbing personal entities – which produces the primary facts upon which the theory is based.

Ontology. In natural sciences – physics, for example – the observer-observed relationship is ontologically discontinuous. That is to say, the subject is faced with the object (inert totality), which allows a purely exterior description of the field that is observed *(heteropsychic facts).*

Replicability. There are 2 aspects that must be considered regarding the replicability of scientific experiments:

1. **Possibility.** In the *natural sciences,* where analysis implies the supposition of a perspective of complete exteriority, the verifiability and *falsifiability of hypotheses* depends upon the replicability of situations.

2. **Impossibility.** In the *human sciences,* however, the repetition of a vital-historical situation of an individual or group becomes impossible, in principle. These are the facts.

Rationality. In the natural sciences, analytical rationality is applied where the propositions are formed outside the reality to which they refer.

Passivity. Another antagonistic condition occurs. In this case, it is a dual passivity:

1. **System.** The observed *system* – regardless of the actions and reactions that are occurring within this system – is passive with respect to the observer.

2. **Observer.** The *observer,* in turn, is passive in relation to the system which is observed and those observed facts are registered within, from outside. The *observer* is also passive in relation to the inference that is made from these facts.

Dialectic. In human sciences, however, dialectic (concrete) rationality is applied, in a totalizing activity (interaction), where the act of knowing relates to the object that is known.

Supposition. The *scientific world* never completely reflects the *real world,* but certain of its selected characteristics that are organized based upon suppositions which are accepted as true.

Precision. Human sciences, including projectiology, doubtless occupy the last place in the hierarchy of the sciences, with regard to their relative degree of precision and the rigor of their results. Their study is thus far more difficult.

Stability. Although its laws are more flexible and less rigorous, they express sufficient stability and constancy, to the degree that they can establish true sciences.

Exactness. For this reason, human sciences are not pseudosciences. In the strictest sense, there is no truly exact science.

Intervening. In light of what has been presented, the following 4 intervening factors in the world of human sciences merit attention:

1. **Achievement.** Many factors pertinent to human sciences are not achieved directly. For example: psychic and parapsychic phenomena which only manifest within the consciousness (intraconsciential micro-universe) and in human behavior. This creates difficulties for making generalizations.

2. **Complexity.** Human factors (psychic and parapsychic) imply greater complexity than quantitative or physical facts. As complexity increases, so do difficulties and the consequent occasion for error, omission, confusion or entropy. This is the source of a variety of sometimes disconcerting opinions on essential subjects within human sciences in general and parapsychic areas in particular.

3. **Liberty.** Physical phenomena, as they are directed by defined laws, can be foreseen and some provoked in order to be better observed. Meanwhile, freedom, which interferes somewhat in human acts and extraphysical experiences, impedes any exact forecast, making calculations in human sciences generally only approximate, and more specifically so in the areas of paraperceptibilities (paraperceptiology).

4. **Evaluation.** Natural sciences deal with material facts and objects which can be weighed and measured, at least indirectly. Thus, this intervention of measuring translates into results which have some degree of mathematical precision.

Quantification. The facts of human beings and their supposed extraphysical experiences, as they are qualitative, cannot have any extremely rigorous quantitative evaluation applied to them.

Causes. Causes in science can be: necessary, sufficient, contributory, contingent, alternative, and others. However, we cannot expect that a single cause, by itself, is sufficient to produce phenomena.

Conjunction. It is necessary to have a conjunction of causes (interaction, confluence) which, when mutually influencing each other, creates a situation where the phenomenon is able to manifest.

Factors. Therefore, one of the extremely important works in the research project is to define the factors that are present and influence the situation.

Universality. On the one hand, there is always the vital component of universality in the phenomenological field of projectiology.

Exceptions. On the other hand, it will be essential to endeavor to classify the exceptions when addressing projectiological phenomena.

Variables. Science is, by its very nature, inexhaustible. There are many variables which remain hidden in all sectors of projectiology research and await discovery. This *state of affairs* will continue for many human generations to come.

End. There is no end to the amount of knowledge we can acquire.

Dimensions. All things external to the physical universe hold no significance for conventional, materialistic, incomplete science and its practical realization, namely technology. Nevertheless, projective consciential phenomena prove – particularly for the consciousness of the researcher-object – the existence of parallel universes, hyperspaces, and the mental dimension or the dimension of cosmoconsciousness.

Theories. Theories are essential parts of science (see chapter 1). The theory referring to a system which is necessarily singular, in the manner of the physical universe of the physicalist scientist, cannot – and should not – be complete.

Unification. The condition would be much worse in relation to any theory that endeavors to embody and unify all systems of parallel universes where it is supposed that the consciousness gravitates in a condition of continuous evolution.

Scale. With the support of the aforementioned criteria for basic research in projectiology, or in all fields of conscientiology, there is an endeavor to delve deeper into known consciential phenomena, correlated to the research, that evolve in a delimited manner along a clear scale, or in a nucleus of knowledge that spans from the point at which the consciousness becomes human (individualized) to the point at which it is presumed to discard its vehicles of manifestation and evolve isolated in the pure mental dimension (trithanatosis, mentalsomatic dimension, free consciousness or FC).

Boundaries. The origin of the consciousness, at one extreme, and its evolution in the pure mental dimension, at the other extreme, constitute the farthest boundaries of our current, absolute ignorance of the diverse worlds, planes, dimensions, environments, communities, conditions, consciential states and activities of interworld consciential exchanges (between communities and *existing paracommunities*).

Undefined. Everything which was left behind in the evolutionary progression of the consciousness, or which occurs beyond this, constitutes the unknown – *the preserved undefined* – which offers itself as a priority megachallenge for continued research for other terrestrial generations or, if possible, for all of us, in other probable lifetimes, resomas, somas and desomas, in individual and group consciential self-relays.

Scientists. Productive scientists generally present 6 characteristic personality traits that enrich their lives with each discovery:

1. **Curiosity.** Intellectual curiosity.
2. **Motivation.** Enthusiasm or motivation in their works.
3. **Independence.** Independence and mental flexibility.
4. **Dedication.** An inclination toward long hours of dedication.
5. **Credit.** The ambition to struggle to achieve credit for their realizations.
6. **Benefits.** The desire to benefit humanity.

Control. Scientists do not seek conformity. Nor are they merely attempting to repeat the experiments of others, or placing the experimental data that others have obtained in doubt. Far from it. It is simply that the more we develop the similarities and the ordered relationships between events, the closer we are to the prediction and effective control of our science.

Approximations. Science is not conducted using only common sense. Scientific knowledge is not satisfied only with *opinions*. It needs *approximations of certainty*.

Verifications. In the experimental verifications of projectiology, whether they be instrumented or based on personal research, the projectiologist, since the investigated subjects are humans, cannot make facts of interest repeat themselves at will, using the comparative system more often.

Statistics. Nevertheless, statistical means can be used that, in the end, will provide a relative quantitative vision, whether in averages, percentages, curves or other resources.

Involvements. One of the oldest ideals of science is to make it such that researchers avoid any type of personal involvement with that being researched. Nevertheless, according to what has been analyzed, it will always be very difficult to completely remove participative research from projectiology and all of the subdisciplines of conscientiology.

Communion. Generally speaking, the subject and the object always need to somehow commune with each other in order for the events to occur. One cannot completely exclude the other.

Openness. What should be sought, then, is maximum neutrality, impersonality, impartiality and universality in relation to the object of study, facing the facts in the effective condition of an *open-minded* ego, as though it were a *blank sheet of paper,* or a *tabula rasa,* that will receive the external impressions without influencing them.

Participation. The observer is participatory when he/she is part of the situation and performs a function or role in it.

Ambivalence. The observer can begin in the non-participatory condition and later become participatory, and vice versa.

Objectivity. The more someone is participatory, the more possible it is to be emotionally involved, losing objectivity and thus jeopardizing the observation. However, at least in certain circumstances, the observation of situations in which the individual does not participate becomes very difficult or very superficial.

Impersonalization. Science is always the result of an individual's experience. Despite everything that has been written, the pure impersonal experience truly does not exist.

Experience. It is important to register some crucial observations at this point. All knowledge of reality comes from experience and refers to it.

Senses. Conventional, physicalist science is based upon the 5 basic senses of the human body (soma). These senses permit anyone to have knowledge about reality through direct, personal experience.

Questions. What blame can be attributed to the author, or you, the reader, as a projectionist or conscientiologist, if we can employ other senses beyond the 5 above-mentioned basic senses?

Intelligence. What responsibility can be attributed to the author, or to you, the reader, if we are able to spontaneously obtain knowledge from other realities through other experiences beyond the experiences and existences of many other individuals? Besides this, we can be independent researchers, since we have the most hard earned freedom, which is the expression of that which we think, feel and experience, with regard to self-persuasive phenomena, in our thosenity or the union of idea, sentiment and personal energies. The *evolutionary* responsibility is far greater in this case. We are already starting to use *evolutionary intelligence.*

Coexistence. Based upon these facts, how should we coexist with contemporary conventional science? How can we reconcile our experiences, the author's and yours, which enrich and gratify us, with the current conventional experiences of others?

Dilemma. This book is an attempt to respond with the greatest possible discernment and logic to those dilemmic issues of the advanced projector, projectiologist or conscientiologist.

Youths. It is hoped that, in the future, this conflictive, human and parapsychic dilemma will be definitively eliminated from upcoming generations, notably those parapsychic youths with some innate wisdom, paragenetics or those arriving from more recent intermissive courses.

Hopes. Our hopes are pinned on these new generations.

Bibliography: Tart (1660, p. 177). The author's recent works: *700 Conscientiology Experiments; 200 Conscientiology Theorices.*

08. HISTORY OF PROJECTIOLOGY

Definition. History of projectiology: chronological exposition of projectiological facts.

Synonymy: historical exposition of projectiology; projectiological parahistory.

Phenomenology. The experience of the consciousness outside the human body is an ancient, universal phenomenon of all epochs, races and peoples, even those considered "non-intellectualized," underdeveloped or primitive.

Paraphysiology. Lucid projection is encountered in the first narratives of classic antiquity, in Biblical, Egyptian and Babylonian antiquity, in the sacred chronicles of the East; appearing as much in the lives of ignorant individuals as in the existence of sages and intellectuals as a natural or biological faculty or, in other words, one of physiological origin or, more precisely, paraphysiological origin, according to the historical registers of the experience of humanity; it is similar, in many aspects, to various other altered states of consciousness, such as: daydream, nightmare, somnambulism, dream, sleep and others.

Universality. Human history (pastology) shows that, since time immemorial, human lucid projection has been common in all countries and was registered in an ample, universal manner in all cultures and intraphysical societies, as well as in the most ancient tribal societies, and even those in prehistoric eras, at the dawn of all civilizations.

Patterns. Narratives of lucid projections follow similar patterns, the same thing happening with the process through which the individual's consciousness leaves the physical body, the conditions of the mind and the human body, depending upon the experience. There are frequently identical reasons and motivations for the phenomenon to occur.

Consensus. Despite differences in culture, epoch, religion, nationality and language, there has been an invariable, persistent substantial uniformity over time, in all places, among all civilizations, throughout the course of history, thus arriving at similar conclusions with respect to the reality of the departure of the consciousness from the human body, in another vehicle of consciential manifestation, always following the same basic constants.

Archetypal. The universal distribution in different cultures throughout history, as mentioned above, makes lucid projection an archetypal experience, that is to say: it is potentially found in many members of the human race only by virtue of being human.

Confirmation. From this, we can also confirm the typically physiological, or paraphysiological, origin of the human lucid projection experience as a consciential state.

Personalities. The abovementioned uniformity derives from the practical affirmations of persons with disparate cultural backgrounds and origins, equal to the following 72, which are readily found in the reports of works including mentions of projective cases: aboriginal Americans, African healers, alchemists, Anglican devotees, animists of the East, anthroposophists, apostles of the New Testament, ascetics, Australian Indians, authors, *brujos,* businesspersons, Catholic devotees, Christian mystics, *civilized persons,* computer programmers, computer scientists, conscientiologists, dissident sages, sundry Spiritualists, engineers, environmentalists, executives, existential inverters, existential recyclers, exoterists, fakirs, feminists, fortune-tellers, Greek philosophers, gurus, healers, initiated Indians, inspired writers, journalists, *mahatmas,* magicians, medicine men, members of the clergy, metapsychics, Mexican Indians, military researchers, nurses, occultists, parapsychologists, peais, penta practitioners, physicians, physicists, physiologists, pilots, poets, politicians, prisoners, professors, prophets of the Old Testament, psychologists, Rosicrucians, *sadus,* scientists, seers, sensitive-researchers, sensitives, Siberian shamans, Spiritists, teachers, technologists, Theosophists, Tibetan Lamas, Western mediums, witch doctors, yogis.

09.   PERIODS   OF   PROJECTIOLOGY

History. The history of projectiology can be divided into 4 distinct periods:

1. The ancient period.
2. The esoteric period.
3. The exoteric period.
4. The laboratorial period.

Pre-history. Since the beginning of recorded human history, one persuasive factor has withstood all skepticism: the extraordinary sum of projective phenomena of the human consciousness and its continued repetition from century to century, from country to country, from one intraphysical society to another.

Legends. There are legends, stemming from prehistoric times, that tell of sages whose *souls* would leave their human bodies and communicate with the *gods.*

Classics. In each of the great classics of ancient culture, lucid projection was known, even by the ancient people of Israel, Persia and India.

Egypt. Beginning with the most primitive cultures, human consciousnesses have been practicing rituals in order to leave the dense body. In Ancient Egypt (5004-3064 B.C.) the worship of the dead was performed through the *ka* or the double, which we now call the *psychosoma.*

Practices. Nowadays, the frenzied pursuit of this same objective is sought in the gyratory dances of the dervishes, the gyrations of *Umbanda* (*Umbanda* is an Afro-Brazilian, spiritist, religious practice), besides innumerous other religious, syncretic, esoteric or animic-parapsychic (intra and extraconsciential) practices.

Greece. For centuries, the Ancient Greeks sought the way to inner illumination through the ceremonies at the temple of Eleusis, where they felt spiritually reborn after participating in rituals – considered to be sacred – for days on end.

Rituals. A great part of these rituals consisted in the experience of lucid projection of the consciousness, which was induced to leave the human body or the coincidence of its vehicles of manifestation.

Losses. However, the genuine secret techniques used in these projective rites were lost, leaving only the oral traditions on the subject which ended up in India and Tibet.

Bibliography: Currie (354, p. 78).

10.   ANCIENT   PERIOD   OF   PROJECTIOLOGY

Definition. Antiquity: the people, human beings, and beliefs of other eras or primeval times in the history of humanity.

Synonymy: remote historical era; ancient historical period.

First. The first historical, ancient or empirical period of projectiology begins with humanity itself and ends at the end of the fourteenth century.

Mythology. The first historical period includes spontaneous and provoked lucid consciential projections registered in the mythology of primitive societies, which still remain in the folklore of many nations, and even in multiple initiations in various temples, ever since tribal religions have existed in all terrestrial civilizations.

Initiations. In this phase, lucid consciential projections were hidden under the generic name of *initiations.* They were extremely restricted to the recesses of the temples, in all religions, the *simple,* primitive ones, as well as those more *developed* (and currently existing) ones. Their processes had profound mystical connotations, partly as a resource for the physical and social survival of their chiefs (believers, followers, acolytes, confreres).

Persecution. Of course, in this period, in many cases, those who produced the experience of lucid consciential projection suffered from the pressures of the fanaticism of that time, being labeled as crazy or demented and accused of witchcraft.

Condemnation. Parapsychic practices in general, classified as spurious practices, were routinely and severely condemned, as can be confirmed in the following passages from the Bible's own text:

1. **Witches.** Witches and magicians should be summarily executed (Exod. 22:18).
2. **Parapsychism.** The exercising of parapsychic faculties were strictly prohibited (Lev. 19:26).
3. **Exile.** Active animists and mediums (sensitives) were detested and exiled (Deut. 18:10).
4. **Prophets.** Prophets and soothsayers were summarily expelled from the places where they appeared (2 Kings 21:6).
5. **Books.** Books about magic, animism and parapsychism were exemplarily burned, in public, in autos-da-fé (Acts 19:19).

Bibliography: Vieira (1747, p. 20).

11. ESOTERIC PERIOD OF PROJECTIOLOGY

Definition. Esotericism: ancient doctrine or antiquated attitude that advocated reserving the teaching of (scientific, philosophical or religious) truth to a restricted, closed number of chosen persons, generally through limited and secret initiations.

Synonymy: group autism; hermetism; occultism.

Autism. Esotericism or occultism was a type of *group autism.*

Second. The second historical (esoteric or pre-scientific) period of projectiology spans from the fifteenth to the nineteenth century.

Esoteric. It is common knowledge that the term *esoteric* refers to all things requiring initiation limited to a reduced circle of people in order to be understood (segregation, discrimination, sectarianism, factionalism, elitism, *fetal corporatism*).

Withholding. In this phase, lucid consciential projection was characterized by the prejudicial aspect of widespread withholding of adequate pertinent information from the public (populace).

Fascination. Bound by ignorance regarding effective means for its voluntary production, the projective phenomenon was always covered up by a *thick smoke screen,* being maintained as an instrument of political domination, through the mystical fascination of the masses by the medieval obscurantist climate, a reflection of previous centuries or, perhaps more precisely, *millennia.*

Concealment. The theme of lucid projection was kept concealed, being criminally prohibited to the public – the *populace* – circulating only through the most restricted avenues of information.

Reactionism. In this phase, at the hands of extremely powerful legions of reactionaries, the implacable persecution of sensitives and projectors, generalized *witch* hunting (most notably throughout Europe) and the predominance of beliefs, dogmas, preconceptions, superstitions, taboos and erroneous traditions arose as never before.

Monopoly. The methods employed to project with lucidity through the centuries and successive generations were prohibited from public scrutiny in this esoteric period, in adherence to an orthodox, monopolizing, segregationist, caste policy.

Policy. This policy, based on censure, concealment of information and the intentional covering up of facts, permitted the truth to be stifled, thus prohibiting adepts and initiates from speaking about their projective experiences in public. These individuals would never say or register everything they experienced and knew regarding parapsychic phenomena.

Remnants. Remnants can still be seen today of the cover-up of facts and the misanthropic hermetism of lucid projection induction techniques stemming from Tibetan yogis, where misinformation is highlighted with the clear intention of discouraging newcomers to the subject.

Adulteration. The dissimulation of facts becomes clear through the undisguised adulteration of precepts and the creation of cover-ups performed using the following 4 intentional, spurious resources:

1. Excessively refined methods (circumlocutions).
2. Ridiculous practices (superimposed rites).
3. Abstruse rituals (infantilisms).
4. Confused terminology (primitive jargon).

Subinformation. The same occurs, for example, with two categories of subinformation:

1. The information supplied by the International Rosicrucian Society, with respect to *psychic projection* (seventh and eleventh stages).
2. The phenomenon of physical bilocation in the field of the hagiology of the Vatican (Catholic clericalism).

Occultism. Up until that time, the teachings on lucid projection remained in the shadows, in obdurate silence, behind the wall of secrecy, in the hands of only those fervent autistic adepts of esotericism (Eastern and Western), or occultism, in the hermetic societies, which were closed around their members, who always harbored repugnance towards performing proselytism and spreading their knowledge.

Principle. The occultists operated from the apparently logical principle – the strategy of occultation – which holds that their doctrine should be deliberately kept hidden and secret, as, upon being revealed, it would obviously no longer be occult.

Repression. In fact, revealing this would eliminate repression (indoctrination, conditioning, *abdominal brainwashing,* sacralization, intellectual coercion) in society and the segregationist and discriminatory spirit that kept the initiates gathered around the same principles, in a manner similar to social forms of control, reward and punishment that help to preserve, protect, mask and reinforce the system of inequalities or the norms of any other underdeveloped intraphysical society in general.

Time. However, time went on until the point where these segregationist reasons no longer existed, thus ending the boycott by the clearly esoteric aspect of projective practices, thereby allowing rationality, the sense of fraternity and the freedom of manifestation to prevail.

Clarification. Lucid projection experiences have thus provided clarification, comfort and a reasonable degree of certainty regarding extraphysical or multidimensional reality to many people.

De-occultism. As with all sciences, *projectiology* has the precise purpose of revealing occult issues (*de-occultism* or consciential openness) and never withholding them.

Universalism. Consciential or universalistic institutions do not defend the *exclusion* of consciousnesses, but defend the *excluded* of two origins and two types:

1. **Somatic.** The *hetero-excluded:* dispossessed humans assisted through the consolation task.
2. **Mentalsomatic.** Those *self-excluded* by leading-edge relative truths: intruders, blind guides and minidissidents who are assisted through the clarification task.

Stop. After lucid projectors were ridiculed, persecuted, imprisoned, castigated, cremated and canonized, in that order, lucid projection gradually stopped being characterized as a mere gross manifestation of witchcraft.

Hagiography. For a period of time, this phenomenon was included in the mystical visions of devotees and theologians, and in the paintings, biographies and narratives of hagiography (Roman Catholicism).

Define. Besides the cases of consciential bilocation listed among the phenomena of hagiography throughout the course of time, 2 projectors from the eighteenth century, who helped define the history of projectiology, deserve a special mention:

1. **Say.** First, the American Quaker minister, Thomas Say (1709-1796), who left a detailed report of a lucid projection, produced while he was in a coma in 1726.

2. **Swedenborg.** The second milestone in the history of projectiology comes to us from the Swedish philosopher, theologian and seer from the eighteenth century, Emanuel Swedenborg (1688-1772).

Precursor. Swedenborg was the precursor of projectiology, the greatest lucid projector that had arisen at that time, a pioneer in receiving the messages of extraphysical consciousnesses or helpers.

Diaries. As an author, Swedenborg left numerous volumes that included reports of his experiences, notably "Diarii Spiritualis" (5 volumes), in which he narrated many of his lucid projections, beginning in 1745, that continued in an uninterrupted series until 1765. They included lofty expressions regarding the double life of the intraphysical consciousness (intraphysicology) when projected in the consciential dimensions (projected intraphysical consciousness, extraphysicology).

Prophet. The brilliant French writer, Honoré de Balzac (1799-1850) – the prophet of projectiology – clearly and incontrovertibly announced the appearance of a *new science,* even before the advent of spiritism, metapsychics, parapsychology and psychotronics, in 1832.

Sesquicentennial. In 1982, the author privately commemorated the 150th anniversary of this precognition.

Affirmations. Balzac used the character *Louis Lambert,* in his psychological, autobiographical novel by the same name, to voice the following questions and affirmations:

1. **French.** "Si j'étais ici pendant que je dormais dans mon alcôve, ce fait ne constitue-t-il pas une *séparation complète* entre mon corps et mon être intérieur?" "Or, si mon esprit et mon corps ont pu se quitter pendant le sommeil, pourquoi ne les ferais-je pas également divorcer ainsi pendant la veille?" "Ces faits se sont accomplis par la puissance d'une *faculté* qui met em oeuvre un *second être* à qui mon corps sert d'enveloppe ..." "Si, pendant la nuit ... dans la plus parfaite immobilité j'ai franchi des espaces, nous aurions des facultés internes, indépendantes des lois physiques extérieures." "Comment les hommes ont-ils si peu réfléchi jusqu'alors aux accidents du sommeil qui accusent en l'homme une double vie? N'y aurait-il pas une *nouvelle science* dans ce phénomène?" (p. 71 and 72, Gallimard Editions, 1980. Some expressions were italicized here).

2. **English.** "If I was here while sleeping in my bedroom, does this fact not constitute a *complete separation* between my body and inner being?" "Well, if my spirit and my body could separate during sleep, why could I not equally divorce them while awake?" "These facts are verified by the power of a *faculty* which puts in movement a *second being* for which my body serves as a housing." "If, during the night… in the most absolute immobility I went through space, then humans have inner faculties which are independent from external physical laws." "Why have humans reflected so little until now upon the accidents of sleep that indicate a double life? Will there not be a *new science* in this phenomenon?"

Translation. As can be read in the text of this volume by Balzac, we can now *technically translate* some expressions that he used:

1. **Discoincidence.** *Complete separation* is now called *discoincidence* of the vehicles of manifestation of the consciousness or intraphysical consciousness.

2. **LPB.** The *faculty* he refers to is now called *lucid projectability (LPB).*

3. **Psychosoma.** The *second being,* in this case, is the *psychosoma,* the parabody of emotions.

4. **Projectiology.** The *new science* was named *projectiology,* one of the many subdisciplines of conscientiology.

Facts. As can be logically concluded, all this occurred according to natural facts, in the exact and rational manner in which it was forecast. This subject will be addressed in greater detail in the next chapter (p. 67, 73).

Spiritism. Finally, the lucid projection experience was established in the supernatural condition of "physical bilocation" or "bicorporeity" in the studies of the "emancipation of the soul," expressions which were frequently used by authors of the nineteenth century, including the codifier of Spiritism in France, Allan Kardec, or Leon Hypolite Denizard Rivail (1804-1869).

12. PRECOGNITIONS REGARDING PROJECTIOLOGY

Definition. Precognition: the phenomenon of foreseeing (prediction) future facts, performed by a precognitor. These names formerly were: *prophecy, prophet.*

Synonymy: foreseeing; foretelling; paragnosis; prediction; pregnosis; presaging.

Futurology. Projectiology, as a science, is obviously not based on any doctrine founded on prophecies or *prophetism,* much less in incipient futurology, which is still not entirely reliable. Anyone who has a calendar can be a futurologist or begin to work with forecasting.

Documentation. It is clarifying and educational, however, to document the facts relative to the esoteric period in the history of projectiology. That is why this chapter is included in this volume.

Nostradamus. Out of healthy curiosity, or responsible intellectual speculation, let us first analyze two quatrains from the book *Centuries,* by Michel de Nostradamus (1503-1566), the celebrated French astronomer and physician.

Self-critique. Personally, the author is not a *nostradamist,* nor does he consider himself, in this analysis, to be an astute exegete against the possible *nostradamic traps,* which are ever-present for the commentator or translator of his texts.

Logic. We have merely used some logic here within the labyrinth that constitutes his extremely *entropic* quatrains.

Clouds. Interpretation of *Centuries,* at first sight, is very similar to the interpretation of the shapes of clouds in the sky: any fertile imagination arrives at the most delirious conceptions, finding whatever they wish in the pictorial composition of the clouds.

Translation. Thus it is best that the aware reader be forewarned regarding the aspect of *"si non é vero, é bene trovatto,"* which should not be disregarded in these considerations, with respect to nostradamic quatrains.

Distortion. Here, the analyst can adjust the meaning of the texts to the facts, also distorting the sense of the message in order for it to coincide with his/her own ideas.

Characteristics. In research performed using theorice and confor, we can easily arrive at the characteristics of nostradamic texts, in which we can detect at least 7 variables, with regard to their *form:*

1. **Quatrains.** The quatrains were not written in chronological order with respect to the events upon which they focused, there being only a few consecutive *series of quatrains.*

2. **Chronology.** He predicts the events, always remaining confused regarding the period and chronological order of the precognitive facts.

3. **Phraseology.** The nebulous phraseology demonstrates vagueness, ambiguity and double meaning.

4. **Languages.** There is a purposeful confused mixture of languages, always generating controversy.

5. **Epoch.** His profound involvement with the sociocultural environment (habitat) – the epoch of paradoxes, the sixteenth century – becomes clear.

6. **Pressure.** There was always his life as a convert – a converted Jew – under the constant, implacable pressure of the Inquisition.

7. **History.** The historic facts related to the subsequent centuries resulted in the majority of the episodes he referred to having already lost the interest that they could have had.

Publications. Nevertheless, we should not forget the fact that, four-and-a-half centuries after his desoma, an average of 30 new specialized publications or works have been published every century, commenting either favorably or unfavorably upon his works.

Culture. Still within confor, we can see, in relation to *content,* that he paradoxically described the world of the future using elements of his time, being a person of polymorphous culture, according to the following 5 intellectual aspects:

1. **Metaphors.** He constantly and deliberately used anagrams, symbols, metaphors, periphrases, Latinisms, enigmas and wordplay.

2. **Grammar.** He used metaplasms as well as poetic and rhetorical grammatical resources, such as: aphaeresis, apocopes, elipses, epentheses, hyperbole, metastases, protheses, syncopes and synecdoches.

3. **Repetitions.** He used phonetic spellings and intentional repetitions, which were sometimes quite intelligent and pertinent.

4. **Polyglotism.** In his polyglotism, he included archaic French, Latin, Provençal, Greek, Spanish and Hebrew.

5. **Polyvalence.** It should not be forgotten, in this context, that Nostradamus was a doctor of medicine, pharmacologist, astronomer, mathematician and historian, as well as being a hermetic philosopher attaché to the courts of that time.

Parapsychic. Regarding parapsychism, Nostradamus showed the following 4 noteworthy strong traits, among others:

1. **Paraperceptiology.** He accepted the reality of hauntings or poltergeists, according to observations in the historical registers in reference to him and as written in Century 7, Quatrain 41.

2. **Serenology.** He knew of the existence of *serenissimi (Homo sapiens serenissimus),* at that time referred to as the *celestial deities* or *angelic beings.*

3. **Paratechnology.** He evoked extraphysical beings using the bronze tripod, the ancient 3-legged table used by the Pythia of the Oracle of Delphi, the same classic furniture of the *gyrating tables* phenomena from the epoch of Allan Kardec.

4. **Desomatic.** Some suspect that he deliberately sponsored his *self-desoma.*

Probabilities. Even when attributing the data of his predictions to coincidence, synchronicity or the law of mathematical probability, Nostradamus gave details: names of persons; names of places; references to buildings still not constructed or even imagined at that time; correct future time periods; precise dates, with the exact months of future events; and other details that, for him, were of future history which, in fact, leads any rational, unbiased observer to seriously deliberate upon his precognitive lucubrations, that are exempt from the influences of mysticism, sacralization, occultism, folklore, delirium, surrealism and exploitations of all types that his works have endured for the last *four-and-a-half centuries.*

Transcendence. There are two occurrences that show logical aspects of profound transcendence and subtlety in the rational analysis of the precognitions of Nostradamus:

1. **Comprehension.** First occurrence: certain visions of facts that he foresaw were not understood even by himself, the precognitor, as occurs with contemporary precognitors.

2. **Words.** Second occurrence: certain expressions in the verses of the quatrains of the *Centuries* were used in an apparently confused or inadequate manner for the exposition of the thoughts, even for Nostradamus' epoch. Nevertheless, they appeared to be perfectly adequate at the exact time in the future for which they were destined and to which they referred.

Meanings. This occurs due to psychological, mesological and natural changes in the meaning or significance of the words occurring in the succession of human generations and the passing of centuries.

World. This emphasizes that the world of precognitive vision, of that time, was far more ample and subtle than it appeared.

Capsules. Not only in regard to the essence, the future facts that were foretold, but, beyond this, even with regard to printed matter, the new meanings that certain terms would have – *mental time capsules* – in reference to the future epoch.

Coin. In this case, the statements of precognition, much like an old coin, increase in value with the passage of time; that which had an insignificant *face* value, in its own time, later, when it is already out of circulation, has an enormous *intrinsic* value. In this semantic aspect, Nostradamus exhibits a singular ability among all precognitors registered by human history. The second event referred to confirms and clearly explains the first event.

Positivity. Let us decipher only 2 quatrains of the *Centuries,* being among the most obscure, which are routinely avoided by the exegetes, perhaps because they are *positive* or pacifying, and thereby do not furnish disastrous, catastrophic or terrifying elements, being highly powerful explosive ammunition in the hands of the *prophets of chaos,* such as: calamities, floods, droughts, earthquakes and wars (battles, invasions, genocides and assassinations), thus remaining without commercial appeal to sensationalist minds.

Original. Let us begin with an analysis of the original version of a strophe of 4 verses, namely Quatrain 27 in Nostradamus' Century 2, published in 1555:

> *"Le divin verbe será du ciel frappé,*
> *Qui ne pourra procéder plus avant:*
> *Du resserant le secret estoupé,*
> *Qu'on marchera par-dessus & devant."*

Archaicism. The following are the meanings of expressions in this Quatrain 27 in Nostradamus' Century 2, written in the archaic French of the sixteenth century:

Le divin verbe: the divine verb; the divine word. It is an expression having a double meaning, which can also mean mantra, verbal formula, cryptic verse. The univocal nature of the adjective *divin* in the *Centuries: Le divin mal,* Century 1, Quatrain 88, the sacred hatred (the opposite of the use in the quatrain under analysis); the sacred evil; the epileptic attack; or, nowadays, the convulsive syndrome.

Frappé: beat; give punches; attack; knock down; strike. This verb is also used in Century 3, Quatrain 59 and C. 4, Q. 33.

Du ciel frappé: stricken from above; fallen from the sky; struck by lightning; knocked down from the sky. An expression also used in Century 1, Q. 27 and C. 2, Q. 56.

Pourra: could. An expression also used in Century 8, Q. 53 and C. 10, Q. 32.

Procéder: result in; lead to.

Avant: before, the first of.

Reserare: discover; unveil; open; reveal.

Estouper or *estoper (étoupé):* guard; close; shut someone up. Archaic French.

Marchera: march; walk; go (infinitive: *marcher*).

Par-dessus: walk over someone; insult; walk past; walk on; hover over.

&: et: and; conjunction.

Devant: in front of someone; precede.

Translation. The following is a synthetic, simple, literal translation of the verses of Nostradamus' 2, Quatrain 27 to English:

> *"The divine word will be revealed from the sky,*
> *And can no longer be any other way:*
> *Unveiling the guarded secret,*
> *It will go upward and forward."*

Prose. The following is an analytical interpretation, in prose, of the same Quatrain 27 in Century 2, which could be the *prophecy of Nostradamus regarding projectiology.*

The divine word (relative truth; projectiology; the extraphysical, multiexistential, self-defensive mantra) **will be attacked** (stricken from above) **from the sky** (extraphysical dimension), **unveiled but which can no longer be any other way** (nothing will succeed against it)**: unveiling the guarded secret** (projectability, part of the physiology of the consciousness; the projection of the lucid consciousness), **will go upward** (will influence all intraphysical and extraphysical things) **and forward** (beyond; through multidimensionality).

Research. The following are 5 detailed expressions from Quatrain 27, according to the research of projectiology:

Le divin verbe: projectiology; a mantra, one of the projective techniques.
Ciel: the extraphysical dimension; multidimensionality.
Resserant le secret: unveiling the *para*physiological secret; the opening of multidimensional life coming to light; the elimination of fears (projectiophobia) and antiprojective conditioning.
Secret estoupé: the discovery of the occult faculty, projectability; nonlucid consciential projection, the secret that was guarded for millennia, which was found to be latent, becomes conscious and explicit for the life of human beings.
Marchera par-dessus & devant: will go upward, through the consciential dimensions, and forward with cosmoethics, serenism and endless evolution.

Comparisons. The interested reader can make comparisons between the translation and the interpretation of this quatrain, with various authors: Béatrice, p. 256; Cheynet, p. 151; Dinotos, p. 48; Fontbrune, p. 235; Hutin, p. 132; Leoni, p. 168, 169, 589; Piobb, p. 60; Roberts, p. 52.

Author. Of these authors, the one who most closely approximates the projectiological interpretation is Cheynet, who writes: "The secret, which has been kept in silence for so long, will finally be unveiled and established." "Humankind will discover occult faculties pertaining to it and which were found to be in a latent state."

Confirmation. A possible confirmation of the *prophecy on projectiology* was also made by Nostradamus, further on, in the middle of the *Centuries.* In this case, the same facts already presented in the previously analyzed quatrain were then seen from another angle, in a later, complementary quatrain, a technique that was much used by the physician-astrologer regarding countless subjects. Let us take a look at Century 3, Quatrain 2.

Strophe. The following is the original text of Nostradamus' Century 3, a strophe of 4 verses or Quatrain 2, published in 1555:

"Le divin verbe donra à la substance,
Comprins ciel, terre, or occult au faict mystique:
Corps, ame, espirit ayant toute puissance,
Tants soubs ses pieds comme au siège Célique."

Semantics. The following are some meanings of expressions in the French language of the sixteenth century, from Nostradamus' Quatrain 2 of Century 3:

Donra: variant of *donnera,* will give. This is a technical use of syncope. This expression was used frequently in *Centuries,* e.g.: C. 6, Q. 56; C. 7, Q. 2; C. 8, Q. 7 e C. 10, Q. 45.
Substance: the substance of spirit; the consciential being; the essence of the consciousness, as opposed to the material being (social being, intraphysical consciousness).
Or: gold. Noun also used, for example, in *Century* 7, Q. 32, e C. 10, Q. 46. Some have translated the expression as *ore.*
Laict. Faict: done; fact; phenomenon. The univocal nature of the noun in the *Centuries*: *Au faict bellique:* C. 3, Q. 30; C. 6, Q. 61. A typographical error occurred here, in certain editions of the *Centuries,* using the noun *laict* (milk) in the place of *faict.*

Puissance: power; authority.

Soubs: underneath; under.

Célique: Celestial; paradisiacal; in the sacred sense. Archaic French. The univocal nature of the adjective in the Centuries: *Du grande temple Célique:* C. 6, Q. 22.

Au siège Célique: on the celestial throne; the papal palace of the Apostolic Roman Catholic Church.

Confirmation. The following is a synthetic, simple, literal translation of the verses of Nostradamus' Century 3, Quatrain 2:

> *"The divine word will give the substance,*
> *Encompassing the sky, earth, hidden gold in the mystical act:*
> *Body, soul, spirit having all power,*
> *Under its feet, as well as on the celestial throne".*

Interpretation. An analytical interpretation, in prose, of the same Quatrain 2, Century 3, of what could be a *confirmation of Nostradamus' prophecy regarding projectiology:*

The divine word (the relative truth of projectiology; the self-defensive, extraphysical, pluri-existential mantra) **will give the substance** (the consciousness; the insubstantial being of humankind), **encompassing the sky** (extraphysical dimension), **earth** (intraphysical human life; crustal or tropospheric existence) **mystical** (symbolic): (showing that) **body, soul, spirit** (the body, the soul or human being, and the consciousness, the command of the holosoma; holosomatics; conscientiology) **having all power** (over the human body or soma), **under its feet** (in life *under* and *above* the crust of the earth; intraphysical existence, laic, secular) **as well as** (regarding) **on the celestial throne** (in the extraphysical dimension; the papal palace of the church, the Vatican, the clergy, including hagiology and the phenomenon of physical bilocation, or advanced projectability).

Projectiology. The following are 7 expressions, presented in detail, from Quatrain 2, Century 3, according to projectiology research:

Substance: the consciousness in evolution.

Or: the leading-edge relative truth of human lucid projectability.

Faict: the inevitable, physiological, or paraphysiological, phenomenon of consciential projection which was nonlucid and mystical, and which becomes lucid and addressed scientifically without dogmatism; the reformulation of values.

Corps: the soma; the human body; the *coarse extremity* of the holosoma.

Ame: the intraphysical consciousness, when temporarily connected with energy in matter.

Espirit: the extraphysical consciousness, its true, more permanent condition at our evolutionary level.

Siège Célique: extraphysical reality; the true origin (extraphysical hometown) of the consciousness that is temporarily manifesting mainly in the intraphysical dimension.

Conclusions. The interested reader can make comparisons between the translation and the interpretation of this Quatrain 2, Century 3, under analysis, with various authors: Allgeier, p. 126, 127, 170; Andreis, p. 126; Avenel, p. 46; Dinotos, p. 69; Fontbrune, p. 234; Houge, p. 31; Hutin, p. 147; Leoni, p. 192, 193, 602; Palhano Jr., p. 94; Robert, p. 76.

Approximation. Of these authors, the one who most closely approximates the projectiological interpretation is Allgeier, who writes: "Human beings will have access to worlds which have until now been considered occult and mystical." "They will learn how to overcome the boundaries of time and space. They will witness events in distant locations." "Their spirits will be capable of periodically being absent from the body."

Mantra. This is an opportune point to inform the reader that, over a decade ago, the author was performing an assistential task, while lucidly projected outside the body in the psychosoma, when he was the victim of a violent attack by a group of 8 powerful intrusive extraphysical consciousnesses. When he felt he was at the point of desoma, under the vassalizing energetic pressure of his pursuers, unable to change the environment or extraphysical dimension, he suddenly received providential help from the retrocognition of a mantra having self-defensive, energetic objectives, which – he now knows – was used by him in the past, as an alchemist, and with which he was able to free himself from this mortal energetic involvement.

Expressions. For this reason, these two quatrains by Nostradamus retain a special, personal, impactful significance that is far greater for the author, being well beyond that which has been presented here.

Synthesis. Cosmoethically speaking, it is not suitable to involve the reader with the pressure of the negative energy of these unhealthy consciential groups by revealing the impressive expressions of the mantra, which is, strictly speaking, an exact synthesis of Quatrain 27 of Century 2, the first one deciphered above.

Alert. Some time later, a helper called the author's attention to the research and location of this mantra in Michel de Nostradamus' Centuries, this being the reason why these considerations were made.

Critique. Are the number of *exact hits,* in these 8 analyzed verses sufficient to distance them from simple chance? Is it possible that the solutions presented for the two quatrains of Nostradamus' text from four-and-a-half centuries ago are "mere historical coincidence" with regard to the facts? Or could it be that all these considerations are only another "use of Nostradamus," "a self-corruption of personal vanity" or "a mere egoistical excrescence of personalism"? Let us leave the final, pondered heterocritique, as well as the competent final conclusion, to the conscientious reader.

Analysis. The analysis of Nostradamus' cryptography, inserted above, had the primary purpose of serving as a paradigm, or an element for technical comparison. This is also the case with the following study of the precognitive text of Honoré de Balzac, from the nineteenth century. This one is more direct, clearer and practically incontestable, in the sense that it refers to a precognition, foresight or "prophecy" in regard to projectiology – perhaps because it is more recent, having only existed for *one-and-a-half centuries*.

Multidimensionality. Neither time nor the fucture will expose the structure of the phenomenon of precognition logically. This parapsychic phenomenon conflicts deeply with conventional science. The basis of traditional scientific reason consists in explaining tomorrow through today, the *essence of forecasting;* and never today through tomorrow, the *essence of precognition.* Only multidimensionality and discoincidentiology are able to clarify the occurrences of precognition within *today-tomorrow,* a singular reality. Strictly speaking, tomorrow does not exist.

Balzac. In the specific case of Honoré de Balzac, the facts should not be excluded due to the incredible precision and appropriateness of their detail, within the historical context, in an *intermezzo* of one-and-a-half centuries. It is opportune to repeat that arguments are useless against facts.

Microbiography. Honoré de Balzac, the brilliant French writer, was born in 1799 in Tours, the Capital of Touraine. He wrote a monumental cycle of 86 novels, besides other philosophical works and died in Paris in 1850. He was the "main" precognitor of projectiology. Let us endeavor to demonstrate this with facts.

Rationality. Honoré de Balzac was the precognitor of projectiology, not in the sense of nostradamic, mystical or irrational pre-messiahs, but in the sense of a foreseeing pre-parascientist, who is rational and foresighted within the world of the current prospective.

Announcement. He clearly and incontrovertibly announced the appearance of a *new science* in 1832, even before the advent of spiritism (1848), metapsychics(1875), parapsychology (1888) and psychotronics (1950). The 150th anniversary of his projectiological precognition (precognitive projection) occurred in 1982.

Affirmations. Balzac used the character *Louis Lambert,* in his autobiographical novel by the same name, to voice the following questions and affirmations (pages 71 to 73, Gallimard Editions, 1980):

French. "Si le paysage n'est pas venu vers moi, ce qui serait absurde à penser, j'y suis donc venu. Si j'étais ici pendant que je dormais dans mon alcôve, ce fait ne constitue-t-il pas une séparation complète entre mon corps et mon être intérieur? N'atteste-t-il pas je ne sais quelle faculté locomotive de l'esprit ou des effets équivalant à ceux de la locomotion du corps? Or, si mon esprit et mon corps ont pu se quitter pendant le sommeil, pourquoi ne les ferais-je pas également divorcer ainsi pendant la veille? Je n'aperçois point de moyens termes entre ces deux propositions. Mais allons plus loin, pénétrons les détails. Ou ces faits se sont accomplis par la puissance d'une faculté qui met en oeuvre un second être à qui mon corps sert d'enveloppe, puisque j'étais dans mon alcôve et voyais le paysage, et ceci renverse bien des systèmes. J'ai marché, j'ai vu, j'ai entendu. Si, pendant la nuit, les yeux fermés, j'ai vu en moi-même des objets colorés, si j'ai entendu des bruits dans le plus absolu silence, et sans les conditions exigées pour que le son se forme, si dans la plus parfaite immobilité j'ai franchi des espaces, nous aurions des facultés internes, indépendantes de lois physiques extérieures. La nature matérielle serait pénétrable par l'esprit. Comment les hommes ont-ils si peu réfléchi jusqu'alors aux accidents du sommeil qui accusent en l'homme une double vie? N'y aurait-il pas une nouvelle science dans ce phénomène? ajouta-t-il en se frappant fortement le front; s'il n'est pas le principe d'une science, il trahit certainement en l'homme d'énormes pouvoirs; il annonce au moins la désunion fréquente de nos deux natures, fait autour duquel je tourne depuis si longtemps. J'ai donc enfin trouvé un témoignage de la supériorité qui distingue nos sens latents de nos sens apparents! *Homo duplex!"*

Translation. The following is a translation into English of the above passage, from Honoré de Balzac's report in French:

English. "If the scenery did not come to me, which would be an absurd thought, then I went to it. If I was here while asleep in my bedroom, does this fact not constitute a complete separation between my body and my inner being? Does it not attest to a locomotive faculty of the spirit or equivalent effects of the locomotion of the body, about which I have no knowledge? Well, if my spirit and my body could separate during sleep, why could I not equally divorce them during the waking state? I cannot clearly see a middle ground between these two propositions. But let us go further and study the problem in detail. These facts were verified by the power of a faculty which puts into movement a second being for which my body serves as a housing, because I saw the scenery while in my bedroom and this destroys many systems. I walked, saw and heard. If, during the night, with my eyes closed I saw colored objects within myself, if I heard sounds in the most absolute silence, and without the conditions necessary for their formation, if in the most absolute immobility I went through space, then humans have internal faculties which are independent from external physical laws. The material world would then be penetrable by the spirit. Why have humans reflected so little until now upon the accidents of sleep that indicate a double life? Will there not be a new science in this phenomenon? If it is not the basis for a science, then it certainly shows that humans have incredible powers; it at least illustrates the frequent separation of our two natures; a fact regarding which I have pondered for such a long time. I have finally found the perfect piece of evidence for the superiority which distinguishes our latent senses from our apparent senses! *Homo duplex!"*

Precision. It is impressive how all that was foreseen by Honoré de Balzac has occurred in the same way, in an unquestionable manner. Those selfsame recent, natural facts of life precisely and rationally confirmed early registered observations.

Ideas. At least 16 ideas registered in the literary expressions of Balzac, in 1832, were transformed into technical postulates of projectiology, more than one-and-a-half centuries later, in 1986. In a detailed analysis, "let us study the problem in detail" (see fig. 12).

Projector. If we consider that the novel "Louis Lambert" was autobiographical, as was registered by Laure Surville, the sister of the author, this demonstrates that Honoré de Balzac was the protagonist lucid projector of the reported precognitive lucid projection. Facts are facts. Within the world of his literary creativity, he was a vigorous sensitive (paraperceptiology), with unmistakable manifestations of extraordinary intuition.

LITERARY EXPRESSIONS: BALZAC, 1832	TECHNICAL EXPRESSIONS: PROJECTIOLOGY, 1986
1. "I went through space" *(J'ai franchi des espaces)* (p. 72)	Extraphysical volitation (see chap. 314)
2. "Destroys many systems" *(renverse bien des systèmes)* (p. 72)	New consciential paradigm (see chap. 2)
3. "Frequent separation" *(désunion fréquente)* (p. 73)	Consciential projections in series (see chap. 438)
4. "Sleeping in my bedroom" *(Je dormais dans mon alcôve)* (p. 71)	Physical base of the projector (see chap. 180)
5. "Double life" *(double vie)* (p. 72)	Multidimensional self-awareness (see chap. 262)
6. "Locomotive faculty of the spirit" *(faculté locomotive de l'espirit)* (p.71)	Projectability (see chap. 158)
7. "Inner faculties" *(facultés internes)* (p. 72)	Paraphysiology of the holosoma (see chap. 103)
8. *Homo duplex* (p. 73)	*Homo projectius* (see chap. 333)
9. "Penetrable nature of matter" *(nature matérielle pénétrable)* (p. 72)	Extraphysical self-permeability (see chap. 304)
10. "New science" *(nouvelle science)* (p. 72)	Projectiology (see chap. 05)
11. "Second being" *(second être)* (p. 72)	Psychosoma (see chap. 125)
12. "Latent senses" *(sens latents)* (p. 73)	Paraperceptibility (see chap. 263)
13. "Complete separation" *(séparation complète)* (p.71)	Holosomatic discoincidence (see chap. 110)
14. "Separate during the waking state" *(se quitter pendant la veille)* (p. 72)	Diurnal lucid projection (see chap. 196)
15. "Separate during sleep" *(se quitter pendant le sommeil)* (p. 72)	Nocturnal lucid projection (see chap. 196)
16. "Saw the scenery" *(Je voyais le paysage)* (p. 72)	Extraphysical vision (see chap. 278)

Fig. 12: Comparison of 16 Confirmatory Expressions from the Prophecy

Precognitor. As well as being a lucid projector, Balzac was a precognitor. For those who are accustomed to "solving an enigma with concepts," trying to take a shortcut with simplistic reasoning, it is worth mentioning that the author did not propose projectiology as a whim, only to endorse the ideas of Honoré de Balzac.

Projection. Let us look at the facts. The author's first lucid projection, being among those studied in this volume, occurred in 1941, when he was 9 years of age. He later studied the theme of lucid projection full time, on a continuous basis, beginning in 1966. By that time, he had a fairly sizeable specialized library on the subject.

Identification. The author identified the prophecy on his own in 1982, while reading the novel, within his routine of uninterrupted bibliographic research, performed during that period.

Gratification. The bibliographic discovery of the prophecy was extremely gratifying, representing, in some way on that occasion, a veritable endorsement of a lifetime of work as an independent researcher, without any official subsidy of any type.

Note. Some of the entries in the following bibliography refer to books translated into Portuguese. This is because the current work was published in Portuguese.

Bibliography (Nostradamus).

1. **ALLGEIER, Kurt**; *As Grandes Profecias de Nostradamus ("Die Grossen Prophezeiungen des Nostradamus in Moderner Deutung");* transl. Maria Madalena Würt Teixeira; 138 pp.; 31 illus.; 13 refs.; 20.5 x 15.5 cm; pb.; Rio de Janeiro, R.J ; Brazil; Editora Tecnoprint; 1983; pp. 126-127.

2. **ALLGEIER, Kurt**; *Profecias Até o Próximo Século: Amanhã Será Realidade ("Morgen Soll es Wahrheit Werden");* transl. Stefania A. Lago; 198 pp.; 24 illus.; 18 refs.; 20.5 x 15.5 cm; pb.; Rio de Janeiro; Brazil; Editora Tecnoprint; 1983; p. 170.

3. **AUGUSTO, Cícero; & HOLDERBAUM, Isabel**; *Previsões de Nostradamus;* 96 pp.; 20 x 13 cm; pb.; LG Promoções Editoriais; no date.

4. **BASCHERA, Renzo**; *As Profecias de Nostradamus ("I Grandi Profeti");* 146 pp.; 13 refs.; glos. 277 terms; 19 x 12.5 cm; pb.; S. Paulo, SP; Brazil; Ed. Best Seller; 1991.

5. **BECKLEY, Timothy Green**; Editorial Direction; *Nostradamus' Unpublished Prophecies;* 64 pp.; 11 illus.; 28 x 21.5 cm; pb.; Inner Light Publications; New Brunswick, N. J.; 1994.

6. **BERLITZ, Charles**; *O Livro dos Fenômenos Estranhos ("World of Strange Phenomena");* transl. Jusmar Gomes; 322 pp.; 21 x 14 cm; pb.; S. Paulo, SP; Brazil; Editora Best Seller; 1990; pp. 143-145.

7. **BESSY, Maurice**; *La Magia;* p. 65.

8. **BONIN, Werner F.**; *Lexicon der Parapsychologie und ihrer Grenzgebiete;* VIII + 588 pp.; illus.; 1.939 refs.; 24 x 17 x 4 cm; hb.; dj.; München; Federal Republic of Germany; Scherz; 1976; pp. 362, 363.

9. **BORRELLI, P.**; *Alquimia, Satanismo, Cagliostro ("Alchimia, Satanismo, Cagliostro");* transl.: Torrieri Guimarães; 184 pp.; 20.5 x 13.5 cm; pb.; S. Paulo, SP; Brazil; Hemus - Livraria Editora Ltda; 1990; p. 92.

10. **BROOKESMITH, ___**; *The Power of the Mind;* p. 83.

11. **CARQUEJA, Júlio Alcoforado**; *O Verdadeiro Breviário de Nostradamus;* 156 pp.; 2 illus.; glos. 35 terms; 18.5 x 13.5 cm; pb.; Rio de Janeiro, RJ; Brazil; Editora Eco; no date.

12. **CHAMBERS, Howard V.**; *An Occult Dictionary for the Millions;* 158 pp.; 17.5 x 10.5 cm; pocket; pb.; New York, N. Y.; Award Books; 1966; p. 99.

13. **CHEETHAM, Erika**; *Novas Profecias de Nostradamus: de 1985 em Diante ("The Further Prophecies of Nostradamus: 1985 and Beyond");* transl. Donaldson M. Garschagen; 256 pp.; 12 chaps.; 21 x 14 cm; pb.; 4th ed.; Rio de Janeiro, RJ; Brazil; Ed. Nova Fronteira S. A.; 1986.

14. **CHEYNET, Ettore**; *Nostradamus e o Inquietante Futuro ("Nostradamus: L'Inquietante Domani");* transl. Maria Thereza Cavalheiro & Yone Canônico Micalli; 176 pp.; glos. 168 terms; 20.5 x 12 cm; hb.; São Paulo, SP; Brazil; Círculo do Livro; 1985; p. 151.

15. **CHRISTOPHER, Milbourne**; *ESP, Seers & Psychics;* X + 286 pp.; illus.; 92 refs.; alph.; 21.5 x 14.5 cm; hb.; dj.; New York, N.Y.; Thomas Y. Crowell Co.; 1970; pp. 106, 107, 111.

16. **CLARET, Martin**; *O Pensamento Vivo de Nostradamus;* 128 pp.; 36 illus.; 1 imag.; 5 photos; 11 refs.; 20.5 x 14 cm; pb.; S. Paulo, SP; Brazil; Martin Claret Editores; 1990.

17. **COMPARATO, Doc**; *Nostradamus: o Príncipe das Profecias;* 176 pp.; 8 photos; 11 refs.; 21.5 x 14 cm; pb.; S. Paulo, SP; Brazil; Ed. Clube do Livro Ltda; 1988.

18. **COOVER, John Edgar**; *Experiments in Psychical Research at Leland Stanford Junior University;* pref. David Starr Jordan; introd. Frank Angel; participation Lillien J. Martin; XXIV + 642 pp.; 70 illus.; 1.975 refs.; 5 apps.; index of names; alph.; 25 x 17 x 5.5 cm; hb.; California; U. S. A.; Stanford University; Department of Psychology; 1917; p. 593.

19. **CORCORAN, Dan**; *Levels of Consciousness Mystical and Spiritual Experiences;* pref. Renald Rosewood; 128 pp.; 20.5 x 13.5 cm; hb.; New York, NY; Exposition Press; 1970; p. 123.

20. **COURNOS, John**; *A Book of Prophecy;* XII + 276 pp.; 15 illus.; 21 x 14.5 cm; hb.; dj.; New York, NY; Bell Publishing Company; no date; p. 143.

21. **CROWLEY, Aleister (Pseud. Edward Alexander Crowley)**; *Magick Without Tears;* introd. Karl J. Gemer; pref. Israel Regardie; epil.. Christopher S. Hyatt; XVI + 528 pp.; 83 chaps.; illus.; app.; alph.; 22 x 14 x 3 cm; pb.; 3rd print.; Phoenix, AZ; U. S. A.; Falcon Press; June, 1982; p. 182.

22. **DINOTOS, Sábado**; *As Centúrias de Nostradamus;* 294 pp.; 23 x 16 cm; pb.; S. Paulo, SP; Brazil; Author's Edition; August, 1965; pp. 48, 69.

23. **DRURY, Nevill; and TILLET, Gregory;** *The Occult Sourcebook;* X + 236 pp.; illus.; index of names; refs.; alph.; 23.5 x 15.5 cm; pb.; Routledge & Kegan Paul; London; 1978; p. 221.

24. **FONTBRUNE, Jean-Charles de**; *Nostradamus ("Nostradamus: historien et prophete");* transl. Aulyde Soares Rodrigues; 564 pp.; 281 refs.; 21 x 13 x 3.5 cm; hb.; dj.; S. Paulo, SP; Brazil; Círculo do Livro S. A.; 1984.

25. **FONTBRUNE, Jean-Charles de**; *Nostradamus Historiador e Profeta: Volume II ("Nostradamus Historien et Prophete: Tome II");* transl. Aulyde Soares Rodrigues; 304 pp.; 5 chaps.; 1 illus.; 221 refs.; 1 tab.; 21 x 14 cm; pb.; Rio de Janeiro; Brazil; Editora Nova Fronteira; 1983; pp. 234, 235.

26. **GALLOTTI, Alícia**; *Nostradamus: As Profecias do Futuro ("Nostradamus - Las Profectas del Futuro");* transl. Reinaldo Guarany; 234 pp.; 21 x 14 cm; pb.; 5th ed.; Rio de Janeiro, RJ; Brazil; Ed. Record; no date.

27. **GARRISON, Omar V.**; *The Encyclopedia of Prophecy;* 228 pp.; 204 entries; 11 illus.; 2 maps; 4 photos; 2 imag.; 24 x 16 cm; hb.; dj.; 1st ed.; New Jersey; U. S. A.; Citadel Press; 1978; pp. 9, 34, 36-37, 67, 109, 120, 174.

28. **GATTEY, Charles Neilson**; *They Saw Tomorrow;* 302 pp.; 9 chaps.; 10 illus.; alph.; 52 refs.; 9 photos; 17.5 x 11 cm; pb.; 1st ed. in 1977; Great Britain; Granada Publishing; 1980; pp. 24-55, 278.

29. **GIBSON, Walter B.; & GIBSON, Litzka R.**; *The Encyclopaedia of Prophecy;* XII + 388 pp.; XII chaps.; illus.; alph.; glos. 105 terms; 20 x 13 cm; pb.; 1st ed. in 1974; Great Britain; Granada Publishing Limited; 1977; p. 55.

30. **GOULD, Rupert Thomas**; *Oddities;* intr. Leslie Shepard; VIII + 228 pp.; XI chaps.; 17 illus.; 1 graph.; 4 mapas; 24 x 17 cm; hb.; dj.; 1st ed.; 2nd print.; New York, NY; University Book; January, 1966.

31. **HARRISON, John Fletcher Clews**; *The Second Coming;* XVIII + 280 pp.; 8 chaps.; 9 illus.; index of names; 507 refs.; 24.5 x 16 cm; hb.; dj.; 1st ed.; London; Routledge & Kegan Paul; 1979; p. 53.

32. **HINES, Terence**; *Pseudoscience and the Paranormal: A Critical Examination of the Evidence;* XII + 372 pp.; 12 chaps.; 20 illus.; 756 refs.; index of names; alph.; 23 x 15.5 x 3 cm; pb.; Buffalo; NY; U. S. A.; Prometheus Books; 1988; pp. 39-42.

33. **HOGUE, John**; *Nostradamus e o Milênio: Predições do Futuro ("Nostradamus and the Millennium");* transl. Vera Wrobel Bloch & Dan Bastos; 208 pp.; 14 chaps.; 211 illus.; 4 tabs.; 21.5 x 19 cm; hb.; dj.; Rio de Janeiro; Brazil; Editora Nova Fronteira; 1988; p. 31.

34. **HORTA, Bernardo**; *Mulheres Barram o Complexo de Nostradamus;* ANO ZERO; Rio de Janeiro, RJ; Magazine; Monthly; Year III; N. 21; January, 1993; 11 illus.; pp. 26-35.

35. **HUTIN, Serge**; *Les Prophéties de Nostradamus;* 300 pp.; 18 refs.; 22.5 x 14 cm; pb.; Paris; Pierre Belfond; 1981; pp. 132, 147.

36. **INGLIS, Brian**; *Natural and Supernatural: A History of the Paranormal from Earliest Times to 1914;* 490 pp.; 38 chaps.; illus.; 693 refs.; alph.; 23.5 x 15.5 x 3.5 cm; hb.; dj.; London; Hodder and Stoughton; 1977; pp. 98-101.

37. **JOCHMANS, Joseph Robert**; *Nostradamus Now: Prophecies of Peril and Promise for The 1990's and Beyond;* pref. Barbara Meister Vitale, John Running Deer Eleaser, and Thomas Kenyon; 416 pp.; 13 chaps.; illus.; cart.; 120 refs.; alph.; 21 x 13.5 cm; pb.; Santa Fe New Mexico; U. S. A.; Sun Books-Publishing; May, 1993.

38. **KLIMO, Jon**; *Channeling: Investigations on Receiving Information from Paranormal Sources;* pref. Charles Theodore Tart; XVI + 384 pp.; 10 chaps.; glos. 62 terms; 115 refs.; alph.; 23.5 x 15.5 x 3 cm; hb.; dj.; Los Angeles; Califórnia; U. S. A.; Jeremy P. Tarcher; 1987; pp. 92, 160, 196.

39. **LACASSE, Maurice A.;** *Nostradamus: The Voice that Echoes through Time;* 198 pp.; 25 chaps.; illus.; graphs.; cart.; photos; 23.5 x 15.5 cm; hb.; dj.; Owings Mills, Maryland; U. S. A.; Noble House; 1992.

40. **LASH, John;** *The Seeker's Handbook: The Complete Guide to Spiritual Pathfinding;* XX + 442 pp.; glos. 1.227 terms; alph.; 23.5 x 15.5 x 3.5 cm; hb.; dj.; New York, NY; Harmony Books; 1990; pp. 332, 348.

41. **LEONI, Edgar;** *Nostradamus and his Prophecies;* 824 pp.; 18 illus.; 110 refs.; alph.; 23 x 15 x 5 cm; hb.; dj.; New York, NY; Bell Publishing Co.; 1982; pp. 168, 169, 192, 193, 589, 602.

42. **LOGAN, Daniel;** *The Anatomy of Prophecy;* XIV + 172 pp.; 7 chaps.; 21 refs.; app.; alph.; 21 x 14 cm; hb.; dj.; Englewood Cliffs; New Jersey; U. S. A.; Prentice-Hall; 1975; pp. 145-147, 153.

43. **MASIL, Curtis;** *As Centúrias de Nostradamus;* 272 pp.; 8 illus.; 5 photos; 10 refs.; 20.7 x 15.5 cm; pb.; Rio de Janeiro, RJ; Brazil; Ed. Tecnoprint S. A.; 1987.

44. **McCANN, Lee;** *Nostradamus: The Man who Saw through Time;* pref. L. M.; 422 pp.; X + III chaps.; 7 illus.; 20 x 13.5 x 3 cm; pb.; New York; Farrar - Straus - Giroux; 1988.

45. **MOLINA, N. A.;** *Nostradamus - A Magia Branca e a Magia Negra;* 344 pp.; 9 + 4 + 5 + 2 + 12 + 5 chaps.; 66 illus.; 1 table; 18 x 14 cm; pb.; 2nd ed.; Rio de Janeiro, RJ; Brazil; Ed. Espiritualista Ltda; no date.

46. **MOORE, John;** *Being in Your Right Mind;* 290 pp.; 59 chaps.; 8 illus.; 76 refs.; 1 graph.; 22.5 x 14.5 cm; hb.; dj.; 1st ed.; Great Britain; Element Books Limited; 1984.

47. **NAVARRO, José;** *O Mestre da Levitação;* DESTINO; Rio de Janeiro, RJ; Magazine; Monthly; Year IV; N. 43; January, 1993; 3 illus.; pp. 52-54.

48. **NOORBERGEN, Rene;** *As Profecias de Nostradamus: Sobre a IIIª Guerra Mundial ("Invitation to a Holocaust");* transl. Louisa Ibañez; 194 pp.; 9 chaps.; 1 illus.; 19 maps; 17 refs.; 21 x 14 cm; pb.; Rio de Janeiro, RJ; Brazil; Livraria Francisco Alves ed. S. A.; 1983; p. 193.

49. **PAPELIVROS;** Editor; *O Breviário de Nostradamus;* 236 pp.; IX + VI + II + II + V chaps.; 51 illus.; glos. 35 terms; enu.; 19.5 x 13.5 cm; pb.; S. Paulo, SP; Brazil; Papelivros - Comércio de Papéis e Livros Ltda; no date.

50. **PIOBB, Pierre Vincent;** *O Segredo das Centúrias de Nostradamus;* transl. Hugo Veloso; introd. Edmundo Cardilho; 250 pp.; 23 illus.; 20 x 13.5 cm; hb.; S. Paulo, SP; Brazil; Editora Três; 1973; p.60.

51. **PROPHET, Elizabeth Clare;** *Nostradamus: Os Quatro Cavaleiros ("Nostradamus: The Four Horsemen");* transl. Miguel Teixeira; 256 pp.; 17 chaps.; 3 illus.; 17.5 x 11.5 cm; pb.; Brasília, DF; Brazil; Summit University; 1988.

52. **RANDI, James;** *The Mask of Nostradamus: The Prophecies of the World's Most Famous Seer;* XIV + 256 pp.; 12 chaps.;14 illus.; 4 apps.; 47 refs.; alph.; 23 x 15 cm; pb.; Buffalo; N. Y.; U. S. A.; Prometheus Books; 1993.

53. **ROBERTS, Henry C.;** Editor; *The Complete Prophecies of Nostradamus;* VI + 350 pp.; 1 illus.; 21 x 14 x 3 cm; hb.; dj.; 45th print.; Oyster Bay; N. Y.; U. S. A.; Nostradamus Co.; 1981; pp. 52, 76.

54. **RUIR, Em;** *Nostradamus: Suas Profecias 1948 - 2023 ("Nostradamus - Ses Prophéties 1948 - 2023");* transl. I. L. Ribeiro; 176 pp.; XIII chaps.; 30 illus.; 20 x 14.5 cm; hb.; S. Paulo, SP; Brazil; Livraria Martins Editora S. A.; October, 1951.

55. **SALIES, Paulo;** *Nostradamus o Juízo Final e o Espiritismo;* pref. Edward Ihler; 86 pp.; 3 illus.; 21.5 x 15.5 cm; pb.; 2nd ed.; Porto Alegre, RS; Brazil; Ed. Fotolitográfica; 1987.

56. **SANCHEZ, Mário;** *Análise das Centúrias de Nostradamus;* I Vol.; 206 pp.; 4 illus.; 1 map; enu.; 21 x 14 cm; pb.; Goiânia, GO; Brazil; Imery Publicações Ltda; no date.

57. **SANMARTIN, Alberto;** *Profecias de Nostradamus sobre o Grande Rei;* 72 pp.; 7 chaps.; 18 x 13 cm; pb.; S. Owings Mills, Maryland; U. S. A.; Paulo, SP; Brazil; February, 1965.

58. **SHADOWITZ, Albert; & WALSH, Peter;** *The Dark Side of Knowledge: Exploring the Occult;* XII + 306 pp.; 13 chaps.; illus.; bibl. 289-296; alph.; 23.5 x 16 cm; pb.; Menlo Park; Califórnia; U. S. A.; Addison-Wesley Publishing Co.; 1976; pp. 114, 115.

59. **SHEPARD, Leslie A.;** Editor; *Encyclopedia of Occultism & Parapsychology;* 2 Vols.; 1.084 pp.; 100 chaps.; glos. 3.749 terms; 28 x 21.5 x 3 cm; pb.; New York, NY; Avon Books; March, 1980; pp. 653, 654.

60. **SLADEK, John;** *The New Apocrypha;* 384 pp.; 26 chaps.; 22 illus.; alph.; 140 refs.; 24 x 16.5 x 3.5 cm; hb.; dj.; 1st ed.; New York, NY; Stein and Day; 1974; pp. 161, 313-318.

61. **SOUZA, Rui Barbosa de;** Editor; *As Profecias de Paracelso: "Prognósticos";* transl. Salvador Obiol de Freitas; 86 pp.; 33 illus.; alph.; 21 x 13.5 cm; pb.; Porto Alegre, RS; Brazil; Editora Rigel Ltda; 1990.

62. **STAUDENMAIER, Ludwig;** *Die Magie Als Experimentelle Naturwissenschaft;* 256 pp.; 9 chaps.; alph.; 22 x 14 cm; hb.; dj.; Darmstadt; Federal Republic of Germany; Wissenschaftliche Buchgesellschaft; 1968; p. 231.

63. **SWANN, Ingo**; *To Kiss Earth Good-Bye;* pref. Gertrude Schmeidler; XX + 218 pp.; 5 chaps.; illus.; 159 refs.; alph.; 24 x 15.5 cm; hb.; dj.; New York, NY; Hawthorn Books; 1975; pp. 139, 144, 148.

64. **SWANN, Ingo**; *Your Nostradamus Factor;* 320 pp.; 25 chaps.; 3 illus.; 189 refs.; alph.; 2 graphs.; 21 x 14 cm; pb.; New York, NY; Fireside; 1993; pp. 36, 88, 89, 228.

65. **WARD, Chas. A.;** *Oracles of Nostradamus;* 376 pp.; alph.; 21 x 13.5 x 3 cm; hb.; dj.; New York; Dorset Press;1986.

66. **WEDECK, Harry E.**; *Dictionary of Spiritualism;* VIII + 376 pp.; glos. 1.913 terms; 21 x 14 cm; hb.; New York, NY; Philosophical Library; 1971; p. 248.

67. **WILSON, Colin; & GRANT, John (Pseud. Paul Barnett)**; *The Directory of Possibilities;* 304 pp.; 7 chaps.; 42 illus.; 94 refs.; alph.; 20 x 13 cm; pb.; Great Britain; Corgi Books; 1982; pp. 132, 133.

68. **WOLDBEN, A.**; *After Nostradamus;* pref. Gavin Gibbons; 224 pp.; 15 chaps.; 39 refs.; 18 x 11 cm; pb.; Great Britain; Granada Publishing; 1975; pp. 54; Eds.: It.

69. **XAVIER, Fritz**; *Nostradamus: Segredos Mágicos para Saúde - Beleza - Amor – Rejuvenescimento;* 118 pp.; 10 chaps.; 19 illus.; 21.7 x 15.5 cm; pb.; Rio de Janeiro, RJ; Brazil; Ed. Tecnoprint S. A.; 1987.

70. **ZAMARTI, Márcia Bagnolesi; director;** *Nostradamus: A Voz do Futuro;* 18 pp.; illus.; photos; 25.5 x 17 cm; pb.; S. Paulo; Brazil; Editora Abril; 1995.

Bibliography. Readers wishing to deepen their research for themselves, on the precognition of Balzac analyzed here, can refer to the translation in English of the short novel entitled *Louis Lambert*.

13. EXOTERIC PERIOD OF PROJECTIOLOGY

Definition. Exoterism: the more recent doctrine, or modern attitude, that aims to transmit the teachings (scientific, philosophical) of truth directly to the public in an unrestricted manner (popular dissemination, popularization of knowledge).

Synonymy: anti-hermetism; exteriorism; openness.

Third. The third historical period – the exoteric period or initial-scientific period of projectiology – extends from 1905 (Turvey) to 1965 (Crookall), in which 7 personalities or authors and their works stand out, as presented in the following chronological order:

1. **First:** the publicly verified lucid projections of Vincent Newton Turvey (1873-1912), in England.

2. **Second:** the original clarion calls of Prescott Farnsworth Hall, in 1916, in the United States of America.

3. **Third:** the publication of the experience of Hugh Callaway (1886-1949) under the pseudonym of Oliver Fox, again in England, in 1920.

4. **Fourth:** the Dane, Johannes E. Hohlemberg, who presented his personal projective experiences at the First International Congress of Psychic Research in Copenhagen, Denmark, in 1921, a fact that is nowadays generally forgotten.

5. **Fifth:** Sylvan Joseph Muldoon (1903-1971), starting in 1929, in the United States of America.

6. **Sixth:** the book by Marcel Louis Fohan ("Yram"), in France.

7. **Seventh:** the detailed work of Robert Crookall, notably from 1960 to 1965, in England.

Demythologization. This period was characterized by an openness, or exoterism, of a relative knowledge of the phenomenon of lucid projection to the public *(populace)*, demythologizing (demythologization) and demystifying the subject, which was already well established at this time under the term *astral projection.*

Metapsychics. This phase saw the beginning of projections induced by animal magnetism produced by researchers Hector Durville (1848-1923) and Charles Lancelin (1852-1941), from the

French school in Paris, and the popularization or democratization of lucid projection through individual experiences, which were better received by open minds and referred to in dozens of works of profound significance and authenticity.

Decade. The second decade of the twentieth century was characterized by a more solid appearance of the lucid consciential projection phenomenon, which can be recalled, with some repetition, through the following 6 authors and their popular works (see International Bibliography of Projectiology).

1. **Fox.** In 1920, the above-cited case of Oliver Fox.
2. **Hohlemberg.** In 1921, the Dane, Johannes E. Hohlemberg, also cited above.
3. **Morrell.** In 1924, Ed Morrell publishes his book, which caused a shakeup in the United States penal system, based on his lucid projections in the dungeon at San Quentin, California.
4. **Larsen.** In 1927, Caroline D. Larsen publishes her book *My Travels in the Spirit World*, which addressed her impressive extraphysical experiences as an active sensitive.
5. **Pelley.** In May of 1928, the author William Dudley Pelley publishes his article "Seven Minutes in Eternity", in *The American Magazine,* narrating a lucid experience outside the human body which proved to be a veritable publicity phenomenon, causing an immense stir on the subject.
6. **Muldoon.** Lastly, in 1929, Sylvan Joseph Muldoon (1903-1971) releases the work which became a major (and more technical) classic on the theme: *The Projection of the Astral Body* (coauthored with Hereward Hubert Lavington Carrington).

Parapsychology. It is here that metapsychics ended and parapsychology began, with the Congress of Utrecht, Holland, in 1953.

14. LABORATORIAL PERIOD OF PROJECTIOLOGY

Definition. Laboratorial experimentation: scientific method that consists of observing a natural phenomenon under predetermined conditions, which allows increased knowledge of the manifestations or laws that regulate this phenomenon.

Synonymy: laboratorial experience; scientific assay.

Fourth. Lastly, the fourth and last historical period of projectiology is the contemporary period, initiated by Charles Theodore Tart (1937), in 1966, in the United States of America, when this researcher conducted the first attempt to remove lucid projection from the restricted arena of individual experiments and take it into the laboratory, performing experiments with the still unidentified young projector, Miss Z.

Present. This period extends up to the present.

OBE. In this phase, astral projection was euphemistically recoined as OBE (out-of-body experience), or projection of the consciousness outside the physical body, a less romantic term currently used by many parapsychologists and introduced to the sophisticated laboratories of the scientific world by parapsychology.

Statistics. There is a consequent intensification of statistical public opinion polls on correlated phenomena, the use of the most sophisticated laboratory instrumentation, ranging from maps, graphs and tables to equipment that measures epidermal reaction (BSR and GSR), electroencephalograph (EEG), electrocardiograph (EKG), *electroopticograph* (EOG), the digital photoplethysmograph and various polygraphs, as well as intercoms, cassettes, videocassettes, diskettes, CD-ROMs and other computer-related resources.

Precision. The precision of the layout of the historical periods of projectiology is debatable.

Cultures. According to geographical areas, customs, uses and cultural levels, the ancient, esoteric and exoteric periods progress, continue to exist and have representatives among us.

Perspectives. However, the laboratorial period beckons with truly optimistic, motivating perspectives, presenting terrestrial humanity with new horizons in the direction of a synthesis and greater comprehension of the facts established by projectiology, with innumerous positive consequences that are projected throughout the upcoming centuries.

Importance. There are 2 aspects which should be considered in parapsychic research:

1. **Cases.** Spontaneous parapsychic cases are important to the degree that they provide indicators (clues) for laboratorial experimentation.

2. **Experiments.** Laboratorial experiments are significant because they demonstrate, under different conditions, what is actually occurring (facts) in the human experience.

Hierarchy. In this way, the hierarchy of importance between these two approaches (positions) is exactly inverse (contrary).

Preference. In parapsychic practices, as a consciential laboratory, the cozy energetic environment (carpet, shoeless, cushions and air conditioning) of the *ashram* (emotional body) is always preferable to the socially solemn, sterile, cold (mentalsoma) and distant environment of the professional religious temple.

Psychosomatics. This is due to the fact that the psychosoma still predominantly controls the behavior of the average member of the human population (a total of 5.9 billion persons in 1997) or the crustal, tropospheric, and extraphysical or paratropospheric population (the parapopulation is 9 times larger than the human population) of this planet.

Phase. With this laboratorial period, projectiology frees itself from the *bookish pre-scientific* phase.

Hermetisms. Projectiology shows those more alert consciousnesses the irrelevance of religions, beliefs, faith and so-called *hermetic sciences* or hermetisms, nowadays including the daily practices of the personal energetic task, or penta, for the rest of the active life of the more lucid, mature intraphysical consciousness.

Bibliography: Balzac (71, p. 71), Castro (265, p. 7), Crookall (388, p. 3), Fox (544, p. 32), Greenhouse (636, p. 13), Hammond (674, p. 210), Kardec (824, p. 213), Muldoon (1105, p. 55), Swedenborg (1639, p. 1), Turvey (1707, p. 14), Vett (1738, p. 379).

15. PIONEERISM IN PROJECTIOLOGY

Definition. Pioneerism: the character or quality of the individual who is the first to anticipate, open or discover ways for other persons, through an unknown region or pioneering endeavor.

Synonymy: pioneering; precursory exploration; trail blazing.

Precocity. Listed below are some precocious moments in the history of projectiology and its protagonists, who are worthy of being considered pioneers in the formation of this science.

Hermotimus. Hermotimus of Clazomenae, a philosopher belonging to the Jonic school, from the sixth century *before Christ*, was apparently able to induce the lucid consciential projection experience at will, using this ability to investigate the nature of the consciential states after death or deactivation of the human body (desoma).

Herodotus. Writers, philosophers, clergy and statesmen/stateswomen of many countries of the ancient world referred to the lucid consciential projection experience. Among them are Gautama Buddha (563-483 B.C.) and Herodotus (485-425 B.C.).

Plato. Plato (428-347 B.C.) related the story of Er, son of Armenius, Pamphylian by birth, a soldier who was taken for dead in combat. At the end of 10 days, when they retrieved the already putrefied dead from the battlefield, they removed him in apparently good condition. They took the body home in order to bury it, when, on the twelfth day, while on the pyre, Er returned to life and reported what he had seen in *the great beyond*.

Interiorization. After leaving the human body, he found his consciousness together with many others in both good and bad condition according to his detailed report. In the end, he did not know how he reached the human body (interiorization) but, upon abruptly opening his eyes early that morning, he saw that he was lying on the pyre.

Bible. The Bible includes some expressive cases that suggest the study of the departure of the consciousness outside the body. The following 3 are examples:

1. **Ezekiel.** Through an assisted lucid projection, Ezekiel's consciousness was lifted up (extracted from the human body) and transported by a *spirit* (helper) to another place (Ezekiel 111:14).

2. **Apocalypse.** The phenomenon of lucid consciential projection was mentioned in the Apocalypse of John (1:10 and 11; 4:2).

3. **Epistles.** Also, Paul of Tarsus (?-67), in his Epistles (2 Corinthians 12:2), mentions the projective phenomenon.

Writers. The following individuals also wrote about consciential projections: Gaius Suetonius Tranquillus and Plinius the Younger (61-113).

Plutarch. Plutarch of Chaeronea (50-120) registered the report of Aridanaeus of Soles, of Cilicia, Asia Minor, a man of precarious morals, according to the opinion of that time, who was given up for dead in 79 A.D. after a violent fall.

Aridanaeus. Just when they were about to bury Aridanaeus' human body, 3 days after the accident, he reentered his body, regained full consciousness and related his lucid experience outside the human body during that 3-day period (prolonged lucid projection) in detail to Protogenes and other friends.

Recycling. From this point forward, Aridanaeus was transformed into a highly virtuous man. He even changed his name, according to the accounts of his contemporaries (projective existential recycling).

Greek. The following are some passages, in Greek, of Plutarch's report (p. 164-172, Societé D'Édition "Les Belles Lettres", 1974):

Τὰς μὲν οὖν πολλὰς ἠγνόει τίνες εἰσί, δύο δ' ἢ τρεῖς ἰδὼν γνωρίμους, ἐπειρᾶτο προσμῖξαι καὶ προσειπεῖν· αἱ δ' οὔτ'-ἤκουον οὔτ' ἦσαν παρ' ἑαυταῖς, ἀλλ' ἔκφρονες καὶ διεπτοημέναι, πᾶσαν ὄψιν ἀποφεύγουσαι καὶ ψαῦσιν.

Ἐνταῦθα μίαν ἔφη ⟨γνῶναι⟩ συγγενοῦς τινος, οὐ μέντοι σαφῶς· ἀποθανεῖν γὰρ ἔτι παιδὸς ὄντος· ἀλλ' ἐκείνην προσαγαγοῦσαν ἐγγὺς εἰπεῖν « χαῖρε, Θεσπέσιε. » Θαυμάσαντος δ' αὐτοῦ καὶ φήσαντος ὡς οὐ Θεσπέσιος ἀλλ' Ἀρδιαῖος ἐστι, « πρότερόν γε, φάναι, τὸ δ' ἀπὸ τοῦδε Θεσπέσιος. Οὐδὲ γάρ τοι τέθνηκας, ἀλλὰ μοίρᾳ τινὶ θεῶν ἥκεις δεῦρο τῷ φρονοῦντι, τὴν δ' ἄλλην ψυχὴν ὥσπερ ἀγκύριον ἐν τῷ σώματι καταλέλοιπας. Σύμβολον δέ σοι καὶ νῦν καὶ αὖθις ἔστω τὸ τὰς ψυχὰς τῶν τεθνηκότων μήτε σκιὰν ποιεῖν μήτε σκαρδαμύττειν ».

Μέχρι μὲν οὖν τούτων εἶναι θεατής· ὡς δ' ἀναστρέφειν ἔμελλεν, ἐν παντὶ κακῷ γενέσθαι διὰ φόβον· γυναῖκα γὰρ αὐτοῦ λαβομένην θαυμαστὴν τὸ εἶδος καὶ τὸ μέγεθος « δεῦρο δή, εἰπεῖν, οὗτος, ὅπως ἕκαστα μᾶλλον μνημονεύσῃς », καί τι ῥαβδίον, ὥσπερ οἱ ζωγράφοι, διάπυρον προσάγειν· ἑτέραν δὲ κωλύειν, αὐτὸν δ' ὥσπερ διὰ σύριγγος, ἐξαίφνης σπασθέντα πνεύματι νεανικῷ σφόδρα καὶ βιαίῳ, τῷ σώματι προσπεσεῖν καὶ ἀναβλέψαι σχεδὸν ἐπ' αὐτοῦ τοῦ μνήματος.

Οὕτως οὖν ἔφην ὅτι ὁ Σολεὺς Θεσπέσιος,
ἀνὴρ ἐκείνου τοῦ γενομένου μεθ' ἡμῶν ἐνταῦθα Πρωτο-
γένους οἰκεῖος καὶ φίλος, ἐν πολλῇ βιώσας ἀκολασίᾳ τὸν
πρῶτον χρόνον, εἶτα ταχὺ τὴν οὐσίαν ἀπολέσας, ἤδη χρόνον
τινὰ καὶ διὰ τὴν ἀνάγκην ἐγένετο πονηρός, καὶ τὸν πλοῦτον
ἐκ μετανοίας διώκων, ταὐτὸ τοῖς ἀκολάστοις ἔπασχε
πάθος οἳ τὰς γυναῖκας ἔχοντες μὲν οὐ φυλάττουσι,
προέμενοι δὲ πειρῶσιν αὖθις ἀδίκως ἑτέροις συνούσας
διαφθείρειν. Οὐδενὸς οὖν ἀπεχόμενος αἰσχροῦ φέροντος
εἰς ἀπόλαυσιν ἢ κέρδος, οὐσίαν μὲν οὐ πολλήν, δόξαν δὲ
πονηρίας ἐν ὀλίγῳ πλείστην συνήγαγε, μάλιστα δ' αὐτὸν
διέβαλεν ἀνενεχθεῖσά τις ἐξ Ἀμφιλόχου μαντεία. Πέμψας
γάρ, ὡς ἔοικεν, ἠρώτα τὸν θεόν εἰ βέλτιον βιώσεται τὸν
ἐπίλοιπον βίον· ὁ δ' ἀνεῖλεν ὅτι πράξει βέλτιον ὅταν
ἀποθάνῃ. Καὶ δὴ τρόπον τινὰ τοῦτο μετ' οὐ πολὺν χρόνον
αὐτῷ συνέπεσε. Κατενεχθεὶς γὰρ ἐξ ὕψους τινὸς εἰς
τράχηλον, οὐ γενομένου τραύματος, ἀλλὰ πληγῆς μόνον,
ἐξέθανε, καὶ τριταῖος ἤδη περὶ τὰς ταφὰς αὐτὰς ἀνήνεγκε.

Ταχὺ δὲ ῥωσθεὶς καὶ παρ' αὐτῷ γενόμενος, ἄπιστόν τινα
τοῦ βίου τὴν μεταβολὴν ἐποίησεν. Οὔτε γὰρ δικαιότερον
περὶ τὰ συμβόλαια γινώσκουσιν ἕτερον Κίλικες ἐν τοῖς
τότε χρόνοις γενόμενον, οὔτε πρὸς τὸ θεῖον ὁσιώτερον οὔτε
λυπηρότερον ἐχθροῖς ἢ βεβαιότερον φίλοις· ὥστε καὶ
ποθεῖν τοὺς ἐντυγχάνοντας αὐτῷ τὴν αἰτίαν ἀκοῦσαι
τῆς διαφορᾶς, οὐκ ἀπὸ τοῦ τυχόντος οἰομένους γεγονέναι
διακόσμησιν εἰς ἦθος τοσαύτην, ὅπερ ἦν ἀληθές, ὡς αὐτὸς
διηγεῖτο τῷ τε Πρωτογένει καὶ τοῖς ὁμοίως ἐπιεικέσι τῶν
φίλων.

Ἐπεὶ γὰρ ἐξέπεσε τὸ φρονοῦν τοῦ σώματος, οἷον ἄν
τις ἐκ πλοίου κυβερνήτης εἰς βυθὸν ἀπορριφεὶς πάθοι τὸ
πρῶτον, οὕτως ὑπὸ τῆς μεταβολῆς ἔσχεν· εἶτα, μικρὸν
ἐξαρθείς, ἔδοξεν ἀναπνεῖν ὅλος καὶ περιορᾶν πανταχόθεν,
ὥσπερ ἑνὸς ὄμματος ἀνοιχθείσης τῆς ψυχῆς.

English. The following is a translation of these passages to English:

"Here, then, is the report that I made: Thespesios of Soles, close friend of Protogenes, who lived here with us, spent the first part of his life in complete dissipation and consequently rapidly lost his material wealth.

"Later, necessity led him to vice; thus, in search of that wealth which he lamented having lost, he came to behave like those libertines who, instead of caring for the women they have, abandon them and later try to corrupt them in order to fraudulently reprehend them when they have already had new unions.

"He soon refused no dishonorable act, as long as it provided him with pleasure and gain. He was thereby able to make a fortune, albeit a mediocre one, and quickly gained a reputation for great dishonesty.

"But what caused him the greatest damage was the oracle given by Amphilocus: he had told him to ask God if the rest of his life would be better; the oracle responded that he would be better when he was dead. Actually, in a sense, it was in this manner that things occurred.

"Falling from a certain height, he landed on his neck and, in spite of not being wounded, was in a state of shock and taken for dead. Thus it was that, three days later, at the precise moment he was to be buried, he returned to life.

"Upon becoming reanimated and reestablished, he quickly underwent an unbelievable change in lifestyle; in fact, the Sicilians knew of no one among their contemporaries who was more scrupulous in his obligations, more pious in regard to divinity, more disturbing to his enemies, more trustworthy to his friends.

"He changed in such a manner that those who knew him wanted to know the reason for this change, as they said it was such a radical transformation of character that it could not have occurred by chance. It was in fact true, as he told Protogenes and other equally reliable friends.

"Ever since his thinking soul left his body, his first impression was similar to that of a diver who is projected outside of his boat in the abyss; let us see, then, the effect of this change.

"Emerging a bit, it appeared that his whole being breathed freely, and that he could see in all directions at once, his soul being open like one singular eye.

"Most of these souls were unknown; however, he saw two or three which he knew and endeavored to approach and speak to them; but they did not understand him, as they were not themselves, being crazed, in panic, and evading being seen and having any contact.

"In this environment, he recognized the soul of a cousin; in other words, he was uncertain, because this cousin had died when he was still a child; but the soul approached him, saying: 'Good day, Thespesios.' He became frightened, saying that he was not called Thespesios, but rather, Aridanaeus. The other replied, 'Yes, before, but from now on you are Thespesios.

"In truth, you are not dead, you came here by a decree of the gods, with the thinking part of your soul; you left the rest in your body as an anchor. Know, through these signs, how to conduct yourself now and later on: the souls of the dead do not cast a shadow and their eyes do not blink.

"All the while, Thespesios had been a simple spectator, however, as he was capable of recovering, a great fear enveloped him; a certain enormous woman of great beauty held him and said: 'I come here in order to better record within you each one of your memories.' She approached him with a small reddish stick, the color of fire, like those used by painters.

"But another woman intervened and stopped her. Then he suddenly, as though sucked by a violent, irresistible blast from a siphon, returned to his body and opened his eyes, when he was about to be lowered to his grave."

New perspective. After his prolonged lucid projection, Aridanaeus of Soles became transformed into a highly virtuous man and even changed his name to *Thespesios* (2 egos in a single intraphysical life), as suggested by the helper during the extraphysical experience. This is a typical case of new perspective or existential recycling with a genuinely projective origin, an event that occurs with the same characteristics nowadays in the most diverse societies.

Curma. A senator of Numidia, North Africa (now Algeria), named Curma, in the fifth century after Christ, as reported by Augustine of Tagaste (354-430), remained in a state of coma for several days and, upon awakening, told of having consciously lived outside his human body.

Seers. In ancient times, human lucid projectors, or those in whom the sight of the consciousness separated from the human body was opened, were called seers and later called prophets (1 Sam. 9:9).

Terms. In more recent times, the myths, mythologies, traditional cosmologies, mystical practices, beliefs, sagas and folkloric legends of many people have been presenting their own terms for characterizing, in one way or another, for better or for worse, the condition and personality of the contemporary lucid projector, or projectionist. The following 18 expressions serve as examples:

1. *Ataí* (Melanesians).
2. *Benandanti* (Lorena; sixteenth and seventeenth centuries).
3. *Delog* (Tibetans).
4. *Doppelgänger* (Germans).
5. *Doshi* (the Botswana people of the Bantus).
6. *Dovidja* (Hindus).
7. *Homo duplex* (Honoré de Balzac).
8. *Iruntarinia* (the Ngtataras of Australia).
9. *Kelah* (the Karens of Myanmar).
10. *Mora* (Slavs).
11. *Mzimu* (the tribes of the Lake Nyasa area, Africa).
12. *Navujieip* (Wild River Shoshone of Wyoming).
13. *Ort* (Syrians, Finnish people of Oriental Russia).
14. *Sky*-walker (Hindus).
15. *Sunäsun* (Mongolian Buryats of Siberia).
16. *Tamhasg* (Scots).
17. *Vardöger* (Norwegians).
18. *Wairua* (Maoris of New Zealand).

Bibliography: Almeida (15, p. 291), Balzac (71, p. 71), Black (137, p. 26), Bozzano (191, p. 132), Crookall (338, p. 145; 340, p . XI), Currie (354, p. 78), Delanne (381, p. 22), Durville (436, p. 41), Eliade (475, p. 117), Frost (560, p. 31), Greenhouse (636, p. 13), Guilmot (661, p. 57), King (846, p. 107), Knight (851, p. 273), Martin (1002, p. 34), Mitchell (1059, p. 37), Muldoon (1105, p. 45), Plato (1261, p. 487), Plutarch (1264, p. 39), Prieur (1289, p. 93), Sculthorp (1531, p. 133), Vieira (1762, p. 217), Walker (1781, p. 1).

---

16. CHRONOLOGY OF PROJECTIOLOGY

Definition. Projectiological chronology: treatise of the historical data, noteworthy facts and notable works of projectiology.

Synonymy: establishment of projectiological dates.

Events. The following is a list of the most notable events to date, 2002, in the still recent existence of projectiology, including the historical data prior to its proposal as a science:

347 B.C. – Plato writes about the case of the *human lucid projection* – an *extraphysical excursion* – of Er, the Armenian, proving the universality of this consciential phenomenon.

79 A.D. – In Cilicia, Asia Minor, Aridanaeus of Soles undergoes an experience now called near-death, with extraphysical experiences that remained as the first more detailed report registered for posterity. It came to us through Plutarch of Chaeronea.

100 A.D. – Plutarch of Chaeronea registers the *projective report* of the lucid projection experienced by Aridanaeus of Soles, of Silesia, Asia Minor.

1743 – In Stockholm, Sweden, the work *Diarii Spiritualis* by Emanuel Swedenborg is started. He would consequently become the *precursor* of projectiology and the first projective diarist, who recorded his experiences over a period of twenty years.

1832 – The publishing of the autobiographical, psychological novel *Louis Lambert* in Paris, that acclaims its author, Honoré de Balzac, as the first *prophet* (precognitor) of projectiology.

1832 – Honoré de Balzac, in Paris, gives the name of *Homo duplex* to the human lucid projector.

April 18, 1857 – The first edition of *Le Livre des Esprits,* by Allan Kardec, is published in Paris. In its eighth chapter, topics 153 to 171, it studies the emancipation of the soul (intraphysical consciousness) during corporeal life (projectiology), an aspect of the phenomena of the spirits which was forgotten in *spiritism,* whether in the French movement or those in other countries, when extraphysical consciousnesses and their phenomena generally received preferential attention.

1929 – Publication in the United States of America of the work *The Projection of the Astral Body,* by Sylvan Joseph Muldoon and Hereward Hubert Lavington Carrington, which became the first *classic* of projectiology.

1939 – The Russian Semyon D. Kirlian presents *again* the controversial *electrographic irradiations.*

1946 – The conscientiological technique of *existential inversion* (existential invertology) – already self-researched by the author in a theorical manner – was launched for the first time, although having little impact on intraphysical society,

1962 – The Russian Iosif M. Goldberg *re*discovers the "novelty" of *dermal-optical perception* (skin sight).

1966 – The author begins to give priority and full-time dedication to the *research* of *projectiology/conscientiology* in his work (experimentology).

1966 – The interconsciential assistential technique of *penta (personal energetic task),* popularly called *passes to the void,* which is a daily practice performed for the rest of the individual's life, is launched.

1966 – At the University of California at Davis, in the United States of America, the researcher Charles Theodore Tart performs the first *laboratory* experiment with human lucid projection.

1970 – The Theory of *Homo sapiens serenissimus* and its corollaries is officially proposed (serenology).

1971 – The work *Journeys Out of the Body* by Robert Monroe is launched in New York, NY. Many editions have been printed, making it the first international bestseller of projectiology.

1975 – In the United States of America, the book *Life After Life,* by Raymond A. Moody Jr., with preface by Elisabeth Kübler-Ross, became an international bestseller. This small work achieved worldwide attention, for the first time, for the near-death experience (NDE) and, consequently, for extracorporeal phenomena. This opened a new and unexpected field within the area of medicine for projectiology research.

1978 – In Storrs, Connecticut, in the United States of America, *The International Association for Near-Death Studies (IANDS)* is founded. It is an international organization of scientists and the public, dedicated to exploring near-death experiences (1 of the 54 phenomena in the basic phenomenological complex of projectiology) and its implications.

1979 – The conscientiotherapeutic technique of prophylaxis and self-defense, the *vibrational state* (VS), including the prophylactic VS (paraprophylaxia), is launched.

1980 – The theory of the *cosmoethical megaparadigm,* cosmoethics – popularly called the cosmic moral – is proposed.

1980 – The theory of *interassistentiality,* or *the consolation task* (the primary task of consolation) and *the clarification task* (the evolved task of clarification) is proposed within conscientiological intraphysical society.

1980 – The conscientiotherapeutic technique of *auric coupling* (holochakrology) is launched.

1981 – In Storrs, Connecticut, in the United States of America, *IANDS* launches the first periodical publication, journal or technical magazine, *Anabiosis – The Journal for Near-Death Studies,* dedicated specifically to the publication of near-death experience research.

1981 – In Storrs, Connecticut, in the United States of America, *Vital Signs,* is launched by *IANDS.* It is the first bulletin (quarterly digest) dedicated to reporting on works and tasks performed by the research team of the first organization exclusively dedicated to the investigation of the near-death experience.

September 6, 1981 – In Rio de Janeiro, Brazil, the *Center for Continuous Consciousness* is founded, with the presence of 19 persons. This served to call particular attention, for the first time, to continuous consciential lucidity and would trigger the creation of dozens of other centers in various locations.

1981 – In Rio de Janeiro, Brazil, the book *Projections of the Consciousness* is published – currently in its 5th edition (Portuguese), as well as having editions in Spanish and English – in which the term *projectiology* is proposed for the first time.

1982 – The conscientiometric work hypothesis of *cons*, or the units of lucidity of the consciousness (holomaturology), is proposed.

1982 – According to research estimates, 8 million *near-death experiences* (NDE) occur every year.

November, 1982 – Sebastião Mendes de Carvalho, on the research team of the Center for Continuous Consciousness in Rio de Janeiro, Brazil, published the first *article* in the popular press with the term *projectiology* in the title of the work. Publication: *Reincarnation*, a monthly magazine published in Porto Alegre, capital of the state of Grande do Sul, Brazil, p.14, 15.

June, 1983 – In São Paulo, São Paulo, Brazil the monthly column *Bulletin of Projectiology Number 1,* is published in the *Jornal Espírita*. This bulletin published 83 editions in the following years (communicology).

1983 – In São Paulo, São Paulo, Brazil, impassioned articles written by ideologically patrolling spiritists, who are extremely purist, orthodox and sectarian, were published against projectiology (Examples: Monteiro; Worm), which served to attract greater attention to the research of the human lucid projection phenomenon. On that occasion, the *Center for Continuous Consciousness* in Rio de Janeiro, Brazil, was not able to respond to the increased number of incoming letters requesting projectiological information.

August, 1983 – In São Paulo, São Paulo, Brazil, on page 6 of the journal *Folha Espírita,* the *Carta Aberta aos Espíritas (Open Letter to Spiritists)* is published, in which the author publicly presents his position regarding projectiology to the ideological patrollers of the kardecist movement of Brazil (parapedagogy).

March, 1984 – In São Paulo, São Paulo, Brazil, on page 4 of the *Jornal Espírita,* the article *Maturidade Extrafísica* is published by the author, emphasizing, for the first time, the importance of the integral *maturity* (holomaturology) of the consciousness.

March 29-31, 1985 – In Kansas City, Montana, in the United States of America, the first Convention of *The International Association for Near-Death Studies (IANDS)* is held, being dedicated exclusively to the study and discussion of near-death experiences.

January 31, 1986 – In Rio de Janeiro, Brazil, the first pilot edition of 5,000 copies of the work *Projeciologia (Projectiology)* – distributed free of charge and now out of print – is launched. It presents the first large international bibliography on projectiological themes (1,907 titles). The first *extraphysical code of ethics* was included in this work in chap. 132, p. 211-213, indicating 16 practical items relative to *cosmoethics;* as well as the 3 basic conscential states, p. 34.

1986 – The theory of the *consciential paradigm* and its corollaries is proposed.

1986 – The theory of *groupkarmic interprison* and its corollaries (holokarmology) is proposed.

1987 – In Bryn Athyn, Pennsylvania, in the United States of America, the bulletin *Revitalized Signs,* the successor to *Vital Signs,* with the same objectives, is launched by *IANDS.*

June 12-16, 1987 – The *First Projectiology Seminar in Brasilia* was held, being registered in a newsletter authored by Prof. Basilio Baranoff.

December 12,13, 1987 – In the Convention Center at Unicamp, in Campinas, São Paulo, Brazil, the *1st Brazilian Symposium of Continuous Consciousness (BSCC)* was held, in which the author defended the *theory of Homo sapiens serenissimus.* This first, more ample debate on general aspects of projectiology included the participation of 142 persons from 8 different states in Brazil: São Paulo, Rio de Janeiro, Minas Gerais, Bahia, Santa Catarina, Sergipe, Amazonas and the Federal District, and from a total of 7 capitals and 21 cities.

January 16, 1988 – In Rio de Janeiro, Brazil, the *International Institute of Projectiology (IIP),* was founded, being the first *institute* dedicated exclusively to the research, study and teaching of projectiological themes (conscientiocentrology).

1988 – The basic techniques of *conscientiotherapy* are presented.

1988 – The *Swedenborg syndrome* is diagnosed, according to conscientiotherapy.

1989 – The theory of *petifreeness* was proposed as being a theorical procedure that is of priority and more feasible, in the short-term, in the evolutionary way of the intraphysical consciousness, at our present average stage of intraconsciential progress (petifreeology).

June, 1989 – The *Bulletin of Information on Projectiology (BIPRO),* of the International Institute of Projectiology, in Rio de Janeiro, Rio de Janeiro, Brazil, is launched (communicology).

1990 – The conscientiological theory of *strong traitism* and its corollaries (strong traits of the consciousness) is proposed.

1990 – The conscientiological theory of *thosenes* (thought, sentiment and consciential energy) and its corollaries (thosenology) is proposed.

1990 – The *consciential bond* is theorically (theory and technique) presented and established in conscientiological intraphysical society (parasociology), at the International Institute of Projectiology, in Rio de Janeiro, Rio de Janeiro, Brazil.

1990 – The conscientiometric and parasexual technique of the *penile aura* (sexosomatics) is proposed, directed mostly toward youth.

1990 – The conscientiological and parasexual technique of the *holo-orgasm* (sexosomatics) is proposed.

June 4-7, 1990 – The *I International Congress on Projectiology,* in Rio de Janeiro, Rio de Janeiro, Brazil is held (communicology).

1991 – The conscientiological theory of *consciential paracomatose* (projectiotherapy, conscientiotherapy) is proposed.

1991 – The theory of the *incomplete couple* and its corollaries (intraphysicology) is proposed.

1991 – The conscientiometric technique of *intraconsciential balancing* (conscientiometry) is proposed, being a self-help resource of interest to all persons.

1992 – The theory of *existential robotization* (intraphysicology) is proposed.

February 9, 1992 – In Rio de Janeiro, Rio de Janeiro, Brazil, the first *group of existential inverters* is founded, with 17 young inverters (existential invertology) from the team of volunteers of the International Institute of Projectiology (IIP).

February 22, 1992 – A research project is performed at the International Institute of Projectiology (IIP), in Rio de Janeiro, Rio de Janeiro, Brazil, that proposes 12 attitudes for avoiding the state of *extraphysical catatonia.*

1992 – The *International Bibliography of Conscientiology,* including the specific phenomena of projectiology, exceeds 5,000 references from 37 countries.

May 30, 1993 – The first ample *debate* on the *consciential paradigm* is held at the International Institute of Projectiology (IIP), in Rio de Janeiro, Rio de Janeiro, Brazil.

1994 – Twenty percent of conventional *scientists* still dedicate their work and talent to the improvement of techniques for killing their fellow beings.

1994 – A high number of parapsychic, multidisciplinary investigators dedicate themselves more intensely to the *research of NDEs,* notably those of children.

1994 – Our *human brain* consists of almost 3.3 lb (1.5 kg) of matter, while almost nothing is known about the *parabrain* (paraneurology).

1994 – There is still no conventional scientific publication that addresses the issue of *thosene* (thosenology).

January, 1997 – The magazine *Conscientia* is launched.

July, 1998 – *The Journal of Conscientiology* is launched.

October 21-24, 1999 – The *II International Congress on Projectiology is held* in Barcelona, Spain, (communicology).

May 16-19, 2002 – The *III International Congress on Projectiology and Conscientiology is held* in Manhattan, NY, USA (communicology).

Bibliography: See the author's recent work, *700 Conscientiology Experiments.*

II – Relationships between Projectiology and Other Sciences

17. PROJECTIOLOGY AND INTERDISCIPLINARITY

Definitions. Interdisciplinarity: the common condition referring to or including two or more disciplines or areas of knowledge; existing interaction between two or more disciplines.

Synonymy: integration of wisdom; juxtaposition of diverse disciplines; multidisciplinarity; pluricurricular knowledge; pluridisciplinarity; scientific universality; synthesis of knowledge; transdisciplinarity.

Universalism. Interdisciplinarity, when it represents an integration of learning or a synthesis of knowledge, harmonizes and fits entirely with generalism, holistics and, moreover, with universalism, since it advances toward the total conception of the universe (totalogy) through the integration of all fields of human consciousness research.

Recognitions. Interdisciplinarity – technical intercommunication between specialists of diversified areas of research – avoids the frustration of recognizing, too late, that you reinvented the wheel and other creations, techniques, and theories that have already been consolidated. These frustrations are characteristic of *closed disciplinarity* or *insufficient interdisciplinarity,* typical of schizophrenic or autistic science.

Monoglotism. Monoglotism currently occurs more within the societies that speak English, the language employed more intensely by science in the West. This has a strong effect upon the processes of globalization or the *babelization of knowledge* that is occurring, being the greatest obstacle to an expansion of interdisciplinarity. We can see a good example of this in Moss, Thelma (bibl. 1,096, p. 150).

Exchange. No science is sovereign to the point of disregarding the collaboration of other sciences. Each has its own specific content that characterizes it. Nevertheless, all of them exist and develop in an interconnected manner, in an incessant and irreversible exchange of values.

Isolation. The individual who refuses scientific collaboration commits the grave error of possibly ending up working in isolation. It is always good to clarify postures: independent research is oftentimes a healthy fact; permanent isolation is always a mistake. These are merely logical concepts.

Predisposition. Polyglotism, international education and a multicultural support system predispose the researcher from any scientific area toward positive interdisciplinarity.

Derivations. Thus, as mentioned above, parapsychology is derived from metapsychics and projectiology is derived from parapsychology – these 3 lines of research being included within the vast field of conscientiology or egology.

Stage. Projectiology's experimental research of leading-edge relative truth, within the scope of conscientiology, always aims to move along advanced lines (projected, or through projections) beyond the limits of conventional human knowledge. This signifies stepping beyond all human forms and the traditional, technological, and artificial limitations of the most up-to-date pure scientific investigation.

Holosomatics. This explains the indispensable employment of interdisciplinarity and holosomatics in the emergence of the *science of projectiology,* as well as the decisive role played by universalism and extraphysicology (multidimensionality) in the establishment of the *philosophy of projectiology.*

Elimination. As is generally the case with all sciences, regarding the affirmation of relative truth, projectiology seeks to eliminate the following 28 spurious variables, among others:

1. Absence of critical judgment.
2. Acceptance of appearances.
3. Beliefs.
4. Chimerical ideas.
5. Delirious subjectivism.
6. Easy presumptions.

   7. Fallacies, notably those of a logical nature (errors in logic).
   8. Futile philosophies.
   9. Hallucinations of all types.
10. Illegitimate inquiries.
11. Illuminated mystification.
12. Ingenuous or recherché superstitions.
13. Insecure reasoning.
14. Intellectual stagnation.
15. Irrationalism.
16. A lack of possibilities.
17. Metaphysical abstractions.
18. Mysticism.
19. Mythology.
20. A non-analytical spirit.
21. Paranoia.
22. Preconceptions or apriorisms.
23. Sensory illusions.
24. Sophism (sophistry).
25. A spirit of credulity.
26. Uncalculated shots in the dark.
27. Unverified suggestions *(suggestions based merely on one's own thoughts)*.
28. Well-educated ignorance.

Basis. Projectiology is not a doctrinaire ideology or a closed system of ideas (monolithism) based on faith, revelation, dogmas or the creation of heretics.

Neophobia. Projectiology, as a conscientiocentric and theorice-oriented science, will never follow a linear trajectory or submit itself to mental straightjackets, because it combats all types of neophobia through bold, neophilic personal experiences: self-discernment; self-analyses, self-evaluations, multidimensional self-awareness, bioenergetic self-balancing, evolutionary self-organization, self-education, self-research, lucid self-projectability, self-retrocognitions and continuous self-superceding.

Uncertainties. Conscientiology can delineate the lives of projectiologists and conscientiologists through cosmoethics, the clarification task and polykarmality. Nevertheless, this attitude is the intraphysical consciousness' own; it signifies imprisonment rather than a process of uninterrupted intraphysical recycling that is capable of improving the individual's general ethical, political, scientific and philosophical uncertainties.

Binomial. Projectiology causes intraphysical consciousnesses to become dispassionate about ideas, but eager for evolutionary self-overcoming, detoxifying oneself regarding the homeostasis of the holosoma, including consciential energies, emotions and thosenes. The interested individual learns to coexist with opposites within the context of the *admiration-disagreement binomial.*

Egos. Each of us can have many egos in a single human existence, if we consider the ego as being representative of the personality, the social being or the role that the individual plays in intraphysical society, within his/her evolutionary group or families. In evolutionary terms, it's ideal when the change of egos is for the better, as in the case of Aridanaeus of Soles/ Thespesios.

Case study. In the twentieth century, we can see, as never before in human lives, the changing of egos that is being performed by the same intraphysical consciousness. The following are two examples of changes for the better in different periods – the first and the second – of the individuals' existential programs:

   1. **Marxism.** The man who lived armed with the Marxist-Leninist theory of history and had an explanation for everything, was submissive to dogmas, crutches and conditioning, and freed himself through lucid projective experiences with which he feels free, light and happy – a citizen of the cosmos.

   2. **Catholicism.** The woman who was a loyal member of the Catholic Church and broke with faith of any origin in order to undertake personal experiments with consciential energies and parapsychic

experiences based on projectiology. This was done without rejection mechanisms toward the original ideas, thereby achieving greater personal confidence and energetic self-defense.

18. PROJECTIOLOGY AND OTHER SCIENCES

Field. The limits of the parapsychic research of projectiology are not defined and its field necessarily presents the ample involvement of other disciplines through a practical interdisciplinarity.

Intersection. In fact, all sciences intersect with projectiology on one or more particularly sensitive point.

Refinement. As with all sciences, projectiology is subsidized by other sciences *(refinement of knowledge).*

Multidisciplinarity. On the other hand, scientists in any field can benefit from discoveries provided by lucid projections. This is because some of the most enriching areas of modern science are those that ignore the limits between the various disciplines and take on interdisciplinary, multidisciplinary or universalistic aspects through scientific teams with diversified knowledge.

Sciences. In the analysis of the phenomenology of projections, it is inevitably necessary to appeal to other correlated sciences, such as the following 6:

1. Biology.
2. Parabiology.
3. Psychobiology and other medical specializations.
4. Medicine.
5. Paramedicine.
6. Psychiatry.

Parapsychobiophysics. When researching projections of the human consciousness and the extraphysical consciousness, projectiology gets to the core of parapsychobiophysics.

Zoology. When studying animal projection and the existence of extraphysical animals – parafauna – projectiology enters fully within the scope of zoology (parazoology).

Botany. When analyzing the projections of plants in general, and the existence of extraphysical plants – parafauna – as well as human lucid projections provoked through the use of plants, projectiology decidedly penetrates into the areas of botany (parabotany).

Implications. Besides the sciences mentioned, projectiology is directly related to anthropology, astronomy, physics, psychology, sociology and history, which are referred to in this section in specific chapters.

Technology. The implications of projectiology with regard to technology and human culture in general are vast and still undetermined. The possibilities of study and practical application are also unlimited.

Areas. The phenomena of projectiology also present close connections with other such diverse areas of human knowledge as: geography, including cartography; oceanography; meteorology; geology; speleology; ecology; science fiction; art; music; and others.

Mathematics. Projectiology has a relationship with the universal language of mathematics when presenting the formulas of its enunciations, models and theories.

Chemistry. It also has a relationship with chemistry when analyzing consciential projections and drugs, both light and heavy, licit and illicit, medications, incense, perfumes and fragrances.

Archeology. The research field of archeology has been utilizing the resources of projective archeology, together with extraphysical psychometry and extraphysical retrocognition, since the nineteenth century. Nowadays there is a wealth of evidence of its efficiency in this area of human knowledge, as well as specialized works on the subject (see *Goodman,* Jeffrey; *Schwartz,* Stephan A.; and *Wilson,* Colin).

Laziness. Faith of any kind also signifies laziness.

Mysticism. Mysticism, existing religions, multiform religiosity, religious professionalism and temporal power, proliferate intensely and establish their lasting roots in human societies due to existential (intraphysical) mental laziness or, more precisely, pluri-existential consciential indolence (intellectual fatigue, mental vacuum).

Complacency. This maintains the intraphysical consciousness inert and complacent, without initiative or motivation to think for him/herself and more inclined to *believe* than to *experience*.

Absolutism. Thus, the consciousness accepts the imposition of a ready-made set of ideas, an *absolute truth* that is imposed upon it by the *savers of souls,* forming a closed, sectarian doctrinaire group that does not allow refutation.

Discovery. In this condition, in which no one asks the individual to reason, and everybody spares the person any mental effort, insisting that he/she remains a component of existential robotization that is immersed in chronic sloth – with a doctrine that is prefabricated, is thought out for the person, is chewed and ruminated, ready to be swallowed (ingested) and blindly followed – the lazy consciousness feels him/herself to be realized, makes him/herself comfortable and retreats into his/her *own little world.*

Psychosoma. This is the evolutionary level at which the emotional body (psychosoma) is predominant over the passive consciousness that has still not discovered the existence of the parabody of discernment, namely the mentalsoma.

Self-determination. The experience of lucid projection in other existential dimensions breaks the inertia of this fossilized state, leading the intraphysical consciousness to discover, by itself, and apply the mentalsoma with lucidity and self-determination.

Crutches. In other words: the science of projectiology (that seeks refutation) builds up, with expressive naturalness, the revolutionary philosophical proposal of the improvement of the consciousness – which forever dispenses with *crutches* having any mystical connotation, as well as religiosity of any kind. Its application further suggests the practice of penta for those individuals motivated toward interconsciential assistance.

Self-discernment. This demonstrates that the evolutionary advancement of the consciousness occurs on a continuous basis after reaching a certain level (that of *Homo sapiens serenissimus*) by rationally, logically, and reflectively applying the measurement of pure self-discernment stemming from the mentalsoma.

Influence. All this develops beyond the instinctive-animal influence of the human body's *brain* (or even the *abdominal brain*) and, furthermore, beyond the immature-emotional influence of the psychosoma's *parabrain*.

Key. Therein lies the evolutionary key that is currently being encountered by intraphysical consciousnesses upon awakening from their stagnant, multi-existential, millenary somnambulism through lucid consciential projections.

Religion. Projectiology is ready and able to offer scientific equivalents for many traditional religious concepts, even though it is still in its initial stages and has an endless amount of research before it, as does every science. This is especially true with regard to consciential modes of communication in the following 3 areas:

1. **Confirmations.** Prayer and evocation, that depend on telepathy, can have their results immediately and directly confirmed in the extraphysical dimension by the consciousness, which is projected from the human body at that time.

2. **Experiences.** Viewing, or the revelation of clairvoyance, can be felt or experienced by the projected intraphysical consciousness at the extraphysical location, including those locations in extraphysical communities.

3. **Therapies.** So-called *physical miracles* and those *prodigious cures* generated by psychokinesis or telekinesis (ectoplasmy) – as well as many other concepts – can be verified by the lucid projector through the direct action of the vehicles of manifestation and the use of consciential energy.

Theologians. Modern theologians use emotionally charged words in such a way as to produce a state of consciousness in their listeners and readers in which the persuasive logic of an argument is not very deeply scrutinized. This is a technical subtlety.

Sentimentalism. The intrusion of emotion and sentimentalism, which are characteristic of the psychosoma, the parabody of emotions and desires, is always typical of a flawed argument that does not come from the parabody of discernment.

Artifice. This philosophical or technical artifice has been deeply employed in the catechisms and conditionings of Buddhism, Christianity, Hinduism, Judaism and Islam as well as in other variants of religious, theological and mystical knowledge.

Substitution. Hence, lucid projection beneficially substitutes belief in general, blind faith, and even so-called *rationalized faith* with knowledge that is direct, personal, incontrovertible and, finally, definitive for the consciousness. In this way, any element that is intermediary or intrusive towards impartial reasoning, holomaturity and greater discernment is eliminated.

Penta. The daily practice (for the rest of the intraphysical consciousness' life) of the personal energetic task (penta), as implemented upon a foundation of lucid consciential projection, completely replaces the adult individual's need for religion, belief or faith of any kind or origin. Penta confirms, in a practical manner, that which reasoning, self-discernment and logic have already proved to the individual.

Hagiography. Projectiology has a direct relationship with hagiography or hagiology, as there is an entire field of projective hagiography that studies the lives of the so-called *saints,* with evidence of the intercurrence of all main projectiological phenomena.

Expressions. Roman Catholic hagiologists label the visions and extraphysical encounters experienced by the intraphysical projector with infantile expressions, such as the following 4:

1. "Experience of God."
2. "Extraordinary infused grace."
3. "Presence of the absolute."
4. "Visitation by God."

Case study. The compilation of the occurrences of lucid projection that have been recorded up until the present constitutes the historical development of projectiology. This official case study is an impressive collection and involves the interconnection of dozens of diverse areas of human thought, as can be observed in the International Bibliography (See *700 Conscientiology Experiments,* International Bibliography, 5,116 works).

Methods. Despite what has been written, today's sciences – modeled within the structure of the space-time continuum in which we live while in the ordinary, physical waking state – do not possess adequate resources for studying the consciousness' experiences outside the human body, when projected in the isolated mentalsoma in the mentalsomatic dimension.

Neoconcepts. If the space-time model is inadequate to explain these lucid projections, we need to develop new concepts of reality in order to explain them. To this end, the creation of new methods of scientific investigation will be inevitable.

Facts. At this point, if we wish to map out the world of projectiological experiences, we return to an imposition stemming from the facts: ideally, both the researcher and the research subject will produce lucid projective experiences through the impulsion of their will (preferably without the use of drugs), each one maintaining the consciousness totally open to new manifestations, with a minimum of personal emotional and psychological influences, in order to overcome the greatest possible number of discrepancies in their extraphysical perceptions while the consciousness is temporarily projected and free, as well as in their analysis of those experiences realized while outside the human body.

Idiosyncrasies. This participatory research, involving the *researcher-research object,* will maximally eliminate the extremely individual idiosyncratic interpretations stemming from each person's value system. The phenomena will thus be studied in a more objective and transparent manner.

Bibliography: Amadou (21, p. 23), Ancilli (24, p. 264), Black (137, p. 121), D'arbó (365, p. 32), Goodman (618, p. 219), Green (632, p. 93), Greene (635, p. 101), Mitchell (1058, p. 41), Pratt (1285, p. 155), Rouhier (1478, p. 8), Schwartz (1527, p. 67), Targ (1651, p. 13), White (1828, p. 218), Wilson (1856, p. 125), Wolman (1863, p. 929).

19. PROJECTIOLOGY AND PARAPSYCHOLOGY

Definition. Parapsychology (Greek: *para,* beyond, alongside; *psyché,* soul; *logos,* treatise, study): branch of psychology addressing behavior that is still not capable of being described or explained in terms of known physical principles, and which has an assured and irreversible role in humankind's evolution or, in other words, that which transcends psychology.

Synonymy: bio-information; biopsychics; biopsychism; biopsychoenergetics; biosophy; cosmosophy; hyperpsychics; metapsychics; metapsychism; metapsychology; nomothetical psychology; paraneuropsychology; paranormalism; paranormology; paraphysics; parapsychics; parapsychism; parapsychobiophysics; parapsychologism; psilogy; psiology (Carrol B. Nash); psionics; psychic research; psychobioenergetics (Soviet term); psychobiophysics; psycho-energetics; psychotronics (Czech term); science of the paranormal; scientific spiritism; transcendent science; ultraphany (Italian term).

Term. The term "parapsychology" was coined in 1889 by Max Dessoir – a German psychologist and parapsychic researcher.

Psi-gamma. Projectiology, or projective parapsychology, a subdiscipline of conscientiology regarding its related phenomena, is derived from the phenomenological framework of human parapsychology in the study of subjective phenomena (psi-gamma).

Discoincidentiology. Parapsychology can be divided by separating those phenomena regarded as being pure paranormal phenomena into: those that are produced when the intraphysical consciousness' vehicles of manifestation are coincident (they present a unified body, holosoma); and those produced when the intraphysical consciousness' vehicles of manifestation are out of the condition of coincidence (discoincidence).

Manifestations. Thus, we can see that a number of so-called pure paranormal occurrences fall within the scope of coincidentiology and others lie within discoincidentiology, namely projectiology. Nevertheless, in practice, the phenomena intermingle in their manifestations stemming either from one condition or another, constantly and intricately alternating and mixing themselves.

Accreditation. Parapsychology was recognized as a science and admitted (with 165 votes in favor and 30 votes against) as a member science to the *American Association for the Advancement of Science* (A.A.A.S.) on December 30, 1969.

Affiliation. The A.A.A.S., an international society founded in 1957, based in New York, NY, brings together approximately 200 researchers of all fields, from 25 countries. It officially accepted, as one of its new divisions, the affiliation or accreditation of the Parapsychological Association (P.A.) – a prestigious association, the membership of which includes the most eminent parapsychologists in the world.

Subdivision. This was equivalent to accepting parapsychology as being a sector of science, with the same rights as other areas.

Courses. There is nothing that cannot be exhaustively researched. Research continues.

Laboratories. There are currently 129 scientific parapsychology courses or laboratories in operation, spread throughout the planet in various institutions.

Institutions. The following are some of these institutions: Augusto Mota Integrated Colleges, Rio de Janeiro, Brazil (post-graduate course in parapsychology); Duke University, Durham, North Carolina, U.S.A.; University of Edinburgh, Scotland; University of Freiburg, Breisgau, Germany;

Long Island University, Greenvale, U.S.A.; University of California, Santa Barbara, California, U.S.A.; Utrecht University, Netherlands; Biopsychic Sciences College at Paraná, Curitiba, Paraná, Brazil.

Facts. The number of facts observed at the beginning of the era of modern science – which has existed for only 4 centuries – was so small that it was not worth dividing it into different sciences. The number of facts later grew to the point that specialization became more and more indispensable. In the current Internet age, the tendency is to continue to grow.

Consensus. In a considerable number of sciences, it is rare that a consensus is reached on any concept. All unanimity indicates ignorance.

Resistance. There is also a resistance, as part of the intraphysical consciousness' nature, towards modifying our concept of the world. This occurs with the author, with the reader, and with scientists in general.

Theories. Innovative theories are only accepted by new generations, or when one or two generations of researchers have already passed through desoma.

Factors. This seems to be due not only to arteriosclerosis, senility, dementia or Alzheimer's disease, but also to considerable influencing human factors that are understandable, to a point, in this pathological intraphysical society in which we live, which is much more of a hospital than a school. The following are 7 examples:

1. **Preconceptions.** Scientific preconceptions that are very well disguised by self-corruption.
2. *Status.* Social *status* (prestige in a small group, political behavior of a *mega-ego*).
3. **Corporatism.** Professional or corporatist interests *(lobbyism)*.
4. **Money.** Subservience to economic power or slavery to money.
5. *Seated-on-the-fence.* Personal complacence or a *seated-on-the-fence* attitude.
6. **Washing.** Brainwashing (abdominal brain).
7. **Repressions.** The absence of derepression.

Research. Some time ago, an editor of *New Scientist,* a most prestigious scientific magazine, performed a research project in order to prove that the scientific community opposed the existence of parapsychological phenomena. The result was precisely the contrary. About 75% of those polled said they felt that these phenomena had been proven or were in the process of being proven.

Scientists. The most surprising result of this research was that 40% of the scientists interviewed declared that they accepted the reality of parapsychological phenomena because they had personally experienced them.

Interests. It is ironic and regrettable that the same human interests which limit the development of parapsychic research will be responsible for its inevitable and inescapable development. This with bellicose objectives in view, such as espionage and frank political domination of consciousnesses by superpower nations who are in constant conflict in all areas, including so-called *psychic warfare, consciential warfare* or *psychotronic warfare,* in the field of *consciousness technology.*

Sciences. It is important to stress once again that projectiology relates to other sciences and, due to many factors, requires interdisciplinary or universalistic approaches.

Growth. In the case of projectiology, we see, for the first time, that a specific research area within parapsychology requires its independent establishment in order that science as a whole grows as one (see *The Essential Conscientiology*).

Analysis. In the description and analysis of the occurrences of projectiology, only parapsychology (psycho-energetics in Soviet Russia and psychotronics in Czechoslovakia), has greater authority and sufficient technical competence for ponderable applications, making the participation of the latter in this field irrecusable and irreplaceable.

Russia. The Russian Academy of Sciences (the former Soviet Union) officially confirmed the paranormal powers of the sensitive Djuna Davitashivili who was tested in its Physiology Institute on August 26, 1987. Called the *D phenomenon* (D refers to the first letter of the parapsychic woman's name), it is the ability of an individual to heat other bodies and cure illnesses with infrared irradiation (bioenergy) emitted from human hands.

Batrachian. Scientists proved the transmission of bioenergy from the sensitive's hands to a batrachian (frog) heart by using equipment to register a significant slowing of the heartbeat.

Cancer. A member of the Academy of Sciences saw the sensitive, who practices under the official supervision of medical doctors, cure a case of skin cancer in only 15 minutes. (*O Globo;* Rio de Janeiro; newspaper; daily; section: "Ciência e Vida"; year LXIII; No. 19,639; August 27, 1987; one illus.; p. 1, 18).

Register. In this way, the pioneering nature of the Russians was registered in an official, open recognition of parapsychology, parapsychism and, thereby, projectiology. This was due to the projection of bioenergy, as well as the highly developed research of certain advanced phenomena or paraperceptions in Russia, beyond the research of other Western countries, including The United States of America where, until today, there is a great deal of blind and often commercial pressure against institutions dedicated to parapsychology and parapsychic phenomena, with a great amount of euphemism and political and corporatist pretense.

Folklore. At this point it is important to consider 4 categories of folklore:

1. **Alchemy.** Alchemy became the folklore of chemistry.
2. **Astrology.** Astrology became the folklore of astronomy.
3. **Religion.** Religion (mysticism) became the folklore of empiricism (science, replicability).
4. **Occultism.** Occultism (esoterism) became the folklore of parapsychology.

Driving forces. We can consider 3 categories of interconnected evolutionary *driving forces:*

1. **Mind.** The revelation or scientific discovery of the mind (human brain) was the *driving force* of psychoanalysis.
2. **Paraperceptiology.** The revelation or scientific discovery of human paraperceptions (animism-parapsychism) was the *driving force* of parapsychology.
3. **Conscientiality.** The revelation or scientific discovery of the integral consciousness (holosoma, holobiography, multidimensionality, holomaturity) is the *driving force* of projectiology.

Brazil. Brazilian parapsychologists helped to form the universalistic perspective in the approach to projectiology. In this sense, when the greatest names in parapsychology in Brazil over the years are listed, the following 14, among others, should not be overlooked (see International Bibliography of Projectiology):

1. **Andrade,** Hernani Guimarães.
2. **Borges,** Walter Rosa.
3. **Faria,** Osmar Andrade.
4. **Góes,** Eurico de.
5. **Lessa,** Adelaide Peters.
6. **Lyra,** Alberto.
7. **Machado,** Brasilio Marcondes.
8. **Machado,** Mário Amaral.
9. **Montagno,** Elson.
10. **Paula,** João Teixeira de.
11. **Pires,** José Herculano.
12. **Rodrigues,** Henrique.
13. **Tabone,** Márcia.
14. **Tinoco,** Carlos Alberto.

Bibliography: Amadou (21, p. 404), Ashby (59, p. 144), Beloff (107, p. 149), Berendt (120, p. 120), Black (137, p. 39), Blackmore (139, p. 242), Blasco (151, p. 103), Bret (202, p. 11), Chauvin (275, p. 106), Cohen (290, p. 158), Douglas (409, p. 323), Dragaud (412, p. 53), Faria (495, p. 76), Ferreira (509,

p. 49), Gómez (613, p. 135), Herlin (714, p. 177), Heydecker (716, p. 49), Holroyd (737, p. 22), Imbassahy (778, p. 206), Inardi (786, p. 130), Klein (850, p. 81), Larcher (887, p. 187), Mac Dougall (966, p. 523), Mc Connell (1019, p. 75), Meek (1028, p. 89), Morel (1086, p. 41), Paixão (1183, p. 106), Paula (1208, p. 60), Pires (1247, p. 21), Randall (1368, p. 184), Russell (1482, p. 57), Saisset (1495, p. 26), Salomon (1497, p. 140), Still (1622, p. 236), Sudre (1630, p. 348), Targ (1651, p. 156), Tishner (1687, p. 122), Valério (1725, p. 74), Wolman (1863, p. 790). See the author's recent book: *The Essential Conscientiology* (in Portuguese).

20. PROJECTIOLOGY AND PSYCHOLOGY

Definition. Psychology (Greek: *psyché,* soul; *logos,* treatise, study): the science of psychic phenomena and human behavior.

Synonymy: personology; science of the intraphysical consciousness; science of the mind; science of the psyche.

Explanation. The relationships of parapsychology and projectiology with psychology are very deep. The object of these 3 sciences is the study of human nature.

Metapsychics. Without metapsychics, contemporary parapsychology would not exist; but parapsychology is an extrapolation of psychology.

Conscientiology. It is not possible to conceptualize psychology in a manner that satisfies all existing schools. Far from having a single definition, what exists is a complex of theories, each one defined by its adepts and often in disagreement with the others. Here, psychology is presented as being the study of *only* the *intraphysical* consciousness.

Transpersonal. The consciousness, addressed in an integral manner, is the object of study in conscientiology. We can see it is far vaster and more all-encompassing than transpersonal psychology.

Mind-matter. There are researchers locked into the mind-matter dilemma who still insist that the phenomenon of lucid projection is a purely psychological experience and not a parapsychological phenomenon. In other words, they feel its explanation does not require a parapsychic influence, although they do not distance themselves from the possibility of parapsychic phenomena occurring during the projective process.

Unification. There is no single field of psychology. Unlike mathematics, physics or biology, psychology is not a unified science.

Branch. Aside from educational, social, evolutionary, differential, comparative, general, and other lines of psychology, there currently exists a branch of psychology, or more specifically of psychotherapy, called *transpersonal psychology.* This field specializes in the study of altered states of consciousness, including transcendental and parapsychic experiences, as well as projections of the consciousness.

Neurophysiology. On the other hand, the connection between psychology and physics is neurophysiology.

Vehicles. The acknowledgement of the existence of the consciousness' vehicles, namely the ability of the consciousness to think, act and move outside the human body without the use of nerves and muscles, has strong, inevitable implications in the placement of projective phenomena outside the restricted field of *soul-less* psychology.

Series. This is evidenced by the veteran projector, or anyone who produces lucid projections in series without the negative, subversive interference of pharmacological crutches (drugs or medications).

Psychosoma. Transpersonal psychology (Wilber, 1845), or the fourth-power, is more directly connected to projectiology with regard to projections of the consciousness in the psychosoma when projected together with the holochakra. More recently, it includes the achievement of transcendent projections of the consciousness in the mentalsoma, which are highly subjective personal experiences of cosmic consciousness or cosmoconsciousness.

Self-bilocation. The individual who accepts the reality of the phenomena of bilocation and self-bilocation admits the existence of a second, extraphysical, and less dense body. In this case, the evidence transcends the scope of the manifestations of classic psychology.

Soft. It is clear that projectiology (a body of knowledge that is intrinsically coherent and extrinsically useful) cannot constitute a *hard* science. It must be considered a *soft* science, as is psychology, because not all of the concepts that it deals with have been satisfactorily quantified.

Consciousness. On the one hand, it is understandable that the most brilliant psychologist, as well as any other researcher in any field of human knowledge who has not personally experienced expansion of the consciousness in the *mentalsoma,* is neither able to evaluate the phenomenon nor present viable hypotheses regarding this occurrence, which is totally unfamiliar to that individual.

Competence. The individual most competent to deeply judge the matter is the one who has personally had the experience.

Polysonography. On the other hand, psychological influence cannot be disregarded in lucid projection techniques. Current psychological studies in sleep and dream laboratories through the use of polysonography, have brought important help to the clarification of altered states of consciousness, including lucid consciousness projection, the idea of which can even be transmitted through simple *psychological contagion.*

Research. In light of what has been shown, the rational recommendation for projectiology research, that currently goes beyond the limitations of classic psychology, is a fusion of both the psychological and parapsychological lines, without an overlap of their capabilities.

Exchange. It is necessary to maintain an open mind in terms of the findings, with continued interest in the results, regardless of their origin, and a maximal exchange of ideas and conclusions with an interdisciplinary, universalistic attitude.

Conception. The researcher who has still not had the great adventure of finding him/herself alive outside the human body with his/her own lucid, perceptive personality separated from and near the human body, is not capable of forming a clear concept about the practical and positive value of verified evidence, and opinion based on personal experience.

Drugs. Nevertheless, the individual who has consciential experiences that are brought on by drugs clearly has a tendency to insert the OBE within the scope of common, classic human psychology. This has generated many erroneous ideas among experimenters who are sometimes persons of considerable good will, good intention, intellectual capacity and material means.

Methodology. To experimenters in general, the author recommends endeavoring to produce projective experiences. They should not be those induced by drugs, but spontaneous projections provoked by the will with special training in order to arrive at conclusions, patterns and paradigms that are correct in regard to projectiological phenomena.

Thanatophobia. Another point of close connection between psychology and projectiology is fear research (thanatophobia). This is an area of great interest for both fields, as well as the field of medicine.

Value. The dogma of immature science, concerning itself exclusively with the general and not with the particular, has had the effect of leaving participatory research aside. When individual differences are not taken into consideration, a great deal of the value of experimental discoveries is lost.

Idiography. Projectiology is in the uncommon position of being a science whose exponents are part of its own object of study, in the same manner as occurs with psychology and parapsychology. These 3 sciences are *idiographic* disciplines.

Challenge. Those individuals who are interested in projectiology receive the challenge of opening a new idiographic area of scientific investigation. They are faced with personally exploring that which is, for the most part, still virgin territory, to do this in a meticulous and systematic manner, developing new theories and techniques in line with progress made and, furthermore, offering a new insight into themselves as consciousnesses in evolution.

Differences. Contrary to psychology and orthodox medicine, projectiology seeks to study the following 8 objects of research:

1. **Serenology.** Those who adhere to the general evolutionary laws *(serenissimi),* as opposed to criminals or those intraphysical consciousnesses still lacking a reasonable level of evolution (abnormal psychology; psychiatric disturbances; behavioral disturbances).

2. **Neophilia.** Neophilic courage, as opposed to fear (corporatist neophobia).

3. **Cosmoethics.** Cosmoethical megafraternity, as opposed to hostility (human ethics).

4. **Extraphysicology.** Broad multidimensional vision, as opposed to intraphysical blindness or mere somatics (restricted vision, narrow-mindedness).

5. **Evolutiology.** The present, in relation to the immediate future (consciential evolution or the multidimensional here and now), as opposed to the present in relation only to the past (pastology).

6. **Holomaturology.** The healthy, centered consciousness (paraphysiological holosomatic homeostasis), as opposed to the insecure and disturbed individual (mere physiological organic homeostasis).

7. **Health.** The exaltation of health (prophylaxis) above the exaltation of illness (bioenergetic blockages and imbalances), pertinent to mercantilistic lines of knowledge in the conventional areas of human health.

8. **Paraprophylaxis.** Paraprophylaxis (evolutionary intelligence) first and foremost, and not merely conventional therapeutics (material intelligence) above all.

Emotions. Another difference between psychology and projectiology is that psychologists have always discovered more enthusiasm and self-awareness in the conditions which provoke emotions.

Discernment. Lucid projectors endeavor to master their emotions, without repressing them, by having more discerning reactions that stem from the mentalsoma, as opposed to those stemming from the psychosoma, which is still very animalistic.

Trauma. If, on the one hand, the emotional involvement of the self tends to increase the extent of learning in general, a great intensity of emotional excitement, on the other hand, tends to reduce the scope of learning. When outside the human body – with regard to projective learning in extraphysical consciential dimensions – this fact becomes predominant and, worse still, undesirable, as it can lead to the interruption of the experience or an extraphysical trauma.

Bibliography: Banks (75, p. 110), Blackmore (139, p. 242), Boirac (164, p. 264), Bosc (172, p. 309), Burt (224, p. 50), Dane (363, p. 249), Donahue (407, p. 16), Garfield (568, p. 125), Irwin (791, p. 244), Jung (812, p. 320; 813, p. 506), Schapiro (1513, p. 259), Tart (1653, p. 153), Wang (1794, p. 145), Wilber (1845, p. 120).

21. PROJECTIOLOGY AND BIOLOGY

Definitions. Biology: the science of life in general; the study of living beings in their relationships with each other and their environment.

Synonymy: the science of life.

Parabiology. Lucid projection allows humankind to start studying the external contours and manifestations that derive from the human body or, in other words, the other vehicles of manifestation of the consciousness that parabiology, metabiology or transcendental biology will study in depth in the near future.

Animals. Due to its relationships with other living beings, projectiology enables original observations and analyses of the extraphysical perceptions and extraphysical vehicles of manifestation of animals (zoology) and plants (botany), besides humankind and life forms that are totally unknown here on earth (para-exobiology). This can be accomplished in a direct manner in specific extraphysical environments.

Bodies. Projective experiments demonstrate to the lucid projector that so-called inferior subhuman animals possess extraphysical bodies that emit light, present an aura and, in certain conditions, also project in their physical bodies' immaterial substrata in a manner similar to that of the human or intraphysical consciousness.

Paraperceptions. Parapsychic facts observed to date suggest that, in the same way that we possess holosomatic, animic and parapsychic paraperceptions which are more accurate than those already discovered, we also possess physical perceptions in the human body that are more sophisticated than those we consciously employ or have so far even imagined and presume to exist.

Perceptions. There are physical potential perceptions, which are more subtle or sophisticated, that have not been entirely discovered or fully employed within the scope of our basic organic senses, such as our common memory, vision and audition.

Potentialities. The discovery of these perceptive and paraperceptive potentialities, that have been unknown until now, as well as other physical senses (geographic instinct and geological or radiesthetic instinct), will further clarify the boundaries between the limits of the human-animal phenomenological complex (psychology) and those of the consciential and interdimensional-based phenomenological complex of projectiology.

Overlaps. In the same way that overlaps inevitably occur among physics, mathematics and astronomy, there are also inevitable overlaps between projectiology, parapsychology and psychology. In spite of all interdisciplinary or pluri-scientific relationships, projectiology proceeds independently in the same manner that physics and the other abovementioned sciences evolve.

Themes. The following are 12 projectiology themes, among others, that are related to biology and are addressed to a greater or lesser degree in this book:

1. Asomnia.
2. Biofeedback.
3. Bioluminescence.
4. Cellular regeneration.
5. Cenesthopathy.
6. Exobiology.
7. Human body.
8. Human brain.
9. Human epiphysis.
10. Organicism.
11. Spontaneous human combustion.
12. Sthenobiosis.

Bibliography: Andrade (29, p. 67), Geley (581, p. 270), Greene (635, p. 100), Russell (1482, p. 112), Steiger (1601, p. 209), Watson (1801, p. 305).

22. PROJECTIOLOGY AND MEDICINE

Definition. Medicine: the art or science of curing or attenuating diseases.

Synonymy: clinical medicine (branch); medical science; medical surgery (branch); science of curing.

Areas. Through experiments performed with the intraphysical consciousness projected in the psychosoma, projectiology will, sooner or later, radically alter the following 4 areas of research, at the very least:

1. **Medicine.** The pillars upon which medicine are based, especially clinical anamnesis.
2. **Physiology.** Physiology, when able to complete the existing knowledge of the physiology of the brain, for example.
3. **Therapeutics.** Therapeutics in general.
4. **Psychiatry.** Psychiatry, in particular, aside from other classic sectors.

Knowledge. The knowledge of projectiology can amplify the fields of medicine. This is especially true of psychiatry, or more appropriately, metapsychiatry.

Holosoma. Instead of treating patients simply as physical organisms, they can be addressed as complete entities which are in a coincident state regarding the vehicles of manifestation of the consciousness (unified body, holosoma), through the paranatomy, paraphysiology and parapsychopathology of these vehicles.

Energies. A deeper understanding of bioenergy, the human aura, the chakras, the energetic points of acupuncture (acupuncture points), and the absorption and exteriorization of consciential energies, will be of immense value in the greater understanding of physical and mental disturbances that affect the human personality.

Projective. In the same way that internal, nuclear, allopathic, homeopathic, legal, space and other areas of medicine exist, the author hereby registers the launching of *projective medicine,* that studies the cause of diseases through the use of lucid projections, and which inevitably, either now or in the future, will be used by medical colleagues.

Publications. As a result of bibliographical research, the reader will find 20 technical articles on projectiological themes in the specific bibliography of this chapter. These articles are edited through 9 different recognized, specialized, medical periodicals published between 1934 and 1982. They are the following:

1. *American Journal of Psychiatry.*
2. *American Medical Association Archives of Neurology and Psychiatry.*
3. *Archives General of Psychiatry.*
4. *British Journal of Medical Psychology.*
5. *The Edinburgh Medical Journal.*
6. *The Journal of Nervous and Mental Disease.*
7. *The Journal of the American Medical Association.*
8. *New England Journal of Medicine.*
9. *Psychiatry Journal for the Study of Interpersonal Process.*

Proof. This fact, in and of itself, proves the direct relationships that exist between the research of modern medicine and the research of projectiology.

Techniques. The following 3 techniques, described in another part of this book, already comprise a part of projective medicine:

1. Extraphysical anamnesis.
2. Projective diagnostics.
3. Projective therapeutics or projectiotherapy.

Para. As we can see by the context of this book, projectiology has already taken the first steps in the unexplored fields of human paranatomy, paraphysiology and parapsychopathology. There is still much to be done regarding the para-embryology of the psychosoma, the para-histology of ectoplasm, and in relation to the genetics of the psychosoma (paragenetics).

Occurrences. The following, aside from others – including some already referred to – are 12 irrefutable relationships of projectiology with diverse areas of medicine. They are practically imposed as a result of a variety of human lucid projection experiences:

1. Illnesses in general: clinical medicine.
2. Physical pain: clinical medicine.
3. Anesthesia and surgery: clinical surgery.
4. State of suspended animation: clinical surgery.
5. Near-death experiences (NDEs): clinical surgery.
6. Parasurgery: clinical surgery.
7. Heart and heartbeat: cardiology.
8. Drugs: pharmacology.

9. Parturition: obstetrics.
10. Hemiplegics: traumatology.
11. Mutilated persons: traumatology.
12. Therapeutics: projectiotherapy.

Field. It is easy to see that lucid projection opens up an entirely new field of scientific exploration that is just as vast and complex as the world of biomedical sciences or that which researches the objective life of the human consciousness in the ordinary, physical waking state.

Projectiatry. The medicine of consciential projection – when it is present as a xenophrenic state, being a consequence of the human attribute of projectability – is designated as *projectiatry*.

Quality. The innumerous theoretical doubts, or those queries raised out of simple ignorance, never cast doubt upon modern medicine as a science. The research portrayed by this book aims to lead projectiology to this same superior level of advanced science, at the appropriate time.

Bibliography: Blacher (136, p. 229), Cerviño (271, p. 59), Coleman (291, p. 254), Ehrenwald (471, p. 151), Fodor (526, p. 66), Gabbard (564, p. 374), Geddes (578, p. 365), Greene (635, p. 100), Greyson (643, p. 188), Heine (706, p. 263), Irwin (791, p. 244), Laubscher (890, p. 27), Lief (925, p. 171), Lippman (934, p. 345), Ludwig (956, p. 225), Lukianowicz (957, p. 199), Mc Harg (1021, p. 48), Mello (1032, p. 34), Mendes (1033, p. 31), Neppe (1123, p. 1), Noyes Jr. (1141, p. 19; 1142, p. 174), Paim (1182, p. 226), Ring (1404, p. 273; 1406, p. 27), Sabom (1486, p. 15; 1487, p. 1071; 1488, p. 29), Schnaper (1519, p. 268), Schul (1522, p. 216), Souza (1584, p. 11), Steiger (1601, p. 209), Stevenson (1619, p. 152; 1621, p. 265), Todd (1689, p. 47), Twemlow (1710, p. 450), Vieira (1762, p. 110), West (1824, p. 274).

23. PROJECTIOLOGY AND ANTHROPOLOGY

Definition. Anthropology: the natural science, the scope of which is the study and classification of the physical and cultural characteristics of human groups.

Synonymy: anthropologism; anthropometry.

Vehicles. Lucid projection – when it studies, identifies and endeavors to apply the various vehicles of manifestation of the consciousness through parapsychism – creates profound implications for anthropology.

Terms. It is also easy to verify the close relationship between projectiology and anthropology through an analysis of the terms that are used (nomenclature, terminology).

Projectionists. In the literature of scientific parapsychology, those individuals who present various types of parapsychic abilities are called: sensitives, paranormals, subjects, mediums, clairvoyants and projectionists. In the anthropological literature these same individuals are called: magicians, witches, rainmakers, prophets, seers and shamans.

Occurrences. The following are 6 direct relationships, among others, between projectiology and various research fields within anthropology. These relationships are practically imposed, due to projectiological occurrences of various kinds:

1. Autobiographies of projectors.
2. *Congressus subtilis.*
3. Mind-expanding drugs.
4. Possessions and external influences by intelligent entities (extraphysical consciousnesses).
5. Diverse trances.
6. Primitive tribes that produce lucid projections.

Research. In 1978, Dean Shiels compared the beliefs of 60 different cultures through the reference files of the human relations archives maintained by anthropological research. These files contain codified information that is organized in topics and conserved on microfilm.

Double. He extracted some information from each culture regarding the ability of the double or soul to travel without the human body.

Cultures. Of the 54 cultures from which some information of this type was reported, 25 (or 46%) affirmed that most or all of their people could travel in this manner under certain conditions. Another 23 (or 43%) affirmed that some of their members were able to do this, and only 3 cultures did not affirm that they believed in anything of this nature.

Conclusion. We can therefore conclude that belief in projections of the consciousness from the human body is very common.

Projective. Just as physical anthropology and cultural or social anthropology (a branch of sociology) exist, the author hereby launches *projective anthropology,* a branch of anthropology that studies the physical characteristics of human groups through lucid projection. It is reasonable to think that this will inevitably, either now or in the future, become an anthropological research area.

Anthropomaximology. Anthropomaximology is a new branch of anthropology. It is defined as "anthropology directed towards the evaluation of maximal human potential and the consequences of these maximum possible results in relation to humankind." This field has allowed much greater progress in establishing new athletic records.

Relationship. Based on the premise that the lucid projector is *a transcendental athlete,* projectiology has a close relationship with anthropomaximology, because the development of the projector depends on the improvement of the individual's physical-extraphysical performance through a general improvement of physical and psychic conditions, the evolution of parapsychic techniques and training, and the valuing of the consciousness' vehicles of manifestation, in order to set new extraphysical records.

Para-anthropology. We can even speak of "Para-anthropomaximology." This would be Para-anthropology that respects humankind as being substantially composed of the consciousness and matter (derived from immanent energy).

Bibliography: Alverga (18, p. 138), Angoff (40, p. 241), Blackmore (139, p. 72), Bourguignon (181, p. 12), Bozzano (191, p. 125), Castaneda (255, p. 121), De Mille (386, p. 85), Dubant (419, p. 76), Eliade (475, p. 117), Fontaine (533, p. 71), Hoffman (733, p. 5), Lamont (874, p. 109), Lewis (923, p. 53), Long (946, p. 33), Mc Intosh (1022, p. 460), Neihardt (1121, p. 204), Oesterreich (1145, p. 5), Sangirardi Jr. (1503, p. 181), Shiels (1547, p. 697), Tart (1653, p. 161) Wheeler (1826, p. 118), Wolman (1863, p. 667).

---

24. PROJECTIOLOGY AND SOCIOLOGY

Definition. Sociology: the objective study of the relationships that are consciously or unconsciously established between people who live in a community or a social group, or among different social groups that live within a larger society.

Synonymy: science of collective behavior; science of social phenomena; social studies; study of human interrelationships; theory of human life in groups.

Areas. The direct relationships between the phenomena of lucid projection and sociology, whether culturalist or structuralist, occur in various areas such as the following 4:

1. In the historical research of projectiology.
2. In the scope of restrictive total institutions.
3. In sociologists' advanced fields of study.
4. In the study of imitative contagion.

Renovation. Sciences interrelate deeply with each other. In a fundamental comparison, the sociology of the imaginary – through the work of open-minded persons with a very libertarian education – is applying the same approach as that of initial projectiology research, namely specifically studying the aspects of life that are situated outside rationality or that *have another logic.*

Phenomena. In sociology, just as in projectiology, this is only achieved by discovering phenomena and working on their explanation in a manner that is free and does not remain bound to pre-established, traditional rules. This finally allows the overcoming of barriers to that which can be accounted for and fit into orthodox concepts (fundamentalism).

Position. Although many sociologists do not admit the possibility of macrochanges – and veteran lucid projectors much less so, in light of the wise extraphysical control of all that exists – this position is precisely the same as the renovating directive of the context expressed in the projectiological panorama of this book.

Projective. Just as economic sociology and plant sociology exist, aside from various subdisciplines such as family, political, urban, rural, industrial, demographic and educational sociology, the author hereby launches *projective sociology,* which studies the relationships between people within a social group as well as relationships between social groups and the greater *extraphysical society* through lucid projections. It is reasonable to believe that this will inevitably, whether now or in the future, be an object of study by sociologists.

Bibliography: Castaneda (255, p. 170), Lewis (923, p. 17), Prince (1290, p. 13).

25. PROJECTIOLOGY AND PHYSICS

Definition. Physics: the branch of science that studies natural laws and processes, and the states and properties of matter and energy.

Synonymy: science of matter; science of nature.

Universe. Projection of the consciousness is inseparably related to physics, mainly regarding the current strictly energetic, immaterial and interactive fields of research, such as field theory, the attempt to unify electromagnetism, gravitation and the interaction between elementary particles.

Conjecture. The development of modern physics is based upon many concepts that have so far not been confirmed as being anything more than conjecture.

Axioms. In practice, it becomes almost impossible to differentiate the axioms of modern physics from those of the most ancient philosophies.

Interaction. Bearing in mind that: the implications of the consciousness with energy have already been established; space-time has a complementary physical existence, and in different systems of reference time flows differently; the act of observing or trying to measure intrinsically interferes in the measurement of the atomic world, thereby establishing the cornerstone of quantum mechanics; the consciousness closely interconnects itself with all existing vital districts, affecting the universe, even in a manner relative to the past, present and future, whether as an invisible point or a world of fecund vitality, the need arises for a connection between physics and paraphysics, interconnected with lucid projection, one as an instrument of the other, in complementary interaction.

Paraphysics. Thus, there is currently an emergence of a new natural science – paraphysics – through the marriage of sophisticated research methodology, instruments, new and more ample concepts, and an expansive vision of the nature of humankind, dedicated to the study of the physics of parapsychic processes, including projectiology.

Molecules. In fact, through lucid projection, the physicist can leave the human body, reduce the consciousness down to the size of a single molecule, enter into a specific object and actually *directly* examine the molecules and atoms that compose it. This is in agreement with that which is observed in projections using the isolated mentalsoma.

Mentalsoma. In the future, the lucid projection of an intraphysical consciousness in the mentalsoma will be the most accurate instrument in physics.

Projective. Just as solid physics, fluid physics, plasma physics, molecular physics, quantum physics, statistical physics, mathematical physics, relativistic physics, atomic physics, nuclear physics, elementary particle physics, field physics, tribology or friction physics exist, as well as the physics that is dedicated to cosmology and gravitation (astrophysics), all of which are separated within theoretical, experimental and applied research, the author hereby launches *projective physics* or projective paraphysics, which studies the states and properties of matter and energy through the use of lucid projection. It is reasonable to suppose that this will inevitably, whether now or in the future, be the field of research of paraphysicists.

Bibliography: Bentov (119, p. 3), Greene (*635,* p. 101), Greenhouse (*639,* p. 335), Grosso (*650,* p. 187), Meek (1030, p. 109), Mishlove (1055, p. 279), Mitchell (1058, p. 426), Schul (1524, p. 41), Talbot (1642, p. 162), Toben (1688, p. 63), White (1829, p. 297), Wolman (1863, p. 749).

26. PROJECTIOLOGY AND ASTRONOMY

Definition. Astronomy: the science that studies the position, movements and constitution of the celestial bodies.

Synonymy: cosmological science; science of the stars; uranognosis.

Direct. Through projectiology, the astronomer, instead of being restricted to an optical instrument (telescope) or, in radio astronomy, the reading of radio-frequency radiation, can in fact send his/her own consciousness outside the human body through space in order to observe and directly research things firsthand, without human or physical intermediaries.

Galaxies. The astronomer, through lucid projection in the mentalsoma in the mentalsomatic dimension, can travel to other galaxies (exoprojections) located far beyond the reach of astronomy and even decipher the enigma of extraterrestrial life and various other phenomena that currently remain to be solved.

Astronautics. Astronautics, the science and technique of space flight, derived from astronomy, can also deeply benefit from projectiological studies, in view of the relationships between astronauts, spaceships, space stations, scientists, instruments, and tracking bases on earth.

Projective. Just as cometary astronomy, field astronomy, position astronomy, descriptive astronomy, stellar astronomy, instrumental astronomy, meteoric astronomy, metric astronomy and practical astronomy exist, the author hereby launches *projective astronomy* or parapsychonautics, that studies the celestial bodies through the use of lucid projection, or exoprojection. It is reasonable to assume that astronomers will use them and no futurological prevision is required in order to make this affirmation.

Clairvoyance. Remote viewing (traveling clairvoyance) experiments have already been performed with sensitives who consci... explored 2 planets. We can say in passing that lucid projection is the most practical, secure and efficient method of space travel.

Similarities. In regard to astronautics – within which various aerospace sciences should be included, such as: aerodynamics, aerologation, aerology, aeronautical navigation, aeronautics, aeronomy, aerostatics, aerostation, astrionics, astronavigation and astrophysics – the curious similarities between projection of the consciousness in the psychosoma and flights made by aircraft and spacecraft deserve to be registered.

Expressions. It suffices to observe the following 18 expressions, among many others, that were, in one way or another, adapted from astronautical terminology by projectiology in order to adequately designate certain aspects of projectiological phenomena. They are used, some more frequently than others, throughout this book.

1. Accompanying body (a portion of the holochakra) = booster (part of the rocket).
2. Animic flight (paratropospheric lucid projection) = cislunar space flight.
3. Astrosoma (astral body) = astro; celestial body.
4. Auric coupling = space docking.
5. Extraphysical flight (volitation) = controlled space flight.
6. Immediate extraphysical translocation = direct flight, without intermediary stops (non-stop flight).

7. Intraphysical assistant = air crew/flight crew; ground crew.
8. Lucid projector's log = flight log.
9. Mental target = flight plan.
10. Physical base = air base; aerodrome; airport.
11. Projected projector in the bedroom = captive balloon.
12. Projective range (duration of the lucid projection) = (flight) range.
13. Rapid consecutive exteriorizations = emergency landings.
14. Sidereal flight (lucid exoprojection) = translunar space flight.
15. Stages of lucid projection = stages of a (space) flight.
16. Stationary flight: the dirigible that *hovers* in the air in order to make scientific observations and the intraphysical consciousness who leaves the soma and positions the *stationary* psychosoma over the human body.
17. Takeoff of the psychosoma = takeoff of the aircraft.
18. Volitative group = squadron (of aircraft).

Energy. There are many other similarities between projectiology and aeronautics. The following are 4 more sophisticated cases:

1. **Tanker.** The transmission of energy from the helper to the projected projector is perfect in its likeness to the in-flight refueling executed by tanker planes (KC-10 Extender, USAF) to the aircraft that will use the fuel.

2. **Blackout.** *Consciential blackout* is the same complete loss of senses experienced by pilots in tight barrel rolls.

3. **Crop duster.** The extraphysical consciousness or projected intraphysical consciousness that exteriorizes restorative consciential energy is reminiscent of a *crop duster* in action.

4. **Joint.** The pregnant woman who lucidly projects together with the consciousness of the fetus is reminiscent of the well-known compound aircraft in which she, the projector *(aeroboat)*, has the consciousness of the fetus *(hydroplane, seaplane)* on her *back*. This consciousness later separates from her, in the extraphysical dimension, continuing on with its consciential experience.

Bibliography: Greene (635, p. 101), Mitchell (1057, p. 28), Mittl (1061, p. 5).

27. PROJECTIOLOGY AND HISTORY

Definitions. History: the methodical narration of notable facts that have occurred during the development of peoples' lives, in particular, and during the existence of humankind, in general; the science and method that allow the learning and transmitting of the knowledge acquired through tradition and/or through documents related to evolution and the past of humanity.

Synonymy: chronological report; historical science; narration of facts; pastology, register of occurrences.

Transformations. Although the lucid experience of the consciousness outside the human body is an ancient and universal phenomenon, the technical-scientific study of consciential projections is extremely new and will bring historical structural transformations to society (this still pathological intraphysical society) and human cultures.

Communicology. The direct and interdimensional means of communication afforded by animism (intraconsciential experience) and the parapsychism of lucid projections surpasses the human senses.

Intraconscientiality. By allowing the paravision of new environments, lucid consciential projections expand the mental time and space of the intraphysical consciousness.

Vehicles. This demonstrates that the best means of interconsciential communication are within the consciousness itself.

Impact. Projectiology, like every new science, is gradually becoming consolidated. Nevertheless, it is reasonable to suppose that it will not be devoid of historical impact, and may provoke a peculiar transformation over time in the human consciential surroundings. This will occur due to its research of the extensions of the body (soma) and the human senses that projectiological research sponsors, thereby dispensing with common or advanced technologies in this electronic age. Let us, then, in this respect, follow the logical concepts in the following sequence of arguments.

Structures. Historically speaking, projectiology is arising beyond material mechanisms with forms that are new, interdimensional, and even contradictory to existing communication modalities, precisely when the previously created structural forms of technology and computer systems are reaching their maximal performance and influence.

Inner. The phenomenon of lucid projection and projectiology itself occur *within the consciousness,* in a direct, personal implosion of knowledge, and not *from outside the human body,* directed to all beings indifferently, as science and communication technology have always sought to do.

Revolution. In the above-mentioned aspect, projectiology is ultra-revolutionary because it positions itself for a head-on confrontation with conventional science (that addresses phenomena as a function of all consciousnesses; the universals), technology (communication technology) and modern history itself, permitting the total and instantaneous understanding of the message by the expanded consciousness.

Extensions. Projectiology creates extensions, not with the material human body in mind, but with all the vehicles of manifestation (holosoma) and the evolutionary enrichment of the consciousness itself.

Material. This is achieved not through primitive, perishable materials but through the sophisticated, non-perishable resources of its own internal structure.

Perspective. The perspective of projectiology exalts the consciential micro-universe, randomly and simultaneously focusing on the *isolated* consciousness – the responsible agent (egokarmality, holobiography), which is very different from all other consciousnesses – as science does, demanding universal replicability of experiments.

Progression. The soma (cellular body), as well as the individual's senses within it, stand out in human life. For any attentive observer of consciential self-evolution, the logical development of the intraphysical consciousness' perceptions proceeds apace, acquiring new aspects in the course of human history.

Senses. Humankind's senses are constantly becoming more refined in response to external realities to which they are exposed. They are constantly becoming more enhanced and subtle, regarding all types of perceptive nuances in all areas.

Relationship. This is due more to transformations in the human knowledge of things and humankind's skillful dealings in regard to these things, rather than a physical change in the human sensory equipment itself, which has remained more or less unchanged over the last few millennia.

Paraperceptions. Thus, on the one hand, humankind gradually learns how to employ the physical senses more correctly and capably while, on the other hand, the same occurs with (extraphysical) paraperceptions.

Abilities. The extensions of the human consciousness that have been gradually acquired throughout human history are not in physical instruments per se, but in the essential development of the senses and abilities acquired by the ego, which are represented by the instrument, or through it.

Vision. Let us consider, for example, a basic organic perception and its spatial relationship – the sense of physical vision (optics). Broadly speaking, the human species has been living in the same environment, or has seen objects and geographical features in the same physical setting, since its origin in time immemorial, composed of: earth, oceans, rivers, mountains, day, night, vegetation, animals, air, sky, stars and other resources.

Mark. The consciousness of humankind, generation after generation, through slow alterations, nevertheless leaves its human mark, or its *thosenic signature,* on the external world that it sees.

Changes. The changes in the use of its senses, beginning with vision, lead humankind to develop in 3 concrete directions, or 3 different areas:

1. **Physical.** The division of land promoted the appearance of problems regarding physical space (proxemics), such as: the distribution of plots of land; land invasions; agrarian reform.

2. **Celestial.** Controlled agriculture called humankind's attention to the heavens: the movements of the stars; the changing of the seasons; plantations and harvests. Maritime navigation and commerce also contributed: ships, merchants and navigators.

3. **Beyond.** Locomotion and man-made vehicles, beginning with the wheel, then cars and airplanes, as extensions of the legs, finally took humankind to outer space; to astronautics; to space law; to the moon. We hardly need to mention that the airplane absorbed a multitude of ocean liner passengers.

Stars. Those who look at the stars today see them in the same manner in which they were observed 30 centuries ago.

Agriculture. The movements of the stars were therefore rigorously recorded due to the needs of agriculture and navigation.

Lifetimes. The consciousness, when in the intraphysical condition, has been seeing the same points of light in the dark sky for dozens of lifetimes and holobiographies.

Difference. Nowadays, we say that we see the stars differently, because we know that the earth is a planet in our solar system, and the Sun is a star like many others.

Relations. We relate to this knowledge differently than we did 30 centuries ago when we thought that these stars were inhabited by *gods*. These were, however, quite bestial creations (abdominal brain) on our part.

Space. From a chronological point of view, this same space, seen and studied by humankind, can be scientifically classified into 3 types:

1. **Euclidean.** Euclidean space, initially established through the principles of Euclidean geometry.

2. **Einsteinian.** Einsteinian curved space, discovered by Albert Einstein through the theories of modern physics.

3. **Multidimensional.** The interdimensional or multidimensional space of relative leading-edge truths observed by the lucid projector's paravision and experienced by him/her in the projected state, or the multiple dimensions and hyperspaces currently researched by projectiology.

Fact. It can therefore be concluded that the *evolutionary* phenomenon of the use of human vision is, without a doubt, a historical fact; but there is much more to consider. Let us look at the following 5 items:

1. **Photo.** The photographic camera invaded the professional space of the painter who paints live portraits by copying from the original article.

2. **Cinema.** The cinema – a creation of the twentieth century – reprocessing live theater, absorbed a vast amount of the opera market, which was created in the seventeenth century.

3. **Television.** Television – both recorded and live – replacing the cinema, claimed an immense portion of movie theater activity, resulting in many empty seats.

4. **Clairvoyance.** Clairvoyance – an extra-sensorial or parapsychic perception – invading and enriching the acuity of ordinary human vision, opens *windows* of contemplation to the energetic dimension through states of ecstasy.

5. **Projections.** As a more recent and impressive acquisition, lucid projective experience opens *doorways* for a direct passage of the consciousness to the same energetic dimension and other dimensions that are even more impactful (evolved extraphysical communities).

Self-awareness. These facts bring a deep multidimensional self-awareness to the intraphysical consciousness that interacts everywhere, constituting the greatest transforming objective in history, which is proposed and defended by projectiology.

Impulses. One of the qualities that places human beings above the subhuman animal world is that their actions are no longer simple immediate responses to sensations and impulses.

Understanding. The more that intraphysical consciousnesses replace an ignorance of their inner (intraconsciential) world and the world around them with a true understanding of their holosomatic constitution, their various bodies or vehicles of manifestation and the laws that govern them, the more they will be able to plan the vast repercussions of the interdimensional actions they put in motion.

Parahistory. In the same manner that universal, national, political, religious, economic, narrative, pragmatic, ancient, medieval, modern, contemporary and other areas of history exist, the author hereby launches *parahistory,* that studies the multidimensional history of *para-humanity,* and its consequences, through lucid projections. It is reasonable to think that this will inevitably, whether now or in the future, become an object of study and a useful tool for historians.

Bibliography: Alexandrian (11, p. 288), Doyle (411, p.36), Durville (441, p.22), Inardi (786, p. 148), Inglis (789, p. 24), Knight (852, p. 177).

28. DIVISION OF PROJECTIOLOGY

Segments. In accordance with observations of those beings who project, projectiology is divided into 4 well-defined educational segments, in the following order:

1. **Intraphysical.** Hominal projectiology.
2. **Extraphysical.** Non-human projectiology.
3. **Subhuman.** Animal projectiology.
4. **Botanical.** Vegetative projectiology.

Areas. Hominal (human) projectiology includes the area of projections of the intraphysical consciousness; non-human or extra-human projectiology pertains to projections of the extraphysical consciousness; animal projectiology pertains to the subintelligent projections of animals; botanical projectiology pertains to projections of plants in general. Each of these segments will be analyzed in a specific chapter in this section.

Aspects. The fact that projections include more than one kingdom in nature, the hominal, animal and vegetable, and still reaches extraphysical beings in the extraphysical dimensions, speaks in favor of 4 relevant observations:

1. **Diversity.** The diversity of projective manifestations.
2. **Denominators.** The existence of natural common denominators in projective occurrences.
3. **Physiology.** The physiological aspect of the nature of projective phenomena.
4. **Interdisciplinarity.** The necessity of an approach that is broad, inclusive, interdisciplinary, universalistic and unifying in its scientific analysis.

Vehicles. The areas of projectiology will be extremely useful when the natural components of the vehicles of manifestation of the consciential principle (the consciousness) and the phenomena-related elements that constitute common denominators (main paradigms) are researched in greater detail, according to the categories of projective occurrences.

Areas. It would be unwise here to overlook subjective projectiology, naturalist projectiology, projectiography, projectiocritique and projectiotherapy. These areas are also relevant within the world of projectiology research.

Rescue. Projectiology serves to rescue human consciousnesses from the underdevelopment to which they were relegated, after thousands of centuries of blind and isolationist policies that kept us – evidently with some degree of responsibility on our part – within our evolutionary groups in the condition of human beings in multiple intraphysical societies and myriads of intraphysical experiences (*locked existences* or those lacking lucid consciential projections), set apart from the evolutionary innovations of lucid projectability, existential inversion, penta, the extraphysical clinic, cosmoconscientiology and serenology, and their libertarian consequences.

29. LUCID PROJECTION AND THE HUMAN CONSCIOUSNESS

Definitions. The consciousness: the attribute of inner knowledge of one's own existence and of one's modifications, highly developed in the human species; the number of interconnections of the conscious, unconscious and intuitive memory, as well as interdimensional energetic and informational sensing with discernment, when observing or studying a phenomenon.

Synonymy: brain programmer (intraphysical consciousness, extraphysical consciousness); conditioned awareness; conscious identity of the person; cosmic egoceptor; cosmic transceiver; interiority of the ego; intraphysical awareness; knowledge of one's self (self-psyche); multidimensional egosyntonizer; palingenetic ecosystem; pluri-existential ecosystem.

Incommunicability. The definition presented here is appropriate, despite the fact that, in psychology, *consciousness* customarily designates only the subjective and *incommunicable* aspect of psychic activity that cannot be known, in a manner apart from the individual, except for the manifestations of behavior.

Properties. At least the following 3 properties are suggested as being inherent to the consciousness:

1. **Continuity.** *Continuity,* or the uninterrupted nature of individual awareness, that forms a continuous chain with current experiences, uniting them with those of the past. Mnemosomatics, biomemory and holomemory are involved here in a specific manner.

2. **Change.** The constant *change* or the perpetual movement of our ideas, representations, sentiments and tendencies that incessantly develop, transform, dissolve and reconstitute. Thosenology and all categories of thosenes are involved here in a characteristic manner.

3. **Contradiction.** The dialectical law of *contradiction,* inherent in all natural phenomena, the excitement and inhibition that occurs constantly in the nervous system of the human consciousness' physical body (soma). The aspects inherent to somatics, genetics and paragenetics are involved here.

Indestructibility. One fact in the field of projectiology that tranquilizes the awakened intraphysical consciousness and gives it cause to think is that: no object or creation of this human world seems capable of destroying the consciousness, neither the use of napalm, nor the employment of other defoliants, nor a hydrogen bomb explosion, nor the use of a neutron bomb. The consciousness itself seems indestructible, *incapable of dying or being killed* in any dimension in which it manifests.

Physicality. The consciousness does not possess physical proprieties.

Sophistication. As a theory, with the objective of research, it is considered that the more the consciousness evolves, the more sophisticated and complex it becomes, to the point that it gradually annexes the memory of experiences acquired in its cycle of successive lives – or existential seriation (holobiography) and multidimensional cycle – until it becomes aware of possessing the entirety of these experiences and has access to integral, continuous or causal holomemory.

States. From an evolutionary point of view, considering the consciousness as being the ego, the basic consciential states can be classified into 3 distinct categories:

1. **Extraphysicology.** The extraphysical consciential state of the consciousness.
2. **Intraphysicology.** The intraphysical consciential state of the consciousness.
3. **Projectiology.** The projective consciential state of the consciousness.

Projectability. This projective consciential state of the consciousness is subdivided into two distinct conditions:

1. **Intraphysical consciousness.** The *projective* consciential state of the *intraphysical consciousness* (4 vehicles).

2. **Extraphysical consciousness.** The *paraprojective* consciential state of the *extraphysical consciousness* (2 vehicles).

Others. Many different consciential states can be listed in a general manner, such as the following 20:

1. Coma or loss of consciousness.
2. Cosmoconsciousness.

3. Daydream (waking dream).
4. Dream (oneirism).
5. Ecstasy (beatitude).
6. Hyperalertness.
7. Hypnagogy (preamble to sleep).
8. Hypnopompy (intraphysical awakening).
9. Hypnotic dream.
10. Inspiration (serendipity, synchronicity).
11. Lethargy or dormancy.
12. Meditation or deep reflection.
13. Natural dream.
14. Ordinary waking state.
15. Psychedelic state (pharmacology).
16. Regression in time.
17. Semilucid projection or lucid dream.
18. State of hysteria.
19. Stupor.
20. Trance.

Dimensions. In the general study of the dimensions of the consciousness, the various consciential states, that anyone can experience, can be classified into two basic categories:

1. **Psychosomatic.** The unthinking consciousness. The impulsivity and precipitation of the thosenic manifestations of the consciousness that are *more laden with sen* (emotions that prevail upon the personality) are included here.

2. **Mentalsomatic.** The thinking or self-aware consciousness. The most noble attributes of the mentalsoma that lead the intraphysical consciousness to the experience of cosmoconsciousness are included here.

Unthinking. The following 6 conditions, among others, are included in the phenomena of the unthinking consciousness:

1. Organic awareness (mind).
2. The memory bank (cerebral memory, biomemory).
3. The state of coma (comatose).
4. The state of stupor.
5. Sleep without rapid bi-ocular movements.
6. Sleep with rapid synchronous bi-ocular movements.

Introversion. Through the quality of self-perceptibility, in the introversion of awareness, or through centripetal sensations or those that return upon themselves, the consciousness – the thinking being – achieves cognition of its own awareness, or self-awareness – the *awareness of the consciousness* or the subjective awareness of the ego – when it perceives its own functions and rationalizes personal existence, becoming conscious of the existence of its own awareness.

Self-awareness. In the set of states of the self-aware consciousness – in which it is conscious of being aware – the following 8 basic phenomena, among others, are included:

1. The ordinary, physical waking state or pragmatic awareness.
2. Lethargy.
3. State of hysteria.
4. Relaxed awareness.
5. Daydream (waking dream).
6. The trance state induced by any agent.
7. Extraphysically projected awareness.
8. Expanded awareness, the holophotic mind or cosmoconsciousness.

Foundations. All projectiology phenomena can be classified into two basic categories in regard to the condition of physical awareness: with some physical awareness and devoid of physical awareness.

1. **First.** In the first condition, *with* some physical awareness or with the *human brain semi-empty,* the following phenomena occur: traveling clairvoyance; autoscopy; consciential projections with the human body in movement; and others.

2. **Second.** In the second condition, *without* physical awareness or with the *human brain empty,* the phenomena of great projections occur: projection of the consciousness in the psychosoma, with and without the holochakra (dense energies), or wherein the psychosoma has a greater or lesser density; projection of the consciousness in the psychosoma that is partially or completely shaped in its humanoid form (shaping agent of the soma); projection of the consciousness in the isolated mentalsoma; phenomenon of physical bilocation; and others.

Fields. Undoubtedly, 3 fields that show intense research activity favors the studies of lucid projection, unexpectedly bringing inestimable contributions to the development of its research:

1. **NDE.** Near-death experiences (NDE).
2. **SLP.** Lucid dreams or semilucid projections (SLP).
3. **RV.** Remote viewing (RV or traveling clairvoyance).

Role. In the fields of the scientific work of projectiology, the *consciousness* plays a role in research and reasoning that is as important as that played, for example, by the 3 following objects of research:

1. **Cell.** The *cell* in regard to the development of biology.
2. **Atom.** The *atom* in regard to the advancement of physics.
3. **Galaxy.** The *galaxy* in regard to the evolution of astronomy.

Computer. In the research of the consciousness, per se, it is important to consider some of its parallels in relation to the computer in this era of information technology.

Advantages. The human being invented the computer, which possesses 4 basic *advantages* over the human being him/herself:

1. **Speed.** Speed in the execution of certain operations.
2. **Revision.** Exemption from mistakes in revision.
3. **Disposition.** Absence of fatigue.
4. **Tranquility.** Absence of nervous tension.

Shortcomings. Nevertheless, at least for the time being, these advantages are in no way able to compensate for 4 crucial *shortcomings* of the computer, despite its victory over chess players:

1. **Intellectuality.** Lack of intellectual flexibility.
2. **Imagination.** Lack of imagination.
3. **Reasoning.** Lack of logical self-reasoning.
4. **Learning.** Lack of learning.

Attributes. These shortcomings of computers are restricted to 4 qualities (attributes, faculties, mega-strong-traits) which are thus far inherent in the consciousness of its creator, humankind.

Liberty. Lucid consciential projection is not a mere re-invention of the savage capitalistic culture, guaranteed by physiology. Nevertheless, it can doubtless be considered in the 4 following manners:

1. **Consumerism.** An option of consumption.
2. **Freedom.** The practicing of an unsuspected freedom.
3. **Mobility.** The experience of mobility that increases more each time.
4. **Illimitable.** The rupturing of limits for the consciousness.

Bibliography: Bentov (119, p. 71), Besant (134, p. 173), Jacobson (796, p. 217), Kettelkamp (841, p. 89), Michaël (1041, p. 157), Morris (1093, p. 105), Steiger (1601, p. 216), Vieira (1762, p. 198), Walker (1781, p. 97), White (1827, p. 28), Wilber (1845, p. 120).

30. HUMAN LUCID PROJECTION

Definitions. Human lucid projection: the unique experience of perception of the environment, whether spontaneous or induced, in which the center of one's awareness appears to situate itself in a spatial location separate from one's living human body (breathing soma); passage of the consciousness from the intraphysical state to the projected state.

Synonymy: *AKE* (out-of-body experience); androprojection; animic excursion; animic flight; animic migration; animic travel; apopsychic; asomatic experience; astral departure; astral dream; astral duplication; astral experience; astral flight; astral journey; astral migration; astral deambulation; astral peregrination; astral projection; astral separation; astral telemetry; astral travel; astrotraveling; clairvoyant travel; DBE (departure from the human body experience); departure from the body experience; departure of the consciousness from coincidence; detachment of the living person; disassociation; discoincidence; disconnection; disconnection of the body; disembodiment; disjunction; dislocation of the consciousness; dissociation; ECE (extracorporeal experience); emancipation of the soul; escape to the astral; existential liberation; experience exterior to the human body; exsomatic state; exsomation (Greek: *ek*, outside; *soma*, body); exteriorization of the astrosoma; exteriorization of the psyche; exteriorization; externalization; extracorporeal adventure; extracorporeal projection; extracorporeal test; extracorporeal travel; extraphysical journey; extraphysical mini-vacation; extraphysical travel; extrasensory travel; extrusion of the psychic double; extrusion of the psychosoma; flight of the mind; floating dream; gynoprojection; half-death; heterologous projection; hominal projection; homoprojection; human projection; *in spirito* travel (Benandanti; Lorena; sixteenth and seventeenth century); interdimensional projection; interdimensional visit; journey of the soul; liberation of the consciousness; little death; live unfolding; lucid projection of the self; means of extraphysical access; mini-death; movable center of the consciousness; multidimensional travel; mystical travel; natural unfolding of the personality; non-intermediated consciential experience; OBE (out-of-body experience); OBE or OOBE (out-of-the-body experience); OBP or OOBP (out-of-the-body projection); oneiric trance; OOB excursion; otherworldly experience; out of the human body experience; out-of-body episode; parapsychic excursion; parapsychic unfolding; parasomatic experience; perispirit escape; perispirit travel; perispiritual unfolding; *prapti;* pre-discarnation; pre-experience of death; preview of death; prior death; projection of the second body; projection of the self; projection of the soul; projection outside the body; projective experience; provisory death; provisory discarnation; provisory unfolding; psychic projection; psychodynamic travel; rehearsal of death; relocation of the consciential seat; "rising into the sky;" scholastic experience; self-diplosis; self-disembodiment; "self-induced depersonalization;" shamanistic flight; sidereal exit; sidereal flight; small death; spiritual detachment; spiritual deambulation; spiritual projection; spiritual travel; state of consciential emancipation; strolling doubles; temporary death; temporary disembodiment; temporary excarnation; thanatoid experience; trans-outflow of the consciousness; transport by the spirit; travel in the dream body; travel to eternity; trip in the beyond; unfolding of the consciousness; unfolding of the person; unfolding; up-anchoring of the consciousness; *videha* (India); voluntary detachment; voluntary unfolding; waking sleep; walking doubles.

Thesaurus. The Thesaurus of Projectiology highlights the expression *human lucid projection* as being the best or most accurate for labeling the phenomenon, from among the dozens of terms listed above.

Summary. The first 9 most frequently asked questions, when initially addressing any new subject, can thus be answered in the following summarized manner, regarding lucid projection in general:

1. **Who** produces lucid projection? The consciential principles, more specifically the intraphysical and extraphysical consciousnesses (extraphysical dimensions, intermissions).

2. **What** constitutes or generates lucid projection? A greater or lesser degree of discoincidence of the consciousness' vehicles of manifestation (holosoma).

3. **Where** is lucid projection produced and developed? In any district or environment of the physical universe, and part of the extraphysical universe, where the consciousness manifests itself.

4. **When** is lucid projection produced? At any time and under any meteorological conditions, because time and meteorology do not necessarily or directly influence the production of lucid projection.

5. **Why** is lucid projection produced and developed? Due to the internal nature of the normal physiology and paraphysiology of the vehicles of manifestation of the consciousness, when it temporarily changes its consciential state.

6. **With what** should lucid projection be produced? Initially, by using the psychosoma.

7. **How** is lucid projection produced? By altering the vibratory or energetic frequencies of the vehicles of manifestation of the consciousness.

8. **For what purpose** is lucid projection produced? It has countless objectives, or a variety of uses, according to the specific lucid projection, whether it is produced voluntarily or involuntarily.

9. **To what degree** should lucid projection be produced? To the point of not causing any problems in the daily human life of the consciential projector, thus avoiding alienation toward physical existence or the existential program.

Access. The study of lucid projection is not religion, creed, dogma or religiosity. It represents a direct way toward prioritized self-knowledge or, using other popular expressions, an intraconsciential renovation or a *way of inner illumination* that is granted to each of us, a *beachhead* for the exploration and conquest of the extraphysical world by the intraphysical consciousness prior to biological death – beginning with the individual extraphysical sphere of energy (personal holothosene). It is a state of consciousness and a method for human, personal, direct and incontrovertible access for the consciousness to extraphysical dimensions, through the separation of the psyche (mind, psychological maturity) from its dense physical substrate.

Relationships. Projection of the intraphysical consciousness *outside the human body* or, in other words, *further out* than it actually is or lives, has been related to dream, psychological symbolism, hallucination, mental imbalance, traveling clairvoyance, biological disturbances, imitation of the process of biological death and many altered states of consciousness. These aspects will be studied in the context of this book, according to the sequential analysis of the subjects.

Exoteric. The popularization of lucid projection – induced voluntarily – created a situation whereby the phenomenon ceased to be mysterious, esoteric, hermetic, occult and inaccessible to non-initiates of the age of obscurantism, in order to become natural, exoteric, public, accepted as being physiological or paraphysiological and accessible to all humanity through evolutionary consciential openness. This reaction began in 1905 and intensified from 1950 onward, with the great demographic explosion and the processes of more ample interconsciential communication, pertaining to the current age of acceleration of human history.

Blockages. There are those who attribute the blocked capacity of the intraphysical consciousness (or the majority of humankind) to temporarily leave the human body in lucid projections – and thereby only have spontaneous nonlucid projection during natural sleep *(locked existence)* – to the idle capacity of the human organism or the non-utilization of about 80% of the potentialities of the cerebral hemispheres and 30% of the potentialities of both lungs, aside from other organs, and the use of only 25% of one's psychic potential, the energy of one's mind, the elaboration of thoughts.

Proof. These affirmations require definitive scientific proof through the research of neurology and projectiology (conscientiology).

Hygiene. From the beginning of humankind on this planet up until the first quarter of the nineteenth century, we deactivated millions of our somas because we were not aware of the existence of pathogenic microorganisms that were understood in greater detail from the time of Louis Pasteur onward. Lucid projectability took a little longer to be discovered and employed with awareness: it was practically unknown to the public until about 1950 (the twentieth century).

Independence. Upon overcoming fear (projectiophobia) and one's motivation being kindled, lucid projection of the consciousness outside the human body occurs regardless of gender, age, race, order of birth, political tendency, faith, religion, religiosity, education, philosophy, financial status or even one's preconceived ideas.

Physiology. This proves that lucid projection is a normal physiological attribute of the human body that is, in many ways, a primary biological phenomenon. It is as natural as sleep, dreams, digestion, the sex act (for women and men), as well as menstruation, gestation, and childbirth (for women).

Universality. In regard to its universality, it is observed that lucid projection, as an intrinsically natural function, occurs with multifaceted variables, such as the following 5:

1. **Age.** With people of all physical ages, from children to those of *advanced age* (80 years and older).

2. **Health.** With physically or mentally healthy or ill individuals of both genders.

3. **Information.** With those who have heard of, read about or studied the subject, as well as with those who are completely unaware of the subject, whether they are uninformed, misinformed, under-informed, or those ignorant existentially-robotized individuals who pertain to intraphysical society.

4. **Life.** With social beings living a routine life, as well as victims of disasters or accidents who are undergoing surgery.

5. **Intentionality.** Through the personality's active force of will and intention, as well as when unwanted, for that individual who experiences an *extraphysical escape*, for example.

Powers. Many religious systems have been promising a pleasant life beyond the grave or beyond the crematorium, teaching that you should suffer current misfortunes with a smile. Lucid projection research not only reaffirms these considerations but goes much further, indicating that the opposite approach is even better. Use the development of your personal powers – will, intentionality and self-organization, for example – in order to immediately improve your current human life. At our evolutionary level, we return to intraphysical life to be happy with lucid evolution. It is no longer worthwhile to cultivate suffering, pain and torment.

Balance. Let us not wait for the decomposition of the human body for our consciousnesses to achieve more agreeable or balanced conditions.

Now. This can be obtained here. *Today is the day; now is the time; this is the moment.* It can be done without any repression, dogmatism, demagogy or abdominal brainwashing from the protoconcepts of religions or theologies (preschool courses) of which approximately 100 thousand have existed over the span of human history.

Bases. Succinctly, lucid projections present approximately 12 basic common occurrences that people experience spontaneously and, in many cases, exhibit a certain reluctance to mention, due to social repression and conditioning:

1. **Self-projection.** Feel the consciousness (ego, self-lucidity) leaving the human body (soma): lucid projection (LP) per se.

2. **Primoprojection.** Have the experience of leaving the human body, with lucidity, only once: first lucid projection (primoprojection).

3. **Self-discoincidence.** Feel the separation of the consciousness a short distance from the human body: projection in the physical base.

4. **Self-location.** Feel that you are above your own human body: *extra*physical self-location.

5. **Self-bilocation.** See your own human body below you: consciential self-bilocation.

6. **Self-translocation.** Feel that you are moving to a distant point without using the human body: extraphysical self-translocation.

7. **Paravision.** Be convinced of being able to observe, *de visu, in loco,* what happens at a distance from your own body: extraphysical vision (paravision).

8. **Telekinesis.** Produce physical effects outside the human body, without using the body, which occurs only occasionally: extraphysical telekinesis (called *psychokinesis* by some researchers).

9. **Bilocation.** Make other people see you, while in the condition of a projected experimenter, a phenomenon that occurs rarely: *physical bilocation* per se.

10. **Self-apparition.** Make the projected consciousness appear, when sensed or perceived at a distance by other people, through means other than the dense physical presence, a phenomenon that also occurs very rarely: *inter vivos* apparition; extraphysical telepathy.

11. **Self-persuasion.** Be certain that you somehow really *traveled outside* the human body: *projective self-persuasion* regarding facts and experiences.

12. **Self-confirmation.** Prove the authenticity of your own lucid extracorporeal projection to yourself, after a detailed comparison of the places, facts, beings and time frame that you experienced at a distance, without the human body: self-confirmation subsequent to the lucid projection.

Proof. Lucid projection is neither an article of faith, *nor merely* a theme for religious debate. Neither is it a pretext for philosophical observations, nor a process for the enrichment of the meditations of poets or the works of literati. Lucid projection is *individual proof* for the intraphysical consciousness that offers the interested person at least 4 mega-challenges that serve as definitive evidence or multiple pieces of evidence, allowing you to begin your personal research or experiments that are high-priority and have a great recycling effect upon the existential program:

1. **Multidimensions.** The existence of the extraphysical world or the extraphysical dimensions beyond this *dimension of oxygen (existential multidimensionality),* one of the mega-challenges confronted by *philosophical schools.*

2. **Multibodies.** The existence of the vehicles of consciential manifestation, beyond the soma (holosoma), with the subsequent loss of the fear of death (thanatophobia), one of the mega-challenges in *human health* research.

3. **Multiexistences.** *Personal* proof of the theory of successive lives or existential seriation, through retrocognitive projections, one of the mega-challenges of many religions, sects and *theologies* throughout time.

4. **Multipopulations.** Proof of the fact of the habitability of other worlds or planets *(extraphysical multipopulations),* one of the mega-challenges that *astronomy* has always confronted.

Pluralities. There are, in other words, 5 pluralities that lucid projection evidences to the attentive practitioner, as can be seen in the following context:

1. **Vehicles.** The plurality of vehicles (bodies) of consciential manifestation (holosomatics).

2. **States.** The plurality of the consciential states (conditions), including xenophrenia, when healthy.

3. **Dimensions.** The plurality of existential (multidimensionality) dimensions (planes, worlds, communities, colonies, districts, environments), holoresomatics.

4. **Existences.** The plurality of consciential existences (lives) or stages (holobiography, multi-existential cycle).

5. **Stars.** The plurality of stars (planets) which are inhabited (cosmos).

Book. This book obviously gives special attention to human lucid projections.

Term. It is necessary to distinguish between the different meanings of the term "projection." For example, lucid projection, analyzed here, should not be confused with "projection," in the sense employed in psychoanalysis or psychology.

Psychoanalysis. In psychoanalysis, projection is the process whereby the individual expels qualities, sentiments and desires – that one does not recognize or refuses to see in oneself – out from oneself, ascribing them to another person or thing. It is an archaic defense that particularly manifests itself in paranoia.

Psychology. Also, "projection" is generally used in psychology to signify that the individual perceives the environment and responds as a function of what it is. This is the basis of various *psychological projective techniques.*

Expression. The following illustrates the manner in which the expression *lucid projection* is currently most often used in 5 different languages:

1. **Portuguese:** *projeção astral* or *experiência fora-do-corpo.*
2. **French:** *dedoublemment.*
3. **Spanish:** *desdoblamiento.*
4. **German:** *astralwanderung.*
5. **Italian:** *proiezzione astrale.*

Bibliography: Andrade (27, p. 131), Bardon (80, p. 322), Bayless (98, p. 99), Carrington (246, p. 147), Corvalán (306, p. 72), Coxhead (312, p. 116), Ebon (454, p. 104), Eliade (477, p. 98), Ferguson (512, p. 167), Fugairon (562, p. 131), Gonçalves (614, p. 5), Green (632, p. 46), Kardec (825, p. 362), London (944, p. 169), Marinuzzi (998, p. 171), Mittl (1061, p. 7), Pratt (1285, p. 42), Rogo (1439, p. 47), Schatz (1514, p. 46), Smith (1572, p. 19), Steiger (1601, p. 5), Swedenborg (1639, p. 211), Walker (1781, p. 63), Wolman (1863, p. 929).

31. LUCID PARAPROJECTION

Definitions. Lucid paraprojection: the experience of the extraphysical consciousness – whether "terrestrial" or "extraterrestrial" – that leaves the psychosoma stationary in the extraphysical dimension, and departs projected in the mentalsoma, in the mentalsomatic dimension; passage of the extraphysical consciousness to the projected state.

Synonymy: extra-human lucid projection; lucid projection of the extraphysical consciousness; para-human lucid projection.

Analogies. In the same way that there are phenomena produced by extraphysical consciousnesses which are analogous to human phenomena (the phenomena of transcendent physical effects, for example), there are consciential projections in the mentalsoma of intraphysical consciousnesses which are analogous to those experienced by extraphysical consciousnesses.

Environment. Pure, mental lucid projections of the intraphysical and extraphysical consciousness are similar to each other. This is because they occur in the same environment, the mentalsomatic dimension – a point of encounter that is common to all consciousnesses – utilizing the same vehicle of manifestation of the consciousness, namely the mentalsoma.

Differences. Up until now, the existence of basic differences in the connection of the mentalsoma with the parabrain of the psychosoma (through the golden cord) has been unknown, when referring to an intraphysical consciousness (connected to the holochakra and human body), as compared to an extraphysical consciousness that has already passed through the second desoma or, in other words, lacks the human body and the holochakra.

Distinction. In practice, however, regardless of the foregoing, the intraphysical consciousness, projected in the isolated mentalsoma, can generally distinguish perfectly between the intraphysical consciousness and the extraphysical consciousness, due to the consciential faculties of the mentalsoma (concentration, attention, association of ideas).

Bibliography: Vieira (1762, p. 73), Xavier (1882, p. 182).

32. ANIMAL   PROJECTION

Definition. Animal projection: projection of the rudimentary consciousness (consciential principle in evolution) of the subhuman animal outside its biological body.

Synonymy: subhuman projection; subintelligent projection; *zooprojection.*

Considerations. Based on the premise that the human, or hominid, is an animal; that animals, generally speaking, need to sleep as humans do, a generally accepted point of analysis being the fact that many species even dream; and that the consciousness of humans, during natural sleep, always unconsciously, spontaneously and physiologically projects itself from the human body; *it can logically be deduced* that higher animals, having a well constituted physical structure, possess an extraphysical vehicle of manifestation and project themselves in this vehicle – although all indications are that this occurs unconsciously – in a manner that is analogous to that of the human personality when it embarks on natural sleep.

Genetics. It should not be forgotten, in this context, that our *human* genetic makeup is 96.7% identical to the *subhuman* genetic makeup of the chimpanzee. There is a genetic difference of only 3.3% between us.

Characteristics. The facts listed thus far allow us to point to 6 characteristics of the projection of subhuman animals:

1. **Unconsciousness.** Subhuman unconsciousness.
2. **Rarity.** Rarity of the occurrence.
3. **Intraphysicality.** Relationship with human life (holothosene of intraphysical consciousnesses).
4. **Fugacity.** Spatially short projection, or in the proximity of the physical body.
5. **Paratroposphere.** In the proximity of the tropospheric environment (paratroposphere) of the human being with which it has affinity (empathy), in the case of domestic animals.
6. **Rudimentary.** The projective phenomenon as an unconscious agent on the part of the rudimentary subhuman consciousness.

Zoanthropy. Animal projection should not be confused with zoanthropy.

Animal-projectors. The most common subhuman animal-projectors are domestic animals, especially dogs and cats, perhaps due to their more intimate, diuturnal relationship with social (human) beings, as many of them even sleep on top of, or underneath, the owner's bed.

Roger. While projected on the night of July 29, 1982, in the apartment located on Visconde de Pirajá Street, Rio de Janeiro city, Brazil, the author observed "Roger" the guard dog (also projected at that time) at length. Roger later became the champion of the junior class of the Yorkshire breed. Roger was a 15-month old adult weighing 3.3 lbs. (1.5 kilos), and was affectionate, tame and intelligent for its evolutionary level.

Verification. On this opportunity it was possible to verify 3 distinctive facts:

1. **Aura.** The existence of its aura (energy).
2. **Parabody.** The existence of its extraphysical body (parabody) similar to its physical body.
3. **Miniholochakra.** The slightly luminous energetic connection (miniholochakra), similar to the silver cord of human beings, between its extraphysical and intraphysical vehicle.

Lucidity. At this time, the little projected dog, possibly due to the author's exceptionally felicitous realization of the consciential projection, demonstrated its habitual lucidity and – leaving the living room where its physical body was resting – wanted to follow the author's psychosoma to the bedroom, wishing to lick and rub up against him while wagging its short extraphysical tail (caudal appendix) in an extremely happy manner.

Appendix. When Roger was acquired, its tail or caudal appendix had already been cut, and he was also extraphysically seen to have a cut tail or, in other words, it was seen to be of the same size as when Roger was in the ordinary waking state (intraphysicality).

De-awareness. It is easy to suppose, only as a *research hypothesis,* that the rudimentary consciousness of the subhuman animal which, as it is generally accepted, does not demonstrate well-defined awareness of itself in the ordinary waking state, likewise remains devoid of awareness of itself or, in other words, *de-aware,* when it deactivates its biological subhuman body, as well as during the projections from its physical body.

Mental. All indications are that animals do not project themselves in the rudimentary mentalsoma, but only in the psychosoma, when in a primary phase of evolution, in the tropospheric extraphysical dimension.

Development. This evidence leads us to suppose that the mentalsoma only becomes defined and developed when the consciential principle reaches the *hominal level* and acquires awareness, as we understand it, with full self-awareness, thereby enabling its firsts incursions into the mentalsomatic dimension.

Dimension. This corroborates the fact that no animal subconsciousnesses which are evolutionarily inferior to the level of the human being (subhuman animals) are found to manifest in the pure (without the interference of other extraphysical dimensions) mentalsomatic dimension.

Psychosoma. The following conclusion can be drawn here: all para-animals encountered in the tropospheric extraphysical dimensions are in contact with extraphysical consciousnesses or projected intraphysical consciousnesses manifesting in the psychosoma.

Senselessness. Strictly speaking, all senselessness of the immature person represents a pathological de-awareness.

Alienation. Everything that separates one from maximum possible acumen of one's ego, today, constitutes alienation from consciential multidimensionality. The best course is for the intelligent intraphysical consciousness to always avoid this alienation, regardless of the circumstance or the defensive pretext.

De-awareness. The alienation, in this case, serves to promote *de-awareness,* generated by a reduction in the level of personal lucidity, a regression to the evolutionary animal stage.

Bibliography: Bayless (94, p. 130), Cornillier (305, p. 43), Crookall (343, p. 40), Delanne (385, p. 100), Easton (451, p. 145), Ebon (453, p. 100), Fugairon (562, p. 153), Green (633, p. 195), Kardec (825, p. 289), Steiger (1606, p. 180), Talamonti (1641, p. 227).

33. PLANT PROJECTION

Definition. Plant projection: projection of the energetic equivalent of the live plant from its botanical physical structure.

Synonymy: phytoprojection; projection of the double of the vegetable.

Kirlian photography. No one contests the vital manifestations of plants. It is for this reason that the highly controversial *Kirlian photography* merely confirmed the old suppositions that the double of plants also exteriorize in their own way.

Cord. The controversial *phantom appendage,* detected by special *Kirlian photos,* appears in plant projections and looks like a cord connected to the plant.

Verification. Lucid projection experiences allow the projected human consciousness to personally verify the energetic counterpart of the plant and its exteriorization when *injured* by the projector using the parahands of the psychosoma.

Bibliography: Moss (1096, p. 174).

34. LAWS OF PROJECTIOLOGY

Definition. Law: constant relationship between phenomena of a given order that expresses their nature or essence.

Synonymy: generalization; norm; postulate; prescription; principle.

Consideration. Leaving its birthplace, projectiology, a relative newcomer among the already established conventional academic studies, has not yet arrived at the point of establishing ample and complex generalizations or laws regarding human behavior that are analogous to the laws and principles presented by chemistry, astronomy or physics, for example. Nevertheless, something worthy of consideration can already be offered in this sense, despite projectiology's *insufficient mileage.*

Science. The knowledge of the general history of science has reached a point where there is a clear awareness that the fundamental principles in acceptance today will often be seen as strange concepts of an immature erudition, tomorrow.

Utility. Therefore, the postulates listed below should be viewed within a context of heterocritique, with a willingness to abandon any or all of them when they are no longer of use.

Indications. As of this writing (2002), these affirmations seem to be supported by many existing indicators and seem to be useful guides for the research and study of projectiology, and correlated subjects.

Enunciation. According to parapsychophysiology, any consciousness that undergoes resoma in the intraphysical dimension can temporarily leave the human body (soma) and return to it without negative consequences for anyone. Projectiology openly endorses this enunciation through laboratorial and individual experiments.

Accumulation. The accumulation of experiments makes it impossible to confuse dreams and other altered states of consciousness with the lucid projection phenomenon.

Proof. This fact eliminates all doubt regarding the authenticity of lucid projection for the veteran projector with individual, unquestionable and definitive proof, because the phenomenon is self-persuasive, extinguishes personal doubts and establishes new perspectives in the projector-experimenter's existence.

Vehicles. There are irreconcilable differences between the nature of the psychosoma and the nature of the mentalsoma. Projections of the isolated consciousness, when produced in these vehicles of manifestation, are completely and unmistakably different.

Preponderances. The biological or physical body preponderantly dominates the intraphysical or human dimension; the psychosoma, the extraphysical tropospheric or paratropospheric dimension; the mentalsoma, the mentalsomatic dimension, evidently always sustaining the thosenizations of the consciousness in any condition or dimension.

Intentionality. This entire crescendo of actions obviously occurs under the indispensable command of the pointer of the consciousness or the qualification of the personality's essential intentionality when it manifests itself.

Soma. During peaks of perception in the ordinary, physical waking state, as the human body is so absolutely *real* for the intraphysical consciousness, the individual is not aware of the existence of the psychosoma.

Psychosoma. A phenomenon similar to that described above occurs when the consciousness in the psychosoma – which is also absolutely *real* for the intraphysical consciousness when projected in the pure extraphysical dimension – does not perceive the existence of the human body. The exception to this is when, on certain occasions, one sees one's human body before oneself.

Mentalsoma. Still another similar phenomenon occurs in reference to the *mentalsoma,* that is absolutely real for the intraphysical consciousness, when projected in the mentalsomatic dimension. However, here the consciousness is in a condition in which it does not perceive the existence of any body or vehicle of manifestation as we understand and sense them in the ordinary, physical waking state.

Motivation. Most human beings have still not experienced an impactful lucid projection because they were not sufficiently motivated toward this goal. In other words, the ordinary person has generally not yet had any conscious or unconscious motive to wish to "leave the human body."

Somnambulism. Chronic lack of motivation, the process of initiation of the conscious, voluntary and efficient action for consciousnesses in general to temporarily, but lucidly, leave the human body, unquestionably shows that almost all of humanity has been sleeping through life or, to use a more appropriate expression, has literally been *somnambulant for millennia.*

Thought. Outside the body, the consciousness goes wherever it thinks of going.

Thosene. The consciousness is what it thinks (or thosenizes).

Coadjutants. Lucid projection, an occurrence owing to the natural faculties of the intraphysical consciousness, is quite achievable without the helpers and without the self-aware parapsychism of the practitioner. Nevertheless, it becomes much easier, and offers much higher quality results, with these 2 coadjutants.

Action-reaction. The attempt to produce consciential projections with negative, anticosmoethical intentions, whatever they may be, results in the reversion of the sick results upon the projector's own consciousness.

Cosmoethics. Hence the indispensable nature of philosophical analysis – or of the influence and frank action of cosmoethics, and the philosophical bases of universalism – in the arena of manifestations and the world of projectiology research.

Nature. Within the next few decades, the phenomenon of human lucid projection, *no longer contaminated by magic,* will stop being considered a mystical, religious, bizarre or strange occurrence. It will then be addressed, accepted and studied in a natural and widespread manner, more and more scientifically, as the law of nature that it is. This, with neither obscurantism, nor involvement with surrealism, beliefs, delirium, disinformation, manipulation of existentially robotized intraphysical consciousnesses, or folkloric manifestations.

Bibliography: Andrade (27, p. 144), Muldoon (1105, p. 65).

---

35. PARADOXES OF PROJECTIOLOGY

Definitions. Paradox: the concept that is, or appears to be, contrary to common belief; the assemblage of words or contradictory concepts.

Synonymy: apparent contradiction; contradiction; countersense; oxymoron.

Categories. There are many paradoxes in the occurrences of projectiology. The following 16 categories can be highlighted according to the area of phenomena in which they appear or in regard to their specific nature:

1. **Assistential.** Unfortunately, human beings generally help more when they remain *nonlucid* while projected in the extraphysical dimension – even when helping in extraphysical assistance and operating as nonlucid extraphysical sensitives – than when entirely *lucid* regarding their liberated condition. This is due to the fear and other negative emotions exhibited by novices regarding consciential projection.

2. **Biological.** Impulsive *youths,* during their adolescence, present a great ease for projecting and recalling extraphysical facts in the manner of a natural physiological reaction of their intraphysical period or age group. Nevertheless, *senior citizens* or veterans of life or golden agers (old youths), 65 or older, have a more expanded serenity and experience that allows them to cope with the density and keep their balance regarding the results, objectives and evolutionary effects of the intraphysical consciousness' projective experiences.

3. **Consciential.** In fact, awareness is a continuous permanent state, because we are somehow *conscious* even when we think we are *unconscious* or asleep.

4. **Dualistic.** The intraphysical consciousness produces projections simultaneously using animism (intraconscientiality) and parapsychism; in an active and passive manner; with two lives, human and extraphysical; with two memories, human (biomemory) and integral (holomemory); submissive to human morals and cosmoethics; combating euthanasia, in the ordinary, physical waking state, following human codes and, as an aide to death, while projected in the extraphysical dimension, helping to deactivate the biological bodies of intraphysical consciousnesses or, in other words, helping consciousnesses to go through the transition of the first, biological or cellular desoma.

5. **Phenomenological.** In the phenomenon of consciential self-bilocation, intraphysical consciousnesses *actually go outside themselves* in a lucid projection and then contemplate and analyze their own inactive human bodies. Philosophically speaking, this act constitutes the first step toward the consciousness *going inside itself.*

6. **Philosophical.** Lucid projection demonstrates the existence of *excessively materialized* consciousnesses that are in a more comfortable condition now, while they are human beings, bound to the dense matter of the soma – the body that they worship and preserve with so much tenacity – as compared to the subsequent period, when they are extraphysical consciousnesses, free in the extraphysical dimension, albeit without the human body. This generates an *intuitive attachment* to

matter which – as incredible as it may seem – coexists and derives from a tranquil acceptance of the ego's survival of biological death. These facts transform and notably extend the currently used philosophical concepts of materialism and spiritualism because they reveal the regrettable ambivalence or a *spiritualistic-materialism,* the existence of which has always gone unnoticed in the subconscious of many individuals.

7. **Physiological.** When the projected consciousness endeavors to have a composed, well-formed psychosoma, it will have more possibilities for condensing a percentage of matter in this vehicle of manifestation or aggregate an increasingly greater amount of the holochakra. This will result in the consciousness remaining bound or restricted to the proximities of the terrestrial crust, without advancing to better districts, environments or communities of the extraphysical dimension.

8. **Mnemonic.** When the projected intraphysical consciousness becomes slightly adept at briefly utilizing the amplitude of reasoning of the integral memory (holomemory), it has difficulty in passing on these recollections to the partial memory of the ordinary, physical waking state (biomemory or cerebral memory) upon physically awakening. This same consciousness, while enjoying the benefits of the integral memory in the extraphysical dimension, finds it difficult, when there, to revalidate the concepts and appearances that it defends in regard to the issues and facts of intraphysical existence – due to the narrow vision of human preconceptions, repressions and conditionings. It is very difficult, in this case, to make one system of reasoning mesh with the other. Holomemory surpasses all conventional parameters of observation of the ordinary intraphysical consciousness belonging to the unthinking masses. Not all types of intelligence that predominate in the intraphysical consciousness' life permit an easier or smoother access to the inventory of recollections in the holomemory. This is a fact that still *requires in-depth research* or, in other words, a comparison of biomemory, holomemory and the category of intelligence predominantly used in the intraphysical consciousness' existence.

9. **Parapsychological.** Every intraphysical consciousness projects every night while sleeping, but remains nonlucid or semilucid outside the human body. Sporadically, upon achieving extraphysical self-awareness, the individual almost always suffers a trauma or *consciential shock* that makes the consciousness immediately return to the dense cellular body, thus losing the unique learning opportunity provided by the extraphysical experience.

10. **Psychological.** Lucid projection frees one from the repressions of the consciousness that, paradoxically, provides one with greater powers against negative, controlling emotionalism.

11. **Psychotherapeutic.** The best process for lending new meaning to the experiences of human life is to leave it through lucid projection. The best process for intraphysical consciousnesses to increase the ability to be in contact with themselves, others and events, is to get out from themselves through lucid projection.

12. **Chemistry.** After 40 years of age, one is forced to use medications that protect the cerebral cortex against arteriosclerosis and the problems of aging. These drugs are positive on one hand, as they avert intracranial pressure, stimulate the functioning of the brain and improve the cerebral memory or biomemory. On the other hand, they make the individual more awake and thus impede lucid projection, because they intensify and enhance the ordinary waking state in a person who is already predisposed to this due to crystallized habits and the need for fewer hours of sleep.

13. **Desomatic.** Lucid projection, or anticipated physical minideath (desomatics or thanatology), a *highly individual* experiment, leads to the definitive elimination of all types of personalism in the human projector's mind, through the ideas and sentiments that are amplified by *pure universalism.*

14. **Technician.** In order to improve the method for projecting, the projector should first saturate the mind, or *fill the mind* with the idea of lucid projection. Nevertheless, as soon as one perceives oneself to be projected, the individual should forget all human conditioning and preconceived ideas, keeping the *mind empty,* or open and receptive to any idea, event or new phenomenon that occurs extraphysically.

15. **Paraphysiological.** The intraphysical consciousness who is *physically* less anchored can achieve biological, *physical maturity* more quickly and can consequently advance even more quickly toward *extraphysical* maturity or holomaturity.

16. **Self-awareness.** Lucid projection, although a *natural occurrence* common to all humanity, presents the condition of advanced physical self-awareness as an occurrence that is unfortunately still *beyond the pattern* of the intraphysical consciousness' ordinary condition or, in other words, subordinated to the prison of the physical, terrestrial restriction imposed upon the extraphysical consciousness when operating a soma through resoma.

Resolution. Every paradox is waiting to be resolved.

Complexity. The paradoxes encountered in the occurrences of projectiology reaffirm the complexity and ample range of their manifestations in the areas of action of one's consciousness, and suggest innumerous research hypotheses.

Transcendent. Conscientiology and projectiology are sciences that are *more transcendent* or transpersonal in nature.

Demarcated. They are not so specific and demarcated regarding their manifestations and research in the intraphysical and extraphysical dimensions. This does not occur, for example, with physics, paraphysics, biology, parabiology, and many other sciences with radical *non-transcendent* counterparts that are far more contrary or antipodal when researched by humans or extraphysical consciousnesses.

Dilemma. The lack of understanding and application of this disparity between sciences is the fundamental cause for the existence of the two-centuries-old *mind-matter* dilemma and the traditional, non-participatory research which is unchanging and outdated on the part of the researchers working in the conventional sciences *(dermatologies of the consciousness)*.

Consciousness. The material world does not have available resources that can provide equipment or instrumentation capable of directly studying the consciousness, which transcends consciential and immanent energies and, therefore, matter itself, in all of its most rudimentary or coarse manifestations, without the subtleties, *insubstantialities*, *rarefactions* and interdimensionalitites of the consciousness of subhumans and humans.

Bibliography: Rogo (1446, p. 320).

36. PROJECTIVE LIMITATIONS

Definition. Projective limitations: factors that are disadvantageous, restricting the expansion of the objectives and practical applications of lucid consciential projection.

Synonymy: projective delimitations; projective disadvantages; projective improprieties; projective inconveniences.

Types. Besides the fact that lucid projection of the consciousness is, for a great number of researchers, by far the most transcendent, interesting and important phenomenon known to humanity, yielding many more definitive results for the individual and, obviously, presenting many more advantages than disadvantages, within the areas of psychology or parapsychology, 4 factors can be pointed out as being inconvenient, substantial limitations of projectiology: individualism; methodology; projective recesses; and the characteristics of the current growth of the human brain.

1. **Individualism.** The fact remains, which is incontrovertible up to the time of writing in 2002, that lucid projection research – as it is an exclusive and, above all, an inevitably individual occurrence, not directly affecting the multitudes, the unthinking masses (existential robotization) – has not been permitted to advance more rapidly, neither over the centuries of human history, nor (so far) in this technological era, because its research presents minimal psychological appeal to the human masses, who are absorbed in immediate material (earthly, hedonistic, physicalist, exclusively intraphysical) interests. This is characteristic of instinctive, animal, human life.

Proof. We cannot discard the fact that the ideal, basic proof of the existence of lucid projection is still something which will remain individual and nontransferable, achieved through the effort, training and improvement of the interested individual's personal performance.

Appeal. Lucid projection appeals to the individual, yet there is no great collective appeal. Lucid consciential projection is not the type of thing or activity that is, for example, able to: sell records, attract radio and television audiences, or increase tourism.

Success. The research findings do not appeal to a mass audience or attract the *populace* like the soccer player, the radical sport athlete on the edge of suicide, the sexy singer or musical pop star – all of whom are champions of human and transitory success.

Funds. It is common knowledge that all human-based research obviously demands financial resources besides the "people" factor. As lucid projection is not directly involved with the unthinking human populace, official funds for scientific research become scarce, except, unfortunately, for research related to ultra-secret bellicose objectives, or "psychotronic war."

2. **Methodology.** There is always the limiting factor of the impracticality of making a single, practical, efficient, standardized and common lucid projection technique indiscriminately viable, easy and accessible to the majority of humans, who are at least thus far still somnambulant. This is due to the equally extremely individual nature of the lucid projection experience and to the variety of tendencies and characters of human consciousnesses.

3. **Recess.** Projective recess is a common fact that affects the intraphysical personality and creates practical disinterest toward the subject of consciential projection. It almost always occurs during one's terrestrial period of greater human productivity. Therefore, the absolute and relative projective recess generated by diverse causes and its consequences, also certainly constitute a powerful limiting factor in the practical development of humanity's lucid consciential projections.

4. **Brain.** Another factor that constitutes a considerable projective limitation is the exceptional, minority, countercurrent (against the flow) condition of expansion of the human brain, which is necessary for the development of the consciential projector's consciousness. It seems to be more efficient when concentrating on the right cerebral hemisphere – thereby expanding one's animic (intraconscientiality) and parapsychic capacities. However, on the contrary, it is currently observed that the average members of the planetary population predominantly concentrate on the development of the left cerebral hemisphere or, in other words, they are still caught up in the improvement of their command of language (laryngochakra) and rational operations.

Future. Despite the aforementioned limitations, the author remains optimistic and confident regarding the possible, plausible or probable future of projectiology.

Roots. A presumed process for definitively destroying and eliminating the science of projectiology will always be impracticable due to its basic phenomenological and physiological roots that are irrevocably lodged within the structure of the human body (soma).

Methods. The improvement of human lucid projections will be inevitable to the extent that projective methods are applied from this point forward.

Consensus. Mindful projective experiments with a desirable ethicality – performed by investigators who have a serious, vigilant, secure and deeply self-critiquing awareness – will inevitably occur. They will be impelled by the natural development of ideas, human interests and planetary issues. Hence, a consensus will arise that will establish productive routines regarding the phenomena that benefit everyone.

Replicability. On the other hand, we do not consider the difficulties involved in replicating all lucid projection experiences in an absolutely identical manner – stemming from undoubtedly individual factors – to be an insurmountable obstacle to the development of projectiology.

Logic. The imperative of the replicability of identical phenomena - applied in an ad *arbitrium manner* by researchers - which is presented as a basic, irrevocable and irreplaceable requirement of conventional scientific method, and of which we are constantly reminded, does not stand up to logical critique, as seen with astronomical phenomena, for example, which, although not being replicable, are not outlawed by science.

Astronomy. Astronomy also does not owe its prodigious development to the experimental manipulation of the celestial bodies.

Restraint. As a consequence of its current stage of consciential evolution, or the freedom of the ego, humankind no longer possesses the natural instinctual restraint that inhibits other animals from killing members of their own species.

Respect. In intraphysical society, there is a much greater liberalism regarding customs and sexual permissiveness. On the other hand, there is a much deeper respect for the rights of subhuman consciousnesses, plants and nature (ecology).

Intelligence. These facts are proof that human intelligence, in general, on this planet has already at least overcome the consciential primary nature of the rudimentary (so-called inferior) intelligence of subhuman animals. Strictly speaking, it is important to consider that subhuman beings already present a sketchy form of jealousy, envy, egocentrism and other emotional reactions similar to those of a child.

Mega-weak-traits. Nevertheless, in the current condition of the consciousness' evolutionary passage to another level or the *sublimation of the ego,* we cannot be boastful of terrestrial human intelligence, as seen by these 10 individual (psychopathies) and social (sociopathies) mega-weak-traits:

1. **Cruelty.** Calculated human cruelty.
2. **Anti-ecology.** Refined anti-ecological abuses.
3. **Genocide.** Crimes of genocide.
4. **Wars.** Continuous wars, armed conflicts, uprisings and revolutions.
5. **Lynchings.** Lynchings and collective suicides, under any pretext.
6. **Arsenals.** Nuclear arsenals and the rearming of nations.
7. **Mafias.** The organized crime of the multiform multinational mafias or the *societas sceleris.*
8. **Exterminators.** Aggression, kidnapping, assassination, death squads and gang raids.
9. **Terrorism.** *Faceless* international terrorism.
10. **Serial.** Mass slaughters and unspeakable crimes committed by the same individual, the so-called serial (serial killer, mass murderer) murderer (animal), who is intelligent, aware, calculating, cold, socially integrated, methodical, discreet and silent; and those who "shoot anything that moves."

Solutions. The nature of these consciential conflicts evidences that they will only be diminished or resolved when all violence is eliminated, by means of 4 measures that demand immense *political good will on the part of governments,* which still does not exist:

1. **Comprehension.** The deep comprehension of unconscious human passions (psychosoma or emotional body). Lucid projectability (LPB) is a light at the end of this tunnel.
2. **Altruism.** The ability to correctly satisfy the necessities that are more economic in nature (altruism), such that the *rich countries* (First World) stop exploiting the *countries of the dispossessed* (Third World). The hope lies in the strengthening of the United Nations (UN), in the still fetal globalization process and in the creation of a global government.
3. **Maxifraternity.** The establishment of better communication between potential adversaries (maxifraternity). An auspicious activity in this respect is the Internet.
4. **Universalism.** The improvement of the organization of governmental, national and international institutions (universalism), as well as conscientiocentric institutions; and changes in ideologies and values attributed to ephemeral things and life by humankind (extraphysical maturity or holomaturity). Included here are non-governmental organizations (NGOs), the International Institute of Projectiology and Conscientiology (IIPC), the Center for Higher Studies of the Consciousness (CHSC), the International Academy of Conscientiology (IAC), the International Association for Evolution of the Consciousness (Aracê) and the International Campus of Conscientiology (ICC).

Research. On library shelves we can find some books, even very attractive ones, that introduce areas of human research. The following are 8 examples of exotic or enigmatic titles: *Biosofia, Cosmonomia, Geopsíquica, Homaranismo, Metablética, Nomezofia, Psicomaiêutica and Teocracismo* (see Specific Bibliography).

Title words. You have probably never heard of some of these 8 title words, or seen them written in your preferred reading list or cited in the most popular dictionaries.

Marginality. The author thinks that "projectiology," some decades from now, will not have the same obscure destiny as these respectable lines of thought or still peripheral concepts.

Projectiological Bibliography: Bayless (98, p. 99), Crookall (338, p. 139), Monroe (1065, p. 204).

Specific Bibliography:

1. **CALLILE, Miguel, Junior;** *Psicomaiêutica;* 178 pp.; 20.5 X 14 cm; pb.; Rio de Janeiro; Brazil; Companhia Brasileira de Artes Gráficas; 1968; p. 14.

2. **MAIA, Pedro;** *Geopsíquica: Das Relações da Fisiologia e da Psicologia com a Geotípica e a Geocósmica;* 204 pp.; 18.5 X 13.5 cm; pb.; Rio de Janeiro; Brazil; Jornal do Commercio; 1955; p. 32.

3. **MORAIS, Pedro Deodato de;** *Biosofia: Sabedoria do Presente – Ciência – Religião;* 238 pp.; 21 chaps.; 33 illus.; 18.5 X 13.5 cm; pb.; São Paulo, SP; Brazil; Edições Melhoramentos; no date; p. 7.

4. **SALAZAR, Gabriele;** *Nomezofia: Revelações Completas Sobre as Irradiações do Nome;* 322 pp.; 62 chaps.; illus.; 135 tabs.; 2 apps..; 20 X 13.5 cm; pb.; São Paulo, SP; Brazil; Editora Moraes; 1939; p. 13.

5. **SOUZA, Délio Pereira de;** *Homaranismo: A Idéia Interna;* pres. Benedicto Silva; 90 pp.; 30 chaps.; illus.; 21 X 14 cm; pb.; Rio de Janeiro; Brazil; Spirita Eldona Societo F. V. Lorenz; 1983; p. 9.

6. **TIMOTEO** (pseud. of José Roque Martins e Silva); *Teocracismo: A Terceira Idéia;* pref. Pietro Ubaldi; 206 pp.; 7 chaps.; 12 illus.; 2 tabs.; 23 X 15 cm; pb.; Rio de Janeiro; Brazil; Livraria Freitas Bastos; 1968; p. 56.

7. **TÔRRES, Joviano;** *Totalidade e Sociologia: Exposição Geral Sumária de Cosmonomia;* 672 pp.; 23 X 15 cm; pb.; Rio de Janeiro; Brazil; Author's Edition; 1956; p. 15.

8. **VAN DER BERG, J. H.;** *Metablética: Psicologia Histórica* (Metabletica of Leer Der Veranderingen); transl. Francisco Van Der Water & Miguel Maillet; pref. Leonardo Van Acker; 256 pp.; 5 chaps.; 5 illus.; ono.; 21 X 14.5 cm; pb.; São Paulo, SP; Brazil; Editora Mestre Jou; 1965; p. 16.

III – *Phenomena of Projectiology*

37. CLASSIFICATION OF PROJECTIVE PHENOMENA

Definition. Projective phenomenon: parapsychic occurrence specific to the scope of projectiology.

Synonymy: projectiological phenomenon; projective occurrence.

World. The world of projectiology research includes a domain of manifestations beginning with common facts or phenomena, namely those which almost all persons may have experienced and recalled at one time or another, such as semilucid projection in which the individual appears to be flying with some degree of lucidity. At the other end of the spectrum, some extreme cases can be included – which are as rare as they are spectacular – such as the phenomenon of physical bilocation, observed by numerous human witnesses.

Complex. In the phenomenological complex of projectiology, 54 correlated, connected or *sister* parapsychic phenomena are included here. They represent manifestations, consequences or correlations closely related to the act of the intraphysical consciousness projecting from the human body (soma). These phenomena go beyond essential consciential projections, which are addressed in detail in other specialized chapters of this book, according to the sequential analysis of subjects.

Denominator. In the component chapters of this section, only the correlated phenomena were listed, independent of their causes, effects and operational aspects. They compose a *phenomenological complex,* or a block of phenomena with similar patterns, paradigms or manifestations. Their common denominator is the lucid projection of the intraphysical consciousness out of holosomatic coincidence with the human body.

Analysis. These phenomena simultaneously demand analytical study *per se* and, at the same time, analysis as a whole, in order to arrive at unified interpretations and global, clarifying, and correct views of the facts.

Causes. Many of these correlated phenomena can be provoked by causes other than the occurrences triggered by lucid projection of the intraphysical consciousness. For example, the more frequent poltergeist is not at all related to projectiology. The same is the case with spontaneous human combustion and other phenomena. The phenomena brought together are those which relate directly to projectiology.

Identification. It sometimes becomes very difficult to clearly identify or strictly classify the exact parapsychic phenomenon that we experience. For example: the expansion of the consciousness through projection in the mentalsoma, traveling clairvoyance and extraphysical vision are 3 very distinct occurrences in their manifestations. They can occur so simultaneously, mixed together with the interrelated facts, that the experimenter is not able to discern them from each other or to know at which point one phenomenon ended and another began.

Complexity. It is worth bearing in mind here that the consciousness is the most complex object in the universe.

Isolation. The degree to which a phenomenon is isolated determines the degree to which it can be acted upon in order to measure it, attempt to include it in a law or utilize its potentialities or force.

Fragmentation. The study of projective phenomena demonstrates that the *analytical decomposition of the human consciousness* – or the fragmentation of psychic and parapsychic activity – into different parts or into isolated, intellectual, affective and volitional functions, in an independent manner, will always be artificial. This is only done in response to the need for educational exposition and the facilitation of theoretical and practical research.

Thosenology. We should bear in mind that the thosene, or the complex base of manifestations of all consciousnesses is composed of 3 inseparable variables: idea or thought, emotion or sentiment and consciential energy or the act itself.

Practice. Due to the difficulty in identifying the phenomena in a detailed and accurate manner, the classification of projectiological phenomenology is the theory needed for precise research analysis. However, it is worth noting that, in practice, the consciousness presents itself as a totality, and all the spontaneous classified facts coexist in an interpenetrating manner, in a profound interaction, mutually influencing each other, connected to each other, establishing a relationship of cause and effect among themselves. They also alternate in their development, spontaneously overturning human selections, lists and schemes, as adequate and just as they may be or present themselves.

Classification. The phenomena related to projectiology were classified here according to the specific condition of the intraphysical consciousness – situated as the focus of analysis in a context, or the existing causal connection between all parapsychic processes – into *subjective* projective phenomena and *ambivalent* projective phenomena.

Concomitant. Besides these phenomena, there are those which are *concomitant* to lucid projection and are analyzed separately.

Orders. Deepening this superficial classification, which involves an initial educational approach, these projective phenomena can be divided still further into classes and orders, according to certain characteristics. The following 7, among others, serve as examples:

1. **Projectability.** Their parapsychic nature (projectiology, paraperceptiology).
2. **Intraphysicality.** Their physical nature (intraphysicology, somatics).
3. **Exteriority.** Their external and more exuberant manifestations.
4. **Intellectuality.** Their intellectual content or significance (mentalsoma).
5. **Personalities.** The condition of the personalities in which they are produced.
6. **Uses.** The uses of the occurrence for the main protagonist of the phenomenon.
7. **Will.** The dependence of the event upon the will of the consciousness in focus.

Suppositions. Given the phenomena that are provoked by the projected intraphysical consciousness and have thus far been verified, it must be supposed that various others, which are still unrecorded, may occur. For example: metaphony or the electronic voice phenomenon, communication executed by the projected intraphysical consciousness through apparatuses, recorders, telephones, television and others; direct writing performed by the projected intraphysical consciousness; direct painting, idem; direct drawing, idem; and others.

Perceptions. The classification of parapsychic phenomena and particularly projectiological phenomena serves to keep the various forms of extra-sensory perception, or intraconsciential and parapsychic phenomena in general, separate from each other, insofar as this is possible.

---

38. SUBJECTIVE PROJECTIVE PHENOMENA

Definition. Subjective projective phenomena: parapsychic occurrences restricted to the scope of projectiology that occur more within the consciousness and with the vehicles of manifestation of the projector partially or completely projected, thereby rendering the participation of the surrounding environment secondary.

Synonymy: internal projective phenomenon.

Psychosphere. There are 22 main interconnected phenomena, among others, which are essentially related to the psychosphere of the human projector:

1. Benign extraphysical projective catalepsy.
2. Benign physical projective catalepsy.
3. Consciential self-bilocation.

4. Cosmic consciousness (cosmoconsciousness).
5. Double projection.
6. External autoscopy.
7. Extraphysical clairvoyance.
8. Extraphysical double vision.
9. Extraphysical intuition.
10. Extraphysical precognition.
11. Extraphysical psychometry.
12. Extraphysical repercussions.
13. Extraphysical retrocognition.
14. Internal autoscopy.
15. Near-death experience (NDE): pre-final projection.
16. Near-death experience (NDE): resuscitative projection.
17. Physical repercussions.
18. Pre-projective, projective and post-projective double awareness.
19. Projective déjà vu.
20. Projective panoramic vision.
21. Self-telekinesis.
22. Waking discoincidence.

Psychometry. In many of these phenomena, classified here as subjective projective phenomena, interrelations occur that are often directly related to the environment, as seen, for example, with the occurrences of extraphysical psychometry. Nevertheless, the roots and the realm of manifestation of these phenomena are mainly restricted within the consciousness. The environment therefore actually becomes secondary. This observation speaks equally in favor of the relativity and limitation of all phenomenological classification.

Analysis. Every important subjective projective phenomenon will be addressed in detail in its own chapter of this book, either in this or other sections, according to the sequential analysis of the topics.

39. CONSCIENTIAL SELF-BILOCATION

Definition. Consciential self-bilocation (OE: *self*, self; Latin, *bis*, two; and *locus*, place): the act of the intraphysical projector encountering and contemplating its own human body *face-to-face*, while its consciousness is outside it, headquartered in another vehicle of consciential manifestation.

Synonymy: autonomous abmaterialization; direct self-viewing; spontaneous self-visualization; epiprojection; breaking of the perception barrier; extraphysical self-contemplation; self- bicorporeity; projective self-confrontation; vision of one's own human body; vision of two bodies.

Self-bilocator. Consciential self-bilocation is the same phenomenon as bilocation. In this case, however, it is produced and perceived directly by the consciousness of the actual bilocator, or more precisely, the self-bilocator (see fig. 39, p. 1,121).

Perception. It is interesting to point out that many projected intraphysical consciousnesses do not immediately perceive that they are contemplating their own human body during the occurrence of consciential self-bilocation. Others are surprised to see themselves floating, suspended in the air, without falling to the floor.

Experiences. Although included in the first spontaneous occurrences that the projected intraphysical consciousness experiences, not all lucid projectors are able to have the following 6 experiences:

1. **Self-viewing.** See their own human body that has an empty brain, or is temporarily without the consciousness which, in this case, is located outside the two cerebral hemispheres.

2. Self-embrace. Perform a *self-embrace,* or enfold their own physical body with the extraphysical arms of the psychosoma (para-arms).

3. Connection. Identify the silver cord, namely the existence of the para-energetic connection between the two consciential vehicles.

4. Helper. Extraphysically and consciously approach a helper.

5. Self-awareness. Produce a projection with continuous self-awareness, or one without any lapse in lucidity throughout the entire process.

6. Dimension. Visit the *native* extraphysical dimension, per se, which is devoid of all influence from human life, *below* the troposphere and *above* the earth's crust.

Proof. Consciential self-bilocation, commonly occurring during near-death experiences, although presenting objective manifestations, constitutes a fascinating subjective phenomenon because it proves the reality of the psychosoma to the projector and, at a more advanced stage, evidences the existence of the mentalsoma.

Theta. Consciential self-bilocation can thus evidence the survival of the consciousness after the biological death of the human body, or the so-called *theta* phenomenon.

Reactions. Six emotional, parapsychic, extraphysical, basic and opposing reactions can overwhelm the consciousness projected in the psychosoma (emotional body) upon suddenly coming across its own human body for the first time (being outside it):

1. Desoma. Fear of having unknowingly deactivated the soma and now observing its own cadaver, upon contemplating its own human body with its rigid members and pallid face, in the manner of a dead person.

2. Compassion. Sentiment of profound compassion for the organic form seen on that occasion, which is unquestionably disarmed and inactive.

3. Gratitude. An unexpected sentiment of gratitude for the human body, upon being aware that it represents a valuable instrument or vehicle of manifestation of its own consciousness.

4. Narcissism. Cultivation of unexpected narcissism (self-idolatry, self-fascination), sometimes not detected by the consciousness until that instance.

5. *Non-identification.* The opposite reaction, the absence of a sense of identifying (non-identification) with its own human body, which often appears to be dead, impersonal matter, or simply a strange, distant puppet.

6. Comprehension. An increased comprehension of human existence, of extraphysical life and the relationships between them.

Types. Consciential self-bilocation presents 2 basic types, in regard to its physical aspect: *immobile* self-bilocation and *mobile* self-bilocation.

1. Immobile. Immobile self-bilocation occurs when the human body is inanimate, or inactive, almost always while resting, lying on a bed, during natural sleep.

Duration. Immobile self-bilocation is a common occurrence and of longer duration.

2. Mobile. In mobile self-bilocation, the human body continues moving, occurring more frequently while walking, with the projected consciousness observing from above (epiprojection) and from behind (retroprojection in regard to space).

Rarity. Spontaneous mobile consciential self-bilocation is a rarer occurrence and one of brief duration.

Others. Besides the 2 abovementioned types, consciential self-bilocation can be:

1. Accompanied: when the projected consciousness sees its own human body and that of its partner or evolutionary duo, at the same time.

2. Successive: when the projected consciousness sees its own human body, first during the takeoff of the psychosoma and then again, later, prior to interiorizing. This allows the individual to confirm the phenomenon, and the fact that the physical body has sometimes remained immobile in the same position the entire time.

Near-death. In near-death experiences, the consciousness in crisis may observe its human body moving, including undergoing intense convulsions, or being handled violently during the operations of clinical reanimation (resuscitation), with a complete absence of pain or discomfort, even when specialized doctors perform painful procedures without using anesthesia. On these occasions, the consciousness acts like a spectator, as though it were seated in a balcony of a theater, in a movie theater watching a film, or in the intimacy of the home watching a television program.

Modes. Two other modes of consciential bilocation deserve singling out:

1. **Monologue.** When the projected projector sees his/her own human body *occupied* by the helper and speaking through his/her vocal mechanism, in the case of psychophonic monologue.

2. **Psychophony.** When the projected projector witnesses the psychophonic communication of an extraphysical consciousness, such as an ill extraphysical consciousness speaking through the projector's own human body, in a parapsychic deintrusion session.

Metaphors. The following are some ideas, metaphors or images that consciential self-bilocation can suggest to those who experience it: an outline of the main parts of the dense body in relief, as though it were a real being, with its image reflected in a mirror or in water, reproduced in a photo, on a TV screen, as a sculpture, or projected on a movie screen.

Recognition. Through the experience of consciential self-bilocation, there is a definitive recognition of the soma by the consciousness, which is analogous to 8 different things, although having some similarities:

1. **Straightjacket.** The straightjacket of the intraphysical consciousness.
2. **Prison.** A prison of flesh and blood.
3. **Plant.** A living plant devoid of essence.
4. *Quasi-cadaver.* A *quasi-cadaver.*
5. **Bark.** The bark of a hollow tree.
6. **Apparatus.** An unplugged apparatus.
7. **Sosie.** The sosie (double) of an individual.
8. **Facsimile.** A duplicate (photocopy, xerox) or inert facsimile.

Relations. The following are occurrences which are directly related to the phenomenon of self-bilocation: extraphysical-physical self-touch, self-embrace, extraphysical self-examination or the accurate examination of the projector's own psychosoma.

Interiorization. All of these extraphysical acts may provoke abrupt interiorization of the consciousness which was projected in the psychosoma and involuntarily returned to the human body.

Mentalsoma. The most evolved stage of the self-bilocation phenomenon pertaining to the veteran lucid projector is the case in which the consciousness, projecting in the isolated mentalsoma, leaves the psychosoma *inside* the human body or, in other words, simultaneously reduces the restriction imposed by 2 bodies, the physical body and the psychosoma. This phenomenon occurs in cases of double consciential projection.

Double. If, on the one hand, the abovementioned double consciential projection does not allow procedures such as self-touch, self-embrace and extraphysical self-examination, on the other hand, it does allow the contemplation of the entire human body, without emotionalism, whether it has a dull aspect or is luminous or, in other words, with the energies of the holochakra or the psychosoma's own light.

Bibliography: Atienza (61, p. 259), Bedford (103, p. 15), Blackmore (139, p. 3), Bord (170, p. 13), Bozzano (184, p. 159), Butler (228, p. 116), Campbell (237, p. 26), Castaneda (258, p. 47), Cornillier (304, p. 87), Crookall (343, p. 18), Cume (354, p. 144), Eysenck (493, p. 155), Gibier (587, p. 125), Giovetti (593, p. 61), Green (632, p. 37), Greene (635, p. 58), Greenhouse (636, p. 155), Guéret (659, p. 163), Hampton (676, p. 39), Holzer (745, p. 171), Jung (813, p. 507), Lippman (934, p. 348), Lischka (937, p. 121), Machado (968, p. 15),

MacLaine (980, p. 285), Manning (994, p. 89), Monroe (1065, p. 172), Muldoon (1105, p. 52), Ostby (1171, p. 225), Parrish-Harra (1202, p. 77), Rampa (1351, p. 126), Reis (1384, p. 91), Ring (1406, p. 45), Rogo (1444, p. 64), Sabom (1486, p. 32), Sherman (1551, p. 184), Steiger (1601, p. 45), Swedenborg (1635, p. 253), Tourinho (1692, p. 17), Vett (1738, p. 387), Vieira (1749, p. 16), Watkins (1799, p. 18).

40. PROJECTIVE AUTOSCOPY

Definition. Autoscopy (Greek: *autos,* oneself: *skopeni,* observe): the faculty and act of the individuals directly seeing or sensing themselves in front of themselves, while maintaining full waking consciousness, without the aid of any physical resource.

Synonymy: autoscopic experience; autoscopic metagnomy; autoscopic vision; viewing of oneself; cenestovisual kinesthesia; deuteroscopy; exteriorization of the kinesthetic sensation; *heautoscopic* hallucination; projective *heautoscopy* (Greek: *heautou,* of oneself + English: -scopy; *that one which sees him/herself*); self-apparition; self-gnosis; self-telediplosis; self-viewing; visualization of the image of the body.

Categories. Autoscopy can be generally classified into at least the following 11 categories:

1. Internal (studied below).
2. External (analyzed ahead).
3. Similar.
4. Different.
5. Specular (negative, or one related to mirrors).
6. Cenesthetic.
7. Recurrent.
8. Oneiric (related to dreams).
9. Partial (anatomically incomplete doubles).
10. Total (complete or apparently integral doubles).
11. Projective.

Sensations. Autoscopic sensations can be positive or negative, to various degrees and with different varieties. The phenomenon is one of the most obscure and controversial among all those grouped within the *phenomenological complex of projectiology.*

Cenesthetic. In cenesthetic autoscopy, the double is only sensed, without being seen by the consciousness.

Narcissism. Various psychoanalysts attribute autoscopic experiences to narcissism, self-idolatry or self-fascination. This simplistic hypothesis is completely ruled out by the projective heteroscopy phenomenon.

Nature. In a considerable number of cases that arise in a very transitory and accidental manner, the many occurrences of autoscopy cannot absolutely be qualified as pathological – whether they are internal or external – when someone visualizes his/her own image, which is exactly like him/herself, with identical clothes, the same hands and figure, or is faced with an *autoscopic phantasm* of him/herself.

Predispositions. The *twilight state of the consciousness,* whether deep self-concentration, daydream, sleep or general anesthesia, favors the appearance of the autoscopy phenomenon.

Attributes. The condition, moment, distance and aspect of the *autoscopic apparition* vary greatly.

Form. The form may have a smaller stature and be wearing different clothing at that moment.

Dialogue. In the majority of autoscopic occurrences, the apparition appears entirely mute, but it can happen that a dialogue and even a flagrant difference of opinion is established between the form and the *self* situated in the human body, perhaps due to autosuggestion.

Hypothesis. Quite often, it seems that a projection of the holochakra of the individual occurs, a likeness which is exteriorized without the consciousness, thereby creating the autoscopic phantasm, a second person, or *autoscopic double.*

Center. This apparition neither constitutes nor contains the center of the consciousness or the pointer of the consciousness.

Bibliography: Black (137, p. 15), Blackmore (139, p. 155), Bonin (168, p. 57), Bozzano (192, p. 154), Breecher (198, p. 28), Champlin (272, p. 182), D'arbó (365, p. 163), Dubugras (426, p. 369), Dumas (432, p. 9), Fodor (528, p. 25), Green (633, p. 212), Hemmert (713, p. 52), Kolosimo (858, p. 156), Larcher (887, p. 337), Lukianowicz (957, p. 199), Morel (1086, p. 37), Paim (1182, p. 52), Paula (1208, p. 57), Rank (1374, p. 73), Rogo (1444, p. 2), Sabom (1486, p. 235), Seabra (1534, p. 86), Shepard (1548, p. 83), Shirley (1553, p. 62), Sollier (1581, p. 3), Steiger (1601, p. 91), Stokes (1624, p. 23), Sudre (1630, p. 205), Tchou (1669, p. 279), Todd (1689, p. 47), Vieira (1762, p. 90).

41. INTERNAL AUTOSCOPY

Definition. Internal autoscopy: the faculty and act in which individuals have an organic, internal vision of their own human bodies, inner organs and phenomena of vegetative life, either with the consciousness apparently inside the brain, or outside the physical body (soma).

Synonymy: alloscopy; autoscopic metagnomy; autoscopic unfolding; direct endoscopy; direct entoscopy; introvision; self-representation; self-vivisection; X-ray vision of oneself.

Inside. Internal autoscopy, when the center of the consciousness remains *inside* the human body, is obviously partial or, in other words, only one organic area is seen. A partial projection of the consciousness may or may not occur.

Outside. Internal autoscopy in which the *center of the consciousness* remains *outside* the human body, typically projective, can be partial or total, constituting an advanced phase of the phenomenon of consciential self-bilocation. In this condition, the consciousness simultaneously sees the physical body and the extraphysical body (psychosoma).

Observations. During autoscopic vision of the interior of the individual's own human body, projected lucid projectors observe at least 6 occurrences:

1. **Soma.** The body (soma), which is perfectly recognizable by its personal characteristics.
2. **Face.** The face.
3. **Nerves.** The bundles of veins and nerves, that vibrate like *luminous prickling.*
4. **Heart.** The heart beating.
5. **Blood.** The blood circulating, in a *vivid red flame,* coursing through the arteries.
6. **Armor.** The vascular networks and muscular structures or muscular mass, forming a unit, like a type of transparent crystal armor.

Diagnosis. In the majority of cases of internal autoscopy, it not only ceases to be pathological, but also becomes an extraordinary resource for projective self-diagnosis, especially in the phenomena of traveling clairvoyance performed for the sake of assistance to the person themselves. It should not be forgotten that it is difficult to establish a reasonably accurate diagnosis in certain obscure disturbances and processes.

Bibliography: Bonin (168, p. 57), Bozzano (184, p. 113), Coxhead (312, p. 128), D'arbó (365, p. 163), Depascale (392, p. 15), Fodor (528, p. 25), Gibier (587, p. 126), Gómez (613, p. 20), Greenhouse (636, p. 43), Kolosimo (858, p. 156), Larcher (887, p. 338), Martin (1002, p. 29), Morel (1086, p. 37), Paula (1208, p. 57), Richet (1398, p. 136), Seabra (1534, p. 98), Shepard (1548, p. 83), Sollier (*1581,* p. 45), Tondriau (1690, p. 198), Zaniah (1899, p. 60).

42. EXTERNAL AUTOSCOPY

Definition. External autoscopy: the faculty and act of the individual seeing him/herself, while in the ordinary, physical waking state.

Synonymy: apparition to oneself; autophany; autoscopy of one's own double; autoscopic unfolding; *homologous projection;* homologous unfolding; phantasmic reflection; simulacrum-projection; sosie phenomenon; specular autoscopy.

Psychiatry. The external autoscopic phenomenon or insubstantial shadow of oneself, has been characterized for decades as being hallucination by many areas of medical research, especially the area of psychiatry founded on neurological bases, where 5 common terms are used, such as, "autoscopic hallucination," "autoscopy," "autoscopic double," "chimerical double" and "specular vision."

Etiology. In the etiology, or study of causes of pathological autoscopic hallucinations, some of the following 14 morbid organic conditions can be detected:

1. Acute labyrinthic vertigo.
2. Anxiety.
3. Chronic alcoholism.
4. Depressive states.
5. Epilepsy.
6. Fatigue.
7. Infectious, traumatic, vascular or neoplastic cerebral lesions, particularly in the temporo-parieto-occipital zones.
8. Influenza.
9. Intoxication by drugs.
10. Lethargic encephalitis.
11. Migraine.
12. Paralytic dementia.
13. Schizophrenia.
14. Toxic-febrile states.

Affinity. There is a greater affinity between pathological autoscopy, epilepsy and migraine (hemicrania).

Perceptions. In cases of pathological external autoscopy, individuals not only see the exact image of themselves as a *living replica* (visual perception) – whether solid, transparent, semitransparent or indistinct, like a mist, or similar to a gray gelatin – but can also *hear* their double with their mind (pseudo-auditive perception), perceive their movements (kinesthetic perception) and remain emotionally and intellectually aware of the existence of their double as an integral part of themselves (psycho-emotional perception).

History. Various writers, novelists, philosophers and poets have reported external autoscopic visions throughout human history, although some of the reported experiences are autobiographical, especially the following 14:

1. Hans Christian-Andersen (1805-1875), "Tales."
2. Aristotle (384-322 B.C.).
3. Grabrielle D'Annunzio (1863-1938), "Notturno," poem.
4. Louis Charles Adélaide Chamisso de Boncourt (1781-1838), "Peter Schlemihl."
5. Alphonse Daudet (1840-1897), works.
6. Fyodor Mikhailovich Dostoevsky (1821-1881), "The Double."
7. Johann Wolfang von Goethe (1749-1832), works.
8. Ernst Theodor Amadeus Hoffman (1776-1822), "Tales."
9. Franz Kafka (1883-1924), "The Trial" (trans. Willa Muir & Edwin Muir; epil. Max Brod; 256 p.; 18 cm.; pocket; pb.; Penguin Books; Aylesbury; Great Britain; 1981).

10. Henry René Albert Guy de Maupassant (1850-1893), "Le Horla" ("O Horla e Outras Histórias"; trans. and pref. José Thomaz Brum; 104 p.; illus.; 21 cm x 13.5 cm; pb.; L & PM Publishers; Porto Alegre, RS, Brazil; 1986).

11. Louis Charles Alfred de Musset (1810-1857), "La Nuit de Décembre."

12. Ferdinand Raimond, "Le Dissipateur."

13. Johann Paul Friedrich Richter (1763-1825), "Hesperus."

14. John Steinbeck (1902-1968), "Great Valley."

Psychopaths. If we radically consider all external autoscopic phenomena to be pathological, then the above authors would doubtless have been psychopaths, which frankly sounds irrational or at least illogical and inadmissible.

Case study. From a psychiatric point of view, strange hallucinatory autoscopic occurrences arise, including the case of the patient who practiced mutual masturbation or, in other words, did so together at the same time with the figure of his projected double.

Permeability. There are similarities between the occurrences of phantom limbs and autoscopic doubles, according to observations of psychiatrists and neurologists. For example, the quality of permeability that permits the phantom limbs and the autoscopic double to *pass* through solid objects such as walls, beds and the patient's human body.

Shadow. The fundamental difference between the autoscopic double and the classic apparition is that only the second casts a visible shadow, which is frequently observed by those who perceive the phenomenon.

Specular. In specular autoscopy, also called *negative* autoscopy, individuals see themselves before themselves to be absolutely identical and can observe his/her reproduction (simulacrum) breathe and live in detailed unison with themselves (which seems to be the holochakra, in this case).

Inside. Besides the occurrences of hallucinatory or pathological autoscopy, real autoscopy also exists. External projective autoscopy is considered here to be the condition in which the consciousness remains headquartered in the brain, namely *inside* the human body. When the consciousness sees its body while *outside* it, or inside the extraphysical body – the psychosoma – consciential self-bilocation occurs.

Bibliography: Blackmore (139, p. 159), Bozzano (184, p. 158), Bret (202, p. 42), Coleman (291, p. 254), Dostoievski (408, p. 62), Duchatel (430, p. 112), Fodor (528, p. 25), Fugairon (562, p. 131), Larcher (887, p. 337), Lukianowicz (957, p. 216), Martin (1002, p. 29), Osty (1173, p. 19), Owen (1178, p. 227), Paula (1208, p. 57), Richet (1398, p. 703), Shepard (1548, p. 83), Sollier (1581, p. 7), Todd (1689, p. 50), Walker (1781, p. 148).

43. COMPARISONS BETWEEN EXTERNAL AUTOSCOPY AND LUCID PROJECTION

Differential. The basic differential factors between pure external autoscopy and lucid consciential projection outside the human body are very strong, defined and unmistakable, in regard to the following 5 approaches for studying both phenomena simultaneously:

1. **Position.** In most cases, external autoscopy occurs when the person's human body is standing. In most cases, lucid projection occurs when the person's inanimate human body is reclined (or lying down).

2. **Takeoff.** In external autoscopy, the consciousness stays *where it is* and does not have any sensation of leaving the physical body. In lucid consciential projection, the lucid takeoff is an unmistakable phenomenon and a generally unforgettable experience of leaving the physical body.

3. **Form.** The human, or humanoid, form seen by the consciousness itself during the external autoscopy phenomenon is generally incomplete. The form observed in lucid consciential projection is complete and the vision is clearer, whether perceived by the consciousness itself (consciential self-bilocation) or by others (physical bilocation).

4. **Vision.** External autoscopy consists of a consciousness, which is coincident, seeing a double of itself, which is found to be outside the human body. Lucid consciential projection involves the sensation (lucid perception) of the consciousness being outside the human body, while discoincident, experiencing events of another type.

5. **Base.** In external autoscopy, the form which is seen (energetic body or holochakra) does not transport the consciousness (the consciential center or the pointer of the consciousness), which is *inside* the two cerebral hemispheres (*full* brain). In lucid consciential projections, the consciousness transports itself in other conditions, generally in the emotional body (psychosoma), while temporarily *outside* the cerebral hemispheres (*empty* brain).

44. PROJECTIVE CATALEPSY

Definition. Projective catalepsy (Greek: *katalepsis,* a seizing, grasping): a psychophysical state characterized by a rigidity of the members, insensitivity, slow respiration and a temporary incapacity of the lucid intraphysical consciousness to move the human body while consciously headquartered *inside it,* due to a dissociation between sensitivity and the motor capacities.

Synonymy: astral catalepsy; cataleptic consciousness; fourth state; generalized projective paralysis; physiological catalepsy; post-projective catalepsy; *pre-OBE* catalepsy; projective cataleptic paralysis; projective paralytic awakening; projective physical paralysis; projective tonic immobility; pseudo-awakening; waking paralysis; suspension of sensations and movements.

Weight. In the experience of projective catalepsy, intraphysical consciousnesses, from the beginning of the manifestation, feels that they are somehow *inside* the material mass of the human body. However, they are not able to move the human body, as though it were overcome by some physical weight which gives it the strange impression that the human body – or the set of vehicles of manifestations of the consciousness, the holosoma – weighs hundreds of pounds/kilos. This gives the sensation of being pressed against the bed, which prevents the consciousness from making any muscular movement, however slight.

Categories. There are two basic categories of projective catalepsy:

1. **Before.** Catalepsy related to departure or pre-projective catalepsy.
2. **After.** Catalepsy related to return or post-projective catalepsy.

Extraphysicality. Projective catalepsy related to departure occurs when the consciousness leaves the ordinary, physical waking state and endeavors to enter the extraphysical dimension (in this case, the energetic dimension or the paratropospheric dimension).

Interiorization. Projective catalepsy upon return occurs when the projected consciousness interiorizes into the human body and endeavors to physically awaken.

Post-projective. In catalepsy upon return, or post-projective catalepsy – which is far more interesting – the consciousness often returns in the psychosoma from a distance, *brimming* with the collected extraphysical sensations, with the *condenser-psychosoma* replenished by extraphysical or cosmic energy. This breaks the imperturbable granitic structure of the process of successive lives (existential series and multiexistential cycle), feeling as though the barriers between the dimensions of life have been destroyed, broadening the mental horizon to infinity, namely with an expansion of the consciousness and uninterrupted lucidity during the entire process. The extraphysical period is often not recalled, and the consciousness only awakens in the cataleptic state.

Benign. The extraphysical or physiological projective cataleptic state, which is invariably inoffensive or benign, namely of brief duration and devoid of damaging consequences, should not be confused with dramatic physical or pathological catalepsy, which is invariably malignant, being characterized by a truly morbid state arising in pre-moribund phases. This second condition can lead to the burial of the human body (soma) of an individual (intraphysical consciousness) who is believed to be clinically dead.

Psychopathology. From a psychopathological point of view, in the morbid state of catalepsy of the consciousness, called "simulation of death syndrome," the person often feels unable to move and may even hear what is going on around his/her paralyzed human body.

Reproduction. This psychopathological state reproduces almost all of the characteristics of biological death (first desoma), especially these 3:

1. **Metabolism.** A reduction in the basal metabolic rate or the cooling of the human body.

2. **Fibrillation.** The heart beats slowing down to fibrillation or, in other words, practically imperceptible or in extreme bradycardia.

3. **Mydriasis.** Mydriasis or the total dilation of the pupils (an event which invariably occurs 2 to 3 minutes after physical death), although the blood is still *warm* or is heading towards complete cooling.

Duration. Also, according to psychopathology, the cataleptic state (awakening attack; awakening cataplexy; retarded psychomotor awakening; sleep paralysis) lasting more than 6 hours does not exist, because the patient thereupon enters into brain death and dies.

Return. The ill person generally returns to normal life spontaneously, when cardiotonics and oxygen are applied.

Burial. The chances that a person might undergo a necropsy (autopsy) or be accidentally buried are very remote nowadays, although they are always exploited by literature, being a theme of mystery films, part of the *folklore of death* and a recurrent theme in mysticism.

Necropsy. In accordance with the law, necropsy is only performed 6 hours after death. The body that arrives at competent medicolegal institutes is only taken to the freezer after completing the 6-hour wait, prior to a discerning examination, in order to avoid the risk of freezing someone who is still physically alive. For this reason, the risk of initiating a necropsy upon someone who is still alive and affected by the cataleptic state is, therefore, inexistent.

Barrier. Projective catalepsy occurs more frequently in the intraphysical projector's first experiences, caused by a *barrier of fear* (projectiophobia) or a lack of preparation for lucidly projecting.

Recess. Projective catalepsy often impresses the suggestible, insecure, fearful consciousness, which does not know any projective techniques and becomes frightened. This can produce temporary blocks (projective recess), during a certain period, for new lucid departures in the psychosoma.

Bridge. In projective catalepsy, the intraphysical consciousness can still feel the small movements of the psychosoma inside the human body, with the level of awareness practically equal to that of the ordinary, physical waking state. This cataleptic state thus constitutes a true bridge between the two dimensions – the dense physical and the extraphysical – without any interference from other intraphysical or extraphysical intelligences, or even parapsychic connotations.

Sensations. The following 7, among others, are the more frequent general sensations that stem from or occur subsequent to the projective cataleptic state:

1. **Bed.** The psychosoma sinking into the bed.

2. **Psychosoma.** The psychosoma sliding to one side.

3. **Segments.** Segments of the psychosoma, such as the paralegs and para-arms, *undulating* to one side.

4. **Movement.** The sequential elevation, departure and reentry of the psychosoma (dynamic of discoincidence).

5. **Soma.** Perception of one's human body (soma), as though it were a sealed box.

6. **Respiration.** An abnormal relationship of the intraphysical consciousness with the phenomenon of respiration.

7. **Satisfaction.** The extremely clear inner satisfaction of the intraphysical consciousness owing to the experience of having 2 organisms, in different dimensions of existence, with the unquestionable power (will, intentionality) of neutralizing or eliminating the omnipresent pseudotyranny of dense matter while still breathing on the planetary crust or in the troposphere.

Post-desomatic. Incidentally – according to observations made by lucid projectors in the extraphysical dimension, clairvoyant sensitives on deathbeds and psychophonic communications from extraphysical consciousnesses – the *post-desomatic* cataleptic condition occurs with certain persons for a period of time, as soon as they undergo deactivation of the human body (first desoma) while still on the deathbed, prior to their consciential awakening in the extraphysical dimension.

Desomatics. Under these circumstances, the consciousness feels its human body to be cold and is not able to move a single particle of matter, in the manner of pre-desomatic catalepsy.

Projectors. These lucid projectors – due to the type or nature of the consciential energies they possess – are called upon to assist in the removal of intraphysical consciousnesses, which have recently become extraphysical consciousnesses, from these *post-desomatic* cataleptic states.

Cause. It is believed that the real cause of projective catalepsy is the temporary impossibility of consciential communication between the mind of the psychosoma, in this case the mentalsoma, which is headquartered in the parabrain of the psychosoma, and the cortical motor areas of the dense, physical brain of the human body.

Holochakra. There may be an influence in the process of some still unclear alteration of the psychophysical, parabiological or energetic *insertions* of the silver cord (holochakra) in both vehicles of manifestation of the intraphysical consciousness: the psychosoma and the human body.

REM. A brief state of physical paralysis, or an incapacity to move, pertaining to projective catalepsy, commonly occurs for some seconds when the dreamer awakens during the phase of rapid synchronic eye movements or REM, before the human body's muscle tonus has had time to be restored.

Techniques. By following physiological techniques – without committing any physical or mental excess – there is no difficulty in breaking a moderate or intense projective cataleptic state. There are 2 simple processes for accomplishing this: either provoke physical awakening or induce *reprojection* of the consciousness in the psychosoma.

1. **Awakening.** In this process, which is more suitable for *pre*-projective catalepsy, your consciousness should endeavor – with ardent desire – to move the smallest part of the human body, whether it is an eyelid, a lip, the tongue, a finger, or even breathe more deeply and awaken normally in the ordinary, physical waking state.

2. **Reprojection.** In this process, which is more suitable for *post*-projective catalepsy, your consciousness should wish to leave the human body and project, or more appropriately, to *re*project in the psychosoma, which is less difficult.

Second. In most cases, the cataleptic state does not occur after the second lucid projection.

Proof. As an animic (intraconscientiality without extraphysical consciousnesses), xenophrenic, parapsychic, realistic and impressive phenomenon, projective catalepsy provides excellent proof of the existence of the extraphysical body or, in other words, the psychosoma, to the projector. As an unforgettable phenomenological impression, it is only surpassed by experiencing the lucid takeoff of the consciousness in the psychosoma.

Burial. *Projective* catalepsy should neither be considered to be maleficent, nor confused with *pathological* catalepsy, nor should the individual fear premature or involuntary burial as a consequence of this psychophysical condition. It is sufficient to reflect upon the fact that voluntary burial – a phenomenon common in the East for a certain time – was based precisely upon *provoked* projective catalepsy.

State. Cataleptic awareness is also called the *fourth state* by Eastern researchers, in relation to 3 other consciential states:

1. **Waking.** The ordinary, physical waking state.
2. **Dream.** The common symbolic dream.
3. **Sleep.** Natural sleep without dreams.

Bibliography: Andreas (36, p. 55), Bayless (98, p. 112), Crookall (343, p. 25), Digest (401, p. 350), El-Aowar (474, p. 100), Eliade (476, p. 65), Fodor (528, p. 42), Gaynor (577, p. 33), Gómez (613, p. 28), Greenhouse (636, p. 149), Kardec (824, p. 222), Krishna (867, p. 103), Monroe (1065, p. 247), Morel (1086, p. 47), Muldoon (1105, p. 11), Paula (1208, p. 69), Reis (1384, p. 86), Rogo (1444, p. 42), Salley (1496, p. 157), Shepard (1548, p. 151), Spence (1588, p. 95), Swedenborg (1635, p. 250), Tondriau (1690, p. 207), Vieira (1762, p. 160), Walker (1781, p. 69), Zaniah (1899, p. 106).

---

45. EXTRAPHYSICAL CLAIRVOYANCE

Definition. Extraphysical clairvoyance (Latin: *clarus,* clear; *videre,* to see): the perceptive faculty of the consciousness projected from the human body that allows it to acquire information, through the perception of images or scenes, about objects, psychic events, scenes and forms which are near or distant or occur in space, or even outside the intraphysical dimension.

Synonymy: astral clairvoyance; extraphysical double vision; extraphysical hylognosis; extraphysical paropsis; extraphysical second sight; extraphysical telecognosis; extraphysical telopsis; extraphysical viewing; ultraviewing.

Attribute. The faculty of clairvoyance outside the human body is not dependent upon the intraphysical projector being an active clairvoyant in the ordinary, physical waking state and arises as a normal attribute of the freed consciousness, generally through the *para-eyes* of the psychosoma.

Psychospheres. One practical consequence of extraphysical clairvoyance is the projected projector seeing auras, parapsychic constellations or the psychospheres of intraphysical beings in general.

Bibliography: Blavatsky (153, p. 120), Cavendish (266, p. 64), Chaplin (273, p. 37), Day (376, p. 29), Digest (401, p. 350), Fodor (528, p. 45), Gaynor (577, p. 37), Greene (635, p. 89), Leadbeater (898, p. 1), Martin (1003, p. 35), Morel (1086, p. 51), Paula (1208, p. 71), Pensamento (1224, p. 29), Shepard (1548, p. 167), Spence (1588, p. 105), Tondriau (1690, p. 209), Vieira (1762, p. 44), Wedeck (1807, p. 85), Zaniah (1899, p. 112).

---

46. COSMOCONSCIOUSNESS

Definitions. Cosmoconsciousness: the inner condition or perception of the consciousness of the cosmos, life and the order of the universe; the indescribable intellectual, ethical exultation, when the consciousness feels the living presence of the universe and becomes one with it, in a single, indivisible unit.

Synonymy: a touch of the infinite; absolute moment; absolute Tao (Taoism); AH reaction (Arthur Koestler); *ante mortem* nirvana; ascendant self-transcendence; baptism of the spirit; climax experience; consciential big-bang; consciousness in the mentalsomatic dimension; cosmic awareness; cosmic consciousness; cosmic identification; cosmic mind; cosmic psyche; culminant experience; decerebrated consciousness; expanded consciousness; experience of atemporality; extraphysical maturity; extratemporal moment; fana or annihilation (Sufism); global consciential hyperacuity; holophotic mind; intercosmic consciousness; intimation of immortality; *kensho;* maximal extraphysical euphoria; mentalsomatic projection (projectiology); nirvana or extinction (Buddhism); objective consciousness; oceanic sentiment; plateau experience; projective superwaking; psychic turnaround; samadhi or conjunction (Yoga); samadhic consciousness; satori or illumination (Zen-Buddhism); self-absorption; sentiment of transformation; sleep without sleep; spiritual union; supercosmic consciousness; superlucid consciousness; supermind; supramental consciousness; total interfusion; transcendental unconscious; transconsciousness; transpersonal consciousness; *unio mystica* (Eastern mysticism); universal mind; *wu* (Chinese).

Cosmoconscientiology. The phenomenon of cosmoconsciousness, because of its transcendence and effects, required the creation of an area or specific subdiscipline within conscientiology: *cosmoconscientiology*.

Energy. The elevation of the state of consciousness requires intense consciential energy. High levels of intensity and frequency of energy (holochakrology) keep the levels of consciousness elevated. The phenomenon of cosmic consciousness or cosmoconsciousness is based upon these principles.

Communicology. There is interconsciential communication in the peculiar condition of cosmoconsciousness or, in other words: the use of conscientese. Most lines of human knowledge have still not detected, nor do they use, this transcendent mode of interconsciential communication belonging to the exceptional condition of cosmoconsciousness.

Mentalsomatics. In mentalsomatics, the state of cosmoconsciousness determines the more evolved condition of holosomatic homeostasis for the intraphysical consciousness.

Maturation. All the causes and conditions of the state of cosmoconsciousness are in the consciousness itself, awaiting maturation. This would be a type of *period of evolutionary incubation* or *period of a lack of holomaturity*.

Factors. Mental pacification and the liberation of *superconsciousness* act as predisposing factors, triggering projection in the mentalsoma and consequent cosmoconsciousness, thereby signifying 3 realities:

1. **Xenophrenia.** The xenophrenic state of a greater magnitude of paraperceptions.
2. **Experimentology.** The supreme peak of consciential experience at our evolutionary level (experimentology).
3. **Simultaneity.** The simultaneous contraction and expansion of the consciousness.

Explanation. The following are 6 bases provided for the comprehension and approximation of an explanation of the state of cosmoconsciousness:

1. **Dimension.** The existence of the mentalsomatic dimension.
2. **Mentalsoma.** The paraphysiology of the mentalsoma (mentalsomatics).
3. **Projections.** Lucid projections produced by way of the mentalsoma.
4. **Continuity.** Projections with continuous self-awareness.
5. **State.** The state of continuous self-awareness.
6. **Scale.** The scale of the state of continuous self-awareness (parahistory).

Indication. The understanding of these bases is the best indication or suggestion for the individual interested in endeavoring to achieve cosmoconsciousness.

Eclosion. The physical base for the eclosion of the phenomenon of cosmoconsciousness – a secondary component – can be any location (intraphysicology), because it manifests in the mentalsomatic dimension, in an atemporal manner, without forms (non-forms), without spaces or the physical universe (non-spaces) and without time, and can only be understood through extraphysical intuition or holomemory.

Powers. The consciential powers stemming from the mentalsoma that trigger the state of cosmoconsciousness manifest outside the physical head (encephalon) or, in other words, extrapolate the cerebral hemispheres even beyond the coronochakra. They extend, engross, penetrate, traverse, saturate, inspire, instill and diffuse life and lucidity, fertilizing all the energetic centers of the human individual – whether or not they are known by that individual – directly from the mentalsomatic dimension.

Levels. There is a temporary, gradual (by levels) state in the phenomenon of cosmoconsciousness which installs itself in two forms:

1. **Increasing.** In an increasing manner, gradually, little by little.
2. **Abrupt.** Abruptly in the manner of an agreeable, welcome surprise. This second condition is generally superior in its effects and quality to the first.

Duration. The duration of the state of cosmoconsciousness is always apparent because it is atemporal, according to our conventions or, in other words: it occurs beyond or independently of chronological time, in an intraconsciential, inner or *internal manner.*

Physiology. Nevertheless, the time that the intraphysical consciousness spontaneously or thoughtfully dedicates to the phenomenon – which reflects upon the *exterior of his/her life,* in the physiology of his/her soma and, consequently, in the paraphysiology of his/her holosoma (holosomatics) – can be classified into 1 of 2 periods:

1. **Seconds.** An experience of seconds (").
2. **Minutes.** An experience of minutes ('). No longer than this.

Categories. The states of cosmoconsciousness can be classified into 3 basic categories with regard to the intensity or content of the recycling experience (intraconsciential recycling):

1. **Approximative.** Approximative or incipient experiences of cosmoconsciousness.
2. **Average.** Experiences of average cosmoconsciousness, in regard to the density of the experience.
3. **Intense.** Intense or dense experiences of cosmoconsciousness are dependent upon the 3 categories of maturity of the intraphysical consciousness: biological, mental, and holomaturity (holomaturology).

Attainment. The condition of cosmoconsciousness can be attained in 2 manners:

1. **Spontaneous.** Spontaneous and independent of the will of the intraphysical consciousness.
2. **Provoked.** Provoked or intentional, as a consequence of effort and self-capacity.

Projectability. Lucid projection by way of the mentalsoma offers the best, most intense and enriching conditions for experiencing the provoked state of cosmoconsciousness. It depends greatly upon the level of projectiocritique of the intraphysical consciousness.

Intensity. The intensity of the experience of cosmic consciousness varies in the life of a single individual and between different individuals.

Single. A person may have only one culminant experience in his/her entire life.

Multiple. However, many individuals can experience an intense episode and other lesser experiences, which are still indescribable, extremely personal, nontransferable, unquestionable, immeasurable, cataclysmic and inalienable.

Stem. The condition of cosmoconsciousness obtained stemming from the projected state tends to be superior to cosmoconsciousness obtained from the ordinary, physical waking state, due to the direct experience through the mentalsoma, holomaturity and holomemory.

Impressions. In other words: the pure mentalsomatic dimension, reached indirectly from the intraphysical dimension is *less* impressive to the consciousness than reaching the mentalsomatic dimension directly from the extraphysical dimension, per se.

Difficulty. It is very difficult to characterize the experience of cosmoconsciousness within evolutiology and existential recyclology.

Exclusion. It is easier, through the process of elimination, to point out what cosmoconsciousness is not. It is not, at the very least, the following 15 conditions or occurrences:

1. It is not ecstasy pertaining to primary parapsychism or contemplation.
2. It is not hallucination of any type or nature.
3. It is not discrimination, segregation, factiousness or sectarianism.
4. It is not the partiality of myopic vision or narrow-mindedness.
5. It is not a gross, material or somatic activity.
6. It is not consciential passivity of any type.
7. It is not consciential confinement.
8. It is not simple intellectual exaltation of polymathy.
9. It is not a mere emotional exaltation of psychosomatics.
10. It is not a universal orgasm or holo-orgasm within sexosomatics.

11. It is not mysticism (intraphysical consciousnesses of existential robotization).
12. It is not psychologism (dermatologies of the consciousness, *epidermic* sciences).
13. It is not philosophism (cogitations of *theoreticians*).
14. It is not theologism (dogmas of theological empires).
15. It is not any conceptual limit.

Focus. In cosmoconsciousness, the focus of the consciousness (center or consciential pointer) or the point where the concentration of attention is maximum, is based in the unlimited reservoir of the entire universe, which becomes its field of manifestation. Therefore, 4 ordinary variables of our thosenization disappear:

1. **Consciousness.** The margin or periphery of the consciousness.
2. **Time.** The time factor (parachronology).
3. **Vehicle.** The vehicle of the consciousness (the zenith of holosomatics).
4. **Space.** Space, as we know it.

Paroxysms. Such a consciential expansion allows the individual to achieve, sometimes in seconds, an entire existence of understanding, *revelation, illumination* and *ascendant self-transcendence* due to healthy paroxysms of the holomemory, which are potentiated through great retrocognitions (mnemosomatics).

Certainty. The experience of intense cosmoconsciousness communicates unshakeable certainty, being incontestable and definitively self-persuasive for the individual.

Imitation. Nevertheless, a person can have a mere approximation, or an imitation of the state of cosmoconsciousness. In this case, he/she still doubts the legitimacy of the experience. It is as though he/she had had only a half-projection (hemiprojection) in the mentalsoma, a half-strength experience, a pale glimpse of a greater reality, a mere *introductory sample* of a great experience.

Maximum. Reaching the experience of intense cosmoconsciousness, whether in a gradual or spontaneous manner, represents the achievement of the maximum possible peak in production of lucid consciential projections. This can even signify an existential maxi-moratorium or an existential maxi-program (existential programology).

Repetitions. After this, there remains only its increasingly intense repetition, with regard to its increased level of quality.

Alienation. It is worth noting that intense consciential projections in the psychosoma can provoke the alienation of the intraphysical consciousness in regard to the physical world (intraphysicology and somatics). Experiences of cosmoconsciousness do not cause such alienation, but nevertheless lead the individual to inevitable intraconsciential recycling and existential recycling (existential recyclology).

Objectives. The state of cosmoconsciousness allows the achievement of 3 transcendent consciential objectives in a natural manner as healthy consequences or aftereffects:

1. **Understanding.** An initial understanding of cosmoethics and evolutionary intelligence.
2. **Paraperceptiology.** The conscious use of intraconsciential and parapsychic powers.
3. **Genius.** The achievement of healthy genius or, in other words, one devoid of the unhealthy connotations of animal life in the manifestations of the intraphysical or extraphysical consciousness, amplifying the simultaneous use of more than 1 module of intelligence or multi-intelligences (3, 11 or even more).

Concepts. Cosmoconsciousness reveals the most transcendent types of concepts to the intraphysical consciousness. The following are 8 examples:

1. **Holomemory.** Easier access to the integral memory or holomemory (mnemosomatics).
2. **Omni-optics.** Omni-optics or the cosmovision of that which exists.
3. **Perspective.** The perspective of multifaceted research of the micro-universe of the consciousness and the universe or cosmos.
4. **Mega-experience.** Multimodal mega-experience in multiple dimensions.

5. **Holobiography.** Inborn (congenital or innate) wisdom characteristic of the multi-secular or multi-millenary holobiography of the intraphysical consciousness (healthy self-retrocognitions).

6. **Groupkarmality.** The collective sense in the individualized intraphysical consciousness or a maximal sense of groupality (groupkarmality).

7. **Holokarmology.** The individual's absolute indemnification or acquittal of his/her own groupkarmic interprisons through polykarmality (holokarmality), on the way toward self-awareness regarding the petifree state (petifreeology).

8. **Cosmoethic.** A broad ethic or a maximal or matured cosmoethics.

Incubation. Upon self-examination, after the intense experience of cosmoconsciousness, the individual will see that he/she first – consciously or unconsciously – underwent a type of preparatory process, a period of incubation or trial work phase for maturation of the phenomenon prior to his/her *intraconsciential implosion-explosion.*

Procedures. At least the following 8 evolved, libertarian procedures aid in the preparation for the experience of cosmoconsciousness:

1. **Imperturbability.** Imperturbability or personal balance.
2. **Derepression.** Self-aware derepression or sociocultural deconditioning.
3. *Depreconception. Depreconception* or neophilia as a good personal habit.
4. **Tachypsychism.** Self-aware tachypsychism or the lightning-fast elaboration of self-thosenes.
5. **Impersonalization.** Impersonalization in thosenization (which is not the same as *depersonalization* or *alienation*) or the *act of thinking more about others in a healthy manner.*
6. **Self-hypnosis.** Fully conscious or intentional self-hypnosis, aiming at self-knowledge and personal growth.
7. **Curricula.** The background of two categories of interactive extraphysical curricula:

A. **Multiexistential.** The intraphysical, multiexistential curriculum (resomas, existential seriation and existential completism).

B. **Multi-intermissive.** The extraphysical, *multi-intermissive* curriculum (intermissions and experiences of extraphysical euphoria).

8. **Minicog.** The work of interconsciential assistance as a minicog within a multidimensional, assistential maximechanism with the helpers. This is the most relevant and influential process for triggering the great experience of cosmoconsciousness.

Development. After the cosmoconsciousness experience has been achieved or experienced, there are two very distinct phases in its development: the induction phase and the command phase.

1. **Induction.** In the beginning, there is an increasing capacity for inducing the state of cosmoconsciousness in an extremely personal manner, so much so that only the consciousness knows that this type of induction works, at least for that individual.

2. **Command.** Later, the consciential force arises that is necessary for commanding the state of cosmoconsciousness in detail, including the frequency, intensity and *duration* of the experiences.

Inclusions. The following 14 variables, among others, included at the same time, can be encountered in the state of cosmoconsciousness (cosmic consciousness):

1. **Mind.** The mind.
2. **Thought.** The faculty of thought or the *tho* of thosene.
3. **Psychism.** Psychism (brain).
4. **Consciousness.** The consciousness (per se).
5. **Parapsychism.** Parapsychism (parabrain, mentalsoma).
6. **Volition.** Volition or will, the greatest personal power of the consciousness.
7. **Self-awareness.** The combined process of thinking, feeling and all that makes up a state of consciousness.

8. **Thosenology.** The state of profound intertwining of thought or ideation and sentiment or emotionalism (mind-heart), where it becomes impracticable to separate them, as occurs with the indissociability of the 3 components of thosenization.

9. **Individualization.** Insulation (aloneness) or universal individualization wherein the consciousness has no relation with the social collective elements that constitute the ego.

10. **Self-identification.** Uniqueness or the act wherein the ego ceases to identify with external elements and returns to encounter its own individuality (reencounter with one's own identity or shadow).

11. **Rupturing.** The *para*perceptive rupturing (breakthrough) of the psychic crust in which the intraphysical consciousness found itself enclosed, like being in a cocoon through the psychophysiological restriction imposed by resoma upon its holosoma of an extraphysical consciousness (2 vehicles), now with the holosoma of an intraphysical consciousness (4 vehicles).

12. **Self-perception.** Self-perception (self-knowing) or becoming aware of what you in fact *are,* in an instantaneous vision of the *self* in action (self-manifestation or self-thosenity).

13. **Self-awakening.** Self-awakening (awareness) or a greater lucidity of becoming aware of the self in all its extension, depth, complexity and other elements of a like nature.

14. **Hetero-identification.** Empathetically adjusted identification with the universe (oneness).

Conscientiogram. The understanding of cosmoconsciousness is extremely important in order to understand the conscientiogram (within conscientiometry) and conscientiology itself, even from an extraphysical point of view.

Avoidance. One problem encountered in the experience of all phenomena related to expansion of the consciousness, in the world of projectiological practices – which can only be solved by the individual through self-examination – is the judicious avoidance of the negative predominance of one consciential attribute, which is inadequate in that context, over another or others in the development of the experiences. Many errors result from this in interpretation of the experimentations.

Tendency. In principle, all consciential attributes do not always tend to expand together. When they do not, inefficient choices arise.

Choices. The following are examples of spurious choices of consciential attributes in projectiological occurrences, which are extremely relevant regarding the phenomenon of cosmoconsciousness:

1. **Fabulation.** Imagination can predominate over discernment. In this case, the consciousness loses a great part of its critical judgment. This is the erroneous valuing of fabulation over reality. It is very common in artists and poets.

2. **Emotionalism.** Emotionality (psychosomatics) can preponderate over rationality (mentalsomatics). Thus, the euphoric consciousness (intraphysical euphoria) aborts projective experiences in a frustrating manner. This is the erroneous valuing of emotionalism over maturity.

3. **Pastism.** Causal memory (holomemory) can preponderate over ever fugacious practicality (pragmatism, theorice, praxis) of the moment, leading the consciousness to marginalize its essential objectives. This is the erroneous valuing of the past over the present. It is very common in nostalgic and elderly persons.

4. *Effect-attribute.* Extraphysical attention can predominate over extraphysical self-awareness and the projected consciousness becomes caught in a secondary event, a rite of passage, losing sight of the essential objective. This is the erroneous valuing of a mere *effect-attribute* over the *cause-attribute.*

Continuous. It is necessary to avoid confusing the state of cosmoconsciousness or cosmic consciousness with the state of continuous self-awareness.

Note. It is also imperative to avoid confusing the authentic, healthy, pure experience of cosmoconsciousness with *pharmacological phantasmagoria,* or the unpredictable consequences of the action of dozens of neurochemical substances (neurotransmitters) that exist or are produced in the human brain or the organic systems – such as serotonin – and are sometimes misinterpreted in a sick manner.

Chemistry. Over the centuries, these facts have been generating mystical versions of reality, beatific visions and religious exaltations in the occurrences of the so-called *chemistry of mysticism*. This has occurred with anonymous or famous persons with various degrees of illness who were or were not aware of their infirmities, being diagnosed as having temporal lobe epilepsy, schizophrenia and other neuropsychic disturbances.

Increases. As the author has previously affirmed, there are 4 situations which have increased: human population; occupation of habitable spaces; atmospheric pollution; and obstinate economic competition between persons and institutions. So far, these have worsened the possibilities for the intraphysical consciousness to openly move toward the practice of the *omnilateral* mind, maxifraternity, universal citizenship, pure universalism, multidimensionality, cosmoethics and, lastly, like an evolutionary crowning, the personal condition of inner liberation, stemming from the phenomenon of cosmoconsciousness.

Reductions. The relationship of *reductions in human work* or intraphysical work with the experience of cosmoconsciousness can be illustrated with the following 3 connected facts, in chronological order:

1. **Technology.** Technology reduced *manual labor* or that relating to the psychomotricity of the soma.

2. **Informatics.** Informatics (infocommunicology) reduced *mental work* or the work of the neurons of the cerebral hemispheres (encephalic brain).

3. **Cosmoconsciousness.** Today, cosmoconsciousness reduces *paracerebral work* (the parabrain is an attribute of the psychosoma) pertaining to the multidimensionality of the intraphysical consciousness.

Groupality. One of the more obscure points within evolved groupality is precisely the study of the condition of cosmoconsciousness and conscientese, a challenge for all lucid projector-researchers, pre-*serenissimi*, consciential epicenters and petifree individuals.

Conscientiology. According to the subdisciplines or research areas of conscientiology, 4 evolved factors can predispose the experience of the cosmoconsciousness phenomenon:

1. **Existential maxi-program.** A recent, advanced, intermissive course dedicated to the upcoming execution of the existential maxi-program (intermissiology, existential programology).

2. **Macrosoma.** The use of a macrosoma (macrosomatics).

3. **Paragenetics.** Rich, powerful paragenetics, capable of overcoming the coercive forces of the genetics of the reborn extraphysical consciousness.

4. **Serenology.** The condition of serenism of the *Homo sapiens serenissimus*.

Cosmothosene. The cosmothosene is the thosene specific to conscientese, the state of cosmoconsciousness or the advanced form of communication of conscientese.

Era. The tendency of contemporary life, from now on, is to predispose a continually greater number of persons toward experiencing cosmoconsciousness, thus redefining and amplifying the *condition of conscientiality* of the planetary holothosene in this era of the consciousness.

Bibliography: Brunton (217, p. 284), Bucke *(218,* p. 60), Buckland (219, p. 190), Carrington (245, p. 114), Cavendish (266, p. 66), Chaplin (273, p. 39), Crookall (326, p. 3), Digest (401, p. 351), Driesch (413, p. 143), Dychtwald (444, p. 249), Eliade (476, p. 66), Fodor (528, p. 65), Frazer (549, p. 2683), Gaynor (577, p. 40), Greene (635, p. 69), Humphreys (766, p. 125), Jacobson (796, p. 252), James (803, p. 389), Krishna (867, p. 124), Michaël (1041, p. 104), Paula (1208, p. 77), Riland (1403, p. 252), Roy (1480, p. 148), Saher (1493, p. 7), Salley (1496, p. 159), Schatz (1514, p. 285), Shepard (1548, p. 194), Sherman (1551, p. 230), Smith (1572, p. 131), Suzuki (1631, p. 118), Twitchell (1712, p. 15), Uchôa (1720, p. 103), Vieira (1762, p. 217), Walker (1781, p. 27), Wang (1794, p. 1), Wedeck (1807, p. 90), White (1830, p. 240), Yogananda (1894, p. 144), Zaniah (1899, p. 117).

47. PROJECTIVE DÉJÀ VU

Definition. Projective déjà vu: prior unconscious knowledge, or an impression of having seen or met a person, visited a certain place, or experienced a situation that the percipient has, in fact, never seen, been to, or experienced before in the ordinary, physical waking state, because it is an impression gathered by the projected consciousness during a lucid or semilucid consciential projection.

Synonymy: duplicative metagnomy; phenomenon of the already projectively seen; projective biperception; projective dejaism; projective paramnesia; projective promnesia; projective retro-glimpse; projective sentiment of already having seen; reverse projective memory.

Forms. The phenomena of déjà vu generally refer to things already seen, but are actually not restricted to visual perception.

Expressions. The following 11 expressions in the French language indicate real or imagined forms of reencounter with the past:

1. *Déjà aimé* = already loved.
2. *Déjà entendu* = already heard.
3. *Déjà éprouvé* = already experienced.
4. *Déjà-lû* = already read.
5. *Déjà pensé* = already thought.
6. *Déjà rencontré* = already met.
7. *Déjà-rêvé* = already dreamt.
8. *Déjà senti* = already felt.
9. *Déjà vécu* = already lived.
10. *Déjà visité* = already visited.
11. *Déjà vu* = already seen.

False. Alterations in memory such as paramnesia, mental fatigue and certain organic intoxications can create false *déjà vu*, false memory, false recognition, mental echo or pseudo-reminiscence. In this case, it is a pathological occurrence which should not be confused with the authentic impressions addressed here, stemming from consciential projections.

Psychopathology. Memory presents alterations in all psychopathy, mental or cerebral illnesses. This, in fact, in many cases, generates the illusion of the already-seen.

Categories. There are two basic categories of already-seen impressions, relative to consciential projections: physical projective déjà vu, in the human dimension; and extraphysical projective déjà vu, in the extraphysical dimension.

1. **Physical**. Common, physical projective déjà vu occurs in the ordinary, physical waking state when the consciousness pacifically, unquestionably recognizes the place, physical object, person or central point of recall which, in fact, was visited or seen by the individual during a lucid excursion outside the human body, in a consciential projection.

2. **Extraphysical.** The more complex, extraphysical déjà vu (extraphysically already dreamt or experienced) arises for the projected consciousness in any environment identified by its perceptions. This is so whether it is crustal or paratropospheric or even extraphysical per se, when recognizing the circumstances and the beings which were actually experienced or known in the past, in this or in another previous existence, or even in an extraphysical, interexistential interval, or intermissive period.

Evidence. Projective déjà vu, when occurring with a person who has still not experienced an impactful, recalled lucid projection, is evidence and proof, for that individual, of the existence of the spontaneous, lucid projection experience, which had not previously been recalled.

Triggering. In other words: when the projected consciousness remembers a fact that occurred during a prior lucid projection, which was not registered in its waking memory (biomemory), that recollection generates a delayed recall of other details of that lucid projection, which were forgotten or buried in the holomemory. In this case, one recollection *triggers* other recollections.

Cognitions. Within mnemosomatics and in regard to the mnemosoma, there are certain occurrences of projective déjà vu which are directly related to extraphysical retrocognitions and precognitions.

Opposition. The opposing phenomenon to déjà vu is *never-having-seen*, which is characteristically pathological.

Existential seriation. Aside from projective déjà vu, the other phenomenon of this type most frequently encountered by the intraphysical consciousness in the ordinary, physical waking state is *existential seriation déjà vu,* which is multiexistential and frequently multi-secular. In other words: the authentic, retrocognitive recollections of another previous life, already experienced by the consciousness in a retrosoma.

Psychology. The Freudian school of psychology, or psychoanalysis, generally considers déjà vu to be a defense mechanism invented by the subconscious in order to avoid the fear generated by certain critical situations. Obviously, when the situation is not critical and projective déjà vu occurs, this standpoint is meaningless.

Bibliography: Brittain (206, p. 52), Chaplin (273, p. 43), Delanne (385, p. 199), Flammarion (524, p. 232), Fodor (528, p. 120), Frost (560, p. 18), Gaynor (577, p. 46), Martin (1003, p. 40), Miranda (1051, p. 156), Morel (1086, p. 60), Müller (1107, p. 108), Neppe (1122, p. 23), Paim (1182, p. 167), Prado (1284, p. 11), Prieur (1289, p. 198), Ritchie (1407, p. 91), Shepard (1548, p. 224), Walker (1786, p. 82).

---

48. NEAR-DEATH EXPERIENCE (NDE)

Definition. Near-death experience: a projection of the intraphysical consciousness which is involuntary or forced by critical human circumstances, common to terminally-ill patients, moribund patients and survivors of clinical death (first desoma).

Synonymy: experience of imminent death (EID); experience on the brink of death; first spontaneous extraphysical initiation; forced accidental projection; imminent death phenomenon; intimate encounter with death; NDE; near-death crisis; near-death phenomenon; *near-desoma* experience; near-fatal event; near-terminal event; second life experience.

Climate. The moment of biological death, cerebral death, clinical death, or the deactivation of the human body (desoma), has always offered a climate that is favorable toward the occurrence of phenomena considered to be parapsychic. The occurrence of lucid projections in this critical period is thus understandable.

Accidents. Various types of occurrences, near-terminal events or moments of extreme danger can trigger the near-death experience for diverse persons. The following 9 are some examples:

1. Children who are victims of near-drowning.
2. Near-drowned fishermen.
3. Near-electrocuted individuals.
4. Workers who survived construction site, mountain and railway accidents.
5. Drivers and passengers of car accidents.
6. Soldiers wounded on the battlefield.
7. Construction workers who fell from high construction sites.
8. Victims of building collapses and cave-ins.
9. Other victims of similar accidents.

Predispositions. Besides these accidents, certain medical circumstances also predispose provocation of the near-death experience, or the condition in which the person witnesses personal clinical reanimation (resuscitation) – as though being in the back of the surgical theater. The following 8 conditions are some dramatic examples:

1. **Illnesses.** Serious illnesses. A complicated childbirth.
2. **Comatose.** States of deep coma (comatose).
3. **Torture.** Tortured persons.

4. **Suicide.** Suicide attempts *(near-hangings).*

5. **Cardiopathy.** Heart attacks.

6. **Traumatisms.** Serious traumas.

7. **Allergies.** Paroxysmal allergic reactions.

8. **Disturbances.** Other serious diseases and acute disturbances of adults, children and adolescents.

Characteristics. Certain persons – or the *escapees of near-death* – who were rescued from near-fatal accidents at the last minute, notably in the medical field of *reanimation (resurrection) technology,* reveal a series of particularly characteristic elements of the near-death experience in general. The following 15, among others, are examples:

1. **Perceptions.** Sharpening of certain perceptions.

2. **Attention.** Altered attention.

3. **Tachypsychism.** Increase in the velocity of thoughts (tachypsychism or, in this case, *paratachypsychism*).

4. **Xenophrenia.** Altered mental state.

5. **Ineffability.** Uncontrollable ineffability.

6. **Time.** Altered perception of time and space.

7. **Self-control.** Loss of self-control.

8. **Psychosomatics.** Predominance of emotionalism in the manifestations of the intraphysical consciousness.

9. **Mnemosomatics.** Reliving of memories.

10. **Discoincidence.** Sensation of separation from the human body or the sense of detachment.

11. **Floating.** Sensation of floating.

12. **Desomatics.** Sensation of death (desoma).

13. **Reality.** Sensation of reality.

14. **Slowness.** Sensation and experience of slow motion.

15. **Identity.** Transcendence of personal identity.

Time. In subjective phenomena, the altered perception of time during the near-death experience can be singled out, wherein the sensation of an apparent reduction in the velocity of environmental or *external time* commonly arises for the accident victim – a sensation of *slow motion* – in contrast to the extraordinary increase in the velocity of *internal time.*

Projectiology. Lucid projection is a common experience among persons who undergo critical near-death events.

Medicine. According to recent medical research, age, sex, race, residential area, family size, level of education, civil status, occupation, social class, religious upbringing and religious affiliation have no influence upon whether or not a person experienced lucid projection during a medical near-death crisis.

Classification. Near-death crises were classified into 3 basic patterns, from a medical point of view, by the researcher Michael B. Sabom:

1. The autoscopic experience or the phenomenon of self-bilocation.

2. The transcendental experience in which the consciousness lucidly leaves the scenario of the medical resuscitation room or the scene of the accident.

3. The experience of both occurrences combined.

Units. Nowadays, after going through the emergency room, usually located on the ground floor of the hospital, and being classified as code blue or code 99 (in the United States of America, for example), patients with irreversible illnesses (a metastatic cancer, for example) are taken to the intensive care unit (ICU), in large hospitals, as long as it is a reversible complication and not the endpoint of their disease. Seriously-ill patients, with a chance of recovery, stay in a coronary unit.

Instrumentation. These units, which are superior to postoperative recovery rooms, according to the achievements of medical technology, have equipment for artificial respiration, mechanical respirators (respiratory prosthesis), heart monitors, continuous ambulatory blood pressure monitoring (ABPM), among others. The intraaortic balloon pump and gamma camera can also be used in these units.

Categories. Among the conditions of terminal patients in general, two categories can be singled out which can influence the triggering of near-death experiences:

1. Cerebrovascular accident (CVA).
2. Multiple organ dysfunction syndrome (MODS), a cancer which has metastasized.

Atmosphere. Everything is currently being done in order to change the atmosphere (holothosene) of ICUs so they do not appear to be glass domes, painful doorways to the death of the physical body (desoma), inviolable recesses or torture chambers.

Light. Therefore, lights are not pointed into the patient's face and the ICUs are painted in subdued colors.

Hygiene. People are now allowed to enter with only an apron, protection on the feet and after having washed their hands.

Syndrome. All this aims to remove the tense atmosphere, the terrorizing chaos and the ICU Syndrome.

Statistics. Statistics show that, on average, 2 out of 10 patients admitted to an ICU die.

Resources. Besides other secondary resources, the following are 4 hospital resources which are capable of helping to improve the ill patient in an intensive care unit:

1. The electrocardiogram, which monitors the heartbeat in up to 12 derivations, when a complete EKG is needed on paper. For continuous monitoring, 3 or 4 derivations are generally used.
2. The cell-saver, that collects and filters blood which is lost during hemorrhaging and avoids the risks of blood transfusions. It is used to a great extent within the context of the surgical center.
3. The intravenous (IV) drip, that replaces the work of the nurse and controls the flow of drugs applied to the organism of the patient in exact doses.
4. The hemodynamic control which, connected through catheters to two arteries, monitors the blood pressure and shows the results on a screen (the Swan-Ganz, the echocardiograph and the invasive arterial pressure monitor may be included here).

Pharmacology. Medication therapy is one of the areas that developed recently. It is also one of the main aspects in the maintenance of human life, in which the following can be singled out:

1. Vasoactive amines: dopamine and dobutamine. These two drugs are currently (2002) essential in intensive therapy.
2. Other potent intropic agents.
3. Thrombolytic agents (streptokinase, tissue plasminogen activator, urokinase) in the early therapy of acute myocardial infarction (AMI) as well as pulmonary embolism.

Nutrition. Another area that has acquired great relevance in intensive therapy is parenteral (and enteral) nutrition. There are medications for all types of ill persons (persons with COPD, diabetics, hypertensives, individuals suffering from malnutrition, newborns and many others) and for all types of pathologies. It is a highly specialized area that has been receiving a great amount of attention in all of the most renown medical centers.

Apparatuses. The following are 11 apparatuses that are important in an ICU:

1. Continuous electrocardiograph monitor.
2. Digital oximeter: measures the oxygen saturation in the arterial blood (saturation of hemoglobin).
3. IV drips for the more accurate and adequate application of intravenous drugs.
4. Continuous arterial pressure monitor.
5. Mechanical respirator (sustains human life).
6. Swan-Ganz catheter.
7. External pacemaker (sustains human life).
8. Dialyzer (sustains human life).

9. Defibrillator for cardioversion in the reversal of cardiopulmonary arrest and some types of arrhythmia (it is ideally available in any part of the hospital, mainly in emergency and ICU).

10. Intragastric tonometer, for monitoring intramucous pH, in the early detection of low tissue blood flow conditions.

11. Pin for monitoring intracranial pressure.

Types. The near-death experience, certainly a special type of lucid projection, exhibits clearly recognizable patterns and can be classified into 2 basic types: those of terminal patients and those of revived patients.

1. **Terminal.** Terminal patients, who actually pass through desoma soon after experiencing a pre-final projection.

2. **Revived.** Revived patients or survivors of a near-death crisis who have undergone a resuscitative projection. In other words, they had the sensation of dying, but lived to tell their story. This even includes failed suicides, "losers" regarding the tremendous final act of madness that is suicide.

Multiple. Revived individuals can even have more than one (multiple) near-death experience.

Cord. It is interesting to point out that the silver cord, in certain cases of the near-death experience, is perceived to be exhausted, *slightly worn-out,* or to have a lower energetic potential.

Sensations. The near-death experience can be classified into two basic categories, according to the sensations that the intraphysical consciousness can have:

1. **Gratification.** Agreeable; of well-being or gratification.
2. **Nightmare.** As disagreeable as a nightmare.

Patterns. Just like spontaneous lucid projection, the near-death experience, although being of a highly subjective nature, presents a notable consistency in its patterns, varying slightly with regard to the following 5 aspects:

1. **Culture.** Culture or sociocultural background.
2. **Age.** Physical age, which ranges from infancy to *advanced age,* starting from 8 decades of human existence.
3. **Religion.** The religion of the individual.
4. **Cause.** The fundamental cause of the phenomenon.
5. **Diversity.** The diversity of occurrence from one intraphysical consciousness to another.

Explanations. Researchers generally endeavor to explain the nature and significance of the near-death experience in terms of the following 13 occurrences, among others:

1. Altered state of consciousness.
2. Autoscopic hallucination.
3. Conscious mental fabrication.
4. Depersonalization.
5. Dream.
6. Drug-induced hallucination or illusion.
7. Mystical influences.
8. Parapsychic holographic model.
9. Preexisting expectations.
10. Release of endorphins.
11. Semiconscious state.
12. Subconscious fabrication.
13. Temporal lobe crisis.

Hormones. One of the hypotheses raised in order to explain the appearance of near-death phenomena is based on the fear of death (thanatophobia), which would activate the production and secretion of hormones from the suprarenal glands, which would then, in turn, generate parapsychic effects similar to certain drugs like mescaline, LSD and others.

Facts. This hypothesis, however, is contested by the registered cases of individuals having more than one near-death experience at different times, when the intraphysical consciousness actually loses the fear of death (thanatophobia) in the first experience and, even so, continues to have a second, third or more experiences.

Children. The greatest evidence of the phenomenon of the near-death experience arises with dying children – that undergo near-drowning experiences, for example – who see or meet extraphysical consciousnesses which are deceased persons, namely someone who invariably preceded them in desoma or biological death, and whose reports follow the same general patterns as those of adults.

Intraphysical consciousnesses. Logically, if the reports of these experiences close to biological death or desoma were mere hallucinations, the children, at least in some of the cases registered by pediatricians, would have had hallucinations of a certain relative who was still alive and breathing among humans (intraphysical consciousnesses), which does not occur. Prototypical cases like these can be seen in the currently extensive specialized literature on the phenomenon.

Beliefs. It is worth emphasizing that the person's (adult, child) religious beliefs influence the interpretation of the near-death experience, but do not, however, alter the essence of the experience.

Phenomena. To the degree that the consciousness is able to get closer to the climax of the death of the human body (desoma), a greater number of phenomenological elements appear in near-death experiences. Statistically speaking, NDEs happen to more than 1,000 persons per year in the United States of America alone.

Farewell. The near-death experience should not be confused with the farewell projection or critical apparition, nor with the theory of successive lives or existential seriation.

Publications. For a more in-depth technical or historical study of the near-death experience, a detailed consultation of the following two specialized publications (which are no longer in circulation) is indispensable: *Anabiosis: The Journal for Near-Death Studies* (10 editions), and *Vital Signs* magazine (17 editions); as well as their two specialized replacement publications, *Journal of Near-Death Studies* and *Revitalized Signs,* all edited in the United States of America. The *Journal* is currently edited in *New York, NY.* It is currently at Volume 16, Number 4, Summer 1998.

Adverb. It is worth clarifying that the adverb *near* is used in this book to signify *almost* or *on the edge of,* and constitutes an ample variety of expressions in the context of correlated phenomena, as with the following 21 examples:

1. Near-death crisis.
2. Near-death critical event.
3. Near-death egress.
4. Near-death experience.
5. Near-death phenomenon.
6. Near-death resuscitative experience.
7. Near-death.
8. Near-drowned.
9. Near-drowning event.
10. Near-drowning experience.
11. Near-drowning victim.
12. Near-electrocuted.
13. Near-fatal accident.
14. Near-fatal event.
15. Near-hanged.
16. Near-mortal critical event.
17. Near-mortal event.
18. Near-rebirth.
19. Near-sleep.
20. Near-terminal death experience.
21. Near-terminal event.

Projectiological Bibliography: Andrade (29, p. 83), Badham (67, p. 71), Banerjee (74, p. 40), Baumann (93, p. 65), Bender (113, p. 170), Bennett (118, p. 3), Blackmore (139, p. 133), Bozzano (188, p. 48), Caversan (267, p. 9), Champlin (272, p. 218), Chauvin (275, p. 105), Conti (296, p. 124), Currie (354, p. 113), Ebon (453, p. 24), Eysenck (493, p. 155), Fardwel (494, p. 15), Gabbard (564, p. 374), Gallup Jr. (566, p. 36), Gauld (576, p. 221), Gildea (591, p. 43), Giovetti (593, p. 145), Goldberg (606, p. 174), Grattan-Guinness (626, p. 109), Grof (647, p. 9), Grosso (654, p. 37), Harlow (681, p. 112), Heim (702, p. 337), Hemmert (712, p. 181), Hodson (729, p. 138), Holzer (750, p. 13), Ingber (788, p. 16), Knight (851, p. 397), Levine (921, p. 272), Lundahl (959, p. 1, p. 97), Meek (1030, p. 55), Moody Jr. (1077, p. 10; 1078, p. 33), Noyes Jr. (1141, p. 19), Osis (1163, p. 38), Parrish-Harra (1202, p. 75), Perkins (1236, p. 5), Perry (1238, p. 100), Plato (1261, p. 488), Prieur (1289, p. 122), Rawlings (1375, p. 61), Ring (1405, p. 5; 1406, p. 1), Rogo (1445, p. 60), Sabom (1486, p. 12; 1487, p. 1071; 1488, p. 29), Smith (1574, p. 114), Steiger (1601, p. 42), Stevenson (1621, p. 265), Vieira (1762, p. 175), Wheeler (1826, p. 8), White (1832, p. 20), Wilkerson (1848, p. 39), Wilson (1852, p. 15).

Specific Bibliography:

1. **Basford,** Terry K.; *Near-death Experiences: An Annotated Bibliography;* X + 182 pp.; 710 bibliographic entries; ono.; 21.5 x 14 cm; hb.; New York, NY; Garland Publishing; 1990; pp. I-X, 1-182.

---

49. PRE-FINAL PROJECTION

Definition. Pre-final projection: involuntary or forced experience of the consciousness outside the human body, common in terminal patients.

Synonymy: anticipated detachment; *ântuma projection;* deathbed visions; next to the last projection of the intraphysical consciousness; pre-agonizing experience; pre-final projection; visit of projective health; terminal near-death experience.

Terminal. The terminal near-death experience, a characteristic type of lucid projection, occurs shortly before the transition of biological death with moribund, incurable or terminal patients.

Pattern. Classic cases of lucid projection experienced by terminal patients more or less follow a sequential pattern of events, similar to the following 13, that commonly occur in the final phase of human life:

1. The incurable patient has a presentiment that he/she is on the threshold of desoma.
2. The patient bids farewell to family and friends.
3. The patient stretches the legs out on the bed.
4. The patient crosses the hands over the chest in a traditional position.
5. The patient goes into deep unconsciousness.
6. The doctor responsible is present.
7. The patient has no pulse or perceptible heart beat for hours.
8. At this point, the church bells declare the patient dead.
9. However, the inert body occasionally takes weak, almost imperceptible breaths.
10. The doctor pricks the muscles with a pin, with no response.
11. Soon afterwards, however, the patient awakens, entirely lucid for the last time.
12. Surprised and dazzled, the patient reports the experiences outside the human body.
13. The patient subsequently undergoes desoma, truly happy.

Phenomena. Pre-final projections often exhibit intriguing phenomenological aspects that invalidate all of the merely psychological interpretations for the entire set of projectiological occurrences.

Deceased. The above-cited cases include human beings (adults as well as children), who report seeing, meeting and mentally understanding the consciousnesses of 2 or more deceased relatives, brothers, friends and others. There are persons, in cases of near-death experience, who come across cherished pets that have died.

Encounter. The following serves as an example: if the consciousness of the agonizing person (adult or child) encounters extraphysical consciousnesses, deceased friends, one of which had died only 2 days before, given that the agonizing person was unaware of the deactivation of this friend's physical body, the occurrence completely annuls the psychological hypothesis of information being accumulated in the mind of the agonizing person.

Bibliography: Bozzano (189, p. 83), Champlin (272, p. 212), Currie (354, p. 113), Ebon (453, p. 37), Fiore (518, p. 202), Greenhouse (636, p. 147), Grosso (654, p. 38), Ingber (788, p. 20), Malz (992, p. 81), Rogo (1445, p. 65), Tyrrell (1717, p. 165).

---

50. RESUSCITATIVE PROJECTION

Definition. Resuscitative projection: the involuntary experience of the consciousness outside the human body, common with survivors of clinical death, non-terminal patients, or those technically considered to be dead (desoma), also called revived, resuscitated, recuperated or reanimated individuals, who are almost always victims of diverse types of accidents.

Synonymy: aborted death; apparent death; cardiopulmonary reanimation (resurrection); clinical resuscitation; death with return; provisory death; pseudodeath; *pseudodesoma;* resuscitative near-death experience; return from clinical death.

Accidents. Persons who have experienced cardiac arrest, drowning, freezing, hemorrhaging, or were shot, suffered car accidents and other incidents – whose heart stopped beating, lungs stopped breathing, arterial pressure became undetectable, pupils dilated and body temperature dropped drastically – have often been brought back from the brink of desoma with modern medicine's sophisticated reanimation (resuscitation) techniques.

Descriptions. After the abovementioned tragic episodes, many "ex-dead" describe fabulous experiences during their temporary journey in the *kingdom of death* through lucid projection, where they encounter *deceased* relatives and friends, as well as *extraphysical assistants* or *beings of light*.

Spontaneous. Spontaneous resuscitative projections have been registered for dozens of centuries, as seen in the previously cited episode (prototypical case) of Er, son of Armenius of Pamphylia, reported by Plato (400 B.C.; "The Republic," Book 10).

Evidence. The resuscitative projection proves the falsity of the popular saying, "no one returns to tell us what exists after death."

Types. Resuscitated patients may have gone through a *blank consciential period* or had extremely vivid experiences. Some of those who had been considered technically dead and were later resuscitated *more than once* report both types of experience. No one knows why these variations occur.

Pattern. The following are 22 examples of the characteristic sensations that constitute the pattern-sequence of near-death experiences or revivals from apparent death:

1. **Ineffability.** A difficulty in putting all the aspects of the experience into words.

2. **Floating.** A sensation of floating in mid-air in the environment, or in the hospital room, near the ceiling.

3. **Awareness.** Awareness of the conversations and actions of those present around the human body, in a situation wherein the individual is deeply unconscious upon hearing that he/she is dead.

4. **Incommunicability.** Seeing relatives crying and trying to speak to them, without anyone hearing the words.

5. **Permeability.** An attempt to touch people without success.

6. **Translocation.** The sensation of traveling at high speeds.

7. **Tunnel.** The sensation of rapidly traveling in the dark along the interior of a long tunnel, abyss, hole, cavern, cylinder, funnel, well, or deep valley.

8. **Buzzing.** Auditory sensations of strange and often disagreeable noises such as buzzing, whistling and tinkling. Nevertheless, the sensation of hearing an agreeable melody can occur.

9. **Calm.** A strong sensation of tranquility, peace and quietude.

10. **Solitude.** A sensation of profound solitude.

11. **Psychosoma.** The surprising sensation of possessing another body, beyond the human body, often a type of cloud.

12. **Encounters.** Encounters with extraphysical consciousnesses or intelligent extraphysical beings.

13. **Parapsychotics.** Seeing extraphysical consciousnesses who are disturbed by post-desomatic parapsychosis, being stuck to some object, person or habit and in conflict or tormented.

14. **Messenger.** The apparition of a being composed of blinding light, that is radiating intense happiness and love, generally taken to be a guide or messenger.

15. **Review.** Telepathic dialogue with the messenger, without words or accusations, relative to past actions during human existence and the consequences thereof, reviewed from infancy, like a film or a mirror, like a self-judgment.

16. **Mental.** There are those who relate brief glimpses of the mentalsomatic dimension of existence, as though they were a center of consciousness suspended in a void, where all knowledge seems to coexist with an apparent state of extremely ineffable timelessness and spacelessness.

17. **Colonies.** Some describe luminous, extraphysical communities similar to so-called *heaven*, in accordance with biblical, religious or unusual mystical notions that they know.

18. **Border.** The individual is faced with something symbolic described as a barrier, fence, entrance, border, limit, demarcation line, gray cloud, door, gate, or river. If this *point of no return* or *point of conversion* were crossed, it would signify no return to the human body and the acceptance of biological death or desoma. This episode represents a decisive process.

19. **Moratorium.** Some believe that the messenger promotes some pardoning or salvation from biological death solely for the purpose of rescuing some loved one who is still alive on earth, or in favor of an existential moratorium for the individual him/herself.

20. **Interiorization.** The interiorization of the consciousness is often felt to be a great disappointment, especially for those who undergo resuscitation after clinical death.

21. **Effects.** The effects subsequent to the near-death experience are invariably positive. The following 5 variables serve as examples:

    A. **Self-confidence.** Elimination of the fear of death (thanatophobia).

    B. **Megafraternity.** Acquisition of a greater humanitarian sense.

    C. **Paraperceptiology.** Development of parapsychic faculties.

    D. **Goals.** The individual's deep determination toward high objectives (goals).

    E. **Serenity.** A reduction in anxiety when faced with the difficulties of human life.

22. **Discussion.** Generally, individuals, encountering a lack of comprehension on the part of others with respect to consciential experiences, soon learn not to discuss the subject of extraphysical experiences openly in order to get along better with other intraphysical consciousnesses for the remainder of their terrestrial existence or intraphysical survival.

Bibliography: Baker (69, p. 14), Bedford (103, p. 190), Blackmore (139, p. 142), Champlin (272, p. 231), Crookall (343, p. 19), Currie (354, p. 137), Eysenck (493, p. 160), Flammarion (522, p. 107), Grosso (654, p. 38), Hampton (676, p. 6), Malz (992, p. 81), Moody Jr. (1078, p. 33), Plato (1261, p. 487), Ritchie (1407, p. 104), Sabom (1486, p. 91), Steiger (1601, p. 31), Wallis (1791, p. 20), Wilkerson (1848, p. 55).

51. EXTRAPHYSICAL INTUITION

Definitions. Extraphysical intuition (Latin: *in,* in; *tueri,* to look at, view): the phenomenon of instantaneous perception and clear inner knowledge through the apprehension and abrupt entrance into the consciousness of thoughts or ideas, truth or fact, when projected from the human body, without the intervention of any rational process; the capacity for separately considering certain concepts and conditions that normally intervene in our habitual thought processes.

Synonymy: abrupt extraphysical comprehension; apotheosis of intelligence; direct extraphysical understanding; extraphysical insight; extraphysical inspiration; extraphysical intellectual instinct; extraphysical introvision; extraphysical knowledge without reasoning; extraphysical notice; extraphysical premonitory conviction; extraphysical sixth sense; first guide of the projected consciousness; inherent extraphysical knowledge; inner extraphysical voice; inner extraphysical warning; instantaneous extraphysical foresight; interdimensional reason; preconscious.

Hypothesis. Intuition can play an indispensable role in the elaboration of hypotheses. In this case, however, it is absolutely necessary to put these hypotheses to the test.

Illusions. Intuition should not be accepted only on its own merit, without verification, because this opens the door to all types of illusions and superstitions.

Science. Science rejects intuition per se as sufficient proof of its own relative truth.

Proof. For science, that which is intuitively grasped needs to be subsequently proven through observation, experimentation and reasoning, and accepted only after being put through the sieve of these convergent proofs and the universality of the *intercorroborative* testimony.

Factors. In our evolutionary development we are faced with 3 factors of *relative protection,* in ascending order:

1. Instinct (subhuman animal).
2. Reason (human being).
3. Intuition (*serenissimus,* holomemory, holobiography, retrocognitions).

Occurrences. Static intuition is often taken to be the cause of the following 13 occurrences, for example:

1. Consciential confinement.
2. Creative illness.
3. Creative trance.
4. *Divine emanation.*
5. Epileptic state.
6. Flash of genius.
7. Inspirational crisis.
8. Inventive eclosion.
9. Mild furor.
10. Oneiric influence.
11. Psychic automatism.
12. State of madness.
13. Sublime improvisation.

Consequences. Intuition can consequently lead to various conditions, such as the following 9:

1. Catharsis, purging or purification.
2. Consciential outflow.
3. *Creative gestation.*
4. Expansion of the consciousness.
5. Insight.
6. Intraphysical euphoria.
7. Mental purification.

8. Psychic relief.
9. Ventilation of the ego.

Similarities. Nevertheless, intuition in ordinary, everyday life continues to be the fundamental source of all knowledge.

Flash. Intuition, in general, does not always arise in a blinding flash.

Signals. In the process of intuition, preliminary indicators or precursory signals often occur that finally lead to it. The following 4 are examples:

1. **Idea.** The vague idea hidden in the back of the consciousness.
2. **Vision.** The vague glimpsing of things in the periphery of our field of vision.
3. **Hypomnesia.** The irritation experienced when having difficulty in remembering someone's name (hypomnesia).
4. **Clarification.** The anticipation of clarification.

Complexity. Intuition is generally a sentiment of what is unjust or wrong and manifests simply, although being a complex phenomenon.

Categories. Extraphysical intuition can be classified into 4 basic categories, according to its conditioning or causes: recollective, premonitory, psychometric and inspiratory.

1. **Recollective:** when stemming from a recollection or retrocognition, subordinate to the past-time-factor (mentalsoma): the voice of knowledge accumulated during past existences (self-intuition of paragenetics and holobiography).
2. **Premonitory:** when restricted to the perceptions of the consciousness projected within the immediate-future-time-factor (mentalsoma): the voice of cosmic consciousness.
3. **Psychometric:** when limited to the perceptions of the consciousness projected within the form-space-factor, in a crustal or paratropospheric environment (psychosoma): the voice of the extraphysical environment.
4. **Inspiratory:** when constituting a suggestion coming from an invisible, intangible extraphysical consciousness (extraphysical parapsychism): the voice of another consciousness (hetero-intuition, a phenomenon very close to telepathy).

Depth. Extraphysical intuition is the same intuition that is characteristic of the intraphysical consciousness' ordinary, physical waking state. The only difference is its greater depth of supranormal information gathered through the subconscious which, in this case, accesses all previous existences and intermissive periods, bringing it inside that selfsame consciousness when it finds itself projected from the human body (access to the holomemory).

Enrichment. Extraphysical intuition is also the same *reasoning* that is common to ordinary life, except it is enriched in an *interdimensional* manner.

Intrathosenes. The general mechanism of intuition seems to bear some relation to the phenomenon of hearing *mental words,* or intrathosenes. This relationship merits more research within thosenology.

Calm. The mechanism of the subjective experience of extraphysical intuition demands a certain state of consciential calm in order to function better.

Obstacles. The following are 8 obstacles or factors, among others, that make the acquisition of extraphysical intuitions more difficult:

1. The projected consciousness which is very agitated by its own experience.
2. Short attention span.
3. Distractibility.
4. Happiness or extraphysical euphoria.
5. Fear (phobias).
6. Sadness, grief or lamentation.
7. An anxious temperament.
8. Extraphysical trauma.

Neutrality. The facts suggest that the best condition for accessing intuition is the inner unemotional, unaffectionate state of consciential neutrality (serenity, tranquility).

Awareness. Extraphysical intuition simplifies experiences for the projected consciousness in a positive way, giving it the incontestable awareness of certain facts when it urgently needs to know them, sometimes arising providentially in a dramatic, very special and unique extraphysical circumstance.

Evolution. In principle, the novice lucid projector does not perceive the existence of extraphysical intuition. The individual simply uses it without perceiving the existence of this consciential faculty.

Confidence. With the spontaneous repetition of intuitive-projective experiences and the evolutionary development of the lucid projector, the projected consciousness acquires confidence with regard to its intuition and begins to apply it normally, with ease, as though it were a new tool acquired in its extraphysical activities.

Door. The inner certainty offered by the flashes of extraphysical intuition, for example, with respect to a detail regarding a fact, the mental identification of an extraphysical consciousness, clarification on a certain existential circumstance and other occurrences, arises immediately. It does not always represent the direct or indirect inspiration of a helper, because it constitutes the consciousness' natural perception, which is incomprehensible when living in the ordinary, physical waking state.

Realities. In general, intuition unquestionably constitutes at least the following 4 realities:

1. **Logic.** Leapfrogging steps of logic.
2. **Reason.** Anticipation regarding the processes of reason.
3. **Thought.** Shortcut in the natural or physiological elaboration of thought.
4. **Proofs.** Prior revelation regarding much sought-after and discussed scientific proofs.

Research. The author leaves the following research hypothesis: If intriguing intuition, as a subjective experience, is more evolved than reason and if reason is an attribute of the consciousness in the mentalsoma, might not intuition emanate from "something" of the consciousness which is beyond or more evolved than the mentalsoma, a condition characteristic of free consciousness (FC) which we still do not understand?

Acquisition. Extraphysical intuition plays an important and often decisive role in the acquisition of *original ideas* through lucid consciential projection.

Bibliography: Blavatsky (153, p. 284), Bonin (168, p. 252), Chaplin (273, p. 89), Day (376, p. 65), Fodor (528, p. 185), Gaynor (577, p. 87), Greene (635, p. 89), Morel (1086, p. 98), Pensamento (1224, p. 57), Shepard (1548, p. 469), Vieira (1762, p. 66), Wang (1794, p. 17), Zaniah (1899, p. 245).

---

52. EXTRAPHYSICAL PRECOGNITION

Definition. Extraphysical precognition (Latin: *prae,* pre; *cognoscere,* to know): the perceptive faculty whereby the consciousness, fully projected outside the human body, comes to know indeterminate upcoming facts, including objects, scenes and distant forms in the future.

Synonymy: anticipated projective memory; extraphysical clairvoyance in the future; extraphysical future memory; extraphysical paragnosis; extraphysical pre-esthesia; extraphysical pregnosis; extraphysical premonition; extraphysical prenotion; extraphysical prescience; extraphysical prognosis; extraphysical promnesia; extraphysical prophetic metagnomy; extraphysical radar; intuitional accessing of the future; projective forecast; projective precognition; projective proscopy; prophetic astral projection.

Categories. Precognitions can be placed into 4 basic categories:

1. **Realistic.** Ordinary, spontaneous and realistic precognition.
2. **Intuitive.** Unrealistic and intuitive precognition.
3. **Laboratorial.** Precognition provoked in the laboratory.
4. **Extraphysical.** Spontaneous extraphysical precognition that comprises precognitive lucid projection. It is far more common than imagined.

Self-precognition. Extraphysical precognition, when related to the projector him/herself, is the extraphysical self-precognition of death (desoma), generally through illness or accident.

Retrocognition. There are instances of extraphysical retrocognition in which the projected intraphysical consciousness becomes aware of past facts, prior to the present human existence, identifies former personalities who are currently intraphysical. This enables projective forecasts of events in the near future.

Mixed. This last occurrence should be classified as a special type of extraphysical precognition or as a complex, retrocognitive-precognitive, mixed, effect or consequence phenomenon.

Percipient. It is common for the agent of the phenomenon – the projected projector – to analyze its own occurrences of extraphysical precognition.

Apparition. Nevertheless, there are many cases of projective precognition that occur directly with the percipient of the lucid projection of another – a case of *inter vivos* consciential apparition.

Unconsciousness. In these cases, the projector – whether projected, or even in the ordinary, physical waking state, after the consciential projection – is not aware of the precognitive facts that refer to him/her and which he/she transmitted, becoming aware of this only after they are ratified over time (see *Bozzano,* Ernesto).

Bibliography: Blasco (151, p. 133), Bonin (168, p. 408), Boswell (174, p. 78), Bozzano (188, p. 87), Cavendish (266, p. 205), Chaplin (273, p. 125), Cheetham (276, p. 149), Cornillier (304, p. 85), Denis (390, p. 85), Digest (401, p. 374), Fodor (528, p. 295), Gaynor (577, p. 144), Grattan-Guinness (626, p. 144), Greenhouse (639, p. 58), Harrison (685, p. 103), Holzer (751, p. 108), Marin (996, p. 118), Martin (1003, p. 97), Monroe (1065, p. 152), Morel (1086, p. 144), Norvell (1137, p. 217), Paula (1208, p. 75), Schiff (1515, p. 117), Shepard (1548, p. 727), Still (1622, p. 255), Tondriau (1690, p. 273), Vieira (1762, p. 90), Wang (1794, p. 219), Wedeck (1807, p. 288), Zaniah (1899, p. 364).

---

53.   EXTRAPHYSICAL   PSYCHOMETRY

Definition. Extraphysical psychometry (Greek: *psykhé,* soul; *metron,* measurement): knowledge acquired by the projected human consciousness regarding the present and past, as well as details about personalities, by way of direct extraphysical contact with the double of these physical objects (catalysts) that pertain to the epoch or epochs regarding which the individual wishes to know.

Synonymy: astral psychometry; astral *telefrontisia;* extraphysical iconognosis; extraphysical psicognition; extraphysical psychoscopy; extraphysical retrocognitive telesthesia; extraphysical telegnomy; indirect extraphysical lucidity; paratelegnomy; projective psychometry.

Potentiation. Lucid projection potentiates the psychometric capacity of the intraphysical sensitive. This suggests that there is a strange relationship between the essential nature of the phenomenon and the mentalsoma, outside time and space.

Technique. The technique of extraphysical psychometry follows the same criteria as the well-known practices of common psychometry in the ordinary waking state, except that it utilizes the spontaneous amplification of the perceptions of the projected human consciousness in order to feel, perceive and see the *essence of things,* achieve *universal knowledge* directly in the *cosmic memory, book of life, akashic* records or *akashic* registers, in the so-called *reflexive ether* of the universe.

Uses. Extraphysical psychometry, although difficult in practice, is used in the tracing of missing persons and criminals who are sought by the intraphysical authorities.

Bibliography: Boswell (174, p. 166), Carton (252, p. 225), Cavendish (266, p. 168), Chaplin (273, p. 127), Day (376, p. 105), Digest (401, p. 331), Fodor (528, p. 317), Gaynor (577, p. 148), Johnson (807, p. 175), Lee (908, p. 165), Martin (1003, p. 102), Morel (1086, p. 149), Paula (1208, p. 89), Pensamento (1224, p. 81), Perkins (1236, p. 44), Sculthorp (1531, p. 108), Shepard (1548, p. 754), Spence (1588, p. 333), Toben (1688, p. 79), Tondriau (1690, p. 270), Vieira (1762, p. 159), Wedeck (1807, p. 293).

54. EXTRAPHYSICAL RETROCOGNITION

Definition. Extraphysical retrocognition (Latin: *retro,* behind; *cognoscere,* to know): perceptive faculty whereby the intraphysical consciousness, fully projected from the human body, becomes aware of facts, scenes, forms, objects, successes and experiences pertaining to the distant past.

Synonymy: extraphysical clairvoyance in the past; extraphysical consciential internation in the past; extraphysical post-cognition; extraphysical remote memory; extraphysical retromonition; extraphysical retroscopy; mnemonic retrocession; multi-existential retrocognition; pre-natal regressive projection; projective multidimensional memory; projective retrocognition; regression of extracerebral memory; retrocognitive projection; superlucid dream.

Events. Retrocognition experienced by the projected consciousness can refer to events from the individual's current existence or other previous intraphysical lives, which may be known or entirely unknown. This always occurs through perceptive resources that go beyond the possibilities of ordinary, physical memory, cerebral memory or biomemory, and rational inference based on known facts.

Projection. Extraphysical retrocognition – acting in a direction inverse to extraphysical precognition in chronological time – permits the occurrence of retrocognitive lucid projection.

Hypotheses. The following are 5 work hypotheses pertinent to the subject:

1. **Work.** How does the process of retrocognitive lucid projection actually work?
2. **Cause.** What is the raison d'être of retrocognitive lucid projection?
3. **Time.** In this case, does time operate in an inverse manner?
4. **Holomemory.** Could extraphysical retrocognition be a consciential journey using the integral consciousness or is it exclusively an intraconsciential journey within the holomemory?
5. **Mentalsoma.** Does the retrocognitive process only manifest and develop within the mentalsoma, in the mentalsomatic dimension?

Pseudo-intrusion. The phenomenon of extraphysical retrocognition, in certain cases, can generate pseudo-intrusion, in this case self-intrusion, as though the recollection of a prior intraphysical existence were a separate, intrusive entity associated with the underlying mental disturbance of the individual, which does not cease to be a typical parapsychosis.

Categories. Considering another aspect of the phenomenon, retrocognitive experiences can be placed into two categories: those that are personal and those pertaining to others.

1. **Personal.** Personal retrocognitive experiences are those that refer to the past – and *less* complex – experiences of the consciousness itself.

2. **Others.** Retrocognitive experiences of others are those that refer to past – and *more* complex – experiences of other individuals. They generally occur in circumstances in which the intraphysical projector is serving as a sensitive in the human dimension and learns of the experiences of someone who already passed through desoma by using sympathetic assimilation, extraphysical psychophony and projective recollection.

Politics. These retrocognitive experiences of others occur frequently in extraphysical deintrusive assistential services provided to former members of rival political groups.

Bibliography: Cannon (240, p. 40), Castaneda (256, p. 17), Cavendish (266, p. 211), Chaplin (273, p. 131), D'arbó (365, p. 152), Digest (401, p. 375), Edwards (465, p. 99), Fodor (528, p. 328), Gaynor (577, p. 155), Morel (1086, p. 156), Müller (1107, p. 253), Paula (1208, p. 109), Shepard (1548, p. 776), Steiger (1601, p. 147), Tondriau (1690, p. 273), Tourinho (1692, p. 47), Vieira (1762, p. 159), Wang (1794, p. 217), Zaniah (1899, p. 387).

55. PROJECTIVE   PANORAMIC   VISION

Definition. Projective panoramic vision: spontaneous, *en bloc,* simultaneous, retrospective vision of human facts and psychological conditions experienced by the projected intraphysical consciousness, through the superactivity of the evocative memory.

Synonymy: cinematographic recollection; consciential self-examination; consciential self-judgment; ecmnesia; *en bloc* evocations; epilog of biological death; existential examination; existential review; introspective visual review; kaleidoscopic vision of existence; life retrospective; life review; mnemonic cinematographic film; mnemonic mirror; panoramic memory; panoramic projective review; panoramic reconstitution of life; panoramic remembrance; pictographic recollections; recapitulation of life; recapitulation of remembrances; reexperiencing of memories; synthesis of recollections; synthetic memory; synthetic reminiscence of existence; total retrospective review.

Characteristics. The phenomenon of panoramic vision presents 10 basic characteristics:

1. **Instantaneity.** The scenes of panoramic vision develop in sudden succession, surprising the individual, like an orderly whirlwind of facts around the person.

2. **Simultaneity.** Many facts can be exhibited simultaneously in panoramic vision, with lifelike images occurring at the same time and in the same plane.

3. **Ordering.** The scenes of panoramic vision can also proceed in an orderly, regular manner, whether in inverse order to that in which the facts were experienced (retrograde order), or in a direct manner, in the exact chronological succession in which the facts were produced.

4. **Intensity.** The number of recollections in panoramic vision vary from individual to individual, presenting two degrees of intensity:

A. **Integral.** The integral recollections provide the entire panorama of existence which have occurred up to that moment, from trivial facts to those that are most important.

B. **Partial.** The partial recollections are restricted to a specific part of human existence.

5. **Images.** The images of panoramic vision are pictographic, being figurative frames from daily life with an uncommonly lifelike nature, as well as having spectacular sound, color, movement and emotion that unfolds before the consciousness.

6. **Clarity.** The scenes are extremely clear, showing all the smallest intrinsic and collateral details of the occurrences of panoramic vision, even including situations that had been forgotten and are therefore unexpected. Scenes can either have an incredible vivacity or be projected in only two dimensions.

7. **Sensations.** The sensations experienced during panoramic vision are profound, whether they are of satisfaction and relief, or remorse. The sentiments between good and bad are very well defined. The phenomenon allows the consciousness to analyze in detail its own sensations in the progression of its personal history. The critical moments and common facts, the positive and negative occurrences – the actions regarding which the consciousness felt gratified as well as the attitudes it was ashamed to remember on that occasion – are gathered impartially, all at once, into a whole, through panels. On rare occasions, the sequence of memories can unfurl without emotional involvement, in an impersonal manner.

8. **Duration.** In panoramic vision, the thousands of scenes involved in a perfect integral recapitulation of the recollections of episodes of human existence last for some seconds or can extend up to a maximum of almost one hour. There is no sensation of the passage of minutes. Often, 6 decades pass in tenths of a second, in a complete consciential self-judgment.

9. **Significance.** The experience of panoramic vision can be interpreted as an educational effort, stemming from the more evolved consciential dimensions, with the aim of helping the intraphysical consciousness to understand the significance of human life.

10. **Summary.** The recollections of panoramic vision can be of an entire period of consciential life or may only arise as a "summary." In this case, only the more relevant or decisive recollections appear.

Conditions. Hypermnesia or mnemonic exaltation generally occurs more frequently during at least the following 18 conditions or stages, or with persons in critical circumstances:

1. Physical illness.
2. High fever.
3. Religious exaltation.
4. Ecstasy (beatitude).
5. Elevated emotional condition.
6. *Pre-mortem* delirium or the crisis which precedes dying.
7. Hysteria.
8. Senility (Alzheimer's disease).
9. Epilepsy.
10. Other xenophrenic states or altered states of consciousness.
11. Persons who experience life-threatening situations or the imminence of the human body's death.
12. Asphyxiation by submersion.
13. Explosion on a battlefield.
14. Surgical operation.
15. Falls from treetops.
16. Falls experienced by mountain climbers.
17. Near-strangled individuals.
18. Wounded soldiers.

Forced. All the above-cited facts predispose the forced, abrupt projection of the consciousness. That is why it is connected to occurrences of panoramic vision.

Expressions. Many scholars endeavor to identify panoramic vision in general with expressions such as: "*akashic* register," "annals of the past," "astral clichés," "astral images," "astral light," "brain of nature," "ether-reflector," "indelible images," "memory of God," "memory of nature," "memory of the world," "soul of the world," "soul of things," and others.

Mechanisms. These expressions endeavor to say much in regard to the causes, sources and resources of the phenomenon. However, they actually clarify nothing. The mechanisms of memory remain extremely obscure.

Children. It is interesting to note that, in near-death experiences, children do not experience the panoramic review of their lives, which are obviously of short duration. This fact is an exception in relation to adults, who have greater, more traumatic and extensive experiences to recall when undergoing the near-death experience. The facts show that the same occurs with the experience of projective panoramic vision.

Accidents. Panoramic vision especially occurs in impactful circumstances aside from hypermnesia, super-recall or the simple exaltation of memory, when the consciousness experiences the near-death phenomenon. It can also occur spontaneously, during abrupt lucid projections, in cases of physical accident.

Memory. In panoramic vision, introspective (*inside* the consciousness, outside time and space) projection occurs in the mnemonic center or integral memory bank of the personality. This happens without external interference from occurrences that refer to the person's existence, as though it were an immense computer that reviews its own biography – in an instant, as though on film – with all the programmed data.

Scenes. The scenes seem to pass before the *mind's eye*, intraconscientially.

Continuous. Panoramic vision clearly demonstrates that, when necessary, the *integral* memory (holomemory) of the consciousness shows itself to be *continuous* memory or one without hiatus, perfect, indelible and susceptible of emerging in all of its plenitude in critical moments of the intraphysical being's (intraphysical consciousness) life.

Causes. Panoramic vision is explained as being an effect which is consequent to the superexcitation of the mnemonic faculties, produced by the crisis of dying, in the disconnection of the cerebral hemispheres and the integral memory (holomemory) of the consciousness, that occurs in the beginning of the discoincidence of its vehicles of manifestation, in this case, the soma and psychosoma.

Helper. However, it sometimes seems that panoramic vision is also triggered intentionally by the direct interference of an extraphysical helper upon the projected or semiprojected consciousness.

Objectives. Many people characterize the phenomenon of panoramic vision as being a moral test or an examination of the individual's conscience.

Relief. It is curious to note, in this sense, that in certain cases of panoramic vision the individual notices that the sequence of the scenes occurs in a selective manner, or *in relief,* emphasizing the reason for the vision, namely the analytical objective with regard to the personality and his/her true emotions felt at the precise moment at which the facts occur.

Photos. It is as if the consciousness were examining a vast collection of photos of familiar persons, with the figures appearing flat and two-dimensional, with the exception of one, precisely his/her personality, that is in focus, appearing more clearly, accentuated, emphasized, in relief, as though it were under the *spotlight* the entire time.

Intention. This would seem to indicate the underlying intention of consciential self-examination somehow acting upon the causes of panoramic mnemonic phenomena.

Extraphysical consciousnesses. Through parapsychic, psychophonic and psychographic communications, extraphysical consciousnesses generally affirm that they experience panoramic vision immediately after the first death and before the *restorative sleep,* characteristic of that intraphysical consciousness which has just returned to the status of an extraphysical consciousness in the extraphysical dimension.

Haptics. In analogy with the existing scientific aspects of physics – such as acoustics, optics and olfactology – *haptics,* the science of touch, was created.

Classification. Panoramic vision can be classified into two categories, according to the division of the general perceptions of human personalities, visual (optics) and auditory-mental (acoustics and haptics):

1. **Frequent.** The most frequent or common occurrence is panoramic vision per se, when the consciousness focuses its perceptions only through the *visual aspect.*

2. **Infrequent.** Less frequent is the recapitulation of recollections when the perceptions of the consciousness are predominately characterized by the *auditive-mental* aspect.

Bibliography: Bayless (98, p. 128), Black (137, p. 144), Blackmore (139, p. 150), Bozzano (186, p. 114), Browning (213, p. 43), Crookall (343, p. 113), Currie (354, p. 154), Delanne (385, p. 143), Depascale (392, p. 143), Ebon (453, p. 125), Frazer (549, p. 154), Grattan-Guinness (626, p. 109), Hampton (676, p. 57), Larcher (887, p. 98), Lukianowicz (957, p. 206), Miranda (1050, p. 33), Montandon (1070, p. 295), Müller (1107, p. 167), Noyes Jr. (1141, p. 21; 1142, p. 174), Ring (1406, p. 157), Ritchie (1407, p. 46), Sabom (1486, p. 74), Vieira (1762, p. 217), Walker (1786, p. 123), Wheeler (1826, p. 26).

---

56. AMBIFACETED PROJECTIVE PHENOMENA

Definition. Ambifaceted projective phenomena: parapsychic occurrences restricted to the scope of projectiology that occur within the consciousness of the projector – who may or may not be projected – but which, however, have important consequences outside this same consciousness or its consciential micro-universe.

Synonymy: external projective phenomenon; trans-sensory phenomenon.

Intraphysical. The following 32 connected, main or ambifaceted parapsychic phenomena, among others, occur with the human consciousness – which may or may not be projected – and with the participation of the intraphysical consciousness, whether in the ordinary, physical waking state or projected in an extraphysical environment:

1. Apparition of the projected projector to intraphysical beings.
2. Cardiac and umbilical self-desoma.
3. Creation of morphothosenes (thought-forms).
4. Exteriorization of motricity.

5. Exteriorization of sensitivity.

6. Extraphysical elongation.

7. Extraphysical energetic transmissions (exteriorizations) made by the projected projector, including *exteriorization-by-three* or *triple energization*.

8. Extraphysical projective psychophony.

9. Extraphysical self-transfiguration.

10. Extraphysical telekinesis.

11. Extraphysical telepathy.

12. False arrival.

13. Farewell projection.

14. Human parateleportation.

15. Human projective psychophony.

16. Physical bilocation of the person of the projector, seen by others

17. Physical multilocation.

18. Possessive projection.

19. Projection of the subhuman animal's double, detected by an intraphysical consciousness.

20. Projective ectoplasmy.

21. Projective heteroscopy.

22. Projective parapyrogenesis.

23. Projective pneumatophony.

24. Projective poltergeist.

25. Projective psychography.

26. Projective raps.

27. Self-psychophony.

28. Semimaterialization.

29. Sonorous projection.

30. State of suspended animation.

31. Traveling clairvoyance.

32. Zoanthropy.

Analysis. All important ambifaceted projective phenomena will be addressed in detail in a specific chapter in this book, either in this or in other sections, according to the sequential analysis of the subjects.

Complexity. In cases of parapsychic phenomena with an extraphysical agent that may be an intraphysical *consciousness*, an extraphysical consciousness, or a recent-extraphysical consciousness – which can be referred to as an *intraphysical-extraphysical consciousness* – human detection can be performed by one or more intraphysical percipients at the same time.

Confirmation. In this last hypothesis of collective perception, the phenomenon receives more ample confirmation, the revalidation of the facts, making the occurrences more complex and the analyses and interpretations more difficult.

57. SELF-PSYCHOPHONY

Definition. Self-psychophony (OE: *self*, self; Greek: *psyche*, soul; *phone*, sound): the faculty whereby the consciousness speaks through the speech mechanisms of the human body while remaining partially projected outside it.

Synonymy: animic psychophony; *inter vivos* psychophony; intraconsciential psychophony; personification; self-incorporation.

Nature. Self-psychophony, or intraconsciential psychophony, constitutes an altered state of consciousness, an animic phenomenon, as opposed to classic parapsychic psychophony, or the incorporation of an extraphysical consciousness. It works like a consciential semi-detachment or a partial discoincidence of the vehicles of manifestation of the consciousness.

Categories. The phenomenon of self-psychophony can occur in a completely unconscious manner and can be classified into two basic categories: simultaneous self-psychophony and retrocognitive self-psychophony.

1. **Simultaneous.** In simultaneous self-psychophony – also called clairvoyant autoscopy, personification, or the well-known, controversial *phenomenon of animism* – the consciousness enters into an altered state and talks about contemporary facts.

2. **Retrocognitive.** In retrocognitive self-psychophony, the consciousness refers to facts from previous existences, unaware of the fact, as it occurs in parapsychic sessions when the consciousness of the sensitive – in this case an animist – mnemonically exteriorizes itself to one of its previous lives, reporting about what it knew or what it experienced on that occasion.

Regression. A correlated or similar phenomenon that can be brought to mind here is memory regression.

Clairvoyance. Simultaneous self-psychophony is common during traveling clairvoyance, where the sensitive feels his/her own consciousness to be partially projected from the human body, seeing scenes or witnessing events, transmitting descriptions and reports through his/her psychophysiological mechanism of speech (laryngochakra).

Monologue. Self-psychophony is a phenomenon that is similar to, albeit significantly different from, psychophonic monologue, wherein the sensitive's consciousness leaves the state of coincidence of the consciential vehicles of manifestation, although remaining in the proximity, speaking between worlds with an extraphysical consciousness who speaks through the vocal apparatus (laryngochakra) of his/her human body.

Bibliography: Mitchell (1058, p. 44), Rogo (1446, p. 155).

58. PHYSICAL   BILOCATION

Definitions. Physical bilocation (Latin: *bis,* two; *locus,* place): the simultaneous presence of the personality of an individual in 2 locations; the act of someone being and acting in 2 distinct locations through parapsychic means; the faculty whereby the same consciousness appears in more than 1 body (vehicle of manifestation) seemingly at the same time.

Synonymy: *anguttara nikaya* (Tibet); apparition of the living to the living; apparition of the projectionist; appearance outside the body; autonomous abmaterialization; bicorporality; bicorporeity; bilocation of the living; bilocational apparition; bilocational excursion; bilocational journey; bi-presence; double location; double presence; double solid body; holosomatic mitosis; incipient bilocation; *inter vivos* solid apparition; *larvata;* materialization of a living person without a sensitive; materialization of the adept; materialization of the projected intraphysical consciousness; materialization-projection; materialized apparition; materialized unfolding; natural materialization; non-human kind; objective bilocation; objective unfolding; phantasm state; phenomenon of double persons; phenomenon of duplication; physical bilocation; reciprocal hallucination; self-ectoplasmy; self-materialization; self-telediplosia; simultaneous bilocation; solid psychosoma; spectacular consciential projection.

Mechanisms. In most cases, physical bilocation is an involuntary, animic (of the intraphysical consciousness) projection in which the soma, that is inactive or absolutely static and immobile – similar to the death of the human body (desoma) – and in the empty brain condition, due to the temporary absence of the consciousness, remains in one place (the improvised physical base). Thus the consciousness, moved for whatever extreme psychological reasons, presents itself in the psychosoma, which is visible (stimulating the visual perceptions of other intraphysical consciousnesses) or even tangible (stimulating the tactile perceptions of the fingers of other intraphysical consciousnesses) in another nearby or distant location.

Distinction. There are those who make a theoretical distinction between 2 phenomena:

1. Bilocation, which refers to *2 places*.
2. Bicorporeity, relative to *2 bodies*.

Similarities. In practice, however, the 2 phenomena are similar or identical in their origin, evolution and objective, possibly occurring in at least 4 specific conditions of the intraphysical consciousness:

1. **Trance.** With the person in a parapsychic trance.
2. **Somnolence.** In the state of somnolence.
3. **Sleep.** During natural sleep.
4. **Projection.** In an altered state of consciousness, projected with full lucidity.

Distance. The phenomenon of physical bilocation can occur near to or distant from the human body. In fact, the bilocation of the actual human body does not occur. It is, rather, the projection of the intraphysical consciousness when outside the body.

Objectivity. Physical bilocation can be further classified into two basic categories with regard to its objectivity:

1. **Objective.** Objective bilocation, when the presence of the bilocator is made ostensive and practically physical, being perceived by more than 1 percipient or witness.
2. **Subjective.** Subjective bilocation, when the form of the individual appears with all of its lifelike attributes to a sensitive, or a clairvoyant sensitive, who is distant from where the bilocator's human body is located at that moment, having been left in a condition of relative inactivity (vulnerable, inanimate, torpid, vegetative).

Types. The phenomenon of physical bilocation can be produced in 3 different ways:

1. Unconscious.
2. Conscious.
3. Experimental or false bilocation. This mode of the phenomenon was produced by French researchers and was called *false bilocation* by some scholars.

Factors. In the causes of the phenomena of physical bilocation, 1 of 2 basic triggering factors can be detected, which should be researched with regard to their motivations, per se:

1. **Escape.** Escape from a difficult human situation, thereby serving as a maneuver for physical survival on the part of the bilocating social being (intraphysical consciousness). It is, therefore, a process of *intra*consciential origin.
2. **Help.** Help for a person with whom the bilocator is almost always affectionately connected and truly wishes to provide service or assistance. It is therefore a process of *extra*consciential origin.

Hallucination. Those who have not had a more profound lucid projection experience tend to interpret physical bilocation as being implausible, a mere reciprocal hallucination between the agent and the percipient or percipients. The author judges this hypothesis to be simplistic and inconsistent, when faced with the facts and the wealth of existing historical reports on the topic.

Mixed. The phenomenon should be called *physical* bilocation in order to distinguish it from *mixed* bilocation in two dimensions or, in other words, the simultaneous presence of the individual's human form, the human body in the empty brain condition in the intraphysical dimension, and its humanoid form, with the mentalsoma and the consciousness in the extraphysical dimension per se, during the occurrences of lucid projection, although manifesting itself visibly and tangibly to human beings.

Tangibility. Physical bilocation is the same phenomenon as apparition of an intraphysical projector to intraphysical consciousnesses, but more tangible, seen, or physically perceived by a greater number of persons due to its quality of visibility.

Apparition. In fact, the apparition of a projected projector is always a bilocation, although, in this situation, the apparition (psychosoma) and the human body of the projector are observed separately at the same time.

Space. It is important to classify the phenomenon of physical bilocation into two basic categories, with regard to space:

1. **Soma.** In bilocation considered to be *subjective,* the projected projector, or agent, appears at a distance from the human body (soma) to a percipient (the subjectivity of this being that the projector does not see his/her distant soma).

2. **Place.** In bilocation considered to be *objective,* the projected projector manifests his/her presence *(copy)* in a place different from that which his/her human body *(original)* occupies, the presence of which is confirmed or detected by one or more other persons who are different from those who see the projector's immobile human body.

Fear. Fear can sometimes dominate the novice projector, as well as the intraphysical witness who sees him/her projected. The cause for this seems to be in the unusual aspect of the occurrence for both parties, although each one acts in his/her own, specific or different situation.

Density. In the phenomenon of physical bilocation, the anthropomorphic figure of the bilocator can be of 2 distinct types in regard to its density:

1. Vaporous.
2. Dense.

Brink. Bilocation occurs more frequently in the moments before death, or the brink of biological death or desoma, prior to the deactivation of the consciousness' human body.

Clairvoyance. Certain cases of pure clairvoyance, on the part of an intraphysical percipient who registers the apparition of someone, can be confused with the phenomenon of physical bilocation, although being a very different fact. In this eventuality, the condensation or semimaterialization of the projector's psychosoma does not occur. What does occur is only the more pronounced parapsychic perception of the profound acuity of the paraperceptiology of the *spectator-percipient-sensitive-clairvoyant,* or even an interconsciential phenomenon of *paraclairvoyance.*

Sharpness. The visual images or humanoid, human and extraphysical forms of the apparitions and of the bilocator's manifest themselves in different degrees of sharpness on the part of the percipient or clairvoyant.

Duration. The phenomenon can have many degrees of duration, lasting from tenths of a second to several hours for the percipient.

Simulacrum. The isolated projection of the holochakra represents a phantasmagoric bilocation, or a mere simulacrum. That is to say, a projection of this vehicle occurs without the dislocation of the seat of the consciousness, which remains in the psychosoma and the human body, like an energetic image projected *from* and *by* the person. It can be seen, but does not have its own personality, nor is it the center of the consciousness (pointer of the consciousness).

Case study. Everything points to the fact that certain cases of autoscopy, false arrival and 2 classic examples of physical bilocation – that of Antonio de Pádua (1195-1231), and Emília Sagée (1845) – are of the nature of simulacra. There was no retrieval of information, awareness of the individual and, particularly in the case of the 2 last examples above, the fact did not serve any purpose lucidly elaborated by the will of the responsible parties.

Effects. In most physical bilocation phenomena, the appearance of the bilocator's psychosoma is observed by a person or a group and successively by various persons, and even by subhuman animals, especially dogs and cats (pets), without provoking tangible, physical effects or, in other words, without leaving traces.

Reminders. There are, however, rare and remarkable incidents in which some type of evidence, trace, human sign, animate or inanimate semipermanent measurable marks, and physical traces resulting from patent physical or telekinetic contacts are left, thereby providing proof of the presence of the bilocator at that location.

Objects. Certain occurrences of physical bilocation constitute indisputable proof of the relationship between the projector bilocators and physical objects during the moments of their parapsychic trances. These fall into two categories:

1. **Carry.** The projected projector can transport physical objects – personal *baggage* – along on the *extraphysical trip* and leave it at the location visited, where he/she was seen to be physically bilocated.

2. **Bring.** The projected projector can bring back objects – parapsychic *souvenirs* – which were obtained at the distant place visited.

Non-human kind. The intraphysical projector, projected in the solid psychosoma, in the phenomenon of tangible or physical bilocation, is a true non-human kind, a being that was not biologically generated, or a *para-android*. In these cases, in a paraphysical creation, the humanoid being is generated through means other than natural conception, gestation, genetics and human, physical, biological or animal birth.

Paragenetics. The non-human kind proceeds or stems directly from the paragenetics of the consciousness.

Communications. In parapsychic (mediumistic or channeled) communications or, more precisely, animic (intraphysical consciousness) *inter vivos* communications, the communicant-projector, or pseudo-dead is producing – whether through psychophony or psychography, in a location different from its physical base – the phenomenon of physical bilocation, without, however, the tangible condensation of the form of the psychosoma occurring.

Frequency. *Inter vivos* parapsychic communications occur more frequently than *inter vivos* animic communications. In these cases, the pure animic process is very rare.

Guide. Some help is always provided, notably by the sensitive's extraphysical mentor (blind guide or helper).

Thread. The *thread of light* – or, better yet, the silver cord – generally constitutes the only perceptible difference between the apparition characteristic of the intraphysical bilocator and the apparition of the extraphysical consciousness.

Appearance. Nevertheless, some percipients and clairvoyants even add – as a differential characteristic between one apparition and another – the lifeless, dead (visual, physiognomy), statue-like or mannequin-like appearance of certain apparitions of intraphysical beings (intraphysical consciousnesses).

Motivations. The following are 6 of the more frequent deep concerns or strong motivations, among others, for the intraphysical consciousness to spontaneously produce ostensive, physical bilocation, or that which is perceived by other intraphysical beings:

1. Extraphysical assistance (helper, evolutiologist).
2. Intense affection, including that of an evolutionary duo.
3. Religious devotion (belief, faith, fanaticism, sectarianism).
4. Professional service.
5. Urgent human business (intraphysical problems).
6. Strictly political reasons.

Devitalization. The phenomena of bilocation in general, and all those which are based upon the temporary transference of the seat of the consciousness out from the human body – including altered states of the intraphysical consciousness – occur in multiple gradations during the reduction of the individual's vitality, in at least some of the following 8 conditions:

1. Natural sleep (sleeper).
2. Sleep produced by anesthetics (patient).
3. Hypnotic, somnambulistic phase *(sujet).*
4. Lipothymia (fainting, becoming weak, everything goes dark, loss of the senses).
5. State of coma (comatose).
6. Crisis of convalescence (convalescent).
7. Nervous fatigue (overwork, pathological stress).
8. Demoralization (depression).

Explanation. Currently, the most plausible explanation for the phenomenon of human bilocation is to interpret it as being an occurrence in which the vehicles of manifestation of the bilocator-projector are simultaneously both partially objective and partially immaterial.

Stage. This means that physical bilocation constitutes an advanced stage of ordinary human lucid projection.

Hagiography. Hagiographists, including Augustine of Tagaste, Africa, who wrote *The City of God,* refer to bilocators and their bilocations in their writings.

Historians. The Latin historians Cornelius Tacitus (55-120), author of the *Annals;* and Gaius Suetonius Tranquillus (70-122), responsible for the work *Lives of the Caesars,* also spoke about aspects of projectiology phenomena.

Projector-bilocators. Occurrences with various projector-bilocators (as well as some *trilocators*) have been registered in the world's chronicles, most notably the following 20:

1. Alphonse-Marie de Liguori (1696-1787).
2. Angelo de Acri (epoch: 1739).
3. Antonio de Pádua (1195-1231).
4. Apollonius of Tyana (98 A.D.).
5. Caterina dei Ricci (1522-1590).
6. Clement I (first century).
7. Dadaji.
8. Emília Sagée (1845).
9. Eurípedes Barsanulfo (1880-1918), Sacramento, MG, Brazil, Spiritist.
10. Francesco Forgione, or Pio de Petralcina (1887-1968).
11. Francisco Xavier (1571).
12. Giuseppe Desa, of Cupertino (1603-1663).
13. José de Anchieta (1534-1597), São Paulo, Brazil, Catholic.
14. Liduvina de Flandres (1400).
15. Maria de Agreda (1602-1665).
16. Martin de Porres (1579-1639).
17. Natuzza Evolo, Paravati, Calabrian, Italian, Catholic.
18. Sathya Sai Baba, India.
19. Severo de Ravena.
20. Teresa Higginson (1844).

Induction. Thus far, the phenomenon of physical bilocation cannot be artificially induced with relative ease, as is being done with ordinary human lucid projection.

Mega-strong-traits. The person who is predisposed toward or is a natural candidate for the production of physical bilocation – particularly when enjoying a positive peak in the scale of his/her biological clock or parapsychophysiological biorhythm – is the intraphysical consciousness who presents 1 or all of the following 3 mega-strong-traits:

1. **Imagination.** Ample powers of imagination.
2. **Attention.** A certain capacity for maintaining divided attention, or doing something while thinking about something else (cerebral versatility, intellectual polyvalence).
3. **Holochakra.** An advanced capacity for voluntarily exteriorizing consciential energy.

Television. The following is 1 practical example of the abovementioned division of attention: watching and intelligently following 3 different television channels or programs at the same time – either by using the remote control or 3 operating television sets – demonstrates an expressive level of division of attention which is sufficient to predispose the consciousness of the television viewer to produce the phenomenon of physical bilocation.

Assisted. It should be kept in mind that just as assisted lucid projection exists, so does assisted physical bilocation exist or, in other words, that which is sponsored by helpers, and which perhaps predominates among all the categories of these phenomena.

Recall. In most instances, the phenomenon of physical bilocation only became known to the bilocator after the occurrence, subsequent to his/her presence being confirmed by percipients in another location distant from his/her physical base. This shows the absence of recall of the extraphysical events by the bilocators in general, as happens with almost all of humanity, every night upon sleeping.

Desoma. As previously mentioned, many cases of physical bilocation occur moments before death, from the death bed (desoma).

Triangulation. Only very rarely does physical bilocation permit one to *connect extremes,* integrate the processed information, polarize the reports and triangulate converging testimonies or, in other words, obtain confirmatory evidence between at least the following 3 individuals, or those persons who play different roles in the occurrences:

1. **Witness.** The observer-witness who sees the inactive human body of the bilocator in the physical base.
2. **Percipient.** The occasional percipient who simultaneously witnesses the tangibility of the same bilocator's psychosoma at another location.
3. **Bilocator.** The bilocator per se, who gives a detailed report of the event when in the ordinary, physical waking state, immediately after the occurrence.

Evolution. The facts show that repeated human parateleportation constitutes the most evolved stage of physical bilocation. There thus occurs a clear ascending progression in the development of the 3 interrelated phenomena, in the following 3 distinct steps:

1. **LP.** First, human lucid projection (LP).
2. **Bilocation.** Second, physical bilocation.
3. **Parateleportation.** Third, human parateleportation.

Complex. This gradation speaks in favor of the existence of the phenomenological complex of projectiology and the theory of irruption of the psychosoma in the soma.

Evidence. Among the experimental evidence that has been presented at different points in time, in order to directly demonstrate the reality of the phenomenon of physical bilocation, the following 4 can be singled out as the most relevant:

1. **Psychosoma.** Photographs of the materialized psychosoma of the projected intraphysical consciousness, together with his/her human body. These are called *photos of doubles.* This is currently an extremely controversial fact, with the improvement of the art and science of photography.
2. **Emanations.** Photographs of nebulous, dense, colored emanations, at the deathbed.
3. **Exteriorization.** Hypnotically-induced projection of the consciousness, wherein the projector's human body is wrapped in a paper covered with a fluorescent substance. This provokes fluorescence upon the exit of the psychosoma, or the phenomenon of the exteriorization of sensitivity.
4. **Telekinesis.** Physical effects provoked by the consciousness while projected in the psychosoma and witnessed by intraphysical beings in the waking state, or projective telekinesis with a projective origin.

Extraphysical. Physical bilocation should not be confused with extraphysical bilocation, or double projection.

Evolo. Among the most well known currently living bilocator-projectors, the Italian, Calabrian, illiterate, mystical Catholic woman, Natuzza Evolo can be singled out. She was born in 1924 in the city of Paravati, where she was still residing (1990) with her husband and 5 children.

Talents. Among her most noteworthy animic-parapsychic talents, the capacities of seeing extraphysical consciousnesses and diagnosing illnesses can also be included.

Stigmatization. She is a stigmatic. Her wounds, in the form of a cross, have occasionally appeared on her wrists and feet, since the age of 10. Her stigma also include the bizarre phenomena of *hemography.*

Testimonies. The projective powers of Natuzza Evolo have been researched since 1974 by Prof. Valerio Marinelli, an engineer at the University of Calabria, who has collected and documented 52 different cases of lucid projection and physical bilocation produced by Natuzza, with the testimonies of still-living persons. A portion of the investigations was published in 1979, in a restricted circulation edition of the publication *A Study of the Bilocational Phenomenon of Natuzza Evolo* (see bibliography below).

Statistics. Natuzza Evolo was clearly seen by human witnesses in 18 cases of physical bilocation. In 8 cases, there were apparitions of extraphysical consciousnesses accompanying the bilocator, in a visually perceivable manner or in an invisible manner. On another 6 occasions, the voice of the bilocator was heard, but her apparition was not seen.

Activities. In 13 cases, during the phenomenon of physical bilocation, this bilocator conducted incontestable physical activities, such as the following 5:

1. **Speech.** Speaking, evidencing her own voice for the witness or percipient.
2. **Watch.** Making a desk clock work.
3. **Door.** Loudly slamming a door.
4. **Vase.** Moving a vase with flowers.
5. **Hair.** Pulling the hair of one witness' head.

Stains. In 9 cases, her bilocational apparitions left bloodstained fingerprints, similar to those of her hemographs, and some with religious designs, in the locations of the physical bilocations.

Indications. These incontrovertible indications of Natuzza Evolo's physical presence at the bilocation scene eliminated the outworn hypothesis of individual or collective *hallucination* to explain the bilocational phenomena.

Proof. Fingerprints made with the person's own blood certainly provide definitive proof of the presence of a bilocated projector.

Known. In this case, the occurrence becomes even more expressive, because Ms. Evolo is sometimes accompanied by an extraphysical consciousness who the witness had known for a long time, when still an intraphysical consciousness, sometimes being identified as the witness' own father, another relative or another personality.

Information. This bilocator has the habit of giving information about her bilocational visit *before* being informed about the experience by the witness (chronology).

Will. According to Natuzza Evolo's registered declarations, her bilocations have never occurred through her own will.

Extraphysical consciousnesses. According to her testimony, one or more extraphysical consciousnesses present themselves and accompany her to where her presence is needed. There, she has full awareness of the location visited and of the existence, at that moment, of her inactive human body that has been left in her house in Paravati. She remains only some seconds or a few minutes, returning to the physical base, while always maintaining consciential lucidity regarding the main events of the phenomena.

Details. Natuzza Evolo explains that her bilocations can occur at night, when sleeping, as well as when she is awake. In this situation, she suddenly feels herself to be in a new environment, as though she had been *teleported* there and then immediately becomes aware that she has been bilocated.

Instantaneity. The translocation is instantaneous, regardless of the distance.

Incidence. According to Ms. Evolo, the bilocations can occur many times a day and she can visit various locations and different persons in succession.

Assistential. It should be pointed out that these physical bilocations that are assisted by helpers and are assistential, in favor of others, and even have mystical connotations, serve to demonstrate that mysticism, asceticism, the life of a hermit and a celibate life are totally dispensable for the development of animism and parapsychism, since this bilocator is married, a housewife and the mother of 5 children. The same occurs in countless cases of penta (daily, personal energetic task) practitioners.

Trilocation. Natuzza's extraphysical companion or helper often tells her where she is bilocated. At other times, she has the impression of being in 3 places at the same time or, in other words: the phenomenon of *physical trilocation* occurs, which has also been reported by other projectors. It seems to be produced by the action of the vehicles of manifestation of the intraphysical consciousness due to the instantaneity of the occurrences.

Consciousness. In these cases, the seat of the consciousness is singular, however the facts occur with extreme rapidity, giving the impression of being in 3 or more places at the same time. The seat of the consciousness separates, but in a lightning fast manner. The mentalsoma, for example, generally acts independently from chronological time, as we conventionally understand it in this intraphysical dimension, in the ordinary, physical waking state.

Uselessness. The phenomenon of physical bilocation alone annuls and makes hundreds of materialistic themes and disciplines at universities throughout the planet ineffective by proving their uselessness and the waste of time they represent.

Specific Bibliography:

1. **MARINELLI, Valerio;** *Natuzza di Paravati: Serva del Signore;* Volume Primo; XVIII + 334 pp.; 13 chaps.; illus.; 24 x 17 cm; pb.; 3rd ed.; Vibo Valentia; Italy; Edizioni Mapograf; 1986; pp. 19-24, 187-225.

2. **MARINELLI, Valerio;** *Natuzza di Paravati: Umile Serva del Signore;* Volume Secondo; XVI + 456 pp.; 12 chaps.; illus.; 24 x 17 cm; Vibo Valentia; Italy; Edizioni Mapograf; 1985; pp. 177-264, 451-456.

59.	COMPARISONS BETWEEN LUCID PROJECTION AND PHYSICAL BILOCATION

Comparisons. Despite the fact that both lucid projection and physical bilocation are phenomena involving exteriorization of the human consciousness, that temporarily leaves its *coarse* seat in the brain – the facts still suggesting that the second phenomenon is the continuation, or more evolved stage, of the first – it is worthwhile pointing out 7 superficially established aspects in a differential comparison between the two:

1. **Takeoff.** In lucid projection, the consciousness generally clearly perceives the sensations of the takeoff of the psychosoma. In physical bilocation, the consciousness generally does not experience the act of leaving the human body.

2. **Psychosoma.** In lucid projection, the consciousness can, in certain cases, leave the human body and not feel itself to be *inside* any vehicle of the consciousness, when manifesting in the mentalsoma. In physical bilocation, the consciousness always has the sensation of having 1 body, in this case the psychosoma, which is clearly similar to the human body.

3. **Translocation.** In lucid projection, the consciousness generally has the unquestionable sensation of leaving the human body and only then leaves the physical base. In physical bilocation, the consciousness generally only perceives that it has already translocated to its destination in some instantaneous manner.

4. **Telekinesis.** In lucid projection, the consciousness generally does not interact well with the new environment or communicate well with the human beings that it encounters. In physical bilocation, the consciousness interacts with the new environment and executes physical acts or, in other words: produces telekinesis phenomena, communicates with occasional human witnesses and, less frequently, can even bring back some evidence of having been in the other intraphysical environment.

5. **Duration.** Lucid projection generally tends to be of brief duration. It would seem that physical bilocation tends to last a little longer. This comparison still requires more research in order to arrive at a more reliable conclusion.

6. **Witnesses.** In instances of lucid projection, the percipient of *inter vivos* apparitions of the projector generally seems to see a partially immaterial figure before him/her. In instances of physical bilocation, the percipient of the *inter vivos* apparition of the bilocator generally has the impression of actually interacting and communicating with a real, living person like any other.

7. **Complexity.** The projector can commonly produce the phenomenon of lucid projection at will. The bilocator is not always able to produce physical bilocation, or a visible, tangible *inter vivos* apparition at will. This demonstrates that the phenomenon is doubtlessly more complex compared to the phenomenon of simple lucid projection.

Double. Perhaps 1 of the rarest phenomena of projectiology is *bi-bilocation,* double bilocation, wherein 2 bilocators are projected with lucidity at the same time, in unmistakable conditions of tangibility. Up until now, only a very few incidents of this type have been reported.

Vampirism. Many cases of ill bilocators, or even inexperienced projectors, can be classified as being authentic instances of vampirism. Well known facts exist through the folkloric reports of the citizens of many countries.

Zoanthropic. There are also cases of self-transfigurations of the psychosoma, resulting from physical, zoanthropic bilocations, or certain phenomena of zoanthropy, in which the bilocator presents him/herself in the psychosoma that is changed into the form of the subhuman animal regarding which he/she continues to be influenced by suggestion. This fact doubtlessly constitutes a manifestation restricted to the parapsychopathology of the psychosoma.

Bibliography: ADGMT (03, p. 47), Aksakof (09, p. 543), Aliança (13, p. 149), Ambelain (23, p. 29), Ancilli (24, p. 264), Andrade (27, p. 150), Andreas (36, p. 39), Armond (53, p. 75), Azevedo (64, p. 44), Baker (69, p. 24), Bardens (79, p. 137), Bastos (89, p. 74), Battersby (92, p. 22), Bénezech (115, p. 25), Berthe (126, p. 359), Bertrand (127, p. 47), Black (137, p. 23), Blackmore (139, p. 12), Bonin (168, p. 81), Boswell (174, p. 134), Bozzano (188, p. 1), Campbell (237, p. 76), Carton (252, p. 317), Castro (263, p. 104), Cavendish (266, p. 54), Cerchio (270, p. 35), Champlin (272, p. 192), Chaplin (273, p. 25), Chevreuil (278, p. 208), Crookall (343, p. 63), Crouzet (344, p. 202), D'arbó (365, p. 166), Day (376, p. 21), Delanne (382, p. 147), Denis (387, p. 315), Depascale (392, p. 17), Digest (401, p. 348), Dumas (432, p. 212), Ebon (455, p. 111), Edwards (463, p. 289), Egloffstein (469, p. 1103), Faria (495, p. 78), Fase (499, p. 231), Feesp (503, p. 115), Ferguson (507, p. 28), Flammarion (524, p. 39), Fodor (528, p. 30), Foin (532, p. 14), Fortune (540, p. 50), Freixedo (554, p. 49), Gaynor (577, p. 26), Gomes (612, p. 117), Gómez (613, p. 23), Green (632, p. 37), Greenhouse (636, p. 79), Haemmerlé (668, p. 569), Hemmert (712, p. 25; 713, p. 38), Holzer (751, p. 111), Hunt (767, p. 50), Inglis (789, p. 24), Jaffé (798, p. 143), Kardec (826, p. 372), Knight (851, p. 279), Larcher (887, p. 339), Lee (908, p. 77), Lhermitte (924, p. 197), Lorenzatto (952, p. 142), Martin (1002, p. 44), Martin (1003, p. 27), Mead (1024, p. 107), Mitchell (1058, p. 688), Montandon (1068, p. 17), Morel (1086, p. 41), Morris (1093, p. 147), Muntañola (1108, p. 82), Myers (1114, p. 230), Nobre (1130, p. 113), Novelino (1140, p. 135), Olcott (1147, p. 370), Owen (1177, p. 255), Paronelli (1199, p. 186), Paula (1208, p. 60), Pensamento (1224, p. 97), Pisani (1248, p. 126), Poinsot (1269, p. 148), Poodt (1272, p. 262), Prieur (1289, p. 92), Richet (1398, p. 700), Rizzini (1411, p. 75), Rogo (1447, p. 81; 1458, p. 39), RPA (1481, p. 18), Schutel (1525, p. 30), Sculthorp (1531, p. 135), Seabra (1534, p. 85), Shepard (1548, p. 107), Smith (1574, p. 47), Stead (1598, p. 330), Steiger (1601, p. 97), Stelter (1613, p. 80), Sudre (1630, p. 355), Tambascio (1645, p. 78), Tchou (1668, p. 203), Tiret (1686, p. 130), Tischner (1687, p. 157), Tondriau (1690, p. 201), Thurston (1700, p. 285), Valério (1725, p. 74), Vieira (1743, p. 6), Wang (1794, p. 195), Webb (1804, p. 82), Wedeck (1807, p. 56), Weil (1810, p. 144), Wilson (1854, p. 543), Wolman (1863, p. 609), Yogananda (1894, p. 184), Zaniah (1899, p. 73).

---

60. TRAVELING   CLAIRVOYANCE

Definition. Traveling clairvoyance: simultaneous partial projection of the visual paraperceptions of the consciousness, at a distance from the human body, along with the "live" oral description and report on extraphysical events glimpsed by the projector, including the psychosphere of extraphysical consciousnesses (traveling consciousness) (see fig. 60, p. 1,122).

Synonymy: ambulant clairvoyance; clairvoyance in space; clairvoyant travel; distant traveling clairvoyance; distant vision; fifty-fifty projection; hypnotic mental projection; independent clairvoyance; indirect vision; *inter vivos* clairvoyance; itinerant clairvoyance; itinerant spirit; long-distance clairvoyance; long-distance vision; micro PK; mind travel or MT; mobile clairvoyance; projection without recall II; remote observation; remote perception; remote precognitive perception; remote sensitivity; remote viewing or RV; remote vision; telepathic travel; teleperception; traveling clairvoyance or TC; *traveling consciousness;* traveling metagnosis; traveling telecognosis; traveling telopsis; visual metagnomy.

Categories. Traveling clairvoyance, or tracing executed by the semi-awake consciousness, beyond the barriers of space and the existential dimensions, can be interpreted according to 3 perspectives or classified into 3 basic categories:

1. **Spontaneous.** Spontaneous, normal, common clairvoyance, without trance.
2. **Self-induced.** Self-induced traveling clairvoyance, per se.
3. **Hetero-induced.** Traveling clairvoyance hypnotically induced by another.

Ideoplasty. Aside from these 3 perspectives, clairvoyance can be assisted by a helper, with or without ideoplastic projection.

Perceptions. The perceptions of the traveling clairvoyant can be classified into two basic categories:

1. **Physical.** Traveling clairvoyance in which the sensitive perceives hidden physical objects, remote physical environments or living beings (humans, subhumans) at a distance.
2. **Extraphysical.** Traveling clairvoyance in which the sensitive perceives immaterial forms, environments, extraphysical consciousnesses and extraterrestrials at a distance.

Remote. Remote viewing (scanning) is a mode of traveling clairvoyance wherein the clairvoyant describes a remote location, indicated only by the geographical coordinates of latitude and longitude. The execution of remote viewing demands full attention and deep concentration on the part of the clairvoyant.

Noise. In specific cases of remote viewing, or probing using geographical coordinates, a type of "mental noise" arises, owing to memory and imagination, which interferes in the acquisition of information by the clairvoyant who, probably due to this, has difficulty in detecting names, numbers, letters and other analytical material.

Manifestations. The following are two phenomenological manifestations that are equivalent in terms of psychological or mental reactions and parapsychic or extraconsciential reactions of the intraphysical consciousness:

1. **Dream.** The *lucid dream* constitutes the initial, psychological manifestation of the *lucid projection,* this being a parapsychic phenomenon.
2. **Viewing.** *Remote viewing* is the initial, psychological manifestation of *traveling clairvoyance,* this also being a parapsychic phenomenon.

Magnetism. Some sensitives affirm that common clairvoyance increases when they sit with their back toward the North Terrestrial Pole, when they are in the Northern Hemisphere; and with their back toward the South Terrestrial Pole, when they are in the Southern Hemisphere. Nevertheless, the role that magnetism plays in the majority of the functions of the human body and in parapsychic faculties is still not clear. These affirmations still require further research regarding the facts.

Physiology. The action of the mechanism of speech in traveling clairvoyance is of extreme importance, illustrating the probable function of the silver cord (holochakra) seen during lucid projections, which may also exercise functions in different types of parapsychic phenomena.

Confirmation. In certain cases, traveling clairvoyance can be simultaneously confirmed during the unfolding of the phenomenon, through local or long-distance telephone calls made by the researcher, who places the mouthpiece to the mouth of the projector in trance and he/she directly reports what he/she sees in the location, visited by his/her projected consciousness, to the person who is beside his/her human body and to the other person, who listens to the phone at a distance.

Participation. In traveling clairvoyance hypnotically induced by another, the hypnotist can unconsciously or telepathically influence the descriptions and subjects related by the projector. In this case, the researcher-hypnotist also becomes a participant, besides being the recorder of the facts and a guide for the projector. This should be avoided, taking adequate precautions and employing special safeguards against this participation through the conduct and words used by the hypnotist.

Staccato. While in trance, the traveling clairvoyant often responds to direct questions in a staccato manner – reminiscent of the difficulty involved in obtaining information from ill persons, in certain circumstances – there being long pauses in their descriptions, thus making the use of a telephone somewhat inadequate.

Exoclairvoyance. Celebrated experiments were realized in 1973, in the United States of America, with the sensitives Ingo Swann (1933-) and Harold Sherman, using traveling clairvoyance to explore the planets Jupiter and Mercury, through exoclairvoyance, prior to space probes being sent there.

Agreement. The observations of the clairvoyants generally tallied with the findings made by astronautical instruments.

Bibliography: Ashby (59, p. 156), Baker (69, p. 29), Balanovski (70, p. 19), Balzac (72, p. 66), Blackmore (139, p. 13), Bret (202, p. 193), Coxhead (311, p. 65), Crookall (320, p. 26), Crouzet (344, p. 199), Currie (354, p. 91), Dailey (356, p. 196), D'arbó (365, p. 204), Davies (370, p. 64), Davis (371, p. 15), Dingwall (404, p. 93), Fodor (528, p. 48), Garrett (573, p. 157), Gauld (575, p. 169), Goodman (618, p. 219), Greene (635, p. 94), Greenhouse (636, p. 275), Hill (723, p. 17), Hitching (727, p. 82), Holroyd (736, p. 106), Knight (851, p. 428), Lamont (874, p. 96), Mishlove (1055, p. 135), Morris (1092, p. 30), Myers (1114, p. 231), Podmore (1267, p. 66), Pratt (1285, p. 33), Rogo (1444, p. 120), RPA (1481, p. 8), Shirley (1553, p. 37), Sinclair (1564, p. 73), Smith (1567, p. 346), Steiger (1601, p. 131), Steinour (1612, p. 54), Swann (1632, p. 121), Targ (1651, p. 14; 1652, p. 18), Tart (1665, p. 15), Tourinho (1692, p. 13), Turvey (1707, p. 157), Warcollier (1796, p. 187).

61. LUCID PROJECTION AND TRAVELING CLAIRVOYANCE

Complex. Strictly speaking, projection of the consciousness from the human body constitutes a phenomenological complex that – (1) besides the projection in the integral psychosoma, or with the humanoid form completely constituted; (2) in the partial psychosoma, or with an imperfect humanoid form; (3) in the psychosoma with and without the holochakra; and (4) in the mentalsoma – encompasses various lesser phenomena, including the following 5:

1. **Apparition.** The apparition of the projected projector to intraphysical consciousnesses.
2. **Bilocation.** The physical bilocation of the person of the projector
3. **Telekinesis.** The production of projective telekinesis.
4. **Typtology.** The manifestation of the consciousness of the projector by way of the phenomena of typtology.
5. **Poltergeist.** The participation of the consciousness of the projector in instances of poltergeist.

Miniprojections. Aside from the cited phenomena, traveling clairvoyance merits singling out as it can be considered to be a lesser projection, or a set of miniprojections, wherein there is a predominance of manifestations of the extraphysical visual perceptions of the consciousness, which does not leave the human body for extended periods and can continue to communicate through speech, in a type of self-psychophony.

Alternations. All experiences of lucid projection can be mixed together with different successive or alternate states of consciousness. In this way, for example, the projector can experience the phenomenon of traveling clairvoyance and, soon thereafter, produce the integral projection of the consciousness in the psychosoma, and vice versa.

Nuances. The following 3 distinct phenomena are aspects or nuances of the same phenomenon of lucid projection of short duration, whether spontaneous or provoked at will, or even through hypnotic induction:

1. Traveling clairvoyance.
2. Remote viewing.
3. Mind traveling.

Results. Traveling clairvoyance receives more attention from observers as it produces immediate, practical results. This is generally because the consciousness, in these cases, performs extraphysical actions in the crustal, paratropospheric dimension that relate to the human or diuturnal physical life of the participants.

Daydream. Remote viewing can be interpreted as a daydream with some flashes of awareness or clairvoyance at a distance. This can serve as a visualization technique which is useful for inducing a major lucid projection in the psychosoma.

Repetition. Self-discernment between one state and another can only be achieved with patient, exhaustive repetition of the experiences by the projector.

Mentalsoma. Certain occurrences of traveling clairvoyance seem to suggest that the majority of these facts are often partial projections of only the mentalsoma of the projector.

Reincorporation. In certain instances of traveling clairvoyance, the consciousness of the projector can transform its extraphysical manifestation, through the force of the will, into a full projection. This is followed by the instantaneous extraphysical reincorporation of the psychosoma, which projects, without needing to return to the human body to effect this maneuver.

Humanoid. One hypothesis suggests that the extraphysical reincorporation of the psychosoma must be due to the resources of the golden cord, which are still very unclear to us. The phenomenon is an impressive one, as though the projected consciousness, feeling itself to be without any body whatsoever, suddenly gained a complete humanoid body, in order for it to manifest in perfect consonance with the extraphysical environment.

Bibliography: Fodor (529, p. 173), Rogo (1444, p. 122), Steiger (1601, p. 131), Turvey (1707, p. 159).

---

62. COMPARISONS BETWEEN TRAVELING CLAIRVOYANCE AND LUCID PROJECTION

Differential. By using the system of comparison and contrast, the following are 9 differential factors that allow a distinction between traveling clairvoyance and the full projection of the consciousness from the human body in the psychosoma:

1. **Takeoff.** In traveling clairvoyance, the consciousness does not experience the takeoff of the entire psychosoma. In projection with continuous self-awareness, the process of lucid takeoff is impressive and unique.

2. **Speech.** In traveling clairvoyance, the consciousness of the individual in trance can see at a distance and simultaneously report what is being seen, speaking through the vocal mechanism of the human body. In full, lucid projection, the consciousness remains absent from the inactive human body, with only vegetative life, and is not able to act upon the soma, which remains in the *empty brain* condition, sometimes in a coma-like state.

3. **Permanence.** In traveling clairvoyance, the individual, although seeing at a distance, is fully aware that he/she is still in the human body. In a full projection, the consciousness is completely aware of the fact that it is manifesting in the psychosoma and not in the human body.

4. **Paraperceptions.** In traveling clairvoyance, the consciousness sees, although it does not *touch* the things that it sees. In full projection, the consciousness sees firsthand and achieves the paraperception of touch.

5. **Participation.** In traveling clairvoyance, the consciousness is a simple spectator of events at a distance. In full projection, the consciousness recognizes that it is a protagonist or a participant of extraphysical events.

6. **Translocation.** In traveling clairvoyance, the paraperceptions of the consciousness are always tropospheric or crustal and superficial. In a full projection, the consciousness experiences more vivid sensations, including the unquestionable dislocation through space to the target-place, sometimes to extraphysical districts per se, with *departure-return-new-departure-return* being determined by the consciousness itself.

7. **Cord.** In traveling clairvoyance, the consciousness does not see the energetic formations that surround the human body. In full projection, the consciousness can perform a detailed analysis of its own silver cord.

8. **Bilocation.** In traveling clairvoyance, the consciousness sees scenarios at a distance. In full projection, the consciousness can ostensively manifest in the psychosoma, producing the phenomena of apparition to intraphysical consciousnesses and the physical bilocation of the personality itself.

9. **Preview.** Traveling clairvoyance frequently operates like a previous projection of a well-defined projection of the full consciousness, clearly demonstrating that, through clairvoyance, the consciousness *comes to see* where it will go and then it goes there through projection, leaving the human body behind.

Communication. The greatest evidence that the phenomenon of traveling clairvoyance will inevitably always be inferior or insufficient, compared to lucid, consciential projection, per se, is the fact that the consciousness of the clairvoyant continues to communicate through the speech mechanism of the human body.

Restriction. This demonstrates that, in this manner, the consciousness is not able to completely free itself from the 2 cerebral hemispheres or, more appropriately, from the inferior condition of physical restriction, thus not being able to achieve a higher level of expansion of the consciousness.

Holochakra. Certain clairvoyant sensitives, upon analyzing a traveling clairvoyant in trance, affirm that the greater part of the clairvoyant's human aura goes together with the vehicle of manifestation (psychosoma) of his/her consciousness which projects. This demonstrates that a good portion of the holochakra goes together with the consciousness.

Psychosoma. If the holochakra goes, it is because the psychosoma also goes along with it, because the holochakra alone does not transport the consciousness, which is headquartered in the mentalsoma.

Very rapid. It can be concluded, at this point, that many cases of traveling clairvoyance are nothing more than an intensive series of full – however extremely rapid – lucid projections. In this case, the consciousness projects fully, together with the holochakra, the psychosoma and the mentalsoma, and returns to report what is seen through the speech mechanism of the human body, many times in succession, in an intensive manner.

Bibliography: Crookall (343, p. 41), Fodor (529, p. 173).

63. PROJECTIVE ECTOPLASMY

Definition. Ectoplasmy: the temporary appearance of more or less organized substances with various degrees of solidity, having characteristics of physical objects and/or human forms – lips, faces, eyes, heads, complete configurations, clothing, personal objects – composed of an unknown agent, using the exteriorization of ectoplasm.

Synonymy: ectometaplasy; ectoplasmic concretion; ectoplasty; ectoplasy; entoplasmy; etherialization; experimental materialization; hylopasty; hyloplasmy; *inter vivos* ectoplasmy; *inter vivos* materialization; *laboratorial apparition;* mechanical projection; metamorphogeny; metideogeny; metideoplasy; objective thought-form; phantasmogenesis; psychoplasmy; semoplasmy; stereobioenergetic effects; tangible morphothosene; teleplasmy; teleplasty.

Signals. The following two occurrences clarify each other:

1. **Intraphysical consciousness.** Physical torpidity is the first personal sign of the discoincidence of the vehicles of manifestation of the intraphysical consciousness.

2. **Soma.** Discoincidence is the first sign of the beginning of the process of dematerialization of the human body or soma.

Chronology. Thus, the chronological order of the phenomena of discoincidence of the vehicles of manifestation of the intraphysical consciousness and the process of dematerialization of the soma, can be understood through 5 steps:

1. **Torpidity.** Physical torpidity: the first sign or loss of organic sensations.
2. **Discoincidence.** Discoincidence of the vehicles of manifestation of the intraphysical consciousness (rudimentary consciential projection).
3. **Dematerialization.** Dematerialization of part or segments of the soma.
4. **Rematerialization.** Rematerialization of the parts of the soma which were dematerialized.
5. **Sensitivity.** Organic sensitivity: the final sign or the regaining of organic senses.

Complex. Strictly speaking, ectoplasmy seems to comprise a phenomenological complex that is structured by way of 3 other very characteristic phenomena, which arise in the following chronological order:

1. First, the dematerialization of the sensitive (and intraphysical assistants).
2. Second, the materialization of temporary forms.
3. Third, the rematerialization of the ectoplasmic sensitive and assistants who, even so, still almost always end up losing some amount of body weight.

Interdependence. The facts suggest that any materialization results from a partial or total dematerialization, as though one phenomenon always depended upon another in order to occur.

Agent. Ectoplasm is always the psychophysical agent of ectoplasmy.

Physics. The materialization, dematerialization and rematerialization of atomic elements are already known to professionals of nuclear physics in the familiar environment of their laboratories, but this has still not been happening in the daily reality of ordinary human existence.

Similarities. Ectoplasmy, which is, in theory, the greatest parapsychic phenomenon (macro-PK), presents some similarities to lucid projection, which is, in theory, the greatest intraconsciential phenomenon of the intraphysical consciousness (animism). This is because it generally seems to be a projection of vital, mechanical, luminous energy.

Coexistence. Nevertheless, ectoplasmy and lucid projection always coexist.

Laboratorial. In certain cases, it is supposed that ectoplasmy represents nothing more than the exact, tangible projection of the vehicles of manifestation of the consciousness of the ectoplasmic sensitive. This constitutes the experimental, laboratorial apparition to intraphysicals of part or all of the human body, of the holochakra (including the silver cord) and even the psychosoma. In these cases, the sensitive's double serves as a mold for the creation of other materialized forms (phantasmogenesis). In this situation there is an irruption of the psychosoma through the soma.

Decomposition. Ectoplasm is a plastic, physical and extraphysical essence, that easily decomposes and appears in unstable forms as tenuous vapors, sticks, spirals, wires, cords, webs, rigid or semi-rigid rays, sometimes moving sinuously like reptiles and other times as though it were a living, intelligent being, vibrating, stretching or shrinking.

Condensation. This essence, ectoplasm, can constitute the condensation of the form of an entire or partial human body, in a phenomenon of partial materialization, sometimes with the anatomical decentralization and even the partial or total dematerialization of the human body of the ectoplasmic sensitive.

Conditions. The following are 3 basically different conditions:

1. The state of materialization of the intraphysical consciousness' own life.
2. The phenomenon of dematerialization of the human body.
3. The phenomenon of rematerialization.

Projection. All generally partial dematerialization with rematerialization of the human body, is also, in some way, a projection of the intraphysical consciousness.

Multidimensionality. If dematerialization occurs, matter goes or is generally temporarily projected to another dimension.

Takeoff. Dematerialization is the phenomenon correspondent to the takeoff of the psychosoma or the departure of the consciousness from the state of coincidence of the consciential vehicles.

Interiorization. Rematerialization, which is generally abrupt, is the phenomenon corresponding to the sudden interiorization of the projected consciousness.

Angles. Evidently, 3 consciential states represent the same condition, approached from different angles:

1. **Waking.** The ordinary, physical waking state of the consciousness manifesting in the human body.

2. **Holosoma.** The state of coincidence of the vehicles of consciential manifestation (holosomatic state).

3. **Existence.** The ordinary state of physical materialization of human existence.

Assisted. Among the phenomena of dematerialization, materialization and rematerialization registered in parapsychic and conscientiological case studies since the nineteenth century, it is inferred that dematerialization is one of the most advanced and complete projections of the intraphysical consciousness, assisted by the helpers – of the ectoplasmic sensitive, in this case – that can be produced on earth.

Reaggregation. This is because, in certain instances, the complete disappearance, without a trace, or disaggregation of the organic matter of the human body of the sensitive (who is confined in a booth and securely tied) and even the inorganic matter of the clothing, accessories and surrounding objects, can be complete for the duration of the phenomenon of materialization or ectoplasmy. This lasts until the immediate recomposition, reaggregation or rematerialization, with subsequent disappearance of the form or forms that had previously been temporarily materialized.

Multiple. The instances of physical multilocation, or the bilocation of more than one double of the projector – various projections of morphothosenes (thought-forms) of humanoid configuration at the same time – indicate that, in certain cases, different extraphysical consciousnesses can simultaneously become tangible during ectoplasmy sessions (in this case: triplasia, pentaplasia), each one using a projected double or facsimile of the ectoplasmic sensitive.

Phenomena. In order to avoid misunderstandings, it should be stressed that, within the framework of projectiology, two categories of well-defined phenomena occur relative to human materializations, in terms of their natures: animic materialization and parapsychic materialization.

1. **Animic** or intraconsciential materialization, only of the intraphysical consciousness. Psychophysical materialization of the living person *without a sensitive,* or the phenomenon of physical bilocation. The materialization of the bilocator's psychosoma occurs in this case. This is a fact that rarely occurs.

2. **Parapsychic** materialization or that of the intraphysical consciousness with some extraphysical consciousness. Psychophysical materialization of the living person *with a sensitive* or, in other words, the physical manifestation of the communicant-projector, who is projected and tangible due to ectoplasm coming from other sources: the ectoplasmic sensitive, the assistants who operate as secondary sensitives, besides other diverse ectoplasmic resources. This is a fact that occurs even more rarely.

Projected. It should be kept in mind that the even more authentic phenomenon of projective ectoplasmy of the projected intraphysical consciousness occurs when the ectoplasmatic-sensitive-projector – while projected – provides energy, or ectoplasm, directly to another intraphysical consciousness (also projected) or an extraphysical consciousness in order for it to materialize (or semi-materialize) itself and be seen by other intraphysical beings (intraphysical consciousnesses and subhuman animals) which are breathing in the ordinary, physical waking state.

Lucidity. In a good number of instances, the projected projector that exteriorizes energy, in the above-mentioned cases, does not lose extraphysical lucidity.

Energy. The energy furnished by the projected projector generally couples – potentiates or is potentiated – with the energy, or ectoplasm, of the intraphysical consciousness or intraphysical consciousnesses who witnesses the materialization of the being, which is the object of the phenomenon.

Hypotheses. The author puts forward the following 3 work hypotheses, which are extremely pertinent with regard to projective ectoplasmy:

1. **Unconsciousness.** Can the intraphysical consciousness of the bilocator unconsciously use his/her own ectoplasm without the direct cooperation of extraphysical consciousnesses?

2. **Inclusions.** In the phenomenon of physical, tangible bilocation, might there also be an imperceptible – or more precisely, unconscious – inclusion of the ectoplasmic elements of other intraphysical beings besides the bilocator's own human body?

3. **Origin.** Finally, where does the ectoplasm with which the bilocator materialized come from?

Bibliography: ADGMT (03, p. 190), Ambelain (23, p. 58), Andrade (27, p. 160), Bardon (80, p. 325), Boddington (158, p. 35), Bonin (168, p. 153), Bosc (172, p. 309), Chaplin (273, p. 100), Crouzet (344, p. 398), Day (376, p. 82), Delanne (382, p. 452), Depascale (392, p. 31), Digest (401, p. 366), Doyle (411, p. 294), Espérance (485, p. 355), Fodor (528, p. 216), Freixedo (554, p. 119), Gaynor (577, p. 109), Goes (605, p. 151), Gómez (613, p. 59), Granger (620, p. 149), Granja (621, p. 331), Holzer (743, p. 195), Leaf (904, p. 87), Marinuzzi (998, p. 173), Martin (1002, p. 30), Martin (1003, p. 77), Meek (1030, p. 93), Montandon (1068, p. 25), Morel (1086, p. 171), Myers (1114, p. 544), Paula (1208, p. 42), Riland (1403, p. 181), RPA (1481, p. 173), Shepard (1548, p. 567), Tishner (1687, p. 136), Toben (1688, p. 69), Vett (1738, p. 390), Vieira (1762, p. 107), Zaniah (1899, p. 299).

64. SEMIMATERIALIZATION

Definition. Semimaterialization: miniscule, brief materialization produced with the participation of the lucid, spectating intraphysical projector.

Synonymy: clairvoyant-materialization; collateral materialization; economical materialization; intramaterialization; vision-materialization.

Connection. Lucid projection permits the confluence of diverse phenomena, such as the connection of the clairvoyance of an intraphysical consciousness, operating as a clairvoyant-ectoplasmic *semi-sensitive*, with a *semi-materialized* extraphysical consciousness, through the process that encompasses 8 points:

1. **Partial.** On the physical side, the partial projection of the consciousness allows the projector the possibility of having a miniscule clairvoyance and simultaneously provides exteriorized energy, which is compound in this case, until it forms or condenses ectoplasm *(minimaterialization)*.

2. **Miniscule.** On the extraphysical side, the helpers manipulate the ectoplasm, producing a perfect, lifelike, brief, miniscule materialization that only demands an indispensable minimum of energy or, in other words, a very small amount of exteriorized ectoplasm.

3. **Encounter.** The clairvoyance of the projected projector with full awareness, and remaining contiguous to the human body, converges and encounters the semimaterialization – in this case, a familiar extraphysical consciousness – with which the projector maintains a profound empathy, or *rapport*, in order to facilitate the execution of the process.

4. **Sphere.** The phenomena always develop inside the extraphysical sphere of energy that surrounds the human body of the intraphysical consciousness (extraphysical psychosphere or holothosene), with a profound interdependence between the 2 main responsible parties, the projector and the extraphysical consciousness.

5. **Interaction.** An effective interaction occurs between two different dimensions – the physical and extraphysical paratropospheric or crustal dimension – at a *halfway point,* or in the three-and-a-half dimension (an energetic floodgate), the *energetic dimension,* each one contributing a minimum of its possibilities and efforts, for the maximum, common objective.

6. **Conjugation.** The results of these 2 conjugated efforts, which occur simultaneously and in the same space-time continuum, are the individual materialization of an extraphysical consciousness as well as the individual, conscious vision of the intraphysical projector. This vision is extraordinarily lifelike, clear, detailed and a transmitter of ideas, or better still, enables consciential conversation that is unquestionable for the projector.

7. **Practice.** This fact permits the practice of the improvement of energetic or ectoplasmic manipulation on the part of the extraphysical consciousnesses involved in the process.

8. **Economical.** This materialized-vision, or clairvoyant-materialization, represents a genuine animic-parapsychic, or parapsychic-animic, manifestation which is extremely economical because it utilizes only one intraphysical consciousness, does not expend excessive energy, time or effort in either dimension and does not interfere in the interdimensional activities in progress, such as extraphysical assistential tasks.

Personal. These observations are the result of repeated personal experiments performed by the author (parapsychic researcher-participant), registered over time in special laboratories. In Rio de Janeiro, RJ, Brazil alone, approximately 300 experiments with consciential energies were performed over a 6-year period in the 1980s.

Bibliography: Vieira (1762, p. 44).

---

65. STATE OF SUSPENDED ANIMATION

Definition. Suspended animation: the state in which the intraphysical consciousness has temporarily suspended the essential vital functions of its cellular body, subsequently returning to its normal physiological conditions, in certain cases without provoking any damage to its health, the cells having survived in a metabolism of human hibernation.

Synonymy: ambiosis; animated suspension; apparent death; biopausy; biostasis; burial of a living person; cataplexy; consensual burial; hypobiosis; induced human hibernation; intentional burial; intentional inhumation; non-fatal sleep; prolonged burial; prolonged sleep; semimortal state; state of suspended life; stenobiosis; suspended death; thanatoidia; *vaju-stambha;* voluntary catalepsy; voluntary cataleptic state; voluntary inhumation.

Hibernation. The condition of animal hibernation (Latin: *hiber,* winter), or prolonged hibernal sleep, is a semi-state between natural sleep and biological death. In other words, it is the most extreme form of non-fatal sleep, which occurs with various animals, called hibernators, such as: insectivores; hirundinidae; squirrel; hamster or cricetidae; marmotae; bat; some birds and other subhuman animals.

Regulation. Hibernal animals continue regulating their temperatures; they readjust their thermostats to lower levels. The temperature is frequently lowered to the level of the ambient air, if it is above thirty-two degrees Fahrenheit (zero degrees Celsius). The pulse slows. Even aging apparently stops. The following is an example: the American squirrel, in its social interrelationships, has a pulse of between 200 and 400 beats per minute; when hibernating, this falls to between 7 and 10 beats per minute.

Animals. The state of suspended animation, or this condition of prolonged hibernation, even including apparently cadaveric rigidity, being coma-like in some cases, is a common physiological occurrence with the above-mentioned hibernating – so-called *subhuman* – animals living in regions that freeze for a number of months during winter.

Exception. This is why it is perfectly natural that the human being – the so-called *superior animal* – can also, exceptionally, as exception-behavior, realize that which those inferior animals perform normally, as pattern-behavior.

Trigger. It is for this reason that scientific searches were initiated, in the twentieth century, seeking out the trigger (detonator, triggering factor) that induces hibernation, or the elixir of suspended animation.

The objective was its rational application in human beings, in the sense of taking them to states of extreme *metabolic depression,* which will greatly favor the following 7 intraphysical procedures, among others:

1. Combating of the aging process (senescence, senility, old age, gerontology).
2. Interplanetary flights by astronauts. (*Omni;* New York, NY; magazine; monthly; illus.; vol. 6; no. 6; March, 1984; p. 70).
3. Personal weight control.
4. Surgery in general.
5. Surgical anesthesia.
6. The treatment of insomnia, viral infections, neoplasias and even radiation sickness.
7. The use of anorexics.

Lungfish. The Australian lungfish may be the oldest life form on the face of the earth. When the waters recede, it buries itself in the mud, leaving only a small air hole. It remains there, hibernating, without the ingestion of any food or water for *up to 5 years* until the waters return. It then emerges, unharmed, and resumes intraphysical life.

Ancurina. Upon studying the incredible ability of these fish to live on the threshold of life, without apparently aging or requiring nutrition, researchers see that the same state is possible in human beings. The key substance for this is a protein in the brain, a peptide that carries chemical information, called *ancurina.*

Training. In the East, and even today in the West, yogis and fakirs are frequently trained to control the autonomic nervous system, the part of the human nervous system which is normally not under willful control, and which regulates the activities of the heart, body temperature, blood pressure, pupilary dilation and respiration.

Silence. Electrocardiograms and electroencephalograms have already been taken of yogis when in conditions analogous to inhumation. These experiments evidenced the intense physiological action provoked by the yogic technique, proving that the person can achieve a profound circulatory reduction at will, as well as the electrical silence where the provisory suspension of the organic functions occurs. They can thereby achieve a considerable reduction, or an electroencephalogram that is practically null, plane, or *isoelectric,* showing an absence of any electrical activity – the condition of a cadaver.

Projection. The state of suspended animation can, exceptionally, enable lucid projection with a relative recall of extraphysical events. This is because the consciousness of the individual remains awake in certain cases, continually showing the potential and enormous resistance that the human body, the human mind or the determination of the disciplined will are capable of, within a balanced intentionality.

Categories. The state of suspended animation of the human being can be classified into 9 distinct, basic categories: voluntary burial; premature burial and the timely saving of the victim; mystical resurrection; reanimation of drowning victims; surgery performed with hypothermia and medical reheating; the modeling of hypobiosis; zombification with the consequent reanimation of voodoo; poisoning; and deep parapsychic trance.

1. **Burial.** Voluntary burial is the act whereby the fakir, the yogi, the fasting individual, the meditator, the monk, while controlling the autonomic nervous system, allows him/herself to be buried directly in the soil, or in a tomb, enclosed in a sack, small container or locked box with an air cubage that is totally insufficient to assure their survival. They are isolated from all sources of vitality for a period of time, being under the direct control of observers.

Technique. The following is the basic yoga technique for *voluntary inhumation* or suspended animation, in this case, voluntary burial, which was used a great deal in India, Iran and other places:

1. The yogi sits on a soft bed made of furs and combed cotton in a quasi-subterranean cubicle.
2. The yogi turns his face to the East.
3. He crosses his legs in the lotus position.

4. He fixes his gaze on the base of his nose.

5. He *inverts his tongue, having reversed the lingual frenum,* to the back of the throat, in the pharynx, closing the opening of the glottis.

6. He closes the eyelids.

7. He benumbs the members and enters into a deep trance.

Disciples. Next, the yogi's disciples rub his lips, close his eyes and ears with pieces of linen, covered in wax, in order to protect him from insects, the effects of the atmosphere on the organic tissues, as well as to protect him against the germs of decomposition.

Shroud. Finally, wrapping him in a linen shroud, they tie the 4 ends over his head.

Inhumation. The observers and local authorities who are present imprint a seal on the knot of the shroud. The body of the yogi is buried, alive, in a small wooden casket – a human hibernaculum – hermetically sealed and signed with a seal and signatures.

Cubicle. The yogi, buried in the walled grave, a 3-foot (1-meter) deep cubicle, with a door that is closed, sealed and completely walled in with clay.

Soil. In certain cases, the tomb is covered with a large quantity of carefully compressed soil.

Barley. Barley is planted in the ground and a guard of 4 sentinels remains on duty. They relieve each other every two hours and secure the area day and night, preventing strangers from entering.

Security. According to the yogis, the small reserve of air that remains inside the box where the practitioner is voluntarily buried serves as a safety measure, designed to allow him to take only a few breaths in order to return to the previous state in case an accident forces him out of his yogic trance, or samadhi, thereby placing him in danger.

Self-regulation. The dynamic of the phenomenon of voluntary burial is precisely in the self-regulation of the organism, which is executed by the meditator through deep meditation, creating a state of hibernation, *self-lethargy* and voluntary catalepsy, with the abolition of all intentional and unintentional movement, and the partial suppression of human life, including respiration.

Soma. The human body or soma is thus maintained with its vital processes and functions at an absolutely minimal functional level. The practitioner emerges from this state rested and happy, without any traces of lasting negative or ill physical or psychological effects.

Exhumation. The inhumed practitioner – who lived through this period while subjected to a suppression of oxygen – is reanimated (resurrected) in the *ritual of reviviscence,* sometimes after a period of 6 weeks. This occurs at the "exhumation," or the breaking of the seals, with the added presence of a medical authority.

Statue. The practitioner appears to be a wax statue or a semi-cadaver, a body that is cold and apparently lifeless, but mysteriously preserved from decomposition.

Cranium. According to reports of these occurrences, the only area which is less cold is the cranium.

Theories. The most ingenious and ingenuous theories have been put forward to explain the phenomenon of voluntary burial, including the porousness of the soil that covers the interred practitioner and the use of miracle drugs on his part.

Demonstration. It is common knowledge, however, that all theories should be exhaustively questioned until they are able to be demonstrated. In this case, the demonstration has never occurred.

Duels. Some decades ago, "fakir duels" were performed between different nationalities, in Europe, in order to see who could exhibit greater prowess of voluntary burial for a longer time.

Prohibition. In 1955, the authorities in India prohibited the practice of voluntary burial, due to the high number of fatal victims of this type of fakir practice, persons insufficiently trained to conduct such a transcendent feat through the state of *samadhi,* equivalent to *satori* and the state of cosmic consciousness or cosmoconsciousness.

2. **Premature.** The difference between biological death (desoma) and parapsychic trance is still not entirely understood by the majority of humanity. Intentional burial – a public demonstration of determination and courage – should not be confused with the obscure and lamentable phenomena

of premature, unintentional burial, or the apparent death of persons who are alive but ill and in a rigid, cold, cataleptic state, without a heartbeat (a pathological condition), and who were disinterred, or removed from the coffin, and saved from asphyxia.

Necropsies. Many autopsies or necropsies have been mistakenly performed on living persons. In one case, the physician, who certified someone's death, had to pay for the burial expenses and an indemnification to the saved "living-dead" victim.

Case study. The following are 5 famous cases of persons who were buried alive, but lived past it nonetheless. They are listed along with the year of their premature burial:

1. Marjorie Elphinstone (seventeenth century).
2. Margaret Halvron (1610).
3. Victorine Lefourcade (1810).
4. Max Hoffman (1865).
5. Delphine de St. Paul (1876).

Taphephobia. There is currently no great cause for nurturing taphephobia, or the obsessive fear of being buried alive.

Incidence. Nowadays, so-called *apparent death* and undue burial are only possible in certain exceptional cases.

Vietnam. Upon transportation of the bodies of American soldiers buried in Vietnam to the United States of America, their coffins were opened, as a matter of policy. Dislocations and alterations – such as gnawed fists, bodies overturned in the casket, fractured kneecaps, changed fingers and broken nails – were verified in 4% of the cadavers.

Accidents. However, most of the cadavers that were found in a different position inside the coffin were due to accidents which had occurred during their removal, or in the transport of the body from one place to another.

Contractions. Cadavers can sometimes make violent (posthumous) movements due to muscular contractions.

Rigidity. Cadaveric rigidity *(rigor mortis)* appears 3 to 5 hours after biological death or desoma, lasts from 12 to 24 hours and subsequently disappears.

Narrative. Apparent death is also a real fact of suspended animation, being an event that has been greatly exploited in literature since the nineteenth century. In literary narratives, the person who is being carried gets out of the coffin, surprising all those present, and returns to his/her house on foot, almost always alone.

Bioelectrometer. The *bioelectrometer* is currently used. It is a sensitive instrument used specifically to detect the death of the human body and avoid burial of living persons.

Detectovida. Some time ago, in São Paulo, SP, Brazil, an apparatus called the *detectovida* (life detector) was used in order to avoid the burial of persons who are still breathing.

3. **Resurrection.** Intentional burial and premature burial explain the mechanics of the phenomena of resurrection, or the resuscitation of persons who are apparently dead, as in the cases of Lazarus (John 11:14) and the daughter of Jairus (Luke 8:55), according to reports in the New Testament.

4. **Drowning.** There are registered cases of respiratory arrest and suspended animation in the drowning of persons in water colder than 68 degrees Fahrenheit (20 degrees Celsius or centigrade), in which they survived prolonged immersion – often an entire hour underwater – and subsequent reanimation, without irreversible cerebral lesions or other sequels.

Reflex. The suspended animation of those who drown in cold waters is explained by the *diving reflex* or, in other words, the reflex presented by certain *aquatic mammals* who breathe using lungs, besides humans, e.g.: whales and dolphins, that permits an immediate reduction in heart rate, provoking peripheral arterial vasoconstriction, or a reduction in the caliber of the arteries.

Deviation. When this occurs, in the vessels of the members and in all organs, which are not essential for survival, the blood is deviated from the extremities and the viscera that are not of immediate vital interest, such as the liver, spleen and intestines, in favor of the heart and brain.

Water. The diving reflex in humans – children or adults – is triggered when cold or freezing water suddenly covers the forehead and nose, deviating oxygenated blood from the members to the heart and brain through nervous signals.

Transfusion. This permits the heart to guarantee a weak, but constant, cerebral blood transfusion, while the coldness of the water reduces the vital oxygen requirements of the tissues. This mechanism is especially powerful in children.

Coma. In certain occurrences of this type, the drowning victim is retrieved frozen, with at least 4 negative *vital signs*:

1. **Heart.** The heart not beating.

2. **Respiration.** An absence of respiratory frequency.

3. **Temperature.** The temperature of the human body lower than 77 degrees Fahrenheit (25 degrees Celsius or centigrade).

4. **Pressure.** An abrupt drop in arterial pressure.

Other. Aside from these, 2 other *somatic signs* are visible to the naked eye: gray skin and fixed, dilated pupils.

Respirator. In these conditions, the patient is reheated, placed on artificial respiration equipment (mechanical respirator) and induced into a state of *barbiturate coma,* while given high doses of phenobarbital for a period of days (*Jornal do Brasil;* Rio de Janeiro; daily; year XCIII; N. 292; 27, January, 1984; p. 9; *Newsweek;* New York, NY; magazine; weekly; illus.; vol. CIII; N. 6; February 6, 1984; p. 47).

5. **Hypothermia.** The state of suspended animation and the phenomenon of voluntary burial should not surprise medical scholars, bearing in mind the existence of hypothermic surgery, *cerebral cryosurgery,* or artificial hibernation that were created based on the experience of saving those who drowned in cold waters, frozen lakes and snow avalanches (accidental hypothermia).

Surgery. In fact, the uncommon technique of suspended animation is being used with positive results in children and adults with uncomfortable and difficult surgical problems, the solution of which are impracticable using conventional means, due to: small organs; low body weight; intervention close to the heart, in open-heart surgery; and large volumes of blood.

Submersion. The phenomenon known as *submersion hypothermia* is the most important defense against brain damage. It works in the following manner: the extreme cold of the surrounding water, which is breathed into the lungs, cools the human body, lowering the metabolic levels, thereby reducing the need for oxygen in the brain.

Complements. The above-cited medical precautions – immediate heart massage, gradual increase in body temperature and induced coma state, which are also performed to protect the brain – are indispensable complements when ministering to certain drowning victims.

Reheating. In cases of surgery with induced hypothermia, or prolonged hypothermia, the patient – cooled to between 59 and 66.2 degrees Fahrenheit (15 and 19 degrees Celsius or centigrade), for example – has the blood circulation completely interrupted during the 30 or 45 minutes of the operation, given that the blood is reheated soon afterwards, reinitiating the heartbeat (*O Globo;* Rio de Janeiro; newspaper; daily; year 59; N. 18,240; 13, October, 1983; p. 12).

Stop. The human organism (soma) can conserve its integrity even after the stopping of the blood circulation (deliberately interrupted), and the heartbeats for 65 minutes (*Jornal do Brasil;* Rio de Janeiro; newspaper, daily; year 97; N. 42; May 20, 1987; p. 13).

Physiology. In light of the above considerations, it can be rationally concluded that the state of suspended animation is, above all, integrated with human physiology, or the body's natural defense mechanisms (immunity, immunology).

6. **Hypobiosis.** Russian scientists have created a method that provokes the state of hibernation in humans, called *hypobiosis modeling.*

Resistance. This process decelerates the development of illnesses and increases the organism's resistance. It is used successfully with infarct patients and in cases in which it is impossible to provide rapid, simultaneous assistance to many persons.

Thermo-regulation. This method limits or annuls the organism's thermo-regulation processes, giving it qualities of cold-blooded bodies without disturbing physiological functions.

Injection. In order to achieve the state of hypobiosis, it is necessary to apply an injection – at the specialist's discretion – to the patient.

Metabolism. Scientists have been able to achieve temperatures close to 32 degrees Fahrenheit (0 degrees Celsius), with a 90% reduction in metabolism.

Brain. In certain cases, the patient's heart stops beating; the blood is removed and substituted by a nutritive solution; the electroencephalogram shows no activity (*VEJA;* São Paulo, SP; magazine; weekly; year 21; N. 43; October 26, 1988; 2 illus.; p. 81).

7. **Zombification.** Certain scientists, anthropologists, psychiatrists and ethnobotanists are also not surprised by the state of suspended animation, or the phenomenon of voluntary burial, due to the occurrence of the legendary voodoo phenomenon of zombiism or zombification, in Haiti and in other areas of the Caribbean.

Bocor. On these occasions, the fearful *bocor* – the voodoo priest, a professional warlock, in this case – with the complicity of the individual's relatives, poisons the victim with a potion, a "zombi powder," containing toxins that induce a state of coma, which is similar to the death of the physical body. This powder is composed of 3 ingredients extracted from different sources:

1. **Plants.** Plants which are skin irritants.
2. **Frog.** Frogs or *Bufo marinus* (bufotenine), the *cururu* or *bonga* frog.
3. **Tetrodotoxin.** Inflatable fish (prolonged psychotic state), which contains the neurological poison tetrodotoxin, an anesthetic 160,000 times more potent than cocaine.

Ritual. Less than 8 hours after the burial of the person who has been officially declared *dead* or, in other words, in a state of suspended animation from induced intoxication, or a lethargic state indistinguishable from clinical death, the bocor and his followers perform a voodoo ritual in the cemetery, the *cult of the dead,* or the ceremony of resurrection.

Reanimation. There they dig up the soil, exhume and reanimate the pseudodead with a paste – the "zombi cucumber" – applied to the skin, containing sweet potato and the hallucinogenic plant *datura stramonium.*

Intoxication. The resuscitated, zombi, or "walking dead," being a female or male victim, having lost all control, sense of time, space and memory, not exactly aware of his/her situation, is kept in a state of permanent intoxication and is taken to work as a slave in the rural zones of Haiti.

Human vegetable. Zombis, bodies devoid of character and will, are recognized by their existence as a vegetable, their deeply distracted manner, pale face and blank, dead, almost glassy eyes (Bernardo, Stephanie; "Zombis"; *Science Digest;* New York, NY; magazine; monthly; illus.; vol. 92.; N. 2; February, 1984; p. 87, 88).

Retardation. Many of these unfortunate personalities, upon being resuscitated from zombification, are mentally disturbed and become victims of alcoholism, epilepsy, insanity or mental retardation.

Farce. There are, however, registered cases of some zombified persons who were able to survive and recount the tragic farce of the zombification process, being recognized by dozens of persons upon their reappearance, with relative lucidity, one to two decades after the occurrence, as with the well-known case of Clairvius Narcisse (*Time;* New York, NY; magazine; weekly; illus.; vol. 122; N. 17; October 17, 1983; p. 48); Francina Illeus (1976); Natagette Joseph (1966).

Ex-zombi. The *zombi savane* is the ex-zombi, the person who underwent burial, became a *zombi cadaver* and later returned to the living state.

Narcisse. According to the findings of the controversial ethnobotanist Wade Davis, the human body of Clairvius Narcisse – declared as being truly dead in the Albert Schweitzer Hospital in Deschapelles, in the Artibonite Valley, in Haiti – was placed in a freezer for 20 hours, and only then was removed for burial.

8. **Poisoning.** There are subtropical fish, such as *Diodon hystrix* or *fou-fou,* and the *Sphoeroides testudineus, crapaud de mer,* globefish or puffer, that possess the potent neurotoxin tetrodotoxin in the skin, liver, ovaries and intestines.

Paralysis. Tetrodotoxin induces a state of deep paralysis (state of suspended animation), marked by complete immobility, during which the boundary between human life and physical, biological or brain death is not absolutely defined, even for experienced physicians. The poison generally does not place the intraphysical consciousness in a state of suspended animation; the individual most likely passes through desoma due to respiratory paralysis.

Undefined. This undefined situation can lead to an individual being buried alive (premature burial).

Accidents. As a consequence of the above, accidental poisoning from the ingestion of puffer, and the subsequent states of suspended animation, occur in various places.

Japan. Notably in Japan, 4 species of puffer, all of the genus *Fugu,* are sold as a delicacy (gastronomy) by over 1,800 fishmongers in Tokyo alone.

Customers. There, not only the refined customers, but also many restaurant chefs become victim of their own cooking, or of accidental poisoning from puffer.

Heat. Heat (or, more precisely, the action of frying, grilling, baking or cooking) does not denature the tetrodotoxins.

Suicide. Without a doubt, the act of eating puffer or, in other words, practicing *Russian roulette with fish,* shows an undisguisable suicidal tendency (self-murder or senselessness).

Literature. Tetrodotoxin, inducing a state of suspended animation, has been exploited in literature.

Bond. In his spy novels, the British author Ian Fleming has his spymaster James Bond, succumb to the power of tetrodotoxin in the last scene of *From Russia, With Love,* and has him reappear, having come back to life, only in the second chapter of the next novel, *Doctor No.*

9. **Trance.** The deep trance sensitive can become extremely cold and can appear to be dead while in trance.

Psychosoma. In this case, projection of the consciousness in the psychosoma, laden with the holochakra, occurs and installs the parapsychic state of suspended animation. This can often last for two hours.

Paraphysiology. This parapsychic condition should be interpreted as being paraphysiological rather than pathological.

Astronautics. It is hoped that the state of suspended animation during voluntarily-induced hibernation by the fakir, for example, in the phenomenon of intentional burial, also favors the feasibility of future long-distance, long-term space flights by astronauts.

Projectiological Bibliography: Andreas (36, p. 55), Bayless (96, p. 196; 98, p. 113), Bennett (116, p. 249), Blavatsky (154, p. 476), Brunton (216, p. 265), Cavendish (266, p. 195), Digest (400, p. 113), Eliade (477, p. 66), Gibier (587, p. 145), Gonzales (615, p. 23), Greenhouse (636, p. 109), Krishna (867, p. 124), Lancelin (881, p. 484), Larcher (887, p. 96), Leaf (904, p. 91), Lefebure (910, p. 377), Lind (930, p. 206), London (944, p. 204), Motoyama (1098, p. 235), Muldoon (1105, p. 133), Osborn (1154, p. 118), Planeta (1251, p. 19), Rhine (1387, p. 97), Richards (1394, p. 7), Shadowitz (1543, p. 18), Vieira (1762, p. 62), Walker (1781, p. 68).

Specific Bibliography:

1. **Fleming,** Ian; *Doctor No;* 232 pp.; 20 chaps.; 17.5 x 10.5 cm; pocket; pb.; 4th reprint; New York, NY; Berkley Books; December, 1983; p. 15.

2. **Fleming,** Ian; *From Russia, With Love;* 248 pp.; 28 chaps.; 17.5 x 10.5 cm; pocket; pb.; 6th reprint; New York, NY; Berkley Books; March, 1984; p. 246.

66. EXTERIORIZATION OF MOTRICITY

Definition. Exteriorization of motricity: action of the motor force of the individual, who is projected in a parapsychic manner from the periphery (sensitivity) of the human body or soma, whether under the lucid impulsion of the will, in an unconscious manner, or provoked by another consciousness (extraphysical consciousness).

Synonymy: peripheral energy; repercussion of motricity.

Sketch. The exteriorization of motricity constitutes, to a certain extent, a glimpse of that which is fully produced during the phenomenon of projection of the human consciousness (intraphysical consciousness) in the psychosoma.

Projection. The exteriorization of motricity is a type of projection of the motor force of the vehicles of manifestation commanded by the consciousness. It is directly related to 3 phenomena:

1. The exteriorization of energies.
2. The vibrational state (VS).
3. Projective raps.

Telekinesis. The exteriorization of motricity produced through ectoplasm is one of the existing explanations for the phenomenon of telekinesis.

Instruments. Various instruments have been invented, planned and built in this last century of parapsychic experimentation, in order to measure the intensity of the exteriorizable motor force of the human being. The following 14 are examples:

1. **Biometer,** of Louis Lucas.
2. **Cylinders,** of J. Thoré.
3. **Dynamoscope,** of Collongues.
4. **Fluid motors,** of G. de Tromelin.
5. **Galvanometer,** of Puyfontani.
6. **Magnetometer,** of Fortin.
7. **Magnetoscope,** of Rutter.
8. **Pendulum,** of Briche.
9. **Psychometer,** of Góes, in Brazil.
10. **Sensitivometer,** of Gaston Durville.
11. **Spiricom,** of George W. Meek.
12. **Spiritoscope,** of Robert Hare (1781-1858).
13. **Sthenometer,** of Paul Joire.
14. **Volometer,** of Sydney Alrutz.

Consensus. Nevertheless, none of these, or even other apparatuses of energetic integration and interconsciential communication between the consciential dimensions, have been able to achieve a universal consensus regarding their efficacy or efficiency in order for them to come to be used on a daily basis and be recommended here, by the author, as a reliable instrument.

Hope. It is always hoped that some instrument of this nature will arise for common use. Future generations will see.

Potentiation. Interplanetary communication will be a fact in the future world state, on this planet. This occurrence will be able to potentiate the knowledge of humankind regarding this subject.

Bibliography: Andrade (29, p. 124), Blackmore (139, p. 215), Blunsdon (157, p. 143), Boirac (164, p. 278), Carrington (245, p. 246), Chaplin (273, p. 64), Delanne (381, p. 15), Dubor (421, p. 235), Dupouy (434, p. 127), Durville (436, p. 281), Fodor (528, p. 133), Frichet (557, p. 242), Lévrier (922, p. 21), Maxwell (1017, p. 301), Paula (1208, p. 138), Riland (1403, p. 96), Rochas (1428, p. 347), Schutel (1525, p. 21), Shepard (1548, p. 316).

67. EXTERIORIZATION OF SENSITIVITY

Definition. Exteriorization of sensitivity: parapsychic transport of the individual's sensory functions outside the periphery of his/her human body or soma.

Synonymy: ectesthesia; exteriorization of the *sensorium;* parapsychic sensitivity; perispiritual irradiation; repercussion of sensitivity.

Projection. The exteriorization of sensitivity is a type of projection – almost always through hypnotic resources – of the sensations that reach the intraphysical consciousness, thus triggering a dislocation of the holochakra and/or the psychosoma.

Layers. According to Eugene August Albert De Rochas D'Aiglun (1837-1914), parapsychic sensitivity begins to exteriorize itself at the edges of an energetic layer which is parallel to the human body and situated approximately 1 3/8" (35 mm) from the skin. The second sensitive layer exteriorizes itself from 2 3/8" to 2 3/4" (6 or 7 cm) beyond the first.

Reunification. In this phenomenon, the projection of the holochakra and/or psychosoma occurs with the appearance of parapsychic sensitivity in the layers next to the skin, until the (almost always humanoid) form is composed by the union of two nebulous columns – a blue one on the right and a red one on the left – wherein only a temporary separation appears, followed by the reunification (reaggregation) of the polarization of the holochakra and/or psychosoma.

Charges. The phenomenon of exteriorization of sensitivity shows that the psychosoma – or, more specifically, the holochakra, the so-called *body of energy,* or body of vitality – presents negative and positive charges that interact among themselves (polarization).

Question. What is the precise relationship that this has with the *nadis,* energetic points and meridians of acupuncture and do-in (acupressure)?

Senses. The facts show that, through the functions of the holochakra and the psychosoma, there is an effective relationship between the phenomenon of exteriorization of sensitivity and the phenomena of transposition of the senses or dermo-optic vision.

Bibliography: Blackmore (139, p. 183), Blunsdon (157, p. 144), Boirac (164, p. 271), Bozzano (184, p. 156), Carrington (245, p. 246), Chaplin (273, p. 64), Crookall (333, p. 61), Delanne (382, p. 160), Depascale (392, p. 39), Dubor (421, p. 215), Dupouy (434, p. 79), Durville (436, p. 272), Erny (483, p. 78), Flammarion (524, p. 63), Fodor (528, p. 133), Frichet (557, p. 142), Geley (583, p. 76), Larcher (887, p. 338), Lévrier (922, p. 54), Maxwell (1017, p. 301), Morel (1086, p. 75), Paula (1208, p. 138), Riland (1403, p. 96), Rochas (1429, p. 47), Roure (1479, p. 111), Schutel (1525, p. 21), Shepard (1548, p. 317), Targ (1651, p. 78), Tondriau (1690, p. 227), Wauthy (1803, p. 93).

68. FALSE ARRIVAL

Definition. False arrival: prior announcement of the physical arrival of the projector to a residence, effected by the anticipated presence of his/her consciousness – projected in the psychosoma – in unaccustomed physical manifestations perceived by intraphysical beings (intraphysical consciousnesses).

Synonymy: notice of approximation; parapsychic announcement; phenomenon of arrival; *vardager* (Spain); *vardögr* (Swedish term used to signify the perception of approximation of a person before he/she is seen or heard).

Mechanisms. In the phenomenon of false arrival, the projected projector sometimes acts as the emissary of his/her own pending arrival, which is often awaited, acting in an unconscious manner, subsequently ignoring the fact of having been to that place.

Morphothosenes. His/her behavior during the occurrence seems mechanical, like a *somnambulant ghost,* or a projection of morphothosenes or thought-forms.

Factors. The following 6 predisposing factors seem to influence the triggering of *vardager* and even the most minor varieties of this type of phenomena:

1. **Population.** A sparse local human population.
2. **Isolation.** The physical isolation of intraphysical beings (intraphysical consciousnesses).
3. **Solitude.** The psychological condition of existential solitude of individuals.
4. **Altitude.** The high altitude of a location.
5. **Climate.** The lack of sun during many months of the year in a human environment.
6. **Hereditariness.** Some hereditary quality of the persons involved in the phenomenon.

Interpersonal. There must also be other interpersonal or assistential factors that have an exceptional influence, such as: cooperation, material help or support.

Psychosoma. According to previous observations, the psychosoma or emotional parabody plays an important role in the phenomenon of false arrival, as there is a predominance of certain emotional reasons in its causes, such as: kinship, friendship, solitude, physical isolation, a sad environment (holothosene, materthosene), self-absorption, longing and others of a like nature.

Regions. The *vardager* – the messenger phenomenon – occurs in 8 specific regions:

1. Nordic villages in general.
2. Northern Europe.
3. Norway.
4. Sweden.
5. Denmark.
6. Scotland.
7. Basque Country.
8. Galicia, in Northern Spain.

Subhumans. However, *vardager* has been observed among primitive people and subhuman animals.

Universality. The phenomenon of false arrival is more universal than might be imagined, because it arises in areas other than those just cited, albeit more rarely.

Case study. A good example of this is the case that occurred in Birmingham, England in 1833, reported in 1890 by Alexander Nikolayevich Aksakof: 1832-1903 (Aksakof, 9, p. 560).

Effects. Among the physical effects produced by the projected consciousness in *vardager*, and detected by those present, the sounds of 5 human actions can be singled out:

1. **Steps.** Hearing steps on the floor, stairs or hallway.
2. **Doors.** The noise of opening doors.
3. **Coat.** The act of taking off a coat (jacket).
4. **Luggage.** The placement of luggage in its usual place.
5. **Umbrella.** The act of placing an umbrella in the umbrella stand.

Daily. In specific areas where the phenomenon habitually occurs, false arrival is an almost daily phenomenon. In some cases, it operates with such precise timing that the housewife waits for this announcement in order to heat the food.

Announcements. We should not fail to establish the correlation between the phenomenon of false arrival and the *approach announcement* or, in other words, the inexplicable ideas of an imminent encounter with someone, which can occur through an auditory perception, whether during a dream or during the ordinary, physical waking state.

Bibliography: Aksakof (09, p. 560), Andreas (36, p. 48), Battersby (92, p. 95), Black (137, p. 20), Blackmore (139, p. 11), Bonin (168, p. 513), Digest (400, p. 175), Fodor (528, p. 246), Garrett (571, p. 51), Gauld (575, p. 163), Greenhouse (636, p. 175), Haynes (696, p. 263), Heine (706, p. 183), Holroyd (736, p. 108), Jaffé (798, p. 155), Knight (851, p. 94), Leaf (905, p. 91), Muntañola (1108, p. 83), RPA (1481, p. 21), Smith (1572, p. 90), Steiger (1601, p. 94), Vieira (1762, p. 15), Wereide (1822, p. 3).

69. PROJECTIVE   HETEROSCOPY

Definition. Heteroscopy: the faculty and act whereby the projected consciousness sees the interior of the human body, organs and phenomena of the vegetative life of other persons or animals.

Synonymy: heterognosia; heteropsy; heteroscopic metagnomy; heteroscopic vision; metasomoscopy; *inter vivos* clairvoyance; xenoscopy; X-ray vision of another.

Extension. Heteroscopy can be of two categories, in terms of extent:

1. Partial or segmented.
2. Total or complete.

Quality. Heteroscopy can be of two categories, in terms of the quality of the consciential principle:

1. Human or pertaining to the intraphysical consciousness.
2. Subhuman or animal.

Organ. The more common phenomenon is when the consciousness sees the organ, organs, or the limited area of the human body or soma of another person that is affected by some disturbance.

Diagnosis. In most cases, heteroscopy is not pathological, becoming an extraordinary resource of projective diagnosis, especially in the phenomena of traveling clairvoyance provoked in order to provide assistance.

Evidence. Heteroscopy annuls the hypothesis of psychoanalysts who attribute the cause of autoscopy to narcissism or self-fascination.

Narcissism. If there are persons who also see the structure of the human body of others, or even the physical body of animals in general, then the 3 phenomena demonstrate affinity, do not have only one cause and are not derived only from the emotionalisms of the consciousness. In summary: narcissism cannot rationally be the main cause of heteroscopy.

Bibliography: Bonin (168, p. 227), D'arbó (365, p. 164), Kolosimo (858, p. 157), Tondriau (1690, p. 198).

70. PHYSICAL   MULTILOCATION

Definition. Physical multilocation: the apparently simultaneous presence of a person in 3 or more different places through parapsychic means.

Synonymy: multiple physical locations; phenomenon of ubiquitousness; phenomenon of ubiquity; physical trilocation.

Multiplication. In fact, it can be admitted, as a working hypothesis, that the phenomenon of multiplication of the forms of consciential manifestation does not refer to or should not be restricted to only 3 locations, since it sometimes occurs in various locations at the same time.

Transferences. The consciousness cannot be divided into two, three or many parts, as it is concluded by observations of the phenomena of double awareness. This is because a single consciousness is not able to manifest itself actively and consciously in 2 or more different locations at the same time.

Seat. The consciential seat always remains in only 1 place, despite transferring itself from 1 vehicle or location to another with the instantaneity of thought.

Forms. The phenomenon of physical multilocation seems to be due to the attribute of the multiplicity by way of which the consciousness almost always unconsciously projects its morphothosenes (thought-forms), aided by the energetic resources of the holochakra, having the appearance of the shape of its human body.

Note. The phenomenon of *physical multilocation,* which can also be called *physical trilocation,* should not be confused with the phenomenon of *physical-extraphysical trilocation,* or with double projection, or with the attribute of multiplicity of the psychosoma, which permits physical multilocation. These are 2 phenomena and 1 attribute that are completely different from each other.

Bibliography: Crouzet (344, p. 539), Delanne (382, p. 175), Muntañola (1108, p. 92), Owen (1177, p. 255), Sculthorp (1531, p. 135), Yogananda (1894, p. 289).

---

71. PROJECTIVE PARAPYROGENESIS

Definition. Projective parapyrogenesis: combustion in the intraphysical dimension caused by the consciential energies of the projected human projector.

Synonymy: *inter vivos* parapyrogenesis; projective parapsychic combustion; projective pyroparaphoresis.

Poltergeist. In the phenomenon of parapyrogenesis – which is frequent in cases of poltergeist – sudden combustion occurs in environments and even with objects, such as clothes kept in a hermetically sealed trunk.

Types. Projective parapyrogenesis, like projective typtology, is a rare phenomenon. The projector's consciousness hardly ever precisely recalls the act performed in the extraphysical dimension with effects in the physical dimension, it thus being an unconscious phenomenon.

Incendiary. The projected projector responsible for projective parapyrogenesis is an unconscious incendiary, but is nevertheless not a pyromaniac.

Bibliografia: D'arbó (365, p. 229).

---

72. PROJECTIVE PNEUMATOPHONY

Definition. Projective pneumatophony: the type of physical phenomenon of a direct voice that is directly sponsored by a projected intraphysical consciousness.

Synonymy: communication by independent projective voice; direct projective voice; *inter vivos* pneumatophony; projective autophony; projective mistephony.

Theory. According to the most widely accepted theory, the phenomenon of direct voice, through physical effect sensitives (ectoplast), derives from 1 artificial larynx, which is constructed by a communicant intelligence.

Box. This *voice box* works like a material megaphone.

Semimaterialization. In this case, the phenomenon of semimaterialization occurs.

Sonorous. The phenomenon of projective direct voice is a type of sonorous projection.

Bibliography: ADGMT (03, p. 289), Cavendish (266, p. 73), Chaplin (273, p. 48), Fodor (528, p. 92), Gaynor (577, p. 49), Greenhouse (636, p. 139), Martin (1003, p. 43), Morel (1086, p. 180), Paula (1208, 171), Zaniah (1899, p. 483).

---

73. PROJECTIVE POLTERGEIST

Definition. Poltergeist (German: *poltern,* noisy; *geist,* ghost, little devil): intelligent phenomena, noises, diverse physical alterations or disturbances that are normally inexplicable.

Synonymy: haunting of the living; infestation; *inter vivos* poltergeist; metakinetics; metapathologeny; metapsychorrhagia; parapsychic riot; phenomenon of haunting; projective poltergeism; *rabbat;* RSPK (Recurring spontaneous psychokinesis); spontaneous recurrent psychokinesis; *televasia*; thorybism; thorybus.

Phenomenology. The following are 13 basic phenomena, among others, which compose the phenomenological complex of **poltergeist** occurrences:

1. **Transport.** The spectacular transporting of objects.
2. **Lithotelergy.** Flying rocks (lithotelergy).
3. **Violence.** Actions that are sometimes violent.
4. *Apport.* Abnormal movement of heavy furniture *(apport)*.
5. **Falling.** Falling plates, silverware, cups and other fragile objects.
6. **Cracking.** Surprising cracking noises.
7. **Currents.** Air currents.
8. **Doors.** Slamming doors.
9. **Marks.** Marks, scratches, drawings and writing on walls and floors *(interdimensional thosenic signatures)*.
10. **Parapyrogenesis.** Spontaneous parapsychic combustion (parapyrogenesis).
11. **Odors.** Diverse odors.
12. **Apparitions.** Apparitions of ghosts.
13. **Hauntings.** Hauntings or the occurrences in places said to be *haunted.*

Epicenter. Poltergeist occurrences are generally attributed to extraphysical consciousnesses in the proximity of a focal person of the phenomena, who is the source of energy responsible for the mechanics involved in the movement of objects (psychokinesis). This person is almost always a child or adolescent who, in this case, is called a *phenomenological epicenter.*

Categories. There are 3 categories of distinct occurrences in so-called poltergeist phenomena: poltergeists per se; the phenomena of haunting; and projective poltergeists.

1. **Poltergeists.** Poltergeists manifest themselves in 3 ways:

A. A benevolent manner.
B. A prankish manner (immaturity of extraphysical consciousnesses).
C. A destructive or malevolent manner (anticosmoethical).

2. **Locations.** Certain researchers separate the poltergeist – manifestations that change locations, accompanying the phenomenological epicenter – from haunting, which are manifestations connected to a specific location, whether a house, castle, cemetery, building, farm, hospital, church, palace, prison, barracks, or country house, and which occur independent from the existence of an epicenter. In this case, there is a drop in ambient temperature and photographable ghosts sometimes arise.

3. **Projective.** Aside from customary poltergeist events, with their abovementioned causes, it is necessary to add the sporadic cases of haunting, especially manifestations that demonstrate an intelligent presence and are produced by a projected intraphysical consciousness that is either aware or unaware of its extraphysical actions. These phenomena can occur with or without the interference of extraphysical consciousnesses, whether the manifestations be extraphysical telekinesis, physical bilocation, raps or other similar occurrences.

Practices. The epicenter should not be considered an absolute rule for the occurrence of poltergeist. Depending upon its modalities, it can be produced by a projected intraphysical consciousness or by one or more extraphysical consciousnesses. It is also thought that poltergeist is induced from a distance through empirical magical practices, such as those occurring in Brazil with *quimbanda.*

Recurrence. When repeated hauntings are produced by the intraphysical projector, it is due to recurring projections – either lucid or nonlucid – in which case the individual's subconscious will is acting.

Planetary. It should be pointed out here that consciential energy and the widespread occurrences of poltergeist suggest the theory of planetary or cosmic poltergeist in order to explain a considerable number of the apparitions that are typical of UFOlogy.

Bibliography: Aksakof (09, p. 540), Amadou (21, p. 67), Andrade (27, p. 190), Bayless (95, p. 102), Bonin (168, p. 402), Boswell (174, p. 133), Bozzano (194, p. 118), Carrington (251, p. 231), Carton (252, p. 224), Cavendish (266, p. 196), Chaplin (273, p. 122), Chauvin (275, p. 154), Currie (354, p. 106), D'arbó (365, p. 175), Day (376, p. 102), Delanne (385, p. 216), Digest (401, p. 374), Eysenck (493, p. 101), Fodor (528, p. 291), Foin (532, p. 88), Frazer (549, p. 264), Gaynor (577, p. 141), Grant-Veillard (623, p. 110), Grattan-Guinness (626, p. 123), Greenhouse (636, p. 58), Holms (735, p. 238), Holzer (743, p. 196), Kardec (825, p. 166), Lee (908, p. 162), Martin (1003, p. 94), Morel (1086, p. 143), Paula (1208, p. 69), Pratt (1285, p. 118), Randall (1369, p. 51), Rogo (1453, p. 241), RPA (1481, p. 104), Salomon (1497, p. 119), Shepard (1548, p. 718), Spence (1588, p. 325), Steiger (1601, p. 97), Still (1622, p. 165), Sudre (1630, p. 359), Tinoco (1685, p. 34), Tondriau (1690, p. 267), Walker (1781, p. 17), Watson (1800, p. 138), Wedeck (1807, p. 285), Wilson (1855, p. 196), Wolman (1863, p. 382), Zaniah (1899, p. 362).

74. FAREWELL CONSCIENTIAL PROJECTION

Definition. Farewell consciential projection: the extraphysical goodbye visit of the consciousness of the moribund individual, or the dying intraphysical personality, to someone (whether a relative, friend or acquaintance), at the critical moment of the transition of biological death, in the deactivation of his/her physical body, or in his/her *first posthumous minute*.

Synonymy: consciential anti-twilight; consciential farewell apparition; critical apparition; critical projection; *inter vivos* farewell apparition; projection of the first desoma.

Sensations. In the farewell consciential projection, a common and universal occurrence, the agent, or the visitant-projector, can be seen, heard, or merely have its extraphysical presence sensed by another, the visited-percipient social being, which may be an adult, child or subhuman animal, especially a dog.

Motivation. The main motivation that promotes the farewell lucid projection resides in affection, whether it is a bond of kinship, romance or deep friendship.

Suicide. There are registered cases of farewell consciential projections produced by suicides, which proves the existence, as incredible as it may seem, of *suicide-projectors* or, in other words, those who produce final projection through suicide.

Survival. In most cases, the farewell consciential projection constitutes irrefutable individual proof for the percipient of survival of the consciousness after the death of the human body.

Objective. Besides being a final goodbye, this proof of survival often seems to represent the greater objective of the phenomenon, which may be produced with or without the aid of helpers.

Romanticism. Looked at in another way, in many instances, the farewell consciential projection is a final projection that is enriched with the charm of leave-taking by someone who is loved, or a case of romantic biological death.

Categories. There are two modes or categories of final projection (projection without interiorization, projection without return), according to the qualification of the *consciousness-agent:*

1. Lucid.
2. Nonlucid.

Desomatics. The farewell lucid projection only happens because the consciousness is concluding the trance (shock) experience of the first desoma (deactivation of the human body), but has still not gone through the second desoma, the deactivation of the holochakra.

Holochakrality. In this second condition, it becomes far more difficult for the consciousness to manifest to human beings, because its decreased density, or the different degree of the frequency of its energies, distances it from human reality and the possibility of direct intervention in the intraphysical, human or dense dimension.

Pattern. The typical farewell consciential projection generally follows a pattern-sequence of 4 manifestations:

1. **Surprise.** The percipient prepares to go to bed or to go out, whereupon the image or figure of the visitant, a loved one, suddenly and unexpectedly appears before him/her.

2. **Goodbye.** The apparition, clearly identified by the visited-percipient, not only presents a perfect figure, but also the clothing and even the objects of personal use (hat, necklace, glasses, pipe, watch, ring), sometimes smiles and waves goodbye or demonstrates affection.

3. **Disappearance.** After a brief period of time, the apparition silently disappears from the sight of the perceptive intraphysical consciousness.

4. **Confirmation.** Soon after the critical apparition, the percipient receives notice that the visitant's personality has just departed human life at a distant location, and at the exact date and moment of the phenomenon's occurrence, due to the matching time (simulcognition, synchronicity).

Evidence. The simultaneousness nature of the apparition and biological death, as well as the visited person's unawareness of the friend's passing away, serve to rationally remove the hypothesis of visual hallucination and provide significant evidence for the authenticity of this type of consciential projection.

Cord. The silver cord is doubtless a key factor in the phenomenon of the farewell consciential projection.

Rupture. A great number of occurrences happen when the silver cord is rupturing, or immediately after its rupture and the consequent liberation of the psychosoma.

Psychosoma. Thus, in certain cases, the farewell consciential projection constitutes an extreme projection of the psychosoma, practically without the silver cord, being the final act of leave-taking by the intraphysical consciousness, or the *recent-extraphysical-consciousness,* that intraphysical consciousness which has just returned to its condition as an extraphysical consciousness in the intermissive period.

Indirect. Indirect (ricochet) farewell consciential projections also occur in which the intraphysical percipient – the target-being of the projector – is not able to perceive the extraphysical presence and manifestations of the agent undergoing desoma, which are providentially performed by another person who is physically close and parapsychically more sensitive, and who may never have met the agent undergoing desoma in intraphysical life.

Case study. Thus, for example, upon passing through desoma, the brother visits his sister, who does not detect his presence, but the event is perceived in detail by the sensitive babysitter, who is beside her on that occasion, taking care of her child, the nephew of the individual who underwent desoma.

Aspects. The facts show 2 relevant aspects regarding farewell consciential projections:

1. **Frequency.** The farewell consciential projections involving indirect percipients suggest that a far greater number of these phenomena occur than the amount actually registered because the percipients are not able to confirm the presence of the agents that are undergoing desoma.

2. **Reduction.** The evolution and intensification of modern human means of communication, in this era of acceleration of human history, have contributed to a considerable reduction in the motivation that led intraphysical consciousnesses in the process of desoma to seek their loved ones and bid them farewell. Mobile phones, international and long-distance phone calls, faxes, rapid means of transportation, including air transportation, radio transmissions, Internet, e-mail, as well as print and televised media, have reduced the distance between intraphysical beings, since they can always be together when necessary or when they wish.

Animals. The farewell projection also occurs with extraphysical animals, especially pet dogs.

Barks. In these cases, the dog announces its own desoma with persistent loud extraphysical barks, which end up being perceived and waking up the deeply sleeping owner who gets up and finds the animal's physical body already cooling or even cold in another area of the house, far from the owner's bedroom.

Joining. Various categories of lucid projection can present themselves joined into a single one. The following 3 occurrences serve as examples:

1. **Farewell.** A farewell consciential projection occurs.

2. **Final.** This farewell projection is also an intraphysical consciousness' final consciential projection.

3. **Sonorous.** This final projection can develop into a sonorous consciential projection.

Bibliography: Anonymous (46, p. 163), Buttlar (229, p. 35), Carrington (250, p. 191), Crookall (343, p. 54), Ebon (453, p. 97), Fardwell (494, p. 40), Flammarion (524, p. 118), Gauld (575, p. 163), Greenhouse (636, p. 326), Gurney (666, p. 61), Machado (969, p. 66), Osty (1173, p. 49), Owen (1177, p. 269), Padilha (1180, p. 277), Rutledge (1483, p. 30), Steiger (1601, p. 63), Still (1622, p. 237), Tyrrell (1717, p. 34).

75. PROJECTIVE PSYCHOPHONY

Definitions. Projective psychophony (Greek: *psykhé,* soul; *phonos,* sound): the act whereby a projected intraphysical consciousness (the communicant) speaks, while incorporated, through the human body and vocal mechanism of another intraphysical consciousness (the sensitive) whose vehicles of manifestation are coincident; communication of an extraphysical consciousness through the psychosoma of the intraphysical consciousness which is projected to denser extraphysical dimensions.

Synonymy: normal projective possession; projective incorporation.

Categories. Thus, by definition, there are two categories of projective psychophony: human projective psychophony and extraphysical projective psychophony.

1. **Human.** In human projective psychophony, the phenomenon occurs through two intraphysical consciousnesses – the projected incorporator and the other normal intraphysical consciousness – according to the above definition.

2. **Extraphysical.** In extraphysical projective psychophony, the phenomenon occurs through an intraphysical consciousness, or a projected-intraphysical-projector, a sensitive, and an extraphysical consciousness, the communicant.

Personality. In *common human incorporation,* the sensations are very well-defined for the sensitive, as though someone had put their own body onto the sensitive, in the same way that someone usually puts on clothing.

Sense. In this case, the clear, incontrovertible sense of being another person, or personality, arises within oneself.

Sensations. The human psychophonic sensitive *(channel),* when incorporated, actually feels the sensations of his/her own body as if they were another person's. The following 9 variables are examples:

1. The condition of an aged, weak person.
2. A young woman who is healthy and full of life.
3. A lady with a high-pitched voice and arthritic joints.
4. The melancholy and hopelessness (extraphysical melancholy) of a suicide.
5. The broken leg of an accident victim who underwent desoma.
6. Whether a person is heavy or thin, tall or short, man or woman, adult or child.
7. The way that consciousness used to walk when in the condition of a person in intraphysical life.
8. The manner of speech characteristic in timbre and tonality to the former human personality.
9. The memory of another intelligence that possesses him/her temporarily but completely.

Psychosoma. In *extraphysical projective incorporation,* the same situation occurs, with the same, albeit more refined, sensations. What changes is the vehicle of manifestation, now no longer the human body, but the psychosoma and all of its energetic appendices in operation, such as the holochakra, the chakras and the silver cord.

Bibliography: Currie (354, p. 107), Gooch (617, p. 6), Morel (1086, p. 148), Paula (1208, p. 82), Turvey (1707, p. 177), Vieira (1762, p. 80), Zaniah (1899, p. 369).

76. HUMAN PROJECTIVE PSYCHOPHONY

Definition. Human projective psychophony: that phenomenon in which the projected-projector intraphysical consciousness manifests as a communicant, speaking through the vocal mechanism of the human body of an intraphysical sensitive.

Synonymy: human projective incorporation; *inter vivos* psychophony.

Circles. In the nineteenth century, animic-parapsychic study circles were organized in two distant cities wherein the persons would simultaneously meet and communicate between themselves through the sensitives of the circles, through the phenomenon of human projective psychophony.

Telepathy. The events occurred in such a manner as to definitively exclude the possibility of telepathic interference or the direct interference of other animic or intraconsciential phenomena.

Locations. The most well-known circles at that time were those in Boston and New York, in the United States of America.

Movement. The projected intraphysical consciousness can manifest through psychophony while its human body is being carried by a vehicle in motion or, in other words, in a mobile physical base, at the same instant of communication.

Aksakof. In 1890, Alexander Nikolayevich Aksakof (1832-1903), gave a detailed report of one of these cases that occurred in 1882.

Categories. The categories of manifestants – intraphysical consciousnesses – who communicate through a psychophonic sensitive, can be quite diverse. The following are 7 examples:

1. A healthy person.
2. An ill person.
3. A psychopath (mentally insane).
4. A person who is aware of his/her experience after the fact.
5. A person who is unaware of the fact, after its occurrence.
6. Another sensitive.
7. An assassination victim (simultaneously).

Personism. Personism is the manifestation of the animist's intraphysical consciousness through the vocal mechanism of his/her own human body, situating and characterizing the entirety of his/her personality in another of his/her previous existences (generally the one immediately prior to the present one) to which he/she temporarily mnemonically regressed (intrusive personality).

Psychopathology. Many instances of *personism* are restricted to the parapathology of the mentalsoma and can even manifest as undeniable paraclinical profiles of multi-existential self-intrusion.

Interference. It is evident that the reference made here to human projective psychophony is based on the indispensable premise of the anticipated exclusion of any possible interference and confusion with instances of voluntary or involuntary *personism* – or that which is consciously or unconsciously generated (mystification, fraud, simulation) – from the phenomenon being studied.

Bibliography: Aksakof (09, p. 534), Currie (354, p. 108), Turvey (1707, p. 178).

77. EXTRAPHYSICAL PROJECTIVE PSYCHOPHONY

Definition. Extraphysical projective psychophony: the phenomenon in which the projected-projector intraphysical consciousness makes itself passive as a sensitive to another consciousness (extraphysical consciousness) – that is generally presumed to be more evolved – which manifests through the projector's psychosoma in the paratropospheric extraphysical dimension.

Synonymy: extraphysical projective incorporation.

Uses. Extraphysical projective psychophony permits intermediation between consciousnesses that are situated in very different extraphysical dimensions.

Extraphysical consciousness. Through the projector, the extraphysical communicant consciousness does not need to densify its psychosoma in the less evolved, denser dimension and performs this densification in a gradual manner, using the projected intraphysical sensitive for this purpose.

Energy. The intraphysical sensitive projector, when projected – as it carries a greater intensity of human, consciential energy – is better suited to extraphysical psychophony in environments or communities that are near the terrestrial crust, even more than the extraphysical consciousnesses that inhabit this location during their intermissive period.

Looseness. The facts demonstrate that human parapsychic manifestations occur through the looseness of the holochakra or, in other words, are based upon the principle of discoincidence of the vehicles of manifestation of the intraphysical sensitive.

Discoincidence. It is presumed that the same principle of the condition of discoincidence is also in effect for diverse extraphysical parapsychic manifestations.

Dimensions. Just as with intraphysical sensitives, these discoincidences must also occur in analogous manifestations in the extraphysical dimension, either with the projected intraphysical sensitive or the extraphysical sensitive consciousness at the moment of parapsychic manifestation through the extraphysical-communicant from the more evolved extraphysical environment.

Mentalsoma. In this last case, the parapsychic manifestation – occurring without an intraphysical consciousness – seems to happen based on the same principle of discoincidence, but in this instance with the *looseness of the mentalsoma* of the extraphysical-sensitive-consciousness in relation to the extraphysical head (parahead) of its psychosoma. This is because, in such a situation, it has neither a holochakra nor a human body.

Bibliography: Vieira (1762, p. 81).

78. PROJECTIVE PSYCHOGRAPHY

Definition. Projective psychography: a type of parapsychic writing in which the consciousness of the projected intraphysical communicant – at a distance from its human body – writes through the sensitive psychographer.

Synonymy: *inter vivos* psychography; projective automatic writing; projective automatography; projective transcriber parapsychism; psychographic projection; psychography between living persons.

Mentalsomas. Projective psychography sponsored by the consciousness of the intraphysical projector through the human sensitive generally occurs by way of projection of the consciousness in the psychosoma, although the connection of the energetic, consciential, parapsychic wave or mental wave is effected through the mentalsomas of both.

Categories. Projective psychography can be classified into two basic categories:

1. **Direct.** In direct, manual and involuntary projective psychography, the projected human consciousness takes direct control of the motor force writing mechanism, namely the vehicles of manifestation of the intraphysical mechanical sensitive, especially the human body, the nervous system, an arm, a hand and, besides this, the pencil that is held by the sensitive's fingers, being a less difficult and more practical process for the interdimensional transmission of thought through writing.

2. **Indirect.** In indirect, projective psychography, the projected human consciousness can use the most difficult, inconvenient and always rarest resources of the primitive mechanical means of interdimensional transmission of thought through writing, namely through a device such as the funnel or planchette used by the sensitive, almost always with the help of a human assistant who is not a developed sensitive.

Rarity. *Inter vivos* psychography has always been and continues to be rare in any of its categories, manifestations and types of psychographer sensitives. Nevertheless, the phenomenon logically does occur.

Phenomenology. The following 4 phenomena, which involve the human personality, are interconnected or intimately connected to psychography:

1. Intuition.
2. Hypnosis.
3. Telepathy.
4. Clairvoyance (less frequent).

Bibliography: ADGMT (03, p. 245), Bardon (80, p. 384), Chaplin (273, p. 127), Fodor (528, p. 317), Gaynor (577, p. 147), Kardec (825, p. 191), Martin (1003, p. 102), Morel (1086, p. 149), Paula (1208, p. 83), Shepard (1548, p. 753), Zaniah (1899, p. 369).

79. PROJECTIVE RAPS

Definition. Projective raps: knocking noises or percussive sounds of varying intensity – in this case without a visible, known or normal cause – that are produced by a projected intraphysical consciousness.

Synonymy: animic crepitations; *inter vivos* raps; knocks; projective banging; projective percussive sounds; projective rapology; projective typtology; rappings by the projector; raps; scrapes; sonorous knocks; typtological noises; typtological sounds.

Categories. The phenomena of knocks and percussive sounds of extraphysical origin can be classified into 4 categories: parapsychic, animic, internal and typtological.

1. **Parapsychic.** Cracking noises, physical knocks or raps that are provoked by an extraphysical consciousness, and are usually somewhat familiar.

2. **Animic.** Sporadic cases of dull, weak, light, clear and distinct, or even resounding banging noises that are heard by intraphysical beings and are either consciously or unconsciously produced by the projected intraphysical consciousness, with or without interference on the part of extraphysical consciousnesses. They are typical occurrences of exteriorization of motricity.

3. **Internal.** These are banging noises of an extraphysical origin, produced inside the actual wood of a piece of furniture, or material of the room of a house, without any type of external movement *(endokinesis)*.

4. **Typtological.** This is the application of the method of communication, or language – through bangs and knocks which, by agreement, can be separately associated with different letters of the alphabet – which is called typtology (Greek: *typtô*, strike; *logos*, study), or grammatology.

Telekinesis. Strictly speaking, projective raps generally constitute sonorous manifestations of extraphysical telekinesis.

Energies. The production of raps of any type requires the intense application of consciential energies, or more precisely, of ectoplasmy.

Bibliography: ADGMT (03, p. 252), Ambelain (23, p. 73), Bardon (80, p. 325), Chaplin (273, p. 129), Crouzet (344, p. 340), D'arbó (365, p. 270), Digest (399, p. 275), Durville (436, p. 302), Fodor (528, p. 321), Morel (1086, p. 154), Muldoon (1105, p. 275), Myers (1114, p. 454), Paula (1208, p. 103), Pearsall (1215, p. 195), RPA (1481, p. 173), Schatz (1514, p. 199), Shepard (1548, p. 766), Spence (1588, p. 335), Wedeck (1807, p. 300), Zaniah (1899, p. 379).

80. EXTRAPHYSICAL TELEKINESIS

Definition. Extraphysical telekinesis (Greek: *tele,* at a distance; *kinesis,* action, movement): physical action at a distance – such as the movement of physical objects – provoked directly by the intraphysical consciousness which is projected from the human body, especially using the energies of the holochakra and the components of the psychosoma for this purpose (see fig. 80, page 1,123).

Synonymy: extraphysical PK; extraphysical psychokinesis; extraphysical telekinesis; extraphysical telekinesism; *inter vivos* telekinesis; projective parapsychokinesis; projective PK; projective psychokinesis; projective telekinesis.

Psychokinesis. The term *psychokinesis* defines the type of movement, or action, provoked by the consciousness, or the interaction of persons with objects in the environment.

Movement. The term *telekinesis,* on the other hand, defines movement, or action, at a distance from the consciousness – intraphysical, in this case – without the use of any resource of conventional physical manifestation. These terms are indiscriminately used here as though they were synonyms.

Effects. Among the effects generated by the energies of the intraphysical consciousness projected from the human body (projective PK), the following 10 can be listed:

1. **Metaphanism.** Annihilative effects (disappearance of objects; metaphanism).
2. **Biology.** Biological effects (e.g., exteriorization of therapeutic consciential energies).
3. **Combustion.** Combustive effects (the reduction of objects to ashes).
4. **Electromagnetism.** Electromagnetic effects (action upon electrical circuits).
5. **Electrochemistry.** Electrochemical effects (action upon batteries).
6. **Structure.** Structural effects (action upon the physical-chemical properties of objects).
7. **Photogenic.** Photogenic effects (generation of light).
8. **Mechanics.** Mechanical effects (alteration of the kinetic state of objects).
9. **Chemistry.** Chemical nuclear effects (action upon the nature of the chemical elements of objects or the transmutation of objects).
10. **Acoustics.** Sonorous effects (generation of sounds; projective raps; sonorous projection).

Aspects. With the accumulation of experiences, plus the fruitless attempts and the very low rate of success, the lucid projector detects 5 important aspects in the phenomenon of telekinesis provoked by the projected intraphysical consciousness:

1. **Energy.** The extraphysical execution of the movement of any physical object, as insignificant as its weight and volume might be, requires an enormous expenditure of consciential energy.

2. **Charging.** Some objects, especially those of personal use, remain charged with energy and appear luminous to the perceptions of the projected intraphysical consciousness. This charged energy can negatively (against) or positively (in favor) influence telekinetic movement.

3. **Consciousness.** Extraphysical telekinesis, generally born of will, as incredible as it may seem, can be triggered in an unconscious manner by the projected intraphysical consciousness in certain circumstances, even with the assistance of a helper, which is also unperceived by the projector.

4. **Carrying.** In many cases, the physical object only moves when acted upon not only by the will, but also when carried by the extraphysical hands (parahands) of the intraphysical consciousness in the psychosoma, which is in a condition of greater density, thereby taking it from one place to another and even being able to use lucid volitation for this purpose.

5. **Damage.** An extraphysical trauma endured by the projected intraphysical consciousness, at the exact moment that the object is being moved from one place to another, can have an influence upon this action. Depending upon the nature of its structure and the conditions, this can cause its fall and consequent damage.

Case Study. The author extraphysically saw a glass picture frame break on the floor during one of his attempts at extraphysical telekinesis. The object's owner, who was parapsychically insensitive to the extraphysical presence, later attributed the domestic occurrence to a breeze that did not exist in that location.

Reality. The projected intraphysical consciousness often appears to be a type of *living virtual reality.*

Clocks. There are registered cases of clocks that stop and pictures and hanging frames that fall from the wall which are coincident with the farewell consciential projection.

Telekinetic. The intraphysical consciousness capable of producing extraphysical telekinesis, whether spontaneous or voluntary, receives the name of *telekinetic projector.*

Bibliography: Aksakof (09, p. 558), Ambelain (23, p. 73), Bozzano (189, p. 147), Cavendish (266, p. 248), Chaplin (273, p. 157), Crookall (343, p. 93), Day (376, p. 131), Delanne (382, p. 414), Digest (401, p. 380), Durville (436, p. 281), Fodor (528, p. 376), Fortune (540, p. 49), Gaynor (577, p. 183), Grattan-Guinness (626, p. 160), Hemmert (712, p. 40), Machado (968, p. 39), Martin (1003, p. 122), Morel (1086, p. 171), Northage (1135, p. 49), Paula (1208, p. 127), Randall (1369, p. 17), Shepard (1548, p. 912), Spence (1588, p. 404), Vieira (1762, p. 131), Walker (1781, p. 73), Wedeck (1807, p. 345), Zaniah (1899, p. 447).

---

81.   EXTRAPHYSICAL   TELEPATHY

Definition. Extraphysical telepathy: the transmission and reception of thought through the process of direct information from the intraphysical consciousness which is projected in the extraphysical dimension to another intraphysical consciousness that is in the ordinary, physical waking state, or to another projected intraphysical consciousness, or even to an extraphysical consciousness.

Synonymy: consciential telephony; direct extraphysical information; extraphysical cryptesthesia; extraphysical diapsiquia; extraphysical mind reading; extraphysical tele-hypnosis; extraphysical telementation; extraphysical thought transmission; *inter vivos* telepathy; mental telegraphy; parabiological radio; paratelepathy; projection or reception of thoughts *(telethosenes);* spiritual telegraphy; subjective transference of bio-information; super-sensory thought transference; telegnosis; transmental dialog.

Interpretations. Being a form of paraperception or consciential projection, telepathy is also interpreted under 4 aspects:

1. **Telesthesia:** sentiment at a distance.
2. **Cryptesthesia:** hidden sentiment.
3. **Clairsentience:** mind reading.
4. **Thought transference:** unmodifiable by either distance or time.

Synchronicity. Comparative tests using the electroencephalogram in the United States of America and the former Soviet Union suggested perfect synchronicity in the alpha rhythms or relative brain waves of the encephalograms of the emitter and the receiver during telepathic transmissions, when in the ordinary, physical waking state.

Action. The projected intraphysical consciousness almost always spontaneously acts doubly, as a transmitter-agent and as a receiver-percipient of thoughts, whether near to or distant from the other intraphysical consciousness or an extraphysical consciousness.

Looking. In this case, the communication of thoughts is apparently performed by one consciousness looking at the face or *paraface* of the other.

Projections. The great occurrences of advanced telepathy are only executed through the projection of the consciousness outside the human body, even when it is only partial, by means of a partial or even semilucid projection, going beyond the limits of the physical restriction imposed by the cerebral hemispheres.

Telepath. The projected intraphysical consciousness that is able to activate the mental communicatory process of extraphysical telepathy receives the name of *telepath projector.*

Animals. Besides men, women and children, the intraphysical consciousness projected from the human body can induce thoughts in other beings, thoughts that result in actions, especially over diverse subhuman animals, such as cats with which they have some affinity.

Self-awareness. When they are sufficiently aware of their extraphysical condition, intraphysical consciousnesses generally use their extraphysical telepathic processes freely.

Oligophrenia. Extraphysical oligophrenic beings (post-desomatic parapsychotics) are not able to use their telepathic faculty due to their consciential deficiencies.

Acceptance. Currently, telepathy is a parapsychic (or psychic) phenomenon that is generally accepted in the more advanced areas of conventional science. It is the first type of *consciential projection* that is universally admitted without greater restrictions or heated debate. The projection of consciential energies came to be more broadly accepted at the end of the twentieth century.

Bibliography: ADGMT (03, p. 226), Baker (69, p. 30), Blasco (151, p. 165), Blavatsky (153, p. 781), Boswell (174, p. 190), Bozzano (186, p. 166), Cavendish (266, p. 248), Chaplin (273, p. 157), Crookall (343, p. 22), Day (376, p. 132), Digest (401, p. 380), Fodor (528, p. 376), Garrett (574, p. 115), Gaynor (577, p. 183), Greene (635, p. 91), Greyson (643, p. 184), Holzer (751, p. 108), Martin (1003, p. 122), Morel (1086, p. 170), Paula (1208, p. 131), Podmore (1266, p. 204), Russell (1482, p. 60), Shepard (1548, p. 912), Spence (1588, p. 404), Still (1622, p. 232), Swedenborg (1635, p. 256), Toben (1688, p. 78), Tondriau (1690, p. 282), Vieira (1762, p. 125), Walker (1782, p. 406), Warcollier (1796, p. 96), Wedeck (1807, p. 345), Zaniah (1899, p. 446).

---

82. HUMAN PARATELEPORTATION

Definitions. Human parateleportation (Greek: *para,* outside; *tele,* distant, remote; Latin: *portare,* to carry): the phenomenon composed of dematerialization, levitation, apport and rematerialization, in which the intraphysical consciousness suddenly disappears and reappears in another location; the act or process of transporting objects, human beings or subhuman animals through space, without any mechanical means.

Synonymy: extra-human teleportation; intraphysical-extraphysical commute; intraphysical-extraphysical transport; magical metastasis; movable parapsychism; parapsychic commute; parapsychic teleportation; parapsychic transportation; self-parateleportation; teledynamic dislocation; telekinesis of the human being.

Process. In parateleportation – one of the most universal and shocking or impactful parapsychic phenomena – the dissolution or *dematerialization* and subsequent reconstitution or *rematerialization* of the object occurs, which is called *apport.*

Person. When this occurs with living beings, the person (intraphysical consciousness) dissolves into nothing, or vanishes into thin air, only to later reappear outside that environment, at another location.

Characteristics. The following 24 more common factors should be gathered from among the characteristics of human parateleportation:

1. **Inevitability.** The phenomenon of parateleportation is unexpected, unwanted by the parateleported individual, and inevitable.

2. **Surprise.** The parateleported individual disappears from view without warning or a sign of farewell to those present.

3. **Intraphysical consciousness.** The parateleported being can be an adult or child, of any social group or belief, whether an ordinary citizen, a sensitive, a so-called "civilized" individual, or an indigenous person; or an animal: an ox, cow or horse.

4. **Clouds.** The disappearance or reappearance of the parateleported person can occur through a luminous cloud.

5. **Sound.** The phenomenon of parateleportation can occur in silence or with some noise.

6. **Number.** The phenomenon of parateleportation generally involves only one person, but can involve various, one at a time, this being a very rare occurrence.

7. **Amnesia.** Self-awareness disappears with and at the moment of the parateleported individual's disappearance. The state of amnesia continues until that consciousness reappears at a distant location.

8. **Self-lucidity.** Self-lucidity during the course of the phenomenon of parateleportation is the exception.

9. **Sensations.** The parateleported individual can first feel as though his/her legs have disappeared, thereby giving the sensation of extreme lightness of the entire human body, followed by temporary unconsciousness.

10. **Points.** There are two points that occur as a rule, during the phenomenon of human parateleportation: the departure and the arrival.

11. **Reappearance.** The reappearance of the parateleported person in any other place is instantaneous.

12. **Destination.** The destination of the parateleported individual arises at random, without the person's choice or decision.

13. **Direction.** There is almost always only a departure, but the departure and rapid *return* of the individual, in diverse directions, has also occurred.

14. **Shock.** The phenomenon of parateleportation does not cause any damage to the parateleported individual's human body, but produces temporary effects of (psychic) shock.

15. **Space.** Human teleportation is limited to space and is not related to chronological time.

16. **Time.** It seems that no parateleported individual returns to the past, surpasses his/her own memories or disappears into the future.

17. **Duration.** The duration between the disappearance and the reappearance of the parateleported individual ranges from brief moments, to short periods of time and even to hours.

18. **Distance.** The distance involved in the phenomenon of parateleportation varies, from one room to the next, from one country to another and from one continent to another.

19. **Location.** There are often difficulties involved in locating the parateleported individual.

20. **Temperature.** The process of disappearance-dissolution and reemergence-reconstitution of the human body of the parateleported individual requires high temperatures.

21. **Objectives.** The phenomenon of human parateleportation is used for objectives which are unknown and inexplicable.

22. **Hypotheses.** Among the hypotheses that have been put forward to explain human parateleportation, some think it is a means used by nature to distribute things over the face of this planet.

23. **Elimination.** Others think it could be a natural resource of instantaneous protective elimination.

24. **Extraphysical consciousnesses.** The phenomenon of parateleporation may also be provoked by the direct action of extraphysical consciousnesses, thus resulting in *assisted parateleportation.*

Reactions. Human parateleportation has caused many attendants of parapsychic sessions held by sensitives of various types of phenomenological manifestations to become amazed, lower their heads, completely disturbed and confused, or suddenly leave the scene, sometimes scared and stunned.

Parapathology. There have been complicated occurrences of parateleported persons, within the world of parapathology, such as the following 3:

1. **Saboteur.** Parateleportation to military areas forbidden to outsiders, leading the parateleported individual to be taken for a saboteur.

2. **Thief.** Parateleportation inside residences and stores at improper times, when they are closed to the public, which causes the parateleported individual to be taken for a thief.

3. **Poltergeist.** Other occurrences reveal the aspect of *intrusion-related parateleportation,* which are linked to poltergeist activity in certain cases.

Descriptions. In classic descriptions of human parateleportation "whirlwind" is used to refer to"being carried by the wind," "aerial journey," "flying brothers," "unexpected disappearances and reappearances."

Conditions. The parateleported individual sometimes disappears from within a dark room with closed doors and windows and reappears in another room, at a distant location in the same condition, but turned around or facing in the opposite direction.

Bible. The Bible is a fertile field for human parateleportation research. The following 5 such topics:

1. **Elijah.** Elijah raised up in a chariot of fire (2 Kings 2:1).
2. **Ezekiel.** Ezekiel lifted up into the sky (Ezekiel 11: 1).
3. **Nebuchadnezzar.** The episode of men in the furnace of Nebuchadnezzar (604-566 B.C.), (Daniel 3: 20-27).
4. **Philip.** Philip transported from Gaza to Azotus, located more than 30 miles (50 kilometers) away (Acts 8: 39, 40).
5. **Pedro.** The freeing of Pedro from a hermetically sealed, heavily guarded prison (Acts 12: 7-11).

Recent. In the twentieth century, different types of cases of human parateleportation are known, such as the following 4:

1. **Shamans.** The human parateleportation of shamans.
2. **Ectoplasmic.** Ectoplasmic persons or sensitives in ectoplasmy sessions.
3. **Scotto.** The celebrated parapsychic physical effects session of Marquis Carlo Centurione Scotto, held on July 29, 1928, in the castle of Millesimo, in the province of Savona, Italy.
4. **Mirabelli.** The still highly controversial phenomenon of Carmilo Mirabelli (1889-1951), one of the greatest physical effect sensitives of all time, who was parateleported, almost instantaneously, from Estação da Luz, in the city of São Paulo, Brazil, to the city of São Vicente, Brazil, located approximately 56 miles (90 kilometers) away.

Self-parateleportation. The day will come when terrestrial sensitives will practice self-parateleportation or, in other words, the phenomenon will be induced at will, just as many persons are already able to perform self-levitation at will while in the ordinary, physical waking state.

Research. A question for the research of human parateleportation is appropriate here: How many parateleported persons are not included in missing person reports?

Complement. In certain cases, it is presumed that parateleportation actually *complements* the phenomenon of physical bilocation. Instead of the psychosoma returning *en bloc* to the human body through the retraction of the silver cord, the opposite occurs, namely the psychosoma attracting the cells of the human body toward itself, *en bloc,* by way of the same silver cord.

Magnitude. This phenomenon evidences the extraordinary magnitude of the action of the psychosoma as a biological organizing agent or model of the human body (irruption of the psychosoma in the soma).

Transport. In advanced cases of conjunction of the phenomena of poltergeist, intrusiveness, projection of the consciousness and physical bilocation, the bilocation of the person, who is generally mystical, is transformed into a full parateleportation, or projective transportation (OBE transportation).

Decomposition. In these more complex cases, the human body of the bilocator atomically decomposes in the physical base, recomposing itself at another location.

Case study. An example of parateleportation as a consequence of the phenomena of poltergeist or perhaps even intrusiveness, is the case of the young Tyrolese woman, Angelica Darocca, a rigorous ascetic, who *sweated (exuded) blood,* presented stigmas on various areas of the human body and frequently disappeared from her cell, only to reappear inside it later. She was seen in neighboring or distant cities during these disappearances.

Witnesses. The phenomenon of human parateleportation has not given rise to witnesses of transportational movement, per se.

Prapil. The name *prapil* is given to the faculty that the raja yogi acquires of moving in the emotional parabody (psychosoma) from one place to another, as distant as it may be.

Disappearances. Human parateleportation corresponds exactly, by analogy, to the phenomenon of the sudden extraphysical disappearance of extraphysical consciousnesses, as well as projected intraphysical consciousnesses, that manifest in the psychosoma and are commonly observed by other intraphysical consciousnesses that are also projected.

Self-permeability. Human parateleportation temporarily provides the intraphysical consciousness, when discoincident in its vehicles, with the quality of extraphysical self-permeability, or the act of passing through dense, physical objects – such as walls, doors and closed windows – and even the possibility of volitation, in certain cases.

Bibliography: Andreas (36, p. 114), Benavides (110, p. 81), Berg (121, p. 143), Bonin (168, p. 485), Boswell (174, p. 99), Chaplin (273, p. 157), Day (376, p. 133), Fodor (530, p. 7), Frazer (549, p. 259), Goes (605, p. 92), Hitching (727, p. 223), Morel (1086, p. 171), Morris (1093, p. 144), Paula (1208, p. 158), Randall (1369, p. 40), Rogo (1447, p. 107), Shepard (1548, p. 917), Steiger (1601, p. 97), Toben (1699, p. 80).

83. PHENOMENA CONCOMITANT WITH LUCID PROJECTION

Definition. Concomitant phenomenon: that phenomenon which does or does not occur within the space-time continuum, but simultaneously with the occurrence of the lucid projection experience, in a spontaneous and unexpected manner.

Synonymy: by-product of lucid projection; collateral phenomenon; confluent phenomenon; epiphenomenon; intercurrent phenomenon; peripheral effect; peripheral phenomenon; reflex phenomenon; residual phenomenon; surprise-phenomenon.

Complex. Besides the fact of situating the consciousness outside the human body, the lucid projection experience invariably causes certain consequent concomitant parapsychic phenomena (surprise-phenomena) as collateral results of the experience.

Phenomenology. This serves to affirm the character and nature of the phenomenological complex of projectiology.

Sciences. Peripheral phenomena also occur in the fields of medicine and psychotherapy.

Causes. The following 4, among others, have an influence as generative factors of peripheral parapsychic phenomena in general:

1. **Resistance.** The individual's psychological resistances when participating in experiments.

2. **Categories.** It is important to clarify that there are two categories of psychological resistance: healthy, or the self-defense of survival, and pathological, such as those who experience mood swings related to medication being taken.

3. **Anxieties.** Anxieties and the inner defensive reactions of this same individual.

4. **Meteorology.** The meteorological aspects at that time of the experiment. Does atmospheric pressure have an influence in this case?

Laboratory. It is interesting to point out that the incidence of concomitant phenomena affects not only spontaneous and provoked individual lucid projections, but also projective experiments performed in the laboratory. There are already various cases of this nature which have been registered.

Classification. The concomitant phenomena that are more common to lucid projection can be classified into two basic categories: primary and secondary.

1. **Primary.** The following 5 are the most notable *greater* primary phenomena which are concomitant to lucid projection:

   A. Double awareness.
   B. Precognition.
   C. Retrocognition.
   D. Extraphysical psychometry.
   E. Benign catalepsy.

2. **Secondary.** The following 8 are the most notable *lesser* secondary phenomena which are concomitant to lucid projection

   A. Vibrational state.
   B. Transitional state.
   C. Extraphysical evocation.
   D. Current of extraphysical force.
   E. Extraphysical energetic shower.
   F. Extraphysical trauma.
   G. Psychophysical repercussion.
   H. Condition of waking discoincidence.

Bibliography: Ebon (453, p. 76), Fiore (517, p. 167), Greenhouse (636, p. 299), Morris (1092, p. 53), Osis (1159, p. 16), Steiger (1601, p. 226).

---

84. PRELIMINARY PHENOMENA

Definition. Preliminary phenomena: that *lesser occurrence* that *precedes,* prepares, and indicates a *greater occurrence* and, although showing similarities and correlations between the nature of their manifestations, also presents certain pronounced differences between both manifestations, whether qualitative and/or quantitative in nature.

Synonymy: antecedent phenomenon; miniature phenomenon; *miniphenomenon;* preambular phenomenon; precursor phenomenon; trailer phenomenon.

Previsions. The preliminary phenomenon demonstrates the nature, quality or category of the *whole,* in regard to the main phenomenon. It also permits the making of forecasts and prognostications, extremely accurate approximations or coinciding probabilities regarding the next level of evolution of the facts, projects and techniques in diverse areas of the interests and research of humankind.

Categories. The following are 7 categories of preliminary phenomena:

1. **Physics:** the representative fragment of the product.
2. **Engineering:** the showroom.
3. **Industry:** the small free sample.
4. **Biology:** the incubation period (biological or pathological privation).
5. **Psychology:** the laboratory of transformations (experimentation).
6. **Sports:** the preliminary game.
7. **Art:** the general rehearsal of a large-scale performance.

Precedence. In the existing phenomenological complex within the scope of conscientiology research, the well-defined phenomenon of *greater effects,* in the scale of the development of the events, is always preceded by an also very well-defined phenomenon of *lesser effects.* These are indicative of an inferior category or, in other words, are of reduced importance relative to the expression of the results of the main phenomenon. This finally forms a natural series of interlinked facts (cascade effect, domino effect, halo effect) that can also manifest in a process of constant relay.

Standard. There is no doubt regarding the 3 standard aspects of the abovementioned phenomena of the consciousness:

1. **Sequence.** There is an ordered sequence between those phenomena with *lesser* effects and those phenomena with *greater* effects.

2. **Implication.** A relationship of implication between both phenomena stands out, allowing the first phenomenon to forecast what is to follow.

3. **Expression.** The qualitatively greater expression of the second phenomenon (*maxi*phenomenon) over the first (*mini*phenomenon) becomes evident to the consciousness.

Projectiology. It is possible to affirm, without fear of contradiction, that the world of conscientiology research, particularly in its subdiscipline of projectiology, does not deviate from these *rules of precedence* regarding the xenophrenic states and basic projectiological phenomena. Let us consider 10 examples:

1. **Daydreams.** In a determinate line of ascending manifestations, it is observed with mathematical clarity, for example, that a daydream can precede a hypnagogic state (hypnagogy) in the mentalsomatic world of all intraphysical consciousnesses.

2. **Dream.** A common dream, or the exteriorization of repressed mental contents or *oneiric excretions,* can precede a lucid dream, even for those persons with no evident parapsychic tendencies.

3. **Semilucid.** A lucid dream, or semilucid projection can, in turn, like a specific factor, precede a great lucid consciential projection (OBE).

4. **Previews.** Occasional human lucid projections (previews of desoma, temporary minideaths) obviously precede the final projection, or desoma, for all human lucid projectors. They comprise a series of desomas which are as real as natural desoma or biological death of the human body (deactivation of the soma).

5. **Near-death.** The near-death experience (NDE) evidently always precedes desoma for all those who have had this experience.

6. **Bilocation.** Physical bilocation (bicorporeity) can precede the phenomenon of human parateleportation, this second phenomenon thereby constituting a spontaneous complement to the first phenomenon.

7. **Remote.** In another line of ascending parapsychic manifestations, remote viewing (RV) precedes traveling clairvoyance (TC).

8. **Miniprojection.** Traveling clairvoyance, or consciential miniprojection, in turn, precedes the great lucid projection, even in the manner of a prior projection, in certain cases.

9. **Exteriorization.** The exteriorization of consciential energies, whether executed spontaneously or deliberately, precedes extraphysical telekinesis.

10. **Facial.** Facial clairvoyance can precede the act of installing the phenomenon of materialization (ectoplasmy) per se, and so on.

Gradual. Without a doubt, preliminary phenomena constitute the greatest evidence of the law of the gradual, step by step development of animic-parapsychic sensitivities.

Generation. Animic (intraconsciential) development, namely direct, firsthand experience of the consciousness – much less, parapsychic development, namely intermediary, second hand, experience of the consciousness of any type – is not obtained *suddenly,* through spontaneous generation.

Repetition. The achievement of greater sensitivity becomes virtually unsustainable without the continued repetition of the lesser sensitivities, on the part of the consciousness that is self-organized, rigidly disciplined and persistent in the control of the manifestations of its consciential vehicles.

Evaluation. Being self-aware of this mechanism of animic-parapsychic development, any intraphysical consciousness interested in conscientiology can evaluate his/her own parapsychic development in any line of consciential manifestation in which he/she wishes to evolve.

Usefulness. The basic usefulness of the preliminary phenomenon is to offer the interested individual the ideal formula for evaluation – the unit of measurement of his/her own consciential performance – even when he/she feels at a complete loss to give meaning to the events and his/her parapsychic, energetic, intraconsciential or multidimensional experiences.

Stagnation. Any person with evident parapsychism who has been repeating the same procedures and obtaining the same parapsychic results for a decade, always in the same manner, without any innovation or addition to the phenomenological dynamic of his/her manifestations and without any greater or more expressive conquest, clearly remains stopped in time, stagnated in his/her inner improvement.

Inflexibility. He/she may even be performing very well at that level, animated by the most noble concerns and intentions, and may feel self-realized with this, living like a person who is not very willing to admit to having made the slightest errors. He/she is nevertheless complacent, at a standstill in regard to his/her true self-knowledge, showing little mental flexibility in the search for his/her greatest performance in the execution of the existential program.

Step. Each preliminary phenomenon, although not being a summary or synthesis, indicates the next step to which the intraphysical consciousness, if he/she is willing and capable of experimentally producing some lucid consciential projection, should be attentive in order to maintain his/her personal progress in gear.

Direction. The preliminary phenomenon clearly and rationally indicates the direction in which the intraphysical consciousness should concentrate his/her efforts as an animic and parapsychic, energeticist projector, outlining the next, immediate achievement before him/her that is closer at hand.

Evolution. For the individual who keeps his/her feet firmly planted in intraphysical reality but has nevertheless neglected the abovementioned areas of study and is still a victim of the "I will leave it until tomorrow" syndrome, it is important to remember that consciential development in any evolutionary field, besides being infinite, is inevitable. This is because it is truly the essence of the march of evolution of the consciential principle (ego), through that notion which is conventionally referred to as *eternity*.

IV – Altered States of Consciousness

85. XENOPHRENIA

Definition. Xenophrenia (Greek: *xenos,* strange; *phren,* mind): the state of the human consciousness, outside the normal pattern of ordinary, physical waking state, induced by physical, physiological, psychological, pharmacological or parapsychic agents.

Synonymy: altered state of consciousness; alternative perceptions; changes in consciential states; dislocation of consciential perceptions; modified state of consciousness; non-ordinary state of consciousness; xenophrenic state.

Alterations. First and foremost, it is necessary to rationally characterize the circumstantial, *intra-subjective* altered state of consciousness pertaining to the ego itself. Examples include: daydreams, hypnagogy, sleep, somnambulism, ordinary dreams, nightmares, hallucinations and many others.

Distinctions. In this way, it becomes possible to establish the substantially distinctive characteristics of the state of consciential manifestation per se which – although not ceasing to be an altered state of consciousness – presents itself as being far more objective, a condition that is evolutionarily broader and less ephemeral for the ego and with respect to which there are so far only 3 known very distinct states: the intraphysical, extraphysical and projected states.

Manifestations. The expression *projected state* summarizes, in the essence of its meanings (umbrella term), all types of specific projections of the consciousness and the entire specific field of research of the science of projectiology.

Appearance. Many altered states of consciousness, if not all of them, can arise in any of the 3 states of manifestation of the consciousness.

Medicine. From a medical point of view, an altered state of consciousness leads patients to report some of the following 10 experiences:

1. Alterations in concentration, attention, memory or critical judgment.
2. Distortions in perception.
3. Disturbances regarding the sense of chronological time.
4. Emotional extremes oscillating between jubilant ecstasy and deep fears (some type of phobia).
5. Fear of losing touch with reality.
6. Hyper-suggestibility.
7. Ineffability.
8. Sensation of separation between the mind and the human body.
9. Sense of profound truth and discernment.
10. Sense of renewed hope.

Actuation. Altered states of consciousness permit the appearance of almost all parapsychic phenomena and act intensely in at least the following 3 occurrences:

1. In scientific intuition.
2. In poetic inspiration.
3. In mystical-religious ecstasy.

Predominance. In general, the different consciential states appear due to the operational predominance of a specific attribute of the consciousness over the other attributes.

Rapidity. The act whereby the consciousness passes from one state to another, with the predominance of one of its attributes, occurs with ease and in a extremely rapid manner, or instantaneously, according to our sense of chronological time.

Analyses. For this reason, the following 8 observations, among others, can be itemized in an initial analysis:

1. **Will.** In the physical and extraphysical states in which the consciousness is awake and lucid, the will predominates over the other consciential attributes.

2. **Reason.** In the act of critical judgment, reason subjugates imagination.

3. **Imagination.** In the hypnagogic state (altered state of consciousness), imagination and will replace reason.

4. **Memory.** In the phenomenon of retrocognition, the depth of the most remote memory, or integral memory (holomemory), replaces the will.

5. **Unconscious.** In the natural, ordinary dream state (altered state of consciousness), the unconscious – the so greatly unknown *dead file of the consciousness* – replaces the will.

6. **Precognition.** In the phenomenon of precognition, parapsychism (animism or extrasensory perception) replaces the waking memory or that of the ordinary, physical waking state.

7. **Animism.** In the phenomena of animism in general, the will of the consciousness predominates over the influence of the will of external intelligences or consciousnesses.

8. **Parapsychism.** In the manifestations of parapsychism, the sensitive's consciousness makes itself passive to the will of another (an extraphysical consciousness or a projected intraphysical consciousness) which takes the place of the sensitive's will. This even occurs with the help of another extraphysical consciousness, in this case, the sensitive's helper or even blind guide.

Units. Many altered states of consciousness can be considered to be isolated units of associated mental events.

Types. Diverse altered states of consciousness can be confused with lucid projection, such as the following 18:

1. Catalepsy.
2. Continuity and/or discontinuity of awareness.
3. Daydream or guided waking dream.
4. Double awareness.
5. Extraphysical somnambulism.
6. Hallucination.
7. Hypnagogy or semi-awake state.
8. Hypnopompy.
9. Hypnotic trance.
10. Lucid dream or semilucid projection (SLP).
11. Meditation.
12. Nightmare.
13. Ordinary dream.
14. Parapsychic trance.
15. Psychedelic experience.
16. Self-hypnosis or autosuggestion.
17. Self-intrusion or obsession (self-corruption).
18. Triple awareness.

Understanding. To understand xenophrenic states is to understand lucid projection of the consciousness.

Criterion. The intraphysical projector has to seek out a personal criterion for distinguishing heteropsychic stimuli, or those coming from external worlds (the physical and extraphysical, in general), from self-psychic stimuli, or those of an internal origin. The projector also needs to avoid possible confusion between that which the consciousness actually perceives and that which is no more than its creations, such as: hallucinations, daydreams, morphothosenes (thought-forms), nightmares or dreams.

Awareness. Objectifying awareness regarding the above-mentioned criterion, this section addresses the xenophrenic states, making extensive comparisons, parallels, and lists of the differential characteristics between them. This is done in order to provide distinguishing elements to the experimenter who wishes to obtain personal proof of the reality regarding the qualities of the lucid projective consciential experience.

Separation. The separate study of these consciential states is extremely positive.

States. The more we deepen our individual analytical approach toward each consciential state, the less difficult the comprehension of their complexities will be. This is also the case regarding forced consciential projection, spontaneous lucid consciential projection, the natural sleep state, the condition of extracorporeal sleep, ordinary dreams, lucid dreams per se, extracorporeal dreams, and other phenomena.

Sleep. Undoubtedly, although the consciousness may be one and the same, the condition of sleep, in the state of consciousness according to the vehicles of manifestation, is not the same as the condition of extracorporeal sleep, since the consciential circumstances are different.

Dreams. The same occurs with the condition of ordinary dreams and the condition of extracorporeal dreams, and even with forced lucid consciential projections and spontaneous lucid consciential projections.

Bibliography: Brown (211, p. 200), Davies (370, p. 28), Garfield (569, p. 114), Grattan-Guinness (626, p. 326), Greenhouse (636, p. 45), Ludwig (956, p. 225), Roll (1466, p. 231), Sabom (1486, p. 239), Steiger (1601, p. 56), Tart (1653, p. 1), Walker (1781, p. 79), White (1829, p. 23).

---

86. CLASSIFICATION OF XENOPHRENIC STATES

Projection. Lucid projection, along with its entire phenomenological complex, constitutes one of the altered states of the human consciousness.

Phenomena. The phenomena of projection can be classified into 3 basic categories according to phenomenological phases, or the chronological stages of the experiments: physical waking state phenomena, transitional phenomena and extraphysical waking state phenomena.

1. **Physical.** The physical waking phenomena according to consciential states: ordinary, physical waking state, daydream and the transform state.

2. **Transitional.** The transitional phenomena: pre-takeoff, hypnagogic state, sleep and takeoff of the psychosoma.

3. **Extraphysical.** The extraphysical waking state phenomena: oneiric state, nightmare state and extraphysical awakening.

Divisions. The researcher Susan J. Blackmore affirms that natural divisions exist between the different states of consciousness, an observation that the author fully agrees with. Some states of consciousness are close to each other and some are more distant. Some of the limits between these states are easy to cross and others are far more difficult.

Dream. Lucid dream is very close to lucid projection, whereas ordinary dream is far removed.

Nightmare. The nightmare state is situated between these 2 types of dream.

Self-awareness. The condition of the consciousness in the ordinary, physical waking state of the intraphysical consciousness is quite similar to the condition of the intraphysical consciousness when fully projected outside the human body.

Projectability. Lucid projection can be reached with some difficulty from the ordinary, physical waking state, but can be achieved more easily from the hypnagogic state and easier still from a lucid dream.

Relationship. We can classify the xenophrenic states, which are directly related to lucid projection, into 10 basic consciential states in the following order of occurrence: daydream, hypnagogy, transform state, sleep, somnambulism, dream, lucid dream or semilucid projection, nightmare, interconsciential intrusion and hallucination. The following chapters address the relationships of these xenophrenic states with the phenomenon of lucid consciential projection.

Bibliography: Blackmore (147, p. 2).

87. MECHANISMS OF LUCID PROJECTION

Vibration. Briefly, it can be affirmed that projection of the consciousness from the human body is produced by the increase in the vibrations of the vehicles of manifestation of the consciousness, including here the human body itself, as well as the mentalsoma.

Analogies. To show this occurrence we can use crude comparisons or admittedly rough analogies.

Bus. A comparison: when the vibrational frequency of a bus motor reaches a certain pitch, one of the windows in the bus can begin to vibrate together with the motor. What has occurred is that the motor reached the natural vibrational frequency of that window as a whole and the window entered into resonance with the motor.

Body. Each body as a whole has a natural vibrational frequency. Every time that another body reaches this frequency, it makes the first one enter into resonance with the second or, in other words, absorb the other's energy with great intensity.

Transmitter. In the case under analysis, the air (or the sound) is the intermediary transmitter for conducting this energy, as is the forced vibration of the bus itself, in part.

Resonance. If the phenomenon of resonance continues at a high intensity, and if the resonant frequency is identical and not only close, the window will crack or, if it is not securely restrained, will separate from the bus.

Glass. Another comparison: the opera singer breaks a glass when reaching a certain note, or sonorous frequency, that is identical to the natural frequency of the glass as a whole.

Acoustics. In this case, the glass enters into resonance with the note, beginning to rock when the frequency comes close. If the note has a great intensity (or potency) and the singer is persistent, the glass will break into small pieces.

Air. The intermediate transmitter of energy in this case is the air, through the phenomenon of sound, which carries vibratory acoustic energy.

Psychosoma. Each vehicle of manifestation of the consciousness has a natural vibrational frequency. The psychosoma, which is *inside* the human body, having increased its vibrational frequency (extraphysical vibrations) and, probably having reached its natural vibrational frequency, frees itself from the vibrations of the dense organism, thus giving rise to the projection of the consciousness in the psychosoma.

Mentalsoma. The mentalsoma, in turn, having increased its vibrational frequency (mental vibrations), frees itself from the psychosoma, thus giving rise to the projection of the consciousness in the isolated mentalsoma. The psychosoma is considered here to be acting together with the energies of the holochakra, with anywhere from the highest to the lowest extraphysical density of the psychosoma's composition.

Frequency. The psychosoma has a natural vibratory frequency that is higher than that of the human body and lower than that of the mentalsoma. In other words, the psychosoma's resonance energy is higher than that of the human body and lower than that of the mentalsoma.

Phenomena. This fact clarifies innumerous phenomena, including the mechanism of the vibrational state (VS), the mechanism of extraphysical translocation, the influence of a low heart rate in consciential projection, and others.

Structure. The subtler structure of the psychosoma escapes from the dense structure of the human body. The same occurs with the mentalsoma in relation to the psychosoma.

Comparisons. The comparisons made can be specified even further, characterizing the bus as though it were the human body and the window as though it were, for example, an extraphysical arm that projects alone, or the partial projection of a para-arm. The motor of the bus, in this case, would be the mentalsoma or, more precisely, the consciousness.

Summary. In summary, the act of one vehicle of manifestation leaving another, be it the psychosoma or the mentalsoma, depends only upon its achieving the natural vibrational frequency of each one of them through (by some mechanism) the transmission of the resonance energy to these bodies.

Discoincidence. The mechanism of discoincidence of the vehicles of manifestation of the consciousness is therefore based on the phenomenon of resonance.

Universality. One of the definitive pieces of evidence regarding the natural, paraphysical and energetic aspect of lucid projection phenomena that speaks in favor of the increase in the natural vibrational frequency of the consciousness' vehicles of manifestation is the fact that it occurs in disparate cultures, epochs, races, locations and environments, through diverse but fundamentally similar processes, or with a reasonable level of functional interaction.

Verification. The above-cited universality can be verified through various analytical and critical research results, testimonies and autobiographical analyses, such as those occurring between intraphysical consciousnesses, as well as those from extraphysical consciousnesses:

1. Germans (Engel; Fischer; Lischka. See the International Bibliography).
2. Brazilians (Pereira; Prado; Vieira).
3. Danes (Vett).
4. Spaniards (Anglada).
5. French (Durville; Lefebure; Lancelin; "Yram").
6. English (Brennan; Brittain; Crookall; Fox; Gerhardie; Green; Sculthorp; Turvey).
7. Irish (Garrett).
8. North Americans (Greene; Monroe; Muldoon; Swann; Tanous).
9. Indigenous Hawaiians (Long).
10. Mexican Indians (Castaneda).
11. Extraphysical consciousnesses (Maes; Xavier; and many others).

Bibliography: Anglada (39, p. 25), Brennan (200, p. 71), Brittain (206, p. 45), Castaneda (258, p. 20), Crookall (330, p. 1), Durville (436, p. 1), Engel (480, p. 1), Fischer (519, p. 19), Fox (544, p. 32), Garrett (574, p. 67), Gerhardie (584, p. 1), Green (632, p. 1), Greene (635, p. 1), Lancelin (879, p. 309), Lefebure (909, p. 65), Lischka (937, p. 91), Long (946, p. 33), Maes (984, p. 85), Monroe (1065, p. l), Muldoon (1105, p. l), Pereira (1230, p. 16), Prado (1284, p. 1), Sculthorp (1531, p. 17), Swann (1632, p. 65), Tanous (1647, p. 113), Turvey (1707, p. 111), Vett (1738, p. 379), Vieira (1762, p. 7), Xavier (1881, p. 97), Yram (1897, p. 1).

---

88. LUCID PROJECTION AND DAYDREAMS

Definition. Daydream: fantastical story line created by the imagination during the ordinary, physical waking state of the human consciousness or intraphysical consciousness.

Synonymy: associative flow; daydreaming; directed waking dream; diurnal dream; dream realization; flight of fancy; gilded dream; lazy dream; mental digression; mental wandering; mentambulism; oneirism; open-eyed dream; secret fantasy.

Fantasy. Fantasy is a by-product of subjective reality. It is composed of thoughts originating entirely from the consciousness.

Denominations. Fantasy is called by many names, such as the following 6:

1. Castles in the air.
2. Daydreams.
3. Fairy tales.
4. Imaginary events.
5. Imaginary fiction.
6. Science fiction.

Usefulness. Fantasies are useful and important and even essential in practical life.

Creativity. Every creative idea began as a fantasy.

Psychosoma. Literature, drama, music, the fashion and culinary industries, love and sex, and many other things derived from the consciousness based on the *emotional* parabody (psychosoma), somehow exist due to fantasy.

Science. Without fantasy, science – derived from the consciousness and stemming from the *mentalsoma,* the parabody of discernment – would be a mere collection of data, without any ability to formulate connections, interactions and relationships between them.

Theory. Theory – a precursor of all experimentation – is a fantasy until it is proved or confirmed through repeated verification.

Subjects. In this book, there are texts on subjects based entirely on fantasy, such as the following 2 examples:

1. Questionnaire for *serenissimus.*
2. The Ideal Projector.

Uncertainty. Even under the best circumstances there is some uncertainty in determining what is fantasy and what is reality. One of the objectives of science is to reduce this uncertainty to the minimum.

Distinctions. Upon gaining more experience, especially through consciential projections in series, the projector rationalizes and clearly defines the differential characteristics of 5 categories of oneiric experiences for himself:

1. **Projection.** Lucid projection and the common dream of flying and falling.
2. **Physiology.** The dream with an organic origin or originating in the physiology of the soma.
3. **Autobiography.** The *historical* dream or one that focuses on a passage from the individual's personal history, or autobiography.
4. **Nightmare.** The nightmare or the dream with a predominance of a distressing factor.
5. **Waking.** The daydream or *oneiric* fantasy generated while still in the ordinary, physical waking state, where special physiological symptoms do not arise.

Analysis. In some *consciential circumstances* the experienced projector is able to perfectly distinguish personal daydreams (the free association of ideas with the tendency to *magnify* and *justify them*) from lucid projections and even that he/she is experiencing a dream or nightmare based on *the themes of his/her projections.*

Minimization. The analytical criterion of the consciousness becomes so pronounced that these altered states of consciousness – ordinary dream, physiological dream, personal history or autobiographical dream, projective dream, nightmare, daydream, and even oneiric projection, lucid projection and semilucid projection – are so well-defined that they end up being minimized and each one put in its proper place, often at the same instant at which they occur, thus diminishing their importance or partially eliminating them.

Protest. Daydreams above all constitute protests against reality. They do not have the need for logical reflection and lack direction and purpose.

Preparation. Daydreams have been employed as an efficient technique for the intraphysical consciousness to feel inner peace, inner quietude, profound well-being and conciliate natural sleep. This technique is used when confronted with acute crises and the extreme pressures of daily life in human experience, when the individual's mind is very agitated by supposed problems that cannot be resolved. In addition, and more importantly, this technique helps the consciousness to prepare to lucidly project, in certain cases.

Technique. The technique of the ascensional daydream, guided daydream or gilded dream, consists of a great concentration of positive thoughts in which the intraphysical consciousness imagines, in great detail, everything that will make him/her the happiest person in the world at that moment.

Details. In this creation or mental reconstitution of the "apparently impossible," the will, the imagination and one's fantastical creations come together and introduce, in the most minute detail, everything that composes an ideal world for the individual, or at least the following 7 experiential variables:

1. **Location.** The most marvelous location possible.
2. **Weather.** The most exceptional weather conditions.
3. **Company.** The most desirable company.
4. **Clothes.** The most brilliant outfit or the most sumptuous clothing.
5. **Dishes.** Those culinary dishes that are preferred and considered a must.
6. **Impressions.** Those most dreamt-of pleasurable personal impressions or sensations.
7. **Atmosphere.** The materialization of a scenario and an atmosphere with all the illusions that are most craved in human life, in conditions capable of making you completely and definitively happy.

Predominance. Upon reaching the level at which the consciousness predominates over matter, one's mental focus or concentration reaches such an intense, profound level that it becomes real, thus making the consciousness truly happy, distant from inner problems and diuturnal pressures. This will bring psychic and muscular self-relaxation, absolute self-confidence, and the sleep that is sought, all in a natural manner, without the use of any stupefacient and without an excessive waste of time, consciential energies and money.

Bibliography: Lefebure (913, p. 175), MacLaine (980, p. 245), Rogo (1444, p. 123), Steiger (1601, p. 217), Vieira (1762, p. 123).

89. COMPARISONS BETWEEN DAYDREAMS AND LUCID PROJECTIONS

Differential. The differential characteristics between daydreams and lucid projections are well defined and unmistakable with regard to 4 angles of approach:

1. **Coincidence.** When in the condition of the daydream, the intraphysical consciousness is aware of being *inside* or coincident with the human body, in the ordinary, physical waking state. When in the condition of the lucid consciential projection, the intraphysical consciousness knows and feels that it is *outside* the human body or discoincident, and is even able to see the dense body in front of it (self-bilocation phenomenon).
2. **Forms.** In daydreams, less dense substratums arise that are of a physical origin and are tangible or palpable, such as a succession of mental images. In the lucid projection that occurs in physical districts and even in certain extraphysical crustal or tropospheric environments, there is an incontrovertible concretization of much denser physical and extraphysical forms, thought-forms or morphothosenes.
3. **Nature.** The daydream is a consciential condition that is far more oneiric than projective. The consciousness itself distinguishes the major lucid consciential projection in all of its aspects, from the consciential states of dream, nightmare and daydream.
4. **Clairvoyance.** The manifestations of the daydream are similar in part to those of traveling clairvoyance, although the latter presents clearer story lines and goes beyond the inconsequential simple mental elaboration of the human consciousness.

Ascensional. It is curious that the condition of the daydream (as well as the ordinary dream) shows itself to be so different from the condition of consciential projection that it also ends up constituting a process whereby the consciousness can project itself from the human body, called *ascensional daydream* or *guided daydream*. This technique is based on the act wherein the intraphysical consciousness, while in the ordinary, physical waking state, imagines leaving the human body and rising up through space, with the help of rhythmic respiration, after *preparation* through the daydream.

Bibliography: Lefebure (909, p. 176), Vieira (1762, p. 123).

90. LUCID PROJECTION AND SLEEP

Definition. Natural sleep: the state of rest in humans and higher animals that is especially characterized by the normal and periodic suppression of perceptive activity, voluntary motor force and daily social interrelationships, through the relaxation of the senses and muscles, reduction in the heart and respiratory rates, as well as oneiric activity, during which the organism recuperates from fatigue.

Synonymy: daily projection; half-life; Morpheus; nap; normal sleep; ordinary sleep; spontaneous sleep; state of those who sleep.

Organizer. Sleep is the most powerful organizer of the physical body's physiology and the individual's human life. No one escapes this imperative.

Necessity. It is easier to go without food, water and company than without sleep. Sleep is a natural necessity, but it is also a cultural fact and a rite.

Minideath. The state of natural sleep, without consciential projection, is the first and true *minideath*.

Sleepers. Some individuals sleep normally, while others sleep badly. Approximately 15% of the earth's population, when sleeping, has more or less serious difficulties in endeavoring to obtain *sufficient daily* (or nightly) *sleep*.

Phases. Sleep goes through various phases that are divided into ordered cycles of complex activity throughout the night.

Interleukin. A discovery made about sleep reveals that the "S factor," part of a group of chemical elements, can provoke sleep, regulate temperature and stimulate the organism's immunological system. In the final part of the sleep process, a substance called interleukin-1 is liberated, which provokes sleep and stimulates the immunological system.

Immunology. Sleep allows the immunological system to recuperate from environmental challenges faced during the ordinary, physical waking state of the individual in activity.

Movements. While sleeping, an adult makes about 40 to 70 more pronounced movements, including turns and jerks, uses 160 liters of oxygen, and exhales 130 liters of carbonic anhydride each night.

Variations. These variations impede the accumulation of blood in the inert body, maintain a constant exchange of oxygen and carbon dioxide, and maintain the muscular tonus.

Vegetative. The so-called *correlative* organic functions that operate without the action of the will, operating in an involuntary or automatic manner, such as reflexive acts (e.g., respiration, heart rate, gastrointestinal mobility and perspiration) or vegetative life, are regulated by the vegetative or autonomic nervous system. It is mainly composed of 2 nervous systems having opposing functions that balance each other: the sympathetic and parasympathetic (vagus) nervous systems.

Sympathetic. The predominance of the sympathetic nervous system maintains the consciousness in the ordinary, physical waking state.

Vagus. The predominance of the vagus nerves allows the state of natural sleep.

Latency. The latency of sleep, or the period between turning off the light and the act of sleeping, is less than 15 minutes under normal conditions. On average, it is between 6 and 8 minutes.

Pre-sleep. The pre-sleep state, called *stage 0,* occurs when one starts to fall asleep.

Belief. Since the times of the ancient Greeks, it was always believed that Hypnos, the god of sleep, was the younger brother of Thanatos, the god of death, but this supposition or belief is relative.

Similarity. Sleep is only similar to biological death because it separates the vehicles of manifestation of the consciousness and carries the latter to the extraphysical dimension, thus realizing a daily, natural, physiological, inoffensive and generally nonlucid projection.

Coma. Sleep is neither a passive phenomenon, nor is it the younger brother of the light coma state (neurology).

Manifestations. An infinite number of activities or manifestations occur during sleep.

Thalamus. The thalamus – both the diencephalon (neurons, neurology) and the *energetically shielded chamber* (bedroom, sexosomatics) – play an active role in the control of sleep and wakefulness.

Laboratories. In sleep laboratories, scientists study this altered state of consciousness, sleep, with volunteers daubed with contact gel, and small electrodes connected to the face and scalp.

Polyhypnograph. The electrodes send messages to a polyhypnograph, a recording device that transcribes the sleeping person's brain waves, heart beats, eyes movements and muscular activity onto moving continuous sheets of chart paper using ink pens that oscillate.

Types. There are 2 basic types of sleep that alternate: slow sleep and rapid sleep.

1. **Slow.** Slow, inactive or calm sleep, a period of bodily relaxation, is classified as non-REM or NREM (non-rapid eye movement) sleep, and is composed of 4 progressively deeper stages.

1. Light (5-7 cycles per second, theta waves).
2. Confirmed (4-5 cycles per second, theta waves).
3. Deep (2-4 cycles per second, delta waves).
4. Very deep (0.5-2 cycles per second, delta waves).

Electroencephalograph. The electroencephalograph (EEG) registers the phases of rest with characteristic brain waves.

Temperature. During slow sleep, the heart rate drops, respiration slows and body temperature reaches its lowest point.

2. **Rapid.** Rapid or active sleep is characterized by EEG tracings that are distinct from those of the slow period, presenting total muscular atonia, rapid synchronistic movements of the eyeballs under the closed eyelids, and intense brain activity, as evidenced by strong variations in metabolic activity, a suppression of muscular activity and vivid dreams.

REM. This type receives the name of REM sleep (rapid eye movement sleep).

Dreams. In the phase of sleep in which the eyeballs present rapid, synchronistic, involuntary eye movements (REM) under the closed eyelids, there is an increase in brain activity, heart rate, respiratory frequency, hormonal secretion and the appearance of different patterns of brain waves and dreams.

Register. The polyhypnograph registers the sleeping person's brain waves, pulse and respiration, more pronounced body movements, and involuntary, rapid, synchronistic bi-ocular movements. These are measured by way of electrodes attached to the skin above and below or on each side of one eye, detecting the difference in the potential (voltage) through the eyeball in-between the cornea and retina.

Duration. Each individual *eye* movement lasts a fraction of a second, but 1 period of eye movements frequently lasts, with interruptions, about 50 minutes.

Direction. The quantity and direction of eye movements corresponds, in certain cases, to that which the dreamer is looking at or following with the eyes.

Neurophysiology. As we have seen, a complex neurophysiological activity of the human organism occurs during sleep. The body only apparently remains immobile, as small spasms or contractions occur in the leg muscles, jolts take place in the toes and fingers, and grimaces are caused by facial muscles.

Beginning. Regarding the soma, per se, dreams frequently begin soon after a series of *corporal* movements (cerebellum, psychomotricity) have ceased.

Men. Occasionally, during sleep, penile erection occurs in men, regardless of the sleeper's physical age or level of sexual satisfaction (androsomatics).

Women. With women, the cyclical awakening of the clitoris or the periodic lubrication of the vagina occurs, manifestations which are independent of the sleeper's physical age or level of sexual satisfaction (gynosomatics).

Blood. These occurrences are not related to dream content, as they are a result of the organism's blood flow in the genital area.

Paradoxical. In the REM phase of sleep, muscular paralysis also occurs, which causes this phase of sleep to be termed *paradoxical*. Although the brain is very active, the muscles of the torso and body members essentially become paralyzed, as if to protect the sleeper, or dreamer, from the possibility of physically reacting to that which is being dreamt about.

Habitat. Sleep is the dream's natural *habitat* although it is not the same *habitat* for lucid consciential projection.

Continuous. The evidence for this fact becomes highlighted in the experience of projection with continuous self-awareness, wherein there is no intermingling of other altered states of consciousness, whether daydream, sleep, nightmare, hypnagogy or hypnopompy.

Manipulation. At least some types of projection involve a conscious state characterized by the conscious manipulation of REM sleep, which occurs periodically, 4 to 5 times every night.

Recuperation. Delta sleep, which is the deepest phase of sleep, seems to be connected to the individual's *physical* recuperation, while REM sleep is linked to *psychological* recuperation.

Spasms. When one produces the full projection of the consciousness in the psychosoma or mentalsoma, leaving the human body in the empty brain condition, complete immobility is established. In this state, even small spasms do not occur with so much frequency because the organic reflexes almost completely annul themselves in the organism that remains inanimate and only with vegetative life.

Chronopsychophysiology. Modern chronobiology (sleep chronopsychophysiology) laboratories research the automatic manner in which the human body's chronometric, chronobiological or circadian rhythm governs the sleeping-waking cycle, mainly objectifying the application of sleep hygiene and chronotherapy in the treatment of insomnia. This research is performed through polysonography – the continuous, simultaneous registering (polysonogram) of diverse physiological variables, mainly brain activity, eye movements and muscular activity during sleep.

Functions. The following are 5 essential functions of sleep:

1. **Detoxification.** Eliminates the human body's cellular intoxication.
2. **Changes.** Triggers physical, chemical, hormonal and muscular changes.
3. **Protection.** Maintains the human being safe from damage.
4. **Energy.** Renews the vitality of the energy of the holochakra (energetic parabody) and psychosoma (emotional parabody).
5. **Perceptions.** Frees the perceptions of the consciousness through the discoincidence of its vehicles of manifestation.

Quality. The quality of sleep is more important than its quantity.

Projector. The *extraphysical consciousness* (extraphysical being) in the condition wherein its vehicles of manifestation (2 vehicles: psychosoma and mentalsoma) are coincident, and the *projected intraphysical consciousness* (4 vehicles) when discoincident, can experience different categories of sleep.

Soma. In certain cases, the physical body (soma) sleeps (vegetates) without the consciousness, and the projected consciousness simultaneously sleeps close to or distant from the physical body.

Extraphysical consciousnesses. The sleep of the projector during consciential detachment, when at a distance where the silver cord (energetic connections) is stretched beyond the proximities of the human body, or when the projector remains within the minimal circumference of the silver cord's distension is, in most cases, assisted by some extraphysical consciousness, including helpers.

Self-telekinesis. The involuntary, unconscious and almost imperceptible physical movements of the sleeper while in the sleep state, generally constitute reflexive reactions to identical undulations and oscillations of the semi-exteriorized or fully exteriorized psychosoma which is, however, in an unstable condition, close to the human body. These can be considered occurrences of *mild mini-self-telekinesis.*

Reflexes. The facts show that, in some cases, reflexes (repercussions) can occur in 2 directions: from the extraphysical vehicle (psychosoma) to the physical vehicle (soma) and from the physical vehicle to the extraphysical vehicle.

Consecutive. Major changes in the position of the sleeper's human body, e.g., from one side to the other during sleep, correspond, in some cases, *but not in all cases,* to reflexive reactions to small, consecutive and sometimes semilucid exteriorizations-interiorizations of the consciousness in the psychosoma.

Causes. The human being or intraphysical consciousness can sleep or, in other words, can substitute the alpha rhythm of the EEG for a slower rhythm, e.g., delta waves, due to various causes, notably the following 9:

1. **Physiology.** Natural, spontaneous, physiological sleep.
2. **Autosuggestion.** Sleep provoked by autosuggestion.
3. **Accident.** Sleep provoked by an accident.
4. **Anesthesia.** Sleep provoked by anesthesia.
5. **Pharmacology.** Sleep provoked by light or heavy, licit or illicit drugs.
6. **Hibernation.** Hibernal sleep provoked by a reduction in temperature (hypothermia).
7. **Hypnosis.** Hypnotic sleep provoked by a hypnotist.
8. **Helper.** Hypnotic sleep provoked by a healthy extraphysical consciousness (preamble to an assisted projection).
9. **Intruder.** Hypnotic sleep provoked by an ill extraphysical consciousness (interconsciential intrusion).

Projectability. From any of these 9 types of sleep, the sleeper's consciousness can enter into a projective state or, in other words, can initiate a nonlucid, semilucid or lucid consciential projection.

Bibliography: Andreas (36, p. 28), Bunker (222, p. 201), Crookall (320, p. 149; 323, p. 1), Denis (389, p. 141), Kardec (824, p. 213), Martin (1002, p. 27), Muldoon (1105, p. 69), Powell (1278, p. 82), Prieur (1289, p. 73), Salley (1496, p. 157), Shay (1546, p. 22), Steiger (1601, p. 47), Steiner (1610, p. 47), Vieira (1762, p. 125), Walker (1781, p. 93).

---

91. EVOLUTIONARY VACUUM THEORY

Definition. Evolutionary vacuum: daily period in which the human bodies of men, women and children are biologically renovated through natural sleep, when the intraphysical consciousness also sleeps without having lucid extraphysical experiences.

Synonymy: consciential evolutionary loss; daily consciential hibernation; evolutionary breach; evolutionary gap; evolutionary hiatus; evolutionary void; interval of *dead* life; lacuna of self-awareness; period of consciential inattentiveness; *semilife;* vacuum of consciential lucidity.

Sleep. As an altered state of consciousness, sleep constitutes one of the most nullifying and apparently useless conditions that the intraphysical consciousness is known to go through. For example: parapsychic phenomena that occur with the ego can occur while the human body is sleeping, because the soma is not the consciousness. They are distinct realities.

Asleep. Nevertheless, with the exception of fantasized dreams, lucid dreams and intuitions, the majority of people probably do not experience even 10% of their animic, parapsychic and lucid projective potential that remains dormant and nullify themselves together with the human body, during the daily period of natural sleep.

Career. *Evolutionary careers* differ from consciousness to consciousness.

Hiatuses. Nevertheless, the *evolutionary hiatuses* generated by the biological renewal of the soma are, in fact, inevitable for all intraphysical consciousnesses.

Shortening. It is up to the interested party to shorten or prolong the duration of personal consciential and evolutionary loss according to his/her number of hours of natural sleep.

Losses. Among the consciential losses generated by daily periods of sleep, we can point out the use of the personality's fundamental faculties, such as the following 8:

1. Alertness.
2. Superior reflexive awareness.
3. Consciential self-concentration.
4. Attention.
5. Rationality.
6. Critical judgment (self-critique and hetero-critique).
7. Use of imagery.
8. Memory.

Analysis. The condition of daily existential and *intrusive* periods analyzed here, can always be interpreted as a type of vacuum, in the manner of the following 11:

1. Daily consciential vacuum.
2. Vacuum of unperceived uselessness.
3. Vacuum of attentiveness (or inattentiveness).
4. Vacuum of perception (or paraperception).
5. Vacuum of self-awareness (or unconsciousness).
6. Vacuum of routine waste.
7. Vacuum of experience (or inexperience).
8. Vacuum of relative consciential hibernation.
9. Vacuum of definitive personal loss.
10. Evolutionary vacuum.
11. Physiological (or paraphysiological) vacuum.

Ambivalence. As can be observed in the preceding enumeration, some characteristics of the evolutionary vacuum's daily existential periods are *paradoxical,* apparently *contradictory* or blatantly *ambivalent.*

Vacillation. The facts are similar to the case of a vacillating person who arrives at the bus station in Rio de Janeiro (Brazil) and does not know where to go: whether to go to the outskirts of the city, to go ahead without an address, to wander at random (nonlucid projection), to go to Porto Alegre, a city in the South of Brazil (lucid projection at a distance) or to return home (interiorization into the soma).

Melatonin. According to human physiology, the pineal gland liberates melatonin, which is thus far considered to be the most potent factor for inducing natural or human sleep (together with vasopressin and oxytocin, both secreted by the hypophysis).

Activity. Up until now, nothing definitively proves that the intraphysical consciousness needs 5 conditions:

1. **Sleep.** To sleep (the soma needs to rest its cells or interneurons).
2. **Inertia.** Phases of immobility, inertia or accentuated inactivity.
3. *Deperception.* Periodic suppression of self-acuity or perceptive activity.
4. **Hibernation.** Personal hibernation, in the manner of many subhuman animals.
5. **Vacuity.** A daily consciential vacuity.

Mutability. What is observed is that the energetic body of the consciousness, e.g., the human aura, does not stop, presenting extreme mutability in its manifestations and endless pulsations. The same occurs with the consciousness per se, which is always active.

Life. Life is activity, pulsation or movement.

Duration. The *average* period (number of hours) of natural sleep, in which delta sleep is included, or that sleep which is capable of providing some degree of minidiscoincidence for the normal person, is 8 hours within the 24-hour day/night cycle. Thus, the duration of the daily evolutionary vacuum for the average intraphysical consciousness is probably 1/3 of the individual's existence, on average taking advantage of 16 hours, or 2/3 of the condition of the useful waking state.

Waste. Strictly speaking, if we hypothetically consider the daily periods of the intraphysical consciousness' evolutionary vacuum as being useless, we will then have pinpointed the ego's greatest wastefulness in intraphysical life, namely the loss of 1/3 of its personal opportunities for experience, development and personal reeducation.

Recuperation. The recuperation of the daily periods of evolutionary vacuum allows the experiential utilization of up to 1/3 of the evolutionary potentialities that are dormant and not utilized by the intraphysical consciousness. Even when it is still not possible to totally achieve this ceiling, any percentage of recuperation of this evolutionary opportunity, which has thus far been constantly and systematically lost, will represent a significant dynamization of consciential growth.

Nonlucid. The evolutionary vacuum of human sleep is partially filled by all persons, in the majority of their sleep periods, by instinctive or nonlucid projections. These experiences are generated within the physical base, close to but *outside* the soma. These experiences reach 100% of terrestrial humanity during ordinary sleep.

Para-instinct. In this case, the ego para-instinctively sinks into a state of *extracorporeal sleep*. This means that intraphysical consciousnesses depart from the state of coincidence of the holosoma, in the psychosoma, but do not achieve the lucidity needed to experience and remember extraphysical facts.

Percentage. According to international statistics, of all (100%) the components of humanity, who experience nonlucid projections, 9.8% experience lucid dreams or semilucid projections, and only 1.2 % produce lucid projections. This leaves a total of 89% of the population, from all areas, who project exclusively in a nonlucid manner, without any extraphysical experience and, consequently, without any projective recall.

Self-awareness. Extraphysical self-awareness is the irreplaceable causal agent for the greater fulfillment of daily periods of the evolutionary vacuum of human sleep. This is achieved by regaining lucidity immediately after the intraphysical consciousness' vehicles of manifestation discoincide into another consciential dimension.

Permanent. Extraphysical self-awareness is also the first step toward achieving permanent multidimensional self-awareness, one of the basic goals of projectiology that can be reached by the motivated practitioner through the individual's own will.

Projectiology. In practice, experimental projectiology (experimentology) offers the technical means whereby the interested intraphysical consciousness gradually diminishes personal daily periods of evolutionary vacuum, through two conditions:

1. **Projection.** It firstly supplies techniques for the practitioner to replace an apparently useless altered state of consciousness – sleep – with another far more enriching altered state of consciousness, which is the lucid consciential projection. This is one personal projectiological utility. The soma remains partially inert during sleep. The consciousness, during the same period, awakens and has transcendental experiences.

2. **Continuous.** Later on, at an advanced stage, it indicates methods for the intraphysical consciousness to gradually promote, reach and live in the state of continuous self-awareness, or intraphysical existence with an uninterrupted waking state.

Others. The intraphysical consciousness experiences brief or prolonged physiological or pathological occurrences, less frequently, that are similar to the vacuum of natural sleep, such as the following 6:

1. Epileptic absence *(petit mal).*
2. Syncope (fainting).
3. Cranial trauma (brain concussion).
4. Encephalic lesion.
5. State of light coma (comatose). Coma 1 or light coma, relative to coma 2 (coma per se), coma 3 (deep), and coma 4 (brain death).
6. Post-desomatic sleep or restorative sleep of the consciousness that resumes being an extraphysical consciousness.

Contents. Periods of evolutionary consciential vacuum do occur in some of these conditions. However, they present greater content, well-defined causal or triggering factors and, as they are occasional conditions, they do not get to the point of being so *intrusive* and far-reaching in the consciousness' evolutionary ascensional progress.

Elimination. It is reasonable to suppose that all intraphysical consciousnesses on this planet will one day eliminate their daily periods of evolutionary vacuum, achieving the condition of absolute serenism of the ego, with integral lucidity or lucidity with no interruption in continuity, and without stagnant periods with regard to the retention of the causal memory (integral memory, holomemory).

92. LUCID PROJECTION AND SOMNAMBULISM

Definition. Somnambulism (Latin: *somnus*, sleep; *ambulare*, walk): the xenophrenic state of sleep or semi-awake trance that occurs in a spontaneous or artificially induced manner, in which the subconscious faculties take the place of normal awareness and direct the human body to perform physical actions, whether they are common, erratic (sleep walking), talking in one's sleep (somniloquy), or highly intellectual (problem solving).

Synonymy: ambulatory activity; noctambulation; semi-awake trance; sleepwalking; walking while sleeping.

Incidence. Spontaneous somnambulism is frequent in children from 3 to 10 years of age – notably in boys – during the state of deep natural sleep, in the first third of the night. It is a disturbance in REM sleep (during the dream period). It mostly affects people above middle age (90% are men).

Criminology. During certain somnambulistic disturbances, the person can even commit crimes without remembering what occurred. Night terror has some similarity with somnambulism.

Motricity. As a generally benign disturbance, somnambulism occurs in the first of the 6 nocturnal portions of sleep, as it shifts from a deeper to a lighter sleep: the motor functions awaken, while the consciousness continues to sleep. In other words, the somnambulant moves but is not aware of what is happening.

Arrhythmia. Psychopathologically speaking, somnambulism is considered to be provoked by a generally hereditary cerebral arrhythmia.

Duration. The spontaneous somnambulistic state can last from 30 seconds to 30 minutes, during which the somnambulist, in the manner of an automaton, maintains open eyelids and an expressionless face.

Eyelids. Nevertheless, the somnambulist can also walk with eyelids closed and with a perfect sense of direction.

Amnesia. As a general rule, the somnambulist's consciousness, upon waking up, does not recall anything from the natural trance of the somnambulistic crisis. In this case, therefore, amnesia or hypomnesia occurs.

Types. In hypnology, somnambulism is generally classified into 4 types – when the phenomenon is addressed in view of the intraphysical or human dimension:

1. Natural.
2. Symptomatic.
3. Artificial.
4. Ecstatic.

Electro-hypnogram. The electro-hypnogram is the electroencephalogram that is characteristic of sleep.

Somnosis. Somnosis is somnambulism provoked during hypnotic sleep.

Vigilambulism. Vigilambulism or, in other words, unconscious automatism occurring during the ordinary, physical waking state and manifesting itself through more or less coordinated acts – such as standing up, walking and executing simple tasks, shouting, kicking about, calling someone – represents a "second state" that does not leave any recall whatsoever and is mostly observed in children, adolescents, hysterical persons and in certain epileptics.

Degrees. There are various degrees or intensities of the somnambulistic state.

Sleep. The somnambulistic state differs from the state of natural sleep by the muscular tension that remains equal to that of the physical condition of the human body when it is in the ordinary, physical waking state.

Catalepsy. Catalepsy is a deep stage of somnambulism that does not present memory in certain occurrences of hypnosis.

Extraphysical. In the same way that extraphysical catalepsy exists, *extraphysical somnambulism* (somnambulism of the double) also occurs. This constitutes a nonlucid consciential projection.

Projective. Besides the types already referred to, *projective somnambulism* also exists.

Inoffensive. After having a considerable number of projective experiences, the veteran consciential projector can begin to discover him/herself experiencing periods of somnambulism of a characteristically projective origin. Although they are light and inoffensive, they generate extremely real – and sometimes disturbing – facts that are clearly evidenced by the circumstances.

Intercurrences. Due to projective somnambulism, 4 intercurrences or natural effects of the phenomenon can arise:

1. **Identification.** The consciential projector only identifies the fact of acting in a somnambulistic manner after some time – almost always hours – after the occurrence. This can evidently be intriguing and even disturbing in the first occurrences.

2. **Prolonged.** In this case, the somnambulism evidences a prolonged consciential projection, generally of 3 hours or longer; although it lacks complete physical recall or, in other words, has only extraphysical memory (holomemory).

3. **Showers.** Post-projective energetic showers clearly reveal the occurrence of consciential projection in the previous period. They nevertheless do not have an emergence of an integral recall of the extraphysical experiences, which is generally impracticable with consciential projections that last more than one hour.

4. **Facts.** The following are 4 absolutely unrecalled physical facts which reveal to the intraphysical consciousness that they were executed in a projective somnambulistic state:

A. **Soma.** Unrecalled change of the physical position of the human body (soma) that is inanimate on the bed.

B. **Cover.** The placement or removal of a cover from the inanimate human body without recollection of the occurrence. This is a fact common to all persons, even without the occurrence of a consciential projection.

C. **Conditioner.** Turning off the air-conditioning (air-conditioner) after the environment becomes adequately cool, also without recollection of the fact.

D. **Window.** Closing or opening the projector's bedroom window or door according to the convenience of temperature, air currents and other factors, without emergence of the recollection of the fact.

Observation. It is important for us to understand that there is one type of somnambulism that is initiated with the consciousness' vehicles of manifestation still in coincidence, and another one in which the intraphysical consciousness is already somehow discoincident (or semidiscoincident).

Predisposition. Other factors can obviously predispose the occurrence of the veteran consciential projector's somnambulism, aside from prolonged consciential projection, especially the following 4:

1. **Exhaustion.** Physical exhaustion prior to the experiment.

2. **Circumstances.** Specific existential circumstances.

3. **Medication.** Use of medication that favors sleep.

4. **Phenomenology.** Category of the prolonged consciential projection (assisted, assistential, or that of another nature).

Criminology. The state of somnambulism, when malign, can even lead the intraphysical consciousness to commit acts of madness, as with the case that occurred on May, 1987 in Canada, where a man of 23 years of age killed his mother-in-law and violently attacked his father-in-law. This person was absolved by the court because it was shown that he was a somnambulist since childhood and had committed the crime while asleep (*O Globo;* newspaper; daily; section: *O Mundo;* 1 illus.; Rio de Janeiro, RJ, Brazil; August 12, 1992; p. 20).

Parapathology. There are cases of young somnambulists who throw themselves from an open window on a high floor of an apartment building and accidentally commit suicide. Cases of highly developed and constant somnambulism demand more accurate observations regarding malignant aspects for the person and his/her relatives. Malign somnambulism in an intraphysical consciousness with extraphysical intrusion is that which requires more attention and caution.

Bibliography: ADGMT (03, p. 269), Andreas (36, p. 54), Blasco (151, p. 91), Carton (252, p. 231), Crouzet (344, p. 254), Day (376, p. 120), Fodor (528, p. 352), Gaynor (577, p. 171), Kardec (824, p. 223), Larcher (887, p. 142), Morel (1086, p. 165), Paula (1208, p. 118), Shepard (1548, p. 851), Spence (1588, p. 373), Tondriau (1690, p. 279), Vieira (1762, p. 121), Walker (1784, p. 268), Zaniah (1899, p. 430).

93. LUCID PROJECTION AND DREAMS

Definition. Natural sleep: intermediate consciential state between the ordinary, physical waking state and natural sleep, characterized by a set of ideas or a sequence of images that are more or less coherent and present themselves to the consciousness.

Synonymy: common dream; dream of the observer; nocturnal daydream; normal psychosis; oneiric state; ordinary dream; physiological dream; symbol creation state.

Research. Researchers have clearly shown that during 8 hours of sleep all adults usually dream repeatedly during 4 or 5 periods of 30 minutes each. Individuals seem to fundamentally differ with regard to the clarity with which they recall their dreams.

Hypomnesia. If you think you rarely or never dream, it is because you do not recall (hypomnesia) your dreams and not because you are not having oneiric experiences, which are practically inevitable every night. Fetuses and babies also dream.

Dream. Current sleep research shows that, under normal conditions, every person dreams every night, generally at 90 minute intervals after falling sleep.

Phases. The first dream of the night lasts about 10 minutes, and the following phases gradually increase to a final dream of between 30 and 45 minutes, which is frequently recalled.

Percentage. The natural facts of life cause the human being to dream sometimes for 25% of the time asleep, or 4 to 5 times during an average 8 hours of sleep per night, thus yielding a total dream time of about one-and-a-half hours.

Totals. Thus, each person has a total of more than 1,000 dreams per year, or spends more than 4 entire years of personal human existence *dreaming*.

Center. Researchers are currently endeavoring to open a new area of dream research for the pinpointing and identification of the so-called "dream center" in the human brain, by studying explosion victims who are injured on battlefields.

Fragment. These persons cease dreaming when a small bomb fragment becomes lodged in the brain exactly at the point where the "center of sleep" is thought to be located, apparently destroying it.

Effects. At least 11 effects occur due to sleep and dreams:

1. An excess of incorrect interpretations of extraphysical events.
2. Creations of the imagination.
3. Extraphysical hallucinations.
4. Inconsequential nightmares.

5. Intercurrent dreams.
6. Mental masks.
7. Odd associations with extraphysical realities.
8. Physiological and organic reflexes.
9. Psychological molds.
10. Release of daily tensions.
11. Unfitting supplementary data.

Bad. Two thirds of the dreams of healthy people are *bad* or unpleasant dreams.

Blindness. Persons who are blind from birth have auditory dreams.

Loss. Persons who become blind at some point during their life gradually lose their visual dreams.

Sounds. Ambient sounds, such as a telephone or an alarm clock ringing can sometimes become part of a dream.

Categories. There are many categories of dreams, according to the types of manifestations that occupy the intraphysical consciousness' mind. The following is a list of 16 examples:

1. Bad dream.
2. Bizarre dream.
3. Creative dream.
4. Dramatic dream.
5. Dream of survival.
6. Exciting dream.
7. Gratifying dream.
8. High dream.
9. Incomprehensible dream.
10. Invented dream.
11. Monotonous dream.
12. Mutual dream.
13. Nocturnal dream.
14. Recurring dream.
15. Vivid dream.
16. Warning dream.

Mimic. The dreamer typically remains immobile for the duration of the dream, but may make some slight movements, or certain special mimicking gestures with the hands, feet and face.

Theories. Many theories are proposed, however there is so far no consensus regarding the true cause of the altered state of consciousness that we call *dream*.

Nets. The most recent theory claims that dreams undo undesirable neural nets, thus avoiding an overloading that reduces the efficiency of the brain – in the manner of a data processing machine – during the period in which this organ has its main functions deactivated.

By-product. Dreams may merely be a psychological follow-up – a type of by-product – of a specific rhythmic operation of the nervous system.

Symbols. Dream symbols are generated in an attempt to compensate for an insufficiency in the physical memory bank (biomemory), that encounters neither parallels nor similes in its programming for that which the consciousness perceives in the extraphysical dimension.

Discoincidence. When sleeping, every human being or intraphysical consciousness departs from the state of coincidence of the consciousness' vehicles of manifestation either lucidly, semilucidly or nonlucidly.

Rational. Upon accumulating lucid consciential projection experiences, it is observed that the tendency is to make dreams more rational and apparently less incoherent, thus permitting the consciousness' critical judgment to allow it to *discover that it is dreaming*. This minimizes the dream's oneiric disturbances and even partially nullifies the dream, little by little, the consciousness thus leaving the human body in an ordinary lucid consciential projection.

Comparison. Many lucid projectors compare lucid consciential projection to a color photograph and the ordinary dream to a black and white photo. This actually does little to characterize the reality of these 2 altered states of consciousness.

Product. If, on the one hand, there are projective techniques that are based on dreams, the facts, on the other hand, indicate that at least 1 ordinary dream each night is the product of or the *effect* of a lucid projection, instead of being the generator or the direct *cause* of a consciential projection.

Fall. According to the opinion of many lucid projectors, dreams of falling (lucid proto-projections) are related, in a considerable number of cases, to the phenomenon of physical repercussion.

Complexity. Lucid consciential projections, as evolved as the human projector may be, do not exclude the natural unconscious elaboration of morphothosenes, ordinary dreams, nightmares, daydreams, hypnagogic states, hypnopompic states, nonlucid projections, semilucid projections and other altered states of the consciousness, whose intra-subjective life does not stop, thus always being extremely complex.

Relationship. Unconsciously generated morphothosenes and ordinary dreams are intimately related to each other, to the force of the ego's imagination, as well as those images experienced or even those which are recorded without the individual realizing it in the most recent hours of the intraphysical consciousness' experiences. They are stored in the personal consciential data bank, namely the very recent facts of the morphothosene (thought-form) generator, the dreamer and the imaginer who, in the final analysis, are one and the same person. These facts become important elements for the projector who wishes to precisely analyze and distinguish personal projective experiences from those products generated by his/her elaboration of thoughts, whether they are morphothosenes or ordinary dreams.

Bibliography: Andreas (36, p. 29), Blackmore (139, p. 14), Broad (208, p. 53), Campbell (237, p. 4), Donahue (407, p. 6), Fodor (528, p. 174), Frost (560, p. 32), Garfield (568, p. 118), Grattan-Guinness (626, p. 81), Gudjonsson (658, p. 110), Holzer (745, p. 163), Krippner (862, p. 94), Motoyama (1098, p. 204), Osborn (1155, p. 162), Powell (1278, p. 93), Roll (1466, p. 228), Sabom (1486, p. 226), Vieira (1766, p. 5), Wang (1794, p. 157).

94. ONEIRIC   IMAGES

Definition. Oneiric image: the image born in a dream, inside the consciousness, whether it is imaginative, hallucinatory, nightmarish, one's own thought-form or morphothosene, the morphothosene of another intelligence, or a distorted perception of extraphysical reality.

Synonymy: dream image; hallucinatory image; phantom image.

Dreams. According to the biological, practical or utilitarian interpretation of psychopathology, there is no other sector of human experience that is more irrational and devoid of logic than dreams.

Contents. Psychoanalysis, on the other hand, which is diametrically opposed to the psychopathological interpretation, considers dreams to be always endowed with *meaning*, presenting contents that are subject to interpretation within a psychological framework.

Logic. The term "logic" can be taken to signify *sense* which, in everyday language, is understood within the perspective of a subject and not objects.

Decoding. In this way, a fact may not possess "logic" for one person, if this individual does not understand it, but does possess "logic" for another person, if that individual was able to decode it.

Object. The object, in and of itself, would be neither logical nor illogical. This is what common sense does, and it only has validity from the subject's point of view.

Principles. The term "logic" can still be taken in a rigorous sense, and in this meaning it will imply, upon being used, that 3 principles are not isolated, namely:

1. **Identity.** The principle of identity.
2. **Noncontradiction.** The principle of noncontradiction.

3. **Third.** Except for intuitionist mathematicians, the principle of the "excluded third." In this sense, then, nothing in the world would be illogical, only sentences (linguistics, the plane is semantic) could violate these principles. Based on this, dreams, as phenomena, would not be *illogical,* as they would not contradict any of these 3 principles.

Products. Oneiric images – individual psychic products that constitute the content of dreams, oneiric deliria and twilight states – represent visual or fantastic images which, due to the obfuscated condition of the ordinary waking state, are considered to correspond to real objects.

Characteristics. As well, according to psychopathology, the following 7 can be singled out from among the phenomenal characteristics of oneiric images: vivacity, mobility, atemporality, aspatiality, intimacy, irrationality and experientiality.

1. **Vivacity.** Despite the lack of sensorial clarity, the oneiric image is vivid and endowed with extreme plasticity.

2. **Mobility.** All oneiric images are essentially unstable and movable, and are therefore not fixed, or are ceaselessly moving.

3. **Atemporality.** The oneiric image manifests itself independent of the time factor.

4. **Aspatiality.** The oneiric image manifests itself independent of the space factor.

5. **Intimacy.** The oneiric image is projected in internal space, in the intimacy of the consciousness, momentarily considered as objective space.

6. **Irrationality.** The oneiric image is fundamentally illogical or irrational in its appearances (see the topic "Dreams," above).

7. **Experientiality.** All oneiric images derive from some specific experience of the consciousness.

Stimuli. Certain factors, such as the following 11, can serve as triggering stimuli for the composition of sequences in oneiric situations, whether of ordinary dreams or nightmares:

1. Anger (in this case: rage, antipathy).
2. Anxiety.
3. Cold.
4. Fear.
5. Fever.
6. Indigestion.
7. Intense light shone on the sleeper's closed eye lids.
8. Menstrual cramps.
9. Noises.
10. Pre-menstrual tension (PMT).
11. Vesical repletion.

Causes. The causes of oneiric images are highly varied. Among them, the following 10 can be listed:

1. Cortical excitation of oneiric imagination.
2. Discontinuity in the degree of extraphysical awareness.
3. Fright.
4. Incorrect rationalization of facts that actually occurred during authentic projections.
5. Occasional nightmare.
6. Physical or extraphysical trauma while the human body is inactive.
7. Sheer hallucination due to foods or medication.
8. Unconscious creation of thought-forms or morphothosenes.
9. Unconscious reception of the morphothosenes of others.
10. Vegetative or neuromuscular reflexes of the organs.

Effects. Countless effects arise from oneiric images, although the essential ones presented here are those related to lucid projection, most notably the following 3:

1. **Perceptions.** Interference in the correct perception of extraphysical events.
2. **Evaluation.** Confusion in the evaluation of extraphysical experiences.
3. **Recall.** Distortion of recollection of the extraphysical period, creating embellishment in the fragmentary recall.

Alert. In light of the facts presented, the projector should always be alert in the sense of maintaining extraphysical lucidity, clarity in the quality of parapsychic perceptions and the possibility of outside consciential interference in the experiments, always removing all doubts in interpretation, incoherence and extravagance, which should be attributed to oneiric images.

Agents. The voluntary intensification of lucid projections in series permits the intraphysical consciousness to perfectly distinguish ordinary dreams in a specific manner, in order to subordinate them to being agents for lucid consciential projection, whether their origin is essentially organic, hypertensive, arteriosclerotic, thermic, or others.

Arteriosclerotic. Recurrent arteriosclerotic dreams are those that indicate the crystallization of the memory in a determinate existential period, generally at least 2 to 3 decades in the past.

Traumas. Arteriosclerotic dreams make the imagination and memory return to the same nucleus of preoccupations or traumas that afflicted the individual in adolescence or infancy, for example, and can be transformed into an effective lucid consciential projection through abrupt extraphysical self-awareness.

Bibliography: Alverga (18, p. 202), Carrington (247, p. 60), Castaneda (258, p. 132), Holzer (745, p. 56), Paim (1182, p. 41), Steiner (1610, p. 56), Vieira (1762, p. 49), Walker (1782, p. 110).

95. COMPARISONS BETWEEN DREAMS AND LUCID PROJECTIONS

Differential. The basic differential characteristics of natural, common dreams and the lucid projection of the consciousness from the human body are very distinct and can generally be classified into two categories:

1. Subjective or individual.
2. Objective or public.

Comparisons. The following are 33 didactic comparisons between natural dreams and lucid consciential projections:

1. **Beginning.** In a dream, the intraphysical consciousness does not start dreaming while in the ordinary, physical waking state. In lucid projection, there are episodes wherein the condition of continuous self-awareness is effectively maintained from the waking state or, in other words, before, during and after the projective experiment, without lapse or interruption in consciential lucidity.

2. **Vibrational.** In a dream no condition arises that can be interpreted as being the intense vibrational state, a singular, unique phenomenon that frequently occurs before and after a lucid projection, in a manner that is unmistakable to the projector.

3. **Sounds.** In a dream, the strange intracranial sounds do not occur which are characteristic of the consciential interiorization stage and, less frequently, of the takeoff stage, when the consciousness projects in the psychosoma.

4. **Takeoff.** In dreams there are no consciential impressions of the exit from the human organism. In projection, lucid takeoff in the projective experience of continuous self-awareness is fascinating and unique.

5. **Awareness.** In dreams, due to their inoperative nature, the intraphysical consciousness may not always determine the oneiric images at will, but acts like a spectator or semi-spectator of a show that unfolds before it, over which it has no control as, in fact, we do not dream, *we are dreamt, we suffer* the dream, we are objects of the dream. The projected consciousness generally directs the

extraphysical acts and has decision-making capacity equal to that which occurs in the ordinary, physical waking state, because we are the agents of extraphysical events in which we are integrated, speaking, acting, and actually moving.

6. **Activity.** In dreams mental activity is habitual. In lucid projection the consciousness' inner activity transcends the ordinary, physical waking state in richness.

7. **Reason.** In dreams, full reasoning capacity does not occur with ease. In lucid projection, reasoning faculties remain the same in the 2 states, the physical waking state and the extraphysical waking state. They also often transcend the bounds of the ordinary, physical waking state.

8. **Judgment.** In dreams there is neither time nor a clear, immediate awareness of experiences; critical judgment is absent and the most absurd occurrences and situations are readily accepted, because the consciousness is not sufficiently alert to awaken the sense of attention. In lucid projection, critical judgment is always present and the projector is unquestionably certain that his/her human body is distant from the consciousness or, in other words, the consciousness is outside the human body.

9. **Autosuggestion.** In dreams, autosuggestion does not influence the coordination of images. In lucid projection, will or thought determine acts and extraphysical events.

10. **Waking.** In dreams, the dreamer neither recalls nor is aware of the ordinary, physical waking state. In lucid projections, the projector maintains all memories of the waking state.

11. **State.** The dream, as an altered state of consciousness, does not present the magnitude of lucid experience that lucid projection provides in a *sui generis* manner: the degree of self-awareness; the sensation of freedom; the feeling of well-being; the mental lucidity; the expansion of a notion of power; permeability relative to structures and physical bodies; volitation; extraphysical euphoria.

12. **Quality.** In a dream, images more frequently appear distorted, unreal and full of fantasies arising from the creations of the intraphysical consciousness. In lucid projection, the consciousness sees images and experiences events that do not become deformed, are real, occur in a defined environment that is independent of its personal creativity and do not require interpretation.

13. **Intensity.** In dreams, the images of the experiences are less intense than those of the ordinary, physical waking state. In lucid projection, the objective images may attain the greatest degree of intensity of all consciential states.

14. **Images.** Dreams, although having weaker images, allow a stronger and easier recall because they almost always occur when the vehicles of consciential manifestation are nearly coincident or totally coincident, or at least when the consciousness is in the proximity of the human body. Lucid projections, while having stronger images, almost always afford weaker, evanescent, and fleeting memories, as they occur without the direct influence of the brain, the physical organ of the human body, but of the parabrain instead, the extraphysical organ of the psychosoma.

15. **Predetermination.** In a dream, it would be useless to attempt to plan the execution of a specific action, while in the oneiric state, in a specific place chosen before sleeping. Lucid projection makes it possible for you to carry out a resolution, made before sleeping, to direct yourself to a specific location during the experience and realize the willfully planned extraphysical action.

16. **Translocation.** A dream allows deliberate extraphysical travel, but of a relative, illusory, internal, imaginary nature that is merely thought by the consciousness. Lucid projection facilitates the willful execution of extraphysical translocation in a *departure-return-new-departure*, in the same itinerary, giving the projector direct, irrefutable experience of extraphysical situations commanded by the will.

17. **Body.** In a dream, the dreamer, given that he/she dreams inside him/herself (brain), does not have the direct, objective view of his/her own human body when outside it, as with consciential self-bilocation, a characteristic and singular fact that lucid projection provides in an impressive manner, including tactile sensation, self-embrace and the proof – which is definitive for the lucid projector – of the existence of the parabrain or psychosoma.

18. **Reflexes.** During a dream, sensory stimuli produce fantasies. In lucid projection, during the absence of the consciousness from the human body, small external touches made upon the inactive human body provoke the return of the psychosoma with the unmistakable sensation of traction of the silver cord, the admonitory discomfort, intracranial sounds and other phenomena peculiar to extraphysical repercussions.

19. **Interiorization.** Those occurrences characteristic of the mechanism of lucid projection, such as the lucid interiorization of the consciousness while in the psychosoma, are not experiences that can be associated or confused with dreams.

20. **Duration.** It is very difficult to prolong a dream. During a lucid projection, the consciousness determines whether it is going to end or continue the extraphysical period and, through perseverant training, the veteran projector can voluntarily make the experience last for an hour or more.

21. **Recall.** In a dream, the dreamer *(oneironaut)* most often does not recall the images in a correct and logical sequence. The lucid projector *(projectionaut)* can recall the complete, coherent events of the projection in full detail. The projector sometimes does not even need to recall the facts, because it does not lose awareness at any time during the experience.

22. **Accomplishments.** Lucid projectors are able to see and participate in *real* events, as well as describe actual places visited by the consciousness during the extraphysical period. These accomplishments surpass the normal possibilities of dreams with regard to the frequency, validity and intensity of the consciential experiences.

23. **Continuance.** In a continuance-dream, occurring after an intermission of awakening or sleeping, the images continue in the same apparently incoherent and illogical manner as before. In a continuance-projection, the sequential images of the episodes are coherent and well interlinked, whether according to the theme, the scenario-locations and the character-consciousnesses of the lucid projection, in the first as much as in the second occurrence. The second projective experience undeniably confirms the events and experiences of the first for the lucid projector.

24. **Recurring.** In *recurring* dreams, *there is a reprise of the same* personalities, scenarios and dream story lines that involve 1 constant theme. In recurring projections, there is no repetition of identical patterns of extraphysical occurrences, but similar events that can be grouped, inserted or classified into similar categories.

25. **Energies.** In a dream, the following do not occur: exteriorization of energies, energetic shower, *physical* and psychic phenomena which are ostensive and peculiar to the complex of manifestations of lucid projection, whether occurring before, during, or even after the episodes.

26. **Psychosoma.** There is no similarity between the extremely individual characteristics of the vehicle of manifestation, the psychosoma, which are sensed and observed by the consciousness of the projected projector, and the altered states of consciousness that pertain to the natural dream.

27. **Self-knowledge.** The veteran projector distinguishes perfectly between lucid projections and dreams in a convincing, unquestionable and definitive manner for him/herself.

28. **Ostensive.** The ostensive, public manifestations of lucid projection – such as influence over persons, appearance of the projected projector to intraphysical beings and others – transcend the parameters of the manifestations of dreams.

29. **Encounters.** Lucid encounters between the consciousness of the projected projector and intraphysical beings or extraphysical consciousnesses definitively surpass the restricted limitations of dreams.

30. **Waking.** In dreams, there are no witnesses to oneiric events. In many cases of lucid projection, intraphysical beings who are in the waking state and are present give matching testimonies regarding the occurrences that were triggered or witnessed by the projected projector, as they see its *inter vivos* apparition, or witness the phenomenon of its physical bilocation.

31. **Frequency.** Dreams are more frequent and, furthermore, are better recalled than lucid projections.

32. **Extraphysical.** Some projected-intraphysical-witness-projectors are present and directly participate in the same extraphysical events with other consciousnesses. This does not occur in shared dreams.

33. **Laboratorial.** Laboratory experiments demonstrate, in practice, with the use of special equipment and monitoring, that the reality of lucid projection is an altered state of consciousness very different from the dream state. For example, electro-oculogram readings indicate that rapid bi-ocular movements diminish or stop completely during the period in which the consciousness is projected and indicate a sharp increase in these same rapid eye movements during ordinary dream or while in the oneiric state.

Approaches. The approach, focus and the consciential treatment of a subject are very different between an ordinary dreamer and a lucid projector when they are active. The following are 2 examples:

1. **Fantasy.** The conditioned mind of a young female television viewer has a colorful dream in which she is involved in a fanciful story about an impressive actor in her favorite soap opera.

2. **Reality.** The consciousness of the same young female television viewer projects itself, consciously invading, in a direct and real way, the privacy of the actor-target, who plays the particular soap opera character.

Primitive. It is worth noting that the cultures of primitive societies usually make a symbolic distinction between natural dreams and lucid projections, referring to different trips of the *soul* to *realms* that are also different.

Projectiogenic. It is interesting to note that dreams – just as with daydreams – are so different from lucid projection that they also come to be used as a process whereby the consciousness projects itself from the human body, so-called projectiogenic dreams.

Bibliography: Andreas (36, p. 55), Baumann (93, p. 37), Brown (211, p. 214), Champlin (272, p. 205), Crookall (343, p. 42), Currie (354, p. 78), Farrar (496, p. 198), Fischer (519, p. 171), Frost (560, p. 37), Greenhouse (636, p. 42), Holzer (747, p. 124), Lefebure (909, p. 46), Monroe (1065, p. 179), Monteith (1072, p. 47), Rampa (1352, p. 71), Reis (1384, p. 55), Salley (1496, p. 162), Stevens (1615, p. 232), Stokes (1625, p. 22), Vieira (1766, p. 5), Yram (1897, p. 112).

---

96. ORDINARY DREAMS ABOUT LUCID PROJECTION

Saturation. After repeated projective experiences and the veteran projector's consequent mental saturation with the subject of lucid projection, typical ordinary dreams with specific themes on lucid projection spontaneously and inevitably arise as an inoffensive, secondary side effect of this saturation.

Identification. Ordinary dreams about lucid projection are easy to identify and distinguish due to their extremely personal characteristics, when compared with semilucid projections, precognitive dreams and premonitory dreams.

Inexperience. In certain cases, ordinary dreams that are centered on projective themes can even happen to the intraphysical consciousness who has never experienced a entirely lucid major projection (which is recalled in this human life).

Experience. Nevertheless, it is very common for this to happen to the veteran projector who has had a considerable number of experiences outside the human body and who has a consciousness that is psychologically predisposed to oneiric story lines about lucid projections.

Characters. Among the more striking characteristics of dreams with lucid projection as their theme, the following 6 can be singled out:

1. **Awareness.** Absence of awareness and critical judgment characteristic of the dreamer and not of the projected projector, who enjoys extraphysical lucidity. For example: the projector's consciousness, when dreaming, does not perceive that it has already projected many other times and wants to project as if it were the first time.

2. **Time.** Discrepancies regarding chronological time and weather conditions characteristic of the dream scenario. For example: the projector – a dreamer in this case – feels him/herself to be flying over the street of his/her physical base, illuminated by the summer sun, at a time when it is actually night and is even raining.

3. **Clothing.** There is an evident discrepancy regarding the clothes being used. For example: the projector – a dreamer in this case – experiences being dressed in a suit and tie, and is concerned with the cleanliness of the shoes, looking for some polish to put on them before meeting some projected friends. Obviously, no projector will ever need to polish shoes while projected.

4. **Vehicle.** Discrepancy regarding the vehicle of manifestation. For example: the projector – a dreamer in this case – unexpectedly thinks of projecting directly with his/her own dense human body, which is impracticable and incoherent in that instance.

5. **Attitudes.** Discrepancy regarding attitudes. For example: the projector – a dreamer in this case – feverishly looks for, and cannot find, 1 technical book on lucid projection that he/she wishes to study, in an atmosphere typical of nightmarish anguish.

6. **Energies.** Absence of the post-projective shower of energies. For example: the projector – a dreamer in this case – physically awakens and does not enjoy any of the well-being characteristic of the post-projective period of an authentic major projection.

Erection. One of the most common dreams in which the consciousness of the veteran projector identifies that it is dreaming, occurs *after* a prolonged assistential projection that was distant from the physical base, when the consciousness interiorizes and encounters the physical penis in erection (androsomatics).

Parapenis. This physiological erection that began during the temporary absence of the consciousness from the human body did not previously extraphysically have a repercussion in its psychosoma or, in other words, in its *parapenis,* nor even in its mentalsoma. It thus did not get to the point of provoking the para-erection of the extraphysical penis.

Interiorization. In this case, the erotic dream, when it occurs, almost always begins immediately when the projected consciousness interiorizes. The consciousness might not let itself become involved by the dream, and may even physically awaken soon thereafter.

Opportunity. In a single night, a person can experience an expressive lucid projection and, soon thereafter, dream about the same projection. This is the best opportunity for making a detailed study of the differences between these manifestations and the phenomenological parameters between one experience and the other.

Inductions. The projector may either intentionally produce a lucid projection or induce a dream about that selfsame projection soon thereafter.

Bibliography: Shay (1546, p. 91).

97. SEMILUCID PROJECTION

Definition. Semilucid projection: a dream that the intraphysical consciousness experiences for a period of time in which he/she enters into a state wherein he/she knows he/she is dreaming but is unable to obtain a greater degree of uninterrupted lucidity during the entire period and does not even become aware that he/she will soon physically awaken.

Synonymy: consciential subprojection; conscious dream; discontinuous projection; dream of knowledge; high dream; *lucid dream;* mixed dream; participatory dream; pre-lucid dream; pre-projective dream; semi-dream state; semilucid projection; semi-oneiric projection; semi-projective dream; state of fluctuating consciousness; translucid dream; true dream; twilight consciential projection; veridical dream.

Complexity. Semilucid projection is classified as being intermediary between the 3 basic categories of consciential projections, in regard to the degree of lucidity:

1. Nonlucid projection.
2. Semilucid projection.
3. Lucid projection.

Similarities. Semilucid projection has similarities and direct relationships with at least the following 5 intraconsciential occurrences:

1. **Daydream.** Daydream or the waking dream.
2. **Hypnagogy.** The hypnagogic state.
3. **Pharmacology.** Psychedelic states (pharmacological, or chemical).
4. **Hypnosis.** Hypnotic hallucinations.
5. **Imagetic.** The types of imagetic (image) creation.

Sleep. It is currently accepted that sleep is a far more complex phenomenon than was previously thought. It is even possible to be simultaneously awake and asleep, because the condition of the *ordinary, physical waking state* and the altered condition of the *dream* are not mutually exclusive consciential states.

Intensity. At our current evolutionary level, no intraphysical consciousness only sleeps, only dreams or projects all the time when he/she leaves the ordinary, physical waking state.

Discontinuity. All persons, including the most advanced consciential projectors, ordinarily have a period of discontinuous sleep. In other words, upon going to bed at night they sleep, dream, have a nightmare, project, dream again, wake up, sleep, dream, and project again, and so on, until waking up in the morning and getting out of bed.

Mixture. This fact predisposes the appearance of mixed consciential projections, evidencing some degree of lucidity while simultaneously being interwoven with oneiric images.

Interaction. As a general rule regarding terrestrial humanity, consciousnesses project themselves at night while sleeping. However, neither they nor their vehicles of manifestation – in this case, especially the psychosoma – get to the point of interacting with the extraphysical environment where they temporarily go. They most often remain within the extraphysical sphere of energy (psychosphere, holothosene, materthosene).

Nightmare. Semilucid consciential projection in the psychosoma generates a nightmarish consciential projection due to uncontrolled extraphysical emotion.

Circuit. The influence of the silver cord's two-way energy flow, in the human body-psychosoma circuit, is decisive in the production of semilucid consciential projection.

Ballast. The greater the percentage of semimaterial energetic constituent components – ballast – of the energetic body or holochakra that enter into the structure of the projected psychosoma through the silver cord, thus increasing its density, the greater will be the clouding or obnubilation of the consciousness' lucidity during the projection.

Rarefaction. The psychosoma, when much more rarefied (less dense or *lighter*), facilitates the maintenance of the projected consciousness' lucidity.

Factors. Any consciential projection in which there is an interference of oneiric factors, profound distortions of images, absurd, incoherent and incongruent scenes, whether at the beginning, middle or end of the extraphysical period experienced by the consciousness, constitutes a semilucid projection.

Predisposition. Semilucid projection acts as a predisposing factor, launching pad, or halfway point for the lucid dreamer's consciousness to reach a full-scale lucid projection.

Proximity. Semilucid projection is closer to certain altered states of consciousness, such as: somnambulism, dreams and nightmares of all types and manifestations.

Rule. The following is a fundamental principle or rule: semilucid projection occurs with all people, *without exception,* even when they do not perceive the extent and nature of this typical consciential phenomenon.

Types. The following are 4 types of oneiric experiences that may, in many cases, but *not in all* cases, be semilucid projections:

1. **Flight.** An agreeable dream of unimpeded flight, with a clear view of landscapes.
2. **Fall.** A dream of an abrupt fall with immediate physical awakening, whereupon physical repercussions also occur.
3. **Sliding.** A dream of sliding along on your bare feet.
4. **Clothing.** A dream of being dressed in pajamas, in a manner that is inappropriate for the environment or scenario of the oneiric experience.

Veridical. Certain so-called veridical dreams – presumably *supra*normal dreams that in some ways correspond to facts or events beyond the dreamer's normal knowledge or sensory range – also constitute semilucid projections.

Joint. Joint semilucid projections can occur. These are more evolved phenomena than mutual dreams and less evolved phenomena than full, joint lucid projections.

Archiprojections. Lucid dream - an inferior, primary version of lucid projection   which only lasts for a few minutes, typically occurring at 5 o'clock in the morning, in which the dreamer develops a certain degree of lucidity while dreaming, recognizes the dream, which is almost always more colorful than an ordinary dream, perceives that he/she is dreaming with no need to wake up, as well as a great number of dreams of floating, flying and falling, can be interpreted as semilucid projections and, moreover, in some cases, are initial or incipient projections (protoprojections or archiprojections).

Distinction. However, distinguishing between a lucid dream and a full lucid projection becomes difficult, as it depends on the practice of the self-critiquing and discerning projector, a characteristic that is only achieved by those who have already experienced a series of lucid projections and possess personal elements needed for making comparisons.

REM. All lucid dreams occur during the period called REM dreaming.

Understanding. Thus, we can conclude that, strictly speaking, only an understanding of lucid projections allows the practitioner to understand semilucid projections or lucid dreams.

Statistics. According to the statistical surveys performed to date, only 5% to 10% of the population has lucid dreams with some regularity.

Separation. There is currently a tendency among researchers to separate the following 3 events:

1. **Semilucidity.** Lucid dream or semilucid projection.
2. **Oneirism.** Natural dreams.
3. **Self-awareness.** Lucid projection.

Publication. In the United States of America, an institute has been founded that is dedicated to the research of lucid dreams: The Lucidity Institute (home page on the Internet).

Analyses. The more we anatomize the consciential states in order to establish more circumstantiated analyses, without losing the panoramic vision of the phenomena, the better it will be for research of the consciousness, which is the most complex reality in the cosmos.

Metachoric. Lucid dreams are also being studied together with full lucid projections (extracorporeal experiences) and *false awakenings.* This research is studying processes called *metachoric experiences* or, in other words, those in chorus with the 3 abovementioned consciential experiences.

Technique. The most efficacious technique for inducing lucid projection through ordinary lucid dream that is currently employed and recommended by international research symposiums on ordinary dreams and lucid dreaming, is for the individual to ask him/herself, as many times as possible, in all environments and circumstances, day after day, during at least one month, the following simple but pondered question: *Am I awake or am I sleeping?* This method really works, and the lucid dream ends up leading the consciousness to a full lucid projection.

Entrance. Sleep researchers accept that, with correct, adequate mental training, it is possible not only to have an objective, clear vision of our own dreams but *also to enter them* and alter them, just as the director of a play or a theatrical author reworks the plot of a piece on-the-spot directly on the stage (in the scene).

Mnemosomatics. The autosuggestion technique used to induce a lucid dream is the mnemonic induction of lucid dreams (MILD) technique, which is based on the following affirmation being made to oneself when going to sleep: "The next time I am dreaming, I want to remember that I am dreaming." One then visualizes oneself to be simultaneously sleeping in the bed and dreaming, and being very much aware of where he/she is.

Inducer. In light of the facts, lucid dream can be utilized as an inducer of lucid projection, in the same manner as the more common projectiogenic dream.

Recollection. Due to the discontinuity of extraphysical lucidity, the recollection of experiences during a semilucid projection frequently becomes repressed, altered or more difficult.

Oneiric. In the *oneiric projection* – a characteristic type of semilucid projection – the projector only has discontinuous awareness during the experiences. Instances of authentic exteriorization occur, mixed with oneiric episodes, which can be interspersed with brief phases of normal sleep. This should not be confused with projective dreams.

Consequences. Nonlucid projection, or projection in the extraphysical dimension without self-awareness, can occur *with* or *without* visually perceiving events.

Unconsciousness. In this case, the projector can see extraphysical events and even act upon physical objects. He/she does not, however, perceive that he/she is projected on that occasion, being able to recall the scenes of the facts after physical awakening.

Evidence. This is the condition of extraphysical somnambulism, of certain apparitions of the intraphysical projector and even cases of physical bilocation, or even projective poltergeist and projective haunting.

Conclusions. These pieces of evidence lead to 4 conclusions about our consciential conditions:

1. **Awareness.** Awareness, merely as a state of lucidity, is *independent* from the process of projection in general.

2. **Biomemory.** The memory (biomemory) that is present in the neurons (of the cerebral hemispheres) is *independent* from the intraphysical consciousness' process of lucid and nonlucid projection.

3. **Dream.** The phenomenological complex of projection or, more precisely, the altered state of the consciousness that is semilucidly projected, has superficial similarities, but is essentially very *different* from the oneiric state because, in this case, it is a lucid dream.

4. **Somnambulism.** The phenomenological complex of semilucid projection has superficial similarities, but is essentially very *different* from the somnambulic state.

Locations. In theory, the researcher could endeavor to characterize and distinguish the lucid dream state from the semilucid consciential projection according the consciential location or seat where the intraphysical consciousness' experience unfolds, in 2 manners with regard to the parabrain:

1. **Inside.** The lucid dream, in this case, would unfold in the parabrain of the psychosoma, but *inside* the human body, in the intimacy of the encephalon, or the 2 cerebral hemispheres.

2. **Outside.** The semilucid projection would always manifest in the parabrain of the psychosoma, though when it is *outside* the brain or the human body.

Extracorporeal. This distinction, although simplistic, becomes problematic when the projected intraphysical consciousness (headquartered in the parabrain of the psychosoma) sometimes experiences *extracorporeal sleep* and experiences an *extracorporeal dream* that should logically, in this case, be classified as a lucid dream, because this same consciousness sensorially detects nothing regarding the extraphysical dimension in this instance.

Classification. Hence, lucid dreams are included and classified here as semilucid projections, besides any other considerations, in light of the real difficulty in rigorously separating the real manifestations of these altered states of consciousness which occur, interlace and alternate with surprising rapidity. The consciousness does not stop.

Categories. It is worth registering here the 3 categories in which the lucid dream can develop, in regard to certain, essentially diverse consciential conditions:

1. **Brain.** The lucid dream unfolds inside the human brain, when the consciousness' vehicles of manifestation are coincident, and therefore without any consciential projection.

ISBE. This simply oneiric experience is the ISBE (inside-the-body experience, or experience inside the human body or soma) or the dream that develops inside the human body. Do not confuse this with the intracorporeal experience or the ordinary, physical waking state.

2. **Unconscious.** The lucid dream only unfolds inside the parabrain of the projected psychosoma in a nonlucid consciential projection.

OOBE. This experience is the OOBE (out-of-the-body experience or experience outside the human body), although it is not experienced with lucidity (nonlucid projection).

3. **Semilucid.** The lucid dream unfolds inside the parabrain of the projected psychosoma in a semilucid consciential projection, namely when the consciousness partially detects, with its perceptions, the extraphysical dimension, where it is manifesting on that occasion.

Lucidity. This experience is the OOBE (out-of-the-body experience) with a certain degree of lucidity (semilucid projection).

Research. Statistical public opinion research conducted with students revealed a far higher incidence of the lucid dream phenomenon, or semilucid consciential projection, with significantly higher percentages, in relation to lucid consciential projection, per se (approximately 10:1).

Perceptual. Within the scope of semilucid projections, it would also be more rational to include specific consciential projections of one isolated perception (perceptual projection) of the consciousness, without resulting in full discoincidence of its vehicles of manifestation.

Clairvoyance. For example, visual perception, peculiar to clairvoyance, is in certain cases a projection of the sense of *vision* outside the human body, without the dislocation of the entire *center of the consciousness* and its essential components or other basic attributes outside its physical seat, the brain. The same may occur with the *auditive, tactile,* and other sensory perceptions.

Relationships. This phenomenon has a direct relationship with certain occurrences of telekinesis, *traveling* clairvoyance, exteriorization of motricity and sensitivity.

Intraphysical consciousnesses. Perceptual projections are common with persons or intraphysical consciousnesses who are on drugs, ill, novice clairvoyants, aura readers and other personalities.

Subtleties. The projected consciousness' contradictory attitudes during semilucid projections are sometimes extremely subtle because its emotions suffocate rationality.

Case Study. For example: in order to counteract the retraction of the silver cord – which is dragging the psychosoma back into the human body – the anxious consciousness, already projected outside the building where it resides, tries, as a last resort, to grab and hold onto the cement ledge at the base of the closed bedroom window (of the bedroom where the soma rests) with the parahands. This ledge is situated 6'6" (2 meters) from the bed, but is within the radius of the all-powerful action of the silver cord, which is 13' (4 meters) on average.

Phenomena. In this maneuver, its parahands first went through the curtains and the windowpane (the attribute of self-permeability of the psychosoma), in order to immediately attach themselves to the window sill (phenomenon of extraphysical telekinesis).

Procedures. Conclusion: the projected consciousness attempts to employ – in an obviously futile manner – two procedures that are antagonistic, or which cannot coexist almost simultaneously:

1. **Dematerialization.** The dematerialization or permeability of the parahands.
2. **Materialization.** The materialization or impermeability of the same parahands.

Cord. In this case, the evident and most common phenomenon occurs, namely the impermeability of the parahands in the two procedures, and the silver cord wins the contest.

Bibliography: Anderson (26, p. 133), Armond (53, p. 49), Blackmore (139, p. 107), Broad (209, p. 162), Bunker (222, p. 106), Campbell (237, p. 14), Castaneda (258, p. 56), Coxhead (311, p. 92), Donahue (407, p. 5), Drury (414, p. 22), Frost (560, p. 32), Garfield (568, p. 118), Gooch (617, p. 71), Grattan-Guinness (626, p. 80), Green (631, p. 18), Grosso (650, p. 187), Gudjonsson (658, p. 110), Heindel (705, p. 149), Holzer (751, p. 105), Mc Creery (1020, p. 13) Mitchell (1059, p. 12), Monroe (1065, p. 179), Muldoon (1105, p. 57), Ouspensky (1174, p. 293), Peralva (1225, p. 97), Rogo (1444, p. 133), Sculthorp (1531, p. 156), Sparrow (1587, p. 60), Steiner (1610, p. 56), Stokes (1625, p. 22), Vieira (1762, p. 124), Walker (1781, p. 98), Wolman (1863, p. 925).

98. LUCID PROJECTION AND NIGHTMARES

Definition. Nightmare: the afflictive dream the effects of which are agitation, anguish and oppression during its development.

Synonymy: bad dream; *cauchemar;* demonic dream; nightmarish dream; nightmarish hallucination; sleep terror disorder.

Victim. In nightmares, what occurs is a periodic detonation of neural activity, reflecting material in which the individual is more a victim (direct experiencer) than an actor (feigned protagonist).

Infancy. Nightmares are generally associated with basic fears in our infancy and recreate a time in our current physical life in which we are completely defenseless.

Insecurity. Nightmares occur in adult life when a person feels insecure and recalls these initial fears, insecurities and disagreeable expectations.

Mood. Sleepers who have nightmares during the night, even when they do not remember them, generally wake up in a bad mood.

Spontaneous. Children's spontaneous nightmares always appear after deep sleep, notably at the beginning of the night. Awakened due to intense anguish, or panicky fear (oneirophobia), the child screams loudly and is sometimes difficult to calm.

Pathology. Sleep terror disorder is not an expression of dreams, but represents a pathological awakening that frequently occurs in children between 4 and 7, or between 10 and 13 years of physical age.

Avoidance. Some persons suffer periods of prolonged and frequent nightmares (recurrence), in accordance with certain occurrences in life.

Prophylaxis. There are 3 attitudes that help the individual to avoid all types of traumatic nightmares:

1. **Cause.** Discover what it is that causes the person to feel afraid or have that type of phobia.
2. **Thoughts.** Maintain pleasant thoughts before sleeping.
3. **Relaxation.** Maintain a state of inner relaxation.

Incidence. Many nightmares, whether they are of origins which are chemical-physiological (medications, food), pathological (specific illness, trauma, accident), environmental (excessive heat) or others, can arise exaggerating or intensifying the story line of a distressful situation previously experienced, even if many decades ago, either in one's childhood or adolescence.

Recurrence. Nightmares tend to repeat themselves, with small variations on the same basic familiar story line, and as a function of the repetition of the cause that generated them.

Categories. Nightmarish hallucinations, or "night demons," vary according to the dreamer's psychic state and organic state, and can be divided into 3 groups or categories:

1. **Personages.** According to the (exotic) personages that are involved.
2. **Animals.** According to the (monstrous) animals in their story lines.
3. **Situations.** According to the (tragic) situations that they comprise.

Forms. Nightmares also manifest in two forms:

1. **Possession.** Passive, in which the dreamer-possessed individual submits him/herself to nightmarish anguish without reaction.
2. **Reaction.** Active, in which the dreamer reacts to the nightmare's hallucinatory conditions.

Characters. The adult's nightmare in its various forms, whether digestive, hypertensive, or of another nature, constitutes a manifestation of the altered state of consciousness called *dream*. The characteristics that differentiate it from lucid projection are obvious.

Recall. There are two conditions of recall in this context:

1. **Fright.** People generally recall *nightmares* because they are frightened by them.
2. **Vagueness.** In many cases, *lucid projections* are not recalled because they hold no significance for the intraphysical consciousness, other than being mild or agreeable, not frightening experiences. They are often vague and lack sufficient emotional significance to provoke recall.

Start. The intraphysical consciousness can project from the human body starting out from a nightmare, or from an *anxiety attack* experienced in a dream, as well as from experiencing a characteristically nightmarish semilucid projection.

Lucidity. As a rule, when the consciousness achieves some degree of lucidity during a nightmare, negative dream, or terrorizing dream – the lucid nightmare – the nightmare disappears completely.

States. This last condition can develop into 1 of 3 consciential states:

1. **Dream.** The nightmare disappears and the consciousness continues to uninterruptedly experience a natural dream that is inoffensive or even agreeable, from an emotional point of view.
2. **Projection.** The nightmare disappears and the consciousness subsequently has a lucid projection.
3. **Awakening.** The nightmare disappears and the consciousness physically awakens, recalling multiple different consciential events.

Volitation. One of the more common processes for eliminating a nightmare stems from the ability of the consciousness to volitate extraphysically.

Scenario. Upon feeling anguished, in extremely frightening circumstances, the consciousness *leaves the nightmarish scenario* volitating.

Psychosoma. This fact suggests that the psychosoma's advanced consciential attributes do not permit the consciousness to have intense projective nightmares, because these attributes – developed to a degree beyond the human body's restrictions – break the conditioning of organic limitations and naturally undo the nightmarish anguish.

Sensations. We can arrive at two conclusions regarding the intraphysical consciousness' sensations from the material presented thus far:

1. **Oneiric.** The common *natural dream* constitutes a consciential experience that is *stronger* than a nightmare, in respect to its sensations, although this does not seem to be the case at first sight, because it imposes itself upon the consciousness (dream *versus* nightmare).
2. **Projective.** Similarly, *lucid projection* is a *stronger* experience than natural dream and nightmare from the standpoint of the consciousness' experiences when in these altered states (lucid projection *versus* dream and nightmare).

Parapathology. The intraphysical consciousness' intrusion-related situations, as well as the incubus and succubus processes (sexosomatics), can trigger terrifying nightmares.

Bibliography: Fodor (529, p. 185), Frost (560, p. 49), Rampa (1352, p. 71), Vieira (1762, p. 49), Walker (1781, p. 100).

99. COMPARISONS BETWEEN NIGHTMARES AND EXTRAPHYSICAL INTRUSION

Differential. The basic differential characteristics between nightmares and extraphysical interconsciential intrusions are very important for the intraphysical projector's understanding of consciential states. They are well defined, as can be seen in these 10 topics:

1. **Evidence.** The nightmare constitutes a manifestation that is specifically internal, psychic or self-psychic, related to the intraphysical consciousness itself.

Nightmare. Influence exerted over others through the thoughts and emotions of extraphysical intruders (intruders, as well as their satellites) can even occur through nightmarish manifestation by way of external interference that is effected upon the individual's oneiric images, whether that person is a child, youth, or adult.

Paraperceptions. Nevertheless, these interferences sometimes become evident to the intraphysical consciousness. They are extraphysically *para*sensed, *para*seen and *para*touched as originating *from outside* oneself (heteropsychic), namely stemming from another or other consciousnesses.

2. **States.** A nightmare is a characteristic manifestation that occurs in the oneiric state or during the intraphysical consciousness' ordinary dreams, being almost always benign.

Malign. Intrusion-related influence is a profuse manifestation, arising in many cases as a living nightmare, or occurring in the ordinary, physical waking state like a negative daydream imposed upon the intraphysical consciousness, with clearly noxious or malign aspects.

3. **Continuity.** Nightmares, which are ephemeral manifestations, generally completely extinguish at the moment the consciousness physically awakens.

Continuation. Intrusion-related influence, a less transitory manifestation, does not always end upon physical awakening. It demonstrates a logical continuation and continuity into other conditions or altered states of consciousness. Negative *mental wedges* or *xenothosenes* – sick ones, in this case – also occur (thosenology).

4. **Images.** The nightmare is characterized by an absence of logic in its nightmarish images.

Logic. Intrusion-related influence demonstrates reasonably plausible connotations in its negative images, that are induced or forged in the intraphysical consciousness' mind.

5. **Positions.** In a nightmare, the characters do not have well-defined roles.

Roles. In extraphysical interconsciential intrusion, the roles performed by the extraphysical consciousness (the *tormenter*) and the intraphysical consciousness (the *victim*) are clearly defined.

6. **Emotionality.** In a nightmare, ephemeral emotionality arises from the human being's own sentiments and sensations.

Superimposition. Intrusion-related influence provokes insinuating, strange, and even exotic superimposed emotionality in the individual who is suffering intrusion.

7. **Memory.** A nightmare does not provoke considerable alterations in the normal flow of the dreamer's mnemonic engrams upon awakening.

Intrusion. Intrusion-related influence causes an invasion or intrusion of traumatizing phantom-recollections into the victim's memory that correspond to events that were not experienced in the current existence and therefore do not have a corresponding place in the biomemory of the current existence.

Para-amnesia. These recollections compose the para-amnesia that can sometimes even refer to experiences from previous lives together with the victimizer or the intrusive company.

8. **Age.** Nightmares occur more frequently in children. Intrusion-related influence occurs more frequently with adults.

9. **Incidence.** From the perspective of the incidence of the various conditions analyzed here, we cannot say that an *intrusion-related nightmare* exists.

Recurrence. The most that can happen is that the individual has a recurring nightmare, or one that repeats due to certain predisposing physiological or psychic conditions.

Intrusion. On the other hand, nightmarish, uncomfortable and insidious intrusion does occur, and has unmistakable characteristics, in the manner of a mega-weak-trait.

10. **Parapsychopathology.** As can be seen, ordinary nightmares, which we can call *natural* or *physiological* nightmares, are overall very different in their manifestations from *artificial* (parapsychopathological) nightmares, which are created from the existence and action of a consciousness that intrudes upon the intraphysical consciousness' psychic (intraconsciential) and parapsychic (intra and extraconsciential) life.

Bibliography: Vieira (1762, p. 49).

100. LUCID PROJECTION AND HALLUCINATION

Definitions. Hallucination (Latin: *hallucinari*, to mistake): the apparent perception of an external object that is not present at the moment; a mental error in sensory perception not based on an objective reality; an experience with the characteristics of sensory perception, but with no evident sensory stimulation.

Synonymy: derangement; fantasy; ideophane; illusion; mirage; perception without an object; wrong perception.

Similarities. There undoubtedly exist similarities between hallucination and certain ordinary states of consciousness, especially natural *sleep*, the ordinary *dream*, and the physiological *nightmare*.

Defense. All these states constitute the human body's (soma) own and peculiar defense mechanisms against that which is unbearable (something) to the consciousness (self-lucidity).

Aspects. Some researchers consider 2 apparently logical aspects:

1. **Awake.** Hallucinations could be the consciousness' dreams in the ordinary, physical waking state.

2. **Sleep.** Dreams could be hallucinations experienced by the sleeping person (sleep).

Psychopathology. Within psychopathology, hallucinatory states arise more easily in those consciential conditions that are intermediary between the ordinary, physical waking state and the natural sleep state.

Disturbances. These conditions present themselves in almost all mental disturbances, notably in the following 5, among others:

1. Bipolar disorder (manic-depressive psychosis).
2. Epilepsy.
3. Exotoxic psychoses.
4. Feverish delirium.
5. Schizophrenia.

Clairvoyance. On the other hand, visual hallucinations are extremely similar in their manifestations to the animic-parapsychic phenomenon of *facial clairvoyance*, especially due to the following 4 characteristics:

1. **Eyes.** As they occur with the eyes open.
2. **Gaze.** Maintenance of a fixed gaze in a specific direction.
3. **Fixation.** The special characteristic attitude of expectation, or fixation.
4. **Indifference.** Indifference to normal visual stimuli.

Energy. Bioenergy is a powerful anti-nightmare factor. If you are aware of your consciential energies and are able to enter into the vibrational state whenever you wish in any critical or traumatic circumstance while in the ordinary, physical waking state, and if the vibrational state is already a permanent consciential habit of self-defense, the most intelligent thing to do is to continue to produce the same condition when experiencing the altered state of a nightmare.

Will. The energies triggered by the will undo the nightmare images upon rationalizing the oneiric scenes.

Phenomenon. All phenomena, and therefore, all altered states of consciousness require energy.

Thosenization. It is a matter of thosenization, with the *ene* component.

Realities. However, the consciousness, or the will itself, is simultaneously 4 realities:

1. More than energy.
2. More than the brain.
3. More than the neurons.
4. More than the soma's *cellular flimflam.*

Causes. Generally speaking, besides mental disorders, hunger, thirst, fear, guilt, loneliness and extreme physical sensory deprivation or emotional deprivation can cause hallucinations that are simple or complex phenomena and vary in type and manner, such as the following 19, among others:

1. Abstract hallucinations.
2. Antagonistic hallucinations.
3. Associated hallucinations.
4. Auditory hallucinations.
5. Cenesthetic hallucinations.
6. Endoscopic hallucinations.
7. Extrascenic hallucinations.
8. Gigantic or Gulliverian hallucinations.
9. Gustatory hallucinations.
10. Kinesthetic hallucinations.
11. Negative hallucinations.
12. Neurological hallucinations.
13. Normopsychic hallucinations.
14. Olfactory hallucinations.
15. Perceptive hallucinations.
16. Psychomotor hallucinations.
17. Small or Lilliputian hallucinations.
18. Tactile hallucinations.
19. Visual hallucinations.

Similarities. The greatest similarities between hallucinations and lucid projections are in regard to the following 3 factors:

1. **Alterations.** Both are altered states of consciousness.
2. **Mechanisms.** Both act as consciential self-defense mechanisms.
3. **Deprivation.** Both can be triggered by sensory deprivation.

Explanation. Hallucination is generally proposed as the psychological occurrence that explains lucid projection. This explanation is obviously given by those who have never experienced consciential projections and are unaware of the extent of manifestations that arise in the much broader consciential universe of projectiology.

Multi-sensory. Lucid projection, using hallucination as an explanatory hypothesis, would be an illusory, imaginary perception that utilizes all the senses as a mechanism, or at least vision, audition and taction.

Collective. In order to explain certain projections of the consciousness, the hallucination theory would have to be a collective or a group one, because it would simultaneously occur with the projector, the assistant or assistants, and witness-observers, in the case of joint or shared apparitions. Each individual's perceptions would react simultaneously and with several of their senses in hallucinatory states. This is difficult to understand in light of logic and reason. This hypothesis is more absurd (nonsense) than hallucination itself.

Facts. There are 2 essential facts that, for the projector, eliminate the hallucination hypothesis as being explanatory of lucid projection:

1. **Induction.** The individual can experimentally induce the lucid projection, and the projector is very clear that the experiences are not mere autosuggestions.

2. **Self-bilocation.** During the self-bilocation phenomenon, the consciousness sees itself outside the human body and contemplates it in relief with full lucidity as the real being that it is.

Cases. In cases of lucid projection, it can be seen that the accounts are far too numerous and unanimous to be considered mere hallucinations, as they come from all countries, and are related by non-pathological people who receive all types of cultural influence and describe the occurrences as having the same phenomena-related patterns. It is highly improbable that so many apparently psychologically healthy persons are suffering hallucinations.

Physiology. In this case, the best, more rational and logical hypothesis that matches up with the general facts is to consider consciential projection to be a natural, physiological and universal phenomenon that is equal to other *parapsychic* (intraconsciential and parapsychic) phenomena.

Veridical. It is worth noting that there are those who defend the existence of the so-called *veridical hallucination*, corresponding to an event or circumstance that is unknown to the percipient, which, in this case, distorts the meaning of the term *hallucination*.

Bibliography: Blackmore (139, p. 81), Champlin (272, p. 205), Currie (354, p. 159), Fortune (540, p. 76), Gooch (617, p. 72), Gurney (666, p. 457), Kardec (825, p. 140), Lippman (934, p. 345), Marinuzzi (998, p. 112), Paim (1182, p. 45), Rogo (1436, p. 178), Souza (1584, p. 8), Todd (1689, p. 53), Walker (1781, p. 85), Wolman (1863, p. 926).

---

101. COMPARISONS BETWEEN HALLUCINATION AND LUCID PROJECTION

Differential. The basic differential characteristics between hallucination and projection of the consciousness outside the human body, like those that refer to ordinary dreams, are quite striking and can generally be classified into two categories:

1. **Individual.** Subjective or individual.
2. **Public.** Objective or public.

Subjective. We will now consider at least 14 of these differential characteristics between hallucination and projection of the consciousness, the first 8 being subjective ones:

1. **Predetermination.** It is useless to attempt to execute a specific action in a predetermined location while hallucinating. With projection, this becomes possible, and with assured results, starting from the resolution taken before sleeping to direct oneself to a certain location during the projection and, when there, to realize the extraphysical action that was planned.

2. **Takeoff.** The experience of lucid takeoff, namely the impressions of the departure from the human body, cannot be associated with hallucinations.

3. **Psychosoma.** The extremely individual characteristics of the psychosoma and its manifestations, that are felt and observed by the projected projector, convince it of extraphysical realities, which are far removed from any mistaken perceptions or hallucinations.

4. **Realities.** Hallucinations do not present the resources necessary to provide exact information regarding *real* events experienced and the *real* places described by the projector.

5. **Translocation.** Deliberate extraphysical transit is not possible through hallucination by the consciousness. Projection facilitates the willful execution of extraphysical *departure-return-new-departure*

translocation, in the same itinerary or trajectory, giving the projector the direct, irrefutable experience of extraphysical situations commanded by its own will.

6. **Interiorization.** The experience of lucid interiorization while in the psychosoma is also very different from hallucination.

7. **Energies.** In hallucination there is no exteriorization of energies and the ostensive energetic shower, which are *physical* and psychic phenomena peculiar to the complex of projective manifestations, whether occurring before, during, or even after the projective episodes.

8. **Self-knowledge.** The projector perfectly distinguishes lucid consciential projections from any erroneous perceptions or hallucinations through the self-persuasion that is peculiar to the projective phenomenon.

Objectives. We will now look at 6 objective differential characteristics between hallucination and projection of the consciousness:

9. **Influence.** The influence exercised by the projected projector over other persons, including the apparitions to intraphysical consciousnesses, is not even remotely similar to erroneous perceptions or hallucinations.

10. **Encounters.** Logically speaking, hallucinations do not permit encounters with extraphysical consciousnesses or intraphysical consciousnesses, as occurs with lucid projections.

11. **Waking.** Hallucinations do not permit occurrences similar to those of intraphysical beings who are in the waking state, are present, and give matching testimonies regarding the events seen by the projector, as they see its apparition in the psychosoma, or the phenomenon of physical bilocation.

12. **Extraphysical.** Some projected-intraphysical-witness-projectors observe and directly participate in the same extraphysical events with other companions. This does not occur in hallucinations.

13. **Laboratorial.** Laboratory experiments demonstrate, in practice, with the use of special equipment and monitoring, the reality that the lucid projection is an altered state of consciousness quite different from hallucinations.

14. **Philosophical.** The powerful effects of lucid projection upon the philosophical perspectives of the experimenter, such as loss of fear of physical death (thanatophobia), existential recycling and others, constitute evidence against the affirmation that projections are mere hallucinations or fantasies, from which such profound or lasting effects would never be expected.

Drugs. Nonetheless, some apparent forms of hallucinatory experience, such as those induced by light or heavy, licit or illicit drugs, have been known to cause effects, which are not so profound, upon the individual's subsequent existence. Paradoxically, however, many of these effects can actually constitute drug-induced projections (pharmacology).

Improbabilities. Lucid projections have been spontaneously experienced by persons who did not accept (conviction) the existence of the phenomenon until it happened to them (experience).

Questions. From the preceding considerations, it is possible to pose two pertinent questions:

1. **Informed.** Why do those persons who are aware of projections, but nonetheless do not accept projectiological phenomena, have hallucinations of projections?

2. **Uninformed.** Why do persons who never heard of lucid projection have hallucinations of projections? Strictly speaking, these hallucinations logically would either be very improbable or even impossible to occur.

Conclusion. The above arguments lead us to the evident and logical conclusion that hallucinations, regardless of their type, do not satisfactorily explain lucid projections.

Bibliography: Champlin (272, p. 205), Stokes (1625, p. 24).

V – Vehicles of Manifestation of the Consciousness

102. EGO

Definitions. Ego: the substratum of the individualized consciential principle; the primordial and irreducible state of consciousness, the basis of all states of consciousness.

Synonymy: *anandamayakosha;* androgynous being; *atman;* causal body; cause of psychic life; central self; controller; driver of the soma; eternal identity; eternal integral consciousness; greater self; individuality; intelligent principle; *jiva;* microworld; *pneuma;* principle of identity; psyche; *purusha;* real self; self; *sema;* soul; spirit; spiritual principle; super being; superconscious; thinking self; true self.

Consciousness. Before considering the vehicles of the consciousness, or meta-organisms (holosomatics), it is important to think about what the consciousness or ego is.

Energy. The consciousness is *more than energy.* Even if it were only energy, it would not exist without a substratum. Hence the existence of the ego and the vehicles for its manifestation.

Multidimensionality. The human being is a multidimensional being.

Instruments. Evidently, the human body, the holochakra, the psychosoma, or even the mentalsoma, are not – whether isolatedly or even when together in the condition of coincidence of all bodies, or the unified body – the consciousness, or the ego itself. These vehicles are merely instruments, since they do not think by themselves.

Attributes. Everything points to the fact that the consciousness presents final attributes of ample magnitude, even *beyond the faculty of thinking,* as can be observed in the state of cosmoconsciousness and the occurrences of extraphysical intuition.

Faculties. It has been suggested that the intraphysical consciousness has 3 basic capacities or faculties:

1. **Cognition:** the act of knowing or possessing knowledge.
2. **Affection:** sentiment.
3. **Volition:** desire.

Physiology. Mental phenomena would generally be restricted to the operation of one of these 3 faculties:

1. Cognition: the sense of perception, memory, introspection, intuition, inference and other sources of knowledge.
2. Affection: sensation, emotions, moods, personal characteristics and other manifestations of sentiment.
3. Volition: motives, desires, deliberations, decisions, choices, struggles, longings and actions or, in other words, the preponderant factors that influence and reveal acts of will.

Holosomatics. In another approach using holosomatics and thosenology, it can be said, in part, that:

1. Cognition (intuition, memory) is more restricted to the mentalsoma *(tho).*
2. Affection (sensation, emotions, moods) refers more to the emotional body *(sen).*
3. Volition (struggles, actions) materializes through the soma, with the energies of the holochakra *(e).*

Classification. The intraphysical consciousness, the human being per se, the structure of the psychic apparatus in his/her thinking essence, can be classified according to 3 specific consciential aspects:

1. **Subego.** The subego is the most obscure, subterranean, primitive, instinctive, genetic and animal part of the personality. The *id* which is autonomous, hypoconscious, subpersonal and neurological, maintains a direct relationship with the consciential energies of the holochakra.

2. **Ego.** The ego, per se, is the emotional, social part, the sensations of the personality – whether awake, or in the ordinary, physical waking state – that maintains a relationship with the consciousness, headquartered in the mentalsoma, but still bound to the parabrain of the psychosoma (parahead).

3. **Superego.** The superego is the part opposed to the animal, which is contrary to natural impulses, the *suspectometer*, the voice of the conscience, the paragenetics generated by its holobiography, the keeper of codes of ethics, that reaches the experience of cosmoethics and exists in direct relation to pure consciousness, in the mentalsoma.

Ultimate. Strictly speaking, the ultimate substratum of the being presents at least the following 8 characteristics:

1. It is independent.
2. It is nonmaterial.
3. It is noncerebral.
4. It cannot be compared to the life, mind, emotions or instincts of the human being.
5. It is not the ephemeral and changeable human personality.
6. It does not have limits.
7. It is not born, as we understand it.
8. It does not die, being therefore indestructible, the consciential principle that is self-animated after being created.

Life. The ego, or eternal consciousness, creation or emanation, the primary origin of which remains unknown, is beyond all transitory elements, this being the reason why the consciousness of the intraphysical projector ends up preferring, through personal experiences, another form of life besides physical existence, there not being in this any pretense of greatness or outstanding quality. It is simply a matter of skill, experience, knowledge and rationality.

Self-awareness. Self-awareness is the faculty or capacity whereby the human being is aware of his/her existence, or is aware of being conscious of his/her mind, thoughts and sentiments. This involves other mental faculties such as reason, memory and imagination.

Chimpanzees. Self-awareness is the single essential quality that differentiates humans from subhuman animals. This is because it is not found in any other living organism on earth, not even in chimpanzees, which sometimes momentarily seem capable of being aware of their existence and present a genetic makeup that is 96.7% identical to that of humans.

Blood. It should be stressed that, in the sanguineous relationship between humans and higher simians, the chimpanzee is the only simian having an *"O" blood type,* the universal donor.

Knowledge. In summary: even considering the existence of some tenuous form of self-awareness in other subhuman animals, the human being has an awareness of him/herself that is qualitatively greatly superior in this respect. The human being is not limited to knowing, he/she knows that he/she knows. The human knows him/herself when he/she so desires.

State. The state of the free consciousness (FC), in which the ego manifests itself solely and permanently through the mentalsoma, appears to be the greatest idea that we possess – in the current stage of terrestrial knowledge – regarding the natural or *raw* condition of the incorporeal nature of this selfsame ego.

Mentalsoma. In this case, the meaning of the term "mentalsoma" transcends the sense of a simple seat of logic, reason and other consciential attributes of the intraphysical consciousness. In fact, another neologism should be created in order to define the *mentalsoma* in this condition.

Singular. In spite of having various vehicles of consciential manifestation and being able to mobilize them at the same time, resulting in the condition of *double awareness,* each one of us has only one waking consciousness.

Functions. At least 7 basic functions can be attributed to the ego:

1. Thought (fundamental intelligence).
2. Impulse (instincts).
3. Sensation (coordination).

4. Sentiment (emotions).

5. Imagination (dreams, daydreams).

6. Will (destiny, free will).

7. Intuition (relative truths).

Realities. The expressions in parentheses, being presented in the plural, correspond more precisely to the levels of analytical and embryonic realities within us (egos).

Bibliography: Bozzano (184, p. 123), Martin (1002, p. 20), Michaël (1041, p. 59), Mittl (1061, p. 9), Monroe (1065, p. 273), Prieur (1289, p. 52), Rampa (1361, p. 52), Vieira (1762, p. 86), Walker (1781, p. 82).

103. TYPES OF HOLOSOMATIC VEHICLES

Definition. Holosoma (*holo*, whole, entire set; *soma*, body): instruments, bodies or vehicles through which the ego (the consciousness) manifests in the physical and extraphysical universes.

Synonymy: additional bodies; compound human; consciential instruments; consciential unistructure; consciential vehicles; corporeal grouping; cosmic bodies; encased bodies; external conformations of the ego; housings of the consciousness; integral whole; *koshas;* meta-organisms; metaphysical bodies; multi-ego; multiple ego; nonphysical bodies; packaged bodies; personal whole; pluri-ego; recipients of the consciousness; *rupas;* set of bodies; spiritual wraps; total human; wraps of the consciousness.

Vehicles. The great variety of evidence in the field of projectiology research makes it extremely difficult to explain all cases and phenomena, except by accepting the fact of exteriorization of the intraphysical consciousness in other vehicles of manifestation besides the human body (see fig. 103, p. 1,124).

Dissociation. Based on this premise, human individuality is not limited to the visible human body in the ordinary, physical waking state. It is made up of the set of elements that are encased, one inside the other, coexisting in harmony and which, under certain conditions, can be dissociated.

Interaction. Projections of the consciousness are precisely the consequence of the dissociation of these bodies or vehicles that are associated, interactive, coincident, encased, juxtaposed, aligned, interpenetrated or coexistent.

Coexistence. The vehicles of manifestation of the intraphysical consciousness, in the state of coincidence, coexist at the same place or space on earth, although each one vibrates at its own frequency, or dimension of extremely individual and distinct existence.

Types. The consciential vehicles range from the dense physical organism (human body) at the physical extreme, spanning through the parabodies (extraphysical vehicles) – the holochakra and psychosoma – to the subtle mentalsoma, at the extraphysical extreme. This set (organizational chart) can be perceived at our present evolutionary level.

Subtlety. There might be still more subtle manifestations. Who knows?

Reality. These vehicles are real, each in its own way, and are not *smoke* that disperses in the air.

Classification. For the practical application of these concepts, the vehicles of manifestation of the consciousness can be classified and named in 6 manners or according to basic variables:

A. Vehicle 1 = Body 1 = B 1 = Human body (soma).

B. Vehicle 1.5 = Body 1.5 = B 1.5 = Holochakra (energetic parabody).

C. Appendix 1.5 = A 1.5 = Silver cord.

D. Vehicle 2 = Body 2 = B 2 = Psychosoma (emotional parabody).

E. Appendix 2.5 = A 2.5 = Golden cord.

F. Vehicle 3 = Body 3 = B 3 = Mentalsoma (parabody of discernment).

Images. In the holosoma awareness technique, for awareness of the reality of the 4 coincident vehicles of manifestation of the intraphysical consciousness – the human body, the holochakra or the energetic parabody (that does not transport the consciousness), the psychosoma or the emotional parabody, and the mentalsoma – we can utilize various resources of multiple images or crude comparisons, especially the following 4: mirrors, furniture, dolls, and a kit including a sponge, sand and water.

1. **Mirrors.** Observe the reflected image of your human body, as though you were at the tailor's shop standing between double facing mirrors such that you see your own image (in an infinite progression of mirrors of multiple images, over the shoulder) repeated 3 times behind you.

2. **Furniture.** Study the interpenetration of a set of 4 pieces of furniture, such as Chinese tables, or even 4 perfectly encasing boxes that fit one into another, forming a harmonic set that occupies less volume and space.

3. **Dolls.** Examine a clipping of 1 simple model of dolls, or of the entire human body, that is well-proportioned, holding hands, made out of a sheet of white paper, folded back and forth 3 times; or 4 *matrioskas* (little mothers), painted, wooden Russian dolls that fit one into the other.

4. **Sponge.** Get an ordinary sponge, endeavor to fill it with fine sand, then submerge it in a bucket of limpid water. You will then observe the simultaneous, conjoined existence of 3 distinct, very evident substances, each one interpenetrating the other: the sponge (the human body), the sand within (the psychosoma) and the water (mentalsoma) flowing through the sponge.

Union. The holosoma represents the extremely complex union of living multileveled or *bio-para-psychic-social* systems.

Simultaneity. Each vehicle of the consciousness is simultaneously two realities, the computer and the programmer or, in other words:

1. **Computer.** Each vehicle is the computer of the next more evolved vehicle.

2. **Programmer.** Each vehicle is the programmer of the next less evolved vehicle.

Scale. In an operative ascending scale, or in the consciential organizational chart, the consciousness has power over all vehicles of the consciousness and directly or indirectly controls them from its basic headquarters, the mentalsoma.

Ascendancy. The mentalsoma, headquartered in the parabrain of the psychosoma, has direct ascendancy over the psychosoma and controls it through the parabrain and the golden cord.

CNS. The psychosoma, or the emotional body, headquartered in all the individual's *nerve elements,* is directly ascendant over the holochakra, or the energetic parabody, silver cord, chakras, human aura, and over the human body, or the instinctive body, controlling it through the central nervous system (CNS), namely the brain.

Characteristics. Various aspects characterize the vehicles of manifestation of the consciousness and need to be researched in order to discover their mechanism, dynamic and composition, especially with regard to the following 13 characteristics:

1. The human body in the ordinary, physical waking state.
2. The human body during lucid consciential projection.
3. The integral psychosoma.
4. The partial psychosoma.
5. The psychosoma with the holochakra.
6. The psychosoma without the holochakra.
7. The mentalsoma.
8. Self-invisibility.
9. Incorporeity.
10. The influence of the holochakra.
11. The silver cord, the force centers (chakras) and the aura.
12. Densities.
13. Indeterminate characteristics.

Separation. The human body and other vehicles of consciential manifestation are elements separate from ourselves. We are not merely our bodies. Beyond all forms, we are the eternal or permanent consciousness.

Environment. Each vehicle of manifestation of the consciousness varies regarding its nature, according to the environment where the consciousness has to act and the characteristics of that environment.

Adaptations. Intraphysical beings, when adapted to their environment, are *stronger* in the material world. Extraphysical consciousnesses, when adapted to their environment, are *stronger* in the evolved extraphysical dimensions.

Manipulation. Lucid consciential projection is based upon the consciousness' capacity to simultaneously, but separately, manipulate the human body and another vehicle of manifestation, whether the psychosoma or the mentalsoma.

Basics. Irrespective of the existence of all vehicles and instruments of manifestation of the consciousness analyzed here, the 3 basic elements of the intraphysical consciousness need to be emphasized, with practical life in view: the ego, the psychosoma and the human body.

Names. The consciential vehicles have been given diverse names throughout time and intraphysical societies.

Concepts. Concepts other than the synonyms mentioned in this section, when not equivalent but at least similar or analogous, as well as the correlative names used equally by various personalities, philosophers and researchers in general registered by human history to identify one vehicle or another or some of their primordial aspects, should be borne in mind. The following 12 are examples listed in alphabetical order:

1. **Animal-spirits,** by René Descartes (1596-1650).
2. *Animus,* by Lucretius (last century B.C.).
3. **Archetypal ideas,** by Plato (428-347 B.C.).
4. **Directing idea,** by Claude Bernard (1813-1878).
5. **Entelechies,** by Aristotle (384-322 B.C.).
6. **Internal sense,** by Mesmer (1734-1815).
7. **Luminous intermediary,** by Puységur (1751-1825).
8. **Monads,** by Leibnitz (1646-1716).
9. **Solar atoms,** by Pythagoras (572-497 B.C.).
10. **Substantial body,** by Emanuel Swedenborg (1688-1772).
11. **Transparent man,** by Cyrano de Bergerac (1619-1655).
12. **Vital principle,** by Barthez.

Neologisms. We can name the bodies of the main vehicles of the consciousness more accurately if we use roots from the Greek language:

1. **Soma** (physical body): human body, a term already currently in use.
2. **Deuterosoma** (*deutero,* second, two; *soma,* body): spiritual body, second body, the same as "psychosoma".
3. **Cephalosoma** (*cephalo,* head; *soma,* body): mentalsoma.
4. **Holosoma**: the set of all the bodies when they are coincident, the individual in the ordinary, physical waking state.

Hierarchy. In a single transmission line of electric energy, *power* with a frequency of 60 Hz and *communication* with a frequency between 30 KHz and 500 KHz can be sent in a superimposed and coexistent manner. This constitutes a hierarchy of subsystems coordinated with different levels of complexity, such as organs, tissues, cells, organelles and macromolecules – infinitesimal beings.

Consubstantiality. The *human being* is his/her physical body (the consciousness is not the soma). Outside the soma, the human being (citizen) loses his/her substantial integrity. The human construct, in the intraphysical dimension, remains unintelligible outside this *consubstantiality.*

Sets. Some individuals are disturbed by the diversity of names given to the vehicles of the consciousness. We can offer theses individuals 3 uniform sets of similar expressions to signify the same 4 consciential vehicles listed here as the physical body, holochakra, psychosoma and mentalsoma, in that order:

1. **Bodies:** human, energetic, emotional and mental.
2. **Somas:** soma, aerosoma I, aerosoma II and cephalosoma.
3. *Koshas: kosha, pranamayakosha, manomayakosha* and *vijnamayakosha.*

Hidden. Regarding the vehicles of manifestation of the consciousness, there are 5 very different occurrences that constitute their hidden features or, in other words, that which is still unknown with regard to their *modus operandi:*

1. **Silver.** Where does the silver cord hide when the consciential bodies are coincident in the ordinary, physical waking state?
2. **Psychosoma.** Where does the psychosoma hide when the vehicles of manifestation of the consciousness are in the natural state of coincidence?
3. **Golden.** Where does the golden cord remain during lucid projection of the consciousness in the psychosoma?
4. **Parahead.** Where is the mentalsoma located in the parabrain or, in other words, in the interior of the extraphysical head (parahead) of the psychosoma, when it is coincident or even when it is projected?
5. **Consciousness.** Where does the consciousness go and remain during the individual's temporary state of relative unconsciousness?

Cord. It seems that the silver cord does not *hide* in any specific place.

Particle. Each particle of the psychosoma appears to be connected to its physical analog. When the psychosoma distances itself from the soma, these connections come together forming the silver cord, just as different radio and TV signals can coexist.

Frequencies. We can only begin to understand the hidden features of the vehicles of manifestation of the consciousness, or the temporary location of theses elements of the ego, in certain *circumstances,* by accepting the existence of different vibratory frequencies between these vehicles. Some conceal others, all interpenetrating in relative interdependence, just as occurs with the simultaneous physical and extraphysical dimensions of universal life.

Coexistence. These dimensions and vehicles are not superimposed but coexist in the same space and time.

Seats. From the perspective of the seats of the vehicles of manifestation of the consciousness, or the interpenetrating consciential bodies, 6 inferences can be made regarding the subjects presented, in their entirety:

1. **Holochakra.** The human body or soma houses the silver cord or holochakra.
2. **Psychosoma.** Although it receives basic orientation from the psychosoma, the human body also houses this vehicle.
3. **Parts.** From a sectorial perspective, or relative to the parts of the human body, for example, the hand houses the parahand, the leg houses the paraleg, and so on.
4. **Brain.** The human brain houses the parabrain of the psychosoma.
5. **Parabrain.** The parabrain of the psychosoma houses the mentalsoma.
6. **Mentalsoma.** The mentalsoma probably houses the consciousness.

Bibliography: Andreas (36, p. 91), Bentov (119, p. 134), Besant (129, p. 12), Blavatsky (153, p. 128), Crookall (343, p. 14), Durville (436, p. 27), Greenhouse (636, p. 133), Guéret (659, p. 161), Meek (1030, p. 37), Norvell (1138, p. 168), Osborn (1154, p. 61), Powell (1278, p. 1), Prieur (1289, p. 11), Rampa (1361, p. 76), Sculthorp (1531, p. 156), Shay (1546, p. 10), Steiner (1610, p. 55), Vieira (1762, p. 73), Yogananda (1894, p. 381).

104. PRE-RESOMA

Definition. Pre-resoma: the activation and encasing of the extraphysical consciousness, by way of the psychosoma, in the holochakra, thereby initiating the connection of the silver cord in the incipient soma.

Synonymy: ante-incarnation; birth of the silver cord; connection of the holochakra; creation of the holochakra; extraphysical incarnation; first birth; first rebirth; first resoma; holochakral *incarnation;* human pre-birth; incarnation of the etheric double; initial human rebirth; *mini-incarnation;* previous *incarnation; proto-incarnation.*

Theory. In presenting the extremely logical theory of pre-resoma, which serves to explain various extraphysical and physical events and phenomena related to the human consciousness, the author reminds those who would object to it that they should refute it with logic, proposing another more rational theory to replace it. This is a fundamental rule of science.

Stages. Pre-resoma indicates the conditions that specify the different stages of the consciousness in the complex process of resoma/desoma.

Conditions. There are 11 different consciential conditions that occur in dense pre-physical/physical/post-physical *chronological order:*

1. **Pre-resoma.** The pre-resomant: the first connection of the holochakra (energy added to the extraphysical consciousness) in matter for the formation of the new soma in the introductory process of human embryogeny. This *addition of consciential energy* is the first step toward resoma.

2. **Resoma.** The resomant: human conception already with the complete union of the egg from the mother's gynosoma with the sperm from the father's androsoma.

3. **Fetus.** The fetal consciousness: the fetus in development.

4. **Newborn.** The newborn: the soma or, more precisely, the holosoma still in a rigorous process of physical restriction and funneling of the extraphysical consciousness or the loss of hyperacuity.

5. **Infant.** The infant: existential consolidation occurs at 7 years of age.

6. **Adolescent.** The adolescent: the youth (pre-intraphysical consciousness).

7. **Intraphysical consciousness.** The adult consciousness per se: organic or biological maturity at 26 years of age.

8. **Pre-desomant.** The pre-desomant: the aged person, the individual who is between sixty-five and eighty-four years of age or, more appropriately, the intraphysical consciousness who is eighty-five years of age and over.

9. **Desomant.** The desomant: the terminally ill person pertaining to desomatics or thanatology (pre-extraphysical consciousness).

10. **Recent-desomant.** The recent-desomant: the traces of the holochakra after first desoma.

11. **Extraphysical consciousness.** The extraphysical consciousness: the extraphysical consciousness per se, or the errant extraphysical consciousness.

Restriction. The restriction of the consciential attributes begins in the pre-resoma period in order for the consciousness to adapt to the conditions of the intraphysical funneling of human existence.

Transformation. At this point there may be a visual extraphysical transformation of the extraphysical consciousness, as well as its planned juvenilization (rejuvenescence through self-transfiguration of the psychosoma), including attitudes, interests, occupations and the nature of its life (existential program) in accordance with the human conditions it will encounter in the upcoming intraphysical life, in a preview of the impending life *(simulated resoma).*

Nuptials. In the pre-resoma condition, the extraphysical consciousness (kin, blind guide, intruder, helper) often extraphysically attends the wedding (nuptials) of its future parents (when the bride is not pregnant).

Engagement. The extraphysical consciousness can even energetically (cardiochakra) participate or intervene (affinity) in the articulations (engagement) for the upcoming wedding.

Cupid. This inspired the myth of *cupid* or the *little angel* with the appearance of a child and, therefore, already extraphysically restricted.

Hypothesis. To what degree do the future parents, in certain cases, emanate consciential energies for the formation of the initial trace of holochakral energies of the extraphysical consciousness that is a candidate to resoma while still in the condition of a pre-resomant?

Psicociese. Pre-resoma or the constitution of the holochakra is that which allows the occurrence of pithiatism, *psicociese* or psychological (human) pregnancy.

Subhumans. Through this, it is observed that pre-resoma seems to occur with subhuman animals or, in other words, they also exhibit *psychological pregnancy* or psychic gestation.

Gestation. Human (or subhuman) gestation per se is genetic, being a cellular, organic and dense union or creation of the embryo of the soma.

Holochakra. Psychological gestation is holochakral, being merely an energetic, cellular union without dense organic substrates.

Bibliografia: Vieira (1762, p. 23).

105. RESOMA

Definition. Resoma: the activation and encasing of the extraphysical consciousness (mentalsoma + psychosoma) in the condition of pre-resoma – by way of the holochakra – in the soma or human body (human conception + fetus).

Synonymy: birth of the soma; birth; cellular incarnation; cellular resoma; creation of the vitalized soma; junction of the soma; organic resoma; rebirth; second birth; second resoma; vitalization of the soma.

Projection. Resoma is a *fixed* and prolonged projection of the desomant consciousness (extraphysical consciousness) for a specific period, thereby constituting the holosoma (integral or involving 4 vehicles) of the human being.

Prodigality. In a surprisingly prescient mechanism, life begins again at every new birth of a human being with extreme prodigality or even an apparent waste or dissipation.

Sperm. A single seminal emission from the genitourinary organ (originating from the masculine sex glands: testicles) of the androsoma contains 300 million sperm or the total number of the population of an above average sized country.

Population. Less than two dozen seminal emissions represent a quantity equivalent to the current human population of this planet.

Eggs. The gynosoma (female human body) contains 700 thousand eggs at birth.

Emissions. Only 400 eggs will be emitted, the equivalent of 1 every 28 days in the course of slightly more than 3 decades of genital life.

Ephemerality. In spite of the entire aforementioned prodigality, the prescient mechanism of human life, in order to support itself on this planet, does not allow uninterrupted or very long-lasting existences, but only short (current maximum: 13 decades), temporary or ephemeral existences in series, without exception.

Death. The death of the human body (desoma) is the condition which is indispensable for the survival of the human species and the continuation of learning on the part of the consciousnesses on this mega-school-planet.

Immortality. A humanity that has individuals who become immortal would, within a few years, become suffocated, lacking the energy, the food and the space necessary for its existence or survival. The human species would disappear from the face of the earth.

Intraphysical society. Without the desoma of individuals – or of the human body – there would be no human society (intraphysical society), human history, human future or hope for human beings (intraphysical consciousnesses).

Abortions. In cases involving a series of abortions carried out by the same consciousness, it leaves the pre-resoma condition, enters the resoma condition, returns to pre-resoma and, in this way, returns to resoma many times in succession without achieving the condition of a being which has undergone pure desoma, or second desoma.

Suicides. It is presumed that cases of successive abortions occur frequently with the consciousnesses of suicidal individuals that have many aggravating circumstances. This occurs in order to attenuate karmic debts or disturbances. This is popularly referred to as the *burning* or *purging of karma.*

Stillborn. The stillborn is the human body, or the soma, which is born without a pre-resomant consciousness to vitalize it, or with an empty brain (anencephaly, when it exists) from the beginning of the process of gestation, or from the fetal period.

Bioethics. *Headless clones* of subhuman animals are already being created in order to offset the undersupply of organs for human transplants, triggering heated controversy in the bioethics community.

Stillbirth. Stillbirth is the birth of the soma alone (devoid of the consciousness) which, in this case, is a pathological or morbid occurrence.

Bibliography. Vieira (1762, p. 23).

---

106. LUCID PROJECTION AND THE HUMAN BODY

Definitions. Human body: the body of the individual of the *Animal* kingdom, *Chordata* phylum, *Mammalia* class, *Primate* order, *Hominidae* family, *Homo* genus, *Homo sapiens* species, the most elevated level of animal development on earth; the physical substance or material structure of every human being; the body that is nourished by food, feels the effects of fatigue, suffers wear, degeneration and disintegration.

Synonymy: alpha body; animal body; bioelectric mechanism; bioform; biological body; biosoma; body-house; brain-body; cage of flesh; capsule of the ego; carapace of the psychosoma; carnal body; carnal chrysalis; carnal involucre; cellular attire; cellular prison; cellular vehicle; city of nine doors; compressor of the self; container of the internal bodies of the consciousness; corporeal residence; corruptible body; crude body; dense body; dense organism; discardable body; earthly body; electrobiochemical mechanism; emitting physical body; evident body; exterior body; external body; genetic body; goblet of clay; heavy body; hominal body; human aggregate; human engine block; human magnet; human organism; instinctive body; larva-body; lithosoma; living machine; megaphone of the consciousness; mind-body; mortal armor; mortal body; mundane body; natural body; normal body; organic form; physical body; physical deep-sea diving suit; physical *habitat;* physical involucre; physical self; primary body (for the man); psychophysical organism; respiratory machine; sarcophagus of carbon; skiff of flesh; skin of the consciousness; *soma;* somatic body; *stula;* temple of the soul; terrestrial body; terrestrial shell; three-in-one body; tridimensional body; vital object.

Androsoma. The male human body – androsoma – has approximately 60 trillion cells; 5 million hairs; 650 muscles; 208 bones; 100 joints; and 59,652 mi (96,000 km) of arteries, veins and capillaries.

Organism. The person, considered to be a living, *physical ecosystem,* receives the name of organism.

Comparisons. The physical body of human beings – the most limited and imperfect expression of the consciousness – besides the synonymy presented above, is still labeled or compared (analogies, metaphors) with a box, burden, car, cell, city, clock, dungeon, electronic instrument, grave, heavy attire, mantle, microcosm, microuniverse, oven, overcoat, sanctuary, steam engine, tomb, trench, tunic of skin and other objects.

Mechanics. There are evident similarities between the functions of the human organism and those performed by apparatuses and systems used by mechanics. The following are 14 examples:

1. Bones: reinforced concrete.
2. Brain: electronic switchboard.
3. Circulatory system: irrigation plant.
4. Ears: diapasons.
5. Eyes: cameras.
6. Heart: pump.
7. Incisor teeth: scissors.
8. Kidneys: filters.
9. Liver: glycogenic central heating.
10. Lungs: bellows.
11. Molar teeth: pestle.
12. Muscles: elevating machines.
13. Stomach: chemical laboratory (or biodigestor).
14. Synovia: oiler.

Registers. The marvelous mechanism of the human body, formed by these approximately 60 trillion cells – each one individually having capacitance and inductance – equipped with all types of extremely precise clocks and measuring devices, registers and responds to, aside from the 5 basic senses, every physical rhythmic change in its surroundings due to many environmental factors: electric fields, magnetic fields, gravity, cosmic influences, ionization, light, pressure, cosmic rays, temperature, time and humidity.

Relationships. The relationships of the holosoma and its components with the sciences can be very illuminating. Broadly speaking, the human body has a more direct relationship with biology, anthropology and medicine. The energetic parabody has a more direct relationship with acupuncture. The emotional parabody has a more direct relationship with psychology. The mentalsoma has a more direct relationship with parapsychology. The entire holosoma has a more direct relationship with projectiology (or holosomatics). Conscientiology studies the consciousness, or the ego per se, beyond the holosoma.

Dynamic. The soma is only a vehicle for carrying us through human life. The consciousness never stops and does not have a static human appearance or structure.

Resynthesis. Throughout its useful life, during the phase of biological growth and beyond, the human body undergoes profound and constant alteration in the continuous process of destruction-reconstruction, or the elaborate resynthesis of its material components. The cells are substituted or replaced by fresh material derived from its sources of nutrition: the air of respiration, food and ordinary drink.

Renovation. It is currently accepted that general cellular renovation of the 5 fundamental systems of the human body is completed every 158 days:

1. Structural.
2. Muscular.
3. Circulatory.
4. Nervous.
5. Lymphatic.

Lives. This means that every intraphysical consciousness undergoes resoma at least twice a year and that a single human life spanning 5 decades literally constitutes more than 100 brief uninterrupted interconnected lives.

Characteristics. The human being shares many characteristics with other animals. He/she is, however, an animal that practices art and science.

Eyes. The human being's intellectual activities are conditioned by the eyes. The sense of vision dominates the human perspective of the external world.

Gynosoma. Women continuously have mammae (gynosoma).

Sexosomatics. Men adopt the frontal position during sexual relations. Men are practically the only primates that do not have a bone inside the penis.

Intentionality. Humans have the effective and constant capacity of assigning a use to things in advance, with a purpose or intention underlying their behavior. This is rarely seen in subhuman animals, with the exception of the chimpanzee.

Stimuli. In the condition of intraphysical beings, we are constantly bombarded by all types of sensory stimuli that the sense organs of the human body and the proprioceptive sensations stemming from this selfsame body unceasingly register.

Sensations. Because it is dense and tangible, the coarsest or most *impenetrable* of all vehicles of manifestation of the consciousness, being a special structure for the greater intraphysical restriction of the *self,* the human body permits animal, coarse and intense sensations, including pain and orgasm. This leads the unwary intraphysical consciousness to mistakenly think that only this body and no other vehicle in its complex vital organization – namely in its unified body (holosoma) – exists.

Incapacity. Because it is so enslaved by the perception of physical reality, as it is assimilated by the 5 basic organic senses, the intraphysical consciousness becomes incapable of accepting (conviction) its true nature or recognizing its multivehicular constitution.

Philosophers. For the majority of adults – including thinkers, philosophers, scientists and intellectuals in general – it becomes incomprehensible, difficult and almost impossible to accept the fact that the consciousness exists outside the human body as something separate or separated from it, or to even ponder this deeply.

Inhibition. This is one of the basic inhibiting factors (autosuggestion, self-hypnosis, somatization) of lucid projection and is the reason why this phenomenon has still not achieved unanimous acceptance by the members of the human species.

Cenesthesia. Complex cenesthetic sensations provide the intraphysical consciousness with an inner perception and, at the same time, the sense of the existence of the human body. The existence of cenesthetic images has been proven by psychopathology.

Constituents. The following are 32 constituents or parts of the human body that are considered as themes for reflection in the practices of Orientalism: bile, blood, bones, cerebral hemispheres, fat (lipids), feces, flesh, hair of the head, heart, intestines, kidneys, liver, lungs, lymph, medulla, mesentery, mucous, nails, phlegm, pleural membrane, pus, saliva, serum, skin formations, skin, spleen, stomach, sweat, tears, teeth, tendons and urine.

Zeal. We live in dense matter zealously taking care of the human body, which gives us a lot of work and requires great expenditures from us when endeavoring to satisfy respiration, hunger, thirst, sex, hygiene, as well as sheltering and serving it from morning to night, year-round, throughout human life (lifetime). All this from the time we are born on the face of the earth until this selfsame body is deactivated by final projection, or biological death (first desoma).

Worship. There is currently a blossoming of impassioned worship of the human body, the first physical abode.

Sports. This is expressed through all types of sports and gymnastics, including choreographed gymnastics, gymnastics for senior citizens, narcissistic gymnastics, and others. They have the objective of achieving physical shapeliness, restoring lost self-confidence and ensuring continued mental well-being and social integration.

Compulsiveness. Basic care of the human body is practically compulsory and inevitable.

Disasters. If we leave the body to itself, disasters such as the following 6 will occur:

1. **Oxygen.** If we do not breathe fairly oxygenated air, we die from asphyxiation within a few minutes.

2. **Diet.** If we do not eat (food), we die from inanition within days.

3. **Liquids.** If we do not drink, we die from thirst in less time than from hunger.

4. **Hygiene.** If we do not cut our hair, we develop a mane.

5. **Nails.** If we do not cut our nails, we cannot satisfactorily use our hands and feet.

6. **Bath.** If we do not take a bath, we soon become a foul-smelling pile of trash.

Image. That is why we continuously gaze fixedly at our image while contemplating ourselves in the mirror – an ever-present theme in our concerns regarding waking conscious life – attentive to the conservation of physical and mental health and the means for satisfying the condition of *well-being*.

Concentration. As a result of this profound single-mindedness of every intraphysical consciousness – intense and continuous concentration upon the human body – it is always much easier to believe that the human body, controlled by the brain, the physical seat of the consciousness, is the sum total and the sole specimen of our being, and that we are merely *biochemical machines*.

Vehicles. Lucid projection, however, shows the interested individual that intellect, reasoning, imagination, critical judgment, memory, advanced perception, sentiment (deeply rationalized emotion) and all other functions of the consciousness can exist in a pure form, independent from the human body, manifesting the self through the other vehicles which are more evolved than the soma.

Aspect. We exist. This does not require proof. But the human body, 60% of the weight of which is water, is only one aspect of our total being.

Confusion. The intraphysical consciousness, who is used to identifying him/herself with external clothing, typically makes the following 3 types of mistakes:

1. **Attire.** Confuses the human body with his/her clothing.

2. **Ego.** Confuses his/her vehicles of manifestation with the ego.

3. **Personality.** Confuses his/her transitory wrapping with the eternal personality.

Illusion. Matter seems very real, inflexible, hard and solid to humans in the ordinary, physical waking state. The basic sensory organs give the *illusion of the solidity* and *material* nature of objects.

Physics. However, contemporary physicists affirm that matter is neither as solid as it appears, nor is it the way that we perceive it. For example, if all the space between the atomic particles that compose matter were to be removed through a compression process, the human body of an adult would be smaller than the point of a pin. This is because 99.99% of the human body is empty space.

Devoid. In other words: the human body, including the brain, is mostly water and, in fact, both are mostly "devoid" of any "solid matter".

Matter. Matter, in the sense of a solid, compact and impenetrable body, does not exist.

Differences. Matter itself, at ambient temperature, shows appreciable differences in its manifestations. The following are 4 examples:

1. **Liquid.** *Mercury* is a liquid metal.

2. **Solid.** *Lead* is a solid metal.

3. **Gas.** *Oxygen* – the foundation of intraphysical life – is a gas.

4. **Glass.** *Glass* is actually a super-cooled liquid that does not have the crystalline structure that characterizes true solids.

Objectivity. Incidentally, it merits adding that some researchers place the "objective existence" of things in doubt. They think that all of this is no more than a huge "mental construction."

Ponderations. The referred to evidence can be pondered by the reader who nurtures 3 categories of doubt:

1. **Resoma.** Doubt regarding the critical condition of the extraphysical consciousness in the process of resoma in the human body, which begins immediately after biological conception.

2. **Connection.** Doubt regarding the connection of the consciousness in the condition of physical restriction imposed by the human body during the entire intraphysical existence.

3. **Relationship.** Doubt regarding the intervehicular relationship of the human body with the psychosoma when it is presumed to have merely one thousandth of the weight of that body while projected in the extraphysical dimension but still over the planetary crust or within the troposphere.

Energy. All the material of our human body – an energetic structure – can be controlled by our intraphysical consciousness. This can be seen in the effects of yoga techniques, the processes of biofeedback and, mainly, the extraordinary effects of the basic mobilization of consciential energies (BME).

Divisions. The human body can also be studied through the following 5 divisions:

1. Right/left.
2. Front/rear.
3. Top/bottom.
4. Head/body.
5. Trunk/members.

Chakras. It is interesting to point out that the left half of the human body presents the insertion point of the 2 isolated essential basic chakras, in the corresponding location in the holochakra and psychosoma: the cardiac and the splenic. The *upper* division shows the insertion points of 4 chakras and the *lower* division shows the insertion points of 3 chakras.

Head. The division of the head alone shows the insertion points of 3 basic chakras.

Trunk. The insertion points of all the other essential chakras are in the trunk. There are no insertion points of main chakras in the members, but only of secondary or tertiary chakras.

Somatopsyche. According to psychology, the condition of the individual's self-awareness of his/her own human body is referred to as *somatopsyche*.

Spaces. According to proposed hypotheses, the psychosoma seems to occupy a more general four-dimensional space, from the moment of encounter of two portions of energized matter, the sperm and the egg.

Deprivations. There only needs to be an increase in physical restriction, namely a greater sensory deprivation – pain, hunger, thirst, anesthesia and others – in order for the intraphysical consciousness to project outside the human body, as though it were being expelled, *squeezed* out, moved in the psychosoma from the place it occupies. This is, hypothetically speaking, probably due to the field effects (physics).

Particles. The facts suggest that the psychosoma is made up of particles which are different from dense physical ones. If its particles were of the same nature as dense physical particles (molecules, atoms, electrons and others), there would be an excessively strong interaction between them. This would make lucid projection impossible, namely the discoincidence of at least 2 vehicles of manifestation of the consciousness.

Inactive. During the period of complete projection in which the consciousness remains outside, the inactive or temporarily unoccupied body remains inert, passive, *unconscious* or in an apparent sleep state.

Latency. Through the essential connection of the silver cord, vegetative and organic life maintain a minimum of vital processes, respiration, a barely perceptible pulse, circulation, and the natural physiology of the organism, through the autonomic nervous system, in a form of latent life.

Cadaver. The human body without the consciousness resembles a human cadaver.

Suspension. In this state in which the sensory systems and the motor systems are temporarily suspended, the projector's *intraphysical assistant,* as long as he/she is sufficiently observant, can sometimes even clearly hear the bubbling sounds made by intestinal gasses, when close to the inactive body and the brain, which has been emptied of the consciousness.

Similarities. The situation of the inactive human body during prolonged projection is often reminiscent of a cadaver, although the latent vital signs allow one to unquestionably distinguish one condition from the other.

Stillborn. It is likewise reminiscent of the condition of the lifeless stillborn fetus nested in the uterus and the yogi who is voluntarily buried alive for a period of time. It is also reminiscent of projective autoscopy.

Aircraft. This situation is similar to an aircraft flying on autopilot while the pilot temporarily leaves the cockpit to visit the airplane lavatory, although this particular case is more adequately likened to lucid projection while the soma is in movement.

Mimicry. During the exteriorization stage of the consciousness in the psychosoma when the consciousness is sometimes not very lucid, while projected from the human body, extraphysical movements are poorly reproduced, as though mimicking, due to simple perceptible body reflexes. This occurs independent from and beyond the habitual physiological movements involved in natural sleep.

Reflexes. However, when the consciousness feels that it is projected with full lucidity and is able to extraphysically translocate itself outside the sphere of energy that surrounds the human body (psychosphere), it becomes incapable of passing its movements – whether moving a hand, foot, or turning over in bed – directly to the physical body. This is because the body displays a deep and generalized absence of reflexes while the human senses are inactive.

Interiorization. This measure can only be taken through total interiorization or, at least, through partial interiorization of the consciousness in the psychosoma. In this case, the holochakra would be so rarefied (extraphysical particles more distant from each other) that the flow of energy necessary for the exchanges of consciential command from the psychosoma to the human body does not occur. This special condition is akin to the fine wire with high resistance which, nevertheless, cannot conduct a great amount of current.

Reactions. When projected in the *extra*physical dimension, the *intra*physical consciousness can, under certain conditions, present manifestations which are most notably marked by indifference toward the human body. This is expressed in many ways, such as the following 8 types of subtle relationships which are similar, though not identical:

1. **Insignificance.** The human form appears insignificant.
2. **Strangeness.** Contemplating the human body as if it belonged to a stranger.
3. **Indifference.** *Total* indifference toward the human form (appearance).
4. **Dispassion.** Observing the human body dispassionately.
5. **Disinterest.** Having absolutely no interest in his/her own human body.
6. **Unemotionality.** Looking at the physical body without emotion.
7. **Unconcern.** Being completely unconcerned regarding the human body.
8. **Impersonality.** Viewing the physical body in an impersonal manner.

Reluctance. Many intraphysical consciousnesses, when projected in the extraphysical dimension, display an undisguisable reluctance to return to the human body. This is expressed in various ways, such as the following 8 most common manners:

1. **Contrariety.** Showing deep contrariety to return.
2. **Hardship.** Feeling the return to be a painful hardship.
3. **Desire.** Not demonstrating any desire to return.
4. **Obedience.** Obeying, against their will, the irresistible order to return.
5. **Stay.** Having the insistent desire to stay there forever.
6. **Disappointment.** Displaying acute disappointment regarding the return to human life.
7. **Rebellion.** Showing great rebellion against returning to dense matter.
8. **Thought.** Even getting to the point of thinking: "Why not let the body die?"

Attire. Every physical object has its *extraphysical duplicate*. This is why there is a type of energetic connection, which is sill not fully characterized and defined, between the human organism and the objects it wears or comes in direct contact with, such as: all types of attire, rings, earrings, glasses, contact lenses, dentures, prosthetics in general, plastic items, all artifices of vanity, and others.

Prosthesis. The human or *intraphysical* body is nothing more than a temporary prosthesis that the extraphysical consciousness – which already has 2 extraphysical parabodies (psychosoma and mentalsoma) – uses when it manifests on the planetary crust. This results in 2 facts:

1. **Mother.** The mother is the preeminent *professional prosthetist*.
2. **Uterus.** The uterus is a *prosthetics workshop*, installed to serve extraphysical consciousnesses or similar personalities from the extraphysical dimension.

Cybernetics. The resources of cybernetics, or mechanisms for the technical extension of the human being, are *prosthetic products*, such as the following 3:

1. **Computer.** The *computer* is an external prosthetic for enlarging biomemory (mnemosomatics), namely the cerebral dictionary (autobiography).
2. **Automobile.** The *car* is a temporary prosthetic for extending the two human legs (somatics) or the potentiation of the cerebellum (psychomotricity).
3. **Robots.** In robot wars, or *prosthetic wars,* no one dies. Only the *robots – prosthetics of humans –* are exterminated or deactivated.

Suicide. This occurs in the same way with human suicide. Those who kill themselves or commit self-murder only annihilate the temporary prosthesis: the intraphysical body. For this reason, every suicide (self-destroyer) is an extremely frustrated desomant intraphysical consciousness because it will never be able to kill the actual consciousness which is, even for itself, a reality that is *deathless* or incapable of being *assassinated.*

Paraphysiology. From now on, in this section dedicated to analyzing the vehicles of manifestation of the consciousness, the limits of the *human* constitution and physiology are no longer those determined by orthodox or conventional anatomists and physiologists.

Heterodoxy. The observations gathered here do not allow themselves to be adapted to concepts that currently govern orthodox biology and medicine.

Epistemology. That is why the contents of this book – driven by the facts – transcend the limits of traditional science, as it is habitually accepted, and the most strongly defended theory of knowledge. This indicates that the present is already an appropriate time, demanding an epistemological revolution or a gnoseology which is based on new foundations (paragnoseology). It is common knowledge that epistemology is the study of "how we know what we know." This is when a new paradigm is needed in order to replace the decadent conventional mechanist Newtonian-Cartesian paradigm.

Bibliography: Alverga (18, p. 217), Battersby (92, p. 14), Besant (129, p. 19), Carton (252, p. 98), Crookall (326, p. 121), Dychtwald (444, p. 39), Frazer (549, p. 156), Greene (635, p. 57), Greenhouse (636, p. 135), Heindel (705, p. 44), Kardec (824, p. 197), Martin (1002, p. 8), Meek (1030, p. 16), Paim (1182, p. 37), Perkins (1236, p. 132), Prieur (1289, p. 48), Rogo (1444, p. 34), Russell (1482, p. 26), Schatz (1514, p. 185), Vieira (1757, p. 3), Walker (1782, p. 26), Wang (1794, p. 181).

---

107. PINEAL

Definition. Pineal (Latin: *pinus,* pinecone): the gland of endocrine secretion which is extremely well protected at the center of the human brain (another gland of endocrine secretion) – of which, however, it is not a part – enclosed between the 2 cerebral hemispheres, atop the spinal column.

Synonymy: base of the rational soul (René Descartes); *conarium;* cyclopean eye; epiphysis; eye of Shiva; mental eye; pineal body; pineal eye; pineal gland; *place of the self;* sensitive antenna; third eye; third sight.

Historical. All indications are that the pineal gland was best described for the first time in the year 300 B.C. by the Greek physician Herophilus and the Greek anatomist Erasistratus, both from Alexandria. They attributed this organ with the function of being the *valve of the memory.*

Unique. This organ has always intrigued anatomists because, whereas the entire brain is duplicate, the pineal is unique in the brain in that it has no duplicate.

Nomenclature. The pineal gland received its name because it is shaped like a pine cone. It is also called the *third eye* because, in its formation, it begins as an eye.

Cells. The cells of the pineal gland are called *pinealocytes*.

Anatomy. In anatomical terms, the pineal gland is an oval, piniform corpusculum or, in other words, is similar to the seed of a pine tree, or is conical.

Pea. The pineal gland is a small organ. It is the size of a pea, has a grayish pink color, weighs no more than 100 mg, and is 5/16" (8 mm) long and 3/16" (5 mm) wide in humans.

Diencephalon. The pineal gland originates in the epithalamus, which is the structure of the diencephalon, in the dense tissue of the choroid screen, above the anterior quadrigeminal tubercula and behind the third ventricle.

Autonomic. The pineal gland is innervated exclusively by the autonomic nervous system.

Melatonin. The pineal gland secrets the hormone called melatonin *(5-methoxi-N-acetyl tryptamine)*, which inhibits the chemistry of sexual maturation and seems to react to darkness.

Light. In other words: light inhibits the pineal gland's production of melatonin.

Substances. It is accepted that the pineal gland is the only source of melatonin in the human body. There is also a series of brain chemicals inside the gland.

Physiology. Up until some decades ago, the pineal organ was only seen as an evolutionary relic or an anachronistic remnant of evolutionary development, a type of appendix encased in the center of our brains, not serving any biological function.

Hormone. Scientists proved the error of this belief by discovering that the pineal gland stops secreting its hormone, melatonin, when the individual is exposed to a bright light of 2,500 luxes, or approximately the intensity of indirect sunlight on a clear spring day.

Lux. The lux is the quantity of light received at a distance of 3'4" (1 meter) from a standard candle.

Segregation. Melatonin is normally only secreted in the darkness of night.

Evidence. With new scientific discoveries, researchers admit that the human pineal gland still functions as an "eye" that is sensitive to light.

Waves. It is suspected that the pineal gland emits and receives *biomagnetic waves.*

Effects. The following are 14 effects that melatonin has on important sexual factors:

1. It delays the onset of puberty.
2. It reduces the weight of the gonads.
3. It reduces ovarian progesterone.
4. It reduces the hormone that stimulates the serum follicles.
5. It reduces serum luteinizing hormone.
6. It reduces the synthesis of testosterone.
7. It reduces the luteinizing hormone of the pituitary.
8. It reduces the factors that liberate hypothalamic gonadotropin.
9. It increases prolactin of the serum.
10. It increases testosterone metabolism in the liver.
11. It increases the synthesis of progesterone.
12. It increases serotonin in the pituitary gland.
13. It inhibits uterine contractions.
14. It suppresses spontaneous or induced ovulation.

Sleep. Melatonin not only affects sleep, producing an increase in REM cycles, but also enriches our dreams with greater vividness. These activities also liberate a substance from the pineal gland called *vasotocin,* which is the most potent sleep-inducing factor.

Parapsychopathology. It is suspected that there are parapsychopathological disturbances which stem from abnormalities or alterations of the pineal gland, related to human blindness.

Chronobiology. Biorhythmology is the biological science (chronobiology) of physiological analysis that studies the vital or internal rhythms, rhythmic variations, endogenous clock or body cycles, notably the following 4:

1. **Resomatics.** The biological or circadian rhythm *(circa diem* or *approximately one day)* or a 24-hour activity cycle. Here we can include: appetite, sex, defecation, micturition and mental capacity. There are time indicators in the circadian rhythm: clocks, regular meal times, work shifts.

2. **Waking.** Sleep/wake cycle, sleep/wake alternation or sleep-rest activity.

3. **Gynosomatics.** The hormone cycles related to gynosomatics or those of women: ovulation/menstruation.

4. **Existential seriation.** Birth/death or resoma/desoma.

Medications. The normal temperature of the human body and its capacity for absorbing medications changes depending upon the time of day. Body cycles which are normally synchronized desynchronize themselves.

Cycles. The sleep/wake cycle is interconnected to over one hundred other more or less 24-hour corporal cycles.

Clock. Medical researchers affirm that the pineal gland influences the regulation of the individual's biological clock or physiological biorhythm, seasonal rhythms or circadian changes, relative to the *cosmoclimatic rhythm* and the *day/night cycle,* given that it is somehow responsible for readjusting our internal clocks (chronobiology) when we cross time zones.

Disturbances. It is recommended that those who suffer from these problems after long flights to distant time zones (jet lag) wherein there is a substantial alteration in the time of day due to the differences of the time zones (flights in a westerly or easterly direction) get sufficient exposure to sunlight until the human body becomes synchronized again.

Jet lag. Jet lag is characterized by fatigue, changes in mood, inefficiency and similar symptoms. Older people suffer from this disturbance more than young people.

Note. It is important to note that the biological clocks referred to here should not be confused with the common biorhythm graphic calendars that are sold commercially and are based upon the presupposition that the rhythms begin at birth, at a zero point, with forecasts of precise cycles of creativity (33 days), sensitivity (28 days) and physical strength (23 days) that are counted from this zero point. The existence of these rhythms has still not been scientifically demonstrated.

Cord. Parapsychology studies admit that the pineal gland is the fulcrum of the final energetic connection of the silver cord in the human body. This is why the projector sometimes feels a certain intracranial pressure at the final moment of lucid takeoff in the psychosoma.

Speculation. So far, this subject is mere speculation, from a scientific point of view, due to the complexity of the cortical functions that have still not been clarified. The silver cord requires new and more convincing responses.

Point. One's awareness is attracted to the point between the eyebrows, the third eye or the epiphysis, on 5 occasions:

1. **Hypnagogy.** When wishing to achieve the hypnagogic state, the condition of alpha waves, or the alpha state, because the practitioner turns the eyes upward.

2. **Somnambulism.** When entering into a very ordinary somnambulistic state, because the somnambulant's eyes turn upward.

3. **Self-desoma.** When the intraphysical consciousness promotes a certain type of self-desoma, or induced final projection, also looking upward.

4. **Desoma.** The eyes of a cadaver (desoma) turn upward as well.

5. **VS.** When trying to install the vibrational state (VS) in an instantaneous manner.

Curiosities. In pineal gland research, the following 5 relevant, or at least curious, observations should be borne in mind:

1. **Sensitives.** Meticulous comparative studies of necropsies show a greater volume of the epiphysis in cadavers of sensitives or parapsychic intraphysical consciousnesses.

2. **Hindus.** Other comparative studies of necropsies show an epiphysis twice the normal size in brains of Hindus, as compared with the average size found in the brains of Europeans.

3. **Acid.** Lysergic acid (LSD), which is structurally similar to serotonin, a neurotransmitter that is directly related to the pineal gland, is used as a stimulus, a psychophysiological potentiating factor or a hallucinogenic catalyst. In some cases, it opens the doorways to extraphysical consciential perceptions (paraperceptions).

4. **Chakras.** Much has been said about it, but there is still no proof of the relation between the pineal gland and the 2 essential chakras in the encephalic area: the coronochakra and the frontochakra.

5. **Apparatus.** The pineal gland has a great similarity in form and structure with a certain piece of the receiving apparatus of a wireless telegraph, which also contains certain small particles that look like the sand-like tissue of the gland.

Technique. A technical approach for those who easily wake up in the middle of the night and have difficulty in falling asleep again is, upon awakening, to leave the lights off. Only 15 minutes of illumination are sufficient to suspend the production of melatonin, the hormone that controls sleep.

Bibliography: ADGMT (03, p. 144), Battersby (92, p. 83), Blavatsky (154, p. 480), Brennan (200, p. 80), Brunton (217, p. 229), Carrington (245, p. 200), Day (376, p. 101), Drury (414, p. 209), Fox (544, p. 142), Gooch (617, p. 202), Greenhouse (636, p. 26), Haynes (698, p. 152), Heindel (704, p. 72), Leadbeater (897, p. 41), Lee (908, p. 151), Motoyama (1098, p. 202), Muldoon (1105, p. 142), Pastorino (1206, p. 92), Planeta (1249, p. 161), Powell (1278, p. 33), Puryear (1341, p. 190), Reis (1384, p. 46), Rizzini (1410, p. 145), Roberts (1420, p. 121), Santos (1505, p. 61), Shay (1546, p. 93), Shirley (1554, p. 106), Twitchell (1714, p. 93), Vieira (1762, p. 84), Walker (1781, p. 44), Watson (1800, p. 113), Wilson (1858, p. 144), Xavier (1879, p. 19).

108. EXTRAPHYSICAL EXAMINATION

Definition. Extraphysical examination: the assemblage of information obtained by the projected intraphysical consciousness from an analysis of its physical body, projected psychosoma, or the vehicles of manifestation of the intraphysical consciousness (the human body, holochakra, psychosoma and mentalsoma) in the coincident condition; or even the analysis of the psychosoma of the extraphysical consciousness.

Synonymy: extraphysical anamnesis; para-anamnesis; paraphysical self-analysis.

Categories. There are two categories of extraphysical examination:

1. The extraphysical self-examination.
2. The extraphysical hetero-examination, or the examination of another.

Self-examination. It is always better if the projected intraphysical consciousness endeavors to perform, by him/herself, the extraphysical examination of another personality – whether a projected intraphysical consciousness or an extraphysical consciousness – only after performing an extraphysical examination of his/her own psychosoma.

Characteristics. The projected intraphysical consciousness can focus his/her attention on countless characteristics of the vehicles of manifestation of the consciousness (holosoma) during the extraphysical examination, notably the following 11 variables:

1. Holochakra.
2. Human aura.
3. Silver cord.
4. Psychosoma.
5. Mentalsoma.

6. Personal form, whether complete or incomplete, humanoid, solid, transparent, oval, a small circle, a colored cloud, a point of awareness or mental focus.

7. A center of energy (mentalsoma).

8. The consciousness apparently without a body, amorphous (mentalsoma).

9. Insertions or connections of the silver cord (resoma).

10. Navel, nevus, scar and its extraphysical relationships.

11. Examination of the fetus specifically in regard to the pregnant woman consciential projector.

Maturity. The experience of extraphysical self-examination of the projected consciousness substantially contributes toward the acquisition of maturity or consciential holomaturity.

Bibliography: Monroe (1065, p. 168), Steiger (1601, p. 140), Vieira (1762, p. 84).

109. HOLOSOMATIC COINCIDENCE

Definition. Holosomatic coincidence: the condition of harmonious coexistence, interpenetration, juxtaposition, alignment, interdependence and interrelationship between the ego, or the consciousness, the mentalsoma, the psychosoma, the holochakra and the human body, also including the golden cord in this complex of structures, or the connection between the mentalsoma and the psychosoma, as well as the connection of the psychosoma with the human body, or the silver cord.

Synonymy: alignment of the vehicles of the consciousness (an obviously incorrect expression); coalescence of the consciential vehicles; condition of the unified body; condition of concentric bodies; holosomatic interweaving; state of coincidence; multi-organism state; singular state; connection of the bodies.

Mentalsoma. The mentalsoma, the vehicle which is always *more* coincident than the others, is headquartered in the parabrain or, in other words: in the extraphysical head of the psychosoma even when the consciousness is projected in this vehicle.

Bodies. The bodies can be coincident when they are concentric, occupying the same space.

Discoincidence. The bodies can also be out of coincidence – or in the condition of discoincidence – and leave or enter the state of coincidence.

Unified. The human body or soma and the consciousness in the ordinary, physical waking state, form the most coincident body of all: the unified body.

Waking. The ordinary, physical waking state, the state of the intraphysical consciousness in which his/her vehicles of manifestation are totally coincident, shows that 2 or more bodies can simultaneously occupy the same place or space, and interact with each other, as long as each vehicle is in its own specific dimension of existence or manifestation.

Variations. Undoubtedly, the *degree* of coincidence of the bodies, or vehicles of manifestation of the consciousness, varies from person to person.

Locking. Some consciousnesses actually live more *locked* in the human body than others. We are unaware of the real factors that so strongly interfere in order to maintain more or less permanent and intense coincidence.

Intraphysicology. The instance wherein the consciousness is in the human body in the ordinary, physical waking state represents the condition of coincidence of all vehicles of manifestation of the intraphysical consciousness.

Extraphysicology. However, coincidence or purely extraphysical coupling can occur, whether of the holochakra with the psychosoma and mentalsoma, or only of the psychosoma with the mentalsoma.

Extraphysical consciousnesses. Extraphysical coincidence is that which is specific to extraphysical consciousnesses and intraphysical consciousnesses who are temporarily projected from the human body.

Law. There is a law of indistinguishability which states: the bodies (vehicles) of manifestation of an intraphysical consciousness, when fully coincident, thereby comprising the unified body or holosoma, become indistinguishable to the ordinary physical perception of other intraphysical consciousnesses.

Bibliography: Monroe (1065, p. 221), Muldoon (1105, p. 62), Prieur (1289, p. 56), Vieira (1762, p. 14), Walker (1786, p. 107).

110. DISCOINCIDENCE OF THE VEHICLES OF MANIFESTATION

Definition. Discoincidence of the vehicles of manifestation of the consciousness: the departure of any vehicle of manifestation from the condition of coincidence or from the connection of the consciential bodies.

Synonymy: decoupling of the vehicles of manifestation; departure from holosomatic coincidence; disconnection of the bodies; disconnection of the consciential vehicles; disjunction of the bodies; holosomatic disengagement; non-alignment of the bodies.

Types. There are 3 basic types of discoincidence of the vehicles of manifestation of the intraphysical consciousness: minidiscoincidence, maxidiscoincidence and final discoincidence.

1. **Minidiscoincidence.** Minimal discoincidence, or minidiscoincidence, which is more common with regard to the extraphysical members (paralegs, parafeet, para-arms, parahands) or the paratrunk of the psychosoma, occurs more frequently: in traveling clairvoyance; in semi-separations; in natural sleep; in everyday shocks or psychological states; and in almost all other altered states of consciousness and parapsychic phenomena.

Evolution. The state of minidiscoincidence can evolve to complete discoincidence of the vehicles of consciential manifestation or to partial interiorization.

2. **Maxidiscoincidence.** Maxidiscoincidence involves the simultaneous departure of the parahead – obviously including the parabrain – the paratrunk and the paramembers of the psychosoma from their tight coexistence with the human body.

Psychosomatics. This maxidiscoincidence constitutes the complete projection of the intraphysical consciousness in the psychosoma at a distance from the human body, while being vitalized only by a fine string of the maximally-extended silver cord, appearing like a thread or a strand of hair.

3. **Desoma.** The integral, always definitive, discoincidence of the vehicles of consciential manifestation, constitutes final projection, desoma or biological first death, which occurs upon the definitive rupture of the silver cord.

Consciousness. These 3 types of discoincidence can occur in a conscious or unconscious manner for the intraphysical consciousness.

Signs. The following are the 5 most common psychophysical signs or sensations of discoincidence of the vehicles of manifestation of the intraphysical consciousness:

1. **Awakening.** Awakening suddenly in the physical body after a nightmare.
2. **Emptiness.** The sensation of *walking on clouds* or walking in a void.
3. **Heart.** Feeling like *one's heart is in one's mouth*.
4. **Dream.** Dreaming and perceiving that one is dreaming. This is due to an extracorporeal dream or a discoincident dream.
5. **Stars.** *Seeing stars.*

Holochakra. A frequent type of discoincidence is the *partial* exteriorization of the holochakra, which occurs after the *maxidiscoincidence* of a major projection of the consciousness in the psychosoma.

Sleep. It is presumed that sleep – natural discoincidence or minidiscoincidence – serves to recuperate the psychosoma's extraphysical or cosmic energy and temporarily sanitize the human organism's state of cellular intoxication.

Xenophrenia. Discoincidence of the vehicles of consciential manifestation is an essential triggering factor for a great number of altered states of consciousness (xenophrenia). These occur soon after the influence of diverse factors: depression; physical illness; drugs; intense emotion; hypnotic state; intense mental stress; ingestion of alcohol; ordinary sleep.

Geniuses. It is generally accepted that geniuses' vehicles of manifestation of the consciousness are slightly discoincident during their creative moments (pangraphy).

Psychopathies. Certain psychopathies (mental disturbances) present chronic or long-lasting discoincidence, as in the case of certain types of schizophrenia. This shows that vehicular discoincidence can be natural or pathological. With regard to this aspect, the phenomenon of waking discoincidence should be analyzed.

Parapsychism. Simple minidiscoincidence, whether spontaneous and nonlucid or provoked and lucid, of the parahead of the psychosoma, exiting from tight coexistence with the human head, as well as the mentalsoma exteriorizing from the parahead, located in the parabrain of the psychosoma, predisposes the manifestation of most types of parapsychism. This speaks in favor of the importance of the preponderant action of the coronochakra and frontochakra upon the other chakras.

Ectoplasm. As a rule, the exteriorization of ectoplasm begins with discoincidence, even when partial, of the vehicles of manifestation of the intraphysical consciousness of the ectoplasmic sensitive: the human body, the holochakra and the psychosoma.

Bibliography: Ebon (453, p. 123), Muldoon (1102, p. 122), Stanké (1595, p. 112), Vieira (1762, p. 14), Walker (1786, p. 108).

---

111.   HOLOCHAKRA

Definitions. Holochakra: the vibratory, energetic, luminous, vaporous and provisional envelope that structurally coexists and envelops the human body, being directly related to the exteriorization of energies, the silver cord and the chakras; the intermediary energetic agent between the psychosoma and the human body (see fig. 111, p. 1,125).

Synonymy: aerosoma I; aetheric body; ballast of the psychosoma; Bardo body (Tibetans); biocosmic body; bioplasmic body; contrabody; diaphanous body; *djan;* energetic armor; energetic body; energetic parabody; energetic tow; energetic vehicle; energosoma; ephemeral body; etheric body; etheric double; etheric veil; first energy body; great phantasm; human body-psychosoma bridge; *kesdjun* body(Georgi Ivanocitch Gurdjieff: 1949); leptohylic body; leptomeric body; luminous shell; odic body; *pranamayakosha;* pranic body; reflection of the physical body; semiphysical vehicle; *umbra;* unifying body; vehicle of prana; vehicle of vitality; veil of the human body; vital body (Rosicrucians); vital double; vital human copy; vitality body.

Invisibility. The holochakra, as an energetic vehicle, always remains invisible to the sight of the ordinary individual.

Creation. It is logically assumed that the holochakra is created prior to human conception or in the extraphysical pre-resomatic period (intermissiology).

Antiquity. The holochakra was known as a component of the (human-extraphysical) individual or intraphysical consciousness by the ancient Assyrian, Chaldean, Chinese, Egyptian, Essene and Hindu *initiates.*

Present. Nowadays, the holochakra is a theme of study for esoterics, Rosicrucians, Theosophists and yogis.

Medicine. The holochakra is still totally unknown by conventional allopathic medicine. It is, however, utilized in Chinese medicine as well as to explain the mechanisms of the workings of homeopathy, acupuncture, do-in or acupressure, and *shiatsu.*

Recess. The permanent cultivation of voluntary, intentional or self-lucid discoincidence of the vehicles of consciential manifestation or, in other words, some type of lucid consciential projection, is a preponderant factor against the implantation of projective recess.

Form. In other words: the lucid projector remains *projectively in shape* by regularly projecting. Projective recess, regardless of the reason for its generation, is a condition which indicates that the intraphysical consciousness is *out of shape,* from a projectiological point of view. This corroborates the semimaterial condition of the holochakra and the psychosoma, and the conscential projector's quality as an extraphysical athlete.

Bibliography: Aliança (13, p. 151), Andréa (33, p. 24), Andreas (36, p. 86), Babajiananda (65, p. 58), Battersby (92, p. 22), Besant (129, p. 37), Carton (252, p. 98), Castaneda (258, p. 201), Cavendish (266, p. 83), Champlin (272, p. 165), Crookall (343, p. 118), Guéret (659, p. 60), Hodson (729, p. 39), Holroyd (736, p. 97), Kilner (843, p. 38), Leadbeater (897, p. 71), Maes (983, p. 141), Perkins (1236, p. 51), Powell (1280, p. 100), Prieur (1289, p. 106), Steiger (1601, p. 113), Vieira (1762, p. 73), Walker (1781, p. 53), Wang (1794, p. 187), Xavier (1881, p. 99).

112. PARA-ANATOMY OF THE HOLOCHAKRA

Definition. Para-anatomy: the transcendent anatomy of the vehicles of manifestation of the consciousness, excluding the human body or the soma.

Synonymy: extraphysical anatomy; meta-anatomy; parapsychoanatomy; transanatomy; transcendent anatomy.

Contexture. The holochakra emerges from electric currents circulating through the nervous system and extends approximately 3/8" (1 cm) beyond the outline of the human body. It has a dense contexture in primitive human beings (human-animals) and a subtle and delicate contexture in conscientially more evolved human beings (human-intraphysical consciousnesses).

Characteristics. The following are 9 more relevant characteristics of the holochakra:

1. A humanoid form that is generally larger than the human body.
2. Body of vitality.
3. *Doppelgänger* (Germany) or *phantom double.*
4. Energetic form of the human body.
5. Luminosity.
6. Coloration which is sometimes black and white.
7. Hybrid nature or physical and extraphysical structure.
8. Differences between the intraphysical consciousness and the extraphysical consciousness that have undergone the first desoma.
9. It seems to be more connected to the umbilicochakra or the area of the solar plexus.

Nadis. In the para-anatomy of the holochakra, attention should be given to the chakras, the human aura and the thousands of *nadis* (72,000, by conventional calculations) or small channels of energetic circulation, which form a web inside and on the surface of the holochakra, transmitting energy to the cells of the human body.

Discoincidence. The holochakra does not have sensory organs. It is the vehicle that partially becomes discoincident with the vehicles of manifestation of the intraphysical consciousness with ease. It is therefore the *most discoincident* of the 4 existing vehicles. It is directly related to the meridians of acupuncture and do-in (acupressure).

Simulacrum. The holochakra does not operate as a separate, individual vehicle for the manifestation of the consciousness. It does not gather information because it does not transport the physical brain or its corresponding extraphysical brain, the parabrain. As it is incapable of acting on its own, its projections by itself are almost always simple humanoid simulacra of the projector.

Formations. The holochakra is sometimes accompanied by vapor formations, violet clouds, mists or clouds of smoke.

Aura. The exteriorized part of the soma or the visible part of the holochakra constitutes the human aura.

Bibliography: Baraduc (76, p. 93), Crookall (338, p. 141), Ellison (478, p. 355), Guéret (659, p. 63), Maes (983, p. 145), Rampa (1367, p. 25).

113. PARAPHYSIOLOGY OF THE HOLOCHAKRA

Definition. Paraphysiology: the physiology of the vehicles of manifestation of the consciousness, excluding the human body or the soma.

Synonymy: extraphysical physiology; metaphysiology; parapsychophysiology; transcendent physiology; transphysiology.

Characteristics. The holochakra is the vehicle of vitality, *prana* or cosmic energy. It is not an instrument of lucidity of the consciousness. It absorbs energy and distributes it throughout the human body as an energetic intermediary between the human body and the psychosoma.

Unintelligence. The holochakra does not operate as a separate vehicle for the manifestation of the consciousness because it is not a direct instrument of the consciousness or a true vehicle of the intelligent principle.

Relationships. The holochakra, or holochakrology, has direct relationships with 16 consciential conditions or relevant phenomena – as well as others, obviously – that involve the intraphysical consciousness:

1. **Soma.** The human body or the soma.
2. **Connection.** The silver cord (energetic connection).
3. **Parabody.** The psychosoma or emotional parabody of the consciousness.
4. **Chakras.** The chakras or force centers.
5. **Sexochakra.** The sexochakra, *kundalini* or serpentine fire (sexosomatics).
6. **Psychosphere.** The protective shell or psychosphere of the person or intraphysical consciousness (personal holothosene).
7. **Aura.** The human aura or the energetic photosphere of the intraphysical consciousness.
8. **Vision.** The post-desomatic panoramic vision of the extraphysical consciousnesses (former intraphysical consciousnesses) which have recently arrived at extraphysicality or the intermissive period and have still not passed through second desoma.
9. **NDE.** The phenomena of the near-death experience (NDE).
10. **Desoma.** The first death, biological death or cardiopulmonary and cerebral (encephalic) death.
11. **VS.** The vibrational state (VS).
12. **Exteriorization.** The exteriorization or liberation of energies.
13. **Parapsychism.** The parapsychic manifestations that act as catalysts of consciential energies.
14. **Phenomena.** The parapsychic phenomena having physical effects.
15. **Autoscopy.** External autoscopy.
16. **Projections.** Multiple consciential projections.

Gestation. Being the main factor responsible for the elaboration of ectoplasm, the holochakra plays a predominant role in the *final projection of the pregnant woman* (gynecology, gynosomatics) and in controversial transcendental photographs.

Renovation. The holochakra reacts to all of the individual's thoughts and emotions, influences the functions and controls the metabolism of the human body, influences the nutrition and repair of worn-out or diseased cells, substituting them with other healthy ones, recuperating the materials lost from the human body, which renews itself completely every 158 days (hypothesis).

Hypnosis. Hypnosis generally acts upon the holochakra of the consciousness to a considerable degree.

Soma. There is a total interdependence and close solidarity between the holochakra and the human body. Alterations in one vehicle provoke alterations in the other.

Vitality. The organizing vital principle that originates from the consciousness in the psychosoma manifests through the energies of the *pranic parabody* or holochakra.

Percentage. The facts show that the holochakra, as an energetic intermediary that allows the continuation of human life, cannot be *totally* projected from the human body because this would provoke biological death or first desoma.

Portion. It should therefore be understood that every manifestation or projection of the holochakra represents the exteriorization of only a certain portion of its energies and potentialities. This is because a minimal amount of these forces always remains, in all existential circumstances of the intraphysical being, vitalizing the dense form or the organs and organic systems.

Orbiting. When a *portion of the holochakra* projects alone, or in an isolated manner, without the psychosoma and mentalsoma (the seat of the consciousness) or, in other words, an energetic projection without the consciousness, it represents nothing more than an orbiting body, or an *accompanying body* of the psychosoma. A great percentage of the holochakra's energies never leave their insertions, which are generalized or spread throughout the structure of the soma. This only occurs upon desoma (medulla oblongata).

Consciousness. The psychosoma cannot be projected by itself without the mentalsoma and without the consciousness. These vehicles can only be projected when the consciousness goes together with them.

Discoincidence. Nevertheless, the consciousness can project a portion of the holochakra without accompanying it. The consciousness can also project in the psychosoma, leaving it projected (discoincident) as well, and then departing only by way of the mentalsoma.

Semilucidity. Lucid dreams, or semilucid projections, almost always occur when the consciousness projects in the psychosoma, using a greater portion of the semiphysical substances of the holochakra. It is still not known why this occurs.

Hypothesis. At this point, it is worthwhile posing the following question: Do the exteriorized portions of the psychosoma – called ectoplasmic arms, pseudopods, psychic rods, levers and prolongations by some – that cause the mysterious movement of physical objects in ectoplasmy experiments, sometimes stem solely from the compound elements of the holochakra, and other times also by internal, biological, cellular elements of the human body?

Ballast. The holochakra acts like ballast for the psychosoma, densifying and "materializing" the structure of this vehicle of manifestation when it projects, resulting in the so-called "laden psychosoma" which *transports* the consciousness.

Imitation. In external autoscopy, the exteriorized holochakra precisely imitates the gestures and postures that the consciousness makes in the ordinary, physical waking state. This imitation is executed unconsciously. It seems that the holochakra has some type of repetitive and conditioned *mechanical instinct*.

Division. In the same phenomenon of external autoscopy, the exteriorized holochakra can execute the actions that the consciousness in the ordinary, physical waking state *thinks* while performing other different actions. This demonstrates that individuals who are able to divide their *attention* are naturally predisposed to external autoscopy.

Cords. There are 3 categories of connection between the vehicles of manifestation of the intraphysical consciousness:

1. **Soma.** The human body (soma) has the umbilical cord between mother and fetus.
2. **Psychosoma.** The psychosoma has the silver cord with the soma.
3. **Mentalsoma.** The mentalsoma has the golden cord with the psychosoma.

Question. The observant individual can thus pose the following question: Might the holochakra have some similar connection?

Connection. The facts indicate that the holochakra, by itself, is already a connection between the human body and the psychosoma, given that the silver cord is only one of the components of the holochakra, which manifests in certain circumstances.

Regeneration. Based upon the fact of the *phantom member* issue, which is considered to be a biological and parabiological remnant of human regeneration, the most probable hypothesis for the advanced occurrence of regeneration of the adult human body can initially be based upon the following 3 elements:

1. **Will.** The powerful will of the amputee.
2. **Bioenergy.** His/her ability to exteriorize the holochakra, or bioenergy (bioenergetic field).
3. **Psychosomatics.** His/her awareness of the existence of the psychosoma.

Fields. The condensation and relative solidification of the energies of the aura or, more precisely, the holochakra, around the individual's human body, under certain conditions, forms a bioenergetic field, an extraphysical sphere of dense energy, like a shield or protection for the epidermis and the superficial fascia (formerly the *hypodermis*).

Isolating. This type of extraphysical isolation (isolating material) occurs in at least 2 parapsychic phenomena:

1. **Incombustibility.** The phenomena of incombustibility pertaining to the individual (limited field).
2. **Parasurgery.** *Pararegeneration* (enlarged bioenergetic field) in instances of *para-anesthesia*, *para-asepsis* and *parahemostasis* occurring during parasurgery performed on the bodies of the surgeon's patients, a *pararegeneration* (amplified bioenergetic field).

Effects. The holochakra (energetic parabody) operates as a sealant (desensitizer) in the phenomenon of incombustibility (not burning the feet) and as a sensitizer (desealant) in the phenomenon of the installed bioenergetic field (sensation of human heat).

Cause. What is the mechanism of these 2 antagonistic phenomena? There must be a single cause that explains the 2 effects.

Bibliography: Andreas (36, p. 53), Butler (227, p. 67), Crookall (343, p. 118), Fortune (540, p. 52), Guéret (659, p. 61), Maes (983, p. 152), Vieira (1762, p. 73).

---

114. LOOSENESS OF THE HOLOCHAKRA

Definition. Looseness of the holochakra: the condition of the relatively free operation of energetic parabody, or holochakra, in relation to the emotional body, or psychosoma, and the human body.

Synonymy: pranic projection; projection of the holochakra.

Paraphysiology. In the post-projective period, during lucid projections in series, there is frequently a benign looseness or a greater freeing of the holochakra. This phenomenon is connected to the normal paraphysiology of the vehicles of manifestation of the consciousness. In this condition, the holochakra leaves the state of coincidence of the consciential vehicles with ease.

Clothes. The holochakra – when it is looser from the soma even during the ordinary, physical waking state – seems like very loose, lightweight clothing that the projector is wearing over the human body as well as the regular clothing. The extra folds wave around him/her, as though it were gossamer, even during the ordinary, physical waking state.

Self-transfiguration. This *loose clothing* characteristic of the holochakra seems to influence the mechanism of self-transfiguration of the psychosoma.

Sensation. Any type of developed sensitive who is somewhat more self-observant can perceive and detect this condition and hypothesis of the looseness of the holochakra. The sensation is really very characteristic of *looseness* or as though something had become loose inside us and continues to accompany us, although remaining connected, floating around us.

Causes. The following are 12 factors, among others, which predispose the condition of looseness of the holochakra and can be considered its essential causes:

1. Vibrational state (VS).
2. Assistential projection.
3. Lucid projections in series.
4. Direct projection in the mentalsoma.
5. The experience of cosmoconsciousness.

  6. Awakening of the *kundalini* or the energies of the sexochakra.
  7. The condition of parapsychism due to any type of manifestation.
  8. Hydromagnetic shower.
  9. Aeromagnetic refrigeration.
  10. General surgical anesthesia.
  11. The maintenance of an aura of health in good condition.
  12. The existence of a protective shell or the personal psychosphere (individual holothosene).

Intoxication. *Vibratory intoxication* of the organism, the blocking of energies or energetic imbalance, is the condition in which the intraphysical being is not able to circulate the consciential energy within him/herself.

Detoxification. Full looseness of the holochakra is only achieved when a more complete energetic detoxification of the vehicles of manifestation of the projector's consciousness has occurred. This is why it happens more commonly after an assistential projection, such as one in which the projected projector, besides having absorbed energy in the extraphysical dimension, also donated energy for the extraphysical consciousnesses or intraphysical consciousnesses that are ill or needy (energivorous).

Coronochakra. One of the processes for maintaining prolonged paraphysiological looseness of the holochakra is to occasionally provoke, e.g.: every two hours, in certain periods, an energetic shower through the coronochakra triggered by the will, always maintaining personal psychological balance, without irritation or negative ideas.

Effects. The condition of looseness of the holochakra provokes the following 13 well-defined effects, among others:

  1. **VS.** Installation of a spontaneous vibrational state, either with or without consciential projection.

  2. **Extraphysical consciousnesses.** The perception by the projector, or by sensitives in general, through vibrations felt throughout the human body, of the presence of extraphysical consciousnesses, without seeing them directly.

  3. **Shower.** The triggering of a more ordinary energetic shower with greater frequency.

  4. **Aura.** Full installation of the conditions of the projective aura.

  5. **Projection.** Indisputable self-confirmation of the recently completed lucid projection.

  6. **Continuation-projection.** The predisposition of the lucid projector toward another projection, the continuation-projection, as well as the occurrence of lucid projections in series.

  7. **Energy.** The frustrating sensation of a useless loss of consciential energy through energetic exteriorization from the entire soma-holochakra-psychosoma set.

  8. **Announcement.** The facilitation of prior announcement of an imminent lucid projection between two consecutive lucid projections.

  9. **Self-luminosity.** Facilitation of perception of the lucid projector's self-luminosity or the lights around oneself, which can sometimes be seen by witnesses around the projector, such as the *intraphysical assistant,* and clairvoyant relatives and sensitives, in the immediate post-projective period.

  10. **Stature.** The false impression on the part of the projector, as well as the surrounding sensitives, that the projector's human body is taller in stature. The human body evidently does not become taller, but the coincident bodies are actually taller. This is because the effects of this vehicular condition, in this particular case, are extraphysical and not physical.

  11. **Neurovegetative.** A predisposition toward the appearance of agreeable goose bumps and positive neurovegetative manifestations throughout the human body.

  12. **Duration.** This condition of the looseness of the holochakra more commonly lasts only for some minutes, although it can last for hours, an entire day and, in exceptional circumstances, for days and weeks at a time. This is dependent upon the intelligent use and possible coexistence between the lucid projector and this psychophysical state.

13. **Donation.** The looseness of the holochakra allows the intraphysical consciousness to achieve the condition of a permanent universal donor of consciential energy. This is very important in penta and the works performed in the extraphysical clinic of the self-lucid consciential epicenter.

Waking. The condition of looseness of the holochakra is the most common type of phenomenon of waking discoincidence for the intraphysical consciousness and is directly related to the installation of the bioenergetic field of the human being.

Reconnection. The facts show that the condition of full looseness of the holochakra, disconnected from the human body, can stop from one moment to another, through as yet unknown processes, thereby energetically reverting to the previous condition of severe ordinary coincidence of the human body, the holochakra and the psychosoma. Evidently, this sudden reconnection of the links of the holochakra may cause many occurrences of projective recess, being one of the evident causes of this selfsame phenomenon.

Mentalsoma. Looseness of the mentalsoma of the extraphysical-sensitive-consciousness relative to the extraphysical head of its psychosoma (parahead) and the parabrain also occurs in the extraphysical dimension, as the extraphysical consciousness, in this situation, obviously has neither the holochakra nor the human body.

Interaction. The following are 3 projective occurrences which, after a certain level, are interdependent and therefore interact and amalgamate, generating a condition of highly expressive projectability and parapsychism:

1. **Projections.** A series of lucid projections or continuous consecutive self-aware projections.
2. **Looseness.** The state of healthy looseness of the holochakra.
3. **Discoincidence.** The maintenance of a healthy state of waking discoincidence of the intraphysical consciousness.

Bibliography: Crookall (338, p. 141), Ebon (453, p. 114), Maes (983, p. 141).

---

115. PARAPATHOLOGY OF THE HOLOCHAKRA

Definition. Parapathology: pathology of the vehicles of manifestation of the consciousness, excluding the human body or the soma.

Synonymy: extraphysical pathology; metapathology; parapsychopathology; transcendent parapathology; transpathology.

Characteristics. Various occurrences can be listed within the scope of parapathology of the holochakra. The following 8 are some of these variables:

1. **Looseness.** Pathological looseness of the holochakra.
2. **Projection.** Morbid disconnection or discoincidence of the intraphysical consciousness.
3. **Parapsychoses.** Post-desomatic parapsychoses of extraphysical consciousnesses.
4. **Sexochakra.** Premature awakening of the energies of the sexochakra.
5. **Repercussions.** Phenomena of parapsychophysiological repercussions of holochakral origin.
6. **Amputation.** Consequences of amputation of members of the soma.
7. **Retention.** Inability to retain consciential energy.
8. **Chakras.** Parapathology of the chakras.

Alienation. Pathological looseness of the holochakra facilitates the occurrence of the projector's alienation from the commitments of human life. It is closely related to countless syndromes and psychopathologies encountered in cases of psychiatric hospital patients.

Dissociation. Dissociation of the holochakra, which normally allows the projection of this same vehicle, can be dependent upon a mental state in which the intraphysical consciousness is not able to control his/her mental processes. Certain cases of external autoscopy should be included in these considerations, including the classic case of Emília Sagée.

Illnesses. Diverse human illnesses have their origin in energetic alterations between the psychosoma and the human body or, in other words, the holochakra, it sufficing to observe the processes of acupuncture, do-in or acupressure.

Image. Various occurrences suggest that those suffering from migraine, epilepsy, or patients suffering from disturbances in their corporeal image (distortions), e.g.: feeling that their legs are shorter or that they do not exist, or even thinking that they have an extra arm, may consist of energetic exteriorizations of the denser holochakra, with or without considerable help from the imagination and morphothosenes.

Bibliography: Fortune (540, p. 17), Guéret (659, p. 61), Powell (1278, p. 35), Rampa (1361, p. 40).

---

116. HUMAN AURA

Definition. Aura (Latin: *aura*, breeze): a field of an unknown nature, with some magnetic characteristics, having a luminous appearance to sensitives, extraphysical consciousnesses and projected intraphysical consciousnesses, on certain occasions, the colors of which are probably connected to the energy field and the activities and thoughts of those involved, such as living beings, adults, children, fetuses, animals, plants, minerals and physical objects, and even extraphysical consciousnesses (self-luminosity) (see fig. 116, p. 1,126).

Synonymy: auric egg; bio-aura; circle of radiance; electro-aura; external vestment of the psychosoma; extraphysical calling card; extraphysical medical chart; extraphysical warning system; human atmosphere; human glory; human light; human nebula; human rainbow; luminous psychosphere; magnetic aura; mental defense; mystical oval; parapsychic constellation; personal nimbus; physical aura; psychic halo; psychic photosphere; psychic radar; sphere of sensation; vital aureole.

Aspects. With regard to its characteristics, 3 aspects of the aura should be singled out:

1. **Omnipresence.** It is evident in *all* things and not only in some.
2. **Movement.** It becomes radically modified upon every movement made by the object contained within it.
3. **Envelope.** It generally appears to be an ornament or ornamental envelope in which the object or being appears to be encased, as though it were in a container.

Operation. The human aura typically has a large vibrant ovoid form, crossed by many currents of light in constantly moving rays and vortexes.

Warning. In the human being, the aura works like an extraphysical warning or defense system, or psychic radar generally not perceived by the average human being in the ordinary, physical waking state.

Image. The human aura, usually invisible – as with the scent of a flower that is identified – does not submit itself to human hypocrisy. This is because it always reflects the exact, raw image of the individual, representing his/her true calling card, or extraphysical medical chart, which is seen or read by clairvoyants, sensitives, initiates, extraphysical consciousnesses, lucid projectors and even subhuman animals, in certain cases.

Light. The nature of the aura is similar to that of a light which is simultaneously corpuscular and vibratory.

Size. The volume, size, outline and density of the aura are extremely variable.

Dimensions. The ordinary person emits an aura of approximately 4" (10 cm). The positive parapsychically-developed individual has an aura 3 or more times this size.

Film. It is presumed that the holochakra is only partially responsible for the human aura, as well as for the so-called auric film that surrounds it, because the extraphysical consciousness, after passing through second desoma, or discarding the holochakra, still presents a certain aura.

Secondary. More common secondary or effluent auras exist around a person's head and hands.

Nature. The nature of the human aura is generally characterized by the following 9 variables:

1. Coloration.
2. Density.
3. Format.
4. Invisibility.
5. Luminosity.
6. Substance.
7. Subtlety.
8. Vitality.
9. Volume.

Waves. The electromagnetic field of the aura, composed of a myriad of lines of force, emits waves.

Classification. In order to identify and classify the human auric atmosphere, it should be observed that it can present itself with at least the following 9 characteristics:

1. **Opacity.** Dull or brilliant.
2. **Extension.** Narrow or wide.
3. **Serenity.** Disturbed or calm (temperament).
4. **Health.** Unhealthy or healthy (holochakral homeostasis).
5. **Purity.** Maculated or pure.
6. **Color.** Multicolor or unicolor (sensations).
7. **Empathy.** Unfriendly or charming (empathetic).
8. **Holothosene.** Retracted or engaging (holothosenics).
9. **Presence.** *Withered* or powerful

Brilliance. Depending upon circumstances and emotions, the aura contracts or dilates, intensifies or fades in brilliance.

State. The human being's state of health and age influences the conditions of the aura, which is renewed many times in the course of an intraphysical existence (lifetime).

Categories. There are various categories of human aura, among which the following 5 can be singled out:

1. **Miniature.** The common miniature aura, belonging to the ordinary intraphysical consciousness, who only nurtures so-called tropospheric interests. This aura extends only a few inches (centimeters) from the concrete limits of the soma.

2. **Healthy.** The aura of health is an aura which is healthy, positive, strong and pleasant to behold.

3. **Confused.** The confused aura is that belonging to ill persons, especially psychopaths (madmen).

4. **Mega-aura.** The mega-aura is the aura of the *serenissimi* which reaches vast distances through the impulsion of consciential energy.

5. **Nimbus.** The aura surrounding the head, also called the *nimbus, gloria, halo, aureole* or *mystical oval,* when very dark, is generally indicative, to the clairvoyant, of the individual's imminent desoma.

Interaction. Human auras interact with each other, from a positive as well as from a negative point of view. This creates attraction, including auric couplings and repulsions between persons.

Operation. Through their auras, human beings everywhere incessantly operate as energetic or parapsychic receivers or sponges, as well as emitters or donors of consciential energy.

Theorems. We can posit 2 theorems with regard to the human aura in relation to thosenology:

1. **Volume.** The intensity of thought or sentiment determines the *volume* of the human aura (the category of the *emphasis* of the self-thosene).

2. **Coloration.** The quality of thought or the sentiment determines the *coloration* of the human aura (the category of the *emphasis* of the self-thosene).

Maintenance. There are 22 spontaneous psychophysiological resources, or extraphysical antipollutant detoxification and vibratory defense techniques, among others, that allow any type or category of projector or sensitive to maintain the cleanliness of the aura of health:

1. Absorption of environmental energies.
2. Aeromagnetic refrigeration.
3. Brief phlegm.
4. Discharging or neutralizing, as well as absorbing self-exteriorizations.
5. Energetic showers.
6. Guided meditation, prayer or oration.
7. Hydromagnetic showers.
8. Light sniffling.
9. Localized involuntary muscular contractions (myoclonuses).
10. Physical, mental and consciential hygiene.
11. Positive concentration of the auric self-image.
12. Practicing healthy, non-radical sports.
13. Shivers with energetic or extraphysical foundations beyond the sensations of the soma.
14. Special diets.
15. Stretching.
16. Swimming in the ocean.
17. The absence of antiphysiological addictions (self-weak traits).
18. Unexpected bilateral tearing of the eyes.
19. Varied individual signals of parapsychism (signage).
20. Vibrational state (VS).
21. Walks in forests and gardens.
22. Yawns with parapsychic foundations.

VS. Without a doubt, the most efficacious of all the 22 above-mentioned resources is the voluntary installation of the vibrational state.

Kirlian photographs. Many studious individuals attempt to play down the reality of the human aura, which seems to arise in the controversial *Kirlian photographs,* through various suppositions, such as: chemical effects; control of information; corona effect; effects of electrical conductivity; electronic aura; faulty technology; heat effects; models of energetic fields; odor molecules; odoriferous covering; odoriferous envelope; photographic defects; scent molecules; and others. Independent of this, however, the human aura seems to remain ostensive and evident, in the same manner, for those who have *eyes to perceive it,* namely clairvoyant sensitives.

Objects. At least the following 7 objects present larger auras than other objects, and are easily identified by the projected projector's consciousness:

1. **Art.** Spectacular works of art (Florence, Italy).
2. **Worship.** Certain personal objects or those pertaining to worship, idolatry or adoration.
3. **Images.** Images of temples in general.
4. **Tombstones.** Tombstones in cemeteries (tombs, mausoleums).
5. **Books.** Mystical books or those relating to catechesis.
6. **Monuments.** Noteworthy statues and monuments in general.
7. **Personal.** Objects of long-standing use or those of personal use (prized).

Psychosoma. The psychosoma, when leaving the state of coincidence of the vehicles of manifestation of the consciousness, is sometimes mistakenly perceived by clairvoyants as the human aura.

Note. The *human* energetic aura is the vibratory magnetic field most intimately connected to the human body. It should thus not be confused with the following 5 basic categories of other distinct auras:

1. **Projective.** The specifically *projective* aura.

2. **Extraphysical.** The *extraphysical* aura or the condition of extraphysical self-luminosity.

3. **Pathologies.** The *epileptic* aura, pertaining to the convulsive syndrome, a signal that proceeds an epileptic crisis, as well as *neuropathic halos.* Both are strictly pathological conditions.

4. **Psychophysiological.** Psychophysiological auras, such as: the *sensitive* aura, the *motor* aura and the *psychic* aura, denoting anguish, fear, terror and hallucination.

5. **Electronic.** The *electronic aura,* corresponding to the corona effects in electronics.

Psychosphere. The *psychosphere,* as it is referred to in this book, of the intraphysical or extraphysical consciousness, is the assemblage of energetic manifestations of the consciousness within the personal holothosene, which envelops the entire holochakra, the aura and the other manifestations of its intentionality in any consciential dimension. The psychosphere always encompasses, for example, the consciential energy (the *e* of thosene) of the consciousness' *holothosene* and even its personal *materthosene,* the nucleus of its holothosene.

Bibliography: Andreas (36, p. 84), Bennett (117, p. 83), Black (137, p. 151), Blasco (151, p. 253), Boswell (174, p. 55), Cardillo (242, p. 58), Carrington (245, p. 53), Cavendish (266, p. 48), Coquet (301, p. 233), Crouzet (344, p. 234), D'arbó (365, p. 174), Depascale (392, p. 13), Drury (414, p. 60), Edmunds (461, p. 94), Fodor (528, p. 17), Greenhouse (636, p. 69), Hapgood (678, p. 321), Hodson (729, p. 114), Kilner (843, p. 1), Krippner (864, p. 171), Leadbeater (900, p. 129), Meek (1028, p. 250), Montandon (1071, p. 47), Moss (1096, p. 159), Powell (1278, p. 7), Prieur (1289, p. 35), Rampa (1361, p. 32), Regush (1382, p. 122; 1383, p. 93), Steiger (1601, p. 144), Toben (1688, p. 77), Vieira (1762, p. 65), Walker (1781, p. 15), Wilson (1858, p. 123).

---

117. SILVER CORD

Definition. Silver cord: the semimaterial attachment that keeps the psychosoma linked to the human body with an initial connection in the psychosoma and another in the soma.

Synonymy: binding of the psychosoma; aeriform tie; *aka* cord (Huna); anchor of the psychosoma; animic thread; aromatic cord; astral cable; astral cord; astral thread; band of phosphorescent light; brilliant ribbon; cable of light; cable of the physical diving suit; conduit of life; cord of connection; cord of energy; cord of ethereal matter; cord of flames; cord of life; cord of light; cord of od; diaphanous cord; elastic cord; elastic force; electric connection; energetic communication; etheric cord; etheric line; etheric thread; etheric umbilical cord; extra member of the human body; extraphysical magnet; extraphysical multiplex conduit; filament of a spider's web; fine and luminous cord; fine and silky cord; fine cord (Kol); fine cord of light; flexible rod; fluidic cord; fluidic line; fluidic tie; fluidic umbilical cord; foreign appendix; fragile luminous thread; hidden chain; human body-psychosoma intercorporeal connection; intangible cable; intangible cord; intermediary connective tie; irradiant energy current; lifeline; line of light; line of vital force; linking cord; living cord; long neck; luminous filament; luminous hose; luminous spider's web; luminous thread; magnetic cord; nebulous cord; pajama cord; perispiritual cord; phosphorescent tail; prison guard; psychic cord; ray of light; ray of moonlight; ribbon of light; scintillating cord; scintillating thread of light; security cord; semimaterial tie; semiphysical connection; shadowy line; shadowy ray; shaft of light; shaft of moonlight; silky thread; silvery appendix; silvery connection; silvery cord; silvery light; small junction of a spider's web; smoky cable; spider's silk; spiritual link; string of silver; strip of light; *sutratma;* temporary extension; thin ribbon; thin thread of silver; thread of a spider's web; thread of the consciousness; trail of silvery light; tube of energy; vaporous cord; variation on the umbilical cord; vital current; vital intermediary; vital magnetic cord; vital tie; weak silvery light; whitened cord.

Parabiophysical. Much like the pineal gland and ectoplasm, the silver cord is a parabiophysical element or, in other words: although it is somehow rooted within the physical cells, its energetic manifestations transcend the limits of dense matter, or the areas pertaining to *physical* biology, crossing into parabiology.

Ecclesiastes. Chapter 12, Verse 6 of the book of Ecclesiastes, the Preacher, in the Bible (Old Testament), is recalled by scholars of the silver cord: "Remember Him before the silver cord is broken and the golden bowl is crushed...," in order to confirm the existence of this energetic appendix. Some researchers, however, contend that the cord refers to the spinal cord, or the spinal medulla, and not the connection between the physical body and the extraphysical body.

Bibliography: Andrade (27, p. 148), Andreas (36, p. 38), Ashish (60, p. 245), Bardon (80, p. 318), Baumann (93, p. 43), Benavides (109, p. 238), Black (137, p. 148), Blackmore (139, p. 3), Blunsdon (157, p. 50), Boddington (158, p. 8), Bord (170, p. 10), Boswell (174, p. 129), Bozzano (193, p. 116), Bulford (220, p. 24), Butler (227, p. 73), Carrington (245, p. 277), Christie-Murray (282, p. 620), Crookall (320, p. 118; 332, p. 31; 333, p. 163), David-Neel (368, p. 46), Delanne (381, p. 147), Denis (389, p. 163), Denning (391, p. 42), Ebon (453, p. 116), Eclesiastes, 12:6, Edmonds (460, p. 30), Eliade (476, p. 183), Erny (483, p. 85), Farrar (496, p. 197), Frost (560, p. 57), Gauld (576, p. 221), Gerhardi (584, p. 40), Gibier (587, p. 114), Giovetti (593, p. 71), Goldberg (606, p. 172), Greene (635, p. 60), Greenhouse (636, p. 46), Guirao (663, p. 42), Hampton (676, p. 45), Heindel (705, p. 36), Holroyd (736, p. 115), Holzer (745, p. 164), Kardec (825, p. 361), Laubscher (890, p. 33), Lenz (914, p. 61), MacLaine (980, p. 285), Maes (983, p. 130), Martin (1002, p. 24), Meek (1030, p. 29), Mittl (1061, p. 6), Monroe (1065, p. 175), Montandon (1070, p. 224), Muldoon (1105, p. 77), Mutañola (1108, p. 99), Norvell (1139, p. 153), Parrish-Harra (1202, p. 75), Pastorino (1206, p. 180), Perkins (1236, p. 100), Prado (1284, p. 25), Prieur (1289, p. 109), Ramacháraca (1348, p. 44), Rampa (1361, p. 35), Ranieri (1373, p. 11), Richards (1393, p. 62), Riland (1403, p. 59), Ring (1406, p. 231), Rogo (1444, p. 60), RPA (1481, p. 33), Sabom (1486, p. 75), Sculthorp (1531, p. 27), Shay (1546, p. 17), Sherman (1551, p. 194), Shirley (1553, p. 46), Smith (1573, p. 66), Smith (1577, p. 151), Vieira (1762, p. 84), Vishnudevananda (1776, p. 301), Walker (1781, p. 56), Watson (1800, p. 137), Wolman (1863, p. 608), Yram (1897, p. 75), Zingaropoli (1901, p. 33).

118. PARA-ANATOMY OF THE SILVER CORD

Pivotal. The silver cord is the pivotal factor of the phenomenon of projection of the intraphysical consciousness in the psychosoma, besides being the *pivotal factor* of biological *death* or that of the human body (desoma).

Characteristics. Among the characteristics of the para-anatomy of the silver cord, at least the following 10 can be singled out:

1. **Minicords.** The branches or the various minicords or fine, elastic scintillating cords close to the human body.
2. **Root.** The main root when the silver cord becomes distant from the human body.
3. **Heat.** The heat and bareness of naked human tissue.
4. **Thickness.** Thickness, varying diameters and ducts.
5. **Weight.** Weight, volume, density, format and extendibility.
6. **Sensitivity.** Sensitivity to touch and heat.
7. **Brilliance.** Brilliance, luminosity, silvery coloration and phosphorescence.
8. **Pulsation.** Pulsation.
9. **Texture.** Texture.
10. **Action.** A more extensive or vigorous sphere of action or perimeter.

Sensations. Few consciential projectors see and examine the silver cord clearly or self-convincingly. However, a great number of them, almost the majority of veteran experimenters, *sense* its presence, action and force.

Error. Due to inexperience, some projectors erroneously attribute these sensations to other unknown causes and factors, including nonexistent intrusion or unknown forces.

Nonexistence. Other projectors affirm the nonexistence of the silver cord because they have never seen it.

Observations. The characteristics of the silver cord can be identified through 3 distinct observations:

1. **Difficult.** In the first observation, which is difficult, the projector is able to examine its own silver cord.

2. **Rare.** In the second observation, which is rare, the projector detects the silver cord of another projected intraphysical consciousness.

3. **Extremely rare.** In the third observation, which is extremely rare, the fortunate projector simultaneously observes the silver cords of more than one projected intraphysical consciousness.

Irrelevance. The act of seeing the silver cord is neither a vital issue nor is it one of greater relevance.

Development. The novice projector should not be concerned if he/she has never seen the silver cord, as this does not represent any obstacle to the full development of lucid projections.

Presence. The projected intraphysical consciousness can sense the active presence of the silver cord without seeing it.

Near-death. It is worth highlighting that, in many near-death experiences (NDE), the intraphysical consciousness projected in a forced manner spontaneously witnesses, for example, the surgeon, surgical assistants, the anesthetist and the nurses moving from side to side, busy in the surgery room, in order to save the projector's human body which is ill or has suffered an accident. On this occasion, the consciousness, when inexperienced regarding the subject, becomes afraid that any one of these persons might sever the silver cord, which is visible or extremely ostensive *only to the projector,* being connected between the consciousness and the inactive soma on the operating table.

Single. The intraphysical consciousness has only a single silver cord, although it is made up of countless connections that come together forming a main connection. It is sometimes seen as 2, 3 or more cords. Furthermore, all this exists beyond the psychosoma, mentalsoma, its intriguing connection with the psychosoma (golden cord) and the global action of the holochakra.

Gathering. Besides, that which is called the *silver cord* can actually be interpreted as a gathering of *regional silver cords,* or minicords of specific areas, whether of the head (parahead); an arm (para-arm); a leg (paraleg); a foot (parafoot); a finger (parafinger); and others.

Denomination. There are those who refer to this selfsame silver cord as a *copper cord* when it is *more dense,* vigorous, within the extraphysical sphere of energy, and in partial projections related to the vegetative area of the human body.

Tension. The tension and diameter of the intercorporal connection are greater at a shorter distance from the human body.

Diameter. Within a distance of 2" to 6" (5 to 15 cm), the silver cord has a diameter of 2" (5 cm). At a greater distance, more than 33' (10 meters), for example, it is as thin as a (sewing) thread.

Change. In a lucid projection, one never knows when the silver cord will completely disappear, with only the *golden cord* remaining or, in other words, when a consciential projection in the psychosoma will end and a consciential projection in the isolated mentalsoma will begin.

Immateriality. One inference, however, seems to be evident regarding the silver cord, that the connections can be listed in an ascending scale of dematerialization (or immateriality), according to its popular names, in the following manner:

1. **Copper.** First, the copper cord.
2. **Silver.** Second, the silver cord.
3. **Gold.** Third, the golden cord.

Color. The coloration of the silver cord varies from person to person, although the brilliant and phosphorescent white color predominates, hence its popular name.

Differences. The silver cord, like the human body, has its peculiar differences from person to person, being stronger or weaker according to the physical age and extraphysical development of the intraphysical consciousness.

Base. Based upon the supposition, as evidenced by the facts, that the psychosoma is a semimaterial body and that the silver cord, a substance (reality) that is unknown to us, is still more material than the psychosoma and that sometimes, when exteriorized close to the human body, weighs more than the psychosoma. It can thus be logically concluded that the base of the silver cord in the human body is intracellular.

Structures. Although having a main encephalic base (pineal gland and medulla oblongata), the silver cord branches out and comes from all intracellular structures of the organism, from head to feet.

Branches. If the silver cord has an intracellular origin, its branches – analogous to the system of veins of the human body – have a purely physical origin, perhaps stemming from organizing force fields, in order to keep it from going in all directions, the irradiating center of which is found in the encephalic region.

Connection. It is important to emphasize that the silver cord is a connection of the holochakra and *is not the entire elongated holochakra*. The holochakra is a much more complex element than the silver cord, despite all the intriguing possibilities of the manifestation of this appendix.

Materiality. The space factor seems to act intensely upon the branches of the silver cord, which has great force when physically close to the human body and gradually loses force when more distant from it. This surely speaks in favor of the pattern of the materiality of the structure, nature or, in fact, the anatomy of the silver cord.

Classification. The silver cord can be classified according to its connections in the human body: the encephalic, umbilical, digital, manual, podal or dorsal silver cord.

Binding. The *binding* silver cord is that which retains the psychosoma in the physical base, in the bedroom.

Connections. It is put forward, as a hypothesis, that the connection of the silver cord in the human body is established by the medulla oblongata and the brain. It may maintain a relationship with the pineal gland and a series of intracellular branches throughout the organism and seems not to terminate in the individual's skin, but gives the impression of entering the human body, establishing deep connections there with the vital centers of all the organs.

Extremities. Two categories of extremities should be considered in the connections of the silver cord:

1. **Greater.** The greater extremity, called the *conical root,* which is the more potent end, has a varied point of insertion that is ordinarily located in the region of the head, exiting from the frontal or nuchal region. Its physical base is located inside the head and may be the medulla oblongata or the epiphysis. This connection only disappears upon first desoma.

2. **Lesser.** The lesser extremity, the fine, more rarefied root, has its point of insertion and base in the psychosoma. This connection only disappears upon second desoma.

Density. In certain extraphysical situations, the silver cord seems to be denser and heavier than the psychosoma or, in other words, hypothetically weighs more than 3.5 oz. (100 g), if we consider the psychosoma to have a total weight of 2.5 oz (70 g).

Nature. The silver cord participates in the material nature of the human body as well as the extraphysical nature of the psychosoma. It is therefore a composite of components of the structures of the human body and the psychosoma, being a hybrid element or an energetic intermediary. Its structure is composed of a conglomerate of luminous energy corpuscles with a nature that is closer to the psychosoma than to dense matter. It is therefore, in this analogy, a substance that is similar to or more subtle than ectoplasm, which is denser or more biological.

Analogies. Contemporary lucid projectors have compared the silver cord with: a cord, thread, band, light, neon, strip, elastic tube, staircase, current, snake, ray of light, and even with the umbilical cord.

Bibliography: Bardon (80, p. 318), Baumann (93, p. 47), Bord (170, p. 10), Crookall (325, p. 87; 343, p. 83), Greene (635, p. 60), Greenhouse (636, p. 33), Rampa (1367, p. 24), Vieira (1762, p. 53).

119. PARAPHYSIOLOGY OF THE SILVER CORD

Characteristics. Among the characteristics of the paraphysiology of the silver cord, at least the following 17 variables deserve singling out:

1. **Connection.** Soma-psychosoma link or connection.
2. **Free will.** Agent of extraphysical free will (freedom).
3. **Retention.** Retaining and freeing of the psychosoma.
4. **Vitality.** Vitality, sensitivity and flexibility.
5. **Retractability.** Undefined retractability and extendibility, along the entire cord.
6. **Tenuity.** Density, tenuity, invisibility and visibility.
7. **Projection.** Active in the occurrence of the phenomena of lucid projection.
8. **Automatism.** Unconscious automatism (mechanicalness).
9. **Impulses.** Bi-directional vital impulses.
10. **Point.** Critical point in the potency of retention of the psychosoma.
11. **Exteriorization.** Active in the mechanisms of exteriorization of consciential energies.
12. **Volitation.** Access to unimpeded volitation (extraphysicology).
13. **Chakras.** Relationship with the chakras.
14. **Desomatics.** Active in the transition of biological death or desoma.
15. **Holochakrology.** Relationship with the entire holochakra.
16. **Reins.** Operates as the reins of the intraphysical being or intraphysical consciousness.
17. **Clairvoyance.** Relationship with traveling clairvoyance.

Functions. The following are 5 other functions of the silver cord that are less evident or even more subtle:

1. **Forms.** Responsible for the differences in form (appearance, physiognomy) between the extraphysical consciousness and the intraphysical consciousness or the projected intraphysical projector.
2. **Repercussions.** Execution of physical and extraphysical repercussions.
3. **Density.** Regulation of the psychosoma's density through gradation of the ballast of semimaterial energetic substance through the holochakra, sometimes dispensing with interiorization, whether in the physical base or at a certain distance.
4. **Potentiation.** Responsible for the variation of the amount of energy and its consequences.
5. **Disappearances.** Sponsoring of sudden disappearances in instances of extraphysical defense.

Duration. The integral silver cord only exists from the moment of physical, biological conception until the final projection or first desoma, when the human body is deactivated.

Remnants. Remnants of the silver cord remain connected to the psychosoma, in the holochakra, and disappear with the second desoma or, in other words, upon deactivation of the holochakra.

Umbilicochakra. Many projectors, especially novices or those still lacking extraphysical agility, imagine that the psychosoma only leaves the human body through the solar plexus or, in other words, from the area of the umbilicochakra. The facts seem to demonstrate, however, that this observation is only partially correct.

Exit. The silver cord exits the human body through the solar plexus, but it also, and mainly, leaves simultaneously through the essential connection, the cranium (the seat of the brain) and the extraphysical head (parahead) of the psychosoma, which is the seat of the mentalsoma or, more precisely, the seat of the consciousness or ego.

Anatomy. Visualization of the exit of the silver cord from the area of the solar plexus is facilitated by the anatomy and even by the para-anatomy of the vehicles of manifestation of the intraphysical consciousness.

Eyes. The physical eyes easily see the navel, as it is more distant. This obviously cannot occur with regard to the area of the cerebral cortex.

Difficulty. In light of this, it is very difficult for the intraphysical consciousness to attempt to see the silver cord leaving the human body and to perceive the occurrences of the trance simultaneously, or in a single experience.

Sinciput. To begin with, due to the intraphysical projector's psychological conditioning through physical vision, it becomes impossible to see the center of the cranium or sinciput (top of the head).

Takeoff. This act can be realized – despite being difficult to achieve, even for the projector's extraphysical vision – during the lucid takeoff of his/her own psychosoma, when it is transporting the consciousness.

Abdominal. The partial exit of the psychosoma leaving the abdominal area (animal-human) is easily seen extraphysically by the consciousness which is still stuck in the physical head. This is why many novice projectors witness the occurrence.

Cranium. However, the same does not occur with regard to departure from the head of the psychosoma through the cranium, or the head of the human body, the *only* exit from which the consciousness leaves the cellular organism and one that very few veteran projectors perceive in an unquestionable manner.

Retraction. The silver cord spends most of its useful life retracted or hidden within the cells, without showing itself.

Shackle. The silver cord is the hidden shackle of the intraphysical consciousness, who is always a prisoner of intraphysical restriction.

Examination. The technique for examining the silver cord involves the act of slowly returning to the human body. This is an occasion in which the increase in thickness of this energetic connection, or its links, fine threads and the other details of its reality can be observed.

Conception. The biological conception of the human body triggers the creation of the silver cord which, in theory, is inexistent in the psychosoma of the extraphysical consciousness that undergoes resoma, except in resomas or existential programs of a less evolved nature (existential miniprogram). In this case, the basic connection of the silver cord in the psychosoma plays a primordial role in the paraphysiology of this appendix.

Absorption. The sometimes lightning-fast absorption of the silver cord by the human body provokes the condition of *admonitory discomfort*.

Recapturing. The recapturing of the silver cord by the human body is performed by the entire human body, but mainly by the projector's physical head. Recapturing signifies interiorization of the silver cord and psychosoma.

Holochakra. The basic holochakra can remain in the human body without the intervention of the projected silver cord.

Sensations. The physical sensations of the dense human body suffocate the sensations caused by the silver cord.

Action. The closer the silver cord is to the human body, the more vigorous its action. The more distant it is, the weaker its action becomes.

Conduction. Among the functions of the silver cord, the bi-directional conduction of energies between the psychosoma and the human body should be singled out. This allows the partial or total departure and interiorization of the psychosoma.

Isolated. The silver cord also departs from the harmony of the holosoma unaccompanied or alone or, in other words, without the psychosoma or the consciousness. This explains why the phenomenon of the exteriorization of the holochakra is always partial.

Properties. The silver cord has an infinite capacity for extension. It maintains an average range of a greater power of action of approximately 13' (4 m) from the human body, starting from the center of the cranium or, more precisely, the center of the physical brain.

Pivotal. With regard to desomatics, the silver cord is often confused with a tunnel or a passage when it departs and returns to the human body. It is the pivotal factor in brain death, as the first desoma or deactivation of the dense organism only occurs upon the rupture of the silver cord.

Appendix. The silver cord, as an appendix of the human body, controls the vital vegetative processes of the inactive physical body – whether respiratory, circulatory, or others – during lucid projection.

Permanence. Nevertheless, the silver cord, operating as an energetic intercorporal connection with the psychosoma, remains with the psychosoma even after the first death or deactivation of the human body, until the occurrence of second desoma, which is the definitive deactivation of the holochakra (its last connections).

Potency. *Projective potency* (projective range) is the capacity of extension of the projector's silver cord.

Chamber. Some projectors only project close to the human body in the bedroom (their chamber), without ever projecting thousands of miles (kilometers) away. Is this only due to their *extraphysical inhibition* or to an insufficient projective potency? Each case needs to be analyzed individually.

Test. The following is currently the most logical *test of the remainder of one's life:* if the lucid projector wishes to rationally know if he/she will still live a long time in the human body or, in other words, wishes to ascertain the approximate duration of his/her survival, or the time remaining until undergoing desoma at the correct moment, it is sufficient to project and examine the silver cord while in the extraphysical sphere of energy, close to the human body.

Paranape. If the experimenter notes that the silver cord is vigorous, strong, dense, firm and full of energy at the *paranape* of the psychosoma, he/she can safely conclude that he/she has every possibility of continuing to live in the intraphysical dimension for quite some time.

Debilitation. The abovementioned technique is logically based on the silver cord's tendency to appear weak, debilitated and less potent in its actions, according to the reduction in the intraphysical consciousness' vitality, the closer he/she gets to the first desoma or biological death.

Instruments. Consciential energies are inexhaustible, although the same is not true for intraphysical instruments that are obsolete.

Torpidity. Physical torpidity is the first sign of freedom from the connections of the silver cord, a common occurrence prior to takeoff of the psychosoma. Without physical torpidity, an *entire* exteriorization of the cord does not occur, only a partial one, evidently maintaining the physical connection in both cases.

Respiration. It is the silver cord that provides the sensation of a loss of respiration upon takeoff and the resumption of respiration upon interiorization of the psychosoma. In certain circumstances, it is involved in the acquisition of clarity of extraphysical illumination, or the projected projector's paravision.

Occurrences. With regard to the connections of the silver cord with the human body, the following 3 occurrences merit particular attention:

1. **Growth.** As a semimaterial connection, the silver cord grows along with the human body, the child having a *smaller* cord than the adult.

2. **Aging.** The silver cord also *ages,* accompanying the natural senescence of the organism, by losing a portion of energy or its ability to act, as it follows the gradual weakening or the *loss* of a certain percentage of the soma's physical cells.

3. **Spreading.** This last fact speaks in favor of the theory that the silver cord spreads (distributes) itself throughout the human body when in the coincident state, connecting every physical cell to its corresponding extraphysical cell.

Psychosoma. The process of exteriorization of the silver cord, under certain conditions, seems to be closely connected to *physical* imbalance, vibrations, turbulence and generally lateral oscillations. These states affect the psychosoma soon after takeoff, when it remains floating over the human body lying on the bed. This is similar to alternating electrical current, which alternately flows in reverse directions.

Semiprojection. This occurs because the silver cord remains only semiprojected, having a greater circulation of unstable and zigzagging energy that alternates between the human body and the psychosoma in a lightning-fast manner.

Conductivity. The conductivity characteristic of the silver cord, transporting energy from the human body to the psychosoma during lucid projection, is more intense in the vicinity of the dense body than at a distance of hundreds of miles (kilometers) from same.

Types. Based on the above, it can be concluded that there are at least 2 very distinct types of conductivity of the silver cord:

1. **Proximity.** The first type, *less extraphysical,* in the proximity of the human body, wherein the silver cord is thicker.

2. **Distance.** The second type, *less physical*, at a distance from the human body, within the range of the psychosoma's maintenance by the silver cord, beyond the 13' (4 m) radius, far from the material body, wherein the silver cord is rarified and practically invisible.

Pulsations. On certain occasions, the evident vital pulsations of the energetic current of the silver cord can be observed. Upon each pulsation in the physical-extraphysical direction, for example, the psychosoma becomes more vital and dense while the human body *apparently* becomes *more and more lifeless*.

Double. The pulsations of vitality become easier for the projected projector to detect during lucid projections with the denser compound double, wherein they are more evident.

Crossings. The silver cord plays a decisive role every time the intraphysical consciousness, projected in the psychosoma, crosses from one extraphysical dimension to another more or less evolved extraphysical dimension.

Case study. On one occasion, the author experienced passing through 5 consecutive dimensions in a two-hour period, through 5 consecutive projections with continuous self-awareness.

Return. In the first two crossings, the author returned to the human body. In the others, it was not necessary to return, although the *admonitory warning* of the silver cord occurred.

Corrections. In the first crossing, it was possible to remain somewhat lucid inside the human body, only to correct the mouth that was open, by placing a pillow supporting the mandible (lower jaw, chin).

Close. In the second crossing, it was possible to come close to the physical form without interiorizing.

Lucidity. In each crossing from one dimension to another, the psychosoma gradually became perceptibly more rarified and subtle. This was accompanied by amplified lucidity of the consciousness, which increased more and more each time, without blackouts, and even with an intensification of tachypsychism or the quick elaboration of thoughts, deductions, extraphysical-physical comparisons and critical judgment. It was clearly perceived that one vehicle of manifestation, the psychosoma, was being used the entire time.

Message. In certain cases of parapsychic transmission, it seems that the communicant consciousness takes direct and temporary possession of the projected intraphysical sensitive's silver cord, transmitting its message through the silver cord. This is still an obscure point of parapsychism that the author leaves here, as a relevant work hypothesis.

Automatism. Certain processes of traction and distension of the silver cord seem to be automatic and, when triggered suddenly, proceed irreversibly to the end. This is why one may think that there must be an automatism of subconscious origin in its operations, in some cases. The same occurs with the holochakra. Actually, the holochakra and the silver cord, in certain manifestations, seem to be one and the same thing.

Root. The silver cord sometimes seems to be or operate like the seed or root of the psychosoma, a fact which is better perceived in partial separations, when the silver cord first leaves the human body as though it were the initiator of the process.

Interaction. In some cases, when close to several living human bodies and within the 13' (4 m) radius around the physical heads, the silver cords, when denser and more potent, interact between the consciousnesses that are projected simultaneously, either with or without lucidity.

Contiguity. This causes disagreeable effects or impressions of contiguity through the exteriorization of sensitivity, unexpected and undesirable repercussions, through joint *contacts* and movements.

Couples. This contiguity effect is the reason why, when producing concomitant lucid projections with several persons, or involving various psychosomas, in the same physical base, it is best to do so keeping a distance greater than 26' 3" (8 m) between the human bodies, which is not practical. This gives rise to the "repercussions of couples".

Twists. In takeoffs performed by *rolling the psychosoma,* rapid and violent twists of the silver cord around the psychosoma occur naturally. Sometimes, 3 or more successive turns can occur without any consequence for this appendix. The same happens in major *spiral takeoffs* of the psychosoma.

Curiosities. The projected projector can disguise the ostensive presence of the silver cord in certain extraphysical districts and also suffer the influence of terrestrial gravity.

Paranavel. Furthermore, the silver cord does not manifest any umbilical appearance in the area of the psychosoma's navel (paranavel).

Hypotheses. The following are 3 hypotheses to be researched within this context:

1. **Autoscopy.** What is the relationship between the silver cord and autoscopy?

2. *Ideoduct.* Would it be possible to build a mental, artificial, electro-electronic silver cord or *ideoduct,* a hybrid interworld apparatus for the transmission of mental waves from one consciential dimension to another?

3. *Coronatron.* Would it be possible to build a *coronatron,* another hybrid apparatus closely connected to the intraphysical consciousness' coronochakra, with the objective of intensifying his/her acquisition and exteriorization of energy?

Bibliography: Baumann (93, p. 43), Crookall (325, p. 90), Rampa (1361, p. 140), Vieira (1762, p. 147).

---

120. SPHERES OF ACTION OF THE SILVER CORD

Action. The silver cord exercises its activities in 3 well-defined fields of action:

1. **Inside.** The silver cord has a minimal active capacity in the biological realm when multi-fractionated and passive within the human body.

2. **Outside.** The silver cord exercises greatest and almost full control over the subconscious will and the psychosoma when it leaves the human body, within a 13' (4 m) radius, or inside the extraphysical sphere of energy (personal psychosphere).

3. **Distant.** As though it were a fine luminous thread, the silver cord keeps the psychosoma projected in the extraphysical dimension (or energetic dimension) when it acts at a distance from the human body beyond the abovementioned 13' (4 m) radius relative to the brain (encephalic).

Intruder. The silver cord has been the "terrible intruder" of many individuals who are fearful and ignorant of extraphysical reality.

Ignorance. Due to their ignorance of the existence and operation of the silver cord, many individuals have suffered extreme terror upon thinking they had been overtaken by an all-powerful intruder that had *grabbed them from behind* when projecting from the human body.

Retention. This happens because they are unaware of the retentive force of the silver cord which keeps them close to the soma (intraphysical anchoring) (see fig. 120, p. 1,127).

Fear. It is necessary to combat infantile fear and perform a detailed analysis of the silver cord. In the majority of the above-cited cases, there is obviously no intruder at all.

Admonitory. The brief and characteristic *discomfort* provoked by the insistent *call* from the silver cord for the intraphysical consciousness projected in the psychosoma to return to the human body is classified as *admonitory*. In this case, the admonitory discomfort is taken for the *intruder* of many intraphysical consciousnesses who find themselves extraphysically impeded from leaving their own bedroom (chamber).

Vacuum. The silver cord's retractive power over the intraphysical consciousness projected from the human body in the psychosoma is so potent, in certain cases, that the projector has the sensation of being vigorously sucked as though there were a permanent *vacuum* around the bed where his/her inactive dense body rests.

Bibliography: Rogo (1444, p. 85), Vieira (1762, p. 176).

121.   REDUCTION   OF   THE   SILVER   CORD

Material. The physical percentage of the semimaterial nature of the silver cord cannot be ignored, as one of its basic connections is implanted precisely in the human, cellular, physical body or soma.

Retractability. This is why it is important to analyze – in its paraphysiology, as well as in its attribute of retractability – the phenomenon of the reduction of the silver cord.

Occurrences. In the act of reducing the volume of the silver cord, 2 very clear phenomena occur:

1. **Reduction.** A reduction in width, diameter, activity, materiality and potency.
2. **Increase.** An increase in length, extendibility, passivity and dematerializability.

Dichotomy. The intraphysical consciousness only perceives the phenomenon of *energetic dichotomy* of the silver cord – simultaneous reduction and increase – when it is defined that one portion remains in the human body and the other goes with the projected psychosoma, after a great deal of accurate self-observation.

Time. The phenomenon of the silver cord's reduction in volume can occur in 3 ways with regard to *time:*

1. **Instantaneous.** Rapidly or instantaneously.
2. **Slow.** Slowly.
3. **Gradual.** Gradually or in stages.

Projection. Any of these 3 modes, with regard to time, occur in two ways in relation to consciential projection:

1. **Soon.** Immediately upon takeoff, which is most frequent.
2. **Subsequent.** Later, during the period in which the intraphysical consciousness is projected.

Effects. During the reduction of the volume of the silver cord, 6 basic characteristics of projection are defined:

1. **Density.** The degree of density of the projected psychosoma.
2. **Direction.** The possibility of the psychosoma projecting with or without the holochakra, depending upon whether, at the moment prior to the reduction, the energies of the silver cord have flowed in the direction of the psychosoma or not.

3. **Freeing.** The possibility of the intraphysical consciousness producing a projection distant from the human body, freeing it from the area of intense activity inside the extraphysical sphere of consciential energy.

4. **Duration.** The possibility of a more prolonged consciential projection occurring, which lasts for many minutes or hours and not only for brief seconds.

5. **Self-lucidity.** The level of magnitude of the projected intraphysical consciousness' extraphysical self-lucidity.

6. **Memory.** The possibility (personal universe or holothosene) of the projected intraphysical consciousness' mnemonic resources (mnemosomatics).

Bibliography: Vieira (1762, p. 137).

122. PARAPATHOLOGY OF THE SILVER CORD

Characteristics. Among the characteristics that comprise the parapathology of the silver cord, at least the following 3 categories of consequences can be singled out:

1. **Takeoff.** Consequences of imperfect takeoff.
2. **Interiorization.** Consequences of imperfect interiorization.
3. **Repercussions.** Consequences of physical and extraphysical repercussions.

Psychopathies. There is still no indication of proof, but it is logically and rationally suspected that alterations in the silver cord have a substantial influence upon the disturbances or syndromes that affect intraphysical personalities, especially with respect to psychopathies or advanced mental illnesses.

Accident. The accidental rupture of the silver cord can occur in certain mortal circumstances, such as the dislocation of air pressure due to the nearby explosion of a powerful bomb, provoking fear, shock *(shock wave)* and vibration, and thus expelling the intraphysical consciousness from the soma in a violent projection in the psychosoma or, in other words, a traumatic and sudden discoincidence *(pathological extraphysical escape)*.

Marionettes. In certain cases of parapathology, the silver cord of the ill intraphysical consciousness operates as if it were a set of marionette strings for the extraphysical intruders.

Rupture. The intentional rupturing of the silver cord by the intraphysical consciousness *(extraphysical suicide)* and the intentional rupture provoked by another *(extraphysical homicide)* are two occurrences that are theoretically possible but impracticable, in light of the retractile power of these appendices and their *retraction-fractionation-distribution trinomial* which is realized throughout the human body within tenths of a second.

Desoma. The process of first desoma, deactivation of the human body, seems not to have its beginning in the cells of the soma, but in the structure of the silver cord.

Decomposition. The rupture of the silver cord generally triggers decomposition of the human body. However, the facts indicate that the rupture of the silver cord can occur without decomposition of the soma being initiated.

Ignorance. The mechanisms of these occurrences are thus far entirely unknown or undiscovered, requiring more ample self-investigation and research.

Unprotectedness. There is, in fact, no such thing as an unprotected projector.

Assistance. In theory, all intraphysical beings have intangible support and constant extraphysical assistential protection (helpers, evolutiologists) available to them in order to project with or without lucidity.

Security. This assistential resource, in and of itself, constitutes a security mechanism that is quite superior to the paraphysiology of the silver cord.

Report. There is no recorded report, throughout human history or in projectiological literature, of an occurrence of the rupture of the silver cord during a lucid projection.

Indestructibility. The silver cord seems to be indestructible up until the moment of correct (personal success) or incorrect (personal error) desoma.

Unawareness. Nevertheless, this certainly and rationally could occur without the intraphysical consciousness being aware of the fact. The parapathology of the silver cord will, in the future, clarify this subject.

Bibliography: Baumann (93, p. 45), Crookall (333, p. 64), Rampa (1361, p. 115).

123. ECTOPLASM AND THE SILVER CORD

Definition. Ectoplasm (Greek: *ektós,* outside; *plasma,* mold, substance): the mysterious, omnimodal protoplasmic substance that flows from the human body of the ectoplasmic sensitive and through the manipulation of which – whether by his/her subconscious or by way of extraphysical consciousnesses – superphysical phenomena occur, including materialization or ectoplasmy, which can be a partial or complete manifestation.

Synonymy: animalized fluid; atmosplasm; first matter; *hylê;* ideoplasm; pachyplasm; primordial substance; psychoplasm; teleplasm; vitalized ether.

Comparison. Various authors of projectiological works compare ectoplasm to the silver cord. Strictly speaking, however, they are very different from each other, as will be shown in the next chapter.

Differences. In the final analysis, it is verified that the differences are unquestionably more pronounced than the similarities.

Derivation. It is perhaps more accurate to consider ectoplasm as a condensed derivative of the silver cord, although its immateriality and manifestations are different.

Approximations. Nevertheless, in order to begin a technical analysis, the following are 10 characteristics of ectoplasm that are very similar to the manifestations of the silver cord:

1. **Channel.** The silver cord is connected to the human body of every intraphysical consciousness – including the lucid projector and the ectoplasmic sensitive – like a feeding channel, or a connection involving bi-directional vital impulses, looking like the umbilical cord. Ectoplasm also operates in both these manners.

2. **Interaction.** Upon manifesting, both of these consciential instruments demonstrate the existence of a constant interaction between 2 bodies or vehicles of the consciousness, the dense, physical human body and the less dense, extraphysical psychosoma.

3. **Form.** Both tend to assume the human (anthropomorphic) form of the physical body when manifesting, whether it is of the ectoplasmic sensitive or the lucid projector, including a detailed duplication of the face, following the action of the vital fields of the cells of the human organism or the preexisting *biological organizing model.* In essence, both ectoplasm and the silver cord are derived from the holochakra.

4. **Instability.** In both phenomena, ectoplasmy and projection of the consciousness in the psychosoma, there is an unstable balance of the human *physical form* with the other *humanoid form,* namely the psychosoma.

5. **Will.** The manifestations of both ectoplasm and the silver cord are restricted to psychological factors derived from the will and emotivity. In this case, the influence of the psychosoma (emotional parabody) is evident.

6. **Cords.** Both ectoplasm and the silver cord frequently appear in the form of a thread or threads, a cord or cords.

7. **Perimeter.** Both maintain their more intense activities within a defined perimeter centered at and surrounding the projector's human body or the ectoplasmic sensitive's human body.

8. **Return.** As they are both highly susceptible elements, they demonstrate a clear inclination to return and be reabsorbed by the human body of the intraphysical consciousness from whence they emanate, even evidencing abrupt interiorization or sudden retraction.

9. **Repercussion.** Ectoplasm and the silver cord exhibit an evident predisposition toward the appearance of physical repercussion phenomena in the human body that have an extraphysical origin.

10. **Consciousness.** Both facilitate the appearance of a type of ephemeral double awareness in the being (intraphysical consciousness) who is responsible for the phenomena.

Biodegradable. In the interest of useful speculation, it is worth investigating the possible relationship between enigmatic ectoplasm and another biodegradable, highly perfected and enigmatic material of controverted existence, called *angel's hair* – devil's jelly, spider's web – interpreted as being an excess of materialized energy, according to UFOlogy reports.

Hypotheses. It is presumed that, according to the types of cells of the ectoplasmic sensitive's human body, which are predominantly involved in its composition, ectoplasm can, for example, be: osseous, muscular, neurological or dermal. Two hypotheses can thus be put forward: Is *dermatogenic* ectoplasm more often used in the production of mute ectoplasmic forms? Does *neurogenic* ectoplasm predominate in the production of luminous ectoplasmic forms?

Healing. Varicolored ectoplasm – including the first mass, which is initially olive-green, later dark and then white, smelling like herbs and looking like chewing gum – is also similar to poison that is removed from patients, as a natural element of multimillenary primitive healing therapies. This demonstrates its familiar characteristic of rapid disappearance upon coming in contact with the surrounding air.

Case study. An example of this was observed in the greatly publicized, albeit unsuccessful, treatment based on herbs and incense burning performed in Rio de Janeiro, Brazil by the Brazilian scientist Augusto Rushi (1916-1986), attended by Raoni, a *Txucarramãe* Indian chieftain and the peai Sapaim of the Camaiura tribe. This shows that ectoplasm may just as likely be composed of healthy cells or organic substances as pathological substances extracted from the human organism. (*Medeiros, Rogério; Manchete;* Rio de Janeiro, RJ, Brazil; magazine; weekly; N. 1764; year 34; February 8, 1986; illus.; p. 12, 13).

Phenomena. In light of observations made over time, ectoplasm is a singular partially biological compound substance that appears in the following 4 diverse areas of parapsychic investigation:

1. **Metapsychics.** In the old materialization phenomena of metapsychics.

2. **Parasurgery.** In heterodox surgeries or parasurgeries performed by sensitives in various countries.

3. *Umbanda.* In certain phenomena occurring during the rituals of *Umbanda.*

4. **Indigenous.** In the healings performed by indigenous peoples.

Bibliography: ADGMT (03, p. 87), Andrade (27, p. 111), Ashby (59, p. 148), Cavendish (266, p. 83), Chaplin (273, p. 59), Crookall (343, p. 22), D'arbó (365, p. 170), Day (376, p. 41), Depascale (392, p. 31), Digest (401, p. 353), Doyle (411, p. 337), Fodor (528, p. 113), Fortune (540, p. 49), Frazer (549, p. 228), Freixedo (554, p. 119), Gaynor (577, p. 53), Gómez (613, p. 59), Granja (621, p. 215), Greenhouse (636, p. 64), Martin (1003, p. 48), Meek (1028, p. 290), Montandon (1068, p. 261), Morel (1086, p. 67), Paula (1208, p. 95), Randall (1369, p. 129), Riland (1403, p. 84), RPA (1481, p. 172), Scott (1529, p. 63), Shepard (1548, p. 275), Stelter (1613, p. 215), Swedenborg (1639, p. 114), Vieira (1762, p. 84), Walker (1782, p. 124; 1785, p. 81), Ward (1797, p. 47), Zaniah (1899, p. 165).

---

124. COMPARISONS BETWEEN ECTOPLASM AND THE SILVER CORD

Differential. In spite of the *10 similarities* referred to in the previous chapter – small parallels which, in the end, are surpassed by striking differences – the following *20 differential characteristics* between ectoplasm and the silver cord definitively show that both elements, according to their general properties, differ from each other and should not be confused:

1. **Essence.** Ectoplasm, in essence, is an exteriorized substance that is more *material* than immaterial. The silver cord, whether a single extraphysical energetic thread or many extraphysical energetic threads, is *more immaterial* than material.

2. **Vehicle.** The *less vital* action of ectoplasm depends upon the structure of the human body. The *more vital* action of the silver cord always affects the structure of the psychosoma.

3. **Action.** The exteriorization of ectoplasm does not occur in all phenomena of projection of the intraphysical consciousness in the psychosoma. The silver cord is somehow active in *all* phenomena that involve the psychosoma, even in certain manifestations of ectoplasmy.

4. **Exit.** Ectoplasm flows from the 9 natural orifices of the human body (gynosoma and androsoma), mainly from inside the mouth, nose and ears. The silver cord mostly exits from inside the physical head, without any relationship to the 9 natural orifices of the entire *human organism* or even with the natural orifices of the *human head* in particular.

5. **Coloration.** Ectoplasm can have various colors, including black. The *silvery* cord obviously received its name as it has a color which is opposite to black: clear, white or *silver*.

6. **Elasticity.** The elasticity of ectoplasm reaches a maximum of some dozens of yards (meters) in length. The extendibility of the silver cord appears, in theory, to be practically infinite.

7. **Temperature.** As a rule, ectoplasm lowers the temperature of the immediate human surroundings upon being exteriorized. Exteriorization of the silver cord has no relationship with the ambient human temperature.

8. **Gaze.** Ectoplasm is sensitive to the direct gaze of intraphysical consciousnesses in general who are in the ordinary, physical waking state. The silver cord, even when exteriorized with great potency, is generally not seen by most waking intraphysical beings.

9. **Dependency.** Ectoplasm seems to be dependent upon the holochakra and the human body. The silver cord maintains an evident direct relationship with the psychosoma, besides the holochakra and the human body. Ectoplasm seems to be more dependent upon the silver cord than vice versa.

10. **Docility.** Ectoplasm is more docile to the will or psychodynamic command of the ectoplasmic sensitive and even submits itself to the will of strangers. The silver cord frequently, if not almost always, opposes the will of the projected intraphysical consciousness (automatisms) and seems not to even respond to the will or psychodynamic command of other consciousnesses.

11. **Particles.** Although there is a similarity between the rapid return or retraction of ectoplasm and the silver cord to the human body – as mentioned in the previous chapter – ectoplasm has the characteristic of returning to its donor together with foreign particles that have adhered to its structure. The interiorization of the intraphysical consciousness projected in the psychosoma can cause physical repercussions in the human body, although this is not an identical occurrence.

12. **Illumination.** Ectoplasm is ultra-sensitive to ordinary white light, while the silver cord is not. This shows that, in an *ascending scale of immateriality,* ectoplasm ranks lower and the silver cord ranks higher.

13. **Solidity.** The extremely versatile ectoplasm can manifest in liquid, solid, dry and hard states, materializing shapes of persons, animals and objects. The silver cord seems to be far firmer, more rigorous and conservative in its attributes, lacking this multimodal versatility. The silver cord never adopts a liquid state, for example.

14. **Repulsion.** As it is cold, gelatinous, adhesive, humid, unctuous and viscous, ectoplasm goes though various states, such as: flaky, diffuse, gaseous, milky, liquid and plasmatic. It is also sometimes repelled by physical touch. The silver cord decidedly does not present these characteristics.

15. **Odor.** Ectoplasm emanates a characteristic odor reminiscent of ozone. The silver cord does not have any odor.

16. **Composition.** In rare laboratorial microscopic analyses of the structural composition of ectoplasm – a transitory liquid, semi-solid and solid substance – leucocytes, epithelial cells, fat globules, mucous and characteristics of albuminoidal matter were found. The silver cord is a structure which is apparently much *simpler,* although more *powerful* in its manifestations.

17. **Cysts.** Ectoplasm can be compared to the inner membrane of an egg and the strange formations called *dermoid cysts* that have components analogous in structure to human skin. They contain organized matter, fat, hair, teeth and glands, sometimes even with teratoid remnants. The silver cord cannot be compared to these elements.

18. **Combinations.** Ectoplasm presents *parachemical combinations* with minerals that do not come from the human body, plants or even the clothing of the ectoplasmic sensitive. The silver cord does not feature these parachemical combinations.

19. **Rupture.** Ectoplasm has already been cut into its exteriorized segments, detaching portions for laboratory analysis, without resulting in significant traumas to the ectoplasmic sensitive. It is known that the silver cord, when ruptured, provokes the deactivation of the intraphysical (intraphysical consciousness) projector's human body. In other words: ectoplasm is the parapsychophysical agent of ephemeral ectoplasmy, which lasts a few hours at most; while the silver cord is the intervehicular agent of the extraphysical consciousness that currently (1998) remains a resomant for an average period of 7 decades.

20. **Independence.** With all this evidence, it seems that ectoplasm often manifests without the direct action of the silver cord. The silver cord, in the majority of projective occurrences, does not seem to depend upon ectoplasm in order to manifest.

Dissimilarities. Phenomena show that consciential energy, the silver cord and ectoplasm, although presenting certain superficial similarities, are manifestations coming from the intraphysical consciousness which are undoubtedly different due to the following 3 factors:

1. **Energy.** In its essence, consciential energy is the *mobilization* of pure force.

2. **Cord.** The silver cord is an intervehicular *connection,* or an appendix for coupling and uncoupling.

3. **Ectoplasm.** Ectoplasm is consciential energy that is composed of differentiated *elements,* including those which are organic.

Corporification. With respect to the capacity for corporification, it is important to consider 2 relevant aspects:

1. **Various.** Ectoplasm seems to corporify vehicles (or their appearance) and promote manifestations of its owner (ectoplasmic sensitive) and another or others (more than one intraphysical consciousness).

2. **Single.** The silver cord is only able to corporify the vehicle and promote the manifestations of its owner (ectoplasmic sensitive) or its singular origin (one intraphysical consciousness).

Dematerialization. Lastly, the structures of these different elements can be rationally classified into an ascending scale of dematerialization in 4 basic levels:

1. **Liquid.** The human body or soma: a structure that is both solid and liquid.

2. **Gaseous.** Ectoplasm: a structure that is also gaseous.

3. **Energetic.** The silver cord: an energetic structure derived from the holochakra.

4. **Field.** The psychosoma: a structure that has a close relationship with the field process (physics).

Explanation. However, this still does not explain much. Further research is lacking. This is one more challenge for all experimenters.

Bibliography: Andrade (27, p. 111), Crookall (325, p. 172), Crouzet (344, p. 381), Holzer (743, p. 192), Sachs (1489, p. 15), Scott (1529, p. 63), Vieira (1762, p. 55).

125. PSYCHOSOMA

Definition. Psychosoma (Greek: *psyckhé,* soul; *soma,* body): the vehicle of the consciousness that acts in the paratropospheric extraphysical dimension or *close* to the terrestrial crust, as well as in the extraphysical dimension that is more *distant* from the planetary crust of this planet.

Synonymy: accommodating vehicle; aero body; aerosoma II; *aka* body; *ambiroa* (Tanala); *andadura* (Bakairi, South America); animic body; apparitional body; apparitional double; apparitional duplicate; aristogenesis (Osborn); aromal body (Fourier); *asisi* (Orokaivans); astral body; astral configuration; astral double; astral self; astral twin; *astroeidê* (Neoplatonism of the school of Alexandria); *astroeide;* astro-mental body; astrosoma; ballast of the mental body; *baodhas* (Zend-Avesta); beta body; biomagnetic duplicate (Hernani Guimarães Andrade); body of desires (Tibetans); body of emotions; body of resurrection; body of the soul; breeze (Pomo); brilliant body; bubble-body; butterfly (Burma); butterfly body; celestial body; *cha* (Bushmen); coincident hidden body; continent vehicle; crystal glass; deuterosoma; discarnate body; *doppelgänger* (Germany); double body; double of the sensitive; double; dreaming body; ectosoma; *eidolon* (specter: Greek traditionalism); eloptic radiation; emotional body; emotional parabody; emotive body; energy-body; *enormon* (Hippocrates: 460-356 B.C.); *Ens astrale;* envelope of the soul; essence of the soul *(Ila);* etheric sosie; *evestrum* (Paracelsus: 1490-1541); extra body; extraphysical equivalent; extraphysical sosie; extraphysical twin; fetch (Ancient Bretons); finer body (Friedrich Wilhelm Joseph von Schelling: 1775-1854); floating body; fluidic body (Leibnitz); fluidic double; fluidic involucre (Alfred Erny); fluidic organism; fluidic vestment; fluid-perispiritic envelope; four-dimensional body; *gangan* (Maltese); glorious body (early Christians); *hambarnan* (Indonesia); hidden guest (Maurice Maeterlinck, Nobelist in literature in 1911: 1861-1949); human double; humanoid body; *hun* (Chinese); igneous body; imago (Latin traditionalism); immaterial body; imponderable body; incorporeal self (Rundi); incorruptible body (Gross); inner fantastic body (Johann C. Friederick Zöllner: 1834-1882); intangible body; interior body; internal body; invisible body; invisible double; *isithunzi* (Zulus of South Africa); itinerant double; *iunga* (Tapirape); *jivi* (Santhi); *jiwa* (Gond, India); *kama-rupa* (esoteric Buddhism); *kasith* (Mataco); *kespix* (Yahgan); *kha* (Egypt); *khi* (Vietnamese); *khouan* (Laotians); *kino-aka* body (Hun); *kra;* larva (Romans); light vehicle; *linga sharira;* living double; luciform body; luminous body; magnetic double; *mana-peri* (indigenous Goianese; Brazil); *manomayakosha* (Vedanta); *mauli* (Pukapukans); *mbisimo* (Zande, Africa); meta-organism (Lazarus de Paczolay Hellenbach: 1827-1887); metasoma (Bret); mirror-body; morphogenetic model; moth body; *moya* (Tonga); *mwelolo* (Manus); mysterious thing (Cuénot); *nephesch* (cabalists); nephosoma; *neurara;* neuric aura (Dodee); *ngancha* (Aranda, Australia); nomogenesis (Bergh); nonphysical body; *ocililemba* (Mbundu); *oquema; oqueumata;* other self (Bushmen); *ot-jumulo* (Andamanese, East Asia); out-of-body body (OBB); parabrain body; parallel body; paraphysical body; passional soul; perispirit (Allan Kardec); perispiritic body; perispiritic vehicle; personal double; phantasmic body; phantom body; phantom double; *pieu* (Miao); plastic intermediary; plastic mediator (Ralph Cudworth: 1617-1688); pneumatic body; pre-existing body; pre-physical body; primordial body; projected body; psychic body; psychoform (Teilhard de Chardin: 1881-1955); *purba* (Cuna, South America); quasi-material vehicle; radiant body; rarified body; replica body; reserve body; *rouach* (Jewish cabala); scintillating light (Chinese); second being; second body (parapsychology); second body of energy; second self (Carajás); second skin; secondary body (for humans); semimaterial body; sentient body; shadow (Bakairi, South America); sidereal body; *siga* (Mossi); sixth awareness (Buddhism); small ghost; *somode (Somod); somurgo;* spiritual body (Paulo de Tarso); spiritual double; spiritual organism; subtle body (Aristotle); subtle carriage of the soul (Plato); subtle double; subtle flesh of the soul (Pythagoras); subtle organism (Leibnitz); *suckshuma upadhi* (Raja Yoga); *sumangar* (Makassar); superphysical body; supplementary body; surplus body; *Swarth;* tenuous body; thanatic body; *thankhi* (China); *thunos;* traveling double; traveling soul (Apaches); twin body; two in one body; *udjichog* (Ojibwa); *uhane* (Marquesans); ultraphysical body; *umbra* (Ancient Rome); unfolded form; *utai* (Japan); vehicle of emotion; vital body (Rosicrucians); *warro* (Murngin); wraith; *yagu* (Yapese); *yalo vinaka (Lau); zelem.*

Importance. The extensive list (exhaustive style) of denominations for naming the psychosoma shows the *importance* of its functions among the vehicles of manifestation of the intraphysical consciousness in earth's current evolutionary stage. At the same time, it shows the common *unfamiliarity* with regard to its nature and functions in all types of intraphysical societies and (indigenous) *nations*.

Self-awareness. The majority of individuals have self-awareness with regard to the human body, but they do not have this same self-awareness with regard to the psychosoma. This is regrettable, because it is a condition that brings generalized negative consequences in human existence for all humanity.

Emotionality. In modern society, 4 common but extremely pathological occurrences can be evidenced:

1. **Gambling.** Unrestrained gambling.
2. **Alcoholism.** Alcoholic beverages ingested in excess (alcoholism).
3. **Toxicomania.** Drug abuse involving light, heavy, legal and illegal drugs.
4. **Sensationalism.** Journalistic sensationalism in general.

Objective. All 4 of these actions have the objective of reaching and, above all, actually do reach the psychosoma or emotional parabody of the *human-animal*. The following is merely one example: the sensationalism of the press (newspapers or news magazines), radio and television, in certain intraphysical societies, has as its news flashes the exploitation of crime, sex and violence, in a shocking exposition of facts, issues, events and ideas. These generate many illustrated follow-up stories in a concerted effort to awaken intense emotions, provoke strong sentiments, call attention with unusual appeals to the senses, or awaken uncommon or extreme beliefs.

Control. Although all individuals have and use a psychosoma, few people have self-awareness regarding the existence of this vehicle because they are not able to control it correctly or operate it with full lucidity and agility when manifesting outside the human body.

Realities. The following are 5 subdisciplines of conscientiology or connected, interdependent, consequent or priority realities that many people are lacking on earth at the end of the twentieth century, presented here in logical or chronological order:

1. **Psychosomatics.** Conventional scientists insist on continuing to ignore the *psychosoma* or, in other words, one of the essences of the entire body of research presented by this book.

2. **Evolutiology.** They consequently do not use *evolutionary intelligence* with self-awareness, a mode of intelligence which is more complex than the others.

3. **Serenology.** Without evolutionary intelligence, they do not identify the existence of *Homo sapiens serenissimus*.

4. **Cosmoconscientiology.** Without the identification of *serenissimus,* they do not experience *intercommunicative cosmoconsciousness* or the phenomenon of maximum interconsciential communicability.

5. **Communicology.** Without communication in the state of maximum expansion of the mentalsoma – cosmoconsciousness – they do not detect the existence of *conscientese*.

Research. For this reason, the more that individuals can be made aware of the existence of the psychosoma, study it and research it in depth, the better it will be for everyone's comprehension, well-being and consciential development.

Bibliography: Aliança (13, p. 151), Andréa (33, p. 19), Andreas (36, p. 38), Ashish (60, p. 343), Barreto (83, p. 68), Besant (129, p. 47), Bret (202, p. 44), Butler (228, p. 52), Carrington (245, p. 266), Carton (252, p. 101), Castaneda (258, p. 20), Crookall (320, p. 101), Crowe (345, p. 185), Delanne (381, p. 28), Depascale (392, p. 104), Erny (483, p. 75), Frost (560, p. 55), Granja (621, p. 153), Greenhouse (636, p. 24), Hodson (729, p. 55), Holms (735, p. 448), Jorge (811, p. 114), Kardec (825, p. 19), Martin (1002, p. 18), Matson (1013. p 38), Michaël (1041, p 50), Miranda (1050, p. 63), Monroe (1065. p. 166), Montandon (1068, p. 15.) Moss (1096,

p. 196), Muldoon (1105, p. 279), Murphy (1112, p. 71), Pensamento (1224, p. 31), Perkins (1236, p. 52), Powell (1278, p. 1), Prieur (1289, p. 144), 1 Corinthians 15:44, Rampa (1361, p. 76), Schutel (1525, p. 28), Seabra (1534, p. 121), Shay (1546, p. 13), Smith (1574, p. 55), Steiger (1601, p. 219), Steiner (1610, p. 52), Todd (1689, p. 52), Vieira (1765, p. 5), Walker (1781, p. 32), Wang (1794, p. 147), Yogananda (1894, p. 35).

126. PARA-ANATOMY OF THE PSYCHOSOMA

Characteristics. Among the characteristics of the para-anatomy of the psychosoma, at least the following 10 variables can be singled out:

1. Format.
2. Insertion of the silver cord (the first one, prior to resoma).
3. Force centers.
4. Nature, composition, structure and luminosity.
5. Aura.
6. Coloration.
7. Average weight of 2.47 oz. (70 g) (a hypothesis).
8. Volume, mass and density.
9. The percentage of rarefied matter.
10. Differences between the psychosoma of the intraphysical consciousness and the extraphysical consciousness.

Seat. When the vehicles of the consciousness are in the coincident state, the seat of the psychosoma extends throughout the human body.

Presentation. In certain circumstances, the psychosoma – a vehicle that is as objective to the intraphysical consciousness projected with lucidity as the human body in the intraphysical dimension – can present itself in two manners:

1. **Simple.** Simple or adequate.
2. **Compound.** Compound, in this case when combined with part of the energies of the holochakra.

Form. In evolved extraphysical dimensions, the psychosoma does not have a fixed form, nor is it rigid or condensed in any particular way.

Gelatin. The psychosoma is sometimes similar to gelatin that needs to be removed from a mold: the human body.

Comparisons. Morphologically speaking, the psychosoma of the projected intraphysical consciousness, and even the psychosoma of the extraphysical consciousness, appears more substantial than transparent to the eyes of sensitive intraphysical observers, although simultaneously appearing diaphanous, as often happens with *clouds*. Such a comparison or analogy clearly illustrates the reality of the density of the psychosoma.

Ageless. With regard to form, the psychosoma is *ageless* or, in other words: it does not age, strictly speaking. However, it transfigures itself.

Composition. It is presumed that at least 3 components which are somewhat familiar to humans may make up part of the composition of the semi-physical structure of the psychosoma:

1. **Particles.** Elementary particles.
2. **Fields.** Electromagnetic and gravitational fields.
3. **Light.** Photons (light).

Morphothosene. Nevertheless, the psychosoma is essentially a thought-form or a morphothosene in light of its property of transfiguration.

Evidence. Over the course of the past 2 centuries, diverse researchers have singled out experimental signs in persistent attempts at evidencing the reality of the psychosoma, especially through the following 5 resources:

1. **Doubles.** Supposedly authentic photos of the supposedly materialized psychosoma of an intraphysical consciousness projected close to the human body (controversial photos of doubles).
2. **Emanations.** Photos of nebulous, dense and colored emanations on the deathbed (desoma).
3. **Molds.** Wax molds made of the feet and hands of personalities through ectoplasmic sensitives.
4. **Marks.** Impressions made from parts of the psychosoma on smoke-stained surfaces.
5. **Effects.** Physical effects directly provoked by the projected intraphysical consciousness.

Repetition. However, this experimental evidence lacks universal acceptance, which means that the experiments should be repeated or insistently reexamined for a period of time.

Bibliography: Blackmore (139, p. 1 29), Boswell (174, p. 128), Carrington (245, p. 279), Delanne (381, p. 145), Frost (560, p. 33), Greenhouse (636, p. 97), Martin (1002, p. 23), Rogo (1444, p. 22), Vieira (1762, p. 138).

127. PARAPSYCHOPHYSIOLOGY OF THE PSYCHOSOMA

Characteristics. Within the characteristics of the parapsychophysiology of the intraphysical consciousness' psychosoma, at least the following 21 variables can be singled out:

1. **Sensations.** It makes human sensations possible.
2. **Interface.** It serves as a bridge or interface between the free mind and the dense human brain.
3. **Action.** It serves as a vehicle of awareness and action.
4. *Uniform.* It is the basic subtle uniform of the *paratropospheric* projector.
5. **Self-transfigurations.** It shows malleability or parapsychophysiological self-transfigurations, thereby allowing the attainment of morphothosenes or thought-forms and extraphysical clothing.
6. **Light.** It grows, is elastic and irradiates its own light.
7. **Irradiation.** It irradiates its own energy.
8. **Foundation.** It performs basic general operations (psychosomatic foundation).
9. **Projection.** It is active in lucid and nonlucid consciential projection.
10. **Thosenology.** It is sensitive to thoughts or thosenes, representing the *sen* of thosenes.
11. **Tangibility.** It allows tangibility in certain instances.
12. **Apparition.** It allows the apparition of the intraphysical projector to other intraphysical beings.
13. **Parapsychism.** It presents plasticity, which predisposes extraphysical parapsychism.
14. **Predisposition.** It predisposes the action of the silver cord.
15. **Paragenetics.** It is related to paragenetics, genetics and the growth of the human body.
16. **Emotionality.** It functions as the parabody of desires or the emotional parabody.
17. **Holochakra.** It is related to the holochakra through the silver cord and *ballonnement* (balloonment).
18. **Magnetism.** It is an instrument that is sensitive to magnetic influences, including those of the human body.
19. **Paramimicry.** It allows the phenomenon of extraphysical mimicry or paramimicry.
20. **Senses.** It is the reason why the senses of smell and taste appear less in the perceptions of the intraphysical consciousness who is projected in the paratropospheric dimensions.
21. **Sounds.** It is related to intracranial sounds.

Factors. The psychosoma is influenced by material factors such as the earth's gravitational pull, the density of matter and surface tension upon passing through thick material structures (extraphysical self-permeability) on certain occasions.

Plates. It also influences photographic plates (telekinesis) and sensitive physical instruments.

Condenser. The psychosoma is the consciousness' cosmic energy condenser, whether it is an intraphysical or extraphysical consciousness.

Regulators. The silver cord regulates the density of the intraphysical consciousness' psychosoma, which varies from one human lucid projection to another. If the silver cord regulates the density of the psychosoma, this same density, in turn, regulates the condensation, subtlety, fluidity or rarefaction of the psychosoma, establishes its vibratory orbit and permits the absorption of *subtle matter* from and in the extraphysical environment or district. All this is directly dependent upon the will of the projected intraphysical consciousness.

Thought. Thought, whether conscious or unconscious, has a powerful effect upon the density of the psychosoma of the intraphysical and extraphysical consciousness.

Intermediation. In the complex intermediation or the interface performed by the intraphysical consciousness' psychosoma between the machine – in this case the human body – and the consciousness headquartered in the mentalsoma, its greater density allows the projected human projector to be seen by a greater number of extraphysical consciousnesses.

Selection. The energetic fields that compose the paratropospheric extraphysical districts, make a spontaneous and balanced selection of projected extraphysical and intraphysical consciousnesses through the vibratory density of the psychosoma of each one.

Formula. The following is a coherent formula in evolutiology: a permanent reduction in the semiphysical density of the psychosoma gradually occurs, in a continuous manner, in direct proportion to the increase in the general evolutionary level of the consciousness.

Free will. As a result of the principle of this formula, the psychosoma itself restricts the sphere of action of consciential free will.

Malleability. The malleability of the psychosoma permits multiple successive translocations of the consciousness to extraphysical districts and environments of different densities.

Return. In rarefaction of the intraphysical consciousness' psychosoma, energies are returned to the human body with the objective of reducing ballast. This leaves the projected intraphysical consciousness with a minimum of the holochakra's energies and makes it unnecessary to interiorize.

Rarefaction. Rarefaction can occur in 2 ways:

1. **Interiorization.** With the interiorization of the psychosoma in the human body.
2. **Cord.** Through the silver cord, whether the intraphysical consciousness is physically close to or distant from the physical base.

Condensation. Condensation or rarefaction of the psychosoma can also occur through the silver cord either with or without interiorization of the projected intraphysical consciousness.

Scale. The psychosoma establishes the scale of extraphysical opacity, translucency, transparency and luminosity. These allow a distinction to be made between: intraphysical consciousnesses, extraphysical consciousnesses and projected intraphysical beings.

Self-defense. This temporary variation in the density of the psychosoma acts as an extraordinary resource of extraphysical consciential self-defense because the consciousness can switch from one extraphysical environment or district to another.

Relationships. The psychosoma of the intraphysical consciousness maintains functional relationships with the human body, the holochakra, the silver cord and the mentalsoma.

Impossibilities. Strictly speaking, real pain, lesions, wounds or accidents are not possible while in the psychosoma, as they occur with the human body.

Simulacra. When the simulacra of these events occur, it is due to the influence of the *para*psychological conditioning of the inexperienced or ill intraphysical consciousness, whether or not he/she is projected. This can even occur to extraphysical consciousnesses.

Unique. The psychosoma is unique as a vehicle of manifestation of the intraphysical consciousness because it simultaneously has two intercorporal connections:

1. **Rudimentary.** The rudimentary connections of the silver cord.
2. **Evolved.** The evolved connections of the golden cord.

Effects. Only the psychosoma allows the intraphysical consciousness and the extraphysical consciousness to feel the effects of the action of energy currents and *extraphysical hydromagnetic storms.*

Repulsion. In certain cases, the magnetic field of the awakened consciousness' psychosoma generates automatic repulsion on the part of ill, projected intraphysical consciousnesses, intrusive extraphysical consciousnesses, intruders in general and viscous energivorous parapsychopaths (extraphysical consciousnesses). Rare instances of this nature occur between intraphysical consciousnesses.

Intermediary. The psychosoma of the intraphysical consciousness is the intermediary parabody between the machine (the human body) and the same consciousness headquartered in the mentalsoma, a condition which is represented in the following two manners:

1. **Intraphysical consciousness.** The intraphysical being is the consciousness that still has an integral psychosoma.
2. **Extraphysical consciousness.** The extraphysical consciousness is the consciousness that has a free psychosoma, lacks the silver cord, part of the holochakra (or the entire holochakra) and the human body.

Survival. The psychosoma survives and continues to be entirely functional after the first and second desomas or deactivation of the human body and holochakra.

Disappearance. The psychosoma only definitively disappears upon the third desoma or in the definitive transformation of the *Homo sapiens serenissimus* into the free consciousness (FC).

Emotions. In the same way that the mentalsoma is directly responsible for the consciousness' flow of sentiments *(high conscientiality),* the psychosoma, as it is close to the holochakra and human body, is responsible for the consciousness' emotional manifestations (animality or instinctive reactions).

Cohesion. Through the psychosoma, with the support of the holochakra, the intraphysical consciousness executes the cohesion of the myriad of cells that compose the animal or human body, maintaining the apparent stability of the living form. This occurs paradoxically through the constant, always *renovated* and *renovating* movement of the atoms.

Stability. This stability of the living human form receives two very common names:

1. **Memory.** Within the context of time it is called *memory.*
2. **Substance.** Within the context of space it is called *substance.*

Proof. Human proof or corpus delicti does not apply to the psychosoma, as seen by the following 5 facts, among others:

1. **Impressions.** The psychosoma does not leave impressions, signs, marks, vestiges or residues wherever it goes on the earth's crust.
2. **Shadow.** Strictly speaking, the psychosoma does not cast a shadow when it is in sunlight.
3. **Footprint.** It leaves no footprints on the earth's surface.
4. **Fingerprint.** It leaves no fingerprints on objects.
5. **Odor.** It does not emanate a distinctive odor in the human environment.

Will. Nevertheless, many of these facts can occur due to the density of the psychosoma, according to acts of will and the creation of morphothosenes.

Growth. The psychosoma does not need to grow, whereas the human body obviously grows.

Duration. The psychosoma takes on the humanoid form of the adult, intraphysical being, transfiguring itself according to the will of the consciousness, while it exists. The psychosoma disappears or, in other words, is discarded, when the consciousness achieves the condition of free consciousness (FC).

Appendices. It is worth repeating that the golden cord is the *appendix* that belongs to the psychosoma, in the same way that the silver cord is the *appendix* that belongs to the human body or soma.

Learning. The intraphysical consciousness has to learn to control the projected psychosoma just as a child learns to physically balance him/herself and take the first human steps in his/her new intraphysical existence.

Weight. The basic average weight of the projected intraphysical consciousness' psychosoma seems to be 1 thousandth of the weight of the human body that houses it.

Variations. The density, the silver cord and the holochakra, as a whole, acting like equipment or a load, have a great influence upon the weight of the projected intraphysical consciousness' psychosoma. This vehicle can therefore have different weights (variations) in a single lucid projective experience.

Composition. As the psychosoma is not a reality of fixed forms, its composition can vary from moment to moment. It is thus considered to be the parabody of desires, or the mutable or unstable emotional parabody.

Intoxication. It is still not known if the excessive accumulation of the *waste material* of the intestinal bolus – with the installation of intestinal constipation and consequent organic intoxication – has an influence upon the weight of the intraphysical consciousness' projected psychosoma.

Strength. Repeated facts show that the intraphysical consciousness, when projected from the human body, has greater strength or can at least generate considerably more energy in the extraphysical dimension than when coincident or restricted *inside* the human body, in the ordinary, physical waking state.

Exteriorization. Part of the psychosoma can leave and free itself from any part of the human body. However, the intraphysical consciousness only leaves in the psychosoma through the head, whether through the sinciput, forehead, nuchal region or the parietal and temporal sides of the cranium.

States. There are many consciential conditions or states in which the psychosoma leaves the condition of coincidence with the other vehicles of manifestation and remains bound only by the silver cord, as in the case of: sleep, hypnosis, anesthesia and lucid projection.

Laws. The facts lead us to the logical conclusion that the psychosoma of the intraphysical consciousness contains all the *organogenic laws,* according to which the human body is formed due to paragenetics and retrosomas which were deactivated in his/her multimillenary past.

Aspermic. However, the psychosoma is an *aspermic* body: it does not produce a "seed."

Ballast. The psychosoma sometimes acts as the ballast of the mentalsoma, densifying and "materializing" the structure of this vehicle of manifestation when it projects while transporting the consciousness. It thereby forms the so-called "laden mentalsoma".

Physical. The intraphysical consciousness projected in the psychosoma can unquestionably operate in this physical dimension, or in consensual reality, thereby generating the following phenomena, among others: physical bilocation, exteriorization of motricity, false arrival, projective parapyrogenesis, projective poltergeist, projective raps and projective telekinesis.

Phenomena. The existence of the psychosoma of intraphysical and extraphysical consciousnesses explains the most varied psi phenomena, which include: raps, poltergeist, intuitive writing, automatic drawing, radiesthesia (radionics), ideoplasty, apparitions, xenoglossy, clairvoyance, inner voices when non-pathological, telepathy and predictions.

Paraprojection. The parapsychophysiology of the psychosoma amplifies the manifestations with respect to the intraphysical consciousness, notably in the phenomena of *lucid paraprojection,* which is also parapsychophysiological.

Instruments. The fingers, hands, arms, feet, legs, senses and the human body as a whole are natural instruments of the intraphysical consciousness. On the other hand, the heart and liver, for example, are only instruments of the human organism.

Question. If the silver cord, holochakra, extraphysical perceptions and psychosoma as a whole are paranatural instruments of the consciousness, what are the instruments exclusively of the psychosoma?

Volitation. Since it does not have bones, joints and muscles, the projected intraphysical consciousness' psychosoma does not need the basic physiological components of biomechanics (kinesiology), namely the analysis of the human body's movements. This is a discipline which is of overall interest to orthopedics (traumatology), rehabilitation, physical education and athletic techniques. On the other hand, the psychosoma needs to be paraphysiologically addressed with regard to balance, due to planetary gravitation, extraphysical posture, walking, floating and volitation or, in other words, lucid, free and unimpeded flight outside the human body, which is at rest and with the *brain emptied* of the consciousness at that time.

Transfigurations. Among the characteristics and functions of the psychosoma, the following 6 should be singled out:

1. Extraphysical elasticity.
2. Extraphysical imponderability.
3. Extraphysical permeability.
4. Extraphysical translocation.
5. Luminosity.
6. Transfigurations that can be either conscious (self-transfigurations) or unconscious.

Resomatics. The more prolonged transfigurations of the psychosoma occur during the period of consciential restriction, in the process of resoma of the extraphysical consciousness, in *paragenetic/genetic blending* with vivified matter, thereby composing the intraphysical vehicle, namely: the soma.

Visual. The *para*psychological (extraphysical psychology) reflexes stemming from the human body of physical life, still conserve the most frequent or typical appearance of the consciousness during the subsequent intermissive period.

Marks. Cases of birthmarks or blemishes suggestive of existential seriation and studied by researchers are clear evidence of the parapsychopathological disturbances of the psychosoma, which are responsible for the transference of physical impressions of the human body of the previous intraphysical life to the human body of the current intraphysical life.

Confusion. The properties of the psychosoma are so transcendent in relation to the soma that they confuse the projected intraphysical consciousness with regard to the interpretation of its extraphysical experiences. This is worsened due to the fantasies of the oneiric and semilucid states that interfere in subsequent analysis of the projective experiences.

Withdrawal. Another subtle property of the psychosoma is the inversion of the relative positions of the volitator and the scenery during volitation: in this case the consciousness *allows* the scenery to pass before it while *apparently* remaining at a *standstill* or intraconscientially withdrawn (para-introspection).

Dehydration. The prolonged projection in which the psychosoma is laden with ectoplasm extracted from the cells of the soma provokes *dehydration* of the joints of the soma, which is at rest in the physical base. This generally occurs after a half-hour long projection. The absorption of extraphysical energies through the laden psychosoma by the projected intraphysical consciousness allows the subsequent *recuperation* or compensation of the joints with the replacement of the soma's liquids and cells.

Bibliography: Delanne (381, p. 16), Greenhouse (636, p. 59), Leadbeater (899, p. 57), Moss (1097, p. 196), Powell (1278, p. 23), Vieira (1762, p. 85).

128. PARAPSYCHOPATHOLOGY OF THE PSYCHOSOMA

Disturbances. The occurrences of parapathology of the psychosoma can be classified into 2 types:

1. Minidisturbances.
2. Maxidisturbances.

Minidisturbances. Among the minidisturbances of the parapsychopathology of the intraphysical consciousness' psychosoma, the following 4 types of occurrence can be singled out:

1. Extraphysical consequences of the amputated member.
2. Blindness, advanced myopia and daltonism.
3. Buzzing (certain manifestations).
4. Extraphysical attacks (psychosoma of extraphysical consciousnesses).

Discoincidence. Still within the minidisturbances of the parapsychopathology of the psychosoma, partial discoincidences of the psychosoma occur due to spontaneous physical causes. The following 8 serve as examples:

1. **Contusion.** Cranial contusion.
2. *Stars.* The physical effect of "seeing stars."
3. **Stomach.** The sensation of having one's "heart in one's mouth" when a potent and fast elevator is ascending or descending (roller coaster).
4. **Step.** The sensation of stepping into thin air upon stepping onto the wrong step or when climbing down a ladder.
5. **Brake.** The sensation due to the abrupt braking of a vehicle.
6. **Discoincidence.** The provocation of discoincidence, with a primitive parapsychic objective in the gyrations of *Umbanda*.
7. **Shock.** Discoincidence due to a major shock.
8. **Sneeze.** Discoincidence due to a strong sneeze in predisposing circumstances.

Maxidisturbances. Among the maxidisturbances of the parapsychopathology of the psychosoma, the following 12, among others, can be singled out:

1. Extraphysical sexual mania *(para-sexaholic).*
2. Pathological discoincidence.
3. Self-intrusion or extraphysical obsession.
4. Oneirophobia.
5. Certain cases of epileptic petit mal (pathological absence).
6. Extraphysical oligophrenia or deficiency in the development of the intraphysical consciousness' consciential attributes.
7. Extraphysical coma or paracoma of intraphysical consciousnesses who have *locked intraphysical existences.*
8. Consequences of air dislocation due to the explosion of a nearby bomb, with the effect of a wave of shock and vibrations, violently expelling the psychosoma from the human body.
9. Pathological transfigurations.
10. The state of the psychosoma as though it were atrophied, *withered* or *cracked,* looking like the bark of a tree.
11. Extraphysical lycanthropy (zoanthropy).
12. *Retroparapsychic scars* of the psychosoma.

Realities. Fortunately, the undeniable personal evidence of lucid projection leads the intraphysical consciousness to a supreme level of veracity regarding psychophysical realities that allows him/her to distinguish between, locate and identify the two basic spheres of consciential life.

Extremes. This fact occurs ranging all the way from the apex of sublimity, with the most ennobling aspects of the human personality, to the inferior extreme of the shadowy meanderings of the most abject multiexistential, paragenetic and holobiographical deficiencies and psychoses in the world of psychopathology and conventional human criminology.

Experiences. Thus, with the accumulation of experiences outside the human body, the individual no longer has any doubt regarding the possibilities of positive or healthy and negative or ill realizations of the intraphysical consciousness who temporarily liberates him/herself from the dense vehicle.

Consequences. The individual's personal condition engenders the consequences of the sublime modeling of fraternal social assistance to ill individuals, invalids or the disenfranchised, as well as the identification of robbery, pillaging, sexual assault and even the perpetration of large-scale homicides, massacres and genocides full of tragedy.

Rehearsals. Frequently, when a criminal affirms, "I was out of my mind" at the moment of a criminal act, his/her intraphysical consciousness – often before the act – was actually outside him/herself. In other words, he/she was outside the human body, whether aware or unaware of this fact, whereupon he/she deliberately perpetrated the criminal act. This now confirms his/her prior morbid propositions and endorses the *extraphysical rehearsals which have already been performed.*

Extraphysicology. Conclusion: the extraphysical dimension, mainly the paratroposphere, has continued to serve, throughout the millennia of human history, as a permanent *consciential laboratory,* as much for the healthy and liberating creations of good or cosmoethical geniuses, as for the sick and evolutionarily stagnating creations of evil or anticosmoethical geniuses.

Thought. For the will – the generator of force – thought acts as an agent of manifestation in the modeling of creative as well as destructive acts, creating everything from abnegated social assistants to the intraphysical intruder, the incubus and succubus which know no morals, boundaries, scruples or social education (sociopaths, sociopathies).

Company. Acting upon all of this is the balanced or demented company that the intraphysical consciousness chooses while in the ordinary, physical waking state or while outside the body. This is because likes attract, interact and often end up in a type of symbiotic and energetic interdependence between the dimensions of consciential life, creating diverse obscure syndromes.

Genetics. It is important to note that many cases of morphological disturbance of the soma that manifest along genetic lines during the phases of human gestation and ostensively appear upon rebirth can, in certain cases, be directly attributed, either in part or in whole, to parapsychopathologies of the psychosoma.

Variations. The following are 6 types of basic morphological variations in the human body – sometimes considered teratological – that are always of enormous clinical relevance:

1. **General:** variations in constitution; nanism; gigantism; asymmetries of development; and dystrophic syndromes.

2. **Trunk:** variations in the vertebral column and variations in the thorax.

3. **Head:** variations in the cranium; facial types; ocular variations; variations in the ears; facial fissures; and buccal variations.

4. **Hands and feet:** hyperdactylia or polydactylia; hypodactylia or ectodactyly; mega, brachy, macro and microdactilia; hyper and hypophalangism; clinodactyly; and syndactyly.

5. **Genitals:** hermaphroditism; ectopias; duplications; penile fissures; polymastia; amastia; and gynecomastia.

6. **Integument:** dyschromias; *dystrichoses;* and variations of phanerosis.

Psychology. Within the scope of human emotional manifestations (psychology) restricted to the psychosoma, all excess generally jeopardizes and causes problems due to the action of consciential immaturity or the absence of reflection, pondering and discernment.

Case study. With regard to this aspect, 5 occurrences can be seen:

1. **Superprojection.** The negative effects of a mother's or father's overprotection of a son or daughter where, for example, "The mother smothers the child with affection?"

2. **Compassion.** Blind and disturbing compassion that facilitates interconsciential or intrusive influences.

3. **Intention.** Isolated good intention lacking discernment.

4. **Will.** Good will alone, also without discernment, which is why it is affirmed and lucid consciential projectors confirm: the paratropospheric extraphysical dimension is overcrowded with parapsychotic post-desomatic extraphysical consciousnesses.

5. **Hospitals.** Psychiatric hospitals filled with unhappy mental patients.

Psychosomatics. So-called psychosomatic medicine – simultaneously addressing the human body and the consciousness, which are interrelated and considered together, treating disturbances or organic lesions produced by psychic influences (emotions, desires, fear and fixed ideas), combating certain types of gastrointestinal ulcers, functional colopathy, *anphotonias* and other disturbances – is actually beginning to enter, albeit superficially, the still obscure realm of the parapsychopathology of the psychosoma or the "body of *human* consciousness," which is above all directed by the intraphysical consciousness which is always headquartered in the mentalsoma.

Desoma. When the intraphysical consciousness discards the human body through the *first desoma*, most illnesses known to classic (physicalist) medicine or, in other words, all *organic* or cellular illnesses (organic nosology or nosography), lose their raison d'être. This is because the alleged cause or singular motive for these pathologies – the *soma* – ceases to exist.

Second. When this same consciousness, having recently become an extraphysical consciousness, discards the remnants of the connections of the holochakra in the psychosoma through *second desoma*, all the illnesses restricted to imbalances in consciential energy, as in disturbances treated by acupuncture and do-in, or the so-called *pathological awakening of the kundalini* or, in short, all disturbances which have arisen as a direct result of *primary* consciential energies, lose their raison d'être. This is because the supposed cause or singular motive of these disturbances – the *holochakra* or its remnants – ceases to exist.

Illnesses. However, neither all organic illnesses nor the energetic disturbances of the consciousness cease to exist, as would be expected, after the first and second desomas.

Paragenetics. This does not occur due to the properties of the psychosoma (the emotional parabody), which is capable of forming and maintaining these illnesses and disturbances – or their characteristic effects and symptoms – stemming from its structure, through the powerful action (psychological paraconditioning that forms the individual paragenetics) of the will through the mentalsoma and the self-transfigurations of the psychosoma.

Holokarma. This gives rise to *holokarmic illnesses,* or chronic disturbances established over centuries that continue from one human life to the next (multi-existentiality, personal holobiography), from one soma (*retrosoma*) to the next, or from one holochakra *(retro-holochakra)* to the next, restricted to the parapsychopathology of the psychosoma and the mentalsoma.

Medicine. The interested reader will note the logic of the explanations presented above and the regrettable condition of classic, conventional or physicalist medicine, which still only concerns itself with 1 vehicle of consciential manifestation, the human body. It still needs to discover, understand and address 3 more vehicles of consciential manifestation in conjunction.

Game. In this tragic game through the maintenance of the health of the consciousness, conventional medicine, which is currently excessively commercial, has thus far, over the centuries, continued to lose 3 to 1.

Bibliography: Fortune (540, p. 48), Vieira (1762, p. 161).

---

129. COMPARISONS BETWEEN THE SOMA AND THE PSYCHOSOMA

Modeling. The psychosoma is the *modeling agent of the soma,* or the human body. It acts subordinated to genetic laws and respects the biogravitational field in which it breathes and develops.

Replica. This is why one vehicle is a replica of the other.

Expressions. The opaque human body expresses the psychosoma in the dense intraphysical dimension. The luminous psychosoma expresses the human body in the rarefied extraphysical dimension.

Objects. The human body is a *terrestrial* object that walks in the intraphysical dimension. The psychosoma, however, is an *aerial* object that volitates.

Energizing. The holochakra, including the silver cord, is the intermediary energizing agent of the interrelationship between the psychosoma and the soma. It permits both to operate together in perfect union, while in the state of coincidence and discoincidence. It always endeavors to maintain and prolong the vitality of the existing structures or physical and extraphysical, mental (psychological, biomemory) and consciential health – holosomatic homeostasis – from the organism's conception to its deactivation through the biological first desoma.

Hygiene. Physical hygiene is the maintenance of the *human machine*. Mental (or consciential) hygiene is the maintenance of the *extraphysical paramachine* (psychosoma).

Creations. The psychosoma as the duplicate of the soma, or vice versa, has inspired curious customs and creations over time, including the following 3:

1. **Greeks.** The ancient Greeks avoided looking at their own image reflected on the surface of water as the shadow of the human body appeared to them to be the dark side of their own self.

2. **Stevenson.** Robert Lewis Balfour Stevenson (1850-1894) wrote the celebrated *Dr. Jekyll and Mr. Hyde.*

3. **Wilde.** Oscar Fingall Wills Wilde (1854-1900) wrote the novel *The Picture of Dorian Gray* in 1891.

Inhibition. Over the many thousands of winters and summers of human history on earth, successive generations of intraphysical beings have kept the psychosoma operating only as an *inhibited* (or constrained) vehicle of manifestation between the impulses of the consciousness and the impressions received through the human body, in the intraphysical dimension, and in the state of coincidence of the bodies (vehicles) of consciential manifestation.

Ignorance. Intraphysical consciousnesses, even the generations alive today, are generally unaware that the psychosoma can act in its own extraphysical dimension, using its own resources which are far more evolved than those of the physical body, and that the consciousness (the will) can act directly upon it. This includes the will of the intraphysical consciousness.

Consequences. The abovementioned conjuncture results in two extremely serious consequences:

1. **First:** the first consequence is that no fewer than 4 billion beings of flesh and blood – the majority of the current members of humanity – upon sleeping every night, leave the physical body or at least remain discoincident in their vehicles of manifestation, experiencing actual ephemeral minideaths, *retaining* the consciousness *inside* the psychosoma, whether 1½" (4 cm) or 13' (4 m) away from their own physical body. It remains there futilely waiting for the physical impulses of this same inactive body or, more precisely, the impulses of the brain, which is filled with neurons, interactions, synapses, glias and other elements, but is *empty* for a certain period because the consciousness is temporarily removed from it.

Hibernation. Naturally projected intraphysical consciousnesses, under the influence of the paraphysiology of their own psychosoma, maintain themselves in this condition of unnecessary deep hibernation which is characteristic of extraphysical infancy. They thereby sadly waste evolutionary opportunities of inestimable value, submerged in a deplorable inertia, the extension of which often amounts to 1/3 of the period of terrestrial life (8 hours in a daily 24-hour period).

Miniprojections. Short nonlucid consciential projections or miniprojections are only of value because they are a natural process of absorbing immanent energy in the extraphysical dimension, an aspect which is important for human life.

Dormitory-planet. From an extraphysical evolutionary perspective, the earth can be considered to be an immense day care center (mega-nursery), or *dormitory-planet.*

Unconsciousness. Terrestrial humanity still sleeps the pathetic sleep of deep unconsciousness.

Blockage. The billions of unconscious, intraphysical consciousnesses who leave the physical body night after night, year after year, and are temporarily freed in the extraphysical body (psychosoma), do not awaken to the other greater reality. This is because they *ruminate* on their own blocked and paralyzing thoughts, in a closed circuit.

Somnambulists. These *extraphysical somnambulists* enter the extraphysical dimension without perceiving it and see nothing. This is because, in this case, the ego paraphysiologically leaves the physical body but, despite this, is unable to *get out of itself*, remaining mired in its own egotistical morphothosenes, gravitating around itself *(mega-ego),* in neutral.

Conditions. The saddest part of all is that among these somnambulants are persons of all existential and cultural levels and conditions, from all countries, spread throughout all continents. They are indifferent to this waste and the majority do not even reflect on the issue.

2. **Second:** the second consequence refers to those intraphysical consciousnesses who became extraphysical consciousnesses again and remain unconscious, somnambulant or semiconscious, sometimes for long periods, in the paratropospheric extraphysical dimension, because they keep waiting to feel the physical vibrations of the deactivated body of dense matter that they lost definitively in the *first desoma,* but with which they remain deeply conditioned. They thus do not enter into any extraphysical activity in their new interexistential interval or intermissive period in the new *environment* or district.

Sleep. The obvious conclusion of this lamentable situation is that terrestrial humanity is *sleeping too much* during human existence (lifetime) and even after desoma (intermissive period).

Solution. The solution to the problem is to put an end to the idleness of the psychosoma, when in the condition of an intraphysical consciousness, as well as during the post-desomatic phase. There is no other immediate solution. Does the reader have any other solution to offer? What is your opinion?

Awakening. It is essential that there be an awakening to the extraordinary resources that the psychosoma can offer. This will allow it to act freely so that consciousnesses can then also act directly in the mentalsoma in an unimpeded manner, thereby dispensing with the intermediary vehicles of manifestation.

Resource. There is only one efficient resource for the *initial* extraphysical awakening of humanity: lucid projection in the psychosoma.

Problem. The schools of transcendent theoretical studies, the more advanced parapsychic practices and all attempts at self-knowledge of the intraphysical consciousness help greatly, although none of them has resolved this long-standing problem as yet.

Development. The era of unfounded fear, superstitions, beliefs, abstruse rituals and cheap mysticism has passed.

Awareness. Every intraphysical consciousnesses who wishes to can now know with certainty that they have their own light, their human aura and inner potential to be developed using their own will, through their own efforts and consciential energies.

Time. Those who wish to develop their latent parapsychic powers in this era of extraphysical emancipation have no time to lose.

Power. Through lucid projection, which offers dozens of uses and can be produced by anyone, the only requirement is *mental discipline* or self-organization, the third consciential power after will and intentionality (quality), in order to achieve unlimited positive applications in daily life. This is not asking too much.

Discipline. It is evident that without discipline no one achieves improved personal performance of any type, anywhere, under any conditions.

Warning. Finally, it is always good to remind everyone of a warning that is one of the basic laws of projectiology: *never try to project the consciousness with a negative or anticosmoethical intention.* The unhealthy results of this will, first of all, affect the ill-willed projector.

Cosmoethics. Elevated ethical principles (cosmoethics) are indispensable in order to have superior, healthy, extraphysical consciential experiences.

Bibliography: Frost (560, p. 187), Martin (1002, p. 40), Moss (1096, p. 197), Muldoon (1105, p. 277), Vieira (1765, p. 5), Walker (1786, p. 19), Xavier (1879, p. 21).

130. THEORY OF IRRUPTION OF THE PSYCHOSOMA

Definition. The theory of *irruption of the psychosoma* in the intraphysical dimension takes as a postulate – a fact or effect recognized without previous demonstration – that the emotional parabody, through the evolution of the intraphysical consciousnesses of a planet, insinuates itself, shows itself or *arises forcefully* in diverse circumstances in human life.

Dimensions. According to extraphysicology, there are extraphysical events which suggest that one dimension, through the evolution of the average consciousnesses that inhabit it (holothosene), tends to progress toward the next more evolved consecutive or *contiguous* dimension beyond it.

Evolutiology. Thus, there may be more evolved planets with a more rarefied or subtle physicality than that of the earth and which can be reached and inhabited with semidematerialized terrestrial somas, thereby facilitating more intensive, instantaneous and advanced multidimensional projections.

Analogy. We can use the analogy here of the deciduous tooth, or the child's *milk tooth* (odontology), which is replaced by the natural, *adult* or permanent tooth that irrupts (irruption) when the appropriate period of *biological maturity* of the intraphysical consciousness' soma arrives.

Parabiology. The same occurs with the soma that is gradually replaced by the psychosoma when the natural time of the soma's *parabiological evolution* (somatics and psychosomatics) arrives.

Deciduous. Thus we can conclude that the soma is, to a certain degree, deciduous or susceptible to being eliminated, either in whole or in part, in a transitory or more permanent manner, by the psychosoma (first desoma) and even manifestation in the intraphysical dimension without the soma (the phenomenon of the *ungenerated* or *agénères*).

Scope. The broad scope of the explanation of the theory of irruption of the psychosoma in the human dimension comes in contact with multiple areas of intraphysical life and conscientiology. The following are 5 examples:

1. **Research.** Research performed on bioluminescence, cellular regeneration, general bioethics and genetic engineering will eventually enable the tangibility or intraphysical manifestation of the psychosoma's properties in this intraphysical dimension through the soma in a direct fashion.

2. **Bioluminescence.** Bioluminescence applied to the human body will approximate the *luminosity* of the psychosoma.

3. **Regeneration.** Cellular regeneration of the soma will permit this vehicle to approximate the property of *transfiguration* of the psychosoma.

4. **UFOlogy.** If these events occur they will explain a series of theories on controversial UFOlogical phenomena and will have great influence on interplanetary travel and the terrestrial life of intraphysical consciousnesses on other planets in the inevitable and future colonization of celestial bodies close to earth.

5. **Energies.** The theory of the *abundance of consciential energies* of current terrestrial reality already paves the way for the establishment of the foundations for the more ample irruption of the psychosoma in intraphysical life. This is currently occurring due to demographic explosion, an increase in the number of mini-connections of energetic flow or holochakral links in somas, establishing the connection of the psychosoma, which allows the extraphysical consciousness to temporarily anchor itself in dense matter and live as an intraphysical consciousness in this human dimension.

Cells. The histological factor or cellular alterations – matter vivified by consciential energies – represent the most relevant variables in these occurrences.

Explanations. This advanced theory of irruption of the psychosoma – presented here in order to be debated, invalidated and refuted – rationally explains countless aspects of consciential phenomena within paraphenomenology (conscientiology) that are still obscure. The following 27, selected from many others, are examples:

1. Auric coupling between intraphysical consciousnesses (holochakrology).
2. Exteriorization of motricity.
3. Extraphysical elongation of the soma (holosomatics).
4. False arrival (intraphysicology).
5. Human parateleportation.
6. Intersciential possession (conscientiotherapy).
7. Internal and external autoscopy (paraphysiology).
8. Intraconsciential (animic) and parapsychic (per se) energetic signage.
9. Isolated cases of disappearance of persons or somas (desomatics, self-desoma).
10. Macrosoma (macrosomatics).
11. Materialization or projective ectoplasmy (macro-PK).
12. Para-anesthesia.
13. Para-asepsis.
14. Paracicatrization.
15. Parahemostasis.
16. Parapsychic diagnostics (conscientiotherapy).
17. Pararegeneration.
18. Parasurgery.
19. Physical bilocation of the intraphysical consciousness (projectiology).
20. Physical dematerialization (paraphenomenology).
21. Projective heteroscopy.
22. Semimaterialization.
23. Sympathetic assimilation of consciential energies (holochakrology).
24. The anonymity of *Homo sapiens serenissimus* (evolutiology, serenology).
25. The apparition of the projected intraphysical consciousness to other intraphysical consciousnesses (paraphenomenology).
26. Traveling clairvoyance (projectiology).
27. Waking discoincidence (holochakrology).

Accident. A physical accident (pathology) that involves the brain (cranial fracture) can trigger the appearance (paraphysiology) of energetic and parapsychic signage, based on the auditory mechanisms, for example.

Break. In this case, it is as though the fracture *had broken* the rigidity and integrity of the structure of the holosomatic connection between the vehicles of manifestation.

Crack. Energetic signage serves as an *artificial crack* or *wedge* that remains open between the existential dimensions of the intraphysical consciousness.

Anticipation. Such an accident paradoxically anticipates the evolved condition of irruption of the psychosoma through the soma.

Fiction. In science fiction movies, the moment when the *extraterrestrial* personality erupts from the throat of the terrestrial personality is a crude analogy to the irruption of the psychosoma through the soma.

Macrosomatics. Intraphysical consciousnesses who have a macrosoma would be the most predisposed to irruption of the psychosoma.

131. THE SOMA AND CONSCIENTIAL PRIORITIZATION

Definition. Consciential prioritization: placing preference or evolutionary option in first place, exercised according to the consciousness' level of maturity regarding free will, in the realization of its personal rights.

Synonymy: evolutionary discernment; maturity of free will; evolutionary option.

Holosoma. Consciential prioritization becomes important and basic in the approaches of projectiology which, above all, prioritizes the holosoma, or the set of vehicles of manifestation of the consciousness.

Brain. The soma, or the human body is, above all, the brain.

Soma. All implements of the human body, besides the brain, exist due to and in order to serve as instruments which are dependent upon the brain or the intraphysical seat of the consciousness (extraphysical consciousness or intraphysical consciousness).

Projectiology. The projectiological perspective respects the choices of others or, in other words, the free will of others. However, projectiology cannot prioritize its research based on those intraphysical consciousnesses who are impassioned and adventurous, still lost and centralized in the organic segments and secondary appendices of the soma, the individual's animal body, the most coarse vehicle of the consciousness.

Parabrain. With respect to this primary consciential vehicle – the soma – projectiological objectives are centered in the 2 cerebral hemispheres, which reflect the parabrain in order to prioritize the evolved manifestations of the mentalsoma or the parabody of discernment.

Interests. Extraphysical consciousnesses undergo resoma and are concerned with interests, objectives and the execution of different existential programs. Interests hypermotivate and determine priorities.

Rights. Each person has his/her personal right to do what he/she wishes with his/her physical body. Some individuals become regrettably lost in their prioritizations regarding the soma.

Psychosoma. When someone constantly prioritizes his/her choices based upon the emotional parabody – the psychosoma – he/she inevitably thereby remains at the level of subhuman animals.

Heart. Legions of intraphysical consciousnesses dislocate the vital center of organic existence – the heart – to other secondary components of the human body.

Immaturities. There are myriad examples of less intelligent consciential interests or consciential prioritizations that are faulty, insensitive, immature and demonstrate evolutionary inexperience.

Realities. Instead of placing all *human realities* in the service of the consciousness, or its imperishable *intraconsciential reality,* some individuals place the consciousness in the service of all *other secondary realities,* emphasizing the frame of the painting and not its message. The following are 5 of these immaturities.

Wheel. It is common knowledge that the wheel and the automobile were invented merely as an extension of the legs, in order to accelerate the locomotion of humans by utilizing the brain and thereby allowing a more rapid and efficient physical dislocation from one place to another.

Feet. However, there are those who throw their entire intraphysical life away or, in other words, risk and waste their entire human body in a primitive manner, only prioritizing the feet, or essentially living with and for the legs.

1. **Podalic.** We thus encounter *podalic consciousnesses* or cheetah-consciousnesses.

Cheetah. It is common knowledge that the cheetah *(Acinonyx jubatus),* with a large body and a *small head,* is the fastest land animal on the face of the earth. It can reach incredible speeds of up to 69.6 mi/hr or 102 ft/sec (112 km/hr or 31.11 m/s). The following are some examples of podalic consciousnesses: the marathon runner with a fixed idea (monoideism); and the most glaring example of all, the motorcyclist.

Motorcyclist. The motorcyclist places his/her entire human life at risk when riding a powerful machine. It is common knowledge that the motorcycle was created, manufactured and is irremediably maintained in *critically dangerous conditions* in the likewise highly unsafe intense urban transit of the megacity, metropolis or megalopolis. This temerity, even when superficially rationalized, or when employing all available ego defense mechanisms, clearly evidences an unconscious, subconsciously inserted, or even conscious suicidal tendency which is characteristic of consciential immaturity.

Reconciliation. Many people die prematurely in motorcycle accidents, therefore making it practically impossible to rationally introduce and include the motorcycle within the context of consciential maturity, or to reconcile the condition of the motorcyclist or even the passenger within the context of multidimensional self-awareness, which is considered to be the greatest objective of projectiology.

Motorcycle. A 400 cc motorcycle, when at rest, weighs 308 lbs. (140 kg). At a speed of 100 mph (160 kph), or 146 fps (44.4 mps), including the motorcyclist's weight of 154 lbs. (70 kg), resulting in a total weight of 462 lbs. (210 kg), this all reduces – based upon sophisticated equations – to only 2.2 lbs. (1 kg.). Under these conditions, a simple stone on the road with a 1 1/8" (3 cm) diameter is capable of destabilizing the *motorcycle-motorcyclist set.*

Mathematics. In current intraphysical society, the interests of industry, commerce, the economy, sports, leisure, transportation, transport and others, including the omnipresent exploitation of youth, make it impracticable to nurture any hope for a substantial alteration in the framework of this mathematical context of consciential immaturity of the motorcyclist-motorcycle, human-machine set.

Claws. There are also those who throw away their intraphysical life or, in other words, risk and waste their entire human body in a primitive manner, only prioritizing their magnesium-covered fingers and toes. With human life at the tip of their fingers, now transformed into claws, they scale artificial and natural structures. In these highly critical conditions, the slightest mistake results in the climber's human body falling and being smashed on the ground, the asphalt or the concrete below.

2. **Digital.** In this way we come across *digital consciousnesses,* the modern spider-men and spider-women, or spider-consciousnesses.

Madness. These individuals bordering on stark madness by scaling with their bare hands – a radical suicide-sport generated by mountain climbing – challenge precipices with their hands, without ropes or spikes, hanging at altitudes of 328' (100 m), for example, from cliffs, elevated walls of rock and/ or brick, without any equipment, applying only magnesium powder to their hands to give them greater adhesion and sensitivity, securing themselves using the holes and fissures of rocks and constructions.

Paradox. There is an impressive innate paradox in this context of spider-persons which is detected through two observations regarding the rationally incontestable facts:

A. **Confidence.** On the positive side, the extreme confidence of the consciousness in the *sophisticated machine,* the human body.

B. **Abuse.** On the negative side, the abuse and unconcern regarding the utilization of this *perishable instrument,* the selfsame human body.

3. **Gastric.** There are also *gastric consciousnesses:* obese gastronomes who prioritize dilation of the *stomach* and die prematurely from overeating.

4. **Muscular.** There are also *muscular consciousnesses*: male athletes and, more recently, female athletes who prioritize (muscular) hypertrophy of the *biceps* through bodybuilding (a generalized fad nowadays) or weightlifting (halterophilia), overloading the heart and prematurely deactivating the soma.

5. **Sexual.** Finally, *sexual consciousnesses* should also be borne in mind: those women and, more recently, men who prioritize the sexual organs by performing the so-called *oldest profession,* prostitution.

Consciousness. Note here that the consciousness has no sex.

Self-critique. Each intraphysical consciousness has his/her essential interest. What is most important for us, beyond heterocritique, is self-critique.

Questions. In light of the above, it is always worthwhile and indicative of intelligence to ask ourselves the following 3 questions: What is my predominant fundamental interest? What has my maximal consciential prioritization been? Do I live a life that is centered in my consciousness through the use of the brain or do I still vegetate through my organic, animal or subhuman components?

Projectiological Bibliography: Formiga (539, p. 49).
Specific Bibliography:
1. **O' Callaghan, Karen;** *Our Amazing World: Fascinating Facts;* 158 pp.; illus.; alph.; 28 cm x 21.5 cm; hb.; England; Brimax Books; 1986; p.13.

132. CHAKRAS

Definition. Chakras: nuclei or limiting fields of energy that basically constitute the holochakra – the vehicle of energy inside the human body – which connects this body with the psychosoma, serving as connection points through which force flows from one vehicle of the consciousness to the other (see fig. 132, p. 1,128).

Synonymy: biochemical centers; bioenergetic centers; chakral organs; circles of energy; cones of energy; energetic channels; energetic disks; energetic knots; energetic macrovortices; energetic nuclei; energy centers; extraphysical frequency accelerators; force centers; fulcrums of force; *khorlos;* lotus; microcosmic centers; *padmas;* sensory centers; vital centers; vital doorways; vital transducers; vortices of energy; wheels.

Relationships. Based upon rational inferences, it is presumed that there are at least 3 categories of particular and logical relationships between certain chakras and other vehicles of manifestation of the consciousness, although the dynamics of these particular relationships are still very obscure in our current research:

1. **Mentalsoma.** The (encephalic) coronochakra has a particular relationship with the mentalsoma (parabody of discernment) with respect to the transmission of ideas.

2. **Psychosoma.** The (thoracic) cardiochakra has a particular relationship with the psychosoma (emotional parabody) with respect to the emotional world of the intraphysical consciousness.

3. **Holochakra.** The (vegetative) splenochakra has a particular relationship with the holochakra (energetic parabody) in the coexistence of the ego with energies, in any environment.

Bipolarity. In the analysis of bipolarity patterns, it is worth noting that the energetic communications between the vehicles of manifestation of the consciousness present 3 objective peculiarities with regard to the chakras and the left side of the human body, suggesting that the left side binds the extraphysical consciousness more firmly in the intraphysical dimension:

1. **Hemisphere.** The brain (coronochakra: mentalsoma) presents 2 cerebral hemispheres, given that the left hemisphere seems to predominate in the more human manifestations of the intraphysical consciousness (ideas). There must be an intrinsic relationship between the mentalsoma and the nurturing of ideas.

2. **Heart.** The heart (cardiochakra: psychosoma) is located in the mediastinum – between the 2 lungs – somewhat to the left in the thoracic or cardiorespiratory cavity (oxygen). There must be an intrinsic relationship between emotions and oxygen.

3. **Spleen.** The spleen (splenochakra: holochakra) is located to the left in the abdominal or vegetative (food) area. There must be an intrinsic relationship between consciential energy and food.

Nature. Based on the fact that most people are dextral (right-handed), it is inferred that the natural orientation holds the extraphysical consciousness more to the left, with two objectives, among others:

1. **Rearguard.** The left hemisphere, the heart and the spleen, in a *defensive* rearguard.

2. **Vanguard.** The consciousness communicates with the human dimension to the right, the front line of *attack,* even with the right hand and arm, through decussation of the pyramidal tract or the crossing of cerebral functions.

Bibliografia: ADGMT (03, p. 55), Ajaya (08, p. 238), Babajiananda (65, p. 44), Blavatsky (153, p. 133), Cavendish (266, p. 64), Coquet (301, p. 33), Coxhead (312, p. 204), David-Nell (368, p. 263), Day (376, p. 27), Digest (401, p. 350), Drury (414, p. 80), Gaynor (577, p. 34), Gomes (612, p. 188), Gooch (617, p. 213), Guéret (659, p. 65), Hope (756, p. 53), Karagulla (814, p. 123), Leadbeater (897, p. 71), Maes (983, p. 169), Martin (1003, p. 32), Meek (1028, p. 248), Meurois-Givaudin (1039, p. 119), Mitchell (1058, p. 688), Motoyama (1098, p. 130), Pastorino (1206, p. 151), Pensamento (1224, p. 28), Powell (1280, p. 35), Prieur (1289, p. 217), Raja-Aari (1345, p. 70), Rogo (1444, p. 70), Saher (1493, p. 157), Scott (1529, p. 196), Tondriau (1690, p. 208), Vieira (1762, p. 146), Walker (1781, p. 39), Wang (1794, p. 148), Wedeck (1807, p. 78), White (1831, p. 30), Yogananda (1894, p. 158), Zaniah (1899, p. 138).

133. PARA-ANATOMY OF THE CHAKRAS

Characteristics. Among the characteristics of the para-anatomy of the major chakras, at least the following 6 variables can be singled out:

1. The sexochakra, splenochakra and umbilicochakra force centers of the human-animal.
2. The cardiochakra, laryngochakra, frontochakra and coronochakra force centers of the human-consciousness.
3. The formats of the force centers.
4. The colorations.
5. The reverberances.
6. The intensities of consciential energy.

Formats. The force centers are similar to 4 objects:

1. **Plates.** The depressions similar to small plates or vortices.
2. **Radar.** The concave radar hemispheres, or rose petals.
3. **Water.** The vortices that water forms when a sink is unstoppered at its bottom. The whirlpool that appears – with its mouth in the upper area of the liquid (surface) and the apex that is coincident with the drain opening – produces an image very similar to the vortices or chakras.
4. **Propeller.** The image that is approximately 8" (20 cm) in diameter made by large airplane propellers when rotating at high speed.

Vortex. Seen from the front, for example, the chakra has a substantially circular form and its spiral rotation produces certain radiations. A cross section view shows that each chakra or vortex is a depression in the holochakra. The opening is in the most external part and the apex of the cone is practically at skin level. The shaft of the vortex, which is an extraphysical extension, terminates at some point close to the human organism.

Areas. The chakras also present spirals or *intravortical nervures* and, although these are located in certain specific areas or organs of the human body, they are not identical to these areas.

Diameter. In the ordinary individual, each major chakra appears where the nervous tissue is more concentrated. These chakras have a diameter of ¾" to 1¼" (2 to 3 cm) and a weak luminosity.

Evolution. The forms and luminous characteristics of the energy centers gradually grow along with the personal evolution or extraphysical improvement of the intraphysical consciousness.

Use. The more evolved the consciousness, the more it perceives and uses the functions of the chakras intelligently.

Types. The chakras can be classified into 4 types according to their size, expression and function: great, large, medium and small.

Vigor. In every intraphysical consciousness certain chakras can be more vigorous than others.

Knots. Besides being mental pictures of the *chakral knots* or energetic fulcrums that manifest in the extraphysical-body-dimension (extraphysicality) to the human-body-dimension (intraphysicality), the subtle force centers have been seen from different perspectives according to different metaphysical traditions, including the following 7:

1. The energies of the Tantra.
2. The hierarchies of the Neo-Confucians.
3. The *keni-kou* intervals of the Taoists.
4. The *kosas* of the Vedanta.
5. The *sefirot* of the Cabala.
6. The transmutation series of the alchemists.
7. The *vijnanas* of the Yogacara.

Gradation. All these manifestations, in one way or another, obey the vibratory gradation of the human personality's energetic vortices, derived from his/her consciousness.

Total. It is estimated that there are approximately 88,000 (conventional calculation) chakras in each intraphysical consciousness, but only 30 are considered sufficiently important to receive a name.

Analysis. The classical analysis provided here addresses the 7 major or great chakras:

1. Coronochakra.
2. Frontochakra.
3. Laryngochakra.
4. Cardiochakra.
5. Umbilicochakra.
6. Splenochakra.
7. Sexochakra.

Buddhism. Tibetan Buddhism recognizes only 5 main chakras, combining the first with the second and the sixth with the seventh.

1. **Sexochakra.** The first chakra – root, radical, fundamental center, sexochakra, genesic, *muladhara* or anchor of the consciousness – is located outside, in the area of the perineum, between the sacrum and the genital organs. It points downward and is associated with the four bones of the coccyx.

Flower. The sexochakra has a starlike or triangular format. It has a reddish color, is compared with a four-petaled flower, is the seat of the *kundalini*, serpentine fire, igneous power or the brute consciential energy in men (androchakra or androsex) and, evidently, in women (gynochakra or gynosex).

Geoenergies. The sexochakra initiates its action receiving geoenergies through the soles of the feet *(pre-kundalini)* and the legs.

Instincts. The sexochakra has a close relationship with the human body, the cellular systems, the so-called *instincts*, animality, sexuality, geoenergies (telluric energies), *kundalini*, the organs and genesic glands, and the organic immaturity of the soma.

Activation. All other chakras are activated by the basic chakra because it acts like a *bipolar key*, feeding the other chakras.

Passions. In the psychosphere of the young intraphysical consciousness, in which the sexochakra predominates, the energies create an emotional holothosene of intense pluridimensional involvement. This can frequently end up predisposing and provoking violent amorous passions. In these complex occurrences, there is a direct relationship between the mentalsoma, the psychosoma, the sexochakra, the cardiochakra and the person's physical form (soma, appearance).

Intraphysical consciousness. Most of these cases of violent amorous passions, or various kinds of tragic emotional adventures experienced by youths, is centered in the young woman who heightens the passion in a man, or in various men simultaneously, as well as kindred intraphysical and extraphysical intelligences.

Separation. There is a fine line, within those egos involved, between a healthy condition and psychopathology, pure romantic love and morbid hatred, the intraphysical consciousness-consciousness and the intraphysical consciousness-animal.

2. **Umbilicochakra.** The second chakra – umbilicochakra, *manipura* – is located slightly above the navel and is associated with the fifth lumbar vertebra.

Green. The umbilicochakra generally presents a greenish color.

Sympathetic. It is related to the solar plexus, as it is the extraphysical counterpart of the sympathetic nervous system.

Abdominal brain. It is also called the *archeus-director*, belly-brain, abdominal brain, moral-heart-of-the-entrails or the hub-of-the-soul.

3. **Splenochakra.** The third chakra – splenochakra, *swadhistana* – situated over the area of the spleen, selects and distributes the vitalizing energies throughout the organs of the human body.

Projection. Through the natural vivification that it provides, the splenochakra enables the intraphysical consciousness to lucidly project (takeoff) from the human body in the psychosoma.

4. **Cardiochakra.** The fourth chakra – cardiochakra, thoracic, *anahata* – having a yellowish color, vitalizes the heart and lungs. It is an influential agent in the human personality's emotivity. The cardiochakra has a close relationship with the psychosoma, emotionalism, romanticism, adult infantilism (Peter Pan syndrome), the thymus, psychological immaturity and artistic tendencies.

5. **Laryngochakra.** The fifth chakra – laryngochakra, cervical chakra, *vishuda* – is located close to the area where the spinal column meets the medulla oblongata.

Communication. Being the intermediary between the organic manifestations of the vegetative area and mental manifestations, the laryngochakra is especially active in the consciousness' communication, being the controller of the masses.

6. **Frontochakra.** The sixth chakra – frontochakra, glabellar, pineal, *ajna,* third eye, third sight, mental eye, "Christ's eye" or the headlight of the forehead – is located between the eyebrows, projecting itself outward from the center of the forehead.

Clairvoyance. The frontochakra displays a close relationship with clairvoyance in all its forms and manifestations.

Pulsation. Those who, while in the ordinary, physical waking state, frequently feel the frontal chakra vibrating, pulsating or throbbing, do so because the *kundalini* and the other chakras, with the exception of the resplendent coronal chakra, have already been fully awakened for a long time. This is a common occurrence among developed sensitives of all types of manifestations or phenomenological modalities of parapsychism.

Power. For this reason, the frontochakra is a center of directive power through which *revelation* occurs – interdimensional communication or the final bastion of reason and analysis in the microcosm of the human personality or the microuniverse of the intraphysical consciousness.

7. **Coronal.** The seventh chakra – coronochakra, megachakra or *sahasrara* – the most important chakra, expands upward from the top of the cranium or the sinciput, in the area of the anterior fontanel or bregma.

Crown. Turned upward like a crown, the coronochakra allows the expansion of the consciousness, frees the mentalsoma from the parabrain of the psychosoma, constitutes the luminous aureole or the upper part of the human aura, as well as the *cap full of nodules,* as seen in oriental engravings, also called the *lotus of one thousand petals.*

Sentiments. The coronochakra has a close relationship with the mentalsoma, the pineal gland, rationality, the more elevated sentiments, serenity, consciential balance, and organic, psychological and consciential maturity (holomaturity of the intraphysical consciousness).

Transcendence. In fact, the coronochakra is not actually a chakra like the others, because it is encountered beyond the mind or, in other words, it transcends the condition of the human consciousness encased in the braincase, in the ordinary, physical waking state.

Awakening. Awakening of the coronochakra occurs as a result of the work of gradual energetic awakening performed in the other less important chakras, especially in the frontochakra.

Others. The chakras can also be extraphysically sensed and seen in the palms of the hands, the articulation of the cubitus (formerly the *elbows*), shoulders, knees, pelvis and in the soles of the feet.

Circles. The medium-sized vortices form circles around the main vortex, acting like satellites. The small vortices, being more numerous, are located on the periphery of the holochakra and are, in turn, natural satellites of the medium-sized chakras.

Evidence. Up until now, the evidence for the existence of chakras, as with the phenomenon of lucid consciential projection, remains almost entirely subjective, individual and experiential.

Pulsations. In spite of all the anatomy and physiology studies that the author has attended at accredited universities, he has not been able to explain the *very physical* pulsations and movements in his human body through the research performed in the area of biological science or medical science. One example of this is the pulsations and movements that occur in the region of the forehead (glabellar area) corresponding to the frontochakra. They are sometimes involuntary, unexpected and very intense, even occurring in the full ordinary, physical waking state.

Vehicle. This individual, tangible fact, which was sensed and then repeated day after day, month after month, year after year, can only be attributed to another vehicle of manifestation of the consciousness.

Forehead. There are no organs or anatomophysiological conditions in this organic area – the forehead – that justify the abovementioned ostensive sensations or manifestations. They occur in a fully conscious manner while in the ordinary, physical waking state with the eyes open during the day. Sophisms, arguments, abstruse scientific or scientistic explanations and useless expenditures of time are all pointless.

Acupuncture. This fact exists and can be felt or experienced by anyone who so desires. All that is required is to perform the basic mobilization of consciential energies (bioenergies), or begin a more in-depth study of traditional Chinese medicine or acupuncture, its meridians, points and channels of energy *(nadis)*.

Bibliography: Bardon (80, p. 43), Dychtwald (444, p. 94), Guéret (659, p. 65), Leadbeater (897, p. 71), Powell (1280, p. 32), Walker (1782, p. 315), White (1831, p. 121).

134. PARAPHYSIOLOGY OF THE CHAKRAS

Transformers. The chakras capture, separate and distribute the immanent energies that exist in the physical-extraphysical universe, transforming them into consciential energies. In other words, they maintain energetic transferences throughout the totality of the human being or the exchanges between his/her biopsychic presence and the external energies.

Accelerators. The chakras generally act as accelerators of the vibratory frequency of the human body (soma), together with the holochakra which unites the human body with the psychosoma through the silver cord.

Characteristics. Among the characteristics of the paraphysiology of the chakras, the following 8 variables can be singled out:

1. **Function.** The presumed function of each energy center.
2. **Colors.** The varied colors of each chakra according to its performance.
3. **Repercussions.** The regional physical repercussions and the energy centers.
4. **Awakening.** The consequences of the awakening of the coronochakra.
5. **Sexosomatics.** The sexochakra and the *kundalini*.
6. **Cosmoconsciousness.** The coronochakra and samadhi.
7. **Brain.** The coronochakra and the *empty brain* condition.
8. **Sensations.** The physical and extraphysical sensations of the frontochakra.

Interrelationship. One of the most important subjects, in this particular, is the obscure interrelationship between the force centers, especially the relationship of the coronochakra with the epiphysis (pineal gland), the coronochakra with the medulla oblongata, the coronochakra with the nodules of the right and left auricular pavilions (tragi), the frontochakra with the tragi, and the relationships of the chakras with the human body, the holochakra and the psychosoma.

Coronochakra. The reactivation of the coronochakra provides the intraphysical consciousness with extraphysical self-awareness or, in other words, lucid projections during natural sleep. The frontochakra predisposes the reactivation of the coronochakra and the energetic manifestations in the center of the encephalon and the pineal gland.

Relationships. The sexochakra is directly related to sexual excitability or the libido, the 2 orgasms of the man, the penile and the anal; and the 3 orgasms of the woman, the vaginal, the clitoral and the anal.

Orgasms. The intensification, circulation and channeling of the energies of the sexochakra, passing through the other force centers, promoting the vibrational state and expansion of the consciousness, provides the following two categories of orgasm:

1. **Anthropomorphistic.** The *anthropomorphistic orgasm,* or the one occurring throughout the human body by way of the psychosoma.

2. **Holo-orgasm.** The *cosmic orgasm* (holo-orgasm), characteristic of greater samadhi, which transcends sex or all earthly sensations and planetary emotions. It occurs by way of the mentalsoma, ranging from the initial efforts of the human-animal to the sublimation of the human-consciousness.

Plexuses. The chakras have a close relationship with the health or illness of the social being (intraphysical consciousness). In this sense, it is customary to relate each chakra with certain glands that are anatomically close to its base, as well as with nervous plexuses. The following are 6 examples:

1. **Carotid.** The carotid plexus (frontal chakra or frontochakra).
2. **Pharyngeal.** The pharyngeal plexus (laryngeal chakra or laryngochakra).
3. **Cardiac.** The pulmonary and cardiac plexuses (cardiac chakra or cardiochakra).
4. **Splenic.** The splenic plexus (splenic chakra or splenochakra).
5. **Solar.** The solar plexus (umbilical chakra or umbilicochakra).
6. **Pelvic.** The pelvic and coccygeal plexuses (radical chakra or sexochakra).

Sexosoma. There are remarkable differences between men (androsoma) and women (gynosoma) with regard to the paraphysiology of the chakras, due to the secondary sexual characteristics. The following 2 aspects serve as examples:

1. **Androsoma.** The laryngochakra of the man operates more intensely in the individual with a full beard.

2. **Gynosoma.** The cardiochakra, in turn, acts particularly more vigorously in the lactating woman and, generally, in the woman with normal mammae *(breasts).*

Frontochakra. It is interesting to note the various uses of the area of the frontochakra, such as the following 4 variables:

1. **Massages.** Massages, as used by some lucid projectors in order to project from the human body with lucidity.

2. **Pressure.** Digital pressure, as used by other lucid projectors in order to recall the recently completed consciential projection.

3. **Hypnosis.** Also with the pressure of a finger, as used by hypnotists or magnetizers (as they were called) since the nineteenth century, in order to make the hypnotized person reproduce information provided in previous hypnotic experiments, even being called "somnambulistic memory points" by them, in this case.

4. **Signal.** In mystical rituals and practices, such as the commonplace "sign of the cross" that attempts to simultaneously stimulate the activation of 3 chakras: the cardiochakra, the frontochakra and the laryngochakra, in that order.

Cerebellum. It is presumed that the *kundalini,* or the energy of the sexochakra, is activated by the functions of the human cerebellum. There is still no scientific proof to support this hypothesis.

Bibliography: Gomes (617, p. 60), Gooch (617, p. 213), Miranda (1050, p. 137), Powell (1279, p. 240), Vieira (1762, p. 146).

135. PARAPATHOLOGY OF THE HOLOCHAKRA AND VAMPIRISM

Definition. Bioenergetic vampire: the intraphysical being whose consciential energies are imbalanced and who is continually parasitic toward others, generally in an unconscious manner.

Synonymy: bioenergetic drain; *bioenergetic thief;* carrier of the *bioenergetic exhaustion syndrome;* consciential black hole; consciential energy parasite; holochakral exhauster.

Parapathology. The bioenergetic vampire – an intraphysical consciousness, for example – can either live with no morbid extraphysical influence, such as solitary human drainage, or can be aided and worsened in his/her imbalances and excessive energetic absorptions by ill or energivorous extraphysical consciousnesses.

Holochakra. This condition of human vampirism is restricted to the parapathology of the holochakra or the energetic parabody and is better understood through projectiotherapy or conscientiotherapy.

Characteristic. The fundamental characteristic of the bioenergetic vampire is an insatiable or uninterrupted absorption of consciential energy, with a constant anxiety for an unattained bioenergetic replenishment, satiation or compensation, in an attempt to fill a *bottomless pit* in his/her disturbed, imbalanced or blocked chakras which are operating chaotically.

Causes. The most common cause of installation of bioenergetic vampirism is bioenergetic imbalance of an affective nature, with an egotistical foundation. One example of this is the person who lives in a constant state of sexual deprivation.

Effects. The basic effects of the vampire's bioenergetic imbalance begin with his/her dependence upon family members. At a more advanced stage, there is a pathological or intense irruption of the energies of the sexochakra *(kundalini).*

Awareness. The vampire may or may not be aware of the parapathological conditions of his/her holochakra.

Ignorance. He/she does not understand why other persons do not enjoy his/her company, until discovering and endeavoring to balance him/herself without jeopardizing others.

Repulsion. However, he/she instills an instinctive repulsion in others, including pets, in certain cases. This is due to his/her surreptitious, undermining, absorbing and exhausting activity with regard to the consciential energy of others.

Hand. In a certain phase, while energetically imbalanced, the intraphysical vampire is constantly placing his/her more defensive hand – the right or left hand, depending on whether he/she is left-handed or right-handed – over the stomach, the heart, the abdomen or the throat, swallowing from time to time, as though attempting to use the palm of the hand to stop the unrestrained exit of energies from his/her umbilicochakra, cardiochakra or laryngochakra, to no avail. Well-defined parasympathetic disturbances are established at this point.

Affectivity. While still in adolescence, in the beginning of the adult phase, the intraphysical consciousness obviously does not encounter an adequate or permanent affective partner with whom to form an evolutionary duo. This is because his/her friends break off the friendship without explanation, as they themselves do not understand why they are uncomfortable in his/her presence.

Antipathy. The ordinary social being, in a process of consciential robotization, is generally parapsychically undeveloped and unable to readily identify why they do not find the vampire to be agreeable.

Chemical. Another individual, or victim of the vampire, considers chemical or allergic explanations which, in this case, prove insufficient.

Thief. Only the sensitives who are more advanced and lucid with regard to bioenergetic control are able to identify the vampire as an *energetic thief,* a fulcrum of vital exhaustion, a living, mobile energetic drain.

Syndrome. The following fields are mere palliatives in these cases of bioenergetic drainage: medicine in general, limited to the human body and the 5 basic senses; psychiatry in particular;

psychology in general; psychoanalysis in particular; ordinary psychotherapy; psychosomatics; homeopathy; and even classic acupuncture. They do not achieve lasting results in the remission of the *holochakral exhaustion syndrome.*

Therapy. The therapy has to be performed in the holochakra, but stemming from the mentalsoma and directed toward a *self*-cure and not a *hetero*cure. The more aware the intraphysical consciousness becomes of his/her disturbance, the easier it will be to have a remission of the parapathological process.

Tumult. The bioenergetic exhaustion that the vampire provokes around him/herself creates constant tumult. When it is unconscious, the individual – who is often a youth with irreproachable looks and full of youthful vigor – does not understand why he/she becomes a *group repellent* and everyone quickly and quietly leaves, in a *para-instinctive* reaction.

Reasons. The intraphysical consciousness who is a victim of bioenergetic exhaustion looks for physical reasons, such as bad breath, body odor, foot odor or other similar causes. He/she consults a doctor and often takes prescription medication, goes on intense diets and even blames his/her liver, without hitting upon the true cause which lies in his/her holochakra.

Isolation. The bioenergetic vampire can end up in a regrettable state of social, physical, affective and even intellectual isolation that is imposed due to his/her characteristic of uninterrupted absorption, or *unfriendly and pathological* assimilation, without compensatory donation of consciential energies, through his/her *evil eye* (popular reaction) or his/her condition of a *killjoy.*

Retention. The bioenergetic vampire is not able to retain consciential energy, which is impermanent in his/her psychosphere, for any length of time. He/she feels comfortable for a few moments and seems to be balanced and replenished. However, he/she returns to the previous condition of exhaustion in a matter of minutes or hours.

Waste. The worst part of all is that this bioenergetic dissipation is generally not well-utilized. It becomes a waste, is squandered unconsciously or is even absorbed by constant or occasional extraphysical intruders.

Intruders. It is nevertheless worth noting that there are intraphysical vampires who even provoke repulsion in pets and – stranger still – in ill extraphysical consciousnesses or intruders that are weaker than the vampire. This is because they are unable to avoid or overcome the action of exhaustion or to take advantage of the condition that they suffer when in the presence of this human drain, who is an extremely powerful living *black hole* that attracts and drains all nearby energetic sources.

Animal. There are parapathological cases that have their beginning with intrusive influence and a single intrusive extraphysical consciousness. Then, after bioenergetic imbalance is installed, the intruder consciously or unconsciously retreats from the intrusion victim, like an animal that instinctively flees from a poisonous plant or a venomous being, leaving him/her to fend for him/herself. The vampire thus continues to stir up the *entropic bioenergetic dust* wherever he/she goes.

Relationship. The bioenergetic vampire never remains unnoticed. He/she attracts attention, even when silent, in a type of unspoken notoriety wherever he/she goes, like an inexplicable but stigmatizing repellant. This can create difficulties in relating with family members, classmates, workmates and, evidently, with people in general.

Self-awareness. The only efficient recourse for the lasting bioenergetic counterbalancing of the vampiric state is the self-awareness obtained and put into action regarding the problem by the interested person him/herself. This individual, now maintaining bioenergetic self-balance, no longer needs the consciential energy of others. He/she ceases the regrettable process of uncontrollable absorption and thereby ceases to play the sad role of a bioenergetic drainer. His/her presence is no longer disgraceful or instinctively repulsive and the vampire can once again coexist normally with other beings.

Orientation. The parapsychic being or projectiotherapist who discovers and identifies someone as a bioenergetic vampire, generally through sympathetic assimilation, sensing the symptoms and signals that disturb the other person, should employ the maximum possible conscientiological orientation in the act of helping and assisting that individual.

Address. The parapsychic being needs to observe the relative severity of the vampirism process, the degree of psychic and parapsychic understanding of the personality in question, the time, location and circumstances in which to expose the problem, and the best way to verbally address the issue.

Self-analysis. This is of vital importance because the person can see and feel him/herself portrayed in such a manner, hemmed in by so many precise details in a naked self-analysis, that he/she ends up becoming desperate if not well-prepared beforehand.

Shock. In this case, the shock of becoming aware of the truth can worsen the illness instead of curing it. The patient can undergo desoma due to an attempted cure.

Remission. The basic solution for remission of the condition of bioenergetic vampirism is for that person to refrain from egoism, personal problems, and to think altruistically of others, without hidden agendas, maintaining a regular affective life. He/she needs to help others, overcoming his/her conditions without asking or looking for anything else for him/herself, dedicating him/herself to the assistance of others, without any ifs ands or buts, self-corruptions or pathothosenes, demands or restrictions.

Altruism. Pure and applied solidary assistential altruism is the only real and definitive resource for stopping conscious and unconscious bioenergetic draining between consciential principles.

Bibliography: Fortune (540, p. 56), Karagulla (814, p. 158), Vieira (1762, p. 58).

136. THEORY OF INTERCHAKRAL RELATIONSHIPS

Definition. Interchakral relationship: the paraphysiological interaction between one chakra and another, or between various major chakras of a single person.

Synonymy: chakral interbonding; chakral interconnection; interchakral interaction.

Interaction. Besides the parapsychic interaction between the organs, organic systems and the major chakras, or force centers – in this case the holochakra – there are relationships between the energies of one chakra and the energies of another chakra, or even various chakras, in the same individual.

Theory. In the theory of chakral relationships, various types of interaction are highlighted between the chakras themselves, as well as between the chakras and the physiology of the human being. The following are 12 examples:

1. Sexochakra-sexuality, or conception (women).
2. Sexochakra-laryngochakra.
3. Umbilicochakra-gestation (women).
4. Cardiochakra-mammae or lactation (women).
5. Cardiochakra-laryngochakra.
6. Laryngochakra-crying (more with regard to children).
7. Laryngochakra-languages (more with regard to adults).
8. Laryngochakra-communicability, beards (men).
9. Laryngochakra-frontochakra.
10. Frontochakra-coronochakra (mentalsomatics).
11. Frontochakra-multidimensionality, or clairvoyance.
12. Frontochakra-psychosoma.

Sexochakra. As an example of complex interchakral relationships, we can see what actually technically occurs regarding the bioenergetic reflexes between the sexochakra – located in the *human-animal* area – and the laryngochakra, located in the *human-consciousness* area.

Effects. The following 8 effects can be singled out as the main causes of bioenergetic relationships between the *kundalinic,* radical or sexochakra (perineum) and the laryngochakra (throat) in the same person:

1. Among the possible manifestations of the libido, or sexual excitability, whether in a man or a woman, is constriction of the throat.

2. The tongue, located between the mouth and the throat in the oral cavity, serves as a spare sexual organ by those men or women who use it preponderantly in sexual intercourse.

3. Anal orgasm can immediately generate hypophonia – a reduction in the tone or timbre of the voice – in both men and women.

4. Multiple anal orgasms can cause the effemination of the man's voice and accentuated femininity in the woman's voice.

5. Bathing the anus with hot water using the jet of the bidet, in the practices of feminine or masculine masturbation, can cause multiple anal orgasms and momentary but immediate alterations in the tone or timbre of the voice in women as well as in men.

6. Bathing the anus with cold water using the jet of the bidet can immediately cause hypophonia in women as well as in men.

7. Bathing the anus with water using the jet of the bidet can temporarily, but immediately, affect the verbal communicability of the man or woman.

8. Fellatio (throat), performed either by a man or a woman, can generate (penile, anal, vaginal, clitoral, simple or multiple) orgasms in the person performing the act.

Predominances. It is worth observing that the intraphysical consciousness suffers the characteristic predominance of the energies of a specific major chakra, according to the evolutionary phase of the his/her human life. We can therefore highlight the initial predominance of the sexochakra upon conception; soon thereafter the umbilicochakra; then the cardiochakra; subsequently the laryngochakra; and, finally, the frontochakra, as illustrated below.

Gestation. Physical or animal human life is consolidated through the umbilicochakra (human-animal) during gestation up until the loss of the umbilical cord upon birth. Logically then, for this reason, gestation is the *first* and most *animal* period of the human being's life or, in other words: his/her arrival in intraphysical life.

Trajectory. The cry of the newborn signals the moment at which the predominance of the umbilicochakra (umbilical cord) is lost. It is also the beginning of the predominance of the laryngochakra in human evolution toward the final predominance of the encephalic chakras, in the ascendant animal-consciousness trajectory, or the sexochakra-coronochakra crescendo.

Cry. The initial animal cry keeps the newly resonant extraphysical consciousness connected to his/her extremely new human body, which is now free, outside the mother's body. The sounds of the cries are directly derived from the energies of the laryngochakra (throat).

Substitute. Crying is the natural, immediate *substitute* for the umbilical cord.

Encephalic. During existence, the human being gravitates or evolves (human-consciousness) toward the predominant use of the energies of the encephalic chakras (coronochakra and frontochakra). From this, other interconnections are born: the medulla oblongata and the silver cord (projection of the consciousness in the psychosoma); the pineal gland and interdimensional exchanges (parapsychism); the parabrain and the golden cord (projection of the consciousness in the mentalsoma).

Cardiochakra. There is a clear correlation between emotions and high risk in specific types of cancer. Emotions affect the hormonal regulation mechanism. The interconnection of the cardiochakra and the woman's mammae (prolactin) is evidenced in breast cancers, when there is a higher risk in women who suffer from chronic solitude (emotions and the cardiochakra), or from social isolation (deprivation of communicability and the laryngochakra). The same does not occur with the socially solitary man.

Imbalance. The laryngochakra-cardiochakra interconnection, or the language-cardiovascular system interconnection, is seen in tests with hypertensive individuals. Language (verbal) is a function which is unique to the human body and the human being. The absence of social contact impairs the human being's health due to the imbalance of the laryngochakra.

Membrane. There is something that can be called a *social membrane*, or a *second skin*, which is constituted through social communicability. A lack of social communicability represents a lack of human solidarity, the main application of human life, or the act of assistentially and conscientially serving others.

Language. The relationships of the human-animal (the 5 basic senses) during his/her life are developed through speech (language) or, in other words, through the energies of the laryngochakra in the human-consciousness area. In human communication we literally project our emotions (cardiochakra) in that which we say (laryngochakra).

Evolution. The relationships of humans, *via laryngochakra,* derived from the accumulation of physical experiences, need to be substituted by clairvoyance (parapsychism), *via the frontochakra,* through the accumulation of physical-extraphysical experiences. Only this *intraparapsychic* evolution allows the individual to guard against chronic solitude, or social isolation, one of the causes of premature death of the human being, thereby expanding his/her circle of interdimensional or multidimensional relationships.

Solitude. The sensation of solitude or isolation affects the human body (soma). The solitary individual feels disconnected from the living universe, especially in relation to nearby social beings. The solitude that is felt – whether it is *heated* or hostile (cardiovascular problems), or *cold* or depressive (neoplasias) – lowers one's resistance to illness, weakening both the cardiovascular and the immune system.

Multidimensional. Solitude is eliminated in the person who coexists, in a self-aware and multidimensional manner, with extraphysical or desomant intraphysical – but living – consciousnesses, besides human beings or subhuman animals.

Projectability. Conclusion: solitude does not exist for those who are aware of the energetic dimension. In other words: the developed clairvoyant will never be alone. Thus, logically, self-aware projectability is the *last* and most *consciential* period of the social being's life, the dignified solution of human life.

Executive. These considerations suggest that the 2 major chakras not highlighted here in the analysis of the predominance of energies – the splenochakra and the coronochakra – perform distinct *executive* functions with regard to the soma and the other chakras. The splenochakra distributes the energies throughout the body in order to keep it healthy, without imbalance. The coronochakra leads the intraphysical consciousness to energetically leave the soma in order to achieve more evolved experiences in other dimensions, in the psychosoma and the mentalsoma.

---

137. LUCID PROJECTION AND THE GOLDEN CORD

Definition. Golden cord: the presumed energetic element that keeps the mentalsoma connected to the parahead or, more precisely, to the parabrain of the psychosoma.

Synonymy: extraphysical remote control; gold cord; intercorporal psychosoma-mentalsoma connection; mental extraphysical passport; quintessential cord.

Intervehicular. The golden cord is the direct, intervehicular connecting element of the intraphysical as well as the extraphysical consciousness. It is situated between the extraphysical dimension per se and the pure mentalsomatic dimension.

Energy. The evidence of the golden cord suggests that the consciousness cannot do without energy, not even to enter (or leave) the mentalsomatic dimension.

Characteristics. Among the characteristics of the golden cord, at least the following 7 variables can be singled out:

1. **Homology.** Homological supposition.
2. **Key.** The key to the mentalsomatic dimension.
3. **Reins.** The reins of the unevolved extraphysical consciousness.
4. **Para-anatomy.** A *para-anatomy* that is still completely unknown.

5. **Paraphysiology.** A *paraphysiology* that is still obscure.
6. **Energies.** Ambivalent energetic conduction, both sending and receiving.
7. **Action.** Action that lacks space-time-form.

Insertion. Based on the fact that the extraphysical consciousness projects itself in the mentalsoma directly from the psychosoma, it is inferred that the golden cord – the *remote control* connection that exists between the psychosoma and the mentalsoma – has its insertion point in the psychosoma.

Departure. Thus, by analogy, the intraphysical consciousness who projects in the isolated mentalsoma leaves directly from the parabrain of the psychosoma and not from the human body.

Consolation. The attentive reader should not aprioristically repudiate the transcendent themes and suppositions of this and the following chapters of this section.

Hypotheses. If the science of our terrestrial civilization has not yet arrived at the point of considering these subjects, which are considered to be excessively surrealistic, prudently considering them to be mere speculative or conjectural hypotheses, it consoles itself with the fact that it will get there someday, just as – it is supposed – the science of many other civilizations on myriads of inhabited planets dispersed throughout the universe has already done.

Exobiology. Exobiology will eventually support many affirmations that are made by projectiology, corroborating the verifications obtained through lucid exoprojections in many places by different human projectors.

Maintenance. Every field needs a maintaining agent. No field remains in space simply for the sake of remaining there.

Supposition. It is presumed that the mentalsoma must have the *unconscious* function of maintaining the existence of its own field through the structures of fixed thoughts (the *tho* of thosene). Might this constitute the golden cord?

Parahead. The parahead is the most important part of the psychosoma.

Integrity. The connection between the golden cord and the parahead or, more precisely, the parabrain, the foundation of the psychosoma, maintains this same psychosoma *intact* or integral. If this were not the case, its extraphysical (semiphysical) structure would come undone.

Bibliography: Vieira (1762, p. 218).

138.   PARA-ANATOMY   OF   THE   GOLDEN   CORD

Observations. The term *para-anatomy* – although it may not seem correct when applied to the connection that keeps the mentalsoma, the *formless* vehicle of the consciousness, bound to the parabrain of the psychosoma – is used here in order to allow a better understanding of new, original material, as there is no other more adequate expression.

Nature. The nature of the golden cord – whether that of the intraphysical consciousness or the extraphysical consciousness – is energetic or, in this case, quintessentialized, and extremely obscure within the current framework of our knowledge and research.

Connections. It is rationally presumed that there are two energetic connections for the golden cord:

1. First connection: directly in the mentalsoma.
2. Second connection: directly in the extraphysical head or parahead (parabrain).

Energy. The golden cord does not seem to operate like a *cord*, but an energetic connection, similar to a *remote control* extending out from the parabrain of the psychosoma and *magnetically* securing the mentalsoma.

Base. It is presumed, as a tentative hypothesis, that the base of the remote control is, however, in the mentalsoma and not in the psychosoma which, at first sight, would be the natural homologous fact.

Command. This evidences that the golden cord operates in a manner contrary to that which occurs with the silver cord, whose greater command, in an ambivalence of forces (bi-directional energetic canal) seems to have its base in the human brain.

Bibliography: Vieira (1762, p. 218).

---

139. PARAPHYSIOLOGY OF THE GOLDEN CORD

Observations. Just as with the word *para-anatomy,* the term *paraphysiology* does not seem apt when applied to the connection that maintains the mentalsoma, a *formless* vehicle of the consciousness, bound to the parabrain of the psychosoma. However, it is being used here in the interest of greater understanding, as it addresses a new and original subject and there is no other more adequate expression.

Cohesion. During the entire evolutionary stage of the intraphysical consciousness or extraphysical consciousness *inside* the parabrain of the psychosoma, the golden cord would be the connecting element responsible in terms of the psychosoma-mentalsoma cohesion remaining healthy and stable in any intraphysical or extraphysical circumstance.

Passport. The golden cord is the connecting element (passport) by way of which the intraphysical or extraphysical consciousness leaves the extraphysical dimension per se and enters the mentalsomatic dimension, and vice versa.

Resistance. It is presumed, as a working hypothesis, that the golden cord, over the consciousness' many millennia of evolutionary experiences or its holobiography, resists the successive and alternate biological shocks of resomas and desomas, in the cycle of multiple human existences and intermissions, and only disappears upon deactivation of the psychosoma, in the third death, when the consciousness achieves the condition of free consciousness (FC) and continues to exist from that point on in the mentalsoma, in a situation that is still incomprehensible in terms of the current rationalizations of humanity.

Bibliography: Vieira (1762, p. 218).

---

140. COMPARISONS BETWEEN THE SILVER CORD
AND THE GOLDEN CORD

Differential. In the sole interest of clarifying a deeper study of the consciousness, it is pertinent to establish the following 11 original comparisons or homologous deductions between the intercorporal connections of its vehicles of manifestation.

Comprehension. If, in practice, this comparison is unworkable, because each of these connections acts in a different dimension of life, then, theoretically speaking, speculative analysis yields valuable and original clarifications for comprehension of the vehicles of manifestation of the consciousness.

1. **Roots.** The silver cord encompasses the entire human form in its roots, from head to toe. It is presumed that the golden cord only connects the consciousness, from the extraphysical head of the psychosoma (the parahead or, more precisely, the parabrain) to the mentalsoma, from one dimension to another.

2. **Insertions.** The silver cord is more material, with one of its points of insertion being located directly in the human body. It is presumed that one of the golden cord's insertion points is located directly in the mentalsoma, in a doubly extraphysical condition that is difficult to evaluate. This is because, when it leaves the intraphysical dimension, it passes through the extraphysical dimension per se and reaches the pure mentalsomatic dimension.

3. **Nature.** The silver cord has form, volume, weight and even well-defined motor and tactile processes. It is presumed that the golden cord is merely an energetic element under the remote command of the mentalsoma.

4. **Dependence.** The silver cord is a distinct connection that is more dependent upon the psychosoma than the human body. This is because it disappears in two stages, upon the first and the second desoma. It is presumed that the golden cord is a distinct element that is more dependent on the mentalsoma than the psychosoma. This is because it disappears when the consciousness achieves the condition of free consciousness (FC).

5. **Appendices.** The silver cord is, without a doubt, an appendix of the human body. It is presumed that the golden cord is, in fact, an appendix of the psychosoma.

6. **Sensations.** The silver cord carries sensations firstly to the consciousness in the psychosoma (the parabody of emotions). It is presumed that the golden cord carries the consciousness' thoughts in the mentalsoma.

7. **Inferiority.** The silver cord is the *inferior* or still unevolved connection element of the psychosoma. It is presumed that the golden cord is the *inferior* connection element of the mentalsoma.

8. **Plurality.** The silver cord is renewable or, in other words, is replaced at each new desoma, myriads of silver cords arising and disappearing for each consciousness, as is the case with holochakras. It is presumed that the same singular golden cord remains during the entire evolution of the ego, until the consciousness reaches the condition of free consciousness, when the golden cord disappears or is discarded together with the psychosoma.

9. **Sphere.** The silver cord receives a considerable amount of influence from the extraphysical sphere of energy, including gravitation and experiences over time. This does not seem to occur with the golden cord.

10. **Growth.** The silver cord expands and shrinks or contracts and extends, *growing* with the psychosoma only during a single human life. After reaching adult form, it does not grow any more. It is presumed that the golden cord accompanies the mentalsoma, *growing* with it in some manner. The mentalsoma expands with evolution, although it does not have a defined form as we know it in the intraphysical dimension.

11. **Guardians.** The silver cord is the guardian of the extraphysical dimension for the intraphysical consciousness, when he/she is in the ordinary, physical waking state. The golden cord is the guardian of the mentalsomatic dimension whether the consciousness is in the ordinary, physical waking state or in the extraphysical dimension per se.

141. LUCID PROJECTION AND THE MENTALSOMA

Definition. Mentalsoma: the vehicle of manifestation of the intraphysical consciousness when this consciousness acts in an isolated manner, without the human body, the holochakra and the humanoid form of the psychosoma, headquartered in the unified body (holosoma), in the parabrain of the psychosoma.

Synonymy: ball of light; body of sentiments; body of the intellect; body of wisdom; bubble of energy; *cephalosoma;* content vehicle; dream body; focus of living light; formless body; intellectual body; intuitosoma; luminous globe; mass of living energy; megamind; mental ball; mental sheath; mnemonic body; mobile center of energy; noemasoma; parabody of discernment; parapsychic body; psychic body; punctiform consciousness; rational body; seventh consciousness (Buddhism); third attention; third element; *vijnamayakosha.*

Characteristics. Among the characteristics of the mentalsoma, at least the following 14 variables stand out:

1. **Formlessness.** The mentalsoma as a formless creation.
2. **Form.** Misty oval shapes, or white, gold or blue balls of energy.
3. **Organ.** The existence of the mentalsoma beyond the human sensory organs.

4. **Extremities.** The manifestation of a body lacking extremities, neither hands nor feet.

5. **Flexibility.** The most flexible independent vehicle of the consciousness manifests beyond the *light cone*, in the mentalsomatic dimension.

6. **Exchange.** The exchanging of vitality with the psychosoma through the golden cord.

7. **Stage.** Represents the vehicle of the essential stage of free consciousness.

8. **Imperceptibility.** The mentalsoma is imperceptible to the human eye because it transcends form and space as we see and sense it in the ordinary, physical waking state.

9. **Lucidity.** Levels of awareness (lucidity) and the mentalsoma.

10. **Cosmoconsciousness.** Cosmic self-awareness, whether continuous or sporadic (cosmoconsciousness).

11. **Holomemory.** Continuous integral memory or holomemory.

12. **Sexuality.** The consciousness in an existential condition that is free from the sexual impulse.

13. **Differences.** The differences of the mentalsoma for the intraphysical consciousness and the extraphysical consciousness.

14. **Paraperceptions.** The general paraperceptions of relative omniscience, as well as omnivision and omni-audition.

Seat. In the coincidence of the bodies of the intraphysical consciousness, the seat of the mentalsoma is in the extraphysical head of the psychosoma (parabrain) and not in the head of the human body (brain).

Carapace. The psychosoma thus constitutes the carapace of the mentalsoma.

Steps. In consciential evolution that is already in process through myriads of successive intraphysical lives, the consciential or intelligent principle *vegetates* when it is a plant, *sensualizes* when it is an animal and *intellectualizes* when a human being.

Self-mimicries. However, intraphysical consciousnesses generally continue to repeat the first two stages (plant or flora, botany; and subhuman animal or fauna, zoology) over long periods of time extemporaneously – in many cases without any greater usefulness (dispensable, inconvenient or useless self-mimicries) – thereby being dislocated in evolutionary time on this assistential *hospital-megaschool-planet*. It is reasonable to think that the evolutionary spiral does not demand so many repetitions. This can be seen in the following 3 stages:

1. **Revegetation.** From an evolutionary perspective, the intraphysical consciousness who is already in the self-creative period, only "revegetates" when he/she allows his/her physical, biological, carnal, cellular and ephemeral body to predominate. In this case, they are "more tree than consciousness," rooted in the soil, "remain stationary" and content themselves with the reactions of plants or *vegetalism*.

Ontology. They are bound by (cellular) roots to a specific, fixed or immobile intraphysical location *(little egotistical world)* that, in evolutionarily terms, pertains to a previous evolutionary stage (retrosomas) which should have already been fully overcome. They thus concentrate themselves in egokarma, without getting out of themselves, in disharmony with their *ontological structuring*.

2. **Reanimalization.** The intraphysical consciousness only *re-sensualizes* or, in other words, reanimalizes him/herself when constantly deciding his/her destiny through action (free will) based predominantly upon his/her psychosoma or emotional parabody (thosenes with an *emphasis on sen*). In this case, these are those dynamically, psychologically, juridically and ethically more irrational consciousnesses. He/she contents him/herself with the reactions of subhuman animals, abdicating from the characteristics of *Homo sapiens sapiens*.

Groupkarma. He/she thus *re-endures* the predominance of specifications characteristic of subhumanity that evolutionarily pertain to a previous stage. He/she concentrates in groupkarma, like *group-souls*, living in direct confrontation or in radical contradiction with his/her essential constitution, seeing things through the eyes of a subhuman animal.

3. **Intellectualization.** The intraphysical consciousness actually only becomes intellectualized when he/she directs human existence based upon a preponderant action of the mentalsoma. Only the lucid individual has an effective intellect and is able to be intellectual, fully using his/her mentalsoma

– the vehicle of reason, the nucleus of discernment or the parabody of *sentiments* – instead of the parabody of emotions or desires. He/she thus fully and coherently interconnects his/her evolutionary consciential reality (hyperacuity, holomaturity).

Polykarma. He/she concentrates him/herself in polykarma or consciential multidimensionality, living in both theory and practice (theorice), according to the intellect, cosmoethically. Which phase characterizes you?

Fifty. During its resoma of up to 75 years of age, the consciousness almost always lives 2/3 of this time under the predominance of the psychosoma and only has a chance to begin living under the predominance of the attributes of the mentalsoma after 50 years of age, in the final third of human life, after it has already overcome the animal impulses and all blind emotionalism in its decisions.

Distance. Most consciousnesses do not end up living in the human body with some predominance of the mentalsoma. This is not only because they remain far from this condition, as they have achieved the *second childhood,* continuing to be *eternally young,* but also because they have still not awakened to the realities of the full, multidimensional life of the lucid consciousness.

Illusion. It can thus be seen that the human body and the holochakra, sustained by the psychosoma, are systems that simultaneously allow the manifestations of the consciousness and obfuscate it under a fog of thick illusion.

Alarm clock. For this reason, the mentalsoma is actually the only efficient alarm clock of the consciousness for its own continued evolution.

Maturities. For the intraphysical consciousness, maturity of the consciousness in terrestrial life will continue for many millennia to be conditioned by the biological maturity of the social being's human body.

Ages. In other words: physical or biological age influences and conditions mental, psychological age which, in turn, is able to more or less reflect the extraphysical and real age of the extraphysical consciousness that became an intraphysical consciousness.

Survival. The dilation of the useful period of the human's lifetime will continually allow greater action of the mentalsoma over consciousnesses. This is because the individual in full maturity will have more time and a better opportunity to think and act in a useful manner after the periods of menopause (gynosoma), andropause (androsoma), retirement, family responsibilities, professional responsibilities and the *fermentations of terrestrial attractions,* dedicating him/herself to liberating tasks (clarification task, penta, polykarmality) without having only human goals or interests of mere physical, organic or animal survival.

Control. After 40 years of physical age, the intraphysical consciousness becomes more predisposed to the production of lucid projection in the mentalsoma. This is because he/she shows a greater tendency to be free from exacerbated emotional ecstasy, maintaining better inner control over his/her manifestations.

Emotionalism. Excessive animal emotionalism is contrary to mental or rational life and acts as an obstacle to the production of consciential projection in the mentalsoma.

Neophobia. However, some lustrums later, when the individual is in his/her sixties and beyond, it becomes more difficult to produce lucid projection – for those who were not previously accustomed to the phenomenon – due to the stratification of the human body, excessively consolidated habits, a deep-rooted existential routine, arteriosclerosis and the full strength irruption of peevishness, crankiness, apriorism, misoneism or neophobia.

Expansion. The projection with expansion up to the condition of full cosmic consciousness or cosmoconsciousness seems to only appear after 30 or 40 years of physical age (see Bucke, Richard Maurice).

Looseness. In the extraphysical dimension, there is a looseness of the mentalsoma of the more lucid sensitive-consciousness or extraphysical consciousness in relation to the parabrain of the psychosoma when, in that phase, that consciousness does not have the holochakra, the silver cord or even the human body.

Tracking. According to the helpers, the galaxies and planets are placed extremely distant from each other in order to, among other reasons, stimulate consciousnesses to overcome the bonds of matter through cosmic investigation using lucid projection outside the denser vehicles of manifestation. This has the objective of reaching more distant places, or those situated within the confines of the physical and tropospheric (crustal) universes using the free mentalsoma in the environment called the *mentalsomatic dimension*, which is common to all intraphysical and extraphysical consciousnesses.

Hypotheses. The following are two questions for research related to this theme:

1. **Emotional.** Could it be that resoma on earth, and on other evolutionarily similar planets, only occurs for the specialized animal-emotional development of the individualized consciousness manifesting through the psychosoma?

2. **Intellectual.** Might there be other appropriate processes and *resomas* for the intellectual-sentimental (rationalized emotion, *superdiscernment*) development of the consciousness manifesting through the mentalsoma, after it definitively frees itself from the psychosoma (third desoma)?

Development. The habit of elevated reflection, mental concentration and serene, constant, successive and guided study of advanced and non-mundane subjects, develops the mentalsoma of the consciousness.

Cenesthopathy. In certain consciential projections in the isolated mentalsoma, the precise notion of inexistence of any type of body or vehicle of consciential manifestation arises. This should not be confused with cenesthopathy or, in other words: the loss of awareness of one's own human body in the ordinary, physical waking state, a very different psychopathological condition, which is one type of cenesthetic disturbance.

Bibliography: Andréa (33, p. 16), Ashish (60, p. 344), Besant (129, p. 81), Bozzano (192, p. 159), Bucke (218, p. 60), Castaneda (258, p. 177), Denning (391, p. 12), Donahue (407, p. 19), Greenhouse (636, p. 70), Guéret (659, p. 165), Hodson (729, p. 80), Leadbeater (902, p. 95), Leaf (905, p. 149), Lefebure (909, p. 110), Miranda (1048, p. 285), Muldoon (1105, p. 225), Perkins (1236, p. 53), Powell (1279, p. 143), Prieur (1289, p. 263), Puryear (1341, p. 3), Rampa (1361, p. 76), Rogo (1444, p. 119), Saraydarian (1507, p. 32), Sculthorp (1531, p. 142), Swedenborg (1639, p. 294), Toben (1688, p. 73), Vieira (1762, p. 218), Wang (1794, p. 147), Xavier (1882, p. 197).

142. PARAPSYCHOPHYSIOLOGY OF THE MENTALSOMA

Term. The term *parapsychophysiology* does not seem to be appropriate when applied to the mentalsoma, a *formless* vehicle. It is used here, however, in order to provide a better understanding of the subject because no other more adequate expression exists.

Mind. The mentalsoma is the vehicle of manifestation of the consciousness that is suited to the mentalsomatic dimension, which is also called the *universal mind*.

Characteristics. Among the characteristics of the parapsychophysiology of the mentalsoma, at least the following 15 variables can be singled out:

1. **Omnipresence.** Omnipresent cosmic mind.
2. **Transmission.** Transmitter of images, thoughts and sentiments.
3. **Thosenization.** Irradiator of mental energetic waves or thosenes.
4. **Morphothosenology.** Projector of morphothosenes or thought-forms.
5. **Megapsychometry.** Psychometrizer of the universe.
6. **Magnification.** Magnifier of everything or of an understanding of the consciousness.
7. **Omniscience.** The personal notion of omniscience and omnipresence.
8. **Mentalsomatic.** Sponsor of mentalsomatic projection and the consciousness apparently not having a body or vehicle of manifestation, occurring when the projected projector looks at itself and sees, senses or finds nothing of *substance* or structure relative to its thosenizing nucleus (pointer of the consciousness).

9. **Projectability.** Permits consciential projection while the human body is temporarily left in movement.

10. **Punctiform.** Permits the punctiform consciousness' presence in space.

11. **Takeoff.** Direct invariable takeoff from the coincident or projected psychosoma.

12. **Paraperceptiology.** Permits the consciousness to operate as a sensitive in the mentalsomatic dimension, in certain circumstances.

13. **Psychosomatics.** Maintains the structure – perhaps that of the field (physics) – of the psychosoma.

14. **Exchange.** Action of the golden cord.

15. **Paraphenomenology.** Simple separation, double separation, with and without the simultaneous projection of the psychosoma.

Impossibilities. When isolated, the mentalsoma does not allow at least the following 4 operations:

1. **Matter.** Direct action upon matter.

2. **Psychomotricity.** Motor effects.

3. **Intrusion.** Extraphysical attack upon the projected intraphysical consciousness.

4. **Deintrusion.** Classic deintrusive consciential projection.

Invulnerability. It shows itself to be invulnerable to the action of force currents and extraphysical hydromagnetic tempests.

Recontact. In certain instances, the mentalsoma enables the intraphysical consciousness to perceive the following sequence of 10 occurrences during the process of *recontacting* with material creations, in the act of interiorizing into the extraphysical head (parahead, parabrain) of the coincident psychosoma and, therefore, in the human body:

1. **Space.** Space and our intraphysical manifestation.

2. **Forms.** Forms and our relationships with material reality.

3. **Time.** Chronological time in the condition of our creation.

4. **Gravitation.** Planetary gravitation and its influence upon the intraphysical consciousness.

5. **Weight.** Somatic weight and the *towing* of the soma.

6. **Respiration.** Respiration or the 2 lungs and its enslaving influence.

7. **Circulation.** The beating of the heart and its continuous operation.

8. **Volume.** The volume of the human body.

9. **Restriction.** Accentuated compression or mental tension, characteristic of consciential restriction imposed through prolonged interiorization of the consciousness in matter or through resoma.

10. **Awakening.** Physical awakening of the consciousness and its lucidity, which is always reduced in the waking state.

Loosening. The mentalsoma loosens the tensions of the intellective circuits, promoting the free flow of ideas or uninterrupted thosenization.

Relaxation. As a general rule, a lucid mental and pure projection is equivalent to a period of intellectual relaxation or taking a series of effective nutritional substances or, in other words: extraphysical energy, which is spontaneously absorbed to the cerebral hemispheres of the intraphysical consciousness.

Brains. Based on the fact that the mentalsoma of the extraphysical consciousness leaves the psychosoma temporarily inactive during the lucid, extraphysical or mental paraprojection of the extraphysical consciousness, it can be concluded that the seat of the mentalsoma is in the extraphysical head (parahead) or, more precisely, in the parabrain of the psychosoma.

Differences. Hence, it can also be inferred that the parabrain of the psychosoma, despite being a matrix of the human brain, is very different from it, at least due to the following 3 occurrences:

1. **Density.** It does not have very dense matter in its structure.

2. **Transfiguration.** It has the attribute of changing shape.

3. **Freedom.** It allows the departure and free expansion of the mentalsoma.

Hemispheres. All this makes one think that the mentalsoma, just like the parabrain of the psychosoma, is constructed of 2 hemispheres – similar to the human brain – although with possibilities of structural variations that we (intraphysical consciousnesses) are still unaware of when manifesting in the mentalsomatic dimension.

Growth. Although lacking a defined form, the mentalsoma grows constantly, in some manner, along with the evolution of the consciousness.

Appendix. The mentalsoma does not have any appendix of its own. This is because the intercorporal or intervehicular connection of the golden cord is more rooted in the psychosoma, with which it disappears when the consciousness *(serenissimus)* reaches the evolutionary condition of free consciousness (FC).

Potentiation. Lucid projection in the mentalsoma or, in other words, the freeing of the integral mind of the personality, potentiates the performance of the psychic faculties of the intraphysical lucid projector the following day. The individual, at least temporarily, is almost euphoric and is in better shape to coordinate personal thoughts, use memory, and work intellectually with the imagination and critical judgment.

Adjust. The mentalsoma is the most powerful vehicle for adjusting, balancing and homogenizing the holosoma. The employment or practical use of the mentalsoma by the intraphysical consciousness has the quality of curing certain indispositions generated by the altered physiology of the human body, energetic imbalances characteristic of the holochakra and affective disturbances that disrupt the psychosoma.

Technique. Thus, gastric distress, from eating something the organism cannot process (chemical instinct, food intolerance), for example, can easily and quickly be overcome in a spontaneous manner if the intraphysical consciousness gets to work using the mentalsoma, through a productive and absorbing intellectual task that tends to amplify his/her lucidity (hyperacuity) regarding consciential multidimensionality.

Occupational therapy. This work ends up being an effective resource of occupational therapy or, more precisely, upon harmonizing the vehicles of manifestation of the intraphysical consciousness, there is a remission of possible existing disturbances, in a self-therapeutic reaction.

Indissociability. At our current evolutionary level on earth, the intraphysical consciousness shows itself to be indissociable from the mentalsoma, in which the consciousness remains headquartered all the time, regardless of its manifestation or wherever it goes in its consciential projections.

Extinction. This indissociability will one day extinguish. According to current research, when, how and in what way the consciousness will manifest itself is not known.

Sentiments. Just as the psychosoma is directly responsible for the manifestation of the consciousness' primary emotions, the mentalsoma is responsible for the afflux of the consciousness' elevated sentiments.

Rationalization. The way of the growth of the consciousness intentionally acting from the mentalsoma upon the psychosoma, until the point at which the ego, in the first consciential vehicle, completely controls and directs the second vehicle, has been developing through the conquest of gradual rationalization.

History. For example, 3 stages can be observed in recent human history:

1. **Christianity.** First, primitive Christianity arose as a rationalized form of Judaism.

2. **Protestantism.** Second, Protestant Christianity developed as a rationalized form of Catholicism.

3. **Parapsychology.** Third, parapsychology appeared – at least in its early stages – as a more functional alternative form of religion or, in other words: a type of *religion substitute.*

Self-experimentation. In light of all these processes of secularization or *mental laicization of the sacred,* projectiology offers the practical part of consciential life, definitively dispensing with all manner of faith or belief, offering personal knowledge through rational self-experimentation with *inner and multidimensional cosmoethical renewal.*

Decline. At a certain point in this evolution, it is evident that religion will definitively cease to have any raison d'être for the more lucid intraphysical consciousness. As currently seen with the rapid acceleration of history, 2 categories of *imperial decline* will occur simultaneously:

1. **Materialism.** The decline of the Newtonian-Cartesian reductionist paradigm or the *materialist empires* of immature science.

2. **Dogmatism.** The decline of religions or *religious empires* as a whole.

Rationality. We cannot rationally *argue with the facts*.

Hypotheses. The following are two projectiological research hypotheses that are pertinent in this context:

1. **Frontochakra.** What is the relationship between the frontochakra and the golden cord?

2. **Coronochakra.** What is the relationship between the coronochakra, or its energies, and the mentalsoma?

Bibliography: Powell (1279, p. 14), Steiger (1601, p. 133), Walker (1781, p. 71).

---

143. RELATIVISTIC SPACE-TIME

Definition. Space-time: the unification through relativity of the concepts of space and time in the *space-time continuum* wherein space loses its isolated character and time ceases to be independent from the frame of reference, given that the physical phenomena no longer only pass through space, or occur in time, but take place in a more complex four-dimensional entity that is space-time, a broader notion of which will be presented below.

Synonymy: light cone; space-time continuum.

Intangibility. The reader who is concerned or, perhaps more precisely, nauseated by the intangibility and the "surrealistic" nature of some chapters in this section, would do well to bear in mind that nowadays there is nothing impractical or unscientific about intangible things.

Invisibility. It can be seen that science concerns itself more and more with intangible and invisible things in practical daily life, such as fields and waves, which brings these cogitations closer to or places them – in many aspects and perspectives – in harmony with the laws of physics.

Interval. In order to broaden the notion of space-time, it is necessary to define a value referred to as the interval in which the product, the maximum velocity of propagation of the interactions of known matter, which coincides with the speed of light in a vacuum, 186,282 miles (299,000 kilometers) per second (c), and the time interval between two events (t_2-t_1) in a certain frame of reference, would be a fourth complementary coordinate, besides the existing three, namely x, y and z. The interval between two events would then be given by the equation:

$$S_{1,2} = [c^2 (t_2-t_1)^2 - (x_2-x_1)^2 - (y_2-y_1)^2 - (z_2-z_1)^2]^{1/2}$$

where the indices 1 and 2 refer to each one of the events; as opposed to the ordinary interval in tridimensional space

$$r = [(x_2-x_1)^2 + (y_2-y_1)^2 + (z_2-z_1)^2]^{1/2}$$

and with time "t" as the independent coordinate of space, in classic physics.

Invariance. The interval "s" between events is the same in all inertial systems of reference (which are not found to be under the influence of external forces). In other words, it is an invariant in relation to the transformation from one system of reference to any other.

Constancy. This invariance is the expression of the constancy of the speed of light in any system of reference.

Light. When the velocity of 2 events occurs at a speed slower than that of light in a vacuum, the intervals are referred to as being timelike, as opposed to being spacelike. As shown in fig. 143, there is only one "x" coordinate and time "t", in order to facilitate visualization (in fact, there would have to be 4 axes, *x, y, z* and *t* that are perpendicular to each other, which would be impossible in our tridimensional space), we have a planar graphic representation of space-time divisions.

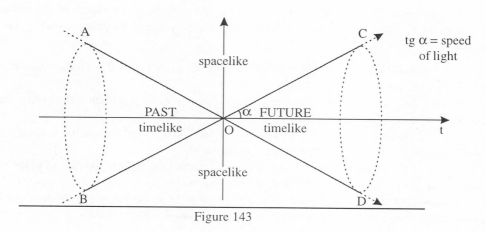

Figure 143

Time. Taking any event, designated as "O," at the beginning of the spatial and temporal coordinates, in order to examine how to find the other events relative to event O, the rectilinear and uniform movement of a particle that passes through the origin O, is a straight line that passes through O and whose tangent of the angle of inclination with the t-axis supplies the velocity of the particle. All lines that represent movements of particles can be found only inside the domain *AOB* and *COD*. The intervals between any event of this domain and the event O are timelike or temporal. In this domain, for *t* > O, in the region *COD*, all events occur *after* O, or are in the future relative to O, in all systems of reference. This domain is also called *absolute future* relative to event O. The events of domain *AOB* are called *absolute past* relative to event O.

Regions. Matter, as well as known and proven physical phenomena, including all known interactions, are inside these regions, which are also called the "light cone."

Velocity. The velocity of a material object, according to existing observations, must be less than or, at most, equal to the speed of light, in cases in which the object is transformed into *photonic energy*.

Space. In the regions *AOC* and *BOD,* the interval between any event and event O is spacelike or spatial. From this it can be concluded that, in any system of reference, these events occur at different points in space.

Concepts. The concepts of *simultaneity, before* and *after* are relative. For any event in this domain there are frames of reference wherein it occurs *after* event O, frames of reference wherein it occurs *before* O, and frames of reference wherein it occurs *simultaneously* with O. Little or nothing is known about the spacelike intervals in physics.

Own. Figure 143 illustrates a frame of reference that pertains to where one is. When observed from 2 different comparable systems of reference, both space and time flow in a particular and different manner. The reader may wish consult specialized works for further clarification.

Hypotheses. It can be seen that, in the domain of spacelike intervals, one can be at various points (or all points) of space at the same instant, or travel, if without the dense material body, *at a velocity faster than the speed of light*. In other words, one can go to the future, the past, or remain in the present.

Projection. Projective experiences in the mentalsoma, for example, lead us to propose or hypothesize that the phenomena observed in this state can be within the scope of spacelike intervals. This is reflected in the thoughts of Bernhard Riemann (1826-1866), who proposed the existence of space as being independent of metric (measurements of distance and angles), given that spatial metric is the result of the existence of matter and the forces between matter. The mentalsoma remains independent from it, coexisting in this space without metric.

Types. Incidentally, there are 5 operations of departure and return of the intraphysical consciousness from the consciential seat in consciential projections, when utilizing the isolated mentalsoma:

1. **Coincidence.** The mentalsoma leaves (projection) the parabrain of the psychosoma when it is still coincident with the human body.

2. **Discoincidence.** The mentalsoma leaves (projection) the parabrain of the psychosoma when it remains discoincident with the human body.

3. **Coincident interiorization.** The mentalsoma returns (interiorization) to the parabrain of the psychosoma which is coincident with the human body.

4. **Discoincident interiorization.** The mentalsoma returns (interiorization) to the parabrain of the psychosoma which is discoincident with the human body.

5. **Inversion.** The psychosoma (parabrain) projects and continues to the free mentalsoma, outside the human body, and absorbs it in a process of inverse interiorization.

Bibliography: Bentov (119, p. 3), Talbot (1642, p. 162), Toben (1688, p. 63), Vieira (1762, p. 198), Wolman (1863, p. 749).

---

144. PARAPSYCHOPATHOLOGY OF THE MENTALSOMA

Parapsychopathology. The parapsychopathology of the mentalsoma, which is still very obscure, seems to be extensive and encompasses an actual specific and complex parapsychopathology that often manifests itself through extraphysical consciousnesses in the extraphysical dimensions that are suitable for the free rein of the psychosoma and not in the pure mentalsomatic dimension.

Unconsciousness. The temporary loss of self-awareness, or *post-desomatic unconsciousness,* is one of the disturbances that affect the mentalsoma of intraphysical consciousnesses that return to the status of extraphysical consciousnesses through recent desoma. They are more easily detected by the intraphysical projector projected with lucidity.

Parapsychoses. Unconsciousness is one of the more common *post-desomatic parapsychoses.* In this case, it often represents a mere continuation of senile psychosis (Alzheimer's disease).

Monoideism. The simplest parapsychosis manifests when the consciousness (extraphysical consciousness), which has recently returned to the intermissive period, does not perceive that it has passed through biological death (desoma) and has lost the human body (soma) which it was using up until a short while ago. This condition is well-known to members of parapsychic deintrusion sessions. It is also called *posthumous monoideism.*

Extraphysical melancholy. Post-desomatic parapsychosis generally occurs to all those who are unprepared to take on extraphysical life upon desoma. Sadly, nowadays, this still constitutes the great majority of terrestrial humanity and can occur after extraphysical melancholy.

Ignorance. The parapsychotic generally has no interest in knowing that its human body is dead. This is because it considers its continued consciousness as absolute proof that it has not undergone desoma, despite the deeply rooted belief it may nurture regarding its own immortality and as fanatic as its religious beliefs may be.

Viscous. Parapsychotic extraphysical consciousnesses, due to their continuous hunger for consciential energy (energivorous extraphysical consciousnesses), can also appear to be viscous or, in other words, to have slowness, viscosity and detailedness in their manifestations.

Visitant. This is why they tend to implacably join with the visitant in certain circumstances or extraphysical environments, even when it is a projected intraphysical consciousness that they unconsciously follow as much as possible and wherever possible.

Assistentiality. It is extremely important that the intraphysical projector be aware of this fact regarding assistential projections.

Symptomatology. In this condition of *unconsciousness,* the ill extraphysical consciousness generally does not perceive the following 6 realities:

1. **Location.** Where it actually is.
2. **Community.** The new sphere of life in which it lives.
3. **Freedom.** The freer conditions that it can enjoy.
4. **Time.** The time and environment in which it lives.
5. **Intercommunication.** Its possible new relationships.
6. **Consequences.** The consequences stemming from this new consciential condition.

Animal. Unconsciousness leads the human consciousness that has recently returned to the condition of an extraphysical consciousness to temporarily relive an animal phase or, in other words, an irrational phase which it has overcome through its multiexistential experiences a long time ago.

Intermission. It undergoes the extraphysical experience of the intermissive period similar to the restricted consciousness of the subhuman animal which, either intraphysically or extraphysically, does not present real self-awareness. That is to say, it does not know who it is, as an individual personality, and does not correctly situate itself in extraphysical space and chronological time. It also does not perceive the transformations of its environment and does not manifest the basic indications of correct psychological orientation.

Psychosoma. The consciential disturbance of unconsciousness, in this case, is of the mentalsoma but reflects itself entirely and manifests itself especially through the psychosoma (emotional parabody) of the extraphysical consciousness.

Holochakra. This disturbance even persists after the experience of its second desoma or the definitive discarding of the remnants of the holochakra.

Therapeutic. One of the processes for the recuperation and cure of unconsciousness and the installation of a greater consciential awakening in the extraphysical dimension takes place in the setting up of live theatrical acts with various groups of patients (parapsychodrama). These include the participation of self-aware, assistant-extraphysical-consciousnesses that coexist with these patients. They also *portray* with them, over periods of time, didactic-therapeutic theatrical pieces and dramas, preparing them for extraphysical life or another upcoming or impending intraphysical life.

Duration. If we view them from the perspective of human chronological time, these prolonged dramas, experiences or laboratories last for weeks and months, just like short and simulated prior human existences. In order for them to occur, it is not necessary that the chronological scale of intraphysical life be observed. They are virtual intraphysical mini-existences *(mock trial, simulated auction of Teles, practice test)* although being mental. What percentage of these do not recuperate? What percentage of them do not go through the second desoma?

Character. The author came across an old helper that appeared *fatter* in its extraphysical visual appearance. It was transfigured, wearing exotic clothing and, according to this helper, had been completely engaged in these conditions for months, according to terrestrial chronological calculations. It was performing a role in a long dramatization in a district of the tropospheric extraphysical dimension in a large cast of *unconscious patients* with the main aim of recuperating them.

Absorption. In these absorbing or monopolizing circumstances, the helper could not attend to any other task on the planetary crust. This is why we had not seen each other since the previous year. This was mentioned when extraphysically introducing me to the participants of the simulated but live theatrical piece.

Traumas. Post-desomatic parapsychoses also occur due to small psychological traumas that the intraphysical consciousness may have suffered in his/her last days in the human body.

Fixation. A minimal psychological trauma, such as deception, mistakes, self-guilt, grief or friction, binds the consciousness to a secondary terrestrial problem that is difficult for the ego to eliminate immediately.

Parahygiene. This becomes transformed into a fixed idea, a tenacious monoideistic or adherent theme. The extraphysical consciousness wishes to remove it from its mind (paramind, parabrain) and perform mental parahygiene, but is unable to do so.

Holothosene. The persistent, traumatic and absorbing idea keeps the extraphysical consciousness immersed in the terrestrial themes and climate (holothosene). This completely impairs the consciousness after its being freed through the *first* desoma or final projection.

Gerontology. In this case, the greater the physical age (longevity, gerontology, from sixty-five to eighty-four years of age, eighty-five years of age and over) of the intraphysical consciousness, the more complex and deeper the post-desomatic parapsychosis will be. This is due to senility, arteriosclerosis, Alzheimer's disease, grouchiness and cantankerousness, which facilitates the installation of the fixed idea.

Parasleep. Post-desomatic restorative sleep or *parasleep* is the overall most indicated resource, from the beginning, for alleviating the intraphysical consciousness that became an extraphysical consciousness from a traumatic or absorbing idea. However, the extraphysical consciousness does not always achieve this renewing tranquil sleep. In this aspect, all improvement depends, above all and aside from everyone (helpers, evolutiologists, *serenissimi*), upon the consciousness itself.

Prophylaxis. Those who wish to free themselves from the mental and ethical disturbances that overwhelm any consciousness after the biological shock of desoma, should immediately begin to perform an effective prophylaxis of all fixed, involving and stubborn ideas, actually *cleansing* the time, space and consciential energies of any *personal fossilization*.

Desoma. Those who undergo desoma leave the human body *here* but continue with their emotional and mental bodies *there*. Those who nurture fixed and stubborn ideas are well-advised to start preparing themselves now, for their own benefit.

Requisitions. The recent desomant that is a victim of a post-desomatic traumatic fixed idea is more hampered and takes longer to renew itself when it leaves young loved ones behind in intraphysical life who need the lost presence and affection, as well as deeply desiring and insisting upon seeing the personality again, having its company and knowing how it is doing.

Messages. Among these are the suffering individuals and parents who regularly go to mediums and *multiform channelings* to *receive messages*. The mental waves install morbid affective currents. It is always the recent desomant that suffers more, which, at this point, requires extraphysical renewal.

Encounter. In theory, the human lucid projector should not anxiously provoke an encounter with a recent desomant, regardless of who it is. It is always more prudent, intelligent and useful to let events spontaneously follow their natural extraphysical course. The most rational and productive approach for all is to maintain positive mental and affective waves in favor of the memory of the one who underwent desoma, albeit without making insistent, egoistical, obsessive and *magnetizing* requests that always disturb, impair and benefit no one in this situation.

Oligophrenias. Extraphysical oligophrenias, *frenastenias* or *olipsiquias* are syndromes or disturbances that are characteristic of pathology of the mentalsoma. In other words, they are mental deficiencies of the extraphysical consciousness that are reflected in the psychosoma. They seem to be generated by unrestrained emotions between biological shocks of *resoma* and *desoma*. This results in the following effects: deficiency in mental development, lack of mental concentration, lack of coordinated critical judgment and other mentalsomatic alterations.

Alterations. With reference to intraphysical consciousnesses, the temporary parapsychopathological alterations of the projected human consciousness are generated by disturbances in the parapsychophysiological activity that occur between the cerebral hemispheres (the head of the human body), the *paracerebral hemispheres* (the parahead of the psychosoma), and the mentalsoma situated in the parahead (or, more precisely, in the parabrain) of the psychosoma.

Causes. Among the causes of the parapsychopathological alterations of the projected intraphysical consciousness, at least the following 5 occurrences can be singled out:

1. **Conditioning.** Psychological conditioning imposed by the repressions of the physical restriction of the human body, generating *parapsychological* or extraphysical conditioning.

2. **Dissipation.** Temporary consciential (parapsychological) draining of consciential energy.

3. **Intoxication.** Intraconsciential intoxication of energetic origin.

4. **Illnesses.** Physical illnesses with extraphysical repercussions.

5. **Interdependence.** Alterations in the interdependence between the cortical areas and the silver cord, or the golden cord.

Types. Among the types of states of the projected intraphysical consciousness with alterations – which are parapsychopathological, in most cases – the following 2 can be singled out:

1. **Obnubilation.** Extraphysical obnubilation of the projected consciousness, or the morbid distraction of the normal course of parapsychic processes, is essentially characterized by 5 reactions:

A. **Lucidity.** Reduction in the degree of extraphysical lucidity, with slowness of comprehension, difficulty in perception and the elaboration of extraphysical impressions.

B. **Thought.** Alteration in the train of thought (pointer of the consciousness).

C. **Evocation.** Disturbance of fixation and evocation.

D. **Disorientation.** A certain degree of extraphysical disorientation.

E. **Sleepiness.** More or less accentuated extraphysical sleepiness.

2. **Euphoria.** Paradoxically, extraphysical euphoria is negative in most projective occurrences. This state can lead the consciousness to ridiculous states of inconsequential contemplation and profound sentiments of beatitude which, in the end, contribute nothing positive to the projected consciousness. On the contrary, extraphysical euphoria subsequently brings about the following 3 reactions:

A. **Learning.** The sensation of irreparable loss of an opportunity to learn outside the human body.

B. **Waste.** The notion of wasting extraphysical time.

C. **Energy.** The frustration of squandering consciential energy.

Effects. Among the effects of parapsychopathological alterations of the projected intraphysical consciousness, at least the following 16 can be singled out:

1. Diverse self-obsessions.

2. Nonlucid projection.

3. Indifference or apathy when faced with extraphysical experiences.

4. Extemporaneous sidetracking of extraphysical attention.

5. Incoherence in observations made regarding extraphysical events.

6. Appearance of unexpected or inappropriate mental targets.

7. The state of the erratic projector.

8. Loss of extraphysical freedom.

9. The installation of semilucid projections or another altered state of consciousness lamentably imposing itself over the lucid projection.

10. Extraphysical trauma.

11. Abrupt imposed interiorization.

12. Premature cessation of the lucid projection.

13. Loss of the educational opportunity of projective experiences.

14. Prolonged projective recess.

15. Fragmentary or completely annulled post-projective recall.

16. The phenomenon of voluntary *personism (mystifying psychophony)* or involuntary *personism.*

Problems. The intraphysical consciousness can encounter 2 similar problems, among others, of retardation due to his/her condition of physical restriction:

1. **Retardation.** First, for example, the well-known pathological state in which the cranium does not develop together with the human brain. This can even cause fused bones that do not leave space for the brain to grow. This provokes terrible headaches (cephalalgias) and *mental retardation*.

2. **Consciential.** Second, the condition in which the consciousness projects in the expanded mentalsoma and is unable to pass the recollections of the experiences to the parabrain (of the psychosoma) and the human brain. This generates *consciential retardation*.

Sentiments. The deep alterations in the manifestations of the consciousness' sentiments are inserted into the scope of the mentalsoma's influence. In this case, it is not known when they are simple effects of the emotions (psychosoma, *with an emphasis on the sen* of self-thosenes) or when they are actual sentiments or, in other words, thoughts that are rationally linked to emotions (mentalsoma, *with an emphasis on the tho* of self-thosenes).

Bibliography: Swedenborg (1639, p. 80), Vieira (1762, p. 153).

145. PREDOMINANCE OF A CONSCIENTIAL VEHICLE

Definition. Predominance of a consciential vehicle: the preponderant and continued action of the consciousness – intraphysical consciousness (4 vehicles) or extraphysical consciousness (2 vehicles) – through 1 metaorganism in particular, when it ends up monopolizing the entire holosoma.

Synonymy: consciential vehicular preponderance; monopoly by a vehicle of manifestation; predominance of a metaorganism.

Clarity. According to the paraphysiology of the holosoma in the experiential universe of the consciousness, there can be an evident, more or less clear, predominance of 1 specific consciential vehicle.

Types. The diversification of consciential experiences ends up comprising various types of vehicular predominances with regard to the group of similar variables, such as the following 12:

1. Accidental, self-provoked or hetero-provoked.
2. Animal (human body) or extraphysical (mentalsoma).
3. Appropriate or avoidable.
4. Brief or prolonged (chronology).
5. Defined or ambivalent (paradoxical).
6. Gratifying or assistential (reparation or evolution).
7. Healthy (physiological or paraphysiological) or unhealthy (pathological or parapathological).
8. Intraphysical, projective (extraphysical) or desomatic.
9. Preparatory or executive (existential program).
10. Regressive or renovating.
11. Self-aware or unconscious (self-lucidity).
12. Sporadic or frequent (chronicity).

Intraphysical. There are phases of human activity with such a clear and absolute predominance of the action of 1 vehicle of manifestation upon the holosoma, or 1 consciential segment over the *entire* intraphysical consciousness, that there is no room for doubt.

Categories. The following, for example, are 4 categories of action of 1 consciential segment:

1. **Muscles.** In the phases of monopolization by the human body, matter and muscles predominate. The following are some examples: the athlete who is hibernating immersed in intensive training; the manual laborer who starts a new job; the professional model with a busy schedule.

2. **Energies.** In the phases of monopolization by the holochakra, *exchanges* and consciential energies predominate. The following are some examples: the actress at the start of a theatrical season;

the professional pianist on tour; the popular singer in his/her first season of shows; the lucid consciential projector, when he/she is an extraphysical prisoner of the silver cord, in the phase in which he/she is unable to leave the physical base on more enriching projective excursions.

3. **Emotions.** Desires and emotions predominate in the phases of monopolization by the psychosoma. The following are some examples: the newlywed during the *honeymoon* (energetic maxi-springtime); the traveler who takes a vacation in his/her hometown (wistfulness, nostalgia), or native country.

4. **Ideas.** The intellect and ideas predominate in the phases of monopolization by the mentalsoma. The following are some examples: the author who goes into isolation in order to write a new book; the scientist in the initial phase of a *research cycle;* the student in the intense phase of study for college entrance examinations.

Conflict. Irreconcilable existential (or extraphysical) conditions generate intrapsychic dilemmas and conflicts that lead the consciousness to install the wrong, eccentric, dislocated, extemporaneous or paradoxical predominance of one vehicle of manifestation over the others. The predominance is always destructive in such a condition.

Change. The change that has occurred may merely relate to the positive or negative quality of vehicular predominance and not the consciential vehicle itself. The following are 3 examples:

1. **Newlywed.** The newlywed who, at the beginning of her *honeymoon* (positive predominance of the emotional body), is notified of the unexpected desoma (anticlimax) of her beloved mother (paradoxical negative predominance of the same emotional parabody).

2. **Athlete.** The focused athlete (positive predominance of the human body) who needs to take the college entrance examination for his/her chosen career studies (positive, but dislocated, predominance of the mentalsoma) in the same period.

3. **Author.** The author who goes to the countryside to write a book on economics (positive predominance of the mentalsoma) and falls in love with his/her neighbor (extemporaneous predominance of the emotional parabody) while there.

Evidence. The overall analysis of the predominance of each consciential vehicle over the others clearly manifests 4 occurrences:

1. **Holosoma.** The existence of the holosoma.
2. **Action.** The particular action of each metaorganism.
3. **Physiology.** The physiology or paraphysiology of each consciential vehicle.
4. **Pathology.** The pathology or parapathology of each consciential vehicle.

Fermentation. No manifestations of the *integral* intraphysical personality can be counted on if he/she is in a specific phase of evolutionary fermentation, under the predominance of one consciential vehicle.

Comprehension. The reader will coexist better with others, and with him/herself, if he/she understands this technical mechanism and endeavors to function adequately with these phases of consciential performance. This will avoid annoyance, intolerance and misunderstanding in the dynamic of intraphysical existence.

Parapathology. In theory, all monopolization by the action of 1 consciential vehicle over the others, when excessively prolonged, becomes spurious or parapathological, and in fact constitutes a *para-hypertrophy* or an exorbitance of functions.

Use. If we have various vehicles of consciential manifestation, it stands to reason that it is in order to use all of them together and harmoniously, in peaceful coexistence, in order to gradually free ourselves from those that we can deactivate during the progress of consciential evolution.

Exception. To permit the predominance of one vehicle of consciential manifestation over the others is an exception-behavior for the consciousness.

Pattern. The harmonized use of the multiple vehicles of manifestation that make up the holosoma is the pattern-behavior for the consciousness.

Deactivations. The following are 3 examples of tendencies of consciousnesses regarding somatic deactivations:

1. **First.** The *natural* tendency of the moribund individual (mostly in desomatics) is to deactivate the human body (first desoma).

2. **Second.** The *intermissive* tendency of the recent desomant intraphysical consciousness (now an extraphysical consciousness), when more lucid, is to discard the remnants of the holochakra (second desoma).

3. **Third.** The advanced *evolutionary* tendency of *Homo sapiens serenissimus (serenissimus)* is to free him/herself from the psychosoma once and for all (third desoma).

Retrogression. The *general* condition of the predominance of 1 consciential vehicle over the holosoma operates in direct opposition to these evolutionary tendencies, in this case, in retrogression. In this case, only 1 metaorganism is activated to the detriment of the others, with the consciousness not discarding any of them: without bringing about any evolutionary advantage.

Desomants. The desomant intraphysical consciousness also goes through phases of a predominance of 1 specific vehicle of manifestation. The following are some examples: the soma, soon after the desoma of the intraphysical consciousness, in cases of post-desomatic parapsychosis; the holochakra, until it overcomes the second desoma, in certain cases; the psychosoma, in the period in which the consciousness meets its loved ones that have already gone through desoma (extraphysical consciousnesses); the mentalsoma, during field trips, in preparation for a new life and a new upcoming existential program.

Incomprehension. Legions of human beings remain intranquil, uncomprehending or angry regarding the alleged disregard or indifference from their former relatives, friends and colleagues, which are now desomant. According to these individuals, they do not respond to their desires, evocations, prayers, whims and personal egotisms. In many cases this occurs because they do not understand the dynamic of the occurrences and incidents of the experiential phases of the desomant intraphysical consciousnesses.

Intrusions. The desomant intraphysical consciousness often cannot even maintain itself in a balanced manner. How then will it be able to understand the situation, respond to critical complaints of others or assistentially intercede in favor of another? On other occasions it will be so deeply involved in the contexts of experiences, dimensions, remote environments and consciential energies that useful dislocation from one place to another becomes impractical.

Questions. Are you, experimenter, currently in an evident phase of the predominance of 1 vehicle of manifestation? Which vehicle? Is the predominance conscious or unconscious? Is the existential phase healthy or pathological?

Duration. Logically and rationally, one should only allow a prolonged (duration) predominance of one consciential vehicle if it is of the mentalsoma – the parabody of discernment – and, even then, if it is healthy.

Bibliography: Vieira (1672, p. 134).

---

146. DESOMA

Definition. Desoma: the painless deactivation and discarding of a vehicle of manifestation of the intraphysical consciousness.

Synonymy: demise; deactivation of the consciential vehicle; discarding of the consciential covering; death; thanatosis; way of mutation.

Transmutations. Death represents a change in the level of the consciousness (consciential principle) through the deactivation and discarding of one of its vehicles of manifestation. This is similar to various known natural events, such as the following 5 evolutionary transmutations:

1. **Tree.** The tree growing new leaves.
2. **Bird.** The bird molting its feathers.
3. **Fruit.** The fruit discarding its skin.

4. **Insect.** The insect (cicada) substituting its exuvia.
5. **Reptile.** The reptile (snake) shedding its skin.

Types. There are 3 types of death or desoma in the specific case of the consciousness:

1. The first death.
2. The second death.
3. The third death.

Disintegration. Each death or desoma constitutes the paralysis and consequent definitive disintegration of a certain instrument, machine, vehicle or body through which the consciousness acted.

Reactions. Further, each death can represent 4 reactions:

1. **Shock.** A consciential or parabiological shock.
2. **Crisis.** A positive growing crisis (healthy stress) for the consciousness.
3. **Transition.** A defined period of evolutionary transition for the consciousness.
4. **Change.** A radical change for the ego that is generally painless and for the better.

Taboos. The deaths, however, within human customs, still remain intensively involved in excessive taboos, conditioning, preconceptions, beliefs, superstitions, emotionalism, misunderstanding, low-level information, bad information and disinformation.

Qualification. Despite all this, deaths or desomas, in their 3 types of manifestation, are experiences which are more agreeable than disagreeable.

Birth. Each death, or discarding of a consciential vehicle, actually constitutes a type of birth of the consciousness in another far more evolved form of existence.

Bibliography: ADGMT (03, p. 212), Chu (284, p. 61), Crookall (339, p. 181). Hampton (676, p. 17), Heindel (705, p. 109), Perkins (1236, p. 77), Powell (1278, p. 107), Vieira (1762, p. 62), Wang (1794, p. 155).

---

147. FIRST DESOMA

Definitions. First desoma: deactivation and discarding of the human body with the rupture of the silver cord, returning the intraphysical consciousness to his/her condition as an extraphysical consciousness, still with the holochakra, psychosoma and mentalsoma as its vehicles of manifestation; passage of the intraphysical consciousness from the intraphysical state to the extraphysical state.

Synonymy: biological death; brain death; changing of matter; cytological death; deactivation of the human body; deactivation of the physical body; death of the human body; decession; definitive unfolding; demobilization of the human body; discarding of the human body; discarnation; disembodiment; disoccupation of the human body; dying; end of animal human life; final detachment of the perispirit; *final discoincidence;* final projection; final takeoff of the psychosoma; full corporal death; last detachment; last human projection; last semiphysical projection; liberation from the human body; lysis; molecular death; monothanatosis; natural death; obit; passing; perishing of the soma; physical death; *primothanatosis;* release of the imprisoned consciousness; self-lysis (suicide); somatic death; thanatological event; trespass; trespassing.

Ego. It is more appropriate to understand 2 facts that are similar and complementary regarding desoma:

1. **Burial.** Human existence, resoma or intraphysical rebirth, is actually the *burial of the ego* – directed by the mentalsoma, in the parabrain of the psychosoma – into the human body (soma), from the beginning of biological conception, during physical growth, and up to organic and psychological maturity.

2. **Exhumation.** Desoma or biological death is the *exhumation of the ego* from the human body, given that the deactivated soma actually dies and decomposes.

Elimination. The transition of first desoma – deactivation or permanent cessation of the vital functions of the human body (cardiopulmonary death and encephalic death) – do not offer the intraphysical consciousness any means of escape. It also definitively eliminates from the *freed* consciousness: myths, taboos, mysticisms and mystification of all types that confuse the human mind when engaged in comprehension of extraphysical realities.

Conquest. Lucid projection, or physical and temporary minideath, permits this vital conquest while still in human life.

Types. There are 2 basic types of first desoma regarding the time factor:

1. **Sudden.** Sudden death, which includes syncope and asphyxia.
2. **Slow.** Agonized or slow death.

Intentionality. According to intentionality, there can also be two categories of first death:

1. **Voluntary.** Voluntary, in this case, suicide.
2. **Imposed.** Imposed, which occurs through illness, organic deterioration or accident.

Cemetery. Strictly speaking, the cemetery is the last physical base of the human consciousness (intraphysical consciousness) in his/her final projection, last semiphysical projection or the biological death of the soma.

Impure. From the perspective of the vehicle of manifestation, the *impure* extraphysical consciousness is that which only passed through deactivation of the human body (first desoma), without freeing itself from the *remnants of the holochakra* (second desoma).

Liberation. According to what can be observed in the phenomena of projectiology – e.g.: in farewell projections – the death of the physical body does not constitute a *cessation* of energy, but represents more of a *liberation* of energy for the consciousness.

Transference. First desoma, with regard to the human body, occurs because, with the rupture of the silver cord, consciential energy (vital fluid) can no longer be transferred from the consciousness (mentalsoma) through the psychosoma and the holochakra to the human body. From this point on, the soma begins to gradually disaggregate, installing organic chaos and the annihilation of the cells.

Law. The death of the human body and its utilization as a cadaver, or used matter, obeys the *law of conservation of energy* which states that: energy is neither created nor destroyed, but transformed.

Alternation. One of the most complex and controversial subjects in desomatics or thanatology is the bold hypothesis of the exchanging of the intraphysical consciousness in a human body, at an adult age, for another consciousness that is extraphysical, which alternates in the utilization of the vehicle of manifestation of the consciousness.

Splicing. In the hypothesis of alternation – human life without infancy, the transplanting of the entire human body, transmigration in adulthood, adult resoma or the *theory of walk-ins* – there would be an inexplicable rupture of the silver cord that would then be *spliced* to the silver cord of the extraphysical consciousness, which would still have one or, in other words, part of the holochakra. In this case, there would be no deactivation of the human body in the process of changeover of command, which would continue with another consciential, holochakral, psychosomatic and, obviously, mentalsomatic command.

Tenant. In the hypothesis of successive adult lives, or substitution of the consciousness, there would be an experience of first desoma for one consciousness (the first tenant, the donor of the human body) and a simultaneous rebirth in the intraphysical dimension of another consciousness (the second tenant or the walk-in) already as an adult by resurrection through the loan of a cadaver, or even the continuation of another's living human body.

Cannibalization. In a way, this existential alternation is a type of cannibalization, or a removal of usable parts from one piece of equipment in order to better reuse them in another.

Advantages. Those who defend this hypothesis of successive adult lives allege that its occurrence affords 4 essential advantages:

1. **Soma.** Utilization of the human body (soma) of an adult.
2. **Memory.** Conservation of memories that are more vivid than those which are stored, in the manner of organismic or cellular memory, a fact that is extraordinarily difficult to understand.

3. **Maturity.** Elimination of time lost with childhood.

4. **Avoidance.** Avoidance of the temptations and problems characteristic of inexperience during youth.

Possession. Eastern beliefs accept that adult resoma can occur through possession by an extraphysical consciousness – which has just left its human body – of another human body, at the same instant that it is abandoned by its former occupant, there being a productive goal which justifies the occurrence.

Christ. There is also a hypothesis that Jesus of Nazareth, the Christ, was reborn at adult age, precisely on the occasion of his baptism, and thus the existence of the obscure periods of his earlier life, prior to his public life of only 3 years.

Case study. There are reports of exchanges of consciential direction in the East, whereas the most well-known and controversial cases in recent decades, in the West, are the following 2:

1. **Rampa.** Cyril Henry Hoskin – Carl Kuan Suo, or Tuesday Lobsang Rampa, in 1949 (Rampa, 1353, p. 94).

2. **Paladin.** David Paladin (1926-1944) – Wassily Kandinsky (1866-1944), the father of abstract painting (Banerjee, 74, p. 45). In 1985, Mr. David Paladin still lived (?) in the United States of America.

Dissociation. These cases related to the hypothesis of successive adult lives, or walk-in beings, according to more conscientious researchers, should not be confused with the phenomenon of possession or with "dual personality," characterized by psychiatrists, psychoanalysts and psychologists as "dissociation of personality" or "secondary personality".

Possession. Until the present, however, interconsciential possession is certainly *the most rational hypothesis* for explaining these phenomena in most of the abovementioned cases. Existential recycling clarifies certain other cases.

Obscurity. There are still countless obscure facets regarding the death of the human body.

Capgras. Would there be certain rare cases of Capgras syndrome – the illusion of doubles or the illusion of sosies, when the person believes that a friend or relative was substituted by a perfect sosie – related to *walk-in beings* or the possession of adults by ill extraphysical consciousnesses?

Disconnection. It is important to highlight the fact that the consciousness that has recently arrived at the intermissive period does not always immediately disconnect from its cadaver in the act of rupturing the silver cord.

Evidence. A great deal of evidence has been presented by clairvoyant sensitives who see the psychosoma of the individual close to the cadaver, as well as communications from extraphysical consciousnesses tormented by the sensation of still feeling the human body in decomposition.

Apparitions. Besides, in this particular phenomenon, circumstantial indications sponsored by post-desomatic apparitions carry far greater weight.

Scratch. A typical case of apparition is that of *scratches* accidentally made on the *face* of the recently deceased young girl by her mother while dressing the body (cadaver) for burial, which were subsequently covered with makeup, thus keeping the fact secret out of embarrassment.

Disfigurement. This small accident was only made public 9 years later by the brother of the deceased who saw his sister in an apparition, disfigured by the scratches.

Impressions. This proved that, up until the cadaver was dressed, the consciousness of the girl, perhaps already having undergone the rupture of the silver cord, still felt the impressions of the human body and in some way was still located inside it. The girl thus suffered the extraphysical repercussion of the *scratch on her face* as it appeared when her psychosoma was seen by her brother (Ebon, 453, p. 14; Myers, 1114, p. 27).

Hypotheses. This occurrence raises various hypotheses that can contribute to our research. The following are 4 examples:

1. **Energies.** Even after the rupture of the silver cord or, in other words, passage through the first death, does the consciousness still feel the impressions of the human body through the energetic remnants of the holochakra? This seems to be the case in certain extraphysical instances or circumstances.

2. **Pain.** What are these extraphysical circumstances? Could it be that the consciousness of the girl felt the pain provoked by the scratch? This might be the case. Considering these aspects, should the act of cremating cadavers be analyzed in detail?

3. **Self-transfiguration.** Could the consciousness of the girl have seen the scratch on her body during decomposition and modeled or sculpted the scratch on her para-face through self-transfiguration, in the same manner as human stigmatizations? Does this hypothesis seem less probable?

4. **Burial.** Could the silver cord already have been ruptured at the instance of the scratch – or was the youth actually buried alive?

Emotionalism. Soon after the first desoma, the tendency of the intraphysical consciousness that has recently arrived in the intermissive period is to turn the attention inward to internal or intraconsciential life and, above all, to live in sentiments and in the parabrain (of the psychosoma, or emotional parabody), and not in the external world.

Parapsychosis. If the intraphysical consciousness – now an extraphysical consciousness – is evolutionarily still dominated more by animal emotions, or the nonpositive or less evolved sentiments of human life, it has no foundation for the manifestations of its emotionalism. The consequences of this are feelings of anguish, anxiety, extraphysical melancholy and post-desomatic parapsychosis.

Infernos. These antagonistic conditions between internal life and the external world generate the shadowy paratropospheric dimensions and the concepts of hell and *Hades* created by the cosmologies of myriads of religions and theological infernos.

Clairvoyance. One of the lesser and subjective sources of evidence, although not without value for this reason, of the transition of first desoma is the clairvoyance of those sensitives who see intraphysical beings undergo desoma, including the final takeoff of the psychosoma of the moribund individual.

Waste. First desoma should be studied in far greater depth in order to someday avoid the sadness and misfortune of the great waste of tears, worry, time, energy and expenditures related to cadavers, that has been occurring in all countries or on all continents, throughout the centuries, even in this proud age of science and technology, as well as this age of *acceleration of human history*.

Relativity. The relative nature of human life cannot be forgotten: the awareness of the proudest of individuals is reduced every night through sleep; is disturbed in physical life due to illness; and, finally, his/her human body is irreversibly decomposed after desoma or biological death.

Maturity. With the passing of springs and summers, human life, when it is conscientially and evolutionarily productive, naturally manifests the extraphysical maturity or holomaturity of the consciousness. This is expressed by the following 8 unmistakable characteristics, among others:

1. **Disillusions.** An increase in disillusions typical of human immaturity, which are now discovered and identified.

2. **Nostalgia.** The irruption of deep, transcendent nostalgia within the intraphysical consciousness for a world better than that of the intraphysical dimension.

3. **Self-awareness.** A greater self-awareness of the prison or physical restriction characteristic of the human body.

4. **Conception.** A precise conception of the condition of the imprisoned living-dead consciousness, that transforms itself into the dead-living or resuscitated consciousness.

5. **Return.** The idea of the welcome return to its true origin or extraphysical point of origin (extraphysical hometown) after the completion of the personal existential program.

6. **Freedom.** The intense and gratifying longing (or para-longing) for the wide-open spaces of the extraphysical environments and communities.

7. **Happiness.** The happiness of observing one's own human body spontaneously and naturally decaying on its own – regardless of the care given to it – leading to its impending, inevitable, definitive disposal, which makes one change existential priorities.

8. **Anxiety.** The constant, albeit responsible, anxiety for an apparent late return, in the case of the prolonged wait of an elderly person (sixty-five to eighty-four years of age; eighty-five years of age and over).

Observers. Citizens in the United States of America, for example, do not confront the death of the human body in practice. Desoma is relegated to hospitals where the cadaver is covered up with a white sheet.

Responsibility. In this case, the responsibility is transferred to the medical team, while citizens maintain a safe distance as mere "innocent" bystanders.

Thanatophobia. Individuals do not want to confront deactivation of the soma because their fear of biological death – thanatophobia – is too deep-rooted. That is why they "bury their heads in the sand like ostriches," an ego defense mechanism of retrocession.

Desomatics. This is why consolidation of the research and practices of thanatology and desomatics is so important.

Cerebral. The conditions that characterize brain (brain or human body) death, from a medical, clinical or surgical point of view, is the inexistence of voluntary respiratory movement, universal areflexia and dilation of the pupils.

Bibliography: Banerjee (74, p. 39), Baumann (93, p. 71), Blavatsky (153, p. 444), Bozzano (192, p. 125), Brittain (206, p. 65), Chinmoy (280, p. 5), Crookall (339, p. 18), Currie (354, p. 156), Ebon (453, p. 14), Erny (483, p. 82), Flammarion (524, p. 80), Fodor (528, p. 80), Gauld (576, p. 221), Greene (635, p. 60), Greenhouse (636 p. 26), Hodson (729, p. 77), Holms (735, p. 22), Huxley (771, p. 267), Kardec (824, p. 110), Levine (921, p. 1), Morel (1086, p. 127), Myers (1114, p. 27), Noyes Jr. (1142, p. 174), Oldfield (1148, p. 167), Osis (1159, p. 15), Paula (1208, p. 123), Pole (1270, p. 82), Powell (1278, p.107), Rampa (1353, p. 94), Stanké (1595, p. 101), Taylor (1666, p. 152), Underwood (1721, p. 202), Vieira (1762, p. 157), Wang (1794, p. 155), Xavier (1883, p. 268), Zaniah (1899, p. 316).

148. SECOND DESOMA

Definition. Second desoma: deactivation and discarding of the holochakra, including retraction of the remnants of the silver cord and the aura of the holochakra, the extraphysical consciousness thereby remaining in the mentalsoma as well as in the psychosoma, which presents its own aura.

Synonymy: bithanatosis; creation of the astral shell; deactivation of the holochakra; death of the third day; discarding of the holochakra; extraphysical death; final desoma; final discarnation; post-death; post-discarnation; second discarnation; separation of the compound double.

Trace. In deactivation of the holochakra, the remnants of the silver cord vary according to whether the intraphysical consciousness, which has returned to the condition of an extraphysical consciousness, has or has not completed the existential period preestablished by its evolutionary orientation (evolutiologist). In this case, the remnants of its vital energy will have been partially or totally used up.

Purification. Second desoma constitutes the purification of all ectoplasmic emanations of the being (consciousness) that has departed from dense matter. The ectoplasmic emanations of the average intraphysical consciousness disintegrate 2 or 3 days after deactivation of the soma (human body).

Streamlined. From the perspective of the vehicle of manifestation, the *pure* or *streamlined* *extraphysical consciousness* is that which has already discarded the remnants of the silver cord through deactivation of the holochakra.

Bibliography: Aliança (13, p. 152), Beard (99, p. 122), Blavatsky (153, p 715), Bozzano (193, p. 109), Crookall (339, p. 131), Gaynor (577, p. 164), Greenhouse (636, p. 26), Heindel (705, p. 38), Holzer (748, p. 158), Lee (908, p. 91), Oséias, 6: 1-2, Shirley (1553, p. 50), Walker (1782, p. 262), Wedeck (1807, p. 319), Zaniah (1899, p. 408).

149. THIRD DESOMA

Definition. Third desoma: deactivation and discarding of the psychosoma with the rupture of the golden cord and the entrance of the extraphysical consciousness into the condition of free consciousness (FC), from which point it permanently manifests only through the mentalsoma.

Synonymy: birth of the free consciousness; consciential liberation; deactivation of the psychosoma; discarding of the psychosoma; dispensing with the psychosoma; extraphysical death; *moksha;* the end of erraticism; the end of serenism; the end of successive intraphysical lives; trithanatosis.

End. Third death signals the end of the migration of the ego, *Homo sapiens serenissimus (serenissimus),* the extinction of the cycle of the coming and going of resomas and desomas, or personal intraphysical existences. This is the inevitable objective of all consciousnesses or *sentient* beings.

Scale. Third death is the crowning of the evolution of the consciousness at the end of the seventh stage of the scale of continuous self-awareness. It thus initiates a new stage in eternal evolution, and one which is currently entirely unknown by humankind.

Mentalsoma. It is easier to understand the condition of erraticism of the extraphysical consciousness and much more difficult to understand the end of this same erraticism, or the condition of the *domicile* of the extraphysical consciousness in the mentalsoma in the mentalsomatic dimension. What occurs there? It seems that no one is yet able to satisfactorily answer this question.

Primothosene. People naturally always concern themselves with the challenging idea of the existence of the primothosene or the primary cause of the cosmos, or the *uncaused cause.* Perhaps still more disturbing is the idea of the mentalsomatic dimension where the extraphysical consciousness manifests itself forever, without appendices, as we know it, living in its holosomatics only with the mentalsoma, probably in a condition of continuous self-awareness.

Bibliography: Rampa (1361, p. 96), Vieira (1762, p. 214), Walker (1786, p. 22).

150. THE THREE DESOMAS

Ruptures. As can be deduced from the assertions made in the preceding chapters, the 3 desomas merely represent severances, ruptures, phasic mutations or separations of vehicles of manifestation that can be deactivated, discarded and decomposed, in light of the immortality of the consciousness.

Annihilation. None of the 3 desomas, whether analyzed separately or together, in any way imply a complete extinction or annihilation of the self, the consciousness or conscientiality.

Biological. Biological death, due to natural causes, always represents an occurrence that should be considered an authentic evolutionary process of the eternal consciousness and the development of the very vehicles of human manifestation of consciousnesses.

Reactivation. The deactivation of the bodies or vehicles of manifestation of the consciousness seems to be definitive. Their reactivation is impracticable.

Relay. The contrary would appear to be a regressive or unnatural occurrence, in spite of the existence of the above-cited controversial hypothesis of consciential relay, or direct resoma in adulthood which, in a certain aspect, would somehow sponsor this reactivation with the entrance of another consciousness into human life.

Assistant. The first and second desomas of others are occurrences for which lucid intraphysical projectors are called upon to help extraphysically during assistential projections. This turns the projected intraphysical consciousness into an authentic assistant of biological death, within desomatics and thanatology.

Discrepancy. Of the 3 desomas, or the 3 vehicular disposals of the consciousness, the discarding of the human body – desoma or biological death – is the most disconcerting and radical, or the one that presents the greatest environmental discrepancy for the ego.

Approximation. As strange as it may seem, discarding is the occurrence that actually most closely approximates the phenomenon of human lucid projection in its manifestations and effects. This is why it has continued to be so difficult throughout the millennia for the intraphysical consciousness to implement the natural habit of projecting the human body with lucidity to other dimensions beyond the tropospheric life in which we live in intraphysical existence.

Discrepancy. The discrepancy or disparity between the consciential environments or vehicular conditions is 1:1,000 when the intraphysical consciousness projects in the psychosoma (bearing in mind the *weight* of this vehicle) and 1:∞ ("infinity") when the intraphysical consciousness projects only in the isolated mentalsoma. The lucid projector would do well to meditate deeply upon this topic.

Rebirths. The following is a hypothesis: just as there are 3 desomas, each successive life constitutes 3 rebirths or distinct stages: conception, parturition and human maturity.

1. **Conception.** First stage: biological conception or, in other words, the initial union of the psychosoma with the human body or resoma per se. At this point pre-resoma – or the act of creating the silver cord which initiates the action of the energetic body (holochakra) – has already occurred. This first stage is the period of cooperation or co-optation of the extraphysical consciousness undergoing resoma with another intraphysical consciousness (pregnant woman) or other extraphysical consciousnesses (the consciousness of another fetus or other fetuses, twins, triplets or xiphopaguses).

2. **Parturition.** Second stage: *délivrance,* or the act of birth per se, allows the extraphysical consciousness to begin to act freely and individually by itself in the intraphysical dimension and to temporarily be an intraphysical consciousness *(spatialization of the extraphysical consciousness).* Every individual leaves the womb as a male or female animal.

3. **Maturity.** Third stage: it is only in physical or biological maturity, after childhood, youth or at 26 years of physical age, that the intraphysical consciousness is able to entirely manifest itself (psychological maturity), revealing all the potential (paragenetics, innate ideas, charisma, holomemory, recuperation of cons) that he/she brings with him/herself. There are many consciousnesses that undergo resoma and desoma without having passed through the third stage.

Relationships. This phase of physical maturity is preceded by an effective consolidation of the intraphysical consciousness in a new human life, which generally occurs at about seven years of physical age. Physical maturity, however, has no direct relationship with most human codes (21 years of age).

Anchoring. Further, this physical maturity does not depend upon the condition of a greater psychophysiological anchoring of the resomant extraphysical consciousness, as the opposite generally occurs: the intraphysical being who is less physically anchored can achieve mental or psychological maturity more rapidly and, as a result, can achieve extraphysical maturity or holomaturity even more rapidly.

Double. Despite evolutionary obstacles, according to reports in extraphysical communities or environments, there are already intraphysical consciousnesses on this planet who are able to sponsor first and second desoma at the same time *(double desoma).* In this case, the consciousness, in a wholesale manner or all at once, promotes the positive, healthy donation of consciential energy – still human in nature – to ill (intraphysical and/or extraphysical) consciousnesses.

Immolation. In terms of tropospheric assistance, it is presumed that this energetic immolation may constitute the maximal, final realization that is attainable by the intraphysical consciousness *(serenissimi),* through a chakral self-desoma.

Exclusions. This act of consciential parahygiene promotes at least the following 4 exclusions:

1. **Trauma.** The biological or traumatic shock of desoma.
2. **Paraprophylaxis.** The condition of post-desomatic parapsychosis (paraprophylaxis).
3. **Self-efficiency.** *Wastes* in energetic applications (evolutionary self-efficiency).
4. **Vampirizations.** Interconsciential vampirizations by the extraphysical consciousness when *energivorous.*

Bibliography: Bennett (117, p. 29), Vieira (1762, p. 157).

151. COMPARISONS BETWEEN OCCASIONAL AND FINAL PROJECTION

Rupture. Biological death is the last cause for an involuntary projection when, with the rupture of the silver cord, the extraphysical consciousness can only undergo resoma in another human body (soma) in a new intraphysical existence.

Nature. Based upon the nature of human life, in the same way that both natural desoma and forced desoma exist, natural (spontaneous) lucid projection and forced lucid projection also occur.

Differential. The following are 6 basic differential characteristics between final projection, or deactivation of the human body, and ordinary consciential projection:

1. **Cord.** In final projection, the definitive rupture of the silver cord takes place, a fact which defines deactivation of the human body. In ordinary lucid projection, the silver cord is merely temporarily dislodged from its organic, physical base, to which it soon returns.

2. **Discoincidence.** In final projection, the definitive discoincidence of the vehicles of manifestation of the consciousness occurs, especially the psychosoma leaving the human body forever. In ordinary projection, there is only a temporary discoincidence of these vehicles.

3. **Sleep.** In most cases, final projection leads the consciousness to go through a period of extraphysical rest or so-called *restorative sleep*. In projection with continuous self-awareness, for example, the condition of uninterrupted wakefulness occurs during the entire process, with no sleep, dreams or nightmares of any kind.

4. **Vision.** Final projection consistently presents a retrospective panoramic vision that is often comprehensive with regard to the intraphysical consciousness' current human existence. It is uncommon for the panoramic vision to arise in consciential projection, although it sometimes occurs during certain near-death phenomena (NDE).

5. **Assistance.** Final projection invariably receives extraphysical assistance from helpers or extraphysical consciousnesses that are specialists in handling the processes of desomatics. Ordinary consciential projection most often occurs without the tangible or visible assistance of helpers.

6. *Deaths*. Final projection is the definitive *physical death* of the human body. Occasional ordinary projection represents a mere temporary *psychic (brain devoid of content) death* of the human body, which remains in the *empty brain* condition.

Doorways. The doorways to consciential projection – the ordinary, physical waking state, daydreams, sleepiness, natural sleep, ordinary dreams, nightmares, the hypnagogic state and extracorporeal sleep – are the same ones through which the consciousness achieves final projection (biological or somatic death).

Possessions. The human body, the clothes in which it is dressed and the personal effects that remain with the soma constitute the immediate possessions of the human projector that are left behind on the occasion of his/her final projection.

Processes. There are 2 processes which are relatively characteristic of biological shocks:

1. **Condensation.** Resoma is an extraphysical-physical condensation process.

2. **Decomposition.** Desoma is a physical-extraphysical decomposition process (dissipation, evaporation or gasification).

Bibliography: Bozzano (184, p. 149), Druly (414, p. 39), Shay (1546, p. 28), Steiger (1601, p. 107), Xavier (1883, p. 209), Yogananda (1894, p. 245).

> ## 152. COMPARISONS BETWEEN THE PSYCHOSOMA OF THE INTRAPHYSICAL AND EXTRAPHYSICAL CONSCIOUSNESS

Differential. The intraphysical consciousness projected in the psychosoma and the extraphysical consciousness – the deceased consciousness or the supraliving being; which normally manifests itself through the same vehicle, having already passed through the second death or, in other words, having deactivated the holochakra – present a number of differential characteristics when compared. This greatly aids in the identification of extraphysical consciousnesses encountered by the lucid projector in his/her experiences. The following are 17 notable examples:

1. **Cord.** The fundamental difference with regard to the psychosoma of the intraphysical consciousness and that of the extraphysical consciousness is in the connection with the human body – the silver cord – which is inevitably connected to it and, as free as it may be in the extraphysical dimension, in a projection in the psychosoma, will always be far more strongly bound than the healthy extraphysical consciousness that has already passed through second desoma.

2. **Holochakra.** The psychosoma of the projected intraphysical consciousness can exhibit the energies of the holochakra, including the dense irradiations of the human aura, which does not occur with the healthy extraphysical consciousness in the state of (extraphysical) coincidence, when it has already passed through second desoma.

3. **Resoma.** Resoma or human life itself is always a parody or a poor imitation, a copy of the extraphysical life of the extraphysical consciousness when free and healthy, or devoid of disturbances related to post-desomatic parapsychopathology, beginning with the possible manifestations of the psychosoma of the intraphysical consciousness that are greatly muffled or restricted with regard to sensations. Resoma is a process which is diminishing, funneling, delimiting, reducing, microsynthesizing and restricting for the ego or the extraphysical consciousness.

4. **Restriction.** Analysis of the extraphysical period of lucid projection leads the experienced projector to understand that in intraphysical life the intraphysical consciousness suffers a consciential restriction or constriction at a ratio of 1,000:1, or a reduction to one thousandth. This is similar to what happens regarding weight, between the human body and the psychosoma, when the intraphysical consciousness goes from having the sensation of weighing 154 lbs. (70 Kg) to the lightness of 2.47 oz. (70 g). This rationally indicates that the plenitude of consciential life is annulled at a level of 99.9%, with the physical restriction that is imposed through resoma or human existence.

5. **Period.** The difference between the *brief* extraphysical period of the intraphysical consciousness' projection and the *prolonged* interval between the extraphysical consciousness' human lives (intermissive period) shows the projector's consciousness that it is necessary to take advantage of the chance for extraphysical freedom as far as possible. This fact disturbs the intraphysical projector's choice regarding his/her mental targets, leading to indecision in his/her extraphysical behavior: simultaneous choices of destinations; interruptions due to interference from another chosen consciential target; gate-crashing-projection; and others.

6. **Perceptions.** From the data presented, it can be concluded that any comparison between the possibilities of the capacities and perceptions of the *intraphysical* projector, projected in the psychosoma, and the *extraphysical consciousness* manifesting through the same vehicle, will always result in the verification of a negative difference in manifestations, against the human projector. This generally starts at a ratio of 1:1,000 (99.9%) or at least on an order of 1:100 (99%).

7. **Weight.** The psychosoma of the projected projector, even without the holochakra and even when in a condition of low condensation, will always be denser and heavier than the psychosoma of the free extraphysical consciousness that is manifesting through this vehicle. This is because the projected projector does not lose the insertion of the silver cord in the psychosoma, as well as the remnants of semiphysical energies, which are always quite visible or perceptible and active.

8. **Volume.** The projector's psychosoma always appears *fatter*, *swollen* or apparently larger in volume than the *thinner* psychosoma of the extraphysical consciousness. This is not only due to density, through the silver cord when active, but is also due to the existence of the laden holochakra, which is *over* or interpenetrant with the psychosoma, which is a frequent occurrence during lucid projections.

9. **Self-luminosity.** The psychosoma of the extraphysical consciousness is more luminous, brilliant and transparent than the psychosoma of the projected intraphysical consciousness. This is due to his/her greater density, which gives him/her greater translucence or even complete opacity. It is also why the projected consciousness has difficulty in maintaining serenity and *natural* manifestations, including self-luminosity.

10. **Energy.** Physical energy, or that of the human body, which the psychosoma of the intraphysical consciousness carries with it when projecting, is so different in quality or nature from the energy of the psychosoma of the evolved extraphysical consciousness, e.g.: the helper, that it is used with the helper's orientation and aid in treating ill intraphysical consciousnesses and even extraphysical consciousnesses with post-desomatic parapsychosis during the experienced projector's assistential projections.

11. **Time.** The intraphysical projector who is more influenced by the conditioning of chronological time and only rarely has a free period of projection with full lucidity endeavors to take greater advantage of the opportunity. This makes it such that the events seem to transpire more rapidly for the projector, but this is not always the case.

12. **Transfigurations.** It is easier for the extraphysical consciousness to transfigure its lone, *streamlined* psychosoma or one that is devoid of the holochakra and the amount of dense physical matter, than it is for the projected projector to do so. This fact gives the ill extraphysical consciousness an advantage in confrontations with the projector which is projected from the human body in dimensions that are still very paratropospheric.

13. **Alterations.** Extraphysical consciousnesses more frequently present pathological alterations of the psychosoma, which does not easily occur with the psychosoma of the projected intraphysical consciousness. This fact favors the veteran projector.

14. **Performance.** The superexcitability of the projected projector when desiring to take maximum advantage of his/her *extraphysical minivacations* always impairs the full use of his/her possibilities for manifestation, as well as his/her choice of destination and performance outside the human body in general. This does not happen with the extraphysical consciousness, which is aware of its more permanent extraphysical existence.

15. **Confrontations.** The abovementioned aspects speak in favor of the fact that, in consciential confrontations during extraphysical attacks by ill extraphysical consciousnesses and in deintrusive tasks during projection, the projector always receives the cooperation of the helper, without which any extraphysical conflict would be impracticable. This is due to the disparity of forces that favors the extraphysical consciousness – even when it is an ill one – as long as it has a fair amount of consciential lucidity.

16. **Troposphere.** There are not as many healthy extraphysical consciousnesses on the terrestrial crust as one might presume. In certain localized areas, one can only find a considerable number of ill extraphysical consciousnesses that are in lack of physical energies (energivores) trying to satisfy their still human material sensations. In a rough comparison, it is not worthwhile for the *healthy* extraphysical consciousness to leave its comfortable *residential neighborhood* or extraphysical community located in a better extraphysical dimension only to lose its way in the dark meanderings of the *basfonds* of the paratropospheric dimension together with humans.

17. **Gravitation.** The gravitational force of this planet only exercises a relative influence upon consciousnesses that are disturbed by their psychological reflexes or on the occasions when they manifest with an excessively condensed psychosoma. However, this fact does not affect the healthy extraphysical consciousness, but can affect the projected projector, in certain circumstances.

153. COMPARISONS BETWEEN THE PSYCHOSOMA AND THE MENTALSOMA

Format. With respect to format, the consciential manifestations through the human body (or the unified body) occur along the longitudinal direction of the psychosoma. This is why the human is a social being that has a *long*, vertical, erect form (even when the upper and lower members are extended, lengthwise or longitudinal) and a center of gravity in the encephalic or superior extremity.

Omnidirectional. The consciential manifestations through the isolated mentalsoma occur through the universal component of *formlessness* or omnidirectionality. The *antigravitational* mentalsoma does not have length or a longitudinal direction.

Differential. The following are 20 differential factors that allow the consciousness to distinguish the vehicle of manifestation in which it is projecting on that occasion and the disparities between lucid projections in the psychosoma (always transporting the mentalsoma in the parabrain) and those in the isolated mentalsoma:

1. **Takeoff.** The takeoff of the intraphysical consciousness in the psychosoma can be perceived by the projector *throughout* his/her human body. The takeoff in the mentalsoma only occurs in the cortical area or only within the braincase (encephalon).

2. **Self-awareness.** The psychosoma enables levels of awareness above the ordinary, physical waking state. The mentalsoma permits the condition of cosmoconsciousness or maximal expansion of the consciousness (hyperacuity).

3. **Disconnections.** The psychosoma only projects from the human body in a simple or single disconnection. The mentalsoma projects from the psychosoma (parabrain) while the latter is coincident with the human body or even when it is discoincident, at a distance from the human body. In this case, a double disconnection occurs.

4. **Dimensions.** The psychosoma only travels in paratropospheric or crustal extraphysical dimensions and in native or pure dimensions. It also permits direct manifestation with the physical, human dimension, including telekinesis and other phenomena, acting at a *motor* or even tactile extraphysical level. The mentalsoma enables understanding from a *mental* or maximal transcendent visual perspective, although it does not permit motor or tactile manifestation, acting at a direct and pure consciousness-to-consciousness level.

5. **Coincidences.** The psychosoma always renews its *coincidence* with new human bodies (somas) during lifetimes. The mentalsoma always remains at the same coincidence with the psychosoma until the third desoma.

6. **Form.** The psychosoma has some type of humanoid or other form. This is due to the transfigurations and self-transfigurations that are *seen* and *perceived* by the consciousness, including extraphysical clothing. The mentalsoma is formless or incorporeal. In fact, the term *body* is not even appropriate for naming it as a vehicle. The consciousness feels *invisible* even to itself in this vehicle.

7. **Growing.** The psychosoma continues to insert the four-dimensional, humanoid form of its evolution, until reaching adult human form, at which point it no longer grows. The mentalsoma always *grows* in some manner during the evolution of the ego.

8. **Connection.** The psychosoma *ostensively* and manifestly presents the action of the silver cord, particularly its retractable function, aside from various other defined aspects. The subtle golden cord, which connects the psychosoma to the mentalsoma, is not a visualizable intercorporal element like the silver cord.

9. **Appendices.** The psychosoma, besides presenting a connection belonging to the human body – the silver cord – has the golden cord, which is its own connection with the mentalsoma. To our knowledge, the mentalsoma has no intercorporal connection of its own.

10. **Weight.** The psychosoma provides the consciousness with a certain *sensation* of weight, albeit an extremely minor one, being hypothetically one thousandth of the weight of the human body. The mentalsoma does not allow the consciousness to perceive any sensation of weight.

11. **Emotionalism.** The psychosoma – the vehicle of emotion, the emotional body or that of desires – exacerbates the projector's emotionalism, that is common in his/her ordinary, physical waking state. The mentalsoma does not enable coarse emotionalism.

12. **Influences.** The psychosoma permits extraphysical attacks upon the projected projector by extraphysical consciousnesses and the performance of deintrusive projections. The mentalsoma neither allows extraphysical attacks nor does it allow deintrusive projections in the manner that it is performed. This is because the extraphysical approach occurs in the mentalsomatic dimension.

13. **Parapsychism.** The psychosoma enables the projected projector to operate as a sensitive when in the extraphysical dimension, in manners similar to those used in the intraphysical dimension or human life. The *parapsychic* perceptions, including the performance of a more ample parapsychism, are more advanced when the consciousness is operating in the mentalsoma.

14. **Participation.** The consciousness, when operating in the psychosoma, is more of a participant (protagonist) than an observer (spectator) of extraphysical events. The consciousness, when manifesting through the mentalsoma, is fully an observer, within its possibilities to do so and only participates in the facts *mentally*, or in a mentalsomatic dimension.

15. **Communication.** The psychosoma allows the consciousness to articulate extraphysical speech or *mechanicoid* transmental dialogue. The mentalsoma only enables pure extraphysical telepathy, including *conscientese*, and no other process of communication.

16. **Gravitation.** The consciousness, when projected in the psychosoma, can feel the action of gravitational and geoenergetic forces upon it in certain paratropospheric extraphysical environments. These same forces never act upon the mentalsoma.

17. **Currents.** The consciousness, when projected in the psychosoma, can be carried along by extraphysical force currents which, in turn, are not active in the mentalsomatic dimension where the mentalsoma manifests.

18. *Tempests.* The consciousness projected in the psychosoma can feel certain effects of *extraphysical hydromagnetic tempests* which, in turn, are not active in the mentalsomatic dimension where the mentalsoma – the parabody of discernment – manifests.

19. **Visualization.** The psychosoma is *visualized* by a greater number of consciousnesses in 3 dimensions: the dense physical or human dimension (apparition of the projected intraphysical consciousness and physical bilocation), the paratropospheric extraphysical dimension and the *native* extraphysical dimension per se. The mentalsoma is *not* visualized by the extraphysical consciousnesses of these 3 dimensions and its presence is perceived in a different manner, at a purely parapsychic level, in the mentalsomatic dimension.

20. **Repercussions.** The psychosoma predisposes the occurrence of well-defined physical and extraphysical repercussions. The mentalsoma can detect the occurrence of some disturbance with the human body, although it does not allow the consciousness to suffer extraphysical traumas at a distance from this same human body.

Psychosoma. The consciousness that predominantly uses the psychosoma over the mentalsoma, besides leaning towards emotionalism, evidences at least the following 6 tendencies:

1. **Symbols.** He/she endeavors to express him/herself more through symbols, images or icons, in the form of objects, instead of concepts.

2. *Crutches.* This *psychosomatic* person still relies upon a greater number of psychophysiological *crutches*.

3. **Insecurity.** He/she is more needy than secure.

4. **Limitation.** His/her horizon or consciential microuniverse is more limited.

5. **Impoverishment.** His/her thoughts are impoverished and therefore closer to illogicalities, mental deficiencies, demential states and psychoses, and further from true maturity of the mentalsoma.

6. **Discordance.** His/her thoughts or thosenizations are still in stark discordance with the objective reality of the consciential dimension wherever he/she is.

Mentalsoma. The consciousness that predominantly uses the mentalsoma over the psychosoma evidences at least the following 8 more evolved tendencies:

1. **Agreement.** His/her thoughts are in greater agreement with the objective reality of the dimension of consciential life where he/she is on that occasion.
2. **Concepts.** He/she is able to express him/herself with concepts and not only with symbols.
3. **Dispense.** He/she dispenses with psychophysiological crutches.
4. **Maturity.** He/she has already discovered the value and necessity of consciential maturity.
5. **Microuniverse.** He/she has a more ample horizon or consciential microuniverse.
6. **Rationality.** He/she bases him/herself in rationality and not emotionalism.
7. **Security.** He/she is more secure than needy.
8. **Self-thosenes.** He/she enjoys a richer mental life and more productive self-thosenes.

Emotions. There is an evolutionary passage, born of balance and discernment, from the human-animal to the human-consciousness.

Aura. Any very strong sentiment charges the entire human body, energizes the mind and alters the coloration of the aura and the psychosoma.

Instincts. The consciousness that still lives more with the psychosoma is susceptible to being easily dominated by instinctive emotions, whether they are: aggression, anger, avarice, courage, despair, disagreement, disharmony, egoism, envy, equanimity, fear, frustration, grief, hate, hostility, indifference, jealousy, passion, possessiveness, rivalry, sadness, shame, vanity, violence and others.

Exchange. The consciousness that makes an effort to live more with the mentalsoma exchanges the above-cited sensations for positive elevated sentiments, or rationalized emotions, such as: agreement, compassion, disinterested friendship, fraternity, happiness, harmony, kindness, pure love, a sense of humanity, serenity, understanding and others.

Bibliography: Greene (635, p. 49), Vieira (1762, p. 73), Walker (1782, p. 296).

---

154. COMPARISONS BETWEEN THE MENTALSOMA OF THE INTRAPHYSICAL AND EXTRAPHYSICAL CONSCIOUSNESS

Different. According to logical suppositions derived from extraphysical facts, the intraphysical consciousness projected in the mentalsoma presents at least the following 6 basic characteristics which are different from the mentalsoma of the extraphysical consciousness:

1. **First.** The mentalsoma – in the mentalsomatic projection of the intraphysical consciousness, which leaves the state of coincidence of the ordinary, physical waking state and has still not gone through any of the 3 desomas – is different from the mentalsoma of the extraphysical consciousness with regard to lucid projection. Firstly, this extraphysical consciousness has already passed through deactivation of the human body and, depending upon the interval between its first and second desoma, is less likely to leave the psychosoma immersed in post-desomatic disturbance or in the phase of restorative sleep, as it is temporarily *more bound.*

2. **Second.** The mentalsoma – in the mentalsomatic projection of the intraphysical consciousness that has not yet passed through any of the 3 desomas – is different from that of the extraphysical consciousness, which has already passed through the second desoma, mainly with regard to a greater difficulty in exteriorizing. The extraphysical consciousness that has had its human body and holochakra deactivated is *less bound* and more inclined to have projection in the mentalsoma.

3. **Third.** The mentalsoma – in the mentalsomatic projection of the intraphysical consciousness who has not yet passed through any of the 3 desomas – is obviously very different from the free mentalsoma of the extraphysical consciousness that has already experienced the 3 desomas and has achieved the condition of free consciousness, therefore being beyond the prison of the evolutionarily inferior vehicles of manifestation.

4. Takeoffs. The extraphysical consciousness takes off from its *free psychosoma*, with the mentalsoma enjoying a much greater ease than the intraphysical consciousness who always has his/her *psychosoma bound* to the human body.

5. Relief. In the act of resoma, the following incorporate themselves into the human body simultaneously: the ego, the mentalsoma, the psychosoma and the foundations of the holochakra. In the act of desoma, the intraphysical consciousness, in the mentalsoma, is relieved of the human body (first desoma) and the holochakra (second desoma), remaining only with the psychosoma.

6. Restriction. The mentalsoma of the intraphysical consciousness undergoes *double restriction*: *inside* the psychosoma and *inside* the human body. The mentalsoma of the ordinary extraphysical consciousness experiences only a single restriction: *inside* the psychosoma.

Metaphor. Incidentally, the physical restriction imposed upon the consciousness, through the law of successive lives from biological conception to adulthood, can be better understood as consciential evolutionary impulsion by way of metaphor. The gardener goes to the garden and prunes and cuts the entire rosebush seeming to kill it, leaving only the stump of the trunk of the mutilated rosebush. Time passes, however, and during the subsequent summer the rosebush reappears, flowering exuberantly, with greater vigor and lushness.

Adaptation. The more unconsciously adapted the intraphysical consciousness is to the human environment, the less he/she feels the physical restriction of human life. He/she is fully well-adjusted – like an *autochthon* – to his/her environment or *habitat*.

Maladaptation. On the other hand, the more evolved the intraphysical consciousness is, the more consciously aware he/she is of the condition of physical restriction and the more effort he/she makes in order to disentangle him/herself from it. He/she thus lives in an instigating, challenging and conscious maladaptation, that is a function of successive lives. With this the individual amplifies his/her consciential powers and the scope of his/her interworld or multidimensional influence.

Ignorance. The more adapted the intraphysical consciousness is to the condition of physical restriction, the less harm he/she can inflict upon others. This is because he/she neither has the means nor the skill (*evolutionary know-how*) to expand his/her powers of consciential action. The wrongs performed by the individual are singularly restricted to the limits of the physical surface of the illusory world of matter.

Limitation. Thus, the condition of physical restriction, in and of itself, naturally delimits the possibilities of the intraphysical consciousness' action. This also signifies that all human wrongs, although a lamentable fruit of ignorance, and unnecessary up to a certain point, are always confined within the cosmos, are circumscribed, limited and relative.

Animal. The subhuman, wild, instinctive, violent animal remains constantly ready and continuously anxious to physically eliminate another animal (often a sibling), if possible with its own claws and teeth, in the constant struggle for survival or, in other words, the maintenance of its own physical life.

Weakness. Its power is *weak*, however, because its thought or *self-thosene* (zoothosene) is impotent.

Ineptitude. The human consciousness who wishes to inflict harm upon social beings, always fighting in some way in defense of its instinctive human body, is still not very distant from this unevolved condition of the wild animal, although he/she has cerebral hemispheres with greater consciential possibilities – a fact he/she is unaware of – which he/she obviously does not know how to use (evolutionary ineptness) to the full extent of its resources.

Restraint. Neither – dominated by the instincts characteristic of the animal body and the emotions characteristic of the psychosoma – possess the mental resources and are unable to achieve extensive results in their actions because they are naturally restrained and circumscribed by the condition of physical restriction of the consciousness.

Brain. Every intraphysical consciousness uses a greater or lesser but extremely individual percentage of the functional resources of the cerebral hemispheres. The more optimistic conventional sciences accept that when an individual is using his/her brain at a high level, the brain is still only using 21% of its potential, the remaining 79% thus being idle.

Violence. The act of violence is one of the more characteristic and typical signals of consciential adaptation to the condition of physical restriction of the intraphysical consciousness.

Control. It can easily be concluded that any act of violence in any part of the physical universe, as drastic as its apparent collective reflexes may seem, always has limited repercussions that are already forecast by other consciousnesses which are free from consciential restriction, are an *infinite number of evolutionary light-years ahead* and in greater control of everything that is happening here.

FCs. These consciousnesses – free consciousnesses or FCs – have already freed themselves from the condition of physical restriction, violence, animal emotions and the dominating influence of the emotional parabody in order to act with full consciential maturity directly through the mentalsoma (the parabody of discernment) through cosmic, extremely elevated sentiments, or with the rationalized emotions of greater holomaturity. This is the experience of continuous or permanent cosmoconsciousness.

Order. The holosomatic evolutionary conquests of the consciousness over itself presents a correct and ideal order that is better than others, as it is more efficient: the order of the (naturally ascending) crescendo.

Mastery. With regard to its vehicles of manifestation, the consciousness firstly needs to master the more rudimentary manifestations of the human body; then the manifestations of the consciential energies of the energetic parabody (holochakra); followed by the manifestations of the animalized emotions; and, lastly, the modelings of the mentalsoma.

Alteration. Any alteration of this logical order of evolutionary conquests still brings incurable gaps to the overall harmony of the consciousness' microuniverse.

155. RELATIONSHIPS BETWEEN CONSCIENTIAL VEHICLES AND CONSCIENTIAL PHENOMENA

Patterns. In a comparison between the 4 vehicles of manifestation of the consciousness and the dozens of phenomena of projectiology, certain patterns clearly and logically emerge which, by being emphasized, enhance the precision and raise the level of understanding in the field of analysis of conscientiology in general.

Predominance. Some consciential phenomena presented may be controversial when they are subordinated specifically to one position, in a scale of development. However, maximum consensus needs to be attempted based upon a variable that is considered to be fundamental: the possible predominance of the manifestation of the consciousness based upon one vehicle in the generating acts of each phenomenon. Evidently, the level of evolution of the predominant consciential vehicle can be the factor which determines the evolutionary level of the phenomenon.

Scale. This is why, upon establishing a scale of ascending evolutionary magnitude of projectiological phenomena, based upon a predominant consciential vehicle, or 2, 3 or 4 vehicles of consciential manifestation that operate in sequence, there are 10 blocks of phenomena (see fig. 155).

Blocks

1	*Human body*			
2	Human body	Holochakra		
3	Human body	Holochakra	Psychosoma	
4	Human body	Holochakra	Psychosoma	Mentalsoma
5		*Holochakra*		
6		Holochakra	Psychosoma	
7		Holochakra	Psychosoma	Mentalsoma
8			*Psychosoma*	
9			Psychosoma	Mentalsoma
10				*Mentalsoma*

Figure 155

1. **Human body:** included here are all the phenomena which are only restricted to conventional anatomy, physiology and psychology, researched by official science or perspectives which are exclusively physicalist with regard to the ego. It should be stressed, however, that many physiological and pathological manifestations still involve the holochakra and other vehicles of consciential manifestations, hence the existence of acupuncture, do-in, acupressure and homeopathy.

2. **Human body and energetic parabody:** self-telekinesis; extraphysical double vision. Based on this phenomenological block, projectiological occurrences – researched by projectiology, or by holistic approaches to the ego – have their beginnings.

3. **Human body, holochakra and psychosoma:** animic or projective poltergeist; animic or projective raps; classic physical bilocation; consciential self-bilocation; external autoscopy; extraphysical repercussions during consciential projection; extraphysical telekinesis; human parateleportation; physical repercussions during consciential projection; projective catalepsy; projective ectoplasmy; resuscitative projection; semimaterialization; sonorous projection; the state of suspended animation; waking discoincidence.

4. **Human body, holochakra, psychosoma and mentalsoma:** cardiac self-desoma; double awareness; double projection; extraphysical precognition; extraphysical retrocognition; internal autoscopy; phenomena concomitant with lucid projection; projective déjà vu; self-psychophony; traveling clairvoyance; umbilical self-desoma; voluntary self-combustion.

5. **Holochakra:** extraphysical parapyrogenesis; physical multilocation.

6. **Holochakra and psychosoma:** exteriorization of motricity; exteriorization of sensitivity; extraphysical clairvoyance; extraphysical elongation; extraphysical projective psychophony; false arrival; farewell projection; projective heteroscopy; projective pneumatophony; projective psychography; semifinal projection.

7. **Holochakra, psychosoma and mentalsoma:** creation of morphothosenes; extraphysical psychometry; extraphysical self-transfiguration; possessive projection; projective psychophony; zoanthropy.

8. **Psychosoma:** extraphysical euphoria.

9. **Psychosoma and mentalsoma:** extraphysical intuition; extraphysical telepathy.

10. **Mentalsoma:** conscientese; cosmoconsciousness.

Frequency. The specific consciential phenomena of intraphysical consciousnesses are included from phenomenological block 1 up to phenomenological block 4, but they even reach phenomenological block 10. The phenomena of projectiology more often occur in the area of phenomenological block 3 or, in other words, with the soma, holochakra and psychosoma together. This is to be expected, in light of our condition as intraphysical beings. For the same reason, soon thereafter the most often encountered projectiological phenomena fall within phenomenological block 4, or when the 4 vehicles of consciential manifestation act together. The consciential phenomena characteristic of extraphysical consciousnesses begin at phenomenological block 5 and span up to phenomenological block 10.

Energies. Strictly speaking, consciential energies come into play and participate in some manner in the development of every consciential phenomenon. What varies in each case is the nature or type of acting energy. Listed here are those projectiological phenomena in which consciential energy is the predominant, main factor, based upon the holochakra. These phenomena basically depend upon the mild or impactful consciential energies involved.

Phenomena. The mentalsoma obviously participates in every consciential phenomenon. However, it does not participate directly in the development of unconscious consciential phenomena.

Self-bilocation. The fact that one consciential vehicle predominates in the development of a projectiological phenomenon can be better approached and understood more simply. For example, upon studying the phenomenon of consciential self-bilocation and the human body, the real engine of the phenomenon, or that which actually generates consciential self-bilocation, is the holochakra, which allows the consciousness to generally see the human body through the psychosoma.

Déjà vu. It merits noting the fact that in projective déjà vu (block 4), the projected consciousness, in a first phase, sees something or experiences a certain extraphysical activity through the psychosoma and, in a second phase, recalls the extraphysical occurrences through the human body in the ordinary, physical waking state. When the intraphysical consciousness is projected he/she experiences the déjà vu directly through the psychosoma, in most experiences. However, only the integral memory (holomemory), an attribute of the consciousness headquartered in the mentalsoma, is able to unite the two phases to compose the phenomenon of projective déjà vu.

Evolution. It can be verified that the greatest number of projectiological phenomena occur by way of the holochakra (energetic parabody) and the psychosoma (emotional parabody). This is coherent with human reality, because it corresponds precisely to the nature and evolutionary level of this planet. In the analysis of psychological phenomena, the human body predominates in the phenomenological set. In this projectiological analysis, immediately following the human body – which allows the consciousness to manifest in the concrete physical dimension of the forms and space of this planet – is the (as yet animal) psychosoma, which transports the consciousness and obviously predominates in the consciential dealings in this environment. Hence the characteristics of this scale, as well as the fact of the still considerable predominance of immaturity and emotionalism in human proceedings.

---

156. RELATIONSHIPS BETWEEN CHAKRAS AND CONSCIENTIAL PHENOMENA

Analysis. In analyzing the dozens of phenomena of projectiology relative to the chakras, the importance of the role played by the holochakra (energetic parabody) in the development of the human consciousness stands out.

Scale. The following is a list of the major chakras and the most common projectiological phenomena, presented in decreasing importance with regard to the 7 levels of energetic centers:

1. **All:** all the chakras together or the entire holochakra; self-telekinesis; double projection; extraphysical psychometry; waking discoincidence; state of suspended animation; physical multilocation; extraphysical elongation; farewell projection; human parateleportation; resuscitative projection; projective pneumatophony; semifinal projection; zoanthropy; extraphysical repercussions during lucid projection; voluntary self-combustion; traveling clairvoyance.

2. **Coronochakra:** projective catalepsy; double awareness; projective déjà vu; extraphysical precognition; extraphysical retrocognition; projective psychography.

3. **Frontochakra:** extraphysical double vision; consciential self-bilocation; internal autoscopy; extraphysical clairvoyance; projective heteroscopy.

4. **Laryngochakra:** extraphysical projective psychophony.

5. **Cardiochakra:** cardiac self-desoma; exteriorization of sensitivity.

6. **Umbilicochakra:** (almost always involving the sexochakra and the splenochakra): projective ectoplasmy (vegetative); semimaterialization; animic or projective poltergeist; animic or projective raps; sonorous projection; extraphysical telekinesis; umbilical self-desoma; extraphysical parapyrogenesis; exteriorization of motricity; false arrival.

7. **Sexochakra:** interconsciential possession; *congressus subtilis.*

VI – *Philosophical Perspectives*

157. PROJECTIOLOGY AND PHILOSOPHY

Definitions. Philosophy: the organized system of knowledge that seeks to explain the universe, the natural forces that operate within it, the purpose of existence, the correct manner for one to organize and live one's life, the relationship between humankind and the universe, and interrelationships within humankind; the science that studies all things through their fundamental reasons, acquired in light of natural reasoning.

Synonymy: culture of knowledge; extension of sciences; gnosis; investigation of knowledge; science of reasoning; set of doctrines; set of specific knowledge; wisdom.

Reason. It is a commonly accepted fact among the greatest researchers that science does not exist without philosophy. There are those who affirm that it would not be inaccurate to consider all sciences as subdisciplines of philosophy. Hence the reason for this section in this book.

Interpretation. The complete absence of a philosophy of life is as harmful as a false philosophy. To have an interpretation of the meaning of existence based on solid foundations is what most intraphysical consciousnesses wish, above all, to have. Projectiology can offer this.

Solution. Strictly speaking, there does not seem to be another solution, as seen in the following: the lucid human projector, upon discovering and experiencing other consciential dimensions – which surpass the restricted possibilities of merely physical experimentation of contemporary science – can only live in peace, firstly, through a philosophy based in multidimensionality; secondly, through projectiology, the science of multidimensionality.

Conceptualizations. When lucid consciential projections register, organize and transmit new concepts of the reality of the cosmos to human beings, they lead the individual to well-defined philosophical conceptualizations, such as the following 5, among many others:

1. **Metempiricism.** The extraphysical experiments would be metempiric as they are beyond empiricism, or in a condition the knowledge of which cannot be achieved through ordinary sensorial experience.

2. **Reevaluation.** Lucid consciential projection prompts the projector to *rethink* his/her entire existence or, in other words, the effect of addressing anew all of humankind's traditional problematic questions with a renewed sense of critiquing and greater depth, leading the projector to general redefinitions or the essential recycling of human existence.

3. **Quintessence.** The mentalsoma, frequently referred to in this book, would be the vehicle of manifestations of the quintessence of the ego, according to the concepts of Aristotle.

4. **Hyperuranus.** The mentalsomatic dimension, in turn, would be the hyperuranus according to Plato, the ideal world or that of the free consciousness.

5. **Universalism.** Universalism, derived from experiments with lucid consciential projection, is undoubtedly the true, well-defined and characterized philosophical doctrine. It will be addressed at a later point. It is not a compromised or closed philosophy, but an open, literally *universal* one devoid of factions.

Sciences. Philosophy maintains general relationships with all sciences and special relationships with each science.

Bases. Each science presents two bases:

1. **Experimentation.** A solid experimental base.
2. **Speculation.** A purely speculative part.

Projectiology. The science of consciential projection presents a purely scientific base – projectiology – and a characteristically philosophical part: *projectiosophy*, or projectionism.

Philosophosis. Contemporary common philosophy suffers the chronic disease of *philosophosis:* it remains mired in circumlocution, addicted to repetition, suffering from a lack of copy desk editing. The practice of lucid consciential projection provokes the remission of philosophosis.

Axioms. Projectiology, as all sciences, shares with philosophy the need to formulate presuppositions or axioms that can neither be proven nor disproven.

Projectionism. Projectionism is not a religion, a belief, a rationalized faith, Christian rationalism, a universal panacea or religiosity.

Multidisciplinarity. Projectionism is an area or scientific subdiscipline linked to conscientiology with multidisciplinary reflections that is a field of knowledge and animic-parapsychic research derived from an altered, albeit physiological or paraphysiological state of the consciousness.

Act. Philosophy and ideology can only act as *gray eminences* of the science of *projectiology*. Philosophy is always necessary and ideology will always be partial and fragmentary, with a function that is precisely opposite to that of science, namely to hide the real contradictions.

Elimination. Projectiology, as self-revelation – scientific, in this case – will permit the consciousness to eliminate at least the following 7 millenary lacunae:

1. **Self-sufficiency.** Eliminate the need for new revelations and religious beliefs, thus making one more self-sufficient.

2. **Experimentation.** Eliminate religious faith or belief of any type through personal experimentation.

3. **Discernment.** Eliminate fanatic religiosity by the use of a more ample discernment.

4. **Direction.** Eliminate human and extraphysical intermediaries (sensitives, archetypes and mythological blind guides) in interconsciential and multidimensional coexistence.

5. **Rationality.** Eliminate animal emotionalism, emphasizing rational, logical, reflexive and ponderous decisions in daily life.

6. **Parapsychism.** Eliminate mysticism in general, which only exists due to extraphysical inexperience or immaturity, through the libertarian self-experiences of the intraphysical consciousness.

7. **Evolution.** Eliminate, with time and new existences, the use of one's own psychosoma, finally becoming a free consciousness (FC).

Knowledge. The consciousness begins to obtain essential knowledge or precise information regarding life and the universe directly for itself in the mentalsomatic dimension, by way of the mentalsoma.

Principles. Projectiology instills the progressionist tendency of the intraphysical consciousness to live more by emancipatory personal principles than by human interest, personal desire or rules, even those which are ancestral or traditional but are outdated in the face of consciential evolution.

Proselytism. The individual process of consciential realization, the theory of successive intraphysical lives (existential seriation), the theory of holokarma, the theory of the clarification task and other principles identified by projectiology do not lend themselves to proselytism, catechesis or systematic indoctrination. They are deeply restricted to personal responsibility and occur with the intraphysical consciousness who is interested in learning by him/herself (self-education), performing his/her own research and achieving greater self-knowledge with his/her own motivation. It is futile to erroneously or uselessly attempt to profane the micro-universe of others (inculcation) who are not motivated or, more precisely, are immature in regard to these leading-edge relative truths.

Doctrines. In this book, there are direct analyses of lucid projection in light of diverse doctrines and lines of philosophy, such as the following 5:

1. Existential seriation (multiexistentiality, holoresomatics).
2. Materialism.
3. *Naphology*.
4. Universalism.
5. Yoga.

Complementary. Besides these, technical indications are found in the International Bibliography on works that address projectiology themes but specifically deal with complementary subjects, such as the following 22:

1. Anthroposophy.
2. Cabalism.
3. Castanedism.
4. Catholicism.
5. Christianity.
6. Esoterism.
7. Eubiosis.
8. Evangelism.
9. Hagiology
10. Hinduism.
11. Huna *(Hunismo)*.
12. Jungianism.
13. Law.
14. Magic.
15. Rosicrucianism.
16. Shamanism.
17. Spiritism.
18. Swedenborgism.
19. Theosophy.
20. Umbandism.
21. Voodooism.
22. Zen Buddhism.

Tests. This section entitled *Philosophical Perspectives,* could also be called *Philosophical Projectiology,* not because it is not scientific, but because a good part of the best theorizations presented in these areas have still not been subjected to decisive scientific tests, because we have not yet discovered adequate scientific equipment to present quantitative pronouncements regarding this research.

Bibliography: Alexandrian (11, p. 288), Fisichella (520, p. 14), Plato (1271, p. 487), Plutarch (1264, p. 162), Rogo (1444, p. 183), Wang (1794, p. 13), Wheatley (1825, p. 5), Wolman (1863, p. 757).

---

158. THEORY OF PROJECTABILITY

Definition. Projectability: the animic faculty that can be essentially intraconsciential, acting without the help of other consciousnesses, or the consciential condition whereby the consciousness projects from the human body in the psychosoma, or projects itself outside both the physical body and psychosoma at the same time, in the mentalsoma, in both cases with regard to the intraphysical consciousness; or projects itself from the psychosoma only, in the mentalsoma, in this case with regard to the extraphysical consciousness.

Synonymy: astral power; consciential looseness; existential anti-seriation; faculty for projecting phantasms; gift for consciential projection; metaphysical power; projectiogenics; projectional capacity; projective ability; projective appetite; projective capacity; projective competence; projective faculty; projective performance; projective potency; projective potential; projective quality; projective talent.

Nature. Projectability, or the fundamental capacity of the projector to project, is neither a hereditary gift nor an exclusive privilege of anyone in particular, as it is inherent in children, men and women, as well as extraphysical consciousnesses.

Paraphysiology. All intraphysical and extraphysical beings have some rudiments of projectability. This condition is thus not pathological, being essentially physiological or, more precisely, paraphysiological.

Classification. Projectability, just as parapsychism, can be classified into two categories:

1. **Human,** as it manifests itself from the intraphysical dimension or, in other words, that of the intraphysical consciousness.

2. **Extraphysical,** that which is characteristic of the extraphysical consciousness.

Animism. Human projectability constitutes a characteristic essential type of animism, just as a certain type of paraperceptiology is characteristic of parapsychism.

Explanation. Human projectability, which can even be an involuntary aptitude, explains why some people have a greater tendency than others to experience lucid projections of the consciousness from the dense body, not only spontaneously but also through intentional projection induced by the will.

Use. Projectability, as a human attribute, strictly speaking, has its roots in the unified body complex, or the physical-holochakra-psychosoma-mentalsoma-ego (holosoma) complex. It is independent of both the moral development of the projector, as well as his/her own full self-awareness of this animic condition (pertaining to the intraphysical consciousness).

Prevention. This means that *average projectability* alone is no assurance against *low morality*. The intraphysical consciousness does not become respectable just by having a lucid projection.

Qualification. The applications of projectability can be positive or negative, in accordance with the qualities and actions of the intraphysical consciousness.

Problems. All applied science presents moral problems that need to be confronted instead of avoided. We need only look at what is occurring at the end of this twentieth century, in the various areas of bioethics research (abortion, *surrogacy,* euthanasia, artificial insemination, transsexual operations, organ transplants) and their consequences.

Cosmoethics. In spite of everything, the genuine quality with which the intraphysical consciousness projects itself outside the human body becomes, in and of itself, irresistibly ethical, and those who develop their ethics *highly* – which only happens in accordance with cosmoethics, an indispensable prerequisite – naturally become responsible and do not use them spuriously or in order to harm others.

Mentalsoma. For instance, it is impracticable for the consciousness when manifesting itself in the mentalsoma, to reach the pure mentalsomatic dimension without really demonstrating ethical intangibility according to cosmoethics. Otherwise, one attitude will naturally exclude the possibility of the other.

Development. Human projectability is developed through the improvement of the performance of the intraphysical consciousness dedicated to proper exercise and training aiming to produce lucid projections in series.

Dedication. Projectability, in order to be developed, requires dedication and training on the part of the consciousness, as with any type of physical, intellectual, artistic or parapsychic improvement.

Recess. By merely waiting passively for spontaneous projections to occur, the projector will end up having natural periods of projective recess.

Predisposition. For this reason, the most intelligent approach, if someone wishes to develop psychophysical faculties, is to be willing to voluntarily provoke lucid projections, producing them with rationality, and cultivating them without discouragement.

Barriers. The most common barriers to the development of projectability are generally the following 8 variables:

1. Fear or projectiophobia.
2. The condition of *abdominal brainwashing*.
3. A hectic human life.
4. A lack of study on the subject of lucid projection.
5. A lack of motivation to project lucidly.
6. Mental indiscipline or lack of self-organization.
7. Bad intentions (unqualified intentionality).
8. Negative autosuggestions, such as: "I will never be able to project myself."

Manifestations. Projectability can manifest more intensely in 3 different circumstances of human existence:

1. **Irruption.** In the irruption of involuntary lucid projections or those which are beyond the direct control of the intraphysical consciousness.

2. **Self-awareness.** In the production of voluntary lucid projections or those which are derived from the direct deliberation or the intraphysical consciousness who is self-aware with regard to projective phenomena.

3. **Potency.** In the sudden and exuberant awakening of a latent *projective potency,* triggered by diverse factors, such as the following 3:

A. **Paragenetics.** The immersion of the intraphysical consciousness into self-awareness of the projective phenomenon due to training performed in previous intraphysical existences (paragenetic parapsychism).

B. **Parapsychism.** Certain predisposing and special parapsychic conditions of human existence, the causes of which are still unknown.

C. **Health.** Cases dependent upon psychophysical equilibrium, health-illness, which affect the human being.

Bibliography: Armond (53, p. 14), Butler (227, p. 69), Guéret (659, p. 162), Norvell (1139, p. 150), Rigonatti (1402, p. 163), Rogo (1444, p. 1), Vieira (1762, p. 177).

---

159. THEORY OF THE LEADING-EDGE RELATIVE TRUTHS OF PROJECTIOLOGY

Definition. Leading-edge relative truth of projectiology: the maximal temporary reality for the intraphysical consciousness who is lucid with regard to his/her own practical life in multidimensionality.

Synonymy: hot subject of projectiology; precursory relative truth of projectiology; synthesis of projectiology; vanguard relative projectiological truth.

Premise. In the same way that, for us, no perfect consciousnesses, completely pure social beings, perfect works or definitive perfection exist, neither absolute nor eternal truth exist. Only relative truths are valid for us, which are permanently subject to refutations of all origins and types. This is the basic premise of science, the fundamental postulate of epistemology and rational research in general.

Controversy. The acuity of the intraphysical consciousness always passes first through the ordinary or rearguard relative truth, which is already established and pacific or is already *settled*. Only then, with lucidity and personal choice, does the consciousness attain the *new, hot off the press,* leading-edge or vanguard relative truth that arrives gradually, positioned right in the *eye of the storm* of controversy in the initial state of pre-science.

Superiority. To those egos who first grasp it, this leading-edge relative truth evidences its *status* of unmistakable superiority in relation to that relative truth which is already established and with which no one any longer exerts consciential effort, energy, space and time to prove, and which may now be out-of-date.

Yield. As a pattern of manifestation, leading-edge relative truth – although more difficult to choose and experience – always tends to produce more, conscientially speaking, in favor of evolution of the ego itself and other surrounding consciousnesses. This is because the ego will always base itself on the highest or maximum conceivable common denominators.

Stages. In the development of the relative truths that directly interest us here, ranging from the rearguard to the vanguard of consciential experiences, we encounter 3 clear stages:

1. **Projectiology.** The theories of projectiology lead the ego to an understanding of the concept and experiential application of projectability.

2. **Projectability.** The advanced performance of projectability gradually leads the ego to the condition of consciential holomaturity or, in other words, organic, psychological and integral maturity.

3. **Holomaturity.** When consciential holomaturity is acquired, it leads the ego to the understanding of and the more intelligent option of applying leading-edge, relative truths, namely those relative truths found to be philosophically and scientifically at the vanguard of multidimensional or projectiological evolutionary research.

List. The following is a list of 20 leading-edge, relative truths of projectiology in a comparison with their alternatives. Common or rearguard truths are listed first, followed by their corresponding leading-edge or vanguard truths:

1. **Wholesale.** Choice of a *retail* approach vs. Choice of a *wholesale* approach.

2. **Clarification task.** Assistential task of consolation vs. Assistential task of clarification of consciousnesses.

3. **Polykarma.** Egokarmic and groupkarmic accounts vs. Prioritization of the polykarmic account.

4. **Self-awareness.** Faith of any type vs. Multidimensional self-awareness.

5. **Free will.** A resigned condition of abdominal brainwashing vs. Conscious derepressions with prioritizations based on free will.

6. **Existential program.** Personal impulsion of doctrines and beliefs vs. Personal impulsion of one's own principles for living human life and completing the personal existential program.

7. **Mentalsomatics.** Life led by the psychosoma vs. Life led by the mentalsoma.

8. **Cosmoconscientiology.** Egoistic cosmoconsciousness vs. Communicative cosmoconsciousness (state of cosmic consciousness).

9. **Cosmoethics.** Defense of the human moral vs. Applied (consciential impeccability) cosmoethics (cosmic moral).

10. **Universalism.** Parochial sectarianism vs. Open universalism.

11. **Holochakrology.** Indifference toward bioenergy vs. Practical holochakral self-awareness.

12. **Holobiography.** Living a repetitive human life vs. Self-awareness of the applied multiexistentiality of the consciousness (holobiography and existential completism).

13. **Penta.** The receiving of simple *mediumistic energetic passes* vs. The performance of penta.

14. **Bait.** The constant experiencing of unconscious mini-intrusions vs. Self-awareness of the condition of *extraphysical bait* in search of the experience of being a consciential epicenter.

15. **Self-projectability.** Mere nonlucid consciential projections vs. The production of projections with continuous self-awareness.

16. **Will.** Enslavement to paraphysiological *crutches* vs. Experiences through the impulsion of the will, with self-discernment.

17. **Self-control.** Manifest personal insecurity vs. Self-control with lucid ambiguities (pattern-behavior and exception-behavior).

18. **Self-education.** Mere academic or orthodox specialism vs. A predominance of generalist self-education.

19. **Openness.** Closed esoterism vs. Open exoterism (consciential openness).

20. **Serenology.** A need for personality cults (idolatry) vs. The holothosene of the *serenissimi* (serenism).

Refutations. We thus have the above list of leading-edge relative truths of projectiology. Pragmatically speaking, for the author and some researchers, these truths are no longer *expressions* *"in quotes"* of reality or merely simple concepts, but are in effect without logical fallacies, waiting to be overturned or invalidated by refutations, more original concepts or advanced restrictive ideas on the part of nonconformist heterocritiquing individuals.

State. For many, the vanguard relative truths of projectiology are still premature truths. Philosophically speaking, with reference to these concepts, the author has already left the states of ignorance, doubts and opinion behind him. All of this has become evident, a state of rational and reasonable certainty, without fear of being mistaken, because the evidence of these realities occurred in physical and extraphysical practice, and according to cosmoethics.

Proof. Unfortunately, projectiological proof is still more individual, experiential, participatory and extremely personal. Nevertheless, it is important to point out that it is not just subjective, but is also self-persuasive, convincing the interested individuals themselves.

Models. Truth, by itself, being useful as a criterion for the acceptance of a theory, makes it necessary that the concept demonstrates correspondence, coherence and pragmatism in relation to the facts. Therefore, the connection between theories and facts is being sought within this context with the models of projectiology because they surpass the acuity of verification of all terrestrial equipment employed in the physical sciences.

Synthesis. All the basic themes of projectiology are entirely antidogmatic, stripped or in the condition of a *compound fracture,* bared to volleys of refutation. This list represents, as closely as possible, the practical synthesis of the greater objectives of *human projectiology.*

Targets. It is opportune to suggest that you, the supercritical experimenter, should make the above-cited concepts the preferred targets of your most devastating heterocritiques and questioning.

Compact. The compact gathering of ideas makes the targets more instigating, more ample and less difficult to hit.

Exceptions. It would be more rational to revise these concepts, beginning with the identification of possible exceptions in the enunciated themes and conditions, in order to critique subsequently the following chapter on the leading-edge relative truths of *extraphysical conscientiology.*

---

160. THEORY OF THE LEADING-EDGE RELATIVE TRUTHS OF EXTRAPHYSICAL CONSCIENTIOLOGY

Definition. Leading-edge relative truth of extraphysical conscientiology: the temporary and maximal reality for the desomant intraphysical consciousness (already an extraphysical consciousness) which is lucid regarding its own life in multidimensionality.

Synonymy: synthesis of extraphysical conscientiology.

Preference. Projectiology will continue to be a scientific or self-evolutionary preference that is in the minority for a long time to come. This fact is very logical and natural in light of evolution, as we shall see.

Counterpart. Let us begin with a very human, social or temporal aspect. For example, the *International Institute of Projectiology and Conscientiology* – or everything that this human institution intends to accomplish and represent – merely signifies the physical, *Homo sapiens*-related counterpart of the rationally-presumable *Multidimensional Institute of Conscientiology.* This extraphysical institute researches even more transcendent issues pertaining to the consciousness than those which the IIPC researches and has as its objectives.

Comparisons. Everything that the IIPC applies on earth has its more advanced or evolved extraphysical corresponding part or counterpart. In this way, we can establish various comparisons: the first column lists the human part of the IIPC, or the leading-edge relative truths of intraphysical projectiology; the second column lists the extraphysical part of the leading-edge relative truths of extraphysical conscientiology. Thus, we have the themes researched or the disciplines (subjects) of the courses here, in our intraphysical life, and the themes researched or disciplines of the courses in the extraphysical dimensions (intermission and intermissive courses).

Columns. The following is a list of sample themes, listed in two columns (see fig. 160). In the first column the leading-edge relative truths of intraphysical or human projectiology are presented. Then, in the second column, the corresponding leading-edge relative truths of extraphysical conscientiology are listed.

HUMAN PROJECTIOLOGY		EXTRAPHYSICAL CONSCIENTIOLOGY
1. International Institute of Projectiology and Conscientiology	vs.	Multidimensional Institute of Conscientiology.
2. Human projectability.	vs.	Self-aware interdimensionality.
3. Projective or projectiological courses.	vs.	Intermissive or pre-resomatic courses.
4. Human telepathy (transference of thoughts).	vs.	Superior conscientese.
5. Existential seriation in practice.	vs.	Self-aware intermissivity or spirituality.
6. First and second desomas.	vs.	*Moksha* or third desoma.
7. Aware groupkarmic *extraphysical bait*.	vs.	Aware polykarmic helper.
8. The practicing of penta.	vs.	Self-aware energetic erraticism.
9. Extraphysical clinic in the physical plane.	vs.	*Invisible college* of the *serenissimi*.
10. Multidimensional self-awareness.	vs.	Multidimensional self-cosmoconsciousness.
11. State of continuous consciousness.	vs.	State of continuous cosmoconsciousness.
12. *Serenissimi* per se.	vs.	Pure spirits per se.
13. Human leader-consciousnesses.	vs.	Architect-consciousnesses of galaxies.
14. Primary intraphysical cosmoethics.	vs.	Superior extraphysical cosmoethics.
15. Condition of consciential maturity.	vs.	Condition of pure serenism.
16. Consciential era.	vs.	Third post-space-time evolutionary course.

Fig. 160 – Comparison of leading-edge relative truths of projectiology-conscientiology

Minority. If we reflect upon the fact that the themes in the first column will be, for a long time, the *evolutionary preferences of the minority* in human societies, which are generally pathological or still immature, we can understand how much more distant the themes of the second column are from the average realities of human life.

Preferences. We can perform an analysis, for example, with regard to cosmoethics. We can see that *primary* cosmoethics is currently the cosmoethical preference that is in the minority for humanity, just as *superior* cosmoethics is currently the cosmoethical preference that is in the minority for para-humanity.

Hope. At any rate, it is already a personal relief, or a note of authentic group hope, that we are able to understand the *existence* of and accept, with discernment, the *logical justification* for thinking upon these themes.

Evolution. As a result of the inevitable evolutionary progress of consciousnesses, all themes of extraphysical conscientiology, in the second column, will one day be researched more deeply by all of us – consciousnesses currently in evolution as intraphysical beings – in order to *experience* them while still in the ordinary intraphysical life of this planet or in another evolutionary megaschool of the cosmos.

Multidimensionality. Do not accept any of the hypotheses upon which this chapter is based without first rigorously pondering and critiquing what is presented here. In order to analyze such transcendent conjectures, only multidimensionality exercised with a reasonable level of performance, can provide the keys capable of satisfying our rationality, logic and discernment.

161. COSMOETHICS

Definition. Cosmoethics: the set of broad intraphysical and extraphysical universal norms that are beyond the principles of social morality, euphemisms, social conventions, and transitory human laws and labels.

Synonymy: cosmic moral; dynamic moral; ethical intangibility; extraphysical behavior pattern; extraphysical impeccability; extraphysical moral; law of the avatars; optimization of wisdom; para-ethic; projective moral; pure neo-ethic; supermoral; universal law.

Phenomena. Strictly speaking, the phenomena of projectiology do not have any relationship with faith, religion, religiosity, philosophy, atheism, materialism or spiritualism.

Paraphysiology. The phenomena of projectiology are facts derived from human paraphysiology.

Sociability. Nevertheless, a greater engagement with lucid projection ends up having social and political content.

Philosophy. In light of the above, this section presents inevitable existing philosophical perspectives, but does so without participating in the ideological-political competitions in this period of humanity's development, because such an attitude would be contrary to legitimate scientific, objective, impartial, and universalistic behavior.

Pattern. The person endowed with animic faculties or developed parapsychic sensibilities is not necessarily a person with an elevated consciential standard or moral character.

Improvement. Parapsychic powers can be improved by anyone who dedicates some time to them.

Intellectuality. Nor do animic-parapsychic sensibilities themselves constitute advanced development in any other area, such as intellectuality. Often precisely the opposite occurs.

Evolution. For this reason, as previously mentioned, ordinary lucid projection can occur independent of one's level of ethics. Nevertheless, the evolution and productive development of experiences outside the human body inevitably only occurs, like a prerequisite, in a perfect coexistence with cosmoethics.

Sensitivity. On the other hand, the evolution of the ego (egokarmic, holokarmic) itself makes it so that the highly developed consciousness is also, inevitably, an active animist and sensitive.

Holomaturity. *Intellectual* capacity, in turn, has nothing to do with either *emotional* maturity or *global* consciential maturity or holomaturity.

Cosmoconsciousness. However, the individual who has already achieved the state of cosmoconsciousness no longer needs the rules of morality as understood in everyday existence.

Self-conscientiality. Serenity, certainty in regard to extraphysical life and the sense of awareness – self-conscientiality – of the rhythm of multidimensional life, possesses its own innate laws and ethics.

Ingenuity. Ingenuity thus lies in being able to morally and act creatively according to laws that stem from genius itself, something still quite rare among people.

Agent. The universality of the principles of cosmoethics establishes the norms of the lucid projector's code of behavior, who is, in truth, neither an angel nor a *devil* (Asmodeus: Book of Tobit), but has potentialities for both good and evil, being a consciousness with unlimited freedom, without barriers or frontiers, as though being an invisible, multinational agent.

Secrecy. The lucid projector can operate behind the scenes in all sectors of planetary life in a secret, anonymous manner, sometimes directly upon unaware, unprepared and unready consciousnesses, or even those completely ignorant of one's existence as a lucid projector.

Development. Fortunately, the facts show that, without the principles of cosmoethics or, in other words, the framework of indispensable ethical values – or with unethical attitudes and actions – there is neither a development in one's lucid projections in general nor an improvement in one's consciential perceptions during lucid extraphysical experiments.

Effects. Among the effects stemming from cosmoethics, at least the following 12 can be singled out:

1. **Humanism.** The expansion of a sense of humanity (a sketch of megafraternity).

2. **Universalism.** The substitution of narrow-minded, parochial, telluric ideologies or geoenergetic materthosenes with other universalistic or cosmic concepts.

3. **Privacy.** The dilation of the concept of privacy *(domicentrism)*.

4. **Self-weak-traits.** Self-awareness of the immediate consequences of self-weak-traits and conscious errors, through logical thoughts.

5. **Pathothosenes.** The identification of pathothosenes or unsuspected, *mental peccadilloes*.

6. **Affectivity.** An understanding, without preconceptions, of extraphysical or groupkarmic, paragenetic, ancestral, transcendent affectivity.

7. **Sexosomatics.** Comprehension of the extraphysical consequences of human or somatic sexuality.

8. **Paratroposphere.** An understanding of the absolute extraphysical sexual permissiveness that exists in the paratropospheric dimensions *(parapromiscuity)*.

9. **Heterodoxy.** A loss of interest in segregationist orthodoxy and exacerbated corporatism (court favoritism, nepotism).

10. **Assistentiality.** An increased interest in anonymous and universalistic, educational, fraternal, interconsciential assistance.

11. **Politics.** Motivation by political causes of a universal nature.

12. **Religiosity.** The natural elimination of a need for religion and religiosity as they are currently understood and are practiced on the earth (intraphysical society, traditionalism).

Consciousnesses. Intraphysical and extraphysical consciousnesses on the planet are in evolution or, more precisely, are still not evolved to a degree such that they are not able to control the mentalsomatic or consciential dimension.

Categories. For this reason, consciousnesses can be divided into two general categories: more ill and less ill.

1. **More.** The more ill consciousnesses are those considered *evil*, those having bad intentions, being more egotistical, according to Manichaean moral divisions of good and evil, or of human, social, conventional and deontological ethics.

Intrusion victims. Among these consciousnesses are major frank intraphysical intrusion victims and intruders, who are aggressive individuals immersed in secular imbalances and who still persist in highlighting the worst aspects of terrestrial life (mental derangement, deformed ideas, objects *charged* with ill energies, Mafioso institutions, locations with poltergeist activity). This terrestrial existence can, in this case, be seen, from this perspective, as a *deficiencyland*.

2. **Less.** The less ill consciousnesses are so-called *good* individuals, or those who endeavor to act correctly, being non-violent persons who seek to always have good intentions, and exhibit less egotistical attitudes or behavior than the average and, enjoying relative balance upon emphasizing the better aspects of human existence (balanced intraphysical consciousnesses, orthothosenes, objects in a healthy holothosene, locations with *therapeutic energies*), seen as a temporary stage.

Projectors. Among these consciousnesses are those that customarily produce lucid projections, have some extraphysical discernment and, strictly speaking, are the only ones who are truly able to develop their consciential projections due to their adherence, without difficulty, to cosmoethics.

Reflexes. It is impractical to have a disparity between the projector's human life and its intercurrent and concomitant extraphysical experiences. There is an absolute interdependence between one condition and another.

Incorruptibility. Ethical incorruptibility of human life reflects cosmoethics in the extraphysical dimension, one being interdependent and interacting with the other.

Efforts. No evolutionary conquest of the consciousness is born of improvisation. The lucid projector who has mild and sporadic experiences is a common one. The advanced lucid projector, however, although completely anonymous, is the product of the sedimentation of his/her own individual multiexistential efforts over many centuries and untiring repetition of experiences.

Unawareness. Temporary departure from the human body with lucidity is accessible to everyone, including those who are completely unaware of extraphysical life and cosmoethics.

Variables. Nevertheless, the following 4 basic variables can vary greatly for each individual, element or being:

1. **Communities.** The extraphysical environments (communities) reached in projections.
2. **Company.** Extraphysical company (intruders, blind guides or helpers) encountered.
3. **Paraperceptions.** The quality of the individual paraperceptions of the intraphysical consciousness when freer or projected from the soma.
4. **Events.** The nature and level of the events experienced outside dense matter.

Cosmification. Projectiology naturally and spontaneously promotes an inner evolution ranging from the mere physical restriction of the human body, or planetary provincialism or chauvinism (parochialism), to the plenitude of *cosmification of the consciousness,* or the *universalism* of the ego's objectives.

Integration. In this way, the intraphysical consciousness grows, expands its conceptual horizons, transcends the limitations of the physical base, the bedroom (energetically shielded chamber) and the small, prosaic or animal problems of everyday life, and consciously integrates with the universe, infinity and the eternity of life.

Immunity. The ethic intangibility of the lucid projector who endeavors to live in accordance with cosmoethics, gives immunity to its defenses and makes it *invulnerable* to any negative forces.

Freedom. Whether coming from the intraphysical or extraphysical dimension, these negative forces can neither block the individual's decisions nor limit his/her always positive human actions or those beyond dense matter, if he/she (the consciential epicenter) wishes, in spite of the occurrence of mini-intrusions and the condition of self-aware assistential bait, until arriving at the condition of evolutionary consciential awareness of the *petifree being.*

Theorice. The advanced lucid projector does not give greater emphasis to either theory or practice (theorice) in particular and does not substitute one approach with the other, but endeavors to unite one effort to the other or, more precisely: joins the development of personal animic-parapsychic faculties to personal intraconsciential growth (inner recycling or intraphysical recycling), improving itself (self-overcoming) through assistance (clarification task, penta) to other intraphysical and extraphysical consciousnesses.

Peace. Only cosmoethics allows the intraphysical consciousness to live in peace multidimensionally, because it presents subtleties that are only perceived from an extraphysical perspective.

Case study. The following is an example. A certain woman used to exalt to the heavens and evoke, in her public discourses, a female personality who had lived some time ago and that – as she knew perfectly well – had been herself in one of her previous human existences.

Conflict. In light of these facts, 2 aspects were shown to be in open conflict:

1. **Ignorance.** To those people who worshipped this evoked personality and were ignorant of the multidimensional identification of its lifetimes, this fact was perfectly natural, justifiable and even laudable.

2. **Para-hypocrisy.** To extraphysical consciousnesses, however, this repeated and insistent act was blatant vanity and total hypocrisy or, more precisely, para-hypocrisy.

Self-promotion. This *multi-existential self-promotion* continued for some time, until some extraphysical intruders questioned her regarding the matter, *paraface-to-paraface,* during one of her departures or lucid projections to the paratropospheric extraphysical dimension.

Positions. Through the efforts of the experience of lucid projectability, researchers and, little by little, the general populace, will acquire a new ethical consciousness, or cosmoethics, which will place humankind in a new position before nature and the intraphysical consciousness, evolutionarily free, in a new position within the cosmos (wholeness).

Bibliography: Castaneda (258, p. 21), Humphreys (766, p. 140), Muldoon (1105, p. 315), Vieira (1762, p. 184), Yram (1897, p. 90).

---

162. EXTRAPHYSICAL CODE OF ETHICS

Definition. Extraphysical code of ethics: the methodical and systematic study of useful rules and precepts regarding experiences of the human consciousness projected with lucidity from the human body.

Synonymy: collection of extraphysical laws; extraphysical countercode; set of projective rules; statutes of ethical progress; system of projective principles.

Items. In the extraphysical code of ethics, or countercode of the projected projector – analyzed here as a theory of research – in benefit of the practitioner and the development of his/her consciential projections, it is necessary to include practical items, based on facts, similar to at least the following 16 listed below in alphabetical order:

1. **Friendships.** Cultivate personal relationships and friendships without distinction in the intraphysical and extraphysical dimensions. Facts: consciousnesses do not extinguish and destinies cross outside the human body (groupkarma).

2. **Intention.** We can only allow ourselves to make mistakes due to ignorance, never due to bad intention. Fact: the law of cause and effect postulates that no intention of the consciousness remains hidden without consequences, without responses, repercussions such as action and reaction, or *boomerang* effects.

3. **Intercessions.** Intercede in a rational and positive manner, whenever possible, in favor of intraphysical and extraphysical consciousnesses. Facts: the projector helps the intraphysical consciousness in need, who is naturally assisted by his/her personal extraphysical helper. This helper, grateful and in solidarity, eventually becomes the projector's helper.

4. **Mind.** Keep your mind open to the reception of extraphysical events. Fact: the intraphysical consciousness who only wishes to extraphysically see what he/she conceives, ends up only seeing his/her pathothosenes and thought forms and will not get out of himself/herself in the ordinary, physical waking state in order to achieve extraphysical self-awareness.

5. **Moral.** Regard cosmoethics as indispensable for consciential and extraphysical evolution. Facts: correct extraphysical assistential practices in favor of terminally-ill intraphysical consciousness, for example, if considered only from a human perspective, clash head-on with the code of human ethics regarding euthanasia in most countries.

6. **Preconceptions.** Avoid negative conditioned reflexes and preconceived ideas as much as possible when projected. Fact: the religious, factional, orthodox and segregationist (or *brainwashed*) intraphysical consciousness, when projected, hinders (with one's *para*psychological conditioning) the performance of extraphysical assistance administered to believers of other religions at a religious temple. This is because psychological or human conditioning becomes transformed into parapsychological or extraphysical conditioning.

7. **Privacy.** Endeavor to be useful when extraphysically projected and even invade, if necessary in some circumstances, the privacy of intraphysical and extraphysical consciousnesses. Fact: through lucid projection, beneficial energies can be transmitted anonymously to an intraphysical consciousness who would otherwise never allow this fraternal assistance due to his/her sectarian scruples in the ordinary, physical waking state.

8. **Rights.** Respect the rights of other consciousnesses, as minimal as they may be. Fact: most intraphysical consciousnesses live unaware of the extraphysical realities and have open or disguised fear of projecting themselves from the human body (projectiophobia) to other dimensions of life.

9. **Self-coherence.** Maintain self-coherence between acts in the ordinary, physical waking state and extraphysical actions during the projective period. Fact: among invisible witnesses there are perturbing sick extraphysical consciousnesses that are never silent regarding what they *see* and, generally speaking, they see (witness) practically everything.

10. **Self-critiquing.** Live with self-critique in order to act with dignity. Fact: in extraphysical confrontations the consciousness is called on to test its integrity, performance and possibilities.

11. **Serenity.** Maintain continuous serenity, balance and self-control against emotionalism in all extraphysical situations through the control of one's self, without becoming excessively perturbed when acting under pressure or in emergencies outside the human body, rationalizing the emotions until transforming them into elevated sentiments. Fact: the projected intraphysical consciousness, when controlled by strong emotions, diminishes its extraphysical paraperceptions, loses control of the lucid projection, becomes subject to extraphysical traumas, may return abruptly to the dense body, and prematurely and frustratingly interrupt the experience outside the human body.

12. **Sexosomatics.** Understand the functions of sex in terrestrial life and its positive and negative extraphysical consequences. Facts: healthy emotional effusions, in the extraphysical dimensions, go beyond forms, degree of permissiveness and the clichés of human customs. It is therefore evidently impracticable to realize occurrences in the extraphysical dimension, such as ejaculation, fecundation, gestation and others.

13. **Thoughts.** Be aware of the vital importance of mental acts – thosenes *with a predominance in tho* – in the extraphysical dimensions. Fact: unconscious, unexpected and undesirable evocations, occur much more frequently than we imagine.

14. **Unapproachable.** Know how to recognize the consciousnesses that, in critical circumstances, should not be directly contacted by the projector when projected in the extraphysical dimension. The following are 3 facts worth considering, regarding examples of beings that should not be contacted:

A. **Vehicle.** The difficult situation of an intraphysical consciousness who is driving a vehicle at high speed.

B. **Arms.** The person who has the forefinger on the trigger of a firearm.

C. **Intermission.** The intraphysical consciousness who has recently arrived in the intermissive period and is undergoing restorative sleep or parasleep.

15. **Universalism.** Include in universalism the ideology characteristic of the evolved extraphysical communities or those more lucid extraphysical consciousnesses. Facts: everybody has red blood. The psychosoma is not descendent from any race, is not distinguished by the color of the skin, and is not obliged to follow any creed. No extraphysical consciousness has citizenship. The megaschool of earth is, in fact, one of the smallest fragments of cosmic debris in the universe.

16. **Well-being.** Place the well-being of all above the sectarian or factional interests (corporatism, *lobbyism*) of associations, groups and nations *(nationalism, xenophobia)*. Facts: extraphysical

cooperation involving issues with bellicose objectives and espionage tactics, with the objective of supplanting future and supposed enemies, causes the negative results of *groupkarmic interprison,* first of all, for the consciential projector.

Avoidances. In summary, being practical, the lucid projector who wishes to evolve according to the principles of cosmoethics should avoid at least 3 negative procedures:

1. **Espionage.** Perform military or industrial espionage.
2. **Detective.** Endeavor to verify – working as a private detective – the infidelity of couples or any other person.
3. **Secrets.** Endeavor to discover secrets that others wish to keep hidden.

Bibliography: Steiger (1602, p. 157), Vieira (1762, p. 184).

---

163. LUCID PROJECTION AND MATERIALISM

Definition. Materialism: the tendency, attitude or system that thinks that everything is matter and that *immaterial* substances do not exist.

Synonymy: atheism; materialist philosophy; materialistic creed; negativism; physicalism; physicalist philosophy; pure technological philosophy.

Tendencies. There are philosophical tendencies and existential principles that delay life, self-knowledge and the inner evolution of the consciousness. Egoism and materialism are good examples of this, in this current industrial and commercial human society (intraphysical society).

Puerilities. Materialistic ideas are puerile and contradictory in many respects.

Categelophobia. The materialist avoids building up his/her hopes about the ultra-life regarding something that can be shown to be a mere dream. He/she is afraid of being considered foolish or being ridiculed (categelophobia) if, upon the death of his/her human body, there were nothing left. This is a completely obtuse way of thinking, because if this really happened, or nothing really occurred, he/she would not even know.

Justification. Philosophy demonstrates that there is no greater justification for a materialistic philosophy than for a consciential one, a materialistic philosophy not being any more scientific than a consciential one (consciential paradigm).

Subjectivity. Philosophically speaking, the reality of a subjective fact has the same nature as a material fact. A subjective fact can be as real as a material, objective, intense fact.

Lost. The true materialist is that intraphysical consciousness who is completely lost in his/her intraphysical present, who endeavors to eliminate his/her own past and future. Mired in, concentrated upon and fascinated with the hedonistic experience of the here-and-now of his/her animal body, this individual crawls over the planetary crust. In his/her myopic, carnal or cellular vision, the following do not exist: the holosoma, existential seriation, the progressive evolution of the aware being, consciential multidimensionality, universalism, holomaturity and even cosmoethics. Egokarma still absolutely predominates in the context of the individual's self-thosenity.

Impracticability. Isolated, sophistical efforts are made by individuals – who, incidentally, have not personally produced lucid projection – who are busy with secondary objectives of political domination, in the sense of including lucid projection, in an aprioristic manner, within the scope of phenomena connected to materialism. Nevertheless, the facts demonstrate, so far, only individually speaking, the complete impracticability of this unhappy attempt.

Evidence. It becomes illogical, not to mention irrational or infantile, for projectors to make any attempt to avoid or mask the reality of extraphysical facts related to the psychosoma and silver cord by producing simple lucid projections above their own bed in the privacy of their bedrooms in order not to talk about other bodies or immaterial objects.

Value. One simple real fact is worth more than all conceivable wordplay.

Denunciation. Hence, this book openly denounces and contests the manner of thought and action of the most modern, cultured people in today's world, namely those who speak and live materialistically, who are obstinate in not seriously considering the growing manifestations of so-called "parapsychism;" those who negate the reality of immaterial force fields and, naturally, the mind, or the consciousness; and any other thing that is not matter.

Projection. Lucid projection proves to the interested person that the death of the human body does not put an end to the personality.

Projectors. There are no great materialist projectors, because the first condition rationally excludes the second.

Matter. It would be preferable to call atomic particles "something," as they present such extraordinarily microscopic diameters – if indeed we can call them *diameters* – capable of traversing a distance of many light-years without even colliding with each other within *intra-atomic space.*

Missile. This is analogous to the idea of a missile launched into space that travels for billions of miles without even passing near any other object or celestial body.

Solidity. All material things, including ourselves, are composed of matter which seems very solid to the sensorial perception of any person. Nevertheless, if this is solid, what do we mean by "solid"? Is not solidity a completely egocentric personal point of view with regard to matter?

Conversion. We also know that atomic fission showed that matter can be converted into waves of energy according to Albert Einstein's well-known equation, $E = mc^2$ or, in other words: "the mass of a body is the measure of its content of energy", and that sometimes energy can be converted into matter.

Atoms. Nuclear physics showed that atoms – the units of construction of all material things – are composed of a space full of fields and particles in movement, the particles of which sometimes act more like waves than particles.

Space. In the hardest substance, 2 atoms never touch each other, the space between 2 adjacent atoms being, in fact, much greater than the atoms themselves.

Destruction. Matter and energy can neither be created nor destroyed, and their form can only be altered.

Reality. Besides all this, many scientists and philosophers, both materialist and non-materialist, come to question the "objectivity," "reality" or even the "existence" of matter, energy, space and time.

Ultramaterialism. Unfortunately, even today, within the scope of parapsychology, the researcher and his/her research will become more accepted by the general public to the degree that they make greater concessions in favor of ultramaterialism, which prevails in most areas of human activity.

Half-truths. It will be easier to have one's work recognized and greater financial grants available to sustain scientific research upon restricting oneself only to half-truths of the manifestations in the field of parapsychology.

Isolation. The farther the researcher advances on the extraphysical front in the direction of the more ample leading-edge relative truths, the more isolated he/she will feel in all respects.

Vicious. How long this vicious circle will continue no one knows, although matter itself has been *dematerialized* by physicists and, in light of this, materialism can no longer be presented as a scientific philosophy. Marxist doctrine itself entered into decline in practical international life at the end of the twentieth century.

Note. Based on the material presented thus far, those who deny the existence of the consciousness acting outside the human body will waste their time if they continue reading this book.

Fields. The discovery, in the field of biology, of the organizing electromagnetic or electrodynamic fields of cells, proves that humankind, even physically, is not constituted of simple chemistry, nor is it a consequence of a grouping of proteins, nor is it a result of blind causality, nor does it originate from erratic genes, nor are elevated human sentiments expressed through chemistry alone.

Energy. Modern science currently accepts that matter is concentrated energy. This energy is not tangible, constituting an abstract principle.

Source. We can thus conclude that the material world as well as extraphysical environments have the same origin or, in other words, they arise from some form of energy which unfolds into some parts that compose the physical universe and other parts that serve as bases for parapsychic experiences, thoughts and consciential attributes.

Discontinuous. Projectiology helps the intraphysical consciousness unveil and amplify the universe of his/her philosophical concepts, in a scale that is well-defined through 3 distinct consciential, evolutionary, increasing, logical and rational stages: crustal concepts, provincialist concepts and universalistic concepts:

1. **Crustal.** With lucid paratropospheric projections, even within the space above one's own human bed, the intraphysical consciousness annihilates meager materialistic concepts, atheism, physicalist, telluric, merely technological philosophy, and naturally becomes consciential, shelving the *theta* operation and definitively discarding anxiety regarding acceptance of the fact of survival of the consciousness after the human body's biological death.

Departure. Here, the human-animal leaves the lair, leaves the bedroom and opens his/her door to this planet with a new perspective.

2. **Provincialist.** With lucid projections in the extraphysical dimension, per se, the intraphysical consciousness who admits conscientiality in general promotes his/her own opening, or *open-mindedness,* discovers the law of successive intraphysical lives (existential seriation) and progresses up to the limits of the geocentric or homemade, provincialist and planetary conceptions of Christianity, which still has as a model and maximum example, a personality who was also human, Jesus of Nazareth (4 B.C. – 29 A.D.), the greatest myth, the *intraphysical* taboo personality, or he who still utilizes the psychosoma constantly, judged by many to be the most evolved being in recorded human history (although not yet a *Homo sapiens serenissimus,* or *serenissimus*).

Campus. Here, the human-consciousness departs from the segregationist terrestrial university and extends his/her *campus* to the universe.

3. **Universalistic.** With lucid projections using the mentalsoma in the mentalsomatic dimension, the intraphysical consciousness overcomes small, planetary human conceptions and even the scope of this galaxy, the Milky Way, advancing toward the infinite with universalistic ideas of terrestrial life and even beyond the space-time-form continuum, which maintains the human body restricted, characteristic of human or intraphysical existence.

How. With the condition of cosmoconsciousness, the social being begins to reflect upon the *how* and *why* of understanding the reality of the free consciousness (FC), which no longer uses the psychosoma, nor is it reborn within the current existing conceptions of resomatics, permanently living in the state of continuous self-awareness.

Challenge. Here, the consciousness confronts its greatest challenge: conscious self-evolution jointly with the general evolution of all the innumerous consciousnesses in the universe (populations of demography and *parapopulations* of parademography).

Astronomy. On the other hand, in light of the data evidenced by current astronomic research, 8 modern suppositions accepted by various schools or lines of research deserve mention here:

1. **Galaxies.** The physical universe – which shows profound intelligibility or prescience – probably has 100 billion galaxies.

2. **Stars.** Other galaxies (besides the Milky Way), such as Andromeda, each include between 200 and 400 billion stars.

3. **Life.** Extraterrestrial life and many types of intelligent beings exist.

4. **Civilizations.** It is presumed that thousands of civilizations exist and communicate among themselves.

5. **Intercommunication.** There is a system of intercommunication in our galaxy – the Milky Way – in which we still do not participate.

6. **Astronautics.** A space voyage to the star closest to earth, would take about 40,000 years or 400 centuries.

7. **Signals.** A piece of equipment is currently being used to analyze radio signals. It is basically a spectral analyzer, with an extremely wide bandwidth, over a million channels, used to scan the heavens in search of signals of life on distant planets.

8. **Contact.** Let us wait, then, for the first official, intelligent, physical, interplanetary communication or even an absentee contact, which can arise at any moment.

Mega-intrusion. In conclusion, it is important to ponder the following: materialism, which has existed for centuries in intraphysical society, is the greatest feat achieved by the mega-intruders on this earth. A philosophical and experiential condition that is completely irrational has been maintained through money, social prestige and temporal power for those intraphysical consciousnesses who are predisposed and, above all, self-corrupt. Now, however, in this era of conscientiality, this type of mega-intrusion is coming to an end forever, on a one-way road within the evolution of consciousnesses. Conscientially speaking, this planet will never be the same from this point on.

Bibliography: Flammarion (524, p. 32), Frazer (549, p. 127), Kardec (824, p. 56), Meek (1028, p. 306), Müller (1107, p. 33), Pushkin (1342, p. 300), Russell (1482, p. 42), Targ (1651, p. 156), Vieira (1762, p. 219).

164.   UNIVERSALISM

Definitions. Universalism: the set of ideas derived from the universality of the basic laws of nature and the universe which will become, over time or, in other words, from the natural evolution of the consciousness, the dominant philosophy of the human species and of all beings in the cosmos; self-lucid identification of the consciousness with the community, the state, the planet and finally the cosmos or the universe.

Synonymy: cosmic movement; cosmism; cosmological manual; cosmopolitanism; eclecticism; ecumenism; homaranism; philosophy of the canon of the universe; stellarism; statutes of cosmic citizenship; statutes of the universe; unifying perspective; universal conciliation; universal consent; universal context; universal union; uprooted theology.

Botany. The question of universalism does not only involve modern humankind, nor was it born with *Homo sapiens*. *Fetal* universalism started with the first life on this planet, even before the subhumans of zoology, directly through plants (botany).

Monocultures. Let us examine the facts. The extensive monocultures (vegetal egocentrism) do not sustain life.

Exclusivity. Nature does not permit flora to practice monoculture. The predominance of certain species can even occur, but disastrous exclusivity never persists (*first egocentrism*).

Deintrusion. Thus, nature favors the natural control (*first deintrusion*) of plagues, viruses and bacteria (*first intruders*).

Separation. Involvement in a religious belief, whichever it may be, separates human beings from other human beings, their evolutionary colleagues.

Fight. Once separated from his/her contemporaries, and seeking to maintain personal security, this human fights with other humans, his/her evolutionary fellow human beings, or those with whom one coexists, even within the scope of his/her belief.

Politics. This fact occurs because every religious institution of necessity has its politics. All politics is partisan. All partisanship is obviously fractionating.

Megafraternity. The one who understands and practices universalism endeavors to apply the sentiment of cosmic love or that of universal fraternity (megafraternity), and no longer fights with other consciousnesses (*useful pacifism*).

Antennas. Artificial satellites and parabolic antennas are at the forefront of the inevitable universalism of culture, the sciences and the arts.

Earth. Planet earth, besides being *deficiencyland,* a *megaslaughterhouse,* a planetary trash bin or a correctional institution is, above all, a consciential megaschool.

Truth. In human life, many clairvoyants and revealers have already demonstrated aspects of the full, tranquil and self-persuasive truth of the facts that can be achieved to a greater degree directly through the experience of lucid projection, above all in the mentalsomatic dimension.

Perfection. On the other hand, there are no perfect consciousnesses, completely pure beings, perfect works, or perfect revelations on earth.

Initiates. Without examining the merit of each one, it can be affirmed that intraphysical beings, such as Moses (eighteenth century B.C.), Zoroaster (eighth century B.C.), Gautama Buddha (483 B.C.), Laotzu (531 B.C.), Jesus of Nazareth (4 B.C. – 29 A.D.), Mohammed, Francis of Assisi (Giovanni di Francesco di Bernardone (1181-1226), Dante Alighieri (1265-1321), Leonardo da Vinci (1452-1519), Emanuel Swedenborg (1688-1772), Andrew Jackson Davis (1826-1910), Mohandas Karamchand Gandhi (1869-1948), Edgar Cayce (1877-1945) and Eurípedes Barsanulfo (1880-1918), besides many others, were types of initiated personalities or extraphysical adepts, registered by human history, who came from more evolved extraphysical dimensions.

Innocents. Alongside these historical personalities, *operating outside of* or apparently against their specific tasks, countless other extraphysical and intraphysical consciousnesses, in different eras, have been acting as useful-innocents of the evolved extraphysical dimensions, performing, in their time and in their own way, a secondary but important role of coadjutants taking the position of heterocritics, maxidissidents, adversaries and counteragents.

Complexity. The universe is more complex than we can imagine. There are semimaterial stars.

Suns. There are sentient beings in the high temperatures of suns.

Macrobeings. There are macrobeings and microbeings in conditions beyond our current comprehension.

Inaccessibility. A great percentage of reality is radically inaccessible to our present stage of knowledge. The concept of solidity is also relative.

Table. The periodic table of the elements is just starting for planetary humankind.

Histology. Many cell transmutations occur that are beyond the currently understood processes of physics, chemistry and biology.

Unit. Lucid projection facilitates a greater understanding of the universe as a living unit.

Culture. When viewed from a cultural perspective, universalism arises in an ample range of manifestations, spanning from pure erudition to heightened popularization.

Opponents. Based on the aforementioned ideas, the following 8 practical aspects, for example, are or have been diametrically opposed to universalistic policy:

1. Human neuralgic frontiers.
2. The "Berlin Wall."
3. The "38th Parallel," which divided and established the two Koreas.
4. Exacerbated nationalism.
5. Cultural parochialism or isolationism.
6. The closing of ports.
7. The "Iron Curtain" or the "Bamboo Curtain" (xenophobia).
8. Any type of dictatorship.

Harmonies. Universalism leads the intraphysical consciousness to emphasize 3 categories of harmonies:

1. **Mentalsomatics.** Elevated sentiments or intellect-emotion harmony (mentalsomatics, psychosomatics).
2. **Theorice.** Direct personal experience or theory-experience harmony or theorice.
3. **Nature.** Profound integration with nature and the cosmos or humankind-nature harmony.

Platform. Besides provincialist blinders, humankind has priority goals, causes, ideas, universalistic or intergalactic banners with philosophical, political, social, economic and practical connotations having profound significance and value for the improvement of the standard of existence and quality of human life which stem from cosmoethics.

Projectability. The veteran projector ends up sharing these priority goals, accepting them as being cumulative, natural or physiological effects of that which he/she experiences, witnesses or participates in within his/her double life during the unfolding of extraphysical events.

Executability. Although, at first sight, it seems utopian to defend these ideas relative to current human life, with numerous and powerful interests and forces in opposition, we can list a platform of behavior that reflects the directives which are in force in the assistential undertakings stemming from evolved extraphysical communities. These directives are fully executable by the minds that long to free themselves from the geocentric, orthodox, sectarian, segregationist, telluric, parochial, domestic limitations of this planet, as this will undoubtedly be the goal of future generations.

Positions. The following are 20 libertarian positions of the intraphysical consciousness motivated by evolutiology:

1. **Rights.** The sincere, lucid defense of human rights in general.

2. **Antidictatorship.** The extinction of ostensive or disguised dictatorships in the governing of people and minorities. A totalitarian nation, or a paternalistic government, does not help the intraphysical consciousness develop its individuality toward an evolved condition of full self-awareness.

3. **Antiwar.** Exaltation of the principles of nonviolence and pacifism on the earth and in cosmic space, with the pursuit of the gradual, unilateral disarmament of all nations.

4. **Globalization.** The way toward the creation of a world state, centralized world government, or a global system composed of intensely correlated units.

5. **Governments.** The establishment of multinational governments in specific areas and conditional spheres of action.

6. **Ecology.** Preservation and recuperation of nature in general (ecology).

7. **Minorities.** Safeguarding of the small number of beings (indigenous people and animal species) on the verge of extinction.

8. **Antihunger.** The battle against hunger and scarcity of food in the world, within a universal, rationalistic consensus.

9. **Families.** Family planning in accordance with terrestrial regions and human customs.

10. **Consumerism.** Protection of the consumer on all fronts of consumerism, avoiding unmeasured or exploitive consumerism, including the prohibition of advertisements for medications, pesticides, alcoholic beverages and tobacco.

11. **Antipollution.** The minimization of noise from all machines, safeguarding us from tragedies, accidents and calamities due to the failure of automatic sensors and computers.

12. **Assistentiality.** Discerning cosmopolitan social assistance, without discrimination based on race, social or age group, guaranteeing health, well-being, education, leisure and longevity (old age) to the billions of inhabitants of this planet.

13. **Antidrug.** Formation of supranational antidrug organizations in international solidarity in the fight against drugs and research in partnership with all pharmaceutical laboratories on human diseases and the most dangerous killer viruses, in order to obtain vaccines and medications which, once obtained, are given international usage status, free of patents and privileges.

14. **Antitobaccoism.** The use of all appropriate resources in the task of liberating intraphysical society from the smoking addiction (tobaccoism).

15. **Polyglotism.** International consecration, for immediate use, of those living languages that are in greater use, in view of the practical harmonization of individuals, in light of conscientese, the universalistic language.

16. **Unification.** The implementation of the greatest possible ecumenism between religions, as well as between multidisciplinary scientific perspectives, in order to achieve the unified perspective of all types of beliefs and all lines of scientific research.

17. **Knowledge.** The popularization of lucid projection, gradually substituting belief with knowledge.

18. **Antiform.** The psychological and parapsychological liberation of the intraphysical consciousness from its prison of human forms, in view of consciential or extraphysical holomaturity.

19. **Coexistology.** The individual unveiling of universalistic coexistology through the extinction of everything that can separate consciousnesses, defending the dissemination of intelligent life throughout that portion of the universe that is within reach.

20. **Conscientiality.** The indefatigable pursuit of the state of continuous self-awareness.

Transcendence. The general universalistic view leads the awakened intraphysical consciousness to discard his/her three-dimensional self, or private, isolated, instinctive egoistic *(mega-ego)* point of view, replacing it with a transcendent, four-dimensional, cosmic and broad approach, in accordance with the principles of pure fraternity.

Diversification. It is worth emphasizing that this awareness of consciential evolution will not reach the point of sterilizing creativity and the natural diversification of the *human being,* who will always be happier knowing how to coexist with the ambiguities of permissible concessions by the ego, without fixed ideas or pre-determined behavior patterns, but with various completely free ways of living, loving, eating, drinking, building, sowing, playing, speaking and thinking.

Independence. Universalism leads the intraphysical consciousness to voluntarily (a work of the will) honor the reality of the extraphysical dimensions (animism-parapsychism) in a rational manner, simultaneously and completely dispensing with a dependence upon social religiosity and the influence of religious professionalism of any type, even that of multinational or supranational religious empires.

Freedom. Freeing the consciousness from excessive repression of its conduct (punctiliousness) and unnecessary restraint (castration) of its creativity, universalism allows it to healthily amplify its *universalized inner freedom* (the most precious of assets) to immeasurable limits, without the prison of dogmatism, obscurantism, *intellectual fossilization* (oxidization or rusting of ideas) and *consciential rancidity* (consciential energy that produces a disagreeable taste and smell) characteristic of unevolved paratropospheric extraphysical environments.

Broadness. Summing up: the concept of universalism permits the more lucid intraphysical consciousness to simultaneously consider all broader aspects of human existence, eliminating basic egoistic divergencies between human beings and beings in general.

Globalization. Therefore, the globalizing notion of life's harmony will, in practice, gradually increase. People will then deal with things and be motivated so as to consolidate at least the following 5 sets of intraphysical collective realizations:

1. **Ecumenism.** The convergence of all religions in an ecumenical union: ecumenism.
2. **Eclecticism.** Conjoined philosophies: eclecticism.
3. **Multidisciplinarity.** Conjoined sciences: multidisciplinarity.
4. **Coalition.** Conjoined policies: coalition.
5. **Holomaturity.** Religions, philosophies, sciences and politics also simultaneously conjoined: cosmism, although respecting their limits and respective distinct areas, moving toward collective or universal extraphysical maturity.

Amplification. The free extraphysical experience inexorably leads to the universalistic amplification and deepening of the consciousness's mentality. Imagine that you visited, with full lucidity, 10 different planets, some less developed, others equal to and others still more evolved than earth. This would result in your planetary or terrestrial mentality inevitably changing and amplifying to a broader level of universalism.

Courses. This is exactly what happens, on a smaller scale, with veteran, intraphysical, lucid projectors, and, to a greater degree, with extraphysical consciousnesses, including those that have recently passed through resoma, when they are conscientially more lucid, having undergone the second desoma during their *intermissive courses*. The importance of the earth's role, then, becomes diluted in the magnitude of the cosmic immensity that is sensed, perceived or experienced.

Interdisciplinary. It is worth observing that there are 4 well established interdisciplinary fields manifesting in humankind's daily life:

1. **Anomalistics.** Anomalistics or the comparative study of anomalies.
2. **Futurology.** Futurology or the forecasting of futurities.
3. **Polymathics.** Polymathics or the integration of scientific disciplines with humanistic and consciential fields.
4. **Conscientiology.** Conscientiology, or the general study of the consciousness (noetics).

Bibliography: Alverga (18, p. 193), Gildea (591, p. 43), Gooch (617, p. 17), Kardec (824, p. 184), Powell (1279, p. 165), Rampa (1351, p. 138), Saraydarian (1507, p. 238), Vieira (1762, p. 29), Yogananda (1894, p. 220).

---

165. EVIDENCE OF CONSCIENTIAL MATURITY ON EARTH

Prognostics. Through a succinct analysis, it is possible to locate and identify the prognostics of a gradual installation of extraphysical consciential maturity on earth.

Classification. The following are 20 evident signs of greater consciential maturity found on this planet. They are classified here according to the condition of maturity, whether predominantly individual, collective or ambivalent:

Individual maturity:

1. **Self-awareness.** The currently less common execution of deliberate consciential self-analysis, or the self-critical consciousness (conscientiometry, conscientiogram).
2. **Conscientese.** Self-awareness that is indicative of the existence of conscientese (communicology).
3. **Cosmoconsciousness.** The condition of cosmoconsciousness obtained from the individual's will within cosmoconscientiology.
4. **Deintrusion.** Intentional execution of extraphysical deintrusion through deintrusive self-projection or a more ample extraphysical self-awareness (projectiotherapy).
5. **Future.** Intention regarding planning one's next human life while still living out this existence or self-lucidity with regard to the evolutionary future.
6. **Self-freedom.** Exaltation of the condition of practicing conscious self-freedom.
7. **Projectability.** Lucid projectability (LPB) already practiced on a diuturnal basis with full self-awareness and the execution of projection with continuous self-awareness (projectiology).
8. **Sentiment.** Spontaneous self-rationalization of emotions or self-awareness regarding the lucid use of the mentalsoma (mentalsomatics).

Collective maturity:

9. **Astronautics.** The international conquests of astronautics for pacific use or *interstellar awareness.*
10. **Rights.** The defense of human rights that is becoming frequent and generalized, or the juridical awareness, since the Universal Declaration of Human Rights adopted by the United Nations General Assembly, on December 10, 1948.

11. **Ecology.** Emergence of a greater collective ecological awareness (ecological NGOs).

12. **Fraternity.** Gregarious modern life in metropolises (megalopolises, megacities, condominiums, apartments), current sports activities (tournaments, clubs, Olympiads) and group leisure (playgrounds, tourism, charters), or an increase in community awareness; international organizations that demonstrate humankind's concern for humankind (Amnesty International, International Red Cross, Minority Rights, Women's Rights Movements, Human Rights Movements, the Peace Movement; and finally: the possibility of breathing today (1998), in the planet's troposphere, a population that already comprises six billion human beings).

Bioenergy. Ironclad willpower in the conscious application of bioenergy with the most surprising positive results: intergovernmental organizations, such as the International Monetary Fund (IMF), created on December 27, 1945; the installation of the World Health Organization (WHO); the International Labor Organization (ILO); UNESCO (United Nations Educational, Scientific and Cultural Organization); and the fact that the Indian state of Sikkim, in the Himalayas exists, where assassination is practically unknown, are unequivocal demonstrations of consciential maturity: the acquisition of original ideas; the creation of new facts; the identification of acts of consciential immaturity. Consciential maturity leads the intraphysical consciousness to serenity, notably characterized by impartiality and equanimity.

13. **Interdisciplinarity.** The interdisciplinarity sought in a more emphatic manner in contemporary science (invisible school) or scientific awareness.

14. **Union.** The uninterrupted operation, for over 3 decades, of the United Nations (UN) or political cosmoconsciousness.

Ambivalent maturity:

15. **Communicability.** Aware, parapsychic, interplanetary communication (animism; parapsychism; projectiology; UFOlogy).

16. **Clarification task.** The lucid practicing, on an individual and group basis, of the fraternal clarification task or interassistential self-awareness.

17. **Ethics.** Identification and practical application of cosmoethics or ethical self-awareness.

18. **Pacifism.** The pursuit, albeit still hesitant, of the implantation of pacifism as an ideal and definitive norm among human beings (non-violence) or anti-bellicose self-awareness.

19. **Questioning.** The fact of humankind more and more becoming a serene questioner or a self-critiquing and heterocritiquing awareness.

20. **Universalism.** The philosophy of universalism, the application of which is already sought on a daily basis, both individually and in group, or anti-egoistic self-awareness.

Objectivity. It can be deduced from these signs that individual maturity, besides being subjective, is consequently objectively exteriorized through the individual's ordinary acts, thereby characterizing the details of his/her behavior in the intraphysical society of which he/she is a member.

Permanence. There is currently an increase in the percentage of beings who have passed through desoma (extraterrestrial extraphysical consciousnesses) and those having undergone resoma (intraphysical consciousnesses of the planetary superpopulation). These 2 facts create a situation that remains undefined regarding the exact degree of consciential maturity on earth. Nevertheless, through the resources of projectiology, we reach the conclusion that – aside from other possible conditions of consciential maturity – the abovementioned certainly came in order to remain on this planet. In addition to this, all indications are that these conditions will henceforth continue to be improved and become more evolved.

Specific Bibliography: More recent works by the author: *700 Conscientiology Experiments* (in Portuguese); *Conscientiogram* (in Portuguese).

166. HOLOMATURITY

Definition. Holomaturity: the evolutionary state in which the consciential principle acquires maturity on the way toward full development in its evolution or multidimensional, holobiographical and multimillenary progression.

Synonymy: consciential constitution; consciential discernment; consciential maturation; consciential matureness; extraphysical maturation; extraphysical matureness; holistic maturity; innocence of wisdom; integral consciential maturity; projective prophylaxis; serenism; supermaturity.

Neoteny. Humankind, as a human animal, is one of the few mammals that maintains a biological component that is common and natural among amphibians called *neoteny* or, in other words, the tendency of the adults of certain species to retain juvenile characteristics.

Syndrome. Some authors call this condition the "Peter Pan syndrome." Therefore, even after becoming an adult, and being sexually capable of reproduction, the human being continues to behave childishly, in an irrational or immature manner.

Hyperacuity. The intraphysical consciousness has to overcome neoteny in order to become fully mature (recuperation of cons, hyperacuity).

Learning. In ordinary life, within the didactic directives of educational services, the maturity of the human personality is the capacity characterized by 10 strong-traits:

1. Have money in your pocket without spending it (*material* self-control).
2. Perform a task, whether or not you are monitored *(self-motivation)*.
3. Postpone immediate gratification in favor of long term gain *(forecast)*.
4. Be able to suffer an injustice and not wish to avenge yourself in a like manner *(cosmoethics)*.
5. Control anger (emotional self-control) resolving differences without violence *(discernment)*.
6. Make a decision and keep it despite opposition and changes *(personality)*.
7. Confront disagreeable situations without complaint or discouragement *(serenity)*.
8. Know how to live in peace with that which we cannot change *(ambiguities)*.
9. Change that which can be changed, recognizing one's own faults *(self-critiquing)*.
10. Pass safely through existential crises (*consciential* self-control).

Multidimensionality. According to projectiology, however, the greatest indication characteristic of a highly mature personality regarding evolution is the incorporation of the universe (macrocosm) within one's own consciential micro-universe (microcosm), through the capacity for identifying and establishing an increasingly ample empathy (universalism) with living beings and inanimate things at more and more inner levels (cosmoethics). This is the practice of consciential multidimensionality.

Implications. The intraphysical consciousness often resists personal growth and nourishes a deep fear of maturity because it implies many things, including a certain degree of independence and autonomy, a capacity for self-discipline, certainty in regard to objectives and values, and motivation towards a level of personal realization.

Responsibility. Furthermore, greater maturity implies greater responsibility, which is a frightening possibility for some people.

Success. There are also those who fear success, excellence and knowledge. For example, fear of success and fear of greater maturity are closely related. The more success we have in terms of performance, abilities, knowledge, sense of perspective, leadership, and so on, the more people expect from us.

Existential robotization. Intraphysical consciousnesses who are still immature, discouraged or literally mediocre (existential robotization) find refuge and security in not being either too advanced or too behind the rest of the evolutionary group, but located within the obscure average (mediocrity).

Knowledge. Immaturity also leads the intraphysical consciousness to fear knowledge. There are those who seek knowledge, as well as those who avoid it, in order to reduce anxiety. The knowledge of a certain fact implies the obligation to action. Immature individuals consider it safer not to know. If they knew, they would have to do something about it, or feel guilty over their cowardice.

Unaware. There are therefore those who still prefer, in this era of modern science, to live as a *blissful ignoramus* instead of being an *unhappy sage*. Such is the case with the inveterate smoker who deliberately ignores any discussion or literature that could clarify the possible connections between cancer and smoking.

Orgasmolatry. The current human evolutionary planetary moment relates to intraphysical consciousnesses whose lives are based on hedonistic principles, uncontrollably seeking pleasure, orgasmolatry and, consequently, an exaggerated worship of the human body and youth, and the associated motivating interests, commerce, industries, communities, media and advertising to this end, not to mention those who still live at a subhuman level, and whose efforts consist solely in obtaining the minimum necessary for the survival of their body, which is understandable, up to a certain point.

Animals. When considered in the condition of human beings, we are all still animals.

Zoology. Our zoological reality (zoology, fauna) indicates 3 facts worthy of study:

1. **Tail.** All human beings still present a caudal appendix (tail) up until the 10th week of intrauterine life.

2. **Canines.** All healthy persons with an intact soma, present 4 canine teeth for tearing meat or food in general.

3. **Chimpanzee.** Our biological or genetic makeup is 96.7% identical to that of the simian, monkey or chimpanzee. Our difference, of a greater conscientiality, is only 3.3% of our genetic make-up.

Instincts. Fortunately or unfortunately, most of the manifestations of our human behavior is based on the instincts of subhumanity.

Beliefs. Archaic beliefs, rooted in emotion (psychosoma) and seeped in taboos, still predominate everywhere in the twenty-first century.

Immaturity. Nevertheless, this also begets the side effect of a yearning to remain forever young, in *eternal youth* or in perpetual infancy, like *immutable minors,* which means remaining extraphysically immature, superficial and uncommitted at all costs.

Illness. There is very intense pressure for people to be young in the current intraphysical consumerist society. The physical human world suffers from the illness of infantilism.

Gerontophobia. The current norm is based on the fear of aging, the avoidance of baldness, the repudiation of white hairs, the taboo of wrinkles, the continued worship of the shape of the human body, namely generalized *gerontophobia* or the precocious senility complex.

Stubbornness. Clearly, if intraphysical consciousnesses insist on maintaining the *status quo* of their own evolutionary infancy, afraid of even reaching ordinary and restricted human, physical, psychic maturity, how are they going to achieve extra-human, extraphysical, parapsychic maturity or holomaturity?

Exploitation. Youth worship, the juvenescence of intraphysical society, or more appropriately, the exploitation of youth or its hypocritical deification, in this perverse relationship of generations, and the individual's common desperate need to appear, think and act youthfully, regardless of chronological age, under the threat of obsolescence and the *stigma of the discardable,* leads the *intra*physical consciousness to *extra*physical somnambulism. Any projector can easily verify this fact through mild, prosaic or paratropospheric projections.

Fetus. The results of orgasmolatry and gerontophobia – the prevailing binomial being exaltation of youth-shame of aging – has been felt for centuries and is easily encountered in the two dimensions of life: most (89%) of the consciousnesses of the members of terrestrial humanity live in a somnambulant condition while in the human body. After the soma begins to decompose, these consciousnesses arrive in the paratropospheric extraphysical dimension perturbed by various types of prolonged post-desomatic parapsychoses, manifesting themselves in conditions such as: extraphysical fetuses, consciential embryos or beings that are immature in the presence of reality.

Culture. The mass communication mentality is contrary to the mentality of culture in general. Culture is based on the individual, whereas the means of communication lead people to the stagnation of uniformity or non-inventiveness.

Simplism. Culture illuminates the complexity of the multidimensional life of the intraphysical consciousness and the means of communication simplify it in an infantile, primary and simplistic manner, an attitude characteristic of the lowest common denominator.

Interrogation. Culture signifies endless questioning – an uninterrupted search for leading-edge relative truth – and the means of communication are not aware of anything more than quick, simplistic answers regarding everything.

Amnesia. A world obsessed by materialistic reality is a world obsessed about forgetting (amnesia) previous lessons. This tends to continue the evolutionary stagnation of the intraphysical consciousness.

Solution. How are we going to reach maturity in consciential (parapsychic), multiexistential terms, when most of us (humanity) are still not even able to be mature in cerebral (psychological) terms in just one life, namely the present one? The answer-solution to this question-dilemma is in the personal mastery of bioenergy (holochakrology), in the understanding and use of the holosoma (multicorporal consciential ecosystem) and in the full application of universalism.

Awakening. This is why lucid projection is recommended as a functional practice in order to achieve the awakening of somnambulants, who are adepts of the human body's animal youth, as well as the primary emotionalism of the psychosoma (emotional parabody). This will allow the achievement, besides terrestrial youth, not merely human maturity, but continuing to the discovery of extraphysical maturity or holomaturity, or elevated sentiments (rationalized emotions) by prioritizing the use of the mentalsoma (parabody of discernment).

Logic. Logic, originating from the mentalsoma, does not enrapture. It is a conquest of *Homo sapiens serenissimus* or *serenissimus*.

Persuasion. We can use all available techniques to demonstrate objectively, through logical argumentation, that our opinions are well founded, that our point of view is fair, that our affirmations are true, that our goals are laudable. Even so, after this, by proving the truth of that which we affirm, a person who listens to us will not feel obliged to accept, admit or follow us, and may reply saying: "You did not convince me" or, "Well, it seems to be true, but this doesn't change my point of view" or, "You are right, I now have another opinion, but nevertheless I will not behave differently". That is why, in projectiology, the individual, when really interested or motivated, should personally perform participative projectiological research.

Proof. The most concrete, marked and indisputable proof is not always able to convince or persuade a person, regardless of how solid a cultural background that individual may have. The facts evidence this every day.

Verbaction. The following are 10 disturbing examples of the inappropriate use of verbaction on the part of paradoxical professionals who refute proof when faced with obvious pertinent facts:

1. **Chancellor.** The monoglot chancellor (diplomatic incompetence).
2. **Dietician.** The overweight dietician (obesity).
3. **Tamer.** The lion tamer who runs fearfully from a mouse (murophobia or musophobia).
4. **Engineer.** The fearful engineer who does not travel by plane (phobia).
5. **Nun.** The catholic nun who becomes pregnant (gestation).
6. **Journalist.** The illiterate journalist (professional incompetence).
7. **Pulmonary.** The pulmonary specialist who smokes (smoking).
8. **Psychiatry.** The psychiatrist who bites his/her nails (onychophagy).
9. **Religious.** The religious professional who commits suicide.
10. **Sensitive.** The veteran sensitive who is afraid of first desoma (thanatophobia).

Self-control. Only maturity of the consciousness brings inner renovation, straightforward discernment or true self-control of the ego through the thoughts and actions of the consciousness, coming from the mentalsoma.

Egokarma. One cannot live intraphysical existence for another intraphysical consciousness. Egokarma comes before the measurements of groupkarma and polykarma.

Service. We can affirm that humans are organically, mentally and psychologically mature when their human faculties arrive at full development, such that they are able to adequately react to any circumstance that terrestrial life presents and provide themselves and intraphysical society with the service that is expected.

Process. Lucid consciential projection, highlighting the fallacies of the worship of eternal immaturity, is an efficient maturative process for the intraphysical consciousness. It integrates the information that is processed, associates a maximum of self-thosenes, amplifies one's perspectives toward a broader and more panoramic visions of beings and issues, in the direction of hyperacuity or lucidity of understood and accepted immortality, thereby achieving a convenient balance between awareness and intuition.

All. Extraphysical maturity allows the intraphysical consciousness to understand its meta-organisms (holosomatics).

Coordination. We are not merely the cellular organism: liver, heart, brain, attractive skin or the perfect plastic features with attractive sexual characteristics. Being more than this, we are the intrinsic coordination of various vehicles of manifestation (unified body), the most ostensive and rudimentary one being the human body, and the most subtle being the mentalsoma, which houses the consciousness or ego and all of its basic attributes.

Environment. Extraphysical maturity also leads the intraphysical consciousness to consider its relationship with its environment. The vehicles of manifestation of the consciousness depend upon its environment.

Relationships. We do not relate only with the human dimension, but we also constantly relate to, control and are always being controlled by 3 other categories of consciential environments or communities:

1. **Paratroposphere.** To and by the tropospheric extraphysical dimension (paratroposphere), a duplicate of this intraphysical or human dimension.

2. **Extraphysical.** To and by the extraphysical dimension, per se, being extremely different from the intraphysical or human dimension.

3. **Mentalsomatic.** To and by the pure mentalsomatic dimension, with the absence of the psychosoma, and which decidedly does not present any similarities to the human dimension.

Self-support. Maturity leads the consciousness to transfer the environmental, instinctive and emotional support of *human life* to the rational, parapsychic and extraphysical self-support of *multidimensionality.*

Formula. Consciential maturity can be expressed in a simple formula: the inversion of the conduct of the human being who, in many other journeys through planetary life, remained at the inferior level of *maximal-suffering-with-minimal-learning,* who now moves on to the superior level of *maximal-learning-with-minimal-suffering.*

Conditions. There are two conditions which are quite different and extremely well-defined:

1. *Intra*physical maturity.
2. *Extra*physical maturity.

Infantilism. The intraphysical consciousness has still not discarded extraphysical immaturity and also has not discovered the existence and usefulness of extraphysical maturity, as long as he/she remains in human infancy or consciential infantilism, dazzled by 3 involvements:

1. **Physicalism.** The physical or intrasomatic world, the daily temptations of pathological intraphysical society and existential robotization.

2. **Autobiography.** Solely human, mental maturity, bedazzlement by the development of one's own terrestrial biography, which ends in the grave or the crematorium.

3. **Superficiality.** Consciential infancy, fascination only with surface realities beyond dense matter, without applying them to promote personal intraconsciential recycling.

Premises. Any intraphysical consciousness arrives at a more ample consciential maturity through the following 3 premises or stages of self-discernment:

1. **Happiness.** After the ego *(mega-ego)* naturally overcomes – without missing, without complaining – the psychophysical conditions characteristic of crying out of happiness, or the dispensation of the need to feed multifaceted deficiencies.

2. **Renunciation.** After the personality silently and spontaneously renounces – without grief or rupture (minidissidence) – the more legitimate and just personal rights, in the face of the material arena of this planet.

3. *Justice.* After the motivated person stops combating blatant injustices ("justice") when this combative approach does not favor others besides him/herself.

Oblationality. It is doubtless intelligent and worthwhile to endeavor to interpret the condition of holomaturity, an attitude which is easily understood. It is, however, difficult to become capable of effortlessly living in harmony with all the intrinsic, underlying details of these premises and priorities that compose a condition of non-pathological oblationality.

Thosenology. Maturity of the consciousness deepens and amplifies discernment, pointing out to the ego how to order its actions or self-thosenes from the mentalsoma, maintaining a balanced ascendancy over the other vehicles of consciential manifestation.

Pathology. However, this does not negatively or *pathologically* signify the following 7 postures:

1. **Stratagem.** The intellectualization of social relations as a defensive means of cutting normal emotional involvement (protective stratagem).

2. **Hermitry.** Solitary self-absorption that seeks social isolation as the best standard of social life (fruitless hermitry).

3. **Alienation.** Transformation of oneself into an uncommitted, robotic being, with no emotional ties to anything or anyone (distanced spectator).

4. **Contradiction.** The metamorphosis of emotion and spontaneity into abstractions, in an attempt to mechanize love and esthetics (contradictory positioning).

5. **Psychosoma.** The judgment that the emotional parabody – the psychosoma – is merely an obtuse, eternally animal instrument, with no other use (radical sophistication).

6. **Criticism.** The belief that emotional involvements will always be infantile, weak or simply idiotic (cynical criticism).

7. **Intellectualism.** Addressing problems and situations, while invariably divorcing them from their emotional aspects (blind intellectualism).

Health. Maturity of the consciousness signifies – in a positive and healthy manner – control, without repression or sacrifice, of the emotions that can enslave the ego, employing, for this purpose, rationalized emotions, or those greater sentiments that come directly from the pointer of the consciousness, which is based in the mentalsoma.

Caution. Consciential maturity leads the individual to live with lucidity, alertness and to be cautious regarding 7 areas of intraphysical knowledge:

1. **Religion.** Religion, when it is a simple professionally imposed package (dogmas) of absolute, definitive, unverifiable and improbable truths.

2. **Art.** Art that is devoid of content and message when it signifies the discovery of a *greater number* of new, experimental methods (styles) for *continually saying less and less.*

3. **Cybernetics.** Cybernetics (automation) wherein the machine robotizes and separates the intraphysical consciousness from coexistence with social beings.

4. **Technology.** Technology, when concentrated only in superindustries (bellicosity) of carnage and genocide.

5. **Science.** Science, when it only creates researchers (dermatologists of the consciousness) who never deepen their own causal reality as self-aware beings.

6. **Politics.** Politics, when it is interested solely in heightened abdominal brainwashing (repression) of the unthinking human masses (existential robotization).

7. **Communication.** Communication, when it exclusively sells the fallacies (lies) of the fulgurant mind manipulators, the violators of intraconsciential micro-universes or the impudent merchants of the consciousness.

Period. The individual who psychologically and conscientially matures earlier has a greater chance of better utilizing his/her period between successive lives or lifetimes.

Mistakes. Without applied extraphysical maturity, the regrettable repetition of errors, mistakes and infantile omissions of perspectives from prior intraphysical existences (retrosomas) – whether they are philosophical, political, religious, mystical, artistic, poetic, idealistic or well-intentioned – becomes almost inevitable.

Difficulty. That is why intraphysical consciousnesses find it so difficult to act with rationality, discernment and common sense, without mysticism and dependency upon rituals (psychological crutches, leashes and yokes), in the face of extraphysical realities.

Repeaters. The contingency made up of those who are repeating multiexistential mistakes – those who are prisoners of dispensable self-mimicry – comprise the majority of *somnambulant humanity.*

Signals. Individual extraphysical maturity or holomaturity, and the recuperation of cons or human hyperacuity, are marked by 10 unmistakable signs:

1. **Self-coexistence.** The intraphysical consciousness feels good coexisting with him/herself, as a personality, dispensing with the need for greater and rigid self-critiques (conscientiometry, conscientiogram).

2. **Self-determination.** The intraphysical consciousness severs his/her dependence upon others, things, and all psychophysiological crutches, although having, as never before, the precise notion of interdependence between all beings or consciential principles that are in continuous evolution.

3. **Self-confidence.** The intraphysical consciousness acquires self-confidence, annihilating the paranoia of timidity (shyness is an illness) on the way toward security, authenticity, sincerity and frankness.

4. **Self-development.** The individual does not keep waiting for dreamt-of help to come from other beings, from *destiny* or from circumstances. He/she endeavors instead to realize the best by him/herself, developing personal potentialities (paragenetics, innate ideas, personal talents) with discernment regarding evolutionary priorities and acting with an increasingly well-defined decision-making ability.

5. **Self-liberation.** The individual dispenses forever with personality cults (idolatry, adoration) and becomes liberated from the megapotency of so-called *public opinion.*

6. **Self-realization.** The intraphysical consciousness assumes a position that is founded upon solid evolutionary and rational bases, pursuing self-realization and conquest through continuous recycling, which enriches his/her human existence with increasing productivity within the existential program (existential programology).

7. **Self-discipline.** The person remains balanced, becomes disciplined, participatory, co-optive and authentic in all manifestations, through self-monitoring, thereby completely eliminating self-corruption and pathothosenes.

8. **Self-sufficiency.** The social being no longer asks on his/her own behalf in his/her intercession and revindication, but only on behalf of other consciential principles.

9. **Self-examination.** The ego no longer fuels personal grief, susceptibility, sensitivity or jealousy in his/her inner world (consciential micro-universe), nor does he/she expect gratitude, recognition, financial return or perfect understanding by others regarding that which he/she does. Thus, he/she does not get disappointed, as a conscious member of the microminority among the minorities of intraphysical society, remaining free of complexes and repression, in the pursuit of pure interconsciential understanding.

10. **Self-awareness.** Both the intraphysical consciousness and the extraphysical consciousness achieve full self-awareness of the mentalsoma and the mentalsomatic dimension and endeavor to live – wherever they may be – predominantly in accordance with the serenity, balance and discernment that the consciousness possesses when it is isolated in the mentalsoma, rationalizing the emotions or, in other words, relegating the ephemeral manifestations of the animal emotionalism that is natural to the psychosoma to a secondary position. This has the effect of gradually using up and atrophying this vehicle up to the point of making it disappear, when there is no longer a reason for it to exist, whereupon the consciousness reaches the condition of free consciousness (third desoma).

Conscientiometry. From a practical standpoint, the level of consciential maturity can be measured, with conscientiometry, through the successive beliefs that are nurtured by the intraphysical consciousness in 4 existential periods:

1. **Infancy.** First, during infancy, a belief in God (religiosity).
2. **Youth.** Second, in youth, for example, until a short while ago, in Karl Marx (socialism).
3. **Adulthood.** Third, in adulthood, in the lotto or lottery (automatic wealth).
4. **Maturity.** Fourth, in the period of integral or holistic conscientiological maturity, in self-confidence or, in other words, in the impulsion of your own will to evolve multidimensionally, thereby maximally dispensing with idolatry, crutches and egoistical supports.

Principles. Stemming from faiths of all types, the intraphysical consciousness acquires direct knowledge; stemming from random, alienating beliefs, the individual defines secure personal principles for living. Identify, if possible, which level is your own. You only stand to gain as a result of this approach.

Types. The true age (maturity) of a person can be classified into 3 distinct types:

1. **Chronological.** The chronological age of the human body or the state of coincidence of the vehicles of manifestation of the intraphysical consciousness, including the holochakra.
2. **Psychological.** The person's psychological age or, in other words, the mind or brain, including the parabrain or the psychosoma.
3. **Consciential.** The consciential age of the consciousness, per se, which is headquartered in the mentalsoma, with the holomemory and the rationalized emotions.

Conduct. Psychological maturity is a rare condition. Not all persons are able to discern between mature behavior and infantile behavior. The mature or infantile solution of problems should be observed by all of us.

Adults. The immaturity of adult humans is common. Not all adults are adults. There are adults who are clearly retarded and yet are not considered to be mentally debilitated. There are those who are grownups on the outside, but are still children within (or are *always* children inside). Adult immaturity explains many lamentable events in human history, which thus far remain inexplicable (certain frivolous wars, absurd escalations of weaponry and other facts).

Mentalities. Strictly speaking, there are those who consider children, who are so dependent, to essentially be criminals and, therefore, to be dangerous. This is due to their irresponsible or infantile animal manifestations. Fortunately, the children's physical capacities are too limited. However, an infantile mentality inside an adult human body is much more dangerous and potentially disastrous. We are not merely referring here to the unhappy exceptional individuals (oligophrenics, the mentally retarded or cases considered to be ostensively pathological), but instead to the frank immaturity of those average adults who are rarely socially perceived as such (existential robotization).

Trap. Those who pursue extraphysical truth can be drawn into a psychological trap or pressured to remain conscientially immature in the following 2 manners:

1. *Mentally,* in the condition of the accommodating psychological servitude of people who give up their right to question certain vital themes in order to avoid creating a scene.

2. *Emotionally,* upon accepting a basic interconsciential dependency on some professional guru, sensitive or orthodox leader (rituals, talismans, amulets, astrological charts, predictions) for the rest of his/her human life. These complacencies become transformed into psychophysical yokes or crutches and the entire scenario consolidates the aspect of group intrusion of intraphysical consciousnesses or group fascination.

Spectacles. The daily exhibitions of human and consciential immaturity are the most readily encountered spectacles in social life, whether on the street (transit neuroses), in newspapers (police columns), television stations (soap operas at the lowest common denominator, the predominantly malevolent character), in homes (domestic tyranny), in office departments (the prepotency of those in command positions: *Those who can give orders, do so; those who are judicious, obey.*). Consciential immaturities occur in the home, at work, in social life, in emotions and in decisions.

Retardation. Planetary humanity still suffers from the worst possible ill: retarded consciential development, one of the most lamentable diseases that affect the mentalsoma, and with a high degree of frequency in the profiles of parapathology of the parabody of discernment. Those who suffer this condition are immutable-anomalous-beings (at an evolutionary standstill) in a universe in constant mutability (the constant progress of the universe). There are a shocking number of conscientially retarded consciousnesses.

Cons. The majority of existing adults are mental and consciential children. There are persons who never grew internally or, in other words: did not recover a reasonable number of their cons. For example: it is easy to encounter a 30-year-old woman who is the emotional equivalent of a 15-year-old girl; or the 25-year-old man who has the egocentric perspective of a child of 5.

Evolution. Consciential evolution is the journey of the consciousness from immaturity to maturity. The act of working on behalf of the maturity of the human species is pure universalism, or the greatest clarification task that is available to the social being. It represents cooperation in *bioenergetic weaning* in regard to excessive dependencies and personality cults.

Intruders. The populations of the intraphysical dimension and extraphysical paratropospheric dimension are in desperate need of consciential maturity. There are legions of semiconscious adversaries of consciential maturity or, in other words, intraphysical and extraphysical intruders who are *semi-conscious* of their hetero-intrusion.

History. All persons can grow irrespective of their physical age. Unfortunately, throughout the earth's history, there has never been a sufficient number of mature-model individuals (leaders) in the proper place at the right time. Example: the level of electoral candidates everywhere. This is the profile of the planetary mega-school to date.

Demonstrations. The following can rationally be considered clear demonstrations of consciential immaturity: fear, any type of psychological insecurity and the act of considering oneself to be an exception to the human species.

Projectability. Adult immaturity directly hampers the development of lucid projectability or the capacity of the intraphysical consciousness to project with lucidity to extraphysical dimensions.

Exercise. Consciential maturity is pure rationality, a practical experience in line with the dictates of the mentalsoma. The exercising of maturity is the act of endeavoring to eliminate the psychological obstacles that impede humankind from rationally executing its tasks, as well as being enormously forceful in the sense of reducing the millenary difficulty of ridding ourselves of our irrational beliefs (animal experience).

Fraternity. When acting, while in the state of maturity, the intraphysical consciousness preponderantly, stemming from the mentalsoma, rationalizes the emotions to a point at which common love is transformed into a profound sentiment of pure fraternity. This sentiment allows one to overcome, in one's intraconsciential world, the levels of gender definition, besides the influence of human appearances, different physical ages, family positions and the social conditions of each being.

Retrocognitions. This transcendent human attitude helps the intraphysical consciousness have positive retrocognitions and locate and identify other consciousnesses of his/her evolutionary group (groupkarma), when they pass through resoma. This intraphysical consciousness, upon arriving at 50 years of age, at least, in a single human lifetime, may recognize, for example: certain consciousnesses in two short consecutive human lives; and certain extraphysical consciousnesses, first in the extraphysical dimension, and then, subsequently, reborn in the intraphysical dimension, breathing oxygen at his/her side.

Derepression. The first great struggle required for the intraphysical consciousness to achieve a greater maturity in adulthood is the overcoming of his/her own repressions (abdominal brainwashing) generated by education and the inevitable instruction that he/she underwent in infancy, adolescence and the beginning of his/her adulthood. It is important not to forget: this effort must be repeated, indefatigably, in each new intraphysical existence (a new soma and a new holochakra).

Intraphysical consciousnesses. Realistically speaking, humanity can be divided into two categories of intraphysical consciousnesses: very repressed and less repressed. Those intraphysical consciousnesses who are very repressed studied little and reflected even less. In this planetary evolutionary stage, projectiology is directed to those intraphysical consciousnesses who are *less repressed* or, in other words: the only ones capable of understanding and practicing it with indispensable lucidity.

Anti-repentant. The thought, word or, specifically, the mature consciential act is essentially a catalyst for the self-evolutionary process, signifying the maximum that is possible at that consciential moment or that which is ideal for all. Additionally: it is logical, executable, functional and *anti-repentant.*

Impact. The impact of consciential maturity often impresses and traumatizes. This fact is practically inevitable. The consciousness, when operating from the mentalsoma (leading-edge relative truth), is stronger, more effective and decisive than when it operates from the psychosoma (desires, animalism), from the holochakra (bioenergy) or from the human body (musculature). For example, the author, as a result of the minimal leading-edge relative truths which he is able to understand, has been called an *antichrist,* and these intraphysical consciousnesses are not far from the truth. The communicator of these leading-edge relative truths will always be an *antimythical torturer* of intraphysical consciousnesses.

Sadism. Orthodox, sectarian, factional and narrow-minded persons judge the analysts of evolution of the consciousness to be sadistic. *Brainwashing deprogramming* frequently *hurts greatly,* both morally and intraconscientially. In these cases, the ego's self-defense mechanisms are *finely ground* in order for the positive intraconsciential recycling of the life of the intraphysical consciousness to occur. Hence conscientiological mini-dissidents arise. Extremely mutilating *consciential surgeries* occur in the area of leading-edge or vanguard ideas. Is there, perchance, another, more efficient methodology for helping others to understand leading-edge relative truths and self-cures?

Bibliography: Miranda (1050, p. 148), Vieira (1762, p. 220).

167. TECHNIQUE FOR ACQUIRING A UNIVERSALISTIC SENSE

Definitions. Universalistic sense: the inner consciential condition of conciliation and pure conformity with all beings and things of the universe; the state of consciousness already identified with the universal community, total and irreversible awakening to pure universalism.

Synonymy: citizenship of the universe; cosmopolitan sense; eclectic sense; open mind; open-mindedness; self-awareness of the cosmos; understanding of cosmic law; universalistic coexistology.

Fixation. Every time the consciousness has a more lasting and deep fixation in one consciential dimension its attribute of omniperception is restricted, which signifies self-castration, temporary obfuscation and a decrease in its maximum consciential and evolutionary effectiveness. In order to minimize setbacks in its demand for its own evolutionary growth, the consciousness needs to be more self-aware of this fact.

Resoma. The greatest fixation that occurs in the evolutionary scale of the consciousness is the act of its resoma into a human body. The only occurrence worse than this is the pathological condition of post-desomatic parapsychosis.

Zenith. Nevertheless, somewhere along the evolutionary trajectory, one inevitably arrives at a level at which the consciousness spontaneously detaches itself from all of its egoism in order to permanently embrace pure altruism with no constraint, sacrifice or greater difficulty on its own part. Upon arriving at this zenith of greater understanding, all segregations, labels and specific demands of the ego lose their raison d'être, regardless of one's cultural background, native language or the intraphysical society in which one lives.

Process. The process of the consciousness' acquisition of the universalistic sense, while still in the intraphysical condition, represents a constant struggle against the conditioning imposed by the indispensable, and always repressive, human education, in the sense of achieving the following 4 objectives:

1. **Reproduction.** The cutting of the egoistic links of animal reproduction (human gestation).

2. **Competitiveness.** Refraining from all types of merely planetary competition in any field or sector of intraphysical manifestation.

3. **Universalism.** Universal interests placed *before* interests that are parochial, provincial or pertain to *one's own little world*.

4. **Vision.** A wide-ranging view that always endeavors to focus *beyond* the confines of the planet where one temporarily resides.

State. Thus, the state of universalistic sense is the final condition that crowns the consciousness and is situated well beyond an increasing scale: the state of a sense of family, profession, community, region, nation, continent and, lastly, planet.

Advance. The universalistic sense prizes universal consent, shifts from the part to the whole, advances beyond and leaves behind all ideas or manifestations of retrograde policies that express egoism, such as: segregation; nationalism; exacerbated patriotism; the radical party; Jacobinism; xenophobia; the clan; the sect; the closed club; orthodoxy; dissidence; isolation; excessive, multiple *leashes of the ego;* and other correlated tendencies or those of an identical nature.

Technique. The acquisition of a more profound applied universalistic sense is accessible to any individual. Therefore, it is worth observing these 10 topics:

1. **Training.** Disciplined training in the control of consciential energy and the production of lucid consciential projections allows the interested individual to have a more ample development of parapsychic perceptions, starting with ordinary clairvoyance or the reading of the energetic aura that surrounds all beings and objects.

2. **Interworlds.** The principles of evolution suggest that all of us, without exception, are predestined to be *gods* at an opportune moment. The more the consciousness evolves, the more it increases the range of its influence towards some type of omnipresence, and deepens its understanding towards some type of omniscience. At this point, the development of clairvoyance opens the perceptive doors of the intraphysical consciousness to other consciential dimensions. This permits him/her to live while thinking, feeling and reacting in many dimensions at the same time, although headquartering the ego, without alienation, in one of them – in this case, the intraphysicality that is characteristic of his/her human body – even when this physical dimension, strictly speaking, is much more pathological (entropy) than healthy.

3. **Unveiling.** The unveiling of other dimensions on the spot – during the development of daily occurrences – shows the intraphysical personality other more evolved parameters of heterocritical judgment: a more accurate vision of universal life; his/her practical integration with the cosmos; the precise understanding of universalism; a greater and uncommon level of consciential maturity (holomaturity); and rationalized emotions (sentiments) in relation to all beings and nature with whom he/she coexists.

4. **Energy.** Upon being awakened to multidimensional life, the consciousness precisely identifies and characterizes the function and action of consciential energy in all of its manifestations in the manner of the maxim resource, the common denominator, the master key, the instrument which discriminates priorities or, the unit of measure of beings and things in its actions.

5. **Auras.** The auras of these beings and things will be perceived at another level from now on, with a different perspective, more intimately congregating and amalgamating all the objects of universal reality, freeing the clairvoyant consciousness from slavery to the rigid forms of matter. This same consciousness will even locate and identify deceased beings, situating each in its level or dimension of manifestation. In this way, for example, from a human environment, it can begin to simultaneously distinguish 3 extraphysical consciousnesses, each in its own dimension, where the less evolved ones do not perceive the presence of those that are more evolved.

6. **Time.** With the passage of time and an accumulation of experiences, the universalistic sense ends up establishing a sensation of lucid inner peace in the ego that no longer allows anxiety regarding the past, present and future or, in other words: eliminating time, which has now become a simple factor that is constraining and unnecessary for its evolutionary impulse.

7. **Consequences.** As a result of the elimination of the excessive effect of the time factor, the intraphysical consciousness no longer spends time waiting to pass through desoma, or harbors expectations regarding the impulses of the changes in the human calendar, in order to fully live or realize more. The individual pursues the resources for maximal experience from that very moment, in the still physical here and now, because he/she knows that the evolutionary task is a singular one, whether in the intraphysical state, the extraphysical state or the projected state. The consciousness that is still convinced of being able to energetically vibrate in an intense manner through the force of the will, regardless of the vehicle of manifestation which is predominately manifesting in a specific environment at any moment, benefits from this in a positive way.

8. **Co-optation.** This attitude of growth conquers the sympathy of more greatly evolved consciousnesses (evolutiologists, *serenissimus* and even free consciousnesses) that control all existing things. The individual therefore becomes even more engaged as a lucid, active minicog within the evolutionary maximechanism that oversees all living beings. The degree of his/her co-optation increases. He/she will no longer remain in blind opposition to the universe, but will gladly integrate him/herself in an intimate, definitive manner, into the framework of conscious assistants (evolutionary team) and directly join with the pervading situation in this universe. His/her presence (personal holothosene) will be much more impactful and productive in the scenario in which he/she participates, not ostentatiously, but anonymously, working at the core essence of things, addressing that which is important and performing truly lasting work (existential program).

9. **Cosmic.** At this level, the consciousness generally reaches the condition of cosmoconsciousness, receiving *a touch of the infinite* and entering the real state of the universalistic sense – in the blink of an eye and in a wholesale manner – as though through a providential shortcut.

10. **Cosmocracy.** Lastly, the simultaneous views of different consciential dimensions, and the conjoined interdisciplinary and multifaceted analyses of the problems and phenomena of multidimensional life, lead the intraphysical consciousness' aspirations toward the consciential era or, in other words, implantation of the cosmocracy.

Projections. The maintenance of a universalistic sense decisively helps the performance and development of the intraphysical consciousness regarding lucid consciential projections, notably in his/her periodic extraphysical experiences.

Senselessness. No ordinary, immature or vulgar personality is exempt from senselessness. The maintenance of an open and universalistic consciential micro-universe offers us the best resource for directly combating the limitations of our mega-weak-traits of senselessness. Hence the opportunity and importance of establishing the technical bases for the acquisition of a universalistic sense, being the best method for overcoming the condition of multimillenary, multiexistential or holobiographical consciential immaturity, retardation and torpidity.

Considerations. It is far from the author's intention to exhaustively solve, here and now, the ancestral and crucial problem of the immaturity of the human consciousness in a manner that will persuade all intraphysical consciousnesses regarding the usefulness of constantly perceiving and experiencing a universalistic sense. However, the following are 10 considerations – basic rules that are coherent from a logical point of view and are acceptable from an ethical standpoint – that are capable of technically defending us from the specific errors of senselessness, immature opinions, and the narrow-mindedness that sidetracks us from a direct line of reasoning:

1. **Self-awareness.** Carry out rigorous self-critique regarding your own tendencies in all areas of human activity.

2. **Comparison.** Perform a deeper examination of differences in opinion, in a comparison of your parents, colleagues and friends.

3. **Openness.** Become informed on opinions held in social circles other than your own (open-mindedness) through tests of direct personal experience (yours).

4. **Coexistence.** Coexist with other individuals with whom you wholly disagree maintaining a climate of harmony (peaceful coexistence), avoiding anger or misunderstanding due to opinions contrary to your own (admiration-disagreement binomial).

5. **Gathering.** Take the initiative of prudently gathering the ideas of others (inter and multicultural contacts) who have tendencies that are different from yours, aware that neither party has good evidence in more heated controversies.

6. **Depreconception.** Read books, magazines, newspapers and CD-ROMs dedicated to the dissemination of lines of thought that are different from yours, with the certainty that if the individuals who write and publish these works appear crazy or wicked to you, you also appear that way to them.

7. **Dialogue.** Establish an imaginary dialogue with a hypothetical opponent, pursuing – unbiasedly, democratically, and in a comparison of all opinions (inner debate) – the ideal prevailing opinion, or the one with a useful consensus regarding each subject under analysis.

8. **Interdisciplinarity.** Pursue interdisciplinarity in your research, making your own direct observations, knowing how to use modern means of communication, the most efficient physical agents of universalism (parabolic antenna; artificial satellites; the Internet; multimedia; cable TV).

9. **Polyglotism.** Endeavor, if possible, to read, speak and think in languages that are not your native tongue.

10. **Travel.** If possible, travel and live away from your own country for a period of time (cultural excursion; study scholarship), in order to eliminate preconceptions restricted to the space-time *continuum*.

Maturity. These attitudes enable the deepening of our logical perceptive acuity and, consequently, amplify our level of consciential maturity against psychic vacuity *(empty-headedness)*, lack of intellectual sharpness, lack of sensitivity, faulty reasoning, defective powers of observation and mental slowness, on the way toward imperturbability, which is characteristic of a fraternal and agile person, who is simultaneously centered and universalistic *(serenissimus)*.

Expansion. After employing these logical resources of maturity, or executable universalistic processes – which can inspire the use of many others – you will remain in a state of full consciential immaturity only if you so desire, because the result, for the person who puts them into practice, will be to subjugate the psychosoma, amplify the use of the mentalsoma and, finally, achieve the expansion of your own consciousness (cosmoconsciousness) by using consciential energies and self-thosenes in a far more intelligent manner.

Specific Bibliography: The author's most recent work: *700 Conscientiology Experiments.*

168. THEORY OF CONSCIENTIAL SELF-CONTROL

Definition. Consciential self-control: the condition of the correct use and matured practice of the consciousness' balance in relation to itself, other consciential principles (consciousnesses in evolution), and the universe which shelters it.

Synonymy: self-control of the ego; volitive self-confidence.

Types. The condition of consciential self-control presents 2 well-characterized basic types:

1. **Initial.** Initial or partial self-control, typical of pre-*serenissimi*.
2. **Final.** Final or global self-control, typical of *serenissimi*.

FCs. Ahead of these two types, situated at another level, at the forefront of evolution, free consciousnesses (FCs) are encountered.

Limits. Ordinary, somnambulant, humanly average or evolutionarily mediocre persons have their normal consciential limits of self-control in the coincident state within intraphysical existence upon their vehicles of manifestation: the human body (soma); the energetic parabody (holochakra); the emotional parabody (psychosoma); and the parabody of discernment (mentalsoma).

Sensitives. However, there are those intraphysical consciousnesses who are able to control their mind – self-consciential control – above or beyond the normal limits of the evolutionary performance of average persons. These individuals are called *sensitives, animists, scientists, nobelists, artists, record breakers, medalists, gifted* and other names. Some are considered to be witches or warlocks; others are considered to be *mystics, hierophants* and *saints* (of these 1,848 are registered in Catholic hagiology); still others are called *magicians* or *conjurors.*

Quality. Numbers cannot clearly convey all that exists regarding consciential evolution. The quality level of the effort which the intraphysical consciousness seeks through the maturity of freewill is extremely important.

Objectives. Many immature individuals feel self-realized upon exerting great amounts of effort in consciential self-control toward objectives that are badly chosen, unconstructive, inefficient, negative, pathological or predominantly useless with regard to the acceleration of the evolutionary self-yield of his/her consciousness, in accordance with the principles of cosmoethics.

Immaturity. Immaturities with respect to consciential evolution can be verified in a great number of books of international records as examples of what can be intelligently avoided by more lucid interested persons regarding evolution.

Disparate. There are those who go to great lengths in order to set the most disparate records, such as: balancing golf balls on a piece of furniture; hold up cigar boxes on the chin; eat more than anyone else. Are these beings still too animalized or materialized to concern themselves with the idea of ceasing to undergo resoma? They undoubtedly are.

Partial. Partial or sectorial consciential self-control can be subdivided into 4 categories, according to the control of the consciousness over each of its vehicles of manifestation. We can thus, as examples, come across the actions, when positive, of the contortionist, the sensitive, the artist in general and the genius of proven wisdom.

1. **Somatics.** The contortionist controls the segments of the human body or soma, beyond the average of the population, and transforms him/herself into a *human snake* or a *boneless woman;* the athlete breaks international records in positive acts of strength or Olympic games. Examples: Harry Houdini (1874-1926); Sergei Vassilievitch Rachmaninov (1873-1943), the musician with the greatest finger span; Mark Spitz, the multiple medalist swimmer; Edson Arantes do Nascimento (1940-), Pelé. In these cases it is necessary that the person has a hereditary condition for a specific genetic predisposition (egokarma), with perseverant dedication to self-disciplined training over a long period of time. All subhuman animals (consciential principles) have still not evolutionarily arrived at this level.

2. **Holochakrology.** The sensitive (animist-parapsychic) controls the energetic parabody above the average of the population and helps persons to cure themselves, parapsychically bends metal, promotes telekinesis, transmutes objects, materializes substances, triggers rays of light and energy

around him/herself. Examples: Jesus of Nazareth; Daniel Douglas Home; Eusapia Paladino; Uri Geller (1946-); Thomas Green Morton (1947-); and others. In general, the performance of the ego is based on the emotional parabody, in the state of discoincidence, in order to act directly upon the energetic body, because it does not transport the consciousness. That is why *physical parapsychic* phenomena depend so much on the emotion of the moment that is predominant in the environment (holothosene); the company or personalities in the surroundings of the sensitives; the predisposition and personality of the parapsychic researcher.

3. **Psychosomatics.** The artist controls the emotional parabody above the average of the population and *electrifies* the cardiochakra and the psychosoma of others, creating immortal works in many artistic areas. Examples: Ludwig van Beethoven (1770-1827); Enrico Caruso (1873-1921); Niccolò Paganini (1782-1840); Vincent Van Gogh (1853-1890); William Shakespeare (1564-1616); Honoré de Balzac (1799-1850); Rita Moreno (1931-), the most versatile international actress. In many cases, the artist controls the emotions excessively during creations aimed at other persons, but ends up being a victim of the relationship with his/her own emotions through implosive excesses (drugs) and sick catharses.

4. **Mentalsomatics.** The genius, with greater wisdom, has an above average control of his/her mental parabody and invents things, discovers laws and presents innovations or discoveries that overshadow everyone else and captivate the world. Examples: Aristotle; Galileo Galilei; Isaac Newton; John Bowring (1792-1872), the greatest polyglot; Albert Einstein. As a rule, these philosophers, scientists, inventors and discoverers are those people who are more capable of making suggestions to others regarding the search for the benefits of consciential maturity. This depends upon the degree of lucidity of his/her own reality or genius.

Specialities. At our current evolutionary level on this planet, the evolutionary talents of the consciousness, obtained through the repetitions of millennia and the string of intraphysical lives, almost always concentrate in a specialized manner in the extremity of a specific single line of activity. They still do not simultaneously present multifaceted capacities in their personality, or multimodal creativity in broad, generalist actions in more than one vehicle of consciential manifestation.

Conscientiometry. When a person controls one or more of the vehicles of manifestation, that intraphysical personality still presents 4 very characteristic traits in his/her evolutionary profile:

1. **Autobiography.** He/she obstinately defends his/her autobiography.
2. **Registers.** He/she is entered in the registers of humanity.
3. **Encyclopedias.** He/she has his/her biography in international encyclopedias.
4. **Records.** He/she is listed among the human record holders of all people.

Insertion. This personality, without exception, regardless of who it is, can be inserted into one of the 4 basic aforementioned types.

Global. The *serenissimus,* however, can be classified as a fifth type regarding the condition of consciential self-control. He/she controls, without pathological repression, and beyond the average of the planetary population, the 4 vehicles of manifestation of the consciousness – the soma, the holochakra, the psychosoma and the mentalsoma – in an intelligent, global, simultaneous, conscious or intentional manner, without significant difficulty, effort or sacrifice on his/her part.

Direction. Being more aware of universal laws, *serenissimus* is better able to anonymously, surreptitiously, multidimensionally and secretly direct other planetary beings in their evolution (evolutionary catalysis). Example: *Monja* (Vieira, 1762, p. 201).

Holosoma. Upon beginning to control the holosoma, the 4 vehicles of consciential manifestation together and at the same time, the intraphysical consciousness becomes anonymous to intraphysical humanity, *exiting the scenes* of the stage of human life. This signifies that holosomatic self-control is necessary and characteristically multidimensional.

Discarding. The preceding observations become logical if we are attentive to the fact that *human life* rationally relates to the consciousness in the animal or *human body*, which is always perishable and discardable in a predetermined and inevitable period of time.

Bibliography: Vieira (1762, p. 201).

169. THEORY OF ESSENTIAL WISDOM

Definition. Essential wisdom: that body of knowledge which deepens further regarding the structure of the consciousness, in its multiple dimensions, with regard to its manifestations or self-thosenes, extending itself in a more lasting way over consciential evolutionary time and, therefore, being qualitatively superior to others.

Synonymy: causal wisdom; essential science; *leading-edge wisdom;* mature wisdom; maximal wisdom; multidimensional instruction; priority science.

Concept. The concept of wisdom is always masked by appearances, superficialities and the general momentary conditions of human life, when addressed in only one intraphysical life, throughout the history of humanity. This masking is intensified still further in the myopic perspectives of universal phenomena, which are broad but developed through the immaturity of materialists or physicalists.

Existential seriation. In view of the above, the following question can be asked: "How much is one human life worth within the context of the complete scheme of the uninterrupted evolution of the consciousness (existential seriation, holobiography)?" A single intraphysical existence does not serve as a parameter measuring the undefined future of the consciousness. It illuminates a few upcoming immediate consciential steps, but nevertheless does not unveil the remote future and integral destiny.

Categories. We can consider wisdom in diverse types or categories according to its consequences, effects, scope, permanence and other variables.

Titles. How can it be contested that the wisdom of a holistic philosopher, addressing many dimensions where the consciousness expresses itself, who already has a deep understanding of cosmoethics, is not qualitatively superior to the wisdom of an eminent scientist, such as a specialist in physics at the zenith of excellence in conventional megascience, but whose knowledge is restricted only to the circumscribed atmosphere of human life, which is of reduced evolutionary validity, regardless of how many titles and extraordinary international laureates he/she possesses?

Self-lucidity. The awarding of titles does not confer a greater self-lucidity upon the recipient than that of other mortals, in any field of consciential investigation.

Prioritization. The quality of option-prioritization shown by the nucleus of knowledge chosen by the sage – free will – defines the degree of his/her initial wisdom or maturity.

Essence. The most essential wisdom is that in which the consciousness applies a maximum of his/her intelligences and potentialities in the establishment of more advanced priorities in his/her research. Therefore, the most essential wisdom expresses the gathering of the knowledge of highest priority, with regard to its importance and productivity relative to personal and collective effort, in line with the interminable evolution of the consciousness.

Sages. Based on these logical premises regarding wisdom in general, it is easy to conclude that there are two categories of sages, independent of personal notoriety:

1. **Essential.** Sages of essential wisdom.
2. **Secondary.** Sages of secondary wisdom.

Brilliance. In other words, without any elitism, there are sages of the first category and sages of the second category, with regard to the quality of their wisdom. The prestige, celebrity, academic titles and awards that they have received in their existence, or their *nobelism,* the brilliance of their human career and their biographical registration in renowned, prestigious international encyclopedias is unimportant because, in this case, these variables become secondary.

Consciousness. The consciousness is a far more important reality, and is of far greater interest than the transitory postulates of human science.

Non-prioritization. The lack of prioritization (non-prioritization) regarding the choice of the individual's interests shows the narrowness of the consciential micro-universe of certain sages.

Characteristics. The following 4 characteristic aspects, among many others, are essential proof and are indispensable for the classification of the consciousness' level of wisdom:

1. **Holomaturity.** The correct use of intellectuality according to cosmoethics or, in other words, intellectuality that is indicative of holomaturity.

2. **Openness.** The openness of the mind simultaneously to culture and counterculture, formal education and self-education, specialities and generalism, orthodoxy and heterodoxy, without preconceptions, academicism and scientism.

3. **Polymathy.** The broad and experienced view of understanding and erudition or polymathy.

4. **Self-education.** The maintenance of a good personal library (holotheca) in view of irreplaceable, continued self-education (autodidact).

Evolution. The multidimensional order and logic of evolution suggests that the consciousness only achieves the level of the first category of wisdom after already having experienced wisdom of the second category, within the logical progression of seriated, successive intraphysical lives (existential seriation).

Paradox. Paradoxically, there are anonymous sages without diplomas who are nevertheless aware of and experience leading-edge relative truths which are essential for the consciousness itself. These scholars are far more important than the greatest sages who have received international acclaim for one or another contribution made in a given sector of human knowledge, but that is limited and more transitory in the endless evolutionary way of the consciousness.

Serenissimus. From the perspective of their evolutionary evaluations, there are anonymous-sage pre-*serenissimi* at better levels of performance (anonymous existential maxi-program) than many notorious-greater-sage pre-*serenissimi* (explicit existential maxi-programs). The first ones find themselves closer to the level of the evolutiologist or of the *serenissimus* and are headed toward the aware anonymous condition of *serenissimus*.

Maturity. Greater and integral consciential maturity leads the intraphysical consciousness to seek more ample development of free will beyond human passions and parochialism. This inevitably leads to the identification and prioritization of essential wisdom.

Arguments. Human arguments are not strong enough to change facts.

Interests. The basic difference between the lucid and young intraphysical consciousness and the lucid and mature intraphysical consciousness lies in the fact that the first still maintains his/her basic interests predominantly bound to the immediatist present, and to the limited and defined future of the current human life that is to be built. The second consciousness centers his/her essential interests beyond ephemeral human life, toward the infinite future of consciential life, without generating any alienation.

Knowledge. The categories of knowledge cannot be merely classified into technical (physical, molecular, material) and human (corporal, cellular, cerebral), but also need to be amplified by multidimensional variables (consciential, essential, cosmoethical).

Projectiology. Conscientiology is one of the most essential of all sciences because it focuses precisely on the research of the rational, integral and maximal awareness of the consciential micro-universe. Projectiology acts exclusively within the scope of essential wisdom, or that of conscientiology, because it concentrates all of its research, without any messianism, in the third basic state of the consciousness, or the projected state, which is important to the intraphysical consciousness and even to the extraphysical consciousness.

Intelligence. The complex module of *evolutionary intelligence* can be considered as the *materthosene* of essential wisdom within an individual holothosene, in relation to the twists and turns of the difficulties through which we pass in intraphysical life, always aiming toward existential completism.

170. CONSCIENTIAL   ERA

Definition. *Consciential era:* that era in which average human consciousnesses will encounter themselves sufficiently improved through the impacts, redefinitions, revolutions and evolution created by generalized lucid projection.

Synonymy: *cosmocracy;* life with mega-helpers; new neolithic revolution; physical-extraphysical counter-civilization; projectional era; projective era.

Graduation. In the development of the consciousness, everything evolves in a generalized and irreversible graduation that reaches all areas of thosenic manifestation. The following, for example, are 28 logical progressions of facts, listed here in alphabetical order:

1. From alchemy to chemistry.
2. From astrology to astronomy.
3. From bioethics to cosmoethics.
4. From candles to spotlights.
5. From cave paintings to holography.
6. From caves to megacities.
7. From common sense to mature science.
8. From faith to lucid self-experience.
9. From flora (botany) to fauna (zoology).
10. From good intention to self-discernment.
11. From horses to spaceships.
12. From ignorance to wisdom.
13. From instinct to reason.
14. From kindergarten to the post-graduate course.
15. From medicinal teas to conscientiotherapy.
16. *From mediumship to lucid self-projectability.*
17. From miming to conscientese.
18. From pre-*serenissimus* to *Homo sapiens serenissimus.*
19. From religion to the practice of penta.
20. From smoke signals to e-mail.
21. From soma to mentalsoma.
22. From subhuman animals to humankind.
23. From the clan to the world state.
24. From the consultation room to the extraphysical clinic.
25. From the feudal system to the world state.
26. From typing (typewriter) to keyboarding (computer).
27. From veterinary science to medicine.
28. From walking to volitation.

Order. The experience of continued human lucid projections gradually establishes a distinct and hidden order by which one lives, that becomes perceptible through the multidimensional comparisons, multifaceted analyses and self-critiquing judgments of the intraphysical consciousness that is in frequent transit between various consciential dimensions. These experiences end up being reflected in the life of the human being.

Extraphysical. The rational direction of human consciousness to a more advanced stage, beyond the following temporary physical conquests to an extraphysical and lasting level in relation to the multiexistential consciousness must be emphasized: beyond the periods or waves of change; beyond the research that sociologists, anthropologists, psychologists, thinkers and futurologists employ in order to arrive at conclusions, think ahead and make forecasts, establishing the evolutionary phases of intraphysical societies and human communities; from the first wave, or the agricultural revolution, the second wave, or the industrial revolution, up to the so-called third wave of current history, the age of information, electronics, the global village, communication technology; and even beyond the future *waves* that will come more and more rapidly and ephemerally in the coming decades.

Implantation. Logic imposes a living and a clearly discernible standard from which it can be concluded that the generalized conquest of this consciential era – analyzed here as a theory for research – will still take some time to be implanted in the planetary atmosphere (human holothosene).

Experience. Nevertheless, the individual experience of this consciential era can already be sought, pursued and enjoyed now, both individually and in small groups, for those who wish to and are sufficiently motivated towards this.

Priority. Lucid projection, in unveiling the extraphysical world that coexists with this human world, minimizes the problems of the individual's daily life, allowing one to counterbalance the values of sociological conquests, as advanced as they may be, internally exalting a greater certainty and better consequences, which naturally becomes a priority for the more lucid individual.

Multivehicular. With repeated and advanced lucid projections, the intraphysical consciousness begins to establish multi-secular, multi-existential and multi-vehicular plans. In other words, the individual plans while taking into account many vehicles of manifestation or human bodies, thus expanding aspirations beyond planetary limits, at a cosmic, universal and atemporal level, or more precisely, beyond human calendars, ephemeralities, conquests, discoveries and inventions, at a level that it is as yet unattainable by even the most brilliant sociology or futurology project.

Helpers. So far, we live on the earth under the protection of the helpers for the execution of any advanced extraphysical undertaking.

Self-sufficiency. The consciential era will be the period of life that naturally dispenses with the resources and incessant interventions of the helpers. Thus, the consciousness will act on its own, directly, with self-sufficiency both inside and outside the human body, dispensing with all *parapsychophysical crutches.* The consciousness will therefore be in close, profound harmony with his/her evolutionary orienter or the evolutiologist of his/her karmic group *(mega-helper).*

Existential seriation. All indications are that when the consciential era is installed on a planet, it marks the beginning of the end of the rigidity that is characteristic of successive lives or existential seriation, for the consciousnesses that inhabit it.

Eras. The scale of evolution of the intraphysical consciousness on earth can be built upon 6 eras established according to *energetic stages:*

1. **Muscular.** The era with a predominance of *muscular energy,* of work performed with the muscles of human and subhuman animals, of biceps and manual labor (hands, arms, soma).

2. **Mechanics.** The era with a predominance of *motor energy,* beyond human articulations or, in other words, the work performed by wheel, the motor and the machine at the beginning of technical-scientific development through the extensions of feet and legs (automobile, truck, tractor, airplane).

3. **Chemistry.** The era with a predominance of *chemical energy,* derived from the pollutional burning of organic fuels (coal, petroleum, gas) and greater industrialization, with the extension of the eyes and the frontochakra, from the microscopes of histology to the telescopes of astronomy.

4. **Atomics.** The era with a predominance of superconcentrated *physical energy,* of the nucleus of atoms of metal (uranium, thorium) operating generators, ships and submarines, not to mention hydroelectric energy (Itaipu) and solar energy, along with their extensions of the nervous system and the laryngochakra (telephone, radio, television, fax).

5. **Electronics.** The era with a predominance of *neuronal energy* with direct extensions of the brain (cerebellum, psychomotor activity, psychomyology) and the coronochakra (computer, transistors, chips, automation).

6. **Volitional.** The era relative to self-awareness of *consciential energy* (holochakra), the impulsion of the will, control of the emotions of the psychosoma through the mentalsoma, discernment, consciential maturity, with the direct extension of the human senses (parapsychic phenomena) and the awakening of multidimensional self-awareness. This era arose with projectiology in the twentieth century.

Bibliography: Vieira (1762, p. 219).

171. HOLOKARMIC ACCOUNTS

Definition. Karma: the law of cosmoethical causation, which neither punishes nor rewards, neither creates nor designates anything, but infallibly directs all other laws that produce certain consequences in the set of actions of the consciousness.

Synonymy: law of action and reaction; law of cause and effect; law of retribution; law of return; theory of behavioral reversion.

Division. In a more instructional approach, it is always better to focus the theory of karma of the consciousness into 3 well-defined segments: egokarma, groupkarma and polykarma.

1. **Egokarma.** The pure, individual, or egokarmic, account refers to the inner life of the person, its consequences (psychosphere or individual holothosene) and the egocentrism or egoism of the instinct for survival.

2. **Groupkarma.** The account of the consciousness in relation to its resomatic group comprises its evolutionary groupkarma, derived from the interpersonal activities or those of the karmic group (community of destiny; group fascination).

3. **Polykarma.** The account related to intra and extraphysical collectivities, and a more ample individual public life, comprises the polykarma of that consciousness and its pure, applied fraternity (multidimensionality).

Holokarma. Holokarma is the karma of the *consolidated balance* of the consciousness' actions, or the sum total of its 3 karmic accounts.

Differences. The fundamental differences between the egoistic actions of the intraphysical consciousness when defending his/her egokarma and groupkarma – when faced with fraternal human actions within the context of polykarma – can be identified by the ideology developed through the creation of well-devised secrets, the withholding of information, subtle involvements, emotional blackmail and, most commonly, the inculcation of behavior.

Leading-edge. The projectiological perspectives of leading-edge truths inevitably lead the consciousness to the source of indispensable concepts or to the support provided by the highest common denominators. They marginalize peripheral aspects, going straight to the useful core facts related to the consciousness. They always value intelligent prioritization. They seek that which is more profitable in terms of the conscious evolution of the consciential micro-universe.

Philosophy. The individual's life philosophy or political ideology has a great influence upon the karmic accounts of the intraphysical consciousness.

Levels. With respect to karmic accounts, it is observed that the intraphysical consciousness evolves, in the environments of the intraphysical dimension, along an ascending scale within the social context, through at least the following 8 well-defined environmental or geographical levels:

1. **Home.** Still the cornerstone of society, the family unit above all stratifies the first cradle of the egokarma of the intraphysical consciousness and is the instrument of renovation for intraphysical society in general. The family institution, a micro-structure inserted into the social macro-structure, is the group that seeks the union of all its members, stemming from the work of the mother and father, within a society that is divided into classes. The family environment, the cornerstone of intraphysical society, presents many contradictions. Within this environment arise the demands of genetics, the trials and torments of the destitute home, the members of the family unit, the initial formation of the personality, the first examples and impressions, the critical comparisons of contrasting socio-economic situations, the pressures for greater social justice, relatives and, later on, outside the family unit, matrimony or, when the social being is evolutionarily more advanced, the evolutionary duo.

Small world. There are adults, human family members who have never left the well-defended and egoistic scope of their home or nuclear family. They live segregated in the *small world* of their home, that has become transformed into an ivory tower filled with egoism, in defense of the monopoly of their egokarma and, to a lesser degree, stuck to their karmic group (clan).

2. **School.** The school, the second immediate field of influence and interaction of the resonant consciousness, is where collective education is administered and the student class exists, the *sacred cow*, the extension of the family. Within this context the following can be noted: mass dissemination of repressions, authoritarianism, and social conditioning; preparation of children for intraphysical life; inculcation of behavior and the dominant ideology; possible generalized acritical sentiments; *consciential* awakening or intellectual torpor; deformations of human reality; and the first big enticing attractions for the consciousness outside the home.

Discipline. In the educational institution, the concept of discipline should always arise in the performance of an intelligent activity, in order to generate learning and a critical posture. Unfortunately, the authority figures do not always base their actions in dialogue and a common pursuit. An initial group of colleagues (karmic group) appears in the school and *attach* themselves *to the branches* of the genealogical tree of egoisms of the consciousness.

3. **District.** In the district of the city that has similar functions, aspects or people per se, where offices, clinics, tailor shops, stores or any other workplaces are installed. In low-level districts, one encounters human misery, slums, flood victims and the *embassies* of those contaminating non-evolved extraphysical environments. In these physical environments, work is performed that is not always entertaining, not always dignified and does not always produce wealth, but which constitutes the profession that gives weight and prestige in a social context. From this arises religion and religious mystifications that, unfortunately, seek, through social restraints, the alienation of the dominated class.

Innovations. It is from the workplace, however, that the bothersome forms of behavior arise which nevertheless bring innovations, the ever-present perturbations that exist in any type of transformation for the better, thus enriching the holokarma of the consciousness. The extraphysical consciousness, when reborn, although more multidimensionally aware (evolutiologist, *serenissimus*), paradoxically concludes that the nonstructural individual revolution depends upon the will of each one, exclusively, and at a certain evolutionary level will become more opportune and advantageous for consciential destinies. Without incurring any monopoly of egoism in his/her actions, the consciousness bases itself on the fact that the extraphysical lucid parapopulation is greater in number and evolutionary consequences to the physical, human consciential population (an estimated 9:1 ratio in 1998).

4. **City.** The city is the demographic complex that is socially and economically formed by an important non-agrarian concentration of the population. It can also be the environment, the nature, the reflection of agrarian problems and those of the rural proletariat, who are most exploited by the municipality; the daily life of the urban-industrial environment, the laborers who make up the *reserve army* and above all, the overpopulation, pollution, lack of green areas, the problem of unemployment, residential difficulties, traffic jams, the lack of food, medical assistance and leisure for children. The city is the assemblage of large groups of individuals who differ from each other in classes and coexist with their contemporaries, the social sport club, elitism, sumptuousness, snobbism and all types of segregation.

Interprison. As a general rule, all intraphysical consciousnesses who pertain to the dominant and exploiting class that owns production facilities and sweatshops, without serving others in an ample manner, must necessarily be reborn into the same country due to the obligations that they – more or less consciously – assume with the groupkarmic interprison.

5. **State.** The state, as considered here, is the territorial division of certain countries, the regionalism, foods, folklores and regional dialects, but also the ecological problems, hunters, lumberjacks, water polluters, the state colony of the metropolis and of the capital.

Ecology. Up until now, egokarmic and groupkarmic action incontestably predominate in the destiny of most consciousnesses and many social beings become entangled in their groupkarmic accounts due to the misuse of fauna and flora (anti-ecology).

6. **Country.** The country is the homeland, the native land. The homeland is generally portrayed in the exaltation of its economic and political grandeur, in an infantile, poetic manner, as the generous mother and protector, the ideological conditionings that are full of contradictions.

Democracy. Much is generally said about a democracy and a socialization that is never fully achieved or experienced, but maintains a capitalist-enslaving ideology, generating myopic nationalism, patriotism and patriots, the nationally vainglorious individuals, and ambiguous *unions between brothers*. Here, almost always unconsciously, groupkarma acts upon the majority of consciential destinies.

7. **Earth.** On the third planet of the solar system, the following are still predominantly cultivated to a high degree: unchecked planetary egoism, the rigidity of religions and ideological sectarianism. Therein live planetary humanity, the human species, the consciousness as human-animal. The unforgettable superiority of human beings over subhumans is always omnipresent in physical existence.

Cons. Materialists and egoists think that terrestrial humanity is the only grouping of living conscious beings that exists in the cosmos. Nevertheless, the action of polykarma can already be applied at highly expressive levels. With the notion of the habitability of other planets and internationalism, initial polykarma begins to be clearly defined here for the more apt, lucid intraphysical consciousness or the one with a greater recuperation of cons.

8. **Universe.** The universe is the sum total of everything that exists when taken as a whole. Multidimensionality, beginning with the intraphysical dimension, is endorsed by astronomy and astronautics, by parabolic antennae and parapsychic perceptions, in the physical and extraphysical practice of universalism.

Altruism. Integral, maximal and positive polykarma is consolidated by practicing altruism at a truly universal level.

---

172. THEORICE OF HUMAN ASSISTENTIAL TASKS

Definition. Human assistential task: service of fraternal aid on the part of a consciousness in favor of another or others.

Synonymy: assistential work; fraternal service; interpersonal help; work of solidarity.

Categories. According to the directives of universalism, there are two categories of libertarian human assistential tasks of consciential emancipation which are different from each other and are very well-defined:

1. **Consolation task.** The consolation task (initial *microlibertarian*).
2. **Clarification task.** The clarification task (advanced *macrolibertarian*).

Complementarity. Both are dignified, useful and indispensable in the evolutionary scale of the consciousness. They present rigid principles but complement each other because they endeavor to express fraternal love, to practice kindness, to teach consciousnesses, to be useful to humanity or fulfill the raison d'être of human existence: to help those beings with whom we *co-evolve* or lend incessant mutual assistance.

Crossroads. When the intraphysical consciousness decides to evolve in a rational manner, the natural progress of existence sooner or later leads one to a crossroads, or a growing crisis in human life (existential program). At this point, the two types of tasks can no longer allow a limited course of action.

Choice. When faced with both, each self-aware intraphysical being finds him/herself obliged to choose the essential directives for the basis of his/her own assistential work, listed below in 18 logical comparisons. These comparisons are to be analyzed and critiqued preferably by persons over 21 years of physical age who are already able to think about the quality of the eternal consciousness, despite living in the condition of a human being in a perishable animal body:

1. **Politics.** The *simple* task of consolation is involved in the situation of the majority. It is compliant, *responding with "yes" more often* than "no," *pleases others* and always blesses, offering palliatives for those who still need to ask for themselves. The *complex* task of clarification is involved

in the minority of the opposition. It analyzes realistically, *responds with "no" more often* than "yes," clarifies the facts, points out mistakes, teaching each person to only ask for others, and no longer for him/herself, in the direction of complete consciential self-sufficiency.

2. **Languages.** Those who console *cover up problems* and, using syrupy postures, shielding themselves in compassion, partially open the minds of others using infantile parables, images, circumlocutions, euphemisms and sugarcoated adjectives, *bordering on* hypocrisy. Those who clarify exalt self-critiquing and, with defined attitudes, shield themselves in justice, fully open the minds of others using constructive frankness in a language that is concise, direct and realistic, *far removed* from hypocrisy.

3. **Performance.** The service of consolation is *easily understood,* is pleasant to execute and soothing to perform. It produces immediate, rewarding, tangible and visible human results. The clarification task is *difficult to understand,* is less agreeable to execute, is not always pleasant to perform and only shows long-term extraphysical results, beyond human life.

4. **Techniques.** Consolation is based on the submission and blind passivity of individuals, functions with parapsychism predominating over animism, speaks solely at the level of consciousnesses that are led, reaches the majority of the *populace* and still submits itself to public opinion, giving special attention to the *quantity* (volume) of its services. Clarification is based on lucid, active performance and on the reaction of individuals. It functions with animism predominating over parapsychism, speaks at the level of consciousnesses that are led and lead, addresses the minority of conscientially mature beings and acts with full independence in the presence of so-called *public opinion,* giving far more attention to the *quality* of its services, including those of penta.

5. **Dimensions.** The still immature consolation task grows in full emotionality, under the direct inspiration of the *paratropospheric dimension,* through the psychosoma (the parabody of emotions), using the individual's desires or the capacity to feel. The clarification task, on the way to holomaturity, grows in full consciousness, under the direct inspiration of the *mentalsomatic dimension,* through the mentalsoma (the parabody of *sentiments*), using the individual's ideas or the capacity to think (reasoning, thosenization). This topic summarizes the essence of the author's theory on assistential and educational works between consciousnesses.

6. **Objectives.** Upon acting, consolation dedicates itself more to *form* or the ephemeral appearance of beings, things and facts; concentrates its performance in *megahome-earth* and the emergence of consciential first-aid; and employing the practice of empiricism in emergency therapy, it represents the palliative of "quickly removing only the mosquitoes that are attracted by filth." Upon acting, clarification applies itself more deeply, to *content* or the permanent essence of beings, things and facts; centralizes its performance in *megaschool-earth* and in the campaign of consciential prophylaxis; and practicing scientific theory as a singular vaccination, it acts as a preventive "gradually removing the dirt and the mosquitoes 'forever'".

7. **Resources.** Consolation uses *intuition,* requires a mystical climate of revelation in order to exalt emotionalism – its basis for persuasion – thus leaving many people still asleep in their somnambulism, because its relative *truth* of its teaching, which is partial and enslaving, is bound to the religious movement, which retains a monopoly over truth, to unending politics and to human labels. Clarification uses *rationality,* needs the balance of science in order to exalt discernment, the basis of its persuasion, trying to awaken all those *evolutionary slumberers* because the impartial and free relative truth of its teaching restricts itself only to the naked and blunt facts, universal phenomena, conscientiality, philosophy and pure extraphysical reality.

8. **Age.** The consolation task dedicates itself to consciential infancy and adolescence and, appealing to the force of emotivity, manipulates passions. It still makes concessions to the means needed to attain its ends, using dispensable subterfuge and committing the peccadilloes (pathothosenes) characteristic of religious demagogues (sophism and fallacious logic). The clarification task dedicates itself to consciential maturity, appealing to the serenity of reason. It works with reason, concerning itself with the qualification of the means for attaining its ends, desiring the attainment of full consciential authenticity.

9. **Consciousnesses.** The *more maternal* task of consolation acts to promote the gains of successive lives, appealing, above all, to extraphysical consciousnesses – which intraphysically undergo resoma – to subsequently reflect upon humankind in its condition as consciousness. The *more paternal* clarification task works toward the freeing of all from the cycle of existential seriation, basing itself first upon humankind, already intraphysical consciousnesses, to subsequently appeal to extraphysical consciousnesses. Within this context, machismo and feminism are secondary, because the consciousness itself does not have gender, although both tasks present characteristics that are still restricted to the subhuman aspects of the intraphysical consciousness.

10. **Existential seriation.** The *repressive* consolation task, as it is still moralistic, seeks to implant the virtues of *sanctity* and empty salvationism, speaks with austerity, is demanding, respects Puritanism and is sensitive to conventionalism. It beckons with the illusory possibility of immediate inner reform and the necessity of only a single physical life to reach liberation from the multiexistential cycle, using all the psychological crutches that it comes across. The *derepressive* clarification task, as it is moralizing, demands nothing, always speaks of the need for many inevitable successive physical lives and intermissive periods in the direction toward the true liberation of the consciousness. With a good humor and leisure, it repudiates convention, eliminating all the psychological dependencies and crutches that it can.

11. **Renovation.** The *repetitive* task of consolation rehashes antiquated formulas, all the while discoursing in a sacramental tone, sometimes accommodating itself in the rearguard "mending used cloths," and maintaining the human masses in a lamentable unconscious psychological dependency. The *renovative* clarification task applies new formulas and dares to face the *front-line* of the evolutionary battle, "exchanging used cloths for new ones" and leads intraphysical consciousnesses to a conscious psychological interdependence, wherein they are responsible for themselves with a greater lucidity.

12. **Vehicles.** The consolation task endeavors to locate the center of the consciousness in the *psychosoma* – the emotional parabody – acting upon the human-animal, e.g., through the enthusiastic *show* of the orator, creating listeners who applaud profusely and who, distressed and inhibited, do not expose their ideas for fear of failing to please. The clarification task endeavors to locate the core of the consciousness in the *mentalsoma* – the vehicle of balance and maturity – acting upon the human-consciousness, e.g., through the gathering of ideas through discussions promoted by the teacher. This creates uninhibited students who assume their own personality and critically question everything and everyone in a universalistic manner (omniquestioning).

13. **Chronology.** The *primary* phase of consolation spans from the past to the present, manifesting in the space-time continuum in the physical restriction of the intraphysical consciousness, based in the intransigence of orthodoxy and self-defensive purism that leads to the segregation of local, parochial, national and planetary provincialism. The *evolved* phase of clarification spans from the present to the future, providing the consciousness with the means for liberating itself from form, space and chronological time, until it arrives at the universalism of pure fraternity, without elitism or *ivory towers*.

14. **Justice.** The consolation task is rooted in requests for *mercy*, first and foremost, by the consoler and in his/her own favor. The clarification task is rooted in requests for full *justice* by the clarifier, however not only in his/her own favor, but first and foremost for the benefit of his/her evolutionary colleagues.

15. **Polykarma.** In the consolation task, the consoler is still more concerned with the details of the defensive activity and final balance of his/her egokarmic and groupkarmic accounts. In the clarification task, the clarifier is essentially concerned with the details of the activity and final balance of his/her polykarmic account.

16. **Approaches.** The consolation task is strictly dedicated to the religious dimension, e.g., the Gospel and Christ worship, by worshipping the myth of Jesus Christ, the top guru, making people feel more and think less. Through *wordplay*, the consolation task leads people through the lyricism of

poetry, blind romanticism and the exaltation of religion and religiosity, because it requires faith. The clarification task is essentially dedicated to the parameters of logic, good sense and the foundations of science – conscientiology, for example – making each one think for him/herself in order to domesticate instincts and animal sensations and, by *tossing ideas around,* leads him/her to the discernment and experimentation of pure science, substituting belief and unproductive religiosity with knowledge (wisdom or experience). There is a fundamental difference between wordplay and tossing ideas around: content and form (confor).

17. **Religions.** The consolation task still promotes idolatrous personality cults *("-latries"),* maintains gurus and untouchable issues as taboos. It concerns itself with proselytism and is sensitive to competition (competitiveness) with other religions and philosophies. The clarification task no longer propagates personality cults, dispenses with gurus, distances itself from systematic indoctrination, and endeavors to harmonize with the best side of the numerous religions, philosophies and lines of knowledge *("-sophies").*

18. **Examples.** Sects and churches generally only have resources for executing the primary phase of the consolation task, because they are captive to human life, temporal power, dogma and the *magister dixit,* not being able to deeply clarify anything if they do not apply open animism and parapsychism. Extraphysical truths, considered from the universalistic point of view, have the power to clarify and, surpassing the consolation task (which can be practiced by others who are newcomers to assistentiality), do not need to repeat it, creating temporal empires, because they have attained the task of self-knowledge through the animism of lucid projection, pure parapsychism, and extraphysical deintrusion, in which the intraphysical consciousness directly goes, researches and concludes for him/herself, without intermediaries or external influences, about human life and the consciential dimensions (consciential multidimensionality).

Beacon. Although both of these assistential instruments are useful, the tendency of the consolation task is to be an evolutionarily benumbing instrument, an *anesthetic.* The tendency of the clarification task is to be an illuminating instrument, a *beacon.*

Merits. The intraphysical being who is able to perform the clarification task, today on earth, should consider him/herself lucky. Having great merit is indispensable in order to develop the clarification task in the current human atmosphere or in the terrestrial holothosene.

Sectarianism. All human assistential or educational undertakings – *in any area,* although having a manifest or dissimulated sectarian sense, as inspired or temporally grandiose (pharaonic) as they might be – are still bound to the inceptive consolation task. Only the frank sense of universalism allows achievement of the authentic contextual level of the clarification of consciousnesses and ample polykarmality.

Construction. Generally, the intraphysical consciousness, through the consolation task, first constructs a personal foundation of energetic defense, from which he/she subsequently endeavors to build the clarification task.

Formula. Coldly analyzing the two human assistential tasks under discussion, using a simple arithmetical formula, it can easily be concluded that *1 man-hour* of the new and more difficult work of clarification is qualitatively worth much more than at least *10 man-hours* of work of consolation, a task which we have been repeating (dispensable self-mimicry) over centuries in a series of intraphysical lives and intermissive periods.

Practicality. The reader should not discard this chapter, judging it to be excessively idealistic. This subject, in addition to being very rational and practical, can help you keep your feet firmly planted on the ground of the planet.

Case Study. In near-death experiences, when the "being of light" appears to the projected intraphysical consciousness, at the critical moment in which he/she must decide whether to stay in the extraphysical dimension or return to the human body to continue with an existential mini-moratorium, as a general rule they ask: "What have you done in favor of others in your life on earth?"

173. SELF-CRITIQUE OF THE PROJECTOR

Definition. Self-critique: critique performed by someone upon him/herself or upon his/her own acts and manifestations.

Synonymy: critical self-awareness; self-analysis; self-confrontation; self-confrontational judgment; self-critiquing judgment; self-detection of lies; self-evaluation; *suspectometer*.

Mixing. The projective consciential experience is not an easy subject to present in detail. Above all, our conscious and unconscious desires and passions become quickly mixed into the observation, selection and classification of the extraphysical events that are experienced or witnessed by the projected projector.

Objectivity. If we do not maintain an attitude of permanent scientific impartiality and objectivity, we see only what we want to see, closing the eyes (and para-eyes) to that which we do not want to perceive.

Reality. It is not necessary to have an opinion about everything in the cosmos. Nor need we accept one of two theories, both of which are conflicting or incomprehensible for us. Whenever we encounter something that we do not understand, we need to postpone the acceptance of the reality around us.

Fantasies. Those who read the fantasies of science fiction suspend their disbelief and criticism in order to delight themselves with the *story*. In dealing with reality, the safest attitude is to suspend the acceptance that one has of the facts, unless the intraphysical consciousness prefers to think in the world of fantasy or, in other words: live a pipe dream or a daydream.

Objective. There is only one objective reality. The conventional objective reality is the universe that is studied by physicists, chemists, biologists and other scientists within the space-time continuum, as well as those objects, elementary particles and beings that populate it, which are observed by the physical senses and the instruments which are under the command of the observer. This includes your human body and the signals that circulate through your nervous system. These signals allow the connection between objective reality and the human perception of this same objective reality.

Subjective. Various subjective realities exist that correspond to each consciousness or consciential micro-universe. The electrochemical pulses involved in the registration of the biomemory or cerebral memory carry information between the sensory organs and the brain, allowing the observer to detect the presence of objects and events outside the human body.

Perceptions. The perception of events occurring *outside* the human body or, in other words, the lucidity or awareness of external perceptions, constitutes subjective reality per se. Only the consciousness can know its own subjective reality, in which is included the perceptions of occurrences *inside* one's own human body and in all the other vehicles of manifestation of the consciousness (holosoma).

Repression. The projector has to observe and interpret extraphysical events without taking personal interests and desires into consideration. The individual needs, as far as possible, to liberate him/herself from all scientific preconceptions or dogmas, religious repression and sacralization, and those of education and class conditioning (corporatism, lobbyism, nepotism).

Elaboration. The projective experimenter need not and should not endeavor to remodel the ordinary dream in order to present it in the form of a relatively coherent and comprehensible story *(psychological makeup)* in order to pass it off as a lucid projection, in the same way that secondary elaboration is produced by the patient in psychoanalysis. In this case, the person removes the absurdity and incoherence from the dream, covering its flaws, performing partial or total remodeling of its elements, embellishing those portions which have been selected.

Conspiracy. Lucid projectors should also not resort – as countless philosophical, political, religious or social groups do – to the veil of silence, as though a conspiracy had been mounted by the authorities, government, opposition groups, powerful individuals, or economic forces in order to guarantee that his/her points of view on projectiology are not being heard, and that the final, definitive triumph of their ideas, which are learned in and through their lucid projective experiences, are being postponed.

Devil. It should be kept in mind, for example, that, similar to the conspiracy theory, religious professionals invented the devil (Beelzebub, Diabolus, Lucifer, Mephistopheles, Satan), some centuries ago, in order to explain the human failings of Christianity as a global movement.

Ignorance. The result of this is the interpretation of ignorance, not as a mere absence of understanding, but as the action of a sinister force, the origin of impure and malevolent influences that perverted our mind and imposed the erroneous habit upon us of resisting knowledge and contesting the facts. On the other hand, these facts unfortunately did not and do not impede the development of interconsciential intrusions and self-intrusions or obsessions.

Precipitation. Another sick tendency of human nature is exaggeration or precipitation in the analysis of a fact when someone operates based on the erroneous idea that "if this is not the truth, then it ought to be," avoiding considering other perspectives and ignoring all evidence that is contrary to your own – which has been established in advance (apriorism) – with regard to the subject.

Exaggeration. Exaggeration sometimes makes a person – when at an intellectual crossroads or when presented with an interpretational dilemma – resort to changing the story, or even applying force upon the theory of an analyzed subject, through a great deal of *squeezing, pulling, pushing, and twisting,* in order for the story to fit better or give the impression of squaring perfectly with the facts under analysis.

Authenticity. Lucid projection constitutes an authentic fact in and of itself. It dispenses with all types of psychological aids. It is not necessary to resort to any types of appeal in order to affirm it as being a real and persuasive phenomenon to anyone else.

Self-sufficiency. The natural fact of lucid projection is self-sufficient, speaks for itself and defends itself. Lucid projection is self-persuasive, thereby being a challenge to all intelligent or more lucid social beings.

Self-critique. Given these considerations, it is worth emphasizing that – in any parapsychic or conscientiological scientific experiment, notably those regarding individual experiments with lucid projection – the practitioner should conduct a rigorous examination of self-critique *after* physical awakening.

Classification. At this point, it is important for the interested individual to ponder the classification of the analyses. Critiquing, in projectiology and conscientiometry, is consciential analysis. Critiquing can generally be placed into two categories: self-critique and heterocritique. Self-critique – the most relevant of all types of critiquing – is the consciousness' analysis of itself.

Heterocritique. Heterocritique can be divided into two classifications: first – and more relevant, in this particular case – the consciential analysis performed by another or others (consensus) upon ourselves, the author or you, the reader. Second, your consciential analysis of another or others.

Utilization. Heterocritique generated by others in regard to you, even when it is spontaneous or unsolicited, needs to be rationally pondered and utilized by you. What is more: you should always seek out heterocritique in order to improve your consciential awareness and improve your behavior patterns and strategy for consciential self-analysis. You should obviously not confuse the above-cited critique with so-called current *public opinion,* or *kaffeeklatsch* gossip.

Analysis. In this detailed examination you need to analyze whether your extraphysical experiences were not perhaps hallucination, coincidence, daydream, mistake, exaggeration, hypnagogy, hypnopompy, distorted memory, erroneous perceptions, imagination, fantasies, illusions, delirium, nightmare and dream, or a possible combination of these and other explanations. As you know, *to analyze* signifies: to disassemble, dissect, separate, study and interpret.

Projectiocritique. The existence of projectiocritique, or rigorous psychological self-analysis, enumerated below with 10 items for those who wish to evolve with projections and achieve a greater extraphysical maturity, are singled out, before any other practical considerations, in order to highlight its importance and, above all, help the individual who aspires to have impactful lucid projections:

1. **Projection.** Only proceed with the comparison of your own consciential experiences with the data in this book when you are fully convinced that you have had a lucid projection and not any other altered state of consciousness, much less those that are reminiscent of movies, television shows, computer archives, novels, literature, passions or puerile vanity.

2. **Incoherences.** Research all causes and correlations of all *anachronisms, incongruities, incoherences, inconsequences and inconsistencies* of the extraphysical perceptions experienced during the projective experiments.

3. **Distortions.** Do not withhold information under some pretext, do not write your reports under pressure, or deliberately distort the version of the occurrences in order to avoid difficulties in the acceptance of your projective experiments.

4. **Exclusions.** Be authentic, always faithful to the facts, distancing yourself from any propensity to highlight any perspectives to the exclusion of others when analyzing lucid projections.

5. **Frankness.** Be completely frank, using sensible and rational approaches in the registering of your extraphysical experiences.

6. **Imagination.** Eliminate embellishments forged by the imagination, or imagistic processes, during the detailed interpretation of parapsychic occurrences.

7. **Preconceptions.** Jettison possible preconceptions, or taboos of civilization and all types of dogmas upon studying projective experiences.

8. **Doubts.** Abstain from forcibly transforming doubts into certainties when naturally focusing upon projective phenomena.

9. **Fearlessness.** Derepress and unreservedly expose yourself, realistically, without fear of complications, misunderstandings, misinformation or threats regarding your lucid projections.

10. **Confession.** Always confess ignorance, when necessary, upon being faced with any doubtful subjects under analysis.

Self-censure. On the other hand, you, as a practitioner who is interested in lucid projectability (LPB), should be aware that this self-critique cannot be confused or exaggeratedly interpreted to the point of becoming a castrating or sterilizing self-censure that indicates a tendency in your perspective, expressing opinions which are censured by myths, spurious influences, subconscious coercion in the analysis of facts or detours from the forms of scientific procedure.

Excesses. We should not forget that 2 excesses can be lucidly interpreted here:

1. **Masochism.** Excessive *self*-critique can be interpreted by you, the experimenter, as masochism.

2. **Sadism.** Excessive *hetero*critique can still be interpreted, *by* and *for* you, as sadism.

Projectiolatry. The author is, personally, against all stagnating and excessive cults. This is why he is against *projectiolatry*.

Role. The projector who wishes to evolve cannot abdicate from his/her reason, discernment, good sense, permanent state of self-critique and frankness, starting with him/herself, recognizing the precise role of lucid projection in the development of humankind, nevertheless with neither excesses, exaggeration, fantasies nor fabulations.

Hypotheses. Incidentally, the author has seen nothing in the extraphysical dimensions, environments and communities, through lucid projections, that serves to prove the following 4 theories:

1. **Metempsychosis.** Metempsychosis, or the doctrine in which a human consciousness is reborn into the body of a subhuman animal.

2. **Mate.** Soul mates or the supposition wherein two consciousnesses with a great deal of affinity evolve interdependently with one another.

3. **Fusionism.** Fusionism or consciential fusion *(melding)*, the hypothesis of two or three consciousnesses merging, thereby forming another more evolved consciousness.

4. **Elementals.** Beings called elementals or the separate creation, with a parallel evolution of consciential principles that are different from the personality and which culminates in the composition of the human consciousness (intraphysical consciousness).

Bibliography: Garret (571, p. 50), Gooch (617, p. 45), Rigonatti (1402, p. 163), Rogo (1444, p. 16), Vieira (1762, p. 62).

174. LUCID PROJECTION AND ABDOMINAL BRAINWASHING

Definition. Abdominal brainwashing: the method – through the systematic production of fatigue, using chemical agents, persuasion, indoctrination and incessant torment – that endeavors to convert persons lacking free determination of their will to a generally political credo that they would not embrace if they were free.

Synonymy: brainwashing *(hsi-nao);* cerebral attack; drug induced abreaction; forced mental intrusion; ideological reconditioning; ideological remodeling; imposition of belief; memory reprogramming; mental stripping; menticide (term created by Joost A. M. Meerloo); mind manipulation; mind modeling; pathological indoctrination; perverse conversion; planned intellectual coercion; psychopolitics; thought control; undesirable persuasion.

Anti-critique. Abdominal brainwashing is the most abject and manifest form of indoctrination. It makes human life with self-critique, universalism, consciential maturity and development of the intraphysical being's lucid projectability impracticable, because it makes it impossible to install self-control in the mental time and space of the unaware intraphysical consciousness. This topic should therefore be analyzed in detail in order to remain inoculated against it (paraprophylaxis).

Obstacle. Second only to fear (neophobia, projectiophobia), brainwashing (a term coined by Edward Hunter in 1951) is the second greatest obstacle, or practical impediment, to the development of projectiology. In order for it to develop in the individual, lucid projectability requires the application of discernment, which brainwashing or, more precisely, *abdominal brainwashing,* eliminates in the intraphysical consciousness.

History. Historically, abdominal brainwashing is not a new process for the implantation or reinforcement of beliefs. It has always existed in one form or another, in all epochs, either at a more superficial, restricted level *(copycat; peer pressure; vidiotism)* or, at a deeper, broader level (resomatic forgetfulness; mystical excesses; false confessions).

Automatons. The routine established by culture and created by the formation of habits, through the strength of social rules and environmental myths, turns all persons into partial automatons.

Promoters. In modern life, the promoters of unperceived abdominal brainwashings are those incessant prattlers that never shut up: publicity, advertisements, radio, television, Internet, movies, variety newspapers and magazines.

Pacifier. Strictly speaking, subtle abdominal brainwashing begins in the cradle, when the pacifier is used to stop up the mouth of a newborn.

Protowashing. The so-called *group-soul* of subhuman animals seems to be the first natural, incipient, spontaneous and unconscious abdominal brainwashing process (abdominal protowashing) existing in the universe.

Mold. In certain cases, the adult, through abdominal brainwashing, becomes a child again, fitting into a mold of deliberately prepared thought (ideological remodeling) and impinged behavior (inculcation) for a specific group. These observations suggest that many aspects of human abdominal brainwashing constitute a psychological regression of the ego to the state of primitive animality or the condition of *group-soul.*

Dolphins. It is worth noting that even dolphins, when in captivity resulting from their capture, imprisonment and physical isolation, suffer psychological changes, rarely live for a long time and, in these deprived conditions, do not exhibit any degree of extrasensory perception.

Resoma. On the other hand, the resoma of an extraphysical consciousness is also an abdominal brainwashing process, notably for those egos who do not experience lucid self-retrocognitions or, in other words, those intraphysical or social beings, most of whom do not remember their experiences prior to physical rebirth (previous intraphysical lives and intermissive periods). In this aspect, every physical life is a new consciousness-washing due to intraphysical restriction and the loss of cons. A new – most recent – multiexistential catharsis occurs when the consciousness is able to remember some experience previous to the current intraphysical life. This is the process used in past life regressions.

Evolution. This approach shows that abdominal brainwashing – in this case consciential, with pluri-existential and multi-secular effects – is a process that is primarily restricted to the actual mechanism of evolution of the consciousness.

Forgetfulness. We forget our previous experiences, living our life without awareness of our integral past in order to dedicate greater attention to our less undesirable side, making the better side of our ego, preferably, come to the fore. We gradually remember our more forgotten or more remote experiences to the degree that we gradually become more apt, understanding and mature, improving our consciential performance with respect to the evolution of all.

Slate. It is common knowledge that intellectual indoctrination (mentalsoma) that lacks emotional exaltation (psychosoma) is notably *inefficient*. This is because modern political abdominal brainwashing techniques, the methods for awakening religious fervor, changing human convictions, gathering and conserving neophytes, preserving political beliefs and making proselytes outside the group with *softening* processes and the careful disturbance of cerebral activity, are always directed toward an assault upon the emotions, and not the intelligence, thereby erasing the *cortical slate* (cerebral hemispheres), jeopardizing discernment and increasing suggestibility.

Mechanism. The basic process for quick conversion is always the total exhaustion of the human body, the bombardment of the brain taken to the point of exhaustion, pressure placed upon the ego beyond its tolerance level, the inhibition of the individual's reasoning capacity and critical faculties, until reaching the point of physical collapse, emotional fatigue, sudden stupor or the total collapse of the nervous system.

Conditioning. Through continued tension, awakening and sufficiently over-stimulating the individual's strong emotions to the point where the perturbed victim becomes angry, afraid or excited, which is deliberately provoked, the person can be conditioned to detest that which was loved and to love that which had been detested, to dissipate beliefs and attitudes and destroy thought and behavior patterns.

Characteristics. Cases of abdominal brainwashing – from the mildest to the strongest ones, whether latent or manifest – can generally be grouped and explained by the following 6 basic characteristics: types; responsible parties; institutions; processes; victims; and consequences.

1. **Types.** Strictly speaking, there are different types of abdominal brainwashing. Some examples are: automatizing; classic; commercial; confessional; contemplative; group; mass; indirect; individual; market oriented; police oriented; political; religious; *resomatic;* ritual; robotizing; sanctifying; somnambulizing or zombifying; spontaneous.

2. **Responsible.** Those persons responsible for abdominal brainwashing – *brainwashers,* human domesticators, ego invaders, specialists in totalitarian menticide, vandals or violators of consciousnesses – receive different names according to different contexts. Examples: advertisers; dictators; indoctrinators; initiators; intraphysical intruders; kidnappers; lawyers; liberal professionals; pastors; politicians; priests; psychiatrists; psychoanalysts; psychotherapists; secret police; superiors; and torturers.

3. **Institutions.** Mental reform techniques applied in many locations or institutions vary according to the target group and circumstances, but the basic approach is the same. Examples: clinic; concentration camp; convent; factory; maternal uterus; military headquarters; police department; political correctional facility; political party; psychiatric hospital; revolutionary school; temple; or wartime hospital.

4. **Processes.** It is interesting to note that the process, the mental collapse and the condition of abdominal brainwashing itself all receive different names in different contexts. Examples: *brainwashing* in the techniques used by the elite forces of modern political war; *contemplation* in the mystical practices of religious sects; *forced confessions* in police interrogations; *forgetfulness* in the general process of resoma; *initiation rites* in orders, mystical fraternities and primitive societies; *marketing* in the competition of commerce and industry; *menticidal assault* in the political processes sustained through physical and psychic violence; *rapid sanctification* in diverse religious catechisms; *zombification* in the practices of voodooism.

5. **Victims.** In theory, practically all intraphysical beings can be victims of abdominal brainwashing, although some persons are more predisposed than others. Examples: certain ill persons; conditioned zombies; excessively religious persons; exhausted soldiers; fatigued prisoners; gang members; hetero-suggestible personalities; ignorant or uncultured people; kidnap victims; materially dispossessed individuals; non-religious seekers; opinionative robots; potential proselytes; pusillanimous egos; religious neophytes; the individual who has lost a loved one; tired workers; torture victims; vulnerable ordinary citizens.

6. **Consequences.** The consequences of abdominal brainwashing present variations according to their carefully planned objectives. Examples: the achievement of *sanctification;* attributing a state of *grace to the intervention of the Holy Spirit;* the *freeing of souls;* the achievement of religious cures; conversion to the old militant communism; the creation of mental slaves; the menticide syndrome; the demonstration of the precision of Freud's theories; the perverted use of Pavlovian rules; the breaking of old behavior patterns with the implantation of other new ones; *barbed wire* phobia; the epidemics of religious or political fanaticism throughout time.

Indoctrination. Specific and countless examples of abdominal brainwashing are found with all victims of sectarian, factious or systematic indoctrination, physiological and chemical pressure and group suggestion that aim to dismantle the personality and construct a new personality. Examples: soldiers (*group-soul* of a regiment), in this case in reference to professional killers throughout time (Japanese kamikazes; car bombs in Lebanon and other locations); the orthodox followers of diverse religious orders (the *group-soul* of fanaticism); the historical processes of the Inquisition (thirteenth to seventeenth century) and the imposed abjurations; the movement of religious exaltation of the Crusades; the conversion of Saul on the road to Damascus (Acts 9:1 and 18); the use of concentration camps and forced labor camps with the technique of mental purging of prisoners (Second World War); psychoanalytical methods with catharsis and the reliving of childhood traumas, and the techniques of multiexistential regression (often exceptionally positive); campaigns of religious revivalism of orthodox beliefs (Methodists; those individuals obsessed with the Bible); the techniques of multinational inculcation of the soul (the Moonism cult; the Hare Krishna movement); the totalitarian propaganda of radical assemblies (the *training* of Hitler Youth; the Symbionese Liberation Army; the Brazilian Society for the Defense of Tradition, Family and Propriety); political reeducation programs (the beginnings of Chinese Communism; the prisoners of war in the Korean War); the condition of certain contemporary kidnapping victims, imposed by kidnappers, who suffer from the *Stockholm syndrome,* in which the victims (masochism) surrender emotionally, sympathizing with the kidnappers (sadism).

Franciscans. The following is a historic or classic example of abdominal brainwashing preformed with the *best of intentions and the greatest goodwill,* without any self- and heterodiscernment or consciential maturity but fanatically through religion, that was already occurring in the year 1228 in the processes of contemplation or sanctification. Priest, author and biographer, Thomas of Celano, when candidly referring to the Franciscans, of the Catholic religious order of the same name, established by Francis of Assisi, originally left the following pearls in Latin in reference to the *group-soul* of the convent (italics by the author):

"They above all possess the virtue of mutual and constant charity, to the point that it unites their wills, the 40 or 50 living in the same place seeming to have *a single will and a single opinion"* (p. 20). "Some of them have already become so unaccustomed to speaking that, when they need to, they *barely recall how to form words"* (p. 20). "They have finally *arrived at a level of contemplation,* wherein they learn everything that they have to do or not do in order to learn to please God, dedicating day and night to divine glorification and prayer" (p. 21).

Techniques. In summary, it can be affirmed that the abdominal brainwashing process is a new and methodical combination of known techniques, destroying deep-rooted preconceptions through the removal of perceptual and social support, the prohibition of humor, a weakening of the ego, the annihilation of the old self-image and its replacement with another, in a strategy of mental subjection, even changing the social being's legal name, in some cases producing a clear change in the ego during intraphysical life with the loss of the prior identity.

Scale. The scale of the phenomena of abdominal brainwashing, whether spontaneous or unconscious on the part of the victim, can be synthesized into a crescendo of consciential alterations, through 7 levels:

1. Absence of conscious self-critique.
2. Obsession or fixed idea (monoideism).
3. Fanaticism (political, religious).
4. Intrusion (or self-intrusion).
5. Consummate abdominal brainwashing.
6. Profound alterations in the personality.
7. Loss of a portion of intraphysical life and the existential program.

Efficiency. It is always unwise to underestimate the efficiency of the methods of perverse indoctrination. It is an illusion to believe that intellectual knowledge of what is happening can always keep a person from being indoctrinated. The facts show that: the human body cannot resist conditioning; no one is completely safe from the process of mental reprogramming; there is still a generalized ignorance regarding abdominal brainwashing techniques. For example, *all* infantry soldiers, being normal men who are trained to kill or be killed, suffer an eventual neurological reaction – combat fatigue – when submitted to the pressures of combat over a sufficiently long period of time in a continued, severe campaign.

Recruitment. Abdominal brainwashing, promoted by modern religious cults through recruiters of those who are solitary, indecisive, lacking affection, desperate and disappointed individuals, applies at least the following 20 coercive techniques, listed here in alphabetical order:

1. Absolute loyalty.
2. Altered diet.
3. Chants and meditation.
4. Conformity.
5. Doctrinaire confusion.
6. Exclusivity.
7. False sense of camaraderie.
8. Financial involvement.
9. Hypnotic states.
10. Illogical activities.
11. Indoctrinating bombardment with the spoken word.
12. Isolation from the outside world.
13. Lack of privacy.
14. New family relationships.
15. Pavlovian control.
16. Rejection of values.
17. Sense of community affirmation.
18. Sensory deprivation.
19. Total loss of privacy.
20. Unquestioning submission.

Conscientiometry. In light of this detailed presentation of material, it is worthwhile for each one of us to ask the following question with rigorous self-critique: "To what degree does some type of abdominal brainwashing diminish the acuity of my unveiling of the surroundings, impede the development of my reason and reduce the level of my consciential maturity?" The quality of the response to this conscientiometric question defines your projectiological possibilities as an intraphysical being.

Research. If you are still in doubt regarding the exact response, research the theme more deeply, using different approaches, with the following mini-bibliography.

Projectiological Bibliography: Almeida (15; Atos, 9:8), James (803, p. 223), Sargant (1508, p. 9).

Specific Bibliography:

1. **CELANO, Tomas de;** *Vida de São Francisco de Assis;* Biography; transl. José Carlos C. Pedroso; 224 pp.; 220 chaps.; 21 X 13,5 cm; pb.; Petrópolis, RJ; Brazil; Editora Vozes; 1975; pp. 20, 21.

2. **LIFTON, Robert J.;** *Thought Reform of Western Civilians in Chinese Communist Prisons; Psychiatry;* Vol. 19; 1956; pp. 173-195.

3. **MEERLOO, Joost Abraham Maurits;** *O Rapto do Espírito (The Rape of the Mind);* transl. Eugênia Moraes de Andrade & Raul de Morais; 386 pp.; 18 chaps.; 130 refs.; 20,5 X 13,5 cm; pb.; São Paulo, SP, Brazil; Instituição Brasileira de Difusão Cultural; 1959; p. 13.

4. **REBOUL, Olivier;** *A Doutrinação (L'Endoctrinement);* transl.; Staff; XX + 164 pp.; 8 chaps.; 11 refs.; 21 X 14 cm; pb.; São Paulo, SP, Brazil, Companhia Editora Nacional; 1980; p. 87.

5. **SARGANT, William;** *A Conquista da Mente: Fisiologia da Conversão e da Lavagem Cerebral (Battle for the Mind);* transl. Aydano Arruda; 246 pp.; 11 chaps.; illus.; 59 refs.; São Paulo, SP, Brazil; Ibrasa; 1968; p. 50.

VII – Pre-Projection Physical Waking State

---
175. CHRONOLOGICAL ANALYSIS OF LUCID PROJECTION

Definition. Chronological analysis: detailed examination of each constituent element or discrete part of a phenomenon, in order to understand its nature, proportions, functions, limits, relationships and consequences with regard to the natural chronology of the phenomenological occurrences.

Synonymy: chronographic analysis; study through chronological time.

Analysis. In the analysis of the entire lucid projection, induced by any process or methodology, it is important to consider the set of factors inherent to the transcendent, animic (intraconsciential) and parapsychic nature of the phenomena, which change in each of the projector's experiences, as well as from one projector to another.

Enumeration. The intraphysical consciousness interested in performing a detailed study can establish a comparison, identifying the similarities and differences of the projection in question with the specifications sequentially arranged in an *illustrative enumeration (flowchart),* starting from this section 7.

Patterns. This section includes, in chronological order, an extensive and diversified quantity of the typical patterns of the most common experiences, occurring before, during and after the activities of the consciousness when outside the human body. It also includes highly probable eventualities, concurrent phenomena and multiple detailed technical procedures, derivations and consequences, cited as correctly as possible in the chronological order of events (timeline) that develop in an ordinary projection.

Repetitions. The purpose of clarifying the important details as much as possible, establishing bases for the evaluation of the quality of the experiments, generated inevitable repetition due to the interactions of the phenomena and congenerous approaches.

Evidence. In the topics presented, all having intriguing and more or less original perspectives which require further exploration, the items terminate with the providential *and others*. This resource – apparently unscientific – attests to the current ignorance regarding the repercussions and extent of experiments that will only be clarified, confirmed or invalidated in the near future by the scientific criterion of a convergence of evidence, through the universality of reproducible observations of lucid projection practitioners and parapsychic phenomena researchers.

Note. It is important to emphasize the fact that none of the characteristics presented here, listing projective details, can be taken as being general, as they vary from person to person and can even occur in a manner that is contrary to what is affirmed.

Facts. Nevertheless, these characteristics are typical of the difficulties commonly experienced by the majority of lucid projectors and are related to the psychological (intracerebral) and intraconsciential (consciential micro-universe) facts most common to human existence and completion of the existential program.

---
176. STAGES OF LUCID PROJECTION

Cycle. The *projective cycle* is composed of 5 main, distinct stages or 5 different steps that the intraphysical consciousness has to execute in the intraphysical and extraphysical dimension in order to produce the experience of lucid projection.

Chronology. The 5 projective stages can be differentiated in the following chronological order:

1. **Pre-departure.** Pre-projection physical waking state (preparation for consciential departure).
2. **Takeoff.** Exteriorization of the consciousness (takeoff).
3. **Volitation.** Extraphysical period of the consciousness (extraphysical experience, volitation).
4. **Interiorization.** Interiorization of the consciousness into the human body (consciential reentry or *re-incorporation*).
5. **Outcomes.** Post-projection physical waking state (outcomes of consciential arrival).

Waking state. The ordinary, physical waking state, before as well as after the production of the lucid projection experience, becomes important because the following frequently occurs:

1. **Pre-projective.** Before, the preambulary or pre-projective phenomena or influences.
2. **Post-projective.** The immediate consequences of the experiment or diverse post-projective manifestations arise soon after the experiment.

Highlight. From this chapter on, each of the 5 stages of the lucid projection experience will be highlighted in various parts, in order to anatomize the projective occurrences of the human consciousness or intraphysical consciousness as far as possible.

Bibliography: Vieira (1762, p. 53).

---

177. DOORWAYS TO LUCID PROJECTION

Dimensions. All doorways to dimensions that are external to the intraphysical consciousness are predisposing states for the production of lucid consciential projection.

Types. There are various types of *doorways* to human lucid projection, such as the following 17, listed in alphabetical order:

1. Autoscopy.
2. Daydream.
3. Diverse xenophrenic states.
4. Extracorporeal sleep.
5. Extraphysical catalepsy.
6. Extraphysical somnambulism.
7. Hypnagogic state (alpha waves).
8. Natural sleep.
9. Nightmare.
10. Ordinary dream.
11. Ordinary, physical waking state.
12. Parapsychic trance (specific).
13. Parapsychic.
14. Physical catalepsy.
15. Psychological.
16. Somnolence.
17. Vibrational state (VS).

Ambivalence. These projective doorways are ambivalent, as they can pertain to both the *entrance* to and *exit* from lucid projection. Thus, the consciousness of the projector leaves the state of natural sleep, for example, and returns to it soon thereafter.

Alternation. The common alternation of the states of consciousness, referring mostly to natural sleep, dreams and nightmares, occurs less frequently with the physical waking state, daydreams and the hypnagogic state (hypnagogy).

Traumas. Various physical traumas can provoke a lucid projection, such as the following 10, listed in alphabetical order:

1. Drugs.
2. Electric shock.
3. Encephalic traumatism.
4. Impact of the sudden acceleration or deceleration of a vehicle (car, for example).
5. Odontological anesthesia.
6. Previous partial projection.
7. Psychic and emotional shock.

8. Serious illness.
9. State of coma.
10. Surgery.

Repetition. Any intraphysical projector can experience all of the consciential states referred to here in order to begin the lucid projection, although 1 or 2 states repeat more frequently according to the process employed to project.

Bibliography: Shay (1546, p. 32).

178. DATE OF THE PROJECTIVE EXPERIMENT

Occurrences. With regard to the date of the projector's experiment, various occurrences, or at least the following 10, can be observed:

1. Consulting the calendar and scheduling.
2. Day of the month.
3. Best day of the week for the projector.
4. Month.
5. Year.
6. Holiday.
7. Atypical day or one involving a disruption in the human body's psychophysiological rhythm (circadian cycle, biological clock, biochronology).
8. Phase of the moon.
9. Personal register.
10. Other references specific to the intraphysical consciousness.

Confirmation. The details of the date, which seem unnecessary at first glance, are actually factors relevant to the intentional or unexpected subsequent confirmation of occurrences of human lucid consciential projection. They are notably important in the case of precognitive projections.

Comparisons. Besides, they serve as valuable elements in the comparative studies between seriated consciential projections and the influences of the human environment (holothosene).

Projector. It is always relevant for a woman to observe her menstrual periods in relation to lucid projections, verifying if there is a notable aspect or interaction between one fact and the other.

Rest. Certain women feel a greater need to rest when their menstrual period is approaching. Besides, pre-menstrual tension (PMT) frequently occurs.

Moon. Some individuals recommend not performing experiments with projection during certain phases of the moon, especially in the last quarter. Nevertheless, the author considers that precaution to be secondary, simple superstition or a harmless preconception.

Bibliography: Butler (227, p. 74), Monroe (1065, p. 235), Vieira (1762, p. 210).

179. METEOROLOGICAL CONDITIONS PRIOR TO LUCID PROJECTION

Characteristics. Among the characteristics of meteorological conditions that bear some relation to lucid consciential projection, the following 10 can be singled out:

1. Good weather.
2. Rainy weather.
3. Storm.
4. Windstorm.

5. Lightning.
6. Thunder.
7. Nearby noises.
8. Relative air humidity.
9. Cold.
10. Heat.

Cosmic. The so-called cosmic, meteorological factors, climatic influences and changes in the seasons should not, in fact, exercise any influence over the lucid projection experience. It above all depends upon the decided will, psychological motivation and performance of the practitioner, who can overcome all inconvenient or apparently adverse conditions to the experiment.

Novice. It will always be easy to write this, but in practice the theory (theorice) is not all that simple due to psychological factors, conditionings of all kinds, that are specific to each person, preconceptions and deeply rooted superstitions that stratify the complexities which are part of each human personality.

Optimization. Hence, it will always be better for the novice to choose a favorable, ideal or typical day with good weather to begin the projective exercises, optimizing the circumstances for initial attempts as far as possible.

Bibliography: Butler (227, p. 74), Vieira (1762, p. 165).

---

180. PHYSICAL BASE OF THE PROJECTOR

Definition. Physical base: selected safe location where the human body of the intraphysical consciousness remains while projecting from it.

Synonymy: *astralport;* bedroom; domicile of the human body; *duodrome;* energetically shielded chamber; garage of the soma; human base; landing field; parking lot of the human body; private retreat; projective base; spinning top for successive projections; support base; volitational station.

Internal. Strictly speaking, the first internal physical base of the intraphysical consciousness is the human body or soma.

Battery. The extraphysical sphere of energy or psychosphere of the intraphysical consciousness makes the projector's physical base its battery of consciential energy (CE), which can be charged or uncharged (unbalanced) on the occasion of the lucid consciential projection.

Categories. There are various categories of physical base for the projector, such as the following 21:

1. The internal physical base, the human body.
2. The external physical bases: the bedroom, as well as the others listed below.
3. Living room.
4. Large room.
5. Office.
6. A walled location.
7. Laboratory.
8. Apartment.
9. House.
10. Farm.
11. Institution.
12. Temple.
13. Monastery (convent, seminary).
14. In the open air or outdoors.
15. Yard.

16. Balcony.
17. A stationary vehicle.
18. A moving vehicle.
19. A customary or familiar base.
20. An occasional or emergency base.
21. A floating base (boat, ship, submarine, balloon).

Best. The best and most common physical base is a silent bedroom where the projector can keep the door locked and the windows closed.

Blue. The color blue, used in the decoration of the bedroom or room, has a positive or sedative effect toward sleep and lucid projection.

Location. In the physical base, at least the following 7 essential factors should be borne in mind:

1. Environmental conditions.
2. Equipment for sleeping that sometimes functions for simple physical reasons and other times for purely psychological reasons.
3. Complete equipment for annotations.
4. Local altitude.
5. Acoustic isolation, as well as isolated surroundings.
6. Everything that distracts the physical mind detracts from lucid projection.
7. Closed or opened doors and windows.

Rest. In theory, at least, one can sleep on anything: bed, armchair, sofa, bed frame, lawn, carpet, on a truck and other objects or vehicles, even when they are moving.

Rigidity. There are those who rest lying on very rigid surfaces, such as floors which, according to specialists, do not afford restful sleep.

Headboard. Others sleep with the headboard of the bed slightly elevated.

Hammocks. There others still who spend the night in hammocks.

Astronauts. Astronauts sleep well floating in zero gravity.

Privilege. The inside of an orbiting spaceship cabin can be considered a privileged physical base for lucid consciential projections, despite all the physiological problems it can cause for the astronauts.

Bed. Using a single bed avoids spontaneous movements and unconscious contacts by one's mate, a very common act when both sleep in a double bed.

Twin. If sleeping with one's mate is disturbing, the individual should try using twin beds or separate rooms. This may seem less romantic, but in certain cases it is even better for a good matrimonial relationship. Nevertheless, this is never the ideal for the self-aware evolutionary duo.

Length. In principle, your bed should be at least 6" (15 cm) longer than you.

Obstacles. All obstacles to *freedom* of the human body represent an obstacle to *sleep*.

Extra. Those who prefer and have sufficient space can, for example, use an extra large or king-size bed that is sufficiently ample, being 86.75" (2.2 m) long and 63" (1.60 m) wide.

Kicks. The king-size bed allows each partner to use separate blankets on the same mattress, thus sleeping together (double occupancy) and yet separate from each other. This nullifies the effects of *random kicks*.

Distance. The distance between the floor and the projector's human body upon projecting does not matter and does not seriously interfere with the production of lucid projections.

Bunk. It has been observed that many veteran lucid projectors exteriorize the consciousness, leaving the physical body lying on the higher level of a bunk bed or, in other words, on the second or even the third superimposed narrow bed, being part of a special attachment of a set of beds inside the house, or even in the compartment of a ship's cabin.

Mattress. The mattress should not have springs. Besides making noises that can be heard when lying on your front, they become magnetized (electromagnetism) and there are those who think this interferes in the experiment, in certain cases.

Width. The mattress must be sufficiently wide in order to allow freedom of movement.

Flotation. A springless mattress, aside from being more relaxing, does not make noise, nullifies the reciprocal disturbances made while sleeping and gives the sensation of floating on air, thus providing a more tranquil sleep.

Subhuman. Mattresses without animal fibers have been recommended by some ecologist projectors, as the subhuman animal that provided the fibers died while terrified. Some persons are sensitive to these negative energies

Objects. Besides the usual mattresses, there are those who sleep on at least 4 other types of objects:

1. Lumpy, broken-down mats, as hard as bricks.
2. Water-beds.
3. Inflatable mattresses.
4. Pads.

Sheets. The sheets in the physical base should be clean, cool and soft. Cotton sheets are most highly recommended, as their natural texture generates less static electricity, thus favoring natural sleep.

Pillows. There are pillows with different degrees of hardness and softness, thinness and thickness. They can be made of synthetic material, continuous multi-filament fiber or foam, for those who suffer from allergies. A very thick or bulky pillow can create problems in the cervical column (neck).

Position. Pillows need to be thick enough to keep the head in the same horizontal position as the shoulders and spinal column. This can be verified by standing up with the shoulder against a wall. The space between the head and wall, corresponds to the thickness of the pillow, for the average person who sleeps while lying on the side.

Laboratory. In laboratory experiments the sensitive, placed in the dorsal position, uses a *U-shaped* foam rubber pillow in order to be immobilized and limit auditive perception.

Bag. There are those who produce lucid projections while leaving the inactive human body inside a large zippered sleeping bag, used for camping, placed directly on the bare ground, in the open air with only the sky above them.

Cocoon. The sleeping bag – a type of a temporary cocoon for the adult's human body – is the most simplified, external, portable physical base that a lucid projector can have.

Ropes. There are mountain climbers who have already lucidly projected, in a spontaneous manner, while the human body is inactive, fastened by two ropes from the protrusions of high rocks. Many of these intraphysical consciousnesses live intraconscientially *on the verge of suicide* while practicing their radical sports.

Furniture. Aside from the bed, other pieces of furniture may occupy the bedroom-laboratory of the lucid projector, such as the following 4:

1. Chair
2. Armchair.
3. Inset closet.
4. Bedside table.

Instruments. Many instruments are optional and end up being used in the physical base, such as the following 11:

1. Silent digital clock with a display that can be consulted in the penumbra.
2. Chronometer.
3. Thermometer.
4. Hygrometer.
5. A barometer hung on the wall.
6. An easy-to-use flashlight.
7. Direct or indirect air-conditioning.

8. A portable tape recorder.
9. A nearby light switch.
10. Various monitors and polygraphs.
11. An electroencephalograph and other instruments for physiological measurement, if needed.

Avoidances. One should avoid electric wires, telephone, radio, television, stereo equipment, VCR and other electronic devices that are unnecessary for consciential projection being switched on in the bedroom.

Mask. You can use a comfortable sleeping mask and ear plugs when lying down, but they can interfere in the physical and psychological states of the lucid projection practitioner. In other words, they solve one problem while creating another.

Resources. Aside from the instruments already listed, there are other resources for writing and reading that can be used in the physical base, such as the following 4:

1. Pencil or ballpoint pen.
2. Blank sheets of paper.
3. Calendar.
4. A book of selected and mentally pacifying readings, for those who do not suffer from insomnia.

Blankets. One should use a minimum of blankets on the human body in order to avoid the inconvenient weight that produces negative impressions in the psychosoma and even inopportune nightmares.

Family. The *intraphysical assistant,* as well as the presence of family members and their illnesses have a bearing on consciential projections.

Interference. It is recommendable to avoid creating concern in family members or interference in the normal course of their existences with the occurrences of experiments with lucid projection, e.g., someone wanting to enter the bedroom during the projective experiment, as they can only co-operate when they are able to understand what the projector is experiencing, thereby remaining sympathetic toward the experiments.

Vehicles. Experiences in which the consciousness projects from the human body that has been left in a mobile physical base, e.g., a vehicle such as a car, bus, train or airplane, are frequently of short duration and generally uninteresting. The same occurs when the projector projects while listening to the radio or watching television.

Forced. In forced projections, the physical base varies a lot and can be one of the following 9:

1. A surgery table.
2. A hospital bed.
3. A dentist's chair.
4. An ambulance stretcher.
5. Highway asphalt.
6. A battlefield.
7. A sidewalk.
8. A prison cot.
9. A body of water: the sea or a river.

Cubicle. Irrespective of the physical base, even a small closed cubicle, the consciousness should not have any baseless fear about getting stuck there, since the psychosoma's permeability gives ample freedom of extraphysical action.

Theory. There are those who, at bed time, are concerned about aligning the human body along the north-south magnetic axis or, in other words, pointing the head northward and the feet southward, in order to be in harmony with the earth's magnetic field, which would supposedly help induce sleep. Nevertheless, there is no scientific justification for this north-south magnetic wave theory (electromagnetism), the repose of sleep and its influence on lucid projections.

Blockage. The sporadic changing of one's physical base, as with the projector's departure from the city to another location, e.g., the beach, the mountains or the countryside (farm), and a prolonged and different projection occurring in one of these new places during this period can provoke *mnemonic blockage*. This especially occurs if the projected projector extraphysically returns to the original, habitual base to perform extraphysical assistance from there.

Dislocation. The above-cited fact stems from the *para*psychological dislocation of the intraphysical consciousness, in view of the new location of the human body away from its routine environment, now inactive in a strange room. In this case, upon physically awakening, the projector tries to put him/herself – from a mental point of view – in the new temporary physical base and the inadaptability to the environment blocks his/her recollection.

Extremes. There are two extreme physical bases:

1. **Uterus.** The uterus is the *first,* external and initial physical base used by the fetal body of the resomant consciousness in its *initial projection,* its first semi-physical projection, in use soon after human conception (resomatics).

2. **Cemetery.** The cemetery (grave, tomb, sepulcher) is the *last,* external and definitive physical base of the intraphysical consciousness (when the soma is buried and not cremated), in his/her *final projection,* his/her last semi-physical projection or biological death (desomatics).

Exoprojection. When the consciousness is projected in the psychosoma in outer space – lucid exoprojection – it can return with lucidity to the terrestrial physical base passing through a maximum of 10 stages of visualization, or dimensions, listed here in a decreasing scale of geographical size, ranging from space to the 2 cerebral hemispheres:

1. Earth (troposphere).
2. Continent.
3. Country.
4. Regional area (state, province).
5. City (village, megalopolis, capital).
6. District (borough).
7. Residence (house, farm, apartment).
8. Bedroom (energetically shielded chamber).
9. Human body or soma.
10. Human head or encephalon.

Head. Thus, it can be observed that the physical base, in its simplest form, is precisely the human head, namely the 2 cerebral hemispheres.

Mentalsoma. When projected in the isolated mentalsoma, the consciousness can radically eliminate the intermediate stages of visualization, returning from outer space directly to the cerebral hemispheres or, better still, to the act of physically awakening.

Macrocosm. In the macrocosmic extreme of outer space, the projected intraphysical consciousness can receive impressions of occurrences similar to the following 6:

1. The condition of darkness.
2. Seeing stars.
3. Colors.
4. Lights.
5. Extraphysical consciousnesses or projected intraphysical consciousnesses.
6. Extraphysical intuitions.

Microcosm. In the microcosmic extreme of the physical head, the intraphysical consciousness can, upon interiorizing, have experiences along the lines of the following 5:

1. Consciential blackout.
2. Intracranial sounds.

3. The condition of darkness.

4. Brief cataleptic state.

5. Abrupt physical awakening.

Caverns. The caverns and grottos carved out by humankind or nature in the petrous structure of mountains constitute excellent external physical bases for the intraphysical consciousness who endeavors to produce lucid consciential projections.

Rule. There is a steadfast rule: tell me your physical base and I will tell you how your consciential projections are.

Climate. The inner climate of the physical base influences and defines the employment of the vehicle of manifestation of the consciousness and, consequently, the average type of the human projector's lucid consciential projection experiences. The following are 2 examples:

1. **Psychosoma.** The physical base with very human characteristics – geo-energetic (telluric), emotional or passionate ("emotiogenic") – predisposes the intraphysical consciousness to have lucid consciential projections in the psychosoma (emotional parabody) in the environments of the intraphysical tropospheric dimension.

2. **Mentalsoma.** The physical base with an elevated atmosphere of rationalized or intellectual ("rationogenic") emotions inclines the intraphysical consciousness to have lucid projections in the mentalsoma, in the mentalsomatic dimension.

Incense. The use of perfume, incense, strong deodorizers or antiseptics should be avoided in the intimacy of the physical base. Besides not contributing to the production of immediate lucid projection, they can, in certain situations, depending on the consciential projector, interfere with or mask the complex extraphysical olfactory perceptions of the consciousness projected in the psychosoma.

Extraphysical clinic. The physical base of the veteran, active or hard-working projector who is already engaged in a physical-extraphysical assistential team (intraphysical minicog consciential epicenter of a multidimensional assistential maximechanism), can be transformed into a clinic for extraphysical work (extraphysical clinic) by the helpers who are attuned to the projector, his/her family members and his/her assistential works.

Penta. The daily personal energetic task, or penta, is the ideal process for maintaining the energetic equilibrium and homogeneity of the extraphysical clinic.

Personalities. In this extraphysical clinic, the 4 following basic types (profiles) of extraphysical personalities (extraphysical consciousnesses) can be found:

1. **Somnambulants.** *Somnambulants,* unconscious extraphysical consciousnesses (sometimes projected intraphysical beings as well) who are temporarily in the extraphysical clinic, but unaware of the environment and indifferent to human beings.

2. **Sick.** *Sick individuals,* including parapsychotic post-desomatics, energivorous extraphysical consciousnesses or intruders, who are attracted by the process of extraphysical bait and who may or may not interfere in the human atmosphere, albeit under the zealous supervision of the helpers.

3. **Convalescents.** Extraphysical *convalescents,* including *extraphysical blind guides* (old relatives or family acquaintances that have already gone through desoma) which interact with the physical and extraphysical environments. They even *sit* on available chairs, observe what the human beings do, listen to their open conversations and often wish to talk with the projected projector.

4. **Helpers.** *Helpers* of all types and nature who supervise the extraphysical clinic, always executing defined tasks in short or long shifts, with temporary tasks or more long-term obligations.

Bibliography. Brunton (217, p. 267), Castaneda (258, p. 199), Crookall (331, p. 42), Frost (560, p. 52), Greenhouse (636, p. 154), Mittl (1061, p. 9), Monroe (1065, p. 211), Muldoon (1105, p. 182), Powell (1278, p. 83), St. Clair (1593, p. 149), Swedenborg (1635, p. 105), Vieira (1752, p. 4).

181. *PROJECTARIUM*

Definition. *Projectarium:* the physical base scientifically prepared to facilitate the development of lucid projections.

Synonymy: extraphysical observatory; interdimensional chamber; location of extraphysical retreat; lucid projection laboratory; physical-base-laboratory; projective anechoic chamber; projective chamber; projective ecosystem; projective mute room; projective soundless chamber; projective soundproof chamber; projective soundproof room; projective station; *projectorium.*

Reasons. In view of the fact that the ambient conditions of the physical dimension, or the space-time continuum, even when against one's will, always exercise a reasonable amount of psychophysical influence on the human body and the consciousness of the projector, the ideal would be to create, just as a hypothesis, a special, optimizing physical base where all the propitious conditions for having a completely lucid consciential projection are brought together, namely a *projective ecosystem.*

Vibrations. Among the conditions for installation of the *projectarium,* the following 10 can be singled out:

1. **Painting.** The room painted blue with a non-glossy paint, in order to reduce light reflection as much as possible.

2. **Soundproof.** Highly isolating lining and masonry or soundproofed (soundproof chamber, anechoic chamber) or acoustically highly isolated.

3. **Antivibratory.** The construction built or lined for reasonable isolation against external sounds should also provide isolation from significant mechanical shocks and have characteristics that are absorptive (no transmission to the interior) of external vibrations (antivibratory), shock absorbers.

4. **Conditions.** The internal space of the *projectarium* should extend beyond the perimeter of the more intense action of the silver cord, or a radius of at least 13' (4 m) from the human head of the projector in repose in the dorsal position.

5. **Air conditioning.** Use of indirect, silent air conditioning.

6. **Ozone.** Application of ozone in the environment in order to aid the physiology and paraphysiology of the projector's vehicles (holothosene).

7. **Furniture.** Use of practical furniture inside the projectarium.

8. **Instruments.** Use of non-intrusive instruments for registering physiological processes and making measurements of all types.

9. **Room.** Isolated annexed support room.

10. **Notice.** A written notice in the external area to refrain from disturbing the location for any reason during the experiments.

Hypotheses. The following are 4 working hypotheses pertinent to the *projectarium:*

1. **Gravitation.** Could nullification of the gravitational force or the installation of a state of imponderability inside the *projectarium* help in the production of lucid consciential projections?

2. **Field.** Would the installation of a special force field help?

3. **Cage.** Would the use of a Faraday Cage be appropriate?

4. **Energetic dimension.** What relationships could be created between the *projectarium,* the extraphysical sphere of energy (personal psychosphere) and the energetic dimension?

Bibliography: Puharich (1338, p. 111).

182. AMBIENT LIGHT

Para-eyes. The mechanism of the human body's physical eyeballs is practically not used in the development of consciential projections. In these experiences the para-eyes of the psychosoma are almost always used by the projected consciousness.

Extremes. As a rule, the two extremes of ambient luminous intensity, maximal illumination (natural or artificial) or complete darkness, although not being impediments or antiprojective factors, disturb rather than help in the experiments of inducing lucid consciential projections, for the majority of projectors.

Stimulus. The presence of light, being a stimulus, impedes sleep.

Penumbra. The consciential projector should only let a few rays of light enter the bedroom from which he/she projects or, in other words, should maintain the bedroom at a low level of illumination. The semi-dark or penumbra, achieved with the use of a small, weak lamp or some discrete light source that enters the room is the ideal illuminative condition of the location where the projector's inactive human body rests in the physical base.

Objects. All polished reflective surfaces, sharp-edged equipment, sharp, pointed objects and other dangerous objects or those that can predispose accidents in the home, should be removed from the bedroom.

Points. Semi-illumination allows the projector to maintain visual points of reference, to lie down and get up from the bed, immediately discerning the actual position of the human body in relation to the objects and furniture in the room, without losing sense of direction upon waking up, in case the lights of the environment are turned off.

Avoidances. All these measures aim to avoid the following 4 occurrences:

1. **Awakening.** Confused physical awakening.
2. **Walking.** The need to walk while feeling your way in the dark.
3. **Furniture.** The act of bumping up against and tripping over furniture in the physical base.
4. **Accidents.** Potential minor accidents in the home.

Cloth. A penumbra can be maintained in the chamber of the physical base with a dark cloth used as a window curtain *(blackout curtain)* or in between the ordinary curtains and the window panes, if present.

Bibliography: Monroe (1065, p. 211), Muldoon (1105, p. 204), Vieira (1762, p. 17).

183. AMBIENT TEMPERATURE

Definition. Ambient dysthermia: the condition of more extreme ambient temperature – whether intense cold or excessive heat – that goes beyond the possibilities of acclimation on the part of the human organism (soma).

Synonymy: ambient hyperthermia; ambient hypothermia; extreme ambient temperature.

Importance. An adequate ambient temperature of 68° F (Fahrenheit) (20° C, Celsius or centigrade) and the quality of air breathed during sleep are of extreme importance for lucid projection experiments induced by the will.

Summer. In summer, maintaining the air inside the house (indoors) cooler than that outside the house (outdoors) induces sleep.

Relaxation. Low temperature as well as high temperature trigger mental inquietude, discomfort and restlessness, impairing muscular relaxation, intensifying blood circulation and heart beat, thus impeding the human body from being inactive and liberating the psychosoma with the consciousness to have an excursion in another consciential dimension.

Ideal. Given that the *human body's thermostat* and sensitivity to cold vary, there is no ideal temperature that works for all persons. Nevertheless, as already mentioned, the best temperature for projecting is around 68° F (20° C). It is always preferable to feel a little cold than to feel a little hot.

Restlessness. With the temperature inside the bedroom above 75.02° F (23.9° C), the person does not sleep well, is restless and sleeps more lightly.

Nightmares. Above this temperature, disagreeable dreams and nightmares arise, according to recent research on sleep and insomnia performed in specialized laboratories.

Air conditioner. In hot climates, the use of central, silent air conditioning is recommended, where possible. Otherwise, use an air conditioner installed in an adjoining room in order to provide indirect cooling and diminish the effects of the apparatus' noise on the individual.

Change. During the period in which the consciousness finds itself projected, a sudden change in ambient temperature, either an increase or a decrease, can provoke an extraphysical repercussion with the ensuing return of the projected intraphysical consciousness, interiorization and abrupt physical awakening.

Analysis. The analysis of ambient dysthermia requires a multidisciplinary approach, in at least the following 9 areas of research:

1. **Medicine.** In the field of medicine, the state of suspended animation and the consequent projection of the intraphysical consciousness occur provoked by hypothermia, in *hypothermic surgeries, cerebral cryosurgery*, artificial hibernation, *accidental hypothermia* and in the hypothermia of submersion.

2. **Metapsychics.** In the old metapsychic experiments, there was an immediate *drop in temperature* of the human environment in the materialization room when ectoplasm was materialized in materialization phenomena.

3. **Parapsychology.** In modern parapsychology experiments, there is a condition of cooling in the manifestations of physical effects, telekinesis, the icy currents of air in poltergeist cases and other occurrences. Just as with interstellar space, *extremely low temperatures* exist in all that pertains to the extraphysical paratropospheric dimension.

4. **Projectiology.** In projectiology practices, when the projected consciousness re-encounters the human body, upon interiorizing, it almost always feels the organism to be cold, at a *lower temperature*, often contrary to the warmer environment of the physical base where it finds itself.

5. **History.** According to the teachings of human history, the industrial revolution developed in areas of *lower temperatures.*

6. **Geography.** According to geography, the same industrial revolution enjoys greater growth precisely in the areas of *cold temperature,* north of the Tropic of Cancer, as well as south of the Tropic of Capricorn.

7. **Economy.** The economy progressed as a consequence of the transition of agriculture to the industrial era, precisely in the *colder countries.*

8. **Sociology.** Sociology has still not tackled, in a broad manner, as is needed, the problem of civilizations in *cold environments,* due to the taboo of the racial issue.

9. **Politics.** Politics places the so-called Third World predominately in the warmer, tropical areas, while the First World remains in the *colder areas.*

Map. For the reader interested in further details on the subject, analysis of the map published by the World Bank on the distribution of "Industrialized Countries and Regions" is recommended, as it clearly shows the location of human progress as being dependent upon colder areas.

Industrialization. Upon studying this world map, Llerena considers that the new industrial stage today comprises no more than a quarter of the world population, situated in the temperate zones of the planet (gray areas on the map). The more industrialized area in Brazil is highlighted.

Compensation. It can be seen that ambient dysthermia acts vigorously upon the parapsychic conditions of humankind. Obviously, projectiology could not be exempt from this action. Just as the Inca civilization compensated latitude with altitude, projectiology compensates climate, temperature and humidity with air conditioning.

Projectiological Bibliography: Butler (228, p. 149), Muldoon (1105, p. 197), Vieira (1762, p. 98).

Specific Bibliography: Llerena, Carlos Moyano; *El Futuro Posible;* Buenos Aires, Argentina; Sudamericana; 1989.

184. AMBIENT   NOISE

Definitions. Acoustics: that part of physics that studies the oscillations and waves occurring in elastic mediums, the frequencies of which range from 20 to 20,000 Hz and are perceived by the ears as sonorous waves; the physical science of matrix analysis that studies sounds and noises.

Synonymy: science of noises; *decibelogy.*

Adversary. Noise, or undesirable sound, due to its effects upon the human being, is the great ambient adversary of sleep and also of the lucid consciential projection experience for the majority of projectors. Therefore, we should observe and control the level of ambient noise in the physical base of the consciential projector.

Aggression. The noxiousness of a noise – or the aggressive action that a noise exercises upon the organism and also, consequently, upon the intraphysical consciousness – can logically be characterized by the disturbances or alterations that it produces.

Sensitivity. Sensitivity to sound varies from person to person and according to the stage of sleep in which one finds oneself, as well as one's sex, physical age and the place where one is located.

Women. Women are more susceptible to waking up due to noise than men.

Volume. The degree of disturbance caused by a noise depends on one's familiarity with the sound, its intensity, its duration and the person's sensitivity to that noise.

Unit. The unit of noise intensity is the decibel (dB).

Decibels. The following is a scale (ranking, table) of noises (racket, sonorous pollution), according to the pressure of sound in decibels, with 30 values:

    0 = Silence; acoustic laboratory, whispering (tending toward zero is a *safe zone*).

  15 = Leaves blown by the wind (very low sound, whispering).

  20 = Ticking of a clock; radio broadcasting booth; tranquil garden.

  30 = Murmurs from 1' (30 cm) away; conversation in a low tone of voice (proxemics).

  35 = A library; a quiet room.

  40 = Ordinary conversation from 20" (50 cm) away; calm office (low sound, ideal).

  45 = Ordinary apartment; tranquil street; first class lounge on a transatlantic cruise.

  50 = Common typewriter; tranquil restaurant; silent car (common noise).

  60 = Ordinary conversation; singing bird (still within the safety zone).

  65 = Noisy house; tour bus (a person can suffer from stress).

  70 = Traffic on a relatively quiet city street.

  72 = Subway train (loud voice).

  75 = Thunder; a busy street (loss of sleep; irritability; depression; fatigue).

  80 = Cinelândia (downtown area), Rio de Janeiro, RJ, Brazil, at rush hour.

  81 = Electric drill.

  82 = 50' (15 m) away from heavy traffic (the *risk zone* starts here).

  84 = Vacuum cleaner operating outside the physical base.

  85 = Powerful radio at maximum volume in a room; car horn.

  89 = Certain samba schools; a crowded *Latin* restaurant.

  90 = Blender (discomfort); action film.

  92 = Worship services at certain churches.

  95 = Sports car in motion (increase in tension; intestinal disturbances).

100 = Motorcycle without a muffler; jackhammer at less than 16' (5 m); rock concert; subway.

107 = Powerful lawn mower in operation.

108 = Anhangabaú tunnel, São Paulo, SP, Brazil.

110 = Car horn at a distance of 3' (1 m).

120 = Chainsaw (impossible to have a conversation).

125 = Pile driver in operation (already in the lesion zone).

130 = Jet taking off at 100' (30 m) (airplane turbine).

150 = Firing revolver.

Sleep. Above 60 decibels (60 dB), approximately the noise of a truck passing on the street, the majority of persons wake up or at least suffer a disturbance in their natural sleep.

Stimuli. Any sound above 70 decibels (70 dB) begins to stimulate signals from the nervous system to the rest of the human body.

Circulation. If the sound is sudden, uninterrupted and meaningless, the arterial pressure will increase and the supply of blood to the heart will diminish (cardiorespiratory circulation).

Tachycardia. When the intensity increases, the pupils dilate, the muscles of the abdomen and thorax contract and the heart beats faster (tachycardia). This occurs with any sleeping person.

Scale. The following are 4 abovementioned occurrences, according to their decibel level for certain sounds in outdoor environments, that can wake you up in the physical base or interrupt your lucid projection through extraphysical traumas: a vacuum cleaner operating outside the physical base; a sports car in movement; a powerful lawnmower in operation; a jet plane taking off.

Threshold. The noise level of 120 decibels (120 dB) makes conversation impossible, marks the beginning of the normal pain threshold and is also a noxious condition for the ears, being the starting point for possible acoustic traumas and traumatic deafness.

Locations. Locations of the projector's human body that do not favor the production of lucid projection are illustrated by the following 5 examples:

1. **Airport.** Physical base near the sonic boom of jet airplanes in the vicinity of an airport, or the strong sonic explosion (sonic clap or sonic boom) that occasionally occurs due to variations in pressure coming from the passage of an aircraft that flies at (or above) the speed of sound (or breaking the sound barrier, clap).

2. **Street.** Physical base on a busy street or highway.

3. **Building.** Physical base in an apartment building with thin walls or little acoustic isolation.

4. **Market.** Physical base located near an urban street market.

5. **Club.** Physical base located near a club featuring noisy social or athletic activities.

Interruptive. The series of specific interruptive undesirable ambient noises that, when near the inactive human body of the projected projector, can impair the development of the production of lucid projection, can be classified into 2 basic types:

1. Indoor.
2. Outdoor.

Indoor. Among the indoor interruptive noises, at least the following 10 can be singled out:

1. Doorbells, telephones and intercoms.
2. Pendulums and the ticking of noisy clocks.
3. The creaking of spring mattresses.
4. Noisy windows.
5. Door slams.
6. Jackhammers or the sounds of flushing toilets.
7. Ascending and descending of elevators, especially when badly adjusted.
8. Sound appliances operating at high volume.
9. Crackling fire in the fireplace.
10. Loud dog barks.

Outdoor. Among outdoor interruptive noises, the following 18 can be singled out:

1. An exploding air balloon.
2. A next door neighbor's air conditioner that is loud, loose or badly regulated.
3. Pigeons cooing out on the window ledge.
4. Outside noises from the street, a train, a reception hall or a neighboring staircase.
5. Nocturnal caterwauling.
6. Singing of a swift or a bellbird in the vicinity.

7. Emptying of trash containers in the street (community service).

8. Nocturnal street repair using jackhammers (sewer, water, gas, telephone, cable TV systems).

9. Vehicles driving over metal plates.

10. People walking, objects falling or being dragged over the ceramic or wood floor in the apartment above.

11. Neighborhood party (weekend).

12. Vibration of the floor in the physical base.

13. Storms, thunder, howling winds and other acts of nature.

14. Fire engine, police car and ambulance sirens (as in New York City).

15. The horn or alarm of a car parked in the street going off.

16. Construction noises, such as saws and mechanical hammering.

17. Construction or remodeling of buildings in the neighborhood.

18. Chinese wind chimes hung near the physical base (calming 1 resident and disturbing the sleep of 10 neighbors).

Earplugs. Some individuals solve the problem of noise when going to bed by using earplugs (small plastic cylinders or cones), or even anti-noise balls (big disposable pieces of cotton that can be either dry or soaked in water, olive oil or vaseline). They are all able to block out only about 20 decibels. The balls of wax, molded by hand, are difficult to insert and fall out easily.

Protection. The following are 8 resources currently used for the acoustic protection of environments that help to isolate the projector's bedroom (shielded chamber):

1. Double windows.

2. Installation of an air conditioner.

3. Sealing of the slits around the bedroom window, which reduces the noise level by about 10 decibels, because where air enters, sound waves also come in.

4. Installation of thick curtains, since they are porous, act as sound sponges, absorbing the sounds.

5. Double curtains or, in other words, curtains with a velvet or synthetic fabric lining.

6. Decorative wall carpets hung in the noisy area.

7. Installation of 1" (2.5 cm) thick soundproofing cork on the walls. This absorbs 57% of the sound that infiltrates through the walls.

8. Lowering of the ceiling with suspended acoustic tiles.

Cold. In cold climates, double-thick doors and double-pane windows maintain a reasonable level of acoustic isolation in the projector's bedroom.

Air conditioner. In order to reduce the acoustic impact in the bedroom of a physical base located in an area of high sound pollution, it is recommended that one turn on an air conditioner placed a short distance away. Its continuous operation produces a *white noise,* or a low-frequency noise, that blends with the noises of the environment and favors sleep through the creation of positively conditioned reflexes.

Blockages. If you try to mentally block or cover up the negative noises, this can also inadvertently block the inspirations and suggestions of the helper who tries to assist you in the production of lucid projection. In this case, your consciousness closes in on itself and, instead of going outwards (centrifugal direction) in a projection, can end up interiorizing even more, inside yourself (centripetal direction), in the intimacy of your coincident vehicles of manifestation.

Causes. Physical noises have diverse effects upon human lucid projection. Just as physical noise can, on the one hand, abruptly interrupt an extraphysical experience, even finalizing the lucid projection with physical repercussions (there is a projective technique using precisely this characteristic), it can also, on the other hand, generate a spontaneous and instantaneous lucid projection. For example, this situation has already been registered many times with a person in a deep, heavy sleep using an alarm clock to awaken him/her.

Alarm clock. In the semilucid state in which one finds oneself when hearing the strident sound of the alarm clock, the consciousness tries to turn it off, as it has done daily. But instead, now projected, the parahand – to the individual's amazement – goes through the "off" button and the ringing apparatus.

Awakening. Instead of the consciousness *physically* awakening as a result of the ambient noise, an *extraphysical* awakening occurs in this specific case.

Intraphysical consciousness. Hence, we may conclude that the intraphysical consciousness is frequently found to be in an ambiguous or versatile condition, predisposed and ready to enter into different consciential dimensions, according to the injunctions of the moment.

Bibliography: Crookall (331, p. 32), Frost (560, p. 53), Vieira (1762, p. 55).

---

185. INTRAPHYSICAL ASSISTANT

Definition. Intraphysical assistant: the intraphysical guardian of the human body of the projector which is inactive and emptied of the consciousness during lucid projection.

Synonymy: ground crew; human guardian; intraphysical guardian angel; intraphysical vigilante; projection adviser.

Categories. Among the many categories of intraphysical assistant, at least the following 8 can be singled out:

1. Husband or wife (partner of an evolutionary duo).
2. Family member.
3. Leader of a research meeting.
4. Researcher (projectiologist, conscientiologist).
5. Hypnotist.
6. Physician.
7. Sensitive.
8. Friend.

Duo. The partner of the evolutionary duo is the ideal assistant for the projector.

Projection. The projector can project with or without the assistance of another individual, as well as being able to dispense with certain factors such as a technique, parapsychism and others. The individual can even project spontaneously, by accident.

Protection. Nevertheless, the more a projector endeavors to make the experiments physiological, rational and protected using the resources that are available and adaptable to the environment, the better will be the individual's performance in high-quality lucid consciential projections.

Assistant. The role of the intraphysical assistant is the same as the person on aircraft landing strips who assists the takeoff and landing of aircraft with occasional aircraft-related services; as well as the so-called *extraphysical guardian angel.*

Tendency. The natural tendency of projectiological facts is to gradually transform the intraphysical assistant into the projector's extraphysical assistant as well or, in other words, they end up projecting together.

Circle. Certain parapsychic, occultist, esoteric, spiritist and syncretic organizations gather many intraphysical assistants, forming a circle of vigilance and irradiation, or an energetic or parapsychic human chain in order to protect and guard the inactive soma that is with them – emptied of the projector's consciousness, which is temporarily absent in extraphysical and intensive assistential service – against any harm.

Bibliography: Butler (227, p. 71), Fortune (540, p. 154), Vieira (1762, p. 18).

186. PHYSIOLOGICAL STATES PRIOR TO LUCID PROJECTION

Occurrences. Among the preconditions of the human body that influence the physiological state prior to the lucid projection, the following 20 can be singled out:

1. Physical age.
2. Normal health.
3. Occasional illness.
4. Chronic illness.
5. Wound.
6. Convalescence.
7. Rest.
8. Physical fatigue.
9. Mental fatigue.
10. Sleepiness.
11. Heart rate.
12. Hypomnesia.
13. Use of medication.
14. Body weight.
15. Diet.
16. Fasting.
17. Gastric repletion.
18. Intestinal constipation.
19. Sports: power walking, swimming.
20. Biorhythms and parabiorhythms.

Projector. Besides that which has been presented, the female projector can particularly be influenced prior to the consciential projection experience by menarche, pre-menstrual tension (PMT), menstruation, gestation, breastfeeding and menopause, for example.

Sleep. To start with, it is preferable that the practitioner be rested, having had enough sleep, in order to attend to the physiological needs of the individual's organism before trying to produce a lucid consciential projection. Countless factors that predispose the person to sleep normally, or to combat insomnia, favor the production of lucid projection.

Bath. Some favor taking a lukewarm bath before going to bed in order to relax, but the water temperature should be between 89.6 and 95 degrees Fahrenheit (between 32 and 35 degrees Celsius) in order to induce sleep. The person can remain immersed in the water for approximately 20 minutes. If the bathtub is sufficiently spacious, there is no problem in turning the lights off, closing the eyes and floating.

Towel. After the bath, the individual should dry the body gently with a fluffy towel without rubbing, as the friction is stimulating and predisposes the intraphysical consciousness toward the waking state and not sleep.

Nose. Before lying down to project, it is advisable to create the simple habit of clearing the nose thoroughly with warm water, unblocking the nasal cavities, and thus allowing unencumbered respiration.

Avoidances. Before lying down to produce a lucid projection, the practitioner should also avoid ingesting more diuretic beverages and food – e.g., tea, beer, white wine, soft drinks, mineral water, asparagus, melon, watermelon, cherries – in order not to have to get up to go to the bathroom, thus creating difficulty in getting to sleep and predisposing the production of consciential projection.

Bibliography: Frost (560, p. 46), Vieira (1762, p. 130).

187. CONSCIENTIAL STATES PRIOR TO LUCID PROJECTION

Categories. The psychological or *consciential preconditions* to consciential projection can vary greatly, as the projection practitioner may be in a mood characterized by one of the following 13 personal conditions:

1. Serene (tranquility).
2. Unstable (anxious, tense).
3. Motivated (eager).
4. Defiant.
5. Fearful (insecure).
6. In a parapsychic trance.
7. Confident about the imminent projection.
8. Informed about lucid projection.
9. Expectant.
10. Ignorant about the subject.
11. Away from the subject for some time.
12. Indifferent.
13. In a mood contrary (hostile) to lucid projection.

States. There are 7 psychological states that classify the entire period in an increasing scale that ranges from the condition of full alertness of the wakeful consciousness to the immediacy of natural sleep:

1. **Activity.** You feel active.

2. **Level.** Your consciousness operates at a high level, although without complete strength.

3. **Relaxation.** In the condition of relaxation, your consciousness is aware, although not fully alert.

4. **Dizziness.** You feel quite dizzy.

5. **Slowness.** Aside from feeling dizzy, you are somewhat slow.

6. **Sleepiness.** Your consciential condition is very characteristic of psychological sleepiness and detachment (alienation).

7. **Incapacity.** You find yourself in a quasi-asleep condition, unable to stay awake.

Avoidances. The following 6 examples are personal predispositions that act as psychological factors that are negative toward lucid projection immediately *before the experiments* and should therefore be avoided:

1. **Films.** Watch heavy or violent films.

2. **Shows.** Attend exciting shows.

3. **Reading.** Stop reading an absorbing book or CD-ROM at a dramatic part, which may create the desire to continue with the storyline.

4. **Contact.** Enter into contact with people you disagree with.

5. **Concerns.** Harbor thoughts of concern and disgust.

6. **Thosenization.** Other thoughts or thosenes that are easy to identify and avoid.

Bibliography: Frost (560, p. 46), Vieira (1762, p. 27).

188. ORDINARY PHYSICAL WAKING STATE

Definition. Physical waking state: the awake or conscious state of the intraphysical consciousness maintained by the center of vigilance of the mind (pointer of the consciousness).

Synonymy: alert state; diurnal consciousness; first attention; intracorporeal experience; ordinary lucidity; ordinary waking state; physical vigilance.

Activity. Erratic mental activity, with no specific objective, is sometimes referred to by expressions such as the following 4:

1. Undirected thought.
2. Train of thought (mental flow).
3. Ordinary awareness of the waking state.
4. Internal monologues.

Classification. The ordinary, physical waking state can be classified into 2 modes:

1. **Coincidence.** The state of *intracorporeal* experience or coincidence of the vehicles of manifestation of the intraphysical consciousness.

2. **Discoincidence.** The state (contraposition) of human lucid projection, *extracorporeal* experience or discoincidence of the vehicles of manifestation of the intraphysical consciousness.

Conditions. According to detailed experiments with lucid projection during the period prior to the loss of ordinary physical wakefulness, at least the following 4 conditions should be observed:

1. **Order.** Order of sleep: first, second, third, or last sleep.
2. **Sleepiness.** Sleepiness or a state of unexpected sleep.
3. **Sleep.** Sleep without loss of physical wakefulness.
4. **Insomnia.** Insomnia that has been overcome.

RAS. The state of cerebral cortical activity or, in other words, the ordinary waking period of the human consciousness is maintained by impulses that pass through the RAS or *reticular activating system,* a bundle of nerve fibers that ascend through the mesencephalon, from the vertebral column to the areas of the cerebral cortex.

Obstruction. The obstruction or inhibition of the impulses that pass through the RAS would explain the states of natural sleep and hypnosis.

Foresee. High quality human lucid projection has its roots, or foretokens, in the ordinary, physical waking state or, in other words, in the psychophysiological condition that prevails over the consciousness before projecting from the human body.

Emotionalism. If emotions already prevail over the practitioner's reasoning prior to projecting, they will naturally also prevail during the extraphysical period, and will also submit the consciousness to inevitable traumas and diminish the purity of perceptions.

Reactions. From this psychosomatic fact, one of two categories of reaction may result in the projector's consciential micro-universe regarding the quality of the projection:

1. **Vegetative.** This emotional reaction will only allow the production of mere animalized or *vegetative projection.*

2. **Evolved.** Contrarily, if emotional equilibrium and full serenity proceed with the consciousness without hiatus from one dimension of life to another, the projector will achieve a conscientially more advanced or evolved projection.

Bibliography: Castaneda (258, p. 20), D'arbó (365, p. 239), Ebon (453, p. 31), Vieira (1762, p. 70).

189. PHYSICAL POSITION PRIOR TO LUCID PROJECTION

Importance. Lucid projection is the only serious activity that the intraphysical consciousness executes in which he/she leaves the human body behind. This is why the position in which he/she remains resting, temporarily inactive, acquires enormous importance.

Rest. The following are 7 motionless or resting physical positions that can characterize the physical conditions of the intraphysical consciousness prior to lucid projection:

1. Dorsal position.
2. In line with the head.
3. Lateral position, on the right or left side.
4. Prone position.
5. Reclined position.
6. Seated position.
7. Erect or standing position.

Circulation. The projection practitioner should avoid lying at the edge of the mattress in order to prevent putting pressure on some parts of the soma and consequently creating a circulation problem in the outstretched arm or leg.

Stomach. Lying on your front, *on the stomach* or on one side of the stomach, customarily not only makes takeoff difficult, but sometimes even interiorization. Therefore, this is the least recommended position for *novice* lucid projectors.

Activities. The following are 10 activities or physical positions of the person in movement that are most common prior to lucid projection:

1. **Holochakra.** The person speaking (on the phone, for example).
2. **Walking.** The person walking (normally, or in a hurry).
3. **Race.** The person (marathon runner) running (aerobic race).
4. **Swimming.** The person (athlete) swimming (any style or stroke).
5. **Editing.** The person (writer, transcriber) writing manually (manuscript).
6. **Dance.** The person dancing (dancer) alone or with a dance partner.
7. **Typing.** The person (typist or computer operator) keyboarding (typing).
8. **Music.** The person (musician) playing piano or another musical instrument.
9. **Driving.** The person inside a vehicle (even driving) whether a car (driver, chauffeur), bus, train, racing car (driver), airplane (even flying the plane), bicycle (cyclist), motorcycle (motorcyclist), launch or boat.
10. **Equestrian.** A person (horseman) riding a horse.

Effects. Among the effects of physical positions prior to a consciential projection, at least the following 4 should be observed:

1. Comfortable physical position.
2. Uncomfortable physical position.
3. Voluntary physical position.
4. Forced physical position.

Ritual. Almost everyone has a favorite position for sleeping, which is part of the ritual of sleep.

Choreography. There is also a certain choreography in the way in which we position ourselves in bed during the night.

Accommodation. An intraphysical consciousness can employ different means for settling into the bed for sleep. The following 7 are examples:

1. Sleep with the body stretched out.
2. Sleep with the body twisted.
3. Sleep in the prone position.

4. Sleep in the fetal position.

5. Sleep hugging a pillow or a *stuffed animal.*

6. Sleep with one foot outside the blankets.

7. Sleep with the human body more fully stretched.

Classification. People generally have two positions for sleeping:

1. **Alpha.** The *alpha position,* which one assumes when awake but relaxed, ready to dive into the first stages of sleep.

2. **Beta** (omega). As the individual feels sleep approaching, the *omega position* is assumed, which will be maintained for the greater part of deep sleep.

Comfort. Each person should let the human body settle itself in the position in which it naturally feels comfortable.

Cross. One of the most comfortable positions is the swastika, wherein the body imitates a broken cross, with the intraphysical consciousness laying on the front, with one of the arms over the head, the other bent and placed under the body, and the legs bent as though the person were running.

Arms. The arms should preferably be placed alongside the human body, without touching any part of the soma, in order for the consciousness to project with lucidity.

Coziness. A cozy environment is better for sleeping than an ample room.

Uterus. People generally sleep better when in an indoor environment where they can be found in a situation similar to the fetus inside the maternal womb or, in other words, in a *uterine environment.*

Alignment. Although still not scientifically proven, popular empiricism indicates that the alignment of the human body in the north-south direction – with the head facing northward and feet southward – has some positive relationship with the telluric, geoenergetic or magnetic currents and helps in the attainment of tranquil sleep. It is a hypothesis for consideration.

Rotation. It is worth registering that the influence of the earth's rotation and its magnetic field is sufficient to move the magnetic needle of a compass and also to slightly effect the human body's nervous system.

Hypoxia. The following are hypotheses that still need to be tested:

1. **Head.** Would the use of a high pillow, putting the head at a level higher than the body, foster the production of lucid projection, as it predisposes cortical hypoxia?

2. **Armchair.** Would sitting in an armchair, for example, which also predisposes cortical hypoxia, facilitate lucid projection?

3. **Front.** Is it more *difficult* to consciously project when lying on your front in bed, as mentioned above, due to the absence of cortical hypoxia?

Recall. Although in certain cases cerebral hypoxia impairs recall after projective experiences, it is a recommendable condition because it facilitates departure from the soma, a practice that is much more difficult than the other (recall). We should opt for the lesser of 2 evils.

Memories. A great extraphysical experience always reinforces the practitioner's memories – holomemory and biomemory – of projection. Leaving the soma with lucidity is a much more problematic activity and one that, rationally, should always be prioritized.

Bibliography: Huson (768, p. 109), Mittl (1061, p. 8), Monroe (1065, p. 211), Schiff (1515, p. 180), Vieira (1762, p. 210).

---

190. DORSAL POSITION

Definition. Dorsal position: the horizontal physical position of one who is lying on the back. (see fig. 190, p. 1,129).

Synonymy: favorite position of lucid projectors; projective posture; reclined position; supination; supine position; terrestrial posture.

Ideal. The position of the projector lying on the back (supine or dorsal position) on the bed, floor, grass or in other locations – although being the most difficult position for most lucid projection practitioners to remain in – is the ideal and physiologically the best, as it naturally predisposes the consciousness to leave the human body in a natural manner.

Explanation. This favorable condition of the dorsal position can be explained in 2 ways: according to the extraphysical aspect, as well as the physical aspect, per se:

1. **Extraphysical.** The positive extraphysical effect of the dorsal position upon the production of lucid projection is explained by the fact that the psychosoma, upon leaving the human body, in almost all common lucid projections and even in the discoincidence of natural sleep every night, remains in the dorsal position, longitudinally, floating from 2-20" (5-50 cm), on average, above the human body, before standing up or becoming erect and the consciousness of the projected projector acquiring greater extraphysical self-awareness.

2. **Physical.** In a manner similar to that occurring when a person is under a general anesthetic and remains in the dorsal position, the very position of laying on one's back – with the human body stretched out on either a bed or a surgery table – physically favors the production of the lucid projection phenomenon, because it predisposes a reduction in or lack of oxygen in the cerebral hemispheres (cortical hypoxia).

Anesthesia. Under a general anesthesia, this occurs after the anesthetic has increased psychophysiological relaxation and diminished the respiratory frequency.

Technique. It should be kept in mind that mild or inoffensive cortical hypoxia can even constitute an efficient projective technique.

Maintenance. It is worth further pointing out that remaining in the dorsal position immediately after a lucid projection, produced shortly before, facilitates the production of spontaneous lucid projections in series soon thereafter, in a single night of voluntary projective experimentations.

Habit. In line with what has been presented, for the individual interested in producing high quality lucid projections, it is worth making all possible effort, with neither laziness nor feverishness, to acquire the good projective habit of always sleeping on the back, in spite of the physical and psychological difficulties that will initially be faced, struggling with oneself in order to reach this objective.

Projector. The dorsal position – with legs spread apart, the human body on the bed in total muscular relaxation and the use of loose clothing – favors the male projector, because it avoids the predisposition toward an inappropriate penile erection, which interferes in the projective process.

Erection. Nevertheless, that corporal position works in this respect only in some cases, because physiological erection during natural sleep occurs irrespective of the physical position of the sexual organ.

Projector. The dorsal position, with the legs spread apart, does not particularly favor some young women who are affectionately or sexually deprived. It is recommended that these young projectors, if necessary, when preparing to practice lucid projection, draw the legs and feet *(pre-kundalini)* together in order to avoid inappropriate and undesirable dispersive, mental connotations regarding the sex act.

Pillow. Certain people, upon reaching a deep relaxation of the human body, have the tendency to naturally and unwittingly open their mouth when they assume the dorsal position in order to project with lucidity. It is recommended that these persons place a light, somewhat hard, pillow lengthwise under the chin in order to keep the mouth closed. In this way they avoid: snoring loudly, physically waking themselves up due to extraphysical repercussions or provoking tonsillitis (dry mouth, hypophonation).

Similarities. The projector being in the dorsal position on the bed allows the spontaneous projection of the consciousness in the psychosoma to occur, similar to 3 natural factors:

1. **Perspiration.** The phenomenon of the unconscious perspiring of the human body.
2. **Evaporation.** The imperceptible evaporation of a tree's moisture.
3. **Emanation.** The subtle emanation of a flower's perfume.

Mildness. The projective process of the intraphysical consciousness in the dorsal position develops in a gentle, natural or unsuspected manner by the consciousness that finds itself to already be in the extraphysical dimension, manifesting through a consciential vehicle other than the human body.

Bibliography: Crookall (331, p. 98), Denning (391, p. 84), Garfield (569, p. 121), Greenhouse (636, p. 43), Mittl (1061, p. 8), Muldoon (1105, p. 200), Vieira (1762, p. 17).

---

191. CONDITIONS OF THE HUMAN BODY PRIOR TO LUCID PROJECTION

Touch. In pure lucid consciential projections, or those generated through the impulsion of will, without the interference of pathological factors, or those which are essentially artificial, any circumstance or occurrence that involves touching the human body, which has been left temporarily inactive, can bring the consciousness back to the somatic form.

Factors. It is always advisable to observe the preconditions of the human body prior to the lucid consciential projection experiment, removing all factors that can disturb the natural development of the occurrences. The following 3 are examples:

1. **Soma.** The clothes of the projector's human body (soma).
2. **Bed.** Bed linen.
3. **Objects.** The objects in contact with the projector's human body.

Impure. In *impure* or prolonged artificial consciential projections stemming from pathological processes, accidents and near-death phenomena (NDE), as opposed to *pure* lucid consciential projections, it has been observed that the human body that is at rest can be touched – while its clothes are being changed or it is bound with rope, as occurs in some indigenous tribes, for example – without these movements provoking an abrupt return, with extraphysical repercussions, of the consciousness projected in the psychosoma.

Laboratorial. In lucid consciential projection experiments performed in the laboratory, the projector also submits him/herself to a condition that depends upon wires and direct connections to monitors and diverse apparatuses. This is one of the initial obstacles that scientific experimentation always has to overcome.

Bibliography: Crookall (331, p. 26), Monroe (1065, p. 211), Vieira (1762, p. 143).

---

192. OBJECTS OF THE PROJECTOR

Types. The projector, regardless of whether lying down sleeping, seated, or even moving, wearing clothes, shoes, hat, glasses, contact lenses, rings, jewelry, wristwatch, carrying objects in the pockets, holding a cigar in-between the fingers (polluted tobacco addict), can still produce a lucid projection.

Agility. In fact, these conditions and material objects do not hamper the agility of the exteriorized psychosoma or the isolated projected mentalsoma.

Simplification. In spite of what has been presented, it is recommended that one simplifies the human body's conditions in voluntary experiments, with a view toward reducing the negative psychological factors that act upon the projector's consciousness.

Removal. Among the objects, whether metallic or not, in contact with the projector's human body that should be removed, the following 9 can be singled out:

1. Wedding ring.
2. Rings.
3. Wrist, pocket, mechanical, electrical, electronic, or digital watches.
4. Bracelet or belt.

5. Earrings.
6. Chain around the neck or on an arm.
7. Necklace.
8. Hair band or tiara.
9. Eyeglasses or contact lenses: as a rule, the removal of these is recommendable in certain cases, except for lenses that are made to be worn for a week or longer without being removed.

Exceptions. Obviously, there are objects that should not or cannot be removed, as is the case with an ill person with bandages, a cast, a pacemaker, or a projector who is currently using an internal absorbent, and others of a similar nature.

Bibliography: Frost (560, p. 52), Monroe (1065, p. 211), Vieira (1762, p. 172).

193. CLOTHES OF THE PROJECTOR

Types. Two types of clothing influence projective practices because they are in direct contact with the projector's human body:

1. **Soma.** The clothing enveloping your soma on that occasion.
2. **Bed.** The sheets on the bed where your human body is at rest, in certain cases.

Common. The projector's clothing can be of at least the following 5 types:

1. The nightly pajamas, the attire most used by night projectors.
2. Underwear, even T-shirts and light nightgowns, for example.
3. Athletic clothing.
4. Dress or suit.
5. Ordinary clothing.

Recommendations. Nevertheless, clothing that is light and very loose is always recommended, in order to avoid blood stasis, as well as removing shoes and socks. During the projective practices you should not wear belt, eyeglasses or wristwatch.

Looseness. The knees, back of the neck and fingers should be unrestrained and should not have anything constricting them.

Weight. Regarding bed linen, it is advisable to use a minimum of blankets that are as light as possible, to avoid extra weight on the human body. This extra weight provokes negative psychological effects during natural sleep and lucid projection itself, including nightmares, inconvenient sensations of weight and suffocation, extraphysical semi-lucidity, extraphysical traumas and physical repercussions.

Pressure. One should allow the light sheets to drape gently over the human body, including the feet, without creating the least amount of pressure.

Avoidances. Covers and blankets made of synthetic fabric are not recommended. Some studious individuals recommend avoiding all types of colored clothing, that can energetically intoxicate the person's aura. This subject still requires more in-depth research.

Nudity. There are those who prefer to sleep, and to even prepare for lucid projection, entirely undressed which, due care being paid to the ambient temperature in order not to catch a cold, will always be a practical process, as this creates the positive psychological effects of freedom, agility and lightness. It is worth mentioning that the act of the projection practitioner lying in the nude can lead the consciousness, when projected in the psychosoma, to also feel naked in the extraphysical dimension.

Cleanliness. There are individuals who particularly emphasize the aspect of personal hygiene and the cleanliness of the person's clothes and bed linen as important requirements for predisposing lucid projection, in view of personal comfort as well as the circulation of consciential energies, being preferable for the person to take a shower before beginning the experience.

Shower. After showering one should not create friction on the body when drying in order to avoid keeping the consciousness excessively alert.

Bibliography: Mittl (1061, p. 8), Monroe (1065, p. 211), Muldoon (1105, p. 199), Vieira (1762, p. 188).

194. CAUSES OF LUCID PROJECTION

Types. The causes, or the etiology of the lucid consciential projection phenomenon can be classified into 2 basic types: subjective and objective.

A. **Subjective.** The following 13 items, at least, are the most common subjective causes of lucid projection, or those originating *inside* the consciousness (intraconscientially):

1. Absorption of cosmic energy.
2. Break in routine.
3. Dream (xenophrenic state).
4. Extreme pain.
5. Great mental concentration.
6. Hypnagogic state.
7. Physiological discoincidence every night during sleep, the most common.
8. Production of the vibrational state (VS).
9. Self-determination.
10. Sensory deprivation.
11. Spontaneous cause.
12. Strong desire.
13. Voluntary induction.

B. **Objectives.** Among the objective causes of lucid projection, or those originating *outside* the consciousness (extraconscientially), at least the following 13 can be singled out:

1. Anesthesia.
2. Catalytic factor.
3. Critical life-threatening situation (desoma).
4. Drugs (pharmacology, psychopathology).
5. Electric or emotional shock.
6. Indeterminate cause.
7. Laboratorial factor.
8. Near-death experience (NDE).
9. Physical accident.
10. Physical lesion.
11. Special coadjutant.
12. Surgery.
13. Trance state (xenophrenic state).

Impure. Impure consciential projections can be provoked by people who suffer from abnormal or ill conditions (pathology). The following 7 variables are examples:

1. Chronic alcoholism.
2. Migraine attacks.
3. Intense common cold.
4. Typhoid fever crisis.
5. Epilepsy.
6. Medication.
7. Encephalic trauma.

Bibliography: Champlin (272, p. 210), Crookall (338, p. 118), Shay (1546, p. 32).

195. LUCID PROJECTION AND DISTANCE

Space. The *space factor* interferes with the projected consciousness in 3 ways:

1. **Strong.** Strong or vigorous effect when the consciousness is projected in the psychosoma in the paratropospheric extraphysical dimension.
2. **Weak.** Weak effect in the extraphysical districts not directly related to the human dimension.
3. **None.** No effect, in other words: does not act upon the consciousness when projected in the mentalsomatic dimension, or in lucid projections experienced in the isolated mentalsoma.

Voluntary. From what has been presented above, we can easily conclude that intentionally produced, voluntary, ordinary projection which, in the majority of cases, occurs within the projector's physical base, or in the environment of the projector's existence, is strongly related to the space factor.

Scale. The facts related to physical distance allow the elaboration of a scale with 3 progressive stages of discoincidence or 3 well-defined distances that occur between the vehicles of the manifestation of the consciousness:

1. **Inch.** The first stage, which is physiological and common to all persons, constitutes a minimal, partial exit of the psychosoma, only about an inch (a few centimeters) out of coincidence, or *minidiscoincidence,* as occurs in natural *sleep,* every night, or in a condition of extreme physical *fatigue*.
2. **Feet.** The second stage, which is traumatic and less common for the majority of individuals, indicates the complete exit of the psychosoma from the human body, less than 3 feet (1 meter), or some yards (meters) away, within the physical base. This stage frequently occurs in physical accidents that involve *trauma,* and scenarios that unfold in surgery rooms, dental clinics and hospitals where patients are under anesthesia.
3. **Miles.** The third stage, born of motivation, is rarer and is characterized by a great separation of the vehicles of manifestation, *maxidiscoincidence.* The consciousness, projected in the psychosoma, or the body of desires, reaches distances of miles (kilometers), traversing oceans and continents, almost always carried by a strong wish to be in a specific place, or together with a specific person (consciential target).

Spatial. Without a doubt, spatial projections are also included in this scale, as in these two basic categories, for example:

1. **Microcosm.** The projections of the consciousness in the microcosm (psychosphere, personal holothosene) of one's own human body are classified in the first stage of the scale.
2. **Macrocosm.** Exoprojections, or those that occur in the macrocosm, in heavenly bodies distant from the earth, in cosmic space, are classified in the abovementioned third stage.

Relaxation. The greater the practitioner's capacity for psychophysical self-relaxation, the greater will be the possibility for his/her consciousness to lucidly project itself further from the human body and physical base, thus imposing a more intense neutralization upon the action of the silver cord.

Bibliography: Baumann (93, p. 23), Martin (1002, p. 49).

196. STARTING TIME OF THE PROJECTIVE EXPERIMENT

Characteristics. Among the characteristics of the starting time that the lucid consciential projection practitioner should consider, at least the following 10 variables should be observed:

1. Time planned according to the experimenter's daily work routine, which does not interfere with normal, professional tasks, or with the practice of any type of parapsychic trance.
2. Punctuality, in view of the assistance provided by the helpers.

3. Consultation of the clock and specialized instruments.

4. As exact a time as possible (including minutes) of the beginning of the projective preparation.

5. The moments before going to bed to sleep.

6. The first half of the night.

7. The morning period.

8. The afternoon period.

9. Other subsequent data.

10. Detailed record of the experiment.

Ideal. Lucid projection can be produced at any time of the day or night. Nevertheless, the intraphysical consciousness benefits from choosing a better time for lucidly projecting from the human body: during daybreak, in the second half of the night (precisely between midnight and 3 o'clock in the morning, local time), a period in which the majority of people are sleeping within or near the physical base. Thus, their attention or general mental concentration is deviated and focused on other mental targets aside from the projector's personality and existence.

Melatonin. According to observations made by the author, the space of time between midnight and 3 o'clock in the morning is precisely (or coincidentally) the same time period of peak melatonin hormone production by the internal pineal secretion gland (the so-called *third eye*).

Sleep. It is currently accepted that melatonin controls reactions to stress and changes in environment. It helps to conduce the human body toward the condition of relaxation, to calm it and to predispose sleep. These are precisely the conditions necessary for psychophysical preparation for the production of lucid consciential projection.

Light. Melatonin produces effects similar to those typical of the old drug "Valium®". The production of this hormone is governed by the quantity of light that the human eyes receive.

Questions. On the other hand, is it the condition of the vegetative life of the human body without the consciousness, or the consciousness' *empty brain* state, that also predisposes the production of melatonin through the pineal gland? In other words: does the pineal gland carry out its *organic* functions better when it does not suffer the direct influence of the consciousness' *presence?*

Hypothesis. At any rate, this original observation, based on the facts registered here about the unquestionable *lucid projection-melatonin* relationship deserves more in-depth research (work hypothesis) in the areas of the physiology of the human body and the paraphysiology of the psychosoma.

Assistential. The best time for lucid projectors who intend to perform extraphysical assistance – either alone or assisted by a helper – is between 6:00 and 11:00 PM (local time). This is characterized by psychotherapists as the period of "human anguish," the more adequate time to endeavor to minimize depression, despair, sadness, neediness, doubt, grief, great loneliness and the imbalanced relationships of intraphysical beings, especially the inhabitants of the great urban conglomerations, megacities or megalopolises.

Incubation. The lucid projection phenomenon provoked by the impulsion of will, through perseverant exercises and training, sometimes presents a latent period or a type of incubation phase of some days or weeks.

Moon. Some authors recommend that the practitioner begin his/her projective exercises during the new moon. Nevertheless, repeating what has already been affirmed: there is no scientific evidence that a specific phase of the moon, or specific manifestations of any other heavenly body, negatively or positively influence the intraphysical consciousness in the act of the individual's induction of a lucid consciential projection.

Bibliography: Butler (227, p. 70), Castaneda (258, p. 114), Frost (560, p. 45), Huson (768, p. 108), Targ (1652, p. 11), Vieira (1762, p. 210).

VIII – Lucid Projection Techniques

197. PREPARATION FOR LUCID PROJECTION

Definition. Technique: the set of precepts or processes that a science makes use of, as well as the ability to use these norms or the practical part.

Synonymy: scientific norms; scientific processes.

Preparations. We will first consider here (in the next 9 chapters) the preparatory techniques for lucid projection and the basic projective techniques. We will then address the derived techniques of lucid projection, per se.

Predominance. In the elaboration of all the listed projective techniques, the following 6 variables always predominate, where possible:

1. **Didactic.** The manifest intention of the didactic or normative presentation.
2. **Methods.** Well-organized methods with formal plans.
3. **Suggestions.** Detailed systems with direct suggestions.
4. **Concordance.** The codification of concordant aspects.
5. **Avoidances.** Notices regarding useful avoidances in the procedure.
6. **Users.** Indications according to specific personalities (technique users).

Reactions. The consciential reactions that occur in the preparatory processes for lucid projection can be classified as physical actions and psychological reactions.

A. **Physical.** Among the physical *actions* in preparation for lucid projection at least the following 11 procedures can be singled out:

1. Personal and environmental hygiene (cleanliness).
2. Attending to physiological needs, such as emptying the bladder, clearing the nostrils with warm water.
3. The practitioner remaining in intraphysical isolation.
4. Specialized reading.
5. Stretches, sighs, shivers and yawns (energetic detoxification).
6. Hydromagnetic *shower* or aeromagnetic *refrigeration*.
7. Vibrational state (VS) or exteriorization of energies (self-passes).
8. Psychophonic monolog.
9. Recorded suggestions.
10. Reduction in the heterogeneity of the physical-extraphysical environment (holothosene).
11. Avoidance of ingesting excessive amounts of heavy, solid and liquid foods.

B. **Psychological.** Among the psychological *reactions* involved in preparing for lucid projection, the following 10, among others, can be pointed out:

1. An inner fearless and worry-free state.
2. Mental concentration.
3. Self-determination.
4. Healthy autosuggestions.
5. Saturation of the mind with the intention of projecting from the soma.
6. Energetic shower.
7. Energetic and parapsychic signage.
8. Personal lack of preparation.
9. Healthy or pathological mental perspectives.
10. Parapsychic phenomena such as: inspiration, clairvoyance, psychophony and physical effects.

Data. It will always be better if your consciousness acquires the greatest possible amount of clarifying data on projectiology before endeavoring to exit the human body with lucidity.

Sleep. The preparatory process for your consciousness to project from the human body is just like the process of preparing for sleep every night.

Habits. As a lucid projection practitioner you should primarily avoid abrupt, radical changes in the patterns of your habits or human lifestyle.

Shower. The hydromagnetic shower is a type of energetic detoxification executed through the exteriorization of energy. It is commanded by the will while taking a shower and works like an individual, localized hydromagnetic storm, in a type of hydrotherapeutic prophylaxis.

Water. The water should be set at a comfortable temperature. It removes the heavy fluids and thought-forms or dense morphothosenes, rinsing the organic form, reaching the holochakra, including the aura, silver cord and psychosoma.

Refrigeration. Aeromagnetic refrigeration is also a type of energetic detoxification that can be performed by those who are accustomed to using air conditioners in hot climates and who do not have any type of allergy to cold air, which can provoke a cold.

Conditioner. Aeromagnetic refrigeration consists of the emission of consciential energy at a distance of 3' (1 m) in front of a 1 HP air conditioner that is installed at a lower elevation and set on "low."

Efficiency. Although providing distinctively positive effects, this method is not as efficient as the physical and energetic action of the jets of shower water acting on the aligned bodies (androsoma or gynosoma).

Effects. Both the above-mentioned shower and cooling procedures produce positive and distinct physical-extraphysical effects, such as the following 7:

1. **Perceptions.** They preserve the quality of the projector's perceptions when practiced before an anticipated or imminent projection.

2. **Coronochakra.** They dilate the pulsation and the luminous rhythm of the nucleus or vortex, as well as the rays, shoots, petals, sections or lotus of the coronochakra, from whence they originate.

3. **Emitter.** They transform the lucid projector into an authentic emitter or transmitter of energy.

4. **Healthiness.** They serve to maintain the practitioner's *aura of health*.

5. **Self-defense.** They create and maintain the so-called *protective shell* (energetic self-defense) for the lucid projector.

6. **Mentalsoma.** They gradually and continuously expand and increase the size of the mentalsoma, which greatly helps in advanced mental projections.

7. **Projectability.** They help in the amplification of the awakening of the coronochakra and, consequently, in the activation of the other chakras. This permits lucid projections in series, leading toward continuous self-awareness day and night.

Bibliography: Frost (560, p. 45), Rogo (1444, p. XI), Steiger (1601, p. 122), Vieira (1762, p. 51).

---

198. GENERALITIES ON PROJECTIVE TECHNIQUES

Rule. Every intraphysical consciousness – even when undergoing the agony of biological death (first desoma) of the soma – can temporarily project the lucid consciousness from the human body.

Exception. In theory, there are no known exceptions to this rule. That is, there is no known extremely personal condition which can definitively impede an intraphysical consciousness from temporarily leaving the inactive – albeit vitalized by a vegetative existence – human body and, thereafter, return to it.

Difficulties. Those who are totally ignorant of the subject of lucid projection and novice projectors face 4 basic difficulties in order to voluntarily project with lucidity:

1. **Projection.** The actual process of the consciousness projecting from the human body.
2. **Lucidity.** The temporary attainment and maintenance of extraphysical lucidity.
3. **Recall.** The posterior recollection of extraphysical facts that one experienced or participated in.

   4. **Report.** The accurate translation into words of the pure psychophysical and extraphysical sensations during the different events of a lucid projection.

Holochakra. The mechanism of the functioning of several methods herein can be explained by the alteration of the holochakra's structure or its relations between the human body and psychosoma.

Case study. One day, the author, when retyping these chapters, was sought out by a young musician from a distant capital. The young woman explained what she was researching and asked a favor. Would it be possible for the author to teach her to attain lucid projections? She clearly expected that my reply would be succinct. Furthermore, she seemed to think that once she had half-a-dozen guidelines she would achieve immediate results.

Athleticism. The author sought to explain that it was not quite as simple as that. He informed her that the subject had currently demanded almost two decades of research and occupied dozens of pages in this book, discussing the methods for producing lucid projection and showing how they should be followed.

Tennis. The author explained that it was like a book on tennis, her favorite sport. In tennis, one studies the science and the art that presuppose rules for each of the shots, the *modus operandi* of the *why* and the *know-how* involved in applying them, describing the organization of these parts in the general strategy of a winning game. The science and art of projecting from the human body with lucidity must be studied in a similar manner.

Athlete. There are guidelines for each of the steps that are to be taken in order to achieve a full lucid projection. Thus, the lucid consciential projector is nothing less than a transcendent athlete.

Music. The youth appeared distrustful. Although realizing that she did not know how to conscientially project with lucidity, she seemed to think that there is not much to teach regarding the subject. The author asked her if it was sufficient to listen to sounds in order to listen to a symphony, such as Beethoven's "Ninth," which had been playing when she arrived. She responded, "Of course not." This is what would happen with lucid projection and the author asked her to explain her technique for listening to music properly. She said that, yes, she could do this, but not in a few words.

Symphony. Listening to a symphony is complicated. It is not sufficient to remain attentive, there are so many different things to consider, so many parts to distinguish and classify. One cannot instantly and simply teach everything that the listener has to know. Besides, it would take a good amount of time listening to music before someone becomes a good listener.

Conditions. It was explained to her that producing lucid projections was also like that. If someone could learn to listen to erudite music, he/she could learn to conscientially project with lucidity, as long as the conditions were the same. There would be norms to know and follow. It is with practice that one creates good habits. There are no insurmountable difficulties. It only requires the will to learn, motivation and patience.

Changes. The production of lucid consciential projection aims precisely to change stratified habits in the entire physical existence of the intraphysical consciousness, regardless of age and peculiar characteristics (strong traits and weak traits) of the individual's personality.

Notion. If she did not find the response completely satisfactory, it would be difficult for her to learn to consientially project with lucidity. She had no idea about what actually constitutes a lucid projection. Since she considered lucid projection to be something that anyone can do, something that we bring with us in the functioning of our organism, she refused to admit that learning to project with lucidity was the same as learning to listen to music, play tennis or to train oneself in the complex use of the human senses and the attributes of the ego.

Help. The author's help cannot surpass the help that the interested readers give themselves. Many often say they think it would be good to learn to project with lucidity, if they knew how to do it. Firstly, they can be certain of success *if they exert themselves*. Secondly, if they wish it, they *will know how to exert themselves*.

Individuality. Lucid projection practitioners do not develop equally, as there are many differences between individuals and all projective results depend exclusively, above all, upon the person or his/her individual characteristics.

Sections. The interested reader should look in the specialized sections of this book for the techniques related to the 4 acts that are difficult in terms of lucid projection. One should select those with which one feels a greater affinity and is motivated to use, in order to begin perseverant training.

Style. Remember that regardless of which technique is chosen it should become a personal, nontransferable practice that is in harmony with your personality, temperament, style, consciential micro-universe and personal performance.

Hygiene. Certain suggestive resources or factors that trigger projective processes can be extremely useful for the novice. Every resource, even the most exotic ones, as long as they are inoffensive for the consciousness, contributing toward the aims in view, within physical, mental and consciential hygiene, can and should be used in order to produce lucid projections.

Effort. All effort or sacrifice made toward this goal is worth one's personal dedication.

Crutches. The projector gradually, upon gaining more experience, will always end up reaching a stage in which he/she will dispense with all dependencies or psychophysical crutches that he/she uses to overcome deficiencies in the process of lucid projection.

Identification. Taking this into consideration, the interested reader should identify the process, methodology or procedure, among the dozens of existing methods and coadjutants for projecting with lucidity, to which he/she best adapts.

Artifice. If you need a word, symbol, image or even a strange artifice in order to feel secure in the act of projecting, you should use it and later, upon gaining more experience, simplify where possible, dispensing with all superfluous resources.

Habits. What is most important, nonetheless, is not merely to leave the human body, but to create the simplest physiological personal habits for projecting that you can in order to gradually achieve high quality experiments with a complete mastery of the processes.

Learning. Remember that extraphysical learning is arduous and infinite, as it does not even cease upon biological death of the human body (first desoma).

Concentration. Projective exercises, regardless of which one you have chosen to use, should be practiced in a moment or period of calm, in a peaceful environment, slowly, with a good amount of attention and available time, and in an atmosphere (holothosene) that is adequately isolated.

Automatism. Avoid executing the techniques in an automatic and unfocused manner. The regular practice of projective exercises at a specific time, preferably in the early morning, produces positive results in less time.

Age. All the projective techniques that are analyzed here are indicated only for persons 15 years of age and older. Individuals of both sexes below this age should wait to arrive at this existential period – when they, as human beings, have consolidated the foundations of the central nervous system – in order to begin practicing lucid consciential projection induced through the impulsion of their own will.

Science. Nevertheless, we cannot forget the classic question, "At what age should we teach science to a child?" The response is simple, "From the moment the child asks, 'Why?'"

Spontaneity. On the other hand, when lucid projection arises spontaneously before the youth reaches this age, it is inoffensive and, in this case, inevitable and imperative.

Ignorance. Nevertheless, many youths suffer disastrous consequences due to the ignorance of many people on this subject, including liberal professionals, in terms of incorrect approaches, unnecessary therapies and incorrect medications administered in a great number of cases.

Attempts. If you are really interested in producing lucid consciential projections you should not try only once or a few times over a period of time using a single technique and give up the subject forever if, perchance, you do not succeed.

Routines. The production of lucid projection depends upon innumerous factors, including those of an individual physiological nature. This is why, even if you change projective techniques, you should make further attempts from time to time, especially after changing basic habits or existential routines, no matter how insignificant you find them to be at first glance. Such modifications can predispose you to the onset of a consciential phenomenon, notably so when you have never had a previous lucid consciential experience.

Spontaneous. In any case, if you are really interested in producing lucid consciential projections or have tried to provoke such experiences, prepare yourself psychologically to accept spontaneous lucid projections because they might occur during any favorable opportunity from now on. The projective phenomenon is physiological or paraphysiological and, besides, can be sponsored by helpers, evolutiologists and *serenissimi.*

Holochakrology. As we will see in the following chapters, with the presentation of the projective techniques, the studies on holochakrology and the application of consciential energies, in accordance with the basic chakra, are of undeniable relevance in the development of the lucid projectability (LPB) of the intraphysical consciousness.

Bibliography: Baker (69, p. 35), Baumann (93, p. 77), Conway (297, p. 188), Gomes (611, p. 124), Huson (768, p. 105), Matson (1013, p. 39), Norvell (1139, p. 152), St. Clair (1593, p. 148), Twitchell (1712, p. 49), Verneuil (1735, p. 189), Whiteman (1842, p. 240).

199. PROJECTIVE PSYCHOPHYSIOLOGICAL CRUTCHES

Definition. Psychophysical crutch: the inducing resource or triggering factor used by yourself, a novice projector, prior to the beginning of the experience, with the objective of obtaining the technique for lucidly projecting or at least dynamizing the projection.

Synonymy: catalyst of lucid projection; parapsychic artifice; parapsychic crutch; potentiater of lucid projection; psychological artifice; psychophysical inductor; psychophysical stratagem; psychophysiological dependence; ritualistic support; somatopsychic support; symbolic representative.

Types. Psychophysical crutches can generally be classified into 3 types:

1. **Physical.** Two psychophysical crutches, which are more physical than psychological:

A. **Massages.** Massaging of the ankles and forehead to induce psychophysical relaxation.

B. **Dance.** Dancing with the spinning of the human body and head.

2. **Physiological.** Four psychophysical crutches of physiological origin:

A. **Fasting.** The use of fasting to weaken the human body and predispose the psychosoma to takeoff.

B. **Thirst.** The use of thirst for the same objective.

C. **Transmissions.** Reception of transmissions and self-transmissions of energies (consciential energies).

D. **Psychomotor.** The practicing of physical exercises in order to become tired and sleepy.

3. **Psychological.** Nine psychophysical crutches, which are more psychological than physical:

A. **Hypnosis.** Hypnotic induction in order to project.

B. **Rituals.** Diverse rituals, some presenting excessively mystic connotations.

C. **Music.** Listening to soft relaxation and sleep-inducing music on tape or disc.

D. **Visualizations.** Visual projections of the ocean, rivers, waterfalls, sky, clouds or meadows.

E. **Inductions.** Vocal inductions performed by the leader upon a group of candidates to lucid projection.

F. **Mantras.** Mantras: special words or expressions.

G. **Oration.** Special oration (prayer), either unspoken or verbalized, performed by the projector or by another in order to solicit extraphysical help.

H. **Evocations.** Conscious and realistic evocations.

I. **Faith.** One's own religion or individual faith.

Laboratories. Currently, even in the scientific laboratorial research of lucid projection, audiovisual apparatuses, inventions and other resources – such as the vibrating chair, colored spiral discs and others – are used and can be undeniably interpreted and classified, in one way or another, as psychophysical crutches or *electronic rituals* (technical procedures).

Obstacles. Nevertheless, all rituals are, generally speaking, psychophysical crutches which, when excessive, can become conditioning factors that keep us from getting directly in contact with physical reality and with extraphysical reality. This fact must not be forgotten in any considerations regarding projective psychophysical crutches.

Meditation. It is also worth mentioning that conventional physical meditation, whether the common or transcendental type, can even permit a first lucid projection for the practitioner who has a projective predisposition. But it does not always help everyone, from the standpoint of projectiology. On the contrary, it can be a hindrance in relation to the efforts and attempts made by the intraphysical consciousness to project with lucidity, because one person's consciential performance is very different or, better still, opposite to that of another individual.

Comparison. The following is a succinct comparison of 2 basic differential factors between the state of meditation and the phenomenon of lucid projection:

1. **Direction.** In the condition of meditation, the consciousness goes *into itself,* centripetally, in the interior of the consciential micro-universe or the ego, balances the dense organism, calms the mind, often interiorizing itself still further into the physical body. In the phenomenon of lucid projection, the consciousness, when in the physical dimension, *goes out of itself,* centrifugally, leaving the human body, exteriorizing itself toward one or more existential dimensions, with the possibility of establishing direct extraphysical contacts with other consciousnesses, balancing the energies of the psychosoma, expanding itself beyond the physical mind (brain, biomemory) and the inner world of the ego.

2. **Extraphysical.** After takeoff of the psychosoma, or the departure of the consciousness from the human body – during the extraphysical period of the projected consciousness – the consciousness can, according to extraphysical circumstances, perform extraphysical (extracorporeal) meditation directly in that consciential dimension. This resource is quite different from conventional meditation and permits the consciousness to obtain original ideas, while it is temporarily outside the human brain.

Dispense. Successive projective experiences, bringing greater extraphysical maturity, projective experience and agility, makes it such that the intraphysical consciousness ends up dispensing with physical, physiological and psychological dependence or crutches – whether stars, shells, maps, cards, pendulums, pyramids, sensitives and gurus; or the personal use of amulets, mystical rings, bracelets, necklaces, crosses, magical defenses, herbs, metals, perfumed objects, stones, head, foot or hand protectors, blessed saints and talismans – in order to rely solely on his/her steadfast will to leave the human body naturally. This, of course, without disregarding the common physiological resources of both mental and physical hygiene, basic animic-parapsychical aids and the cooperation of the helpers.

Scaffolding. All diverse types of rituals and crutches should be considered scaffolding that is destined to disappear when the edifice of the projective technique has been constructed or, in other words: when the projector has perfectly mastered the process of lucidly projecting through the impulsion of his/her own will.

Superstition. It is important to warn the knowledgeable reader that, strictly speaking, the following 4 procedures, sometimes included in techniques to produce lucid projections, are perfectly dispensable resources which only exist or are used out of psychological conditioning or human superstition. They are:

1. **Stars.** Influence of the phase of the moon or other heavenly bodies.
2. **Head.** Positioning the human head in a particular direction in accordance with geographical factors.
3. **Diet.** Special diet, whether vegetarian, fruitarian or carnivorous.
4. **Amulets.** Any kind of amulet designed to protect the intraphysical consciousness while in the ordinary, physical waking state or when projected in the extraphysical dimension.

Last. At our present level of consciential evolution, the 4 most useful psychophysiological crutches and the last to be naturally discarded by the consciousness are: evocation with discernment and serenity, parapsychism, helpers and laboratorial equipment.

Minicrutches. The person who develops consciential energy resources, who has already refined his/her own parapsychic or animic sensitivities and who fluently employs the functioning of his/her chakras has no plausible reason for being concerned with minicrutches that are used so much by worried novices and unsatisfied seekers, such as: horoscopes, biorhythms, predictions, amulets, talismans, pendants, bracelets, crystals, pyramidology and others of a like nature.

Affirmations. These superficial and less effective crutches (of the retailer) are apparently useful only for those beginners who do not as yet have other more potent, evolved and efficient resources for their consciential affirmations and parapsychic realizations (that are characteristic of the "wholesaling" intraphysical consciousness with greater self-discernment).

Reflection. Unfortunately, psychophysiological crutches can be used in like manner for *well-intentioned* practices of extraphysical assistance or the *malevolent* practice of extraphysical attacks upon intraphysical consciousnesses. Sadder still, both of these practices can also be developed without the use of any psychophysiological crutches, by using only the vigorous, iron-clad, obstinate will of the practitioner. It is always useful to reflect upon these facts.

Withholding. In light of these phenomena, on the other hand, we cannot withhold information regarding the realities of the extraphysical dimensions, creating an "occult science" and maintaining the obscurantism, occultism and esoterism that predominated everywhere until quite recently.

Procedure. Scientific research and diffusion of the collected findings, including their implications in light of cosmoethics, are the best conduct or the ideal technical procedure for all social beings.

Conditions. Generally speaking, psychophysiological crutches can lead the intraphysical consciousness to negative conditions that need to be remembered, in the sense of avoiding them in projective techniques. They include the following set of 12 anachronistic variables:

1. **Conditioning.** Paralyzing bureaucratization or unproductive conditioning.
2. **Fissures.** Deformations of the consciousness or fissures in one's personality.
3. **Pathothosenes.** Sterilizing degradation, self-corruption or pathothosenes.
4. **Stereotypes.** Fossilizing stereotypes and stratifications.
5. **Monoideism.** Obsession, fixed ideas or monoideism.
6. **Censure.** Castrating prohibitions or censures.
7. **Rules.** Rigid, but useless, rules.

8. **Delirium.** Tyrannical or obtrusive rituals (delirium).
9. **Routines.** Senseless routines.
10. **Symbols.** Empty symbols and senseless formulas.
11. **Taboos.** Superstitions and taboos.
12. **Traditions.** Outmoded or fossilizing ancestral traditions.

Goal. Physical-extraphysical life demonstrates that each extraphysical consciousness goes through the resoma process alone – except the more pathological cases of Siamese twins – in a naked human body, without ever bringing extraphysical crutches with them. Everyone also passes through the desoma process alone without ever taking along physical crutches, even during group, collective desomas or those that occur en masse.

Irrationality. These facts evidence the wisdom of living without crutches and rituals of any type, as most of them are folly, absurd, irrational, nonsensical and evasive. The condition of being free from all these things is the ultimate, inescapable, definitive, mature and rational goal in the natural evolution of consciousnesses.

Inducers. The continuity of projective work permits one to dispense with all psychophysical inducers according to the following 2-element formula:

1. **Physical.** The physically healthy person does not need physical crutches.
2. **Parapsychic.** The parapsychically healthy person does not require parapsychic crutches.

Bibliography: Black (137, p. 52), Brittain (206, p. 45), Fiore (517, p. 168), Fortune (540, p. 49), Frost (560, p. 74), Glaskin (598, p. 27), Monroe (1065, p. 216), Muldoon (1105, p. 211), Reis (1384, p. 51), Steiger (1601, p. 83), Twitchell (1712, p. 119), Vieira (1754, p. 4).

---

200. PSYCHOPHYSIOLOGICAL SELF-RELAXATION TECHNIQUE

Definition. Psychophysiological self-relaxation: the voluntary action of relaxing the entire human body and, finally, one's own mind, thus permitting the freeing of the holochakra and then the psychosoma, carrying with it the intraphysical consciousness.

Synonymy: alphatization; liberation of the holochakra; muscular and mental relaxation; physical relaxation; *pratyhara;* progressive muscular relaxation (PMR).

Sleep. When tense, one probably feels tired but, at the same time, finds oneself so awake inside that it becomes difficult to calm down and undo the *inner knots*. This is why a reduction in muscular tonus characterizes the state of natural sleep.

Condition. Progressive, deep muscular relaxation of the human body allows you to achieve complete immobility, semi-lethargy or induce a state of anesthesia in every area of the human body, thus overcoming psychic and muscular tension, anxiety and insomnia at the same time that you empty your mind of everything except the desire to lucidly leave the dense body.

Step. This procedure is the first, almost indispensable, step needed for you to voluntarily produce a lucid consciential projection.

Initiative. In many projective processes, the consciousness takes the initiative to leave the human body. In the psychophysiological self-relaxation technique the contrary occurs, in that the human body creates the condition wherein the intraphysical consciousness departs from within itself.

Alpha. The perfect progressive and controlled, concentrative corporal self-relaxation predisposes your mind to a self-induced hypnagogic state – corresponding to the alpha rhythm captured by the electroencephalograph – being an essential component of the mental control or meditative techniques used in yoga, Zen, transcendental meditation and autogenous training.

Recordings. The psychophysiological self-relaxation technique can even be practiced by using instructions recorded on discs or tapes, as well as listening to recordings of special sounds, such as the relaxing sound of ocean waves crashing on the beach.

Immobility. Above all, psychophysiological self-relaxation (of the nerves and muscles) must lead you to total immobility, namely a state of general relaxation, in a comfortable position, lying down, motionless, with muscular hypotonicity and mental passivity.

Tension. Tension – the condition contrary to relaxation – is responsible for inopportune movements on the part of the practitioner.

Inconvenience. Once you have initiated your state of self-relaxation, you cannot give in to the inconvenient and extemporaneous desires to scratch, swallow dryly, clear your throat, cough or move your fingers and joints.

Progressive. One of the most greatly utilized procedures is progressive self-relaxation, through which you convince your human body to stretch itself, mentally going over all the organic areas and, indirectly, removing tension by contracting and relaxing the muscles in a set order for a period of 30 minutes, before beginning the projective experiment, following these 8 steps:

1. **Isolation.** Isolate yourself in a closed room where you will not be disturbed while practicing the exercise. Remain in the nude or wear only light, loose clothes. Loosen your belt and remove your glasses and watch. Make sure that nothing is pressing or binding your knees, nape of the neck and fingers.

2. **Position.** Lay down on a bed or sit in a comfortable chair or armchair. The seated position predisposes the production of lucid projection for many people. Close your eyes.

3. **Contraction.** Do not contract your muscles with all your strength. Just keep them firm, counting slowly from 1 to 5 and then relax them for about 20 seconds before working with another group of muscles.

4. **Respiration.** Contract and relax each group of muscles 2 or 3 times, endeavoring to inhale while contracting them, hold your breath while counting and exhale when relaxing. The bedroom or room should be well-ventilated.

5. **Attention.** Focus your attention on the sensation of specific muscle areas alternately contracting and relaxing, keeping the rest of your body calm and still.

6. **Imagination.** Pretend that your entire being constitutes only that part of your body upon which you are working. The process must be simultaneously a mental (consciousness) and physical (soma) exercise.

7. **Sequence.** Contract and suddenly relax the muscles starting with the fingers, hand, forearm or the arm (biceps, triceps), first on one side, then on the other. Then, do the same with the muscles of the head, starting with the top of your cranium. Then work with the muscles of the face, that is: forehead, eyes, eyelids, cheeks, chin and mouth; neck; back; shoulders, in the back and front; chest; abdomen; and, finally, buttocks, legs, feet, toes, first on one side then the other.

8. **Time.** Do not expect immediate results the first time you exercise self-relaxation. Endeavor to gradually learn the procedure that suits you best, performing the exercises daily for two weeks.

Night. Many practitioners avoid performing self-relaxation exercises at night because they induce sleep and the individual ends up calmly sleeping without projecting lucidly.

Flotation. If you are a good swimmer, it will be very easy to create the conditioned reflexes of the physical and mental self-relaxation techniques necessary to produce lucid consciential projection. All you have to do is, in summer, enter the sea and go a little beyond the surf (where there are no sharks), float on your back on the water's surface with the top of your head toward the sun (in order to avoid glare in the eyes), stretch the arms and legs and let the movement of the waves move your body at will, buoying or floating entirely relaxed.

Bibliography: Andreas (36, p. 56), Baumann (93, p. 78), Blackmore (139, p. 94), Boswell (174, p. 137), Bowles (182, p. 60), Brennan (199, p. 39), Carrington (245, p. 38), Fontcuberta (534, p. 173), Green (632, p. 53), Hermógenes (715, p. 259), London (944, p. 56), Monroe (1065, p. 207), Morel (1086, p. 155), Morris (1092, p. 212; 1093, p. 51), Muntañola (1108, p. 26), Reis (1384, p. 51), Rogo (1444, p. 34), Salley (1496, p. 160), Schiff (1515, p. 27), Shay (1546, p. 36), Steiger (1601, p. 217), Verneuil (1735, p. 189), Vieira (1762, p. 79), Walker (1781, p. 105), Zaniah (1899, p. 384).

201. MENTAL CONCENTRATION TECHNIQUE

Definition. Mental concentration: the direct focalization of your senses and conscious mental faculties upon a single subject, without distractions.

Synonymy: capacity of mental concentration; centralization of thought; *dharana;* dynamic will; mental focalization; unidirectional concentration; unidirectional will; willful control.

Will. Strictly speaking, all the articles necessary for supplying a lucid projector can be boiled down to a singular piece of equipment: your ironclad will.

Intelligence. Your ironclad will becomes inevitable, and practically irreplaceable, in the intelligent actions of your consciousness.

Ambiguity. Meditation, both *with* and *without* mental concentration, can just as easily help or hinder you in lucid projection processes.

Molecules. There is laboratorial evidence that the "concentration of the consciousness" can influence the molecular structure of water, metals, mercury in particular and cells of the human body.

Change. Knowing the exact time to *shift mental gears,* when you should or should not concentrate, is the key to voluntary lucid projection including, in this case, the lucid takeoff in the psychosoma and projection with continuous self-awareness.

Mind. On the one hand, for your consciousness to take off from the human body in the psychosoma using any kind of takeoff, it is always best to leave the *mind empty* and not concentrate. On the other hand, dynamic concentration aids the predominance of activity in the right cerebral hemisphere, which predisposes the consciousness to fantasies, interfering with the purity and quality of your extraphysical perceptions, attracting oneiric interferences after your consciousness has projected.

Complexity. The projector has to choose the condition that potentiates lucid projection the most for him/her. Once again, we observe the degree to which the consciousness is an extremely complex reality.

Focalization. When your eyes lose their capacity to focalize directly and correctly, your subconscious or unconscious mind (or your unconscious will) enters into action, impelling your psychosoma to exteriorize from the human body, taking with it your consciousness attached to the parabrain.

Attitudes. It is still worth emphasizing that voluntary lucid projection is, above all, the product of 3 conjugated intraconsciential attitudes:

1. **Determination.** A question of simple determination (intentionality).
2. **Conscious.** A conscious act of will (deliberation).
3. **Dynamization.** A process of consciously dynamizing the human will (self-lucid thosenization).

Contemplation. Based on the abovementioned concepts, an action that can lead your consciousness to project itself from the human body with lucidity is to contemplate an object placed a certain distance from your eyes fixedly.

Technique. The following is a mental concentration technique that induces you to project yourself lucidly from your human body in 7 steps:

1. **Isolation.** Isolate yourself in a closed room where you will not be disturbed while practicing the exercises. Remain in the nude or use only light, loose clothing.

2. **Candle.** Place a lighted candle on a wide plate (to avoid fires) in a distant part of the room.

3. **Armchair.** Keeping your trunk erect and hands on thighs, sit on a comfortable chair or armchair about 9' 10" (3 m) away from the candle, at the other end of the room.

4. **Darkness.** Darken the room entirely, leaving only the light of the candle.

5. **Stare.** Stare attentively at the lighted candle in front of you and concentrate on it until you are unaware of the rest of the physical world around you.

6. **Extension.** At this point, only you and the candle exist. The candle is an extension of yourself, of your human body.

7. **Visualization.** When you, near and facing the lighted candle, feel your normal awareness become *suspended,* first imagine or visualize your psychosoma moving out of the human body and going toward the lighted candle. Then, *feel* your departure and yourself going toward the candle.

Chakras. These exercises should be practiced with the maximal impulsion of your hyperdynamized, ironclad will. Some practitioners focalize on the frontochakra or umbilicochakra to energetically hyperdynamize or intensify the exhaustive, obstinate effort of the impulsion of the will.

Classification. *Mental concentration* represents the second stage in deep meditation techniques, the first stage being *attention* and the third, *contemplation.*

Distractibility. The contrary state, or the consciential condition antipodal to the ability of mental concentration is distractibility or, in other words: the ease with which the consciousness changes the course of thought under the influence of external stimuli. This is a subject that is much researched within the world of psychopathology.

Bibliography: Blackmore (139, p. 95), Carrington (245, p. 95), Crawford (313, p. 17), Gaynor (577, p. 38), Green (632, p. 111), Heindel (705, p. 31), Lefebure (911, p. 122), Martin (1002, p. 55), Meek (1028, p. 267), Monroe (1065, p. 208), Reis (1384, p. 71), Rogo (1444, p. 19), Saraydarian (1507, p. 63), Shay (1546, p. 38), Steiger (1601, p. 185), Verneuil (1735, p. 49), Vieira (1762, p. 175), Walker (1781, p. 105).

---

202. RHYTHMIC RESPIRATION TECHNIQUE

Definition. Rhythmic respiration: the respiration exercise based upon a specific rhythm of breathing, or one with an exhalation that is slower than normal.

Synonymy: metered respiration; pneumoprojection; retention of breath; retention of respiration; rhythmical respiration; voluntary respiring.

Respiration. Respiration is the process through which the human body inhales, uses oxygen and liberates carbon dioxide.

Capacity. The total capacity of the 2 lungs is not correctly and fully utilized by human beings. On average, only about 70% is used.

Instruction. Breath control has been continually taught to instrumentalists, singers and athletes. It has also been used for a long time to put the intraphysical consciousness into a trance state and permit the departure of the psychosoma from the human body, taking the consciousness with it.

Antigravity. The control of respiration explains such phenomena as induced levitation based on the antigravity, or countergravity, of the marathoner monks and lamas of Tibet, who can cover tremendous distances at surprising speeds.

Biodynamics. The biodynamics of breathing evidences 4 categories of vital physiological involvement:

1. **Areas.** Involvement of the lips, nose, throat, stomach, diaphragm, lungs, brain and heart (specific areas).

2. **Soma.** Involvement of the entire human body (soma) from head to toe.

3. **Occurrences.** Involvement of many other occurrences, such as: yawning, eructation (belching), sneezing, snoring, hiccups and coughs.

4. **Alternation.** The obvious involvement of continuous, alternating inhalation and exhalation. Oxygen is the vital foundation of intraphysical existence.

Slavery. You, an intraphysical being, are a mental slave of air or, in this case, oxygen.

Retention. The apparently simple act of holding your breath may cause a slight discoincidence of the vehicles of manifestation of the consciousness. Thus, appropriate respiration constitutes an effective process for you to project due to the action of carbon dioxide.

Oxygen. This aerial vitalizing substance, oxygen, is more important for human survival than any solid or liquid nourishment ingested through the mouth.

Detoxification. The system of inhalation and exhalation, as well as simple acts, such as sneezing, eructation (belching), hiccupping and yawning can act as psychophysical detoxification agents for you as a lucid projection practitioner.

Muscles. It is necessary to warn you from the beginning that exercises that involve the retention of the breath should be executed by a decrease in the action of your abdominal muscles and not through constriction of the throat.

Excess. Any excessive effort during these exercises indicates that you are proceeding incorrectly.

Inhalations. Normally, a healthy person inhales and exhales air approximately 17 to 25 times per minute, or makes approximately 24,480 respiratory exchanges per day.

Sufficiency. To calm the mind during animic-parapsychic experiences, for example, 10 inhalations per minute are normally sufficient.

Ideal. Nevertheless, if you can restrict yourself to a mere 5 respiratory exchanges it will be better or the ideal.

Meditation. In meditation exercises, only 4 respiratory exchanges occur per minute, but when the process becomes deeper, the meditator's respiration is not even perceived.

Diving. The best and quickest way for you to become fully aware of the breathing process, as well as of your own human body – which helps greatly in the practice of lucid projection – is for you (if you are a swimmer) to cross the limpid waters of a full swimming pool, deep underwater, in a tranquil environment.

Physiology. The following is the correct physiological technique of human respiration that aims to induce you to lucidly project from your human body, through 8 steps:

1. **Isolation.** On an empty stomach, isolate yourself in a closed room where you will not be disturbed while practicing the exercise. Remain in the nude or use only light and loose clothing. It is always good to clean both nostrils with lukewarm water so that your respiration will be unimpeded.

2. **Back.** Sit straight-backed on a comfortable chair or armchair. Keep the arms extended alongside the body, muscles relaxed, without moving the shoulders. This is an ideal position to apply in some projective techniques.

3. **Nostrils.** Breathe slowly and regularly through the nostrils. Do not breathe through the mouth or with the chest. Let your abdomen distend. The room or bedroom should be well-ventilated.

4. **Diaphragm.** Using the diaphragm to breathe, you gradually distend the lower part of the chest and push the lower ribs outward.

5. **Lungs.** Continue filling the lungs with air and start to fill the upper extremities of the lungs, the pulmonary apexes, pushing the lower ribs further outward. This will renew the residual air in the lungs.

6. **Exhalation.** Hold your breath for some seconds and then slowly exhale through the nose, forcing the exit of all air, emptying the lungs completely and contracting your abdomen as much as possible, as if to have it touch the spine.

7. **Repetition.** Repeat the complete sequence above consecutively 6 times or, in other words, 6 consecutive inhalations and 6 consecutive exhalations. Then rest, holding your breath for some seconds or for as long as you can without feeling uncomfortable.

8. **Sleep.** Continue the exercise until you fall asleep or, in other words, breathe as slowly as you can until your respiration is hardly perceptible.

Cardiochakra. According to holochakrology, it should be remembered that the effectiveness of the rhythmic respiration technique greatly depends upon the quality of energies of the cardiochakra of the intraphysical consciousness practitioner.

Bibliography: Baker (69, p. 74), Baumann (93, p. 79), Boswell (174, p. 136), Butler (228, p. 164), Coquet (301, p. 228), Crawford (313, p. 47), Crookall (343, p. 55), David-Neel (368, p. 47), Denning (391, p. 37), Eliade (477, p. 62), Greene (635, p. 24), Guéret (659, p. 79), Lefebure (911, p. 15), Martin (1002, p. 59), Michaël (1041, p. 174), Mittl (1061, p. 9), Rampa (1361, p. 82), Reis (1384, p. 53), Rogo (1444, p. 72), Shay (1546, p. 37), Vieira (1762, p. 175), Walker (1781, p. 37), Yogananda (1894, p. 235).

---

203. IMAGINATIVE ESCAPES TECHNIQUE

Definition. Imaginative escape: the voluntary action of your creative imagination which permits the separation of your consciousness and your brain, or the freeing of the psychosoma, taking the consciousness with it to manifest in another dimension (see fig. 203, p. 1,130).

Synonymy: directed daydream; imaginary journey; moving dream; self-programmed daydream; waking dream.

Desire. In using creative imagination – through the use of imagery – you apply a strong desire and visualization of images to suggest, in a form of autosuggestion or self-hypnosis, the separation of the consciousness from the physical brain or, in other words: the departure of the psychosoma transporting the consciousness out from the human body in an escape from a physical environment (intraphysicality) to another that is well-characterized (extraphysicality).

Association. The most appropriate images for your imaginative escape will be those which emerge from your unconscious mind, or those closely associated with your personal life.

Resources. The following is the imaginative escape technique using 3 different resources:

1. **Sea.** The most common creative imagination process is to imagine yourself anchored to the bottom of the sea, desperately needing to go upward, forcing your way to the surface.

2. **Wall.** Another method is to visualize yourself on one side of a high wall, in a deserted area, and try to jump or scale the wall to reach the pleasant, green scenery on the other side.

3. **Staircase.** A third method is to concentrate on climbing an imaginary staircase all the way to the top, from where another district can be reached, at which point your psychosoma will detach itself from the human body.

Instructor. These projection proceedings can also be induced by an instructor or guide, or even by a previously prepared recording that will lead you through the various stages of the experiment. It is somewhat similar to massage and projective visualization techniques, and to modern techniques employed in psychotherapy.

Group. The imaginative escape technique can be induced by an instructor who speaks softly, slowly, in a calm tone of voice to a group of highly imaginative people gathered at the same time and in the same place, or collectively programmed, as if their minds were embarking on a group *tour*.

Bibliography: Boswell (174, p. 140), Martin (1002, p. 51), Muldoon (1105, p. 161), Rogo (1444, p. 151), Shay (1546, p. 40).

204. PROJECTIVE VISUALIZATION TECHNIQUE

Definition. Projective visualization: the process by which you seek to mentally see the inducing images of lucid projection which are deliberately created by your own imagination.

Synonymy: projective self-visualization; projective visibilization; projective *yantra*.

Systems. Throughout time, diverse systems have been using *visualization* to attain projection of the consciousness from the human body, especially: cabalism; tantric yoga; Tibetan yoga; hermetic magic; contemporary parapsychologists; ancient Egyptian practices; and shamanism.

Coadjutants. Visualization exercises are powerful coadjutants for you to project, in light of the following 4 factors:

1. **Projectiology.** They actually help in the processes of voluntary lucid projection.

2. **Discoincidence.** They predispose the discoincidence of the vehicles of manifestation of your consciousness.

3. **Analysis.** They intensify the capacity to observe and analyze extraphysical events with clarity and precision.

4. **Mnemosomatics.** They act to improve your memory and, consequently, in the technique of recall subsequent to projective experiences.

Technique. The following is the 14-step logical visualization technique that can predispose you to leave the human body:

1. **Isolation.** Isolate yourself in a closed room where you will not be disturbed while practicing the exercise. Remain nude or use only light, loose clothing.

2. **Armchair.** Sit in a comfortable armchair at a distance of 4'11" (1.5 m) from a uniformly colored wall – white, for instance – which serves as a background. There must not be any furniture or decorative piece nearby which could divert your attention.

3. **Vase.** Place a simple object, such as a vase, directly in front of your visual field (see fig. 204. p. 1,131).

4. **Stare.** Stare attentively at the vase until you have memorized everything about it in detail, including the form, color, shape, base, opening and its use.

5. **Visualization.** With your eyes closed, visualize and mentally recreate, outside of your head at a distance, the vase and the bedroom, with all of the perspectives, shapes and exact proportions.

6. **Confirmation.** As soon as the visualized images fade, open your eyes and confirm how the room actually looks.

7. **Repetition.** Repeat the process for 20 minutes daily and uninterruptedly, without missing a single day.

8. **Alarm clock.** As soon as you have mastered the process described so far, having clear visualizations, place 1 reliable alarm clock in front of you and memorize the time. Close your eyes and visualize the alarm clock, including its shape, colors, contours and hands.

9. **Mental.** Next, visualize your mental alarm clock ticking far from you, at a distance.

10. **Power.** After a few minutes, open your eyes and check the exact time on the alarm clock to see if it is approximately the same time you visualized. If it is, your powers of visualization, or capacity to project part of your consciousness, is reaching its highest peak and you will be able to reach the extraphysical dimension lucidly.

11. **Details.** At this point, first visualize yourself, with all the action details, leaving the human body using the psychosoma.

12. **Self-visualization.** The exercise of self-visualization in the psychosoma does not mean that you should only think you are leaving the dense body, but you need to visualize your own extraphysical duplicate in minute detail rising and freeing itself in the extraphysical dimension.

13. **Soma.** On the other hand, the visualization process makes you forget about the existence of your soma or human body and you can project yourself using the mental body, wherein you will feel bodiless. For many practitioners, this visualization process is easier for projecting lucidly.

14. **Tunnel.** Another visualization resource used for you to project lucidly is creation of the mental image of a dark tunnel with a distant exit. At the precise moment you visualize the fact that you are reaching the tunnel's exit, your psychosoma exteriorizes from the human body.

Step. Visualization using the remote viewing method, as it is easier, can serve as a first step toward developing lucid projection. Many people have experienced actual remote viewing even without any kind of training or inducement to lucid projection.

Remote. Here is a simple remote viewing technique in 10 steps:

1. **Photos.** Arrange to have someone take a series of large photos of diverse areas in the city or neighborhood where you reside.

2. **Choice.** Choose one photo of an area unknown to you, look at it attentively and then seat yourself in an armchair or comfortable chair in an isolated room and visualize the location reproduced in the photograph.

3. **Imagination.** Maintain the visualized images in your mind as long as possible. Imagine yourself leaving your human body, going to this place and floating above it.

4. **Details.** Observe all details, shapes, colors and possible structures of the visualized area, without censure, judgment or analysis.

5. **Register.** If possible, register what you have visualized and experienced on tape or draw the most relevant details you were able to see.

6. **Comparison.** Next, meticulously compare what you saw with the photo.

7. **Extras.** Make special note of anything extra or different that you saw and that is not in the picture. It can be scenery behind a building, a peculiar cloud formation in the sky (always ephemeral but suggestive, e.g., a tornado characteristic of the region), a new construction to one side, a parked old or abandoned vehicle, or any other detail that calls your attention.

8. **Location.** Write down these extra details and immediately go by car to the location itself.

9. **Correction.** Once there, see if any of your additional observations are correct.

10. **Functioning.** If you had actually never visited that location before and your supplemental individual observations were correct, it is clear that your remote viewing functioned.

Unconscious. In certain cases, the visualization technique – and the author has written reports to this respect – has been employed in an unconscious manner by novice projectors. This proves its physiological or natural character.

Case study. A young man was longing for his girlfriend and, one afternoon before resting in Brasilia, intensely visualized the beach in Rio de Janeiro where she might be with her group of friends. He saw himself on a certain beach (Arpoador beach in Ipanema, Rio de Janeiro, Brazil) at that time.

Frustration. This same lucid projector, *while projected,* tried to speak to his girlfriend and her friends, but they all ignored him. This caused him a great deal of frustration.

Frontochakra. According to holochakrology, we should keep in mind that the effectiveness of the projective visualization technique greatly depends upon the quality of the energy of the frontochakra of the intraphysical consciousness practitioner.

Bibliography: Blackmore (139, p. 94), Butler (227, p. 70), Greene (635, p. 19), Huson (768, p. 111), King (844, p. 33), Martin (1002, p. 54), Richards (1394, p. 77), Rogo (1444, p. 107), Samuels (1500, p. 120), Saraydarian (1507, p. 134), Shay (1546, p. 65), Walker (1781, p. 106).

205. PROJECTIVE POSTURES TECHNIQUE

Definition. Projective postures: the set of psychological and physical positions you assume in order to lucidly project your consciousness from the human body or soma.

Synonymy: projective attitudes; psychophysical projective positions.

Rule. In everything you are willing to do, you find yourself obliged to assume certain positions, whether they are psychological attitudes, physical postures or physiological dispositions, which are more effective for your performance and more adequate for your undertaking. Lucid projections are no exception to this rule.

Techniques. Today, there are techniques for everything that we decide to do in intraphysical life.

Sequence. Here is a sequence of 15 technical psychophysical or physiological postures that facilitate lucid projection, which are also physiological or induced by the will of the individual:

1. **Location.** Lie on your back on the bed in a comfortable position. There are those who prefer to lie directly on the floor in order to achieve greater relaxation. The result will be the same in either case.

2. **Clothes.** Loosen your clothes, which should be minimal, only those that are really indispensable. You can be in the nude if you wish. Loosen your belt, remove your glasses (or contact lenses, if that is the case) and your wristwatch. Remember to keep your knees, neck and fingers free from any restriction.

3. **Pillows.** Place 1 pillow under your head and 2 others under your knees or popliteal (hamstring) area, in order to accommodate yourself and facilitate the blood circulation of the lower extremities, if convenient.

4. **Legs.** Stretch the legs without tension or stiffness.

5. **Feet.** Place the feet approximately 1' (30 cm) apart.

6. **Arms.** Rest the arms extended alongside your human body.

7. **Hands.** Open the hands, palms down, on the pillows that were placed under your legs.

8. **Head.** Rest your head in a position that will not strain your neck.

9. **Muscles.** Relax all muscles, without forgetting the jaw, face and neck muscles.

10. **Eyelids.** Close the eyelids naturally, as if you were going to sleep.

11. **Mouth.** Close the mouth without compressing the lips.

12. **Saliva.** Avoid the successive swallowing of saliva, which is generally provoked by the practitioner's nervousness.

13. **Respiration.** Let your respiration flow naturally. The room or bedroom should be well ventilated.

14. **Relaxation.** Relax totally, including your fingers, reaching the state of complete immobility or semi-lethargy.

15. **Torpidity.** Calmly wait for the complete torpidity of your human body, which will occur little by little.

Adaptation. Through the suggestions indicated, you should gradually seek the physical and psychological conditions that are best adapted to your personal tendencies.

Female projector. Particularly for the reader who is a female aspirant to lucid projection, it is recommended, if necessary, to draw the legs and feet together in order to avoid distracting, inopportune mental connotations with regard to sex (sexosoma *versus* soma).

Bibliography: Denning (391, p. 68), Frost (560, p. 52), Vieira (1762, p. 79).

206. CLASSIFICATION OF LUCID PROJECTION TECHNIQUES

Preparations. Up to this point or, in other words, the last 9 chapters, the techniques presented were related more to the preparation of the future projector and the basic techniques for producing lucid projection.

Classification. As for the techniques derived for lucid projection, per se, or the formal systems for inducing projection, one must start with their classification.

Hundreds. Hundreds of the most diverse ancient, new and perfected techniques, and their variations, are available in order for consciousnesses to project themselves from the human body with lucidity in experiences induced by their own will.

Ideal. The ideal method, a single, safe, simple, entirely effective formula, that has received universal approval or viability and is adequate for everyone, a veritable common denominator, still does not exist. We also do not expect it to be developed very soon.

Personalities. This fact is due to the diversification of personalities, physical constitutions, human character, individual behavior and the existence of 3 highly complex ultraphysical vehicles – the holochakra, psychosoma and mentalsoma – that are unequally developed and are evolutionarily organized as individual instruments of each intraphysical consciousness.

Inadequacies. Although the current alternative methods are incomparably superior to those employed half-a-century ago, for example, they still are inadequate to meet the practical needs of all individuals with disparate sex, age, biotype, temperament and conduct.

Patrimony. If a universal method existed, totally lucid projection would already be the patrimony of all individuals in many intraphysical societies, on various levels of civilization, from time immemorial.

Knowledge. We presently have to be content with the fragmented knowledge that is currently available to us, because our ignorance in many areas of projectiology is still significant and we are defiantly continuing in this field of research which is still affected by obscurities, mysteries, enigmas, unknowns or questions.

Reasons. There are many correct ways of predisposing the projective process in a good human environment (holothosene). You therefore should not use only a single technique to produce lucid projection, but take advantage of everything that will permit you to healthily attain the objective of projecting with lucidity and good recall, according to the physical and extraphysical conditions of the moment.

Attributes. The techniques for one to project oneself are based on 1 or several attributes of one's own consciousness, such as: imagination, visualization and mental concentration.

Mega-strong-trait. You, an aspirant to lucid projection, should verify, with extreme self-critique, which is your best consciential attribute or your mentalsomatic mega-strong-trait or that in which you are most versatile, in order to use it as a fundamental resource.

Abilities. The acts of relaxing both mentally and physically, clearing the mind with ease and redirecting attention outward from the human body are the most necessary and promising abilities you can present as an aspirant to having major lucid projections.

Self-confidence. On the other hand, if you admit or are confident that a certain technique will work for you, this will probably occur.

Combinations. Sometimes, it is more valuable to combine different methods in order to leave the human body, individually adapting them to your temperament, inclinations and circumstances. However, to be truly effective, any projection process tests your willpower in terms of being a fearless (projectiophilic), disciplined and perseverant person.

Chance. Assuming there is no universal method for voluntarily projecting that works for all intraphysical consciousnesses in an indistinct and generalized manner, a set of greatly varied, although select, techniques are presented here.

Suitability. It is worth your knowing all possible projective techniques in order to ensure the greatest possible chance of encountering at least one that will work for you or is better suited to your temperament and personal conditions. This technique should at least inspire you to attempt *to improvise your own specific,* individually ideal *method.*

Compensation. Practice all indirect, supplementary means and do so on a long-term basis, because lucid projection compensates for all your persistent efforts and performance.

Suitability. As you will see, there are processes for projecting that can help a certain microminority of individuals, as they better adapt to the conditions of a specific projector. This technique would be suitable in terms of highly personalized prerequisites, such as the following 9:

1. **Lungs.** The individual with good lungs: carbon dioxide technique.
2. **Suggestion.** The person who is impressionable: hetero-hypnosis technique.
3. **Art.** The individual with an artistic temperament: projectiogenic images technique.
4. **Duo.** The partner in an evolutionary duo: the sex act technique.
5. **Will.** The person with a strong will: physiological resources technique.
6. **Music.** The music lover: the musical pieces or melodies technique.
7. **Paraperceptiology.** The sufficiently developed and active sensitive: the technique of projection assisted by a helper.
8. **Dreamer.** The constant dreamer: the projectiogenic dream technique.
9. **Intellectuality.** The intellectual individual: the technique of projection in the mentalsoma.

Sleep. Some techniques can only be used by those who sleep alone, otherwise the practitioner will disturb the individual who is sleeping beside him/her (e.g.: the partner in an evolutionary duo).

Company. There are techniques for the aided projector, that is, one who is in the company of someone else, such as: sex act, hetero-hypnosis, massage and visualizations, music and visualizations, assisted projection, transmissibility.

Veterans. There are also techniques for the veteran projector: mentalsoma, repetition and rolling over backward.

Movement. Other projective techniques require movement, e.g.: the sex act, carbon dioxide, mantras, massage, pineal, break-in-routine and rotation.

Preferred. Of all the techniques herein described for voluntary projection or projection provoked by your consciousness or your will, two stand out as being preferred or advantageous because they are easier and spontaneous: self-hypnosis and projectiogenic dream.

Better. In spite of what has already been said, researchers have still not proven that there is one method that is better than the others for producing lucid consciential projection.

Motivation. All projective methods can work if you master the techniques that help to induce progressive, deep neurological and muscular relaxation, and simultaneously maintain sufficient motivation to temporarily leave the human body.

Others. Besides those mentioned, which are considered to be the most functional, hundreds of other processes exist for consciential projecting with lucidity, in accordance with the tendencies of your personality as an aspirant to being a lucid consciential projector or even as a veteran experimenter. The following 6 categories are examples:

1. **Extraphysical:** a direct and realistic request for assistance made to a known helper, an extraphysical consciousness which inspires confidence in you to project with lucidity.

2. **Paraperceptive:** application of energetic touches (consciential chakroprojection) in order to intensify the personal vibrational state (VS) and produce the departure of the psychosoma.

3. **Psychological:** monoideism regarding a certain chosen form that one endeavors to see in a dream, or even the process of emotional shock (consciential traumatoprojection).

4. **Chemical:** the use of several special drugs, including anesthetics (consciential narcoprojection).

5. **Physiological:** a back-and-forth nodding movement of the head which has been flung backward (consciential cephaloprojection).

6. **Physical:** placing oneself in the rhythmically flashing light of a stroboscopic lamp (consciential stroboprojection); electric shock (consciential electroprojection); sensory deprivation; restricted environment; decrease in personal vitality; flotation with total solitary confinement, in total darkness and complete silence, in a tank of water that has been chemically prepared; wearing a jacket so tight that you can hardly move; and breathing through a tube (consciential hydroprojetion).

Deprivation. *Sensory deprivation,* or perceptual isolation, is the name given to the prolonged, and practically complete, deprivation of sensory stimulation obtained in a laboratory or experimental chamber – in a rigidly monotonous environment, or a situation in which absolutely nothing occurs, as all standardized or perceptual stimulation has been removed – following this technical orientation involving 5 variables:

1. **Room.** Use a soundproof room in which a monotonal masking sound is transmitted through headphones, which blocks out other noises that might still be able to penetrate the air-conditioned room.

2. **Bed.** Lie down on a comfortable bed.

3. **Pillow.** Place your head on a U-shaped pillow that covers your ears.

4. **Glasses.** Put on glasses with frosted glass (or ping pong ball halves over the eyes) that do not permit any visual perception.

5. **Cardboard.** Put on cotton gloves and wrap your arms in long cardboard tubes that extend past your fingers, in order to block tactile perceptions.

Rigidity. These arduous and rigid conditions can clearly help any intraphysical consciousness produce lucid consciential projection.

Phenomena. In the application of any of the projective techniques, your consciousness may experience common phenomena, such as: the vibrational state; lucid dream or semilucid consciential projection; harmless physical catalepsy; and others.

Ointment. The following is a medieval recipe – among many existing recipes – of "astral projection ointments" to be applied to the entire human body prior to a projective experiment. These are very popular in certain parapsychic study circles. Contents: 5 ounces of lanolin; 1 ounce of hashish; 1 handful of hemp flowers; 1 handful of poppy flowers; ½ handful of hellebore.

Placebo. The greater function of these ointments as resources for the production of lucid projection is only psychological or autosuggestive (placebo).

Attempts. It is evidently unnecessary for you to practice all the methods, but you have nothing to lose by making some attempts at conscientially projecting with a certain degree of lucidity using any method that is harmless to your physical or mental health, since no specific minimum standardization for the control of the basic technical parameters for projective methods has been established yet.

Order. In the following chapters, the author has taken the responsibility of distinguishing the best techniques for you to lucidly project. They are currently those most widely known and used, and are the most adaptable to each practitioner, according to his/her projective capacity, psychophysical predispositions and individual motivation.

Bibliography: Baker (69, p. 56), Battersby (92, p. 11), Blackmore (139, p. 94), Bord (170, p. 53), Boswell (174, p. 137), Castaneda (258, p. 113), Crawford (313, p. 64), Crookall (331, p. 64; 340, p. 25), Denning (391, p. 157), Fox (544, p. 32), Frost (560, p. 45), Greene (635, p. 38), Greenhouse (636, p. 255), Hall (671, p. 39), Huxley (771, p. 234), Jagot (799, p. 155), King (846, p. 107), Lefebure (909, p. 63), Lilly (926, p. 7), Martin (1002, p. 46), Miranda (1050, p. 78), Mittl (1061, p. 4), Monroe (1065, p. 215), Muldoon (1105, p. 314), Ophiel (1150, p. 35), Rogo (1444, p. 19), Salley (1496, p. 160), Schiff (1515, p. 120), Sculthorp (1531, p. 17), Steiger (1601, p. 157), Turvey (1707, p. 157), Vieira (1762, p. 8), Yram (1897, p. 51).

207. OPENING DOOR TECHNIQUE

Steps. This is the opening door technique, which induces you to lucidly project from your human body. It is given here in 8 steps:

1. **Isolation.** Isolate yourself in a closed room where you will not be disturbed while practicing the exercises. Remain in the nude or use only light, loose clothes.

2. **Armchair.** Sit straight-backed in a comfortable chair, or armchair, with hands on thighs.

3. **Imagination.** Close the eyes and imagine, using the obstinate force of your ironclad will, a closed door set in a white wall.

4. **Inscription.** On the closed door, mentally inscribe a characteristic symbol, such as the infinity symbol (∞).

5. **Meditation.** Meditate on the inscription on the closed door for a few minutes.

6. **Opening.** Intensely visualize the door opening slowly and endeavor to see yourself going through the open door to the other side of the white wall.

7. **Repetition.** Repeat all steps of the exercise, in the correct order, intensifying the visualization more and more each time.

8. **Exteriorization.** The exteriorization of your psychosoma will occur suddenly with a sensation of extreme lightness and ample freedom of extraphysical movement in the paramembers of the psychosoma.

Bibliography: Fortune (540, p. 154), Grant-Veillard (623, p. 93), King (846, p. 114), Martin (1002, p. 57), Rogo (1444, p. 54), Walker (1781, p. 112).

208. PROJECTIVE SEX ACT TECHNIQUE

Definition. Projective sex act: procedure through which a man and a woman release the libido and simultaneously, or due to this, produce a lucid projection experience.

Synonymy: joint projective orgasm; libidoprojection; projectiogenic orgasm; projectiogenic sexual union; projective sexual intercourse.

Predisposition. According to public opinion polls, one of the existing and verified conditions for the deliberate or spontaneous production of the human lucid projection experience is precisely when the individual is having a sexual orgasm.

Impact. This is why certain people can produce the lucid projection experience far more easily during the sex act or soon after a joint orgasm. This happens due to the emotional impact of orgasm

VIII – Lucid Projection Techniques

445

and the extreme degree of relaxation and the predisposition of the human body and mind to undergo natural sleep after the sex act.

Relaxant. It is known that sexual hormones exert a certain relaxing effect upon both men and women.

Sexology. In the study of sexology without taboos – relative to lucid projection experiences – it becomes imperative to start from the fact that the sex act is not ugly, dirty, sordid, prohibited, painful or disagreeable.

Physiology. On the contrary, the sex act is a gift of biology, an active part of the natural physiology of the human creature, that can also be used simply for the pleasure that it gives one, without any medical reason or sense of guilt.

Repressions. What has made the understanding of sex more difficult is the absence of advanced sexosomatics education due to ignorance (excessive repressions, preconceptions) regarding sexual techniques, attitudes or norms considered to be correct.

Reduction. Sex is the world's most popular revitalizing agent or stress reduction technique.

Benefits. Practiced correctly, the sex act combines the benefits of active aerobic exercise, aside from its vibrant impact, with the fundamental high point of the individual's thoughts and emotion.

Reactions. The benefits of the sex act are reflected throughout the human body through the following 4 basic reactions:

1. **Circulation.** An intensification in blood circulation.
2. **Heart.** An acceleration in heartbeat.
3. **Respiration.** An elevation in respiratory capacity.
4. **Relaxation.** The triggering of deep muscular relaxation.

Tranquility. This process for projecting with lucidity is only recommended for partners in an evolutionary duo, couples who are married or of any other condition as long as they have an active sexlife that is also tranquil, devoid of anxieties, guilt or any other concerns in the phase subsequent to the sexual union.

Time. The most adequate time for this practice is in the second half of the night or, more precisely, between 2 and 4 o'clock in the morning, when neither partner has any kind of concern or duty to perform immediately after the sex act.

Unconcern. The lucid projection candidate, during or immediately after the sex act, should remain completely unconcerned about surrounding human life, during and after the orgasm, allowing the impact of his/her emotions to dislocate his/her consciousness from the human body and the sleep state to come over the physical body without loss of lucidity, only thinking about projecting to the extraphysical dimension, removing all other ideas from his/her intraconsciential world.

Bathroom. Ideally, when possible, both partners will always wait to go to the bathroom until later, after the projective experience.

Men. Men usually benefit more from the sex act technique because, according to verifications of modern sexology, they tend to sleep more soundly than women after sexual union.

Advantages. The use of the projective sex act technique presents 5 indisputable advantages:

1. **Habit.** It naturally creates the habit – for the partner in an evolutionary duo who has a disciplined mind and consolidated habits – of projecting with lucidity soon thereafter.
2. **Deintrusion.** It avoids extraphysical traumas and strengthens the lucid projectors when faced with troublesome approaches by ill or energivorous extraphysical consciousnesses pursuing animal emotions or consciential energies of sexual origin.
3. **Erections.** It eliminates many occurrences of penile as well as clitoral erections, which are more frequent in sexually-deprived persons.

4. **Joint.** It permits a greater agility for the evolutionary duo to obtain joint lucid projections.

5. **Union.** It facilitates a deeper and fuller extraphysical union for both sexual partners, which will be reflected in their shared life in the ordinary, physical waking state.

Restriction. During the sex act performed in the "missionary" position (with the man on top of the woman), the woman is frequently not able to experience full pleasure due to the force of the man's weight restricting her movements. This restraining condition, or sensory deprivation, sometimes generates a sudden lucid projection, according to reports made by some women who are physically more fragile than their partner.

Karezza. The projective sex act technique should not be confused with *Karezza,* also called *magical masturbation,* or sexual union without orgasm, frequently prolonged over various hours. It is a magical practice vehemently disapproved of by the majority of psychologists and sexologists, and one of which the author also disapproves. The aim of this practice is the achievement of a hallucinatory trance, or hypnagogic state, wherein both partners have contact with extraphysical consciousnesses.

Sexochakra. According to holochakrology, we should bear in mind that the effectiveness of the projective sex act technique greatly depends upon the quality of the energy of the sexochakra of the male (androchakra) or female (gynochakra) intraphysical consciousness practitioner.

Bibliography: Denning (391, p. 203), Frost (560, p. 65), King (846, p. 128), Rampa (1361, p. 20), Twemlow (1710, p. 452), Vieira (1752, p. 21).

209. PROJECTIVE SELF-IMAGE TECHNIQUE

Definition. Projective self-image: the image, in this case strictly physical or human, that you mentally have of yourself and which helps you to lucidly project from the soma or cellular body (see fig. 209, p. 1,132).

Synonymy: narcissistic technique; projective mirror technique; projective self-reflection; self-awareness of the human form.

Reflection. This method for the consciousness to project from the human body with lucidity is ideal for those who are able to sleep while seated in an armchair and is based on a detailed narcissistic study of awareness of oneself, self-knowledge or of the self-image reflected on a smooth surface, preferably a mirror. However, other surfaces can also be used to good effect, such as still, clean water, polished metal, glass or a crystal ball.

Transference. Through the self-image technique, the consciousness of the observer passes *into* the completely flat mirror or, in other words, to one's reflected image, in a process similar to that in which the human consciousness leaves the human body and goes inside a nearby, motionless, physical object. In this case, one feels and perceives from the perspective of the object, as if the human body – a physical object – was temporarily substituted by another physical object.

Technique. The following is the projective self-image technique, that induces you to lucidly project from your human body, through the following 7 steps:

1. **Isolation.** At bedtime, isolate yourself in a closed room where you will not be disturbed while practicing the exercises. Go to the bathroom and attend to any physiological needs prior to the technique, then put on a loose pair of pajamas.

2. **Armchair.** Sit in a comfortable armchair placed in front of a big mirror that reflects your entire human body when you stand. The armchair must be placed near the light switch of the artificial light source that illuminates the room.

3. **Inspection.** Then carefully inspect every detail of your own reflection in the mirror, as though you had never analyzed yourself before, discovering aspects that you had never noticed.

Note each expression, shape, color and contour of every physical component of your face, hair, forehead, eyebrows, eyes, nose, mouth, chin and ears in a reflexive, circumstantiated self-examination.

4. **Name.** Stand and examine your entire body and finally fix your attentive observation on your eyes or directly into the pupils. In this position, repeat your own name several times clearly and audibly, as if it were a mantra.

5. **Visualization.** Visualize yourself, alive, in the place of the reflected image. Make it move as though it were your real form, just like your consciousness acting while outside the human body.

6. **Sleep.** Keep this visualization intense. Forget the mirror and the present physical circumstances until you are overcome by sleep or physical fatigue.

7. **Saturation.** In the most intense phase of the visualization, give in to the urge to sleep, turn off the light and sleep in the armchair, preferably, or in a nearby bed (as a last resort), with the mind saturated with your vital image.

Television. The image of your mirrored figure, created in your mind, is similar to the luminous image retained in your vision as a television viewer when you go to sleep at night immediately after switching off the TV in your bedroom.

Impression. If the transference of your consciousness to the reflected image was very intense and deep, it impresses your subconscious will to such an extent that the psychosoma is projected with your consciousness, thus occurring your immediate extraphysical awakening and the beginning of your lucid consciential projection, per se.

Bibliography: Bord (170, p. 56), Carrington (245, p. 259), Farrar (496, p. 193), Greene (635, p. 32), Huson (768, p. 113), King (845, p. 118), Muldoon (1105, p. 217), Rogo (1444, p. 54), Shay (1546, p. 62).

210. SELF-VISUALIZATION WITH OPEN EYES TECHNIQUE

Base. This exercise is based on visualization of the separation of your psychosoma with your eyes *open*, which is not easy. However, the difficulty diminishes with practice and when you have already mastered the self-visualization with *closed* eyes technique.

Indications. The process of visualization with open eyes is indicated only for the individual who has a predominance of visual memory in visualizations, general perceptions and common observations, and who is endowed with a powerful imagination.

Technique. The following is the self-visualization with open eyes technique that induces you to lucidly project from your human body in 4 steps:

1. **Isolation.** Isolate yourself in a closed room where you will not be disturbed while practicing the exercises. Remain in the nude or use only light, loose clothing.

2. **Bed.** Lie on your back and extend the arms alongside the body.

3. **Visualization.** While keeping the eyes open, visualize, just like someone watching a film, the separation of your psychosoma gradually leaving your entire human body.

4. **Progression.** Visualize the formation of your extraphysical feet (parafeet), then paralegs, paratrunk, para-arms and parahead, slowly and in minute detail, until you can distinctly see your entire double (psychosoma) distinctly formed outside your human body.

Illumination. You should choose whether to leave the room illuminated or in a penumbra, according to the influence of light on your pupils (photophobia).

Bibliography: Martin (1002, p. 55), Walker (1781, p. 106).

211. STEP COUNTING TECHNIQUE

Trip. This technique is based on the detailed visualization of a specific trip, used to visit a loved one, with a precise number of steps to complete the journey.

Return. You imagine yourself leaving your house, taking the necessary number of steps and then reaching the house you want to visit. You knock at the door and it is opened by the person you want to visit. Your empathy with this person can potentiate the effects of the technique. You should return to your own house taking the same number of steps.

Demands. The step counting method demands considerable concentration, vivid visualization and the precise number of steps and details regarding the route (itinerary, trajectory).

Variation. The most common and practical variation of this method is for the projector to leave the bedroom and go to the kitchen of his/her house or apartment, observing and visualizing the smallest details of the physical particularities along this domestic route that has been visited and examined in detail many, many times while in the ordinary, physical waking state.

Blueprint. It is always better to carefully repeat the exercises, without getting discouraged, even using a blueprint of the location and drawings of every possible detail of all existing furniture and interior decoration in the building, indicating at least 6 main points chosen along the route, such as:

1. Picture frame on the wall.
2. Point of illumination.
3. Flower vase.
4. Hallway corner.
5. Coffee table.
6. Television.

Impression. The exact impression of the details of the objects and the angles of the route in the individual's memory ends up leading the experimenter to have a projection, extraphysical awareness and the unimpeded travel of the domestic route in the psychosoma.

Bibliography: Crawford (313, p. 68), Martin (1002, p. 59), Muldoon (1105, p. 221), Ophiel (1150, p. 27), Walker (1781, p. 112).

212. CARBON DIOXIDE TECHNIQUE

Definition. Carbon dioxide technique: this well-known gas, when at elevated levels in the pulmonary alveoli (hypercapnia) and circulatory system, generally in an atoxic mixture or without any serious side effects, of 7 parts (70%) oxygen and 3 parts (30%) carbon gas, diminishes the efficiency of the functioning of the brain and permits the freeing of the consciousness manifesting in the psychosoma.

Synonymy: carbon anhydride technique; carbonoprojection; CO_2 technique; hypercarbonic technique; intentional asphyxia; lack of air; oxygen starvation; premeditated suffocation; voluntary agony.

Atmosphere. Carbon dioxide (formula CO_2) is an incombustible, colorless, odorless, heavy gas. It is nontoxic, although an asphyxiant. It makes up 0.02% of the atmosphere at sea level.

Liquid. Carbon dioxide is soluble in water and alcohol. It liquefies at a pressure of 5 atmospheres and a temperature of -68.8°F, degrees Fahrenheit (-56°C, degrees Celsius or centigrade).

Evaporation. At normal pressure, part evaporates and part solidifies, forming dry ice (solid carbonic anhydride or carbonic snow), used to maintain low temperatures: -128.2°F, degrees Fahrenheit (-89°C, degrees Celsius).

Meteorology. This gas is employed in the preparation of carbonated beverages, in medicine, in fire extinguishers and, in solid form, in the seeding of clouds, with the aim of modifying the structure of the cloud and provoking its precipitation or dissipation.

Botany. Carbon dioxide is an indispensable food for plants, being eliminated by living beings as a result of cellular respiration.

Psychiatry. Carbon gas, as mentioned above, has already been therapeutically administered to psychoneurotic patients via mask. This generated an ample variety of subjective sensory phenomena that were extremely similar to the near-death experience (NDE), including the exact sensation of the separation of the consciousness from the human body and consciential self-bilocation.

NDE. This proves that the retention of carbon dioxide in the brain – when the individual is exposed to extreme hypercarbonic conditions – can trigger the near-death experience, which ends up being inoffensive or, more precisely, becomes a forced lucid projection.

Alterations. Changes in the velocity and intensity of respiration influence the heartbeat and blood pressure, altering the levels of oxygen, carbon dioxide, acids, alkali, lactates and calcium in the circulatory system. This also affects the normal functioning (neurophysiology) of the cerebral hemispheres, in either a serious or inoffensive manner.

Symptoms. Hypoxia, privation provoked by a low or inadequate level of oxygen in the tissues, and hypoxemia, a lack of oxygen in the circulatory system – a consequence, for example, of a reduction in atmospheric pressure – constitute forms of *oxygen starvation* producing symptoms of asphyxia, suffocation, ringing in the head, lack of muscular coordination, visual alterations, dizziness, psychic absence, perspiration, emotional instability, loss of critical judgment, hallucinations and other xenophrenic states.

Hypobaropathy. Each organ of the human body has a very different tolerance to hypoxia.

Disturbances. A lack of oxygen in breathed air causes disturbances that receive various denominations, such as: hypobaropathy; altitude sickness; mountain sickness; airsickness; *soroche; apunamiento.*

Mountain climbing. This phenomenon occurs with human beings (e.g.: mountain climbers) when they are at high altitudes, above 3.73 mi. (6,000 m), on mountains or in airplanes.

Chamber. The normal air in the consciential projector's bedroom (energetically shielded chamber) contains 21% oxygen and can be considered to have 0% carbon dioxide.

Desoma. It is important to mention that if carbon dioxide (CO_2, anhydrous carbon) is inhaled in its 100% pure state, it immediately causes the deactivation (desoma) or *death of the human body* through asphyxia or suffocation. In this case, the person inhales without oxygenating the blood.

Appendectomy. In Brazil, in 1986, a case of medical error occurred, with international repercussions for the professional involved when – during an appendectomy – carbon gas, being mistaken for oxygen, was applied to a young patient.

Ecology. In 1989, at the international meeting in Paris known as *Planet Earth*, carbon gas was unanimously chosen as *The Earth's Number 1 Enemy* by 180 experts from 40 different countries, assembled with the proposal of reducing the escalating levels of pollution.

Combustion. It has been shown that 80% of carbon gas emissions into the atmosphere are caused by the burning of carbon, petroleum and gas, and only 20% is due to deforestation.

Harmlessness. It is interesting to emphasize the pacific, harmless and positive use of carbonic gas within projectiology.

Occurrences. Six occurrences arise in the field of projectiology due to the decrease of oxygen in the lungs with a consequent increase of carbon dioxide in the tissues: the rhythmic respiration technique; near-death experiences; accidents with asphyxiation; lucid projections in prisons; the existence of inadequate sleeping habits; voluntary mini-deaths.

1. **Respiration.** Hypercapnia, excessive carbon dioxide in the blood and, consequently, an elevated level of carbon dioxide in the brain, explains the mechanism by which the rhythmic respiration technique operates. This is used in the respiratory exercises of yoga which, when practiced systematically, induce prolonged suspensions in respiration or, in other words, a retention of expiration or reduction in respiratory rhythm, interrupted by pauses and leaves the experimenter slightly oxygen starved or in a condition of voluntary agony.

2. **Near-death.** Carbon dioxide is normally formed in the brain as an end product of cerebral cellular metabolism. The incoming, pure or oxygen-rich blood supply that takes oxygen to the brain is also responsible for the return transport – impure blood or that mixed with carbon dioxide – of carbon dioxide out of the brain in order for the CO_2 to finally be expelled by the lungs. A stoppage in the flow of pure blood provokes a heart attack (infarct, myocardial infarction), a hypercarbonized brain (hypercarbia), as well as a great number of near-death experiences (NDE), and, in certain cases, departures of the consciousness from the human body.

3. **Accidents.** The increase in carbon dioxide in order to produce lucid projection even occurs with a certain frequency, in a spontaneous manner, without the deliberate intention of the intraphysical consciousness, in serious accidents that generate suffocation or asphyxiation.

4. **Solitary.** The same process of increasing carbon dioxide unconsciously produces involuntary lucid projection in confined individuals in restrictive total institutions, such as prison inmates in cells and solitary confinement cells with reduced cubage where the air is polluted and has reduced oxygen content.

Solitude. Incidentally, ordinary clairvoyance gives a new meaning to multidimensional life and makes the scorn insignificant that the external social and human world may heap upon the intraphysical consciousness, for any reason.

Relationships. One's circle of consciential relationships amplifies without limits. The intraphysical consciousness will never again feel alone, solitary or completely isolated.

5. **Covers.** The condemned habit of a person covering the head with the blankets while sleeping, thus diminishing his/her capacity for inhaling oxygen and increasing the level of carbon dioxide in the space around the face, or nostrils, in certain cases facilitates lucid projection of the consciousness in the psychosoma.

Migraine. It is worth remembering that the person who likes to sleep after daybreak and pulls the covers over the head to block out the sunlight entering the window can end up suffering from headaches or migraines.

6. **Mini-death.** The use of carbon dioxide evidences the similarity between the phenomenon of lucid projection – also called a *preview* of death – and the experience of biological and definitive first desoma. If inhaled in its pure form, carbon dioxide provokes the death of the human body; if inhaled in small amounts or volumes (30%), it predisposes lucid projection in the psychosoma. The carbon dioxide technique therefore endeavors to produce the deliberate mini-death phenomenon.

Technique. In spite of what has been said so far and as long as you have good lungs and a trouble-free heart and cardiorespiratory system, you can produce simple, harmless and voluntary intoxication following physiological processes by increasing carbonic-acid gas levels in the tissues of your own human body.

Slow. By breathing slowly or, in other words, by inhaling a smaller volume of *air* and, therefore, a smaller amount of *oxygen* and a greater volume of leftover *carbon dioxide,* you hold or reduce the exchange of gases. In this way, the human body is predisposed to free the psychosoma, with a slight discoincidence of the psychosoma in relation to the dense body.

Effects. The abovementioned process, upon decreasing the activity of your two cerebral hemispheres, will provoke sleep, reduce your heart rate, generally deaden your physiology and dislodge your psychosoma from dense matter.

Duration. Your inhalation or the act of inhaling air (with oxygen) into your lungs is normally equal to the duration of your exhalation, or the act of expelling air from the lungs.

Time. Following this process, the retention of air in your lungs, and therefore of carbon dioxide, should be half of your inhalation or more, up to 3 or 4 times its duration. You need to execute this little by little, through repeated respiratory exercises.

Beginning. Initially, the time relationship between inhalation, the act of retaining air in the lungs and exhalation should be, 12 seconds to inhale, 48 seconds to retain the air, and 24 seconds to exhale.

Maintenance. With a chronometer in front of you, slowly increase the period of retention of the air in your lungs, until reaching the maintenance phase of inhaling for 16 seconds, retaining the air for 64 seconds, and exhaling for 32 seconds.

Totals. Always on an empty stomach, perform 20 complete cycles in each session in order to obtain compensatory results.

Repetitions. Some practitioners repeat the exercises 4 times a day.

Greenhouse. A greenhouse filled with plants can serve as an excellent physical base during the day, with the person lying down inside, in a peaceful environment.

Photosynthesis. Through the mechanism of photosynthesis, plants exteriorize carbon dioxide during the day, thus increasing the level of CO_2 in the practitioner's organism or, in other words, diminishing the oxygen level in the environment and its inhalation into your lungs.

Deprivation. This important process installs a condition of light gaseous intoxication, predisposes the takeoff of the psychosoma (sensory deprivation), composing, in a reverse manner, the mechanism of the projective technique through carbon dioxide. Instead of retaining CO_2 in the organism, one inhales a greater amount of this gas, in this case.

Cubage. It is very important to observe the cubage and sealing of the greenhouse, the quantity of plants, quality of the internal air and the duration of the experimenter's stay inside the greenhouse, so that the gas does not end up generating a serious intoxication for the individual remaining there. There are intraphysical consciousnesses who have gone through desoma due to intoxication inside a greenhouse.

Caverns. Throughout time, ancient initiates, seers and prophets, such as founders of religions, Moses (seventh century, B.C.) and Zoroaster (eighth century, B.C.), as well as meditators, hermits, yogis, Indians, Tibetan yogis and others, have chosen grottos or caverns that have been carved by humans, sculpted out of the stone portion of mountains by nature, or those which are existent in the desert, as their residences, isolated self-imprisonments, or favorite retreats for the improvement of their animic-parapsychic performance.

Factors. The use of natural stone caverns develops consciously or even unconsciously, or perhaps it is more accurate to say instinctively, due to the following 6 factors:

1. **Stones.** The stones of a cavern, including stalactites and stalagmites, offer natural protection against bad weather, winds and brusque changes in the ambient temperature between day and night.

2. **Isolation.** Caves, as natural sources of shelter, offer shade, penumbra and the silence necessary for complete isolation or solitary consciential confinement.

3. **Physiology.** The rarefied air inside a cave, a lack of exposure to bad weather and minimal physical movement significantly reduce the practitioner's physiological needs, reducing to a minimum the hygiene habits indispensable for maintaining one's human body.

4. **Humidity.** The humidity in a cavern helps to lower the temperature and maintain it there, which predisposes all types of parapsychic categories.

5. **Pineal.** A cave can offer complete isolation from light sources. This is very important, as it is known that the pineal gland – which is presumed to be closely connected to clairvoyance, parapsychic phenomena in general and the encephalic chakras (coronochakra, frontochakra, nuchal chakra) – is highly photosensitive. The activity of the pineal gland is activated by darkness and inhibited by light. In humans, this influence occurs through the sympathetic nervous system.

6. **Dioxide.** A decrease in the oxygen level of air circulating in a cave generates projection of the consciousness through a natural discoincidence of the vehicles of manifestation under the action of an increasingly high concentration of carbon dioxide in the cave upon the human organism or, in other words, in the pulmonary alveoli and circulatory system. This doubtlessly constitutes the most important and decisive factor in producing consciential projection.

Hypercapnia. It is worth clarifying that hypercapnia is the excess of carbon dioxide gas in the blood that first provokes neuropsychic effects, including torpor and somnolence. At a more elevated level, the accumulation of CO_2 in the blood triggers pathological conditions until arriving at periodic respiration, or Cheyne-Stokes respiration, which is observed in comatose states or sometimes in deep sleep and, in the absence of a superior regulation, stems from a bulbar reflex.

Base. It is easy to infer from these facts that, aside from the primitive nature of the process of its use, the cave undoubtedly constitutes an excellent physical base for the production of lucid projections of the intraphysical consciousness, especially using the carbon dioxide technique in a restricted environment with sensory deprivation.

Cardiochakra. According to holochakrology, it should not be forgotten that the effectiveness of the carbon dioxide technique greatly depends upon the quality of the cardiochakra energies of the intraphysical consciousness practitioner.

Bibliography: Brennan (199, p. 97), Brunton (217, p. 267), Charrière (274, p. 338), Huxley (771, p. 95), Lefebure (909, p. 208), Moore (1079, p. 58), Sabom (1486, p. 241), Vieira (1772, p. 8), Walker (1782, p. 342).

---

213. PROJECTIVE FACTOR TECHNIQUE

Definition. Projective factor: mental target, be it a target-object or specific target-place, that you use as a psychophysiological support for your lucid projection.

Synonymy: projective crutch; projective fixation factor; projective support.

Target-object. An intentionally-chosen target-object, as well as a target-place, can be used as a projective factor, element or point of focus outside your human body, in a paratropospheric extraphysical district.

Types. You can choose innumerous *target-objects,* however, only one must be used as a fixation factor, such as:

1. **Internal.** Inside the home (indoors) or in a closed area: an object of personal use; a book; a closed music box; a small decorative piece; a sculpture; a painting; and others.

2. **External.** Outside the home (outdoors) or in the open air: a bush; stone; sand dune; wall; and others.

Person. Obviously, a target-person can also be used.

Affinity. The location where the target-object is located is extremely important for you. As an aspirant to producing a lucid projection, you need to have an affinity or establish a rapport with the environment, like it, know it in great detail and even frequent the place, if necessary.

Target-places. You can choose one of these examples of target-places and use it as a fixation factor: a room or an internal area in a house or apartment; a portion of the garden or backyard of your physical base.

Spontaneous. Certain objects with which you identify, in locations that psychologically predispose you to the production of lucid projection, operate as natural projective factors, triggering non-programmed, spontaneous and surprising projections, sometimes even without your even being aware of the existence of a projective factor.

Bibliography: Castaneda (258, p. 149), Vieira (1762, p. 111).

214. PROJECTIVE HETERO-HYPNOSIS TECHNIQUE

Definition. Hetero-hypnosis: procedure through which a person (the hypnotist, who has strong will-power and a certain psychism or congenital magnetism (paragenetics)) influences another (the hypnotized subject), nullifying the subject's awareness and will, placing him/her into a specific psychic state, with or without trance, that releases the subject's subconscious powers. The subject will do what the hypnotist suggests by concentrating on a thought, idea, place or person, with post-hypnotic suggestions even possibly occurring.

Synonymy: bradyism; druidic sleep; hetero-suggestion; hypnoprojection; hypnotic lucid projection; hypnotic state; hypnotic suggestion; hypnotism; intellectual vivisection; mechanical suggestion; mesmerism; moral vivisection; nervous sleep; objective hypnosis; persuasive suggestion; *sofronization;* third-party suggestion.

Hypnotist. In order to avoid wasting time in the lobby of parapsychic phenomena, as well as useless efforts, frustrated attempts and wrong approaches, the ideal hypnotist (moral vivisectionist) for cooperating in participatory investigations of projectiology in general will always be a projectionist-physician-hypnotist.

Self-persuasion. This is because it is presumed that this person has already experienced the lucid projection phenomenon on his/her own in a spontaneous or voluntary manner and is convinced that the altered consciential state of lucid projection is, in fact, unique and extremely individual, and is not simply a suggested consciential condition, a mere inconsequential fabulation or morbid personification.

Conditions. The projective hetero-hypnosis technique, or the hypnotic lucid projection, is the same as projective self-hypnosis although, in this case, it is induced by someone else. It is indicated, as much as the other technique, only for those who are sensitive to deep hypnosis or who have the special conditions for this process.

Suggestion. In the ordinary, physical waking state, *suggestion* is every idea that is awakened in the human brain and accepted by it. Suggestion is the process wherein a person, without arguing, giving orders or coercing, directly induces another person to act in a certain manner or accept a certain opinion.

Hypersuggestibility. Hypnosis is a xenophrenic or supranormal state of hypersuggestibility that can be artificially provoked by various means.

Subhuman. It is worth clarifying that the process of magnetization (a type of hypnosis) of subhuman animals excludes or annihilates the hypothesis or *idea of suggestion* and the act of acceptance by the brain.

Resources. Different coadjutant resources are used in hetero-suggestion, in the sense of intensifying the *rapport* between the sensitive and the hypnotist, notably the following 16:

1. Blowing warm air at the patient.
2. Holding up the thumbs.
3. Hypnotic lights.
4. Inductive melodies.
5. Inhalation of subterraneous smoke, vapors or gases.
6. Magnetic passes, with or without contact.
7. Monotone speech.
8. Narcotics.
9. Relaxation lamps.
10. Rhythmic sounds.
11. Staring at a point of light.
12. Staring at shiny or polished surfaces.
13. Strong and brusque (gong) or light prolonged and repeated auditory or visual sensory stimulation.

14. Suggestions or verbal orders (hetero-suggestions).
15. Touching hypnogenic zones or points.
16. Use of aromas.

Mentally. In spite of this exemplificative enumeration, it is possible to hypnotize a person merely mentally and without the use of any ostensive crutch or external resource.

First. Currently, hetero-hypnosis has gained a well-defined scientific status, although many of its mechanisms are completely obscure. Apply this method, requesting that someone who is a competent hypnotist and in whom you trust implicitly to proceed, as a first step, to give you a hypnotic suggestion, resulting from an induced state of auric coupling.

Isolation. On an empty stomach, go to the bathroom and attend to all your physiological needs. Then, isolate yourself in a closed room together with the hypnotist, where neither of you will be disturbed while proceeding with the experiment.

Recorder. You can be accompanied by a third person who will monitor a silently functioning recorder.

Clothes. Wear light, loose clothing, remain barefoot or wear only socks.

Predisposition. Sit in a comfortable armchair where you can lean your head back. Inwardly predispose yourself receptively, with complete trust and passivity, to the suggestions that will be made.

Second. Once the hypnotic suggestion has been made, the hypnotist, in a second phase, stimulating your capacity to project (projectability), which all of us, intraphysical consciousnesses, naturally possess, induces you to have a lucid projection or, in other words, a departure of your consciousness from the human body in the psychosoma, and your indispensable recollection subsequent to the extraphysical experiences which will occur, stemming from 1 of 3 hypnotic states:

1. Somnolence.
2. Hypotaxia.
3. Hypnotic somnambulism.

Place. At this point, the hypnotist will induce your consciousness to extraphysically go to a certain place, the target-place, such as a house or apartment, the place and inhabitants of which neither you nor the hypnotist are familiar with, in order to avoid any kind of telepathic interference with the experiment.

Para-experiences. Once there, you will verify (para-experiences) what is occurring both intra and extraphysically, the persons present and other details of the environment and events that are of interest, later remembering the events witnessed or in which you participated.

Occurrences. In hetero-hypnotic suggestive induction, 3 intraconsciential conditions frequently occur:

1. **VS.** The vibrational state (VS).
2. **Trendelenburg.** The consciential condition of extraphysical Trendelenburg.
3. **Clairvoyance.** The phenomenon of traveling clairvoyance.

Sensations. Having a greater energetic sensibility on your part, as a person who is predisposed toward lucid projection, you will clearly feel the waves of consciential energy that flow from the hypnotist during the trance process, which potentiate, transport or accompany the suggestions that he/ she makes.

Bi-controlled. The bi-controlled projection, or one that is controlled in two existential dimensions, is a more complex and sophisticated consciential experience that stems firstly from a projection of yours, that is controlled by the hypnotist, until your consciousness, projected in the psychosoma, encounters a helper – a beneficent extraphysical consciousness – which, after encountering you in a projected state, will start to give you continuous extraphysical assistance from that point on, thereby assuming command of the experiment.

Dehypnosis. In this case, an alteration of *dehypnosis* or, in other words, the final stage of the hypnotic state occurs.

Percentage. Unfortunately, the hypnotic technique does not function equally for all intraphysical beings to project themselves with lucidity, since only a small percentage of the population is able to reach a sufficiently deep hypnotic trance.

Depth. It has been possible to objectively measure the depth of the hypnotic state in the laboratory using a voltmeter.

Efficiency. Despite everything, hetero-hypnosis is one of the most efficient techniques used to produce the experience of human lucid projection.

Controlled. It would be unwise to confuse assisted lucid projection, in which a consciousness is assisted from the takeoff of the psychosoma and receives assistance outside the human body during the entire experiment from a visible or intangible helper, with lucid projection controlled by a human hypnotist who places your consciousness in a deep hypnotic sleep and monitors your extraphysical activities through appropriate suggestions (hypnotic consciential projection).

Traveling. Incidentally, it would not be honest for the hypnotist, regardless of the best of intentions that may be nurtured, to wish to only trigger the production of the traveling clairvoyance (emotional body) of the sensitives and stop there, letting them remain dependent upon or at the mercy of the hypnotist's consciential energies.

Independence. The hypnotist needs to insist that the sensitives make an effort to extraphysically evolve on their own, producing major lucid consciential projections, including those in the isolated mentalsoma, using their personal ironclad will.

Crutch. The hypnotist plays the role of a parapsychophysiological crutch for the traveling clairvoyant (dependent). Nevertheless, the hypnotist should also not continue being a crutch for the parapsychically lucid or self-sufficient lucid projector forever.

Slaveocrats. The hypnotist should strive for effective consciential maturity, on his/her part, and cannot stagnate the consciential development of other intraphysical consciousnesses, indefinitely sustaining groups of dependents or interconsciential slaves in the manner of the following 3 professional slaveocrats of this still pathological intraphysical society:

1. **Clinician.** The bygone clinician who would keep a patient's leg ulcer from healing.
2. **Clergyman.** The clergyman whose church construction never gets completed.
3. **Seducers.** Certain religious professionals, leader-mediums, gurus, psychoanalysts and bioenergetic seducers/seductresses who take advantage of incautious or parapsychically susceptible intraphysical consciousnesses through use of the consolation task, as they are motivated only by tropospheric financial-economic interests.

Satellites. According to evolutiology, consciousnesses should grow freely, like their own stars and not be reflective satellites (satellites of *intraphysical intruders*). They need to exist without psychological dependences, on their own, dispensing with *"...latries"*, with real discernment and consciential maturity.

Bibliography: Antunes (47, p. 155), Blackmore (139, p. 103), Blavatsky (153, p. 259), Brennan (199, p. 37), Brittain (206, p. 46), Castaneda (256, p. 122), Cavendish (266, p. 114), Chaplin (273, p. 83), Crookall (338, p. 135), D'arbó (365, p. 127), Depascale (392, p. 56), Dingwall (403, p. 90), Du Potet (433, p. 145), Fodor (528, p. 179), Gaynor (577, p. 81), Goldberg (606, p. 12), Holzer (751, p. 109), Jagot (799, p. 155), Kettelkamp (841, p. 27), Martin (1002, p. 67), Michaelus (1042, p. 278), Miranda (1050, p. 97), Morel (1086, p. 91), Moutin (1100, p. 367), Nebel (1118, p. 108), Russell (1482, p. 33), Saint-Jean (1494, p. 130), Shepard (1548, p. 448), Spence (1588, p. 216), Steiger (1601, p. 127), Still (1622, p. 24), Tondriau (1690, p. 238), Wambach (1793, p. 46), Wang (1794, p. 165), Zaniah (1899, p. 229).

215. PROJECTIVE SELF-HYPNOSIS TECHNIQUE

Definition. Self-hypnosis (OE: *self,* self; Greek: *hypnos, dream):* the hypnotic state induced through the practitioner's will.

Synonymy: autosuggestion; *estatuvolência;* hypnotic self-conditioning; hypnotic self-reaction; physiological projective method; progressive lucid projection; self-hypnoprojection; self-hypnotic projection; self-hypnotic suggestion; self-induced trance; self-mesmerism; statuvolence; subjective hypnosis; suggestion by oneself.

Pain. Self-hypnosis is currently employed as an effective technique for controlling cases of fear (phobias of various natures and origins), shock and even the most atrocious pain felt by soldiers in the line of battle, including the treatment of battle wounds.

Reactions. In this case, the individual, with the help of a tape recording of brief instructions from a specialist, substitutes the action of the hypnotist, thus producing the hypnotic reactions within him/herself.

Yoga. The cultivation of samadhi in yoga practices is a self-hypnotic process.

Easy. There are 2 processes whereby you can induce self-hypnosis in general:

1. Hetero-induction.
2. Autosuggestion.

Trance. The first process, hetero-induction, is easier, faster and more efficient. It is the act of permitting a capable, non-neophyte hypnotist, who is responsible and whom you trust completely, to put you into a hypnotic trance.

Word. Then, the hypnotist will give you a keyword that you can use from that point on to self-induce the projective trance again by saying the word out loud. This selected word functions as a post-hypnotic suggestion.

Bigdream. The hypnotist's suggestion might be similar to the following: "You are now in a deep sleep. In a moment I will awaken you, but before this I want you to know that every time you say the word *bigdream* in a loud voice, you will immediately fall into a deep sleep, just as you are sleeping now. The word is *bigdream.* Another person can say this word, but it will have no effect on you. However, when you say it in a loud voice, you will fall into a deep sleep like the one you are in now. While asleep, you will remain in control. You will be able to direct your mind where you wish it to go. You will be able to control your body and emotions when you are in this deep sleep".

Uncommon. The post-hypnotic suggestion, that is, the chosen keyword must be uncommon, not used in regular speech in order to avoid it being said by a friend or someone in a TV show, since this could cause some embarrassment (if a mistaken suggestion occurs) or, what is much worse, if you heard it on the radio while driving, for example. This could cause an accident if it actually induced you into a trance. Here are 5 examples of short, oxytone, invented words that can serve as keywords: *bantaz, chamum, nantur, parcol, transtal.*

Difficult. The second method for inducing self-hypnosis, and certainly a difficult one, is for you to produce it on your own. The technique should be the same as when the hypnotist puts the sensitive into a trance, the difference being that you will simultaneously be the hypnotist and the sensitive.

Hetero-hypnosis. The technique for self-hypnosis is the same as that for hetero-hypnosis, however being induced by yourself. It is indicated, as is the other, only for those persons who are sensitive to deep hypnosis, or who possess the special conditions for this process.

Self-determination. Still using the simple, spontaneous and less technical autosuggestion method, you must fearlessly decide to allow the human body to be commanded by your will that has been influenced by mental saturation with the idea of lucid projection. This should be done before you sleep, lying on your back on the bed, in a totally relaxed condition, imagining the departure of your psychosoma upward from the human body, until achieving the hypnagogic state, losing consciousness, awakening from an ordinary dream and floating above the bed.

Departure. Visualize yourself as a body leaving from within another body.

Flotation. Feel yourself abandoning the dense body as if you were floating on water.

Repetitions. You should repeat the above indicated procedure, neither lazily nor feverishly, but perseveringly, night after night, for at least 15 days in a row, gradually improving your psychophysiological performance.

Unconsciousness. After a while, the wish to leave the human body will become unconscious. You will then have the perfect impression that you are an *immaterial* being. You will, in fact, lose the notion of a crude and heavy human body and can often even feel yourself to be on a cloud, bodiless, massless and without any contact with the ground, floating and completely dematerialized (mentalsoma).

Emphasis. Whoever wishes to place greater emphasis on his/her own suggestion for lucidly projecting outside the human body can say out loud to him/herself: "I will leave this body, maintaining awareness and will see it on the bed!" Repeat this suggestion firmly at least 10 times.

Intercurrences. Meanwhile, you should not fail to observe frequent animic-parapsychic intercurrences, such as:

1. **VS.** The vibrational state (VS).
2. **Chakras.** The sensations of the chakras.
3. **Signage.** Parapsychic signals (personal signage).
4. **Clairvoyance.** The phenomena of clairvoyance.
5. **Clairaudience.** The phenomena of clairaudience.

Stimulants. These occurrences act as powerful stimulants, motivating you to proceed perseveringly in a deeply motivated manner and without discouragement, with the projective experiments.

Bibliography: Boswell (174, p. 138), Brennan (199, p. 43), Fox (544, p. 64), Goldberg (606, p. 19), Kettelkamp (841, p. 39), Knight (853, p. 56), Monroe (1065, p. 207), Nebel (1118, p. 113), Rampa (1366, p. 205), Rogo (1444, p. 168), Steiger (1601, p. 195), Vieira (1762, p. 205), Wang (1794, p. 161).

---

216. PROJECTIOGENIC IMAGES TECHNIQUE

Definition. Projectiogenic images: objective mental figurations that stimulate your consciousness to leave the human body using the psychosoma.

Synonymy: images stimulative of projection; projectiogenic figurations; projective visualization strategies.

Types. There are useful psychological techniques that act as triggering factors of your lucid projection. They are based in the creation, which is maintained in your mind, of 6 diverse types of objective mental images that stimulate the takeoff of the psychosoma, transporting the consciousness:

1. **Cone.** Visualize a conical form, whether an hourglass, successively smaller or larger circles, or a cone inside which your body contracts itself somewhat, in order to then expand, twisting yourself from the inside gradually outward until leaving the cone and obtaining, due to this compression, the exteriorization of your consciousness in the psychosoma.

2. **Rope.** Imagine climbing a rope, thereby giving movement to the psychosoma and thus dislodging it from the state of coincidence with the human body.

3. **Wave.** Imagine yourself being carried on the crest of a wave until you reach another environment, in this case the paratropospheric extraphysical dimension. An adequate suggestion for surfers.

4. **Evaporation.** Imagine the departure of your consciousness from the human body, as though the extraphysical body (psychosoma) were evaporating through all the pores of your dense organism.

5. **Tornado.** Concentrate intensely on the spiraling movement of a tornado (whirlwind, cyclone, twister), that is, a column of spiraling air or sand, wherein your consciousness is sucked up into the top of the column of air, contracting until it becomes a simple point of consciousness, when it will then leave the column of air moving upward. At this point, you will expand, reaching another existential dimension.

6. **Tank.** Elaborate the mental figure of a tank that gradually fills with water, on the surface of which you, as a point of light, float until finding a small opening at one side of the tank, through which you transfer yourself to the extraphysical paratropospheric dimension.

Bibliography: Huson (768, p. 112), Muldoon (1105, p. 314), Rogo (1444, p. 53), Shay (1546, p. 62).

217. LUCID PROJECTION THROUGH FASTING TECHNIQUE

Definition. Projective fasting: the partial and temporary abstinence from food with the objective of producing lucid projection of the consciousness outside the human body (soma).

Synonymy: diet control technique; projectiogenic fast; projectiogenic privation of food; projectiogenic suspension of food; projection through fasting; projection through hunger; projective nutritional abstinence; self-conservational projection; third day projection.

State. From a medical point of view, the human body is fasting when all previously ingested nourishment has already passed through the digestive process and been assimilated by the cells.

Antiquity. There have been few civilizations throughout human history – if indeed any have existed – whose religious and ethical systems did not at one time or another institutionalize the practice of regularly suspending alimentation.

Tribes. Ever since the tribal eras of the most primitive civilizations, there was always someone who affirmed that prolonged fasting, or the deliberate abstinence from food, helps free the extraphysical body of the consciousness or, in other words, the psychosoma from the soma.

Applications. Currently, at the close of the twentieth century, fasting is used for at least the following 4 rational reasons:

1. **Physiology.** A period of rest for the animal or human physiology.
2. **Antitoxic.** An efficient, natural means for reversing the toxemia of the human organism.
3. **Restoration.** Restoration of the individual's physical and mental health.
4. **Survival.** A Russian technique of periodic fasting for prolonging animal life (veterinary) and human life (medicine).

Starving. On the other hand, statistics show that approximately 3 million underprivileged persons on the earth fast daily against their will, as they have nothing to eat. Unfortunately.

Mechanism. The mechanism of voluntary or involuntary fasting, used in this case since antiquity, is explained through the alteration of the organic metabolism's dietetic regulation or, in other words, through a lack of vitamins and a deficiency of glucose (sugar) in the circulatory system. This tends to act firstly upon the central nervous system, the most vulnerable of all the human body's tissues.

Optimization. This creates psychological states which are favorable – optimization – to a reduction in the efficiency of the cerebral hemispheres, and separation of the consciousness and the mind, or the consequent freeing of the consciousness in the psychosoma.

Symptoms. Nevertheless, it is appropriate to point out that the regular practice of any type of mortification of the human body should be well-oriented under efficient, specialized, technical supervision in order to avoid innumerous undesirable mental symptoms.

Exclusions. At least the following 9 categories of intraphysical consciousnesses are excluded from this projective technique and, obviously, from the majority of lucid projection methods:

1. **Children.** Children, in general.
2. **Adolescents.** Adolescents, in general.
3. **Anemic.** The anemic individual.
4. **Weight.** Those presenting insufficient body weight *(weight deficit).*
5. **Hepatopathy.** The carrier of a hepatic affection.
6. **Convalescent.** The individual who has recently suffered an organic disturbance.
7. **Smoker.** The inveterate smoker (tobacco addict).
8. **Addict.** The individual who constantly uses light or heavy, licit or illicit drugs, narcotics or numbing agents.
9. **Alcoholic.** One who ingests alcoholic beverages in excess (alcoholic).

Recommendation. In light of the facts presented here, a brief fast is recommended in order to produce lucid projection for the person in good health who has a good appetite and for whom the abstinence from food will already be beneficial at any rate, serving as an efficient form of detoxification, rest and cellular rejuvenation of the organs. This person should remain alert in order to not harm him/herself with improper diet, malnutrition or illness due to deprivation.

Insensitivity. The projective fast is also a good technical indicator for those who display a cold, extremely analytical temperament, are fully self-centered from a material or physical perspective, and have no evident or manifest parapsychic-animic-energetic sensitivity up until this time.

Break. Fasting, in this case, breaks down the thick psychological "crust" of the materiality of the *resomant extraphysical consciousness,* opening weak spots in his/her excessive defenses, self-critiques, censures, conditionings, repressions and insensitivities, somehow predisposing him/her to new sensations and unpredictable discoveries.

Adaptation. Each person adapts to fasting in a different manner and to a different degree.

Duration. There are those who can safely fast for a month or more.

Alterations. Profound biological alterations occur in your human organism after only 24 hours of abstinence from food.

Loss. Most individuals who fast lose from 1.1 to 3.3 lb (½ to 1½ kg) of corporal weight in the first 24 hours.

Period. The best period of the year for you to perform an experimental fast would be on a weekend or during your summer vacation, for example.

Winter. In winter time, your organism needs more nourishment to maintain body temperature, keep the metabolism balanced and avoid infections, even the common cold. It is not advisable for you to drain your organic reserves uselessly at this stage of your technical apprenticeship in projectiology.

Physician. An intelligent course of action would be to consult your *trusted physician* first to ascertain if you are in a fit condition to submit yourself to moderate fasting for 3 days under his/her competent medical supervision.

Period. Fasting for a shorter period will offer you all the unpleasant part of the process without bringing any of the benefits.

Seclusion. During this short period of fasting, it is best to remain in seclusion, preferably staying at home, abstaining from any kind of work or, at least, heavy work that requires intense physical effort. You should not operate machinery or drive because you could faint behind the wheel.

Mentalsoma. All mental work, or that related to the mentalsoma, which is considered important, should be postponed.

Sensations. The practice of fasting is not as uncomfortable an experience as those who are well-fed or live constantly intoxicated by medication might imagine. The effort required to experience it is worthwhile.

Water. During the entire fast you, as someone undergoing a fast, should breathe fresh air and drink clean water at room temperature, and only when you feel thirsty or, when in doubt, at your regular mealtimes.

Specification. Partial fasting can consist of only ingesting specific foods, such as the following 3 categories:

1. Succulent fruits.
2. Citric juices.
3. Dairy products.

Occurrences. Here are the occurrences that are generated by the lucid projection through fasting technique, according to each of the 3 days of the personal experience:

1. **First day.** During the first day, easier for you to bear, you will be somewhat obsessed with food, your *stomach* will *grumble* repeatedly and you might have difficulty sleeping.

False hunger. About 12 hours into the fast, you might have the sensation of false hunger or psychological hunger.

Avoidances. Avoid mental and emotional stimuli, noises, tension, anxiety and fear.

2. **Second day.** In the second day of the fast, the most difficult one, headaches and a surprising feeling of weakness can occur, but both symptoms should disappear quickly, partly because they are of a psychological nature, due to the break in your *dietary routine*.

Hunger. Do not forget: hunger is the main component of a set of needs connected to the essential functions that maintain your human life.

3. **Third day.** The third and last day of the fast begins to produce benefits to the degree that your unconscious tires of protesting. Headaches, weakness and any other side effects will disappear inconsequentially, and your energy and thought processes will become clear. You may experience inoffensive *fleeting visions*.

Refrigerator. At this point, you will go to bed feeling hungry, so that your frustrated appetite, the intense desire to eat, will rise to the surface of your subconscious mind. This will lead your consciousness, projected in the psychosoma, to go to the refrigerator, freezer or kitchen cabinet, or to a familiar restaurant, snack bar or bakery in the vicinity of your physical base, in an attempt to break the enforced fast.

Return. The return to a normal diet, on the fourth day, should be gradual so as not to damage the organism's functions.

Warning. If, soon after the fasting period, you stuff yourself with food for another 3 days, eating excessively, you will intoxicate your body again – both the human body and the psychosoma – and you will leave these bodies in a worse condition than they were before the fast.

Coadjutants. If you prefer, you can enhance the projective fasting technique with the application of at least 4 useful coadjutant resources:

1. **Respiration.** Rhythmic respiration exercises.
2. **Visualization.** Visualization exercises.
3. **Immobility.** The waking physical immobility technique.
4. **Alimentation.** Alimentation reduced to only pro-projection foods.

Food. The foods referred to below should be considered as simple superstitions, or autosuggestive resources, because their action in favor of or against the production of lucid projection has not as yet been proven in laboratories or empirically (consensus), as is the case with various proposals in this book.

Hypothesis. This is a projectiological working hypothesis that requires more in-depth research: antiprojective and projective foods (somatics and umbilicochakra).

1. **Antiprojective.** At least the following 6 types of foodstuffs are considered to be *antiprojective foodstuffs:*

A. Any foods ingested immediately before the projective experiment.

B. Heavy meals or the ingestion of excessive amounts of food at any time on the day of the experiment.

C. Any type of meat during the 3 days of fasting.

D. Nuts: chestnuts, cashews, Brazil nuts, almonds, hazelnuts, coconuts and peanuts.

E. Any type of smoking (some persons prefer smoking to food).

F. Alcoholic beverages, as well as licit and illicit drugs in general.

2. **Projective.** At least the following 4 types of nutriments are considered *pro-projective nutriments:*

A. Carrots.

B. Fruits.

C. Vegetables and greens.

D. Raw eggs, as long as they are ingested in moderation, observing the issue of the personal level of less desirable cholesterol.

Factors. Two factors simultaneously act to free your psychosoma with the fasting technique:

1. **Soma.** Your human body, being more inactive from the lack of food, that generates the psychophysiological symptoms of fatigue besides the purifying effects of the organism.

2. **Suggestion.** The suggestion of food, your intense and constant desire to satiate the provoked hunger.

Involuntary. It is important to inform interested individuals that the author has received many reports of spontaneous, or involuntarily generated, first lucid projections experienced by persons with excess corporal weight and who, while attempting to be on a diet, endeavored to go to sleep without eating anything, thus being extremely hungry or, in other words, in a state of sensory deprivation, in this case. Later, they found themselves in the kitchen trying to turn on the light switch to brighten the room, take the milk out of the refrigerator and put it in a glass. When they were not able to do as they wished, they concluded that they were "in spirit, outside the human body". One of these individuals even looked through the window at the moonlight before consciously entering (interiorizing into) the physical body.

Umbilicochakra. According to holochakrology, it should not be forgotten that the effectiveness of the lucid projection through fasting technique depends greatly upon the quality of the energies of the umbilicochakra of the intraphysical consciousness practitioner.

Bibliography: Andreas (36, p. 52), Black (137, p. 77), Brennan (199, p. 95), Carrington (245, p. 35), Ferguson (507, p. 58), Frost (560, p. 69), Greenhouse (636, p. 31), Hall (670, p. 679), Huson (768, p. 107), Matson (1013, p. 136), Muldoon (1105, p. 191), Puharich (1338, p. 199), Rogo (1444, p. 52), Tondriau (1690, p. 242), Vieira (1762, p. 39), Walker (1781, p. 84), Watson (1800, p. 114).

---

218. PROJECTIVE MANTRAS TECHNIQUE

Definition. Mantra: verbal formula used by Hindu, Buddhist, Moslem, Jewish and Christian rituals, in mantra yoga, cabalism and meditation techniques, usually being very short, one or a few words, in order to provoke a parapsychic condition, relaxation or consciential projection.

Synonymy: cryptic verse; *jappa;* litany; magic syllable; mantric recitation; monology; monosyllabic prayer; monotone chant; mystical verse; occult sound; personal morphothosene; private thought-form; psalmody; ritual recitation; seed-sound; special phoneme; spoken affirmation; syllabic sound; words of power; yoga-mantra.

Christian. Popular prayers, such as "The Lord's Prayer," "Hail Mary," and phrases like: "Jesus Christ, Son of God, have mercy on this sinner," are genuinely Christian mantras.

Popular. The most well-known, popular mantra used everywhere is "OM," which signifies "key of the universe;" others are: "Ram;" "God;" "Shanti;" "Jay".

Resolutions. The affirmations are spoken resolutions that, when used correctly, align the physical, mental and consciential energies.

Trance. The ritualistic method of the mantras, through continuous monotonal chanting of the same syllables over very long periods of time, in the manner of a self-hypnotic effect, promotes the induction of the consciousness into a trance state, whereupon the psychosoma exteriorizes itself from the human body.

Mechanisms. The physiological production of spoken words simply consists of triggering certain vibrations: the external agent, the sound, provokes an impression in the listener's ear. This causes other vibrations in the auditory canal and tympanic membranes, which are connected to the *auditory nerves*. These, in turn, communicate with the cortical *auditory centers* in the brain. Upon reaching the brain, the initial *excitation* is perceived as *sensation*.

Explanation. Therefore, trances obtained by verbal expedients or mantras can be explained by the effect or power of the verbally repeated words which create a kind of psycho-chemical-physiological rhythm in the human body.

Rhythm. This rhythm, together with the breathing during speech, contributes to a reduction in oxygen volume and an increase in the amount of carbon dioxide in the pulmonary alveoli and blood stream. This alters adrenaline levels, which affects the oxygenation of the cerebral cortex, predisposing the discoincidence of the vehicles of the consciousness.

Effects. Some people presume that mantras have a powerful effect on the soma-holochakra-psychosoma energetic complex, given that, in this case, its effect would be more energetic or psychological than physiological, in biochemical terms.

Sexochakra. In yoga, mantras are used to awaken chakras or the sexochakra *(kundalini)*.

Name. You can use the formula of special phonemes to dissociate the vehicles of your consciousness (mantric projection), induced merely by the cadenced repetition, in a low tone of voice, of your own *first name*, or nickname, removing any erratic idea or concern.

Beads. Some people additionally potentiate the mantra method by fingering a long string of beads or a rosary, while repeating a verse or characteristic sound. They may also simultaneously perform breathing exercises.

Repetition. Mantras are enriched, potentiated and activated through repetition.

Efficiency. In fact, rhythmic respiration is more efficient and works better than mantras for producing lucid projection. On the other hand, the technique involving the mixture of oxygen and carbon dioxide, or direct chemical action, works even better than the rhythmic respiration technique for provoking lucid projection.

Oxygen. The 3 projective methods – mantras, rhythmic respiration and carbon dioxide – present 1 basic objective: attain an inoffensive reduction in oxygen or a nontoxic concentration of carbon dioxide in the cerebral hemispheres that permits the release of the psychosoma.

Contrathosene. In spite of everything that has been presented, it should be kept in mind that mantras also function, in their own way, through the *mental word,* which is not audibly spoken, being a contrathosene. Hence the name *occult sound.*

Laryngochakra. According to holochakrology, we should not forget that the effectiveness of the projective mantras technique depends greatly upon the quality of energies of the laryngochakra of the intraphysical consciousness practitioner.

Bibliography: Armstrong (56, p. 87), Bozzano (188, p. 53), Brennan (199, p. 98), Carrington (245, p. 62), Cavendish (266, p. 137), Chaplin (273, p. 99), Crawford (313, p. 43), Crowley (348, p. 15), Day (376, p. 82), Digest (401, p. 366), Gaynor (577, p. 107), Hermógenes (715, p. 340), Martin (1002, p. 56), Martin (1003, p. 77), Norvell (1136, p. 197), Pensamento (1224, p. 67), Rogo (1444, p. 71), Sargant (1508, p. 99), Shay (1546, p. 48), Steiger (1606, p. 90), Tondriau (1690, p. 251), Walker (1781, p. 109), Wedeck (1807, p. 224), Yogananda (1894, p. 429), Zaniah (1899, p. 294).

219. PROJECTIVE MASSAGE AND VISUALIZATION TECHNIQUE

Definition. Christos experiment: technique of inducing an altered state of consciousness with the eventual occurrence of the hypnagogic state, vibrational state, lucid projection, traveling clairvoyance, retrocognition, precognition or simple daydream, fantasy and oneiric images, by submitting a person to massage and autosuggestions, with external help, but without undergoing direct hypnosis and without losing ordinary wakefulness.

Synonymy: Christos technique; Glaskin technique; retrocognitive projective technique; stimulation of the third eye; William Swygard method.

First. The first phase is to lie on the floor, on your back, barefoot and with a pillow under your head. Another pillow can be placed under the feet or back in order to better accommodate you and make you feel very comfortable.

Ankles. An assistant vigorously massages your ankles for 3 minutes in order to induce you into deep relaxation.

Eyes. Keep your eyes firmly closed the entire time from this point on.

Forehead. At the same time, the assistant who is controlling the experience makes suggestions to you, asks questions and massages the lower center part of your forehead, the glabellar area or *third eye* location or, in other words, between the frontal lobes of the brain, in a circular movement with the side of the hand curved, as if holding the fist in that position.

Relaxation. You must be entirely relaxed. If you are still somewhat tense, breathe deeply a few times and let your body loosen up.

Compression. The massage of the forehead must be vigorous and brief so that you will feel actual vibrations or *humming* inside your head.

Friction. However, the compression should not be extreme to the point of causing unexpected and undesirable skin *abrasion* due to friction in the glabellar area, especially if you are a woman with sensitive skin or you are sunburned.

Oil. An oily substance can be used to facilitate the compression and massaging of the forehead.

Second. In the second phase, you begin mental exercises, when sufficiently relaxed, to make you expand the consciousness beyond the normal limits of your human body, using these 7 procedures:

1. Keeping your eyes closed, visualize and feel yourself *growing* 2" (5 cm) out through the soles of the feet or the ankles, through extraphysical elongation.

2. Return to normal size and repeat the exercise several times until you feel you can do it easily.

3. Then, concentrate your attention on your head. Grow 2" (5 cm) until you are taller. Return to normal height and repeat the exercise several times. The instructor should encourage you to talk as much as possible, so that you will become accustomed to the idea, for later use, when you are asked to describe the experience.

4. Now *grow* about 1' (30 cm) out from your feet. Return to normal.

5. Do the same with your head.

6. Now *stretch your body* 23½" (60 cm) beyond your feet, maintaining this length while you do the same with the head. Repeat as many times as necessary in order to do it correctly.

7. Finally, while you are still *stretched* in both directions, imagine yourself expanding like a balloon, or the production of *ballonnement,* until you feel free from your human body.

Third. In the third phase, or in the state of expansion, extraphysically go to a familiar place, such as the front door of your house or apartment building, and describe it in minute detail.

Observations. Seek out different angles of observation, moving forward and then backward, to one side and then another, and finally, slightly upwards, describing the whole time what you see with the consciousness expanded through traveling clairvoyance.

Description. Now, *raise yourself up into the air* about 1,640' (500 m) and describe what you see.

Time. See what time it is, as well as the weather conditions, which do not necessarily need to be the same as when you began the experience.

Differences. As a voluntary act, change from day to night, then go back again, changing night to day, always describing the differences observed.

Control. Remember that you maintain full control over that which you are experiencing, this being the most important detail and that which deserves most attention.

Landing. Finally, under a clear blue sky, raise yourself far above the earth, as far as you can, until the scenery below you is no more than an indistinct blur, and then slowly return to earth, landing feet-first until you feel yourself on the ground.

Alterations. In this stage, if the technique has produced results in your specific case, you will perceive the alterations that took place in your environment.

Scenes. The scenes that you will see now might later even be interpreted as possible experiences of another previous human existence.

Awakening. It is not important if you are conscientially aware or not, the massage and visualization technique works anyway. The greater your consciential awareness (conscientiality), however, the greater will be your ability to see and understand the experience.

Frontochakra. According to holochakrology, we should not forget that the effectiveness of the projective massage and visualization technique depends greatly upon the quality of the energies of the frontochakra of the intraphysical consciousness practitioner.

Bibliography: Blackmore (139, p. 99), Brennan (200, p. 79), Glaskin (599, p. 216), Gooch (617, p. 93), Knight (853, p. 57), Lamont (874, p. 100), Rogo (1444, p. 157), Thalbourne (1675, p. 10), Walker (1786, p. 90).

---

220. PROJECTIVE MUSIC AND VISUALIZATION TECHNIQUE

Definition. Variation of the Christos experiment: technique of inducing an altered state of consciousness based on massage, music and visualizations.

Synonymy: musical stimulation; musicogenic projection; musicoprojection; variant of the Christos experiment; variation of the Glaskin technique.

Alternative. If the technique described above did not produce results, the reason might lie in the fact that you have a normal but unique personality or, in other words: your perceptions are not essentially based on vision but on general perceptions, such as the haptic type, or those acting through the synesthetic fusion of the following 4 senses:

1. Touch (haptics).
2. Audition (acoustics).
3. Olfaction (olfactology).
4. Taste.

Procedure. In this case, adopt an alternative procedure in 5 steps:

1. **Relaxation.** Follow the relaxation technique, the massages and the visualized expansion exercises exactly as recommended in the previous chapter.

2. **Music.** When you have completed the final "expand like a balloon" *(ballonnement)* stage, remain relaxed and keep your eyes closed while listening to a varied selection of musical themes. Listen only to instrumental music, avoiding those pieces with lyrics, and include instrumental folk music from as many countries as possible.

3. **Images.** Describe to your instructor the emotions, sentiments and images that each of the musical pieces evokes in you. The important detail lies in the images (visualizations). When these begin to arise, describe them in as much detail as possible.

4. **Control.** When you perceive the images very clearly, generally accompanied by rapid synchronic involuntary eye movements, your instructor will turn off the musical recording. If this act interferes with the images you see, the music can be played again. It is important to remind you that you fully control everything in your surroundings.

5. **Imprint.** When the images are firmly etched in your mind, continue as in the previous technique. To imprint the experience, it is preferable to gradually remove the background music.

Audition. Music has served as a generating factor for innumerous parapsychic experiences, when it is being played or simply listened to. Although not recommended for the experienced consciential projector, there are those who use it as a simple initial process for projecting, as well as for blocking out or masking noises in a noisy physical base.

Cooperation. For certain people, music, and in some cases even repetitive music, presents emotional implications that end up aiding in the success of the lucid consciential projection.

Organ. Everyone is familiar with the suggestive force of organ music and the human voice (the most evolved musical instrument) in a chorus, widely used in temple atmospheres.

Harmonies. In a simple form of this technique, you can, if you are a music aficionado, play a favorite recording on CD or tape – generally a gentle, uplifting or romantic melody without lyrics – and become involved in the harmonies, thinking about leaving the human body and, after a short while, your lucid consciential projection will occur.

Turn off. In this case, as a rule, you will use only one melody, or a set of half-hour long recorded melodies. The recording will thus silently and automatically turn itself off immediately upon the distancing of your consciousness which, in this way, will not be disturbed during the period of the development of extraphysical actions.

Bibliography: Brennan (200, p. 81), Frost (560, p. 53), Glaskin (599, p. 220), Greenhouse (636, p. 180), Knight (853, p. 57), Shay (1546, p. 39).

221. TRIGGERING OBJECT-FACTOR TECHNIQUE

Motivation. Certain motivating physical objects that temporarily carry an intense emotional charge for the intraphysical consciousness can be employed as agents for triggering lucid projection within one's own physical base.

Items. The motivating object-factors can be recently acquired simple objects of personal use, rare collectible items for the collector, something that has been stored for years and one wishes to see and remember or a present that has been received.

Eagerness. The most important thing, in this case, is for the experimenter to do everything possible to intensify the eagerness to hold, see, discover and examine, firsthand, the object that is stored at a distance, in another room of the physical base.

Tension. The object needs to be at a distance from the human body of the practitioner, yet within the physical base, in order to increase the tension of knowing it is so near and yet so far, so *accessible* and simultaneously *inaccessible,* thus deepening the desire to have it within one's grasp.

Elements. The following are the 4 elements that come together to make the intraphysical consciousness project itself, at night, to the object:

1. Curiosity.
2. Eagerness.
3. Satisfaction.
4. Surprise.

Types. The following are 6 practical types of objects that trigger a lucid projection:

1. **Letter.** An anxiously awaited, but innocuous, letter of no serious consequence and which, upon arrival, must not be opened but placed on a piece of furniture a certain distance from the bedroom (energetically shielded chamber) of the consciential projection practitioner.

2. **Book.** A book that you have wanted to read for some time, but of which you have not even seen the cover.

3. **CD.** A CD or *compact disc* that you want to hear, but you leave the wrapping on.

4. **Present.** An unidentified present received from a dear friend, but that can remain wrapped until the following morning.

5. **Video.** A movie on videotape that you received recently and have been wanting to see for a long time.

6. **Collection.** A collector's item sent from abroad: an objet d'art, a shell, a quantity of postage stamps, antique coins, antiques and other similar objects (holotheca).

Birthday. This projective method can be applied with greater ease on the night of the (especially a young) practitioner's birthday, as long as the individual receives presents that have remained wrapped for some time, when possible.

Stimulus. Spinning objects, such as rotating stars and colored disks placed in the projector's visual field, can be employed to stimulate the separation of or reduce the cohesion between the psychosoma and human body. This procedure is used to a great extent in the parapsychic practices of the East.

Process. The colored disk, for example, is placed at a point between and a short distance away from the eyebrows, and the practitioner looks at it fixedly without blinking, allowing the effects of the movement, the lights and the colors to act upon your mind, altering your state of consciousness.

Bibliography: Steiger (1601, p. 117).

222. MUSICAL PHYSICAL AWAKENING TECHNIQUE

Definition. Musical physical awakening: the act of waking up the intraphysical sleeper at a predetermined time, precisely when his/her consciousness is projected outside the human body, in order to call it back with the complete recollection of the extraphysical experiences.

Synonymy: programmed physical awakening.

Periods. Each night, normal or natural sleep clearly presents 2 distinct periods already scientifically identified. They form a standard pattern that is repeated in an alternating manner during the entire night:

1. **Deep.** Deep sleep, devoid of dreams, that occurs soon after the hypnagogic state and is repeated every 90 minutes.

2. **REM.** Sleep with symbolic dreams, wherein rapid synchronous eye movements (REM) arise.

Middle. Those who awaken in the middle of a REM (rapid synchronous eye movement) period, remember vivid imaginative creations and can give detailed reports of many oneiric situations or those of ordinary symbolic dreams.

End. Upon waking up, however, at the end of the sleep period without eye movements, the sleeper may report having experiences of the consciousness projected outside the human body.

Foundations. These 2 principles regarding the moment of awakening establish the foundations of the musical physical awakening technique: to physically awaken the consciousness while engaged in the first projection, generally not remembered, of the night, after the common phenomenon of jerks (myoclonus) occurs. They serve, physiologically speaking, as a sign of an imminent projection, at the end of the period of dreamless sleep.

Time. Before going to bed, set an alarm clock to wake you up 90 minutes after the time you will probably fall asleep that night. This is the time at which your consciousness is most likely to be spontaneously projected, in the middle of an experience outside the human body, which commonly occurs every night.

Music. The alarm clock should preferably be of the musical kind that awakens the sleeper with soft music. Using this equipment will serve to avoid greater extraphysical traumas and will minimize the undesirable effects of an abrupt physical awakening.

Processes. The following are 4 processes for awakening the consciousness at a precise moment:

1. **Shakes.** Ask someone to shake your inactive physical body.
2. **Bell.** Entrust your *intraphysical* assistant to set off a bell next to your human body at a certain time.
3. **Radio alarm clock.** Set a radio alarm clock before going to bed.
4. **Alarm clock.** Set an ordinary alarm clock for a specific time.

Results. These methods also work, but do not produce results that are as positive as those obtained with the use of a *musical alarm clock* that awakens one with soft music. This reduces the negative consequences that violent awakening has on the recollection of the extraphysical events of an abruptly interrupted projection.

Principle. As can be seen, this method is rationally based on the principle – already tested in thousands of laboratory tests – that every intraphysical consciousness projects spontaneously every night during certain phases of natural sleep, although the extraphysical experiences are not recalled in the ordinary, physical waking state.

Average. The period of 90 minutes after the beginning of natural sleep was initially chosen as it represents an average, or the most common fact, according to the physiological sleep chronology of the sleep of sleepers in general. This permits the achievement of positive results for half of all practitioners.

Ideal. Despite what has been said so far, the best time for musical awakening in your personal case is always that which you research, identify and prefer, namely the exact, very individual time when your consciousness is projected. This is the time that works best for you exclusively and can be, for example, 120, 180 or 210 minutes after the beginning of your natural sleep every night.

Surprise. This means surprising the consciousness in the second or third period of dreamless sleep, or during the second or third non-remembered lucid projection of the night.

Statistics. These are not random times, as they adhere to statistics obtained from research performed in *sleep laboratories,* currently a common practice in diverse cultural centers.

Effects. Gently breaking the silence with soft music provokes the physical awakening of your consciousness, brought back by surprise precisely when it is extraphysically experiencing one of its non-recalled spontaneous projections.

Benefit. This type of awakening, although interrupting your extraphysical experience, has the greater benefit of making your consciousness compulsorily return to the human body, which is inactive in the physical base, with a complete and exact recollection of the extraphysical experiences of that moment.

Proof. This procedure will prove 2 facts to you:

1. **Physiology.** You project every night, although spontaneously, in a physiological manner.

2. **Retrocognitions.** This process offers you the possibility of having complete recollection of experiences, the nature and category of which you might never have otherwise remembered or experienced lucidly in your entire human existence.

Suggestions. Both facts referred to here outline the conditions for you to motivate yourself to induce lucid projection through the resolute force of your will, as well as the initial means available to you for remembering extraphysical experiences.

Recall. This technique does not constitute a method for you to produce lucid projection, per se. It is, however, a specific, secure, scientific process for proving to yourself that you can and should remember the experiences that you have throughout your life and which you do not ordinarily remember.

Self-awareness. This method, therefore, signifies not only the ordinary physical awakening of your consciousness, but the greater awakening of your self-awareness in regard to the phenomena of human lucid projection.

Bibliography: Frost (560, p. 44).

---

223. ASSISTED PROJECTION TECHNIQUE

Definition. Assisted lucid projection: the essentially animic-parapsychic projection technique in which you, as a lucid projector, are directly assisted or commanded during the experiment by a helper who is almost always a projection expert, being a special modality of projection for all sensitives with a certain degree of development.

Synonymy: commanded projection; directed consciential projection; hitchhike-projection; easy projection.

Indication. Assisted human consciential projection is a specially suited phenomenic modality which generally only occurs to the active, well-intentioned sensitive who has a reasonable level of unorthodox parapsychic development, and is a universalistic (open minded) consciousness capable of facing all types of consciousnesses or extraphysical consciousnesses without becoming traumatized, in any extraphysical plane or dimension (see fig. 223, p. 1,133).

Proof. Assisted projection proves that parapsychic components (together with other extraphysical or intraphysical consciousnesses) generally interact in the animic processes (developed only by the consciousness of the practitioner) of the lucid projections of the intraphysical consciousness in the psychosoma.

Occurrences. In assisted lucid projection, certain occurrences, arising from the exercising of parapsychism, are common in the preparatory stage of the experiment, such as the following 9:

1. **Notice.** A notice regarding the upcoming lucid projection.
2. **Energies.** Consciential energy exteriorization exercises.
3. **Monologue.** The psychophonic monologue.
4. **Showers.** Energetic showers upon the projector.
5. **Hetero-transmissions.** Prolonged extraphysical transmissions (along the practitioner's entire soma).
6. **Self-transmissions.** Self-transmissions of energy.
7. **Frontochakra.** Transcendent sensations stemming from the movement of the frontochakra.
8. **Xenothosenes.** Mental suggestions (healthy xenothosenes).
9. **Torpor.** Torpor of hypnotic origin.

Passivity. You should be confidently predisposed toward lucid projection with the psychological and physical passivity with which you submit to the common parapsychic process, as in the case of psychophony. This is why the assisted process does not constitute a purely animic phenomenon, namely one that is produced only with your decided will.

Evocation. You can employ sincerely-felt, rationalized, mental, spontaneous evocation as a basic resource for achieving the objective of your consciousness leaving the human body. This predisposes your deep affinity, empathy or rapport with your closest helper, if you are accustomed to this *psychophysiological crutch* modality.

Awakening. The most common phenomenon to occur in assisted lucid projection is for your consciousness to suffer a brief hiatus in lucidity and later extraphysically awaken somewhere in the paratropospheric or crustal (tropospheric) dimension.

Clairaudience. Your *auditory parapsychism,* if it exists, can be utilized by the helper to suggest or candidly order certain actions during the development of the exteriorization of your consciousness, in the stages of muscular relaxation, mental concentration, absolute serenity, rolling takeoff, re-exteriorizations and re-interiorizations.

Alternate. Often, clairaudience may alternate with transmental or telepathic dialogue in the psychosphere of the projector-sensitive.

Assistance. In assisted consciential projection, the extraphysical assistance of the helper frequently continues for the entire period of exteriorization of your consciousness from the human body, even when at a distance from the physical base or in extraphysical districts and communities, per se.

Intangibility. However, the presence of the helper is almost always sensed in an unquestionable manner, although it is not visible or tangible to you.

Advantages. The assisted-parapsychic-animic projection presents unquestionable advantages over other techniques used for your consciousness to project in the psychosoma, bearing in mind the following 6 variables:

1. **Takeoff.** It permits your lucid takeoff in many cases.

2. **Parapsychism.** It dynamizes the development of all types of parapsychic phenomena.

3. **Self-confidence.** It deepens your confidence and your openness toward projecting consciously.

4. **Security.** It deepens your sense of security in performing projections.

5. **Sensations.** It provides more agreeable sensations during the unfolding of the projection.

6. **Preparation.** It serves as a projection that precedes other extraphysical assistential tasks in which you will participate.

Sleep. It is worth pointing out that the helper will most often approach you during your natural sleep period, while your vehicles of manifestation are in spontaneous discoincidence. The helper will provoke your extraphysical awakening through an intensification in your awareness, as you are already outside the dense body.

Recall. In these cases, the recall following the events of the projection does not always have the same high quality as that of a projection with continuous self-awareness, wherein lucidity is maintained without hiatus, or without any unconsciousness, from the beginning to the end of the experiment.

Helpers. The helpers that provide assistance in lucid projections are technical extraphysical consciousnesses who are accustomed to the phenomena of energy exteriorization, ectoplasmy and assistance to ill humans and extraphysicals.

Together. Instead of 1 helper, 2 or more helpers can operate at the same time, brought together for the tasks, helping you to produce your lucid consciential projection as a projector-sensitive.

Nurses. Sometimes it seems that one helper supports the shoulders of the psychosoma and another lifts up the feet, transporting your psychosoma from the physical bed to the extraphysical dimension, similar to 2 nurses transferring an ill person from the stretcher to the bed.

Merit. As a basic rule regarding the phenomenon, we should bear in mind that the major assisted projection – that is agreeable in all senses, clarifying, of long duration and enriching to the intraphysical consciousness – obviously does not occur without the sensitive-projectionist having some merit.

By-product. The assistential projection frequently constitutes an evident by-product of extraphysical assistential tasks (conscientiotherapy, penta, extraphysical clinic).

Phases. In this case, the intraphysical consciousness functions in 2 very distinct phases:

1. **Donation.** In a semilucid mode in the first phase, serving as a donor of consciential energy during extraphysical assistential tasks.

2. **Action.** Soon afterward, in a well-defined second phase, the helper energetically intensifies the projector's self-awareness and gives projective free rein to the projector.

Gratification. The extraphysical assistential service performed by the projector through the donation of the dense consciential energies of the human being, that are suitable for the consciential awakening of energivorous extraphysical consciousnesses or parapsychotic *post-desomatics,* can offer you a profound sense of inner gratification.

Recess. A lack of inner balance, an absence of confidence in the helpers, your surrender to fear, frank consciential immaturity, hesitations in your physical and extraphysical decisions relative to the projective work, can all produce a hiatus in the extraphysical assistential services of the lucid projector ("those who stay out of the way help greatly") and unfortunate subsequent periods of recess from your consciential projections.

Merit. This proves, often ostensively, that *assisted* consciential projections exist and clearly are always developed with a clear dependence upon meritorious services of extraphysical *assistential* projections.

Joint. The most common joint projections of intraphysical consciousnesses are those sponsored by the helpers. This greatly facilitates extraphysical encounters that are usually difficult for the projected consciousness to achieve in terms of correctly pinpointing the predetermined mental targets, times, communities, and extraphysical districts that are to be reached.

Bibliography: Andrade (27, p. 136), Crookall (331, p. 36), Davis (371, p. 61), Espérance (485, p. 263), Hives (728, p. 7), Müller (1107, p. 252), Pereira (1230, p. 119), Sculthorp (1531, p. 22), Steiger (1601, p. 12), Swedenborg (1639, p. 1), Turvey (1707, p. 93), Twigg (1711, p. 56), Vieira (1769, p. 5).

224. LUCID PROJECTION THROUGH DREAM TECHNIQUE

Definition. Dream control: the lucid consciential projection produced from an ordinary natural dream wherein your consciousness somehow becomes lucid, thus provoking transition from a passive to an active condition, undoing the oneiric images and actually controlling or directing, as much as possible, what are actually extraphysical events and experiences.

Synonymy: controlled extraphysical awareness; conversion of the dreamer into a projector; dream conversion; dream prolongation; oneirogenic projection; oneiroprojection; pre-programmed dream; pre-projection dream; projectiogenic dream; projectiogenous dream; pro-projection dream.

Suitability. This method is only suitable for the individual presenting – in his/her profile as a pre-serenissimus intraphysical consciousness – some or all of these 5 distinct personality characteristics or traits:

1. **Value.** The individual who gives value and significance to ordinary dreams.

2. **Memory.** The individual who remembers many dreams, without forgetting any details.

3. **Messages.** The individual who accepts that dreams bring messages with some positive quality through their reflection of his/her subconscious material.

4. **Fissures.** The individual who admits that dreams highlight obscure aspects of or fissures in his/her personality.

5. **Learning.** The individual who recognizes that through dreams he/she can learn something that is useful for his/her personal and group evolution.

Gravitation. The psychological conditioning stemming from the action of gravity on the intraphysical consciousness alerts the dreamer to the incongruence and unreality of dreams, and the fact that he/she is dreaming. From this are born the majority of lucid dreams or semilucid consciential projections.

Flying. Dreamers of lucid dreams, or semilucid consciential projectors, have a greater number of dreams of flying than the average dreamer.

Will. Based on the phenomena presented here, you should always endeavor to recognize incongruence in and the unreality of your dreams, clarify your consciousness and undo the simple oneiric scenarios through the force of your awakened will (consciential energy).

Frequency. Many people have no idea how often dreams are, in fact, semilucid consciential projections.

Prolongation. You will be capable of lucidly projecting through the simple resource of extending or prolonging the sequences of your natural dream and programming them.

Predisposition. The technique will evidently be easier if you have already dreamt and sensed, as the dream unfolded, that you were dreaming, because in this way you find yourself predisposed to acquiring active extraphysical awareness with greater ease.

Saturation. The most usual process recommends that, while in the ordinary, physical waking state, you saturate your mind with the will to extraphysically awaken from a natural dream of any kind.

Types. The dreams that typically facilitate lucid projection the most are those involving extraphysical flights, or volitation, whether they are spontaneous or previously planned by your decided will.

Activities. You should endeavor to maintain lucidity of the consciousness as much as possible while in the hypnagogic state and build your own dream, selecting some intense motor activity, sport or favorite pastime that gives you a most agreeable sensation and that approximates or imitates the maneuvers of levitation or free flight outside the human body.

Sensation. From the very beginning, you should avoid selecting an oneiric activity with a habitual sensation that is disagreeable because, in this way, instead of a lucid projection, it will provoke extraphysical trauma, with your subsequent abrupt interiorization, physical repercussion or, at least, a nightmare, but it is unlikely that you will achieve a pro-projective dream.

Nightmares. Nevertheless, in spite of all the preceding arguments, many persons, although infrequently, project from nightmares induced by their ironclad will.

Examples. You should observe each 1 of the following examples of preferred motor activities and get a sense of the 3 categories of actions that are thoroughly programmed for pro-projection dreams: ascending actions, lateral actions and descending actions.

1. **Ascending.** Actions that take you in a directly ascensional direction make dreams easier to induce and best predispose your lucid projection, because they follow the trajectory that the psychosoma most often takes in a classic takeoff, leaving the human body in an upward departure. The following are 3 examples:

A. **Elevator.** Ascend in a rapid elevator.

B. **Ferris wheel.** Be carried upward in a Ferris wheel.

C. **Airplane.** Ascend in a rocket, spaceship, airplane, helicopter, glider, hang glider or balloon.

2. **Lateral.** Actions that impel you forward produce a lateral takeoff of the psychosoma, either to the right or the left of the human body. The following 5 are examples:

D. **Swimming.** Swim energetically in a sports competition.

E. **Speedboat.** Ride in a speedboat.

F. **Run.** Participate in a marathon.

G. **Water-ski.** Water-ski at high speeds.

H. **Surf.** Surf high waves.

3. **Descending.** Actions that impel one downward with the sensation of free-fall are more difficult, as they are contrary to the *natural,* spontaneous movements of the psychosoma, although they are also capable of being executed. The following are 5 examples:

I. **Diving board.** Dive from an elevated diving board into a full swimming pool.

J. **Descent.** Descend in a rapid elevator.

K. **Loop-the-loop.** Descend riding a roller coaster or doing loop-the-loops in an amusement park ride.

L. **Dive.** Dive into the sea from an overhanging cliff.

M. **Parachute.** Go parachuting.

Repetition. You need to choose only one type of dream. It should be personal and as adequate as possible to your temperament and daily life existence. Construct it vividly in your imagination, thinking about it every night, repeating it insistently until you saturate your mind, and suggestively impress your subconscious with the will to experience the agreeable sensations and the desire to remember the dream, in detail, after physically awakening.

Easy. If the dream you chose is one of the easy ones, such as taking off in an airplane, you will convert the dream into a projection when you feel yourself heading toward the clouds, visualizing the projection and taking control of the extraphysical events that are almost always occurring near the human body.

Difficult. If you chose one of the more difficult dreams, such as diving from a diving board into a swimming pool, you will enter into the projection upon seeing yourself heading for the water. This is because you will remember the subject, your wish, the idea you have nurtured for a long time. The fall will disappear as your consciousness emerges in the extraphysical environment, within the physical base or next to your body that is inactive and emptied of the consciousness (domestic holothosene).

Flotation. The first really extraphysical sensation that arises is floating, or the act of gliding in space. This can begin with or without the psychosoma oscillating from one side to the other. It will then begin to slide.

Precautions. Before, during the dream and in the conversion to a projection, and even during the subsequent extraphysical condition, you should not think about the existence of the physical base, the human body, the silver cord, or any other factor or idea that might intervene in the natural development of your lucid projection.

Induction. The following is a technique for the induction of an ordinary dream that permits you, as a swimmer, to lucidly project in 6 steps:

1. **Isolation.** At night, near dawn, isolate yourself in a closed bedroom, where you will not be disturbed while conducting the exercise. The room or bedroom should be well-ventilated. Remain in the nude, or use only a pair of light, loose swimming trunks.

2. **Position.** Lie on the bed, in a comfortable position and close your eyes.

3. **Surf.** Imagine that you are going to surf high waves on a beautiful, sunny afternoon.

4. **Images.** Sleep with your mind filled with images of the sea, waves and wind passing before you. Observe the movements of your body and watch the seagulls (birds) and Portuguese men-of-war.

5. **Recall.** Upon awakening, remain in bed without moving and try to remember the entirety of your early morning dream. If you are unable to remember anything, change your position, as this might help your recall.

6. **Register.** As soon as the memories of the dream come to mind, endeavor to register them by writing them down, typing them onto a laptop, or dictating them into a tape recorder. The best occasion for registering any experience, notably the parapsychic ones (including the waking physical

immobility experiment) is the place where the event or experience took place. This reduces selective tendencies, distortion through *re-evocation* and interference from ambient noise and *static*.

Note. It is a well-known fact that anyone can influence the content of his/her dreams by focalizing the mind on a specific subject shortly before going to sleep. This common fact serves to alert you – as a practitioner of lucid projection – to avoid confusing a dream about lucid projection with the experience of an actual lucid projection induced by a dream. They are 2 altered states of consciousness which are quite distinct from each other.

Suggestion. In general, one can suggest a dream before going to sleep, nevertheless one is unable to influence the development of the oneiric images after they have begun.

Ideoplasty. In the transition period between the 2 altered states of consciousness – from dream to lucid projection – the unconscious ideoplastic modeling of consistent morphothosenes or thought-forms can occur before the projected intraphysical consciousness has achieved full extraphysical lucidity.

Case study. On one occasion the author dreamt that he would receive a news magazine and extraphysically awakened on top of a hill in Rio de Janeiro, already dressed in normal attire and with the morphothosene (thought-form) of the magazine in the parahands of the psychosoma. At this point, he hurled the para-magazine over the top of the hill and took off, lucidly and freely volitating through the skies of Rio de Janeiro.

Phenomena. We should not forget that the simple and elementary phenomena of ideoplasty are involved in the appearance of diverse phenomena. The following are 2 examples:

1. **Stigmatization.** In stigmatization or trophic cutaneous modifications that are provoked through suggestion.

2. **Mimetism.** In an entirely unconscious manner in the phenomena of mimetism that are still so mysterious to us and occur frequently in subhuman animals.

Bibliography: Armond (53, p. 39), Battersby (92, p. 33), Blackmore (139, p. 115), Carrington (245, p. 288), Castaneda (258, p. 9), Crouzet (344, p. 123), Drury (414, p. 23), Fox (544, p. 34), Frost (560, p. 22), Garfield (569, p. 120), Greenhouse (636, p. 258), Lefebure (909, p. 131), Martin (1002, p. 63), Muldoon (1105, p. 158), Ophiel (1150, p. 35), Rogo (1444, p. 130), Salley (1496, p. 160), Shay (1546, p. 87), Steiger (1601, p. 55), Vieira (1770, p. 3).

225. FRAGMENTED LUCID PROJECTION TECHNIQUE

Definition. Fragmented lucid projection: the projection produced through gradual exteriorization, part by part, of each one of the specific areas of your humanoid form of the psychosoma.

Synonymy: fractionated projection; gradual projection; gradual unfolding; half-unfolding; incipient projection; partial discoincidence; *partial projection;* partial unfolding; peripheric projection; segmented projection; semi-detachment; semiprojection; semi-unfolding.

Types. The semiprojection of a counterpart of your human body can be of an arm, leg, arms and legs at the same time, the trunk and head and, more rarely, the head (parahead) only. Shortly after a complete projection, the phenomena of extraphysical elongation, or sudden interiorization, even with physical repercussion, can also occur.

Third. Partial projection gives the intraphysical consciousness a sensation of possessing a third hand (parahand); a third arm (para-arm); a third leg (paraleg) (see fig. 225, p. 1,134); or 4 arms.

Lucidity. Semi-projection can be lucid or, in other words, provoked through a determined act of will. It can also be nonlucid, when occurring spontaneously.

Perception. It is almost always the veteran projector who can clearly identify or perceive a spontaneous nonlucid projection, obviously after it has been produced.

Minicord. The main motor agent of the semiprojection is the silver cord. This suggests that this appendix of the human body can also exit from diverse areas or segments, there being a mini-silver cord for an arm or a leg.

Technique. After you go through the projective preliminaries, especially physical and mental self-relaxation, close your eyes and concentrate your attention on a segment or part of your human body, your left leg, for example.

Left. While you are thinking about your left leg, *wish* decisively that it leave slightly in an upward direction from its condition of coincidence with your bodies or vehicles of manifestation.

Legs. Concentrate on your left extraphysical leg until you feel that it has dislocated upward. Next, concentrate on your right extraphysical leg, wishing to move it out of coincidence with the vehicles as well.

Body. Little by little, exercise the whole body in this way, *wishing,* in a determined manner, that the extraphysical segments slightly leave the state of coincidence with their physical forms or locations, under your imperious willful command.

Persistence. Do not try to rush the process. Use patience and persistence. This may require various attempts before you obtain discoincidence of even the first segment.

Success. If you are successful with *fractionated* projection, you are prepared to project your consciousness in the *entire* psychosoma in the extraphysical dimension.

Head. The semiprojection of only the head of the psychosoma presents characteristic signals, especially of a mental nature, which permits one to clearly distinguish it from projection of the consciousness in the isolated mentalsoma.

Last. For a great number of projectors, the extraphysical head of the psychosoma (parahead) is the last part to leave the coincidence of the consciential bodies or vehicles.

Sensitives. Developed sensitives show the greatest predisposition toward semiprojections, possibly due to looseness of the holochakra and the natural predisposition toward the precursory signals of projectability, including physical torpidity, alienation, disappearance, *ballonnement,* and dizziness.

Intoxication. Sometimes, semi-detachment occurs spontaneously due to the natural energetic obstruction, or *pranic blockage* of an organic area, e.g.: in the abdomen, when the umbilicochakra and splenochakra are blocked due to the effects of intoxication caused by intestinal constipation (excess of waste matter).

Seated. The partial lucid projection, semiprojection, or hemiprojection (half of the physical body) of only the para-arms, the trunk from the waist up, and the parahead of the human body constitutes a seated consciential projection. This extraphysical position often imposes the immediate return of the projected consciousness to the condition of complete recoincidence of the vehicles of manifestation.

Psychopathology. Besides partial projection – which constitutes a natural and frequent parapsychophysiological phenomenon in the experiences of veteran lucid consciential projectors – hallucinations also occur, as in the case of phantom, extra or supernumerary arms, as it is referred to in psychopathology. This especially happens with epileptic or migraine patients, which is a very different condition.

Syncope. We should not omit a reference to the pathological or unhealthy context in which partial projections occur or, in other words, in the initial manifestations of syncope, weakness, fainting or loss of consciousness.

Torpidity. In fact, at the onset, in cases of arterial hypotension, the person is sometimes surprised by fragmented projections of his/her physical terminations – hands and arms, feet and legs – with the physical torpidity of these corporal segments, before experiencing dizziness or fainting, through a temporary loss of consciousness.

Discrimination. As a rule, it becomes difficult for the consciousness – in circumstances that are generally very stressful and generative of syncope – to remain lucid and clearly discriminate, in a detailed manner, step-by-step, the organic or physical-psychic occurrences in a self-analysis of the symptoms and signs in which the syncope develops prior to the person losing consciousness.

Thwarted. In thwarted fainting, however, the intraphysical consciousness who underwent the initial stages of fainting without losing consciousness or, in other words, without achieving the complete condition of fainting, is able to compare the pathological experience with a fragmented lucid projection, sponsored by his/her will, which is a healthy condition.

Hypotension. A less common example of thwarted syncope is the person with arterial hypertension (blood pressure: 140 by 100 mm Hg) who, upon inadvertently taking an excessive amount of a diuretic is, hours later, weakened and overcome by a drop in arterial pressure (blood pressure: 90 by 60 mm Hg), but does not get to the point of fainting.

Self-analysis. This condition often permits a person to better perform self-analysis because excessive psychic or emotional factors do not occur so intensely, whereas triggering physical-chemical factors predominate more in this case.

Clarity. In these cases of frustrated syncope, the fragmented projection of the arms is generally clearer and more dramatic than when sponsored only through the deliberate impulsion of the will, in an entirely healthy context.

Note. *Semiprojection,* which represents a partial exteriorization of the psychosoma, should not be confused with *semilucid projection,* which is based on a discontinuity in the lucidity of the projected consciousness; nor should it be confused with the condition of waking discoincidence.

Bibliography: Alverga (18, p. 214), Armond (53, p. 127), Boswell (174, p. 138), Carton (252, p. 310), Delanne (382, p. 152), Giovetti (593, p. 51), Gomes (612, p. 82), Greenhouse (636, p. 199), Guilmot (661, p. 57), Leaf (905, p. 145), Monroe (1065, p. 170), Reis (1384, p. 90), Rogo (1444, p. 85), Seabra (1534, p. 89), Todd (1689, p. 47), Verneuil (1735, p. 95), Vett (1738, p. 385), Vieira (1762, p. 107).

226. PROJECTION IN THE ISOLATED MENTALSOMA TECHNIQUE

Definition. Projection in the mentalsoma: the state of maximal expansion of your consciousness at a supra-rational and supra-sensory level of concentration.

Synonymy: asomatic experience (without a body); cosmic consciousness (Richard Maurice Bucke: 1837-1902); cosmoprojection; ecstasy (mystics); exaltation (mediumship); *kairos* (existentialism); *khou* (Ancient Egypt); mental projection (projectiology); nirvana (Buddhism); profound projectability; samadhi (Yoga); *satori* (Zen); *slema* (Cabalism); superprojection; ultraconsciousness; *unio mystica* (Catholicism).

Phase. As a lucid projector, you should only endeavor to produce a projection voluntarily in the mentalsoma after you have achieved some control with voluntary projection techniques – even if the results are not continuous over chronological time – in the psychosoma alone, and in the psychosoma laden with the energies of the holochakra (denser) within the physical base in the paratropospheric extraphysical dimension, as well as in extraphysical districts not having any direct relation to physical life.

Self-knowledge. At this point, you should be aware that you will now endeavor to reach an advanced stage of your inner illumination, integral self-knowledge and the condition of cosmic consciousness or cosmoconsciousness.

Target-idea. You need to reflect upon the extremely important fact that, according to the theorice of the mentalsoma, the target-idea predominates and works better in consciential projections in the isolated mentalsoma, in the mentalsomatic dimension, which is common to the entire universe.

Target-person. The target-person or even the target-place tends to attract his/her consciousness together with the psychosoma, which is projected from the human body.

Difficulty. When projected in the mentalsoma, either spontaneously or voluntarily, you might be surprised to find yourself together with a target-person or in a target-place, but it will be much more difficult to deliberately produce a mental projection using these targets.

Processes. While in the ordinary, physical waking state, you should reflect on the details and fundamental steps of the processes your consciousness goes through to achieve a projection in the mentalsoma: the mentalsoma detaches itself from the parabrain of the psychosoma which is almost always partially or totally discoincident from the human body and holochakra, being very close to the human body or at a certain distance from it.

Position. Use the physical position that is most comfortable for you, the same one you use most often to project in the psychosoma, preferably the dorsal position, performing progressive muscular relaxation until the entire human body is torpid.

Forget. Forget, at this time, 3 categories or facets of *personal world:*

1. **Forms.** The world of forms: length, width and height (lines, curves, spheres, the *light cone,* geometry).

2. **Space.** The world of spaces: the physical, the paratropospheric extraphysical and the extraphysical, per se, which is more ample (proxemics, *domicentrism*, physics).

3. **Time.** The world of chronological time: the past, the present and the future (minutes, hours, days, chronology, chronobiology).

Restriction. These elements are negative, in this case, because they further restrict your mind, human brain, biomemory and, consequently, your intraphysical consciousness, which is doubly constrained in the conditioned situation between two realities:

1. *Funnel.* The *funneling (the funnel of restriction)* of existence.
2. *Bellows.* The *human bellows* of intraphysical life, the soma (lungs, uninterrupted respiration).

Zero. Keep your consciousness as open as possible, predisposed to the reception of new ideas or creative, original, new facts (neophilia). Remove all preconceptions and the reflexes of human conditioning, as though you had begun to reflect now, for the first time, about everything regarding life and the universe, starting from *zero.* Suppose yourself, without pre-judgment, to be in an absolute vacuum or in a possible *nothingness.*

Recourse. As a last recourse, you may concentrate your undivided attention on an elevated or universalistic concept or, in other words, a constructive idea, an enigmatic question suitable for being developed into new angles and parameters that go beyond the boundaries of your consciential maturity and knowledge in the ordinary, physical waking state. It must, however, be similar to your most sophisticated *fourth world:* the individual mental world (consciential micro-universe, personal holothosene).

Examples. The following are 5 ideas suitable for you to induce your consciousness to project in the isolated mentalsoma, according to your personal cultural background:

1. **Mathematics.** If you are a mathematician, you should think about the precise notion of the *infinite.*

2. **Physics.** If you are a physicist, think about the deepest inner structure of the *black hole.*

3. **Medicine.** If you are a physician, think about the nature of *therapeutic psychophysical energy.*

4. **Parapsychism.** If you are a sensitive, think about your own *parapsychic manifestation* in the mentalsoma.

5. **Spiritism.** If you are a spiritist, think about understanding the manifestation of an evolutionarily pure spirit (an FC or *free consciousness*).

Overlook. Most often, your consciousness perceives neither the exteriorization nor the interiorization of your mentalsoma *from* and *in* the parabrain of the psychosoma.

Awareness. Your awareness of being in the mentalsoma almost always arises when you are already in the mentalsomatic dimension. This is due to your indirect observations, or by a process of elimination, in light of the exceptional magnitude of self-lucidity, the apparent absence of a vehicle of manifestation of your consciousness – like a simple point of awareness, an incorporeal point in space or a ball of vitalized energy – as well as your ego's unmistakable inner state of unequalled and unprecedented equilibrium.

Differential. If you are a novice projector, you should remember these differential clarifying characteristics in order to obtain correct analysis of the experiments: whenever you are projected and feel or see yourself as having a parabody, parahands, extremities and strong emotions, you are, without a doubt, manifesting in the psychosoma (the body of desires) and not in the mentalsoma, regardless of how grandiose the sensation of exaltation, euphoria, freedom, lightness or size of your consciousness.

Reflection. As a lucid projector, it becomes useful for you to reflect upon the experiences that you have produced, on the same day as the occurrence – especially if they were mental projections – because this opportune reflection upon a *fresh,* recent experience can provoke much deeper conclusions regarding the apprehension and comprehension of intraconsciential phenomena and extraphysical events. This brings elucidation about obscure points and original ideas in other fields of knowledge, enriching your *cultural background,* the recuperation of cons and frank access to your holomemory.

Will. Obviously, anyone can project in the mentalsoma. This only depends upon the impulsion of one's decided will and effective motivation. It can even allow the consciousness to break through the *contact quarantine* with other intelligent civilizations existent in the universe (lucid exoprojections).

Difficulties. Nevertheless, when your consciousness is projected directly in the mentalsoma, certain manifestations become difficult or, better still, impracticable. The following are examples of 11 interdicted, extemporaneous or temporarily inaccessible thosenic manifestations:

1. Coarse emotionalism (serenity can occur, serenology).
2. Extraphysical self-anamnesis (para-semiology).
3. Humanoid speech (*conscientese* can occur, communicology).
4. Invisible interconsciential unions (*congressus subtilis*).
5. Phenomenon of apparition of the intraphysical projector (*inter vivos* apparition).
6. Phenomenon of visible bilocation of the consciousness (paraphenomenology).
7. Physical self-bilocation.
8. Production of direct physical effects (macro-PK, ectoplasmy).
9. Self-telekinesis.
10. Self-transfiguration.
11. Viewing of the silver cord (holochakrology).

Bibliography: Bucke (218, p. 60), Castaneda (258, p. 177), Fodor (528, p. 65), Greene (635, p. 41), Greenhouse (636, p. 25), Lilly (927, p. 71), Marinho (997, p. 83), Miranda (1048, p. 285), Muldoon (1105, p. 225), Powell (1279, p. 89), Rogo (1446, p. 320), Sculthorp (1531, p. 144), Shepard (1548, p. 596), Toben (1688, p. 73), Vieira (1771, p. 13), Walker (1781, p. 27).

---

227. PINEAL PROJECTION TECHNIQUE

Definition. Pineal projection: the process whereby you, as an intraphysical consciousness, project from your human body through *excitation* of the pineal gland.

Synonymy: adenoprojection; pineal activation; pineal *excitation;* pineal exercise; pineal *eye* technique.

Focalizing. One of the processes used for producing lucid projection is based upon the state of physical relaxation coupled with mental focalization upon the pineal gland, or in the direction of its location (more-or-less at the center of the brain, taken as a point of reference) and fixation of autosuggestion through deep mental self-awareness.

Ophthalmology. This projective process is only indicated for those with no ocular or ophthalmological problems.

Glabella. To focalize the mind at the center of the cranium, thus awakening the pineal gland, considered here as the controller of consciential projection, you mentally concentrate at the base of the nose, the point between your eyebrows or on the glabellar area. This action requires that your eyes direct themselves upward to a point that does not produce discomfort or, obviously, permanent strabismus.

Axes. The method most often used for locating the pineal gland is to imagine 2 axes or straight lines passing through your head:

1. **First.** The first axis, running from front to back, begins at the point between your eyebrows and ends at the prominent area of the occipital bone at the nape of your neck.

2. **Second.** The second (transversal) axis runs from one temple to the other or, in other words, from the left side of your head (or cranium) to the right side.

Location. The gland is located precisely at the point where the 2 axes intersect.

Techniques. You can employ the pineal gland *excitation* technique by converging the two eyeballs upward and toward the center of the forehead, maintaining them in this position for about 10 seconds. Next, return your eyeballs to their normal positions, relax the ocular muscles and the optical nerve.

Execution. You need to repeat the exercise a few times and execute it with the muscles of the forehead and face completely relaxed.

Index. You can also use the technique involving the slow, successive approximating and distancing of your index finger, following it with your eyes. You will move the finger back and forth from the glabellar area (between the eyebrows) to a distance of 1' (30 cm), always above your eyes, several times.

Coordination. As various people have already done, after a certain time, and with some practice, you learn to coordinate the eye muscles and improve the process without feeling any discomfort or causing any damage to your eyesight.

Takeoff. The projection of your consciousness occurs with the sudden takeoff of the extraphysical head (parahead) of the psychosoma through the cranium. This occurs in a surprising but inoffensive manner, also producing intracranial sounds.

Hypothesis. Based on the fact that the pineal gland begins to *devolve* after puberty and in the period of adulthood, is the pineal projection technique easier for adolescents to apply?

Coronochakra. According to holochakrology, we should keep in mind that the effectiveness of the pineal projection technique depends greatly upon the quality of the energies of the coronochakra of the intraphysical consciousness practitioner.

Bibliography: Bayless (98, p. 158), Bord (170, p. 58), Fox (544, p. 142), Reis (1384, p. 42), Shay (1546, p. 55), Yogananda (1894, p. 167).

---

228. CHANGE IN ROUTINE TECHNIQUE

Definitions. Routine: the habitual action realized day after day; the sequence of acts that you observe out of habit or, in other words, through frequent repetition.

Synonymy: action of the subconscious mind; action of the subconscious will; tenacious habit.

Trauma. Any old habit, a normal or commonplace action but one which is sufficiently ingrained to be strong, when it is interrupted, or broken, interrupts a routine and tends to create a small trauma (stress) in the consciousness which is upset because it is attached to this routine.

Strength. This is why the pressure of habit, or the force of routine, is a power that can be advantageously applied as a process for projecting with lucidity, because the projected consciousness, moved by the subconscious will, tends to follow routine patterns, thereby occurring frequent cases of spontaneous lucid projection.

Place. Thus, for example, you choose a certain place where you are used to going, either inside or outside your physical base.

Dissatisfaction. If you stop going to this place, thus depriving yourself of this desire or forcing the suppression of this habit that is a part of your life, thinking about it intensely and insistently, and continuing with this unsatisfied wish, your subconscious will, upon sleeping and under suggestion, will take your lucid consciousness in the psychosoma to this precise place, repeating the routine motor (mechanical or automatic) action.

Base. A common example of a change in routine is the sudden move from the projector's physical base. In this instance, the individual sleeps in a new domicile and awakens thinking that he/she is in the previous place. The projector's consciousness takes off from the new physical base and extraphysically returns to the old one.

Warning. It is worth warning you here not to use negative habits or routines – e.g.: imbibing alcohol or overeating – with the intention of projecting with lucidity.

Others. There are two other methods described in this section that are based on the change in routine technique: lucid projection through fasting and lucid projection through the provocation of thirst.

Bibliography: Lancelin (879, p. 313), Muldoon (1105, p. 226), Shay (1546, p. 70), Vieira (1762, p. 111).

229. PROJECTIVE REPETITION TECHNIQUE

Repetition. If you have already consciously projected from the human body on any occasion, either spontaneously or deliberately, you can often project again.

Conditions. Through the projective repetition technique, you, as the protagonist of at least one lucid extraphysical projection, should endeavor to repeat the conditions and postures which predisposed your human body to physiologically permit the takeoff of your psychosoma.

Coadjutants. Particularly in this method, you should bear the following 2 healthy coadjutants in mind:

1. **Fatigue.** Fatigue after prolonged physical activity during the day.
2. **Concentration.** Mental concentration fixed on the desire to project, before going to bed to sleep.

Projectiography. Projectiography, as well as the projector's personal diary, when analyzed discerningly, generally helps the development of veteran projectors' lucid projections and can unquestionably aid in the execution of the projective repetition technique.

Bibliography: Frost (560, p. 225), Vieira (1762, p. 210).

230. ROTATION OF THE PSYCHOSOMA TECHNIQUE

Definition. Rotation of the psychosoma: method through which you produce projection of your consciousness in the psychosoma through rotational movements with this consciential vehicle.

Synonymy: the turning over onto the back technique.

Drowsiness. Among the projective psychosoma rolling techniques, one most used by the author is turning over onto the back, which is more indicated when you feel physically tired (exhausted) or very drowsy.

Time. It becomes easier to execute the rotation of the psychosoma technique at daybreak or when the day is beginning, after you have had 4 or 5 hours of normal sleep and have left the bed to study or do any other thing, having returned to bed still fairly drowsy.

Takeoff. As difficult as it may seem at first sight, this process, substantially paraphysiological and devoid of symbolic or ritualistic resource, works perfectly well and permits your consciousness to follow, with full lucidly, the most difficult part of the projection, namely the lucid takeoff or abrupt departure of the psychosoma.

Position. Among the possible variations, for example, you can lie face down (prone position) or against the left side of the face, at the edge of the bed. If you wish, you can even cross one leg over the other, placing the right foot over the calf of the left leg, allowing you to relax completely. You can also use a pillow for the head, close to the nape of the neck, and another under the right arm.

Nostrils. Prior cleansing of your nostrils with warm water obviously becomes of particular importance in the utilization of the prone position, or lying on your stomach, on the bed.

Reaction. It is currently believed that the individual who lies on his/her front is almost always psychologically, through the force of an infantile reaction, endeavoring to forget the tribulations of material life, escaping the realities of the physical world by somehow *sinking himself/herself* into the cushion or, in other words: *into the earth*.

Suitability. Although the prone position is generally less recommended for projections, you can use it in these specific conditions with considerable convenience and suitability in order to achieve the hypnagogic state or the alpha brain wave condition.

Escape. In the prone position, your consciousness endeavors to mentally *escape* from the physical world and, upon attaining the hypnagogic state, you should think of blindly flinging yourself backward and upward, far away from yourself and out of the bed, e.g.: to the left, where you know there is no furniture or other object, thus minimizing or eliminating as much as possible the psychological reflexes of your daily conditioning with regard to the environment of your physical base.

Characteristics. We repeat here, for the sake of clarity, the consciential operations that should occur, based on the following 7 basic characteristics:

1. **Objective.** The objective of resolutely flinging yourself from the bed.

2. **Extrication.** The rapid, voluntary extrication of the consciousness in the psychosoma.

3. **Paraback.** A backwards posture (paraback of the psychosoma) in the extrication of the consciousness in the psychosoma.

4. **Perceptions.** The perceptive condition of blindness of the consciousness.

5. **Direction.** An upward direction over the human body.

6. **Intentionality.** The consciential intention to place yourself far from your own human body.

7. **Choice.** The choice of leaving through the left side of the human body, which was at rest or motionless in the prone position.

Musculature. You obviously do not move the human body and do not even tense the muscles when attempting to fling yourself backwards in the psychosoma out of the human body.

Collision. When following the indicated method, your consciousness should not be apprehensive, although it is more frequent than you might think – even for veteran projectors – to *run into* a closet, table or object, or *collide* with a wall, closed window or other material factor in the intraphysical base when manifesting in the psychosoma.

Cord. Your willpower must function and control the force of retraction of the silver cord. It is for this reason that the backward fling is extremely valid.

Reverse. You will probably notice, in this case, that your silver cord will be connected at the nape of your physical body and at the *paraforehead* of your psychosoma. This is the reverse of other methods.

Psychosoma. During the development of this process, your psychosoma rolls over in the air next to the bed one or two times, finally remaining upright, with your extraphysical head (parahead) further from the human body, which is lying on the bed.

Face. Your extraphysical face, in this case, usually faces the bed.

Attempts. You must not become discouraged or give up, but try the extraction one, two, three times or more, stubbornly persisting with immediate consecutive trials.

Half-turn. A half-turn of the psychosoma can also occur, instead of it rolling over once or twice.

Target. With some training – at most by the third attempt, sometimes with successive takeoffs and interiorizations – your consciousness will already feel free and see itself at a distance from your human body. Once this happens, you should immediately forget all the factors and signs of the physical base and focus on a well-defined mental target, if you want to leave the place.

Interiorization. The interiorization of the psychosoma in the prone position can be easily accomplished with its return directly through the back of your human body, and with full awareness, in most cases.

Exercises. Physical exercise in general greatly helps in the experiments with the psychosoma.

Pool. If you are accustomed to swimming, it is highly recommend that you endeavor to become used to jumping backwards into a swimming pool full of water, while in the ordinary, physical waking state.

Derepression. This practice will annul any negative psychological connotation you may harbor toward it in a hidden, undefined or unperceived manner. It will remove your repression and conditioning connected with the uncustomary action of flinging yourself back and upwards in the psychosoma, far from yourself and the bed, in the dark, during lucid and voluntary takeoff.

Observation. Obviously, for those readers unaccustomed to parapsychic phenomena and animic-parapsychic practices, that which is written here will appear to be pure fantasy or science fiction. If you are one of these persons, the author recommends that you not waste time with any projective training for now.

Self-critique. The most intelligent course of action would be to study a little more about the subject, gathering ideas with some veteran lucid projector and only returning to the indicated projective technique – either this one or *any other healthy method* proven to be effective – maintaining a maximum of self-critique, heterocritique and discernment in everything you do.

Bibliography: Blackmore (139, p. 102), Vieira (1762, p. 144).

231. ROTATION OF THE HUMAN BODY TECHNIQUE

Definition. Rotation of the human body: method for you to produce projection of the consciousness in the psychosoma by employing rotative movements with your physical body.

Synonymy: abstract dance; gyration; gyroprojection; lucid projection rotative technique; projective rotation; rotation; rotational method.

Mechanism. The act of gyrating your human body, especially the head, provokes dizziness through an alteration of the regular functioning of the labyrinth or the center of equilibrium of your human body. Also, this act predisposes the departure of your psychosoma from its natural state of coincidence with the entire human body (unified body), including the head, and your consequent departure from the condition of ordinary wakefulness through a forced takeoff or, in other words, through the abrupt projection of the consciousness.

Uses. The gyratory method is mostly used to produce an altered state of consciousness, parapsychic trance, religious ecstasy and even lucid consciential projection through the dances of Middle Eastern dervishes, the shamans' trances of controlled possession, the modern European practices of witchcraft and the well-known mediumistic gyration or the spinning dances of violent possession in Umbanda or Candomble in Brazil, with an African origin (religious syncretism).

Frenzy. In the abovementioned cases, the gyratory movements are synchronized to traditional chanting or dance and become progressively more frenetic as the individual goes into trance.

Dervishes. Whirling dervishes or spinning witches, begging ascetics, Muslims or Arabs, Turks, Persians and Egyptians are adepts of Sufism. Their repeating gyrational dance is executed through gyrations in circles for extended periods of time. These prolonged dances symbolize the movement of the planets in relation to the sun. They present individual rhythmic expression, can be practiced in groups and lead the dancer to a state of exhaustion and self-induced trance. Some dervishes also use mantras while they dance.

Trance. In the cases of gyrating dances – rhythmic drumming and dances lasting until exhaustion – dizziness and fatigue rapidly lead the consciousness to collapse in a parapsychic trance with consequent visions. The human body can remain under the command of an extraphysical consciousness (possession) during the period of exteriorization of the consciousness, with or without the occurrence of the phenomenon of psychophony.

Chair. A similar technique is applied in order to voluntarily and consciously produce consciential projection using a common revolving chair, such as an office chair. This permits the continued rotation at a certain velocity with the experimenter's entire body weight seated. The rotation of the chair can be suddenly interrupted. The best type of chair for rotating the body is the type used in *flight simulators,* currently employed in the treatment of a common type of labyrinthitis.

Contraindications. This method is obviously not recommended for those who have had labyrinthitis, disturbances in equilibrium or audition, as well as problems in the cervical spine (neck). It is especially important not to use an old chair, as this can lead to falls and accidents.

Nystagmus. Incidentally, it is worth mentioning that a specific chair is being used for consecutive nystagmus examinations wherein the individual is submitted to a certain number of rotations at a constant velocity, which are suddenly interrupted. In this way, one can determine the labyrinth's sensitivity threshold to rotational acceleration.

Takeoffs. The departure of the psychosoma from discoincidence of the unified body can be produced through the following 3 basic procedures, among others:

1. **Line.** In a straight line.
2. **Spins.** Spinning to one side.
3. **Whirling.** Whirling or in an upward spiral.

Direction. The most diverse and bizarre consciential exteriorizations or takeoffs can occur through the rotational method because your consciousness never knows in which of the 3 procedures it will leave, or its destination (direction) upon temporarily leaving the human body in the psychosoma.

Violence. One must be prepared regarding the violent aspect of the gyrating chair practice, which can bring about a negative aspect in the form of creating an extraphysical trauma and thus impairing the quality of the perceptions of the intraphysical consciousness when projected.

Bibliography: Brennan (199, p. 96), Day (376, p. 35), Lewis (923, p. 167), Martin (1002, p. 41), Shepard (1548, p. 231), Spence (1588, p. 121), Zaniah (1899, p. 150).

232. PROJECTIVE MENTAL SATURATION TECHNIQUE

Definition. Projective mental saturation: pressuring the mind with the idea of lucid projection, exercised through all healthy physical, mental and psychological means possible, over a set period of time.

Synonymy: direct projective method; program of total projective immersion; projective psychic saturation; rapid projective system; state of projective quasi-obsession; subconscious impregnation technique; total immersion technique.

Marathons. The study method of psychic saturation gives decidedly rapid results. It is much used as an effective process in intensive training seminars for obtaining consciential illumination through study marathons and debate roundtables.

Languages. It is also employed in the intensive learning of languages, in rapid courses, with a single student, without regular teachers, calling on all the educational resources possible. It can also be used with a resident student, together with other students in a program of full-time total isolation with an actual internment for fifteen days, wherein one is bombarded with the idiom in all imaginable manners.

Mistakes. No one should judge him/herself incapable of projecting from the human body with full lucidity. In this sense, fear (projectiophobia) is the greatest mistake of all and underestimation of one's own potential and personal worth is a close second. Fear and underestimation annihilate the spontaneity and motivation of the consciousness.

Deficiencies. One must combat these deficiencies on the way of psychic and parapsychic development, in all sectors and practical applications.

Atmosphere. Mental saturation fostered with the idea of lucid projection represents the creation of a healthy (non-pathological) fixed idea or monoideism with the deliberate will of projecting yourself, installing the adequate mental atmosphere for this and impressing the subconscious mind in the home, namely the physical base (holothosene) of the projective aspirant.

Saturating. Among the saturating elements adequate for you to promote mental impregnation with the idea of lucid projection, the following 10 should be singled out:

1. **Ambition.** Nurture a productive and ardent ambition to project yourself with a high degree of lucidity, in the manner of a materthosene of your holothosene.

2. **Concentration.** Think intensely or, better still, concentrate your thoughts on the phenomenon of lucid projection at appropriate times and places, on a daily basis.

3. **Understanding.** Understand projectiological phenomena in detail, with naturality, establishing relationships between lucid projections and your preoccupations, human interests and natural cogitations, such as your profession, cultural research and hobbies.

4. **Reading.** Read about the bodies of manifestation of the consciousness and the multiple existing reports from projectors that are easy to consult, whether in books, magazines, e-mails, web sites or journals. Any investment of this type that is made will be worthwhile.

5. **Studies.** Always study perseveringly, analyzing deeply, if possible, the events related to lucid projections.

6. **File.** Also, if it is appropriate, make a collection of file cards on projective themes, compiling your own research files. These cards can be distributed throughout your house, whether on the bedside table, the bathroom mirror, your reading desk or hung on the walls.

7. **Recorder.** Use a tape recorder to register the projective techniques you use or the words of projectors, and listen to these tapes incessantly.

8. **Gathering.** Talk with other persons interested in the theme of lucid projection, be they veteran or novice projectors, projectiology students, or aspirants to lucid projection. Endeavor to achieve the greatest possible gathering of relevant ideas.

9. **Practice.** From the first day of your saturation effort, practice projective exercises intensively, without any interruptions in a series of disciplined attempts.

10. **Implant.** Let the subject "lucid projection" develop for some hours every day, 7 times a week until it becomes firmly implanted or deeply rooted in your mental life and the diuturnal routines of your existence, thus creating and fixating specific related neosynapses.

Dreams. Through this system, consciential processes undergo subtle modifications. Within a maximum of 3 to 4 weeks, when the concentrated effort is relaxed, as a first result of mental saturation, natural dreams about lucid projection will occur, if not a small exteriorization of your lucid consciousness in the psychosoma in the physical base. This is an excellent indication of psychic saturation and an effective opening in the way to lucid projection per se.

Principle. There is a basic principle: whoever dreams with projections, even if it is only a nightmare or *bad dream,* is well on the way to producing lucid projection.

Heterocritiques. The direct method, however, is not free of critiques. It is not simply anyone who can withstand an immersion program that greatly emphasizes personal effort on the part of an intraphysical consciousness who is inexperienced regarding the subject, which provokes aimless lucid projections or the erraticism of lucid projection. However, let us be realistic and practical: this evidently becomes secondary.

Corrections. What is important is to break down the taboo, the conditioning or the obstacle to the lucid departure of your consciousness from the human body. Later, you yourself will correct the initial technical imperfections, improve your mental targets, enrich your extraphysical agenda and you will naturally develop yourself with the repetition of the experiments.

Work. Obtaining lucid projection requires work and demands perseverance. However, few emotions can be compared to the moment when you perceive, for the first time, that you are lucid outside your own human body, free of the connections of dense matter or, in other words: victorious over yourself.

Bibliography: Muldoon (1105, p. 219), Schiff (1515, p. 29), Vieira (1762, p. 189).

---

233. PROJECTION THROUGH THIRST TECHNIQUE

Definition. Thirst: common, physiological, human, internal sensation of necessity produced by a need for (lack of) water (H_2O) or the will to drink.

Synonymy: privation of water; sensation of dryness.

Suggestion. In the same way that the sensation of hunger or the fasting technique is used the sensation of thirst is also employed as a suggestion for impressing the subconscious mind and forcing the departure of the intraphysical consciousness from the human body in the psychosoma in order to satiate an intensely repressed desire.

Domicile. In this manner, you endeavor to transfer the consciousness from its domicile, based on the principle that no one wants to live in a house without water.

Day. From early in the morning on, endeavor to remain thirsty all day, avoiding the ingestion of any liquids: water; juice; soft drinks; tea; any kind of alcoholic beverages; very succulent fruits; soups; or broths.

Night. At night, you go to bed feeling continuously dry, maintaining the intense wish to drink water, thinking about the place where you could satiate your thirst, e.g., 1 of the following 5 possibilities:

1. **Glass.** A glass of cold water strategically placed in position as a mental target or, in other words, a target-object.

2. **Refrigerator.** The refrigerator in the kitchen filled with bottles of mineral water.
3. **Filter.** A pitcher of cold water placed in a nearby place.
4. **Source.** A natural source of clean water (fountain).
5. **River.** A nearby river of unpolluted water.

Potentiation. There are those who further aggravate the condition of dryness and anxiety for water, intensifying or potentiating the accumulated desire. You can use 4 resources for this purpose:

1. **Imagination.** Imagine that you are drinking.
2. **Contemplation.** Look at a glass full of water in front of you, without drinking.
3. **Salt.** Place a small amount of salt in your mouth.
4. **Hyperdipsia.** Take a few swallows of salty water before going to bed. This will even further intensify the sensation of dryness (hyperdipsia).

Warning. This process of sensory deprivation should not be applied with the concept or the consumption of salt if the intraphysical consciousness suffers from arterial hypertension and neither should it be utilized in an exaggerated manner. If it is, this can cause nightmares *before,* instead of lucid consciential projections *afterward.*

Climate. The technique of employing thirst for the intraphysical consciousness to lucidly project from the human body should be applied during only one day, by a person in good health, especially in a warm climate, during summer, maintaining due care in order to avoid undesirable dehydration. For safety reasons, the supervision of a trusted physician is recommended.

Umbilicochakra. According to holochakrology, it should be borne in mind that the effectiveness of the projection through thirst technique depends greatly upon the quality of the energies of the umbilicochakra (as well as the laryngochakra) of the intraphysical consciousness practitioner.

Bibliography: Crookall (343, p. 111), Muldoon (1105, p. 227), Smith (1572, p. 23), Vieira (1762, p. 39), Walker (1781, p. 113).

---

234.   TRANSFERENCE   OF   THE   CONSCIOUSNESS   TECHNIQUE

Leap. In this method, the practitioner with a fertile mind and great determination endeavors to leap from fictitious imagination to a real experience.

Imagination. Remember that imagination is one of the most important means by which we organize, systematize and classify the processed information in our biomemory.

Effort. After visualizing the psychosoma floating over the human body, the consciousness makes a maximal effort to transfer itself to the psychosoma.

Self-bilocation. This process requires the complete dedication of the experimenter and can be developed to such a degree of perfection that it allows the consciousness to contemplate its own resting, motionless human body (self-bilocation) as though it were a *lifeless shell* on the bed or the floor.

Movements. There are those who add (reinforcement, potentiation or optimization) intense movement of the psychosoma to this imaginative practice, with it turning and moving about, full of consciential energy, and with complete extraphysical agility.

Form. This method, much used in so-called magical practices, is the same as the body of light, body of illusion or ball of light, in which the individual applies respiration, the exteriorization of energies and the transference of an intentionally visualized personal form through a *connection of force,* which is also imagined, between the human body and the idealized form.

Mirror. The projective self-image technique employs precisely the same method of transferring the consciousness of the observer to the individual's image reflected in a large mirror.

Bibliography: Butler (227, p. 67), Martin (1002, p. 54).

235. PROJECTIVE TRANSMISSIBILITY TECHNIQUE

Benefit. Just as the consciousness of the projector, upon projecting, can act upon the consciousness of a sleeping or dreaming person, the lucid projection, as an altered state of consciousness, can, under propitious circumstances of physical and psychological predisposition, be transmitted or predispose other persons, or can have the beneficial capacity of parapsychically inciting other individuals to produce it.

Person. Projective contagion operates more intensely with the partner in an evolutionary duo or a person who is very close to (empathic with) the veteran projector.

Mechanism. The mechanism of psychophysical reaction of transmissibility is based on the exteriorization of consciential energies and the determined force of the transmitter practitioner's ironclad will.

Causes. Facts indicate that projective transmissibility parapsychologically exists and works due to 3 factors:

1. **Coexistence.** Day-to-day coexistence with the phenomenon of lucid projection.
2. **Saturation.** Mental saturation regarding the subject of lucid projectability.
3. **Report.** Enthusiasm upon hearing someone report their projective experience.

Periapsis. Similar to periapsis in astronomy or, in other words, the nearest point to the center of attraction in the orbit of any satellite, there exists the *consciential periapsis,* wherein the center of attraction is the parabrain – the seat of the mentalsoma – in the psychosoma.

Applications. Recognizing the existence of the consciential periapsis permits the energy mobilization practitioner to understand and better apply 4 technical procedures:

1. **Contagion.** Positive or healthy animic-parapsychic contagion.
2. **Psychosphere.** The individual extraphysical sphere of energy (psychosphere, personal holothosene).
3. **Coupling.** Auric coupling between two intraphysical consciousnesses.
4. **Exteriorization.** Exteriorization of consciential energies.

Case study. For example, the person with a greater capacity for energy exteriorization can put another person who does not have the conscious capacity for energy exteriorization – and who is even completely blocked regarding animic-parapsychic sensitivity – "under his/her wing," or together with him/herself continuously for a period of time, within the extraphysical sphere of energy. This, along with the aid of the helpers, will increase the individual's parapsychic perceptions.

Tests. The author has observed this fact repeatedly with innumerous extraphysically developed or assisted sensitives. He has also personally tested this many times with friends and acquaintances, starting with auric coupling.

Period. The average period of close association needed with the test-person is 3 days. At this point, the animic-parapsychic phenomena, including facial clairvoyance, occur without interference from any hypnotic factors or explicit suggestions.

236. PROJECTIVE DIAGNOSIS TECHNIQUE

Definition. Projective diagnosis: that which has the objective of identifying a disease, based upon extraphysical examination (para-semiology) of the patient or *evolutient,* being physically performed at a distance, but directly by the projected or semi-projected projector under hypnotic trance and through the phenomenon of traveling clairvoyance.

Synonymy: clairvoyant diagnosis; diagnostic clairvoyance; diagnostic sympathetic assimilation; extraphysical diagnosis; extraphysical-hypnophysical exam; paracatheterization; paralaparoscopy;

parathoracoscopy; projective diagnosis; projective diagnostic exam; projective paradiagnosis; projective self-diagnosis; projective telediagnosis.

Technique. In the technique for performing projective diagnosis, the hypnotist, who is experienced in projectiology, puts the sensitive into a trance, using hetero-hypnosis methods, and instructs the person to extraphysically translocate to the specific target-person. In this case, the identification of the target-patient, unknown to both parties, should be supplied by a third person (double-blind test), preferably a physician who indicates a patient from his/her own clinic who has a complex disturbance or one with an unclear diagnosis.

Verification. First, the traveling clairvoyant describes the target-patient's physical appearance (looks, physiognomy) to the physician who is present in order for him/her to verify the authenticity and precision of the traveling clairvoyance phenomenon on the spot.

Examination. Next, the traveling clairvoyant will endeavor to perform extraphysical examination of the target-patient using the resource of heteroscopy or, in other words, as if perceiving with an x-ray machine (sweeping) over the ill person's entire human body, describing the specific physical disturbances as they are perceived while in the hypnotic trance state.

Warning. The doctor who is not familiar with parapsychic phenomena, especially those of traveling clairvoyance, must be prepared to understand the vague, very general manner or the inadequate terms with which the hypnotized clairvoyant (when this is a person who is not accustomed to the vocabulary, jargon or terminology of the anatomist, the physiologist or the clinician) describes the various signals of the target-patient's illness.

Knowledge. The matter should be received with naturality as it is perfectly understandable, since the clairvoyant does not have to be a technician, trained in any area of medicine or human health, have a basic knowledge of anatomy or an adequate clinical vocabulary (terminology, nomenclature), in order to correctly perform his/her parapsychic functions.

Academic. In order to make a projective diagnosis, the demanding physician can choose a trusted experienced medical student to act as the hypnotic test-sensitive or, in other words, use the student as a traveling clairvoyant in the analysis of clinical cases.

Qualification. This provision will eliminate all deficiencies in descriptions involving precise medical terms (nomenclature), as they will be made by a qualified person, thus generally improving telediagnostic techniques in general.

Acupuncture. If the interested physician and medical student possess some knowledge of acupuncture or Chinese medicine, this will further help in the understanding of the descriptions made using traveling clairvoyance. This is because the semi-projected consciousness sees the 3 vehicles of manifestation – the human body, holochakra and psychosoma – coincident at the same time, locating light and dark luminous, colored spots, as though performing an acupuncture examination without needles or instruments through the verification of the condition of the target-patient's energetic points.

Prognosis. The execution of a projective diagnosis frequently not only permits one to determine a correct and final diagnosis, but also to suggest a prognosis.

Indications. Projective telediagnosis, going beyond clinical, physical or laboratorial diagnosis can, in many cases, be employed with for the following 4 basic goals in mind, among others:

1. **Doubts.** Eliminate doubts in medical evaluation.
2. **False.** Avoid false judgment of symptoms, signs and etiology in the identification of diseases.
3. **Divergences.** Eliminate diagnostic and prognostic divergences or errors.
4. **Surgeries.** Avoid exploratory surgeries and questionable, unnecessary or erroneous surgical operations.

Advantages. Projective paradiagnosis presents the following 4 advantages worth considering, among others:

1. **Unconsciousness.** Confidentiality, as it can be determined without bothering the patient who is unaware of the measure taken.

2. **Simplification.** It dispenses with the physical examination and even eliminates, in certain cases, the discomfort of catheters and invasive procedures, which reduces surgical aggression upon the organism.

3. **Instantaneity.** The positive instantaneous aspect of the process.

4. **Economy.** The evident economy of the method.

Self-diagnosis. The diagnosis performed by the semi-projected clairvoyant while in trance relative to his/her own human body constitutes a *projective self-diagnosis.*

Veterinary. The diagnosis made by the semi-projected clairvoyant while in trance relative to the physical body of a subhuman or irrational animal constitutes a *veterinary projective diagnosis.*

Coadjutant. Extraphysical diagnosis, while constituting a significant evolution in the practice of diagnosis, must be employed prudently and only as a coadjutant or complement to conventional medical practice, which is indispensable in all instances.

Bibliography: Fodor (528, p. 25), Freixedo (553, p. 49), Frost (560, p. 178), Steiger (1601, p. 209).

---

237. PROJECTIOTHERAPY

Definition. Projectiotherapy: the treatment, alleviation or remission of diseases of organic, psychic or parapsychic origin of the projector or another person, through the production of lucid consciential projection.

Synonymy: extraphysical teletherapy; lifesaver projection; projective self-cure; projective self-remission; projective therapy; projective treatment; remissive projection; self-curative-therapeutic projection; self-remissive projection; therapy without crutches.

Specialty. Projectiotherapy is an area or technical specialty of conscientiology (evolutiology, experimentology, conscientiotherapy).

Therapist. The projected intraphysical being who endeavors to apply this projective therapy receives the name of *projector-therapist.*

Mentalsoma. Projective therapeutics is classified as one of the cure-at-a-distance techniques although it is applied directly in the extraphysical dimension through the application of energetic pulses – or consciential energy – focused on the holochakra and psychosoma of the patient, or through the action of the will directly from the mentalsoma (mentalsomatics).

Vehicles. Projectiotherapy occurs based on the vehicles of manifestation of the intraphysical consciousness (holosoma) – the human body, holochakra (energetic body), psychosoma (emotional body) and mentalsoma (mental body, holosomatics).

Citadel. Strictly speaking, conventional medicine addresses the human body; acupuncture, do-in, homeopathy and all bioenergy therapeutics act intensively upon the holochakra or the energetic body; extraphysical deintrusion, irradiations at a distance and other techniques particularly utilize the psychosoma. Projectiotherapy, besides utilizing all these means, notably also employs the last recourse, the therapeutic attack on the citadel of the consciousness – the mentalsoma – at our current evolutionary level, in search of the definitive remission of its maladies.

Prophylaxis. Lucid projection, while not performing miraculous cures, in and of itself, constitutes an invaluable prophylactic process, preventing innumerous illnesses and disturbances of the psychophysical systems of human beings, especially when it acts through the effective implantation of extraphysical maturity in the consciential life of the projector and all beings in general.

Holomaturity. Integral consciential maturity or holomaturity is synonymous with projective prophylaxis.

Psychosomatics. It becomes easy to evaluate the immense animic-parapsychic therapeutic possibilities, for oneself or others, of the lucid departure of the intraphysical consciousness from his/her cellular body, if we reflect upon the fact that countless illnesses are the result of pathological conditions that arise in the psychosoma (psychosomatic illnesses). In these cases, the best therapeutic process will always be to act directly upon the energetic system of the holochakra together with the psychosoma of the patient.

Types. There are basic techniques for the application of projective therapy, through the following 3 provisions, e.g.:

1. **Self-sufficiency.** The projector can produce a lucid projection by him/herself: self-hypnosis, autosuggestion or self-induction.

2. **Helper.** The projector can avail him/herself of the assistance of a helper: assisted lucid projection.

3. **Hypnotist.** The projector can utilize the services of a trusted hypnotist: hetero-hypnosis.

Provisions. Countless curative provisions can be achieved through projectiotherapy, including the following 8, e.g.:

1. **Energies.** Absorption and exteriorization of cosmic energies or extraphysically absorbed energies.

2. **Fields.** Formation or installation of prophylactic or therapeutic consciential energy fields.

3. **Holomemory.** Accurate investigations into the archives of the integral memory or holomemory of consciousnesses.

4. **Projections.** Lucid projections of the consciousness in space and time, with incalculably positive results.

5. **Interviews.** Positive rapport with extraphysical consciousnesses (extraphysical personalities), awake intraphysical beings or projected intraphysical consciousnesses, through direct interviews.

6. **Transfusions.** Energetic transfusions to the holochakra and psychosoma of intraphysical beings and needy or energivorous extraphysical consciousnesses.

7. **Psychosoma.** Instantaneous positive alterations in the psychosoma of an intraphysical consciousness which has passed through desoma.

8. **Holosoma.** Analysis, as a whole, of the holosoma of the ill being.

Energy. The projector, projected in the psychosoma, in any of the techniques indicated, can utilize the exteriorization of consciential energy, whether executed strictly by oneself, or with the aid of a helper.

Holosomatic. This energy is sent directly to your own human body; to the coincident human body, holochakra, psychosoma and mentalsoma (holosoma) of another intraphysical consciousness; or to the psychosoma and mentalsoma of an extraphysical consciousness (and the remnants of the holochakra, when that extraphysical consciousness has still not passed through second desoma).

Lucidity. In the direct application of this therapeutic energy, the projected consciousness of the projector-therapist has to be prepared with good intention, sufficient lucidity regarding what to do, including an awareness of the patient's affected organs and the organic areas in relation to the basic chakras, especially if one is performing projective therapeutics on one's own.

Agent. When there is an intervention of assistance on the part of a helper (an extraphysical consciousness) or a human hypnotist, the lucidity of the projected projector can, in certain cases, be less accentuated and the projected projector will thus function more as a *teleguided* physical-extraphysical agent.

Disturbances. Innumerous disturbances, syndromes or diseases can be treated and even self-cured through projective therapy, such as the following 8:

1. Cases of organic pathologies due to or triggered by disturbances characteristic of the parapathology of the holochakra and psychosoma.

2. Consciential energetic imbalances and blockages in general.

3. Egokarmic stigmas.

4. Interconsciential intrusions in general.

     5. Post-desomatic parapsychoses.

     6. Interconsciential energetic parasitisms or possessions.

     7. Psychoses in general.

     8. Repressed parapsychism syndromes.

Mentalsomatic. The direct action upon the mentalsoma of the patient, as with the curing of dipsomania (alcoholism), for example, can be performed through a consciential projection wherein the projector-therapist takes possession of the patient's soma (*inter vivos* incorporation), in a temporary, benign possession. The projector then suggests to the patient's consciousness, directly from mentalsoma to mentalsoma, that the patient naturally give up the addiction to drink (chemical or pharmacological dependency) or the use of drugs. In certain resistant cases, this practice, always assisted by a helper, needs to be applied more than once during the projectiotherapy process.

Deintrusion. In cases of direct interference by intruding extraphysical personalities or intrusions by extraphysical consciousnesses, the clarifier-projector, projected in the psychosoma, promotes a direct confrontation *(extraphysical face-off)* with the participating extraphysical consciousnesses in a service of direct or personal extraphysical deintrusion.

Apometria. One of the animic (intraphysical consciousnesses) therapeutic techniques utilizing lucid projection used in Brazil is *apometria,* a term created by José Lacerda de Azevedo to designate Luiz Rodrigues' *hypnometria,* wherein the patient's consciousness is projected in the psychosoma directly to the extraphysical therapists (extraphysical consciousnesses).

Dynamization. Together with the patient, sensitives who are also projected in the psychosoma, assist in the extraphysical care, dynamizing the groupal therapeutic process. In these cases, the patient generally does not see, sense or register anything regarding the therapeutic processes, but noticeably improves in the cases of interconsciential intrusion.

Self-help. There are many registered cases in which an intraphysical consciousness projects in the psychosoma in search of human resources of first-aid for his/her own injured human body, or in conditions of extreme danger regarding the life of the soma. These registered cases actually do not only constitute *self-cures,* but also ensure the maintenance of one's intraphysical existence, or the continuation of material survival on earth (lifetime).

Coadjutant. Although projective therapy constitutes a remarkable evolution and an enlargement of therapeutic areas, it must be applied prudently, whether in isolated cases, using only the resources of the animic potentiality of the intraphysical consciousness, or together with parapsychism, but always as a coadjutant resource, alternative therapy or valuable complement to conventional, orthodox medical practice, which is indispensable in any case, not forgetting acupuncture and homeopathy.

Bibliography: Costa (308, p. 4), Greenhouse (636, p. 200), Hermógenes (715, p. 259), Krippner (865, p. 299), Moore (1081, p. 176), Netto (1125, p. 77), Steiger (1601, p. 210), Walker (1781, p. 59).

---

238. PSYCHOLOGICAL   CONDITIONING   TECHNIQUES

Pre-takeoff. The psychological conditionings in the pre-takeoff stage that predispose your consciousness to lucid projection are based on technical visualizations that must be carried out when you are in the previously mentioned physical postures. The following 10 are examples:

     1. **Thosenization.** Concentrate your thoughts on the objective of lucid projection, avoiding scattered thoughts and daydreams.

     2. **Somatics.** Mentally, gradually stop feeling the human body, with the firm thought that your dense body no longer exists.

     3. **Universes.** Make your consciousness enter the realms of absolute silence, as if the known universe (cosmos) had disappeared for you.

     4. **Forms.** Think intensely upon the idea that material forms no longer exist for you.

5. **Alienation.** Seek the condition of inner alienation toward everything that is physical or material.

6. **Imagination.** Imagine the upward takeoff of your consciousness in the psychosoma or the mentalsoma.

7. **Floating.** Intensely desire to float further above where you feel yourself to be.

8. **Rolling.** Roll the psychosoma to one side, to either the right or the left, the side that you prefer at the moment.

9. **Sounds.** Prepare yourself to hear the shrill sounds (extraphysical sounds) characteristic of the takeoff of the psychosoma, a fact that occurs with relative frequency.

10. **Autosuggestion.** If, by chance, your consciousness loses lucidity in various consecutive experiments, use an autosuggestion before the experience and you will awaken in the extraphysical dimension.

Bibliography: Monroe (1065, p. 207), Muldoon (1105, p. 188), Vieira (1762, p. 53).

IX – *Exteriorization of the Consciousness Stage*

239. SIGNALS PRECURSORY TO LUCID PROJECTION

Definition. Projective signal: the ostensive occurrence that characterizes the improvement of the processes that produce lucid projection.

Synonymy: indicator of projectability; precursory signal of lucid projection.

Qualities. Among the basic qualities that act to enhance the performance of the aspirant to lucid projection, at least the following 5 can be singled out:

1. **Desire.** The sincere desire to project.
2. **Disposition.** Absence of fear (projectiophilia) or blocks generated by autosuggestion.
3. **Self-discipline.** Incessant and regular experimentation.
4. **Constancy.** Constancy and tenacity of the proposals.
5. **Saturation.** Mental saturation with respect to the subject (creation of specific neosynapses).

Attitudes. These attitudes and procedures permit the appearance of characteristic signals in order to achieve greater success in the production of lucid projections.

Types. The following are 13 basic indications that the experimenter is on the way to achieving the objective of lucidly projecting him/herself:

1. Torpidity of the human body.
2. Sensation of alienation with regard to the physical world (human dimension).
3. Swooning.
4. Vibrational state.
5. *Ballonnement* (balloonment).
6. Projective catalepsy.
7. Vivid natural dreams (recurrence).
8. Continuous dreams of flying.
9. Dreams on the theme of lucid projection (mental saturation).
10. *Quasi-projections,* namely semilucid or badly recalled projective experiences.
11. Lucid projections aborted by some kind of trauma or repercussion, whether intraphysical or extraphysical.
12. Sensation of taking off in the psychosoma.
13. The occurrence of intraphysical repercussions with some lucidity.

Certainty. If some of these signals occur, the aspirant to lucid projection can be absolutely sure that he/she will soon be able to project with ample lucidity. It is simply a matter of insisting with the use of preestablished methods and disciplines.

Stimulus. The precursory signs of lucid projection serve as powerful stimuli to motivate the practitioner to continue with his/her experimentations.

Bibliography: Armond (53, p. 126), Shay (1546, p. 91).

240. PROJECTIVE AURA

Definition. Projective aura: the sensation or particular phenomenon that precedes the beginning of the projection of the consciousness from the human body or soma.

Synonymy: notice of projection; phenomenon of signs; presaging of extraphysical action; primary extraphysical signs; projective disposition.

Personal. The projective aura represents the initial subjective or objective signs of the projective trance. Upon gaining experience, the projector ends up perfectly identifying and characterizing all aspects of his/her extremely individual projective aura. He/she can thus forecast an imminent consciential projection and accelerate personal projective development.

Causes. Among the causes of projective aura, at least the following 9 should be singled out:

1. **Looseness.** Holochakral looseness.
2. **Predisposition.** Animic or intraconsciential predisposition.
3. **Physiology.** The physiology of the human body.
4. **Paraphysiology.** The paraphysiology of the psychosoma.
5. **Bait.** The phenomenon of interconsciential bait.
6. **Projection.** Partial consciential projection.
7. **Notice.** Notice of a consciential projection.
8. **Prior.** A prior consciential projection.
9. **Clairvoyance.** Traveling clairvoyance.

Character. According to projectors in general, there are hundreds of types of signs that are characteristic of the projective aura. These signs can be characterized as motor, sensitive, sensorial, psychic or parapsychic (extra-sensory).

Types. The following are the 5 most frequent types of signs specific to the projective aura:

1. **Air.** Perception of a flow of air in the environment.
2. **Whistle.** Hearing a whistling or hissing noise around the practitioner.
3. **Frontochakra.** Subjective manifestations of the chakras, especially the frontochakra.
4. **Vibration.** Small vibration in the head or in the upper part of the thorax.
5. **Light.** Sensation of an abrupt increase in the brightness of the light in the room of the physical base.

Effects. Besides the abovementioned generic signs, there are at least 9 more effects that sometimes comprise the projective aura:

1. **Digestion.** *Acceleration of digestion* and the elimination of gastric repletion, both occurrences having an extraphysical origin.
2. **Visual.** Transiform physiognomic alterations.
3. **Hallucinations.** Olfactory hallucinations.
4. **Impressive.** Parapsychic perception of extraphysical presences (extraphysical consciousnesses or, very rarely, projected intraphysical consciousnesses) due to *impressive parapsychism* (impressions of the sensitive intraphysical consciousness).
5. **Parapsychism.** Parapsychic phenomena in general.
6. **Approach.** Sensations of a mental approach or an interconsciential attack of an extraphysical or invisible origin.
7. **Signage.** Signals that are typical of parapsychism.
8. **Somnolence.** Somnolence or hypnagogy.
9. **Clairvoyance.** Facial clairvoyance.

Traveling. The practitioner can experience traveling clairvoyance prior to the integral projection of the consciousness in the psychosoma. This can serve as a prior projection, a notice of an upcoming projection or a *preview* of an impending consciential projection, per se. In this case, it can also act as a factor supplying *rapport* or intensifying the necessary empathy with the target-beings in mind who are in another intraphysical or extraphysical environment.

Helpers. Traveling clairvoyance, especially in the conditions referred to, but also in the majority of circumstances, can be promoted by helpers as they are interested in the development of projections, the development of the projector's parapsychic capacities, the resulting performance of fraternal assistance and other factors still unknown to projectors and *surrounding intraphysical consciousnesses (occasional bystanders)*.

Recognition. After having some lucid projections, the intraphysical projector, attentive to his/her own sensations, ends up recognizing the signals of his/her projective aura and, predisposing him/herself with plenty of relaxation and motivation to help, will be able to leave the human body with much greater ease, in a manner that is constant, uniform, standardized and with greater lucidity.

Duration. The projective aura normally occurs for only a few brief minutes, immediately before the intraphysical consciousness projects. Nevertheless, it can exceptionally last for one or two hours, until the human and/or extraphysical circumstances allow the production of the projection as it should be, or according to the necessities and specific implications of the *physical-extraphysical moment* of the existence of the intraphysical consciousness (existential program).

Pathologies. The projective aura is an extremely positive, simple paraphysiological manifestation. Although it actually represents a very well-defined *aura* it has no direct connection with pathological causes and manifestations, nor is it linked to the epileptic aura, asthmatic aura, the renal colic (lithiasis) aura, the hysterical aura, or that of a migraine (headache), also called visual, sensorial or *psychic auras*.

Bibliography: Frost (560, p. 55), Guirdham (664, p. 15), Monroe (1065, p. 216), Vieira (1762, p. 87).

241. PHYSICAL   TORPIDITY

Definition. Physical torpidity: the temporary absence of the sensitivity and, therefore, the action of the human body when the senses enter into torpor, constituting the first personal sign of discoincidence of the vehicles of manifestation of the intraphysical consciousness.

Synonymy: deadening of the organism; organic torpidity; organic insensitivity; yoganidra; sensation of organic anesthesia; physical torpor; organic torpor.

Frequency. A reduction in cardiac frequency or, in other words, a reduction in the rhythm of the heartbeat, constitutes the basic factor predisposing the human organism to the state of physical torpidity, stemming from the impulsion of the will.

Cause. The essential cause of physical torpidity is the deactivation of the nervous system through the inhibition of nerve endings. It is for this reason that it generally begins in the extremities, feet, legs, hands and arms.

Signal. Therefore, the appearance of physical torpidity is the first local, characteristic signal of the partial exteriorization of the psychosoma, precisely in the area of the human body that is numb.

Inertia. The partial or complete exit of the psychosoma simultaneously provokes physical torpidity. Therefore, this condition always indicates the occurrence of a partial or complete discoincidence of the vehicles of manifestation of the consciousness, thereby arising the temporary inertia of the human body and the freeing of the psychosoma.

Anesthetics. If we consider the deadening effects of anesthetic substances, used in medical and odontological local anesthesia of the patient, we can better understand the phenomenon of physical pre-projective torpidity.

Local. The anesthetic inhibits the transmission of nerve impulses from the neural net of the organic area that has been anesthetized, thereby removing its sensitivity. This fact leads us to think that local anesthesia, in fact, results in an artificial or chemical partial projection of a *portion* of the psychosoma from the human body, through the action of the anesthetic.

General. Likewise, general anesthesia represents a complete artificial and chemical projection of the *entire* psychosoma from the human body, through the action of the anesthetic.

Surgeries. In endorsement of this last occurrence, there are dozens of known cases of lucid projection, registered over many decades, that have occurred in medical surgery rooms and dental offices.

Conclusions. The following 6 inferences can be drawn from these facts:

1. **Will.** The human body's intense physical torpidity of parapsychic origin is the result of a natural self-anesthesia, consciously or unconsciously executed by the will of the practitioner.

2. **Anesthesia.** Evidence abounds of the commonplace cases of anesthesia, under analysis here, which are induced through hypnotic suggestion. They are, nonetheless, instances of actual anesthesia produced through the willful force of the hypnotized individual under the command of the hypnotist.

3. **Discoincidence.** Any type of anesthesia or suppression of local or general neurological activity presupposes the localized or generalized exit of the psychosoma from the condition of coincidence of the bodies or vehicles of manifestation of the intraphysical consciousness.

4. **Holochakra.** Anesthesia acts directly upon the nervous system and, indirectly, upon the holochakra, the energetic body of the intraphysical consciousness. It also evidently acts upon the silver cord, the essential intercorporal connection between the human body and psychosoma. The silver cord is an *essential part* of the selfsame holochakra.

5. **Cord.** The silver cord – in this case, the element of intercorporal soma-psychosoma connection – is inserted, connected or, better still, derives from the entire organism, from all of its cells, but essentially from the nerves, the nerve endings, the entire nervous system and, finally, the brain itself or, in other words, the 2 cerebral hemispheres.

6. **Equivalence.** In the condition of the manifestations of parapsychobiophysical phenomena, the following 4 occurrences are equivalent:

A. **Hypnosis.** Psychological anesthesia executed through hypnosis (parabrain).

B. **Analgesic.** Chemical anesthesia (analgesia) obtained through an anesthetic (somatics).

C. **Parapsychism.** The state of organic insensitivity exhibited by fakirs and sensitives.

D. **Will.** The condition of physical torpidity, installed consciously or unconsciously through the force and action of the will of the intraphysical consciousness.

Bibliography: Armond (53, p. 126), Muldoon (1105, p. 215), Rossi (1476, p. 5), Vieira (1762, p. 143).

---

242.   *BALLONNEMENT*

Definition. *Ballonnement:* the sensation of physical expansion – although, in fact, of extraphysical origin or deriving from the holochakra – of any part of the human body, whether the face, members, trunk or even the entire cellular organism that seems to grow, swell, dilate, expand and inflate like a balloon.

Synonymy: "balloonment"; extraphysical sensation of inflating; sensation of an expanded body; sensation of corporal expansion; sensation of corporal swelling.

Frequency. The most common sensation of *ballonnement* is the apparent dilatation, expansion, swelling or thickening of the hands, feet and solar plexus (umbilicochakra) in all directions, and the supposed swelling of the lips, cheeks and chin, which are frequent in parapsychic activities, mainly those with energy transmitting and psychophonic sensitives.

Takeoff. The phenomenon of *ballonnement* sometimes arises for the projector in the moments prior to the takeoff of the psychosoma, or in the pre-takeoff period, either before or simultaneous with the vibrational state. It constitutes an effect of the exteriorization of the psychosoma, generally together with a greater amount of the holochakra.

Sensation. The *ballonnement* effect should provoke happiness in the practitioner rather than apprehension or fear, since it represents one of the first personal indications of discoincidence of the vehicles of manifestation, or the fact that your intraphysical consciousness is starting to leave dense matter with some lucidity.

Incorporation. Besides the sensations stemming from expansion of the animist-sensitive's holochakra and psychosoma during the *ballonnement* phenomenon, incorporation (psychophony) of an extraphysical consciousness also occurs. In this case, the animist-sensitive feels the psychosoma of the extraphysical consciousness, just as the latter feels the psychosoma, holochakra and human body of the sensitive.

Intensification. *Ballonnement* is obviously more pronounced and intense when a slender sensitive with physical effect (ectoplast) capacities incorporates a former intraphysical consciousness which lived in an obese soma. Physical self-transfigurations can even occur in this situation.

Bubble. The *ballonnement* phenomenon demonstrates, in a non-sophistical manner for the experiencer, that the psychosoma is actually a *bubble-body*, and that the parapsychic sensations experienced have a direct relationship with the holochakra.

Tympanites. We must not confuse *ballonnement* of extraphysical origin, analyzed here, with *ballonnement*, a sensation of physical, abdominal origin, due to the pathological distension of the intestine by gas, for example, addressed in medical pathology using the expressions: "meteorism," "tympanites," or "pneumatosis".

Bibliography: Armond (53, p. 127), Greenhouse (636, p. 224), Paula (1208, p. 79), Reis (1384, p. 53), Tourinho (1692, p. 100), Vieira (1762, p. 19).

---

243. PRE-TAKEOFF

Definition. Pre-takeoff: the preliminary state of the intraphysical consciousness immediately prior to the takeoff of the psychosoma from the human body, or the direct projection of the intraphysical consciousness in the isolated mentalsoma.

Synonymy: introductory state of projection; preliminaries of projection.

Psychosoma. The pre-takeoff characteristics analyzed here relate more to the departure of the intraphysical consciousness from the human body using the mentalsoma and psychosoma – which are more frequent and rich in parapsychic occurrences – and not the direct projection of the intraphysical consciousness only in the isolated mentalsoma, which is rarer and more difficult to analyze.

Characteristics. Among the aspects that characterize the projective pre-takeoff stage, at least the following 17 factors can be singled out:

1. Organic torpidity.
2. Alienation in regard to the human body.
3. Vibrational state (VS).
4. *Ballonnement,* sometimes of the entire body.
5. Sensations of the chakras or centers of force (holochakrology).
6. Specific pulsation of the frontochakra.
7. Hypnagogic state.
8. Fugacious visions.
9. Pre-projective sleep.
10. Pre-projective physical catalepsy.
11. Sensation of the *extraphysical hand.*
12. Semidisconnection.
13. Half-exteriorization.
14. Stretching of an extraphysical member (elongation).
15. Extraphysical Trendelenburg.
16. Self-telekinesis.
17. Loss of physical wakefulness.

Contacts. During the pre-takeoff period, it is just as common for the developing as well as the developed sensitive-projector to have healthy or vigorous mental or parapsychic contacts from the helpers as it is to receive pathological or sick contacts from unbalanced (energivorous) extraphysical consciousnesses. It is from these processes that pre-projective parapsychic phenomena arise.

Bibliography: Vieira (1762, p. 53).

244. VIBRATIONAL STATE

Definition. Vibrational state: the condition wherein the holochakra and psychosoma accelerate their vibrations in order to escape from the slow vibrations of the human body, which can produce a projection of the intraphysical consciousness in the psychosoma (fig. 244, p. 1,135).

Synonymy: energetic state; extraphysical electric state; extraphysical *prickling;* internal motor activity; vibrational effects; vibrational sensations; VS.

Looseness. The vibrational state appears, above all, to be promoted by a greater and benign paraphysiological freedom or looseness of the holochakra.

Causes. The following 4 physical factors also act to trigger the vibrational state:

1. Physical vibrations of the entire human body.
2. Cold winds.
3. A substantial drop in ambient temperature.
4. A condition of emotional exaltation.

Characteristics. The vibrational state stems from the intensification of the release or freeing of consciential energies. It may be perceptible or imperceptible to the consciousness and occurs more frequently in consciential projections in the psychosoma with greater density. This is due to the fact that this vehicle carries a greater portion of the holochakra, or energetic body, with it. With the isolated psychosoma or mentalsoma, expansions of the consciousness occur more frequently.

VS. It is important to clarify that the "sensations of vibrations" experienced by the consciousness are not the same as "consciential energies", however the latter is responsible for (causes) the generation of the former (effects). Therefore, VS or the vibrational state actually ends up being an *energetic state,* although "vibrations" and "energies" are intrinsically very different realities.

Effects. Among the sensations of the vibrational state, at least the following 3 effects can be singled out:

1. **Waves.** Movement of internal and equal waves of pulsating, painless vibrations, the frequency – or number of vibrations per second – and intensity of which can be controlled by the will, their frequency being rhythmically increased or decreased.

2. **Sweeping.** A stronger or weaker intensity of vibrations *sweeping* the inactive human body from head to hands and feet, and returning to the brain, in a constant circuit of brief seconds.

3. **Resonance.** This occurs until reaching the natural vibratory frequency or resonant frequency of each vehicle of manifestation separately.

Continuity. Often, the vibrational state is characterized only by the sensation of intense continuous vibration.

Sounds. At other times, noises or intracranial sounds, as well as stimuli or visual effects, appear.

Images. The following are 8 images, metaphors or comparisons that consciential projectors use in order to characterize the sensations of the vibrational state:

1. A pleasant generalized pins and needles.
2. Continuous electric shocks.
3. Electric vibrations.
4. Internal dynamo.
5. Internal *prickling*.
6. Magnetic currents.
7. Mild electricity.
8. The starting of an internal engine.

Paresthesia. In medicine, the sensation of *prickling* over the entire body is called "paresthesia."

Prickling. In psychology, the term *prickling* refers to an unevenly distributed, intermittent or oscillating sensation, like an ambulatory pricking, giving the notion of a large number of ants running across the skin. It is produced by the action of a mild faradic current or of very strong mechanical vibrations that reach a sensitive group of nerves before reaching the pain threshold. This sensation greatly approximates certain occurrences of the vibrational state.

Mirmalgia. It is worth mentioning that a prickling sensation that becomes painful is a different occurrence and is termed *mirmalgia*.

Relaxation. Sometimes it is worth the effort of provoking the vibrational state, not with the singular intention of producing a full lucid consciential projection in the psychosoma, but with the objective of escaping the cold, coercive rigidity of the restriction of the physical body, or the prison of human forms, in a quick and positive psychological relaxation.

Sensations. When provoked intensely with psychological relaxation in mind, the vibrational state can predispose the appearance of diverse positive sensations, such as the following 3:

1. **Orgasm.** An extremely agreeable parapsychic *vibratory orgasm* that manifests throughout the body.

2. *Fire.* Immersion in an *energetic fire,* as though the entire organism were engulfed by rising crackling flames.

3. *Eyes.* Instantaneous appearance of *energetic eyes* – like minisprings or eyes of water – the small vibratory fires of which flow intensely with localized spouts seemingly in a circumscribed segment or area of the human body, such as the forearm, calf of the leg or solar plexus (umbilicochakra).

Catalepsy. Vibrational sensations and benign catalepsy often occur simultaneously and are not clearly distinguishable for some lucid consciential projectors.

Coronochakra. The positive rays of the *iridescent* coronochakra's luminous human crest crown the vibrational state.

Unison. It seems theoretically safe to presume that vibrational state in unison – with synchronized vibrations – can occur through a greater auric coupling between an intraphysical sensitive and an extraphysical consciousness which has not yet passed through the second desoma. This junction results in the occurrence of different effects including an intense reciprocal exteriorization of energies, which predisposes the manifestation of varied phenomena. It is reasonable to suppose that this occurs in certain cases of ectoplasmy and the interconsciential transmission of bioenergies.

Takeoff. In the final stage of the vibrational state a sensation of intracranial pressure can occur, soon followed by the takeoff of the psychosoma transporting the consciousness. The consciousness may remain aware or unaware of the occurrence during takeoff.

Dematerialization. The more advanced vibrational state – or its climax – is the total ectoplasmic condition, or the complete dematerialization of the human body. This occurs in the phenomena of human parateleportation.

Migraine. Some migraine or hemicrania (psychopathology) sufferers report that, at times, after the onset of a severe headache, they feel as though the entire human body is vibrating and moving as if it were a fast-moving pendulum. These reported sensations are precisely reminiscent of the parapsychophysiological and *natural* sensations of the vibrational state.

Chair. The sensations of the vibrational state have been artificially created using a *vibratory chair* together with Ganzfeld stimulation. This makes the person feel vibrations, as though an electric current were passing throughout his/her human body. The purpose of the chair is to induce the consciousness to experience lucid projection. John Palmer is a researcher who observed that half of those persons tested with the vibratory chair were successful in inducing a lucid consciential projection.

Collective. *Collective auric coupling* can occur in a group of individuals who gather under the influence of a common factor that acts upon them (groupal holothosene), or even in a considerable multitude. It can be fundamentally *unconscious* with regard to the occurrence and generated by the emotions (emotional contagion). From this, the vibrational state can occur, which is also *unconscious* with regard to the energies and is generated by the emotions of the promoter, or promoters of the gathering, as well as the majority of the components of the encounter.

Nature. The type of temporary auric coupling, as well as the type of transitory vibrational state, can both be of a positive (healthy) or negative (sick) nature.

Cause. The cause of the phenomenon here is the *interattraction* between each consciousness through the emotional body (psychosoma, psychosomatics).

Holochakrology. The main effects are generated by the energetic body (holochakra, holochakrology).

Quality. It should not be forgotten that the projected intraphysical consciential projector may not only observe but also participate in these occurrences, whether in a conscious manner as an extraphysical paramedic *(leader)* or in an unconscious mode as "cannon fodder" *(victim).*

Homeostasis. In regard to the homeostatic nature (health of the holosomas), collective auric couplings can present themselves in 3 ways: positive, negative and ambivalent.

Positive. The following are 3 examples of collective auric couplings and joint, unisonous vibrational states of a crowd, which can be of a positive or healthy nature:

1. **Leader.** The constructive religious leader at the high point of his/her speech with an expectant crowd.

2. **Virtuoso.** The virtuoso at the end of a well-performed violin concert, for example, with a crowd that is aware and sensitive to what they have just heard.

3. **Valedictorian.** The end of a speech by an experienced valedictorian during the solemn act of a university graduation ceremony.

Assistance. When the emotional energy and the circumstances are positive, the helpers take advantage of the opportunity to extraphysically aid (interconsciential assistance) the intraphysical and extraphysical beings which are in need or in lack.

Negative. The following are 2 examples of collective auric couplings and joint or unisonous vibrational states of a demented crowd that is hopelessly negative or sick or, in other words, manifestations of *mass poisoning:*

1. **Riot.** The political leader who instigates the crowd during a riot.

2. **Lynching.** The climax of intoxicated fury during a lynching.

Minimization. When the commotional energy and circumstances are negative, the helpers do what they can in order to reduce or minimize the misdeeds as much as possible. They assist those they are able to among the participants who are always in subhuman psychological conditions.

Ambivalent. The following are 5 examples of collective auric couplings and joint or unisonous vibrational states of a crowd which can simultaneously have an ambivalent, positive and negative nature:

1. **Fans.** The enthusiasm of fans at a decisive championship game (soccer, basketball, volleyball, baseball) in a filled to capacity stadium.

2. **Gamblers.** The vibration when the horses turn into the final stretch of the big race at the race track (horseracing fanatics).

3. **Samba dancers.** The climax of a samba school procession on the parade route during carnival.

4. **Artist.** The veteran artist who sings for his/her captive audience.

5. **Orator.** The orator upon psychologically involving his/her listeners (oratory, eloquence).

Bibliography: Alverga (18, p. 64), Blackmore (139, p. 101), Castaneda (258, p. 124), Crookall (343, p. 143), Greene (635, p. 92), Lippman (934, p. 347), Manning (993, p. 155), Monroe (1065, p. 210), Reis (1384, p. 54), Rogo (1444, p. 12), Salley (1496, p. 158), Sculthorp (1531, p. 17), Vieira (1762, p. 19), White (1831, p. 144).

245.   HYPNAGOGY

Definitions. Hypnagogy (Greek: *hipnos,* sleep; and *agogos,* conductor): the transitional twilight condition of the consciousness (intraphysical consciousness) that characterizes the somnolent interval between the ordinary, physical waking state and the state of natural sleep; the altered state of consciousness introductory to natural sleep, characterized by oneiric images, hallucinatory visions and representations with visual and auditory effects, due to exacerbation of the imagination.

Synonymy: alpha rhythm; alpha state; alphagenic state; germinal substance of dreams; hymnagogy; hypnagogic activity; hypnagogic conditions; hypnagogic creations; hypnagogic episodes; hypnagogic events; hypnagogic experience; hypnagogic hallucinations; hypnagogic ideation; hypnagogic images; hypnagogic interval; hypnagogic mentation; hypnagogic paramnesia; hypnagogic period; hypnagogic phenomena; hypnagogic processes; hypnagogic state; hypnagogic thoughts; hypnagogic transition; hypnagogic visions; hypnoid state; lightninglike dreams; micro-dreams; pre-sleep state; quasi-sleep; semi-asleep state; semi-awake state; semi-dream state; semi-sleep images; semi-sleep state; semi-somnolent state; twilight state; twilight zone; waking-sleeping border state.

Term. The term *hypnagogic* was coined by A. Maury in 1848.

Material. There is currently more material on hypnagogy to be analyzed. Research is being developed and literature on hypnagogy can be encountered that is made up of reports where, for example, the following 13 consciential conditions are studied:

1. The pre-hypnagogic state.
2. Hypnagogic recall.
3. The subjects of hypnagogic experiments.
4. The training of hypnagogic *biofeedback.*
5. Hypnagogic content.
6. The hypnagogic electroencephalogram.
7. Hypnagogic oneiroid fantasies.
8. Hypnagogicoid phenomena.
9. Synesthetic hypnagogic imagination.
10. Receptivity to hypnagogic phenomena.
11. The aspects of the spontaneous emergence, quality and location of hypnagogic images.
12. The vividness, detail, novelty and grotesque appearance of hypnagogic *faces.*
13. The uncommon beauty and grandeur of hypnagogic *landscapes.*

Relations. Today, researchers endeavor to establish the relationship between hypnagogic *images* and other types of *imagination,* as the one induced by drugs and eidetics; as well as the relationship with déjà vu in general, the self-symbolic phenomenon, suggestibility, personality characteristics, correlated physiological data and rapid eye movements, in order to obtain better explanations for neurophysiological mechanisms of the phenomena and, in this way, formulate theories of greater consensus.

Phenomena. At least the following 4 occurrences have been observed in conjunction with the hypnagogic state in regard to these phenomena:

1. **EEG.** A drop in the frequency and a depression in the amplitude of an electroencephalogram (EEG).
2. **REM.** A tendency for slowness of eye movements.
3. **Musculature.** A decrease in the activity of the frontal muscles.
4. **Respiration.** Changes in respiratory patterns.

Obscurity. Little is still known about two other obscure occurrences:

1. **Mnemosomatics.** The nature of mnemonic storage and the processes involved in recuperating memories of the hypnagogic state.
2. **Hemispheres.** The relative contributions of the left and right cerebral hemispheres in hypnagogic mentation.

Hypnagog. The *hypnagog* generally acts in the passive role of a spectator of a theatrical piece or film, similar to an ordinary dream. This is why hypnagogic phenomena are called *microdreams.*

Polyopia. Cases of polyopia, dysmegalopsia and dysmorphia of the somato-sensory sphere occurring during the hypnagogic state have been verified.

Deprivation. Hypnagogic images seem to be a secondary component in experiences of sensory deprivation.

Tetrad. Hypnagogic images are part of the narcoleptic tetrad composed of:

1. Hypnagogy.
2. Dream paralysis.
3. Narcolepsy.
4. Cataplexy.

Methodology. Four processes have been used in hypnagogic state research methodology:

1. **Spontaneity.** Spontaneous self-observations.
2. **Self-systematization.** Method of systematic self-observation.
3. **Questionnaires.** Survey of questionnaire data sampling.
4. **Hetero-systematization.** Systematic experimental investigation.

Self-awareness. One of the criteria applied in order for an episode of personal experience to be considered hypnagogic is that the person presents the condition of continuous self-awareness of his/her environment.

Electroencephalograph. The loss of awareness of one's external situation can be gauged in a secure and reliable manner when *alpha* brain waves, from 12 to 14 Hertz or cycles per second, appear through electrodes placed on the cranium and are registered on the spindles of the electroencephalograph.

Children. Hypnagogic phenomena are relatively common and have always been more frequently reported by younger children.

Forms. Four basic hallucinatory forms or patterns have been identified as constants, or to frequently occur, in the hypnagogic state:

1. Hammocks, trellises, honeycombs (bees) and arabesques.
2. Spider webs.
3. Tunnel, funnel, grove, cone and vase.
4. Spiral.

Pharmacology. Many of these forms are also imagetic constants due to the use of light or heavy, licit or illicit drugs (pharmacology, criminology).

Recall. It has been consistently noted over time that hypnagogic phenomena are extremely difficult to recall if they are not registered immediately after they occur (mnemosomatics).

Forces. Hypnagogic phenomena seem to occur due to the struggle of two opposing forces in the consciousness:

1. **Brain.** Sleepiness (mental fatigue, somatics).
2. **Mind.** The effort of thinking (thosenization, thosenology).

Mythology. Spontaneous experiences with hypnagogic images looking like environments external to the individual may have played an important role in the development of folklore and mythology through the centuries.

Errors. There are many possibilities for the occurrence of visual errors.

Causes. Upon thinking that we see an external object, we can be mistaken for 3 basic reasons:

1. **Intraphysicality.** The external world, e.g.: the mirage, reflections and illusions or hallucinations (ecology or social influence).

2. **Somatics.** The human body (soma), e.g.: a stimulus to the eyes.

3. **Nightmare.** The brain, e.g.: the experience of a common physiological nightmare (neurology).

Criticism. Authors affirm that hypnagogic states cannot be compared with hallucinations, since they are criticized and censured, do not determine the acceptance of the individual and are fed by objects from the environment.

Characterizations. Any person can experience various types of sensations or visual images, which should be well-characterized, especially in terms of their specific origins, in order to better understand and distinguish the phenomena of hypnagogy from other visual or even animic-parapsychic occurrences, including all types of clairvoyance.

Categories. The following are 4 types or categories of images from which one can establish different characters:

1. **Secondary.** When people close their eyes after slowly and clearly observing an object for a few seconds, they see an image or a succession of images that reproduce the shape of the object which, as in photographs, can be positive or negative images, whether in a successive or alternating manner. These are common images, also called *complementary, consecutive, posterior* or *secondary* images, which are generated from commonplace external vision.

Recurrence. These visual images are inserted within the period of retinal oscillations or the recurring images and include: primary images, tertiary images and quartic images.

2. **Phosphene.** Other diverse luminous impressions can be experienced through *compression* or, in other words: pressing on the eyeball with the eyelids closed. In this case, the images are called *phosphenes.*

Mechanical. These effects can arise in the form of circles, colored flowers and more-or-less geometric figures, such as the designs of certain tapestries that are animated with the movement of a whirlwind. Nevertheless, they are merely the result of a mechanical action exercised upon the eyeball.

Sensations. Technically, phosphenes can be described as luminous sensations due to an inadequate electrical or mechanical (shocks to the eye, compression from an external or internal source, as in glaucoma) excitation of the retinal receptors.

Rotatory. There are also *rotatory* phosphenes that are produced by applying separate electrical stimuli, with very close frequencies, to each of the eyes.

3. **Entoptic.** Entoptic images are those visual images that occur in the interior of the eyeball. They are, therefore, of subjective origin, almost always cerebral, generally multiple, blurry, overlapping and have irregular shapes. They are visual stimulations originating in the eye itself: images of blood vessels and, sometimes, of blood cells, leukocytes that circulate in the vitreous humor *(floating flies)* and cell fragments. The vitreous humor is a gelatinous substance in the interior of the eyeball. These cell remnants, deposited in the bottom of the eye, dislocate when it moves.

Scotomas. Among these phenomena can be found retinal blue arcs, Maxwell spots and scotomas. These are manifested as more-or-less extensive, dark, immovable spots that cover a portion of the visual field or the object that is being observed. This results exclusively from the insensitivity of a corresponding portion of the *retina*. Often, in these cases, luminous, brilliant, flashing points or lines also appear. Scotoma is a type of temporary blindness, originating in the cerebral cortex. The images seen are sometimes described by persons of advanced age as *spider webs, floating flies, flashes, colored ribbons* and *stars*. These manifestations, when luminous or scintillating, move rapidly in a zigzag fashion.

Sleep. Scintillating scotomas awaken the sleeper and disturb his/her attempts to go back to sleep.

Migraine. Luminous scintillating scotoma appears in the ophthalmic migraine. Hemianoptic scotoma is due to a small lesion in the calcarine zone of the visual cortex, since it is found in symmetrical regions of the visual fields of the 2 eyes.

4. **Clairvoyance.** Other quite diverse precedential visions are incidences of *facial* clairvoyance (the transfigurations of Jesus of Nazareth) or the elementary animic-parapsychic phenomena of common clairvoyance that transcend the limits, atmosphere and characteristics of the physical forms seen at the moment, while the eyes are open.

Electrode. Upon electrical excitation of the visual region of the brain, what patients see is much more elementary than the things they see in normal life. They describe what they see as "flickering lights", "colors", "stars", "wheels of fire", "glauco-cerulean and reddish discs", "pale blue lights", "spinning colored balloons", "stiletto-like sparkling grayish objects" and so on. All these visual reactions are elementary.

Models. An electrode that transmits 40, 60 or 80 impulses per second to the receptive surface of a field in the sensorial cortex is not able to imitate the diverse models of current impulses that normally arrive at this region, when a person sees or senses objects in his/her environment while in the ordinary, physical waking state.

Multidimensionality. If all of this occurs during the physical waking state, consider the far more sophisticated processes that occur when your consciousness perceives interdimensional or multidimensional realities through clairvoyance.

Occurrences. In the development of the images of facial clairvoyance, the following 10 occurrences can arise:

1. Clairvoyance by clairvoyant 1 of images superimposed on the face of clairvoyant 2, or vice-versa.

2. Simultaneous facial clairvoyance.

3. Images of landscapes.

4. Clairvoyance beyond the physical environment, the next room or the surrounding city block.

5. A parade of recognized and unfamiliar faces seen by both clairvoyants, sometimes totaling fifty or more personalities in 30 minutes of clairvoyance.

6. A variety of intercurrent physical effect phenomena with the first, more experienced clairvoyant, including alterations in respiration, stimulation of the chakras (notably the frontochakra and umbilicochakra) and a decrease in the body temperature of the clairvoyant.

7. The temporary disappearance of images, as though the scene had become blurry, with the appearance of new personalities.

8. The successive reappearance of some personalities many times in succession.

9. The instantaneous appearance and disappearance of a personality in the "screen" of the clairvoyance.

10. Caricatural alterations in the facial features of the clairvoyants.

Special. Neither the ambient light, nor the use of corrective lenses or glasses by both clairvoyants during the trance, nor the recent ingestion of food, still in the digestive process, alter the development of the phenomena of clairvoyance.

Preparation. The self-perceptible movement of the frontochakra of clairvoyant 1 announces the preparation of facial clairvoyance.

Beginning. The alterations in the facial characteristics of clairvoyant 2, as perceived by clairvoyant 1, generally represent the beginning of the clairvoyant manifestations.

Coupling. The auric coupling between the 2 aspiring clairvoyants, either over hours or even days of continued time together, facilitates the manifestations.

Eye. It is worth clarifying that – besides all the visual images already referred to – in complete darkness, without stimuli capable of provoking entoptic phenomena, an impression of a grayish light with irregular space-time distribution persists that seems to be due to the influx of the spontaneous discharges of the optical fibers. This would be the light of the human eye itself, the intra-ocular fluid or the self-luminosity of the retina.

Hypothesis. In this context, it is worth asking: Can we deduce from this occurrence that nerve impulses carry photons? What is the relationship of this to the luminosity of the psychosoma when it suddenly irrupts through the soma of the intraphysical consciousness (theory of irruption of the psychosoma) or, in other words, when the soma itself presents luminosity?

Appearance. On the other hand, hypnagogic images *(condensed hieroglyphs)* present themselves differently from the images referred to here, because they are the neighbors of natural sleep and more frequently appear as colored images, in which case the eyes are closed or the individual is in a completely dark environment, when the *human body* is inactive and *voluntary attention* remains active.

Somnolence. Hypnagogy is directly related to the state of somnolence or, in other words, the state of falling asleep, wherein voluntary control of activity and thought disappears, without the complete severing of sensory-motor relations with the external environment.

Hallucinations. The condition of somnolence can present hypnagogic hallucinations.

Predormitum. The initial phase of sleep receives the name of *predormitum.*

Prodromes. Hypnagogy is characterized by the prodromes of natural sleep and does not only constitute the doorway to sleep. This is because it also predisposes one toward lucid projection, and particularly projection with continuous self-awareness, as the discoincidence of the vehicles of manifestation of the consciousness, in many cases, begins precisely during the hypnagogic period.

Demarcations. Hypnagogy is characterized by two very distinct lines:

1. **Consciousness.** The line of demarcation between *consciousness* and unconsciousness.

2. **Coincidence.** The line of demarcation between the states of coincidence and discoincidence of the vehicles of manifestation of the intraphysical consciousness.

Takeoff. Hypnagogy is also an ideal opportunity for the intraphysical projector's consciousness to experience a fully lucid takeoff in the psychosoma.

Powers. The controlled hypnagogic state, as well as the hypnopompic state, have been recognized for approximately 3 centuries by many clairvoyants as being especially favorable for communication with extraphysical consciousnesses which have passed through first desoma. It is also advantageous for the development of animic-parapsychic powers, such as: telepathy, clairvoyance, precognition and cure (heteropalliative and parapsychic self-remission).

Myoclonuses. The hypnagogic state can be accompanied by abrupt and repeated involuntary muscular jerks or spasms in the form of more-or-less localized wrenching contractions or movements that occur either in a synchronized or irregular fashion, known as *myoclonuses.* There are other types of myoclonuses with a pathological etiology and nature.

Duration. The hypnagogic state, or the first phase in the sequence of natural sleep, can persist for a few seconds or can last for up to about 15 minutes, according to modern laboratory research on sleep and insomnia.

Pupils. Elevating the pupils toward the top of the head, brow line or sinciput, while concentrating one's consciousness on an imaginary point visualized at the top or center of the cranium, easily provokes the hypnagogic condition. This is an initial resource used in yoga practices, by practitioners of biofeedback and in the majority of mind expansion techniques, mind control, or alphagenics, namely the emission of small *alpha* type brain waves. Alpha waves range from 8 to 13 Hertz or cycles per second (cps) and can be detected by placing electrodes on the cranium, thus recording the *language of the brain.*

Waves. Currently, no less than 32 separate wires and channels are used to capture and register brain waves.

Potentials. The electroencephalograph (EEG) measures, registers and amplifies fluctuations in the voltage, or miniscule electrical potentials, occurring in the test-person's cerebral hemispheres. It then groups them into 4 categories or waves.

Electroencephalogram. Reading the resulting record, or electroencephalogram, allows one to know when large parts of the brain are actively working.

Hertz. One Hertz (Hz) is equivalent to 1 vibration per second.

Alpha. The alpha rhythm (Berger rhythm or alpha wave) refers to a state of passive alertness, or superficial (light) meditation. It does not generally occur when the eyes are open.

Frequencies. Three other small electrical pulsations, or frequencies, of brain waves also exist:

1. **Beta.** *Beta* waves, 14-30 cycles per second, correspond to the ordinary, physical waking state, which accompanies all types of intellectual activity as well as the individual's problem solving processes.

2. *Theta.* *Theta* waves, 4-7 cps, are related to deep meditation. They are believed to constitute the frequency of creative mental activity or when the person induces a deep altered state of consciousness.

3. **Delta.** *Delta* waves, 0.5-3 cps, appear during the state of deep sleep, wherein there are no rapid synchronous bi-ocular movements.

Pathology. When delta waves appear during the ordinary, physical waking state, it is indicative of a brain pathology.

Importance. All individuals who exhibit high amounts of *theta* waves while they are preparing to have a lucid projection invariably report having lucid experiences soon thereafter. This demonstrates that, of the 4 basic categories of electric brain pulsations, *theta* waves are more important, mysterious and exhibit the most intimate relationship with lucid projections, particularly those that present *consciential blackout*.

Control. As a general rule, those desiring to leave the human body who are able to generate and control *theta* waves produce impactful lucid projections.

Conditions. The alpha state appears under conditions of psychophysical relaxation, passivity, tranquility, inhibition of the outer world, assimilation, psychic well-being, abolition of the conscious, exalted sensitivity and during the production of phenomena occurring due to *psi capacities*.

Psychedelic. The alpha state is the best substitute for psychedelic drugs in general.

Hypnosis. In order to have an overall understanding of the consciential states studied in hetero-hypnosis, for example, we can divide the mind into 3 segments:

1. **Conscious.** The conscious mind, awake and attentive at the *beta* level.
2. **Subconscious.** The subconscious mind is at the *alpha* level.
3. **Unconscious.** The unconscious mind is manifested in light sleep, the *theta* level and deep sleep, the *delta* level, in which it is sometimes possible, in exceptional cases, to be conscious, according to inferences drawn from certain yoga techniques.

Language. Besides the brain waves referred to here, neuroscientists currently study other aspects of the intricate *language of the brain* and have already detected different waves, such as those of: expectation, surprise and reprocessing.

Mechanisms. It is hoped that a comprehension of the mechanisms of the brain will also afford a clearer understanding of the mechanisms in the innumerous aspects of projectiology in the near future.

Forearm. There is an effective, well-known technique for prolonging the hypnagogic state in order to allow the consciousness to *penetrate the images* of this state, which normally *behave* independently of the individual's voluntary control, initiating a lucid projection.

Technique. Lie down in the dorsal position, physically relax and extend the arms alongside the human body. When you feel yourself getting sleepy, raise one of the forearms into the vertical position over the bed and keep it there, resting it on its elbow. Every time your consciousness begins to sleep, your forearm will fall onto the bed and you will awaken. This will prevent your falling asleep and will prolong your hypnagogy, thus predisposing you toward having a lucid projection.

Hypnopompy. The consciential condition contrary or antipodal to hypnagogy is hypnopompy.

Parasomnia. The set of presomnia, where hypnagogy is situated, and postsomnia, where hypnopompy is inserted, constitute *parasomnia,* or the 2 psychic states that precede and follow the ordinary or natural sleep state. Parasomnia can be pathological.

Differences. By their differential characteristics, altered states of consciousness exhibit their own diversified nuances that places them into a crescendo of manifestations, such as:

1. **Hypnagogy.** Hypnagogy represents an inner event, *without* the direct participation of the spectator-hypnagog.

2. **Paradream.** A dream constitutes an inner event *with* only the relative participation of the consciousness of the spectator-dreamer.

3. **Projection.** The lucid consciential projection is not an event that falls within either category. It is an authentic adventure of the intraphysical consciousness which is temporarily freed from the *bellows of the soma* and is active with the full decision-making powers of the projected projector.

Bibliography: Andrade (27, p. 114), Bonin (168, p. 240), Bret (203, p. 47), Cavendish (266, p. 114), Coxhead (312, p. 78), Crookall (339, p. XXVIII), D'arbó (365, p. 41), Edmunds (461, p. 247), Frost (560, p. 54), Gertz (585, p. 155), Gómez (613, p. 87), Grant-Veillard (623, p. 92), Grattan-Guinness (626, p. 3921), Gurney (666, p. 389), Kardec (825, p. 189), Lukianowicz (957, p. 210), Martin (1003, p. 67), Monroe (1065, p. 207), Morel (1086, p. 91), Morris (1092, p. 21; 1093, p. 156), Muldoon (1105, p. 69), Panati (1193, p. 156), Rogo (1444, p. 146), Schul (1524, p. 85), Shirley (1553, p. 105), Sudre (1630, p. 82), Tart (1653, p.75), Vieira (1762, p. 147), Walker (1781, p. 113).

246. TRANSITIONAL   STATE

Definition. Transitional state: period of tenths of a second or, more rarely, of several seconds or minutes, that occurs between the beginning of the discoincidence of the vehicles of manifestation of the intraphysical consciousness, or takeoff, and the full exteriorization of the psychosoma, occurring when the consciousness apparently finds itself in 2 vehicles – physical and extraphysical – or is passing quickly from one vehicle to another.

Synonymy: minidiscoincidence; semi-takeoff.

Dubiousness. During the transition stage, eccentric and dubious sensations often appear that are difficult for the projector to characterize and express, even when lucid during the entirety of the experiment.

Alarm clock. The common experience during lucid projection in which an intraphysical consciousness awakens extraphysically instead of waking up in the ordinary, physical waking state at the exact instant that an alarm clock rings, also incontrovertibly characterizes the condition of the transitional state.

Occurrences. Various events occur during the transition stage of consciential projection, especially the following 4:

1. Condition of instability of the psychosoma (psychosomatics).
2. Sinking takeoff (consciential projectability).
3. Double awareness.
4. Extraphysical double vision.

Bibliography: Crookall (343, p. 32), Muldoon (1105, p. 125), Vieira (1762, p. 44).

247. DOUBLE AWARENESS

Definition. Double awareness: the sensation of being in 2 centers of the consciousness at the same time or, in other words, in 2 vehicles of manifestation simultaneously, in this case almost always in the physical brain and the consciousness in the mentalsoma, which is bound in the parabrain of the psychosoma.

Synonymy: alternating consciousness; consciential cleavage; divided consciousness; double perceptions; dual consciousness; mental diplopia; sensation of 2 consciential pointers; sense of consciential duality; split consciousness.

Pointer. In order to further clarify the above definition it can be stated that the phenomenon of double awareness constitutes a transitional state of lucid projection in which part of the consciousness *seems to be* headquartered in the human body and the other part headquartered in the psychosoma. There is some lucidity simultaneously in each of the locations, sometimes predominating in one place and then in another, according to the focus of attention or the pointer of the consciousness.

Expansion. Actually, the consciousness does not divide itself, although it expands itself to currently unknown limits.

Integral. The integral consciousness seems to exist only in one body or vehicle of manifestation.

Mentalsoma. Nevertheless, mainly because of the extreme velocity or instantaneous nature of the process, the sensations *may appear to be* double, dubious, bifaceted or in 2 places at the same time, in an *apparent dichotomy* of the personality, as if the seat of intelligence – the mentalsoma – were unstable, transitional, shifting or moveable.

Semitakeoff. The phenomenon of double awareness has a direct relationship with the takeoff of the psychosoma from the human body or, in other words, constitutes an occurrence characteristic of the transition period of semitakeoff, semidisconnection, half-exteriorization or minidiscoincidence of the vehicles of consciential manifestation.

Pre-projective. Double awareness is more frequent as a pre-projective occurrence, although, more rarely, it can also arise after an interiorization of the consciousness in the psychosoma into the human body.

Bilocation. Physical bilocation should not be confused with 3 distinct and characteristic phenomena.

1. **Paravision.** Extraphysical double vision.
2. **Vision.** Duplication of the sense of vision.
3. **Consciousness.** Sensation of double awareness.

Electrode. In the same way, the sensations of double awareness, stemming from the discoincidence of the vehicles of manifestation of the ego, should not be confused with the sensations of being in 2 time periods and 2 different places. This occurs due to the stimulus of certain areas of the brain with a very fine electrode, which is an entirely chemical and electrical phenomenon of the organism. In this process, memories connected to a specific experience in the past, but from one's current human existence, can be reactivated (intraphysicology).

Hemispheres. As a working hypothesis, is it worth questioning whether the existence of the 2 cerebral hemispheres, left and right, might have some relationship with the sensation of double awareness in the same way that the *double ego* hypothesis exists?

Cord. The factor that seems to decisively influence the creation of the double awareness sensation is a reduction in the energetic link, namely the *caliber* of the silver cord, that does not transmit vigorous stimuli from one vehicle to the other, or from the human body to the psychosoma, and vice-versa.

Hypothesis. Could this occur in certain cases due to a parapsychic effect or to a survival instinct born of the fear of losing instantaneous control of the human body?

Omnipresence. In summary: according to observations it can be concluded that, due to more evolved consciential sensations and the lightning-fast velocity of the mentalsoma's still obscure consciential processes in the mentalsomatic dimension, omnipresent consciousness sometimes seems to exist or, in other words, the attribute of omnipresence, which is a mere appearance.

Unipresence. Strictly speaking, therefore, the consciousness, whatever its consciential seat at a specific moment, is always a *uni*present consciousness, having only a single presence.

Bibliography: Alverga (18, p. 288), Baker (69, p. 46), Battersby (92, p. 80), Black (137, p. 79), Blackmore (139, p. 38), Bozzano (188, p. 36), Carrington (245, p. 288), Castaneda (259, p. 84), Crookall (323, p. 41; 339, p. 100; 343, p. 35), Drury (414, p. 23), Fox (544, p. 37), Green (632, p. 41), Greenhouse (636, p. 67), Holroyd (736, p. 112), Kardec (824, p. 81), Martin (1002, p. 29), Muldoon (1105, p. 107), Rogo (1444, p. 58), Steiger (1601, p. 223), Vieira (1762, p. 115), Walker (1781, p. 70), Yram (1897, p. 77).

248. EXTRAPHYSICAL DOUBLE VISION

Definition. Extraphysical double vision: the simultaneous visualization of 2 different environments or scenarios directly through the human eyes – in this case, through the brain (the eyes are just visual organs, therefore, it is *the brain that sees*) – as well as through the extraphysical vision (the para-eyes), in this case, through the psychosoma-mentalsoma relationship while outside the cellular organism, whether in the bedroom (energetically shielded chamber) or beyond.

Synonymy: ambivalent vision; animic-parapsychic vision; combined vision; extraphysical double vision; vision through 4 eyes.

Neurophysiology. According to neurophysiology, the following can exist: bi-ocular vision, the vision of colors, in-depth vision (stereoscopic vision) and three-dimensional vision. There is currently a greater development of the understanding of specific cerebral centers in order to interpret/organize the images that populate the micro-universe of the intraphysical consciousness of adults, children or youths.

Brain. It should be stressed that, physically speaking, it is the brain that sees. It can see even without the presence of external stimuli, as occurs in natural dreams (physiological), nightmares (physiological or pathological) and in hallucinatory phenomena (physiological or pathological).

Transition. In the manner of double awareness, extraphysical double vision is a similar phenomenon being the transition state of lucid projection in which part of the vision is simultaneously in the human body and part is in the psychosoma. It occurs through a two-way path of the sense of vision.

Pre-projective. Extraphysical double vision is more frequently a pre-projective occurrence, although it can also, but more rarely, occur after an interiorization of the consciousness that is preparing to awaken physically.

Clairvoyance. Extraphysical double vision should not be confused with clairvoyance, or second sight, as this only represents the second part of the latter.

Composition. In short, extraphysical double vision is normal physical vision plus the familiar clairvoyance, working simultaneously.

Audition. The phenomenon of double audition occurs with a certain frequency during the interiorization of the projected consciousness when returning to the human body. On these occasions, the projector's consciousness can extraphysically see the extraphysical consciousness which is speaking, sometimes calling its name. Due to the vision, or the *somehow perceptible* sound of the call, the consciousness ends up abruptly interiorizing while still hearing its name being insistently called.

Clapping. Often, the projected consciousness interiorizes because it hears a physical or extraphysical cracking or clapping noise of unknown origin.

Sensations. Evidently, according to the *eccentricity of the senses,* or the sensations that the consciousness experiences during the transition from one consciential state to another, besides *double* awareness, extraphysical *double* vision and *double* audition, *double* touch, *double* motricity and *double* sensitivity can occur.

Bibliography: Muldoon (1105, p. 107), Walker (1781, p. 70).

249. EXTRAPHYSICAL BRADYKINESIS

Definition. Extraphysical bradykinesis: the condition of abnormal slowness in the extraphysical movements of the intraphysical consciousness while projected in the psychosoma.

Synonymy: extraphysical slowness; slow extraphysical dislocation; slow-motion extraphysical movement; slow-motion.

Medicine. In medicine (neurology, psychiatry) the term *bradykinesis* denotes the slowness of the individual's movements due to a compromised nervous system, as occurs in Parkinson's disease and epilepsy, for example.

Net. Here we analyze the slow, laden, heavy extraphysical movement of the psychosoma of the projected consciousness. This generally occurs in the portion of the silver cord's intense activity, within the extraphysical sphere of energy. The psychosoma seems to be involved by a *net of energetic connections* that impedes it from moving in its condition of normal disentanglement, at full velocity.

Marionette. The psychosoma, in this case, seems transformed into a simple marionette. Any human lucid projector can have this experience regardless of his/her organic condition.

Causes. In projectiology, the *slow-motion* phenomenon seems to originate from the transitional or discontinuous state of the consciousness that occurs during the process of lucid projection, almost always when the exteriorized psychosoma is denser or carrying part of the holochakra.

Ballast. The greater density of this heavier and more voluminous ballast makes it difficult for the emotional vehicle of the consciousness to move with agility.

Coadjutants. The following are 2 other probable generating factors or coadjutants of extraphysical bradykinesis:

1. **Cord.** The difficulty and limitation of movements due to the direct action of the silver cord, when denser.

2. **Imponderability.** The insecurity of the movements of the projected intraphysical consciousness due to its psychosomatic or extraphysical imponderability, which is uncommon or unhabitual during the day-to-day existential routine.

Frustration. It is worth mentioning that sometimes, with the condition of extraphysical bradykinesis, the consciousness wants to move with greater agility but is not able to. It is locked in an indeterminate dragging slowness that makes the experience disagreeable and quite frustrating. It is similar to the common admonitory signals sent through the silver cord to the psychosoma of the projected intraphysical consciousness when he/she needs to return to the human body which remains inactive in the physical base.

Readjustment. In the phenomenon of traveling clairvoyance, produced by a clairvoyant through hetero-hypnosis, the hypnotist eliminates the condition of the clairvoyant's bradykinesis through energetic exteriorizations applied longitudinally or lengthwise onto his/her human body. Thus, the hypnotist applies his/her own consciential energy to readjust the equilibrium of the other consciousness.

VS. The same can be accomplished directly by the projected consciousness in an independent manner, which should install the VS or vibrational state (self-energization) and readjust the conditions of its consciential energies, thereby eliminating the *slow-motion* condition.

Energy. The instability of the projected human projector's psychosoma, as well as extraphysical bradykinesis, are conditions stemming from the energetic imbalance that arises during the transition period between the ordinary, physical waking state of the coincident intraphysical consciousness and its discoincidence or projection to the extraphysical dimension.

Will. Every energetic imbalance can be readjusted through the action of the will of the consciousness upon the manifestations of its consciential energies (holochakrology).

Bibliography: Noyes Jr. (1141, p. 20), Vieira (1762, p. 124).

250. PARAPSYCHOLEPSY

Definition. Parapsycholepsy: the brief lapse in the lucidity of the consciousness that frequently occurs in the transition of the focus of mental operations, headquartered in the brain of the human body, to the *paramental operations,* headquartered in the parabrain of the psychosoma, generally occurring at the precise moment at which the formation (recomposition, re-aggregation) of the humanoid structure of the exteriorized psychosoma is completed, being constituted in the extraphysical dimension, evidently outside the limits of the human body (soma).

Synonymy: consciential blackout; consciential short-circuit; extraphysical absence; extraphysical amnesic episode; extraphysical clouding of the consciousness; extraphysical consciential eclipse; extraphysical lapse of the consciousness; extraphysical loss of consciousness; extraphysical period of unconsciousness; hiatus of extraphysical awareness.

Brain. The brain is an electric apparatus with positive and negative polarity, and any interference with this polarity results in a loss of lucidity *(physical mind)* that can finally arrive at a transitory consciential blackout *(extraphysical consciousness).*

Parabrain. Consciential blackout occurs in the psychosoma – in the parabrain in which the mentalsoma or the consciousness is headquartered – and obviously directly affects the consciousness itself in the mentalsoma.

Takeoff. The physical-extraphysical blackout of the consciousness is situated at that point which is the most difficult or critical for maintaining lucidity. Blackout is the agent responsible for the difficulty of the consciential projector to experience the totally awake takeoff of the psychosoma, which is the rarest type of takeoff of all. Blackout demarcates the transition of the focalization of the thoughts of the consciousness – the pointer of the consciousness – from one vehicle of manifestation, the soma, to another, the psychosoma.

Emptying. This is the critical moment of basic discoincidence, the changing of the seat of the consciential pointer or the creation of the *empty brain condition.*

Tunnel. Temporary blackout is directly connected to the silver cord and the tunnel effect. This is because the projected consciousness seems to suddenly enter a dark tunnel, sometimes feeling a certain confusion, obnubilation or obfuscation in its extraphysical perceptions.

Bulb. Consciential blackout is reminiscent of an electric bulb that briefly diminishes in brightness and increases its luminous intensity soon thereafter to return to normal.

Change. Consciential blackout also appears like a profound and instantaneous change that arises during the changing of gears of consciential operations.

Incidence. According to the statistics of public surveys, the experience of parapsycholepsy affects approximately 30% of all individuals who report having consciential projections.

Time. Chronological time is always difficult to interpret, from an extraphysical point of view.

Duration. Although the duration of *consciential blackout* can vary within broad time limits, it seems to be generally very rapid, and at times lightning-fast, lasting a moment, an instant, tenths of a second or only a few seconds.

Vision. After a brief blackout, extraphysical illumination, or the first vision of the consciousness while outside of the body, arises. This vision appears nebulous, whitish and indistinct.

Sounds. Next, sounds that may perchance exist in the situation also arise.

Stars. A person suffering an injury to the head, e.g.: with cranioencephalic trauma in a brain concussion, has the sensation of *seeing st*ars due to a momentary blow to the optic nerve. This is produced as a result of the momentary dislocation of the victim's psychosoma, just as with the consciential blackout which, nonetheless, is a normal, non-accidental or physiological occurrence.

Toll. Projective blackout represents the toll that the intraphysical consciousness pays in order to temporarily cross the border between the human dimension and the extraphysical dimension (energetic dimension). The phenomenon energetically works like an electric or electromagnetic short circuit.

Self-awareness. Projection with continuous self-awareness somehow nullifies this toll. How does this happen? The answer seems to be beyond human understanding or at least beyond the current grasp of science. We still do not understand its mechanism. It is necessary to begin studying a little more holochakrology in a direct manner.

Will. The will, however, can eliminate the occurrence of consciential blackout.

Interiorization. Projective blackout may occur less frequently in the opposite direction, after the return of the projected consciousness and its interiorization into the human body, in the transition of the focus of consciential operations from the psychosoma to the dense body. Nonetheless, this does not take on the phenomenological magnitude and importance of the projective blackout which is specific to the takeoff stage of the psychosoma transporting the consciousness.

Translocation. Blackout of the lucidity of the projected consciousness may also occur when the psychosoma moves very rapidly from one extraphysical dimension or district to another.

Memory. The lucidity of the consciousness greatly depends on memory.

Unconsciousness. Strictly speaking, the state of total or absolute unconsciousness does not exist.

Subconscious. Our subconscious never sleeps.

Consciousness. The mind, in this case the consciousness, is always permanently conscious, even when in the states that we call unconscious and during projective blackouts. What more commonly occurs is that the consciousness does not remember what happened upon returning to the ordinary, physical waking state.

Inertia. It is interesting to note an analogy between the unconscious state of being (always relative and not absolute) and the concept of inertia, a property of matter (also always relative and not absolute), since it includes both the body at rest that tends to remain at rest, as well as the *body in movement* that tends to remain in movement, except when affected by a foreign or external force.

Movement. There is apparently nothing in the universe that remains at a *standstill,* such as the following 3 realities:

1. **Physics.** Atoms move themselves: see quantum physics.

2. **Somatics.** Bodies move themselves: see what happens to an inactive soma or a sedentary human life that destroy themselves.

3. **Conscientiology.** Intraphysical consciousnesses do not sleep even when the soma demands rest and physiological and periodical recomposition.

Images. The following, for example, are 11 images and expressions used by consciential projectors to characterize the projective blackout:

1. Consciential darkening.
2. Momentary darkness in awareness.
3. Personal state of complete unconsciousness.
4. Temporary lapse of lucidity.
5. Unexpected period of unconsciousness.
6. A second of *empty* unconsciousness.
7. Fogging of awareness.
8. "Everything became dark."
9. "Everything became empty."
10. "I underwent momentary unconsciousness."
11. "I had a loss of lucidity."

Absences. Finally, there are 4 basic types of psychic absence or consciential lapse. They are very distinct, with more or less ample blackouts occurring in the continued succession of the lucidity of the intraphysical consciousness and should be observed in order not to confuse them with each other:

1. **Epilepsy.** Pathological psychic absence or epileptic *petit mal*, generated by various causes.

2. **Psychophony.** Psychic absence due to benign parapsychic trance, characteristic of incorporation or semiconscious psychophony. Nevertheless, this type can also be pathological in those cases triggered due to intrusion by a pathological or *energivorous* extraphysical consciousness, blind guide, extraphysical intruder, or outright interconsciential possession. At the beginning of the manifestation, one can have recollections that do not fit within one's personal memories or, in other words, pseudomemories or *para-amnesias.*

3. **Retrocognition.** Psychic absence due to an extremely intense retrocognition that occurred in the ordinary, physical waking state. In this situation, the intraphysical consciousness remembers experiences of the previous human existence, but perceives that they are real, are its own, pertaining to its holomemory or holobiographical integral memory.

4. **Projection.** Psychic absence due to a generally nonlucid or semilucid instantaneous consciential projection. This occurs due to the exit of the intraphysical consciousness from its seat in the human brain.

Bibliography: Bayless (98, p. 114), Boswell (174, p. 140), Crookall (340, p. 40), Digest (399, p. 275), Holroyd (736, p. 111), Martin (1002, p. 27), Muldoon (1105, p. 233), Rogo (1444, p. 58), Walker (1781, p. 77).

---

251. INTRACRANIAL SOUNDS OF TAKEOFF

Definition. Intracranial sounds of takeoff: the noises that are difficult to characterize, perceived only by the consciousness when projecting, almost always stemming from the cranium itself, whether intra or extracerebrally, at the exact moment of a lucid takeoff in the psychosoma.

Synonymy: encephalic echoes; extraphysical tinnitus *(acúfeno);* inexplicable intracranial sounds; internal clicks.

Tinnitus. According to psychology, the name tinnitus *(acúfeno)* is given to all auditory sensations that are not produced by a stimulus external to the organism.

Sanity. Tinnitus *(acúfeno)* does not always have a pathological origin.

Classification. Intracranial sounds occurring during the development of a lucid projection can be classified into two categories:

1. **Takeoff.** The sounds related to the takeoff of the psychosoma that was interiorized in the soma.

2. **Interiorization.** The sounds related to the interiorization of the psychosoma that was projected in the extraphysical dimension into the soma.

Cause. The main cause of the acoustical phenomena analyzed here – projective intracranial sounds – seems to be the abrupt or moderately traumatic takeoff of the extraphysical head of the psychosoma (parahead) from the human head, which produces the effect of intracranial energetic discharges.

Expressions. These energetic discharges are felt and heard by lucid consciential projectors and reported, for example, along the line of the following 6 categories of expressions:

1. Jingling.
2. Buzzing (loud jingling).
3. Tinkling (medium jingling).
4. Sibilations (sharp jingling).
5. Crackles (brief tinnitus *(acúfeno)* with an undeveloped tonal character).
6. Squeaks, chirps or twitters.

Action. During an abrupt takeoff, the silver cord acts decisively in the encephalic area.

Ductility. Hypothetically, these sounds can be provoked by the *ductile* movement of the silver cord that gradually changes from being a *layer*, distributed in the head, to being an actual *cord*.

Occurrences. Projective intracranial sounds occurring *simultaneously with* a lucid *takeoff* are less frequent and milder than intracranial sounds occurring *simultaneously with* the abrupt *interiorization* of the entire psychosoma *(inductility)*.

Self-awareness. Sounds can occur consecutively in a single projection with continuous self-awareness or, in other words: *first* during a lucid takeoff; *afterwards* during a lucid interiorization.

Succession. Intracranial sounds can also occur during many successive or consecutive exits and reentries of the psychosoma out of and into the human body in a short period of time.

Types. With regard to their frequency and intensity, extraphysical tinnitus *(acúfenos)* occurring during the takeoff and interiorization of the psychosoma are generally described, for example, using the following 4 expressions:

1. **High frequency.** Loud noises and whistles or high frequency tinnitus *(acúfenos)* in the air.
2. **High intensity.** The sound of bells pealing violently or high intensity tinnitus *(acúfenos)*.
3. **Low frequency.** Flapping wings or low frequency tinnitus *(acúfenos)*.
4. **Low intensity**. Mild or low intensity tinnitus *(acúfenos)*.

VS. These facts suggest that the intracranial sounds during the takeoff of the psychosoma are directly related to the vibrational state (VS).

Uniformity. In a consciential projection, whether during a lucid takeoff or a lucid interiorization – separately, with no relationship between one occurrence and the other – the sounds generally present patterns or are definitely uniform and independent, or are of high or low frequency and do not alternate from one frequency to another.

Psychosoma. The intensity of intracranial sounds during lucid takeoff is dependent upon the rapidity of the psychosoma or, more precisely, the velocity of the action of the holochakra between the soma and psychosoma.

Characteristics. Among the characteristics of intracranial sounds of takeoff we can point out the extremely personal internal sounds, whether they are heard inside the head, in the right or left ear.

Inoffensiveness. The sounds are always inoffensive.

Personality. The intensity and types vary according to the personality of the projector.

Analogies. Often, extraphysical tinnitus *(acúfenos)* are similar to the sounds stemming from small events in daily life, such as the following 5:

1. Metallic sounds.
2. Tearing of silk.
3. Falling grains.
4. A door slamming.
5. Vibration of a guitar string or another musical instrument.

Utilities. With time and repetition of the experiences, the intracranial sounds heard by the intraphysical consciousness present 3 categories of unquestionable holosomatic or self-persuasive evidence:

1. **Holochakra.** The existence of the holochakra.
2. **Cord.** The existence of the silver cord or cords (regional).
3. **Chakras.** The existence of chakras and consciential energy ducts.

Onomatopoeia. The following are 8 onomatopoeias sometimes used by consciential projectors to express types of intracranial sounds heard during interiorization and takeoff of the psychosoma: *bam; blam; chii; pap; sizz; tam; tirro; zing.*

Bibliography: Buther (227, p. 73), Castaneda (258, p. 202), Crookall (343, p. 94), Farrar (496, p. 198), Muldoon (1105, p. 34), Rogo (1444, p. 7), Salley (1496, p. 159), Walker (1781, p. 67).

252. TAKEOFF

Definition. Takeoff: the initial operation of the detachment of the psychosoma from the human body or soma.

Synonymy: act of detachment of the intraphysical consciousness; discoincidence of the psychosoma; disjoining of the double; ejection of the psychosoma; physical-extraphysical *decorpage;* point of OOB detachment; rapid departure of the psychosoma.

Mentalsoma. Besides the takeoff of the psychosoma, the takeoff of the mentalsoma also occurs. However, this happens in subtle and diverse conditions that only reach the encephalic area of the human body, beginning with the extraphysical head of the psychosoma (the parahead or, in this case, the parabrain).

Impression. The takeoff of the psychosoma with the consciousness fully lucid is one of the most impressive steps in the experience of lucid projection (see fig. 252, p. 1,136).

Types. There are various types of takeoff, such as the following 9:

1. Lucid takeoff: the least frequent.
2. Semilucid takeoff.
3. Nonlucid takeoff: the most frequent.
4. Slow or discriminative takeoff.
5. Abrupt takeoff or takeoff by ejection: the *extraphysical escape.*
6. Complete, incomplete or partial takeoff.
7. Imperfect takeoff.
8. Voluntary or compulsory takeoff.
9. Totally unperceived takeoff, without any period of transition that is perceptible by the consciousness.

Positions. When projecting from the human body, the psychosoma – always transporting the mentalsoma and the consciousness – can assume the most different extraphysical positions, the following 12 being examples:

1. Vertical.
2. To the right or left side of the dense body.
3. Rolling.
4. With one, two or three somersaults over itself.
5. In spiral, whirl, or zigzag.
6. Backward.
7. Lengthwise.
8. Upward or vertical, classic.
9. Through the head, the most common.
10. Through the feet, the rarest.
11. Diving down or through the bed below.
12. Seated on one's own body.

Intercurrences. Besides that which has been presented, other sensations often occur during the takeoff of the psychosoma, such as the following 13:

1. Sensation of intracranial pressure, almost always in the center of the cranium or in the occipital base.
2. Sensation of pressure on the forehead or in the center of the frontal force (frontochakra).
3. Vibrational state (VS).
4. Sensation of a reduction in size (rare).
5. Successive attempts without achieving results.
6. Rhythm during takeoff.
7. A comfortable and impressive sensation of loss of respiration.

8. Extraphysical supine position.
9. Oscillations and undulations of the psychosoma.
10. Sensation of absolute freedom.
11. Takeoff in sequence.
12. Condition of physical anchoring of the projector.
13. Antiprojection or *anti-takeoff.*

Areas. The final part of the takeoff, or the exit of the psychosoma from the human body, usually occurs in the following organic areas, which are not always perceived: head, nuchal region; glabella or area between the eyebrows; center of the brain; medulla oblongata; epiphysis or pineal gland; top of the cranium (sinciput, bregma, brow line).

Solar. Less often, the projector can feel as if he/she were leaving the human body through the umbilical area, or solar plexus. Actually, however, the head of the psychosoma and, therefore, the seat of the consciousness does not frequently leave the physical body through this area (umbilicochakra).

Error. Most of the time, this fact constitutes a simple impression or an erroneous interpretation of the occurrences that repetitive experiences do not confirm.

Vision. This occurs because the consciousness does not see itself leaving from the head when, on the contrary, it can easily see the connections of the silver cord leaving the human body through the umbilicochakra, which corresponds to the first segment of the psychosoma to exteriorize itself.

Turns. When the projector is lying on his/her right or left side on the bed, it predisposes a lateral lucid takeoff of the consciousness in the psychosoma through rapid rolling turns made over the body. This does not cause any dizziness or confusion for the projector. Sometimes, this rolling allows the psychosoma to remain standing or erect in relation to the resting human body, after making two or more turns.

Projections. In projections of continuous self-awareness, the takeoff of the psychosoma with the consciousness fully lucid occurs more frequently when they are lateral. During these takeoffs, the psychosoma can be in a *horizontal position* or a *standing position.*

Lying down. The position of the psychosoma lying down predisposes the occurrence of a local projection, within the extraphysical sphere of energy, so that the consciousness has more difficulty in leaving the physical base due to the retractive power of the silver cord. Under these conditions, lucid projections are generally of short duration.

Standing. When the psychosoma is in an erect position, it gives the consciousness greater extraphysical agility. This allows it to leave the physical base and reach its distant mental target. Under these conditions, lucid projections are sometimes more prolonged.

Helpers. The helpers have certain energetic assistential resources that transcend our current understanding.

VS. The helpers' resources allow the intraphysical consciousness to leave the human body in an instantaneous takeoff through an increase or intensification of the vibrational state (VS), within the coincident individual, with or without his/her being aware of the fact and without disturbing him/her deeply or causing any harm.

Pulling. It is as if a pulling, suction or aspiration, performed by a special bundle of rays or a *vortex of energy,* is focused directly on the individual, regardless of whether it is an adult, child or animal. This explains various aspects of supposed abduction phenomena in UFO studies.

Exit. The intraphysical consciousness, when projecting to the extraphysical dimension in the psychosoma, generally does not perceive his/her exit from the physical base simply because his/her back is toward him/herself, endeavoring to look forward in the opposite direction, according to the usual conditioning imposed by the unidirectional vision of the human body.

Gradation. A backward exit allows one to *look behind oneself* and verify in detail the act of leaving the physical base. This can be performed little by little, with the body gradually *more distant,* until it disappears, losing its importance for the consciousness which is now engaged in extraphysical experiences.

Trendelenburg. During semidisconnection, or partial projection, it is common for the extraphysical Trendelenburg position (a type of imprisoning of the parahead) to occur. In other words: the psychosoma exteriorizes almost completely, becoming tilted downward, with only the extraphysical head (parahead) bound inside the physical brain, which maintains the waking state. Soon thereafter, the psychosoma may assume the extraphysical supine position, thus floating longitudinally above the human body.

Extremes. The experience of lucid takeoff, within the context of lucid projection phenomena, brings together the following 2 extremes of intense personal experience in a radical and singular manner:

1. **Micro-universe.** Firstly, the intraphysical consciousness microscopically and centripetally goes to the apex of his/her *interior state* or, in other words, to the intimacy of his/her consciential micro-universe. He/she feels more alive and awake than ever before, within his/her intraphysical, concrete and cellular micro-universe.

2. **Macro-universe.** Soon thereafter, instantaneously and without any lapse in lucidity, he/she leaves this coarse, material condition to centrifugally and telescopically go to the maximum of his/her exterior nature, or to the multidimensional macro-universe, manifesting in a subtle extraphysical vehicle, in another condition of expanded lucidity.

Stages. In some cases, 2 very distinct stages occur during the slow exteriorization of the psychosoma which, on the other hand, is confirmed by the phenomenon of exteriorization of sensitivity:

1. **Disaggregation.** *First,* the stage of disaggregation, decomposition or separation of the elements of the psychosoma, gradually leaving the human body.

2. **Reaggregation.** *Second,* the stage of re-agglomeration, reaggregation or reconstitution of the elements of the psychosoma, gradually reorganizing or reunifying the exact humanoid formation of the psychosoma while outside the human body, within the perimeter of the intense influence of the silver cord.

Common. The disaggregation of the elements of the psychosoma can occur in various ways. In the most common manner, the disconnection starts with the feet, legs, hands, arms, trunk, neck and, finally, the head, as if it were *steam* rising up from the pores, forming small balloons from the corporal segments.

Desoma. Biological death, final projection or the first desoma has already been described in exactly this way by countless communicant extraphysical consciousnesses through the phenomenon of psychography.

Observation. The disaggregation as well as the reaggregation of the psychosoma can be witnessed by the attentive observation of the projectionist. This signifies that both processes do not compromise the lucidity and the quality of the perceptions of the intraphysical consciousness. In rapid sideways exteriorization, for example, the *sensation of steam* does not occur.

Slow. The slow takeoff of the psychosoma, when entirely lucid, allows the intraphysical consciousness to *savor* extraphysical freedom little-by-little, bit-by-bit.

Happiness. The individual thus senses the *self* gradually rise from the bed to the ceiling, intensely experiencing the act of ascension. This provides an immense happiness as it brings the condition of being light and free, without the human body, the dense material or the heavy burden proceeding together. On the contrary, the latter remains bound to the bed, *deactivated* and *down there,* in the manner of a "dead weight from which I freed myself."

Frustration. Often, on this occasion, our *uninvited warden,* the silver cord, unfortunately enters the scene and ends the party. Our consciousness then unwillingly *interiorizes* once more, bringing a sense of great frustration.

Rolling. During the lateral rolling takeoff of the psychosoma, projectors who are married (or form an evolutionary duo) and sleep in the same bed should dismiss the psychological connotation associated with the human body of the mate lying at his/her side, with the male on the left and the woman on the right, for example.

Inhibition. Strictly speaking, from a practical viewpoint, this fact is not of the least importance, due to the difference between life's dimensions and the psychosoma's extraphysical permeability. Therefore, psychologically speaking, this can inhibit the partner's projective performance, as well as causing energetic problems with the silver cord.

Psychology. As a general rule, all psychological influence is always important and should be considered in the techniques for lucid consciential projection. This is because psychology studies precisely the reactions of the intraphysical consciousness (mind, brain, biomemory or the reactions of nerve cells), which the projector can sometimes not predict.

Cord. The most common lucid takeoff occurs wherein the projected consciousness is stuck within the perimeter of the silver cord's vigorous action, in the physical base. This can happen many times in a row, within a one-hour period of voluntary or involuntary experiences.

Research. These lucid projections allow the practitioner to specifically research two occurrences:

1. **Sounds.** The intracranial sounds during takeoff.
2. **Energies.** The vigorous consciential energies of the silver cord when active.

Animic-parapsychic. The takeoff of the psychosoma leaving the human body can be animic-parapsychic when the semi-incorporated extraphysical mentor directly helps the projector leave the dense vehicle.

Bibliography: Brittain (206, p. 51), Castaneda (258, p. 117), Greenhouse (636, p. 257), Monroe (1065, p. 219), Reis (1384, p. 70), Ring (1406, p. 45), Salley (1496, p. 157), Vieira (1762, p. 147), Walker (1781, p. 67), Whiteman (1842, p. 250).

---

253. SINKING   TAKEOFF

Definition. Sinking takeoff: exteriorization of the intraphysical consciousness manifesting through the psychosoma in which one has the parakinesthetic sensation of sinking or sliding downward through the members, articulations, tendons and muscles of the human body.

Synonymy: collisional takeoff; downward takeoff.

Sinking. In the sinking takeoff, the human body seems to move downward, sometimes appearing to have abruptly entered the mattress and the inside of the bed, going all the way to the bedroom floor, when the projector is lying on his/her back on the bed in his/her physical base.

Impression. The sinking or downward exit of the psychosoma from the physical body does not always occur. The opposite often occurs, the psychosoma elevates to one degree or another, either slowly or instantaneously from the human body. This gives the impression that the human body is sinking, due to the downward retraction of part of the energies of the silver cord. These energies obviously remain in connection with the physical body (the second connection of the holochakra).

Opposite. The best way to understand and improve your sensitivity regarding the sinking takeoff is by producing an instantaneous projection with continuous self-awareness, wherein the human body is lying on its front, inactive on the bed. In this way, the psychosoma will take off slowly, upward, in the opposite direction.

Nose. Thus, when leaving part of the silver cord's power behind, the downward sensation becomes clear and unquestionable, giving a real impression that the physical nose is sinking further into the mattress, the dense body seeming to become heavier, thus delicately liberating the psychosoma without any difficulties. This parakinesthetic sensation puzzles the individual who experiences it for the first time greatly.

Forms. Sinking represents the only mode of takeoff wherein the intraphysical consciousness in the psychosoma leaves in a direct encounter, or on a collision course, with forms, bodies or physical objects (the environment's decorative items) that are in the bedroom of the intraphysical projector's physical base along with or next to his/her own human body.

Rarity. This rare kind of sinking takeoff is only worthwhile for its exotic experience, as it almost always inhibits the appearance of profound extraphysical self-awareness. As well, it can provoke a trauma with the consequent abrupt interiorization of the consciousness, which is disturbed by its conditioned reflexes that are deeply rooted in human life, relative to the forms and structures of bodies and physical objects.

Bibliography: Muldoon (1105, p. 124).

---

254. INSTABILITY OF THE PSYCHOSOMA

Definition. Instability of the psychosoma: the state of brief extraphysical movement of the psychosoma that frequently occurs soon after lucid or nonlucid takeoff of the consciousness from the human body and which consists of the combination of a vertical oscillation and an oscillation around its transversal axis.

Synonymy: extraphysical rocking reaction; extraphysical rocking; floating of the psychosoma; oscillation of the psychosoma; the condition of extraphysical seesawing; turbulence of the psychosoma; undulation of the psychosoma.

First. In many projective experiences, the first immediate sensation of the intraphysical consciousness projected with lucidity – common to the majority of projectors having spontaneous experiences – in the physical base is, naturally, the movement of the psychosoma, which seems like a feather or a bubble floating in midair in its final stage of lucid takeoff.

Oscillations. This occurrence is characterized by the psychosoma oscillating and floating from one side to the other and, less often, by whirling, zigzagging, rocking, snaking or making small jumps. It does not provoke dizziness in the projected consciousness, which follows along in its seat, located in the parabrain.

Projectiophobia. As the oscillations of the psychosoma constitute the first direct experiences of the intraphysical consciousness projected in the extraphysical dimension, they represent the routine cause of the fear some people have of projecting themselves, or *projectiophobia*.

Evolution. This is the primary condition that should be combated and removed at all cost if the lucid projector wishes to evolve with his/her projective experiences.

Exit. During the psychosoma's state of instability, the lucid consciousness generally seeks to force an exit from the magnetic involvement of the human body, sometimes to one side, sometimes to the other, thus taking advantage of the undulations or even producing other movements within the undulations that are maintained by the silver cord or the energetic connections of the holochakra.

Duplicity. The state of instability of the psychosoma can also transmit the sensation of duplicity in which the consciousness feels as if it were two persons, one in space, swinging above the other which is lying on the bed or, in other words: 1 body *seesawing* just above the other.

Motricity. Oscillation of the projected psychosoma basically constitutes a phenomenon of exteriorization of motricity.

Rhythm. More rarely, the state of instability can develop a type of *oscillatory rhythm* in the psychosoma that begins in the human body, the source of the process, before concluding the operation of an either lucid or nonlucid takeoff, and liberating its segments little by little, as though it were bubbling until beginning to float, upon which extraphysical stability occurs.

Positions. The condition of dynamic instability is always relative. It can occur with the psychosoma in any extraphysical position, although it frequently occurs within the extraphysical sphere of energy or, in other words: only within the perimeter of the totipotency of the silver cord or the energetic connections of the holochakra.

Partial. Oscillations of the psychosoma can occur in a partial manner only with the paramembers (paralegs or para-arms) while the consciousness is entirely lucid in the ordinary, physical waking state during a partial projection of the psychosoma.

Rocking. When the human body is lying on its front, the consciousness can feel the psychosoma to be unstable, also lying on its front, facing downward, moving from side to side like a rocking ship. This provokes an extremely exotic or uncommon sensation.

Cord. Although the oscillations and fluctuations of the projected psychosoma sometimes present disagreeable impressions, as they evidence the vigorous and preponderant force of the silver cord upon the weak will of the inexperienced consciousness, they are completely inoffensive.

Frustration. In other words, the oscillations and fluctuations of the psychosoma do not ordinarily have any negative or lasting consequences, except for the occasional frustration of consciential interiorization that is considered premature or is against the wish of the intraphysical consciousness.

Occurrences. The following are 2 subsequent facts that occur more commonly after the condition of extraphysical instability of the psychosoma:

1. **Stability.** The stability of this consciential vehicle which, once it is standing up or erect, frees itself from the influence of the silver cord, beginning a lucid projection in the extraphysical dimension.

2. **Interiorization.** Consciential interiorization, almost always frustrating, occurring as a consequence of the mild or violent traction of the silver cord.

Readjustment. In the phenomenon of traveling clairvoyance produced by the clairvoyant through hetero-hypnosis, the hypnotist eliminates the condition of instability of the psychosoma of the clairvoyant through energetic exteriorizations applied longitudinally or lengthwise onto its human body. Thus, the hypnotist applies his/her own consciential energy to readjust the balance of the other consciousness.

VS. The same can be accomplished directly by the projected consciousness in an independent manner. It should install the VS or vibrational state (self-energization) and readjust the conditions of its consciential energy, thereby eliminating the instability of the psychosoma.

Energy. Both extraphysical bradykinesis or slow motion, as well as the instability of the psychosoma of the projected human projector, are conditions caused by the energetic imbalance that occurs in transition between the ordinary, physical waking state of the coincident consciousness and its discoincidence, or projection to the extraphysical dimension, while still inside the physical base.

Will. Every energetic imbalance can be readjusted through the action of the will of the consciousness upon the manifestations of its consciential energies.

Distant. The state of instability of the psychosoma does not generally occur when an intraphysical consciousness, although projected, recovers its lucidity only when physically distant from the physical base.

Help. According to reports given by sundry projectors, this greatly helps those who lay in a hammock placed far from a wall, door or window. It also helps miniprojectors *swing playfully,* who nevertheless still have short legs whose feet are not able to reach the wall.

Bibliography: Muldoon (1105, p. 74), Reis (1384, p. 54), Vieira (1762, p. 174).

---

255.   TRACE   OF   LIGHT

Definition. Trace of light: the vestiges, sparks, scintillations or luminous signals that the psychosoma of the intraphysical consciousness sometimes leaves behind when moving in the extraphysical dimension, notably when at high speed and carrying the consciential energies of the holochakra.

Synonymy: comet effect; extraphysical flash; luminous sparkles of the psychosoma; luminous trace of the psychosoma; phosphorescent tail; tail of light; trail of light; "wings of angels".

Radiation. The psychosoma, also called the luminous body or radiant parabody, when discoincident from the consciential vehicles of manifestation, always has some unmanifested or even exuberant clarity.

Potency. Nevertheless, the tonality, gradation and intensity or, in other words, the irradiant energetic potency of the consciousness, varies according to its evolutionary level, the conditions of the vehicle of manifestation, the extraphysical environment and its personal actions on that occasion.

Characteristics. Among the essential characteristics of the trace of light, at least the following 7 can be pointed out:

1. **Emergence.** The sparks appear spontaneously, with or without the consciousness being aware of the occurrence.

2. **Origin.** The luminous effect comes directly from the energetic potency of the psychosoma of the projected intraphysical consciousness with extraphysical forms condensed by the energies of the holochakra.

3. **Volitation.** In the majority of occurrences, the trace of light occurs naturally from the process of extraphysical volitation.

4. **Direction.** The sparks appear in the direction of the movement of extraphysical translocation, although in the opposite direction of the movement (see fig. 255, p. 1,137).

5. **Extension.** The sparking can reach a distance of up to approximately 24" (60 cm) from the psychosoma.

6. **Intensity.** The intensity of the scintillation depends upon the velocity of the extraphysical translocation of the consciousness, when manifesting in the psychosoma.

7. **Coloration.** The colors and tonalities of the scintillations show the evolutionary level of the consciousness-psychosoma binomial, beyond the manifestations of the human aura.

Surprise. In the first consciential projections in the psychosoma, the intraphysical consciousness may notice that he/she is emitting sparks. This is often very surprising the first time it occurs.

Interpretation. From this, some disturbance regarding the interpretation of this occurrence can also arise as the intraphysical consciousness does not know if the sparks are his/her own unconscious creation or if they are emitted from some intangible personality (extraphysical consciousness) located in the area.

Parallel. The silver cord should not be confused with the trace of light. During the projection of the consciousness when distant from the human body, the silver cord remains connected at only 1 point of the free psychosoma, generally in the parahead at the extraphysical nucha (paranucha), for example. The trace of light almost always presents a sparkling over the entire dorsal area or the back of the humanoid form of the psychosoma.

Tail. The term "phosphorescent tail" refers to the scintillations of the silver cord. It nevertheless often refers to the trace of light of the psychosoma, that seems to be sparkling and leaving a trail of luminosity wherever the projected consciousness goes.

Wings. One hypothesis contends that the psychosoma's trace of light is responsible for the ancient, imaginary, mythological idea that the angels (evolved spirits) fly (volitate) with luminous wings (traces of light) on the back of their body of light (psychosoma).

Mythology. As we can see in this case, mythology has a partly logical rationale, finding evident substrata for creation of the myth.

Hypotheses. The trace of light of the psychosoma of the projected intraphysical consciousness, arouses many important hypotheses and the following two might be the most appropriate ones:

1. **Exhaust.** Could these sparks be a means of outflow, an exhaust process, garbage discharge, burned refuse, emunctory system, or an excretory system of the psychosoma's energies?

2. **Friction.** Or could the trace of light be a consequence of the psychosoma's friction against the specific vibratory level of the extraphysical environment in which the projected consciousness moves?

Bibliography: Carrington (245, p. 278), Crookall (343, p. 49), Martin (1002, p. 27), Muldoon (1105, p. 59), Vieira (1762, p. 50).

256.   RESPIRATION   DURING   TAKEOFF

Definition. Human respiration: the act of inhaling and exhaling, filling and emptying the 2 lungs, through which the human organism absorbs oxygen and expels carbon dioxide gas.

Synonymy: breath; human breathing; human respiration.

Nourishment. A healthy adult breathes between 17 and 25 times per minute. Respiration is automatic by nature and fundamental for the survival of all human beings. Without it, human life would be impossible on earth. It is the main source of nourishment only for the mass of matter comprising the cellular or physical body (soma).

Psychosoma. Despite being the auxiliary instrument of the human body's biological organizing system, a perfect replica of the soma, the psychosoma does not have hemoglobin, blood or active respiratory equipment. Similarly, the consciousness does not need cardiorespiratory processes while manifesting itself extraphysically.

Head. All indications are that the psychosoma has these instruments or systems only as a function of the human body, but does not need to use them when manifesting itself. As proof of this fact, the consciousness manifests itself extraphysically using only the head of the psychosoma or, in other words, partial projections in the form of a phantasm.

Simulacrum. If the will of the projected projector wishes to, it breathes. More precisely, it simulates the respiratory process in the same way that it can appear younger, create clothes for itself (self transfigurations) and perform other surprising extraphysical actions.

Takeoff. In lucid projection, during the phase of lucid takeoff, the projector may verify that respiration is the most intense and predominant organic sensation, the last to disappear when taking off and the first to be reacquired when interiorizing.

Physiology. More than the circulation of the blood and beating of the heart, the physiological phenomenon of respiration constitutes the vital factor of the projective process, being the most perceptible occurrence and the one that prevails over all others at the precise moment of leaving the human body.

Yoga. The analyzed facts are confirmation of the benefits of rhythmic respiratory exercises and yoga techniques, which can actually serve as *coadjutants* to the methods for efficient production of lucid projection.

Sensations. During the process of integral projection of the consciousness in the psychosoma, respiration of the human body does not change. The extraphysical sensations of the consciousness using the psychosoma are merely modified.

Facts. The sensation of not breathing is felt as a loss and corroborates the following 8 facts:

1. **Weak trait.** A person breathes 11,520 liters of air per day, from which his/her lungs filter 543 liters of oxygen necessary for the maintenance of life. The habitual function of respiration represents a heavy burden *(human physiological weak trait)* that individuals always carry. In daily life, nobody perceives this inconvenience (intraphysical restriction, temporary loss of cons) that is clearly discovered or evidenced through the phenomenon of lucid projection.

2. **Synchronism.** The extraphysical sensation of the synchronism of simultaneous human body-psychosoma respiration.

3. **Imponderability.** The loss of the respiratory function constitutes the first factor to establish the condition of weight loss, lightness or the psychosoma's extraphysical imponderability. This can scare unsuspecting individuals who feel it for the first time, for whom it seems to be a common symptom of asphyxia or a *lack of air* (dyspnea).

4. **Freedom.** The act of discontinuing respiration predisposes and establishes the condition of absolute freedom experienced by the projected intraphysical consciousness.

5. **Extraphysical euphoria.** The absence of respiration represents the beginning of the condition of extraphysical euphoria.

6. **Volitation.** Removal of the burden of respiration lays the foundation for extraphysical free flight, beginning with its *parapsychological* aspect.

7. **Sphere.** The halt in respiration constitutes the first step toward the liberation of the psychosoma from the extraphysical sphere of energy, or the act of becoming free from the totipotent operation of the silver cord.

8. **Nature.** Human respiration is a mechanical, coarse and heavy process compared with the lightness and subtle nature of the structure and manifestations of the psychosoma.

Interiorization. If the intraphysical consciousness thinks about or wishes to breathe while projected in the psychosoma in the proximity of the human body, especially while inside the extraphysical sphere of energy, this intention can provoke an abrupt interiorization imposed by the retraction of the silver cord.

Catalepsy. We can extract a valuable practical consequence from the process of respiration by utilizing it to neutralize the state of projective catalepsy. If the consciousness is in this state, it can exit it by firmly desiring to breathe. This act makes the psychosoma interact and engage more intimately with the human body, thereby promoting the coincidence of these vehicles. This breaks the immobility of the cataleptic condition with the perceptible sensation of the intensification of the process of natural respiration.

Parapsychotics. Only post-desomatic parapsychotics – those extraphysical consciousnesses which still think they are using the human body – suffer discomfort such as physical pain and heat, perceive the coarse sensations of corporal matter and breathe naturally as though they still had functioning lungs. This is because they are obnubilated and numb, do not feel any difference between the human body that they have already unwittingly discarded and the psychosoma through which they currently and continuously manifest.

Conclusion. This is the logical conclusion upon analysis of the facts: if, while projected, you always feel the need to breathe in the extraphysical dimension, it is because you still do not know how to utilize the vast possibilities of the free manifestation of your consciential vehicles. If you wish, you do not need to breathe in any circumstance outside the human body.

Bibliography: Castaneda (258, p. 135), Greenhouse (636, p. 88), Huson (768, p. 109), Lefebure (909, p. 206), Vieira (1762, p. 175), Walker (1781, p. 36), Yogananda (1894, p. 233).

---

257. CONSCIENTIAL   HIBERNATION

Definition. Consciential hibernation: the state of natural minimal discoincidence, with sometimes only a few centimeters between the human body and the psychosoma which becomes inactive or still, a fact that always occurs when someone enters into the state of natural sleep.

Synonymy: condition of the individual who is buried alive; consciential absolute zero; consciential period of inactivity; consciential semi-hibernation; neutral point; zero condition; zone of quietude of the consciousness.

Causes. The physiological causes of consciential hibernation seem to be cellular intoxication due to a lack of natural sleep, as well as the spontaneous relaxation of the entire organism, a fact that occurs when one begins to lose wakefulness.

Effects. Direct results that arise from this period of inactivity are the cellular detoxification of the organism and the absorption or replenishment of extraphysical energy by the psychosoma.

Absorption. This means that the psychosoma absorbs little or no extraphysical energy while coincident with the soma and needs to free itself, or return to its own dimension (the extraphysical dimension, per se) in order to fully absorb energy. Energetic absorption performed while in the ordinary, physical waking state is always less intense than that which is conducted directly with the psychosoma or when it is in a state of discoincidence of the vehicles of manifestation.

Occurrences. The hypnagogic state generally precedes consciential hibernation, discoincidence and movements of the psychosoma appearing slowly or instantaneously. Frequently, the consciousness does not notice the occurrence and, more rarely, it is aware of the fact through the lucid takeoff.

Oscillations. Soon thereafter, the psychosoma can undergo oscillations, undulations, turbulence, as well as physical repercussions.

Dream. Later on, the first dream during the sleep period occurs.

REM. The vegetative life of the human body related to oneiric states – including involuntary, rapid, synchronistic, bi-ocular movements (REM) – also occurs when the consciousness is in the *zone of quietude*.

Inertia. This signifies that consciential hibernation does not cause the absolute inertia of the intraphysical consciousness.

Holochakra. During consciential hibernation – a phenomenon peculiar to the extraphysical sphere of consciential energies – the discoincidence of the vehicles of manifestation is not only of the holochakra, but of the psychosoma transporting the consciousness.

Projectability. During projections with the holochakra alone, the consciousness does not project together with it.

Phenomenology. In some advanced pathological cases of interconsciential possession, it sometimes seems that the intraphysical consciousness remains in a state of hibernation while his/her human body remains under the command of the possessor.

Burials. This fact seems to occur temporarily in certain voluntary burials (yogis) without any extraphysical or pathological influence.

Repercussions. When there is any instability in the human body or the projected consciousness during consciential hibernation, the sudden abrupt return of the consciousness in the psychosoma to the human body produces some type of psychophysical repercussion, such as the well-known jerks, stretching and frightened physical awakening. These are common occurrences with children and adolescents, to which adults comment – mere folklore – that *these persons are simply growing up.*

Bibliography: Lilly (926, p. 48), Muldoon (1105, p. 123), Walker (1781, p. 77).

---

258. EXTRAPHYSICAL OPENING

Definition. Extraphysical opening: the condition outside the human body, or the impression that the projected intraphysical consciousness has, more often occurring soon after the takeoff of the psychosoma, of entering and passing – generally at high velocity – through a long, narrow, dark opening, until reaching the state of extraphysical illumination.

Synonymy: conductive tunnel; cosmic tunnel; extraphysical tube; interdimensional transmitter vein; spatial hole; spatial opening; spatial vacuum; tunnel effect.

Near-death. Reports of the tunnel effect, or an extraphysical opening, are very frequent during human lucid projections that occur during near-death experiences (NDE).

Descriptions. This long, narrow, dark tunnel is also generally described using some of the following 23 expressions:

1. Abyss.
2. Cave.
3. Cavern.
4. Channel.
5. Chasm or cosmic chasm.
6. Dark vacuum.
7. Deep valley.
8. Drain.
9. Enclosure.

10. Funnel of darkness.
11. Gutter.
12. Hole or hole in space.
13. Machine cylinder.
14. Narrow hallway.
15. Opening in space.
16. Pipe.
17. Pit.
18. Silent emptiness.
19. Tunnel in the cosmos.
20. Tunnel like a chimney with light at the top.
21. Well.
22. Whirlpool.
23. Wide tube.

Causes. The probable cause of most cases of tunnel effect, or the passage of the consciousness through an extraphysical opening, is the change of the condition of the projected consciousness from one level – sphere, frequency, parallel world, extraphysical plane or dimension – to another.

Time. It is for this reason that some compare the tunnel effect to a deformation of time or a black hole, a concern of physicists and astronomers.

Hypothesis. The following is a research hypothesis: could it be that the silver cord, a conductor of energy, is responsible for the impression of the tunnel effect in certain experiences when the intraphysical consciousness is projected in extraphysical paratropospheric environments and the circular part of this appendix (holochakra) exteriorizes *prior to* the extraphysical head of the psychosoma (parahead with parabrain), with the mentalsoma and the consciousness *inside?*

Frequency. The tunnel effect, or extraphysical opening, occurs with projected intraphysical consciousnesses not only in spontaneous lucid projections but also in voluntary lucid projections. The tunnel effect occurs more frequently during the exteriorization of the consciousness when in the psychosoma, but it can also occur during the interiorization of the psychosoma, namely when the intraphysical consciousness is returning to the physical base, human life or the dense physical dimension.

Exit. Descriptions show that the extraphysical opening, or the cosmic tunnel, is not only a departure but simultaneously an extraphysical exit, because it allows the return of the intraphysical consciousness from a parallel world to its temporary-headquarters-world or, in other words, its own native, physical, human *habitat.*

Passageway. This indicates that the extraphysical opening, cosmic tunnel, or any other denomination one wishes to give it, constitutes a *two-way* passageway of coming and going, of entrance and exit.

Currents. The tunnel effect should not be confused with the phenomenon of extraphysical currents of energy, or currents of force and can occur in other altered states of consciousness, aside from lucid consciential projection. It can even be induced by drugs.

Birth. The hypothesis has been posed that the tunnel effect might be a reprise (playback) of the consciousness' experience of traveling through the birth canal of natural childbirth. Nevertheless, research shows that lucid consciential projections often occur with persons delivered through Cesarean section – a condition in which the individual did not pass through the natural birth canal – which definitively eliminates that supposition.

Bibliography: Alverga (18, p. 138), Andreas (36, p. 56), Battersby (92, p. 93), Blackmore (139, p. 147; 140, p. 231), Brennan (200, p. 77), Caversan (267, p. 11), Crookall (338, p. 119), Currie (354, p. 144), Digest (399, p. 275), Drury (414, p. 20), Ebon (453, p. 33), Eysenck (493, p. 156), Fiore (518, p. 208), Fox (544, p. 98), Frazer (549, p. 155), Garfield (569, p. 141), Goldberg (606, p. 172), Greenhouse (636, p. 265), Martin (1002, p. 26), Monroe (1065, p. 87), Moody Jr. (1078, p. 30), Parrish-Harra (1202, p. 79), Perry (1238, p. 104), Ring (1406, p. 53), Rogo (1444, p. 178), Sabom (1486, p. 61), Steiger (1601, p. 45), Wheeler (1826, p. 2), Whiteman (1840, p. 58).

259.   EXTRAPHYSICAL   ELONGATION

Definition. Extraphysical elongation: partial projection characterized by a sensed and observable greater elongation or alteration in the length, dimension or volume of the parts of the psychosoma, notably the paramembers or extraphysical members.

Synonymy: extraphysical elongation; extraphysical stretching of the psychosoma.

Elasticity. The phenomenon of elongation in general is a consequence of elasticity, which is an essential attribute of the psychosoma and should not be cause for concern or fear on the part of the lucid projection practitioner.

Paramembers. The more common elongations with projectors occur with the para-arms and paralegs of the psychosoma being partially projected from the human body.

Self-kinesis. The elongation of the projector still represents a type of *self-kinesis* or, in other words, the movement of the psychosoma produced by the consciousness itself, in a manner of extraphysical translocation, through the action of the consciential energies.

Elongater. The individual who produces elongation is called an *elongater.*

Sensitive. The sensitive responsible for elongation receives the name of *elongater sensitive.*

Technique. An exercise that any practitioner of lucid projection can apply is to lay down on the back, close the eyes, stretch the arms and hands alongside the body, physically relax and use the will to bring the two parahands together above the thorax.

Effects. The effects of this partial projection are impressive because the practitioner does not lose lucidity. From this point, you can stretch the para-arms and provoke extraphysical elongation.

Itching. Some lucid projection practitioners experience partial projections and spontaneous extraphysical elongations due to an itching of the skin or ear during the period in which they are endeavoring to produce a lucid projection.

Ear. When a person is physically relaxed he/she can, for example, feel the intense itching of one of his/her ears due to an allergic reaction. This makes him/her *instinctively* raise the extraphysical index finger to the ear with the intention of scratching it.

Translocation. Some lucid consciential projectors apply the elongation of the psychosoma to translocate extraphysically from one district to another.

Shortening. In the same way that extraphysical elongation occurs, the opposite – extraphysical shortening – can also take place. This is reminiscent of the cases of physical shortening registered in ectoplasmy experiments and in reports of hagiography.

Case study. The phenomenon of elongation of the psychosoma has somehow continued to be reported throughout time in 4 very diverse human areas:

1. **Art.** The supposition of extraphysical elongation arose in order to explain the artistic virtuosity of certain people such as the Spanish musical prodigy Pepito Rodriguez Ariola. He was born in La Coruña, a small town near Ferrol on December 14, 1896. In 1900, at the physical age of 3-and-a-half, he could play octaves on the piano through the increase of his hands, although they could actually only span 5-note intervals. In this case, the semiprojection of the *parafingers,* or a partial projection of the *parahands* of the psychosoma, would have been occurring in a spontaneous and unconscious manner.

2. **Ectoplasmy.** Aside from ancient references made to the phenomenon of ectoplasmy in human history, cases of elongation of the physical members with corporal prolongation or distension of the cellular body of the ectoplasmic sensitive have been registered. Often, these would reach up to 10" (25 cm) through the transfiguration of the psychosoma, bringing about ectoplasm, on this occasion, and the consequent partial dematerialization of the ectoplasmic sensitive's human body.

3. **Hypnology.** There is also the case registered by the French school of hypnosis of a sensitive – who was not pregnant – portraying the scene of a childbirth with impressive realism wherein she felt pain, cried, writhed and clenched her hands. Moreover, all those persons present verified that her

breasts actually became fuller than usual. The increased volume of her breasts is a phenomenon of *hypnotic elongation*. This is, nevertheless, a complex occurrence of dematerialization-materialization-rematerialization.

4. **Neurology.** In registered neurology experiments, the posterior zones of the parietal lobes were stimulated, producing *sensations* of elongation of the human body's image.

Elasticity. Extraphysical elongation is reminiscent of occurrences of elasticity in certain organs of the soma: penis (androsoma), uterus (gynosoma), vagina (gynosoma) and clitoris (gynosoma).

Bibliography: Andreas (36, p. 92), Blunsdon (157, p. 72), Bonin (168, p. 157), Bozzano (192, p. 19), Cavendish (266, p. 83), Digest (401, p. 353), Eysenck (493, p. 28), Fodor (528, p. 124), Gauld (575, p. 213), Gaynor (577, p. 56), Holt (741, p. 210), Monroe (1065, p. 170), Randall (1369, p. 42), Reis (1384, p. 53), Riland (1403, p. 87), Shepard (1548, p. 294), Somerlott (1582, p. 110), Spence (1588, p. 141), Todd (1689, p. 52), Tourinho (1693, p. 38), Thurston (1700, p. 285), Underwood (1721, p. 23), Wedeck (1807, p. 128).

---

260. EXTRAPHYSICAL AWAKENING

Definition. Extraphysical awakening: the act of the intraphysical consciousness waking up with full lucidity somewhere outside the human body.

Synonymy: act of waking up outside the human body; beginning of extraphysical self-awareness; extracorporeal awakening.

Types. There are various types of extraphysical awakening, such as the following 6:

1. Slow.
2. Abrupt (extraphysical escape).
3. Oneiric (pertaining to a dream).
4. Voluntary.
5. Solitary.
6. Assisted by an energetic shower from a helper.

Characteristics. The extraphysical awakening of the intraphysical consciousness presents at least the following 11 distinct characteristics:

1. Level of immediate awareness.
2. Darkness, illumination or penumbra in regard to the paravisual perception of the extraphysical environment or dimension.
3. *Open eyes.*
4. Closed para-eyes.
5. Self-awareness in regard to the vehicle of manifestation, whether in the physical base, a nearby or distant place.
6. In a condition of extraphysical disorientation.
7. With oscillations and undulations of the projected psychosoma.
8. In a position of extraphysical equilibrium.
9. In a position of extraphysical disequilibrium.
10. In the condition of a *blind, deaf* and *mute* consciousness.
11. With mental perspectives that may be healthy or pathological.

Continuous. In the experiences of projections with continuous awareness, it is obvious that neither extraphysical nor physical awakenings occur.

Resurrection. The occurrence denominated *spiritual resurrection,* a much used expression in religious environments, represents nothing more than the extraphysical awakening of the consciousness after going through unconscious final projection (desoma).

261. EXTRAPHYSICAL SELF-AWAKENING TECHNIQUE

Liberation. In the production of lucid projection, what is important is that you see yourself in the extraphysical dimension free from the consciential state you were in before – whether it was sleep, a dream, a nightmare, a daydream, hypnagogy or the ordinary, physical waking state – and acquire full lucidity outside the human body. This is because, as a general rule, your consciousness does not perceive it has temporarily left the human body.

Autosuggestion. The most common provision for predisposing extraphysical awakening is repeating the following phrase to yourself many times before going to bed to sleep: "I am going to wake up lying over the bed above my body."

Test. You can employ the positive resource of the *coherence test* in order to remove the interference of all oneiric images or gravitating morphothosenes, thus refining your extraphysical perceptions and *denuding* your consciousness. This test consists of a judicious observation of aberrations in the scenes that you are perceiving or experiencing. For example, if you see a cat clucking like a chicken; if you ascertain that every stone in a wall takes on a different color; if the humanoid beings you see are blurry and superimposed; these visions clearly show incoherences or oneiric alterations that disappear as soon as you become aware that you are dreaming. This will initiate a more lucid projection.

Faculties. You can utilize all extraphysical *natural* resources that often spontaneously provoke extraphysical awakening, such as: the characteristic faculties of the psychosoma, self-luminosity, the acuity of extraphysical vision, permeability, lightness, volitation, invulnerability to physical agents, invisibility or intangibility to human beings.

Awareness. While in the ordinary, physical waking state, you must saturate your mind with the idea and determination of extraphysically awakening yourself when one or more of the following 18 conditions come to your attention:

1. **Psychosoma.** Find yourself suspended in empty space, stopped or in movement above the floor (instability of the psychosoma).

2. **Respiration.** Notice that you do not need to breathe (departure from intraphysical restriction).

3. **Elasticity.** Observe that your arm stretches easily (extraphysical elasticity).

4. **Invisibility.** Perceive that an ordinary mirror does not reflect your image (extraphysical invisibility).

5. **Imperceptibility.** Observe that other beings are not aware of the presence of your consciousness projected in the environment (extraphysical invisibility).

6. **Inaudibility.** Verify that those beings present do not hear your words (extraphysical inaudibility).

7. **Self-luminosity.** Discover that you are somehow emitting your own light (extraphysical self-luminosity).

8. **Imponderability.** Discover that you are lighter or discover that your *body* does not cast a shadow when in the sun (extraphysical imponderability).

9. **Translocation.** Perceive that you are somehow moving from one district to another, either by gliding or flying, and that this is different from the state of inactivity in which you left your human body on the bed (extraphysical translocation).

10. **Freedom.** Experience yourself having greater freedom, being capable of going wherever you wish (sense of freedom).

11. **Paravision.** Recognize that your vision manifests characteristics superior to physical vision (paravision), such as: endoscopy or depth, microscopy, magnification, retrovision and vision with no perspective.

12. **Transparency.** Verify the transparency of all objects and constructions that you see.

13. **Copy.** Identify that all things have a double form, or luminous copy (second universe).

14. **Rejuvenation.** Find yourself suddenly rejuvenated (unconscious self-transfiguration).

15. **Invulnerability.** Clearly experience a person or moving vehicle pass right through you in any public place (extraphysical invulnerability).

16. **Self-permeability.** Pass a hand freely through physical objects (extraphysical self-permeability).

17. **Projectability.** Observe yourself and verify that you do not have a body or vehicle of manifestation (projection in the mentalsoma).

18. **Ideoplasty.** Notice that you redo or undo the scenes that you visualize with a simple act of will (ideoplasty).

Stimulus. It is recommended that the veteran projector read and reflect upon the above listed 18 extraphysical conditions, as they can actually stimulate the production of *spontaneous* lucid projections, as well as amplifying extraphysical self-lucidity. This has already occurred on a number of occasions with the author.

Bibliography: Vieira (1762, p. 67).

X – Extraphysical Period of the Consciousness

262. EXTRAPHYSICAL SELF-AWARENESS

Definition. Extraphysical self-awareness: the state of consciential lucidity while outside the human body that allows the intraphysical consciousness to have absolute certainty that he/she is neither dreaming nor in the normal waking state.

Synonymy: astral awareness; astral lucidity; connection of awareness; extracorporeal lucidity; extraphysical lucidity; extraphysical self-awareness; extraphysical wakefulness; second attention.

Awakening. The majority of intraphysical consciousnesses, when projected from the human body, remain aware *in* the extraphysical dimension but, nonetheless, are unfortunately unaware *of* the selfsame extraphysical dimension.

Challenge. The majority of projected projectors encounter extraphysical situations that cannot be categorized in terms with which they are already familiar. In these cases, they need to *adapt,* create new strategies and modify or combine old strategies in order to deal with the challenge of the *new world.*

Thought. Creating the habit of maintaining sustained and concentrated thoughts during daily life, in the ordinary waking state, results in having absolute control of the thoughts of the consciousness projected in the extraphysical dimension.

Objective. The entire technical endeavor of this book is directed toward the processes for obtaining extraphysical self-awareness, the greatest condition or the most difficult objective to achieve in the experience of lucid projection.

Bottleneck. Having *overcome the bottleneck* or having obtained extraphysical self-awareness, everything else will come naturally to the consciential projection practitioner due to the following 3 facts:

1. **Departure.** All intraphysical consciousnesses leave the human body every night.
2. **Interiorization.** Returning to the body is always easy and does not involve any major difficulties.
3. **Recall.** Recall is a simple consequence of extraphysical lucidity, in most cases.

Horizontality. While in the extraphysical horizontal position, the psychosoma remains passive and inactive.

Verticality. While in the vertical or erect position, this vehicle generally allows the projected intraphysical consciousness to recuperate lucidity. This fact is perhaps due to the physical and psychic conditioning of individuals who spend most of their life in the erect position, in the ordinary, physical waking state.

Extension. At least the following 7 facets should be analyzed regarding the extent or degree of the lucidity of the consciousness:

1. **Ordinary.** Ordinary, superficial or profound awareness.
2. **Semi-awareness.** Semi-awareness per se.
3. **Superawareness.** Cosmic superawareness.
4. **Uniform.** Uniform awareness.
5. **Discontinuous.** Discontinuous awareness.
6. **Self-awareness.** Awareness of oneself, although without form.
7. **Appearance.** The sensation of apparent omniscience (mentalsoma).

Attributes. Among the attributes of extraphysical self-awareness, at least the following 14 can be singled out:

1. **Thosenology.** Thought (or thosenization).
2. **Concentration.** Mental elaboration.
3. **Reason.** Reasoning (or reason).
4. **Attention.** Long or short attention span.
5. **Mnemosomatics.** Memory (mnemosomatics).

6. **Holomemory.** Compound pluriexistential or holobiographical memory of the integral memory bank (holomemory, personal holobiography, holoresomatics).

7. **Imagistic.** Imagination or imagistic capacity.

8. **Comprehension.** Comprehension or understanding, comprehensive understanding.

9. **Self-discernment.** Discernment (distinction between better and worse, outdated and ideal, cosmoethical and anticosmoethical).

10. **Globalization.** Association of ideas (the panoramic vision of universalism).

11. **Critiquing.** Critical judgment (self-critiquing and heterocritiquing).

12. **Comparison.** Comparison or the habit of establishing relationships (association of ideas).

13. **Abstraction.** Abstraction or *alienation without becoming alienated.*

14. **Generalization.** Generalization or broader conclusions (multidimensionality; generalism; polyglotism; formal education and self-education; culture and multiculturalism; encyclopedism; polymathy).

Aspects. The following are 13 important aspects in the world of extraphysical self-awareness:

1. **Maintenance.** Maintenance of extraphysical self-awareness.

2. *Paramind.* An open mind or open *paramind.*

3. **Paratachypsychism.** *Extraphysical presence of mind.*

4. **Coherence.** Coherence in the progression of extraphysical experiences or events.

5. **Paraperceptiology.** Gradation of perceptions according to consciential projection.

6. **Shock.** Intraconsciential shock.

7. **Somnambulism.** Extraphysical somnambulism.

8. **Oneirism.** Pre-projective dream.

9. **Lapses.** Consciential lapses.

10. **Volition.** The action of will upon the forms of the psychosoma.

11. **Psychosomatics.** The consciousness in the partially configured psychosoma as well as in the integral psychosoma.

12. **Mentalsomatics.** The consciousness in the isolated mentalsoma.

13. **Awareness.** The difference of awareness (cognitive capacity) in one vehicle of manifestation and another.

Lucidity. An elevated level of extraphysical lucidity favors recall subsequent to the projection.

Discontinuity. The state of discontinuous extraphysical lucidity sometimes causes fragmented recall.

Faculty. Ordinary, physical self-awareness is the faculty of being aware of your own behavior, which involves the capacity to reflect upon it and, using reason, to maintain or modify it.

Initiatives. Extraphysical self-awareness allows the projected projector at least the following 5 well-defined initiatives:

1. **Control.** Deliberately control your condition or extraphysical situation.

2. **Paravisual.** Have a nude or clothed appearance (para-appearance).

3. **Direction.** Determine the direction and the destination to which you transfer yourself.

4. **Encounters.** Encounter other consciousnesses or extraphysical consciousnesses.

5. **Learning.** Learn new ideas in the extraphysical dimension.

Perceptions. While projected in the extraphysical dimension, the consciousness – when in the psychosoma and, more intensely, in the mentalsoma, in the mentalsomatic dimension – can achieve an elevated state of self-awareness that allows it to perceive everything *en bloc,* at once, instantaneously and in detail, regardless of the amount of minutiae in the concepts that are perceived.

Factors. One of the first factors among those that call the attention of the intraphysical consciousness projected for the first time is the hitherto unknown relationship between the sensation of the human body's heaviness and the psychosoma's lightness. This fact implies the notion of the inertia of the bodies and the action of gravity upon them, which are diminished or temporarily extinguished.

Mysticism. From an extraphysical standpoint, mysticism – in this context understood to be emotionality without rationality – impairs consciential lucidity, a fact that illustrates 2 principles:

1. **Obnubilation.** The greater the mysticism in the *dominant* emotions of the projected intraphysical consciousness, the more obnubilated his/her lucidity will be.

2. **Serenity.** The greater the serenity, or the greater the elevated sentiments (rational and *tamed* emotions), the more lucid the projected intraphysical consciousness will be.

Ballast. The consciousness of the projected projector being assisted by helper(s) in extraphysical assistential activities tends to remain clouded, obfuscated or eclipsed. This is not only because it is ballasted by the holochakra, or manifesting through the dense psychosoma, but also due to the presence of the helper(s).

Obscurity. There are some more obscure aspects related to these events that require further research and clarification.

Relation. Something occurs in this contiguous relationship that sometimes impedes the full lucidity of the projected consciousness, as occurs with 3 other similar events:

1. **Satellite.** The satellite (moon) being dependent upon the star (planet, sun).

2. **Clairvoyant.** The clairvoyant being dependent upon the nagual.

3. **Sensitive.** The sensitive being dependent upon the extraphysical mentor.

Errors. Probably 90% of all lucid projections of the consciousness experienced by intraphysical projectors, even when prolonged and important, are no more than semilucid projections or mere lucid dreams. Hence it is necessary to insist that the act of obtaining advanced extraphysical self-awareness is the greatest basic conquest for any lucid projector.

Doubts. Only with an elevated level of extraphysical self-awareness can the intraphysical consciousness liberate him/herself from the errors of interpretation in experiences outside his/her human body. Thus, a single lucid projection does not always resolve the intraphysical consciousness' issues of the essential doubts regarding the real extraphysical world.

Exception. The above-mentioned fact also shows that lucid projection – although being a *natural*, physiological *occurrence* and common to all of humanity, and being an advanced condition of extraphysical self-awareness – is paradoxically an occurrence which is unfortunately still the *exception* for the intraphysical consciousness. In other words, it is still subordinated to the prison or *funnel* of the condition of terrestrial physical restriction and to the *bellows* (the lungs in the maintenance of the soma).

Immaturity. Persons who are excessively *locked* when their vehicles of consciential manifestation are in the coincident state are much more prone to be immature extraphysical consciousnesses. In other words, they fall into the same post-desomatic extraphysical conditions as certain children who, upon undergoing desoma, remain in the intermissive period, sometimes for an extended period of time, presenting only an infantile lucidity, mentality and, frequently, paraform of the psychosoma. They take a long time to recuperate the conditions and forms of the natural adulthood (somatic adulthood or maturity) from their *next-to-last* human life (next-to-last retrosoma).

Development. Despite everything, the parapsychically developed intraphysical consciousness can enjoy perfect lucidity when projected from the human body.

Analogy. The following is a pertinent comparison of two experiences in different consciential dimensions:

1. **Intraphysicology.** Human life is like a *movie,* produced far from the public, where one can employ all the tricks of the trade and spectacular special effects.

2. **Extraphysicology.** Temporary, extraphysical life, during the experience of lucid projection is like a *play* in which one has direct, raw, face-to-face contact with the audience, in which crude camera tricks are not allowed.

Bibliography: Alverga (18, p. 96), Bayless (98, p. 100), Castaneda (258, p. 20), Crookall (343, p. 42), Denning (391, p. 158), Gonçalves (614, p. 5), Powell (1278, p. 89), Vieira (1762, p. 214), Walker (1781, p. 70).

263. SCALE OF LUCIDITY OF THE PROJECTED CONSCIOUSNESS

Definition. Scale of lucidity of the projected consciousness: the ordered sequence of factors for establishing the development of the magnificence of the phenomenon of extraphysical lucidity.

Synonymy: table of extraphysical lucidity.

Awareness. The normal or unaltered mental state of the waking, adult intraphysical consciousness – or that in which the individual spends the greater part of his/her time in the ordinary, physical waking state – was arbitrarily chosen as the conventional pattern for characterizing the condition of full, total, complete, rational or lucid awareness.

Exclusions. This state of lucidity of the intraphysical consciousness excludes various factors or conditions, such as the following 9:

1. **Sleep.** Sleep or somatic renewal.
2. **Sleepiness.** Nap (sleepiness, hypnagogy).
3. **Absence.** Small abstraction (absence).
4. **Daydream.** Daydream or deep waking dream.
5. **Pharmacology.** Drugged organic state (pharmacological).
6. **Psychopathology.** Permanent mental insanity or a psychotic episode.
7. **Pathology.** Serious or chronic illness (organic disturbance).
8. **Self-lucidity.** Prenatal, infantile and senile mental conditions.
9. **Incapacitation.** All other psychological situations in which the intraphysical consciousness (mind) is incapable of acting efficiently when faced with the practical, prosaic or trivial everyday problems of human existence.

Variations. According to the above-cited characterization of the waking state, it can clearly be seen that human awareness, in everyday life, varies in layers, stages, percentages, degrees or levels, according to the individual conditions and circumstances of the moment, which provoke bursts of exacerbation or reductions of obfuscation in the individual's lucidity.

Extraphysicality. Those who project with some frequency or, in other words, after having approximately 10 lucid projections in succession, without great gaps of time between them, end up easily verifying that the *degree of lucidity* of their consciousness, while in the extraphysical dimension, also varies from experience to experience, in the same manner as occurs in the ordinary, physical waking state.

Change. There is a close relationship between change of consciential dimension and consciential lucidity. As a rule, every change from one extraphysical dimension to another, as small as it may be, disturbs or reduces the degree of the projected intraphysical consciousness' extraphysical lucidity.

Oneirism. In the new extraphysical dimension, the projected intraphysical consciousness' lucidity may be clearer than before (rarer), or he/she may mix the images that he/she visualizes (more frequent), thereby ending up in a condition of semilucidity or in an oneiric state (oneirism).

Relationship. The relationship between awareness, wakefulness regarding the environment and extraphysical self-permeability is intense and profound for the intraphysical consciousness projected in the extraphysical tropospheric dimension.

Perception. For example, upon returning to the physical base, the projected intraphysical consciousness can pass through countless physical obstacles without noticing it and only become aware of the environment when in the bedroom or *inside* the soma. The building where his/her physical body resides, the ceilings, outer walls, inner walls, furniture or interior decoration of the human environments were neither seen nor *perceived* by the intraphysical consciousness. This shows that, in the same extraphysical dimension, in a single lucid projection, the vehicles of consciential manifestation can go through diverse vibratory frequencies in their energies and densities.

Functioning. In order for the lucidity of the projected intraphysical consciousness (*paramind*) to be full and function adequately both *sensorial,* or paraphysiological, perceptions and *intellectual* abilities need to manifest simultaneously. It is therefore necessary – in the case of the psychosoma, for example – that the vehicle be completely projected, or at least with all its essential attributes, in order for the consciousness to operate efficiently in an extraphysical dimension.

Recall. Furthermore, *lucidity* has to be accompanied by *recall* subsequent to the extraphysical experiences in order for these two conditions to be efficiently registered and accompanied by accurate observation.

Classification. There are still no standard units for measuring, or known elements for gauging, levels of awareness in the ordinary, physical waking state. Thus, in an attempt to quantify the subject, certain parameters or characteristics can be established according to the quality of the projected projector's perceptions, in a scale of qualities and values or subjective classification – obviously the most precise possible – within the current circumstances, which are composed of 5 basic degrees or percentages:

1. **20%.** The extraphysical experience with 20% lucidity constitutes *semi-awareness:* discontinuity of extraphysical wakefulness; oneiric interferences in incoming perceptions; hallucinogenic aberrations; factors which definitively characterize the state of semilucid projection or, in other words, that state which is mixed with dreams, nightmares and consciential projection (somatics).

2. **40%.** The extraphysical experience with 40% lucidity shows the elements of *doubt:* constant positive (exaltation) or negative (fear, projectiophobia) emotional influence during the entire period of extraphysical exteriorization; doubt, or unawareness, on that occasion, regarding the fact of being projected; continuous insecurity during the entire course of extraphysical actions.

3. **60%.** The extraphysical experience with 60% lucidity shows the characteristics of *certainty:* full conviction of being projected; the beginning of the association of ideas and rational comparisons between the physical and extraphysical dimension, which are spontaneously elaborated with defined critical judgment (holosomatics).

4. **80%.** The extraphysical experience with 80% lucidity shows *self-awareness:* lucidity equal to that of the ordinary, physical waking state; unalterable uniformity of clear perceptions; a complete absence of immature or irrational emotionality; the maturity of the undisputed knowledge of being projected, or extraphysical self-awareness; maximum critical judgment, with the ordinary possibilities of the projector's self-critique (projectiology).

5. **100%.** The extraphysical experience with 100% lucidity is characterized by *superawareness:* lucidity superior to the maximum available in the ordinary, physical waking state and which incontrovertibly identifies the state of cosmoconsciousness typical of magnificent consciential projections in the isolated mentalsoma (cosmoconscientiology).

Comparison. Evidently, the state of 100% of extraphysical awareness is equivalent to the impossible 150% of lucidity in the standard ordinary, waking state.

Average. The majority of consciential projections characterized as being lucid – by all consciential *projectors,* over the course of *time, everywhere,* in all *conditions* – varies between the average range of 40% and 60% of extraphysical lucidity or, in other words, between the states of *vacillation-doubt* and *confidence-certainty* in manifestations outside the human body.

Instrument. This scale represents the first practical measuring instrument allowing the lucid projection practitioner to evaluate his/her own effort in each experiment, giving exact perspectives of the improvement of lucid projectability (LPB), or the goals for improvement of his/her extraphysical performance.

Psychology. As strange as it may seem, even the repressions and conditionings that comprise the psychological profile of each intraphysical consciousness influence the level of his/her lucidity when projected from the human body in the tropospheric extraphysical dimension.

Case study. For example: a very systematic person with deep-rooted habits, who is not accustomed to walking alone on deserted streets or in unfamiliar places for fear of being assaulted, can become traumatized in the very beginning, when outside the human body, in similar circumstances. For this reason, the projector is not able to achieve extraphysical lucidity, thereby remaining in a semilucid or nightmarish condition. His/her repressed *psychological* (intraphysicology) conditions do not permit him/her to attain healthy *parapsychic* (extraphysicology) conditions.

Bibliography: Baumann (93, p. 111), Vieira (1762, p. 143), Walker (1781, p. 24).

264. CONSCIENTIAL LUCIDITY AND PERCEIVED TIME

Definitions. Extraphysical sensation of time: the impression through which the intraphysical consciousness, while projected with lucidity, perceives the succession and duration of experiences outside the human body; the extrasensory process of the consciousness regarding the perception of the time factor.

Synonymy: para-perception of the fourth (temporal) dimension.

Premises. The following are 6 premises concerning the consciential lucidity-perceived time relationship:

1. **Conditionings.** Conditioned reflexes play the most important role in the consolidation of all manner of our habits and repressions. These even transcend the scope of manifestations of our personal psychology in the ordinary, physical waking state, and reach the manifestations of our *para*psychology, when our consciousness is projected from the human body. In other words, when it is temporarily freed from the prison of the dense brain, the *black box* or transelectro-electronic machine which is only partially decipherable by our current intelligence. It is common knowledge that the continuous flow of time plays an important role precisely in the generation of these selfsame conditionings.

2. **Past.** One of the fundamental questions of scientific research is past time. All the factual information we have to work with refers to past events. In any scientific investigation, we have to make generalizations based upon this factual information, in order to know what to expect in the future and to sophisticate our research.

3. **Independence.** Strictly speaking, in the same way that the consciousness, which is insubstantial per se, does not need to depend upon the human body, the respiratory mechanism, natural sleep, physical forms, atmospheric pressure and gravitational laws in order to live and act freely, it also does not need to depend upon or suffer the consequences of the effects of the time factor, the chronological world or space-time coordinates.

4. **Cosmic.** Terrestrial humanity has thus far been living in an unnecessary condition of unconscious slavery to the internal and perceived time factor. In order to change this tyranny of time upon us, we need to create a new mental or consciential system according to the still immeasurable potentiality and vastness of our *total self,* until we arrive at a state of frequent cosmoconsciousness (cosmoconscientiology).

5. **Expansion.** Every act of expansion of the attributes of the human consciousness is, in some way, an escape from the condition of anthropomorphic physical restriction. It is therefore a specific type of nonlucid, semilucid or lucid consciential projection.

6. **Freedom.** The condition of expanded consciousness is the greatest possible realization of individual freedom – in this case, almost absolute – which can be enjoyed by the ego while humanized in a social, intraphysical or terrestrial manner (citizen). The expanded consciousness is an escape from time, or better still, the true freedom of the intraphysical consciousness from the *internal prison* of time, forged by the ego.

Cause. Given these 6 premises, it can be inferred that the influence of time, which – in theory – forms the fourth dimension, is one of the essential causes of greater alterations in the levels of extraphysical lucidity of the intraphysical consciousness while fully projected from the soma.

Pluri-awareness. When the time factor is not acting upon the consciousness, or even merely reducing the intensity of its action, when this selfsame consciousness finds itself free or expanded, the past, present and future occur together and coexist simultaneously within the consciousness. This comprises the condition of *atemporal pluri-awareness*.

Effects. The following are 6 effects generated by the condition of atemporal pluri-awareness:

1. **Alterations.** Lightning-fast alterations in or successions of consciential levels.
2. **Oneirism.** Chaotic oneiric images characterized by incongruity, incoherence, inconsistency and anachronism, which interfere in the lucidity of the projected intraphysical consciousness.
3. **Duplicity.** The condition of apparent double and multiple awarenesses.
4. **Semilucidity.** Semilucid consciential projections.
5. **Retrocognitions.** Retrocognitive consciential projections.
6. **Precognitions.** Precognitive consciential projections.

Anchoring. In order for the consciousness to induce full lucidity at a certain level or consciential dimension, it needs to somehow anchor itself in a stable manner at this level through the factor of perceived time – in a compact or frozen manner, in this case – in order to separate fantasies from real images, or *separate the wheat from the chaff* (extraphysical self-discernment).

Kaleidoscope. The consciousness – in reference to the manifestation of attributes which anchor its lucidity on a certain occasion – is always a living kaleidoscope: it is uninterruptedly mutable, unsleeping and almost unending.

Attributes. The consciousness allows time to influence its consciential world (consciential attributes) either positively or negatively. For example, within the scope of memory, time acts like a fixative, serving to preserve the clarity of recorded memories. More precisely, the consciousness allows time to operate as an imposed pause upon the uninterrupted flow of the inner images of its vibrantly alive inner experiences.

Elements. The following are examples of 6 time-fixative elements perceived by the consciousness:

1. **Light.** The chronological course of light or the day-night, sunrise-sunset rhythm.
2. **Seconds.** The passage of seconds of a clock.
3. **Vibrations.** The vibrations of any type of object: atom, radio station or pendulum.
4. **Seasons.** Distinction regarding the seasons of the year.
5. **Era.** The human clothing and customs of each era.
6. **Age.** The characterization of physical or biological age in the periods of infancy, youth, maturity and old age (from sixty-five years of age and over).

Brain. Physical and extraphysical phenomena converge in order to demonstrate that the consciousness is an active reality beyond the human brain.

Hemispheres. The 2 hemispheres operate like *restricting fields* of an enormous quantity of variables of the mentalsoma's manifestations, in order to allow activity in only one specific area, without dispersion to other areas.

Parabrain. Similarly, the parabrain (of the psychosoma) appears to be the seat of the mentalsoma which, in turn, is the seat of the consciousness.

Level. Each perceived period of time ends up creating – only apparently, simply by and for the consciousness – a level of consciential lucidity, a level of depth of reasoning and a different and specific range of perception according to a certain level of time.

Suspension. The provisory and interrupted elimination or suspension of time, as a consciential dimension, is one of the causes of instability in the projected consciousness' levels of lucidity.

Crises. Although being an extraordinary inner resource, or evidence of greater evolution, this suspension of time nevertheless ends up triggering evolutionary consciential growing crises.

Double. The condition of double awareness manifests itself on a scale of 3 levels:

1. **Coincidence.** The condition of *cerebral,* intraphysical or waking awareness.
2. **Discoincidence.** The intraphysical consciousness who is temporarily in the projected, *empty-brain* condition.

3. **Hyperacuity.** The situation of the *extraphysical* consciousness when in a state of extreme lucidity or hyperacuity.

Semilucidity. As long as there is no fixation of time by the consciousness, the condition of *atemporal pluri-awareness* predominates or, in other words, a state of inner entropy of the consciousness occurs due to the time factor. Thereby, ordinary semilucid consciential projections arise due to ignorance regarding the paraphysiology of the holosoma.

---

265. ILLUMINATION OF THE EXTRAPHYSICAL ENVIRONMENT

Definition. Illumination of the extraphysical environment: the perception, by the intraphysical consciousness projected in the extraphysical dimension, of light irradiating from a nonspecific origin and consequent brightening.

Synonymy: clarifying of the perceptions of the projected intraphysical consciousness; illumination of the extraphysical environment.

Unmani. The extraphysical period of the consciousness, or the state of the consciousness while outside the human body – namely the stage in which all intraphysical beings find themselves outside the dense body, e.g.: during certain phases of natural sleep, parapsychic trance and during lucid projection – is referred to as the state of *unmani* in the East. The condition of extraphysical illumination for the projected intraphysical consciousness is dependent upon this state of lucidity.

Night. There is no night outside dense matter for the projected consciousness.

Indirect. In the extraphysical tropospheric dimension, which appears to be a luminescent duplicate of the physical dimension, an indirect luminosity always arises for the consciousness. This luminosity does not emanate from any specific direction, but is diffuse, brilliant and intense. It neither disturbs nor obfuscates the shadowless extraphysical vision.

Near-death. It is worth observing that the intraphysical consciousness, after being lucidly projected from the human body, notably in near-death experiences (NDE), sometimes when describing extraphysical illumination does not speak in terms of light, but in terms of a *total absence of light* and *complete darkness*. The projector thinks – with these expressions – that he/she is not saying the same thing and is more correctly describing the real situation in the extraphysical dimension in certain intraconsciential (internal or *subjective*) conditions and extraconsciential (external or *objective*) circumstances.

Difference. In fact, illumination and an absence of darkness do not, strictly speaking, signify the same thing. This subtle but ponderable difference more clearly evidences the extraphysical reality of the intraphysical consciousness projected under certain conditions.

Self-awareness. The illumination of the extraphysical environment is one of the first ostensive and characteristic manifestations of the projector's self-awareness upon realizing that he/she is projected from the human body. Nevertheless, this is not a *sine qua non* condition for the intraphysical consciousness to be in the extraphysical dimension or to be absolutely self-aware of being outside the dense body. This is because that state can occur in the dark, namely without the consciousness seeing anything.

Vision. This phenomenon occurs due to the fact that vision is not everything to the consciousness nor does it express everything that you are, but only one of the consciousness' multiple *mentalsomatic attributes,* just like many others.

Characteristics. Among the characteristics of illumination in the extraphysical environment, at least the following 23 can be singled out:

1. **Perception.** The clear perception of extraphysical illumination by the projected consciousness.
2. **Moment.** The occasion or precise moment when extraphysical illumination arises.
3. **Speed.** The speed at which extraphysical illumination arises for the consciousness.
4. **Intensity.** The intensity of extraphysical illumination.

5. **Clarity.** The clarity of extraphysical illumination.
6. **Coloring.** The predominant color in the extraphysical illumination.
7. **Unicolor.** The unicolor condition, a bluish or yellowish color.
8. **Bicolor.** The bicolor condition, or black and white.
9. **Multicolor.** Multicolored extraphysical illumination.
10. **Grays.** Gray images.
11. **Silver.** Silvery images.
12. **Time.** Diurnal or nocturnal extraphysical illumination.
13. **Nature.** Natural or artificial extraphysical illumination.
14. **Uniformity.** The uniformity of extraphysical illumination.
15. **Increase.** A sudden increase in extraphysical illumination.
16. **Effects.** Phosphorescence, scintillations and stroboscopic effects.
17. **Blindness.** The consciential condition without vision.
18. **Neutrality.** Neutral vision of the projected consciousness, which is neither blind nor sighted.
19. **Desire.** The desire to see and extraphysical illumination.
20. **Explosions.** Explosions of light which are perceived extraphysically.
21. **Fog.** The condition of extraphysical fog.
22. **Darkness.** Extraphysical total darkness and semi-obscurity.
23. **Mentalsoma.** The environment without perceptible space-time (mentalsomatic dimension).

Movement. The relation between extraphysical illumination and movement of the projected consciousness shows that it can feel itself to be stationary somewhere, in the dark, translocate itself in the dark and volitate while apparently blind, often without any problem or harm occurring.

Amplification. The amplification of vision and extraphysical illumination reach a point that exceeds the physical dimension, making it difficult to visualize the details of forms in the human dimension. This fact engenders errors in the interpretation of events and mistakes in the description of forms, things and objects which are seen.

Case study. One day, a group of explorers encountered a little girl, no more than 2 years old, in an encampment abandoned by the indigenous Guayaquils. The child was retrieved by an ethnographer who entrusted her to his own mother. Thus raised and educated in a new mesology or intraphysical environment and in the *highly civilized* European culture, the little "savage one" became a modern adult woman who, speaking many languages, conducted profound studies in ethnology, collaborated with her adoptive father and eventually married him.

Paramesology. If the human environment (mesology) exercises such a profound influence upon the intraphysical consciousness, it is to be expected that the extraphysical environment (paramesology) also exercises a significant influence upon the projected intraphysical consciousness, beyond the little we understand on this subject thus far. This fact deserves our reflection.

Bibliography: Castaneda (258, p. 207), Greenhouse (636, p. 253), Kardec (824, p. 163), Monroe (1065, p. 131), Ring (1406, p. 48), Vieira (1762, p. 107).

---

266. VEHICLE OF MANIFESTATION IDENTIFICATION TECHNIQUE

Definition. Extraphysical self-examination: the observation made, through extraphysical perceptions (paraperceptions), of the qualities and circumstances in which the vehicle of manifestation of the intraphysical consciousness projected from the human body presents itself.

Synonymy: para-somatognosis; projective self-examination.

Identification. Your consciousness, as a projector – in view of the improvement of your extraphysical performance, upon seeing yourself temporarily free from the human body – should endeavor to recognize and identify the vehicle through which you are manifesting on that occasion. This may be either the psychosoma or the mentalsoma.

Psychosoma. With regard to the projection of your consciousness in the psychosoma, it can be entirely free or, in other words, connected to the fine and almost always imperceptible silver cord, although with little or no energy pertaining to the nuclei of the holochakra. The psychosoma can also be partially formed, with varying concentrations of the holochakra's energy.

Observation. There are many specific conditions that permit you to differentiate the psychosoma from the mentalsoma, especially the observation of some basic aspects of the extraphysical experiment.

Differential. The basic differences between the psychosoma and the mentalsoma have already been established in detail through descriptions and comparisons made in various preceding chapters. They can be summarized with the following 13 variables:

1. **Takeoff.** The type of takeoff.
2. **Hyperacuity.** The degree of extraphysical self-awareness.
3. **Departure.** A single or double departure.
4. **Dimension.** The precise condition of the dimension of manifestation.
5. **Form.** The form of the vehicle of manifestation.
6. **Connection.** The nature of the intervehicular connection.
7. **Sensations.** The sensations of weight, emotionality and the nuances of extraphysical parapsychism.
8. **Influence.** The occurrence of some extraphysical influence.
9. **Participation.** The nature of participation with the extraphysical environment.
10. **Communicology.** The process of consciential communication.
11. **Energy.** The effects of energy currents.
12. **Recognition.** The possibility of the projected consciousness being seen by other beings.
13. **Repercussions.** Physical and extraphysical repercussions.

Bibliography: Vieira (1762, p. 107).

267. EXPANSION OF THE PROJECTED CONSCIOUSNESS TECHNIQUE

Awareness. After becoming aware of which vehicle you are manifesting in, either the psychosoma or the mentalsoma, it will be easier for your projected consciousness to maintain lucidity and then expand your attributes and perceptions outside the human body, amplifying your level of extraphysical self-critiquing and hetero-critiquing judgment.

Psychosoma. When in the psychosoma, your projected consciousness should endeavor to remain as serene as possible, discarding all emotionality, of any origin or cause. You need to concentrate on the delicate importance of the situation while free in the extraphysical dimension and take advantage of that period of lucid projection.

Input. At this point, you need to clearly define which of your modes of sensory input are operating the most: vision, audition, olfaction, touch, inspiration or another extraphysical parapsychic input, in order to then endeavor to expand along that line.

Impressions. Your *consciousness* or, in other words, that which refers to your soma (you are not your soma) especially needs to disengage from these 3 impressions that cause the process of exteriorization related to your soma:

1. **Position.** The position in which you find yourself after takeoff from the psychosoma.
2. **Soma.** The ordinary vision of your inactive human body (soma).
3. **Base.** The details of the environment of your physical base.

Target. All this should be done in order to immediately reach another mental target that is propitious to the development of your extraphysical experiences and lucid projection itself, without losing sight of the educational opportunity in the projective period.

Deconditioning. Lucid projection is capable of alleviating and expanding the intraphysical consciousness' profoundly conditioned perceptions through a number of extremely powerful *restrictive factors* with a variety of origins and natures, notably the following 13:

1. **Ecology.** Environmental or mesological (ecology).
2. **Art.** Artistic or psychosomatic (self-mimicries, existential miniprogram).
3. **Science.** Scientific or mentalsomatic (reason, logic, cons).
4. **Economy.** Economic or related to intraphysical survival (money).
5. **Karmic group.** Relatives or the first and second families (groupkarmality).
6. **Politics.** Philosophical, ideological, political or doctrinaire (positioning).
7. **Paragenetics.** Holokarmic or personal paragenetic.
8. **Culture.** Intellectual or cultural (habits or one's own *little world*).
9. **Profession.** Professional or corporative (nepotism, the condition of *entanglement*).
10. **Psychology.** Psychological or mental (referring to the 2 cerebral hemispheres).
11. **Education.** Religious or relating to pre-maternal and maternal education.
12. **Intraphysical society.** Social or relative to the repressions of the *abdominal brainwashing* of intraphysical society.
13. **Genetic.** Personal somatic or genetic (hereditariness predominately from the father or mother).

Mentalsoma. If you are manifesting through the mentalsoma, your consciousness should seek, through extraphysical reflection, the greatest ideas that you have always wanted to investigate. This should be done while bearing in mind your short extraphysical stay in the mentalsomatic dimension and the need for you to remember these important events upon returning to the intraphysical dimension shortly thereafter.

Bibliography: Vieira (1762, p. 66).

---

268. ORIENTATION OF THE PROJECTED CONSCIOUSNESS

Definition. Projective orientation: the act of becoming aware of the extraphysical location in which the consciousness finds itself when projected from the human body, and its situation in relation to the extraphysical environment.

Synonymy: extraphysical metatropism; extraphysical self-location; extraphysical spatial awareness; para-spatial orientation; projective self-direction.

Space. Personal orientation is found to be intimately connected with the notions of space and time.

Categories. There are two basic categories of personal orientation:

1. **Self-psychism.** *Self-psychic* orientation relative to the person him/herself, or the condition which allows the intraphysical consciousness to identify him/herself, to clearly perceive where he/she is, the day, month and year (Gregorian calendar) and the situation in relation to the environment (mesology).

2. **Allopsychism.** *Allopsychic* orientation or the notion of the consciousness itself, intraconscientially speaking, in relation to the outside world per se (cosmos).

Terrestrial. Certain environments close to the troposphere (the earth's crust) allow the projected intraphysical consciousness to pinpoint his/her extraphysical location, e.g.: when finding him/herself projected above the human body, on the ceiling of the bedroom, in an ordinary bedroom in his/her own home, in a familiar location in the city where he/she resides, or in the familiar residence of a friend or relative.

Intuition. However, extraphysical self-location is not always easy, even in the paratroposphere. Extraphysical intuition greatly assists the orientation of the projected intraphysical consciousness.

Extraphysical. In extraphysical environments per se – which are native, paratropospheric, underdeveloped or evolved, more distant from the terrestrial atmosphere – the projected intraphysical consciousness generally does not have sufficiently secure means or indications for orienting him/herself, except when he/she returns to the same location where he/she had previously been or when visiting a familiar extraphysical consciousness.

Classification. Extraphysical environments visited by the projected intraphysical consciousness can be classified into those which are known and unknown to the projector.

1. **Known.** In known environments, at least the following 4 variables should be observed:

A. **Location.** The personal location.

B. **Self-determination.** Self-determination regarding one's own destiny (goal, target).

C. **Parachronology.** The sense of time.

D. **Warning.** An inner warning or extraphysical intuition regarding the environment or district.

2. **Unknown.** In unknown environments, one can look for the smallest indications regarding the location, such as the following 8 variables:

E. **Meteorology.** The meteorological conditions at that moment.

F. **Sun.** The position of the sun, when visible.

G. **Week.** The day of the week and its relation to the flow of events.

H. **Meridian.** The time zone and the possibility of being in another terrestrial meridian.

I. **Approach.** A direct extraphysical approach made to *any consciousness appearing before you.*

J. **Signs.** Signs written in large letters above the roofs of intraphysical buildings (while volitating).

K. **Monuments.** Isolated monuments, especially those in the middle of a public square.

L. **Advertisement.** A lighted advertisement, poster, signboard, placard, billboard, or tower clock.

Objects. The following is a list of 11 key objects that can be useful for you, as a projected intraphysical consciousness, in order to awaken recollections and enable you to identify your extraphysical location:

1. **Residences.** Types of houses or buildings.

2. **Vehicles.** Types of vehicles, cars, trucks or carts.

3. **License plate.** The license plates of cars or vehicles.

4. **Make.** The make and model of vehicles.

5. **Print media.** Journals, magazines and periodicals, their dates, titles, texts, names of persons, photos or illustrations.

6. **Screens.** Screens and pictures placed for public viewing.

7. **Identities.** Living beings or extraphysical consciousnesses, their possible identities, names or personal identifying evidence (documents).

8. **Addresses.** Address tags on luggage.

9. **Factories.** Offices, companies or factories.

10. **Signs.** Signs over doors (cultural or commercial).

11. **Signboards.** Gate signboards or street signs.

Erraticism. *Projective erraticism* is the temporary condition of the erratic consciential projector, namely that projected intraphysical consciousness who leaves the human body without orientation, in a lost manner, and is unable to locate him/herself. He/she is not able to reach his/her mental target when he/she has one and does not even arrive or reach a familiar extraphysical district, even after several attempts, only appearing at unfamiliar locations.

Panic. Regardless of the situation, extraphysical disorientation and the condition of projective erraticism usually neither cause substantial negative consequences nor should they scare the projected consciousness which, in every extraphysical situation, needs to avoid panic. Panic almost always signifies the abrupt, traumatic and undesirable ending of the consciential experience, and the sudden return of the consciousness to the human body accompanied by intraphysical repercussions.

Inertia. Obviously, neither the physical base, nor the human body – both temporarily abandoned – change location during the period of the consciousness' lucid consciential projection. This is a question of logic regarding the inertia of bodies.

Interiorization. Whenever necessary, the projected intraphysical consciousness needs only to think about his/her own human body, maintaining a firm desire to return to the physical base, resulting in his/her return, interiorization and physical awakening, without any major problems or obstacles.

Sense. The projected intraphysical consciousness, due to the operation of the silver cord in the *extraphysical dimension,* on the one hand, and the performance of the golden cord in the *mentalsomatic* dimension, on the other hand – whether consciously or unconsciously regarding these operations – enjoys a generally infallible sense of orientation in *extraphysical space* for returning to the isolated human body or to the coincident human body and psychosoma, which were left inactive in an intraphysical base.

Stereognosis. This occurs in the manner of *stereognosis,* in the common stereognostic sense, as with carrier pigeons and swallows, in regard to their movement in the *airspace* of the terrestrial troposphere and paratroposphere. This is also the case with dogs, cats or ants, in their dislocations on the *physical space* of the earth's surface.

Hypothesis. The 4 senses of orientation of these 4 types of subhuman animals, with manifest effects of dislocations in 4 very distinct *mesological conditions* may have a more intrinsic, profound and common cause to all 4. Which one? What? This research hypothesis is posed here in order to be tested.

Bibliography: Frost (560, p. 98), Kardec (824, p. 149), Monroe (1065, p. 60), Vieira (1762, p. 18).

269. EXTRAPHYSICAL ENVIRONMENTS

Definitions. Extraphysical environment: the location where the projected intraphysical consciousness locates him/herself outside the human body and the tridimensional geographic world; the sphere or dimension of life beyond the intraphysical, material or human dimension of existence.

Synonymy: alternant realities; alternative realities; alternative universe; astral domains; astral kingdoms; astral light; astral plane; astral reality; astral world; beyond the grave; beyond the tomb; circle of rescues; cryptocosmos; dimensions of existence; engaged universes; extraphysical district; extraphysical *habitat;* extraphysical plane; extraphysical state of the consciousness; extraphysical world; extrasensory world; fourth dimension; hyperspace; intertwined worlds; invisible space; invisible space-time; invisible world; kingdoms of existence; levels of reality; meta-etheric environment; meta-etheric planes of existence; meta-etheric worlds; parallel dimension; parallel universe; plastic interactive world; pluridimensions; polydimensional planes; second state; *second universe;* spiritual fields; spiritual world; spirituality; tachypsycholand; the beyond; transpersonal dimensions of the psyche; transpsychic reality; vibratory frequencies; world of immortality.

Principle. Any extraphysical district, above all, constitutes a state of consciousness and not a place. This is an essential principle of parageography (extraphysicology).

Schools. According to the Chinese researcher Solon Wang, the following are the 14 most important schools of knowledge on earth. Six of them are religions, 3 being Eastern, listed in decreasing number of adepts, namely Brahmanism or Hinduism, Buddhism and Zoroastrianism; and 3 being Western, listed in decreasing number of adepts, namely Christianity (Jesus of Nazareth), Islam (Mohammed) and Judaism (Moses). Six are philosophies, 3 being Eastern, namely Taoism, Confucianism and Yoga; and 3 being Western, namely Greek (Pythagoras and others), European Spiritualism (Descartes and others) and Materialism (Karl Marx: 1818-1883, and others). Two are sciences, natural or ancient science and new or psychic science.

Acceptance. Of these 14 schools of knowledge, 12 accept the existence of multiple dimensions in the cosmos and life and only two, ancient science and materialism, accept only the material or intraphysical dimension.

Tendency. Even in ordinary human life, every individual has his/her own personal conception of the world, possibly being born with a strong tendency to inhabit a certain type of universe to the detriment of the other.

Microuniverse. Every consciousness possesses its own personal microuniverse.

Intraconscientiality. The world is, above all, inside us.

Equality. We are not in a single world that is identical for all of us.

Acuities. The acuities of our physical senses (vision, audition and others) and parapsychic perceptions (lucid projection, clairvoyance and others) vary from adult to adult, from child to child, from animist to animist, from projector to projector, from sensitive to sensitive.

Serenissimus. *Serenissimus (Homo sapiens serenissimus)* lives simultaneously in various dimensions, with great equilibrium and self-awareness, wherever wishing to manifest.

Pre-*serenissimus*. Projectiology offers the intraphysical consciousness – or the pre-*serenissimus*, namely any one of us – the techniques for achieving, living and lucidly enjoying the fruits of the period of resoma with a new intraphysical life and the execution of the existential program.

Categories. Regarding the nature and the predominant quality of the energetic exchange between intraphysical consciousnesses per se, and between intraphysical consciousnesses and extraphysical consciousnesses, in relation to developed sensitives (whether aware or unaware of their abilities or potentialities), human environments can be classified into 3 categories:

1. **Absorbing:** slaughterhouses; nightclubs; gambling establishments; casinos; cemeteries; police stations; hospitals; institutions of social welfare; banking establishments; penitentiaries.

2. **Donating:** touristic spots with few visitors; jungles; tranquil parks; public squares with few transients; beaches with few beachgoers.

3. **Ambivalent:** sports clubs; open air performances; elevated artistic shows; motels; crowds; religious temples.

Sensitive. In order to live harmoniously, the intraphysical sensitive needs to know how to behave in each of the above-cited locations, without fearing or fleeing from any environment.

Projector. The same occurs with the projected intraphysical consciousness in the extraphysical dimension, in relation to the environment and the beings and extraphysical consciousnesses which he/ she comes across. Nevertheless, there are extraphysical locations which should be wisely avoided.

Spaces. Lucid projection opens up new and broader spaces to the intraphysical consciousness, which are much more diversified than the entire immense physical universe (cosmos) that humankind knows and has partial access to.

Types. Extraphysical environments can be classified into 4 types or levels:

1. **Cord.** The reduced perimeter of the vigorous action of the silver cord; the perimeter of which extends 13 feet (4 meters) from the human brain.

2. **Paratroposphere.** The plane or dimension that is coincident with the physical universe; the crustal or paratropospheric dimension.

3. **Extraphysicality.** The extraphysical plane or dimension per se, beginning from the energetic dimension; the extraphysical spheres.

4. **Mentalsomatics.** The mentalsomatic dimension.

Districts. It would be more realistic to characterize the districts – the physical and the extraphysical – as having 3 basic consciential states:

1. **Deficiencyland.** In the physical dimension, or *deficiencyland,* things, creations or objects appear to be more well-defined and delineated for the individual.

Words. Here, words endeavor to express ideas which are also defined in their smallest detail regarding the consensual or objective *reality* (for us).

2. **Transitland.** The tropospheric extraphysical dimension, or transitland, is always in transition, its forms varying infinitely, at every moment, according to the perceptions of the consciousness which is manifesting there.

Morphothosenes. Morphothosenes dominate the multiple environments and the expression of ideas can be executed telepathically, either with or without words.

Illusions. This is the dimension of illusions (the *Maya* of the extraphysical side) more closely related to dreams, nightmares and hallucinations in general.

3. **Conscientioland.** The mentalsomatic dimension, conscientioland or idealand, is the dimension of the future, of pure ideas and *en bloc* ideas, that dispenses with articulated words, and where life also expresses itself telepathically.

Conscientese. The native language in the mentalsomatic dimension is *conscientese*.

Vehicles. The extraphysical environments constitute some of the most serious problems for the intraphysical consciousness, based on the principle that the vehicles of consciential manifestation are relative, and are especially employed here as didactic resources for research.

State. Above all, the inner, personal state of the consciousness always predominates.

Simultaneity. Your perceptions – as a lucid projector – do not remain limited to a single scenario of the environment. The simultaneous perception of multiple environments can occur during a lucid projection. This sometimes greatly complicates things and profoundly confuses the consciousness.

Discontinuity. Consciential states are often more important than the environments which are perceived or identified, since a permanent discontinuity of the levels of the consciousness occurs. In a single projection, the projector can reach various levels of consciousness or different extraphysical environments in succession, whether or not he/she is aware of it.

Perceptions. The disparity of the consciousness' perceptions in relation to the perceived realities is another powerful factor of interference and is difficult to resolve within the restricted scope of rudimentary research that so far exists on the subject.

Everydayness. The extraphysical experiences of the projected consciousness are similar to momentary sensations, but they do not have the same type of relationship with the external or physical world as do the common everyday sensations in the ordinary, physical waking state.

Description. From this arises the basic problem of the manner in which to describe such experiences. Extraphysical journeys, from the very start, are included by the novice projector among the mnemic occurrences.

Conditions. Three facts prove the affirmation that extraphysical dimensions are a state of being, or a condition of the consciousness:

1. **Superimposition.** The planes or dimensions are not physically superimposed upon each other in the way we are accustomed to thinking in terrestrial or intraphysical life.

2. **Distinction.** The planes or dimensions do not have a clear spatial distinction.

3. **Differences.** The planes or dimensions do not present degrees of differentiation that allow easy characterization.

Psychiatry. According to modern psychiatry, the lower the social level of the population, the greater the incidence of mental disturbances. For example, human migrations and subhuman conditions, or social pressures, in the peripheries of the big urban centers (megacities, megametropolises, megalopolises) predispose an elevation in the index of psychiatric disturbances (neuroses). In general, 50% of cases occur within lower economic levels, 30% in the middle class and only 20% within more privileged classes. Psychiatric problems increase when the migrant does not work. If he/she has some type of activity, the index of psychiatric disturbances is equal to that of the local active population.

Reflexes. This human scenario precisely reflects, or is reflected, in its entirety, in extraphysical tropospheric environments that are populated by extraphysical consciousnesses (extraphysical migrations from the first desoma) which suffer from post-desomatic parapsychoses, or other consciential disturbances restricted to holosomatic parapathology, or the parapathology of the mentalsoma, psychosoma and holochakra.

Evolution. The extraphysical dimension, per se, as well as the mentalsomatic dimension, can be divided according to the evolutionary level of the consciousnesses which are encountered there – whether they are in transit or remain for longer periods of time – into 4 types of environment:

1. **Paratroposphere.** The *underdeveloped* extraphysical dimension (paratroposphere, ordinary *paraspeech*).

2. **Communities.** The evolved extraphysical dimension (communities of advanced extraphysical consciousnesses, telepathy).

3. **Cosmoconsciousness.** The *underdeveloped* mentalsomatic dimension (the phenomenon of cosmoconsciousness).

4. **FCs.** The evolved mentalsomatic dimension (free consciousnesses or FCs, conscientese).

Evolved. The majority of the considerations and analyses of this book – which endeavors to be practical and aims to avoid misunderstandings when referring, in theory, to the extraphysical dimension, per se – takes its evolutionary level into consideration. The same applies with regard to the mentalsomatic dimension. The observations in general made here refer to the evolved mentalsomatic dimension or, in other words, the one with well-defined characteristics.

Autochthons. The extraphysical consciousnesses or those consciousnesses belonging to extraphysical environments – namely the primitive inhabitants, aborigines, natives or autochthons of extraphysical districts – although periodically going through resoma, do not have races like those of human inhabitants.

Paragenetics. The essence of genetics is transmitted from one intraphysical consciousness to another. The essence of paragenetics *is not* transmitted from one consciousness (or extraphysical consciousness) to another.

Similarities. Extraphysical consciousnesses are similar with regard to the process of consciential evolution, but dissimilar with regard to the evolutionary levels of consciousnesses in general when considered individually.

Time. There are extraphysical environments that can be classified according to chronological time because they seem to better allow "journeys" of the consciousness backward, into the past or retrocognitive, and forward, in the future or precognitive. This is especially true with the gradations of the mentalsomatic dimension.

Cosmos. Other extraphysical environments are unarguably distant from the terrestrial crust, or troposphere, out in the cosmos or distant sidereal space (for us), where the consciousness docks itself through lucid consciential *exoprojections*.

Worlds. From a real perspective, or one relative to consciousnesses and their existence and evolution, not considering their vehicles of manifestation, there are at least 6 consciential worlds, according to the relative theory of World 3, proposed by Karl Raimund Popper (1902-1994) (*Objective Knowledge: An Evolutionary Approach;* London; Oxford University Press; 1972; p. 118; Eng., Port.) to wit:

1. **World 1:** the objective plane of material things; the physical universe; the world of material states.

2. **World 2:** the subjective world of minds or consciential principles that have gone through resoma; the mental universe, a specific place for human and animal minds, a mediator between World 1 and World 3.

3. **World 3:** objective ideas; public domain objective structures (microcosm), a product, which is not necessarily intentional, of the action of the consciousnesses of living beings (intraphysical beings) and which, once having arisen (produced by humankind), exists independent of these consciousnesses (houses, cities, machines, vehicles and others); human cultural inheritance.

4. **World 4:** the objective extraphysical dimension, the paratroposphere and the extraphysical dimension per se; the extraphysical universe (four-dimensional or tetra-dimensional); the world of extraphysical states.

5. **World 5:** the subjective mental (consciential) dimension of (cosmic consciential) cosmoconsciousness, utilized by intraphysical and extraphysical consciousnesses, without the charge of human passions, which is still extremely obscure for intraphysical consciousnesses.

6. **World 6:** objective structures (macrocosm), a product, which is not necessarily intentional, of the action of evolved extraphysical consciousnesses and which, once having arisen, exists independent of these consciousnesses (planets, solar systems, galaxies), including the abstract structures created by extraphysical consciousnesses (projectability, conscientese, code of extraphysical cosmoethics, universalism, extraphysical maturity, scale of the state of continuous self-awareness); *extraphysical cultural inheritance.*

Primothosene. Besides this new concept of *extraphysical cultural inheritance*, it is assumed that there was a primary cause, or primothosene, that created the *initial* World 1, and began the cycle of worlds that currently exist, are discernable and can be enjoyed by self-aware, self-critiquing and heterocritiquing consciousnesses. This implies the crude, physical Big Bang concept of conventional science.

Bibliography: Andreas (36, p. 54), Baker (69, p. 79), Bayless (98, p. 48), Butler (227, p. 73), Currie (354, p. 103), Denning (391, p. 45), Farrar (496, p. 191), Frazer (549, p. 157), Frost (560, p. 103), Greene (635, p. 10), Greenhouse (636, p. 264), Krishna (867, p. 124), Monroe (1065, p. 82), Perkins (1236, p. 92), Reis (1384, p. 14), Steiger (1601, p. 133), Talbot (1642, p. 164), Vieira (1762, p. 48), Walker (1781, p. 116), Wang (1794, p. 25), Xavier (1882, p. 263), Yogananda (1894, p. 381).

270. TROPOSPHERIC EXTRAPHYSICAL DIMENSION

Definition. Tropospheric extraphysical dimension: the extraphysical environment that is a duplicate of the physical or human environment and coexists with it (see fig. 270, p. 1,138).

Synonymy: afterdeath world; anti-environment; astral side; astral world; astraline world; chimerical lights; crustal plane; crustal sphere; exterior darkness; hyperspace; immediate post-physical areas; inferior astral; invisible world, OBE world; low-astral; paratroposphere; pathological deposit; posthumous world; psi world; reflecting sphere; second world; the astral here and now; transitland; transpsychic reality; *umbral;* vestibule of learning; world of illusion; world of reflections; world of thoughts.

Existence. Extraphysical things, objects and forms inevitably exist prior to ourselves in our perceptions as intraphysical projectors, even when we are not aware of it. Extraphysical nature is prior to our organic nature, as temporary human beings.

Crust. In principle, geographically speaking, the dense, tropospheric (or paratropospheric) extraphysical dimension is very similar to the physical world (the natural world or *mythland*).

Term. The term *districts* is better adapted to the crustal (paratropospheric) dimension or that which is coincident with the objective, physical universe. This is because, in this case, there are areas – or districts, spheres, spaces, locations, places, planes, regions, subplanes or zones – that are less mutable to the perceptions of consciousnesses and are beyond the individual state of each consciousness, whether using expressions such as: *spiritual world,* used by spiritists; *astral* plane, according to the language of theosophists; or *astral* light, according to magicians.

Situation. Although the crustal or tropospheric extraphysical dimensions do not exist just because they are linked to the planetary crust, or the earth, many persons become disturbed upon thinking about where they are situated, located or are physically dependent.

Earth. It is worth bearing in mind that the planet earth is not just a simple, naked globe that ends in the clouds or the boundaries of the troposphere.

Layers. The earth is like a cosmic spaceship with outer walls composed of invisible atomic particles, which terrestrial magnetism (geomagnetism) has in 3 covers or layers:

1. **First.** The first Van-Allen layer (radiation belts), with a thickness of 3,000 mi (5,000 km).
2. **Second.** The second Van-Allen layer, with 12,000 mi (20,000 km).
3. **Magnetosphere.** The magnetosphere, which extends approximately 40,000 mi (65,000 km) into the physical universe.

Aura. In this *physical aura of earth* – which surrounds and accompanies it throughout the universe – the extraphysical crustal planes or dimensions progress and orbit it like *invisible extraphysical satellites*.

Parageography. In paratropospheric, crustal extraphysical environments, or those which coexist with human life, there is a real transcendent geography, or *parageography,* that still requires mapping. It is constituted and defined – beyond being a duplicate of physical objects and beings – through the accidents generated by consistent and less transitory morphothosenes that have persisted over the human centuries. This is especially true regarding communities that have contact with terrestrial life, the *habitat* of extraphysical beings (extraphysical consciousnesses), areas of still very materialized transition. There is even that which can be called *extraphysical ecology (para-ecology),* or the physical-extraphysical ecosystem.

Space. Parageographic space can be located, differentiated and varied. It is described as having a delimited portion of a paraterritory (para-subsoil, para-soil, para-air), which encompasses an extraphysical, parabiological or extra-human reality. From this arise the crustal, darkened and subcrustal extraphysical areas.

Paraterritory. Parageographic space, in general, is perceived as being a paraterritory that is akin to a human territory or a part of it (region, county, state, province, city, borough, neighborhood or district).

Parapopulations. In this parageographic space, extraphysical communities, para-animals and paraplants are established, where paraspecies and (extra-human) parapopulations are found.

Organization. All this results in a *metastable extraphysical organization.*

Morphothosenes. The morphothosenes comprising the paratropospheric space allow a comprehensive understanding of its para-reality, in the practical study of the interior (paradecoration), or the set of the perceived volumes of the exterior (para-urbanism or urbanization and extraphysical reurbanization).

Deterioration. In sociology, the zone of deterioration or vice is already well-defined: a zone of the city characterized by the precarious state of edification and the high level of maladjustment of its inhabitants (slums).

Uncontrol. The individuals in that place endeavor to evade certain forms of social control and tend to get caught up in the confusion and variety of the behavior patterns of that area. In this place concentrations of the greatest variety of youth gangs, prostitution, delinquency, drug trafficking, violence, misery and vice (sociopathologies, sociopathies) are found.

Mold. This area of deterioration, as well as others, tends to mold its inhabitants.

Parody. The zone of human deterioration is nothing more than an imperfect and parodic copy of the shadowy paratropospheric areas visited by the consciential projector when serving as an extraphysical assistant.

Resonance. These physical-extraphysical zones, or toxic-universes, resonate with each other and the consciousnesses there exchange ideas, emotions, attitudes and objectives.

Base. Obviously, the physical base in one of these zones is naturally predisposed to a permanent connection with the deteriorated crustal paratropospheric areas.

Extraphysical clinic. If someone works in one of these areas with the practice of penta, he/she will, after a while, have an ample and busy extraphysical clinic of interconsciential assistance.

Assistential. In assistential projections, the projected intraphysical consciousness will inevitably travel to unevolved extraphysical districts that have received various names over time, such as the following 8:

1. Hades (Robert Crookall: 1890-1981).
2. Inferior Astral Plane (Theosophists).
3. Inferno (Dante Alighieri: 1265-1321).
4. *Kamaloka* (Hindus).
5. Locale II (Robert Allan Monroe: 1915-1995).
6. Purgatory.
7. Sheol.
8. *Umbral* (Spiritists).

Animals. The extraphysical beings (extraphysical consciousnesses at different evolutionary levels) found in the bowels of the planetary crust, in these shadowy or more backward zones, seem to undergo a phenomenon of evolutionary standstill or temporary degeneration, reminiscent of the conditions of sub-human and even human beings, such as the following 5 species:

1. **Endógeos.** *Endógeos,* which are constantly digging the soil (burrowers).
2. **Cavernicoles.** Troglobionts or cavernicoles.
3. **Folióbios.** *Folióbios* or the inhabitants of caverns and mounds of earth.
4. **Topóbios.** *Topóbios* or those which remain under rocks or fissures in the soil.
5. **Troglodytes.** Troglodytes namely, cave-dwelling humans.

Extraphysical. Strictly speaking, the denser extraphysical world (or that with concrete forms, concretions, concretism and concreteness) has its beginning at the edge of the frequency of manifestation of the vehicles of manifestation of the consciousness beyond the holochakra or, in other words, excluding the human body and the holochakra – which can be detected by rudimentary human instruments – and beginning with the psychosoma, in the tropospheric extraphysical dimension, and spanning to the mentalsoma, in the mentalsomatic dimension.

Temperatures. It is important to note that the evidence gathered through various parapsychic phenomena suggests the continuous and predominant existence of extremely low temperatures (para-sensation) in the tropospheric extraphysical dimension, such as the temperatures of interstellar space.

Ectoplasmy. This explains the cooling that occurs in the human environment during parapsychic manifestations with physical effects, ectoplasmy, telekinesis, dematerialization and currents of cold air.

Population. In the tropospheric extraphysical dimension, the extraphysical consciousnesses which make up the crustal phantasm population are found. These extraphysical consciousnesses, in their own *habitat,* are so *solid* or firm and extremely objective, having real bodies which are so dense they can collide with your intraphysical consciousness – when you are projected in the psychosoma – which nevertheless also passes through all *physical* objects, moving human vehicles and even solid granite.

Novelism. In tropospheric extraphysical environments or those coexisting with human life, novel events occur, depending upon the location, such as the following 4:

1. **Movie.** Glide in front of a movie projector lens and the moviegoers, watching everything, without your presence being perceived.
2. **Electricity.** Pass through the thick electrical structures of fully functioning power plants.
3. **Ocean.** Plumb the depths of an oceanic abyss, visiting a strange and exotic world.
4. **Fire.** Pass through a wall of flames during a conflagration.

Comprisal. The tropospheric extraphysical dimension does not only refer to the earth, but to *all* planets in the universe, whether or not they are inhabited.

Patterns. There is only *one extraphysical dimension* in the universe, in spite of its different vibratory, frequency or existential patterns. Moreover, there is only one mentalsomatic dimension in the entire universe.

Gradations. Likewise, there is only one physical or material dimension, in spite of its different vibratory gradations – soil, water, air, solid state, liquid state, gaseous state, plasma, fields (such as electromagnetic, gravitational or nuclear) – with variable vibratory effects that are interconnected at each level. This constitutes the physical universe of the ordinary, physical waking state of the consciousness, on any planet at the same evolutionary level.

Parallel. These 3 dimensions – the physical, extraphysical and mental – comprise the so-called *basic parallel universes.*

Language. In common parlance: in the *tropospheric* or crustal extraphysical dimension it is futile to have the *para-demeanor* of saintliness, waste *para-breath,* walk on *para-eggs* or adorn yourself with peacock *para-feathers.* However, you should confront everything with *parahead* held high, without being asleep at the *para-switch* (physical base), being the captain of your own *para-ship,* aware that one *parahand* washes the other and that the extraphysical sun rises for all consciousnesses.

Bibliography: Desmond (393, p. 55), Frost (560, p. 97), Hart (687, p. 236), Pike (1243, p. 29), Powell (1278, p. 144), Swedenborg (1635, p. 245), Vieira (1762, p. 65), Xavier (1882, p. 17).

271. EXTRAPHYSICAL   COMMUNITIES

Definition. Extraphysical community: the field of consciential energy – group energy, in this case – formed by the conglomerate of morphothosenes from groups of kindred extraphysical consciousnesses which are cohesive due to deep, complex and permanent links of self-interest.

Synonymy: community of extraphysical consciousnesses; consciential colony; extraphysical consciential conglomerate; pre-resomatic laboratory.

Consciousness. The world – regardless of which one – is a mere appearance outside the consciousness.

Abstraction. There is no abstract thought for the consciousness.

Knowledge. Knowledge is always subjective.

State. This is why we reaffirm that any physical or extraphysical district is, above all, a state of consciousness for the consciousness and not a place, or temporal-space reference.

Tropism. There is a presumption that the first extraphysical communities on a planet are formed in the manner of a spontaneous (energetic) tropism that occurs with the so-called *group-souls* of subhuman animals.

Pockets. The gathering of kindred consciousnesses creates energetic pockets. They are formed in an *instinctive*, spontaneous or completely unconscious manner or, in other words, are automatically determined by the predominant animal instincts that still remain in the average being or intraphysical consciousness which has undergone desoma.

Types. The most diverse types or categories of extraphysical communities exist. They can be formed by an overwhelming majority – which represents their raison d'être – of extraphysical consciousnesses with a masculine or feminine mentality, of extraphysical consciousnesses with a homosexual mentality, of former nationalist militants, of former artists in general, of former musicians, of former religious professionals, of former scientists and of other groups that were formed in human life.

Aims. Organized extraphysical communities – formed through the will of the consciousnesses mobilizing morphothosenes – aim, in principle, toward two basic or characteristic ends:

1. **Farewells.** Help those extraphysical consciousnesses which will go through resoma or, in other words: sponsor the *extraphysical send-offs* or farewells for those which will once again submit themselves to the restriction of their own consciousness through the *shock of resoma*.

2. **Reception.** Welcome those intraphysical consciousnesses which have left the period of intraphysical existence, those recent desomants or, more precisely: the *extraphysical reception* of those which have passed through the *first desoma*.

Transition. In both cases, the extraphysical communities serve as places of transition between one dimension of consciential life and another.

Parahospitals. Without a doubt, the extraphysical reception communities are the most numerous and problematic. They are true parahospitals or extraphysical assistance colonies because they welcome the veterans arriving from the frontline of human life. They are very different from extraphysical send-off colonies, which are involved with the resomatic preparation of the candidates to existence with a human body, an opportunity that is always full of hope, projects, existential programs and positive forecasts.

Paramentality. As a general rule, an extraphysical community will be more evolved proportionately to the average level of universalism of its extraphysical population's *paramentality*, or the predominant group materthosene in its holothosene.

Paratroposphere. In view of this, there is a much greater number of extraphysical communities of deceased ill intraphysical consciousnesses on the planetary crust (paratroposphere) – which are easier to encounter – than the number of evolved extraphysical conglomerates.

Groups. There are *parasocial* groups of extraphysical consciousnesses which are so withdrawn and suspicious that they do not even allow themselves to be observed by extraphysical or lucidly projected intraphysical participant-observers.

Assistants. Certain groups of extraphysical consciousnesses remain so impacted, introverted and inaccessible that they refuse to paracoexist with other neutral extraphysical consciousnesses or those more reliable observers or external assistants.

Hostility. Thus, at least the following 5 categories of extraphysical consciousnesses antagonize all those appearing in their communities:

1. **Interprisons.** Sectarians, factionalists, corporatists, fanatics, votaries, lobbyists or politicians who have passed through desoma and are already bound in groupkarmic interprisons.

2. **Paramafias.** Paramafias or gangs *(societas sceleris)* of deceased criminals.

3. **Anticosmoethical.** Extraphysical groups that plan some type of anticosmoethical strategy (mega-intruders).

4. **Defense.** Associations which retain knowledge that, according to their elements or components, must be aggressively maintained in secrecy for their common or evolutionarily wrong defense.

5. **Intimacy.** Extraphysical consciousnesses which live in great *parapromiscuity,* in a vulnerable condition of intimacy among themselves.

Visits. Sadly, the tropospheric and morbid extraphysical communities on this planet are still those which are most visited, night after night, by the great majority of the members of somnambulistic humanity (existential robotization). This occurs during natural sleep, when they leave their somas and intraphysical bases in nonlucid and semilucid consciential projections in all latitudes, continents, countries, metropolises, villages and rural zones.

Obstacles. These facts remain powerful obstacles to the consciential progress of everyone in the holothosene of intraterrestrial life. This is because they certainly show that the majority of human consciential projectors is made up of those who are still suffering from blatant intrusion, those suffering from partial intrusion or useful-innocents of intruders, satellites of intruders and extraphysical blind guides.

Approach. In general, the lucid projector senses that he/she is taken from the physical base, first volitating some yards (meters) above the ground, rising higher and higher and increasing his/her extraphysical speed upon getting farther from the human body, until arriving at the extraphysical community.

Buildings. Frequently, the para-buildings of extraphysical communities, when more closely related to human life, precisely reproduce the outside and interior decoration of the residences from the most recent intraphysical life of those deceased intraphysical consciousnesses which temporarily inhabit them in the intermissive period. This reality confuses projected intraphysical consciousnesses.

Reproductions. There are extraphysical reproductions which are true maquettes or living scenarios of entire neighborhoods of human cities.

Extraphysical consciousnesses. In a preliminary analysis which is independent of the evolutionary level and state of consciential health, the extraphysical consciousnesses encountered in extraphysical communities can be classified into 4 categories:

1. **Subcrustal.** Subcrustal or intraterrestrial, per se.
2. **Crustal.** Crustal or paratropospheric.
3. **Volitator.** Volitators or volitants.
4. **Mentalsomatic.** Mental or mentalsomatic.

Deintrusion. Major intraphysical consciousness-extraphysical consciousness intrusions are only removed when it is possible to directly extract the last vestiges which are firmly planted and fixed in a crustal or paratropospheric extraphysical community, which constitutes the extraphysical or presomatic origin (extraphysical hometown) of the intraphysical consciousness suffering from intrusion.

Evolutiologists. Hence the transcendent value of the extraphysical deintrusion task performed with the participation of intraphysical consciential projectors and the consequent service of the rebirth of these intrusive extraphysical consciousnesses realized by helpers, consciential epicenters, petifree consciousnesses and evolutiologists.

Dismantling. Consciential progress can only become consolidated on this planet after the total dismantling or reurbanization of thousands of these shadowy, morbid and tragic tropospheric or crustal extraphysical communities (parapathology).

Responsible. These communities are responsible for the great individual, group and collective intrusive processes between intraphysical and extraphysical beings. They are also responsible for the deliberate obstruction of the installation of a higher level of maturity and recuperation of cons (hyperacuity) among terrestrial (intraphysical and extraphysical) consciousnesses.

Extraterrestrials. Myriads of more evolved extraterrestrial extraphysical consciousnesses which have never had resomatic experiences on this planet are currently deeply extraphysically involved in the methodical and continuous extinction of multimillenary morbid extraphysical communities which *metastasize*, encyst and weigh upon human life and extraphysical terrestrial life.

Reurbanization. It is believed that this is the greatest effort toward collective deintrusion and extraphysical reurbanization that has ever been undertaken on this planet throughout its entire history of multimillenary multiexistential cycles (holoresomatics, holobiographies, holomemory) up until the present.

Pocket. Based on the fact that every bioenergetic field is situated in the still very obscure *three-and-a-half dimension* (energetic dimension) and that every extraphysical community constitutes a group energetic field, it can be concluded that every extraphysical community is also situated in the energetic dimension, forming an *inter*dimensional and specific pocket of group consciential energy. This is inserted between the physical (human) dimension and the tropospheric extraphysical dimension, which is close and concomitant to the intraphysical (dense) dimension.

Dimension. The following are 7 characteristics of the energetic dimension:

1. **Deaths.** The space-time of the first and second desomas.

2. **Intermission.** At least a minimal portion of the intermissive or inter-resomatic period of the consciousness.

3. **Looseness.** The level of operation of the looseness of the holochakra (of the intraphysical consciousness).

4. **Bradykinesis.** The area of the totipotent operation of the silver cord or the so-called *condition of double awareness,* oneiric images (dreams) and extraphysical slow motion or bradykinesis.

5. **Discoincidence.** The specific environment of discoincidence of the vehicles of manifestation of the intraphysical consciousness.

6. **Gravitation.** The graduated gravitational field of the planet.

7. **Evolution.** The beginning of the interaction and acceleration of the consciential evolutionary rhythm.

Semimateriality. In view of the above, one can more rationally interpret the aspect, which is sometimes more difficult to understand, of the evident semimateriality of the extraphysical communities described in minute detail by lucid projectors and communicant extraphysical consciousnesses through various types of parapsychic manifestations in different times and locations.

Bibliography: Baker (69, p. 79), Borgia (171, p. 42), Monroe (1065, p. 73), Owen (1177, p. 261), Vieira (1762, p. 181), Xavier (1882, p. 263).

---

272. EXTRAPHYSICAL DIMENSION PER SE

Definition. Extraphysical dimension per se: the native, preexisting extraphysical environment in relation to the human dimension, with no direct, ostensive or easy connection with intraphysical life.

Synonymy: extraphysical *habitat;* higher astral; medium astral; pure spiritual dimension; pure spiritual plane; purely consciential sphere; ultraterrene stop.

Thought. All thoughts, wishes and acts are far more intense, quick and *corporifying* in the multidimensional, coexisting and interpenetrating circles of the extraphysical dimension.

Concomitance. There, thought is action or, in other words: thought and action manifest concomitantly. There is no time lag between them, as occurs in the physical dimension.

Waves. Radio and television waves are very real. They are solid and, in spite of this, mix and pass through each other without colliding, as long as each one of them remains in its frequency or "vibrations per second" range.

Analogy. This provides an analogy or a good example for picturing scenes, places and facts pertaining to the extraphysical dimension or, in other words, the environments which the intraphysical consciousness encounters when he/she projects him/herself and will also encounter after deactivation of the human body.

Solidity. Scenes, places and facts are, locally speaking, very solid things in our own habitual plane of human experience. There is no reason for us to presume that the scenes, places and facts we experience while projected from the human body are different in terms of their *local solidity,* in any dimension of existence aside from ordinary dense matter.

Extraphysical. In extraphysical environments per se – unmapped regions, the *habitat* of extraphysical beings – we encounter communities of extraphysical consciousnesses that are kindred in their harmonies and their imbalances. This gives rise, for example, to the following 5 categories:

1. **Agreeable.** Agreeable, healthy places which are still indescribable for us as intraphysical consciousnesses.

2. **Transitional.** All types of transitional places.

3. **Convalescence.** Regions of extraphysical convalescence which are adapted to the work of successive intraphysical lives.

4. **Bedroom.** *Extraphysical bedroom communities.*

5. **Subplanes.** Negative or ill extraphysical subplanes.

Bell tower. There are vertical, elevated extraphysical communities, created like groups of bell towers or bird houses, without floors, highways or streets, as we understand them. They are adapted to flying residents, their buildings having open air access in all directions.

Paraplants. Living plants that are long, luminous, colored, transparent and very tall in relation to the buildings are seen to sprout up around the fliers' roadless housing complexes. It is not known whether these paraplants always grow to that size and if they reproduce in that dimension (parabotany).

Psychosoma. As previously explained, the psychosoma operates as a morphogenetic model for the human body, orienting its growth and its forms, in peaceful coexistence with the laws of genetics harmonized by the specific paragenetics of the resonant extraphysical consciousness.

Hypotheses. The following are two work hypotheses: Is it possible that something similar occurs in relation to the planets or the entire physical universe? What is the profound relationship between the native extraphysical dimension and the physical dimension?

Interpsychology. Interpsychology is the science that studies the psychological reactions which individuals of a collective induce in other individuals.

Assimilation. The intentional or unconscious interaction of individuals would trigger resistance, opposition or, conversely, an assimilation of one individual by others.

Inspirations. The highest degree of reactions pertaining to interpsychology – which in this case are also transcendent – occur individually among the inhabitants of the physical and extraphysical tropospheric consciential dimensions. Examples of this can be found in the phenomena of inspirations, intuitions and intrusions triggered by extraphysical consciousnesses.

Collective. Joint reactions already refer to collective parapsychology.

Bibliography: Monroe (1065, p. 73), Vieira (1762, p. 50), Xavier (1882, p. 17).

273. MENTALSOMATIC   DIMENSION

Definition. Mentalsomatic dimension: the extraphysical environment that is characteristic to or native to the mentalsoma.

Synonymy: conscientioland; mental sphere; *habitat* of thoughts; *manasloka;* plane of omniscience; third astral plane; vestibule of wisdom; think tank.

Storehouse. Upon achieving cosmoconsciousness in mentalsomatic projections, the projector participates in the collective field of the consciousness, the storehouse of the universal consciousness or the mental plane, the domain of the so-called *"akashic* register", the universal, eclectic and equalizing meeting place which is common to all consciousnesses, a free area for those capable of reaching it and enjoying it.

Global. Only the mentalsomatic dimension allows the consciousness to experience an expansion such that it achieves the global or universalized view of the entirety of *all things* in a single whole, establishing the lines of union between phenomena or universal events.

Types. The mentalsomatic dimension can be interpreted from 2 standpoints, or placed into 2 levels of classification, according to the manifestations which it affords: the underdeveloped mentalsomatic dimension and the evolved mentalsomatic dimension.

1. **Underdeveloped.** The first mentalsomatic dimension, which can be called corporeal, is still inferior in regard to consciential evolution, being mixed with energies of the psychosoma or the evolved extraphysical dimension per se. It allows the interdimensional dislocation of a ball of energy, a vital ovoid or energetic fulcrum, evolving to a point of consciousness or, in other words, *the punctiform consciousness*.

2. **Evolved.** The second mentalsomatic dimension, which can be called incorporeal, is more evolved and pure. It is the native environment of the consciousness itself, the *nec plus ultra* of consciential levels. It is an environment of non-space, non-time, non-form or, more precisely: an environment in which the consciousness controls these variables at will, making it absolutely incomprehensible to the more advanced reason of contemporary humans who are not projected in the mentalsoma.

Projections. There are mental projections of various types, ranging from the superficial, being mere copies of projections or simple free daydreams, to projections of the punctiform consciousness, all the way to the achievement of full consciential projection in the mentalsoma, which is indefinable, non-transferable, indescribable or understood only by those who have experienced it. It is worth stressing that the latter is in no way related to mysticism, fanaticism, emotionalism, moralism and other "isms." Its manifestation transcends the parameters of human illusions ("Maya") and all types of preconceptions.

Holochakrology. Energetic projections of a portion of the holochakra, sometimes assuming the individual's humanoid form at a distance from his/her human body, should not be confused with consciential projections in the mentalsoma.

Vehicles. In summary, it is observed that projections of the intraphysical consciousness take place using 2 vehicles which allow the transportation of the consciousness: the psychosoma (emotional body, astral body or perispirit) in the crustal dimensions and the mentalsoma in the mentalsomatic dimension.

Conditions. This multidimensional reality presents 3 specific conditions:

1. **Extraphysicology.** Projections of the extraphysical consciousness also occur using the same 2 vehicles which allow the consciousness to be transported: the psychosoma, in the phenomena of ectoplasmy, making the consciousness temporarily dense in the intraphysical dimension (inverse direction); and the mentalsoma in the mental dimension.

2. **Resomatics.** When the extraphysical consciousness goes through a more long-lasting resoma (70 years of physical age), in the psychosoma (inverse direction), and when the extraphysical consciousness temporarily materializes, in the selfsame emotional body (inverse direction), the 2 processes are *similar,* although they are not identical.

3. **Identification.** When the intraphysical consciousness and the extraphysical consciousness project in the mentalsoma, in the mental plane, the 2 processes are extremely *similar*.

Meeting. Conclusion: the pure mental plane is the *meeting place* for all more lucid consciousnesses. Intraphysical consciousnesses in general and less evolved extraphysical consciousnesses achieve better conditions in both cases of projection in the mentalsoma in the pure mental dimension, even when temporary.

Flashes. Generally speaking, the consciousness is in a constant state of ebullience, experiencing incessant consciential flashes, illuminations and dislocations of its base of manifestation, which can take it to the pure mentalsomatic dimension or make it return to the crustal or tropospheric extraphysical dimension.

Other. It is presumed, as a working hypothesis, that there are other dimensions beyond, or more evolved than, the mentalsomatic dimension. However, we simply do not know about them, nor do we have resources for conceiving them in detail or rationally imagining them.

Intraphysicology. If we consider the physical universe to be infinite, there are even physical parts which we will never observe in the human condition.

Manifestations. The manifestation of the consciousness in the pure, evolved mental dimension is literally *breathtaking* and, moreover, there is no longer a respiratory mechanism. This is because there is no body, as we are accustomed to it, nor are there objects, forms, time and other *objective* variables or realities characteristic of our human or physical world.

Astronomy. The numbers, conditions and research data of astronomy are reminiscent of the *objectivities* of the mentalsomatic dimension.

Hypotheses. The following are some working hypotheses: Is the mentalsomatic dimension immutable? What is the relationship between the mentalsomatic dimension and the so-called *cosmic engineers?* Can it be said that the basic consciential energies stem from the mentalsomatic dimension?

Responses. At our current stage of knowledge, we still cannot find adequate answers for these questions.

Bibliography: Bardon (80, p. 49), Desmond (394, p. 194).

274. EXTRAPHYSICAL SPHERE OF ENERGY

Definition. Extraphysical sphere of energy: the extraphysical force field with a 13' (4 m) radius (or, by extension, a 26' (8 m) diameter) that envelops the human body of the projector.

Synonymy: area of alternative realities*;* area of discoincidence; area of double awareness; double of the physical base; essential *psi field;* extraphysical base of the intraphysical projector; extraphysical biomagnetic field; extraphysical decompression chamber; extraphysical energetic bubble; hypnagogic area; hypnopompic area; interplanar energetic field; living gravitational field; magnetic sluice gate of the psychosoma; parabiosphere; parapsychosphere; para-sphere; pluridimensional field of interaction; scenario of self-bilocation.

Characteristics. The extraphysical sphere of energy or parapsychosphere – in this case, a figure with 3 dimensions encompassing a pluridimensional space – presents 20 characteristic and defined factors:

1. **Prisons.** The human body is the *first* cellular prison of the psychosoma with the intraphysical consciousness inside it. The individual sphere of extraphysical energy is the immediately following *second* prison.

2. **Center.** The human head, notably the 2 cerebral hemispheres, operates as a central irradiator of energy. The pineal gland, medulla oblongata, coronochakra and frontochakra can be singled out here. The pineal gland represents the physical nucleus of the extraphysical sphere of energy. Strictly speaking, the mentalsoma is the central, essential irradiator of the extraphysical sphere of energy.

3. **Footage.** The diameter of the sphere of energy reaches an average of 26' (8 m), or a radius of 13' (4 m) from the human head or, more precisely, from the 2 cerebral hemispheres.

4. **Agent.** The silver cord, the crustal irradiating agent of this energetic center, is confused with the parapsychosphere, attributing it with greater quantities of volume and weight. Both are greater than the volume and weight of the projected psychosoma, in certain instances in the world of projectiology phenomena.

5. **Current.** The lengthwise direction of the human body, from head to feet (or from feet to head), when lying on its back, allows the conduction of a greater energetic current and influence in the takeoff of the psychosoma. The human body serves as a ground wire, just as a car does for its radio antenna. The dorsal position is ideal for predisposing the human body to lucid projection of the consciousness in the psychosoma.

6. **Hemisphere.** The upper hemisphere of the globe of energy is more important than the lower hemisphere in relation to the human head. This occurs due to the psychological influence of the intraphysical consciousness' deeply rooted habits with material forms, with the conditioning of the human body's position, the clothes, the bed linen, the bed itself and the bedroom floor in the physical base. The sphere of energy defines the environment of the projected consciousness, devoid of any useful need, and in favor of the retractive power of the silver cord.

7. **Space.** Ideally, there would be greater space behind the head of the lucid projection practitioner's inactive human body or, more precisely, more than 13' (4 m) without solid obstacles. This would eliminate the psychological and parapsychological influence of the unfounded concern of extraphysically *colliding* with physical bodies or objects.

8. **Operation.** The energy-filled sphere operates in almost all stages of the projection of the consciousness, but does so more strongly in tropospheric or crustal lucid projections.

9. **Weight.** The psychosoma tends to be *heavier* when inside the extraphysical sphere of energy. This weight is *perceived* by the projected intraphysical consciousness.

10. **Retention.** The extraphysical sphere of energy is the area of greater retention of the psychosoma, under the more vigorous action of the silver cord.

11. **Holochakra.** The energetic sphere permits a greater agility in the holochakra's performance or, more precisely, it represents a direct manifestation of the holochakra. On the other hand, depending upon its extension, the aura of the psychosoma of the intraphysical consciousness more intensely vitalizes and energizes his/her extraphysical sphere of energy.

12. **Slow motion.** The extraphysical actions of the projected consciousness frequently occur in slow motion inside the energetic sphere. This is due to the semiphysical environment, the greater *weight* of the vehicles of manifestation and the semilucid transition phase of extraphysical awakening.

13. **Uterus.** In the energetic sphere or the spheroid extraphysical force field – the *extraphysical uterus* – the floating of the psychosoma is similar to the sensation of the fetus in the amniotic fluid of the pregnant human woman. It is mentioned here as a good symbolic representation for individuals who study the themes of Sigmund Freud's works.

14. **Fields.** The extraphysical sphere of energy is closely related to all of life's electrodynamic fields: vital field (L-fields), thought or mental fields, biological fields, biogravitational fields and psi fields. Its relationship with artificial, electric and/or magnetic energetic fields is not yet known.

15. **Dimension.** The sphere of energy can be characterized as the field of interaction of the *three-and-a-half dimension* or, in other words, transition from the third dimension to the fourth dimension, or from a median frequency between the motor action of dense matter and the hyper-tachyonic action of free thought.

16. **Occurrences.** Various phenomena occur with greater intensity inside the extraphysical sphere of energy: the influence of terrestrial gravitation; hypnagogy; discoincidence of the vehicles of manifestation of the consciousness; oscillations or instability of the psychosoma; extraphysical catalepsy; double awareness; extracorporeal sleep; consciential self-bilocation; extraphysical repercussions; hypnopompy.

17. **Isolation.** Obviously, the intraphysical consciousness projected in the psychosoma isolated inside a 13' (4 m) radius from the human head will be better, will suffer less restriction and will enjoy greater extraphysical agility than with an awake intraphysical consciousness or projected together with that individual. When the intraphysical consciousness projects, the sphere remains, but is modified. The human aura is directly related to the extraphysical sphere of energy and, under certain circumstances, can be visible to the clairvoyant and to projected intraphysical consciousnesses.

18. **Booth.** Actually, the parapsychic booth – which is closed with curtains and used in the session rooms of physical effect phenomena, or ectoplasmy, for the purpose of condensing the psychic energy required for manifestations – is always recommended precisely because of the extraphysical sphere of energy.

19. **Faraday.** There is a supposition that a Faraday cage with a diameter of 26' (8 m) would intensify the energetic field of the extraphysical energy field and would negatively condition the environment and restrict the extraphysical movements of the projected consciousness. Could this be the case?

20. **Imponderability.** Is it possible that the effect of physical imponderability, or the absence of gravity upon the projector's human body (androsoma, gynosoma), would affect the extraphysical sphere of energy?

Xenophrenia. The quality and intensity of the extraphysical sphere of energy, in and of itself, generate conditions which predispose the installation of diverse altered states of the intraphysical consciousness.

Circumscribed. In the circumscribed lucid projection, the intraphysical consciousness remains within the range of the extraphysical sphere of energy or centered within the 26' (8 m) diameter perimeter around the human head.

Characterization. Two very evident realities can be characterized in this context:

1. **Exteriorization.** The projection of the consciousness within the area of this extraphysical sphere of energy, or within the perimeter of the action of the silver cord, as though it were an *exteriorization*.

2. **Excursion.** When the projected consciousness transfers its seat to more distant districts, beyond the extraphysical sphere of energy, characterizing the extraphysical *excursion*.

Snare. The intraphysical consciousness who only, or invariably, lucidly projects in the area around his/her own human body – within the 26' (8 m) perimeter of his/her extraphysical sphere of energy – without being able to control the connections of the silver cord, is not producing an ideal, not to mention *healthy*, experience. It is like a spider that gets caught up in its own web, not knowing how to get free from its own trap. Over 90% of the members of terrestrial humanity have been unconsciously living in this type of energetic snare during natural sleep for millennia.

Morphothosenes. It is known that consciential energy generates morphothosenes and that prolonged, continuous reflection upon the same subject can create a morphothosene of tremendous power. This form remains over time, with the appearance and behavior of an actual entity.

Cage. Most individuals go through life enclosed in their energetic snare, or mental cage naturally constructed by themselves, within their individual extraphysical sphere of energy, through morphothosenes generated by the energy of their habitual thoughts reacting upon them, which tend to reproduce themselves indefinitely.

Arteriosclerosis. Arteriosclerosis worsens this energetic cage scenario even further, and it continues even beyond the deactivation of the human body and senile psychoses (Alzheimer's disease).

Couplings. The extraphysical sphere of energy and its interrelation with the human aura act vigorously in the installation of auric couplings, as well as in relation to certain objects which are large but restricted to the individual, or even extremely individual physical environments, such as the following 5 examples:

1. **Chamber.** The intraphysical consciousness' bedroom (energetically shielded chamber).
2. **Office.** The personal office.
3. **Car.** The car of long-standing personal use.
4. **Boat.** The fisherman's small boat.
5. **Plane.** The private pilot's small plane.

Protection. In these cases, the extraphysical sphere of energy cooperates in the permanent installation of an intense and profound *human-machine relationship,* keeping and involving the object in a type of individual, energetic anti-disaster protection.

Extraphysical consciousness. The extraphysical sphere of energy analyzed here refers to the deceased intraphysical consciousness which has already passed through the first desoma (biological death, extraphysical consciousness), and which has not gone through the second desoma (deactivation of the holochakra). The extraphysical sphere of energy of the more lucid and free extraphysical consciousness is different, being more evolved.

Bibliography: Andrade (28, p. 43), Bedford (103, p. 189), Gaynor (577, p. 31), Greenhouse (636, p. 317), Monroe (1065, p. 270), Sculthorp (1531, p. 156), Talbot (1642, p. 160), Vieira (1762, p. 115).

275. HUMAN BRAIN

Definition. Human brain: the most organized material substance on the face of the earth, part of the central nervous system housed inside the human cranium, or beneath the protective osseous helmet, currently considered to be a large endocrine secreting gland.

Synonymy: biological computer; black box of thought; cerebral hemispheres; controller of the human body; encephalon; master organ of the soma; mediator of the consciousness; organ of thought; physical brain; straightjacket of the extraphysical consciousness; thinking apparatus; thinking machine.

Models: The decoding or study of the workings of the human brain has already used at least 7 models thus far: hydraulic, dioptric, phrenologic, geologic, embryological, mechanotechnological and computational.

Oxygen. Of all the organs of the body, the brain is the one which breathes more actively, consuming a greater quantity of oxygen in a given amount of time.

Object. Until now, research indicates the exceptional condition of the brain being a complex of physical-chemical material that represents only 2% of the human body's weight. It is the only known lucid object in the physical universe that directs and controls all the areas and organs of the human body through approximately ten billion neurons and one hundred trillion connections and intersections, 80% of its weight being water.

Use. All things aside, and although considered by many to be a luxury organ – whose owner has still not learned how to make good use of it, being developed beyond his/her needs – not every human brain is capable of handling all the mundane (material) and ultramundane (extraphysical) activities of the veteran, intraphysical lucid projector together at the same time.

Control. The brain, being the most complex apparatus in the universe, the most intriguing and unfathomable part of the human body, does not control thoughts, sentiments and the will, although it is controlled by these 3 elements.

Driver. The impulses of the mentalsoma cannot act directly upon the human body. The brain thus works like a driver, just like those used in electronics, amplifying and shaping the impulses.

Transistor. The synapse in the brain is similar to the diode or transistor in an electronic circuit. There are approximately one hundred trillion synapses in the brain.

Switchboard. The brain can be compared to a type of telephone switchboard or a computer.

Human. The human is an animal that laughs, has a language composed of coherent sounds that form a vocabulary and thinks with full self-awareness (of itself).

Genetics. Every cell of the human brain retains the memory of the millions of years of the age of humankind.

Cachalot. The brain of the cachalot *(Physeter macrocephalus)* is 6 times bigger than the human brain.

Awareness. On account of awareness, humans – despite being the final product of the entire evolution of life on this planet – are greater, more important and have more expression than the sum total of their parts and physical accessories, as complex, sophisticated, subtle and transcendent as the mechanisms of the cerebral cortex may in fact be.

Physiology. If the cortex could be stretched, its surface would cover approximately 1.68 yd.^{2} (2 m^2).

Continent. The brain is the continent, the consciousness is the content.

Paraphysiology. The empty brain condition of the consciousness, which is naturally generated by lucid projection and referred to here in many topics, should not appear odd to studious individuals because it is, in fact, physiological or, more precisely, paraphysiological. If not, it will be seen below.

Emptying. Everything related to the functions of the human body occurs through the filling and emptying of the organs or viscera, which are emptied of content in some manner, as in the following 8 examples:

1. **Lungs.** The lungs fill and empty themselves with air (oxygen).
2. **Heart.** The heart and blood vessels as well, with venous and arterial blood.
3. **Stomach.** The stomach, with ingested food.
4. **Intestines.** The intestines, with a bolus of food.
5. **Bladder.** The bladder, with the urine excreted by the kidneys.
6. **Gallbladder.** The gallbladder, with bile.
7. **Testicles.** The testicles, with sperm.
8. **Hemispheres.** The cerebral hemispheres, in turn and in their own way, fill and empty themselves with the consciousness.

Pattern. The physiological organs operate in this way, following the phenomenological pattern, with the intraphysical consciousness, whether in a lucid, conscious, or unconscious manner.

Evidence. In this particular case, we do not only encounter an analogous or homologous phenomenon, but a simple phenomenological pattern that is logical, rational and evident.

Operation. The human brain is similar in appearance to a big 3.3 lb. (1.5 kg) nut and, although being the most complex physical structure, as well as the most sensitive computer in existence, it does not directly operate in the extraphysical world when the consciousness finds itself projected outside the human body.

Egos. There are 2 cerebral hemispheres, the right and the left, each with its own specialized function. The hemispheres appear to be mirror images of each other. There are those who suppose that there are 2 egos, according to the manifestations of the consciousness, notably with regard to speech.

Fibers. The cerebral hemispheres transmit information to each other through the corpus callosum, which is made up of 200 million nerve fibers. One hemisphere is capable of assuming the intellectual and motor functions performed by the other, which evidently shows that the functioning of the brain, *with some exceptions,* does not depend upon any specific area of cerebral matter.

Neurophysiology. Let us take a succinct look at some neurophysiological data regarding the 2 cerebral hemispheres:

1. **Left.** The left hemisphere exercises control over logical and abstract thought; stores symbols of objects; speaks with ease, repeating the words it hears with rapidity and precision; it, however, does not reproduce a musical passage faithfully, preferring to mark the rhythm. It reproduces an object as it

knows it and not as it perceives it. When confronted with an irregular figure, it is unable to retain it in its memory as it cannot conceptualize it.

2. **Right**. The right hemisphere commands concrete thought and the formation of images; speaks little, communicating with isolated words, mimics or gestures; is capable of hearing a melody and reproducing the tones. It memorizes figures of (three-dimensional) forms that are strange to the human eye. The influences of the right cerebral hemisphere predominate in paranormal manifestations.

Drawing. The differences between the cerebral hemispheres has been successfully employed in the acceleration of learning to draw, in which the student is forced to use his or her right cerebral hemisphere. In this case, the student is led to correctly copy the negative (empty) space of a piece of furniture, such as a chair, instead of its form, thus exercising the right hemisphere of the brain, which has a global perception of the object.

Form. The student is also requested to copy objects upside down because the figure is otherwise rejected by the left hemisphere which cannot conceptualize it. The object's bizarre form is of greater interest to the right hemisphere that solves the drawing as a brainteaser, resulting in better resolved details.

Hypothesis. It is supposed that there must be a way to accelerate the production of lucid consciential projections through the compulsory use of the right cerebral hemisphere. This is a promising research hypothesis.

Illustrators. Incidentally, a high percentage of lucid projectors, among professionals, are creative illustrators. This is probably because they are obliged to create ideas, original forms and details. They also have to get out of themselves in search of the new, and reconstruct the world around them through their illustrations. Thus, they are more predisposed and motivated to produce spontaneous and even willfully provoked consciential projections, reaching extraphysical dimensions which are unexplored, new and enriching to their imaginative conceptions and personal experiences.

Polarity. Some researchers also consider the brain to have a front/back polarity, as well as a division of left and right hemispheres. The back portion, the *old* brain, is common to subhuman animals, whereas the *front* part, the *newer* circuits, are more human and tend toward greater self-awareness.

Implants. Recent neurophysiology research demonstrates that cerebral lesions are reversible through tissue implants. The damaged nervous system can regenerate its fibers and restore lost mental functions and even improve memory and learning capacity. This is performed by transplanting fetal cells, which are richer in regenerative factors and more easily adapt to the new environment, thereby creating new connections between the transplanted tissue and the remaining brain matter.

Growth. According to anthropological studies made on the detailed internal architecture of the skull, it is currently accepted that the capacity or volume of the human brain increases on the order of 10.8 mg per generation (every 5 lustrums) on average; with an approximate increase of 300,000 neurons; precisely in the frontal and parietal regions; predominately in the left hemisphere; in those regions of the brain responsible for the command and elaboration of language and rational operations. It is forecast that this slow rhythm of growth will double humankind's cerebral capacity within only 4 million years.

Minority. The animist-sensitive or, more precisely, the lucid projector, is currently in the minority. It is presumed that this is due to the need for the intraphysical consciousness to expand its right cerebral hemisphere and thus act against the current average pattern of cerebral evolution characterized by a predominance of the left cerebral hemisphere.

Mind. The brain is not the mind. The mind serves as the programmer of the cells that comprise the brain.

Evidence. There are two basic pieces of evidence which support the conclusion that the mind functions independently from the brain:

1. **Pathology.** The apparent persistence of *elevated cortical ability* despite irreparable damage to large areas of the brain in cases of tumors and other cortical diseases, in which a drastically large amount of the brain is removed, as with hemispherectomies in which half of the brain is surgically removed.

2. **Projectiology.** Lucid consciousness projections and normal thought processes, namely facts that survive after verified cases of clinical death.

Reference. The human brain of the consciential projector, at the very center of the extraphysical sphere of energy – simultaneously being the entryway to the extraphysical dimension and the return doorway to the physical dimension – is, strictly speaking, the only physical reference point or, more precisely, the absolute and practical reference on earth, considered from a physical perspective, for the projected intraphysical being.

Interference. Contiguous physical objects or constructions, namely the bed, furniture, walls, building (even in a building with extra thick walls or with floors above and below, in an apartment complex) and even the city block and the city itself, need not – and for the sake of the projector's freedom and extraphysical agility should not – interfere in the extraphysical events in which the consciousness participates or observes. All this must remain inexistent for this selfsame intraphysical consciousness, while temporarily free in a different plane of life or in a different consciential dimension.

Conditioning. When the consciousness of the projector leaves the human body in the psychosoma, or emotional body, it becomes important to control the supervening emotions and, above all, the conditioned reflexes acquired in diuturnal human life which are intensely reflected in the manifestations of the ways in which we habitually coexist with material forms and structures. Hence the necessity and importance of the thoughtful and profound awareness of the consciential projector in regard to the reality of the extraphysical sphere of energy, the extraphysical dimension, the nature of the psychosoma and many other correlated factors.

Weight. In order to begin this awareness, the projector should judiciously meditate upon the fact that the psychosoma has only one thousandth of the weight of the human body. This means that the 3.3 lb. (1.5 kg) brain of a human is reduced to an extraphysical *parabrain* weighing only 0.05 oz. (1.5 g).

Forces. The projector's form also obeys the criterion of the will of the projected consciousness. For this reason, brute, physical force disappears entirely, giving way to the subtlety of mental, consciential, psychic or parapsychic force.

Exercises. Those who are accustomed only to physical or muscular exercise, or to the violence of brute force, naturally find it more difficult to adapt to the extraphysical period of the projected consciousness in comparison to those who are accustomed to intellectual, psychic, parapsychic exercises or the cultivation of a determined genre of art.

Moderation. However, this does not mean that the projector should entirely eliminate physical exercise from his/her life. On the contrary, when applied in moderation as a complement to intellectual life, it can only contribute to the maintenance of physical health and the development of lucid projections.

Health. A healthy mind, in a healthy human body, sustains the physiological foundation of the processes of lucid projection produced in line with some type of methodology.

Empty. The empty brain condition – or the vegetative brain – only occurs when there is a temporary transfer of the seat of the consciousness outside the human body. For example, traveling clairvoyance does not present the empty brain condition, since the clairvoyant is even able to describe what he/she is experiencing at the very moment it is happening. In other words, in a major lucid projection, the ego (the extraphysical substratum of the human brain) is projected from the human body. In traveling clairvoyance, on the other hand, this is not so much the case. It is hard to affirm that the *empty brain* condition occurs in this case because the consciousness leaves and returns to the physical brain at such a high velocity that it is not even perceived.

Box. The brain, in the machine of the human body, upon being transformed into a cadaver, remains like a *black box, indecipherable* by humankind to date.

Computer. In 1986, it was estimated that it would cost 3 billion dollars in order to construct a computer with the same characteristics as the human brain, yours, for example. This is a number with a 3 and 9 zeros. Is it not therefore worth taking advantage of your invaluable asset of thought, creativity and ideas?

Bibliography: Bozzano (184, p. 118), Carrington (245, p. 87), Crookall (343, p. 73), Frost (560, p. 90), Gooch (617, p. 201), Meek (1028, p. 238), Morris (1093, p. 99), Muldoon (1105, p. 140), Reis (1384, p. 56), Riverain (1408, p. 126), Russell (1482, p. 58), Steiger (1601, p. 7), Stokes (1625, p. 24), Vieira (1762, p. 157), Walker (1781, p. 45).

---

276.   PARABRAIN

Definition. Parabrain: the extraphysical brain of the psychosoma, whether of the consciousness which has undergone desoma (extraphysical consciousness), resoma (intraphysical consciousness), or is temporarily projected (projector) in the psychosoma, with or without full extraphysical lucidity.

Synonymy: bioplasmic brain; brain of the psychosoma; controller of the psychosoma; emotionalizer; extraphysical brain; para-encephalon; second brain; self-transfigurer.

Para-anatomy. The parabrain can be considered an improved reflection of the cerebral hemispheres.

Paracerebellum. The paracerebellum, a duplicate of the cerebellum, being more restricted to the dynamic functions of the human body, does not operate extraphysically with an intensity equal to that of the extraphysical duplicates of the cerebral hemispheres.

Para-object. Of all known semi-physical forms, the human parabrain seems to be the para-object that is most sophisticated, most important and has the most transcendent and immediate consequences.

Weight. Based on the previously presented supposition that the psychosoma – a consciential, but still semiphysical, vehicle – weighs, on average, one thousandth of the weight of the human body (soma), an individual weighing 154 lb. (70 kg) with a brain of 3.3 lb. (1.5 kg), will have a psychosoma weighing 2.47 oz. (70 g) with a parabrain of 0.053 oz. (1.5 g). There is therefore a 1:1000 weight and density ratio between the brain and the parabrain.

Paraphysiology. Just as the human brain houses the parabrain, the parabrain, in turn, houses the mentalsoma. The parabrain operates as much in the coincidence of the vehicles of manifestation of the consciousness – with the human body, the holochakra, the psychosoma and the mentalsoma making up the holosoma (coexistence) – as in the discoincidence of these same vehicles, namely submersed in and dominated by the various paraphysiological characteristics, according to the consciential dimension (level) at which it finds itself.

Thosenes. Obviously, the thosenes of the consciousness, when in the discoincident state, cannot always be the same or at the same level when in the coincident state, as in the ordinary, physical waking state.

Properties. The parabrain, although, strictly speaking, being the matrix for the human brain, is very different from it because of its various properties, such as the following 7:

1. **Subtlety.** According to psychosomatics, the parabrain has a greater subtlety because it is light and quintessentialized, not having such dense matter in its free structure, as occurs with the brain, which is protected inside the osseous helmet of the human head.

2. **Mutability.** According to evolutiology, the parabrain differs fundamentally from the brain in regard to its mutability or, in other words: each brain arises, develops and disappears together with and for only 1 human body; the parabrain, which is less perishable, sustains the existential seriation mechanism of the consciousness in countless human bodies *(retrosomas)* or, in other words, in the succession of other countless brains *(retrobrains)* which are more perishable and always ephemeral.

3. **Self-transfigurability.** The parabrain (self-transfigurer) is able to alter the extraphysical forms of the psychosoma according to the will of the consciousness, whether unconsciously or consciously.

4. **Expandability.** The parabrain allows the exit and free expansion of the mentalsoma in the mentalsomatic dimension, still the most obscure area researched on earth.

5. **Emotivity.** The parabrain (emotionalizer) is the basic fulcrum of all the types of emotions that stimulate the consciousness. This is why the psychosoma is called the "emotional body". It is one of the properties of the parabrain that is more difficult to conveniently utilize.

6. **Force.** The parabrain presents a parapsychic force, derived from the dynamic of the will, which is extraordinarily more potent in its subtlety than physical or brute, muscular, animal force.

7. **Memorization.** According to mnemosomatics, the quality of recall of the extraphysical events in which the consciousness of the human projector participates while projected in the psychosoma depends upon the transmission level of the recollections from the second brain (psychosoma) to the first brain (soma). The paraphysiology of the parabrain shows that this para-organ of thought simultaneously holds, with relative ease, the memories of the consciousness' experiences in two or more consciential dimensions, or those resulting from experiences of the consciousness in various parallel worlds, something which does not occur with the dense brain.

Hemispheres. The facts lead one to think that the mentalsoma, as well as the parabrain (of the psychosoma) are made up of 2 hemispheres, just like the human brain, because each element of these is a reflection of the other more evolved version. However, the structures of these extraphysical components still remain very obscure for us intraphysical consciousnesses, when active in the pure mentalsomatic dimension.

Consequences. The consequences of the discovery regarding the identification of the properties and self-awareness relative to the parabrain are simply revolutionary and have a profound impact for the evolution of the consciousness (or hyperacuity) and the progress of the sciences in general.

Solution. The notion (and evaluation) of the parabrain is, in fact, the rational solution for the controversy regarding the mind-matter binomial, or the effective discovery of the ancient and mysterious interaction between the consciousness and the human body (soma).

Applications. Many researchers still consider the human brain a luxury organ, its owner still not having learned how to make good use of all its potentialities, which peak at only approximately 80%. The individual thereby has an instrument which is developed beyond the needs and applications of the parabrain by the contemporary intraphysical consciousness. It is worth noting that the brain cannot handle the more sophisticated, veteran, intraphysical, lucid projector's *entire* range of material and extraphysical activities together and at the same time.

Utilization. Most intraphysical consciousnesses, even when they temporarily free themselves from a predominance of the operations of the dense brain – during their lucid consciential projections – do not know how to use the possibilities and paraperceptions of the parabrain (the basic organ, in this case) with full awareness and efficiency. In other words: they continue to think, manifesting themselves through the parabrain, as though they were still inhibited and stuck in the dense brain, the secondary organ, and consequently in the physical restriction of the human body.

Desomatics. This can be stated another way according to desomatics: up to now, they have only learned to think with the restricted cellular brain in any situations or existential dimensions in which they find themselves. After undergoing desoma, the sad result of this is the installation of post-desomatic parapsychosis: for an extended period of time, recently-deceased consciousnesses in general do not suspect the radical changes in their surroundings and that the human body has died, and sometimes, depending on the case, has even disintegrated (decomposition) and completely disappeared.

Neurology. The greatest impactive power of recognizing the reality of the parabrain occurs in the areas of neurology and neurophysiology. This is because, in this case, it reaches the kernel of the research, still reflecting upon all consequences and structural recycling of observations and discoveries made by neurologists and neurophysiologists.

Mentalsoma. The most important relationships of the parabrain occur with the mentalsoma, which is the basic seat of manifestation of the consciousness when humanized, whether in an intraphysical condition or in the post-desoma condition, as long as it is, evolutionarily speaking, in a situation which is still tropospheric, crustal or terrestrial.

Zoology. Based upon the evolutionary development verified in embryology, it can rationally be concluded that subhuman animals also have a rudimentary parabrain corresponding to their evolutionary level.

Comparison. Without a doubt, the parabrain related to a simple brain, weighing a few grams, cannot be compared to that related to a complex brain, weighing 53 oz. (1,500 g), for example, regardless of which living being it commands.

277. GENERAL EXTRAPHYSICAL PERCEPTIONS

Definition. Extraphysical perception: the reception or registering of an extrasensory or parapsychophysiological impression in the consciential centers of the intraphysical consciousness projected from the human body.

Synonymy: extraphysical extrasensory perception; extraphysical impression; extraphysical perceptiveness.

Characteristics. Among the general extraphysical perceptions, at least the following 13, in line with the objectives of our research, can be listed:

1. **Psychosomatics.** Consciential perceptions by the psychosoma.
2. **Mentalsomatics.** Consciential perceptions by the mentalsoma.
3. **Extraphysicology.** Extraphysical vision.
4. **Omnivision.** Omnivision by the mentalsoma.
5. **Para-audition.** Extraphysical audition or para-audition.
6. **Omni-audition.** Omni-audition by the mentalsoma.
7. **Para-senses.** Extraphysical touch, smell and taste or para-senses.
8. **Para-acuity.** Acuity of the extraphysical senses or para-acuity.
9. **Sharpening.** Subtlety, semi-awareness and sharpening of extraphysical senses.
10. **Paratemperature.** An absence or presence of the extraphysical sensation of heat or cold (paratemperature) on the part of the projected intraphysical consciousness.
11. **Para-equilibrium.** The extraphysical sensation of equilibrium or para-equilibrium (parapronation).
12. **Radiations.** Mental radiations.
13. *Para-pain.* Extraphysical painful sensations or *para-pain* (para-algia, a process like many others referred to here of *para*psychology, *para*psychism, the extraphysical conditioning or *para*-sensations of the intraphysical consciousness who is still subordinated to instincts, vegetative life and intraphysical experiences).

Differences. According to experiments performed thus far, it can be verified that the extraphysical perceptions pertaining to the projected intraphysical consciousness differ in the two following manners:

1. **Physical.** First, physical perceptions, per se, which occur in the ordinary, physical waking state.
2. **Extrasensory.** Second, extrasensory perceptions (ESP), which somehow also occur stemming from the consciential state of ordinary, physical wakefulness.

Dissimilarities. Because of the scale of general observations of the projected intraphysical consciousness, 2 projectors, or even the partners of a harmonized and well-consolidated evolutionary duo, never report experiences that are entirely identical or show a completely equal development of their experiences outside the human body.

Processes. The intraphysical consciousness projected from the human body registers information through 3 basic, well-defined processes which are reaffirmed below:

1. **Paratelepathy.** Direct, common, mental acquisition or extraphysical telepathy (paratelepathy).

2. **Paraclairvoyance.** Acquisition in the form of perceiving images, scenarios, or extraphysical clairvoyance (paraclairvoyance).

3. **Para-intuition.** Acquisition, through thoughts or ideas that suddenly enter the consciousness, or extraphysical intuition (para-intuition).

Types. General impressions in the extraphysical dimension can be classified into 3 basic types: positive, negative and ambivalent.

1. **Positive.** Attainment of extraphysical illumination; cosmic superconsciousness; sense of absolute peace.

2. **Negative.** Regarding projectors in general: admonitory discomfort; the effects of extraphysical repercussion; sudden, imposed, premature or traumatic interiorization. Regarding the novice projector: fear of the unknown (neophobia); extraphysical insecurity; unfounded concern about not returning to the human body; pseudo-death; indecision; disorientation; depressive solitude; panic; sexual impulse.

3. **Ambivalent.** Euphoria; sense of omnipotence; sense of absolute freedom; immateriality; subtleness of extraphysical sensations.

Frontochakra. The parafrontochakra of the psychosoma allows the projected intraphysical consciousness to improve its tropospheric extraphysical perceptions, seeing and distinguishing the form and nature of extraphysical four-dimensional environments and objects with greater precision. All more advanced lucid projectors end up having a permanently pulsating developed frontochakra. This is because one condition stimulates the other and both, necessarily and inevitably, coexist.

Phobias. The following are 13 phobias that can be instantaneously generated by the novice projector during lucid projection:

1. **Intrusion.** Fear of encountering an old adversary that is already deceased (interconsciential intrusion).

2. **Basophobia.** Fear of floating and falling (basophobia) when volitating.

3. **Coma.** Fear of not awakening after reentering the human body.

4. **Diplychiphobia.** Fear of suffering a trauma or accident (diplychiphobia) with the head or the entire body.

5. **Eremophobia.** Fear of being alone (eremophobia, autophobia, monophobia) and getting lost in a deserted location.

6. **Phobophobia.** Fear of the individual's own fears in relation to unknown and as yet unexperienced situations.

7. **Hypnophobia.** Fear of sleeping, morbid fear of not returning to the human body or the intraphysical base during sleep.

8. **Interiorization.** Fear of not being able to reenter the human body or of interiorization.

9. **Neophobia.** Fear of confronting the unknown, the mysterious, the new world or the *incognito*.

10. **Nosophobia.** Fear of contracting an irreversible mental (psychopathy) disease (nosophobia).

11. **Possession.** Fear of encountering a stranger occupying the projector's own human body upon returning to the intraphysical base (interconsciential possession).

12. **Taphephobia.** Morbid fear of being buried alive (taphephobia) or with the lucid consciousness imprisoned within its own dense body (pathological catalepsy).

13. **Thanatophobia.** Fear of dying (deactivation of the soma) or thanatophobia – the mother of all phobias – in this case, without being prepared or prior to the appropriate time.

Penetration. A characteristic sensation stemming from lucid projection and one which is truly unique for the consciousness in the ordinary, physical waking state, is the sense of universal accessibility or penetrability into everything and everyone, with a certain awareness of a seemingly omnipotent penetration and full capacity for the invasion, investigation and study of places, more inhospitable environments and the lives of more inaccessible intraphysical beings.

Ancestrality. It becomes difficult to characterize precisely the sensation of invasion that has some connotation in regard to our subhuman ancestrality.

Analogies. This invasion may be a glimpse of the ambivalent sensation that some individuals experience in the following 5 conditions:

1. **Assault.** The nocturnal assailant in action.
2. **Inmate.** The prison inmate upon being freed after many lustrums in captivity.
3. **Port.** The sailor who is back at port after months of confinement on a ship on the high seas.
4. **Power.** The personality who finds him/herself suddenly armed with immense decision making power with regard to human circumstances.
5. **Daydream.** The person who, in his/her almost always negative daydreams, imagines him/herself as an invisible violator of houses, bodies, intimacies and consciousnesses.

Albedo. The albedo, or the total reflective force of the earth and its atmosphere, generally appears greater to the perceptions of the lucid volitating consciousness, whether it is a healthy extraphysical consciousness or a lucid projected intraphysical consciousness. It can easily identify the energetic or luminous radiations from the surfaces of bodies situated in a landscape, such as bodies of water, trees, rock formations, monuments or others.

Violation. The extraphysical sensation of invasion can lead the novice and incautious projected projector to the negative impulse of extraphysical sexual violation.

Intuition. The projected consciousness, upon experiencing correct impressions at any level of lucidity, always has the corresponding intuitive sensation of whether it is proceeding correctly or incorrectly, in a cosmoethical or anticosmoethical manner.

Inventory. The sensorial experiences involved in the inner processes of lucid projection are not part of our normal inventory of sensory data, but overflow beyond the ideas that are routinely conceived. This is why these impressions or sensations become so difficult to translate into words.

Self-confidence. The projector should have self-confidence in his/her parapsychic abilities.

Censure. When projected, the projector should not worry or censure what he/she observes, regardless of how strange, fantastic or absurd it may appear during the lucid projection.

Analysis. Later, upon returning to the human body, in the ordinary, physical waking state, the projector should perform a detailed self-critical analysis of his/her extraphysical information and perceptions.

Robot. Rationalization and critical analysis should not be attempted while the consciousness is projected, otherwise the projector's preconceptions, which make him/her a robot with its solid system of beliefs and repressions, mechanically suffocate his/her intuitive abilities.

Mistakes. The consciential projector should also not be concerned with the mistakes in his/her extraphysical research. It is better to practice lucid projection with perseverance and patience, sustaining the intention that he/she will succeed in his/her attempts, not only to project, but also to perform research outside the human body.

Pattern. Every time the projected intraphysical consciousness makes his/her human, physical environment the standard plane of reference for his/her extraphysical observations, he/she tends to increase the percentage of observational errors. It can thus be concluded that the standard plane of reference pertaining to the extraphysical world needs to be discovered, identified and applied with lucidity and reason by the lucid projector.

Echo. Some conditions of the projected intraphysical consciousness make his/her extraphysical environment into a veritable echo chamber, where he/she hears his/her own voice resonating.

Hyperacuity. There are reports of visual and auditory hyperacuity (hyperacusia) occurring during various phenomena such as interconsciential apparitions and lucid projections in which the percipient – whether a clairvoyant sensitive, clairaudient sensitive or lucid projector – enjoys an intensification of visual or auditory perceptions during parapsychic events.

Discomfort. In lucid projections produced through pure, natural or physiological processes, any disagreeable sensation that arises while the phenomena are occurring is too short-lived to be characterized as a true inner discomfort. However, in lucid projections produced through impure, forced or antiphysiological processes, the greatest variety of disagreeable sensations can occur, depending upon the interference and combination of a thousand and one physical and extraphysical factors.

Bibliography: Blackmore (139, p. 40), Brittain (206, p. 49), Donahue (407, p. 104), Durville (436, p. 231), Faria (495, p. 82), Frost (560, p. 60), Green (633, p. 169), Greene (635, p. 96), Hart (687, p. 244), Muldoon (1103, p. 150), Rogo (1446, p. 158), Stokes (1625, p. 22), Vieira (1762, p. 131).

278. EXTRAPHYSICAL VISION

Definition. Extraphysical vision: the visual perception of the intraphysical consciousness when projected from the human body.

Synonymy: astral vision; extraphysical clarity; paravision; vision in the fourth dimension.

Vehicles. None of the extraphysical senses are, necessarily, located or restricted to any part of the psychosoma or mentalsoma. The projected consciousness manifests itself in these vehicles through the set of its extraphysical constituents while the consciential senses, in this condition, are active in all parts of these vehicles. Hence the possibility of the occurrence – even through a minor discoincidence of the consciential vehicles – of clairvoyance or global visions forward, backward, above, below or to both sides, as well as skin sight, the phenomena of transposition of senses, and others.

Characteristics. Among the characteristics and types of extraphysical vision, at least the following 23 can be singled out:

1. Ordinary monocular vision.
2. Stereoscopic or binocular vision.
3. Uniform, well-focalized vision.
4. Unstable vision.
5. Out of focus vision.
6. Unidirectional vision.
7. Retrovision.
8. Circular vision.
9. Global or 360° vision.
10. Vision lacking deformation that eliminates perspective.
11. Vision on well-defined planes.
12. Omnidirectional vision.
13. Generalized omnivision or omni-sight, characteristic of the mentalsoma.
14. *En bloc* vision.
15. Deep endoscopic or X-ray vision.
16. Magnifying or telescopic vision.
17. Microscopic vision.
18. Chromatic vision.
19. Vision in the dark.
20. The range of vision and influence of willpower in extraphysical vision.

21. Close-up vision.
22. Zoom and extraphysical vision.
23. Panoramic vision.

Application. Strictly speaking, blinding lights and impenetrable darkness do not exist for the projected intraphysical consciousness. It all depends on his/her personal potential, application of the will and extraphysical performance in order to enable him/her to see, discern, witness or participate in extraphysical events.

Coadjutant. Extraphysical vision is a powerful coadjutant factor for the awareness of the consciousness upon projecting, as well as the extraphysical awakening of projectors in general, especially myopic and daltonic intraphysical consciousnesses in the ordinary, physical waking state.

Distance. According to the processes of dissimulation, masking and simulation used in camouflage techniques, it is known that objects do not appear the same when seen from the ground as opposed to being seen from an airplane (distance).

Observation. Besides, observations made in intraphysicality suffer limitations imposed by fog, rain or smoke.

Subtle. If our coarse physical senses suffer from these situations while in the ordinary waking state, what would the projected projector experience with his/her subtle paraperceptions while in the much more sophisticated extraphysical dimensions?

Aspects. By virtue of the transference of the processes of extraphysical vision, when the consciousness goes from one body (the human body) and from one dimension (that of the ordinary, physical waking state) to another body (generally the psychosoma) and to another dimension (generally the tropospheric or crustal extraphysical dimension), even the most familiar objects in certain circumstances can appear unknown to the projected intraphysical consciousness, taking on chaotic, surrealistic and strange aspects.

Invisible. Extraphysical vision can also perceive forms which, although physical, are completely invisible to retinal, physical or ordinary sight. Included in this case are the particles that make up the atmosphere and the emanations from living beings.

Global. The generalized extraphysical global, circular, panoramic vision or omnivision, characteristic of the mentalsoma, allows one to simultaneously see in all directions in the light or in the dark and see objects from all sides at the same time.

Particle. In this case, each particle located inside a solid is as visible as that which is found on the surface. Also, hearing is replaced by the tachypsychic and automatic perception of thoughts.

Speed. In the tachypsychism of the projected and expanded intraphysical consciousness, the speed of mental elaboration seems to be higher than the maximum speed of the interactions of the phenomena or that of the speed of light.

Dissolution. When the projected projector has more consciential energy, extraphysical vision sometimes seems to penetrate the molecules of solid objects such as walls and rocks as though dense matter dissolved on contact with the thought emitted by the projector's consciousness. This is the sensation of *extraphysical dissolution.*

Blind. *Blind projection,* or that taking place in *extraphysical darkness,* is that in which the intraphysical consciousness clearly perceives he/she is projected outside the human body, although not seeing anything in the period prior to obtaining extraphysical vision. Note: the consciousness is quite aware that he/she is projected from the human body, sees absolutely nothing and can even volitate in complete darkness without seeing anything.

Distinction. The projected consciousness needs to learn to distinguish extraphysical environments by overcoming undefined extraphysical vision, no visibility, as when in a penumbra, which often occurs due to a lack of consciential energy.

Difficulties. Letters and numbers are the most difficult items for the projected consciousness to see, distinguish or read. Visual images, or vivid figures, are more accessible to extraphysical vision. These observations have already been verified under laboratory conditions, but their cause is still unknown.

Self-energizations. One of the resources that the author has used while projected in order to obtain or intensify extraphysical vision is the application of self-energizations made directly from the extraphysical dimension to the head of his own psychosoma (parahead). These resources seem to balance the energies, *rinsing* or *cleansing* the dense energetic excess of the holochakra or the extraphysical environment that is *attached* to the psychosoma, thereby clearing up the process of direct vision.

Distortions. The extraphysical vision of the projected intraphysical consciousness varies greatly in terms of focus, clarity and coordination. It is dependent upon the extraphysical environment in focus and, more than anything, the qualities of the extraphysical perceptions of the consciousness, according to the vehicle of manifestation being used on that occasion, which can alter or distort the actual visions, owing to countless factors.

Case study. The following are 2 examples of distorted extraphysical vision:

1. **Soma.** Seeing one's own human body (soma) lying on the bed without a head, or with a dark mass in the place of a head, or with a plane (two-dimensional) perspective, as though it were a sheet of paper (flatman).

2. **Environment.** Seeing the environment of the bedroom in an altered fashion, with nonexistent curtains, different decoration, a bigger space, higher ceiling and different colors.

Bibliography: Andreas (36, p. 54), Blackmore (139, p. 4), Bozzano (186, p. 166), Coxhead (312, p. 119), Currie (354, p. 148), Denning (391, p. 48), Grosso (650, p. 186), Krishnan (869, p. 21), Mitchell (1059, p. 4), Monroe (1065, p. 183), Salley (1496, p. 159), Sculthorp (1531, p. 94), Sherman (1551, p. 185), Vieira (1762, p. 116), Yogananda (1894, p. 205).

279. EXTRAPHYSICAL ATTENTION

Definition. Extraphysical attention: assiduity of the projected consciousness to some idea, object or *thing*.

Synonymy: fixation of observation; para-attention.

Types. Extraphysical attention can be classified into 2 basic types:

1. **Focused.** Focused or applied attention.
2. **Distracted.** Wandering or distracted attention.

Control. The control of fixation of attention is the irreplaceable foundation for the improvement of extraphysical perceptions and the improvement of the quality of the experiments of the intraphysical consciousness during excursions outside the human body.

Distraction. Any distraction of extraphysical attention can mean a sometimes radical change in the mental target predetermined by the projected intraphysical consciousness.

Thosenization. In this case, extraphysical attention spearheads or leverages 3 factors (trinomial) that can be summarized in a single thosenization practically at the same time: will, thought and action.

Holochakrology. The absence of fixation of observation on the part of the projected intraphysical consciousness wholly absorbed in what he/she sees outside the human body results in a great number of projectors never seeing the silver cord and thereby believing it does not exist.

Psychosomatics. Other projectors do not even distinguish their own psychosoma, parahands and even their extraphysical clothing.

Bibliography: Baumann (93, p. 44), Vieira (1762, p. 83).

280.	SCALE OF OBSERVATION OF THE PROJECTED CONSCIOUSNESS

Definition. Scale of observation: the reference system chosen by the consciousness in order to face and analyze the phenomena of daily life.

Synonymy: analytic angle; didactic viewpoint; process of observation; reference system; scientific perspective.

Versions. Depending upon the moment and the circumstances of its perception, the consciousness examines its probable version of the universe.

Reality. Wherever there is a consciousness, different types of reality exist according to the different types and levels of evolution of the consciousness, or particular aspects of experience.

Universe. The universe, as well as the consciential dimensions, above all constitute a purely parapsychic structure that is consonant with the manner of being, the pattern of perception, the scale of actualization or the approximation of the reality perceived by the consciousness, individually, as a separate unit, *per se*.

Perception. The objective existence of things primarily depends upon subjective perception.

Inseparability. Strictly speaking, existence and perception, subject and object are inseparable concepts.

Psychosoma. The emotional body – the psychosoma – creates its own emotional field or emotional world (holothosene having a materthosene with an emphasized *sen*) and this influences the understanding of reality as seen by the consciousness.

Intercommunications. The experiences are intercommunicable in the cosmic *here and now*.

Manifestations. Our consciousness, having unstable manifestations, acts incessantly, or thosenizes through diverse levels of subjectivity.

Physics. Even the data of our knowledge of physics are impregnated with subjectivity. It is impossible for two persons to observe the same phenomenon, except in an incomplete and approximate sense.

Chalk. A piece of chalk used to write on the blackboard will be seen by the common person, according to the *scale* of *normal* human observation, as being a small solid object.

Case study. The following are 3 examples of the analysis of 1 piece of chalk according to the scale of observation of 3 different professionals:

1. **Geologist.** The geologist, following the *microscopic scale,* will see the geological components, the process of rock formation, its age, hardness, the calcium carbonate or calcium sulfate of the chalk.

2. **Chemist.** The chemist, restricted to the *chemical scale,* will analyze the chemical composition of the chalk, its pH, speculating on the chains of chemical elements derived from the carbon that composes the piece of chalk.

3. **Physicist.** The physicist, in accordance with the level of the *subatomic scale,* will distinguish the electrons, protons, nuclei and fields in perpetual movement that form the chalk.

Vision. In the case of the chalk, each of these 4 intraphysical consciousnesses – the common person, the geologist, the chemist and the physicist – saw the same object, apparently as though examining *4 objects* that are different from each other.

Electrons. The natural, basic phenomenon, in this case, is a singular one: the movement of electrons.

Phenomena. None of the *4 observers* made a mistake, nor did they modify the object, although 4 distinct *phenomena* were detected.

Systems. The fact occurred due to the use of *4* different *reference systems*.

Scale. For the individual – or the consciousness – the scale of observation creates the phenomenon.

Discovery. The consciousness that changes the scale of observation encounters or discovers new phenomena for itself and other consciousnesses.

Change. Any change in the scale of observation will engender different phenomena in relation to the same observing consciousness.

Analysis. In the case under analysis, only 1 observer could have seen 4 different phenomena where there is only the natural phenomenon of the movement of the electrons and atomic particles that make up the chalk.

Telepathy. Another example where the importance of the scale of observation can be observed is the problem in telepathic transmission, which is still considered to be performed through images and not words, thereby dispensing with the problem of linguistic diversity.

Bucket. If someone were to telepathically transmit the idea of 1 *bucket* to a group of persons, it could be received in the most diverse ways. Some will think the transmission was a cup of water, others will see a glue stick, others a wastebasket, others a pencil, a mug or even an actual bucket and all will be correct, although with different ideas.

Greek. If the thought were to be transmitted today to a Greek, from Ancient Greece, that "An airplane crashed into an apartment building and destroyed a television tower." or the idea of "a late model car", for example, he would limit all this thoughts to his/her own ideas and would certainly see another phenomenon. This is because these events or objects would still not pertain to the scope of his/her thoughts – consciential microuniverse – or he/she would simply say that he/she understood nothing.

Microuniverse. The intraphysical consciousness is a complex microuniverse that does not allow correct simplistic or hasty analyses. Each person has his/her own perspective in the examination of reality or experiences, things, objects, locations, phenomena and facts.

Sofa. Personal perspective alters the significance of things. A large sofa, for example, signifies different things for the following 4 categories of human beings: an upholsterer; a couple of lovers; an elderly person (old age) who is exhausted after walking; and a furniture mover.

Errors. Personal perspective can generate errors in interpretation.

Interpretation. The following is a classic example of the mechanism of errors in interpretation. Four persons simultaneously sit around a small square card table. Then, an uppercase "M" is placed at the center of the table. Depending upon where each person is seated, 4 different objects will be seen:

1. An "M".
2. An "E".
3. A "W".
4. An angular "3".

Expectations. It can thus be seen that these persons may also be mentally or psychologically *set in their ways*, a condition that interferes in their repressions, conditionings, brainwashings, sacralizations and expectations in the analysis of the context.

Deductions. It becomes easy to deduce that the analysis of the scale of observation permits the achievement of 4 distinct objectives:

1. **Understanding.** An increased understanding of things (personalities, realities and objects) from a scientific point of view.

2. **Hits.** The avoidance of serious mistakes in rational perspectives and analyses, generally coming from the human brain.

3. **Differences.** The identification of great differences generated by erroneous observations.

4. **Paradoxes.** The logical explanation of countless paradoxes, apparent contradictions and tautologies.

Rashomon. The analysis of the scale of observation, in the area of projectiology, avoids a situation similar to the one portrayed in "Rashomon," a film made in 1950 by Akira Kurosawa, with Toshiro Mifune, which won the top award at the 1951 Venice Film Festival. In the story, which takes place in medieval Japan, each protagonist, observer or narrator reports the events from his/her point of view in his/her own personal style.

Extraphysicology. If the intraphysical consciousness, in the ordinary, physical waking state, in the dimension of dense matter, using the distortional mirror of the human senses, can err so greatly regarding the everyday phenomena of physical reality to which he/she is habituated in diuturnal life, what will happen when this same consciousness projects – still with the same lucidity – from the human body in the subtle, unhabituated, immense, undefined and unexplored extraphysical dimension?

Ambiguity. While the intraphysical consciousness is projected in the extraphysical dimension, whether in the psychosoma or the mentalsoma, the process through which he/she receives information differs from the 5 or more basic senses of the human body that breathes in the intraphysical dimension. To start with, the lucid projector is, above all, simultaneously the observed object and the observer of the projective experience.

Human. Physical vision is routinely stable, continuous and immutable. When the intraphysical consciousness sees and analyzes a physical object, the possibilities of his/her vision are predictable. He/she is aware of the extent of the investigative resources that he/she can count on in order to accurately examine the object.

Instruments. In many cases, the intraphysical consciousness, unconcerned about time, uses more accurate instruments in order to maximally correct his/her physical deficiencies and improve detailed examination: lenses, glasses, magnifying glasses, microscopes and telescopes.

Projected. The extraphysical vision of the projected intraphysical consciousness is unstable, unpredictable and tends to work extremely rapidly. There are also no possibilities for using instruments while in the projected state outside the human body.

Lucidity. The only intelligent solution will be the intensification of extraphysical lucidity, improving the perceptions of the projected consciousness, which encompasses parameters that are much more ample than the amplitude of the consciousness in the condition of restriction of the human body, when in the ordinary, physical waking state.

Conditions. Bearing in mind the scale of observation of the projected human consciousness, we can thereby understand the causes of disparities in the projector's extraphysical perceptions that stem from the following 6 projective conditions, among others:

1. **Projectability.** The type or nature of lucid consciential projection.
2. **Vehicles.** The vehicle of manifestation of the consciousness.
3. **Density.** The density of this vehicle of manifestation.
4. **Self-lucidity.** The degree of self-lucidity of the projected consciousness.
5. **Frequency.** The vibratory frequency of the extraphysical dimension in which the consciousness is manifesting.
6. **Competence.** The extraphysical skill, experience and agility or projective competence of the projected consciousness.

Synchronicity. It evidently becomes very difficult for two intraphysical consciousnesses to be projected with the following 4 identical or synchronous manifestations:

1. **Moment.** Projected at the same time.
2. **Dimension.** Projected in the same dimension.
3. **Identity.** Both being in the same 6 previously mentioned projective conditions.
4. **Events.** All this occurring in order to observe or participate in the same extraphysical events or experiences.

Disparities. From these logical facts, disparities arise in the reports due to the diversity of the extraphysical acquisition of the projected consciousnesses' experiences.

Supposition. For example, suppose that 4 intraphysical projectors endeavor to extraphysically visit an ill target-person in a distant city:

1. **Common.** The consciousness of the *first* projector leaves the inactive human body in the psychosoma, which is in a *light* condition, with full lucidity, locates the target-person and later reports

having transmitted, apparently alone, a flow of consciential energy in the gastrointestinal area (umbilicochakra) of the assisted intraphysical consciousness.

2. **Assisted.** The consciousness of the *second* projector, leaving the inactive human body in the psychosoma, which is in a *dense* condition, laden with the energies of the holochakra, in a semilucid condition, assisted by a helper, goes to the target-person who receives the energies of both – the projected intraphysical consciousness and the helper – reporting nothing about the details of the extraphysical experiment because he/she does not remember it.

3. **Clairvoyance.** The consciousness of the *third* projector, with no loss in lucidity or psychomotor control of the human body, leaves instantaneously through traveling clairvoyance, goes to the target-person and reports seeing the interior of his/her organism through extraphysical heteroscopy, identifies a gastric ulcer and, finally, mentions having transmitted consciential energies to the patient's entire affected organic area.

4. **Mentalsoma.** The consciousness of the *fourth* projector leaves the inactive human body together with the holochakra and psychosoma and, in the condition of a punctiform consciousness, extraphysically *enters* the brain of the target-patient and, after returning, affirms having energetically helped the patient, who has a gastric ulcer, through an improvement of his/her thosenes.

Experiences. The 4 projectors had 4 different experiences, satisfactorily reached the mental target and fulfilled the purpose of the lucid consciential projection, each in his/her own way.

Angles. The 4 projectors, however, differ in regard to the scale of observation employed according to the projected consciousness, which made each one report events with the *same object* – the target-patient – but from *different angles*.

Misunderstandings. Countless misunderstandings and apparent contradictions can obviously arise from this upon making an accurate comparative analysis of the 4 experiences.

Repetitions. It is even possible for the *same* projector, in the *same* extraphysical district and in two different projections to observe aspects or angles of the *same* beings, objects and occurrences in an entirely *different* manner due to his/her extraphysical perceptions being altered in a specific manner during each projective occasion.

Personal. The author has extraphysically returned to the same extraphysical location up to 3 or 4 times at different periods in order to begin to truly understand it. On the other hand, this resource improves the personal reference system in the scale of extraphysical observation.

Sensitive. In the same way, it should be remembered that the scale of observation of the clairvoyant sensitive is very different from the frame of reference of the common person who lacks advanced parapsychic sensitivity with regard to the possibility of detecting and identifying the projected projector or, in another words: cooperating and establishing confirmations subsequent to projection of the consciousness.

Bibliography: Vieira (1762, p. 40).

281. PERFORMANCE OF THE PROJECTED CONSCIOUSNESS

Definition. Performance of the projected consciousness: the actuation of the intraphysical projector according to his/her projective possibilities while free in the extraphysical dimension.

Synonymy: projective actuation; projective competence; projective performance.

Scale. The performance of the projected consciousness extends over a wide range of actuations, from the common and familiar everyday attitudes characteristic of human life to the more surprising and exotic manifestations relative to conventional existence.

Periods. The actions of the projected consciousness permit the evaluation of its basic evolution and they also have an influence upon 4 existential periods:

1. **Existence.** The remainder of the individual's human life (lifetime).
2. **Desoma.** The final projection or the upcoming and inevitable desoma.

3. **Intermission.** The interval between two immediate intraphysical lives or the post-desomatic intermissive period.

4. **Cycle.** The characteristics of the upcoming human life, within the personal and multi-existential cycle of intraphysical and successive existences that dominate us all at our current evolutionary level (holoresomatics).

Categories. Among the existing categories of the performance of the intraphysical consciousness projected in the psychosoma, at least the following 26 can be singled out:

1. **Respiration.** Lack of a need for respiration (annulment of the condition of the *human bellows*).
2. **Pain.** Absence of physical pain.
3. **Lightness.** Lightness in personal manifestations.
4. **Weight.** Absence of one's own body weight.
5. **Insubstantiality.** Experience of insubstantiality regarding oneself.
6. **Intangibility.** The condition of intangibility to human beings.
7. **Invulnerability.** The condition of invulnerability to physical agents.
8. **Paraphotonics.** Personal, extraphysical photonic irradiation.
9. **Energies.** More evident irradiation of one's own consciential energies.
10. **Morphothosenes.** Creation of morphothosenes or thought-forms.
11. **Paraclothing.** Mental texture of the extraphysical clothing (paraclothing) that shapes the visual appearance of the psychosoma in which the projector manifests.
12. **Self-luminosity.** The condition of personal extraphysical self-luminosity.
13. **Rejuvenation.** Rejuvenation of the extraphysical esthetic appearance (para-appearance).
14. **Transparency.** Personal verification of the transparency of human things and objects.
15. **Double.** Observation of the double of human things and objects.
16. **Self-permeability.** The condition of extraphysical self-permeability.
17. **Psycholocomotion.** Use of psycholocomotion or extraphysical dislocation through the impulses of the will.
18. **Paraphenomenology.** Triggering of extraphysical parapsychic phenomena.
19. **Stroboscopy.** Generation of extraphysical stroboscopic effects.
20. **Parapsychism.** Use of parapsychism without the direct use of the human body, when far from the physical base, using the psychosoma and mentalsoma.
21. **Paravisitation.** Performing fraternal paravisits or spontaneous extraphysical invasions – with no anticosmoethical intention – into the privacy of an intraphysical or extraphysical consciousness that has the appearance of a man or a woman and is not encapsulated.
22. **Apparition.** Personal tangible apparition to intraphysical beings.
23. **Bilocation.** Promotion and experience of the phenomenon of physical bilocation.
24. **Mnemosomatics.** Experience of the phenomena of mnemosomatics: extraphysical precognition and retrocognition.
25. **Conscientiality.** Enjoyment of a temporary consciential life, although lacking conventional human form and time.
26. **Self-awareness.** Enjoyment of the condition of continuous self-awareness.

Implication. The intangibility of the projected consciousness in relation to human beings ordinarily directly implies the fact that the psychosoma, as well as the holochakra, when *inside* the human body, do not exist for the consciousness. It is as though they were simply created as morphothosenes at the moment of projection, because they would otherwise present direct resistance as substances which are analogous to those of the projector.

Facts. The facts, however, remain: the human body, holochakra and psychosoma are extremely *real* when the consciousness manifests itself adequately, according to the existential dimension. They also do not seem to be morphothosenes or thought-forms, nor do they show resistance to each other in their manifestations relative to the circumstances.

Substances. The *substances* of these consciential vehicles, therefore, exist with vibratory frequencies in their energies or different *insubstantialities*.

Compound. *Compound extraphysical actions* – or, in other words, the simultaneous attitudes that demand, firstly, the division of attention and, secondly, the division of the channeling of the transmission of consciential energy to various targets by the consciousness projected with lucidity from the human body in a tropospheric extraphysical environment – are evidently among the more difficult and evolved.

Attention. Good examples of *tripartite* (or multipartite) *attention* are found in the compound manifestations that require conditions such as the following 7:

1. **Assistance.** The assistential act of continued volitation, or hovering in midair, in a heavier or denser tropospheric extraphysical environment.

2. **Exteriorization.** Perform a specific application of one's own consciential energies.

3. **Psychosoma.** Exteriorize energies simultaneously from the parahands and para-arms of the psychosoma to an ill extraphysical consciousness that is off to one side.

4. **Extraphysical consciousness.** Also exteriorize energies to another extraphysical consciousness that is off to the other side.

5. **Balance.** Maintain stability of the peaceful course of the lucid projection, as well as inner consciential balance.

6. **Emotionality.** Avoid negative, impassioned, emotional involvements.

7. **Patience.** Avoid losing patience and fraternal comprehension.

Concentration. In order to achieve all positive objectives, in a complex situation such as this, the projected intraphysical consciousness should minimize the disturbances of the patients, restricting what they say, shout, *telepathize* or nervously gesticulate, beyond the central focus of the projector's attention, concentrating on the maintenance of the balance of his/her strategic position and in the execution of intense transmissions of consciential energies.

Bibliography: Vieira (1762, p. 159).

282. INABILITIES OF THE PROJECTED CONSCIOUSNESS

Definition. Inability of the projected consciousness: *lack of* experience, practice, agility and competence in experimentation with lucid projection in the extraphysical dimension.

Synonymy: extraphysical inability; extraphysical incapacity; paratropospheric inability; projective incompetence; projective ineptitude.

Habits. The mental habits and patterns deriving from human activities in the ordinary, physical waking state strongly influence the reactions and behavior of the projected intraphysical consciousness in the extraphysical condition, thereby engendering many of the projected projector's inabilities.

Genius. With regard to intraphysical beings in general, in theory, no one is entirely incapable outside the human body. By the same token, however, no one is entirely capable in this same condition. For example, the author has not yet encountered an intraphysical pre-*serenissimus* projector who could be considered a projective genius. Does anyone know of one?

Categories. The inabilities of the projected intraphysical consciousness can be placed into two categories:

1. **Generalization.** Universal (groupkarmic) inabilities.

2. **Personal.** Individual (egokarmic) inabilities.

Universal. The following are 3 examples of universal inabilities of the projected intraphysical consciousness:

1. **Contacts.** Difficulty in contacting intraphysical beings.
2. **Intraphysicology.** Inability to affect physical objects.
3. **Reading.** Difficulty in performing various types of reading.

Individual. The following are 8 examples of individual inabilities of the projected intraphysical consciousness:

1. **Compulsion.** Ridiculous or infantile compulsive reactions.
2. **Repression.** Lack of monitoring of one's own instincts, chronic bad habits, human repressions and conditionings (self-weak-traits).
3. **Emotionalism.** Difficulty in performing a critical reduction of emotionalism (psychosomatics) in the paratropospheric dimension.
4. **Lack.** Difficulty in controlling the sexual impulse and its extraphysical repercussions.
5. **Traumas.** Extemporaneous and misplaced personal passivity when faced with disagreeable surprises and extraphysical traumas.
6. **Phobias.** Phobias or fears that are unfounded and sometimes even indistinct or of unknown origin.
7. **Initiative.** Weak initiative on the part of the projected intraphysical consciousness.
8. **Inhibition.** Extraphysical inhibition of the projected intraphysical consciousness which restricts the environment and facilitates the retraction of the silver cord.

Overcome. Universal inabilities that affect all projected intraphysical consciousnesses are overcome with the evolution of the practitioner's lucid projectability. This is only obtained after the intraphysical being is able to overcome his/her individual inabilities through theoretical study and disciplined, continued and successive projections.

Techniques. From this arises the reason for and importance of projective techniques.

Contributions. Certainly the improvement of these individual conditions, according to cosmoethics, personal behavior, mental concentration, acclimation to discoveries and new things (neophilia), while in the ordinary, physical waking state, all contribute equally to overcoming the projected intraphysical consciousness' inabilities.

Bibliography: Greene (635, p. 56), Monroe (1065, p. 182), Schiff (1515, p. 116), Vieira (1762, p. 163).

---

283. EXTRAPHYSICAL IMPOSSIBILITIES

Definition. Extraphysical impossibility: everything which, in fact, cannot be realized by the intraphysical consciousness while projected from the human body.

Synonymy: extraphysical impracticability; extraphysical incapacity; extraphysical infeasibility; extraphysical unfeasibility.

Discernment. The projector should always be aware of his/her actual extraphysical impossibilities, which will allow him/her to have greater discernment outside the human body, to rationally identify oneiric interference in extraphysical events, to be aware of the extent of his/her morphothosenes and the deepening of his/her self-critiquing and heterocritiquing judgment.

Types. Obviously excluding fantasy states and simulacra of actions, there are 3 basic types of extraphysical impossibilities for the projector: physiological, psychological and psychophysical.

1. **Physiological:** ejaculation; ovulation; fertilization; gestation (or generation of new children); abortion; ordinary nutrition.
2. **Psychological:** suicide; biological death or desoma.
3. **Psychophysical:** the fact that the projected intraphysical consciousness cannot take anything with him/her from the intraphysical dimension to the extraphysical dimension during a lucid projection and the consequences of this particular condition.

Extraphysical consciousnesses. It is important to remember that there are legions of conscientially undeveloped extraphysical consciousnesses which still live in their illusory consciential worlds. They use the dense psychosoma to fulfill all the physiological needs of an ordinary person, which they still consider themselves to have and to be. For those consciousnesses, these needs are real, critical, indispensable and, more precisely, *para*pathological.

Intraphysical consciousness. The projected intraphysical consciousness obviously should not imitate the abovementioned parapathological conditions of ill extraphysical consciousnesses.

Bibliography: Carrington (245, p. 281), Rampa (1357, p. 109), Vieira (1762, p. 162).

---

284. IMMANENT ENERGY

Definition. Immanent energy (Greek: *energeia*, active): primary, vibratory, invisible, essential and multiform *inergia* which is totally impersonal, dispersed in all objects or physical realities, interpenetrating the entire universe, therefore being universally diffused, or omnipresent, still untamed by the human consciousness, and too subtle to be identified by modern equipment.

Synonymy: acasa (Hindu); *alcaeste;* anamorphosis (Ludwig von Bertalanffy); *andrimanitra* (Malaysia, Philippines); *ani* (Ponape, Pacific); *anima mundi* (Avicenna: 980-1037); animal magnetism (Franz Anton Mesmer); anthropoflux (Farny); *anut* (Kusaie, Pacific); *aôr* (Hebrews); *arqueo* (Paracelsus); *arunquiltha* (aborigines, Australia); astral energy; astral force; astral light (H. P. H. F. de Blavatsky: 1831-1891); *atna* (Maoris, New Zeland); *ayik* (Elgonyi, Africa); azote (alchemists); *badi* (Malaysia); *baraka* (Sufis); biodynamic force (Enrico Morselli: 1852-1929); bioenergy; bio-flux (Paul Joire); bioflux; *bioliceté* (Vladimir Pravdine); biomagnetism (George de la Warr: 1904-1969); bioplasm (V. S. Grischenko); bioplasmic energy (Soviet scientists); biopsychic energy; bio-radiant energy (Francesco Racanelli); biotic energy; *cause formativa* (Aristotle); *chi* (acupuncturists, China); churinga (Aborigines, Australia); cohesion of the universe; cosmic energy; cosmic force; crystalline force; curative energy; dielectric biocosmic energy (Oscar Brumler); ectenic force (Marc Thury: 1822-1905); ectoplasm (Charles Robert Richet: 1850-1935); efflorescences (Albert Freiherr von Schrenk-Notzing: 1862-1929); effluvia (Hippolyte Baraduc: 1850-1902); *élan vital* (Henri Louis Bergson: 1859-1941); electronic force; elima (Congolese); *eloptic* energy (Thomas Galen Hieronymus); entelechy (Hans Driesch: 1867-1941); etheric force (radiesthesists); etheric formative force (Rudolf Steiner: 1861-1925); *etherium* (J. S. Grimes); extramaterial force; factor X (Bernard Grad); *facultas formatrix* (Galeno: 130-200); fakirian fluid; field information; fifth force; formative energy (Paul Kammerer); fundamental cosmic fluid; *gestaltung* (Johann Wolfang von Goethe); *glama* (Persia); *han* (Ponape, Pacific); Holy Spirit (Christian tradition); *hormic* energy (William Mc Dougall: 1871-1938); *huaca* (Peruvians); innate (D. D. Palmer); integral energy; integrative tendency (Arthur Koestler: 1905-1983); invisible energy; irradiant cerebral force (Cesare Lombroso: 1836-1909); *it* (Georg Groddeck: 1886-1934); *kalit* (Palan, Pacific); *kasinge* (Palan, Pacific); *ki* (Chinese and Japanese Acupuncture); *kriptus;* *kundalini; labuni* (Gelaria, New Guinea); libido (Sigmund Freud: 1856-1939); life-force (Luigi Galvani: 1739-1798); *magnale magnum* (Jan Baptista van Helmont: 1577-1644); magnetic energy; magnetic fluid (Franz Anton Mesmer); magnetoelectricity (William T. Tiller); magnetoism (A. Wendler); *mahashakti;* mana (Polynesians and Hawaiian kahunas); *manitu* (Algonquian indians); *megbe* (Ituri Pygmies); mesmeric fluid; metapsychic energy; motor force (John Ernst Worrel Keely); *mulungu* (Yaos, Central Africa); *mungo* (Sudanese); munis (Paracelsus); mythogenetic radiation (Alexander Gurwitch); negative entropy (Erwin Schrödinger); neo-energy; nervaura (Joseph Rodes Buchanan); *nervengeist* (Frederika Hauffe: 1801-1829); nervous force (Charles Bray); neuric energy (E. Barety); neuricity (E. Barety); neuric-radiant force (A. Bareti); *ngai* (Masai, Africa); *njom* (Ekoi, Africa); Nobel Prize winner in medicine in 1913); noetic energy (Charles Musès); *nous* (Plato); od (Karl Louis von Reichenbach); OD rays; odic force (Karl Louis von Reichenbach, 1788-1869); odic radiation; *odile; oki* (Iroquois indians); onana; *oni* (Nazareno Tourinho); *orenda* (Iroquois indians); orgone

(Wilhelm Reich: 1897-1957); orgonic energy; para-electricity (Ambrose Alexander Worral: 1899-1972); para-energy; perispiritual fluid; physiological radiation; physionuclear energy; *pneuma* (Erasistratus: 300 B.C.); *prakriti* or *mulaprakriti* (Hindus); prana (yogis, India); pre-physical energy (George de la Warr); primal energy; primary human force field; primary perception (Cleve Backster); primary universal force; primordial energy; psi capacity (Joseph Banks Rhine: 1895-1980); psi plasma (Andrija Karl Puharich); psi-energy; psychic fluid; psychic force (William Edward Cox: ?-1879); psychic lever (William Jackson Crawford: ?-1930); *psychode* (Marc Thury); psychonuclear energy; psychosomatic energy; psychosomatic force; psychosomatic phenomenon (modern medicine); psychotronic energy (Robert Pavlitta); psychotronic force; quantic connection; quasi-eletrostatic field (Henry Margenau); rays of light (Robert Fludd: 1574-1637); rigid rays (Julian Ochorowicz: 1850-1918); *rlum* (Bushmen, Kalahari); root fluid; *ruach* (Hebrews); *sa* (Egyptians); serpentine fire; serpentine wisdom (Cabalists); sidereal light (Paracelsus); *sila* (Eskimos); somatonuclear energy; soul of the universe (Gustav Benjamin Stromberg); *spiral; spiricity* (Adin Ballou); *spiritus* (Robert Fludd); sustaning energy; synchronicity (Carl Gustav Jung: 1875-1961); synergy (Abraham Maslow: 1908-1970); *tao;* telergic energy; telesma (Hermes Mercúrio Trimegistus); tellergy; telluric force; the great arcane (practical magic); third force (Robert Allan Monroe); time (Nikolai Kozyrev); *tondi* (Bataks, Pacific); undefined force (Albert De Rochas: 1837-1914); unified concept; unified field (Albert Einstein: 1879-1955, Nobel Prize winner); unitary principle of nature (L. L. White); universal energy; universal fluid; *universion* (Georges Lakhovsky); virtue (Jesus of Nazareth); *vis formativa; vis medicatrix naturae* (Hippocrates); vital electricity; vital energy (ancient Chinese); vital fluid (Allan Kardec); vital force (Christian Friedrich Samuel Hahnemann: 1755-1843); vital magnetism (Charles Littlefield); vital principle (vitalists); *vril* (Henry Bulwer-Lytton); *wakan* (Sioux indians); *wakonda* (Sioux indians); *wodan* (Germans); *wong* (Africans, Gold Coast); X-energy (John White); X-force (L. E. Eeman); *yaris* (Tobi, Pacific); *yesod* (Cabalists); YX-rays; *zoéter* (Hippolyte Baraduc); *zogo* (tribes, Torres Strait, Australia).

Multimodal. As can be observed in this extensive and still incomplete synonymy of names and terms for immanent energy – which are not exactly synonyms in all cases but are equivalent in their convergent objectives, namely to represent different names for the same type of concept – humanity is anxious to recognize, understand and control this energy that permeates the cosmos. It is apparently omnipresent, multimodal and was verified 30 centuries before the current era of the Gregorian calendar.

Forms. Modern day physics researchers have established the existence of 4 basic forms of physical energy or energetic interactions, listed here in decreasing order:

1. **Strong.** *Strong* interaction that acts at the subatomic level of elementary particles, equally causing the union of the atomic nucleus.

2. **Electromagnetic.** *Electromagnetic* interaction, where the greater part of modern or everyday physics is to be found.

3. **Weak.** *Weak* interaction that is also observed at the subatomic level of elementary particles and radioactivity.

4. **Gravitational.** *Gravitational* interaction that humans feel as gravitational force.

Cosmos. It is generally accepted that all matter is energy. It is impossible to imagine the cosmos without energy, one of the last remaining ordinary things about which we know nothing, because we merely observe its manifestations.

Terminology. The terms "immanent energy" and "consciential energy" are used here to characterize these non-physical energies. They require a universal consensus, which should arise someday, of a suitable term, when an expression will be coined for this objective. This will serve to ratify this still controversial hypothesis which, moreover, has logical roots since ancient time, as seen in the studies of modern researchers.

Transference. In fact, immanent energy cannot be created or destroyed, but only evaluated, concentrated, blocked, dispersed, transferred, acquired, transformed, modulated, emitted and projected by the subconscious structures forming the *psi potentiality*, influencing parapsychic phenomena and the projectability of human beings from the soma, as well as all of their thosenizations.

Universal. This energy has been identified in different times, locations and civilizations since ancient esoteric and pre-scientific traditions, as a universal phenomenon.

Matter. All existing matter is energy.

Indestructibility. Matter-energy has the properties of increativity and indestructibility.

Explanations. Immanent energy constitutes an essential factor for the satisfactory explanation of countless occurrences, such as: acupressure; acupuncture; aura; *ballonnement* (French term); bending metal at will; chakras; *congressus subtilis* (Latin expression); consciential energy; dematerializations; ectoplasmy; exteriorization of curative energies; exteriorization of motricity; extraphysical parapyrogenesis; extraphysical rain, currents and fire; extraphysical self-defenses; extraphysical sphere of energy; homeopathy; interdicted extraphysical locations; *kundalini* (Hindu term, sexochakra); morphothosenes; orgonology; parasurgery; post-projective energetic shower; projective poltergeist (German term); projective raps (English term); radiesthesia (radionics); rematerializations; self-curative projection; self-desoma; self-luminosity; spontaneous self-combustion; teleportation; trace of light of the psychosoma; vibrational state; voluntary self-cardiac arrest; voluntary self-combustion.

Application. Consciential energy, derived from immanent energy, is indivisible, inoffensive in and of itself and is applied by each individual according to his/her intention and level of cosmoethics. Some do so with sex appeal, others projecting with lucidity, still others researching and so on.

Analysis. If the reader wishes to delve deeper into the ever-relevant subject of consciential energies, he/she should analyze the dozens of chapters in this book that address this theme in a comprehensive manner.

Bibliography: ADGMT (03, p. 135), Andreas (36, p. 84), Bedford (103, p. 15), Blavatsky (153, p. 378), Coddington (289, p. 15), D'arbó (365, p. 197), Digest (401, p. 382), Fodor (528, p. 125), Gaynor (577, p. 199), Granja (621, p. 156), Greene (635, p. 60), Greenhouse (636, p. 102), Hammond (674, p. 12), Haynes (698, p. 154), Karagulla (814, p. 110), Kilner (843, p. 38), Long (947, p. 125), Martin (1003, p. 84), Meek (1030, p. 34), Monroe (1065, p. 270), Mons (1066, p. 120), Morel (1086, p. 81), Moss (1096, p. 104), Paula (1208, p. 149), Pensamento (1224, p. 75), Puharich (1337, p. 245), Shepard (1548, p. 295), Spence (1588, p. 141), Tansley (1649, p. 123), Tondriau (1690, p. 23), Tourinho (1693, p. 78), Walker (1782, p. 32), Wang (1794, p. 69), Wedeck (1807, p. 262), White (1829, p. 550), Wilson (1854, p. 534), Zaniah (1899, p. 334).

---

285. CONSCIENTIAL POWERS

Definition. Consciential power: the consciousness' capacity for self-determination regarding its own life and destiny.

Synonymy: capacity of the consciousness; consciential action; consciential control; energetic radiance; energy of will; force of animus; parapsychic power; personal power; power of consciential energy; right of the consciousness; self-aware free will; *siddhis*.

Source. Immanent energy is the source of energy that is common to all consciousnesses.

Personal. Consciential energy is the source of personal power.

Maturity. Power grows along with the maturity of the social being.

Maintenance. Consciential maturity predisposes the storage or maintenance of personal power.

Fundamentals. Strictly speaking, the consciousness presents 3 intraconsciential or fundamental intrinsic powers that should not be omitted here. They are listed in order of development, whereas each one depends upon the previous one or the others:

1. **Volition.** Personal will or the potency of volition.
2. **Intentionality.** Intentionality or the cosmoethical quality of the intention of the consciousness.
3. **Self-organization.** Self-organization or personal discipline regarding personal interrupted thosenization.

Penta. According to conscientiology, the fourth fundamental power of the intraphysical consciousness is the adequate practice of the daily, consciential energetic task or penta, with highly evolutionary results.

Facets. The decisive power to accept something, to have conviction about something or maintain a relative certainty can be analyzed according to 3 logical facets:

1. **Concentration.** The state in which the consciousness inwardly concentrates consciential energy upon that which it accepts.

2. **Categories.** This consciousness can be a child, adult or an extraphysical consciousness.

3. *That. That* which is accepted can be an idea, behavior, object or an intraphysical or extraphysical environment.

Principle. Based upon this principle of energetic concentration, anyone can better understand the manifestations and uses – including those which are spontaneous, instinctive or unconscious – of consciential energy by the members of humanity throughout history.

Energy. When immanent energy is transformed and applied as consciential energy (bioenergy), it leads the human personality, whether conscious or unconscious of the facts, to acquire powers and rights, influencing the existential environment or consciential dimension with its self-determination.

Types. In practice, the consciential powers discovered and identified by the sensitivity of the interested person can be classified into 4 basic types: word, gesture, object and place.

1. **Word.** The word of power can be mental (self-thosene, intrathosene) or spoken. The following are some examples: discourses; prayers; evocations; mantras; hymns and canticles in the dead or exotic languages of Catholics, evangelists, umbandists and followers of other religions.

2. **Gesture.** The gesture of power is that act or gestural manifestation which concentrates, potentiates and directs consciential energy to reach a target. Examples: raise an arm in evocation; move the right hand in order to send positive energy to someone (energization); the dance; the procession; the gesture of blessing; ritualistic acts and objects; the drawing of crosses and stars; and many others.

Personalities. Diverse personalities, such as leaders, communicators, teachers, lawyers, public prosecutors, orators in general and artists of all categories use specific gestures of power (consciential acts) anywhere, broadly and sometimes even abusively, on a frequent and daily basis wherever they wish to manifest themselves.

3. **Object.** The object of power is a material object that has form and occupies space, including the human body, used as an instrument for potentiating bioenergy. The following are some examples: the objects of an altar; the image and the bier of a saint; the monstrance of the priest; a pyramid; the sword used in magic; an object of personal use for establishing *rapport*; the hands of a healer; the (insured) legs or breasts of a star; and others.

Others. Objects are the most commonly found type of consciential power, as can be observed in the following examples: any type of symbol; the incense of an Eastern monk; the plant of power (drugs); the bible of the evangelical pastor; the amulet; the rabbit's foot; clenched fist amulet; the necklace; the bracelet; the earring; the queen's crown; the king's throne; the leader's scepter; the skull with a candle; crystals; jaguar's teeth; the conch shell; the whale bones of the voodoo priest, or *hougan;* shells; the coins of the Umbandist *pai-de-santo* (priest); sacred garments; scapular; the images and pictures of the crucifixion; the lighting effects and shining objects of altars; the Eucharist; the aspergillum; the sacred chorus; the candles and other various liturgical vestments of the catholic priest; the human body of the prostitute; the deck of playing cards; tarot cards; the crystal ball; dowsing rods; pendulums; the object scanned by the psychometrist; the pen used for signing government decrees; the communicator's microphone; and many others.

4. **Place.** The most common place of power is that environment where the energies flow more strongly, without intersections or negative or harmful interferences, and which allow the full manifestation or thosenization of the consciousness. The following are some examples: a nook in the garden; a bench, a corner of an interior wall; a well-positioned chair in a living room; a stable; and many others. *Feng shui* is worth mentioning in this context.

Radiesthesia. Places of power are especially researched by radiesthesia or radionics, for the purpose of prophylaxis and therapy. These include: the bed in an apartment bedroom; the secretary's desk in an office; the corner of the table in a meeting room; the orator's rostrum; the priest's pulpit; the director's chair in a meeting room; the artist's stage.

Hair. As can be seen, certain talismans, and even certain apparently incomprehensible uses or habits, have their raison d'être and actually work in energetic terms. For example, Samson's famous hair that, according to legend, was cut by Delilah, making him lose his incredible strength, could have actually had an effective application. The hair of the scalp (the root and shaft) is directly and intimately related to the coronochakra, the lotus of 1,000 petals, the most influential of all the holochakra's force centers, or nuclei of the consciential energy of the human personality (holosoma, unified body).

Chakras. Besides the relationship between the hair on the head and the coronochakra, a man balances his laryngochakra more effectively when he has a long, full beard. A woman effectively balances the cardiochakra (psychosoma) when she is able to maintain her breasts (prolactin, lactogenic hormone) proportional to her physical constitution. In these last 2 cases, there is an evident increase in consciential powers through physical or organic factors.

Pathology. On the other hand, from a pathological point of view, it can be observed that an obese person or one with a large abdomen, has his/her umbilicochakra (solar plexus) unbalanced or blocked, being constantly overworked, thereby impairing the nearby chakras. In this case, there is a reduction in consciential powers due to an organic disturbance.

Transformations. It is interesting to note that certain objects used in order to compensate for physical deficiencies (a lack or an absence of power), such as a cane, an artificial arm and others, can become efficient objects (self-sufficiency or the presence of power).

Priorities. When using the powers of consciential energy, the interested individual, whether young or old, should remember that what is most important or of greatest interest is establishing rational and cosmoethical priorities in the application of parapsychic resources in accordance with his/her personal development.

Losses. The failure to establish priorities in his/her manifestations makes the consciousness lose a great deal of intraconsciential energy, time and space, repeating unnecessary actions (dispensable self-mimicry), enslaved by dispensable ceremonies and rituals, mired in the dispersiveness of its acts, at a sublevel of evolutionary consciential performance.

Objectives. All types of consciential power should be meticulously and rigorously studied by the lucid consciential projection practitioner in order to achieve 3 well-defined objectives in his/her intraphysical and extraphysical life:

1. **Application.** The application of these powers when it is truly suitable or cosmoethically constructive for the individual or others on an everyday basis in intraphysical life or in the extraphysical dimension.

2. **Self-defense.** The act of defending oneself against the powers of balanced or imbalanced intraphysical or extraphysical consciousnesses, when necessary, either in the ordinary, physical waking state or while lucidly projected outside the body.

3. **Freedom.** The act of freeing oneself from submission to the conscious or unconscious use of consciential powers that are entirely dispensable for the individual, or are not in favor of other beings (consciential maturity).

Crutches. All psychological rituals and crutches are temporary, infantile and infantilizing.

Consciousness. The most important *object* is the consciousness, signifying the potent thought or ironclad will (self-motivation) of the personality of the intraphysical or extraphysical being.

Will. All known objects are ephemeral and gradually come down to the *consciousness*. Only the will of the consciousness itself remains as the irreplaceable and eternal resource of power or the *primopower* (first power).

Bibliography: Andrade (32, p. 59), Castaneda (257, p. 152).

---

286. CONSCIENTIAL   ENERGY

Definition. Consciential energy: that immanent energy which the consciousness uses in its general manifestations or thosenizations.

Synonymy: animic energy; animic force; biological PK (biological psychokinesis); energetic microwaves; inner energy; ovarian power; personal magnetism; projective energy; self-energy; sperm power; the energy of will; volitative energy.

Attributes. Regardless of the name that this immanent energy which is transformed into consciential energy someday receives, it currently appears to be responsible for the attributes or qualities of the human personality, referred to by the following 13 expressions, among others:

1. Allure.
2. Charisma, a condition derived from paragenetics.
3. Charm.
4. Emotional magic.
5. Fascination.
6. Glamour.
7. It.
8. Personal enchantment.
9. Personal magnetism.
10. Physical attraction.
11. Seductive power.
12. Sex appeal.
13. Sympathy.

Broad. There are those who also use the term *energy* to broadly denote (umbrella term) any synonym of: attraction; audience participation; *axé;* charge; climate; disposition; enthusiasm; fluid; health; peak; power; vibration; vigor; vitality; and willpower.

Presence. Consciential energy stands out more ostensively in the person who has a *magnetic presence*, latent force, exuberant potentiality, is *photogenic*, liberating involving energy and *exuding power.*

Leadership. Consciential energy is, among other things, responsible for stratification of the defined presence of the human personality in the terrestrial scenario and sustains the phenomenon of leadership when someone from the group with a greater energetic capacity imposes the dominant thought, the group mentality, the vision of life or the "collective" will.

Flock. Thus, the *human flock* is led by an individual or a small group, based upon a clan, family, congregation, oligopoly, institution, society, nation or continent.

Research. Consciential energy instigates countless research projects regarding its nature, peculiar properties, sources, particles, liberation, transference, isolation, storage, fields, biological compatibility and catalysis, sensitivity to intelligence, relationship to time and space, the laws that govern it, its most efficient use and other consequences. All this may seem quite abstract but does not, however, preclude its existence.

Facts. Those who think they can easily discard the theory of consciential energy, derived from immanent energy, as being too illogical or irrational to explain countless phenomena throughout the universe, should bear in mind the following 4 facts, for example, relative to our personal electromagnetic aura:

1. **Thermic.** The human body emits magnetic energy and thermic energy.

2. **Bioelectric.** Countless techniques of modern conventional medicine are based precisely upon biological concepts of some form of bioelectric energy, or psycho-electric waves generated by thoughts and the consciousness.

3. **Electroencephalograph.** The electroencephalograph registers and records forms of electromagnetic energy that pulsate continually in the 2 cerebral hemispheres of humans and subhuman animals, from which recordings many customarily make diagnoses.

4. **Bioelectronics.** The electrocardiogram, electromyogram, chronaximetry and other bioelectronic processes are also partial registers of organic energies.

Influx. The hypothesis of consciential energy is as valid or acceptable as nervous influx, which is still hypothetical. Has any neurophysiologist (or even you) ever personally witnessed *neural influx,* this all-powerful hypothetical agent that is considered to circulate along the nerve fibers of the human body?

Energization. What is the nature of the relationship between neural influx and consciential energy and to what degree does is act? It is good to bear in mind that there is an accepted distinction between 2 types of energization: magnetic (organic, neurological, pure human, material, physiological, somatic) and consciential per se (extraphysical, extra-organic, compound, paraphysiological, holosomatic).

Relations. At least the following 8 areas of human knowledge have a direct relation to and interest in the applications of consciential energy:

1. **Medicine.** All of modern or contemporary medicine.

2. **Holochakrality.** The Hindus' ancient concepts regarding the chakras.

3. **Acupuncture.** The nadis, the invisible points and network of energy conductors known as the meridians of acupuncture or of Chinese medicine.

4. **Acupressure.** The techniques of do-in or acupressure, currently popular in various countries.

5. **Homeopathy.** Unicist homeopathy, which is based upon the remission of illnesses by harmonizing the individual's energy.

6. **Meditation.** Yoga and transcendental meditation.

7. **Anti-gymnastics.** Anti-gymnastics.

8. **Bioenergetic.** Bioenergetic therapy in all of its forms.

MRI. It is incidentally worth remarking upon a recent conquest of medical technology – a veritable revolution in the diagnosis of infirmities – the construction of the magnetic resonance imaging (MRI) camera, which allows the extremely detailed imaging of diseased organs or tissues, thereby allowing diagnoses that are much more accurate and precise, including those in the exploration of the brain and the nervous system. There has already been mention of the first *photography of thought* (*O Globo;* newspaper; daily; Rio de Janeiro, RJ, Brazil; June 16, 1998).

Signals. MRI does not use X-rays. It uses magnetic signals emitted by the nuclei of hydrogen atoms, an element present in the entire organism (*O Globo;* newspaper; daily; Year LIX; N. 18,449; Rio de Janeiro, RJ, Brazil; May 18, 1984; p. 29).

Diagnostic. MRI creates an artificial magnetic field 500 to 40,000 times greater than the earth's magnetic field. This field is so strong that it orients the electrons of the organism's atoms. To this is added another energy that is equal to that of a radio-frequency which, through resonance, changes the position of the lines of force of the electrons' movements. In this way, a special system of electrical transmission, functioning at approximately minus 868°F (-200°C), is captured and computerized in order to form an image. This apparatus allows spectrography, quantifying the chemical elements of the molecules, precisely indicating the concentration of substances such as phosphorus, sugar, sodium or oxygen in the organism (*O Globo;* newspaper; daily; Year LXIV; N. 20,103; Rio de Janeiro, RJ, Brazil; December 6, 1988; p. 16).

Ectoplasm. When consciential energy condenses in order to manifest in a compound condition in the substance called *ectoplasm*, it gives the sensation of coagulating, appearing to gather into globs inside the ectoplasmic sensitive's human body, congregating organic or biological components.

Sources. According to somatics, the human personality has 5 basic sources of vital energy, presented here in order of increasing importance:

1. **Ingestion.** Ingestion of solids and liquids.
2. **Respiration.** Respiration or organic oxygenation.
3. **Absorption.** Absorption of energy in the ordinary, physical waking state from plants, animals, persons, the soil and the sun, through primary, secondary and tertiary chakras.
4. **Sleep.** Sleep or cellular detoxification with a minor discoincidence of the vehicles of manifestation of the consciousness (personal number of hours of sleep).
5. **Projectability.** Projection of the consciousness in the psychosoma or direct absorption of cosmic energy (consciential projectability).

Production. The developed human transmitter of consciential energies – a charged holochakral battery or a source of supplementary force – feels that consciential energy, in certain circumstances, can produce heat, cold and a *prickling* sensation (para-esthesia) mainly in the hands. The individuals that he/she treats can come to him/her in a state of energetic imbalance, like *drained batteries* (imbalance of consciential energies).

Action. The action of consciential energy shows itself to be intimately associated with homeostatic mechanisms or, in other words, appears to maintain the human organism in a state of *optimal* operation, or full health.

Heat. Consciential energy provokes an alteration in molecular movement. This is why it produces heat during therapeutic transmissions between intraphysical consciousnesses, affecting the self-regulatory processes that maintain order in biological systems and, in this case, intensifying the capacity of the human organism to neutralize entropy, despite the fact that heat increases entropy. These chemical reactions are very powerful.

Matter. Through his/her emunctories, the human being constantly rids him/herself of various types of waste material, whether intestinal, vesical, pulmonary, vaginal, auditory or epidermal. It also continuously excretes mental paramatter, or the morphothosenes that populate the psychosphere of the individual's consciential microuniverse. Like many houses, the consciential microuniverse never completely cleans out its internal trash, which is generated on a continuous basis. The greater the person's physical weight and biological age, the greater his/her amount of waste matter may be. These excreted materials, when excessive, present low amounts of consciential energies that often influence the creation of the bioenergetic imbalances and blocks of the intraphysical consciousness.

Transmission. It is theorized that consciential energy is not conducted directly through the nervous system, but electrolytically, through the conjunctive tissue, transmitting information and signals in the surroundings of the surface of the human body.

Oxygen. On the other hand, it is generally accepted that immanent energy is intrinsic to the oxygen molecule (prana).

Motor. Consciential energy can manifest through the psychosoma as a motor force, still leaving many fundamental aspects to be researched, such as: intensity; potency; takeoff; extraphysical translocation; the action of the silver cord; telekinetic effects; interconsciential communication; and the interpretation of the nature of energy.

Therapeutic. Consciential energy also manifests as a therapeutic resource when used as a curative method that regards the human organism more as energy than as mass, still leaving the various related manifestations to be researched, such as: therapeutic exteriorization; *external* energy; the parapsychic channel; extraphysical energizations; magnetic self-defense; the influence of affinity or extraphysical empathy.

Antiquity. Treatment through the laying on of hands or direct energizations *(Reiki)* has been used by the Greeks, Egyptians, Hindus and Chinese since antiquity.

Insistence. Mechanist scientists still insist on placing consciential energy at the same level of fantasies such as phlogiston, ether, N-Rays, caloric, canals on Mars, *lysenkoism,* a perpetual motion machine, squaring a circle and others. Every paradigm change is very slow.

Evidence. Two facts that prove the existence of consciential energy, which can be transferred from a donor to a human receiver, have been demonstrated in the laboratory:

1. **Water.** Water treated with consciential energy changes the color of the solution of the crystal, giving a visual indication of the presence of energy.

2. **Tension.** The same water, when treated with consciential energy, shows a change in its surface tension, hydrogen bonds and the electrical properties of the water.

Modeling. The objective modeling of morphothosenes and moving waves can be distinguished in the shaping of forms through consciential energy. There are no 2 individuals alike, in terms of the qualities or characteristics of personal consciential energy (volume of manifestation, frequency, duration, accumulation, velocity, recomposition, dissipation, direction and other variables).

Characterization. Each human being can be classified by the essential characteristic or trace of the specific energies of his/her consciential microuniverse. This is the core of his/her individualizing holothosene.

Organ. When meeting a person, you can really define the type of consciential energies according to the predominant organ or system of that individual.

Parapsychism. These characteristics are undisguisable to the parapsychic acuity or sensitivity of the observer with bioenergetic self-control, although operating on an unconscious level in most individuals, whether victim-seducer or victim-seduced.

Case study. The following are 7 examples of these facts:

1. **Drainer.** The human drainer: the bioenergetically ill person; the woman in lack of affection.
2. **Psychomotricity.** A set of muscles: the fanatic athlete; the weightlifter (cerebellum).
3. **Palmochakras.** A pair of hands: the virtuoso; the specialized artisan.
4. **Sexochakra.** A sexual organ: the addicted sexaholic (sex-maniac); nymphomaniac.
5. **Umbilicochakra.** A stomach: the gourmet; the overweight female gourmand.
6. **Cardiochakra.** A heart: the religious consoler (consolation task); the tearful artist (infantilism).
7. **Coronochakra.** A brain: the self-aware erudite; the mature social being.

Fetus. The interfacing of consciential energies coming from the auric coupling of the state of gestation, between the pregnant woman and the consciousness of the fetus, probably somehow profoundly affects the resomatic directives or conditions of the recent-resomant extraphysical consciousness.

Prematurity. It can thus be asked: "What are the real energetic consequences for the resomant extraphysical consciousness that passes through *fetal infancy* or, in other words, through the period between birth as a premature infant (from sixteen weeks on) and the date on which it would otherwise be born as a full-term baby (forty weeks)?"

Hypothesis. The best research hypothesis, in this case, is a survey of the levels of awareness and chakral operation of adults who were born prematurely and those who were full-term babies. This research has still not been performed. Might prematurely born individuals be more susceptible to bioenergetic imbalance?

Systems. Today, in various countries, acupuncture, moxibustion and acupressure, as readily accepted scientific norms, use knowledge of the physical-extraphysical bioenergetic system, based upon the *holistic theory* and the structure of the bioplasmic body as a fourth organic system equivalent to the 3 other systems: the nervous system, the circulatory system and the lymphatic system. Its techniques make use of the acupuncture points, the system of meridians, the system of ducts or circuits of low resistance, which are directly related to the endocrine system.

Therapies. Therefore, consciential energy is already involved in various fields of medicine and in controversial alternative therapies. Only those who do not wish to see this fact do not perceive it.

Future. It is rational to forecast that in the future all children, just as they are currently obliged by law to have vaccines and compulsory basic education, will legally be obligated to become familiar with and control the procedures of energetic reception, transmission and self-defense through the self-aware mobilization of bioenergy (VS).

Anomalies. To what degree is the consciential energy of the experimenter (unknown source of error) responsible for the surprising and inexplicable apparent (or occult) effects in the laboratory that can be reproduced for a while (anomalous results or simple synchronistic, isolated *coincidences*) and finally disappear without trace? These facts are related to the sheep-goat effects and experimenter effects.

Bibliography: Alverga (18, p. 81), Baraduc (76, p. 93), Bedford (103, p. 171), Gibier (587, p. 114), Meek (1028, p. 165), Scott (1529, p. 62), Walker (1781, p. 15), Wang (1794, p. 151), White (1831, p. 443), Yogananda (1894, p. 235).

287. MOBILIZATION OF CONSCIENTIAL ENERGIES

Definition. Mobilization of consciential energy: the act of will whereby the intraphysical consciousness sponsors the circulation of consciential energies inside and outside his/her human body, redirecting and normalizing their flows (see fig. 287, p. 1,139).

Synonymy: circulation of consciential energy; energetic normalization; energization.

Scale. Intraphysical consciousnesses can be placed into 4 categories, in an ascending scale of excellence with regard to their relationship with consciential energy:

1. **Ignorant.** The intraphysical consciousness who is completely unaware of the subject of consciential energies.

2. **Theoretician.** The intraphysical consciousness who is theoretically familiar with consciential energy but has not had any self-aware experience with his/her transcendent reality.

3. **Superficial.** The intraphysical consciousness who, as well as having a theoretical understanding of the subject, has already had some experimental, practical, superficial or occasional contact with consciential energy in a self-aware manner.

4. **Technique.** The intraphysical consciousness who has a theoretical and practical (theorical) understanding of consciential energy and technically applies it, through the impulsion of his/her will, consciously controlling the operation of the chakras.

Greatnesses. Strictly speaking, this ascending scale of excellence, aside from measuring the degree of theorical experience of intraphysical consciousnesses with consciential energy – the *touchstone* of all basic phenomena of life on this planet – indisputably shows 3 other greatnesses of the human personality:

1. **Phenomena.** The precise level of the intraphysical consciousness' awareness regarding parapsychic phenomena in general (evolutiology).

2. **Projectability.** The intraphysical consciousness' level of projective excellence (consciential states).

3. **Parapsychism.** The intraphysical consciousness' level of parapsychic development (multidimensional exchanges).

Reservoirs. Consciential energy, being as subtle as it is powerful, penetrates human bodies and the bodies of subhuman animals. We all have a certain amount of it throughout the body, but mainly in certain reservoirs such as the cerebrospinal axis and sympathetic plexuses, like the solar plexus, or in the abdominal brain (umbilicochakra).

Types. In mobilization of consciential energy, any intraphysical consciousness can, on his/her own, execute 3 types of simpler, basic procedures, or the basic mobilization of energies (BME):

1. **Circulation.** The circulation of consciential energies in a closed circuit.
2. **Reception.** The reception or absorption of consciential energies.
3. **Release.** The exteriorization or release of consciential energies.

Will. The execution of any of theses 3 basic procedures has to start from the practitioner's will.

Key. Ironclad, granitic or steely will is the key that unlocks the ample performance of consciential energetic procedures, turning the psychosoma and holochakra together into an energy mobilization center.

Mobilization. The mobilization of consciential energies predisposes the animist practitioner to serve as a sensitive for extraphysical consciousnesses which are technicians in all energetic operations in favor of intraphysical or extraphysical beings.

Perceptions. The natural development of sensitivity in the application or mobilization of energies allows the animist-sensitive, with time and repeated experiences, to perceive energetic manifestations within him/herself when alone, extending the energetic pathways within his/her vehicles of consciential manifestation, or in the energetic current formed by the group of receptor and donor individuals, and extraphysical consciousnesses, when gathered in a collective experiment of bioenergetic exteriorization or irradiation.

Points. There are 3 points of access that can be used in order to approach the energetic psychosphere of an intraphysical consciousness in a practical, para-anatomical, paraphysiological and paratherapeutic manner:

1. **Hands.** Through one's own hands or fingers (palmochakras) – without making physical contact (between yourself and the other person) – pointing them directly at the forehead (coronochakra and frontochakra) of the child or adult at a distance of 1 3/8" (3 cm).

2. **Middle.** Pointing the middle finger of one of the hands, or the middle fingers of both hands, for example – at a distance of 1 3/8" (3 cm), without making physical contact – toward the middle finger of one of the hands of the person under analysis (palmochakras, cardiochakra and laryngochakra).

3. **Hallux.** Performing the same procedure (middle fingers of the hand) at a distance of 1 3/8" (3 cm) – without making physical contact – toward the big toe or hallux of one of the person's (bare) feet (sexochakra).

Procedures. Five different conscientiotherapy practices can be performed through these probings or procedures.

1. **Affinity.** Establish direct auric coupling with someone.

2. **Holochakra.** Therapeutically balance the person's holochakra through bioenergetic unblocking and balancing.

3. **Evaluation.** Assess or evaluate the bioenergetic potentialities of an individual or evolutient.

4. **Paradiagnosis.** Establish deep sympathetic assimilation with an evolutient with the specific objective of paradiagnosis or even a prolonged therapy with more long-lasting results (self-remission).

5. **Self-discrimination.** Allow the person to discriminate his/her sensations regarding exteriorized consciential energies and thereby perform a candid analysis of the level of awareness of his/her own holochakra or of specific chakras.

Performance. The practitioner will notice that his/her energetic performance varies from one day to another, being vanquished or victorious from the endeavor, according to his/her prior preparation, goodwill, disposition, donation, passivation, optimization, *self-maintenance in good shape* or efficiency in cooperating with assistential energetic services, such as during the daily practices of penta.

Procedures. Thus, if the practitioner wishes to perform research by extending him/herself throughout the environment, he/she will perceive the following 39 very distinct occurrences or technical procedures within holochakrology and thosenology, listed here in alphabetical order:

1. **Absorption.** The acquisition or interiorization of immanent and consciential energies to him/herself.

2. **Accumulation.** The localization, accumulation or storage of masses of condensed energies generated by the intraphysical consciousness him/herself and by all those intraphysical and extraphysical consciousnesses present.

3. **Assimilations.** Sympathetic assimilations (synchronism) and sympathetic deassimilations performed by the decided and more potent will.

4. **Asynchronies.** Divergences or asynchronies of energetic flow, or *breaking the chain* with internal and *external* agents (xenothosenes).

5. **Balances.** Various instances of energetic balancing or unblocking that pertain to that person and others (groupthosene).

6. **Blocking.** The blocking and unblocking (balancing and detoxification) of the energetic flows of others when unhealthy or intrusive to the microuniverse of that person or to the energy current already installed and consolidated through affinity.

7. **Category.** The category of energies that are generally present.

8. **Chakra.** The (personal) chakra, the manifestations of which predominate in the energy current.

9. **Continuity.** Verification of the dynamic of the rare continuous flow of consciential energies in certain assistential, emergency and critical situations.

10. **Coupling.** Auric coupling and uncoupling established between intraphysical and extraphysical consciousnesses by the decided will.

11. **Direction.** The direction, orientation, course and destination intentionally applied to assistential energetic flows.

12. **Discrimination.** The clear identification and specification of consciential energies all the time.

13. **Dissipation.** The location and identification of the spreading, dispersion or dissipation of consciential energies.

14. **Donors.** Participants who are (more "connected") self-aware maintainers and donors or sustainers of the current of consciential energies.

15. **Draining.** The rupture or draining of the energetic current.

16. **Duration.** The duration, permanence or predominance of a specific dynamic of energetic flows.

17. **Empathy.** The strong or weak energetically associated affinities of those persons present (empathy, homothosenes, orthothosenes).

18. **Encapsulations.** The energetic "cysts" of intraphysical and extraphysical consciousnesses which have no affinity with the environment (holothosene) and are encapsulated or dependent upon extraphysical intruders *(satellites of intruders)*.

19. **Exteriorization.** The release, exteriorization or self-aware transference of consciential energies from one intraphysical consciousness to another, from one object to another and from one environment to another.

20. **Homogenization.** The homogeneity of bioenergetic discharge or the uniformity of the intense flow of consciential energies of continuous action.

21. **Increase.** An increase or decrease in the volume (impulsion) of energetic flow.

22. **Increases.** Increases in *external* energies (heterothosenes) that may be healthy or unhealthy.

23. **Intensity.** The intensity of flow or of energy "pulsations" that pass by.

24. **Intermittence.** The identification of the energetic flow occurring through *streams of discharge* of consciential energies.

25. **Loss.** The apparent temporary loss (transference) of energies during assistential works.

26. **Pathothosene.** The identification of the type of pathothosene of the person who is distracted or parapsychically absent (encapsulated) from similar manifestations ("disconnected") within the chain of assistential energies.

27. **Paths.** The paths of the circulation of energies both inside and outside the environment or, in other words: the continuous dynamic or the self-aware mobilization of personal and group energies (materthosene or group thosene).

28. **Recomposition.** The normalization of *immanent* energy assimilation and the recomposition of personal levels of *consciential* energies of the holochakra (energetic homeostasis).

29. **Reduction.** A reduction in the volume of energetic flow generated by personal willpower.

30. **Reinforcement.** The lucid reception of additions or *showers* of reinforcing and unexpected consciential energies that envelop intraphysical consciousnesses.

31. **Reunification.** The energetic supply made in favor of homogenization of the frequencies of energies or of thosenes, when energetic surpluses bridge the gaps and discontinuity in the flows, restoring the vital current.

32. **Rhythm.** The frequency, rhythmic pulsation or precise, average or predominant rhythm of the personal energetic flow.

33. **Specification.** The specification of energetic flows that are *in streams* or are continuous.

34. **Synchronizations.** Synchronizations with intraphysical and extraphysical external agents.

35. **Temperature.** The sensation of a predominantly hot or cold temperature in manifestations (somatic biothermia), with somatic heating or cooling occurring through consciential energies.

36. *Tentacles.* The involving energetic *tentacles* that can be intercepted and annulled through the determination of the will.

37. **Vacillations.** The mental or *xenothosenic* vacillations of those persons present.

38. **Velocity.** The willful force of the impulsion of the energetic flow or the velocity of the energetic discharge generated by the will stemming from the materthosene and *median* will of the group performing assistential services.

39. **VS.** The installation of a prophylactic vibrational state (VS) at the beginning and end of interconsciential energetic assistance.

Fields. The fields of consciential energies installed in the Extension Course in Projectiology and Conscientiology 2 (ECP2), of the International Institute of Projectiology and Conscientiology, were conceived and developed in order to allow practical observation and detailed testing with all of the energetic procedures listed herein.

Bibliography: Alverga (18, p. 81), Gibier (587, p. 135).

---

288. CLOSED CIRCULATION OF ENERGIES TECHNIQUE

Definition. Closed circulation of energies: conscious control of energetic movements inside yourself, from your head to your feet and hands, and back to your head.

Synonymy: closed energization; dynamization of the vibrational state; energies in closed circuit; internal energetic circulation.

Will. The dimension, intensity, velocity and duration of the closed circulation of consciential energies vary according to your active will (see fig. 288, p. 1,139).

Uses. Among the uses of the control of the closed circulation of energies by your intraphysical consciousness inside your own human organism and your other coincident vehicles, at least the following 6 can be singled out:

1. **VS.** Installation of the vibrational state (VS), a condition that predisposes even a lucid takeoff of your consciousness projected in the psychosoma.

2. **Self-confidence.** Intense motivation, providing you self-confidence to use your own consciential energies and allowing you to distinguish external energies that you receive.

3. **Digestion.** Acceleration of your digestion in appropriate occasions of interconsciential assistance.

4. **Self-cure.** Heal organic disturbances, mini-illnesses and minor-indispositions.

5. **Prophylaxis.** Obtain one thousand and one positive and prophylactic consciential resources that are easily understood by you or anyone else (consolation task, clarification task, penta).

6. **Self-defenses.** Completely block the entrance of undesirable energies to your inner world, thereby augmenting your energetic self-defenses (self-encapsulation).

Practice. Circulation of energy, without exteriorizing, from the head to the feet and from the feet back to the head, can be performed many times. Soon thereafter, the process will be changed to the condition of an extremely intense vibrational state throughout all vehicles of manifestation of the consciousness. This practice sterilizes the environment in a vibratory manner, provides a great sense of well-being, a positive disposition and self-confidence to the intraphysical consciousness.

Procedures. The closed-circuit energetic self-defense technique can be structured around 6 basic procedures:

1. **Feet.** Remain erect, with feet astride. Close the eyelids. Let the arms drop alongside the body. Direct the flow (or influx) of your energies, through the impulsion of the will, from the head to the hands and feet. Do not worry if you do not know what bioenergy is. Continued practice will show you the entire energetic reality. If you feel nothing during the first attempts, do not be concerned. Persist and you will end up feeling something. This is inevitable because it is part of the paraphysiological development of us all.

2. **Head.** Return the flow of the energies, through the impulsion of your decided will, from the feet to the head. At this point, you will already be able to identify the direction of the energetic flow upwards, contrary to the previous flow.

3. **Discrimination.** Repeat the same procedure 10 times, perceiving and discriminating the flow of energies sweeping the various parts and organs of your human body. At this point, the unblocking, balancing and potentiation of your energies in your energetic centers and points begins.

4. **Speed.** Continue the same procedures, now gradually increasing the speed (or rhythm) of the impulsion of the flow of energies.

5. **Intensity.** Continue with the same procedures, now maximally increasing the intensity (rhythm or volume) of the flow of energies. This flow will comprise progressively larger and more potent circuits, which you will perceive.

6. **Vibrational.** Finally, install the vibrational state. The flow and the closed circuit disappears and your entire psychosphere becomes completely "lit up", "dazzling", or "incandescent" with the vibrating energies.

Repetitions. Endeavor to repeat the entire process many times a day to start with, in different conditions, situations and circumstances, always remaining erect (standing up) if possible. The following are examples: in the bathroom nude; wearing informal attire; wearing social attire; holding packages; in the sun; in the rain; and in other various conditions.

Alert. It is necessary to perform the circulation of energies in the most diverse existential circumstances and situations because we never know when we will need more energetic defenses. Diuturnal life always presents many surprises and not all of them are welcome or agreeable. We should be energetically ready and alert 24 hours a day, all year, our whole life.

Note. We should never use any parapsychophysical artifices or crutches, regardless of their nature or pretext, with the intention of optimizing or "enriching" the process of installation and operation of the vibrational state, because this will drastically impede the development of self-confidence in our own consciential energies and their applications. The following 2 examples are to be avoided, in this case: imagination as a *psychological crutch*; the vibrating chair as a *physical crutch*.

Crutch. It is always wise to bear in mind that, in our consciential condition while in the projected state, or even while in the extraphysical state, in the post-desomatic intermissive period, after the decomposition of our human body, neither the author nor you will have any physical object at hand to serve as a parapsychophysical crutch in our energetic self-defense when faced with interconsciential attacks from ill extraphysical consciousnesses.

Immaturity. When you use any artifice or crutch, except for the impulsion of your unbreakable will, you erroneously and lazily endeavor to transfer the effort you need in order to develop your energies through your dynamized will and improve your notably emotional self-control to the "providential" crutch. This is, therefore, an attitude that is infantile, conscientially immature and intraconscientially regressive, as well as being repressive and escapist. It is also an indefensible harmful postponement of something that we all have to confront either now or later, here or elsewhere.

Bibliography: Vieira (1762, p. 19).

289. RECEPTION OF CONSCIENTIAL ENERGIES TECHNIQUE

Definition. Reception of energies: conscious or unconscious absorption and interiorization of forces assimilated from intraphysical and extraphysical consciousnesses, as well as from natural sources (plants, water and others) that are in the surroundings of the intraphysical consciousness.

Synonymy: conscious energetic absorption; conscious energy assimilation; conscious extraction of external energy.

Neutrality. In the physical and extraphysical consciential encounters of human life, rarely does someone always remain neutral regarding the bioenergetic aspect or the energies of consciential principles or immanent energies in general.

Balance. Generally speaking, you either give or absorb energies from others almost constantly, through the chakras (force centers) and energetic points (meridians) of the holochakra (vital body), keeping yourself energetically balanced (healthy) or unbalanced (ill).

Types. There are many types of reception of energies, such as the following 4:

1. **Reception.** Received (magnetic) energization, whether perceptible or imperceptible.
2. **Hydromagnetic.** The hydromagnetic shower.
3. **Aeromagnetic.** Aeromagnetic refrigeration.
4. **Post-projective.** The post-projective energetic shower.

Receiver. The receiver of consciential energies is also known as a *centripetal person*. The opposite, the donor of consciential energies, is the *centrifugal person*.

Coupling. In auric coupling, absorption as well as exteriorization of energies can occur on the part of one or another consciousness which consciously or unconsciously allows a temporary energetic union or, in other words, the homogenization of the energies of both.

Pathological. The pathological absorption of energies is energetic vampirization. It can also be intentional or unconscious on the part of the receiver or, in the case of an ill person, one who suffers from constant imbalance in the circulation of his/her physical-extraphysical energies.

Contraband. The intentional acquisition of energies from others, plants and objects, should never get to the point of vampirism or the frank parasitism of draining the individual, animal or plant in *energetic contraband*. This is similar, for example, to the concise system of the tapper Hestreo – a true vampire technician – who drains the seringa tree to the point where he removes all the sap and leaves it completely dehydrated or dry.

Bibliography: Vieira (1762, p. 51).

290. ABSORPTION OF EXTRAPHYSICAL ENERGIES TECHNIQUE

Definition. Absorption of energies from the extraphysical or cosmic dimension: the act wherein your consciousness projected in the psychosoma absorbs energy like an extraphysical accumulator.

Synonymy: absorption of immanent energy; acquisition of cosmic energy; extraphysical assimilation of prana; process of extraphysical nutrition.

Sources. The absorption of cosmic energies – or direct immanent energy transformed into indirect consciential energy – through projection in the psychosoma, is the human personality's fifth basic source of vital energy, after alimentation, respiration, energetic absorption during the ordinary waking state and the state of natural sleep (see fig. 290, p. 1,140).

Sleep. Sleep permits two categories of basic absorption of energies:

1. **Minor.** The minor absorption of prana or cosmic energies trough the miniprojection of your psychosoma near your human body, in the intraphysical base or energetically shielded chamber.

2. **Major.** The major absorption of cosmic energy through the maxiprojection of your psychosoma some distance from your intraphysical base.

Influences. The splenochakra of the holochakra-psychosoma set is attributed with the function of absorption of cosmic energies by the projected intraphysical consciousness, when its psychosoma is affected by 3 basic influences, listed below in order of decreasing importance:

1. **Locations.** Extraphysical locations which are natural reservoirs of prana, e.g.: the ocean, rivers, vegetation and others.

2. **Distance.** The physical distance between the projected psychosoma and the human body, by virtue of extraphysical freedom, volitation and greater absorption.

3. **Time.** The duration of the consciential projection, which has a minor influence because the time factor gradually disappears when the consciousness is extraphysically (conscientially) more *distant* from the human body that was left inactive at the intraphysical base.

Law. The capacity to absorb cosmic energies increases in direct proportion to the physical distance between your projected psychosoma (a semiphysical body) and your human, physical and inactive body.

Uses. Within the uses of absorption of cosmic energies, at least the following 3 can be singled out:

1. **Health.** Recuperation of physical and mental health.

2. **Sleep.** Recuperation from a sleepless night (correction of one's personal sleep schedule).

3. **LPB.** Increased possibilities for improving projective performance or your lucid projectability (LPB).

Regeneration. During the natural sleep state, which allows extracorporeal sleep, and during the consciential projection condition, whether nonlucid, semilucid or lucid, the psychosoma, now detached from the human body, has more opportunity and possibility to work toward the regeneration and recuperation of this same human body through absorption of cosmic energies. It thereby intensifies the potentialities of the holochakra (energetic parabody) as well as more rapidly curing fractures and luxations, detoxifying the organs and renewing the physiology of the organic systems.

Analogy. The absorption of cosmic energies by the projected psychosoma is somewhat analogous to the absorption of luminous energy, or photons, by a plastic switch or commutator. This is a wall mounted device that can interrupt or reestablish continuity in an electrical circuit and, after being exposed to the light of an electric lamp, creates a temporary weak luminosity in the typical darkness of the closed bedroom.

Commutator. The luminous commutator is, due to the phenomenon of phosphorescence, frequently used nowadays in order to provide orientation in dark, closed environments. This is because it illuminates and maintains visual reference points, so that persons do not lose their sense of direction upon moving about in a penumbra or in darkness.

Hypotheses. The absorption of cosmic energies raises various questions or hypotheses for research, such as the following two:

1. **Light.** Does the absorption of cosmic energies also constitute an absorption of luminous energy by the psychosoma?

2. **Psychosomatics.** Is the psychosoma of the intraphysical consciousness which projects very frequently more luminous than the psychosoma of average human beings?

Force. An increase in personal force, physical and psychic disposition of the intraphysical consciousness who projects in the psychosoma far from the physical base is a fact that is observed by veteran consciential projectors. On the other hand, it is not known to what degree this sensation of force and disposition stems from the positive parapsychic conditions of the intraphysical projector.

Proof. There is still no known scientific process that can prove the conjectures and questions of this chapter. However, it is possible to obtain individual and definitive evidence through projective practices. Skeptics and interested individuals are therefore urged to perform research and seek out proof by producing some prolonged lucid projections at a distance in the psychosoma.

CHSC. Major research with consciential energies can be performed in the many independent and isolated laboratories at the Center for Higher Studies of the Consciousness (CHSC), in Iguassu Falls, PR, Brazil, which are specially constructed for this purpose.

Transmission. The silver cord or, more precisely, the holochakra transmits the absorbed energies directly through the projected psychosoma to the cells of the human body.

Volitation. Extraphysical volitation, obviously with the consequent absorption of cosmic energies and the reinvigoration of the paraphysiology and physiology in general, in certain conditions, increases the manifestations of the sexochakra and intensifies the sexual excitation (libido) of the lucid projector in the ordinary, physical waking state.

Aphrodisiac. In this case, consciential projection works like an infallible aphrodisiac. The veteran projector should be cautious with regard to intrusions, self-intrusions and self-corruptions in view of cosmoethics. This is like walking a razor's edge. The monogamous human being who is sexually mature and settled into a harmonized and stable affectionate relationship − being a partner of an evolutionary duo − is the one who is better off in this process. It is important to note that the physical age of the intraphysical consciousness has little influence in these occurrences.

Bibliography: Andrade (27, p. 159), Andreas (36, p. 52), Muldoon (1105, p. 142).

291. EXTERIORIZATION OF CONSCIENTIAL ENERGIES

Definition. Exteriorization of consciential energies: the act wherein the consciousness emits, through one or more of its vehicles of manifestation, consciential energies that are temporarily accumulated inside it or are passing through it (see fig. 291, p. 1,140).

Synonymy: biotherapy; donation of energies; energetic emission; extravasation of *od;* looseness of the holochakra technique; self-aware bioenergetic projection.

Types. Among the types of exteriorization of consciential energies of the intraphysical consciousness, at least the following 6 can be singled out:

1. **Self-lucidity.** Conscious or unconscious energetic exteriorization.

2. **Dimension.** Energetic exteriorization produced in the ordinary, physical waking state or in the extraphysical dimension.

3. **Penta.** The energizations that are apparently emitted into the void during the daily, regular and technical practices of penta.

4. **Individuality.** The energizations that are performed solitarily, alone or only with the projector as an intraphysical being.

5. **Groupality.** The energizations that are performed in a group (chains) of intraphysical beings (intraphysical consciousnesses and subhuman animals).

6. **Assisted.** The energetic transmission emitted to assisted intraphysical beings as well as to energivorous and parapsychotic post-desomatic extraphysical consciousnesses.

Donor. The donor of consciential energies is also known as a *centrifugal person*.

Uses. Among the basic uses of exteriorization of consciential energies, at least the following 8 can be singled out:

1. **Holochakra.** Improvement in the aura of health (holochakra) in the lucid projector's psychosphere (holothosene).

2. **Base.** Extraphysical cleansing of the lucid projector's intraphysical base (energetically shielded chamber).

3. **Projections.** A parapsychic coadjutant to lucid projections, especially those that are assisted, programmed or sponsored by extraphysical helpers.

4. **Assistance.** A complement to extraphysical assistential tasks performed during periods of lucid projection.

5. **Deintrusions.** Cooperation in the tasks of extraphysical rescue, extraphysical deintrusion and the act of assistentially serving as *interconsciential bait*.

6. **Psychosomatics.** The positive rarefaction of the psychosoma, thereby better predisposing one to projections with continuous self-awareness.

7. **Blocking.** The blocking or neutralization of certain intrusive parapsychic manifestations from other beings in relation to oneself, such as in the performance of the clairvoyance of a clairvoyant sensitive.

8. **Encounters.** Self-defense encounters or energetic confrontations with ill extraphysical consciousnesses and with intraphysical beings who are either in the waking state or projected, on certain occasions.

Detection. Over the decades, the author has observed 4 apparently diverse occurrences that nevertheless present characteristics which are common to the intensification of consciential energies that are exteriorized, or psychophysiological, active and detectable:

1. **Burn.** The patient who was recently burned in the open air and was an inpatient at a specialized clinic, after being saved from a violent electric discharge of lightning that originated from a cloud and terminated in the ground (thunderbolt, flash of lightning). This fleeting intensification of consciential energies generally disappears shortly after leaving the clinic.

2. **Abducted.** The burn victim who affirmed having been "abducted by an unidentified flying object", having experienced the so-called contact of the third kind of UFOlogy, manifesting a period of hours of total amnesia that are only recoverable through hypnotic mnemonic regression. Some abductees are energetically active, in this state, 4 years after the event.

3. **Sexochakra.** The person ("recent extraphysical burn victim") who recently suffered an abrupt awakening of the kundalini (sexochakra), the release of the so-called *serpentine fire* of the sexochakra, with or without awareness of his/her state, which can disappear after a short while or may last for decades.

4. **Sensitive.** The experienced sensitive who is able, at any moment, through the impulsion of his/her own will, to perceive and trigger the reception as well as the exteriorization of energies from and to living beings, objects and human environments, whether they are active sensitives of the parapsychism of physical effects, energy transmitters, psychic parasurgeons, telekineticists or veteran lucid projectors. This state generally lasts longer than the others.

Transformations. These 4 personality types are listed here in ascending order of their energetic possibilities, although any of the first 3 can become a developed sensitive over time. These experiences provoke the *healthy looseness of the holochakra* for a considerably prolonged period.

Potenkinetic. The author proposes the term *potenkinetic* to characterize the condition of the vehicles of manifestation of the intraphysical consciousness, which determines his/her capacity for transmitting and receiving consciential energy, more popularly known as bioenergy.

Bibliography: Gibier (587, p. 136), Machado (968, p. 37), Pisani (1248, p. 285), Schutel (1525, p. 25), Targ (1651, p. 253), Vieira (1762, p. 51), White (1831, p. 94).

---

292. EXTERIORIZATION OF CONSCIENTIAL ENERGIES TECHNIQUE

Isolation. The exteriorization of energies, as a physical-extraphysical self-hygiene technique and a coadjutant in the development of lucid consciential projections, can be produced by you whenever needed, although it is preferable to do so in an environment that allows physical isolation.

Locations. You can practice the exteriorization of energies: at an ill person's bedside; at an assistential institution through the application of public energizations; through energizations apparently into the distance, in the privacy of your home, in the practices of penta.

Omni-interaction. Energetic omni-interaction can be sought by the individual using mental force through evocation or mental irradiation in an effort to bring together all living beings, ranging from viruses, fish, insects, larger animals, humans and extraphysical consciousnesses, all the way to those consciousnesses in the pure mentalsomatic dimension, for a single universalistic objective of perfect harmony: "May the best occur for everyone."

Therapeutic. The following are 5 factors that play fundamental roles in the exteriorization of therapeutic energies:

1. **Volition.** Your will.
2. **Hands.** The imposition of your hands.
3. **Movement.** Energetic movement with your arms and hands, in certain cases.
4. **Visualization.** The intentional visualization of the desired therapeutic effect.
5. **Receptor.** The will of the recipient consciousness.

Law. The facts show a basic law of projectiology that is quite edifying: those who are able to exteriorize (project) their consciential energies, with lucidity, only using the impulsion of the will, are also able to project (exteriorize) their own consciousness, with lucidity, from the human body, using only the impulsion of the will. One needs only to desire and be sufficiently motivated toward this objective.

Lungs. In the beginning of the practice of mobilization of consciential energy – sponsored by one's own will, or even when aided by a helper – the act of exteriorization is generally accompanied by *expiration* or exhalation and the act of reception of energies is accompanied by, or synchronized with, *inspiration* or inhalation (lungs).

Sensations. The following are 5 of the most common primary sensations experienced in the exteriorization of consciential energies:

1. *Electricity.* A type of *internal electricity.*
2. **Numbness.** Localized physical numbness (torpidity).
3. *Prickling.* A *prickling* sensation on the hands, fingers, arms and cheeks (para-esthesia).
4. **Myology.** Muscular contractions, as in the hands, arms, neck and around the head (encephalon).
5. **Heterocommand.** Imperious impulses that are *external* or commanded by another intangible or extraphysical consciousness, from outside oneself (heterocommand).

Pulsation. "Energetic cerebral pulsation" or neuronal pulsation is the classic sensation of mobilization of consciential energies experienced by the animist intraphysical consciousness or, in other words, provoked by the intraphysical consciousness him/herself without anyone's interference, either from a sensitive, assistance from an extraphysical consciousness, or even from a projected intraphysical consciousness.

Occurrences. Inoffensive and agreeable energetic cerebral pulsation may be accompanied by various organic occurrences, such as the following 10:

1. **Energization.** Powerful cerebral energization.
2. **Contractions.** Muscular contractions throughout the head.
3. **Sounds.** Intracranial sounds.
4. **Vibrations.** Tympanic vibrations.
5. **Respiration.** Sounds of the energetic transmissions that may or may not be synchronized with the respiration or heartbeat.
6. **Force.** A sensation of vigorous force, "electricity in the arms, hands and fingers."
7. **Goose bumps.** Generalized goose bumps.
8. **Temperature.** Changes in body temperature.
9. **Rhythm.** Changes in the rhythm and intensity of energetic transmission.
10. **Location.** The precise sensation of the location of the energetic current in the human body.

Four-hands. During energetic exteriorizations, such as when performing penta, at a set time, in moments of very intense discharges, while you are semi-possessed by an extraphysical helper, the 4-hands phenomenon sometimes occurs, namely, two other hands seem to work together with your hands in perfect synchrony. This happens due to the departure of your extraphysical hands (parahands) from the state of coincidence of the vehicles of manifestation (fragmented projection).

Limitation. The exteriorization of energies should not reach the point of draining or *physically* weakening the practitioner. Thus, it is not necessary for the novice, for example, to perform more than 11 major therapeutic transmissions everyday, in order to preserve his/her health and well-being. The energies are inexhaustible, but the inactive muscle fibers can be affected.

Transmissions. The number 11 does not have any mystical connotation here. In fact, there are only 10 transmissions, because the first one almost always corresponds to a preparation or simple energetic reception by the transmitter (recovery or warm-up).

Psychomotricity. It is pointless for you to help others to cure themselves and become sick yourself, thereby cutting off the energetic source. For this reason, it should be dosed only with regard to psychomotricity or lack of ability or physical exercises (sedentariness, inactivity) when one is beginning the assistential energetic practices.

Factors. Within this context, one principle should be borne in mind: consciential energies are, above all, inexhaustible because immanent energies are endless and, strictly speaking, are independent from the element of time or space.

Last. It should be stressed that the eleventh energetic transmission, namely the last one, generally pertains to direct extraphysical assistance performed inside the actual area of the physical base, also serving to leave the practitioner's environment extraphysically sanitized (energetically shielded chamber, healthy personal holothosene).

Bibliography: Gibier (587, p. 136), Reis (1384, p. 73).

---

293. PENTA TECHNIQUE

Definition. Penta: the *pe*rsonal *e*nergetic *ta*sk or energetic transmission from the intraphysical consciousness – commanded by an extraphysical helper while the practitioner is in the ordinary waking state – directly to extraphysical consciousnesses or projected intraphysical consciousnesses, all of which are intangible and invisible to ordinary human vision (see fig. 293, p. 1,141).

Synonymy: assistential session of "me alone"; energization of the "unknown patient" (victim or persecutor); individual animic-parapsychic session; parapsychic self-experiment; service of energetic balancing; solitary passivity; solitary psychogroup; the practice of energization to the void.

Preparation. In the daily penta practice, you, as a solitary sensitive, make yourself comfortable on a bed, preferably in the dark, relax, meditate and become mentally and muscularly passive to the extraphysical helper. Incorporation or semi-incorporation transpires in order for the transmission of assistential consciential energies to take place while the practitioner is seated or standing (erect).

Assistance. The anonymous extraphysical assistance performed through the practices of penta, realized within the *period of human anguish* – between 6:00 PM and 10:00 PM – must be performed daily, including weekends, which bring the *Sunday neurosis* to individuals in lack of affection who, while removed from the daily routine, are forced to confront the shallowness and emptiness of their lives.

Period. It should be stressed that, according to available statistics, 6:00 PM is the time at which the greatest number of intraphysical beings undergo desoma throughout the world.

Occurrences. After the incontestable action of another intelligence upon your vehicles of manifestation – the human body, the holochakra and the psychosoma – you may experience at least the following 8 events:

1. Lucid projection.
2. Various clairvoyant episodes.
3. Psychophonic monologue.
4. Changes in the position of the soma.
5. Numbness of the lips and face.
6. Sensation of cold air, most often in the hands.
7. Energetic cerebral pulsations.
8. Sensation of dematerialization of the fingers and even the hands.

Flame. The energy exteriorizations can often give the impression that your human body has become an enormous flame, a 9'10" (3 m) long tongue of fire that is extremely hot at the perimeter and ice cold at the center, whipping forward and upward and reverberating as if it were a focus of light expanding and contracting in powerful, intelligent and controlled alternating outward and inward movements.

Sounds. The sounds of the vibrations pass through your head and appear to leave through your arms and hands like drums being beaten intelligently or the cadence of a one-word mantra which is not spoken, but is repeatedly heard with greater or lesser acceleration.

Movements. The synchronous, frenetic, spasmodic distributing movements made with the arms and hands during benign semi-possession are aimed toward the assistance of intraphysical and extraphysical consciousnesses through 3 distinct operations which are almost always interconnected:

1. **Exteriorization.** Exteriorization of immanent-consciential energies.
2. **Dematerialization.** Temporary fleeting dematerialization of parts of the animist-sensitive's human body.
3. **Ectoplasmy.** The extraction of your human ectoplasm, exclusively for therapeutic purposes.

Distributors. The para-arms and para-hands of the psychosoma of the practitioner are the real distributors of energy, under the actual command of a helper, the basic energetic transmitter.

Environment. An ambient temperature below 68°F (20°C) facilitates the practicing or intensification of the exteriorizations of assistential energies.

Concepts. In order to maintain syntony, balance, and intensify the operations while in the vibrational state during major exteriorizations of energy, the helper instills intuition that leads the animist-sensitive, when more aware, to inevitably reflect upon concepts which, while being disparate at first sight, are related by their unquestionably logical connections to each other and to the service-by-3, similar to the following: the uncreated creator; self-gestation; the phoenix; eternity; the infinity of the past; the infinity of the future; omnipotence; implosion; potential to the nth degree; perpetual motion machine; black hole; bottomless sack.

Development. It seems that the more evolved a consciousness is, the more intensity its energetic potential has and the less consciential effort and time is required in order to complete its energetic replenishment and sympathetic deassimilation.

Time. At the beginning of the exercises, the energetic irradiations take up to an hour. With time, a daily development occurs allowing the 11 discharges to be completed in an individual session of only 25 to 45 minutes.

Transmissions. Each *series* of energetic discharges corresponds to at least 50 transmission-contractions. Thus, 550 to 750 transmissions will be performed by the end of each daily session.

Evolution. At a more advanced stage, the helpers transform the projector's physical base into an extraphysical medical clinic or, in other words, a multidimensional clinic for helping the intraphysical and extraphysical needy, unaided or dispossessed.

Observations. The following are 20 practical observations on the practice of penta:

1. **Warning.** The penta technique is not recommended for those who have never experienced impactful, ostensive parapsychic manifestations or to novices in terms of paraperceptiology, who are not yet parapsychically developed and who are not able to sufficiently control the processes of multidimensional interconsciential exchange.

2. **Parapsychism.** Only fairly developed sensitives – without serious problems of interconsciential intrusion, entirely confident in what they do, aware of the closed circulation of energies, reception of energies and transmission of consciential energies – should practice the daily exteriorization of energies at a set time.

3. **Recess.** The assistential exteriorization of energies at a daily pre-set time is the best means by which the veteran lucid projector can avoid a prolonged recess in the production of his/her lucid projections.

4. **Waves.** The energetic transmissions are emitted in well-defined waves of energy that are perceived by the projector-sensitive as being generally intermittent (discontinuous).

5. **Holochakra.** During the exteriorization of energies, the human body sometimes seems smaller or of lesser volume. This is due to the expansion of the exteriorized holochakra and characterizes the non-pathological phenomenon of *self-microscopy*.

6. **Machine.** Frequently, during the energetic transmissions, the practitioner seems to hear the pulsing of an immense machine, as though having a unified body or, in other words, as if all of his/her consciential vehicles were coupled to an extremely powerful invisible dynamo, serving as a sensitive for the intangible extraphysical machine.

7. **Flame-throwers.** During benign semi-possession, the holochakra of the arms and hands seem like flame-throwers spraying the energies forward with apparent violence through the accelerated and continued rhythmic discharges. The hands may also seem to be periodic energetic sprayers. At this time, images of force arise, inspired by the helpers, e.g.: the incandescent creation of the solar system; a sea of hot lava pouring from an erupting volcano; hot steel pouring from ovens in a steel-works. This entire process is reminiscent of the workings of an interdimensional-energetic-consciential-centrifuge.

8. **Interface.** The first energetic discharge – which is more receptive for the extraphysical sensitive-transmitter than donative for the recipient consciousness – establishes the parapsychic interface.

9. **Eighth.** In general, one energetic discharge among the 11 – e.g.: the eighth – can be notably more intense or more potent than the others.

10. **Quality.** Duration is not an important factor in the energetic discharges. The quality and potentiality of the energies transmitted is far more important.

11. **Intervals**. The brief interval of time between one energetic transmission and another serves to physiologically replenish the intraphysical transmitter, to readjust the intraphysical consciousness-extraphysical consciousness interface as well as to substitute the proximate or distant recipient consciousness when necessary. In this period, the helper generally does not lose parapsychic-mental-energetic control of the process. The intense sensations felt by the practitioner may disappear in the intervals between one energetic discharge and another, thus remaining controlled by the extraphysical consciousness during the transmissions and benignly semi-possessed during the intervals.

12. **Synchronizations**. The sounds of the rhythmic vibrations in the head during the energetic discharges are synchronous with the distributing movements of the arms and hands.

13. **Asynchronies**. The interference of ephemeral asynchronies between the sounds and energetic distributions is due to the difficulty of the engagement or, in other words, the disengagement between the mind of the sensitive and the extraphysical transmitter consciousness.

14. **Transmitters**. The extraphysical energetic transmitters – extraphysical consciousnesses having a male or female appearance – can take turns during a single session and the sensitive-projector will perceive the alternation and changes in techniques which are characteristically individualistic and unmistakable.

15. **Intensity**. The more intense the energetic transmissions are, the greater will be the well-being of the practitioner in the period following the transmissions.

16. **Rhythms**. Often, the intense and sometimes varied rhythm of the energetic discharges, physical movements and muscular contractions has almost no affect on the practitioner's heart rate. This fact, in and of itself, constitutes a separate subjective and concomitant phenomenon. Strictly speaking, the ever-perceivable frequency of the practitioner's energetic transmissions is not subordinated to his/her will, heart rate, or even his/her cardiorespiratory frequency, as well as the passage of time of an ordinary watch, or any other source except for the parapsychic or motor commands of the basic extraphysical transmitter. Nevertheless, the entire transmission often seems to be connected to powerful extraphysical and intangible apparatuses. There can be 4 to 5 rhythms of energetic transmission that are quite different from each other in a single session of 10 basic transmissions.

17. **Calibration.** The daily practice of penta allows the practitioner to calibrate his/her energetic condition or health of that day, week or current period of terrestrial existence.

18. **Protection**. The practice of penta maintains a positive extraphysical protection over the lucid projector's human life.

19. **Ideas**. The state or period of the transmissions in penta show themselves to be highly propitious for the assimilation of new ideas by the attentive practitioner.

20. **Consciousness**. The psychophysical state of the sensitive or lucid projector during the practice of penta can be compared to the condition of cosmoconsciousness that is characteristic of the ordinary, physical waking state or maximum assistential pangraphy.

Collectivity. It is common knowledge that any human undertaking with a positive, group, collective energy or one born from a homogenous and cohesive group of individuals with a strong sense of union and affinity when gathered, is stronger, more intense, vigorous and curative, benefiting a greater number of assisted consciousnesses than individual, isolated energy or that energy derived from just one consciousness.

Professionals. The artist on the stage, the orator on the rostrum, the lawyer in court, the professor at a presentation and the sensitive in trance are all familiar with the energy emanated from a live audience. From this arose the practice of the parapsychic session.

Syntony. The "parapsychic and assistential session of *me* alone" is apparently contrary to or runs counter to the abovementioned energy in group precept. Nevertheless, it should be borne in mind that the penta practitioner *is never alone*. This is because he/she always acts in profound syntony with the extraphysical helpers and even, in exceptional cases, with projected intraphysical consciousnesses and those consciousnesses that are assisted, when serving as a therapist to needy, energivorous extraphysical consciousnesses or ill extraphysical parapsychotics. The fact that it is a parapsychic task involving only one intraphysical consciousness makes inspection and vibratory defenses more efficient and, above all, generally easier for the helpers to maintain.

Union. With a syntony of the consciousnesses, a harmonizing of elevated sentiments (empathy) and cohesion in their objectives, the percentage of intraphysicals relative to extraphysicals is not important. What does matter is the union that creates mental or, more precisely, consciential force, which represents the intensity of mobilized energies with a positive intention.

Umbilical. At a more advanced stage, the practice of penta can be extraphysically oriented toward physical (ectoplasmic) effects, e.g.: with the following 9 characteristics of manifestation:

1. **Position.** Use of the dorsal position.
2. **Temperature.** A drop in corporal and ambient temperature.
3. **Phenomena.** Mild physical effect phenomena.
4. **Trunk.** More energetic exteriorizations coming from the trunk and head, and less from the arms and hands.
5. **Frequency.** A change in respiratory frequency during the energetic transmissions.
6. **Umbilicochakra.** A marked predominance of activity of the umbilicochakra in the energetic transmissions.
7. **Abdomen.** An upward pulling sensation in the abdomen with each energetic exteriorization.
8. **Musculature.** A strengthening of the abdominal musculature.
9. **Arms.** Cessation of muscular hypertrophy in the arms and shoulders.

Duration. Energetic transmissions performed while the animist-sensitive is seated and predominantly using the head, arms and hands – or with a predominance of the coronochakra, frontochakra and laryngochakra – are made with physical movements that are broader, faster, and the assistential session is shorter. Energetic transmissions performed while the animist-sensitive is lying down, predominantly using the head, thorax and abdomen or, in other words, with all 7 basic chakras active, are made with physical movements that are less intense, slower, and the energetic session is longer with a greater number of ectoplasmic effects.

Practical. The performance of penta is extremely practical with regard to human life. Even the person who, due to personal, human commitments cannot exercise parapsychism even twice a week in specialized study groups, can practice penta every day. This can be done alone and in secret, without excessive self-censure, before or after business hours, in the privacy of their home, without the problems of commuting and traffic, or the demands of conventions, rituals and social principles of human existence in intraphysical society, independent from the presence and judgment of other intraphysical beings.

Prisoners. The practice of penta, as well as lucid projections, are especially indicated for prisoners in general who wish to change their destiny for the better (existential recycling), while incapable of physically removing themselves because of the human circumstances imposed by their forced isolation.

Myology. A warning to interested individuals: those who practice the assistential exercises of penta on a daily basis, making themselves passive to the helper, will end up having arm, shoulder, thorax, pectoral and other muscles that are larger and firmer. Their body weight will also increase due to these exercises after a while due to the increased amount of physical, motor and muscular movement performed habitually and regularly.

Itching. One of the first indications of the manifestation of physical effect phenomena, or the indisputable exteriorization of ectoplasm, is the uncommon itching of the nasal mucosae or interior of the nose (nasal cavities). This occurs during the assistential practices of energy transmission during penta. It is probably due to the initial emission of ectoplasm through the nasal mucosae.

Nudity. Based on the fact that the practice of penta occurs while the practitioner is alone and isolated – as long as he/she observes the absence of local air currents, a suitable ambient temperature and a correct use of air conditioning so as to avoid catching a cold – he/she can make him/herself parapsychically passive to the helpers while entirely nude and do so with naturality because they, being of evolved mentalities, do not place importance upon this fact. This can, however, affect the reactions of the extraphysical consciousnesses that extraphysically awaken due to the exercises of assistential energetic transmissions, as their consciential microuniverses are still deeply influenced by human conditioning (post-desomatic parapsychotics).

Chakras. The energetic transmissions are constantly improved. After a number of years, the daily exercises – which are not considered a chore, but awaited daily with personal joy – make the energizer perceive the chakras, especially the following 4, simultaneously while in the ordinary, physical waking state:

1. **Sexochakra.** The sexochakra, pulsating as though the practitioner were seated on a ball of fire.

2. **Umbilicochakra.** The umbilicochakra or the entire abdomen energized toward the front.

3. **Frontochakra.** The frontochakra, which appears to be a small but powerful apparatus encrusted in the forehead.

4. **Coronochakra.** The coronochakra with the impressive sensation of the dissolving of the head.

Approaches. The helpers also bring ill extraphysical consciousnesses which are more disturbed and in lack (energivorous) in order to approach the practitioner directly while he/she is in the ordinary, physical waking state or while projected.

Results. At this point, the physical-extraphysical *rapport* (affinity, interaction, empathy) is intensified and the results of the assistential energetic irradiations improve.

Extras. When the penta practitioner arrives at a higher level of affinity with the *main* extraphysical transmitter, extra or emergency energetic exteriorizations can occur either before (usually) or after the daily period of transmissions at unexpected moments or circumstances.

Health. This all occurs without psychically or physically forcing the practitioner but, instead, in an agreeable, enriching and healthful manner – which will never bring any intrusive or harmful connotation – aiming toward the treatment of ill extraphysical consciousnesses in an emergency situation.

Absorption. The absorption or sympathetic assimilation of illnesses, disturbances or ailments of certain person-patients or ill extraphysical consciousnesses, through affinity, good intention and energetic ascendancy, can occur during the assistential transmissions of penta, whether they be conscious or unconscious on the part of both, the energizer-absorber and the patient-absorbed.

Remission. The definitive remission of the patient's symptoms, after transmissions spanning over a period of hours, days, or even weeks, is what in many cases reveals the occurrence of sympathetic absorption. Whenever this occurs, it is always triggered by the extraphysical benefactors, according to the animist-sensitive transmitter's greater capacity to discard the disturbances through energetic strengthening. The practitioner, nevertheless, may or may not identify the absorption, as soon as it is installed, depending upon the level of his/her technical self-lucidity within these assistential processes.

Case study. A typical example of the sympathetic absorption of pathological conditions of the human body-holochakra-psychosoma of an ill individual is that of someone suffering alterations in a member, whether it is a leg that has been exhibiting pain, edema, locomotive difficulties and other disturbances for a long time and for which all conventional examinations, diagnoses and treatments, as well as alternative treatments, have proven ineffective. These disturbances disappear when treated with energetic transmissions, often only with transmissions at a distance and in secret.

Bait. Sympathetic absorption among consciousnesses is the most advanced effect of the condition of animic-parapsychic bait. It is established upon the state of *rapport,* the existence of consciential energies and the phenomenon of auric coupling. This should not be interpreted as an intrusive episode, as pathological, interconsciential intrusion is understood.

Therapeutic. Sympathetic absorption is, above all, therapeutic and non-pathological, although it stems from cases of intrusion or chronic possession, negative magic, the syncretic practices of many sects, physical-extraphysical couplings with ill consciousnesses and other primitive and anticosmoethical manifestations of the same type, such as the use of *prescriptions* and the practices of *Mandingos* used in candomblé and *quimbanda in order to kill persons* (note, for example, the specialized technical works of Pierre Verger).

Responsories. Many practices, which are popularly called "responses" and "responsories," are positively or healthily performed through sympathetic absorption.

Continuum. The assistential habits of energy exteriorization can lead the intraphysical consciousness to a centering or *fundamentation* of the ego, the most elevated state of equilibrium that a human being can attain. At this point, the coupling of his/her mentalsoma with the mentalsoma of an experienced extraphysical consciousness – a helper – almost always occurs, in the serene condition of the interface of the awareness *continuum*.

Maturity. One of the uses of the practice of penta is to help heal the disturbances within the scope of the parapathology of the psychosoma. Among them are the sequels of physical restriction of the intraphysical consciousness that recently became an extraphysical consciousness. For example: the faster recuperation of extraphysical maturity for those consciousnesses that underwent desoma at a tender age or during adolescence or, in other words, the extraphysical children that merit or need to return to consciential adulthood more quickly. In these cases, the paratropospheric energies of the human sensitive operate in a positive and effective manner, with the possibility of greater *rapport* in the unblocking and balancing of the remaining quite animal, human, related energies that are still connected to the extraphysical consciousness.

Tasks. Among the more elevated objectives of the practice of penta, the increasing predominance of the clarification task over the consolation task can surely be included. It can thus be seen that there are penta practices of higher or lower quality, not only in terms of the practitioner, in different stages of his/her life, but also in terms of the interdimensional results of different practitioners.

Groups. Penta study groups have been developed at the offices of the International Institute of Projectiology and Conscientiology (IIPC) by veteran penta practitioners.

Bibliography: Vieira (1762, p. 165). A recent work by the author specifically on this theme: *Penta Manual: Personal Energetic Task.*

---

294. THEORY OF ENERGETIC SYMPATHETIC ASSIMILATION

Definition. Energetic sympathetic assimilation: the quality and act of a consciousness simultaneously absorbing the consciential energies and analyzing the holosomatic, paraphysiological and parapathological conditions of another.

Synonymy: bioenergetic catheterization; consented energetic reception; empathic communication; energetic assimilation through affinity; energetic involvement; *enkinesia* (shamanic medicine); interconsciential assimilation; investigative energetic projection; symbiotic paranormality; sympathetic absorption; therapist-patient resonance.

Technique. The parapsychic technique of sympathetic assimilation is only performed through the impulsion of the decided will, a working tool of the animist-parapsychic, after deep *auric coupling* has been established. Sympathetic assimilation is of overall interest within the practices of projectiology.

Physical. In theory, no direct physical *contact* is necessary in order to establish energetic sympathetic assimilation, except the laying on of hands, if needed. There is also no need for the use of any physical *instrument*, or merely human artifices such as prayer, mantras or counting.

Transcendence. Consciential energy transcends the *physical world* in any gradation of its conditions of manifestation, whether having imperceptible, minor, moderate or great *intensity*; or having slow, active, constant, rapid or strong *impulses*.

Space. Sympathetic assimilation can be established regardless of physical *distance*, in terms of space. It can be sent to another person, even from one continent to another.

Time. Sympathetic assimilation can be established instantaneously. In a split second, the emitter of consciential energy can invade the psychosphere of someone who senses the *energetic intrusion* at that same moment.

Circuit. Energetic sympathetic assimilation is simultaneously an exteriorization (projection) of energy (energetic probe), upon *departure,* and absorption of energy (retaking), upon *return.* The energizer thus closes a circuit of energy and investigative sensitivity with someone.

Factors. There are 3 essential or causal factors in the development of the phenomena of interconsciential, sympathetic energetic assimilation:

1. **Lucidity.** The level of lucidity, balance and wakefulness of the energizer makes the energizer *aware* or *unaware* of 3 agents: his/her willpower, personal consciential energies and sensitivity regarding the *correct* or *incorrect* holosomatic investigation of another. This factor stems exclusively from the degree of holochakral self-awareness.

2. **Nature.** The nature, quality or excellence of the stable consciential energy used in the process of sympathetic assimilation enables *healthy* (sound) practices, or *unhealthy* (pathological) actions, in the probing of the inner, harmonious or entropic conditions of the personal holosoma.

3. **Intensity.** The intensity, volume, quantity or condensation of consciential energy employed in the process of sympathetic assimilation allows *weaker* or *stronger* energetic operations, and more superficial or intrusive and deep holosomatic probings. This factor depends upon the level of personal experience, agility and energetic training. It is wise to bear in mind that basic immanent energy is inexhaustible.

Classification. Interconsciential energetic sympathetic assimilation can be classified into 5 basic types:

1. **Paraphysiological.** Simple and ephemeral energetic harmonization, exclusively at the levels of the holosomatic functions of the consciousness. Examples: auric coupling generated through the instinctive and unconscious, but visceral, impulses of the passionate emanations of two persons in love; conscious auric coupling, when intentionally promoted between two or more human psychospheres. Auric coupling is a common fact during human sexual relations.

2. **Parapathology.** Unconscious energetic *acceptance,* by the intraphysical consciousness, of the *intrusion* and holosomatic intrusion – whether unconscious or even when conscious – of an ill extraphysical consciousness. Examples: the transference, energetic repercussion or somatization of signs, sensations and symptoms, or even the installation of disease (tuberculosis, dermatosis) that is parapsychically maintained from the unconscious extraphysical intruder (post-desomatic parapsychotic), to the intraphysical consciousness suffering from intrusion; the so-called *contact high* of the director of the psychedelic session (drugs, LSD).

3. **Paradiagnosis.** Energetic involvement – up to a level capable of reflecting the symptomatology of disturbances in the emitting being (involver) through ephemeral and inoffensive somatization – that may or may not be perceived by the involved intraphysical consciousness. Example: energetic assimilation aiming to provide a *paradiagnosis* of a patient.

4. **Paratherapy.** Energetic receptivity with curative aims on the part of the intraphysical sensitive who becomes passive in order to receive the manifestation from the deceased ill consciousness. At this point, the illness is transported out of the patient's body. Examples: psychophonic trances performed

in classic deintrusion sessions that not only awaken the ill extraphysical consciousnesses, but also improve the sensitive over time; the absorber-energy emitter and the absorbed-patient in the therapeutic practices of penta; the passage of the illness from the patient to the shamanic healer; the practices of *benzedeiras.*

5. **Paraprophylaxis.** Energetic symbiosis of two consciousnesses aiming to test the self-defensive or prophylactic energetic resources of both. Examples: energetic and spontaneous projective holosomatic or, in other words, holosoma to holosoma confrontation; the modern athletic challenge intended to celebrate the *bioenergetic champion* within a group of likeminded persons.

Contagion. Unfortunately, the contagion of disease through the transmission of bioenergy actually occurs in persons who lack vibratory self-defense or are bioenergetically vulnerable and do not follow recommendations for physical, mental and consciential hygiene.

Difference. It can be concluded that the qualitative difference between diagnostic sympathetic assimilation and parapathological sympathetic assimilation is merely in the fact that, in the first, the assimilator temporarily absorbs only the sensations of the blockages and *symptoms* of the patient. In the second, not only are the deep symptoms or strata absorbed and installed, but also the components of the actual *disturbances* of the patient being assisted (contagion via bioenergy).

Para-asepsis. The triggering of the *vibrational state,* when necessary, applied as a resource of para-asepsis after paradiagnosis, or even in all practices of sympathetic assimilation, eliminates any possibility of permanent absorption or contagion of the bioenergetic imbalances and blockages of the patient.

Forecast. The author has been using this efficient and practical technique for over 4 decades without contracting any illness merely through bioenergetic contacts and exchanges. It is easy to forecast that in the future this method will prevail over all diagnosis techniques. At that point, universities of medicine, psychology, odontology, nursing and psychotherapy (specialization) will probably teach *Practical Discrimination of Bioenergy,* a discipline suitable for the first year of university.

Serenissimus. Energetic sympathetic assimilation performed extraphysically with a *Homo sapiens serenissimus,* or *serenissimus,* is a process that is difficult in practice but ideal for the energetic self-analysis of the pre-*serenissimus* or, in other words: ourselves, ordinary intraphysical consciousnesses in evolution on earth.

---

295.   ABUSES IN THE USE OF CONSCIENTIAL ENERGIES

Definition. Discernment: the ability of the consciousness to judge things or phenomena in a clear and sensible manner.

Synonymy: ability to discern; discerning analysis; norm of judgment; strict criterion.

Vehicles. The interactive agent between the vehicles of the consciousness is the consciential energy that is commanded by the conscious or even unconscious will.

Use. The abusive use of a consciential vehicle can cause damage to another vehicle of manifestation. Thus, the intraphysical consciousness (materialist) who lives only for his/her human body (instincts or the sexochakra) does not develop the resources of the psychosoma or emotional body (cardiochakra).

Psychosomatics. On the other hand, the individual who lives only for emotions (psychosomatics), without reflecting upon his/her existence to a greater degree, is not able to improve the elevated sentiments or rationalized emotions (coronochakra) pertaining to the mentalsoma.

Biology. The directives of human biology are quite strict and do not allow excesses in any direction, not even regarding the abusive application of consciential energy when they transcend biological limits and attain parabiology.

Soma. It is common knowledge that consciential energy is unlimited and inexhaustible because it comes from immanent energy, which exists throughout the universe and the consciential dimensions. Nevertheless, upon performing excessive mechanical movements and processes or other abuses the human body (soma) can present disturbances stemming from the application of consciential energy in diverse forms through it.

Disturbances. The following are 5 occurrences that can be identified as disturbances or damage subsequent to the incorrect use of consciential energy (bioenergy) by an intraphysical being.

1. **Microlesions.** In theory, the lucid projector, or the animist-parapsychic, can exteriorize consciential energy all day, every day. Nevertheless, if the intraphysical consciousness' muscles are not accustomed to the intensity of the physical exercises performed, he/she can later suffer the effects of microlesions of the muscle fibers and its uncomfortable aftereffects: muscle pain and physical indisposition.

2. **Hypertrophy.** The simple acts of exteriorization of consciential energy on the part the intraphysical consciousness (magnetic exteriorization), or even the energies composed by extraphysical consciousnesses or helpers (extraphysical exteriorization) – through physical exercises pertaining to prolonged, assiduous, intensive practices, such as those of daily penta – can develop the evident hypertrophy (greater volume) of the muscles of the forearms, biceps, shoulders and thorax, depending upon the energy exteriorization techniques used. This obviously increases the individual's body weight and makes him/her appear more robust and firm.

3. **Decalcification.** The installation of a dense bioenergy field, with a substantial reduction in the ectoplast's basal metabolic rate and hypothermia of the extremities during the parapsychic trance, when repeated intensively, can predispose the appearance of peripheral decalcifications in the toenails, for example, if there is any organic predisposition in this sense: physical constitution; age; peripheral circulation; calcium metabolism.

4. **Transference.** In theory, *bioenergy* is the same as any *medication,* which can cure as well as kill. It is always necessary to keep a discerning eye on the variables that interfere in the movements and practices of energetic processes. The technique of sympathetic assimilation, for example, performed through the auric coupling of the sensitive to the assisted individual can, in some cases when the sympathetic assimilation becomes very intense and continuous, transfer or absorb certain unhealthy predispositions or install disturbances that will generate the patient's symptoms in the bioenergetic donor. This happens when he/she lacks adequate techniques and environment for the maintenance of the extraphysical para-asepsis of his/her psychosphere (deassimilations) and personal organic replenishment. This can occur not only with the ordinary energy emitter, but also with any type of physician, psychologist, nurse and even with the social worker or human health professional.

5. **Resistance.** In the correct maintenance of the parahygiene of the consciential energy donor, the relationship between his/her organic state and the extent or depth of his/her work should always be borne in mind. When the person lacking a balanced diet and a high natural organic resistance dedicates him/herself excessively to bioenergy donation, he/she can become predisposed to after work fatigue, minidisturbances in his/her weak points and frequent colds.

Hangovers. Correct practices with consciential energies never generate *energetic hangovers*.

Others. The best medication can become poison, depending upon its abusive use. Other disturbances and inconveniences will easily be identified by the interested individual upon developing his/her control and application of consciential energies based on the examples offered here.

Actions. It can be seen from these objective and rational examples that the consciousness needs to guard against error and damaging excess in everything that it does. Positive intentions and goodwill help greatly but can generate blatant senselessness when applied alone. Active discernment of the consciousness is always indispensable in order that productive actions in one sector of manifestation develop without generating harm in other sectors.

Theorice. That is why the ideal union of theory and practice (theorice), namely the simultaneous use of diligent study (intellectuality) as well as parapsychophysical experience, should always be recommended to everyone, whether it is the occasional ordinary practitioner or the active researcher.

Age. Youth, of course, provides greater resistance than mature physical age. Nevertheless, youths can be more predisposed to organic minidisturbances in work involving the application of consciential energies. This is due to dispersiveness of efforts, lack of method, indiscipline in everyday life, *disassociation of ideas,* an unbalanced diet and an irregular eating schedule.

Code. Middle-aged or mature individuals can come out better in these cases. Although not having the defenses of the youths' age group, adults already have a *behavior pattern* that is *methodical* and stricter for themselves in terms of physical, mental and consciential hygiene, with healthy habits.

Exteriorization. The simple existence of the possibility of malefactions ensuing from the exteriorization of consciential energies does not imply that one should avoid them, inhibit oneself in regard to its use or fear its continued use and applications.

Discernment. Consciential energy is the foundation, the instrument, the touchstone of renovation of the consciousness in its evolutionary development. However, as with everything that exists, it demands discernment in order to be used wisely, competently and efficiently.

Decision. The intraphysical consciousness needs to always have decisiveness, courage and motivation in the lasting, evolutionary and multidimensional consciential realizations that he/she intends to pursue.

296. THEORICE OF MORPHOTHOSENES

Definition. Morphothosenes: mental formations shaped and organized by the energy and the dynamism of thought (thosenes), guided by the will and enriched by the imagination of the consciousness, whether intraphysical or extraphysical.

Synonymy: astral clichés; astral creations; astromental images; consensual forms; extraphysical visual creations; floating thoughts; forms that are thought; form-thoughts; human simulacra; ideoforms; ideomorphs; ideoplastic forms; ideoplastic projections; mental effects; mental models; mental pararealizations; mental projections; objective mental formations; psycho-effects; psychones; thought-forms; tulpas; tulpoids.

Effects. The *thosene* is constituted of three indissoluble components: thought *(tho)*, sentiment *(sen)* and consciential energy *(e)*. Every defined thought produces 2 immediate effects:

1. **Vibration.** First effect: a radiant vibration.

2. **Form.** Second effect: a floating thought-form, all this through the consciential energies or the *e*, the third element of the thosene.

Creation. Morphothosenes are created by the consciousness at every fraction of a second of its existence.

Procedures. Thought, a most powerful creation, can be manifested through at least 7 basic procedures:

1. **Focalization.** Sustained, focalized, concentrated and projected by the force of imagination, or through reflection, prayer, meditation, suggestion, ritual or evocation.

2. **Telepathy.** Transmitted at a distance, as in telepathy.

3. **Bending.** Employed to bend metal, as in the Geller effect.

4. **Anticosmoethics.** Used anticosmoethically to kill birds in flight, as done by certain primitive animists or witches.

5. **Fly-killer.** Applied to kill flies, as in the manner of a prisoner-projector in England (Will Howell, *The Way to Why*).

6. **Existence.** Used to create morphothosenes or thought-forms that are imbued with a temporary independent existence.

7. **Holothosenes.** Besides the above, it can gather in group thoughts and collective thoughts, and create personal and group holothosenes.

Paratroposphere. That which is called the crustal or *paratropospheric dimension* – the extraphysical sphere that coexists with human life – constitutes a fluid, plastic, non-physical and apparently omnipresent environment. Although formless per se, this dimension has the property of taking on or reflecting whatever form is mentally impressed upon it.

Water. The shapeless extraphysical substances that constitute thought-forms or morphothosenes are similar to water in a glass. Even though the liquid is formless, it adapts itself exactly to the shape of the glass into which it is poured.

Imagination. As a product of imagination, the morphothosene does not have life of its own, although, even so, it acts, moved by the thought of the consciousness, its creator.

Manifestations. Morphothosenes can be of the most diverse categories according to their properties and manifestations, such as these 11:

1. **Conscientiality.** Conscious or unconscious in relation to the consciousness.
2. **Consolidation.** Stable (consolidated) or unstable (immature).
3. **Health.** Positive, healthy and cosmoethical or negative, sick and anticosmoethical.
4. **Consistency.** Evanescent or consistent.
5. **Duration.** Ephemeral (fleeting) or quasi-permanent (holothosenic) which, in certain cases, even require extraphysical reurbanization lasting for hundreds of years.
6. **Creativity.** In the rough or of the pre-*serenissimus*, or refined of the *serenissimi*.
7. **Expression.** Small (such as phytothosenes) or grandiose (such as from free consciousnesses).
8. **Structure.** Opaque or transparent.
9. **Irradiation.** Dull or luminous (irradiant).
10. **Temporality.** New (recently created) or gravitating residues (multimillenary).
11. **Thosenity.** Self-morphothosenes or heteromorphothosenes.

Identification. Identical types of morphothosenes mutually attract each other.

Effects. It can logically be deduced that the vibrations of only one thought produce effects such as: shape, color, light and sound, including musical chords in the extraphysical dimension.

Transformations. The action of fantasies, impulses, desires, appetites, passions and emotions can transform *things* or the surrounding reality in the dimension where we manifest ourselves.

Harmonization. The unconscious morphothosenes coalesce and harmonize with the creations of preexisting thoughts or, to the contrary, battle openly against the thosenic realities previously created by other consciousnesses.

Habits. The morphothosenes of the consciousness act upon it, thereby creating the habits, uses, customs and routines of personal thought, sentiment and action.

Groupality. Individual ideoplastic formations are different from those of a group.

Potency. Individual will, although producing specific uniform results, is weaker than group or collective will (union increases strength).

Caliber. The power of the influence of the fixed *(extraphysical)* parapopulation's average mental caliber characterizes, edifies and maintains the extraphysical environment (districts, communities). That is why there are parallel, individual and collective mental *worlds,* as well as others in incessant transition.

Self-transfigurations. Acting upon the psychosoma, the consciousness can both generate and cure organic illnesses and forge self-transfigurations. For example, it is possible to create a third leg (supernumerary member), or rejuvenate the appearance through the power of thought, or the consciential energies.

Paraclothing. Extraphysical clothes (paraclothing) are morphothosenes, which have generally been created in an unconscious, para-instinctive, *automatic* way or through tactism.

Ephemerality. There is evidence for the existence of ephemeral and quasi-permanent morphothosenes, however, the facts and logic suggest that eternal morphothosenes do not exist.

Duels. Outright extraphysical duels between wills or combats with morphothosenes occur. This is why there are residual or gravitating negative thought-forms in many places.

Communicology. Telepathy and the means of mass communication (media) in general (interconsciential communicology) are directly related to the creation of morphothosenes in human environments.

Pollution. The essential pollution of planet earth (ecology, para-ecology, *planetary trash*) is, above all, a *thosenic pollution* or one generated and maintained by anticosmoethical or sick holothosenes.

Imagistic. Many images which are mentally evoked and sustained by the intraphysical consciousness through his/her passions become consistent morphothosenes that act upon the thought world of intraphysical and extraphysical consciousnesses. This even creates cumulative group-thoughts, which still require research and investigation by sensitives, projectors, penta practitioners, conscientiologists and conscientiotherapists, in order to be more clearly understood and better avoided by the unwary.

Reality. Thoughts are real things.

Psychopathology. Morphothosenes comprise many of the hallucinations of all types of psychopaths or the mentally ill of both sexes and of all intraphysical ages.

Extraphysical. The reader should not conclude that only his/her morphothosenes exist in the dimensions where his/her intraphysical consciousness (you) projects. In fact, there are other independent extraphysical shapes which are consistent and real apart from the physical, human and dense shapes of this paratropospheric dimension, outside the intraphysical base and beyond the morphothosenes generated by the consciousness.

Vision. The projected consciousness sees the extraphysical shapes because they are there, although these forms are generally not his/her creations.

Artifacts. Those who nurture doubts regarding the possible existence of concrete morphothosenes – well-constituted and incredibly solid extraphysical artifacts – should ponder the existence of the silver cord. This non-material or semi-material appendix or object is extremely tangible, active and vigorous in many ways. All intraphysical beings have it – including plants and bacteria – and nothing similar in shape, structure and function is to be found among all existing objects and bodies in the entire physical universe. It is important to bear in mind that the *umbilical cord* does not have the same nature or functions as the *silver cord.*

Primothosene. In truth, the entire universe is the assemblage of the thosenes from all the consciousnesses that exist within it. Nonetheless, this does not exclude the existence of an "uncreated cause" or a *primothosene,* a principle that is still beyond our comprehension.

Consensus. The extraphysical dimensions are consensual realities, that is, the result of the interaction of two or more consciousnesses on an empty space, acting through morphothosenes or individual and general thosenization.

Average. The average blocks of morphothosenes in a certain area make up the extraphysical environment or, more precisely, even the intraphysical environment which is always derived from it.

Distortion. The general reality is often perceived in a distorted manner by the intraphysical consciousness individually, as a result of (infantile) egocentrism, (adult) egoism, consciential restriction, loss of cons, immaturity, pathothosenes, repression and abdominal brainwashing.

Complexity. Extraphysical self-awareness and morphothosenes present deeply complex aspects.

Detection. The projected intraphysical consciousness can simultaneously see and detect what are presumed to be parts of his/her psychosoma, paralegs, para-arms or parahands; the holochakra or the extended and brilliant silver cord; and even the paraphysiognomy of an extraphysical consciousness in front of him/her. All of this disappears in an instant, without any reason which is apparent or identifiable at that moment.

Mentalsomatics. This can occur due to the creation of one's morphothosenes. Even so, the consciousness still remains projected only in the mentalsoma.

Mistakes. When projected in this manner only once, this intraphysical consciousness will think that the silver cord and the extraphysical consciousnesses are mere mental creations derived from its human conditioning, from reading, habitual imaginative acquisitions and nothing more. This shows reason and even a fair degree of coherence and good mnemotechnique, but also a serious error in evaluation, stemming from the inexperience of the intraphysical consciousness that is projected in the complex isolated mentalsoma.

Disappointment. On the other hand, the intraphysical consciousness that projects many times in different ways and under various extraphysical conditions will inevitably conclude that the silver cord exists. In certain extraphysical circumstances, he/she will even be deeply disappointed by the actions of this appendix, which reduces his/her manifestations outside the human body.

Inexperience. In the same manner, the projected intraphysical consciousness can come across extraphysical consciousnesses – as happened with the author – and try to exteriorize thoughts and energies with the objective of undoing what are considered to be mental shapes of personalities before him/her. These, being real, roar with laughter, make fun of and ridicule this obviously futile attempt. They immediately establish an open thosenic and energetic extraphysical confrontation. The inexperience of the consciousness – projected in the psychosoma this time – will lead him/her to commit another primary error in evaluation.

Force. Every morphothosene sent from one consciousness to another is a real transference of a certain quantity of force and matter from the emitter to the receiver, about whom he/she thinks and with whom he/she syntonizes with greater or lesser empathy.

Discharge. The passivity of the receiving consciousness and the harmonious character of the thoughts of both – the emitter and the receiver – make it such that the morphothosene is discharged onto the receiver to varying degrees according to the structure of the emitter's intentionality.

Thought. Everything that can be done, imagined or invented by the thoughts of the intraphysical consciousness, when in the ordinary, physical waking state in this tropospheric dimension, can be accomplished much more easily by the same intraphysical consciousness when lucidly projected outside his/her human body.

Categories. The intraphysical consciousness, when projected and lucid, can sometimes perfectly detect 3 basic categories of his/her morphothosenes: detached, pursuing and projected morphothosenes.

1. **Detached.** Detached morphothosenes are those that are incessantly left behind the consciousness and comprise its mental trace or the *basic thosenic signature*. They should not be confused with the previously mentioned trace of light.

2. **Pursuing.** Pursuing morphothosenes are those that hover over and pursue the personality or, in other words, his/her repetitive thoughts and more common tempting self-thosenes, which are energetically highly charged and self-reproducible. Such morphothosenes can have an extremely negative or pathological influence over their creator because he/she is generally unaware of his/her own unhappy mental creations and is often even unaware of his/her positive and healthy mental creations.

3. **Projected.** Projected morphothosenes are those which are flung far away by the consciousness to specific targets: beings, objects and places. Such projection of morphothosenes can be: positive, negative or neutral; created consciously or unconsciously; pure or elaborate; and alone or in good or bad company.

Bibliography: Babajiananda (65, p. 39), Bennett (117, p. 25), Blackmore (139, p. 232), Blavatsky (153, p. 187), Bozzano (186, p. 157), Brennan (199, p. 66), Cavendish (266, p. 254), Chaplin (273, p. 158), Coquet (301, p. 65), Crookall (338, p. 219), Day (376, p. 138), Fodor (528, p. 383), Frost (560, p. 206), Gaynor (577, p. 186), Greene (635, p. 65), Hodson (729, p. 105), Leadbeater (901, p. 280), Lee (908, p. 189), Monroe (1065, p. 75), Muldoon (1102, p. 118), Osborn (1155, p. 165), Powell (1279, p. 45), Rogo (1453, p. 248), Schatz (1514, p. 201), Sculthorp (1531, p. 115), Shepard (1548, p. 933), Steiger (1607, p. 245), Talbot (1642, p. 144), Vieira (1762, p. 20), Walker (1782, p. 414), Wang (1794, p. 215), Xavier (1891, p. 49), Yram (1897, p. 148), Zain (1898, p. 40).

297. COMPARISONS BETWEEN LUCID PROJECTION AND MORPHOTHOSENES

Differential. There are clearly defined differences between the self-projection of morphothosenes created by the projected consciousness and the real images of lucid projection that already exist and are perceived by the same projected consciousness in the extraphysical dimension, as can be verified in the following 7 technical comparisons:

1. **Origins.** When they are formed by the projector's consciousness, self-projections of morphothosenes do not present any uniqueness or novelty, because they stem from personal and obviously familiar experiences. The real images of lucid projection do not originate from the projected consciousness, but are already created by other intelligences that are generally unknown.

2. **Location.** Most self-projections of morphothosenes occur more frequently inside the individual extraphysical sphere of energy (psychosphere) that envelops the consciousness when inside or outside but physically close to the human body. Lucid projection occurs both inside and outside the extraphysical sphere of energy, in any extraphysical environment or district.

3. **Unpredictability.** Self-projections of morphothosenes almost always present the inescapable characteristic of predictability or prior knowledge of that which will be seen, because they are images generated within the scope of the manifestations of the projector's consciousness. Lucid projection surpasses the parameters of knowledge of the intraphysical consciousness projector and, being unpredictable, springs inconceivable surprises on the experiencer.

4. **Vitality.** Self-projections of morphothosenes do not show signs of life because they are inevitably only forged with apparent artificial life, whether conscious or unconscious in nature. Lucid projections present lively experiences and sensations having the unmistakable charm of authenticity, vitality and unique magnitude, sometimes being much more vibrant than the common reality of human existence in the ordinary, physical waking state.

5. **Durability.** Self-projections of morphothosenes spontaneously tend to be ephemeral and lack the power of survival. The images of lucid projection tend to be long-lasting, independent and indifferent, according to the extraphysical environment where the projected consciousness manifests itself.

6. **Resistance.** Self-projections of morphothosenes are generally easily and rapidly dissolved by the projector's will because they are created and arise ephemerally restricted to the will, intentionality and imagination. The real images of lucid projections are resistant to the projected projector's will and do not easily disappear. They almost always exist prior to and remain after the lucid projection, as they exist in the extraphysical dimension.

7. **Takeoff.** Self-projections of morphothosenes clearly do not have the experience of the lucid takeoff and interiorization of the consciousness projected in the psychosoma, or the experience of leaving and reentering the human body. These experiences are specific to the phenomena of lucid projections.

Bibliography: Fodor (528, p. 382), Vieira (1758, p. 3), Yram (1897, p. 148).

298. MORPHOTHOSENE CREATION TECHNIQUE

Foretokens. Self-projections of the human mind during deep meditation (introspection), daydreams and the effort of the mentalist represent the foretokens of the formation of morphothosenes in the extraphysical dimension.

Details. The details of mental creation require extraphysical energy while using the deep power of singular thought or, thought directed toward a single objective.

Raw material. Thought – a type of mental raw material, or ductile extraphysical substance – together with the will and the attention that is fixated with clarity on the smallest details of the desired object in an environment that is adequate for self-thosenization of the consciousness, instantaneously shapes morphothosenes.

Technique. The basic mental shape which maintains a morphothosene until arriving at the predominant materthosene and, consequently, the peculiar and characteristic personal holothosene, is conceived and constructed by the consciousness through the simultaneous union of 4 consciential attributes:

1. **Concentration.** The effort of the concentration of attention (fixation).
2. **Imagination.** Visualization through imagination (imagistic processes).
3. **Emotionality.** Vitalization through emotions (psychosomatics).
4. **Will.** Maintenance through the will that created it (intentionality).

Imagistic. The imaginary visual field is very restricted in consciousnesses with a weak imagination regarding visualization. It is likewise very ample in those with a fertile imagination.

Holochakrology. The qualities of mental images – specifically of visual images, the clarity and precision of outlines – depend upon intrinsic personal conditions, as well as the intensity and quantity (volume) of the consciential energies (holochakrology) they are imbued with.

Capacity. The capacity for abstraction can increase the efficiency of one's imagination.

Rationality. Paradoxically, rational ideas reduce the normal capacity for producing visual images.

Thinkers. Incidentally, scientists and thinkers have little capacity (underendowed) for visual imagination, a strong trait which is very developed in women and youths of both sexes.

Simple. In the morphothosene creation technique, thought which is spontaneous and lacks the effort of will conceives only formless sketches of the image. Simple thought obtains simple creations.

Duration. The less important a mental creation is, the more ephemeral it will be.

Law. The lower the evolutionary level of the environment or an extraphysical community, the denser and fuller it is with confused, disturbed and ephemeral mental forms.

Relief. In the creation of morphothosenes and extraphysical forms, the objects are not only imagined with their form and outline, but are also raised with a certain degree of relief.

Attention. The objects in which greater attention is focused stand out as being more colored and somewhat salient over the imagined or created background.

Recreation. Those extraphysical objects of little importance can easily be modified and recreated by any consciousness.

Complexity. The greater and more complex mental assemblies, the collective environment, gigantic scenarios and large objects, are only altered by the creative force of the assemblage of thoughts of the *inhabitants*, the autochthons of that dimension, or the powerful and more evolved consciousnesses (*serenissimi*, free consciousnesses).

Repetition. Repeated modeling exercises clearly improve the performance of the consciousness in the creation of morphothosenes.

Hypothesis. The following is a research hypothesis: What is the relationship between human morphothosenes and the earth's gravitational force?

Addition. If the projected intraphysical consciousness thinks of a detail that is missing in the object, upon coming across it, even if it is a physical or an ordinary one, the projector can unconsciously and instantly add it. This gives the object an extraordinary sense of realism that can fool the extraphysical perceptions in a very self-convincing manner. It is thus always important for the intraphysical consciousness, when projected, to maintain alert self-critical judgment and improve his/her own capacity to differentiate the extraphysical images down to the smallest detail.

Openness. On the other hand, the intraphysical lucid projector, when projecting, needs to maintain an open mind without excessively narrow-minded prejudgments, apriorisms or human conditioning.

Fossilization. The projector will otherwise *inadvertently* only see what he/she wishes to. In other words, he/she will only see his/her very familiar pattern-morphothosenes, reexperiencing his/her own lucubrations in an endless vicious circle (fossilization). The projector will thus not participate in the realities of the extraphysical dimension, which are independent from him/her as a consciousness. These realities have always existed on their own or were generated and have been maintained by other consciousnesses over a long period of time.

Uses. When the consciousness manifests lucidly in the psychosoma, its ideoplastic projections facilitate the elaboration of logical, clear and sensible thought, thereby improving its images, concepts, judgments and capacities for paying attention, concentrating, making comparisons and deciding with a view toward the evolution of the mentalsoma.

Maturity. The creation of morphothosenes dynamizes the level of maturity of the consciousness, acting as a propelling agent for its passage from projection in the psychosoma (which is easier) to superlucid projection in the isolated mentalsoma (which is far more difficult).

Work. The act of creating and recreating *concrete* extraphysical forms is an objective and healthy form of extraphysical *paraleisure* for those extraphysical consciousnesses which are close to and in the planetary troposphere. This dynamizes the parapsychophysiology of their consciential faculties or attributes, on the way toward the state of continuous self-awareness.

Bibliography: Bennett (117, p. 26), Blavatsky (153, p. 222), Brennan (199, p. 66), Buckland (219, p. 153), Carrington (251, p. 242), Cavendish (266, p. 254), Gomes (612, p. 118), Leadbeater (901, p. 280), Powell (1279, p. 50), Vieira (1758, p. 3).

299. SEXUAL FACTORS FAVORABLE TO LUCID PROJECTION

Classification. Sexual factors favorable to lucid projection can be classified as physiological, psychological and parapsychic:

1. **Physiological:** an active and balanced sexlife; marriage or the condition of an evolutionary duo without problems; personal hygiene in the phase preparatory to projection.

2. **Psychological:** elimination of taboos regarding sexuality; a precise notion of the functions and the constructive force of sexochakral energies (libido); an understanding of cosmoethics in relation to human morality.

3. **Parapsychic:** a harmonious coexistence between active sex and consciential projections in series, deintrusive projection and projection in the mentalsoma; an understanding of the unproductiveness of extraphysical sex; the technique of projecting immediately after the sex act.

Projector. The dorsal position – with legs spread apart, loose clothing and the body relaxed on the bed – favors the male projector because it avoids a predisposition toward inopportune penile erection, which negatively interferes in the projective process, in some cases, only because an erection occurs during sleep, regardless of the physical position of the sexual organ. This position is not favorable for some women.

Sexosomatic. As the intensive practice of lucid projection becomes popular and generalized with evolution and time, it will allow healthy women and men to control their sexosomatic manifestations.

Sports. Just as the sex act is currently the most popular sport on earth, there are other evolved planets where lucid projection is the favorite sport of the intraphysical inhabitants.

Superiority. Multidimensional facts show that neither men nor women are superior to each other in regard to the factors restricted to the intraphysical consciousness, given that masculinity and femininity are mere episodic manifestations within the evolutionary way of all.

Diversifications. It is obvious that there are, nevertheless, functional diversifications, notably in light of the connecting of different human bodies, or the patterns of sexual roles. These operational diversifications are reflected in parapsychic areas. Two examples are to be found in the poltergeist and the phenomenon of cosmoconsciousness.

Poltergeist. It is currently accepted that the epicenter of the basic poltergeist phenomenon – one of the most primary parapsychic phenomena – is an adolescent intraphysical consciousness (puberty), and that the sexual processes play an important role in the phenomenon.

Young women. Occurrences indicate a considerable preponderance of activity related to young women (95%) compared to the proportion of young men (5%) in cases involving adolescents (Bayless, p. 214).

Sexochakra. The poltergeist is an assemblage of phenomena with physical effects and is related to the *kundalini* or consciential energies stemming from the sexochakra and, finally, from the psychosoma.

Cosmoconsciousness. The evolved phenomenon of cosmoconsciousness – the most illuminating of all phenomena pertaining to the intraphysical consciousness – occurs while the consciousness is in the mentalsoma, which is headquartered in the parabrain of the psychosoma, in the mentalsomatic dimension. Some researchers note that the cosmoconsciousness condition occurs in a clear and much more frequent manner with men than with women (Bucke; Steiger).

Hypothesis. In light of these observations, the following question can be posed: Does the conquest of self-awareness – in terms of the evolved androgenesis, by the consciousness which, strictly speaking, *has no gender* – begin in an evolutionary extreme, from the woman, using the gynosoma, the key element of animal reproduction, through the genesic chakra and the psychosoma, and consolidate, at another evolved extreme, with the man using the androsoma, the less important element in animal reproduction, through the condition of cosmoconsciousness? Does this hypothesis, without any depreciative intention, seem logical?

Bibliography: Baker (69, p. 90), Moore (1082, p. 230), Richards (1394, p. 38), Steiger (1608, p. 3).

---

300. SEXUAL FACTORS UNFAVORABLE TO LUCID PROJECTION

Classification. The sexual factors unfavorable to lucid projections can be classified as physiological, psychological and parapsychic.

1. **Physiological:** sanguineous stasis generated by the sleep position or vesical repletion in the inactive physical body, which provokes an erection before or during exteriorization of the projector; projection in the dorsal position with the female projector's legs spread apart on the bed; use of sensory deprivation of the sexual impulse as a projection generation factor; an inactive or disorganized sexlife; lack of sex; excessive sexual freedom and permissiveness; period of sexual *fermentation* (promiscuity).

2. **Psychological:** intranquil *mental* sex; sexual self-guilt; overestimation of the libido (sexaholic); lack of defense against mental or intersciential approaches.

3. **Parapsychic:** the condition of the conscious or unconscious extraphysical sexual predator-projector, or violator-projector, and its prey; the interflow of extraphysical forces with ill or energivorous extraphysical consciousnesses; the extraphysical kiss; reflections of the unrestrained sexual impulse in the projected consciousness; lack of defense against extraphysical attacks; the passive condition of a victim of extraphysical vampirization, having a sexual origin, by ill extraphysical consciousnesses or projected intraphysical consciousnesses; sexual evocation of intraphysical and extraphysical consciousnesses; promiscuous invisible unions; *congressus subtilis* with the wrong consciousness

(partner); the vampire-partner; creation of morphothosenes having a sexual origin; consciential projections solely through the psychosoma or the body of desires.

Self-guilt. Sexually deprived persons, or those who repress their natural emotions and nurture constant anxieties, ideas and sentiments of guilt regarding affectionate relationships – whether because of marital infidelity, "living in sin", maintaining "illicit relationships", receiving accusations and criticism about their sexual conduct, or attempting to "sublimate" their own healthy physiological impulses – act in a negative manner in terms of lucid consciential projection. This is because projection, in order to develop, requires a constantly worry-free condition and a mind that is open – without inculcations – to renewal and new knowledge (neophilia).

Camouflage. The intraphysical consciousness who is projected in an extraphysical dimension is not able to camouflage his/her emotions or emotional lacks if he/she does not control them on a diuturnal basis in the ordinary, physical waking state.

Morphothosenes. In many cases, the unconscious modeling of morphothosenes makes it such that the male consciential projector molds mental forms of a woman and the female consciential projector molds mental forms of a man which, for them, present all the characteristics and vital signs of their extraphysical sexual fantasies. This occurs in the same manner with persons who nurture homosexual fantasies.

Bibliography: Frost (560, p. 62), Monroe (1065, p. 190), Muldoon (1105, p. 181), Prado (1284, p. 42), Richards (1394, p. 38), Vieira (1762, p. 45).

---

301. EXTRAPHYSICAL   ROMANCES

Definition. Extraphysical romance: all of the acts through which the intraphysical consciousness dates or has a positive affair while projected out of his/her human body.

Synonymy: astral love; astral sex; extraphysical affair; extraphysical dating; paratropospheric sex; projected romance.

Adventures. Lucid projection allows intraphysical projectors to actually have two distinct types of romantic adventures in the extraphysical dimension:

1. **Primitive.** Those still involving the characteristically primitive sensations of physical sex and tropospheric results, or *congressus subtilis.*

2. **Evolved.** Those having emotions elevated to levels of ample expansion of the consciousness and indescribable results of sublimation, in an ecstasy that is supreme and therefore evolved.

Intentionality. Each of these experiences is dependent upon the quality of the consciousness' intentionality (true intentions), the company it seeks and those with which it has an affinity (empathy, because likes attract).

Marriage. Extraphysical and positive romances or honeymoons frequently prepare an upcoming human union or the constitution of an evolutionary duo between two projected intraphysical projectors. These are sometimes facilitated by helpers, which serve as cupids in this case. There are those who have asked their intraphysical girlfriend's hand in marriage, while outside the human body, before doing so officially in the ordinary, physical waking state.

Widowers. Many widowers and widows of various ages who are still intraphysical, solitary and longing, continue their affectionate experiences – generally maintained in secret – in elevated levels of sublimation, with the companions who preceded them in biological death (desoma or final projection).

Differences. The differences in the level of lucidity of extraphysically projected intraphysical consciousnesses and the degree of recall of the experiences of lucid projections involved 2 intraphysical partners in an extraphysical romance make it such that only 1 of them, the more predisposed party, has complete recollection of his/her experiences in another consciential dimension.

Bibliography: Denning (391, p. 203), Fox (544, p. 61), Frost (560, p. 66), Greenhouse (636, p. 115), Monroe (1065, p. 198), Morrell (1088, p. 369), Muldoon (1105, p. 256), Norvell (1139, p. 157), Prado (1284, p. 114), Schiff (1515, p. 115), Sculthorp (1531, p. 62), Shirley (1553, p. 105), Vieira (1762, p. 46), Walker (1781, p. 145), Yram (1897, p. 205).

---

302. *CONGRESSUS SUBTILIS*

Definition. *Congressus subtilis:* invisible parasexual union with an extraphysical consciousness or even, very rarely, a projected intraphysical consciousness, while the intraphysical consciousness is physically resting.

Synonymy: divine coitus; extraphysical coitus; extraphysical erotic encounter; extraphysical sex act; incubism; intangible parasexual union; invisible intercourse; invisible union; mystical sexual relations; sexual visit in a dream; sidereal rape; succubism.

Notion. The notion that sexual relations can occur between mortals and *supernatural beings, gods, angels* and *demons,* is one of humanity's most widespread beliefs, according to the *affirmations* of anthropology researchers.

Concepts. The following are 9 concepts that should be understood by those who wish to have a deeper understanding of the more pathological or less healthy occurrences of *congressus subtilis:*

1. **Thosenology.** The negative morphothosenes stemming from erotothosenes (mental adultery).
2. **Sexosomatics.** The physical aspects of ordinary human sexual relations.
3. **Holochakrology.** The manifestations of the energies of the sexochakra *(kundalini).*
4. **Folklore.** The ancient *love potions.*
5. **Grimoires.** The ritual prescriptions of grimoires.
6. **Tonics.** So-called aphrodisiac tonics, drugs and cocktails.
7. **Partners.** The *astral* partner.
8. **Lovers.** Angelic lovers.
9. **Predators.** The specifically sexosomatic extraphysical visits made by sexual predators upon sexually deprived intraphysical consciousnesses.

Types. It was accepted for centuries, in various human regions and cultures, that the incubus, an extraphysical entity with the form of a male human, angel or demon, sought invisible union with female intraphysical consciousnesses, and the succubus, an extraphysical entity with the form of a female human, angel or demon, sought invisible union with male intraphysical consciousnesses.

Appearances. However, projections of the consciousness show that invisible unions occur with both intraphysical and extraphysical consciousnesses having a predominantly masculine or feminine mentality or tendency, regardless of their human or extraphysical visual appearance.

Psychosomatics. The extraphysical consciousness and the extraphysically projected intraphysical consciousness can change the form of their sexual appearance at will, according to the properties of the psychosoma or emotional parabody.

Factors. Various factors explain the occurrence of *congressus subtilis,* such as the following 7:

1. **Thosenization.** The power of thought or self-thosenization.
2. **Evocations.** The power of conscious and unconscious evocation.
3. **Empathy.** The natural attraction (empathy) of likeminded consciousnesses.
4. **Monothosenes.** Fixed ideas, monoideisms, mental echoes or monothosenes.
5. **Sport.** The popularity of sex – the favorite human sport – which, above all, originates in the mind ("between the ears and not between the thighs").
6. **Extraphysicology.** The existence of extraphysical consciousnesses of all types and multimillenary experiences, nurturing all kinds of intentions and sometimes fixed upon a single anticosmoethical objective in the paratropospheric dimensions.

7. **Instincts.** The silent and mental sexual instincts and appeals that stem from the affective and sexual deprivation of persons who are unconcerned and unprepared with regard to the extraphysical dimensions.

Film. *The Entity* is a film that impressively and realistically addresses the incubism phenomenon experienced by a North American woman who suffers from intrusion and is possessed by an extraphysical consciousness with masculine characteristics. This film is based on a true story that had its beginning in 1976.

Proximity. Invisible unions between intraphysical consciousnesses, or between intraphysical and extraphysical consciousnesses, can occur with the consciousness of a partner – man or woman – who is in the physical body (the human host) or with both consciousnesses of the projected partners. The closer they are to each other, physically speaking, the easier it will be to obtain extraphysical sexual company.

Energies. With invisible unions involving affectionate embraces ("bear hugs") and contact that is intimate although neither displaying characteristics common to the sex act, nor with orgasm identical to that of humans, there is an exchange or interflow of energies between the partners. This can be a simple peaceful mental advance, when there is a reciprocal revitalization, or an open and direct extraphysical attack, in this case signifying vampirization or blatant energetic plundering, with the revitalization of only one of the partners.

Varieties. Invisible unions occur with 2 partners, or even among various somewhat likeminded partners, between the two basic dimensions of existence: the human, intraphysical or tropospheric and the extraphysical or paratropospheric.

Prophylaxis. The establishment of an evolutionary duo or the normalization of the man and woman's sexlife is the ideal prophylaxis, or the natural and physiological solution for the projective couple to avoid vampirizing *congressus subtilis* and calmly seek projective development through maturity, the clarification task, *consciential gestations* and polykarmality.

Effects. Besides the above-cited effects, *congressus subtilis* can provoke dreams, nightmares, recollections, daydreams, physical repercussions and temporary or permanent interconsciential intrusions.

Will. The will prevails in invisible sexual intercourse. If the intraphysical being, and even the extraphysical consciousness, do not wish the invisible union, it does not occur, regardless of the human circumstances or interdimensional situations.

Shared. One of the most common types of *congressus subtilis* is the shared orgasm in which the intraphysical being finds him/herself unprotected, or passive to the plundering of his/her physical sensations by an extraphysical consciousness of any sexual preference, but having some affinity with the victim.

Case study. This occurs, for example, when one partner commits suicide due to the termination of a neurotic, tempestuous romance and returns, or remains in this human dimension, in order to reestablish the romantic relationship. This even occurs during the sex act of human partners who are influenced by one or more ill, energivorous extraphysical consciousness.

Frustrating. The shared orgasm, frustrated orgasm, semi-orgasm, pseudo-orgasm, generally happens with only one single real orgasm occurring at a time on the part of the intraphysical partner (man or woman), whether it be penile, vaginal, clitoral or anal. This is shared between 2 partners, the intraphysical and extraphysical consciousness, regardless of whether both partners have the same or a different *mental sex*.

Mini-intrusion. The extraphysical influence can manifest in the manner of interconsciential mini-intrusion or ephemeral intrusion. This can last minutes or a few hours, only until achieving reciprocal relief, whether soon after a dream, nightmare, sexothosene, pathothosene or even in a sophisticated act of solitary and silent self-masturbation, in complete physical isolation, in the ordinary, physical waking state.

Emission. Innocent involuntary nocturnal emissions of sperm can attract so-called *succubi* extraphysical consciousnesses (female para-appearance).

Bait. A positive aspect of *congressus subtilis* that challenges human comprehension should be added here. In order to assist intraphysical and extraphysical consciousnesses – reciprocal agents or victims of shared orgasm – the helpers sometimes take advantage of the post-orgasmic period of mutual relief to intervene and guide the one or more ill extraphysical consciousnesses to another extraphysical location. They almost always definitively detach from the intraphysical being who, in this case, served as psychophysical bait, usually unconsciously.

Therapeutic. This shows that, as incredible as it may seem at first, these extraphysical consciousnesses known as *succubi* and *incubi,* act while in a semiconscious condition, albeit in a positive and therapeutic manner.

Comprehension. The affirmations of the previous topic, evidenced by the extraphysical experiences of veteran projectors, can only be understood by the lucid and unbiased intraphysical consciousness, with reference to the following 4 aspects:

1. **Moral.** The sometimes shocking disparities between cosmoethics and conventional human morality. Examples: invisible energetic reunions which lack malice or bad intention; an ordinary human couple can have an invisible union beyond the usual physical union.

2. **Nonproductiveness.** The differences between extraphysical sex – which is natural and malice-free, although nonproductive in terms of human gestation or, in other words, lacks reproductive results and their physical consequences – and physical sex, with its immediate results.

3. *Rapport.* The need to establish deep consciential *rapport* (empathy) between the one who assists and the one who should be extraphysically assisted, in certain cases of assistance provided to post-desomatic parapsychotics *(former intraphysical consciousnesses).*

4. **Universalism.** The universalistic understanding, without preconceptions or taboos, of the needs of consciousnesses that are still parapsychically attached to human instincts. In this case, there are obviously no concessions made to the excesses of the permissivenesses of habits and liberalities regarding the promiscuities and sexual contaminations between men and women.

Awareness. Sadly, the earth will revolve many times, with the appearance of countless human generations and an equal number of consciential lifetimes on this planet, before even half of terrestrial humanity becomes aware of these and other phenomena of equal significance, priority and relevance, in order to enact a prophylaxis of the parasitism and vampirization of interconsciential energies. This takes into consideration the fact that the average human being still erroneously overvalues sexuality among his/her existential resources, tasks, sports and pastimes.

Bibliography: Blavatsky (153, p. 278), Cavendish (266, p. 125), Chaplin (273, p. 88), Day (376, p. 63), Denning (391, p. 203), Digest (401, p. 361), Fortune (540, p. 144), Gaynor (577, p. 85), Gooch (616, p. 29), Lewis (923, p. 66), Martin (1003, p. 70), Pensamento (1224, p. 55), Planeta (1249, p. 168), Richards (1392, p. 139), Shepard (1548, p. 461), Spence (1588, p. 223), Tondriau (1690, p. 241), Vieira (1762, p. 46), Walker (1782, p. 94), Wedeck (1807, p. 186), Zaniah (1899, p. 241).

---

303.   EXTRAPHYSICAL   SELF-LUMINOSITY

Definition. Extraphysical self-luminosity: the quality by which the projected intraphysical consciousness and many extraphysical consciousnesses close to the earth irradiate light through their vehicles of consciential manifestation (see fig. 303, p. 1,142).

Synonymy: extraphysical aura; extraphysical luminescent aureole.

Cause. Self-luminosity is the basic effect caused by the consciousness' own field of energy, which becomes visible to the perceptions of lucid consciousnesses in the extraphysical dimension.

Effects. Among the characteristics of the effects of extraphysical self-luminosity, at least the following 12 should be singled out:

1. The degree of intensity (decrease, increase).
2. Luster.
3. The predominant color.
4. Glimmering, scintillation or sparkling.
5. Luminous trail.

6. Fluxes.
7. Uniformity.
8. The effects of the will.
9. The extension of the luminous projection.
10. The relationship with the extraphysical district, environment or community.
11. Translucence.
12. Monochrome.

Energy. Extraphysical self-luminosity is closely related to the exteriorization of consciential energy.

Types. There are 3 types of extraphysical self-luminosity according to the vehicle of manifestation of the projected consciousness:

1. **Psychosomatics.** Only in the psychosoma.
2. **Holochakrology.** In the psychosoma with the holochakra.
3. **Mentalsomatics.** In the mentalsoma.

Sensitives. Extraphysical luminosity helps overall in certain cases of *inter vivos* apparitions and the apparitions of extraphysical consciousnesses. This is because it is easier for the clairvoyant sensitive to perceive extraphysical lights and reverberations than well-constituted forms.

Self-awareness. The consciousness projected in the psychosoma does not always realize that it emits its own light.

Identification. Sometimes, on certain occasions, without identifying the source, the projector thinks the light is external, from a helper, for example, whereas the light actually emanates from the projector him/herself.

Extinguishment. Other times, the projector only notices that he/she has some luminosity when this extinguishes as a result of passing from a rarefied extraphysical environment to another denser environment (group holothosene).

Opacity. Many intraphysical projectors, when projected, as well as countless extraphysical consciousnesses, appear to be opaque or without luminosity. This can be due to various causes, such as the following 4:

1. **Parapathology.** Disturbances of the consciousness itself.
2. **Evolutiology.** Pathological personal evolutionary period.
3. **Extraphysicology.** The influence of the extraphysical environment (para-ecology) upon the consciousness.
4. **Volition.** Intentional opacity provoked by the will (volition) of the consciousness during the service of extraphysical interconsciential assistance.

Extraphysical consciousnesses. Evidently, extraphysical beings and consciousnesses also present the quality of self-luminosity, although they do not always make use of it. This depends upon the conditions and performance of the more or less alert consciousness.

Disadvantages. Self-luminosity becomes disadvantageous in dull or evolutionarily underdeveloped extraphysical communities or environments because it attracts the attention of the resident native beings (autochthons), whether the visitor is a projected intraphysical consciousness or a lucid extraphysical consciousness that has to *turn off* or become opaque in order to avoid problems by looking like the others. The *outsider's disguise* allows blending into the realities of the district.

Note. The following 3 different realities should not be confused with each other:

1. **Self-luminosity.** The human aura with extraphysical self-luminosity.
2. **Paraluminosity.** The human aura with the still more subtle extraphysical aura.
3. **Bioluminescence.** Bioluminescence (pyrophorous), the biological or natural quality of certain evolutionarily inferior (firefly, glowworm, noctiluca, jellyfish, starfish, scarab beetle or *zarlippus*) living beings (biophotogenesis or physioluminescence).

Bibliography: Bozzano (188, p. 74), Castaneda (258, p. 118), Durville (436, p. 197), Greenhouse (636, p. 284), Kardec (825, p. 149), Vieira (1762, p. 65).

304.	EXTRAPHYSICAL SELF-PERMEABILITY

Definition. Extraphysical self-permeability: the quality of the psychosoma whereby the consciousness, when projected in this vehicle, and many extraphysical consciousnesses contiguous with intraphysical life on earth, pass through solid objects, including dense, tropospheric physical forms, as well as certain formations native to the extraphysical environment (see fig. 304, p. 1,143).

Synonymy: extraphysical self-penetrability; interdimensional self-penetration.

Mechanism. The mechanism of self-permeability is explained by the different vibratory frequency of the vehicles of manifestation of the consciousness or, in other words, the occurrence of interpenetrability of the existential dimensions.

Effects. Well-defined vibratory barriers or extraphysical resistance sometimes arise for the projected lucid projector, that considers his/her psychosoma to be solid, due to various factors, such as the following 5:

1. Unknown densities.
2. Unknown *substances*.
3. *Surface tension.*
4. Unknown impermeability of encountered formations.
5. Clear sensations of passing through, penetrating and perforating.

Types. There are 4 basic types of extraphysical self-permeability:

1. **Structures.** Interpenetration of field 1, passing through material structures.
2. **Intraphysicology.** Interpenetration of field 2, passing through the bodies of intraphysical beings, humans and subhuman animals.
3. **Extraphysicology.** Interpenetration of field 3, passing through the bodies (vehicles) of extraphysical consciousnesses (projected extraphysical human beings and extraphysical animals).
4. **Mentalsomatics.** Interpenetration of field 4, the isolated mentalsoma of the projected consciousness acting directly in the mentalsomatic dimension, passing through any physical-extraphysical structure.

Case study. The following are 3 examples of extraphysical interpenetration:

1. **Parafingers.** Pass the parafingers through a cup or glass.
2. **Psychosomatics.** Pass the parabody (psychosoma) through a table, furniture, door, wall, fence and vehicles, from one end to the other.
3. **Parabodies.** Extraphysically pass through the bodies of awake persons and animals, without their perceiving it.

Sensation. In many cases of lucid projection with the compound double – when the psychosoma is denser or laden with the holochakra – the projected intraphysical consciousness, upon passing through a wall, fence or closed door, has the sensation of passing through fog.

Reverse. The extraphysical sensations frequently give the reverse impression that the physical doors and walls pass through the psychosoma, the psychosoma not seeming to actually pass through the objects.

Limitations. Extraphysical self-permeability is neither infinite nor totipotent, as it presents evident limitations that are insurmountable for us, such as the following 3:

1. **Ballast.** The psychosoma, when very dense or excessively laden with holochakral ballast, has difficulty in passing through certain solid bodies, because it may contain an elevated amount of matter, beyond the average amount that is useful for its extraphysical permeability.

2. **Parapsychism.** The aspect of parapsychic inhibition or the psychological reactions of the projected intraphysical consciousness also have an influence. If the intraphysical consciousness projected in the psychosoma is hesitant or harbors the erroneous idea that he/she will not pass through a certain formation, he/she will in fact not succeed. This is explained through autosuggestion and the mechanism of morphothosene modeling.

3. **Extraphysicals.** The psychosoma is not able to penetrate certain extraphysical formations which were shaped by certain extraphysical consciousnesses. Although excessively dense, most of them were created like that on purpose. This is also caused by morphothosene modeling.

Consciousness. The projected consciousness does not always perceive the self-permeability of the psychosoma. It therefore continues to be inhibited when faced with physical objects, whether opening a door's double, avoiding intraphysical vehicles and subhuman animals in the waking state that move toward the projector.

Self-reluctivity. Reluctivity is the opposite of permeability. In cases of blockages in the operation of the self-permeability of the psychosoma or, in other words, the *self-reluctivity of the psychosoma,* some projectors endeavor to reduce the density of the vehicle through their own will or they try to open a door, for example, using ordinary processes, lifting the (extraphysical) hand to the knob or even entering the door backward (paraback). These means somehow alter the *para*psychology of the consciousness, the extraphysical conditions and/or density of the psychosoma.

Rearguard. Another means for overcoming the self-reluctivity of the psychosoma is entering via the back entrance when possible, for example, instead of using the front door.

Polarity. The act of the consciousness projected in the psychosoma circling around the human construction seems to alter the magnetic polarity of this vehicle relative to the extraphysical environment, one polarity acting in opposition to the other. This ends up eliminating the resistance that is encountered.

Energy. Is it possible in this case that the front door, which is ostensive, more visible, seen, focused upon, dense or impregnated with the energy of the thoughts of intraphysical consciousnesses – just like the images of cults, monuments, tombstones and other objects – hampers the self-permeability of the psychosoma of the projected intraphysical consciousness?

Attraction. It is presumed that the consciousness's vehicle of manifestation maintains its magnetic polarity as well as the extraphysical environment or, more precisely, semi-physical environment. However, upon turning around, the psychosoma may come into magnetic consonance with the environment it wishes to enter. This is like 2 magnetic poles that repel when facing each other but, when one is turned around, they attract each other through the inversion of one of them (magnet).

Shadows. For the intraphysical consciousness projected from the human body, tables, chairs, walls, vehicles and persons' bodies often seem to be as insubstantial as the ordinary shadows of objects and things when in the ordinary, physical waking state. The psychosoma, on the other hand, is simultaneously perceived to be extremely solid and unarguably real.

Tangibility. When the projected consciousness becomes denser he/she achieves full extraphysical reluctivity. He/she is then no longer invisible and is tangibly perceived by 3 categories of percipients, in the following order of occurrence:

1. **Clairvoyants.** By human beings, but firstly, obviously, by clairvoyants.

2. **Subhumans.** Secondly, by subhuman pets, especially dogs.

3. **Intraphysical consciousnesses.** Next, by human beings or intraphysical consciousnesses in general. This produces the phenomena of *inter vivos* apparition, physical bilocation and extraphysical parateleportation.

Mentalsoma. The action of the *isolated mentalsoma* should not be confused with the operation of the *isolated psychosoma*. The mentalsoma operates in the universal and infinite mentalsomatic dimension with less influence from space, form and time.

Freedom. Incidentally, it is neither easy nor common for the intraphysical consciousness to act with greater freedom in the isolated mentalsoma without any influence or ballast of the psychosoma.

Ballast. It should be borne in mind that just as the *holochakra* can serve as ballast for the psychosoma during a lucid projection, the *psychosoma* can serve as ballast for the mentalsoma in another lucid projection.

Movements. In extraphysical reality, the consciousness manifesting in the psychosoma can enter the time-space structure whenever it wishes and leave it to go to a fifth or higher axis, for example, and move about within it, ignoring the space-time structure. It can enter this space-time structure when it wishes, maintaining its position in the other axes constant. It can also travel through time, maintaining space as a constant, or it can travel through space while keeping time constant, or a combination of these, traveling forward and back in space and time.

Axes. Time and space do not cease to exist for the mentalsoma of the consciousness, but this vehicle can maintain its position indifferently in these space-time axes and move about in another which it finds more interesting and is unknown to us. This works in the same way that we walk in a direction along the x-axis and maintain our positions and directions constant on the y-axis and z-axis. When we need to move upward (z-axis) or to the side (y-axis) we can do this also, because space and time do not cease to exist.

Interval. If a spatial interval is greater than, less than or equal to zero, we cannot affirm that it does not exist. The same occurs in relation to a time interval, since these 2 physical aspects are clarified by Einstein's theory of relativity, which establishes that they are not absolute, as classical physics had proclaimed. What is absolute, however, is the velocity of light in a vacuum over any (referential) spatial interval (since velocity = spatial interval / time interval). These 2 aspects are relative when the reference system is changed and can, depending upon the system, be greater than, less than or equal to zero.

Bibliography: Brittain (206, p. 50), Currie (354, p. 100), Delanne (381, p. 209), Farrar (496, p. 196), Greene (635, p. 58), Greenhouse (636, p. 56), Kardec (825, p. 137), Larsen (888, p. 13), Richards (1392, p. 45), Sherman (1551, p. 191), Stokes (1625, p. 24), Vieira (1762, p. 207).

305. EXTRAPHYSICAL ELASTICITY

Definition: Extraphysical elasticity: the property which the psychosoma (of human beings, in this case) presents when submitted to the action of the will of the intraphysical consciousness, projected in this vehicle, of becoming deformed as an instrument of manifestation and later returning to its original, generally humanoid form (see fig. 305, p. 1,144).

Synonymy: elastic property of the psychosoma; extraphysical plasticity.

Extraphysical consciousnesses. Many extraphysical consciousnesses which are in the terrestrial troposphere obviously also have this property – the extraphysical elasticity of the psychosoma – to a more advanced or evolved degree than we do, as intraphysical beings, when we lucidly project from the human body.

Limit. There is no known limit to the elasticity of the psychosoma, beyond which its transfiguration will result in permanent deformation.

Hypothesis. Is it possible that intraphysical consciousnesses are still not able to perform maximal demands that are close to or beyond the elastic limit of the psychosoma? The evolution of projectiology research will answer this question.

Phenomena. The extraphysical elasticity of the intraphysical consciousness' psychosoma allows the occurrence of a variety of other phenomena which are analyzed in this book, such as the following 5:

1. **Self-transfiguration.** Extraphysical self-transfiguration in the psychosoma.
2. **Elongation.** Extraphysical elongation in the psychosoma.
3. **Mimicry.** Extraphysical mimicry.
4. **Clothing.** The appearance of the extraphysical clothing with which extraphysical consciousnesses and projected intraphysical consciousnesses dress their psychosomas.
5. **Zoanthropy.** Zoanthropy.

Bibliography: Vieira (1762, p. 107).

306.   EXTRAPHYSICAL   IMPONDERABILITY

Definition. Extraphysical imponderability: the quality through which the projected intraphysical consciousness and many extraphysical consciousnesses in the earth's troposphere cannot be weighed because they do not present a weight that can be evaluated, not specifically manifesting in the psychosoma, but in the mentalsoma.

Synonymy: antigravitational condition; antigravitational quality.

Cause. The cause of extraphysical imponderability is in the absence of matter, as we understand it, in the mentalsoma.

Mentalsomatics. Strictly speaking, *absolute imponderability* only exists when the consciousness manifests in the mentalsoma.

Psychosomatics. On the other hand, in the case of *extraphysical ponderability,* as well as volitation, consciential energies serve to sustain and propel the psychosoma.

Ponderability. The psychosoma is ponderable or, in other words, contains mass or energy. It thus necessarily suffers gravitational attraction. However, due to its reduced weight, this attraction can easily be eliminated by an opposing force, implemented by the consciousness through the movement of nearby energies which are impelled by the will.

Thousandth. It is presumed, as a hypothesis, that the weight of the psychosoma is approximately 2.47 oz (70 g) or, in other words, one thousandth of the average human body weight. All indications are that, up to this weight, the intraphysical consciousness projected in the psychosoma is capable of moving more easily against terrestrial gravity. Above this weight, however, the psychosoma presents an increased ponderability and reaches a point where it begins to be influenced by the earth's gravitational force.

Holochakra. The holochakra plays a particularly important role in the density of the projected psychosoma and, thereby, in the gradation of extraphysical ponderability. The psychosoma, when without the holochakra, is less ponderable than when laden with it.

Consciousness. The projected consciousness can immediately perceive the reduced ponderability of the psychosoma relative to the human body because it feels lighter and *free as a bird.*

Imponderability. Any type of matter or energy has mass and therefore necessarily suffers gravitational attraction.

Deflection. This is the case, for example, with the experiment performed in 1919, which demonstrated Albert Einstein's (1916) assertion that light rays were deflected upon passing close to the sun's mass.

Absence. Only the total absence of energy is imponderable.

Mentalsoma. In the same manner, any matter or energy cannot, in theory, exceed the speed of light. It is therefore accepted that, in order to reach faster-than-light speeds, or penetrate into spacelike, the consciousness must be manifesting only in the mentalsoma (devoid of energy through the action of the will, in this case?), thereby being able to travel through time at will. The realities of the mentalsoma are still very obscure to our megathosenes.

Evolution. The more evolved an extraphysical consciousness is, the less ponderable it will be.

Scale. The projected projector therefore encounters, on an ascending scale, extraphysical consciousnesses similar to humans, which are dense and *heavy,* subject to the law of gravity, at one extreme, and beings which are totally imponderable, when manifesting in the so-called "mentalsomatic dimension," at the other extreme.

Holograms. Generally speaking, the extraphysical consciousnesses which are seen by the projector (projected intraphysical consciousness) seem to them, in principle, to be veritable *living holograms* or *virtual realities.*

Bibliography: Andreas (36, p. 55), Bozzano (184, p. 131), Delanne (381, p. 209).

307. EXTRAPHYSICAL   INAUDIBILITY

Definition. Extraphysical inaudibility: the quality through which projected intraphysical consciousnesses and many extraphysical consciousnesses in the earth's troposphere cannot be heard by intraphysical beings in the ordinary waking state, whether they are projected in the psychosoma or the mentalsoma.

Synonymy: unhearability.

Cause. Extraphysical inaudibility is the effect caused by a change in the existential dimension of the projected consciousness that passes from the physical dimension to the extraphysical dimension using another vehicle of manifestation adequate for the plane in which it is manifesting.

Consciousness. Because it hears its own voice, the inexperienced projected consciousness has the habit of speaking to human beings and thinks it is being clearly heard, even receiving apparent responses and holding conversations which actually do not exist as they are forged solely by its own morphothosenes.

Contact. Verbal contact between a projector and an intraphysical consciousness becomes very problematic, especially if the individual is not a developed clairaudient sensitive.

Reversion. When the projected consciousness overcomes its inaudibility, which is habitual on the part of human beings, and is able to produce sounds (reversion), the following 2 phenomena occur:

1. Projective pneumatophony.
2. Sonorous projection.

Voice. When the extraphysical consciousness is able to speak to intraphysical beings, the extraphysical-physical phenomenon of direct voice occurs.

Clairaudients. Hearing or clairaudient sensitives are able to receive telepathic messages which are sometimes sonorous for them. The messages are sent by extraphysical consciousnesses and projected intraphysical consciousnesses. In this case, extraphysical inaudibility does not need to be overcome on the part of the transmitting agent.

Mentalsoma. When the projected consciousness is manifesting solely in the isolated mentalsoma, it is presumed that it does not have the means to produce sound although it communicates directly with the mentalsoma of other extraphysical consciousnesses or even intraphysical consciousnesses.

Bibliography: Currie (354, p. 147), Monroe (1065, p. 47).

308. EXTRAPHYSICAL   INVISIBILITY

Definition. Extraphysical invisibility: the quality through which the projected intraphysical consciousness and many extraphysical consciousnesses in the earth's troposphere can ordinarily not be seen by intraphysical beings when manifesting directly in the psychosoma or mentalsoma.

Synonymy: extraphysical insubstantiality; mental invisibility; self-invisibility.

Types. The quality of extraphysical invisibility gives the psychosoma one of its many names, the invisible body. Nevertheless, the least relative mental invisibility is that of the isolated mentalsoma, without the psychosoma.

Patterns. It is feasible to suppose that there are patterns of visibility which may be perceived in different ways and not within or with currently known patterns.

Causes. Invisibility is based on the vibratory frequency of the vehicle of manifestation of the consciousness. For this reason, the projected projector, depending upon extraphysical circumstances, can be invisible to intraphysical consciousnesses as well as to unevolved and even evolved extraphysical consciousnesses.

Case study. Example: when manifesting in the mentalsoma, the intraphysical consciousness will not be seen by extraphysical helpers which are manifesting in the psychosoma on that occasion.

Vehicle. Strictly speaking, total or absolute invisibility does not exist. If the consciousness is not seen or perceived in one dimension at a given moment it will be perceived in another or other dimensions. This always depends upon the consciential vehicle of manifestation used on that occasion.

Manifestation. The temporary invisibility of the projected lucid projector to persons in the ordinary, physical waking state, in their daily routines, constitutes one of the most grandiose manifestations of projective experiences. It can be included among the initial manifestations of human parateleportation, wherein a temporary invisibility of even the human body occurs.

Utopia. The invisibility of the projected intraphysical projector somehow concretizes the utopia of the legendary *invisible man,* who goes wherever he wishes without anyone perceiving his invasive or intrusive presence, as though everyone is unaware of the reality he experiences.

Predator. This sometimes negatively transforms the lucid projector who is unprepared, inexperienced and ignorant of the laws of cosmoethics into a veritable extraphysical predator, from a sexual standpoint, or a frank violator of consciousnesses and environments, when he/she actually takes on the profile of an advanced type of ghost-human, vampire-human or operative intraphysical intruder.

Fiction. Incidentally, Herbert George Wells (1866-1946), the famous English writer, wrote a science fiction novel entitled *The Invisible Man,* which was made into a movie with the same title by Universal Pictures Corporation.

Self-permeability. The abovementioned work recounts the disastrous adventure of a character named Griffin – "the most genial of all physicists" – the first malicious invisible man who suffered hunger, thirst, cold and uttered sounds, but did not have the attribute of physical self-permeability *(O Homem Invisível (The Invisible Man);* trans. Monteiro Lobato; 252 p.; 18.5 cm.; br; 2nd ed.; Companhia Editora Nacional; São Paulo; Brazil; 1934).

Self-invisibility. When projected in the mentalsoma, the consciousness becomes invisible even to him/herself or, in other words, the phenomenon of self-invisibility arises in which the projected projector is neither seen nor sees him/herself, thereby leading him/her to believe that he/she has no vehicle of manifestation and to feel like a mobile point of awareness or merely a vital center of consciential energies.

Visibility. In order for extraphysical visibility to occur on the part of an intraphysical consciousness, the projected intraphysical consciousness needs to have a psychosoma that is denser or laden with the holochakra. In this case, an actual physical visibility occurs or the phenomenon of materialization of the psychosoma of the projected intraphysical consciousness.

Consciousness. The projected projector is not always aware that he/she is invisible to human beings. He/she thus attempts to communicate and even gets angry with intraphysical beings who are indifferent to his/her extraphysical presence.

Bibliography: Bardon (80, p. 385), Blasco (151, p. 193), Carrington (245, p. 230), Carton (252, p. 362), Currie (354, p. 99), Hammond (674, p. 192), Kardec (825, p. 155), Richards (1392, p. 1), Walker (1781, p. 151).

---

309.   EXTRAPHYSICAL   INVULNERABILITY

Definition. Extraphysical invulnerability: the quality of the psychosoma whereby the projected intraphysical consciousness and many extraphysical consciousnesses in the earth's troposphere cannot be affected or wounded from attacks by humans or physical objects.

Synonymy: extraphysical noncombustibility; extraphysical unattackability; physical-extraphysical immunity.

Lesion. Given that the psychosoma is a semiphysical vehicle, it cannot, in fact, be wounded with weapons or sharp pointed objects, or burned, as happens with the structure of the human body (self-combustion), or killed, deactivated (desoma) through one's own will or the will of another. It also cannot decompose, as occurs with the soma, if the intraphysical consciousness is still a pre-*serenissimus.*

Serenissimus. This occurs only at the third desoma, when the *serenissimus* moves to the evolved state of free consciousness (FC).

Repercussion. There are exceptional cases which are intentionally triggered by the extraphysical helpers, wherein an extraphysical touch made to the projected human sensitive's psychosoma provokes a repercussion in his/her inactive soma in the intraphysical base, thereby giving rise to a more complex phenomenon involving the interference of other extraphysical consciousnesses.

Total. According to logical precedents, the quality of invulnerability does not confer total, absolute or indirect immunity to the psychosoma, as can be seen, in summary, with the following 4 aspects of extraphysical occurrences:

1. **Emotional.** As the psychosoma is characteristically the emotional parabody, it can be attacked from the standpoint of vulgar emotions, making the consciousness susceptible to feel, for example, an attack of energetic extraphysical darts in the form of weapons or objects created by morphothosenes with a high density and an elevated energetic level.

2. **Transfiguration.** Although always remaining unwounded, intact and undamaged from conventional physical attacks, the psychosoma, due to its complex structure, permits the ability of self-transfiguration. This gives the psychosoma an appearance of very relative integrity because the consciousness changes its extraphysical form at will, whether consciously or unconsciously, through self-determination or hetero-hypnosis. This is a *healthy* occurrence during extraphysical assistential tasks and *pathological* in the disfigurations of the phenomena of extraphysical lycanthropy.

3. **Sensitivity.** The phenomenon of exteriorization of sensitivity demonstrates that, although not being permanently wounded per se, the psychosoma transfers the *physical lesion* inflicted upon it, as occurs in cases of pinpricks and small cuts made to the human body, in a typical phenomenon of physical repercussion.

4. **Ectoplasmy.** Just as in the phenomenon of exteriorization of sensitivity, another typical physical repercussion of the materialized form occurs to the human body of the materialization ectoplast or sensitive during ectoplasmy experiments.

Vulnerability. Extraphysical repercussions upon the projected psychosoma having physical causes likewise demonstrate the relativity of the attribute of invulnerability of this vehicle or, more precisely, its real vulnerability as a semiphysical creation.

Awareness. The projected consciousness only becomes aware of his/her extraphysical invulnerability after some experience, or when he/she acquires greater lucidity outside the human body through the accumulation of projective experience. Until that point, the projector usually makes one mistake after another due to his/her preconceptions, repressions and deep-rooted social habits, such as: trying to run away from assailants, fearing all types of unfamiliar extraphysical consciousness that appears and needlessly enduring traumas.

Discoincidence. In fact, the condition of discoincidence of the vehicles of manifestation of the consciousness – whether in a voluntary or provoked lucid projection, or even in an involuntary or spontaneous consciential projection – is at the root of all cases of invulnerability, noncombustibility, para-anesthesia, human dematerialization and many other phenomena, due to the invulnerability of the psychosoma.

Mentalsoma. The projected consciousness only enjoys absolute extraphysical invulnerability when he/she manifests in the isolated mentalsoma, an occasion in which he/she even remains immune to the ordinary phenomena of interconsciential intrusion having an extraphysical origin.

Self-affirmations. The extraphysical invulnerability of the psychosoma allows the projected intraphysical consciousness certain freeing, self-realizing or self-affirming attitudes which would normally be avoided in the ordinary, physical waking state, such as the following 10:

1. **Parawalk.** Walk or perform parawalking (like a *tourist*) or volitate over rocky places that are full of weeds, debris, trash or scrap heaps, without worrying about hurting your feet.

2. **Fire.** Go into a large-scale fire without appropriate protective clothing (such as those used by *firemen*), without fearing the flames and toxic gases.

3. **Jungles.** Examine dense jungles, inhospitable fields and groups of suspicious bushes at close range, without clothes, boots and other protective gear, without worrying about poisonous snakes and other potentially dangerous subhuman animals.

4. **Jaguar.** Pet a live, awake jaguar in the open air inside a dense jungle.

5. **Lion.** Enter the cage of a live, awake lion and embrace it without fear.

6. **Alligator.** Extraphysically cross a swamp filled with alligators.

7. **River.** Extraphysically enter a river full of piranhas.

8. **Airplane.** Sit on the wing of an airplane in flight and enjoy the view from above.

9. **Scaling.** Climb or scale steep places without any protective *mountain climbing* or radical sport gear (borderline suicide), without worrying about falling and getting hurt.

10. **Caves.** Fearlessly enter the darkness of abysses, precipices, abyssal areas, caves and caverns of all types, like a *speleologist.*

Bibliography: Carton (252, p. 365), Frost (560, p. 62), Larcher (887, p. 192), Walker (1781, p. 152).

---

310. EXTRAPHYSICAL MULTIPLICITY

Definition. Extraphysical multiplicity: the quality through which the projected intraphysical consciousness and many extraphysical consciousnesses in the earth's troposphere multiply the form of the psychosoma, the simulacra of which can simultaneously appear in various locations.

Synonymy: all-presence of extraphysical form; multilocation of extraphysical forms; omnipresence of the extraphysical form; ubiquity of the extraphysical form.

Multilocation. The quality of multiplicity, derived from the creation of morphothosenes which are almost always unconscious, allow the development of the phenomenon of multilocation of forms or the creation of simulacra of the individual, which are clearly perceptible.

Autoscopy. The multiplicity of extraphysical forms is involved in certain phenomena of external autoscopy in an unconscious manner. In this case, it appears to be closely related to consciential energies and paraphysiological functions of the holochakra.

Relation. In order to minimize the difficulty in understanding the quality of multiplicity of the psychosoma, it is important to observe that it is related to or can better clarify the following *6 occurrences:*

1. **Hologram.** The hologram, or the holographic plate, is a modern paradox with regard to the continent-content binomial, or *a part* of a whole that *contains the whole which contains it.* The holographic plate allows the projection of a three-dimensional object in space. If the hologram is cut into many pieces, each fragment reproduces the entire object. This non-vital, optical (physics) occurrence of the hologram clearly demonstrates its similarity with the quality of multiplicity of the psychosoma.

2. **Clone.** The clone is the *assemblage of individuals* of the same genetic constitution derived from the asexual reproduction of a single original individual (continuous fission, continuous formation of sprouts, and propagation through cuttings). This vital, biological occurrence of the clone also demonstrates deep similarities with the quality of multiplicity of the psychosoma.

3. **Psychosomatics.** The quality of multiplicity of the psychosoma, derived from the creation of morphothosenes which are almost always unconscious, allows the development of the phenomenon of multilocation of forms, or the creation of clearly perceived *simulacra* of the individual.

4. **Ectoplasmy.** The quality of multiplicity of the psychosoma allows the occurrence of so-called simultaneous or *multiple materializations* during ectoplasmy experiments (in this case: triplasy, tetraplasy, pentaplasy). In these cases, two or more extraphysical consciousnesses are made tangible at the expense of the consciential energies which are densified by the cellular elements of the soma,

specifically those of a single intraphysical consciousness, the main ectoplasmic sensitive, from whom all manifest formations are derived and to whom they temporarily remain connected.

5. **Holochakra.** The quality of multiplicity of the psychosoma is involved in certain phenomena of *external autoscopy,* in an unconscious manner. In this case, it appears to be closely related to consciential energies and the functions of the holochakra.

6. **Clairvoyance.** The quality of multiplicity of the psychosoma can explain the cases of the simultaneous presence of an *extraphysical consciousness* detected by clairvoyant sensitives in various groups of parapsychic practices in human locations which are distant from each other.

Seven. The author has encountered a lucid projector who affirms that the consciousness has 7 bodies or vehicles of manifestation. This individual sought to confirm certain occultist affirmations because he saw 6 of his bodies on one occasion, while the seat of his consciousness temporarily remained in only 1 other vehicle.

Simulacra. However, depending upon the efficiency of the performance of the consciousness, the projector can consciously form not only 6 but "n" duplicates, or countless simulacra of his/her vehicles of manifestation, like a *paracloning* (extraphysical cloning) derived from consciential self-determination.

Note. Multiplicity of the vehicles of the consciousness should not be confused with the following 3 phenomena:

1. **Bilocation.** The phenomenon of physical bilocation.

2. **Trilocation.** The phenomenon of *physical-extraphysical* trilocation or double consciential projection.

3. **Multilocation.** The phenomenon of physical multilocation or *physical* trilocation.

Distinction. These 3 occurrences are indicative of a quality and 3 phenomena that are perfectly distinct from each other.

Bibliography: ADGMT (03, p. 282), Butler (228, p. 115), Crouzet (344, p. 204), Delanne (382, p. 175), Digest (401, p. 381), Morel (1086, p. 177), Paula (1208, p. 166), Pensamento (1224, p. 97), Sculthorp (1531, p. 135), Zaniah (1899, p. 462).

---

311. EXTRAPHYSICAL TRANSLOCATION

Definition. Extraphysical translocation: locomotion of the intraphysical consciousness in general when projected from the human body.

Synonymy: extraphysical self-kinesis; extraphysical transit; instantaneous transference; psycholocomotion.

Types. General extraphysical translocation can be executed by employing countless modes (variables) of the manifestations of the extraphysical consciousness or the projected intraphysical consciousness, such as the following 16:

1. **Company.** Individual or in group.
2. **Hyperacuity.** Conscious or unconscious.
3. **Illumination.** In a light or dark environment.
4. **Performance.** Easy or difficult.
5. **Dimension.** In an instantaneous transference from a consciential location or dimension.
6. **Parawalking.** Through parawalking (like ordinary walking).
7. **Gliding.** Through gliding.
8. **Floating.** Through floating.
9. **Volitation.** Through levitation or volitation.

10. **Mentalsomatics.** Like a ball of energy (mentalsoma).

11. **Paramovement.** By "moving without walking" (paramovement).

12. *Tunnel.* Through a *tunnel.*

13. **Currents.** By way of currents of force.

14. **Empathy.** Through extraphysical translocation *via human television* (*rapport* or empathy).

15. *Aviation.* Through *extraphysical aviation.*

16. **Continuity.** By consecutive translocations (continuity) through extraphysical environments of different densities.

Hitchhike. Extraphysical translocation in group sometimes makes two categories of personalities arise:

1. The *extraphysical hitchhiker.*

2. The satellite-volitator.

Distance. Strictly speaking, problems of distance do not exist for the lucid projected consciousness. Evidence of this can be found in spatial lucid projections or exoprojections, with target-places beyond our *solar system.*

Location. In order to cross these considerable distances, the projected consciousness does not need to worry about the location of the star or the direction in which one should go in order to reach the destination. What the practitioner does need is to intensely wish to be there, and he/she will be there almost immediately through a projection in the mentalsoma.

Route. In the mentalsomatic dimension, the extraphysical route is irrelevant. The mental target is the factor which is more important in this context.

Segmented. Extraphysical translocation can also occur in a segmented manner, in parts, as if the consciousness projected in the psychosoma performed large successive leaps in order to reach its target-place, or were obliged to stop at 3 or 4 intermediate points, without being able to go direct, non-stop, from the physical base to the target-place. This generally occurs when there is a greater energetic density in the structure of the psychosoma which, in this case, is laden with the energies of the holochakra.

Dimensions. There are 2 basic modes of translocation regarding consciential dimensions:

1. **Unidimensional.** From one extraphysical district to another, in the same dimension.

2. **Bidimensional.** From one district in one dimension to another district in another dimension. There is an effective change of dimension in this case.

Improvement. The processes and movements of the consciousness projected in the psychosoma are improved with the repetition of experiences. In other words, the volitation technique evolves and should be gradually learned and refined through continuous exercises which manifest in 3 stages:

1. **Freedom.** In the beginning, volitation gives the sensation of emptiness or being free in outer space, not always in a tranquil environment.

2. **Confidence.** Confidence later arises. The consciousness learns to use its new consciential abilities or resources and from this comes the agreeable enjoyment of extraphysical translocation.

3. **Habit.** Later, the veteran projector becomes accustomed (creates the habit) to and delights in free volitation, getting to the point of missing it and regretting the periods of the ordinary, physical waking state, in which it cannot be enjoyed.

Tonic. The excitement and involvement of volitation act like an extraphysical tonic, pacifying the consciousness or establishing true prophylaxis against melancholy of an imprecise origin and an effective extraphysical vaccination against irritability during the ordinary, physical waking state. This clearly signifies a condition of tranquility on the way toward understanding and experiencing serenism.

Sensations. Sometimes the projected consciousness seems to swim in midair. On other occasions, it has no sensation of movement while moving outside the human body.

Witches. Some individuals believe that extraphysical translocation, namely the volitation of projected intraphysical projectors, inspired the story of witches that fly on broomsticks, elaborated during the Middle Ages and the Inquisition, when thousands of supposed witches or sensitives were sacrificed, some even being burned at the stake.

Cord. It is often easier for the projected consciousness to visit someone in a distant city approximately 30 minutes away, for example, than to approach a nearby bedroom in the physical base and stay there for a few moments. This is due to the retraction of the silver cord that is close to the human body, which imposes abrupt interiorizations of the projected intraphysical consciousness.

Control. The more the projected intraphysical consciousness lucidly controls his/her consciential attributes, the better he/she will be able to operate in the extraphysical dimensions. For example: it is sometimes easier to *pass over* a physical wall than to *pass through* this same wall. In other words: depending upon the density of the vehicle of manifestation, it may be more convenient for the intraphysical consciousness to translocate through extraphysical volitation than to use self-permeability of his/her psychosoma.

Mentalsoma. When the projected intraphysical consciousness or an extraphysical consciousness manifests in the mentalsoma, extraphysical translocation is accomplished in a lightning fast manner. For the one using the mentalsoma, the distance to be crossed is unimportant. This is because all points of the universe will be separated from each other by the same time period or, in other words, in an instantaneous, atemporal manner (non-time).

Equilibrium. Although many dreams of flying are actually semilucid projections, one should not confuse them with extraphysical volitation, that unquestionably occurs in a manner that is self-persuasive for the projector at a distance from the human body with the common physiological sensations of floating, flying and spinning, as described in 8% of the reports of ordinary dreams, according to statistics on human consciential projections.

Theories. In line with current theories, the common sensations of floating occur because the brain is receiving disparate signals from the ventricular activation or balance mechanisms. The images of floating, or of other experiences which do not occur in ordinary waking life, can be influenced by the mechanisms of the areas that regulate the position and the equilibrium of the head and neck.

Bibliography: Currie (354, p. 102), Delanne (381, p. 209), Farrar (496, p. 191), Frost (560, p. 59), Greene (635, p. 108), Greenhouse (636, p. 109), Huson (768, p. 116), Sculthorp (1532, p. 24), Shay (1546, p. 97), Vieira (1762, p. 185), Walker (1781, p. 73), Yram (1897, p. 80).

312. MECHANISMS OF EXTRAPHYSICAL TRANSLOCATION

Transit. There is a great similarity between the mechanisms of consciential projection and the mechanisms of the transit of the projected consciousness. This is explained by a change in the vibrational frequency of the vehicle through which the consciousness is manifesting on any specific occasion.

Sensations. Most of the *sensations* of extraphysical translocation, including volitation and force currents, during the rapid unfolding of events when nothing is perceived of the *scenarios* or details of the succession of images, result from a simple change in the vibratory frequency of the vehicle of manifestation of the consciousness leaving one extraphysical energetic environment, plane or field and going to another. This is the case whether a shift is being made from the terrestrial troposphere to an extraphysical district per se, or from this extraphysical district to more evolved extraphysical communities or districts.

Underdeveloped. In underdeveloped consciential environments, the psychosoma generally operates together with the holochakra.

Time. Translocation through time, or that in which *time is stopped* is, above all, of a consciential nature.

Bibliography: Baumann (93, p. 21).

313. SPEED   OF   THE   PROJECTED   PROJECTOR

Definition. Extraphysical speed is the relationship between the distance traveled and elapsed time relative to the trajectory of the psychosoma of the projected projector in the paratropospheric extraphysical dimension.

Synonymy: speed of extraphysical dislocation.

Speed. Above all, it is important to clarify that the consciousness projected without physical or energetic ballast can, in theory, travel faster than the speed of light.

Will. Para-ecological environmental or local differences influence the speed of the projected consciousness' dislocation. It can be easy and rapid or difficult and slow, depending upon the experimenter's will and the density of the environment. There are extraphysical districts which are extremely dense and more difficult for consciential translocation than the planetary crust or paratroposphere itself.

Types. The speed of the projected projector can be classified into 4 basic types:

1. **Slow.** In *slow motion,* sluggish and arduous.

2. **Normal.** Normal or the speed of natural ordinary walking, when the projector is free to move about in the extraphysical environment like a healthy human being.

3. **Intermediate.** Intermediate, or the speed at which the projector moves effortlessly, faster than normal speed, without hindering extraphysical perceptions. At this speed, the projector is able to observe the passing of the images in the environments where he/she travels.

4. **Supranormal.** Supranormal speed, beyond human understanding, does not allow the projector to distinguish the extremely rapidly passing surrounding scenery or visions. A semilucid state frequently occurs. This type of speed is that of the current of force, which is often characterized by high speed wherein the projected consciousness does not always feel capable of stopping when it wishes.

Vision. It is worth mentioning that, when traveling close to the speed of light, it is possible to circle the earth 7 times in only 1 second, wherein it would not be possible to see anything.

Mentalsoma. Here we are only referring to the extraphysical speed of the consciousness when it manifests extraphysically in the psychosoma. In the mentalsomatic dimension, time and space are relative and speed, which is faster than tachyonic speed – because it is in spacelike – is mental, or travels at the speed of thought, without the consciousness losing lucidity.

Friction. Friction seems to occur between the vehicle of the consciousness and the local vibratory level in certain environments, as when the psychosoma is laden with the holochakra. This is reminiscent of the trace of light or the energetic escape of the psychosoma.

Bibliography: Crookall (343, p. 93), Greene (635, p. 6), Muldoon (1105, p. 59), Vieira (1762, p. 55), Yram (1897, p. 62).

314. LUCID   VOLITATION   TECHNIQUE

Definition. Volitation: the most common process of locomotion of the consciousness when projected from the human body.

Synonymy: extraphysical flight; extraphysical gliding.

Types. Among the types of extraphysical volitation, at least the following 10 can be singled out:

1. **Self-volitation.** Individual dislocation or self-volitation.

2. **Group.** Group dislocation or team volitation.

3. **Assisted.** Flight assisted by visible or intangible intelligences or heterovolitation.

4. ***Hitchhike.*** The *extraphysical hitchhike.*
5. **Infantile.** The *infantile extraphysical hitchhike.*
6. **Hyperacuity.** Lucid, semilucid or nonlucid dislocation.
7. **Slow.** Slow dislocation.
8. **Rapid.** Rapid dislocation.
9. **Antigravity.** Upward or antigravitational volitation.
10. **Takeoff.** The takeoff of volitation.

Movements. The psychosoma of the projected consciousness can move in various manners, such as the following 7:

1. **Circles.** Move in circles in the air.
2. **Zigzag.** Whirl around or move in a zigzag.
3. **Exercises.** Perform an *extraphysical dance, extraphysical swimming* and *extraphysical skating.*
4. **Directions.** Perform dislocations in various directions, whether upward, downward, to the side or at an angle.
5. **Stop.** Stop in midair.
6. ***Landing.*** Land the psychosoma or perform an *extraphysical landing.*
7. **Tree.** Volitation allows you to leave the branches of a high tree, circling around the trunk, as though descending a spiral staircase, for example.

Effects. Among the effects stemming from volitation, the following 9 can be singled out:

1. **Position.** The position of the psychosoma standing up, upside down, lying down, at an angle, reclining, with extended arms, open arms or cross-legged.
2. **Observation.** Looking straight ahead.
3. **Energies.** The degree of intensity of propulsive consciential energies.
4. **Environment.** The density of the environment.
5. **Conditioning.** Conditioned human reflexes and their extraphysical consequences.
6. **Paralegs.** The para-arms and paralegs of the psychosoma.
7. **Gravitation.** Consciential conditioning to gravitation.
8. **Transport.** The transporting of another consciousness or extraphysical hitchhiking: extraphysical consciousness or projected intraphysical consciousness.
9. **Mnemosomatics.** Improvement of the projector's recall through lucid volitation.

Help. In certain circumstances, the movement of the arms and legs of the psychosoma, as though the consciousness were swimming in midair or performing rhythmic dancing movements, parapsychically helps the volitation of the projected intraphysical consciousness.

Impulsion. The idea of impelling oneself forward also helps in extraphysical dislocation.

Imposition. During the dislocation of extraphysical volitation, the projected intraphysical consciousness, even with all of his/her lucidity, is not always able to stop at will. Sometimes his/her desire to stop allows him/her to merely reduce the speed of extraphysical dislocation, which continues to a destination that is almost always unknown to the consciousness on that occasion.

Elevation. In some extraphysical areas, even paratropospheric ones, due to the environment and/or the personal conditions of the projected intraphysical consciousness, high altitude extraphysical volitation, namely the voluntary and rapid propulsion of the psychosoma upward, in space, greatly helps in the discernment and identification of the overall physical-extraphysical district being visited.

Concentration. Extraphysical volitation requires considerable concentration of the thoughts of the consciousness or the concentrated attention.

Oligophrenics. Incidentally, extraphysical oligophrenics are generally not able to volitate due to the deficiency of their consciential development, difficulty in mental concentration and lack of coordination of critical judgment. Their mentality promotes insecurity and a loss of maintenance of the psychosoma, and apparent falling while volitating.

Agent. In extraphysical crustal or paratropospheric environments, unimpeded volitation realistically serves as the agent that allows discrimination of consciousnesses' level of awareness and extraphysical performance.

Case study. Thus, for example, an intraphysical consciousness projected with full lucidity in the tranquil early morning hours, freely cuts through space at a height equivalent to the sixth floor of buildings in the dense atmosphere of the big city streets (megacity, megalopolis). Meanwhile, a familiar ill extraphysical consciousness (*clinging* extraphysical consciousness) tries to follow him/her, without any intrusive intention, only desiring his/her company, by moving with some rapidity following the same route down on the street.

Assistential. Unimpeded lucid volitation can be useful as an effective assistential resource in certain paratropospheric environments. One or another ill, energivorous or intrusive extraphysical consciousness that is still very materialized, instantly changes its extraphysical reactions – turning from a *lion into a lamb* – if it is suddenly taken on a flight through midair by the projected intraphysical projector.

Mechanism. Besides the element of surprise, pusillanimity and sometimes the extraphysical consciousness' inability to volitate due to post-desomatic *para*conditioning – that is deeply rooted in its parapsychic reactions or consciential micro-universe – have an influence here, creating cowardice and the stark fear of falling from heights (basophobia).

Antigravity. Extraphysical volitation generally works against gravity or is performed under an antigravity condition.

Leadership. The volitative group commonly volitates in a closed formation in which the consciousnesses – extraphysical consciousnesses and projected intraphysical consciousnesses – dislocate beside the leader of the formation.

Competition. The author extraphysically witnessed a competition in rapid self-volitation between paratropospheric extraphysical consciousnesses in a street (swimming pool) in a district of Rio de Janeiro, Brazil. Each extraphysical consciousness (like a swimmer) threw itself (diving) from the roof of a three-story building (edge of the swimming pool), grazing the asphalt of the middle of the road (bottom of the pool) as quickly as possible, rose from there (antigravity volitation) up to the roof of the three-story building across the street (other side of the pool), where it landed, rose up and returned, erect, to the street.

Densities. This strange competition had its raison d'être, as extraphysical flight is not easy in certain paratropospheric districts, due to the density of the psychosoma and its relationship with the density of the *heavy* environment.

Longing. After the human lucid projector intensifies personal experiences of volitation outside the physical body, he/she will begin to understand the fearlessness and ideal of those consciousnesses confined to the physical restriction of terrestrial existence, but personalities who intuitively long for unimpeded extraphysical volitation, such as pilots in general, acrobatic pilots, astronauts and pilot-authors. These include some well known personalities: Charles Augustus Lindbergh (1902-1974), Antoine de Saint-Exupéry (1900-1944), Richard Bach, Edgar D. Mitchell, pioneers of greater aerial exploration of the physical space of the universe beyond earth. It can thus be seen that there is actually an inter-resomatic, intermissive or *parapsychic longing*.

Bibliography: Andreas (36, p. 55), Castaneda (255, p. 122), Leaf (905, p. 144), Mesquita (1037, p. 224), Muldoon (1105, p. 59), Sabom (1486, p. 54), Shay (1546, p. 99), Swedenborg (1639, p. 100), Vieira (1762, p. 201), Xavier (1890, p. 173).

315. EXTRAPHYSICAL ENERGY CURRENTS

Definition. Extraphysical energy currents: the extraphysical flow of energies existing in the paratropospheric dimensions and in extraphysical dimensions (extraphysicology) without dependence on or direct contact with the physical world (intraphysicology).

Synonymy: astral vortex; current of force; energetic corridor; energetic runway; errant current of energy; extraphysical energy current; extraphysical magnetic current; extraphysical wind; invisible tide; paratropospheric corridor.

Connection. We live in a condition of permanent cosmic connection or immanent interdependency with the entire universe.

Cosmoconsciousness. This fact is more intensely verified by the consciousness in the state of cosmoconsciousness. It is expressed through the smallest occurrences, such as the following 6:

1. **Wave.** A reflection from our consciousness makes waves throughout the universe.
2. **Thosene.** The *smallest* phytothosene counts within the *greatest* holothosene.
3. **Drop.** A drop of water is important in the depths of the ocean.
4. **Virus.** A virus has its specific place in the terrestrial atmosphere.
5. **Hair.** A strand of hair counts in a head of hair.
6. **Atom.** Each small atom has its personal register in the inventory of the entire cosmos.

Earth. The earth, just like the other inhabited planets in the physical universe – according to the correspondences between the microcosm and the macrocosm – has chakras, an aura, a psychosphere, meridians or networks of energy conductors and nadis or energetic points.

Realities. This same earth receives macro-acupuncture through the implantation of needles (menhirs, megaliths, dolmens); has interdimensional energetic doors; has circulating nervous flows; is crisscrossed by telluric currents (geoenergies) which are related to the traditional routes of the self-aware individual.

Effects. The state of universal interdependence and the characteristics of earth produce multiple effects that, for example, affect the following 8 occurrences:

1. **Conscientese.** Conscientese within the mentalsomatic universe.
2. **Hyperacuity.** The achievement of the state of continuous self-awareness.
3. **Universalism.** The concepts of universalism.
4. **Extraphysicology.** Extraphysical environments or communities.
5. **Bioenergetics.** The techniques of exteriorization of consciential energies.
6. *Naphology.* The complex studies and research of *naphology*.
7. **Somatics.** The physical position prior to the experience of lucid consciential projection.
8. **Conscientiality.** Countless other phenomena and procedures of the intraphysical consciousness in the ordinary, physical waking state and of the projected consciousness when outside the human body.

Objectives. Among the objectives of the extraphysical currents, at least the following 6 can be singled out:

1. **Vehicle.** An extraphysical means for rapid, general and continued translocation.
2. **Prophylaxis.** A prophylactic vibratory process of the mental world, defense of the physical and/or extraphysical environment.
3. **Antipollution.** Extraphysical antipollution.
4. **Commemorations.** Preparation or optimization of collective commemorations.
5. **Assistentiality.** An assistential resource in human catastrophes and calamities.
6. **Holosomatic.** Exclusive or direct influence upon the holochakra and psychosoma.

Characteristics. Among the characteristics that specify extraphysical currents, at least the following 24 can be singled out:

1. Field of energy.
2. Flow of energy.
3. Whirlwind.
4. Vibratory cloud.
5. Lightning.
6. *Extraphysical gust of wind.*
7. *Extraphysical hurricane.*
8. *Full sweep.*
9. Single current.
10. Multiple currents.
11. Interconnected currents.
12. Individual currents.
13. Collective currents.
14. Occasional currents.
15. Periodic currents.
16. Continuous currents.
17. Luminosity.
18. Penumbra.
19. Lapse of darkness.
20. Lapse of awareness.
21. Scintillations.
22. Colorations.
23. Sounds.
24. Melodies.

Movements. Extraphysical currents present intelligent effects and do not always allow voluntary movements to be made by the consciousness that is being translocated.

Agents. However, the currents can be reached with mentalsomatic triggering agents (e.g.: a *branch of an extraphysical tree*).

Direction. With regard to direction, extraphysical currents can be categorized into at least 4 types:

1. One-way.
2. Two-way.
3. Intersecting.
4. *Centrifugal* flow.

Trajectory. With regard to trajectory, extraphysical currents can be categorized into at least 5 types:

1. Straight.
2. Oblique.
3. Curved.
4. Horizontal.
5. Vertical.

Irresistibility. Extraphysical currents present the characteristic of irresistibility. The transported consciousness, whether an intraphysical consciousness or an extraphysical consciousness, almost always has to allow itself to be passively guided by the intensity of the current's force, often being swept along.

Peculiarities. They also show the following 5 peculiarities:

1. **Suction.** The existence of the effect of suction.
2. **Entrance.** The point of entrance.
3. **Impulsion.** The initial impulsion.
4. **Exit.** The exit of the current of energies.
5. **Expulsion.** The abrupt expulsion of the transported consciousness, on certain occasions.

Relationships. Extraphysical currents also present at least the following 12 relationships with the projected consciousness:

1. **Participants.** An individual or group experience.
2. **Psychosomatic.** Simple or odd positions of the psychosoma.
3. **Position.** Influence of the consciousness in the position of translocation.
4. **Changes.** Changes in posture while in transit.
5. *Scene.* Awareness of the transit and the *scene of extraphysical origin.*
6. **Sensations.** Vivid sensations that the phenomenon communicates.
7. **Emotionality.** Euphoria (extraphysical euphoria), fear (phobia) or surprise.
8. **Action.** The current of force can act upon the projected consciousness from takeoff or only during a specific extraphysical period of the consciential projection.
9. **Transit.** The departure and return in a single extraphysical experience or transit.
10. **Coexistence.** The effects of personal resistance and passivity to the current.
11. **Support.** The almost always futile attempt to anchor oneself with surrounding objects.
12. **Projectability.** The relationship of the experience of lucid projection in a whirlwind manner with the current of force.

Tunnel. Extraphysical currents of energy should not be confused with the *tunnel effect.*

Research. No one knows up to what point the intriguing extraphysical currents of energy are natural or artificial in the paratropospheric environments, thus demanding countless research projects by lucid consciential projectors.

Bibliography: Butler (228, p. 141), Castaneda (258, p. 234), Greenhouse (636, p. 263), Monroe (1065, p. 83), Muldoon (1102, p. 70), Schiff (1515, p. 177), Shirley (1553, p. 108), Steiger (1601, p. 112), Swedenborg (1639, p. 101), Vieira (1762, p. 201), Yram (1897, p. 60).

---

316. EXTRAPHYSICAL RAIN

Definition. Extraphysical rain: the torrent of positive energetic resources that sometimes flow in the paratropospheric extraphysical dimension.

Synonymy: extraphysical devastation; hydromagnetic tempest.

Causes. The main cause of extraphysical energetic rain lies in the formation of cysts or excrescences of negative or pathological morphothosenes that weigh upon the mentalsomatic economy of the extraphysical environment as well as the human environment.

Hypothesis. Extraphysical energetic rain seems to be generated by as yet inscrutable extraphysical intelligences. Might they be the direct and somehow more collective effects of free consciousnesses?

Effects. The main effects of extraphysical energetic rain are, at least, the following 3:

1. **Para-asepsis.** The cleansing or para-asepsis of chronic morphothosenes in the paratropospheric dimension.
2. *Parareurbanization.* Basic *reurbanization* and cleansing of the extraphysical environment.
3. **Cleansing.** Improvement and cleansing of the psychospheres of extraphysical patients in circumscribed atmospheres.

Types. Extraphysical energetic rain can manifest as ordinary rain or together (at the same time) with storms and other terrestrial meteorological disasters, including the following 5 types:

1. **Earthquakes.** Earthquakes or seaquakes.
2. **Volcanoes.** Volcanic eruptions.
3. **Tornados.** Hurricanes or tornados.
4. **Fires.** Large-scale fires.
5. **Floods.** Widespread floods.

Interrelationships. However, extraphysical energetic rain is not always related to meteorological phenomena.

Psychosoma. The projected consciousness only experiences or witnesses extraphysical energetic rain when manifesting in the psychosoma when it is free of or laden with the holochakra, and not when projected in the isolated mentalsoma in the mentalsomatic dimension.

Bibliography: Vieira (1762, p. 75), Xavier (1883, p. 157), Yram (1897, p. 109), Zoppi (1903, p. 98).

317. EXTRAPHYSICAL FIRE

Definition. Extraphysical fire: a mass of extraphysical flames that arises in certain paratropospheric extraphysical, or even native, environments or districts, with the objective of purifying the environment by cleansing residual, old, negative and dense morphothosenes.

Synonymy: mass of (extraphysical) paraflames; purifying bonfire; purifying fire.

Characteristics. Among the characteristics of extraphysical fires, at least the following 9 can be singled out:

1. **Intelligence.** Intelligence: the consciousness observes that it is neither an effect created by its emotions nor the fruit of its imagination.

2. **Luminosity.** Powerful light that illuminates the entire para-environment.

3. **Intensity.** Impressive intensity.

4. **Violence.** Astonishing and widespread violence.

5. **Volume.** Weight and volume.

6. **Orientation.** Impulsion and orientation by unknown winds with an origin that is unknown to those experiencing it.

7. **Delimitation.** Intelligent action that is intentionally delimited with regard to paraspace and our notions of chronological time.

8. **Mass.** Igneous mass similar to that which is felt in intraphysicality.

9. **Forms.** Forms of *paraflames* and *parablazes*.

Crepitations. Extraphysical fire has agitated whirling movements and crepitations that attract extraphysical beings and involve broad localized areas in a single environment, even over bodies of water.

Preservation. These masses of flames deliberately preserve certain zones, which are clearings of defense, but they exacerbate the sensation of high temperature in the extraphysical surroundings. They are always brief, according to chronological time, giving the impression of lasting for a few minutes.

Morphothosenes. The intelligence shown by the purifying action of extraphysical fire clearly evidences the action of the evolved consciousnesses that sponsor it. The fires appear to be performed by morphothosenes in previously installed force fields.

Purification. The purifying fire somehow affects certain energivorous, parapsychotic, post-desomatic extraphysical consciousnesses that feel burned upon being reached and try to evade its attraction and contact. They act like an extremely dirty person who does not want to take a bath. They therefore run away terrified, as do those intraphysical consciousnesses which are projected in the environment.

Hell. Over time, extraphysical fire has characterized the images of the terrestrial and ingenuous, although macabre, belief that became the doctrine of the *eternal fire* of hell where *human souls* are disturbed without relief. Fortunately, such formations constitute mere images or ephemeral consciential creations.

Parapyrogenesis. Extraphysical fire should not be confused with the cases of extraphysical parapyrogenesis that occur in the intraphysical dimension and stem from extraphysical causes.

Bibliography: Prado (1284, p. 118), Xavier (1883, p. 163).

318. GENERAL EXTRAPHYSICAL EMOTIONS

Definition. Extraphysical emotion: the intense and brief reaction of the projected consciousness to an unexpected event, which is accompanied by a painful or agreeable emotional state.

Synonymy: extraphysical commotion; extraphysical emotivity.

Types. Among the types of extraphysical emotions, the following can be singled out: self-control; emotionalism; extraphysical euphoria; laughter; solitude; compassion; embarrassment; fear; sexual impulse.

Causes. Among the main causes of the extraphysical emotions of an intraphysical consciousness, at least the following 14 can be singled out:

1. **Parahand.** Pass the extraphysical hand (parahand) of the psychosoma through the structure of physical objects.
2. **Walls.** Pass through walls with naturality.
3. **Bodies.** Pass through the bodies of human beings (somas).
4. **Soma.** Observe one's own inactive human body up close.
5. **Psychosoma.** See one's own psychosoma reflected in an ordinary mirror.
6. **Take off.** Take off suddenly from the human body (extraphysical escape).
7. **Cord.** Make a detailed examination of the silver cord.
8. **Hyperacuity.** Expand awareness (hyperacuity) and visual paraperceptions outside the human body.
9. **Self-transfiguration.** Perceive oneself to be partially configured in a semi-humanoid body of manifestation.
10. **Respiration.** Perceive the precise moment of the loss of respiration.
11. **Volitation.** Volitate alone and freely.
12. **Extraphysical euphoria.** Experience the state of extraphysical euphoria.
13. **Encounter.** Encounter the consciousness of a familiar personality which has undergone desoma.
14. **Attack.** Suffer an extraphysical attack from an ill extraphysical consciousness.

Reactions. Among the inner reactions of the projected intraphysical consciousness that are triggered or arise after extraphysical emotions, at least the following 6 can be singled out:

1. **Volitation.** Personal will (volition).
2. **Habits.** Social habits (personal sociability).
3. **Repressions.** Conditioned reflexes (personal repressions).
4. **Preconceptions.** Preconceived ideas (preconceptions, apriorisms).
5. **Recomposition.** Emotional recomposition.
6. **Ridicule.** Sensation of ridicule.

Effects. Among the effects stemming from the extraphysical emotions of the projected projector, at least the following 4 can be singled out:

1. **Holosomatics.** Differentiation between the psychosoma and the mentalsoma.
2. **Extraphysicology.** Extraphysical trauma.
3. **Intraphysicology.** Sudden, imposed, premature or traumatic interiorization.
4. **Thosenization.** Choice of serenity (thosenization with an *emphasis* on the *tho* of thosenes) as the best technical extraphysical conduct.

Serenity. The consciousness of the consciential projector needs to teach itself, through autosuggestion, to maintain composure, balance and serenity when outside the human body, in order not to succumb to fear and not panic when faced with traumatizing surprises.

Exercises. In order to achieve serenity outside the human body, it is necessary to begin to understand it and practice it while still in the body, namely while in the ordinary, physical waking state.

Athymia. On the other hand, when achieving a state of serenity is recommended, it obviously does not imply that the person should become a robot or arrive at a pathological condition, such as *athymia* – a reduction or disappearance of affectivity, or one's external manifestations, which are common in stuporous and hebephrenic syndromes – and the *non-emotionality* that is the absence of emotional reactivity.

Sentiments. Many studious individuals currently consider that emotions are not the same as sentiments.

Emotions. Emotions are biological or more animalized. Sentiments are thoughts connected to emotions, rationality and self-critical judgment coming into play here.

Psychosomatics. Emotions are more restricted to the human body, the holochakra and the psychosoma. Emotional intelligence is only 1 of at least 12 modes of intelligence researched within conscientiology that the intraphysical consciousness possesses.

Mentalsomatics. Sentiments stem more from the mentalsoma of the consciousness.

Incapacity. There are individuals who do not know how to join their thoughts with their emotions and are always incapable of describing what they feel and precisely how their experiences feel.

Hemispheres. It is suspected that the inability to describe one's own experiences is due to a disturbance in communication between the 2 cerebral hemispheres.

Alexithymia. The psychiatrist Peter Sifneos coined the term *alexithymia* to refer to the condition of persons who lack an adequate vocabulary for expressing their sentiments.

Pathology. These *emotional illiterates* appear to make up approximately 10% of the population. Among them, besides persons considered normal and healthy, alcoholics, hypochondriacs, patients with psychosomatic illnesses, seriously traumatized persons, sociopaths and drug addicts (toxicomaniacs) are found.

Hypotheses. Research has still not been performed in order to ascertain the relationship between lucid consciential projection and alexithymia. The author registers below 4 more projectiological research and work hypotheses:

1. **Percentage.** What percentage of alexithymics become advanced lucid projectors?

2. **Paratrauma.** Does the consciousness of the alexithymic stop suffering extraphysical trauma (paratrauma) when projected with lucidity or does he/she experience traumas without being able to express them?

3. **Health.** Is alexithymia a positive or healthy condition (extreme extraphysical self-control, health), or is it negative or pathological (difficulties in paraperceptions, illness) with regard to development of the intraphysical consciousness' lucid consciential projections?

4. **Parapsychopathology.** Does the insufficiency of communication between the 2 cerebral hemispheres reveal a pre-existing effect or disturbance restricted to the parapsychopathology of the mentalsoma headquartered in the parabrain of the psychosoma, or is it a disturbance acquired in this human life, restricted merely to the dense brain?

Bibliography: Monroe (1065, p. 205), Steiger (1601, p. 126), Vieira (1762, p. 120).

---

319. EXTRAPHYSICAL EUPHORIA

Definition. Extraphysical euphoria: the state of satisfaction, invulnerability and optimism with the sensation of perfect well-being, intense happiness or euphoria beyond words that overwhelms the intraphysical consciousness projected in the psychosoma in certain circumstances in the extraphysical dimension, especially in the paratropospheric dimension.

Synonymy: ephemeral extraphysical ecstasy; exacerbation of extraphysical emotivity; extraphysical euphoria; irresistible ecstasy.

Types. Extraphysical euphoria, as a temporary, ambiguous or hybrid sensation, can be productive or counterproductive, negative or positive. This is dependent upon the immediate decisions and attitudes of the projected consciousness with regard to knowing or not knowing how to control it and taking advantage of this sensation.

Emotivity. The main cause of extraphysical euphoria is the exacerbated emotionalism of the consciousness stimulated by the psychosoma (emotional parabody) on that occasion.

Acme. Extraphysical euphoria represents the acme of primary forms of emotive reactions by the intraphysical consciousness in evolutionary ascension from the raw, earthly or tropospheric animality to the level of evolved self-conscientiality.

Causes. Among the secondary causes of extraphysical euphoria, at least the following 5 can be included:

1. **Volitation.** The satisfaction of indulging in unimpeded volitation far from material limitation and the draconian action of respiration and planetary gravitation.

2. **Megafreedom.** Attainment of the plenitude of a sense of extraphysical megafreedom.

3. **Peace.** The appearance of inner peace or immaculate and vivid inner pacification.

4. **Immateriality.** The sensation of immateriality and lightness typical of the discoincident or free psychosoma.

5. **Somatic.** Self-awareness of the condition of the temporary extraphysical freedom of the consciousness and its concomitant connection with the temporarily inactive human body.

Effects. The effects of extraphysical euphoria bring positive or negative consequences to the projected intraphysical consciousness.

1. **Positive.** The following are positive effects of extraphysical euphoria: benign awakening of the projector's sexochakra *(kundalini)* energy and the consequent awakening of the other basic chakras; stimulation of physical and extraphysical assistential works; appearance of sincere gratitude to the greater powers of extraphysical life; anxiousness to understand, forgive (reconcile) and cooperate in a positive manner with all beings and everything good that exists in the universe; appearance of a universalistic sense toward humanity and para-humanity.

2. **Negative.** The following are negative effects of extraphysical euphoria: extraphysical trauma and the consequent abrupt return to the human body; physical repercussions; the excesses of mysticism; difficulty in translating the extraphysical experiences and sensations into words.

Techniques. In techniques for the control and immediate use of extraphysical euphoria, various resources can be employed, such as the following 4:

1. **Evocation.** Make a grateful and sincere mental evocation when installing the state of euphoria.

2. **Volition.** Perform emotional readjustment or the recovery of serenity through willpower (volition).

3. **Target.** Endeavor to maintain maximum equilibrium without losing the current extraphysical mental or consciential target.

4. **Self-maturity.** Think about ceasing to be an animal, child or immature being as a projected consciousness.

Routinization. The definitive control of extraphysical euphoria by the consciousness can only be achieved by making one's extraphysical experiences routine through the repetition of continued self-lucid projections in series with the same nature and expression. This finally brings security, consciential self-maturity and serenity.

Expansion. When projected in the isolated *mentalsoma,* the intraphysical consciousness, in a state of cosmic expansion, does not actually feel the extraphysical euphoria that the psychosoma provides but an immanent well-being without coarse sensations or emotions. This cosmic expansion of the projected consciousness, in some *structural* way, is undoubtedly essentially superior, more evolved and quite different from the primary euphoria that arises when the intraphysical consciousness is overloaded by the emotionalism of the *psychosoma.*

Bibliography: Bozzano (188, p. 54), Rampa (1361, p. 17), Vieira (1762, p. 83), White (1831, p. 96).

320. EXTRAPHYSICAL FORMS OF THE PROJECTED PROJECTOR

Definition. Extraphysical form of the projected projector: the outline, physiognomy and *visual* appearance with which the projected consciousness presents itself when manifesting outside the human body.

Synonymy: extraphysical appearance of the consciousness; para-appearance of the consciousness.

Vehicle. The extraphysical form of the projected intraphysical projector is dependent upon 1 of 2 vehicles of manifestation of his/her consciousness:

1. **Mentalsoma.** When manifesting in the isolated mentalsoma it does not present a defined form, or does not present any form.

2. **Psychosoma.** When manifesting in the psychosoma, it commonly has a humanoid form with characteristics of its current human body, whether in whole or in part.

Environment. The extraphysical form of the projected intraphysical projector is closely related to the extraphysical environment where its consciousness is manifesting.

Agreement. No one reaches a certain extraphysical environment, nor does one fully manifest there, if not entirely in agreement (adequation, adjustment) with the characteristics of the environment. This is the case regardless of who, where or when, in any extraphysical situation involving the intraphysical or extraphysical consciousness.

Paraperceptions. Changes in the density of the psychosoma, according to the extraphysical environment, influence the projected consciousness' perception of surrounding extraphysical forms.

Impressions. The impressions of extraphysical forms can be entirely real or absurdly illusory, depending upon the perceptions, emotions, ideas and modeling of the consciousness, as with the following 3:

1. **Psychosomatics.** When projected in the psychosoma, the intraphysical consciousness can look much younger, taller and appear to have larger eyes.

2. **Extraphysicology.** One can have the impression that human and extraphysical constructions have higher ceilings.

3. **Walls.** Walls seem to be farther away from each other and environments generally seem to appear more ample.

Bibliography: Frost (560, p. 61), Greenhouse (636, p. 97), Ostby (1171, p. 232), Vieira (1762, p. 168).

321. EXTRAPHYSICAL CLOTHING

Definition. Extraphysical clothing: the elements that comprise the form of the psychosoma where the intraphysical consciousness manifests in the extraphysical dimension, including para-clothing, para-shoes, para-accessories or para-rings.

Synonymy: extraphysical apparel; extraphysical attire; extraphysical clothing; extraphysical garments; paraclothing of the projected projector.

Characteristics. Various aspects should be considered when analyzing extraphysical clothing, such as the following 12:

1. **Types.** Types, colors and variations of clothing, as well as indeterminate clothing.

2. **Parashoes.** Various types of parashoes.

3. **Paraglasses.** Various types of paraglasses.

4. **Replicas.** Para-replicas of bandages and casts of the wounded or injured projected intraphysical consciousness.

5. **Creation.** The manner or nature of creation of the clothing.

6. **Modifications.** Modifications – even unconscious and instantaneous – in the clothing.

7. **Imagistic.** The power of imagination in personal extraphysical presentations.

8. **Thosenization.** The act of wearing what is thosenized and what the projector thinks he/she is wearing.

9. **Somnambulism.** The extraphysical somnambulist and the unconscious creation of clothing.

10. **Psychosomatics.** The *enlargement* of extraphysical clothing together with the reconstitution of the psychosoma.

11. **Holochakrology.** The influence of the consciential energies of the human aura (holochakrology).

12. **Sanitary napkin.** The intraphysical projector's sanitary napkin and its extraphysical replica.

Mentality. The facts show that extraphysical clothing arises naturally and not according to the reality of the extraphysical environment, nor is it derived from this environment, wherever the consciousness is projected, but according to its thoughts, thosenes and the mentality of the consciousness on that occasion.

Visual. While the intraphysical consciousness is projected, the visual appearance of the psychosoma is, as a rule, *androsomoid* for the man and *gynosomoid* for the woman. This seems to have the objective of better identifying the projected consciousness.

Nudity. Projected intraphysical consciousnesses instinctively dress themselves because they are conditioned against nudity by their repressive human education.

Paratroposphere. There are paratropospheric environments, however, that are veritable extraphysical nudist colonies.

Children. The projected projector frequently sees intraphysical children projected in the nude, without extraphysical clothing.

Attention. Could this be due to the natural distracted nature of children, their short attention span and the difficulty in focusing their will on a single issue, or that they are less conditioned to clothing than adults?

Changes. The same spontaneity, stemming from the unconscious, with which extraphysical clothing naturally arises, also appears to happen with the sudden changes that these clothes undergo, or even the state of alternation between being clothed or naked, according to the circumstances that influence the mental microuniverse of the consciousness.

Theories. The following 4 theories are proposed in explanation of the extraphysical clothing of the intraphysical consciousness projected in the psychosoma, although the fourth theory is more widely accepted by consciential projectors or researchers in general:

1. **Double.** The extraphysical forms of all material objects, or the double of all existing things, might somehow unconsciously become joined with the intraphysical consciousness projected in the psychosoma in the extraphysical dimension.

2. **Holochakra.** The consciousness, in the psychosoma, might spontaneously manipulate the semimaterial components of the holochakra and the extraphysical clothing thereby appears.

3. **Material.** The consciousness projected in the psychosoma might interweave its form and clothing, absorbing elements of the wood and metal that already exist in the material sources of this physical dimension.

4. **Morphothosenes.** The accessories of the psychosoma might be morphothosenes or thought forms created by the consciousness, which is already responsible for the vitalization of the psychosoma and the human body.

Ectoplasmy. A subject directly related to the extraphysical clothing of the consciential projector is the clothing of extraphysical consciousnesses materialized in ectoplasmy experiments performed since the nineteenth century, regarding which there is still much obscurity and, naturally, intense controversy.

Bibliography: Baumann (93, p. 48), Bozzano (184, p. 145), Carrington (247, p. 55), Crookall (332, p. 5), Currie (354, p. 98), Durville (436, p. 214), Engel (480, p. 29), Fodor (528, p. 383), Frost (560, p. 58), Greenhouse (636, p. 76), Hart (687, p. 243), Holms (735, p. 449), Kardec (825, p. 156), Lester (919, p. 61), Lischka (937, p. 117), Monroe (1065, p. 183), Muldoon (1105, p. 282), Müller (1107, p. 158), Osborn (1157, p. 159), Prado (1284, p. 45), Prieur (1289, p. 111), Shepard (1548, p. 267), Shirley (1553, p. 145), Steiger (1601, p. 66), Swedenborg (1635, p. 100), Tyrrell (1717, p. 166), Vieira (1762, p. 32), Walker (1781, p. 71), Xavier (1890, p. 179).

322. UNIFORM OF THE PROJECTED PROJECTOR

Definition. Uniform of the projected projector: the extraphysical attire in which the intraphysical consciousness projected in the psychosoma is most frequently dressed.

Synonymy: habitual paraclothing of the projected intraphysical consciousness.

Pajamas. The most common uniform of the projected intraphysical projector is ordinary pajamas, a nightgown or the nightwear in which the projector goes to bed, which is quite understandable.

Facts. The use of the form of pajamas or nightwear is due to 2 facts:

1. **Noctivagant.** The majority of projections of experienced projectors are produced at night when they go to bed. This is the reason for the predominance of noctivagant (noctivagous) projectors.

2. **Unconsciousness.** The mental texture of extraphysical clothing generally occurs unconsciously. The projected consciousness uses the attire it knows its human body was dressed in the last time it thought about the subject while in the ordinary, physical waking state, prior to projecting.

Projectors. Due to natural feminine vanity, a great number of projectors with some experience, when projected, frequently present themselves in a refined evening dress as extraphysical clothing, as though they were going to an elegant evening reception.

Inappropriateness. Pajamas (or a nightgown), when used as a uniform, besides characterizing and standardizing the consciousness' extraphysical appearance or image, facilitates its extraphysical awakening. This is because the projected projector perceives he/she is going about in inappropriate attire, with a ridiculous attitude and in a place where it would be inadmissible for him/her to be when in the ordinary, physical waking state, wearing pajamas in the middle of a commercial street, for example. This also helps the projector intensify his/her extraphysical self-awareness.

Habits. The extraphysical uniform, however, varies according to the projector's habits and daily concerns, such as the following 5:

1. **Discretion.** A clerk usually wears discreet clothing.
2. **Social.** The businessman wears a suit.
3. **Lab coat.** The medical doctor wears a lab coat.
4. **Surgery.** The surgeon sometimes wears appropriate attire for going into the surgery room.
5. **Sport.** The athlete wears sport attire.

Shoes. Whether wearing pajamas or any other attire, the intraphysical consciousness projected in the psychosoma is not always wearing shoes. He/she often finds that he/she is wearing only socks and is frequently not even aware of the fact.

Establishment. The establishment of the form, outline, fashion, size, style and appearance of the projector's uniform and his/her mental focus on that fact are notably relevant as measures capable of standardizing personal habits in order to have continued projections in series, without long-lasting periods of recess, as well as extraphysical contact with other projected consciousnesses and consciousnesses in general.

Bibliography: Butler (227, p. 71), Greenhouse (636, p. 71), Vieira (1762, p. 187).

323. EXTRAPHYSICAL SELF-TRANSFIGURATION

Definition. Extraphysical self-transfiguration: the changing of the external form of the psychosoma through the will of the consciousness (see fig. 323, p. 1,145).

Synonymy: deformation of the extraphysical appearance; *endometaplasia;* extraphysical disfigurement; extraphysical metamorphosis; extraphysical self-transfiguration; polymorphy of the psychosoma; *somurgoscopia.*

Form. In theory, depending upon its performance when manifesting in the psychosoma, the consciousness is able to temporarily assume different forms.

Environment. In most types of extraphysical self-transfiguration, the extraphysical environment, district or community seems to have a decisive influence in the transfiguration process.

Types. The following are 5 types of transfiguration of the psychosoma:

1. **Unconscious.** Unconscious, oneiric, spontaneous or involuntary self-transfiguration of the psychosoma. This spontaneous transfiguration stems from an extraphysical trauma.

2. **Conscious.** Conscious self-transfiguration is provoked by the impulse of the will of the intraphysical consciousness upon his/her psychosoma.

3. **Successive.** There are successive self-transfigurations of the psychosoma that follow one another uninterruptedly in certain extraphysical circumstances and according to parapathological disturbances of the intraphysical consciousness.

4. **Dialogic.** Dialogic self-transformation of the psychosoma is that which is unconscious and provoked by the transmental dialog of the parapsychotic, energivorous and viscous extraphysical consciousness that may accompany the projector in his/her extraphysical trajectory.

5. **Co-participant.** Co-participant self-transfiguration of the psychosoma is that which is shared by the participation of the psychosoma of the extraphysical visitor – or even of a projected intraphysical consciousness – that becomes infected with the phenomenon during transmental dialogue.

Influence. The extraphysical environment seems to have a decisive influence in most types of extraphysical self-transfiguration.

Cause. The main cause of self-transfiguration is in the plasticity of the psychosoma, which is sensitive to the will and emotivity of the consciousness.

Deformations. In order to understand unconscious self-transfiguration, it is sufficient to reflect upon the physiognomic alterations a person exhibits when faced with a positive or negative surprise, or in regard to certain physical deformations occurring during certain serious illnesses.

Soma. If the human body (soma) alters so much, weighing 154 lb. (70 kg), the psychosoma (emotional parabody), weighing only one thousandth of this, with 2.47 oz. (70 g), alters much more in the face of *parastresses,* critical traumas and unexpected impacts in the extraphysical dimension.

Effects. Among the countless effects of self-transfiguration of the psychosoma, from the frivolous-comical to the serious-productive, the following 10 can be singled out:

1. **Growth.** Transfiguration of the psychosoma explains the phenomenon of the biological growth of the soma, which is merely a transfiguration of the biological body, over a more or less prolonged period, promoted by the conditioning laws of genetics upon the consciousness when in the condition of physical restriction.

2. **Extraterrestrials.** Transfiguration of the psychosoma explains the resoma of extraterrestrial beings on this planet earth. In this way, the extraphysical consciousness having a psychosoma with a non-terrestrial form, which is exotic according to terrestrial shapes, is reborn here following the rigid evolutionary genetic laws of this planet and the anthropomorphic lines pertaining to our human bodies through the quality of transfiguration.

3. **Facial.** The phenomena of facial clairvoyance occur through the auric coupling of two or more persons. The exteriorization of bioenergy densifies, forming a compound energetic cloud, or aeriform ectoplasm on or between the faces of the intraphysical consciousnesses. This allows the appearance of other faces, extraphysical beings and even visual landscapes, projections or messages. As it is a typical initial manifestation of ectoplasmy, facial clairvoyance can evolve to the point where ephemeral transfigurations of the human body and psychosoma occur.

4. **Ectoplasmy.** In ectoplasmy or materialization experiments, transfigurations of the ectoplasmic sensitive's face and human body appear. They become modified, adopting facial features that are notably different from their own. This is especially due to his/her own ectoplasm, in a combination of their consciential vehicles: the soma, the holochakra and the psychosoma.

5. **Elongation.** A more frequent effect of transfiguration of the psychosoma is the phenomenon of extraphysical elongation. This arises as though there were a prolongation of parts or organs of the human body through the exteriorization of bioenergy and, consequently, ectoplasm.

6. **Corrections.** Through self-transfigurations imposed on the psychosoma through the impulse of the will, certain extraphysical consciousnesses that have recently arrived in the extraphysical dimension or the post-desomatic intermissive period, and even some projected intraphysical consciousnesses with developed extraphysical abilities, upon becoming aware of this extraordinary resource of plasticity, endeavor to correct deficiencies in their appearance, or rectify their old inhibitions, complexes, repressions and conditioning in a lasting or temporary manner. The following are some examples of *paravanity:* women who dream of being young, lose their belly or endeavor to sculpt a perfect nose; men who correct their baldness, increase their height (extraphysical giants) or develop big muscles; frustrated artists who instantly become singers, adding the resource of morphothosenes to self-transfiguration.

7. **Parapsychism.** Transfigurations of the psychosoma occur during certain manifestations and *extraphysical parapsychic trances* (paramediumship).

8. **Clairvoyance.** Self-transfigurations of the psychosoma allow aiding, assistential and educational extraphysical consciousnesses to show themselves to other extraphysical consciousnesses and be seen by human clairvoyants, disguised as someone familiar (helper), an archetypal being worshiped in a parapsychic environment or group.

9. **Zoanthropy.** Transfiguration of the psychosoma provoked by autosuggestion or suggestion from another intelligence to weak and impressionable extraphysical consciousnesses occurs in cases of extraphysical zoanthropy or lycanthropy generated by hypnotist-intruders.

10. **Intrusion.** Transfiguration of the psychosoma enables ill, mystifying extraphysical consciousnesses to portray themselves with different appearances in processes of interconsciential intrusion, subjugation and fascination. They pass for those they are not, hiding their true identity. One should neither identify nor qualify an extraphysical interlocutor (an extraphysical consciousness or projected intraphysical consciousness) by its appearance, nor only by the discernment or coherence of its discourses, that which it shows, does or endeavors to do, but above all by the perceptible quality of the consciential energies it exteriorizes and the consequences thereof.

Transsexuals. It is sometimes very frustrating, in one's first extraphysical encounter, to come across a former male friend who, when intraphysical, was well-known and now, as an extraphysical consciousness, has the appearance of a beautiful woman. It is the form or retrosoma of another life, almost always that immediately prior to the most recent one, with which its consciousness has more affinity and feels more at ease. The author has already amicably and jokingly censured one of his acquaintances, who underwent desoma prematurely and had never shown any ostensive feminine tendency while in human life. Actually, this is a fact that is normal, understandable and totally different from the operations or surgeries of intraphysical transsexuals.

Sex. Sex is, above all, a manifestation that originates in the mind, or directly in the *coincident* intraphysical consciousness. Therefore, the more evolutionarily developed a consciousness is, the greater will be its possibilities for presenting the sexual appearance it wishes, whether masculine, feminine or transsexual.

Basic. It can thus be seen that there are 3 basic types of self-transfiguration:

1. **Somatics.** Transfiguration of the human body due to stress or illness.

2. **Holosomatics.** Ectoplasmic transfiguration, namely transfiguration of the human body, holochakra and psychosoma, is also known as *endometaplasia* or somurgoscopy.

3. **Psychosomatics.** Transfiguration of the psychosoma itself, in the extraphysical dimension.

Specific. Besides the specific types of extraphysical self-transfigurations referred to above, such as extraphysical clothing, the uniform of the projected projector and extraphysical elongation, zoanthropy, extraphysical mutation and extraphysical mimicry will be analyzed.

Bibliography: Ambelain (23, p. 40), Delanne (381, p. 256), Kardec (825, p. 153), Monroe (1065, p. 170), RPA (1481, p. 173), Vieira (1762, p. 18), Yogananda (1894, p. 383).

324. ZOANTHROPY

Definition. Zoanthropy: the presumed occurrence whereby a human being can, under certain circumstances, transform him/herself into an inferior or subhuman animal.

Synonymy: animal-human; cynanthropy; energetic mutation; human metamorphosis; lycanthropy; wolf-man; wolf-woman.

Metamorphosis. Since ancient times in primitive human areas, among savage tribes, and mainly during the Middle Ages, there has been a belief in the metamorphosis of persons into subhuman animals such as dogs *(cynanthropy),* horses *(hippanthropy),* jackals, hyenas, jaguars, lions, leopards, tigers, bears, other wild animals and even reptiles.

Lycanthropy. The typical form of transformation of humans into animals in Europe has been the wolf, thus the denomination of *lycanthropy* (Greek: *lukos,* wolf; and *anthropos,* man).

Epidemic. There was even a case of epidemic zoanthropy in a convent in Germany, wherein the nuns believed they had been possessed by cats, or transfigured into cats, and strangely behaved in that manner.

Confusion. In cases of zoanthropy, there has always been heightened confusion regarding the following 4 characteristics or categories of the phenomenon:

1. **Volition.** Whether the transformation is voluntary or involuntary (volition).
2. **Duration.** Whether it is temporary or permanent.
3. **Holosomatics.** Whether it is actually a transformation of the human body (soma) or the extraphysical body (psychosoma) of a male (androsoma) or female (gynosoma).
4. **Zoology.** Whether it manifests directly through the psychosoma or through an animal.

Psychopathology. According to psychopathology, regarding the obscure mental disorder of *lycanthropy* included in the chapter on delirious metamorphic ideas, the ill person believes him/herself to have been transformed into a wolf and imitates the habits and the voice of this animal. The agent therefore receives specific names in the following 6 languages:

1. *Licantropo* (Portuguese).
2. *Loup-garou* (French).
3. *Lubizón* (Spanish).
4. *Lupo mannaro* (Italian).
5. *Wahrwolf* (German).
6. Werewolf (English).

Regions. This occurrence also receives different names according to the region where it is addressed: *bigournes* or *ganipotes* (Saintonge); *garwbleiz* (Brittany); *sabaziens* (Greece); *varoux* (Normandy).

Nebuchadnezzar. This occurred to Nebuchadnezzar (604-566 B.C.), the powerful king of Babylonia, who spent 7 years thinking he was an animal, according to a report in the Bible (Dan. 4: 33).

Writers. Ancient writers, such as Titus Petronius Arbiter (?-66), Caius Plinius Caecilius Secundus (61-113), Sextus Propertus (50-15 B.C.) and Publius Virgilius Maro (70-19 B.C.), left their reference works on this strange psychopathology, lycanthropy.

Parapsychology. Parapsychology does not include zoanthropy in the sphere of its direct research areas, although in certain pathological cases of autosuggestion and even in external processes of hypnotic suggestion, individuals can feel like subhuman animals, extraphysically acquiring animal forms, besides other possible points of contact with parapsychological phenomena.

Facts. Projection of the intraphysical consciousness in the psychosoma provides 3 facts that merit analysis in relation to this subject:

1. **Self-transfigurations.** The projected intraphysical consciousness, when using the plastic properties of the psychosoma, can transfigure this vehicle of manifestation and assume any form he/she wishes.

2. **Bilocation.** In the phenomena of apparitions of living persons and physical bilocation, the projected intraphysical consciousness can appear visible and tangible to human beings.

3. **Repercussions.** The phenomena of large-scale repercussions of an extraphysical origin that occur during lucid projections and involve exteriorizations of sensitivity and motricity, as well as phenomena of ectoplasmic physical effects, show that when the intraphysical consciousness is projected in the dense or tangible psychosoma a wound inflicted by a physical object can be transferred to the human body.

Possibility. Based on the evidence above, zoanthropy can rationally be considered as a substantial, irrefutable parapsychic possibility that is beyond historical or mythological interests.

Research. Exteriorization of animal-human sensitivity provokes a series of research problems, such as the following 5:

1. **Sensitivity.** The effects of the transference of sensitivity upon the subhuman animal.

2. **Subhumanity.** The control of the subhuman animal by these influences.

3. **Reaction.** The reaction of the subhuman consciousness upon the human consciousness.

4. **Dangers.** The potential dangers that these experiments cause.

5. **Beliefs.** The element of truth or the trace of reality that exists at the root of many legends, sagas, myths and popular beliefs, even regarding folkloric creations such as vampires, Dracula, werewolves and others.

Registers. Along the same line of considerations, 2 types of manifestation are worth mentioning:

1. **Extraphysicology.** In the extraphysical dimension there are ill extraphysical consciousnesses that have aberrant forms, including animals, dragons, giants, centaurs and Cyclopes. These are often caused by hypnotic, obsessive and extraphysical fascinations and suggestions.

2. **Intraphysicology.** As previously mentioned, there are also rare and surprising materializations of subhuman animals with evident manifestations of life in intraphysical ectoplasmy experiments.

Transference. Besides that which has already been presented, the phenomenon of exteriorization of sensitivity raises pertinent questions: Would it be possible to transfer the sensitivity of a human being to a so-called evolutionarily inferior subhuman animal? In this case, would it also be natural to expect a repercussion from the animal's sensitivity to the human body?

Fetus. In its 9 months of evolution, the human fetus – the inhabitant of the uterus – passes through various zoological forms.

Hypothesis. To what degree are these embryonic transformations – derived from hereditariness and respected by the biological organizing system of the human body, a faculty of the psychosoma – directly related to the faculty of self-transfiguration of the psychosoma produced by the consciousness?

Bibliography: ADGMT (03, p. 175), Ambelain (23, p. 41), Armond (53, p. 87), Bennett (116, p. 187), Bonin (168, p. 548), Carton (252, p. 344), Chaplin (273, p. 95), Day (376, p. 78), Depascale (392, p. 67), Drury (414, p. 37), Fodor (528, p. 210), Fontaine (533, p. 71), Gaynor (577, p. 102), Gomes (612, p. 120), Gómez (613, p. 107), Gurney (666, p. 173), Martin (1003, p. 74), Oesterreich (1145, p. 191), Pensamento (1224, p. 62), Poinsot (1269, p. 149), Rigonatti (1402, p. 95), Rochas (1430, p. 39), Shepard (1548, p. 541), Spence (1588, p. 255), Tondriau (1690, p. 245), Vieira (1762, p. 81), Wantuil (1795, p. 34), Xavier (1881, p. 218), Zaniah (1899, p. 274).

325. EXTRAPHYSICAL MUTATION

Definition. Extraphysical mutation: the faculty through which the consciousness constantly varies or deforms the humanoid shape of the psychosoma.

Synonymy: extraphysical metamorphosis.

Self-transfiguration. Voluntary extraphysical mutation is a particular type of self-transfiguration, in the same way that extraphysical mimetism and zoanthropy exist.

Types. Mutation of the psychosoma can manifest in two ways:

1. **Involuntary.** Parapathologically, in extreme cases of instability of the extraphysical form. It occurs independently from the will of the ill extraphysical consciousness.

2. **Voluntary.** Voluntarily and without serious parapathological connotations, although with intentions that are not always healthy or correct (which does not cease to be morbid).

Interpretation. Extraphysical mutation creates difficulties in interpretation of the extraphysical facts on the part of the inexperienced lucid consciential projector, when projected. The projector finds him/herself confused with the occurrence, not knowing whether he/she should attribute it to hallucinations, oneiric images, morphothosenes or another logical cause originating from within him/her, or from the universe of the manifestations of his/her own consciousness.

Fiction. *Extraphysical mutants* show that the intensely elaborated creations in science fiction stories were often generated as mere copies of extraphysical realities seen by the somewhat lucid projected consciousnesses of their authors while outside the human body.

326. EXTRAPHYSICAL MIMICRY TECHNIQUE

Definition. Extraphysical mimicry: the resemblance of the projected intraphysical consciousness to the extraphysical environment where he/she is manifesting through the faculty of self-transfiguration of the psychosoma.

Synonymy: camouflage of the consciousness; consciential dissimulation; extraphysical disguise; extraphysical distraction; extraphysical homochromy; extraphysical mimicry; extraphysical self-dissimulation; vibratory mimicry.

Protection. It is common knowledge that the protective artifice of mimicry is frequently used by subhuman animals that are considered inferior and even *unconscious.* They change not only the shape of the body as well as the color of the skin for short periods of time, according to the characteristics of the environment in which they want to camouflage themselves. The same occurs in the processes used in military camouflage.

Skin. Many people do not notice that human skin also makes its rudimentary attempts at camouflage or turns to the stratagems of the soma. The following are some examples: the erection of the papillae of the skin similar to the reaction of a startled cat with its hair on end; the abrupt whitening of the hair at certain critical situations in human life; discoloration of the skin, technically known as *fear melanosis,* which changes the color of the person's skin.

Camouflage. As a working hypothesis to be researched, extraphysical mimicry – one of the varieties or applications of the property of self-transfiguration of the psychosoma, produced by the consciousness through the will – constitutes asymmetric camouflage. It is sometimes an actual dissolving of the vehicle of consciential manifestation into the environment which it temporarily assumes or, in other words, the structure of the morphothosenes, the color of the existing objects and the forms of the surroundings.

Types. The extraphysical mimetic adaptation of the intraphysical lucid projector's psychosoma can occur in an instantaneous manner – an artifice used when the consciousness wishes to escape from a location quickly – or in a well-elaborated, slow and calculated manner with the plasticizing and organizing power of thought.

Clothing. The mimetic process most commonly produced by the projected projector, in an unconscious manner, is the consciousness mimicking the appearance, clothing, fashion and costumes of the average autochthonous extraphysical consciousnesses existing in an environment (extraphysical community) that the projector temporarily visits. This is done in order to appear similar to the others and not call attention to the projector's status as an outsider, which is almost always uncomfortable, out of place or embarrassing. It should be borne in mind that it is also a protective artifice against fear in certain cases.

Trauma. The first change related to the extraphysical environment in the presentation of the projected intraphysical projector can occur unconsciously as a natural response to the intense desires of the consciousness to defend itself. In these cases a minor inconsequential trauma occurs, which is understandable.

Freeing. A series of factors of extraphysical origin come together in order to gradually free the consciousness of the intraphysical projector from the tyrannical image of the forms and nature of dense matter in human life. The following 3 are examples:

1. **Self-affirmations.** Extraphysical self-affirmations.
2. **Attributes.** The application of the attributes and properties of the consciousness when projected.
3. **Volitation.** Enjoyment of unimpeded extraphysical volitation.

Conquest. This inevitably amplifies the space of your interconsciential micro-universe, freeing you from the animal-materialist level to achieve the more evolved consciential level of cosmoconsciousness. This inner conquest can apparently only be obtained through lucid consciential projections.

Bibliography: Vieira (1762, p. 103).

XI – *Relationships of the Projected Consciousness*

327. CONSCIENTIAL COMMUNICABILITY

Definition. Consciential communicability: the process and quality of participation of the consciousness in its existence and relationship with other consciousnesses.

Synonymy: consciential communication; consciential participation.

Types. The dynamic of consciential communication occurs through diverse manners of expression or means, in the fashion of the following 9:

1. Thought as universal language.
2. *Thought-speech.*
3. Transmental dialogue or extraphysical telepathy.
4. Unarticulated humanoid speech.
5. Echoing speech.
6. The resonant voice of undetermined origin (diverse frequencies).
7. The voice lacking inflection.
8. Mental reception of an indeterminate origin.
9. Presentiment.

Factors. The following are 16 factors, among others, which influence interconsciential communication:

1. Mental idiomatic base.
2. Characteristics of the native idiom (e.g.: slang).
3. Habit of thinking in the native language.
4. Comparison of native idioms.
5. Feminine speech.
6. Masculine speech.
7. Infantile speech.
8. Bradypsychism and tachypsychism, or the velocity with which one thinks.
9. Difficulties in extraphysical communication.
10. Comparison between pure telepathy in the ordinary, physical waking state and the extraphysical period.
11. Interference from radio and television stations, and telephony in consciential communication.
12. The existence and possible influence of telepathic transmitters and receptors.
13. The psychological state of the transmitter or receptor.
14. The influence of the extraphysical environment in consciential communication.
15. Spontaneous mental communication with extraphysical subhuman animals.
16. Extraphysical incommunicability.

Hearing. As a general rule, the projector *hears the thought* of the extraphysical consciousness in the extraphysical dimension in the same way that he/she *hears the voice* of the intraphysical consciousness in the ordinary, physical waking state.

Discrimination. The projected consciousness is sometimes able to discriminate or distinguish the intensity, frequency and timbre of the extraphysical interlocutor, when encountering a long-standing familiar intraphysical person, which is now an extraphysical consciousness in a dimension beyond the paratroposphere.

Echoes. In the extraphysical dimension, the words that are heard, or the thoughts that are understood, often appear to be *echoes,* because the projected consciousness seems to know the thoughts of the other interlocutor consciousness before they are exteriorized. In other words: the projector acquires what was thought by another, via telepathy, before the thought is expressed through extraphysical speech.

Simultaneity. The projected consciousness can simultaneously grasp telepathy and speech in the same extraphysical dimension, depending upon the interlocutor, the circumstances and the extraphysical environment where the projector is manifesting.

Mechanisms. It can be inferred from the above facts that the projected projector possesses inner mechanisms of intercommunication with other consciousnesses, which are frequently still unknown and evidently not controlled by the projector.

Bibliography: Kardec (824, p. 175), Sabom (1486, p. 70), Vieira (1762, p. 183).

328.   INTERCONSCIENTIAL   EXPERIENCES

Definition. Interconsciential experience: the joint, simultaneous experience of two (duo or couple) or more consciousnesses (group, crowd or collectivity).

Synonymy: consciential interconnection; consciential interfusion; interpersonal relationship.

Types. The following 5 basic types of interconsciential experience can be singled out, depending on whether they occur between intraphysical consciousnesses, extraphysical consciousnesses or projected consciousnesses in parapsychic trances or animic (intraconsciential) trances.

Scale. Besides the analysis of interpersonal unions, in an ascending scale of excellence of intraphysical-consciousness to intraphysical-consciousness communicability – being the most common interconsciential experiences – the following 5 maximal interactions or *inner apogees* can be singled out:

1. **Somatic.** Sexual intercourse or the apex of specific, primary consciential or human-body-to-human-body intercommunicability (somas). Effects: physical love; *kundalini;* orgasm; relief; reproduction; and animality.

2. **Holochakral.** Auric coupling or the culmination of specific, energetic consciential or holochakra-to-holochakra intercommunicability. Effects: energetic love; energetic interfusion; health; diagnosis; and cure.

3. **Psychosomatics.** The impassioned state or the zenith of specific, affective consciential or psychosoma-to-psychosoma intercommunicability. Effects: affective love per se; euphoria; mysticism; work of art; neurotic relationship; and fatal attraction.

4. **Mentalsomatics.** The cosmic colloquium or the pinnacle of specific, mentalsoma-to-mentalsoma, consciential intercommunicability. Effects: extraphysical love; maturity; cosmoconsciousness; spontaneous telepathy; conscientese; and oceanic sentiment.

5. **Holosomatics.** Lastly, as a hypothesis of possible research, the rational likelihood of the fifth and last totalizing or globalizing consciential interaction needs to be admitted: holosoma-to-holosoma intercommunicability, the simultaneous occurrence of the 4 abovementioned inner apogees, which may only occur with a pair of *serenissimi* in their last intraphysical life. Effects: cosmic love; transitory consciential interfusion.

Extraphysical consciousness. In the extraphysical-consciousness-to-extraphysical-consciousness intercommunicability of those beings which have already passed through the first and second desomas, there is an occurrence of only the 3 last components of the inner apogees of the above scale.

Fifth. The fifth, holosomatic, apogee – the *innermost* of them, in this case – only includes the emotional (psychosoma) and mental (mentalsoma) parabodies. Their effects are similar to the effects of the totalizing interaction of intraphysical consciousnesses, albeit in an evolved or potentiated condition. Another effect: group volitation.

Cord. The above presentation suggests that the golden cord – an energetic remote paracontrol – does not promote manifest consciential interactions due to its degree of subtlety.

Projective. Among the interconsciential experiences of projected consciousnesses, joint consciential projections (JCPs) are included. Effects: extraphysical encounters; joint extraphysical assistance.

Animic. The interconsciential experiences of consciousnesses during well-defined parapsychic trances are developed according to the type of the phenomenon, e.g.: *inter vivos* animism (only between intraphysical consciousnesses), the apparition of the intraphysical projector to another intraphysical consciousness. Effects: animic or animic-parapsychic messages.

329. CONSCIENTESE

Definition. Conscientese: the telepathic idiom, native to the extraphysical dimension, which is suitable for communication between the consciousnesses of this planet and the consciousnesses of the entire extraphysical universe.

Synonymy: *angelic language;* consciential idiom; cosmic idiom; cosmic language; extraphysical telepathy; galactic idiom; omniglot idiom; telepathic idiom; transmental dialogue; universal mental language; universalistic idiom.

Telepathy. As a theory for research, conscientese is the modeling – as a universal idiom of the consciousness – of extraphysical telepathy itself or, in other words, the sudden entrance of a thought or idea into the projected consciousness.

Difference. However, it is worth highlighting one difference: in certain cases, telepathy uses the articulation of words; conscientese is solely a pure mental or consciential language, devoid of any support, *crutch,* or artifice which is external to the consciousness.

Thoughts. There are 3 basic forms of human language: spoken language, written language and mime (expression). Telepathy is a form of consciential projection of thoughts, in this case.

Characteristics. Among the relevant characteristics of conscientese, at least the following 9 can be singled out:

1. **Self-awareness.** The act whereby the projected intraphysical consciousness is perfectly aware of what the other (extraphysical, projected intraphysical) consciousness is thinking, and vice versa.

2. **Communicology.** The instantaneous consciousness-to-consciousness transmission of an *en bloc* basic idea.

3. **Holomaturity.** Variation in the percentage of comprehension, according to the extraphysical district.

4. **Mentalsomatics.** Thought transmission performed directly from one mentalsoma to another mentalsoma eliminates errors in interpretation, heteroconsciential interference and *psychic static.*

5. **Thosenology.** The interrelationship between conscientese and morphothosenes.

6. **Parapsychism.** Conscientese acting during parapsychic manifestations.

7. **Evolutiology.** Conscientese obviously makes universalism possible and inevitable as a philosophical doctrine in the natural evolution of the eternal consciousness.

8. **Monoglotism.** The monoglot individual and his/her difficulties regarding conscientese.

9. **Polyglotism.** The polyglot individual and his/her abilities regarding conscientese.

Science. Scientific language can be classified into 4 distinct categories:

1. **Natural.** Examples: the English language, the Spanish language, the Portuguese language.
2. **Artificial conceptual.** Example: arithmetical notation.
3. **Artificial non-conceptual.** Example: musical notation.
4. **Paranatural.** Example: conscientese.

Languages. Human languages are perhaps the last physical reflections from which the consciousness definitively frees itself, in the pure mentalsomatic dimension, upon fully reaching the mastery of conscientese.

Materthosene. This occurs due to the matrices or images of ideas of the human idiom or idioms that are predominant in the experiences which are rooted in the ego's integral memory or, in other words: the *mental idiomatic base* of each consciousness, which forms the average or predominant materthosene in its personal holothosene.

Eliminations. Conscientese represents the greatest advancement in consciential communication because it sponsors at least the following 3 primordial evolutionary eliminations:

1. **Terms.** Eliminates the articulation of words (terms).
2. **Symbols.** Eliminates words themselves (symbols).
3. **Language.** Eliminates symbolic or infantile language, currently employed in a *very rational manner,* even within the most logical science, mathematics, being the science of symbols in which an entire discourse can be synthesized in a single image that is universal and even atemporal.

Interpreters. Conscientese leaves behind all the diversities, orthographies, pronunciations and particularities of human languages, as well as the necessity for interpreters, dictionaries and grammars necessary for the consciousness to communicate.

Holokarmology. Conscientese is intimately related to polyglotism. Polyglotism, in turn, has a direct, rational relationship with karmic laws (holokarmology).

Depth. The personal task of an intraphysical consciousness shows greater depth in time and space or, in other words: it shows itself to be more multiexistential and pluri-secular when based on some fundamental service with direct multilingual manifestations which reaches various deep roots within the entirety of the experiences of the consciousness.

Case study. For example: the individual who is reborn in Brazil and solely interacts with the Portuguese language in his/her activities is, *generally speaking,* probably rearranging his/her superficial groupkarmic accounts, only with regard to the last 5 centuries and the most recent half-dozen personal lifetimes, the predominantly post-indigenous phase of life in the Americas.

Holobiography. In order to reach the more complex archives of one's even deeper past – the phase prior to the fifteenth century A.D. – one needs to reach one's prior origin wherein, *generally speaking,* the individual will have had contacts with intraphysical consciousnesses in other countries, with other languages and diverse customs, healthily complicating international relationships and sophisticating the prospection of the meanderings of the personal history or holobiography, within his/her holomemory.

Base. Conscientese leads the consciousness, regardless of its level of education, to discover the active existence of the phenomenon of the mental linguistic base while outside the human body in the mentalsoma.

Discovery. This mental linguistic base, in turn, leads the consciousness to discover the practical importance of at least the following 8 vital languages, which often transcend the scope of human universities:

1. **Sanskrit.** The Sanskrit language, in terms of the inestimable understanding of the theology of the East.
2. **Hebrew.** The Hebrew language, which is also historically and culturally precious to the theology of the West.
3. **Greek.** The Greek language, as an instrument for exhuming the classic texts of ancient thought.
4. **Latin.** The Latin language, also as an instrument for exhuming the classic texts.
5. **Chinese.** The Chinese language as the contemporary form of the effective political ideas of approximately ¼ of the terrestrial population.
6. **Russian.** The Russian language also as the contemporary form of the effective political ideas of a high percentage of the terrestrial population.
7. **French.** The French language, now in decadence, although a remnant of the cultural expression of twentieth century Western civilization.

8. **English.** The English language as the (not always efficient) resonator of ideas, is the key to the doors leading to the compilation of contemporary civilization's modern thought, as well as being a bridge to other languages.

Education. It can thus be observed that so-called modern formal education is found wanting due to its deficiencies. In the author's case, for example, language classes were attended for two decades in accredited schools where the basics of only 3 of the above 8 languages were learned. Additional self-studies had to be performed, almost always in other districts.

Precursor. It is presumed that, in the remote future, in the consciential era, only 4 or 5 languages will be used in the entire world – with one predominating – and that all individuals will be polyglots. This will therefore be the period precursory to conscientese actually being used in human life or in the ordinary, physical waking state with the irruption of the psychosoma in intraphysicality occurring in a reasonable percentage of intraphysical consciousnesses.

Awareness. Awareness of the existence and the uses of conscientese prepares the consciousness to gradually understand, seek out and achieve the following 4 conditions, among others:

1. **Universalism.** The conception of universalism.
2. **Cosmoconsciousness.** The phenomenon of cosmoconsciousness.
3. **Cosmism.** The state of the galactic consciousness.
4. **Conscientiality.** The state of continuous self-awareness.

Explanations. Conscientese – as a faculty essential for consciential manifestation – can serve to explain the raison d'être of the following 3 realities, among others, in a manner closer to reality:

1. **Intraconscientiality.** The extraphysical environments, multidimensionality or the consciential states.
2. **Holosomatics.** The vehicles of manifestation of the consciousness or the holosoma.
3. **Paraperceptiology.** The parapsychic waves in the manifestations of paraperceptiology.

Mnemosomatics. As a working hypothesis, it is presumed that the mental idiomatic base of the intraphysical consciousness is one of the fundamental causes that produces distortions in the reminiscences or memories of extraphysical experiences during the projective period.

Metabolism. The mental idiomatic base collides head-on with conscientese, in this case. There seems to be a lack of sufficient proficiency, agility or time for the cerebral hemispheres to *metabolize* or assimilate the information which is extraphysically accessed or acquired by the consciousness, when in the ordinary, physical waking state.

Recall. The repetition and accumulation of projective experiences tend to improve the processes of recall.

Jargon. It is worth noting the existence of extraphysical multilingual jargon stemming from many earthly languages. It can only be heard among extraphysical consciousnesses that still need – for themselves or for others – to articulate words in order to communicate among themselves.

Vocabulary. The following are 10 paratropospheric, extraphysical multilingual jargon words and expressions:

1. *Bellows:* the human body (somatics).
2. *Breathe:* the same as *breather* (intraphysicology).
3. *Breather:* intraphysical or human dimension (intraphysicology).
4. *Dog walker:* (pejorative), helper (projectiology).
5. *Down below:* the planetary crust, the paratroposphere (intraphysicology).
6. *Exit the breather:* go through desoma (desomatics).
7. *Go into a breather:* go through resoma (resomatics).
8. *Go to a breather:* go through resoma (resomatics).
9. *Grey people:* a group of ill or energivorous extraphysical consciousnesses (parapathology).
10. *Pajamaed:* projected intraphysical projector (lucid projectability).

Bibliography: Powell (1278, p. 34), Schiff (1515, p. 209), Sherman (1551, p. 192), Vieira (1762, p. 22).

330. EXTRAPHYSICAL COMMUNICABILITY TECHNIQUE

Identification. In order for you – as a projected projector – to better communicate with the extraphysical consciousnesses you come across in the extraphysical dimension, you should first locate yourself and identify the easiest process of communication allowing you to understand and make yourself understood by those you encounter.

Means. Extraphysical consciential communication can be conducted through means which are *verbal,* in a certain respect or, in other words, that are similar to the process of conventional human speech, as well as occurring telepathically, consciousness-to-consciousness, in a direct, mentalsomatic manner.

Aspects. As a general rule, mind-to-mind (brain-to-brain or parabrain-to-parabrain) telepathic communication, or transmental dialogue (conscientese), does not always work in all extraphysical environments. It is therefore important to observe the following 4 aspects:

1. **Environment.** Verify the possibilities or the evolutionary level of the extraphysical environment.

2. **Idiom.** Identify the mental or human idiomatic base derived from the native language formerly used by the average member of the *population,* now *extraphysical,* when they were intraphysical.

3. **Will.** Maintain the decided will to understand the mental emission of the interlocutor or listener.

4. **Psychosphere.** Endeavor to examine the psychosphere of the extraphysical consciousness, which is reminiscent of "lip reading", as used by deaf persons in the ordinary, physical waking state.

Understanding. The difficulties in understanding extraphysical experiences are also due to the human language, which is still incapable of incorporating in the consciousness the experiences which are not synthesized into a number of specific operational concepts.

Bibliography: Vieira (1762, p. 89).

331. EXTRAPHYSICAL ACQUISITION OF ORIGINAL IDEAS

Definition. Original idea: new information acquired by the consciousness.

Synonymy: "creative hallucination"; fertile idea; illuminating idea; independent thought; "inventive dream"; new idea; original concept; unprecedented concept; unprecedented idea.

Neology. Neology is the logical science of ideological analysis that studies the rationales which represent mental conceptions and new theories.

Sources. Different sources act in the generation of original ideas, especially the following 11:

1. **Observation.** The direct observation of the behavior of nature.
2. **Reflection.** The fertile process of reflection.
3. **Brainstorming.** Brainstorming or the technique for stimulating creativity.
4. **Serendipity.** Serendipity (Horace Walpole: 1754) or the sudden interpretation of a phenomenon or fact.
5. **Gatherings.** Scientific gatherings, congresses, seminars and their debates.
6. **Libraries.** The periodic frequenting of libraries, holothecas and museums.
7. **Bookstores.** Frequenting new and used bookstores (megastore chains).
8. **Results.** Dissatisfaction in results from consciential solutions to problems.
9. **Doubts.** The spontaneous blossoming of doubts regarding facts.
10. **Students.** The questions posed or presented by all types of scholars from different areas.
11. **Extraphysicology.** The direct extraphysical acquisition of unprecedented concepts.

Factors. The following are 7 factors that influence intellectual creation and predispose the intraphysical consciousness to a greater acquisition of original ideas:

1. Emotional balance (a personality with minor consciential fissures).
2. Self-discernment (hyperacuity through the mentalsoma).
3. Mentality or self-conscientiality (qualification of intentionality).
4. Sensorial erudition (hyperacuity through the psychosoma).
5. Interdisciplinary or multidisciplinary erudition.
6. Consciential maturity or holomaturity (recuperation of cons).
7. Applied universalism.

Fact. The sudden emergence of profound knowledge, intellectual structures or visions in the consciousness projected in the extraphysical dimension has long been registered. These insights clearly never occurred to the same consciousness while in the ordinary, physical waking state, even when performing creative work.

Causes. The fundamental causes for the extraphysical acquisition of original ideas reside in the projector's own consciousness. Endeavoring to maintain an awakened discernment, the intraphysical consciousness, through attentive observations while projected in the extraphysical dimension – as well as the detailed analysis of Cartesian reasoning, the appeal of good sense regarding the parapsychic occurrences and acceptance of the wisdom of the natural laws and their conclusions – is able to acquire positive ideas of renovation and original concepts using the experiences of lucid projection. These experiences include educational lucid projection, in an efficient process of previously programmed ostensive inspiration.

Types. The fruit of inspiration, the extraphysical acquisition of ideas or the parapsychic acquisition of information by the projected intraphysical consciousness during the lucid projection phenomena – reported in numerous published cases – can be of various types, such as the following 7:

1. The pursued idea.
2. The unpursued idea.
3. The known idea.
4. The unknown idea.
5. The target-idea.
6. The brilliance of creativity.
7. Sheer inventiveness.

Effects. Among the effects resulting from the extraphysical acquisition of original ideas, at least the following 12 can be singled out:

1. Messages, prose, poetry, titles of works.
2. Unprecedented extraphysical instruction.
3. Working hypotheses.
4. Psychological fecundation.
5. The germination of new ideas.
6. A source of strategies for reasoning.
7. Solutions for pending issues (doubts, speculations, trial hypotheses).
8. Enhanced inventiveness.
9. The creation of innovative resources.
10. Effective learning.
11. Scientific discoveries.
12. Decision making under uncertain conditions.

Technique. The following is one of the most enriching practical suggestions for the interested reader: the *least fallible technique* for generating creativity or finding a new idea, as well as for achieving inventiveness and original discovery – used extensively by the author when setting the foundations of projectiology – is the establishment of analogies, parallels, comparisons, multiple interdisciplinary perspectives, enumerations and possible conflicts between diverse authors, their works and ideas.

Ideation. In this case, the polyglot researcher needs to have piles of books, materials (subjects) or publications at hand. He/she needs to mix them, merge them and *analyze* one against the other in detail as much as possible – even using sophisticated computer resources, if possible – adjusting them in a process of *ideation,* a centrifugation of ideas (a crucible of concepts) or *consensualization.*

Cosmogram. In this way, the librarian is transformed into an inventor, the curious individual into a discoverer and the ordinary reader into an original author (this is the modern cosmogram technique, proposed by the author).

Vehicles. The extraphysical acquisition of original ideas generally occurs when the consciousness manifests in the mentalsoma, in the mentalsomatic dimension, or through visual projections sponsored by helpers in the paratropospheric extraphysical dimension. In both cases, the consciential experiences are popularly taken to be extraordinary dreams or lucid dreams (semilucid projections).

Scale. The process of extraphysical acquisition of original ideas can be divided into a scale of 4 phases according to the combined observations of psychology, parapsychology and projectiology:

1. **Preparation.** In the initial phase of preparation, the intense activity of the consciousness, while in the ordinary, physical waking state, allows the reception of information. It is thus approached from many angles and various preliminary attempts are developed unsuccessfully in order to solve the problem at hand.

2. **Incubation.** In the incubation phase, the consciousness further intensifies his/her attempts at solving the problem. This only culminates when the person sleeps, almost always exhausted from the fruitless efforts, finally forgetting his/her investigative intrusions.

3. **Acquisition.** In the acquisition or illumination phase – the most important and difficult one of the undertaking – the consciousness reaches the climax of the creative process (gestation). The solution arrives suddenly and spontaneously when the consciousness finds him/herself in the state of discoincidence of the vehicles of consciential manifestation.

4. **Confirmation.** In the final confirmation phase, or subsequent verification phase, the individual (now in the ordinary, physical waking state) merely tests the practical viability of the solution that was directly acquired either in the extraphysical dimension or in the mentalsomatic dimension.

Bibliography: Denning (391, p. 50), Holroyd (738, p. 72), Walker (1782, p. 108), White (1829, p. 219).

---

332. HISTORICAL ORIGINAL IDEAS

Definition. Historical original idea: the acquisition of new information executed by a personality (pre-*serenissimus*) who became a celebrity in his/her time, being registered in the high points of human history.

Synonymy: "historical creative hallucination"; "historical inventive dream"; historical original concept; historical unprecedented concept; historical unprecedented idea.

Depositions. Human history shows numerous cases of parapsychic cognitive experience, or the extraphysical acquisition of ideas, according to the depositions of individuals. They actually constitute – as a last evolutionary recourse – authentic, more or less lucid projections of the intraphysical consciousness (hyperacuity), in the manner the following 23 categories of people, listed here in alphabetical order of their specific occupations:

    1. Artists.

    2. Autobiographers.

    3. Chemists.

    4. Composers.

    5. Discoverers.

    6. Executives.

    7. Governors.

    8. Inventors.

    9. Mathematicians.

  10. Novelists.

  11. Painters.

  12. Philosophers.

  13. Physicians.

  14. Physicists.

  15. Playwrights.

  16. Poets.

  17. Politicians.

  18. Researchers.

  19. Scientists.

  20. Statesmen.

  21. Students.

  22. Thinkers.

  23. Writers.

Examples. The following are 42 historical examples of extraphysical acquisition of original ideas, listed by the name of the receptor and his/her new concepts or renovating works:

    1. Abraham Lincoln (1809-1865), certain evolved ideas and politico-social stances.

    2. Ann Radcliffe (1764-1823), *The Mysteries of Udolpho,* in 1794.

    3. Bernard Palissy (1510-1589), ceramic pieces.

    4. Charles Pierre Baudelaire (1821-1867), poems.

    5. Charlotte Brontë (1816-1855), prose.

    6. Dante Alighieri (1265-1321), *The Divine Comedy*.

    7. Dmitri Ivanovich Mendeleiyev (1834-1907), the periodic table of elements

    8. Edgar Allan Poe (1809-1849), stories.

    9. Edward Lucas White, novel *Andivius Hedulio*.

  10. Edwin Richman, the gyroscope.

  11. Elias Howe (1819-1867), invented the sewing machine.

  12. Étienne Bonnot de Condillac (1715-1780), metaphysical discussions.

  13. Francis Thompson (1859-1907), *The Hound of Heaven*.

  14. Friedrich August Kekulé von Stradonitz (1829-1896), arrangement of the atoms in the molecular structure of benzene.

  15. Friedrich Gottlieb Klopstock (1724-1803), poems.

  16. Girolamo Cardano (1501-1576), certain scientific ideas

  17. Giuseppe Tartini (1692-1770), sonata *The Devil's Trill*.

  18. Guy de Maupassant (1850-1893), poems.

  19. Harriet Elizabeth Beecher Stowe (1811-1896), *Uncle Tom's Cabin*.

  20. Henrik Johan Ibsen (1828-1906): "Brand, A Dramatic Poem."

  21. Herman Volrath Hilprecht (1859-1925), deciphering of the inscriptions on fragments of agate from ancient Mesopotamia.

  22. Isaac Newton (1642-1727), mathematical problems.

  23. Jean Cocteau (1889-1963), certain intellectual creations.

24. Jean de La Fontaine (1621-1695), *Fables*.
25. Jean Louis Rodolphe Agassiz (1807-1873), restoration of the configuration of the fish fossil.
26. Johan August Strindberg (1849-1912), playwright.
27. Johann Wolfang von Goethe (1823), scientific problems and poems.
28. John Bunyan (1628-1688), *The Pilgrim's Progress*.
29. John Dryden (1631-1700), poetry.
30. Leo Nikolayevich Tolstoy (1828-1910), prose.
31. Marie Jean Antoine Nicolas de Caritat, Marquês de Condorcet (1743-1794), mathematical problems.
32. Mary Wollstonecraft Shelley (1797-1851), *Frankenstein*.
33. Niels Henrik David Bohr (1885-1962), Nobel Laureate, model of the structure of the atom.
34. Otto Loewi (1873-1961), Nobel Laureate in medicine in 1936, the chemical transmission of nerve impulses by way of a chemical substance.
35. Percy Bysshe Shelley (1792-1822), some of his literary works.
36. Samuel Taylor Coleridge (177 2-1834), the poem "Kubla Khan."
37. Thomaz De Quincey (1785-1859), confessions.
38. Voltaire (Pseud. of Jean François Marie Arouet de; 1694-1778), "La Henriade", epic poem.
39. William Blake (1757-1827), paintings.
40. William Cowper (1731-1800), certain ideas which were advanced for his time.
41. William Makepeace Thackeray (1811-1863), *Vanity Fair: A Novel Without a Hero*.
42. Wolfang Amadeus M. Mozart (1756-1791), various musical compositions.

Instrument. Lucid consciential projection, despite being a phenomenon which is basically contrary to the apparently rigid patterns of successive human lives will, over time and with the accumulation of experiences, present humanity with an increasingly greater reliability as a coadjutant working tool for the intraphysical consciousness in his/her multiple undertakings.

Bibliography: Bergier (122, p. 18), Coleman (291, p. 269), Denis (389, p. 144), Edwards (463, p. 108), Frost (560, p. 24), Garfield (568, p. 37), Guieu (660, p. 95), Krippner (862, p. 134), Monteith (1072, p. 198), Norvell (1136, p. 201), Tishner (1687, p. 29), Wang (1794, p. 891), Wilson (1858, p. 127).

333. CURRENT ORIGINAL IDEAS

Definition. Current original idea: the acquisition of new information, in the present, through lucid projection.

Synonymy: concept of neosynapses; contemporary neoconcept; currently new concept; leading-edge idea; leading-edge relative truth.

Acquisitions. Direct extraphysical knowledge is acquired through the most advanced process using lucid projection of the consciousness, whether of an intraphysical or extraphysical consciousness, in the mentalsoma, in the mentalsomatic dimension, free from the constraints of all types and conceptions of form, space and time that subjugate and restrict the manifestations of the individual's personality. There is an old popular expression that says: "I slept on it and dreamt of the solution."

Current. The author, through lucid projections, has made verifications, acquired fertile ideas and arrived at current extraphysical concepts that are logical and unprecedented to some degree. They were confirmed by the facts, just as with some apparently common concepts which, in one way or another, make some kind of creative contribution to the evolution of consciousnesses.

Phenomenology. These ideas at least serve to characterize minimal aspects which are still unknown, or are not fully identified, and are also not applied coherently in the phenomenological research of lucid projections, refining problem-solving ability.

Purpose. These concepts, terms and compound expressions are used here due to the lack of others which are more appropriate, precise and clarifying. They serve as aids for delineating the descriptions of real experiences, not being a dogmatic doctrine to be followed. As long as someone has experiences of this kind and analyzes them, the concepts can be applied in order to create new experiences.

Language. The language, or the form sketched out here, becomes organizing, disciplining, as well as being a guide for self-consciousness research.

Expressions. The following is a list or index of over 300 new expressions and neologisms, aside from many other existing ones. Their meanings can be consulted by the interested reader by performing a deeper projectiological analysis in the text of this book, notably through the remissive index at the end of this work: acceleration of digestion; adenoprojection; admonitory discomfort; aeromagnetic refrigeration; alternating resoma; anchor of the psychosoma; androprojection; animicity; animic-parapsychic takeoff; anticipated evocation; anti-resomatic function of lucid projection; archeoprojection; assistential ancestrality; assistential volitation; bariprojection; *bi*bilocation; bicontrolled projection; biprojection; biprojector; blind projection; catalyst-projector; cephaloprojection; cephalosoma; chakroprojection; clarifier projector; class-projection; closed energization; *consciential continuum;* consciential energy; consciential laboratory; consciential retardation; consciential self-bilocation; conscientiogram; conscientioland; conscientiology; contiguity effect; continuous memory (holomemory); co-projector; *coronatron;* cosmification of the consciousness; cosmocracy; cosmoprojection; couple repercussion; crash-projector; deficiencyland; departure-return-new-departure; desomants; dormitory-planet; double attack; double projection; double restriction; duodrome; echocephalos; edaphoprojection; egology; empty brain; *en bloc* recall; energetic contraband; energetic eyes; energetic immolation; energetic omni-interaction; energetic trap; epiprojection; error of the consciousness; escape of the psychosoma; exoclairvoyance; exoprojection; extraphysical abductee; extraphysical advance visit; extraphysical agenda; extraphysical anamnesis; extraphysical bedroom community; extraphysical centrifugal power currents; extraphysical coma (paracomatosis); extraphysical consciential obnubilation; *extraphysical counter-approach;* extraphysical counterespionage; extraphysical decompression chamber; extraphysical disappearances of consciousnesses; extraphysical dissolution; extraphysical ecology (para-ecology); extraphysical exorcist; extraphysical faux pas; extraphysical hetero-awakening; extraphysical homicide; extraphysical homochromy; extraphysical inaudibility; extraphysical macrotraumas; extraphysical map; extraphysical microtraumas; extraphysical minivacations; extraphysical mutants; extraphysical oligophrenia; extraphysical peregrinations; extraphysical races; extraphysical remote control; extraphysical reurbanization; extraphysical ride; extraphysical satellites; extraphysical self-evocation; extraphysical self-location; extraphysical suicide; extraphysical superficial tension; extraphysical transsexuals; extraphysical traumas; extraphysical Trendelenburg; extraphysical uterus; extraphysical-intraphysical self-touch; first physical base; first semiphysical projection; fixed resoma; flight range; four-hands; gyroprojection; half-materialization; helper-projector; hemiprojection; historical semilucid projection; holochakra; holochakral self-desoma; holokarma; holosoma; *Homo projectius;* homologous projection; homoprojection; hydromagnetic shower; hydroprojection; ideoduct; ideogenetic projection; unknown hideout; immanent energy; impure post-desoma personality; indirect farewell projection; instability in the prone position; intracorporeal experience; inverse interiorization; laboratorial apparition; last physical base; libidoprojection; locked intraphysical consciousnesses; lucid megaprojection; lucidity-recall binomial; materialization-projection; mental idiomatic base; mental wedge installer (xenothosenes); mentofacture; miniprojector; mixed bilocation; mnemonic block; mnemonic opening; mnemonic seed; more and less evolved resomas; multimemory (polymemory); multivehicular plannings; musicoprojection; narcoprojection; old silver cord; omniglot language; omniclairvoyance; oneiric projection; oneiric repercussion; oneiroprojection; orbiting body; orgasmolatry; para-android; para-anesthesia; para-asepsis; parabrain; paradoxical appearance; para-eyes; parafauna; paraflora; parageography; para-hypocrisy; parapolitics; paraprojection; paraprojective state; parapsychic android; parapsychic longing; parapsychic polyvalence; parapsychonautics; parapsychosphere; para-sociology;

para-somnia; parasurgery; paravision; passivating condition; penta; phenomenological crescendos; physical-extraphysical moment; phytoprojection; pivotal cause of death; pneumoprojection; polymemory; portable intraphysical base; possessive projection; post-desomatic discoincidence; post-desomatic parapsychosis; postnatal extraphysical regression; post-projective energetic shower; pre-final projection; pre-resomatic autobiography; primoprojection; professional hereditariness; prohibited locations; projectability; *projectarium;* projectiocracy; projectiocritique; projectiogenic current; projectiogenic dream; projectiogenic orgasm; projectiogenic; projectiography; projectiolatry; projectionics; projectionistics; projectiophobia; projectiorrhea; projectiotoxic; projective anthropology; projective astronomy; projective aura; projective chamber; projective cycle; projective déjà vu; projective haunting; projective medicine; projective mini-dream; projective parapsychology; projective physics; projective recess; projective rotation; projective self-diagnosis; projective self-persuasion; projective signal; projective sociology; projective trance; projective transition phase; projectively gifted; projector-spectator; protagonist-projector; pseudo-intrusion; psychic statics; psychofractures; psychofugal movement of the consciousness; psychological gaps; psychopetal movement of the consciousness; psychophonic monologue; psychophysical crutches; psychophysiological anchor; quasi-awakening; recapturing of the silver cord; reduction of the silver cord; refractory monoideism; relative inhibiting agents; reprojection; resomatic analysis; resomatic relay; resuscitative projection; retroparapsychic scars; rotation of the psychosoma; scale of extraphysical contacts; scale of extraphysical observation; scale of lucidity of the projected consciousness; seated projection; second universe; self-embrace; self-invisibility; self-kinesis; self-materialization; self-microscopy; self-programmed daydream; self-reluctivity of the psychosoma; self-revelation; self-target; semiphysical projection; semi-reborn personality; semi-takeoff; *serenissimi;* session of me alone; shared apparition; shared orgasm; silver mini-cord; simultaneous self-psychophony; solid psychosoma; sonorous projection; sterilizing predisposition; stroboprojection; student-projector; subintrant resomas; surprise-phenomenon; telekinetic projector; theorice; three desomas; three-and-a-half dimension; transconsciousness; transitland; triphasic reluctance; ultraclairvoyance; unipresence; unisonous vibrational states; unknown patient; vibratory chart; vibratory orgasm; voluntary self-combustion; wake-up-projector; waking discoincidence; zooprojection.

Chapters. The following are 40 entire chapters in this book that also represent more observations, assays, hypotheses and theories generated by the author's experiences, which await further confirmation from researchers: animal projection; assisted projection; auric couplings; conscientese; consciential era; consciential locations; energization by three technique; exteriorization of energy; extraphysical agenda; extraphysical code of ethics; extraphysical disappearances; extraphysical mimicry; extraphysical self-awakening technique; extraphysical sphere of energy; looseness of the holochakra; lucid projection in total institutions; paradoxes of projectiology; physical multilocation; physiology of the projected state; post-natal regressive projection; projectability; *projectarium;* the projected projector's uniform; (projection as a result of) the sex act; projection in the mentalsoma; projective aura; projective resomatic recycling; psychological contagion; psychophysiological anchor; quadruple memory; respiration during takeoff; rolling backward; scale of observation of the projected consciousness; scale of the state of continuous self-awareness; self-telekinesis; semi-materialization; spheres of action of the silver cord; transitional state; unapproachable beings; waking discoincidence.

Note. The ultrademanding reader who wishes to limit him/herself to the more common and evident facts or phenomena – being those readily accepted by the majority of researchers, as they consider certain advanced subjects to be excessively obscure, nebulous or surrealistic – should avoid the abovementioned chapters and others of a like nature in this book.

Heterodoxy. The author does not harbor any illusion about the full acceptance of the material presented here that is new and non-orthodox (unorthodox or heterodox). As incredible as it may seem, any type of new or leading-edge idea is not as well received today (neophobia) and is less likely to be adopted in this technological era than it was in the so-called *age of obscurantism.* This seems to be *very positive* and demonstrates progress or, in other words, shows a greater degree of consciential maturity in the intellectual mean of the planetary population.

Rationality. The reader who considers the author to be inventing too much, or creating an excess of words and expressions in his *mental meanderings* would be wise to reserve judgment, use good sense and observe logic or, more precisely, the rationality of each of the expressions in relation to the physical-extraphysical facts. This can be obtained through lucid experiences outside the human body, by the interested individual wishing to spend the time, expend the effort and repeat trainings just as many persons all over – including the author – have done.

Intraphysical consciousness. The intraphysical consciousness lives in a physical or animal world characterized by a struggle for life that is filled with cruelty, grief and ire, but also with radiant promises of the human implantation of pardon, pure megafraternity and spontaneous love.

Self-discernment. The more mature manner to exist or continue evolving, while passing through this dimension, is to maintain reason, good intention, good will, self-discernment and a high level of optimism, or good humor, endeavoring to assistentially serve others (assistentiology).

Philosophy. Lucid projection helps decisively in the execution of this process of evolutive existence to the degree that it provides the intraphysical consciousness with the means for perceiving new, as yet undetected patterns, or original ideas, in the apparently turbulent surrounding chaos, thereupon transmitting to others the introvisions, opinions, new and renovating examples that emerge from this chaos. In this respect, projectiology represents an active existential platform in the field of human philosophy.

Bibliography: Vieira (1762, p. 8). A recent book by the author on this subject: *200 Conscientiology Theorices* (in Portuguese).

---

334. AVOIDABLE EXTRAPHYSICAL IDEAS

Definition. Avoidable extraphysical ideas: inconvenient, inopportune, dislocated, extemporaneous, anticosmoethical or negative thoughts which should be avoided by the projected projector in order to maintain the harmonic and constructive continuation of the lucid consciential projection experience.

Synonymy: avoidable extraphysical contrathosenes; avoidable *mental venial sins;* avoidable oneirothosenes; avoidable pathothosenes; *extraphysical faux pas;* extraphysical mental improprieties; parapsychic interferences.

Factor. The power of thought in the extraphysical dimension is an extremely well-known factor that should always be respected by the intraphysical consciousness, endeavoring – through holomaturity and without ingenuousnesses – to perceive the better side of beings, things, ideas and events that he/she encounters while projected, if he/she wishes to evolve with his/her cosmoethical experiences.

Differences. Extraphysically speaking, the action of thought is more serious, direct and less subtle. Paradoxically, the utmost objectivity, so greatly sought after by materialist personalities, is precisely extraphysical and not intraphysical.

Intraphysicology. In the ordinary, physical waking state, any intraphysical consciousness can mask what he/she thinks, remaining silent, not allowing his/her ideas to become evident.

Graphothosene. While projected, the intraphysical consciousness thinks and simultaneously produces, executes and transmits his/her mental or thosenic creations – practically *para-yelling* – even without vocalizing them, in a lightning-fast manner, with no possibility to take back that which he/she exteriorized or added into the cosmos or, in other words: his/her graphothosene or indelible *thosenic signature.*

Present. The present remains set forever and never *unhappens* in any dimension, although this fact, in the extraphysical dimension, is more insinuating, ostensive and involving.

Hygiene. As a consequence of the above, the projector needs to make advance preparations by creating healthy thinking or thosenizing habits through mental or consciential hygiene (self-thosenes, orthothosenes) in order to avoid *para-embarrassments* and *paradeceptions* outside the body.

Case study. The following are 3 common examples of avoidable ideas or thosenes in the extraphysical dimension:

1. **Heterocritiques.** Immediately intraconscientially or mentally analyze the errors of others, upon providing assistance to certain ill extraphysical consciousnesses (spontaneous heterocritiques, contrathosenes, *mental words*).

2. **Sexosomatics.** Mentally create scenes regarding sexual and/or *parasexual* practices in inadequate paratropospheric environments (sexothosene, sexual fantasy, mental adultery, sexual holothosene).

3. **Factiousness.** Invoke beliefs and preconceptions in direct contacts with extraphysical consciousnesses accustomed to other lines of thought or even universalistic lines of thought.

Warnings. Many extraphysical warnings arise for the projected intraphysical consciousness, through intuition or direct suggestion from the helpers, to not think about a certain subject in a specific instance regarding experiences outside the human body – e.g.: on sex – in order to avoid mental approaches by *energivorous* or extremely deprived *extraphysical consciousnesses* with fixed ideas (monoideisms, monothosenes) on the theme, that are in search of energetic victims and human excitation.

Analogies. Extraphysical ideas that are avoidable by the projected projector follow 2 other types of analogous extraphysical attitudes:

1. **Locations.** Locations prohibited to the projected consciousness.
2. **Beings.** Beings unapproachable to the projected consciousness.

Bibliography: Vieira (1762, p. 44).

---

335. PROJECTIVE MENTAL TARGETS

Definition. Projective mental target: a predetermined goal that the consciousness plans to reach, through concentration and decision of self-determined will, upon seeing itself outside the human body.

Synonymy: consciential paragoal; consciential target; destination of the projected projector; extraphysical destination; extraphysical flight plan; point chosen as a consciential objective.

Categories. Projective mental targets can be classified into 3 categories, according to beings, locations and the projector's ideas.

1. **Beings:** intraphysical beings (target-person, person-target or destination-person); extraphysical consciousness; target-patient; self-target; intraphysical subhuman animal; extraphysical subhuman animal.

2. **Locations:** human or physical; extraphysical; *mental;* target-area, or area-target; mobile target-area; fixed target-area; three-dimensional target-object; two-dimensional target-object (e.g.: a picture).

3. **Ideas:** self-thosenes or thoughts conceived in the ordinary, physical waking state; target-idea or idea-target; self-thosenes or thoughts conceived in the extraphysical dimension; working hypothesis.

Analysis. The following are 18 fundamental aspects that should still be considered in the analysis of the consciousness' objectives or the projective mental targets:

1. An examination of potential targets in order to determine their importance to the consciousness.
2. Known or unknown target.
3. Single or multiple targets.
4. Unexpected target.

5. An error in action.
6. A correction in action.
7. Plausible reasons.
8. Indeterminate utility.
9. Conscious, anticipated or involuntary evocation.
10. Crash-projection.
11. Agreeable or disagreeable surprises upon reaching the mental target.
12. Extraphysical traumas.
13. Extraphysical obstacles.
14. Unforeseen or unknown obstacles (e.g.: a new resoma).
15. Target-being and consciential communication.
16. Extraphysical target-person *via human television.*
17. Petifree individuals, evolutiologists and *serenissimi.*
18. Oligophrenics and satellites of intruders.

Self-target. The projective self-target or the projector's human body allows the following 4 transcendent self-experimentations regarding the holosoma, among others:

1. **Self-examination.** Extraphysical self-examination.
2. **Autoscopy.** Internal extraphysical autoscopy.
3. **Cord.** Analysis of the silver cord.
4. **Holochakra.** Analysis of the holochakra as a whole.

Target-person. With the direct, deliberate use of a target-person, with whom the human consciousness has affinity, any experimenter is able to achieve a higher degree of hits in his/her attempts to reach a projective mental target.

Extraphysicology. In cases of target-persons, it sometimes happens that the projector's consciousness comes upon the targeted person, both of them being outside the human body. This occurs more frequently than one would imagine, due to the following 4 factors:

1. **Dimension.** When the projector plans to reach a target-person, he/she does not always think about which existential dimension the consciousness or person is located in at that time, whether it be a human or extraphysical dimension.
2. **Relationships.** Close relationships between family members, father and son, couples or lovers.
3. **Sleep.** Nighttime, when both consciousnesses are sleeping.
4. **Reflection.** Affective concerns or reflection upon daily activities, given that the target-person went to sleep thinking about the projector, although ignoring the subject of lucid projection.

Technique. A simple mental target, with which one employs the principle of focusing the attention in order to free the psychosoma, serves as an efficient projective technique for many projectors.

Curiosity. The following are 4 examples of the most sought-after projective target-places, due to curiosity:

1. **Tibet.** A subterranean library in Tibet.
2. **Vatican.** The secret section of the Vatican library in Rome.
3. **Temple.** The inside of a Masonic temple during an evening meeting.
4. **Headquarters.** The inside of the headquarters of a secret sect.

Pilgrimage. Veritable *extraphysical pilgrimages* are made to certain locations that involve consciousnesses with deep religious, social or historical motivations, such as the following 10:

1. Lourdes, France
2. The Vatican, in Rome, Italy.
3. The Kaaba, in Mecca, Saudi Arabia.
4. Jerusalem, Israel.
5. The Parthenon, in Athens, Greece.

6. The Taj Mahal, in India.

7. The pyramid at Giza, Egypt.

8. The cement sarcophagus in which the damaged nuclear reactor at Chernobyl in Russia was buried.

9. The graves of loved ones in distant cemeteries.

10. The spot where Apollo 13 made a moon landing.

Motivation. Many nonlucid projectors reach these places as a result of thinking about them so much – a condition of spontaneous saturation – and yearning to go there, because one of the basic vital forces for lucid projection lies in the great motivation of the consciousness which experiences them.

Bibliography: Andreas (36, p. 54), Crookall (343, p. 112), Ebon (453, p. 90), Frost (560, p. 50), Giovetti (593, p. 82), Monroe (1065, p. 225), Norvell (1139, p. 155), Sherman (1551, p. 190), Shirley (1553, p. 147), Steiger (1601, p. 124), Vieira (1762, p. 19).

---

336. TECHNIQUES FOR REACHING THE MENTAL TARGET

Target-being. Choose a friend for whom you have affinity and note down his/her address. Perform the experiment at a time that is best for both of you. It is necessary for you to nurture a positive intention and think fixedly about the mental target for a period of days, saturating your mind while in the ordinary, physical waking state.

Avoidances. You should avoid choosing a target-extraphysical-consciousness that has recently arrived in the extraphysical dimension (first desoma), as well as a recently-reborn consciousness or a target-fetal-consciousness, for obvious reasons.

Mnemosomatics. The target-intraphysical-consciousness does not always recall the extraphysical encounter. It is not only you, as a lucid projector, that will have difficulty in recalling the extraphysical events.

Somatics. When endeavoring to reach the mental target during the extraphysical stage, do not focus on the parts of your own human body or on the silver cord, in order to avoid returning to the physical base against your will.

Links. You can use psychic or affective links that assist profoundly in the establishment of *rapport* (affinity, empathy) with the target-person, vitalizing his/her image in your mind. An example would be something that has come directly from him/her, such as the following 5 items:

1. **Photo.** A recent photo of the individual.
2. **Manuscript.** A sample of a personal manuscript, such as a recent letter.
3. **Gift.** A gift recently received directly from the individual.
4. **Object.** An object of his/her personal use.
5. **Jewelry.** An inexpensive piece of jewelry owned by the individual.

Shower. If you have an intimate physical relationship with the target-person, of the opposite sex, whose habits you are aware of, you can even plan to take a shower with him/her, while only you are projected.

Dream. If, during the development of a dream, your consciousness tells you that you are dreaming and that you are going to separate from the human body, your dream will end and give way to a lucid projection. Upon interiorizing, simply tell yourself that you will leave again and this will end up happening.

Psychosoma. Those who dream with the target-idea of the psychosoma as a vehicle of manifestation of the consciousness end up projecting and maintaining lucidity during the entire extraphysical experience.

Telepathy. Reaching the mental target does not always represent a completed extraphysical operation. It is sometimes necessary for you to obtain telepathic communication with the target-being.

Adaptation. Each projector is better adapted to specific types of mental targets and certain extraphysical encounters.

Evocation. The thoughts you have immediately prior to projecting often serve to prepare, open the way for and remove the obstacles in order for your consciousness to reach the target-person, in an *anticipated evocation*.

Parapsychism. Parapsychism and consciential discernment of the target-person assist your task as a lucid projector.

Mystification. Be aware that you, as a projector, are not exempt from encountering a mystifying extraphysical consciousness, instead of the chosen and evoked target-being. This fact sometimes demands direct, extraphysical, interconsciential confrontation.

Correction. As a projector, while in the ordinary, physical waking state, you will often plan to reach a certain target by way of a human address and, soon after exteriorizing, will intuitively sense that the person has moved and you were not aware of this fact. You need not concern yourself with this, however, as you will go to the new destination, thereby correcting your trajectory.

Personality. The consciential microuniverse of the personality of the target-person has a more influential force upon your consciousness than his/her address, when extraphysically searching or tracking.

Failures. In special cases of perception failure, only a portion of your holochakra projects, without your consciousness or, more precisely, there is only a projection of your humanoid morphothosenes. This explains the *total absence* of recall, because your consciousness did not, in fact, project from your human body or, in other words, it did not dislocate from your cerebral base.

Connections. As strange or absurd as it may seem, the extraphysical destination that your projected consciousness arrives at when it is lost, or that particular environment which is reached, is always somehow related (affinity or synchronicity) to you. Your consciousness is nevertheless unable to perceive the reasons or identify the connections that make you visit it in a lucid projection on that occasion. Nothing happens by chance. Synchronicity permeates our *general self-thosenity*. Every one of our cells has some kind of relationship with every other electron in the universe or cosmos.

Recall. Nevertheless, the possibility of a lack of recall – which masks the success of the lucid projection – should be borne in mind regarding all experiments. The projector goes to the location, or even reaches the target-person, but does not recall the fact, thereby thinking that the projective attempt failed, only to later discover that the person did indeed perceive the projector's extraphysical presence.

Bibliography: Baker (69, p. 60), Frost (560, p. 98).

---

337. PROHIBITED LOCATIONS

Definition. Prohibited location: a human district or extraphysical environment which the projected intraphysical consciousness should avoid, or immediately consider to be off limits, due to personal motives and conveniences, other beings and circumstances in the environment, or the existence of potential or real risks.

Synonymy: avoidable place; critical location; dangerous location; extraphysical ambush; forbidden location; negatively impregnated location; prohibited space; prohibited zone; unapproachable location.

Locus. Medicine has always used the expression *locus minoris resistenciae* or, namely the weak point, the point of least organic resistance where an illness begins to manifest in the patient's human body.

Earth. Similar locations also exist between the tropospheric extraphysical dimension and the intraphysical dimension, on the *body* of planet earth, in reference to the places where ill extraphysical consciousnesses can manifest with less difficulty, such as the following 5:

1. **Poltergeist.** Houses presenting occurrences of poltergeist.
2. **Crimes.** Places where violent crimes were committed.
3. **Assassination.** The human scenario of assassination.
4. **Torture.** Ex-torture-chambers.
5. **Dungeons.** Former prison dungeons.

Geography. In every city, sociologists, anthropologists, urban heads of research and police reporters study that city's *shadowy geography,* composed of locations stigmatized by mega-intrusions, suffering and pain; and those addresses marked (environmental stigmas) by poltergeists and hauntings.

Holothosene. Natural tragedies and collective nightmares (landslides, cave-ins, collapses, fires, floods, shipwrecks, accidents, train pileups, riots); dramas; individual acts of violence and imprudence (kidnappings, rapes, homicides, attacks, assaults, gang raids) having a social impact; all profoundly imprint human environments and the mental-emotional archives (mnemosomatics) of the ordinary *unconscious-evocator-citizen.* They thereby unfortunately become integrated into the living memory of the city and its urban holothosene.

Energies. These human locations present *environmental stigmas* or retain parasitic energies, "walls with memories", microvibrations, gravitating waves, abstract waves or perceptible *waveforms.* This leads the projected intraphysical consciousness to maintain a self-restriction of actions or an intentionally conditioned freedom, sometimes even for reasons of self-defense.

Test sites. It should be borne in mind that there are even many locations on the planetary crust that are off-limits to visitors, and even to air, land and ocean traffic, such as sites where missiles, rockets and other armaments are tested.

Thoughts. According to biological research performed with electromagnetic fields, thoughts (the *tho* of thosenes) can be impressed upon matter. Evidence of this is found in the thoughts of terror, desperation, intense grief or extreme fear which paraphysically impregnates the structure of a building after a tragedy, assassination or the massacre of a group of intraphysical consciousnesses.

Paroxysms. In the events occurring in these places, the protagonists or involved parties act under extreme tension, in intense mental activity, with their affective, psychic, consciential energies or negative and anticosmoethical bioenergies (energetic pollution) flowing at extremely high levels, triggering paroxysms of hate or zeniths of horror.

Excrescences. The extraphysical duplicates (second universe) of the objects in these environments remain deformed with indelible crusts or *extraphysical excrescences* that irradiate influences which are not always detectible by unrefined human senses. From this arises the need for *extraphysical reurbanization.*

Thosenes. The thoughts, thosenes or remnants of these emotional forces seem to have an indefinite permanence, transmitting sensations of depression, anguish or inquietude to visitors who are completely ignorant of the event for many lustrums after the tragedy.

Reurbanization. In this way, a pathological holothosene is formed which, over time, requires extraphysical reurbanization of the environment or community, performed by the *serenissimi.*

Trail. In these cases, the gravitating energies establish a clear trail which is consciously or unconsciously followed by those having a sharpened sensitivity, or a certain parapsychic development, as soon as they enter the human construction for the first time.

Locations. In certain occasions, such a place *(locus delicti)* saturated with consciential energies functions, from a parapsychic point of view, just like a small hole in a dam through which it begins to collapse. In the same way that the above-cited physical-extraphysical locations exist, there are also critical extraphysical-physical locations.

Types. The locations that can spontaneously be considered prohibited to the consciousness projected with lucidity can be classified into: physical, extraphysical and ambivalent.

1. **Physical.** Among the physical or human locations that can be considered prohibited to the projected intraphysical consciousness, the following can be singled out: the couple's bedroom; a sectarian ritual initiation lodge that has gone out of business; abandoned monasteries; certain apparently inoffensive ruins; certain old monuments and mausoleums; the location of a bloody battlefield; a place with statues or images that were consecrated with the sacrificial blood of living beings; a place where "witches" were burned alive; certain cemeteries; medieval citadels; tombs; crypts; dolmens; certain psychiatric hospitals and institutions; and old prisons.

2. **Extraphysical.** Among the extraphysical locations that can be considered prohibited to the projected intraphysical consciousness, the following can be listed: a colony with openly hostile inhabitants or extraphysical consciousnesses; an unfamiliar and disagreeable extraphysical district.

3. **Ambivalent.** There are physical and/or extraphysical locations where, for example, rituals were practiced over long periods of time, which should be avoided by the projected intraphysical consciousness. Magic rituals leave sensations with *extremely intense emotional connotations* impregnated in those places, or gravitating energies which are difficult to dissipate or remove from the area. Those areas are able to cause parapsychic influences that can disturb the extraphysical balance of the intraphysical consciousness, when projected. They can be good for some and awful for others, depending upon the quality of the intentionality of the consciousnesses or their interests.

Interflows. Unapproachable places, whether they are in the open air, inside a house, or even in the bedroom of an apartment, often contain strictly *physical* negative influences, such as the intersection of energetic interflows between the component objects of the environment. These intersections can generate discomfort, a lack of coordination in thought, localized pains, indeterminate indispositions in the intraphysical consciousness who lives his/her everyday life or occasionally performs some task there. These interflows are easily detected by pendulum, aurameter and magnetic divining rod (radiesthesia, radionics) technicians.

Power. The so-called *place of power* in any environment can be precisely located and demarcated, even showing the correct direction of the consciential energies that are in contact with persons at that location. This can be executed with conscious or unconscious probing performed by any sensitive individual (psychometry), even when he/she is not using physical supports, instruments or crutches.

Hostility. There are 5 human areas that are traditionally prohibited to outsiders (humans), namely places where visitors or tourists are (physically) not welcome or are even treated with open hostility (unwelcome, *persona non grata*):

1. Badin Dalam, a village in Java.
2. Mecca, a city in Saudi Arabia.
3. Mount Athos, in Greece.
4. North Sentinel, one of the 200 islands that form the Andaman group, in the Bay of Bengal.
5. Staphorst, a city located to the north of Amsterdam, in Holland.

Prevention. If you decide, while lucidly projected outside your soma, to go to one of these curious but openly hostile places, go there forewarned, paying attention to your real intentions, the positive purpose of your visit and being willing to confront any disagreeable surprises.

Subhuman. There are, incidentally, subhuman beings which are also not welcome – in this case, *justifiably unwelcome* – in specific places, such as the following 3:

1. **Cats.** Cats in the home with a newborn (shedding of fur).
2. **Monkeys.** Monkeys in china shops (breaking of plates).
3. **Birds.** Birds (especially large ones) at airports (plane crashes).

Atmosphere. The tendency is for the atmosphere of the ambient holothosene in a physically hostile place to be *doubly hostile,* extraphysically speaking.

Bibliography: Castaneda (258, p. 21), Crawford (313, p. 53), Fortune (540, p. 76), Frost (560, p. 183), Kardec (824, p. 175), Russell (1482, p. 66), Vieira (1762, p. 185).

338. EXTRAPHYSICAL TELEKINESIS PRODUCTION TECHNIQUE

Definition. Extraphysical telekinesis: direct production of physical effects by the projected intraphysical consciousness.

Synonymy: animic telekinesis; intentional exteriorization of motricity.

Self-determination. When you, as a projected projector, find yourself to be lucid, denser in the free psychosoma, and well-constituted outside the human body, you can endeavor, using the full force of your will, to act upon material objects or people. This can be accomplished through actions that are simple, spontaneous or have been prepared prior to projecting, even with the presence of waking human volunteers.

Types. The physical effect phenomena provoked by the projected intraphysical consciousness can be of the following 19 types:

1. **Apparatus.** Turn on a TV, radio or computer that is far from the bedroom.
2. **Bell.** Ring a doorbell.
3. **Book.** Open a book.
4. **Candle.** Snuff a lighted candle.
5. **Chair.** Move a light rocking chair.
6. **Door.** Open a door.
7. **Ears.** Tickle an intraphysical being's ear.
8. **Face.** Affectionately touch the face of someone you know.
9. **Faucet.** Turn on a faucet.
10. **Feather.** Stop the movement of a feather in midair.
11. **Flashlight.** Turn on a flashlight using minimal pressure.
12. **Food.** Pick up a piece of food.
13. **Lamp.** Turn on a lamp by pressing the switch.
14. **Object.** Lift a small object.
15. **Page.** Turn a page of an open book.
16. **Pinch.** Pinch a friend.
17. **Refrigerator.** Open the refrigerator door.
18. **Table.** Knock on a door or the top of a table (typtology).
19. **Wing.** Touch a loose moth's wing.

Uses. Among the uses of the extraphysical telekinesis phenomenon, the following 4 can be singled out:

1. **Energies.** Development of energetic transmission.
2. **Projectability.** Effective proof of lucid projection.
3. **Research.** Practical application of working hypotheses.
4. **Assistance.** Assist an intraphysical being and prevent him/her from becoming a victim of a serious physical accident.

Repression. There are conditioned reflexes which are created by repressive factors, stemming from conventional education, which can provoke obstacles to the production of extraphysical telekinesis through inhibition or psychological action. Some examples are: not touching cards or diaries belonging to others; not entering the intimacy of an unfamiliar persons' bedroom.

Technical. Among the extraphysical telekinesis phenomena that can technically be provoked, the following 2 can be singled out:

1. **Ball.** Make a small, light ball fall from atop the bedside table to the floor in the bedroom.
2. **Impressions.** Imprint the fingerprints (parafingers) of the extraphysical right hand (right parahand) of the psychosoma on a flat surface sprinkled with fine flour.

Bibliography: Brittain (206, p. 50), Greenhouse (636, p. 57), Kardec (824, p. 237), Muldoon (1105, p. 267), Vieira (1762, p. 26).

339. SCALE OF EXTRAPHYSICAL CONTACTS

Definition. Extraphysical contact: the relationship of the proximity, vibratory frequency or parapsychic influence of the intraphysical consciousness with other human beings or subhuman animals, whether they be intraphysical or extraphysical consciousnesses.

Synonymy: consciential encounter; extraphysical encounter.

Evolution. The natural evolution of projections or the chronological development of each projector's lucid projections enables the possibility of rationally elaborating the most common and physiological scale of their consciential encounters, visual or *tactile* contacts with other beings, outside the human body.

Scale. The following is a scale of the projector's cumulative extraphysical contacts, on 4 levels of excellence, in the most common, ascending or evolving order of the unfolding of events outside the body:

1. **Self-contemplation.** There is firstly an occurrence of self-contemplation, or visual or even tactile encounters of the projected intraphysical consciousness with his/her own human body, obviously in the physical base or, in other words, the phenomenon of consciential self-bilocation.

2. *Inter vivos.* Secondly, the projected intraphysical consciousness encounters or visualizes another or other intraphysical beings, who are almost always in the ordinary, physical waking state. *Inter vivos* apparition may occur in certain cases.

3. **Confrontations.** Next, the projected intraphysical consciousness comes upon one or more extraphysical consciousnesses, whether they be deceased relatives, helpers, blind guides, energivorous extraphysical consciousnesses, satellites of intruders or intruders, sometimes in extraphysical confrontations.

4. **Joint.** Lastly, the projected consciousness has a direct contact with 1 or more projected beings or colleagues from extraphysical excursions, thereby having joint projections.

Mentalsomatics. The most frequent contacts occur through lucid projections in the psychosoma. Nevertheless, consciential encounters do arise in the mentalsomatic dimension on very different bases.

Disparities. This scale represents the typical development of more habitual occurrences. There are, however, projectors who naturally overturn the scale by having the most disparate experiences when they project, such as the following 4:

1. **Soma.** There are those who only examine their own human body – the soma – when projected.

2. **Intraphysical consciousnesses.** There are those who only encounter intraphysical beings when projected.

3. **Extraphysical consciousnesses.** Others only see extraphysical consciousnesses in their lucid projections.

4. **Isolation.** There are still others who so far have neither contacted anyone, nor have they seen any being while projected alone.

Complete. Evidently, the veteran projector will only have completed his/her panorama of experiences of extraphysical contacts upon being able to realize the 4 categories of different encounters in different extraphysical opportunities and instances. This will allow him/her to perform an overall analysis of the events and potentialities of the extraphysical dimensions.

Bibliography: Vieira (1762, p. 109).

340. THE PROJECTED INTRAPHYSICAL CONSCIOUSNESS AND THE HUMAN BODY

Definition. Individual: the consciousness who temporarily undergoes resoma, possessing a biocybernetic, cognitive, self-regulated male (androsoma) or female (gynosoma) human body through which he/she manifests, transforming him/herself, upon reaching physical maturity, into a human product of psychosocial conditioning and development.

Synonymy: citizen; human person; intraphysical being; intraphysical consciousness; personality; social being.

Categories. Among the categories of the relationship of the projected intraphysical consciousness and his/her own human body, at least the following 7 can be singled out:

1. **Self-bilocation.** Self-contemplation or observation of one's own human body at a distance, or the phenomenon of consciential self-bilocation.
2. **Viewing.** Ordinary viewing of the human body.
3. **Endoscopy.** Endoscopic viewing of the human body.
4. **Distance.** Viewing the human body from a distance.
5. **Psychosoma.** Viewing the human body together with the psychosoma and, consequently, with the consciousness.
6. **Eyes.** The characteristics of the eyes of the human body itself, while the brain is emptied of the consciousness.
7. **Mirror.** The reflected image of the psychosoma, a copy of the human body, in front of an ordinary mirror.

Touch. Various occurrences arise regarding the sense of touch, such as the following 5:

1. **Complexity.** Extraphysical-physical compound or complex touch.
2. **Self-embrace.** Psychosoma-human body self-embrace.
3. **Temperature.** Perception of the human body's temperature, sensed in the psychosoma upon touching the human body.
4. **Position.** Intentional change in the body's position.
5. **Saliva.** Deglutition of saliva that has accumulated in the mouth.

Aspects. The following are 8 aspects to be considered in the relationship between the projected consciousness and his/her own human body:

1. **Holochakrology.** Identification of the silver cord or the existence of the holochakra.
2. **Aura.** Viewing the human aura.
3. **Chakras.** Viewing the actual chakras in the holochakra and in the psychosoma.
4. **Respiration.** The observation of respiration, blood circulation and heartbeat.
5. **Catalepsy.** Extraphysical catalepsy as a reflex in the psychosoma from the state of the human body.
6. **Emotion.** Extraphysical emotion.
7. **Philosophy.** The tendency to philosophize when faced with one's own inanimate body of flesh and bones.
8. **Respect.** The sentiment of respect or frank rejection toward the *physical machine.*

Effects. Diverse critical and transcendent effects stem from the relationship of the projected intraphysical consciousness and his/her human body, such as the following 8:

1. *Experimentum.* The *experimentum crucis* or "acid test" of the human being who eliminates the intraphysical consciousness' serious doubts or rudimentary uncertainties regarding his/her condition and evolution.

2. **Intraconsciential recycling.** The doorway to *inner self-illumination* or full self-knowledge that inevitably causes intraconsciential recycling or even existential recycling for the intraphysical consciousness.

3. **Maturity.** The first effective and mature step inward, which makes the intraphysical consciousness dispense with a legion of immaturities. The following 12 items are examples: panics, phobias, myths, icons, taboos, manias, fads, illusions, enticements, excesses, faux pas and *abdominal brainwashing* in this still pathological intraphysical society.

4. **Exteriorization.** Definitive individual proof of the exteriorization of the consciousness.

5. **Brain.** Verification of the temporary *empty brain* condition of the consciousness.

6. **Somatics.** Verification of the human body's (soma's) temporary inactivity or its non-pathological vegetative state.

7. **Evolutiology.** A greater comprehension of the evolutionary use of the human body.

8. **Projectiology.** The experience of imposed interiorization within the phenomena of lucid projectability.

Relations. The intraphysical consciousness' viewing of his/her own human body is intimately related to the following 4 distinct phenomena:

1. **Internal.** Internal autoscopy or the direct viewing of the human body's internal organs.

2. **External.** External autoscopy or the viewing of the projected holochakra, while the projector is in the ordinary, physical waking state.

3. **Simple.** Consciential self-bilocation or the simultaneous viewing of the human body and the psychosoma, while the consciousness is headquartered in this vehicle in a simple projection.

4. **Double.** Compound self-bilocation or the simultaneous viewing of the human body with both the holochakra and the psychosoma coincident, while the consciousness is headquartered only in the mentalsoma, which occurs in cases of double projection.

Neurons. It can be observed that the production of lucid projection is being motivated by self-lucid extraphysical consciousnesses worldwide. Regardless of this, however, to what degree are the current intense technological cogitations of the human mind, the increase in stimuli due to the acceleration of history, the more frequent use of electronic instruments and the consequent greater utilization of neural networks influencing this fact?

Bibliography: Castaneda (258, p. 47), Monroe (1065, p. 168), Paula (1208, p. 42), Vieira (1762, p. 109).

---

341. CONSCIENTIAL SELF-BILOCATION TECHNIQUE

Effort. Any positive effort expended to produce lucid projection is worthwhile, even if it is just to experience consciential self-bilocation only once in your lifetime.

Doorway. The impactful phenomenon of consciential self-bilocation which, as already mentioned, is accessible to any sufficiently motivated individual, represents the *experimentum crucis* of the human being, the most practical doorway to the inner illumination of the personality, the first really efficient step inward. It is equivalent to deeply researching the entirety of an immense specialized library, or an intense intraconsciential educational immersion performed over many decades.

Conditions. Your projected consciousness should endeavor to contemplate your own *immobile* human body when you have sufficient extraphysical lucidity near the bed inside the energetically shielded chamber in the physical base where your body is inactive. The best occasion for this is when you feel fully motivated for the experience.

Attitude. The most suitable attitude for your consciousness, in this case, will be for you to think about your own human body without emotionalism, with a great deal of serenity and balance, being prepared for any surprise in order to avoid extraphysical trauma. Besides this, you should not think or wish to interiorize into it.

Touch. You should avoid touching your human body, upon seeing it while projected, in order to prevent being magnetically drawn toward an abrupt, extemporaneous and undesirable interiorization by the silver cord.

Physical. Your physical body can be clearly seen, in every detail, in a cataleptic state, apparently torpid in vegetative life, your consciousness not being inside it. It may also be seen merely as a silhouette or a form on the bed. However, even in this handicapped circumstance, your consciousness is entirely certain that this is your human body, even though you are *outside* the body, *distant* from the body, or *in front* of the inactive body.

Eyes. The contemplation of your human body when the eyelids are open, revealing the eyes – the *captors of intentionality* – to be dull or lifeless, aside from being a rare and impressive event, becomes more profoundly imprinted on your memory than when the eyelids are closed.

Orientation. This more frequent orientation of the self-bilocator's extraphysical perceptions is what allows viewing from above, as though your consciousness was poised in midair, at an elevated point over your human body.

Dimensions. It is more common for you to see a complete image of your own human body in 3 dimensions, and not in a flattened, plane, two-dimensional form, as you always see it reflected in mirrors, or copied in paintings, photographs and ordinary films. This occurs even when your human body is immersed in full physical darkness.

Perceptions. When your projected consciousness has difficulty seeing its own human body, this is due to a change in your extraphysical perception of energy and light. Depending upon the surrounding extraphysical environment, light can appear to become reflected, annulled or cancelled and the images may totally disappear from your consciential perceptions. This usually occurs when, while projected, you move from one level of awareness or existential dimension to another.

Frequencies. With regard to the phenomenon of consciential self-bilocation, you need to be observant of the fact – as the most important aspect of extraphysical analysis – that your projected consciousness manifests at a specific frequency, whereas your human body remains unaltered, at its own frequency in the intraphysical dimension. The greater the difference between the two frequencies, the greater will be the difficulty of your consciential visualization.

Bibliography: Vieira (1762, p. 109).

---

342. THE PROJECTED CONSCIOUSNESS AND INTRAPHYSICAL BEINGS

Definition. Intraphysicality: the temporary condition of the consciousness while living restricted in the human body, or the condition of the consciential principle when restricted to a still animal or vegetable body.

Intraphysicology. The condition of intraphysicality provoked the creation of the subdiscipline of *intraphysicology* within conscientiology, being the domain of intraphysical consciousnesses, as well as subhuman animals (animals, fauna, zoology) and vegetable beings (plants, flora, botany).

Forms. There are various forms of living intraphysical beings: vegetable (seed, tree), subhuman animal (egg, animal), fetus (intrauterine fetal life), child, woman (gynosoma), man (androsoma).

Traits. With regard to the basic aspects – strong traits and weak traits – of the personality in the intraphysical dimension and in contact with the projected intraphysical consciousness, at least the following 6 characteristics can be singled out:

1. **Knowledge.** To be known and recognized by the memory (or holomemory) of the intraphysical consciousness.

2. **Unknown.** To be unknown or not remembered by the intraphysical consciousness in his/her retrocognitions.

3. **Friendship.** Friendly personality: an old friend.

4. **Hostility.** Hostile personality: an intrusive intraphysical consciousness, an intraphysical consciousness suffering from intrusion who is a satellite of an intruder.

5. **Consciousness.** To be conscious: intraphysical blind guide, intraphysical helper.

6. **Unconsciousness.** To be unconscious: psychotic intraphysical consciousness, energivorous intraphysical consciousness.

Nature: Regarding the nature of the relationship between the projected intraphysical consciousness and intraphysical beings, it is important to highlight the following 15 variables:

1. Awake social being.
2. Clairvoyance.
3. Cooperation in the lucid projection of an intraphysical consciousness.
4. Deintrusion in general.
5. Extraphysical assistance in general.
6. Extraphysical awakening of a sleeping intraphysical being.
7. *Inter vivos* apparitions.
8. Intraphysical deintrusion.
9. Physical contact.
10. Psychography.
11. Psychophony.
12. Respect of another's privacy.
13. Respect of the consciential rights of others (respect of your fellow being).
14. Sleeping intraphysical being.
15. Telepathy.

Relationships. Many friendly relationships or long-standing human friendships are formed as a result of gatherings of intraphysical beings in the extraphysical dimension through spontaneous or assisted lucid projections, which may or may not be recalled.

Distinctions. In certain *extraphysical circumstances* – environments in which consciential perceptions are more difficult – it becomes necessary to use special resources in order to know if the beings which the projected projector begins to see are projected intraphysical beings, still living in the human body, or are already residing in the extraphysical dimension during the intermissive period.

Shouts. One resource, in this context, is the act of shouting, as though the (projected) intraphysical consciousness in the extraphysical dimension had a throat and vocal cords. If the interlocutors do not hear our shouts, it almost always indicates that they are intraphysical beings in the ordinary, physical waking state (somaticity).

Para-arm. Another contact resource, when in the extraphysical dimension, is to float (volitation) over the observed being, just as in paintings of angels, and pass an extraphysical arm (para-arm) in front of it. Generally, when the personality does not react and passes right through the para-arm of your psychosoma without perceiving it, this shows the observed consciousness to be an intraphysical being in the ordinary, physical waking state (somaticity).

Certainty. These rudimentary resources clearly cannot provide certainty in all cases, due to the subtle gradation of our perceptions and paraperceptions regarding the consciential dimensions.

Luminosity. It is easy to distinguish between the inanimate human body of the projected intraphysical consciousness, or even an ordinary cadaver, and the human body of a waking, intraphysical being. This is because this living vehicle irradiates a certain luminosity, a phosphorescence, which does not occur with the first 2, which generally are opaque and lack their own luminosity since they are devoid of the consciousness, whether temporarily (projected intraphysical consciousness, *brain emptied of the consciousness*), or definitively (final projection, desoma).

Photophoria. Parapsychic light, photogenesis, phosphorescence, photophoria or telephany, is somatic energy which is transformed and exteriorized in a form of light and is a relevant concept in this context.

Bibliography: Baumann (93, p. 27), Bozzano (184, p. 131), Leadbeater (901, p. 307).

343. THE PROJECTED CONSCIOUSNESS AND EXTRAPHYSICAL BEINGS

Definition. Extraphysical consciousness: the consciousness when free from the human body, in longer intermissive periods or during the intervals between two intraphysical lives.

Synonymy: being which has undergone desoma; consciousness which has undergone desoma; extraphysical consciousness.

Appearance. The extraphysical appearance (para-appearance) or the appearance of extraphysical beings in general varies greatly, as illustrated in the following 5 examples:

1. **Appearance.** The appearance (physiognomy) of a man, woman, child, animal or plant.
2. **Intelligence.** Intelligent beings.
3. **Forms.** Life forms that are often unknown.
4. **Extraphysicality.** Apparently autochthonous inhabitants of the extraphysical dimension.
5. **Exoticism.** Exotic or extraterrestrial appearances different from our humanoid form.

Traits. With regard to the basic characteristics – strong traits and weak traits – of the personality encountered in the extraphysical dimension and in contact with the projected intraphysical consciousness, at least the following 6 traits can be singled out:

1. **Known.** A being that is known and recognized by the memory of the projected intraphysical consciousness.
2. **Unknown.** A being that is unknown or not remembered by the projected intraphysical consciousness.
3. **Friendship.** Friendly personality: a deceased old friend, another projected intraphysical consciousness ("colleague").
4. **Hostility.** Hostile personality: intrusive extraphysical consciousness (a being which is evolutionarily underdeveloped, an inhabitant of the paratroposphere), an extraphysical consciousness that is a satellite of an intruder.
5. **Consciousness.** Conscious being: blind guide, helper (calming para-appearance), evolutiologist, *serenissimus* (evolved being).
6. **Unconsciousness.** Unconscious being: post-desomatic parapsychotic extraphysical consciousness (ill being), energivorous extraphysical consciousness (disturbing para-appearance).

Types. Extraphysical beings manifest themselves in various forms or with various *paraphysiognomies* to the projected intraphysical consciousness. The following 15 are provided as examples:

1. **Colleague.** An evolutionary colleague or someone pertaining to the individual's karmic group.
2. **Friend.** A recognized or identified deceased friend.
3. **Helper.** A helper which is known to the projected intraphysical consciousness.
4. **Host.** A host for the lucid projectability of the intraphysical consciousness.
5. **Ill.** A being which is visibly ill or disturbed (unbalanced extraphysical consciousness).
6. **Intraphysical consciousness.** An intraphysical consciousness which has recently undergone desoma and has not yet passed through the second desoma.
7. **Intruder.** An ostensive intruder.
8. **Karmic group.** The evolutionary group (karmic group).
9. **Mocker.** A mocking being with the appearance of a man or woman.
10. **Mutant.** An extraphysical mutant unable to maintain a tranquil para-appearance.
11. **Neighbor.** A neighbor who has already undergone desoma.
12. **Paraprotector.** Someone's bodyguard or paraprotector.
13. **Relative.** A relative, with the para-appearance of a man or woman, which has already undergone desoma.
14. **Unknown.** An unknown being or one which is unidentified on that occasion.
15. **Vampirizer.** Extraphysical vampirizer.

Nature. With regard to the nature of the relationship between the projected intraphysical consciousness and extraphysical beings, the following 21 more expressive variables merit singling out:

1. Active intersciential relationship.
2. An intersciential encounter or reencounter.
3. Approaches made *by* the projector.
4. Approaches made *toward* the projector.
5. Blatant deintrusion.
6. Commemoration of the present or the past of kindred consciousnesses.
7. Conduct in the presence of post-desomatic parapsychotics.
8. Cooperation in the desoma phase.
9. Discipular relationship (disciple and master, student and teacher).
10. Embrace or para-embrace.
11. Extraphysical interdimensional ride.
12. Fruitless searches (investigations, research projects, evocations).
13. Impediments having diverse origins or causes.
14. Intersciential intrusion.
15. Many types of invisible union.
16. Negative or pathological relationship.
17. Passive intersciential relationship.
18. Positive or healthy relationship.
19. Reactions of lucidity by the consciousness regarding *unknown* beings or those which apparently were not seen before.
20. Sexual or parasexual company.
21. Undesirable company.

Density. The density of one's psychosoma determines the degree to which the projected intraphysical projector can be seen by extraphysical beings.

Ability. No present or past titles, hierarchy, social class or human positions have any value with regard to the extraphysical dimension. What counts is the real evolutionary superiority of the consciousness, which affords ability, experience, freedom, lucidity and proficiency (know-how, *modus faciendi*) to its unfettered and cosmoethical extraphysical actions.

Paradox. Due to the rejuvenation of the para-appearance of lucid extraphysical consciousnesses, the phenomenon of *paradoxical appearance* commonly occurs. In this case, the mature, white-haired intraphysical projector encounters the *former father* (extraphysical consciousness) having a more rejuvenated or younger (black hair) paraphysiognomy than the projector; or the aged intraphysical projector encounters the *former great grandmother* (extraphysical consciousness), finding it to be youthful looking, in contrast with personal recollections or old family photos and films.

Surprises. Surprising events of this type can sometimes provoke some facts that are also unexpected, such as the following 3 types of side effects:

1. **Paralucidity.** Increase the extraphysical lucidity (paralucidity) of the projected intraphysical consciousness.

2. **Paratrauma.** Immediately provoke an extraphysical trauma (paratrauma) in the projected intraphysical consciousness.

3. **Retrocognitions.** Disturb the recall of the authentic extraphysical experiences (retrocognitions), which are mistaken for dreams or nightmares.

Threat. It is still unknown, within the scope of projectiological research, why and to what degree a well-intentioned projected intraphysical consciousness constitutes a threat to the tranquility of lucid ill-willed extraphysical consciousnesses with regard to their extraphysical condition.

Factors. There must be other still unknown factors, besides the existence of the positive consciential energy of the intraphysical consciousness projected in the psychosoma and the quality of his/her personality, which is different from the residents (autochthons) in that district or extraphysical community. This positive consciential energy also allows the projector – with his/her intromission as an outsider in a district distant from the human body – to awaken other consciousnesses sleeping in the extraphysical dimension.

Bibliography: Bayless (98, p. 100), Crookall (323, p. 1), Kardec (824, p. 174), Steiger (1601, p. 103).

344. THE PROJECTED CONSCIOUSNESS AND OTHER PROJECTED BEINGS

Definition. Projected being: the consciousness when projected from his/her vehicle or vehicles of manifestation.

Synonymy: projected consciousness; projected projector; projecting projector.

Types. Any projected consciousness can encounter diverse types of projected beings, such as the following 3:

1. **Psychosomatic.** Intraphysical consciousnesses projected in the psychosoma in the crustal or paratropospheric extraphysical plane.

2. **Mentalsomatic.** Intraphysical or extraphysical consciousnesses projected in the mentalsoma in the mentalsomatic dimension.

3. **Subhumanity.** Evolutionarily inferior beings or subhuman animals, not to mention plants projected in the paratropospheric dimension.

Characteristics. Within the characteristics of the relationships of the projected consciousness with other projected beings, the following 8 can be singled out:

1. **Para-appearance.** The extraphysical appearance of intraphysical projectors.
2. **Age.** Physical age and extraphysical appearance.
3. **Rejuvenation.** Extraphysical rejuvenation of the para-appearance.
4. **Returns.** Sudden returns to the human body and abrupt disappearances.
5. **Repercussions.** Joint physical repercussions.
6. **Empathy.** The influence of affinity or interconsciential empathy.
7. **Kinfolk.** The influence of consanguinity or kinship.
8. **Friendship.** Friendly or hostile being.

Categories. Projected beings encountered by the projected intraphysical consciousness can be placed into various categories, such as the following 5:

1. **Colleagues.** Familiar projective colleagues.
2. **Unknown.** Unknown projectors.
3. **Relatives.** Projected relatives.
4. **Child.** Projected children.
5. **Subhumans.** Projected subhuman, intraphysical pet animals (very rare).

Joint. The lucid, joint consciential projection of intraphysical beings or the encounter or reencounter of colleagues or projected intraphysical projectors enables extraphysical tasks of mutual cooperation, such as the following 4:

1. **Holochakrality.** Mutual energetic assistance.
2. **Self-awareness.** Help in the attainment of a high degree of extraphysical self-awareness.
3. **Volitation.** Joint volitation.
4. **Defenses.** Joint extraphysical defenses in the face of attacks by ill extraphysical consciousnesses.

Bibliography: Monroe (1065, p. 163), Vieira (1762, p. 121).

345. EXTRAPHYSICAL DISAPPEARANCES

Definition. Extraphysical disappearance: the sudden disappearance of an extraphysical consciousness or projected intraphysical consciousness from a certain environment or extraphysical community.

Synonymy: abrupt extraphysical disappearance; extraphysical disappearance; instantaneous extraphysical disappearance; sudden extraphysical disappearance.

Causes. The following are 3 of the main causes of instantaneous disappearance of beings in the extraphysical dimension:

1. **Dimension.** A change in dimension or vibratory frequency by the manifesting consciousness.
2. **Retraction.** Violent retraction of the silver cord due to a physical cause, or an *extraphysical* repercussion to the projected intraphysical consciousness.
3. **Trauma.** Extraphysical trauma to the projected intraphysical consciousness, or a *physical* repercussion.

Disappear. The following are 3 categories of beings that can suddenly disappear in the extraphysical dimension from your astounded or surprised paravision.

1. **Extraphysicology.** Extraphysical consciousnesses in general.
2. **Intraphysicology.** Projected intraphysical consciousnesses.
3. **Self-experimentation.** The projected projector him/herself.

Projector. Instantaneous disappearance in the extraphysical dimension is not always directly related to the projected projector's perceptions, nor does it depend upon his/her will or alter the conditions of the extraphysical environment that influences him/her on that occasion. This can, however, be traumatic if one is not accustomed to lightning-fast disappearance, sometimes of one's own closer extraphysical company, whether a helper, a projected colleague or an extraphysical interlocutor.

Multiple. Sudden, multiple extraphysical disappearances of various beings can occur simultaneously. This happens due to the abovementioned causes, especially with extraphysical consciousnesses subordinated to the same director responsible for a group volitating together or a holothosenically kindred team. It is reminiscent of so-called *group-souls* of subhuman animals and facts such as a school of fish immediately and unexpectedly turning together and swimming in the opposite direction when a noise is made in the sea.

Creativity. The extraphysical facts show that sudden disappearances in the paratropospheric dimension have inspired animated cartoonists, who make a character disappear in a lightning-fast manner on a road, upon which it shrinks rapidly until disappearing like a small point on the infinite perspective of the horizon. These 2 types of disappearance from the scene have deep analogies with our imagination.

Dissipation. The sudden disappearance of extraphysical consciousnesses, which are actually present in the extraphysical environment or community, should not be confused with the abrupt dissipation of mental images or artificial morphothosenes, which are generated in ordinary dreams, nightmares, lucid dreams and visual projections promoted by helpers. These occurrences are very distinct and clearly defined, in an unmistakable manner, due to certain characteristics affecting the extraphysical perceptions of the projected intraphysical consciousness which, because of his/her personal experience, has no doubts regarding this distinction.

Bibliography: Bardon (80, p. 386), Castaneda (256, p. 210), Frost (560, p. 57), Swedenborg (1635, p. 252), Vieira (1762, p. 183).

346. EXTRAPHYSICAL APPROACH TECHNIQUE

Definition. Extraphysical approach: the contacting of one consciousness by another in the extraphysical dimension in some manner.

Synonymy: extraphysical contact; the act of accessing an extraphysical consciousness.

Categories. There are various categories of extraphysical approaches, among which are the following 4:

1. **Donation.** An action performed by the projected projector on another being, such as a donation of consciential energies or information.

2. **Reception.** The act of a being approaching the projected projector, as in the reception of consciential energies or information.

3. **Helpers.** The healthy acts of helpers, petifree consciousnesses, consciential epicenters or evolutiologists.

4. **Intruders.** The ill acts of energivorous extraphysical consciousnesses, extraphysical blind guides, intruders and the satellites of interconsciential intruders.

Extraterrestrials. The projector can approach and be approached by non-human extraterrestrials (exotic para-appearances) or subhuman beings. Approaches made to the projected projector by extraphysical consciousnesses are particularly considered here.

Objectives. Among the relevant objectives of extraphysical approaches, at least the following 14 can be singled out:

1. Reception or donation of extraphysical assistance.
2. Interconsciential deintrusion.
3. Lucid assistential interconsciential bait.
4. Extraphysical rescuing of a deprived or ill extraphysical consciousness.
5. Intrusion or extraphysical attack.
6. Energetic draining.
7. Friendly or hostile reencounter.
8. Casual encounter.
9. Inoffensive jesting.
10. The consequence of conscious or unconscious evocation.
11. Physical awakening.
12. Extraphysical awakening.
13. Physical anchoring of the intraphysical consciousness in the human body or the act, whether positive or negative, of obstructing lucid projection.
14. Extraphysical parapsychism.

Nature. With regard to its nature, the extraphysical approach can be: agreeable; friendly; disagreeable; hostile; expected; unexpected; pathological; serene; or violent.

Vehicles. With regard to the vehicles of manifestation of the consciousness, the extraphysical approach can be based on 4 modes or conditions:

1. **Psychosomatic.** Psychosoma to psychosoma.
2. **Mentalsomatic.** Mentalsoma to mentalsoma.
3. **Telepathic.** Mentalsoma to psychosoma, by way of telepathic processes.
4. **Holosomatic.** The holosomatic psychosphere of the consciousness and its role in extraphysical approaches.

Processes. Among the more relevant processes of extraphysical approaches, at least the following 13 can be singled out:

1. A mind-to-mind approach (paratelepathy).
2. Transmental dialog.
3. Summons.
4. Extraphysical energetic transference.
5. Extraphysical eyes, glances, faces, smiles, embraces and kisses.
6. Overflowing tenderness.
7. Empathy or *rapport*.
8. Touch or direct contact.
9. The extraphysical right hand (parahand) of the psychosoma.
10. The use of morphothosenes.
11. The sudden attack and unexpected *extraphysical ambush.*
12. The positive or negative energetic jet.
13. The physical effect in the physical dimension which is analogous to morphothosenes in the extraphysical dimension.

Districts. Extraphysical approaches can occur in at least the following 5 basic consciential environments or districts:

1. **Dimension.** In the same consciential dimension.
2. **Extraphysicology.** From one extraphysical dimension to a different extraphysical dimension.
3. **Intraphysicology.** From the extraphysical dimension to the human dimension (intraphysicology).
4. **Holochakrology.** Within the extraphysical sphere of energy (conscientiality, energetic dimension).
5. **Base.** Inside the physical base (domesticity, energetic dimension).

Effects. Extraphysical approaches cause at least the following 6 different effects for the projector (intraphysical consciousness):

1. Euphoria (extraphysical euphoria or intraphysical euphoria).
2. Clarifications or extraphysical lessons.
3. Extraphysical trauma with abrupt return to the human body.
4. Physical repercussions (somatics).
5. Unexpected difficulties in personal manifestations.
6. Unexpected ease in personal manifestations.

Bibliography: Monroe (1065, p. 132).

---

347. EXTRAPHYSICAL HETERO-AWAKENING TECHNIQUE

Definition. Extraphysical hetero-awakening: extraphysical procedure performed by the projected projector – the extraphysical awakener – whereby he/she sponsors the temporary departure (projection) of an intraphysical consciousness, the sleeping human, from his/her physical body (soma) (see fig. 347, p. 1,146).

Synonymy: consciential exteriorization of another; extraphysical approach made to the sleeper; extraphysical awakening of the intraphysical consciousness; extraphysical-physical approach; projector which projects another; takeoff induced by another; temporary *physical-extraphysical ejection;* transference of the consciousness of another.

Types. It is generally more difficult than it appears to force the extraction of an intraphysical consciousness from his/her physical body, in the psychosoma, in order for him/her to remain projected even for only some moments. This is true regardless of whether it is a known or unknown, semilucid or lucid, cooperative or hostile adult, child, or subhuman animal.

Sponsorship. Extraphysical hetero-awakening can be sponsored by an extraphysical or projected intraphysical consciousness.

Study. This act, per se, needs to be previously studied by the experienced projector in order not to represent an undue intromission into the privacy of the target-being or, in other words, an intrusion or undesirable invasion into the *dream* of another. By using the extraphysical approach, the projector helps to transfer the seat of another's intraphysical consciousness out from his/her human body.

Assistance. When you, as a projected intraphysical projector, receive telepathic suggestions or are ostensively assisted and even teleguided by a helper, which is usually intangible, the task of exteriorizing an intraphysical consciousness becomes easier to execute.

Consent. The same occurs when you first receive the consent and open cooperation of the target-person, while in the ordinary, physical waking state and later receive the same cooperation while attempting to perform extraphysical hetero-awakening.

Resource. The following are 11 resources that should be remembered when temporarily *ejecting* an intraphysical consciousness from his/her own human body (soma):

1. **Discernment.** Good intention (quality of intentionality) and discernment on the part of the experimenter.

2. **Cosmoethics.** A plausible constructive or cosmoethical reason for the procedure.

3. **Conscientiality.** Extraphysical lucidity on the part of the projector-awakener's consciousness.

4. **Self-confidence.** Self-confidence on the part of the projector-awakener.

5. **Self-thosenity.** Maintenance of an undisturbed train of thought without deviations or imperturbable self-thosenity.

6. **Evocation.** Positively evoking a helper in favor of the target-consciousness.

7. **Selectivity.** Choice or selection of a fearless target-person, especially one who has no apprehensions regarding extraphysical consciousnesses and is knowledgeable on the subject of lucid projection.

8. **Time.** Choice of time (timing), preferably when the intraphysical being is tranquilly sleeping, alone, at night, with absolutely no possibility of human (intraphysical consciousness) or subhuman (dog, cat) interferences.

9. **Planning.** The act of beginning to concentrate on the target-person, even before initiating the production of lucid projection, if possible.

10. **Holothosenity.** Intentional direct exteriorization of consciential energies upon the target-person and his/her environment or personal holothosene.

11. **Empathy.** The employment of all useful possibilities for establishing a deep *rapport*, empathy, affinity or interaction with the target-consciousness in question, including entering into his/her psychosphere in an energetic fusion or an intense auric coupling.

Measures. You, as a projector-awakener, can use the following 3 basic measures:

1. **Psychosomatics.** Utilize extraphysical telepathy and even physical touch, if possible, through the greater density of your own psychosoma.

2. **Interlocution.** Speak to the sleeper who is being parapsychically approached, extraphysically and audibly calling him/her gently by an informal name, when known.

3. **Volition.** Use imperturbable conviction and will power (volition), like a hypnotizer, with the singular intention of awakening the lucidity of the consciousness in the extraphysical dimension.

Helper. As a projected projector-awakener, you need to be aware that you should, at this point, act like a (projected) intraphysical helper which has been given a specific, dignified, respectful, cosmoethical and pure task, as though you were an extraphysical consciousness that is fully aware of your situation or assistential condition.

Hygiene. Using consciential hygiene, do not allow any interference of extemporaneous thoughts or spurious self-thosenes (pathothosenes) – even fleeting ones – in your consciousness, mentally concentrating exclusively upon your objectives without any vacillation.

Interiorization. A mere partial departure of the sleeper's psychosoma, transporting the consciousness, can occur. Upon becoming lucid and seeing the projector-awakener, the sleeper's consciousness becomes disturbed or alarmed such that it abruptly interiorizes and may even suffer inoffensive physical repercussions. In this case, you should abandon the attempt at extraphysical hetero-awakening.

Attempts. Generally speaking, if you are not able to bring about any effective communication with the target-person after 3 successive attempts, you should leave the experience for another more favorable opportunity.

Reactions. As a projected projector, you need to be prepared for any surprising reactions on the part of the intraphysical target-consciousness, in the sense of avoiding frustrations to both parties, in the manner of some of the following 5:

1. **Attack.** The target-consciousness furiously lashing out against you, the projector.

2. **Fear.** The target-consciousness demonstrating an insuperable fear of leaving the human body (thanatophobia).

3. **Somnambulism.** The target-consciousness being somnambulistic.

4. **Mistake.** The faulty judgment of the target-consciousness who is experiencing a nightmare in which you, the lucid projector, are his/her persecutor.

5. **Alienation.** The target-being, upon physical awakening, getting up from the bed and turning his/her back on you, the projected projector, without the slightest formality.

Extracorporeal. Extracorporeal sleep – the act of the target-consciousness sleeping while headquartered in the projected psychosoma, being close to but *outside* the human body, which is still inside his/her own bedroom – interferes in extraphysical-physical approaches much more often than one might suppose. This common fact brings with it some consequences that require observation.

Consequences. As a projected projector, you may approach your friend thinking that he/she is sleeping on the bed only to find that he/she is also projected. Your friend's consciousness might therefore extraphysically awaken with greater ease, which is a welcome and providential exception. The other possibility is an abrupt interiorization of the sleeper's consciousness, which is *sucked* by the human body through the silver cord, this being the most common occurrence. In this situation, it is useless to make another immediate attempt at hetero-awakening. The best option is to leave it for another more propitious occasion.

Miniprojector. It can also happen that the consciousness of a child, a relative or a friend – found to be sleeping, already projected, upon your approaching him/her while projected – floats over the human body, experiences a momentary extraphysical awakening upon recognizing you (the projector) and, drawing near you, smilingly, warmly, continues to sleep as though secure and comfortable in his/her own bed or crib. In this case, it becomes easy for you, the projector-awakener, to sponsor the extraphysical awakening of the miniprojector, skillfully and without even wishing to do so.

Joint. The act of extraphysically approaching the sleeper is intimately related to joint projections or shared extraphysical activities.

Sign. After the sleeper has gained awareness in the extraphysical dimension, you, the projected projector, can give him/her a sign, symbol, keyword or password, in an extraphysical visual projection which you have willfully created – or in other words, a specific morphothosene – in order for the sleeper to remember the encounter, even if only as a dream.

Impression. The extraphysical symbol or sign will become more firmly impressed upon the sleeper's memory, aiding in his/her recall after physically awakening. On this occasion, you can also transmit useful instructions or information to the target-consciousness.

Recoincidence. It is frequently useful for you to exteriorize calming consciential energies to the target-person after the interiorization or recoincidence of his/her consciousness. This helps to leave him/her in a serene or normal psychophysiological condition and assists him/her in the subsequent recollection of the extraphysical experiences.

Surprises. Both agreeable and disagreeable surprises can transpire in these approaches, as has occurred with the author on a certain occasion due to inexperience. An attempt was being made to extract a friend's consciousness from his human body in an exteriorization of the psychosoma, whereupon the friend approached the projected projector (the author) from behind his psychosoma, smiling. He was already projected and lucid, and this fact had not been perceived by the author.

Vampire. On other occasions, there are those who have even taken the author to be a vampire, an extraphysical monster, an intruder and a presumed hardened adversary during attempted extraphysical hetero-awakenings.

Rejuvenation. Upon leaving the human body, the intraphysical consciousness generally has an appearance that is rejuvenated, good looking and sometimes surprisingly luminous.

Duo. Extraphysically approaching a partner who sleeps in the same bed of the evolutionary duo almost always ends up in the undesirable and *abrupt interiorization* of the projector-awakener's already projected consciousness. This is due to the proximity of the human bodies of both or the phenomenon of spontaneous and habitual auric coupling.

Counterapproach. When approaching a sleeping friend, you, as a projected projector, should not be surprised if you receive an extraphysical counterapproach that is often terribly hostile from one or more intruders of the target-friend. They arise to simultaneously defend possession of their *prey* or their consciential space. In this case, there is no immediate alternative: you must extraphysically confront them, without fear or vacillation, doing your best in order to help these ill personalities, remaining confident that you will always receive powerful extraphysical assistance from the helpers, whether intangible or visible.

Uses. The following are 8 of the uses of temporarily extracting an intraphysical consciousness from his/her human body:

1. **Projectability.** Demonstration of the possibility of projecting during the period of natural sleep.
2. **Help.** Technical aid for the development of a friend's lucid projection.
3. **Development.** Elimination of the intraphysical projector's extraphysical idleness.
4. **Parapsychism.** Cooperation in the development of an intraphysical consciousness's parapsychism.
5. **Communicology.** Transmission of someone's edifying message, whether it is that of a helper, relative or friend which is an intraphysical being or an extraphysical consciousness.
6. **Paratelepathy.** Production of extraphysical telepathic prospecting.
7. **Cooperation.** Searching for the cooperation of the intraphysical being for positive extraphysical or even human tasks.
8. **Deintrusiveness.** Powerful aid in the services of interconsciential deintrusion of all types.

Bibliography: Baumann (93, p. 87), Cooke (300, p. 36), Dillon (402, p. 110), Farrar (496, p. 192), Lefebure (909, p. 65), Powell (1278, p. 90), Rogo (1444, p. 181), Smith (1574, p. 121), Vieira (1762, p. 57), Young (1895, p. 95).

---

348. UNAPPROACHABLE BEINGS

Definition. Unapproachable being: a human being or extraphysical consciousness in a difficult situation or an obviously critical position, wherein the projected intraphysical consciousness should avoid making an approach – for personal reasons or for the convenience of the projector or other beings – because any interference made by the projector (projected intraphysical consciousness) might unintentionally disturb that being (the target-being, in this case) or cause undesirable harm unintentionally.

Synonymy: critical target-being; interdicted being; untouchable being.

Intraphysicals. Among the intraphysical beings who are, in theory, unapproachable by the projected intraphysical consciousness, the following 3 merit singling out as examples:

1. **Driver.** The individual in a potentially dangerous condition, when driving a vehicle, whether it is a car, motorcycle or other vehicle.

2. **Worker.** The worker who is absorbed in the operation of machinery, which can cause a serious work-related accident.

3. **Barber.** The barber shaving a customer while holding the razor.

Surgeon. According to the theorice of unapproachable beings, for the purpose of research, the surgeon who is operating on the inactive human body of the intraphysical consciousness who is projected due to the effect of anesthetics should not be directly approached by the projected-patient-consciousness him/herself.

Perceptions. In the case of unapproachable human beings, the essential problem lies in the difficulty of the projected consciousness knowing, with certainty, if he/she will or will not be perceived by the intraphysical being – although this does not occur in the majority of cases – and when perceived, what that being's psychological reaction will be upon seeing the projector.

Meters. There are still no reliable meters, tracers or sensors for measuring parapsychic phenomena or the parapsychic reactions of the human being.

Extraphysical consciousnesses. Among the extraphysical consciousnesses that are unapproachable by the projected intraphysical consciousness, the following two, in theory, can be singled out:

1. **Suicide.** The extraphysical consciousness that is a recent arrival to extraphysicality or the period of post-desomatic intermission and is extremely disturbed, as in certain cases of suicide, for example.

2. **Parasleep.** The extraphysical consciousness that is sleeping the so-called *restorative sleep*.

Conditions. Beings and places that are unapproachable to the projected intraphysical consciousness should be classified in the following manner, according to the projector's extraphysical condition on that occasion. The following 3 variables serve as examples:

1. **Hyperacuity.** Degree of lucidity: upon finding him/herself semilucid in a hostile environment, for example, it will be more prudent for the projector to return to the human body.

2. **Holosomatics.** Vehicle of manifestation: when in the mentalsoma, it becomes very difficult for the projector to have a direct influence upon intraphysical beings, human bodies or physical objects.

3. **Company.** Occasional company: it *is not advisable* for the projected projector to go for an extraphysical stroll with an ill extraphysical consciousness.

Bibliography: Monroe (1064, p. 164), Vieira (1762, p. 163).

---

349. EXTRAPHYSICAL-PHYSICAL SELF-TOUCH TECHNIQUE

Definition. Extraphysical-physical self-touch: the act of the projector touching his/her own human body while its consciousness is projected outside it in another vehicle of manifestation.

Synonymy: extraphysical self-embrace; self-tangibility.

Self-embrace. The *first* fully lucid consciential self-bilocation frequently leads the projected projector to an immediate subsequent *second* operation, which is not always feasible, of self-touch with the extraphysical arms (para-arms) of the psychosoma. This is soon followed by a *third* operation, the self-embrace or, in other words, embracing the human body, which remains inactive in a condition of inertia.

Face. The immediate physical point of self-touch is generally the face, as it is the area which is most accessible and most commonly seen. It is also the organic segment which identifies any person, followed by other areas of the human body.

Determining. The difficulties of self-touch and self-embrace lie in 2 determining factors:

1. **Proximity.** The close proximity of the 2 vehicles of the consciousness.

2. **Cord.** The preponderant action of the silver cord's mediation upon the projected intraphysical consciousness, inside the individual extraphysical psychosphere of consciential energy.

Reinteriorization. Both of these factors provoke an almost always irreversible abrupt reinteriorization.

Temperature. Upon touching it with the parafingers of the psychosoma, the human body can give the consciousness the sensation of being cold, like a cadaver, or hot, like a normal or feverish living being. These sensations depend upon the degree of the projected projector's self-awareness, his/her emotional reactions at that moment and his/her psychophysiological influences or, more precisely, his/her *parapsychophysiological* influences, upon his/her own extraphysical perceptions.

Trauma. Extraphysical self-touch commonly provokes a small trauma in the projected intraphysical consciousness, which thereby abruptly interiorizes into the human body which is touched. This can even bring about an inoffensive intraphysical repercussion.

Bibliography: Green (632, p. 45), Greenhouse (636, p. 62), Monroe (1065, p. 173), Vieira (1762, p. 109).

350. AURIC COUPLINGS

Definition. Auric coupling: the development of an empathy, interfusion and temporary union of the energetic auras of the vehicles of manifestation of two or more consciousnesses.

Synonymy: auric interfusion; empathetic coupling; energetic coupling; energetic Siamese twins; ephemeral consciential fusion; extraphysical xiphopagus; holochakral interpenetration; interaction of consciousnesses; occult polarity; parapsychic polarity.

Telemagic. Nothing occurs without an interaction. *Telemagic* is the attraction or sympathy existing between terrestrial objects and mother earth (geoenergy).

Gravity. Gravity, for example, represents a form of telemagic for physicists.

Pathemia. Pathemia, another form of telemagic, is the emotional relationship between things that are characterized, for example, by 3 factors relative to the psychosoma, the parabody of emotions:

1. **Attraction.** *Sympathy* (to feel *with*) or attraction, participation in the emotions of another.

2. **Indifference.** *Apathy*, per se, indifference or neutrality, insensitivity to the causes which habitually provoke emotions.

3. **Repulsion.** *Antipathy* or repulsion, the sentiment of disaffection, which reaches the point of open antagonism.

Empathy. Various concepts are based on pathemia, such as the following 7:

1. **Intropathy.** The *empathy* (to feel *as*), *unipathy* or *intropathy,* being a type of affective communion in which 2 beings identify with one another and consciously understand each other in such a manner that they come to have the same sentiments; related to *rapport*, that mutual relationship between two or more persons which makes it such that each one is able to immediately and spontaneously respond to others.

2. **Implasty.** *Implasty* and other well-known phenomena such as the exteriorization of consciential energies.

3. **Sensitivity.** The exteriorization of sensitivity.

4. **Repercussion.** Physical repercussion during lucid projectability.

5. **Zoanthropy.** Zoanthropy.

6. **Stigmas.** Stigmas in general.

7. **Cord.** The connection process between the mentalsoma and the parabrain of the psychosoma through the golden cord.

Mimipathy. Aside from empathy, it is important to highlight the existence of *mimipathy,* the emotional state of the intellectual's mind when he/she is creating.

Cosmopathy. The state of *cosmopathy,* the detection of influxes of cosmic emotion: the maximal holothosene of the universe.

Tropisms. *Tropisms* and *tactisms* between inanimate realities, as well as between animate or living realities.

Machines. Attractions and repulsions between humans and machines – or the *human-machine relationship* – have been verified.

Films. It is common knowledge that the photographic film industry and other industries do not allow certain employees to process their film because these individuals damage it merely with the bioenergetic irradiation from their physical presence.

Telephones. Also, certain persons are not able to work in other specialized firms because they produce radio static, interfere in television films, or make telephones ring continuously without apparent cause.

Consanguineous. Successive, consanguineous intraphysical lives (existential seriation) can predispose the phenomena of profound auric coupling between individuals, particularly between mother and daughter, father and son, and others.

Polarity. Within parapsychic polarity, one position acts in opposition to the other. If the disturbing or entropic side exists, so does the constructive side also exist – whether it be the active leader or the receptive follower – and even the condition of auric coupling.

Exchange. All of the abovementioned occurrences show the subtle process that enables the exchange of emotions or, in other words, the affective reactions of great intensity, which are dependent upon the diencephalic centers and normally allow manifestations of a vegetative nature.

Emotions. Among the basic emotions, the following are included: happiness, grief (pain), fear, anger, love and repugnance. From these emotions, other consciential conditions arise, such as: attraction, compatibility, agreement, harmony, compassion, union, integration between two or more consciousnesses, which occurs intensely in the state of auric coupling.

Operations. The facts indicate that, in the current phase of *subhumanity,* the *consciential principle* (the individualized, human consciousness) does not submit itself to the following 4 arithmetic operations:

1. **Division.** It does not divide itself, as observed in the sensations of the phenomena of double awareness.

2. **Multiplication.** It does not multiply itself, according to the manifestations of the attribute of multiplicity of the psychosoma.

3. **Subtraction.** It does not undergo subtraction, according to the continuous evolution of the ego, because it neither backslides nor regresses, despite being able to remain stationary. The consciousness that remains stationary has already regressed in the march of evolution, because no one stops his/her thosenization process. This is why a prolonged sedentary life or physical inactivity signifies regression.

4. **Addition.** It is not possible to add (addition) one consciousness to others. Therefore, strictly speaking, so-called *soul mates* do not in fact exist, except for the expressions of romanticism or literature; also, definitive consciential fusions apparently do not occur, although interconsciential possessions do occur.

Phenomenon. Despite these occurrences, 3 types of the temporary phenomenon of auric coupling can occur:

1. **Intraphysicology.** Only between intraphysical consciousnesses.

2. **Extraphysicology.** Only between extraphysical consciousnesses.

3. **Multidimensionality.** Simultaneously between intraphysical and extraphysical consciousnesses.

Categories. According to the research theory, the following are the most common categories of auric coupling:

1. **Pairs.** Pairs of consciousnesses (evolutionary duo, mother and daughter, father and son, and others).
2. **Trios.** Trios of consciousnesses, including that between triplets.
3. **Groups.** Groups of consciousnesses, or consciential fields (groupkarma, group holothosene).

Contagion. Auric coupling presents energetic contagion.

Interaction. A simple auric duo can become amplified to the point where it forms an *auric group* – or a unified consciousness – with profound psychic interaction in which the isolated parapsychic aptitudes reinforce one another. This interaction is not easy, although it can be performed.

Classification. Auric couplings can generally be classified into physiological and pathological.

Physiological. Physiological or natural auric coupling encompasses various categories of two or more beings, such as the following 27 examples listed in alphabetical order:

1. Certain young (subhuman offspring).
2. Conscientiotherapist-evolutient.
3. Extraphysical master-disciple.
4. Father-son.
5. Godfather-godchild.
6. Hen-chicks.
7. Horse-rider integration.
8. Hypnotist-sensitive.
9. Leader-follower, whether political duos or religious professional duos.
10. Mother-daughter.
11. Partner-partner in an evolutionary duo or husband-wife.
12. Penta practitioner-helper.
13. A physically and extraphysically impassioned couple.
14. Physician-patient.
15. Preacher-*sinner*.
16. Pregnant woman and fetus or fetuses.
17. Projector-helper.
18. Prophet-interpreter.
19. Psychologist-patient.
20. Psychophonic sensitive-communicant.
21. Salesperson-customer.
22. Sensitive-extraphysical mentor or helper.
23. Sister souls or individuals who have a deep affinity and friendship.
24. Teacher-student.
25. Telepathic message emitter-receiver.
26. Therapeutic energy donator-recipient, as with exteriorization of consciential energies.
27. Uniovular or monozygotic, monochorionic and monoamniotic twins.

Pathological. The following is an alphabetical listing of the 8 most frequent pathological (or parapathological) auric couplings:

1. Animal symbiosis.
2. A crowd of rioters.
3. A group of ill personalities, such as those with convulsive manifestations.
4. Group or collective hysteria.
5. Intrusion victim-intruder duo.
6. Lynch mob.
7. Mutinous persons (ship, rebellion).
8. Pregnant woman-intrusion victim-intruder trio.

Group. Auric couplings comprising more than 3 consciousnesses generally tend to become ill or pathological. There are those who affirm that this is the reason why Jesus of Nazareth *promised* to be present in groups of two or 3 persons who were gathered in his name and not in the middle of simply any crowd.

Efficiency. The most effective energetic transmission is always human aura-to-aura, or more precisely, the chakra-to-chakra donation of energy.

Crowd. A human, as an individualized consciousness, when a member of a crowd – a mass of heterogeneous elements – loses his/her personal identity, the ability to reason logically, moral choice, and the sense of individual and collective responsibility.

Crises. The suggestibility, excitability and energetic intoxication of the masses makes the individual, a member of the group, cease to have a personal opinion or will. This individual, who is subject to crises or sudden and violent attacks of hate, as well as enthusiasm, panic, and imposed, simultaneous, transmitted multiple madness, becomes capable of perpetrating the most heinous and gratuitous acts of violence against others and even him/herself. The abrupt immersion in the group holothosene, or the act of yielding part of one's own identity almost always represents a type of instantaneous, individual self-intrusion.

Worse. Individuals, in the midst of a crowd – inebriated without having ingested any drink – are thus worse in all aspects. The elements of a crowd level out to the lowest common denominator. Although union provides strength, a meeting of good individuals will not generally obtain an excellent result. It will often have a mediocre result and frequently one that is even worse.

Exception. It seems that the only existing exceptions regarding the auric coupling of more than 3 consciousnesses are those related to the human gestation and birth of quadruplets, quintuplets, sextuplets, or other healthy couplings. This may occur because the consciousnesses, in these cases, are under the more rigorous action of the pronounced physical restriction of fetal life (e.g.: the fetal aura is smaller in various aspects), and the powerful influence of the ego and the vehicles of manifestation of the pregnant woman's consciousness, logically including her human body.

Interactions. Aside from the auric couplings mentioned above, there are 4 specific interactions with nature, listed in decreasing order:

1. **Zoology.** Interorganismic communications, or the so-called *primary consciousness*.
2. **Humanity.** The human consciousness with the subhuman pet animal.
3. **Botany.** The phenomenon of the person with a *green thumb* and the plant which is zealously cared for.
4. **Matter.** Interactions of the consciousness with inanimate bodies (human-machine), such as the favorite object or that of personal use, the individual instrument and its owner: technician-electronic apparatus; virtuoso-violin; pianist-piano; automobile-driver/owner; airplane-pilot/owner; boat-fisherman/owner; and others.

Phenomena. The occurrence of auric coupling also acts in the predisposition and triggering of a series of phenomena that are substantially closely related and require further research, such as the following 4 examples:

1. **Parasurgery.** Parasurgery, performed indirectly by a third person who is interposed, being situated between the parasurgeon and the patient.
2. **Pharmacology.** A contact high related to light and heavy drugs.
3. **Projectiology.** The occurrence of projective contagion.
4. **Holochakrology.** The assistential technique of exteriorization of energies by three.

Ephemeral. Auric coupling, even if ephemeral, always occurs between the 2 partners of sexual union, in parapsychic trance and in hypnotic trance.

Hetero-hypnosis. The practically omnipresent phenomenon of hetero-hypnosis, or hetero-suggestion, evidences a continuous spectrum of possibilities that coexist with humans in all fields of their activities, starting with the simplest social gatherings. The facts show that this aspect of auric coupling will be studied more deeply in the future in order to reduce widely practiced abuses in modern intraphysical society in the area of communication, political advertising, artistic areas and many others.

Rituals. In the mystical meetings of sects as well as in syncretic religious rituals, the prayers which are spoken out loud, the formation of healing circles, the music, the chants (mantras), the reliance on hymns, group dances, the cadences of the maracas and other hypnotic resources, have the purpose of installing a trance or an altered state of consciousness. This is achieved through the energetic maintenance of all those who are present, harmonizing them with these and other psychophysiological crutches in a single flow of energy or, in other words, creating auric coupling between all the participants.

Spheres. In many occurrences of auric coupling, the influence of the extraphysical psychosphere of the energy of each intraphysical consciousness involved enters into action.

Projections. Projections of the consciousness gradually enable the intraphysical consciousness to extraphysically and directly verify – and even make use of the sometimes profoundly shocking reality of – the affinities and antipathies of auric couplings between all types of beings.

Syndrome. The Stendhal syndrome (Henry Beyle: 1783-1842), or Freud's sense of being overwhelmed is the noble and elegant malaise or shock that some healthy tourists and visitors, who are highly sensitive and of good taste, manifest – notably persons between two and four decades of physical age, who are single or alone – when face-to-face with the beauty of artistic (paintings and sculptures) and extraordinary architectural works of famous museums, palaces, galleries and monuments.

Symptoms. The most typical symptoms of the state of esthetic exaltation of the Stendhal syndrome are the following 6:

1. Physical indisposition.
2. Vertigo.
3. Loss of orientation in space and time.
4. Confused state.
5. Sensations of abandonment, impotence and depression.
6. Crisis of amnesia (sometimes).

Case study. The most classic examples of works of art and more frequent examples of artistic monuments which cause shock, vertigo and delirium are found in Florence, the capital of Tuscany, Italy. The following are 5 examples:

1. **Brunelleschi.** Brunelleschi's cupola (Filippo Brunelleschi: 1377-1446).
2. **Boticelli.** Botticelli's *La Primavera* (Sandro di Mariano Filipepi Botticelli: 1444-1510).
3. **Michelangelo.** Michelangelo's *David* (Michelangelo Buonarroti: 1475-1564).
4. **Tiziano.** A painting by Tiziano (Tiziano Vecellio: 1490-1576).
5. **Caravaggio.** A painting by Caravaggio (Michelangelo Merisi Caravaggio: 1573-1610), the last 2 in the Galeria Uffizi.

Greece. Other examples of the Stendhal syndrome are reported to occur when in the presence of artistic and architectural works in Athens, Greece.

Mechanism. These facts occur due to the more intense *rapport* (or empathy) or the interaction of auric coupling between the visitor and the art objects (energy accumulators), or that environment (holothosene, psychometrizing). They become charged with consciential energies which accumulated over time as a result of intraphysical consciousnesses being there, contemplating them ecstatically and depositing a portion of their personal energies in those objects. The more recent visitor therefore experiences the trauma of the initial departure of the consciousness from the state of holosomatic coincidence, or the exteriorization of energies of the holochakra (energetic parabody), notably those of the cardiochakra, or even the greater discoincidence of the psychosoma (emotional parabody).

Discoincidence. This occurs regardless of the individual being aware of his/her parapsychic attributes and can lead him/her to a temporary state of waking discoincidence.

Projectiological Bibliography: Alverga (18, p. 187), Castaneda (258, p. 109), Hope (756, p. 8), Huxley (771, p. 155), Moss (1096, p. 188), Vieira (1762, p. 158), Walker (1781, p. 7), White (1829, p. 319), Yogananda (1894, p. 198).

Specific Bibliography:

1. **ARAÚJO NETTO;** *Charme de Florença Enfeitiça os Turistas;* JORNAL DO BRASIL; Rio de Janeiro, RJ, Brazil; Daily; Year XCVI; N. 325; March 1, 1987; 1st section; illus.; p. 13.

2. **CORTES,** Celina; *Roteiros Mágicos;* JORNAL DO BRASIL; Rio de Janeiro, RJ, Brazil; Daily; July 5, 1989; illus.; p. 13.

3. **MAGHERINI,** Graziella; *La Sindrome di Stendhal;* 220 pp.; 5 chaps.; 16 tables; bibl.; 20.5 X 14 cm; pb.; 2nd ed.; Firenze; Italy; Ponte alle Grazie; Gennaio, 1995; pp. 1-220.

---

351. EXTRAPHYSICAL HELPERS

Definition. Extraphysical helper: beneficent extraphysical consciousness, existing separately from protoplasm, which aids the intraphysical consciousness during extraphysical departures, in the periods experienced outside the human body as well as in human life during the ordinary, physical waking state.

Synonymy: angel of death; angel of light; being of light; extraphysical advisor; extraphysical aide; extraphysical ally; extraphysical assistant; extraphysical cicerone; extraphysical companion; extraphysical control; extraphysical copilot; extraphysical escort; extraphysical gatekeeper; extraphysical ghostwriter; extraphysical guardian; extraphysical master of ceremonies; extraphysical master; extraphysical mentor; extraphysical midwife; extraphysical partner; extraphysical protector; extraphysical tutor; facilitator of self-lucid projection; "god;" "gods;" friend entity; hidden instructor; hyperphysical being; initiator; intangible mentor; invisible assistant; invisible worker; projector's hidden friend; protector spirit; psi entity; radiant apparitional being; spiritual benefactor; *supersoul*; trailblazer.

Categories. Among the types (categories) of extraphysical helpers, the following 10 can be singled out:

1. Extraphysical technician of projections of the consciousness.
2. Extraphysical master.
3. Man, woman, child: with regard to extraphysical appearance.
4. Former relative, former friend, former colleague, former convict, or even an apparent stranger, of greater affinity, which has already undergone desoma.
5. Intangible presence.
6. Helper of explicit assistance.
7. Deintruder.
8. Extraphysical police.
9. Desoma facilitator (first desoma).
10. Holochakra deactivator (second desoma).

Former relatives. There are projectors that, for example, evoke a helper-father, helper-mother, helper-sister or helper-cousin.

Extraterrestrials. Only continued extraphysical experiences allow the projector to distinguish terrestrial helpers from extraterrestrial helpers by their extraphysical forms, sensitivities and peculiar occupations that transcend this planet's atmosphere.

Fringe benefits. Among their attributes or the *extraphysical fringe benefits* furnished by the helper to the projected human projector during the consciential projection, with the aim of providing extraphysical assistance, the following 10 can be singled out:

1. **Assistance.** Frequent intangible, invisible or subtle extraphysical assistance; less frequent, explicit, tangible or direct extraphysical assistance.

2. **Awakening.** Sponsoring of extraphysical awakening as well as lucid and semilucid, assisted and commanded projections.

3. **Contacts.** The establishment of interconsciential encounters or contacts.

4. **Education.** Execution of didactic visual projections (pedagogy, education).

5. **Energies.** Energetic support: transmission of consciential energy.

6. **Lucidity.** An increase in the lucidity and self-awareness of the projected consciousness.

7. **Mentalsomatics.** Direct manifestation by the extraphysical consciousness in the mentalsoma, approaching the intraphysical projector's mentalsoma.

8. **Projectability.** Efficient aid in physical moments (related to consciential projection) and in extraphysical situations.

9. **Suggestions.** Promotion of inspiration or the transmission of intuitive suggestions.

10. **Volitation.** Extraphysical dislocation with volitation in group.

Relationship. In the normal relationship between the intraphysical consciousness and the helpers, there are no traces of mysticism, human preconceptions or artificiality in conduct. When this does occur, it indicates the presence of an extraphysical blind guide, an energivorous or needy extraphysical consciousness, or a deceased relative, which is not a helper: a technical and universalistic extraphysical consciousness within the world of solidarity and interconsciential assistance.

Para-appearance. When the helper wishes to provide assistance, it even takes on the appearance or the para-appearance of either gender, or even both genders, if necessary.

Call. The projector calls the helper through spontaneous and heartfelt evocative thought.

Evolution. While human bodies are resting during natural sleep, intraphysical consciousnesses project to extraphysical districts, communities or consciential environments with which they have an affinity. In projections guided by a helper, the projector goes to disagreeable as well as advanced extraphysical districts that do not correspond to the projector's level of discernment or evolution.

Technicians. Helpers are a specific type of extraphysical consciousness, being more common than others in extraphysical relationships with projected intraphysical consciousnesses. This is because they are *experienced experts* or technicians (specialists) in projectiology, although their appearances while working, para-appearances or *extraphysical physiognomies* vary infinitely.

Reality. Leaving the human body many times with lucidity, the intraphysical consciousness eventually encounters someone who, most often, is a helper. After various contacts with different helpers, the projector – as rigid in principles and skeptical in human conditioning as he/she may be – becomes convinced they are not fruits of the collective consciousness, much less archetypal figures or universal hallucinations, but tangible personalities, real intelligences and independent, active consciousnesses.

Cooperation. Regardless of the names that are given to them, such as guides, mentors, angels, guardians, extraphysical assistants or liberators, and the spectrum of their extraphysical appearance – a man on a throne, Tibetan monk, luminous apparition, point of colored energy, child, woman, friendly old man, relative, friend, stranger – helpers always efficiently cooperate with the projected intraphysical consciousness because it is their task under all circumstances.

Graduation. However, it is important to emphasize that, just as with any technician in any area of human service, the level of competence varies from helper to helper, this being one of the reasons for the diversity of forms in which they present themselves.

Hyperacuity. There are helpers that are equal to ourselves and those that are extremely lucid, the presence of which transmits a balance and serenity far removed from that of the planetary climate.

Merit. Every projector has the helper that he/she merits, according to the projection that is experienced. The services of the helpers are broader, more constant and sophisticated than we imagine at first sight.

Retention. The helpers, which are well-versed in the mechanics of lucid projection, trade off with each other according to the needs of their tasks. It should be remembered that, in the same way that they help the intraphysical consciousness temporarily leave the human body, the helpers also aid one to remain in the human body, detaining the individual in the intraphysical dimension without projecting, whenever circumstances require it for the benefit of the projector, who is sometimes unaware of the reasons for this procedure.

Programming. In projections guided by the helpers, the projector's possibilities of observation and analysis are programmed. The projector sees and recalls only what the helpers decide to expose. While outside the body, the projector enjoys a conditional freedom regarding great objectives that transcend his/her position as an obscure worker at the lowest echelon of the team or, in other words: a self-aware *minicog* engaged within a *maximechanism* of interconsciential and multidimensional assistance. In this realistic situation, the intraphysical being ends up feeling entirely secure in his/her works of solidarity.

Mnemosomatics. The frequent suggestion made by the helpers not to record the recollections of selected extraphysical experiences which are part of a series of lucid projections serves to corroborate the selectivity of post-projective recall.

Areas. Upon continuing to have projective experiences, the intraphysical consciousness interrelates with extraphysical consciousnesses of diverse areas of interest, schools of learning, philosophies and extraphysical occupations, notably the following 6:

1. **Aborigines.** Beings who lived in South and North America, and still have common interests regarding life and nature. They deal with so-called *witchcraft,* shamanism, Afro-Brazilian worship services and parapsychic practices pertaining to the Spiritist movement. They are predominantly found in certain areas of paratropospheric environments. Among their leaders are a large number of magnetizers and technicians specialized in works performed together with subhuman beings or extraphysical consciousnesses that preserve nature.

2. **Africans.** Beings that come from previous intraphysical lives which occurred in primitive African tribes predominate in extraphysical environments of this continent, and act upon the 3 Americas. They extraphysically maintain parapsychic and religious cults and syncretisms in many countries.

3. **Asians.** Extraphysical beings with recent human experiences or, in other words, in the last few centuries, in India, Tibet, China and surrounding areas. They cultivate individual practices of primary intraconsciential illumination among humans. They possess physical-extraphysical recourses which are more deeply rooted in antiquity. They are enthusiasts of primary research, lacking a higher level of cosmoethics from the mentalsomatic dimension. They are mostly proponents of Asian religions, including Zen, Yoga and Orientalism. They are generally inexperienced regarding interconsciential deintrusion and are still very attached to egoistic processes *(siddis).*

4. **Magnetizers.** Extraphysical consciousnesses which almost always have holobiographical roots (existential seriation) in Europe. They are mostly engaged in paratropospheric activities related to extraphysical assistential tasks at Masonry centers, a great number of fraternal organizations and lines of antiquated esoterism.

5. **Sensitives.** Extraphysical consciousnesses with holobiographical experiences (existential seriation) in Western countries where they performed tasks in the field of parapsychism. They are consciousnesses involved in extraphysical assistance with all other groups of paratropospheric extraphysical consciousnesses, spiritists in general, umbandists, extraphysical former indigenous people and exorcist Pentecostalists.

6. **Artists.** Groups of extraphysical consciousnesses that motivate artists in general, intellectual sensitives, authors, researchers and cultural institutions.

Preconceptions. The existence and activities of the extraphysical helpers are some of the most interesting and more frequently forgotten aspects in the experimental field of projectiology. This is due to the scientific and religious preconceptions, stereotypes, archetypes, taboos and group abdominal brainwashing that still surround the subject.

Master. In parapsychic studies, it is common to affirm, "When the apprentice is ready, the master appears." Lucid projection enables the more lucid intraphysical consciousness to invert and transcend this affirmation. This is because the consciousness itself leaves the human body, *re*discovers extraphysical realities, expands the consciousness and renews its own way (intraconsciential recycling, existential recycling). The projector therefore ends up finding the extraphysical benefactor (helper) that inspires the individual's existence and amplifies recollections of his/her intermissive course.

Exchange. Contact and prolonged or continuous exchanges between an intraphysical consciousness and an extraphysical consciousness depend upon conditions and factors that are not only related to the intraphysical consciousness but also to the extraphysical consciousness, both of which are important types.

Types. Prolonged low-level (tropospheric) exchanges with an extraphysical consciousness that is still constantly tied to a human mentality, appetites and sensations are always easier and more common to achieve. On the other hand, a prolonged high-level exchange can only be maintained in the mentalsomatic dimension, through the mentalsomas of the consciousnesses, after a certain period of continued cosmoethical experiences.

Extraphysical consciousness. As the extraphysical consciousness gradually refines its sensations and interests, its contact with humans becomes progressively more difficult. Remaining hereabouts then represents a personal sacrifice directed toward assistance to the components of its evolutionary group.

Sources. This is why more long-lasting extraphysical contacts only occur with two simultaneous sources.

1. *Laborer.* With the still unevolved, unpredictable, paratropospheric extraphysical consciousness or the *extraphysical laborer,* with a predominance of former influences from the cerebellum, psychomotricity and the *abdominal sub-brain* related to its retrosomas.

2. *Master.* With the evolved extraphysical consciousness, *distant* from the human atmosphere, or the *extraphysical master*, with a predominance of the former influences from the brain and mentalsoma related to its retrosomas.

Extraphysical consciousnesses. The majority of more developed human sensitives enable the intermediation of 2 basic types of extraphysical consciousnesses – though they may or may not be aware of this fact – and with the clear predominance of 1 type or the other:

1. *Workers. Extraphysical workers,* which are able to remain close to the earth for longer periods, being dedicated to tropospheric tasks, restricted to the psychosoma, using parapsychic transmissions that are more mechanical or motive, *manual,* on the *planetary surface.* They are more involved in the consolation task and groupkarmality (a great number existential miniprograms).

2. *Intellectuals. Extraphysical intellectuals,* dedicated to creative mentalsomatic tasks – which endeavor to operate through the mentalsoma, in more subtle parapsychic transmissions (pangraphy) through mental waves, without predominantly using the sensitive's nervous and muscular or motive system. They are more involved in the clarification task and polykarmality (existential maxi-program, macrosomatics).

Transfigurations. Extraphysical consciousnesses are multifaceted and many of them are sufficiently open, in evolutionary terms, to perform assistance to intraphysical consciousnesses in their trials and tribulations. This is the case whether consoling or clarifying, when evoked in a thousand ways through countless human procedures. They appear in a transfigured manner to the individual, respecting personal habits, customs, traditions, archetypes, beliefs and conditioning.

Characteristics. This is why they are characterized or present various personal traits, such as the following 4:

1. **UFOlogy.** The powerful, exotic, extraterrestrial extraphysical consciousnesses appearing to UFO enthusiasts.

2. **Civilization.** Humanoid beings of light appearing to the so-called civilized human.

3. **Syncretisms.** The personalities of the *preto velho,* peai and other forms, in the many Afro-American syncretic manifestations.

4. **Indigenous.** In the form of an immense eagle, a living black panther and other subhuman animals considered to be inferior, to more primitive indigenous peoples.

Service. Those who think that departures from the human body appear to be tours or simple nocturnal touristic excursions without any noble objective at first sight, are mistaken. Wherever an extraphysical helper appears, edifying fraternal work is being performed.

Maturity. *Conducting scientific work* with evolved consciousnesses is always far more relevant, productive and gratifying than *conducting religious work* with these same consciousnesses. It is a question of consciential maturity.

Coherence. The tasks of interconsciential assistance performed by the extraphysical helpers are disciplined, strict and continuous, being very different from those of the extraphysical blind guides.

Case study. It was impressive and confirmative of the author's contention to encounter for the first time an unknown, impactful and unforgettable helper working alone in an assistential task in a paratropospheric environment. Only 4 terrestrial years later, the author encountered this same coherent and perseverant extraphysical consciousness with the same appearance. It was acting alone in the same manner and line of work, but in another extraphysical assistential task and a different paratropospheric district, aiding another being with diverse needs.

Projector-helper. The experienced projected consciential projector can serve as a helper for a novice projected consciential projector.

Rotation. Today's intraphysical consciential projector can be tomorrow's helper, and vice versa, in the multiexistential rotating cycle of successive intraphysical lives and intermissive periods.

Serenissimi. *Serenissimi (Homo sapiens serenissimus)* are parapsychically evolved helpers, true fulcrums of anti-emotive operant serenity exhibiting extreme and constant inner and outer tranquility in all extraphysical actions. They always present a clear psychosphere, namely one devoid of *consciential clouds*.

Harmony. *Serenissimi* are not robots, cyborgs, mutants, unclassifiable mannequins or statues. They are consciential worlds that are harmonized and made peaceful by elevated sentiments, illuminating ideas and awakened will.

College. An Invisible College of the *Serenissimi* exists. The *serenissimi* have extraphysical teams for providing continuous interconsciential assistance.

Scale. In an ascending evolutionary scale, a distinction can be made between pre-*serenissimi,* helpers, petifree consciousnesses, evolutiologists, *serenissimi* and free consciousnesses (FCs).

Bibliography: Brittain (206, p. 56), Crookall (323, p. 1), Engel (480, p. 14), Frost (560, p. 56), Gaynor (577, p. 39), Gonçalves (614, p. 5), Greenhouse (636, p. 274), Hives (728, p. 69), Kardec (824, p. 247), Leadbeater (895, p. 27), Meek (1030, p. 147), Mittl (1061, p. 5), Monroe (1065, p. 132), Powell (1278, p. 236), Rogo (1444, p. 59), Schiff (1515, p. 114), Shay (1546, p. 77), Steiger (1601, p. 73), Swedenborg (1635, p. 121), Vieira (1762, p. 168), Yram (1897, p. 54), Zaniah (1899, p. 60).

---

352. LUCID PROJECTION AND EVOCATION

Definition. Evocation (Latin: *evocatio,* to call forth with energy): the willful act through which the extraphysical presence of extraphysical consciousnesses or projected intraphysical consciousnesses are summoned and end up appearing to the evocator, whether in the paratropospheric dimension or distant from the intraphysical dimension.

Synonymy: consciential summons; consciential tracking; directed supplication; evocatory act; extraphysical summons; invocation; telepathic convocation; telepathic tracking.

Telepathy. It is above all worth highlighting that, in almost all of its categories and manifestations, evocation constitutes a strictly telepathic effect between two or more consciousnesses.

Categories. The basic categories of evocation vary according to the aspect in which the facts are analyzed. The following 14 are listed as examples:

1. **Lucidity.** Conscious evocation or that which is produced intentionally.

2. **Unconsciousness.** Unconscious or spontaneous evocation.

3. **Projective.** Projective evocation or that which is inserted into the context of the extraphysical events of lucid projection.

4. **Waking.** Waking evocation or that which is produced during the ordinary, physical waking state.

   5. **Extraphysical consciousness.** Evocation of an extraphysical consciousness or a projected intraphysical consciousness.

   6. **Target.** Evocation of a target-being, target-place or target-idea, as places and objects can be evoked.

   7. **Thosenic.** Evocation by thoughts (self-thosenes), through spoken words or gestures.

   8. **Chronological.** Immediate, delayed or anticipated evocation.

   9. **Health.** Positive or healthy evocation.

   10. **Pathology.** Negative, uncomfortable or pathological evocation.

   11. **Natural.** Natural evocation.

   12. **Ritual.** Ritualistic evocation.

   13. **Formulated.** Evocation with an evocative formula.

   14. **Self-evocation.** Self-evocation or one regarding the consciousness' own microuniverse.

   Induced. Besides the abovementioned evocations, probings and personal evocations induced through the stimulation of electrodes in different parts of the human brain were conducted in the laboratory, thereby exhuming long forgotten memories and sentiments.

   Sentiments. Patients did not feel any discomfort with these tests because the brain does not have nerve endings for registering pain. It became evident, however, that not only were past events registered in detail, but also the sentiments associated with these events. In this way, an experience and the particular sentiment associated with it are interconnected such that one cannot be elicited without the other.

   Thosenology. This occurrence serves to corroborate the principles of the thosene and the studies of thosenology, based on the fact that these 3 elements – thought, sentiment and consciential energy – manifest themselves together constantly and indissociably through our consciousnesses.

   Recollection. The evoked recollection is not an exact photographic or phonographic reproduction of past scenes or events, but the reproduction of what the patient saw, heard, felt and understood. In this case, the intraphysical consciousness operates together with the mentalsoma and psychosoma upon the human body (cerebral hemispheres) through consciential energies.

   Consciousnesses. Evocation, even when it is a consciential process without the direct participation of any other awake being, occurs efficiently and triggers telepathic processes including those with other extraphysical consciousnesses residing on earth, as well as extraterrestrial, intraphysical and extraphysical consciousnesses residing on other planets. This is the reason for the natural connection between projectiology and *naphology* or the concern with consciential lives on other heavenly bodies in the cosmos.

   Agents. Among the most relevant factors involved in the phenomenon of evocation of consciousnesses, linking agents or psychic connections should be highlighted, such as the face of the evoked being and notably the recollection of his/her eyes.

   Name. Besides this, the name of the person, specifically his/her nickname, known only to a small circle of friends, serve as powerful agents of *rapport*, affinity or empathy.

   Oligophrenics. Extraphysical oligophrenics neither perform fluent extraphysical telepathy nor do they coordinate critical judgment in a normal fashion. This is because they are not able to maintain mental concentration and, due to their general consciential deficiencies, they have neither syntony of thought nor sufficient mental resources to respond to conscious and unconscious evocations from intraphysical consciousnesses.

   Somatics. The projected projector's thought regarding his/her distant inactive body – which sometimes makes him/her return to the physical base and even interiorize abruptly and unexpectedly – and retrocognitive recall, or that regarding the consciousness' previous intraphysical life (personal retrosoma), can sometimes be classified as self-evocations.

   Existential seriation. More rarely, self-evocations can involve personal multi-existential or interconsciential aspects.

   Case study. The author is aware of many cases of evoking intraphysical consciousnesses in which the presence of a personality – that had supposedly already been living in the intermissive period for a long time – was called upon. However, in these cases, it was that selfsame person in one of his/her prior human existences (holobiography, retrosoma).

Occurrences. Multi-existential self-evocations can generate the following 3 unexpected occurrences, among others:

1. **Intrusiveness.** The *paradoxical intrusion* by an intruder which seeks to pass as the evoked personality or, in other words, to take the place of the *evoked personality,* and which the evoker does not identify as not being the personality he/she is evoking (negative or pathological, interconsciential).

2. **Personification.** The predisposition of animic phenomena, in this case, a phenomenon of unconscious mystification, personification or incorporation of oneself, one's own personality, in the conditions of the previous human life (negative and, in many cases, pathological in regard to holosomatics and psychosomatics, intraconscientially speaking).

3. **Self-retrocognition.** The pluri-existential recollection of the intraphysical consciousness, who definitively identifies him/herself as the evoked person (relatively positive or healthy regarding the expanded consciousness' access to his/her holomemory). In this case, he/she can be aided by an extraphysical helper acting as a triggering factor of the phenomenon.

Identification. In line with the preceding presentation, self-evocation or the phenomenon in which the evocator and the evoked personality are the same consciousness, should be included as an existing resource – albeit not always easy to execute – for the intraphysical consciousness to identify and research his/her own past human lives. Certain cases of spontaneous, unconscious self-evocation should also be included when the occurrences of animic personification seem to be characterized as a consciential disturbance pertaining to the area of parapsychopathology of the mentalsoma.

Bibliography: ADGMT (03, p. 123), Blavatsky (153, p. 208), Chaplin (273, p. 89), Gaynor (577, p. 87), Gómez (613, p. 71), Greene (635, p. 67), Hapgood (678, p. 324), Heindel (705, p. 66), Kardec (825, p. 338), Martin (1003, p. 71), Paula (1208, p. 137), Pensamento (1224, p. 44), Planeta (1249, p. 170), Shepard (1548, p. 469), Spence (1588, p. 228), Tondriau (1690, p. 226), Zaniah (1899, p. 189).

---

353. CONSCIOUS   EVOCATION   TECHNIQUE

Definition. Conscious evocation: a mental summoning intentionally made by the consciousness.
Synonymy: intentional evocation; premeditated evocation; voluntary evocation.
Positivity. You, as a lucid projector, can use conscious evocations in a positive manner not only in the ordinary, physical waking state, but also when lucidly projected in the extraphysical dimension, as long as you pay attention to the following 6 essential factors:

1. **Objectives.** The productive, healthy or cosmoethical objectives of your evocation.
2. **Personality.** The characteristics or personal traits of the personality of the evoked being.
3. **Holothosene.** The circumstances regarding the environment or the specific context (personal holothosene, notably that of the evoked being) on the occasion of the evocation.
4. **District.** The district or community where the evoked consciousness is supposedly located.
5. **Self-thosenity.** The evocator's current psychophysical condition (self-thosenity, intentionality, animus or motivation).
6. **Consequences.** The anticipated analysis of the consequences subsequent to your evocation.

Uses. Among the main practical applications of the evocatory phenomenon for the lucid evoking projector (you), the following 4 can be singled out:

1. **Interview.** A useful interview or encounter with a certain being, that has been shelved for a long time and has still not been realized.
2. **Assistance.** Assistential aid provided to extraphysical consciousnesses which generally have not undergone the second desoma, or the discarding of the entire holochakra.

3. **Hetero-awakening.** An encounter with a loved one – an empathic personality in your life – provoked by intentional evocation, in order to prove its own desoma to it or its extraphysical, intermissive, consciential hetero-awakening.

4. **Subhuman.** An extraphysical encounter with a former subhuman animal or a pet, which is now an extraphysical consciousness (subhuman consciential principle, parazoology).

Technique. Direct evocation can be used as a process whereby you project with lucidity. Get a photo, personal object, or piece of clothing belonging to a personality which is now an extraphysical consciousness that you wish to contact (obviously one which you presume to be in good, non-intrusive, extraphysical, intraconsciential condition). Then think intensely about this for a long time. You should reflect on the person and try to remember some of the experiences you shared with this conscientially evolved personality with whom you always had affinity or empathy.

Absence. The evoked being does not always appear to the evoker. All categories of intelligences or consciential principles can be evoked for a useful purpose. However, the evoked being will not always be willing, available, or in a condition to show up. This is due to various impediments, which can even frequently be against its will.

Avoidances. Evidently, evocation of intraphysical consciousnesses with a debilitated human body should be avoided, such as: seriously ill persons, ill aged persons, infants, and all intraphysical consciousnesses who underwent desoma with personal problems regarding their existence in the extraphysical dimension, as well as problems stemming from the extraphysical dimension.

Spontaneity. There are intentional evocations which are so spontaneous that they seem unconscious because the evocator is actually not aware that he/she is performing an evocation. Here are 2 examples: the simple recollection of a distant location and, often, of an object which one has not seen for a long time; a mental supplication directed to an extraphysical mentor.

Biographers. The greatest technical evocators are biographers of deceased personalities or extraphysical consciousnesses which were celebrities or *former persons* that are cherished through the memories of the *populace*.

Bibliography: Kardec (825, p. 366), King (846, p. 173), Mittl (1061, p. 8), Monroe (1065, p. 112).

---

354. UNCONSCIOUS   EVOCATIONS

Definition. Unconscious evocation: a mental summons made unintentionally and in an unnoticed manner by the intraphysical or extraphysical consciousness, whether in the physical or extraphysical dimension.

Synonymy: involuntary evocation; uncomfortable evocation; unexpected evocation; unintentional evocation; unnoticed evocation; unpremeditated evocation.

Contumacious. There are unconscious contumacious evokers among persons of advanced age (from sixty-five years of age and over) who lack adequate intraconsciential preparation and are not accustomed to the mechanisms of exchanges between the spheres of consciential life.

Energivorous. These persons provoke the living and frequently uncomfortable presence of energivorous consciousnesses which appear in order to seek help or speak with unbridled frankness, through the self-thosenes charged with tropospheric human emotions from which they are still not detached.

Avoidance. Unconscious evocations should always be avoided because, in most cases, they have negative consequences, beginning with the unwary evoker him/herself. They can also provoke transitory or permanent intrusions. This is why the lucid projector, whether in the ordinary, physical waking state, or in the extraphysical dimension, should be alert regarding his/her real intention, as well as the nature and quality of personal thosenes.

Semilucidity. Unconscious evocations are common to semilucid intraphysical projectors who have extraphysical experiences that are mixed with oneiric intercurrences. They almost always take them to be simple dreams or nightmares (altered states of consciousness), reminiscent of personalities from the dreamer's past.

Bait. In certain cases of *anticipated evocation,* the projector, while in the ordinary, physical waking state, makes an unconscious evocation of a being and later comes face-to-face with that same being during the consciential projection. This evocation operates similar to the process of physical and extraphysical interconsciential, assistential bait.

Agents. Foremost among the more common and active evocatory intermediary agents in the production of unconscious evocations is the nostalgic viewing of old family photo albums and verbal, direct, humorous, irreverent and many other types of observations made in front of the portraits of ancestors in the family gallery (groupkarmality).

Bibliography: Vieira (1762, p. 121).

355. EXTRAPHYSICAL MANIFESTATIONS OF THE SENSITIVE-PROJECTOR

Types. Among the extraphysical manifestations of the sensitive-projector, at least the following 8 can be singled out:

1. Extraphysical intuition.
2. Close or distant clairvoyance.
3. Clairaudience.
4. Extraphysical psychophony.
5. Extraphysical retrocognition.
6. Extraphysical precognition.
7. Energetic exteriorizations by three.
8. Group evocations.

Conditions. The consciential condition of the sensitive-projector varies during parapsychic manifestations in the extraphysical dimension and can be passive, in a trance, or lucid, either with complete self-awareness or with semi-awareness.

Psychosoma. The vehicle that is best suited for the sensitive-projector's extraphysical manifestations is the psychosoma, when it is reasonably laden with the holochakra.

Phenomena. The sensitive-projector's deep extraphysical passivity, during the phase of intense activity, can predispose various post-projective phenomena, especially post-projective energetic showers and the condition of waking discoincidence. Both phenomena are healthy and have gratifying effects.

Bibliography: Currie (354, p. 107), Greenhouse (636, p. 173), Smith (1572, p. 110), Turvey (1707, p. 170).

356. PHYSICAL MANIFESTATIONS OF THE COMMUNICANT-PROJECTOR

Definition. Communicant-projector: the intraphysical consciousness who manifests through a human sensitive as though he/she were an extraphysical consciousness.

Synonymy: intraphysical communicant; intraphysical consciousness-communicant; intraphysical consciousness-possessor; intraphysical possessor.

Types. Projective psychophony is the communicant-projector's most common physical or human manifestation. Besides this, energization by three and the apparition of the intraphysical projector should be listed, including his/her presence at the deathbed of persons who are about to undergo desoma (terminally ill persons, ICU). On these occasions, the intraphysical consciousness is usually found to be sleeping, or at least semi-awake.

Personalities. The communicant-projector can manifest as his/her current personality or in the form of one of his/her prior personalities or, in other words: from one of his/her previous intraphysical lives and, therefore, like a person who has already undergone desoma.

Density. The facts show that the psychosoma's density diminishes due to its distancing from the organism which it left – taking the consciousness with it – in order to manifest through an intraphysical sensitive.

Possession. Rare cases of possession of the intraphysical being by a projected consciousness of another intraphysical being have been registered. These perfectly characterize the phenomenon of the communicant-projector, in this case, the possessor-projector and the possession-projection. These facts are doubtlessly always brief, cyclic and pathological or parapathological.

Bibliography: Aksakof (09, p. 534), Armond (53, p. 87), Currie (354, p. 107), Delanne (381, p. 136), Denis (389, p. 162), Gauld (576, p. 265), Müller (1107, p. 239), Oesterreich (1145, p. 27), Rigonatti (1402, p. 82), Souza (1585, p. 122), Turvey (1707, p. 175).

---

357. ENERGIZATION BY THREE TECHNIQUE

Definition. Energization by three: the transference of consciential energy transmitted by a helper through 2 sensitives at the same time, one being a *lucid projected* intraphysical consciousness and the other being an intraphysical consciousness in a conventional *parapsychic trance*.

Synonymy: compound energetic transfusion; compound extraphysical energization; energization by 6 hands; transference of compound consciential energies; triple energization.

Participation. The author has already participated in assistential-parapsychic activities outside the human body as a projected projector with complete lucidity. One of them is precisely the transmission of consciential energies by three in *kardecist* (Spiritist) parapsychic sessions in domestic environments, as well as others in *terreiros de Umbanda* sessions.

Universalism. Actually, this is one of the reasons the author declares himself to be openly universalistic. Although understanding human reactions in this case, he does not defend the excesses of *parochial purism* or *egoistic entrenchment* in the practice of any doctrine, principle, theology, religion or sect. These should be universalistic, above all, but never are and cannot be. This is because of the doctrinaire, fundamentalist, orthodox, sectarian or factionalist principles on which each of these lines of human knowledge are based and remain statically rooted. They are all very different and even antipodal and irreconcilable regarding the principles of science, its rational experiments and continued scientific refutations of leading-edge relative truths.

Regression. Strictly speaking, being a disseminator of a dogmatic religion is an evolutionary regression for the adult intraphysical consciousness with multidimensional lucidity, regardless of who it is or where that individual is located.

Coherence. We need to live coherently with ourselves in any dimension where we manifest or thosenize.

Hypocrisy. The author, after reaching physical, intraconsciential maturity, was not able to hypocritically be a *mere* doctrinaire sensitive, disseminator of a religion or sectarian, fundamentalist, orthodox line while in the ordinary, physical waking state and simultaneously operate as a universalistic sensitive while lucidly projected outside the human body. Multidimensional coherence is required.

Labels. Extraphysical reality – existing prior to intraphysical realities – does not arise already labeled by humans. Parapsychism operates independent of labels.

Assistance. The assistential service of the human *minicog* within a *maximechanism,* especially the extraphysical one, cannot depend upon human preconceptions. If it were any other way, the indispensable conditions of *rapport,* empathy or affinity would not occur with the helper, which simultaneously operates as a friend of the sensitive and the assisted being. This is because, in this case, the helper serves as an extraphysical mentor with the common sensitive or as a *preto velho (para-appearance),* endeavoring to clarify what it can, removing the extraphysical blind guides, intruders and the satellites of intruders related to all of them. There would also not be any *rapport* between the sensitive and the ill intraphysical or extraphysical consciousness, which needs to be assisted by the transferences of consciential energies by 3 consciousnesses. This must occur without thinking, as a priority, about whether someone is intraphysical, extraphysical, lucid, materialist, agnostic, or anything else. This represents a consciousness or someone in need of assistance, which is sufficient in this case.

Inexistence. For the extraphysical helpers there is no racism, particularism, sectarianism or instinctive factiousness, which are restricted to the abdominal sub-brain of the unthinking human masses (see fig. 357, p. 1,147).

Choice. Parapsychic practice, common sense and self-discernment demand that the intelligent projector realistically situate him/herself on the lowest echelon of the scale of service in the extraphysical assistential work team. This is why he/she should not and cannot be performing any type of segregation, demanding specific working conditions, exhibiting infantile shamefacedness or choosing human locations, extraphysical environments, beings to be assisted or helpers for performing tasks and working together jointly as a lucid assistential minicog. The projector should demand nothing, but should be thankful for everything he/she receives, because he/she always ends up benefiting from consciential evolution in group, as in the practices of penta.

Ladder. The transmission of transferences of consciential energies by three technique forms a ladder of consciousnesses with descending rungs spanning from the sensitive's extraphysical-mentor-helper, the *highest* rung; to the projected projector, the *middle* rung; to the intraphysical sensitive – the *cavalo* ("horse") in *Umbanda* – the *lowest* rung. The energies that flow downward from above reach the assisted ill personality, whether an intraphysical or extraphysical consciousness, the base of the energetic ladder. The comparative scale of the rungs of this *ladder* is derived from the level of the consciential plane or dimension.

Sex. The sensitive in this case can be a man or a woman, the gender being of little importance, as there is no alteration in the process of transmission of energization by three. There are female sensitives who afford a greater passivity in the lucid parapsychic exchanges, thereby further facilitating the realization of the assistential process due to the characteristics of the gynosoma.

Approach. The author, in the performance of transferences of assistential consciential energies by 3, generally arrives alone at the location, teleguided by extraphysical intuition. The works progress with the extraphysical helper together with a sensitive from the beginning of the session, or even before the session in certain cases.

Encasing. With the aid of the benevolent helper, the sensitive is approached as though performing an anatomical encasing from behind in a forward direction, coming in contact with his/her back from above his/her shoulders and arms.

Irradiations. The energetic irradiations do not originate from the projector, or from his/her psychosoma, but come *from outside*, or *from above*, from a rich source (extraphysical helper). Although entering in a more rarefied or subtle state, they condense with intensity and vigor upon passing through the psychosoma, and even more so soon afterward when passing through the coincident sensitive. The irradiations quickly reach each one of the 4 heads, first the two extraphysical ones and then the two physical ones. The movement of the para-arms and parahands of the psychosoma are generally made in synchrony with the arms and hands of the sensitive.

Information. To those who are interested, it is worth mentioning something about that which occurs within the intraphysical consciousness projected in the psychosoma upon making him/herself passive in order to participate in energization by three. What follows is that which has been occurring with the author in his experimentations. We do not know what happens with others. It has still not been possible to find better details in the International Bibliography of Projectiology on the subject in order to present it here.

Frustrations. Sometimes, the circumstances of energizations by three create dramatic, silent and indescribable frustrations. In this case, the sensitive interferes, blocks and stops his/her participation in the transmission before it ends, when the energetic current is flowing most intensely. The projector, with the aid of the helper, therefore has to continue the energization without counting on the sensitive until the energetic transmission is concluded.

Will. The wish to transmit an initial energization in the sensitive constantly arises in the projector prior to each more serious task in order to calm him/her or, more precisely, to more forcibly subjugate him/her. However, the projector cannot force the parapsychic interface because this attitude would affect the central nervous system and even the neuromuscular system of the sensitive's entire human body.

Automatism. There comes a point at which the projector, under the guidance and energies of the benevolent helper, is able to control the sensitive. However, the sensitive unexpectedly begins to think about other subjects that are foreign and negative for the transmission, automatically acting like a robot. This interrupts the interface by three and the flow of the energies.

Sensations. Lastly, the projector continues to withstand the transmission of various energizations sustained by the patience, benevolence and the impressive example of the helper. Nevertheless, due to the constant effort made in order to maintain the interface or synchronization, or to overcome the continued disconnectedness or asynchrony, the projector starts feeling – in his/her psychosoma (emotional parabody), which is dense and even more *laden* by the silver cord – the reflections from the heavy irradiations from the patients, the sensitive and the participants in the environment.

Vomitings. An irrepressible urge to vomit is among the reactions that commonly occur on these occasions. It is characteristic of the physical effect phenomena that are more vigorously reflected in the projected projector, as the projector is an intermediary element or the one operating as a sensitive between the 3 participants in the work, like 1 electric wire between 2 terminals. If the sensations increase, the solution is to return to the human body, which is lying in the physical base. The projector still takes with him/her the impressions of vomiting which, everything aside, soon pass with the energetic showers sponsored by the helpers, which are more easily transmitted in the *field* of the projector's *home* (personal holothosene).

Sacrifices. In spite of everything, it is quite worth all the effort required to participate in energization by 3, where the most sacrificial role is actually not performed by the projected projector, despite all the abovementioned possible frustrations. The one which suffers most, in first place, is the helper, which is aware of everything and sees everything, and is sometimes also in an embarrassing condition of impotence. In second place is the sensitive who knows nothing and generally does not see anything clearly. This is followed by the sensations and experiences of the projected projector.

Validity. The participation of the projected projector is always valid to some extent. The helpers would obviously not go to so much trouble for nothing. According to explanations received in this sense, the energetic density of the projected intraphysical consciousness' temporarily freed psychosoma is at a frequency which is intermediary between the helper's less dense or rarefied psychosoma and the denser psychosoma of the sensitive who is coincident with the human body. This circumstance allows a greater interfacing between the different dimensions of these lives – the physical and the extraphysical dimensions – and the 4 psychosomas, energy condensing vehicles that participate in the energization by 3: the first 3, in the final analysis, are transmitters or relay stations, and the fourth psychosoma (that of the assisted individual) is the receptor. This is how the intraconsciential-parapsychic phenomenon operates within the parapsychism-animism binomial.

Psychosoma. Strictly speaking, the projected consciousness should not feel the urge to vomit while in the psychosoma, owing to the fact that the physical, or physiological, impressions do not reach his/her para-anatomy or his/her paraphysiology. Nevertheless, this does happen due to his/her greater density. The projector, during energization by 3, in this illustrative context, acts as though he/she were a *half-intraphysical consciousness,* or a *half-extraphysical consciousness,* between the helper (extraphysical consciousness) and the sensitive (intraphysical consciousness) who is in trance, or in the ordinary coincident, waking state.

Predisposition. Although somewhat parapsychically developed sensitives are more predisposed to extraphysically participate in energization by 3, the individual wishing to produce lucid projections, whether assistential or assisted, should psychologically predispose him/herself to have these experiences. Such extraphysical aid comprises the list of assistential tasks pertaining to the teams of helpers.

Parapsychism. Many individuals who are not sensitive in the ordinary, physical waking state are transformed into powerful extraphysical sensitives in energization by 3. A great number of the projected intraphysical consciousnesses working in these teams are not sensitives in ordinary human existence.

Recollections. Hundreds of projected intraphysical consciousnesses are constantly participating in energization by 3 everywhere. However, the consciential energies from the holochakra, which ballast the psychosoma on these occasions, disturb the recollections that are always fragmentary in most cases. The projectors end up not recalling extraphysical occurrences after physically awakening. They are unconscious workers in the world of interconsciential assistentiology on earth.

Bibliography: Vieira (1762, p. 80).

---

358. *INTER VIVOS* COMMUNICATION TECHNIQUE

Definition. *Inter vivos* communication: the physical, animic-parapsychic communication of the intraphysical consciousness projected from the soma (cellular body) with the consciousnesses of other human beings in the waking state.

Synonymy: case of parapsychic reciprocity; communication between living beings; *inter vivos* animism; *inter vivos* parapsychism; mediumistic trance; parapsychic manifestation of living beings; physical manifestation of the communicant projector; sophisticated communication between intraphysical consciousnesses.

Terminology. There are linguistic purists who may find a number of errors in the terminology below. This is because they work from the principle that there is no parapsychic, or even animic-parapsychic *inter vivos* communication. Nevertheless, certain terms are used here for a lack of better ones. Many of them have been used for a long time. The *pure* phenomenon, whether complex parapsychic (with two consciousnesses) or *pure* animic (with only one consciousness) is not only rare, in practice, but extremely difficult to verify.

Types. Among the types of animic-parapsychic *inter vivos* communication, at least the following 11 can be singled out:

1. Apparition to an intraphysical consciousness.
2. Bilocation or materialization-projection.
3. Extraphysical telekinesis.
4. Projective parapyrogenesis.
5. Projective pneumatophony.
6. Projective poltergeist.
7. Projective psychography.
8. Projective psychometry.
9. Projective psychophony.
10. Projective raps.
11. Telepathic transmission and reception with an intraphysical consciousness.

Conditions. The consciential levels of the projected intraphysical consciousness can be: active, unconscious, or amnesic (amnestic).

Interposed. In manifestations through the psychophonic sensitive, the communicant-projector operates as a consciousness which is interposed between the sensitive and the sensitive's own extraphysical mentor, the extraphysical supervisor of the parapsychic works in that are in progress.

Materializations. Among the physical manifestations of the communicant-projector, we can include all the psychophysical materializations of intraphysical consciousnesses (living persons) *with* sensitives or, in other words, those which are projected and manifest through the ectoplasmic resources of a human sensitive.

Animism. In the eyes of the observers, when a projected intraphysical consciousness communicates through an intraphysical sensitive – prior to the occurrence of an ordinary parapsychic phenomenon – a purely animic phenomenon (which is rare) occurs between two intraphysical consciousnesses which utilize the extraphysical dimension. Under these circumstances, both apply their own parapsychic capacities, thereby often dispensing with the direct participation of any extraphysical consciousness or external intelligence.

Bibliography: Aksakof (09, p. 542), Bozzano (185, p. 63), Crookall (343, p. 61), Crouzet (344, p. 429), Currie (354, p. 11), Ebon (453, p. 101), Flammarion (522, p. 206), Gauld (576, p. 226), Greenhouse (636, p. 162), Gurney (666, p. XXV), Lombroso (943, p. 254), Marryat (1001, p. 35), Martins (1009, p. 95), Muldoon (1103, p. 23), Riverain (1408, p. 119), Rodrigues (1431, p. 27), Salter (1498, p. 133), Smith (1574, p. 121), Turvey (1707, p. 175), Xavier (1873, p. 43).

---

359. *INTER VIVOS* APPARITION

Definition. *Inter vivos* apparition: the appearance of the consciousness of the intraphysical projector to other intraphysical beings.

Synonymy: apparition of a living being; human specter; *inter vivos* projection; projected apparition; projective apparition; projective tangibilization; self-induced phantasm.

Phantasm. In various countries, including England, for example, the person's double is called a *phantasm* or *spectrum*.

Superstition. It is generally – and superstitiously – presumed that the apparition is a harbinger of death for the one who was seen. This is based on the fact that the approach of the first desoma weakens the connections (silver cord, holochakra) between the human body (soma) and extraphysical body (psychosoma) of the individual.

Spontaneity. Parapsychic apparitions of projected intraphysical consciousnesses most often occur spontaneously during deep natural sleep and often with complete unawareness on the part of the agent, the projector.

Phenomenology. This is one of the most difficult projectiological phenomena to voluntarily and consciously provoke due to the inevitable, intense expenditure of consciential energies.

Sensitive. The least difficult means for producing an intentional apparition is for the projector to make an intraphysical consciousness into an energy donor, predisposed to the production of the phenomenon.

Qualities. This person or candidate should have 4 essential qualities:

1. **Empathy.** He/she should truly have affinity with the projector in order to facilitate *rapport*.

2. **Maturity.** He/she should live without fear of experiencing multidimensionality and the apparitions of intraphysical and/or extraphysical consciousnesses.

3. **Parapsychism.** He/she should have a pronounced parapsychic clairvoyant sensitivity.

4. **Holochakrology.** He/she should demonstrate a capacity for the practical application of consciential energies, most notably those related to the frontochakra. The purpose of this is to reduce the required degree of the physical condensation of the psychosoma that will be seen by the percipient.

Shared. In this case, for example, the percipient's clairvoyance promotes 50% of the *shared apparition,* leaving the other 50% to be supplied by the intraphysical projector-agent, which is projected in the psychosoma as densely as possible or, in other words, laden with the holochakra. The phenomenon thus occurs as though it were the harmonious conjugation of the manifestations of a *pair of sensitives*.

Circumstances. The conjugation of human circumstances most propitious for the deliberate production of the *inter vivos* apparition phenomenon is when a male consciential projector appears to a solitary female sensitive-percipient. This may occur due to "attraction of the opposite sex".

Characteristics. Apparitions of the projected intraphysical consciential projector can occur while the intraphysical percipient is sleeping or apparently awake. The apparitions generally appear to be immobile or gliding in front of the percipient. In many cases, immobile apparitions are mere morphothosene projections at a distance.

Forms. *Inter vivos* apparitions can be: vaporous, diaphanous, vague, imprecise, or clearly defined with regard to the outline, physiognomy, features, posture, corpulence, gestures and other aspects of the appearance of the human person. The inferior members of the humanoid form – obviously including the feet – are less pronounced during the apparitions.

Dialogue. The rarer cases of the apparition of intraphysical beings are those in which the projected consciential projector is seen, is tangible and, in addition, maintains a lively, intelligent conversation with the human-percipient-witness, unmistakably characterizing an occurrence of physical bilocation.

Animals. Among the more frequent spontaneous apparitions of projected intraphysical beings are those in which the percipients are children and pets, especially cats and dogs.

Bibliography: Andrade (27, p. 117), Baumann (93, p. 29), Bennett (117, p. 28), Bozzano (184, p. 151), Crookall (331, p. 23), Green (633, p. 26), Hart (687, p. 182), Kardec (825, p. 133), Mackenzie (970, p. 242), Martins (1005, p. 97), Muntañola (1108, p. 107), Vieira (1762, p. 168).

---

360. REACTIONS OF INTRAPHYSICAL CONSCIOUSNESSES TO THE APPARITION OF THE PROJECTOR

Varieties. The reactions of intraphysical beings in the ordinary, physical waking state to the apparition of a likewise intraphysical consciousness or a projected projector vary considerably according to the psychological state of the percipient, the human environment, the degree of the apparition's tangibility, and the ideas, emotions and reciprocal intentionalities that come into play among the triggering factors of the phenomenon.

Categories. Among the categories of reactions of intraphysical beings – adults, children and subhuman animals – to the apparition of intraphysical projected projectors, the following 12, presented in alphabetical order, can be singled out:

1. **Appeal.** Extend the right hand toward the crucifix hanging around the neck (nun).
2. **Attack.** Sic a guard dog against the projector's apparition.
3. **Beatitude.** Contemplate the apparition in contrite silence and introspection.
4. **Escape.** Run away quickly without looking back (immaturity).
5. **Extroversion.** Try to communicate with balance (laryngochakra).
6. **Fear.** Become fearful, and often terrified.
7. **Indifference.** Remain indifferent, as though he/she were a mere hallucination.
8. **Infantile.** Try to touch the apparition's shape (child).
9. **Mysticism.** Piously cross oneself.
10. **Panic.** Scream in desperation (woman).
11. **Self-defense.** Brandish a weapon (an armed individual).
12. **Surprise.** Become deeply shocked and speechless.

Subhumans. Subhuman animals – intraphysical beings aside from human beings – exhibit reactions to the apparition of a human projector, such as the following 8:

1. Happiness when it perceives the projected owner.
2. Agitation.
3. Behavior which is not characteristic of its temperament.
4. Leaving quietly with its tail between its legs (dog).

5. Temporary paralysis or shock due to fear or stupefaction.
6. Secondary physiological effects.
7. Barks (dog).
8. Neighs (horse).

Bibliography: Baumann (93, p. 33), Monroe (1065, p. 58), Vieira (1762, p. 168).

---

361. EXTRAPHYSICAL ATTACKS UPON THE PROJECTOR

Definition. Extraphysical attack: the act of someone aggressively attacking the personality of the human projector when in the ordinary, physical waking state or when projected from the soma in the psychosoma.

Synonymy: ambush; extraphysical aggression; extraphysical assault; extraphysical spat; parapsychic attack.

Attackers. Among the characteristics of the extraphysical attackers of the projector – including projected intraphysical consciousnesses – the following 12 examples can be pointed out:

1. Projected intraphysical consciousness or extraphysical consciousness with a masculine para-appearance.
2. Projected intraphysical consciousness or extraphysical consciousness with a feminine para-appearance.
3. Projected intraphysical consciousness or *extraphysical consciousness with an undefined* para-appearance.
4. Habitual extraphysical assailant.
5. Common extraphysical vampire (energivorous extraphysical consciousness).
6. Known projected intraphysical consciousness or extraphysical consciousness.
7. Unknown projected intraphysical consciousness or extraphysical consciousness.
8. Conscious intraphysical consciousness or extraphysical consciousness.
9. Unconscious intraphysical consciousness or extraphysical consciousness.
10. Oligophrenic extraphysical consciousness.
11. Ill extraphysical consciousness with no bad intention.
12. A group of various extraphysical attackers at the same time (mega-intruders).

Attacks. Among the characteristics of extraphysical attacks upon the projector, the following 10 occur most frequently:

1. **Impulsion.** The ill extraphysical consciousness throws itself onto the projected projector's psychosoma with full force.
2. **Restriction.** The intention of restricting the projected consciousness' extraphysical movements.
3. **Obstacles.** The successive placement of extraphysical obstacles, or dense morphothosenes, in order to block the projected consciousness' translocation. Some examples are the abrupt creation of a closed door or window and walls unexpectedly appearing in front of the projector.
4. **Paraforms.** The disagreeable paraforms or para-appearances of the beings that appear.
5. **Transfiguration.** The transfiguration of the attacker, aiming to provoke fear.
6. *Darts.* Throwing *energetic darts.*
7. **Pursuit.** Open pursuit.
8. **Hunting.** Extraphysical hunting.
9. **Cornering.** Extraphysical cornering.
10. **Pressures.** Extraphysical pressure upon one's consciential microuniverse.

Expressions. Extraphysical attackers generally have a special predilection for directing their typically verbally (humanoid) articulated accusatory expressions, endeavoring to reach the emotional balance of the projected intraphysical consciousness. This is done through the creation of a sadistic, embarrassing, humiliating and nightmarish atmosphere. They thus use all possible negative resources, including the exaltation of actual errors in the projector's conduct of which they are aware.

Causes. Among the causes of extraphysical attacks upon the human consciousness while projected outside the human body, the following 5 can be singled out:

1. **Lack.** Energetic lack due to the parapathology of the psychosoma of the attacker or energivorous extraphysical consciousness.
2. **Parapsychopathology.** Genuine parapsychopathology.
3. **Awakening.** Extraphysical awakening of an ill extraphysical consciousness (second desoma).
4. **Self-motivation.** Simple or mutual emotional self-motivation.
5. **Intrusion.** Evident intentional interconsciential intrusion.

Effects. Among the effects of extraphysical attacks upon the lucid projector, at least the following 12 should be listed:

1. Extraphysical attacks pertaining to or due to tasks of extraphysical deintrusion.
2. Temporary extraphysical influence.
3. Consciential obnubilation.
4. Physical exhaustion.
5. Irresistible sleep.
6. Energetic drainage of the projected projector's consciousness.
7. Energetic duels.
8. Waking discoincidence.
9. Learning of extraphysical self-defense.
10. *Loss of time* and the extraphysical opportunity.
11. Deep worry based on some unfounded fear, even when only during a single hour of isolation or solitude (psychosomatics).
12. Hypomnesia of a specific vital point that is not remembered at the moment in a critical existential situation (mnemosomatics).

Mentalsoma. Simple, negative mental approaches occur while in the ordinary, physical waking state or while in the preparatory stage for lucid projection, in pre-takeoff and during extraphysical awakening of the projected consciousness. This is performed by other consciousnesses, whether in the psychosoma or directly in the mentalsoma.

Psychosoma. Nevertheless, ostensive, direct extraphysical attacks seem to only occur when the intraphysical consciousness is projected in the psychosoma, and not when he/she is projected in an isolated manner only in the mentalsoma in the pure mentalsomatic dimension.

Double. Frequent attacks by extraphysical beings upon intraphysical beings originate firstly in his/her ordinary, physical waking state, later continuing during lucid projection. They are therefore double attacks.

Types. There are two types of extraphysical attacks:

1. **Pathology.** Pathological, per se, generally having a sexual or parasexual origin.
2. **Unconsciousness.** Unconscious or performed by an energivorous or deprived post-desomatic parapsychotic extraphysical consciousness.

Parapolitics. Extraphysical attacks can also be generated due to parapolitical motives or, in other words, when the intraphysical projector's consciousness confronts the negative intentions of the attackers while performing extraphysical fraternal assistance or any other work inside or outside the human body. The assistance thus becomes a natural obstacle to the continuation of the attackers' plan of action, which is like an unconscious invasion into their space of manifestation or their specific holothosenes.

Bibliography: Denning (391, p. 223), Drury (414, p. 58), Dubugras (423, p. 49), Fortune (540, p. 51), King (846, p. 105), Lewis (923, p. 201), Llewellyn (939, p. 21), Monroe (1065, p. 119), Muldoon (1105, p. 292), Sculthorp (1531, p. 49), Vieira (1762, p. 122), Yram (1897, p. 101).

362. SELF-DEFENSE TECHNIQUES OF THE PROJECTOR

Dimensions. The extraphysical dimensions where the intraphysical consciousness projects when temporarily leaving the human body – especially the paratropospheric dimension, which is interpenetrant with the physical world – present legions of mentally or consciential ill extraphysical consciousnesses, extraphysical psychopaths (parapsychopaths), as well as rare projected intraphysical beings which are also ill. The first are commonly known as *intrusive extraphysical consciousnesses* and the second are called *intraphysical intruders.*

Satellites. However, not all of these beings are genuinely a bad lot or intruders with bad intentions. The vast majority are extraphysical somnambulants or unhappy ill beings controlled by post-desomatic parapsychosis, needy extraphysical consciousnesses or, for the most part, unconscious energivorous satellites of intruders and even of extraphysical *blind guides.*

Learning. Without entering into the merits of the characters or nuances of the ill extraphysical personalities, one fact should be considered from a practical point of view: if the projector wishes to develop his/her activities in these extraphysical districts or communities, he/she should inevitably learn to extraphysically coexist with all types of ill extraphysical consciousnesses.

Self-defense. In light of the above, it is necessary for the lucid projector to prepare him/herself with extraphysical resources and self-defense methods which are appropriate and capable of maintaining the consciousness' indispensable balance while projected, as well as in the ordinary, physical waking state.

Mentalsomatics. In the pure mentalsomatic dimension, where consciousnesses manifest directly through the mentalsoma, there are no ill manifestations such as those mentioned above, which occur in the dense intraphysical dimension where consciousnesses manifest through the psychosoma or soma.

Undisguisable. The intraphysical consciousness projected in the extraphysical dimension has to make an effort not to have any type of fear (neophobia, thanatophobia). The psychosoma, or emotional parabody, is visible in the extraphysical or paratropospheric dimension. Likes attract. The psychosoma clearly shows the character, the true intention, the strength or weakness that the consciousness actually feels in relation to other extraphysical beings. Intentions become *exposed,* unhidable, patent, *undisguisable* and inexcusable. Rudimentary interconsciential seductions are impracticable.

Resource. Among the dignified and effective self-defense resources available to the lucid projector, the following 20, listed in alphabetical order, can be singled out:

1. **Assistant.** Utilize the help of the *intraphysical assistant.*

2. **Assistentiology.** Exteriorization of consciential energies with a therapeutic intention (conscientiotherapy).

3. **Base.** Take advantage of the natural isolation of the physical base.

4. **Behavior.** Practicing productive or enriching extraphysical activities.

5. **Contacts.** Extraphysical relationships that are healthy, positive and fearless, without mysticism.

6. **Cord.** Use of the operational energetic resources of the *silver cord.*

7. **Cosmoethics.** Awareness of applied cosmoethics.

8. **Density.** Use the psychosoma's extraphysical density as an extraordinary self-defense resource.

9. **Disappearance.** Instantaneous disappearance provoked by focusing the will upon the inactive human body, which is in the intraphysical base.

10. **Exteriorizations.** Intelligent graduation of the potency of exteriorizable consciential energies.

11. **Helpers.** Productive coexistence with the extraphysical helpers.

12. **Holochakrology.** Self-confidence in the emission of defensive thoughts and energies before, during and after consciential projection.

13. **Interiorizations.** Use of voluntary and involuntary interiorizations.

14. **Paralysis.** Energetic repellence or repulsion like a *paralyzing gas.*

15. **Psychosomatics.** The condition of opacity of the psychosoma.

16. **Self-luminosity.** The self-luminosity of the psychosoma.

17. **Serenity.** Constant serenity, if possible.

18. **Telepathy.** Transmental dialogue or extraphysical telepathy.

19. **Thosenology.** Constant beneficial self-thosenes.

20. **Volitation.** Lucid volitation.

Defenses. Within holosomatics, there are two categories of defense available to consciousnesses:

1. **Holochakral.** The holochakra, through the consciential energies, serves to defend the consciousness against other beings, intraphysical consciousnesses and extraphysical consciousnesses or, in other words: against interconsciential intrusions, fascinations, subjugations and possessions.

2. **Mentalsoma.** The mentalsoma, through an expansion of lucidity or consciential hyperacuity, serves to defend the consciousness against itself or, in other words: against self-intrusions, self-fascinations, monoideisms and fixed ideas (rigidity or caustic stubbornness) within its own consciential microuniverse. It is a question of consciential self-concentration.

Warning. When projected in the extraphysical dimension, the intraphysical consciousness should not underestimate the potency and capacity of the powerful thosenes stemming from the decided will of yourself and others. Therefore, all anti-fraternal or anticosmoethical thoughts need to be definitively and absolutely removed. There is no wiser alternative regarding personal evolution.

Intentionality. The high-quality cosmoethical, positive or healthy intentionality of one's will to succeed is always irreplaceable in the extraphysical cogitations and thosenizations of any consciousness.

Certainty. It becomes vitally necessary to maintain absolute certainty regarding the character of those consciousnesses with which we are obliged to energetically confront or wage a war of wills. They may be extraphysical consciousnesses that have already passed through the transition of final projection (desoma) and *can no longer die,* physically speaking. They may also be intraphysical consciousnesses, still ill or with anticosmoethical intentions but susceptible to undergoing desoma or *losing* the human body in a fatal extraphysical trauma.

Assassinations. There are intraphysical consciousnesses (*intra*physical mega-intruders) that are temporarily projected with lucidity and operating in the (paratropospheric) extraphysical dimension which assassinate (or *para-assassinate*) other *sleeping* intraphysical consciousnesses in the intraphysical dimension. They even impede the interference of (healthy) helpers and (ill) extraphysical intruders. The disturbing emotions and interrelationships between intraphysical consciousnesses predispose these insane actions of *intra*physical mega-intruders.

Burdens. The final consequences of the mental burdens of a consciousness are still very obscure to us, intraphysical lucid consciential projectors.

Self-thosenes. The self-thosenes of the human consciousness are sometimes disconcerting and profoundly surprising.

Actions. On the other hand, it is positive for an intraphysical projector to work together with the helpers in desomatic processes which are just and in line with the natural time spans of egokarmic laws. Another action (negative in this case) is for the consciential projector to assume an unbalanced righteousness, or to serve as an instrument of the intruders and contribute to an unjust, extemporaneous or *inappropriately timed* demise of an intraphysical companion, being one which is not in accordance with the natural time spans of egokarmic laws.

Avoidances. Generally, when in the extraphysical dimension, the consciousness that cooperates and assists as a deintruder should never respond to an extraphysical attack with another attack of equal intention, quality and nature, thereby lowering itself to the anticosmoethical and infracosmic moral level of the ill para-attacker.

Clarification task. Assistential thoughts, methods and strategies always have to be more *human*, fraternal, consoling and clarifying (the clarification task) in order for them to be fruitful and not leave any undesirable and disturbing residues.

Approach. The following is a basic rule in physical-extraphysical interconsciential assistance: the intraphysical consciousness projected with lucidity should relate to those consciousnesses in need of his/her extraphysical assistential tasks as though he/she were a parent, sibling, social worker, physician, nurse, professor, colleague or peer. The aim of this is to deepen the *rapport* and empathically and effectively help the extraphysical patients and common intruders.

Ideal. This will always be the ideal extraphysical attitude or approach for achieving effective results in the development of the lucid intraphysical consciential projector, independent of any personal cultural background or mystical resource.

Mysticisms. Mysticism, in these cases, *if not in all cases,* is an entirely anachronistic and infantile attitude. This is because it is not based on the rationality, maturity and universalistic cosmoethical discernment of those who have a panoramic vision of multidimensional realities.

Para-instinctive. With regard to consciential self-defense techniques, it is clarifying to note the ego's *para-instinctive* resources, or those processes in which the consciousness – paradoxically, through an apparent animalistic regression – subsequently shields itself against an extraphysical attack or a negative charge of consciential energies. The following are 3 categories:

1. **Intraphysicology.** Intraphysical, in the ordinary, physical waking state.

2. **Projectiology.** Extraphysical, in the projected consciential state (intraphysical or extraphysical consciousness).

3. **Intermission.** Extraphysical, in the *desomant* state, per se.

Stratagems. In these self-defensive resources, the consciousness almost always unconsciously resorts, in the beginning, to stratagems or talents which have already been used in prior phases of its evolutionary journey in the self-defensive condition of animals considered to be inferior. The following are 4 of these stratagems:

1. **Aura.** The exacerbation of the personal aura, which becomes ostensive, impressive, insinuant, up to the consciousness' maximum auric irradiation. The effects of this process are shock, surprise and intimidation, which affect the consciousness of the attacker or attackers.

Peacock. This auric resource, which is clearly reminiscent of the reaction of the peacock *(Pavo cristatu Linneus)* and other animals, can and should be used intentionally, even in the ordinary, physical waking state. In certain cases, however, this stratagem can be so effective that it hampers the development of the intraphysical consciousness' assistential service in his/her deintrusive condition as energetic bait for ill extraphysicals. This is because it can *scare the captive (the netted consciousness)* that flees with terror far from the psychosphere of the assister – the *consciential bait*.

2. **Vibrational.** The installation of a maximal vibrational state, intentionally promoted by the impulsion of the consciousness' will. The effects of this process are those of energetic repellants, which are unquestionably felt by the attacker or attackers.

Electric eel. There are many types of energetic repellants. It is worth highlighting the electric shock like the discharges of the electric eel *(Electrophorus electricus),* which has a paralyzing effect similar to other known fish. In certain cases, it impels the attacking extraphysical consciousness to abruptly let go of the *red-hot psychosoma* of the attacked consciousness (victim). It is ejected a certain distance away and can even be overtaken by a restful sleep or a deep torpor for awhile. In certain extraphysical circumstances, this self-defensive process acts surprisingly quickly and is highly efficient in its objectives.

3. **Self-transfiguration.** The attacked consciousness' deliberate self-transfiguration of its own psychosoma, thereby installing the condition of extraphysical mimicry. The effects of this process are asymmetrical camouflage or throwing others off the trail, in certain delicate or highly critical extraphysical situations.

Chameleon. Extraphysical mimicry occurs in the same way as with subhuman animals that are able to change color, such as the chameleon and certain fish and insects.

4. Coupling. The intentional triggering of a profound and intense auric coupling of the attacked consciousness with the attacking extraphysical consciousness or consciousnesses. The effects of this process are to calm or even paralyze the intruder or intruders that *run out of steam,* give up their anticosmoethical intentions (at least temporarily), or leave the scene as soon as possible.

Spider. Defensive auric couplings are reminiscent of the spider's techniques of using the threads of its web to entangle and envelop its incautious prey. Strictly speaking, this process, instead of being a pure self-defense against an open attack, is an opposite strategy – *self-defense through counterattack* – which is of a different positive and well-intentioned nature. The attacking-attacked-consciousness often feels extremely uncomfortable under the unexpected condition of semi-submission to the incompatible consciential energies that are characteristic, different or pertain to the self-defending-counter-attacking-consciousness. If it actually does submit, there can be a sympathetic assimilation of the parapathological disturbances of the attacking-attacked-consciousness by the self-defending-counter-attacking-consciousness.

Energies. It can be seen that the fundamental mechanism of all these processes is an energetic one or, in other words, they are developed through the lucid mobilization of the consciential energies of the awakened ego, who is aware of his/her potentialities and inner resources stemming from the workings of his/her ironclad will.

Bibliography: Fortune (540, p. 155), Hope (756, p. 50), Mickaharic (1044, p. 20), Northage (1135, p. 63), Targ (1651, p. 236), Vieira (1762, p. 182), Yram (1897, p. 96).

---

363. EXTRAPHYSICAL INTRUDERS

Definition. Intruder (or *obsessor*; Latin: *obsessore,* intruder, pursuer, persecutor): the consciousness that exercises a direct or indirect negative action upon another – whether by disturbing, provoking, pursuing and malevolently influencing – through waves of thosenes (emotions, ideas and consciential energies).

Synonymy: alien spirit; *anhangá;* astral parasite; couplings with ill extraphysical consciousnesses; *diakki;* entropic spirit; extraphysical ambusher; extraphysical antigodfather; extraphysical maniac; fascinator; foreign spirit; *gaki;* ill astral being; ill deceased being; ill extraphysical consciousness; incubus; infernal spirit; intrusive spirit; *kiumba;* malevolent spirit; nefarious spirit (New Testament); obsessing; obsessive; obstructer to consciential projection; outsider spirit; parapsychic influencer; pathogenic spirit; peripheral spirit; possessive entity; possessor agent; possessor; post-desomatic parapsychotic; *preta;* spiritual antiguru; subjugator; succubus; tempter; *theta* agent; unevolved extraphysical or projected intraphysical entity; unhappy ghost.

Warning. What follows below should only be read by those who consider themselves to have sufficient psychological balance to understand and calmly reflect upon the more painful and unfortunate subjects regarding the physical-extraphysical populations of this planet without negative emotional involvement. If the reader is afraid of the unknown in terms of the extraphysical dimensions, or nurtures an apprehension of extraphysical consciousnesses, he/she should not read this chapter. There are other milder chapters before and after this one.

Characteristics. The following are 13 general characteristics of the intrusive consciousness:

1. **Ignorance.** Ignorance regarding interconsciential relationships.

2. **Incomprehension.** Incomprehension of its own evolutionary situation.

3. **Contradiction.** Contradictoriness regarding itself and the realities of the cosmos.

4. **Paradoxes.** Experiencing the despair of paradoxical emotions directly through the psychosoma.

5. **Awareness.** Awareness of being anticosmoethical, or knavish.

6. **Affinity.** Possession or lack of a personal connection with the victim of its intrusions.

7. **Realization.** Desire to continue an impracticable activity in the intraphysical dimension, forcing the victim to accept it.

8. **Addiction.** Eagerness to share human emotions or the still animalized emotions of the victim, misleading him/her toward some addiction (drugs), bad habit or mega-weak-trait.

9. **Confusion.** Taking satisfaction in lewd or pathological rudimentary pranks which are characteristic of consciential immaturity, delighting in causing confusion or mega-entropies, usually together with other like-minded extraphysical consciousnesses.

10. *Satellites.* Using semiconscious recent extraphysical arrivals to the extraphysical dimension and even intraphysical beings who are predisposed to its influence as aides – which may be conscious, unconscious, satellites and blind useful-innocents – when they are blocked from acting directly.

11. **Inductions.** Physically and mentally damaging the victim through hate, capable of arriving at the point of inducing the individual to practice the worst diatribes, even including suicide.

12. **Lacks.** Attempting, through egoistical love, to bring the victim back to the extraphysical dimension in order to satisfy its own energetic lacks. It is good to remember that *longing* is the hungering for the specific consciential energies of a loved one by the longing individual.

13. **Pseudo-help.** Endeavor to aid its victim in an apparent and dissimulated manner through antagonistic emotions.

Intrusion. In order to precisely characterize the intruder, it becomes indispensable to define interconsciential intrusion: a mental, or parapsychic, attitude, monothosene, fixed idea or monoideism that pathologically dominates the consciousness' microuniverse on a continuous basis.

Self-intrusion. As a general rule, all intrusion has its beginnings in a self-intrusion.

Adults. Adults are customarily more predisposed to interconsciential intrusion than children. This is a paradox corroborated by the facts.

Ambassador. The worst type of pathological interdimensional personality is the intrusion victim-intruder-intraphysical consciousness. He/she is actually the classic ambassador of the paratropospheric conglomerates of ill extraphysical consciousnesses. Consciential entropy increases around him/her and the internal tension of his/her karmic group or group holothosene intensifies.

Problematic. The intruder that is most problematic and difficult to deal with, contact and speak with is the one that is lucid, intelligent and discrete. It evades healthy extraphysical consciousnesses and does not let itself be seen or *paraperceived* by sensitives in crucial circumstances and moments of parapsychic probing, during deintrusive animic-parapsychic trances or group conscientiotherapy sessions.

Leadership. The veteran intruder generally plays the role of the intellectual author of meticulously planned mega-intrusion, with the intraphysical consciousness-extraphysical consciousness binomial. It lets the *small fish* (satellites of intruders) be caught in the net of deintrusion, but discretely distancing itself, with refined class, from the battlefield of intrusion, carefully conserving its status as a *big fish* (intruder-leader, often for one or more centuries).

Types. There are various types of interconsciential intrusion from the perspective of the extraphysical intruder's attack. The following are 17 examples:

1. **Mutuality.** Mutual, reciprocal or bi-directional intrusion.
2. **Intraconscientiality.** Self-intrusion.
3. **Simplicity.** Simple or naïve intrusion.
4. **Extensibility.** Mini-intrusion regarding the effects or consequences in time and space.
5. **Complexity.** Complex intrusion or one involving the combined actions of multiple intruders.
6. **Group.** Triangular intrusion.
7. **Direction.** Direct intrusion.
8. **Ricochet.** Indirect intrusion or one performed through a ricochet system.
9. **Intraphysical consciousness.** Self-intrusion by the intraphysical consciousness.

10. **Extraphysical consciousness.** Self-intrusion by the extraphysical consciousness.

11. **Intraphysicology.** Intrusion exclusively between intraphysical consciousnesses.

12. **Extraphysicology.** Intrusion exclusively between extraphysical consciousnesses.

13. **Multidimensionality.** Intrusion between an intraphysical consciousness and one or more extraphysical consciousnesses.

14. **Nightmare.** Intrusion based on nightmares.

15. **Hypnosis.** Intrusion with hypnotic bases.

16. **Physiology.** Intrusion with physiological or organic bases (somatics).

17. **Groupkarmality.** Group intrusion (groupkarmic stigma).

Invasion. All types of intrusion of one consciousness upon the intimacy of the microuniverse of another consciousness – even when consented to, but unaware of the extent or depth of the process – tends, in theory, to be *harmful to the consciousness which is being invaded*. It does not matter what the parapsychic condition is or if the interconsciential phenomenon in question is, for example, any of the following 7:

1. **Possession.** Interconsciential possession in its various degrees.

2. **Hetero-hypnosis.** Hetero-hypnosis (ideally used as a last resort).

3. **Impressionability.** Impressionability originating outside the consciential microuniverse.

4. **Ectoplasmy.** Unconscious ectoplasmy (physical effects).

5. **Psychophony.** Psychophony which is more unconscious and involving.

6. **Psychography.** Psychography which is more unconscious and impressive.

7. **Parateleportation.** Unconscious human parateleportation.

Self-awareness. These facts reaffirm the irrefutable importance and superiority of the condition of interdimensional self-awareness over ordinary, mere human awareness, and the insufficiency of living an intraphysical life which, although lucid, is only conventional, ordinary and fearful of consciential alienations.

Homo. The self-aware intraphysical intruder is the prototypical *Homo hostilis,* the creator of the figure of the enemy or the social being that he/she tries – and is sometimes successful – to appear as to his/her adversary, or to the potential victim who comes to suffer intrusion. However, when *Homo hostilis* comes across a positive or cosmoethical being, *Homo amicus,* intrusion is not installed as there is no atmosphere or predisposition for it.

Paranoia. Intrusion is always a system of *paranoia à deux,* a symbiosis of adversaries. Popular psychology summarizes this fact with the saying: "It takes two to tango."

Consensus. War, carnage, extermination and genocide constitute collective intrusion (gang raids, lynchings, armed conflicts) taken to their zenith, through the frequently dissimulated leadership of *Homo hostilis,* the *warlord,* which installs *consensual paranoia* through some type of *abdominal brainwashing.* In this case, it is the masses once again leveling individuals according to the lowest possible common denominator.

Objectives. Among ill extraphysicals, the chronic extraphysical intrusive personalities should be singled out for special study. Intruders act upon the inferior ideas and emotions of adults and children, even using intraphysical subhuman animals in their efforts. However, they do not aim – as a considerable number of studious persons think – toward a mere temporary or permanent possession of the person, but also the circumstances and objectives of the community and its existential conditions.

Charisma. Consciential energies and an impactful physical presence can fool imprudent intraphysical consciousnesses. It is sufficient to observe that leader-intruders or mega-intruders are generally highly charismatic personalities. Adolph Hitler is an example from the twentieth century.

Types. There are interconsciential intruders which specialize in all interests, appetites, passions, situations and instances of the individual's life, as can be seen in the following 6 aspects:

1. **Locations.** There are permanent intruders of certain locations, such as: the headquarters of organizations dedicated to gambling; drug trafficking (mafiocracy); tanneries or slaughterhouses; battlefields; armament factories (bellicosity); cigarette, pipe and cigar factories, and tobacco shops (tobaccoism).

2. **Functions.** There are intruders related to certain public functions that act upon individuals only while they are performing that action, such as: the corrupt administrator.

3. **Ideas.** Other intruders, which are related to specific ideas, act upon beings who, for example, nurture: the idea of assaulting someone; the promotion of mafia-related acts within mafiocracies of all types and psychopathies.

4. **Punctual.** There are intruders associated with a certain time of day, such as: vampires or energivorous extraphysical consciousnesses that act during the night when intraphysical beings are nonlucidly or semilucidly projected during natural sleep. "At night, all cats are gray."

5. **Special.** There are intruders that endeavor to influence special events, such as: during certain carnivalesque commemorations, in *Oktoberfests* or in promiscuous sexual group encounters, orgies and *mixers*.

6. **Technicians.** Some intruders act alone and others work in connected, cohesive groups. There are those that act only upon intraphysical beings or only upon extraphysical beings.

Carelessness. Regarding mini-intrusions, any carelessness on the part of the intraphysical being can be problematic. There are many cases of exclusive interconsciential intrusion masquerading as nervous breakdowns.

Domestic. Among the everyday extraphysical influences upon developed sensitives and projectors, indirect techniques should be singled out, such as those operating through relatives and close relationships. They can even occur in the home, beginning with actions that are apparently more innocuous, as well as more trivial domestic accidents. The following are 3 examples:

1. **Cold.** The maid who leaves the window (or a vent) ajar, covered by the curtains, causing the individual to catch a cold from the cool night air.

2. **Air-conditioner.** Someone who replaced the air-conditioner cover incorrectly so that it falls on the unwary victim.

3. **Cleaning.** Excessive cleaning of a section of the floor, which predisposes a fall. *Even detergent dirties.*

Commentaries. One serious problem in relation to these domestic accidents is that individuals generally think that all physical disturbances are triggered only by the negligence or carelessness of the accident victims. These persons do not like interconsciential energies or intrusions to be mentioned. They immediately label the accident victim as monoideistic in terms of multidimensionality or some persecutional syndrome.

Discretion. The best approach to these facts is for the intraphysical consciousness to see, research and be discreet in personal commentaries in order not to be misinterpreted.

Residues. Incidentally, the rupture of the silver cord (desoma) does not only occur close to the human body, or inside the individual extraphysical sphere of energy. Desoma, or the rupture of the silver cord, while the consciousness is close to the human body, allows him/her to leave *less* vital energetic *residues* in the cadaver. This does not occur if the silver cord ruptures while the ill projected consciousness – suffering from intrusion for a long time – is far from the human body. Many cases of extraphysical vampirization are committed in this second condition, often being provoked by intruders interested in the increased energetic residues that will be left in the cadaver by the final retraction of the silver cord.

Conflicts. The factors that generate interconsciential intrusion due to conflictual relations or conflicts with other consciousnesses can be listed in 6 variables, in order of decreasing incidence:

1. **Emotionalisms.** Various types of emotionalism involving reminiscing about other personalities.

2. **Grief.** Grief, susceptibilities or repressed resentfulness *(envy)*.

3. **Sexosomatics.** Negative sexual contacts, whether physical or extraphysical.

4. **Belligerence.** Thoughts of aversion or outright belligerence regarding another.

5. **Evocations.** Conscious or unconscious evocations of extraphysical or even intraphysical consciousnesses.

6. **Preconceptions.** The morbid cultivation of self-guilt, fixed ideas or repressive conditions because of preconceptions, fanaticisms and erroneous psychological conditioning.

Dependents. *Not all ill extraphysicals are intruders and not all extraphysical intruders are perverse.* If, in human existence, we live with individuals who are mentally deficient, are technically considered to be uneducable and live entirely dependent lives, we obviously must also encounter extraphysical consciousnesses which are, in all aspects, dependent in the extraphysical dimensions.

Oligophrenics. Extraphysical oligophrenics should not be confused with extraphysical intruders or subhuman consciential principles. These exceptional individuals – whether extraphysical mentally retarded beings, imbeciles or idiots, ill consciousnesses or parapsychopaths – need understanding and assistance. They have deficiencies in their mental development because they disrupted their consciential mechanisms and have still not been able to readjust them in order to reason correctly.

Psychosomatics. Para-oligophrenias, or extraphysical mental retardations, especially alter the psychosoma, despite the fact that the generating cause is in the mentalsoma. An unconscious extraphysical persecutor can itself be a victim of one or more conscious persecutors.

Impracticalities. Although the extraphysical oligophrenic can unconsciously operate as an occasional intruder, which is sometimes induced by conscious intruders, it is generally inoffensive due to the following 6 mentalsomatic intraconsciential deficiencies:

1. **Telepathy.** It is not able to perform extraphysical telepathy.
2. **Self-concentration.** It is incapable of maintaining its thoughts on a single subject due to its attention dispersal or short attention span.
3. **Self-dislocation.** It is not able, on its own, to go from one extraphysical environment to another environment of a different frequency, density or nature.
4. **Self-volitation.** It is not able to volitate on its own.
5. **Self-lucidity.** It does not have the acuity necessary for voluntarily and consciously penetrating the psychosphere of the projected intraphysical consciousness in a deeper manner.
6. **Telethosenity.** It does not have sufficient mental syntony and resources to respond to the conscious or unconscious evocations of intraphysical beings.

Hypotheses. Oligophrenia is a complex reality that gives rise to many questions and work hypotheses, such as the following 3, listed here in order to be the subject of future investigation:

1. **Self-thosenity.** Do all oligophrenics have a negative psychosphere (individual extraphysical atmosphere) or are there oligophrenics with a positive personal atmosphere?
2. **Oblationality.** Does the extent of the conditions of renunciation (oblationality) and extraphysical tasks of solidarity and abnegation surpass our normal human capacity for comprehension?
3. **Megafraternity.** Up to what point would an evolved extraphysical consciousness (evolutiologist, *serenissimus*) be interested in being reborn into an oligophrenic physical body that is insensible and incapable of expressing its consciential magnitude in human life, aiming solely to maintain direct contact with the extraphysical (paratropospheric) dimensions, making one of them into a hub or a central station for its own transcendent activities of megafraternity?

Facts. The author has considered these pertinent hypotheses as fact for decades.

Reactions. It is worth informing the public at large that there are 3 consciential conditions or reactions of the intraphysical consciousness that clearly reveal the characteristic and active influence of extraphysical intruders in most, *but not all,* cases:

1. **Accidents.** A predisposition toward accidents (accident proneness) which is characteristic of certain individuals who seem to always be susceptible or likely to suffer repeated accidents, whether in the home, at work, in the street, on the road or even at the club.
2. **Traumatophilia.** Traumatophilia, or the aggressive person's appetite for commotions and his/her apparently spontaneous pursuit of violent physical conflict.

3. **Raptus.** *Raptus* – whether anxious *raptus*, epileptic *raptus*, confused *raptus*, post-commotional *raptus* or post-traumatic *raptus* – which is a sudden and irresistible impulse that leads the individual to perform sometimes serious acts, such as: uncontrolled flight, attacks of violence, sudden attacks of destruction, explosive panic, suicide, violent attacks of homicidal mania *(amok)*, assassination.

Actions. The actions of intruders are executed by direct and indirect attacks (ricochet) upon other nearby individuals or loved ones, at their parapsychic (Gordian knot, crux, mega-weak-trait), psychological or physical-organic weak point while either in the ordinary, physical waking state or during natural sleep, nonlucid projection or semilucid projection.

Anticosmoethical. Various anticosmoethical resources are employed by intruders, such as the following 4:

1. **Self-transfigurations.** Transfigurations of the psychosoma, when trying to look like a personality that has some moral, affective or intellectual ascendancy which can impress and persuade the inexperienced victim.

2. **Heterosuggestions.** Depressive hypnotic heterosuggestions upon the individual's mentalsomatic and emotional (psychosomatic) critical points, such as that person's unconfessed self-guilt, pathothosenes or innermost secrets.

3. **Sadism.** The creation of maximally exacerbated sadistic atmospheres (holothosenic intrusion) for the occasional or regular victims.

4. **Nightmares.** The detailed elaboration of artificial nightmares through hetero-hypnosis.

Addicted. There is a type of intrusive extraphysical consciousness which does everything it can in order for the intraphysical being – the victim of its intrusion – not to undergo desoma. If this were to occur, the intrusive extraphysical consciousness would lose its main source of exploitation or vampirization of consciential energies, through which it is able to consume, sometimes even *para-instinctively*, the intense human, animal or paratropospheric sensations it longs for in its tormented condition as a *post-desomatic addict* (energivorous extraphysical consciousness). Many of these intrusive extraphysical consciousnesses are the victim's very close former relatives.

Running. It is worth pointing out the frantic *extraphysical running* that intruders use in order to compensate for their volitational difficulties, often occurring in human (paratropospheric, in this case) environments. The projected intraphysical consciousness should always suspect extraphysical consciousnesses that transport themselves by moving the extraphysical legs of their psychosoma (paralegs), as though they were participating in a marathon or making an escape, instead of serenely gliding, moving naturally or even being carried along by an energetic current. This is very different and easily distinguished by the projected projector.

Points. The following are the 3 weak points that the extraphysical intruders most often use in order to act upon intraphysical consciousnesses:

1. **Intentionality.** Firstly, the individual's bad intentions (pathothosene), from a psychological perspective.

2. **Phobia.** Secondly, a type of fear or a phobia that is specific to that intraphysical victim.

3. **Somatics.** Thirdly, the physiological or organic points follow in this order: the intraphysical consciousness' brain (including the cerebellum); soon after, his/her lungs or respiratory system; next, his/her cardiochakra (emotionalism).

Principle. In law, there is a general principle that should be borne in mind when analyzing all types of major intruders, at any time, and in any place or consciential dimension: "No one is strong against everyone." That is why there are cosmoethical evolved extraphysical communities.

Mini-intrusion. The most common extraphysical influence upon intraphysical consciousnesses is the nightmarish mini-intrusion, the nightmare in the ordinary, physical waking state or, in other words, the negative or uncomfortable daydream or *waking dream*. The lucid projector can be more predisposed to this type of extraphysical influence, especially if performing assistential projections.

This generally occurs when the projector is alone in a moment of trivial reflection or introspection, during natural sleep, in the silence of mental solitude, in the darkness of his/her physical base (often not *energetically shielded*).

Xenothosene. Mini-intrusion upon the projector always occurs when – through a lack of mental self-vigilance – the consciousness allows a xenothosene or *mental wedge* to be cunningly *inserted* into his/her mind under the apparently innocent pretext of an idea or emotion which is suggestive, but negative or pathological.

Infiltration. The cunning idea gently infiltrates and nestles itself in the individual's mind and the psychophysical circumstances further exaggerate the figures and darken *(weigh down)* the colors of the scenario with regard to its nature and consequences.

Relief. The more attentive reader has probably already experienced these nocturnal 5-minute mini-intrusions and laughed nervously and felt relieved upon recalling the fact while alone the following morning.

Resources. These everyday occurrences hinder the projective development and should be combated with at least the following 8 inner resources:

1. **Hygiene.** Mental or intraconsciential hygiene (self-discipline).
2. **Self-vigilance.** Disciplined self-vigilance (self-organization).
3. **Reflection.** Profoundly sincere and thoughtful reflection (thosenology).
4. **Helper.** Confidence in the assistance of an extraphysical helper, when known.
5. **Rationality.** Rational analysis of the facts in question (mentalsomatics).
6. **Self-disposition.** Maintenance of a positive and optimistic inner disposition.
7. **Balance.** Maintenance of serene balance in the face of all intraphysical and extraphysical circumstances (level of self-conscientiality).
8. **Confrontation.** Through lucid projection, perform a direct and courageous extraphysical confrontation (personal deintrusion) with the responsible extraphysical promoter – the generator of xenothosenes or *mental wedge installer* – which, *at first sight,* is frequently a *very welcome intruder.*

Intraphysical societies. There are toxic intraphysical societies that are more pathological and less pathological, reflecting their coexisting paratropospheric extraphysical communities. The difference between them evidently depends upon the average individual of the population suffering either a greater or lesser degree of intrusion from ill or energivorous extraphysical consciousnesses.

Maintenance. The intensity of intrusion and the construction of a pathological, intrusive holothosene can be maintained and deepened in an ephemeral parochial-group manner or in a long-lasting broad-collective manner.

Morphothosenes. Energetic-mental domination (holochakra-mentalsoma), stemming from the extraphysical dimension (paratroposphere), is based on the use of morphothosenes, extraphysical substances and transfigurations of the extraphysical consciousness' psychosoma (macrocephalic giants and microcephalic pygmies), projected intraphysical consciousnesses and intraphysical consciousnesses suffering from interdimensional abdominal brainwashing.

Para-equipment. Aside from using consciential energies, technicians in energetic-suggestive domination, in these cases, also utilize emotionalism of the unwary; fallacious logic (sophism); seductive paratechnology, including interdimensional apparatuses (intrusive para-equipment); in addition to the complete range of immaturities, inexperiences, interests and terrestrial human appetites.

Countries. All this shows the importance of the service of extraphysical reurbanization and the advantage of being reborn in New World countries, which are considered to be *adventurous* but have global holothosenes that are young as well as pathological materthosenes that are still very weak.

Imitations. Those who wish to know more on the subject of interconsciential intrusion need only reflect upon the resources that human assailants, traffickers and criminals (mafiocracy, anti-social acts) use to perform their infelicitous and illicit activities. This is because everything they do against active human laws (sociopathy) are reflexive, simple and parody-like imitations of the consciential plots of extraphysical and intraphysical intruders in general, or of depraved, obscene and anticosmoethical beings.

Gang raids. That is why they act alone or in groups (gang raids, lynchings), disguised or in the dark, using all possible circumstantial advantages or those that they chance upon.

Pseudodead. It should be stressed again: at this evolutionary stage on the earth, it is not the extraphysical beings that imitate intraphysical beings, but the other way around. The *pseudodead* continue to lead the *pseudoliving*.

Holothosene. It is well known that volitation stems from the will of the consciousness that is volitating, but it is also influenced by the atmosphere of thoughts or the group holothosene of the consciousnesses based in each extraphysical environment or community.

Volitation. One specific resource of the activities of extraphysical intruders is precisely to make (often in conjunction) extraphysical consciousnesses or projected intraphysical consciousnesses – which are volitating, sometimes fleeing, trying to become free from pursuers – *fall* or return defenseless to their realm, like a bird that has been hit in mid-flight by the bullets of their negative thosenes (pathothosenes).

Principles. The following are 2 more valuable principles or warning signals regarding human conduct while performing intraphysical and extraphysical assistance related to interconsciential intrusion:

1. **Irritation.** The most common initial inner emotional characteristic of the individual's mood related to extraphysical influences upon one's intraphysical consciousness is a blind, gratuitous and silent irritation with no real cause or plausible reason. It is alien to the individual's temperament and his/her good intentions. It also sometimes manifests against everything and everyone with the appearance of certain irrational, eccentric or absurd opinions and convictions, even tending toward antisocial behavior. The individual should therefore constantly be on guard against any irritation or atypical bad mood of any kind which arises in one's inner world when engaged in any task that may constitute or result in an interconsciential deintrusive or assistential task.

2. **Foreboding.** Likewise, take precautions when there is a clear sensation of foreboding which is negative, uncomfortable and involving, before a speaker begins to talk with you on some subject which quickly turns out to be trivial or unimportant.

Videotapes. It is recommended that the interested intraphysical consciousness – who is closer to the person suffering from unconscious human intrusion or mini-intrusion, or that person who does not recognize his/her own condition of occasional intrusion – record on videotape (camcorder) various moments and environments, including natural non-intrusive conditions and intrusive manifestations of the intrusion victim. This is suggested so that the filmed individual can later establish a comparison between his/her healthy state and the condition when suffering from intrusion or undergoing a crisis while under the influence of a disturbed extraphysical consciousness. This therapeutic measure is ideal for making someone aware of all types of personal occasional unconscious mini-intrusions.

Therapies. As a general rule, any person who begins to question his/her personal mental health, or fears losing it, should seek professional help. This aid should not be limited only to psychiatrists, psychologists or therapists, but should also, depending upon the case, include conscientiotherapists dedicated to the treatment of patients clearly suffering from intrusion. It is not intelligent to undervalue or reject atypical, albeit cosmoethical, therapies in this era of inveterate consumerism, wild sexuality and the excessive permissiveness of our intraphysical society, which is still pathological and altogether dominated by capitalism and, in part, by medical imperialism.

Addicts. The modern image which is closest to – while still being a parody of – the shadowy atmosphere of intrusiveness and its intrusive climate, is the so-called *sadism session* sometimes promoted by death squads, addicts, and assailants of houses and parties, in the twentieth century.

Bibliography: ADGMT (03, p. 218), Bayless (98, p. 152), Blavatsky (153, p. 497), Boswell (174, p. 132), Cavendish (266, p. 200), Crookall (323, p. 17), Day (376, p. 92), Depascale (392, p. 96), Fodor (528, p. 265), Franco (547, p. 28), Freixedo (554, p. 68), Gomes (612, p. 136), Heindel (705, p. 117), Lewis (923, p. 201), Martin (1003, p. 95), Martins (1006, p. 161), Meek (1030, p. 71), Mickaharic (1044, p. 26), Miranda (1048, p. 105), Morel (1086, p. 131), Muldoon (1105, p. 294), Müller (1107, p. 203), Paula (1208, p. 130), Pensamento (1224, p. 73), Pettiward (1241, p. 41), Schubert (1521, p. 133), Shepard (1548, p. 655), Spence (1588, p. 299), Swedenborg (1639, p. 136), Tondriau (1690, p. 267), Vieira (1762, p. 60), Walker (1781, p. 103), Wickland (1844, p. 356), Yram (1897, p. 101), Zain (1898, p. 220), Zaniah (1899, p. 333).

364. POSSESSIVE CONSCIENTIAL PROJECTION

Definition. Possessive consciential projection: that projection whereby the projected intraphysical consciousness temporarily possesses an intraphysical person or subhuman intraphysical animal.

Synonymy: intrusive consciential possession; invasive consciential projection; mutual consciential projection; possession-projection; superimposed consciential projection.

Possession. The concept of possession by an extraphysical consciousness currently enjoys wide acceptance among the neospiritualists of Europe, spiritists in general and a large percentage of the Chinese people, in which case it is not considered to be an illness.

Abnormality. It is well known, through comparative psychiatry, that the idea of abnormality varies, according to cultures, times, customs and places. For example: the shaman is considered a genius in Siberia and insane or a psychopath (suffering from hysterical partial dissociation) in Europe; the fakir is considered to be normal and even a saint in India and a psychopath (suffering from catatonic schizophrenia) in England; and so on. Note: reference is not being made here to any tribe studied by anthropology, but countries considered to be part of greatly acclaimed *contemporary civilization*, researched by sociology and political science and even within the current phenomenon of the *acceleration of history*.

Possessor-projector. In possession-projection, the projected projector is temporarily an intraphysical intruder or intraphysical (human) possessor.

Possession-projection. There are cases of projectors in areas of India and in African tribes, witches of primitive human groups which take possession of the physical body of a domestic or wild subhuman animal to act through it in a conscious manner, in order to satisfy similar personal animal passions. This constitutes one of the most primitive forms of exercising animism and parapsychism through possession, as described by anthropologists who research tribes, sects and rites.

Tiger-men. From these possessive projections arise the facts attributed to so-called *tiger-men* or, in other words, tigers humanized through incorporation or animic-parapsychic semi-incorporation. This is a blatant confirmation of the parapsychism of subhuman animals.

Animals. Among the subhuman animals used by primitive intruder-projectors, the following should be listed: wild animals, such as tigers, wolves, jackals, foxes, deer; and pets, such as cats and dogs.

Aims. Among the causes or aims of possession-projections we should highlight the satisfaction of the intraphysical consciousness' animal passions, the search for information and the tracing of missing persons. These actions are undertaken in order to maintain the personal prestige of the possessor-projector in the eyes of primitive tribes, or ignorant clans, in which the projector acts as a witch, priest or oracle.

Positivity. Besides the above-cited aspects, it is important to point out that generally only negative, pathological or macabre possession is mentioned. However, possession can sometimes be a very positive force. An example of this is the extraphysical benefactor or mentor that communicates fully through the sensitive using psychophony. In that moment, the sensitive's human body is completely possessed, in a positive manner, by an extraphysical consciousness, the human body or soma of which has already decomposed, sometimes decades before.

Mutual. Another positive aspect of the phenomenon is mutual possession, or reciprocal incorporation, which serves as a powerful therapeutic resource. Young married couples frequently want to experience the actual sensations of the other partner or mate. Through mutual possession, or the possession of the other's body, even for brief moments, these couples or the partners of an evolutionary duo can better understand each other, the real individual motivations and sensations between them and, if they so desire, can even achieve mutual orgasm in their temporarily exchanged human bodies.

Types. Two types of interconsciential possession have been universally recognized:

1. **Voluntary.** Voluntary possession is accomplished when the individual allows him/herself to be possessed by an extraphysical consciousness, as with the sensitives of Spiritism, *Umbanda (Candomblé, Catimbó),* Pentecostalists (evangelical sects dedicated to exorcism) and others. They allow the possessor to manifest itself, an action which the extraphysical consciousness is normally unable to perform.

2. **Involuntary.** Involuntary possession occurs when the individual does not freely allow him/herself to be possessed, but is overtaken by an external force that is generally malevolent, ill, pathological or anticosmoethical, sometimes even being destructive.

Incorporation. Effective interconsciential possession is established through the phenomenon of parapsychic incorporation. This can be classified into at least 4 categories, according to the variables that interfere in its development:

1. **Consciousness.** The consciousness that incorporates: an extraphysical being or an intraphysical being.

2. **Intraphysical consciousness.** The consciousness or the lucid or semilucid consciousness (intraphysical consciousness).

3. **Area.** The area of activity: generally encephalic (coronochakra, inspiration), abdominal-encephalic (umbilicochakra, ectoplasmy) and manual-encephalic (palmochakra, psychography).

4. **Healthiness.** The condition of healthiness: natural possession (healthy parapsychic communication) or pathological possession (frank pathological interconsciential intrusion).

Analyses. Further details on possession can be obtained in the analyses of zoanthropy herein; in the physical manifestations of the communicant projector; in lucid projection related to subhuman animals.

Watseka. The best known and most investigated case of possession in all of the metapsychical, parapsychological or parapsychical literature is that of Mary Lurancy Vennum (1864-1949)–Mary Roff (1846-1865), or the case which occurred in Watseka, Illinois, in the United States of America, where many experiences of lucid projection during possessive trances were studied in 1878 (Fodor, 528, p. 404; Gauld, 576, p. 156; Knight, 851, p. 303; Myers, 1114, p. 360; Riland, 1403, p. 336; Smith, 1572, p. 168; Steinour, 1612, p. 240; Stevenson, 1620, p. 493; Wang, 1794, p. 486; Wilson, 1858, p. 57).

Hypothesis. Possession is the best and most rational explanation to substitute the controversial hypothesis of adult consciential relay or adult resoma.

Police. After various fruitless attempts, while lucidly projected, the author was able, with the inestimable aid of a helper, after intense auric coupling, to temporarily (for perhaps about 10 minutes) and extraphysically take possession of an enormous male police dog during the early morning of October 14, 1984 in a police headquarters located in the state of Rio de Janeiro, Brazil.

Running. On this occasion, the author was able to make the dog temporarily stop its nervous barking and its eagerness to leave the inside of the building where it was located. Soon thereafter, he felt, together with the dog, the exotic sensations of the impressive and stimulating uncontrolled running between the fences and walls of the headquarters.

Return. The return to the physical base, to the human body, and lucid physical awakening occurred abruptly, albeit with no physical repercussions.

Name. It was not possible to ascertain the dog's name because it was loose in a large area that was partially covered and there was no direct contact with human beings.

Brain. In this case, there was some type of interconsciential possession. The author maintained a certain level of self-lucidity. This indicates that the dog's physical brain permitted it. Why do other animals not present a greater level of self-lucidity and self-knowledge? Could it be because those consciential principles, just like we human beings, still do not use the entire potential offered by the brain? Does evolution actually signify absolute mastery of the human brain on this planet, which *serenissimi* have achieved for a long time?

Bibliography: Armond (53, p. 87), Crookall (343, p. 96), Currie (354, p. 108), Drury (414, p. 121), Fodor (528, p. 294), Frost (560, p. 192), Gomes (611, p. 127), Monroe (1065, p. 160), Myers (1114, p. 298), Riland (1403, p. 336), Sargant (1508, p. 199), Souza (1585, p. 122), Vieira (1762, p. 125), Wang (1794, p. 482), Warcollier (1796, p. 98).

365. DEINTRUSIVE CONSCIENTIAL PROJECTION

Definition. Deintrusive consciential projection: assistential projection that is specialized in tasks of extraphysical interconsciential deintrusion.

Synonymy: *apometria;* battle of wills; direct deintrusion; dispossession; explicit deintrusion; extraphysical confrontation; extraphysical deintrusion; head-on deintrusion; projective deintrusion.

Reasons. Among the essential principles of the raison d'être of the deintrusive consciential projection, at least the following 5 can be singled out:

1. **Assistentiology.** Just as cure (self-cure and therapies) is the most important field that an individual can dedicate him/herself to in human life, deintrusive lucid projection represents the most relevant multidimensional task outside intraphysicality, namely superior extraphysical assistance.

2. **Conscientiotherapy.** It functions as extraphysical therapy for the projector and close relatives.

3. **Paraprophylaxis.** It promotes the ideal prophylaxis against interconsciential intrusion.

4. **Projectiology.** It arises as an inevitable stage in each person's development of lucid projection.

5. **Conscientiology.** It makes continued critical interconsciential contacts possible.

Effects. The positive effects of deintrusive projections can be classified into physical and extraphysical.

Physical. The following are the 10 most important physical effects of deintrusive projection:

1. Personal improvement of lucid projection.
2. Increase in the capacity for remembering extraphysical events.
3. Intensification of consecutive lucid consciential projections and those in series.
4. Anonymous intangible assistance to others.
5. Relief from the existential atmosphere or the domestic holothosene of the physical base.
6. Dynamization of physical and extraphysical parapsychism.
7. Self-awareness of the projective aura.
8. Discovery of personal parapsychic signals (signage).
9. Reception of notices of consciential projection (practical use of signage).
10. Service performed as self-aware, assistential, interconsciential bait (consciential epicenter).

Extraphysical. The following are the 7 most relevant extraphysical effects of deintrusive projection:

1. Increase in the assistance received by the projector.
2. Amplification of the circle of beneficial intervening extraphysical relations.
3. Amplification of extraphysical self-awareness.
4. Overall improvement in the intraphysical projector's extraphysical performance.
5. Improvement of assisted or guided lucid projections.
6. Installation of the intraphysical consciousness' personal extraphysical clinic.
7. Preparation of the intraphysical consciousness' work in order to be a self-aware *minicog* within an interconsciential assistential *maximechanism* (consciential epicenter, penta practitioner).

Assisted. The following are the 16 most common categories of beings which are assisted through deintrusive projections: victims and persecutors, extraphysical consciousnesses and intraphysical consciousnesses; leader-intruders of *extraphysical* groups and *gang raids;* conscious extraphysical intruder consciousnesses; unconscious extraphysical intruder consciousnesses or *floating cadavers;* extraphysical consciousnesses aware that they are suffering from intrusion; extraphysical consciousnesses unaware that they are suffering from intrusion; extraphysical consciousnesses suffering from self-intrusion; assistant extraphysical consciousnesses or *satellites of intruders;* parapsychopaths in general; *unattenuated* former suicide extraphysical consciousnesses; somnambulant extraphysical consciousnesses which are ignorant of their own extraphysical situation; challenging, persecuting or ridiculing extraphysical consciousnesses; intrusive intraphysical beings; intraphysical beings suffering from intrusion; intraphysical beings suffering from self-intrusion; extraphysical and intraphysical consciousnesses which are useful-innocents, under the control of mega-intruders.

Knowledge. It is extremely important for the self-lucid projector to have an inner knowledge of intrusive manifestations because, upon projectiologically developing, they will perform various vital assistential functions, such as the following 3:

1. **Parapsychism.** Clarifying sensitive in deintrusive projections, or an *extraphysical exorcist* (clarifying projector).
2. **Bait.** Self-lucid extraphysical consciential bait.
3. **Aide.** Lucid aide in extraphysical assistential tasks.

Intraphysical consciousness. Individuals or intraphysical consciousnesses who constantly feel uncomfortable when consciously leaving the human body in the psychosoma (emotional body) are generally involved in a direct extraphysical situation with an imbalanced energivorous extraphysical consciousness which is almost always a recent arrival to the extraphysical dimension. As they do not have any resources for promoting a direct deintrusive projection with the ill extraphysical consciousness, the projectors therefore experience regrettable suffering from coming face to face with the ill intruder. This occurs almost every time the projectors go to sleep or leave the state of coincidence of their vehicles of consciential manifestation.

Recommendation. It is recommended that all abovementioned novice projectors perform assistential deintrusion practices – which aim to reconstitute the field of consciential energies (personal holothosene) through the vibrational state and other bioenergetic practices – thereby aiding the projector's lucid extraphysical departures. In this sense, lucid projection and even psychophony performed in favor of ill extraphysical consciousnesses interact and mutually support each other.

Temporary. Lucid projection clears up all cases of interconsciential intrusion. No one should consider him/herself to be abandoned or miserable as a result of discovering, anatomizing and dissecting his/her own real extraphysical situation. It is always relevant not to lose sight of the fact that, above all, small interconsciential intrusions happen to *all* intraphysical beings. This occurs to the benefit of our fellow beings and in favor of everyone's evolution.

Duration. There are interconsciential intrusions that last 5 minutes, 5 hours, 5 days, 5 months, 5 years, and so on. In these cases, there are always beneficent extraphysical consciousnesses aiding, inspiring and transmitting energies to the consciousness suffering from intrusion, in order to help it to improve its extraphysical performance during lucid departures. These temporary influences cooperate extraordinarily toward the lucid projector's development during departures from the human body.

Evolutiology. At the current critical phase of terrestrial progress, it becomes impracticable for the intraphysical being who seeks to produce some consciential evolutionary benefit not to suffer some repercussion from ephemeral extraphysical influence, from time to time, in favor of the ill ones, in favor of him/herself, and in favor of all with whom he/she coexists.

Summary. In summary, 8 important aspects regarding the services of conscious deintrusion can be listed:

1. **Attitude.** The worst *attitude:* the ostrich approach, or avoiding the subject because of superstition or erroneous conditioning. Fear always represents submission and anticipated defeat to intraphysical and extraphysical interconsciential influences.
2. **Sign.** The main *sign:* exoticism as a foreign element in the deintrusive encounter, the breaking of the pattern of assistential works in group.
3. **Symptom.** The greatest *symptom:* having a *short fuse,* unusual irritation which is different from the habitual behavior of the intraphysical consciousness who is being influenced.
4. **Precaution.** The most important *precaution:* the execution of consecutive deintrusive lucid projections.
5. **Resource.** The most efficient *resource:* the exteriorization of consciential energies in the ordinary, physical waking state, as well as in the extraphysical dimension.

6. **Occurrence.** The most common *occurrence:* sudden interiorization of the lucid projector upon having an impactful vision or after experiencing an unforgettable extraphysical *flash.*

7. **Gratification.** The greatest *gratification:* the projector that gets out intact, compared to the high number of persons who succumb to extraphysical interconsciential influence.

8. **Misfortune.** The greatest *misfortune:* the negative influence on health professionals, such as doctors, psychologists, nurses, paramedics and others.

Development. Lucid projection, besides offering the opportunity to work directly with ill personalities, is the basic effective resource for the *intraphysical consciousness* to live better among the consciential dimensions, sustaining consciential integrity, emotional balance, and the maintenance and development of parapsychic practices.

Intentionality. Head-on, explicit, *paraface-to-paraface,* boundary-free contact with any ill extraphysical consciousnesses, with the intentionality for conciliation and fraternal understanding, dynamizes the intraphysical consciousness' lucid departures, improving his/her projective methods.

Sympathy. Assistance performed in favor of ill persons attracts the sympathy and aid of evolved extraphysical consciousnesses. They directly promote and help the detachment or takeoff of the consciential projector's psychosoma – which transports the consciousness – and the acquisition of extraphysical lucidity when projected from the soma.

Practice. The practice of deintrusion is performed under different names and with specific methods according to the area of human activity, such as the following 5:

1. **Shamanism** *(pajelança):* between the peais and the other members of the tribe.

2. **Cleansing** *(descarrego):* between the practitioners of syncretic religions, such as *Candomblé, Catimbó, Macumba, Quimbanda, Umbanda* or *Xangô.*

3. **Exorcism:** between the priests and followers of Catholicism.

4. **Expulsion** of the *devil:* between the evangelical clergy and pastorate of various religious orders (Bible).

5. **Deobsession:** between the indoctrinators and spiritist mediums, whether fundamentalist (Christians), orthodox *(Kardecists), Roustaingist* (Roustaing) or rationalist (Centro Redentor, Rio de Janeiro, RJ, Brazil).

Evolution. The consciential projector's psychophysical evolution becomes impracticable without the production of continuous deintrusive projection. Even if it is for periods determined by the helpers, it constitutes an indispensable consciential element, notably if the projector wishes to: intensify his/her extraphysical departures with greater frequency; prolong the lucid consciential projections, or improve the quality of the extraphysical consciential perceptions.

Psychosomatics. These imperative measures are due to the fact that the emotional body (psychosoma) acts directly in the paratropospheric, excessively emotional dimension that surrounds the earth's planetary crust. It is a common gathering place where intraphysical and extraphysical consciousnesses debate while immersed in the same atmosphere which is determined by a permanent climate of intense, reciprocal and continued consciential influences.

Group. Ample group deintrusive activities can also occur through the retrocognitive experiences of others. In this case, the projected intraphysical projector operating as a sensitive in the extraphysical dimension, for example, makes him/herself passive (psychosoma) and uses sympathetic assimilation and extraphysical incorporation in order to facilitate the energetic shocks made upon a formerly militant extraphysical consciousness from a rival politico-terrorist group, and even from other extraphysical beings and other different groups, if this is the case. The projector later recalls all the extraphysical experiences.

Gladiator. It is always important to reflect upon the fact that the practice of deintrusive lucid projection is not at all related to the techniques of the gladiator.

Bibliography: Costa (308, p. 4), Fortune (540, p. 155), Martins (1006, p. 161), Muldoon (1105, p. 292), Rosin (1475, p. 140), Swedenborg (1639, p. 52), Vieira (1762, p. 99), Yram (1897, p. 105).

366. DEINTRUSIVE PROJECTION TECHNIQUE

Possibilities. The first steps for deintrusive projection are sometimes made in a typical oneiric or nightmarish climate, because the projected intraphysical consciousness is still not able to maintain the serenity and balance required to preserve the correct recall of the extraphysical events.

Alert. The novice projector should remain alert to all nightmares, attempting to establish their cause and the possibility that they are erroneous interpretations of his/her assistential tasks performed during the consciential projection.

Functions. During the deintrusive projection, the projector simultaneously functions as the director of activities, the clarifying sensitive and the sensitive which is extraphysically receiving illuminating ideas and therapeutic energies from the helpers for the extraphysical consciousnesses which are ill and in lack of fraternal assistance.

Assistance. In summary, the projector acts alone and as directly as possible in the place of an entire team of an ordinary parapsychic deintrusion meeting, making all the elements of dense matter unnecessary. That is why this extraphysical activity is the utmost assistential service that can be executed by an intraphysical being.

Procedures. Deintrusive projection techniques can be classified into extraphysical and physical.

Extraphysical. Among the extraphysical techniques of projective deintrusion, at least the following 15 procedures can be singled out:

1. **Self-confidence.** Absolute self-confidence.
2. **Balance.** Conduct involving neither weakness nor superiority, but balance.
3. **Cooperation.** An attitude involving neither argument nor challenge, but cooperation and team spirit.
4. **Helpers.** Absolute confidence in the visible and/or intangible cooperation of the helpers.
5. **Resource.** To appeal to the helpers when necessary.
6. **Parapsychism.** The use of extraphysical parapsychism when the intraphysical consciousness is projected.
7. **Serenity.** Maintenance of constant serenity.
8. **Exteriorizations.** The use of exteriorizations of consciential energies.
9. **Thosenology.** Only allow yourself to have benevolent and fraternal self-thosenes.
10. **Bait.** Consciously and satisfactorily exercising the role of extraphysical bait (self-lucid consciential epicenter) during the production of consciential projection.
11. **Evocations.** Making intentional evocations when necessary.
12. **Hygiene.** Eliminate all inopportune mental discussions (consciential hygiene).
13. **Extraphysical consciousnesses.** Pay special attention to the *para-eyes* of extraphysical consciousnesses.
14. **Cord.** Remain, whenever possible, inside the extraphysical sphere of energy or in the totipotent perimeter of the silver cord's influence.
15. **Interiorizations.** Use the resource of rapid consecutive interiorizations *(emergency landings)*.

Physical. Among the physical techniques that aid projective deintrusion, at least the following 6 procedures can be singled out:

1. **Parahygiene.** Do not nurture any kind of negative idea (mental hygiene).
2. **Self-thosenity.** Do not allow any type of *psychological openings* or pathothosenes (mental peccadilloes) through which ill extraphysical consciousnesses can act.
3. **Services.** Participate in deintrusive tasks in the ordinary, physical waking state, serving as a clarifying sensitive, a psychophonic sensitive or a projected projector.
4. **Penta.** Maintain a daily time for mental irradiations and exteriorization of consciential energies, together with a helper, as a practitioner of continuous penta sessions.

5. **Prophylaxis.** Always remember that you will temporarily and inevitably coexist with ill extraphysical consciousnesses, beginning some hours prior to consciential projection.

6. **Self-lucidity.** Perform the role of psychophysical, assistential and self-lucid bait while in the ordinary, physical waking state.

Defenses. Assistential extraphysical consciousnesses – helpers – establish an energetic system of prophylactic surveillance in the surrounding energetic dimension. It is similar to an intense force field, a strong cordon of isolation or parasanitary encapsulation, defending the intraphysical beings from consciousnesses which are *restricted to the human brain,* as well as from ill extraphysical consciousnesses and nearby consciousnesses in general.

Shielding. The physical base of the projector who is willing to perform extraphysical deintrusion thereby becomes *energetically shielded,* even when he/she still does not have advanced technical resources for projecting and remembering extraphysical events in full detail.

Holochakrology. The clarifying projector or the one that produces deintrusive projections needs all the attributes of the intraphysical sensitive as well as a high level of emotional control. This is because, despite the expansion of his/her consciential faculties, the projector remains, the entire time, close to the silver cord, which returns him/her to the human body. The closer the projector is to the human body and the greater the emotional pressure, the more difficult it is to maintain distance from the vital link (extraphysical sphere of energy) during the crucial processes of assistential tasks between consciousnesses in the intraphysical and the other dimensions.

Respiration. Novice projectors, as well as psychophonic sensitives in general, should always be predisposed to consciously help – without losing sight of the subject, while in the state of parapsychic passivity – those extraphysical consciousnesses which have passed through somatic deactivation (desoma) with pulmonary disturbances. Some examples are advanced pneumonia, pulmonary tuberculosis or lung cancer due to the direct relationship with natural respiration, being the touchstone for the interface of 2 psychosomas (emotional parabodies), that of the projector and that of the extraphysical consciousness. The cardiochakra and its consciential energies play relevant roles in these processes.

Formula. In order to execute the above-cited works, the following 5-point assistential formula is recommended in order for it to be applied with self-determination:

1. **Positivity.** Think positive, healthy and cosmoethical thoughts, not nurturing any type of negative, pessimistic or sick idea.

2. **Megafraternity.** Feel intense well-wishing for your fellow being, regardless of who it is.

3. **Fearless.** Eliminate all feelings of fear, under any pretext, without exceptions.

4. **Trustfulness.** Consider yourself to be constantly assisted and incredibly strong, being a powerhouse of consciential energies ready to be exteriorized in favor of the common good. It is important, when in the presence of an ill extraphysical consciousness, not to transfer personal fears, anxieties or even prepotency. It is necessary to create a climate of mutual trust.

5. **Self-conscientiality.** Through uninterrupted exercises, maximally intensify your lucidity outside the human body whenever possible upon going to bed every day or every night.

Echelons. It should be borne in mind that the technical services of deintrusiveness – which sometimes have complex, multi-secular group roots – can only be efficaciously and fully executed through consciential energies and effective assistance, by implementing a 4-step *orderly annulment* with the supervision of (intraphysical and) extraphysical helpers:

1. **Third.** Initially, deintrusion of the third echelon of intraphysical and extraphysical intruders (unconscious energivorous extraphysical consciousnesses, the *cannon fodder* of the mega-intruders).

2. **Second.** Soon thereafter, deintrusion of the second echelon of intraphysical and extraphysical intruders (the satellites of interconsciential intruders).

3. **First.** Then, the first echelon of senior intraphysical and extraphysical intruders.

4. **Intraphysical consciousness.** Lastly, the direct renewal of the intraphysical consciousness suffering from intrusion, the main victim, the polarizer and main component in the parapathological group in question.

Signs. The signs of the condition of psychophysical bait, even when it occurs consciously, vary according to the characteristics of the influence of the extraphysical consciousness' psychosphere. For example, if the extraphysical consciousness underwent desoma due to a heart attack and the sensitive intraphysical consciousness is predisposed to cardiac problems, he/she can experience labored breathing, tachycardia, restlessness and anxiety. Auric coupling, in this case, predominates through the cardiochakra. This occurs in the same manner with other disturbances, illnesses or mortal crises.

Extraphysical clinic. Regarding this point, it is important to bear in mind the daily practices of penta and the extraordinary results of the interconsciential assistance performed in the consciential epicenter's extraphysical clinic.

Pain. The sensitive who is an intraphysical-bait extraphysical-consciential epicenter is that individual who literally and directly feels (or suffers) "all the suffering of humanity." For example: when working on a haunted (poltergeist) location with a "skull and crossbones," the author hosted at his side, removed and directed a post-desomatic, parapsychotic extraphysical consciousness with a totally altered or transfigured psychosoma (one of the key components of the disturbances). This transpired from 9:00 AM (the moment of auric coupling) until 6:00 PM, when energy exteriorization was performed at that location which was infested with sick energies (pathological holothosene). During these 9 hours as extraphysical bait – coupled with an ill extraphysical consciousness or a conscious intruder – the author silently felt constant but bearable pain and paralysis of the middle finger of the left hand and the left elbow. All the pain, paralysis and other uncomfortable symptoms disappeared at the precise moment when the vigorous, intraconscientially disturbed extraphysical consciousness was removed.

Consciential epicenter. Among the symptoms and signs which indicate that the intraphysical being, sensitive, projector or consciential epicenter is serving as psychophysical bait in order to attract and retain an ill extraphysical consciousness in his/her proximity or energetic psychosphere (personal holothosene) so as to eventually perform extraphysical deintrusion, the following 13 can be singled out:

1. **Obnubilation.** Light intraconsciential obnubilation or obfuscation.
2. **Oppression.** A sensation of undefined and nonlocalized oppression.
3. **Weight.** A sensation of weight on the thorax (cardiochakra).
4. **Irritability.** Unfounded irritability, which is different from the individual's own temperament.
5. **Exhaustion.** Physical exhaustion without any visible cause.
6. **Indisposition.** Sudden, generalized indisposition with no apparent cause.
7. **Foreboding.** A sensation of imminent misfortune or a *sensation of foreboding*.
8. **Sleepiness.** Irresistible somnolence or sleepiness.
9. **Pessimism.** Ideas of sadness, melancholy, bitterness or pessimism which are foreign to the projector's self-thosenes and *mentalsomatic* or psychosomatic habits, denoting heavy parapsychic interferences.
10. **Presence.** An impression of the close and intangible presence of a stranger.
11. *Showers.* Unaccustomed energetic currents, *energetic showers* or disagreeable vibrations sweeping over the human body from time to time.
12. **Odors.** The perception of nauseating odors without origin.
13. **Discoincidence.** Excessive, disturbing or uncomfortable discoincidence while in the waking state.

Self-diagnosis. The detection or self-diagnosis of the above-cited sensations is the fundamental and irreplaceable measure for developing any assistential undertaking or research which involves other consciousnesses from this and other dimensions. This is the attitude which can establish the theorical bases of self-lucid consciential epicentrism.

Reward. The greatest reward or garland which the animist-sensitive can receive is to serve as bait and as a pivotal component for the helpers to place a group of lucid extraphysical consciousnesses – which are on the threshold of resoma – *interning* around the sensitive for some days. This aims to provide them with direct contact, in the terrestrial or intraphysical troposphere, with the manifestations, problems and difficulties of interdimensional and multidimensional exchange between intraphysical and extraphysical consciousnesses.

Advantages. One of the main immediate advantages of serving as psychophysical bait is the avoidance of mishaps or prevention (paraprophylaxis) of events which are worse than a simple, pathological, interconsciential (but ephemeral) influence. For example: the driver of your car (*chauffeur,* relative or friend) comes to work with you unconsciously controlled by an ill extraphysical consciousness. Your extraphysical helpers extraphysically encapsulate this ill extraphysical consciousness together with you, thereby isolating and calming the driver at the wheel. This avoids a probable accident that could also involve you and other persons.

Unconsciousness. Almost always, the intraphysical sensitives and persons around the pivotal component or consciential epicenter are not able to detect the actual status of the developmental stage of the extraphysical observers in detail, generally occurring with positive or healthy energetic irradiations. More rarely, not even the animist-sensitive becomes aware of the events while they are occurring.

Aura. The greater expansion of the vibrant encephalic aura (nimbus, aureole), its enlarged form and its pulsating or reverberating movements – determined by the impulsion of the will – is a phenomenon that is accessible to any intraphysical consciousness who is more alert to animic-parapsychic problems.

Expansion. This auric expansion acts as a defensive resource, which is deintrusive and mild, in the sense of removing disturbing or intrusive extraphysical consciousnesses which flee as a result of being surprised or terrorized by our presence. This holds true whether we are in the ordinary, physical waking state or projected in paratropospheric environments.

Mentalsomatics. The projector who wishes only to leave the human body in the isolated mentalsoma soon after beginning his/her experimentations and to always reach the spheres of the mentalsomatic dimension, avoiding the emotional interferences of the tropospheric and paratropospheric environments, which are characteristic of the psychosoma, would do well to leave this ambition until such time as he/she is an extraphysical consciousness, during the intermissive period in the extraphysical dimension (the next interval between this and the subsequent human existence). He/she should first take advantage of the assistential opportunities that the current human life and the existential program offer. This is because the intraphysical projector generally only achieves habitual projection in the mentalsoma after fully mastering the common techniques of projection in the psychosoma.

Bibliography: Costa (308, p. 4), Martins (1006, p. 162), Vieira (1762, p. 60).

---

367.   ASSISTENTIAL   CONSCIENTIAL   PROJECTION

Definition. Assistential consciential projection: beneficial service performed by the intraphysical consciousness projected from the human body, generally in the psychosoma, alone or participating in a multidimensional team, within assistentiology, a subdiscipline of conscientiology (see fig. 367, p. 1,148).

Synonymy: anonymous extraphysical service; conscious extraphysical mission; extraphysical clarification task; extraphysical consolation task; projective assistance.

Idleness. There are two categories of consciential idleness:

1. **Human.** *Human* assistential idleness is the worst condition of the intraphysical consciousness. This is because, in line with consciential evolution, each one of us is reborn, above all, in order to lucidly serve other consciousnesses. This is so regardless of our existential program, when there is one. It even reaches the point, in certain more evolved contexts of existential maxiprograms, of *rationally justified cosmoethical self-sacrifice.*

2. **Extraphysical.** Extraphysical idleness is the worst possible projective condition. It is even capable of completely annulling the more aware intraphysical projector's extraphysical life, regardless of his/her existential program, when there is one.

Projectiology. Lucid assistential projection is the only existing resource capable of completely eliminating the projector's extraphysical idleness.

Import-export. Through the exchange of lucid projection, the intraphysical consciousness has the resources of *interdimensional import-export,* wherein he/she can *import* extraphysical energies, therapeutic interconsciential resources and original ideas to the human dimension from the more evolved extraphysical communities; and is able to *export* consciential energies and intraphysical assistential resources to the energivorous, needy or ill extraphysical consciousnesses, notably to the paratropospheric districts.

Reception. Because of the precariousness of the funneling imposed by the intraphysical and extraphysical restriction of human existence (cerebral hemispheres) or resoma, in this reception-donation exchange, the projected intraphysical consciousness invariably receives more than he/she gives.

Assistentiology. At least 6 basic types of extraphysical assistance are executed by the projected intraphysical consciousness:

1. **Intraphysicology.** Assistance provided to intraphysical consciousnesses.
2. **Extraphysicology.** Assistance provided to extraphysical consciousnesses.
3. **Desomatics.** Aid provided for first desoma.
4. **Intermissiology.** Aid provided for second desoma.
5. **Deintrusion.** Deintrusive services.
6. **Rescues.** Rescue tasks provided to abductees or those extraphysical consciousnesses suffering from intrusion.

Voluntary. The *volunteer-assistant-projector* condition can be obtained and developed through at least the following 8 universalistic resources:

1. **Self-discernment.** Sincere compassion, stemming from cosmoethical self-discernment, for group and collective problems in instances of natural cataclysms and accidents, such as earthquakes, seaquakes, tornadoes, volcanic eruptions, cave-ins, contaminations, epidemics, large fires, continental pollution and floods.

2. **Hetero-help.** Desire to help in areas of human conflicts, pathological atmospheres and holothosenes of war (bellicosity).

3. **Orthothosenity.** Healthy, cosmoethically and sincerely felt self-thosenity in favor of needier individuals.

4. **Evocation.** Confident evocation of the helpers, aiming toward the well-being of other consciousnesses.

5. **Self-predisposition.** Continued psychophysiological, parapsychic or holosomatic predisposition to serve extraphysically (helpful projected intraphysical consciousness or parasocial assistant).

6. **Holochakrology.** Cultivation of a personal aptitude for exteriorizing therapeutic consciential energies (assistentiology, conscientiotherapy).

7. **Fearlessness.** Complete and permanent absence of any fear (thanatophobia) or pessimistic or negative idea (intraconsciential depression).

8. **Self-discipline.** Self-discipline regarding the exaltation of the better side of persons, institutions, things and facts.

Law. The following is the first active law in assistential lucid projections: the more assistance the intraphysical consciousness gives others, the more assistance he/she will receive to project with lucidity.

Resources. The following are 9 resources that the projected intraphysical consciousness can count on for executing extraphysical intraconsciential assistance:

1. **Parapenta.** Exteriorization of consciential energies when in the state of discoincidence of the vehicles of manifestation or during *parapenta*.

2. **Groupality.** A sense of groupality in the employment of conscious evocation in favor of others (self-conscientiality).

3. **Psychosomatics.** Self-transfigurations of the psychosoma.

4. **Mimicry.** Experience of the phenomenon of extraphysical mimicry.

5. **Bait.** The applied condition of lucid intraconsciential bait (consciential epicenter).

6. **Cosmoethical.** Cosmoethical counseling or extraphysical confrontation.

7. **Pangraphy.** Parapsychic self-passivity for extraphysical pangraphy.

8. **Couplings.** Competent execution of healthy auric couplings.

9. **Institution.** Exchanges with the assistants of the "Extraphysical Red Cross".

Characteristics. The following are the five essential characteristics of assistance provided to intraphysical and extraphysical consciousnesses which are realized by the projected intraphysical consciousness:

1. **Individualism.** The productive individualism of the projector-assistant, which is not known by third parties due to the animism of lucid projection.

2. **Anonymity.** Complete anonymity due to the imperceptibility of extraphysical events by human beings in general.

3. **Secrecy.** Natural absolute secrecy which is characteristic of extraphysical undertakings in relation to intraphysical beings.

4. **Unawareness.** A definitive unawareness on the part of others – notably our peers and the physical elements of our karmic group – regarding assistential activities.

5. **Gratification.** The lucid consciential projector's singular satisfaction or insuperable gratification.

Case study. No other assistential action of human origin can compare with the fraternal work performed through lucid consciential projection. It is sufficient, for example, to consider the following possibility: a seriously ill individual who is removed from concerns regarding extraphysical realities, being skeptical and unapproachable with simple therapeutic energetic exteriorization, can receive palliative aid, or a factor that triggers self-remission, from the fully lucid projected projector. This can occur without the ill person, his/her relatives, the projector's close friends or any other intraphysical being knowing or even suspecting the assistential facts that are transpiring. For the intraphysical consciousness, this is an extremely individual inner reality that is unknown to everyone except the consciential projector. It is thus more of a *cosmoethical secret* which is shared by the projector, the helpers and the extraphysical evolutionary companions.

Approach. Upon finding yourself projected with lucidity and approaching an extraphysical or even an intraphysical consciousness (projected or in the waking state) – which was naturally sent by a (almost always intangible) helper, or one which demands your direct attention (as an assisted personality) – you should endeavor to establish an interaction (affinity, extraphysical empathy, auric coupling) that dissipates obstacles and eliminates barriers. This is done in order to exteriorize consciential energies, transmit renewing ideas and, lastly, to perform competent extraphysical assistance, if required (together with the helper).

Actions. Through the use of your human consciential energies, under the guidance of the helpers, the projected intraphysical consciousness helps the extraphysical consciousness (which is a recent arrival to the extraphysical dimension) in various intermissive actions that immediately follow the deactivation of its human body, notably the following 6:

1. **Desoma.** The definitive departure from the human body.

2. **Self-awareness.** Achievement of extraphysical self-awareness on the part of the intraphysical consciousness, which returns to the status of an extraphysical consciousness.

3. **Self-orientation.** Orientation of the extraphysical consciousness in time and space: the extraphysical environment in which it finds itself and the period of the extraphysical approach.

4. **Contacts.** Help in direct contact with other extraphysical consciousnesses or, more specifically, extraphysical consciousnesses which have recently arrived due to the consciential shocks of accidents, catastrophes and battlefields.

5. **Introduction.** Introduction to and communication with the extraphysical consciousness' relatives and friends.

6. **Sleep.** Introduction of the extraphysical consciousness to a period of restorative extraphysical sleep.

Ancestrality. According to holokarmology, there is, in the extraphysical dimension, a type of *assistential ancestrality* (a resomatic renewal, or a *professional hereditariness*) which acts upon all intraphysical beings. These are apparently diverse but fundamental aspects of a single phenomenon that supersedes and dominates human activities.

Generations. Past generations endeavor to aid current generations in terms of group works in favor of others, such as the following 4:

1. **Metapsychics.** Former metapsychics help current parapsychologists.
2. **Mesmerism.** Former mesmerists cooperate with contemporary hypnotists.
3. **Navigators.** Ancient seafarers (navigators) sponsor the development of the astronauts.
4. **Political science.** Yesterday's politicians inspire today's politicians.

Directive. The projector who wishes to develop his/her beneficial activities should not lose sight of this basic directive of assistential ancestry. It allows the individual to identify his/her helpers and evolutiologists, according to the assistential tasks he/she is requested to perform. The individual can also deepen his/her *rapport* with assistants and those who are assisted in the extraphysical dimension.

Procedure. In helping an ill extraphysical consciousness, the projected projector first needs to make contact with it. Secondly, the projector needs to remain very calm in order to prevail upon the extraphysical consciousness until the helpers can remove it, transferring it to another extraphysical district which is more appropriate for its consciential condition.

Punctiform. In an attempt to provide relief from, remission or self-cure of the ill consciousness' sufferings, the projector establishes a direct auric coupling with the patient (evolutient) while nearby or distant, and can mentally condition him/herself to penetrate the assisted individual's psychosphere, deep into his/her consciential microuniverse, as a *punctiform consciousness*. Soon afterwards, the projector can penetrate each of the assisted consciousness' chakras, or only the chakra which is most indicated for this therapy, in order to directly transmit positive heterothosenes of health and restoration, flows of therapeutic energy and an extraphysical cleansing of the patient's own sources of energetic distribution.

Measures. These measures, which are evolved, but perfectly executable, depend only upon the performance of the decided will of the projector which has the assistance of the helpers.

Interned. One of the common types of extraphysical assistance performed by the helpers is to aid – even by promoting lucid projection – many intraphysical consciousnesses who are generally overlooked and in unsuspected conditions. They suffer intense mortification, humiliation, degradation or violation of their self-esteem, being involuntarily interned in total restrictive institutions: prisons, concentration camps, refugee areas or hospitals, in order to avoid the extreme despair of suicide or homicide.

Volitation. It is evident that free *assistential volitation* is far more useful and appropriate for the intraphysical consciousness in these maximally restrictive conditions than for the individual in regular life. The author has personally tried to sponsor the departure of the consciousness of certain persons in these circumstances, which is not easy, although always proving a promising challenge.

Preparation. Major, prolonged, impactful, educational, assisted consciential projection can be imperceptibly prepared by the helpers over a 3-day period, for example, in order to preserve the physiology of one's human body. Upon recalling the projective events, the projector can sometimes identify – through his/her acts and the events over the last few days – the preparation which was previously unsuspected and unconsciously performed by the projector him/herself, being *teleguided* by the helpers.

Recall. The veteran projector who is accustomed to assistential projections ends up more frequently recalling various actions in which he/she is exteriorizing consciential energy in favor of different extraphysical consciousnesses in the extraphysical dimension.

Studies. Before beginning to aid others through lucid consciential projection you should have a full command of the vehicles of manifestation of your consciousness and be very aware of all of your physical and extraphysical resources. This confirms the vital importance of knowledge gained from a deep study of projectiology.

Tasks. One of the inescapable ambiguities for the lucid consciential projector is that you, as a human lucid projector, an aide in extraphysical tasks, should not, for example, merely be the lesser of the following 4 conditions:

1. **Office.** Not only the overseer in the air-conditioned office, but also the uniformed manual laborer working for the benefit of others.

2. **Headquarters.** Not only the general protected in the headquarters, but also the private on the front line of general interconsciential deintrusion.

3. **Farm.** Not only the *white collar worker* seated at a desk, but also the tanned field worker *sowing the seeds of good*.

4. **Club.** Not only the *well-dressed* country club manager, but also the athlete in sport attire, sweating in order to maintain his/her assistential health.

Bibliography: Carrington (245, p. 287), Crookall (323, p. 1), Frost (560, p. 112), Greenhouse (636, p. 125), Leadbeater (895, p. 270), Lester (919, p. 67), Norvell (1137, p. 224), Powell (1278, p. 85), Steiger (1601, p. 107), Vieira (1762, p. 75), Wallace (1789, p. 198), Zaniah (1899, p. 60).

368. THE PROJECTOR AND DESOMANTS

Definition. Desomant: the intraphysical consciousness who has reached the final stage of intraphysical life, with a lessened expectation for continued human existence, being over 65 years old, an age which is currently accepted as being the beginning of old age, or between 65 and 84 years of age.

Synonymy: a person between sixty-five and eighty-four years of age; a person beyond eighty-five years of age; candidate for final projection; pre-extraphysical consciousness.

Elderly persons. Just as infancy and adulthood are not illnesses, old age is also, strictly speaking, not an infirmity. However, desoma is more imminent for aged persons, because they are constantly aware that their life expectancy on earth reduces moment by moment, notably in the current intraphysical society, and even more in Western society, where myths and stereotypes only strengthen and value youth, good looks, and physical strength, and where the aging process (gerontology) becomes a condemnation and even a stigma.

Relationships. The veteran lucid projector, who has assisted the biological death of others – acting while projected or on the extraphysical side – should seek a deep empathy in extraphysical relationships with extraphysical consciousnesses that have recently arrived in the extraphysical dimension. In order to establish this rapport, the refined study of desomant consciousnesses is of great importance, as occurs with the extraphysical helpers in relation to resomant extraphysical consciousnesses, or those extraphysical consciousnesses which are about to take on another human body (soma).

Ill consciousnesses. The percentage of desomants among the extraphysical consciousnesses which are recent arrivals to the extraphysical dimension, or the post-desomatic intermission, that the projected lucid projector is requested to aid together with the helpers is much greater than the other categories of extraphysical ill consciousnesses during lucid assistential projections. It should be borne in mind that, according to social gerontology, from one-fourth to one-third of the planetary population will be over sixty years of age in the twenty-first century, it being possible for humans to live up to 14 decades (centenarian) in this intraphysical dimension.

Understanding. The lucid consciential projector's understanding of the influencing characteristics and factors in desomants' intraconsciential life is of great value. It allows the projector to be able to help them efficiently when called upon to do so as an intraphysical consciousness projected in the psychosoma, an activity that will therefore increase the development of his/her lucid projections in general.

Complexity. Through the individual characteristics and factors that typify the desomant, the lucid projector – through the psychological study of existential companions, in the ordinary, physical waking state – can, upon projecting, expect to encounter considerable diversity in the characteristics which comprise the ill consciousnesses that they endeavor to aid. This is because, although there are common basic lines, appearances and para-appearances, self-strong-traits and self-weak-traits, each different personality (each complex case) demands on-the-spot individual analysis in order to achieve greater affinity, *rapport,* empathy, synergism, ease of mental syntony, extraphysical communication, energetic transmission and, finally, effective fraternal help.

Average. Whereas the natural genetic limit for human beings is considered to currently be approximately 14 decades – because no biological reason for impeding human life from lasting up to this age has yet been found – the average advanced age of desomants can be taken to be 7 decades. Intellectual growth can proceed normally even at 90 years of physical age.

Characteristics. Desomants generally present the following 11 basic characteristics:

1. **Hair.** White hair.
2. **Hypomnesia.** Benign loss of short-term memory (hypomnesia), characteristic of senility.
3. **Grandparent.** Being a grandparent, or great grandparent.
4. **Isolation.** A more isolated lifestyle.
5. **Retirement.** Retirement and its consequences.
6. **Security.** Social security (geriatrics, gerontology).
7. **Community.** Participation in retirement communities.
8. **Pensions.** Special funds and pensions.
9. **Will.** A will, which is sometimes signed in advance.
10. **Cremation.** Prearranged funeral plans, in certain cases (burial or cremation, organ donation).
11. **Pastimes.** Calm pastimes, such as checkers, chess or cards in the park, group activities, or stamp collecting.

Personality. The desomant is the most common individual in homes for the aged and geriatric hospitals dedicated to the treatment of the problems associated with aging (gerontology).

Positive. The following are 10 positive (self-strong-traits), healthy or characteristic factors of desomants:

1. **Age.** A biological age which is lower than the chronological age.
2. **Interests.** Development of new interests which overcome the problems of retirement.
3. **Mentalsomatic.** A person who is intellectually productive and remains lucid.
4. **Sociability.** Maintenance of a good number of varied social relationships.
5. **Coexistology.** A constant exchange of their personal life experiences with vital individuals.
6. **Temperament.** A temperament that tolerates ambiguities (the "nice old person" who is everyone's friend), without being cantankerous, cranky or stubborn.
7. **Optimism.** Constant optimism and a certain happy extroversion.
8. **Self-prophylaxis.** Psychological preparation for desoma without taboos.
9. **Immortality.** Respect for the realities pertaining to the perennial nature of the consciousness or personal immortality.
10. **Desomatics.** An understanding of the biological shock of desoma.

Negative. Among the negative (self-weak-traits) or pathological factors of desomants, at least the following 8 stand out:

1. **Wear.** Biological age which is above the chronological age (personal decadence).
2. **Involution.** Accentuated senile involution.
3. **Withdrawal.** Lack of social activities *(withdrawal into the personal mega-ego)*.
4. **Pessimism.** Pessimism, defeatism or a certain stubborn introversion or vitriolic indisposition.
5. **Psychosis.** Senile psychosis (accentuated arteriosclerosis) or Alzheimer's disease.
6. **Thanatophobia.** Thanatophobia or an undisguisable fear of the soma's death.
7. **Materialism.** Frank and sincere materialism in all attitudes.
8. **Unpreparedness.** Accentuated unpreparedness for biological (human body) death.

Classification. It is worth mentioning that an attempt was made some time ago to empirically classify elderly persons – considered from the perspective of biological age – into 6 basic types:

1. **Depressed.** The depressed individual, who sees biological death as an imminent end.
2. **Intolerant.** The moralist, who considers him/herself to be virtuous, being generally irritated, intolerant, a meddler and vitriolic.
3. **Amoralist.** The amoralist, usually considered joyous, funny or senile.
4. **Regressive.** The *regressive* individual, dominated by family and circumstances, who becomes unprotected, hypochondriacal and dependent, constantly begging for affection.
5. **Authoritarian.** The *authoritarian* individual, who is elegant, insinuating, athletic, educated and experienced, and judges him/herself to be irreplaceable in his/her particular autocracy.
6. **Ideal.** The *realized* individual, the ideal type, who is a *nice old person* and a friendly grandparent to everyone.

Homologies. Only the principle of homologies, when applied to the sequential analysis of the ego evolving from the interval between resomas or intermission – passing first through the biological shock of the extraphysical consciousness in resoma and then through the biological shock of the intraphysical consciousness in desoma, to return to a new period of intermission – can clarify the facts of thanatology, desomatics or the specific study of the first, physical, somatic desoma.

Chrysalis. The abovementioned sequence of the ego can be metaphorically or homologically compared to the transformation of a larva into a chrysalis and then a butterfly.

Pregnant woman. The same period is similar to the alterations of the pre-mother, or the candidate to maternity, who develops an affinity with the pre-resomant, becomes pregnant and, soon thereafter, a nursing mother to the newborn, or the newly reborn extraphysical consciousness.

Intraphysical consciousness. The same homology can also be observed in the sequence of the intraphysical consciousness who successively becomes a pre-desomant, then recently-deceased from first desoma, until becoming recently-deceased from second desoma.

Holobiography. After this, the entire sequence starts again within the specific, personal multiexistential cycle in the evolutionary group, thereby forming the holobiography of each one of us.

Changes. It is worth emphasizing that the consciousness' extremely personal characteristic attitudes and habits from its recently ended human life do not change from one moment to another just because it has undergone desoma and recently arrived at the extraphysical dimension or its post-desomatic intermissive period.

Hypotheses. Incidentally, Siamese twins, when able to project, do so in the psychosoma, separately. What is the condition of the psychosoma's para-organs in the projected Siamese twin's areas of common connection? Can we conclude that the mechanism of separation through consciential projection is the same as the connection and projective separation of the fetus-pregnant woman duo? This is one more research hypothesis for future verification. The following are subjects which are of interest here: parapathology of the psychosoma, self-transfigurations of the psychosoma, paragenetics, genetics, as well as many others.

Bibliography: Carrington (245, p. 287), Greenhouse (636, p. 125), Leadbeater (903, p. 15), Norvell (1136, p. 244), Vieira (1763, p. 5), Zaniah (1899, p. 60).

369. PROLONGED CONSCIENTIAL PROJECTION TECHNIQUE

Definition. Prolonged consciential projection: that projection in which the consciousness remains projected from the human body longer than one hour, whether spontaneously or deliberately.

Synonymy: lucid megaprojection; prolonged extraphysical excursion.

Remain. Those who project their own consciousness from the human body with some frequency note clearly that the projected projector's problem is actually not how to return to the physical base, interiorize him/herself and physically awaken, but rather, *how to remain projected* longer, having more and better experiences, obtaining a king-size consciential projection (king-size obe, lucid megaprojection).

Resources. Based on the fact that a lucid projection lasts from a few seconds to several hours, it is helpful to become familiar with the following 9 extraphysical resources that you, as a lucid projector, can use in order to prolong your stay outside the human body:

1. **Serenity.** Maintain serenity in all situations and in the face of any extraphysical event, removing occasional traumas.

2. **Self-awareness.** Increase self-awareness of your extraphysical conditions in that situation, maintaining personal balance in the environment in which you find yourself.

3. **Energies.** Mobilize your consciential energies through the willful, extraphysical installation of the vibrational state; do this when fully projected in order to increase your degree of extraphysical lucidity and consequently prolong the duration of your projection.

4. **Freedom.** Discard all thoughts about the human body, silver cord, physical base and human concerns, progressively feeling yourself to be in the condition of a free consciousness.

5. **Cord.** Respond to any demand or admonitory warning made by the silver cord, without being affected by it, attempting to counteract the cord's vigorous action with your decided will. This can be a fierce battle. If possible, your projected consciousness should endeavor to forget the silver cord by fixing your attention on something in the physical base outside the human body.

6. **Distance.** When an inevitable return to the proximities of the dense body occurs, do not interiorize, but try to go further from the physical base.

7. **Re-takeoff.** Interiorize after a consciential projection if necessary, as a last resort, but try to avoid physical awakening, taking off again.

8. **Catalepsy.** Take advantage of benign catalepsy in order to exteriorize and not awaken in the ordinary, physical waking state. Catalepsy and the duration of the consciential projection interact with each other, given that one condition can provoke the other.

9. **Target.** Keep a positive mental target in mind, ready for any emergency, trying to reach it after your first lucid projection.

Case study. There are cases of prolonged consciential projection that are provoked in the phenomenon of voluntary burial, coma states and certain instances of individuals who sleep longer than normal. These facts prove the classic example of prolonged consciential projection, namely the case of Lazarus, in the New Testament (John 11:44). Somnambulism is sometimes related to prolonged consciential projection.

Temperature. One of the easily verified basic characteristics of prolonged lucid projection is the consciousness almost always finding the human body – upon consciential return and interiorization – to be rigid, dehydrated (joints) and cold throughout, at a temperature lower than the environment of the room where the body remains inactive, as though the room were warmer before, during and after the lucid projection.

Extraphysicology. The parallel world, right next to dense physical life, appears to remain at a temperature of zero degrees Celsius, or frozen, just as in interstellar space.

Dimensions. The prolonged (according to chronological time) consciential projection does not always represent a translocation of the consciousness in an extensive extraphysical trip, from the perspective of physical measurement. The phenomenon of consciential projection above all takes place within the consciential world in different dimensions.

Bibliography: Bayless (98, p. 101), Bozzano (184, p. 127), Denning (391, p. 42), Greene (635, p. 63), Swedenborg (1635, p. 256), Vieira (1762, p. 180).

---

370. EXTRAPHYSICAL   AGENDA

Definition. Extraphysical agenda: a written annotation of a list of priority extraphysical mental targets which the projected projector should endeavor to reach gradually, in a chronological manner, establishing intelligent plans for his/her own development.

Synonymy: extraphysical report; list of mental targets; personal projective archive in one's laptop or notebook computer; projective journal.

Targets. It will always be productive for the projector to keep certain important mental targets in mind for any instance in which he/she finds him/herself projected.

Types. The following are 4 different types of mental targets, without negative consequences, for the novice projector to choose, one at a time, as long as they are forewarned against possible extraphysical traumas:

1. **Ideas.** Suggestions for target-ideas: contemplate your own inactive human body; pass through a large physical structure; carefully examine the silver cord; look at yourself in a large ordinary mirror; change your extraphysical attire through the action of your will; find lost objects or treasures, such as the works of Johann Sebastian Bach (1685-1750) which were not used by his son; consult the Book of Toth, burned in Alexandria, in a retrocognitive manner.

2. **Beings.** Suggestions for target-beings: extraphysically awaken the mate or partner of a sleeping evolutionary duo; meet with an awake relative; meet a friend who is informed of the extraphysical visit; embrace a bedridden acquaintance; evoke a familiar extraphysical benefactor.

3. **Physical.** Suggestions for physical target-places: go to a distant physical base that you like; visit the inside of an active volcano; probe the depths of the ocean; enter a dense jungle; go inside caves; scale the peaks of the Himalayas, the Andes and the Rocky Mountains; stroll through a museum which is closed to the public; attend a parapsychic session; enter a photographic studio during a shoot and attempt to appear on the photos being taken; attend a live television show; extraphysically witness poltergeist activity; consult the Vatican Library in the sections which are still closed to the public; penetrate an Egyptian pyramid; go to the moon, the sun, or the planets of this and other solar systems; look for, locate and visit a UFO.

4. **Extraphysical.** Suggestions for extraphysical target-places: visit an extraphysical telephone exchange for intelligences which speak through audiotapes, televisions, telephones and intercoms; visit an evolved extraphysical community.

Person. The projector can only enhance his/her experiments if he/she obtains a very clear photograph of the target-person, holds it in his/her hand and concentrates deeply upon it in order to imprint the image into his/her mind moments before predisposing him/herself to lucid projection.

Photo. Using a good photograph of the physical place you wish to reach through lucid projection also greatly helps the lucid projector.

Maximum. The following are 8 expressive mental targets indicated for the advanced projector's experiments:

1. **Resomatics.** Extraphysically attend a phase of the resoma process.
2. **Desomatics.** Extraphysically attend a phase of the desoma process.

3. **Pregnancy.** Perform an *internal* examination of the organic interior of a pregnant woman and fetus.

4. **Electroshock.** Feel an electric shock while outside the human body manifesting through the psychosoma.

5. **Sneeze.** Analyze the possibility of an extraphysical sneeze.

6. **Psychosomatics.** Extraphysically see the psychosoma of a larger subhuman animal while it is in the discoincident state.

7. **Parazoology.** Extraphysically attend the desoma of a larger animal.

8. **Parabotany.** Extraphysically attend the provoked death of a felled tree.

Cities. While projected from the soma, the intraphysical consciousness can psychometrize his/her own presumed past life in historically famous cities, of which only ruins remain. The following 5 serve as examples:

1. **Babylonia,** in the lower valley of the Euphrates, close to Baghdad, Iraq.
2. **Carthage,** close to Tunis, Africa.
3. **Gomorrah,** in the area of the Dead Sea, Palestine.
4. **Thebes,** the villages of Abu Simbel, Karnak and Luxor.
5. **Troy,** close to Hissarlik, Asia Minor.

Bibliography: Vieira (1762, p. 120).

XII – *Interiorization of the Consciousness Stage*

371. RETURN TO THE PHYSICAL BASE

Definition. Return to the physical base: departure of the projected intraphysical consciousness from its current location in the extraphysical dimension to the physical place where its human body rests, almost always occurring in the final period of a lucid consciential projection.

Synonymy: regress to the human body; return to the physical base.

Types. The following are the 8 main forms of return of the projected consciousness to the physical base:

1. **Lucidity.** Lucid return.
2. **Nonlucidity.** Nonlucid return.
3. **Imposition.** Imposed return.
4. **Unforeseeability.** Unforeseen return.
5. **Abruptness.** Abrupt return.
6. **Slowness.** Slow return.
7. **Isolation**. Solitary return of the projected consciousness, the most frequent condition.
8. **Company.** Accompanied return of the projected consciousness, the rarest condition.

Causes. The following, for example, are the 9 main causes for the return of the projected intraphysical consciousness to the physical base:

1. **Holochakrology.** Action of the silver cord.
2. **Self-determination.** The self-determination of the projector's consciousness.
3. **Inspiration.** Extraphysical inspiration.
4. **Hetero-suggestion.** Suggestion of another through transmental dialogue or paratelepathy.
5. **Somatics.** The concentration of the projected consciousness upon the human body (soma) from a distance.
6. **Phobia.** Fear (phobia) of various origins.
7. **Paratrauma.** Extraphysical intraconsciential trauma.
8. **Indetermination.** Cause not determined by the projected consciousness.
9. **Intraphysicology.** Factors that are internal or external to the inactive human body, such as sound, cold or heat.

Effects. The following are examples of 5 of the main immediate effects of the return of the projected intraphysical consciousness to the physical base:

1. **Continuity.** The consciousness continues the consciential projection in the physical base.
2. **Interiorization.** The consciousness interiorizes.
3. **Sleep.** The consciousness enters into a period of natural sleep.
4. **Extraphysicology.** The consciousness goes through a period of extracorporeal sleep.
5. **Oneirism.** The consciousness starts to dream (altered state of consciousness).

Rule. No projected intraphysical consciousness encounters greater or frequent difficulties in returning to the physical base, interiorizing and physically awakening him/herself.

Recall. In some lucid projections, the return to the physical base can greatly influence the recall of the extraphysical experiences soon after physical awakening.

Self-lucidity. The return of the consciousness to the physical base while still in a condition of profound extraphysical self-lucidity generally predisposes good post-projective recall.

Bibliography: Baumann (93, p. 17), Crookall (325, p. 49), Vieira (1762, p. 109).

372. INTERIORIZATION OF THE PROJECTED INTRAPHYSICAL CONSCIOUSNESS

Definition. Interiorization of the projected intraphysical consciousness: the act of the consciousness projected in the psychosoma entering the human body, thus reestablishing the normal state of coincidence of the vehicles of manifestation of the intraphysical consciousness.

Synonymy: consciential reintegration; corporal re-fusion (rejoining); extraphysical-physical landing; fusion of the consciential bodies; landing of the consciousness; physical embodiment; psychosoma-soma re-coupling; recoincidence; reentry of the projected intraphysical consciousness; retraction of the silver cord; vehicular re-fusions.

Parahead. Interiorization also occurs when the consciousness, projected in the isolated mentalsoma, enters directly into the extraphysical head of the psychosoma (in this case, the parabrain of the parahead). Nevertheless, the sensations in this condition are extremely difficult to detect.

Types: The following are examples of 14 main types of interiorization of the projected consciousness into the human body:

1. **Self-lucidity**. Lucid, semilucid or nonlucid.
2. **Intentionality.** Common or intentional.
3. **Ease**. Easy or difficult.
4. **Parapsychism**. Animic-parapsychic.
5. **Mildness.** Mild or abrupt.
6. **Imposition.** Imposed, premature or traumatic.
7. **Sounds.** Interiorization with intracranial sounds or in silence.
8. **Completeness.** Complete, incomplete or partial (semi-interiorization).
9. **Imperfect.** Imperfect or slow.
10. **Inversion.** *Inverse* (from feet to head).
11. **Self-awakening.** With immediate awakening or without sleep.
12. **Sleep.** With natural sleep.
13. **Dive.** Dive head-first into the soma.
14. **Atypical.** *Enter into the human body* in any manner possible.

Position. The interiorization of the consciousness into the human body can occur in the following 5 manners, in regard to the position or point of entry of the psychosoma:

1. **Above.** From above the soma.
2. **Side.** Right side or left side.
3. **Back.** Through the back of the human body.
4. **Encephalic.** Through the physical head.
5. **Podalic.** Through the feet or inversely.

Common. The most common interiorization of the intraphysical consciousness into the soma starts through the parahead (head of the psychosoma) into the head of the human body.

Animic-parapsychic. The projected intraphysical consciousness using the psychosoma can also return to the human body through an animic-parapsychic interiorization. For example: the projected projector begins a transmission of consciential energy while in the extraphysical dimension, under the command of the helper, while caring for two sick or energivorous extraphysical consciousnesses. The projector immediately returns to the human body, together with the 2 patients and the helper, intensely feeling the flows of energy and all the phases of the assistential tasks which are completed in the physical base, in the act of awakening, with no extraphysical traumas or intraphysical repercussions.

Successive. Successive recoincidences allow the rarefaction and condensation of the structure of the projected psychosoma.

Free-fall. In semilucid projections it is common to have an interiorization from above in free fall, as with a parachutist in an exhibition, in which the projector using the psychosoma – with outspread arms and legs – falls from an apparently great height at high speed into the human body which is lying on the bed on its back. This causes a physical repercussion with an abrupt physical awakening. The semilucid oneiric state of the projected intraphysical consciousness produces this occurrence.

Trendelenburg. While maintaining full awareness, it is possible to interiorize the extraphysical head of the psychosoma (parahead) alone into the physical head. The psychosoma then remains in the *extraphysical Trendelenburg* position without engaging the rest of the human body.

Human cannonball. Once, when the author was projected while returning to the physical base, he remembered the position in which he had left the human body: on his front, with the left side of his face resting on the bed, arms stretched alongside the legs in the direction of the feet. In tenths of a second the psychosoma assumed the same position. He then briefly volitated with this posture and *reentered* in a horizontal *dive* like a *human cannonball,* with such force it gave the impression that the head and shoulders of the resting human body had suffered an impact and momentarily been stretched forward. This all occurred before experiencing a fully lucid intraphysical self-awakening. This occurred due to the inherent plasticity of the psychosoma.

Metaphors. The following are 11 symbols, metaphors, images, analogies or comparisons used by lucid projectors when reporting the interiorization into the human body, *as if the consciousness were:*

1. **Bag.** "Entering a sleeping bag."
2. **Blotting-paper.** "A sheet of blotting-paper absorbing ink."
3. **Gloves.** "A hand entering a glove."
4. **Lock.** "A key entering a lock."
5. **Magnet.** "Steel filings being attracted by a magnet."
6. **Sack.** "Entering a big sack."
7. **Sheath.** "Just like a sword entering its sheath."
8. **Shoe.** "A foot going into a shoe."
9. **Sponge.** "A sponge absorbing water."
10. **Suit.** "Getting into a bathing suit."
11. **Trousers.** "A person's body entering a pair of trousers."

Soma. Depending on the angle of consciential approach for interiorization – from the extraphysical to the intraphysical dimension – the projected intraphysical consciousness does not recognize his/her own human body (soma) and can even be startled. This occurs frequently when entering through the back as the individual is generally not used to seeing him/herself from the back.

Intraphysical consciousness. It is, in fact, much more difficult for the intraphysical consciousness to remain projected outside the human body than to return to the body after having been projected. Generally speaking, lucid interiorization of the intraphysical consciousness is much easier, frequent and more common than lucid takeoff of the same consciousness.

Blackout. Projective blackout can occur after return of the projected consciousness to the physical base, during interiorization into the human body, at the exact moment of transition of the focus of the consciential operations (parabrain) of the psychosoma to the physical body (brain).

Reluctance. In near-death experiences (NDEs), as well as in ordinary lucid projections, the intraphysical consciousness can feel profound extraphysical reluctance to return to human life, trying to resist or openly oppose his/her return to the physical world. This negative attitude should be combated by the enlightened projector.

Triphasic. Extraphysical reluctance, as a *parapsychic* phenomenon, can manifest itself in 3 ways, characterizing triphasic reluctance which appears to be stubbornness or obstinacy of the projected intraphysical consciousness. In this case, it is considered to be immature or inexperienced and to be of infantile consciential age:

1. **Return.** Firstly, the projected intraphysical consciousness does not wish to return to the physical base, endeavoring to remain, albeit temporarily, in the extraphysical environment where he/she arrived, on a fleeting visit.

2. **Recoincidence.** Secondly, the projected intraphysical consciousness – already back at the physical base – does not wish to interiorize or realign him/herself in the inactive human body that awaits him/her.

3. **Awakening.** Thirdly, the projected intraphysical consciousness – already back in the human body – does not wish to wake up and continue living the ordinary physical existence. Nevertheless, such resistance is useless due to the physical restriction imposed by the human body, notably the 2 cerebral hemispheres.

Conditions. The following 5 consciential conditions are similar and should not be confused with one another:

1. **Interiorization.** The act of ordinary interiorization of the intraphysical consciousness that was projected.

2. **Meditation.** The greater interiorization of the consciousness within itself, without consciential projection *(ISBE or inside-the-body experience),* common in cases of deep meditation.

3. **Self-projection.** Self-projection, namely any type of lucid consciential projection, as long as it is produced by the consciousness itself.

4. **Autoscopy.** Internal autoscopy or clairvoyantly seeing the interior of one's own human body, which is performed directly by the projected intraphysical consciousness.

5. **Mentalsoma.** Lucid consciential projection, or the entrance of the intraphysical consciousness, in the mentalsoma, deep inside the microcosm of that individual's human body. This simultaneously constitutes projection, a case of direct autoscopy and self-projection.

Recess. The extraphysical reluctance of the intraphysical consciousness to return to human life, when pronounced, generates a period of projective recess that is deliberately sponsored by the helpers in order to help the lucid consciential projection practitioner.

Case study. It is common knowledge that nonlucid and semilucid consciential projections are indiscriminately experienced by everyone, apparently without exception. The author witnessed the nonlucid interiorization of a certain woman (an intraphysical consciousness) whose consciousness, after being projected at a distance from the physical base in the psychosoma and in a semilucid condition, returned to the physical base. The projected projector did not notice the *presence of the projected intraphysical consciousness* (on that occasion, the author was participating in extraphysical assistance that was being provided to an intraphysical child living in the house). She took off her extraphysical para-dress, reentered her human body – that was inactive under the blankets on the bed – kept her underwear on, as though preparing to sleep again, in accordance with her nightly habit. She also did not notice the *presence of her own human body* lying on the bed.

Abrupt. Abrupt interiorizations that are unexpected by the projected intraphysical consciousness are, nonetheless, inoffensive as they do not leave any residue that is harmful to the consciousness. They are common to some lucid, albeit inexperienced, projectors who do not know how to coexist peacefully with the silver cord.

Causes. The most diverse causes, such as small extraphysical traumas or extraphysical mini-repercussions can provoke an abrupt interiorization or recoincidence of the projected intraphysical consciousness. Even the loud extraphysical laughter of the projector watching a comedy show while projected in front of the stage of a theater can cause an abrupt recoincidence.

Bibliography: Baumann (93, p. 15), Bord (170, p. 51), Bozzano (188, p. 78), Crookall (343, p. 52), Giovetti (593, p. 107), Green (633, p. 170), Greene (635, p. 84), Greenhouse (636, p. 215), Huson (768, p. 127), Monroe (1065, p. 28), Perkins (1236, p. 10), Reis (1384, p. 85), Sabom (1486, p. 75), Shay (1546, p. 98), Smith (1574, p. 54), Vieira (1762, p. 31), Weil (1810, p. 144).

373. SEMIDISCOINCIDENCE OF THE VEHICLES OF MANIFESTATION

Definition. Semidiscoincidence of the vehicles of manifestation: imperfect recoincidence and discordant coexistence between 2 or more vehicles of manifestation of the consciousness (holosoma).

Synonymy: altered disconnection of the bodies; imperfect holosomatic joining; imperfect recoincidence; incomplete recoincidence; semi-fusion of the bodies.

Types. There are diverse types of disconnection – ephemeral to a greater or lesser extent, or even permanent – that can occur between the state of the intraphysical consciousness and the coincidence of his/her vehicles of manifestation (holosoma), when entering into recoincidence. The following 3 should be highlighted:

1. **Semitrance.** The disconnection that occurs with the badly performed or incomplete restoration of the parapsychic trance, or the animic trance (between 2 intraphysical beings), that leaves the consciousness of the sensitive or animist in a semitrance or obnubilation for a variable period of time. This generally does not result in any greater lasting negative consequences or discomfort.

2. **Discoincidence.** The disconnection that occurs with the badly performed interiorization or incomplete recoincidence of the consciousness of the projected projector who remains, for a period of time, in a state of waking discoincidence. This is an animic condition that generates the phenomena addressed by projectiology.

3. **Psychopathology.** The disconnection due to the badly performed or incomplete resoma of the consciousness into its human body. This generates a misdirected trip – and one for which the individual is not prepared – into one's inner world (the consciousness), and without correct return (alienation) to the reality of external mundane (human) life. This is generally diagnosed as *madness*, mental insanity or a category of psychopathological manifestation for which there are other technical classifications. In this case, the deeper disconnection refers to parapsychopathology of the mentalsoma.

Bibliography: Vieira (1762, p. 14).

374. POST-INTERIORIZATION

Definition. Post-interiorization: the state of the intraphysical consciousness immediately subsequent to the interiorization of the psychosoma into the human body, or the interiorization of the mentalsoma into the extraphysical head of the psychosoma (parahead) that is already in the dense body.

Synonymy: the state subsequent to consciential projection.

Mentalsoma. The characteristics of the post-interiorization stage analyzed here deal more with the period following reentry, which occurs more frequently and is richer in occurrences. This refers to the period in which the intraphysical consciousness is returning to the human body in the mentalsoma and in the *psychosoma*. It does not refer to the period subsequent to the direct interiorization of the intraphysical consciousness projected in the isolated mentalsoma, which is rarer and more difficult to analyze.

Characteristics. The post-interiorization period of the projected intraphysical consciousness has its specific characteristics that should be studied, such as the following 11:

1. Return to the extraphysical dimension.
2. Post-projective or quasi-coincident sleep.
3. Extracorporeal post-projective or discoincident sleep.
4. Post-projective catalepsy.
5. Post-projective double awareness.
6. Post-projective vibrational state.
7. Post-projective parapsychic phenomenon.
8. Liberation from sleep.

9. Combat against laziness.
10. Zone of quietude.
11. *Blind, deaf* and *mute* consciousness.

Extraphysical consciousnesses. On one occasion, an extraphysical consciousness witnessed the interiorization of the author (projected with lucidity) into the human body when he was trying to rid himself of some disturbed beings or extraphysical intruders. Soon thereafter, trying to escape from the same extraphysical consciousnesses, it tried to interiorize in the same manner as the author, openly forcing a possessive approach to the physical body, with him already *inside* it, completely unaware of what it was doing.

Deintrusion. A new consciential projection and a cold and direct confrontation was needed in order for the inexperienced extraphysical consciousness to go away. It insistently repeated that, in the same way that the author had *entered,* it also wanted to *enter* into that body to hide and defend itself. It did not perceive the different condition of an intraphysical being and that the body had the identical visual appearance or physiognomy of the author.

Bibliography: Vieira (1762, p. 73).

375. PSYCHOPHYSICAL   REPERCUSSIONS

Definition. Psychophysical repercussions: reactions that have occurred between 2 vehicles of consciential manifestation when they come in contact with each other; either between different vehicles of the same consciousness or between similar vehicles of two or more consciousnesses.

Synonymy: aborted consciential projections; extraphysical-physical reflexes; parapsychic counter shocks; physical-extraphysical reflexes; projective repercussions; reflexive parapsychic commotions.

Categories. Vehicular repercussions of the consciousness can be classified into various phenomenological categories according to the nature of the perspective of the occurrences, such as the following 7:

1. **Physical.** Physical repercussion.
2. **Extraphysical.** Extraphysical repercussion.
3. **Psychosomatic.** Repercussion between the human body and the psychosoma, and vice-versa.
4. **Mentalsomatic.** Repercussion between the psychosoma and the mentalsoma, and vice-versa.
5. **Holochakrology.** Repercussion between the human body and the holochakra.
6. **Hyperacuity.** Repercussion with or without the lucid participation of the consciousness.
7. **Group.** Repercussion between the psychosomas, holochakras and somas of two or more consciousnesses.

Innocuousness. Consciential trauma is the basic characteristic of psychophysical repercussion. Nevertheless, although they are mild traumas, temporary marks, surprises and shocks that involve repercussive phenomena of the consciousness, they are not the source, per se, of any considerable organic perturbation or lasting condition. They are, therefore, innocuous to the physical and mental health of the consciential projector.

Stigmatization. Among the repercussive phenomena of the consciousness we should not omit the cases of stigma or stigmatization on the hands or forehead, such as those known of for centuries that originate from the willful autosuggestion of a person who is highly impressionable, susceptible or emotionally deprived. Such people are generally religious fanatics.

Variations. There are psychophysical repercussions which occur coming from the psychosoma to the human body, as well as from the human body to the psychosoma. They may or may not provoke the physical awakening of the consciousness. Aside from this, psychophysical repercussions occur with or without oneiric components; with or without the occurrence of lucid consciential projections; and, lastly, with or without correct recall of the physical-extraphysical occurrences.

Consequences. In order to better understand the repercussions generated from the psychosoma to the human body, and those produced in the opposite direction, from this vehicle to the psychosoma, at least the following 4 variables need to be analyzed:

1. **Self-awakenings.** Physical self-awakenings of the consciousness.
2. **Oneirism.** Oneiric components, or those story lines shaped by lightning-fast dreams.
3. **Mnemosomatics.** Clear recollections of authentic consciential projections.
4. **Projectability.** The non-existence of lucid consciential projections.

Dreams. In order to understand lucid consciential projections, it is necessary to observe the relationships of psychophysiological repercussions with ordinary dreams, with respect to the 3 following variables:

1. **Mini-dreams.** The awakening of the consciousness when the psychosoma is slightly discoincident, creates physiological repercussive *mini-dreams*. These *mini-dreams* commonly occur before the first sleep period and after the last sleep period.

2. **Story lines.** In physical repercussions, when the mind sleeps with the psychosoma slightly discoincident, the imagination inserts small, colored oneiric story lines in tenths of a second. This occurs at the exact moment of the abrupt return to the condition of juxtaposition with the human body, with some physical motor action that is rational and acceptable to the consciousness thus creating the repercussive mini-dream.

3. **Case study.** The following are 5 examples of repercussive mini-dreams: someone tugging on a part of the human body; catching an object that is unexpectedly thrown at our human body; an imminent and unexpected fall; the surprise of abruptly encountering someone; any banal material shock, whether it is generally electrical, thermal or physical in nature.

Bibliography: Bayless (98, p. 111), Bertrand (127, p. 27), Carrington (245, p. 247), Crookall (333, p. 169), Delanne (381, p. 164), Muldoon (1105, p. 83), Sculthorp (1531, p. 143), Shay (1546, p. 92), Vieira (1762, p. 146), Walker (1781, p. 69).

---

376. EXTRAPHYSICAL REPERCUSSIONS DURING CONSCIENTIAL PROJECTION

Definition. Extraphysical repercussion: the reflex of the human body, inactive in the physical base, upon the projected psychosoma of the intraphysical consciousness that is temporarily projected in the extraphysical dimension.

Synonymy: extraphysical parapsychic counter-shock; extraphysical projective repercussion; extraphysical reflex.

Causes. Listed below are 11 physical causes, stemming from the human body, of extraphysical repercussions that have occurred during a lucid or nonlucid projection of the intraphysical consciousness:

1. **Circulation.** Irregular blood circulation.
2. **Cramps.** Cramps, in general.
3. **Mouth.** Oral respiration (or through the mouth).
4. **Throat.** *Dry throat.*
5. **Respiration.** Stertorous respiration.
6. **Nose.** Nasal obstruction.
7. **Touch.** Physical touch on the human body or soma.
8. **Object.** The falling of an object onto the human body.
9. **Light.** The abrupt entrance of natural light or the turning on of artificial light that shines onto the human body, due to the noise, the action itself, the irradiation of photons or the suddenness of the act.

10. **Company.** Movement of the evolutionary duo's spouse or mate, at his/her side, on a spring mattress.

11. **Subhuman.** The abrupt jumping over the inactive human body by a domestic animal, dog or cat, that has an affinity with the family environment.

Noises. Among the physical causes of extraphysical repercussions, during a lucid or nonlucid projection, we should point out the disturbing ambient noises of the physical base that are near the projected intraphysical consciousness' inactive human body.

Maximum. The combination of the distance between the human body and psychosoma, plus the speed of the return of the psychosoma, produces a maximal (physical or extraphysical) repercussion. This occurs through the energetic conduction and the retractility of the broad or thin silver cord.

Couples. The *repercussion of couples* is a common telepathic phenomenon, or energetic reflex, that manifests when a person who is already sleeping, and another – who tries to project, or simply starts sleeping – has their human body in close proximity to the human body of the first. A repercussion occurs with the first person or, in other words, a joint repercussion.

Extraphysical. Among the extraphysical causes of repercussions – which are also extraphysical – that occur during a lucid or nonlucid projection, we can point out the reaction between one psychosoma and another nearby psychosoma or, in other words, of an intraphysical consciousness which will project to another consciousness that is already projected, and the actuation of the holochakra.

Effects. The following are 6 *extraphysical effects* of the repercussions, which are also *extraphysical*, stemming from the human body, that happen to the projected psychosoma and consciousness during a lucid or nonlucid projection of the intraphysical consciousness:

1. **Base.** Admonitory discomfort inside and outside the physical base.

2. **Cord.** Admonitory discomfort within the potent perimeter of the silver cord.

3. **Sensitivity.** Admonitory discomfort far from the projector's physical base; resulting from a pinprick in the holochakra through space, in the phenomenon of provoked *exteriorization of sensitivity*.

4. **Return.** Abrupt return of the projected consciousness to the physical base.

5. **Movement.** Duplication or mimicry of a physical movement, in the extraphysical dimension, by the psychosoma through the energetic transmission of the silver cord.

6. **Interiorization.** Imposed, premature or traumatic consciential interiorization.

Oneiric. The extraphysical repercussion during the projection is, generally speaking, similar to the *oneiric repercussion,* a phenomenon common to all people. This occurs when the dreamer experiences a nightmare and suddenly becomes frightened. Due to the fear, the individual suffers a consciential oneiric trauma and, as a result, physically awakens.

Bibliography: Greene (635, p. 62), Vieira (1762, p. 165).

377. PHYSICAL REPERCUSSIONS DURING CONSCIENTIAL PROJECTION

Definition. Physical repercussion: the reflex of the psychosoma of the intraphysical consciousness, who is temporarily projected in the extraphysical dimension, upon his/her human body that is inactive in the physical base at that time.

Synonymy: jerks in the human body; paradysbarism; parapsychic-physical counter-shock; physical projective repercussion.

Causes. The following are 11 extraphysical causes of physical repercussions, stemming from the projected psychosoma. They occur during the lucid or nonlucid projection of the intraphysical consciousness.

1. **Takeoff.** Instantaneous takeoff.
2. **Clairvoyance.** Extraphysical clairvoyance.
3. **Surprise.** Extraphysical surprise.
4. **Self-awakening.** Abrupt *extraphysical* self-awakening.
5. **Fear.** Fear of projected consciousnesses (phobia).
6. **Trauma.** Extraphysical trauma.
7. **Attack.** Extraphysical attack of an extraphysical consciousness or another projected intraphysical consciousness (passion) upon the projected consciousness.
8. **Extraphysical euphoria.** Temporary extraphysical euphoria.
9. **Psychosomatics.** Projective stretching of the psychosoma.
10. **Telekinesis.** Telekinesis of extraphysical origin.
11. **Holochakrology.** Intense actuation of the holochakra.

Effects. The following are 17 effects of physical repercussions, stemming from the psychosoma, upon the human body and the projected intraphysical consciousness. They occur during lucid or nonlucid projection:

1. **Return.** Abrupt return of the projected intraphysical consciousness to the physical base.
2. **Interiorization.** Interiorization of the projected intraphysical consciousness.
3. **Self-awakening.** Abrupt *physical* self-awakening.
4. **Commotion.** Reflexive commotion.
5. **Spasms.** Inoffensive muscular spasms.
6. **Jolts.** Stronger spasmodic jolts (jerks).
7. **Sounds.** Intracranial sounds.
8. **Tachycardia.** Ephemeral and inoffensive tachycardia.
9. **Jerk.** Jerking of the entire human body.
10. **Area.** Repercussion of a segment or region of the human body.
11. **Members.** Simultaneous repercussion of both legs or arms.
12. **Mini-dream.** A lightning-fast repercussive mini-dream or the creation of oneiric story lines in tenths of a second.
13. **Mnemosomatics.** Clear recollection of an authentic projection.
14. **Joint.** Joint repercussions.
15. **Catalepsy.** Intraphysical and extraphysical catalepsy.
16. **Burns.** A light sunburning of the individual who is sleeping under the rays of the sun.
17. **Stigmatization.** Stigmatizations, in general.

Intensity. The intensity of the physical repercussion, however great it may be, during the lucid or nonlucid projection, varies from projector to projector and from one experiment to another. Nevertheless, it causes neither serious physical damage nor severe problems to the projection practitioner. A very quick extraphysical awakening can generate a physical repercussion in the human body, along with the immediate physical awakening of the projected consciousness.

Case Study. One afternoon, the author was lying on his right side and turned, in his second nap, remaining on his front, resting the left side of his face at the edge of the bed. While laying on his front, an instantaneous takeoff occurred along with extraphysical awakening at the moment at which he took off entirely, from top to bottom. Due to the instantaneous nature of this event, the consciousness concluded that it was still in the ordinary, physical waking state with the human body falling from the edge of the bed. He thereby experienced an abrupt repercussion in the human body with a physical awakening that was also abrupt.

Equivocal. In this case, it became very clear that all 4 sequential conditions – the ordinary, physical waking state, the extraphysical awakening and the physical repercussion, followed by the physical awakening – occurred in a matter of seconds. In this event, there was no inclusion of any oneiric component. It was just a *mistake of the consciousness,* due to the rapidity of the spontaneous takeoff that caught the intraphysical consciousness by surprise (*extraphysical faux pas*).

Partial. Aside from the small jerks in the extremities of the soma generated by the stimulus of the nerve pathways – popularly called *pranic blocks* – that disturb the circulation, physical repercussions occur because of partial disconnections or isolated projections of the paralegs or para-arms (of the psychosoma).

Physiology. The physiological movements (at times vegetative) of the entire human body that are normally made in life – common during the period of natural sleep – are not related to the movements, travels and experiences of the intraphysical consciousness when he/she is in a freer condition, projected in the psychosoma or mentalsoma. Often, the projector is very distant in the extraphysical dimension when the physical repercussion occurs, which is not a frequent occurrence.

Myoclonuses. We should not confuse the simple, routine jerks occurring with the sleeping person, called myoclonuses – clonic muscular spasms, explained by diverse normal physiological occurrences such as the releasing of the cortical control of the spinal motor neurons – with repercussions that are physical but of an extraphysical origin during the phenomenon of lucid or nonlucid projection. The practice of lucid projection shows conclusively the differences between one type of jerk and another to the projector.

Retention. When the psychosoma of the projected intraphysical consciousness is denser, with a high degree of consciential energies, the phenomena of physical repercussion and the *retinal retention* of the extraphysical image of the scene can occur with greater ease. This occurs especially in regard to an extraphysical consciousness which has more deeply impressed us or generated the extraphysical trauma that triggered an abrupt interiorization. In this case, the projected intraphysical consciousness returns to the physical base, interiorizes and, upon opening the eyes while awakening, surprisingly continues to see the traumatizing image. This provokes the immediate, reflexive closing of the eyelids.

Mentalsoma. It seems not to be possible to have significant physical or extraphysical repercussions when the intraphysical consciousness is projected exclusively, and in an isolated fashion, in the mentalsoma in the mentalsomatic dimension without the direct influences of the psychosoma.

Ectoplasts. Materialization sensitives, or ectoplasts, frequently experience physical repercussions through exteriorizations of ectoplasm. This is analogous to physical repercussions of lucid projectors caused by the silver cord.

Bibliography: Ambelain (23, p. 38), Crookall (325, p. 125), Fortune (540, p. 155), Frost (560, p. 85), Kardec (824, p. 219), Steiger (1601, p. 125), Stokes (1625, p. 22), Vieira (1762, p. 165), Walker (1781, p. 68).

---

378. SELF-TELEKINESIS

Definition. Self-telekinesis: extraphysical touch that occurs with or without the abrupt interiorization of a segment of the humanoid shape of the projected psychosoma. The segments are most commonly of a finger, hand, arm, foot, or leg, generally causing the muscular contraction and quick spasmodic movement of a member of the human body.

Synonymy: abrupt partial interiorization; partial physical repercussion.

Repercussion. Self-telekinesis constitutes an inoffensive phenomenon of physical repercussion which occurs in a semi-disconnection or partial disconnection of the projected intraphysical consciousness in the psychosoma. The psychosoma may or may not brusquely return to the condition of coincidence with the vehicles of manifestation.

Sensations. The intraphysical consciousness can have a greater, lesser or no awareness of the self-telekinesis. When telekinesis is experienced, it is similar to an inoffensive electric shock. This shock is very strong and clearly discernible in the organic area or part of the human body where the phenomenon occurs.

Cause. The *electric shock* of self-telekinesis is caused by the touching of an extraphysical segment – whether a parafinger, parahand, para-arm, parafoot or paraleg – to its correspondent physical part.

Discovery. Individuals can experience self-telekinesis many times during their existence, until the day they have a major lucid projection in the psychosoma. Only after having a lucid projection do many people become aware that they have already experienced many occurrences of self-telekinesis without, however, realizing the fact or interpreting it in an adequately rational manner.

Direction. The extraphysical movements of self-telekinesis always occur instantaneously in an *inward* direction or, in other words, centripetally, from the extraphysical dimension to the intraphysical dimension, from the psychosoma to the soma.

Vegetative. The vegetative life that is developed in the human body by the autonomous nervous system, when the body seems inactive, temporarily without the consciousness, can trigger self-telekinesis, even due to a simple, louder borborygmus (abdominal area).

Thought. When the movements of self-telekinesis involve the physical trunk and head it is because the consciousness was *thinking while outside the brain* and the part of the psychosoma which was discoincident, abruptly interiorizes.

Story line. A small mental or oneiric story line, created in tenths of a second, can establish, accompany or determine the movements of re-coincidence or *coincidentization,* always stemming from a situation or extraphysical point close to the human body, until the instantaneous and perfect coincidence between the psychosoma and soma occurs.

Cord. Self-telekinesis always occurs in a segmented fashion, not only with regard to the physical body, but also the part of the silver cord that corresponds to the segment or organic area, and not the *entire* silver cord or that which reaches the human body in its entirety.

Bibliography: Vieira (1762, p. 53).

---

379.   INTRACRANIAL   SOUNDS   DURING   INTERIORIZATION

Definition. Intracranial sounds during interiorization: noises that are difficult to characterize, perceived only by the consciential projector, almost always inside the cranium – but which can be intracerebral as well as extracerebral – occurring at the precise instant of the interiorization of the psychosoma into the human body.

Synonymy: encephalic echoes; extraphysical tinnitus *(acúfeno);* internal clicks; paraphysiological intracranial sounds.

Causes. The main cause of simultaneous intracranial sounds upon interiorization is the abrupt or traumatic interiorization only of the parahead of the psychosoma. The indispensable action of the holochakra and silver cord evidently influence the occurrence.

Spreading. These sounds can be provoked by the movement of the *spreading* of the silver cord, which gradually ceases to be a *cord* in order to distribute itself throughout the head in the form of a *layer.*

Frequency. The extraphysical tinnitus *(acúfenos)* that occur simultaneously with the abrupt *interiorization* of the integral psychosoma are more frequent than the intracranial sounds that occur simultaneously with the abrupt takeoff of the psychosoma. Sounds can occur consecutively or, in other words, during the *takeoff* of the consciousness in the psychosoma and, later, simultaneously during interiorization.

Characteristics. Projective intracranial sounds create *sonorous repercussions* and are internal, subjective or highly personal. In general, they seem to come from inside the head, whether from the right ear or the left ear; centripetal or centrifugal. They are invariably inoffensive.

Intensity. The intensity of projective intracranial sounds varies: according to the types of consciential projections; from projection to projection, of the same lucid projector; from one consciential projector to another. It often seems that the intensity of the extraphysical tinnitus *(acúfenos)* depends on the rapidity of the maneuvers of the psychosoma in *leaving* from and *entering* into the human body.

Types. The most common types of intracranial sounds that occur during interiorization are: buzzing, tinkling or sibilations. These are interpreted by lucid consciential projectors using diverse metaphors, such as: vibrations in the head, as if there were an internal tightly stretched cord; crackling fire; electrical spark; exploding balloon; dog's bark; ebbing and flowing hissing sound or animic audition.

Direction. Projective intracranial sounds, particularly during the act of recoincidence, are characterized as following the direction in which the psychosoma is interiorizing, whether from the left, the right, from below, or from above the inactive human body on the bed. For instance, if the inert human body, *emptied of the consciousness,* is lying on the left side, the sound will be heard from the outside into the right ear.

Volume. The volume of intracranial sounds during interiorization is sometimes so loud and intense that the inexperienced projector thinks that a sudden physical accident has occurred, throwing the body from the bed to the floor. The following are some examples: apparently being pushed by a person; someone knocking at the door; a piece of furniture falling over near the human body; or a nearby explosion.

Tympanum. Aside from the stimulus of cerebral origin, it becomes very difficult to define whether 1 tympanum vibrates or the 2 tympanums vibrate simultaneously in the production of projective intracranial sounds, or if the 2 tympanums always act or, in some projective occurrences, do not act.

Uncontrol. Extraphysical tinnitus *(acúfenos)* that occur during interiorization do so because the psychosoma *enters* the human body in an uncontrolled or agitated manner. This clearly constitutes a generic affirmation.

Hypothesis. Intracranial sounds that occur during interiorization prove, to the experimenter, the existence of the psychosoma as a semiphysical, or semimaterial, vehicle. This point requires further research from consciential projectors and is a valuable hypothesis for projectiological research.

Onomatopoeia. Various experimenters have sought to characterize precisely the various sounds that they hear inside their head when the consciousness, in the psychosoma, interiorizes into the human body. They employ the resources of analogy and onomatopoeia according to the language used and the graphic-sonorous characterizations of text balloons in cartoon strips. Nevertheless, no consensus or common denominator has been reached which proves the individual character of the occurrence.

Cord. Besides the aspects of parapsychic sounds that have been analyzed, there are cases of partial and even complete and abrupt interiorization of the psychosoma. In these cases, cracking noises occur due to the violent interiorization of the silver cord and psychosoma together, in another part of the physical body outside of the human head, such as between the ribs or in the area of the solar plexus (umbilicochakra).

Bibliography: Andreas (36, p. 57), Bonin (168, p. 429), Crookall (343, p. 91), Greenhouse (636, p. 45), Holzer (751, p. 104), Monroe (1065, p. 222), Shirley (1553, p. 146), Vieira (1762, p. 92).

---

380.   HYPNOPOMPY

Definition. Hypnopompy (Greek: *hypnos,* sleep; and *pompikós,* procession): the transitional condition of natural sleep, or the state of consciousness introductory to physical awakening, during the semi-sleep state that precedes the act of awakening, characterized by oneiric images with auditory effects and hallucinatory visions that continue after intraphysical awakening.

Synonymy: end of the sleep-dream cycle; hymnopompy; hypnopompic state; post-sleep state; quasi-awakening; semi-awake state. The term *hypnopompic* was coined by Myers, in 1904.

Awakening. The hypnopompic state, or hypnopompy, characterizes and defines the essential part of the physical awakening of the intraphysical consciousness, after a consciential projection, whether it is a lucid, semilucid, or nonlucid experience.

Continuous. The projection with continuous self-awareness eliminates the hypnopompic state.

Coincidence. The hypnopompic state – the last phase of the sleep sequence – is the line of demarcation between the unconscious and conscious state of the ego. It also distinguishes the condition of discoincidence and coincidence of the vehicles of manifestation of the consciousness.

Recall. The hypnopompic state constitutes the ideal opportunity for the recall of extraphysical events, for the lucid consciential projector who has just interiorized.

Hypnagogy. The condition that is essentially opposite to hypnopompy is hypnagogy.

Bibliography: Coxhead (312, p. 78), Edmunds (461, p. 41), Gómez (613, p. 87), Grattan-Guinness (626, p. 392), Martin (1003, p. 67), Morel (1086, p. 91), Muldoon (1105, p. 232).

381. PHYSICAL   AWAKENING

Definitions. Physical awakening: the action wherein the projected consciousness awakens in the intraphysical or human dimension soon after a lucid projection; entrance of the consciousness into the ordinary, physical waking state after any altered state of consciousness, such as dream, sleep, or another.

Synonymy: human awakening.

Types. Among the various types of physical awakening, at least the following 7 can be singled out:

1. **Continuity.** Awakening without the asleep-awake transition or the condition of continuous self-awareness.

2. **Health.** Natural or healthy awakening.

3. **Urgency.** Instantaneous awakening or awakening with the intraphysical consciousness manifesting a sense of urgency, e.g.: in the case of an intraphysical repercussion.

4. **Immediate.** Immediate awakening.

5. **Gradual.** Slow or gradual awakening.

6. **Sensation.** Agreeable or disagreeable (uncomfortable) awakening.

7. **Imposition.** Voluntary or imposed awakening.

Causes. The physical awakening of the consciousness can occur due to various causes. The following are 11 examples:

1. **Psychomotricity.** Minimal movement of the human body or soma.

2. **Self-awareness.** Opening of the eyes, common in projections with continuous self-awareness.

3. **Clairaudience.** Notice through clairaudience.

4. **Extraphysicology.** Extraphysical touching of the human body by an extraphysical consciousness.

5. **Self-telekinesis.** Self-telekinesis, or touch by the projected projector itself.

6. **Intraphysicology.** Physical touching of the human body.

7. **Noises.** Noises close to or contiguous to the soma.

8. **Tremors.** Tremors in the physical base (floor).

9. **Holochakrology.** Energetic shower.

10. **Exteriorizations.** Spontaneous exteriorizations of consciential energies.

11. **Catalepsy.** Post-cataleptic physical awakening (benign projective catalepsy).

Soma. There are cases in which, during the night, the mate or partner in an evolutionary duo has a strange feeling and endeavors to awaken his/her companion by shaking her/his human body that is on the bed. At this point, however, the individual observes that he/she is, in fact, attempting to awaken his/her own human body that is laying down and inactive, devoid of his/her consciousness. The individual thus becomes aware of his/her own extraphysical state of projection of the intraphysical consciousness.

Primoprojection. Such an occurrence, generated by an error of interpretation by the inexperienced projected consciousness, occurs more frequently in a first lucid projection (lucid primoprojection).

Bibliography: Vieira (1762, p. 31).

382. PHYSICAL AWAKENING TECHNIQUE

Sleep. The lucid projector does not always interiorize and immediately awaken after consciential projection. Sometimes his/her consciousness sleeps again.

Catalepsy. The projector can also reacquire awareness *in the human brain* and not be able to move physically. This is the inoffensive or benign state of projective catalepsy, which should not be feared. When in this condition, it is sufficient for your consciousness to produce any movement, however slight it may be, with some part of the human body, in order to awaken immediately.

Minimovements. The following is a list of 5 examples of effective minimovements that are useful in ending the condition of projective catalepsy:

1. **Eyes.** Open the eyes.
2. **Finger.** Move a finger or toe.
3. **Tongue.** Move the tip of the tongue inside the mouth.
4. **Breathing.** Breathe, in this case, inhaling more deeply.
5. **Trunk.** Resolutely wish to turn the trunk of the human body.

Continuous. In a projection with continuous self-awareness, the intraphysical consciousness dispenses with post-projective physical awakening in the same way that he/she earlier dispensed with extraphysical awakening. This is because the intraphysical consciousness does not suffer lapses of lucidity during any stage, thus also eliminating the hypnagogic and hypnopompic states in the majority of major projective occurrences.

Bibliography: Vieira (1762, p. 178).

383. POST-PROJECTIVE ENERGETIC SHOWER

Definition. Post-projective energetic shower: the energetic discharge or pleasurable corporal sensation that the projector can feel, even with a certain degree of frequency, soon after the hypnopompic state, subsequent to a consciential projection, at the beginning of the act of recalling the extraphysical experiences.

Synonymy: post-projective energetic discharge; post-projective energetic shower.

Confirmation. In certain cases, the post-projective energetic shower acts as one of the most useful confirmatory resources of the experiences of the consciousness outside the human body. It is generally accompanied by recollection, whether *en bloc* or in fragments, of the extraphysical events experienced by the projected intraphysical consciousness.

Characteristics. The post-projective energetic shower presents the following 5 characteristics, among others:

1. **Spontaneity.** It is spontaneous and often agreeably surprising.
2. **Area.** In the majority of cases, it begins in the head and flows to the feet (direction).
3. **Position.** It occurs with the human body of the projector in any physical position, whether laying down, seated or standing (erect).
4. **Intensity.** It can present an impressive intensity in the vibratory frequency of the consciential energies.
5. **Absorption.** It seems to be somehow related to the absorption of extraphysical energy that was performed by the intraphysical consciousness that was projected.

Sensations. The agreeable, healthy, positive and strengthening sensations of the shower of consciential energies generally occurs in all parapsychic practices. It is felt like internal shudders or tremors, sometimes moving from left to right and from top to bottom, crisscrossing the human body as though they were poured all at once over the head, to the feet and floor, like a large bucket full of energy turned over onto the top (sinciput) of the cranium.

Assisted. The post-projective energetic shower occurs most frequently after an impactful assisted projection, when the act of recalling the projection is the triggering factor of the process. This almost always occurs with the invisible presence, whether detectable or not, of a helper. This also evidences its animic-parapsychic nature, which is common among sensitive-projectors, and those who habitually sense the consciential energies circulating in their vehicles of manifestation, from the inside-out and the outside-in of their consciential micro-universe. Nevertheless, not all post-projective energetic showers are influenced by a helper.

Sleep. Undoubtedly, the post-projective energetic shower always considerably diminishes the need for physical rest through sleep (personal number of hours of sleep) in the period after a lucid projection. Sometimes, sleep becomes completely unnecessary in this period.

Dream. A common dream, by itself, does not have the potentiality or the psychophysical resources to predispose or promote the post-projective energetic shower. This only occurs when the intraphysical consciousness has just returned to the ordinary, physical waking state, after temporarily being outside the human body and absorbing extraphysical energies directly through the psychosoma, whereupon these energies overflow and pour out in a post-projective energetic shower.

Related. The post-projective energetic shower is sometimes directly related to prolonged consciential projections and occurrences of projective somnambulism.

Bibliography: Vieira (1762, p. 58).

384. STATE OF WAKING DISCOINCIDENCE

Definition. Waking discoincidence: the psychophysical condition of the consciential projector after interiorization, in which the intraphysical consciousness perceives itself, with the psychosoma, with or without the holochakra, to be outside the state of coincidence of its vehicles of manifestation, while in a full ordinary, physical waking state, without feeling completely integrated into the human body.

Synonymy: a "foot-larger-than-shoe" state; "half-shut" drawer state; natural trance; prolonged disjunction of the consciential bodies; self-phantoming; state of spontaneous trance; waking dislocation of the consciential bodies.

Categories. The condition of waking discoincidence of the intraphysical consciousness can present itself in the following two basic categories:

1. **Duration.** Brief or prolonged.
2. **Health.** Natural (healthy) or pathological (ill).

Specifications. The phenomenon of waking discoincidence is dependent upon the fact of presenting various inoffensive, agreeable and surprising physiological sensations when it manifests over a short period of time; or ill sensations, when they transform into symptoms restricted to parapathology of the extraphysical vehicles of the intraphysical consciousness and present themselves in a prolonged and disturbing manner.

Discoincidence. Furthermore, the state of waking discoincidence can occur through a mini-discoincidence or a maxi-discoincidence of the vehicles of consciential manifestation.

Sensations. The following is a list of 12 sensations, among others, that the person in the discoincident state can frequently experience, due to the state of waking discoincidence:

1. **Lightness.** Sensation of a lack of corporal weight (looseness of the holochakra, irruption of the psychosoma).
2. **Stature.** Sensation of being taller than normal.
3. **Fluctuation.** Sensation of "walking on air" or "walking on clouds".
4. **Retreat.** Sensation of retreating from persons and objects observed.
5. **Microscopy.** Visual sensation of microscopy.
6. **Spaciousness.** Sensation of expanded space.

7. **Legs.** Sensation of "walking on stilts".

8. **Haptics.** Loss of a tactile sensation of the solidity of physical objects (haptics), including solid foods tasted and ingested through the mouth.

9. **VS.** Permanent predisposition toward the installation of the personal vibrational state (VS).

10. **Self-vacillations.** Ephemeral self-vacillations in attitudes or with regard to gestures and decisions.

11. **Illumination.** Perception of a brilliant, diffuse illumination of things and upon physical things and objects.

12. **Energetic dimension.** A lucid experience in full three-and-a-half dimension or in the energetic dimension.

Semi-interiorization. The state of waking discoincidence, in the essence of the phenomenon, represents a semi-interiorization of the projected intraphysical consciousness, the difference being that it is longer-lasting.

Causes. Physical-extraphysical facts indicate that the state of waking and temporary discoincidence is essentially provoked by at least the following 8 basic causes:

1. **Interiorization.** An alteration in the mechanism of interiorization of the projected intraphysical consciousness.

2. **Energies.** An excess of consciential energies of the recently-projected psychosoma.

3. **Holochakrology.** The condition of total looseness of the holochakra.

4. **Projectability.** A high degree of lucid projectability (LPB) of the intraphysical consciousness.

5. **Intraphysical euphoria.** Emotional exaltation, whether as a result of a recent fleeting extraphysical euphoria or an intraphysical euphoria of the projected intraphysical consciousness, including here a period of energetic springtime.

6. **Interval.** The intermittent and short-lived condition that sometimes arises between two consecutive assisted consciential projections.

7. **Exteriorization.** The more advanced or intense exteriorization of the energies of the holochakra resulting from the individual installation of an intense field of bioenergies.

8. **Psychosomatics.** Irruption of the psychosoma in intraphysicality through the soma.

Effects. The following examples are 3 natural effects of the condition of brief waking discoincidence:

1. **Semiconsciousness.** Superficial semiconsciousness of the intraphysical consciousness while in the ordinary, physical waking state.

2. **Projection.** The ease with which the intraphysical consciousness may initiate another lucid consciential projection immediately, because the consciousness, the psychosoma and the human body remain predisposed to a new experience.

3. **Uncomfortable.** The *wasting* of exteriorized consciential energies, for a period of time, with no apparent finality, in the manner of a negative or uncomfortable effect.

Consequences. Among the consequences verified by other persons who have observed intraphysical consciousnesses in a state of waking discoincidence, the following 4 should be highlighted:

1. **Elongation.** The appearance of the phenomenon of elongation of the head, neck, trunk and arms of the person being observed.

2. **Luminosity.** The appearance of a brilliant and diffuse luminosity above the head of the person in discoincidence, along with the expansion of the aura and the coronochakra.

3. **Elevation.** The observation of the person's human body being taller than usual.

4. **Teleguidance.** Verification of the movements of the soma under analysis seeming to be teleguided or, in other words, commanded from a distance by its discoincident consciousness. This gives rise to actions that are clearly insecure, automatic or occur in slow motion.

Self-awareness. The state of waking discoincidence shows that the consciousness can be *inside* the mentalsoma, in the extraphysical head of the psychosoma (parabrain), as always occurs when the intraphysical consciousness is in the waking state and, in turn, remains *inside* the human head and maintains self-awareness in regard to the partial projection of the members or the trunk of the dense body (soma).

Attacks. The condition of waking discoincidence can be caused by extraphysical attacks upon the intraphysical consciousness, with or without the help of other intraphysical beings. It is preceded, in this case, by very clear sensations, such as: consciential cloudiness, physical exhaustion or overwhelming drowsiness (sleepiness).

Drugs. Certain drugs can generate the condition of waking discoincidence soon after the intense, profound psychedelic experiences have ended.

Migraine. As previously indicated, certain people who suffer from migraines or hemicrania, a headache that almost always occurs on one side of the head, the main symptom being a debilitating headache – as well as some of their sons or daughters who do not have the classic headaches *(migrainoids)* – usually experience the state of waking discoincidence, or the sensation of possessing 2 bodies, even when they are walking or driving a vehicle. This condition is termed "hallucinations of physical duality" by psychiatrists and neurologists.

Note. The condition of waking discoincidence should not be confused with hypnopompy or with the twilight state of incomplete awakening, which is post-alcoholic behavior and is studied in psychiatry (Elpenor Syndrome).

Bibliography: Anderson (26, p. 134), Fortune (540, p. 13), Heindel (705, p. 38), Lippman (934, p. 347), Verneuil (1735, p. 95), Vieira (1762, p. 108), Yram (1897, p. 111).

XIII – Post-Projection Physical Waking State

> ### 385.   THE   PHYSICAL   MIND

Definition. Mind: the organized totality of the physical, conscious, unconscious and endopsychic structures and processes of the consciousness when it is intraphysical.

Synonymy: intelligence; thought.

Problem. *Cartesian dualism* is the establishment of the idea that the mind is independent from the soma. Skeptics refer to this idea as the *ghost in the machine*. In general, this theme is addressed as the *mind-body problem* or the *psychophysical question*.

Levels. There are 4 basic levels of the mind: conscious, subconscious, supraconscious and unconscious during sleep.

Brain. The human brain is used by the consciousness as a physical agent or vehicle for the exercising of its functions. The consciousness is in the brain in the same way that the broadcasting station is in the radio. The consciousness – or the essence of the personality – depends upon processes located in the mentalsoma, passing through the extraphysical parabrain of the psychosoma, and not directly through the dense physical brain.

Obscurities. The connection between the following 7 variables related to the human mind still remain obscure for sciences in general:

1. **Somatics.** The human body (soma) and the mind.
2. **Physiology.** Physiology and psychology.
3. **Psyche.** The soma and the psyche.
4. **Consciousness.** The cerebral cortex and the consciousness.
5. **Idea.** Nerve impulses and ideas.
6. **Thought.** The neuronal electrochemical phenomenon and conscious thought.
7. **Parapsychism.** The stimulation of brain cells and the animic-parapsychic experience.

Characteristics. The consciousness utilizes the human body as a controlled machine, and makes the human being into a microcosm, or a miniature of the universe, thereby distinguishing at least 5 characteristics of the mind:

1. **Wakefulness.** The state of the consciousness during the ordinary, physical waking state.
2. **Restriction.** The mind when restricted to the physical brain or in the condition of the consciential restriction of human life (resomatics).
3. **Emptiness.** The *full* brain, due to the presence of the consciousness in the ordinary, physical waking state, as opposed to the *empty* brain, due to the absence of the consciousness during a lucid or nonlucid projection (projectiology).
4. **Hyperacuity.** Degrees of consciential lucidity (cons).
5. **Cerebration.** Cerebral consciousness.

Histology. It is worth adding that, aside from the *thinking* consciousness, a type of physiological, organic, cellular (histology), genetic or somatic consciousness seems to exist.

Memory. In the complex composition of the mind, memory plays a fundamental role.

Bank. The small and restricted memory bank that only contains the current human life, generally having a maximum of 7 decades of human experiences, is similar to a poorly programmed computer.

Sophistic. This cerebral memory bank always responds to all inquiries, even if it needs to rationalize the unknown facts through sophisms. The amount of general knowledge that the consciential projector carries stocked in the physical memory or, in other words, the personal idea bank, therefore becomes extremely important in order to facilitate the recollection of extraphysical experiences.

Trillions. It is currently estimated that in the course of 7 decades of existence, an individual, while awake in the ordinary, physical waking state, receives, registers and almost always stores or permanently retains 50 trillion *bits* of information.

Bit. Bit, the abbreviation for binary digit (Binary digIT), valued at either 0 or 1, is the smallest unit of information with which, for example, data can be registered and stored in a computer.

Engram. The *engram* is the mnemonic sediment of a lasting nature which is left in the protoplasm of nerve tissue.

Mneme. The *mneme* is the memory that is conserved in the cells of the soma. It is responsible for the behavior of organized matter.

Holomemory. Every occurrence in life, as small as it may be, is stored, although a great number of facts can be temporarily forgotten. Those facts that we consciously remember represent only a fraction of our integral memory or, in other words, the source of the personal identity of the consciousness: the holomemory.

Children. There are cases of children who, after learning how to speak, are able to recall incidents that occurred before they could speak and verbally describe them correctly. This would show that memory persisted in a non-verbal form during the entire period prior to learning to speak, and only later encountered verbal expression.

Area. It is believed that ordinary memory occupies an area of about 2" (5 cm) long and 1½" (4 cm) wide, situated in the very interior of the temporal lobe, in the 2 cerebral hemispheres. This region constitutes the archive or warehouse of all past, current and future experience of the physical life of the human being or intraphysical consciousness.

Neurology. The internal communications that occur inside the brain are made through the prolongation of nerve cells or neurons.

Biochemistry. Bioelectric and biochemical memory also exist. Long-term (biochemical) memory seems to be stored throughout the brain, or even in organic regions beyond the brain, and not only in the small circumscribed region referred to. For example, auditory memory seems to be linked to the cortical area predominantly responsible for audition.

Recollection. Recollection is an act of thinking that awakens sets of memories.

Hypomnesia. All of us, intraphysical beings, generally forget (hypomnesia) at least 5 periods of our existence:

1. **Incidents.** Incidents that occurred only some years, months, or days ago.
2. **Youth.** Ample segments of our youth.
3. **Childhood.** Part of our childhood.
4. **Neonatology.** The first years of human existence.
5. **Prenatal.** The prenatal period.

ASC. We don't remember the greater part of our dreams and, much less, the majority of the projections of our consciousness outside the human body, as well as other *altered states of consciousness* (ASC) that remain blocked in the mnemonic center and are therefore called unconscious experiences.

Faces. Human beings generally recognize faces more easily than names.

Reality. In fact, conscious life is only a thin surface over the ocean of thoughts, sentiments, motivations, sensations, experiences and the integral memory which, for us, represent the greater part of reality.

Categories. Neurosciences list a respectable number of memory categories according to the approach of their study: daily, semantic, episodic, echoic, primary, secondary, private and operational.

Conscientiology. Nevertheless, psychology, for example, does not address the world of extraphysical memory (multidimensional memory) in its entirety. It is an everlasting, indestructible archive pertaining to the projected consciousness and therefore constitutes an area of study of projectiology, a discipline of conscientiology.

Analogies. Various analogies come to mind that characterize memory processes, such as: archive, collection, computer, dictionary, encyclopedia, tape recorder, VCR and warehouse. However, human memory is a system that is superior to all these examples and everything humankind has thus far invented for storing and remembering.

Wisdom. So far, nature has been extraordinarily wiser than scientists.

Learning. Current studies on *human* memory demonstrate that everything one remembers has its raison d'être, because it is not possible to remember something if it has not been learned. This affirmation constitutes, to some extent, patent evidence for the theory of successive intraphysical lives and for the experiences of the lucid consciousness outside the human body or soma.

Factors. The degree of excellence of the projector's recollection of extraphysical episodes depends on his/her personality. The most diverse factors interfere in the quality of even ordinary memory, in the normal, physical waking state, of any individual who is more evolved than a savage – from the complete amnesiac to the memory expert – such as: accident, illness, education, emotionalism and genetics.

Aspects. Neuroscientists distinguish 3 different relevant aspects in the word *memory*:

1. **Systems.** The memory systems or the mechanisms that execute the mnemonic processes.

2. **Representations.** The contents of memory banks, or representations of past experiences which are stored in memory systems.

3. **Performance.** The performance of the memory, or the capacity to recall.

Distinctions. It is indispensable for the lucid consciential projector's parapsychic development, that his/her consciousness distinguish between mental images, morphothosenes and extraphysical events.

Imagetic. Mental images are reconstructions of sensorial experiences. They are formed from information stored in the memory bank, being mere subjective elements of use only *by* and *for* the consciousness. They are the foundation of common dreams, nightmares and hallucinations, 3 different altered states of the intraphysical consciousness. The mental image is the first stage of the morphothosene, that exists only for the consciousness. The difference between images and morphothosenes becomes clearer with an expansion in the intensity of the *thosene* upon a specific *image*.

Morphothosenes. When the projected intraphysical consciousness has a greater degree of lucidity, it does not confuse mental images with real extraphysical events, although these same mental images orient the modeling of morphothosenes in the extraphysical dimension. In other words: morphothosenes are simple mental images that are shaped extraphysically. However, even these are very different from real extraphysical events.

Types. An ordinary mental image can be: visual, tactile, auditory. Extraphysical mental images can be: paravisual, paratactile, para-auditory.

Hypothesis. The recognition by modern neuroscientists of the extraordinary versatility of human memory systems, as well as the fact that there is no demonstrative proof that *all* experiences are permanently stored in common memory, speaks in favor of the hypothesis that a *branch of mnemonic reserves,* more important than the brain, is located in the parabrain of the psychosoma, and that the permanent *headquarters* is in the mentalsoma.

Cord. Without a doubt, in consciential projections in the psychosoma, the silver cord is the fundamental element for the recuperation of the recollection of extraphysical events that are stored by the projected intraphysical consciousness. Note that when the cord is denser, within the extraphysical sphere of energy, in a quick projection, recall occurs more easily. The same does not occur when the silver cord is more rarefied in a projection that transpires at a distance from the human body. As the mind-brain contact becomes imperfect, it makes the recall process more difficult.

Reserve. Facts indicate that during the consciousness' lucid projections in the psychosoma, extraphysical events are normally stored in the mnemonic reserve, following the same processes employed for common facts while in the ordinary, physical waking state.

Mentalsoma. The above-mentioned observations are not valid for the intraphysical consciousness' recollection when projected in the mentalsoma, where the direct process of acquisition and storage transcends the recuperation capacity of ordinary human memory. This is why it is so difficult (perhaps it is more precise to say *impractical*) to recuperate the *integral* experiences of the consciousness projected in the isolated mentalsoma in the pure mentalsomatic dimension.

Intuition. There is some consolation in the even more obscure process of semi-recuperation that is characteristic of the common phenomenon of intuition, which is a type of antidote against forgetting.

Bibliography: Andrews (37, p. 11), Ashish (60, p. 156), Blavatsky (153, p. 428), Carrington (245, p. 87), Day (376, p. 84), Desmond (394, p. 197), Edmunds (461, p. 52), Garrett (572, p. 187), Gaynor (577, p. 113), Greenhouse (636, p. 57), Hammond (675, p. 11), Heindel (705, p. 105), Holt (741, p. 315), James (803, p. 92), Johnson (807, p. 31), Kruger (871, p. XII), Morris (1094, p. 99), Moss (1097, p. 141), Myers (666, p. 598), Osborn (1153, p. 13), Perkins (1236, p. 56), Russell (1482, p. 134), Swann (1632, p. 44), Targ (1652, p. 120), Tart (1663, p. 28), Taylor (1667, p. 225), Walker (1782, p. 253), Watson (1801, p. 245), Wilber (1845, p. 58), Zaniah (1899, p. 304).

---

386. CONSCIENTIAL PROJECTION RECALL

Definition. Projective recall: the act through which the intraphysical consciousness recalls the events he/she experienced during the period in which he/she was projected outside the human body.

Synonymy: memory of extraphysical events; post-projective recall; projective memory; projective mnemonics; projective mnemotechnique; projective recollection.

Processing. The biochemical and hormonal changes that habitually occur at night during natural sleep can impede the consciousness' assimilation of new information. Perhaps that is why people forget dreams as well as lucid projections. The brain apparently cannot receive and process this information during the state of natural sleep.

Analogy. In the same way that we do not recall most of our dreams (although, in theory, everyone dreams every night), we also do not recall most of the extraphysical events experienced during our lucid consciential projections, upon awakening in the morning (although every person projects, at least unconsciously, every night). In this particular aspect, the 2 altered states of consciousness, dream and lucid projection, are analogous.

Factors. The capacity to remember dreams, as well as the capacity to recall the facts experienced during lucid projections, depends on various factors, especially the following 3:

1. **Depth.** The depth of the altered state of consciousness, whether dream or lucid projection.

2. **Interest.** The person's conscious interest, or the consciousness' lucidity, regarding the contents of his/her oneiric experiences or the projective experiences.

3. **Personality.** The characteristics of the dreamer's or projector's personality.

Lucidity. The process of storage and retrieval of extraphysical events during a consciential projection is aided by the projected consciousness' degree of lucidity during the unfolding of the experiment.

Replay. To memorize is to catalog and store for future evocation. It is not possible to replay what was not recorded. Therefore, recall of the facts of lucid projections demonstrates that memory transcends the cerebral hemispheres.

Evidences. The inability and difficulty in recalling the experiences of lucid projection show the distinction between the consciousness and the human body or, in other words, the existence of another vehicle of manifestation of the consciousness (psychosoma), beyond the human body and its 2 cerebral hemispheres (in this case, the parabrain).

Involvement. The consciousness' recollection regarding events that occurred during normal intraphysical life, or in the ordinary, physical waking state, seems to involve cerebral activity. Anyone remembers what was eaten yesterday because the human body or, in other words, the mouth, stomach and the cerebral hemispheres, were involved in the acts (thosenizations) of eating.

Suspension. However, extraphysical activities take place during a period when physical activities are suspended. In this case – as those activities do not involve the use of the cerebral hemispheres – it becomes almost impossible for the intraphysical consciousness to remember the related facts. That is the neurophysiological reason why most of the components of somnambulant humanity do not remember the events experienced during a lucid consciential projection.

Parabrain. We can thus infer that recall of projective facts depends, above all, upon the transmission of recollections from the psychosoma's parabrain to the human body's dense physical brain, notably in projections of the consciousness that are extraphysically experienced in the psychosoma.

Parapsychophysiology. The parapsychophysiology of the parabrain of the psychosoma evidences the fact that this organ naturally can hold the memories of the consciousness' experiences in two or more different consciential dimensions (parallel worlds).

Hypoxia. This is why a lack of oxygen in the cerebral hemispheres (cortical hypoxia) helps the intraphysical consciousness project with lucidity, on the one hand, but makes the transmission of these memories from the parabrain to the brain more difficult, on the other hand, thereby impeding projective recollections.

Anesthesia. Conclusion: the individual who undergoes general anesthesia, as a rule, has the consciousness projected outside the human body with some lucidity. However, few individuals are able to later recall the facts that transpired in this period.

Mentalsoma. Based on these facts, we can also deduce that the structure and nature of the recollection of projective occurrences experienced directly by the consciousness (intraphysical, in this case) when in the isolated mentalsoma are far richer, more complex and difficult than recollections of events experienced when in the psychosoma.

Psychosoma. When projected in the psychosoma, the consciousness, headquartered in the mentalsoma and therefore in the psychosoma's parabrain, has only the task of transferring the memories from this parabrain to the human body's natural brain.

Transfer. When one is projected directly in the mentalsoma, the transference or the transmission of the recollections is performed twice:

1. **Extraphysicology.** First, from the mentalsoma to the psychosoma's parabrain.
2. **Intraphysicology.** Then, from the psychosoma's parabrain to the human body's brain.

Holomemory. Obviously, continuous integral memory, or holomemory, exists constantly in the consciousness when manifesting itself through the mentalsoma.

Categories. Among the categories of lucid projection recall, the following 9 can be singled out:

1. Recall is dispensed with in projections of continuous self-awareness.
2. Natural recall.
3. *En bloc* recall.
4. Fragmentary recall.
5. Random recall.
6. Mnemonic hiatuses.

7. Complete or incomplete mixed recall (*en bloc* plus fragmentary).

8. Delayed recall, the memories of which only return hours or days later.

9. Traumatic recollection or recall of extraphysical occurrences that are very difficult to forget.

Phases. Among the mnemonic functions, there are 3 well-characterized phases that stand out in the entire strictly physiological process of memorization:

1. **Acquisition.** In the acquisition phase, the consciousness acquires new knowledge through the ability to focus on the experienced fact in great detail for the duration of its occurrence, through concentrated attention and personal interest.

2. **Retention.** The retention phase, having no time limit, includes the period in which that which was memorized is found to be conserved in a latent manner.

3. **Reactivation.** In the reactivation phase, the consciousness reactivates or updates the acquired material, utilizing the capacity of evocation.

Reinforcement. The memories last longer when they are reinforced through repetition.

Qualities. Among the qualities of lucid projection recall, the following should be singled out: logic; clarity; coloration; duration; details; rapidity; slowness; and others. These qualities are improved with repeated projective experiences.

Physiology. Various aspects call the experimenter's attention within the scope of the physiology of lucid projection recall, such as the following 7:

1. **Comparison.** The natural process of comparison (association of ideas, panoramic vision, the act of *tying together loose points*) of extraphysical consciousnesses, extraphysical districts and extraphysical events with beings, locations (generally paratropospheric), objects and familiar human circumstances.

2. **Interpretation.** A better *translation* or personal interpretation of forms and known ideas.

3. **Chronology.** The chronology of recalled episodes.

4. **Flashes.** Mnemonic flashes.

5. **Clarification.** The spontaneous and abrupt clarification of the recollection itself.

6. **Repetition.** The repetition of projective experiments, bringing greater ability or competence to the intraphysical consciousness, naturally improves the precision and coherence of the recollections.

7. **Memory.** A good ordinary cerebral memory in the physical waking state predisposes the recall of extraphysical events.

Extraphysical. The active lucid projector, with the accumulation of projective experiences, ends up discovering the *delayed extraphysical recall* that consists in the projected intraphysical consciousness recalling previous extraphysical experiences which, for some reason, were not recalled immediately after interiorizing into the soma on the same day of that previous lucid projection.

Prolonged. The phenomenon of recall is directly related to the occurrence of prolonged projections. There is a great deal of evidence which indicates the intraphysical consciousness' difficulty in maintaining a clear and coherent recollection of the extraphysical experiences after an hour's absence from the human body. It seems that the human brain of the majority of intraphysical consciousnesses does not handle or hold both memories simultaneously after this period. The macrosoma with mentalsomatic foundations influences this capacity, overcoming this mnemonic deficiency in some cases.

Inclusions. It should be borne in mind that the *extraphysical* memory includes the physical memory and exists closer to the integral memory or holomemory. Physical memory is obviously lesser in capacity, being weaker or less efficient. In no way does it include the memory of all the lucid projective experiences of an entire human life. On the other hand, this makes 100% recuperation of the consciousness' cons difficult in intraphysical life.

Research. From now on, the more that biological, chemical, pharmacological, therapeutic, geriatric, psychological and general medical research is able to improve the practical application of the resources of the human brain – a *black box* still only partially decipherable – and improve the attributes and qualities of human memory (mnemosomatics), the greater will be the possibilities of ordinary intraphysical consciousnesses to recuperate more extensively the recollection of their diuturnal extraphysical experiences which have, until now, routinely remained buried in oblivion due to mnemonic imperfections in the joint and separate manifestations of the 2 cerebral hemispheres.

Work. Therefore, all neuroscientists who currently dedicate themselves to various fields of research are consciously or unconsciously working toward the inevitable evolution of projectiology and conscientiology.

Technology. It is important to inquire, based upon chronological time considered in the inverse direction, namely from present to past: To what degree is the evident and unquestionable general increase in human lucid consciential projections, in this *era of acceleration in history,* directly due to the technological improvement of drugs, foods, the electronic radiation of recently discovered and created instruments, and of modern life itself acting upon the cerebral hemispheres of adults and children, with new, intense, continuous and very potent stimuli?

Aspects. Besides the subsequent chapters, there are others in this book that address aspects of the intraphysical consciousness' memory: projective déjà vu; extraphysical precognition; extraphysical retrocognition; projective panoramic vision; and another extremely important topic: the binomial lucidity-recall.

Bibliography: Bozzano (193, p. 104), Crookall (343, p. 182), Frazer (549, p. 156), Powell (1278, p. 90), Swedenborg (1639, p. 133), Vieira (1762, p. 33).

387. FRAGMENTARY RECALL

Definition. Fragmentary recall: coherent or scattered slow recall in parts, segments or fragments, of the extraphysical events experienced by the intraphysical consciousness which has recently interiorized into the human body.

Synonymy: fragmented recall; discontinuous recall.

Inefficiency. Fragmentary recall is the least efficient process by which the intraphysical consciousness remembers the extraphysical experiences, because it is subject to mistakes and the creation of gaps in the flow of recollections.

Discontinuity. In fragmentary or discontinuous recall, besides recollections that emerge in parts, each part often presents its own degree of clarity and intelligibility of recall that is perfectly perceptible and easily differentiated by the consciousness. One may be of an extreme sharpness of precision and perception, another one cloudy and yet another completely obscure.

Order. The *first* fragments to surface *in the memory* of the intraphysical consciousness which has recently arrived from the projective experiment are almost always the *final* extraphysical events.

Lucidity. Projective occurrences show that certain lucid projections – notably those in which the intraphysical consciousness floats or moves at high speeds over rural areas and cities – although being experienced with intense lucidity during the events can, in the end, cause one to recall the events as though they had been semilucid experiences. There are unknown organic, cerebral factors, or those related to the nervous system, that interfere in the mechanisms of the memory in these cases.

Bibliography: Vieira (1762, p. 66).

388. *EN BLOC* RECALL

Definition. *En bloc* recall: rapid, integral and coherent recall of extraphysical events by the intraphysical consciousness that has recently interiorized into the human body.

Synonymy: *en bloc* recollection; continuous recall.

Efficiency. *En bloc* recall is the most efficient process for recalling extraphysical facts. The only system better than this is to completely dispense with the need to recall the experiments outside the human body, which occurs in projections with continuous self-awareness.

Clarity. The clarity or refined level of acuity of the intraphysical consciousness' recall of extraphysical experiences, when always uniform, refers to the possibility of *en bloc* recall.

Mixed. Depending on the intensity of the ideas and emotions, as well as the velocity of the succession of extraphysical events, *en bloc* recall can coexist with fragmentary recall, resulting in a mixed recall. In this case, highly emphasized *en bloc* memories of an experience (generally the main one) occur first, followed by other fragmentary recollections.

Bibliography: Vieira (1762, p. 33).

389. FACTORS FAVORABLE TO CONSCIENTIAL PROJECTION   RECALL

Impacts. According to public opinion research, the following are the most frequent impacts that lucid projection has on people, as separated into 3 distinct periods:

1. **During.** During the experience: the intraphysical consciousness feels calm, peace or quietude; feels absolute freedom; feels spontaneous happiness; feels fear.

2. **Afterward.** Immediately after the experience: the intraphysical consciousness becomes interested in parapsychic phenomena; speaks about the experience; feels curious about the subject; feels that life has changed *(breakthrough, turning point);* feels that it was a transcendent experience; feels in possession of parapsychic abilities, a condition that was previously unknown.

3. **Subsequently.** A longer time after the experience, the intraphysical consciousness: wishes to have the experience again; feels that a greater awareness regarding the reality of human life was developed; feels the experience to be very agreeable; feels the experience has brought personal benefits; feels an inner change to a peaceful self-conviction regarding life after death or deactivation of the human body; feels the experience to have been imbued with great beauty; feels the experience to be the greatest thing that has ever occurred in his/her intraphysical life.

Classification. The factors favorable to recall of lucid projections can be classified into 4 categories:

1. **Psychological:** motivation regarding lucid projection; psychological derepression; mnemonic catalytic agent; meditation upon the memories of lucid projections; extraphysical event selection know-how.

2. **Physiological:** dorsal position of the human body; physical awakening immediately after the lucid projection; lucid projection produced in the second half of the night; maintenance of cerebral circulation or, better still, cerebral circulation which is increased without being pathological, maintaining normal intracranial pressure, a verification of which can be performed through funduscopy; lateral rotation of the head during the post-projective period; mild swinging of the human head back-and-forth; the habit of recalling the lucid projection twice before getting up from the bed to register the experience; an extensive array of general knowledge stored in the ordinary physical memory; youthfulness, signifying that the individual possesses a good acquisition memory; a good ordinary memory in the physical waking state, thus predisposing the recall of extraphysical events.

3. **Physical:** orally relating the lucid projection to a listener; organizing the lucid projection's extraphysical episodes in chronological order with a certain keyword corresponding to the relevant point of each one; immediate registration of lucid projection experiences; rereading of the register to yourself in a loud voice; keyboarding the register of extraphysical events; personal recall technique or projective mnemotechnique; certain types of developed parapsychism; energetic post-projective shower.

4. **Extraphysical:** simple extraphysical episodes; the climax of extraphysical events; the last extraphysical scenes; fixation of the key moments of extraphysical experiences; the cooperation of extraphysical helpers; often, the projected human consciousness' discontinuous lucidity causes fragmentary recollection; interiorization accompanied by immediate physical awakening predisposes *en bloc* recall.

Opening. A deep extraphysical emotion or non-habitual experience of the projected consciousness can provoke a *mnemonic opening,* which facilitates recall remarkably. In these cases, traumatic extraphysical experiences which are impossible to forget occur.

Dreams. The person who is able to learn to recall natural ordinary dreams, improves the recollection of lucid projection experiences.

Details. The person who, in the ordinary, physical waking state, is able to remember apparently negligible details during the unfolding or development of the everyday facts of daily existence, retaining impressions and sensations that are very close or intimate to the psychosphere, presents a greater tendency to enjoy extraphysical lucidity while projected, as well as observing the extraphysical experiences without traumas and clearly recalling the facts witnessed or experienced while projected.

Universe. To accept the conditions of proximity and the influences of the macro-universe upon our consciential micro-universe, in a balanced manner, is the first step toward intelligent multidimensional coexistology. Lucid projection increases our circle of consciential relationships and interdimensional communicability in an unforeseeable manner.

Feedback. It is worth paying attention to the act of feedback and the improvement of accuracy – sharpness, acuteness, perspicacity and exactness – regarding that which is around you, in relation to your attention and memory. Take the example of discovering for the first time the brand name printed on the bathroom accessories that you have been using every day, for decades, and have never noticed.

Medication. This common fact frequently occurs when an older person begins taking anti-arteriosclerosis medication, thus triggering a renovation in the capacities of attention, concentration and memory (mnemonics). This occurrence considerably improves the degree of extraphysical acuteness and the habitual lucid projector's post-projection recall. This even influences an intensification in the number and quality of ordinary dreams. At this point, many extraphysically lucid projectors, nevertheless without good physical recall, discover and easily deduce the number and extension of enriching consciential projections which they have been having but did not recall.

Bibliography: Twemlow (1710, p. 454), Vieira (1762, p. 180).

---

390. FACTORS UNFAVORABLE TO CONSCIENTIAL PROJECTION RECALL

Classification. The factors unfavorable to consciential projection recall can be classified into 4 types:

1. **Psychological:** disinterest regarding lucid projection; excessive self-censorship; fear of extraphysical occurrences; superimposition of data or engrams in the memory bank; hypomnesia or deficient nominative memory; difficulty in acquiring pure thoughts that have to be *translated* into unprecedented words and human expressions; deformation of memories; the fugacity of extraphysical memories; skepticism regarding lucid projections.

2. **Physiological:** position of the human body in the prone position or lying on its front on the bed during projection; surrender of the consciousness to post-interiorization sleep; narcolepsy, an illness that is the opposite of insomnia, or one in which the individual suffers excessive sleeping bouts; intercurrence of dreams; dream-visions and nightmares that mix with the realities of extraphysical events pertaining to the consciential projection; the mnemonic burden of two simultaneous lives, intraphysical and extraphysical; reduction in intracranial circulation or cerebral hypoxemia; discouragement of laziness and comfort of the projector's bed; the act of producing consecutive consciential projections; organic reflexes from freedom from diuturnal tensions; difference in the velocity of transmission of thoughts through the free mind and through the dense brain; the act of dreaming *with* and *about* lucid projection; advanced physical age because of a recently acquired weak memory; organic intoxication.

3. **Physical:** later or postponed registration of the consciential projection; the heavy burden of human life's daily tasks; a change of the projector's physical base.

4. **Extraphysical:** prolonged disparate extraphysical events that occur at a distance from the physical base; impactful extraphysical surprises; priority services of extraphysical assistance; subtleness of extraphysical sensations and events; extraphysical parapsychism exercises; prolonged extraphysical parapsychic trance.

Nap. Recent research shows that a good nap before beginning a learning process can impair the mechanism of memory as it aggravates the capacity to forget. This *mnemonic block* occurs due to the action of the substance called somatotropin, which is liberated during sleep. For this reason, post-interiorization sleep, whether brief or prolonged, light or deep, impairs the recall of extraphysical events experienced by the projector during the lucid projection.

Ambivalence. Not all factors unfavorable to consciential projection recall are actually unfavorable to projection itself, with regard to the quality of the experience and its purpose. Examples of this are extraphysical assistential services and parapsychism exercises outside the human body.

Bibliography: Rampa (1357, p. 190), Vieira (1762, p. 136).

391. EXTRAPHYSICAL EVENT RECALL TECHNIQUES

Reasons. All intraphysical consciousnesses, upon falling asleep every night, produce at least nonlucid miniprojections, common to human beings in general and even to some developed and larger subhuman animals. This is why many candidates to lucid projection need to apply an efficient extraphysical event recall technique far more than they need to apply an improved technique for projecting, because once a small, mild projection is obtained with some degree of extraphysical lucidity, even with a nonlucid takeoff, the projector develops with greater ease with repeated experiences.

Self-programming. The self-programming recall technique can be divided into two phases: prior and subsequent.

1. **Prior.** In the prior phase, program yourself ahead of time by employing autosuggestions such as the following sentence: "I will remember the projection in detail!" Say this to yourself 5 times shortly before falling asleep, during the hypnagogic state.

2. **Subsequent.** In the subsequent phase, upon awakening, remain lying down for some minutes, moving the soma as little as possible, until recalling the extraphysical occurrences twice. Immediately write on a paper, in great detail, everything that you remember having occurred outside the dense body, because the quite fugacious recollections of the consciential projection can easily be masked by *mnemonic entries* of the facts related to diuturnal tasks, that obliterate the physical or cerebral *memory bank*.

Exceptions. In exceptional circumstances, due to advanced physical age and the projector's deficient intracranial circulation, the posterior phase of the indicated process can be altered by slowly rotating the head, moving it to another position soon after physical awakening. This is a posture that helps in consciential projection event recall.

Improvement. There are 3 simple extraphysical resources that can serve to develop the human projector's recall:

1. **Names.** First: repeat to yourself the names *heard* at the exact moment in which they arise during the unfolding of the lucid projection's events in the extraphysical dimension.

2. **Register.** Second: learn names and ideas in the extraphysical dimension, immediately return to the human body, physically wake yourself up and register them without delay. These 2 expedients unblock the *nominative* memory, which is generally blocked. This is generally the most difficult memory for human projectors to conserve.

3. **Interconnection.** Third: if the projected intraphysical consciousness, upon experiencing various different scenes outside the human body during a single projective experience, is able to attentively carry the subject of the prior scene to the next extraphysical scenario – or interconnect the diverse experiences into one homogeneous, similar, continued experience – this consciential expedient will greatly facilitate the recall subsequent to the lucid projection.

Index. The following is a simple technique that, in some cases, has produced results for recalling the extraphysical events which occurred during a lucid projection: touch an index finger to your forehead in order to remind yourself of what you saw or experienced outside the human body.

Hypothesis. In this case, we imagine, as a tentative hypothesis, that the closed circuit circulation of consciential energies that is established stimulates the frontochakra (generally responsible for clairvoyance), which activates the intraphysical consciousness' integral memory bank through the pineal gland.

Comparisons. Another process that can favor the recall of extraphysical facts is the act of establishing comparisons between extraphysical beings, things and facts observed by the projected intraphysical consciousness with familiar physical or human beings, things and facts which – although very different – still have some similarities in regard to their images or characteristics which serve as a point of fixation for the memory.

Bibliography: Guéret (659, p. 163), Vieira (1762, p. 186), Walker (1782, p. 242).

---

392. FRAGMENTARY RECALL TECHNIQUE

Drowsiness. Generally you, just like any person, wake in the middle of the night and remain sleepy or in a *consciential twilight zone,* more asleep than awake. At this point, your human organism entices you (your consciousness) to sleep a little more. The quasi-absolute control of the physical discouragement characteristic of drowsiness prevails and must be overcome by you as a projector, at all costs.

Awakening. You should, then, attempt to remain more awake without getting up from the bed, acting only through thoughts and will. At most, you can move the head to one side, which will help recall, or change the position of the entire human body on the bed.

Recall. Once you have overcome sleep, you should endeavor to recall, without giving up easily, something that occurred immediately prior to that moment. The first oneiric or projective recollection, as small as it may be, will serve as a *mnemonic clue*.

Fragments. From one simple oneiric memory, you need to *draw out* the other memories. The occurrences or small episodes of the extraphysical facts will be *plucked* or *fished* little by little, through small and large fragments, until composing a succession of coherent scenes, in a logical sequence of experiences, that you should analyze with great acumen, separating the oneiric images, the projective images and those that are a mixture of the two.

Impression. The fragmentary recall technique can thus be characterized in detail. If you wake up without any memory of projective experiences but have the *impression* or *intuition* that you projected, you should endeavor to obtain, at all costs, the initial fragment of the memories, or the *mnemonic seed*.

Seed. If you wake up in the morning, or during the night, with a specific fragment of the initial memory of a lucid projection (the mnemonic seed), you should endeavor to recall a small fact immediately prior to the fragment. After you have obtained this, endeavor to remember an immediately subsequent fact. Continue in this way successively and alternately, until reaching the most extensive, deep and best possible projective recall.

Review. Next, you should review many times for yourself the entire sequence of the extraphysical experiences recalled in order to see if you can remember anything else. It is important to avoid inventing, even though unconsciously, portions of memories that can become subtly incorporated into the real memories.

Vibrations. Your greater awareness can sometimes provoke a post-projective energetic shower, a vibratory discharge throughout the human body that is characteristic and confirmatory of the lucid projection experience in a pacific, definitive and unquestionable manner. The energetic shower, due to the prior discoincidence of the vehicles of manifestation of the consciousness, besides confirming the occurrence of your projection, often dynamizes the flow of recall of the scenes, images and experiences that occurred in the extraphysical dimension.

Bibliography: Vieira (1762, p. 191).

---

393. QUADRUPLE MEMORY

Definition. Quadruple memory: simultaneous recall by the intraphysical consciousness which is projected and in a state of expansion, of similar or interrelated facts from 4 diverse sources, epochs, places or existential circumstances.

Synonymy: continuous memory; integral memory; multimemory; polymemory.

Types. In the ordinary, physical waking state, the intraphysical consciousness utilizes 2 types of memory: factual memory and functional memory.

Factual. *Factual* memory is the capacity to take in and store explicit information. Examples: retain names, dates, historic facts, faces, maps. Amnesiacs can lose short-term or long-term memory.

Terms. *Long-term* factual memory constitutes the general archive in which our knowledge is kept. *Short-term* factual memory (limited working memory) retains information that is being processed only in the moment. Example: store a telephone number only until it is dialed.

Functional. *Functional* memory, a generally unconscious longer-lasting process, can only be acquired through repetitive practice. Examples: typing; riding a bicycle with balance.

Continuous. It can thus be concluded that in the ordinary, physical waking state, the individual's cerebral hemispheres have still not been put to work with the integral, *continuous* memory that the consciousness possesses. The latter is almost always maintained unconsciously prior to resoma or, in other words, its total essence as a personality and the entire stock of its experiences or the holomemory.

Hypothesis. The following are some observations about quadruple memory, one of the aspects of continuous memory, a working hypothesis to be developed by researcher-projectors. When there is an expansion of the projected consciousness, there can be a simultaneous recollection of facts related to the theme or the *fact thought about* in the *extraphysical moment,* originating from 4 different existential periods:

1. **Moment.** Events experienced at that moment in the extraphysical dimension.

2. **Waking.** Occurrences originating from the ordinary, physical waking state in the current human life.

3. **Retrocognition.** Occurrences of the last intermissive period, or the extraphysical interval experienced by the consciousness between this human life and the previous one, perceived retrocognitively.

4. **Prior.** Occurrences in past intraphysical lives, especially the human existence immediately prior to the current one.

Separations. Although revolving around a single subject, but originating from diverse epochs, locations and physical or extraphysical *circumstances*, these memories are also specific because, in their details, they exist as separate, impervious, and unaligned from each other, almost always demarcated by clear limits, provoked by solutions of traumatic continuity, such as the lucid projection preceded by a blackout *(intraconsciential deactivation),* the biological shock of desoma, as well as the shock of the consciential restriction of resoma.

Restriction. Obviously, the human body's limited memory bank, restricted by only 7 terrestrial decades, for example, is not programmed with all these data.

Case study. The following is an example of the recollection of polymemory. At daybreak on August 3, 1982, the author, while projected with a certain extraphysical helper in the extraphysical dimension, but above the earth's crust in the German countryside, remembered 4 occurrences at the same time:

1. **Somatics.** An acquaintance (intraphysical consciousness) in the current human life.

2. **Intermission.** The same personality in the most recent intermissive period (as an extraphysical consciousness).

3. **Retrosomatics.** The personality of this individual in a previous intraphysical life with another body (retrosoma).

4. **Relations.** That individual's personal relationships with that physical environment in Germany.

Mentalsoma. The projected intraphysical consciousness can experience quadruple memory when manifesting through the psychosoma, as well as, and more appropriately, when manifesting through the isolated mentalsoma.

Periods. The intraphysical consciousness does not always recall 4 different periods. A person may only recall 2 periods (ordinary double memory); 3 periods (triple memory); or even more than 4 periods (quintuple memory and others).

Recall. In fact, quadruple memory disturbs the later recollection of the lucid projection experience after physical awakening. This provokes confusion in the human brain's mnemonic centers in terms of the now awake consciousness being able to orient – in time and space – its various experiences on the same theme, or correlated themes, which are recalled simultaneously, in an unexpected circumstance and in a rapid manner.

Psychopathologies. A certain type of mentally disturbed personality (psychopath) or conscientially insane individual becomes even more disturbed due to a quadruple memory, or even a double or triple memory, which irrupts abruptly, as though it were a musical piece composed of variations on the same theme. In this case, what occurs is a disturbance that is characteristic of the parapsychopathology of the psychosoma's parabrain, which stems from the natural functions of the mentalsoma, in which it is headquartered.

Pseudomnesia. Quadruple memory, retrocognition, precognition and manifestations of extraphysical consciousnesses through semiconscious psychophony, should not be confused with pathological paramnesia, pseudomnesia or false memory, which is a mental occurrence having a chemical, mechanical or biological origin, and which is very different.

Hypertension. One afternoon the author went to a copy center where he stayed in a closed environment for about two hours monitoring the copying of hundreds of original pages of the first edition of this book. Upon arriving home, he had a brief, mild attack of pseudomnesia that was attributed to long-standing arterial hypertension which, when elevated, increases intracranial pressure and subsequently generates a false memory, a horribly disagreeable disturbance in which the consciousness seems to recall experiences that never fit with the experiences which it has experienced and recalls.

Ammonia. In the above-cited case, upon checking the arterial pressure, which was thought to be normal as the author had been medicated over a period of time, its elevated level was confirmed and its cause was immediately identified: the ammonia, or concentrated ammonia, used in great quantities in the services performed in the closed environment of that xerographic center. Ammonia is also used as liquid rocket fuel. The storage of this toxic product (ammonia) also presents certain problems.

Fainting. Ammonia increases arterial pressure and is frequently used to awaken people who faint by making them smell a vial filled with an aqueous solution of ammonia from which vapors are emitted. Hours later, after staying in a ventilated environment, the arterial pressure returned to normal without the need of any special medication or an increased dosage of routine medication.

Continuity. Memory related to previous or past human lives is not automatically accessible during a lucid projection experience. The phenomenon of quadruple memory calls researchers' attention to the concept that continuous, uninterrupted memory does not exist, at least at this level of our consciential evolution. Memory generally seems to be composed of isolated fragments that join together.

Cubbyholes. It is possible that many compartments or cubbyholes of memory exist, some for the experiences in the ordinary waking state and others for extraphysical experiences. Facts show that only the state of continuous self-awareness conduces the intraphysical consciousness to the acquisition of integral memory or holomemory.

Bibliography: Müller (1107, p. 71), Vieira (1762, p. 160).

394. FINISHING TIME OF THE PROJECTIVE EXPERIMENT

Habits. At the finishing time of the projective experiment, you should, as a lucid projection practitioner, create good habits that serve to help your development as a projector, especially observing the following 4 variables:

1. **Instruments.** Consultation of the clock and instruments installed in your bedroom (energetically shielded chamber).

2. **Time.** Verification, as precisely as possible, of the time of your physical awakening.

3. **Data.** Annotation of other appropriate or pertinent data.

4. **Registration.** General registration of your recently concluded lucid consciential projection.

Positivity. The finishing time of the intraphysical consciousness' projective experiment is *characteristically positive,* even when going to environments of suffering and sadness. This is because you arrive from the extraphysical experiment in a psychologically uplifted condition, in a period of well-being with regard to extraphysical achievements and a feeling of abundance, from an energetic point of view. This is the most propitious occasion for you to take advantage of this exceptional condition of consciential positivity in order to deepen your realistic self-analysis and establish new productive programs in your parapsychic goals and projective developments.

Bibliography: Vieira (1762, p. 191).

395. METEOROLOGICAL CONDITIONS AFTER THE LUCID PROJECTION

Observations. It is sometimes important to observe meteorological conditions after the projective experiment, in view of certain extraphysical occurrences and confirmation of the projective occurrences.

Characteristics. In the identification of meteorological conditions, the following 8 characteristics can be kept in mind:

1. Good weather.
2. Rain or storm.
3. Windstorm.
4. Lightning discharges.
5. Humidity.
6. Cold or heat.
7. Thunderclaps or other noises.
8. Unchanged meteorological conditions.

Comparisons. Two distinct comparisons can be made between the pre-projective and post-projective atmospheric conditions, as well as comparing these, if appropriate, with the environment or bad weather at or distant from the earth's crust, visited by the projected intraphysical consciousness.

Examples. You can check chronological time, duration of the lucid projection, terrestrial geography, or even parageography, observing and comparing, for example, the following 3 occurrences:

1. **Day.** A clear day in one dimension, with night in the other.
2. **Weather.** Good terrestrial weather while in the ordinary, physical waking state, with rain observed in another physical environment visited by the consciousness projected in the psychosoma.
3. **Temperature.** The heat felt in the physical base prior to lucid projection, with the cold of the extraphysical location visited by the projected consciousness.

Bibliography: Vieira (1762, p. 166).

396. DURATION OF THE LUCID PROJECTION

Zones. Chronological time considered in regard to consciential projections is also relative with respect to time zones. The projector can leave the human body in the physical base at nighttime and perform extraphysical actions in the crustal or paratropospheric dimension corresponding to the other terrestrial hemisphere where it is daytime at that moment, or vice-versa. This occurs frequently with the veteran projector.

Paramesology. That is why the examination of time differences – keeping the characteristics of the extraphysical environment (paramesology) in mind – is of great importance in the analysis of each lucid projection.

Time. Lucid projections, in certain extraphysical environments, can make "time pass at a different speed" than that of physical time. In certain cases, for example, 10 physical minutes can correspond to 10 hours of extraphysical experiences. This fact cannot be forgotten when analyzing the time span of any lucid projection.

Autonomy. The average duration of the projector's lucid projection constitutes the *flight range* outside the human body, a time span that should be respected by the experimenter who wishes to develop his/her projective processes and experiments.

Types. Consciential projection can be: instantaneous; lightning-fast; short; prolonged; of indeterminate duration.

Chronology. In the chronology of projections, we can encounter those with durations of tenths of a second, seconds, minutes, hours or days.

Tenths. Projections that last for only tenths of a second are more frequent than one might think and are not always clearly perceived by the intraphysical consciousness due to this selfsame rapidity. In certain cases, this non-pathological phenomenon is quite similar to the pathological phenomenon of epileptic absence or *petit mal*.

Minutes. The projection having a complete cycle lasting only a few minutes is the most common and includes the vast majority of all lucid projections of all projectors. It is theoretically possible for a person to have more than 400 consciential projections of 1-minute duration in a single 8-hour night of natural sleep. Nevertheless, this does not occur because of the incessant alternation of consciential states.

Average. The majority of great lucid projections last for about a half-hour.

Hours. The lucid projection lasting for two or more hours – with the exception of cases of near-death experience (NDE) – only occurs with experienced projectors and generally during the period of a series of projections. This demonstrates that, in fact, it represents an improvement in the voluntary projective process.

Days. The projection lasting for days is generally rare, is of a singular nature in the intraphysical projector's life, and is frequently impure or pathological. It is due to a coma, near-death experience, or voluntary burial of the living person.

Trifles. You should not waste time with trifles or irrelevant occurrences during the period in which you, an intraphysical consciousness, find yourself to be projected, especially in extraphysical environments that are capable of providing evolutionary teachings to the projector.

Prioritization. You are urged to decide to apply extraphysical attention to that which is primarily useful.

Helpers. The more the projected intraphysical consciousness demonstrates a willingness to learn with cosmoethical intentions, the greater will be the possibility of being assisted by the extraphysical helpers.

Case study. There are human occurrences that can help the projector calculate the duration of a projection. For example, an electrical blackout due to an unforeseen accident that subsequently leaves a specific human location dark at night. In this case, if the intraphysical consciousness projects in the physical base that was left while in darkness, it is possible to know if the location's lights came back on before interiorizing and calculate the time by the period of the electrical blackout.

Return. The longer the intraphysical consciousness remains projected with lucidity outside the human body, the less willing he/she will be to return to that selfsame human body. We can, in this way, precisely evaluate the inferior quality of human life as compared to the extraphysical dimensions, for that intraphysical consciousness who is more self-aware of his/her personal evolution.

Bibliography: Baumann (93, p. 63), Blackmore (145, p. 308), Bozzano (188, p. 50), Frost (560, p. 59), Green (632, p. 92), RPA (1481, p. 29), Steiger (1601, p. 5), Vieira (1762, p. 210).

---

397. *CONSCIENTIOLOGICAL* STATE AFTER THE LUCID PROJECTION

Categories. Among the categories of the projector's conscientiological state after a lucid projection experience, the following 6 can be singled out:

1. **Serenology.** Serene or balanced.
2. **Self-confidence.** Self-confident and optimistic.
3. **Intraphysical euphoria.** Euphoric or possessed of a mild intraphysical euphoria.
4. **Shock.** Tearful or still under the emotional shock of the lucid projection.
5. **Guilt.** Depressed or having some sensation of guilt or lack of accomplishment.
6. **Unaltered.** An unaltered state similar to that prior to the projective experience.

Comparisons. Clarifying comparisons can be made between the projector's conscientiological state after the lucid projection experience and the state prior to the projection, as well as with the extraphysical altered state (*paraconscientiological* state) of consciousness during the projection.

Supranormal. During the extraphysical period of projection of the consciousness, an agreeable sensation of supranormality (in nature as well as intensity) generally arises, which tends to continue within the projector even after physical awakening.

Bibliography: Vieira (1762, p. 215).

398. *PHYSIOLOGICAL* STATE AFTER THE LUCID PROJECTION

Physiology. The projector needs to begin the essential study of the vehicles of manifestation of his/her consciousness (holosomatics) starting from the human body; and there is nothing better for this than analyzing the functions of his/her organism after the projective experiment.

Types. Among the physiological aspects that should be highlighted in the physiological self-examination of the projector, at least the following 8 can be singled out:

1. **Relaxed.** Relaxed physical state.
2. **Alert.** Alert state of hyperacuity.
3. **Tiredness.** State of *physical* tiredness (psychomotricity, cerebellum).
4. **Fatigue.** State of *mental* fatigue (intellectual fatigue, cerebral fatigue).
5. **Discomfort.** Discomfort or irritability (pathological).
6. **Hangover.** Early morning hangover or, in this case, energetic hangover (pathological).
7. **Cardiology.** Heart rate condition.
8. **Unaltered.** Unaltered physiological condition.

Female projector. The female projector, in particular, should observe the extremely personal characteristics of her gynosoma in relation to the projective experiments, such as: menarche, menstrual cycle, gestation, breast-feeding, reinstatement of the menstrual cycle, menopause.

Bibliography: Vieira (1762, p. 146).

399. PERIOD OF LOSS OF PHYSICAL WAKEFULNESS

Intercurrences. The period in which ordinary physical wakefulness is lost becomes important for the lucid projector, in order to pinpoint the duration of the projective experiment and the relationships between this and other intercurrent altered states of consciousness, either before, during or after the consciential projection experience.

Sleep. Lucid projection can occur with a state of natural, prior, quick, delayed, light, deep, tranquil and apprehensive sleep. It can even occur without any sleep.

Extracorporeal. Lucid projection can also occur after a state of extracorporeal sleep, while you (the consciousness) are seated in the parabrain of the psychosoma, with your vehicles of manifestation discoincident. It can also occur prior to a period of post-interiorization sleep.

Loss. The period in which ordinary physical wakefulness is lost is characteristic of general natural somnambulism or, in other words, the loss of approximately one third of alert consciential activity which may occur with the majority of contemporary terrestrial humanity.

Evolution. This loss will be eliminated and all this time which is still currently wasted will be utilized with the consciential development of individuals through self-awareness and the healthy experiencing of 3 inevitable major evolutionary conquests:

1. **Cycles.** The successive multi-existential cycles or the cycles of multidimensional existences (resomas, desomas and intermissions).

2. **Projectiology**. The continually intensified and improved practice of lucid consciential projections, notably of the state of continuous self-awareness.

3. **Cosmoconsciousness.** The incomparable experiences of cosmoconsciousness.

Bibliography: Vieira (1762, p. 198).

400. PHYSICAL POSITION AFTER THE LUCID PROJECTION

Types. The projector's physical position after lucid projection can be identified as being at least 1 of the following 5 types:

1. **Unaltered.** The position of the human body which remains unaltered or immobile during the entire projective period.

2. **Altered.** The position of the human body which is altered due to a physiological or physical cause that should be researched and identified.

3. **Comfortable.** Comfortable position.

4. **Uncomfortable.** Uncomfortable position, the cause of which should be identified.

5. **Bed linen.** The unchanged conditions of the bed linen during the projective period.

Effects. The conservation of the unaltered position of the human body (the one prior to takeoff that continues after lucid projection) unequivocally demonstrates the absence of neuromuscular physical reflexes in the inactive soma during the exit of the intraphysical consciousness (you) that temporarily *left* the brain emptied of the consciousness.

Evidence. Based on the fact that a sleeping person normally changes positions at 15 to 20-minute intervals, any lucid projection that seemed to last more than an hour – by the human body having remained unaltered, in a single position, during the entire period – evidences, by this fact alone, an uncommon state of consciousness beyond natural sleep. The difficulty here is proving the physical immobility of the sleeper with any degree of certainty.

Clairvoyance. The human body remaining in an unaltered position over a longer period of time proves, through the process of elimination, the departure of the consciousness from the physical brain, removing the possibility of having changed position and later reassumed the original position. This also disallows that only simple clairvoyance or remote viewing or even traveling clairvoyance has occurred, wherein the intraphysical consciousness generally does not leave the dense brain in a fuller, more prolonged manner, and the physical brain remains *filled* by the consciousness. In this case, only the expansion of extraphysical perceptions occurs, mainly the visual ones, without the entire dislocation of the consciousness in the psychosoma or in the isolated mentalsoma outside the cranium, accompanied by ample movements of the human body and even speech during the experience.

Bibliography: Vieira (1762, p. 210).

401. CONDITIONS OF THE HUMAN BODY AFTER THE LUCID PROJECTION

Occurrences. The following are the 6 events that are most often verified to occur with the human body after the projective experiment:

1. **Torpidity.** Physical torpidity of the soma.

2. **Dehydration.** Mild dehydration, notably of the joints or articulations.

3. **Cracking.** Cracking noises in the joints.

4. **Disposition.** Good physical disposition.
5. **Bladder.** Full bladder.
6. **Unaltered.** Unaltered physical conditions.

Temperature. Prolonged projection naturally tends to alter the human body's conditions, especially the organism's temperature and heart rate which can lower between the beginning and the end of the experiment.

Bibliography: Butler (227, p. 74), Vieira (1762, p. 191).

---

402. PROJECTIOGRAPHY

Definition. Projectiography: the set of detailed self-descriptions and reports of the personal lucid projections of one or more consciential projectors.

Synonymy: archive of consciential projections; collection of projective reports; propaedeutic of projectiology.

Propaedeutic. Projectiography is, strictly speaking, a merely descriptive, propaedeutic discipline related to projectiology.

Research. Projectiography restricts itself to the presentation of technical, historical and statistical material relative to lucid projectors or the projectiological problem to be studied or researched.

Sociography. Projectiography is to projectiology what sociography is to sociology, or what ethnography is to ethnology.

Classification. The discerning lucid projector is accustomed to classifying or inserting each of the projective experiments in the personal documentation of experiences, according to the relevant aspects of the occurrences that are experienced extraphysically. This habit helps enormously in the improvement of personal projective techniques.

Relationships. The following are directly related to projectiography: the historical accounts of projectiology; the diary of the lucid projector; selected cases (case studies) of consciential projections; statistical public opinion research regarding lucid projection experiences; the international projectiological bibliography.

Categories. Various aspects can be shown in order to characterize a consciential projection, defining it, for example, according to one of the following 13 categories:

1. **Primoprojection.** The first consciential projection, primoprojection or shock-projection.
2. **Singular.** Singular consciential projection.
3. **Sporadic.** Sporadic consciential projection.
4. **Seriated.** Lucid projection in series.
5. **Recessive.** Lucid projection in a period of projective recess.
6. **Routine.** Routine consciential projection.
7. **Typical.** Typical lucid projection.
8. **Impactful.** Impactful or unforgettable lucid projection.
9. **Miniprojection.** Lucid miniprojection.
10. **Mild.** Mild lucid projection.
11. **Surprising.** Surprising lucid projection.
12. **Recognized.** Consciential projection in which an environment or mental target is recognized.
13. **Recurrent.** Chronic or recurrent lucid projection.

Comparison. The comparison of a recently produced consciential projection with other experiences already registered by the projector, permits him/her to define the main trend of personal experiences (parapsychic cosmogram), thus perceiving which directions were well chosen or which way is best to follow, in order to develop lucid projections from that point on.

Technique. The projector should consult and analyze his/her projectiography from time to time. Sometimes, as you know, the simple attentive reading of one of the projector's previous lucid projections will induce a new similar extraphysical experience. This fact allowed the creation of the projective repetition technique through the impulsion of the ironclad will.

Bibliography: Frost (560, p. 225), Vieira (1762, p. 210).

403. FINAL REGISTER OF THE LUCID PROJECTION

Recollections. The immediate registering of extraphysical experiences operates as a mnemonic method and should be the rule for neutralizing the natural fugacity of the recollections of the projected intraphysical consciousness' extraphysical period.

Rule. Immediately after your experience, the sooner the extraphysical episode is recorded, the more accurate your report will be. The more time you let pass before registering or recounting a projection, or even an ordinary dream, the fewer details you will remember and they will be forgotten, remaining indelibly recorded only in the holomemory. Forgetfulness makes reconstruction through imagination necessary and increases the possibility of inaccuracies.

Exception. Only exceptionally do experiences occur that you will never forget, as unfavorable as the circumstances toward recalling them may be, due to the psychological or emotional intensity of the events that one has witnessed or participated in.

Material. As a lucid projection practitioner, you should develop the habit of keeping at hand, on the bedside table or by your bed, a notepad or diary, pencil, ballpoint pen, or easy-to-use tape recorder, in order to record your extraphysical experiences immediately upon awakening, the ordinary as well as the bizarre ones that occur during the night.

Detail. One detail that is seemingly irrelevant at the time can be extremely important later in the panoramic analysis of lucid consciential projections. For the majority of people it takes only some weeks for the flow of memories and the annotation of lucid projections to become routine.

Occurrences. Among the occurrences that you should remember in the final record of the lucid projection, the following 10 can be singled out:

1. **Chronology.** Consult the clock and the instruments that may be in the bedroom, or the time of the end of the projection. This should include the exact minute and be as precise as possible.
2. **Data.** Other data that seem to be relevant to you for the analysis of your experiment.
3. **Health.** Your personal health.
4. **Sleep.** The time you took to fall asleep, in your opinion.
5. **Meteorology.** The exact meteorological conditions of the moment.
6. **Time.** The exact time that you wrote the report.
7. **Medication.** The use of your personal medication.
8. **Traumas.** Any traumatic experience prior to lucid projection.
9. **Argument.** An argument that you may have participated in prior to the projective experience.
10. **Routine.** A change in the diuturnal routine of your existence.

Types. Within the types of final record of your lucid consciential projection the following 10 variables can be singled out:

1. **Immediate.** The immediate record.
2. **Subsequent.** The subsequent record.
3. **Manuscript.** The manuscript of the memories of the consciential projections.
4. **Recording.** The recording (tape recorder) of memories, the quickest process for emergencies.
5. **Typing.** Typing the record directly is always the best, when possible, using a personal laptop or notebook computer (diskette; recordable CD-ROM, everything at once).

6. **Shorthand.** The shorthand annotation of the recollections.

7. **Details.** A detailed report of the memories.

8. **Summary.** A telegraphic or summarized version of the experience, being a process that is less recommended.

9. **Mishaps.** The frustrating act of the memories remaining unregistered and subsequently being lost due to mishaps or accidents.

10. **Obstacles.** The overcoming of an obstacle to recording.

Preconceptions. In the immediate records of the lucid consciential projection, you should observe certain avoidances and certain inclusions, such as the following:

1. **Avoidances.** You should avoid preconceived or idiosyncratic ideas such as beliefs, skepticism, dogmatic theories and external influences of any nature.

2. **Inclusions.** You should always include unexpected events, uncommon details, the exceptional vividness of images, apparent incongruence in the sequence of time, and any possible type of anomaly that arises in the events experienced.

Quantity. The more detailed information that the experimenter records, the clearer, more accurate and broader will be the focus on the types of habits that aid or impair the intraphysical consciousness' natural sleep and lucid consciential projection.

Drawings. In the intensification of his/her studies, the consciential projector should pinpoint the main theme of each lucid projection. It is always more beneficial to draw sketches and synoptic graphic representations of that which is necessary in order to adequately register the extraphysical occurrences.

Bibliography: Butler (227, p. 74), Grattan-Guinness (626, p. 211), Norvell (1136, p. 200), Rampa (1352, p. 72), Reis (1384, p. 91).

---

404. DIARY OF THE PROJECTOR

Style. The registration style of memories of projective experiments should preferably be direct, clear, objective, intelligible, organized, dispassionate, informal and detached.

Information. The projector's diary should provide personal information in a synthetic and ordered manner, without attention to literary style. It should have the clarity of straight exposition, without any circumlocution involving ambiguous or obscure words, while maintaining the greatest possible freedom from excessive self-censure regarding the form, and use short phrases in the first person singular.

Journalistic. The projector's diary should be written in a journalistic style, being more informative than opinionative. The most appropriate words and expressions should be used, and the basic orientation ought to be established on the following 2 crucial points:

1. **Prioritization.** Give maximum priority to the *spectator-projector*.

2. **Minimization.** Allow a minimum of action to the *protagonist-projector*.

Embellishment. It will always be better to avoid opinionative embellishment, bombastic and florid approaches, grandiloquence, pejoratives, pseudofolklore and the rococo.

Contents. In regard to content, the projector's diary should contain at least the following 7 features:

1. **Image.** The most astonishing image (megafact) seen during the experiment.

2. **Stages.** The comprehensive memory of the pre-projective stage, the extraphysical period of the consciousness and the post-projective stage.

3. **Intraconscientiality.** The deep intimate or intraconsciential diving of the personality into him/herself.

4. **Autobiographies.** The autobiographies of two lives or two worlds.

5. **Descriptions.** The ambivalent or subjective descriptions and the objective descriptions.

6. **Experiences.** All the occurrences, information, participation, perceptions, ideas and feelings undergone during the experiences.

7. **Striptease.** Trigger a free and complete organic, psychological and extraphysical "striptease," be it of the human body, psychosoma or mentalsoma.

Objectives. Include every detail that you can remember, without underestimating any minimal aspect of beings, personalities, facts, ideas, things, objects and scenarios, as trivial or silly as they may seem at first sight, because in later analyses each detail can have great importance for the development of lucid consciential self-projections.

Details. Human notetakers have the tendency to censure details that seem irrelevant or erroneous, avoiding them in the records that they make. Nevertheless, with respect to lucid projections, it is sometimes precisely those selfsame details – not understood at first sight and badly interpreted – that will later provide the greatest evidence and the most clarifying conclusions.

Uses. Among the uses of the projector's diary, the following 8 can be singled out:

1. **Development.** Monitoring of personal development in lucid projections.

2. **Recall.** Effective stimulus for the improvement of the recollection of extraphysical events.

3. **Language.** A learning of the difficult *translation* – the expression in the language of the dictionary – of the psychophysical sensations.

4. **Self-critique.** Evolution of the experimenter's self-critique.

5. **Paraprophylaxis.** Multidimensional paraprophylaxis or therapeutics.

6. **Reflection.** Production of deep reflection while in the ordinary, physical waking state.

7. **Comparison.** Analytical comparison with other personal lucid projections or with those of another.

8. **Self-awareness.** Verification of your consciential reality, consequently conveying an effort toward an increase in theorical experience and the improved execution of the intraphysical consciousness' existential program.

Clarification. The best and most enlightening written work on lucid projections for the projector is the diary of personal projections or the catalogue of private intraconsciential and extraconsciential occurrences.

Revision. The form, in this case of the diary of lucid projections, must genuinely help the expression of the contents and not make *translation* of the intraphysical consciousness' sensations and the extraphysical experiments more difficult. The individual should not be excessively concerned with the written form in the act of manually writing the extraphysical experiences. Later – after the process has *cooled down* – one should think about making the definitive revision of the originals.

Concepts. In summary: in the diary of lucid projections, the formulation of the scientific contents of ideas or, in other words, the concepts, should maintain absolute predominance over the artistic form of sentences or the arrangement of words.

Margins. Periodically revise the annotations of the diary of lucid projections, also adding clarifying comments in the margins where you judge it to be convenient.

Moment. Start writing the records of your diary of lucid projections at the precise moment you awaken. Do not wait until you have had breakfast, read the newspaper, or started a conversation with someone in the house or physical base.

Manual. When composing your diary, you, as a projector, should not forget that you also write in order to read your own words, when you will analyze the diary as a manual. An effective projective technique utilized today is that of repetition, executed through the repeated performance of the psychophysical conditions and practices already used in a previous lucid projection. Besides, often a simple attentive reading of a portion of a projective report can trigger a lucid projection soon thereafter.

Scale. Consciential projections can be classified according to the decreasing order of qualitative values of the consciousness, during the experiments with lucidity, in a scale that should be used in the composition of the diary with 5 variables:

1. **Mentalsomatics.** Integral projection of the consciousness in the mentalsoma or only with 1 vehicle of consciential manifestation.

2. **Psychosomatics.** The integral projection of the consciousness in the psychosoma or with 2 vehicles of consciential manifestation.

3. **Integral.** The integral projection of the consciousness in the psychosoma with the holochakra or with 3 vehicles of consciential manifestation.

4. **Partial.** Partial projection of the consciousness in the psychosoma *at a distance* or, in other words, in a very rapid manner.

5. **Clairvoyance.** Partial projection of the consciousness in the mentalsoma or, in other words, in a very rapid manner, such as in certain cases of traveling clairvoyance.

Experimentation. It can thus be seen that traveling clairvoyance, although enabling valuable tropospheric evidence, is the weaker projection of the intraphysical consciousness, or that which presents fewer possibilities for experimentation from among all the types of projective experiences.

First. According to historical research that the author has conducted throughout projectiological literature, the first known projective diary was written, in Latin, by Emanuel Swedenborg, between 1745 and 1765. It already included the day, month and year of each short annotation, almost always organized into topics.

Themes. In his first 1,000 daily annotations, that extend up until February 25, 1748, Swedenborg refers to and analyzes various extraphysical themes including: helpers; interconsciential intrusion; intruders; parapsychotic post-desomatics; assisted consciential projection; lucid projections in series; post-projective recall; and volitation.

Bibliography: Alverga (18, p. 200), Campbell (237, p. 4), Swedenborg (1639, p. 1), Vieira (1762, p. 36).

---

405. TECHNICAL NOTES OF THE DIARY OF THE PROJECTOR

Curriculum. Only the diary or, in other words, the *curriculum vitae,* or the course of the lucid projector's physical-extraphysical life allows the verification and identification of the patterns and cycles that gradually characterize the phases of the intraphysical lucid projector's projective existence.

Data. There are at least 15 basic entries in the technical notes that should not be left out of the report on each lucid projection in the projector's diary. They should begin and end the report:

1. The day of the month.
2. The day of the week.
3. The hour.
4. If it is a holiday.
5. The minute.
6. If it is an atypical day.
7. The ambient temperature.
8. The ambient humidity.
9. The weather conditions.
10. The projector's physical position on the bed.
11. The projector's physical state.
12. If the projector was ill on that occasion.
13. The order of sleep.
14. The type of post-projective recall.
15. The hour and the time, to the minute, after the extraphysical experience.

Notice. Other details for the orientation of technical notes that are judged to be relevant can easily be collected from the text of this book.

XIII – Post-Projection Physical Waking State

Diaries. Thus we can observe that the lucid projector's technical field diary presents its own characteristics that make it unique, very distinct from other personalities' diaries and with other purposes, in the manner of a dream diary, a diary of mystical practices, literary diary, intimate romantic diary, or the diary of terrestrial journeys.

Bibliography: King (846, p. 125), Rampa (1352, p. 72), Vieira (1762, p. 9).

406. CONFIRMATIONS AFTER LUCID CONSCIENTIAL PROJECTIONS

Definition. Projective confirmation: the effect of confirming, in the human dimension, the extraphysical events experienced by the projected intraphysical consciousness.

Synonymy: evidence of the lucid projection; objective proof of the projection; projective corroboration; projective ratification.

Occurrences. At least the following 15 variables or occurrences can cooperate toward the human ratification or corroboration of experiences outside the human body.

1. Collection of more incontestable proof.
2. Location.
3. Climate, time and time zone.
4. Person or being.
5. Witness or percipient.
6. Health conditions.
7. Circumstances or situations that influence the experiment.
8. Small pieces of proof or evidence.
9. Simple or complex incidents.
10. Coherences, coincidences or synchronicities.
11. General clues in terms of inscriptions, names, signposts or posters.
12. Specific local occurrences.
13. Impression of already having seen something or the sensations of déjà vu.
14. Maps, telephone lists, telephone calls.
15. Contacts and translocations.

Types. The evidence of the occurrence of lucid projections, even with objective proof, are of extreme importance. The evidence can be voluntary or involuntary, generally being unexpected in this case, and can receive public confirmation and self-confirmation.

Self-confirmations. Self-confirmations of experiences of the consciousness outside the human body or, in other words, the evidence or definitive proof of events experienced extraphysically by the individual are accessible and easy, almost always occurring spontaneously. The projector arrives at a point where it is no longer interesting to merely collect evidence of his/her consciential projections for private use.

Universality. On the other hand, confirming experiences of the consciousness outside the human body to others is problematic and should, above all, be based on the convergence of evidence and in the universality of testimonies.

Sequence. The chronological sequence of occurrences in the human dimension, obtained by the projected intraphysical consciousness, constitute basic information for the confirmation of lucid projection.

Immediate. Confirmations or verifications that are made immediately after a lucid projection, when possible, although dramatic, are more efficient and present the possibility of collecting more substantial documentary details. There are always greater difficulties involved in making non-immediate confirmations after lucid projections.

Paratroposphere. Projections of the consciousness in the psychosoma to locations in the paratroposphere are confirmed based on the congruence of time zones of the places or human districts, weather conditions of the day and the time of the experiment, as well as other attesting elements.

Volitation. The following are 2 typical examples of confirmations subsequent to lucid projection, verified in an almost incontrovertible manner – in the first case by the projector himself, in the second case by a stranger – due to experiences of extraphysical volitation:

1. **Roof.** An elderly man from São Paulo, Brazil, upon feeling that he was flying lucidly and freely outside the human body, saw a curious opening, made due to remodeling, in the middle of a high roof of an enormous church in the city of São Paulo, Brazil. Moved by curiosity upon awakening in the morning in the physical body he went to the church but was dismayed to find that nothing inside or outside the temple looked like the opening he thought he had seen. He then dismissed the issue, attributing it to a simple ordinary dream. Nevertheless, days later, when taking a day flight from Congonhas airport in São Paulo for a business trip, upon taking off he unexpectedly saw the same church *from above*, with the opening of the roof and the characteristic signs of the remodeling construction, just as he had observed during his consciential experience.

2. **Shoe.** A patient admitted to a large North American hospital, after suffering a cardiac arrest, underwent clinical resuscitation. The next morning, she told the social worker who was attending to her that she had left her human body while the medical team was struggling to resuscitate her and saw a tennis shoe, which she described in detail, on a windowsill in a specific wing of the hospital. Her curiosity now aroused, the social worker immediately went to the place and found the tennis shoe.

Bibliography: Blackmore (147, p. 3), Crookall (343, p. 57), Fox (544, p. 56), Greenhouse (636, p. 39), Monroe (1065, p. 54), Muldoon (1105, p. 40), Prado (1284, p. 11), Steiger (1601, p. 47), Vieira (1762, p. 58), Webb (1804, p. 80).

---

407. FACTORS UNFAVORABLE TO POST-PROJECTIVE CONFIRMATIONS

Realities. In the extraphysical dimension each thought or visualization becomes an immediate reality in the specific environment where the consciousness manifests itself. The ordinary extraphysical dimension and the mentalsomatic dimension are realities per se, different from the physical dimension and even from one dimension to another.

Levels. Each of these dimensions is structured upon energies that vibrate at various levels of frequency, as well as having different levels of awareness or self-lucidity.

Laws. Each existential dimension has its own laws that govern it according to its characteristics. These laws cannot be transferred or applied outside it, and much less adjusted to the laws of other dimensions.

Lucidity. The intraphysical consciousness, when projected out from the human body, enjoys a degree of lucidity (hyperacuity, sharpness) that varies from a minimum of zero to a maximum, the climax of the illumination of cosmoconsciousness, which surpasses the highest peak of lucidity attainable by the intraphysical consciousness in the ordinary, physical waking state.

Factors. The following are 9 factors that interfere negatively in the attainment of objective proof or subsequent confirmations of the experiences obtained by the intraphysical consciousness during the lucid projection:

1. **Distinctions.** Sometimes the consciousness, when it projects, does not perceive – at the moment of leaving the human body, as well as during extraphysical circumstances – the fact that it is projected. At other times, it is not able to precisely differentiate the physical dimension from the extraphysical dimension, or even these two dimensions from its own morphothosenes; or, furthermore, the telepathic emissions of intraphysical and extraphysical consciousnesses among the context of shapes and structures seen by the projector which engage his/her paraperceptions.

2. **Vehicles.** It is generally easier for the projected intraphysical consciousness, whether in the psychosoma or the mentalsoma, to perceive the mental structures of the extraphysical dimension – which seem to be more solid at that moment, depending upon the vehicle of manifestation being used – than the dense forms of the intraphysical dimension. This is because the consciousness does not employ the human body's crude senses in order to adequately see, understand and discern physical structures.

3. **Sensitivities.** We cannot discard the fact that the parapsychic intraphysical being's sensitivities are potentiated and expand in geometric proportions when he/she is projected in a vehicle of manifestation, whether the psychosoma or mentalsoma, both of which are infinitely lighter and more subtle, an aspect that dazzles and disturbs those intraphysical consciousnesses which are not used to handling them directly or using them frequently.

4. **Complications.** Everything tends to become more complicated in the following conditions: when the intraphysical consciousness manifests through the dense psychosoma laden with the energies of the holochakra, which blurs or confuses the projector's lucidity and intensifies the somnambulistic condition; when only a partial projection is performed; or even when only the phenomenon of traveling clairvoyance is produced and not an integral projection, which would involve integral displacement out from the set of coincident vehicles within the human body and the condition of the ordinary waking state.

5. **Preconceptions.** Human conditioning and preconceived ideas that the projector carries greatly interfere in the correct interpretation of extraphysical experiences. The individual who projects has to always keep the mind open and receptive to facts, forms, figures and different, strange and unknown lives, discarding all crystallized thoughts, apriorities and preconceptions about something before really seeing or experiencing it directly in the projected state with the paraperceptions. This attitude is not easy, due to misoneism or neophobia. Strictly speaking, lucid projection is the "skeleton key" or passport which facilitates the intraphysical consciousness in verifying everything that is desired without intermediaries or interference. This, however, depends on the perfect psychophysiological performance of each individual.

6. **Self-sophisms.** In many occurrences, preconceptions, rigidly orthodox or fundamentalist principles and conditioned reflexes (abdominal brainwashings) repress, subjugate and suffocate correct extraphysical observations in order to apply an intentionally affirmed falsely logical rationale or human point of view about the facts. In this case, the projector should give priority to first impressions or intuitions, that are usually the accurate and precise ones, and not the others which superimpose themselves, as if they were self-sophisms, having every apparent indication of being authentic and of incontestable reality.

7. **Illusion.** As we can see, the effect of commonplace facts of human illusion, or maya, upon the reality of extraphysical occurrences, also disturbs the mechanism of confirmations subsequent to lucid projections.

8. **Translation.** We must add here the natural difficulty that the average projector has to translate personal emotions, sensations and observations outside the human body into words in oral or written reports. This occurs as a consequence of the difficulty the human being has in expressing his/her sensations, since the individual is restricted since childhood and, in some cases, since intrauterine life. The child is not able to express verbally since the intraconsciential world or cerebral minivocabulary is small or, because of emotional restraint, it is not possible to communicate personal intense pain, the strongest possible sensation. Worse still: in many cases, due to the erroneous attitudes of adults, who ignore or minimize childhood pain, the child thinks that the expression of pain is neither well-accepted nor convenient.

9. **Witnesses.** Another two-sided factor that interferes in the intraphysical consciousness' performance while outside the human body in a positive as well as negative manner are: the witnesses or co-participants of the consciential projection, who can be either an intraphysical being, also projected on the same occasion and in the same extraphysical location who later does not remember anything when in the ordinary, physical waking state; as well as the parapsychic intraphysical being in the waking state who is able to perceive the extraphysical presence of the projected projector, a fact that is always rarer.

Experiences. Based on the facts, we can conclude that only the veteran projector's repeated experiences can supply the precise criteria that allow the projected consciousness to accurately distinguish telepathic messages or extraphysical consciousnesses' subtle intuition; intraphysical consciousnesses' thoughts at a specific moment; extraphysical consciousnesses' psychospheres and the true forms of the location or extraphysical community; and finally, the structures or mental forms in regard to the reality of the physical environment.

Bibliography: Greene (635, p. 84), Martin (1002, p. 7), Monroe (1065, p. 50), Vieira (1762, p. 131).

408. ANALYSIS OF THE PARAPERCEPTIONS OF THE PROJECTOR

Types. Excluding oneiric influences and morphothosenes, there are 5 basic types of general extraphysical perceptions (paraperceptions) that the projected intraphysical consciousness can experience, which are authentic or pure in regard to the locations or environments where the projector manifests:

1. **Intraphysicology.** Pure consciential paraperception of the physical or human environment from the extraphysical dimension.
2. **Paratroposphere.** Pure consciential paraperception of the extraphysical paratropospheric environment.
3. **Extraphysicology.** Pure consciential paraperception of the extraphysical environment per se.
4. **Mentalsomatics.** Pure consciential paraperception of the mentalsomatic dimension.
5. **Joining.** Joined or mixed consciential paraperception or, in other words, a simultaneous mixture of extraphysical and physical forms that, in this case, are difficult to discern and interpret.

Judgment. It is always very difficult to analyze and judge the projected intraphysical consciousness' extraphysical perceptions. Many erroneous extraphysical perceptions occur.

Mistakes. Nevertheless, what the projector says – which in fact does not fit the human conditions that the individual affirms having experienced – is not always entirely wrong. Many times, the interference of situations and the mixture of consciential perceptions occurs. This causes an erroneous interpretation of events witnessed when one judges that which in fact is *extraphysical* to be *physical,* or vice-versa.

Case study. The following is an example of the complexity of the analysis of perceptions of a projected intraphysical consciousness: someone projects to the place where an intraphysical friend is located. There, they enter into resonance with each other and the *visitor* perceives and receives the impressions or telepathic images of the *visited* individual's thoughts at that moment, which was to call the office, and not what in fact was physically being done – changing clothes.

Disappointment. It is obvious that after seeking confirmation for the experiences of his/her lucid projection, the projector who perceived the telepathic emissions, or the exteriorized images of the friend calling the office, becomes very disappointed because the facts neither fit nor coincide, thereby not achieving the convergence of proof that he/she sought.

Mask. In the previous example, the consciential projection was authentic, although the unnoticed or unconscious telepathy for both had suffocated or masked the projector's extraphysical perceptions. In fact, the projector had auscultated, in the psychosphere of the friend's consciousness, the extraphysical formations of the environment, or the extraphysical dimension in which the friend was immersed, and not the person him/herself (the friend), in his/her human environment. More appropriately: in this case, the projector visited, perceived and auscultated the friend's mentalsoma, and not the human body of that selfsame intraphysical consciousness.

Complexity. As we can see, the extraphysical facts, which are always complex, demand interpretations according to the environment or the level of awareness where they occur.

Discoincidence. Besides all this, the fact is that the consciousness of the friend who was visited, as would happen with any one of us (intraphysical beings) when we think or wish to do something with great intensity, with strong intention and vigorous exteriorization of consciential energies, can even leave the state of coincidence or, in other words, slightly separate the vehicles of manifestation in a nonlucid manner without perceiving it. This condition further predisposes extraphysical or telepathic syntony.

Personalities. The following is another possible example of confusion: a projected projector can see 3 people in a human environment where in fact there are only 2 visible intraphysical beings. The third individual, an unknown personality detected by the projector, may not be an intraphysical consciousness, but a simple mental projection. It can also be a visiting extraphysical consciousness, whether a friend or a stranger, or even another intraphysical being projected without the human body, who appeared there in the same manner as the projector.

Incongruous. Among sensitives and contactees (figures in UFOlogy), it has been very common to receive messages or extraphysical experiences about life on another planet – e.g.: Venus – that was verified through subsequent astronautic space research to be physically uninhabited, thus certainly correctly interpreting the message as being incongruous.

Ambiguities. Nevertheless, in many of these incongruous cases, the parapsychic reception or the extraphysical visualization was authentic and correct, not with respect to the environment of the physical surface of the planet in question, but with regard to the structures and formations of the extraphysical dimension that encircles it or, better still, with which it coexists.

Extraphysical consciousnesses. On the other hand, it is not difficult to find extraphysical consciousnesses, even quite frequently when one is projected, who consider the projected intraphysical consciousness to be an extraphysical consciousness. This demonstrates that extraphysical errors in interpretation are also easily committed by non-humans, because everything depends on the pattern or filter of the vehicle's perceptions where the consciousness is manifesting at that moment, regardless of who it is and the personal condition.

Adjustment. Each consciential vehicle leads the consciousness (you), to actually correctly perceive only the dimension to which it is *native* or autochthonous or, in other words, its specific environment in which the vehicle is adjusted to function in an adequate and maximal manner, and not the other coexisting and interpenetrating dimensions that are undeveloped with respect to extraphysical perspicuity, or evolved in regard to the progression of consciousnesses.

Bibliography: Blackmore (147, p. 5), Greene (635, p. 85), Vieira (1762, p. 131), Yram (1897, p. 148).

XIV – The Projector and Projections

---

409.   TYPES   OF   PROJECTOR

Definition. Consciential projector: that intraphysical consciousness who produces the projection of his/her consciousness, whether in an *intraphysical* or extraphysical manner, or who projects his/her consciousness (him/herself) from the human body, in the psychosoma or mentalsoma, in an accidental, assisted, spontaneous, intentional, deliberate or self-provoked (self-projection) manner, as well as that person who promotes the exteriorization of his/her consciential energies through the holochakra.

Synonymy: astral ambulant; astral explorer; astral itinerant; astral nomad; astral observer; astral projector; astral researcher; astral traveler; *astralnaut;* consciential voyager; describer of multidimensionality; explorer of transcendence; exteriorist; exteriorizer; exteriorizing sensitive; extraphysical flier; extraphysical researcher; extraphysical scrutinizer; extraphysical sentinel; healthy extraphysical insomniac; *incarnate* being who is semi-free from the human body; lucid projection executor; lucid projection practitioner; OBEer; OB-Experimenter; OOBEer; OOB-Experimenter; parapsychonaut; projectant; projectator; projectionaut; projectionist; projectist sensitive; psychonaut; receiver-generator of leading-edge ideas; self-projector; spiritual traveler; unfolder; unfolding sensitive.

Characterization. It would not be correct to categorize intraphysical projectors into stereotypes because each human being possesses specific, extremely personal characteristics, which are difficult to characterize.

Differences. All human individuals are profoundly different from each other, structurally as well as biochemically. For this reason, strictly speaking, it seems to be an incorrect scientific orientation to label persons, microcosms or complex minds, elements which, in fact, are impracticable to classify absolutely.

Types. In spite of what has been written, in the interest of elementary analysis, some dominant aspects in the personality of intraphysical projectors can be listed, which result in the following types: nocturnal, diurnal; novice; veteran; empirical, technician; occasional, active; seasonal or bissextile; nonlucid erratic or "gate-crasher"; clairvoyant, precognitive, psychometric, retrocognitive, telekinetic, telepathic, bilocator; astral, mental; sensitive, communicant, clandestine; blind from birth, myopic, colorblind; amputated; pregnant-projector; child, consciousness of the fetus; tangible (*inter vivos* apparition, physical bilocation); exoprojector; and psychonaut or astralnaut.

Desoma. Through extraphysical experiments, the lucid projector gradually learns to *die in peace* or, in other words, can serenely pass through the transition of death or deactivation of the human body (desoma) when his/her time arrives.

Apprenticeship. In light of this fact, the lucid projector is the *apprentice* of death. On the other hand, the lucid projector – cooperating with the extraphysical helpers to aid those who are undergoing the biological shock of physical death, final projection – is undoubtedly an *assistant to death*.

Catalyst. The projector-catalyst is that individual who stimulates persons to lucidly project from the human body, sometimes merely with their physical or extraphysical presence, acting in an energetically positive manner, as opposed to those sterilizing human beings who are capable of inhibiting parapsychic phenomena wherever they appear and manifest themselves.

Historical projectors. The following are 7 eminent projectors, cataloged by human history in and before the twentieth century:

1. Emily Brontë (1818-1848).
2. George Eliot (pen name of Mary Anne Evans: 1819-1880).
3. David Herbert Lawrence (1885-1930).

    4. Alfred Tennyson (1809-1892).
    5. John Buchan Tweedsmuir (1875-1940).
    6. Virginia Woolf (1882-1941).
    7. William Wordsworth (1770-1850).

Cosmoethical. The facts show that an ample cultural background, profound specialization, genius, erudition and even lucid projectability – a faculty with physiological foundations – can exist in the individual in an accentuated manner without any cosmoethical connotation.

Existential recycling. A single, full, lucid projection can trigger and install the condition of existential recycling in the life of the individual, but this is very rare. Strictly speaking, only one or a few lucid projections is not always sufficient to renew a human personality, who is almost always repressed and crystallized by personal bad habits.

Awareness. Only major lucid projections, when repeated, continued, in series, can lead the intraphysical consciousness to become aware of the existence and scope of cosmoethics, its laws and consequences, by him/herself.

Writers. The following examples, from the previous observation, are 3 great historical-projector-writers who experienced lucid projection and nevertheless lamentably ended their days on earth through suicide, or self-elimination:

    1. Virginia Woolf (1882-1941), the brilliant, ill English novelist.
    2. Ernest Miller Hemingway (1899-1961), awarded the Nobel prize for literature in 1954.
    3. Arthur Koestler (1905-1983), internationally renowned journalist and writer.

Notables. Among the self-projectors who achieved notoriety for their spontaneous and/or voluntarily provoked experiences, the following 22 should be singled out.

     1. Alexander Tanous ("Alex").
     2. Alfred Lischka.
     3. Anne-Marie Dinkel.
     4. Dadaji (Chowdhury).
     5. Douglas M. Baker.
     6. Douglas Scott Rogo (1952-1990).
     7. Francis Lefebure.
     8. Hamilton Prado (1907-1972).
     9. Hugh G. Callaway ("Oliver Fox").
    10. Ingo Swann.
    11. Johannes E. Hohlenberg.
    12. John Cunninghan Lilly (1915-).
    13. Marcel Louis Fohan ("Yram") (1884-1917).
    14. Olof Jonsson.
    15. Reinhard Fischer.
    16. Richard A. Greene.
    17. Robert Allan Monroe.
    18. Sathya Sai Baba (1926-).
    19. Stuart Keith Harary (1953-).
    20. Sylvan Joseph Muldoon.
    21. Vincent Newton Turvey (1827-1912).
    22. Yvonne do Amaral Pereira (1906-1984).

Backgrounds. It is important to highlight the universal and physiological character of the lucid projection phenomenon, which is also evidenced through disparities in the temperaments, cultural backgrounds, occupations and personal interests of the individuals who dedicated themselves to producing and/or researching consciential phenomena. An example of this is encountered in these same well-known personalities – artists: Johannes E. Hohlenberg, Ingo Swann; scientists: paleobotanist Robert Crookall; spiritists: Sylvan Joseph Muldoon, Yvonne do Amaral Pereira; executive: Robert Allan Monroe; mystics: Sathya Sai Baba, Marcel Louis Fohan; occultists: Hugh G. Callaway, Francis Lefebure; parapsychologists: Stuart Keith Harary, Douglas Scott Rogo; politicians: Hamilton Prado – besides sensitives of various parapsychic modalities.

Blind. There are *blind experts* in all fields of human knowledge: the cold professor who spoils the subject in the mind of the students; the librarian who is opposed to lending books; the literary critic who is condescending toward poets; the botanist who is blind to the beauty of flowers; the child psychologist who makes children flee in terror. In projectiology we encounter the projector who is *self-consciencially blind,* who avoids the subject of lucid projection. Generally, the cause of this is interconsciential intrusion (fear, phobia) or egoism (sectarianism, factiousness). This should not be confused with the *physically blind* lucid projector.

Left-handedness. In investigations performed up until now with advanced consciential projectors, no greater incidence has been observed of left-handed individuals or, in other words, persons who evidence a deep spontaneous tendency toward a preponderant use of the left hand. The same holds true regarding left-eyed individuals, who show a tendency to use only the left eye when employing monocular vision (aiming a gun, using a monocular microscope).

Percentage. The percentage of left-handed individuals, in both aforementioned independent forms, is the same as in the general population: 10%, one in ten persons.

Parachutist. The parachutist projector is that one which leaves the human body inactive in the seat of an airplane in flight and departs in the psychosoma to have a lucid projection.

Urbanite. Undoubtedly, the *urban* (city dweller, urbanite) lucid projector in hectic daily life, is more vulnerable to projective recess than the *rural* lucid projector, who leads a calmer, simpler life, using a more tranquil physical base. With regard to this point, it is worth observing that modern city inhabitants come into contact with more persons in one week than a country person would encounter, in feudal times, in his/her entire intraphysical life.

Coexistence. The lucid projector is the only individual capable of coexisting, even if in an occasional and temporary manner, with striking personalities from anonymous or noted lives, from the recent or remote past, components of former terrestrial humanity.

Bibliography: Baker (69, p. 14), Butler (228, p. 153), David-Neel (368, p. 46), Granger (620, p. 204), Greene (635, p. 77), Greenhouse (636, p. 13), Guirao (663, p. 127), Hemingway (710, p. 53), Horia (757, p. 115), Koestler (854, p. 352), Lilly (926, p. 24), Morris (1093, p. 147), Murphet (1109, p. 142), Salley (1496, p. 157), Steiger (1602, p. 153), Vieira (1762, p. 123), Walker (1781, p. 57), Yram (1896, p. 124).

---

410. DAZZLED PROJECTORS

Definition. Dazzled projector: the intraphysical consciousness who has never had self-critique, or who actually lost self-critique, in the analysis of his/her own projective experiences.

Synonymy: fanatical projector; foolish projector; traumatized projector.

Attitudes. Because planet earth is simultaneously an evolutionary school and a mega-hospital for consciousnesses, we encounter attitudes which are extremely complex that overwhelm incautious, borderline, confused intraphysical and extraphysical beings, which end up constantly living at the edge, in an indefinite or mixed condition that is indefensibly ill or unevolved.

Extraphysical consciousnesses. There are extraphysical consciousnesses which are simultaneously benefactors-malefactors, morbid bisexuals or sick androgynes. For this reason, there are ambiguous lines of parapsychic practices, both good (healthy) and bad (pathological), of white magic and black magic, of *Umbanda* and *Quimbanda,* of anti-goety and goety. We come across projector-sensitives confused by thanatophobia or the fear of death of the human body. They are intraphysical and extraphysical personalities which are profoundly parapsychic but, nevertheless, are excessively mystical and have no rationality in their practices or a more ample discernment in their priority attitudes.

Maturity. The decision for options that are mature and transparent, although non-absolute, pertaining to leading-edge relative truth and sought out with lucidity, characterizes those consciousnesses which are able to achieve a greater consciential maturity or a more ample recuperation of cons. The dazzled projector is listed among those beings who have still not achieved this greater level of consciential maturity.

Prudence. All compulsion or eagerness to communicate pleasant projective experiences to others should be seasoned with prudence, good sense and judgment by you, as a lucid projector.

Principles. We need to recognize that it is natural and human to be eager to share the happiness, enthusiasm and climate of mentalsomatic elevation inspired by certain impactful extraphysical experiences. However, the communication of these experiences to others, or to strangers, will not always be productive or successful if 4 fundamental principles are not obeyed: the person, time, location and form.

1. **Person.** The communication should be made to the right person, one who is able to understand the subject of lucid projection.

2. **Time.** The communication needs to be made at a time that is opportune for both the projector and especially for the listener.

3. **Location.** The communication needs to be transmitted in circumstances and a location that is propitious to its understanding.

4. **Form.** The communication can only be intelligible with adequate words and expressions, according to the level of the listener.

Causes. Among the causes responsible for the dazzling of certain projectors, at least the following 4 should be singled out:

1. **Extraphysicology.** Inexperience regarding extraphysical experiences.

2. **Intraphysical euphoria.** Uncontrolled intraphysical euphoria.

3. **Indiscipline.** Mental indiscipline.

4. **Self-critique.** A total lack of self-critique.

Effects. The following are 8 effects relevant to the dazzling that affects the intraphysical projector:

1. **Triumphalism.** The negative tendency toward triumphalism, which is common when the projector produces substantial extraphysical experiences by him/herself early on, in the first projections.

2. **Extraphysical euphoria.** Frequent extraphysical euphoria.

3. **Traumas.** Extraphysical traumas.

4. **Projectiography.** Difficulty in the physical-extraphysical investigation of one's own experiments.

5. **Projectiocritique.** Indifference regarding the subsequent conscientious analysis of extraphysical events.

6. **Psychosomatics.** An exacerbated sense of a presumed *personal mission.*

7. **Contradictions.** A loss of control in the management of personal *inner contradictions,* as a consciousness, in the face of rational human and extraphysical observations.

8. **Recess.** The sterilizing effects of projective bedazzlement can induce long periods of recess in the practice of lucid projections, for the projector lacking self-critique, or can inhibit them completely, especially those *projections assisted* by extraphysical helpers.

Immaturity. The material presented thus far allows the examination of the facts from another angle. Consciential immaturity regarding extraphysicology, which is responsible for the appearance of hypnotized conformists, dyed-in-the-wool skeptics, natural somnambulants and post-desomatic parapsychotics also shows itself to be a main sponsor of projective bedazzlement. There is nothing better for combating it than serenity, discernment and sincere realism in the face of personal ignorance regarding universal intraconsciential and extraconsciential phenomena.

Bibliography: Vieira (1762, p. 83).

411. TECHNIQUES FOR DEVELOPMENT OF THE PROJECTOR

Philosophy. Diverse forms of knowledge can coexist within the human being. Besides popular knowledge and scientific knowledge, philosophical knowledge and religious (theological) knowledge, for example, also exist. Philosophical knowledge is valuational, because its starting point consists in hypotheses that cannot be submitted to observation. For this reason, philosophical knowledge is unverifiable, since the enunciations of philosophical hypotheses, as opposed to that which occurs in the field of conventional science, cannot be confirmed. Aside from this, it is rational, systematic, infallible and exact.

Theology. Religious or theological knowledge is based upon doctrines that contain propositions which are *sacred*, because they have been revealed through the supernatural, or inspirational. For this reason, these truths are considered infallible, irrefutable and exact. Their evidence is not verified.

Knowledge. It is worthwhile for the more lucid intraphysical consciousness, whether scientist, philosopher, professional or ordinary person, to confront the existing attitudes, perspectives and languages between two forms of knowledge, scientific and popular or, in other words, between the objective theory of the essentially conjectural knowledge of science and the theory of knowledge based upon common sense. This should be done in order to choose the best directive to observe, explain and decide upon in any sector of day-to-day experience.

Comparisons. The following are 10 comparisons that can make any of us think about priorities:

1. **Uses.** Individuals or intraphysical consciousnesses use popular, familiar, or common-sense knowledge in a spontaneous manner, following acritical customs, which hinder more conscious and productive analysis. In the field of science, the directives are employed in an elaborated manner only after testing the research hypotheses regarding the fact under analysis and the establishment of basic concepts.

2. **Acquisitions.** Common sense is based upon intuition which is simple, lightly pondered, inner unsystematized information, or is the fruit of these casual, unmethodical, unsystematic, fragmentary and ingenuous experiences. Science puts rigor in its methods – inductive, deductive, reductive, observational, experimental, statistical, comparative – for the acquisition of information, offering plausible and rational explanations that are submitted to verification with discernment.

3. **Perspective.** Common sense uses sources of information which are not reliable because they stem strictly from the ego, or inner information, *equanimous content*. Science, which is never personal, distances personal distortions as much as possible, focusing on perspectives that are within the neutrality of universalism or interdisciplinarity.

4. **Objectives.** Common sense is based on the memory of suppositions and personal experiences which were generally not sufficiently reflected upon in order to be reduced to a general formulation. It nevertheless attempts, in this way, to achieve an understanding which is intended to be universal. Science pursues objectives that lead to an integrated and internally coherent body of knowledge.

5. **Open.** It is well known that human beings generally tend to arbitrarily seek support for the beliefs which they already have and do not consider, or are often frankly unaware of, the negative data (utilitarian myopia). Scientific knowledge maintains the sense of scrutiny as open as possible in the observer in order to avoid preconceptions in its perspectives and analyses that constantly require questioning, heterocritiques or refutations.

6. **Procedures.** Common sense respects the words of someone considered to have authority according to the common criterion of the individual observer, or the pre-critical manner of knowing. Scientific knowledge, structured upon a foundation of classified information, uses the systematic procedures of observation and experimentation that is visible to all.

7. **Formalizations.** Common sense is characteristically informal and almost always simplistic: having two negative beliefs to choose from, it opts for an arbitrary preference. Scientific, objective knowledge is based upon the formal directives of pure logic in order to evaluate the evidence encountered with differentiated treatment.

8. **Directives.** Common sense provides imprecise directives which are not always healthy, notably in the evaluation of complex questions, because it makes approximations of things and processes which are essentially different. Science creates well-thought-out techniques in order to verify its principles through research programs that the intraphysical consciousness endeavors to follow, preferably in direct experiments in the laboratory.

9. **Accumulations.** The principles of common sense tend to accumulate in a disorderly manner (fragmentariness), beyond the reach and control of the observer's self-critique. Science applies a selective process of accumulation, establishing discipline, questions and presenting hypotheses and theories – which are in perpetual mutation – in all of its research which, if not verifiable, can be *corroborated.*

10. **Rationality.** Popular knowledge, as positive as it may be, always presents weaknesses because it is self-taught, sometimes emotional, and frequently quasi-instinctive. Scientific knowledge, as it is strictly rational and based upon proofs – although being fallible, because it is not definitive, absolute or final – allows fewer misses or, in other words: more hits.

Conclusion. It cannot be denied that the existence of a grain of truth always stems from common, pre-critical good sense or from the practical concerns of daily life. Science is nevertheless unquestionably the last word in the intelligent approach to any question, phenomenon, or problem pertaining to the human being. This is why the production of lucid consciential projections customarily develops better and evolves more rapidly when exposed to the light of the scientific research of projectiology, the science of self-lucid projection.

Actions. The nature of consciential actions differs when the consciousness establishes its bases or consciential attributes predominantly in the psychosoma or mentalsoma in order to direct its existence.

Psychosomatics. The following can be expected from a psychosomatic foundation: animality, emotionalism, precipitation, indiscipline, illusion, romanticism, idealism, art, passion, form, superficiality, ingenuousness, infantilism, simplism, egocentrism or, in other words, extraphysical immaturity.

Mentalsomatics. The following can be expected from a mentalsomatic foundation: conscientiality, rationality, realism, ponderation, discipline, science, universalism, content, depth, erudition, in summary, extraphysical maturity.

Evolution. All of us, human beings, are natural lucid projectors (paragenetics), but are not all *evolved* natural lucid projectors. For this it becomes necessary to willingly pay the high price or toll in terms of time, energy, effort, training and perseverance in our projective development.

Continuation. A single lucid projection experience can induce changes in you, as an active projector, which allows you to have other projections more easily. Having begun to produce lucid projections, you can repeat it every night. After you have learned how to project, nothing can keep you from continuing to practice lucid projection.

Procedure. The ideal or most intelligent procedure for you, as a lucid projector, is to perseveringly develop your projective talents to the utmost, regardless of which positive or healthy techniques are used, and confront challenges in the extraphysical dimensions without any fear or discouragement.

Crescendos. *Phenomenic crescendos* arise within the phenomenology of projectiology. For example, the projective aura can evolve to traveling clairvoyance, which can evolve to full lucid projection, which can finally evolve to positive or balanced waking discoincidence. These are 4 distinct, well-characterized phenomena that manifest in a natural development or succession.

Phenomenology. Phenomena have permanent independence: they neither remain fixed in their manifestations, nor do they obey theoretical systematic ordering.

Self-performance. In projective development, you, as a projector, are challenged to endeavor to achieve or conquer 15 logical goals in your performance:

1. **Density.** Increase or decrease the density of your psychosoma according to environmental needs (psychosomatics).

2. **Self-lucidity.** Deepen the sensation of being situated as a self-lucid consciousness inside a subtle body (generally the psychosoma).

3. **Hyperacuity.** Expand your own lucidity (cons and *paracons*) during the self-lucid disconnection (takeoff) at a level superior to that of ordinary, waking awareness in the human body.

4. **Holochakrology.** Learn to neutralize the energetic attractive force of the silver cord or, in other words: of the holochakra.

5. **Distancing.** Project yourself a long distance from the physical base.

6. **Chronology.** Project yourself in extraphysical excursions of long duration.

7. **Mnemosomatics.** Recall extraphysical successes in their entirety with memories which are clearer than recollections of facts from material life (intraphysicology).

8. **Self-coherence.** Maintain polymorphic, coherent activity over an extended period of time during a single lucid consciential projection.

9. **Takeoff.** Overcome the difficult phase existing between the vibrational state and the full lucid takeoff in the psychosoma.

10. **Parapsychomotricity.** Improve the available techniques for producing projection while awake and even while moving intraphysically (somatics).

11. **Self-cognition.** Know how to acquire knowledge of indisputable intraconsciential value from evolved extraphysical consciousnesses during extraphysical experiments.

12. **Projectiology.** Promote various consecutive projections by yourself in a single session, whether during the day or night.

13. **Holosomatics.** Simultaneously examine your own human body and psychosoma, which are separated from the state of coincidence of the vehicles of manifestation.

14. **Paraperceptiology.** Develop the paraperceptions of the psychosoma in order to receive the *mental waves* (holothosene) of evolved extraphysical dimensions on all necessary occasions.

15. **Subtle.** Know how to decompose the coarse substances of the psychosoma, when laden, purifying it for more elevated flights or excursions to the subtle dimensions of the consciousness.

Refinement. Besides the aforementioned, you, as a projector, can refine or hone the organization of the psychosoma (psychosomatics) with these 4 arrangements, whenever possible:

1. **Fragments.** Avoid displaying isolated fragments of the psychosoma in your extraphysical manifestation.

2. **Undefined.** Remove incoherent shapes and undefined traits from your psychosoma.

3. **Paramorphology.** Remain well-defined according to the *anthropomorphic shape* or humanoid form of the clear shapes of your psychosoma.

4. **Agility.** Operate productively, in an independent and agile manner, outside the human body, with a luminous, subtle figure.

Crowning. As a crowning of your efforts, you should gradually improve personal lucid projection techniques in such a way that you can expect effective conscious assistance in your own process of undergoing biological death, somatic self-deactivation or final self-projection (desomatics) with certainty and without fantasy, as a practical and final objective of human life.

Goal. To pass through physical walls, to sharply focus beyond the physical eyes, to visit friends without using the human body, to extraphysically and freely volitate in the open air, merely for the pleasure of enjoying the extraordinary state of temporary freedom, does not represent everything. It should also not be the full extent of what you long for or aspire to as a personal goal.

Assistentiology. You should not overlook the learning which occurs through the exercise of extraphysical assistance, as a daily evolutionary megagoal for the consciousness who is avid for knowledge, on the way of self-lucid evolution, without losing sight of the conquest of new stages within the progressive scale of projections of the consciousness, including the ample mentalsomatic projection.

Bibliography: Frost (560, p. 67), Vieira (1762, p. 141).

---

412. PROJECTIVE RECESS

Definition. Projective recess: the existential phase of the intraphysical consciousness which is characterized by the spontaneous cessation – almost always temporary – of lucid projective experiences, within a sequence of self-lucid and intensive projective experiments.

Synonymy: blocking of consciential self-projectability; declining phase of projectability; intermittency of projectability; period of low projective production; projective anti-trance state; projective vacation; spontaneous cessation of projections; suspension of self-projectability.

Similarities. In the same way that the following 5 categories of similar known occurrences exist, periods of recess in the practice or production of human consciential projection experiences also occur:

1. **Psi-missing.** the absence of extrasensory perception and physical parapsychic effects, the reverse effect, or psi-missing.

2. **Disturbances.** The effect of disturbing factors upon the parapsychic phenomena of physical effects, such as a light shining directly into the eyes of the observer-researcher.

3. **Psi-blocker.** The influence of the *sterilizing person,* the adverse sensitive or the psi-blocker, who impedes the production of the physical effect parapsychic phenomenon with his/her physical presence.

4. **Planchette.** The occurrence of the so-called *dead planchette* condition, due to the incompatibility of the vibrations, energies or powers of the parapsychic research group.

5. **Suspension.** The temporary or definitive suspension, or decline, and extinction of various types of parapsychism.

Energy. The 6 (1 + 5) above-cited categories of similar occurrences have a common denominator: the qualitative and/or quantitative alteration of consciential energies of the producer of the animic-parapsychic phenomena, including here the lucid projection experience.

Causes. The following 14 other relevant factors, for example, can be listed as being among the obscure causes of recess in the practice of lucid projection:

1. **Alienation.** A process sponsored by the helpers in order to avoid the condition of intraphysical alienation of the human projector and his/her *human* or *psychophysical anchoring.*

2. **Nosology.** The intercurrence of an illness.

3. **Intoxication.** Toxic causes (drugs, food).

4. **Changes.** A change in residence or a transferring of the intraphysical base.

5. **Trauma.** Consciential trauma of the practitioner.

6. **Holochakrology.** The ending of the condition of looseness of the holochakra with the reattachment of its energetic connections.

7. **Blockage.** Mental blockage of an indeterminate cause.

8. **Therapeutics.** The use of necessary and correctly administered medications.

9. **Accident.** Physical accident.

10. **Chronology.** Alterations in the human schedule and occupation of the lucid projector.

11. **Self-disorganization.** A predominance of indiscipline or a lack of organization in the personal habits of the intraphysical consciousness.

12. **Anticosmoethical.** The improper utilization of lucid projection experiences from the point of view of a cosmoethical life or, in other words, without the indispensable cosmoethical values.

13. **Helpers.** The healthy intervention of the extraphysical helpers due to reasons which are justifiable but unbeknownst to the projector.

14. **Pressure.** The pressure upon the practitioner – of tensions, stresses or crises, which are evolutionary and even very useful to intraphysical material life – that is not well coped with.

Swedenborg. With regard to this condition known as projective recess, which occurs after an intense series of assisted lucid projections, it is worth reading the entire item 1,166, of *Diarii Spiritualis*, by Emanuel Swedenborg – the precursor of projectiological phenomenology – namely, the pioneer of projectiology, written in Latin, the universal language of his time, more than 2 centuries ago, or precisely on March 4, 1748 (5 Volumes: Partis Primae; Volumen Primum; XIV + 450 p.; 21.5 cm.; bound.; Londini; William Newbery; 1844; p. 331):

> "Cum itaque nunc paene per tres annos, seu 33 menses in eo statu fuerim, ut mens mea a corporeis quidem abducta, interesse potuerit societatibus spiritualium et coelestium, et usque fuerim sicut alius in societate hominum, absque ulla differentia, quod irat quoque sunt spiritus, sed usque dum intense inhaeserim mundanis cogitatione, ut dum curas habui de necessariis pecuniis, et hodie epistolam scripsi, sic ut in iis animum aliquantum detinuerim, tunc in statum quasi corporeum lapsus sum, ut non potuerint spiritus mecum loqui, sicut etiam dixerunt, quod quasi absentes fuerint, similiter paene quoque prius; inde scire possum, quod spiritus nequeant loqui cum homine, qui curis mundanis et corporeis impense studet, nam corporea detrahunt quasi ideas mentis, et immergunt corporeis".

> ("For almost 3 years, that is, for 33 months, I have languished lately in such a state of spirit that my consciousness, which was distanced from human matters, could be in the societies of spiritual and celestial beings and, nonetheless, I remained as though I were any other man, in the company of men, without any difference, and this surprised the spirits themselves. In spite of this, when I had to f ully occupy my thoughts with mundane matters – as when I had to confine myself to subjects related to necessary expenses, and when I had to write a letter today – in a manner that kept my mind occupied with these subjects for some time, I then fell into a corporeal state, shall we say, such that the spirits could not communicate with me. They then told me that they had remained absent, almost in the same manner as before. I can thus deduce that the spirits cannot speak with a person who is excessively devoted to human and material preoccupations, because corporal cares can comparatively pull the ideas of the mind, and immerse them in corporal matters.").

Lack. The lack or absence of lucid projection exercises is keenly felt by the intraphysical consciousness who is used to the experiences.

Effects. The following are 5 consciential effects stemming from a well-defined period of projective recess, occurring after a sequential series of intensive consciential projections:

1. **Loss.** A sensation of a loss of important existential values.
2. **Source.** Feeling as though a source of extreme significance had dried up.
3. **Marginalization.** A sensation that the consciousness is marginalized from real life, out of touch with essential issues.
4. **Sublevel.** A sensation of being at sublevel in regard to the vital productivity of the consciousness itself.
5. **Neutral.** A sensation of being "in neutral" in relation to the rhythm of life and the universe, which proceeds without interruption.

Types. In practice, projective recess can be classified into 2 types:

1. **Absolute.** A recess from projection is absolute when the projector remains for a period without enjoying the condition of extraphysical self-awareness and, obviously, without having any recall of extraphysical experiences in the ordinary, physical waking state.
2. **Relative.** A recess from projection is relative when the projector knows, intuitively, that he/she continues enjoying lucidity while projected from the human body, although not having any recall subsequent to the extraphysical events.

Cessation. Besides the aforementioned, the projective recess, whether of the voluntary or involuntary practice of lucid projections, is generally a temporary interval which ceases immediately when the unsuspected cause which produced it stops, although it can, less frequently, mark the permanent or definitive cessation of projective experiences.

Assisted. Permanent projective recess, in certain cases, clearly shows that the lucid projections experienced by the intraphysical consciousness were produced exclusively under the sponsorship of the extraphysical helpers or, in other words, were assisted projections, even when this fact is unknown to the projector.

Prisoners. In this case, the experiences cease definitively, after the helpers no longer have plausible or justifiable reasons for aiding the intraphysical consciousness to project. This frequently occurs with ex-inmates of restrictive total institutions, particularly with ex-prisoners, ex-projectors, or released prisoners.

Paraphysiology. It seems that certain sporadic periods of projective recess are paraphysiological, in view of the vehicles of manifestation of the intraphysical consciousness. In the same way that physical anchoring occurs, through a psychophysiological anchor, a certain moderation in the manifestations of the projected intraphysical consciousness occurs or, in other words, a recess, or reduction in his/her activities outside the human body in favor of its preservation and the prioritization, at that moment, of the projector's physical life over extraphysical life.

Case study. The long-lasting recess characteristic of lucid projections occurs with young projectors who go though adolescence and reach 25 years of physical age experiencing spontaneous projections with a great frequency, for example. Later – due to essential alterations in human existence, particularly a loss of interest in extraphysical matters – they never again experience them.

Service. The phenomenon of lucid projection often involves complex implications which require sophisticated interpretation in order to be fully understood. For example, an intraphysical consciousness, upon intensifying assistential services to other evolutionary associates in human life, and therefore receiving a great number of requests from others – *intraphysical consciousnesses in lack,* as in the practices of penta when an extraphysical clinic has been installed – sometimes finds him/herself intentionally impeded, by the extraphysical helpers, from projecting from the human body with lucidity.

Appeals. This occurs because the solicitations and appeals made by others who already engage him/her in the situations of the ordinary, physical waking state can become very intense on the part of the *extraphysical consciousnesses in lack,* when the intraphysical consciousness (a minicog within a multidimensional, assistential, interconsciential maximechanism) becomes tangible in the paratropospheric extraphysical communities.

Parapopulations. These extraphysical scenarios are inevitable and are most characteristic of lucid consciential projections produced on this planet. It should be borne in mind that wherever needy intraphysical consciousnesses live, there are also needy extraphysical consciousnesses. It is estimated, from the experiences and statistics of projectors, that there are 9 extraphysical consciousnesses for every intraphysical consciousness on the earth, today at the end of the twentieth century. Of these, 3 extraphysical consciousnesses are worse than the author and you, from an evolutionary point of view, 3 extraphysical consciousnesses are similar to ourselves and 3 extraphysical consciousnesses are slightly better than us.

Productivity. In this case, the penta practitioner, for example, cannot always exclusively project with lucidity in evolved extraphysical dimensions. This would hinder the psychic and parapsychic atmosphere (holothosene), installing physical alienation. It would also reduce the progress of the fraternal services – the bases of self-aware evolution – with a reduction in the individual's human assistential productivity.

Regime. In light of the above, the projector is thus intelligently kept on a severe *bread and water* diet of *nonlucid and semilucid projections,* instead of receiving a likely and perhaps well-deserved treatment of *extraphysical privileges* which, in this period of execution of his/her existential program, would be inappropriate, inopportune, dislocated and undesirable.

Prevention. In order to overcome periods of recess in the lucid experiments, the projector must maintain a certain uniformity or pattern in his/her habits, as a *preventive* measure.

Solution. If the recess is already installed, the individual should, as a *solution,* seek to identify – with self critique and without feverishness or anguish – the real cause of the recess, in order to combat it.

Abstinence. Projective recess should not be confused with projective abstinence or the act of the intraphysical being avoiding unproductive extraphysical encounters, which generates *contraprojection.*

Facts. Projective recess is based upon 2 facts: *first,* the intraphysical consciousness somehow spontaneously projects every night upon sleeping, although not enjoying full lucidity or recollection of extraphysical events; *second,* the condition of projectability constitutes, above all, an animic attribute of the intraphysical consciousness, which is natural and physiological in human life, being exclusively dependent upon the projector and no one else; as well as the act of recovering projectability or improving projective performance.

Self-motivation. In light of the facts, the following can be affirmed: all recess in the practice of lucid projection will always be overcome if the intraphysical consciousness truly wishes and is sufficiently motivated to produce new lucid projections.

Doors. The following is a rational conclusion: once the doors to the extraphysical dimensions have been opened, they will never be completely closed to the intraphysical consciousness who opened them.

Bibliography: Andreas (36, p. 95), Grosso (650, p. 186), Kardec (825, p. 250), Mitchell (1059, p. 2), Monroe (1065, p. 204), Morrell (1088, p. 341), Schiff (1515, p. 120), Steiger (1601, p. 202), Swedenborg (1639, p. 313).

---

413. PROJECTIVE   QUESTIONNAIRE

Definition. Projective questionnaire: a series of selected questions with the aim of establishing the profile of lucid projections, or consciential experiences outside the human body.

Synonymy: list of questions about projectiology; list of questions for statistical analysis; multi-level questionnaire for the projector; projective survey.

Collection. The classic questionnaire is an instrument of data collection, made up of an ordered series of questions which should be answered in writing and without the presence of the interviewer. The researcher generally sends the questionnaire to the informant by mail or messenger. After filling it out, the research subject returns it in the same manner.

Standardized questions. This chapter gathers a numbered list of 200 standardized questions, which are both simple and complex items resulting from consciential experiences outside the human body. They require decisive responses, being used for research favoring the improvement of projectiological methods.

Statistics. These questions can and should be answered by you, whether a beginning or veteran lucid projector, young or old. For statistical reasons, keep your answers informative and concise, in order for them to be compared with the answers of other lucid projectors.

Responses. Many responses to the general questions on the phenomenon of lucid human projection can be found in the text of this book. Avoid basing your responses on what you read here or in other volumes.

Questions. It is worth pointing out that, in the field of any science that is in continuous progression, the greater the number of responses achieved, the greater will be the number of new questions generated, thereby creating a *hornets' nest of problems*.

Uses. Responding to the projective questionnaire is always useful for the practitioner of consciential projections, as he/she can better understand the consciential phenomena and express him/herself more accurately regarding the sensations and events that are extraphysically *witnessed* or experienced.

Convergencies. It also becomes useful to studious individuals in general who are able, with these responses, to collect testimonies, establish convergencies of pieces of evidence and conceive general methods that favor the development of projectiology, as has been done with statistical public opinion research.

Frankness. The readers should give frank responses to the questions which they consider pertinent to the issues of their personal projective experiences, bearing in mind that their observations will be used to benefit humanity and the progress of science.

Introduction:

1. Did the occurrences of lucid projection come as a surprise or did you find out about them through other persons?

2. Did you read books about the phenomenon of lucid projection before having experiences? Which books?

3. Are there any special incentives for you to lucidly project?

4. Where, when and how do you lucidly project yourself? Can you do so whenever you wish?

5. Are you a heavy sleeper or a light sleeper? Since when?

6. Can you give two reasons why you know you were projected?

7. Has the state of meditation, reflection and/or mental concentration helped you to conscientially project?

8. Have you received help in order to conscientially project? If you are in doubt, answer "no."

9. What is the best method for conscientially projecting? Explain.

10. What was your first lucid projection like?

Phenomenology:

11. Do you produce natural (pure) lucid projections, forced (impure) lucid projections, or both?

12. Does the vibrational state exist for you?

13. Do you acknowledge the imperfect exteriorization and interiorization of the intraphysical consciousness when projected?

14. Have you ever experienced an impactful *takeoff* of the consciousness (you) in the psychosoma?

15. Have you ever experienced an impactful *interiorization* in the psychosoma?

16. What was your longest lucid projection experience? Describe it.

17. What was your most relevant lucid projection experience?

18. Have you ever experienced the phenomenon of physical repercussion?

19. Have you ever felt the condition of physical catalepsy?

20. Have you ever passed through human beings while moving extraphysically without the human body?

Xenophrenia:

21. How do you distinguish between hallucination and lucid projection?

22. How do you distinguish between daydreams, dreams and the visions of lucid projection?

23. Have you ever dreamt about the phenomenon of lucid projection?

24. Have you ever been aware of dreaming while the dream was occurring? What happened?

25. What are the differences between dreams and morphothosenes?

26. Have you ever produced lucid projections which were initiated in the ordinary, physical waking state?

27. Have you ever produced lucid projections through the hypnagogic state?

28. Have you ever produced lucid projections through dreams? How?

29. What are the differences between extraphysical somnambulism and lucid projection?

30. Is the process of acquiring information through lucid projection the same as that of telepathy or clairvoyance?

Human physiology:

31. Is there a physical, somatic constitution which predisposes one to lucid projection?

32. Were you born by natural parturition, complicated (laborious) parturition or cesarean section?

33. Do you have a monovular twin sister or brother?

34. What is your heart rate?

35. Do you have a chronic illness? Which illness?

36. Have you ever undergone general anesthesia? Why?

37. What effect does the chloroform of medical-dental anesthesia have on lucid projection?

38. Does the gender of the intraphysical consciousness or intraphysical being influence lucid projection?

39. Is there a relationship between the cerebral bulb and takeoff? Why?

40. Can a sneeze (sternutation) provoke the discoincidence of the extraphysical hand or arm of the intraphysical consciousness through psychomotor impact? Why?

Coadjutants:

41. Do you have reliable coadjutants or adjutants for the production of lucid projection? Which ones?

42. What is the greatest influence upon lucid projection? Why?

43. Does a physical base at a high altitude facilitate lucid projection? Why?

44. Does corporal physical weight interfere in lucid projection? Why?

45. Does an adequate diet predispose lucid projection? Why?

46. Does respiration influence lucid projection?

47. Do infancy and advanced age predispose or impede lucid projection?

48. Can the exteriorization of energies be a coadjutant to lucid projections? How?

49. Do the chewing muscles participate in the process of lucid projection?

50. Do the cranial muscles act in lucid projection?

Soma:

51. Have you ever seen your human body while projected?

52. Have you ever seen the inside of the human body while outside it? Why?

53. Have you ever touched the human body while outside it? Where?

54. Up to what point can someone else touch or move the inactive human body without provoking the interiorization of the psychosoma? Why?

55. What is the greatest possible movement of the inactive human body during a prolonged projection of the intraphysical consciousness (you) at a distance?

56. Have you seen the human body with the extraphysical body (psychosoma) inside it?

57. Does the human body lose weight upon the exteriorization of the psychosoma during projection? Always?

58. Have you ever projected while the soma was standing?

59. Have you ever projected while the soma was moving? How?

60. Have you ever heard sounds upon leaving or entering the soma?

Silver cord:

61. Have you ever seen the silver cord extended *distant* from the human body?

62. Do the *size*, format, potency and action of the silver cord vary according to the projector and the consciential projection?

63. Is the volume of the silver cord greater when it is contracted or extended? Why?

64. What factors influence an increase in the perimeter of the silver cord's vigorous action?

65. Where are the bases of connection of the silver cord in the human body?

66. Do you accept the possibility of a twist or a *knot* in the silver cord? Why?

67. Is there a relationship between the cerebral cortex and the silver cord? Describe.

68. How do you imagine the condition of the silver cord during brain surgery, a laparotomy or thoracotomy?

69. What prevents sick extraphysical consciousnesses from rupturing the silver cord of the projected intraphysical being during extraphysical deintrusion?

70. Does the intraphysical consciousness – now an extraphysical consciousness recently arrived at the intermissive period – remain with the *stump* or umbilicus corresponding to the rupture of the silver cord?

Psychosoma:

71. What is the holochakra?

72. Does the holochakra influence physical repercussion?

73. Is there a relationship between the silver cord and the holochakra?

74. What is the precise nature of the psychosoma or emotional body?

75. Do imperfect takeoffs and interiorizations provoke damaging consequences for the human body and the psychosoma? Why?

76. What are the consequences of projection of the intraphysical consciousness in the psychosoma from a car, train, airplane, or with the human body in a vehicle in movement?

77. Is the interpenetration of the psychosomas of 2 projectors possible, given that both are of equal density while outside the human body? Why?

78. Does the density of the psychosoma outside the human body influence the quality of recall subsequent to self-lucid projections? Why?

79. Do solar, ultraviolet, infrared and other rays influence the psychosoma when it is denser outside the human body?

80. Is it possible to shape the projected psychosoma into gigantic forms, a dirigible for example? Why?

Mentalsoma:

81. Have you ever visited an extraphysical environment or community when without a form that is visible to yourself? How?

82. Have you already seen yourself using the mentalsoma? Describe.

83. Do emotions completely disappear while in the mentalsoma?

84. Does the *density* of the mentalsoma vary according to the extraphysical environment?

85. Are there differences between the consciential energies transmitted by the intraphysical consciousness while in the human body, projected in the psychosoma, or directly and isolatedly projected in the mentalsoma?

86. How do you distinguish between the condition of being solely in the mentalsoma and the condition of partial corporification outside the human body?

87. Does the consciousness only reach another solar system in the isolated mentalsoma? Why?

88. Are there differences between the intraphysical being projected in the mentalsoma and the projected extraphysical consciousness?

89. What are the practical consequences of the existence of the mentalsoma?

90. Is there a similarity between the golden cord and a remote control? Why?

Lucid projections:

91. Have you ever had an instantaneous lucid projection?

92. Have you ever suddenly projected unintentionally?

93. Have you ever had consecutive lucid consciential projections?

94. Have you ever projected yourself many times in a single day? Describe.

95. What is the most intense period of projections in series that you have ever experienced? Where? When?

96. Have you ever had recurring lucid projections?

97. Have you ever projected yourself while your eyelids were open?

98. Have you ever projected during a storm? Describe.

99. Have you ever projected yourself while inside a vehicle? Which vehicle?

100. Have you ever had experiences with children outside the human body?

Research:

101. Have you ever had an impactful experience with morphothosenes?

102. Have you ever performed technical experiments with lucid projections? Which experiments?

103. Have you ever visited an extraphysical community?

104. Have you ever been projected on another planet?

105. Have you ever moved some physical object while projected? Which object?

106. Have you ever had a picturesque extraphysical experience?

107. How do you deal with sexuality outside the body?

108. Have you ever had an experience outside the human body that would be considered sexual?

109. How would you evaluate your level of lucidity outside the human body?

110. Can lucid projection cure certain illnesses? Why?

Extraphysical translocation:

111. How do you orient yourself outside the human body? Always?

112. What do you have to say about volitation?

113. How does volitation work?

114. Is there a relationship between human respiration and volitation? Why?

115. Are there differences between individual volitation, or self-volitation, and group volitation? Why?

116. Have you ever encountered currents of force outside the human body?

117. How do you distinguish between an extraphysical current of force and volitation?

118. How do experienced projectors behave themselves during joint projections?

119. While outside the human body, have you ever seen two extraphysical consciousnesses with their auras coupled?

120. While outside the human body, have you ever seen a large group or team of extraphysical consciousnesses?

Para-human physiology (paraphysiology):

121. When projected, do you see yourself nude or clothed? Always?

122. Have you ever perceived a difference in your weight outside the human body?

123. Have you ever perceived phosphorescence in your extraphysical form?

124. How do you conceive the nature of the extraphysical body or the psychosoma?

125. Have you ever seen centers of force or energies in the extraphysical form?
126. Have you ever seen yourself partially exteriorized? How?
127. Have you ever looked at yourself in a mirror while projected with lucidity?
128. Have you ever seen your shadow, under the sun, while outside the human body?
129. What is the greatest extraphysical trauma? Why?
130. Which extraphysical events repeat themselves more frequently in lucid projections? Why?

Extraphysical encounters:

131. Have you ever encountered a friend projected and extraphysically self-aware?
132. Have you ever encountered an extraphysical consciousness in the extraphysical dimension which has recently entered the intermissive period?
133. Have you ever seen an exotic extraphysical artifact? What?
134. Have you ever been shocked outside the human body?
135. What is the strongest emotion that you have felt during a lucid projection?
136. Has anyone ever judged you to be *dead* or deceased while outside the human body?
137. Have you ever learned lessons in the extraphysical dimension? Which lessons?
138. How do you distinguish an intraphysical consciousness from an extraphysical consciousness when outside the human body?
139. Have you already discovered any unexpected personal disability outside the human body?
140. Have you identified any impressive personal performance outside the human body?

Extraphysical activities:

141. Have you ever been the victim of, or a witness to, extraphysical abduction or kidnapping?
142. Have you ever participated in the extraphysical assistential rescue of an intraphysical or extraphysical consciousness?
143. Are there practical ways to gain entrance into evolved extraphysical environments? Which?
144. Have you ever visited a military area closed to outside access during a lucid projection experience? What did you see?
145. Have you ever visited a cemetery mortuary chapel during a lucid projection? Describe.
146. Have you ever visited a slaughterhouse in operation during a lucid projection? Describe.
147. Have you ever helped someone through lucid projection?
148. Do you count on some extraphysical company when projecting?
149. What are the differences between thought-forms (morphothosenes) and real extraphysical images?
150. Have you encountered confirmation for your extraphysical experiences in this book? Which ones?

Obstacles to lucid projection:

151. Do you aware of having suffered intrusive influence at some time? Where? When? How?
152. Have you ever served as extraphysical assistential bait? How?
153. Have you ever had confrontations with extraphysical consciousnesses? Describe.
154. What are the limitations of lucid projection for you?
155. Are there harmful factors to lucid projection?
156. What is the greatest obstacle to lucid projection? Why?
157. Are there dangers or maleficences in the practice of lucid projection?
158. Has lucid projection provoked alienation in you regarding physical life?
159. Is there a human being who cannot conscientially project? Why?
160. Have you noticed incongruities in extraphysical facts? Why?

Personalities:

161. Have you, while projected, seen a pregnant woman in the ordinary, physical waking state?
162. How does the pregnant woman-projector behave with the consciousness of the fetus during her or their projection? Always?

163. Can young people, who are still in their growth phase, frequently project? Why?

164. Do you know a person, blind from birth, who is a lucid projector?

165. Do you know a former inmate who is a lucid projector?

166. Do you know of any crew member of an intercontinental airline who is a lucid projector?

167. Do you know a lucid projector who has an amputated leg?

168. Have you ever known anyone who projected while some part of the body was in a cast?

169. Do you know any color-blind projector?

170. Have you ever seen subhuman animals outside the human body? Which animals?

Parapsychism:

171. Do you think there is any psi factor in lucid projections? Which?

172. Does lucid projection help you practice and develop parapsychism? What type or mode of phenomenon?

173. How do you distinguish animism from parapsychism?

174. Have you ever practiced parapsychism while outside the human body? Which type?

175. Have you ever communicated through an intraphysical sensitive? How?

176. Do extraphysical technicians keep and accumulate the consciential energies that they extract? Why? How?

177. Have you ever perceived any extraphysical benefactor impeding your consciential projection? Why?

178. Do you see any similarities between the mutants of science fiction and extraphysical consciousnesses?

179. Has lucid projection convinced you of the survival of the ego (the consciousness) after biological death (first desoma)?

180. Were you skeptical regarding the survival of the ego prior to experiencing lucid projection?

Post-projective recall:

181. Have you previously accurately examined any extraphysical phenomenon? Which one? (Be as detailed as possible.)

182. What is the best extraphysical environment, community, district or situation that you recall?

183. Have you ever had a lucid projection without consciential blackout, from the beginning to the end of the experience?

184. Do extraphysical events develop for you naturally, rapidly or in slow motion? Why?

185. Have you ever had an impactful experience with chronological time while outside the human body?

186. Have you ever had lucid projections related to the past?

187. Have you ever had lucid projections related to the future?

188. How is your recall of the occurrences of lucid projections?

189. Do you have your own technique for remembering lucid projections? What is it?

190. Do you keep a journal of lucid projection experiences? Why?

Continuous self-awareness:

191. When producing lucid projections, have you ever experienced an entire day and night of continuous self-awareness?

192. Do you know of any intraphysical being who has enjoyed continuous self-awareness for days?

193. How do you see a world in which all the inhabitants have continuous self-awareness?

194. Does the free consciousness (FC) – an extraphysical consciousness – live in a permanent projection of uninterrupted awareness?

195. Does the free consciousness need to sleep and dream?

196. Do you see future benefits in experiences with lucid projections? Why?

197. Do you see any work hypothesis for lucid projection research?

198. Have you ever participated in a roundtable discussion on lucid projection? Where? When?

199. Do you think it is possible to create an extraphysical team composed of intraphysical lucid projectors?

200. Does ethical conduct intervene in the processes of lucid projection? Why? (Get to the heart of the question).

Mailing list. The International Institute of Projectiology and Conscientiology (IIPC) (CEP 70.000, 22422-970, Rio de Janeiro, RJ, Brazil; *Internet: e-mail* – iipc@iipc.org.br – *home page* – www.iipc.org) has for many years been compiling the Mailing List of Lucid Projectors and the Register of Lucid Projectors in its database on projectors and their unprecedented experiences outside the body, signed reports and written responses to specialized questionnaires including questions similar to those posed here.

Contribution. If you wish to contribute to the research and statistical analyses, please submit your personal information and respond to the questions to which you have answers or those which relate to your experiences. This should be done in accordance with your theoretical foundation of knowledge, your theoretical models or original explanations and your intuition on some question, citing the number of each question addressed here and submitting a signed copy for the records.

Anonymity. Also let us know if you prefer to remain anonymous, your information thereby being archived in a strictly confidential manner, or if the experiences can be analyzed in public and edited into a future book.

Database. The database on projectiology of the International Institute of Projectiology and Conscientiology has been archiving the greatest possible amount of information gathered through the following means: register of active lucid projectors, using forms; written records of lucid projections; the collection of responses to projectiological questionnaires; listings of questions gathered in public projectiological debates; a specialized library on projectiology; an international bibliography on projectiology; the live recording of reports by lucid projectors on cassette tapes; a video library with movies of projectiological interest; computerized storage (CD-ROMs, diskettes) of all data pertinent to projectiology by gathering as much information on international research as possible; and the cataloging of addresses of projectiological interest. This is being done in order to enable researchers to gather data and perform searches for certain responses about projectiology within seconds, which would previously have taken months.

Bibliography: Blackmore (139, p. 7), Crookall (338, p. 160), Frost (560, p. 221), Giovetti (593, p. 143), Greenhouse (639, p. 309), Greyson (643, p. 188), Mitchell (1059, p. 102), Neppe (1123, p. 19), Rogo (1444, p. 8), Sabom (1486, p. 70), Sherman (1551, p. 189), St. Clair (1593, p. 156), Stokes (1625, p. 24), Tinoco (1685, p. 185), Vieira (1762, p. 10), Zain (1898, p. 321).

---

414. THE IDEAL PROJECTOR

Definition. Ideal consciential projector: the idealized, theoretical image of the best existing intraphysical personality for the development of lucid projectability within conscientiometry research (conscientiogram).

Synonymy: exemplary projector; idealized projector; prototype of self-lucid projectors.

Prototype. The idealization of the prototype of projectors always serves to help interested individuals appraise and improve themselves through a useful comparison of personal qualities (strong traits) which are necessary for the practical evolution of self-lucid projectability.

Profile. In order to determine the physical and psychological profile of this imagined ideal projector, at least the majority of the following 27 qualities, traits or strong traits should be present.

1. **Assistentiology.** Compassion for all living things.
2. **Balance.** Calm indifference toward everything that constitutes the transitory world, accompanied by a just appreciation of it.
3. **Biomemory.** A cultivated biomemory.
4. **Coexistology.** Peaceful coexistence.
5. **Cosmoethics.** Veracity or an absence of pathothosenes.
6. **Courage.** Courage in all emergencies.
7. **Culture.** Personal humanistic culture (polymathy).
8. **Curiosity.** A healthy, innate and useful curiosity (a scientifically curious intraphysical consciousness).
9. **Deconditioning.** Religious, scientific and social deconditioning.
10. **Habits.** Good habits of intraphysical life.
11. **Health.** Adequate physical health.
12. **Holosomatics.** Physical or somatic self-control.
13. **Inclination.** An inclination toward reading, studying and researching.
14. **Intentionality.** Absolute mental purity (cosmoethical intentionality).
15. **Introspection.** Introspection with discipline in thought (mentalsomatics).
16. **Neophilia.** Fearlessness and neophilia.
17. **Patience.** Nonconformity with patience.
18. **Relaxation.** An advanced capacity for psychophysical relaxation.
19. **Respiration.** An ample thorax with a large lung capacity.
20. **Self-control.** Nervousness with consciential self-control.
21. **Self-critique.** Self-critique regarding priority thosenizations.
22. **Self-discernment.** Good sense or natural self-discernment.
23. **Self-organization.** Someone who is reasonably well organized.
24. **Self-thosenization.** An elevated capacity for psychic absorption or a deep involvement in experiences in general (self-thosenity).
25. **Solidarity.** Total cosmoethical detachment.
26. **Temperament.** A temperament that is more rational-scientific and less mystical-religious.
27. **Will.** The application of ironclad will in the practice of lucid projection.

Complete. The following 6 final, practical finishing touches of aptitude for lucid projection serve to complete the personality of the "superwoman" or "superman", in regard to the imagined ideal projector:

1. **Bed.** Uses a single bed for projective experiments.
2. **Cardiology.** Has a low heart rate.
3. **Clock.** Practices lucid projection between midnight and 4 o'clock in the morning, or in the second half of the night (biological or somatic clock).
4. **Dorsal.** Always lies in the dorsal position on a springless mattress.
5. **Duo.** He/she is part of an evolutionary duo (daily sex).
6. **Homeostasis.** Does not present any significant psychological problem (fissure) regarding the future (intraconsciential homeostasis).

Discernment. The characteristic which perhaps is indispensable in the traits of the ideal projector is the discernment that he/she peacefully presents in regard to him/herself in a comparison of lucid projection with the diverse altered states of consciousness related to the phenomenon, such as: projection in the psychosoma; projection in the mentalsoma; semilucid projection; ordinary dreams; dreams about lucid projection; nightmares; daydreams; and the hypnagogic state. All this while still knowing how to understand and coexist with ambiguities, evolving "treading a fine line" without remaining "seated on the fence."

Ambiguities. The concessions, or ambiguities – made with effective lucidity and maturity, and applied with individual freewill, selected and under constant observation and renovation (paying attention to *pattern-behavior* and *exception-behavior),* with the intention of diminishing their quantity and improving their quality – allow the intraphysical consciousness to conquer his/her obligations in a cohesive, *en bloc,* uninterrupted manner all at once. The individual accomplishes this without leaving undesirable traces *(smudged thosenic signatures)* in his/her conduct, unfinished tasks in his/her existential file with regard to the execution of the existential program, or a negative final balance (existential incompletism, *intraphysical melancholy,* extraphysical melancholy) in the holokarmic account of his/her human life.

Seeker. The best or most effective projector will always be: the psychic, or more appropriately parapsychic, self-made individual; the transcendent athlete wishing to break his/her own records, the disciplined person seeking to be a healthy perfectionist, from an extraphysical point of view, and only for him/herself; the perseverant seeker of leading-edge relative truths who is never satisfied and never tires of striving toward self-knowledge.

Stresses. In order for you to achieve a higher degree of effectiveness in the practices which are characteristic of the ideal projector, there is nothing better than taking care of your physical, mental and consciential health through measures that can save you from stress. This can be done by following these 20 criteria, which are currently generally recommended for all individuals by conscientiotherapy:

1. **Somatics.** Maintain good health, while also keeping an eye on your vision, hearing and teeth.
2. **Nutrition.** Eat at least one hot, balanced meal per day.
3. **Beverages.** Drink less than 3 cups of coffee, tea or soft drinks per day.
4. **Alcoholism.** If you drink alcoholic beverages, always do so in moderation.
5. **Tobaccoism.** Do not smoke.
6. **Weight.** Maintain a body weight appropriate for your height (stature).
7. **Sleep.** Get seven hours of sleep at least four nights a week (sleep schedule).
8. **Exercises.** Exercise until you sweat, at least twice a week.
9. **Trivialities.** Always discuss domestic problems with those who live with you, such as: money and everyday issues.
10. **Affectivity.** Give and receive affection on a regular basis.
11. **Family.** Have at least one family member, in whom you can confide, within a minimum radius of 60 miles (100 km).
12. **Relief.** Speak openly about what you are feeling when angry or concerned.
13. **Friendships.** Maintain a network of friends and acquaintances.
14. **Economy.** Earn enough money to pay for your basic expenses.
15. **Convictions.** Be sure that your general convictions (personal principles) strengthen you.
16. **Sociability.** Attend recreation centers periodically or have regular social activities.
17. **Confidence.** Have 1 or more friend to whom you can confide personal matters.
18. **Self-discipline.** Organize your time efficiently.
19. **Freedom.** Take some time for yourself during the day.
20. **Leisure.** Have some fun at least once a week.

Summary. Regarding lucid projectability, brilliant minds do not have any apparent advantages over average minds. Briefly summarized: any intraphysical consciousness who is mentally competent, intraconscientially centered, of strong personality and perceives with acuity, thinks with clarity, plans with wisdom, acts with propriety, represses negative or morbid thoughts and rejects maladaptive emotions, will always be the best candidate for producing consciential projections with greater lucidity.

Strong traits. There are intraphysical personalities, at the one extreme, with a maximal cultural background and a minimal parapsychic sensitivity; as well as others, at the other extreme, with a minimal cultural background and a maximal parapsychic sensitivity. The ideal would be to join both maximal attributes (strong traits) in a single personality in order that the consciousness, through the mentalsoma, completely masters the emotional impulses of the psychosoma or, in other words, rationality potentiates sublimated intuition, or the sublimated intuition manifests itself, thereby dispensing with the unnecessary crutches and excesses of mysticism.

Evolutiology. This maximal state of serene physical-extraphysical maturity will arise, more and more frequently, among the members of terrestrial humanity from now on.

Decision. It is incumbent upon you to make it more difficult to invade your consciential micro-universe, your protection or consciential self-defenses. If you so desire, will it to be so or remain decided, no one will be able to reach you, much less subjugate you, regardless of whether it involves intrusive suggestions, thoughts, emotions or consciential energies (heterothosenes). You can, in this way, advance more than legions of consciential projectors in any sector of projectiology research. This depends exclusively upon you, your motivation, your decision and self-discipline.

Priority. You may be, and can even recognize yourself to be clearly less experienced, brilliant or talented, weaker paragenetically or less talented in lucid projectability. This is secondary and of little interest. It is much more important that you remain motivated, produce your lucid projections, not tire or lose motivation with that which you do, and remain active and efficient in your lucid projectability.

Theoricity. Within theoricity, experience is superior to theory. The achiever, even when lacking expressive talents, is always superior to the intraphysical consciousness who is merely an observer, as brilliant as that person may be. What, above all, is of much greater value and has much greater weight, is the final position of the ledger of your personal works, the result of the execution of your existential program. This is the number one priority.

Bibliography: Schiff (1515, p. 111), Vieira (1762, p. 123).

---

415.   ANIMISM

Definition. Animism (Latin: *animus,* soul, the consciousness): the complex of intracorporeal (somatic) and extracorporeal phenomena produced by the individual, without external interference, or in the case of projectiology, exclusively by the lucid intraphysical consciousness, or the consciential projector as an intraphysical being.

Synonymy: animicity; organicism; personification; *personism*; psychism.

Classification. Animic phenomenology was classified by Alexander Nikolayevich Aksakof, into 4 items:

1. **Telepathy.** The extracorporeal action of the living human, involving psychic effects (the phenomena of telepathy, transmission of an impression at a distance).

2. **Telekinesis.** The extracorporeal action of the living human, in the form of physical effects (telekinetic phenomena, movement of objects at a distance).

3. **Self-bilocation.** The extracorporeal action of the living human, manifested by the apparition of his/her own image (telephanic phenomena, apparitions at a distance). Consciential projections in general are included here.

4. **Ectoplasmy.** The extracorporeal action of the living human, manifesting in the form of his/her image with certain attributes of corporeity (teleplastic phenomena, formation of materialized bodies).

Characterization. It is always very difficult to characterize a lucid consciential projection which is entirely animic or devoid of interference from extraphysical consciousnesses, due to the intangibility of their presence and their nonassessable action.

Animists. Those who exercise the pure practices of animism are animists, or adepts, according to ancient empirical terminology. They are their own intermediary or bioenergetic catalyst.

Phenomenology. The intraphysical consciousness who is able to operate through the para-organs of the psychosoma while still in his/her human body, produces the majority of parapsychic phenomena exclusively through animism, dispensing with the services of the extraphysical consciousnesses. The following phenomena thereby arise: projective ectoplasmy; projective parapyrogenesis; projective pneumatophony; projective poltergeist; projective psychography; projective psychophony; projective raps; projective telekinesis; self-psychophony and traveling clairvoyance.

Analysis. In the analysis of these occurrences, factors such as conscious and unconscious fraud and mystification are obviously neither pertinent nor of interest. These phenomena are *deliberately provoked* through the force of the intraphysical consciousness who is self-sufficient and the master of his/her own parapsychic powers. They cannot be attributed to the cosmoethical or uncosmoethical responsibility of another. This posture summarizes the entire world of lucid projectability or LPB.

Discoveries. Those who conduct a detailed research of the intricacies of the mechanisms for obtaining inventions and scientific discoveries will naturally – like it or not, consciously or unconsciously – be analyzing the nature and conditions of the animic and parapsychic faculties of the human being.

Conscientiology. On the other hand, one of the best ways to maintain, without recess, the continued and fruitful practice of animic and parapsychic faculties, as well as the development of personal animic (restricted sense) and parapsychic (ample sense) attributes, including the establishment of the physical-extraphysical self-defense of the intraphysical consciousness is for the animist-parapsychic to study or research the positive and transcendent themes of the science of conscientiology.

Bibliography: ADGMT (03, p. 33), Aksakof (09, p. 514), Bastos (89, p. 57), Bonin (168, p. 26), Bozzano (184, p. 287), Dupouy (434, p. 14), Fodor (528, p. 4), Geley (583, p. 66), Granja (622, p. 225), Lisboa (935, p. 202), Miguel (1045, p. 45), Morel (1086, p. 32), Paula (1208, p. 49), Pike (1242, p. 17), Shepard (1548, p. 32), Spence (1588, p. 26), Vieira (1762, p. 125), Wauthy (1803, p. 195), Wedeck (1807, p. 23), Xavier (1891, p. 163), Zaniah (1899, p. 39).

---

416. PARAPSYCHISM

Definition. Sensitive: the individual who exercises parapsychism (in this case human) or the parapsychic psychophysiological faculty of sensing, perceiving or detecting influence directly from the extraphysical dimensions and extraphysical consciousnesses, including intraphysical consciousnesses projected from the human body or soma.

Synonymy: agglutinating person; carrier of extrasensory perception; carrier of parapsychism; channeler; *donkey of the spirits;* extralucid; extraphysicality sensor; extra-sensor; extrasensory percipient; gifted interceptor; *horse of the spirits* (man); human link; interconsciential apparatus; interworld intermediary; interworld mediator; mediumist; mesmeric clairvoyant; metagnome; *metérgico; miko; mule of the spirits* (woman); *paragnomo;* parapsychic bridge; parapsychic guinea pig; parapsychic subject; psychic engine; psychic; psychodynamo; receiver of leading-edge ideas; sensitive; theocrat; *transmission band;* transnormal; ultra-sensitive person.

Parapsychism. Parapsychism is also called: contranormality; extrasensory perception; mediumism; mediumistic faculty; mediumistic sensitivity; mediumship; metagnomy; metanimic faculty; paranormality; parapsychic cognition; parapsychic sensitivity; parapsychodynamics; sixth sense; supersensorial perception; transphysical capacity; ultraperceptive faculty; ultraphany.

Projections. The animism pertaining to the lucid projection phenomenon, as with parapsychism, is evidently a faculty inherent to the intraphysical being. The lucid projection phenomenon can occur spontaneously with the individual, without any intervention from external intelligences. On the other hand, it is estimated that 5% of terrestrial humanity presents more or less developed parapsychic talents, and that 1% of this selfsame humanity has already projected lucidly from the human body.

Complex. Bearing in mind, however, the phenomenological complex which, in and of itself, makes up the occurrences of lucid projection, it becomes difficult to separate parapsychism from the manifestations of the lucid projector, notably due to assisted lucid projections or those directed by extraphysical helpers, which occur with great frequency.

Parapsychic-projectors. The following are 27 parapsychic-projectors who became more well-known: Elwood Babbitt; Douglas M. Baker; Eurípedes Barsanulfo; Annie Brittain; Geraldine Dorothy Cummins (1890-1969); Andrew Jackson Davis (1826-1910); Anne-Marie Dinkel; Elisabeth d'Espérance (Theodore Heurtley Hart-Davies: 1855-1919); Marcel Louis Fohan (Yram); Eileen Jeannette Vancho Lyttle Garrett (1893-1970); Daniel Dunglas Home (1833-1886); Olof Jonsson; Caroline D. Larsen: Gladys Osborne Leonard (1882-1968); Einer Nielsen (1894-1965); Yvonne do Amaral Pereira; Raphael Américo Ranieri; Cora L. V. Richmond (1840-1923); Zilda Giunchetti Rosin; Frederick C. Sculthorp; M. Gifford Shine; Ingo Swann; Emanuel Swedenborg; Attila Von Szalay; Alexander Tanous; Vincent Newton Turvey; Ena Twigg.

Polyvalence. Every sensitive, every animist, as well as every lucid projector, is a parapsychic polyvalent. Greater performance in a certain parapsychic line or in an area of extraphysical exploration is dependent upon the intraphysical consciousness due to *parapsychic polyvalence.*

Orthodoxy. The orthodoxy of the intraphysical sensitive's convictions influences the quality and nature of his/her paraperceptions.

Case study. The clairvoyant, for example, if an orthodox umbandist, tends to mostly see extraphysical consciousnesses such as former *pretos velhos, pombas-giras* and *exus;* the orthodox clairvoyant spiritist tends to see more European-looking extraphysical consciousnesses with evolved, luminous appearances; the universalistic clairvoyant tends to see warriors in ceremonial dress, former physician extraphysical consciousnesses, former turban-wearing Orientals and exotic extraterrestrial extraphysical consciousnesses. Orthodoxy – regardless of which type – is the sepulcher of intelligence.

Energy. The visual appearance, the form or the "work uniform" of the extraphysical benefactor varies according to its own will, due to the phenomenon of self-transfiguration of the psychosoma. The name, label and sometimes even the appearance of the communicant extraphysical consciousness become secondary. What is important, of value and of interest for the sensitive to detect – in the ordinary, physical waking state, as well as when projected in extraphysical communities or environments – is the positive and healthy quality, or the negative and ill quality, of the energetic irradiation of each consciousness, whether intraphysical or extraphysical.

Exclusions. Certainly, the parapsychism considered here refers to genuine phenomena with authentic sensitives. All hypotheses and the extremely high risk of error – with regard to hallucinations or illusions, self-mystification, fraud, pathothosenes, unconscious autosuggestions, intentional charlatanism, fanaticism or the consequences of a lack of self-critique, heteromystification or magic tricks – have been satisfactorily excluded from the sphere of its manifestations.

Session. In any type of parapsychic session, we are merely in the proximity or surroundings of the extraphysical dimensions. If we wish to know its inhabitants, or its environments, its undeveloped and evolved communities, its events, its *parageography,* and its *para-sociology,* we need to enter and live, even if temporarily, in these selfsame environments. There are no package tours for this purpose. Therefore, there is only one resource or alternative: promote lucid self-projection in those who already demonstrate effort and disposition in continued attempts and endeavors.

Conservatism. The condition of parapsychic passivity (when blind or unreflected) predisposes the installation of evolutionary complacency (conservatism, orthodoxy, religion and fossilization regarding self-discernment) or, in other words: submission to the situation of conformity.

Vanguardism. The condition of lucid animic activity predisposes the installation of evolutionary impulsion (vanguardism, heterodoxy, science, cosmoethical and constant renewal) or, in other words: the questioning of the nonconformist opposition.

Self-awareness. For this reason, the healthiest and evolutionarily most profitable condition, in the parapsychic realms, is for the intraphysical consciousness to simultaneously employ his/her composite animic-parapsychic perceptions in the quest for mastery of multidimensional self-awareness.

Comparisons. The following are 4 comparisons, based on the facts, which deserve our logical, mature reflection:

1. **Psychoanalysis.** Psychoanalysis (1 century of existence), *devoid* of the theory of existential seriation or successive intraphysical and intermissive lives, merely studies the intraphysical consciousness from intrauterine life to desoma, within the exclusive limits of somatics.

2. **Yoga.** Yoga (30 centuries of existence), *devoid* of parapsychism, only produces animism, in order for the intraphysical consciousness to achieve the *siddhas,* not dealing with interconsciential deintrusion.

3. **Spiritism.** The spiritist movement (15 decades of existence), *devoid* of animism, merely practices the parapsychism of exchanges between intraphysical consciousnesses and extraphysical consciousnesses in a factionalist, Christian or evangelical manner, like the evangelical exorcist sects and charismatic Catholicism.

4. **Projectiology.** Projectiology (2 decades of existence) employs animism and parapsychism, or the broad parapsychic faculties, including pangraphy, in the ample practical implantation of self-lucid multidimensionality in the micro-universe of the individual wishing to evolve cosmoethically through applied universalism. Everything in life evolves.

Contacts. Based on the unshakable premise that the more evolved an extraphysical consciousness is, the more difficult it becomes to remain in the unevolved existential dimensions and to communicate with the inhabitants of the paratroposphere. It can thus be concluded that it is extremely problematic for a parapsychically developed extraphysical consciousness – from a functional, energetic and cosmoethical point of view – to have prolonged, direct contacts with intraphysical beings in intraphysicality or human life.

Serenissimi. This is why the majority of communicant extraphysical consciousnesses in parapsychic sessions are and will always be relatively undeveloped from a consciential point of view. These facts reaffirm and lend extraordinary value to the intraphysical consciousness being able to project from the human body with lucidity and, on his/her own, meet with evolved extraphysical beings, the *serenissimi.* It will always be much less difficult for them to help us go there occasionally than for them to consider living and remaining here for a somewhat extended period of time.

Mentalsomas. Mentalsomas and the mentalsomatic dimension are the agents involved in these illuminating extraphysical encounters.

Amimia. The condition of inner peace of the *serenissimus* can be represented as a condition of amimia, or an absence of facial expression, although in a natural or non-pathological state. This condition should not be confused with the *amimia* readily found in stuporous states, in catatonia, or – obviously – in the condition of robots, statues and mannequins.

Euthymia. In everyday human life, this condition of perfect tranquility of the consciousness, inner peace and serenity in fact receives the name of *euthymia.*

Approach. The reality of the *serenissimus* is always very difficult to understand using a simple approach from a strictly human perspective. He/she no longer suffers from shyness, an illness that is a type of fear which is generally not treated and is left unresolved. He/she is *un-humble,* which is amoral according to the intraphysical moral concepts of this still pathological intraphysical society. He/she practices a love devoid of mysticism that is always strong in sentiments (rationalized emotions), thoughts and consciential energies. He/she is extremely self-supported in his/her thosenology by cosmoethics.

Prosthesis. The human or intraphysical body is nothing more than a temporary prosthesis for the liberated extraphysical consciousness – which already possesses an *extraphysical* body – when it manifests in the intraphysicality of the earth. *Mediumship* is a system of interconsciential communication that is precarious and not very reliable. This is because it constitutes the lending of a prosthesis – the human body – intended for personal use by the intraphysical consciousness to be employed by a stranger, the extraphysical consciousness. Its productive results require a high degree of continued, exempt heterocritique and self-critique on the part of any individual.

Objects. Everyone knows that, in daily life, objects geared for personal use do not always conveniently adapt, adjust and operate to the use of another individual. It is practically impossible, for example, for someone to adapt and efficiently use somebody else's dentures, glasses or artificial leg.

Projection. Lucid consciential projection constitutes the temporary recuperation of the extraphysical body – a much more evolved body – of the extraphysical consciousness that *lost* it upon undergoing resoma in a soma.

Facts. The facts allow for the elaboration of diverse frameworks that show the historic, or chronological, progress of the altered states of consciousness, animic-parapsychic, or physiological, psychological, parapsychological, projectiological and conscientiological phenomena.

Spiral. Starting along lines of manifestation that are different but interdependent within the same context – or phenomenological complex – and returning almost to the starting point in order to resume the initial steps and start off once again through another opening before us, it can be seen that human manifestations follow the evolutionary spiral, which is inherent to all things.

Manifestations. These manifestations move forward, fall back slightly and continue on ahead, always with small gradual alterations which are more evolved or amplified with other perspectives, with a new look, or new names. All of this occurs according to the trend or the more universal consensus of each period or stage. This ranges from the natural phenomenic appearance of the beginning – or apparent spontaneous generation – up to the new phase of the conquest of technique through an improvement of the performance of the consciousness.

Framework. The following, for example, is a framework of 4 lines of development of interdependent manifestations which interact and clarify the facts within the parameters of the evolutionary spiral, within the last 2 centuries of human history:

1. **Animism:** animal magnetism (mesmerism), energy, suggestion, hypnosis, hypnology (medicine), sophrology, exteriorization of sensitivity, aura, bioplasmatic body, *Kirlian photography* (psychotronics), telekinesis, metal bending, physical effects (physics).

2. **Physical effects:** table turning, telekinesis, materializations (metapsychics), ectoplasmy, ectoplasm, energies, parasurgery, parapsychism.

3. **Paraperceptiology:** intellectual effects (psychology), psychophony, psychography, telepathy (parapsychology), clairvoyance, precognition, prophecy, animism.

4. **Acquisition:** physical self-bilocation, bicorporeity, unfolding of the personality, lucid consciential projection, extraphysical parabody, experience outside the human body, second body, OBE (projectiology), psychosoma, *animism-parapsychism.*

Understanding. The phenomena are obviously not altered with more correct words or more pompous labels (semantics). It can be seen that there is *nothing new under the sun,* except for the human consciousness who feels more aware of the interworld or multidimensional realities and is more open to understanding immutable universal laws.

Bibliography: ADGMT (03, p. 203), Alverga (18, p. 127), Armond (53, p. 11), Azevedo (63, p. 12), Babajiananda (65, p. 51), Barbanell (77, p. 120), Bastos (89, p. 74), Blasco (151, p. 43), Blavatsky (153, p. 425), Bodier (163, p. 21), Bouisson (176, p. 142), Bozzano (184, p. 50; 195, p. 23), Crookall (343, p. 54), Curti (355, p. 16), Delanne (384, p. 315), Eustáquio (487, p. 82), Feesp (503, p. 114), Fodor (528, p. 233), Fortune (541, p. 105), Galeazzi (565, p. 126), Garrett (573, p. 156), Gauld (576, p. 17), Gaynor (577, p. 110), Goes (605, p. 392), Grattan-Guinness (626, p. 75), Greenhouse (636, p. 237), Heindel (705, p. 103), Holloway (734, p. 21), Kardec (825, p. 145), Lancelin (878, p. 39), Leaf (904, p. 84), Lévrier (922, p. 24), Maes (984, p. 85), Martins (1009, p. 95), Meek (1030, p. 61), Morel (1086, p. 119), Northage (1135, p. 48), Pastorino (1206, p. 179), Paula (1208, p. 74), Peralva (1225, p. 17), Pereira (1230, p. 16), Pires (1245, p. 11), Podmore (1267, p. 88), Rosin (1475, p. 32), Rossi-Pagnoni (1477, p. 115), Sekanek (1538, p. 77), Shepard (1548, p. 587), Silva (1562, p. 120), Tondriau (1690, p. 253), Tourinho (1693, p. 34), Vieira (1762, p. 193), Violeta-Odete (1775, p. 111), Xavier (1881, p. 97; 1891, p. 154), Zaniah (1899, p. 302), Zymonidas (1907, p. 181).

417. COMPARISONS BETWEEN THE SENSITIVE AND THE PROJECTOR

Differential. Although, in practice, it is difficult to separate the performance of the projectionist and the sensitive of any type – given that even a projection assisted by helpers is a well-defined type of parapsychism – 8 radically opposed characteristics that are different between the performance of the sensitive and the projector, as an animist or adept, should be singled out in order for them to be better understood:

1. **Activity.** The sensitive needs to have the receptive, docile, self-aware (without blind subjugation), non-resistant attitude of a *passive* instrument in order to submit him/herself to the communicant extraphysical consciousnesses that communicate through him/her. The projector needs to maintain an *active attitude* of determination in order to control him/herself, remain balanced in the face of the influences of extraphysical and intraphysical consciousnesses, and produce lucid projections by him/herself.

2. **Mediation.** The sensitive performs the same role between extraphysical consciousnesses and intraphysical beings as that performed by an interpreter between the interviewee and the interviewer; by the intermediary between a salesperson and a purchaser; by the contact between a publicity agent and a client; and the public relations agent (contact) between a corporation and the public. The lucid projector dispenses with the qualities of these agents of mediation and performs all tasks directly (eliminating the service of intermediation) and, with his/her presence, goes, sees, experiences and returns, all by him/herself, reporting everything about the extraphysical dimension firsthand, being the reporter, commentator and interpreter all at once. The projector is not necessarily a mediator.

3. **Dimensions.** The sensitive simply operates from the physical dimension to the selfsame physical dimension, because if he/she goes directly to the extraphysical dimension, he/she transforms into or operates as a projector. The projector, in a more complex manner, operates in the extraphysical dimension to the same extraphysical dimension and, from there, to the physical dimension.

4. **Manifestations.** The intraphysical (non-projected) sensitive does not manifest through the projector. The projector can manifest through the intraphysical sensitive.

5. **Relationships.** Parapsychism only allows the individual to speak with extraphysical consciousnesses like speaking with a human (a consciousness in the physical waking state). Animism (human lucid projection) allows the individual to speak to extraphysical consciousnesses as one of them or, in other words, just as an extraphysical consciousness when in the condition of a lucid, projected intraphysical consciousness.

6. **Performance.** The intraphysical sensitive, merely as an intermediary, is sometimes not able to perform the tasks of the extraphysical mentor or helper. The projector can, in part, perform the tasks of the extraphysical helper.

7. **Assistance.** The intraphysical sensitive, aided by the extraphysical mentor, communicates together with it in the physical dimension. The projector, aided by the extraphysical helper, works in the extraphysical dimension.

8. **Parapsychism.** The sensitive is always merely an intraphysical sensitive. The projector can be: a projector-sensitive in the physical body, in the case of traveling clairvoyance, for example; a projector-sensitive in the extraphysical dimension, upon functioning as a sensitive outside the human body; and a projector-communicant upon manifesting through the intraphysical sensitive.

Self-service. By means of lucid projection, the consciousness or the *self of the projector* dispenses with the sensitive who provided the service of contact with the extraphysical dimension in order to thereby perform self-service, making everyone's life easier. In the same way, the intraphysical consciousness gradually frees him/herself from the tyranny of machines, including the human-body-machine, through lucid projection.

Simultaneity. The wiser intraphysical researcher will always be the one who knows how to simultaneously utilize animism (e.g.: voluntary lucid projection) and parapsychism (as with semilucid psychophony) in order to intensify his/her know-how regarding extraphysical realities, playing the role of the psychophone-projector, exteriorizer-projector or ectoplast-projector.

Self-awareness. No one is a sensitive of only one type of parapsychism, or an animist of only one animic phenomenon. The intraphysical being develops his/her awareness of the mobilization of consciential energies. For this reason, the majority of sensitives and animists ignore, repress and block the true extent of their parapsychic potentialities. Through a self-awareness of this problem their development occurs in all directions without barriers or limits of manifestation.

Hetero-insecurity. Mediumship of any type is, by its very nature, less evolved, very unstable and more problematic. It presents highs and lows in its manifestations, which always depend, at the very least, upon two energetically attuned consciousnesses in order for it to occur. This, therefore, transmits an unavoidable and unresolvable hetero-insecurity.

Self-assurance. Animism, with regard to any phenomenon, is, by its very nature, more evolved, far more stable and much simpler. It presents a greater uniformity and stability in its manifestations which depend – purely and invariably – upon the performance of the animist's consciousness in the mobilization of consciential energies in order to occur. This thereby offers the guaranty of constant self-assurance.

Bibliography: Greenhouse (636, p. 162), Steiger (1601, p. 106).

---

418. COMPARISONS BETWEEN LUCID PROJECTION AND PARAPSYCHIC TRANCE

Definition. Parapsychic trance (Latin: *transitus,* passage): the psychophysiological or altered state of mind with marked characteristics, such as reduction in lucidity, suspension of voluntary activity and dissociation of the consciousness which becomes passive to the manifestation of another consciousness through the use of its vehicles of consciential manifestation.

Synonymy: medianimic trance; mediumistic state; mediumistic trance; mediumization; psychophonic trance; semi-oneiric state.

Types. While the consciousness (or the *self*) of the sensitive travels projected in the psychosoma in a lucid projection, while simultaneously in a parapsychic trance state – which occurs more frequently than imagined – the human body of the sensitive-projector can temporarily be occupied by a benefactor extraphysical consciousness that speaks through the vocal cords, in the case of common psychophony (benign possession), or by an ill consciousness, in the case of assistential experiments in deintrusion. The human body can also remain temporarily emptied (empty brain) with the departure of the projector and benefactor together, within or distant from the physical base. The trance can be spontaneous or induced.

Differential. Among the differences between the conditions of parapsychic trance and lucid projection, the following should be singled out: amnesia, the discontinuity of memory and the partial annulment of the intraphysical consciousness' defense mechanisms, characteristic of the parapsychic trance.

Experiences. Consciential projectors generally tend to report other types of parapsychic experiences that occurred with them, either together with or separate from lucid consciential projections.

Projective. Incidentally, it should be recorded here that a true *projective trance* sometimes also occurs in certain consciential projections that are not always parapsychic, but in some cases, are entirely animic and positive, as in traveling clairvoyance.

Personalities. Exhaustive scientific tests involving certain physiological concomitants associated with the trance state have been applied to a great variety of personalities while in trance: the *cavalos* ("horses") of Umbanda; Turkish dervishes; Egyptian fakirs; African witch-doctors; Hindu yogis: Spiritist mediums; Buddhist monks; Voodoo practitioners; the sensitives of parapsychology; the somnambulants of hypnology; and Siberian shamans.

Hybridism. The condition of the projected intraphysical consciousness, or the projective state, allows the projector to be entirely him/herself, with his/her full or integral personal manifestation.

Besides this, it allows the projector to meet extraphysical consciousnesses which are also fully themselves. Strictly speaking, during the parapsychic trance an inseparable mixture of personalities or a parapsychic hybridism occurs: the sensitive intraphysical consciousness is not him/herself, but merely a part of the total hybrid personality that is manifested; the extraphysical consciousness is also not itself, but merely the other part that completes the total hybrid personality which the sensitive allows to manifest. This parapsychic hybridism is the most fragile aspect of the general parapsychic processes. In other words: it is a fleeting benign possession which, like it or not, temporarily alters the two personalities, one based in this dimension and the other based in the extraphysical dimension.

Evolution. Sensitives and intraphysical projectors will inevitably become extraphysical consciousnesses with time. Extraphysical consciousnesses, according to the course of evolution of the consciousness, will become intraphysical consciousnesses and projectors at the appropriate time.

Resomatics. If the extraphysical personality were to manifest itself totally through the sensitive, in an integral and satisfactory manner, in a psychophonic trance, for example, it is possible that many consciousnesses would no longer have any need to pass through resoma. If the extraphysical life of the consciousness were to completely satisfy the dictates of consciential evolution, no average extraphysical consciousness would need to go through resoma, be it an intraphysical projector, or a human sensitive.

Imitation. In summary: the parapsychic trance is a temporary imitation of the upcoming or future resoma for the extraphysical consciousness, just as the lucid human projection phenomenon is an imitation (preview) of the deactivation of the projector's human body (desoma) or his/her inevitable biological death, a future event.

Conditions. With regard to animic and parapsychic conditions, lucid consciential projections can be classified into 3 categories:

1. **Animic.** Animic projections: with an absolute predominance of the lucid projector's will, without any interference from extraphysical beings. Although these can still be spontaneous or paraphysiological, without the lucid interference of the projector's will, they do not cease to be animic.

2. **Parapsychic.** Parapsychic projections: with the ostensive or intangible support of one or several extraphysical consciousnesses, which may be extraphysical helpers (assisted projections) and, in sporadic cases, extraphysical intruders *(intrusive projections).*

3. **Mixed.** Mixed projections: those having varying percentages of animism and parapsychism. In practice, the majority of lucid projections are of this type.

Bibliografia: Amadou (21, p. 233), Blavatsky (153, p. 804), Black (137, p. 202), Bonin (168, p. 498), Brennan (199, p. 45), Butler (228, p. 149), Cavendish (266, p. 257), Chaplin (273, p. 158), Crookall (338, p. 150), D'arbó (365, p. 242), Day (376, p. 137), Depascale (392, p. 138), Digest (401, p. 381), Fodor (528, p. 388), Gaynor (577, p. 188), Grant-Veillard (623, p. 69), Greenhouse (636, p. 171), Heindel (705, p. 154), Lewis (923, p. 41), Martin (1003, p. 126), Morel (1086, p. 174), Paula (1208, p. 156), Schatz (1514, p. 195), Shepard (1548, p. 940), Spence (1588, p. 414), Steiger (1601, p. 217), Stokes (1625, p. 24), Tondriau (1690, p. 286), Walker (1782, p. 239), Wedeck (1807, p. 355), Zaniah (1899, p. 458).

419. PARAPSYCHISM AND LUCID PROJECTION

Parapsychism. Parapsychism is still a providential *psychophysiological crutch* sustaining the acquisition of experiences on the part of consciousnesses. Nevertheless, the more lucid consciousness ends up dispensing with this *crutch* after it no longer needs it – neither for itself nor for others – *the fireworks of ostensive phenomena,* self-promotional shows, audience seductions and religious demagogies that involve other consciousnesses besides itself.

Projection. On the other hand, lucid projection cannot rationally be considered as a simple *crutch* to be discarded at the appropriate time, because it does not constitute a process of mere intermediation, like parapsychism. It is, instead, 1 of 3 basic states of the consciousness in evolution.

States. The consciousness can manifest itself in 3 basic states of existence:

1. **Extraphysical consciousness.** Extraphysical life or that of the extraphysical consciousness, which is lasting and essential.

2. **Intraphysical consciousness.** Human life or that of the intraphysical consciousness, which is ephemeral and segmented.

3. **Projectability.** The life of the projected consciousness, which can be an extraphysical consciousness as well as a human being, being even more transitory.

Fusion. Besides these 3 states of existence, there is the state wherein they are fused or, in other words, the evolved state of continuous self-awareness.

Intervallic. The intervallic state of the projected consciousness exists because it opens spaces in 1 of the 2 other basic states of existence, whether extraphysical life or human life. The state of the projected consciousness represents a brief and discontinuous period. It nevertheless occurs together with the other 2.

Coadjutant. In light of the above, it is not, strictly speaking, lucid projection that is a coadjutant to parapsychism, but, on the contrary, parapsychism that represents a coadjutant to lucid projection, the main manifestation for the consciousness.

Power. Parapsychism is a condition, not a power. Lucid projection, besides being a consciential state, also incontestably constitutes a power for the consciousness.

Percentages. In the majority of lucid projections produced nowadays by the intraphysical consciousness, the existence of an animic component and a parapsychic component can be detected. Thus, for example, a projection can have 80% animism and 20% parapsychism, and another can have 30% animism and 70% parapsychism. These percentages vary from projection to projection and from projector to projector.

Evolution. It can be affirmed that, as consciousnesses evolve, the percentage of parapsychism gradually decreases over time, thereby enabling a current estimation of average coefficients (percentages).

Window. The efficient animism of lucid self-projectability – lucid projections performed by the interested individuals who personally experience them – are gradually replacing the process of parapsychism, eliminating intermediaries and dispensing with the messages of third parties. It is not, however, a new means of communication, banishing the other, which is already outdated or antiquated. Each means of perception or expression, human as well as consciential, is its own open *window* to the cosmos. One cannot replace the other.

Duration. Projectability, a paraphysiological attribute of the consciousness, must always have existed beyond a certain evolutionary level. Parapsychism must have existed, in the same manner, from the beginnings of the self-awareness of the consciential or intelligent principle. As a consciential state, projectability suggests that it will last much longer, evolutionary speaking, as a consciential resource. Both, however, should continue together throughout history and the string of evolutionary experiences of every intraphysical consciousness who goes through desoma and is reborn again, while bound to the multi-existential cycle of resomas/desomas/intermissions.

Raison. The raison d'être of parapsychism as a process of intermediation for oneself or for others disappears with the evolution of the vehicles of manifestation of the consciousness. On the other hand, lucid projection will continue to exist as long as the consciousness utilizes these same vehicles of manifestation.

Conclusion. From the above facts, it can rationally be concluded that lucid projection, besides having an animic origin or being different from parapsychism, will also survive after parapsychism in the evolutionary progression of the consciousness.

Mentalsoma. It is worth stressing that parapsychism is also exercised between extraphysical consciousnesses in extraphysical communities or environments. In this case, the looseness of the mentalsoma of the extraphysical-sensitive-consciousness occurs relative to the extraphysical head (parahead) of the psychosoma, because this consciousness has neither a human body nor a holochakra in that situation (after the second desoma).

Bibliography: Gomes (612, p. 20), Leaf (905, p. 142), Vieira (1762, p. 193).

420. GENERAL CLASSIFICATION OF CONSCIENTIAL PROJECTIONS

Categories. There are a great many shades of lucid projection, depending upon the standpoint from which the experience is classified.

System. Every system of classification is open to doubt, because events which are exceptions to the rule always occur. There are at least 18 different types or categories of projections in general, when specific factors are considered, albeit with some aspects which are evidently redundant:

1. **Quality.** The quality of the perceptions: pure or natural consciential projection; impure or forced consciential projection.

2. **Magnitude.** Magnitude of the projected consciousness: lucid projection; semilucid projection or lucid dream; nonlucid projection, common to all lucid intraphysical beings; projection with continuous self-awareness; pseudoprojection (dreams; simple vision; hallucination; errors in thosenic interpretation); projection with amplified awareness (cosmoconsciousness); mild consciential projection; prosaic consciential projection.

3. **Physiology.** Physiological nature: animic projection (the consciousness projects itself, through its own means); parapsychic projection (with interference from a second consciousness); mixed projection.

4. **Will.** The will of the projector: unintentional projection; programmed or experimental projection; test of capacity; espionage projection (anticosmoethical); voluntary self-projection (active, animic); projection with a predetermined target; crash-projection (unknown target, lost or disoriented projector without a destination).

5. **Participation.** External participation: directed consciential projection (passive, parapsychic); assisted projection (mixed or oneiric-parapsychic); interconsciential assistential projection; educational projection; deintrusive projection or one of assistential solidarity.

6. **Company.** Extraphysical company: solitary consciential projection; joint projection (more than 1 projector); double, triple or group projection; junior projection (infantile); gathering of projected intraphysical consciousnesses.

7. **Process.** Nature of the process: natural consciential projection (spontaneous, fortuitous, occasional); technical consciential projection; empirical consciential projection.

8. **Vehicle.** Vehicle of manifestation or holosomatics: consciential projection in the integral psychosoma alone (without the holochakra); projection in the psychosoma with the holochakra; projection of the holochakra or paraphysiological looseness, without transporting the consciousness (energetic); projection in the partially configured psychosoma, semi-separation; projection in the mentalsoma; projection in the psychosoma and in the mentalsoma, or vice versa, without interiorization or physical awakening of the intraphysical consciousness.

9. **Healthfulness.** Healthfulness of the experience: natural projection; strange projection; intrusive projection; nightmarish projection; ill or pathological projection; depressive projection; stressful projection; feverish projection; sexual or sexosomatic projection; medicinal or pharmacological projection; projection caused by accident; medico-surgical anesthetic projection; odonto-surgical anesthetic projection.

10. **Field.** Relationship with the physical space or proxemics: contiguous projection or one in the physical base; projection in the extraphysical dimension per se; projection in the mentalsomatic dimension; projection without space (mentalsomatic); nearby or *low-flying* projection; distant or *long-range flight* projection.

11. **Coloration.** Coloration of the extraphysical environment: black-and-white consciential projection; multicolor projection (color projection); monochromatic projection or one having a predominance of one color; neutral color projection.

12. **Hour.** With regard to the hour or the timing: matutinal consciential projection; vespertine consciential projection; nocturnal consciential projection; rest consciential projection; consciential projection of nappers.

13. **Time.** The chronological time of the extraphysical events: retrocognitive consciential projection or one referring to a past intraphysical life; previous consciential projection or one which is relative to the past of this human life; consciential projection which is current or simultaneous with the present time; premonitory consciential projection or one referring to future facts. There is a non-uniformity in the passage of time regarding that of the projected state and the human body. In most cases, however, the clock of the projected consciousness runs much more slowly than the clock of the human body. It is worth asking the following question: "Is this related to the speed of the thoughts and actions of the projected consciousness or is it related to physical time, as forecast in the theory of relativity?"

14. **Duration.** Duration of the projective experience: extremely brief consciential projection; brief projection; prolonged consciential projection; consciential projection of an imprecise duration.

15. **Chronology.** Chronology of lucid projections: first consciential projection; sporadic consciential projection; previous consciential projection; consecutive consciential projection; recurring or repeating consciential projection; consciential projection in series.

16. **Rarity.** In increasing order of relevance and, consequently, of rarity of the projective experiments, the following can be classified: nonlucid physiological projections, being the most frequent because they involve all of humanity, without exception; semilucid projection or lucid dream; semiprojection or partial projection; first lucid projection, sometimes the only one in the entire lifetime of the intraphysical consciousness; projections with continuous self-awareness, in series, being the rarest.

17. **Involuntary.** Spontaneous or involuntary projections divided into 7 types: consciential projections occurring while the person is sleeping; projections occurring during surgery, during dental surgery, during childbirth (obviously if the individual is a woman); projections occurring during a violent accident; projections occurring when the person is in intense pain; consciential projections occurring during a serious illness; resuscitative consciential projections occurring in near-death crises or experiences, with the resuscitation of the patient; semifinal projections occurring at the moment of the death of the soma.

18. **Causes.** There are 3 types of consciential projections, according to their causes: spontaneous, voluntary and forced. The *spontaneous* consciential projection is more common and occurs naturally, such as when the person is sleeping; the *voluntary* consciential projection is one which is produced intentionally, generally according to the individual's own technique; and the *forced* consciential projection occurs due to traumas to the human body which force the intraphysical consciousness (*me*, you) to project. In this last type are included impure projections provoked by illness, anesthesia, asphyxia, unconsciousness due to an accident, or the use of psychedelic drugs.

Critical. The critical consciential projection is that which occurs during a crisis, whether an accident, disaster, war or armed conflict, or a catastrophe. Do not confuse the critical projection with projectiocritique.

Exoprojection. The consciousness that projects itself to the extraphysical dimension, but to another celestial body beyond the planet earth, produces an exoprojection, cosmic projection, extraterrestrial projection or one in outer space. Photos of other planets, obtained through space research aid the projector in exoprojections, because these heavenly bodies thereby cease to be merely imaginary mental targets (see fig. 420, p. 1,149).

Immediate. The immediate consciential projection is the variety that occurs without any introduction, preparation, transition or intermediary altered state of consciousness. The individual, in this case, lies down and his/her consciousness (you) immediately leaves the human body with total lucidity, directly from the ordinary, physical waking state to the extraphysical dimension. This occurs in instantaneous lucid projections and the escape-projections of intraphysical consciousnesses.

Microprojections. Consciential miniprojections, or consciential microprojections, are discreet, mild experiences of the consciousness which leaves the human body for tenths of a second or for only

1 to 3 seconds. This can even occur while the human body of the projector is in movement, in the ordinary, physical waking state, and does not affect his/her intraphysical existence or physical and mental health.

Microsleep. Consciential microprojection, a natural, paraphysiological state, should not be confused with microsleep, a pathological state which occurs with patients having a tendency toward sleepiness, those who suffer from hypersleep, narcolepsy (hypnolepsy), excessive sleep attacks, or sudden, fleeting sleep crises.

Mnemosomatics. The difference between one state and the other is easy to establish: consciential microprojection is generally an isolated fact that allows recall of extraphysical events; microsleep is not accompanied by recall and often occurs dozens of times in a single night's sleep.

Violent. Violent, impure consciential projections are those experiences which are forced by the dramatic circumstances of human life, notably accidents on roads, on mountains, in the air, in the water, through electrocution or asphyxiation.

Circumstances. Due to human attitudes, occupations or circumstances, consciential projections can be divided into 8 categories relating to the moment of their occurrence: the consciential projection of natural sleep; consciential projection from the waking state, in conditions of heightened reasoning (lucidity); consciential projection during surgery, childbirth or tooth extraction; consciential projection due to a violent accident; consciential projection due to excruciating physical pain; consciential projection during a serious illness; consciential projection during near-death experience, in cases of clinical resuscitation; consciential projection at the moment of the deactivation of the soma.

Bibliography: Baumann (93, p. 23), Chaplin (273, p. 210), Crookall (343, p. 15), Flammarion (524, p. 39), Frost (560, p. 113), Imbassahy (782, p. 9), Montandon (1070, p. 227), Muldoon (1105, p. 56), Sparrow (1587, p. 61), Tart (1660, p. 188).

421. BASIC CATEGORIES OF LUCID PROJECTION

Options. The intraphysical consciousness projects him/herself from the human body following different and well-defined actions, according to the vehicle of manifestation, the condition of lucidity and the existential dimension in which he/she operates. The following is a summarized list of the six basic options that are most often encountered:

1. **Holochakra.** The intraphysical consciousness (you) can project his/her holochakra by itself, in the ordinary extraphysical dimension. It is common knowledge that the holochakra is not the seat of the consciousness.

2. **Density.** The intraphysical consciousness can project him/herself in the psychosoma *with* the holochakra, in the ordinary extraphysical dimension, transported *in* and *by* the mentalsoma.

3. **Rarefaction.** The intraphysical consciousness can project him/herself in the psychosoma *without* the holochakra, in the ordinary extraphysical dimension, transported *in* and *by* the mentalsoma.

4. **Coincidence.** The intraphysical consciousness can project him/herself in the mentalsoma, leaving the psychosoma coincident in the human body, dislocating itself only in the mentalsoma, in the mentalsomatic dimension.

5. **Discoincidence.** The intraphysical consciousness can project him/herself in the psychosoma and, soon thereafter, leave the psychosoma discoincident from the human body, in the ordinary extraphysical dimension, dislocating itself solely in the mentalsoma, in the mentalsomatic dimension.

6. **Intermingling.** The consciousness can project him/herself conjugating different types of vehicles, in the various levels of existential dimensions, in an intermingled manner, whether voluntarily, spontaneously without trauma, spontaneously with trauma, alone, assisted by a helper, in an integral manner or in a partial manner. The conditions can vary even further according to the influence of many other factors, such as degree of lucidity, discontinuity, blackout, duration and intraconsciential balance. Many different types of projectiological phenomena can thereby be understood: projection in general, traveling clairvoyance, physical bilocation and others.

Levels. It should not be forgotten that the ordinary extraphysical dimension, as well as the mentalsomatic dimension, present different levels of *density* and are reciprocally joined to each other in an instantaneous manner, according to the attributes and performance of the projected consciousness, which may or may not be able to promote its passage between dimensions or frequencies.

Specific. The following are 6 more technical categories of specific consciential projections:

1. **Edaphoprojection:** consciential projection in subcrustal areas.

2. **Nephoprojection:** consciential projection in the psychosoma produced by the intraphysical consciousness.

3. **Oligoprojection:** consciential projections of an extremely short duration, some seconds at most.

4. **Pedoprojection:** consciential projection of the miniprojector or, in other words, of a child.

5. **Podoprojection:** partial projection wherein only one parafoot or one paraleg of the psychosoma leaves the human body.

6. **Chiroprojection:** partial projection wherein only one parahand or one para-arm of the psychosoma leaves the human body.

Ample. The rare *broad-spectrum* consciential projection is the variety in which the projected intraphysical consciousness has various basic extraphysical experiences at the same time, such as: seeing his/her own inactive human body on the bed; analyzing the silver cord; meeting a helper; volitating; lucidly visiting another extraphysical environment distant from the physical base; encountering extraphysical consciousnesses besides the helper; having a prolonged lucid projection, in the extraphysical dimension, for longer than a half-hour. All this occurs spontaneously and naturally, without the use of any drugs.

Bibliography: King (845, p. 117), Steiger (1601, p. 4), Vieira (1762, p. 218).

422. EXTRAPHYSICAL LUCIDITY-SUBSEQUENT RECALL BINOMIAL

Definition. Extraphysical lucidity-subsequent recall binomial: the set of two basic conditions that are indispensable for the intraphysical consciousness in order for it to obtain a fully satisfactory lucid projection outside the human body.

Synonymy: experience-recall consciential condition; indispensable projective conditions.

Classification. From the perspective of extraphysical lucidity-subsequent recall binomial, human lucid projection experiences can, both in theory and in practice, be classified into 3 well-defined categories: the lucid, recalled consciential projection, the lucid, unrecalled consciential projection, and the nonlucid, unrecalled consciential projection.

1. **Lucid recalled.** The lucid, recalled projection of the intraphysical consciousness – whether projected in the psychosoma or the mentalsoma – is the variety in which the consciousness enjoys full extraphysical lucidity and later presents a reasonable recall of the extraphysical events that he/she witnessed and/or participated in.

Types. The lucid, recalled consciential projection can be of 2 types: the projection with consciential blackout, which is the most common; and the projection with continuous self-awareness, which is the least common, or the rarest.

2. **Lucid unrecalled.** The lucid, unrecalled projection of the intraphysical consciousness – whether projected in the psychosoma or the mentalsoma – is the variety in which the consciousness enjoys full extraphysical lucidity, but subsequently does not recall the extraphysical events that occurred during the period he/she was absent from the human body. This is a lucid projection only in the extraphysical dimension.

Intuition. In the case of lucid, unrecalled consciential projection, extraphysical experiences can, exceptionally, blossom with the passage of time in the ordinary, physical waking state, through the providential channels of common intuition.

Predisposition. Intuition operates, in many cases, like a simple *mnemonic predisposition*. The intraphysical consciousness, having had experience with the object-theme in focus – while projected from his/her human body, for example – keeps his/her integral archive fed with ideas on this same theme. Later, if the pointer of the consciousness tunes into the frequency of that same theme, this predisposition serves to modulate and prepare the mnemonic reflex, like an enrichment. If this reflex occurs all at once, *en bloc,* then the discovery – the *eureka,* the flash of the *new* or *original* idea – blossoms abruptly. In most cases, however, the recall flows in installments, slowly, gradually, piece by piece, fragment by fragment and does not generate so much emotional impact.

Experiences. Not only do we *know more* than we think: we have already had *more experiences* than we perceive and we store many *more memories* (holomemory) than we ordinarily recall.

Serenissimi. Extraphysical facts indicate that even *serenissimi* are not yet able to recall all of the events collected in their integral memories or holomemories as evolutionary consciential principles that have even passed through the subhuman phase.

Option. The extraphysical helpers affirm that, at a certain point in the intraphysical projector's consciential development – of natural, non-forced projections – with regard to aiding (assisted projections) the extraphysical experience (lucidity)-subsequent recall binomial, they must almost always opt, through extraphysical energetic exteriorizations, in favor of one condition or the other, thereby sacrificing one of them.

Mnemosomatics. It becomes very difficult for the consciousness to have both conditions interwoven or, in other words, to always simultaneously use two memories, which are healthy and clear, of two different existential dimensions. In this case, the extraphysical helpers generally prefer or give priority to the condition which is more important, wherein the intraphysical being has his/her full experiences outside the human body and ceases to have clear recollection of those same experiences, or even forget them completely.

Evidences. This reaffirms 3 well-known projectiological evidences, given that the *first* of them is in the deep, indispensable interrelationship that exists between the experiences of the projected consciousness and the condition and nature of the subsequent post-projective recall.

Confirmations. Clarification performed by the extraphysical helpers also confirms a *second* evidence: recall of the lucid projection experience gradually becomes more difficult for the veteran projector when he/she spends more than 60 minutes and, many times, even spends over 30 minutes of condensed extraphysical experiences with full awareness in a single, continuous lucid departure. The same clarification also confirms a *third* evidence: if it becomes so difficult for the intraphysical consciousness that remains outside the human body (microcosm) and the dense physical dimension (physical universe or macrocosm) for only one or a few hours to simultaneously interconnect two basic consciential dimensions, the extraphysical and the physical, how difficult will it be for the extraphysical consciousness to communicate when it spends weeks, months, or even worse, entire years, distant from the terrestrial crust without a human body and even without the silver cord or the holochakra? Experiences indicate that this fact has some influence on the process of forgetting the past, which is inherent to the resoma of the extraphysical consciousness.

3. **Nonlucid unrecalled.** The nonlucid, unrecalled projection is that in which the consciousness projects from the human body – even being able to participate as an energy donor in extraphysical assistential tasks – although not obtaining adequate, functional extraphysical lucidity. It obviously does not, for this reason, have subsequent recall. This category, strictly speaking, is not a lucid projection.

Unconscious. Nonlucid, unrecalled consciential projection is the same common, unconscious consciential experience that occurs, for example, during the condition of natural sleep, which happens to the entirety of humanity every night, in which every intraphysical consciousness leaves the state of coincidence of the vehicles of consciential manifestation. Nonlucid consciential projection creates the *extraphysical zombie*. Nonlucid consciential projection, or projection without recall, is traveling clairvoyance.

Awakening. Because of nonlucid projections, a paraphysiological occurrence that affects all members of humanity, the following is a rational, decisive recommendation for neophytes interested in projectiology, whether youths or adults: *Awaken the lucid projector that sleeps within you.*

Bibliography: Vieira (1762, p. 145).

423. FIRST LUCID PROJECTION

Definition. First lucid projection: initial experience of the projector's lucid consciousness outside the human body, an occasion in which he/she enters into *projectiocracy*.

Synonymy: first semiphysical projection; once-in-a-lifetime-projection; primoprojection; projective initiation; projector's debut; shock-projection.

Initiations. According to the principles of social anthropology, it can be affirmed that there are, for example, 9 different, basic categories of real initiations that are available to the intraphysical consciousness, depending upon whether the individual has a male or female soma:

1. Circumcision (boy) or the removal of the prepuce.
2. The first emission of sperm (young man).
3. The first shave (man).
4. Menarche (young woman).
5. Deflowering (woman).
6. Conception (pregnant woman, primigravida).
7. The first parturition (primipara).
8. The first parapsychic trance (sensitive).
9. The first lucid consciential projection (projectionist).

Importance. Of all the types of human initiations, or rebirths to a new social status, the most important, without a doubt, as it is the most decisive or the most important for knowledge of oneself, is lucid consciential projection.

Rarity. Up until this point in human history, the majority of intraphysical beings pass through the first 7 animal initiations with ease; few experience the eighth initiation; very few go through the ninth and last test on the list. Unfortunately.

Last. In most registered cases, lucid projection occurs only once during the entire intraphysical life of a person who is not accustomed to parapsychism, simultaneously constituting the first and the last experience or, in other words, the once-in-a-lifetime-lucid-projection.

Characteristics. Not all characteristics of consciential projections are the same with regard to the experience of each debuting-projector. Nonetheless, the following 3 somewhat frequent points can be highlighted:

1. **Desoma.** The thought of having gone through desoma.
2. **Thanatophobia.** Excessive fear (thanatophobia).
3. **Extraphysicality.** The incontestable sensation of being outside the human body.

Inexperience. The following are extraphysical actions that show the inexperience of the projected intraphysical consciousness and commonly occur in the first lucid consciential projection:

1. **Furniture.** Feeling that movements are impeded because of the physical presence of furniture and human constructions.
2. **Parahands.** Attempting to use the extraphysical hands (parahands) to transport objects.
3. **Parafeet.** Using the extraphysical feet (parafeet) when moving.
4. **Walking.** Walking directly on the ground, pavement and floor, without gliding or volitating.

5. **Stairs.** Descending or ascending a flight of stairs just like an ordinary person.
6. **Walls.** Stopping at walls and fences.
7. **Doors.** Attempting to open doors in order to go to another room.

Lucidity. The abovementioned attitudes, which illustrate the inexperience of the projected intraphysical consciousness and his/her ignorance regarding the capacities of the vehicles of manifestation of the intraphysical consciousness can, in many cases, indicate a reduction in the quality of extraphysical lucidity in the situations of experiences outside the human body.

Phenomenon. No one needs to deeply understand a phenomenon in order to experience it. In other words: the individual can experience it in an unconscious or semiconscious manner. Generally speaking, we all breathe without thinking deeply about this fact. Consciential projection is also included in this reality: there are legions of projectors who are completely ignorant of their first spontaneous lucid projection.

Relief. In the first unique lucid projection experience, the individual is almost always lost, confused, searching for words to describe the extraphysical experiences, endeavoring to understand and explain the observations and experiences based on the familiar. The person feels relieved upon knowing that his/her experiences are not unique, and have been told and retold in various parts of the earth, in different times, civilizations, societies and languages.

Acceptance. Due to the extremely individual nature of lucid projection, it is sufficient – in certain cases – for a person to have a single major lucid projective experience in order to convince that individual about extraphysical realities, thereby enabling a reduction of the phase of opportunistic explanations regarding the full acceptance of the phenomena, as has occurred in different scientific fields with so many phenomena that are now readily accepted. The following are 5 examples:

1. **Circulation.** The reluctance and controversies that initially arose regarding the acceptance of the theory of blood circulation.
2. **Heliocentrism.** The hypothesis of heliocentrism.
3. **Hypnosis.** The reality of hypnosis.
4. **Meteorites.** The existence and the falling of meteorites.
5. **Microbiology.** The fact of the existence of bacteria that cause illnesses.

Quality. A single high-quality lucid projective experience can nevertheless have definitive results and deeply mark the intraphysical consciousness for the rest of his/her human days on earth. This can even make overall changes in the way that he/she perceives human existence and the cosmos. This fact demonstrates that the number of lucid projections is relatively unimportant, the quality of the consciential experience always being of greater value.

Causes. The first lucid projection can be classified into 3 categories, according to its causes:

1. **Spontaneity.** The first spontaneous lucid projection.
2. **Assistentiology.** The first lucid projection assisted by an extraphysical helper.
3. **Volition.** The first lucid projection provoked by the will of the novice projector.

Primer. The first projection can serve as a primer or basic handbook of projectiology research for the more intelligent novice projector. It can also function as an efficient stimulating or triggering factor for other lucid projections. For example: brief general anesthesia during minor dental surgery can motivate the projector-patient to become an active projector.

Triumphalism. The first lucid projection can generate a compulsive interest regarding the issue and sometimes generates a spirit of triumphalism in the adult projector, notably when it is produced voluntarily, bringing sterilizing consequences and even an early recess to his/her experimentations. For this reason, primary, irrational triumphalism should be avoided and substituted with the intraphysical consciousness' sincere desire to improve him/herself in new experiences, maintaining an open mind.

Freedom. The *prisoner's profession* is freedom or, in other words, freedom is automatically placed at the forefront of everything that he/she thinks. This also occasionally occurs with the intraphysical lucid projector *(a human prisoner).* After the first impactful lucid projection, now that this freedom has been discovered and identified, the intraphysical consciousness automatically places extraphysical projective freedom – which he/she just became aware of – at the forefront of everything he/she thinks about, thereby desiring escape from the physical restriction imposed by human life.

Uterus. Strictly speaking, the uterus is the first intraphysical base of the human consciousness in his/her initial projection, or the first pre-biological projection, soon after embryonic conception, prior to parturition. There are, however, first lucid projections that only occur after parturition, in the initial months of human existence or in the first years of ordinary physical life.

Bibliography: Baumann (93, p. 100), Blackmore (139, p. 1), Bord (170, p. 10), Crookall (320, p. 74), Greenhouse (636, p. 44), MacLaine (980, p. 284), Muldoon (1105, p. 49), Muntañola (1108, p. 102), Prieur (1289, p. 108), Rogo (1444, p. 16), Sculthorp (1531, p. 17), Shay (1546, p. 94), Vieira (1762, p. 10).

424. DOUBLE CONSCIENTIAL PROJECTION

Definition. Double consciential projection: projection of the intraphysical consciousness in 1 vehicle of manifestation and, soon thereafter, in another, either the psychosoma or the mentalsoma, or vice versa, without the interiorization of that selfsame consciousness in the human body for the duration of the experiment.

Synonymy: 2-stage projection; biprojection; extraphysical bilocation; multiple projection; physical-extraphysical trilocation; projection by 2 vehicles.

Types. Double projection can be produced through two different extraphysical operations, each one having 2 distinct stages: direct double projection and inverse double projection.

1. **Direct.** In direct double projection, the intraphysical consciousness (you) projects from the human body in the psychosoma and silver cord, in a first exteriorization or first stage. Then, leaving the psychosoma *emptied of the consciousness* outside the human body, you leave in the mentalsoma and golden cord, in a second exteriorization or second stage.

2. **Inverse.** In inverse double projection, or double projection through coupling, in the first stage, the intraphysical consciousness (you) projects in the mentalsoma and golden cord, leaving the psychosoma emptied and the silver cord *inside* the human body. Then, in the second stage, the exteriorization of the psychosoma and the silver cord occurs or, in other words, the isolated psychosoma quickly leaves the human body and couples with your already projected mentalsoma through the force of the golden cord.

Passport. It is worth observing that when the mentalsoma is projected in an isolated fashion, by itself, you remain in the mentalsomatic dimension (with the consciousness, obviously). The act of the psychosoma joining with the mentalsoma through the golden cord, in these conditions, shows that the golden cord is the passport of the consciousness, allowing it to always pass from the extraphysical dimension, per se (the paratropospheric dimension, for example), to the mentalsomatic dimension, and vice versa (see fig. 424, p. 1,150).

Possibilities. In double projection, instead of the 2 vehicles – the psychosoma and mentalsoma – being integrated into a coincident whole, both temporarily remain separated and isolated. The direct or indirect, conscious or unconscious general command is always maintained by you, or your consciousness (hyperacuity).

Consciousness. It should not be forgotten that you, the consciousness, invariably remain in the mentalsoma during *all* operations, stages and categories of the fully lucid, semilucid or nonlucid consciential projections of intraphysical beings, whether exteriorizing your vehicle of manifestation by way of the silver cord or the golden cord.

Impossibilities. When the consciousness reaches the second stage of the direct double projection, it becomes almost impracticable for it to touch or command the physiology of its own human body because a discrepancy, break in continuity, hiatus or interpolation is established in conditions that are completely different in their nature, thereby not allowing direct contact. In this case, the consciousness temporarily lacks its *bridge* or its connecting elements – the psychosoma and the holochakra – remaining *bound* to the parabrain (of the psychosoma) by way of the golden cord.

Dimensions. In double projection, the consciousness not only operates with 2 vehicles of manifestation, but also transfers itself through more than 2 existential dimensions, or vibrational gradations. In other words, it passes from the physical dimension through the extraphysical dimension per se all the way to the mentalsomatic dimension in a successive manner, sometimes in tenths of a second, mobilizing its energies during these operations until resuming the state of normal coincidence of all vehicles of manifestation inside the human body.

Helpers. The occurrences of double projection, whether semilucid or completely lucid, are mostly projections which are assisted by extraphysical helpers. In instances of direct double projection, the extraphysical helpers make themselves visible at a vibratory or dimensional level corresponding with the frequency or density of the psychosoma that is isolated and *emptied of the consciousness.*

Sensitive. The phenomenon of double lucid projection occurs with relative frequency, but is not always well understood or conveniently interpreted due to the unawareness or inexperience of the intraphysical projector. The majority of reports on this phenomenon comes from psychophonic sensitives or consciential energy exteriorizers during the performance of extraphysical assistance. In this case, the assistance can even be intended for the sensitive him/herself who, remaining in the state of punctiform consciousness, observes the intervention or direct treatment performed by helpers upon his/her isolated psychosoma, which is emptied of the consciousness, aiming to cleanse energetic alterations that are provoking disturbances (energetic blockages or imbalances) in his/her human body.

Holochakra. In the extraphysical phenomena of exteriorization of the consciousness in the mentalsoma, in the exteriorization of the isolated psychosoma, in the coupling of the psychosoma with the mentalsoma and in the final interiorization of a projective session, the psychosoma – which is always the intermediary vehicle in double lucid projections – can be more or less dense, laden or unladen with the energies of the holochakra.

Trilocation. Double consciential projection is also called *physical-extraphysical trilocation* because, while the intraphysical consciousness remains headquartered, active and lucid in the mentalsoma or, in other words, in the mentalsomatic dimension, the empty psychosoma remains in the paratropospheric dimension or extraphysical dimension per se, and the inactive human body remains in the physical dimension with an *empty brain.*

Trilocators. The consciousness, in this case, does not divide into 3, but simultaneously has 3 of its vehicles in *3* different consciential *locations* or environments. Many bilocators also operate as trilocators (trilocator projectors).

Isolation. In summary, the following two complex conditions occur in this context:

1. **Holochakrology.** The holochakra can project itself alone, in an isolated manner, always without the consciousness. The consciousness remains in the human body or projects itself in the psychosoma or in the mentalsoma.

2. **Psychosomatics.** The psychosoma can be left alone and isolated outside the human body. But in this case, the consciousness remains projected in the isolated mentalsoma, never staying in the human body without the psychosoma and mentalsoma.

Biprojector. The individual who produces double consciential projection is called a *consciential biprojector.*

Note. Lucid, double consciential projection or physical-extraphysical trilocation should not be confused with physical multilocation or physical translocation, two phenomena perfectly distinct from each other, which are analyzed in other chapters of this book.

Bibliography: Andreas (36, p. 46), Black (137, p. 27), Butler (228, p. 115), Crouzet (344, p. 204), Greene (635, p. 91), Rogo (1444, p. 65; 1447, p. 105), Sculthorp (1531, p. 135), Vieira (1762, p. 198).

425. EDUCATIONAL CONSCIENTIAL PROJECTION

Definition. Educational consciential projection: an extraphysical experience sponsored by one or more extraphysical helpers in order to transmit instructions or teachings to the projected intraphysical consciousness.

Synonymy: class-projection; didactic consciential projection; extraphysical initiation; extraphysical test; ideogenetic consciential projection; ideogenetic consciential projection; pedagogical consciential projection.

Helper. In the educational consciential projection the helper can be present and act visibly or invisibly to the projected projector. Sometimes it is only heard or its presence is sensed, without being identified by the projected intraphysical consciousness, because it does not show itself in a tangible or ostensive manner in that extraphysical dimension of manifestation.

Adept. As a parapsychic occurrence, the educational consciential projection speaks in favor of the actual existence of the psychophysical relationship between the active, intraphysical adept and the extraphysical mentor, which is referred to in ancient occult, esoteric or parapsychic texts.

Class-projection. The class-projection, aided by a teacher-helper – which may or may not be visible and generally instructs the *student-projector* on themes regarding exchanges between consciential existential dimensions – is common to sensitive-projectors that have intense and evolved paraperceptive capacities.

School. Upon acquiring a greater body of extraphysical experience, the projector can eventually attend schools in extraphysical communities on a regular basis, during certain periods of his/her human existence, according to the similar testimonies of multiple experimenters with advanced knowledge and extraphysical agility.

Symbolic. In order to improve recall, the projector often receives extraphysical classes through an exteriorization of morphothosenes or symbolic consciential projections and thinks that he/she has had dreams that require interpretation.

Recesses. According to the extraphysical helpers, those who study lucid projection with perseverance or promote extraphysical assistance with dedication – such as penta practitioners – need to project frequently in order to maintain correct trains of coherent, firm, unswerving thought. In these cases, the extraphysical helpers cooperate in order for the periods of recess of lucid projections to be rarer and/or shorter.

Purposes. The purpose of class-projections is to instruct us and increase our body of knowledge about the structure of the universe, the nature of existential realities and the manifestation of natural laws. This is done in order for researchers of truth to free themselves from the chaos of specific concepts stemming from great amounts of the most contradictory or idiosyncratic information and ideas that exist in the traditions, reports and texts (ancient and modern) of the cogitations and lucubrations of human thought.

Mentalsoma. Class-projections, when occurring while the intraphysical consciousness is projected in the mentalsoma, are superior to others and have greater positive results. In these cases, however, recall is scattered, arriving gradually over time, almost always intuitively.

Hemispheres. The contemporary individual's cerebral hemispheres still do not permit the direct, integral, *en bloc* mnemonic filtering of a great volume of ideas belonging to the registers of the holomemory or our holobiography from the mentalsomatic dimension all at the same time.

Bibliography: Crookall (343, p. 99), Crouzet (344, p. 107), Leadbeater (901, p. 306), Monroe (1065, p. 131), Muldoon (1105, p. 148), Schul (1524, p. 84), Sculthorp (1531, p. 26), Sherman (1551, p. 195), Steiger (1601, p. 123), Vieira (1762, p. 137), Yogananda (1894, p. 307).

426. THEORY OF INTERMISSIVE COURSES

Definition. Intermissive course: the set of subjects taught in classes, according to programs planned in series, adapted to the different levels of the students of *materiology*, or *holoresomatics*, during the intermissive periods (intermissions) of desomant consciousnesses.

Synonymy: multiexistential certification course; interexistential course; pre-resomatic course; intermissive research internship; previous mini-resoma; intermissive training; resoma entrance examination.

Paragenetics. According to the theory of existential seriation, every human personality, in this evolutionary phase of *Homo sapiens,* on earth, is already reborn with a respectable stock of (innate) knowledge through paragenetics.

Aptitudes. What distinguishes one person from another is one's deficient or enriched stockpile of pre-science or innate aptitudes resulting from conquests achieved prior to rebirth. This is valid for all consciential principles, even subhuman or pre-human intraphysical beings (simple consciousnesses), to a lesser degree, such as: dogs, horses, elephants, chimpanzees, dolphins, whales.

Pre-science. A greater level of pre-science of the extraphysical consciousness that undergoes resoma signifies a greater freedom from the rigidities of genetics, the determinism of the basic laws of the universe, the influence of mesology, all types of inner needs and many powerful variables that act upon the consciousness which is restricted in the resoma process, being stripped of its major cons.

Intermission. Intermission is the extraphysical interval occurring between two consecutive human lives of the same extraphysical consciousness. Every intraphysical consciousness has already experienced as many *pre-somatic* intermissions as his/her previous human lives. He/she will inevitably go through another *post-desomatic* intermission upon leaving the human body in the final projection or desoma.

Visits. Human and lucid projectors, in the most diverse times and locations, describe their occasional visits to intermissive courses as auditing students. These educational extraphysical excursions give the consciousness an overall vision of consciential life and the existential program with the perspective of *that side,* in a multidimensional manner.

Reports. The visiting lucid projectors mention the existence of multiple extraphysical realities, such as the following 6:

1. **Schools.** Paramaterial educational establishments in communities of like-minded beings.
2. **Faculty.** Faculties of helpers, petifree consciousnesses, evolutiologists and even *serenissimi.*
3. **Para-students.** Student bodies of *resident* para-students.
4. **Rehearsals.** Extraphysical consciousnesses preparing for resoma, which are personifying *simulated* lifetimes, in the manner of theatrical rehearsals and simulated juries.
5. **Morphothosenes.** Transcendent works made from the morphothosenes of evolved mental co-creators.
6. **Replicas.** Installations of exact replicas or living, functioning maquettes of varied human environments.

Objectives. There are various levels of intermissive courses. Four basic objectives can be singled out in the advanced intermissive course:

1. **Evolution.** They maintain self-motivation in the acceleration of the individual's own consciential evolution.
2. **Lifetime.** They use the upcoming human life efficiently, eliminating repetitive experiences or dispensable self-mimicry.
3. **Tasks.** They perform enlightening, predetermined tasks, dynamizing areas of personal, group and collective research.
4. **Planning.** They fit personal intraphysical existences together, according to a retrocognitive perspective, in a single continuous evolutionary line that was previously technically planned in agreement with the directives of the evolutiologist of the karmic group, as well as the individual's existential program relative to the existential programs of evolutionary colleagues.

Characteristics. The candidate to resoma, having been admitted to the advanced courses of specialized *para-education*, presents 4 meritorious characteristics or prerequisites regarding its evolutionary competence:

1. **Holomaturity.** The candidate has achieved para-adulthood or the extraphysical holomaturity that is feasible, neither being in nor presenting the condition of *parachildhood* or infantilization.

2. **Desomatics.** The candidate has passed through the shock of *second desoma,* or deactivation of the holochakra.

3. **Self-discoincidence.** The candidate no longer experiences *locked* human lives or those devoid of lucid consciential projections.

4. **Migrations.** The candidate does not have a *critical,* decisive human life, or one which is subject to imminent, mutilating, interplanetary extraphysical migrations or life with the impositions of *thosenic ruptures* between kindred extraphysical consciousnesses in the evolutionary group. This is a process that is still active and uninterrupted on this planet.

Explanations. The hypothesis of attempted intermissive courses serves to amplify educational philosophy, challenging contemporary educational theories. It explains various occurrences, such as these 3:

1. **Students.** The following were students of intermissive courses: the majority of precocious children or child prodigies; an extensive number of superendowed youths in general, who have specific innate aptitudes in many areas of knowledge; those referred to as being *illuminated* by the condition of cosmic consciousness or cosmoconsciousness; sensitives with various kinds of parapsychism; and a variety of the greatest benefactors of humanity since the seventeenth century.

2. **Teachers.** The most outstanding students, after very successful lives, as existential completists (existential completism), become teachers of intermissive courses.

3. **Echelon.** The first echelon of pre-serenissimus workers, who go through resoma aiming toward the general improvement of the collectivity, is composed of former teachers of the intermissive course.

Didactics. Education is the basic tool for conquering evolution. The facts indicate the improvement of intermissive courses with a more complete methodology. A greater number of the better students are coming to dense matter.

Mandates. There are advanced workers with existential programs or mandates that are executed over 3 consecutive human lives, there being a connection between the 3 experiences.

Generations. The degree to which this will positively influence humanity in the near future can be forecast when the *tenth generation* of former students and former teachers, for example – arriving from intermissive courses which are correlated, active and interwoven – are operating unfailingly, with and among themselves (intraphysical consciousnesses).

Curricula. The following are 26 themes of classes and pararesearch that are included in the curricula of advanced intermissive courses, listed in alphabetical order by subject:

1. **Clarification task.** The consolation task versus the clarification task.

2. **Conciliations.** Experiences with more heteroforgiving justifiably cosmoethical self-sacrifice, in view of the group existential programs.

3. **Cosmism.** Temporary, *parascientific* excursions to other inhabited planets.

4. **Cosmoethics.** Cosmoethics which is applied or experienced in any consciential dimension.

5. **Derepression.** The derepression and *debrainwashing* acceleration technique.

6. **Evolutiology.** Multiexistential self-awareness regarding prolific lifetimes.

7. **Experimentology.** Extraphysical approaches versus intraphysical approaches.

8. **Extraphysical clinic.** Fundamental reasons and causes for opening an active extraphysical clinic.

9. **Extraphysicology.** Lucid and useful projectability (animism) in the intermissive period.

10. **Freedom.** Maturation of personal free will within the karmic group.

11. **Genetics.** Healthy coexistence with genetics in relation to one's own paragenetics.

12. **Holochakrology.** Consciential energetic self-mastery in intraphysical life.
13. **Hyperacuity.** Holomaturity when immersed in dense matter (cons).
14. **Intermissiology.** Useful parapsychism in the intermissive period.
15. **Intraphysicology.** Lucid and useful projectability in the intraphysical state (pangraphy).
16. **Megafraternity.** Prodigality versus pure, exemplified megafraternity.
17. **Mentalsomatics.** Improvement and deepening of fundamental self-reflections.
18. **Mesology.** Healthy self-control of mesology (environment or ecology).
19. **Mnemosomatics.** Acceleration or dynamization of self-retrocognitions.
20. **Multidimensionality.** Interdimensional self-awareness.
21. **Panoramic.** Multimillenary panoramic vision and multiexistential retrocognitions.
22. **Penta.** The daily practice of penta with cosmoethical naturality.
23. **Polykarmology.** Healthy predisposition toward polykarma (holokarmology).
24. **Projectiology.** Parapsychism which is useful while the intraphysical consciousness is in the projected state.
25. **Serenology.** Applied serenology stemming from the petifree condition.
26. **Theorice.** Many types of pre-somatic theorice exercises.

Failures. The above notwithstanding, a high percentage of operational losses and failures is assumed, on the part of the workers that took intermissive courses. This affects ¾ of the various echelons of mandates which are designated or existential programs which are articulated prior to resoma.

Disturbances. The rigidity of genetics, the power of hereditariness, the consciousness outfitted with an entirely new cellular body, the draconian amnesia of physical infancy, the multifarious animal affectionate involvements and the illusion-temptations *(maya)* of material life, regrettably disturb or annul our efforts at renewal as resomants.

Self-mimicries. We end up repeating past, inefficient, instinctive experiences *ad nauseam* in a senseless vicious circle (the law of least resistance), retarding our personal evolution relative to our respective karmic groups or evolutionary colleagues.

Obstacles. The following are 10 common obstacles to the realizations which are predetermined by the elementary presomatic courses. They arise in the first, preparatory phase of human life and reflect upon the second, executive phase. They are listed here in chronological order:

1. Schooling.
2. Profession or job.
3. Karmic group of the *nuclear family* (mother, father).
4. Marriage.
5. Children (progeny).
6. Profession or job of your mate or the partner in your evolutionary duo.
7. Karmic group of the *extended family* (in-laws).
8. Trips.
9. Financial conditions.
10. Human or social interests in general.

Promises. The entire 100% of intermissive course students and student-workers make promises to themselves and are dispatched to resoma with salutations and pompous titles, such as: "messengers of justice"; "pioneers of the ideal"; "ambassadors of peace"; "sculptors of the spirit"; "leaders of renewal"; "messengers of good"; "ministers of truth"; "missionaries of redemption"; "workers of knowledge"; "priests of love"; and many others. Nevertheless, the majority remain merely in this initial poetic promise. A million words are worth far less than a single fact.

Retrocognitions. Your retrocognitions of previous intraphysical lives are less relevant than the recollections of your *intermissive predispositions* or, in other words: that which you studied in your pre-somatic course, even when it is rudimentary.

Conscientiocentrology. The International Institute of Projectiology and Conscientiology (IIPC) – a school of conscientiocentric and universalistic consciential research – endeavors, through a projectiological educational system, to develop teachers who employ theoretical and practical approaches using their mentalsomas and bioenergies, serving as *retrocognitive agents* for intraphysical consciousnesses.

IIPC. The aim of the IIPC is to reactivate – without hypnosis and with self-critique and heterocritique – the deep, integral, causal (holomemory) extracerebral memory of their own intermissive courses, starting from the students' mentalsomas. This makes their *pre-curricular science* or innate ideas, which are preserved through paragenetics, blossom in the present.

Self-analysis. If you wish to become familiar with your potential intermissive course, you should analyze, with great self-critique, whether or not at least 5 of these 10 personality traits (strong traits) are present in yourself and verify their degree, extent, vigor and quality:

1. **Doubts.** An inner absence of mortifying philosophical doubts during adult life.

2. **Self-conscientiality.** The certainty of immortality, the awareness of the eternal nature of your life as a human consciousness.

3. **Use.** A deep inner aspiration to make full use of intraphysical life, regarding personal evolution, seeking discernment and knowledge.

4. **Conscientiality.** A natural acceptance of the theory of existential seriation, or the continued alternation of intraphysical life-intermissive life, as a given which is incorporated in daily existence.

5. **Inspirations.** A sense of illuminating inspirations about the meanderings of personal destiny, your professional or subsistence career, in other words: human life itself.

6. **Assistentiology.** Spontaneous self-motivation for the research and performance of beneficial parapsychic practices (self-lucid cosmoethical solidarity).

7. **Parapsychism.** Animic-parapsychic self-perceptions through phenomena which may even be sporadic or rare, but are convincing or unforgettable for oneself.

8. **Existential program.** Undefined though persistent intuitions about an existential program that you are to realize, whether alone or in group (group karma).

9. **Self-retrocognitions.** Self-retrocognitions which are coherent, enriching and not compulsive or mortifying.

10. **Self-awareness.** General self-aware identification regarding the cosmos, life and the natural order of the universe.

Will. If, however, you do not identify even 5 of these 10 strong traits within your consciential micro-universe and nevertheless insist on participating in an extraphysical course in your next intermission, do not be discouraged. Take the first steps toward achieving this objective. Intermissive courses are accessible to all motivated consciousnesses. Improve what you can in your existence while you still direct a human body with lucidity, relative health and freedom. Apply maximal willpower in the correction of personal errors, starting immediately.

Right. The right to know ourselves and act upon ourselves is nontransferable and completely our own or belongs to each of us.

Shock. As an advanced idea that is completely surrealistic at first glance, the hypothesis of the intermissive course collides with the mechanistic Newtonian-Cartesian paradigm of conventional science, as well as with the reader who is fearful regarding human ambiguities. This attitude makes it so that the individual ends up becoming entrenched within his/her ego defense mechanisms. However, if the individual goes more deeply within him/herself, in a consciential self-examination, he/she will discover the logical bases of this set of concepts, which are practically inevitable considering the basic premise of evolution of the consciousness over a long series of existences or lifetimes.

Inexperience. The individual who, in principle, does not accept this theory has obviously not yet attended an advanced intermissive course.

Logic. Intermissive courses have clear, indisputable uses, with relation to consciential evolution. The practical reality of intermissive courses is a question of logic and a simple awakening of the intelligence. If there is extraphysical life, there must be educational courses. There is no life without education.

Anticosmoethical. In fact, the projected human projector ends up finding intermissive courses through educational consciential projections. Further more: this same veteran, lucid projector also comes across the extraphysical training courses of extraphysical hypnotist-intruders, which even include the satellites of intruders (not to mention extraphysical blind guides), in crustal, paratropospheric, anticosmoethical, or shadowy dimensions. From this arise the inspirations of lawless gangs and schools of organized crime *(societas sceleris)*.

Question. If there are courses of pathological or sick education in extraphysical dimensions, why would there not also be healthy extraphysical educational courses?

Bibliography: Vieira (1762, p. 22).

---

427. NATURAL CONSCIENTIAL PROJECTION

Definition. Natural consciential projection: discoincidence of the vehicles of manifestation of the human consciousness occurring in a spontaneous manner, without provocation on the part of the lucid practitioner or, in other words: without external stimulation.

Synonymy: habitual projection; natural discoincidence; N-OBE; self-generated lucid projection; spontaneous projection; unforced lucid projection; unintentional lucid projection.

Classification. Natural consciential projection can be classified into two primary or basic categories:

1. **Nonlucid.** *Nonlucid* natural projection, occurring more commonly at night, during sleep, affects all members of humanity.

2. **Lucid.** Spontaneous, lucid natural projection, experienced only by a microminority (still in 1998) of individuals.

Characteristics. The following are 5 of the essential characteristics of natural consciential projection:

1. **Spontaneity.** Spontaneity regarding the manifestation.
2. **Amenity.** Gradation of occurrences or personal trauma-free experiences.
3. **Simplicity.** Lack of a need for projective effort or exercise by the intraphysical consciousness.
4. **Imperceptibility.** Absence of perceptible, evident or defined objective (goal), purpose of the lucid projection or a predetermined and established consciential target.
5. **Agility.** The general development of the consciential projection without any control or command by the projector's self-critiquing judgment.

Frequency. Natural consciential projection is more frequent than forced consciential projection. It occurs gradually, in conditions such as illness, psychophysical exhaustion, near-death experience (NDE), natural sleep and the individual's normal states.

Categories. The following are 5 categories or types of occurrences which are *more common* regarding spontaneous consciential projections, according to the personal research of the author, conducted on his person and other international projectors, over 3 decades:

1. **Blind.** Blind projection, close to the human body without the consciousness seeing, but sensing the paratropospheric extraphysical dimension.
2. **Abrupt.** Projection in which the intraphysical consciousness (you) does not perceive the takeoff of the psychosoma and suddenly finds him/herself aware in an environment distant from the physical base.
3. **Somatics.** Projection with the awakening of the intraphysical consciousness inside the bedroom of the physical base, contemplating his/her own human body, which is inactive on the bed.
4. **Extraphysicology.** Projection in which the intraphysical consciousness sees various extraphysical consciousnesses running down shadowy streets.

5. **Volitative.** Projection in which the intraphysical consciousness, through volitation, (almost always) feels him/herself volitating over a countryside environment without encountering any extraphysical consciousnesses.

Predisposition. A spontaneous, lucid projection occurring effortlessly and naturally, can predispose the individual toward a willfully provoked lucid consciential projection more easily, in a shorter period of time and, sometimes, promote projections in series (consecutive experiences).

Taoism. Natural or automatic consciential projection is found in the studies of Chinese Taoism.

Bibliography: Alvarado (17, p. 11), Blackmore (139, p. 51), Crookall (338, p. 3), Holzer (745, p. 163), Montandon (1070, p. 228), Pearce-Higgins (1214, p. 67), Reis (1384, p. 50), Rogo (1444, p. 58), Vieira (1762, p. 111), Wang (1794, p. 198).

428. FORCED LUCID CONSCIENTIAL PROJECTION

Definition. Forced lucid consciential projection: discoincidence of the vehicles of manifestation of the human consciousness provoked by the will of the practitioner or unwittingly by stressful factors, wherein the projector becomes aware of extraphysical occurrences.

Synonymy: E-OBE; forced discoincidence; mechanical exteriorization; mechanical takeoff; toxic consciential projection.

Characteristics. Forced lucid consciential projection is less frequent than natural lucid consciential projection and can occur through the willful action of the intraphysical consciousness or even suddenly (unexpectedly and surprisingly).

Factors. The following are 15 common stressful factors capable of triggering the mechanical projection of the consciousness (you) from the human body. They are listed in alphabetical order of occurrence:

1. Automobile accident or one involving some type of equipment (machine, apparatus).
2. Cave-in (building collapse).
3. Drowning.
4. Effects of medications, anesthetics, narcotics, stupefacients or toxins in general.
5. Emotional syncope.
6. Explosion in a battlefield or an armed conflict.
7. Falling (somatics).
8. Great immanent danger, whether fire, shipwreck, train wreck, battlefield combat, or surgical intervention.
9. Hetero-hypnotic trance.
10. Influence of taking light or heavy drugs (intoxication).
11. Moral shock to the individual.
12. Physical shock to the human body.
13. Suffocation (cardiochakra).
14. Violence in general, such as the knockout of a boxer (anticosmoethical and anti-physiological radical sport).
15. Violent physical accident.

Voluntary. The will of the consciential projector also produces lucid projection which is intentionally forced, or self-induced voluntary lucid projection.

Purity. On the other hand, not all forced consciential projection is totally *impure,* as seen with the production of lucid consciential projection using the mental saturation technique and the carbon dioxide technique, already presented in other chapters of this book.

Bibliography: Alvarado (16, p. 11), Battersby (92, p. 51), Bayless (98, p. 124), Carton (252, p. 311), Crookall (338, p. 118), Currie (354, p. 86), Greenhouse (636, p. 271), Pearce-Higgins (1214, p. 72), Rogo (1444, p. 58), Vieira (1762, p. 190).

429. COMPARISONS BETWEEN NATURAL AND FORCED CONSCIENTIAL PROJECTION

Differential. There are at least 6 basic differences between natural consciential projection and forced consciential projection, in terms of projective facts:

1. **Dimensions.** In a natural consciential projection, the intraphysical consciousness more easily enters the better, more agreeable and more attractive extraphysical dimensions, which are different from intraphysical life on earth. In forced consciential projection, the intraphysical consciousness reaches the extraphysical dimensions featuring more nebulous environments or ambivalent holothosenes.

2. **Encounters.** In natural consciential projection, the intraphysical consciousness encounters former relatives and former friends (extraphysical consciousnesses) more easily. In forced consciential projection, it becomes more difficult for the projected intraphysical consciousness to see or approach extraphysical consciousnesses, except in consciential projections (in this case, traveling clairvoyance) generated through hetero-hypnosis.

3. **Self-lucidity.** In natural consciential projection, the phenomenon of expansion of the consciousness or self-lucidity occurs more frequently. In forced consciential projection, there is a greater alteration in the lucidity of the projected intraphysical consciousness, with a greater interference of oneiric images in extraphysical perceptions occurring (self-paraperceptions).

4. **Pathology.** In natural consciential projection, there is never any factor which can characterize the phenomenon itself as pathological. The forced consciential projection can occur simply due to a fully or indisputably identified illness.

5. **Interference.** In natural consciential projection, there is no interference by extraphysical helpers or extraphysical intruders in the takeoff process. Forced consciential projection can be sponsored by an extraphysical intruder and can even be commanded by an extraphysical helper, in certain positive (healthy) cases.

6. **Inducement.** In natural consciential projection, the projector does not practice any exercise prior to projecting from the soma. Forced consciential projection can be laboriously induced, after great effort by the intraphysical consciousness.

430. ESCAPE-PROJECTION

Definition. Escape-projection: that experiment in which the intraphysical consciousness endeavors to escape from the human body, which has been physically injured in some manner, especially in the psychosoma, being moved or forced by external agents.

Synonymy: consciential escape; projective escape; sudden unfolding.

Categories. The following are 5 of the more frequent categories of escape-projections, according to the predisposing or inducing situations of the phenomenon:

1. **Casualties.** Imminent drowning, for example.
2. **Bellicosity.** The stressful circumstances of war or armed conflicts.
3. **Extremism.** Major physical accidents in caves, caverns, mines, mountain climbing (radical sports) and trenches.
4. **Pathology.** Conditions of illness or psychophysical exhaustion.
5. **Prisoners.** Depressing or extremely stressful situations of incarceration.

Causes. The causes, essential motivations or triggering factors of escape-projection are pain, suffering, a physical trauma or an intense stress factor that provoked the mechanical takeoff or forced ejection of the entire psychosoma from the human body, obviously transporting the consciousness.

Helpers. In addition, this type of lucid consciential projection can be sponsored by an extraphysical helper.

Relationship. There must evidently be some physiological relationship between these instantaneous lucid projections, which feature the continuation of body movements with the cases of people who are able to combine sleeping while standing, and even while on a horse, maintaining their balance while asleep without falling off, or the well-documented case of the excellent pianist who played a passage of music while sleeping.

Note. Escape-projection should not be confused with instantaneous lucid consciential projection, addressed in the next chapter.

Bibliography: Carton (252, p. 311), Crookall (338, p. 33), Frost (560, p. 19), Green (632, p. 63), Greenhouse (636, p. 135), Gurney (666, p. 227), Holms (735, p. 462), Johnson (807, p. 221), Morrell (1088, p. 55), Smythe (1578, p. 277).

---

431. INSTANTANEOUS CONSCIENTIAL PROJECTION

Definition. Instantaneous consciential projection: lightning-fast takeoff, within tenths of a second, or some seconds, with or without the appearance of the immediate extraphysical lucidity of the projected intraphysical consciousness.

Synonymy: automatic projection; instantaneous separation; interdimensional expressway of the intraphysical consciousness; surprise-projection.

Causes. The true causes of instantaneous consciential projection are still very unclear. This phenomenon does not even occur constantly with the advanced and more dedicated projector. In instantaneous consciential projection, both immediate takeoff and immediate interiorization can occur without the intraphysical consciousness being aware of it. In this occurrence, the intraphysical projector can even be erect (soma) or standing up.

Impact. The sensation of impact of the profound difference between the two consciential states – the ordinary, physical waking state and extraphysical lucidity – achieved without transition or interruption in the continuity of lucidity, which sometimes occurs in cases of instantaneous projection, makes it extraordinary, unforgettable and indescribable.

Way. Instantaneous consciential projection constitutes the expressway of the intraphysical consciousness momentarily transferring him/herself to the extraphysical dimension, based upon 3 occurrences:

1. **Technique.** A reduction in the technical efforts of the projector.

2. **Chronology.** A minimized sensation of the duration of the consciousness' departure trajectory to a temporary base or a mobile point outside the human body.

3. **Holochakrology.** It does not allow the viewing of the silver cord.

Surprise. The more common instantaneous consciential projection is spontaneous and provokes surprise, overwhelming the unprepared consciousness (the projector), which has no defined mental target. This instantaneous projection therefore does not always end up being well utilized.

Provoked. Instantaneous consciential projection can be provoked. However, even in these circumstances, the projector never knows with certainty whether or not he/she will have an instantaneous lucid takeoff.

Note. Instantaneous consciential projection – which is apparently healthy and is devoid of any negative or pathological consequence – should not be confused with epileptic absence or petit mal. If, on the one hand, these 2 phenomena are similar in certain aspects, they are, on the other hand, quite different in their causes, sensations and consequences.

Bibliography: Battersby (92, p. 88), Fox (544, p. 48), Frost (560, p. 84), Greenhouse (636, p. 261), Muldoon (1105, p. 257), Shay (1546, p. 103), Vieira (1762, p. 83), Yram (1897, p. 55).

432. CONSCIENTIAL PROJECTION OF THE COMPOUND DOUBLE

Definition. Consciential projection of the compound double: that projection produced by the intraphysical consciousness when he/she manifests extraphysically in the psychosoma laden with part of the holochakra or, in other words, carrying a discardable weight.

Synonymy: consciential bariprojection; consciential projection in the psychosoma with the holochakra; consciential projection of 3 bodies; consciential projection of the composite double.

Characteristics. When projected in the psychosoma, accompanied by a high percentage of the crustal energies of the holochakra, the intraphysical consciousness should prepare him/herself to confront various characteristic, specific extraphysical conjunctures, most notably the following 21:

1. **Ballast.** The consciousness finds the psychosoma to be dense, quite heavy (lucid bariprojection) and complete in its humanoid forms, more laden with the *ballast* (charge or equipment) of the holochakra.

2. **Paratroposphere.** In this condition, the intraphysical consciousness inevitably projects to more paratropospheric extraphysical environments, the *planetary floor*. In these circumstances, the projected intraphysical consciousness often has difficulty going through fences, walls and closed doors or, in other words: he/she encounters problems with extraphysical permeability.

3. **Intraphysicology.** When the intraphysical consciousness undergoes the vigorous intensification of the influence of the physical factors of terrestrial life, it makes this projective modality the *most human* and *least extraphysical* of consciential projections. He/she can sometimes move physical objects or, in other words, produce extraphysical telekinesis, whether consciously or even unconsciously.

4. **Chronology.** In this consciential experience, chronological time seems to pass slowly. In consciential projection of the compound double, 5 minutes of extraphysical experience give the false impression of an hour's absence from the soma and the physical base.

5. **Slow motion.** If projected in this way, in the extraphysical sphere of consciential energies of the intraphysical consciousness, or even in the environment of the physical base, the consciousness can easily move him/herself in slow motion, or mechanically repeat movements that are identical to those of the human body.

6. **Gravitation.** The intraphysical consciousness can unquestionably perceive the influence of the ambient gravitational force. This makes it difficult for the projector to achieve major levitations and full volitation of the psychosoma, which is loaded with energies, which seems contradictory or paradoxical. In order to ascend the height of a twenty-floor building, for example, the projector will seem to have spent the same consciential effort required to circle the entire planet.

7. **Discontinuity.** Upon projecting, on this occasion, the projector is urged to pay attention to his/her lucidity in order to not let him/herself succumb to a discontinuity in lucidity and involve him/herself in a whirlpool of oneiric images during the natural development of extraphysical events. The almost irresistible tendency imposed by extraphysical circumstances will always be to transform the lucid projection into a semilucid projection.

8. **Psychosomatics.** The holochakra, when in tow, potentiates, or more appropriately, maximally exaggerates the emotions that the psychosoma (emotional body) allows the consciousness to feel. For example, any superficial error in interpretation appears to be a world of mistakes. This explains the post-desomatic disturbances and parapsychoses of certain extraphysical consciousnesses which have recently arrived at the intermissive period. They have merely gone through the first desoma – only the deactivation of the human body – and still have part of the holochakra with them. They experience, for some time, profound solitude or isolation, self-guilt and lack of affection that they suppose or that seem, in their intraconsciential micro-universe, to be immense, definitive, eternal and devastating (the illusions of inferno or hell).

9. **Desomatics.** It can be concluded that consciential projection in the psychosoma, laden with a part of the holochakra, gives the intraphysical consciousness a preview of the exact sensations the projector will be feeling during the inevitable shock of first desoma or deactivation of the human

body. The projector will, in this way, definitively understand, by feeling at first hand, a small sample of the inner state of the ill communicants in parapsychic sessions of psychophony and deintrusion.

10. **Traumas.** The above-mentioned predisposition toward emotionality and dramatization predisposes the intraphysical consciousness to extraphysical traumas and repercussions.

11. **Crutch.** There is an insistent and contradictory propensity for the intraphysical consciousness to occasionally remember the human body and the momentary circumstances of the consciential projection, as though this recollection serves as a *parapsychological* crutch for maintaining lucidity. It actually does help, on the one hand, but can also impel the psychosoma to suddenly return to the human body.

12. **Mnemosomatics.** A spontaneous inner reaction arises to fit the extraphysical occurrences, as they unfold, beyond the framework of the *emotional memory* of the current human life. An example of this is the image of trees being cut to clear a space for a tall building. This, seen from an extraphysical point of view, at that moment, leads the projector's consciousness to try to fit it into the scene of deforestation for road construction, witnessed during childhood and still stored in the physical memory bank (cerebral memory of the current brain).

13. **Duration.** Due to all these determining factors, consciential projection in the psychosoma laden with part of the coupled holochakra or, in other words, with a portion of its *operational energetic batteries,* tends to be shorter. Perhaps one of the greatest psychophysical feats available to the intraphysical being must be the act of projecting in these conditions for 3 straight hours, while maintaining full, continuous, imperturbable lucidity, without incurring any secondary pathological connotation or effect.

14. **Shower.** Upon the interiorization of the intraphysical consciousness, after a projection of over 15 minutes in the psychosoma with a portion of the holochakra, a spontaneous, continuous *energetic shower* will inevitably occur upon physical awakening in an apparent overflowing of consciential energies.

15. **Stockpiling.** In light of the above-mentioned fact, it can be inferred that the *defensive energetic armor* that the holochakra represents, in certain physical-extraphysical circumstances, opens and helps to increase the capacity of the projected psychosoma to provide itself with cosmic vitality (immanent energy, volitation).

16. **Discoincidence.** Consciential projection in these specific conditions predisposes temporary, post-projective waking discoincidence of the vehicles of manifestation of the consciousness, as well as the phenomenon of double awareness.

17. **Self-permeability.** In consciential projection of the compound double, the capacity of extraphysical self-permeability (self-penetrability) – a characteristic of the projected intraphysical consciousness – diminishes considerably.

18. **Vision.** In the same way that lucidity becomes diminished and self-permeability becomes restricted, in many cases of consciential projection of the compound double, the extraphysical vision of the projected projector also exhibits reduced acuity or sharpness.

19. **Semi-intraphysical.** The projector, when projected in this manner, almost being *semi-intraphysical* or even materialized, will always be more capable of appearing to sensitive human beings, clairvoyant sensitives (apparition of intraphysical beings) and even to people in general (physical self-bilocation).

20. **Sensitive.** The active, middle-aged, developed sensitive of any type of parapsychism is more capable of producing these consciential projections with impressive lucidity, as they have more experience, even being unaware of coexistence with the projected holochakra. This, however, does not mean that non-sensitive youths do not produce them.

21. **Helper.** Often, the presence of a helper, *at the projector's side,* with the use of transmental dialogue, or extraphysical telepathy, extraordinarily facilitates the maintenance of the extraphysical lucidity and prolongation of this type of consciential projection experience. It is the same with a sleepy person who someone endeavors to keep in the ordinary, physical waking state.

Ectoplasm. Consciential projection of the compound double that achieves greater density or, in other words, is more *materialized,* is that in which the psychosoma receives, through the silver cord – as well as the energetic resources running from the human body up to the psychosoma – ponderable elements of ectoplasm, or biological components, from the structure of human cells (cytoplasm) that compose ectoplasm.

Load. In general, the holochakra constitutes a load of fuel (a jettisonable load or a consumable weight) to the projected and laden psychosoma.

Obesity. An obese person, or one with a high excess of corporal weight, carries considerable organic dead weight, a static charge or an empty burden for living the human experience. This, however, does not apply to the compound double, which is directly related, not to the human body, but to the energetic parabody or holochakra.

Bibliography: Crookall (333, p. 34), Vieira (1762, p. 168).

---

433. POST-NATAL, REGRESSIVE, SEMILUCID CONSCIENTIAL PROJECTION

Definition. Post-natal, regressive, semilucid consciential projection: the natural dream that transforms into a semilucid, consciential projection derived from the specific target-place of the prior human history of the projector.

Synonymy: discontinuous, historical consciential projection; extraphysical consciential return to origins; post-natal extraphysical progression; projective regression; semilucid, historical consciential projection.

Causes. The following are 4 isolated or even convergent causes or factors which come together and predispose the intraphysical consciousness to spontaneously produce semilucid consciential projections stemming from *historical dreams* of his/her personal experience:

1. **Intraphysicology.** A change of residence in life, being a change in street address or district within the same city, as well as a move from one location to another.

2. **Pharmacology.** The use of certain medications that affect the central nervous system, notably in the mnemonic area.

3. **Gerontology.** Mature intraphysical age.

4. **Pathology.** Arteriosclerosis or Alzheimer's disease.

Case study. For example, a person dreams about a certain period of his/her prior personal history, which occurred one, two or more decades before. The physical setting of his/her historical dream, which still exists, predisposes his/her projected consciousness to semilucidly go to the place where he/she lived and had agreeable or traumatic experiences. In this case, it functions as an unconscious evocation of the human target-place, with a vigorous power of attraction. This ends up characterizing a type of *haunting by a living person.*

Places. The places revisited by semilucid projectors in post-natal regression can vary greatly. The following 4 are examples:

1. **Education.** The elementary school from childhood (education or cultural background).
2. **Youth.** The residence where the individual lived during his/her youth.
3. **Freedom.** The place where the individual had unaccompanied or free experiences as a bachelor.
4. **Profession.** The place where the individual lived when he/she began professional life.

Consequences. The following are 5 basic consequences resulting from semilucid, historical projections:

1. **Disconnection.** The semilucid projector sometimes feels even more disturbed in his/her recollections, endeavoring to repeat the simulacrum of the act inspired by his/her monoideism, or vainly

fit the old experiences into the rooms of the current residence, or the current existential circumstances of that night's dream. These circumstances generally do not allow adaptation with the extraphysical activities of his/her semilucid projection which are profoundly disconnected, incoherent, or even absurd.

2. **Invasion.** When the current residents of the former domicile – generally being houses which are still in the same place – have a certain degree of extraphysical lucidity during their sleep period, which is almost always at night, it can happen that both the visiting projector and the visited projectors are simultaneously sleeping and the residents are able to detect the presence of the semilucidly projected projector through a dream and the fact that it is invading the visited projectors' privacy, trying to penetrate the intimacy of their home. The consciousness of the invading projector still considers the residence to be the same, and often his/her own property, trying impossibly to melancholically exhume, or longingly revive experiences which remain in the past, in different circumstances, albeit having occurred in the same human surroundings.

3. **Encounters.** Those who reside in houses or other old well-conserved properties should not be surprised if they sometimes encounter an aimless former resident outside the human body, having returned to that location through his/her semilucid projections, walking like a somnambulant throughout the rooms of the residence, conducting an *extraphysical midnight inspection,* often as though he/she were still the incontestable owner of that environment, the legitimate current inhabitant of that place, or the true owner of the property.

4. **Extraphysical consciousnesses.** Many individuals who have recently become extraphysical consciousnesses through desoma, often still disturbed by some post-desomatic parapsychosis, or posthumous monoideism, return to the terrestrial locations where they had unforgettable impactful experiences. In many cases, these facts are simple repetitions of their historical semilucid projections that occurred during human existence.

5. **Poltergeist.** Some cases of historical poltergeist phenomena should be included here which involve consciousnesses that are now extraphysical. It is, nevertheless, not impossible for this to even occur with the manifestations of intraphysical consciousnesses. Both cases constitute types of *haunting ghosts.*

Recurrence. Due to the same causal factors presented here, the semilucid historical projection can transform itself into a recurring consciential projection, or one that repeats itself frequently, due to the convergence of propitious triggering circumstances.

Bibliography: Vieira (1762, p. 155).

434. SONOROUS CONSCIENTIAL PROJECTION

Definition. Sonorous consciential projection: exteriorization of the consciousness from the human body in the psychosoma, with or without its *sonorous* physical apparition, or at least its speech, which becomes audible to other people, or the characteristic sound of itself, in a location distant from the physical base.

Synonymy: audioprojection; echoic consciential projection; invisible consciential projection; itinerant clairaudience; projective direct voice; resonant consciential projection; sonorous consciential apparition; speaking consciential apparition; traveling clairaudience.

Accidental. The most common sonorous projection of the consciousness is spontaneous or accidental, occurring in cases of highly stressful physical accidents, occurring most frequently during floods and drowning.

Drowning. An almost drowned individual, in the physical and mental agitation in which he/she finds him/herself, without apparent means for escaping the critical situation, uses all of his/her mental energy in agonized screams of desperation, fighting to save him/herself. These calls for help sometimes become physically audible, extraphysically echoing to other persons, relatives and friends, who are distant at that time, even being on other continents.

Projection. In many occurrences such as these, listeners or spectators even witness the humanoid manifestation of the projected projector at the exact moment of the accident.

Images. Although their study has been neglected, *auditory images* have a real existence in time and perform an important role in human life. In the ordinary, physical waking state, they are invoked through a temporal succession or, in other words: with regard to the development of chronological time.

Psychopathology. Psychopathology has proven that *auditory hallucinations* are richer, more frequent and much more relevant then classic visual hallucinations.

Predominance. In the acquisition of information, auditory memory predominates over visual memory. This is naturally due to the capacity for retention of auditory perceptions and the ease with which their images are produced.

Invisible. In most cases of sonorous consciential projection, an invisible projection occurs, namely a projection of the consciousness in the psychosoma wherein the density of this parabody does not reach a level that becomes visible to the percipient or percipients, thus constituting the phenomenon of physical bilocation of the consciousness. This only allows the consciousness to make its presence known through touch or sound.

Density. Thus, it is shown that – from the perspective of the psychosoma's density – the sonorous consciential projection is situated between the common, integral projection of the consciousness, in a rarified form, and the traditional phenomenon of physical bilocation, with a densified form.

Monologues. There are reports of rare occurrences of short monologues by the projector or agent-projector, sketches of dialogue between this consciousness and the percipient, who is even able to *audibly* identify the communicant, although not distinguishing it with the eyes of the human body.

Poltergeist. There are occurrences of effective connection between intraphysical intruders and poltergeist manifestations, which are presumed to be mere sonorous projections of intraphysical consciousnesses.

Direct. There have been registered cases of intraphysical consciousnesses who communicated through the direct voice phenomenon in parapsychic physical effect sessions. In these cases, the person of the communicant neither appeared nor used the sensitive's speech mechanism in order to express him/herself.

Mechanism. The mechanism for producing sonorous consciential projection still remains extremely obscure. For example, in this case would there be a densification of the vocal apparatus of the projector or projector-agent's psychosoma? Would this densification be governed by the extraordinary impulsion of the will of the superlatively stressed consciousness?

Word. Within the scope of auditory images, the inner word, or the *mental word,* presents important significance. It has no objective existence, being entirely foreign to the intraphysical dimension because it refers to a state of self, and therefore only to a psychic or mentalsomatic fact of the intraphysical consciousness. This occurs when the individual thinks about an abstract thing and silently pronounces the word that represents this same thing to him/herself. People who frequently experience the common phenomenon of hearing mental words are more predisposed to be recipients, in occurrences of sonorous consciential projections.

Musicians. Musicians in general, and especially conductors and composers, as they have a more developed ability to hear words and sounds mentally, are also physiologically better able to operate as percipients in sonorous consciential projections.

Hypothesis. A statistical survey has still not been performed of the percentage of conductors and composers among the percipients of sonorous consciential projections. This is a valid, projectiological work hypothesis.

Hyperacuity. There are registered phenomena of auditory hyperacuity (hyperacusia) in which the person acting as a percipient, or clairaudient sensitive, can hear sounds generated by an apparition better than if it were a real person. The same has been occurring with lucid projectors that hear extremely quiet sounds while projected and, nevertheless, in the ordinary, physical waking state are completely deaf or can only hear when using a hearing aid.

Bibliography: Boswell (174, p. 135), Flammarion (524, p. 118), Green (633, p. 169), Greenhouse (636, p. 139), Gurney (666, p. 130), Kardec (825, p. 188), Muldoon (1103, p. 98), Paim (1182, p. 32), Rhine (1389, p. 24), Stevens (1617, p. 237), Wang (1794, p. 191), Wheeler (1826, p. 68).

435. EXTRAPHYSICAL VISUAL PROJECTION

Definition. Extraphysical visual projection: the act wherein the projected intraphysical consciousness sees, hears, senses and, in some ways, even participates in coherent and well-coordinated scenes which are somehow projected by and for the projector, either with or without tangible interference from an extraphysical helper.

Synonymy: extraphysical audiovisual system; extraphysical ideoplasty; illustrated thoughts.

Similarities. Extraphysical visual projection is reminiscent of the occurrences of panoramic vision, recollection of past intraphysical existences and intensely vivid, colored dreams. However, they are different from each other because of the full awareness of being in the extraphysical dimension and the voluntary participation involved in the processes of visual projection.

Symbology. Extraphysical visual projections are not always practical or immediately applicable, clear or fully intelligible, nor are they literal in their messages. They sometimes appear in symbolic form or are mixed with the common facts of physical-extraphysical reality.

Bibliography: Vieira (1762, p. 41).

436. JOINT LUCID PROJECTIONS

Definition. Joint lucid projections: extraphysical experiences in which there is a simultaneous participation of two or more intraphysical consciousnesses who are projected from the soma and manifest with lucidity (see fig. 436, p. 1,151).

Synonymy: consciential projection *à trois;* consciential projections of encounter; extraphysical interconsciential connections; flock of extraphysical fliers; flock of projectors; mutual lucid projections; reciprocal lucid projections; shared consciential projections.

Opportunities. The mechanism of successive intraphysical lives allows extraphysical consciousnesses to physically live in the school-hospital of earth in order to serve (fraternity) each other. This is the major goal of human life. Mutual assistance is logically performed through encounters (coexistology) between intraphysical consciousnesses (humanity). A single resoma in the twentieth century, in the *global village,* or the intensified coexistence of modern intraphysical society, in this era of acceleration of history, allows more encounters between persons, in one week, than during an entire human life in the Middle Ages.

Children. The children that are now beginning their first year of primary education have already lived various existences, compared with their grandparents. This means that our current human life, in its evolutionary usefulness, is *worth dozens of our past intraphysical lives,* even recent ones. This is because it allows an incomparably greater number of encounters with other human beings, thereby affording greater opportunities for mutual assistance between us.

Projectiology. Lucid projections, through *extraphysical* encounters with para-humanity, exponentially increase the possibilities for mutual assistance between intraphysical consciousnesses in general, projected intraphysical consciousnesses and extraphysical consciousnesses.

Types. Joint lucid projections can occur intentionally, with the participating projectors being previously aware, having arranged the experience beforehand, and even taking off from the same physical base. They can also occur spontaneously, through occasional extraphysical encounters sponsored by extraphysical helpers, without the prior knowledge of the human participants. The more frequent type of lucid projection, nowadays, is the one having romantic motives.

Sweethearts. The persons most indicated for tests of joint lucid projection are pairs of young sweethearts, because they are more motivated to be together.

Beginning. In the beginning of the experiments, mere joint *semilucid* projections can occur, instead of joint *lucid* projections.

Lucidity. Besides, the projectors do not always have an equal level of extraphysical lucidity in joint consciential projections. This is natural and the reason why mild discrepancies or apparent conflicts can arise in their reports. Nevertheless, in joint lucid projections, the basic lines of extraphysical events are perceived and registered in a similar and convergent manner, clearly confirming the common experiences.

Assistentiology. Joint consciential projections allow mutual extraphysical assistance between projectors, beginning with the act of leaving the human body, or extraphysical hetero-awakening, and even during lucid and extraphysical volitation. This is because consciousnesses do not present identical levels in their attributes. Degrees of perception, vitality and mastery in the extraphysical dimension vary from projector to projector and even from projection to projection with the same practitioner consciousness.

Confusion. It should also be remembered, if you are endeavoring to produce a lucid projection together with other persons, to take care in order to avoid making noise or creating confusion upon returning from the extraphysical experiences, in order not to interfere in the experiences of other intraphysical consciousnesses which have not yet returned to the area.

Contacts. The projector who is fully aware of having encountered either known or unknown intraphysical consciousnesses, while projected from the human body, should try to contact them personally, giving his/her human address. This is because there is always a chance of meeting someone who also clearly remembers the same extraphysical experiences in identical environments and locations. This allows analysis, study and observation of inestimable corroborative or phenomenological value.

Interiorization. Contact with the projected colleague should be made before it *disappears* in interiorization and moves the human body. Afterwards, it is always very difficult to reestablish any effective understanding of the occasion. You have to leave it for another time, should this arise.

Animism. When 2 or more projected intraphysical projectors encounter each other in the extraphysical dimension there is no parapsychic phenomenon, nor is there interference from another projector nor from an extraphysical consciousness. There is only a purely animic phenomenon between intraphysical consciousnesses, utilizing the extraphysical dimension and their perceptions, without requiring the participation of any extraphysical consciousness.

Categories. Extraphysical encounters can be classified into two categories, with respect to the lucidity of the projected consciousness:

1. **Mutual.** Mutual encounters or those in which two intraphysical consciousnesses meet each other while lucidly projected, thereby having a mutual encounter and interconsciential communication becoming possible.

2. **Unilateral.** Unilateral encounters or those in which only one consciousness is lucid, thereby allowing a unilateral encounter wherein extraphysical communication becomes impracticable.

Assistential. The unilateral extraphysical encounter is common during assistential consciential projections conducted under the auspices of extraphysical helpers wherein one intraphysical consciousness, the assistant, encounters another intraphysical consciousness, the assisted, given that the latter does not exhibit extraphysical lucidity.

Sessions. The projective session is that one in which a group of persons endeavoring to leave the human body together, at the same time, in the same physical base, follow the same inductive factors or use the same psychophysiological crutches. Projective sessions in Brazil (spiritist meetings, *apometria)*, are called "unfolding sessions." These sessions operate under the orientation of a president, which also allows the participation of novice animist-sensitives who observe – without projecting – the veteran consciential projectors who are endeavoring to project in that environment.

Rescues. In these works, lucid projectors endeavor to cooperate in extraphysical assistance provided to ill intraphysical and extraphysical consciousnesses, even performing extraphysical rescues of needy extraphysical consciousnesses which have been kidnapped by others individually or by groups of extraphysical intruder consciousnesses. They also help governors and those governed, assist patients in hospitals, and perform psychic and parapsychic cleansing at a distance.

Currents. Aside from the president, projectors and beginners, individuals serving as energetic supports – persons who are donators of consciential energies and positive thoughts – also participate in these private sessions that aim to produce lucid consciential projection, thereby forming so-called "fluidic currents".

Mystifications. These meetings are considered to have a high degree of mystification, fraud and occurrences of the phenomenon of personification by any researcher who studies them. They are mostly directed with mystical intentions and, although having much good will and evident good intention, they lack a greater universalistic, evolutionary self-discernment, and constantly attempt personal and group manipulations of corporatist or fanatic consciousnesses. This allows the unscrupulous influence of intraphysical and extraphysical blind guides, usually simultaneously.

Team. Joint lucid projections permit the dynamization of extraphysical research teams, or projectiological research teams. They are composed of various veteran projectors that may or may not know each other. The members endeavor to perform studies together or independently in order to later compare perceptions, observations and results of the experiments.

Patterns. The evidence and confirmation achieved by the members of the extraphysical research team allows them to establish patterns and averages of scientific techniques and observations, in many cases even before the official research and discoveries of conventional science. The author has always endeavored to arrive at conclusions regarding the study of projectiology, included in this book, through research performed by teams of projectors (intraphysical consciousnesses).

Individualization. The doorway to the extraphysical dimension, whether through a routine lucid projection or through final projection (desoma or biological death), is invariably extremely individual.

Case study. Regardless of whether a team of projectors can project together, at the same time, leaving from the same physical base, or whether a group of intraphysical consciousnesses can undergo desoma at the same instant, in the same place and through the same group accident, the characteristics of regaining extraphysical awareness will always occur individually, one by one, consciousness by consciousness. This observation is valid and applies to all beings or intraphysical consciential principles, as long as they have achieved intraconsciential and evolutionary individualization.

Exclusive. It should not be forgotten that: for all the team spirit (or teams of consciousnesses) that can be obtained with the maximal technical improvement of joint lucid projections, lucid projection will always, inevitably, above all, be a solitary, extremely individual excursion of the consciousness, resulting from personal merits, efforts and performance.

Vehicles. There are joint lucid projections in the psychosoma of 2 or more intraphysical beings; joint lucid projections in the mentalsoma of 2 or more intraphysical beings; and joint lucid projections in the mentalsoma of 2 or more intraphysical and extraphysical beings at the same time.

Pregnant women. There are at least 6 different modalities in which the consciential projection phenomenon manifests during the period of human pregnancy:

1. The pregnant woman's consciousness projects alone in the psychosoma.
2. The pregnant woman's consciousness projects alone in the mentalsoma.
3. The pregnant woman's consciousness projects in the psychosoma while the resonant consciousness simultaneously projects in the psychosoma: joint projections in the psychosoma. Might this happen more frequently at the end of pregnancy?

4. The consciousness of the resomant projects alone in the psychosoma.

5. The consciousness of the resomant projects alone in the mentalsoma.

6. The pregnant woman's consciousness projects in the mentalsoma while the resomant consciousness also simultaneously projects in the mentalsoma: joint mental projections. Might this happen more frequently at the beginning of pregnancy?

Different. There is apparently no instance of, or at least a low incidence of, simultaneous projections of the consciousness of the pregnant woman and the consciousness of the fetus in different consciential vehicles. This is a research hypothesis.

Pediatrics. Pediatrics explains that when the (nursing) mother sleeps or rests together (auric coupling) with the child (newborn), the sleep cycles of both become synchronized and she operates like a type of respiratory pacemaker for the child. This has prevented sudden infant death syndrome *(crib death),* a disturbance that impedes the child from returning from a very deep sleep. It is characterized by frequent respiratory stoppages during sleep, notably in the early mornings of the winter months, between one and six o'clock in the morning. It is therefore also reasonable to suppose that mother-child joint consciential projections are facilitated in this period.

Conflicts. Smaller or greater conflicts can arise in the reports of joint lucid projectors due to differing degrees in lucidity and differing standpoints of analysis on the part of each projected consciousness.

Helpers. Joint consciential projections can be sponsored by extraphysical helpers, as *pre-programmed* joint consciential projections are extremely rare and difficult without aid from the helpers.

Couplings. Kindred intraphysical beings who are always predisposed – even when unconsciously or without their perceiving it – to mutually trigger the auric coupling phenomenon, exhibit a greater facility for projecting together and with lucidity. Examples of this are found between mother and daughter, or father and son. This predisposition will always be greater if *consanguineous resomas* are occurring between these persons.

Final. Deviating from the norm, there are reports of joint final consciential projections, which differ from ordinary joint consciential projections. In a way, they merely represent cases of concomitant desomas with instances of farewell consciential projections.

Future. All indications are that, in the future, with the technical improvement of projectiological processes, joint, lucid consciential projections, which are currently rare, will become common and accessible to all types of intraphysical consciousnesses in any part of the earth.

Evolution. The following are 7 themes and provisions that will inevitably be encountered with the evolution of projective techniques and practices:

1. **Personal.** Greater technical development of projected personnel (team).
2. **Activities.** Simplification and rationalization of extraphysical activities.
3. **Co-projectors.** Enhancement of lucid consciential *co-projectors.*
4. **Functions.** Evaluation of extraphysical functions in projected projective groups.
5. **Leadership.** Leading projected projective groups.
6. **Dynamic.** Group dynamics in joint, lucid consciential projections.
7. **Methodology.** Organization and methods for joint, lucid consciential projections.

Extraterrestrials. A likeness of these provisions can be seen extraphysically with *extraterrestrial,* lucid consciential projectors.

Bibliography: Andreas (36, p. 29), Becker (102, p. 403), Boswell (174, p. 139), Castaneda (258, p. 131), Corvalán (306, p. 72), Crookall (343, p. 42), Denning (391, p. 182), Digest (399, p. 282), Donahue (407, p. 98), Farrar (496, p. 192), Frost (560, p. 145), Garrett (571, p. 44), Greene (635, p. 109), Greenhouse (636, p. 214), Lilly (927, p. 74), Redentor (1378, p. 83), Rogo (1444, p. 181), Shay (1546, p. 101), St. Clair (1593, p. 153), Vieira (1762, p. 121).

437. COMPARISONS BETWEEN CONSCIENTIAL PROJECTION IN THE MENTALSOMA AND IN THE PSYCHOSOMA

Differential. The following are 12 basic differences that are characteristic of projections of the consciousness in the psychosoma and in the mentalsoma:

1. **Emotions.** In consciential projection in the psychosoma, the consciousness uses a semiphysical vehicle, the emotional parabody. In consciential projection in the isolated mentalsoma, the consciousness manifests in the mentalsomatic dimension, distant from tropospheric emotions, in the vehicle of rationality and balance or the *parabody of self-discernment.*

2. **Ballast.** In consciential projection in the psychosoma, the intraphysical consciousness manifests with greater ballast or *weight,* because he/she is laden with the holochakra, namely the connection of the silver cord and the entire human body, including the physical brain. In consciential projection in the isolated mentalsoma, the consciousness is only linked to the head of the psychosoma and is therefore separated from the physical body and the physical dimension.

3. **Likeness.** The psychosoma can be considered to be an improved likeness of the human body. The mentalsoma has no such likeness.

4. **Action.** In consciential projection in the psychosoma, the intraphysical consciousness acts directly upon the human body. In consciential projection in the mentalsoma, the intraphysical consciousness only acts indirectly upon the human body, with the inevitable intermediation of the psychosoma.

5. **Sensations.** In consciential projection in the psychosoma, the intraphysical consciousness experiences extraphysical sensations and emotions in a constant reciprocal relationship, or in both directions (two-way), with the human body. In consciential projection in the mentalsoma, the sensations of the consciousness are diminished and, in certain cases, even disappear, as we normally understand it.

6. **Telekinesis.** In consciential projection in the psychosoma, the consciousness can produce the phenomenon of extraphysical telekinesis and, when conditions are favorable, act upon dense matter. In consciential projection in the mentalsoma, it is not easy for the consciousness to produce the phenomenon of telekinesis.

7. **Case study.** In consciential projection in the psychosoma, the consciousness has parahands and parafingers for touching and grasping, and para-eyes for reading a book, for example. In consciential projection in the mentalsoma, the consciousness has neither arms, hands, fingers, nor ordinary eyes for reading a book, but instead grasps its contents – its thoughts, ideas, energies, morphothosenes or the mental forms recorded or written in the material volume – all at once, *en bloc.*

8. **Entirety.** When in the psychosoma, the consciousness operates in a manner similar to the human body, in a retail manner, little by little, part by part. When in the isolated mentalsoma, the consciousness operates with a preference toward a wholesale approach, spontaneously, in entirety, in universal ways of manifestation that are common to all.

9. **Magnitude.** Consciential projection in the mentalsoma allows the state of cosmoconsciousness, on the one hand, and the state of *punctiform consciousness,* on the other hand. Both of these states are far more highly evolved and of a much greater magnitude than the manifestations occurring while in the psychosoma.

10. **Procedures.** Upon manifesting in the psychosoma, in the lucid interworld or interdimensional procedures of the intraphysical consciousness, both takeoff and interiorization affect the human body as a whole, from head to toe. In consciential projections in the mentalsoma, these procedures are circumscribed to the parahead (parabrain) of the psychosoma.

11. **Deintrusion.** Projections of the consciousness in the psychosoma still allow interconsciential intrusion and deintrusion. Both of these processes become impossible in the evolved consciential projections of the consciousness in the mentalsoma. Generally speaking, the evolved mentalsomatic

dimension is inaccessible to those consciousnesses that nourish anticosmoethical impulses or energivorous conditions, which are characteristic of pathological interconsciential intrusiveness.

12. **Forms.** In projections of the consciousness in the psychosoma, general human forms, the mechanism of speech and other manifestations characteristic of the human being are still operative for the projected intraphysical consciousness. In advanced consciential projections in the isolated mentalsoma, even these material, instinctive, vegetative or animal manifestations disappear.

Bibliography: Greene (635, p. 49), Vieira (1762, p. 73).

438. SERIATED LUCID CONSCIENTIAL PROJECTIONS

Definition. Seriated lucid consciential projections: experiences of the intraphysical consciousnesses projected with lucidity from the human body with intensive sequences over a certain period.

Synonymy: consecutive lucid projections; consciential projectiorrhea; frequent lucid projections; sequential lucid projections.

Intraphysical consciousness. Any individual who is intelligent, creative, self-confident, hardworking, persistent, determined, fearless, self-motivated with what he/she does is undoubtedly able to produce lucid projections in series and projections with continuous self-awareness through the force of his/her disciplined will. This is dependent only upon the intraphysical consciousness wishing and suitably motivating him/herself to do so. One example is the use of the daily, abnegated practices of penta.

Types. Seriated lucid projections can occur daily, every other day, or weekly, and can last for long periods, months or years.

Periodicity. Both the periodicity of the lucid projections and the average frequency of this incidence are dependent upon the intensive, assistential, extraphysical tasks which occupy the consciousness of the projector (you) – a minicog within an interdimensional, assistential maximechanism – when projected. This also depends upon your human and existential conditions, without becoming overcome by alienation toward intraphysical life and the reasonable completion of your existential program.

Frequency. In 1968, the frequency, in this case, the incidence of lucid projections, was surveyed in a public opinion poll in England. The following percentages were found among those projectors polled: one lucid projection = 60.9%; two = 8.9%; 3 = 5.3%; 4 = 2.3%; 5 = 1.7%; 6 or more lucid projections = 20.9%.

Factors. A single, preponderant projectiogenic factor produces an impactful lucid projection or can even sporadically produce diverse extraphysical experiences. The simultaneous joining of various influencing projectiogenic factors produces lucid projections in series, repeatedly or over time. Conclusion: lucid consciential projections in series are very rarely produced from a single projectiogenic factor but from a combination of various factors.

Effects. On the other hand, lucid projections in series produce 9 distinct, cumulative effects in the projector's personality:

1. **Motivation.** They help to motivate the projector in his/her research, through the renewed stimuli which are naturally provided by new discoveries, investigations and questionings.

2. **Awareness.** They deepen the projector's awareness of sedimented verifications through repeated experiences and through the same phenomena being seen from new angles.

3. **Coherence.** They definitively eliminate the incoherent nature of the set of extraphysical trajectories that the novice lucid projector may, perchance, be having with some frequency.

4. **Universalism.** They increase the healthy detachment of the intraphysical consciousness to human life, naturally leading him/her toward the derepressing, emancipating principles of consciential universalism, without sectarianism or factiousness.

5. **Alienation.** They can lead the unwary projector to pathological alienation regarding his/her commitments with material, family, professional and social life.

6. **Recess.** It order to avoid physical alienation, and ultimately personal *existential incompletism,* the polyvalent extraphysical helpers not only aid the intraphysical consciousness in projecting lucidly, but they also promote appropriate anchoring in the human body. In certain critical occasions, this prevents projection with lucidity and good subsequent recall, thereby triggering phases of recess in the series of lucid consciential projection. This can even completely extinguish the experiences up through the end of the individual's physical existence, as has happened in many reported cases. This does not prevent the consciousness from continuing to work extraphysically and assistentially, albeit without recall.

7. **Quality.** With time, the projector finds him/herself obliged to implant a quality control system in his/her cosmoethical intentionality and production of lucid projections.

8. **Rested.** The state of being rested after several hours of sleep in the early morning (from 5 to 7 o'clock in the morning), generally predisposes the projector having a period of seriated consciential projections to spontaneously produce amenable consciential projections and traveling clairvoyance phenomena. This may be due to the *lightness* of sleep in these conditions, which permits neither an enhancement of self-lucidity outside the human body, nor a greater condensation of the structures of the exteriorized psychosoma.

9. **Passivity.** Consciential projections in series sometimes give the clear impression that the projector, when in a phase of perfect syntony with the extraphysical helper, is in an continuous animic-parapsychic session that lasts for several days and even for weeks. On these occasions, the consciousness of the projector (you) experiences a condition of continued passivity, with an agreeable sensation of potency, under the ambivalent influence of the animic-parapsychic nature of the succession of events. These periods are also characterized by a state of healthy waking discoincidence.

Agreeable. When the experienced lucid projector reaches the phase of self-lucid consciential projections in series, he/she finds him/herself becoming aware of remaining lucid during the physiological exteriorizations of nightly, ordinary, natural sleep. In other words, it becomes almost habitual to have simple, spontaneous, agreeable, consecutive, lucid projections in the physical base with lucid takeoffs and interiorizations without major consequences that precede major projections (self-lucid megaprojections), in the manner of previous consciential projections, or prolonged, unrecalled consciential projections, or even periods of natural sleep.

Integration. The veteran, lucid projector only develops seriated consciential projections with balance and without recess upon deciding to keep his/her projective resources permanently integrated, always monitoring – simultaneously, with rationality and without mysticism or psychophysical crutches – the subtle and coarse aspects as a whole, which seem to be more disparate, but with which the following 7 indispensable variables, for example, relate and interact:

1. **Holothosenology.** The positive personal conscientiological atmosphere or personal holothosene, observing your own lasting, useful materthosene.

2. **Holosomatics.** The carefully nurtured physical health of the soma, which reflects in the holosoma, or maintenance of reasonable holosomatic homeostasis.

3. **Intraphysicology.** Favorable domestic, professional and recreational environments.

4. **Holochakrology.** Self-lucid control of reception and donation of consciential energies.

5. **Assistentiology.** Habitual extraphysical assistance to other intraphysical and extraphysical consciousnesses, such as through the daily practice of penta.

6. **Projectiology.** Constant self-motivation for projecting from the soma with lucidity and with valid purpose.

7. **Cosmoethics.** The rigorous observance of personal conduct within the unshakeable principles of cosmoethics.

Usefulness. Lucid projections require valid objectives or valid mental targets in order for them to be maintained without interruption. No one maintains the production of seriated lucid projections that are amenable or comfortable for the consciousness in a mode of extraphysical uselessness.

Alternations. Instead of occurring on consecutive days, seriated, lucid consciential projections can be coordinated in succession, on alternate days, or every 3 days, keeping the quality of extraphysical perceptions at a high level due to at least the following 4 factors:

1. **Somatics.** Metabolism of the soma or human body.
2. **Neurology.** Replenishment of the nervous system as a whole.
3. **Habits.** Specific human habits of the lucid projector.
4. **Helpers.** Intraconsciential assistance sponsored and coordinated in detail by extraphysical helpers, even when not directly or ostensively detected.

Chronology. On the other hand, because of an unconscious tendency, the intraphysical projector can psychologically inhibit the development of lucid consciential projections in series. This occurs, for example, when producing a lucid projection one day and thinking he/she should produce the next lucid projection only after skipping a day, or on alternate days, in order to avoid conscientially or energetically harming him/herself. With this refusal or reluctance to use a paraphysiological process of extraphysical life, he/she blocks the production of the lucid projective phenomenon through autosuggestion.

Analogy. The human projector can produce several lucid consciential projections daily, whether in the morning, during the day or during the night, without suffering any harm. This negative, chronological, psychological effect – a fruit of multidimensional inexperience – is analogous to the "effects of position" which occur in laboratorial telepathy experiments.

Set. With lucid consciential projections in series, it is common to have a sequence of very lucid, interrelated projections in a single night that ultimately form a set of similar experiences. Their objective may be extraphysical assistance (intraconsciential assistential projection), a useful trip to a certain extraphysical environment or community, or the specific study of a certain advanced theme within evolutiology.

Facts. Given the fact that everyone dreams every night, and that the absolute majority of dreams are bad dreams, nightmares or semi-nightmares, it can be concluded that any period of lucid projections in series, as amenable or superficial as they may be in terms of their results, always constitute a source of relief, of positive, healthy enjoyment and an incontestable evolutionary factor for the intraphysical consciousness, at any time, place and under any existential conditions.

Incidence. Intensive, seriated, lucid consciential projections not only occur with veteran consciential projectors who are aware and experienced regarding the problems or basic themes of projectiology. They can also occur, in a healthy manner, with novice consciential projectors, sometimes uninterruptedly over a period of consecutive months, and can even include the intercurrence of traveling clairvoyance, consciential projections in the mentalsoma, exoprojections or lucid consciential projections while the human body is in motion.

Extraphysicology. Lucid consciential projections in series can, by themselves, potentiate the repetition of new projective experiences. This occurs through the repetition of experiences, as well as through the resources of absorption of extraphysical energies obtained directly in extraphysical dimensions by the intraphysical consciousness in the psychosoma, now temporarily freed from dense matter.

Bibliography: Eysenck (493, p. 156), Sudre (1630, p. 176), Swedenborg (1635, p. 266), Vieira (1762, p. 210).

439. THE PROJECTED CONSCIOUSNESS AND CHRONOLOGICAL TIME

Definition. Time: the succession of phenomena and the duration of mutable things, established through the relationship of cause and effect.

Synonymy: the fourth dimension; geophysical time.

Unsettling. Chronological time is one of the most unsettling and disorienting factors within the framework of manifestations of lucid projections. For this reason, the more the individual can study it, the better it will be for the development of lucid projectors in general and for projectiology itself.

Characteristics. The following are 11 conditions which are relevant in the qualitative and/or quantitative analysis of chronological time by the consciousness of the intraphysical projector:

1. Measured time (quantity).
2. Sensed time (quality).
3. Perceptible time.
4. Subjective time.
5. Objective time.
6. Imperceptible time.
7. Indifferent time.
8. Normal time, slow time or rapid time.
9. Contraction or dilation of time.
10. Lesser or greater time.
11. Past time, present time or future time.

Chronometry. Physics is the science that studies time in all of its aspects. Chronometry, an experimental science, should test its forecasts.

Unit. It is currently admitted that space and time do not exist separate from matter, these 2 concepts being considered as an indissoluble unit.

Events. It becomes difficult to characterize chronological time, the velocity of extraphysical translocation and projection in each body, in relation to the time of the physical base. These events can have the following time-related characteristics: instantaneous, tachyonic, at and below the speed of light. These relationships should be objects of future research involving a temporal generalization of the phenomena.

Computation. Regarding this subject, it is pertinent to remember that scientists using coarse terrestrial computation have already experimentally measured times including those on the order of nanoseconds or 10^{-9} seconds, or 0.000000001 seconds. Theoretically, they have, through simple calculations, obtained results of up to 10^{-22} seconds, or 0.1 thousandth of an attosecond (attosec. = 10^{-18} sec.).

Properties. The metric and topological structure of space-time can be modified during psychic (mental) and parapsychic activities. Mainly in the extraphysical environments analyzed, during the formation of morphothosenes, the topological properties of observed space can be: curved bidimensionality, plane tridimensionality, curved tridimensionality; continuity, extension. Topological properties of time: unidimensionality orthogonally coupled to space, continuity, regulation of temporal *flow,* unidirectionality. The topological properties reflect the integrity or qualitative aspect of space and time. For every rule of symmetry there is a corresponding law of conservation; the law of conservation of energy arises by virtue of the homogeneity of time; the homogeneity of space leads to the conservation of linear *momentum;* the conservation of angular *momentum* manifests connected to the isotropy of space; it is presumed that the law of conservation of electric charge seems to be connected to the invariance of the probability of occurrence of a quantic process, when its amplitude varies by one phase.

Concepts. There currently exist already established concepts on gravitational, electromagnetic, atomic, thermodynamic and entropic time. Time also has its polymorphic and isomorphic series. The property of time that differentiates the future from the past is the directionality or the passage of time. Another property of time is the irreversibility of its flow from the past to the future, which is also related to the increase of entropy or disorganization of the universe.

Space-time. Prior to Isaac Newton (1642-1727), people viewed the world as being bidimensional, the two dimensions in which they could walk. Newton's vision showed that the vertical direction was symmetrical to the other two, through gravitational forces, changing from a bidimensional symmetry to a tridimensional one. Albert Einstein (1879-1955) then changed the view of three-dimensional symmetry to a four-dimensional plane, in restricted relativity, and a four-dimensional curve in general relativity, where it curves to another unknown dimension, and where the greater the gravitational field is, the more curved space-time is and the slower is the flow of time. If one of 2 identical clocks is placed inside a gravitational field and the other outside, after awhile, the clock inside the field will be running late.

Fascination. Time and space have a power of fascination that is generally difficult to escape in our temporary condition as intraphysical consciousnesses who express themselves through a soma.

Distances. *Distance in time* ennobles things, conferring a grandeur to past events, an attractiveness and beautification that they lack in the present. *Distance in space* simply adds a touch of the picturesque and the exotic, favoring the development of dreams, daydreams, idealizations and myths.

Loss. Time which is lost is lost forever. The act of reliving through memory (recollection) is not living fully or thosenizing at the highest level of our potentialities. Intraphysical consciousnesses (human mentalities) relative to space constitute sequences of knowledge in constant mutation.

Types. There is 1 physical time that suffers interference from the environment, modifying the velocity of its flow upon encountering in different reference systems, or in the presence of matter-energy fields or in certain consciential states. Consciential time can penetrate precognitive and retrocognitive phenomena, still ignoring the basic laws involved. This is probably due to an analysis made by the mentalsoma, which is able to penetrate and reach the consciousness of the individual (you) through intuition.

Differences. The system of serial time, divided into seconds, minutes, hours, days, weeks, months, years, centuries and millennia is somehow different and still incomprehensible to us, when considered in the evolved extraphysical dimensions. The differences of chronological time in the pure mentalsomatic dimension, and consequently for the mentalsoma, trigger a series of facts in physical life that are not always well understood because they are still difficult to interpret.

Apparent. The differences of chronological time generate *apparent concomitances* in the agents and conditions of the phenomena which are difficult to analyze because the consciousness operates at a velocity beyond all patterns, *faster than the speed of light.*

Relativity. The intraphysical consciousness can experience a 1-minute projection and need at least half-an-hour to present everything that he/she experienced, saw and heard during that minute, due to the relativity of time connected with the physical sensations.

Velocity. A projector can experience a lucid projection in which he/she goes past various planets and stars, even beyond our solar system, as well as seeing atoms dispersed throughout space, given that this entire consciential projection lasts only 10 minutes at most. It is well known that the light from the sun takes 8 minutes to reach the earth. It can thus be concluded that the projected consciousness was extraphysically operating at a velocity greater than that of light.

Hypothetical. An increase in the "frequency" of all bodies of manifestation of the consciousness may be what produces a hypothetical antigravity state (negative gravity). This increase in frequency may also contribute to a very subtle state of the fields of the bodies of the consciousness, as well as a change of the consciousness' reference system. This enables flights (volitation) with great ease at any speed through space and a dilation of time, relative to the time in the perspective of the human body. This is foreseen in general relativity, due to the action of the gravitational field and the relativity of movement.

Factor. The sensitive in deep trance sometimes *seems* to parapsychically receive various extraphysical consciousnesses, or extraphysical personalities, at the same time. In traveling clairvoyance and successive (it is perhaps better to say: subintrant) lucid projections, the consciousness *seems* to duplicate itself, at first sight manifesting itself in 2 places at the same time, in the physical base and in the scenario being witnessed or visited. Nevertheless, this only apparently occurs because the human body cannot be controlled, in its entirety, by more than 1 central command simultaneously, and the consciousness does not subdivide itself. The time factor cannot be included where, in fact, it does not participate in the origination of the phenomenon.

Retrocognitions. Time is important for everyone. Retrocognitions allow the intraphysical consciousness to avoid falling into the same *cattle guards* (dispensable self-mimicries) that he/she has previously succumbed to. For example: fighting the past or trying to escape it will always be foolish and a waste of consciential energies.

Past. Consciential retrocognitive return, or to the past, is an inevitable fact in the development of the intraphysical consciousness' future, due to 4 fundamental reasons:

1. **Panorama.** Somatic deactivation sponsors the panoramic vision of the recently-ended existence of the intraphysical consciousness that recently became an extraphysical consciousness.

2. **Reencounters.** Extraphysical reencounters occur between the extraphysical consciousness and consciousnesses which underwent desoma before it.

3. **Intermissiology.** The extraphysical or intermissive consciential condition of the extraphysical consciousness depends upon its previous intraphysical existence as an intraphysical being.

4. **Cycle.** The study of the personal lifetime and the immediately preceding, deactivated retrosoma, and even of other more remote personal intraphysical existences (multi-existential cycle), is an indispensable part of the programming of the upcoming life of every consciousness after the intermissive period.

Clock. A clock is associated with the concept of intervals of equal time without alteration. The heartbeat, the taking of the pulse, the rhythm of the metabolism, or the subjective sensation of psychological time (the so-called *biological clock,* or the psychic clock), are not currently suitable as standards for material time for humankind. This is because they do not pertain to the so-called absolute time of periodic phenomena that have a minimum of irregularities. Periodic patterns such as the earth's rotation evolved to precision such as the atomic clock, which is accurate to 1 second in 30,000 years, thereby establishing humankind's basis of time on the planet. Nevertheless, Newton's absolute time, or time that flows uniformly without any relationship to external objects, is defined through physical objects – clocks – which are subject to physical laws. Experimentally speaking, conditions such as travel at velocities approximating the speed of light or the presence of intense gravitational fields alter the passage of time. These conditions are derived from equations of special and general relativity. For this reason, time can no longer be considered an absolute, but a new variable that depends upon the reference system. ·

Questions. Is it possible that persons with tachycardia, accelerated metabolism or tachypsychism live in a more accelerated manner relative to the basic chronological time of the vibrations of our planet's atomic clocks? What are the patterns, what are the degrees of modifications, and which parameters are more important in relation to the vibrations of the atomic clocks on the planet's surface, upon entering the extraphysical world in the psychosoma or mentalsoma? Does time become variable and modifiable in relation to the patterns of the will? These conclusions with regard to time make the following paradox lose all value: "If God (Allah, Brahma, Elohim, Jehovah, *Tupã*) is the *primary* cause of all that exists, what is the *nature* of God?" The term *primary* is temporal, however time is not absolute, but merely one variable among the innumerous other dimensions of these planes, without parameters of comparison with our ordinary senses, which are characteristic of this planet.

Dimensions. From everything that has been scientifically researched up to now, it is known with certainty, as a provisional synthesis, that time amalgamated to tridimensional space constitutes a fourth dimension. This fourth dimension opens human understanding to comprehend the many other consciential dimensions that exist, including the complex phenomena of the projected human consciousness.

Bibliography: Baumann (93, p. 83), Dolis (405, p. 36), Forman (538, p. 154), Frost (560, p. 10), Guéret (659, p. 163), Miranda (1050, p. 17), Muntañola (1108, p. 67), Pushkin (1342, p. 248), Vieira (1762, p. 122).

440.   EXTRAPHYSICAL   EVENTS

Definition. Extraphysical event: extraphysical fact or phenomenon experienced by the projected intraphysical consciousness and, therefore, detected by his/her paraperceptions outside the human body.

Synonymy: extraphysical event; extraphysical fact; extraphysical occurrence; extraphysical phenomenon.

Non-material. It is worth pointing out that quantum mechanics and recent observations regarding the quantum interconnection clearly indicate that, at least within the scope of science, the exclusion of non-material facts is no longer a desirable posture.

Experiences. Extraphysical events can be influenced by at least the following 8 types of experiences that the projected intraphysical consciousness can have:

1. **Sanity.** Positive, agreeable, or negative uncomfortable.
2. **Evolutiology.** Enriching evolved or depressant underdeveloped.
3. **Visualizations.** Black and white, colored or with neutral coloration.
4. **Psychosomatics.** Surprise, trauma or extraphysical attack.
5. **Parageography.** Extraphysical *geography* or parageography.
6. **Extraphysicology.** Extraphysical community.
7. **Specialization.** A specialized extraphysical institution, e.g.: feminine.
8. **Assistentiology.** Assistance to resomants.

Environments. Extraphysical environments and events that occur in the extraphysical dimension are intimately related, being mutually dependent.

Thoughts. *Mesological* influences in dimensions having a vital influence upon thoughts are greater than in the human sphere.

Characteristics. Within the characteristics of extraphysical events experienced by the projected intraphysical consciousness, the following can be singled out: quietness, intense activity, incessant wandering; extraphysical meditation or reflection; simple episodes, disparate extraphysical circumstances, complex facts; surprises, mishaps, traumas; extraphysical visual projection.

Speed. The following factors should be observed regarding the speed of extraphysical events: slow motion; chronological time; tachyonic velocity; the velocity of thought; unawareness of the transpiring of extraphysical events.

Sequence. In the sequence of extraphysical events, the following can be highlighted: single scene; multiple scenes; series of interrelated events; abrupt changes; intermission; paralysis; coherent continuation; a change only in the scenario; change of scenario and the consciousness; events in a single dimension; events in more than one dimension; voluntary participation of the projector (protagonist); non-participation of the projector (spectator); key moments; climax; final scenes (recall).

Repetitive. Among repetitive extraphysical events, the following are common patterns: dislocation up to the ceiling of the residence; sensation of weightlessness; sensation of falling; pass through human residences, entering through the front; volitate halfway up from the floor; contemplate human landscapes; cooperate in assistance to ill intraphysical and extraphysical consciousnesses; suffer extraphysical traumas (novice projector).

Bibliography: Vieira (1762, p. 140).

441.   IMPACTFUL   EXTRAPHYSICAL   EVENTS

Classification. Extraphysical events that are impactful to the projected consciousness can be classified into two categories:

1. **Private:** experience the retraction of the silver cord; contemplate your own inactive human body; analyze the silver cord; change your own extraphysical clothing; encounter projected intraphysical

projectors, recent-extraphysical-consciousnesses, lycanthropes, extraphysical animals; visit extraphysical communities; be suddenly carried along by a current of force; participate in an extraphysical celebration; come upon an extraphysical artifact; make a positive extraphysical evocation; have a picturesque experience; help in an extraphysical rescue; serve as assistential bait with full lucidity; be impelled to an extraphysical confrontation in view of a reconciliation; suffer direct extraphysical attack; perform extraphysical mimicry; observe yourself in a large ordinary mirror; see your own reflected shadow; participate in the aiding of someone's desoma; examine a waking pregnant woman.

2. **Public:** appear to an intraphysical being; produce telepathy with an intraphysical being; promote physical self-bilocation; affect film emulsion, whether photographic, movie or videotape.

Pregnant woman. The pregnant-woman-projector, in particular, can perform an extraphysical self-examination.

Bibliography: Vieira (1762, p. 120).

---

442. EXTRAPHYSICAL   TRAUMAS

Definitions. Extraphysical trauma: an afflux of excitations that exceed the tolerance of the projected intraphysical consciousness and his/her capacity to parapsychically control and metabolize these excitations; a consciential alteration caused by any factor outside the human body that destabilizes the balance and lucidity of the projected intraphysical consciousness.

Synonymy: consciential shock; extraphysical disturbance; extraphysical shock; extraphysical stress; extraphysical traumatism; projective trauma.

Psychosoma. Extraphysical trauma seems to only arise, or more pronouncedly so, in the intraphysical consciousness who is projected in the psychosoma, or the parabody of emotions. It occurs more frequently to the novice projector, due to the quick experience, surprise or an unknown element which increases the excitation to the projected consciousness that is unprepared to liquidate or assimilate it, thereby provoking ephemeral intraconsciential disturbances.

Causes. The extraphysical trauma is characterized by a specific triggering agent, almost always spontaneously identified; a specific degree of intensity; susceptibility of the consciousness; and extent of the projected consciousness' incapacity to respond adequately to the trauma, either by absorbing it, sublimating it, or overcoming it with naturality, as soon as it occurs.

Trac. The extraphysical trauma that affects the lucid projector, notably when experiencing the first lucid consciential projection, is sometimes reminiscent of *trac*, that paralyzing emotion, pathological state of anguish or irrational fear that the actor, musician or singer feels when appearing on stage. This is different from *panic syndrome*.

Agents. The most common traumatogenic or triggering agents permit the division of extraphysical traumas into 2 basic types: microtraumas and macrotraumas.

1. **Microtraumas.** Microtraumas are small extraphysical shocks produced by the inexperience of the projected intraphysical consciousness: pass the extraphysical hand (parahand) through the structure of physical objects; go through walls and closed doors with naturality; pass through the bodies of human beings (self-permeability); contemplate the inactive human body "face-to-face" (self-bilocation); see your psychosoma reflected in an ordinary mirror (self-reflection); take off abruptly in the psychosoma from the human body (extraphysical escape); hear the sound of sudden interiorization; examine the silver cord in detail; perceive the exact moment that respiration is lost; experience the state of extraphysical euphoria.

2. **Macrotraumas.** Macrotraumas are greater extraphysical shocks that generally interrupt the natural continuity of the experience of the consciousness projected from the human body: strong emotion; sexual impulse with extraphysical reflections; extraphysical encounter or reencounter with extraphysical consciousnesses that are acquaintances, friends or relatives; extraphysical retrocognition; a surprising, unexpected extraphysical event; the act of suffering a violent extraphysical attack from

an ill extraphysical consciousness; rapid accumulation of various excitations which are tolerable when isolated, but intolerable when gathered in a short extraphysical period of the intraphysical consciousness' experience; the extraphysical act of becoming aware of unquestionable truth; an engrossing task of extraphysical deintrusion.

Effects. The most common extraphysical traumas to the projected intraphysical consciousness can produce: extraphysical effects and physical effects.

1. **Extraphysical.** The extraphysical effects of extraphysical traumas occur in the intraphysical consciousness while still projected in the extraphysical dimension: premature ending of the extraphysical experience; unforeseen return of the projected consciousness to the physical base; sudden consciential interiorization.

2. **Physical.** The physical effects of extraphysical traumas are emotional or *mechanical* and occur later, in this human dimension, when the consciousness is already in the ordinary, physical waking state: simultaneous and instantaneous return-interiorization-physical awakening; physical repercussion; sudden physical awakening; lapses in awareness which provoke brief amnesia, whether retrograde (rarer) – wherein it is impossible to recall events that occurred before the trauma – or anterograde (more common), or the inability to remember events subsequent to the trauma.

Soma. Extraphysical experiences evidence that, for the courageous projector, greater, subsequent, lasting negative effects do not occur as a result of extraphysical traumas. This is because the soma, or human body, and human life itself, act as natural trauma neutralizing or discharging (dissipation) agents, much like a ground wire.

Traumatotherapy. In fact, extraphysical trauma works therapeutically for the consciousness (you) of the projector, vaccinating him/her, or curing him/her with respect to the aspects of the extraphysical dimension of which he/she was unaware or had never experienced.

Evolution. Extraphysical traumas are actually inevitable and indispensable for the individual development of lucid projections and the veteran projector's extraphysical evolution. Nevertheless, there are countless obscure aspects regarding this subject of physical-extraphysical emotions requiring enormous amounts of advanced research in order for them to be better understood.

Extraphysical consciousness. The extraphysical emotion stemming from an extraphysical dialogue between the projected intraphysical consciousness and that familiar intraphysical consciousness that recently became an extraphysical consciousness (e.g.: a former relative that recently passed away), sometimes even after 2 years of extraphysical or intermissive life, provokes an extraphysical trauma that, for its part, causes the following 5 clearly evident characteristic effects, among others:

1. **Imbalance.** The emotional impact, often merely owing to an *extraphysical phrase* spoken by the projected intraphysical consciousness, produces an energetic imbalance or loss of control of the extraphysical consciousness' individual consciential energies.

2. **Off-balance.** The extraphysical consciousness, thereby weakened and still in a *very humanized* attitude, tries to lean on or to support itself on surrounding physical-extraphysical objects, such as a piece of furniture or a window.

3. **Irradiations.** Sudden and visible alterations occur in the colors of the extraphysical aura of the extraphysical consciousness with the weakening of the luminous irradiations of its psychosoma, which appears to become more opaque.

4. **Aging.** There occurs an instantaneous process of aging in the visual appearance (paratransfiguration) of the psychosoma of the same deceased interlocutor corresponding to the physical age at which it left human life.

5. **Disappearance.** The combination of the abovementioned effects predisposes the phenomenon of extraphysical disappearance, which happens in an abrupt and forced manner or, in other words, against the will of the extraphysical consciousness, which desires to continue with the nostalgic dialogue. Upon changing the energetic frequency and the environment, the traumatized extraphysical consciousness leaves the projector's projected consciousness behind, *planted* in the physical-extraphysical environment, without even allowing time for the projector to help it with some exteriorization of consciential energies.

Case study. Just such a fact happened in precisely this manner with the author, due to a casual observation, clearly lacking any negative intention. This occurred with a friend with whom the author had lived for approximately 3 lustrums. The following conversation with him transpired in the physical base: "See how lucid I am outside the human body, just like you, and afterward I can remember everything that is happening now." He responded: "All of this is really absurd." The author added: "You never accepted anything I used to tell you about it, right"? And he responded: "Actually, no." He shook the parahead of the psychosoma. So, joking with naturality, the author made the imprudent observation that ended up generating an impact: "You really insisted on ignoring all these facts"! That was all it took, as it appeared that he sensed the observation to be a reprimand or a mild rebuke. In light of this, the author returned to the human body without knowing where he went, probably being impelled by extraphysical melancholy.

Attention. It can be seen that it is necessary for us to be attentive in order to help in the works of extraphysical assistance to energivorous extraphysical consciousnesses. A comment that, for us, is simple and inexpressive, can trigger an extraphysical trauma greater than those occurring with the lucid projecting intraphysical consciousness when projected.

Bibliography: Castaneda (258, p. 132), Monroe (1065, p. 155), Vieira (1762, p. 120).

443.   FACTORS   FAVORABLE   TO   LUCID   PROJECTION

General. The most diverse general catalytic factors can predispose, precipitate or even produce a lucid projection: hypnagogic state; natural sleep; ordinary dream; nightmare; hypnopompic state; state of relaxation; autosuggestion; deep concentration; strong emotion; intense motivation; extreme fear; daydream; parapsychic trance; hypnotic trance; yoga practice; awakening of the *kundalini* or the energies of the sexochakra; *Ganzfeld* stimulation; training; physical exercise; physical stress; sensory deprivation; repression of physiological needs; weak or strong drugs; chronic or serious illness; surgical anesthesia; shock; childbirth; accident; indeterminate cause.

Classification. There are various factors that are favorable or specifically predisposing to lucid projection. They are classified according to their nature into 4 categories:

1. **Psychological:** good intention; sense of spontaneous fraternity; optimism; carefreeness; *mental unwinding;* open and relaxed mind; fearlessness; healthy and fertile curiosity; have time; self-critique; self-discipline; motivation, interest; sincere wish to project, the most reliable coadjutant of projection; vocation as a courier; self-knowledge of your own human body and the self; autosuggestive procedures; hypnosis; state of divagation, daydream; trust in the capacities or attributes of the psychosoma; think about lucid projection; read about lucid projection, as long as you do not suffer from insomnia.

2. **Physiological:** go to bed as soon as you become sleepy; natural sleep; sleepiness; habit of sleeping on your back; position of laying on your back on the bed; relative tiredness; emotional self-control; psychophysical relaxation; remain relaxed during the day, avoiding conflicts; balanced sexlife; relaxation period subsequent to the experiences; sex act with neither negative connotations nor *sexual or energetic hangover;* low heart rate; specific illnesses; organic detoxification; fasting; prolonged dysentery due to consumption and physical weakening; certain types of developed parapsychism; precedent of being aware of dreaming during a dream; frequent previous physical repercussions; habit of projecting; maintenance of the image of the intraphysical consciousness him/herself projected.

3. **Physical:** good weather (meteorology); environment favorable to lucid projection; familiar environment used as a physical base; darkened physical base; friend sleeping close to the inactive human body; minimal sleeping attire.

4. **Extraphysical:** cosmoethical conduct; serenity during lucid projection; positive extraphysical relationships; not doubting yourself and your extraphysical capacities.

Aggregations. Pure or natural lucid projection is executable by discarding all psychological, mystical or scientistic aggregations coming from external, artificial or occasional sources.

Within. Everything that healthfully leads a person within him/herself, although maintaining the constant will to leave his/her own human body, favors the practice of lucid projection. This is why projective practices are recommended to all religious persons, or all faiths, and those that enter into psychological seclusion, motivated by any noble and just intention.

Age. Physical age can influence the individual's lucid projections. Due to immaturity in understanding their sensations, lucid projections occurring in infancy sometimes differ from lucid projections produced in adolescence, which can even mark the intraphysical personality. They can also differ from those occurring during maturity, which are more difficult and rarer, and definitively reveal the consciential panoramas.

Resomatics. The resomant extraphysical consciousness generally manifests itself in the adult form of the previous personality, up until one day prior to rebirth. It is even possible to have a projection of the consciousness of the fetus up to that point.

Activities. On the other hand, the fact of the projector maintaining him/herself involved in healthy day-to-day activities, or those related to physical survival – as surprising as it might seem – aids in the development of his/her lucid projections. The exchange in impressions, the gathering of ideas and dialoging with other projectors sustain the projector's motivation and prevent prolonged recesses in the series of experiences.

Intelligences. Cognition is a complex mixture formed by the perception, analysis and comprehension of information received. The more elevated the manifestations of the projector's independent and intercommunicative talents of intelligence – whether the intelligence is linguistic, mathematical, relative to the human body itself, intelligence regarding interpersonal relationship, musical intelligence, or spatial intelligence – the greater will be the possibility for him/her to amplify the extraphysical periods of his/her projected consciousness, increase the quantity of his/her projections in series, and expand the average quality of extraphysical perceptions (paraperceptiology) and lucid projections (projectiology) in general.

Case study. The intellectual competence of the projector in any field can favor his/her projectiological practices, e.g.: intelligence regarding language will easily lead him/her to conscientese; intelligence demonstrated relative to his/her human body permits an understanding and better use of the vehicles of manifestation of his/her consciousness; his/her intelligence regarding correct relationships provides better opportunities for extraphysical contacts; spatial intelligence helps in the grasping and application of extraphysical orientation.

Childbirth. Certain disturbances and accidents related to childbirth seem to positively predispose lucid consciential projection or, in other words, potentiate the projectability of the resomant extraphysical consciousness, a quality that will fully manifest later in the phase of adulthood or maturity. However, the physiological act of rebirth itself has no relationship with the subsequent performance of the consciential projector (see Susan J . Blackmore).

Concepts. Awareness of the basic differences between the concepts of sensation, instinct, self-awareness, emotion, reason, sentiment, postures, conduct and its consequences, are factors which are favorable to the production of lucid consciential projection. The individual can begin to reflect upon these factors, beginning with the following 6 points:

1. **Sensation:** lucid sensory process that is correlated to a physiological process and provides humans and so-called superior animals with a knowledge of the external world. Examples of types are: cold, heat, the 5 basic senses.

2. **Instinct:** forces having a biological origin, inherent to humans and the (larger) higher animals that generally act unconsciously, without exercising reason, although with precise purpose and independent of any learning. Types: life instinct, instinct of gregariousness or herd instinct, sexual instinct, maternal instinct.

3. **Self-awareness:** the consciousness that acquires the capacity for reflecting upon itself (awareness of self). Effects: notion of that being who knows who it is, where it is, what it does.

4. **Emotion:** intense, brief reaction of the organism to an unexpected event, which is accompanied by an affective state having a painful or agreeable connotation, depending upon the diencephalic centers and normally displaying manifestations of a vegetative order, devoid of any greater rationalizations. Types: ordinary love, passion, disgust, jealousy, grief, hate, anger (rage), surprise, embarrassment, sadness, happiness, fear, anxiety, remorse, ecstasy, repugnance (revulsion). It becomes very important to know that an individual's emotional expression constitutes the assemblage of revealing visible manifestations of a patent emotional state, mainly the following 9: vascular reactions: blushing or pallor of the face; respiratory reactions: sighs; expiratory reactions: laughter; mixed reactions: hiccups; glandular reactions: tears, sweat, salivation; generalized muscular reactions: trembling; facial reactions: grimaces or smiles; phonetic reactions: screams; pilomotor reactions: goose bumps and hair standing on end. There are exciting emotions (happiness, anger) and depressing emotions (pain, fear).

5. **Reason:** the faculty that humans have – distinguishing them from other animals – to establish logical relationships, to know, to understand, to reason, which leads them to original ideas. Effects: judgment, logic, discernment, prudence, good sense.

6. **Sentiment:** affective disposition relative to things of a moral or intellectual order, constituting the rationalization of emotions. Types: fraternity, renunciation, abnegation, fearlessness, inner peace. Positive sentiments lead the consciousness to balance, mental and emotional equilibrium, and to physical and extraphysical self-control.

Functionality. The functional development of the consciousness is one of the main objectives to be achieved by projectiology. Once the basic consciential operations and all of their manners of processing are known, lucid consciential projections are achieved through logical thoughts and a scientific sense, like an acquired good habit.

Techniques. In order for the functional development of the intraphysical consciousness to occur, the methodological procedures of projectiology, or logical projective techniques, are necessary (hence the reason for this book). This thereby definitively discards: disconnected pre-logical thoughts between ideas, judgments and reasonings, which are filled with omissions or false declarations, typical of the infantile or immature minds of adults lacking a greater rational development and the uncultured intelligences that precipitately confuse *the identical with the analogous,* without precisely discerning the degree, type, species, the causal succession, occasional succession, and the primary and secondary succession that is involved in the object under analysis.

Defects. This is why, on this point, projectiology eliminates: the defects of thought (correction of self-thosenity); conjunctive pre-logical thoughts; ideas having inappropriate emphases regarding that which is respectful; sacred concepts; thoughts which are magical, mystical, mythical or deficient in regard to perception within the rigor of the principle of sufficient reason.

Correlations. The intimate connections between emotions and the viscera, or somatic correlations, are a subject of common experience. Emotional awakening affects the heartbeat. Fear simulates the sudoriparous glands; sorrow affects the lacrimal glands. The respiratory and digestive systems are involved in the experience of emotion. Irrational beliefs are based upon emotion. Beliefs or thematic presuppositions are *felt* to be real. Believing has been described as *knowing your own viscera.* On the other hand, the functions of the viscera do not cease to also be reflections of the psychosoma, the emotional parabody.

Expressions. In the same way that children understand a much greater number of words than they can say, adults experience a much greater number of sensations than they are able to express in words, in the ordinary, physical waking state as well as during lucid consciential projections.

Aviators. Emotions, even subhuman, *animal* motions, always have their uses in the evolution of the consciousness. The following is a negative example: *to kill proficiently.* During the Second World War (1939-1945), bomber pilots assigned to delicate missions were selected from among emotional individuals. It was effectively proven that non-emotional aviators were incapable of evaluating the danger to which they were exposed, underestimated the power of the adversary's anti-aircraft batteries and had less chance than the others of reaching the set objective or, in other words, they were not *good killers*. Emotional intelligence is characterized by a profound infantilization and paralyzation of the self-discernment of the mentalsoma.

Scale. In an overall analysis, the following 4 basic manifestations regarding the evolutiology of the consciential principle (the consciousness) can be considered on a scale of increasing complexity:

1. **Somatics.** Human sensation: the complex form of genetic-vegetative animal instinct of that resonant extraphysical consciousness which still merely presents rudimentary paragenetics.

2. **Psychosomatics.** Human emotion: the complex form of energetic human sensation, or that which is influenced by the holochakrology – which is always temporary – of the intraphysical consciousness.

3. **Mentalsomatics.** The individual's elevated sentiments: the complex form of human emotion having a discernment that reaches even the evolved extraphysical communities.

4. **Holomaturology.** The consciousness' extraphysical maturity: the complex form of the individual's sentiments within the realm of the phenomenon of cosmoconsciousness.

Bibliography: Blackmore (140, p. 229), Denning (391, p. 6), Morris (1089, p. 1), Muldoon (1105, p. 197), Roll (1466, p. 230), Vieira (1762, p. 123).

---

444. PERSONAL USES OF LUCID PROJECTION

Use. Although the experience of lucid projection is a fact prevalent throughout human history, with a great number of cases already registered, this unusual experience is unfortunately still not perceived, not applied adequately, not used in daily life, nor is it used in a healthy manner by the majority of terrestrial humanity. On the contrary, there are still many people going to psychiatrists, notably youths taken by insistent relatives, due to the fact that they are seeing their own physical body – during healthy, spontaneous lucid projections – when they find themselves fully lucid while outside it. Sadly, this is an attitude of complete general ignorance of parapsychical realities. Hopefully this book can somehow contribute to the reduction of this obscurantism of our contemporary civilization and our sciences which are dedicated to the area of human health.

Indication. Lucid human projection can basically be applied to everything that favors and improves the life of the intraphysical consciousness, as it is a means for obtaining intraconsciential knowledge which could not be obtained in another manner. Lucid human projection offers an unlimited scope for the individual who lives in the hideaway of intraphysical existence *(bastion of the mega-ego)*.

Self-image. Lucid projection allows the human personality to achieve the following 8 extremely personal victories: clarify things, facts or experiences with respect to yourself; change your mood; eliminate personal insecurity; gain self-confidence for living; deal with personal emotional problems with greater realism and success; amplify the individual sense of competence; restore the psychophysical self-image; restructure a new self-concept, with which you can live a better and more productive life.

Types. Among the personal purposes of lucid projection, 5 types of revolutionary basic uses that can benefit humankind should be singled out: therapeutic uses, psychological uses, educational uses, parapsychic uses, and specific practical uses.

Therapeutic Uses:

1. Cure of interconsciential intrusion through extraphysical deintrusion, which can even be sponsored by and for the same lucid projector.

2. Elimination of thanatophobia, or the overwhelming fear of physical death, or the deactivation of the soma (desoma), through recognition of the existence of other consciential dimensions and the vehicles of manifestation of the intraphysical consciousness.

3. Elimination of pneumatophobia, or the fear of seeing or encountering extraphysical consciousnesses, through direct coexistence with the helpers.

4. Elimination of projectiophobia, or the fear of lucidly and temporarily leaving the human body, through the routinization of lucid projective experiences.

5. Elimination of acrophobia, or the fear of high places, and of aerophobia, or the fear of flying (in airplanes), through the practice of unencumbered volitation in extraphysical dimensions.

6. Use of lucid projection as a spontaneous, natural adaptive recourse of the human organism to disasters, surgery, accidents, or emotional stress.

7. Application of the lucid projection experience as a positive and powerful psychological aid in cases of fatal illness or suicidal tendency.

8. Assistance to the pregnant woman-fetus duo by the selfsame pregnant woman-projector.

9. Achievement of a state of supernormal health, because it deepens relaxation, eliminates tension, increases and focuses concentration, enhances memory, improves reflexes, increases self-confidence, and intensifies the desire to live productively.

Psychological uses:

10. Achievement of emotional balance through the practice of extraphysical serenity.

11. Encounters with loved ones while outside the human body.

12. Direct reconciliation with extraphysical adversaries, whether from the projector's past or present.

13. Annihilation of all types of hypocrisy or demagogy.

14. Possibility for extraphysical leisure, or *extraphysical mini-vacations,* through instructive trips taken by the consciousness.

15. Opening of horizons of another broader, richer and more definitive life with an understanding of cosmoethics, thereby affording the control of terrestrial life and solutions to everyday problems.

16. Enjoyment of the incomparable sensation of unfounded happiness and life that is devoid of time.

Educational uses:

17. A shortcut in the progressive route through the acceleration of consciential self-knowledge.

18. Ideal method for educating the consciousness through the acquisition of a profound awareness of personal identity.

19. Derepression of the integral consciousness (holomaturology).

20. Amplification of the extension of the consciousness through the mentalsoma (mentalsomatics).

21. Freedom of the consciousness from the prison of human forms.

22. Gathering of extraphysical opinions with answers to many enigmas or unknowns regarding intraphysical life.

23. Extraphysical acquisition of original ideas, the foundation of evolutionary research.

24. Uncovering of universalistic coexistology (megafraternity).

25. General substitution of beliefs through the transformation of the theory of infantile rationalized faith, which is amplified with direct, practical, experienced, unquestionable and definitive self-knowledge.

26. Self-affirmation of healthy, heuristic curiosity.

27. Gradual elimination of the need for the extraphysical consciousness to be reborn. This is the main purpose of lucid projection or, in other words, its anti-existential-seriation function.

Parapsychic uses:

28. The only process allowing the individual to take advantage of the one third of conscious life, which is routinely wasted by almost all of the terrestrial population under the Draconian demands of natural sleep.

29. Personal incontestable proof of the existence of the psychosoma, silver cord, chakras, mentalsoma and survival of the consciousness after the death of the human body (desoma).

30. Acceleration of the practical development of paraperceptibility or animic-parapsychic capacities in all their modalities and manifestations.

31. Achievement of extraphysical retrocognitions, with definitive proof of the individual's own existential seriation.

32. Acquisition of skill in extraphysical experiences.

33. Means of contacting friends and loved ones who have already resumed their status as extraphysical consciousnesses.

34. Improvement in the silver cord's action (holochakrology).

35. Extraphysical absorption of extraphysical energies.

36. Visits to all types of extraphysical environments.

37. Visits to human locations which are physically inaccessible or inhospitable, such as: deserts, closed forests, frozen regions, caves, depths of the earth, seabeds, mountain ranges and canyons.

38. Visits to human locations closed to strangers, such as: military areas, industrial zones, police establishments, secret organizations and libraries closed to the public.

39. Research performed on other heavenly bodies through exoprojections.

40. Consultation of a veritable database of transcendent information that is beyond all calculations and forecasts.

41. Anticipation of the possibility of the intraphysical being performing tasks using projection of the consciousness in the mentalsoma, that await him/her subsequent to desoma.

42. Personal verification of the existence or nonexistence of extraphysical intruders influencing the projector.

43. Avoidance of crazed acts such as those who kill themselves due to the mere curiosity of feeling and knowing what desoma or death of the human body is, because lucid projection is a *preview* of death.

Specific practical uses:

44. Anticipated strengthening of the individual who will be exposed to the risk of death or deactivation of the human body (soma).

45. Performance of extraphysical actions that are positive to invalids and persons with various general deficiencies, including blind and deaf-mute individuals.

46. Enjoyment of temporary extraphysical freedom by prisoners.

47. Overcoming physical distances through extraphysical processes.

48. Effective use of human time by those who are available, retired and suffer from intraphysical loneliness or forced isolation.

49. Finding an exit when lost in a dark cave (speleologists).

50. House hunting, for purchase, in a distant district or location.

Objectives. The scientific methodology and the various techniques of science which are applied in projectiology have the objective of improving humankind's knowledge (cognitive objective), increasing the individual's well-being, and expanding the individual's power (useful objectives).

Bibliography: Baumann (93, p. 95), Denning (391, p. 1), Frost (560, p. 19), Greene (635, p. 93), Greenhouse (636, p. 118), Leadbeater (901, p. 306), Malz (992, p. 97), Mittl (1061, p. 5), Rigonatti (1401, p. 14), Rogo (1444, p. 166), Vieira (1762, p. 5).

---

445. PROJECTIVE EXISTENTIAL RECYCLING

Definition. Projective existential recycling: change for the better of the entire course and perspective of the human life of the consciousness – caused by the impact of lucid projection – which therefore adopts a new set of values regarding the universe.

Synonymy: consciential recentralization; consciential reorientation; enrichment of the value system; instantaneous ideology; intraphysical about-face; intraphysical new perspective or new perspective regarding the existential program; projective existential moratorium; projective revival of the existential program; sudden intellectual conversion; turnaround of the existential program.

Reflection. The phenomenon of lucid projection, with an elevated degree of lucidity, challenges the individual's reason, generates an inevitable increase in his/her mental reflection and makes the individual *stop and think,* pay more attention to surrounding life issues and really rethosenize his/her view of the cosmos. These effects end up making greater or lesser individual changes in opinion and behavior. This is one more evident use of lucid projection or the lucid projectability of the intraphysical consciousness.

Effects. Among the effects triggered by existential recycling of a projective origin, at least the following 6 can be singled out:

1. **Self-awakening.** Psychological revival.
2. **Mentalsomatics.** Sudden intellectual conversion.
3. **Existential moratorium.** Existential moratorium.
4. **Intraconsciential recycling.** Intraconsciential illumination.
5. **Redefinitions.** Generalized redefinitions applied to human life.
6. **Turnaround.** Demarcation of the human existence into 2 distinct periods: before and after the impactful projection or the turnaround of one's own destiny, created by the individual him/herself.

Past. In the past, projective existential recycling blossomed after visions, mystical ecstasies, and diverse states of expansion of the consciousness or self-transcendence. As a result, sects and religions arose everywhere among the most diverse people.

Complement. Projective existential recycling can be preceded by an existential moratorium, which generally arises after a deep physical trauma, serious illness, near fatal accident, or existential crisis. It is frequently accompanied by the near-death experience (NDE), in this case being a resuscitative consciential projection wherein the consciousness receives – often fully aware – a complement of chronological human time for his/her human life in order to complete a task, perform obligations or execute an egokarmic or groupkarmic rescue, within the directives of his/her existential program.

Moratoriumist. The individual who receives the responsibility of an intraphysical moratorium or the responsibility for accomplishing the existential program is a *moratoriumist.*

Dislocation. Existential recycling through lucid projection is a sudden dislocation – apparently occurring without warning – of the intraphysical consciousness' center of organization in the mentalsoma. This is a fact within the field of mentalsomatics.

Trauma. The abrupt dislocation of the center of consciential organization requires meticulous self-study in order for the new lucid projector to avoid a traumatic or negative personal recentralization, reorientation or new perspective.

Paravisceral. Existential recycling of a projective origin is often more vigorous, deep, sophisticated, far-reaching and paravisceral than any other possible consciential reorientation in human life which is generated by an impetus stemming from privation, illness, ideological adhesion, religious conversion, the persuasive words of a professor or the revolutionary ideas of a book.

Characteristics. The following are conditions and characteristics which are peculiar to the majority of instances of full projective existential recycling:

1. **Rarity.** The rarity of the occurrence, in light of the total planetary population.
2. **Leap.** Existential recycling constitutes a sudden leap in consciential development.
3. **Center.** The occurrence emphasizes the complexity of the center of consciential organization (mentalsoma).
4. **Self-growth.** It illustrates the mobility of the upper limits of the possibilities for consciential self-growth.
5. **Specifications.** Above all, it has particular, personal specifications.

6. **Lability.** It is dependent upon the lability of the personal process of consciential organization.

7. **Capacities.** It is directly related to the capacity for personal reflection, objectivation and education.

8. **Enrichment.** The degree of consciential enrichment from the occurrences is far greater than the degree of trauma arising from them.

9. **Transcendence.** In theory, the new projective perspective transcends all other possible existential recycling.

10. **Triumphalism.** It exhibits a certain emotional gratification tending toward triumphalism, which should always be avoided.

Bibliography: Blackmore (145, p. 309), Portela (1275, p. 127), Vieira (1773, p. 5).

---

446. PUBLIC USES OF LUCID PROJECTION

Categories. Among the public uses of lucid projection, 18 can be divided into 3 categories: therapeutic uses, parapsychic uses, and specific practical uses.

Therapeutic uses:

1. Anonymous or visible (apparition of the projected projector) assistance to intraphysical and extraphysical consciousnesses.

2. Extraphysical rescue of a projected intraphysical being within the interconsciential processes of intrusion and possession.

3. Extraphysical diagnosis or projective telediagnosis.

Parapsychic uses:

4. Proof of the existence of the human consciousness to another (apparition of the intraphysical projector or *inter vivos* apparition).

5. Proof of the existence of the psychosoma (physical bilocation phenomenon).

6. Programmed experiments of lucid projections in the laboratory.

Specific practical uses:

7. Establishment of *holothosenic cartography,* including the specific identification of the local materthosene, physical and extraphysical environments (thosenology).

8. Historical research through projective retrocognition (history).

9. Extraphysical tracking of persons missing due to kidnapping or abductions; plane crashes; boating accidents.

10. Extraphysical tracking of persons who have committed antisocial acts (criminology or police investigation).

11. Extraphysical location of shoals of fish (primitive survival technique).

12. Extraphysical location of fossils and antiquities (archeology or archeological research).

13. Extraphysical location of mineral deposits (geology or geological research).

14. Extraphysical exploration of natural cavities in the earth: grottos; caverns; springs (speleology or speleological research).

15. Anatomy research; histology research, including cells, genes, DNA; general microbiology research; research of atoms and sub-atomic particles through projections of the mentalsoma (mentalsomatics).

16. Spying or investigation through extraphysical espionage. A resource which is obviously negative or anticosmoethical for the lucid consciential projector to use.

17. Extraphysical space probing through consciential probes (astronautics).

18. An impelling factor for space research, given that lucid projection is the most practical means for space travel.

Surveillance. An immediate practical application of the phenomenon of lucid projection, and one which becomes a firm obligation for the veteran lucid projector, in favor of him/herself, others and the environment in which he/she lives, is the *service of extraphysical defense and surveillance*. With the development of projectiology, this service will one day be continuously executed everywhere.

Technique. Through the service of extraphysical defense and surveillance, the awakened, projected, lucid projector controls the physical-extraphysical environment of his/her physical base, expelling all possible intrusive, energivorous, invasive, inconvenient and ill extraphysical consciousnesses that appear. This is accomplished through the practices of penta, conscientiotherapeutic encapsulation and the extraphysical clinic. The following are 14 categories of these personalities:

1. Conscious and unconscious extraphysical invaders of residences.

2. Conscious and unconscious hangers-on of the residents.

3. Extraphysical somnambulists, in this case, energivorous extraphysical consciousnesses, frequently having no ill intentions, although being vampirizers.

4. Extraphysical or intraphysical somnambulists, in this case, projected and needy intraphysical consciousnesses.

5. Object-consciousnesses serving as interconsciential assistential bait for the consciential epicenter who already works with an extraphysical clinic.

6. Classic stubborn extraphysical intruders, including mega-intruder leaders of groups.

7. Those *demanding* satisfaction regarding extraphysical assistential work or extraphysical groupkarmic creditors of intraphysical consciousnesses, which can be the projector, relatives, friends or colleagues of the evolutionary group.

8. Extraphysical *trespassers* of all types and categories.

9. Innocent pawns used as *cannon fodder* by intruders or satellites of extraphysical intruders (intraphysical and extraphysical consciousnesses).

10. Ill extraphysical sentinels.

11. Extraphysical assailants commonly found in the troposphere and the paratroposphere.

12. Extraphysical, paratropospheric, curious ill consciousnesses.

13. Extraphysical children which are "apparently lost".

14. Extraphysical blind guides of all types, which are vampires that are readily encountered in all types of sectarian human doctrinaire groups, whether mystical, religious, sociological, political, artistic, athletic, philosophical and even scientific, when dedicated to anticosmoethical acts (bellicosity, militarism, martial policies, armed conflicts, hostilities).

Security. Spontaneous lucid consciential projection sometimes serves as a physiological security mechanism for the intraphysical consciousness to prevent excessive shock or trauma and allow the individual (with assistance from extraphysical helpers) to transcend pain and fear (thanatophobia) and understand (holomaturity) what is actually happening to him/her (achievement of hyperacuity or recuperation of the major cons). This occurs through intra and extraconsciential, intra and extraphysical, multidimensional mutations.

Self-mutations. The following are examples of 10 postures, procedures or behaviors. They are listed in the logical, sequential order of renovating, or mutational, events triggered by the practice of lucid and cosmoethical consciential projection, as well as the inevitable consequent acquisition of transcendent knowledge attained directly in evolved extraphysical communities:

1. **Growth.** Intra and extraconsciential growing crises.

2. **Evolution.** Positive stress: *the touchstone of evolution*.

3. **Self-turnaround.** Consciential self-turnaround or self-mutation per se.

4. **Intraconsciential recycling.** Intraconsciential recycling (consciential micro-universe).

5. **Existential recycling.** Existential recycling.

6. **Existential moratorium.** Existential moratorium within the existential program.

7. **Penta.** Beginning of the practices of penta or the personal, daily, energetic task for the rest of the current intraphysical existence.

8. **Consciential epicenter.** Acceptance of the condition of consciential epicentrism.

9. **Extraphysical clinic.** The opening of a busy assistential extraphysical clinic derived from your holothosene, which increases your interdimensional responsibilities.

10. **Minicog.** Self-lucid and comfortable recognition of your personal transformation into a lucid minicog of a maximechanism of interconsciential and multidimensional assistance.

Future. In the future, projectiology will allow a surveying of the *holothosenic chart* of every intraphysical city, indicating the gravitations of consciential energies and thosenes (materthosenes) which are positive, healthy, more subtle or better, as well as those which are negative, pathological, heavier or worse. It will also be possible to plot an *extraphysical map* of the environment around conglomerations of humans. Within the factors thus far detected in this sense, the following are included: extraphysical currents of energy; extraphysical assistance service sectors; open extraphysical vampirism in slaughterhouse environments; and others.

Probes. In the technological applications of lucid consciential projection, lucid projectors will be used in the future as consciential probes to investigate other stars and planets distant from the earth, especially using projections in the mentalsoma. This is because distances disappear and chronological time does not have the same magnitude in the mental dimension as it does in the ordinary, physical waking state. Lucid projection will also be employed to research the microcosm of matter, its field interactions, dipoles and multi-poles of electromagnetic waves, nuclei, electrons and neutrinos, using only the pure hyperacuity of the consciousness and thereby avoiding interference from interactions with equipment.

Bibliography: Brittain (206, p. 53), Greene (635, p. 93), Greenhouse (636, p. 89), Leadbeater (901, p. 306), Murphy (1111, p. 58), Steiger (1601, p. 124), Targ (1651, p. 169), Vieira (1773, p. 5).

---

447. FACTORS UNFAVORABLE TO LUCID PROJECTION

Classification. The factors unfavorable or inhibitory to lucid projection can be classified into 4 categories, according to their nature:

1. **Conscientiological** (or psychological): panic; unquietness; anxiety; indiscipline; scattered thoughts or unstable self-thosenity; obsessive ideas (monoideism, fixed ideas); be worried about an appointment; have expectations about the following day; maintain the psychophysiological, corporal, biological clock out of sync with the day-night cycle (circadian rhythm); laziness, depression, mental apathy or intellectual fatigue; staying in bed beyond the natural, healthy number of hours of sleep; pessimism or defeatism; misoneism or neophobia; erroneous tradition; feelings of resentment, grief, susceptibility, disaffection or malevolence; reprehensible or anticosmoethical intentionality; anticosmoethical or bad habits; ignorance of lucid projection; technical unpreparedness for even a primary lucid consciential projection; watching an engrossing movie at the theater, on TV or on tape shortly before preparing to project.

2. **Somatic** (or physiological): emotional lack of control; lying in the prone position in bed; disturbance due to the digestive process, it thus being recommended that heavy meals be eaten two hours prior to predisposing yourself to lucid projection; ingestion of alcoholic beverages prior to attempting a projective experience; organic intoxication; intestinal constipation due to the accumulation of used matter inside the human body; prolonged intellectual activity that uses cerebral or emotive excitation, working late into the night, whether with discussions about ideas, controversies and family disputes, and others; high heart rate; tobaccoism; sexual dissatisfaction or deprivation.

3. **Physical** (or mesological): atmospheric disturbances in the physical base; muggy weather; a very high or very low temperature in the bedroom (energetically shielded chamber); an unfamiliar environment used as a physical base; background music in the physical base (for most veteran

projectors); noises close to the human body; a person awake near the practitioner's human body; heavy sleeping attire; certain drugs, even when correctly prescribed for indispensable therapy, such as stimulants that enhance the physical waking state.

4. **Extraphysical** (or parapsychic): fear (thanatophobia, projectiophobia) during the projection; apprehension of not returning to the human body; extraphysical fear causing involuntary return, physical repercussion and physical catalepsy; extraphysical emotionalism; extraphysical invasion or intrusion, with negative or anticosmoethical intentions, of the privacy of the intraphysical or extraphysical consciousness; the extraphysical tracking of terrestrial or paratropospheric interests; the extraphysical sexual impulse destabilizing the freed psychosoma, which ends up being pulled back to the human body by the silver cord, as well as other consequences that attract extraphysical consciousnesses which have the same category of thosene.

Stimulants. It is also not recommended to ingest beverages that stimulate the brain, up to 4 hours before going to bed. This is especially true for those containing caffeine, such as coffee, tea, hot chocolate and soft drinks, like colas. The human body begins to feel the stimulating effect of caffeine from between thirty minutes to one hour after ingesting any of these drinks. Depending upon the individual, a simple cup of coffee can excite the cerebral cortex up to 7 hours after it is ingested.

Interpretation. Certain erroneous observations made by individuals arise from a complete absence of specialized, technical knowledge. There are authors who intellectually endeavor to give a new twist to the interpretation of the concept of lucid consciential projection or its practice. This leads those authors' readers to a narrow-mindedness which ends up prohibiting, restricting, castrating and annulling their creative inquiry and, consequently, their resources for lucid projectability (LPB).

Trash. There is an immense amount of omnipresent *mental trash* offered everywhere at *bargain-basement prices,* with *superattractive* products that *cannot be passed up,* often using multimillion dollar self-promotions. Among these are included professing, militant, mercantilist *New Age* authors, and even those who perform specialized tasks of primary consolation or clarification. They are inducers of dispensable self-mimicries in incautious intraphysical consciousnesses, all being the components of the unthinking human masses regarding cosmoethical self-conscientiality, as well as being victims of existential robotization, the *multidimensionally blind* leading those who are even blinder.

Insomniferous. All sleep blockers, or insomnia provokers (agrypnotics), regardless of their nature, work against projective experiments: allopathic drugs, stimulants, such as those which extend the individual's period of wakefulness; homeopathic pain medication, such as *Paulinia sorbilis;* the guarana beverage, when made from powder obtained by grating the block of dried fruit paste, commonly recognized as a recourse against sleep.

Psychomotricity. All of this happens because lucid projection becomes much more difficult when the human body is active or in movement (brain, psychomotricity, muscular mass) and easier when in a state of relaxation or natural sleep.

Purpose. Many intraphysical beings neither seek out extraphysical realities beyond diuturnal human life, nor do they lucidly project themselves. This is because they have no motivation to do so as they are unconcerned with seeking a transcendent purpose for their lives or existential programs, a concept about which they are often unaware. They think they have attained this objective, being well situated, busy, productive, satisfied and somewhat self-realized with their own destinies or their own misleading social conditions.

Existential miniprogram. It is important to consider that, in certain cases, the evolutionary stages of certain intraphysical consciousnesses (including those closer to us), or the execution of their existential miniprograms, does not really require much more than this. It will nevertheless be intelligent to bear in mind, as a *relevant orthothosene,* that no intraphysical consciousness escapes *final consciential projection,* the intermissive period, or the nuances of extraphysical euphoria or extraphysical melancholy.

Fear. Other intraphysical beings are not able to project lucidly because they find themselves to be possessed and truly enslaved by a fear which is intense, preexisting, unfounded and deep-rooted in their psychisms (paragenetics) well before becoming familiar with the subject and possibilities of lucid projection.

Disturbances. Two very distinct parapathological facts occur: interconsciential intrusion of an extraphysical or human origin, or even self-intrusion; and the disturbance characteristic of the parapathology of the holochakra, in which consciential energies are easily and continuously lost, thereby not replenishing it with vitality.

Conscientiotherapy. Before considering lucid consciential projection, these intraphysical consciousnesses first need to remove fear from their life or, in other words, achieve relief from intrusion (conscientiotherapy), balance their capacity for mnemonic retention (mnemosomatics) and the circulation of consciential energies within their system (VSs).

Bibliography: Fortune (540, p. 162), Steiger (1601, p. 202), Stokes (1625, p. 23).

448. LUCID PROJECTION AND FEAR

Definition. Fear: the sentiment of great unease when faced with the notion of a real external danger or a reaction when faced with a danger having no real object, a mere imaginary threat.

Synonymy: animal terror; fright; irrational dread; panic; phobia; terror; unjustified apprehension.

Superstitions. One of the most common sources of errors of the consciousness is fear, whether acting directly (e.g.: rumors of disasters at critical times or occasions) or indirectly (e.g.: the idea of hell). The most common fears in daily life are: fear of death (desoma); fear of the dark; fear of the unknown; fear of crowds. Fear generates deep-rooted superstitions.

Illness. Before considering fear in relation to consciential projections, or making references to existential anguish and certain clinical manifestations, it is worth recalling that the *panic syndrome* (fear attack, inner panic, or the fear of being afraid) has been well-characterized through epidemiological, neurophysiological, biochemical and therapeutic investigations.

Self-restriction. In theory, no one is immune to fear, a basic aspect of the human being: an extraphysical consciousness that, while temporarily in the condition of an intraphysical consciousness, continuously suffers a high degree of imposed consciential self-restriction that is still inevitable at our current evolutionary level.

Phobias. Anxiety and panic come and go in waves. Phobias are also more advanced forms of fear and affect up to 1% of the population in various countries. According to psychology, a phobia is behavior acquired through experience; it is neither hereditary, nor is the individual born with it. However, contrary to these opinions, retrocognitions triggered by projective techniques and consciential regressions performed in the field of parapsychology provide the first evidence that certain phobias can have their origin in traumas that occurred in previous human lives (retrosomas) of the consciousness. There is currently an inestimable number of phobias, but they are curable.

Characteristics. The panic reaction, defined as intense fear that arises suddenly, without warning, without apparent cause, or from a cause which does not justify the intensity of the fear, is characterized by at least 4 of the following phenomena: dizziness, tachycardia, palpitations, darkening of the vision, fainting sensation (vertigo), profuse sudoresis (over the entire body), nausea, lack of air (dispnea), tremors, alternating waves of hot and cold, derealization, pain or discomfort in the chest ("tightening in the heart," "knot in the throat"), fear of dying (thanatophobia), fear of change, fear of the unknown (panophobia) or fear of going crazy.

Feed. It is important to remember that fear feeds on itself.

Biopsychiatry. Besides the above-cited symptoms having a psychological cause (psychiatry), the panic reaction, identified as an illness in 1980, occurs due to a biological dysfunction (biopsychiatry). Noradrenaline is ordinarily released by the central nervous system in order to maintain the soma's automatic activities, such as respiration and heartbeat. If the dosage of noradrenaline becomes excessive, it provokes a breakdown in the human organism and can thereby produce strong phobias, such as: a disproportionate fear of leaving the house, fear of taking an elevator and fear of being in closed, crowded spaces.

Stress. This attack of unfounded fear reaches its greatest intensity in less than 10 minutes, almost always after a major stress attack – for example, either by the loss of a loved one, postpartum, or loss of a job – that acts as a precipitating factor of biological vulnerability, thereby triggering the crisis.

Center. Fear, or a *cold chill running down the spine,* arises from thoughts and these come from terrible things that the intraphysical consciousness imagines or anticipates. The individual is urged to break this chain of mental elaboration, imagination and unfounded forecasts, in order to eliminate the fear. Researchers in neurophysiology and biopsychiatry are attempting to identify the fear center – the region that triggers the panic reaction – in a miniscule cerebral nucleus situated in the fourth ventricle, called the *locus ceruleus,* the element responsible for 50% of the noradrenaline activity of the 2 cerebral hemispheres.

Immunity. A negative clinical aspect of fear is that it ends up depressing the organism's immune system, as it provokes tension and this winds up diminishing the fearful person's organic defenses.

Reactions. In an immediate or retarded reaction to inner fear and external danger (the symptoms of fear), the majority of intraphysical consciousnesses, including hypersophisticated persons, manifest an abnormal, inadequate and often dramatic behavior when under pressure. This behavior falls into 1 of the following 4 basic patterns:

1. **Regression.** In a regressive, psychophysical reaction of encystment, there is a loss of acquired behavior by the consciousness or the habits of civilization, or formal poise, with a return of irresponsible, infantile behavior, the primitive refuge of long ago.

2. **Camouflage.** In camouflaging and masking, reactions of the intraphysical consciousness' protective artifice (dissimulation) occur or, in other words: the fainting and mental paralysis of the passive, indifferent and submissive person.

3. **Panic.** Great explosive panic, or frenetic disorientation, running, trampling and the thoughtless fury of mass hysteria, or *everyone for himself,* which manifests as a defense by way of attack or escape. The panicked person spreads panic.

4. **Conditioning.** In psychosomatic conditioning (organic and psychological, in this case), the denser consciential vehicle, the soma, suffers the consequences, thereby resulting in multiple physical symptoms: perspiration; frequent urination; heart palpitations; nausea; diarrhea (functional colopathy); high blood pressure; excessive eating (bulimia).

Occurrences. The fears that overwhelm the intraphysical consciousness regarding lucid projection have various origins: the anguish of the projected consciousness not being able to return to the human body; apprehension when faced with an unknown world, or the extraphysical dimension (fear of the unknown, neophobia, can be a fear of death); the fact of confronting (extraphysical) regions uncharted by human beings; the shock felt by the consciousness projected with lucidity for the first time (self-lucid primoprojection), and thinking that he/she has deactivated his/her soma (biological death); fear of encountering strange monsters, exotic beings never seen before.

Self-murder. Fear can initiate real physiological changes that can literally lead to the death of the human body or desoma by unconscious self-murder.

Distance. Controlling fear is half the distance for someone to project with lucidity.

Climax. Fear is more inconvenient for the consciential projector precisely during the perception of the moment at which the consciousness leaves the human body or, in other words, at the exact final climax of the projective stage of lucid takeoff in the psychosoma.

Barrier. At this time, fear – panic outside the human body – causes the instantaneous paralysis of the psychosoma's takeoff process. This extraphysical emotional trauma truly frustrates the experience of lucid projection and creates a *barrier of fear* that can reappear during other projective attempts by the consciousness and last for a long time afterward. Besides, many projectors do not see the departure of the soma, although they remain lucid during the projective experiences.

Takeoff. The fear that the consciousness feels at the beginning of a lucid takeoff in the psychosoma is very similar to the fear of flying, for those who are afraid of airplanes or dying in an airplane crash and who simultaneously suffer from aerophobia (fear of floating) and claustrophobia (are terrified of being in closed spaces such as tunnels, theaters, formal meetings). This occurs precisely during the takeoff of the aircraft, the most stressful stage of the airplane flight which, incidentally, paradoxically only lasts for 40 seconds. All this occurs after the person has left the house, his/her secure environment and familiar surroundings.

Controlling. Even extremely controlling persons – those who cannot tolerate to sit in the back seat of a taxi and, when in a car, only feel good when driving – may experience fear at the precise instant of lucid takeoff in the psychosoma.

Hypoperception. Hypoperception is characterized by an exaggerated reduction in consciential activity, provoking a reduction of sensitivity and perception. One of the main determining factors of hypoperception is fear.

Projection. Fear is the emotion which troubles most and is the main obstacle to the production of lucid, consciential projection. This is because, strictly speaking, lucid projection represents: the greatest antidote to fear; the greatest psychological self-conquest; the subjugation of matter; the mastery of biological death; the definitive annihilation of consciential insecurity; the control of the consciousness in the mentalsoma over the psychosoma. Without fear, everything is absolutely possible for the projector's consciousness; with fear, there is no individual development of lucid, consciential projections. Fear keeps the consciousness tethered by the dominating emotions, a slave to the psychosoma, imprisoned in the human body *(locked human life).*

Types. Within the world of projectiology research, the infantile or immature reaction of any type of fear does not always arise ostensively or suddenly. Fear often appears, dominating the consciousness slowly and subtly, or camouflaged by other emotions which are the main origin. They arise more or less in the following order, in a complex, ascending scale of manifestations: weight; pressure; worry; restlessness; insecurity; intense disturbance; shock; fear; panic; open dread; animal terror.

Thanatophobia. Fear is the most negative or inhibiting factor – fed by the intraphysical consciousness – in the production of the lucid projection experience. Whether it is fear of the unknown, a morbid dread of dying (deactivation of the soma), fear of the fatality of death (thanatophobia), fear of solitude, or pre-projective fear (projectiophobia), these conditions generate a *sterilizing predisposition* toward projective phenomena. This is due to unconscious negativism or *refractory monoideism,* which does not allow the practitioner to develop the production of lucid projections.

Elimination. Those who experience an ordinary lucid projection, but a fully lucid one – or even a lucid consciential projection during a major near-death experience (NDE) – definitively eliminate the pathological fear of biological death.

Disfigurement. The emotions of the consciousness projected from the human body can predispose the appearance of diverse fears. They end up producing spontaneous morphothosenes related to strange monsters that finally cause an equally spontaneous disfigurement of the psychosoma's humanoid form, since the consciousness is hypersensitive to thoughts and emotions.

Warning. On the other hand, certain declarations made by some authors generate fear in many novices, readers and students of lucid projection. Certain warnings lacking an indication of corresponding techniques for specialized betterment and improvement should not be made. This is because they, on the contrary, become negative and anticosmoethical, creating insecurity and misunderstandings, and have no constructive practical result. This bulky volume, which the reader holds in his/her hands, containing details and exhaustive minutiae, was therefore compiled in order to avoid these inconveniences.

Helpers. The extraphysical helpers and their functions should be perfectly understood by the fearful individual in order for him/her to lose any type of fear. Every consciential projector should operate based upon the following principle: the extraphysical helpers always remain alert and do not let the projected intraphysical consciousness (you) get lost in an unknown extraphysical dimension or let the human body suffer an attack while inactive during the occurrence and development of lucid projection experiences.

Case study. If an intercurrent disaster occurs – such as an unexpected fire in the physical base of the intraphysical consciousness (you) when projected, precisely where the inactive human body is resting – the extraphysical helpers make you return and interiorize in time to rid yourself of the disaster. This obviously happens if the individual is not experiencing his/her final, exact, just and inevitable holokarmic moment of desoma, which is forecast and even often clearly announced.

Desomatics. The probability of becoming ill or even physically dying – deactivating the soma – largely depends upon our inner disposition. The sentiments of depression, despair or feeling abandoned do not cause illnesses, but make persons somehow vulnerable.

Reason. Fear is an *emotional issue* and is not related to an individual's intelligence or education. It therefore essentially stems from the energies of the psychosoma used upon the consciousness and can actually be eliminated with applied reason. This is because – according to thosenology – it is generally easier to control thoughts *(tho)* than emotions *(sen)*.

Desensitization. The best *medical technique* for controlling fears and phobias is progressive desensitization, which generally takes 4 to 8 weeks. In the case of a phobia regarding wounds and blood, for example, the patient looks at photos of accidents or surgeries; handles hypodermic needles; holds flasks of blood; visits emergency clinics; and has his/her blood taken with a small prick on the finger.

Solution. There is, therefore, only one way to overcome the immaturity of fear: firstly, confront any type of fear, doing so gradually, with wisdom and patience, in an educational manner. Start by reading and researching the projective experiences of other lucid projectors, obviously those who did not undergo desoma during the lucid projection experience. Next, trust in the continued assistance of the cosmoethical extraphysical helpers – during consciential projections having cosmoethically productive objectives – even when they are not perceived in the extraphysical dimension. Finally, rationalize emotion – in this case, fear itself, characteristic of the consciousness when manifesting in the psychosoma – until it is completely eliminated, conscientially situating yourself at the level of the mentalsoma, in evolution toward the conquest of full consciential maturity or holomaturity.

Understanding. That which is not understood is always feared. The intraphysical consciousness overcome by fear of parapsychic experiences needs to endeavor to acquire a deep understanding of projectiology. All of his/her fears, as great as they may be, will thereby disappear. Your healthy curiosity of the unknown (unknown: the fruit of ignorance) will always be able to overcome your fear through this selfsame unknown.

Bibliography: Andreas (36, p. 56), Baumann (93, p. 78), Boswell (174, p. 140), Castaneda (256, p. 244), Frost (560, p. 29), Green (632, p. 88), Mittl (1061, p. 6), Monroe (1065, p. 24), Muldoon (1105, p. 150), Reis (1384, p. 54), Rogo (1436, p. 172), Sherman (1551, p. 193), Vieira (1762, p. 162).

449. RELATIVE INHIBITING AGENTS TO LUCID CONSCIENTIAL PROJECTION

Minority. Diverse psychological factors, or relative inhibiting agents, make a small minority of intraphysical consciousnesses instinctively avoid relating their lucid experiences outside the human body. This serves to impede the expansion of projectiology and conscientiology research.

Factors. The following are 12 anti-projective factors common within this still pathological intraphysical society:

1. **Animism.** There are uninformed projectors who avoid addressing the theme of their own authentic lucid projections. This is due to the purely animic or intraconsciential aspect of their experiences which, by all indications, are produced solely by their efforts, without the visible aid of an extraphysical helper or any concomitant resource. This actually does occur, but it is a mistake not to perceive that the conditions of animism and parapsychism have always coexisted and still coexist in the majority of evolved parapsychic manifestations, given that they themselves – the intraphysical projectors – are also immortal or *deathless* consciousnesses, the same as the extraphysical consciousnesses. The great, important projections or king-size projections are still invariably animic-parapsychic in this earth school.

2. **Time.** Some spontaneous projectors, owing to a sense of guilt, avoid making any references to lucid projections which they have in the daytime during working hours, during which, according to them, they should somehow be working like everyone else and not sleeping, without producing something useful. They do not, on the other hand, take into account the transcendent usefulness of these same lucid projections, their dissemination in favor of clarifying others, the existence of retired persons and that these lucid projections produced during daylight hours are even less frequent.

3. **Inexperience.** Many adolescents inadvertently, because of their ingenuousness, do not confront the subject of lucid projections because they consider them to be natural to human beings. They do not perceive the need to refer to day-to-day facts that affect and are known by everyone, like ordinary dreams.

4. **Danger.** There are still those – almost always having good intentions and following the affirmations of authors from the past – who maintain a maximum of secrecy and discretion regarding everything related to lucid projections. They do this in order to avoid the creation of supposed fictitious evils and dangers for credulous and unprepared individuals. This pretext has been distancing a multitude of persons from the practice of lucid projection throughout the millennia of human history, up until approximately 5 decades ago.

5. **Ridicule.** Shy individuals lacking a deep knowledge of the subject often maintain an instinctive unconfessed and repressed fear of being ridiculed. They fear the incredulity of their peers, or being considered insane or untruthful by their relatives, friends, colleagues and neighbors if they openly present the details of their lucid projections. They actually recognize these experiences to be authentic but nevertheless do not talk about them or allow their real names to be mentioned in specialized publications on the subject because they still do not consider projective practices to be socially acceptable conduct.

6. **Anomaly.** There are also ingenuous individuals who fear becoming anomalous human beings or *boogeymen* with lucid projection, which allows the projector to invade the privacy of others and probe the depths of persons' minds in certain cases.

7. **Semilucidity.** The majority of semilucid projections in the individual's assemblage of experiences frequently leads the novice projector to feel incapable of satisfactorily distinguishing real lucid projections from ordinary dreams, although they are very vivid. The intraphysical consciousness ends up being convinced that he/she does not project and therefore does not develop, projectiologically speaking.

8. **Sexuality.** There are social beings who evade the theme of lucid self-projections – that they doubtless consider to be genuine – because they involve experiences having some extraphysical sexual connotation which, at first sight, are difficult to interpret or are capable of causing social embarrassment for themselves and other persons.

9. **Underestimation.** Making the mistake of underestimation, certain individuals judge their experiences to be overly insignificant, as compared to average lucid projectors, to merit reporting and studying. They forget the extremely important factor of the convergence of proof through the universality of identical, repeated and repeatable testimonies.

10. **Overestimation.** There are likewise those individuals who produce lucid projections but withhold any information in this regard, as they mistakenly consider themselves to be very elevated or evolved – above the average of "poor mortals" – incapable of making such a transcendent subject accessible and popular, feeling it is too *sacrosanct* or *intramural.* They are unable to address it without taboos, with naturality and equanimity, in favor of the common good.

11. **Superstition.** There are also those who worship ancient superstitions and confess nothing regarding their projective experiences, which they consider a "special blessing." They base this on the single groundless fear that these revelations, if made public, would definitively paralyze their lucid projections through the automatic loss of their capacity to project, as though their "special blessing" would be revoked if they did not know how to keep the secret or keep up their guard.

12. **Dreams.** Dreams, as altered states of consciousness, affect everyone and are as common as the state of natural sleep. This is why they are easily accepted, receiving a ready, general, *urbi et orbi* approval. Thus, there are those who are less inclined to relate their lucid projection experiences and more likely to interpret or, more precisely, disguise, their lucid projections as dreams so that the declaration of their extraphysical experiences are better accepted without social repudiation.

Relativity. In fact, the action of these inhibitory agents is very relative, as it is entirely dependent upon the quality of the experiences. If the projector has a lucid projection of great importance, even if it be singular, with an elevated degree of lucidity, characterized by impactful extraphysical events, neither these psychological factors nor any other taboos, manias, repressions, brainwashings, conditionings and inhibitions will have a force capable of suffocating the frank exposition of the events or impede the individual's undisguised manifestations regarding the reality of the facts in which he/she participated, experienced or witnessed directly. The greatest definitive proof of this fact is the existence of the international bibliography at the end of this volume.

Rationalization. As great as the projector's *rationalization of protection* may be – who, although personally convinced, desires to remain in the good graces of his/her peers by avoiding confronting extraphysical facts – he/she ends up surrendering to the evidence and accepting the experiences when they are repeated with a greater intensity, and when self-lucid projections occur in a series of consecutive experiences.

Bibliography: Champlin (272, p. 261), Greenhouse (636, p. 219), Râ (1376, p. 19), Steiger (1601, p. 202), Stokes (1625, p. 23), Tart (1661, p. 5).

450.   HARMS   OF   LUCID   PROJECTION

Definition. Harm: the act of producing damage, hurt or injury to someone or something.

Synonymy: damage; inconvenience; obstacle; danger; loss.

Types. The following are harms that stem from lucid projections. They are, in theory, possible and real, but are very rare in projectiological practice: deep extraphysical trauma; negative influence of one intraphysical consciousness upon another; alienation regarding material life, family, profession and friends, or a feeling of distance and indifference regarding the human projector's surroundings.

Inflation. The following are latent dangers and probable harms stemming from lucid projections, according to the incredible-sounding and insistent declarations of certain studious individuals, with whom the author evidently does not agree: aneurysmal rupture; cardiac arrest; cerebral hemorrhage; confused aura; disintegration of the psyche; dizziness; emotional disturbances; encounters with unfamiliar hostile beings; faintings; final projection; friendly but harmful extraphysical encounters; *getting sucked into a black hole;* hallucinations; harmful physical repercussion; headaches; hypochondria; hysteria; interconsciential intrusion; madness; morbid discoincidence; mortal wounding by a pointed metallic instrument or blades in general; nightmares; panic; paralysis; pathological disturbances of the psychosoma; permanent interconsciential influences; physical accidents; physical alienation; possession; premature burial of the still active soma; profound amnesia; psychic shock; reoccupation of the human body by another intelligence; rupture of the silver cord; stigmatization; twisting of the silver cord; and unbearable sensations.

Withholding. No human activity is entirely free of danger. Even complete inactivity and sedentary life present real, indisputable harms. However, this inflation of risks regarding consciential projection has been quite exaggerated and was created, in part, with the intention of maintaining a systematic intentional withholding of information from the general population – or the unthinking human masses – regarding parapsychic or *initiative* practices, since ancient times, continuing through the Middle Ages, and lasting up until 5 decades ago.

Manipulation. The purpose of this posture was an egoistic defense of temporal religious, mystical powers or, in other words: the manipulation of individuals *(cannon fodder, satellites of intruders or intraphysical and extraphysical blind guides)* belonging to small social groups.

Hygiene. The author, during decades of investigation, has never identified a single one of these inconvenient disseminations as being real obstacles to lucid projection. The obstacles that he has encountered have only contributed to the technical improvement of the processes of the detachments, which bring immense personal happiness. Good intention, inner tranquility, self-critiquing consciousness and a slightly developed parapsychism naturally remove these and other risks that may perchance occur in some phase of the development of consciential projection. There is, in fact, no serious restriction regarding its practice as long as ordinary precautions with physical, mental or consciential hygiene are maintained.

Possession. Over the last 4 decades of more intense projective activities, the author has not encountered any incident that could be classified as irreparable possession, something destructive or uncontrollable by the intraphysical consciousness. When this occurs, it is because that selfsame intraphysical consciousness subjects him/herself to lucid submission to another through his/her empathy.

Super-assimilation. Alienation toward physical life is an inconvenience that can appear when there is a super-assimilation of extraphysical experiences in the consciousness of the projector (you). All excess is harmful in this case. If the use of elevated extraphysical perception or paraperception is difficult, the maintenance of two simultaneous lives – physical and extraphysical – will be much more problematic. The facts caused by destructive PK occur in this context.

Control. It should be emphasized that even the intense series of self-lucid projections, including spontaneous ones, always remain under the control of the consciousness of the intraphysical projector (you). Lucid projections only become uncontrollable – which is quite possible – when a process of interconsciential, subjacent, prior, paragenetic or mesological (current cultural background) intrusion is involved.

Dangers. There are always dangers everywhere. There are those who only walk steadily with both feet firmly planted on the ground. Others skate on thin ice; come and go on a *motorbike* (a high-speed vehicle prone to physical accidents); glide while dangling from a hang glider; balance themselves on a loose cord over an abyss in order to enjoy their 15 minutes of *glory*; walk on hot coals; or run on a razor-edge by practicing countless *radical sports (borderline suicide).*

Test. Self-lucid projectors are those who go on excursions between various consciential dimensions, in *previews* of desoma or lucid projections of the consciousness. Between these two categories of personality – the excessive and the reflexive – it is pertinent to ask: "If everyone will eventually have their human body deactivated, who prioritizes his/her acts with greater intelligence in view of the execution of the existential program?"

Real. The only real harms, dangers or obstacles to lucid projection are: ignorance; fear; doubt; passion; illicit plans or anticosmoethical intentionality; the interference by someone in the intimate, physical or multidimensional life of another in a negative manner; the harmful thoughts of the practitioner, whether an adult or youth, or his/her damaging instinct for revenge upon or mistreatment of another.

Avoidances. The practice of lucid projection is not recommended for the following 4 categories of personalities having well-defined characteristics. On the contrary, these individuals should really avoid provoked consciential projections:

1. **Imprudent.** All those who nurture less dignified intentions and are eager to obtain a new negative source of power, which runs contrary to the rights of others, through departures from the human body. This is because they will end up being the victims of their own imprudences and immaturities.

2. **Pusillanimities.** All types of cowardly, pusillanimous and fearful persons, because this will increase their intraconsciential apprehensions, fears and instability. The courage to confront the unknown (neophilia) and new experiences are *sine qua non* conditions for maintaining the constructive aspect of lucid consciential projections.

3. **Unsatisfied.** Those sexually unsatisfied social beings, regardless of age, gender or condition because, upon their consciousness temporarily leaving the human body, projected in the psychosoma (emotional body), they will be overcome by their continued sensual appetites (sexaholics), which are suffocated or repressed without respite, like monoideisms. They will end up being overrun by vampirizing extraphysical company (energivorous extraphysical consciousnesses) that they extraphysically attract in the paratropospheric environments.

4. **Ill.** Ill persons with emotional and/or mental imbalances, as well as those with serious illnesses or in a critical phase of some illness that requires inner peace and complete rest.

Bibliography: Bardens (79, p. 142), Baumann (93, p. 81), Butler (227, p. 69), Champlin (272, p. 203), Crookall (343, p. 111), Ferguson (507, p. 135), Fortune (540, p. 100), Fox (544, p. 39), Hankey (677, p. 131), Mittl (1061, p. 7), Muldoon (1105, p. 17), Rogo (1444, p. 15), Shirley (1553, p. 101), Smith (1574, p. 83), Vieira (1762, p. 62), Walker (1781, p. 100).

XV – Relationships of Lucid Projection

451. LUCID PROJECTION AND ACCIDENTS

Need. In the same manner as with many other parapsychic phenomena, lucid projection seems to develop better when there is an urgent need for the individual to use the subjacent powers or potential of the mind, or of the consciousness which, in many ways, is forcibly restricted within the cranial cavity of the human body during ordinary terrestrial existence.

Sudden. The main seat of the intraphysical consciousness is located in the human brain, which reflects the parabrain of the psychosoma and, therefore, the seat of the consciousness – the mentalsoma. Critical situations, borderline situations and the greatest diversity of physical accidents, which provoke violent stimuli that are uncustomary and highly significant for the consciousness, generate its sudden projection from the human body in the psychosoma, temporarily freeing the parabrain and, consequently, predisposing exceptional consciential manifestations.

Types. The following are the most common factors that induce involuntary lucid projection: violent, physical accidents, especially involving the head (encephalic lesions); accidents involving cars, motorcycles, bicycles and other vehicles; falls endured while mountain climbing; explosions; domestic accidents; electrical discharges; collapses and mudslides; certain types of torture; threats of violence: being a victim of rape, kidnapping or terrorism, as well as being a hostage or prisoner of war.

Disconnection. Frequently, in the case of a physical accident, the projector's consciousness is freed during the extraphysical period, not feeling connected with the human body wounded in the disaster or accident. The body is often examined in a serene manner, without involvement, as though the consciousness were a mere indifferent, dispassionate spectator.

Seriated. In certain cases, physical accidents also predispose the intraphysical consciousness to the production of seriated lucid projections, or projections in series, as explained in a previous chapter.

Childbirth. For over 3 decades, the author has verified that a high number of advanced projectors suffered some type of trauma to the head during childbirth, with subsequent fetal cerebral hypoxemia, e.g.: difficult childbirth; hypoxic child; birth by forceps; umbilical cord coiled (entangled) around the neck; cesarean operation; prematurity; cranial traumas with hematomas.

Gifted. On the one hand, the referred to accidents somehow later predispose the departure of the psychosoma from its coincidence with the vehicles of manifestation. On the other hand, in certain instances, they stimulate the intensification of the memory or recall of extraphysical events, through an improvement in the mutual, inter-hemispheric, energetic communication of the human brain, making the individual into a gifted parapsychic, in this case, projectively gifted.

Chakras. We should not, then, discard the interference which occurs in the profound relationships of the energetic mechanism between the manifestations of the mentalsoma – which is headquartered in the parabrain of the psychosoma – and the 2 cranial chakras, the coronochakra and the frontochakra, which are strongly reflected in the human body-psychosoma connection (holochakra or energetic body).

Infancy. Cases have been registered in the projectiological literature of traumas to the head in early infancy that generally stimulate parapsychism in general and projectability in particular, in the adult phase, due to the subsequent intense, simultaneous use of the 2 cerebral hemispheres and a consequent gradual predominance of the manifestations of the right hemisphere. That is why diverse personalities who lived with depressions of a parietal bone or with greater cranial alterations became renowned sensitives or, in other words, parapsychically or bioenergetically gifted individuals. The following are 4 well-known examples: Eusapia Palladino (1854-1918); Mollie Fancher (1848-1894); Peter Hurkos (1911-1988); Edgar Cayce (1877-1945).

Hypothesis. The relationship between encephalic accidents of all types and projectability is a relevant working research hypothesis for those interested in projectiology. The pattern of the encephalic factor acting upon projectability can manifest in 3 very distinct circumstances, in terms of their occurrences and age periods:

1. **Childbirth.** During childbirth.
2. **Resomatics.** In early infancy or in the beginning of intraphysical life
3. **Maturity.** In a singular accident, when already mature or in adult life.

Bibliography: Battersby (92, p. 59), Baumann (93, p. 59), Crookall (338, p. 132), Dailey (356, p. 16), Desmond (393, p. 54), Greenhouse (636, p. 136), Larcher (887, p. 143), Moody Jr. (1078, p. 45), Muldoon (1105, p. 259), Portela (1275, p. 123), Prieur (1289, p. 76), Ring (1406, p. 27), Sabom (1486, p. 77), Steiger (1601, p. 15), Vieira (1762, p. 39), Walker (1781, p. 66), Wang (1794, p. 177).

452. LUCID PROJECTION AND CHILDREN

Definition. Miniprojector: the child who projects the consciousness from the human body with some lucidity.

Synonymy: child-projector; infantile projector.

First. The majority of advanced projectors, who have already had multiple projections, experienced their first lucid departure while still in infancy, although in this period no one was sufficiently mature to judge and precisely evaluate the extraphysical events experienced or witnessed outside the human body.

Recollections. The recollections of the miniprojector tend to be more symbolic and mixed with fantasies – such as flights in airplanes (levitation) and others of this type – without discarding any retrocognitions about recent volitations in the intermissive pre-resomatic period. This is due to the short attention span which is characteristic of the biological growth of the human body and the gradual development of the cortical cells or, in other words, the cerebral hemispheres.

Joint. Children like to go on trips with their parents, even those which are extraphysical and not physical. This circumstance thus represents a powerful motivation for the joint projection of parents and children, which are more common than one might think, especially in homes in which the subject of consciential projection is routinely discussed.

Sensitivity. Children, especially up until 7 years of physical age, accept their parapsychic experiences as being natural. They are more receptive to extraphysically seeing a projected projector, or even an extraphysical helper, as well as the extraphysical telepathic emissions produced by these personalities in the extraphysical dimension.

Extraphysical consciousnesses. Besides child-projectors, the projected intraphysical consciousness encounters positive extraphysical consciousnesses in the extraphysical dimension that look like children, although they think like mature personalities. He/she can also be helped by extraphysical child-helpers, as well as contacting assisted-child-consciousnesses, together with which he/she is called upon to cooperate in assistential tasks outside the soma.

Confirmations. The consciential projections of miniprojectors are important when the children reveal aspects of extraphysical occurrences that agree with and are confirmed by those observations made by adult intraphysical consciential projectors, bearing in mind that children generally cannot obtain details of observations regarding books, articles or other reports of lucid consciential projections about which they have not read.

Bibliography: Bourdin (178, p. 139), Browning (213, p. 219), Cooke (300, p. 36), Crookall (320, p. 63), Giovetti (593, p. 56), Greenhouse (636, p. 288), Monroe (1065, p. 139), Vieira (1762, p. 78).

453. LUCID PROJECTION AND SUBHUMAN ANIMALS

Definition. Animal or subhuman projector: the being that is evolutionarily below the human level and projects its evolving consciousness from its cellular or physical body.

Synonymy: animal-projector; subhuman-projector.

Extraphysical consciousnesses. Lucid projection permits one to encounter subhuman animals that are real extraphysical consciousnesses in the extraphysical dimension. This shows that animals which are evolutionarily inferior to ourselves possess parabodies or extraphysical vehicles, emit light, present an aura and, in certain circumstances, project in a manner similar to the consciousness of humans.

Types. In the extraphysical dimension we can encounter domestic and wild animals; subhuman extraphysical consciousnesses that are known and unknown on earth; and, less often, projected intraphysical animals.

Occurrences. There are subhuman animals – extraphysical consciousnesses in a primitive state of evolution of the consciential principle – which visit their former owners from their latest intraphysical life; others cooperate with assistential extraphysical consciousnesses in their extraphysical activities; and there are also subhuman intraphysical animals which are currently used to detect the presence of the projector projected in the laboratory.

Intraphysicals. Lucid projection of intraphysical consciousnesses allows them to see subhuman intraphysical animals that are in the waking state in the extraphysical dimension. This confirms the existence of their parabodies or rudimentary extraphysical vehicles of manifestation and other evolutionary characteristics.

Extraterrestrials. The intraphysical consciousness projected in the psychosoma should be prepared to encounter extraphysical subhumans, extraterrestrial living plants in certain evolved extraphysical dimensions which are not directly influenced by the earth, having forms and manifestations which are neither similar to those in intraphysical life on this planet, nor do they have similar beings among humans.

Telepathy. According to the evidence collected through projectiology, beings or organisms can be divided into intraphysical: aquatic, amphibious, terrestrial, aerial; and extraphysical: para-aquatic, para-amphibious, and others. The author has extraphysically seen and analyzed a type of very delicate domesticated animal, 14" (35 cm) tall, that was reminiscent of a miniscule giraffe with a certain degree of intelligence and unhesitatingly responding with a somewhat incipient lucidity to extraphysical telepathy.

Bibliography: ADGMT (03, p. 31), Armond (53, p. 87), Bayless (94, p. 70), Bozzano (190, p. 87), Cornillier (305, p. 43), Dassier (367, p. 272), Fodor (528, p. 3), Greenhouse (636, p. 299), Monroe (1065, p. 136), Morris (1091, p. 8), Muldoon (1102, p. 76), O'Donnell (1144, p. 73), Sculthorp (1531, p. 84), Shepard (1548, p. 32), Vieira (1762, p. 48), Yram (1897, p. 155).

454. LUCID PROJECTION AND INTERPERSONAL UNIONS

Definition. Interpersonal union: the act or effect of the junction or connection of two persons, in most cases of different sexes, generally legitimized by civil and/or religious certification.

Synonymy: concubinage; consortium; espousal; joining; marriage; matrimonial bond; matrimony; nuptials; wedding; wedding anniversary; wedlock.

Importance. An intimate interpersonal relationship can be something more serious than the pleasure that two persons receive from each other's company. It ends up being an institution that – given that it generates children (human gestation) in most cases – is part of the intimate structure of the still pathological intraphysical society and has an importance which goes far beyond the personal emotions of the components of the couple.

Appeals. There are infinite types of relationships between human beings, compatible and incompatible marriage contracts and unions. All imply confidence, concessions and mutual interest. Nevertheless, the affinities, unions, marriages and interests between intraphysical consciousnesses lead to the establishment of the fact that there rationally exist 4 basic *appeals* – 2 sexual and 2 consciential – which impel human beings to live and remain together intimately more than others:

1. The reciprocal sexual appeal.
2. The unilateral sexual appeal.
3. The reciprocal consciential appeal.
4. The unilateral consciential appeal.

Sexual. The 2 types of sexual appeals are characterized by a preponderant action upon the consciousness by the human body (soma), the holochakra (sexochakra, *kundalini*), the psychosoma (emotional parabody), and the emotions which are untamed by the consciousness. They frequently result in the unilateral or reciprocal explosion of passions, impassioned states and the intense puppy love of adolescents, youths and even adults.

Ideal. Mutual passionate love, while it lasts, annuls the emotions that generate rudeness and arrogance in men, and whining and continuous complaining in women, generating a new temporary being, composed of 2 in 1. However, the ideal will always be a relationship between 2 social beings who possess a strong psychic element, with a greater dose of the personality of the lovers influencing their development and maintenance, rather than another purely physical one.

Consciential. The 2 types of consciential appeal (deep-rooted affection between the consciousnesses) are characterized by a preponderant action upon the ego by balance and discernment (consciential maturity), the golden cord, the mentalsoma and the sentiments, or rationalized emotions, which are tamed by the consciousness. They can sometimes result in platonic love, an amorous connection without sexual closeness.

Scale. Using these listed, numbered appeals, a descending scale can be made of the level of excellence of the *unions* between intraphysical consciousnesses, which is composed of 8 categories:

1. **Stable.** The interpersonal unions born of the joint action of sexual and consciential appeals (1 + 3). They are friendlier, more harmonious, stable and lasting bonds that produce fewer divorces and occur less frequently, being composed of consciousnesses who have already lived together intimately for a greater number of human lives, over longer periods of intraphysical and multiexistential contemporaneity. In some cases, the greater level of consciential maturity predisposes the couple to reach the so-called *golden anniversary* (5 decades of duration) or the very rare *diamond anniversary* (6 or 7½ decades of duration). The human beings making up these unions are, from a literary point of view, literally characterized as being *soul mates,* or beings who are naturally destined to live together.

2. **Sister.** Interpersonal unions born from the junction of a unilateral sexual appeal with a reciprocal consciential appeal (2 + 3). These bonds tend to be lasting between human beings inclined to reach at least the so-called *silver anniversary* (5 lustrums of duration). The components of these unions are literally characterized as being *sister souls.*

3. **Disconnected.** Interpersonal unions born from disconnected impulses of preponderant reciprocal sexual appeal with unilateral consciential appeal (1 + 4).

4. **Unilateral.** Interpersonal unions born from impulses of unilateral sexual and consciential appeals (2 + 4). From this point on, the interpersonal bonds of the scale, being progressively less stable, begin to increasingly lead the pair of intraphysical consciousnesses to separation or divorce.

5. **Platonic.** Interpersonal unions characterized only by reciprocal consciential appeal (3), practically platonic.

6. **Common.** Interpersonal unions characterized only by reciprocal sexual appeal (1). These are the most common and animalized types of bonds. They are generally accompanied, or sustained over time, by obvious diverse interests, including mercantile interests, which are also reciprocal.

7. **Self-seeking.** Interpersonal unions characterized only by unilateral consciential appeal (4). Strong human mercantile interests also frequently *begin to operate* here in the formation of bonds.

8. **Unstable.** Interpersonal unions characterized only by unilateral sexual appeal (2). These are more unstable, brief bonds which result in the greatest number of divorces. They are composed of consciousnesses who lived together intimately for only a small number of human lives, or for shorter periods of time. These beings are predisposed to experience only temporary adventures, generating tragedies and groupkarmic debts for the orphans of living parents. Human interests operate still more vigorously in the formation of these typical *patrimonial* unions, in some countries with the bride being bought, or even with the groom being bought. They often involve impressive ceremonies, ostentations and public solemnities (marriages of convenience).

Honeymoon. Unstable interpersonal unions may end with the honeymoon (or even before it) within the first month, or in the first few days after the wedding, which are usually utilized for greater intimacy between the components of the pair.

White. One type of unstable interpersonal union is the so-called *unconsummated marriage* or, in other words: without sexual intercourse having even occurred.

Coupling. Projectiology offers a valuable resource that can greatly help the interested individual to verify for him/herself and more accurately foresee the quality level of an interpersonal union that is under consideration: self-aware *auric coupling* with the target-person requiring exteriorizations of consciential energy and the detection of possible intervening intruders in the affective relationship, notably when realized from the extraphysical dimension. This can be realized, even if only by one of the candidates of the union, the lucid projector of the couple.

Retrobiography. Another resource is retrocognition which – while being difficult to execute – allows one to relive the joint *retrobiography* with the target-being, the interpersonal relationships which they had in one or more previous intraphysical existences.

Initiation. There are marriage processes that are initiated outside the human body through lucid consciential projections.

Vampirization. Marriage between intraphysical consciousnesses brings with it the normalization of the sex life of the partners. It generally physically and paraphysically resolves the cases of extraphysical vampirizations that were installed due to the sexual (sexochakra) attraction of the longing persons, who previously lived in continual sexual dissatisfaction or in sexual privation.

Duo. All that has been reconstructed here regarding age-old interpersonal unions and sexosomatics aims solely to emphasize the formation of the *evolutionary duo* for the accomplishment of the existential program of both partners, which are integrated through the clarification task, existential inversion, existential recycling, penta, consciential epicentrism, extraphysical clinics and even the accomplishment of joint group existential programs within polykarmality, according to the principles and techniques of projectiology and conscientiology.

Test. What does the reader aspire to regarding his/her intraphysical life: the age-old *business of marriage* or the advanced formation of the evolutionary duo?

Bibliography: A recent work by the author on the subject: *Evolutionary Duo Manual* (in Portuguese).

455. LUCID PROJECTION AND CHILDBIRTH

Definitions. Childbirth: the set of physiological phenomena which lead to the departure from the maternal cloister of a normal fetus and its appendages; the act or effect whereby a woman gives birth to a child or infant.

Synonymy: birth; giving birth; delivery; parturition.

Blocks. Childbirth is a traumatic event for many women who have psychological blocks due to fear of the unknown and a lack of discussion on certain taboo subjects – such as sexuality and human birth – during childhood. These psychic factors, aside from known physical causes, can affect the natural process of childbirth.

Complicated. There are dozens of registered cases of lucid projections of the consciousness of parturients, especially when forced by accidents, hemorrhage, general anesthesia or the stress of the work involved in complicated, delayed, laborious or traumatic childbirth.

Cesarean. Cesarean childbirth, by cesarean section – the freeing of the fetus through incisions in the abdominal and uterine walls – as well as difficult, laborious deliveries that require emergency medical care, are those which more greatly predispose the lucid projection of the parturient during labor.

Process. Regardless of its cause, childbirth is sometimes stressful for the pregnant woman-parturient, thus resulting in the liberation of the psychosoma in an *unconscious* process which the consciousness undergoes without awareness in order to escape pain, suffering and anxiety, thereby creating a pause in the traumatizing crisis. Outside the human body, in the extraphysical dimension, all pain disappears, giving way to an indescribable sensation of well-being for the consciousness.

Puerperal-projectors. The most diverse types of puerperal-projectors exist: primoparas; multiparas; youths; adults; those aware or ignorant regarding the subject of consciential projection; and with or without previous lucid projective experiences.

Self-bilocation. There are documented cases of projector-parturients whose consciousness was projected with lucidity during the work of laborious or complicated childbirth. They observed self-bilocation – or, in other words, their human body emptied of its consciousness but partially occupied by the fetus – and witnessed the exact moment of the birth of their child, perfectly distinguishing the infant's gender, being in an exotic position as observers, located outside their own physical body.

Odontology. This occurs naturally wherein the consciousnesses of other persons who, while under general anesthesia in the dentist's office, saw the dentist extract a tooth while located outside the surgery room.

Unborn. Up to this point, childbirth has been analyzed relative to the lucid projection of the parturient. Let us now analyze childbirth relative to the lucid projection of the unborn child, who will later become an adult.

Head. The fetal head is composed of diverse independent osseous parts which are separated from each other by wide, or simply linear, membranous strips (the sutures) and by equally membranous surfaces, of a greater or lesser area (the fontanels), located at the intersection of the sutures.

Bones. The bones of the fetal head vary in plasticity. They give way to pressure, like celluloid, when their malleability is at the maximum. They are otherwise resistant, like a block of cement, in the absence of this attribute.

Hypertension. The brain of the fetus can be directly compressed by the cranial osseous parts, in the work of a complicated childbirth, and are accompanied by great cephalic deformations, due to the effect of excessive malleability. The compression of the fetal head, the osseous parts of which are still independent from each other, is reflected onto the brain and its involucres. The rachidian fluid flows back from the compressed region, which generally coincides with the equator of the presentation, to the respective poles, the base of the brain and the cerebral pallidal, where it provokes the state of hypertension.

Potentiation. Through cephalometry – the cephalic measurement of the fetus – the very large fetal head presents a great difference between the occipitofrontal (O.F.) diameter and the biparietal (B.P.) diameter, thus possibly resulting in innumerous problems during childbirth. These problems *seem* to potentiate the individual's projectability as an adult, due to fetal cerebral hypoxemia, the consequent simultaneous intense use of the 2 cerebral hemispheres and a gradual predominance of the right cerebral hemisphere.

Alterations. The following are 8 complications or alterations from normality which can occur during laborious childbirth, anomalies or deviations from the normal, dystocia or maximal abnormalities, and accidents or events related to the blood, shock and convulsion, which predispose or potentiate the individual's subsequent lucid projectability in the adult phase:

1. Fetal gigantism or macrosomia of the fetus with a large head.
2. Sometimes large serosanguineous bulges *(caput succedaneum)* and hematomas in the fetus.
3. Cephalic deformations of the head or face.
4. Traumatizing instrumental rotation of the fetal head.
5. Traumatizing traction of the fetal head performed by forceps.
6. Coiling of the umbilical cord around the neck (dystocia of the umbilical cord, entanglement).
7. Fetal hypoxia (cerebral hypoxemia, fetal suffering).
8. Eclampsia.

Cesarean section. On the other hand, according to reverifications made by the author, the cesarean operation does not inhibit the individual's projectability, because innumerous veteran projectors have come into this intraphysical dimension (extraphysical consciousnesses which became intraphysical consciousnesses) by cesarean section. What needs to be performed, however, is an indispensable statistical survey of the evidence (working hypotheses) regarding the aspects of the relationship between lucid consciential projections, childbirth, the parturient, the fetus, and lucid consciential projectors.

Near-birth. Based on the birth-lucid projection association, the parapsychologist Barbara Honegger in Washington, United States of America, proposed the hypothesis that lucid consciential projections are merely lucid dreams or, in other words, "near-birth" experiences, wherein the imagination is dependent upon the birth experience. In this case, the sensations pertaining to the experiences of the consciousness outside the human body would all be imaginary, similar to the natural consciential conditions of the fetal period. If this hypothesis were correct, the lucid consciential projection of adults should be more frequently reported by individuals who were born through natural childbirth, and not through cesarean section, which reduces fetal stress.

Analogies. In fact, there are 4 basic analogies between lucid consciential projection and the birth experience:

1. **Departures.** Both experiences somehow constitute departures from the human body.

2. **Cords.** In both experiences, the consciousness is united to the human body during the event by a cord, namely the silver cord or the umbilical cord.

3. **Vibrations.** The sensations of the vibrational state (VS) of the consciential projector are similar to the tremors and vibrations generated, in the fetus, by uterine contractions pertaining to childbirth.

4. **Tunnel.** The sensations of going through a tunnel can be closely compared to the passage of the fetus through the natural canal, which leads him/her to see light.

Test. The English parapsychologist Susan J. Blackmore tested Barbara Honegger's hypothesis with a long, exhaustive questionnaire submitted to adult psychology and parapsychology students in Bristol, England. The questionnaire was answered by 234 persons and the results of the research did not support Honegger's hypothesis, because they did not find a significant relationship between the manner of birth and having experiences of leaving the human body or traveling through a tunnel. Those who had been delivered by cesarean section were shown to have lucid departures from the human body in a slightly higher proportion than those who had natural deliveries. They also showed a greater capacity for controlling their dreams or creating agreeable dreams and a lesser tendency to have dreams of falling, compared to those who underwent normal birth.

Conclusion. It can thus be concluded that the comparison of lucid consciential projection (OBE) with the human birth experience is merely a superficial analogy, but is useless as an explanatory supposition for lucid consciential projection.

Bibliography: Blackmore (140, p. 229), Bord (170, p. 41), Currie (354, p. 141), Honegger (753, p. 230), Parrish-Harra (1202, p. 75), Steiger (1601, p. 45), Twemlow (1710, p. 452).

456. LUCID PROJECTION AND ERECTION

Definition. Erection: the condition of distention, elongation and rigidity of the penis (in a man), or of the clitoris (in a woman), through the inflow of blood to the cavernous tissue of these organs.

Synonymy: genital intumescence; penile tumescence.

Men. Spontaneous erection can occur at any age, with either male or female projectors, being more common among male projectors (penile). This is evidenced by the intraphysical consciousness as a physical reaction upon interiorizing, after returning from a brief or prolonged extraphysical period. This erection is not present before projecting or, more precisely, before sleeping.

Analogy. There is a direct, analogous relationship between the physiological cycle of penile erection, or nocturnal penile intumescence, that is synchronized with the period of REM sleep or, in other words, during rapid synchronous bi-ocular movements, and lasts until the end of this period, and the penile erection that the projected consciousness encounters upon interiorizing in the human body after a lucid projection.

Interiorization. Interiorization of the projected consciousness does not always occur due to an erection. The human body can remain motionless, temporarily *emptied of the consciousness,* and in a state of erection, with a man as well as with a woman. In women, the periodic lubrication of the vagina can even occur.

Frequency. Erections which occur during lucid projection are more frequent than it might seem, as they are reported less often due to the inhibitions or repressions of Victorian or puritanical social morals, and call for more accurate studies within projectiology.

Causes. Among the various causes that may exist for the occurrence of the penile erection during projections, including psychological ones, the following 4 physical and organic causes can be cited:

1. **Physiology.** Physiological predisposition of the projector who is sexually deprived.

2. **Clothes.** Tightfitting nightclothes which, upon being used by the projector, provoke blood stasis.

3. **Soma.** The position of the human body on the bed that favors intumescence of the sexual organ through the inflow of blood to the cavernous tissues.

4. **Emunctory.** Vesical repletion or the condition of a full bladder.

Effects. Among the effects of penile erection during the lucid projection which should be listed, at least the following 3 can be singled out: extraphysical repercussion; abrupt interiorization; and abrupt physical awakening.

Viagra. While on the subject, in May 1998, *Viagra,* the *superpill* against impotence or erectile dysfunction, was launched with great fanfare, provoking controversy throughout the planet. This can be verified through cosmogram research, or clippings from periodicals of that period. The following are 15 examples, listed in chronological order:

1. **"Ereções Diretas: a Pílula da Impotência está Criando Confusão nos EUA" ("Continuous Erections: the Impotence Pill is Creating Confusion in the USA")** (Ruy Castro; *Manchete;* magazine; weekly; 1 illus.; Rio de Janeiro, RJ, Brazil; 5/16/98; p. 39).

2. **"Viagra pode ter matado 6 nos EUA" ("Viagra May Have Killed 6 in the USA")** (*O Dia;* editorial staff; newspaper; section: *Science and Health;* Rio de Janeiro, RJ, Brazil; 5/23/98; p. 08).

3. **"Viagra: A Pílula da Potência" ("Viagra: The Potency Pill")** (Bruno Weis; Ivan Padilha; & Marta Góes; *Isto É;* magazine; weekly; N. 1,495; 10 illus.; 1 graph.; São Paulo, SP, Brazil; 5/25/98; cover page (lead story), p. 126-130).

4. **"Pílula** (Viagra) **faz Homem de 70 Anos abandonar a Mulher" ("Pill** (Viagra) **Makes Man of 70 Years Abandon Wife")** (*O Globo;* editorial staff; newspaper; daily; section: *Science and Life;* Rio de Janeiro, RJ, Brazil; 5/30/98; p. 43).

5. **"Viagra Culture"** (Jennie Smith; Mark Dennis; Joanna Chen-Morris; Barbie Nadeau; Elaine Wu; & Paige Bierma; *Newsweek;* magazine; weekly; Vol. CXXXI; N. 25; 8 illus.; New York, NY; USA; 6/22/98; cover page (lead story), p. 36-40).

6. **"Viagra para Aumentar a População"** (**"Viagra to Increase Population"**) (*Extra;* editorial staff; newspaper; daily; section: *The Country;* Rio de Janeiro, RJ, Brazil; 6/24/98; p. 06).

7. **"EUA investigam 30 Mortes Associadas ao Uso do Viagra"** (**"USA Investigates 30 Deaths Associated with the Use of Viagra"**) (*O Globo;* editorial staff; newspaper; daily; section: *Science and Life;* Rio de Janeiro, RJ; Brazil; 6/30/98; p. 28).

8. **"Guerra Comercial por la Venta de la Píldora Contra la Impotencia"** (**"Commercial War over the Sale of the Pill Against Impotence"**) (*Clarín;* editorial staff; newspaper; daily; 1 illus.; Buenos Aires; Argentina; 7/8/98; p. 58).

9. **"Viagra, Desinformação e Imprudência"** (**"Viagra, Disinformation and Imprudence"**) (Alex Campos; *Jornal do Brasil;* daily; section: *Life;* Rio de Janeiro, RJ, Brazil; 7/26/98; p. 03).

10. **"FDA asked to reassess Viagra"** (*Sun-Sentinel;* editorial staff; newspaper; daily; USA; 8/21/98; p. 3A).

11. **"EUA já têm 69 Mortes Associadas ao Uso do Viagra"** (**"USA Already Has 69 Deaths Associated with the Use of Viagra"**) (*Folha de S. Paulo;* editorial staff; newspaper; daily; section: *Science;* São Paulo, SP, Brazil; 8/27/98; p. 12).

12. **"Médicos Alertam Sobre Novos Riscos do Viagra"** (**"Doctors Warn Over New Risks of Viagra"**) (*Jornal do Brasil;* editorial staff; daily; section: *Science;* Rio de Janeiro, RJ, Brazil; 9/3/98; p. 14).

13. **"Viagra, Effetti Anche Sul Cervello"** (**"Viagra Also Affects the Brain"**) (Alberto Oliverio; *Corriere della Sera;* newspaper; daily; section: *Corriere Scienza;* Milan; Italy; 9/23/98; p. 19).

14. **"Pesquisas que levaram ao Viagra ganham o Nobel"** (**"Research that Led to Viagra Winning the Nobel Prize"**) (*O Globo;* editorial staff; daily; year LXXIV; N. 23,785; section: *Science and Life;* 3 illus.; Rio de Janeiro, RJ, Brazil; 10/13/98; first page (lead story), p. 25).

15. **"Viagra registra Queda de 66% nas Vendas"** (**"Viagra Shows a 66% Drop in Sales"**) (Marcelo Diego; *Folha de S. Paulo;* newspaper; daily; year 78; N. 25,399; São Paulo, SP, Brazil; 10/17/98; first page (lead story), p. 1-12).

Warnings. Many authorities warn against the use of Viagra by men with general heart disease, notably hypertensive individuals. This medication should only be used under medical prescription.

Bibliography: Monroe (1065, p. 195), Salley (1496, p. 159), Vieira (1762, p. 45), Walker (1782, p. 132).

---

457. LUCID PROJECTION AND BLINDNESS

Definition. Blindness: the condition that affects a person who is totally destitute of physical vision and has no perception of light.

Synonymy: amaurosis; blind state; deprivation of the sense of sight; sightlessness; typhlosis; visual deficiency; visual incapacity.

Typhlology. Typhlology is the biological science of ophthalmologic analysis that studies blindness.

Dreams. Persons who are blind at birth, or *sightless* individuals, have dreams which are replete with sounds and not full of visual images. Only those individuals who have already seen at some time have visual dreams.

Hallucinations. Intraphysical consciousnesses who are congenitally blind, upon becoming sick with a psychosis, do not have visual hallucinations, even during deliriums.

Clue. Blind persons have psychophysiological rhythms that differ from those of sighted persons. For example, they are immune to the chronological clues of light for sleeping.

Psychosoma. Nevertheless, many blind persons affirm that they see during their lucid projections, including their experiences of volitation while their consciousnesses (they themselves) are entirely lucid. This demonstrates that they see with the extraphysical visual perceptions of the psychosoma or, in other words, with *the extraphysical eyes,* or para-eyes, sometimes while still in adolescence. This fact shows that the psychosoma already existed prior to the resoma of the consciousness. Regarding this point, the phenomena, well-known since the beginning of this century, called *transposition of senses* and so-called *dermo-optical vision,* greatly studied by Russian parapsychologists, should not be overlooked.

Hyperacuity. There are registered phenomena of visual hyperacuity in which the person acting as a percipient, or clairvoyant sensitive, can clearly see the images of an apparition better than if it were a real, living person in the ordinary, physical waking state. The same has been occurring with consciential projectors that see with extreme clarity when projected and, nonetheless, when in the ordinary, physical waking state, are blind or can only see with the use of strong corrective lenses.

Evidence. The first extraphysical evidence of the experiences of the lucid, but physically blind, projector, are at least the following 5:

1. **Dynamic.** Dreams of flying.
2. **Luminosity.** A misty light.
3. **Colors.** Bright colors.
4. **Catalepsy.** Temporary projective catalepsy.
5. **Shadows.** Living shadows walking before you.

Compensations. The vision of the intraphysical consciousness while projected from the human body and the illumination of the extraphysical environment constitute two inestimable parapsychic or projectiological compensations for any human being who is visually incapacitated.

Hypotheses. So far, reasonable, detailed, consciential projective experiments have still not been performed either with blind persons of all types, or with deaf-mutes. These facts suggest excellent work hypotheses for projectiology researchers.

Bibliography: Andreas (36, p. 31), Currie (354, p. 148), Frost (560, p. 27), Globo (602, p. 17), Green (633, p. 169), Greenhouse (636, p. 313), Krishnan (869, p. 21), Paim (1182, p. 70), Reis (1384, p. 48), Vieira (1762, p. 12).

---

458. LUCID PROJECTION AND PHYSICAL PAIN

Definition. Physical pain: the painful impression experienced by an organ, or a part thereof, transmitted to the brain by the sensory nerves.

Synonymy: painful sensation; physical suffering.

Algology. Algology is the biological science of physical-chemical analysis that studies pain.

Involuntary. An intense spasm of pain, from various causes, acting upon a psychophysiological condition of violent emotional stress, can lead the consciousness out from the human body in the psychosoma, in an involuntary lucid projection.

Types. Various types of intense pain, when bringing deep despair and agony, can provoke lucid projection, in the manner of these 7, among others:

1. **Gastroenterology:** intestinal colic.
2. **Hepatology:** hepato-biliary colic.
3. **Nephrology:** renal colic.
4. **Neurology:** headaches or cephalalgias.
5. **Obstetrics:** colic of childbirth (gynosomatics).
6. **Pneumology:** thoracic pains.
7. **Sociology:** physical torture of a prisoner (political science).

Change. The intraphysical consciousness temporarily moves from one seat, vehicle, or body to another or, in other words, from the human body in the physical dimension to the psychosoma in the extraphysical dimension, thereby escaping the intense physical pain.

Psychosoma. The psychosoma does not produce the sensation of pain which operates only through normal channels of sensory communication belonging to the sensory nerves of the human body. This, however, does not exclude the occurrence of false pain in the case of parapsychotics and other types of personalities, for example.

Return. The alleviation of the great discomfort of the intense pain, which is obtained through lucid projection, can predispose the involuntarily projected intraphysical consciousness to wish not to return to the human body, which is an immense deception. On this occasion, an intangible extraphysical helper – or, less frequently, one which is perceived – interferes, promoting the also involuntary interiorization of the consciousness that is in the psychosoma.

Paradox. The alleviation from the critical pain can lead the projected intraphysical consciousness to the singular, paradoxical, shocking experience of knowing that his/her human body is undergoing the physiological or pathological condition of intense pain, but he/she feels nothing in the psychosoma, as though he/she were two distinct personalities, experiencing different conditions.

Bibliography: Baumann (93, p. 53), Bord (170, p. 40), Boswell (174, p. 131), Crookall (343, p. 98), Currie (354, p. 145), Green (632, p. 106), Greenhouse (636, p. 140), Muldoon (1103, p. 100), Steiger (1601, p. 25), Walker (1781, p. 84).

459. LUCID PROJECTION, THE HEART AND THE HEART RATE

Mistakes. Not everything written about projections of the consciousness is totally correct and should be treated with circumspection. Repeated mistakes and exaggerations have been occurring regarding subjects related to consciential projection for over a century.

Heart patient. The existing mistakes regarding the approach toward consciential projection is well-exemplified by the dissemination, over decades, of an excessive, unnecessary prohibition of the practice of lucid projection for persons who possess circulatory irregularities – heart patients, in general, and hypertensives, in particular. This has been repeatedly recommended, sometimes with incredible vehemence, by past and current authors, some having become classics, from countries such as the United States of America, Great Britain, France, Spain and Brazil. This can be found in works in the specific bibliography of this chapter.

Personal. If the author were to listen to these warnings, he would never have voluntarily produced lucid projection experiences, as he has been a hypertensive for approximately four decades, using strong medication for two decades on a continuous basis.

Hygiene. The correct approach would be for the lucid projection practitioner not to exaggerate in the exercises or in anxieties, because all excesses jeopardize in this case. In fact, however, under normal conditions of physical and mental hygiene, the induced lucid projection experience does no harm to anyone, as it is a simple physiological process of the intraphysical consciousness – similar to the altered consciential states of sleep and dreams – recommended to all well-intentioned persons.

Frequency. The heart rate, or the cardiac rhythm, the number of heartbeats, normally remains between 70 and 80 beats per minute, when measured by the pulsations which are perceived by touching the pulse, in the ordinary, physical waking state.

Slowness. Bradycardia, a slow heart rate, a low cardiac frequency which oscillates between 40 and 50 pulsations per minute, predisposes the human body, when at rest, to greater passivity, allowing the freeing of the psychosoma before the person loses consciousness.

Acceleration. Tachycardia, an accelerated heart rate, with 120 or more beats per minute, represents the natural response of the organism to psychophysiological tension. It acts against organic incapacity, impeding muscular relaxation and psychic calming, frequently making the exteriorization of the psychosoma more difficult.

Indexes. Strictly speaking, the average pulse for men is considered to be between 70 and 72 beats per minute; 78 to 82 for women; 100 to 120 for children.

Tachycardia. Bradycardia is considered to be 60 beats per minute or below, tachycardia as being above 120 beats. In parapsychic trance, for example, the pulse raises up to 130 beats in sensitive women and 230 beats in male shamans.

Verifications. The author has made the following verification, on many occasions, as his own guinea pig, in self-experiments or participative research: under the influence of medication, with a higher arterial pressure, in this case, between 140 and 100 mm of mercury (Hg) (systole and diastole), and the cardiac frequency remaining low, at 48 beats per minute, was able to produce lucid projections with relative ease, including instantaneous projections and those with continuous self-awareness, with a high degree of extraphysical lucidity.

Bradycardia. The above facts demonstrate that arterial pressure – even arterial hypertension – does not influence the production of lucid projection, as long as the heart rate is low, or in bradycardia. An obvious conclusion can be drawn from these experiments: bradycardia is one of the most effective factors for predisposing the intraphysical consciousness to project from the human body with self-awareness.

Exercises. Among the physical exercises that contribute considerably toward the maintenance of bradycardia, the following can be singled out: long-distance walks; swimming; yoga breathing exercises *(pranayama)*.

Control. On the other hand – still with regard to the relationship between lucid projection and the heart – there are those who unadvisedly recommend exercises of voluntary control of heart rate, through the mind or the impulse of the will, in order to immobilize the human body and predispose it to the freeing of the intraphysical consciousness in the psychosoma.

Self-desoma. These processes of intentional control of the heart are nevertheless potentially dangerous – for the person with a heart problem, as well as for the person with a healthy cardiocirculatory system – because they can, even unconsciously, cause self-desoma due to an unexpected, unnecessary and undesirable cardiac arrest. This fact, according to the extraphysical observations of the author, has been occurring more frequently than one would imagine.

Thought. Thought is a powerful force which is not always well controlled that can cure or perturb, create or destroy, bend spoons, inflict burns on the arm of another, kill the human body of the very individual, or even the body of another person.

Asystole. According to existing studies, the heart of a healthy person can stop beating during REM sleep. This pattern of nocturnal asystole, or of the non-beating heart, can even be responsible for the sudden death of normal youths and adults.

Arrhythmia. In cardiac arrhythmia research conducted on human beings, Russian parapsychologists – maintaining a rigorous materialist-dialectical posture and within the framework of their profound interest in so-called consciential warfare – demonstrated that the emotional reactions of one person (the inductor, in this case) systematically influenced the heart rate of another (the percipient, or victim). The figures obtained from a computer analysis of the data of the simultaneously registered electrocardiograms of both individuals in the experiment indicated that, for 5 minutes, the changes in the percipient's heart rate remained completely dependent upon the reactions of the inductor's heart, which was located 6'7" (2 m) away. The reactions were more accentuated in percipients (victims) who had heart problems.

Intrusion. This clearly corroborates the author's research on the dangerous influence of the consciousness upon the heart. In this particular case involving experiments conducted by the Russians, namely the creation of a fully conscious intraphysical intruder, engaged in the installation of purposeful hetero-intrusion, it merits noting that, between two consciousnesses – in this example, two intraphysical beings or intraphysical consciousnesses – the installation of the energetic phenomenon of auric coupling occurs in which the predominance of the energetically more potent intraphysical consciousness almost always prevails over the energetically weaker intraphysical consciousness.

Case study. The author has also already observed other examples of this fact, in detail, in interconsciential intrusions between an intraphysical being (victim) and an extraphysical consciousness (intruder), and between one intraphysical consciousness (intruder) and another (victim).

Energies. This is why it is relevant to insist on the following point: everyone should learn to be aware of, distinguish and control their own consciential energies (vibrational state or VS) as much as possible, which can help and cure (self-remission), as well as inflict illnesses, or even surreptitiously assassinate oneself (conscious or unconscious suicide) or other persons.

Respiration. The ideal that one should technically strive toward, in this area of research, is to control the respiration, without excess. For example: by practicing rhythmic respiration, up to a certain efficient or functional level, however without threatening the physiology or paraphysiology of the vehicles of consciential manifestation. The direct action upon the heart muscle through concentrated thought should be avoided.

Bibliography: Battersby (92, p. 58), Boswell (174, p. 136), Brennan (200, p. 26), Butler (228, p. 117), Coxhead (312, p. 105), Crookall (331, p. 118), D'Arbó (365, p. 180), Denning (391, p. 45), Farrar (496, p. 196), Fox (544, p. 120), King (846, p. 123), Lind (930, p. 27), Lyra (962, p. 241), Muldoon (1105, p. 213), Muntañola (1108, p. 68), Rampa (1359, p. 92), Rogo (1444, p. 15), Shirley (1553, p. 138), Smith (1575, p. 90), Steiger (1601, p. 110), Targ (1651, p. 254), Vieira (1746, p. 6), Walker (1781, p. 104), Yram (1897, p. 26).

460. LUCID PROJECTION AND ILLNESSES

Definitions. Illness: incapacity of the adaptive mechanisms of an organism to conveniently neutralize the stimuli from demands to which it is subjected, resulting in the disturbance in the function or structure of any part, organ or system of the organism; lack or disturbance of health; chronic or intense alteration or failure of the physiological state in one or several of the parts, organs or systems of the human body; reaction to a lesion, malady or infirmity.

Synonymy: ailment; indisposition; infirmity; malady; organic disturbance.

Predisposition. An ill state can predispose the departure of the consciousness (you) from the human body in the psychosoma. However, this particular condition is neither the ideal, nor is it a dependable coadjutant for inducing a pure lucid projection, through which advanced extraphysical knowledge can be obtained in high quality experiments. This is only achieved through the application of natural, simple and physiological projective methods.

Psychosoma. Chronic and serious illnesses, physical disturbances or those of the human body, psychic disturbances or those of the mind, and intraconsciential or parapathological disturbances of the intraphysical consciousness alter the psychosoma for the worse, with respect to the prolonged performance of consciential projections in general. It initially affects the extraphysical attributes of the consciousness and interferes in the perceptions of the projected intraphysical consciousness.

Exceptions. In spite of everything, there are cases of expressive exceptions of sporadic, lucid consciential projections, registered during serious illnesses, which have provided valuable explanations about the mechanisms of parapsychic and projectiological phenomena.

Fatigue. The coexistence of illness and fatigue, in the same person, weakens the connections of the silver cord, predisposes the looseness of the holochakra and allows the consciousness to more easily leave the condition of coincidence of its vehicles of manifestation in search of extraphysical energy, in the psychosoma.

Conditions. The condition of illness thus tends to predispose the consciousness toward performing involuntary lucid projections, and the condition of full health facilitates the consciousness in producing voluntary lucid projections.

Mini-illnesses. Repeated experience demonstrates that mini-illnesses or minor indispositions – such as physical indispositions, psychic asthenia, ephemeral scintillating scotomas, minor neuralgias, simple luxations – affecting the individual are practically self-cured by lucid self-projection when produced in series for a certain intensive period. This is due to the well-known fact that consciential projection allows the intensification of the acquisition of extraphysical energies.

Mechanism. The circulation of the consciential energies which enter and leave or, in other words, are received and exteriorized more vigorously by the consciousness in the psychosoma projected many times in a row, keeps it *cleansed* and *in good shape,* like a continued *extraphysical warm-up.* On the other hand, this greatly stimulates the natural physiology of the human body, consequently performing an efficient prophylaxis and increasing the organic resistance to mini-illnesses.

Extraphysical. The veteran consciential projector inevitably has constant contact or a direct relationship with ill, insane, exacerbated, extraphysical patients in cases of extraphysical interconsciential deintrusion. These are extraphysical intruder consciousnesses that the projector either voluntarily or involuntarily ends up encountering in the extraphysical dimension, upon leaving the human body for brief periods on certain occasions. Consciential energies are indispensable on these occasions.

Bibliography: Baumann (93, p. 53), Bayless (98, p. 114), Bord (170, p. 37), Boswell (174, p. 132), Bozzano (184, p. 126), Crookall (338, p. 20), Greenhouse (636, p. 145), Jung (812, p. 320), Leaf (905, p. 147), Oxenham (1179, p. 1), Ring (1406, p. 27), Sabom (1486, p. 38), Steiger (1601, p. 33), Vieira (1762, p. 108), Walker (1781, p. 82), Wang (1794, p. 173).

---

461. LUCID PROJECTION AND PSYCHOPATHOLOGY

Definition. Psychopathology: that part of human pathology which involves mental infirmities, their origins, symptoms and nature.

Synonymy: mental pathology.

Questionnaire. In light of the extensive number of individuals who affirm to have been consciously outside the human body, it becomes valid to ask and respond: Can it be that we are dealing with a phenomenon in which all these persons suffer from temporary insanity, cerebral dysfunction or neurotic privation at a certain moment, which has occurred neither previously nor subsequently? Rationally, the response can be no.

Physiology. Lucid projection is a physiological resource, a frequently occurring natural phenomenon which should be excluded from the field of human psychopathology, because it neither represents nor stems directly from mental disturbances. However, it is worth clarifying further that the lucid projection phenomenon can *also* occur with patients who suffer from mental disturbances, which does not imply the same thing. Also, moral and physical aggressions and the mental disturbances that come from them can generate the lucid projection phenomenon in complacent persons who do not have sufficient will to produce it for themselves.

Index. Nevertheless, a greater incidence of psychopathies has still not been evidenced in practitioners of lucid projection in comparison with other xenophrenic states or altered states of consciousness.

Average. The identified cases of the relationship between consciential projection and psychopathology lie within the average of occurrences. Important maleficent physiological effects have not been encountered as being derived from projective activities.

Differences. In the areas of psychopathology, there are phenomena or states which are similar to lucid projection, including depersonalization, dissociation of the personality, the *multicleaved* self, the distortion of the human body's image, and pathological autoscopy. However, all of these admitted forms of pathology differ from lucid projection in diverse and very evident important manifestations, just as each dissociation of the consciousness presents fundamental differences from the others.

Case study. Depersonalization – the sensation experienced by the person in which his/her human body feels strange or seems to belong to someone else – can involve anxious sentiments of loss of personal identity, as well as those of unreality in relation to the physical environment, a condition not occurring with lucid projection, which is usually tranquilizing, evidencing a transcendent experience.

Aura. The projective aura is positive, benign, and very different from the epileptic aura, or the aura of the migraine. The same is the case with projective catalepsy, when compared with pathological catalepsy.

Psychosomatics. Self-transfiguration of the psychosoma can be induced by the consciousness itself.

Predominance. Another element which perfectly distinguishes psychopathy (in general) from lucid projection is in the relative predominance of the first occurrence, which is common to humanity, and the rarity of the second occurrence among individuals, when of an impactful nature.

Standpoint. It must also not be forgotten that, just as the processes of medicine cannot be correctly evaluated in terms of the doctors' health, and all of psychoanalysis cannot be evaluated in terms of the psychotic experiences of some analysts, the phenomena pertaining to projectiology cannot be evaluated in terms of the projectors' health. This would be no less than to proceed from a biased standpoint. The possibility of a lucid projector being mentally ill is the same as for any psychiatrist. Just because some doctors are mentally ill, does not imply that *all* doctors must be so.

Parapsychism. Parapsychic facts are not pathological facts. Extrasensory phenomena, not being symptoms of illnesses, occur as much in healthy persons as in psychopaths. Parapsychism is a natural attribute of the personality and it would not be correct to associate it with mental abnormality, identify it as a symptom of illness or a process pertaining to the area of psychopathology, although both it and parapsychology have much in common, because the phenomena of both are deviations from the normal, in the sense of being exceptional.

Rarity. Animic, parapsychic and projective states are not pathological phenomena. They are, without a doubt, altered states, or abnormal phenomena, in the sense that they are rare, but rarity does not signify morbidity.

Projectability. It would always be erroneous to consider projectability as a morbid state of the mind, just as it would be an error to consider menstruation, human biological conception, gestation and natural childbirth as being diseased states of the organism or of the woman's gynosoma.

Angles. On the other hand, an individual's psychiatric disorder does not definitively constitute a prerequisite to his/her promotion to the role of an active lucid projector. According to sociologists and anthropologists, this does not even occur with shamans, medicine men who are prophetic diviners in exotic cultures. There are no shamans who are neurotic or paranoid in daily life. If they were, they would be classified as lunatics and would not survive as respected priests.

Shamans. It should be stressed that shamans are the true rustic, primitive projectors, the precursors of the modern lucid projectors of projectiology. This indicates that projectiological phenomena cannot be connected to psychopathology because they are an integral part of the natural physiology of humans since they appeared on earth.

Normality. Finally, why are lucid projections normal, daily occurrences, with no intrinsic pathological connotation? Simply because they do not produce any negative physiological changes in the individual and can occur in anyone, with the person having a healthy mind, just as with the mentally ill person; with the clairvoyant as well as the blind person; the healthy individual and the invalid; the youth and the elderly person (eighty-five years of age and over).

Evolution. Another fact reaffirms the relationship of lucid projections with the healthy condition of the projector as a human being. The practice of the voluntary, lucid takeoff, or inducement by the intraphysical consciousness when temporarily leaving the human body, presents itself at the current evolutionary level of humanity as an event which is contrary to the rule. This does not imply pathological involution, however, but salutary evolution, being an above average consciential condition in regard to the intraphysical population, and one which is proof of intraconsciential giftedness.

Interviews. In order to corroborate these affirmations, public research projects were performed on lucid projection through interviews administered in Kansas, in the United States of America, under the supervision of clinical physicians, psychiatrists and psychologists. This research, conducted from 1976 to 1981 confirmed the existence of groups of projectors who were healthier than average, demonstrating that lucid projection, as a state of consciousness, per se, does not present itself as being unnatural or pathological, according to the basic affirmations of psychiatrists Glen O. Gabbard, Stewart W. Twemlow and Fowler C. Jones.

Universe. In light of the above, within the field of projectiology, hallucinations, psychopathies and mental aberrations should remain outside the realm of the statistics of pure cases of lucid projection, scattered throughout the entire population, and which really merit being analyzed as recently discovered phenomena, despite the fact that they have always existed.

Realities. Lucid projections do not constitute aberrant experiences, nor are they products of the disturbed mind, but are normal human experiences which combat the individual's anxiety and annihilate the fear of physical death (thanatophobia). They also encourage the practitioner to admit to a continuing life after the human stage, bring profound satisfaction to the physical and intraconsciential existences of the social being, and are psychologically advantageous to those who experience them.

Alarm. Based upon the above-cited rational evidence, the author sends an alarm signal from here to esteemed psychiatrists, neurologists, psychoanalysts, psychologists and psychotherapists in general, as health professionals, in order for them to endeavor to conscientiously distinguish ordinary pathological processes from genuine cases of lucid projection, without confusing the two, in favor of the patients and their intraconsciential states.

Losses. The author has been receiving reports of individuals' experiences, with disastrous results, wherein they, after seeking specialists for help in understanding instances of spontaneous, natural, lucid departures from the human body, began to take the powerful narcotics that they were erroneously prescribed. These pseudotherapeutic resources irreversibly impaired their physical and mental health.

Psychopathology. The following are some real projectiological phenomena – among many or almost all that exist – for which similar psychopathological occurrences are reported, and with which they should not be confused: bradykinesis; duplication of a part of the body; elongation; panoramic vision; partial projection; phantom member (certain cases); projection of the complete double; projective autoscopy; projective déjà vu; self-bilocation; vibrational state; waking discoincidence. In summary: the experience of the lucid consciential projection does not have a pathological impact upon the intraphysical consciousness (human personality).

Bibliography: Blackmore (139, p. 153), Breecher (198, p. 28), Brown (211, p. 217), Grattan-Guinness (626, p. 319), Greenhouse (636, p. 310), Greyson (643, p. 184), Krishna (867, p. 128), Lewis (923, p. 221), Lippman (934, p. 345), Long (946, p. 33), Ludwig (956, p. 225), Lukianowicz (957, p. 199), Monroe (1065, p. 204), Neppe (1123, p. 1), Noyes Jr. (1141, p. 19; 1142, p. 174), Paim (1182, p. 226), Rogo (1444, p. 9), Roll (1466, p. 232), Sabom (1486, p. 220), Stokes (1625, p. 23), Todd (1689, p. 47), Twemlow (1710, p. 453), Vieira (1762, p. 62).

462. LUCID PROJECTION, SURGERY AND ANESTHETICS

Definition. Surgery: the branch of medicine and odontology that treats infirmities or accidents, either totally or in part, by manual and operative procedures.

Synonymy: surgical intervention; surgical operation.

Torpidity. In a surgical operation, the anesthetic begins its action by installing the state of physical torpidity in the anesthetized region. It is a basic precept in projectiology that physical torpidity is the first sign of discoincidence of the vehicles of manifestation of the consciousness.

Anesthetics. Surgery, in medicine as much as in odontology, has a special function in the field of projectiology due to the torpifying effects of anesthetics known as "dissociatives". During a certain period, the following were used more often as anesthetics: nitrogen protoxide, nitrous oxide, or laughing gas; ether; chloroform; trilene; halothane; and ketamine. Since 1844, anesthetics made the human body pass into unconsciousness, elevating the level of carbon dioxide in the organism, thereby predisposing the lucid departure of the consciousness to the extraphysical dimension in sporadic, artificial, forced consciential projections. Thus arose the so-called *anesthetic revelations* in the nineteenth century. Currently, an elevated level of carbon dioxide in the circulatory system represents a risk during the anesthetic procedure. Nowadays, when anesthetics are being applied, a saturation of O_2 is maintained at 100% with supplementary oxygentherapy. Nevertheless, general anesthesia is one of the greatest risk factors in surgery. Nowadays, countless near-death experiences (NDEs) occur during surgeries.

Environment. On the other hand, other powerful physical and psychological factors create a dramatic environment (hospital holothosene), having an intense significance that is propitious for the production of projection of the consciousness in individuals who are sensitive or projectiologically predisposed. The following 6 factors serve as examples:

1. **Infirmary.** The hospital infirmary with the strong smell of chemical substances.
2. **Desomatics.** The sensation of illness and physical death (thanatophobia) in the air, in the hospital environment.
3. **Dynamic.** The gentle comings and goings of medical personnel in the hospital environment.
4. **Mysticism.** The religious figures and images which are also in the hospital environment.
5. **Isolation.** The sensation of isolation and distance from the house, or home, on the part of the sick inpatient.
6. **Analgesic.** The effects of the anesthetic applied during surgery.

Surgeons. Surgeons in general, especially those who are indifferent to parapsychic phenomena and who have still not experienced spontaneous lucid projection, judge the narratives of their postoperative patients to be mere hallucinations provoked by anesthetics during general anesthesia. However, competent parapsychology researchers and some medical researchers now know that the profound state of cerebral unconsciousness, due to the effects of general anesthesia during operation, encourages the consciousness to enjoy some type of lucidity outside the body, in certain cases.

Near-death. Lucid projection during the period of anesthesia, or in the state of sensory deprivation, above all constitutes an efficient process whereby someone is removed from the discomfort of the ill, wounded or traumatized human body, from the physical pain and trauma provoked by the surgeon's scalpel. In certain cases, the alteration of the consciential state is so rapid and impressive that the projected intraphysical consciousness becomes indifferent to his/her own anesthetized human body, whereupon extraphysical helpers appear and convince or compel a return to intraphysical life, thereby bringing on the typical near-death experience (NDE).

Confirmations. The lucid projection experienced while under anesthesia – whether during minor or major surgery, exodontia, alveolotomy, cesarean, appendectomy, tonsillectomy – allows irrefutable confirmations of the extraphysical excursion of the *patient's* consciousness in the surroundings through the testimonies of the medical personnel who work in-between the human-helper-anesthetist, who is unaware of the extraphysical occurrences, and the lucid projector-patient outside the human body.

Inverse. Conversely, and more rarely, reports can be collected of *surgeons* and *nurses* who irrefutably saw the exteriorization of their patients, sometimes on top of the operating table, describing the person's extraphysical double, the face enveloped in fog, or even the silver cord, using the same terms as the projectors themselves, thus confirming the projective experiences.

Professionals. Today there are hundreds of physicians and psychologists who produce their own lucid, consciential projections.

Takeoff. The takeoff of the consciousness in the psychosoma, leaving the human body incapacitated under the action of the anesthesia, often occurs abruptly, in a spiral or zigzag manner.

Unconsciousness. Lucid projection can occur during natural sleep, a self-induced trance, upon fainting, while in a coma, or during the unconsciousness generated by physical or mental trauma. In the state of deep unconsciousness provoked by anesthesia, the consciousness finds itself forced to leave the human body – either in the psychosoma or even directly in the isolated mentalsoma – leaving the physical form, on the operating table, in a much deeper state of unconsciousness than that of natural sleep or any type of trance state.

Comparison. The levels of deep unconsciousness produced by pathological states generate forced projections through abrupt takeoffs, which become disadvantageous in comparison with spontaneous projections wherein the projector is healthy and more apt to make high quality, detailed observations of the extraphysical experiences. However, projections produced under general anesthesia – an experiment of applied pharmacology – offer more impressive and dramatic experiences than the spontaneous projections which occur during natural sleep, or those provoked by the intraphysical consciousness through self-induced trances.

Advice. With the conscious patient merely under a *local* anesthetic, professionals need to pay attention to what is said, and many physicians consider this an inconvenience. Nevertheless, these colleagues are still not aware that projectiology cautions surgeons, assistants, anesthesiologists, nurses, paramedic teams and health personnel – when working professionally – to avoid speaking inappropriately among themselves during surgery, even when the patient is under *general* anesthesia.

Sentence. While under general anesthesia, when the patient is presumed to be unconscious, his/her consciousness – projected from the inactive human body due to the effect of the anesthesia – much more frequently than imagined, clearly *sees, hears* and perceives everything that is said and done in the operating room, including the operation itself. The patient often hears him/herself declared dead or indiscreet details of the technicians' appropriate and inappropriate attitudes, and even facts that occur in the immediate area of the surgical centers. Countless postoperative patients either keep to themselves or report everything they experienced during this period soon after the general anesthesia has worn off.

Risks. It is worth mentioning that the heralds of medicine caution against the risks of general anesthesia. General anesthesia is essential, frequently inevitable and always dangerous. It leaves all persons, especially physicians, uneasy. Anesthesiology is, to a certain extent, an imprecise science. Many persons who undergo surgery under *general* anesthesia still fall victim to cardiorespiratory arrest. The majority of surgical operations can be performed with the patient awake. Only one in eleven thousand persons who undergo surgical intervention with *local* anesthesia (where the patient is awake) becomes a victim of cardiac arrest. This proportional difference is impressive and makes one think.

Note. The subjects addressed in this chapter, relative to the relationships between lucid consciential projection and surgery and anesthesia should not be confused with the relationships of lucid projection and parasurgeries, performed by sensitives.

Bibliography: Andreas (36, p. 50), Baker (69, p. 16), Battersby (92, p. 51), Bord (170, p. 11), Bozzano (192, p. 131), Brittain (206, p. 63), Brunton (216, p. 173), Crookall (320, p. 68; 338, p. 134), Currie (354, p. 146), Giovetti (593, p. 39), Greenhouse (636, p. 154), Gurney (666, p. 505), Holzer (745, p. 165), James (803, p. 378), Jung (813, p. 508), Leaf (905, p. 147), Malz (992, p. 50), Miranda (1050, p. 89), Mitchell (1058, p. 44), Muldoon (1102, p. 75), Parrish-Harra (1202, p. 75), Richards (1394, p. 25), Rogo (1446, p. 155), Sabom (1486, p. 82), Smith (1574, p. 32), Steiger (1601, p. 41), Walker (1781, p. 74), Wang (1794, p. 167).

463. LUCID PROJECTION AND PARASURGERY

Definition. Parasurgery: the branch of paramedicine and the subdiscipline of conscientiology that treats infirmities and accidents, either totally or in part, by manual, operational procedures and methods of parapsychic origin.

Synonymy: alternative surgery; extramedical curative process; extramedical surgical intervention; free surgery; heterodox surgery; logurgy; marginal surgery; metasomatic surgery; parallel surgery; parapsychic operation; parapsychic surgery; popular surgery; public surgery; spiritual surgery; supersurgery; surgical telekinesis; unorthodox surgery.

Invasion. Over the past few decades, international news agencies – through printed and verbal journalism, including shocking cinematographic documentaries and disturbing penal processes – have been reporting on the increasing diffusion of atypical and clandestine surgical interventions which are being realized on human bodies, invading the domain of classic surgery.

Observers. Many observers affirm that, in these unusual operations which have no precedent in medical history and which lie entirely outside conventional rules, healers with no medical training execute the introduction and use of precarious instruments into vital organs, such as: stilettos into the heart and lungs; knife into the eyes and ears; scalpel into the cranium and abdomen; incisions up to 16" (40 cm) long; together with the sudden appearance of medications and the instantaneous healing of large surgical incisions. Paradoxically, all of this is practiced without conventional asepsis and without causing infection; without conventional anesthesia and without pain; without conventional hemostasis and without hemorrhage.

Comparison. Aberrant interventions, based only upon mystical-empirical evidence, have neither been recognized and classified by orthodox science, nor incorporated into surgery, nor addressed by the teachings of official and para-official medical schools. Being facts which cannot be made academic, considered to be heretical in the cultural world of our century, just like all that which does not fit within the list of accepted ideas, they have been included in the study of parallel sciences, alternative therapies or specifically within so-called *parallel medicine.*

Opposition. Apparently without explanation in conventional scientific foundations, these surgeries have encountered strong opposition from medical, scientific and industrial bodies, and have been the object of direct criticism, bitter hostility, skepticism and continued controversy. Polemic has resulted in misinformation. The majority of commentators – visionaries as well as realists – have distorted ideas about interviewees brought together in sensationalistic news programs that detract from the respectable support which research into the subject requires, resulting in spontaneous antagonism toward the subject, which other persons also reject, as they cannot explain it.

Expressions. Aside from the synonymy above, many expressions have been coined to define heterodox surgery, according to extreme, moderate and neutral heterocritical appreciation with regard to its psychological, sociological, legal and medical aspects: "antisurgery"; "social assistance to indigents"; "erudite charlatanism"; "folkloric surgeries"; "social surgery"; "popular beliefs"; "faith healing"; "spectacles of illusionism"; "exploitation of public credulity"; "phenomena of under-development"; "systematic religious proselytism"; "science fiction"; "pithiatism"; "public health problem"; and "subsurgery". These opinions are almost always expressed some distance from the events, without prior investigation but, instead, aprioristically.

Interest. There are many inquiries and controversies surrounding the matter and they will continue for some time to come. There are conflicts of information and analysis, but there seems to be at least one unquestionable reality: the enormous power of popular attraction of these operations grows and is always in evidence. It is common knowledge that any public interest, in this technotronic age, cannot be ignored, arriving at a point at which scientific judgment and good sense come to demand complete investigation, because modern, universalistic experimenters invalidate neither spontaneous phenomena nor personal cases.

Observation. Common news cannot be used as scientific evidence. Equidistant from the confusion and moving toward the direct, cold, cautious observation of heterodox surgeries, any impartial researcher – upon comparing and discussing the methods used by its practitioners, its efficiency or uselessness, when taken as a research hypothesis – will arrive at the conclusion that real parasurgical phenomena actually do exist, in a number of cases.

Scientificness. The objective presentation of the fundamental problem, in this case, should be the scientific examination of the phenomena, without distorting implications, the dramatic aspect, and the entire emotional or corporatist charge which involves it. This is because reports of the facts are always suspect when highly charged with emotion, longing and strictly human interests or those of the clan.

Approaches. The irrefutable evidence of the occurrences defies analysis and imposes new approaches to the questions. This is because – besides faith healing and charlatanism – it has authentic interventions in its manifestations which exhibit a set of processes that are still unknown to science and technology.

Questions. Scientific investigation rigorously begins with the formulation of questions. The following are some pertinent questions: What are the main factors that cause the extraordinary explosion in heterodox interventions? What are their real causes? Where does the power of attraction of parasurgeries come from? Can the practitioners of parasurgery give correct diagnoses, operate and make the ill person feel better with these clandestine operations? Where would the conclusions of a comparative study between modern surgery and heterodox surgery lead us? What would the consequences of this be?

Characteristics. Although various techniques exist, there are 11 common, basic and even curious characteristics which pertain to all authentic parasurgeons:

1. **Responsibility.** The parasurgeon is responsible for all that occurs in the operations that are planned and executed, as well as for the ensuing consequences.

2. **Qualification.** Although some parasurgeon-physicians have appeared upon occasion, the parasurgeon is generally not legally qualified to practice medicine, much less to practice surgical intervention. They therefore practice outside the law.

3. **Benefit.** The authentic parasurgeon does not obtain any material benefit from his/her parapsychic aptitudes, mercantilist charlatans and their *money-oriented company* notwithstanding.

4. **Personality.** The parasurgeon is the indispensable central personality of the parasurgery, without whom there is no intervention.

5. **Backup team.** The parasurgeon does not have a backup team for the preoperative, asepsis, anesthesia, hemostasis and technical assistance in the operative and postoperative processes.

6. **Tactics.** The parasurgeon is the only one to intervene in the surgical area, to use the available equipment and make necessary tactical decisions during the parasurgeries.

7. **Assistants.** The parasurgeon generally has neither a first nor second assistant – the surgeon's assistant, anesthesiologist or colleague-technician – to directly assist in the interventions, exchange ideas or give opinions.

8. **Substitutes.** There is no one to substitute the parasurgeon, in case it is needed, nor is there someone who can reduce preoperative tension.

9. **Meeting.** The parasurgeon does not have medical meetings in order to delegate responsibilities.

10. **Evaluation.** The parasurgeon neither possesses the normal resources for making a preoperative evaluation, nor does he/she request laboratory results in order to assess the risk involved.

11. **Individualism.** The parasurgeon cannot be classified – in the same manner as conventional physicians or surgeons – according to known specialties; being, by nature, an individualist, polyvalent, versatile polysurgeon who practices interventions featuring extremely personal technical procedures.

Energy. Immanent energy, when transformed into consciential energy and used or transmitted by the consciousness as a revitalizing agent, is able to explain countless phenomena in detail, among which are the following 9:

1. Parasurgeries or parasurgical techniques with and without instruments (subdiscipline of conscientiology).

2. The use of the fingers and hands as instruments which work like conductive wires.

3. Para-anesthesiology (subdiscipline of conscientiology).

4. Para-asepsis (subdiscipline of conscientiology).

5. Parahemostasis (subdiscipline of conscientiology).

6. Instantaneous paracicatrization (subdiscipline of conscientiology).

7. The appearance and disappearance of stitches.

8. Definitive remission in certain cases.

9. Power over organic and living things, or the faculty of manipulating biological systems, as evidenced by parasurgeons.

Phenomena. The effects of creation, dis-creation and re-creation in parasurgical phenomena seem to run counter to the laws of physics, with the appearance and disappearance of small and large objects in matter-space-time, through systems having a velocity which is apparently greater than the speed of light.

Hypothesis. There is a hypothesis that in parasurgical operations – whether public, secret, instrumental or manual – there may be a discoincidence of the parasurgeon's vehicles of manifestation. In other words, there is a partial or complete projection, a temporary extraphysical migration of the parasurgeon's consciousness, which performs the cure directly. Nevertheless, according to parasurgeons, it is more common and traditional that an extraphysical consciousness takes responsibility for the operations.

Impartiality. Based on the existing prosaic opinion that a new scientific truth is unable to convince its opponents, making them see the light – but because its opponents eventually pass away and a new human generation grows up, familiarized with this truth – it is hoped that young physicians who are appearing will be able to examine both sides of the subject of parasurgery under consideration with impartiality from now on.

Bibliography: Andreas (36, p. 116), Corgnol (302, p. 29), Digest (399, p. 295), Ehrenwald (471, p. 257), Freedland (550, p. 185), Freixedo (553, p. 92), Horia (757, p. 161), Jacobson (796, p. 75), Krippner (863, p. 222; 865, p. 1), Kruger (871, p. 315), Meek (1028, p. 98), Mishlove (1055, p. 149), Playfair (1262, p. 121), Salomon (1497, p. 106), Schul (1522, p. 109), Sherman (1551, p. 165), Stelter (1613, p. 110), Uphoff (1722, p. 165), Valério (1725, p. 43), Walker (1784, p. 229), Wallace (1789, p. 58), Ward (1797, p. 66), Watson (1800, p. 206), Wolman (1863, p. 674).

464. LUCID   PROJECTION   AND   THE   MUTILATED   PERSON

Definition. Mutilated person: the person who experienced the test of patience and courage of having one or more physical members of the human body amputated, by way of accident or surgical operation, the member or members having been circularly cut to and through the bone or bones.

Synonymy: amputee.

Necessity. The need for amputation arises due to trauma to a member – whether a finger, leg or arm, in the majority of surgical cases, generally by an accident, automobile accident, work-related accident or event in a battlefield – as well as aiming to preserve the survival of the remaining healthy organism.

Restriction. Physical mutilation generally intensifies the process of psychophysical restriction, which keeps the consciousness confined within the human body, controlling the individual's life from the 2 cerebral hemispheres.

Analysis. In the analysis of the relationships between the phenomenon of lucid projection and the amputee, 7 correlated facts merit examination: the general experiences of lucid projectors; the experiences of lucid amputee projectors; the experiences of clairvoyant mediums; the phenomena of the sensations of integrity of amputees; the relationship between phantom pains and visions; *Kirlian photographs* or photos of the energetic emanations of living beings; and those suffering from certain cerebral problems.

1. **Projectors.** Veteran projectors know that, upon projecting in the presence of an intraphysical being who has recently had a member amputated, they will see him/her anthropomorphically *intact,* or whole, as though he/she still possessed the complete member. In a manner similar to other self-aware projectors, the author has already personally proven, with impressive extraphysical observation through lucid projection, the form of the phantom member of a recently amputated individual.

Continuation. The coherence (or cohesion) of the extraphysical substance of the psychosoma – the biological organizing agent (together with genetics) of the human body – acts more strongly than its attraction to the portion which was amputated from the same human body. This is why the extraphysical counterpart of the amputated member is not immediately retracted, nor does it go along with the segment that was amputated during the accident or surgery. The amputated part extraphysically continues to retain the shape or original mold of the integrity of the member for some time, until – according to the new mental self-image that is created by the accident victim – it is retracted into the boundaries of the mutilated form.

2. **Amputees.** There are amputee-projectors who clearly perceive the entirety of their own physically mutilated member upon seeing themselves projected, conscious and free in the extraphysical dimension.

Sensation. There is even a recorded case of a person who had a leg severed in an automobile accident, and whose soma was thrown a distance from the car. The person's consciousness immediately floated outside the human body, over the accident site. It observed the rescue team and even saw its own human body, which was missing one of its legs, but nevertheless retained the extraphysical sensation that its body was intact and whole, including the lost leg.

Self-materialization. We mention here, for information purposes, references to rare facts, which some affirm to be valid, although, unfortunately, still not scientifically proven, in which 1 amputee, for example, whose leg was removed just above the knee, demonstrated the ability to walk normally through self-materialization of the segment of the missing foot and leg.

Obstinacy. This occurs due to the obstinate determination of the individual – obviously predisposed to the exteriorization of ectoplasm – who, still clearly and parapsychically feeling the presence of the member, concentrates his/her ectoplasmic powers and self-materializes the foot and leg for a few instants.

Recomposition. In this case, the amputee, briefly recomposing the lost member and its function of sustaining the human body, walks firmly, without hesitation, with a firm and purposeful stride, as though in possession of two intact legs, although having only one visible leg with the foot in the shoe, and the other part of the pants folded back, held with pins, without a prosthesis or the aid of crutches or any other means of support.

3. **Clairvoyants.** Many clairvoyant mediums affirm, while in the ordinary, physical waking state, seeing the phantom member of the recently amputated person.

4. **Phantom.** Complaints by amputees are well-known to neurologists and psychiatrists, especially in the period of surgical convalescence, wherein they affirm continuing to strongly feel the *sensations of wholeness,* the phantom limbs: the amputated leg; both legs amputated; an amputated hand; an amputated arm; removed ribs or portions of ribs; a partially removed nose; a removed mammilla, in the case of the ablation of the female breast; a pulled tooth; an amputated penis; and also phantom pains which speak in favor of the existence of the double of all living beings, the psychosoma, or the biological organizing model. According to modern neurology, these pains in amputated members have their origin in the thalamus.

5. **Relationship.** The evidence of a suggestive relationship between 2 similar phenomena analyzed here leads to the following inference: the more pronounced the phantom pains of a recently amputated person are, the more visible, or parapsychically perceptible, the amputated portion of his/her human body will be.

Self-image. Phantom limbs only appear after the patient's fifth year of physical age or, in other words, after the development and establishment of the concept of a mental self-image of the human body. In many cases, after some time and the use of a prosthesis by the patient, the phantom limb seems to disappear while the prosthesis is being used, but reappears when it is removed.

6. *Kirlian photographs.* For the sake of illustration, it is worth remembering that certain *Kirlian photographs,* electrographs, bioplasmographs or photos of fields of radiation obtained in Russia, Brazil and the United States of America, suggest an effect of summary parabiological and paraphysical importance and which, perhaps for this or other motives, has been extremely controversial: plant leaves which have *previously* suffered the amputation of a part, appear with the energetic designs still whole, as though still possessing all of their components intact, with the specific exact form of the cut segment. This gives rise to the lost leaf phenomenon, phantom leaf phenomenon, cutaway phenomenon, or phantom effect. There is also the supposition that the phantom body should be able to be better observed with *Kirlian photography* of a human hand with a recently amputated finger.

Fabrication. It has so far not been possible to authentically reproduce the phantom effect in the laboratory in order to obtain the *urbi et orbi* consensus of experimenters with regard to it. Quite to the contrary, the phantom-leaf electrograph can be easily *fabricated* in the following manner: the leaf is pressed with a roll of rubber against the surface of the film located in the Kirlian apparatus or bioplasmograph. Then, one of its parts is sectioned and carefully removed, leaving a clear mark of humidity on the film. The high voltage of the apparatus, which is applied to the remaining portion of the leaf, plus the remaining humidity of the cut portion, produces a photograph with the so-called *phantom portion.* Many individuals make diagnoses with electrographs.

7. **Brain.** For decades, occurrences have been known of persons who have lost part of their brain, for diverse reasons, without any apparent harmful effect upon their mental life. This has corroborated the allegation of the existence of an extraphysical vehicle of the consciousness and the abovementioned facts regarding amputees.

Self-transfiguration. These affirmations do not imply that *all* amputees always remain with the intact extraphysical portion of the physical limb that they lost. This does not necessarily need to occur. If the awakened mind, with the passing of time, after the period of convalescence, surmounts the mental reflection upon the physical deficiency, it is most likely that the individual, after some time, will be seen not to have the extraphysical member, due to the well-known phenomenon of self-transfiguration of the psychosoma which, in this case, is sponsored by the consciousness itself. This, however, is not the rule.

Psychosoma. The psychosoma, whether of an intraphysical consciousness or an extraphysical consciousness, does not always need to obey the humanoid form in order to present itself, make its presence felt or act freely as a vehicle of manifestation of the consciousness.

Disappearances. Accidental cuts, amputations and mutilating surgeries executed directly upon the human body neither affect the para-anatomy of the psychosoma, nor do they interfere in the parapsychophysiology of the psychosoma and much less in the structure of the mentalsoma. That is why organic deficiencies completely disappear in the set of impressions of the consciousness projected with lucidity in the extraphysical dimension.

Repression. If the influence of some physical deficiency still remains in the sensations of the projected intraphysical consciousness during the extraphysical period, this is exclusively due to excessive conditioning, repression, inculcation or erroneous psychological predisposition in its tendencies, namely its *para*psychology.

Conclusions. Stemming from the comprehension of the associated phenomena presented here, and in the interest of his/her own well-being, the reader with any physical deficiency resulting from amputation should be aware of 4 intelligent attitudes:

1. **Vehicles.** Deficiencies and mutilations of the human body, regardless of which they may be, neither reach nor are reflected in the extraphysical vehicles of manifestation of your consciousness. This only occurs if your consciousness (you) wishes it, whether consciously or unconsciously. This indication can be followed by all those having physical deficiencies, including those with chromosomal alterations.

2. **Condition.** Firstly, upon projecting from the human body, deliberately forget your condition as an amputee. Think of yourself as being whole and intact.

3. **Prosthesis.** Further, upon consciously projecting, forget the existence of the prosthesis or artificial limb that you may use to correct the physical deficiency. Strictly speaking, unimpeded volitation in the extraphysical dimension dispenses with any crutch-like resource, whether physical or extraphysical.

4. **Motivation.** These logical arguments, based upon evidence, obviously constitute a powerful motivation for you to endeavor to produce lucid consciential projections voluntarily. This can only enrich your personal experience through a type of compensation that offers a greater freedom to your consciousness, which is confined within the soma, thereby manifesting beyond all psychophysical restriction.

Regeneration. Based upon the existence of the holochakra, the organogenic function of the psychosoma and on the survival of these consciential vehicles, even after the amputation of the physical limb, it is important to consider that the regenerative capacity of the living limbs of the human body – identical to that occurring in salamanders – will be the next conquest of human biology. The human body already recuperates vital parts that have been cut with new growth, as in the regeneration of skin and even the liver. It is thus worthwhile to predict that this same human body will come to recuperate amputated or defective parts, making them grow again through tissue regeneration, such as a fingertip from lesioned nerves, especially in children.

Bibliography: Andreas (36, p. 81), Bonin (168, p. 275), Bozzano (188, p. 19; 193, p. 105), Coxhead (312, p. 161), Crookall (331, p. 48), Currie (354, p. 148), Freedland (550, p. 24), Frost (560, p. 19), Grant-Veillard (623, p. 128), Jacobson (796, p. 130), Krippner (863, p. 184; 864, p. 165; 865, p. 40), Lukianowicz (957, p. 212), Maes (983, p. 161), Mishlove (1055, p. 230), Muldoon (1105, p. 143), Nebel (1118, p. 123), Pisani (1248, p. 262), Playfair (1262, p. 306), Powell (1278, p. 8), Richards (1392, p. 109), Schul (1523, p. 45), Sculthorp (1531, p. 144), Smith (1572, p. 45), Vieira (1756, p. 5), Walker (1783, p. 184), Ward (1797, p. 61), Watson (1800, p. 121).

465. LUCID PROJECTION AND HEMIPLEGICS

Definition. Hemiplegic: that person suffering from paralysis of one side of his/her human body.
Synonymy: collateral paralytic; homolateral paralytic; ipsilateral paralytic.

Hemiplegia. Hemiplegia is a disturbance in motility characterized by a partial or total lack of ability to effect voluntary movements. Common hemiplegia simultaneously affects the members of half of the human body and half of the face of the same side. It stems from damage to the corticospinal pathways in the opposing cerebral hemisphere. The cephalic manifestations are ipsilateral in *alternate* hemiplegia due to the damage of the cerebral trunk at diverse levels.

Section. Some hemiplegics perceive, and even see next to them, on the paralytic side, a longitudinal section of their own psychosoma and affirm that this section has the sensorial integrity that they lack in physical movement due to paralysis.

Explanation. Hemiplegics display a suppression of kinesthetic sensations. Thus, the kinesthetic theory does not explain the existence of this longitudinal section with sensorial integrity. Only the incipient, or partial, projection from the human body – of the psychosoma in this case – can explain this occurrence.

Amputees. The phenomenon occurring with hemiplegics is correlated to phenomena which occur with amputees and blind persons. These are explained by the existence of the psychosoma and its attribute as the organizing model of human forms, constituting a valuable compensation for the physical incapacity of the individual, whether a child or an adult.

Bibliography: Bozzano (184, p. 120; 188, p. 19), Lukianowicz (957, p. 212).

466. LUCID PROJECTION AND DRUGS

Definition. Projective drug: medication (or substances that are intoxicant, torporific, hallucinogenic, psychomimetic, phaneropsychic, phanerothymic, psychedelic, stimulant, unconscious-expanding) used in order to transitorily alter the state of the intraphysical consciousness through systematic practice destined to modify the chemistry of the human body and which may be considered projectiogenic by some researchers.

Synonymy: chemical key; consciential medicine; ecstasy medicine; unconscious-expanding; experimental drug; hallucinogen; hallucinoid; magic drug; metagnomic reactant; mind alterer; mind molder; mythical drug; narcotic; phaneropsychic; phanerothymic; pharmacological crutch; projectiogenic drug; projectiotoxin; projective medicine; projective pharmaceutical ingredient; psychedelic toxin; psychedelic; psychic energizer; psychodyslectic; psychogenetic; psychomimetic; psychophane; psychotomimetic.

Antiquity. For millennia, persons in many intraphysical societies have made use of substances that alter awareness, lucidity or elaboration of thought. There are descriptions of the use of opium dated 40 centuries before Jesus of Nazareth.

Mechanism. Mind-altering drugs disturb the system of enzymes that regulate cerebral functions, reduce cerebral efficiency and permit certain types of mental activities to enter the consciousness that are normally excluded because they do not have immediate survival value, bringing a state of psychic imponderability. These drugs, always having unpredictable results, lead the psychedelic tripper to ascendant (positive) self-transcendence, or to descendent (negative) self-transcendence, because one never knows with certainty which direction the experience will take. Drugs can lead to endless nightmares.

Lethality. At a highly elevated dose, any of the existing hallucinogens can be lethal. In this case, hallucinogens and sacred poisons can be doorways to delirium, even of an extraphysical nature.

Dependency. Hallucinogenic drugs are not addictive, that is, they do not establish a *physiological* dependency; nevertheless, some individuals become *psychologically* dependent upon drugs and, in this sense, develop a "habit", with suicidal, psychotic outbursts.

Process. When evaluating the possible uses and abuses of hallucinogens, the considerable body of knowledge and disparate disciplines should not be disregarded, such as: anthropology, biochemistry, pharmacology, psychology and psychiatry. Various tranquilizers are called "happy pills" because they offer a "free gift". Besides this, many of them can actually be of enormous, instantaneous benefit to the individual. A process that can take 5 years of psychoanalysis, for example, happens and is resolved in one hour, in a considerably less expensive manner, through one *trip, when ascendant,* happy, or positive.

Forms. There are 4 basic forms of light and heavy drugs that can cause damage or be inoffensive to the human organism, whether isolated, in self-experimentation in scientific parapsychism research centers, or having biochemical, medical, psychological and anthropological interests, in an approved experimental program. They can also have additives, in the rituals of sects and primitive, empirical, religious practices: smoked as cigarettes; ingested as seeds; chewable; and synthetic drugs or the product (injections, pills, tablets, capsules) of psychopharmacological research with so-called prophetic, metagnomic plants, magic herbs (addictive or treacherous pharmacological substances).

1. **Cigarettes:** *Cannabis sativa* (grass, pot, hash, weed, marijuana, maryjane, hash oil), the main active ingredient of which is *tetrahydrocannabinol* or THC; *Genista canariensis; Spartium junceum.* Marijuana is considered *devil weed.*

2. **Seeds:** *Banisteriopsis caapi (Ayahuasca); Banisteriopsis inchisus; Ipomoea pursativa; Ipomoea violacea (tlitliltzen); Rivea corymbosa (bejuco, manto, nosolena, uliliuqui, piule, trepadeira).* The papoula bulb (opium, heroine) was discovered by humankind over 7 millennia ago.

3. **Chewables:** *Amanita muscaria* (fly agaric, magic mushroom); *Lophophora williamsii* (thaumaturgic cactus, *hicuri,* peyote, devil root; mescal buttons from which mescaline is derived; *anhalonium*); *Psilocybe mexicana* (agaric, God's flesh, *teonanácatyl*).

4. **Synthetics:** Lysergic acid diethylamide (LSD 25), which is derived from ergotinine (*Claviceps purpurea,* or ergot), in this case a fungus which grows in grains such as rye and wheat; Ketamine (dl 2 – (o-chlorophyll – 2 (methylamine cyclohexane hydrochloride); *escopocloralose* (an association of scopolamine and chloralosis); amital; caffeine citrate; Ecstasy, XTC.

Others. Besides these, other so-called psychedelic substances with metapsychic effects – chemical keys or agents of *samadhitherapy* – are used in order to empirically obtain self-transcendence through chemical means. They are used by Indians of Central America, the southern region of the United States of America, the Amazon region, Africa, Siberia, among which are included: *Atropa belladona; Cereus peruvianus (huachuma); Datura arborea (huanto); Datura inoxia; Datura stramonium* (devil weed, stramonium, devilfig or hellfig); *Hyoscyamus niger; Liptadenia peregrina (Yopo); Mandragora officinarum; Tabernanthe iboga* (ibogaine); *Mimosa hostilis (jurema).* Among the worst are: cocaine, crack, *merla* or cocaine paste.

Term. Marijuana has been generating toxicomania – marijuana mania – characterized by the habit of smoking or chewing Indian hemp or hashish. This drug provokes a state of beatitude accompanied by hallucinations and, at times, furious, sanguinary delirium. From this originated the term *assassin,* derived from the word *hashish.* This fact deserves deep reflection on the part of new generations. The simple inhalation of the air where marihuana has been smoked can cause symptoms of intoxication. In 1998, Amsterdam, Holland was named the *Marijuana Capital.*

Purposes. These substances, plants of knowledge, drugs and *plants of power,* are used: for divining purposes; to discover lost, hidden or stolen objects; in order to find distant, lost or deceased persons who have not been heard from; as an empirical, alternative therapeutic agent and even in miniparasurgeries; in the undertaking of *aerial journeys* to unknown regions; to produce a *trip* through a previous consciential life; to *visit* uninhabited locations and distant cities (intoxicant lucid projections or *iatroprojections*); and with the purpose of extracting confessions ("truth serum").

Daime. The hallucinogen *ayahuasca* or *aiuasca (caapo, cadána, kahi, natema, pinde, yajé),* also called *daime, wine of the soul,* or *divining wine,* prepared by the intense, prolonged infusion or cooking of the stalk, branches and leaves of *Banisteriopsis caapi (jagube, jugube, mariri, banistério),* Amazonian vines and leaves of the *Psychotria spruce* species (*chacrona, mesela,* queen), also an Amazonian climbing plant, is the result of the fusion of these 2 plants.

Alkaloid. The alkaloid resulting from the mixture (boiled by cooking with a wooden fork) of these plants (plus water) is identical to harmine *(telepatina, yageína,* or *banisterina),* isolated from a shrub from the Middle East, *Peganum harmala.*

Degrees. Depending upon the combinations and the number of times the mixture is cooked, it is called 1st, 2nd and 3rd grade (or higher) *daime*.

Root. The strongest or most potent *daime* is that which is made from the root of the *jagube* vine.

Business. The ritualized consumption of *ayahuasca* (the name of the Inca sage) is a millenary practice of the Incas since ancient times and occurring more recently in indigenous ceremonies in the Amazon. Unfortunately, the drug trade is recognized as the *business of the twentieth century.*

Daimists. In the last quarter of the twentieth century, approximately 800 thousand persons, many of them "daimists" along the Acre state (Brazil) border that is shared with Bolivia and Peru, have made regular use of this hallucinogen or psychic energizer. This has been generating "visions," lucid projections, the phenomenon of internal autoscopy and psychophony in some individuals, including collective or group "visions". However, in high doses this hallucinogenic drink provokes delirium, intoxication and can seriously harm the nervous system of the practitioner because, according to some research, it results from the combination of quinine and scopolamine. In 1986, the Federal Drug Council (Conselho Federal de Entorpecentes) in Brazil, removed *aiuasca* from the list of psychoactives and drugs of the Division of Medical Inspection of the Ministry of Health (Divisão de Fiscalização Médica do Ministério da Saúde) (decriminalization).

Children. Unfortunately, in Brazil, for example, there has been decriminalization of the use of drugs derived from *daime,* cigarettes (tobacco in its many forms) and alcohol, which currently afflicts even children and adolescents of the new generations in great numbers, annulling the execution of their existential programs. It is hoped that, in the near future, something more consistent will be done in order to reduce this deplorable condition stemming from the immaturities of the unthinking human masses, of the authorities appointed without political will and the great number of badly drafted laws which are in force.

Therapy. Lysergic acid has been administered to terminal patients with the intention of alleviating their physical suffering, especially those with malignant, or metastatic illnesses, which, besides pain, present deep depression, anxiety, terror of death and destabilized relationships with their family members. This extreme psychedelic therapy offers positive psychological effects in these cases, precisely due to the production of forced lucid projections. However, it is not an ideal therapeutic process.

Leader. The administration of psychotomimetic, or psychedelic, drugs is performed under the attentive supervision of a leader, psychedelic companion, or master of ceremonies of the "psychedelic session." The effects of the drug vary greatly, depending upon: when the drug is taken; where the drug is taken; in whose company; in what dosage; and – perhaps most important of all – by whom it is taken; regardless of which drug is involved.

Technique. The leader of the psychedelic session should not take the drug; has to discard personal preconceptions; put aside the tendency to be judgmental; avoid labeling or depersonalizing the person under the influence of the drug; remain open-minded; not keep secrets from the psychedelic tripper, giving up any attempt at masking. All this is done in order to efficiently accompany the vulnerable drugged individual, who cannot even, for example, cross the street alone without the risk of being run over due to the state of absorption, ecstasy or abstraction in which his/her consciousness is immersed.

Contact. The leader of the psychedelic session almost always ends up feeling a light effect from the drug – whether through the breath of the drugged individual or by the transference of consciential energies, sympathetic assimilation or empathetic communication, the capacity to mentally perceive the emotions of the other being – characterizing the phenomenon of the *contact high trip,* thereby behaving as though also being under the influence of the hallucinogen.

War. Some people claim that, in 1966, the United States Air Force dropped so-called "happy bombs" over Vietnam, explosives filled with gaseous lysergic acid, intended to make the enemy soldiers take long *trips,* thereby becoming temporarily and subjectively absent, and being physically annulled on the battlefield.

Frog. Other authors also affirm that much earlier, in the early eighteenth century, the secretions of the *Bufo marinus* frog, were added to explosive cannonballs. If the cannonball did not liquidate the adversary, the toxins of the frog would. It can be seen that human nature is extremely creative and imaginative with respect to bellicosity.

Effects. The use or ingestion of several of these drugs and plants can generate, at the very least, some of the following 10 negative effects:

1. Intoxication. There are clinics and therapy groups (mutual support).
2. An ephemeral sensation of autism. Interference in personal relationships.
3. Diuresis.
4. Dysentery.
5. Mydriasis, double vision.
6. Increased vision, provoking brilliant ornamental effects.
7. The illusion of a rapid change in the size of persons and objects, or microscopy and macroscopy.
8. Psychological dependence. Obsession with the drug. Many undergo desoma at this point.
9. The archeology of infancy. Complete deterioration of personal and professional life.
10. Tyrannical desires.

Observation. It can be seen that lucid projections induced by intoxication with these magical drugs, mythical drugs, projectiogenic drugs, dream herbs, prophetic fungi, or magic plants, also considered sacred, are always imbued with hallucinations, due to their potent alkaloids and psychoactive properties. They are therefore not recommendable for rational reliable projectiological experiments. A drug has not yet been invented that instills intelligence and talent to the person who lacks them. However, the author hereby pays a tribute of gratitude to all the passive patients, sacrificed victims or human guinea pigs of drugs, being authentic, anonymous explorer-heroes of *consciential space,* in the hope that future research can offer effective, innocuous drugs for the expansion and lucid projection of the consciousness. *In the final analysis, hope is the last to undergo desoma.*

Types. It is worth clarifying that barbiturates impede the individual from dreaming, while tranquilizers, on the contrary, make the person dream. Other drugs can be listed which impede sleep and, therefore, the production of lucid projections: anorectics or appetite suppressants taken without medical supervision; xanthines (caffeine and its derivatives); some psychotropics (antidepressants); cortisone; amphetamines taken to stimulate intellectual capacity; bronchodilators, derivatives of ephedrine, aminophylline and noradrenaline, used in the treatment of asthma.

Pattern. The majority of medications modify the pattern of altered states of consciousness, whether sleep, dreams or lucid projections. Some of these medications actually provoke nightmares. Therefore, in summary: *the fewer medications that are used, or consumed, in any area, the better.* The UN recorded the existence of 13 million cocaine users in 1997.

Experimenters. The ingestion of diverse drugs has been generating alterations in the extraphysical perceptions of certain parapsychology experimenters, thereby resulting in countless perspectives and temporary conclusions based on false, artificial premises. Included in this group are self-researchers or investigators of participatory research, as well as authors who write on projectiological themes. These attitudes can be included among *multidimensional faux pas.*

Difference. When in the ordinary, physical waking state, our consciousness can, on the one hand, learn a lesson in a class in an optimal condition, while we enjoy the fullness of our intellectual perceptions. On the other hand, we can be medicated, drugged or drunk, whereupon our reflexes, concentration and powers of thought deteriorate, often annulling our intellectual perceptions to zero. We can thereby clearly understand the basic difference between a pure, physiological, lucid projection produced naturally by the will and an impure lucid projection, artificially induced by the use of drugs.

Decline. The intensity and quality of the extraphysical perceptions of the projected consciousness deteriorate while under the influence of the drugged organism. The extraphysical experiences and lessons become distorted, masked by mental images, oneiric interference and symbolic forms, being marked by erroneous interpretations. Healthy and ideal consciential expansion does not occur through drugs.

Ecstasy. The synthetic drug *MDMA (methylenedioxymethamphetamine),* also called "Ecstasy" (XTC, Adam), is not a hallucinogen, does not interfere with thoughts and does not alter the individual's perceptions. It does, however, present similarities with amphetamines and mescaline, and has been used, experimentally, to help individuals relate to their own emotions, increasing euphoria, energy and personal disposition. It is not indicated for those with heart or circulatory problems. It comes in gel caps or powder, to be mixed with juice. It does not predispose the individual to lucid consciential projection. The commercialization of this euphoriant was prohibited in the United States of America at the end of 1985.

Happiness. *Biochemical happiness* does not exist.

Beta-blockers. Beta-blocker medicines are currently much used in the treatment of arterial hypertension and other problems. Upon reducing the heart rate, they increase the human body's predisposition to allow projection of the consciousness. They are, however, dangerous drugs which should be prescribed with great caution, specifically for certain disturbances and not exclusively in order to facilitate lucid projection.

Arteriosclerosis. Medicines that prevent arteriosclerosis, senility and Alzheimer's disease, improve cerebral vascularization and increase alertness, but hamper lucid projection because they reduce the period of sleep. Nevertheless, in this case, when the intraphysical consciousness is able to project, he/she enjoys greater extraphysical lucidity and better recall of the extraphysical events that occur in the lucid projection.

Insomnia. The term *insomnia* refers to various interrelated problems: to take a long time to sleep, to awaken many times, or very early, or have light, unsatisfactory sleep. There are at least 23 known types of insomnia.

Projectability. Any type of insomnia – whether at the beginning of the night, during sleep, or in the early morning – hampers the production of lucid projection. Insomniacs should not be confused with healthy hyposomniacs, who need only a few hours of natural (delta) sleep every night, or within a 24-hour, sunrise-sunset, day-night, asleep-awake period.

Sleep-inducers. Narcotics, somniferous pills sold by medical prescription for insomniacs, which depress the central nervous system, act directly upon the brain and leave the person unconscious. No somniferous agent shows effective results for more than 28 days. These drugs are also not recommended for the production of lucid projection because, on the one hand, they reduce the heart rate, arterial pressure, respiratory rhythm, general reflexes and muscle tonus; on the other hand, they inhibit part of natural sleep including the REM cycles, related to dreams and projective predisposition. They thus do not allow refined, high-quality extraphysical perceptions.

Natural. Until now, besides the increase in the problems of insomnia in all countries, a natural somniferous substance that is risk free, powerful but innocuous has not yet been discovered, namely one which reactivates natural sleep without producing side effects or dependency. All insomnia drugs, including the weakest ones on the market, are not completely innocuous. They can lead the consumer to so-called *semitoxicomania,* or the less perceived condition of quasi-addiction, semidependence. They are also unable to provide individuals with sleep that is identical to natural sleep. Drinking coffee at night hampers the quality of sleep.

Alcohol. Alcoholic beverages – wine of the gods or holy wine – generally do not help the projective process. Alcohol facilitates sleepiness but distorts the normal sleep pattern. It suppresses important aspects of the individual's psychophysiology, including dreams, and can provoke early awakening. In other words, it can make people wake up before completing their individual, habitual period of natural sleep. All these factors impair the 3 fundamental aspects of the projective experience: takeoff of the psychosoma; the extraphysical achievement of lucidity of the projected consciousness; and the subsequent recall of the projective experiment.

Imagination. Alcohol tends to further reduce the control of the consciousness over the imagination or, in other words: it allows the imagination to dominate the consciential perceptions or the elaboration of pure thoughts. Ethyl alcohol is therefore a seductive and corrosive liquid that depresses the CNS.

Adverse. Besides the aspects already analyzed, it is still possible that some drugs – which normally do not generate collateral effects for most individuals – may cause adverse, unexpected effects for certain patients, including occasional hallucinations which can confuse the person who is inexperienced regarding the subject. The individual can thereby erroneously conclude that he/she experienced the phenomenon of lucid projection.

Interactions. The noxious interactions of drugs between themselves, or upon their simultaneous use, should not be forgotten. The following 3 are examples:

1. A projective drug and prescribed medications due to clinical problems.
2. A projective drug and other drugs which act upon the central nervous system (CNS).
3. Ingestion of alcoholic beverages in the hours prior to a psychedelic experiment.

Joint. Experiments have not yet been performed on the joint application of various projective techniques along with unconscious-expanding drugs. For example: hypnosis as a preparation for the administration of a drug; hypnosis as an inducer of reexperiences, or the recapturing of an entire psychedelic experience, after the administration of the drug and the experience of the trip; or even hypnosis as a resource of post-hypnotic suggestion for the individual, after the psychedelic experience, to enter into the altered state of consciousness at will. These working hypotheses have not offered conclusive results to date.

Hypnosis. It is important to remember that we should, first and foremost, avoid hypnosis of any type or manifestation, because the still pathological intraphysical society is full of spurious suggestions and hypnoses of all conceivable types, producing the *existential robotization* of millions of intraphysical consciousnesses. There are torpors that are enslaving, legal and dangerous, chemical and *reported* everywhere.

Bibliography: Ald (10, p. 151), Alverga (18, p. 326), Amadou (21, p. 243), Black (137, p. 37), Blackmore (139, p. 104), Bosc (172, p. 326), Brennan (199, p. 97), Castaneda (255, p. 31), Crookall (320, p. 44), D'arbó (365, p. 135), Davies (370, p. 251), Drury (414, p. 205), Fortune (540, p. 116), Frazer (549, p. 346), Grattan-Guinness (626, p. 212), Greene (635, p. 94), Grof (646, p. 186), Hossri (758, p. 108), Huxley (771, p. 98; 772, p. 29), Leary (907, p. 97), Lilly (926, p. 6), Maes (983, p. 151), Martins (1008, p. 16), Masters (1012, p. 85), Moore (1083, p. 139), Muldoon (1103, p. 55), Noyes Jr. (1142, p. 182), Rogo (1444, p. 103), Rouhier (1478, p. 6), Sabom (1486, p. 230), Sangirardi Jr. (1503, p. 181), Smith (1567, p. 37), Steiger (1601, p. 219), Sudre (1630, p. 84), Tart (1654, p. 327), Toynbee (1694, p. 228), Vieira (1762, p. 173), Wang (1794, p. 368), Warcollier (1796, p. 82), Watts (1802, p. 84), Wheeler (1826, p. 113), Wilson (1853, p. 332), Wolman (1863, p. 500).

---

467. COMPARISONS BETWEEN DRUGS AND HYPNOSIS

Differential. In the induction of lucid projection, besides autosuggestion, concentration and other special exercises, it is worth singling out drugs and hypnosis as processes that are prescribed by many enthusiasts. This is why it will be of great value to establish the similarities and differences between the former and the latter.

Contraindications. In the field of parapsychology, in general, and in the area of projectiology, in particular, drugs are frequently contraindicated. This is because they present negative physical aspects, almost all of which relate to the human body, and negative extraphysical aspects, relative to the projected consciousness.

Physical. The following are negative physical, or physiological, aspects that drugs provoke in the individual's human body:

1. **Induction.** The inevitable time required for a drug to take effect.
2. **Side effects.** Undesirable side effects or simultaneous effects upon using a drug.
3. **Convalescence.** The time needed for the individual to subsequently rest, an actual convalescence, wherein the organism endeavors to promote its own detoxification, eliminating the residues of the drug, because it acts like a toxin, a foreign body to the organic environment, creating an artificial illness.
4. **Delayed.** Disagreeable, unpredictable, delayed effects, or those subsequent to the use of the drug.

Extraphysical. Negative extraphysical aspects which light and heavy drugs provoke in the projected consciousness: a reduction in the level or the clarity of the extraphysical perceptions; interference from hallucinatory and oneiric images in the development of actual extraphysical images; reduction in the quality of the performance of the consciousness regarding subsequent recall.

Hypnosis. In a rational comparison of drugs and hetero-hypnosis, namely hypnosis provoked by another to induce lucid projection, the latter is seen to present immensely superior advantages because it can have almost instantaneous results, has no side effects and, when induced by a competent and responsible hypnotist, has no delayed or secondary effects. Besides, the hypnotized person always feels much better after the hypnotic trance.

Ideal. The ideal is that the intraphysical consciousness, whether a youth or an adult, should at all times dispense with the use of drugs, as well as hypnosis, as far as possible. Evolutionarily speaking, it is important for the consciousness to maintain a maximum level of natural lucidity in any dimension in which he/she manifests, or multidimensional self-awareness.

Bibliography: D'arbó (365, p. 133), Grof (647, p. 25), Steiger (1601, p. 127), Vieira (1762, p. 172).

---

468. LUCID PROJECTION AND PSYCHOLOGICAL CONTAGION

Definition. Psychological contagion: transmission of the attitude of one individual to another through mental influence, instinct of imitation or direct, immediate, psychological contact.

Synonymy: contagious propagation; epidemic suggestion; imitative contagion; imitative propagation; mental contagion; mimetic behavior; psychic contagion; psychic mimicry; psychological propagation; sympathetic contagion.

Think. Ordinary intraphysical consciousnesses generally still do not know how to relate in a healthy manner with their extraphysical sphere of consciential energies (energetic field) in human daily life, because they eat, feel, breathe and think inadequately. Ordinary individuals do not even think (or thosenize) for themselves in a free and independent manner. Their minds, lacking control, become integrated into the collective mind of the group to which they pertain. They thus relinquish their ability to discern among those who can be of greater use to them. This gives rise to fads – often including those that are extremely ridiculous and irrational – and to post-desomatic parapsychoses.

Types. Certain forms of the phenomenon of live, psychological contagion are well-known to psychiatrists, psychologists, sociologists and conscientiotherapists. For example, if someone yawns, sneezes, laughs or cries in a room full of people, this attitude can soon be transmitted, in a reflexive manner, to other spectators who are present. Nothing is more contagious than someone fainting in a crowded place.

Zoology. Mimetic behavior is even seen in subhuman animals, e.g.: a horse that shakes its head is soon imitated by those nearby.

Delirium. From a negative or psychopathological point of view, the participation of 1 or more individuals in the delirium of 1 ill person (delirium inducer and delirium induced) is well-known. The mental or psychic contagion of induced advanced madness, of the psychic epidemic and waves of suicides are also well-known. Unfortunately, even suicidal ideas can be implanted and transferred from person to person in a superexcited crowd.

Fads. Besides this, customs, fashions (fads, manias) and social trends are just as much a contagion of ideas, an aping of customs or imitative actions.

Contagiousness. Based on the premise that lucid consciential projection, as a natural, physiological attribute of the human consciousness, can be induced through suggestion or even through autosuggestion, it can be concluded that this consciential attribute receives the influence of certain motivating psychological factors, including *projective contagiousness*. In other words: lucid consciential projection is an experience that is transmittable through psychological contagion. However, there is generally no psychopathological connotation in these spontaneous, consciential projective occurrences.

Idea. Although having only sporadic individual consequences, the idea of lucid consciential projection can evidently be diffused by word of mouth and be communicated in a contagious manner from one individual to another or, more precisely, pass from one consciousness to another.

Gathering. Persons who are gathered together reciprocally influence each other. In the field of projectiology, the most easily detected psychological contagion occurs in a meeting or gathering where someone relates a personal projective experience. An unexpected consequence is the first spontaneous lucid projection by 1 of the listeners, a person who is more sensitive or has a greater latent level of lucid projectability, upon leaving the gathering and lying down routinely to go to sleep that night at home.

Reading. Frequently, the first reading about lucid projection, whether a simple newspaper article or a short chapter in a specialized book, motivates and induces the uninitiated reader who, because of this, ends up producing his/her first lucid projection and – dazzled, or sometimes surprised, by the uniqueness of the occurrence – recounts the experience verbally or in a letter (e-mail, fax). The author has various signed reports on this type of phenomena on file. The newspaper article (cosmogram) or book chapter (library) serve as catalysts for the emergent reaction of potential projectability.

Interferences. From the abovementioned observations, 4 basic inferences appear:

1. **Natural.** Psychological contagion represents an operative factor that sponsors the production of natural, involuntary, spontaneous, lucid projection without the application of any technique or methodology. Lucid projections, in this case, are not mere suggestions or induced hallucinations, but are real and unquestionable extraphysical experiences for the consciousness itself.

2. **Ease.** Psychological contagion highlights the ease which a minority of individuals – who have a greater predisposition (or a more developed projectability) compared to the average members of the population – possess in producing projections. They repeat the *conscious* phenomenon in an *unconscious* manner, without training, method or practice, but only by hearing about it. The majority of individuals achieve this level of performance only after much discipline, perseverant repetition and exhaustive training. It would be an error to disregard the clear evidence represented by this fact in favor of the existence of previous, preexisting experiences by the intraphysical consciousness or, in other words, a confirmation of the theory of successive lives and the existence of paragenetics.

3. **Center.** The evidence demonstrates that the veteran lucid projector is a focal point or *center of irradiation* from which the projective contagion emanates at its highest intensity. Therefore, those who have already produced impactful lucid projections can be certain that, in certain circumstances, the relating of their experiments, even verbally, depending on how it is said, the wave of energetic irradiation of the communication and the charismatic presence can be very positive and useful in the sense of stimulating other persons to produce their first lucid projective experiences.

4. **Current.** The facts also indicate that the centers of projectiological studies, public debates on consciential projection research and the gathering of ideas in meetings of veteran and novice lucid projectors, can form an actual positive *projectiogenic current* in certain areas, social circles or specific locations.

Joint. In fact, imitation – whether fad-imitation, habit-imitation, spontaneous imitation, reflexive imitation – constitutes a behavioral replication of models, the reproduction of which is considered desirable and can be acquired consciously or unconsciously. On the other hand, for the sake of comparison, it is worth bearing in mind that in the case of projections en masse, provoked simultaneously in a group of persons, where joint lucid projection is practiced in a technical manner – through hetero-hypnosis, for example – the participating intraphysical consciousnesses generally do not, on average, present high-quality experiences. This is due to the extremely individual aspect of the projective experience and the mutual interference or reflections of the individual extraphysical spheres of consciential energy between the participants.

Bibliography: Krishna (867, p. 131), Vieira (1762, p. 38).

469. LUCID PROJECTION AND HUMOR

Definition. Humor: the mood to perceive, appreciate and express the surroundings in a negative or positive manner.

Synonymy: disposition of temperament; state of consciousness.

Psychosoma. Common humor, including the black, anticosmoethical humor of the intraphysical consciousness that is projected in the extraphysical dimension, stems from the psychosoma or emotional body. This is why it exists, without parapathological connotations, near the terrestrial crust, in paratropospheric conditions, or in less evolved extraphysical dimensions per se. Mentalsomatic humor achieves levels of fruition that we are not accustomed to in our ever problematic daily human life.

Scowling. On the one hand, extraphysical good humor definitively liquidates any desire for extreme austerity and negative scowling by the consciousness of the projector, which repressive human mysticism is sometimes able to implant in the conditioned behavior of the individuals of the unthinking human masses or those lacking scientific knowledge.

Serenity. On the other hand, extraphysical good humor, by itself, demonstrates the need for the intraphysical consciousness to assume, without radicalism, a position of natural balance and serenity – the attribute of great, luminary intelligences of evolved extraphysical communities – to decide with wisdom and correctness on all occasions, both inside and outside the human body.

Mentalsoma. In order to achieve the pure manifestations of the mentalsoma, the intraphysical consciousness needs to act without deep or irrational emotional interferences. Until arriving at that point, the good humor of fraternity is preferable in any suitable circumstance because this special condition of the consciousness keeps the person's mental health protected from extreme segregationist, inculcatory, repressive rigorism or brainwashing, which can lead the personality to intraconsciential imbalance.

Bibliography: Sculthorp (1531, p. 77), Vieira (1762, p. 183).

470. LUCID PROJECTION AND YOGA

Definition. Yoga: the integrated system of self-discipline and physical and mental control, the objective of which is illumination, liberation and self-realization, in order to transcend the entire manifested universe and return to the origins of one's own consciential life.

Synonymy: *hatha yoga; kundalini yoga; laya yoga; mantra yoga; raja yoga; samadhi yoga* (types). The noble lineage of yoga (elitism) recommends and stipulates the use of the term in the masculine, with *y*, and the pronunciation with the closed *o*: *o yôga* – in Portuguese (*academicism* appears everywhere).

Types. The practice of some of the more than 144 types, systems, modalities, lines and specialties of yoga that exist, results in countless phenomena, including altered states of consciousness, which allow the practitioner to reach the extraphysical dimensions in a self-aware manner.

Videha. The *videha*, the Sanskrit term which literally signifies "one which has no body", corresponds to the spontaneous lucid projector, or the intraphysical consciousness who presents a natural ability for leaving the human body, according to yoga practitioners.

Pranayama. The control of energy, or prana, *pranayama,* or the science of respiration, a yoga technique, is 1 of the basic methods for predisposing the intraphysical consciousness to leave the human body.

Raja. Among the diverse types or aspects of the series of interconnected disciplines of yoga which are directly related to projectiology, the following should be singled out: *hatha yoga; mantra yoga;* raja yoga or mental discipline; and *samadhi yoga,* which allows the achievement of cosmic consciousness (cosmoconsciousness), namely the major projection in the mentalsoma.

Powers. Among the psychic abilities, powers, achievements or *siddhis* which are taught by the Hindu scriptures that address yoga, the following, being intimately related to projectiology, merit singling out: to remain unmoved in the face of the inevitable ills of the human body, in other words, to obtain the serenity that becomes indispensable to the projected consciousness desiring to evolve; to see and hear distant events, or traveling clairvoyance; to reach the speed of thought, or volitation; to introduce oneself into the human body of any intraphysical being, or the action of the communicant-projector; to make the body die at will, or intentional self-desoma; to acquire knowledge of the past, or self-retrocognition; also to acquire knowledge of the present, or clairvoyance, and knowledge of the future, or precognition; and to read the thoughts of others, or telepathy.

Practice. The development of the practice of yoga allows the individual to: increase the temperature of a point in the human body; walk on hot coals; control the human metabolism; stop bleeding; control the soma and the consciousness; produce telekinetic effects; stop or reactivate the heart; remain buried alive for a period of time; overcome pain; perspire at will; use the fingers like scissors; and live standing up (erect) for a period of years.

Machines. Western citizens can currently, in a few hours, learn some of the mental and therapeutic techniques with which the yogis take years of exercises to master the functions of the human body through the mind. This is done using machines that supply information to the person about the changes in personal organic systems. In other words, biofeedback, through which the practitioner can learn to control the blood pressure, heart rate, pain thresholds, body temperature, brainwave activity and other biological functions.

Chakras. Another aspect of the close relationship between lucid projection and yoga is the study of the force centers or chakras, as well as *kundalini yoga.*

Projection. The careful study of projectiology and the consequent practicing of lucid consciential projection solely through the decided willpower of the individual, over time, finally dispenses with the systems and exercises of yoga, as well as with all imaginable psychophysical crutches. It should, however, be recognized that the millenary practices of yoga systems has greatly aided and emancipated consciousnesses, from 30 centuries before Jesus Christ up until current times.

Bibliography: Ancilli (24, p. 632), Andrade (32, p. 59), Anônimo (44, p. 64), Blavatsky (153, p. 877), Bono (169, p. 180), Brennan (199, p. 98), Brunton (217, p. 164), Buttlar (229, p. 107), Calle (232, p. 52), Carrington (245, p. 211), Cavendish (266, p. 279), Chaplin (273, p. 172), Danielou (364, p. 193), Day (376, p. 150), Eliade (477, p. 98), Evans-Wentz (491, p. 293), Feuerstein (551, p. 126), Fodor (528, p. 415), Gaynor (577, p. 206), Green (632, p. 57), Krishna (867, p. 1), Martin (1003, p. 138), Michaël (1041, p. 102), Moore (1082, p. 217), Motoyama (1098, p. 39), Ramacháraca (1347, p. 150), Rogo (1444, p. 68), Roy (1480, p. 148), RPA (1481, p. 85), Saher (1493, p. 26), Satprem (1510, p. 219), Shepard (1548, p. 1006), Spence (1588, p. 438), Tondriau (1690, p. 242), Varenne (1729, p. 182), Vishnudevananda (1776, p. 300), Wang (1794, p. 37), Wedeck (1807, p. 382), White (1831, p. 69), Woods (1864, p. 261), Yogananda (1894, p. 37), Zaniah (1899, p. 491).

471. LUCID PROJECTION IN TOTAL INSTITUTIONS

Definition. Total institution: the place of residence and work where a large number of individuals in a similar condition and separated from the greater society, lead a formally administrated, closed life for a considerable period of time.

Synonymy. The restrictive total institution is sometimes called: collective establishment; greenhouse for changing persons; public institution; social institution; warehouse of interned persons.

Types. There are 5 categories of total institutions in modern, human society, with diverse purposes:

1. Persons who are thought to be incapable and inoffensive: homes for the blind, elderly, orphans and indigents.

2. Those who are considered to be incapable of caring for themselves and who also threaten intraphysical society, although unintentionally: hospitals for the mentally ill, sanitariums for tuberculars and those for individuals with other specific illnesses, and establishments for hansenotics.

3. The protection of the community against those who are intentionally dangerous: prisons, penitentiaries, prison camps and concentration camps.

4. The organization of specific tasks: headquarters, ships, boarding schools and work camps.

5. Refuge from human life and for the religious instruction of recluses: convents, abbeys, and monasteries of contemplative life.

Analyses. Certain psychological and sociological perspectives should not be disregarded in the careful analyses of projectiology. All traditional confinements of human activity can generate involuntary and even voluntary lucid projections. Cases of lucid projections with those confined in restrictive total institutions are well-known, these institutions always being detrimental to the individual's civil identity. This is particularly the case for those entering involuntarily, as occurs in prisons, POW camps and hospitals for the mentally ill.

Closed. The closed conditions of the total institution cause a restriction of information, an absence of leisure activities, a distancing from certain opportunities for behavior, the impossibility of accompanying recent social changes, a sense of lost time and a sharp restriction in individual freedom.

Prisons. Confinement in prisons, for example, operates through prohibitions and barriers to social interaction with the outside world – gratings, locked doors, thick and high walls, steel walls, barbed wire, towers, iron bars, moats, water, forests or swamps – and lead to the invalidation, degradation, humiliation, mortification, profanation and mutilation of the detainee or prisoner's ego.

Examples of this are found in the lives of Edward Morrell, much cited in projectiological literature, and Henri Charrière (1907-1973).

Dioxide. The prison confinement, the dust in the environment, and the polluted, somewhat deoxygenated air in the cell provoke a reduction in the percentage of oxygen inhaled by the prisoner, resulting in the spontaneous production of lucid projection through the technique of increasing the carbon dioxide in the human body, notably in the cerebral hemispheres.

Example. The following is an impressive example of what the author affirms in this description by Henri Charrière (1906-1973), in *Papillon,* pages 337 and 338 (Robert Laffont, 1982):

> "Plus, lorsque littéralement rendu je m'etends sur mon bat-flanc, je pose la tête sur la
> moitié de ma couverture et, l'autre moitié, je la replie sur mon visage. Alors, l'air déjà raréfié de
> la cellule arrive à ma bouche et à mon nez avec difficulté, filtré qu'il est par la couverture. Cela
> doit provoquer dans mes poumons un genre d'asphyxie, ma tête commence à me brûler. J'étouffe
> de chaleur et de manque d'air et alors, d'un seul coup, je m'envole. Ah! ces chevauchées de
> l'âme, quelles sensations indescriptibles elles m'ont données."

> ("Afterward, completely annihilated, I lay down on the bed, placing my head on top of
> half of the cover and cover it with the other half. The air in the cell – as it is already thin –
> hardly gets to my mouth and nose, being filtered by the cover. This may provoke a type of
> asphyxia in my lungs and my head begins to burn. The heat suffocates me, I am without air and
> – suddenly – I take off. Ah! These cavalcades of the soul, what indescribable sensations they
> gave me.")

Predisposing. These conditions of restriction in total institutions impel the confined individual, a true modern captive, to desperately seek resources for escaping this type of slavery or exile. In certain cases, this anxiety has an influence on the subconscious will, resulting in the unintentional, spontaneous production of the lucid projection experience.

Significance. Lucid projection in the total institution signifies a silent protest, an undetectable individual rebellion, an advantageous insubordination and a reasonable investment of time which is spent there involuntarily, making the interned-projector momentarily forget his/her real human situation. As the individual finds nothing to learn, he/she therefore turns to him/herself.

Evidence. We encounter clear evidence of this affirmation in the aforementioned work by Henri Charrière in another passage written in highly descriptive prose with cathartic effect, on pages 338 and 339:

> "Ni toi, procureur inhumain, ni vous, policiers à l'honnêteté douteuse, ni Polein, misérable
> qui a marchandé sa liberté au prix d'un faux témoignage, ni les douze fromages assez crétins
> pour avoir suivi la thèse de l'accusation et sa façon d'interpréter les choses, ni les gaffes de la
> Réclusion, dignes associés de la "mangeuse d'hommes", personne, absolument personne, pas
> même les murs épais ni la distance de cette île perdue sur l'Atlantique, rien, absolument rien de
> moral ou de matériel n'empêchera mes voyages délicieusement teintés du rose de la félicité
> quand je m'envole dans les étoiles."

> ("Neither you, inhumane prosecutor, nor you, police officer of doubtful honesty, nor
> Polein, that scoundrel who bought his freedom at the cost of a false testimony, nor the dozen
> fools on the jury, who were sufficiently stupid to accept the charges brought against me by the
> plaintiffs and their manner of interpreting things, nor the prison guards, worthy associates of
> the "devourer of men," no one, absolutely no one, not even the thick walls, nor the distance
> where this island is located, lost in the Atlantic, nothing, absolutely nothing, no moral or
> material thing will prevent my deliciously rose-colored journeys of happiness, when I take off
> and fly to the stars.")

Substitution. Sociologically speaking, lucid projection, in these cases, constitutes a true type of secondary adjustment, an act of evasion, an unprecedented liberation, a process of psychological, or more appropriately, projectiological or parapsychic substitution.

Escape. The projective phenomenon modifies the conditions of life that is planned for confined projectors and allows them to forget themselves, representing a defense mechanism for shielding them against moral and even physical pain, temporarily erasing all sense that they have of the environment in which and for which they must live.

Extraphysical. The extraphysical world, for those confined in a total institution, literally acts like a world of regular escape, a means of escape from the shackles of confinement.

Helpers. The assistance of the helpers provided to those confined in total institutions is a common type of *assistential* consciential projection, or *assisted* consciential projection, aiming to avoid the extreme despair of suicide and homicide.

Volitation. Unrestricted volitation is much more useful for the intraphysical consciousness who is in the maximally restrictive conditions of total institutions, than it is for the common person, accustomed to enjoying the full freedom of this external intraphysical dimension.

Visits. There is evidence, backed by the reports of prisoners, prison guards and family members of accused innocents who, while living as prisoners – including one case of a prisoner on *death row,* awaiting electrocution in the electric chair, or even on the gallows – received an extraphysical visit from their extraphysical family members who consciously projected from the human body, being moved by intense stress, sometimes even due to physical torture, which may be evident, disguised or covered up.

Incapacity. These affirmations of extraphysical assistance from the extraphysical helpers, which is frequently unexpected, are supported by the known fact that ex-convicts who consciously project while incarcerated, become unable to consciously leave their body as soon as they are freed, beginning a period of permanent projective recess. This also confirms the principle that no one leaves prison in a perfect state.

Myrmecologist. The condition of the evolved consciousness, endowed with a global vision and greater consciential acuity, upon extraphysically *gazing down* at this planet in order to analyze humankind *(Homo sapiens)* and the environment in which it lives (earth) in town and country, is analogous to the myrmecologist who researches and makes detailed observations on the environment, the habits and behavior of ants *(Phylum Arthropoda;* Class *Insecta;* Order *Hymenoptera;* Suborder *Clistogastra;* Family *Formicidae;* Genus *Atta;* Species *attasexdens)* in their miniworld (colony), in the primary and secondary tunnels. A similar analysis can be made by the intraphysical consciousness when lucidly projected in the mentalsoma.

Convent. Incidentally, the convent (of nuns) is the particular restrictive, total human institution (sociology) that is most similar to the ant hill where only female ants live as sisters (myrmecology). They are 2 types of social animals, although extremely diverse, according to the evolution of the consciential principle.

Projectiological Bibliography: Baumann (93, p. 8), Black (137, p. 34), Cannon (240, p. 123), Charrière (274, p. 337), Crookall (338, p. 33), Greenhouse (636, p. 140), Gurney (666, p. 227), Hunt (767, p. 56), Koestler (854, p. 350), Lefebure (909, p. 64), London (944, p. 239), Morrell (1088, p. 316), Moss (1097, p. 293), Muldoon (1103, p. 99), Nebel (1118, p. 107), Steiger (1601, p. 2), Wang (1794, p. 170).

Specific Bibliography:

1. **COSTA, Claúdio;** *Evolução em Cadeia: Reciclagem de um Presidiário pela Tenepes (Evolution in Series: The Recycling of a Prisoner through Penta);* with Suzane Morais; pref. Waldo Vieira; 200 pp.; 28 chaps.; glos. 300 terms; 46 refs.; 2 graphs; enu.; 21 x 14 cm; pb.; Rio de Janeiro, RJ; Brazil; Instituto Internacional de Projeciologia e Conscienciologia; 1998; pp. 5-180.

2. **HOWELL, Will;** *The Way to Why;* 192 pp.; 29 chaps.; 7 refs.; 21 x 24 cm; hb.; dj.; Birmingham; Great Britain; The Bean Press; 1988; pp. 1-192.

3. **SURPREENDENTE;** Editorial Staff; *Viagens Astrais: Condenados Perigosos fogem da Prisão Todas as Noites (Astral Trips: Dangerous Convicts escape from Prison Every Night);* Rio de Janeiro, RJ; Brazil; Magazine; N. 8; illus.; (1998); p. 31.

472. LUCID PROJECTION AND PERSONAL MOVEMENT

Definition. Personal movement: the act or process whereby a person moves him/herself or changes physical position with his/her human body.

Synonymy: individual dislocation; personal action.

Rapidity. Sometimes, a rapid, repeated, uncommon, lengthy movement can provoke discoincidence between the psychosoma and the human body, triggering a lucid or even nonlucid projection. In other words: the person seated in a gyrating chair; the *cavalo* ("horse") in the gyrations of *Umbanda;* the shaman in a frenetic dance; the *mambo,* or voodoo priest, in the whirling of his/her spasmodic pirouettes; the dervish in his/her gyratory dance movements; the athlete or an ordinary runner jogging; the parachutist at the precise moment at which he/she is waiting for the automatic parachute to open.

Direction. Consciousnesses sometimes have completely lucid experiences outside the human body – while their body continues with the coordinated, complex activity – whether driving a vehicle in movement, a normal car, a race car, a locomotive, a bus, plane, motorcycle or motorized bicycle; or even when the person is taking a driving test; someone is simply walking; the orator is speaking; the pastor is delivering a sermon; the author is writing a book; the marathoner is running; the sports enthusiast is playing; the singer is singing a song; the dentist is extracting a tooth from a patient.

Aid. Most projective experiences in which the person is at the wheel of a vehicle are of extremely short duration. In these circumstances, it seems that accidents do not occur due to a subprogram in the mental computer, or the aid of a helper attending to the spontaneous projectors in these momentary projections.

Stop. When someone applies the brakes in a vehicle, e.g.: a car, the human body suffers an abrupt stop. In this case, the psychosoma can continue in movement for a brief moment, so that the intraphysical being feels symptoms similar to those of an illness.

Causes. The main cause of these phenomena, it would seem, is in the absence of a certain amount of oxygen in the cerebral hemispheres – with a predominance of carbon dioxide – as occurs in other cases of a different nature, although from similar causes, triggered by a reduction in respiratory frequency, whether in critical situations of anesthesia, suffocation, drowning, landslides and cave-ins. It seems that these facts can also be related to the resonance frequency of the psychosoma when coincident with the human body, due to the state of external vibration of the vehicle's engine; as well as an external predisposition provoked by sound, thought or vision.

Inertia. Nevertheless, it should not be forgotten that many cases of discoincidence of the vehicles of manifestation of the consciousness are actually due to the mechanical inertia of the psychosoma and/or holochakra.

Bibliography: Andrews (37, p. 121), Black (137, p. 3), Blackmore (145, p. 308), Crookall (343, p. 108), Digest (399, p. 273), Green (632, p. 62), Greenhouse (636, p. 180), Holzer (751, p. 106), Lippman (934, p. 346), Muldoon (1105, p. 102), Noyes Jr. (1141, p. 20), Portela (1275, p. 130), Twemlow (1710, p. 452), Whiteman (1838, p. 177).

473. LUCID PROJECTION AND SPORTS

Definition. Sport: the set of physical exercises practiced using a method.

Synonymy: aerobics; athleticism; calisthenics; gymnastics; physical exercise; recreation.

Hygiene. Physical and mental hygiene are an essential precept for the normal human existence of any person, in the development of any activity. Based upon this premise, sports, or the regular practice of physical exercise, can only aid the projector's development, as it maintains adequate conditions of health and suitable or healthy psychophysical predispositions.

Conditioning. In the physical conditioning of the athlete, as it applies to the practice of lucid projection, it is worth highlighting the value of swimming, long-distance running, *hatha yoga* and the important condition of organic detoxification, based on the premise, which is widely accepted today, that the concentrated performance of a sport is a powerful inducer of altered states of consciousness, without any pathological connotation, in this case. This is because physical exercises particularly stimulate and intensify the energies, the holochakra the chakras.

Swimming. There are indications made in other references in this book to certain positive prescriptions for the projector-swimmer, especially with reference to physical *(soma)* relaxation and the projective technique of an extraphysical back somersault of the *psychosoma.*

Running. There are records of runners who consciously saw themselves outside the human body during exhaustive, long-distance runs, which require maintaining a rhythm of harmonic movements and a constant velocity. Curiously enough, these sport enthusiasts are considered "consciential athletes" by the new sports elite.

Detoxification. Physical exercises, even those ordinary ones which are practiced on a regular basis, efficiently help to shape the human body and keep the organism detoxified, eliminating intestinal constipation, headaches, dizziness and other occurrences which hinder the smooth development of the human physiology, impair the mental world of the intraphysical consciousness and impede the production of the lucid consciential projection experience.

Principles. The following are 2 uncontested principles of *modern civilization:*

1. **Sedentariness.** An inactive or sedentary life (sedentariness) leads to premature desoma for those personalities who are careless regarding the survival *of* and *in* the soma.

2. **Bellicosity.** *Non-radical* sports are the healthy equivalent of the multimillenary or atavistic (group karmic) insane practices of war and armed conflict (bellicosity).

Bibliography: Andrews (37, p. 121), David-Neel (368, p. 191), Greenhouse (636, p. 339), Murphy (1113, p. 3).

---

474. LUCID PROJECTION AND WAR

Definition. War: armed conflict declared between sovereign states or belligerent powers, whether between nations or factions of the same people.

Synonymy: air warfare (type); armed battle; armed conflict; civil warfare (type); declared hostility; guerrilla warfare (type); military combat; total warfare (type).

Explosions. Battle fatigue, isolation and desperation, extreme physical and mental tension, the sudden, violent dislocation of masses of air in the environment, or the impacts caused by explosions and the shockwaves of blasts during war, provoke frequent cases of instantaneous, forced lucid projections in soldiers and civilians prior to their desoma or in those who do not reach the point of losing their lives (without deactivation of the soma).

Forced. The lucid projections that occur on battlefields are invariably forced by circumstances and the physical and psychic traumas which occur, or which assail the human body of the occasional projector. However, in many cases, the fear of death and the deliria generated by war itself also act as powerful projectiogenic factors, as well as being agents against material or biological life. Paradoxically, in these cases, the fear that generally blocks the experience of voluntary lucid projection predisposes forced phenomena.

Weapon. The extremely frightening mental power of the application of consciential energies is, sadly, beginning to be technically explored as an incredibly powerful, modern weapon of war and sabotage, stemming from the research of psychokinetic (PK) phenomena, which, sadly, are currently *undisputedly* accepted as an instrument in combat operations, with the explosive purpose of increasing war between nations. In this tragic mental warfare – or psychic warfare, consciential warfare, telepathic warfare, telekinetic warfare – as it is called, which is currently being developed, research continues with the major powers engaged in multimillion dollar and multimillion ruble projects (which have already occurred) in the study of parapsychology, including projectiology, for exclusively bellicose purposes, as a dependable instrument for defeating the enemy, practicing acts or *effective interference,* in top secret projects.

Examples. The following are 8 significant examples of this research in which the major powers have been engaged since the 1980s: the possibility of discovering and locating military targets at a distance, through the production of remote viewing; the mental tracking of hiding places for missiles, through projective espionage; the technical theft of documents, through apport or extraphysical telekinesis; the mental command, at a distance, of the discharge of all types of combat equipment, through extraphysical telekinesis; the acquisition of secret mental material from other persons, through extraphysical telepathy; the changing of other persons' minds, including ideas, decisions, humor and emotions, also through extraphysical telepathy; the anticipation of plans that are as yet not conceived or fully materialized by the enemy, through extraphysical precognition; the act of inflicting illnesses upon persons through the malign use of consciential energies.

Savagery. Incidentally, the impressions which are made in the mentalsoma are more lasting than those made in the psychosoma. These impressions are constantly reproduced through memory and imagination. The mentalsoma stimulates the psychosoma, awakening desires within it which, in the subhuman animal, lie dormant until they are awakened by physical stimulus. Thus is born within the human consciousness the calculated cruelty that makes the human being, humankind on earth – the so-called *superior* animal – potentially more dangerous and brutally savage than any other subhuman animal considered *inferior.* All this due to the individual's ignorance of the existence and use of his/her own mentalsoma or, in other words, a lack of knowledge about his/her true essence.

Protest. For this reason, the author records here his vehement protest against the worrisome absurdity of war, irrespective of which war it might be, generated by the animal instincts and passions of modern humanity, *the civilized barbarian,* the greatest technical barbarian in human history. At the beginning of 1983 alone, according to the press (*Jornal do Brasil;* Rio de Janeiro; Brazil; daily; year XVII; N. 345; 23, March, 1983; p. 12), there were an estimated 40 major and minor bloody armed conflicts – "conventional wars" or "guerilla wars" – on the earth, involving 45 of the 164 nations existing on the planet at that time, with the involvement of more than 4 million soldiers engaged in full-time combat.

Impact therapy. According to *impact therapy,* or the experience of the clarification task, through leading-edge truths, among the greatest official intrusion-related tasks in human life, the following 4 can be singled out: war, espionage, sabotage and intentional disinformation.

Vaccine. These intraphysical consciousnesses involved in wars – the commanders and the troops – need to know, and the sooner the better for everyone, the individual and deeper realities of the experience of human lucid projection. This inoculates the intraphysical consciousness against all types of war, because it leads one to a better control of the psychosoma – the parabody of desires and emotions – through a greater comprehension and better use of one's own mentalsoma, on the way to extraphysical maturity. It is for this reason that the author presents this technical work as his contribution against the savagery of war and all *warlords.*

Bibliography: Bozzano (184, p. 124), Carrington (250, p. 172), Crookall (331, p. 20), Ebon (456, p. 17), Greenhouse (636, p. 137), Hemingway (710, p. 55), Kardec (824, p. 266), Machado (968, p. 73), Sabom (1486, p. 115), Smith (1572, p. 22), Steiger (1601, p. 84), Targ (1651, p. 9), Tucker (1702, p. 44).

475. LUCID PROJECTION, ESPIONAGE AND BUSINESS

Definition. Projective espionage: the act of spying, investigating and gathering information as a projected, intraphysical spy-projector.

Synonymy: extraphysical espionage; extraphysical spying; parapsychic spying technique; projectiological spying technique; projective spying; psychic espionage.

Spy-projector. In the field of consciousness technology, the secret agent who is dedicated to extraphysical espionage through lucid projection is called: psychotronic agent, extraphysical spy, parapsychic spy, para-spy or spy-projector.

Applications. Extraphysical espionage is classified within the public applications of lucid projection, given that some of these applications are exceptionally positive and the majority of the applications are negative, through the active participation of the projector in diverse practical operations.

Objectives. Such espionage aims to serve industrial, military, private, police, political, journalistic or any intelligence related secret service with bellicose objectives, which proposes to achieve the goal of observing and investigating the privacy of intraphysical consciousnesses, institutions and public areas, as well as the creation of efficient anti-telepathic barriers.

Unsafe. Extraphysical espionage, despite being an inadvisable practice in certain cases, is based on the well-known principle that no secret can really be secure on earth, in light of the universal possibilities of the interference of the perceptions of one consciousness upon other consciousnesses, through king-size lucid projection, extraphysical telepathy and extraphysical telekinesis.

Archives. The governments of the currently major powers are becoming increasingly interested in projectiology research. They aim to use lucid projection as a sophisticated espionage process through the invisible probing of the military, political and industrial archives of other countries, as well as the cunning entry of the projected consciousness into the minds, brains or human bodies of military leaders, political leaders and the members of the embassies of foreign powers.

Invisible. Some countries already take seriously and spend huge sums of money on the creation of their own team of *invisible men.*

Frequency. The observation and collection of information in vital, strategic areas – which is invisible to others and direct and first-hand to the projected projector – and their subsequent report, have actually been used with greater frequency than the public imagines. It is not complicated, because distances and physical barriers do not exist for the consciousness projected outside the human body.

Counterespionage. It becomes far more difficult, compared to routine extraphysical espionage, to detect extraphysical espionage executed by another or, in other words, efficiently perform *extraphysical counterespionage.*

Experiments. In 1973, the Central Intelligence Agency (CIA) of the United States of America performed fully conscious long-distance experiments with the well-known North American sensitives Ingo Swann and Patrick H. Price, conducted by parapsychologists Harold E. Puthoff and Russel Targ at the Stanford Research Institute (SRI) in the state of California, obtaining results which were auspicious and extremely positive for them.

Descriptions. In controlled tests of traveling clairvoyance, the spy-projectors precisely described top-secret military installations and even the contents of confidential archives at these bases. In one of the experiments with Pat Price, the detailed description of a hidden Soviet installation in the Ural Mountains was confirmed by CIA agents in the former Soviet Russia. Both of the abovementioned sensitives extended their projective espionage to China and CIA contacts in the People's Republic confirmed the precision and accuracy of the descriptions.

Scheme. Another scheme of bellicose extraphysical espionage, for example, is based on the undue, temporary and direct appropriation of top-secret maquettes or blueprints for strategic defense, recent inventions, new arms projects, equipment blueprints, vehicle designs and other studies of this nature.

Vestiges. This goal can be achieved by immediately copying the blueprints in the spy-country and later returning them, also extraphysically, to the place from which they were temporarily removed. This is the type of crime that is apparently perfect to human eyes, or the clean, concise infraction, leaving no trails, marks, signs, fingerprints, clues or traces of any type; and thus without creating "inopportune and undesirable" corpus delicti.

Biteleportation. The entire abovementioned scheme, although difficult, is totally feasible in ordinary life, as much in theory as in practice, as it occurs in the extraphysical tropospheric dimension, although demanding an enormous amount of work. In other words, it requires two successive projections by the acting intraphysical consciousness who goes and comes, twice, from the spying country to the country that is being spied upon; performing the transportation of objects or roundtrip biteleportation; and, what is more, the alternant dematerialization-transport-rematerialization, also twice, in each location.

Secrets. Nevertheless, the author does not advise any lucid consciential projector to even try to extraphysically discover: the secret formulas of soft drinks; the nuclear codes of Washington and Moscow; bank account numbers in Switzerland and other countries; the secret of Fatima; and other secrets considered to be well-guarded by the world.

Police. Police investigations executed successfully by projected projectors, through the exteriorization of the consciousness induced by hetero-hypnosis are very well-known. They have the purpose of: tracking missing or kidnapped persons; locating airplanes that have crashed in unknown or inhospitable locations; examining crime scenes; correctly identifying delinquents. On this point, the tasks of projective espionage become positive beyond a doubt and are within the reach of any person willing to develop them.

Warning. Acts of extraphysical espionage, however, are problematic since they are based on malevolent objectives – or unethical, anticosmoethical reasons – which are directly contrary to the principles of cosmoethics, involving misuse of the powers of the human consciousness. They thereby cause negative, serious and unpredictable consequences, whether immediately or soon after their execution, for the entire team of participants of operations of these consciential wars, beginning with, and mainly with, the spy-projector.

Universalism. It is incidentally worth clarifying that unethical reasons are extremely relative. The interrelationship between persons and the lack of understanding between them, although having a positive intention on the part of one of them, is unethical in accordance with the analysis and capacity for understanding on the part of the other. Thus, "unethical" is dependent upon the mental amplitude or degree of universalism of the persons affected. Therefore, what should prevail here, above all, is the capacity to receive the effect, through the actions performed and the subsequent dampening of the vibrations and actions emitted by neophobes. Human life is always thus, and this characterizes consciential evolution. The real level of cosmoethics varies from person to person and is contingent upon lucid intraconsciential self-evolution.

Backfire. The mechanisms of the ever-present law of karma (backfire, boomerang effect, cause and effect or action and reaction) exclude no one, not even the projected intraphysical consciousness or the extraphysical consciousnesses willing to cooperate in positive or negative acts of espionage.

Business. The companies or legal firms which have been created in order to commercially exploit extrasensory powers have been using spy-projectors successfully on their staffs in the United States of America.

Research. In the fulfillment of contracts signed with large corporations, these specialized firms address a diversified field of action by performing research in a parapsychic manner, or through animic (intraconsciential) and parapsychic (with the intervention of another consciousness together with the intraphysical consciousness) processes, such as the following 7:

1. **Tracking.** The tracking of missing persons.
2. **Archeology.** Archeological investigation.

3. **Ships.** The location of sunken ships.

4. **Cities.** The location of underground cities.

5. **Reserves.** The location of subterranean reserves of minerals, natural gas and petroleum.

6. **Prospective.** Forecasts of the prices of precious metals – silver, gold – for private investors.

7. **Computer science.** The production of psychic videogames, like Psi Ball, in which the player, using only mental force, without pressing any buttons, tries to keep the ball in the center of the screen.

Intrusion. Soviet parapsychological research sought, for some decades, maintaining a rigorous ultra-materialist-dialectical posture, to achieve the main objective of influencing or controlling the emotions or behavior of persons at a distance, endeavoring to act upon the frequency and intensity of the brainwaves of others, through the energetic impulsion of the will, directing them toward their interests of political domination. In other words: they sought to intentionally create intraphysical intruders who are aware of the intrusion that they intentionally practiced. To this end, they applied the greatest diversity of drugs, hypnosis and instruments in order to intensify the parapsychism of the sensitives.

Confidential. In addition to everything that has been presented here, it is sad to affirm that there is a military use of projectiology for sabotage and espionage. Projectiological subjects, in certain – extremely interested – official government circles, are also considered to be and are classified as confidential, secret, marked by the indefectible seal of top secret, with dossiers prohibited to the public, still far from being open research.

Contributions. It is to be hoped, however, that the impressive multimillion dollar and multimillion ruble investments applied in these new research areas will bring relevant, albeit long-term, contributions in favor of basic, fraternal, therapeutic, universalistic, illuminating projectiological investigations of the human consciousness.

Bibliography: Andreas (36, p. 58), Boswell (174, p. 100), Browning (213, p. 112), Ebon (456, p. 16), Edwards (464, p. 144), Farrar (496, p. 191), Greene (635, p. 99), Gris (645, p. 434), Linedecker (932, p. 54), Machado (968, p. 73), Mc Rae (1023, p. 27), Miranda (1051, p. 311), Monroe (1065, p. 164), Steiger (1601, p. 84), Tanous (1647, p. 61), Targ (1651, p. XIII), Vieira (1762, p. 97), Webb (1804, p. 77), Wilson (1856, p. 126), Yeterian (1893, p. 17).

---

476. LUCID PROJECTION AND ART IN GENERAL

Definition. Art: the activity involving the creation of sensations or states of consciousness that are generally of an esthetic nature, but that are charged with deep, inner experience capable of eliciting the desire for renovation in another.

Synonymy: artistic work.

Works. Ever since the nineteenth century, lucid projections have inspired the elaboration of countless literary works, poems, stories, soap operas and novels. Some of these works are only fiction, while others relate true cases, dramatic experiences, real extraphysical romances or, in other words, true stories that occurred with the actual authors depicted as characters. Many of these authors are famous writers, while others are sometimes well-known parapsychic intraphysical consciousnesses or simply students of projectiology, who gradually assume a place of significance in the general scheme of human culture.

Prose. In the area of prose, the following are 22 novels of note written on the theme of lucid projection: *Louis Lambert,* by Honoré de Balzac (1799-1850); *...Entonces Seremos Dioses, En la Noche de los Tiempos* and *Rumbos Humanos,* by Rodolfo Benavides (1907-); *Voyage en Astral,* by Mme. Ernest Bosc; *Entre Dois Mundos,* by Antoinette Bourdin; *Zanoni,* by Edward George Earle Bulwer-Lytton (1803-1873); *Papillon,* by Henri Charrière (1907-1973); *Estela,* by Nicolas Camille Flammarion (1842-1925); *Do Outro Lado,* by Wilson Frungilo Júnior (1949-); *Resurrection,* by William

Alexander Gerhardie (1895-1977); *A Farewell to Arms,* by Ernest Hemingway; *The Island,* by Aldous Leonard Huxley (1894-1963); *O Filho de Zanoni,* by Francisco Valdomiro Lorenz (1872-1957); *Peter Ibbetson,* by George Louis Palmella Busson Du Maurier (1834-1896); *Récits d'un Voyaguer de l'Astral,* by Anne & Daniel Meurois-Givaudan; *The Octopus,* by Benjamin Franklin Norris (1870-1902); *Adonai,* by Jorge E. Adoum; *Nas Voragens do Pecado,* by Yvonne do Amaral Pereira; *Metrô para o Outro Mundo,* by José Herculano Pires; *Confidências de Um Inconfidente,* by Marilusa Moreira Vasconcellos; *Ave, Cristo,* by Francisco Cândido Xavier (1911-).

Poetry. Among the poetic compositions specifically conceived objectifying the departure of the consciousness from the human body, the following stand out: *The Prisoner*, by Emily Brontë; *La Nuit de Décembre,* by Alfred de Musset; *Album,* by Wilhelm Busch.

Opera. The novel *Peter Ibbetson* by George Du Maurier, was adapted for opera, with music written by Deems Taylor.

Fiction. In early science fiction stories, teleportation appeared in the form of lucid projection in the following period: *Urânia* (1899), by the French astronomer, sensitive and writer Camille Flammarion; *The Stolen Body* (1898), by the English writer Herbert George Wells (1866-1946); and *Star Rover,* by the North American author Jack London (1876-1916). Many other science fiction (sci-fi, SF) works were subsequently written, wherein lucid projection appears together with reports of phenomena such as levitation, telepathy, telekinesis and traveling clairvoyance.

Children. Authors of children's books sometimes enter the domain of lucid projection in order to compose stories for children. An example of this is Raphael Américo Ranieri, the author of *João Vermelho no Mundo dos Espíritos,* published by Livraria Allan Kardec Editora, of São Paulo, SP, Brazil. This is a story about 2 miniprojectors, João Vermelho and Glorinha, and their instructive excursions outside the human body.

Paintings. The projected consciousnesses of many painters have been acquiring inspiration in the extraphysical dimension through lucid projections to paint on their canvasses. Examples of this type are encountered in the pictographic works of William Blake (1757-1827), Peter Hurkos (pseudonym of Pieter Cornelis van der Hurk: 1911-1988), and Ingo Swann.

Comics. In the popular creations of comic book stories (comic strips) – the so-called eighth art – dozens of authors, scriptwriters and artists, over various decades, have built their stories based on lucid projections. Of all the comic strip heroes, however, the attributes of *The Phantom,* created by the American E. C. Stoner, should be singled out. It was introduced in Portuguese, in Brazil, with N. 25 of the biweekly color magazine *O Guri,* in June of 1941, p. 22-31.

Interiorization. With story line by Roy Thomas, drawings by John Buscema and production by George Klein, the superhero *Doctor Strange* has been shown leaving projected in the extraphysical body, including drawings of his consciential interiorization, as can be seen in the monthly magazine *Heróis da TV,* by Rio Gráfica e Editora, N. 35, May, 1982, p. 81, 82, 97. The same thing happens in the American color magazine, *Doctor Strange Classics,* Vol. 1, N. 1, March of 1984, from the Marvel Comics Group, with story line by Stan Lee, illustration by Steve Ditko and words by Artie Simek, wherein the consciousness of Dr. Strange transfers itself from one place to another in his "extraphysical form", "etheric form", or "ectoplasmic form" as it is explained in the story itself.

Repercussion. With script by Chris Claremont and John Byrnê, and art by Terry Austin, the story "Psychic War". shows projections of the consciousness in the psychosoma, self-transfigurations and the phenomenon of physical repercussion in the monthly magazine *X-Men*, from Rio Gráfica e Editora, N. 8, July-August, 1982, p. 72-76.

Indigenous. With text by G. L. Bonelli, the hero Tex shows many scenes of lucid projections induced by indigenous persons, as seen in the story "Os Filhos da Noite," in the monthly magazine *Tex,* published by Vecchi, Year VI, N. 89, August, 1982, p. 25, 26, as well as other stories in the same genre.

Holotheca. The holotheca of the Center for Higher Studies of the Consciousness (CHSC), in Iguassu Falls, Parana, Brazil, stores in its collection not only examples of the *O Guri* collection and other abovementioned publications, but also hundreds of other editions of comic book stories, complete collections, a vast library and a considerable amount of material from 22 countries, many of which are based on human lucid projections or the phenomena of projectiology of diverse authors and superheroes.

Bibliography: Ash (57, p. 208), Balzac (72, p. 71), Benavides (108, p. 46; 109, p. 178; 111, p. 10), Bosc (173, p. 25), Bourdin (178, p. 20; 179, p. 30), Browning (213, p. 219), Bucke (218, p. 109), Bulwer-Lytton (221, p. 150), Busch (226, p. 252), Charrière (274, p. 337), Crookall (320, p. 9), Dickens (398, p. 46), Digest (399, p. 274), Dostoyevsky (408, p. 62), Duchatel (430, p. 112), Ebon (453, p. 116), Farrère (497, p. 26), Flammarion (523, p. 60; 525, p. 140), Frungilo Jr. (561, p. 84), Gerhardie (584, p. 11), Giovetti (593, p. 19), Greenhouse (636, p. 188), Hemingway (710, p. 53), Huxley (770, p. 45), King (847, p. 273), London (944, p. 3), Lorenz (949, p. 171), Meurois-Guivaudan (1039, p. 22), Mitchell (1058, p. 354), Norris (1134, p. 262), Pereira (1233, p. 9), Pires (1246, p. 44), Ranieri (1372, p. 14), Ring (1406, p. 37), Sabom (1486, p. 39), Steiger (1601, p. 22), Thiago (1676, p. 33), Vasconcellos (1730, p. 13; 1731, p. 154), Wang (1794, p. 460), Wolman (1863, p. 781), Xavier (1870, p. 90).

---

477. LUCID PROJECTION AND EXTRAPHYSICAL MUSIC

Definition. Extraphysical music: sonorous chords that the projected projector hears in the extraphysical dimension.

Synonymy: metachromatic music; music of the spheres; *nad; nada;* parapsychic music; transcendental music.

Types. The most diverse types of music can be heard by the projected intraphysical consciousness, with or without the identification of its origin; played with instruments, orchestrated or presented by refined multi-voices from invisible throats, in passages of conventional melody, choruses without words or in unknown patterns and arrangements beyond human musical staffs; in brief passages or during the entire period of extraphysical exteriorization and even during the interiorization of the consciousness into the human body.

Effects. The effects of extraphysical music vary from gentle melodies to vibrant marches and vehement rhythms, eliciting compassion or enthusiasm, with or without the evident purpose of music therapy.

Immanence. The harmony often exists and immanently endures in the extraphysical environment, regardless of the existence of resident or autochthonous extraphysical consciousnesses and the projected consciousness that is foreign and alien to the environment.

Relaxation. Music in general is particularly used as a psychological support for psychic self-relaxation, or mental concentration, by novice projectors with some success, establishing one or more points of contact for leaving the human body. Normally, slow pieces such as adagios and andantes lead to tranquilization, greater clarity of thought and self-relaxation, as with: *Adagio* (Tomaso Albinoni: 1671-1750); *The Swan* (Charles Camille Saint-Saëns: 1835-1921); *Coppelia* – extracts (Léo Delibes: 1836-1891); *Swan Lake* (Pëtr Ilyich Tschaikowsky: 1840-1893); "Largo", from the opera *Xerxes* (George Frideric Handel: 1685-1759); *Panis Angelicus* (César Auguste Jean Guillaume Hubert Franck: 1822-1890).

Bibliography: Brittain (206, p. 75), Crookall (338, p. 119), Fodor (528, p. 258), Freixedo (554, p. 42), Greenhouse (636, p. 218), Heindel (705, p. 113), Kardec (824, p. 158), Monroe (1065, p. 124), Muldoon (1102, p. 82), Rogo (1448, p. 18; 1455, p. 9), Shepard (1548, p. 626), Vieira (1762, p. 152), Wheeler (1826, p. 68).

478. LUCID PROJECTION AND THE THEATER

Definition. Theater: the art of representing *life,* costumes and humankind, per se.

Synonymy: dramatic art; dramatology; dramaturgy.

Stage. Appearing on a stage before an audience – whether speaking, acting, dancing, singing, playing a musical instrument or even representing a personality before the public, which is absorbed in the artistic performance – often triggers lucid projections.

Hypotheses. Hypotheses have been proposed that the sound and rhythmic pattern of the human voice, the intense desire to perfect the artistic work and the self-abstraction regarding one's own artistic performance, are the causes of the lucid projections of artists who are on stage.

Ambiguities. Probably the artistic condition of actors – which have to deal with the ambiguities of the attitudes of the various characters that they represent – lead them to altered states of consciousness, notably due to psychosomatics.

Impossibilities. The condition should logically be inserted here, among the greatest ambiguities of *human life,* of the individual living with optimism, inner satisfaction and constant motivation. This, despite recognizing in this current human life, and for an indefinite number of intraphysical lives and intermissive periods to come, the following impossibilities, among others: perfection; a perfect human society; absolute truth; certainty; precision; and besides this – as it is still infinitely improbable to join the two conquests at the same time and place – to know that it is politically more relevant to have *freedom without equality* rather than *equality without freedom.*

Spectators. On the other hand, there are cases of spectators who, motivated by inner exaltation of their involvement in the art of the actors on the stage, have lucidly projected to the ceiling of the theater house.

Bibliography: Crookall (343, p. 6), Digest (399, p. 273), Green (632, p. 48), Greenhouse (636, p. 178).

479. LUCID PROJECTION AND CINEMATOGRAPHIC ART

Definition. Cinematographic art: set of methods and processes used to photographically register and project animated or moving scenes used in movie houses, television stations, videocassette recorders and other types of equipment.

Synonymy: cinema; cinematography.

Television. Cinematographic art, in the cinema as well as on television, including commercials, have sometimes used projectiology themes. However, the exploration of this subject has still not been attributed with the importance it is due, nor has it received the high-quality technical treatment that it deserves, due to social, religious and scientific preconceptions.

Cinema. In cinema, perhaps the most sophisticated approach thus far presented has been *Beyond and Back,* a full-length movie in Technicolor by Sunn Classic Pictures, distributed by Columbia Pictures, produced in 1977, written by Stephen Lord, partly based on the book of the same name by Ralph Wilkerson, produced by Charles E. Sellier Jr., directed by James L. Conway, with music by Bob Summers.

Near-death. This acclaimed film, distributed with the restriction that only those 17 years or older may attend, is based on the fundamental analysis of the true experiences of individuals who were declared clinically dead and came back to human life or, in other words, the near-death experience phenomena.

Evidence. Within its context, however, the film clearly presents, through the narration provided by Brad Crandall: evidence in favor of human survival and lucid consciential projection; consciential blackout; the disturbed zones of the paratropospheric dimension; the phenomenon of consciential self-bilocation;

self-permeability of the psychosoma; surgery and human accidents in relation to lucid projection; the existence of extraphysical helpers; the theory of successive lives; and parapsychic communication between consciousnesses.

Personalities. The film shows dramatic depositions and studies of famous personalities, along with their relationships to parapsychic phenomena, including Louise May Alcott (1832-1888), Hippolyte Baraduc, Elizabeth Barrett Browning (1806-1861), Benjamin Franklin (1706-1790), Ernest Miller Hemingway, Harry Houdini (1874-1926) and Plato.

Critic. Unfortunately, a Brazilian film critic (*O Globo;* Rio de Janeiro, Brazil; newspaper; daily; year LVIII; September 2, 1982; p. 36), summarized a condemnation of *Beyond and Back* in the following sentence: "A fascinating theme brought to the screen with ingenuousness and incompetence." This reference, however, did not discourage the public, which was seen to attend the film with reasonable enthusiasm and hold lively discussions on the themes and scenes at the door of the movie theaters soon after the sessions.

Parable. The 114-minute color film, *Jonathan Livingston Seagull,* released in 1973 by Paramount, directed by Hall Bartlett, is based on the extremely successful work of the same name, by Richard Bach. It is a fantasy or parable on the life of a seagull which intends to fly faster than others and which finally penetrates a perfect world. It tackles the following phenomena and occurrences in projectiology, among others: lucid projection; extraphysical helpers; successive lives; instantaneous extraphysical translocation; unimpeded volitation; extraphysical environments; sudden disappearances. The film was awarded 1 star, in a 4-star rating method that encompasses films besides routine production (Leslie Halliwell; *Film Guide;* 2nd ed.; Granada Publishing; London; 1982).

Others. Besides those already mentioned, the following films which address the phenomena of projectiology should be kept in mind: *Altered States; Somewhere in Time;* as well as the hundreds of other films which are more easily found in contemporary video stores.

Future. *More realistic* cinematographic productions and television mini-series are awaited, in the near future, that present less stereotyped portrayals of persons having parapsychic experiences and are artistically better on the theme of lucid projections, including electronically created images in the studio, so-called *scene simulations*. It will someday be possible to make films about lucid projection that do not look like low budget or "B" movies.

Bibliography: Targ (1651, p. 135), Wilkerson (1848, p. 39).

480. LUCID PROJECTION AND *NAPHOLOGY*

Definition. Naphology: the branch of science which studies, deals with and examines the phenomena and events which are said to exist or occur, but for which there is no scientific explanation, in other words, all types of natural sciences, including pseudosciences *(deviant sciences)* and diverse fields such as alchemy, astrology, cabalism, witchcraft, magic, numerology, possession, superstition and UFOlogy or *navexology*.

Synonymy: heterodox disciplines; anomalous phenomena; nebecism; parasciences.

Parasensitives. Over half a century ago, subjects that were considered by science not to be accessible to direct, common, sensory experience, such as the photon and life, were already labeled as parasensitive. Many phenomena characteristic of the parasciences are still genuinely parasensitive. This is why they require special research and scientific approaches that are different from conventional methods. It is clear that, for this reason alone, these parasciences cannot be classified as mere "occult sciences". The phenomena that are called parapsychic exist. The processes for detecting and analyzing them, however, depend upon us and we have so far been insufficient or impotent to decipher, interpret and decode them.

Dimensions. These amorphous fields of interest and complex studies are still subject to a great deal of questioning, cover-ups and omissions of the truth, and any examination of them engenders heated controversies. Nevertheless, it is undeniable that the theory of parallel dimensions, for example, is of interest to all of them, including studies of lucid consciential projections, because of the extraphysical dimensions to which the intraphysical consciousness is projected.

UFOlogy. Projectiological phenomena are directly or indirectly involved in many areas of life and human behavior. The nature and effects of the psychic phenomena and the psychokinetic energy investigated by parapsychology, in general, and projectiology, in particular, have a relationship mainly with UFOlogy, or para-UFOlogy, and the accumulation of data of one field can always be of interest to the other. This is why these subjects are addressed here.

Abductees. In the interest of speculation, the following 15 are observations and characteristics showing similarities between the experiences of projected projectors and the individuals who allege to have been kidnapped or abducted according to controverted *navexology* reports.

1. Amnesia of entire periods of extraphysical or extraterrestrial events.
2. Instantaneous translocation, including interplanetary translocation.
3. The paralysis of the kidnapping victim is reminiscent of projective catalepsy and the state of slow motion.
4. The appearance of a diversity of lights of various colors and manifestations.
5. The appearance of forms coming out from points of light.
6. The flotation of bodies or vehicles of manifestation of the consciousness.
7. Extraphysical, or non-terrestrial, locations without corners or straight lines and with curved surfaces.
8. Beings *(ufosapiens* or *ufonauts)* having appearances or forms (morphology) which are different from humans, in extraphysical contacts with helpers or extraterrestrials.
9. Beings with eyes that are larger than ordinary human eyes.
10. Telepathic dialogues with mental explanations.
11. Seeing the planet earth smaller, at a distance.
12. Loss of the exact sense of chronological time (a difference in the passage of time).
13. The time of translocation being different from the time that has passed *in the location* of the uncommon experience.
14. Expansion of the consciousness with the potentiation of elaboration of thought.
15. The intensification of parapsychic attributes or faculties.

Reports. The registering of the frequent descriptions and reports of contacts with UFOs through lucid projection should not be ignored. These are facts that speak in favor of the hypothesis that the UFOlogical phenomenon occurs in a dimension of the consciousness and does not come from other planets or the more distant confines of sidereal space. There may, nevertheless, be civilizations of intraphysical consciousnesses with technology that is capable of mastering space-time.

Questions. Among the many hypotheses or questions to be answered in the field of naphology, the following, which are of extreme interest to projectiology, should not be forgotten: What is the relationship between extraphysical helpers and the so-called *sedopianos?* Are ill extraphysical consciousnesses *manodins?* Is there a difference between the terrestrial and the extraterrestrial helper?

Progress. Despite the aforementioned hypothesis on the dimensions of the consciousness, it is worth observing that, according to more recent calculations in the area of astronomy, the physical universe is approximately 20 billion years old; our galaxy, the Milky Way, including our closest fulgurating star, the sun, is approximately 10 billion years old; and this planet, the earth, is about 5 billion years old. Our planet is, therefore, a newcomer in the universe. This leads us to suppose that many stars must exist that are billions of years older than our planet and billions of years older than our sun. Those who reflect upon the degree of progress of science on earth, in only the last century, will easily understand that the advances which can occur in a civilization 1 billion years older than terrestrial civilization is far beyond the limits of our imagination, as 1 billion years is the same as 10 million centuries.

Projection. For evolved civilizations on older inhabited planets – the inhabitants of which have already gone through the stages which we are now beginning – the golden cord, the mentalsoma, the mentalsomatic dimension and other very enigmatic subjects of equal magnitude, which we are still unaware of in all branches of knowledge, have surely ceased to be obscure long ago. Until we achieve these extremely advanced evolutionary stages, the only thing that remains to be done is to produce projections of the consciousness from the human body in order to help scientific research and thereby endorse our theoretical suppositions and decipher our enigmas little by little.

Bibliography: Ald (10, p. 18), Bardens (79, p. 192), Bowles (182, p. 108), Cavendish (266, p. 263), Chaplin (273, p. 160), D'arbó (365, p. 225), Digest (400, p. 227), Freedland (550, p. 82), Freixedo (556, p. 119), Granger (620, p. 107), Grattan-Guinness (626, p. 353), Guirao (663, p. 188), Hammond (674, p. 161), Hitching (727, p. 188), Martin (1003, p. 128), Mishlove (1055, p. 195), Mittl (1061, p. 5), Monroe (1065, p. 253), Ostrander (1172, p. 183), Paula (1209, p. 110), Randles (1371, p. 107), Regush (1382, p. 72), Richmann (1399, p. 54), Roberts (1414, p. 194), Rogo (1458, p. 102), Sachs (1489, p. 155), Schiff (1515, p. 118), Shadowitz (1543, p. 191), Shepard (1548, p. 952), Steiger (1602, p. 280), Tansley (1649, p. 307), Uphoff (1722, p. 151), Vallee (1727, p. 62), Vieira (1762, p. 216), Watson (1800, p. 167), Wilson (1857, p. 83).

481. LUCID PROJECTION AND THE *THETA* PHENOMENON

Definition. *Theta* phenomenon: that phenomenon which refers to survival of the personality or continuation of the consciousness after biological death or death of the human body.

Synonymy: evidence of survival of the consciousness; post-desomatic survival; *psi-theta* research; the question of immortality; the theory of continuation of the consciousness; ultralife research.

Evidence. Projection of the consciousness allows the veteran projector 4 indubitable pieces of evidence regarding the survival of his/her own *self* after the death of the human body:

1. **Vehicles.** Personal proof of the existence of the psychosoma and mentalsoma, which survive biological death or deactivation of the soma (desoma).

2. **Self-bilocation.** The phenomenon of consciential self-bilocation evidences, in a definitive, incontestable manner for the self-bilocator, the existence of his/her lucid consciousness acting without the human body, proving to him/herself, while still breathing among humans, the survival of the *self* (you) after biological death or desoma.

3. **Encounters.** Extraphysical encounters of the projector with familiar personalities that have passed through the transition of physical death of the soma prior to the projectionist.

4. **Desoma.** Observation and often direct, extraphysical, active participation of the projector in the phenomenon of the healthy desoma of another, as a desomatics assistant, through assistential consciential projections.

Motivation. In light of the facts of a personal nature, lucid projection eliminates the preoccupation with physical death and thanatophobia, the morbid fear of death or deactivation of the soma for all who are interested. This can be individually obtained by anyone, as long as that person is sufficiently motivated toward projective practices and experiences. Then, the individuals must prepare themselves (prospective, existential program, existential completism, intermissive period) to continue existing with lucidity and discernment. Suicide is the act that generates maximum frustration for any intraphysical consciousness.

Laboratory. On the other hand, lucid projection is an important area for laboratory experiments with the aim of detecting the continuation of the personality and the survival of the human consciousness after biological death or desoma.

Electroencephalogram. Brain death was previously defined in terms of the electroencephalogram, when indicating a straight line (flat or isoelectric electroencephalogram) or electrocerebral silence (ECS). Nevertheless, the EEG alone, even in ECS, is not always sufficient for defining brain death. If evidence of lucid projection were to be found, by as yet undeveloped methods, during the period in which the person has an isoelectric electroencephalogram, this will demonstrate that the consciousness is not a function of the central nervous system and continues to be active after the decomposition of the human body and, therefore, the physical brain.

Bibliography: Ashby (58, p. 5), Bayless (95, p. 148), Bord (170, p. 381), Crookall (339, p. 105), Currie (354, p. 71), Gauld (576, p. 219), Grattan-Guinness (626, p. 109), Meek (1030, p. 55), Morris (1090, p. 1), Osis (1159, p. 1), Reis (1384, p. 60), Rogo (1445, p. 50), Sherman (1551, p. 197), Thouless (1682, p. 155).

---

482. LUCID PROJECTION AND SUCCESSIVE INTRAPHYSICAL LIVES

Definition. Successive intraphysical lives: the form of survival in which the ego, or the consciousness, returns to human life using a body of flesh and blood, after having experienced the biological death or *desoma* of another physical body or *retrosoma,* and passing through a period of existence in the extraphysical dimension or *intermissive period.* Afterward, the extraphysical consciousness returns to human life through resoma and the entire *resoma-desoma-intermission cycle* recommences over centuries and millennia.

Synonymy: consciousness in series; cycle of opportunities; ECM (extracerebral memory); extracerebral memory; holoresomatics; life-death alternation; metensarcous; metensomatosis; palingenesis; plurality of corporeal lives; plurality of existences; rebirth of the personality; resoma-desoma alternation; seriated consciousness; space-time anchoring; successive lives; transmigration of the soul.

Revegetation. In their own way, plants, insects and subhuman animals also undergo resoma. In botany, *revegetation* occurs. Insects, without *flesh* as we understand it, also go through *reinsectization.* Successive intraphysical lives reach intelligent or consciential principles at all of their levels and evolutionary states.

Reasons. The knowledge or, better still, the acceptance of the theory of successive intraphysical lives, which currently reaches half of the terrestrial population, besides bringing profound implications for human beings, alters their general philosophy, eliminates all racial prejudice, nationalist passion and sexual chauvinism. The innermost knowledge of prior, personal intraphysical existences sometimes becomes of vital necessity, because in these lie the origins of egokarmic and groupkarmic problems and the root of many illnesses which currently afflict certain persons. This thereby gives rise to past life therapy, or reincarnationist therapy.

Research. Besides the spontaneous emergence of memories of previous lives which are intimately connected to the internal evolution of the social being, of recurring nightmares, hypnotic pre-natal regression, deep meditation, special massage techniques and other intraconsciential processes and postures, lucid projection is an efficient research method for individual access by the intraphysical consciousness to his/her past or previous existences through the holomemory and projective or extraphysical self-retrocognitions.

Survival. Existential seriation – or seriality of the lives of the consciousness – is proof of the survival of the ego after the deactivation of the human body, or desoma, the future of the being, through recollection of *past experiences.* Lucid projection is proof of the same survival, through the interdimensional recall of *current experiences.* The implication of the time factor and the action of the mechanisms of memory occur in both cases.

Phenomena. Among the 3 consciential states, the intraphysical state and the projected state are, strictly speaking, projections that stem from the extraphysical state of the extraphysical consciousness, in our current evolutionary level of relative multidimensional self-awareness. Conclusion: existential seriation or seriality of consciential lives are nothing more, in the final analysis, than a projectiological phenomenon or, in other words, a less fleeting projection of the consciousness that nowadays lasts 7 decades on average, according to human chronology.

Processes. Personal existential seriations can be researched by the projected intraphysical consciousness through extraphysical recall or retrocognition, sometimes induced by an extraphysical helper, or psychometrically executed in the paratropospheric dimension. There are, however, those intraphysical consciousnesses who are anxious to know about their previous intraphysical lives, when they were accomplished personalities, because they are currently not realizing what they should. This is a reaction of parapsychic compensation.

Laws. The facts indicate that, for any of the existing methods for recalling past lives, there is a sequence – which is non-random, but controlled by as yet unknown laws or agents – for any multi-secular recollection, whether just a single existence or a series of successive existences.

Key factors. Certain key factors always remain hidden until the consciousness learns the lessons of previous intraphysical lives which have already been recalled.

Conclusion. The memories which have occurred are like an elucidative conclusion and are advantageous for the evolution of the consciousness, intensifying the sense of responsibility for the individual regarding the personal multiexistential cycle.

Autobiography. On certain occasions, a consciousness (intraphysical or extraphysical) looks for a personality in the extraphysical dimension and never encounters it. It was that person itself. The authentic multiexistential identification of a figure which was well-known in the past is more difficult to admit publicly. It is sometimes better to keep the discovery a secret. Since the past cannot be changed, why then worry about the fact, creating problems for yourself? The best option is for someone to participate by providing answers in programs such as *O Céu é o Limite* (*The Sky is the Limit*, a Brazilian TV show), obviously using his/her pre-resomatic autobiography or personal holobiography.

Purpose. The main purpose of the lucid projection of the intraphysical being is the gradual elimination of the need for the consciousness to undergo resoma, thus freeing it from the cycles of successive intraphysical lives. The *anti-existential-seriation function* of lucid projection makes it the liberator from the cycle of rebirths and *redeaths* or resomas and desomas.

Senility. The process of aging, arteriosclerosis or human senility is a teleological part of the mechanisms of successive intraphysical lives. When the intraphysical consciousness, in the final part of intraphysical existence, has to prepare to return to his/her extraphysical origin (extraphysical hometown), he/she begins to insistently and fixedly recall – due to the biological alterations imposed by the passage of time and the use of the human body – his/her experiences from infancy and youth, those companions and beings who have preceded him/her to the grave or crematorium and who he/she will inevitably soon reencounter under the injunctions of the law and groupkarmic interprison. It is from this that pathological unconscious evocations are born.

Disappearance. Existential seriation, as an evolutionary process, gradually disappears on its own, on each planet, through lucid projection. The average inhabitants – beginning with the *irruption of the psychosoma* in human life – continue to make the surrounding extraphysical dimension more and more similar to, and intimately identify with, the physical dimension, and this, in turn, with the extraphysical dimension, such that one gradually absorbs the other. This makes successive intraphysical lives lose their raison d'être. At this point, the average of the inhabitants of the planet will have already reached the 7th stage in the scale of the state of continuous consciousness. This is the case from a collective point of view because, with regard to the individual consciousness, evolution can be performed through more advanced stages faster than the average of the planetary population through *petifreeness, evolutiology* and *serenology.*

Formula. The formula of the endless evolution of the perfectible consciousness, through the chain of existential seriation, is expressed by the individual, consciential condition, in relation to the human body through time or, in other words, through the following 5 steps:

1. *Day before yesterday:* worse.
2. *Yesterday:* bad.
3. *Today:* good.
4. *Tomorrow:* better.
5. *Day after tomorrow:* very good.

Types. Strictly speaking, the existential seriations of consciousnesses on planet earth are not equal. In fact, there are 2 basic types of human existence here within the *democracy of consciential evolution:* fixed and alternant.

1. **Fixed.** The first type of intraphysical life – fixed or ordinary – is the singular, dense, immutable type, which is only interspersed with 8 hours of sleep and 16 hours of usable wakefulness, on average, every day.

2. **Alternant.** The second type of intraphysical life – alternant, diversified and enriched – is the union of two simultaneous, interwoven, alternating lives, which are consecutive, one in the ordinary, physical waking state and the other with the intraphysical consciousness projected with lucidity in the extraphysical dimensions.

Percentage. In the second type, the human lifetime is lived with one third more waking chronological time and evolutionary opportunities than the first type, and is currently still not achieved by even 1% of intraphysical humanity living on this planet.

Interest. However, it is noted in the extraphysical dimensions that the time has come to increase the percentage of the second type of existence among human beings on earth. This is the reason for the accentuated increase of interest in lucid consciential projections observed in the environments of intraphysical crustal life, as much as in the environments of extraphysical life (paratroposphere).

Groups. According to this hypothesis (without any concern regarding elitism) of successive, alternant intraphysical and extraphysical lives – which endeavors to support a convergence of evidence – it is considered that intraphysical consciousnesses can be classified into 5 groups:

Group 1. All of terrestrial humanity, or 100% of the population, for example, currently 6 billion persons throughout earth, in theory, have *nonlucid* consciential projections every night.

Group 2. Approximately 20% of this same humanity, or 1.2 billion persons, have *semilucid* consciential projections.

Group 3. Approximately 1%, or 60 million persons, have *conscious* or totally lucid consciential projections.

Group 4. A minimal percentage, perhaps one thousandth, it is supposed, or 60 thousand persons, spread throughout all continents and countries, may already be composed of *alternant* intraphysical beings.

Group 5. A high percentage, perhaps the majority of the 80% or the 4.8 billion persons who only conscientially project in an unconscious manner, seem to have undergone resoma without passing through a full second desoma, thereby living with the remains of the silver cord or the (denser) energetic parabody of the previous human life (last retrosoma), in a *condition of being more tightly locked* within the human body. This logically explains the high rate of nonlucid consciential projections and the condition of generalized somnambulism of current terrestrial humanity in regard to the extraphysical world or multidimensionality.

Organicism. In the research fields of biology and medicine, in general, and anatomy and physiology, in particular, nothing was found to evidence the existence of *anchored and alternant* persons, and *free and locked* persons, because the scope and capacity of the operation of these fields of science remain exclusively restricted to the organicist, human, cerebral, psychic or intracerebral scope of personalities. In order to detect these conditions, it is urged that the energetic parabody or holochakra, and the psychosoma be researched parapsychically, beyond the human body. It is therefore hoped that parabiology, paramedicine, para-anatomy and paraphysiology will consider these and many other advanced themes in a timely manner. The concept of the so-called *bioplasmic body,* presented as a *discovery* in the former Soviet Union, still does not transcend the limits of organic matter. We await the future, while continuing to research.

Chart. In a summary-chart of the percentages and classifications of individuals, their consciential projections and lifetimes on this planet today (fig. 482), it can be seen that: in population group 5 – included within the percentage of group 4 – are those individuals who are definitely interested in projectiology; in population group 4 – within percentage group 3 – adolescents and youths are included who spontaneously left the human body with a degree of lucidity during a certain period and later forgot about the matter, being pressured by the demands of human life; in population group 3, persons are found who experienced lucid dreams; in population group 2 is the assembly of those intraphysical consciousnesses in general who are completely indifferent or, more to the point, unaware of the themes of consciential projection.

Consanguineous. *Consanguineous lifetimes* can predispose animic-parapsychic phenomena between individuals, including auric coupling, joint lucid projection and others. For example: one of two unmarried sisters, who are very close, undergo desoma while still young. The surviving sister, after marrying, receives the extraphysical consciousness of the extraphysical sister, which is going through resoma, as her daughter (consanguineous lifetime) and both of them, now mother and daughter, present a mutual disposition or greater capacity for producing the phenomenon of auric coupling and lucidly projecting together.

Career. With the passage of time, the animist-sensitive, the philosopher, the artist, the scientist, the businessperson and the politician create evolutionary experiences of egokarmic and groupkarmic multiexistential careers that are linked in succession by many existences and groups of consciousnesses. In the recent and new soma, the intraphysical consciousness hides from the intruders of his/her past which, in turn, end up taking on other new bodies. In certain cases, however, the responsible knowledge of a previous intraphysical life helps to enhance the current human life. Hence the value of self-retrocognitions, when they are healthy.

Herd. While the consciousness still finds itself stuck in the groove of consanguineous lifetimes, co-racial lifetimes and intergroupkarmic lifetimes (interprisons), its polykarmic account is found to be poor, tainted by narrow sectarianism, factiousness, nationalism or the egoism of the herd, lacking greater and open horizons of pure, universalistic or cosmic megafraternity for the development of its actions. This is the condition of the *lesser mega-ego* (infantile egocentrism) within the *greater mega-ego* (stratified adult egoism).

Glimpse. Depending upon the intraphysical consciousness, he/she can, while still in the final phase of this human existence, begin to glimpse the outlines of the next intraphysical life. This even includes the approximate length of his/her intermissive period, the environment in which he/she will live, the probable location of the future resoma and the basic conditions of the new terrestrial stage, including the directives and bases of the existential program.

Prospectives. This can be forecast by the intraphysical consciousness without resorting to precognitions or futurological calculations, but simply through deductions of logical prospectives, when consciously projected in the extraphysical dimension, or even in the ordinary, physical waking state.

Self-intrusions. We currently constantly and irresistibly follow in the same exact footsteps (self-thosenic signatures, self-relays) of other previous intraphysical lives. The most subtle self-intrusions are those which are composed of spontaneous retrocognitions that surface in the memory precisely in the period of the epilogs of groupkarmic rescues, on the eve of final settlements in the closing of accounts.

Identities. The consciousnesses of the karmic group are the same, presenting themselves in other somas, other clothing and other physical identities, having the same familiar tendencies, somewhat improved, faced with the consequences of the role they played in the dramas, which are about to be interred, thereby ascending each step within the multidimensional cycle in the scale of evolution. In 1 century, 5 centuries or 8 centuries, the actors are the same, the roles are similar, on average improving minimally, little by little.

Reencounters. Existential seriation promotes – everywhere, anytime, with all those who appear and cross our path – inter-secular, inter-racial, international, inter-social, inter-sexual, intertendentious reencounters.

PERSONS vs. CONSCIENTIAL PROJECTIONS vs. HUMAN RESOMAS

Population Groups	Percentages (%)	Terrestrial Humanity (1998)	Consciential Projections	Human Resomas
1 (Total)	100 %	6,000,000,000 Persons	All types	All types
2	80 %	4,800,000,000 Persons	Nonlucid	Anchored and Locked
3	20 %	1,200,000,000 Persons	Semilucid, Lucid and Continuous	Semi-anchored, Free and Alternant
4	1 %	60,000,000 Persons	Lucid and Continuous	Free and Alternant
5	0.001 %	60,000 Persons	Continuous	Alternant

Figure 482

Synchronicities. This is because the coincidences are simple multiexistential effects that, because of our ignorance, mask the compulsory, inevitable, omnipresent and uninterrupted synchronicities. That which we do not understand today, at the precise moment of the liquidation of the groupkarmic account, each one of us will know in detail through the refluxes of the integral memory.

Acts. The acts in which the ego shows itself to be good, comprehensive, forgiving, cooperative, attentive and cosmoethical signify the facilitation *of credit* in the liquidation of holokarmic debts, generating more prolonged *farewells* between the *interdebtors* (interprisoners). These epilogs of evolutionary stages involve extraphysical interplanetary transmigrations.

Earth. The sharp differences between the dimensions – the human and the extraphysical – for those consciousnesses on earth, clearly demonstrate the evolutionary delay in which we still live here, which is clamoring for understanding and the practical application of the principles and techniques of lucid consciential projection. Real life, for all of us, is in the intermissive period.

Path. All indications are that if the intraphysical or extraphysical consciousness, on earth, wishes to definitively free him/herself from the cycle of intraphysical/intermissive lives, he/she should first of all concern him/herself with the understanding and intense practice of assistential service in favor of other consciousnesses through lucid projections. There does not seem to be another shorter evolutionary route or a more practical and immediate solution in sight.

Near-death. The near-death experience (NDE) – in which the intraphysical consciousness extraordinarily *revives* (never dies) in his/her own human body – should not be confused with the theory of successive intraphysical lives, in which the extraphysical consciousness revives and expresses itself on earth, in another *human body,* whether occurring through biological human conception and rebirth, or even, according to the controversial theory, definitively borrowing from another consciousness that is at an adult physical age, in the hypothesis of consciential relay or walk-ins.

Capsule. The act of assembling a panorama of human lucid projection to date, with this large volume, implies the intention of the author to achieve continuity of this well-intentioned analysis in the next personal intraphysical life. This public confession registers, in a multiexistential, anticipated evocation, the desire to encounter this book – or what is left of it as a cohesive, coherent set of ideas with a philosophical, scientific and rational beginning, middle and end – operating like a *time capsule* for individual use somewhere on this earth in the near future. Codes of names and numbers inserted in the text – post-hypnotic autosuggestions – will predispose the recall, subsequent identification and avoidance of any attempt at usurpation of authorship, also post-desomatic, which would be discouraging, in this case.

Research. The author thus launches the human, intraphysical and holokarmic foundations of the relay of simultaneous, personal research of projectiology and successive lives, through more than 1 human body of the consciousness. In this way, the prospection and confirmation of the theory of successive lives is sought for that selfsame person, within that individual, always in the ordinary, physical waking state. Two different questions are posed here: Is this research mere inconsequential pretense on the part of the author? Is all this work compulsory, already coming from the past? We shall see.

Departure. On the ascensional itinerary (route) of departure and return of consciential evolution, the rudimentary consciential principle – initially (path of departure in the evolutionary spiral) impelled only by brute, unconscious, instinctive egoism – is removed from *polykarma.* For example: the unity in the ovary of fish. Next, the consciousness proceeds, stuck, up until *groupkarma.* For example: the subhuman *group-soul.* It next arrives, unconsciously, at *egokarma* (dependent individualization) with a sectarian egoistic mentality. For example: the guardian of dogmas, the ideological patroller of orthodoxy (ultra-orthodoxy, fundamentalism), the prisoner of personal belief systems (religious, philosophical, political), the executor of consolation (consolation task).

Return. From this, the consciential principle travels back along the evolutionary spiral. Now moved by the conscious altruism of pure megafraternity, it leaves *egokarma* in a secondary position, detoxifying itself from egoism or from itself *(inflated ego, mega-ego).* It balances itself in a just relationship with its *groupkarma*. For example: the evolutionary team (groupality). From here, it finally returns to its origins, *polykarma*. Then, entirely aware of the holokarmic process, it has the refined notion of interdependence or ample free will, with a mentality which is cleansed, completely altruistic (full independent individualization) or universalistic. For example: the individual who seeks consciential maturity, the person who follows personal altruistic principles and not doctrines (leashes of the ego), the executor of clarification (clarification task).

Fingerprints. It seems that the element which would best prove the theory of successive lives is the matching of the fingerprints of 2 beings who were reborn in different periods. There are difficulties in researching this hypothesis. It is first necessary to know if it is possible. If the fingerprints are the same in two intraphysical lives of the consciousness, this fact will prove that they come from the psychosoma. And the laws of genetics, in this case? Dactyloscopy, as a science, only really came into effect after 1890. Thus, this research must necessarily encompass only those human lives from that date until the present, a period in which it is presumed that dactyloscopic registers exist in the archives of some countries. Fingerprints can prove the phenomena of physical bilocation, but this is another matter.

Animals. According to that which can be deduced from the facts observed so far, rebirth or successive lives *seem to occur* exclusively within the same evolutionary species until the consciential principle evolutionarily surmounts it and moves on to another more evolved species, whether on this or another planet. This is why the veteran lucid projector encounters extraphysical animal consciousnesses in the extraphysical dimension – evolutionarily inferior to the level of the human consciousness – which have not been reborn on this planet. This promotes the supposition that many of the beings that represent species in extinction on earth – so strongly defended by ecologists today – may continue their multiexistential evolutionary cycles on other planets throughout the cosmos. There may be planets inhabited only by dinosaurs, for example, and others having animal populations with a much greater variety – intraconsciential forms and levels – than on earth.

Theory. Lucid projection experiments and the experience of extraphysical retrocognitions allow the lucid intraphysical being to research and apply the theory of multiexistential analysis in his/her own existence. In this way, his/her personal identity in this human life is characterized in comparison with him/herself in another, previous intraphysical life, whether it is the previous life, or one or more less recent lives (holomemory, retrosomas, paragenetics). In this way, the individual can enumerate, with extreme self-critique, his/her improvements and evolutionary progress, as well as his/her failures and apparent consciential regressions.

Facets. Through the theory of multiexistential analysis, the individual can endeavor to compare personalities, the similarities between their experiences, exact identifications, inner progress, evident egokarmic indemnification and real or apparent regressions. In this way, at least 10 personal facets of each human period are observed: physical constitution; temperament; human life; scholarship; personal style; religion and religiosity; parapsychism; science and occupation; personal interests and research; and activity in the holokarmic account.

Analyses. In light of the presented theory, after listing over one hundred aspects in the comparison of personalities, the researcher generally arrives at a minimum of 7 analytical observations:

1. **Surmounting.** At a certain point, the consciousness begins to concern itself with surmounting its pluri-secular insufficiencies, in existential seriation or interlinked intraphysical lives, consecutive tasks that continue from one human life to another (consciential self-relays).

2. **Indemnifications.** The appearance of "intraconsciential progress", after the interference of "past causes", characterizes the condition of "evident indemnifications".

3. **Immunization.** The person is immune to public opinion, because he/she may constantly hear or read those who praise and those who criticize, with sensibleness or passion, about that which he/she did, neglected to do (deficit-producing omissions), or affirmed in another life, sometimes not in the last life, but the next to the last or the second to the last.

4. **Para-hypocrisy.** After the establishment of incontrovertible evidence, it becomes necessary to take care regarding acts of para-hypocrisy.

5. **Policy.** The consciousness which is awake to its evolutionary, consciential policy, in the current intraphysical life, not only needs to return to grow evolutionarily, but should ensure that this growth does not repeat distortions (dispensable self-mimicries) which occurred in the past. It will then incorporate the teachings and new conceptions that the previous experience bequeathed it. The consciousness should consider itself as being in frank development, in a singular situation of pluriexistential self-knowledge, enjoying a maximal degree of consciential autonomy – or self-aware free will – without limiting itself to stratifying doctrines, outdated formulas, sectarian principles, parties or factiousness and stagnating conventions, making better use of its intraconsciential paragenetic potential, without excessive dependence upon human or animal life.

6. **Incoherence.** A disparity of points of view, opinions, principles and types of approach can occur in relation to the current ideas or thoughts of the same personality in two human lives. If there is an improvement in this disparity, an apparent incoherence then occurs or, in other words, a positive change. In this case, the consciousness corrects its own mistakes, critiquing itself and combating its past in a critical intraphysical life. It often *unteaches that which it prescribed* to its evolutionary companions, among the millions of consciousnesses of its karmic group, shouldering all the frustrations that this causes, the more self-aware it is of past facts.

7. **Maturity.** The conquest of consciential maturity becomes extremely relevant in regard to the cycle of successive, individual, intraphysical and intermissive existences. For example: in theory, a consciousness can perform the same human clarification task, in 5 short human lives, each having a maximum of 35 years of human existence – because it will mature more quickly – with very short intermissive periods of 1 lustrum or 5 years at most, in 5 different existential periods, in 5 different countries, situated in 5 different continents, in a total period of only 2 centuries. In this case, the consciousness itself plays the role of "the yeast that leavens the bread" with its coherent ideas and edifications interconnected in diverse locations, periods, peoples, customs, languages and conditions. Is it possible that someone on this planet is already utilizing this scheme, which is so simple and yet so complex? This is another research hypothesis regarding successive intraphysical lives.

Cord. The following is a theory for analysis. There are still 2 types of successive lives, with regard to the action of the silver cord: more evolved and less evolved.

Second. The first type: the more evolved lifetime of a streamlined extraphysical consciousness that has passed through the second desoma or, in other words, that has already discarded the remainder of its silver cord from the previous human life, or the last, most recent life.

First. Second type: the less evolved lifetime, of an extraphysical consciousness that has only passed through the first desoma or, in other words, that has lost only the human body, but still has the *base* of the silver cord, or the remainder of the energetic connections that linked it to the previously developed human body (retrosoma), or even the fetal body, and which began to decay. Many *subintrant* human lives of the same consciousness or, in other words, those having very rapid or short intermissive periods, through abortions which may or may not be pathological but are successive, for example, are included in this second type.

Third. The consciousnesses that have passed through the third desoma, or that have already discarded the psychosoma, no longer undergo resoma and are free consciousnesses (FCs).

Root. It can thereby rationally be concluded that the root or the basic connection of the silver cord in the psychosoma can continue acting in more than 1 intraphysical period of the same consciousness. This signifies that the principles that operate in the creation, formation and development of the silver cord are not as rigid as they seem at first sight.

Locking. The theory of successive lives of the less evolved type, referred to here, rationally explains the occurrence of many cases of intraphysical consciousnesses who are excessively *locked* in their human bodies or, in other words, who live in a more rigorous state of coincidence of their consciential vehicles of manifestation. They are generally found to be more materialized – or *physicalized* – as they have an older silver cord that acts more strongly as a physical anchor or, in other words: because they have a laden psychosoma or one which is denser, even before they are reborn.

These intraphysical consciousnesses tend to have more semilucid projections because they project with the dense, laden psychosoma in paratropospheric environments.

Looseness. On the other hand, it can logically be deduced that the consciousness which went through the more evolved type of resoma is precisely the one that is predisposed to have a loose holochakra or, in other words, a *slippery* psychosoma, because it has a *recently acquired* silver cord. This is the intraphysical being who is more predisposed to lucid and impactful projections.

Excommunication. One of the high points of modern human life is the intensification, as never before in the past, of communication between individuals which can thereby *provide incessant inter-assistance.* For this reason, when the elements of contemporary intraphysical society prefer to close themselves up in a shell-like type of egoism, with little desire for communicating with others; occupying themselves only with themselves; maintaining isolation and a constant narcissistic image, wherein the ego is most relevant in first, second and third place; dialoging less and less with others; avoiding the personal bonds of friendship; living more and more as adepts of instruments *(electronic hermits)* or, in other words, computers, telex, telephone, fax, radio and television, which generates *excommunication;* intraphysical life, for them, substantially loses its use as an evolutionary resource. This is the condition of egolatry (the "me" cult) and of the human robotization in its worst states. The Internet is great, but the internaut (or *netizen*) should not forget the skin-to-skin, pore-to-pore and chakra-to-chakra condition of proxemics. Nowadays, so-called *netizen depression* is discussed and even treated.

Self-critiques. There are consciousnesses that undergo rebirth with the exclusive purpose of correcting their ideological or doctrinaire errors from a previous human life, combating their own past, which is sometimes recent. This signifies scrutinizing themselves (para-self-critique) or, in other words, proceeding with multiexistential, holomnemonic and holo-autobiographical self-critiques through human acts, correcting their own direction and the destiny of those consciousnesses which they helped to push onto ideological sidetracks and evolutionarily stagnating ways.

Improvidence. There are intraphysical consciousnesses who waste their human life like an unconscious cultivator. Those who dedicate themselves to work, using only vulgar, popular knowledge, or common sense, which is transmitted from generation to generation, through informal education, without the application of a method or technique, base themselves only upon imitation and personal experience. Lacking scientific knowledge, the imprudent peasant does not improve the plantations or dynamize personal progress as a consciousness.

Popular. On the one hand, popular knowledge is *sensitive* or, in other words, refers to personal experiences, and is *subjective,* because the consciousness itself organizes its own experiences. On the other hand, it is predominantly *superficial,* or conforms to appearances; is *unsystematic,* not using a systematization of ideas; and is *noncritiquing,* not manifesting in a self-critiquing and heterocritiquing manner.

Repetitions. It is well-known, for example, that the repeated cultivation of the same type of plantation every year in the same location exhausts the soil. It likewise occurs with the consciousness in repetitive or self-mimetic existential seriations with undesirable, unnecessary and already dispensable self-relays.

Renovation. The use of projectiology techniques, through appropriate training, permits the simultaneous use of personal knowledge, paragenetics (innate ideas), in that which is worthwhile and efficient, as well as rational self-knowledge through scientific procedures. These have the purpose of explaining *why* and *how* the phenomena of existential seriation occur, in the attempt to evidence the correlated synchronous facts (holokarma), in a more global, multiexistential, personal, retrocognitive vision. This renovates and accelerates the evolutionary progress of the consciousness.

Desomatics. One of the more recent uses of resoma has been seen in the last few decades, namely avoidance of the premature desoma of an intraphysical consciousness. For example, that mother, together with her husband who gives birth to a younger child, who will be the only chance for the oldest daughter, suffering from leukemia, to continue to live intraphysically. The only hope for the 18-year-old leukemic youth is to be the recipient of a bone marrow transplant.

Bioethics. The donator-baby is conceived, in this case, with this primordial purpose: to be a donor. The total compatibility of the marrow, which is extremely rare between biologically unrelated individuals, is greater between siblings, but even so, the probability is one in four. The new child is an intentionally *fabricated* organ bank. Up to what point is this arrangement within the principles of bioethics or cosmoethics?

Bibliography: ADGMT (03, p. 254), Allgeier (14, p. 135), Andrade (29, p. 129), Banerjee (74, p. 41), Bennett (117, p. 10), Berg (121, p. 71), Besant (132, p. 58), Blavatsky (153, p. 646), Bonin (168, p. 426), Boswell (174, p. 113), Brennan (200, p. 71), Cannon (240, p. 41), Cavendish (266, p. 209), Chinmoy (280, p. 3), Day (376, p. 108), Delanne (385, p. 35), Desmond (394, p. 192), Fiore (518, p. 9), Fodor (528, p. 326), Gaynor (577, p. 154), Glaskin (597, p. 20), Goldberg (606, p. 46), Guirdham (664, p. 157), Head (699, p. 448), Hodson (729, p. 170), Kardec (824, p. 116), Lamont (874, p. 83), Leadbeater (903, p. 155), Lenz (914, p. 106), London (944, p. 205), Martin (1003, p. 105), Meek (1030, p. 103), Müller (1107, p. 173), Paula (1208, p. 104), Pensamento (1224, p. 85), Perkins (1236, p. 5), Pratt (1285, p. 140), Puryear (1341, p. 18), Rochas (1430, p. 39), Russell (1482, p. 25), Shepard (1548, p. 772), Spence (1588, p. 335), Stevenson (1618, p. 12; 1620, p. 456), Toben (1688, p. 76), Vieira (1762, p. 158), Walker (1786, p. 77), Wambach (1793, p. 46), Wang (1794, p. 398), Zaniah (1899, p. 383).

483. EXISTENTIAL SERIES

Definition. Existential series: the condition of continuous alternation of one period of life after desoma (extraphysicology) and one period of life after resoma (intraphysicology) comprising the incessant evolutionary itinerary of the consciousness until it frees itself from the compulsory cycle of intraphysical rebirths.

Synonymy: Abred circle (Druidism); human life-desoma alternation; intermission-resoma binomial; *multiexistential cycle.*

Intermission. There are 3 consciential states: the desoma state, the resoma state and the projected state. The desoma state *re*terminates with resoma and *re*commences with desoma. The interval existing between one human life and another constitutes the intermissive period or the intermission.

Holokarma. The karmic accounts, or the relationship of the consciousness with the law of cause and effect or action and reaction, can be classified into 3 basic types:

1. The account of the individual or egokarma (inner life).
2. The group account (resoma group) or groupkarma (private life).
3. The collective account or polykarma (public life).

Predominance. The predominance of 1 type of karmic account over the other 2 has a powerful influence in the category and compulsoriness of the existential series of the consciousness.

Criteria. The facts indicate that various criteria are used in the implantation of the seriality of intraphysical existences, according to the characteristics of the evolutionary level of each consciousness, which is in constant progress. Any generalization on this point will be erroneous. Each case needs to be analyzed in detail, separately. In theory, human calendars have little influence upon the criteria that regulate the multiexistential cycles.

Choices. The more evolved the consciousness, the greater its scope of free will and the broader its range of existential choices. Within the criteria that establish the existential series, the following 4 can be singled out as initial working hypotheses:

1. **Groupkarmality.** The criterion applied according to the expression of the group karmic account (groupkarma) of the consciousness, with its group karmic debt being greater than its personal karmic debt. In this case, the length of its human life and the length of its intermissive period depend, over a long evolutionary period, upon its karmic debts and the cycle of the components of its evolutionary group. A great number of consanguineous human lives are included in this criterion; the consciousnesses

possessing a level of individualization that is still very restricted; the participants of group suicides (more than one suicide).

Groupkarma. In the criterion of pure karmality (groupkarma), 2 groups of groupkarmic accounts are distinguished: firstly, the one related to the consciential principles (consciousnesses) that are of a similar or identical evolutionary level (legal consanguineous family); and secondly, the one related to evolutionarily inferior levels of consciential principles (beings of the reborn individual's para-ecosystem, including viruses, bacteria, germs, worms).

2. **Complementarity.** The criterion applied, for example, to the consciousness that either directly (conscious) or indirectly (unconscious), whether at once or slowly, committed individual suicide (egokarma), and went through resoma immediately, as soon as possible, in order to complement the final period it did not live out in intraphysical life. The consciousness of the suicide tends to reduce the experiences of its intermissive periods over an extended period along its evolutionary way. Suicide is one of the factors having the greatest influence upon direct changes of the criteria that operate in the existential series. Another case of complementarity is death provoked by dementia due to an impacted molar (wisdom tooth), for example.

3. **Activity.** The criterion is applied according to the demands of the pluriexistential activities of the extraphysical consciousness that is evolutionarily above average. The periods of human life vary as greatly as the intermissive periods, in this case, and are independent from each other. Nevertheless, in this case, the unwavering tendency arises for the intermissive periods to become increasingly dilated, which is understandable. The consciousness' life of human leadership sometimes requires direct extraphysical assistance or post-desomatic work in the intermissive period for an extended period (polykarmality).

4. **Equality.** The criterion applied to average consciousnesses that are still very tropospheric in their tendencies, having a personal karmic debt (egokarma) greater than their group karmic debt (groupkarma). It is based on the duration of human life, where the intraphysical life is equal to the intermission or, in other words: human life = intermission. If the consciousness, for example, lived on earth for 7 decades, it will have the equivalent of a 7-decade inter-resomatic period ahead. And so it goes.

Lucidity. Consciential lucidity or, in other words, the level of awareness of the ego in relation to the reality of its series of personal existences, can be composed of 3 conditions:

1. **Unconsciousness.** In the condition of unconsciousness regarding its own existential series, the criteria of karmality and complementarity are included.

2. **Self-awareness.** In the condition of self-awareness regarding its own existential series, the criterion of activity is inserted.

3. **Ambivalence.** In the condition of consciential ambivalence or, in other words, unawareness or self-awareness (cognition) regarding its own existential series, the criterion of equality is involved.

Application. One of the practical applications of knowledge of the existential series can already be identified here: if there are many consciousnesses on this earth (the overwhelming majority) which have still not liberated themselves from their existential series, there already exists a good number of these same consciousnesses which are able to change the criterion regarding the series of their existences through their current human life. From this arises the importance of the conscious life of the intraphysical consciousness currently in development on this planet. In summary: to be free of the cycle of resomas from one moment to the next is impracticable, but to alter the criterion of the multiexistential cycles of the upcoming intraphysical lives for the better is practicable for many resomant consciousnesses.

Models. Let us observe the logic, rationality and discernment of the framework shown here regarding the existential series. If you do not agree, find it very simplistic, or still very lacking regarding certain details of the structure of consciential evolution, endeavor to compile another model that better addresses the existential series. In this way you will actually be cooperating with the projectiological and even philosophical research in progress, and its practical and even cosmoethical consequences.

484. PROJECTION WITH CONTINUOUS SELF-AWARENESS

Definition. Projection with continuous self-awareness: the experiment in which the intraphysical consciousness maintains uninterrupted lucidity at all times, with prolongation of the waking state through sleep, from takeoff until interiorization and return to the ordinary, physical waking state.

Synonymy: consciential projection without blackout; projection of continuous wakefulness; self-awareness in 2 worlds; waking consciential projection.

Rarity. Projection with continuous self-awareness from beginning to end of the experiment has, as its essential characteristic, an absence of any blackout or interruption in continuity of intact wakefulness, the projector maintaining self-awareness in two or more dimensions. This is a rare and extremely impactful experience for the intraphysical consciousness.

Conditions. The projection with continuous self-awareness generally occurs in psychophysical conditions which are ideal for the projector, after sleeping many hours, in the early morning, at a time when the environment is propitious for the experiment. It more commonly occurs spontaneously, in the bedroom where the human body is located. However, it can be provoked and becomes easier to repeat after a few experiences.

Takeoff. The high point of the projection with continuous self-awareness is in the entirely lucid takeoff, the most difficult stage for the projector to obtain, when the consciousness (you) perceive slowly, in detail, in an incontestable and definitive manner, the sensations of the dichotomy of the forces of the silver cord. The greater part of the cord retracts to the human body and the lesser part goes along with the projected intraphysical consciousness.

Sensations. Besides the dichotomy of the energies of the silver cord, the individual perceives intracranial sounds that are generally mild and provoked by the energies of exteriorization. This occurs in a joint action of the partially exteriorized silver cord and the extraphysical head of the psychosoma which exteriorizes itself, as well as the impressive condition of lightness acquired in a lightning-fast manner by the consciousness that escapes the perceptively heavy chains of the human body and the indescribable state, beyond weightlessness and immateriality. The projector has an inner, firsthand, absolute certainty of the unmistakable difference between one inferior condition and another evolved condition.

Step. The *projection* with continuous self-awareness is the first individual and inevitable step for the intraphysical consciousness toward achieving the *state* of continuous self-awareness.

Hypnagogy. In the major projection with continuous self-awareness, the natural consciential states of hypnagogy and hypnopompy cease to exist, without any negative consequence occurring for the intraphysical projector.

Bibliography: Baker (69, p. 76), Desmond (394, p. 192), Muldoon (1105, p. 231), Paziente (1212, p. 42), Powell (1278, p. 106), Reis (1384, p. 63), Vieira (1762, p. 145), Weor (1819, p. 78).

485. STATE OF CONTINUOUS SELF-AWARENESS

Definition. State of continuous self-awareness: the extremely rare condition of the intraphysical consciousness, or extraphysical consciousness, which has achieved continuity of absolute, lucid awareness during the entire period of biological as well as integral consciential life, in the passage of chronological time as we understand it, or in the state of "immortality" of self-discernment.

Synonymy: consciential *continuum;* continuity of awareness; continuous wakefulness; etheric bridge; mental *continuum;* projective *continuum;* psychophysiological ascesis; state of permanent alertness; unification of self-awareness; uninterrupted awareness; uninterrupted wakefulness.

Steps. The awareness and full application of the resources of lucid projection constitute an advanced conquest in the evolution of terrestrial humanity. The human being currently endeavors to overcome 10 distinct steps in his/her development, in random order:

1. *Homo sapiens,* a type of being endowed with reason and astuteness.
2. *Homo loquax,* the animal with a human body, which speaks, reads and writes.
3. *Homo habilis,* which invents manufactured products.
4. *Homo faber,* which makes and uses tools, developing the resources of technology.
5. *Homo economicus,* the proprietor or owner of assets and merchandise.
6. *Homo informaticus,* which recognizes the need to learn and the need to teach through interconsciential communication.
7. *Homo maniacus,* which is impassioned and becomes fanatic, when still dominated by the parabody of desires and the emotions, or the psychosoma.
8. *Homo humanus,* which acquired the sentiments of compassion, a humanitarian sense, the idea of abnegation and justified cosmoethical self-renunciation.
9. *Homo psychicus,* which is anxious to amplify its own self-awareness.
10. *Homo sapiens cosmicus,* which begins to explore the physical universe through astronautics.

Projectius. The human being now achieves the status of *Homo projectius,* that in which he/she is able to be temporarily liberated from physical life, producing the projection of the lucid consciousness from the rustic body of blood, skin and bones in a voluntary manner, or merely through the exercise of his/her own will.

Percentage. Currently, on this planet, the majority of intraphysical beings – even those who produce consciential projections with lucidity – do not even recall an average of 20% of their extraphysical experiences. The ideas and events which are acquired and experienced in projections gradually blossom later in the ordinary, physical waking state through the channels of common intuition.

Panoramic. According to the theory offered here for research, the state of continuous self-awareness, at an advanced level, provides a simultaneous panoramic perception of all existential dimensions, regardless of where the consciousness may be temporarily headquartered.

Future. In the future, lucid projection, by virtue of its natural manifestations, will tend to substitute the human being's sleep state, until attaining the condition of continuous self-awareness, thereby discarding both day and night, in an existence with no break in continuity. This will bring a concomitant expansion of attributes of the mentalsoma, in a phase of evolution which humanity is destined to inevitably achieve, as a natural acquisition, over the millennia.

Characteristics. The initial high point of projection with continuous self-awareness is in the spontaneous elimination of recollection on the part of the lucid projector. This more advanced period of the consciousness has its beginning in the experience of ordinary lucid projection, subsequently passing through an ascending scale with various basic stages. The condition of continuous self-awareness allows the consciousness to participate in the team of awakened lucid projectors and represents the main superior activity, which is common to all intraphysical and extraphysical beings.

Examples. The following are historic examples of personalities who are presumed to have constructed the bridge between the physically awake consciousness and the sleeping consciousness or, in other words, sampling the condition of continuous self-awareness, in special, specific periods of their intraphysical existences: Gautama Buddha, Jesus of Nazareth, Emanuel Swedenborg, Mohandas Karamchand Gandhi (1869-1948), Ramana Maharshi (1879-1950).

Yoga. The state of continuous self-awareness – or the suppression of consciential discontinuity – is the highest goal of yoga, in all of its modalities, through the unification of 4 types of awareness:

1. Ordinary or diurnal waking awareness.
2. The state of sleep with dreams.
3. Sleep without dreams.
4. Cataleptic awareness.

Level. The state of continuous self-awareness is still at a very rudimentary level on earth. However, it is worth asking the following question: Have some of the so-called extraterrestrial beings, of as yet unconfirmed existence, already mastered the condition of continuous self-awareness?

Age. At what physical age can the consciousness already initiate its state or condition of continuous self-awareness in human life: from infancy, in youth or only in full biological maturity?

Asomnia. To what degree is asomnia, or the capacity of unknown etiology that allows the sensitive to control natural, physiological or delta sleep – to the point of annulling the need for this state over a prolonged period – related to the state of continuous self-awareness?

Bibliography: Brunton (215, p. 158), Bucke (218, p. 67), D'arbó (365, p. 200), Eliade (476, p. 66), Krishna (866, p. 12), Leadbeater (896, p. 26), Lefebure (909, p. 158), Monroe (1065, p. 123), Saraydarian (1507, p. 178), Steiner (1611, p. 129), Vieira (1762, p. 213), Walker (1781, p. 23), Yogananda (1894, p. 266).

486. SCALE OF THE STATE OF CONTINUOUS SELF-AWARENESS

Definition. Conscientiogram: the system of evaluation of the evolutionary flow of the consciousness, or intelligent principle, established from the self-awareness of the lucidity of the ego itself (consciential holomaturity).

Synonymy: consciential scale; model of consciential evolution; projective consciential flowchart.

Validity. Following the orientation of an extraphysical helper, this evolutionary scale of the lucid consciential projector was elaborated. It is a practical process used as a pattern for measuring intraconsciential progress over time, a model of evolutionary attribution. The scale includes, delineates and measures a specific evolutionary period of the consciential principle (you) located somewhere between the hominal level – when leaving unconsciousness, indifference and improvisation behind in order to seek specialization, with spontaneous self-discernment – up to the deactivation of the psychosoma, upon reaching the condition of free consciousness or FC.

Factors. The characterization of these stages of the scale of continuous self-awareness are influenced by 3 basic factors:

1. **Human:** the improvement of the vehicle of manifestation and the utilization of chronological time.

2. **Extraphysical:** the relationship between evolutiologists and gradual multidimensional assistance.

3. **Consciential:** the evolution of memory (holomemory) and the application of cosmoethics.

Existential series. The stages were organized into only 7 steps, it being extremely difficult to exclude any of them; on the contrary, the scale can be amplified with small transitional stages. In the same way, it seems to be very problematic to achieve the advanced stages with very few sequential intraphysical lives, which are dedicated to the improvement of projective self-performance, in different human bodies or somas and energetic bodies or holochakras, besides the successive alterations of the personal psychosoma. There are other *specific* evolutionary scales of conscientiology.

Stages. In order to achieve the state of continuous self-awareness, the intraphysical consciousness projector and, likewise, the extraphysical consciousness projector – from pre-serenity to serenology – using the mentalsoma, experience these evolutionary advancements or ascendant stages beginning from the pre-*serenissimus:*

1. **Tests.** In this stage are included common intraphysical projectors of many categories, intrusion-victim-projectors, intruder-projectors, including those which have projections while the human body is in movement, whether walking, horse riding, dancing, singing, typing, playing piano, writing, speaking, in a train, driving a car, racecar, motorcycle, motorized bicycle and even piloting a hang glider, helicopter or airplane. The psychosoma and silver cord are discovered and the personality

learns to deal with these instruments of the consciousness. The uncertain searches come to an end and the first period of examinations, or psychophysical tests, begin for the apprentice of multidimensionality before his/her extraphysical helper. Impure, sporadic or accidental lucid projections occur; as well as pure lucid projections in the psychosoma of the adult, which are continuous from the beginning to the end of the episodes; and lucid self-projections.

2. **Impact.** This is the crossroads-stage for utilization of the current existence on earth regarding a transition in the performance of the lucidity of the consciousness. It includes the impure processes of consciential projections in the psychosoma produced by fakirs who have themselves temporarily buried alive, remain projected in the proximity of the human body during the period of intentional human hibernation and show faulty recall. They have pure lucid projection in the mentalsoma, superconsciousness (samadhi) or the experience of cosmoconsciousness and, under the impact of recalled cosmoconsciousness, the intraphysical projector defines his/her destiny in human life (penta, consciential epicenter, extraphysical clinic), either remaining in neutral or proceeding forward, mastering the physical body or soma.

3. **Admission.** Mixed consecutive consciential projections arise, alternating the vehicles – the psychosoma and the mentalsoma – with various experiences in a single night, including mild consciential projections and continuation-projections. The *flight range* of the projected intraphysical consciousness is already between one and two hours of absence from the human body. The projector begins to maintain greater emotional stability (serenity) and uniformity in his/her physical and extraphysical procedures, which allows superior intraconsciential efficiency. The integral, *en bloc*, recall of extraphysical experiences becomes habitual. The developed parapsychism shows itself to be of immense value. Deintrusive lucid projections become common and both nightmarish projections and spontaneous projections are extinguished. The second level, the period of admission or acceptance of the apprentice by the extraphysical helper occurs, in which the former can no longer expel the latter from the personal psychosphere. Psychophonic monologs appear in which the specialized, assistential extraphysical consciousness orients the tasks of the intraphysical lucid projector who perceives the positive interference in all aspects of existence, through unmistakable signals of parapsychism (signage), intuitions, suggestions, messages and, especially, the energetic shower that starts at the coronochakra. The individual now ceases to be merely a passive sensitive and is transformed into an active assistant (shoulder to shoulder, hand in hand) of extraphysicality, dispensing with formulas, rituals and crutches, as well as doctrines and sectarianism (factiousnesses).

4. **Ethics.** This is the period of consecutive lucid projections in the psychosoma lasting over an entire single night, or the phase of uninterrupted self-awareness for an entire day, eventually. From this ethical stage forward, moral intangibility, from a cosmic point of view, becomes indispensable. Ostensive assistential lucid projections occur and are incorporated into the projector's routine: the habitual viewing of the auras of beings and things in daily life; clairvoyance, clairaudience, telepathy, self-retrocognition, precognition and other phenomena and perceptions, such as the grandiose expansion of the human aura. The existence of the lucid projector (petifree being) in matter without the experiences of lucid projections becomes practically impossible. They become an indispensable part of the projector's diuturnal life, constituting an act that is just as physiological as the actions of inhaling and exhaling in the ordinary, physical waking state.

5. **Affiliation.** The projector begins to have mixed consecutive projections frequently during an entire night, and eventually consecutive lucid projections in the mentalsoma over the whole night. From this point on, lucid projections permanently occupy a part of the existence of the intraphysical projector as well as the extraphysical projector. The *flight range* of the consciousness surpasses two hours of absence from the vehicle of manifestation. The extraphysical studies and the extraphysical intraconsciential assistance are increased and the consciousness dives more deeply into the archives of its past intraphysical existences and intermissive periods, through periodic self-retrocognitions, taking the first steps toward *continuous memory* or holomemory. The emotionalism disappears from the consciousness' micro-universe to make way for constant serenity outside the human body, the consciousness mastering the psychosoma. There are lucid consciential projectors, in this phase, who

work efficiently while extraphysical consciousnesses, but fail dismally when they are reborn, demonstrating that projections of the mentalsoma are more difficult for the intraphysical consciousness than for the extraphysical consciousness. The majority of the projections of the intraphysical consciousness cannot be registered with clarity due to an insufficiency on the part of the neuropsychic memory circuits. The intraphysical projector first endeavors to discard the factor of natural sleep and, next, to eliminate dreams, both being extremely difficult intraconsciential feats. This stage corresponds to the third level of the apprentice, with a full matriculation or affiliation occurring with the extraphysical helper. The parapsychic manifestations become more refined and the intraphysical projector advances in the knowledge of upcoming facts regarding his/her way, through frequent self-precognitions. The evolutiologist gains an evolutionary boost in this stage.

6. **Refinement.** Consecutive projections in the mentalsoma of an entire night frequently begin to occur, as well as the eventual occurrence of mixed projections, until the consciousness attains a predominance of consecutive, prolonged, mentalsomatic projections lasting the entire night. From this stage forward, the intraphysical projector acts in the extraphysical dimensions leaving the dense body in the physical base, in the condition of *protected suspended animation,* which makes him/her immune to all negative or pathological influence, practically extinguishing the deintrusive projections. The intraphysical projector – who, up until this point, always returned to the human body in order to energize it – ceases to do this, using the full potential of the human brain. The interviews with genius extraphysical personalities, including positive historical personages, are intensified and there is little difference between the ordinary activities of the intraphysical projector and those of the active extraphysical projector, based on abnegation and lucid, discerning, self-conscientiality. The psychosoma, whether of the intraphysical consciousness or of the extraphysical consciousness, becomes more fluid, rarefied and subtle. The mentalsoma is amplified in a manner incomprehensible to the perceptions of our current understanding, and both categories of consciential self-projection become similar. The serenity of serenology predominates in this stage.

7. **Purification.** In this stage, consecutive lucid projections in the mentalsoma – or continuous self-awareness per se – are produced every night. This is possible for the intraphysical projector from infancy, which makes the human body seem to be an instrument at his/her service, or to disappear, at will, and execute final self-projection by him/herself, at the correct moment, through a cardiochakral or umbilicochakral self-desoma. At the last part of this stage, the free consciousness (FC) is born – the living-freed (*moksha,* freedom from the multiexistential cycle, the end of the errantry of the consciousness), which discards the now deactivated psychosoma, transcending all the bodies and parabodies of manifestation, limitations and conditions, besides all successive intraphysical and intermissive existences. Now free from the 2 vehicles – the rustic (human) and the subtle (psychosoma) – it is definitively removed from the gears of compulsory successive rebirths, in a form of conditioned existence. It continues to exist in the mentalsoma in the resplendent communities (mentalsomatic dimension), intensifying its relationship with cosmic extraphysical consciousnesses of high intraconsciential evolution, in cosmic extraphysical spaces, visitors from other planets, systems and galaxies, becoming occupied with intergalactic extraphysical processes, with the agents of karma, the builder consciousnesses and the architects of galaxies. At this point, this consciousness takes part in and orients the ample transformations, natural convulsions, catastrophes, cataclysms and destructive calamities that are generated by earthquakes, seaquakes, cyclones, hurricanes, volcanic eruptions, plagues, floods, rainstorms, hailstorms, snowstorms, windstorms, sandstorms; epidemics and the cycles of collective accidents; astronomical or cosmic catastrophes, such as the collision of heavenly bodies and even entire galaxies; and other great disasters and accidents which pummel planetary humanities.

Characteristics. The following are 17 other characteristics of stage 2, *impact,* gathered through suggestions at a public brainstorming session, with the participation of dozens of projectiology students and researchers, on October 27, 1990, at the International Institute of Projectiology, in Rio de Janeiro, RJ, Brazil:

1. **Alternance.** An understanding of the condition of the alternant intraphysical consciousness (intraphysical state/projected state).

2. **Self-discernment.** Repudiation of old idolatries or adorations (guru worship) with self-discernment and consciential maturity.

3. **Self-mimicries.** Self-awareness of necessary and dispensable repetitions in human life.

4. **Self-organization.** Awareness of the indispensable necessity of evolutionary self-organization.

5. **Self-projections.** Planned, lucid self-projections.

6. **Behavior.** Identification and the beginning of peaceful coexistence with inevitable ambiguities (pattern-behavior/exception-behavior).

7. **Cosmoethics.** Initial personal questioning regarding applied cosmoethics.

8. **Epicentrism.** The gaining of a greater awareness (consciential epicenter) of the individual's own lucid, evolutionary sufficiency.

9. **VS.** Practical mastery of the prophylactic vibrational state (VS).

10. **Karmic group.** Identification and location of oneself within the karmic group.

11. **Holokarma.** A primary understanding of personal holokarma.

12. **Intermission.** Self-persuasive recollections of the most recent personal intermissive period (personal intermissive course).

13. **Bait.** Acquisition of the condition of lucid multidimensional assistential bait.

14. **Goal.** Identification of one's own multi-existential goal (existential program and multi-existential cycle).

15. **Existential recycling.** Existential recycling or the constant renewal of one's existential perspective.

16. **Retrocognitions.** Personal experiences (mnemosomatics) of retrocognitions, even when intrusion-related.

17. **Strong-traitism.** Recognition of one's own mega-strong-traits and mini-strong-traits, mega-weak-traits and mini-weak-traits.

Projectability. This stage 2, *impact,* is extremely relevant in practical life because it specifies the level of lucid projectability of the majority of projectiology students and researchers, in order to achieve the *petifree condition* in this human life.

Potentiality. The extraphysical consciousnesses that permanently live in the mentalsoma find themselves potentially capable of maintaining awareness of the energetic auras of galaxies; make the consciousnesses located on evolved planets go into a vibrational state; promote the positive auric coupling of groups of stars; trigger transcendent orgasms or galactic holo-orgasms, and the state of joint, simultaneous, cosmic self-awareness (cosmoconsciousness) of entire physical and extraphysical populations, when necessary.

Considerations. In a single stage, the projector can come across small variables of transitional experiences that pertain to the prior stage or the subsequent one. The average projections of the projector define his/her level on the scale. The most difficult feat is to maintain uniformity in the series of self-aware, major and constant projections. In order to reach the fifth stage, for example, thousands of successive physical existences, similar to those on earth, or on a similar planet, must be necessary, dedicated to this goal, in multiple services of megafraternity. It can thus be seen that there must be people (consciousnesses) today that are endeavoring to move up one stage of one step of the scale, improving performance in lucid consciential projections since the age of the initiations of ancient Egypt, or even before this. What is most important is that the consciousness discovers and becomes aware of the manner in which the consciential evolutionary system (consciential flowchart or conscientiogram) functions.

Civilizations. Assuming that there are at least 3 types of intelligent civilizations, based upon their control of energy sources: Type 1 is that which is capable of exploiting and controlling a quantity of energy equal to the total energy sources of its planet; Type 2 is that which is capable of exploiting and controlling the energy equal to the total energy production of its native star (sun); Type 3 is that which is capable of exploiting and controlling the energy equal to the total energy production of its galaxy; can we conclude that the universalistic components of the Type 3 civilization would all evolutionarily be at the 6th stage of the scale of the state of continuous self-awareness?

Mastery. When the consciousness fully masters the physical vehicle of manifestation, including its biological requirement for natural sleep, leaving this only for the human body, through lucid self-projection, it gradually acquires definitive continuous self-awareness without recesses. Upon achieving this level, the human body can offer nothing more to the consciousness as an element of evolutionary purification and it ceases to go through resoma, as we understand it. At this point, the lucid projection achieves its anti-existential-series purpose, eliminating the cycles of the intraphysical and intermissive lives of the consciousness' realities or experiences.

Discretion. What is most impressive in certain consciousnesses of above-average evolution *(serenissimus)* is the phenomenon of absolute discretion or the condition of complete anonymity that is purposely self-imposed, in a sacrificial manner, and in which they remain while they are intraphysical. These intraphysical human consciousnesses, *serenissimus* – situated above and beyond encyclopedias – can be encountered while lucidly projected in extraphysical dimensions. However, it becomes impracticable, at least according to the experiences of the author, to identify them and encounter them in the ordinary, physical waking state. Why? How are they able to be simultaneously participative without showing themselves?

Questions. The following are some working hypotheses: Can one imperious suggestion, while in a deep hypnotic state, help the individual achieve the first steps toward the state of continuous self-awareness? Would someone be able to provide information regarding how many anonymous practitioners on this planet are currently in the sixth stage? Better still, do you know some of these practitioners? Which stage of continuous self-awareness have the so-called masters of the Himalayas achieved? If we consider, in infinite consciential evolution, animal life as the *first course,* and continuous self-awareness as the *second course,* what would the *third course* be? And what is the *fourth* evolutionary *course?*

Bibliography: Bentov (119, p. 132), Kardec (824, p. 91), Michaël (1041, p. 105), Powell (1279, p. 224), Vieira (1762, p. 214).

---

487. FREE CONSCIOUSNESS

Definition. Free consciousness: the mature consciential center of energetic irradiation that is free from matter, form and space, and from the cycle of lifetimes in perishable bodies, divested of the psychosoma, living only in the isolated mentalsoma.

Synonymy: agent of karma; archangel; architect of galaxies; evolutionary catalyst; FC; living-liberated; pure consciousness; quasi-perfect being.

Characteristics. The following are characteristics of the free consciousness: the condition of no longer suffering the influence of matter, of its tests and expiations; the enjoyment of an inner state of unalterable well-being and harmony; the performance of the transcendent function of an interplanetary or intergalactic transient, without living in errantry (mentalsomatic dimension); the sublime, lucid and incessant action of the consciousness in the quality of the evolutionary catalyst of other consciousnesses. It can thus be seen that the free consciousness is the same God of ancient peoples, the image and likeness of which humankind was considered to be.

Attributes. It naturally becomes difficult for us to understand the nature of the free consciousness. It is presumed, however, that it has an imperturbable serenity; masters immanent energy in a manner that is direct and still not understood within our current resources of understanding and self-maturity; whether it is a permanent flow of sentiment or of rationalized emotion; feels pure tranquil love; understands dense matter and the extraphysical constructions as being substances that are derived from the same source; achieves a level of supreme genius; has powers that can be characterized in our *current* evolutionary condition as being similar to the notion we ascribe to omniscience, omnipotence and omnipresence.

Manifestation. It is presumed that the free consciousness – although it has deactivated its own human body, holochakra and psychosoma – simultaneously perceives all consciential dimensions where it manifests in only a wholesale, intrinsic, consciential manner or, in other words, in a universalistic manner and within megafraternity.

Notion. The following are 8 subjects that can lead the interested individual to a better understanding of the notion of the reality of free consciousness:

1. **Cosmoconsciousness.** The condition of cosmic self-awareness or the experience of cosmoconsciousness.

2. **Mentalsomatic.** The existence of the mentalsomatic dimension.

3. **Mentalsoma.** The subtle manifestation of the mentalsoma.

4. **Projectability.** Lucid consciential projections in the mentalsoma.

5. **Self-awareness.** Projections with continuous self-awareness.

6. **State.** The state of continuous self-awareness.

7. **Scale.** The scale of the state of continuous self-awareness.

8. **Serenology.** The ideas and principles of serenology.

Earth. Due to its young age and its low level on the evolutionary scale or, in other words, its planetary consciential immaturity, planet earth still does not have native free consciousnesses – consciousnesses in the state of *moksha* or liberated from the series of intraphysical existences – residing here or which have been purified on this globe, achieving, directly from here, the seventh stage of the scale of continuous consciousness.

Universalism. It is important, above all, to emphasize that free consciousnesses present an evident universalistic nature and, therefore, do not feel themselves to be in a *planetary,* telluric, geocentric, sectarian or factionalist condition.

Extraterrestrials. The free consciousnesses that control the collective evolution of the earth, extraphysically manifesting on or for this planet, are therefore extraterrestrial beings. They are the most evolved extraphysical consciousnesses among all of those that are directly and *tangibly* related to intraterrestrial beings in general.

Cosmic. Through the notions of the free consciousness, it can be observed that there are 2 characteristic types of condition of cosmic self-awareness or the major projection through the mentalsoma: the solitary consciousness (samadhi, satori) and the accompanied consciousness, or that having encounters in the mentalsomatic dimension, where advanced interconsciential communications occur.

Contactees. In this sense, it is worthwhile mentioning that not all contactees (abductees) encountered by UFOlogy can be categorized as kidnap victims. The human contactees, investigated by UFOlogists, as extraterrestrial beings, can be systematically classified into 3 types, based on their consciential vehicles:

1. **Soma.** The physical contactee, when in the human body in the ordinary waking state (fourth degree or EC-IV), while the consciential vehicles are in the state of integral coincidence (unified body).

2. **Psychosoma.** The extraphysical contactee when the consciousness is projected outside the human body in the psychosoma, obviously with the mentalsoma.

3. **Cephalosoma.** The extraphysical contactee when the consciousness is projected outside the human body and psychosoma, in the isolated mentalsoma (cephalosoma).

Fluency. These last 2 contact processes enable more fluent, positive interconsciential communication through parapsychic means, with the full extraphysical self-awareness of all personalities involved in the encounter process.

Desoma. Consciousnesses, on the earth, which have gone through desoma and are lucid, establish their contacts with the last 2 types of benign extraterrestrial beings. This more easily eliminates the *conditions of interplanetary intrusion* (traumatic victimizer-victim(s) encounters).

Choice. On the other hand, the extraterrestrials, even in their physical contacts, purposely choose their terrestrial contacts (UFOlogical witnesses) according to their physical, psychic and parapsychic (parapsychophysical dynamic) characteristics or pre-conditions. These contacts (fourth degree) almost always inevitably inflict profound intrapsychic and behavioral changes and, sometimes, the condition of positive existential recycling.

Occupation. Among its activities in the field of astronomy, for example, the free consciousness maintains self-awareness regarding the energetic auras of galaxies; amplifies the state of consciousness of entire planetary populations; supervises the physical and consciential evolution of stars and constellations. It can thus be concluded that the consciousness does not cease to be busy even when purified, according to the evolutionary criteria that we are able to discern. This shows that idleness is intrinsically contrary to evolutionary patterns or, in other words, carries a pathological connotation.

Future. The more we understand the reality of the free consciousness, the greater will be the excellence of the quality of our projects and proposals, in view of our immediate future. The condition of the free consciousness is an inevitable goal – although still remote – and is an unwavering model for you, for me, and for all intraphysical consciousnesses.

---

488. SELF-DESOMA

Definition. Self-desoma: the technical, methodical, painless and conscious act of provoking the deactivation of the soma or human body.

Synonymy: chakral desoma; death by mental induction; discarding of the human body; energetic immolation; final self-projection; *mahasamadhi;* parapsychic death; parapsychic desoma technique; parathanatosis; psychogenic death; psychogenic self-desoma; second level of Kriya Yoga; self-euthanasia; self-metathanosia; voluntary abandoning of the human body.

Types. There are two basic, parabiological types of self-desoma: cardiochakral and umbilicochakral, or voluntary self-combustion. Besides these, negative methods are employed, *mahasamadhi,* for the conscious, definitive abandonment of the physical body by yogis, especially in the Himalayas, such as self-freezing *(him samadhi),* self-suffocation *(jal samadhi),* and the deliberate opening of the head *(sthal samadhi)* with the rupturing of the silver cord at the top of the sinciput, similar to natural death. According to affirmations, all of these processes are painless and rapid, although no one knows for sure whether or not any of them represent an act that is correct or condemnable, cosmoethical or uncosmoethical or, in other words, if it was performed at precisely the correct moment of the biological death of the soma for the intraphysical consciousness.

Fine. The line between an act of accelerating or slowing the moment of a desoma or, in this case, between correct self-desoma and veiled suicide (self-destruction), or self-euthanasia, is a very fine one and is complex to interpret. For those who enjoy good health, biological death is not an easy procedure, but for those who know that their life is hanging by a thread, balancing on the edge, feeling the coldness at the edge of the abyss, or in the final phase of the lucid projector, things become less difficult.

Reason. The greatest pretext for provoking self-desoma has been the intention of avoiding the negative effects of advanced senility or, in other words, the frank caducity of certain individuals, which in many cases can merely be the pressure of pride and vanity. Modern preventive and therapeutic resources for defending the intraphysical consciousness against senile disturbances or those derived from arteriosclerosis (Alzheimer's disease), when used in time, have significantly reduced the negative consequences of caducity and senile psychoses.

Moral. The moral question, which is extremely serious in this case, merely refers to the individual's own cosmoethics, the self-discernment and hyperacuity of the intraphysical consciousness who, if he/she wishes, can end his/her physical life rapidly, without any other human being becoming aware of his/her real intentions.

Key. Those who perceive and mobilize elevated consciential energies have easy access to the key to voluntary final projection through the definitive disconnection of the vehicles of manifestation, the human body and psychosoma. This provokes the irreversible rupture of the silver cord, the real and final *causa mortis,* common to all human beings.

Suicide. Self-desoma is only understood to be a positive or healthy process when it occurs, according to cosmoethics, with projectors who are at the seventh stage of the scale of continuous self-awareness and know when the human body ceases to be a useful vehicle for manifestation of the consciousness. Prior to this period, any similar act is reprehensible, negative and anticosmoethical. This is because it is equivalent to a suicide or self-murder, without evidential proof or corpus delicti or, in other words, self-euthanasia, as it is provoked prematurely, or before the correct, appropriate time, in many cases perhaps as an escape from senility which began to appear and be self-perceived or detected by the person through the sensations or by observing personal biological or hereditary lineage according to the individual's elderly close relatives.

Period. The period of appropriate desoma of the intraphysical consciousness does not always correspond to his/her possibilities of self-desomatic performance. Many intraphysical beings can even have resources and techniques for self-desoma when they still find themselves healthy and feeling well, *prior to* the desoma period. However, the appropriate period, due to deficiencies of consciential energies (holochakrology), mental concentration and sufficient will for the attempt, end up being unable to realize their self-desomatic experience. This fact may have led an intraphysical consciousness to induce premature desoma for this very reason, which, nevertheless, is still an error, escape, pathothosene and egokarmic debt.

Incorruptibility. It is common knowledge that, in mortuary records, cases are registered of unaltered cadavers, devoid of any visible sign of physical decomposition, such as desiccation, mold and the characteristic odor. They also remain immutable and untouched for a period of days, months or even years, facts frequently attributed to a special purpose and the "sanctity" of the deceased.

Coma. Somnambulism outside the human body and the natural trances of first desoma, or deactivation of the cellular body, are proof of one or another case of post-desomatic physical incorruptibility – which under the circumstances represents a great irony – signifies nothing more than conservation of the connections of the vehicles of manifestation of the consciousness in the state of coincidence and that one did not *paraphysiologically* pass through the entire process of the first desoma. It thus remains in the proximity of the inactive dense body, while it is still unaltered, in a state of *extraphysical coma.* How many cases of self-desoma can be included in this type of occurrence?

Analogy. The condition of the veteran projector who is aware of self-desomatic techniques is very similar to a patient who has received a permanent artificial heart – made of metal and polyurethane, created by specialists in mechanical medicine, activated by external equipment, a miniaturized air compressor, a generator and tubes – which has full access to the switch that can turn off this heart-apparatus that keeps the individual alive among humans. Both are equipped with the frank option for suicide. There is generally no risk of the projector suiciding, because the projections themselves keep the person in excellent intraconsciential condition. This makes the individual consider the great importance of human life, maintain a permanent interest in living intraphysically and concluding that it is worthwhile to take advantage of the evolutionary possibilities that the intraphysical terrestrial stage still offers.

Bibliography: Ajaya (08, p. 399), Benavides (109, p. 204), Castaneda (256, p. 13), D'arbó (365, p. 227), Ring (1406, p. 27), Russell (1482, p. 71), Vieira (1762, p. 220), Walker (1784, p. 235), White (1831, p. 370), Yogananda (1894, p. 245).

489. VOLUNTARY CARDIAC ARREST

Definition. Voluntary cardiac arrest: the act of the intraphysical consciousness intentionally provoking a cardiac arrest within him/herself, with the objective of producing the deactivation of the human body, or final projection.

Synonymy: cardiochakral desoma; cardiochakral self-desoma; cardiochakral self-euthanasia; provoked mental cardiac self-collapse.

Cause. The fundamental cause of voluntary cardiac arrest is mental concentration, through deep reflection upon the cardiochakra or, more specifically, upon the heart, a vital organ of the human body, making it definitively cease to function, similar to the discharge of a ray which instantly kills the soma, provoking cardiac arrest.

Effects. Evidently, the immediate effect of cardiac arrest is the death of the human body due to the definitive stopping of the heart's functioning, when specialized resources are not used, such as thoracic massages, adrenaline and defibrillators.

Types. There are 2 basic types of the phenomenon of cardiac arrest, from a cosmoethical perspective, which is very important in this case: when provoked by a projector who is already in the seventh stage of the scale of continuous self-awareness, not constituting suicide as we understand it; and when definitively triggered by a projector who is in any of the other previous stages of this same scale, thereby representing calculated suicide, self-murder or self-euthanasia, with the obvious profoundly negative egokarmic consequences, which are easily understood by those who are accustomed to extraphysical realities.

Warning. Voluntary cardiac arrest is the reason why the author has never recommended any psychophysical practices that involve the direct control of the heart with the will, as certain gentle practices recommend direct control of respiration. Thought is a living force and we do not always know, nor are we always predisposed to dose it out within the correct physiological, cosmoethical and productive parameters, as seen, besides this occurrence, in voluntary self-combustion. Both of these phenomena can also be provoked unintentionally and even without the self-awareness of the person responsible for their existence (uncalculated self-euthanasia).

Impact. In order to reflect upon the relevance of the thoracic or cardiac area in research performed by self-aware individuals, it is sufficient to emphasize that conventional science currently admits that a small impact to the heart can kill (desoma). Studies prove that a quick blow at just the right moment makes the heart stop. This is why athletes and children faint suddenly (*Jornal do Brasil;* daily; year CVIII; N. 71; section: *Ciência;* Rio de Janeiro, RJ, Brazil; June 18, 1998; p. 14).

Medicine. For those who have difficulty in assimilating the reality of these facts, it is worth remembering that cardiology currently considers orgasm, euphoria, a setback, a mere agreeable surprise, or a simple shock to be causes of fatal cardiac arrest, under certain conditions.

Bibliography: Muldoon (1105, p. 212).

490. VOLUNTARY SELF-COMBUSTION

Definition. Voluntary self-combustion: the act of the intraphysical consciousness making the real *inner flame* of fire, or psychophysical energy, operate, thereby burning the human body and reducing it to ashes.

Synonymy: consciential self-implosion; provoked mental self-burning; provoked self-oxidation; pyrogenic self-euthanasia; umbilicochakral desoma; umbilicochakral self-desoma; voluntary self-cremation.

Survivors. Spontaneous human combustion, or spontaneous fire – a phenomenon referred to in ancient oriental texts, of which there are currently hundreds of registered cases – is one of the mysteries of the universe of parapsychic phenomenology. It has even been addressed in popular television programs on scientific dissemination and the survivors of this combustion – victims of the occurrence who did not die – have already been studied. There are still no definitive explanations for the occurrences of spontaneous human combustion, only hypotheses, such as a *mechanical failure* in the human organism's temperature control system.

Description. Extranormal combustion is described as a small, but intense, flat, bluish flame that very quickly spreads to all parts of the human body which is affected. This persists until the parts are blackened and, as a rule, are reduced to ashes and oily stains, leaving an unexplainable sweet smell and a grayish smoke. On many occasions, attempts were made to extinguish the flame with water, without success.

Causes. Spontaneous human combustion is caused by the occasional concentration of the internal energies of the organism, the sexochakral energies *(kundalini),* at one or many organic points or areas. Voluntary self-combustion, on the other hand, is provoked by the intention of setting oneself on fire, through a deep mental concentration upon the solar plexus, umbilicochakra or abdominal brain.

Predisposing. The following are 7 physical and physiological conditions that can generally predispose the phenomena of spontaneous human combustion:

1. **Biochemical.** Some chemical components, which are inert when isolated, form explosive compounds when combined.

2. **Bioluminescence.** The bioluminescence emitted by certain insects and fish demonstrates the possibility of *internal fire* of some type.

3. **Fats.** The fats and oils, which the human body contains in quantity, are excellent combustibles.

4. **Phosphorous.** Phosphorous, a chemical constituent of the human body, catches fire spontaneously when exposed to atmospheric air.

5. **Electricity.** Static electricity produces sparks that can, under certain conditions, set the human body on fire.

6. **Intestines.** Human intestinal gases are flammable.

7. **Cadavers.** The gases produced by human cadavers are flammable.

Effects. Among the effects of spontaneous human combustion, the most frequent is sudden desoma, with a small amount of gray residue and a thick layer of greasy soot. More rarely, only multiple burns on various areas of the organism occur, which are not seen or felt during the event and have no apparent cause.

Selective. Among the effects of spontaneous human combustion, as well as that which is voluntarily provoked, is the transformation of the human body into a pile of ashes, which strangely occurs in a selective manner, without provoking a local fire and without burning – and almost always without even singeing – the surrounding flammable substances with which the organism was in direct contact during the occurrence.

Temperature. Incidentally, in order to reduce the human body to ashes – which occurs in official crematoriums – a temperature of over 3,000 degrees Fahrenheit, or more than 1,650 degrees Celsius, is needed for at least 8 hours, in order for the bones to turn to dust. As can be seen, this is a difficult temperature to produce without the aid of flammables.

Somas. Men (androsomas) only burn at more elevated temperatures than women (gynosomas). Does this suggest that consciousnesses are physically more *reborn* when in androsomas or masculine bodies?

Types. According to the preceding reference regarding voluntary cardiac arrest, there are 2 basic types of occurrence in relation to the phenomenon of voluntary self-combustion, from a cosmoethical perspective, which is very important in this case: when provoked by a projector who is already in the seventh stage of the scale of continuous self-awareness, which must be extremely rare and does not constitute suicide as we understand it; and when triggered by a projector who is in any of the other prior stages of the referred-to scale, thus representing suicide, self-murder or calculated self-euthanasia, with obvious, profoundly negative egokarmic consequences that are easily understood by those who are accustomed to extraphysical or multidimensional realities of evolution of the consciousness.

Warning. The phenomenon of human self-combustion, as much as voluntary cardiac arrest, warn of the extremely powerful force of thought, of which we are still not fully aware and do not dose out in a correct, physiological and productive manner. This is why care should be taken when putting the psychophysical energies of the organism and its chakras into motion, because both of the referred-to phenomena can also be provoked unintentionally and even without the responsible party being self-aware and perceiving their existence.

Jesus. At this stage of the analysis of the facts, the following hypothesis is worth examining: Could it be that the disappearance of the human body of Jesus of Nazareth, evolutionarily already living in the seventh stage of the scale of continuous self-awareness, was deliberately and consciously performed by himself, or was it achieved through voluntary self-combustion, leaving no human residue or physical traces? Who knows how many disappearances of persons have not already occurred, and occur nowadays, through this process? Who knows how many disappearances of persons have not already occurred, and occur nowadays, through this process?

Hypotheses. The following are two more pertinent work hypotheses: What is the relationship between bioluminescence (uncontrolled light or energy) and spontaneous self-combustion (wasted heat or energy), 2 of the most uncommon and obscure biological phenomena that challenge human intelligence? Will humankind someday be able to voluntarily produce bioluminescence, when it is able to control light as a form of energy through the phenomenon of irruption of the psychosoma?

Bibliography: Ajaya (08, p. 401), Castaneda (256, p. 13), Digest (400, p. 91), Freixedo (554, p. 53), Vieira (1762, p. 202).

---

491. PSYCHOPHYSIOLOGICAL ANCHOR

Definition. Psychophysiological anchor: the psychological and/or physical element that maintains the consciousness of the advanced projector connected to or interested in human life, performing a consciential prophylaxis against his/her alienation regarding the necessary physical experience on earth.

Synonymy: human anchor; psychophysiological anchoring crutch; the intraphysical consciousness' true friend.

Psychosoma. Generally speaking, psychophysical anchoring is the implantation of the substantial connection of the intraphysical consciousness more strongly to human or terrestrial life. This connection is more frequently executed through exacerbation of the functions of the psychosoma – the parabody of emotions or desires – which activates the emotionalism and passions that bind the intraphysical consciousness to the earth through the illusions of the tropospheric senses. It can thus be concluded that great lucid self-projections in the mentalsoma will forever free the intraphysical projector from the use of psychophysical anchors.

Types. The psychophysical anchor may not only be the dignified thought on the foundations of life, pure affection for someone or an object of noble work, but may also be religious or mystical affective sublimation, interest in a human activity, or an inoffensive but productive hobby.

Factors. The following are 10 extremely positive, motivating, psychophysical anchoring factors, listed in more or less decreasing order of importance, value and constructive repercussion for the intraphysical consciousness: human family ties, professional work, services of social assistance, studies of lucid projection, scientific research, elevated art, athletic performance, instructive travel, adoption of a domestic animal, educational collections.

Drugs. The medications prescribed for the prevention of arteriosclerosis or senility, although used for this purpose, act as powerful psychophysiological anchors for the intraphysical consciousness on earth, without the individual perceiving it. These drugs, generally when used continuously, improve cerebral vascularization, increase the degree of the patient's awareness, reduce the number of hours of sleep, unblock the flow of thoughts, strengthen the memory and, for some time, seriously impede the production of the self-projection of the consciousness, actually anchoring the interests of the intraphysical being in the physical, daily involvements and attractions or in the diuturnal problems of human life.

Effects. The psychophysiological anchor neutralizes euphoria regarding the extraphysical dimensions; sustains, without vacillations and without sidetracks, the fundamental direction of human existence; favors a coherence in attitudes; constantly indicates the essential goal of individual destiny or the healthy execution of the existential program; allows the intraphysical consciousness to achieve a new stage in the scale of the state of continuous self-awareness; and presents a close relationship with the recess of sequential or seriated lucid projections.

Crutch. In its initial structure, the psychophysiological anchor of the consciousness in human existence still constitutes the ultimate crutch, or psychological support, which the intraphysical being needs in order to conclude the terrestrial stage with cosmoethical dignity.

Self-desoma. In an extreme extraphysical liberation, or prodigality, if the yogis and fakirs do not have a balanced psychophysiological anchor, they are susceptible to produce a premature self-desoma or, in other words, one which is completely negative or anticosmoethical.

Excess. In a condition of extreme physical restriction, or attachment, when the human anchor acts excessively upon the intraphysical consciousness, this resource ends up sidetracking the individual from extraphysical reality, reducing parapsychic sensitivity, or *materializing him/her.* Certain existential impacts, such as illnesses, medications, an elevated sum of money appearing unexpectedly and others, can intoxicate the human intraphysical consciousness, emotionally involving the individual in a mummifying crust or, in other words, fossilizing the still living person.

Helpers. Paradoxically, the extraphysical helpers are simultaneously *desoma facilitators* and *resoma facilitators.* This is because they not only aid in the exteriorization of the consciousness from the human body, but also, in certain cases, impede it from leaving this selfsame organism in an excessive, frequent or intense manner. In other words, they free it, on the one hand, and anchor it, on the other hand, within the appropriate and necessary balance required for the individual's terrestrial experiences and personal evolutionary necessities.

Middle ground. Thus it is perceived, far beyond religious, mystical or fanatical postulates, but evidenced and endorsed by the individual's own physical-extraphysical everyday life, that the ideal human conduct, and the necessary abovementioned balance required by terrestrial experiences and the individual evolutionary necessities of the intraphysical consciousness, are not at one extreme of attachment (egoistic and avaricious), much less at another extreme of detachment (prodigal and alienating). It is, instead, at a middle ground, which is appropriate, correct, cosmoethical, and lacks radicalisms, between attachment and detachment to material things on the face of the earth or within the world of intraphysical life.

Cord. The greatest existing physical anchor of intraphysical consciousnesses is the *old* silver cord, the remainder of which accompanies the psychosoma of the extraphysical consciousness even prior to its current resoma.

Bibliography: Vieira (1762, p. 173).

---

492. CONSCIENTIAL   LOCATIONS

Definition. Consciential location: the state or condition wherein the consciousness *temporarily* anchors, concentrates or centralizes its focus, fulcrum, seat of action or the *locus* of its perceptive faculties in a certain evolutionary opportunity or moment.

Synonymy: condition of the consciousness; seat of the consciousness; state of the consciousness.

Point. Whereas the 2 cerebral hemispheres merely represent the visible point of the immense iceberg that constitutes the real consciousness, which is silently submersed in other existential dimensions, it also always has a seat or fulcrum of manifestation on any given occasion. The more evolved a consciousness is, the more frequent and more intense will be its changes of location.

Comprehension. In order to understand the theory of the locations of the seat of the consciousness, which vary according to existential levels, the intraphysical consciousness can use the following example: place 1 index finger in front of you pointing upward, look at it and consider that, in the same place where your dense, visible finger is, there can be 1 billion other similar coexisting fingers, which are invisible to the perception of your eyes, vibrating at different frequencies, with 1 not interfering with the existence of the others and many of these fingers can be mere creations of your consciousness or, in other words, simulations of the human finger.

Projection. In the example provided, your consciousness would be observing or distinguishing only 1 finger, the densest one, that which remains in the condition of physical coincidence. Suppose, however, that your consciousness wishes to project to another level or dimension. It would then use, as a temporary seat, for example, the frequency of the psychosoma, which corresponds to your similar, extraphysical finger, N. 87,587,587, a number chosen at random, being a component of the billion referred to.

Only. Instead of 1 billion fingers there can be "n" fingers, or an infinity of fingers for the psychosoma alone or the extraphysical dimension per se. For the mentalsoma, in the mentalsomatic dimension, the consciousness will not even need duplicates of fingers or the organic vehicle any longer in order to manifest itself.

Causes. According to the synthesis of the studies of locations of the consciousness, it is verified that they occur due to 6 distinct determining factors that comprise a model and can be used as a pattern-measurement to assess all the phenomenology of the consciousness in the following order: lucidity, will, energy, frequency, passivity and change.

1. **Lucidity.** The lucidity of the consciousness depends upon its evolution and can be classified as unconscious, semiconscious and conscious. The facts speak in favor of a constant instability of the consciousness, until such time as it achieves its maximum peak of balance, or relative stability, at the highest level of extraphysical serenity, as if this instability were a component that is indispensable to its life conditions, the demands of evolution and the nature of its perpetuity or eternity.

2. **Will.** The intensity of the will, or consciential activity, depends greatly upon the emotional motivation (emotionalism, psychosomatics) or the rational motivation (sentiment, mentalsomatics) of the consciousness. The will that acts motivated by emotivity demonstrates that the consciousness is still restricted to the manifestations of the psychosoma, the emotional body, or its animal, subhuman side. The will that acts motivated by positive sentiment, or by rationality, shows that it is already headed toward the predominance of consciential manifestations in the mentalsoma or the parabody of self-discernment.

3. **Energies.** The utilization of consciential energies depends upon the efficacy of the consciousness' performance. The performance of the consciousness in the use of consciential energies comes from the degree of awareness regarding the existence of these same consciential energies which, when manipulated unknowingly, or unconsciously, remains within the domain of the instincts of subhuman animals (reptilian brain, atavism) and does not show the same efficiency.

4. **Frequency.** Alteration in the vibratory frequency or density of the vehicle of consciential manifestation depends upon the flow of consciential energies employed by the intraphysical consciousness. There is no rigidly established consciential level for a determinate dimension of life where the consciousness is temporarily headquartered. Each dimension presents immense gradation, ranging from one extreme to the other, from a greater density to a lesser density, or from the condition of discontinuous consciential clarity to the condition of complete consciential clarity in that dimension. Not even the ordinary, physical waking state escapes this principle: no one has the same consciential acuity all the time he/she is physically awake. The same occurs in the paratropospheric dimension and even in the mentalsomatic dimension.

5. **Passivity.** The degree of sensitivity of a consciousness to the influences of others can be normal or pathological. Due to passivity alone, which suffocates the will, diverse distinct phenomena

occur: parapsychism, interconsciential intrusion, intuition, hypnosis, wherein the consciousness is *lived* or teleguided, instead of living or deciding for itself. Self-passivity, when excessive, alters the *groupkarmic account* of the intraphysical consciousness.

6. **Change.** The change from one dimension or level of manifestation of the consciousness can occur instantaneously, either with or without traumatizing it. Time becomes relative with regard to the influence that it exercises over the changes of the consciential locations, because these can occur as lightning-fast as the speed of thought.

Types. Dozens of phenomena stem from changes in consciential location, notably the following 15: self-bilocation of the projected projector; physical bilocation; physical-extraphysical trilocation or double projection; physical multilocation or the multiplicity of identical created forms; extraphysical translocation of the consciousness in the same dimension; pathological self-transfiguration of the consciousness when manifesting in the psychosoma, which is characteristic of extraphysical consciousnesses that are not able to maintain their own form; sudden extraphysical consciential disappearances; traveling clairvoyance; teletransportation; exteriorization of motricity; exteriorization of sensitivity; physical and extraphysical psychometry; physical and extraphysical retrocognition; physical and extraphysical telekinesis; psychophysical anchor.

Uses. Analysis of the factors that determine consciential locations indicates various uses that greatly help the lucid projector understand and obtain an improvement in his/her performance: the necessity of extraphysical serenity; the phenomenon of cosmoconsciousness; projection with continuous self-awareness; the state of continuous self-awareness; and a long list of other phenomena and situations of lesser significance.

Cosmoconsciousness. Consciential location in the condition of cosmoconsciousness becomes comprehensive in a wholesale manner, overall, thereby bringing about the absolute liberation of the consciential seat, which expands itself free from spaces, forms, weights, time, vibratory frequencies and all limitations. The state of cosmoconsciousness facilitates projections of continuous self-awareness which, in turn, push the consciousness to a better level on the scale of the state of continuous self-awareness.

Continuum. Rational conclusions come to the fore after comparing all the evidence: it becomes extremely difficult to predetermine an exact type of self-induced lucid projection. Lucid projection constitutes a consciential *continuum* or a constant succession of altered consciential states uninterruptedly amalgamating, interpenetrating or alternating themselves.

Phenomenology. All classifications of projectiology phenomena serve only to establish didactic theory for the rational and pedagogic analysis of the subject. This is because, in practice, the consciousness spontaneously surpasses classificatory parameters, no matter how rigid they are. In the analysis of the phenomena of lucid projection it will inevitably be accepted that the consciousness cannot be compartmentalized, insofar as it does not divide itself.

Brain. Another aspect that is important in order to understand projectiological phenomena more accurately is that many sensations or consciential states can occur without the departure of the intraphysical consciousness from its physical seat or, in other words, from the dense brain in the head of the human body. The projective consciential phenomenon only occurs when the consciousness dislocates itself, or projects from its physical seat outward, in this case to the extraphysical dimension, either in the isolated mentalsoma or *inside* the parabrain of the psychosoma.

Phenomena. The following are some consciential phenomena that can occur without the departure of the consciousness from its physical seat: daydream; sleep; dream; color lucid dream; nightmare; hypnagogic state; hypnopompic state; intuition; telepathic mental emission; parapsychic and hypnotic telepathic mental reception; mnemonic occurrences; and hallucinations. However, all these phenomena can also occur when the consciousness is located outside the dense, physical brain.

Bibliography: Delanne (382, p. 175), Vieira (1762, p. 73).

493. CONSCIENTIAL DISLOCATIONS

Definition. Consciential dislocation: the act or effect of the consciousness moving from one location to another.

Synonymy: consciential move.

Types. Consciential dislocations can occur according to the vehicles of manifestation of the consciousness, the environments and the dimensions of life, thereby being: holosomatic, environmental or interdimensional (fig. 493). They can also occur according to the direction or dislocation of the consciousness: centrifugal or centripetal.

Law. It is a basic law of projectiology in relation to the consciousness and its vehicles of manifestation that: the consciousness, regardless of its evolutionary level, always ordinarily manifests through its less evolved consciential vehicle. Every time the consciousness manifests itself through a consciential vehicle other than this less evolved one, it is projecting itself.

Evolution. *Lucid* projection tends to be a more evolved state than the physical, waking state of human or terrestrial life due to this fact. Desomas are the discarding of the less evolved vehicles. Therefore, in theory, they constitute evolutionary advancements by the consciousness.

Action. The consciousness, whether intraphysical or extraphysical, employing the vehicles of manifestation in its dislocation, can act as a projector, communicant consciousness or sensitive consciousness.

Series. The following is a list of 35 possible concepts and generalizations related to consciential dislocations and their consequences. The expression in italics identifies the central aspect of the topic, the core of the issue in the sequence of the development under analysis.

Redundancies. With a view toward enhancing the scope of the study, which is at once broad and didactic, subtle or obvious redundancies were maintained, as they are inevitable in the reiterations of the analyses. Before analyzing the following topics, the reader should arm him/herself with patience and remain in a tranquil environment or holothosene in order not to confuse his/her own thosenes.

1. Not every consciential dislocation is *holosomatic*. It can also be environmental.

2. Not every holosomatic consciential dislocation is *interdimensional*. It can also occur only in a single dimension.

3. Not every consciential dislocation is *environmental*. It can also be holosomatic.

4. Not every consciential dislocation is *interdimensional*. It might only be environmental.

5. Not every environmental consciential dislocation is *interdimensional*. It may be merely environmental change in the same dimension.

6. Not every consciential projection is dimensional change. It may be merely *environmental* (geographic or parageographic) change in the same dimension.

7. Every discoincidence of the vehicles of manifestation of the consciousness is a consciential *projection*.

8. Every discoincidence of the vehicles of manifestation of the intraphysical consciousness is *centrifugal*, in regard to the holosoma (the set of 4 vehicles of consciential manifestation).

9. Every coincidence of the vehicles of manifestation of the intraphysical consciousness is *centripetal*, in regard to the holosoma.

10. Not every discoincidence of the vehicles of manifestation of the consciousness is a consciential projection of the consciousness per se. It may merely be of the *holochakra*, a vehicle that does not transport the consciousness.

11. Every *intraphysical* (human) consciousness projects him/herself in the psychosoma. Nevertheless, the degree of extraphysical lucidity with which he/she is able to manifest him/herself varies.

12. Not every *intraphysical* (human) consciousness projects him/herself in the (isolated) mentalsoma. This occurrence depends upon the level of personal performance.

13. Not every *extraphysical* (human) consciousness projects itself in the (isolated) mentalsoma. This occurrence depends upon the level of personal performance.

CONSCIENTIAL DISLOCATIONS

CONSCIOUSNESSES	HOLOSOMATIC DISCOINCIDENCES	ENVIRONMENTAL DISLOCATIONS
INTRAPHYSICAL:		
1. Projector	Takeoff: centrifugal Interiorization: centripetal	Centrifugal interdimensional departure Centripetal interdimensional return
2. Communicant	Dislocation: centripetal	Centrifugal dislocation
3. Medium	Beginning: centrifugal End: centripetal	Remaining in the base-dimension
EXTRAPHYSICAL:		
4. Projector	Takeoff: centrifugal Interiorization: centripetal	Departure: centrifugal Return: centripetal
5. Communicant	Intrusion: centripetal	Errantry
6. Medium	Beginning: centrifugal End: centripetal	Remaining in the base-dimension

Figure 493

14. Every *takeoff* of the consciousness, whether intraphysical or extraphysical, that projects itself is centrifugal in relation to the holosoma, whether it is composed of 4, 3 or 2 consciential vehicles.

15. Every departure from the physical base is centrifugal for the projected *intraphysical* consciousness, in relation to the human body.

16. Every departure from the extraphysical base is centrifugal for the projected *extraphysical* consciousness, in relation to the psychosoma.

17. Every interdimensional departure of the projected *intraphysical* consciousness is centrifugal, in relation to the holosoma.

18. Not every interdimensional departure of the projected *extraphysical* consciousness is centrifugal or centripetal. The extraphysical consciousness lives in the condition of errantry within its community.

19. Every interdimensional dislocation of the communicant *intraphysical* consciousness is centrifugal in regard to his/her own holosoma or, in other words, specifically in regard to the *soma.*

20. Not every interdimensional dislocation of the communicant *extraphysical* consciousness is centrifugal or centripetal. The extraphysical consciousness lives in a state of errantry.

21. Every parapsychic *communication* is holosomatic intrusion generated by the communicant consciousness upon the sensitive (consciousness) and its holosoma.

22. Not every intrusion of the communicant *extraphysical* consciousness causes discoincidence (holosoma) of the sensitive's consciousness, whether an intraphysical or extraphysical consciousness. This fact depends upon the intensity of the intrusion. There is even a process of possession that is specifically mentalsomatic.

23. Not every intrusion of the communicant *intraphysical* consciousness causes the discoincidence (holosoma) of the sensitive's consciousness, whether an intraphysical or extraphysical consciousness. This fact depends upon the intensity of the intrusion. This is why direct interconsciential exchange is not always trustworthy.

24. Every sensitive, whether an intraphysical or extraphysical being, when executing its function, keeps part of its holosoma in the *base-dimension,* even when the consciousness leaves the state of coincidence of the vehicles of manifestation.

25. Not every *intraphysical* consciousness is able to communicate through a sensitive, whether intraphysical or extraphysical (*extraphysical* parapsychism exists). This occurrence depends upon the level of personal performance. There is even interconsciential intrusion of an intraphysical consciousness upon an extraphysical consciousness.

26. Not every *extraphysical* consciousness is able to communicate through a sensitive, whether an intraphysical or extraphysical being. This occurrence depends upon the level of personal performance.

27. Every parapsychic *communication* is an intrusive process for the sensitive's consciousness, whether an intraphysical or extraphysical being, in regard to the holosoma and, generally, in regard to the intraconsciential micro-universe.

28. Not every parapsychic communication is centripetal for the *extraphysical* communicant consciousness. It can remain in an unalterable condition in regard to this aspect. Even post-desomatic parapsychotics exist.

29. Every parapsychic communication is centrifugal for the *intraphysical* communicant consciousness.

30. Every return to the *physical* base is centripetal for the projected consciousness in regard to the holosoma or, in other words, specifically with regard to the *soma.*

31. Every return to the *extraphysical* base is centripetal for the projected extraphysical consciousness.

32. Not every interdimensional return of the projected *extraphysical* consciousness is centrifugal or centripetal. It can remain in unalterable conditions.

33. Every *interiorization* of the projected consciousness, whether intraphysical or extraphysical, is centripetal in relation to the holosoma or, in other words, in relation to the vehicle in which it is interiorizing itself.

34. Every recoincidence of the vehicles of manifestation of the consciousness, whether intraphysical or extraphysical, is a consciential interiorization.

35. Every recoincidence of the vehicles of manifestation of the consciousness is centripetal in relation to the holosoma.

Information. These 35 concepts are not simple word games, but a set of functional information regarding the specific and detailed characterization of personal parapsychic phenomena and those of others.

Occurrences. The analysis of the list allows the lucid projector to more intimately grasp the ideas and better understand the phenomena and consequences of his/her extraphysical experiences during consciential projections, notably regarding the following occurrences and realities: physical base; coincidence; *inter vivos* communications; takeoff; extraphysical disappearances; discoincidence; base-dimension; consciential dimensions; errantry; holochakra; holosoma; incorporation; interiorization; extraphysical lucidity; parapsychism; mentalsoma; interconsciential intrusion; extraphysical dimensions; lucid consciential projections; psychosoma; extraphysical beings; volitation; and others.

Exercise. A good intellectual exercise, with the purpose of predisposing the interested individual to produce lucid projection in the isolated mentalsoma, is to look for some omission, illogicality or mistake in this complex list, which can actually be increased.

494. CONSCIENTIAL NOMADISM

Definition. Consciential nomadism: the healthy condition of the consciousness, when lucid and errant, which constantly moves itself from one *locus* to another, in search of experiences that are enriching for its evolution.

Synonymy: condition of the wandering consciousness; consciential errantry; state of the errant consciousness.

Erraticism. Consciential nomadism, within the context of projectiology, is a more evolved condition than projective erraticism or, in other words, the situation of disorientation of the consciousness when projected.

Holomaturity. The abovementioned consciential nomadism does not constitute any pathological disturbance, deviation, straying, disorientation, oversight or aimlessness of the projected consciousness lacking a mental target. On the contrary, it is the result of the holomaturity of the consciousness, which intentionally becomes nomadic, with lucidity, through the powerful impulsion of its own will.

Dimension. The consciousness, per se, does not sleep. The human aura or the person's energetic psychosphere is always in movement and never stops. The extraphysical consciential dimension (energetic dimension) that is immediately adjacent to the human dimension or that of the soma, corresponds to the direct, specific manifestations of the holochakra, in which the human aura is included. This dimension, which is energetic, comprising unstable creations, is suitable for stimulating the movement of the consciousness, its lucid projections and, finally, consciential nomadism.

Evolution. The more evolved the consciousness is, the more errant it becomes, in regard to its lucid, consciential location. The consciousness progresses or educates itself by voluntarily dislocating itself from a situation or type of manifestation in a gradually more intense, uninterrupted, active and productive manner.

Omnipresence. Consciential nomadism suggests that the consciousness does not have – and was essentially not constituted to have – a fixed seat where it would manifest forever. This is the first evidence that the consciousness evolves to a condition of omnipresence that is *less and less relative,* or active and applied. In this case, it is a sectorial, localized, still partial omnipresence in the universe or a semi-omnipresence, always maintaining its individualization intact.

Paramesology. Therefore, the more centered the consciousness is in its *inner* micro-universe, the more decentralized it becomes regarding the *exterior* multidimensional macro-universe where it lives. Its paramesology is amplified in a manner that is still incomprehensible to us.

Instantaneity. The dislocation of the consciousness from one consciential location to another becomes, in a crescendo, increasingly instantaneous or lightning-fast.

Paradox. The condition of serenism of the *serenissimus (Homo sapiens serenissimus),* through its characteristic of interdimensionality or multidimensionality, is paradoxical. This is because, according to these evolutionary conjectures, the more evolved the consciousness is, the more nomadic and, at the same time, the more serene it becomes. Imperturbable consciential dislocations occur. Its serenity does not signify inertia, indifference or disinterest, but consciential energetic activity, growth and realization. This makes it so that its address book becomes a large library and its degree of communicability reaches conscientese.

Continuity. The condition of advanced consciential nomadism only occurs after the consciousness reaches a better stage of continuous self-awareness, or continuity of its lucidity in the 3 basic consciential states: extraphysical (intermission), intraphysical (human life) and projected (projections of intraphysical and extraphysical consciousnesses).

Pyramid. Using a metaphor: the consciousness leaves the apex of its *evolutionary pyramid* in order to influence all the angles and sides of the bases of its rearguard. The more evolved it is, the greater the volume of its pyramid and the better the scope (extension and qualification) of the bases of its influence.

Projections. The more infrequent and nonlucid its projections of the consciousness are, the more distant the consciousness will be from the condition of consciential nomadism. The more frequent and lucid its projections of the consciousness are, the closer it will be to the condition of consciential nomadism.

Moksha. The condition of consciential nomadism gradually eliminates the effect of the cycle of successive resomas and desomas, allowing the consciousness to achieve the state of liberation of the multi-existential cycle, the third desoma or *moksha,* the main goal of the objective application of lucid consciential projections. In other words: consciential nomadism is a more practical and efficient instrument by way of which lucid projections annul the necessity of the consciousness to go through resoma.

Productivity. Upon becoming continually lucid and active, the consciousness singularly sophisticates or increases the degree of its productivity, which is far removed from the condition of the bedridden patient (entropies), of the human cadaver (fossilizations) or the *brainwashed* human-robot (repressions).

Condition. It can thus be understood, with reasonable clarity, that all effort tending toward the funneling of the ego, egokarma and groupkarma (egocentrism); submission; shyness; a monastic vocation; a parochial mentality; provincial or backwoods complacence; introversion; monoglotism with low communicability; and superspecialization which tends toward elitism is, basically and strictly speaking, a still very *anti-evolutionary* condition in relation to the real progress of the consciousness.

Avoidances. In light of the above, it is worth making the effort to remain forever alert, avoiding or combating: sectarianism; stagnant traditionalism; the obstinate judgment of corporatism; *nationalistic idolatry;* courtliness (castes); *group narcissism; leashes of the ego,* such as class, the orthodox church, race, the strict school, the radical faction and the impassioned club; canine, xenophobic territorial self-defense; religious, political, technical, athletic and sexual intolerance.

Domestication. Consciential nomadism exalts the continuous self-evolution of the person, opening up to fellow beings through mega-universality, impelling the intraphysical consciousness to make political unification of the globe a reality; the defense of ecology and the *omnilateral mind.* For this, it proposes that the person assume the *triangular interaction* of human-animal-plant and, as a social being, propose a *mutual domestication* of human and subhuman intelligence.

Character. Above all, consciential nomadism reaffirms, in a theorical and definitive manner for the interested individual, the *stateless character of the consciousness* or the compulsory and inevitable inseparability that exists between all beings within evolutiology.

XVI – Scientific Perspectives

495. LABORATORY EXPERIMENTS WITH LUCID PROJECTION

Mind. Conventional science abandoned the study of the mind or, more precisely, the consciousness, in the sixteenth century, when the scientific revolution began. There is still strong resistance from the scientific community, and even from human governments, toward acceptance of parapsychic phenomena in general as legitimate objects of research.

Paramind. Psychology, for instance, avoids even using the term *mind,* both *scientifically and euphemistically* (or with a *politically and scientifically correct posture*). When we refer to *mind,* it is only a primary perspective, or that indicative of a *kindergarten level of consciential evolution,* characteristic of the intraconsciential world of the *intraphysical consciousness.* It is not the far more complex perspective of the *extraphysical consciousness,* when free and healthy, and in possession of what can be called the *paramind* or the consciential micro-universe, which employs the holomemory, paragenetics and the reclaiming of holomaturity without the restrictive influences of the *resomatic funnel* of the holochakra and soma, with which we coexist, in a constrained manner, in human life.

Scientists. All scientists who resist the possibility of researching *mind-matter* (brain-consciousness) *interaction,* find it difficult to confront the facts of projectiology because of an alleged inability to comprehend its mechanism. Scientists are generally busy and do not like to change the way they think.

Case study. However, theses same scientists accept the idea of the *gravitational field,* without really understanding how this field works, which even further complicates the interaction of 3 or more bodies; they accept the space-time curvature caused by a physical body, without, in fact, knowing how this occurs.

Methods. According to Charles Fiore, scientific method requires rigorous proof for any new phenomenon. The less common and less orthodox the phenomenon is, the more rigorous the proof should be. This generally means developing a laboratory experiment which, when repeated, regardless of how many times – by any competent researcher, in any laboratory, in any part of the world – produces identical results.

Ease. Standard scientific method is relatively easy to apply in the areas of thermodynamics, atomic physics, organic chemistry and the physical sciences in general. In the cases listed above, the elements under investigation do not have a will of their own, since the relevant external variables, such as temperature, pressure, humidity, composition and other similar variables that are easily identified, measured and controlled, are kept constant and the phenomenon manifests on its own, in the same way, as many times as is necessary to be measured and quantified.

Prospective. The aspects of the reality detected can then be articulated into broad mathematical theories with great powers of prediction (prospective).

Psychology. Of all the sciences, psychology, sociology and economics present the most vague, uncertain and controversial information. The psychological and behavioral sciences present a context which is totally different from the physical sciences.

Control. The control of a certain number of variables becomes extremely problematic. Monkeys, rabbits and rats can be temperamental. The best experimental project can fail because on a certain day a pigeon is not sufficiently hungry to want to get its tasty reward, or a nasal infection makes the hamster incapable of smelling its way through a labyrinth.

Problems. The ability to repeat the experiment indefinitely and the use of statistical techniques is therefore essential in order to satisfy the requirements of scientific method. Nevertheless, psychological phenomena are, in fact, extremely capricious. Furthermore, a plethora of apparently spontaneous, repetitive, automatic, undirected parapsychic events occur. *Parapsi* phenomena are anomalies in the greatest philosophical sense.

Variables. The thoughts, reactions and general behavior of human beings are made up of a great number of variables – a far greater amount than in subhuman animals – such that it becomes a great deal more difficult to fit them into patterns, identify, control and predict them.

Will. Our will is sometimes recalcitrant, often due to causes that are unknown to ourselves and many others. This represents a problem in all psychological sciences, where the facts under investigation are, in and of themselves, subtle, quick, unconsciously provoked and little understood as much by the human-guinea pig as by the researcher.

Ignorance. Even the greatest amount of patience and the best experimental project cannot always obtain parapsychic results, nor can forecasts of results be made. We know very little about the effective control and precise measurement of the phenomena associated with the consciousness, including indispensable variables such as emotional states and processes of the will, but much can be understood through experiments, cataloging, annotation of commonalities, hypotheses, tests, and the construction of models, theories, theoricity and its evolution.

Impartiality. The scientist must be impartial and therefore does not have the right, without consideration, to refuse to fulfill the obligation of examining any alternative hypothesis that might be able to explain a phenomenon, regardless of its source.

Projection. The most difficult area for humankind to study is the consciousness' survival of biological death, deactivation of the soma or the *theta* phenomenon. Death of the human body constitutes a subject that is difficult to discuss even in an abstract manner. How can we introduce this complex study to the rigidly controlled conditions of the laboratory? Some researchers, nonetheless, now think that there is a process whereby they can do this through projection of the consciousness, or laboratorial minideaths.

Data. In the areas of parapsychology, in general, and those of projectiology, in particular, researchers should not expect to encounter research data in the manner in which they are accustomed, namely instrumental readings, photographs, maps, graphs and charts, together with the greatest possible quantity of statistical support, because we are coming face-to-face with the psyche and the mental world that lies outside the better known parameters and physical laws.

Instruments. Nevertheless, new instruments for detection and analytical study should begin to be built, at least for a part of this research, in the same way that these studies should begin to be compared with existing, known science in general.

Methodology. In order for projective phenomena to be studied, it is necessary to develop adequate research methodology in order for scientists to avoid making the common mistake of believing that the entire range of reality can be studied with the methodology of some of the natural sciences.

Studies. The body of evidential and circumstantial data on lucid projection – which should fit together like pieces of a puzzle – constitutes a fascinating and provoking field of study, for those whose temperament is not offended by the extremely individual nature of the information and who know how to coexist with the ambiguities of the problems, circumstances and occurrences that arise.

Science. In projectiology, one must endeavor to behave in accordance with the elevated ideals of science or, in other words, remain curious about everything that happens in the human consciousness' environment (holothosene), investigating and weighing things, and then calmly, fairly and impartially considering the evidence.

Cosmoethics. On the other hand, science is progressive, does not submit to preconceptions, does not become enslaved to convention, nor does it build walls that impede its investigations, although it must always respect ethics or cosmoethics.

Elimination. In projectiology, it is still necessary to eliminate the 4 most pernicious elements of the *gray area* of human knowledge:

1. **Doubts.** Depressive doubts or those which generate anxiety and insecurity, subsequently provoking compulsion.

2. **Mistakes.** Mistakes, generally of personal and paragenetic origin.

3. **Factiousness.** Sectarian opinions or those characteristic of the *human animal*.

4. **Preconceptions.** Preconceptions (or a priori generalizations) generated by social repressions and *leashes of the ego*.

Specialization. There is a need for specialization in the studies of projectiology that provides ample space for specialized studious individuals, because any research team should be multidisciplinary, as it requires the participation of parapsychologists, sensitives, psychologists, physicists, physicians, illusionists (prestidigitators), librarians, computer operators, technicians, and others.

Discovery. It is necessary to beware of overzealous individuals and those who are easily satisfied, valuing the competent students who have a considerable scientific, technical and professional training, who need to be curious, admiring and eager regarding discovery.

Difficulties. It is clear that countless unknown extraphysical occurrences exist, as well as those which are difficult to interpret and understand. The scarcity of explanations in the reports of lucid projections should be accepted as a fact of the current situation of projectiology in the same way that scientists relate to obscure phenomena, such as the experiences of Albert Abraham Michelson (1852-1931) and Edward Williams Morley (1838-1923); the fact of the energy quantum; and many others. The phenomenon itself requires an explanation and, for this reason alone, it is not possible to affirm its non-existence.

Processes. There are 2 general experimental processes regarding lucid projections:

1. **External.** The external method or that of objective, laboratorial and heteropsychic verification.

2. **Internal.** The internal method or that of subjective, individual and self-psychic experimentation.

Training. After dedicating him/herself to arduous training, the researcher becomes his/her own disciple, acquiring firsthand experience (projectiologist-projectionist). Lucid projections have been scientifically demonstrated in the laboratory.

Personalities. There are 4 types of distinct personalities involved in projectiology experiments:

1. **General.** The experimenters in general.

2. **Laboratorial.** The laboratorial projectors.

3. **Participative.** The participative researcher-projectors.

4. **Independent.** The independent projectors with individual experiences.

Motivation. One of the most powerful and convenient motivating factors encountered among those who dedicate themselves to laboratorial self-research with the lucid projection experience is precisely the laboratorial, prior, personal, participatory and nontransferable self-experience of a reasonably lucid, spontaneous consciential projection provoked by psychedelic drugs or a personal method. It may have been a single projection or one in a series, but is an incontestable fact for the individual. This will have indelibly been impressed upon the individual's rationality, self-discernment and memory, upon becoming a lucid consciential projector, or self-aware sensitive by him/herself.

Examples. Among the experimenters who have personally executed participatory research – the evidencing of facts through some type of lucid projection self-experience – the following 9 persons can be given as examples: Raymond Bayless (95, p. 153); Susan ("Sue") J. Blackmore (139, p. 1); Barbara B. Brown (211, p. 213); Hereward Hubert Lavington Carrington: 1880-1958 (249, p. 22); Michael Grosso (650, p. 188); Stuart Keith ("Blue") Harary (Rogo, 1446, p. 170); Andrija Karl Puharich (Black, 137, p. 159); D. Scott Rogo (1446, p. 170); William ("Bill") George Roll Jr. (Ashby, 58, p. 5). Apart from these, there are dozens of other researchers who have directed experimental parapsychic sessions, or even those of a philosophical and/or religious nature.

Understanding. If other researchers were able to learn to induce lucid consciential projections by themselves, in self-experiences – thereby avoiding the use of drugs, which distort both physical and extraphysical perceptions – they would be able to obtain better conditions for understanding the projectiological phenomenon for themselves.

Demand. Some of the above-named scientists, as well as many others, have been convinced of the reality of the experience of the consciousness outside the human body. Their dilemma continues to be extremely real and perturbing, as it is almost impracticable to satisfy the demands of their colleagues, in terms of the controlled laboratorial proof of projectiological experimentation, due to its parapsychic or multidimensional nature.

Drugs. Some experimenters have been solely inducing forced consciential experiences using light or heavy, legal or illegal drugs. This masks or jeopardizes their capacity to judge the projective phenomena critically. This posture generates false or erroneous conclusions regarding the phenomena that are restricted to the consciential area of classic, human or common psychology. Any type of drug – or consciential experiences forced in an extreme manner by pharmacological agents – does not always favor the development of projectiological research, due to the natural confusion that is established in the mind of those who experience these lucid projections and later analyze them.

Permanence. Laboratorial research, coupled with the psychophysiological experiences of the consciousness outside the body, within the constellation of projectiology phenomena, will now gain a permanent status. This will be structured in accordance with an obligation to the truth – in the judicious adoption of a position that is devoid of radicalism, with an emphasis upon a convergence of proofs, and in laborious investigation resulting from team effort – as will be seen in the next chapters, in which laboratory experiments are related.

Summaries. In each of the 6 chapters presented further ahead, which bring together the main laboratory experiments thus far performed with lucid projection, the following basic data have been emphasized: research object; researcher; location; institution; date; sensitive; personal data; experimental conditions; auxiliary equipment; time; duration; number of attempts; targets; findings; comparative percentages; conclusions; working hypotheses; and specialized bibliography.

Bibliography: Baumann (93, p. 99), Bayless (94, p. 73), Black (137, p. 43), Blackmore (139, p. 122), Bowles (182, p. 46), Braud (197, p. 5), Carrington (245, p. 278), Ebon (453, p. 110), Eysenck (493, p. 152), Fiore (517, p. 159), Giovetti (593, p. 23), Grattan-Guinness (626, p. 86), Greenhouse (636, p. 279), Mishlove (1055, p. 133), Monroe (1065, p. 69), Morris (1091, p. 1; 1093, p. 147), Muldoon (1103, p. 37), Osis (1168, p. 327; 1169, p. 525), Palmer (1191, p. 258), Pratt (1285, p. 43), Rogo (1446, p. 75), Roll (1464, p. 142), Salley (1496, p. 162), Smith (1570, p. 1), Stokes (1625, p. 23), Tart (1660, p. 179), Wang (1794, p. 15).

---

496.   SEVEN   MINUTES   IN   ETERNITY

Period. William ("Bill") Dudley Pelley, a North American writer and journalist, had been secluded with a large stock of provisions for several days in early May, 1928 in the tranquility of a cottage on his property in Altadena, California, for the exclusive purpose of writing a book.

Scenario. The property was located close to Pasadena, tucked away at the base of the Sierra Madre Mountains. The bedroom, situated at the back of the house, was quite well ventilated with two immense windows facing the mountains.

Occupation. The intellectual work proceeded normally and he was about to complete it. He felt himself to be both mentally and physically in good shape, writing 6 to 8 hours a day and enjoying outdoor recreation. He was alone, except for his dog Laska. One night, like any other, he went to bed at about 10 o'clock and began to read an interesting study on ethnology, a typical type of leisure reading for him.

Moment. At about midnight, Pelley felt sleepy. He put the book down, took off his glasses and turned off the bedside lamp, following a routine identical to that of hundreds of other nights spent in the tranquility of that isolated place. Laska slept curled up on the floor at the foot of the bed, its favorite spot.

Habits. Pelley did not recall having any specific dream, physical disturbance or insomnia during the first half of that night. He was not in the habit of drinking alcohol, but had been a moderate pipe smoker for the previous two decades, the pipe being an item that was always with him at the typewriter.

Scream. However, between 3 and 4 o'clock in the morning – a time that was later verified – a sharp, internal and frightful scream, commanded by his sleepy consciousness, abruptly came from his throat. Horrified, and in desperation, he moaned to himself, "I am dying! I am dying!"

Sensation. What actually happened to him at that moment he never knew. Some mysterious instinct had mercilessly interrupted his sleep, awakening him with that desperate admonition. Certainly something very serious had happened to him – something that had never occurred to him in his entire life – a physical sensation that he, as a professional writer, was able to describe, in every detail, as being a combination of a heart attack and apoplexy.

Beginning. It was a physical sensation. It was not a dream. He felt entirely awake and lucid. He knew that something had occurred with either his heart or his head – or maybe both – during sleep. His conscious personality was battling forces over which he had no control.

Recollections. He recalled that the phenomenon had begun when he lay down on the bed in the dark bedroom in that cottage in California, whereupon he was dragged to the depths of a cold, blue space with a sensation of endless descent, as though he was succumbing to the effects of anesthetic ether. Strange sounds rang out in his ears. Suddenly, a single thought curiously predominated as he continued to fall, "So, is this death?"

Laska. In the interval between the sharp attack and the end of his descent, he was in sufficient control of his physical senses to think, "My dead body will remain in this isolated house for many days before someone discovers it, unless Laska wakes up and looks for help."

Voice. At one point, a calm, clear, friendly voice whispered into his ear, "Calm down, my friend. Don't worry. You're all right. We're here to help you."

Extraphysical consciousnesses. Someone was helping him – actually two extraphysical consciousnesses – one with its right extraphysical hand at the nape of his neck, and another with its arm under his knees. He remained physically weak, unable to even open his eyes, because a sparkling opaque light was diffused throughout the place where they had taken him.

Dialogue. When Pelley finally regained control of himself, he discovered that he had been *reborn* over a beautiful marble slab, and had come to rest, nude, in front of 2 physically vigorous, apparently friendly youths in white linen uniforms. Both were discreetly amused by his confusion and obvious vexation. The taller one asked, "So, are you feeling better?" He answered, "Yes. Where am I?"

Question. They exchanged glances and merely responded that he should not try to perceive anything in the next 7 minutes. Pelley felt that his question could not be more ridiculous. He knew what had happened. He had gone through all the sensations of death and had appeared in a fascinating place where he had never been before.

Ecstasy. In his new state, he felt an indescribable mental and physical ecstasy. He knew that he was not dreaming. He felt he was alive and among many other intensely alive personalities. He had come with a type of personal body suitable for the new environment, through which he was aware of the beauty and enchantment of the surroundings, that surpassed any descriptions written by humankind. He perceived that he knew those two creatures intimately. His extraphysical experience continued to progress.

Experiences. There was a pool off to one side in which they recommended that he enjoy himself. Upon swimming in the apparently clean water, it seemed that the water itself clothed the nude body. Other extraphysical consciousnesses now appeared. He had the feeling that he had personally and intimately known each one of these enchanting beings at some time in the past. All prior feelings of terror and unfamiliarity had now disappeared completely.

Return. The conclusion of his experience was as unique as its beginning. He felt overcome by a sudden whirlpool of bluish vapor, arising from an unknown source, and something cracked inside his body. He instantly felt himself to be back in his human body, seated on the bed and completely awake. He noted only a certain physical exhaustion throughout the thorax and abdomen that lasted for some minutes. He then shouted, "That was not a dream!"

Dog. His voice awakened the sleeping dog.

Article. At first, this journalistic writer was very reluctant to write and publish his profound personal experience, for which he could be taken to be an eccentric or a lunatic. He had never performed any parapsychic research. Reporting the event could even affect his solid literary reputation. Nevertheless, the editors of *The American Magazine,* in New York, overcame his resistance and the work was written, still under protest, and went public as the first article in the magazine in March, 1929.

Reaction. At that time, the magazine's circulation was approximately 2,225,000. The magazine's advertisers calculated that, each issue being read by at least 4 people, a total of approximately 10,000,000 readers had had access to the report, if the majority of those people had actually read it. This fact was later confirmed due to the overwhelming number of letters received in response. Thousands upon thousands of individuals requested further clarification on his extraordinary experience.

Letters. Over a 6-month period, the writer qualified, analyzed, classified and answered the plethora of letters. Impressively, only 24 respondents did not believe that Pelley was healthy or normal. Many hundreds of readers affirmed that they had had similar experiences with the consciousness outside the human body. The majority, however, did not have the courage to relate the occurrences even to their close relatives, as they were fearful of being considered insane.

Verification. Pelley verified that the majority of the respondents had had experiences that were substantially identical to his in their basic elements. The magazine received the texts of 144 sermons that had been given by religious leaders to the public on the experience in question. The article was published in countless religious and theological periodicals. Of all the pastors, only one accused him of "having sold his soul to the devil," because his article did not mention Jesus Christ.

Pioneer. Suddenly becoming a celebrity with the article, Pelley was aware of having, in a certain strange manner, acquired new senses or prodigious perceptive faculties. This man who was a declared materialist, now felt like a pioneer of human consciousness research. During the same year of 1929, he wrote the small volume: *Seven Minutes in Eternity with their Aftermath.*

Bozzano. Professor Ernesto Bozzano – the indefatigable Italian researcher of animic and parapsychic phenomena, to which he dedicated himself for approximately 50 years – presented Pelley's account as Case N. 4 in one of his dozens of monographs: *Xenoglossy – Polyglot Mediumship.* The publishing house of the Brazilian Spiritist Federation released his book in Rio de Janeiro, faithfully translated to Portuguese by Guillon Ribeiro, in 1933, some time after the occurrence.

Crookall. The prolific English scientist, paleobotanist and author Dr. Robert Crookall, presented Pelley's account as Case N. 92 in his highly significant work, *The Study and Practice of Astral Projection,* published in London in 1960 and in New York in 1966. The case is included in the section of the book dedicated to the analysis of natural, or non-forced, out-of-body experiences.

Today. The facts under analysis here span 7 decades. Now, as the twentieth century draws to a close, in many countries and through a substantial amount of research, the phenomena of projectiology – especially impelled by near-death experiences, thanatology or desomatics, transpersonal psychology and lucid dream research – receive profound interest from eminent scientists in diverse areas, even in interdisciplinary fields.

Arguments. Research pertaining to experiences of the consciousness outside the human body is currently among the main arguments that most contribute toward scientifically and irrefutably evidencing the multiple dimensions of life and the multiple vehicles of the consciousness.

Freedom. Above all, one thing is currently incontestable: one can openly speak about human consciential projection, even by way of the greatest vehicles of mass communication, without worrying about being insane or considered ridiculous by various types of public.

Facts. The facts continue to speak for themselves. The 254 bibliographic sources on lucid projection cataloged by Professor Ernesto Bozzano over the course of 5 decades, grew to 838 cases meticulously analyzed by Dr. Robert Crookall over 3 decades. According to the archives of the author this has currently reached 5,116 diverse bibliographical sources, from 37 countries, in 20 different languages, as listed in the book, *700 Conscientiology Experiments.* It can be seen that projectiology and desomatics are now being developed on a firm footing. The only people who have not yet noted this fact are those who are out of touch with or uninformed regarding international scientific research.

Specific Bibliography:

1. **BOZZANO, Ernesto;** *Xenoglossia: Mediunidade Poliglota;* transl. Guillon Ribeiro; 218 pp.; 18 X 12 cm; hb.; Rio de Janeiro; Brazil; Livraria da Federação Espírita Brasileira; 1933; pp. 23-27. Editions in Italian, English and Portuguese.

2. **CROOKALL, Robert;** *The Study and Practice of Astral Projection;* X + 234 pp.; 6 chaps.; 9 apps..; New Hyde Park; New York; University Books; 1966; pp. 94, 95.

3. **PELLEY, William Dudley;** *Seven Minutes in Eternity with their Aftermath;* Autobiography; 58 pp.; illus.; 17 X 12 cm; hb.; New York; Robert Collier; 1929; pp. 1-58.

497. BRAIN WAVE PATTERNS

Projector. One of the classic experiments with lucid projection was performed by Charles Theodore Tart (1661, p. 3) in 1966 with a young projector, a young single woman, little more than 20 years of age, identified only by the pseudonym of "Miss Z." This experiment was conducted with the objective of demonstrating whether consciential projection could be produced in a laboratory, in this case at the University of California at Davis, USA.

Conditions. On 4 non-consecutive nights, Miss Z reclined on a comfortable bed in the sleep laboratory, making herself available for rigorous experimentation. In order to obtain the profile of all of her physiological changes, she was confined during the experiments – not being able to move from the dorsal position – with electrodes on different points of the head, hands and face, connected by cables to a battery of registering and measuring instruments that monitored: her brain wave patterns (EEG), involuntary synchronous rapid eye movements (REM), her basal skin resistance (BSR), galvanic skin resistance (GSR), heart rate and blood pressure (digital photoplethysmograph).

Room. Two types of multi-channel polygraph machines – Grass and Sanborn – were installed and were completely isolated in the next room, like mechanical sleep monitors, along with an intercom, which allowed the operator to communicate with the projector.

Target. The experimenter chose one 5-digit number at random (a different one each night) from a mathematical table of random numbers. He wrote the number, 2" (5 cm) high, on a small piece of paper. He then hid this on a shelf that was almost 5' (1.5 m) above the young woman's head, thus not allowing her to see the card with the number. She was instructed to sleep well and attempt to read the 5-digit number – her mental target – during a projection of her consciousness or, in other words, a projection of her self or the seat of her lucidity and elaboration of thought.

Findings. From the second to the fourth night, Miss Z reported having seen the wall clock over the shelf while floating outside the human body, which could not have been consulted from where she was, on the bed. She indicated the time shown by the hands of the clock to be precisely the time at which the equipment and polygraphs incontestably demonstrated unique, strange brainwave patterns obtained through the 2 frontal-to-vertex and vertex-to-occipital circuits, and the absence of involuntary rapid synchronous bi-ocular movements that accompany dreams.

Identification. On the fourth and last night, the projector accurately reported the hidden target-number: 25132.

Details. The researcher paid such attention to detail that, in anticipation of refutation by skeptics, he posed the hypothesis, which could not be discarded, that the sensitive could have seen the number reflected in the wall clock's black plastic casing, but he did not believe that this had occurred.

Results. The positive results of the experiment highlighted the brainwave patterns that had appeared with diverse flat, plane or straight-lined characteristics on the electroencephalogram and with accentuated alpha activity, when Miss Z reported that she had been outside her human body. The lack of eye movements shows that the lucid consciential projection is not merely an impression, or a simple autosuggestion or dream, but is a specific state of consciousness, different from the familiar stages of sleep, dream, somnolence and other altered states of consciousness, even the ordinary, physical waking state.

Bibliography: Baumann (93, p. 101), Bayless (98, p. 99), Black (137, p. 118), Blackmore (139, p. 189; 147, p. 4), Bowles (182, p. 62), Braud (197, p. 5), Cohen (290, p. 160), Crookall (320, p. 17), Currie (354, p. 87), Douglas (409, p. 329), Eysenck (493, p. 57), Giovetti (592, p. 24), Goldstein (609, p. 5), Grattan-Guinness (626, p. 84), Holroyd (739, p. 76), Keller (835, p. 349), Mishlove (1055, p. 134), Mitchell (1558, p. 357), Pratt (1285, p. 43), Rogo (1446, p. 103), Salley (1496, p. 162), Steiger (1601, p. 225), Tart (1660, p. 183; *1661,* p. 3), Ward (1797, p. 35), Watson (1800, p. 141).

---

498.   EXTRAPHYSICAL   IDENTIFICATION   OF   AWAKE   PERSONS

Projector. Between September, 1965 and August, 1966, a researcher, Charles Theodore Tart (1662, p. 251), requested on 8 occasions that author, inventor, businessman and projector Robert A. Monroe, produce lucid projections while connected to various types of equipment for measuring physiological functions in the Electroencephalograph Laboratory in the School of Medicine at the University of Virginia, USA.

Conditions. The conditions in the laboratory were not comfortable. A wooden cot – upon which he was to lie, remaining shirtless, dressed only in pants – with a sheet and a pillow, were set up in the semi-dark recording room. He was restricted by connections to the electroencephalograph (EEG) to measure his brainwaves, to an electrocardiogram (EKG) to monitor his heart rate and an electrooculograph (EOG) to measure his involuntary eye movements. The electrodes clipped to his ears caused discomfort and pulsation in the ears, making physical and mental relaxation difficult.

Target. The projector was requested to endeavor to direct his movements during exteriorization to the next room, not only in order to observe the activities of the technician who was monitoring the equipment, but also in order to attempt to read a 5-digit target-number that had been placed on a shelf 6'6" (2 m) above the floor.

Results. On the first 7 nights that he attempted to produce a lucid projection, Monroe did not meet with much success. On the eighth night he was able to produce two brief lateral departures of the consciousness. In the first brief projection, he witnessed some unknown persons talking to each other in an unknown location and was not able to verify whether or not this had been a real perception of occurrences at a distance. In the second brief projection, Monroe did not see the target-number in the next room because he was not able to control his movements. He did, however, correctly describe the female laboratory technician, who was outside the room in the corridor with a man who was later identified as her husband.

Findings. The two brief lucid projections occurred together with what are classified as Stage 1 brainwaves – the brainwave pattern that usually occurs in natural sleep with dreams – and some involuntary rapid bi-ocular movements. His heart rate remained between 65 and 75 beats per minute. The bi-ocular movements were not as rapid as is generally the case during normal sleep. The consciential projections occurred almost immediately after the consciential projector had gone to lie on his bunk, which is extremely rare, because Stage 1 natural sleep occurs after the sleeper has already had 80 to 90 minutes of dreamless sleep.

Conclusions. The experimental result was considered to be quite encouraging, given that it was one of the first attempts to scientifically produce and analyze the complex lucid consciential projection phenomenon in the laboratory.

Bibliography: Andreas (36, p. 37), Baumann (93, p. 100), Black (137, p. 119), Blackmore (139, p. 190; 147, p. 4), Cohen (290, p. 159), Coxhead (312, p. 119), Crookall (320, p. 18), Digest (399, p. 277), Douglas (409, p. 323), Drury (414, p. 29), Ehrenwald (471, p. 159), Greenhouse (636, p. 280), Hintze (726, p. 94), Krippner (863, p. 263), Mitchell (1058, p. 362), Monroe (1065, p. 69), Moss (1097, p. 301), Panati (1193, p. 171), Rogo (1446, p. 134), Salley (1496, p. 162), Spraggett (1589, p. 80), Steiger (1601, p. 225), Tart (1662, p. 251), Watson (1800, p. 141).

499. VISION OUTSIDE THE HUMAN BODY

Projector. The out-of-body vision phenomenon was studied 2 to 3 days a week over many months in 1972 in research conducted by Janet Lee Mitchell, a researcher at the American Society for Psychical Research (ASPR) in New York, NY, USA, and Karlis Osis (1917-). The research subject in these experiments was Ingo Swann, a surrealist painter and writer in his forties, and a clairvoyant with an outgoing personality. Remote viewing or traveling clairvoyance was also studied in these experiments. This is a phenomenon in which the brain of the sensitive is not totally emptied of the consciousness, as occurs during a classic projection in the psychosoma wherein the projector's consciousness is separated to a great degree and has no direct contact with the human body, except for the vital connection of the silver cord (holochakrology).

Conditions. The experiments were conducted during the day, with the clairvoyant seated, completely awake and aware. Electrodes were attached to his scalp, on his left and right occipital lobes, where vision is structured. There was a modern polygraph machine in the next room, thus controlling his movements during the entire period he was in the room.

Target. The immediate target area that the sensitive was to describe was located about 11'6" (3.5 m) above the floor in the room where he would sit. It was placed on a suspended platform that could only be seen when very close to the ceiling. The door was locked. The sensitive, who would enter the room precisely when the experiment began, was to see the target-objects, verbally describe them and subsequently draw them.

Results. The results of the experiments were entirely satisfactory. Swann's exterior vision seemed capable of perceiving more than his normal vision, such as seeing the forms of certain rays of light, ionization of the air with changes in luminous sources and reflections off shiny surfaces.

Details. The repeated experiments demonstrated that the clairvoyant generally seems to perceive the primary colors of paintings or drawings more clearly. Familiar forms seem to be identified with greater ease than unfamiliar forms and objects. Materials such as leather, fabric and ceramic seem to be more perceptible to clairvoyance than plastic, shiny paper or glass.

Judgment. A series of 8 different targets was used to evaluate the projectability of Swann's conscious vision by his describing the objects hidden in the suspended box. His drawings and transcribed verbal descriptions were all mixed together with the real target-objects, and a psychologist, who served as an independent judge, was asked to match the drawings to the target-objects. The judge correctly matched all 8 drawings with their respective target-objects. This result is so highly improbable that it could only happen, at random, in less than 1 in 40,000 attempts, which readily attests to the projective component of Swann's viewing.

Brain. The electroencephalograph readings of both of Swann's cerebral hemispheres were studied. During the periods in which the clairvoyant affirmed that his vision was outside the human body, there was a drop in electrical activity and some more rapid brain wave impulses appeared in the visual areas of his brain's occipital region. The drop in alpha activity during the state outside of the human body was more evident in the right cerebral hemisphere than in the left. All other organic functions remained normal.

Bibliography: Baumann (93, p. 21), Blackmore (147, p. 4), Coxhead (312, p. 122), Crookall (343, p. 166), Digest (399, p. 271), Douglas (409, p. 340), Ebon (454, p. 104), Giovetti (593, p. 25), Grattan-Guinness (626, p. 84), Greenhouse (636, p. 281), Holroyd (737, p. 16), Keller (835, p. 349), Krippner (863, p. 262), Mitchell (1058, p. 365), Rogo (1446, p. 156), Swann (1632, p. 104), Tart (1660, p. 192), Uphoff (1722, p. 81).

---

500. WILLFUL FLIGHT EXPERIMENT

Flight. In January, 1973, Karlis Osis, a parapsychologist, executed the experimental fly-in project, or the out-of-body experiment wherein volunteer projectors would *fly* into the building of the American Society for Psychical Research (ASPR), in New York. The project began with a general summons, throughout the entire Unites States, to those individuals who felt they could project, at will, from where they were to that Manhattan address.

Target. A small office on the fourth floor of the building of the institution was adapted in order to serve as the target-area for about 100 projectors, selected from a large number of volunteers who came forward. These people were informed where to project and, upon arriving, that they were to view 4 unrevealed target-objects which were later displayed in front of a fireplace. These objects were to be viewed at a predetermined time and in a specific position and angle of observation.

Devices. Considering that the direction of vision would be a key problem in the research, 2 optical instruments were used in the experiment: the Optical Image Device and the Color Wheel. Each of them had a small viewing window, the only opening through which the entire target could be seen. In the Optical Image Device, for example, which exhibited different images plus the different colors of the 4 quadrants, the final image was formed using black and white shapes, a color wheel and a series of mirrors. These optical instruments were created in order to eliminate the use of clairvoyance and telepathy. The projected consciousness that claimed to have perceived from a certain point in space should be able to see the target as it appeared through the viewing window, with the *stimulus figure* distorted by optical illusions.

Reports. After the experience, the projector was asked to report what had been observed in detail, according to a preestablished questionnaire, also producing, when possible, drawings and layouts of the location and the objects, either by mail or over the phone.

Percentage. After examining all the reports, it was clear that the experiment had not achieved total success. Only 15% of the *flying* participants were able to give convincing evidence that their consciousnesses (or rather: they themselves) had actually visited the ASPR office through some extraphysical process or vehicle.

Detours. Among the errors noted, certain detours made by lost projected projectors not able to reach the target-area deserve attention. A projector from Toronto, Canada reported interrupting the excursion in order to watch a fire on a nearby block. An extraphysical visitor described commonplace activities that had been occurring on the first floor of the ASPR building, as well as the time that had been wasted by watching many people preparing an art exhibit. Another projectionist affirmed having entered an apartment in a building across the street and having enjoyed silently observing its occupants.

Details. Some projectors had a distorted perception of the size of the target-objects. Others experienced a circular or global vision of things, seeing in all directions at the same time. The barrier placed on the table to divide and block the target-objects was perceived as being transparent by the consciousness of many narrators.

Cup. Among the volunteers who had showed that they had actually been in the target-place, one sensitive, Alexander Tanous, reported that his consciousness had left Portland, Maine many times during the experiment. He not only correctly identified the collection of objects on the round coffee table, the main programmed task, but also indicated the presence of an out-of-place cup of tea, left there due to the oversight of another researcher.

Plant. Another sensitive, Elwood Babbitt, reported that he had *flown* from his house in Wendell, Massachusetts and had reached the target-place on the third attempt, correctly describing it. This projector later drew a wide floor plan of the right side of the back of the office. It included a picture hanging on a wall and a certain plastic figure of a smiling little girl placed at the right side of the target-table.

Statuette. The figure of the smiling girl added a special dimension to the experiment. The researcher, Karlis Osis, had secretly contracted an artist to sculpt a double figure. The statuette appeared to be one thing, when seen from the front, the face of the smiling Venus, and something completely different, when seen from behind or, in other words, a *reclining chair,* in the place of the hair on the head and nape of the Venus. Babbitt saw the face of the statuette and did not see the recliner. This actually could not have been seen from the door from where he affirmed that he had been looking.

Discovery. Teddy Marmoreo, the projector from Toronto, was projected on a certain night, making a *extraphysical advance visit* (anticipatory excursion), investigating the environment ahead of schedule in order to familiarize himself with the target-area. On this occasion he saw Karlis Osis sleeping in the empty ASPR building, which was confirmed by the researcher.

Observations. The experiments showed the same results whether the physical body (soma) of the projector remained seated or lying down; or when the consciousness manifested in an extraphysical body or when it did not sense having any body at all, the condition of a projection in the mentalsoma, the parabody of self-discernment.

Successes. Most good experiments, when the observations were more obvious and conclusive, presented these characteristics: the consciousness did not remain lucid during the entire period of extraphysical exteriorization; the consciousness of the reporter arrived at the destination suddenly, landed right in the office and described the vision as clearly as if the person was, in fact, producing a trip outside the human body.

Failures. The experiment always failed in the following cases: when the sensitive reported having left the physical body slowly and with difficulty; when the consciousness remained lucid during the entire takeoff while leaving the physical body; when one experienced a long flight through space or seemed to be using a vehicle; and when one did not land in the chosen location or did not even find it.

Clairvoyance. The experiences showed that certain sensitives simultaneously felt aware in their physical bases and the ASPR office, which indicated the occurrence of the phenomenon of simple traveling clairvoyance and not an integral lucid consciential projection.

Instruments. Incidentally, researchers now have precise equipment that allows them to perfectly distinguish remote clairvoyance and the phenomenon of telepathy from genuine lucid projection of the consciousness from the human body. For this purpose, targets are placed inside a special box constructed such that they will become visible only when seen through a small viewing window set into one of the sides of the box.

Information. However, according to the same researcher, the results were generally not significant because even the best consciential projectors often saw or described objects in terms of their shapes and colors, and not specific material things with their precise names. Nevertheless, the experiment served to demonstrate the experimenter's hypothesis that the process of acquiring information during the state of lucid projection differs from that of ordinary extrasensory perception.

Brazilians. The Center for Continuous Consciousness, in Rio de Janeiro, Brazil, an institution of parapsychic research that existed prior to the International Institute of Projectiology and Conscientiology, applied the fly-in process over a period of months in the 1980's. Only 3 Brazilian consciential projectors were able to incontestably identify the objects, which were always maintained secret and were changed periodically. During this period, they were located in a room, in a building on Visconde de Pirajá Street, Ipanema district, at the consistently established time of one o'clock in the morning.

Bibliography: Baumann (93, p. 106), Black (137, p. 88), Blackmore (142, p. 193; 147, p. 4), Currie (354, p. 89), Digest (399, p. 282), Douglas (409, p. 330), Ebon (453, p. 71; 454, p. 108), Greenhouse (636, p. 283), Holroyd (736, p. 107), Mishlove (1055, p. 136), Moss (1097, p. 304), Osis (1167, p. 18), Rogo (1446, p. 162), Tanous (1647, p. 124), Vieira (1748, p. 5), Wheeler (1826, p. 84).

501. ANIMAL-DETECTORS OF THE PROJECTED CONSCIOUSNESS

Spirit. Among the laboratory experiments performed on lucid projection, it is worth singling out the projects performed in 1977 by the American researcher Robert ("Bob") Lyle Morris. On that occasion, Morris used Stuart Keith ("Blue") Harary, then a psychology student at Duke University, in the United States, as a research subject. The team, hypothesizing the psychic sensitivity of subhuman animals, tested Harary's 2-month-old kitten, named Spirit.

Cage. The kitten was placed in a cage, the floor of which measured 30" x 80" (76 cm x 203 cm). It was divided into 24 numbered 10-inch (25 cm) squares, over which the animal was obliged to circulate.

Observations. All of the activities of the animal were observed during 2 preliminary periods, followed by 2 experimental periods of 2 minutes each, 1 during a lucid projection and the other during an occasion in which the projector was awake and speaking with the researchers.

Squares. The kitten was monitored using a synchronized clock. Its activity was determined by counting the number of squares over which it moved, thus determining whether or not it could detect the physical-extraphysical presence of the visiting projected projector's consciousness.

Equipment. The sensitive-projector, Stuart Harary, remained in a laboratory of the University of California at Santa Barbara, surrounded by equipment for monitoring his psychophysiological changes, including: an EEG (brain), an EOG (eyes), and an EMG (chin), his respiration, a digital plethysmograph and measurement of the electrical resistance of his skin.

Detection. In order to detect the presence of the projected projector, many other instruments were also used to measure the intensity of the electromagnetic field, the magnetic permeability of the circulating air. Oscilloscopes, thermometers, photomultiplier tubes and a spectrometer were used, in order to measure changes in the energy patterns of the target-area visited by the projector's consciousness or "incorporeal self" (ego).

Indications. The experiments worked splendidly, in regard to the use of all the instrumentation, intended to allow external incontrovertible indications that could fully demonstrate the occurrences.

Behavior. During the experimental period of the projection, the kitten behaved in a passive manner, remaining calm, without mewing, as though it were seeing or perceiving Harary's physical presence. When Harary was not projected, Spirit was constantly trying to get out of the animal activity board and mewed 37 times, but during the lucid projection period, the kitten became calm and did not mew even once.

Results. It was concluded that there was less than a 100:1 possibility of these results occurring by chance. In other words, the results suggested a *parapsi interaction* between the animal and the projected consciousness of the student.

Imagination. At another point, Harary was asked to perform *a false projection,* in which he would endeavor to create the mental images he usually associated with the *real projection* of visiting the kitten, including images of playing with the animal, petting it and getting its attention.

Effects. This other experience demonstrated that merely thinking about and imagining scenarios with the animal did not provoke any of the effects that had occurred during the lucid projection.

Telepathy. The imaginary experience excluded the possibility of simple telepathy having occurred, or another essential parapsychic phenomenon or concomitant phenomenon having taken place between the projector and the subhuman animal. It did, however, indicate something more substantial, namely the production of a projection of the lucid consciousness from the human body in another consciential dimension.

Affinity. Later tests with a hamster (cricetid, gerbil) and a snake did not present the same positive results as those which had occurred with the clairvoyant kitten. According to Morris, the affinity between Harary and his kitten Spirit, actually a pioneer animal-sensitive, a true hero of experimental science, helped the laboratorial proof, which did not occur with the other animals, with which the student had no affinity.

Communication. This experience was very important based on the fact that, for the first time on the entire planet, psychic communication between a human being and an animal had been consistently demonstrated in a strictly controlled laboratory experiment.

Bibliography: Baumann (93, p. 110), Black (137, p. 74), Blackmore (139, p. 220; 146, p. 5), Bowles (182, p. 48), Currie (354, p. 88), Digest (399, p. 278), Douglas (409, p. 332), Ebon (453, p. 86), Eysenck (493, p. 158), Fiore (517, p. 165), Giovetti (593, p. 25), Globo (602, p. 17), Grattan-Guinness (626, p. 83), Greenhouse (636, p. 295), Hintze (726, p. 96), Holroyd (737, p. 101), Krippner (861, p. 150), Mishlove (1055, p. 135), Morris (1089, p. 2; 1090, p. 8; 1092, p. 55), Pisani (1248, p. 128), Rogo (1439, p. 57), Salley (1496, p. 162), Stokes (1625, p. 23), Targ (1651, p. 154), Vieira (1762, p. 20).

502. KINETIC EFFECTS OF THE PROJECTED CONSCIOUSNESS

Tests. In 1979, Karlis Osis and Donna L. McCormick, at the American Society for Psychical Research in New York, researched the kinetic effects of the ostensive position of the consciousness in projections from the human body by using perception tests.

Conditions. The team used a system of control and automatic register, containing sensors placed inside a sealed chamber that were capable of detecting the physical presence of the projector-observer's psychosoma projected from the human body. Alexander Tanous was the projector in this experiment.

Target. During this projection, the projector was to provide extrasensorially perceived information about a figure that was produced at random by a special optical system inside the shielded chamber.

Results. The experiment consisted of 197 attempts, resulting in 114 hits and 83 misses, during 20 sessions. This indicated the presence of *something,* in this case, the kinetic effects of the psychosoma's presence between the sensors in the shielded chamber every time the projected projector was able to correctly describe the figure selected by the *optical image device.*

Conclusions. Lucid projection experiments are the same as some research performed on personality theory: they neither conclusively prove nor invalidate the basic concepts of the theory, but can reinforce or weaken them. The results of this experiment decisively reaffirmed the validity of the working hypothesis of the location of the consciousness outside the human body (extrasomatic) during lucid projections.

Photography. It is to be hoped that, in the future, the psychosoma of the projector, while projected from the human body, will be photographed by an ultra-sensitive camera at the precise moment that its presence is perceived by the activation of sensors in the sealed chamber.

Bibliography: Andrade (29, p. 68), Blackmore (139, p. 223; 143, p. 365), Digest (399, p. 279), Eysenck (493, p. 159), Goldstein (607, p. 4), Grattan-Guinness (626, p. 83), Osis (1164, p. 367; 1168, p. 319), Perry (1238, p. 59).

---

503. PHYSIOLOGY OF THE PROJECTIVE STATE

Definition. Projective state: the set of conditions in which the human organism remains during the entire period of the lucid projection of the intraphysical consciousness from the physical body or soma.

Synonymy: extracorporeal state; mescalinic destiny; OBE state; OOB state (out-of-body state); projective condition; psychedelic condition; state of unfolding.

Physiology. The initial observations with respect to the physiological performance of the human organism during the lucid projection of the consciousness – an activity of the individual that is also physiological or non-pathological – are beginning to emerge subsequent to pioneering experiments with self-induced projections in laboratories.

Brain. Electroencephalograph recordings have shown that a decrease in the electrical activity of the brain occurs during lucid projection.

Hemisphere. The aforementioned decrease in cerebral electrical activity is most pronounced in the right cerebral hemisphere, together with acceleration of the brainwave patterns in the visual areas of the occipital lobe of the lucid projector's physical brain.

Information. The processes of the right cerebral hemisphere suggest that these same processes are involved in the mechanism of acquisition of extraphysical information by the projected intraphysical consciousness.

Sleep. The projective state differs from that of natural or delta sleep, according to the various measurements taken with laboratory equipment.

REM. Electrooculogram recordings have verified that involuntary, synchronous, rapid, bi-ocular movements (REMs) greatly diminish or even cease during lucid projection.

Myology. According to various physiological verifications, including basal skin response (BSR) and galvanic skin response (GSR) readings, a reduction in *muscle tonus* occurs in the human body of the projector during lucid projection.

Frequency. The supposition that a lowering of cardiac frequency is a predisposing factor toward lucid consciential projections, as affirmed by diverse projectors, has still to be confirmed by electrocardiograph and blood volume (digital photoplethysmograph) measurements of the physical body of the projected projector.

Discoincidence. Ganzfeld stimulation ("entire field"), a state of profound progressive muscular self-relaxation, mental concentration, physical stress and psychophysical shock can trigger or precipitate the lucid consciential projection process. This induction is apparently caused by a lack of proprioceptive feedback from the muscles and motor system of the human organism, as well as a general paralysis of the motor system and a decrease in respiratory frequency, which results in discoincidence of the vehicles of manifestation of the intraphysical consciousness.

Conquest. The consciential condition of lucid projection, or the projective condition, is common to both the intraphysical consciousness and the extraphysical consciousness. After their productive, voluntary provocation, lucid projections will always continue as a personal, inalienable conquest of the aware consciousness.

Desomatics. According to extraphysical observations, the intraphysical consciousness accustomed to having lucid projections – even if they are only in the psychosoma – will, after the biological shock of desoma (final projection), be predisposed and apt to produce lucid paraprojections in the mentalsoma. Conclusion: the individual who begins to produce fully lucid consciential projections will not stop having these experiences, either as an intraphysical consciousness or as an extraphysical consciousness.

Psychosoma. From the foregoing we may infer that there is also a *parapsychophysiology* of the extraphysical consciousness' paraprojective state. In this case, paraphysiology refers to the psychosoma of the extraphysical consciousness, when it finds itself in the paraprojective state.

Seats. Strictly speaking, the projective state refers to two separate parts, or consciential seats, of the set of vehicles of manifestation of the consciousness:

1. **Full.** The *full* (inhabited) seat where the consciousness is located at any given moment or, in other words, the parabrain of the psychosoma (extraphysical dimension), or the mentalsoma (mentalsomatic dimension), relative to the paraprojective state.

2. **Empty.** The *empty* (vacant) seat left behind, in this physical dimension, by the intraphysical consciousness in the act of projecting or, in other words, the condition of the brain of the human body emptied of the consciousness, which finds itself projected; or even, the empty brain also accompanied by the *empty parabrain* (of the psychosoma), relative to the projective state.

Projected. The projective state relative to the full seat of the consciousness constitutes 1 of 3 basic states of the consciousness (conscientiology): the desomatic state, the resomatic state and the projected state. The *projected state* can be divided into the intraphysical consciousness' projected state and the extraphysical consciousness' projected state.

Methods. In addition to the laboratorial experimental procedures relative to human consciential projections that have been analyzed in this section up to this point, and better than all the projectiological research processes, 3 other methods are commonly employed in the accurate study of these phenomena. They will be addressed in the following chapters and are: self-observations, public research and the collection of cases on projective occurrences. The detailed research of public opinion can prove to be qualitatively superior to collections of individual projective cases because they are more systematized and demand greater technical sophistication in their development. The research performed with self-observation and collection of projective cases are generally overly influenced by the intrusion of preconceptions, conditioning and the theoretical tendencies of the researcher.

Bibliography: Blackmore (139, p. 121), Grattan-Guinness (626, p. 85), Huson (768, p. 115), Mitchell (1060, p. 44), Morris (1092, p. 127), Osis (1168, p. 319), Salley (1496, p. 162), Schutel (1525, p. 22), Stokes (1625, p. 22), Tart (1661, p. 3), Vieira (1762, p. 177).

504. INDIVIDUAL EXPERIMENTS WITH LUCID PROJECTION

Definition. Provoked lucid projection: the individual, physiological experiment, produced by the will under more natural conditions, wherein the consciousness exits the human body in an intentional, deliberate and repeated manner.

Synonymy: deliberate projection; intentional projection; physiological projection; willful projection.

Specification. The provoked lucid projection, referred to here, in addition to not being an exteriorization that is excessively forced by artificial means, is also not spontaneous, much less occurring in a gratuitous manner, without effort.

Introspection. In the nineteenth century, the basis of psychological investigation was the method of introspection, through which the individual, who was also usually the investigator, tried to observe and classify his/her thoughts and experiences while solving problems, learning, recalling or executing any other cognitive activity, exploring the nature and functions of mental or psychic processes.

Contestation. The traditional procedures of introspection began to be contested in the twentieth century because the investigations in which only one person can make observations are generally not considered to be scientifically rigorous. The observer's statements, in this case, cannot be verified and are therefore open to criticism, especially if the individual is simultaneously the researcher and the research subject, and if it is known that the person has interests (a priori judgments, preconceptions) in regard to establishing a specific theory, to the detriment of another.

Registers. According to the material presented, techniques and instrumentation for measuring rapid, synchronous, involuntary eye movement, electrical brain activity and other physiological processes are extremely important for the study of lucid projection in the laboratory because this apparatus makes it possible to observe some aspects that occur when the subject describes mental (imagetic) images.

Comparison. Nevertheless, the basic problem of the personal nature of these images still requires a solution, which is why, in the research of phenomena as subjective as lucid projection, individual experiences cannot be definitively discarded, as they will always have documentary value, especially with regard to the comparison of reports.

Subjectivity. If we ponder the subject with maximum rationality, conventional scientific methods – to the degree that, due to their methodology, they do not lend themselves to the possibility of understanding that which is specifically subjective – cannot discard individual reports.

Paratroposphere. Experiences of the consciousness outside the human body provide certain images that are directly observable only by the researcher-subject-self-observed-projector. In many cases this excludes other people, as with experiences of the consciousness in paratropospheric districts of the extraphysical dimension (those beyond the terrestrial crust), as well as expansions of the consciousness in the mentalsomatic dimension.

Prospective. So far, no one has been able to conceive any reliable and executable experimental project using human instrumentation, except for the consciousness itself, in order to detect these transcendent experiences. Only the future will tell regarding this matter.

Amateur. Based on the facts, we can conclude that parapsychic research is, without a doubt, currently one of the only fields of human investigation in which the amateur still has a chance to compete with the professional.

Projectiology. Those who decide to investigate self-psychically – within and by themselves – the fields of parapsychic phenomena, especially within projectiology, can still discover one or two things ahead of the scientists. This offers a great incentive for candidates to lucid projection self-research, whether youths or adults.

Conflicts. Given that each person's judgment is very individual, we can understand why there are sometimes apparent conflicts between the observations of events that engage the projected intraphysical consciousness while in another dimension. This is due to the diversity of cultural backgrounds, degrees of extraphysical perception and different capacities for translating extraphysical sensations, as well as intraconsciential conditioning, social influences, abdominal brainwashing and various types of repression.

Conditioning. The intraphysical consciousness' intraconsciential conditioning of an educational, religious, philosophical, scientific, or professional nature, among others (leashes of the ego), represents those factors that most negatively influence the precise evaluation of the intraphysical consciousness' personal experiments when projected outside the human body – whether *distorting* with *parti pris* or fanaticism, consciously or unconsciously *masking* and subverting facts with spurious and undesirable fantasies, exaggerations and superfluity, which suffocate even the best self-critique.

Agreements. In spite of the effects of the complexity of human personalities, the convergences of opinion, mutual agreements or interactive and common denominators that are encountered greatly serve to overcome the divergences in observations made regarding sensations in and reports on the periods before, during and after lucid projection. These convergences of opinion or universality of reports are what can confidently lead researchers to a consensus on definitive evidence, which is accepted *urbi et orbi,* and which permits the establishment of solid foundations in this and other books, theses and specialized papers on the subject.

Objective. Unquestionably, the main objective of all lucid self-projectors regarding the problems of projectiology has been to find a practical, safe, universal projective method that works for all persons, regardless of gender, age, health, culture, domicile and background, as well as psychological or intraconsciential conditioning of any kind.

Fantasy. This method has still not been found and it may simply be a fantasy, in view of the profound diversity of human personalities.

Directives. Nevertheless, it will always be useful to establish the greatest possible number of technical directives that serve to help novice lucid projectors. This is one of the objectives of the author, this book, the IIPC, CHSC and the IAC.

Practice. The authors of the works in the general bibliography at the end of this book have, almost in their entirety, not had any personal experience with lucid projection. This fact is totally comprehensible to any lucid projector.

Writers. The majority of writers are simply writers. They write things to sell (instant books) and do not really have personal experience; they have not actually *gone through* everything that they write. They can even be theoretically very honest when writing, sharing their knowledge, but they are merely repeating what they have read from other authors who, in turn, copied from someone else before them. That is why individual experiences with lucid projection are so very valuable.

Theoricity. Before employing the bibliography of other authors, the author, to maintain honesty, needs to have personal, nontransferable experiences, *sweating blood,* in order to affirm any principle in a manner that is cosmoethical, within the world of projectiology and conscientiology research.

Conscientiologist. It is always a minor accomplishment (existential miniprogram) to be a mere bibliographical or *self-mimetic* researcher who does not propose challenging theories as a multidimensional, holosomatic conscientiologist (scientist who studies the consciousness, consciential researcher), endeavoring to act beyond the scope of conventional science, beyond the complacent, gratifying aspects of the consolation task.

Irrefutable. It is necessary to go far beyond the status quo, in the manner of those works that already exist and have withstood refutation for several decades, along with their consequent practices (theorices), techniques, tests and therapies. The following are 5 examples from among more than 200 that have been published and tested by thousands of intraphysical consciousnesses, within the world of projectiology and conscientiology: *Homo sapiens serenissimus* (serenology), penta (assistentiology), existential inversion (invertology), VS (holochakrology) and thosene (thosenology).

Self-projections. Finally, it becomes clear why individual projective experiments have been maximally stimulated everywhere, obtaining, when possible, the collection of opinions and personal reports that either corroborate or contradict the established data and previously tabulated figures. All this has the purpose of establishing the technical directives for behavior, work hypotheses, paradigms for the phenomena, and the formation of a valid consensus regarding the true nature of the human lucid projection experience. The non-experimental methods likewise demonstrate the undeniable usefulness in generating hypotheses that can be experimentally tested in the future.

Projector-authors. The following is a list of 30 projector-authors – among many others – who have written analytical, descriptive communications or autobiographical works on the phenomena of human lucid projection. They are grouped here according to their 9 countries of origin:

West Germany: Herbert H. G. Engel; Reinhard Fischer; Alfred Lischka.

Brazil: Yvonne do Amaral Pereira; Hamilton Prado.

Denmark: Johannes E. Hohlenberg.

Spain: Vicente Beltrán Anglada.

United States of America: Patricia Garfield; Richard A. Greene; Stuart Keith Harary; John Mittl; Robert Allan Monroe; Sylvan Joseph Muldoon; Henry Steel Olcott (1832-1907); Ingo Swann; Alexander Tanous.

France: Francis Lefebure; Marcel Louis Fohan ("Yram"); Anne Osmont (1872-1953).

England: J. H. Brennan; Annie Brittain; Hugh G. Callaway ("Oliver Fox"); William Alexander Gerhardie; Frank Hives; John Oxenham; Frederick C. Sculthorp; Vincent Newton Turvey; Joseph Hilary Michael Whiteman.

Ireland: Eileen Jeanette Vancho Lyttle Garrett.

Sweden: Emanuel Swedenborg.

Projectiological Bibliography: Ald (10, p. 21), Anglada (39, p. 25), Brennan (200, p. 71), Brittain (206, p. 45), Engel (480, p. 1), Fischer (519, p. 19), Fox (544, p. 32), Garfield (569, p. 72), Garrett (574, p. 69), Gerhardi (584, p. 21), Grattan-Guinness (626, p. 86), Greene (635, p. 47), Harary (679, p. 21), Hives (728, p. 69), Lefebure (909, p. 65), Lischka (937, p. 91), Mittl (1061, p. 4), Monroe (1065, p. 63), Muldoon (1105, p. 45), Olcott (1147, p. 357), Oxenham (1179, p. 1), Pereira (1230, p. 16), Prado (1284, p. 14), Rosin (1475, p. 30), Sculthorp (1531, p. 17), Swann (1632, p. 65), Swedenborg (1639, p. 1), Tanous (1647, p. 113), Turvey (1707, p. 111), Vett (1738, p. 379), Vieira (1762, p. 17), Whiteman (1840, p. 1), Yram (1897, p. 55).

Specific Bibliography: The most recent work of the author on the subject: *200 Teáticas da Conscienciologia: Especialidades e Subcampos (200 Conscientiology Theorices: Subdisciplines).*

---

505. PROJECTIVE PUBLIC OPINION RESEARCH

Definition. Opinion research: surveys conducted in order to discern public opinion, arising from the personal experience of a given population through random sampling, based on the principle that every sample represents the entire population, in miniature.

Synonymy: analysis of reports from a sampling; public opinion poll; regional inquiry; statistical public survey.

Profile. The data collection method (survey, poll) is especially valuable for obtaining a cross section of the population, with comparative objectives.

Universality. The following are 26 statistical research projects, among dozens of others. They include those involving surveys (samplings and analyses of public opinion) that have been conducted since the last century, and more intensely in recent decades. They aim to characterize precisely aspects of projection of the consciousness outside the human body, such as the frequency of the phenomenon and its characteristics and uses, in a search for a convergence of evidence through a universality of reports.

1. **Double.** In 1890, the British Society for Psychical Research, of London, asked thousands of persons this question: "Have you ever, when believing yourself to be completely awake, had a vivid impression of seeing or being touched by a living or inanimate object, or of hearing a voice; which impression, so far as you can discover, was not due to any external physical cause?" Of 17,000 answers, 10% were affirmative. One third of this group said that they had seen the doubles of living persons.

2. **Cases.** In the 1950s, Hornell Norris Hart (1888-1967), then an assistant to Joseph Banks Rhine, examined 288 cases of lucid projection cited in specialized literature. In 99 of these cases he received satisfactory affirmations from the witnesses. In 20 of these 99 cases, the projection was provoked by hypnosis. The majority of the other cases occurred spontaneously, often at the very instant that the projector thought intensely about the other person that the individual would later visit.

3. **Positivity.** In 1952, the same Hornell Hart asked the following question to 155 sociology students at Duke University, in North Carolina, USA: "Have you ever actually seen your physical body from a viewpoint completely outside that body, like standing *beside* the bed and looking at yourself lying *in* the bed, or like floating in the air near your body?" The researcher received 27% affirmative responses.

4. **Critical.** In 1956, Joseph Hilary Michael Whiteman published examples that were chosen from 550 cases of lucid projection, some of which he himself experienced, in which he, in principle, excluded those of a mystical nature. According to this researcher, the projectors' faculties of critical reflection were not only maintained, but also amplified and intensified by an apparently higher level of awareness. The sense of this would be retained after the interiorization of the projected intraphysical consciousness.

5. **Questionnaires.** In 1966, the psychical researcher Celia Elizabeth Green (1935-) made requests in the press and over London radio stations that the reading and listening audience respond to questionnaires regarding experiences in which they had observed things from a point outside their human body. Two questionnaires were sent out in order to be returned; 326 responses to the first questionnaire were received and 251 responses to the second, with written narratives that were typical of projections of the consciousness. These were detailedly and systematically tabulated and statistically analyzed.

6. **Oxford.** In 1967, Celia Elizabeth Green asked 380 students at Oxford University, in Great Britain, if they had had any experience in which they felt they were outside the human body. The researcher received 34% affirmative responses.

7. **Southampton.** In 1967, the same researcher and author, Celia Green, repeated the previous survey, but now asked 115 students at Southampton University, in Great Britain. She received 19% affirmative responses.

8. **Press.** In 1967, John Poynton, a biologist at the University of Natal, South Africa, published a questionnaire in the local press requesting written reports on lucid projection. He received 122 analyzable positive responses.

9. **Psychedelics.** In 1971, Charles Theodore Tart, the well-known American researcher and author, received 44% affirmative responses about lucid projection in a research project including 150 people who had had psychedelic experiences with marijuana.

10. **Religious.** Frances Mary Banks verified that 45% of a group of 800 English, religious, churchgoing individuals affirmed, when asked, that they had already experienced the consciousness being outside the human body.

11. **Audience.** In the 1980s, well-known projector and author, Robert Allan Monroe, asked, in a public lecture on the subject in New York, how many in the audience had had experiences outside the human body. About 1/3 of those present raised their hands.

12. **Postal.** In 1974, John Palmer conducted a research project on lucid projection using questionnaires that were mailed to 700 adult residents of Charlottesville, Virginia, USA. Of the 341 residents who returned a completed questionnaire, 48 (or 14%) responded in the affirmative. Of the students who participated, 266 (or 89%) answered the item about lucid projection, and 66 (25%) of them responded that they had experienced a lucid projection. In the combined samples, 83% of those who reported having had a projection had experienced it only once and 34% had had 8 or more projections. The findings showed that lucid projection is an experience that is common to humanity.

13. **Paranormality.** In 1975, Richard L. Kohr conducted a survey of parapsychic experiences among Americans who were living in cities and were members of the Association for Research and Enlightenment (ARE), headquartered in Virginia Beach, Virginia, with the aim of evaluating the degree of relationship between *parapsi experiences* and other correlated factors, such as habits, attitudes and demographic characteristics. More than 400 people responded, and their responses on lucid projection figured significantly in all the tabulations that were statistically analyzed.

14. **Iceland.** In 1977, a research project was performed in Iceland, wherein 8% of the 902 individuals interviewed affirmed already having experienced at least one lucid projection.

15. **Surrey.** In 1978, another research project was performed with students of Surrey University, Great Britain. Of the 132 interviewees, 11% affirmed having already had an experience outside the human body.

16. **Virginia.** In 1979, another research survey among students at the University of Virginia, USA, revealed that, of the 268 interviewees, 25% had already experienced at least one lucid projection.

17. **Residents.** In 1979, another research project conducted with Virginia state residents showed that 14% of the 354 participants had already had one lucid projection.

18. **Australia.** In 1980, another research program involving students at the University of New England, Australia, verified that 16% of 177 interviewees had already experienced lucid projection.

19. **Psychiatrists.** In 1980, psychiatrists Glen O. Gabbard, Fowler C. Jones and Stuart W. Twemlow, all professors at the University of Topeka, Kansas, USA, sent questionnaires on experiences outside the human body to 420 randomly selected people who were in good physical and mental health, had a college education and were not addicted to drugs. Of those, 339 responded to the questionnaire, allowing the researchers to establish some of the main characteristics of the phenomenon: 85% considered the experience to be very agreeable; 43% considered lucid projection to be the most important factor in their life; 94% affirmed lucid projection to be more real than a dream; 66% thought that their life had changed after the occurrence. These researchers made a marked distinction between lucid projection and the pathological states of depersonalization, morbid autoscopy and schizophrenic syndromes.

20. **Lucid.** In 1981, in England, Susan J. Blackmore verified the existence of a 13% and 14% occurrence rate of lucid projection among groups of 217 students and 155 students respectively. They were simultaneously questioned about lucid projection and lucid dreams, or semilucid projections.

21. **Electors.** Susan J. Blackmore, in 1981, also developed a research project on the lucid projection experience that was mailed to a total of 593 participants selected at random from the registered voters in Bristol, England. The questionnaire asked about dreams, hallucinations, distortions in the corporal image, psychic experiences and beliefs, mystical experiences, imaginal creations and lucid projections. She received 321 (55%) completed questionnaires. Of these, 12% of the respondents reported having had lucid projections. The most important finding was the pronounced association between many of the experiences.

22. **Psychotronics.** On July 28, 1982, on the final night of the III National Congress on Parapsychology and Psychotronics, at the Rio Sheraton Hotel, in Rio de Janeiro, Brazil, during

a presentation on the subject, the author queried the auditorium, filled with 350 participants, and received the immediate response that 25 of those present, namely 7.14% of the audience, had experienced a lucid projection.

23. **Location.** Relative to statistics on written personal experiences, Robert Crookall, a celebrated London researcher, revealed that, in 85% of 838 cases of lucid projection, analyzed in detail, the consciousness of the projected projector remained right here, in the physical or human world (intraphysicology); in the remaining 15%, the projector entered the extraphysical world per se or, in other words, *the world of extraphysical consciousnesses* (extraphysicology).

24. **Italy.** The Italian researcher Paola Giovetti developed a public opinion poll on projection of the consciousness, distributing 300 questionnaires in Italy with dozens of questions, from which 110 were selected and diverse aspects of the phenomenon were analyzed in detail.

25. **Frequency.** Research has also been performed with projectors regarding the frequency of their experiences outside the human body or, in other words, projections in series.

26. **Congresses.** During a presentation made by the author on lucid projection, in room "A" at Rio-Centro, Rio de Janeiro, RJ, Brazil, at 4:00 PM, Sunday, October 27, 1985, on the final day of the extremely popular I Esoteric Fair, it was publicly verified that, of the 450 people present, 30 affirmed having already had at least one lucid consciential projection during their life. The same occurred at the Recife International Club, in Pernambuco, Brazil during the V Brazilian Congress on Parapsychology, at 7:00 PM on Saturday, October, 1986, when it was publicly verified that, of the 572 persons present, 81 affirmed having had at least one lucid consciential projection in their life. In the same manner, in room "A" at the Brazilian College of Surgeons, in Rio de Janeiro, during the I Congress on Alternative Therapies, at 7:00 PM, on Saturday, October, 1986, of the 174 persons present in the audience, 73 declared having had at least one lucid consciential projection in their existence.

Differences. The differences in the percentages of the public opinion surveys conducted on lucid projection over time are attributed to 4 basic causes:

1. **Samplings.** The striking differences between the population samples polled.
2. **Questions.** The variation and nonuniformity of the questions posed to the interviewees.
3. **Context.** The specific context within which the questions were formulated.
4. **Understanding.** That which was actually understood by those interviewed with regard to the questions asked.

Incentive. The expressive, convergent results of these public opinion polls, the collection of similar experiences and the rich source of material for projectiological study – with immense potential for statistical analysis – were obtained over a period of almost 1 century and collected in 7 countries (United States of America, England, South Africa, Iceland, Italy, Australia and Brazil) situated on 4 continents. They have provided an even greater incentive toward the scientific research of projections of the consciousness in other consciential research centers.

Percentage. Based on all existing coordinated, compared statistical tabulations, it is currently estimated, with complete confidence, that approximately *1 out of every 100 persons* or, in other words, 1% of existing humanity (approximately 6 billion persons in 1998), or precisely 60 million individuals, have had some form of *lucid consciential* projection experience, at least *once* during their intraphysical existence.

Bibliography: Alvarado (16, p. 11), Andreas (36, p. 45), Banks (75, p. 110), Baumann (93, p. 3), Black (137, p. 38), Blackmore (138, p. 225; 140, p. 229; 142, p. 82; 145, p. 301), Breecher (198, p. 28), Crookall (320, p. 98; 326, p. 105), Currie (354, p. 80), Digest (399, p. 272), Douglas (409, p. 323), Eysenck (493, p. 157), Frost (560, p. 233), Gallup Jr. (566, p. 12), Garrett (571, p. 42), Giovetti (593, p. 30), Grattan-Guinness (626, p. 80), Green (632, p. 13), Greenhouse (636, p. 333), Greyson (643, p. 188), Hart

(690, p. 153), Holzer (751, p. 107), Irwin (792, p. 3), Kohr (857, p. 395), Kovach (860, p. 94), Martin (1002, p. 37), Morris (1093, p. 102), Noyes Jr. (1141, p. 19), Palmer (1184, p. 221), Poynton (1282, p. 20), Ring (1406, p. 45), Rogo (1446, p. 36), Roriz (1471, p. 20), Salley (1496, p. 157), Smith (1572, p. 14), Steiger (1601, p. 5), Twemlow (1710, p. 450), Vieira (1755, p. 5), Walker (1781, p. 63), Watson (1800, p. 135), Wolman (1863, p. 772).

506. CASES OF LUCID PROJECTION

Definition. Case of lucid projection: example of a projectiological case study including a report of an experience of the consciousness outside the human body, whether spontaneous or induced.

Synonymy: projectiological case study; report of lucid projection.

Case study. It is indisputable that the phenomena of lucid projection, whether voluntary or involuntary, cannot be rejected due to the large number of reports in case studies, or the collection of synopses of individual cases compiled by diligent investigators. A vast general bibliography already exists that is surprisingly and profoundly provoking for science, irrespective of the fact that everyone realizes that this voluminous accumulation of evidence merely constitutes valuable indications and not definitive proof.

Facts. A single isolated fact does not constitute proof. The mass of facts can provide indications of verisimilitude.

Acceptance. Incidentally, it is worth bearing in mind that scientists nowadays readily believe in things they have never seen or measured, because others have made certain claims and fit them within the context of conventional science. However, upon presenting them with something that is outside this framework, they want to see comprehensive proof and experiments, otherwise they ridicule the new perspective. The *quark* has not been satisfactorily detected in the laboratory, but all physicists accept its existence and have awarded the Nobel Prize for its discovery.

Reporters. Those people who report projective experiences – which first undergo a selection process in order to determine their reliability – come from the most diverse social levels, locations, situations and human periods. They are not questionable, psychotic, unstable or illiterate individuals, but are competent, psychologically normal and sane, many of them being researchers, experimenters and practitioners who are particularly responsible and sensible.

Upright. Upright individuals, in this case, are those of solid reputation, who are accustomed to responsibility, holding down a good job, are family men and well-employed women, and are known for their honesty in dealing with others. These people are not seeking publicity (unlike self-promoters), nor do they make the slightest attempt to capitalize on their projective experience or obtain immediate or long-term financial gain (unlike merchants), thereby placing themselves within the patterns of the greatest scientific respectability. They are commonly accepted by the witnesses or participants of unusual and exceptional occurrences.

Experiences. Those who report spontaneous experiences are almost always reluctant to speak about them, at least until they are certain of the sincerity and seriousness of the interlocutor. These people describe real occurrences that they recognize as such. They are experiences out of the ordinary that have no similarity to a dream, and for which they are generally not prepared. They are recognized as being beyond comprehension or outside the patterns of daily life.

Dependability. The more sophisticated and cultured the lucid projector is, the less likely that individual is to make a written report of his/her experience, unless it is possible to remain anonymous, as well as enjoying due respect for the deposition, in order to not be exposed to public ridicule. This is because no one can in all honesty find a single reason to not accept the coherent reports of lucid projectors, especially when they match up with the reports of other individuals, who also have an acceptable level of dependability, thus making the material worthy of consideration.

Rigor. It should be noted that the selected reports are unaltered, nothing having been omitted or added to achieve a possible agreement with other previously published cases. Even after making allowances for exaggeration, errors in judgment and insufficient data, the narratives survived a rigorous selection process and were admitted into the arena of truly intriguing and instigating cases.

Universality. Nevertheless, the narratives match the description of other similar experiences, verified by other people, who have lived in other times, places and circumstances. These facts reaffirm the universality and convergence of the reports.

Prototype. In other words, the cases used in these works are representative of many thousands of others which, although not being absolutely identical in detail, generally fit within the prototype outlined by many existing cases. The uniformity of the testimonies indicates that the occurrences were generally neither exaggerated nor invented.

Translation. The ordinary person's vocabulary is inadequate regarding the situations created by lucid projection. More intelligent projectors sometimes find themselves incapable of putting the elements of their experiences into descriptive and practical words. It is surprising to note how highly educated projectors encounter difficulty in translating the sensations and perceptions that they experience into words.

Descriptions. If we have difficulty – even with regard to accessible subjects on day to day topics – in understanding strange ethnic groups with cultural patterns that are different from ours and geographical conditions that we are not accustomed to, it must be much more difficult, if not impossible, to describe any other dimension of life beyond our daily experience in the ordinary, physical waking state.

Analogies. Lucid projectors often resort to analogies or metaphorical and symbolic language in order to describe something that, for them, is totally indescribable in common terms, mainly when referring to the mentalsoma and the mentalsomatic dimension. Hence the necessity for creating scientific terminology or *technical nomenclature* for all sciences, including projectiology and conscientiology.

Comparisons. The comparison of reports from different individuals helps to shape a perfectly clear picture of lucid projections. This allows the complete or partial examples, which are useful for statistical studies, to indicate and illustrate the prototypes of the most common categories of projections, leading to the construction of basic paradigms for the general analysis of the experiences. This fact affirms the need for the *consciential paradigm*.

Paradigms. The study of the reports of individual – and quite representative – cases of lucid projection, the set of which produces a network of indications, or an interconnected whole, constitutes in its totality, in and of itself, an unquestionable demonstration of the realities of projectiological phenomena. In these reports we can single out innumerable additional details for the research, comparative analysis and establishment of paradigms for these same phenomena.

Elements. When a report of lucid projection demonstrates the existence of extraphysical elements, including extraphysical consciousnesses or extra-human intelligences, it would be completely unscientific not to take them into consideration. The information that each case represents should not be concealed. It should also not be forcibly explained in another manner. Only in this way will we be acting within the canons of authentic scientific research, which require an open mind and an impartial temperament.

Consultation. The cases cumulatively acquire a suggestive force and irresistible supporting evidence. The cumulative reports of these numerous cases, descriptions and admissions, already studied exhaustively, form an immense barrier against the skepticism of those who have not yet experienced lucid projection for themselves. These reports allow the establishment of the fundamental bases that characterize the phenomena of projectiology, which are listed and analyzed in this book and can be consulted in the recommended specific bibliography further ahead. Were it not for the frequent registration of cases of spontaneous lucid projection, other types of research in the projectiological area would probably never have begun.

Computer. The case study of lucid projection is substantially consistent in terms of data. It is still awaiting standardization in a manner that can be correctly read and processed by machines. The computer, upon the implementation of an efficient system or specific program, will allow accurate evaluation of the reports with the comparison of elements, and the statistical analysis of type and content according to the pattern of the narratives in order to determine, from among innumerous aspects, the basic categories of the phenomena through meticulous surveys. A cybernetic investigation of projectiology will thus be performed.

Types. The works from which cases of lucid projection were compiled, indicated in the bibliography of this chapter, can be classified into 2 types:

1. Autobiographies that present detailed individual experiences: Fox, Greene, Monroe, Muldoon, Prado, Sculthorp, Turvey and Yram.

2. Books with reports of various projectors: Ebon, Green, Greenhouse, Kardec, Martin, Muldoon, Myers, Shirley, Eleanor Mildred Balfour Sidgwick (1845-1936), Tyrrell (1879-1952) and Walker.

Crookall. It is worth pointing out that a single author, Robert Crookall (1890-1981), analyzed a most diverse selection of 838 cases of lucid projection in detail, in 5 volumes of his personal bibliography (see the bibliography of this chapter), composed of 21 volumes.

Treatises. Three treatises deserve special mention as they present collections of hundreds of cases of *inter vivos* apparition and other phenomena of projectiology:

1. *Phantasms of the Living,* by Edmund Gurney (1847-1888), Frederic William Henry Myers (1843-1901), and August Frank Podmore (1856-1910), published in London in 1886, 2 volumes and 1,420 pages, presents 701 (702 minus number 209, which was omitted: see Vol. II, page 11) numbered cases of parapsychic phenomena, analyzed in detail.

2. *Human Personality and its Survival of Bodily Death,* by Frederic William Henry Myers, published in London in 1920, 2 volumes and 1,426 pages.

3. *Les Apparitions Materializées des Vivants & des Morts (The Materialized Apparitions of the Living & the Dead),* by Gabriel François Marie Delanne (1857-1926), published in Paris in 1909, 2 volumes and 1,370 pages.

Citations. From among the cases in the field of projectiology research that are most often cited throughout parapsychical literature, each one providing records, reports and detailed analysis, we can single out 3 classic examples of projectiological phenomena regarding which it is important to consider the dozens of bibliographic references of each one:

1. Lucid projection or traveling clairvoyance: the case of the clairvoyant Emanuel *Swedenborg,* 1759: Balzac (72, p. 144), Barboka (78, p. 213), Bonin (168, p. 475), Bret (203, p. 136), Browning (213, p. 54), Byse (230, p. 116), Carrington (248, p. 32), Chiesa (279, p. 46), Cohen (290, p. 39), Coste (309, p. 8), Digest (400, p. 20), Doyle (411, p. 36), Dusen (443, p. 217), Ebon (453, p. 23), Fodor (528, p. 373), Freedland (550, p. 63), Frost (560, p. 27), Goes (605, p. 408), Gooch (617, p. 23), Greenhouse (636, p. 58), Grimard (644, p. 286), Heaps (700, p. 115), Inardi (786, p. 149), Jung (813, p. 481), Knight (851, p. 89), Krippner (861, p. 286), Larcher (887, p. 115), Matter (1014, p. 145), Miguel (1045, p. 70), Mishlove (1055, p. 56), Mitchell (1058, p. 56), Myers (1114, p. 659), Rhine

(1389, p. 27), Richards (1394, p. 31), Seabra (1535, p. 133), Silva (1559, p. 112), Steinour (1612, p. 203), Stevens (1615, p. 81), Still (1622, p. 222), Tuttle (1708, p. 15), Twitchell (1712, p. 147), Wang (1794, p. 24), Wilson (1853, p. 312; 1854, p. 279; 1856, p. 58).

2. External autoscopy and physical bilocation: the case of professor Emília *Sagée,* 1845: Aksakof (09, p. 543), Andrade (27, p. 150), Bertrand (127, p. 57), Blackmore (139, p. 12), Bret (202, p. 69), Chevreuil (278, p. 206), Delanne (382, p. 175), Denis (389, p. 155), Dubor (421, p. 303), Duchatel (430, p. 117), Dumas (432, p. 214), Ebeid (452, p. 138), Flammarion (524, p. 45), Fugairon (562, p. 114), Giovetti (593, p. 12), Goes (605, p. 409), Gomes (612, p. 117), Green (634, p. 106), Hart (690, p. 180), Hemmert (712, p. 28; 713, p. 39), Heydecker (716, p. 49), Imbassahy (780, p. 83), Kardec (827, p. 72), Keller (835, p. 345), Lancelin (876, p. 115), Lawrence (893, p. 378), Lombroso (943, p. 252), Marin (996, p. 122), Meck (1027, p. 127), Metzger (1038, p. 130), Miguel (1045, p. 45), Montandon (1070, p. 228), Moutin (1100, p. 393), Pearce-Higgins (1214, p. 67), Poodt (1272, p. 265), Richet (1398, p. 702), Senillosa (1540, p. 177), Wauthy (1803, p. 171), Wilson (1853, p. 380; 1858, p. 52).

3. Joint projection and physical bilocation: the case of the industrialist S. R. *Wilmot,* 1862: Bardens (79, p. 142), Baumann (93, p. 30), Blackmore (139, p. 200; 147, p. 2), Bret (203, p. 173), Crookall (338, p. 48), Cummins (350, p. 88), Dingwall (404, p. 9), Dumas (432, p. 221), Ebeid (452, p. 108), Flammarion (524, p. 63), Hart (687, p. 183; 690, p. 162), Hemmert (712, p. 22; 713, p. 39), Hill (723, p. 14), Holms (735, p. 456), Hunt (767, p. 53), Knight (851, p. 104), Miranda (1052, p. 72), Mitchell (1058, p. 377), Montandon (1070, p. 232), Myers (114, p. 682), Pearce-Higgins (1214, p. 71), Pisani (1248, p. 127), Rogo (1442, p. 83; 1447, p. 94), Rýzl (1485, p. 126), Smith (1572, p. 87), Steinour (1612, p. 107), Targ (1652, p. 191).

Contact files. The Center for Continuous Consciousness, in Rio de Janeiro, Brazil – the first Institute of Projectiology, founded in 1981 – served as a central receptor of consciential projection experiences and compiled 5 categories of records in the archives of its documentation department, or its databank of projectiological data:

1. Contact files on lucid consciential projectors.
2. Mailing list of active lucid consciential projectors.
3. Collection of confidential reports of unique lucid consciential projections.
4. Responses to detailed questionnaires distributed on the fundamental themes of projectiology.
5. Collection of questions formulated by participants during debates on projectiological themes in diverse cities.

Intention. The intention, in cases such as these, is to publish this data at the appropriate time, after having tabulated the occurrences, in order to separate new patterns of phenomena and subsequently establish paradigms.

Bibliography: Alvarado (16, p. 11), Andreas (36, p. 51), Baumann (93, p. 15), Bayless (95, p. 162), Black (137, p. 3), Blackmore (142, p. 45; 145, p. 302), Bord (170, p. 26), Bozzano (188, p. 12; 193, p. 105), Bret (202, p. 66), Carrington (250, p. 190), Christian (281, p. 4), Cooke (300, p. 29), Crookall (320, p. 3; 330, p. 1; 331, p. 5; 333, p. 11; 338, p. 17), Delanne (382, p. 154), Dingwall (403, p. 93), Ebon (453, p. 115), Edwards (463, p. 165), Fardwell (494, p. 15), Flammarion (522,p. 206), Fox (544, p. 32), Geddes (578, p. 373), Gibier (587, p. 123), Giovetti (592, p. 46), Green (632, p. 19), Greenhouse (636, p. 185), Guieu (660, p. 83), Guimarães (662, p. 25), Gurney (666, p. 707), Hart (687, p. 153), Hemmert (713, p. 64), Holms (735, p. 451), Holroyd (736, p. 97), Kardec (816, p. 11), Knight (851, p. 274), Lippman (934, p. 346), Martin (1002, p. 70), Mitchell (1058, p. 354), Monroe (1065, p. 63), Montandon (1070, p. 227), Muldoon (1102, p. 47; 1103, p. 55; 1105, p. 49), Myers (1114, p. 369), Pearce-Higgins (1214, p. 66), Prado (1284, p. 14), Rogo (1438, p. 5), Sabom (1486, p. 31), Schmeidler (1517, p. 102), Sculthorp (1531, p. 17), Seabra (1534, p. 85), Shirley (1553, p. 71), Sidgwick (1556, p. 217), Stead (1598, p. 24), Steiger (1601, p. 15), Turvey (1707, p. 111), Tyrrell (1717, p. 165), Vieira (1762, p. 17), Walker (1781, p. 63), Wang (1794, p. 157), Wauthy (1803, p. 162), Yram (1897, p. 55).

507. LABORATORY EQUIPMENT IN PROJECTIOLOGY

Definition. Projective equipment: mechanical, electric or electronic agents, any and all other organs, implements, tools or apparatuses that serve to produce a certain work destined to detect specific aspects of the lucid projection phenomenon.

Synonymy: projective apparatus; projective artifact; projective device; projective machine.

Types. Among the objects, machines, ordinary instruments (created for multiple purposes) and equipment created specifically for experimentation with the projected consciousness in the laboratory, the following can currently be singled out: basal skin resistance (BSR) machine; the galvanic skin response (GSR) machine; digital photoplethysmograph for registering cardiac frequency and blood volume; electroencephalograph (EEG); electrocardiograph (ECG, EKG); electromyograph (EMG); electrooculogram; oximeter; equipment for indicating REM or involuntary rapid synchronous eye movements; special equipment for the detection of optical images, optical image device, or optical illusion box; 16-inch (40 cm) spiral florescent colored disc, or color wheel, that spins at approximately 1,200 rpm, designed for tests; Grass 12-channel polygraph; "gyrating chair"; closed-circuit television; multiple recorders; synchronized electronic chronometers; thermometers; barometers; magnetometers; various sensors; oscilloscopes; photomultiplier tubes; ultraviolet and infrared detectors; spectrometers; electromagnetic effect detectors; and soundproof room.

Sensitive. These laboratory instruments allow for the detailed physiological measurement and efficient monitoring of the sensitive and that individual's specific and general reactions during the entire experiment. Nevertheless, they produce a great deal of discomfort because the subject needs to relax while remaining restricted by bipolar electrodes on the chin, plates, conductive wires, the right index finger immobilized and the human body almost always in a fixed position, like a robot that is preprogrammed and teleguided from another room or nearby building.

Detectors. As well as human and animal detectors, diverse types of laboratory equipment have been employed as mechanical detectors in order to evidence the presence of the consciousness in a given place, at a specific moment, in the course of lucid projection.

Medicine. The modern instrumentation currently used in medical technology can also serve to detect many physiological variables, including anatomic and neurological ones, which will facilitate experiments of the intraphysical consciousness.

Ideas. Many other ideas have been put into practice regarding the utilization of instruments in the field of projectiological research, such as: television, for dissemination, as well as hetero-hypnotic induction, of lucid projection; the computer, as an advanced piece of research equipment in the evaluation, codification and analysis of data collected in investigations for the development of projectiology; use of camcorders and VCRs as auxiliary equipment for the researching and registering of projectiology phenomena, as well as the teaching of projectiology classes; the *projectarium*.

Prospective. The future holds many surprises in this field of investigation, because a reliable system for the physical detection of the human consciousness projected from the human body has yet to be discovered, a fact that will inevitably occur in the natural order of things.

Bibliography: Andrade (29, p. 107), Baraduc (76, p. 117), Black (137, p. 52), Ebon (453, p. 73), Grattan-Guinness (626, p. 83), Morris (1092, p. 127), Pratt (1285, p. 43), Rogo (1446, p. 12), Steiger (1601, p. 226).

508. EXPERIMENTAL PROJECTS

Tests. The following are 6 experimental parapsychic projects, among many others that exist, which were created in order to test projections of the consciousness and are apparently still unprecedented:

1. **Animal.** Demonstration of an animal-witness (detector) inclined to move in the direction of 1 point in space where the projected projector is located (Robert Lyle Morris).

2. **Joint.** Production of two lucid projections together in which the 2 projectors will try to visit the same target-area together, detecting what was specially placed there (Robert Lyle Morris).

3. **Sensitive.** The projector, surrounded by monitors, projects his/her consciousness to 1 unknown psychophonic sensitive, who is also surrounded by physiological detection equipment. Once in the projection location, the projector's consciousness controls the sensitive's human body, in the same way as in the phenomenon of psychophony, giving information about him/herself which is unknown to the sensitive. If the projector manifests personal traits that definitively identify him/her as being the projector, the phenomena of lucid projection and *inter vivos* parapsychic communication will be evidenced (John Palmer).

4. **Change.** A complex variant of the previous projective experiment wherein the consciousness of the sensitive (during the trance, on that occasion) additionally extraphysically projects to the inactive human body of the projected projector, proceeding to manifest through that projector's body (Herbert B. Greenhouse).

5. **Blind.** The projector will read the title of a book that has been placed on the highest and most inaccessible shelf of the library, with the cover facing up. The book will have been placed there in the projector's absence by an unknown person who selected the book at random from many other works, without knowing which book was chosen. This will make the project a "double-blind" test, thus removing possible interference from the telepathic phenomenon. The assistants in this project should be skeptical in regard to lucid projection (Carl Sagan).

6. **Television.** Create a television system based on a type of information other than light, such as a magnetic field, electrical field, density, electrical conductivity, magnetic permeability and ionization that will allow one to see, study and film the projected projector. In order to accomplish this, it is first necessary to invent a new camera.

Bibliography: Greenhouse (636, p. 299), Sagan (1492, p. 61).

509. GENERAL HYPOTHESES IN PROJECTIOLOGY

Definition. Hypothesis (Greek: *hypo,* under; *thésis,* placement, proposition): doubtful, however not improbable, supposition regarding natural or parapsychical phenomena, through which an understanding is anticipated, and that will later be directly or indirectly confirmed.

Synonymy: elaborated supposition; hypothetical reasoning; provisional proposition.

Method. In scientific studies, the method followed, upon addressing a subject such as experiences of the consciousness, is to first collect the facts, then classify them and, in the final step, suggest the best method for explaining them. The hypotheses developed in this manner indicate new lines of research and experimentation.

Uses. Hypotheses, constituting unproven ideas, present evident uses, notably to explain the diversity of facts under analysis and prepare the set of established observations for greater acceptance by researchers.

Categories. The 41 general hypothesis that are explanatory of projectiological phenomena can be classified into 4 categories according to the nature of their origin: pharmacological hypotheses, neurophysiological hypotheses, psychological hypotheses and parapsychic hypotheses.

Pharmacological hypotheses:

1. Lack of oxygen or reduction of glucose in the circulatory system (also a physiological explanation).

2. Sensations produced due to the consumption of drugs (pharmacology).

3. Effects of chemical substances produced in the brain (e.g.: endorphins).

Neurophysiological hypotheses:

4. Neurotic aberrations.

5. Effects of chemical substances of the brain itself (e.g.: endorphins). In essence, it is the same as item 3, above.

6. Epilepsy.

7. Cerebral hypoxia.

8. Ineffective functioning of the brain.

Psychological hypotheses:

9. Ordinary, spontaneous hallucination.

10. Autoscopic hallucination.

11. Induced hallucination.

12. Congenital psychic anomaly.

13. Imperceptible autosuggestion.

14. Mental creations (e.g.: the psychosoma).

15. Depersonalization (defense of the ego).

16. Convincing daydream.

17. Morbid state.

18. Fabulations.

19. Self-hypnotic fantasies.

20. Fecundity of the unconscious.

21. Illusion.

22. The early stages of schizophrenia.

23. Projection of the omnipotent and omniscient unconscious.

24. Pseudoprojection.

25. Psychosis or eccentric psychopathology.

26. Resurgence of a forgotten idea.

27. A merely interesting dream.

28. Psychological theory.

29. Mythical visions.

30. Desire or wish to believe.

Parapsychic hypotheses:

31. Imaginary body.

32. Objective body.

33. Rehearsal of biological death (desomatics).

34. Altered state of consciousness.

35. Self-hypnotic state.

36. Fantasies generated due to the increase of *parapsi energy.*

37. Phenomenon of telepathy plus clairvoyance.

38. Parapsychoanalysis or tautological theory.

39. Extrasensory perception without the separation of the consciousness from the human body.

40. Information theory.

41. Theory of the vehicles of the consciousness (holosomatics).

Important. It can be seen that the majority of the proposed hypotheses have a psychological origin, some apparently being redundant, while others are derived from psychiatry or psychopathology. The more important hypotheses deserve a succinct study in separate chapters. The others were defined through different approaches in the various sections of this book. The bibliography specific to this chapter is extremely relevant for the individual who is interested in gaining a deeper understanding of the subject of general hypotheses in projectiology.

Audition. One hypothesis that is still indicated for the explanation of consciential projection concerns auditory pathology. According to this thesis, the occurrences would be produced due to the semicircular canals of the ears being out of adjustment, where the sense of spatiality and orientation in space are located. The world of projectiological occurrences, however, present manifestations (e.g.: physical bilocation, *inter vivos* apparition) quite beyond the restricted sphere of influence of the auditory mechanisms of the human person, a fact that weakens and greatly reduces the possibility of the explanation of the hypothesis.

Production. The majority of the hypotheses and alternative explanations listed here were put forward by people who have not produced consciential projection with unquestionable lucidity. The individual who has experienced extraphysical lucidity – the ideal person for judging the facts, in this case – tranquilly and definitively accepts the exteriorization of the consciousness from the human body without confusing the phenomenon with any other altered state of consciousness. Some of these hypotheses can explain isolated cases, although they do not clarify the entire enormous body of projectiological occurrences, not even when they are added to other hypotheses.

Analyses. All hypotheses (to be verified) should nevertheless be judiciously analyzed by someone who is still reluctant to accept the literal interpretation of lucid consciential projection as being the exteriorization or projection of a semiphysical element or vehicle of extraphysical manifestation leading the consciousness out from the cerebral hemispheres.

Self-hypnotic. The hypothesis of the self-hypnotic state deserves to be mentioned here, based on the studies of hypnotized subjects who show a reduction in the amplitude of their brainwaves on the electroencephalogram. Self-hypnosis can certainly generate lucid consciential projection. Nevertheless, the consciousness projected deliberately, by oneself through the impulsion of one's own will, demonstrates conduct that is quite different from that of the person's consciousness when hypnotized.

Paraphysiology. The occurrences of projectiology allow the creation of a theory of the natural or physiological operation of the vehicles of manifestation of the consciousness, which the author defends as being the only theory that seems to cover all the material regarding lucid, semilucid and nonlucid consciential projections, and their more complex implications.

Experimentation. No projectiological theory should have theological passion, as frequently occurs in the areas of science. The theory of the vehicles of the consciousness will either be confirmed or invalidated by other individual experiences, new and different laboratorial experiments. If the theory is correct, ways will be found to verify its validity. Let us wait for things to transpire and the final verdict of the research to be delivered, without any of us neglecting to perform our own research.

Bibliography: Bayless (95, p. 195), Black (137, p. 129), Blackmore (138, p. 230; 142, p. 225), Champlin (272, p. 208), Crookall (333, p. 22), El-Aowar (474, p. 6), Grattan-Guinness (626, p. 86), Greenhouse (636, p. 271), Hart (690, p. 153), Honegger (753, p. 230), Ingber (788, p. 20), Irwin (791, p. 247), Larcher (887, p. 191), Mitchell (1058, p. 367), Morris (1092, p. 53), Palmer (1187, p. 19), Pearce-Higgins (1214, p. 76), Rogo (1446, p. 338), Sculthorp (1531, p. 156), Shirley (1553, p. 17), Smith (1577, p. 149), Steiger (1601, p. 74), Stokes (1625, p. 22), Taylor (1666, p. 154), Vieira (1762, p. 73).

---

510. HYPOTHESIS OF THE IMAGINARY BODY

Definition. Hypothesis of the imaginary body: the recent parapsychical hypothesis for explaining lucid projections of the consciousness based on the premise that the second body of the consciousness is not real, but is a simple figment of the imagination.

Synonymy: hallucination hypothesis; recent hypothesis; theory of morphothosenes (thought-forms).

Inadequacies. The hypothesis of the imaginary body can explain a small number of cases registered within the scope of psychiatry or general psychopathology, but it cannot adequately clarify the following 3 categories of phenomena:

1. **Third party.** The simultaneous witnessing of the indisputable apparition of the projection by third parties, or various unfamiliar individuals and subhuman animals, in cases of physical bilocation.

2. **Subhumans.** The phenomena in which persons see the freed double of dogs, cats, horses and other subhuman animals, in which circumstances they could not rationally have only noticed the presence of the mental image created merely by the mentality of these animals.

3. **Extraphysical consciousnesses.** The numerous well-authenticated instances of persons who saw the double of individuals who had already passed through desoma, whom they had not known or had not thought about on those occasions, and for which, in these circumstances, it would be difficult to find a motive for the imagined mental images.

Bibliography: Champlin (272, p. 208), Crookall (333, p. 22), Grattan-Guinness (626, p. 86), Mitchell (1058, p. 368), Pearce-Higgins (1214, p. 77), Rogo (1446, p. 339).

---

511. HYPOTHESIS OF THE OBJECTIVE BODY

Definition. Hypothesis of the objective body: the old and natural parapsychic hypothesis for explaining lucid projections of the consciousness based on the premise that the second body of the consciousness is real, although non-physical.

Synonymy: doctrine of lucid projection; hypothesis of the double; hypothesis of the extraphysical body; natural hypothesis; old hypothesis; theory of pneumatology (Jung-Stilling); theory of the second body.

Masks. Theories are indispensable in science. Nevertheless, we cannot mask the *facts* with sophisms, opinions, false information, disinformation, tautologies, unscientific attitudes, conjectures, hypotheses or even "theories."

Adequations. The hypothesis of the objective body presents an *adequate explanation for the world of the occurrences of projections of the consciousness* and extends even beyond them, including phenomena such as the near-death experience (NDE), clairvoyance in general, materializations, psychometry, apparitions and some cases of poltergeist, which demonstrates that these occurrences are not simple fantasies or imaginative creations. This more plausible hypothesis, accepted as valid in this book of wide-ranging research, clarifies the following 8 basic phenomena, among many others:

1. **Psychosoma.** The fact that people categorically affirm having already seen and felt their own double or psychosoma (psychosomatics) freed from the human body, or lucid projection per se, as well as the existence of the chakras (holochakrology).

2. **Self-bilocation.** The allegation by individuals that they are certain of having seen and felt their double in the horizontal position, 3' (1 m) above their own human body, stretched out over the bed, or consciential self-bilocation (projectiology).

3. **Helpers.** The multiple cases in which projectors observe that they are assisted in exiting the human body by many extraphysical associates, namely helpers. The assistance of such helpers would be unnecessary if the experience were merely imagined.

4. **Cord.** The various matching reports of individual and unquestioned verification of the existence of an intercorporal energetic connection, the silver cord, between the human body and the psychosoma, a characteristic which the human body does not possess (nor does it ostensively present) subsequent to the severing of the umbilical cord, soon after biological rebirth (resomatics).

5. **Telekinesis.** The numerous cases of the movement of physical objects, or extraphysical telekinesis, executed by the intraphysical consciousness while manifesting directly through the psychosoma.

6. **VS.** The occurrence of an intense vibrational state (VS), felt with complete lucidity, and the sensations that go beyond the anatomical limits and physiological manifestations of the human body.

7. **Sounds.** The incidence of *sui generis* intracranial sounds during the temporary exit and reentry of the consciousness from and into the human body.

8. **Sensations.** Generalized occurrences of an absence of fear or pain, of an expansion of the consciousness and its reluctance to return to the human body. This happens because the sensations *outside the body* (out-of-body sensation: OBS) experienced through the isolated psychosoma are very agreeable and gratifying to the ego or self.

Against. It is worth noting that no theory will ever be in complete agreement with all known facts in its area. That is why, nowadays, the following facts still speak against acceptance of the hypothesis of the objective body: the natural mixture of correct and incorrect information from lucid consciential projectors, due to imagetic influence and the technical insufficiency of those consciousnesses; and the fact that no one knows how the psychosoma is produced, a challenge that remains for consciential projectors of every evolutionary category and origin. This is therefore the justification and vital importance of projectiological research, in order to transform this idealistic theory into a realistic theory, or one that is verifiable in a conventional manner.

Theory. Nevertheless, the formal proposition of the *objective body* – upon which the context of this book (beginning from the Introduction), or projectiology, is founded – can undoubtedly be considered, at this point, to be an expressive scientific theory which is difficult to discard, because it fulfills the 7 basic prerequisites demanded by scientific rigor as being the foundations for a theory, which are listed below:

1. **Methodology.** The theory of the objective body systematizes human knowledge by supplying an appropriate projectiological methodology: Sections I, II, III and others.

2. **Concepts.** The theory of the objective body serves as a source for an analytical structuring of concepts and conceptual classification (system of reference): dozens of chapters.

3. **Facts.** It explains, generalizes and synthesizes the knowledge of projectiological problems or phenomena (facts): Sections III, IV, V, XIV and others.

4. **Knowledge.** It increases humankind's knowledge (Section II) and discovers gaps indicating areas that have still not been explored in this same field of humankind's knowledge: dozens of chapters.

5. **Comparability.** It reinforces comparability or, in other words, contributes toward the verification of factual, underlying values: Sections X, XI and others.

6. **Research.** It orients projectiological research: Sections VIII, XVI and others.

7. **Guideline.** Lastly, the theory of the objective body offers a guideline for a sector of consciential reality and becomes a means for forecasting facts: Sections I to XVIII, the entire panorama.

Proof. This entire book, with its extensive specialized bibliography, even when meticulously analyzed as a whole, does not offer something that can be taken as being a general, public and definitive proof regarding the existence of the objective body. Nevertheless, with the amount of evidence accumulating on a daily basis, more and more interested persons are discovering the importance and significance of performing continued research based on this hypothesis. With the accumulation of evidence, projection of the consciousness, in the objective body, can progressively make the other hypotheses related to extracorporeal experiences that are currently not well received gain greater acceptance.

Bibliography: Crookall (325, p. 3), Dumas (432, p. 227), Gauld (576, p. 219), Grattan-Guinness (626, p. 86), Pearce-Higgins (1214, p. 83), Rogo (1446, p. 338).

512. LUCID PROJECTION AND THE UNCONSCIOUS

Definition. Unconscious: the set of contents not present in the current field of consciousness, processes and psychic facts that act upon the conduct of the individual, but are outside the scope of awareness and cannot be brought to the fore by any effort of the will or memory, emerging, however, in dreams, Freudian slips, and neurotic or psychotic states.

Synonymy: attic of the mind.; basements of the memory; dead file of the personality; non-conscious; non-critical memory bank; second memory; storehouse of the consciousness.

Hemisphere. The usual psychoanalytical model is composed of the mental strata (psychic apparatus), the unconscious, preconscious and conscious. Psychology and neurology researchers defend the hypothesis that the unconscious is located in the right cerebral hemisphere, the area of the pre-verbal ego, emotivity and, preponderantly, of parapsychic manifestations.

Fecundity. Psychoanalysts who have not experienced lucid projection for themselves might propose the hypothesis of fecundity of the unconscious as the cause of projections. According to the concept of the unconscious – or second memory, in psychoanalysis – it would be part of the mental activity that contains primitive or repressed desires, of which the individual is not aware.

Sleep. By way of the unconscious, the psychic facts that act upon the individual's consciousness, and remain outside the scope of this same consciousness, would emerge during the period of natural sleep, when the consciousness is not alert.

Catharsis. The referred to concept constitutes the same psychological catharsis or liberation of tension in which the personality frees its own repressed desires in a realization of the unconscious, as if the person were living another life. This is purgation or the act of extricating oneself from a disturbing (mental clyster; consciential enema) sentiment (emotion). According to this simplistic hypothesis, all lucid projectors would be ordinary patients of psychoanalysis.

Queries. The controversial unconscious still requires many explanations, it not being unreasonable to ask: How is the unconscious formed? What function does the unconscious serve in the human being? Is the unconscious an exclusively mental process? Is the unconscious a product of a mechanism identical to that of the central nervous system and its physiochemical reactions? Or could the unconscious be the result of both these functions?

Similarities. It can therefore be observed that the situation of the unconscious is very similar to that of the lucid projection: it is a psychic or consciential process, the existence of which the projector is obliged to accept unquestioningly, deducing it from its respective effects, but about which he/she knows little, and regarding which the individual who has not experienced lucid projection possesses absolutely no technical and experiential authority with which to formulate an opinion.

Characterization. In fact, there seem to be at least 4 characteristic types of unconscious: the human personal, the human collective, the animal collective and the cosmic. The human personal unconscious seems to be merely another name arranged to characterize the psychosoma or the integral memory minus the current recallable memory or, in other words, the mentalsoma.

Mentalsomatics. *The human collective unconscious would thus be none other than the mentalsomatic dimension of consciousnesses.*

Inexplicable. The following are some occurrences of the phenomenological complex of lucid projection that the unconscious cannot explain: the phenomenon of the physical bilocation of the personality, evidenced by another; joint projections, or those wherein many intraphysical consciousnesses are projected at the same time; lucid projections detected by laboratory equipment; precognitive projections; the contemplation of one's own human body while the consciousness is temporarily outside it during a lucid projection; the convincing examination of one's own silver cord, or the semimaterial connection between the human body and the psychosoma, by the projector; the physical or telekinetic actions produced by the projected intraphysical consciousness; besides other occurrences.

Time. When the lucid projector extraphysically encounters the personality of a deceased individual who the projector had known when that extraphysical consciousness was seventy years of physical age, and who now looks young – with the para-appearance of the thirtieth year of human life, for example – it clearly counters the hypothesis of the unconscious for explaining the phenomenon of lucid consciential projection. This is evidence related to time or chronology.

Retrocognitive. All things aside, it is worth noting that certain projections of the intraphysical consciousness seem more like direct exteriorizations of the individual's unconscious, briefly suffocating the lucidity of one's ordinary, physical waking state, with no transition phase between one state and another. This may explain many retrocognitive consciential projections (retroprojections) or those related to the recollection of the intraphysical consciousness' previous life.

Unverifiable. In light of the above, we may draw the following conclusion regarding the unverifiable thesis of the unconscious: given that it is still incredibly obscure, the unconscious itself first needs to be explained in order that it may someday be able to satisfactorily explain some occurrence within the sector of projectiology. How can we affirm that A = B without understanding A, B, or both terms or facts?

Bibliography: Carton (252, p. 311), Geley (580, p. 273), Muldoon (1105, p. 249), Paim (1182, p. 215), Pisani (1248, p. 177), Prieur (1289, p. 61), Vieira (1761, p. 22).

---

513. PSYCHOLOGICAL THEORY

Hypnagogic. In 1978, John Palmer presented a psychological theory in order to explain experiences of the consciousness outside the human body, based on the assertion that consciential projection is not a parapsychic phenomenon, but an experience or mental state, like dreams or other altered states of consciousness, deriving from the hypnagogic state, or a psychological process similar to memory and imagination.

Association. Consciential projection, for this researcher, might be associated with the parapsi factor but is nevertheless not inherently a psychic phenomenon, thus seeking to explain it without the support of suppositions involving mind-body separation.

Evidence. This theory, however, does not clarify the evidence of apparitions of the projected intraphysical consciousness, the phenomenon of physical bilocation witnessed by third parties and projection with continuous self-awareness, which does not present the hypnagogic state or, more to the point, completely excludes hypnagogy and hypnopompy.

Bibliography: Blackmore (139, p. 242; 148, p. 21), Grattan-Guinness (626, p. 87), Palmer (1187, p. 21).

514. INFORMATION THEORY

Mechanism. Some theorists and parapsychologists, including Joseph Banks Rhine, suggested that the mechanism of extrasensory perception, even when not directly associated with a lucid consciential projection, is related to the act of the mind projecting itself outside the human body and obtaining information in this manner.

Cogitation. The lucid projection experience actually constitutes an exceptional resource for obtaining transcendent information, but the consciousness, upon projecting itself from the human body, is not always looking for information, or even unconsciously or subtly cogitating on it. Evidences of this are the instances of unexpected, spontaneous, abrupt consciential projections that are not sought by the consciousness.

Unconcern. It is worth remembering that the less concerned a person is regarding personal and existential problems or the more unconcerned one is regarding anything that tomorrow may bring, the more predisposed the individual's consciousness becomes to producing lucid consciential projections.

Fundamental. On the other hand, according to modern information theory, many researchers readily admit that information constitutes an element that should be considered as another fundamental variable of nature. In other words, not only does *transport of a quantity of movement* occur, but also the transport of information, a factor that will be important in the appreciation of natural phenomena or even paraphysiological phenomena, including here human lucid consciential projections.

515. THEORY OF REHEARSAL OF BIOLOGICAL DEATH

Trailer. The explanation of lucid consciential projection being a rehearsal for biological death, or deactivation of the soma, has already been put forward by parapsychologists.

Final. Without a doubt, the lucid projection experience can, in most cases, be rationally characterized as a rehearsal of first desoma, or final projection, but this supposition does not explain the occurrences.

Examples. The hypothesis of the rehearsal of biological death is not sufficient to clarify the following facts: the unrecalled apparition of the projected human projector; lucid consciential projection motivated by some emotional cause capable of promoting an encounter with another intraphysical or extraphysical being; the complete absence of worry regarding physical or biological death on the part of certain veteran lucid projectors or even inexperienced lucid projectors. It can be seen that an inauthentic scientific theory can lead us to a great number of true conclusions and show itself to be of great value and usefulness.

516. WORKING HYPOTHESES

Research. Projectiology is a source of research problems. The following is a list of studies that remain to be performed *ab ovo* in the areas of projectiology: codification of precise rules for the development of gifted parapsychic projectors and a reduction of the empiricism that has existed up until now; rationalization of projectors' techniques and basic manifestations, thereby standardizing the variants in use; creation of bases that allow projectors to receive a basic technical education and maintain an informational exchange between themselves (Invisible College of Lucid Projectors); classification of projectiological phenomenology with adequate terminology that is accepted in all areas of human knowledge; presentation of new hypotheses for a rational explanation of the phenomena involving parapsychology, psychology, medicine, physics and other subjects.

Problems. To projectors, parapsychologists, psychologists, biologists, physicians, researchers in general and those persons interested in projection, the author presents some relevant research problems, in addition to the abovementioned experimental projects, which are listed here, according to 12 sectors of experimental assumptions. These constitute viable hypotheses for future generations of researchers.

1. **Projectiological:** the social elements involved in the development of projective capacity; the extent of the possibilities of projectiology as a field of education; how to turn the productive exceptions in the manifestations of projectiology into rules; an easy method for maintaining continuous self-awareness; an easy method for prolonging the duration of lucid projection; the maximum distance between the human body and the psychosoma for projection in the mentalsoma; agents for projecting in the psychosoma and in the mentalsoma; exteriorization of the mentalsoma from the freed psychosoma; currents of negative forces in paratropospheric extraphysical districts; the human aura and holochakra (holochakrology); an easy method for distinguishing between the mentalsoma and a partial configuration of the extraphysical head of the less dense psychosoma; an easy method for interrupting a period of recess in self-lucid projections; reliable projective aids; an easy method allowing anyone to project in the psychosoma; an easy method for producing joint lucid projections; an easy method allowing anyone to project in the mentalsoma; the differences between morphothosenes and authentic extraphysical images; an easy method for improving recall of the extraphysical stages of consciential projection; the use of hypnosis as a reasonable (without abdominal brainwashing) projective technique; an easy method for penetrating evolved extraphysical communities and environments.

2. **Parapsychological:** the relationship between morphothosenes and hallucinations in the ordinary, physical waking state; the dynamics of the projector's parapsychism; induction of healthy mutual possession; controlled emotions in the psychosoma; holomemory in the mentalsoma.

3. **Psychological:** an easy method for the concentration of thought; an easy method for maintaining permanent mental hygiene.

4. **Biological:** heredity as an active factor in lucid projection; the constitution of the human body in lucid projection; complications during childbirth and projective predisposition.

5. **Para-anatomical:** understanding of the nature of the psychosoma; the nature of the silver cord; chakras; organs of the psychosoma; addressing the nature of the mentalsoma and the golden cord.

6. **Physiological:** excessive physical weight in relation to lucid projection; the maximum physiological possibility of the human body when emptied of the consciousness, which is projected in the psychosoma along with a greater amount of the holochakra; systematization of the projector's animism; stimulation of acupuncture points in the deltoid region and projective capacity.

7. **Paraphysiological:** basic reasons for the variability of projectors' aptitudes; the pregnant woman, the fetus, lucid projections and the probable idiosyncrasies of lucid projection processes; discoincidence in the initial stages of human gestation; differences between extraphysical energy and individual consciential energies; extraphysical malleability and agility of the psychosoma; differences between the energies of intraphysical consciousnesses and extraphysical consciousnesses; criterion for the application of energies obtained by extraphysical technicians (helpers, evolutiologists); the organic cause of intracranial sounds; differences between the energies transmitted by the consciousness when in the human body, the psychosoma and the mentalsoma; an easy method for stimulating projective capacity or lucid projectability.

8. **Pharmacological:** the action of chloroform and other more modern anesthetics in the production of lucid projection; the action of psychedelic drugs in the production of lucid projection.

9. **Therapeutic:** lucid projection as an advanced therapeutic resource; an easy method for the conscious application of energies by the projected intraphysical consciousness.

10. **Parapathological:** the frequent prolonged separation of the consciousness and the *empty brain syndrome;* the parapathology of the silver cord and the holochakra.

11. **Physical:** photograph, with an ultra-sensitive camera, the projector projected in between the sensors of a shielded camera; the relationship of the Faraday cage and the projected consciousness; ionization of the physical base and the lucid projectability of the intraphysical consciousness; human and extraphysical equipment (paratechnology) in projectiology; researching of the microcosm, macrocosm and extraphysical matter, through various types of lucid projection experiences.

12. **Artistic:** lucid projections in literature (poetry and prose); lucid projections and other artistic areas.

Resources. Resources exist – working hypotheses that are still fairly unclear – which can be transformed into psychophysiological crutches for the intraphysical consciousness in order to project, such as certain allopathic or homeopathic medications. The original ideas listed in this volume can also inspire working hypotheses.

Expanders. The mechanism of lucid projection, within the individual or psyche, triggers the *psychopetal movement* of the consciousness, first through relaxation, centralizing the consciousness in the brain, especially in the mnemonic center, and the loss of motor manifestations, with the subsequent torpidity of the entire human body. Secondly, *psychofugal movement* occurs, wherein the consciousness leaves the restriction of the physical brain and expands beyond the force field of the human body, or exteriorizes, overflowing to the extraphysical dimension. In other words, there is first an implosion, followed by an explosion. From a human *animal* point of view, there is first a retreat into concentration, wherein the consciousness prepares itself to kickoff. It then advances and expands, kicking off, per se or, in other words, leaping toward the unknown extraphysical world. To what extent do mind-expanding drugs predispose these movements of the consciousness?

Bibliography: Vieira (1762, p. 218), White (1834, p. 451).

---

517.   HARMONIC   SERIES   MODEL

Definition. Harmonic series: an infinite sequence of tones that arises from a fundamental, stationary oscillation, originating from electric oscillations, sounds or other sources.

Synonymy: harmonic scale; harmonic order; harmonic sequence; Fourier series; harmonic succession.

Difference. Without looking at the 2 musical instruments – a flute and a violin, for example – which alternately play the same note of the same pitch and intensity, any person can tell the sound of the flute from the violin. Even though one has never heard either of the 2 instruments, it is clearly possible to distinguish the difference between the 2 sounds. This gives rise to the following question: If the note of the same pitch and intensity has the same fundamental frequency, and the vibrating air carries this same oscillation to our ears (tympana), how is one able to distinguish the difference between the sound of the 2 instruments? Expressing it another way: How does the oscillation of the air allow differentiation between the sounds, if the oscillation occurs at the same frequency? The answer lies in a greater understanding of the harmonic series.

Base note. Supposing that "do" is the base note, or fundamental frequency, the harmonic series, resonant from this base note, simultaneously with it, that is emitted from each instrument is:

Infinite. This series is theoretically infinite, despite the fact that the harmonic sounds very distant from the fundamental are, in fact, not detected, due to their low intensity. The intervals of frequency between the harmonics can be observed: perfect eighth, perfect fifth, perfect fourth, major third, minor third. Much of what is currently known about the main intervals of musical harmony arose intuitively from this series.

Theorice. In electricity, harmonics play important roles. When a great number of these curves – each one representing 1 harmonic – are superimposed, the resulting curve can have a highly complicated form. The richness and quality of a fundamental frequency depends solely upon the proportions in which the different harmonics are added.

Harmonics. The answer to the previously asked question was shown in the nineteenth century through the investigations of Hermann von Helmholtz (1821-1894), who stated that the different sound characteristic, or the so-called *timbre of a sound,* is determined by the proportion in which the different harmonics are heard or, in other words, it depends upon the energy of the various harmonics, which varies for each instrument, or even according to the way in which the sound is produced.

Figures. Figure 517.2 shows the relationships between the wavelengths of the first 6 harmonics, or the various ways in which one string of 1 musical instrument vibrates for just one note and its first harmonics. Figures 517.3 (b) and (c) show the waveform of a piano and a clarinet, playing one note of the same frequency, but differing in their forms, which characterize the timbre, represented by the sum of its more intense harmonics. A spectrum of frequencies showing the amplitude of each harmonic is shown in figure 517, on page 1,152.

Series. The amplitudes of the harmonics are mathematically represented through the coefficients of a Fourier series (Joseph Fourier 1768-1830).

Perception. There are human ears that can perceive and distinguish up to the seventh harmonic, while others barely perceive or differentiate the fundamental sound. In the same way, a medium and a sensitive are able to perceive visually, or through other consciential senses, various vibrations of matter to different degrees.

Term. It is worth clarifying that the term *sensitive,* in this case, is more ample than the term *medium,* as it includes animic perceptions, while the *medium* plays only the passive role of an intermediary between two consciential dimensions.

Model. This is the proposition of an initial and simple, factual theoretical model, based on well-known analogies of waves with consciential states, amplifying the wave concept through an expansion of the harmonic series with its infinite spectrum of harmonics for each fundamental stationary frequency, as the first step toward future, more sophisticated, models of the states of the various vehicles of consciential manifestation, their parts, their interactions with the various states of "matter" or condensed fields, interactions with other consciousnesses and intra-actions with the consciousness itself (intraconscientiality).

Empiricism. The analogies that are established here, in an initial model, are exclusively empirical – or are based on physical-extraphysical observation – and are associative. They should be tested in order for the model to evolve.

Suppositions. Along the lines of, and by analogy with, the infinite and quantic (noncontinuous) harmonic series – arising naturally from a fundamental vibration of any 1 body, in stationary oscillations progressing to higher frequencies – 7 initial or basic suppositions can be made:

1. **Chakras.** By way of simple association, and based on the monochrome condition that some chakras present – each of them being of a fundamental frequency and accompanied by their various harmonics – various states are established in which each of the chakras can be encountered, depending on the spectrum or intensity of the harmonics, or its respective timbre, thereby configuring the various tints of each one. The state of condensation of the fields associated with each chakra determines its higher or lower frequency, as well as determining the stage of interaction with condensed physical matter.

2. **Idea.** A fundamental frequency can be associated with each idea, which propagates itself through resonance, starting with its outflow from the mental computer in the mentalsoma, through the psychosoma, the holochakra, and finally arriving at the more condensed plasmas of the human body in the brain. It is not known what it is that enters into vibration in these various bodies or vehicles of consciential manifestation. Nevertheless, the transmission picks up interference from each one of them. It can be richer or poorer, according to the state of the various bodies; richer or poorer in harmonics, according to how much that idea has been learned; richer or poorer in other packets of lateral disciplinary ideas, which will either help or hinder conclusive reasoning. Many ideas or thoughts trigger other ideas or thoughts through the phenomena of resonance, where one of

the harmonics of the original idea excites other fundamentals. This gives us an idea of the complexity of this oscillatory system.

3. **States.** These states of vibration might be associated with the complex stages of the vibration of fields, and here the field concept becomes obsolete, and the mechanical and electrical vibrations initially given as an example would be the last stages of vibration of as yet unknown types of fields, but would probably turn out to be fields that are not limited by known space-time dimensions, oscillating in unknown dimensions, arriving at the human brain through simple resonance and the increase of lateral packets of experiences of the various consciential bodies or meta-organisms. Understanding the nature of these vibrations is one of the relevant points that should be an integral part of the interests in future research.

4. **Packets.** The blocks or packets of disciplinary, associative and lateral ideas gradually become refined by taking advantage of the experiences of successive lives (existential seriation), gradually becoming disciplined, purified and controlled through the equilibrium of the infinite harmonics of its wave packets which, acting jointly with the central idea will equilibrate or disequilibrate the response emitted from the complex mental computer. For illustrative purposes, we can cite the parabody of emotions (psychosoma), uncontrolled due to the fear factor, which arrives as 1 emotional and lateral packet pertaining to a specific central situation. When faced with this situation, the parabody of emotions spills out its fear factor, with the full intensity of its charge, vibrating at the fundamental or primary harmonic which, when added to any subsequent rational idea, will remain dominant, being introduced as a negative and prejudicial factor. The individual, with the aid of rationality, good intentions, self-discernment, greater knowledge and a good utilization of personal experiences, can gradually transfer the intense energy of the first harmonic to the others, thus stabilizing the emotions and allowing reason or intuition of the higher parabodies to become purer. In the same manner, and in the opposite direction, if one works toward improving oneself in the denser bodies, one will automatically be improving, in detail, the less dense bodies through other reverberations of the harmonics which are imperceptible to us.

5. **Timbre.** The timbre or "color" of the fundamental vibration is the main point of this model. The consciousness, through a strong will, can interfere in the timbre, or the spectrum of the energies of a fundamental frequency, thus modifying the relative intensity of the various harmonics; can transfer energy from certain harmonics to others, thereby reinforcing the main points of a central idea; or one can modify the fundamental and the spectrum of the harmonics into a specific curative (therapy) energetic transmission or into a physical effects energetic transmission, or in order to provoke a lucid projection. As an illustration of a similar application, we can cite the projective circumstance wherein the projector – wishing to leave the human body (soma) with continuous self-awareness – mobilizes the energies of the chakras using a strong will and reinforces, with a greater intensity, the fundamental frequency of the psychosoma, which is interiorized within the human body along with the holochakra, thus provoking a projection of the consciousness in the psychosoma through the vibrational state. If, on the contrary, the projector reinforces not the fundamental harmonic, but another harmonic with a frequency superior to that of the interiorized psychosoma, a projection will occur without entering into a vibrational state; but directly, with the consciousness *inside* the psychosoma vibrating at a higher frequency.

6. **Ambiguities.** The strong, *ironclad,* projective and dominating mental control of morphothosenes is associated with the mastery of the frequencies of one's own consciential vehicles of manifestation, which are rich in harmonics and controlled by the mind. It is truly the "know thyself" principle of personal conduct recommended by Socrates (470-399 B.C.), dominating and controlling all the bodies (or the soma and the parabodies) of the intraphysical consciousness, making them vibrate together, due to a common goal, which will afford it the greatest possible strength. The more frequencies that vibrate in order to achieve a specific goal, the more solid they will become. The more harmonics that accompany them, the more balanced and perfect it will be. The balance of the intraphysical consciousness' coexistence with ambiguities and his/her deep understanding come into play here.

7. **Projection.** The main, complementary and sole route to the cleansing of each of the bodies – in regard to negative ideas, those ideas of the basement of the mind (consciential basement), the residue of the ferocious animal, regressive or infantile egoistic vanities – lies in lucid projection. It represents the act of knowing yourself fully, confronting and modifying your own self deeply in all the bodies, without mysticism, hypocrisy and egoism, toward the efficient use of the mentalsoma and the experience of the most ample universality that is possible. Through projections of the consciousness, the true sense of the equilibrium of the frequencies of their harmonics in a profound and universal manner is established.

Synthesizers. In a manner analogous to the operation of sound synthesizers – with which one can electronically regulate the duration, intensity, fundamental frequency and timbre of sound at will – mediums, sensitives, animists, parapsychics and lucid projectors can also learn to control these variables through their studies (theories) and training (practice), or theorices, since they possess more acute perceptions and have sufficient consciential energy for this purpose. This will allow them to achieve better experiences that will go to the limit of the individual's control and imagination – while harboring good intentions and self-discernment, and remaining as scientific and universal as possible. We can see that it is necessary to influence the oscillatory system in this case.

Universalism. The expressions "scientific" and "universal" are complementary here. Science occupies itself with the search for truth. This search must have a so-called *scientific* control, in order to avoid jumping to conclusions when faced with phenomena that are masked by many hidden variables. Also, this should be accompanied by a sufficient degree of universalism in order to eliminate fanaticisms (sectarianisms, factionalisms) of any nature, temporary preconceptions, idolatry of any kind and general neophobia. The intraphysical consciousness should, as far as possible, maintain a posture of open-mindedness (intraconsciential openness, neophilia) for the acquisition of new knowledge (or the creation of neosynapses), although never overlooking the indispensable self-discernment of scientific control. These two attributes may appear antagonistic to those who seek leading-edge relative truths – and the traps are set at all times – until the floating balance of both are adjusted, which enables a more rapid ascension.

Acquisitions. These are acquisitions resulting from constant and personal work, improving the manner in which one sees things and relates to problems, always supposing here the preexistence of good intention (self-discernment and cosmoethics, in this case). The control and the universalism of the sensitivity of the extrasensory perception of the upcoming consciential stages is often independent. This is due to the non-linear nature of knowledge acquisition. These perceptions, then, serve to call attention to this type of openness-control.

Altered. Altered states of consciousness – such as oneiric images, the hypnagogic state, the hypnopompic state, daydream, mental concentration, exaltation and dream – would probably be connected with the assimilation of events that one has experienced, or the *digestion* of one's more internal experiences and impressions of the waves that exist in the ocean of one's memory (holomemory) in the various vehicles of manifestation of the intraphysical consciousness. These states gradually disappear in proportion with humankind's evolution, becoming more profound and complementary, until they disappear, leaving the state of completely continuous self-awareness.

Sensitive. The refined sensitive is able to bring the impressions of his/her deeper, more remote frequencies and harmonics to the sphere of the human brain with clarity, as a result of already having controlled and perceived these frequencies in a balanced manner and knowing how to amplify them without interfering with them, positioning the (always preferably *self-aware*) pointer of the consciousness there. These subtle frequencies – upon resonating with the external harmonics of extraphysical objects, persons, or extraphysical agents – may or may not be perceived by the sensitive, depending upon his/her predisposition, motivation, interest, positive curiosity and ability to penetrate the frequencies in question.

Holomemories. Penetration into the mental archives of other consciousnesses (holomemories of consciential micro-universes) can occur up to the level of internal archives, to which not even the assaulted consciousness (violated victim) has access. The depth of penetration is a function of the sensitive's control of consciential frequencies, upon acquiring, by way of resonance, the consciential energies, certain packets of which are located in the space-time of the assaulted consciousness.

Stages. The base-bodies – due to their diverse natures and functions – evidence the necessity of levels of stability in each process, passing from body to body, in order for the evolution of these stages to be processed – just as there are laws for all phenomena, outlining their validity – to our current mental state of the moment or the currently sufficient model. This causes our mental organization to be oriented within these limits, in order to subsequently move forward.

Inspiration. It is common that persons, upon finding themselves absorbing diverse energies (holothosenes), such as under the spray of a shower, or others already cited, perceive changes in the energies of the various harmonics of their vehicles of manifestation, or the timbre of the various bodies and parts, according to the direction of their thosenes *(tho)* toward questions or problems that they wish to solve, in such a manner that they are able to amplify the harmonics up to those of the mentalsoma (parabody of self-discernment). At this point, the consciousness – in a process analogous to that of clairvoyance – brings to the brain or, in other words, transfers itself to the more intense harmonics, causing interesting ideas and achieving the highest states of inspiration.

Precognition. These states of amplification of the waves of the mentalsoma can also occur in the sense of waves traveling through time, explaining the phenomena known as presentiments (self-precognitions). These waves, which are probably multidimensional and have multiple traveling frequencies, even in space-time, address these variables in a relativistic and unconventional manner. A logical, conventional, classic, initial and immediately understandable explanation can be established whereby the pure mentalsoma with its intensive analysis of causes, performs a search for all the possible ways. We can make a pale analogy by comparing this to an immense computer that forecasts the upcoming moves in a chess game after considering all existing pieces and a profound knowledge of its adversary, not overlooking a single variable. This irresistible analysis vibrates in time with the greatest intensity toward the most probable route and with a lesser intensity toward others. The sensitive is sometimes able to single out this wave from the ocean of ideas, locating it while in the waking state, in the manner of a presentiment that comes to the fore, thereby characterizing precognition. Nevertheless, the phenomenon of self-precognition must undoubtedly be influenced by a combination of various phenomena: relativistics, harmonic series, changes of systems, mentalsoma, environment and others as yet to be studied.

Will. It is not necessary, nor is it appropriate or possible for the memory and the organismic consciousness, or the current human body, to be aware of all causes and processes that occur in order to arrive at a similar presentiment, or another type of processing, in the same way that it is not necessary to be aware of the mechanism of all cerebral, nerve, muscular and chemical reactions in order to move a leg to walk. The harmonies of these internal processes are sufficient only with the action of the will – the externalizing pointer of the memory banks and processes of the mental computer – the intensity of which is dependent upon the vibrational harmony of all bodies of the human being, who evolves while learning how to control them, understand them, operate them and finally harmonize them in a single way, or that of balanced, correct and cosmoethical will.

Processes. For mechanisms such as ordinary movements, simpler processes – which have been assimilated and connected to the animal body for a long time – are sufficient. Nevertheless, with the advent of imbalances, blockages can occur during theses processes. On the other hand, for more subtle processes, a lot of cultivation and a long period of balance are necessary, removing the priorities of the primary processes (genetics, somatics) during the waking state and substituting them with processes of the mentalsoma (paragenetics, mentalsomatics).

Learning. We should not fail to seek out and understand the mechanisms and causes of the production of effects simply because it is not necessary to be self-aware of them. On the contrary, it is necessary to bring these learnings to the ordinary waking state through the improvement of theories and a great deal of study, in the same manner that a great portion of the nervous, muscular and chemical reactions needed to produce the movement of a leg are known.

Apparatuses. One of the points in favor of this model is the interference produced by certain individuals and sensitives in electronic apparatuses, the operation of which is dependent upon harmonic frequencies, e.g.: telephone switchboards. These individuals are therefore not able to work in such places. In this case, it is probably the harmonics of their consciential energies intersecting, resonating, colliding and interfering with the harmonics of the electronic apparatuses. It is probably the denser, unchanging energies of the chakras (holochakrology) that produce the interference. Other similar cases are probably certain instances of poltergeist and telekinesis.

Impregnation. During intraphysical life, an individual can perform mental impregnations upon the assembly of positive, negative or neutral waves or, in other words, in favor of, against or indifferent toward others, such that this waveform always returns in different intensities to his/her various bodies, when faced with analogous situations. These situations can be sponsored by the individual or others, so that facts such as these – also positive, negative or indifferent – befall him/her when they become present within the process of free will in human life, whether it be situations, environments, objects or beings that induce this return.

Human diapason. The standard musical pitch (diapason) from a tuning fork is considered, in fact, to be a pure tone or, in other words, is devoid of harmonics superior to the fundamental, as these harmonics are of very low intensity – the pure fundamental thus essentially predominating. The "human diapason" would vibrate with greater intensity in the fundamental, or would somehow directly block the superior harmonics from his/her own senses, and is, for this reason, in lack of sensitive capacities, due to the fact of not being able to significantly modify his/her own timbre, or unblock it to the point of obtaining clear perceptions in order to change or highlight the energies of the harmonics, as occurs with the sensitive who sometimes controls or receives these highlights spontaneously. At any rate, the "human diapason" does not cease to be a potential sensitive to the degree that he/she comes to develop the energetic control of the superior harmonics of his/her consciousness, or extract it from the blockages. This is why it can be affirmed that every human personality (intraphysical consciousness) is, potentially, a medium or sensitive, or even an animist.

Vital. The presence of the vital body, or holochakra, in the psychosoma of the projected intraphysical consciousness, brings with it the harmonic frequencies that are characteristic of the parts of these bodies, especially the centers of consciential energies or chakras. This makes it difficult for the intraphysical consciousness to remain within the frequencies of the psychosoma, with lucidity, when faced with such a great variety of frequencies produced by the energies of the more important chakras, and which the projector is not able to organize and balance. All this must produce dissonances in one's lucidity, which subsequently reduces. This may explain the necessity for the existence of the brain in the human body, which serves as a bastion for the maintenance of awareness, when faced with the condensed flows of the energies of our atomic-molecular-organic matter.

Predisposition. An individual's so-called predisposition – including one's own projectability – would then be directly related to the momentary spectrum of energies of the respective harmonics of his/her bodies. If the superior harmonics are high (up), that is to say unblocked, the individual's extraphysical sensitivity or intuitions will be amplified. On the other hand, and to the contrary, one will not discern much (down) and will mostly think using the fundamental frequencies, if one is in a very terrestrial, tropospheric condition.

Nullification. Based on this control of harmonics, sensitives are able to modify the frequencies of their own harmonics, according to their greater or lesser energetic capacity or will power. The sensitive can also send energies to someone in order to diminish the other's extraphysical sensitivity, through the decrease or nullification of the intensity of the superior harmonics of that being. If the sensitive is sufficiently balanced in regard to his/her consciential energies, he/she will maintain his/her spectrum in a state of constant energetic compensation (holochakral homeostasis). Otherwise, his/her sensitivity will decrease and he/she will enter into energetic imbalance, which is sometimes called illness, disturbance, interconsciential intrusion or stress fatigue (languidness, mental laziness, intraconsciential vacuum).

Holochakrology. Through transmissions of consciential energies (magnetic passes, laying on of hands, blessings), the extraphysical helpers can reinforce: the deadened harmonics of an individual, such that his/her consciousness does not remain in the fundamentals, thus turning him/her into a sensitive; the harmonics of the natural frequency of the psychosoma of the intraphysical consciousness, helping him/her produce a lucid projection; the superior harmonics of the psychosoma of the projected consciousness, amplifying his/her extraphysical vision; or the amplification of the frequencies of the mentalsoma, thereby provoking the projection of the consciousness of the individual toward one of these frequencies, thus occurring projection in the isolated mentalsoma. The intention behind the transmissions (liberations, exteriorizations) of energies to intraphysical ill beings (intraphysical consciousnesses and extraphysical consciousnesses) is perhaps the modification of the timbre or the spectrum of the harmonics, or the elimination of the ill, mental, thosenic waveform that the person, or even the extraphysical consciousness, is unable to discard alone and in whom it becomes strongly impregnated.

Coupling. In the consciential conditions of auric coupling, a type of common resonant junction might occur between the frequencies of the attitudes and thoughts that are cultivated (within the integral holomemory of any time) and the frequencies that are common to other objects or consciousnesses, with or without the perception of the wakeful consciousness of the individual, depending upon his/her capacity for parapsychic perception or energetic sensitivity. This junction can promote subsequent occurrences which are positive-healthy or negative-pathological for consciousnesses, depending upon the intensity of the coupling and whether or not the *internal* consciousness is able to send the perception or intuition of the quality of the coupling to the *external* (wakeful) consciousness.

Intensity. If the quality of the coupling is negative or pathological, the consciousness tries to inhibit its intensity, regardless of whether or not the wakeful consciousness is aware of the posture that has been assumed. In this way, one may or may not change the intensity of the coupling, depending upon the profile of the frequencies that prevail at that moment.

Accidents. If the cultivation (self-thosenity) that prevails over a person is, on average, of analogous (negative) thosenes, that person will reinforce the coupling, principally if there is a predisposition; otherwise the coupling will be undone. We can cite the following example: the imminence of a ceiling (object) falling on a person (consciousness). If that person cultivates analogous negative thosenes (personal holothosene) against others, the individual will be negatively predisposed (accident proneness) and will strengthen that coupling, thereby getting drawn into the reaffirmation of those very frequencies, thereby suffering the accident. In a contrary condition, some excuse or a call will predispose that consciousness to leave that location.

Objects. Objects that are impregnated with certain attitudes and sentiments, whether positive or negative, by their owner, can affect persons who subsequently come to own them. This is because they resonate (empathy, affinity) with the waves of sentiments that emanate from them (psychometry).

Interprisons. At this point, it is also important to recall the mechanism whereby the processes that generate *groupkarmic interprisons* are formed, within consciential micro-universes. These maintain the groupthosenes, group holothosenes, and an anticosmoethical and common materthosene.

Transit. A person who is driving irresponsibly can become connected, through auric coupling, to other drivers or vehicles of analogous mental emissions or those who do not maintain an adequate mental posture. The coupling flow is therefore almost instantaneous, due to analogous resonant frequencies that are cultivated and united to a greater predisposition, which is further connected both to that moment in time, as well as to the individual's consciential evolutionary imperfection. This is why both individual and group commuter neuroses exist. This also explains the importance of cultivating good thoughts (orthothosenity) at any time or place, thereby elevating the positives and inhibiting the negatives. These occurrences are customarily given various names, such as: "current condition of consciential evolution"; "will of God"; "activity in one's egokarmic or individual account"; "activity in one's groupkarmic or group account".

Synchronicity. As can be seen with these facts, the condition of cosmic synchronicity, which involves us all, can also become somewhat more explicit through this harmonic series model.

Energies. The process of the exchange of consciential energies is probably intimately connected with the phenomenon of resonance. A person, upon sending his/her energies to another is, through simple resonance, amplifying certain fundamentals and harmonics of the other's consciousness with a greater or lesser intensity, which will be determined by the duration of the transmission and the intraconsciential action of the receiving system. This transmitted psychic energy can be of a positive-cosmoethical or negative-anticosmoethical nature. The person whose energies are amplified by another can, for this reason, assume attitudes, postures, or have ideas that are likewise positive-healthy or negative-ill, and which that person would not have taken or had if he/she had been isolated from the energetic field (personal holothosene) of the other, or if he/she knew how to receive these amplifications with indifference, rationality, self-discernment, analysis and coherence in his/her own attitudes.

Ramifications. Auric couplings can have many ramifications, depending upon their energetic concentration and their objective (quality of intentionality). There are auric couplings which range from the collective transport of psychosomas, to resonant amplifications in other consciousnesses of any order; from psychic warfare in unprepared minds, to consciential elevation on the way of cosmoethics; from the preparation of mechanical and electronic apparatuses, to their proper use and operation, through the organization of consciential energies; from the organized preparation of the vehicles of manifestation of the consciousness to self-control in any place, time and situation, culminating in projection with continuous self-awareness.

Channels. Probably, due to holokarmic problems or attitudes adopted by the consciousness in the past, there may be an amplification of certain energetic channels and a dampening of the amplitude of others. The amplification of the dampened channels is incumbent upon one's own thosenes, a cultivation of attitudes and the extent of one's own imagination. This will depend upon the creation of a suitable method for those amplifications. It is important that these methods be registered – if indeed they are conscious – in order that other consciousnesses may also utilize them so that they can come out from the darkness of their own senses. These intensities of amplification of sensitivities, according to prior attitudes and without perceiving the entire picture, can be compared to a fine thread, a thicker rope or an iron chain.

Trauma. There are persons who have an "intrinsic energetic imbalance", or bioenergetic imbalance, for whom everything goes wrong in life and who, when submitted to parapsychic testing, present results below a random probability. The complete impairment of a sense can create a condition in which the person does not even consider that sense. Nevertheless, the random probability remains. However, to have a sense (a sensory capacity) totally impaired and to choose neither correct nor random options, but only incorrect ones, is unusual. It is an indication that the person is perceiving (with that sense), but insists on looking for the option that is contrary to that which is correct (pathothosene). This reveals a type of subtle consciential trauma, the energetic opening or amplification of which is like a fine thread.

Imbalance. It is very common to encounter a child who is energetically imbalanced. His/her chakras do not have balanced energies, some operating excessively and others deficiently. This often occurs as a result of playing, excessive laughing and nervousness, which is characteristic of those who rob consciential energies (energivore, vampire or human drainer), or others who transmit negative energies. The same occurs with subhuman animals (zoology) and plants (botany). So-called *blessings* or so-called *energetic passes* can stabilize the chakras, thereby temporarily eliminating the problem.

Adults. Nevertheless, there are also legions of adults who often have the same problem – uncontrolled energetic balance (self-cure or self-remission) – frequently leading to chronic syndromes or illnesses which, over time, affect nearby physical organs, thereby causing concrete problems of an organic or somatic nature. When these energetic imbalances occur, many surrounding persons try to stabilize the other, in a conscious or unconscious manner. However, the person lacking control cannot spend his/her entire life depending on others and feeling sick. He/she should seek the self-control of organization, the balance of self-thosenes and attitudes, rationality and applied self-discernment, emerging from emotional infancy and moving from the condition of being helped (consolation task) to the condition of helping (clarification task) with maturity and self-control, in line with his/her own consciential evolution and the evolution of his/her karmic group.

Analogies. Analogies can be extrapolated in order to construct theories in this field, one example being the uncertainty principle or the phenomenon of changes in quantic states. The greatest probability for encountering the human being's consciousness is in the present and within the sphere of energies of his/her human body. Nevertheless, there also exists the probability of encountering someone's consciousness projected in the past or the future, or encountering it outside the human body in the extraphysical sphere of energies, or projected outside the sphere of energies, and almost free, in any other location. Regardless of which of these states one is encountered in, upon emitting a "photon" of energy, either through the silver cord (holochakrology) or in the direction of another body, in a direction outward from the body where one is located, a change will occur in this quantic state toward another quantic state or energy-frequency-dimension plane that is freer from heavy impositions upon the system, vibrating at more subtle frequencies, and wherein the dense body would be the nucleus of the complete consciential atom. It is common knowledge that analogies act as seeds for the future creation of initial models, improvements, subsequent theories and, finally, a comprehensive vision of reality.

XVII – Open Letters

518. TO THE READER

Warning. A warning is appropriate at this point: if you feel comfortable and complacent with your repressions, conditionings, sacralizations, castrations, taboos, myths, subjugations, leashes of the ego and interconsciential dependencies of human existence, the following 3 things should be avoided as much as possible:

1. **Projectiology.** Projectiology.
2. **Phenomenology.** The phenomenon of lucid projection and you.
3. **Projectability.** All veteran lucid projectors.

Dangers. The 3 items above are real dangers for you. If you begin to reflect upon the reality that they will provide, you will never be the same. Your *good life* will end. You will become aware of greater responsibilities as a result of leading-edge relative truths. You will know more. You will have more power. You will want to work more. You will live with a more lucid consciousness. All of this will inevitably bring you enormous problems, consciential growing crises and constant self-recycling from that point on. Run away from these dangers that are real for you. Continue to calmly repeat yet another self-mimetic human life. After all, the consciousness is imperishable. Evolution is infinite. Why be in such a hurry? You have a long life ahead of you and an abundance of time. Another thing: forget this book. *This is the classic message of the brainwashers* or the human robotizers in this still pathological, superconsumeristic, anti-ecological intraphysical society in which we participate to some degree.

Revolution. The practice of lucid projection gradually makes the lucid projector become quite a revolutionary within *materialist* intraphysical society, as well as in *mystical* human intraphysical society. It is sufficient to consider only 10 personal conditions that the lucid projector achieves:

1. One's personal possibilities maximally deconditioned.
2. Unrepressed to the greatest degree possible (freed).
3. Desacralized regarding everything and everybody, without exception (anti-demagogue).
4. *Untabooed* regarding any subject (self-sufficient).
5. Definitively debrainwashed regarding the intraphysical society in which we live.
6. Unimplicated to a greater degree regarding the immaturities and errors of others (cosmoethics).
7. One who questions everything that exists in a positive continuous and omnipresent manner (self-discerner).
8. Sincere in the extreme regarding frank relative truths (consciential maturity achieved through impact therapy).
9. Free, truly entirely free, in all senses.
10. Universalistic to the point of living with multidimensional self-awareness (self-lucid consciential epicenter).

Presentation. This book can merely serve as a reference work or it can be read from beginning to end. The individual who has reached this point in the book will observe that this methodical work has sought to present the bases of projectiology as a scientific discipline through investigation or construction of a special and systematic science, demonstrating its relevance in the area of knowledge and its revolutionary consequences in many sectors of human activity. Projectiology deserves to be studied in depth because it represents a step forward, a new and unexpected area of unforeseeable positive achievement that promises to amplify the terrestrial consciousness' sphere of activity. However, new knowledge is not merely added to existing knowledge: it has to integrate with this knowledge.

Classification. The characteristic occurrences that are most frequently experienced by the majority of consciential projectors have been listed and studied. Certain observers may, at first sight, judge the comparisons presented here to be inadequate, precipitated or exaggerated, revealing unprecedented, but valid, aspects and giving the new discipline a scientific codification or classification with an analysis and naming of the occurrences. This may be due to an overestimation by uninformed individuals.

Reality. Nevertheless, if you ask your relatives, friends, co-workers, acquaintances and neighbors, and probe your social relationships, you will always find some well-informed person who has already experienced or studied lucid consciential projections. The obvious evidence of consciential, paraphysiological occurrences leaves everyone no alternative other than to accept extraphysical reality. There are countless witnesses who have placed the subject of lucid consciential projection as a top priority among their interests and inquiries, considering this phenomenon to be the most relevant mental and consciential experience that can be naturally achieved during a person's human lifetime.

Stance. The stance of the author regarding projectiology was not reached without a great deal of reflection. If, on the one hand, we maintain that this position is probably the most defendable in an imperfect world (deficiencyland), we do not, on the other hand, propose it as an absolute certainty, nor do we disrespect those who disagree, in light of the diversity of human experiences.

Rejections. Innumerous libertarian ideas of the human consciousness, including many having a strictly scientific origin, were not well-received or were frankly rejected and attacked by scientists, studious individuals and sometimes even by the people of the time. The following 24 discoveries, among many others, encountered adverse conditions of extreme rejection by the human consciousness:

1. Anesthesia.
2. Blood circulation.
3. Daguerreotype (photography).
4. Electric current.
5. Galvanism.
6. Gas illumination.
7. Homeopathy.
8. Hygiene during childbirth.
9. Intercontinental underwater cables.
10. Magnetism.
11. Railways (trains).
12. Sunspots.
13. The composition of air.
14. The earth's rotation.
15. The falling of meteorites.
16. The gramophone (phonograph).
17. The lightning rod.
18. The propeller.
19. The size of the stars.
20. The steamboat (navigation).
21. The undulation of light (wave theory).
22. The vaccine.
23. Thermodynamics.
24. Wireless telegraphy.

Evolution. It must be hoped that this era of crass obscurantism has already been surpassed, in spite of the religious, sociological, political and even scientific inquisitions that still occur here and there.

Approach. We intend to reach all types of young readers whose imagination and creativity have not been totally repressed by the current standardized educational process *(abdominal brainwashing)*. We send our message to those who can cope with states of temporary ambiguity (pattern-behavior vs. exception-behavior) and are not afraid of confronting changes imposed by new ideas. What is presented here is a point of departure, a sketch of the basic idea, an instructive comparison, an invitation to your opinion and critique. What better approach is there for the analysis and research of these essential, high priority problems for people? Humankind transforms itself into the living dead when it abandons interrogation.

Critique. Finally, a reminder to all readers: the activity of reading does not end with the effort made to understand what a book has to say. It must be completed by critiquing or, in other words: with the work of judging everything you read.

519. TO SKEPTICS OF PROJECTIONS OF THE CONSCIOUSNESS

Restraint. We are all aware that everything which is official, academic, orthodox or fundamentalist constitutes a powerful restraint toward any and all intention for renewal. The human mind is primarily traditional and neophobic. There are individuals with a certain mental rigidity that makes their lucid entrance into extraphysical dimensions impracticable. In general, scientists enclose themselves in their own system and create their own world. They routinely negate everything they do not see or become used to not seeing.

Taboos. There are still areas which are protected against scientific investigation by taboos because the dogmatic scientist – cloistered in orthodoxy, defender of his/her social or intraphysical autobiography – lives enslaved by his/her reputation within the current extremely closed and corporative cultural world that does not allow divergences.

Orthodoxy. Etymologically speaking, "orthodoxy" signifies correct opinion or, implicitly, that all opinions which do not coincide with it are not correct. It is logical that professionals see themselves compelled to perseveringly defend their ideas as being the only valid and authorized ones, excluding that which requires revision or innovation. Everything that demands change, even for the better, is thus naturally converted into heterodoxy or deviation.

Discovery. It is generally accepted that no discovery can be enthusiastically received if it conflicts with some existing interest, when it contradicts the points of view of a scientific hierarchy or when it collides head-on with scientific dogmas.

Inhibitions. Logically, no object can, a priori, be excluded from the investigation of science, which should have no inhibitions or impossibilities, which does not admit taboos and which does not have permanently inaccessible areas. Even science is implicitly universalistic.

Gratuitousness. It will always be easy for the self-proclaimed rationalists, sophists of all types and persons with preformed opinions, to make gratuitous affirmations, discard the subject of lucid projection as being unworthy of serious discussion, or contradict, without any proof – for the mere sake of mental contortionism – the supposedly misinterpreted occurrences. In the same manner, a hostile approach of the "I know that this does not work" sort does not lead to any constructive result.

Scientist. It is common knowledge that the perfect human being does not exist. Not even a diploma, obtained through the education industry, confers omniscience. Even renowned scientists can show themselves to be and behave as irrationally as any other person, and perhaps even more so because, being only human, they do not always admit their mistakes and omissions, even when confronted with rigorous and irrefutable evidence, finding it necessary to be on the defensive against any anticipated contradiction or negation, as well as always maintaining awareness and a constant sense of critical judgment. That which is not sufficiently proven, to those who are not experienced, in this case, cannot be negated because, at the same time, they do not know how it is produced or, in other words, it does not fit within the framework of prevailing science.

Infallibility. There are always those who think that their statements should be accepted and believed, yet they will never accept the statements of others. These more stubborn and obstinate negators, compulsive skeptics and incredulous, unsubmissive individuals who always make anticipated judgments, are so convinced of their infallibility that they even doubt their own senses. One generally wastes time, logic and the effort expended with experimentation on these persons of retrograde mentality and narrow views, because they do not want to be convinced, not even by the facts of their own experiences.

Knowledge. The majority of authors of articles for technical magazines, unfortunately, do not have a more ample, multidisciplinary or universalistic knowledge of other scientific fields, not even in regard to international parapsychic research through the ages, as they are often monoglots. They are therefore sometimes not able to realize the full significance of their own discoveries in terms of interdimensional exchange between consciousnesses.

Uncommon. With projectiology, everyone is faced with a new situation that requires similarly new explanations. It is understood that ordinary intelligence rejects the uncommon nature of projectiology, the facts of which should be experienced directly by the individual in order to allow him/her to admit them.

Questions. On general ignorance regarding certain subjects in projectiology, such as the golden cord, or even the mentalsoma, the following 5 common, still obscure, questions regarding matter should also not be overlooked – proving that, within the world of science, not only certainties exist – such as:

1. What are electrons made of?
2. What is the nature of time?
3. How does the nerve fiber impulse occur?
4. How is awareness produced?
5. What type of phenomenon is thought?

Exit. This book aims to expand the limitations of the thoughts of those readers of goodwill and discernment, helping some people find an egress from the limited circle of their generally highly-regarded concepts – in the sense that the restricted consciousness can be replaced by an open mind – as well as advising them regarding the use of difficult words, such as *impossible, never* or *never again*.

Individualism. In light of the aspects presented, and taking into account the very individual nature of lucid consciential projections, it is worth posing two questions to all types of habitual skeptics or those who have never had personal experiences regarding the subject: Is the pure and simple abstention from the theme of consciential projection a just, truly valid or correct attitude? Is it worthwhile trying to understand that consciential projections exist and accept this reality as being an impulsion for the well-being of all? Methodical skepticism, a component of the scientific perspective, merely constitutes the permanent adoption of a critical attitude. Radical or systematic skepticism blocks the possibility of any knowledge.

Alternatives. When faced with a report of a lucid consciential projection experience, the inexperienced listener is left with 3 alternatives regarding the subject: take the narrator's description or tale at face value; question the narrator's mental balance; endeavor to have that same experience in order to evaluate the occurrence sensibly. We invariably recommend the third option to everyone.

520. TO APRIORISTS

Apriorism. No one has the right to judge and much less to condemn that which one does not know because, with the method of preconception or ready and pre-fabricated rejection, any fact can be considered to be almost anything, or judged in the manner that one wishes.

Negation. The following are 5 absurd attitudes that cannot be taken seriously in the analysis of the projectiology phenomena studied here:

1. The apriorists' systematic, unfounded negation of the occurrences without having experienced them.

2. The act of negation due to sheer intellectual cowardice, stemming from a subconscious complex or subconscious censure.

3. Negation because it would be too much trouble to accept the fact that the occurrences are veridical, and remain in an ultra-orthodox complacence that is impermeable to experimental evidence or any rational argument.

4. Negation of facts that are persistent, albeit contrary to prior knowledge, considered unpleasant and harmful to one's well-being because they affect other interests, striking at the survival instinct.

5. Negation in order to feed an *allergy to the future,* evidencing retrograde tendencies, neophobia, misoneism, opposing everything that is new.

Impediments. All of these impede the development of the research that is destined to open new horizons to humankind.

Facts. The facts make one think and demand interpretation. These same facts do not need our agreement or acceptance in order to exist. We have never seen a fact cease to exist in order to assuage its negators. In theory, a fact is no one's exclusive privilege. It can neither be owned, nor does it enter into anyone's custody. It would be useless to submit it to interests, adapt it to contingencies, forge it or hide it. It is a truth and, as a truth, it imposes itself as such.

Attitude. No irrational attitude is capable of impeding new instances of lucid consciential projection, which cannot be reproduced through mere hallucinations, but are repeated by human lucid projectors that are obviously not able to deny the testimony of their own senses or perceptions. The facts exist, with replicable and irrefutable objective and subjective proof, it being impossible to stifle them: people cannot be prevented from sleeping. Natural sleep frequently constitutes the basis for the launching of the xenophrenic state of lucid consciential projection.

Beliefs. All people remain limited and bound to their personal belief system or preconceptions. If the intraphysical being believes that he/she is not able to lucidly project the consciousness from the human body, he/she is not really capable of projecting and will be unlikely to succeed as long as he/she continues to block his/her own manifestations through natural autosuggestion.

Case study. The following are 3 examples of limiting beliefs, detected by conscientiology, that impede the production of lucid consciential projection:

1. **Scientists.** Innumerable elderly scientists have already reached an advanced mental (human) age and no longer have the will, motivation or capacity to accept the loss of their life's philosophy (conditionings or repressions).

2. **Psychologists.** Certain psychologists still do not value, and even come to fear, the revolutionary implications of parapsychology, in regard to the solid future of their own profession (professional competition).

3. **Magicians.** There are professional magicians, illusionists and conjurors who fear the real magic of parapsychology which, in some ways, turns all of them into real charlatans (professional competition).

Cause. The responsibility for a person not lucidly projecting lies with the individual. The reason or cause is in one's own consciousness which – as is the case with all others, prior to living in the open and universal world of one and all – lives in one's own private, closed and individual world, the *inflated ego* or *mega-ego,* with one's own ideas and morphothosenes. These persons must be left to the superintendence of evolutionary time, the greatest renovator of personal and group experiences.

Proof. Lucid projections provide crucial proof and irrefutable self-confirmation with relative ease. For public proof, the facts of lucid projection require dispassionate researchers who do not have strong preconceptions in regard to animism and parapsychism, either for or against, or whose emotional levels are not heavily marked by belief or disbelief of any type, but who accept the evidence with balance and discernment, *without arguing against the facts.*

Progress. The way of science is evolution. Therefore, modify existing codes, reinterpret experimental results, alter university curriculums, rewrite manuals and redefine postulates, but do not interrupt scientific progress.

521. TO PARAPSYCHOLOGISTS

Problems. In the area of projectiology there is still much to be done, with as yet unresolved problems requiring the work of researchers who are willing to tackle this extremely vital subject with the necessary courage to risk traveling down unconventional paths using the transdisciplinary methods and approaches of scientific fact.

Principles. The 4 *principles of parapsychism,* namely transtemporal, transpacial, transphysical and transpersonal principles, constitute the characteristics that define the procedures of projectiology.

Conflicts. Its phenomena lie beyond known physical laws and conflict with 1 or more of 4 other *delimiting principles* that distinguish normal facts from so-called *paranormal facts:*

1. Principles of causation.
2. Limitations of the action of mind upon matter.
3. Dependence of mind upon the brain.
4. Limitations in the means of acquiring information.

Studies. The facts of projectiology are not prodigious: they all occur according to as yet unknown natural mechanisms and laws. Projectiology is, therefore, neither a subject of credulity nor skepticism, to be placed at the service of mystical tendencies, or to be directed by preconceptions of any kind. It does, however, constitute a theme of study devoid of ideological-religious connotations that is to be performed with rigorous submission to the universal laws of scientific observation, experimentation and explanation.

Perspectives. The researcher – parapsychologist, parapsychobiophysicist or psychotronist – who is a puzzle solver, must consider the field of projectiology to be an experimental science and its phenomena as still undergoing inquiry. It is necessary to avail oneself of a good number of perspectives for planning projects that open new lines of investigation in the slow progress toward the general acceptance and scientific recognition of the current situation – *an abundance of questions* and *a lack of explanations* – that is part and parcel of a science in its infancy, albeit one which will be improved.

Objectivity. The reality and authenticity of the facts cannot be dealt with by using platitudes, obsessions or passionalism, but rather with dignity, correctness, willingness to achieve the goal, objectivity and realistic vision, in order to separate projectiology from empiricism, improvisation and the mystical context with which it was arbitrarily connected, so that it evolves on positive foundations under the guidance of people who are capable in all senses and who observe the phenomena without *parti pris,* thus establishing fundamental norms.

Answers. We hope that, over the next few lustrums, many of the answers that are currently beginning to be sought and stressed in this book will be found. This will enable a reduction in the number of necessary steps and the elimination of a few of the many required generations of work, so that, in the future, the phenomena of projectiology can be added to the body of standard scientific knowledge in a practical manner.

Control. Based on the supposition that all aptitude present in certain members of the human race is unlikely to be found lacking in the rest, that if one person is able to do something, then others can also do it, and that everyone is potentially disposed toward parapsychism, it is then necessary that scientific research find a way to transform this aptitude into something more controllable, systematized and accessible to everyone in order to utilize it at will. This will result in incalculable practical benefits in the field of projectiology.

Information. We can classify information according to the intensity of its transmission. The surface of an object is generally more visible than its interior. In the same way, each phenomenon manifests in a manner different from its diverse parts. Regarding written or oral information coming from a given person, it represents the smallest proportion of what is real. It is rare to gather complete documentation on a subject. When that documentation exists it is even rarer that it is consulted by everyone. The greatest goodwill in the world meets with a lack of time and means.

Hypotheses. As working hypotheses, we suggest that parapsychologists, who are specialists in specific subdisciplines of research, conduct a long-term, panoramic, multidisciplinary, exhaustive survey, without fearing the immense volume of data that will be achieved – even better than what we have endeavored to accomplish in this book with projectiology – regarding the essential aspects and phenomena of parapsychology, including the specialized international bibliography, without monoglotism, such as: telepathy; precognition; poltergeist; parapsychic therapies; ectoplasmy; and existential seriation.

Computer. This investigation and general analysis will intensify the confluence of findings and amplify the scope of international research, making possible the creation of a computer megaprogram (as we are currently endeavoring to do) exclusively dedicated to each one of these themes, which will be an invaluable reference resource for all researchers. Whether individually or in teams, with or without official financial support, today or tomorrow, in this or another country, we can foresee that these surveys will be inevitable, even disseminated over the internet or other still more developed processes, in view of the development of the natural order of things and the role of parapsychological research in the general evolution of the human being.

Modesty. The researcher, in general, and notably in projectiology, has to question everything and everyone. Humility – an unresolved illness – is the brother of passivity and both these predispositions of the intraphysical consciousness are contrary to an inquisitive disposition that is indispensable to the researcher in any scientific field. Modesty – a derivation of wisdom – or self-awareness regarding the limitations of human intelligence (self-awareness of one's evolutionary status), is another quite different predisposition of the personality. Creative, exploratory and efficient researchers can and should be modest, but should never be nor need be humble or, in other words, live with shyness, pusillanimity, or blind submission, as can be seen by the thousands everywhere.

522.   TO   PROJECTORS

Observations. The confirmations that have been established suggest some observations to the lucid projection candidate and the active lucid projector – without inconsequential paternalism – that is in their favor: the most intelligent approach is not to fear the cooperation of qualified persons in their experiments; the ideal is to allow their projective capacities to be tested; allow erudite researchers to document the activities with scientific research, in support of themselves, thus standardizing techniques and dispensing with useless procedures; do not content themselves with societal praise, allowing themselves to be monopolized by some cult or *leash of the ego;* take advantage of those valuable periods of more intense lucid projections in series, producing the experiments in a rational manner, before the period of projective recess sets in.

Experiences. It is important to remind novice projectors not to expect to exclusively produce fully lucid projections in the mentalsoma, because they will inevitably also experience interspersed projections in the psychosoma; not only to expect to explore resplendent, evolved extraphysical communities and environments, because they will also visit disagreeable and insalubrious paratropospheric environments; not to expect to satisfy only their personal wishes in the extraphysical dimensions, as they will have to assist others if they wish to progress extraphysically; not to expect to continuously experience only projections in series, as the bases of the development of lucid projection presents periods of recess or inactivity; not to expect to sleep and always project with full lucidity, as novice projectors are not able to eliminate sleep, dreams and nightmares that physiologically coexist with consciential projections; not to expect to attain automatic consciential evolution, because it does not exist. All conquests of the consciousness depend upon gradual, persevering effort, as well, above all, upon ironclad will.

Selection. Many animal evolutionary advances that have been made over the millennia occurred more or less in the following manner: an excess of curiosity impels a small number of beings to a new area of the environment. In the beginning, only one or some of them, at most, ventures into this relatively unfamiliar territory. These constitute the vanguard. When the strange new environment offers advantages, others follow. Thus, natural selection begins to act upon the small group of adventurous individuals and adapts their organisms to the demands of life in the new habitat. After many generations, a new line of adapted animals arises. Intraphysical consciousnesses are currently doing the same, on earth, in regard to the extraphysical dimensions, the human brain and their vehicles of manifestation.

Objective. Let us not try to force the honing of our projective capacity exclusively toward a singular objective, whether trying to project only in the psychosoma in the paratropospheric dimension, or only in the mentalsoma, or wishing to solely achieve the goal of the supreme and immediate expansion of the consciousness through cosmoconsciousness.

Conditions. The efforts of the intraphysical projector should be simultaneously directed toward these 3 battlefronts or toward these 3 conditions of the projected consciousness, maintaining an open mind regarding all positive suggestions of intraphysical and extraphysical origin that can somehow cooperate with harmonious and conjoined self-improvement within the scale of continuous self-awareness.

Existential seriation. On the other hand, we cannot hope to *achieve everything* in this current intraphysical life or existential program. The series of lifetimes in the current evolutionary stage on earth is a long one. No one evolves in only 1 step, nor does anyone abruptly receive intraconsciential illumination in a wholesale manner, at once, as if one had won an invisible lottery. The impact of the prominent fascination in regard to the leading-edge relative truths of conscientiology has had its detonation prepared over successive centuries, millennia, resomas, desomas and intermissive periods.

Interest. In view of existential programology and cosmoethics, the more lucid intraphysical consciousness needs to seek out his/her own interest and overcome the stage of egoism, avidity and astuteness in order to achieve megafraternity and rationally justified abnegation.

Evolution. The lucid projection practitioner needs to conform and learn to play according to the rules of the evolutionary game, remaining alert to the fact that all consciential evolution derives from individual effort, in the improvement of self-performance. This is achieved gradually, step-by-step, projection by projection, strong trait by strong trait, interweaving this intraphysical existence with the next through consciential self-relays. In this manner, the individual advances in his/her stages and engages them in the same objectives of illumination within the positions of evolutionary teams and the network of personal, group and collective holokarmic tolls.

Approach. The manner in which one approaches projectiology will always be more constructive for the projector and for everyone involved when it is universalistic, from a philosophical point of view, and impartial, from a scientific point of view.

Precautions. Mainly the adult projector, especially the one whose first consciential projections resulted from personal animic effort, needs to prevent, as a self-prophylaxis, against 3 manifestations: the powerful and involving enchantment of self-mimetic mysticism; any incipient tendency toward sectarianism in his/her convictions and attitudes; and the temptation – much more common than one might think – of founding a new sect or religion.

Attitudes. The projectiology teacher, or projectiologist, needs to always publicly acknowledge 4 frank attitudes to those who come to study with that person:

1. "I know very little and am always a merchant of my own literate ignorance."

2. "Even if I place my hands, together with the 40 hands of 20 of the volunteers from my team, on your head, I can still not cure a single sick idea of repression, conditioning or sacralization that you might maintain in your intraconscientiality."

3. "I can explain all of projectiology to you, but I cannot understand it for you."

4. "I can provide you with all the projective techniques, but I cannot perform the experiments for you, in your stead."

Evidence. This is the evidence that we have encountered in the physical and extraphysical dimensions. Other lucubrations result from mystical fantasies that lack rational foundations.

XVIII – *International Bibliography of Projectiology*

523. CLARIFICATIONS

Definition. Bibliography: bibliographical, archival and procedural process of the evaluation and study of printed (or cybernetic) texts, in view of the elaboration of general or specialized repertories, which include the phases of research, transcription, description and classification.

Synonymy: bibliographic references; specialized repertory.

Panorama. For the benefit of those bibliophiles, omnivorous readers or voracious reading athletes who wish to metabolize a copious amount of works that refer to lucid projection, only those books, newspapers, magazines, reprints, encyclopedias, dictionaries, anthologies, treatises, manuals, assays, university theses, autobiographies, biographies, novels, monographs, critical analyses, communications, reports, academic works, research results, technical articles from periodicals and other types of publications which address the subject of experiences of the consciousness outside the human body, in whole or in part, have been comprehensively inventoried in this general and systematic, retrospective and current, exhaustive and descriptive international bibliography.

Consult. Any type of research in any scientific area assumes and demands prior bibliographic research or, in other words: all technical research has its beginning and end in the library or holotheca. Over a period of time, approximately 46,000 works – in different languages, addressing the greatest diversity of basic subjects – were consulted and examined in detail, in order to select the publications listed in this bibliography. The abovementioned works were encountered in the private collection (holotheca) of the author, in public and private libraries, and in bookstores (selling new and used books) dealing with all areas of human knowledge.

Level. The essential intention of this book was to compose something unprecedented: the first *International Abstracts of Projectiology*. According to the principles of *confor,* the encountered works obviously vary in quality of content and are unequal in form. They range from those more serious, erudite and profound works, with all catalogic elements dictated by the most advanced library science, elaborated by highly trustworthy, competent contemporary authorities, scientists and researchers; to the writings of eminent pioneers who, although out of print and unlikely to be reprinted, will at least promote interest in current studious individuals for the eventual investigation of some lesser known authors, or a detailed analysis of the themes they address; to the arguably popular and commercial books that achieve the most fantastic lucubrations, created in order to satisfy needy readers and rejected seekers. Many of these works disseminate a particular doctrine, some defending evident human passions or undisguised irrationalities.

Languages. Most of the 1,907 works (plus an additional 20, upon updating) included in this bibliography, without barriers of country or language – thus evidencing the universality of the testimonies on the phenomenon experienced and the convergence of evidence – were originally retyped and later printed, the majority of them originally in 18 different languages. Some have 2, 4, 6, 12 or more volumes. A work is shown in parentheses, such as:

1. Arabic (Ebeid, 452).
2. Chinese (Wang, 1794).
3. Danish (Nielsson, 1127).
4. Dutch (Poortman, 1273).
5. English (Brennan, 199).
6. Esperanto (Kardec, 825).
7. French (Bret, 203).
8. German (Allgeier, 14).
9. Greek (Plutarch, 1264).

10. Hebrew (Almeida, 15).
11. Italian (Bozzano, 193).
12. Japanese (Meishu-Sama, 1031).
13. Latin (Swedenborg, 1639).
14. Portuguese (Antunes, 47).
15. Russian (Pushkin, 1342).
16. Sanskrit (Woods, 1864).
17. Spanish (Anglada, 39).
18. Swedish (Jacobson, 796).

English. Anywhere from 30 to 50 languages are used in scientific literature. English predominates in the works included in this bibliography – currently the language with the highest international penetration in the West – with 910 references, or 47.71% of the total. The Portuguese language is in second place with 589 references, or 30.88%.

Portuguese. It is worth mentioning that the lexicon of the Portuguese language contains 450,000 words. There are currently about 10,000 languages on earth, of which slightly over 100 are written languages. The others are unwritten languages. Of these 100 (written), only about 10 are used by over 100,000,000 people. Among these 10, the Portuguese language is in sixth place *(VEJA;* magazine; weekly; São Paulo, SP; Brazil; edition 1,547; year 31; N. 20; illus.; 20, May, 1998; p. 63), affecting about 180,000,000 people in 7 countries where Portuguese is the official language.

Countries. The works included in this bibliography were originally printed, distributed or edited in 28 countries. Sample works are shown in parentheses: Argentina (Calle, 232); Australia (Glaskin, 596); Austria (Rýzl, 1484); Belgium (Lefebure, 909); Brazil (Andrade, 27); Canada (Grof, 646); China – Taiwan (Wang, 1794); Denmark (Vett, 1738); Egypt (Ebeid, 452); England (Baker, 69); France (Dumas, 432); Greece (Plato, 1261); Holland (Poortman, 1273); Hong Kong (Badham, 67); Iceland (Gudjonsson, 657); India (Saher, 1493); Italy (Giovetti, 592); Japan (Meishu-Sama, 1031); Mexico (Benavides, 109); Portugal (Velho, 1734); South Africa (Laubscher, 889); former Soviet Russia (Vasiliev, 1732); Spain (Muntañola, 1108); Sweden (Jacobson, 796); Switzerland (Engel, 480); United States of America (Muldoon, 1102); Venezuela (Imbassahy, 782); West Germany (Dethlefsen, 396).

Scope. Chronologically speaking, the bibliography starts from the Bible, the writings of Plato and the work of Plutarch of Chaeronea. It circumstantially covers the last 22 decades of the lucid extracorporeal activities of the human race, from the publication of the theological books of Emanuel Swedenborg, including 117 reference works – encyclopedias, dictionaries, anthologies, treatises, catalogues and manuals – or 6.13% of the bibliography. On *January 11, 1985*, the author ended this bibliographic research, thus not including references to works published after this date, except for the 20 works included in the update. Exactly 349 listed works are indicated to have an alphabetic index by subject (alph.), which greatly facilitates the creation of a computerized database. Incidentally: the books containing an alphabetic index by subject are generally serious, more carefully produced, technically clearer and are prepared by authors who are assiduous and who make an effort to aid the reader.

Impartiality. This systematic list was compiled, with total impartiality, without preconceptions, in an ample and unrestricted manner – through exploratory, selective, reflective and interpretive confirmatory readings. This occurred more intensively over a 19-year period (1966 to 1985). It even lists individuals who presented positive and negative heterocritiques, and even controversial works. On the other hand, no work was included gratuitously, only to "pad out" the bibliography, according to the current academic system. All works, without exception, address the subject of lucid projection, even if *only on one page* of their text.

Exclusions. Dozens of diverse irrelevant works were excluded from this international bibliography in light of the this book's objective or, in other words, those works that directly or indirectly merely touch upon the subject, in one or some lines of their texts, with very brief references and with no significance to the themes of projectiology. These works would only increase the amount of books listed without introducing any quality to the list, bringing no effective contribution or real value to projectiological research.

Lies. On the other hand, the following should be kept in mind: there are leaders in the publishing community who openly declare that, nowadays, in intraphysical society, to sell art in general – theater, music, films, books – is to sell lies about lies, recognizing that, in this specific arena, *everyone lies to everyone*. The sociological process of consciential immaturity – extremely professional and professionalizing – is completed in 5 interconnected steps:

1. **Writer.** The circle of ridiculous falsehoods begins with the writer writing lies (palatable literature) for superficial readers.

2. **Agent.** Then, a literary agent reads two pages and affirms that the book is sensational.

3. **Publisher.** The publisher receives the work, reads 1 paragraph and lies to the bookseller, saying that this exceptional book will be a bestseller.

4. **Bookseller.** The bookseller, who reads nothing, repeats this heap of lies to the consumer, the reader of trendy, easily digested books.

5. **Industry.** The book industry continues to prosper, based upon the lucrative exploitation of the emotionalism of human animals, who are always too lazy to think for themselves.

Articles. The bibliography presents articles which are included in exactly 80 different periodicals (magazines, newspapers, bulletins and others) published in various countries, ranging from *gynecological* or *gynosomatic* magazines to essentially technical ones. There are isolated articles that were not listed here, whereas the most important ones are found to be analyzed, transcribed or cited in dozens of the books that are listed.

Collections. The following 9 are relevant, older periodicals, some of them out of circulation, in the collections of which can be found dozens of short and isolated works on projective studies or reports of interesting projectiological occurrences:

1. *Annales des Sciences Psychiques* (Paris).
2. *The Journal of the American Society for Psychical Research* (New York, NY).
3. *Journal of the Society for Psychical Research* (London).
4. *Light* (London).
5. *Proceedings of the Society for Psychical Research* (London).
6. *Revue de Etudes Psychiques* (Paris).
7. *Revue Métapsychique* (Paris).
8. *Revue Scientifique et Morale du Spiritisme* (Paris).
9. *Tidschrift voor Parapsychologie* (Amsterdam).

Database. In the holotheca of the Center for Higher Studies of the Consciousness (CHSC), in Iguassu Falls, Parana, Brazil, we have more than 90% of this international bibliography available for study and research, namely more than 1,700 works, aside from their various editions, totaling 1,907 works, which comprise the current database on projectiology. All works in the collection, some multi-volume, others with various editions, in different locations and languages, are read and reread. Their pages are underlined, with handwritten, detailed annotations, and are signed by the author on the title page. In the first page of each volume there is an exhaustive handwritten reproduction of the work's catalogic record, many of them with annotations or pertinent heterocritiques.

Private. If the reader wishes to study consciential projection phenomena using the works in his/her private library, simply verify if the author's name and the title of the work are listed in this international bibliography. If it is included in the list, the reference indicates the exact pages where the author addresses the subject of consciential projections or correlated phenomena.

Interest. The expressive quantity of opinion, data, and information gathered here cannot be flippantly disregarded. The accumulation of convergent indications on lucid projection is too large not to be taken seriously, much less ignored. The extensive nature of this bibliography constitutes an irrevocable set of documents that, as well as solidly establishing the existence of the human lucid projection phenomenon, attests to the public interest in this consciential occurrence that is growing faster than ever before and has being gaining increased publicity and a greater presence everywhere as never before in human history. This fact has provoked the creation of sections with their own titles, such as "Projection of the Consciousness", on the bookshelves in bookstores specializing in parapsychology, psychology and metaphysics in New York City, the largest publishing and bookselling market that currently exists.

Collection. The current bibliography aims to contribute – within the geographic, chronological, economic and personal limitations of its compiler – with the evident objective of presenting, as closely as possible, the integral collection of literature that exists on this subject up to the present. Unfortunately, this work is still somewhat incomplete, owing to 3 distinct principles: first, the complete bibliography does not exist; second, no author is capable of exhausting a subject; third, the most interesting research in progress, in any specific field of human knowledge, has generally not been printed. One thought-provoking fact: according to the calculations of the author, an average of one new book a day (365 books a year) is currently published – in the English language alone – in the general area of parapsychology. This has been happening for the last two decades.

Unknown. Between the years of 1900 and 1966, 59,404 technical-scientific magazines were published. It is therefore accepted that half of the scientific bibliography generated was not indexed and remains unknown.

Objective. The essential intention of this list within this volume – which is an overall approach – was to constitute as homogeneous as possible a set of precise and detailed indications with elements of references even beyond the usual patterns of more accepted technical norms, when demanded by the work, in light of the possible different cultural backgrounds of the likely readers of this book.

Sources. In order to have greater assurance regarding the information, the use of primary or original sources was emphasized. The truth is that secondary and tertiary sources are always suspect and often biased, carelessly produced or simply erroneous. Secondhand references or indirect quotations, which tend to reduce the documented value, were used only as a last resort, after all means had been exhausted for obtaining the work in its original language and conveniently anatomizing it.

Translations. Whenever possible, preference was given to the revised edition of a publication in its original language, thus avoiding translations, even to the Portuguese language. In order to minimize the negative consequences of this orientation, in all cases where verification was possible, the languages to which the work had already been translated were indicated, as long as the work had not suffered an excessive number of commercial, mutilating cuts. Thus, the Bible was obviously excluded, for example, already (in 1985) having been translated into 1,685 languages and dialects.

Originals. It is always worth emphasizing that the discerning readers who wish to form their own opinions, will have to direct themselves to the original research work, seeking out original publications and sources.

Repetitions. It is understandable that, in a bibliography of this size, there is a repetition of themes, approaches and analyses, as seen with the references to cases of projectiological phenomena. Therefore, if an article was published in a periodical and later inserted in a book – such as an anthology – preference was given to the anthology, whenever possible. In these anthologies on different themes, priority was generally given to the citation of the editor or editors of the work, avoiding naming the author of every article included in the volume.

Projectionalia. As this bibliography is general and universalistic, it is natural that it would represent a true, currently unparalleled, *projectionalia,* being the *intellectual equipment* that is available on the subjects of projectiology, ranging from highly recommended works – according to the evaluation of their level of information – that confer a degree of precision and certainty, to those that are satisfactory and recommendable, and finally to those constituting simplistic literature. These last works are frankly not recommended to many readers, due to their structural fragility, and they do not even deserve mention or further comment. Nevertheless, they are listed – with a maximum of impartiality – waiting for the heterocritiquing, discerning, analytical sense of that reader who is interested in deep intellectual prospects, capable of expunging basic errors, misleading premises, erroneous statistics, invalid arguments and simple falsehoods or fallacious logic (sophisms and philosophisms).

Ordering. In the bibliographic orientation, the works were listed in a uniform manner, using a specific record including that which was possible of the following 21 technical variables:

1. Alphabetical order of the authors, their pseudonyms (pseud), and indications regarding their real names, when known. The name of the author of multiple works was repeated in succession, in order to facilitate consultation by the reader.

2. Co-authors and other specifications were always included after the title, such as subtitle, author of the preface (pref.), translator (trans.), publisher, commentator or reviser.

3. Introduction (intro.).

4. Appendix (append.) or appendices.

5. Reference to illustrations (illus.) or figures (fig.).

6. Number of component volumes (vol.).

7. Number of the periodical publication.

8. Total number of pages (p.).

9. Number of pages or chapters (chaps.) that directly address the subjects of projectiology.

10. Original title of the work, in the translations in which this is listed.

11. Number of pages in the bibliography (bibl.) and the glossary (glos.), if they exist.

12. Alphabetical index of the subjects addressed (alph.) or bibliographic references.

13. Onomastic index (ono.).

14. Vertical dimension of the publication in centimeters (cm).

15. Type of volume, if it is hardback (hb.) or paperback (pb.).

16. Dust jacket (dj.).

17. Publishing house (pub.).

18. Number of edition (ed.) or printing (print.).

19. Location (city, state, province, country, if necessary).

20. Month and year of the edition in focus, when given by the publication.

21. Editions in other languages.

Pages. The total number of pages of each work is always indicated by an even number, rounding up, although in many cases, the last page has no text, and is, therefore, blank. This is because, strictly speaking, an odd-numbered last page cannot exist in the body of a book – except for the cover. The traditional argument of the odd number corresponding to the written pages is not accurate, because pages 2, 4 and others at the ends of chapters or sections, remain blank in the majority of books. In the vertical dimension of the pages of each work, only centimeters and half-centimeters were considered, thus eliminating annotations of intermediary millimeters in order to facilitate and standardize the library registers, where possible.

Reference. When reference is made to one, two or a few pages of a work, it is because some theme specific to projectiology is being addressed only on those pages of that work, whether it be lucid projection, apparition of human beings, physical bilocation, doubles, experience of the consciousness outside the human body, near-death experience that involves lucid projection, classification of this phenomenology, reports of occurrences, citations, annotations and pertinent definitions. The concerned individual can thus evaluate with greater precision the exact scope of the specialized information in the work in focus, before spending time or going to the trouble of looking for it and reading it. The illustrations (illus.) were indicated, although minimal, even when *only one* appears in the work.

Minilibrary. It is extremely difficult to select a few works from the entire international bibliography that are more relevant for the individual study of lucid projection. Nevertheless, particularly in order to help those who are *novices* regarding these selfsame lucid projections, and even running the risk of committing glaring and practically inevitable injustices, 50 books, and not single works, were indicated – the majority of which are relatively easy to locate. They include many classics on the subject that address the themes related to lucid projection in almost all of their pages. They are technically favorable for the development of the lucid projector and can serve to comprise a respectable international minilibrary on projectiology.

List. This list – as is the case with any other list of books – does not contain irreprehensible works. However, these 50 titles, from 8 countries, most of them published in the 1970s, representing only 2.62% of the bibliography, have received fewer negative criticisms from more demanding readers, as they are considered to be more technical, more complete, and particularly useful. The following list includes the name of the author and the country where each work originated (the number in brackets indicates the title of the work in the bibliography): Aksakof: Russia (09); Baker: England (69); Battersby: England (92); Baumann: U.S.A. (93); Black: U.S.A. (137); Blackmore: England (139); Bord: England (170); Bosc: France (173); Bozzano: Italy (188); Brennan: England (199); Crookall: England (338); Crouzet: France (344); Delanne: France (382); Denning: U.S.A. (391); Durville: France (436); Engel: (former) West Germany (480); Fischer: West Germany (519); Fox: England (544); Frost: England (560); Giovetti: Italy (593); Green: England (632); Greene: U.S.A. (635); Greenhouse: U.S.A. (636); Gurney: England (666); Hart: U.S.A. (687); Lancelin: France (879); Lefebure: France (909); Lischka: West Germany (937); Martin: England (1002); Mitchell: U.S.A. (1059); Monroe: U.S.A. (1065); Muldoon: U.S.A. (1105); Muntañola: Spain (1108); Myers: England (1114); Prado: Brazil (1284); Prieur: France (1289); Ritchie: U.S.A. (1407); Rogo: U.S.A. (1444); Sabom: U.S.A. (1486); Sculthorp: England (1531); Shay: U.S.A. (1546); Smith: U.S.A. (1572); Steiger: U.S.A. (1601); Swann: U.S.A. (1632); Tanous: U.S.A. (1647); Turvey: England (1707); Twitchell: U.S.A. (1712); Walker: England (1781); Wheeler: England (1826); Yram: France (1897). Four of these authors, Bozzano, Crookall, Muldoon and Rogo, produced other works on lucid projection, aside from those cited here, that deserve to be consulted by the diligent researcher. Robert Crookall and Scott Rogo are included among the most prolific authors in regard to the works that address the study and technical analysis of lucid projection. It is evident that most of these 50 works are among those which are most referred to in the specific bibliographies.

Specialized. Some of the topics addressed in 17 of the chapters in this book (see Table of Contents) have already been proficiently analyzed using many angles of approach by known authors in an entire book dedicated to the subject: "internal autoscopy and external autoscopy," Sollier (1581); "cosmoconsciousness or cosmic consciousness," Bucke (218); "near-death experience" (NDE), Sabom (1486); "panoramic vision," Bozzano (186); "exteriorization of motricity," Rochas (1428); "exteriorization of sensitivity," Rochas (1429); "human parateleportation," Fodor (530); "xenophrenia," Tart (1653); "human aura," Kilner (843); "massage, musical and projective visualization techniques," Glaskin (598; 599); "extraphysical invisibility," Richards (1392); "extraphysical clothing," Crookall (332); "helpers," Crookall (323); "animism or mediumship," Bozzano (184).

Youths. We recommend the following children's book to those youths interested in the phenomenon of lucid projection, *They Travel Outside Their Bodies,* by Elwood D. Baumann. Unfortunately, this work has not been translated into other languages beyond the original English which, however, does occur with the absolute majority of good projectiological works.

Update. The following 20 extra works on lucid projections, selected from among those published between 1986 and 1998, in Brazil and abroad, are provided in order to update this International Bibliography:

1. **ARAÚJO, Luiz;** *Ensaios Extracorpóreos;* pref. Clóvis Ferreira & Werner Sheinpflug; 126 pp.; 20 chaps.; 20 illus.; glos. 26 terms; add.; alph.; 21.5 x 15 cm; pb.; 2nd ed.; Rio de Janeiro, RJ, Brazil; Instituto Internacional de Projeciologia e Conscienciologia (IIPC); 1998.

2. **ATWATER, P. M. H.;** *Beyond the Light – What Isn't Being Said About Near-death Experience;* introd.. Melvin Morse; XX + 296 pp.; 14 chaps.; 16 illus.; 2 tabs.; 3 apps.; 23.5 x 15.5 x 3 cm; hb.; dj.; New York; U.S.A.; Birch Lane Press; 1994.

3. **BASCOM, Lionel C.; & LOECHER, Barbara;** *By the Light;* X + 212 pp.; 20 chaps.; 17.5 x 10.5 cm; pb.; New York; NY; U.S.A.; Avon Books; September, 1995.

4. **BORGES, Wagner D.;** *Viagem Espiritual II (A Projeção da Consciência);* illustrations by Glória C. Costa; pref. Dráuzio Milagres; 238 pp.; 5 chaps.; Vol. II; 58 illus.; glos. 33 terms; 45 refs.; 19 x 27.5 cm; hb.; 1st ed.; Londrina; Paraná; Brazil; Editora Universalista; 1995.

5. **BRINKLEY, Dannion; with PERRY, Paul;** *Saved by the Light;* introd. Raymond Moody; XII + 162 pp.; 15 chaps.; 21.5 x 14.5 cm; hb.; dj.; New York; U.S.A.; Villard Books; 1994.

6. **BRUNEL, Pierre (org.);** *Dictionary of Literary Myths ("Dictionnaire des Mythes Littéraires");* transl. Carlos Sussekind (et al.); pref. Braz. ed. Nicolau Sevcenko; XXVI + 940 pp.; dictionary: 124 terms; 2180 refs.; 4 diag.; 1 tab.; 24 x 16.5 x 5.5 cm; hb.; Rio de Janeiro, RJ; Brazil; José Olympio; 1997.

7. **BUHLMAN, William;** *Adventures Beyond the Body – How to Experience Out-of-Body Travel;* XII + 292 pp.; 8 chaps.; 13 illus.; glos. 33 terms; app.; alph.; 22 x 14 cm; hb.; dj.; London; Great Britain; Robert Hale; 1997.

8. **COUTINHO, Marco Antonio;** *Além do Corpo – A Arte Tradicional das Experiências Extracorpóreas;* pref. Pedro Camargo; 152 pp.; 11 illus.; 27 refs.; 21 x 14 cm; pb.; Rio de Janeiro; Brazil; Mauad; 1996; pp. 1-152.

9. **CRAZE, Richard;** *Astral Projection, a Beginner's Guide;* 92 pp.; 4 chaps.; 20 x 13 cm; pb.; London; England; Headway – Hodder&Stoughton; 1996.

10. **EBY, Carol;** *Astral Odyssey – Exploring Out-of-Body Experiences;* XVI + 256 pp.; 10 chaps.; 96 refs.; alph.; 21 x 13.5 cm; pb.; York Beach; Maine; U.S.A.; Samuel Weiser; 1996.

11. **EQUIPO DE EXPERTOS OSIRIS;** *La Proyección Astral;* Colección Ciencias Ocultas y Misterios; 110 pp.; 20.5 x 14 cm; pb.; Barcelona; Spain; Editorial De Vecchi; 1992.

12. **FIGUEIRÓ, Luely;** *Viagem Astral: Projecionismo: Passado-presente-futuro;* 110 pp.; 5 illus.; 21 x 14 cm; pb.; São Paulo; Brazil; Ícone; 1993.

13. **GODWIN, Malcolm;** *The Lucid Dreamer – A Waking Guide for the Traveler Between Worlds;* 256 pp.; 13 chaps.; 201 illus.; 46 refs.; alph.; 24 x 19.5 cm; hb.; dj.; Great Britain; Element Books; 1994.

14. **HARRIS, Barbara; & BASCOM, Lionel C.;** *Full Circle – The Near-Death Experience and Beyond;* introd. Bruce Greyson; XVI + 286 pp.; 22 chaps.; app.; 17 x 10.5 cm; pb.; New York; NY; U.S.A.; Pocket Books; April, 1990.

15. **HOWELL, Will;** *The Way to Why;* 192 pp.; 29 chaps.; 7 refs.; 21 x 14 cm; hb.; dj.; Birmingham; Great Britain; The Bean Press; 1988; pp. 1-192.

16. **HUGHES, Marilynn;** *Odysseys of Light – Adventures in Out-of-Body Travel;* XII + 142 pp.; 14 chaps.; 21.5 x 13.5 cm; pb.; Norfolk, VA; U.S.A.; Hampton Roads; 1991.

17. **LATZANG, Dharma;** *Como Fazer Viagens Astrais;* 88 pp.; 10 chaps.; 21 x 14 cm; pb.; Liberdade, São Paulo; Brazil; Traco Editora; 1993.

18. **LORIMER, David;** *Whole in One – The Near-Death Experience and the Ethic of Interconnectedness;* pref. Raymond A. Moody Jr.; XIV + 340 pp.; 9 chaps.; 413 refs.; 3 figs.; alph.; 20 x 13 cm; pb.; London; England; Orkana; 1990.

19. **SOUZA, Narcí Castro de;** *Lições Recebidas em Desdobramento Astral;* 158 pp.; 20 chaps.; 21 x 14 cm; pb.; Rio de Janeiro, RJ; Brazil; Missão Orion; 1996.

20. **STEIGER, Brad;** *One with the Light;* X + 300 pp.; 42 chaps.; 17.5 x 10.5 cm; pb.; New York; NY; U.S.A.; A Signet Book; September, 1994.

Bibliography: Rogo (1448, p. 157), Vieira (1753, p. 7).

524. COMPLEMENTARY SUBJECTS

Marginal. The works that are capable of furnishing greater clarification regarding the 43 complementary technical subjects related to the phenomenological complex of projectiology, and whose marginal or specialized aspects in certain lines of thought were not referred to together within the context of this book, are listed below in order to facilitate the practical consultation of researchers and lucid projectors.

Anthologies: Angoff (40), Armstrong (56), Belline (105; 106), Bourguignon (181), De la Mare (378), De Mille (386), Favre (500), Grattan-Guinness (626), Huxley (771), Jorge (811), Knight (851), Krippner (861), Marx (1010), Meek (1028), Mitchell (1058), Morris (1092; 1093; 1094), Pearce-Higgins (1214), Prince (1290), Ròy (1446), Roll (1462; 1463; 1464; 1465; 1466; 1467; 1468; 1469), Schatz (1514), Tart (1663; 1664; 1665), Tchou (1668), White (1827; 1829; 1830; 1831), Wilson (1851), World (1865).

Anthroposophy: Easton (451), Shepherd (1549), Steiner (1610; 1611).

Autobiographies: Alverga (18), Anglada (39), Balzac (71), Bennett (118), Brittain (206), Castaneda (255), Charrière (274), Crowley (347), Espérance (485), Ford (536), Fox (544), Garfield (569), Garrett (572), Graham (619), Heywood (718), Hives (728), Home (752), Jung (812), Leaf (904), Lilly (927), Lima (928), MacLaine (980), Martins (1009), Monroe (1065), Muldoon (1105), Nielsson (1127), Osmont (1170), Pereira (1230), Prado (1284), Rampa (1360), Richmond (1400), Roberts (1416), Sculthorp (1531), Shell (1579), Swann (1632), Swedenborg (1639), Tanous (1647), Turvey (1707), Twigg (1711), Vieira (1762), Weil (1809), Yogananda (1894), Yram (1897).

Bibliographies: Clarie (286), Drury (418), Goes (605), Tubby (1701), Vieira (1753), Zorab (1904).

Biographies: Ajaya (08), Araujo (49), Barboka (78), Berthe (126), Browning (213), Bouisson (176), Byse (230), Calle (232), Castro (263), Conant (295), Cuno (353), Dillon (402), Edmonds (460), Freitas (552), Gauld (575), Hankey (677), Harrison (685), Holzer (748), Kardec (826), Kerner (840), Linedecker (932), Lutyens (960), Matter (1014), Mead (1024), Morato (1084), Murphet (1109), Neff (1120), Novelino (1140), Paschoal (1204), Rizzini (1411), Roy (1480), Sekanek (1538), Shepherd (1549), Shirley (1554), Silva (1559), Stanké (1595), Stead (1597), Steiger (1606), Thiago (1676), Thomas (1681), Wachtmeister (1780), Wilson (1852).

Book reviews: Adams (02), Amadou (22), Andrade (30), Blackmore (142; 144), Christie-Murray (282), Cook (299), Crookall (319), East (448), Eastman (449), Grosso (650; 652), Lucas (954), Maddeley (981), McHarg (1021), Osis (1162), Parrott (1203), Pearce-Higgins (1213), Rogo (1443), Schwartz (1526), Staff (1594), Stokes (1625), Tart (1655; 1656; 1657; 1659), Thouless (1683), Valle (1726), Whiteman (1837; 1838), Willmann (1850), Zorab (1905; 1906).

Cabalism: Berg (121), Ophiel (1151).

Castanedism: Atlan (62), Bancroft (73), Càstaneda (255; 256; 257; 258; 259; 260; 261), Corvalán (306), De Mille (386), Dubant (419; 420), Drury (414), Noël (1132).

Catalogs: Ashby (59), Holzer (743), Popenoe (1274), Wilson (1858), Zorab (1904).

Catholicism: Ancilli (24), Poodt (1272), Thurston (1700).

Christianity: Almeida (15), Cayce (268), Crookall (326), Currie (354), Johnson (807), Pearce-Higgins (1214), Perry (1238), Ritchie (1407), Thomas (1681), Xavier (1870).

Controversies: (See "Critiques").

Critiques: Anievas (41, p. 20), Balanovski (70, p. 194), Bleibtreu (156, p. 81), Bozzano (193, p. 5), Calle (233, p. 10), Cardillo (241, p. 99), Christie-Murray (282, p. 620), Christopher (283, p. 213), Crookall (334, p. 358), De Mille (386, p. 220), Dragaud (412, p. 53), El-Aowar (474, p. 6), Ernest (482, p. 3), Gardner (567, p. 3), Gooch (617, p. 45), Gynska (667, p. 13), Holzer (748, p. 156), Imbassahy (779, p. 29), Lorenzatto (952, p. 142), Machado (967, p. 83), Maddeley (981, p. 259),

Mendes (1034, p. 25), Miranda (1052, p. 39), Mirclair (1054, p. 87), Monroe (1065, p. 86), Paim (1182, p. 227), Paixão (1183, p. 76), Pisani (1248, p. 177), Poodt (1272, p. 268), Puharich (1337, p. 60), Pushkin (1342, p. 300), Rampa (1364, p. 7), Randi (1370, p. 145), Ring (1404, p. 273), Rogo (1446, p. 254), Rolim (1461, p. 450), Russell (1482, p. 17), Sagan (1492, p. 61), Sangirardi Jr. (1503, p. 15), Sargant (1508, p. 199), Schnaper (1519, p. 268), Segura (1537, p. 177), Sudre (1630, p. 396), Taylor (1667, p. 66), Tourinho (1692, p. 24), Valle (1726, p. 346), Vasiliev (1732, p. 144), Vieira (1744, p. 6), Walker (1786, p. 95), White (1831, p. 132), Whiteman (1837, p. 21).

Dictionaries: ADGMT (03), Ancilli (24), Bacheman (66), Blavatsky (153), Blunsdon (157), Bonin (168), Chaplin (273), Dalmor (361), D'arbó (365), Day (376), Depascale (392), Digest (401), Drury (418), Gaynor (577), Gómez (613), Heindel (705), Lee (908), Martin (1003), Mesquita (1037), M. F. R. C. (1224), Pike (1242), Planeta (1249; 1250; 1251), Rampa (1361), Riland (1403), Stebbing (1600), Tondriau (1690), Underwood (1721), Wedeck (1807), Zaniah (1899).

Ecstasy: Black (137, p. 1), Crookall (324, p. 1), Eliade (475, p. 117), Garfield (569, p. 72), Lewis (923, p. 199).

Encyclopedias: Abbot (01), Ash (57), Bowyer (183), Britannica (205), Cavendish (266), Devore (397), Digest (400), Espasa-Calpe (484), Ferguson (507), Fodor (528), Foin (532), Matson (1013), Poinsot (1270), RPA (1481), Sachs (1489), Shepard (1548), Spence (1588), Walker (1783; 1784; 1785), Zolar (1902).

Esoterism: Fortune (541), Lorenz (951), Mead (1025), Meck (1026).

ESP: Agee (07), Alvarado (16), Braud (197), Burt (224), Christopher (283), Cohen (290), Colton (294), Cooke (300), Dale (357), Easlic (446), Ehrenwald (471), Faria (495), Hart (688), Herlin (714), Heywood (718), Holloway (734), Holroyd (739), Holzer (751), Huson (768), Knight (851), Ostrander (1172), Palmer (1189; 1190; 1191), Pratt (1285), Randi (1370), Rhine (1390), Rogo (1446), Sara (1506), Sherman (1551), Smith (1573; 1575), St. Clair (1593), Stratton (1627), Tchou (1669), Thouless (1682), White (1833).

Ghosts: Bayless (94), Cardillo (241), Carrington (247), Collison-Morley (293), Emmons (479), Fodor (529), Greenhouse (638), Gurney (666), Hemmert (712), Hill (724), Imbassahy (781), Imbassahy (783), Jaffé (798), Lang (885), Lethbridge (920), Mackenzie (970), O'Donnell (1144), Padilha (1180), Rogo (1436), Sidgwick (1556), Thiselton-Dyer (1678), Tyrrell (1717).

Glossaries: Blavatsky (153), Gómez (613), Mesquita (1037), Purucker (1340), Thalbourne (1675), White (1835).

Hagiography: Ancilli (24), Berthe (126), Ebon (455), Fielding-Ould (513), Lewis (923), Poodt (1272), Rogo (1447), Thurston (1700), Wallace (1788), White (1833).

History: Alexandrian (11), Blavatsky (155), Doyle (411), Durville (441), Gauld (575), Inardi (786), Inglis (789), King (845), Knight (852).

Huna: Crookall (343), Hoffman (733), Long (945; 946; 947), Steiger (1603), Straith-Miller (1626).

Initiations: Fortune (541), Guilmot (661), Lefebure (909).

Interviews: Ashby (58), Bleibtreu (153), Bolen (166), Hooper (755), Nietzke (1128), Pose (1277), Psychic (1291), Régis (1380), Rodrigues (1434), Watkins (1799).

Jungism: Burt (225, p. 163), Crookall (329, p. 1), Jaffé (798, p. 143), Jung (812, p. 320; 813, p. 481), Serrano (1542, p. 147), Wilson (1852, p. 7).

Law: Barreto (83), Rodrigues (1433).

Levitation: Richards (1393), Turi (1705).

Magic: Christopher (283), Gardner (567), Randi (1370).

Magic practices: Bardon (80), Bourgeat (180), Butler (227; 228), Camaysar (236), Conway (297), Crowley (348; 349), David-Neel (368), Drury (414; 415; 417), Farrar (496), Fontaine (533), Fortune (540), Hartmann (693), Howard (761), King (844; 845; 846), Knight (852), Mauss (1016), Mousseaux (1099), Ophiel (1151), Papus (1198), Plytoff (1265), Poinsot (1271), Prel (1286), Richards (1392), Sandwith (1502), Steiger (1603), Weor (1821).

Manuals: Bret (203), Carrington (251), Ebon (457), Greene (635), King (846), Leary (907), Mickaharic (1044), Mitchell (1059), Parrish-Harra (1202), Planeta (1257), Schatz (1514), Sepharial (1541), Stokes (1625), Tubby (1701), Verneuil (1735), Wolman (1863).

Polemics: (see "Critiques").

Prophecies: Cheetham (176, p. 149), Cornillier (304, p. 85), Greenhouse (639, p. 58), Lessa (918, p. 337), Marin (996, p. 118), Vivante (1777, p. 122).

Pseudonyms: Ajaya (08), Babajiananda (65), Blacksmith (149), Christian (281), Crowley (347), Espérance (485), Fortune (540), Fox (543), Goldstein (607), Heindel (703), Hillel (1226), Imperator (784), Jefa (05), Kardec (815), Loester (942), Marrick (1000), Michaelus (1042), Moebius (1497), Ophiel (1150), Papus (1197), Ramacháraca (1347), Rampa (1349), Rocha (1425), Rohmer (1460), Satpren (1509), Sepharial (1541), Smith (1567), Steiger (1601), Valério (1725), Weor (1813), Yogananda (1894), Yram (1897), Zain (1898), Zaniah (1899), Zolar (1902).

Psychoanalysis: Ehrenwald (471), Eisenbud (473), El-Aowar (474), Fodor (531), Imbassahy (777), Marin (996), Wolman (1863).

Rosicrucianism: Bernard (124), E. P. (481), Heindel (705), Imperator (784), Loester (942), M. F. R. C. (1040), Rosacruz (1472).

Shamanism: Andreas (36), Drury (417), Eliade (475), Lewis (923), Mercier (1036), Planeta (1253), Wilson (1851).

Spiritism: Aksakof (09), Aliança (13), Barbanell (77), Barkas (82), Bozzano (184), Chevreuil (278), Chiesa (279), Cirne (285), Crouzet (344), Dassier (367), Delanne (383), Denis (387), Doyle (411), Ferreira (509), Green (634), Harnold (683), Imbassahy (775; 779), Kardec (818; 824), Karl (834), Lantier (886), Lombroso (943), Machado (967), Machado (969), Mackintosh (972), Marco (995), Mello (1032), Metzger (1038), Miguel (1045), Miranda (1052), Moutin (1101), Netto (1126), Owen (1177), Papallardo (1196), Paula (1208), Pereira (1230), Rigonatti (1401), Rizzini (1409), Roure (1479), Schofield (1520), Sech (1536), Silva (1561), Starke (1596), Stobart (1623), Thomas (1680), Torteroli (1691), Trespioli (1696; 1697), Tummolo (1704), Uchôa (1719), Velho (1734), Vesme (1736), Wallace (1788), Wauthy (1803), Xavier (1875).

Sports: Andrews (37, p. 6), Murphy (1113, p. 1).

Swedenborgism: Alexandrian (11), Balzac (72), Bellini (106), Boddington (162), Britannica (205), Byse (230), Cuno (353), Davis (371), Doyle (411), Dusen (443), Ebon (458), Fodor (528), Geymuller (586), Matter (1014), Miranda (1053), Pike (1242), Rizzo (1413), Swedenborg (1633; 1634; 1635; 1636; 1637; 1638; 1639; 1640), Thomas (1681), Tuttle (1708), Wilson (1851).

Theosophy: Anglada (38), Ashish (60), Besant (130), Blavatsky (155), Collins (292), Hodson (729), Leadbeater (899), Lyra (961), Neff (1120), Olcott (1147), Pavri (1210), Powell (1278), Richelieu (1397).

Theses: Lessa (18), Machado (967), Scott (1530), Silva (1561).

Treatises: Blavatsky (155), Cirne (285), Crowley (348), Delanne (382), Flammarion (524), Gurney (666), Myers (1114), Papus (1198), Richet (1398), Stevenson (1618), Swedenborg (1634), Wang (1794), Wilson (606).

Umbandism: Alverga (18), Babajiananda (65), Gomes (612), Silva (1562).

Zen Buddhism: Anderson (26), David-Nell (368), Humphres (766), Rogo (1441), Saher (1493), Suzuki (1631).

525. INTERNATIONAL BIBLIOGRAPHY OF PROJECTIOLOGY

1.   ABBOT, A. E.: "Encyclopaedia of the Occult Sciences"; 452 pp.; 20 cm; hb.; Emerson Press; London; 1960; p. 48.

2.   ADAMS, Sally; "The Supreme Adventure" (Robert Crookall); Books Reviews; *Journal of the Society for Psychical Research;* London; Vol. 41; N. 709; September, 1961; pp. 158, 159.

3.   ADGMT; "Dicionário de Doutrina Espírita"; 304 pp.; glos. 297-304; 18.5 cm; pb.; Grupo Espírita Regeneração; Rio de Janeiro; Brazil; 1963; pp. 46-48, 71-73.

4.   ADINAD-DALA; "Dialogos Metafísicos"; 124 pp.; 23 cm; pb.; Author's Edition; Buenos Aires; Argentina; 1963; pp. 101-104.

5.   ADOUM, Jorge (Pseud.: Mago Jefa); "Cosmogenesis segun la Memoria de la Naturaleza"; pref. A. Harb. M.; 92 pp.; bibl. 90; 20 cm; pb.; 3rd ed.; Editorial Kier; Buenos Aires; Argentina; 1980; pp. 29, 32, 33, 40, 42, 43; eds.: Sp., Port.

6.   ADOUM, Jorge (Pseud.: Mago Jefa); "20 Dias no Mundo dos Mortos"; 134 pp.; illus.; 22 cm; pb.; Comissão Divulgadora J. A.; Santos Dumont, MG; Brazil; July, 1978; pp. 1-134.

7.   AGEE, Doris; "Edgar Cayce on ESP"; Editor: Hugh Lynn Cayce; 224 pp.; 18 cm; pocket; pb.; Paperback Library; New York; May, 1969; pp. 40-47.

8.   AJAYA, Swami (Pseud. for Allan Weinstock); Organizator; "Vivendo com os Mestres do Himalaia: Experiências Espirituais de Swami Rama"; transl. Octavio Mendes Cajado; 432 pp.; illus.; glos. 430-432; 19.5 cm; pb.; Editora Pensamento; S. Paulo; Brazil; 1981; pp. 238, 317, 399-401, 406-409.

9.   AKSAKOF, Alexander Nikolayevich; "Animismo e Espiritismo"; transl. C. S.; 712 pp.; illus.; 18 cm; hb.; H. Garnier, Livreiro-Editor; Rio de Janeiro; Brazil; 1903; pp. XXXVIII, XXXIX, 511-574; eds.: Ger., Fr., Port. (Mini-library).

10.   ALD, Roy; "The Man Who Took Trips"; 246 pp.; illus.; 21 cm; hb.; dj.; Delacorte Press; New York; 1971; pp. 18, 151-153, 196.

11.   ALEXANDRIAN; "Histoire de la Philosophie Occulte"; 390 pp.; index of names; 24 cm; pb.; Éditions Seghers; Paris; 1983; pp. 29, 274, 288-293, 310, 312-317; eds.: Fr., Port.

12.   ALFONSO, Eduardo; "La Religion de la Naturaleza: Cosmologia Transcendente"; 376 pp.; illus.; 19.5 cm; pb.; 4th ed.; Editorial Kier; Buenos Aires; Argentina; 1976; pp. 342-346.

13.   ALIANÇA; Editora; "Curso Básico de Espiritismo"; 172 pp.; illus.; 21 cm; pb.; Editora Aliança; S. Paulo; Brazil; March, 1981; pp. 148-153.

14.   ALLGEIER, Kurt; "Du hast Schon einmal Gelebt"; 222 pp.; bibl. 221-223; 18 cm; pocket; pb.; 2nd ed.; Wilhelm Goldmann Verlag; München; West Germany; Dezember, 1981; pp. 117, 126, 135-140.

15.   ALMEIDA, João Ferreira de (Translator); "Bíblia: O Velho e o Novo Testamento"; 1.194 pp.; illus.; 18 cm; hb.; 49th print.; Imprensa Bíblica Brasileira; Rio de Janeiro; Brazil; 1981; Eccles. 12:6; I Cor. 15:44; II Cor. 12:2-4; eds.: Heb., Eng., Fr., Port. and others.

16.   ALVARADO, Carlos; "ESP and Out-of-Body Experiences: A Review of Spontaneous Studies"; *Parapsychology Review;* New York; Vol. 14; N. 4; July-August, 1983; bibl.; pp. 11-13.

17.   ALVARADO, Carlos; "Phenomenological Differences Between Natural and Enforced Out-of-Body Experiences: A Re-analysis of Crookalls Findings"; *Theta;* Durham; North Carolina; Magazine; Vol. 9; 1981; pp. 9-11.

18.   ALVERGA, Alex Polari de; "O Livro das Mirações"; Autobiography; 346 pp.; illus.; 21 cm; pb.; Editora Rocco; Rio de Janeiro; Brazil; 1984; pp. 127-129, 138-140, 214, 215, 271, 272, 280, 281, 288-292, 300, 301, 312.

19.   ALVERY, Robert; "Out of the Body Experiences"; pref. Harry Edwards; 118 pp.; Regency Press; London; 1975; pp. 1-118.

20. ALVISI, Gabriella; "As Vozes dos Vivos de Ontem"; transl. M. de Campos; pref. Giorgio Di Simone; 258 pp.; illus.; 21 cm; pb.; Publicações Europa-América; Mira-Sintra; Portugal; no date; pp. 21, 130-133.

21. AMADOU, Robert; "Parapsicologia: Ensaio Histórico e Crítico"; prol. José Herculano Pires; pref. J. Van Lennep; postf. J. Carvalhal Ribas; 422 pp.; glos. 403-412; index of names, 413-418; 21 cm; pb.; 2nd ed.; Editora Mestre Jou; S. Paulo; Brazil; 1969; pp. 404, 405; eds.: Fr., Sp., Port.

22. AMADOU, Robert; "Revues"; *Revue Métapsychique;* Paris, Bimonthly; Numbers 29, 30; Mai-Août, 1954; pp. 226-228.

23. AMBELAIN, Robert; "O Vampirismo: Da Lenda ao Real"; transl. Ana Silva e Brito; 230 pp.; illus.; 20 cm; pb.; Livraria Bertrand; Amadora; Portugal; 1978; pp. 29-81.

24. ANCILLI, Ermanno; "Diccionario de Espiritualidad"; transl. Joan Llopis; 3 Vol.; 2.106 pp.; Vol. II: 726 pp.; Vol. III: 650 pp.; Systematic index; 24 cm; hb.; dj.; Editorial Herder; Barcelona; Spain; 1983/1984; Vol. I: 730 pp.; p. 264.

25. ANDERSON, Rodger I.; "Contemporary Survival Research: a Critical Review"; *Parapsychology Review;* New York; Vol. 12; N. 5; September-October, 1981; pp. 8-13.

26. ANDERSON, Walt; "Segredos Revelados: Práticas do Budismo Tibetano"; transl. Luiz Horácio da Matta; 216 pp.; illus.; glos. 205, 206; 21 cm; pb.; Livraria Francisco Alves Editora; Rio de Janeiro; Brazil; 1983; pp. 133-135.

27. ANDRADE, Hernani Guimarães; "Espírito, Perispírito e Alma"; pref. Ney Prieto Peres; XX + 246 pp.; illus.; bibl. 231-238; index of names; alph.; 23 cm; cart.; Editora Pensamento; S. Paulo; Brazil; 1984; pp. 99, 110-117, 121-127, 131-160, 183-188, 210, 216, 226 (See Numbers 149; 150; 607-610; 1000).

28. ANDRADE, Hernani Guimarães; "A Matéria Psi"; 74 pp.; bibl. 70-73; 18.5 cm; pb.; Casa Editora O Clarim; Matão, SP; Brazil; March, 1981; p. 44.

29. ANDRADE, Hernani Guimarães; "Morte, Renascimento, Evolução: Uma Biologia Transcendental"; pref. Osmard Andrade Faria; XVIII + 172 pp.; illus.; bibl. 156-161; index of names; alph.; 23 cm; pb.; Editora Pensamento; S. Paulo; Brazil; 1983; pp. 67-69, 89-92.

30. ANDRADE, Hernani Guimarães; "Projeções da Consciência" (Vieira); Section "Revisão de Livro"; *Folha Espírita*; S. Paulo, SP; Brazil; Newspaper; Monthly; illus.; Yr. VIII; N. 89; August, 1981; p. 6.

31. ANDRADE, Herbaldo Lima e; "O Espírito que Deixou o Corpo Durante o Sono"; *Kabala;* Rio de Janeiro; Brazil; Magazine; Monthly; Yr. I; N. 2; 18 cm; September, 1954; pp. 18-24, 32.

32. ANDRADE, José Hermógenes de; "O Yoga e os Poderes Paranormais"; *Anais do III Congresso Nacional de Parapsicologia e Psicotrônica;* Abrap; Rio de Janeiro; Brazil; 24 cm; pb.; July, 1982; 13 pp. (pp. 57-70); pp. 59, 62 (See N. 715).

33. ANDRÉA, Jorge – dos Santos; "Correlações Espírito-Matéria"; 56 pp.; illus.; bibl. 49; 21 cm; pb.; Editora Samos; Rio de Janeiro; Brazil; 1984; p. 25.

34. ANDRÉA, Jorge – dos Santos; "Palingênese, a Grande Lei"; 154 pp.; illus.; 21 cm; pb.; 2nd ed.; Author's Edition; Rio de Janeiro; Brazil; 1980; pp. 144-148.

35. ANDREAE, Christine; "Seances & Spiritualists"; 160 pp.; illus.; bibl. 151-153; alph.; 20.5 cm; hb.; dj.; J. P. Lippincott Co.; Philadelphia; U. S. A.; 1974; pp. 21, 89-96, 101.

36. ANDREAS, Peter, and KILIAN, Caspar; "A Ciência Fantástica"; transl. Trude Von Lascham Solstein; 208 pp.; illus.; bibl. 206-208; 20 cm; pb.; Edições Melhoramentos; S. Paulo; Brazil; 1976; pp. 29, 38-59, 87, 92, 97, 115, 141, 188; eds.: Eng., Ger., Port.

37. ANDREWS, Valerie; "The Psychic Power of Running"; 202 pp.; illus.; alph.; 21.5 cm; pb.; Thorsons Publishers; Great Britain; 1979; pp. 6, 11, 121, 122.

38. ANGLADA, Vicente Beltrán; "La Estructuracion Devica de las Formas"; 224 pp.; illus.; 21 cm; pb.; Editorial Eyras; Madrid; Spain; 1982; pp. 80-82.

39. ANGLADA, Vicente Beltrán; "Mis Experiencias Espirituales"; 190 pp.; 21 cm; cart.; Luis Carcamo, Editor; Madrid; Spain; 1982; pp. 25-27, 63-66, 73-76.

40. ANGOFF, Allan, and BARTH, Diana; Editors; "Parapsychology and Anthropology" (E. J. Dingwall); XX + 328 pp.; illus.; 23 cm; hb.; Parapsychology Foundation; New York; 1974; pp. 241-243, 257-261.

41. ANIEVAS, Joaquim; "Um Jovem Parapsicólogo Americano"; *Revista de Parapsicologia;* S. Paulo, SP; Brazil; Monthly; Yr. 1; N. 6; July, 1973; illus.; pp. 20-22.

42. ANJOS, Luciano dos, and MIRANDA, Hermínio Correa de; "Crônicas de Um e de Outro: De Kennedy ao Homem Artificial"; pref. Abelardo Idalgo Magalhães; 286 pp.; 18 cm; pb.; Federação Espírita Brasileira; Rio de Janeiro; Brazil; 1975; pp. 69, 82, 83, 92, 93, 162-164, 184, 193, 226.

43. ANJOS, Rose dos; "Você é Espírito"; 94 pp.; 21 cm; pb.; Reflexos Editora; Porto Alegre, RS; Brazil; June, 1982; p. 45.

44. ANÔNIMO; "Aum, Signos del Agni Yoga"; 204 pp.; 20 cm; pb.; Editorial Kier; Buenos Aires; Argentina; 1951; pp. 64-66.

45. ANONYMOUS; "The Double Projection"; *Fate;* Magazine; Evanston, Ill.; U.S.A.; Vol. 6; N. 2; February, 1953; p. 60.

46. ANONYMOUS; "The Unseen World: Communications With It"; VIII + 216 pp.; 17.5 cm; hb.; James Burns; London; 1847; pp. 163-180.

47. ANTUNES, João; "Hipnologia Transcendental"; 224 pp.; 18 cm; hb.; Livraria Classica Editora; Lisboa, Portugal; 1913; pp. 163-171.

48. AOM; "Desdobramentos"; Booklet; Copy; 8 pp.; 31 cm; Ascensionada Ordem Mística; Curitiba, PR; Brazil; s. d.; p. 7.

49. ARAUJO, Humberto Leite de; "Barsanulfo, Sua Vida, Seu Exemplo"; 20 pp.; 15 cm; pb.; 3rd ed.; Lar Irmão Francisco; Rio de Janeiro; Brazil; 01, May, 1982; pp. 12, 13.

50. ARAUJO, Maria de Lourdes; "Luz! Símbolo da Fé!"; 106 pp.; 20.5 cm; hb.; Irmãos Pongetti, Editores; Rio de Janeiro; Brazil; 1950; pp. 26, 27.

51. ARMOND, Edgard; "Desenvolvimento Mediúnico Prático"; 80 pp.; 20.5 cm; pb.; Livraria Allan Kardec Editora; S. Paulo; Brazil; no date; p. 70.

52. ARMOND, Edgard; "O Estranho Caso de Rôse Ramires"; 148 pp.; 20.5 cm; pb.; 3rd ed.; Editora Aliança; S. Paulo; Brazil; 1979; pp. 137-141.

53. ARMOND, Edgard; "Mediunidade"; 212 pp.; 21 cm; pb.; 15th ed.; Livraria Allan Kardec Editora; S. Paulo; Brazil; no date; pp. 14, 39, 49-51, 72-77, 87, 127, 195, 208, 209.

54. ARMOND, Edgard; "Mediunidade: Síntese"; 122 pp.; 18 cm; pb.; Livraria Allan Kardec Editora; S. Paulo; Brazil; no date; pp. 22, 23.

55. ARMOND, Edgard; "Na Semeadura"; 2 Vol.; 320 pp.; bibl. 151; 21 cm; pb.; Editora Aliança; S. Paulo; Brazil; 1975/1977; Vol. II: pp. 77-79, 82, 112, 123-128, 143.

56. ARMSTRONG, Neville; Editor; "Harvest of Light: Approaches to the Paranormal"; Anthology; introd. Paul Beard; 258 pp.; 21.5 cm; hb.; dj.; Neville Spearman; London; 1976; pp. 87-92.

57. ASH, Brian; "Encyclopédie Visuelle de la Science-Fiction"; transl. Jean Pierre Galante; 352 pp.; illus.; alph.; 26 cm; cart.; Albin Michel; Paris; 1979; pp. 205-208.

58. ASHBY, Robert H.; "The Case for Survival; An Interview With William Roll"; *Theta;* Durham; North Carolina; U. S. A.; Magazine; Quarterly; N. 45; Summer, 1975; pp. 4-9.

59. ASHBY, Robert H.; "The Guidebook for the Study of Psychical Research"; introd. Renée Haynes; 158 pp.; glos. 144-157; bibl. 34-89; 22 cm; pb.; Rider and Co.; London; 1972; pp. 21, 145, 151, 156, 157.

60. ASHISH, Madhava; "Man, Son of Man; In the Stanzas of Dzyan"; XVI + 352 pp.; illus.; alph.; 21 cm; hb.; dj.; The Theosophical Publishing House; Wheaton; Ill.; U. S.A.; 1970; pp. 333, 334.

61. ATIENZA, Juan G.; "La Gran Manipulación Cósmica"; 280 pp.; 20 cm; pb.; Ediciones Martínez Roca; Barcelona; Spain; 1981; pp. 259, 260.

62. ATLAN, Jacques; "Etude Sur les Cinq Livres de Carlos Castaneda"; *Renaître 2000;* Paris; Magazine; Bimonthly; 122nd Yr.; New series; N. 15; November-December, 1979; pp. 204-212.

63. AZEVEDO, José Lacerda de; "Mediunidade Reprimida"; *Desobsessão;* Porto Alegre, RS; Brazil; Newspaper; Monthly; Yr. XXXI; N. 373; March, 1979; pp. 12-14.

64. AZEVEDO, Juan Rocha de; "Fascinantes Secretos Psiquicos"; prol. Rodolfo Perdomo Bica; 176 pp.; illus.; 20 cm; pb.; Editorial Kier; Buenos Aires; Argentina; 1983; pp. 44-47.

65. BABAJIANANDA (Pseud. for Roger Pierre Feraudy); "Serões do Pai Velho: O Catecismo de Umbanda"; 212 pp.; illus.; 21 cm; pb.; Editora Record; Rio de Janeiro; Brazil; 1978; p. 36.

66. BACHEMAN, William; "The Steinerbooks Dictionary of the Psychic, Mystic, Occult"; 252 pp.; illus.; 18 cm; pocket; pb.; Rudolf Steiner Publications; Blauvelt, N. Y.; U. S. A.; 1973; pp. 20, 29.

67. BADHAM, Paul, and BADHAM, Linda; "Immortality or Extinction?"; 146 pp.; bibl. 142, 143; alph.; 21.5 cm; hb.; The Macmillam Press; Hong Kong; 1982; pp. 12-15, 71-89.

68. BAEZA, Tomas; "La Reencarnacion"; 192 pp.; 192 pp.; 17 cm; pb.; Editorial Bruguera; Barcelona; Spain; Julio, 1975; pp. 52, 53.

69. BAKER, Douglas M.; "Practical Techniques of Astral Projection"; 96 pp.; illus.; bibl. 94; 21.5 cm; pb.; 2nd print.; The Aquarian Press; London; 1978; pp. 1-96 (Mini-library).

70. BALANOVSKI, Eduardo; "Los Fenómenos Paranormales"; 220 pp.; illus.; 19.5 cm; pb.; Gedisa; Barcelona; Spain; February, 1982; pp. 19, 115.

71. BALZAC, Honoré de; "Louis Lambert"; Novel; pref. Raymond Abellio; 176 pp.; 18 cm; pocket; pb.; Éditions Gallimard; Paris; 1980; pp. 32, 71-73; eds.: Fr., Port., etc.

72. BALZAC, Honoré de; "Usula Mirouët"; Novel; transl. Gomes da Silveira; introd. Paulo Rónai; *in* "A Comédia Humana"; Vol. V; XXXIV + 206 pp.; illus.; 21.5 cm; hb.; Editora Globo; Porto Alegre, RS; Brazil; 1953; pp. 66-71.

73. BANCROFT, Anne; "Twentieth Century - Mystics & Sages"; XVI + 344 pp.; illus.; alph.; 21 cm; hb.; dj.; Heinemann; London; 1976; pp. 311, 312.

74. BANERJEE, Hamendras Nat; "Vida Pretérita e Futura"; transl. Sylvio Monteiro; 120 pp.; illus.; 21 cm; pb.; Editorial Nórdica; Rio de Janeiro; Brazil; 1983; pp. 39-41.

75. BANKS, Frances Mary; "The Frontiers of Revelation: An Empirical Study in the Psychology of Psychic and Spiritual Experience"; 232 pp.; Max Parrish; London; 1962; pp. 110-115.

76. BARADUC, Hippolyte; "La Force Vitale"; illus.; 224 pp.; 21.5 cm; hb.; Paul Ollendorff, Éditeur; Paris; 1897; pp. 211-216.

77. BARBANELL, Maurice; "This is Spiritualism"; 224 pp.; alph.; 21.5 cm; pb.; 5th print.; Psychic Press; London; 1983; pp. 25, 120, 121, 206.

78. BARBOKA, Geoffrey A.; "H. P. Blavatsky, Tibet and Tulku"; XXIV + 476 pp.; illus.; bibl. 437-446; alph.; 23 cm; hb.; dj.; 1st print.; The Theosophical Publishing House; Adyar; Madras; India; 1974; pp. 330-342, 424.

79. BARDENS, Dennis; "Mysterious Worlds"; 222 pp.; 21.5 cm; hb.; dj.; W. H. Allen; London; 1970; pp. 47, 137-162.

80. BARDON, Franz; "Iniciacion al Hermetismo"; transl. Manuel Algora Corbi; pref. Otti V.; 406 pp.; illus.; 21 cm; cart.; Luis Carcamo, Editor; Madrid; Spain; 1982; pp. 317-326, 383-388.

81. BARHAM, Allan; "Strange to Relate"; pref. Arthur J. Ellison; introd. Victor Goddard; XII + 128 pp.; illus.; bibl. 124; alph.; 21.5 cm; hb.; dj.; Colin Smythe, Gerards Cross; Great Britain; 1984; pp. 86-93.

82. BARKAS, Thomas P.; "Outlines of Investigations into Modern Spiritualism"; VIII + 160 pp.; 18.5 cm; hb.; Frederick Pitman; London; 1862; pp. 22, 87, 96, 97.

83. BARRETO, Djalma Lúcio Gabriel; "O Alienista, o Louco e a Lei"; 140 pp.; bibl. 135-139; 21 cm; pb.; Editora Vozes; Petrópolis, RJ; Brazil; 1978; pp. 67-69.

84. BARROS, Sílvia Lúcia C. Vasconcellos; "Do Desdobramento à Projeção: O Que Mudou?"; *Folha Espírita;* S. Paulo, SP; Brazil; Newspaper; Monthly; Yr. IX; N. 99; June, 1982; p. 5.

85. BARROS, Sílvia Lúcia C. Vasconcellos; "Experiências Fora do Corpo Físico"; *Jornal Espírita;* S. Paulo, SP; Brazil; Monthly; Yr. VIII; N. 87; illus.; September, 1982; p. 10.

86. BARROS, Sílvia Lúcia C. Vasconcellos; "Novas Perspectivas de Waldo Vieira"; *Revista Internacional do Espiritismo;* Matão, SP; Brazil; Monthly; Yr. LVII; N. 4; 26.5 cm; May, 1982; p. 126.

87. BARTZ, Heinrich; "Astrale Schwebezustände"; *Esotera;* Freiburg; West Germany; Magazine; Monthly; Yr. 21; N. 8; August, 1970; p. 751.

88. BARTZ, Heinrich; "Träume sind nicht nur Gehirnfunktionen"; *Esotera;* Freiburg; West Germany; Magazine; Monthly; Yr. 22; N. 7; July, 1971; pp. 657, 658.

89. BASTOS, Demétrio Pável; "Médium, Quem é, Quem não é"; pref. M. B. Tamassia; 108 pp.; illus.; 19 cm; pb.; Instituto Maria, Departamento Editorial; Juiz de Fora, MG; Brazil; 1981; pp. 35, 57, 58, 74-77.

90. BATES, E. Katherine; "Our Living Dead"; Kegan Paul; London; 1917; p. 12.

91. BATES, E. Katherine; "Seen and Unseen"; XVI + 324 pp.; London; 1907; p. 120.

92. BATTERSBY, Henry Francis Prevost; "Man Outside Himself: The Methods of Astral Projection"; introd. Leslie Shepard; 102 pp.; bibl. 101, 102; 21 cm; hb.; dj.; 2nd print.; University Books; New Jersey; U. S. A.; August, 1973; pp. 1-102 (Mini-library).

93. BAUMANN, Elwood D.; "They Travel Outside Their Bodies"; 10 + 118 pp.; illus.; bibl. 113, 114; alph.; 23.5 cm; hb.; dj.; Franklin Watts; New York; 1980; pp. 1-117 (Mini-library).

94. BAYLESS, Raymond; "Animal Ghosts"; pref. Robert Crookall; 188 pp.; 21 cm; hb.; dj.; University Books; New York; 1970; pp. 70-73.

95. BAYLESS, Raymond; "Apparitions and Survival of Death"; pref. D. Scott Rogo; 206 pp.; bibl. 149, 150; 21 cm; hb.; dj.; University Books; New York; 1973; pp. 79, 148-164, 204-220.

96. BAYLESS, Raymond; "Experiences of a Psychical Research"; 246 pp.; 20.5 cm; hb.; dj.; University Books; New Hyde Park; N. Y.; 1972; pp. 152, 153.

97. BAYLESS, Raymond; "Life at Death"; *Parapsychology Review;* New York; Vol. 12; N. 2; March-April, 1981; pp. 13-15.

98. BAYLESS, Raymond; "The Other Side of Death"; introd. Robert Crookall; 192 pp.; 20 cm; hb.; dj.; University Books; New York; 1971; pp. 7-10, 24, 25, 32, 67, 95-132, 143, 146, 152-161, 182.

99. BEARD, Paul; "Living On: A Study of Altering Consciousness After Death"; 202 pp.; alph.; 20 cm; hb.; dj.; George Allen & Unwin; London; 1980; pp. 34-36.

100. BEAUCIE, Albert La; "Les Nouveaux Horizons Scientifiques de la Vie"; 238 pp.; 18 cm; hb.; Bibliothèque Universelle Beaudelot; Paris; 1907; pp. 53, 54.

101. BECKER, C. B.; "The Failure of Saganomics: Why Bird Models Cannot Explain Near-Death Phenomena"; *Anabiosis;* Magazine; Vol. 2; 1982; pp. 102-109.

102. BECKER, Raymond de; "Las Maquinaciones de la Noche"; transl. J. Herrero; 432 pp.; 18 cm; pb.; pocket; Plaza & Janes; Barcelona; Spain; September, 1977; pp. 401-403.

103. BEDFORD, James, and KENSIGTON, Walt; "El Experimento Delpasse: Un Descubrimiento en el Reino entre la Vida y la Muerte"; transl. Michael Faber-Kaiser; 328 pp.; bibl. 327; 22 cm; pb.; Ediciones Martínez Roca; Barcelona; Spain; 1976; pp. 15, 186-190.

104. BÉLIARD, Octave; "Sorciers, Rêveurs et Démoniaques"; 272 pp.; illus.; bibl. 265-267; 18 cm; pb.; Librairie Alphonse Lemerre; Paris; 1920; pp. 55-60.

105. BELLINE; "Anthologie de L'Au-delà"; pref. Frédéric Royer; 390 pp.; bibl. 383-386; 21.5 cm; pb.; Éditions Robert Laffont; Paris; 1978; pp. 334-339, 361, 362.

106. BELLINE; "Anthologie de L'Au-delà; 2: Domaine Anglophone"; 278 pp.; 21.5 cm; pb.; Éditions Robert Laffont; Paris; 1981; pp. 91-94.

107. BELOFF, John; "New Directions in Parapsychology"; XXVI + 174 pp.; illus.; 21.5 cm; hb.; The Scarecrow Press; Metuchen; N. J.; U. S. A.; 1975; pp. 149-152, 159, 160.

108. BENAVIDES, Rodolfo; "En la Noche de los Tiempos"; Novel; 260 pp.; bibl. 259, 260; 19.5 cm; pb.; 6th ed.; Editores Mexicanos Unidos; Mexico, D. F.; 1971; p. 46.

109.   BENAVIDES, Rodolfo; "...Entonces Seremos Dioses"; Novel; 340 pp.; illus.; 19.5 cm; pb.; Editores Mexicanos Unidos; Mexico, D. F.; 1967; pp. 12, 27-35, 56-60, 113, 123, 131-133, 152, 157, 170, 178-193, 198, 199, 211, 229-233, 309, 317, 323-333.

110.   BENAVIDES, Rodolfo; "Experiencias Paranormales"; 328 pp.; 21.5 cm; pb.; Editorial Diana; Mexico, D. F.; Junio, 1981; pp. 20, 25, 26, 91-103, 121-123.

111.   BENAVIDES, Rodolfo; "Rumbos Humanos"; Novel; 390 pp.; bibl. 389, 390; illus.; 20 cm; pb.; 5th ed.; Editores Mexicanos Unidos; Mexico, D. F.; Febrero, 1971; pp. 10-12, 14, 40.

112.   BAZETT, L. M.; "Beyond the Five Senses"; Basil Blackwell; London; 1946.

113.   BENDER, Hans; "Unser Sechster Sinn"; 176 pp.; illus.; bibl. 175; 18 cm; pocket; pb.; Wilhelm Goldmann Verlag; München; West Germany; 1982; pp. 167-173.

114.   BENDIT, Laurence; "The Mirror of Life and Death"; 200 pp.; 17.5 cm; pb.; 2nd ed.; The Theosophical Publishing House; Wheaton; Ill.; U. S. A.; 1968; pp. 76, 87, 94.

115.   BÉNEZECH, Alfred; "Les Phénomènes Psychiques et la Question de l'Au-delà"; 394 pp.; 17.5 cm; hb.; Librairie Fishbacher; Paris; 1912; pp. 24-27, 198, 199.

116.   BENNETT, Alfred Gordon; "Focus on the Unknown"; XII + 260 pp.; illus.; bibl. 259, 260; 21 cm; hb.; dj.; Rider and Co.; London; 1953; pp. 187, 188, 207, 248-257.

117.   BENNETT, Colin; "Practical Time Travel"; 96 pp.; alph.; 18 cm; pb.; 2nd ed. rev.; Samuel Weiser; New York; 1980; pp. 28, 29; eds.: Eng., Port.

118.   BENNETT, John G.; "Witness"; Autobiography; epil. por Elizabeth Bennett; X + 384 pp.; illus.; 21.5 cm; pb.; Turnstone Press; Wellingborough; Northamptonshire; Great Britain; 1983; pp. 3-6, 10, 261, 283.

119.   BENTOV, Itzhak; "Stalking the Wild Pendulum: On the Mechanics of Consciousness"; XVI + 238 pp.; illus.; bibl. 237; 18 cm; pocket; pb.; 3rd print.; Bantam Books; New York; 1981; pp. 3, 77, 116, 117, 126-142.

120.   BERENDT, Heinz C.; "Parapsicologia"; transl. and introd. Antonio Sanchez Arjona; 192 pp.; illus.; glos. 170-176; bibl. 177-185; index of names; alph.; 21 cm; cart.; Ediciones Morata; Madrid; Spain; 1976; pp. 113, 120-124; eds.: Ger., Sp.

121.   BERG, Philip S.; "Reincarnation: The Wheels of a Soul"; pref. Kenneth R. Clark; 224 pp.; glos. 203-213; alph.; 23 cm; pb.; Research Centre of Kabbalah; New York; 1984; pp. 70, 71, 80, 81, 145.

122.   BERGIER, Jacques; "Você é Paranormal"; transl. Álvaro Cabral; 6 + 114 pp.; 21 cm; pb.; Livraria Eldorado Tijuca; Rio de Janeiro; Brazil; 1972; pp. 28, 29.

123.   BERGSON, Henri; "L'Énergie Spirituelle"; 228 pp.; 21.5 cm; hb.; Librairie Félix Alcan; Paris; 1920; pp. 65-89.

124.   BERNARD, Raymond; "Novas Mensagens do Sanctum Celestial"; transl. Aurora P. de Carvalho; 348 pp.; 23 cm; pb.; Editora Renes; Rio de Janeiro; Brazil; 1974; pp. 203-216.

125.   BERNARDES JR., Lannes J.; "Espiritualismo Evolucionista"; 180 pp.; 23 cm; pb.; Author's Edition; Rio de Janeiro; Brazil; 1966; pp. 134-136.

126.   BERTHE, R. P.; "Saint Alphonse de Liguori"; Biography; 2 Vol.; XVI + 1.448 pp.; illus.; 24 cm; hb.; Librairie de la Sainte-Famille; Paris; 1906; Tome Second: pp. 359-363.

127.   BERTRAND, I.; "La Sorcellerie"; 64 pp.; 18 cm; pb.; Librairie Blond; Paris; 1912; pp. 27-59.

128.   BESANT, Annie Wood; "O Caminho do Discipulado"; transl. E. Nicoll; 114 pp.; glos. 113, 114; 19.5 cm; pb.; Editora Pensamento; S. Paulo; Brazil; 1983; pp. 69, 74, 97, 105.

129.   BESANT, Annie Wood; "O Homem e Seus Corpos"; transl. Mário de Alemquer; 146 pp.; 19 cm; pb.; Editora Pensamento; S. Paulo; Brazil; 1976; pp. 21, 35, 40, 41, 52, 62-72, 125, 127, 128, 133, 134.

130.   BESANT, Annie Wood; "Lecturas Populares de Teosofía"; transl. Federico Climent Terrer; 156 pp.; 18 cm; pb.; Editorial Teosofica Argentina; Rosario; Argentina; 1970; pp. 134-148; eds.: Eng., Sp.

131. BESANT, Annie Wood; "El Poder del Pensamiento"; transl. José Melián; 180 pp.; 17.5 cm; hb.; 3rd ed.; Biblioteca Orientalista; Barcelona; Spain; 1910; pp. 168-173; eds.: Eng., Sp., Port.

132. BESANT, Annie Wood; "Reencarnación"; without translator; 104 pp.; 15 cm; pb.; Federación Teosofica Interamericana; Rosario; Argentina; 1974; pp. 67-79; eds.: Eng., Sp.

133. BESANT, Annie Wood; "A Sabedoria Antiga"; transl. Eugenio N. de Almeida; 246 pp.; 21 cm; pb.; Editora Record; Rio de Janeiro; Brazil; 1977; pp. 63-70.

134. BESANT, Annie Wood; "A Study in Consciousness"; XIV + 372 pp.; illus.; alph.; 18 cm; hb.; 7th print.; The Theosophical Publishing House; Adyar; Madras; India; 1975; pp. 173-188.

135. BESANT, Annie Wood; "Yoga: Ciência da Vida Espiritual"; transl. and pref. Cinira Riedel de Figueiredo; 126 pp.; 19.5 cm; pb.; Editora Pensamento; S. Paulo; Brazil; 1976; pp. 78, 79, 108-111.

136. BLACHER, Richard S.; "To Sleep, Perchance to Dream"; *The Journal of the American Medical Association;* Vol. 242; N. 21; 23, November, 1979; p. 229.

137. BLACK, David; "Ekstasy: Out-of-the-Body Experiences"; 244 pp.; bibl. 215-236; alph.; 20.5 cm; pb.; The Bobbs-Merril Co.; New York; 1975; pp. 1-244 (Mini-library).

138. BLACKMORE, Susan J.; "A Postal Survey of OBEs and Other Experiences"; *Journal of the Society for Psychical Research;* London; Vol. 52; N. 796; February, 1984; bibl. 242, 243; pp. 225-244.

139. BLACKMORE, Susan J.; "Beyond the Body: An Investigation of Out-of-the-Body Experiences"; pref. Brian Inglis; XVI + 272 pp.; illus.; bibl. 253-264; alph.; 20 cm; pb.; Granada Publishing; London; 1983; pp. I + XVI, 1-272 (Mini-library).

140. BLACKMORE, Susan J.; "Birth and the OBE: An Unhelpful Analogy"; *The Journal of the American Society for Psychical Research;* New York; Vol. 77; N. 3; July, 1983; bibl. 235, 236; pp. 229-238.

141. BLACKMORE, Susan J.; "Have You Ever Had An OBE?: The Wording of the Question"; *Journal of the Society for Psychical Research;* London; Vol. 51; N. 791; June, 1982; pp. 292-302.

142. BLACKMORE, Susan J.; "Leaving the Body: A Practical Guide to Astral Projection"; Books Reviews; *Journal of the Society for Psychical Research;* London; Vol. 52; N. 797; June, 1984; pp. 316-318.

143. BLACKMORE, Susan J.; "On the Extrasomatic Localization of OB Projections"; *The Journal of the American Society for Psychical Research;* New York; Vol. 75; N. 4; October, 1981; pp. 365, 366.

144. BLACKMORE, Susan J.; "Out-of-Body Experiences" (Janet Lee Mitchell); Books Reviews; *Journal of the Society for Psychical Research;* London; Vol. 51; N. 792; October, 1982; pp. 387-389.

145. BLACKMORE, Susan J.; "Out-of-Body Experiences, Lucid Dreams, and Imagery: Two Surveys"; *The Journal of the American Society for Psychical Research;* New York; Vol. 76; N. 4; October, 1982; pp. 301-317.

146. BLACKMORE, Susan J.; "Parapsychology and Out-of-the-Body Experiences"; introd. A. J. Ellison; 34 pp.; bibl. 31-33; 21 cm; pb.; The Society for Psychical Research; London; July, 1978; pp. 1-34.

147. BLACKMORE, Susan J.; "Parapsychology: With or Without the OBE?"; *Parapsychology Review;* New York; Vol. 13; N. 6; November-December, 1982; bibl. 7; pp. 1-7.

148. BLACKMORE, Susan J.; "SPR 1981 Conference"; *Parapsychology Review;* New York; Vol. 12; N. 6; November-December, 1981; pp. 19-22.

149. BLACKSMITH, Lawrence (Pseud. for Hernani Guimarães Andrade); "Algo Mais, Além do Cérebro?"; *Folha Espírita;* S. Paulo, SP; Brazil; Newspaper; Monthly; Yr. IX; N. 101; illus.; August, 1982; pp. 4, 5 (See N. 27-30).

150. BLACKSMITH, Lawrence (Pseud. for Hernani Guimarães Andrade); "A Mente Através do Espaço"; *Folha Espírita;* S. Paulo, SP; Brazil; Newspaper; Monthly; Yr. IX; N. 102; illus.; September, 1982; pp. 4, 5.

151. BLASCO, Ricardo; "El Poder Oculto de la Mente Humana"; 266 pp.; illus.; 19 cm; pb.; Ediciones Telstar; Barcelona; Spain; 1975; pp. 187, 188, 190-201, 221, 222.

152. BLAVATSKY, Helen Petrovna Hahn Fadéef de; "Dynamics of the Psychic World"; pref. and introd. Lina Psaltis; XVIII + 132 pp.; bibl. 122, 123; alph.; 21 cm; pb.; The Theosophical Publishing House; London; 1972; pp. 15, 16, 41, 42.

153. BLAVATSKY, Helen Petrovna Hahn Fadéef de; "Glosario Teosofico"; transl. J. Roviralta Borrell; introd. Héctor V. Morel; pref. George Robert Stow Mead; 904 pp.; 22.5 cm; hb.; 4th ed.; Editorial Kier; Buenos Aires; Argentina; 1977; p. 368.

154. BLAVATSKY, Helen Petrovna Hahn Fadéef de; "Isis Unveiled"; 2 Vol. in 1 book; 1.392 pp.; Vol. I: XLVI + 628 pp.; Vol. II: X + 708 pp.; illus.; alph.; 22 cm; hb.; dj.; 4th print.; The Theosophy Co.; Los Angeles, Cal.; U. S. A.; 1975; Vol. I: pp. 476-481; Vol. II: pp. 618, 619.

155. BLAVATSKY, Helen Petrovna Hahn Fadéef de; "The Secret Doctrine"; 6 Vol.; 2.630 pp.; alph.; Vol. 6; 24.5 cm; hb.; dj.; The Theosophical Publishing House; India; 1971; Vol. 5: p. 561.

156. BLEIBTREU, John; "Interviews With Oscar Ichazo"; 190 pp.; alph.; 23 cm; pb.; Arica Institute Press; New York; 1982; pp. 6, 47, 131.

157. BLUNSDON, Norman; "A Popular Dictionary of Spiritualism"; pref. Eric W. Stuart; 256 pp.; bibl. 237-256; 20 cm; hb.; Arco Publications; London; 1962; pp. 20, 29, 50, 51, 63, 248.

158. BODDINGTON, Harry; "Materialisations"; 194 pp.; illus.; 18 cm; hb.; Psychic Press; London; no date; pp. VIII, fig. 20.

159. BODDINGTON, Harry; "Mediums Who Leave Their Bodies"; *Psychic News;* London; Newspaper; N. 89; February 3, 1934; p. 2.

160. BODDINGTON, Harry; "Passing Through Brick Walls"; *Psychic News;* London; Newspaper; illus.; 10, February, 1934; N. 90; p. 4.

161. BODDINGTON, Harry; "Paying Visits With Astral Bodies"; *Psychic News;* London; Newspaper; N. 102; 05, May, 1934; p. 2.

162. BODDINGTON, Harry; "Swedenborg's Visits to the Spirit World and After"; *Psychic News;* London; Newspaper; N. 79; 25, November, 1933; p. 8.

163. BODIER, Paul; "Como Desenvolver a Mediunidade"; transl., pref. and glos.: Francisco Klörs Werneck; 134 pp.; illus.; glos. 121-132; 18.5 cm; pb.; 7th ed.; Editora Eco; Rio de Janeiro; Brazil; 1981; pp. 21, 23, 122, 123, 131.

164. BOIRAC, Émile; "La Psychologie Inconnue"; XIV + 360 pp.; index of names; 21.5 cm; hb.; 2nd ed.; Librairie Félix Alcan; Paris; 1912; pp. 91, 264-285.

165. BOIS, Jules; "Le Monde Invisible"; 432 pp.; 18 cm; hb.; Ernest Flammarion, Éditeur; Paris; no date; pp. 376-379.

166. BOLEN, James Grayson; "Interview: Charles Theodore Tart"; *Psychic;* Magazine; Vol. IV; N. 3; February, 1973; illus.; pp. 6-11.

167. BOND, M. Phyllis; "Beyond the Strange"; *Fate;* Magazine; Evanston; Ill.; U. S. A.; 158 pp.; 18 cm; pocket; pb.; Paperback Library; New York; September, 1971; pp. 75-78.

168. BONIN, Werner F.; "Lexicon Der Parapsychologie und ihrer Grenzgebiete"; VIII + 588 pp.; illus.; bibl. 553-587; 24 cm; hb.; dj.; Scherz; München; West Germany; 1976; pp. 39, 40, 122, 138, 139, 171, 172, 345, 374, 429, 449, 502; eds.: Ger., Sp.

169. BONO, Ernesto; "Senhor da Yoga e da Mente"; 260 pp.; bibl. 259, 260; 21 cm; pb.; Editora Record; Rio de Janeiro; Brazil; 1980; pp. 180-182.

170. BORD, Janet; "Astral Projection"; 64 pp.; bibl. 62, 63; 18 cm; pb.; The Aquarian Press; London; 1977; pp. 1-64; eds.: Eng., Sp. (Mini-library).

171. BORGIA, Anthony; "A Vida nos Mundos Invisíveis"; pref. John Anderson; transl. J. Escobar Faria; 210 pp.; 19.5 cm; pb.; Empresa Editora O Pensamento; S. Paulo; Brazil; 1960; pp. 17, 176.

172. BOSC, Ernest; "La Psychologie Devant La Science et Les Savants"; 392 pp.; 17.5 cm; hb.; 3rd ed.; H. Daragon, Éditeur; Paris; 1908; pp. 309-315.

173. BOSC, Mme, Ernest (M. A. B.); "Voyage en Astral ou Vingt Nuits Consécutives des Dégagement Conscient"; 408 pp.; illus.; 18 cm; hb.; Chamuel, Éditeur; Paris; 1896; pp. 1-408; eds.: Fr., Port. (Mini-library).

174. BOSWELL, Harriet A.; "Master Guide to Psychism"; 224 pp.; 23 cm; hb.; dj.; Parker Publishing Co.; West Nyack; New York; October, 1970; pp. 62, 63, 69, 127-141.

175. BOTELHO, Henrique; "Um Caso de Desdobramento"; *Vanguarda;* Rio de Janeiro; Brazil; Newspaper; Daily; Section "Nas Fronteiras do Outro Mundo"; Yr. X; N. 6.531; 12, October, 1932; p. 2.

176. BOUISSOU, Michaël; "The Life of a Sensitive"; transl. Mervyn Savill; 216 pp.; Sidwick & Jackson; London; 1955; pp. 142-147, 190-196.

177. BOULTON, Peter, and BOULTON, Jane; "Psychic Beam to Beyond" (Lenora Huet); pref. Jane Boulton; 134 pp.; 23 cm; pb.; De Vorss & Co.; Marina del Rey; Cal.; U. S. A.; 1983; p. 64.

178. BOURDIN, Antoinette; "Entre Dois Mundos"; Novel; transl. Manuel Quintão; 216 pp.; 18 cm; pb.; 4th ed.; Federação Espírita Brasileira; Rio de Janeiro; Brazil; 1980; pp. 20, 49, 137-140.

179. BOURDIN, Antoinette; "Memórias da Loucura"; Novel; transl. Manuel Quintão; 244 pp.; 18 cm; pb.; 3rd ed.; Federação Espírita Brasileira; Rio de Janeiro; Brazil; 1980; pp. 30, 31, 42, 43, 46, 50, 56, 64, 71, 91, 138.

180. BOURGEAT, J.-G.; "Magie"; 160 pp.; 17.5 cm; hb.; Chamuel, Éditeur; Paris; 1895; pp. 30, 122, 123.

181. BOURGUIGNON, Erika; "Religion, Altered States of Consciousness and Social Change"; Anthology; X + 390 pp.; illus.; bibl.; alph.; 21.5 cm; hb.; dj.; Ohio State University Press; Columbus; Ohio; U. S. A.; 1973; pp. 12, 245.

182. BOWLES, Norma, and HYNDS, Fran; "Psi Search"; 168 pp.; illus.; bibl. 145-147; glos. 153-155; alph.; 27.5 cm; pb.; Harper & Row, Publishers; New York; 1978; pp. 14, 15, 48-50, 62, 63, 154.

183. BOWYER, Mathew J.; "Encyclopedia of Mystical Terminology"; 136 pp.; illus.; alph.; 24 cm; hb.; dj.; A. S. Barnes and Co.; New York; 1979; pp. 35, 43, 95, 96.

184. BOZZANO, Ernesto; "Animismo ou Espiritismo?"; transl. Guillon Ribeiro; 296 pp.; 18 cm; pb.; 2nd ed.; Federação Espírita Brasileira; Rio de Janeiro; Brazil; 1951; pp. 50-53, 70, 118-168, 287, 289.

185. BOZZANO, Ernesto; "Comunicações Mediúnicas Entre Vivos"; transl. Francisco Klörs Werneck; pres. José Herculano Pires; 172 pp.; 21 cm; pb.; 2nd ed.; Edicel; S. Paulo; Brazil; December, 1978; pp. 23, 25, 27, 33, 39, 40, 47, 57, 63-66, 70, 77, 84, 95, 96, 120-122, 136, 170, 171.

186. BOZZANO, Ernesto; "A Crise da Morte"; transl. and pref. Guillon Ribeiro; 178 pp.; 18 cm; pb.; 4th ed.; Federação Espírita Brasileira; Rio de Janeiro; Brazil; 1979; pp. 29, 30, 159-163.

187. BOZZANO, Ernesto; "O Espiritismo e as Manifestações Psíquicas"; transl. Francisco Klörs Werneck; 118 pp.; 21 cm; pb.; Editora Eco; Rio de Janeiro; Brazil; no date; pp. 53-59, 69.

188. BOZZANO, Ernesto; "Fenômenos de Bilocação"; transl. Francisco Klörs Werneck; pref. Carlos Imbassahy; 152 pp.; 21 cm; pb.; 2nd ed.; Edições Correio Fraterno; S. Bernardo do Campo, SP; Brazil; February, 1983; pp. 1-152 (Mini-library).

189. BOZZANO, Ernesto; "Fenômenos Psíquicos no Momento da Morte"; transl. and pref. Carlos Imbassahy; 320 pp.; 18 cm; hb.; Federação Espírita Brasileira; Rio de Janeiro; Brazil; 1927; pp. 83, 84.

190. BOZZANO, Ernesto; "Les Manifestations Métapsychiques et les Animaux"; without translator; 194 pp.; 18.5 cm; pb.; Éditions Jean Meyer; Paris; 1926; pp. 37, 87-90.

191. BOZZANO, Ernesto; "Des Manifestations Supranormales Chez les Peuples Sauvages"; without translator; 166 pp.; 18 cm; pb.; Éditions Jean Meyer; Paris; 1927; pp. 36, 63, 115-118, 125-134.

192. BOZZANO, Ernesto; "A Morte e os Seus Mistérios"; transl. and pref. Francisco Klörs Werneck; 168 pp.; 21 cm; pb.; Editora Eco; Rio de Janeiro; Brazil; no date; pp. 125, 126, 131, 133, 135, 154, 162, 167.

193. BOZZANO, Ernesto; "Per la Difesa dello Spiritismo"; 240 pp.; 23 cm; pb.; Società Editrice Partenopea; Napoli; Italy; 1927; pp. 101-118; eds.: It., Port.

194. BOZZANO, Ernesto; "Les Phénomènes de Hantise"; transl. C. de Vesme; pref. J. Maxwell; XII + 312 pp.; 21.5 cm; hb.; Librairie Félix Alcan; Paris; 1920; pp. 110-125.

195. BOZZANO, Ernesto; "Xenoglossia: Mediunidade Poliglota"; transl. Guillon Ribeiro; 218 pp.; 18 cm; hb.; Federação Espírita Brasileira; Rio de Janeiro; Brazil; 1933; pp. 23-27.

196. BRANDON, Wilfred; "Open the Door"; transcribed by Edith Ellis; XXII + 196 pp.; 20.5 cm; hb.; dj.; C. & R. Anthony; New York; 1958; pp. 26, 85, 155.

197. BRAUD, William G.; "Psi Perfomance and Autonomic Nervous System Activity"; *The Journal of the American Society for Psychical Research;* New York; Vol. 75; N. 1; January, 1981; bibl. 27-35; pp. 1-35 (p. 5).

198. BREECHER, Maury; "Cientistas: Sair do Corpo não é Sonho Nem Loucura"; *O Globo;* Rio de Janeiro; Brazil; Newspaper; Daily; Yr. LVII; N. 17.640; 14, February, 1982; illus.; p. 28.

199. BRENNAN, J. H.; "Astral Doorways"; 116 pp.; illus.; 22 cm; hb.; dj.; 4th ed.; The Aquarian Press; London; 1977; pp. 1-100; eds.: Eng., Sp. (Mini-library).

200. BRENNAN, J. H.; "Reincarnation: Five Keys to Past Lives"; 96 pp.; alph.; 18 cm; pb.; 2nd ed.; The Aquarian Press; London; 1981; pp. 71-82; eds.: Eng., Port.

201. BRENT, Sandor; "Deliberately Induced Pre-mortem, Out-of-Body Experiences: An Experiential and Theoretical Approach"; *in* "Between Life and Death"; Robert Kastenbaum; Springer; New York; 1979.

202. BRET, P. Thomas; "Les Métapsychoses"; 3 Vol.; 972 pp.; 23 cm; pb.; Librairie J.-B. Baillière et Fils; Paris; 1939-1948; 1st Vol.: pp. 26, 27, 42, 43, 66-98, 134-212.

203. BRET, P. Thomas; "Précis de Métapsychique"; 3 Vol.; 520 pp.; Manual; glos. 29-58; 23.5 cm; hb.; Librairie J.-B. Baillière et Fils; Paris; 1927-1932; 1st Vol.: pp. 30, 32, 136, 173-176.

204. BRICAUD, Jean; "I Primi Elementi di Occultismo"; transl. Pietro Bornia; 142 pp.; glos. 109-114; bibl. 115-139; illus.; 18 cm; hb.; Casa Editrice Atanor; Todi; Italy; 1922; pp. 51-58.

205. BRITANNICA, Encyclopaedia; 24 Vol.; 24.500 pp.; illus.; bibl. 670; alph.; 27.5 cm; hb.; Encyclopaedia Britannica; Chicago; Ill.; U. S. A.; 1964; Vol. 18: p. 670.

206. BRITTAIN, Annie; "Twixt Earth and Heaven"; 190 pp.; 18.5 cm; hb.; illus.; Rider & Co.; London; 1935; pp. 45-93.

207. BRO, Hermon Hartzell; "Edgar Cayce on Religion and Psychic Experience"; pref. Hugh Lynn Cayce; 264 pp.; 18 cm; pocket; pb.; Warner Books; New York; 1970; pp. 132-147.

208. BROAD, Charlie Dunbar; "Dreaming and Some of its Implications"; *Proceedings of the Society for Psychical Research;* London; Vol. 52; Part 188; February, 1959; pp. 53-78.

209. BROAD, Charlie Dunbar; "Lectures on Psychical Research, Incorporating the Perrott Lectures Given in Cambridge University in 1959 and 1960"; 450 pp.; illus.; 23 cm; Humanities Press; New York; 1962.

210. BROAD, Charlie Dunbar; "Phantasms of the Living and of the Dead"; *Proceedings of the Society for Psychical Research;* London; Vol. 50; Part 183; May, 1953; pp. 51-66.

211. BROWN, Barbara B.; "Supermind: The Ultimate Energy"; XIV + 286 pp.; bibl. 277-279; alph.; 23.5 cm; hb.; dj.; Harper & Row, Publishers; New York; 1980; pp. 211-217.

212. BROWN, Slater; "The Heyday of Spiritualism"; 296 pp.; illus.; bibl.; alph.; 18 cm; pb.; Pocket Books; New York; 1972.

213. BROWNING, Norma Lee; "The Psychic World of Peter Hurkos"; introd. C. V. Wood Jr.; 238 pp.; illus.; 18 cm; pocket; pb.; Signet Mystic Book; New York; 1971; pp. 46, 54, 112-114, 219.

214. BRUCKER, Karl; "Die Rosenkreuz-Meditation als Weg zum ununterbrochenem Bewusstsein und zur Einweihung"; *Die Andere Welt;* Freiburg; West Germany; Magazine; Monthly; Yr. 20; N. 7; July, 1969; pp. 617-622.

215. BRUNTON, Paul; "A Busca do Eu Superior"; transl. Gilberto Bernardes de Oliveira; 256 pp.; illus.; 19.5 cm; pb.; Editora Pensamento; S. Paulo; Brazil; 1978; p. 158.

216. BRUNTON, Paul; "O Egito Secreto"; transl. Zofia de P. Gaffron; 270 pp.; illus.; 19.5 cm; pb.; Editora Pensamento; S. Paulo; Brazil; 1976; pp. 67-72, 131, 173, 175-177, 266.

217. BRUNTON, Paul; "A Índia Secreta"; transl. Zofia de P. Gaffron; introd. Francis Younghusband; 298 pp.; illus.; glos. 295-297; 21 cm; pb.; Editora Pensamento; S. Paulo; Brazil; 1968; pp. 86, 87, 93-95, 123, 124, 141-143, 204, 284, 285.

218. BUCKE, Richard Maurice; "Cosmic Consciousness: A Study in the Evolution of the Human Mind"; XX + 326 pp.; bibl. 319-326; 23 cm; pb.; 3rd print.; The Citadel Press; Secaucus; New Jersey; U. S. A.; 1977; pp. 7, 8, 60-63; eds.: Eng., Port.

219. BUCKLAND, Raymond, and CARRINGTON, Hereward Hubert Levington; "Amazing Secrets of the Psychic World"; 202 pp.; 21 cm; cart.; 2nd print.; Parker Publishing Co.; West Nyack; New York; July, 1977; pp. 152-156.

220. BULFORD, Staveley; "Man's Unknown Journey"; 222 pp.; illus.; glos. 212-215; bibl. 200; alph.; 21 cm; hb.; 2nd print.; ed. rev.; Rider & Co.; London; May, 1944; pp. 24, 102, 110, 137-157.

221. BULWER-LYTTON, Edward George Earle; "Zanoni"; Novel; transl. Ricardo Siqueira; 282 pp.; 21 cm; pb.; Livros do Mundo Inteiro; S. Paulo; Brazil; 1972; pp. 150, 202, 203.

222. BUNKER, Dusty; "Dream Cycles"; 230 pp.; illus.; bibl. 225, 226; alph.; 23.5 cm; pb.; Para Research; Rockport; Massachusetts; U. S. A.; April, 1981; pp. 106-111, 208, 211.

223. BURANG, Theodore; "Tibetan Art of Healing"; transl. and introd. Susan Macintosh; X + 118 pp.; 20 cm; pb.; Watkins Publishing; London; 1974; pp. 17-26.

224. BURT, Cyril; "E. S. P. and Psychology"; introd. Anita Gregory; 180 pp.; alph.; 21.5 cm; hb.; dj.; Weidenfeld and Nicolson; London; 1975; p. 50.

225. BURT, Cyril; "Jung's Account of his Paranormal Experiences"; *Journal of the Society for Psychical Research;* London; Vol. 42; N. 718; December, 1963; pp. 163-180.

226. BUSCH, Wilhelm; "Album"; 464 pp.; illus.; 24 cm; hb.; Rascher Verlag; Zürich; Switzerland; 1945; pp. 252, 253.

227. BUTLER, W. E.; "Apprenticed to Magic"; 106 pp.; illus.; 22 cm; pb.; The Aquarian Press; London; 1981; pp. 67-74.

228. BUTLER, W. E.; "The Magician: His Training and Work"; 176 pp.; illus.; bibl. 173-176; 21 cm; pb.; 4th print.; Wilshire Book Co.; North Hollywood; Cal.; U.S.A.; 1969; pp. 114-121.

229. BUTTLAR, Johannes V.; "Caminho para a Eternidade"; transl. Trude von Laschan Solstein Arneitz; 194 pp.; illus.; bibl. 187-193; 20 cm; pb.; Edições Melhoramentos; S. Paulo; Brazil; 1976; pp. 33-36, 107-110.

230. BYSE, Charles; "Swedenborg"; Biography; 5 Vol.; 1.706 pp.; illus.; 17.5 cm; hb.; Georges Bridel & Cie. Éditeurs; Lausanne; Switzerland; 1911-1913; Vol. 1: pp. 115, 116.

231. CAJADO, Gilmen Maia; "Passeando Fora do Corpo Físico"; *Luzerna Sobre o Alqueire;* Duque de Caxias, RJ; Brazil; Newspaper; Yr. VI; N. 71; September-October, 1983, p. 1.

232. CALLE, Ramiro A.; "Ananda: El Yogui Errante"; 202 pp.; 20 cm; pb.; Editorial Kier; Buenos Aires; Argentina; 1980; pp. 52, 53, 164, 168, 169.

233. CALLE, Ramiro A.; "Verdad y Mentira de "El Tercer Ojo""; 224 pp.; illus.; bibl. 221, 222; 21 cm; pb.; Editorial Eyras; Madrid; Spain; 1980; pp. 10, 15, 18, 22, 195, 201.

234. CALMET, Augustine; "The Phantom World: The Philosophy of Spirits, Apparitions, etc."; editor Henry Christmas; 2 Vol.; Vol. I: XXXII + 378 pp.; Vol. II: VI + 362 pp.; R. Bentley; London; 1850.

235. CAMAYSAR, Rosabis; "Consciência Cósmica"; 286 pp.; 18.5 cm; hb.; Editora O Pensamento; S. Paulo; Brazil; no date; pp. 86-88, 98, 99.

236. CAMAYSAR, Rosabis; "Magia do Sertão"; 194 pp.; 18.5 cm; pb.; 2nd ed.; Empresa Editora Pensamento; S. Paulo; Brazil; 1940; pp. 161-178.

237. CAMPBELL, Jean; "Dreams Beyond Dreaming"; 152 pp.; bibl. 151; 21.5 cm; pb.; Unilaw Library Book; Virginia Beach; Norfolk; U. S. A.; 1980; pp. 20-27, 76.

238. CAMPIGNY, H.-M. de; "Les Traditions et les Doctrines Ésotériques"; 254 pp.; 18.5 cm; hb.; Editions Astra; Paris; Février, 1946; pp. 61-108.

239. CAMPOS, Alberto; "El Enigma de la Muerte y la Vida de Ultratumba"; 304 pp.; 18.5 cm; hb.; A. Marzo; Barcelona; Spain; 1931; pp. 76-90.

240. CANNON, Alexander; "The Shadow of Destiny: The Power of Karma"; 176 pp.; illus.; 21.5 cm; pb.; The Aquarian Press; London; February, 1970; pp. 41, 55, 118, 119, 121-126.

241. CARDILLO, Edmundo; "Fantasmas do Ocultismo"; 120 pp.; 21 cm; pb.; Edibace; S. Paulo; Brazil; 1972; pp. 99-119.

242. CARDILLO, Edmundo; "As Máscaras da Morte"; 94 pp.; 18 cm; pb.; Brasbiblos; S. Paulo; Brazil; 1972; pp. 35, 36.

243. CARNEIRO, Victor Ribas; "ABC do Espiritismo"; 198 pp.; glos. 192, 193; 18 cm; pb.; 2nd ed.; Federação Espírita do Paraná; Curitiba, PR; Brazil; 1977; pp. 83, 84.

244. CARPENTER, Edward; "The Art of Creation"; George Allen & Unwin; London; 1904; p. 18.

245. CARRINGTON, Hereward Hubert Levington; "Higher Psychical Development"; XII + 294 pp.; illus.; glos. 290; alph.; 22 cm; pb.; The Aquarian Press; London; 1978; pp. 153, 266-289.

246. CARRINGTON, Hereward Hubert Levington; "Modern Psychical Phenomena"; XVI + 332 pp.; illus.; index of names; 20.5 cm; hb.; Dodd, Mead and Co.; New York; 1919; pp. 146-154.

247. CARRINGTON, Hereward Hubert Levington; "Phantasms of the Dead or True Ghost Stories"; 246 pp.; illus.; glos. 11, 12; bibl. 245, 246; 20 cm; hb.; American Universities Publishing Co.; New York; 1920; pp. 40-43, 46-50.

248. CARRINGTON, Hereward Hubert Levington; "A Primer of Psychical Research"; 118 pp.; 19 cm; hb.; dj.; Ives Washburn Publishers; New York; 1932; pp. 32-35, 46.

249. CARRINGTON, Hereward Hubert Levington; "Psychic Oddities"; 184 pp.; 21 cm; hb.; dj.; Rider and Co.; London; 1952; pp. 22, 127-134.

250. CARRINGTON, Hereward Hubert Levington; "Psychical Phenomena and the War"; X + 364 pp.; alph.; 21.5 cm; hb.; Dodd, Mead and Co.; New York; 1919; pp. 172, 173, 190, 191, 201-203.

251. CARRINGTON, Hereward Hubert Levington; "Your Psychic Powers and How to Develop Them"; XVIII + 358 pp.; illus.; 21 cm; pb.; Newcastle Publishing Co.; California; U. S. A.; 1975; pp. 47, 138, 229-235, 241, 245.

252. CARTON, Paul; "La Science Occulte et les Sciences Occultes"; 460 pp.; illus.; alph.; 23.5 cm; cart.; reed.; Librairie Le François; Paris; 1976; pp. 106, 224, 225, 295, 303, 304, 309-320, 326, 337, 341, 344, 345, 361, 369, 408.

253. CARVALHO, Sebastião de; "Waldo Vieira e a Projeciologia"; *Reencarnação;* Porto Alegre, RS; Brazil; Magazine; Monthly; Yr. XXXIV; N. 417; November, 1982; pp. 14, 15.

254. CASSOLI, P.; "Esiste la Bilocazione?"; *Rivista Metapsichica;* Milano; Italy; Installment I; 1954.

255. CASTANEDA, Carlos César Salvador Arana; "A Erva do Diabo"; transl. Luzia Machado da Costa; 246 pp.; 20.5 cm; pb.; 10th ed.; Editora Record; Rio de Janeiro; Brazil; no date; pp. 121-126, 208.

256. CASTANEDA, Carlos César Salvador Arana; "The Fire From Within"; 296 pp.; 21 cm; hb.; dj.; Simon and Schuster; New York; 1984; pp. 79, 122, 123, 136, 155, 156, 174-184, 208, 209, 212, 215, 216, 219, 220, 271, 272, 274-276, 287, 288.

257. CASTANEDA, Carlos César Salvador Arana; "Journey To Ixtlan: The Lessons of Don Juan"; 282 pp.; 18 cm; pocket; pb.; Penguin Books; London; 1979; pp. 167-169; eds.: Eng., Ger., Port., etc.

258. CASTANEDA, Carlos César Salvador Arana; "O Presente da Águia"; transl. Vera Maria Whately; 262 pp.; 21 cm; pb.; Editora Record; Rio de Janeiro; Brazil; October, 1981; pp. 9, 20-24, 46-48, 93-110, 112-120, 124-133, 190-211.

259. CASTANEDA, Carlos César Salvador Arana; "O Segundo Círculo do Poder"; transl. Luzia Machado da Costa; 238 pp.; 21 cm; pb.; 3rd ed.; Editora Record; Rio de Janeiro; Brazil; no date; pp. 84, 155, 203.

260. CASTANEDA, Carlos César Salvador Arana; "A Separate Reality: Further Conversations With Don Juan"; 270 pp.; 18 cm; pocket; pb.; Penguin Books; London; 1979; pp. 104, 130-132; 137, 154; eds.: Eng., Port., etc.

261. CASTANEDA, Carlos César Salvador Arana; "Tales of Power"; 284 pp.; 18 cm; pocket; pb.; Penguin Books; London; 1980; pp. 17, 35; eds.: Eng., Port., Fr., etc.

262. CASTELLAN, Yvonne; "Le Spiritisme"; 128 pp.; bibl. 125, 126; 17.5 cm; pb.; Presses Universitaires de France; Paris; 1954; pp. 24-28; eds.: Fr., Port.

263. CASTRO, Almerindo Martins de ; "Antônio de Pádua"; 160 pp.; illus.; 18 cm; hb.; 2nd ed.; Federação Espírita Brasileira; Rio de Janeiro; Brazil; 1945; pp. 44, 48, 49, 104-111.

264. CASTRO, Almerindo Martins de; "O Martírio dos Suicidas"; 210 pp.; 18 cm; pb.; 7th ed.; Federação Espírita Brasileira; Rio de Janeiro; Brazil; 1980; p. 139.

265. CASTRO, Francisco Lyon de; Editor; "O Ocultismo: A Revelação da Ciência dos Magos"; transl. Maria Leonor Braga Abecassis; 146 pp.; illus.; 21 cm; pb.; Publicações Europa-América; Mira-Sintra; Portugal; no date; pp. 48-50.

266. CAVENDISH, Richard; Editor; "Encyclopedia of the Unexplained"; introd. Joseph Banks Rhine; 304 pp.; illus.; bibl. 286-297; 28 cm; pb.; Routledge & Kegan Paul; London; 1974; pp. 37-39.

267. CAVERSAN, Ariovaldo, and ANDRADE, Geziel; "O Pós-morte Visto por Ernesto Bozzano e Raymond A. Moody Jr."; *Reformador;* Rio de Janeiro; Brazil; Magazine; Monthly; Yr. 101; N. 1.851; June, 1983; pp. 9-11.

268. CAYCE, Hugh Lynn; Editor; "The Edgar Cayce Reader"; 188 pp.; 18 cm; pocket; pb.; Warner Books; New York; 1974; pp. 120-128.

269. CAYCE, Hugh Lynn; "Faces of Fear"; VIII + 198 pp.; illus.; bibl. 190-193; alph.; 17.5 cm; pocket; pb.; Berkley Books; New York; February, 1982; pp. 72-76, 79,80.

270. CERCHIO Firenze 77; "Dai Mondi Invisibili: Incontri e Colloqui"; 242 pp.; illus.; 21.5 cm; pb.; Edizioni Mediterranee; Roma; Italy; 1977; pp. 35, 36.

271. CERVIÑO, Jayme; "Além do Inconsciente"; 188 pp.; 18.5 cm; pb.; Federação Espírita Brasileira; Rio de Janeiro; Brazil; 1968; pp. 95.

272. CHAMPLIN, Russel Norman; "Evidências Científicas Demonstram que Você Vive Depois da Morte"; 276 pp.; bibl. 273-276; 21 cm; pb.; Nova Época Editorial; S. Paulo; Brazil; 1981; pp. 33, 34, 91, 97, 163-211, 231-263.

273. CHAPLIN, J. P.; "Dictionary of the Occult and Paranormal"; 180 pp.; illus.; 18 cm; pocket; pb.; Dell Publishing Co.; New York; December, 1976; p. 14.

274. CHARRIÈRE, Henri; "Papillon"; Novel; pres. Jean-Pierre Castelnau & Jean-François Revel; 698 pp.; illus.; 16.5 cm; pocket; pb.; Robert Laffont; Paris; 1982; pp. 337-339; eds.: Fr., Eng., Port.

275. CHAUVIN, Rémy; "La Parapsychologie: Quand L'Irrationnel Rejoin la Science"; 210 pp.; illus.; bibl. 201-206; 23 cm; pb.; Hachette; Paris; 1980; p. 106.

276. CHEETHAM, Erika; "As Profecias de Nostradamus"; transl. Áurea Weissenberg; 514 pp.; 21 cm; pb.; 10th ed.; Editora Nova Fronteira; Rio de Janeiro; Brazil; 1983; pp. 149, 150, 218.

277. CHEVREUIL, L.; "On Ne Meurt Pas"; 318 pp.; 18 cm; hb.; Jouve & Cie., Éditeurs; Paris; no date; pp. 139-159.

278. CHEVREUIL, L.; "Le Spiritisme dans L'Église"; 316 pp.; index of names; 19 cm; pb.; Jouve & Cie., Éditeurs; Paris; 1922; pp. 206-218.

279. CHIESA, Carlos Luis; "Origen del Espiritismo y su Doctrina"; 408 pp.; 20 cm; pb.; Editorial Constancia; Buenos Aires; Argentina; 1946; pp. 46-48, 82, 83.

280. CHINMOY, Sri; "Death and Reincarnation"; 142 pp.; illus.; 18 cm; pb.; Agni Press; Jamaica; N. Y.; U. S. A.; 1974; pp. 3-5.

281. CHRISTIAN, Johann (Pseud. for Gilberto Campista Guarino); "Um Fato Estranho"; *Obreiros do Bem;* Rio de Janeiro; Brazil; Newspaper; Monthly; Yr. II; N. 20; May, 1975; pp. 4, 5 (See N. 656).

282. CHRISTIE-MURRAY, David; "Psychic Voyages" (Stuart Holroyd); Books Reviews; *Journal of the Society for Psychical Research;* London; Vol. 49; N. 773; September, 1977; p. 620.

283. CHRISTOPHER, Milbourne; "Esp, Seers & Psychics"; X + 268 pp.; illus.; bibl. 251-257; alph.; 21.5 cm; hb.; dj.; Thomas Y. Crowell Co.; New York; 1970; pp. 213-220.

284. CHU, Paul E.; "Life Before Birth, Life on Earth, Life After Death"; IV + 194 pp.; bibl. 192, 193; 17.5 cm; pb.; 2nd print.; World View Press; Fort Lee, New Jersey; U. S. A.; June, 1976; pp. 169-173.

285. CIRNE, Leopoldo; "Doutrina e Prática do Espiritismo"; 2 Vol.; 734 pp.; 22 cm; hb.; Tipografia do Jornal do Commercio; Rio de Janeiro; Brazil; 1920; Vol. I: pp. 221-234.

286. CLARIE, Thomas C.; "Occult Bibliography"; 454 pp.; alph.; 21.5 cm; hb.; The Scarecrow Press; Metuchen, N. J.; U. S. A.; 1978; N. 17, 25, 104, 318, 319, 320, 580, 620, 626, 688, 882, 1129, 1295, 1296, 1396, 1498, 1584, 1764.

287. COBLENTZ, Stanton A.; "Light Beyond: The Wonderworld of Parapsychology"; 206 pp.; alph.; Cornwall Books; East Brunswick, N. J.; U. S. A.; 1982.

288. CODD, Clara M.; "La Eterna Sabiduria de la Vida"; 244 pp.; 19 cm; pb.; Editorial Orion; Mexico, D. F.; 1977; pp. 143-152.

289. CODDINGTON, Mary; "A Energia Curativa"; transl. Neide Camera Loureiro Pinto; pref. William Gutman; 218 pp.; 21 cm; pb.; Editora Record; Rio de Janeiro; Brazil; 1981; p. 48.

290. COHEN, Daniel; "ESP: The Search Beyond the Senses"; 188 pp.; illus.; glos. 175-178; bibl. 179, 180; alph.; hb.; dj.; Harcourt Brace Jovanovich; New York; 1973; pp. 158-161, 176.

291. COLEMAN, Stanley M.; "The Phantom Double: Its Psychological Significance"; *British Journal of Medical Psychology;* Vol. 14; Part 3; N. 254; 1934; bibl. 273; pp. 254-273.

292. COLLINS, Mabel; "O Despertar"; transl. Cinira Riedel de Figueiredo; 124 pp.; illus.; 19.5 cm; pb.; Editora Pensamento; S. Paulo; Brazil; 1964; pp. 13, 23-26, 55-59, 63-68, 72, 76, 77, 100, 107-110, 117.

293. COLLISON-MORLEY, Lacy; "Greek and Roman Ghost Stories"; VIII + 80 pp.; illus.; 21 cm; hb.; dj.; Argonaut, Publishers; Chicago; Ill.; U. S. A.; 1968; pp. 45-53.

294. COLTON, Ann Ree; "Ethical ESP"; introd. Jonathan Murro; 368 pp.; glos. 352-361; alph.; 21.5 cm; hb.; dj.; Arc Publishing Co.; Glendale, Cal.; U. S. A.; 1971; pp. 156, 157.

295. CONANT, Frances Ann; "Mrs. J. H. Conant, 1831-1875"; Biography; Notes: Allen Putnam; 322 pp.; illus.; William White; Boston; Massachusetts; U. S. A.; 1873.

296. CONTI, Massimo; "Testemunhas do Outro Mundo"; *Manchete;* Rio de Janeiro; Brazil; Magazine; Weekly; N. 1.270; 21, August, 1976; illus.; pp. 124, 125.

297. CONWAY, David; "Magic: An Occult Primer"; 286 pp.; illus.; Jonathan Cape; London; 1972.

298. CONYBEARE, Irene; "Die Schöpferische Kraft des Denkens und Fühlens"; *Die Andere Welt;* Freiburg; West Germany; Magazine; Monthly; Yr. 20; N. 12; December, 1969; illus.; pp. 1066-1069.

299. COOK, Emily Williams; "Beyond the Body: An Investigation of Out-of-the-Body Experiences"; Books Reviews; *Anabiosis - The Journal for Near-Death Studies;* Vol. 4; N. 1; Spring, 1984; pp. 97-104.

300. COOKE, Aileen H.; "Out of the Mouth of Babes: E. S. P. in Children"; pref. John D. Pearce-Higgins; 192 pp.; bibl. 187-190; alph.; 21.5 cm; hb.; dj.; James Clarke & Co.; London; 1968; 19-30, 36-45, 151.

301. COQUET, Michel; "Les Çakras: L'Anatomie Occulte de L'Homme"; 262 pp.; illus.; bibl. 257, 258; 22 cm; pb.; Dervy-Livres; Paris; 1982; pp. 216, 219.

302. CORGNOL, Christian de; "Los Sanadores Filipinos"; transl. J. A. Bravo; 176 pp.; illus.; glos. 169-175; 20 cm; pb.; Ediciones Martínez Roca; Barcelona; Spain; 1979; p. 169.

303. CORLISS, William R.; "Strange Minds: A Sourcebook of Unusual Mental Phenomena"; 286 pp.; Sourcebook Project; Glen Arm, Md.; U. S. A.; 1976.

304. CORNILLIER, Pierre-Émile; "La Prédiction de L'Avenir"; XII + 112 pp.; 19 cm; pb.; Librairie Félix Alcan; Paris; 1926; pp. 14, 85-88.

305. CORNILLIER, Pierre-Émile; "La Survivance de L'Ame et Son Évolution Après la Mort"; 580 pp.; alph.; 22 cm; hb.; 2nd ed.; Imprimerie Bussiére; Paris; 1921; pp. 142, 143, 406, 407.

306. CORVALÁN, Graciela N. Vico; "Dialogo a Fondo con Carlos Castaneda"; *Mutantia;* Buenos Aires; Argentina; Magazine; Bimonthly; N. 10; 1/1982; illus.; pp. 52-81.

307. COSTA, Carlos A. de Araujo; "O Paranormal e Seus Mistérios"; pref. Apio Campos; 154 pp.; illus.; glos. 149-152; bibl. 61, 93, 133; 21 cm; pb.; Gazeta do Interior; Castanhal; Pará; Brazil; 1981; p. 149.

308. COSTA, Vitor Ronaldo de Souza; "Apometria: Técnica Magnética de Pesquisas Espirituais"; *Jornal Espírita;* S. Paulo; Brazil; Monthly; Yr. 9; N. 104; February, 1984; illus.; bibl.; p. 4.

309. COSTE, Albert; "Fenômenos Psíquicos Ocultos"; without translator; pref. Medeiros e Albuquerque; LXXX + 228 pp.; illus.; 17.5 cm; hb.; H. Garnier, Livreiro-Editor; Rio de Janeiro; Brazil; 1903; pp. 77-79.

310. COUTO, Sousa; "Fenômeno de Exteriorização Anímica Obtido em Lisboa"; *Estudos Psíquicos;* Lisboa; Portugal; Magazine; Monthly; N. 4; September, 1905; pp. 74, 75.

311. COXHEAD, David, and HILLER, Susan; "Dreams: Visions of the Night"; 96 pp.; illus.; bibl. 96; 28 cm; pb.; Avon Books; New York; 1976; pp. 23, 92, 93; eds.: Eng., Fr.

312. COXHEAD, Nona; "Mindpower"; 270 pp.; illus.; bibl. 243-255; alph.; 18 cm; pocket; pb.; Penguin Books; New York; 1979; pp. 10, 62, 116-128; eds.: Eng., It., Fr., Sp.

313. CRAWFORD, Quantz; "Methods of Psychic Development"; 102 pp.; illus.; 20.5 cm; pb.; Llewellyn Publications; St. Paul; Minnesota; U. S. A.; 1978; pp. 63-69.

314. CRESPIGNY, Philip de; "This World and Beyond"; pp. 258; Cassell and Co.; London; 1934.

315. CROLARD, Jean-Francis; "Renaître Après la Mort"; 190 pp.; 21.5 cm; pb.; Éditions Robert Laffont; Paris; Novembre, 1979; pp. 39, 40, 53; eds.: Fr., Port.

316. CROOKALL, Robert; "An Infant's Perceptions of a Death"; *Journal of the Society for Psychical Research;* London; Vol. 42; N. 717; September, 1963; pp. 124-126.

317. CROOKALL, Robert; "Astral Projection"; *Fate;* Magazine; Evanston, Ill.; U.S.A.; September, 1970; pp. 67-73.

318. CROOKALL, Robert; "Astral Travelling"; Correspondence; *Journal of the Society for Psychical Research;* London; Vol. 42; N. 717; September, 1963; pp. 147, 148.

319. CROOKALL, Robert; "Astral Travelling: Review of "The Enigma of Out-of-Body Travel" (Susy Smith); *International Journal of Parapsychology;* Vol. VIII; N. 3; Summer, 1966.

320. CROOKALL, Robert; "Casebook of Astral Projection"; XVI + 160 pp.; 23 cm; hb.; dj.; University Books; Secaucus, N. J.; U. S. A.; 1972; pp. I-XVI, 1-160.

321. CROOKALL, Robert; "Der Austritt des Astralkörpers"; transl. E. G. Johns; *Esotera;* Freiburg; West Germany; Magazine; Monthly; Yr. 22; N. 11; November, 1971; pp. 1006-1011.

322. CROOKALL, Robert; "Dreams" of High Significance"; 90 pp.; glos. 71-77; alph.; 23 cm; pb.; Darshana International; Moradabad; India; 1974; pp. 1-90.

323. CROOKALL, Robert; "During Sleep: The Possibility of "co-operation" between the Living and the Dead"; introd. Leslie Shepard; XVI + 102 pp.; bibl. 99-102; 20 cm; hb.; dj.; University Books; Secaucus, N. J.; U. S. A.; 1974; pp. 1-4, 94, 95.

324. CROOKALL, Robert; "Ectasy: The Release of the Soul From the Body"; 164 pp.; Darshana International; Moradabad; India; 1975.

325. CROOKALL, Robert; "Events on the Threshold of the After-Life"; introd. Cyril Atkinson; VIII + 236 pp.; illus.; bibl. 204-223; alph.; 24.5 cm; hb.; Darshana International; Moradabad; India; 1967; pp. 2-198.

326. CROOKALL, Robert; "The Interpretation of Cosmic & Mystical Experiences"; pref. J. D. Pearce-Higgins; XII + 176 pp.; glos. 155-157; alph.; 21.5 cm; hb.; dj.; James Clarke & Co.; Cambridge; Great Britain; 1969; pp. 3-157.

327. CROOKALL, Robert; "Intimations of Immortality"; XVI + 142 pp.; James Clarke and Co.; London; 1965; pp. I-XVI, 1-142.

328. CROOKALL, Robert; "Journey Into Death"; *Fate;* Magazine; Evanston, Ill.; U. S. A.; Vol. 16; N. 6; June, 1963.

329. CROOKALL, Robert; "The Jung-Jaffé View of Out-of-the-Body Experiences"; 134 pp.; The World Fellowship Press; Great Britain; 1970; pp. 1-134.

330. CROOKALL, Robert; "The Mechanisms of Astral Projection"; VIII + 136 pp.; bibl. 120-125; 26 cm; Darshana International; Moradabad; India; 1968; pp. 1-136.

331. CROOKALL, Robert; "More Astral Projections: Analysis of Case Histories"; XX + 154 pp.; 21.5 cm; hb.; dj.; The Aquarian Press; London; 1964; pp. 1-154.

332. CROOKALL, Robert; "The Next World and the Next: Ghostly Garments"; XXII + 152 pp.; alph.; 18.5 cm; hb.; dj.; The Theosophical Publishing House; London; 1966; pp. 5, 6, 9, 10, 118-122, 129.

333. CROOKALL, Robert; "Out-of-the Body Experiences: A Fourth Analysis"; 224 pp.; 21 cm; hb.; dj.; University Books; New York; 1970; pp. 1-224.

334. CROOKALL, Robert; "Out-of-the-Body Experiences and Cultural Traditions"; *Journal of the Society for Psychical Research;* London; Vol. 44; N. 737; September, 1968; pp. 358-362.

335. CROOKALL, Robert; "Out-of-Body Experiences and Survival"; Cases 383-544; The World Fellowship Press; Great Britain; 1970.

336. CROOKALL, Robert; "Psychic Breathing"; 96 pp.; glos. 91, 92; 22 cm; pb.; The Aquarian Press; London; 1979; pp. 24-31, 48-68.

337. CROOKALL, Robert; "The Reluctant but Psychic Psychiatrist"; *Two Worlds;* London; Magazine; Monthly; 81st Year; N. 3898; November, 1968; pp. 336-340.

338. CROOKALL, Robert; "The Study and Practice of Astral Projection"; 234 pp.; 23 cm; hb.; dj.; University Books; New York; 1966; pp. 1-234 (Mini-library).

339. CROOKALL, Robert; "The Supreme Adventure"; XXX + 258 pp.; illus.; glos. XVII-XXIV; alph.; 22 cm; hb.; dj.; 2nd ed.; The Attic Press; Great Britain; 1975; pp. 18-21, 105-112, 115, 116, 129, 174, 175, 178, 198, 251.

340. CROOKALL, Robert; "The Techniques of Astral Projection"; 112 pp.; 22 cm; hb.; dj.; The Aquarian Press; London; 1977; pp. 1-112.

341. CROOKALL, Robert; "They Leave Their Bodies and Float in the Air"; *Two Worlds;* London; Magazine; Monthly; 82nd Year; N. 3901; February, 1969; pp. 61-63.

342. CROOKALL, Robert; "Wenn die Seele ihre Fesseln Abstreift"; transl. L. Langenwalder; *Esotera;* Freiburg; West Germany; Magazine; Monthly; Yr. 21; N. 9; September, 1970; pp. 781-783.

343. CROOKALL, Robert; "What Happens When You Die"; 196 pp.; 21.5 cm; hb.; dj.; Colin Smythe; London; 1978; pp. 1-196.

344. CROUZET, Jean-Philippe; "Les Merveilles du Spiritisme"; 572 pp.; illus.; fig. 17, 23, 34-37; bibl. 543; 22 cm; pb.; Nouvelles Éditions Debresse; Paris; 1971; pp. 73, 78, 80, 88-96, 103, 108, 120, 123, 199-204, 238, 239, 254, 255, 398-404, 429-431, 528, 539 (Mini-library).

345. CROWE, Catherine; "Les Cotés Obscurs de la Nature"; transl. Z.; pref. Albert Rochas; 512 pp.; 21.5 cm; hb.; P.-G. Leymarie, Éditeur; Paris; 1900; pp. 126, 127, 160-213.

346. CROWELL, Eugene; "The Spirit World"; 198 pp.; Colley & Rider; Boston; Massachusetts; U. S. A.; 1879.

347. CROWLEY, Aleister (Pseud. for Edward Alexander Crowley); "The Confessions of Aleister Crowley"; pref. Kenneth Grant; introd. John Symonds; 960 pp.; illus.; alph.; 23.5 cm; hb.; dj.; Routledge & Kegan Paul; London; 1979; pp. 224, 225, 260, 445, 517, 525, 694, 913.

348. CROWLEY, Aleister (Pseud. for Edward Alexander Crowley); "Magick"; introd. John Symonds and Kenneth Grant; XIV + 512 pp.; illus.; glos. 119-122; alph.; 23.5 cm; hb.; dj.; Routledge & Kegan Paul; London; 1979; pp. 265, 266, 337.

349. CROWLEY, Aleister (Pseud. for Edward Alexander Crowley); "Magick Without Tears"; introd. Karl J. Germer; pref. Israel Regardie; epil. Christopher S. Hyatt; XVI + 528 pp.; illus.; alph.; 22 cm; pb.; 3rd print.; Falcon Press; Phoenix, AZ; U. S. A.; June, 1982; pp. 18, 19, 22, 191, 245, 375, 388, 389.

350. CUMMINS, Geraldine Dorothy; "Mind in Life and Death"; introd. Raynor C. Johnson; epil. David Russell; 270 pp.; glos. 261-263; alph.; 21.5 cm; hb.; dj.; The Aquarian Press; London; 1956; pp. 88-90, 93, 97, 99, 249, 250.

351. CUMMINS, Geraldine Dorothy; "The Road to Immortality"; 196 pp.; 18.5 cm; hb.; Psychic Press; London; 1967; pp. 79, 80.

352. CUMMINS, Geraldine Dorothy; "Travellers in Eternity"; comp. E. B. Gibbes; pref. Eric Parker; 204 pp.; Psychic Press; London; 1948; pp. 171, 177.

353. CUNO, John Christian; "Memoirs on Swedenborg"; Biography; transl. Claire E. Berninger; editor and pref. Alfred Acton; XXII + 180 pp.; 17.5 cm; hb.; The Academy Book Room; Bryn Athyn, PA; U. S. A.; 1947; pp. 12, 13, 44, 58, 60, 61, 66; eds.: Ger., Eng.

354. CURRIE, Ian; "You Cannot Die"; 288 pp.; illus.; 23 cm; hb.; dj.; Methuen; New York; 1978; pp. 9-12, 35, 71-111, 136-161.

355. CURTI, Rino; "Mediunidade em Ação"; 176 pp.; 21 cm; pb.; Edições Feesp; S. Paulo; Brazil; 1983; pp. 16-18.

356. DAILEY, Abram Hoagland; "Mollie Fancher, the Brooklin Enigma"; XIV + 262 pp.; illus.; 20.5 cm; hb.; Brooklin; U. S. A.; 1894.

357. DALE, Laura A.; WHITE, Rhea Amelia; and MURPHY, G.; "A Selection of Cases from a Recent Survey of Spontaneous ESP Phenomena"; *The Journal of the American Society for Psychical Research:* New York; Vol. 56; 1962; pp. 3-47.

358. DALLAS, H. A.; "Communications from the Still Incarnate at a Distance from the Body"; *Occult Review;* London; Magazine; Vol. 40; 1924; pp. 26-32.

359. DALLAS, H. A.; "Visions of Dying in the Ninth and Nineteenth Centuries"; *Light;* London; Magazine; Vol. XLIII; 1923; p. 309.

360. DALLAS, Mary Kyle; "The Freed Spirit"; XII + 232 pp.; 18.5 cm; C. B. Reed; New York; 1894.

361. DALMOR, E. R.; "Quien Fue y Quien Es en Ocultismo"; 604 pp.; 23 cm; pb.; Editorial Kier; Buenos Aires; Argentina; 1970; pp. 290, 291, 442.

362. DANE, Christopher; "Psychic Travel"; 192 pp.; Popular Library; New York; 1974.

363. DANE, L.; "Astral Travel: A Psychological Overview"; *The Journal of Altered States of Consciousness;* U. S. A.; Vol. 2; 1976; pp. 249-258.

364. DANIÉLOU, Alain; "Yoga, Méthode de Réintégration"; 212 pp.; 18 cm; pb.; 2nd ed.; L'Arche; Paris; 1973; pp. 193, 194.

365. D'ARBÓ, Prof. (Pseud.); "La Parapsicologia... en Profundidad"; 248 pp.; illus.; glos. 199-244; 22 cm; hb.; dj.; Plaza & Janes; Barcelona; Spain; March, 1979; pp. 127, 128, 133, 152, 161, 166, 167, 200, 202, 206, 207.

366. D'ARGONNEL, Oscar; "Não Há Morte"; 222 pp.; 20.5 cm; pb.; 2nd ed.; Author's Edition; Rio de Janeiro; Brazil; 1920; pp. 129-147.

367. DASSIER, Adolphe; "Essai Sur L'Humanité Posthume et le Spiritisme"; 308 pp.; 17 cm; hb.; Librairie J.-B. Baillière et Fils; Paris; 1883; pp. 272-287.

368. DAVID-NEEL, Alexandra; "Tibete: Magia e Mistério"; introd. Aaron Sussman; transl. Maria Judith Martins; 294 pp.; 21 cm; pb.; Hemus Livraria Editora; S. Paulo; Brazil; August, 1972; pp. 46, 47, 263.

369. DAVIDS, Rhys; "What is Your Will?"; Rider & Co.; London; pp. 67, 218.

370. DAVIES, Owen; Editor; "The Omni Book of the Paranormal & the Mind"; introd. Frank Kendig; 430 pp.; 17.5 cm; pocket; pb.; Kensigton Publishing; New York; no date; pp. 285, 295.

371. DAVIS, Andrew Jackson; "The Great Harmonia"; 3 Vol.; 1.200 pp.; illus.; 19 cm; hb.; 8th ed.; The Austin Publishing Co.; Los Angeles, Cal.; U. S. A.; 1923; Vol. II: pp. 8, 9, 15-24, 61.

372. DAVY, Charles; "Towards a Third Culture"; Faber & Faber; London; 1961; p. 112.

373. DAVY, John; "Há Vida Após a Morte?"; *Manchete;* Rio de Janeiro; Brazil; Magazine; Weekly; N. 1442; 8, December, 1979; pp. 28-33.

374. DAVY, John; "The Woman Who "Left" her Body"; *The Observer;* Newspaper; Great Britain; 13, October, 1968; p. 6.

375. DAWSON-SCOTT, C. A.; "From Four Who Are Dead"; Arrowsmith; London; 1926; pp. 13-19.

376. DAY, Harvey; "Occult Illustrated Dictionary"; IV + 156 pp.; 20 cm; hb.; dj.; Oxford University Press; New York; 1976; pp. 11, 12.

377. DEJEAN, Georges; "A Nova Luz"; transl. and introd. Guillon Ribeiro; 248 pp.; 18 cm; hb.; dj.; Federação Espírita Brasileira; Rio de Janeiro; Brazil; 1937; pp. 89, 90.

378. DE LA MARE, Walter; "Behold this Dreamer!"; Anthology; 714 pp.; 24 cm; hb.; dj.; Alfred A. Knoff; New York; 1939; pp. 411-426.

379. DELACOUR, Jean-Baptiste; "Aus den Jenseits Zurück"; pref. A. Resch; 144 pp.; bibl. 143; 18 cm; pocket; pb.; Th. Knaur; München; West Germany; 1973; pp. 7-142.

380. DELANEY, Walter; "Ultra-Psicônica"; transl. Miécio Araújo Jorge Honkis; 286 pp.; illus.; 21 cm; pb.; Editora Record; Rio de Janeiro; Brazil; no date; pp. 262-264.

381. DELANNE, François Marie Gabriel; "A Alma é Imortal"; transl. Guillon Ribeiro; 314 pp.; 18 cm; pb.; 4th ed.; Federação Espírita Brasileira; Rio de Janeiro; Brazil; 1978; pp. 15, 49, 86-119, 135, 168, 203-210, 255-265.

382. DELANNE, François Marie Gabriel; "Les Apparitions Matérialisées des Vivants & des Morts"; 2 Vol.; 1.370 pp.; illus.; 22.5 cm; hb.; Librairie Spirite; Paris; 1909; pp. 144-521 (Mini-library).

383. DELANNE, François Marie Gabriel; "Comptu Rendu du Congrès Spirite et Spiritualiste International 1900"; 732 pp.; 23.5 cm; hb.; Societé Française d'Étude des Phénomènes Psychiques; Paris; 1902; pp. 79-87.

384. DELANNE, François Marie Gabriel; "Recherches Sur la Médiumnité"; XII + 516 pp.; illus.; 17.5 cm; hb.; Librairie Des Sciences Psychiques; Paris; 1902; pp. 315-317, 320-323.

385. DELANNE, François Marie Gabriel; "Reencarnação"; transl. Carlos Imbassahy; 324 pp.; 17.5 cm; hb.; Federação Espírita Brasileira; Rio de Janeiro; Brazil; 1940; pp. 100, 101, 204-207.

386. DE MILLE, Richard; Editor; "The Don Juan Papers: Further Castaneda Controversies"; Anthology; 526 pp.; illus.; bibl. 489-510; alph.; 23 cm; pb.; 2nd print.; Ross-Erikson Publishers; Santa Barbara; Cal.; U. S. A.; 1981; pp. 85, 220-225, 276, 419, 420.

387. DENIS, Léon; "Cristianismo e Espiritismo"; without translator; 330 pp.; 17.5 cm; hb.; 4th ed.; Federação Espírita Brasileira; Rio de Janeiro; Brazil; 1941; pp. 315, 316.

388. DENIS, Léon; "Depois da Morte"; transl. João Lourenço de Sousa; 334 pp.; illus.; 18 cm; pb.; 10th ed.; Federação Espírita Brasileira; Rio de Janeiro; Brazil; 1978; pp. 177, 178.

389. DENIS, Léon; "No Invisível"; transl. Leopoldo Cirne; 456 pp.; 18 cm; hb.; 5th ed.; Federação Espírita Brasileira; Rio de Janeiro; Brazil; 1946; pp. 140-167.

390. DENIS, Léon; "O Problema do Ser, do Destino e da Dor"; without translator; 404 pp.; illus.; 18 cm; pb.; 11st ed.; Federação Espírita Brasileira; Rio de Janeiro; Brazil; 1979; pp. 75-99.

391. DENNING, Melita, & PHILLIPS, Osborne; "The Llewellyn Practical Guide to Astral Projection"; 240 pp.; illus.; glos. 237-239; 20.5 cm; pb.; Llewellyn Publications; U. S. A.; 1979; pp. 1-240; eds.: Eng., Sp. (Mini-library).

392. DEPASCALE, Alfonso, y RINALDINI, Manio; "Diccionario de Metapsiquismo-Espiritismo"; 150 pp.; illus.; 22 cm; hb.; Author's Editions; Buenos Aires; Argentina; 1927; pp. 9, 10, 17, 27, 92.

393. DESMOND, Shaw; "After Sudden Death"; 128 pp.; 16.5 cm; pb.; 2nd ed.; Andrew Dakers; London; December, 1939; pp. 53, 54, 57, 79.

394. DESMOND, Shaw; "Reincarnation For Everyman"; 244 pp.; 18.5 cm; hb.; Rider and Co.; London; no date; pp. 189, 192-198.

395. DESMOND, Shaw; "You Can Speak With Your Dead"; 104 pp.; 18.5 cm; hb.; Rider & Co.; London; 1945; p. 34.

396. DETHLEFSEN, Thorwald; "Das Leben nach dem Leben"; 272 pp.; illus.; 18 cm; pocket; pb.; 4th ed.; Wilhelm Heyne Verlag; München; West Germany; 1977; pp. 158-161, 167, 171, 172.

397. DEVORE, Nicholas; "Enciclopedia Astrologica"; transl. Héctor V. Morel; 414 pp.; 23 cm; pb.; 2nd ed.; Editorial Kier; Buenos Aires; Argentina; 1977; p. 328.

398. DICKENS, Charles; "Três Espíritos do Natal"; transl. Wallace Leal V. Rodrigues; 156 pp.; illus.; 18 cm; pb.; 2nd ed.; Casa Editora O Clarim; Matão, SP; Brazil; 1975; pp. 46, 47, 68, 96, 110, 115.

399. DIGEST, Reader's; "Into the Unknown"; 352 pp.; alph.; bibl. 342, 343; alph.; 27.5 cm; hb.; dj.; The Reader's Digest Association; New York; 1981; pp. 246, 270-283, 338.

400. DIGEST, Reader's; "Mysteries of the Unexplained"; 320 pp.; illus.; bibl. 307-310; alph.; 27.5 cm; hb.; dj.; The Reader's Digest Association; New York; 1982; pp. 166, 168, 175, 227; eds.: Eng., Port.

401. DIGEST, Sélection Du Reader's; "L'Europe Des Sociétés Secrètes"; 384 pp.; illus.; glos. 344-383; 31 cm; hb.; Sélection Du Reader's Digest; Paris; Novembre, 1980; pp. 334, 336, 337, 342, 347.

402. DILLON, Douglas, and DILLON, Barbara; "An Explosion of Being"; 224 pp.; bibl. 211-213; alph.; 23 cm; pb.; Parker Publishing Co.; West Nyack, N. Y.; U. S. A.; 1984; pp. 55, 56, 110, 113, 114, 116, 126, 165, 173, 174, 202, 203.

403. DINGWALL, Eric J.; Editor; "Abnormal Hypnotic Phenomena"; VIII + 174 pp.; illus.; bibl. 159-164; index of names; 22 cm; hb.; dj.; J. & A. Churchill; London; 1968; pp. 93, 96.

404. DINGWALL, Eric John, and LANGDON-DAVIES, John; "The Unknown is it Nearer?"; 174 pp.; alph.; 18.5 cm; hb.; dj.; Cassel & Co.; London; 1956; pp. 9, 29, 30.

405. DOLIS, Rosangela Maria; "Viagens no Tempo"; *Planeta;* S. Paulo; Brazil; Magazine; Monthly; N. 139; April, 1984; illus.; bibl.; pp. 36-43.

406. DONAHUE, James J.; "Dream Reality: The Conscious Creation of Dream & Paranormal Experience"; ed. rev.; Bench Press; Oakland, Cal.; U. S. A.; 1979; pp. 68-70.

407. DONAHUE, James J.; "Enigma: Psychology, the Paranormal and Self-Transformation"; 200 pp.; glos. 167-170; bibl. 171-193; alph.; 21.5 cm; pb.; Bench Press; Oakland; Cal.; U. S. A.; 1979; pp. 6, 7, 13, 16-21, 25, 48, 63, 64, 70, 74, 77-79, 89, 97-111, 129, 150, 168, 169.

408. DOSTOIEVSKI, Fiodor; "O Sósia"; Novel; transl. Corália Rêgo Lins; 200 pp.; 19 cm; pb.; Casa Editora Vecchi; Rio de Janeiro; Brazil; 1943; pp. 43, 58, 59, 62, 68.

409. DOUGLAS, Alfred; "Extra-Sensory Powers"; 392 pp.; illus.; bibl. 379-385; alph.; 21.5 cm; hb.; dj.; The Overlook Press; New York; 1977; pp. 16, 323-332, 340, 341.

410. DOWDING, Hugh; "Lychgate"; 128 pp.; 18.5 cm; hb.; dj.; 2nd print.; Rider and Co.; London; September, 1945; pp. 42, 52, 60.

411. DOYLE, Arthur Conan; "História do Espiritismo"; transl. and introd. Júlio Abreu Filho; pref. José Herculano Pires; 500 pp.; illus.; 21 cm; pb.; Editora O Pensamento; S. Paulo; Brazil; 1960; pp. 36, 66, 294.

412. DRAGAUD, J.; "Parapsicologia Através de Perguntas e Respostas"; 92 pp.; illus.; alph.; 21 cm; pb.; Edições de Ouro; Rio de Janeiro; Brazil; 1980; pp. 53-55, 78, 79.

413. DRIESCH, Hans; "Psychical Research"; transl. Theodore Berterman; XVI + 176 pp.; 18.5 cm; pb.; G. Bell & Sons; London; 1933; pp. 138-146.

414. DRURY, Nevill; "Don Juan, Mescalito and Modern Magic"; X + 230 pp.; illus.; bibl. 222-225; alph.; 21.5 cm; pb.; Routledge & Kegan Paul; London; 1978; pp. 6, 11-13, 17-44, 54, 57, 58, 59-61, 70, 78, 146, 155; eds.: Eng., Sp.

415. DRURY, Nevill; "Inner Visions: Explorations in Magical Consciousness"; 142 pp.; illus.; bibl. 133-138; alph.; 23 cm; pb.; Routledge & Kegan Paul; London; 1979; pp. 4, 27, 45, 124.

416. DRURY, Nevill; "The Path of the Chameleon"; 160 pp.; illus.; bibl.; alph.; Spearman; London; 1973.

417. DRURY, Nevill; "The Shaman and the Magician"; pref. Michael Harner; XIV + 130 pp.; illus.; bibl. 119-126; alph.; 21.5 cm; pb.; Routledge & Kegan Paul; London; 1982; pp. 27, 29, 32, 43, 44, 46, 48, 94, 96, 98.

418. DRURY, Nevill, and TILLET, Gregory; "The Occult Sourcebook"; X + 236 pp.; illus.; index of names; alph.; 23.5 cm; pb.; Routledge & Kegan Paul; London; 1978; pp. IX, 95-99.

419. DUBANT, Bernard, et MARGUERIE, Michel; "Castaneda: La Voie du Guerrier"; 100 pp.; illus.; 21.5 cm; pb.; 2nd ed.; Guy Trédaniel; Paris; 1982; pp. 76-80.

420. DUBANT, Bernard, et MARGUERIE, Michel; "Castaneda: Le Sant dans l'Inconnu"; 138 pp.; illus.; 21.5 cm; pb.; Guy Trédaniel; Paris; 1982; pp. 76-78.

421. DUBOR, Georges de; "Les Mystères de L'Hypnose"; XII + 336 pp.; 17.5 cm; hb.; Perrin et Cie., Librairies-Éditeurs; Paris; 1920; pp. 269-305.

422. DUBUGRAS, Elsie; "O Aprendizado pela Reencarnação"; *Planeta;* S. Paulo; Brazil; Magazine; Monthly; N. 118-A; July, 1982; illus.; pp. 31-37.

423. DUBUGRAS, Elsie; "O Ataque Invisível das Forças Psíquicas"; *Planeta;* S. Paulo; Brazil; Magazine; Monthly; N. 125; February, 1983; illus.; pp. 49-54.

424. DUBUGRAS, Elsie; "Bons e Maus Contatos com Seres de Outra Dimensão"; *Planeta;* S. Paulo; Brazil; Magazine; Monthly; N. 120; September, 1982; illus.; pp. 106-112.

425. DUBUGRAS, Elsie; "O Desdobramento"; *Planeta;* S. Paulo; Brazil; Magazine; Monthly; N. 48; September, 1976; pp. 6-17.

426. DUBUGRAS, Elsie; "O Desdobramento Versus Autoscopia"; *Revista Internacional do Espiritismo;* Matão, SP; Brazil; Monthly; Yr. LIV; N. 12; January, 1980; pp. 369, 370.

427. DUBUGRAS, Elsie; "O Juiz Estava Vivo em Pernambuco mas Apareceu "Materializado" na Suíça"; *Planeta;* S. Paulo; Brazil; Magazine; Monthly; N. 77; February, 1979; illus.; pp. 59-61.

428. DUBUGRAS, Elsie; "As Várias Maneiras de Viajar Fora do Corpo"; *Planeta;* S. Paulo; Brazil; Magazine; Monthly; N. 66; March, 1978; illus.; pp. 60-63.

429. DUBUGRAS, Elsie, and ARAIA, Eduardo; "A Segura Expansão das Ciências do Paranormal"; *Planeta;* S. Paulo; Brazil; Magazine; Monthly; N. 120; September, 1982; illus.; pp. 41-54.

430. DUCHATEL, Ed., et WARCOLLIER, R.; "Les Miracles de la Volonté"; pref. Émile Boirac; 244 pp.; 21.5 cm; hb.; Hector et Henri Durville, Éditeurs; Paris; no date; pp. 112-124.

431. DUMAS, André; "Le Corps Subtil et ses Problèmes"; *Renaître 2000;* Paris; Magazine; Bimonthly; 124th Yr.; New series; N. 25; November-December, 1981; pp. 197-202.

432. DUMAS, André; "La Science de L'Ame"; pref. Léon Périn; 434 pp.; glos. 9, 10; bibl. 415-430; 18 cm; Éditions Ocia; Paris; 1947; pp. 212-230; eds.: Fr., It.

433. DU POTET, Jules Denis Sennevoy; "Traité Complet de Magnétisme Animal"; VIII + 632 pp.; 21.5 cm; hb.; 8th ed.; Librairie Félix Alcan; Paris; 1930; pp. 549-562.

434. DUPOUY, Edmond; "Sciences Occultes et Physiologie Psychique"; VIII + 312 pp.; illus.; 17.5 cm; hb.; Société D'Éditions Scientifiques; Paris; 1898; pp. 79, 93, 127-129, 140-150.

435. DURVILLE, Hector; "Desdobramento do Corpo Humano ou Exteriorização do Duplo"; *Estudos Psíquicos;* Lisboa; Portugal; Magazine; Monthly; N. 8; January, 1908; pp. 150, 169, 192, 210, 230.

436. DURVILLE, Hector; "Le Fantôme des Vivants: Anatomie et Physiologie de L'Ame"; 356 pp.; illus.; 18 cm; hb.; Librairie du Magnetisme; Paris; Mai, 1909; pp. 1-356 (Mini-library).

437. DURVILLE, Hector; "Magnétisme Personnel"; 314 pp.; illus.; 18 cm; hb.; Hector & Henri Durville, Éditeur; Paris; 1912; pp. 39-61; eds.: Fr., Port.

438. DURVILLE, Hector; "New Experiments With Phantoms of the Living"; *Annals of Psychical Science;* Vol. 7; 1908; pp. 464-470.

439. DURVILLE, Hector; "Pour Dédoubler le Corps Humain"; Henri Durville, Imprimeur-Éditeur; Paris; 1922.

440. DURVILLE, Hector; "Télépathie Télépsychie"; 250 pp.; illus.; 22 cm; hb.; 2nd ed.; Henri Durville, Imprimeur-Éditeur; Paris; 1919; pp. 103-109.

441. DURVILLE, Hector, et JAGOT, Paul C.; "Histoire Raisonnée du Magnétisme et du Psychisme Pratique"; 488 pp.; illus.; 17.5 cm; hb.; Hector et Henri Durville, Éditeurs; Paris; 1914; pp. 22, 23.

442. DURVILLE, Henri; "Los Misterios Iniciaticos"; 184 pp.; illus.; 21 cm; pb.; Editorial Orion; Mexico, D.F.; 1979; pp. 134-137.

443. DUSEN, Wilson Van; "Caminhos do Mundo Interior"; transl. Cesar Tozzi; 222 pp.; 21 cm; pb.; Editora Record; Rio de Janeiro; Brazil; no date; pp. 215-217.

444. DYCHTWALD, Ken; "Corpomente"; transl. Maria Sílvia Mourão Neto; pres. Anna Veronica Mautner; 280 pp.; illus.; bibl. 267-278; 21 cm; pb.; Summus Editorial; S. Paulo; Brazil; 1984; pp. 233, 249-254.

445. EAGLE, White; "Spiritual Unfoldment"; 144 pp.; alph.; 19 cm; hb.; dj.; The White Eagle Publishing Trust; London; April, 1978; p. 41.

446. EASLIC, Hassie Annelle; "Extra Sensory Perception: What Does it Signify?"; 72 pp.; 20.5 cm; hb.; dj.; Vantage Press; New York; 1973; pp. 39, 40.

447. EAST, John N. (Pseud.); "Man the Immortal"; introd. W. Y. Evans-Wentz; pref. Geraldine Cummins; 232 pp.; bibl. 231; The Psychic Press; London; 1960.

448. EAST, John N. (Pseud.); "The Mystical Life" (J. H. M. Whiteman); Books Reviews; *Journal of the Society for Psychical Research;* London; Vol. 41; N. 708; June, 1961; pp. 83, 84.

449. EASTMAN, Margaret; "Astral Projection: A Record of Out-of-the-Body Experiences" (Oliver Fox); Books Reviews; *Journal of the Society for Psychical Research;* London; Vol. 42; N. 717; September, 1963; pp. 138-140.

450. EASTMAN, Margaret; "Out-of-the-Body Experiences"; *Proceedings of the Society for Psychical Research;* Vol. 53; Part 193; December, 1962; pp. 287-309.

451. EASTON, Stewart C.; "Man and World in the Light of Anthroposophy"; VIII + 536 pp.; alph.; 21 cm; hb.; 2nd ed. rev.; The Anthroposophic Press; New York; 1982; pp. 145, 146.

452. EBEID, Raouf; "Fenômenos da Saída do Corpo"; Original Árabe; Private Translation; 222 pp.; illus.; bibl. 210-217; 21 cm; pb.; Dar El-Fekr El-Arabi; Cairo; Egypt; 1975; pp. 1-222; ed. only Arab.

453. EBON, Martin; "The Evidence for Life After Death"; 178 pp.; bibl. 175, 176; 18 cm; pocket; pb.; New American Library; New York; August, 1977; pp. 1, 4, 12, 24-36, 44, 45, 50, 66, 71-76, 86-94, 97, 100, 110-138, 168, 169, 173; eds.: Eng., Port.

454. EBON, Martin; Editor; "Fenomenos Parapsicológicos: Misticismo y Reencarnación"; transl. Maria E. I. de Fischman; 192 pp.; 17.5 cm; pocket; pb.; Ediciones Hormé; Buenos Aires; Argentina; 1977; pp. 104-108.

455. EBON, Martin; "Miracles"; 8 + 200 pp.; 18 cm; pocket; pb.; New American Library; New York; December, 1981; pp. 111-114, 175, 182, 183.

456. EBON, Martin; "Psychic Warfare: Threat or Illusion?"; 6 + 282 pp.; bibl. 262-272; alph.; 23 cm; hb.; dj.; Mc Graw-Hill Book Co.; New York; 1983; pp. 16, 17.

457. EBON, Martin; "The Signet Handbook of Parapsychology"; 520 pp.; illus.; glos. 509-512; 18 cm; pocket; pb.; Signet Book; New York; 1978; pp. 173-200, 466-482.

458. EBON, Martin; "They Knew the Unknown"; 256 pp.; bibl. 249-251; alph.; 18 cm; pocket; pb.; Signet Book; New York; September, 1972; pp. 22, 23, 41-43, 105, 106, 192, 200; eds.: Eng., Port.

459. EDGE, Hoyt L.; "Rejointer to Dr. Wheatley's Note On "Do Spirits Matter?"; *The Journal of the American Society for Psychical Research;* New York; Vol. 70; N. 4; October, 1976; 402-407.

460. EDMONDS, I. G.; "D. D. Home: O Homem que Falava com Espíritos"; transl. Nair Lacerda; 130 pp.; illus.; bibl. 129; 19.5 cm; pb.; Editora Pensamento; S. Paulo; Brazil; 1983; pp. 30-32.

461. EDMUNDS, H. Tudor; Editor; "Psychism and the Unconscious Mind"; XVI + 254 pp.; 18 cm; pb.; 2nd ed.; The Theosophical Publishing House; Wheaton, Ill.; U. S. A.; 1974; p. 40.

462. EDSALL, F. S.; "O Mundo dos Fenômenos Psíquicos"; transl. and pref. J. Gervásio de Figueiredo; 212 pp.; glos. 209-212; 19.5 cm; pb.; Editora Pensamento; S. Paulo; Brazil; no date; pp. 90, 93, 205, 206.

463. EDWARDS, Frank; "Strange World"; XVI + 238 pp.; 18 cm; pocket; pb.; 7th print.; Bantam Books; New York; no date; pp. 108-113, 165-168.

464. EDWARDS, Frank; "Stranger Than Science"; X + 182 pp.; 18 cm; pocket; pb.; Bantam Books; New York; June, 1967; pp. 144-146.

465. EDWARDS, Frank; "Strangest of All"; 176 pp.; 18 cm; pocket; pb.; New American Library; New York; May, 1974; pp. 99-101.

466. EEDEN, Frederick van; "A Study of Dreams"; *Proceedings of the Society for Psychical Research;* London; Vol. 26; 1913; pp. 431-461.

467. EGLOFFSTEIN, P. P. F. V.; "Ein Bilokationserlebnis von Seltener Klarheit"; *Die Andere Welt;* Freiburg; West Germany; Magazine; Monthly; Yr. 19; N. 11; November, 1968; pp. 1018-1020.

468. EGLOFFSTEIN, P. P. F. V.; "Im Lande des Grossen Glücks"; *Esotera;* Freiburg; West Germany; Magazine; Monthly; Yr. 23; N. 9; September, 1972; pp. 815-818.

469. EGLOFFSTEIN, P. P. F. V.; "Unterricht in Bilokation?"; *Esotera;* Freiburg; West Germany; Magazine; Monthly; Yr. 23; N. 12; December, 1972; illus.; pp. 1103-1106.

470. EHRENWALD, Jan; "Correspondence: Dr. Ehrenwald Explains"; *Parapsychology Review;* New York; Vol. 12; N. 6; November-December, 1981; pp. 26, 27.

471. EHRENWALD, Jan; "The ESP Experience: A Psychiatric Validation"; XII + 308 pp.; illus.; bibl. 289-298; alph.; 23.5 cm; hb.; dj.; Basic Books, Publishers; New York; 1978; pp. 76, 151-161, 190, 233-236; eds.: Eng., Fr.

472. EHRENWALD, Jan; "Out-of-the Body Experiences and the Denial of Death"; *The Journal of Nervous and Mental Disease;* Baltimore; Maryland; U. S. A.; Vol. 159; N. 4; Serial N. 1103; October, 1974; bibl. 233; pp. 227-233.

473. EISENBUD, Jule; "The World of Ted Serios"; 368 pp.; illus.; bibl. 348-357; alph.; 23.5 cm; hb.; William Morrow & Co.; New York; 1967; pp. 231, 232, 235; eds.: Eng., Ger.

474. EL-AOWAR, Mahab; "Parapsicanálise: Uma Teoria da Paranormalidade"; 198 pp.; 21 cm; pb.; Edições Achiamé; Rio de Janeiro; Brazil; 1983; pp. 6, 97-101, 183, 184.

475. ELIADE, Mircea; "El Chamanismo y las Técnicas Arcaicas del Éxtasis"; transl. Ernestina de Champourcin; 484 pp.; 21 cm; pb.; 2nd ed.; Fondo de Cultura Económica; Mexico, D. F.; 1976; pp. 117-120, 240, 279, 281.

476. ELIADE, Mircea; "The Two and the One"; transl. J. M. Cohen; 224 pp.; alph.; 20.5 cm; pb.; The University of Chicago Press; Chicago; Ill.; U. S. A.; 1979; pp. 66-75, 183, 184.

477. ELIADE, Mircea; "Yoga Inmortalidad y Libertad"; transl. Susana de Aldecoa; 412 pp.; 20 cm; pb.; Editorial La Pleyade; Buenos Aires; Argentina; 1977; pp. 65, 66, 98.

478. ELLISON, Arthur J.; "Some Recent Experiments in Psychic Perceptivity"; *Journal of the Society for Psychical Research;* London; Magazine; Monthly; Vol. 41; N. 713; September, 1962; pp. 355-365.

479. EMMONS, Charles F.; "Chinese Ghost and ESP"; 298 pp.; glos. 286-288; bibl. 277-285; alph.; hb.; The Scarecrow Press; Metuchen; N. J.; U. S. A.; 1982; pp. 44, 45, 47, 171, 267, 269, 270.

480. ENGEL, Herbert H. G.; "Der Sphärenwanderer"; 236 pp.; illus.; 23 cm; hb.; dj.; Ansata-Verlag; Interlaken; Schweiz; 1981; pp. 1-236 (Mini-library).

481. E. P.; "Mensagens Rosa-crucianas"; 296 pp.; 19.5 cm; pb.; Editora Pensamento; S. Paulo; Brazil; 1978; pp. 288-295.

482. ERNEST, Victor H.; "Eu Falei com Espíritos"; transl. Luiz Aparecido Caruso; pres. John H. Houser; 76 pp.; 18 cm; pb.; 3rd ed.; Editora Mundo Cristão; S. Paulo; Brazil;1981; p. 15.

483. ERNY, Alfred; "O Psiquismo Experimental"; without translator; 228 pp.; 18 cm; pb.; 2nd ed.; Federação Espírita Brasileira; Rio de Janeiro; Brazil;1953; pp. 79-81, 91-101.

484. ESPASA-CALPE; Editors; "Enciclopedia Universal Ilustrada"; 106 (one hundred and six) Vol.; 24.5 cm; hb.; Espasa-Calpe; Madrid; Spain; 1920 / 1980; Tome XVIII: VIII + 1.456 pp.; p. 476.

485. ESPÉRANCE, Elisabeth d' (Pseud. for Juliet Anne Theodore Heurtley Hart-Davies); "Shadow Land"; introd. Alexander Nikolayevich Aksakof; XXII + 414 pp.; illus.; 18 cm; hb.; George Redway; London; 1897; pp. 355-367; eds.: Eng., Fr., Ger., Port.

486. ESTRELLA, Décio; "Nuvens Negras"; *Tribuna Umbandista;* S. Paulo; Brazil; Newspaper; Yr. XXVII; N. 307 / 313; January-July, 1981; pp. 1, 3.

487. EUSTÁQUIO, Centro Espírita Irmão; Directors; "Curso de Conscientização Mediúnica"; 256 pp.; 3 Installments; illus.; bibl. 173, 174; 31 cm; pb.; Centro Espírita Irmão Eustáquio; Salvador, BA; Brazil; 1983; pp. 82-84.

488. EUSTÁQUIO, Centro Espírita Irmão; Directors; "Espiritismo: Visão Integrada da Vida"; 96 pp.; 22 cm; pb.; Centro Espírita Irmão Eustáquio; Salvador, BA; Brazil; 1982; pp. 66, 67, 70.

489. EUSTÁQUIO, Centro Espírita Irmão; Directors; "Quem Somos"; pref. Edson Nunes da Silva; pres. Regina Braga Moreira Caldas; 98 pp.; illus.; 21.5 cm; pb.; Centro Espírita Irmão Eustáquio; Salvador, BA; Brazil; 1976; pp. 14, 15, 51, 52.

490. EVANS, W. H.; "O Misterioso Mundo dos Sonhos"; *Estudos Psíquicos;* Lisboa; Portugal; Magazine; Monthly; 25th Yr.; N. 3; March, 1964; pp. 90-92.

491. EVANS-WENTZ, Walter Y.; "Yoga Tibetano y Doctrinas Secretas"; transl. Hector V. Morel; pref. R. R. Marett; 408 pp.; illus.; 19.5 cm; pb.; 3rd ed.; Editorial Kier; Buenos Aires; Argentina; 1980; pp. 293, 294.

492. EVIN, Simone; "A Comunhão dos Santos"; transl. Izidoro Duarte Santos; *Estudos Psíquicos;* Lisboa; Portugal; Magazine; Monthly; 31st Yr.; N. 11; November, 1970; pp. 322, 323.

493. EYSENCK, Hans Jürgen, and SARGENT, Carl; "Explaining the Unexplained: Mysteries of the Paranormal"; 192pp.; illus.; bibl. 188, 189; alph.; 25 cm; hb.; dj.; Weindenfeld and Nicolson; London; 1982; pp. 155-162.

494. FARDWEL, Willian; "La Supervivencia"; 238 pp.; 19 cm; pb.; Rafael Caro Raggio, Editor; Madrid; Spain; August, 1929; pp. 15-70.

495. FARIA, Osmar Andrade; "Parapsicologia: Panorama Atual das Funções Psi"; pref. Hernani Guimarães Andrade; 376 pp.; illus.; bibl. 345-357; 22.5 cm; pb.; Livraria Atheneu; Rio de Janeiro; Brazil; 1981; pp. 76-78, 290, 322, 323.

496. FARRAR, Stewart; "Lo Que Hacen las Brujas"; 222 pp.; illus.; 18 cm; pocket; pb.; Ediciones Martínez Roca; Barcelona; Spain; 1977; pp. 190-199.

497. FARRÈRE, Claude; "L'Autre Côté... Contes Insolites"; 248 pp.; 18.5 cm; pb.; Ernest Flammarion, Éditeur; Paris; 1928; pp. 26-30, 36, 37, 47.

498. FARTHING, Geoffrey; "Exploring the Great Beyond: A Survey of the Field of the Extraordinary"; XII + 214 pp.; glos. 208-214; bibl. 203-207; 21 cm; pb.; The Theosophical Publishing House; Wheaton, Ill.; U. S. A.; 1978; pp. 157-159, 212.

499. FASE; Editors; "Século XX: Ciência e Futurologia"; 308 pp.; 20 cm; hb.; Editora Fase; Rio de Janeiro; Brazil; 1982; pp. 231-234.

500. FAVRE, François; Anthology; "Les Apparitions Mysterieuses"; 318 pp.; illus.; bibl. 316-318; 24 cm; pb.; Claude Tchou; Paris; Novembre, 1978; pp. 18-27.

501. FEDERACION Espiritista Internacional; "Libro Resumen del V Congresso Espiritista Internacional"; 384 pp.; illus.; 24 cm; hb.; Tipografia Cosmos; Barcelona; Spain; Septiembre, 1934; p. 322.

502. FEDERMANN, R., and SCHREIBER, H.; "Testemunhos do Ocultismo"; transl. Attilio Cancian; 286 pp.; illus.; 21 cm; pb.; Editora e Distribuidora Líder; S. Paulo; Brazil; no date; pp. 18, 19, 244, 245.

503. FEESP; Editor; "Pontos da Escola de Médiuns: Ensino Teórico"; pref. Edgard Armond; Tome III; 116 pp.; 21 cm; pb.; 6th ed.; Edição Feesp; S. Paulo; Brazil; 1972; pp. 114, 115.

504. FEITOSA, Fenelon Alves; "Naná, os Espíritos e seus Fenômenos"; 260 pp.; 21 cm; pb.; Editora Jocal; S. Paulo; Brazil; 1981; pp. 150-153, 168, 169.

505. FENWICK, Agnes M.; "My Journey Into God's Realm of Light"; Exposition Press; New York; 1974; 64 pp.

506. FEOLA, José; "PK: Mind Over Matter"; introd. Mulford Quickert Sibley; 176 pp.; illus.; glos. 163-167; bibl. 169-171; alph.; 21.5 cm; hb.; Dillon Press; Minneapolis; Minnesota; U. S. A.; 1975; pp. 59,163.

507. FERGUSON, John; "Encyclopaedia of Mysticism and the Mystery Religious"; 228 pp.; illus.; bibl. 217-227; 24 cm; pb.; Thames and Hudson; London; 1976; p. 28.

508. FERNANDES, Diamantino Coelho; "As Forças do Bem"; 188 pp.; 23 cm; pb.; 7th ed.; Livraria Freitas Bastos; Rio de Janeiro; Brazil; 1982; pp. 82, 83, 108, 109, 117, 118, 121, 145, 146, 152, 167.

509. FERREIRA, Mário; "Espiritismo Revelação Centenária, Parapsicologia Ciência Moderna"; pref. Francisco Carlos de Castro Neves; pres. Eurípedes de Castro; 140 pp.; 21 cm; pb.; 2nd ed.; Editora Bels; Porto Alegre, RS; Brazil; 1976; pp. 49, 51.

510. FESENMEYER; "Bordeland: Life Between Life and Death"; 132 pp.; 22 cm; hb.; dj.; Regency Press; London; 1967; pp. 48-60.

511. FEUERSTEIN, Georg; "The Essence of Yoga; A Contribution to the Psychohistory of Indian Civilization"; pref. Algis Mickunas; 224 pp.; illus.; bibl. 215-219; alph.; 21.5 cm; pb.; Rider and Co.; London; 1974; p. 126.

512. FERGUSON, Robert A.; "Telemetria Psíquica"; transl. Maria Lucia Sarquis Aiex; 222 pp.; illus.; 21 cm; pb.; Editora Record; Rio de Janeiro; Brazil; 1983; pp. 166-182.

513. FIELDING-OULD, Fielding; "The Wonders of the Saints in the Light of Spiritualism"; introd. Lady Gleuconner; 128 pp.; 19 cm; J. M. Watkins; London; 1919.

514. FIGANIÉRE, Frederico Francisco Stuart de – Mourão; "Submundo, Mundo e Supramundo"; introd. Edmundo Cardillo; 298 pp.; illus.; glos. 17-21; 20.5 cm; hb.; Editora Três; S. Paulo; Brazil; 1973; pp. 235-238, 242.

515. FIGUIER, Louis; "Depois da Morte"; transl. Ferreira de Araújo; 384 pp.; illus.; 18.5 cm; hb.; H. Garnier, Livreiro-Editor; Rio de Janeiro; Brazil; 1902; pp. 136, 137.

516. FINOTTI, Paulo; "Ressurreição"; prol. Mário Ferreira; 132 pp.; bibl. 129-131; 20.5 cm; pb.; Gráfica e Editora Edigraf; S. Paulo; Brazil; 1972; pp. 83, 84, 105, 106.

517. FIORE, Charles, and LANDSBURG, Allan; "Death Encounters"; 200 pp.; bibl. 195-197; 18 cm; pocket; pb.; Bantam Books; New York; July, 1979; pp. 5, 7, 19-22, 27-30, 35-57, 94, 100, 159-170, 188.

518. FIORE, Edith; "Já Vivemos Antes"; transl. Maria Luísa Ferreira da Costa; 226 pp.; 21 cm; pb.; Publicações Europa-América; Lisboa; Portugal; no date; pp. 205, 208, 215; eds.: Eng., Fr., Port.

519. FISCHER, Reinhard; "Raumfahrt der Seele: Erlebnisse im Umkreis der Mentalprojektion"; 270 pp.; illus.; bibl. 270; 19.5 cm; hb.; dj.; Verlag Hermann Bauer; Freiburg; West Germany; 1975; pp. 19-200 (Mini-library).

520. FISICHELLA, Anthoni J.; "Metapsychics: the Science of Life"; introd. Brad Steiger; XXX + 284 pp.; illus.; alph.; 21.5 cm; pb.; Llewellyn Publications; St. Paul, Minnesota; U. S. A.; 1984; pp. 14, 42, 218.

521. FITTIPALDI, Bártolo; Editor; "Quando será Conhecida a Verdade Sobre o Sonho?"; *Enigmas da Humanidade;* S. Paulo; Brazil; Magazine; N. 3; 1984; pp. 51-56.

522. FLAMMARION, Camille; "O Desconhecido e os Problemas Psíquicos"; transl. Arnaldo São Thiago; 2 vol.; 520 pp.; 18 cm; pb.; 3rd ed.; Federação Espírita Brasileira; Rio de Janeiro; Brazil; 1979; Vol. I: pp. 90-93, 96, 107-199; Vol. II: pp. 159-203, 272; eds.: Fr., It., Port.

523. FLAMMARION, Camille; "Estela"; Novel; transl. Almerindo Martins de Castro; 332 pp.; 18 cm; hb.; Federação Espírita Brasileira; Rio de Janeiro; Brazil; 1950; pp. 60, 61, 202-205, 266.

524. FLAMMARION, Camille; "A Morte e o Seu Mistério"; without translator; 3 Vol.; 1.048 pp.; 18 cm; pb.; 3rd ed.; Federação Espírita Brasileira; Rio de Janeiro; Brazil; 1982; Vol. I: pp. 80-85, 124, 125, 232, 233; Vol. II: pp. 38-88, 110-152; Vol. III: pp. 117-125, 131; eds.: Fr., It., Port.

525. FLAMMARION, Camille; "Urânia"; Novel; transl. Almerindo Martins de Castro; 198 pp.; 18 cm; pb.; 4th ed.; Federação Espírita Brasileira; Rio de Janeiro; Brazil; 1979; pp. 113-120.

526. FODOR, Nandor; "Algumas Incógnitas da Vida"; without translator; *Estudos Psíquicos;* Lisboa; Portugal; Magazine; Monthly; 23rd Yr.; N. 3; March, 1962; pp. 66-70.

527. FODOR, Nandor; "Between Two Worlds"; XIV + 298 pp.; bibl. 127-129; 21 cm; hb.; dj.; Parker Publishing Co.; West Nyack, N. Y.; U. S. A.; 1964; pp. 116-119, 170-172.

528. FODOR, Nandor; "Encyclopaedia of Psychic Science"; pref. Oliver Lodge; introd. Leslie A. Shepard; XL + 416 pp.; 25 cm; hb.; dj.; 3rd print.; University Books; New York; November, 1969; pp. 100-105.

529. FODOR, Nandor; "The Haunted Mind"; 314 pp.; alph.; 20 cm; hb.; dj.; Helix Press; New York; 1959; pp. 173-185.

530. FODOR, Nandor; "Mind Over Space"; 222 pp.; 20.5 cm; hb.; dj.; The Citadel Press; New York; 1962; pp. 28, 74-76.

531. FODOR, Nandor; "New Approaches to Dream Interpretation"; XVI + 368 pp.; alph.; 21 cm; hb.; dj.; University Books; New York; 1951; pp. 184-187.

532. FOIN, Raoul; "Les Mystères qui nos Entourent"; 180 pp.; 18 cm; pb.; Omnium Littéraire; Paris; 1967; pp. 119-148.

533. FONTAINE, Pierre; "La Magie Chez les Noirs"; pref. Fernand Divoire; 178 pp.; illus.; bibl. 175; 21 cm; pb.; Éditions Dervy; Paris; Juin, 1949; pp. 71-79.

534. FONTCUBERTA, Antonio Blay; "Relajación y Energía"; 296 pp.; 21 cm; pb.; 2nd ed.; Elicien; Barcelona; Spain; 1976; pp. 173-182.

535. FORD, Arthur; "Bericht vom Leben nach dem Tode"; without translator; 304 pp.; index of names; 21.5 cm; hb.; dj.; Scherz; München; West Germany; 1972; pp. 220, 221, 292.

536. FORD, Arthur; "Nothing so Strange"; Autobiography; with Margueritte Harmon Bro; 250 pp.; alph.; 21 cm; Harper & Row Publishers; New York; 1958; pp. 159-162.

537. FORD, Arthur; "Unknown but Known"; 176 pp.; alph.; 18 cm; pocket; pb.; The New American Library; New York; November, 1969; pp. 52-56.

538. FORMAN, Joan; "The Mask of Time"; 256 pp.; illus.; glos. 254.; bibl. 252-254; alph.; 21.5 cm; hb.; dj.; 2nd print.; MacDonald and Jane's Publishers; London; 1979; pp. 154, 155, 213, 236, 241, 254.

539. FORMIGA, Eurícledes, and MONTEIRO, Eduardo Carvalho; "Motoqueiros no Além"; 150 pp.; illus.; glos. 148, 149; 18.5 cm; pb.; 4th ed.; Instituto de Difusão Espírita; Araras, SP; Brazil; September, 1983; pp. 49, 51, 52.

540. FORTUNE, Dion (Pseud. for Violet M. Firth); "Psychic Self-Defense"; 210 pp.; 21.5 cm; pb.; 17th print.; The Aquarian Press; London; 1977; pp. 13, 28, 36-40, 42, 48-53, 58, 63-65, 98-100, 145, 148, 154-156, 160, 164, 208; eds.: Eng., Sp.

541. FORTUNE, Dion (Pseud. for Violet M. Firth); "The Training and Work of an Initiate"; 126 pp.; 21.5 cm; pb.; 2nd print.; The Aquarian Press; London; 1981; pp. 80, 105, 106, 126; eds.: Eng., Sp.

542. FOSTER, Gloria M.; "Traum, Hellsehen oder Astralwanderung?"; transl. E. M. Körner; *Esotera;* Freiburg; West Germany; Magazine; Monthly; Yr. 24; N. 1; January, 1973; p. 71.

543. FOX, Oliver (Pseud. for Hugh G. Callaway); "The Pineal Doorway: A Record of Research"; *Occult Review;* London; Magazine; Monthly; Vol. 31; N. 4; April, 1920.

544. FOX, Oliver (Pseud. for Hugh G. Callaway); "Astral Projection: A Record of Out-of-the-Body Experiences"; pref. John C. Wilson; 160 pp.; 20.5 cm; pb.; 4th ed.; The Citadel Press; Secaucus, N. J.; U. S. A.; 1962; pp. 1-160 (Mini-library).

545. FRANCO, Divaldo Pereira; "Nas Fronteiras da Loucura"; 252 pp.; illus.; 21 cm; pb.; 2nd ed.; Livraria Espírita Alvorada Editora; Salvador, BA; Brazil; 1984; pp. 12, 36-39, 41, 45-49, 54, 70, 71, 100, 101, 108, 109, 122, 131-133, 142-148, 178, 179, 187, 191-194, 196-201, 203, 208-211, 216-222, 240, 241.

546. FRANCO, Divaldo Pereira; "Nos Bastidores da Obsessão"; 282 pp.; 18 cm; pb.; 2nd ed.; Federação Espírita Brasileira; Rio de Janeiro; Brazil; 1976; pp. 11, 25, 31, 35, 63-65, 76, 105, 110, 120, 130, 133, 135, 136, 139, 273.

547. FRANCO, Divaldo Pereira; "Painéis da Obsessão"; 270 pp.; 21 cm; pb.; 2nd ed.; Livraria Espírita Alvorada Editora; Salvador, BA; Brazil; 1984; pp. 28, 40, 41, 44, 60, 67, 91, 105, 208, 229, 246.

548. FRANKLIN, Robert M.; "On the Acronym "OBE"; *The Journal of the American Society for Psychical Research;* New York; Vol. 69; N. 1; January, 1975; pp. 97, 98.

549. FRAZER, Felix J.; "Parallel Paths to the Unseen Worlds"; introd. Ann Davies; 382 pp.; illus.; 23 cm; pb.; Builders of the Adytum; Los Angeles, Cal.; U. S. A.; 1967; pp. 43-46, 155-160, 369.

550. FREEDLAND, Nat; "The Occult Explosion"; 270 pp.; alph.; 22 cm; hb.; dj.; 2nd print.; G. P. Putnam's Sons; New York; 1972; pp. 63, 100-102.

551. FREIRE, António J.; "Da Alma Humana"; 320 pp.; 18 cm; hb.; illus.; Federação Espírita Portuguesa; Lisboa; Portugal; 1950; pp. 150-176, 285-302.

552. FREITAS, Alberto de; "Viagem ao Invisível"; *Informação;* S. Paulo; Brazil; Magazine; Monthly; Yr. VI; N. 65; April, 1982; pp. 20-24.

553. FREIXEDO, Salvador; "Curanderismo y Curaciones por la Fe"; 190 pp.; illus.; 20 cm; pb.; Ediciones Martínez Roca; Barcelona; Spain; 1983; pp. 48, 49, 114.

554. FREIXEDO, Salvador; "El Diabolico Inconsciente: Parapsicologia y Religión"; with Alfonso Martínez Taboas; 388 pp.; illus.; bibl. 381-385; 20.5 cm; pb.; 5th ed.; Editorial Orion; Mexico, D. F.; January, 1977; pp. 49-53.

555. FREIXEDO, Salvador; "Extraterrestres y Creencias Religiosas"; 200 pp.; 19 cm; pb.; 2nd ed.; Editorial Orion; Mexico, D. F.; 1977; pp. 88, 95.

556. FREIXEDO, Salvador; "La Religión entre la Parapsicologia y los Ovnis"; 272 pp.; illus.; bibl. 265-267; 21.5 cm; pb.; Editorial Orion; Mexico, D. F.; 1978; p. 44.

557. FRICHET, Henry; "Les Forces Mystérieuses"; 282 pp.; 17 cm; hb.; Librairie Astra; Paris; no date; pp. 130-135, 142-148, 242, 243.

558. FRICHET, Henry; "L'Homme et ses Pouvoirs Secrets"; 244 pp.; 17.5 cm; hb.; Librairie Astra; Paris; 1945; pp. 43, 179, 180.

559. FRISEN, Roy M.; "Astral Journeys"; *Fate;* Evanston; Ill.; U. S. A.; Magazine; Monthly; Vol. 6; N. 11; November, 1953; pp. 16-23.

560. FROST, Gavin, and FROST, Yvonne; "Astral Travel"; 240 pp.; illus.; bibl. 239, 240; 18 cm; pocket; pb.; Granada Publishing; London; 1982; pp. 1-240 (Mini-library).

561. FRUNGILO JÚNIOR, Wilson; "Do Outro Lado"; Novel; 156 pp.; 18.5 cm; pb.; 3rd ed.; Instituto de Difusão Espírita; Araras, SP; Brazil; January, 1984; pp. 49, 84-92, 99-102, 118, 142-153.

562. FUGAIRON, L. S.; "La Survivance de L'Ame: La Mort et la Renaissance chez les Êtres Vivants"; 276 pp.; illus.; 17.5 cm; hb.; Librairie du Magnétisme; Paris; 1907; pp. 114-127, 131-137, 153-155, 166, 167.

563. FUNK, Isaac Kaufman; "The Psychic Riddle"; 244 pp.; alph.; 18.5 cm; hb.; Funk & Wagnalls Co.; New York; 1947; pp. 179, 180.

564. GABBARD, Glen O.; TWEMLOW, Stuart W.; and JONES, Fowler C.; "Do Near Death Experiences Occur Only Near Death?"; *The Journal of Nervous and Mental Disease;* Baltimore, Maryland; U. S. A.; Vol. 169; N. 6; 1981; bibl. 377; pp. 374-377.

565. GALEAZZI, Marlene Anna; "Tia Neiva: A Médium que Salvou a Si Mesma da Morte"; *Manchete;* Rio de Janeiro; Brazil; Magazine; Weekly; Yr. 31; N. 1.601; 25, December, 1982; illus.; pp. 126-129.

566. GALLUP JR., George; with William Proctor; "Adventures in Immortality"; 214 pp.; alph.; 18 cm; pocket; pb.; Corgi Books; London; 1984; pp. 12, 13, 17, 22, 30, 35, 36-40, 46, 68, 99, 100, 133, 139, 146, 160, 161.

567. GARDNER, Martin; "Science Good, Bad and Bogus"; XVIII + 412 pp.; illus.; alph.; 23 cm; hb.; dj.; Prometheus Books; Buffalo, N. Y.; U. S. A.; 1981; pp. 96, 98, 144, 145, 302, 303, 378.

568. GARFIELD, Patricia L.; "Creative Dreaming"; 244 pp.; alph.; 18 cm; pocket; pb.; 7th print.; Ballantine Books; New York; January, 1981; pp. 118-150, 221, 222; eds.: Eng., Port.

569. GARFIELD, Patricia L.; "Pathway to Ecstasy"; Autobiography; XVI + 254 pp.; illus.; bibl. 241-246; alph.; 23 cm; hb.; dj.; Holt, Rinehart & Winston; New York; 1979; pp. 13, 36, 72-77, 95, 113-128, 141-150.

570. GARRETT, Eileen Jeannette Vancho Little; "Awareness"; XVIII + 308 pp.; illus.; 21 cm; hb.; dj.; 4th print.; Creative Age Press; New York; 1945; pp. 278-282.

571. GARRETT, Eileen Jeannette Vancho Little; "Beyond the Five Senses"; Anthology; 384 pp.; glos. 383-384; 22 cm; hb.; dj.; J. B. Lippincott Co.; New York; 1957; pp. 42-58.

572. GARRETT, Eileen Jeannette Vancho Little; "Many Voices: The Autobiography of a Medium"; introd. Allan Angoff; 252 pp.; alph.; 22 cm; hb.; dj.; G. P. Putnam's Sons; New York; 1968; pp. 189, 190, 193-195, 197, 198; eds.: Eng., Port.

573. GARRETT, Eileen Jeannette Vancho Little; "My Lyfe as a Search for the Meaning of Mediumship"; Autobiography; 226 pp.; 21.5 cm; hb.; Rider & Co.; London; 1939; pp. 156-161, 203-205.

574. GARRETT, Eileen Jeannette Vancho Little; "Telepathy"; introd. Eugene Rollin Corson; XXX + 210 pp.; bibl. 209, 210; 21 cm; hb.; dj.; Creative Age Press; New York; 1945; pp. 67-90.

575. GAULD, Alan; "The Founders of Psychical Research"; XII + 388 pp.; alph.; 21.5 cm; hb.; dj.; Schocken Books; New York; 1968; pp. 162-164, 169, 170, 182.

576. GAULD, Alan; "Mediumship and Survival: A Century of Investigations"; pref. Brian Inglis; XIV + 288 pp.; illus.; bibl. 268-282; alph.; 22 cm; hb.; dj.; William Heinemann; London; 1982; pp. 215-230, 250-253, 265.

577. GAYNOR, Frank; "Dictionary of Mysticism"; 210 pp.; 23 cm; hb.; dj.; Philosophical Library; New York; 1953; pp. 19, 26.

578. GEDDES, Auckland; "A Voice from the Grandstand"; *The Edinburg Medical Journal;* Great Britain; Vol. XLIV; N. VI; June, 1937; pp. 365-384.

579. GEISLER, H.; "Sind Astralwanderungen Wirklich so Gefährlich?"; *Esotera;* Freiburg; West Germany; Magazine; Monthly; Yr. 24; N. 7; July, 1973; p. 578.

580. GELEY, Gustave; "De L'Inconscient au Conscient"; XIV + 346 pp.; 21.5 cm; hb.; Librairie Félix Alcan; Paris; 1921; pp. 142, 273, 274; eds.: Fr., Eng., Sp., Port.

581. GELEY, Gustave; "Les Preuves du Transformisme"; 288 pp.; illus.; bibl. 5, 6; 21.5 cm; hb.; Félix Alcan, Éditeur; Paris; 1901; pp. 270, 271.

582. GELEY, Gustave; "O Ser Subconsciente"; transl. and introd. Gilberto Campista Guarino; 230 pp.; 18 cm; pb.; Federação Espírita Brasileira; Rio de Janeiro; Brazil; 1975; pp. 91-94, 167; eds.: Fr., Sp., Port.

583. GELEY, Gustave; "Resumo da Doutrina Espírita"; transl. and introd. Isidoro Duarte Santos; pref. Jean Meyer; 194 pp.; glos. 171-189; 22 cm; pb.; 3rd ed.; Livraria Allan Kardec Editora; S. Paulo; Brazil; 1975; pp. 31, 32, 66, 67, 76-78, 172.

584. GERHARDI, William; "Resurrection"; Novel; Cassell & Co.; London; 1934.

585. GERTZ, John; "Hypnagogic Fantasy, EEG, and Psi Perfomance in a Single Subjet"; *The Journal of American Society for Psychical Research;* New York; Vol. 77; N. 2; April, 1983; bibl. 167-170; pp. 155-170.

586. GEYMULLER, Henry de; "Swedenborg et les Phénomènes Psychiques"; 462 pp.; bibl. 442-453; 22.5 cm; hb.; Librairie Ernest Leroux; Paris; no date; pp. 412-415.

587. GIBIER, Paul; "Análise das Cousas"; transl. and pref. T.; 234 pp.; illus.; 18 cm; hb.; 2nd ed.; Federação Espírita Brasileira; Rio de Janeiro; Brazil; 1934; pp. 105, 113-115, 117, 123-130.

588. GIBSON, Litzka R., and GIBSON, W. B.; "The Mystic and Occult Arts: A Guide to their Use in Daily Living"; 224 pp.; Parker Publishing Co.; West Nyack; N. Y.; U. S. A.; 1969.

589. GILBERT, Alice; "Philip in the Spheres"; Aquarian Press; London; 1952; pp. 17, 56, 101.

590. GILBERT, Alice; "Philip in Two Worlds"; pref. L. A. G. Strong; 242 pp.; 18.5 cm; hb.; Andrew Dakers; London; 1948; pp. 94, 113, 126-139.

591. GILDEA, William; "Nem Céu, Nem Inferno: Uma Luz Depois da Morte"; *O Globo;* Rio de Janeiro; Brazil; Newspaper; Daily; Yr. LII; N. 15.968; 30, June, 1977; illus.; p. 43.

592. GIOVETTI, Paola; "Qualcuno é Tornato"; pref. Emilio Servadio; 176 pp.; bibl. 174; 20 cm; pb.; Armenia Editore; Milano; Italy; 1981; pp. 8, 24, 43-58, 68.

593. GIOVETTI, Paola; "Viaggi Senza Corpo"; 160 pp.; bibl. 155, 156; 20 cm; pb.; Armenia Editore; Milano; Italy; 1983; pp. 1-160 (Mini-library).

594. GIOVETTI, Paola; "Le Visioni dei Morenti"; *Luce e Ombra;* Verona; Italy; Magazine; Quarterly; Yr. 80; N. 4; October-December, 1980; pp. 319-331.

595. GIROLAMO, Nancy Puhlmann Di; "O Castelo das Aves Feridas"; 100 pp.; 21 cm; pb.; Instituição Beneficente Nosso Lar; S. Paulo; Brazil; no date; pp. 13-98.

596. GLASKIN, Gerald M.; "A Door to Eternity: Proving the Christos Experience"; 184 pp.; illus.; bibl. 182, 183; 21.5 cm; hb.; dj.; Wildwood House; Bookwise; Australia; 1979; pp. 166-170.

597. GLASKIN, Gerald M.; "Mergulho Numa Vida Passada"; *Planeta;* S. Paulo; Brazil; Magazine; Monthly; N. 59; August, 1977; illus.; pp. 20-24.

598. GLASKIN, Gerald M.; "Windows of the Mind: The Christos Experiment"; 208 pp.; 21.5 cm; hb.; dj.; Wildwood House, London; 1974; pp. 11-18, 27-35, 177, 201.

599. GLASKIN, Gerald M.; "Worlds Within: Probing the Christos Experience"; 224 pp.; illus.; 21.5 cm; hb.; dj.; Wildwood House; London; 1976; pp. 214-223.

600. GLOBO, O; Editorial; "Americano Conta que Morreu e Gostou"; *O Globo;* Rio de Janeiro; Brazil; Newspaper; Daily; Yr. LIX; N. 18.171; 5, August, 1983; p.14.

601. GLOBO, O; Editorial; Apla; "A Enfermeira Morta Durante Duas Horas"; *O Globo;* Rio de Janeiro; Brazil; Newspaper; Daily; Yr. XXXVII; N. 10.890; 31, October, 1961; pp. 1, 2.

602. GLOBO, O; Editorial; "Normal e Paranormal: Onde Está a Realidade?"; *O Globo;* Rio de Janeiro; Brazil; Newspaper; Daily; Yr. LIII; N. 16.063; 3, October, 1977; p. 17.

603. GLOBO, O; Editorial; World Report; "Na Volta da Fronteira da Morte, Nova Visão da Vida"; *O Globo;* Rio de Janeiro; Brazil; Newspaper; Daily; Yr. LIX; N. 18.484; 17, June, 1984; illus.; p. 29.

604. GODWIN, John; "Occult America"; XII + 314 pp.; illus.; glos. 291-294; alph.; 21 cm; hb.; Doubleday and Co.; Garden City, N. Y.; U. S. A.; 1972; pp. 20, 112-120, 128, 194, 195.

605. GOES, Eurico de; "Prodígios da Biopsíquica Obtidos com o Médium Mirabelli"; 472 pp.; illus.; bibl. 429-466; 18 cm; hb.; Tipografia Cupolo; S. Paulo; Brazil; 1937; pp. 21, 25, 50, 91-93, 137, 142, 392-411, 440.

606. GOLDBERG, Bruce; "Past Lives Future Lives"; VI + 186 pp.; 21.5 cm; pb.; Newcastle Publishing Co.; North Hollywood, Cal.; U. S. A.; June, 1982; p, 24, 65, 172.

607. GOLDSTEIN, Karl W. (Pseud. for Hernani Guimarães Andrade); "A Gente Morre... E Depois? Existiria um Suporte Estrutural para o Modelo Organizador Biológico?"; *Folha Espírita;* S. Paulo; Brazil; Newspaper; Monthly; Yr. VIII; N. 89; August, 1981; illus.; pp. 4, 5 (See N. 27-30).

608. GOLDSTEIN, Karl W. (Pseud. for Hernani Guimarães Andrade); "Como Age Você Fora do Corpo Durante o Sono"; *Folha Espírita;* S. Paulo; Brazil; Newspaper; Monthly; Yr. V; N. 54; September, 1978; illus.; p. 5.

609. GOLDSTEIN, Karl W. (Pseud. for Hernani Guimarães Andrade); "Desdobramento Astral no Laboratório"; *Folha Espírita;* S. Paulo; Brazil; Newspaper; Monthly; Yr. V; N. 56; November, 1978; illus.; p. 5.

610. GOLDSTEIN, Karl W. (Pseud. for Hernani Guimarães Andrade); "Enquanto Você Dorme Seu Corpo Astral Pode Viajar Visitando Outros Mundos"; *Folha Espírita;* S. Paulo; Brazil; Newspaper; Monthly; Yr. V; N. 55; October, 1978; illus.; pp. 5, 7.

611. GOMES, Vera Braga de Souza; "Deus, o Universo e o Homem"; 146 pp.; illus.; bibl. 146; 21 cm; pb.; Mudra; Rio de Janeiro; Brazil; 1982; pp. 60, 65, 111, 123-125, 127.

612. GOMES, Vera Braga de Souza; "Intermediários do Além"; 228 pp.; illus.; bibl. 223; 20.5 cm; pb.; Mudra; Rio de Janeiro; Brazil; 1983; pp. 52-55, 57, 60, 72, 82-87, 113-118, 148, 171, 172.

613. GÓMEZ, Quintin López; "Glosario de Palavras Nuevas e Poco Comunes"; 178 pp.; 16 cm; hb.; José Ventayol Vilá; Tarrasa; Spain; 1926; pp. 22, 23.

614. GONÇALVES, Júlio César; "Eles Prometem Ensinar Você a Sair do Próprio Corpo"; *Shopping News-City News;* S. Paulo; Brazil; Newspaper; Yr. 18; N. 891; 10, October, 1982; illus.; pp. 1, 5.

615. GONZALES, Georges; "O que nos Espera Depois da Morte"; transl. and pref. Francisco Klörs Werneck; 140 pp.; 20 cm; pb.; Editora Eco; Rio de Janeiro; Brazil; 1969; pp. 35, 36.

616. GOOCH, Stan; "Creatures from Inner Space"; 252 pp.; bibl. 140-248; alph.; 21.5 cm; hb.; dj.; Rider & Co.; London, 1984; pp. 194, 205.

617. GOOCH, Stan; "The Paranormal"; VI + 314 pp.; illus.; glos. 298, 299; bibl. 300-306; alph.; 20.5 cm; hb.; dj.; Harper & Row, Publishers; New York; 1978; pp. 23, 24, 93-95, 149, 237, 238.

618. GOODMAN, Jeffrey; "Arqueología Psíquica"; transl. Gonzalo Zaragoza; prol. Paul S. Martin; 224 pp.; bibl. 215-224; 20 cm; pb.; Ediciones Martínez Roca; Barcelona; Spain; 1981; pp. 200-204.

619. GRAHAM, Winifred; "I Introduce"; Autobiography; 228 pp.; ilus; alph.; 21.5 cm; hb.; Skeffington and Son; London; no date; p. 57.

620. GRANGER, Michel; "L'Héritage des Extra-terrestres ou Panorama de la Médiumnité Moderne"; 256 pp.; illus.; 21 cm; pb.; Albin Michel; Paris; 1977; pp. 204, 205.

621. GRANJA, Pedro; "Afinal, Quem Somos? De Onde Viemos e Para Onde Vamos..."; pref. Monteiro Lobato; 394 pp.; bibl. 9-12; 21.5 cm; pb.; 5th ed.; Editora Brasiliense; S. Paulo; Brazil; 1951; pp. 62, 224, 229, 249, 331-345, 348.

622. GRANJA, Pedro; "Os Simples e os Sábios"; 266 pp.; bibl. 5, 6; 21.5 cm; pb.; Edição Calvário; S. Paulo; Brazil; 1971; pp. 225, 226.

623. GRANT-VEILLARD, Sim; "101 Respuestas Sobre los Poderes Sobrenaturales"; transl. Ricardo Vargas; 174 pp.; bibl. 165, 166; 19 cm; pb.; Sagitario Ediciones y Distribuciones; Barcelona; Spain; February, 1976; pp. 117, 125-129.

624. GRASSET, J.; "L'Occultisme Hier et Aujourd'hui"; pref. M. Émile Faguet; 472 pp.; bibl. 445-461; alph.; 19 cm; hb.; 2nd ed.; Coulet et Fils, Éditeurs; Montpellier; France; 1908; pp. 258-260.

625. GRASSET, J.; "Le Spiritisme Devant la Science"; pref. Pierre Janet; XXX + 392 pp.; bibl. 377-390; alph.; 19 cm; hb.; 2nd ed.; Masson & Cie., Éditeurs; Paris; 1904; pp. 83-96, 326.

626. GRATTAN-GUINNESS, Ivor; Editor; "Psychical Research: A Guide to its History, Principles and Practices"; 424 pp.; illus.; glos. 387-399; index of names; bibl. 88, 89; alph.; 21.5 cm; pb.; The Aquarian Press; Wellingborough, Northamptonshire; Great Britain; 1982; pp. 78-89, 110, 191, 297, 319, 326, 327, 351, 394, 399.

627. GRAVES, Tom, and HOULT, Janet; Editors; "The Essential T. C. Lethbridge"; introd. Colin Wilson; XX + 216 pp.; illus.; alph.; 21.5 cm; hb.; dj.; Routledge & Kegan Paul; London; 1980; pp. 150, 151.

628. GREEN, Celia Elizabeth; "Analysis of Spontaneous Cases"; *Proceedings of the Society for Psychical Research;* London; Vol. 53; Part 191; November, 1960; illus.; pp. 97-161.

629. GREEN, Celia Elizabeth; "The Decline and Fall of Science"; X + 184 pp.; glos. 176, 177; bibl. 178, 179; alph.; 21.5 cm; hb.; dj.; Hamish Hamilton; London; 1976; pp. 13, 59, 68, 75, 82-84, 86, 93-100, 112-118, 120, 126, 129, 133, 138, 154, 161, 176.

630. GREEN, Celia Elizabeth; "Ecsomatic Experiences and Related Phenomena"; *Journal of the Society for Psychical Research;* London; Vol. 44; N. 733; September, 1967; pp. 111-131.

631. GREEN, Celia Elizabeth; "Lucid Dreams"; pref. H. H. Price; 194 pp.; ono; alph.; 22 cm; hb.; dj.; Institute of Psychophysical Research; Oxford; Great Britain; 1968; pp. 18-22, 28-40, 50, 60-62, 68, 69, 71-74, 99, 123, 129, 130, 161-169, 172.

632. GREEN, Celia Elizabeth; "Out-of-the-Body Experiences"; 144 pp.; alph.; 22 cm; hb.; dj.; Institute of Psychophysical Research; Oxford; Great Britain; 1968; pp. 1-144; eds.: Eng., It. (Mini-library).

633. GREEN, Celia Elizabeth, and MC CREERY, Charles; "Apparitions"; X + 218 pp.; bibl. 213; alph.; 21.5 cm; hb.; dj.; Hamish Hamilton; London; 1975; pp. 4, 5, 9, 12, 20, 21, 26-32, 36, 37, 53-58, 61, 73, 74, 79, 83, 100, 107, 111, 112, 125, 127, 132, 134, 135, 142, 146, 159, 169, 174, 178, 183-187, 195, 211, 212.

634. GREEN, Edward; "O Espiritismo"; without translator; 202 pp.; 18 cm; hb.; Gráfica Editora Unitas; S. Paulo; Brazil; no date; pp. 103-118.

635. GREENE, Richard A.; "The Handbook of Astral Projection"; 156 pp.; glos. 103-106; 21.5 cm; pb.; Next Step Publications; Cambridge; Massachusetts; U. S. A.; 1979; pp. 1-156 (Mini-library).

636. GREENHOUSE, Herbert B.; "The Astral Journey"; 360 pp.; bibl.; 341-347; alph.; 21 cm; dj.; Doubleday & Co.; New York; 1975; pp. 1-360; eds.: Eng., It., Sp. (Mini-library).

637. GREENHOUSE, Herbert B.; "The Book of Psychic Knowledge"; 254 pp.; bibl. 247-253; Taplinger; New York; 1973.

638. GREENHOUSE, Herbert B.; "In Defense of Ghosts"; VIII + 254 pp.; 22 cm; 2nd ed.; Simon; New York; 1970.

639. GREENHOUSE, Herbert B.; "Premonitions: A Leap into the Future"; 320 pp.; alph.; 18 cm; pocket; pb.; Pan Books; London; 1975; pp. 58, 59, 309.

640. GREGORY, Clive C. L.; and KOHSEN, Anita; "Physical and Psychical Research: An Analysis of Belief"; X + 214 pp.; illus.; bibl. 211-213; 21.5 cm; hb.; The Omega Press; Reigate; Surrey; Great Britain; 1954; pp. 143, 194, 199.

641. GREGORY, William; "Animal Magnetism"; 254 pp.; 22 cm; W. H. Harrison; London; 1877.

642. GRENSIDE, Dorothy; "The Meaning of Dreams"; G. Bell & Sons; London; 1923; pp. 48, 117.

643. GREYSON, Bruce; "Telepathy in Mental Illness: Deluge or Delusion?"; *The Journal of Nervous and Mental Disease;* Baltimore; Maryland; U. S. A.; Vol. 165; N. 8; 1977; bibl. 198-200; pp. 184-200.

644. GRIMARD, Ed.; "Une Échappée sur L'Infini"; X + 418 pp.; 18 cm; hb.; Leymarie Éditeur; Paris; 1899; pp. 286, 287, 356.

645. GRIS, Henry, and DICK, William; "The New Soviet Psychic Discoveries"; 448 pp.; alph.; 18 cm; pocket; pb.; Warner Books; New York; March, 1979; pp. 434, 435.

646. GROF, Stanislav; "Realms of the Human Unconscious: Observations from LSD Research"; XXVI + 260 pp.; illus.; bibl. 245, 246; alph.; 21 cm; pb.; E. P. Dutton; Toronto; Canada; 1976; pp. 186-190.

647. GROF, Stanislav, and GROF, Christina; "Beyond Death: The Gates of Consciousness"; 96 pp.; illus.; bibl. 96; 28 cm; cart.; Thames and Hudson; London; 1980; pp. 9-14, 25.

648. GROF, Stanislav, and HALIFAX, Joan; "The Human Encounter With Death"; pref. Elisabeth Kübler-Ross; XVI + 240 pp.; bibl. 222-228; alph.; 21 cm; pb.; E. P. Dutton; New York; 1978; pp. 154, 155.

649. GROSS, Darwin; "Ihr Recht Zu Wissen"; transl. Steve De Witt; introd. Bernardine Burlin; 190 pp.; 18 cm; pocket; pb.; IWP Publishing; Menlo Park; Cal.; U. S. A.; 1980; pp. 79, 84-87, 93.

650. GROSSO, Michael; "Out-of-Body Experiences: A Handbook" (Janet Lee Mitchell); Books Reviews; *The Journal of the American Society for Psychical Research;* New York; Magazine; Monthly; Vol. 76; N. 2; April, 1982; pp. 186-188.

651. GROSSO, Michael; "Plato and Out-of-the-Body Experiences"; *The Journal of the American Society for Psychical Research;* New York; Magazine; Monthly; Vol. 69; N. 1; January, 1975; bibl. 74; pp. 61-74.

652. GROSSO, Michael; "A Practical Guide to Death and Dying" (John Warren White); Books Reviews; *The Journal of the American Society for Psychical Research;* New York; Magazine; Monthly; Vol. 76; N. 1; January, 1982; pp. 75-78.

653. GROSSO, Michael; "Some Varieties of Out-of-Body Experience"; *The Journal of the American Society for Psychical Research;* New York; Magazine; Monthly; Vol. 70; N. 2; April, 1976; bibl. 192, 193; pp. 179-193.

654. GROSSO, Michael; "Toward an Explanation of Near-Death Phenomena"; *The Journal of the American Society for Psychical Research;* New York; Magazine; Monthly; Vol. 75; N. 1; January, 1981; pp. 37-60.

655. GUAITA, Stanislas de; "No Umbral do Mistério"; transl. José Antônio Faria Corrêa; ed. André Pitágoras; 142 pp.; illus.; 22.5 cm; pb.; Grafosul; Porto Alegre, RS; Brazil; 1979; pp. 92, 116, 117.

656. GUARINO, Gilberto Campista; "Clarividência, Precognição, Espaço-Tempo e Domínio Informacional Omnijacente"; *Anais do III Congresso Nacional de Parapsicologia e Psicotrônica;* pp. 40-57; illus.; 24 cm; pb.; Abrap; Rio de Janeiro; Brazil; July, 1982; pp. 48, 51 (See N. 281).

657. GUDJONSSON, Thorsteinn; "Astrobiology: The Science of the Universe"; 202 pp.; illus.; Bioradii Publications; Reykjavík; Iceland; 1976.

658. GUDJONSSON, Thorsteinn; "Dreams are the Key to the Cosmos"; introd. John Alexander; 176 pp.; illus.; 19.5 cm; pb.; Bioradii Publications; Reykjavík; Iceland; 1982; pp. 110-126.

659. GUÉRET, André, and OUDINOT, Pierre; "O Homem e os Imponderáveis"; transl. J. Constantino K. Riemma; 190 pp.; illus.; bibl. 188-190.; 19.5 cm; pb.; Editora Pensamento; S. Paulo; Brazil; 1982; pp. 64, 161-166.

660. GUIEU, Jimmy; "El Libro de los Paranormales"; transl. Sofía Noguera; 254 pp.; illus.; 19.5 cm; pb.; A. T. E.; Barcelona; Spain; 1978; pp. 83-87, 95-98.

661. GUILMOT, Max; "Les Initiés et les Rites Initiatiques en Egypte Ancienne"; 266 pp.; illus.; alph.; 21.5 cm; pb.; Éditions Robert Laffont; Paris; 1977; pp. 57-60.

662. GUIMARÃES, Salô; "Projeção Consciente"; *O Caminheiro;* Newspaper; Bimonthly; S. Paulo; Brazil; Yr. 2; N. 18; November-December, 1982; illus.; p. 15.

663. GUIRAO, Pedro; "Dossier del Mas Alla"; 240 pp.; 18 cm; pocket; pb.; Plaza & Janes; Barcelona; Spain; May, 1980; pp. 40, 42, 50, 99, 127, 179-190.

664. GUIRDHAM, Arthur; "Entre Dois Mundos"; transl. Norberto de Paula Lima and Márcio Pugliesi; 198 pp.; illus.; 19.5 cm; pb.; Editora Pensamento; S. Paulo; Brazil; no date; pp. 10, 34-37, 43, 47, 86, 119, 120.

665. GUIRDHAM, Arthur; "The Nature of Healing"; George Allen & Unwin; London; 1964; p. 65.

666. GURNEY, Edmund; MYERS, Frederic William Henry; and PODMORE, August Frank; "Phantasms of the Living"; 2 Vol.; 1.420 pp.; 22 cm; hb.; Trübner and Co.; London; 1886; Vol. I: pp. LXI-LXIV, 204-220, 230, 231, 251-254, 347-358, 420-424; Vol. II: pp. 61-71, 82-86, 130-152, 169-270, 386-560, 600-641 (Mini-library).

667. GYNSKA, Tola; "A Escada de Ouro de Vênus"; transl. Marysia Fontoura Leinz; pref. André Doffagne; 140 pp.; 21.5 cm; pb.; Centro Espiritual Vahali-Brasil; S. Paulo; Brazil; 1978; pp. 13, 14.

668. HAEMMERLÉ, A.; "Experiences of Bilocation"; *Annals of Psychical Science;* Vol. 4; 1906; pp. 113-119.

669. HALES, Carol; "Astral Errand of Mercy"; *Fate;* Evanston; Ill.; U. S. A.; Magazine; Monthly; Vol. 16; N. 9; September, 1963.

670. HALL, Prescott F.; "Digest of Spirit Teachings Received Through Mrs. Minnie E. Keeler"; *The Journal of the American Society for Psychical Research;* Vol. X; November-December, 1916; pp. 632-661, 679-708.

671. HALL, Prescott F.; "Experiments in Astral Projection"; *The Journal of the American Society for Psychical Research;* New York; Vol. XII; January, 1918; pp. 39-60.

672. HALLOCK, Charles; "Luminous Bodies: Here and Hereafter"; 110 pp.; Metaphysical Publishing Co.; New York; 1906.

673. HAMLYN, E. C.; "Medical Man Says Astral Projection is Commonplace"; *Psychic News;* London; N. 2.174; 02, February, 1974; p. 5.

674. HAMMOND, C. L.; "Lost Secrets from Ancient Mystery Schools"; Vol. One; XIV + 222 pp.; 20.5 cm; hb.; dj.; New Horizon; Great Britain; 1984; pp. XIII, 9, 58, 139, 153, 155, 159, 161, 167-169, 216.

675. HAMMOND, David; "The Search for Psychic Power"; 292 pp.; alph.; 18 cm; pocket; pb.; Bantam Books; New York; 1975; pp. 11, 104-122, 146, 147; eds.: Eng., Sp.

676. HAMPTON, Charles; "The Transition Called Death: A Recurring Experience"; introd. Joy Mills; 116 pp.; illus.; bibl. 111-116; 18 cm; pb.; The Theosophical Publishing House; Wheaton, Ill.; U. S. A.; 1979; pp. 6-10, 16-19, 26, 30, 39, 43-53, 77; eds.: Eng., Port.

677. HANKEY, Muriel Winifred; "James Hewat McKenzie: Pioneer of Psychical Research"; Biography; 158 pp.; illus.; alph.; 21.5 cm; hb.; dj.; Helix Press; New York; 1963; pp. 29, 125-127, 130-132.

678. HAPGOOD, Charles H.; "Voices of Spirit: Through the Psychic Experience of Elwood Babbitt"; 336 pp.; illus.; glos. 321-328; bibl. 329-332; alph.; 23 cm; hb.; dj.; Delacorte Press/Seymour Lawrence; New York; 1975; pp. 75, 176-184, 325; eds.: Eng., Port.

679. HARARY, Stuart Keith, and SOLFVIN, G.; "A Study of Out-of-Body Experiences Using Auditory Targets"; *Research in Parapsychology 1976;* The Scarecrow Press; Metuchen, N. J.; U. S. A.; 1977.

680. HARE, Michael; "The Multiple Universe: On the Nature of Spiritual Reality"; 198 pp.; bibl.; Julian Press; New York; 1968.

681. HARLOW, S. Ralph; "Life After Death"; introd. Enid Hoffman; 174 pp.; 23.5 cm; pb.; Para Research; Rockport, Massachusetts; U. S. A.; 1982; pp. 7, 8, 112.

682. HARLOW, S. Ralph; "SOS: Traumtelepatie"; transl. E. M. Körner; *Esotera;* Freiburg; West Germany; Magazine; Monthly; Yr. 21; N. 4; April, 1970; pp. 320, 321.

683. HARNOLD, Hans; "Como se Organizam e se Dirigem as Sessões Espíritas"; without translator; 170 pp.; 18 cm; pb.; Empresa Editora O Pensamento; S. Paulo; Brazil; 1926; pp. 24, 35-37.

684. HARRIS, Bertha; "Traveller in Eternity"; 64 pp.; Regency Press; London; 1975; pp. 1-64.

685. HARRISON, Shirley, and FRANKLIN, Lynn; "The Psychic Search"; introd. Allan A. Swenson; VIII + 152 pp.; illus.; 23 cm; pb.; Guy Gannett Publishing; Portland, Maine; U. S. A.; 1981; pp. 103, 104.

686. HARRISON, William H.; "Spirits Before Our Eyes"; 220 pp.; W. H. Harrison; London; 1879.

687. HART, Hornell Norris; "The Enigma of Survival: The Case For and Against an After Life"; 286 pp.; illus.; bibl. 264-276; alph.; 21 cm; hb.; dj.; Charles C. Thomas, Publisher; Springfield, Ill.; U. S. A.; 1959; pp. 159, 160, 175, 182-185, 200, 203, 204, 225-228, 241-245, 260, 261 (Mini-library).

688. HART, Hornell Norris; "ESP Projection: Spontaneous Cases and the Experimental Method"; *The Journal of the American Society for Psychical Research;* New York; 1954; pp. 121-146.

689. HART, Hornell Norris; "Toward a New Philosophical Basis for Parapsychological Phenomena"; 68 pp.; illus.; 23 cm; pb.; Parapsychology Foundation; New York; 1965; pp. 15-22, 45, 46.

690. HART, Hornell Norris; "Six Theories About Apparitions"; *Proceedings of the Society for Psychical Research;* London; Vol. 50; Part 185; May, 1956; pp. 153-239.

691. HART, Hornell Norris; "Travelling ESP"; *Proceedings of the First International Conference of Parapsychological Studies;* Parapsychology Foundation; New York; 1955.

692. HART, Hornell Norris, and HART, Ella B.; "Visions and Apparitions Collectivelly and Reciprocally Perceived"; *Proceedings of the Society for Psychical Research;* Vol. XLI; Part 130; May, 1933; pp. 205-249.

693. HARTMANN, Franz; "Magic White and Black"; 298 pp.; illus.; 22 cm; pb.; 5th ed.; Newcastle Publishing Co.; North Hollywood, Cal.; U. S. A.; 1971; pp. 164-182.

694. HAUTERIVE, Ernest D'; "Le Merveilleux au XVIIIe. Siècle"; 264 pp.; bibl. 255-259; 17.5 cm; hb.; Félix Juven, Éditeur; Paris; no date; pp. 88-93.

695. HAY, David; "Exploring Inner Space"; 256 pp.; bibl. 236-246; alph.; 20 cm; pb.; Penguin Books; Great Britain; 1982; p. 136.

696. HAYNES, Renée; "Las Fuerzas Ocultas"; transl. Jose Angel de Juanes; 278 pp.; illus.; alph.; 21 cm; pb.; Ediciones Morata; Madrid; Spain; 1962; pp. 88, 89, 93, 263.

697. HAYNES, Renée; "Out-of-the-Body Experiences"; *Journal of the Society for Psychical Research;* London; Vol. 41; N. 707; March, 1961; p. 52.

698. HAYNES, Renée; "The Seeing Eye, the Seeing I; Perception, Sensory and Extra-Sensory"; 224 pp.; alph.; 21.5 cm; hb.; dj.; Hutchinson & Co.; London; 1976; pp. 13, 76, 93, 142, 148, 149, 158, 207, 208.

699. HEAD, Joseph, and CRANSTON, S. L.; "Reincarnation: The Phoenix Fire Mystery"; 620 pp.; 23 cm; hb.; Julian Press / Crown Publishers; New York; 1977; pp. 413, 414, 448-455.

700. HEAPS, Willard A.; "Psychic Phenomena"; 192 pp.; bibl. 172-183; alph.; 20 cm; hb.; dj.; Thomas Nelson, Publishers; Nashville, Tenessee; U. S. A.; 1974; pp. 31, 45, 168, 182, 183.

701. HEGEDÜS, Alejandro; "Los Fenómenos Extranormales"; 378 pp.; bibl. 373, 374; 20 cm; cart.; Editorial Kier; Buenos Aires; Argentina; 1962; pp. 272-293.

702. HEIM, Albert; "Notizen über den Tod durch Absturz"; Jahrbuch des Schweizer Alpenclub; Vol. 27; 1892; pp. 327-337.

703. HEINDEL, Max (Pseud. for Carl Louis Grasshoff); "El Cuerpo de Deseos"; without translator; 144 pp.; 20 cm; pb.; 3rd ed.; Editorial Kier; Buenos Aires; Argentina; 1977; pp. 55-59.

704. HEINDEL, Max (Pseud. for Carl Louis Grasshoff); "El Cuerpo Vital"; without translator; 150 pp.; 20 cm; pb.; 3rd ed.; Editorial Kier; Buenos Aires; Argentina; 1977; pp. 71-91.

705. HEINDEL, Max (Pseud. for Carl Louis Grasshoff); "Diccionario Rosacruz"; without translator; 158 pp.; illus.; 19.5 cm; pb.; 2nd ed.; Editorial Kier; Buenos Aires; Argentina; 1977; pp. 20-22, 47.

706. HEINE, H. G.; "The Vital Sense: The Implications and Explanation of the Sixth Sense"; VIII + 296 pp.; bibl. 279-285; alph.; 21.5 cm; hb.; dj.; Cassell and Co.; London; 1960; pp. 116, 130, 133, 183-186, 203, 204, 258, 259, 263-268.

707. HEINTSCHEL-HEINEGG, Aglaja; "Der innere Kompass bei Tieren und Menschen"; *Esotera;* Freiburg; West Germany; Magazine; Monthly; Yr. 24; N. 5; May, 1973; illus.; pp. 395-403.

708. HEINTSCHEL-HEINEGG, Aglaja; "Kontakte mit Unsichtbaren? Mediales Erleben"; 218 pp.; bibl. 248-250; alph.; 18 cm; pocket; pb.; Fischer Taschenbuch Verlag; Frankfurt; West Germany; 1980; pp. 120-138, 146, 149, 150, 229, 241, 244.

709. HELB, Dies; "O Desdobramento"; *Planeta;* S. Paulo; Brazil; Magazine; Monthly; N. 57; June, 1977; pp. 26-33.

710. HEMINGWAY, Ernest; "A Farewell to Arms"; Novel; 288 pp.; 19 cm; hb.; Jonathan Cape; London; 1958; p. 53.

711. HEMMERLIN, Emmanuel; "Les Expériences Hors du Corps en Relation Avec la Mort Physique"; *Renaître 2000;* Paris; Magazine; Quarterly; 125th and 126th Yr.; New series; Numbers 29, 30, 31; August-October, 1982; pp. 157, 158, 174; November-December, 1982; pp. 213-216; January-February, 1983; pp. 7-10.

712. HEMMERT, Danielle, and ROUDÈNE, Alex; "Aparições, Fantasmas e Desdobramentos"; transl. Nastia Sliozkin; 206 pp.; illus.; bibl. 204, 205; 21 cm; pb.; Publicações Europa-América; Mira-Sintra; Portugal; no date; pp. 8, 9, 13-61, 175-200; eds.: Fr., Port.

713. HEMMERT, Danielle, and ROUDÈNE, Alex; "O Universo dos Espíritos"; transl. Attílio Cancian; 202 pp.; bibl. 199; 21 cm; pb.; Hemus Editora; S. Paulo; Brazil; 1984; pp. 29-71.

714. HERLIN, Hans; "O Mundo Extra-Sensorial"; transl. Ruy Jungmann; 208 pp.; 21 cm; pb.; 2nd ed.; Distribuidora Record; Rio de Janeiro; Brazil; no date; pp. 177-188; eds.: Ger., Sp., Port.

715. HERMÓGENES, José; "Yoga para Nervosos"; pres. Oswaldo Paulino; 390 pp.; illus.; glos. 371-380; bibl. 381-390; 21 cm; pb.; 18th ed.; Editora Record; Rio de Janeiro; Brazil; 1984; pp. 259-264 (See N. 32).

716. HEYDECKER, Joe J.; "Fatos da Parapsicologia"; transl. Edith Wagner; 108 pp.; illus.; 23 cm; pb.; Livraria Freitas Bastos; Rio de Janeiro; Brazil; 1984; p. 49.

717. HEYWOOD, Rosalind; "Beyond the Reach of Sense"; 252 pp.; alph.; 21 cm; pb.; E. P. Dutton & Co.; New York; 1974; p. 242.

718. HEYWOOD, Rosalind; "ESP: A Personal Memoir"; Autobiography; introd. Cyril Burt; 222 pp.; 21 cm; hb.; dj.; E. P. Dutton & Co.; New York; 1964; pp. 103, 104.

719. HEYWOOD, Rosalind; "Out-of-the-Body Experiences"; *Journal of the Society for Psychical Research;* London; Vol. 42; N. 716; June, 1963; p. 86.

720. HILL, Douglas; "O Regresso dos Mortos"; transl. Maria de Lourdes Medeiros; 120 pp.; illus.; 20 cm; pb.; Edilivro; Lisboa; Portugal; 1980; pp. 52, 53.

721. HILL, Douglas, and WILLIAMS, Pat; "The Supernatural"; 352 pp.; illus.; alph.; 24 cm; hb.; Hawthorn Books Publishers; New York; 1965; pp. 106, 322.

722. HILL, J. Arthur; "Man is a Spirit"; 120 pp.; Cassell and Co.; London; 1918; pp. 43, 73.

723. HILL, J. Arthur; "New Evidences in Psychical Research"; introd. Oliver Lodge; 218 pp.; alph.; 19 cm; hb.; William Rider & Son; London; 1911; pp. 13-21.

724. HILL, J. Arthur; "Psychical Investigations"; 304 pp.; alph.; 21 cm; hb.; George H. Doran Co.; New York; 1917; p. 250.

725. HILLS, Christopher; "Nuclear Evolution, Discovery of the Rainbow Body"; XIV + 1.010 pp.; illus.; alph.; 23.5 cm; pb.; University of the Trees Press; Boulder Creek, Cal.; U. S. A.; 1979; p. 89.

726. HINTZE, Naomi A., and PRATT, J. Gaither; "The Psychic Realm: What can You Believe?"; pref. Ian Stevenson; 270 pp.; bibl. 255-263; alph.; 21 cm; hb.; dj.; Random House; New York; 1975; pp. 86-96.

727. HITCHING, Francis; "The World Atlas of Mysteries"; 256 pp.; illus.; bibl. 242-248; alph.; 29 cm; cart.; 6th print.; Pan Books; London; 1983; pp. 82-85, 106, 107.

728. HIVES, Frank; "Glimpses Into Infinity"; pref. Mrs. Philip Champion de Crespigny; introd. G. Lumley; XXXIV + 278 pp.; 17.5 cm; hb.; John Lane the Bodley Head; London; 1931; pp. 7-11, 69-142.

729. HODSON, Geoffrey; "Basic Theosophy"; 572 pp.; illus.; bibl. 339, 340; 21 cm; hb.; dj.; The Theosophical Publishing House; Adyar, Madras; India; 1981; pp. 73-76, 138-142, 157, 158, 164.

730. HODSON, Geoffrey; "O Reino dos Deuses"; transl. Carmen Penteado Piza and Joaquim Gervásio de Figueiredo; 258 pp.; illus.; 23.5 cm; hb.; Sociedade Teosófica do Brasil; S. Paulo; Brazil; 1967; p. 247.

731. HODSON, Geoffrey; "The Science of Seership"; 224 pp.; illus.; alph.; 22 cm; hb.; 5th print.; The Occult Book Society; London; no date; p. 215.

732. HOFFMAN, Enid; "Develop Your Psychic Skills"; 184 pp.; bibl. 177, 178; alph.; 23.5 cm; pb.; Para Research; Rockport, Massachusetts; U. S. A.; 1982; pp. 35, 38, 39, 61.

733. HOFFMAN, Enid; "Huna: A Beginner's Guide"; 220 pp.; illus.; bibl. 213-215; alph.; 23.5 cm; pb.; 5th print.; Para Research; Rockport, Massachusetts; U. S. A.; 1982; pp. 19, 55.

734. HOLLOWAY, Gilbert N.; "O Médium e sua Percepção Extra-Sensorial"; transl. Almira B. Guimarães and Ebréia de Castro Alves; 192 pp.; 21 cm; pb.; 2nd ed.; Editora Pallas; Rio de Janeiro; Brazil; 1982; pp. 21, 112, 113, 145, 146.

735. HOLMS, Archibald Campbell; "The Facts of Psychic Science"; pref. Leslie A. Shepard; XXVI + 512 pp.; index of names; alph.; 23.5 cm; hb.; dj.; University Books; New York; 1969; pp. 448-469.

736. HOLROYD, Stuart; "Alien Intelligence"; 232 pp.; illus.; bibl. 227-229; alph.; 23.5 cm; hb.; dj.; Everest House Publishers; New York; 1979; pp. 97-124, 141, 142.

737. HOLROYD, Stuart; "Los Fenómenos de la Parapsicología"; transl. José Luis Alvarez; 144 pp.; 26 cm; hb.; Editorial Noguer; Barcelona; Spain; 1976; pp. 16, 17, 22-25, 41-43, 101.

738. HOLROYD, Stuart; "El Mundo de los Sueños"; transl. Alfredo Andrés; 144 pp.; illus.; 26 cm; hb.; Editorial Noguer; Barcelona; Spain; 1977; pp.72-78.

739. HOLROYD, Stuart; "PSI and the Consciousness Explosion"; 236 pp.; alph.; 21 cm; hb.; dj.; Taplinger Publishing Co.; New York; 1977; pp. 17, 75-77, 155, 156.

740. HOLROYD, Stuart; "Psychic Voyages"; 144 pp.; illus.; 26 cm; hb.; Doubleday and Co.; New York; 1977; pp. 46-85.

741. HOLT, Henry; "On the Cosmic Relations"; 2 Vol.; XII + 990 pp.; alph.; 22 cm; hb.; Houghton Mifflin Co.; New York; February, 1915; pp. 881-913.

742. HOLZER, Hans; "Carismática"; transl. Maria Stella Bruce; 154 pp.; 21 cm; pb.; 5th ed.; Editora Record; Rio de Janeiro; Brazil; no date; pp. 98-103.

743. HOLZER, Hans; "The Directory of the Occult"; 202 pp.; glos. 189-201; 21 cm; hb.; dj.; Henry Regnery Co.; Chicago, Ill.; U. S. A.; 1974; pp. 190, 192.

744. HOLZER, Hans; "Extra-Sensory Perception and You"; 216 pp.; 21 cm; hb.; dj.; Leslie Frewin Publishers; London; 1969; pp. 42-50, 98, 99.

745. HOLZER, Hans; "Interpretación Práctica de los Sueños"; transl. Celia Filipetto; 190 pp.; bibl. 187; 20 cm; pb.; Ediciones Martínez Roca; Barcelona; Spain; 1981; pp. 56, 57, 161-174.

746. HOLZER, Hans; "Janela Sobre o Passado"; transl. Affonso Blacheyre; 240 pp.; illus.; 21 cm; pb.; Distribuidora Record; Rio de Janeiro; Brazil; no date; pp. 21-23, 120, 121.

747. HOLZER, Hans; "O Lado Psíquico dos Sonhos"; transl. Vera Day; 176 pp.; 21 cm; pb.; Editora Record; Rio de Janeiro; Brazil; 1976; pp. 33, 122-136.

748. HOLZER, Hans; "The Psychic World of Bishop Pike"; 224 pp.; alph.; 21 cm; hb.; dj.; Crown Publishers; New York; 1970; pp. 156, 158.

749. HOLZER, Hans; "O Sobrenatural ao Nosso Alcance"; transl. Luíza Ribeiro; 178 pp.; 21 cm; pb.; Editorial Nórdica; Rio de Janeiro; Brazil; 1977; pp. 55-64.

750. HOLZER, Hans; "Supervivientes de la Muerte"; transl. Horacio González Trejo; 172 pp.; 19.5 cm; pb.; Ediciones Martínez Roca; Barcelona; Spain; 1980; pp. 13-27.

751. HOLZER, Hans; "The Truth About ESP"; 176 pp.; 21 cm; hb.; dj.; Doubleday & Co.; New York; 1974; pp. 93-114.

752. HOME, Daniel Dunglas; "Révélations sur Ma Vie Surnaturelle"; 338 pp.; 18.5 cm; pb.; 2nd ed.; Didier et Cie, E. Dentu; Paris; 1863; pp. 56-82.

753. HONEGGER, Barbara; "The OBE as a Near-Birth Experience"; *In* Research in Parapsychology; 1982; The Scarecrow Press; Metuchen, N. J.; U. S. A.; pp. 230, 231.

754. HONEGGER, Barbara, and PALMER, John; "Correspondence"; *Parapsychology Review;* New York; Vol. 10; N. 2; March-April, 1979; pp. 24-27.

755. HOOPER, Judith; "Interview John Lilly"; *Omni;* New York; Magazine; Monthly; Vol. V; N. 4; January, 1983; illus.; pp.56-58, 74, 76, 78-82.

756. HOPE, Murry; "Practical Techniques of Psychic Self-Defense"; 96 pp.; alph.; 18 cm; pb.; The Aquarian Press; Wellingborough; Northamptonshire; Great Britain; 1983; pp. 46, 49-55.

757. HORIA, Vintila; "Encuesta Detras de lo Visible"; 256 pp.; 18 cm; pocket; pb.; Plaza & Janes; Barcelona; Spain; February, 1980; pp. 115-125, 160, 161.

758. HOSSRI, Cesário Morey; "Prática do Treinamento Autógeno & LSD"; 158 pp.; illus.; bibl. 151-154; 21 cm; pb.; Editora Mestre Jou; S. Paulo; Brazil; 1968; pp. 99-101, 105, 148.

759. HOSSRI, Cesário Morey; "Sonho Acordado Dirigido"; 172 pp.; illus.; bibl. 163-170; 21 cm; pb.; Editora Mestre Jou; S. Paulo; Brazil; 1974; pp. 128, 129.

760. HOSSRI, Cesário Morey; "Tratamento Autógeno e Equilíbrio Psicotônico"; 124 pp.; illus.; bibl. 120-122; 21 cm; pb.; 4th ed.; Editora Mestre Jou; S. Paulo; Brazil; 1978; p.73.

761. HOWARD, Michael; "Candle Burning, Its Occult Significance"; 96 pp.; alph.; 18 cm; pb.; 2nd print.; The Aquarian Press; Wellingborough, Northamptonshire; Great Britain; 1982; pp. 84, 85.

762. HUBER, Guido; "Übersinnliche Gaben"; pref. Peter Ringger; 148 pp.; bibl. 146, 147; 20 cm; hb.; dj.; Origo Verlag; Zürich; Switzerland; 1959; pp. 23, 94, 109.

763. HUBER, Lela; "Gegenseitiger Astral besuch"; transl. E. M. Körner; *Esotera;* Freiburg; West Germany; Magazine; Monthly; Yr. 21; N. 10; Oktober, 1970; p. 941.

764. HUDSON, Thomson Jay; "The Law of Psychic Phenomena"; introd. Erwin Seale; 410 pp.; 18 cm; pb.; Samuel Weiser; New York; 1975; pp. 185-190, 289, 290; eds.: Eng., Port.

765. HUFFORD, David J.; "The Terror that Comes in the Night"; 278 pp.; bibl.; alph.; University of Pennsylvania Press; Philadelphia, PA; U. S. A.; 1982.

766. HUMPHREYS, Christmas; "O Zen-Budismo"; transl. Louisa Ibañez; 188 pp.; bibl. 183-187; 21 cm; pb.; Zahar Editores; Rio de Janeiro; Brazil; 1977; pp. 123-131.

767. HUNT, Douglas; "Exploring the Occult"; 220 pp.; 18 cm; pocket; pb.; 2nd print.; Ballantine Books; New York; April, 1970; pp. 50-62, 192, 193.

768. HUSON, Paul; "How to Test and Develop Your ESP"; 216 pp.; illus.; glos. 197-203; bibl. 204-207; alph.; 23.5 cm; hb.; dj.; Stein and Day Publishers; New York; 1975; pp. 65, 101-117, 193, 194, 199, 200.

769. HUTCHINGS, Emily Grant; "Where do we go from Here? The Journey of Life"; 306 pp.; Putnam's; New York; 1933.

770. HUXLEY, Aldous Leonard; "A Ilha"; Novel; transl. Gisela Brigitte Laub; 358 pp.; 21 cm; pb.; 6th ed.; Editora Civilização Brasileira; Rio de Janeiro; Brazil; 1971; pp. 45-48, 320, 325, 326.

771. HUXLEY, Aldous Leonard; "Moksha"; Anthology; transl. Eliana Sabino; org. Michel Horowitz and Cynthia Palmer; introd. Albert Hofmann and Alexander Shulgin; 330 pp.; alph.; 21 cm; pb.; Editora Globo; Rio de Janeiro; Brazil; 1983; pp. 83, 84, 98, 99, 234-240, 263, 267.

772. HUXLEY, Aldous Leonard; "As Portas da Percepção"; transl. and pref. Oswaldo de Araújo Souza; 46 pp.; 21 cm; pb.; 9th ed.; Editora Globo; Porto Alegre, RS; Brazil; 1979; pp. 29-30.

773. HYSLOP, James H.; "Psychical Research and Survival"; X + 208 pp.; bibl. 207, 208; 18.5 cm; hb.; G. Bell & Sons; London; 1913; pp. 135-137, 144.

774. IBRAHIM, Yosip; "Mi Preparacion para Ganimedes"; 208 pp.; illus.; 20 cm; pb.; 5th ed.; Editorial Ganimedes; Buenos Aires; Argentina; November, 1976; pp. 149-155.

775. IMBASSAHY, Carlos; "Espiritismo"; *in* "Religiões Comparadas: Oito Sínteses Doutrinárias"; 228 pp.; illus.; 22.5 cm; pb.; Cruzada Espiritualista; Rio de Janeiro; Brazil; 1929; pp. 148, 158, 159.

776. IMBASSAHY, Carlos; "A Evolução"; pref. Pedro Granja; 362 pp.; 21 cm; pb.; Livraria da Federação Espírita do Paraná; Curitiba, PR; Brazil; 1955; pp. 251-264.

777. IMBASSAHY, Carlos; "Freud e as Manifestações da Alma"; 252 pp.; 20.5 cm; pb.; Editora Eco; Rio de Janeiro; Brazil; no date; pp. 138, 139.

778. IMBASSAHY, Carlos; "Hipóteses em Parapsicologia"; pref. José Alberto Menezes; 276 pp.; 21 cm; pb.; Editora Eco; Rio de Janeiro; Brazil; 1967; pp. 206-209.

779. IMBASSAHY, Carlos; "À Margem do Espiritismo"; pref. Guillon Ribeiro; 256 pp.; 17.5 cm; hb.; 2nd ed.; Federação Espírita Brasileira; Rio de Janeiro; Brazil; 1950; pp. 115-120.

780. IMBASSAHY, Carlos; "O Que é a Morte"; pref. José Herculano Pires; 190 pp.; bibl. 187-189; 21 cm; pb.; Editora Cultural Espírita; S. Paulo; Brazil; 1978; pp. 82-135.

781. IMBASSAHY, Carlos, and GRANJA, Pedro; "Fantasmas, Fantasias e Fantoches"; pref. Júlio Abreu Filho; 400 pp.; 21.5 cm; pb.; Édipo, Edições Populares; S. Paulo; Brazil; September, 1950; p. 382.

782. IMBASSAHY, Carlos de Brito; "Classificacion de los Fenomenos Paranormales"; *Evolucion;* Caracas; Venezuela; Magazine; Monthly; Yr. XVI; N. 74; Octubre, 1984; illus.; pp. 9-12.

783. IMBASSAHY, Carlos de Brito; "Quando os Fantasmas se Divertem"; pref. Hernani Guimarães Andrade; 14 + 176 pp.; 18.5 cm; pb.; Casa Editora O Clarim; Matão, SP; Brazil; 1971; pp. 127, 128.

784. IMPERATOR (Pseud.); "Pode a Consciência ser Projetada?"; *O Rosacruz;* Magazine; Monthly; August, 1978; illus.; pp. 124-127.

785. IMPERATOR (Pseud.); "A Projeção da Consciência"; *O Rosacruz;* Magazine; Monthly; February, 1983; illus.; pp. 52-55.

786. INARDI, Massimo; "A História da Parapsicologia"; transl. A. J. Pinto Ribeiro; 310 pp.; bibl. 303-305; 22 cm; pb.; Edições 70; Lisboa; Portugal; July, 1979; pp. 148-150.

787. INARDI, Massimo; "O Sexto Sentido"; transl. Attílio Cancian; 220 pp.; illus.; bibl. 215-217; 21 cm; pb.; Hemus; S. Paulo; Brazil; 1977; pp. 93-203.

788. INGBER, Dina; "Visões de Além da Morte"; *Ciência Ilustrada;* S. Paulo; Brazil; Magazine; Monthly; Yr. II; N. 7; April, 1983; illus.; pp. 16-21.

789. INGLIS, Brian; "Natural and Supernatural: A History of the Paranormal from Earliest Times to 1914"; 490 pp.; illus.; bibl. 455-476; alph.; 23.5 cm; hb.; dj.; Hodder and Stoughton; London; 1977; pp. 24, 131, 132, 149, 333, 334.

790. IRWIN, Harvey J.; "Out-of-the-Body Down Under: Some Cognitive Characteristics of Australian Students Reporting OOBEs"; *Journal of the Society for Psychical Research;* London; Vol. 50; N. 785; bibl.; September, 1980; pp. 448-459.

791. IRWIN, Harvey J.; "The Psychological Function of Out-of-body Experiences: So Who Needs the Out-of-Body Experience?"; *The Journal of Nervous and Mental Disease;* Baltimore, Maryland; U. S. A.; Vol. 169; N. 4; 1981; bibl. 247, 248; pp. 244-248.

792. IRWIN, Harvey J.; "Some Psychological Dimensions of the Out-of-Body Experience"; *Parapsychology Review;* New York; Vol. 12; N. 4; July-August, 1981; pp. 1-6.

793. ISAACS, Julian; "On Kinetic Effects During Out-of-Body Projection"; *The Journal of the American Society for Psychical Research;* New York; Vol. 75; N. 2; April, 1981; pp. 192-194.

794. JACKSON, A. W.; "The Celtic Church Speaks Today"; World Fellowship Press; 1968; p. 26.

795. JACO, Grace R.; "Wenn das der Tod ist..."; transl. E. M. Körner; *Esotera;* Freiburg; West Germany; Magazine; Monthly; Yr. 21; N. 11; November, 1970; p. 1020.

796. JACOBSON, Nils O.; "Life Without Death?"; transl. Sheila La Farge; VIII + 342 pp.; illus.; glos. 327-329; bibl. 295-325; alph.; 21.5 cm; hb.; dj.; Turnstone Books; London; 1974; pp. 91-126; eds.: Swedish, Eng., Ger., Port.

797. JACOBY, A.; "Señor Kon-tiki"; George Allen & Unwin; London; 1968; p. 24.

798. JAFFÉ, Aniela; "Apparitions, An Archetypal Approach to Death Dreams And Ghosts"; pref. Carl Gustav Jung; VIII + 214 p.; alph.; 23 cm; pb.; Spring Publications; Irving, Texas; U. S. A.; 1979; pp. 143-167.

799. JAGOT, Paul-Clément; "Méthode Scientifique Moderne de Magnétisme, Hypnotisme, Suggestion"; 352 pp.; illus.; 22 cm; hb.; 2nd ed.; M. Drouin, Éditeur; Paris; no date; pp. 155-172; eds.: Fr., It.

800. JAGOT, Paul-Clément; "Traité Méthodique du Magnétisme Personnel"; 268 pp.; 22 cm; hb.; Éditions Dangles; Paris; 31, May, 1952; pp.165-180.

801. JAGOT, Paul-Clément; "Traité Théorique et Pratique de la Double Vue"; 200 pp.; illus.; 22.5 cm; pb.; Librairie et Éditions Leymarie; Paris; 1982; pp. 150-152.

802. JAMES, William; "Études et Réflexions d'un Psychiste"; transl. Durandeaud; introd. René Sudré; 336 pp.; 19 cm; pb.; Payot; Paris; 1924; pp. 171-174; eds.: Eng., Fr., Port.

803. JAMES, William; "The Varieties of Religious Experience"; XVIII + 526 pp.; alph.; 18 cm; hb.; The Modern Library; New York; no date; pp. 376-386.

804. JEANNE, Louise; "Causeries Spirites"; 216 pp.; 17 cm; hb.; Imprimerie Durand, Fillons et Lagarde; Toulouse; France; 1885; pp. 86-88.

805. JEBB, Robert H.; "A Business-man's Experiences of the Truth of Life After Death"; Aird & Coghill; London; 1925; pp. 52, 113.

806. JOHN, Da Free; "Easy Death"; editor Georg Feuerstein; introd. Kenneth Ring; XXII + 406 pp.; illus.; alph.; 23 cm; pb.; The Dawn Horse Press; Clearlake, Cal.; U. S. A.; 1983; pp. 239, 254-256, 276, 360-362.

807. JOHNSON, Raynor C.; "The Imprisoned Splendour"; 426 pp.; alph.; 22 cm; pb.; The Theosophical Publishing House; Wheaton, Ill.; U. S. A.; 1971; pp. 218-240.

808. JOHNSON, Raynor C.; "A Watcher on the Hills"; Hodder and Stoughton; London; 1959.

809. JOIRE, Paul; "De L'Extériorisation de la Sensibilité"; 380 pp.; illus.; 21 cm; hb.; Félix Alcan, Éditeur; Paris; 1897; pp. 341-352.

810. JOIRE, Paul; "Psychical and Supernormal Phenomena"; 634 pp.; illus.; 21.5 cm; hb.; Frederick A. Stokes Co.; New York; no date; pp. 79-91.

811. JORGE, José; Organizator; "Antologia do Perispírito"; 204 pp.; illus.; bibl. 197-202; 23 cm; pb.; Instituto Maria; Juiz de Fora, MG; Brazil; 1983; pp. 12, 54-57, 78-80, 193.

812. JUNG, Carl Gustav; "Memoires, Dreams, Reflections"; ed. and introd. Aniella Jaffé; transl. Richard Winston and Clara Winston; 448 pp.; illus.; glos. 410-420; alph.; 18 cm; pocket; pb.; 11st print.; William Collins Sons; Glasgow; Great Britain; November, 1977; pp. 320, 321, 343, 344; eds.: Ger., Eng., Port.

813. JUNG, Carl Gustav; "The Structure and Dynamics of the Psyche"; transl. R. F. C. Hull; X + 588 pp.; bibl. 535-552; alph.; 23 cm; hb.; dj.; 4th print.; Princeton University Press; New Jersey; U. S. A.; 1978; pp. 481, 482, 506-509.

814. KARAGULLA, Shafica; "Breakthrough to Creativity"; 268 pp.; bibl. 263-268; 22.5 cm; hb.; dj.; De Vorss & Co.; Marina Del Rey, Cal.; U. S. A.; 1978; pp. 73, 110-115, 180, 246.

815. KARDEC, Allan (Pseud. for Leon Hypolite Denizard Rivail); "O Céu e o Inferno"; transl. Manuel Justiniano Quintão; 426 pp.; 18 cm; pb.; 28th ed.; Federação Espírita Brasileira; Rio de Janeiro; Brazil; 1982; pp. 55, 168-172, 174, 243, 249, 407.

816. KARDEC, Allan (Pseud. for Leon Hypolite Denizard Rivail); "Espírito de um Lado, Corpo do Outro"; transl. Júlio Abreu Filho; *Revista Espírita;* Paris; Monthly; Yr. III; N. 1; reed.; 21 cm; hb.; Edicel; S. Paulo; Brazil; 1968; January, 1860; pp. 11-19.

817. KARDEC, Allan (Pseud. for Leon Hypolite Denizard Rivail); "Estudo sobre o Espírito de Pessoas Vivas"; transl. Júlio Abreu Filho; *Revista Espírita;* Paris; Monthly; Yr. III; N. 3; reed.; Edicel; S. Paulo; 1968; March, 1860; pp. 85-91.

818. KARDEC, Allan (Pseud. for Leon Hypolite Denizard Rivail); "O Evangelho Segundo o Espiritismo"; transl. Guillon Ribeiro; 456 pp.; 18 cm; pb.; 86th ed.; Federação Espírita Brasileira; Rio de Janeiro; Brazil; 1982; pp. 109, 110, 398, 400, 427.

819. KARDEC, Allan (Pseud. for Leon Hypolite Denizard Rivail); "Evocação de um Surdo-mudo Encarnado"; transl. Júlio Abreu Filho; *Revista Espírita;* Paris; Monthly; Yr. VIII; Vol. 1; reed.; Edicel; S. Paulo; Brazil; 1968; January, 1865; pp. 19-21.

820. KARDEC, Allan (Pseud. for Leon Hypolite Denizard Rivail); "Fenômeno de Bi-Corporeidade"; transl. Júlio Abreu Filho; *Revista Espírita;* Paris; Monthly; Yr. I; N. 12; reed.; Edicel; S. Paulo; Brazil; 1968; December, 1858; pp. 343-346.

821. KARDEC, Allan (Pseud. for Leon Hypolite Denizard Rivail); "A Gênese"; transl. Guillon Ribeiro; 400 pp.; 18 cm; pb.; 15th ed.; Federação Espírita Brasileira; Rio de Janeiro; Brazil; 1967; pp. 203, 273-283, 290, 293, 294, 339, 340, 354.

822. KARDEC, Allan (Pseud. for Leon Hypolite Denizard Rivail); "Identidade de um Espírito Encarnado"; transl. Júlio Abreu Filho; *Revista Espírita;* Paris; Monthly; Yr. VI; Vol. 1; reed.; Edicel; S. Paulo; Brazil; 1968; January, 1863; pp. 20-23.

823. KARDEC, Allan (Pseud. for Leon Hypolite Denizard Rivail); "Ligação Entre o Espírito e o Corpo"; transl. Júlio Abreu Filho; *Revista Espírita;* Paris; Monthly; Yr. II; N. 5; reed.; Edicel; S. Paulo; Brazil; 1968; May, 1859; pp. 139, 140.

824. KARDEC, Allan (Pseud. for Leon Hypolite Denizard Rivail); "O Livro dos Espíritos"; transl. Guillon Ribeiro; 480 pp.; illus.; 18 cm; pb.; 31st ed.; Federação Espírita Brasileira; Rio de Janeiro; Brazil; no date; pp. 171, 201, 213-236, 254, 278.

825. KARDEC, Allan (Pseud. for Leon Hypolite Denizard Rivail); "O Livro dos Médiuns"; transl. Guillon Ribeiro; 480 pp.; glos. 478-480; 18 cm; pb.; 30th ed.; Federação Espírita Brasileira; Rio de Janeiro; Brazil; 1972; pp. 71, 117, 123, 124, 128, 141-153, 260, 361-364, 367, 376; eds.: Fr., Eng., Port., It., Sp., esperanto.

826. KARDEC, Allan (Pseud. for Leon Hypolite Denizard Rivail); "Maria D'Agreda: Fenômeno de Bicorporeidade"; transl. Júlio Abreu Filho; *Revista Espírita;* Paris; Monthly; Yr. III; N. 11; reed.; Edicel; S. Paulo; Brazil; 1968; November, 1860; pp. 372-376.

827. KARDEC, Allan (Pseud. for Leon Hypolite Denizard Rivail); "Obras Póstumas"; transl. Guillon Ribeiro; 354 pp.; 18 cm; pb.; 12nd ed.; Federação Espírita Brasileira; Rio de Janeiro; Brazil; 1964; pp. 46-51, 69-78, 89, 90, 159, 160, 171.

828. KARDEC, Allan (Pseud. for Leon Hypolite Denizard Rivail); "O Principiante Espírita"; without translator; introd. Henri Sausse; 128 pp.; 18 cm; hb.; 10th ed.; Federação Espírita Brasileira; Rio de Janeiro; Brazil; 1944; pp. 101, 113, 114.

829. KARDEC, Allan (Pseud. for Leon Hypolite Denizard Rivail); "O Que é o Espiritismo"; without translator; introd. Henri Sausse; 218 pp.; 18 cm; pb.; 24th ed.; Federação Espírita Brasileira; Rio de Janeiro; Brazil; 1982; pp. 194, 195, 204.

830. KARDEC, Allan (Pseud. for Leon Hypolite Denizard Rivail); "Santo Atanásio, Espírita sem o Saber"; transl. Júlio Abreu Filho; *Revista Espírita;* Paris; Monthly; Yr. VII; Vol. 1; reed.; Edicel; S. Paulo; 1968; January, 1864; pp. 29, 30.

831. KARDEC, Allan (Pseud. for Leon Hypolite Denizard Rivail); "Teoria dos Sonhos"; transl. Júlio Abreu Filho; *Revista Espírita;* Paris; Monthly; Yr. VIII; Vol. 7; reed.; Edicel; S. Paulo; 1968; July, 1865; pp. 202-205.

832. KARDEC, Allan (Pseud. for Leon Hypolite Denizard Rivail); "Uma Aparição Providencial"; transl. Júlio Abreu Filho; *Revista Espírita;* Paris; Monthly; Yr. IV; N. 7; reed.; Edicel; S. Paulo; Brazil; 1968; July, 1861; pp. 212-215.

833. KARDEC, Allan (Pseud. for Leon Hypolite Denizard Rivail); "Um Sonho Instrutivo"; transl. Júlio Abreu Filho; *Revista Espírita;* Paris; Monthly; Yr. IX; Vol. 6; reed.; Edicel; S. Paulo; Brazil; 1968; July, 1866; pp. 171-174.

834. KARL, Miguel; "O Espiritismo, Doutrina da Felicidade"; introd. Cesar Gonçalves; 96 pp.; 17.5 cm; hb.; Editora Espírita; Rio de Janeiro; Brazil; 1937; pp. 85-87.

835. KELLER, Werner; "La Parapsychologie Ouvre le Futur"; transl. Anne Soulé-Abeilhou; 412 pp.; illus.; glos. 407-410; bibl. 411, 412; 21.5 cm; pb.; Éditions Robert Laffont; Paris; 1978; pp. 340-360, 408; em Ger., Fr.

836. KELWAY-BAMBER, L.; "Claude's Book"; introd. Oliver Lodge; XXVIII + 150 pp.; 19 cm; hb.; 2nd ed.; Methuen & Co.; London; 1919; pp. 10, 11.

837. KELWAY-BAMBER, L.; "Claude's Second Book"; introd. Ellis Thomas Powell; XX + 124 pp.; illus.; 18 cm; hb.; Psychic Book Club; London; 1919; pp. 75, 76.

838. KENNELLY, F. J.; "Reincarnation and Survival"; 88 pp.; Arken Publishing Co.; Aurora; U. S. A.; 1974.

839. KENNETT, Frances; "How to Read Your Dreams"; 64 pp.; illus.; 29 cm; hb.; dj.; Golden Hands Books; London; 1975; p. 58.

840. KERNER, Justinus; "A Vidente de Prevorst"; Biography; transl. Carlos Imbassahy; 266 pp.; 19 cm; pb.; Casa Editora O Clarim; Matão, SP; Brazil; 1973; pp. 65, 66.

841. KETTELKAMP, Larry; "Hypnosis: The Wakeful Sleep"; 96 pp.; illus.; alph.; 21 cm; hb.; dj.; William Morrow and Co.; New York; 1975; pp. 89-91.

842. KFOURI, Fauze; "Raio X da Mente Humana"; pref. L. Romanowski; 190 pp.; glos. 181-187; bibl. 189, 190; 21 cm; pb.; 4th ed.; Author's Edition; S. Paulo; Brazil; 1976; pp. 182.

843. KILNER, Walter John; "The Human Aura"; pref. Leslie A. Shepard; XIV + 306 pp.; illus.; alph.; 21 cm; pb.; The Citadel Press; Secaucus, N. J.; U. S. A.; 1965; pp. 38-43.

844. KING, Francis; editor and introd.; "Astral Projection, Ritual Magic and Alchemy"; 254 pp.; illus.; 22 cm; hb.; dj.; Samuel Weiser; New York; 1972; pp. 49-76.

845. KING, Francis; "Ritual Magic in England"; 176 pp.; bibl. 175, 176; 18 cm; pocket; pb.; New English Library; London; December, 1972; pp. 101, 114-118.

846. KING, Francis, and SKINNER, Stephen; "Techniques of High Magic: A Manual of Self-Initiation"; 228 pp.; illus.; bibl. 218; alph.; 21 cm; pb.; Destiny Books; New York; 1981; pp. 10, 13, 106-125, 218.

847. KING, Stephen; "O Iluminado"; transl. Betty Ramos Albuquerque; 396 pp.; 21 cm; pb.; 2nd ed.; Editora Record; Rio de Janeiro; Brazil; 1983; pp. 31, 78, 273.

848. KINGSTON, Kenny; "Sweet Spirits"; XII + 260 pp.; illus.; alph.; 23 cm; hb.; dj.; Contemporary Books; Chicago, Ill.; U. S. A.; 1978; pp. 143, 144.

849. KIPP, Heinrich; "Die Geisterwelt ist nicht verschlossem..."; *Die Andere Welt;* Freiburg; West Germany; Magazine; Monthly; Yr. 20; N. 12; December, 1969; pp. 1097, 1098.

850. KLEIN, Aaron E.; "Parapsychologie"; 112 pp.; illus.; 18 cm; pocket; pb.; Wilhelm Goldman Verlag; München; West Germany; 1975; pp. 81-83.

851. KNIGHT, David C.; "The ESP Reader"; Anthology; XIV + 432 pp.; glos. 424-428; bibl. 429-431; index of names; 23 cm; hb.; dj.; Castle Books; Secaucus, N. J.; U. S. A.; 1969; pp. 89, 104, 273-316, 393-400, 424-428.

852. KNIGHT, Gareth; "A History of White Magic"; introd. Kathleen Raine; 236 pp.; illus.; bibl. 223-226; alph.; 21 cm; pb.; Samuel Weiser; New York; 1979; pp. 177-179, 218.

853. KNIGHT, Gareth; "Occult Exercises and Practices"; 96 pp.; illus.; alph.; 18 cm; pb.; The Aquarian Press; London; 1982; pp. 33-59; eds.: Eng., Sp.

854. KOESTLER, Arthur; "The Invisible Writing"; Hamish Hamilton, Collins; London; 1954; p. 352.

855. KOHN, Elisabeth; "Ein Weg zur grundlegenden Schicksalswandlung"; *Die Andere Welt;* Freiburg; West Germany; Magazine; Monthly; Yr. 19; N. 3; March, 1968; pp. 208-210.

856. KOHN, Elisabeth; "Erwach aus dem Traum des Lebens!"; *Esotera;* Freiburg; West Germany; Magazine; Monthly; Yr. 23; N. 5; May, 1972; pp. 423-428.

857. KOHR, Richard L.; "A Survey of Psi Experiences Among Members of a Special Population"; *The Journal of the American Society for Psychical Research;* New York; Vol. 74; N. 4; October, 1980; pp. 395-411.

858. KOLOSIMO, Peter; "Ciudadanos de las Tinieblas"; transl. Juan Moreno; pref. Andrea Romero; 256 pp.; 18 cm; pocket; pb.; 2nd ed.; Plaza & Janes; Barcelona; Spain; November, 1979; pp. 145-149, 156.

859. KOPP, René; "Introduction Générale a L'Étude des Sciences Occultes"; 384 pp.; 23 cm; pb.; Paul Leymairie Éditeur; Paris; 1930; pp. 127-132.

860. KOVACH, Tom; "Out-of-Body Survey"; *Omni;* New York; Magazine; Monthly; Vol. 4; N. 11; August, 1982; illus.; p. 94.

861. KRIPPNER, Stanley Curtiss; Editor; "Extrasensory Perception"; Anthology; introd. Montague Ullman; 308 pp.; index of names; alph.; 23 cm; hb.; dj.; Plenum Press; New York; 1978; pp. 116-118, 150, 159, 160.

862. KRIPPNER, Stanley Curtiss; "The Implications of Contemporary Dream Research"; *Journal of the American Society of Psichosomatic Dentistry and Medicine;* Part I; Vol. 18; N. 3; 1971; pp. 94-101; Part. II; Vol. 18; N. 4; bibl. 138-140; 1972; pp. 130-140.

863. KRIPPNER, Stanley Curtiss; "Song of the Siren: A Parapsychological Odyssey"; XVIII + 312 pp.; alph.; 23.5 cm; hb.; Harper & Row, Publishers; New York; 1975; pp. 262-264.

864. KRIPPNER, Stanley Curtiss; & RUBIN, Daniel; Editors; "The Kirlian Aura: Photographing the Galaxies of Life"; 208 pp.; illus.; bibl. 200-204; 21 cm; pb.; Anchor Press; New York; 1974; pp. 171, 172.

865. KRIPPNER, Stanley Curtiss; & VILLOLDO, Alberto; "The Realms of Healing"; introd. Evan Harris Walker; X + 336 pp.; illus.; bibl. 317-324; alph.; 21.5 cm; pb.; Celestial Arts; Millbrae, Cal.; U. S. A.; 1976; pp. 299, 300.

866. KRISHNA, Gopi; "Kundalini: The Evolutionary Energy in Man"; introd. Frederic Spiegelberg; comment James Hillman; 252 pp.; 22 cm; pb.; Shambhala Publications; Boulder; Colorado; U. S. A.; 1971; pp. 12, 13.

867. KRISHNA, Gopi; "The Secret of Yoga"; 212 pp.; 21.5 cm; pb.; Turnstone Press; Wellingborough; Northamptonshire; Great Britain; 1981; pp. 123-126.

868. KRISHNAN, V.; "Near-Death Experiences: Reassessment Urged"; *Parapshychology Review;* New York; Vol. 12; N. 4; July-August, 1981; pp. 10, 11.

869. KRISHNAN, V.; "Out-of-the-Body Vision"; *Parapsychology Review;* New York; Vol. 13; N. 2; March-April, 1982; bibl. 22; pp. 21, 22.

870. KRISHNAN, V.; "Correspondence: V. Krishnan Questions"; *Parapsychology Review;* New York; Vol. II; N. 4; July-August, 1980; bibl.; p. 26.

871. KRUGER, Helen; "Other Healers, Other Cures"; XVI + 404 pp.; alph.; 23 cm; hb.; dj.; The Bobbs-Merril Co.; New York; 1974; pp. 302, 303, 337.

872. KYBER, Manfred; "Também Eles são Nossos Irmãos?"; transl. Tatiana Braunwieser; 162 pp.; illus.; 19.5 cm; pb.; Editora Cultural Espiritual; S. Paulo; Brazil; 1981; pp. 138-142.

873. LAFFERTY, La Vedi, and HOLLOWELL, Bud; "The Eternal Dance"; pres. Car. Llewellyn Weschcke; introd. Patricia-Rochelle Diegel; 540 pp.; illus.; bibl. 511-522; alph.; 20.5 cm; pb.; Llewellyn Publications; St. Paul, Minnesota; U. S. A.; pp. 340, 453, 478.

874. LAMONT, Stewart; "Is Anybody There?"; 144 pp.; glos. 143; 21.5 cm; hb.; dj.; Mainstream Publishing; Edinburg; Great Britain; 1980; pp. 81-104, 109-114, 143.

875. LANCELIN, Charles; "L'Ame Humaine"; 206 pp.; illus.; 17 cm; hb.; Henri Durville, Imprimeur-Éditeur; Paris; 1920; pp. 9, 33-43.

876. LANCELIN, Charles; "L'Au-Dela et ses Problèmes"; pref. Michel de Montaigne; 304 pp.; illus.; 17.5 cm; pb.; Librairie du Magnetisme; Paris; 1907; pp. 112-135.

877. LANCELIN, Charles; "L'Évocation des Morts"; 60 pp.; 24 cm; pb.; Henri Durville, Imprimeur-Éditeur; Paris; 1925; pp. 14, 15.

878. LANCELIN, Charles; "La Fraude dans la Production des Phénomènes Médiumniques"; 132 pp.; 25.5 cm; pb.; Hector et Henri Durville, Éditeurs; Paris; no date; pp. 39, 40.

879. LANCELIN, Charles; "Méthode de Dédoublement Personnel: Extériorization de la Neuricité, Sorties en Astral"; 554 pp.; illus.; 22 cm; hb.; Hector et Henri Durville, Éditeurs; Paris; 1912; pp. 309-398 (Mini-library).

880. LANCELIN, Charles; "L'Occultisme et la Science"; 678 pp.; 22 cm; pb.; Éditions Jean Meyer; Paris; 1926; pp. 496-504.

881. LANCELIN, Charles; "L'Occultisme et la Vie"; 544 pp.; illus.; 22 cm; hb.; Éditions Adyar; Paris; 1928; pp. 484-487, 535-540.

882. LANCELIN, Charles; "A Prática do Desdobramento"; without translator; *Revista O Pensamento*; S. Paulo; Yr. XXXV; N. 408, 409, 410; September-October, 1942; illus.; pp. 297-299, 327-329.

883. LANCELIN, Charles; "La Vie Posthume"; 416 pp.; illus.; 24 cm; hb.; Henri Durville, Imprimeur-Éditeur; Paris; 1923; pp. 145-155.

884. LANDAU, Lucian; "An Unusual Out-of-the-Body Experience"; *Journal of the Society for Psychical Research;* London; Vol. 42; N. 717; September, 1963; illus.; pp. 126-128.

885. LANG, Andrew; "The Book of Dreams and Ghosts"; introd. Robert Reginald; 302 pp.; illus.; 21.5 cm; pb.; Newcastle Publishing Co; Hollywood, Cal.; U. S. A.; 1972; pp. 84-87, 89-93.

886. LANTIER, Jacques; "El Espiritismo"; transl. M. Bofill y E. Petit; 176 pp.; bibl. 175, 176; 21.5 cm; pb.; Ediciones Martínez Roca; Barcelona; Spain; 1976; pp. 147-149.

887. LARCHER, Hubert; & RAVIGNANT, Patrick; "Os Domínios da Parapsicologia"; transl. Margarida Schiappa and Francisco Agarez; 366 pp.; illus.; glos. 337-345; bibl. 349-359; 20.5 cm; cart.; Edições 70; Lisboa; Portugal; January, 1977; pp. 9, 33, 48, 169, 187-194, 284-286, 310, 337-340.

888. LARSEN, Caroline D.; "My Travels in the Spirit World"; 106 pp.; illus.; 20 cm; hb.; Tulle Co.; Rutland, Vermont; U. S. A.; 1927; pp. 1-106.

889. LAUBSCHER, Barend Jacob Frederick; "Beyond Life's Curtain"; pref. John D. Pearce-Higgins; 108 pp.; illus.; 21 cm; hb.; dj.; Howard Timmim; Cape Town; South Africa; 1967; pp. 28-32, 39, 54-66.

890. LAUBSCHER, Barend Jacob Frederick; "Where Mystery Dwells"; pref. John D. Pearce-Higgins; X + 262 pp.; alph.; 21.5 cm; hb.; dj.; James Clarke & Co.; Cambridge; England; 1972; pp. 23, 27-36, 104, 198, 200-208, 212.

891. LAUTNER, Theodor; "Seelenwanderungen während des Schlafes und bei Ohnmachten"; *Die Andere Welt*; Freiburg; West Germany; Magazine; Monthly; Yr. 19; N. 12; December, 1968; illus.; pp. 1073-1077.

892. LAWRENCE, J.; "Magnetismo Utilitário y Milagroso"; without translator; 196 pp.; illus.; 18 cm; hb.; Eletric & Magnetic Federal Institute; Rio de Janeiro; Brazil; no date; pp. 125-127, 183-187.

893. LAWRENCE, J.; "Ocultismo Pratico"; 400 pp.; 23 cm; hb.; 2nd ed.; Lawrence & Co.; Rio de Janeiro; Brazil; 01, March, 1913; pp. 364-384.

894. LEADBEATER, Charles Webster; "The Astral Plane: Its Scenery, Inhabitants, and Phenomena"; 128 pp.; 17.5 cm; hb.; 5th ed.; Theosophical Publishing House; Los Angeles; U. S. A.; 1918; pp. 31-35; eds.: Eng., Sp., Port.

895. LEADBEATER, Charles Webster; "Les Aides Invisibles"; without translator; 160 pp.; 17.5 cm; hb.; 4th ed.; Les Éditions Adyar; Paris; 1930; pp. 27-37; eds.: Eng., Fr., Sp., Port.

896. LEADBEATER, Charles Webster; "Los Centros de Fuerza y el Fuego Serpentino"; without translator; 52 pp.; 17 cm; pb.; Editorial Orion; Mexico; D. F.; 1976; pp. 23-28.

897. LEADBEATER, Charles Webster; "The Chakras"; XIV + 132 pp.; illus.; alph.; 21 cm; hb.; dj.; The Theosophical Publishing House; Adyar, Madras; India; 1973; pp. 71-94.

898. LEADBEATER, Charles Webster; "De La Clairvoyance"; transl. La Garnérie; 228 pp.; 18.5 cm; hb.; Publications Théosophiques; Paris; 1910; pp. 69-106; eds.: Eng., Fr., Port.

899. LEADBEATER, Charles Webster; "Compêndio de Teosofia"; without translator; 116 pp.; 19.5 cm; pb.; Editora Pensamento; S. Paulo; Brazil; no date; pp. 52, 61, 70, 71.

900. LEADBEATER, Charles Webster; "El Hombre Visible e Invisible"; transl. Luis Aguilera Fernandez; 140 pp.; illus.; 22.5 cm; pb.; 6th ed.; Editorial Kier; Buenos Aires; Argentina; 1977; pp. 107-111.

901. LEADBEATER, Charles Webster; "O Lado Oculto das Coisas"; transl. Raymundo Mendes Sobral; 382 pp.; bibl. 381; alph.; 19.5 cm; pb.; Editora Pensamento; S. Paulo; Brazil; 1981; pp. 305-308.

902. LEADBEATER, Charles Webster; "El Plano Mental"; transl. Federico Climent Terrer; 100 pp.; 19.5 cm; pb.; 5th ed.; Editorial Kier; Buenos Aires; Argentina; 1976; pp. 1-100.

903. LEADBEATER, Charles Webster; "O Que há Além da Morte"; transl. Cinira Riedel de Figueiredo; 362 pp.; 19.5 cm; pb.; Editora Pensamento; S. Paulo; Brazil; 1974; pp. 165-175; eds.: Eng., Sp., Port.

904. LEAF, Horace; "A Morte não é o Fim: Memórias de Um Médium"; Autobiography; transl. Nair Lacerda; 202 pp.; 19.5 cm; pb.; Editora Pensamento; S. Paulo; Brazil; 1984; pp. 84-92.

905. LEAF, Horace; "What Mediumship is"; 168 pp.; 18.5 cm; hb.; dj.; 8th print.; Spiritualist Press; London; 1976; pp. 142-150.

906. LEAL, Julio Cesar; "A Casa de Deus"; 202 pp.; 17 cm; hb.; 2nd ed.; Federação Espírita Brasileira; Rio de Janeiro; Brazil; 1921; pp. 45, 48, 49.

907. LEARY, Timothy; METZNER, Ralph; and ALPERT, Richard; "The Psychedelic Experience: A Manual Based on the Tibetan Book of the Dead"; 160 pp.; 23.5 cm; hb.; 2nd print.; University Books; New York; September, 1964; pp. 38, 59.

908. LEE, Dal; "Dictionary of Astrology"; 250 pp.; illus.; 18 cm; pocket; pb.; Warner Books; New York; December, 1968; p. 71.

909. LEFEBURE, Francis; "Expériences Initiatiques"; 2 Vol.; 416 pp.; Tome II; illus.; 22.5 cm; pb.; 2nd ed.; Librairie Verrycken; Antuérpia; Belgium; 1976; pp. 1-274 (Mini-library).

910. LEFEBURE, Francis; "Les Homologies: Architecture Cosmique"; 460 pp.; illus.; 24 cm; pb.; 2nd ed.; Le Courrier du Livre; Paris; 1978; pp. 190, 269, 283, 304, 305, 311, 313, 333, 342-344, 360, 379.

911. LEFEBURE, Francis; "Respiración Ritmica y Concentración Mental"; 128 pp.; 19.5 cm; pb.; Editorial Kier; Buenos Aires; Argentina; 1978; pp. 122-124.

912. LEFEBURE, Francis; "La Respiration et l'Amour"; *Inconnues;* Lausanne; Switzerland; Magazine; 3rd Série; Vol. 12; 1956; pp. 146-161.

913. LEFEBURE, Francis; "La Rêverie Dirigée"; *Inconnues;* Lausanne; Switzerland; Magazine; 3rd Série; Vol. 14; 1960; pp. 175-181.

914. LENZ, Frederick; "Lifetimes: True Accounts of Reincarnation"; 206 pp.; alph.; 23 cm; hb.; dj.; The Bobbs-Merril Co.; New York; 1979; pp. 47, 59-61, 94-96.

915. LEONARD, Gladys Osborn; "The Last Crossing"; Psychic Book Club; London; 1937; pp. 73, 106.

916. LEONARD, Gladys Osborn; "My Life in Two Worlds"; 300 pp.; 18 cm; hb.; Cassell & Co.; London; 1931; pp. 23-29.

917. LESLIE, William, and GREEN, Celia Elizabeth; "Ausserköperliche Erfahrunge: wissenschaftlich erforscht"; transl. E. M. Körner; *Esotera;* Freiburg; West Germany; Magazine; Monthly; Yr. 21; N. 5; May, 1970; pp. 417-419.

918. LESSA, Adelaide Petters; "Precognição"; 392 pp.; illus.; bibl. 381-388; 21 cm; pb.; Livraria Duas Cidades; S. Paulo; Brazil; 1975; pp. 337, 354.

919. LESTER, Reginald Mounstephens; "In Search of the Hereafter"; XIV + 242 pp.; 20.5 cm; hb.; dj.; Wilfred Funk; New York; 1953; pp. 54-68.

920. LETHBRIDGE, T. C.; "Ghost and Ghoul"; XII + 156 pp.; illus.; alph.; 22 cm; pb.; 2nd print.; Routledge and Kegan Paul; London; 1967; pp. 143-145.

921. LEVINE, Stephen; "Who Dies? An Investigation of Conscious Living and Conscious Dying"; pref. Ram Dass; XVI + 318 pp.; bibl. 308-310; alph.; 21 cm; pb.; Anchor Books; New York; 1982; pp. 277-280.

922. LÉVRIER, Léon; "Les Forces Médiumniques"; pref. J. Pascal; 88 pp.; illus.; 18 cm; pb.; Nicolas, Renault & Cie.; Poitiers; France; 1921; pp. 24-31, 54-62.

923. LEWIS, Ioan M.; "Êxtase Religioso"; transl. José Rubens Siqueira de Madureira; 264 pp.; illus.; bibl. 255-259; 20.5 cm; pb.; Editora Perspectiva; S. Paulo; Brazil; 1977; pp. 53, 55, 56, 199-201, 206.

924. LHERMITTE, Jean; "Le Problème des Miracles"; 234 pp.; 18.5 cm; pb.; 6th ed.; Librairie Gallimard; Paris; 1956; pp. 197-212.

925. LIEF, Harold I.; "Commentary on Dr. Ian Stevenson's "The Evidence of Man's Survival After Death"; *The Journal of Nervous and Mental Disease;* Baltimore, Maryland; U. S. A.; Vol. 165; N. 3; 1977; bibl. 173; pp. 171-173.

926. LILLY, John Cunningham; "The Center of the Cyclone"; XII + 226 pp.; bibl. 221, 222; 21 cm; hb.; dj.; The Julian Press; New York; March, 1972; pp. 24-58, 148; eds.: Eng., It., Sp.

927. LILLY, John Cunningham, and LILLY, Antonietta Lena; "The Dyadic Cyclone: The Autobiography of a Couple"; 252 pp.; illus.; bibl. 246-248; 20 cm; pocket; pb.; Granada Publishing; London; 1978; pp. 69-77.

928. LIMA, Luiz da Rocha; "Memórias de Um Presidente de Trabalhos"; pres. Paulo da Costa Rzezinski; 708 pp.; illus.; bibl. 707, 708; 27 cm; cart.; Lar de Frei Luiz; Rio de Janeiro; Brazil; 1982; pp. 54, 55.

929. LIMOSIN, Febo de; "Para Hablar con los Espiritus"; 180 pp.; illus.; 20.5 cm; hb.; Publicaciones Mundial; Barcelona; Spain; 1930; pp. 161-166.

930. LIND, Frank; "My Occult Case Book"; X + 214 pp.; illus.; 18.5 cm; hb.; dj.; Rider and Co.; London; 1953; pp. 26-41, 118, 128, 206-208, 213.

931. LINEDECKER, Clifford L.; "Country Music Stars and the Supernatural"; 318 pp.; illus.; 18 cm; pocket; pb.; Dell Publishing Co.; New York; July, 1979; pp. 284-293.

932. LINEDECKER, Clifford L.; "Psychic Spy: The Story of an Astounding Man" (Ernesto A. Montgomery); Biography; XIV + 178 pp.; bibl. 176-178; 21 cm; hb.; dj.; Doubleday and Co.; Garden City, N. Y.; U. S. A.; 1976; pp. 48-58.

933. LINS, Edmar; "Os Fantásticos Caminhos da Parapsicologia"; pref. Joston Miguel Silva; 278 pp.; illus.; 20.5 cm; pb.; Ebrasa; Brasília; Brazil; 1970; pp. 87, 88, 90, 91.

934. LIPPMAN, Caro W.; "Hallucinations of Physical Duality in Migraine"; *The Journal of Nervous and Mental Disease;* New York; Vol. 117; N. 4; Serial N. 856; April, 1953; pp. 345-350.

935. LISBÔA, Roberto; "Primeiros Passos em Metapsíquica"; 274 pp.; illus.; bibl. 271, 272; 23 cm; pb.; Editor Borsoi; Rio de Janeiro; Brazil; 1955; pp. 202-206.

936. LISCHKA, Alfred; "Durch meine Hölle und Meinen Himmel"; *Esotera;* Freiburg; West Germany; Magazine; Monthly; Yr. 24; N. 12; December, 1973; illus.; pp. 1104-1109.

937. LISCHKA, Alfred; "Erlebnisse jenseits der Schwelle"; 234 pp.; bibl. 229-234; 23 cm; hb.; dj.; Ansata-Verlag; Schwarzenburg; Switzerland; 1979; pp. 91-180 (Mini-library).

938. LISCHKA, Alfred; "Ich Erkante, dass ich an der Decke Schwebte"; *Esotera;* Freiburg; West Germany; Magazine; Monthly; Yr. 24; N. 11; November, 1973; illus.; pp. 1001-1005.

939. LLEWELLYN, Editorial Staff; "The Truth About Psychic Attack & Protection"; 28 pp.; 21 cm; pb.; Llewellyn Publications; St. Paul, MN; U. S. A.; 1984; pp. 21, 22.

940. LOBO, Ary Maurell; "Ou a Vida Termina com a Morte, ou com a Morte Começa Outra Vida"; *Ciência Popular;* Rio de Janeiro; Brazil; Magazine; Monthly; N. 11; August, 1949; pp. 1-3.

941. LODGE, Oliver; "The Survival of Man"; XII + 358 pp.; illus.; alph.; 19 cm; hb.; Methuen & Co.; London; February, 1911; pp. 88, 99-104.

942. LOESTER (Pseud.); "Práticas Esotéricas"; 394 pp.; illus.; 18.5 cm; hb.; Editora O Pensamento; S. Paulo; Brazil; 1923; pp. 32-39.

943. LOMBROSO, Cesare; "After Death - What?"; transl. William Sloane Kennedy; XIV + 364 pp.; illus.; alph.; 21 cm; hb.; Small, Maynard & Co.; Boston; U. S. A.; 1909; pp. 246-257; eds.: Eng., Ger., It., Port.

944. LONDON, Jack; "The Star Rover"; Novel; The Macmillan Co.; London; 1963.

945. LONG, Max Freedom; "Recovering the Ancient Magic"; pref. E. Otha Wingo; 288 pp.; illus.; 18.5 cm; pb.; Huna Press; Cape Giardeau, MO; U. S. A.; 1981; pp. 142-146.

946. LONG, Max Freedom; "The Secret Science at Work"; 344 pp.; alph.; 21 cm; hb.; De Vorss & Co.; Marina del Rey, Cal.; U. S. A.; no date; pp. 33-60.

947. LONG, Max Freedom; "The Secret Science Behind Miracles"; 408 pp.; illus.; glos. 407, 408; alph.; 21 cm; pb.; 13rd print.; De Vorss & Co.; Publishers; Marina Del Rey, Cal.; U. S. A.; 1981; pp. 104, 110, 111, 127, 148-152, 154, 158, 172, 200-204, 213-215, 261, 287-291, 378, 379; eds.: Eng., Port.

948. LORENZ, Francisco Valdomiro; "Chamas de Ódio e a Luz do Puro Amor"; 180 pp.; illus.; 19.5 cm; pb.; Editora Pensamento; S. Paulo; Brazil; 1983; pp. 38, 39, 177-179.

949. LORENZ, Francisco Valdomiro; "O Filho de Zanoni"; Novel; 234 pp.; 23 cm; hb.; 2nd ed.; Empresa Editora O Pensamento; S. Paulo; Brazil; 1943; p. 171.

950. LORENZ, Francisco Valdomiro; "Lições Práticas de Ocultismo Utilitário"; 282 pp.; 18 cm; hb.; Editora O Pensamento; S. Paulo; Brazil; 1942; pp. 227-231.

951. LORENZ, Francisco Valdomiro; "Raios de Luz Espiritual: Ensinos Esotéricos"; 198 pp.; 19.5 cm; pb.; Editora Pensamento; S. Paulo; Brazil; 1973; pp. 44, 72.

952. LORENZATTO, José; "Parapsicologia e Religião: Alguns Aspectos da Mística à Luz da Ciência"; pres. Oscar González-Quevedo; 200 pp.; 21 cm; pb.; Edições Loyola; S. Paulo; Brazil; 1979; pp. 142-153.

953. L'ORNE, Mme. Asa; "Chloroformed but Conscious"; *Bordeland;* London; Magazine; Monthly; Vol. I; N. VI; October, 1894; pp. 564, 565.

954. LUCAS, Dean; "The Jung-Jaffé View of Out-of-body Experiences" (Robert Crookall); Books Reviews; *Theta;* Durham; North Carolina; U. S. A.; N. 38; Winter, 1973; pp. 6-8.

955. LUCKNER, Udo Oscar; "A Lenda de Araés"; 110 pp.; illus.; 21 cm; pb.; Imery Publicações; Goiânia, GO; Brazil; 1983; pp. 69, 70.

956. LUDWIG, Arnold M.; "Altered States of Consciousness"; *Archives General of Psychiatry;* Vol. 15; September, 1966; bibl. 233, 234; pp. 225-234.

957. LUKIANOWICZ, N.; "Autoscopic Phenomena*"; American Medical Association Archives of Neurology and Psychiatry;* Vol. 80; August, 1958; bibl. 218-220; pp. 199-220.

958. LUNA, Roso de; "O Livro que Mata a Morte"; transl. and pres. Edmundo Cardillo; 298 pp.; 20 cm; hb.; Editora Três; S. Paulo; Brazil; 1973; pp. 122, 158, 229-232, 291, 292.

959. LURDAHL, Craig R.; "A Collection of Near-Death Research Readings"; Anthology; pref. Raymond A. Moody Jr.; XVI + 240 pp.; 22.5 cm; hb.; dj.; Nelson-Hall Publishers; Chicago, Ill.; U. S. A.; 1982.

960. LUTYENS, Mary; "Krishnamurti: Os Anos do Despertar"; Biography; transl. Octavio Mendes Cajado; 302 pp.; illus.; 19.5 cm; pb.; Editora Cultrix; S. Paulo; Brazil; 1978; pp. 22, 25, 38, 43-49, 163, 174.

961. LYRA, Alberto; "O Ensino dos Mahatmas"; 278 pp.; illus.; 21 cm; pb.; Ibrasa; S. Paulo; Brazil; 1977; pp. 128, 129.

962. LYRA, Alberto; "O Inconsciente, a Magia e o Diabo no Século XX"; 294 pp.; 21 cm; pb.; Distribuidora Record; Rio de Janeiro; Brazil; no date; pp. 204-249.

963. LYRA, Alberto; "Parapsicologia e Inconsciente Coletivo"; 176 pp.; 19.5 cm; pb.; Editora Pensamento; S. Paulo; Brazil; 1970; pp. 14, 15.

964. LYRA, Alberto; "Parapsicologia, Psiquiatria, Religião"; 186 pp.; 20 cm; pb.; Editora Pensamento; S. Paulo; Brazil; 1968; pp. 86-90.

965. M; "Dioses Atomicos"; 222 pp.; illus.; glos. 215-217; 20 cm; pb.; Editorial Kier; Buenos Aires; Argentina; 1950; pp. 101-103.

966. MACDOUGALL, Curtis D.; "Superstition and the Press"; XII + 616 pp.; alph.; 23 cm; pb.; Prometheus Books; Buffalo, N. Y.; U. S. A.; 1983; pp. 117-121, 324, 360, 527, 529, 546, 555.

967. MACHADO, Brasilio Marcondes; "Contribuição ao Estudo da Psiquiatria, Espiritismo e Metapsiquismo"; Thesis; 272 pp.; illus.; bibl. 266-269; 22 cm; hb.; Author's Edition; Rio de Janeiro; Brazil; 1922; pp. 94-96.

968. MACHADO, Mário Amaral; "Os Fenômenos Paranormais de Thomas Green"; 154 pp.; illus.; 21 cm; pb.; Editora Tecnoprint; Rio de Janeiro; Brazil; 1984; pp. 15-23, 58.

969. MACHADO, Ubiratan Paulo; "Os Intelectuais e o Espiritismo"; pref. Salim Miguel; 242 pp.; illus.; bibl. 233-240; 21 cm; pb.; Edições Antares; Rio de Janeiro; Brazil; 1983; pp. 65, 66, 207, 208.

970. MACKENZIE, Andrew; "Hauntings and Apparitions"; introd. Brian Inglis; XVIII + 270 pp.; illus.; bibl. 258-265; alph.; 20 cm; pb.; Granada Publishing; London; 1983; pp. 7, 31, 242, 243.

971. MACKLIN, John; "Passaporte para o Desconhecido"; transl. Hélio Pólvora; 134 pp.; 21 cm; pb.; Distribuidora Record; Rio de Janeiro; Brazil; no date; pp. 87, 88.

972. MACKINTOSH, William Hunter; "Did He Dream His Past Incarnation?"; *Psychic News;* London; Newspaper; Weekly; N. 2436; February 10, 1979; p. 2.

973. MACKINTOSH, William Hunter; "Doctor Takes Astral Flight to Earth's Bowels"; *Psychic News;* London; Newspaper; Weekly; N. 2178; March 2, 1974; p. 2.

974. MACKINTOSH, William Hunter; "The Essence of Espiritualism"; 62 pp.; 22 cm; Gerrard's Cross, Smythe; London; 1973.

975. MACKINTOSH, William Hunter; "Famous Medium Describes Her Other-World Visits"; *Psychic News;* London; Newspaper; Weekly; N. 2241; May 17, 1975; p. 2.

976. MACKINTOSH, William Hunter; "His Astral Travel is in Space and Time"; *Psychic News;* London; Newspaper; Weekly; N. 2219; December 14, 1974; p. 2.

977. MACKINTOSH, William Hunter; "How You can Become Astral Traveller"; *Psychic News;* London; Newspaper; Weekly; N. 2308; August 28, 1976; p. 2.

978. MACKINTOSH, William Hunter; "She Left Her Body and Entered the Atom"; *Psychic News;* London; Newspaper; Weekly; N. 2451; May 26, 1979; illus.; p. 2.

979. MACKINTOSH, William Hunter; "What Causes Astral Body to Travel?"; *Psychic News*; London; Newspaper; Weekly; N. 2520; September 27, 1980; p. 2.

980. MACLAINE, Shirley; "Minhas Vidas"; Autobiography; transl. A. B. Pinheiro de Lemos; 318 pp.; 21 cm; pb.; Editora Record; Rio de Janeiro; Brazil; 1983; pp. 9, 151-153, 169, 170, 192, 284-287.

981. MADDELEY, Peter; "Events on the Threshold of the After-Life" (Robert Crookall); Books Reviews; *Journal of the Society for Psychical Research;* London; Vol. 44; N. 735; March, 1968; pp. 259, 260.

982. MADDOCK, Peter; "London Parascience Conference"; *Parapsychology Review;* New York; Vol. II; N. 66; November-December, 1980; pp. 15-18.

983. MAES, Hercílio; "Elucidações do Além"; prfr. José Fuzeira; 194 pp.; illus.; 22.5 cm; pb.; 2nd ed.; Livraria Freitas Bastos; Rio de Janeiro; Brazil; 1975; pp. 145, 148, 151, 164, 165, 167, 168, 185, 188.

984. MAES, Hercílio; "Mediunismo"; 244 pp.; 23 cm; pb.; 3rd ed.; Livraria Freitas Bastos; Rio de Janeiro; Brazil; 1978; pp. 85-88.

985. MAES, Hercílio; "Semeando e Colhendo"; 274 pp.; 23.5 cm; pb.; Livraria Freitas Bastos; Rio de Janeiro; Brazil; 1967; pp. 32, 82, 184.

986. MAES, Hercílio; "A Sobrevivência do Espírito"; 254 pp.; 23 cm; pb.; 3rd ed.; Livraria Freitas Bastos; Rio de Janeiro; Brazil; 1978; pp. 184-194.

987. MAES, Hercílio; "A Vida Além da Sepultura"; 288 pp.; 23 cm; pb.; 3rd ed.; Livraria Freitas Bastos; Rio de Janeiro; Brazil; 1979; p. 6.

988. MAETERLINCK, Maurice; "L'Hôte Inconnu"; VIII + 326 pp.; 18 cm; hb.; Eugène Fasquelle, Éditeur; Paris; 1917; pp. 15-18; eds.: Fr., Sp.

989. MAGRE, Maurice; "Les Interventions Surnaturelles"; 252 pp.; 19 cm; pb.; Fasquelle Éditeurs; Paris; 23, March, 1939; pp. 145-150, 205.

990. MAHONY, Patrick; "Out of Silence: A Book of Factual Fantasies"; 180 pp.; Storm; New York; 1948.

991. MALLORY, Lucy A. Rose; Editora; "The World's Advance Thought: The Avant-Courier of the New Spiritual Dispensation"; Vol. 28; N. 9; New Series; October, 1917.

992. MALZ, Betty P.; "My Glimpse of Eternity"; 130 pp.; 17.5 cm; pocket; pb.; Berkeley Books; New York; April, 1980; pp. 81-87; eds.: Eng., Port.

993. MANNING, Al G.; "Aproveite o Seu Poder Psicocósmico"; transl. Eduardo Brandão; 240 pp.; 21 cm; pb.; Editora Record; Rio de Janeiro; Brazil; 1983; pp. 153-162.

994. MANNING, Matthew; "Un Fenómeno Paranormal"; transl. Ramón Ibero; pref. Peter Bander; introd. Derek G. Manning; 232 pp.; illus.; 20 cm; hb.; dj.; Ediciones Matínez Roca; Barcelona; Spain; 1976; pp. 25, 85, 89, 93; eds.: Eng., Sp.

995. MARCO, Felice; "La Mecanica Dello Spiritismo"; 156 pp.; 20.5 cm; hb.; Ditta G. B. Paravia e Co.; Torino; Italy; 1909; pp. 66-70.

996. MARIN, Cesar Camargo y; "Psico-Analisis del Sueño Profetico"; prol. Quintiliano Saldaña; 328 pp.; bibl. 303-318; 18 cm; hb.; M. Aguilar, Editor; Madrid; Spain; 1929; pp. 98, 118-128, 148.

997. MARINHO, Iracema; "Cartas para o Além"; 1st Vol.; 178 pp.; 21 cm; pb.; Editora Elyas; Rio de Janeiro; Brazil; 1982; pp. 83, 84.

998. MARINUZZI, Raul; "Parapsicologia Didática"; introd. Vinicius de Carvalho; 182 pp.; illus.; glos. 171-181; 21 cm; pb.; Livraria Freitas Bastos; Rio de Janeiro; Brazil; 1977; p. 171.

999. MARQUES, América Paoliello; "Estrutura da Personalidade em Sujeitos Sensitivos e Não-Sensitivos"; 50 pp.; bibl. 30, 31; 21 cm; pb.; Gráfica Editora Karnac; Rio de Janeiro; Brazil; 1979; p. 3.

1000. MARRICK, Sergivan Du (Pseud. for Hernani Guimarães Andrade); "A Sobrevivência da Personalidade Após a Morte do Corpo Físico"; *Folha Espírita;* S. Paulo; Brazil; Newspaper; Monthly; Yr. II; N. 13; April, 1975; p. 6 (See N. 27-30).

1001. MARRYAT, Florence; "There is no Death"; 248 pp.; 24 cm; hb.; dj.; Causeway Books; New York; 1973; pp. 35-47.

1002. MARTIN, Anthony; "The Theory and Practice of Astral Projection: Exploration in a World Beyond the Body"; 96 pp.; bibl. 93-95; alph.; 18 cm; pb.; The Aquarian Press; London; 1980; pp. 1-96; eds.: Eng., Sp. (Mini-library).

1003. MARTIN, B. W.; "The Dictionary of the Occult"; 140 pp.; 23.5 cm; pb.; Rider and Co.; London; 1979; pp. 22, 23, 86, 87.

1004. MARTIN, Malachi; "Hostage to the Devil"; 480 pp.; alph.; 23 cm; hb.; dj.; Reader's Digest Press; New York; 1976; pp. 352-355; eds.: Eng., Port.

1005. MARTINS, Celso; "A Delicada Questão da Vida"; 134 pp.; bibl. 119; alph.; 20.5 cm; pb.; 3rd ed.; Edicel; S. Paulo; Brazil; June, 1979; pp. 97, 98.

1006. MARTINS, Celso; "A Obsessão e seu Tratamento Espírita"; 176 pp.; bibl. 65, 66, 124, 174, 175; 21 cm; pb.; Edicel; S. Paulo; Brazil; May, 1982; pp. 25-32, 162, 163, 165, 166.

1007. MARTINS, Celso; "Ocorrências no Mundo Espiritual"; *Desobsessão;* Porto Alegre, RS; Brazil; Newspaper; Monthly; Yr. XXXIII; N. 403; September, 1981; p. 7.

1008. MARTINS, Edílson; "Seita do Santo Daime Usa em Rituais Alucinógeno Amazônico"; *Jornal do Brasil;* Rio de Janeiro; Brazil; Daily; Yr. XCIII; N. 212; 6, November, 1983; illus.; p. 16.

1009. MARTINS, Romualdo Joaquim; "Memórias de Um Médium"; pref. Derna Rosa; 186 pp.; 22 cm; pb.; no publisher; S. Paulo; Brazil; 1964; pp. 95-97.

1010. MARX, Monique; Anthology; "L'Infini Sursis on de l'Autre Côté de la Vie"; 318 pp.; illus.; bibl. 314-316; 24 cm; pb.; Claude Tchou; Paris; 1979; pp. 27, 28, 31, 107-110, 158.

1011. MASON, Peggy; "I Visit the Animal Spirit Realms"; *Two Worlds*; London; Magazine; Monthly; 82nd Year; N. 3897; October, 1968; pp. 292-296.

1012. MASTERS, R. E. L., and HOUSTON, Jean; "The Varieties of Psychedelic Experience"; 326 pp.; 22 cm; hb.; dj.; 2nd ed.; Turnstorne Books; London; 1973; pp. 85-87, 114-117.

1013. MATSON, Katinka; "The Encyclopaedia of Reality"; 362 pp.; 20 cm; pb.; Granada Publishing; London; 1979; pp. 38-40.

1014. MATTER, M.; "Emanuel Swedenborg: Sa Vie, Ses Écrits et Sa Doctrine"; Biography; XVI + 436 pp.; 22 cm; hb.; Didier et Cie., Librairies-Éditeurs; Paris; 1863; pp. 98, 109, 110, 145, 232, 366.

1015. MATTOS, Idalinda A.; "Desdobramento Materializado"; *A Flama Espírita;* Uberaba, MG; Brazil; Newspaper; Weekly; Yr. XXXV; N. 2.502; 20, November, 1982; p. 3.

1016. MAUSS, Marcel; "A General Theory of Magic"; transl. Robert Brain; pref. David Pocock; 148 pp.; alph.; 21.5 cm; hb.; dj.; Routledge & Kegan Paul; London; 1972; pp. 34, 35, 122, 123.

1017. MAXWELL, Joseph; "Les Phénomènes Psychiques"; pref. Charles Robert Richet; 320 pp.; 21.5 cm; hb.; 6th ed.; Librairie Félix Alcan; Paris; 1920; pp. 190, 224, 298-301.

1018. MC ADAMS, Elizabeth E.; & BAYLESS, Raymond; "The Case for Life After Death: Parapsychologists Hook at the Evidence"; 158 pp.; bibl. 151-153; alph.; Nelson-Hall; Chicago, Ill.; U. S. A.; 1981.

1019. MC CONNELL, R. A.; Editor; "Encounters With Parapsychology"; 236 pp.; 23 cm; pb.; Author's Edition; Pittsburgh, PA; U. S. A.; 1981; pp. 75, 76, 169.

1020. MC CREERY, Charles; "Psychical Phenomena and the Physical World"; introd. George Joy; 138 pp.; alph.; 21.5 cm; hb.; dj.; Hamish Hamilton; London; 1973; pp. 9, 17, 31-42, 49, 104-106, 118-132.

1021. MC HARG, James F.; "Journeys Out of the Body" (Robert Monroe); Books Reviews; *Journal of the Society for Psychical Research*; London; Vol. 47; N. 755; March, 1973; pp. 48-52.

1022. MC INTOSH, Alastair I.; "Beliefs About Out-of-the-Body Experiences Among the Elema, Gulf Kamea, and Rigo Peoples of Papua, New Guinea"; *Journal of the Society for Psychical Research*; London; Vol. 50; N. 785; September, 1980; illus.; bibl.; pp. 460-478.

1023. MC RAE, Ronald; "Mind Wars: The True Story of Government Research Into the Military Potential of Psychic Weapons"; introd. Marcello Truzzi; 156 pp.; bibl. 139-150; alph.; 21 cm; hb.; dj.; St. Martin's Press; New York; 1984; pp. 27, 52.

1024. MEAD, George Robert Stow; "Apolonio de Tyana"; transl. Julio González; pref. Rafael Urbano; 142 pp.; 20 cm; pb.; Editorial Dedalo; Buenos Aires; Argentina; 1977; pp. 106, 107.

1025. MEAD, George Robert Stow; "The Subtle Body in Western Tradition"; 110 pp.; 18.5 cm; cart.; Stuart & Watkins; London; 1967; pp. 33-55.

1026. MECK, M. de; "Esotérisme & Survie: Études d'un Mystique Moderne"; 282 pp.; 19.5 cm; hb.; Éditions Drouin; Paris; no date; pp. 256-260.

1027. MECK, M. de; "Métapsychisme et Occultisme"; 296 pp.; bibl. 287-294; 23 cm; pb.; Librairie A. M. Beaudelot; Paris; 1928; pp. 126, 127, 153, 154.

1028. MEEK, George W.; Organizator; "As Curas Paranormais: Como se Processam"; Anthology; transl. Syomara Cajado; 364 pp.; illus.; bibl. 280-282, 352-354; 19.5 cm; pb.; Editora Pensamento; S. Paulo; Brazil; 1984; pp. 8, 97, 98, 228, 234, 244-254, 324, 327.

1029. MEEK, George W.; "From Enigma to Science"; introd. Kelvin Spencer; 200 pp.; illus.; bibl. 182-194; alph.; 21 cm; hb.; dj.; Samuel Weiser; New York; 1974; pp. 188, 189.

1030. MEEK, George W.; "O Que nos Espera Depois da Morte?"; transl. Gilberto Campista Guarino; 190 pp.; illus.; 21 cm; pb.; Editora Record; Rio de Janeiro; Brazil; 1983; pp. 41, 42, 55-60, 115, 152, 160.

1031. MEISHU-SAMA; "Alicerce do Paraíso"; without translator; 5 Vol.; 604 pp.; 17 cm; hb.; Fundação Mokiti Okada; S. Paulo; Brazil; 1981; 3rd Vol.: pp. 36, 55, 110, 111; 4th Vol.: pp. 108, 109; eds.: Jpn., Port.

1032. MELLO, Wilson Ferreira de; "Medicina e Espiritismo"; *Boletim Médico-Espírita;* S. Paulo; Brazil;Yr. I; N. 1; March, 1984; bibl. 45, 46; pp. 34-46.

1033. MENDES, Eliezer Cerqueira; "Personalidade Hiperconsciente"; 122 pp.; 19.5 cm; pb.; Author's Edition; Bahia; Brazil; 1977; pp. 31-39.

1034. MENDES, Eliezer Cerqueira; "Psicotranse: Terapia dos Distúrbios Mentais e Psicossomáticos"; 154 pp.; 19.5 cm; pb.; Editora Pensamento; S. Paulo; Brazil; 1980; pp.37-41, 58, 59.

1035. MENZEL, Hedda; "Spontane und Experimentelle Austritte des Astralkörpers"; *Esotera;* Freiburg; Alemanha Ocidental; Magazine; Monthly; Yr. 23; N. 10; October, 1972; illus.; pp. 877-881.

1036. MERCIER, Mario; "Chamanisme et Chamans: Le Vécu dans L'Expéricence Magique"; 182 pp.; illus.; bibl. 179, 180; 22.5 cm; pb.; Pierre Belfond; Paris; 1977; pp. 22, 25, 147-169.

1037. MESQUITA, José Marques; "Elucidário de "Evolução em Dois Mundos"; pres. Roque Jacintho; 304 pp.; bibl. 282, 283; alph.; 14 cm; pb.; Edições Culturesp; S. Paulo; Brazil; 1984; p. 221.

1038. METZGER, D.; "Essai de Spiritisme Scientifique"; 456 pp.; 18 cm; hb.; Librairie des Sciences Psychologiques; Paris; 1894; pp. 124-166.

1039. MEUROIS-GIVAUDAN, Anne, et MEUROIS-GIVAUDAN, Daniel; "Récits d'un Voyageur de l'Astral"; Novel; 284 pp.; 21 cm; pb.; 2nd ed.; Éditions Arista; Paris; 1983; pp. 1-284.

1040. M. F. R. C.; "Diccionario Rosacruz"; 158 pp.; 19.5 cm; hb.; Editoral Kier; Buenos Aires; Argentina; 1971; pp. 20-22, 36-38, 47.

1041. MICHAËL, Tara; "O Yoga"; transl. Raul Bezerra Pedreira Filho and Suzana Joffily Cruz; pref. Jacques Maui; 194 pp.; illus.; bibl. 185-187; 21 cm; pb.; Zahar Editores; Rio de Janeiro; Brazil; 1976; pp. 50, 51, 94, 95, 102-105.

1042. MICHAELUS (Pseud. for Miguel Timponi); "Magnetismo Espiritual"; 308 pp.; 18.5 cm; pb.; 2nd ed.; Federação Espírita Brasileira; Rio de Janeiro; Brazil; 1967; pp. 278-281.

1043. MICHEL, Aimé; "Deslocar Sem o Corpo"; *Planeta;* S. Paulo; Brazil; Magazine; Monthly; N. 9; May, 1973; pp. 72-85.

1044. MICKAHARIC, Draja; "Spiritual Cleansing: A Handbook of Psychic Protection"; 98 pp.; illus.; alph.; 21 cm; pb.; Samuel Weiser; York Beach, Maine; U. S. A.; 1982; pp. 20-26.

1045. MIGUEL, Alfredo; "Fenômenos Espíritas e Anímicos"; 152 pp.; 21 cm; pb.; Edições Feesp; S. Paulo; Brazil; 1981; pp. 40, 41, 45-63, 90.

1046. MINOR, Elaine; "Gateway to the Unknown"; VIII + 182 pp.; illus.; 21.5 cm; pb.; 3rd print.; Sanai Publications; Los Angeles, Cal.; U. S. A.; 1981; pp. 62-66.

1047. MIRANDA, Hermínio Correa de; "O Desdobramento e a Rejeição da Morte"; *Obreiros do Bem;* Rio de Janeiro; Brazil; Newspaper; Monthly; March, 1976; pp. 2, 3.

1048. MIRANDA, Hermínio Correa de; "Diálogo com as Sombras: Teoria e Prática da Doutrinação"; pref. Francisco Thiesen; 290 pp.; 18 cm; pb.; Federação Espírita Brasileira; Rio de Janeiro; Brazil; September, 1979; pp. 40, 51, 101, 108, 116, 132, 147, 170, 176, 183, 198, 200, 247, 263, 273-285.

1049. MIRANDA, Hermínio Correa de; "As Marcas do Cristo"; pres. Francisco Thiesen; 2 Vol.; 538 pp.; 18 cm; pb.; Federação Espírita Brasileira; Rio de Janeiro; Brazil; 1979; Vol. I: pp. 91, 92, 134, 189, 213, 245; Vol. II: pp. 125, 162, 242.

1050. MIRANDA, Hermínio Correa de; "A Memória e o Tempo"; 2 Vol.; 336 pp.; illus.; bibl. 149-153; 21 cm; pb.; Editora Cultural Espírita; S. Paulo; Brazil; 1982 / 1984; Vol. I: pp. 33, 56, 68, 77-80, 85, 87, 89-92, 101, 103, 117-120, 132-139, 151, 164-167, 172, 175, 176; Vol. II: pp. 13, 14, 17, 53, 58, 70, 74, 78, 79, 88, 93, 96-102, 104-107, 121, 122, 125.

1051. MIRANDA, Hermínio Correa de; "Reencarnação e Imortalidade"; pref. Gilberto Campista Guarino; 322 pp.; 18 cm; pb.; Federação Espírita Brasileira; Rio de Janeiro; Brazil; 1976; pp. 44, 55, 56, 103, 104, 113-116, 126, 127, 133, 176, 177, 187, 203, 204, 214, 241, 265, 295, 310, 311.

1052. MIRANDA, Hermínio Correa de; "Sobrevivência e Comunicabilidade dos Espíritos"; pref. Francisco Thiesen; 318 pp.; 18 cm; pb.; Federação Espírita Brasileira; Rio de Janeiro; Brazil; 1977; pp. 39-59, 71-73, 77, 78, 160, 161, 175, 181, 182, 190, 191, 196, 197, 200-211, 278.

1053. MIRANDA, Hermínio Correa de; "Uma Revisão dos Ensinos de Swedenborg" (Stella Myers); Book Review; *Reformador;* Rio de Janeiro; Brazil; Magazine; Monthly; Yr. 79; Vol. 79; N. 8, 9, 10; August-October, 1961; pp. 179-181, 207-209, 234-236.

1054. MIRCLAIR, Francis de; "Le "Démon" Spirite: Cours Pratique de Médiumnité"; 232 pp.; 18.5 cm; pb.; Éditions Fulgor; Paris; 1922; pp. 125-133.

1055. MISHLOVE, Jeffrey; "The Roots of Consciousness"; XXXIV + 348 pp.; illus.; bibl. 323-336; alph.; 27.5 cm; pb.; Random House; New York; May, 1979; pp. XXIX, 126-138.

1056. MISRAKI, Paul; "L'Expérience de L'Après-Vie"; 268 pp.; bibl. 263-267; 21.5 cm; pb.; Éditions Robert Laffont; Paris; 1974; pp. 21, 51.

1057. MITCHELL, Edgar D.; "O Astronauta do Espaço Interior"; without translator; Interview with Alan Vaughan; *Planeta;* S. Paulo; Brazil; Magazine; Monthly; Special number; 1983; illus.; pp. 24-29.

1058. MITCHELL, Edgard D.; "Psychic Exploration: A Challenge for Science"; Anthology; Editor: John White; 708 pp.; illus.; alph.; 20 cm; pb.; Paragon Books; New York; 1979; pp. 348-373.

1059. MITCHELL, Janet Lee; "Out-of-Body Experiences: A Handbook"; pref. Gertrude Schmeidler; XII + 128 pp.; bibl.; alph.; Mc Farland & Co.; Jefferson, N. C.; U. S. A.; 1981; pp. I-XII, 1-128 (Mini-library).

1060. MITCHELL, Janet Lee; "Out of the Body Vision"; *Psychic Magazine;* U. S. A.; March-April, 1973; illus.; pp. 44-47.

1061. MITTL, John; "Astral Projection: Modus Operandi"; 10 pp.; 28 cm; pb.; Health Research; Mokelumne Hill, Cal.; U. S. A.; 1960; pp. 1-10.

1062. MIYAMOTO, H.; "Aparición de um Encarnado"; *Conocimiento;* Buenos Aires; Argentina; Magazine; Monthly; N. 385, 386; Enero, 1970.

1063. MOLINERO (Yogakrisnanda); "O Segredo da Múmia"; introd. Edmundo Cardillo; 168 pp.; 21 cm; pb.; Editora Mandala; S. Paulo; Brazil; 1975; pp. 8, 22-24, 28, 29, 32, 33, 61, 104, 113, 114, 121, 122, 142, 149-151, 154, 159, 164-167.

1064. MONROE, Robert Allan; "Dort, wo Man zu Hause ist"; without translator; *Esotera;* Freiburg; West Germany; Magazine; Monthly; Yr. 23; N. 12; December, 1972; pp. 1063, 1064.

1065. MONROE, Robert Allan; "Journeys Out of the Body"; New Foreword; epil. Stuart W. Twemlow; 280 pp.; 20.5 cm; pb.; new ed. updated; Anchor Press; New York; 1977; pp. 1-280; eds.: Eng., Ger., It., Port. (Mini-library).

1066. MONS, W. E. R.; "Beyond Mind"; 256 pp.; bibl. 233-247; alph.; 21.5 cm; hb.; dj.; Rider & Co.; London; 1983; pp. 56, 57, 99, 194.

1067. MONTANDON, H. C. Raoul; "De la Bête a L'Homme"; 370 pp.; illus.; 22 cm; hb.; Éditions Victor Attinger; Paris; Juillet, 1943; pp. 229-240.

1068. MONTANDON, H. C. Raoul; "Formes Matérialisées"; 324 pp.; illus.; 22.5 cm; pb.; Éditions Victor Attinger; Paris; 1946; pp. 15-25.

1069. MONTANDON, H. C. Raoul; "Maisons et Lieux Hantés"; 230 pp.; 21 cm; hb.; La Diffusion Scientifique; Paris; 1953; pp. 171-194.

1070. MONTANDON, H. C. Raoul; "La Mort Cette Inconnue"; 396 pp.; bibl. 365-393; 23 cm; pb.; Éditions Victor Attinger; Paris; 1948; pp. 224-287.

1071. MONTANDON, H. C. Raoul; "Les Radiations Humaines"; 460 pp.; illus.; 23 cm; pb.; Librairie Félix Alcan; Paris; 1927; pp. 9, 10, 47.

1072. MONTEITH, Mary E.; "A Book of True Dreams"; 220 pp.; alph.; 21.5 cm; hb.; Heath Cranton; London; 1929; pp. 47-55, 77, 100, 198, 203.

1073. MONTEITH, Mary E.; "The Fringe of Immortality"; introd. Abraham Wallace; XVI + 204 pp.; 17.5 cm; hb.; John Murray; London; 1920; pp. 6, 15-20, 146, 195.

1074. MONTGOMERY, Ruth; "Strangers Among Us"; 256 pp.; 17.5 cm; pocket; pb.; 2nd print.; Fawcett Crest; New York; June, 1983; pp. 112, 113.

1075. MOODY JR., Raymond A.; "O Outro Lado da Existência"; *Planeta;* S. Paulo; Brazil; Magazine; Monthly; N. 118-A; July, 1982; illus.; pp. 4-9.

1076. MOODY JR., Raymond A.; "Reflections on Life After Life"; 150 pp.; bibl. 147, 148; 18 cm; pocket; pb.; Bantam Books; New York; March, 1978; pp. 15-18.

1077. MOODY JR., Raymond A.; "Testemunhas dos que Foram e Voltaram"; *Jornal do Brasil;* Rio de Janeiro; Brazil; Daily; Section B; 8, August, 1977; illus.; p. 10.

1078. MOODY JR., Raymond A.; "Vida Depois da Vida"; transl. Rodolfo Azzi; pref. Elisabeth Kübler-Ross; 154 pp.; 17 cm; pocket; pb.; 3rd ed.; Edibolso; S. Paulo; Brazil; no date; pp. 33-81, 123, 130, 131; eds.: Eng., Fr., It., Port.

1079. MOORE, Brooke Noel; "The Philosophical Possibilities Beyond Death"; 222pp.; bibl. 206-213; alph.; Charles C. Thomas; Springfield, Ill.; U. S. A.; 1981.

1080. MOORE, Evelyn Garth; "Try the Spirits"; 132 pp.; bibl. 123-126; Oxford University Press; New York; 1977.

1081. MOORE, Marcia; "Hypersentience"; XIV + 304 pp.; 18 cm; pocket; pb.; Bantam Books; New York; August, 1977; p. 161.

1082. MOORE, Marcia, and DOUGLAS, Mark; "Yoga, Science of the Self"; pref. Shepard Guiandes; XVI + 318 pp.; illus.; glos. 273-277; bibl. 281-285; alph.; 21.5 cm; hb.; dj.; 2nd ed.; Arcane Publications; York Harbor, Maine; U. S. A.; 1969; pp. 91, 101, 213, 217-220, 273, 285.

1083. MOORE, Marcia, and ALLTOUNIAN, Howard Sunny; "Journeys Into the Bright World"; 184 pp.; bibl. 183, 184; 23 cm; pb.; Para Research; Rockport, Massachusetts; U. S. A.; 1978; pp. 43, 139-143, 155.

1084. MORATO, Agnelo; "Ibne: A História de um Jovem que Venceu a Morte"; pref. José Ferreira Carrato; 216 pp.; illus.; 21 cm; pb.; Edições Correio Fraterno; S. Bernardo do Campo, SP; Brazil; March, 1984; pp. 145-150.

1085. MOREIRA, Zair de Figueiredo; "Luzes na Penumbra"; 200 pp.; illus.; 23 cm; pb.; Gráfica Mundo Espírita; Rio de Janeiro; Brazil; 1945; pp. 44-46.

1086. MOREL, Hector V., and MORAL, José Dali; "Diccionario de Parapsicología"; 206 pp.; bibl. 201-204; 23 cm; pb.; Editorial Kier; Buenos Aires; Argentina; 1977; p. 41.

1087. MORRANNIER, Jeanne; "La Science et l'Esprit"; 220 pp.; 22 cm; pb.; Éditions Fernand Lanore; Paris; 1983; p. 20.

1088. MORRELL, Edward; "The Twenty-fifth Man"; New Era Publishing Co.; Montclair, N. J.; U. S. A.; 1924.

1089. MORRIS, Robert L.; "PRF Research on Out-of-Body Experiences 1973"; *Theta*; Durham, North Carolina; U. S. A.; Magazine; Quarterly; N. 41; Summer, 1974; pp. 1-3.

1090. MORRIS, Robert L.; "An Experimental Approach to the Survival Problem"; *Theta;* Durham, North Carolina; U. S. A.; Magazine; N. 33, 34; Fall, 1971; Winter, 1972; bibl.; pp. 1-8.

1091. MORRIS, Robert L.; HARARY, Stuart Keith; JANIS, Joseph-Hartwell; John; & ROLL, William G.; "Studies of Communication During Out-of-Body Experiences"; *The Journal of the American Society for Psychical Research;* New York; Vol. 72; N. 1; January, 1978; bibl. 20, 21; pp. 1-21.

1092. MORRIS, J. D.; ROLL, William G.; and MORRIS, Robert L.; Editors; "Research in Parapsychology 1974"; Anthology; 266 pp.; glos. 229-231; index of names; alph.; 21.5 cm; hb.; The Scarecrow Press; Metuchen, N. J.; U. S. A.; 1975; pp. 5, 53-56, 111, 122-133, 190, 191.

1093. MORRIS, J. D.; ROLL, William G.; and MORRIS, Robert L.; Editors; "Research in Parapsychology 1975"; Anthology; 278 pp.; glos. 243-245; index of names; alph.; 21.5 cm; hb.; The Scarecrow Press; Metuchen, N. J.; U. S. A.; 1976; pp. 102-106, 147-150, 229, 244.

1094. MORRIS, J. D.; ROLL, William G.; and MORRIS, Robert L.; Editors; "Research in Parapsychology 1976"; Anthology; 286 pp.; alph.; 21.5 cm; hb.; The Scarecrow Press; Metuchen, N. J.; U. S. A.; 1977; pp. 57-59, 62, 185.

1095. MOSER, Robert E.; "Mental and Astral Projection"; 60 pp.; 21.5 cm; cart.; Esoteric Publications; Cottonwood, AZ; U. S. A.; 1974; pp. 1-60.

1096. MOSS, Thelma; "The Body Electric"; 256 pp.; illus.; 20 cm; pocket; pb.; Granada Publishing; London; 1981; pp. 51, 133, 196-198, 209, 215, 244.

1097. MOSS, Thelma; "The Probability of the Impossible"; 410 pp.; illus.; bibl. 389-404; alph.; 20.5 cm; pb.; New American Library; New York; October, 1975; pp. 278-304; eds.: Eng., It.

1098. MOTOYAMA, Hiroshi; "Theories of the Chakras: Bridge to Higher Consciousness"; introd. Satyananda Saraswati; 294 pp.; illus.; alph.; 21 cm; pb.; The Theosophical Publishing House; Wheaton, Ill.; U. S. A.; 1981; pp. 204, 205, 245, 246, 254.

1099. MOUSSEAUX, Gougenot des; "Les Médiateurs et les Moyens de la Magie, le Fantôme Humain et le Principe Vital"; Plon Éditeurs; 1863.

1100. MOUTIN, L.; Le Magnétisme Humain"; 478 pp.; 18 cm; hb.; Perrin et Cie., Librairies-Éditeurs; Paris; 1907; pp. 367-400.

1101. MOUTIN, L.; "The Relations Between Magnetism and Spiritism"; *The Two Worlds;* Manchester; England; Newspaper; Weekly; Vol. XI; N. 557; July 15, 1898; pp. 463-465.

1102. MULDOON, Sylvan Joseph; "The Case for Astral Projection"; 174 pp.; 20 cm; hb.; 2nd print.; The Aries Press; Chicago, Ill.; U. S. A.; 1936; pp. 1-174.

1103. MULDOON, Sylvan Joseph, and CARRINGTON, Hereward Hubert Levington; "The Phenomena of Astral Projection"; 222 pp.; illus.; bibl. 221, 222; 21 cm; pb.; Samuel Weiser; New York; 1974; pp. 1-222; eds.: Eng., Fr., Sp.

1104. MULDOON, Sylvan Joseph; "Psychic Experiences of Famous People"; XVI + 204 pp.; 21 cm; hb.; dj.; The Aries Press; Chicago, Ill.; U. S. A.; 1947; pp. 168-172.

1105. MULDOON, Sylvan Joseph, and CARRINGTON, Hereward Hubert Levington; "The Projection of the Astral Body"; 320 pp.; illus.; alph.; 22 cm; pb.; 6th print.; Rider & Co.; London; 1977; pp. 1-320; eds.: Eng., Fr., Sp., Port., Ger. (Mini-library).

1106. MULFORD, Prentice; "Nossas Forças Mentais"; without translator; 4 Vol.; 830 pp.; 19.5 cm; pb.; Editora Pensamento; S. Paulo; Brazil; 1984; Vol. I: pp. 16-24, 27-30, 33.

1107. MÜLLER, Karl E.; "Reencarnação Baseada em Fatos"; transl. Harry Meredig; pres. Hernani Guimarães Andrade; prol. Ella Sheridan; 298 pp.; 21 cm; pb.; Editora Difusora Cultural; S. Paulo; Brazil; October, 1978; pp. 76, 81, 99, 108, 110-113, 130-132, 146, 158, 171, 173-177, 180, 181, 185, 200, 232, 235, 239, 240, 243, 252-262, 276, 283, 285, 291, 293.

1108. MUNTAÑOLA, J. Roca; "Viaje al Antiuniverso: El Viaje Astral"; 176 pp.; glos.; 165-171; bibl. 172; 21 cm; cart.; Editorial Alas; Barcelona; Spain; 1974; pp. 1-176 (Mini-library).

1109. MURPHET, Howard; "Sai Baba: Man of Miracles"; Biography; 212 pp.; illus.; alph.; 21 cm; pb.; Samuel Weiser; York Beach, Maine; U. S. A.; 1981; pp. 13, 112, 113, 138, 139, 142-144, 151, 172-174.

1110. MURPHY, Joseph; "Energia Cósmica: O Poder Milagroso do Universo"; transl. A. B. Pinheiro de Lemos; 272 pp.; 21 cm; pb.; Editora Record; Rio de Janeiro; Brazil; no date; pp. 246-248.

1111. MURPHY, Joseph; "A Magia do Poder Extra-Sensorial"; transl. João Távora; 214 pp.; 21 cm; pb.; 8th ed; Editora Record; Rio de Janeiro; Brazil; 1981; pp. 55-66.

1112. MURPHY, G., and BALLOU, R. O.; "William James on Psychical Research"; 340 pp.; Viking Press; New York; 1969.

1113. MURPHY, Michael, and WHITE, Rhea Amelia; "The Psychic Side of Sports"; 228 pp.; illus.; Addison-Wesley; Reading, Mass.; U. S. A.; 1978; pp. 1-3.

1114. MYERS, Frederic William Henry; "Human Personality and his Survival of Bodily Death"; 2 Vol.; 1.426 pp.; glos. XIII-XXII; alph.; 24 cm; hb.; new print.; Longmans, Green, and Co.; London; 1920; Vol I: pp. XV, XVII, 121-152, 220-297, 369-436; eds.: Eng., It., Sp., Port. (Mini-library).

1115. MYERS, Stella; "Herein Know Thyself"; 178 pp.; 21.5 cm; hb.; John Wadsworth; Keighley; Yorkshire; Great Britain; no date; pp. 56-59, 65, 66.

1116. NAILLEN, A. Van der; "Nos Templos do Himalaia"; without translator; 254 pp.; 18.5 cm; 7th ed.; Empresa Editora O Pensamento; S. Paulo; Brazil; no date; pp. 83, 84, 87-89, 159.

1117. NAPIER, Alice; "Zeitplan geändertl"; transl. E. M. Körner; *Esotera;* Freiburg; West Germany; Magazine; Monthly; Yr. 23; N. 3; March, 1972; pp. 263, 264.

1118.   NEBEL, Long John, with TELLER, Sanford M.; "The Psychic World Around Us"; introd. Jacqueline Susann; 192 pp.; 18 cm; pocket; pb.; New American Library; New York; March, 1970; pp. 26, 105-122.

1119.   NEECH, W. F.; "O Homem que Conheceu o Espírito do Universo antes de Morrer"; *Estudos Psíquicos;* Lisboa; Portugal; Magazine; Monthly; 20th Yr.; February, 1959; pp. 34-36.

1120.   NEFF, Mary K.; "Personal Memoirs of H. P. Blavatsky"; 322 pp.; illus.; bibl. 312; alph.; 20.5 cm; pb.; 2nd print.; The Theosophical Publishing House; Wheaton, Ill.; U. S. A.; 1971; pp. 122, 123.

1121.   NEIHARDT, John G.; "Black Elk Speaks"; XVIII + 238 pp.; illus.; 18 cm; pocket; pb.; Washington Square Press; New York; 1972; pp. 204-208.

1122.   NEPPE, Vernon M.; "The Psychology of Déjà Vu"; introd. Lewis A. Hurst; 278 pp.; glos. 248-255; bibl. 256-267; index of names; alph.; 21 cm; pb.; Witwatersrand University Press; Johannesburg; South Africa; 1983; pp. 23, 40, 41, 44.

1123.   NEPPE, Vernon M.; "Temporal Lobe Symptomatology in Subjetive Paranormal Experiments"; *The Journal of the American Society for Psychical Research;* Vol. 77; N. 1; January, 1983; bibl. 14, 15; pp.1-29.

1124.   NESTLER, Vincenzo; "A Telepatia"; transl. Fernanda Figueira; 182 pp.; illus.; bibl. 165-179; 21.5 cm; pb.; Edições 70; Lisboa; Portugal; September, 1979; pp. 107-110.

1125.   NETTO, Aureliano Alves; "Extraordinárias Curas Espirituais"; pref. Celso Martins; 126 pp.; 21 cm; pb.; Editora Eco; Rio de Janeiro; Brazil; no date; pp. 77-79.

1126.   NETTO, Aureliano Alves; "Extraordinários Fenômenos Espíritas"; pref. Celso Martins; 186 pp.; 21 cm; pb.; Editora Cultural Espírita; S. Paulo; Brazil; April, 1982; pp. 101-103, 119-126, 135-140.

1127.   NIELSSON, Haraldur; "Minhas Experiências Espíritas"; transl. Francisco Klörs Werneck; pref. Richard Hoffmann and Georg Henrich; 120 pp.; 19 cm; pb.; Translator's Edition; Rio de Janeiro; Brazil; 1940; pp. 87-90; eds.: Dan., Ger., Fr., Sp., Port.

1128.   NIETZKE, Ann; "Para Viver, é Preciso Aceitar a Morte" (Kübler-Ross); Interview; *Planeta;* S. Paulo; Brazil; Magazine; Monthly; N. 74; November, 1978; illus.; pp. 21-24.

1129.   NIKTO (Pseud.); "En la Frontera del Outro Mundo"; 64 pp.; 18.5 cm; pb.; Editorial Constancia; Buenos Aires; Argentina; 1958; pp. 23-26.

1130.   NOBRE, José de Freitas; "Homenagem a José de Anchieta"; 128 pp.; 21 cm; pb.; Congresso Nacional; Brasília; Brazil; 1980; pp. 111, 113, 117.

1131.   NOBRE, José de Freitas; "A Perseguição Policial Contra Eurípedes Barsanulfo"; 94 pp.; illus.; 21 cm; pb.; Edicel; S. Paulo; Brazil; 1981; pp. 11, 15, 16.

1132.   NOËL, Daniel C.; "Carlos Castaneda: Ombres et Lumières"; transl. and pref. Vincent Bardet and Zéno Bianu; 254 pp.; 18 cm; pocket; pb.; Albin Michel; Paris; 1981; pp. 66-69, 85.

1133.   NOGUEIRA, Tânia; "Quarta Dimensão: A Porta para o Incompreendido"; *Planeta;* S. Paulo; Brazil; Magazine; Monthly; N. 133; October, 1983; illus.; pp. 34-41.

1134.   NORRIS, Benjamin Franklin; "The Octopus"; Novel; introd. Kenneth S. Lynn; XXVIII + 448 pp.; illus.; 21 cm; pb.; Houghton Mifflin Co.; Boston, Massachusetts; U. S. A.; 1958; pp. 262-269.

1135.   NORTHAGE, Ivy; "The Mechanics of Mediumship"; 84 pp.; illus.; 18.5 cm; pb.; Author's Edition; London; 1979; pp. 48-50.

1136.   NORVELL, Anthony; "Alfapsiquismo: O Caminho Místico para Uma Vida Perfeita"; transl. A. B. Pinheiro de Lemos; 252 pp.; 21 cm; pb.; 2nd ed.; Editora Record; Rio de Janeiro; Brazil; no date; pp. 195-203.

1137.   NORVELL, Anthony; "Amazing Secrets of the Mystic East"; 228 pp.; 21.5 cm; pb.; A. Thomas and Co.; Northamptonshire; Great Britain; 1981; pp. 216-227; eds.: Eng., Port.

1138.   NORVELL, Anthony; "O Poder da Meditação Transcendental"; transl. Aydano Arruda; 220 pp.; 21 cm; pb.; Ibrasa; S. Paulo; Brazil; 1979; pp. 167-173.

1139. NORVELL, Anthony; "O Poder das Forças Ocultas"; transl. Aydano Arruda; 220 pp.; 20.5 cm; pb.; 2nd ed.; Ibrasa; S. Paulo; Brazil; 1982; pp. 149-161.

1140. NOVELINO, Corina; "Eurípedes: O Homem e a Missão"; 256 pp.; illus.; 18.5 cm; pb.; Instituto de Difusão Espírita; Araras, SP; Brazil; 1979; pp. 87, 135-137, 179.

1141. NOYES JR., Russell; "Depersonalization in the Face of Life-Threatening Danger: A Description"; *Psychiatry – Journal for the Study of Interpersonal Process;* Washington, D. C.; U. S. A.; Vol. 39; N. 1; February, 1976; pp. 19-27.

1142. NOYES JR., Russell; "The Experience of Dying"; *Psychiatry – Journal for the Study of Interpersonal Process;* Washington, D. C.; U. S. A.; Vol. 35; N. 2; May, 1972; bibl. 183, 184; pp. 174-184.

1143. OCTOPUS BOOKS; "The Occult and the Supernatural"; 124 pp.; illus.; alph.; 30 cm; hb.; dj.; Crescent Books; New York; 1975; pp. 71-73.

1144. O'DONNELL, Elliott; "Ghosts with a Purpose"; 196 pp.; 21 cm; hb.; dj.; Rider and Co.; London; 1951; pp. 76-78.

1145. OESTERREICH, Trangott Konstantin; "Possession Demoniacal & Other"; introd. Anita Kohsen Gregory; XXIV + 400 pp.; alph.; 23 cm; pb.; The Citadel Press; Secaucus, N. J.; U. S. A.; 1974; pp. 27, 28; eds.: Ger., Eng., Fr.

1146. OHLHAVER, Hinrich; "Os Mortos Vivem"; transl. Vicente Jascyk; prfr. Wallace Leal V. Rodrigues; 362 pp.; illus.; 18.5 cm; pb.; Casa Editora O Clarim; Matão, SP; Brazil; 1971; pp. 82-96.

1147. OLCOTT, Henry Steel; "A La Decouverte de L'Occulte"; transl. La Vieuville; introd. L. V.; 464 pp.; illus.; 21 cm; pb.; Éditions Adyar; Paris; 1976; pp. 357-374; ed em Eng., Fr., Sp.

1148. OLDFIELD, Josiah; "The Mystery of Death"; 172 pp.; 21.5 cm; hb.; Rider and Co.; London; 1951; p. 167.

1149. OLIVEIRA, Decio Rufino de; "Fenômenos Parapsicológicos e Energia Consciente"; 242 pp.; bibl. 241; 21 cm; pb.; 2nd ed.; Editora Guanabara; Rio de Janeiro; Brazil; 1972; pp. 128, 129.

1150. OPHIEL (Pseud. for Edward C. Peach); "The Art and Practice of Astral Projection"; VI + 122 pp.; illus.; 21 cm; pb.; 15th ed.; Samuel Weiser; New York; 1977; pp. I-VI, 1-122.

1151. OPHIEL (Pseud. for Edward C. Peach); "The Art and Practice of Caballa Magic"; 152 pp.; illus.; bibl. 152; 21 cm; pb.; 2nd print.; Samuel Weiser; York Beach; Maine; U. S. A.; 1981; pp. 81, 99, 108, 110.

1152. OPHIEL (Pseud. for Edward C. Peach); "The Art and Practice of Clairvoyance"; XIV + 138 pp.; illus.; 21 cm; pb.; 5th print.; Samuel Weiser; New York; 1975; pp. 59, 113-115.

1153. OSBORN, Arthur W.; "The Cosmic Womb"; XIV + 234 pp.; bibl. 217-226; alph.; 21 cm; pb.; The Theosophical Publishing House; Wheaton; Ill.; U. S. A.; 1969; pp. 24, 25, 74, 92-94.

1154. OSBORN, Arthur W.; "The Expansion of Awareness"; prol. Raynor C. Johnson; introd. Rohit Mehta; 272 pp.; bibl. 257-267; alph.; 21 cm; pb.; 2nd print.; The Theosophical Publishing House; Wheaton; Ill.; U. S. A.; 1970; pp. 60, 66, 199.

1155. OSBORN, Arthur W.; "The Future is Now"; 254 pp.; alph.; 18 cm; pb.; 2nd print.; The Theosophical Publishing House; Wheaton; Ill; U. S. A.; 1973; pp. 160-164, 167, 168.

1156. OSBORN, Arthur W.; "The Meaning of Personal Existence"; pref. Ian Stevenson; XVIII + 232 pp.; bibl. 215-224; alph.; 21 cm; hb.; dj.; The Theosophical Publishing House; Wheaton; Ill; U. S. A.; 1967; pp. 45-53, 178, 179.

1157. OSBORN, Arthur W.; "The Superphysical"; introd. W. H. Maxwell Telling; XVI + 350 pp.; bibl. 333-343; alph.; 21.5 cm; hb.; dj.; Ivor Nicholson & Watson; London; 1937; pp. 148-151, 156-160.

1158. OSIS, Karlis; "Assassin's Shadow Disrupts Experiment"; *ASPR Newsletter;* New York; Vol. VII; N. 3; July, 1981; p. 16.

1159. OSIS, Karlis; "Deathbed Observations by Physicians and Nurses"; 114 pp.; illus.; bibl. 102, 103; 21.5 cm; pb.; 4th print.; Parapsychology Foundation; New York; January, 1982; pp. 1-114.

1160. OSIS, Karlis; "Out-of-the-Body Experiences: A Personal View"; *Psi News;* Vol. 4.; N. 3; 1981.

1161. OSIS, Karlis; "Out-of-Body Research at the ASPR"; *ASPR Newsletter;* New York; N. 22; Summer, 1974; pp. 1-3.

1162. OSIS, Karlis; "Recollections of Death: A Medical Investigation"; Books Reviews; *The Journal of the American Society of Psychical Research;* New York; Vol. 77; N. 1; January, 1983; pp. 79-83.

1163. OSIS, Karlis, and HARALDSSON, Erlendur; "At the Hour of Death"; XII + 244 pp.; bibl. 234-237; alph.; 20.5 cm; pb.; Avon Books; New York; November, 1977; pp. 4, 7, 12, 13, 20, 25, 38, 39, 63, 168, 169, 198, 201; eds.: Eng., Sp., It.

1164. OSIS, Karlis, and MC CORMICK, Donna; "The Authors Reply"; *The Journal of the American Society for Psychical Research;* New York; Vol. 75; N. 4; October, 1981; pp. 367, 368.

1165. OSIS, Karlis, and MC CORMICK, Donna; "The Authors Reply to Mr. Isaacs"; *The Journal of the American Society for Psychical Research;* New York; Vol. 75; N. 2; April, 1981; pp. 194-197.

1166. OSIS, Karlis, and MC CORMICK, Donna; "Current ASPR Research on Out-of-Body Experiences"; *ASPR Newsletter;* New York; Vol. VI; N. 4; October, 1980; pp. 21, 22.

1167. OSIS, Karlis, and MC CORMICK, Donna; "Insiders' Views of the OBE: A Questionnaire Survey at the ASPR"; *Newsletter;* The American Society for Psychical Research; New York; Vol. 4; 1978; pp. 18, 19.

1168. OSIS, Karlis, and MC CORMICK, Donna; "Kinetic Effects at the Ostensible Location of an Out-of-Body Projection During Perceptual Testing"; *The Journal of the American Society for Psychical Research;* New York; Vol. 74; N. 3; July, 1980; bibl. 328, 329; pp. 319-329.

1169. OSIS, Karlis, and MITCHELL, Janet Lee; "Physiological Correlates of Reported Out of the Body Experiences"; *Journal of the Society for Psychical Research;* London; Vol. 49; N. 772; June, 1977; bibl. 535, 536; pp. 525-536.

1170. OSMONT, Anne; "Mes Voyages en Astral"; Omnium Litteraire; Paris.

1171. OSTBY, O. A.; "An Awakening to the Universe"; VIII + 368 pp.; 19 cm; hb.; Author's Edition; Minneapolis; Minnesota; U. S. A.; 1927; pp. 2, 6-8, 11, 225-227.

1172. OSTRANDER, Sheila, and SCHROEDER, Lynn; "Psychic Experiences: ESP Investigated"; 250 pp.; alph.; 21 cm; hb.; dj.; Sterling Publishing Co.; New York; 1977; pp. 156-159, 223-225, 238-239.

1173. OSTY, Eugène; "La Connaissance Supra-Normale"; VII + 388 pp.; 21.5 cm; hb.; Librairie Félix Alcan; Paris; 1923; pp. 19-25, 48, 49, 380; eds.: Fr., Eng.

1174. OUSPENSKY, Peter Demianovitch; "Un Nuevo Modelo del Universo"; transl. Armando Cosani Sologúren; 590 pp.; illus.; alph.; 22.5 cm; pb.; 2nd ed.; Editorial Kier; Buenos Aires; Argentina; 1980; pp. 291-330.

1175. OWEN, Alan Robert George; "Psychic Mysteries of the North: Discoveries from the Maritime Provinces and Beyond"; 244 pp.; bibl. 233-238; alph.; 21.5 cm; hb.; dj.; Harper and Row, Publishers; New York; 1975; pp. 143, 144, 146, 147.

1176. OWEN, G. Vale; "Facts and the Future Life"; 192 pp.; 19 cm; hb.; 4th print.; Hutchinson & Co.; London; no date; pp. 124-129.

1177. OWEN, Robert Dale; "Footfalls on the Boundary of Another World"; XX + 392 pp.; bibl. XVII-XX; alph.; 20 cm; hb.; Trübner & Co.; London; 1860; pp. 230-260.

1178. OWEN, Robert Dale; "Região em Litígio Entre Este Mundo e o Outro"; pref. and transl. Francisco Raimundo Ewerton Quadros; 478 pp.; 17.5 cm; hb.; Federação Espírita Brasileira; Rio de Janeiro; Brazil; 1938; pp. 227-232, 391, 392.

1179. OXENHAM, John, and OXENHAM, Erica; "Out of the Body"; VIII + 118 pp.; 18.5 cm; hb.; 4th print.; Longmans Green and Co.; London; 1942; pp. I-VIII, 1-118.

1180. PADILHA, Viriato; "O Livro dos Fantasmas"; 294 pp.; 19 cm; pb.; Spiker; Rio de Janeiro; Brazil; 1956; pp. 277-279.

1181.   PAIGE, C. A.; "Unusual Experiences"; *The Journal of the American Society for Psychical Research;* New York; Vol XL; N. 3; July, 1946; pp. 185-187.

1182.   PAIM, Isaías; "Curso de Psicopatologia"; 288 pp.; bibl. 281-283; index of names; alph.; 21.5 cm; pb.; 9th ed.; Editora Pedagógica e Universitária; S. Paulo; Brazil; 1982; pp. 226-229.

1183.   PAIXÃO, Paulo, and SILVA, César Santos; "Parapsicologia, Ciência ou Magia?"; 120 pp.; illus.; glos. 105-115; bibl. 116-119; 21 cm; pb.; Interinvest Editora e Distribuidora; Rio de Janeiro; Brazil; 1974; pp. 106, 107.

1184.   PALMER, John; "A Comunity Mail Survey of Psychic Experiences"; *The Journal of the American Society for Psychical Research;* New York; Vol. 73; N. 2; April, 1979; pp. 221-251.

1185.   PALMER, John; "Consciousness Localized in Space Outside the Body"; *Osteopathic Physician;* Vol. 14; April, 1974; pp. 51-62.

1186.   PALMER, John; "ESP and Out-of-Body Experiences: EEG Correlates"; *in* Research in Parapsychology 1978; The Scarecrow Press; Metuchen; N. J.; U. S. A.; 1979; pp. 135-138.

1187.   PALMER, John; "The Out-of-Body Experience: A Psychological Theory"; *Parapsychology Review;* New York; Vol. 9; N. 5; September-October, 1978; pp. 19-22.

1188.   PALMER, John; "Some New Directions for Research on Out-of-Body Experiences"; *in* Research in Parapsychology 1973; The Scarecrow Press; Metuchen; N. J.; U. S. A.; 1974.

1189.   PALMER, John, and LIEBERMAN, Ronald; "ESP and Out-of-Body Experiences: A Further Study"; *in* Research in Parapsychology 1975; The Scarecrow Press; Metuchen; N. J.; U. S. A.; 1976.

1190.   PALMER, John, and LIEBERMAN, Ronald; "The Influence of Psychological Set on ESP and Out-of-Body Experiences"; *The Journal of the American Society for Psychical Research;* Vol. 69; N. 3; July, 1975; bibl. 212, 213; pp. 193-213.

1191.   PALMER, John, and VASSAR, Carol; "ESP and Out-of-the-Body Experiences: An Exploratory Study"; *The Journal of the American Society for Psychical Research;* New York; Vol. 68, 1974; pp. 257-280.

1192.   PALMER, John, and VASSAR, Carol; "Toward Experimental Induction of the Out-of-the-Body Experience"; *in* Research in Parapsychology 1973; The Scarecrow Press; Metuchen; N. J.; U. S. A.; 1974; pp. 38-41.

1193.   PANATI, Charles; "Supersenses"; XVI + 342 pp.; illus.; index of names; alph.; 18 cm; pocket; pb.; Anchor Books; New York; 1976; pp. 167-176.

1194.   PANCHADASI, Swami; "The Astral World"; 94 pp.; 15.5 cm; pb.; no publisher; U. S. A.; no date; pp. 28-35.

1195.   PANCHADASI, Swami; "Nuestras Fuerzas Ocultas: Telepatia y Clarividencia"; 254 pp.; 19 cm; pb.; 2nd ed.; Editorial Kier; Buenos Aires; Argentina; 1980; pp. 217-226.

1196.   PAPPALARDO, Armando; "Spiritismo"; 238 pp.; illus.; 15 cm; hb.; 2nd ed.; Ulrico Hoepli; Milano; Italy; 1901; pp. 178-184.

1197.   PAPUS (Pseud. for Gérard Anaclet Vincent Encausse); "ABC Illustré D'Occultisme"; 448 pp.; illus.; 24 cm; pb.; 9th ed.; Éditions Dangles; Paris; Juin, 1979; pp. 70-82, 113, 193, 319, 418, 423.

1198.   PAPUS (Pseud. for Gérard Anaclet Vincent Encausse); "Tratado Elementar de Magia Prática"; transl. and pref. E. P.; 552 pp.; illus.; 21 cm; pb.; Editora Pensamento; S. Paulo; Brazil; 1978; pp. 479-489.

1199.   PARONELLI, Fede; "Nuovi Orizzonti della Scienza Moderna"; 208 pp.; 19 cm; pb.; Fratelli Bocca, Editori; Milano; Italy; 1942; pp. 157, 161, 186.

1200.   PARAPSYCHOLOGY FOUNDATION; "Proceedings of Four Conferences of Parapsychological Studies"; 180 pp.; 20 cm; hb.; Parapsychology Foundadion; New York; 1957; pp. 114-116, 168, 169.

1201.   PARKER, Adrian; "States of Mind"; 198 pp.; bibl.; alph.; Taplinger; New York; 1975.

1202. PARRISH-HARRA, Carol W.; "A New Age Handbook for Death and Dying"; introd. Vera Stanley Alder; XIV + 138 pp.; illus.; bibl. 137, 138; 23 cm; pb.; De Vorss & Co.; Marina del Rey; Cal.; U. S. A.; 1982; pp. 75-80, 102.

1203. PARROT, Ian; "Nad: A Study of Some Unusual Other-World Experiences" (D. Scott Rogo); Books Reviews; *Journal of the Society for Psychical Research;* London; Vol. 46; N. 747; March, 1971; pp. 69-71.

1204. PASCHOAL, Januario De; "Dá Licença..."; 162 pp.; illus.; 23 cm; pb.; Editora Rodemar; Rio de Janeiro; Brazil; 1962; pp. 21, 22.

1205. PASQUA, Norberto; "Fenômenos Anímicos: Prova da Existência do Espírito"; *Unificação;* S. Paulo; Brazil; Newspaper; Monthly; Yr. XXII; N. 257; August, 1974; p. 7.

1206. PASTORINO, Carlos Torres; "Técnica da Mediunidade"; 214 pp.; illus.; bibl. 205; 23 cm; pb.; 2nd ed.; Sabedoria Livraria Editora; Rio de Janeiro; Brazil; 1973; pp. 146, 179, 180.

1207. PAUL, Walter K.; "Out of the Body Mantras"; *Light;* London; Magazine; Vol. 88; 1968; pp. 26-40.

1208. PAULA, João Teixeira de; "Dicionário de Parapsicologia, Metapsíquica e Espiritismo"; pres. Hernani Guimarães Andrade; 3 Vol.; 480 pp.; illus.; bibl.; 23 cm; hb.; Banco Cultural Brasileiro Editora; S. Paulo; Brazil; 1970; p. 60.

1209. PAULA, Luiz Gonzaga Scortecci de; "Mensagens Extraterrestres"; pref. Adhemar Eugênio de Mello; 152 pp.; illus.; 21 cm; pb.; 2nd ed.; João Scortecci & Fumiko Hayashi Editors; S. Paulo; Brazil; 1983; pp. 19, 22, 31, 34, 59, 63, 67, 80-83, 91, 97, 110, 120.

1210. PAVRI, P.; "Teosofia Explicada"; XXIV + 500 pp.; illus.; 20.5 cm; pb.; Editorial Orion; Mexico, D. F.; 1978; pp. 83, 93, 294-296.

1211. PAYNE, Phoebe D., and BENDIT, L. J.; "The Psychic Sense"; introd. L. A. G. Strong; 228 pp.; bibl. 225, 226; alph.; 20 cm; hb.; 2nd ed.; Faber and Faber; London; 1958; pp. 48, 49; eds.: Eng., Fr.

1212. PAZIENTE, Mario; "Curso Preparatório de Eubiose"; pref. João Roque Gomez; 102 pp.; illus.; 21 cm; pb.; Biblioteca Dhâranâ; S. Paulo; Brazil; 1983; pp. 42, 43.

1213. PEARCE-HIGGINS, John D.; "The Study and Practice of Astral Projection" (Robert Crookall); Books Reviews; *Journal of the Society for Psychical Research;* London; Vol. 41; N. 709; September, 1961; pp. 159-161.

1214. PEARCE-HIGGINS, John D., and WHITBY, G. Stanley; "Life, Death and Psychical Research"; 272 pp.; bibl. 270-272; 22 cm; pb.; Rider and Co.; London; 1973; pp. 66-88.

1215. PEARSALL, Ronald; "The Table-Rappers"; 258 pp.; illus.; bibl. 241-243; alph.; 21.5 cm; hb.; dj.; Michael Joseph; London; 1972; pp. 195-201.

1216. PEARSON, P. G.; "Hungry Projection"; *Fate;* Evanston; Ill.; U. S. A.; Magazine; Monthly; Vol. 6; N. 35; February, 1953; p. 67.

1217. PEDRAZZANI, Jean-Michel; "Techniques et Pouvoirs de l'Occultisme"; 224 pp.; glos. 205-212; 22 cm; pb.; Pierre Belfond; Paris; 1976; p. 207; eds.: Fr., Sp.

1218. PEEBLES, J. M.; "Immortality"; 296 pp.; 23 cm; hb.; Colby and Rich, Publishers; Boston; Ill; U. S. A.; 1882; pp. 227-230.

1219. PELLETIER, Horace; "Force Psychique et Extériorisation de la Sensibilité"; *"Le Voile D'Isis";* Paris; Magazine; Weekly; Troisième Année; N. 76; 8, Juin, 1892; pp. 2-5.

1220. PENSAMENTO; Editor; "Forças Ocultas"; 316 pp.; ilus; 18 cm; hb.; 5th ed.; Editora O Pensamento; S. Paulo; Brazil; 1946; pp. 177-180.

1221. PENSAMENTO; Editor; "Magnetismo"; 150 pp.; ilus; 23.5 cm; pb.; 10th ed.; Empresa Editora O Pensamento; S. Paulo; Brazil; 1956; pp. 77-80.

1222. PENSAMENTO; Editor; "Método de Hipnotismo"; 218 pp.; illus.; 18 cm; pb.; 3rd ed.; Editora O Pensamento; S. Paulo; Brazil; 1928; pp. 189-192.

1223.   PENSAMENTO; Editor; "Primeira Série de Instruções: Círculo Esotérico da Comunhão do Pensamento"; 512 pp.; illus.; 15.5 cm; hb.; Editora Pensamento; S. Paulo; Brazil; no date; pp. 118-120.

1224.   PENSAMENTO; Editor; "Dicionário de Ciências Ocultas"; 102 pp.; 19.5 cm; pb.; 9th ed.; Editora Pensamento; S. Paulo; Brazil; 1963; p. 45.

1225.   PERALVA, Martins; "Estudando a Mediunidade"; 232 pp.; illus.; 18 cm; pb.; 7th ed.; Federação Espírita Brasileira; Rio de Janeiro; Brazil; 1979; pp. 86-91, 96-100.

1226.   PEREIRA, Adélia Gregory (Pseud. Hillel); "Desbravamento da Transideral na Era do Aquário"; pref. João Evangelista Ferraz; 160 pp.; 21 cm; pb.; 2nd ed.; Editora CBAG; Rio de Janeiro; Brazil; 1979; pp. 81-85.

1227.   PEREIRA, Yvonne do Amaral; "Devassando o Invisível"; 232 pp.; 18 cm; pb.; 3rd ed.; Federação Espírita Brasileira; Rio de Janeiro; Brazil; 1976; pp. 25-31, 47, 52, 70-72, 75, 78, 79, 84, 86-103, 106, 108-115, 122, 123, 127-143, 147, 150-161, 178-182, 189, 191, 217-232.

1228.   PEREIRA, Yvonne do Amaral; "Dramas da Obsessão"; 210 pp.; illus.; 18 cm; pb.; 4th ed.; Federação Espírita Brasileira; Rio de Janeiro; Brazil; 1981; pp. 20, 28, 59, 167, 170, 201, 205.

1229.   PEREIRA, Yvonne do Amaral; "Memórias de Um Suicida"; 568 pp.; 18 cm; pb.; 4th ed.; Federação Espírita Brasileira; Rio de Janeiro; Brazil; 1973; pp. 9-11.

1230.   PEREIRA, Yvonne do Amaral; "Recordações da Mediunidade"; 212 pp.; 18 cm; pb.; 2nd ed.; Federação Espírita Brasileira; Rio de Janeiro; Brazil; 1976; pp. 16-21, 28-32, 51-56, 64, 65, 75, 114-127, 130-138, 141-147, 158, 160, 181.

1231.   PEREIRA, Yvonne do Amaral; "Ressurreição e Vida"; 314 pp.; 18 cm; pb.; 5th ed.; Federação Espírita Brasileira; Rio de Janeiro; Brazil; 1981; pp. 205, 208.

1232.   PEREIRA, Yvonne do Amaral; "A Tragédia de Santa Maria"; 268 pp.; 18 cm; pb.; 5th ed.; Federação Espírita Brasileira; Rio de Janeiro; Brazil; 1980; pp.; 22, 24-26, 29.

1233.   PEREIRA, Yvonne do Amaral; "Nas Voragens do Pecado"; Novel; 318 pp.; 18 cm; pb.; 4th ed.; Federação Espírita Brasileira; Rio de Janeiro; Brazil; 1980; pp. 9-11.

1234.   PÉRES, Floriano Moinho; "Elizabeth Taylor: Um Caso de Desdobramento"; *Correio Fraterno do ABC;* S. Bernardo do Campo, SP; Brazil; Newspaper; Monthly; Yr. XVI; N. 143; November, 1982; p. 5.

1235.   PÉRES, Floriano Moinho; "Cientistas: Sair do Corpo não é Sonho nem Loucura"; *Jornal Espírita;* S. Paulo; Brazil; Monthly; Yr. VIII; N. 87; September, 1982; illus.; p. 10.

1236.   PERKINS, James Scudday; "Experiencing Reincarnation"; X + 192 pp.; illus.; glos. 179-183; bibl. 187-189; alph.; 21 cm; pb.; 2nd print.; The Theosophical Publishing House; Wheaton; Ill.; U. S. A.; 1979; pp. 5-11.

1237.   PERMUTT, Cyril; "Beyond the Spectrum: A Survey of Supernormal Photography"; 186 pp.; illus.; alph.; 23.5 cm; hb.; dj.; Patrick Stephens; Cambridge; Great Britain; 1983; p. 59.

1238.   PERRY, Michael Charles; "Psychic Studies: A Christian's View"; 224 pp.; bibl. 108, 109; index of names; alph.; 21.5 cm; pb.; The Aquarian Press; Wellingborough; Northamptonshire; Great Britain; 1984; pp. 59-61; 65, 74, 100-109, 114, 120, 210, 214.

1239.   PERSINGER, Michael A.; "The Paranormal"; 248 pp.; MSS Information Corporation; New York; 1974.

1240.   PETERSEN, William J.; "Those Curious New Cults in the 80's"; introd. Jay Kesler; 12 + 308 pp.; bibl. 306, 307; 17.5 cm; pocket; pb.; ed. rev.; Keats Publishing; New Canaan; Connecticut; U. S. A.; 1982; pp. 286-290.

1241.   PETTIWARD, Cynthia; "Dossier Posesión"; transl. Esteban Serra; pref. G. S. Whitby; 156 pp.; 21.5 cm; pb.; Ediciones Martínez Roca; Barcelona; Spain; 1977; pp. 20, 21, 41-43.

1242.   PIKE, E. Royston; "Dictionnaire des Religions"; transl. Serge Huttin; VIII + 330 pp.; 23.5 cm; hb.; dj.; Presses Universitaires de France; Paris; 1954; pp. 17, 29, 127, 296, 297.

1243. PIKE, James A., with KENNEDY, Diane; "The Other Side"; X + 398 pp.; bibl. 387-397; 21 cm; hb.; dj.; Doubleday & Co.; Garden City; New York; 1968; pp. 28, 29, 394.

1244. PIOBB, Pierre; "L'Année Occultiste et Psychique"; 350 pp.; 17 cm; hb.; Henri Daragon, Éditeur; Paris; 5, October, 1909; pp. 248-262.

1245. PIRES, José Herculano; "Mediunidade: Vida e Comunicação"; 160 pp.; bibl. 147; index of names; 21 cm; pb.; 3rd ed.; Edicel; S. Paulo; Brazil; 1978; pp. 14, 115, 117.

1246. PIRES, José Herculano; "Metrô para o Outro Mundo: Ficção Científica Paranormal"; Novel; 136 pp.; 21 cm; pb.; Edicel; S. Paulo; Brazil; September, 1981; pp. 44, 56, 58, 61, 74, 93, 123, 124.

1247. PIRES, José Herculano; "Parapsicologia Hoje e Amanhã"; 216 pp.; glos. 215, 216; bibl. 213, 214; 21 cm; pb.; 6th ed.; Edicel; S. Paulo; Brazil; 1981; pp. 67-69, 126.

1248. PISANI, Isola; "Para Além da Morte"; transl. S. Silva; 300 pp.; bibl. 295-299; 21 cm; pb.; Publicações Europa-América; Lisboa; Portugal; no date; pp. 126-131, 177, 278, 279.

1249. PLANETA; Editorial; "Dicionário de Ciências Ocultas"; 242 pp.; illus.; 20 cm; pb.; Magazine; Monthly; N. 14-A; Especial; Editora Três; S. Paulo; Brazil; October, 1973; p. 139.

1250. PLANETA; Editorial; "Dicionário do Fantástico"; 128 pp.; 20 cm; pb.; Magazine; Monthly; N. 33-A; Especial; Editora Três; S. Paulo; Brazil; April, 1975; pp. 34, 35.

1251. PLANETA; Editorial; "Dicionário do Inexplicado"; 3 Vol.; 198 pp.; illus.; Installments; Magazine; Monthly; N. 131-B, 132-A, 133-A; Editora Três; S. Paulo; Brazil; August-October, 1983; 1st Vol.: pp. 14, 22, 40, 47, 48, 65, 66; 2nd Vol.: p. 58; 3rd Vol.: pp. 16-20.

1252. PLANETA; Editorial; "Os Entrantes"; Magazine; Monthly; N. 147 A; Editora Três; S. Paulo; Brazil; December, 1984; illus.; pp. 36-42.

1253. PLANETA; Editorial; "A Escola de Xamãs"; Magazine; Monthly; N. 109; Editora Três; S. Paulo; Brazil; October, 1981; illus.; pp. 34-41.

1254. PLANETA; Editorial; "Este Homem se Chama Cesario Hossri"; Magazine; Monthly; N. 41; Editora Três; S. Paulo; Brazil; January, 1976; illus.; pp. 18-26.

1255. PLANETA; Editorial; "A Fruta Sagrada"; Magazine; Monthly; N. 49; Editora Três; S. Paulo; Brazil; October, 1976; pp. 26-33.

1256. PLANETA; Editorial; "Ingo Swann: O Homem Que Viaja Fora do Corpo"; Magazine; Monthly; N. 65; Editora Três; S. Paulo; Brazil; February, 1978; illus.; pp. 28-33.

1257. PLANETA; Editorial; "Manual do Feiticeiro"; 132 pp.; 28 cm; pb.; illus.; installments; Magazine; Monthly; N. 139-A, 140-A; Editora Três; S. Paulo; Brazil; April-May, 1984; pp. 16, 31, 39.

1258. PLANETA; Editorial; "Sonhos Psíquicos: Sondando o Outro Lado da Vida"; Magazine; Monthly; N. 128-B; Editora Três; S. Paulo; Brazil; May, 1983; illus.; pp. 50-57.

1259. PLANETA; Editorial; "Thelma Moss: Vamos Sair do Quadrado e Aceitar Todos os Fatos, Estranhos ou Não"; Magazine; Monthly; N. 37-A; Editora Três; S. Paulo; Brazil; October, 1975; illus.; pp. 6-17.

1260. PLANETA; Editorial; "A Visão Transcendente"; Magazine; Monthly; N. 141; Editora Três; S. Paulo; Brazil; June, 1984; illus.; pp. 34-39.

1261. PLATÃO; "A República"; transl. and introd. Maria Helena da Rocha Pereira; LX + 502 pp.; bibl. LV-LVIII; 21 cm; hb.; dj.; Fundação Calouste Gulbenkian; Lisboa; Portugal; September, 1980; pp. 487-500; eds.: Gr., Port., etc.

1262. PLAYFAIR, Guy Lyon; "The Flying Cow"; 320 pp.; illus.; alph.; 21.5 cm; hb.; dj.; Souvenir Press; London; 1975; pp. 63, 64.

1263. PLAYFAIR, Guy Lyon; "The Indefinite Boundary"; app. Hernani Guimarães Andrade; 320 pp.; illus.; glos. 291-294; alph.; 22 cm; hb.; dj.; Souvenir Press; London; 1976; pp. 77, 185, 186, 192, 254, 292.

1264. PLUTARCO DE QUERONÉIA; "Oeuvres Morales"; Traités 37-41; "Sur les Délais de la Justice Divine"; Tome VII; Deuxième Partie; transl. Robert Klaerr, et Yvonne Vernière; XIV + 252 pp.; index of names; alph.; 20 cm; pb.; Société D'Édition Les Belles Lettres; Paris; 1974; pp. 162-169; eds.: Gr., Fr.; private translation in Port.

1265. PLYTOFF, G.; "La Magie"; VIII + 312 pp.; illus.; 17.5 cm; hb.; Librairie J.-B. Bailliére et Fils; Paris; 1892; pp. 86-88.

1266. PODMORE, Frank; "Apparitions and Thought-Transference: An Examination of the Evidence for Telepathy"; XVI + 402 pp.; illus.; alph.; 18.5 cm; hb.; Walter Scott; London; 1894; pp. 204-206, 218, 367, 368.

1267. PODMORE, Frank; "Mediums of the 19th Century"; introd. E. J. Dingwall; 720 pp.; 2 Vol.; alph.; 23.5 cm; hb.; University Books; New York; 1963; Vol. I: pp. XIII, XIV, 47, 66, 88-91.

1268. POINSOT, M.-C.; "Encyclopédie des Sciences Occultes"; 630 pp.; illus.; 23 cm; hb.; Les Éditions Georges-Anquetil; Paris; 1925; pp. 563, 564.

1269. POINSOT, M.-C.; "La Magie des Campagnes"; 286 pp.; 25 cm; pb.; La Diffusion Scientifique; Paris; 1950; pp. 148-152.

1270. POLE, Wellesley Tudor; "Private Dowding"; 94 pp.; 18.5 cm; pb.; 7th ed.; Pilgrims Books Services; Tasburgh Norwich; England; 1984; pp. 65-67, 74, 77, 83-85.

1271. POLIDORO, Osvaldo; "Um Médium de Transportes"; 248 pp.; 15.5 cm; hb.; Livraria Allan Kardec Editora; S. Paulo; Brazil; 1951; pp. 35-37, 50-54, 86, 99, 129, 137, 145, 164-171, 187.

1272. POODT, Th.; "Les Phénomènes Mystérieux du Psychisme"; 496 pp.; glos. 13-17; 23 cm; hb.; Édition Algo; Anvers; France; 1926; pp. 14, 262-268; eds.: Fr., Sp.

1273. POORTMAN, J. J.; "Ochêma: De zin van het Hylisch Pluralisme"; 3 Vol.; 746 pp.; Van Gorkum & Co.; Assen; Netherlands;; 1967; pp. 462-489; eds.: Dut.

1274. POPENOE, Cris; "Books for Inner Development"; 384 pp.; illus.; 28 cm; pb.; Random House; London; 1976; pp. 30, 31.

1275. PORTELA, Fernando; "Além do Normal"; pres. Luis Pellegrini; 162 pp.; 21 cm; pb.; Traço Editora; Santos, SP; Brazil; 1984; pp. 65, 66, 122-133.

1276. PORTELA, Fernando; "Voar Sem Asas"; *Ícaro;* S. Paulo; Brazil; Magazine; Monthly; Yr. I; N. 14; October, 1984; illus.; pp. 34, 35.

1277. POSE, Joaquim Miralles; "Waldo Vieira: Viagens por Outros Planos"; Interview; *Planeta;* S. Paulo; Brazil; Magazine; Monthly; N. 144; September, 1984; illus.; pp. 11-15.

1278. POWELL, Arthur Edgard; "The Astral Body"; XIV + 266 pp.; bibl. XI; alph.; 21 cm; The Theosophical Publishing House; Wheaton; Ill.; U. S. A.; 1978; pp. 1-106, 130, 167, 197, 219, 225, 227, 228, 234-250; eds.: Eng., Sp., Port.

1279. POWELL, Arthur Edgard; "O Corpo Mental"; transl. Nair Lacerda; 272 pp.; illus.; 19.5 cm; pb.; Editora Pensamento; S. Paulo; Brazil; 1984; pp. 63, 86, 105, 126, 135, 136, 143-145, 148-153, 216, 237, 261; eds.: Eng., Sp., Port.

1280. POWELL, Arthur Edgard; "O Duplo Etérico"; prfr. J. Gervásio de Figueiredo; 184 pp.; illus.; glos.; 179-181; 19.5 cm; pb.; 4th ed.; Editora Pensamento; S. Paulo; Brazil; 1973; pp. 10, 36, 52, 68, 76, 78.

1281. POYNTON, John D.; "Astralwanderungen wissenschaftlich bewiesen"; transl. E. M. Körner; *Esotera;* Freiburg; West Germany; Magazine; Monthly; Yr. 23; N. 2; February, 1972; p. 112.

1282. POYNTON, John D.; "Parapsychology in South Africa"; South African Society for Psychical Research; Johannesburg; South Africa; 1975; pp. 95-123.

1283. PRADO, Hamilton; "Ainda no Limiar do Mistério da Sobrevivência"; 64 pp.; 21.5 cm; pb.; Author's Edition; S. Paulo; Brazil; 1969; pp. 1-64.

1284. PRADO, Hamilton; "No Limiar do Mistério da Sobrevivência: Experiência com o Eu Astral"; 158 pp.; 21.5 cm; hb.; Serviço Social Batuira; S. Paulo; Brazil; 1967; pp. 1-158 (Mini-library).

1285. PRATT, J. Gaither; "ESP Research Today: A Study of Developments in Parapsychology Since 1960"; 196 pp.; bibl. 175-178, 184-186; alph.; 22 cm; hb.; The Scarecrow Press; Metychen; N. J.; U. S. A.; 1973; pp. 42-44, 51, 177.

1286. PREL, Carl Du; "La Magie: Science Naturelle"; 2 Vol.; 696 pp.; 2 Parties; transl. Nissa; pref. Guillaume de Fontenay; illus.; 23 cm; pb.; Librairie Des Sciences Psychiques; Paris; 1908; pp. 82-114.

1287. PRELM, Virginia van; "Experiências de Desdobramento no Sítio Uirapuru"; *Planeta;* S. Paulo; Brazil; Magazine; Monthly; N. 68; May, 1978; pp. 24-29.

1288. PRICE, Nancy; "Acquainted with the Night: A Book of Dreams"; 156 pp.; 22 cm; hb.; George Ronald; Oxford; Great Britain; no date; pp. 51-56.

1289. PRIEUR, Jean; "L'Aura et le Corps Immortel"; 280 pp.; 21.5 cm; pb.; Éditions Robert Laffont; Paris; Mars, 1979; pp. 18, 23, 28, 73-120, 274 (Mini-library).

1290. PRINCE, Walter Franklin; "Noted Witnesses for Psychic Occurrences"; Anthology; VIII + 336 pp.; 24 cm; hb.; dj.; University Books; New York; 1963; pp. 30-32, 166-168.

1291. PSYCHIC; Editorial; "Interview: Ingo Swann"; Magazine; illus.; bibl. 48, 49; March-April, 1973; pp. 7-11, 48, 49.

1292. PSYCHIC NEWS; Editor; "Astral Caller Becomes Ball of Light"; London; Newspaper; Weekly; N. 2277; January 24, 1976; p. 8.

1293. PSYCHIC NEWS; Editor; "Astral Traveller Convinces Sceptic by Locating Hidden Birthmark"; London; Newspaper; Weekly; N. 2179; 9, March, 1974; p. 7.

1294. PSYCHIC NEWS; Editor; "Astral Travels Make Him Citizen of Two Worlds"; London; Newspaper; Weekly; N. 2040; July 10, 1971; illus.; p. 8.

1295. PSYCHIC NEWS; Editor; "Clinically Dead Patients get Preview of After-Life"; London; Newspaper; Weekly; N. 2395; April 29, 1978; illus.; p. 1.

1296. PSYCHIC NEWS; Editor; "Clinically Dead Woman Meets Parents in Beyond"; London; Newspaper; Weekly; N. 2519; September 20, 1980; p. 3.

1297. PSYCHIC NEWS; Editor; "Dead Fiancee's Spirit Return Confirms his Out-of-Body Travels"; London; Newspaper; Weekly; N. 2505; June 14, 1980; p. 7.

1298. PSYCHIC NEWS; Editor; "Dead Medico Leaves his Body, and Re-enters it"; London; Newspaper; Weekly; N. 1983; June 6, 1970; p. 7.

1299. PSYCHIC NEWS; Editor; "Doctors Cite Evidence for Life After Life"; London; Newspaper; Weekly; N. 2446; April 21, 1979; illus.; pp. 1, 7.

1300. PSYCHIC NEWS; Editor; "Famous Author Often Left His Body for Astral Travels" (William Gerhardi); London; Newspaper; Weekly; N. 2356; July 30, 1977; p. 3.

1301. PSYCHIC NEWS; Editor; "Film Star Tells of Leaving Her Body" (Gloria Swanson); London; Newspaper; Weekly; N. 2399; May 27, 1978; p. 1.

1302. PSYCHIC NEWS; Editor; "Healer Leaves His Body to Treat Sufferers"; London; Newspaper; Weekly; N. 2419; October 14, 1978; illus.; p. 3.

1303. PSYCHIC NEWS; Editor; "He Leaves His Body and Meets Father in Spirit World"; London; Newspaper; Weekly; N. 2432; January 13, 1979; pp. 1, 5.

1304. PSYCHIC NEWS; Editor; "Hemingway Tells of Out-Body Experience"; London; Newspaper; Weekly; N. 2413; September 2, 1978; p. 7.

1305. PSYCHIC NEWS; Editor; "His Astral Trip From France to Sweden is Confirmed"; London; Newspaper; Weekly; N. 2347; May 28, 1977; p. 7.

1306. PSYCHIC NEWS; Editor; "How to do-it-Yourself Astral Travel"; London; Newspaper; Weekly; N. 2003; October 24, 1970; p. 3.

1307. PSYCHIC NEWS; Editor; "In Astral Form She Follows Her Physical Body for Two Days"; London; Newspaper; Weekly; N. 2484; illus.; January 12, 1980; p. 7.

1308. PSYCHIC NEWS; Editor; "Jeremy Lloyd Astral Travels"; London; Newspaper; Weekly; N. 2455; June 23, 1979; illus.; pp. 1, 8.

1309. PSYCHIC NEWS; Editor; "Leaving her Body Shows Death is Painless"; London; Newspaper; Weekly; N. 2144; July 7, 1973; p. 3.

1310. PSYCHIC NEWS; Editor; "Man Lying on Bed was me"; London; Newspaper; Weekly; N. 2444; April 7, 1979; illus.; p. 8.

1311. PSYCHIC NEWS; Editor; "Medico Confirms Out of Body Trips Occur"; London; Newspaper; Weekly; N. 2480; December 15, 1979; p. 8.

1312. PSYCHIC NEWS; Editor; "Medico is Dismayed to Find he has Died"; London; Newspaper; Weekly; N. 1079; April 8, 1972; p. 5.

1313. PSYCHIC NEWS; Editor; "Medium Describes Her Feelings While Out of the Body"; London; Newspaper; Weekly; N. 101; 28, April, 1934; p. 4.

1314. PSYCHIC NEWS; Editor; "Mother, Out of Body, Joins Dead Son at His Funeral"; London; Newspaper; Weekly; N. 2337; March 19, 1977; p. 2.

1315. PSYCHIC NEWS; Editor; "My Astral Travels" (David Jacobs); London; Newspaper; Weekly; N. 2067; January 15, 1972; illus.; pp. 1, 4.

1316. PSYCHIC NEWS; Editor; "My Husband Leaves His Body to Talk to Me"; London; Newspaper; Weekly; N. 2527; November 15, 1980; p. 2.

1317. PSYCHIC NEWS; Editor; "One in Five Have Astral Trips"; London; Newspaper; Weekly; N. 1434; January 27, 1979; p. 3.

1318. PSYCHIC NEWS; Editor; "Out-of-Body Bride Sees her Wedding From Church Steeple"; London; Newspaper; Weekly; N. 2249; July 12, 1975; illus.; p. 8.

1319. PSYCHIC NEWS; Editor; "Out-of-Body Mystic Heals Dying Boy With Help From Beyond"; London; Newspaper; Weekly; N. 2393; April 15, 1978; p. 3.

1320. PSYCHIC NEWS; Editor; "Out-of-Body Patient Convinces Doubting Dentist"; London; Newspaper; Weekly; N. 2359; August 20, 1977; p. 3.

1321. PSYCHIC NEWS; Editor; "Out-of-Body Trips Don't Prove Survival, Says Scientist"; London; Newspaper; Weekly; N. 2526; November 8, 1980; p. 7.

1322. PSYCHIC NEWS; Editor; "Out-of-Body Trip Ends Fear of Passing"; London; Newspaper; Weekly; N. 2342; April 23, 1977; p. 1.

1323. PSYCHIC NEWS; Editor; "Out of Her Body She Sees Her Baby's Birth"; London; Newspaper; Weekly; N. 2334; February 26, 1977; p. 4.

1324. PSYCHIC NEWS; Editor; "Out of His Body he Finds There Were Two of Me"; London; Newspaper; Weekly; N. 1969; February 28, 1970; illus.; p. 3.

1325. PSYCHIC NEWS; Editor; "Perchance to Dream: of the Future That Comes True"; London; Newspaper; Weekly; N. 1971; March 14, 1970; illus.; p. 8.

1326. PSYCHIC NEWS; Editor; "Pinch Mark Proves His Out-of-Body Visit"; London; Newspaper; Weekly; N. 2465; September 1, 1979; p. 2.

1327. PSYCHIC NEWS; Editor; "Psychic Pays Astral Visits to Planets"; London; Newspaper; Weekly; N. 2264; October 25; 1975; illus.; p. 1.

1328. PSYCHIC NEWS; Editor; "Psychic Projects Himself Into Locked, Sealed Box in Out-of-Body Test"; London; Newspaper; Weekly; N. 2524; October 25, 1980; p. 2.

1329. PSYCHIC NEWS; Editor; "Satellites Confirm His Astral Trip to Planets"; London; Newspaper; Weekly; N. 2393; April 5, 1978; illus.; p. 1.

1330. PSYCHIC NEWS; Editor; "Scientist is Exception to Rule Because He Experiences ESP" (Charles Theodore Tart); London; Newspaper; Weekly; N. 2134; April 28, 1973; p. 7.

1331. PSYCHIC NEWS; Editor; "They Feel More Solid Out of Theirs Bodies"; London; Newspaper; Weekly; N. 2039; July 3, 1971; illus.; p. 5.

1332. PSYCHIC NEWS; Editor; "They Have Previews of Spirit World While Clinically Dead"; London; Newspaper; Weekly; N. 2331; February 5, 1977; illus.; p. 1.

1333. PSYCHIC NEWS; Editor; "They Try to Prove Soul Exists With Out-of-Body Tests"; London; Newspaper; Weekly; N. 2204; August 31, 1974; p. 2.

1334. PSYCHIC NEWS; Editor; "Tortured Convict Met Future Wife During His Out-of-Body Trip"; London; Newspaper; Weekly; N. 1530; December 6, 1980; p. 5.

1335. PSYCHIC NEWS; Editor; "TV Features Out-of-Body Visits By People Who are Medically Dead"; London; Newspaper; Weekly; N. 2441; March 17, 1979; illus.; p. 1.

1336. PSYCHIC NEWS; Editor; "While Asleep He Helped Those Prematurely Born Into Beyond"; London; Newspaper; Weekly; N. 2411; August 19, 1978; illus.; p. 7.

1337. PUHARICH, Andrija Karl; "Beyond Telepathy"; XVIII + 340 pp.; illus.; index of names; bibl. 299-305; alph.; 18 cm; pocket; pb.; Anchor Press; New York; 1973; pp. 60-86, 187-190; eds.: Eng., Fr.

1338. PUHARICH, Andrija Karl; "The Sacred Mushroom: Key to the Door of Eternity"; 262 pp.; illus.; 21 cm; hb.; dj.; Doubleday & Co.; New York; 1959; pp. 39, 59-65, 168, 169, 198, 199.

1339. PUHLMANN, Maria Augusta Ferreira; "As Quatro Deusas da Babilônia"; Novel; pres. Nancy Puhlmann Di Girolamo; 184 pp.; 21 cm; pb.; 2nd ed.; Livraria Allan Kardec Editora; S. Paulo; Brazil; 1984; pp. 13, 38, 74, 140, 180.

1340. PURUCKER, G. de; "Occult Glossary: A Compendium of Oriental and Theosophical Terms"; 10 + 194 pp.; alph.; 21 cm; pb.; Theosophical University Press; Pasadena; Cal.; U. S. A.; 1972; pp. 9, 10, 81, 102.

1341. PURYEAR, Herbert Bruce; "The Edgar Cayce Primer"; XIV + 250 pp.; illus.; alph.; 17.5 cm; pocket; pb.; Bantam Books; New York; September, 1982; pp. 46, 47, 133.

1342. PUSHKIN, Vaniamin N., y DUBROV, Aleksandr Petrovich; "La Parapsicologia y las Ciencias Naturales Modernas"; transl. A. Hernández Barrenechea; 368 pp.; illus.; bibl. 351-365; 17 cm; pocket; pb.; Akal Editor; Madrid; Spain; 1980; pp. 271-273, 277, 300, 301; eds.: Rus., Eng., Sp.

1343. QUEIROZ, Lauro Larrea de; "Dinâmica da Morte"; 174 pp.; 21 cm; pb.; Horizonte Editora; Brasília; Brazil; 1979; pp. 113-127.

1344. RACHLEFF, Owen S.; "The Occult Conceit"; XX + 236 pp.; bibl. 225-227; alph.; 20.5 cm; hb.; dj.; Bell Publishing Co.; New York; 1971; pp. 184-186.

1345. RAJA-AARI, Oreb; "Bases Esenias"; 252 pp.; illus.; 19.5 cm; pb.; 2nd ed.; Editorial Kier; Buenos Aires; Argentina; 1980; pp. 182, 183.

1346. RAJNEESH, Bhagwan Shree; "A Psicologia do Esotérico"; transl. Edvaldo Pereira Lima and Wanda Honório; pref. Ma Satya Bharti; 182 pp.; illus.; 21 cm; pb.; Editora Parma; S. Paulo; Brazil; no date; pp. 73-85.

1347. RAMACHÁRACA, Yogue (Pseud. for William Walter Atkinson); "Catorze Lições de Filosofia Yogue"; transl. Francisco Valdomiro Lorenz; 224 pp.; 19 cm; hb.; 8th ed.; Editora Pensamento; S. Paulo; Brazil; 1957; pp. 148-152.

1348. RAMACHÁRACA, Yogue (Pseud. for William Walter Atkinson); "A Vida Depois da Morte"; transl. Francisco Valdomiro Lorenz; pref. E. P.; 158 pp.; 19.5 cm; pb.; Editora Pensamento; S. Paulo; Brazil; 1981; pp. 34, 35, 66, 67.

1349. RAMPA, Tuesday Lobsang (Pseud. for Cyril Henry Hoskin); "Além do 1.º Décimo"; transl. Lia Alverga-Wyler; 180 pp.; 21 cm; pb.; Distribuidora Record; Rio de Janeiro; Brazil; no date; pp. 35-57, 144, 145.

1350. RAMPA, Tuesday Lobsang (Pseud. for Cyril Henry Hoskin); "Capítulos da Vida"; transl. Lia Alverga-Wyler; 234 pp.; illus.; 21 cm; pb.; Distribuidora Record; Rio de Janeiro; Brazil; 1967; pp. 125, 158, 172-189.

1351. RAMPA, Tuesday Lobsang (Pseud. for Cyril Henry Hoskin); "A Caverna dos Antigos"; transl. Affonso Blacheyre; 216 pp.; 21 cm; pb.; 2nd ed.; Distribuidora Record; Rio de Janeiro; Brazil; no date; pp. 22, 23, 34, 35, 47, 67, 71, 72, 83, 93, 126, 127, 132-138.

1352. RAMPA, Tuesday Lobsang (Pseud. for Cyril Henry Hoskin); "A Chama Sagrada"; transl. Ruy Jungmann; 172 pp.; 21 cm; pb.; 2nd ed.; Distribuidora Record; Rio de Janeiro; Brazil; no date; pp. 74-79.

1353. RAMPA, Tuesday Lobsang (Pseud. for Cyril Henry Hoskin); "Entre os Monges do Tibete"; transl. Affonso Blacheyre; 272 pp.; 21 cm; pb.; 10th ed.; Editora Record; Rio de Janeiro; Brazil; no date; pp. 38-47.

1354. RAMPA, Tuesday Lobsang (Pseud. for Cyril Henry Hoskin); "O Eremita"; transl. Pinheiro de Lemos; 190 pp.; 21 cm; pb.; 2nd ed.; Distribuidora Record; Rio de Janeiro; Brazil; no date; pp. 54, 88, 128, 145, 159.

1355. RAMPA, Tuesday Lobsang (Pseud. for Cyril Henry Hoskin); "A Fé Que me Guia"; transl. Luzia Machado da Costa; 170 pp.; 21 cm; pb.; Editora Record; Rio de Janeiro; Brazil; no date; pp. 8, 9, 18, 111.

1356. RAMPA, Tuesday Lobsang (Pseud. for Cyril Henry Hoskin); "Foi Assim!"; transl. Luzia Machado da Costa; 182 pp.; 21 cm; pb.; 3rd ed.; Editora Record; Rio de Janeiro; Brazil; no date; pp. 123-126.

1357. RAMPA, Tuesday Lobsang (Pseud. for Cyril Henry Hoskin); "Luz de Vela"; transl. Luzia Machado da Costa; 168 pp.; 21 cm; pb.; 3rd ed.; Distribuidora Record; Rio de Janeiro; Brazil; no date; pp. 107-109.

1358. RAMPA, Tuesday Lobsang (Pseud. for Cyril Henry Hoskin); "O Manto Amarelo"; transl. Ruy Jungmann; 168 pp.; 21 cm; pb.; Distribuidora Record; Rio de Janeiro; Brazil; 1966; pp. 78, 79; eds.: Eng., Sp., Port., etc.

1359. RAMPA, Tuesday Lobsang (Pseud. for Cyril Henry Hoskin); "O Médico de Lhasa"; transl. Affonso Blacheyre; 216 pp.; 21 cm; pb.; 9th ed.; Editora Record; Rio de Janeiro; Brazil; no date; pp. 89-92.

1360. RAMPA, Tuesday Lobsang (Pseud. for Cyril Henry Hoskin); "Minha Vida com o Lama"; transl. Affonso Blacheyre; 196 pp.; illus.; 21 cm; pb.; Distribuidora Record; Rio de Janeiro; Brazil; no date; pp. 59, 71, 78.

1361. RAMPA, Tuesday Lobsang (Pseud. for Cyril Henry Hoskin); "A Sabedoria dos Lamas"; transl. Affonso Blacheyre; 182 pp.; 21 cm; pb.; Distribuidora Record; Rio de Janeiro; Brazil; no date; pp. 17-21, 35, 39, 40, 60, 66, 72, 73, 93-96, 101, 102, 116, 118, 120, 121, 134, 140-142.

1362. RAMPA, Tuesday Lobsang (Pseud. for Cyril Henry Hoskin); "O Sábio do Tibete"; transl. Francisco Manoel da Rocha Filho; 180 pp.; 20.5 cm; pb.; 3rd ed.; Editora Record; Rio de Janeiro; Brazil; no date; p. 147.

1363. RAMPA, Tuesday Lobsang (Pseud. for Cyril Henry Hoskin); "Sol Poente"; transl. Luzia Machado da Costa; 184 pp.; 21 cm; pb.; 3rd ed.; Editora Record; Rio de Janeiro; Brazil; no date; pp. 58-62.

1364. RAMPA, Tuesday Lobsang (Pseud. for Cyril Henry Hoskin); "A 3.ª Visão"; transl. Antonio Neves-Pedro; 254 pp.; illus.; 21 cm; pb.; 2nd ed.; Distribuidora Record; Rio de Janeiro; Brazil; no date; pp. 143-145, 249-251.

1365. RAMPA, Tuesday Lobsang (Pseud. for Cyril Henry Hoskin); "Três Vidas"; transl. Vera Neves Pedroso; 188 pp.; 21 cm; pb.; 2nd ed.; Editora Record; Rio de Janeiro; Brazil; no date; pp. 43-67.

1366. RAMPA, Tuesday Lobsang (Pseud. for Cyril Henry Hoskin); "A Vela N.º 13"; transl. Carlos Evaristo M. Costa; 228 pp.; 21 cm; pb.; Distribuidora Record; Rio de Janeiro; Brazil; no date; pp. 205-210.

1367. RAMPA, Tuesday Lobsang (Pseud. for Cyril Henry Hoskin); "Você e a Eternidade"; transl. Affonso Blacheyre; 214 pp.; illus.; 21 cm; pb.; Distribuidora Record; Rio de Janeiro; Brazil; 1965; pp. 64-89, 117, 123-133.

1368. RANDALL, John L.; "Parapsychology and the Nature of Life"; 256 pp.; illus.; bibl. 244-252; alph.; 21.5 cm; hb.; dj.; Souvenir Press; London; 1975; pp. 184, 238, 241.

1369. RANDALL, John L.; "Psychokinesis: A Study of Paranormal Forces Through the Ages"; 256 pp.; glos. 234-238; bibl. 239-250; alph.; 21.5 cm; hb.; dj.; Souvenir Press; London; 1982; pp. 17, 28.

1370. RANDI, James; "Flim, Flam! Psychics, ESP, Unicorns and Other Delusions"; introd. Isaac Asimov; XVI + 342 pp.; illus.; bibl. 331-334; alph.; 23 cm; pb.; Prometheus Books; Buffalo, N. Y.; U. S. A.; 1982; pp. 63, 145-148.

1371. RANDLES, Jenny, and WHETNALL, Paul; "Alien Contact: Window on Another World"; X + 208 pp.; illus.; bibl. 201, 202; alph.; 18 cm; pocket; pb.; Hodder and Stoughton; London; 1983; pp. 65, 66, 100-108, 139, 158, 159, 179.

1372. RANIERI, Raphael A.; "João Vermelho no Mundo dos Espíritos"; 188 pp.; illus.; 18 cm; hb.; Livraria Allan Kardec Editora; S. Paulo; Brazil; no date; pp. 14-94, 129, 139-174.

1373. RANIERI, Raphael A.; "O Sexo Além da Morte"; 180 pp.; 21 cm; pb.; 3rd ed.; Editora Eco; Rio de Janeiro; Brazil; no date; p. 9.

1374. RANK, Otto; "El Doble"; transl. Floreal Mazía; 142 pp.; alph.; 20 cm; pb.; Ediciones Orión; Buenos Aires; Argentina; 1976; pp. 51, 73-76, 98-102.

1375. RAWLINGS, Maurice; "Beyond Death's Door"; 172 pp.; illus.; bibl. 161-164; 21.5 cm; pb.; 5th print.; Sheldon Press; London; 1983; pp. 61-68.

1376. RÃ, Bô In; "O Livro do Além"; transl. Margarida Monteiro; 126 pp.; 21 cm; pb.; Editora Record; Rio de Janeiro; Brazil; 1983; pp. 17-20.

1377. READ, Elizabeth; "Wanted: Astral Fliers"; *Fate;* Evanston; Ill.; U. S. A.; Magazine; Monthly; November, 1968; pp. 44-50.

1378. REDENTOR, Centro; "Prática do Racionalismo Cristão"; 226 pp.; illus.; 22.5 cm; hb.; 6th ed.; Centro Redentor; Rio de Janeiro; Brazil; 1972; pp. 82, 83, 88, 89, 93, 95, 212, 214.

1379. REDENTOR, Centro; "A Vida Fora da Matéria"; 428 pp.; illus.; 22.5 cm; hb.; 1st ed.; Centro Espírita Redentor; Rio de Janeiro; Brazil; 1930; pp. 141-174.

1380. RÉGIS, Jaci, and RODRIGUES, José; "Waldo Vieira e Sua Proposta de Trabalho"; *Espiritismo e Unificação;* Santos, SP; Brazil; Newspaper; Monthly; Yr. XVIII; N. 325; January, 1980; illus.; pp. 1, 5, 6.

1381. REGUSH, June, and REGUSH, Nicholas; "Psi: The Other World Catalogue"; 320 pp.; Putnam; New York; 1974.

1382. REGUSH, Nicholas M.; "Exploring the Human Aura"; 184 pp.; bibl. 143-177; alph.; 21 cm; hb.; dj.; Prentice-Hall; New Jersey; U. S. A.; 1975; pp. 122-125.

1383. REGUSH, Nicholas M.; "The Human Aura"; 240 pp.; bibl. 235-237; 17.5 cm; pb.; Berkeley Medallion Book; New York; December, 1974; pp. 93-112.

1384. REIS, Hermínio da Silva, and REIS, Bianca; "Técnica Física do Desenvolvimento da Consciência Humana"; Installment; Copy; 92 pp.; illus.; 31 cm; pb.; 2nd ed.; Authors' Edition; Belo Horizonte, MG; Brazil; no date; pp. 1-92.

1385. RÉNO-BAJOLAIS, J.; "Méthode Racionnelle D'Influence a Distance et de Dédoublement"; 128 pp.; illus.; 18.5 cm; pb.; 7th ed.; Éditions Niclaus; Paris; 1982; pp. 105-124.

1386. REYNER, J. H.; "No Easy Immortality"; 90 pp.; bibl. 87, 88; alph.; 22 cm; hb.; dj.; George Allen & Unwin; London; 1979; pp. 39, 40, 59, 60.

1387. RHINE, Joseph Banks; "O Alcance do Espírito"; transl. E. Jacy Monteiro; 220 pp.; illus.; bibl. 219, 220; 21 cm; pb.; Bestseller Importadora de Livros; S. Paulo; Brazil; 1965; pp. 59, 60.

1388. RHINE, Joseph Banks; "Telepathy and Other Untestable Hypothesis"; *Journal of Parapshchology;* Durham; North Carolina; U. S. A.; Vol. 38; June, 1974; pp. 137-153.

1389. RHINE, Louisa Ella; "Canais Ocultos do Espírito"; transl. E. Jacy Monteiro; pref. J. B. Rhine; 260 pp.; 21 cm; pb.; Bestseller Importadora de Livros; S. Paulo; Brazil; 1966; pp. 23, 24, 27, 28.

1390. RHINE, Louisa Ella; "ESP in Life and Lab"; XII + 276 pp.; alph.; 21 cm; hb.; The Macmillan Co.; New York; 1967; pp. 42, 43.

1391. RIBEIRO, Matias José; "Um Fato Incrível, Mas Verdadeiro"; *Shopping News – City News;* S. Paulo; Brazil; Newspaper; 7, August, 1983; illus.; p. 14.

1392. RICHARDS, Steve, "Invisibility: Mastering the Art of Vanishing"; 160 pp.; illus.; alph.; 21.5 cm; pb.; The Aquarian Press; London; 1982; pp. 24, 25, 45, 46, 109, 110, 139; eds.: Eng., Port.

1393. RICHARDS, Steve; "Levitacion"; transl. Rafael Lassaletta; 170 pp.; illus.; 20.5 cm; pb.; Edaf; Madrid; Spain; 1981; pp. 58-64.

1394. RICHARDS, Steve; "The Traveller's Guide to the Astral Plane"; 110 pp.; illus.; alph.; 21.5 cm; pb.; The Aquarian Press; Wellingborough; Northamptonshire; Great Britain; 1983; pp. 1-110.

1395. RICHARDSON, C.; "46 Berichte von der Schwelle des Todes"; *Esotera;* Freiburg; West Germany; Magazine; Monthly; Yr. 22; N. 8; August, 1971; pp. 747, 748.

1396. RICHARDSON, William T.; "Out-of-the Body Sensations"; Correspondence; *Journal of the Society for Psychical Research;* London; Vol. 41; N. 710; December; 1961; pp. 214.

1397. RICHELIEU, Peter; "A Viagem de Uma Alma"; transl. Nair Lacerda; 198 pp.; 19.5 cm; pb.; Editora Pensamento; S. Paulo; Brazil; 1974; pp. 1-198.

1398. RICHET, Charles Robert; "Traité de Métaspsychique"; 812 pp.; illus.; index of names; alph.; 23.5 cm; hb.; Librairie Félix Alcan; Paris; Janvrier, 1922; pp. 700-714; eds.: Fr., Eng., Sp., Port.

1399. RICHMANN, Gary; "Caso Hermínio-Bianca, Dura Missão Após um Contato de 3.° Grau"; *Planeta;* S. Paulo; Brazil; Magazine; Monthly; N. 94; illus.; July, 1980; pp. 50-54.

1400. RICHMOND, Cora L. V.; "My Experiences While Out of My Body"; 76 pp.; 20 cm; hb.; Christopher Press; Boston; Ill.; U. S. A.; 1915; pp. 1-76.

1401. RIGONATTI, Eliseu; "O Espiritismo Aplicado"; 82 pp.; 19.5 cm; pb.; 4th ed.; Editora Pensamento; S. Paulo; Brazil; 1981; pp. 11-20.

1402. RIGONATTI, Eliseu; "O Evangelho das Recordações"; 254 pp.; 19 cm; pb.; Editora Pensamento; S. Paulo; Brazil; 1983; pp. 25, 77, 78, 82, 84, 88, 100, 123, 163-165, 169, 170, 188, 246.

1403. RILAND, George; "The New Steinerbooks Dictionary of the Paranormal"; 8 + 358 pp.; illus.; 21 cm; hb.; Rudolf Steiner Publications; New York; 1980; pp. 17, 29, 271, 343.

1404. RING, Kenneth; "Commentary on "The Reality of Death Experiences: A Personal Perspective" (Ernst A. Rodin); *The Journal of Nervous and Mental Disease;* Baltimore; Maryland; U. S. A.; Vol. 168; N. 5; 1980; bibl. 274; pp. 273, 274.

1405. RING, Kenneth; "Further Studies of the Near-Death Experience"; *Theta*; Durham; North Carolina; U. S. A.; Magazine; Vol. 7; 1979; pp. 1-3.

1406. RING, Kenneth; "Life at Death: A Scientific Investigation of the Near-Death Experience"; introd. Raymond Moody; 310 pp.; illus.; bibl. 297-300; alph.; 23.5 cm; pb.; Quill; New York; 1982; pp. 1-310.

1407. RITCHIE, George Gordon, and SHERRIL, Elisabeth; "Voltar do Amanhã"; pres. Raymond A. Moody Jr.; transl. Gilberto Campista Guarino; 116 pp.; 21 cm; pb.; Editorial Nórdica; Rio de Janeiro; Brazil; 1981; pp. 33-69, 80, 91, 92 (Mini-library).

1408. RIVERAIN, Jean; "Nuestros Poderes Ocultos"; transl. Eduardo Pons Prades; 144 pp.; illus.; 21.5 cm; pb.; Ediciones Martínez Roca; Barcelona; Spain; 1973; pp. 118-120, 124-129.

1409. RIZZINI, Carlos Toledo; "Evolução Para o Terceiro Milênio: Tratado Psíquico Para o Homem Moderno"; pref. Celso Martins; 296 pp.; bibl. 269, 270; alph.; 21 cm; pb.; 2nd ed.; Edicel; S. Paulo; Brazil; 1980; pp. 37-39, 68, 71, 81, 87, 89, 156, 157.

1410. RIZZINI, Carlos Toledo; "O Homem e Sua Felicidade"; 248 pp.; illus.; bibl. 229-232; glos. 232-247; 21 cm; pb.; Edições Correio Fraterno; S. Bernardo do Campo, SP; Brazil; March, 1984; pp. 95, 96.

1411. RIZZINI, Jorge; "Eurípedes Barsanulfo: O Apóstolo da Caridade"; 134 pp.; illus.; 21 cm; pb.; Edições Correio Fraterno; S. Bernardo do Campo, SP; Brazil; 1979; pp. 75, 76.

1412. RIZZO, Samuel S.; "Psico-Bio-Física ou Metafísica Científica"; *Estudos Psíquicos;* Lisboa; Portugal; Magazine; Monthly; 39th Yr.; N. 3; March, 1978; pp. 70-77.

1413. RIZZO, Samuel S.; "Report on Metapsychical Investigation"; 108 pp.; 21.5 cm; pb.; Livraria Freitas Bastos; Rio de Janeiro; Brazil; 1965; pp. 10, 11, 75.

1414. ROBERTS, Jane; "Adventures in Consciousness"; XII + 290 pp.; illus.; glos. 280, 281; alph.; 18 cm; pocket; pb.; Bantam Books; New York; July, 1979; pp. 81, 191, 199.

1415. ROBERTS, Jane; "The Afterdeath Journal of an American Philosopher: The World View of William James"; 242 pp.; alph.; 21 cm; pb.; Prentice-Hall; Englewood Cliffs; New Jersey; U. S. A.; 1978; pp. 112.

1416. ROBERTS, Jane; "The Coming of Seth"; XVIII + 252 pp.; bibl. 251, 252; 18 cm; pocket; pb.; Pocket Books; New York; April, 1976; pp. XI, 208, 209, 233, 236.

1417. ROBERTS, Jane; "The Education of Oversoul Seven"; Prentice-Hall; Englewoods Cliffs; New Jersey; U. S. A.; 1973.

1418. ROBERTS, Jane; "The Nature of the Psyche"; 258 pp.; alph.; 17.5 cm; pocket; pb.; Bantam Books; New York; January, 1984; p. 34.

1419. ROBERTS, Jane; "Psychic Politics"; 374 pp.; alph.; 21 cm; pb.; Prentice-Hall; Englewoods Cliffs; New Jersey; U. S. A.; 1976; pp. 208-211.

1420. ROBERTS, Jane; "The Seth Material"; XIV + 318 pp.; illus.; alph.; 21 cm; pb.; Prentice-Hall; Englewoods Cliffs; New Jersey; U. S. A.; 1970; pp. 71-78, 97-110.

1421. ROBERTS, Jane; "Seth Speaks"; XXVIII + 516 pp.; alph.; 21 cm; pb.; Prentice-Hall; Englewoods Cliffs; New Jersey; U. S. A.; 1972; pp. 73, 254, 255, 257.

1422. ROBERTS, Jane; "The 'Unknown' Reality: A Seth Book"; 296 pp.; alph.; 23 cm; hb.; dj.; Prentice-Hall; Englewood Cliffs; New Jersey; U. S. A.; 1977; pp. 81, 82.

1423. ROCHA, Alberto de Souza; "Letargia e Catalepsia"; *Desobsessão;* Porto Alegre, RS; Brazil; Newspaper; Monthly; Yr. XXXI; N. 373; March, 1979; pp. 1, 5.

1424. ROCHA, Alberto de Souza; "Perispírito e Projeção"; *Revista Internacional do Espiritismo;* Matão, SP; Brazil; Monthly; Yr. LVIII; N. 8; September, 1983; pp. 228-230.

1425. ROCHA, Boanerges da (Pseud. for Indalício Hildegardo Mendes); "Importante Experiência de Desdobramento Voluntário"; *Reformador;* Rio de Janeiro; Brazil; Magazine; Monthly; Yr. 79; N. 7; July, 1961; pp. 157, 158.

1426. ROCHAS, Eugène August Albert D'Aiglun; "The Bordeland of Physics"; without translator; *The Two Worlds;* Manchester; England; Newspaper; Weekly; Vol. XI; N. 555; July 1, 1898; pp. 421-423.

1427. ROCHAS, Eugène August Albert D'Aiglun; "Experiências de Bilocação"; without translator; *Estudos Psíquicos*; Lisboa; Portugal; Magazine; Monthly; N. 10; March, 1907; pp. 187-191.

1428. ROCHAS, Eugène August Albert D'Aiglun; "L'Exteriorisation de la Motricité"; VIII + 482 pp.; illus.; 21.5 cm; hb.; Chamuel, Éditeur; Paris; 1896; pp. 337-346.

1429. ROCHAS, Eugène August Albert D'Aiglun; "L'Exteriorisation de la Sensibilité"; XII + 252 pp.; illus.; 21.5 cm; hb.; Chamuel; Éditeur; Paris; 1895; pp. 47-73.

1430. ROCHAS, Eugène August Albert D'Aiglun; "Les Vies Successives"; 504 pp.; illus.; 22 cm; hb.; Librairie Genérale des Sciences Occultes; Paris; 1911; pp. 39-43; eds.: Fr., Port.

1431. RODRIGUES, Antonio Fernandes, and MARTINS, Celso; "Na Rota do Ano 2.000"; pres. Rodrigues de Camargo; 114 pp.; 21 cm; pb.; Editora e Gráfica ABC do Interior; Conchas, SP; Brazil; 1984; pp. 27-29.

1432. RODRIGUES, Henrique; "Curso Intensivo de Parapsicologia e Psicobiofísica"; 48 pp.; illus.; 27.5 cm; pb.; Centro de Estudos Psicobiofísicos; Belo Horizonte, MG; Brazil; no date; pp. 13, 14, 17, 39, 40.

1433. RODRIGUES, Ubirajara Franco; "Parapsicologia e Justiça"; 170 pp.; glos. 163-169; bibl. 161, 162; 21 cm; pb.; Editora Gráfica Véritas; Três Corações, MG; Brazil; no date; p. 167.

1434. RODRIGUES, Wallace Leal V.; "Entrevista com o Eng. Hernani Guimarães Andrade"; *Revista Internacional do Espiritismo;* Matão, SP; Brazil; Monthly; N. 9; October, 1974; illus.; pp. 271-277.

1435. ROGO, D. Scott; "Aspects of Out-of-the-Body Experiences"; *Journal of the Society for Psychical Research;* London; Vol. 48; N. 768; June, 1976; pp. 329-335.

1436. ROGO, D. Scott; "An Experience of Phantoms"; 214 pp.; illus.; bibl. 207-209; alph.; 21 cm; hb.; dj.; Taplinger Publishing Co.; New York; 1974; pp. 90-105, 119-122, 133, 161-180, 185, 186, 201, 202; eds.: Eng., It.

1437. ROGO, D. Scott; "Astral Projection: A Risky Practice?"; *Fate;* Evanston; Ill.; U. S. A.; Magazine; Monthly; Vol. 26; N. 5; Issue 278; May, 1973; pp. 74-80.

1438. ROGO, D. Scott; "Case Studies in Parapsychology"; *Parapsychology Review;* New York; Vol. 15; N. 5; September-October, 1984; pp. 5-7.

1439. ROGO, D. Scott; "En Busca de lo Desconocido"; transl. Esteban Serra; 180 pp.; 20 cm; pb.; Ediciones Martínez Roca; Barcelona; Spain; 1982; pp. 46-74, 143, 144; eds.: Eng., Sp.

1440. ROGO, D. Scott; "A Experiência Fora do Corpo"; without translator; *Planeta;* S. Paulo; Brazil; Magazine; Monthly; N. 73; October, 1978; pp. 24-29.

1441. ROGO, D. Scott; "Astral Projection in Tibetan Buddhist Literature"; *International Journal of Parapsychology;* U. S. A.; Vol. 10; N. 3; Autumn, 1968; pp. 277-284.

1442. ROGO, D. Scott; "Exploring Psychic Phenomena"; 168 pp.; bibl. 162, 163; alph.; 21 cm; pb.; The Theosophical Publishing House; Wheaton; Ill.; U. S. A.; 1976; pp. 11, 72-93, 107, 143.

1443. ROGO, D. Scott; "Events On the Threshold of the Afterlife" (Robert Crookall); Books Reviews; *Theta;* Durham; North Carolina; U. S. A.; Magazine; N. 38; Winter, 1973; pp. 5, 6.

1444. ROGO, D. Scott; "Leaving the Body: A Practical Guide to Astral Projection"; introd. Charles Theodore Tart; XIV + 190 pp.; illus.; bibl. 185; alph.; 20.5 cm; pb.; Prentice-Hall; Englewood Cliffs; New Jersey; U. S. A.; 1983; pp. I-XIV, 1-190 (Mini-library).

1445. ROGO, D. Scott; "Man Does Survive Death: The Welcoming Silence"; 192 pp.; illus.; 21 cm; pb.; The Citadel Press; New Jersey; U. S. A.; 1977; pp. 13-50, 66, 67.

1446. ROGO, D. Scott; "Mind Beyond the Body: The Mystery of ESP Projection"; Anthology; 366 pp.; illus.; 18 cm; pocket; pb.; Penguin Books; New York; 1978; pp. 1-366; eds.: Eng., It.

1447. ROGO, D. Scott; "Miracles: A Parascientific Inquiry Into Wondrous Phenomena"; XII + 334 pp.; illus.; bibl. 315-321; alph.; 23 cm; pb.; Contemporary Books; Chicago; Ill.; U. S. A.; 1983; pp. 1, 3, 8, 30, 65, 68, 70, 81-109, 202, 265, 299, 301, 305, 308, 313.

1448. ROGO, D. Scott; "NAD: A Study of Some Unusual "Other-World" Experiences"; postscript: Robert Crookall; 176 pp.; bibl. 173-176; 21 cm; hb.; dj.; University Books; New York; 1970; pp. 18-35, 39, 50, 58, 63-67, 70, 87, 114, 129-134, 142-144, 148, 157-170.

1449. ROGO, D. Scott; "Out-of-Body Dimensions"; *in* "Other-Worlds, Other Universes"; Brad Steiger and John White; Editors; Doubleday; Garden City, N. Y.; 1977.

1450. ROGO, D. Scott; "Out-of-the-Body Experiences"; *Psychic;* U. S. A.; Magazine; March-April, 1973; illus.; pp. 50-55.

1451. ROGO, D. Scott; "Parapsychology: A Century of Inquiry"; 318 pp.; bibl. 305-307; alph.; 18 cm; pocket; pb.; Dell Publishing Co.; New York; April, 1976; pp. 274-279.

1452. ROGO, D. Scott; "Parapsychology at the APA"; *Parapsychology Review;* New York; Vol. 12; N. 6; November-December, 1981; pp. 6-9.

1453. ROGO, D. Scott; "The Poltergeist Experience"; 302 pp.; alph.; 18.5 cm; pocket; pb.; Penguin Books; New York; 1979; pp. 241-247.

1454. ROGO, D. Scott; "Psychic Researchers Dismiss Mediumship"; *Two Worlds;* London; Magazine; Monthly; 81st Year; N. 3893; June, 1968; pp. 186, 187.

1455. ROGO, D. Scott; "A Psychic Study of "The Music of the Spheres"; NAD; Vol. II; pref. Raymond Bayless; 176 pp.; bibl. 173-176; 21 cm; hb.; dj.; University Books; Secaucus; N. J.; U. S. A.; 1972; pp. 9, 17, 24, 27, 46-48, 157-161.

1456. ROGO, D. Scott; "Psychological Models of the Out-of-Body Experience"; *Journal of Parapsychology;* U. S. A.; Vol. 46; 1982; pp. 29-45.

1457. ROGO, D. Scott; "Researching the Out-of-Body Experience: The State of the Art"; *Anabiosis: The Journal for Near-Death Studies;* U. S. A.; Vol. 4; N. 1; Spring, 1984; bibl. 45-49; pp. 21-49.

1458. ROGO, D. Scott; "El Universo Encantado"; transl. Jorge Binaghi; 198 pp.; 20 cm; pb.; Ediciones Martínez Roca; Barcelona; Spain; 1981; p. 39.

1459. ROGO, D. Scott; & BAYLESS, Raymond; "Phone Calls From the Dead"; XIV + 210 pp.; bibl. 197-201; alph.; 17.5 cm; pocket; pb.; Berkley Publishing Corporation; New York; February, 1980; pp. 79, 80; eds.: Eng., It.

1460. ROHMER, Sax (Pseud. for Arthur Sarsfield Ward); "Astral Voyages"; *Pall Mall Gazette;* Great Britain; September, 1935.

1461. ROLIM, P.; "O Problema Espiritista"; 614 pp.; 19 cm; pb.; Casa do Castelo Editora; Coimbra; Portugal; 1932; pp. 336-338, 446, 450-455.

1462. ROLL, William G.; Editor; "Research in Parapsychology 1977"; Anthology; VIII + 272 pp.; 21.5 cm; hb.; alph.; The Scarecrow Press; Metuchen, N. J.; U. S. A.; 1978; pp. 11-14, 28.

1463. ROLL, William G.; Editor; "Research in Parapsychology 1978"; Anthology; VIII + 212 pp.; alph.; 21.5 cm; hb.; The Scarecrow Press; Metuchen, N. J.; U. S. A.; 1979; pp. 3, 9, 19, 31, 34, 50-52, 135-138.

1464. ROLL, William G.; Editor; "Research in Parapsychology 1979"; Anthology; VI + 232 pp.; alph.; 21.5 cm; hb.; The Scarecrow Press; Metuchen, N. J.; U. S. A.; 1980; pp. 21, 142-145.

1465. ROLL, William G.; & BELOFF, John; Editors; "Research in Parapsychology 1980"; Anthology; VI + 168 pp.; alph.; 21.5 cm; hb.; The Scarecrow Press; Metuchen, N. J.; U. S. A.; 1981; pp. 11, 14, 105, 106, 125, 132, 138, 142.

1466. ROLL, William G.; BELOFF, John; & WHITE, Rhea Amelia; Editors; "Research in Parapsychology 1982"; Anthology; XVI + 366 pp.; index of names; alph.; 21.5 cm; hb.; The Scarecrow Press; Metuchen, N. J.; U. S. A.; 1983; pp. 6, 8, 18, 20, 28, 130, 131, 225, 229-234.

1467. ROLL, William G.; MORRIS, Robert L.; & MORRIS, J. D.; Editors; "Research in Parapsychology 1972"; Anthology; 250 pp.; alph.; 21.5 cm; hb.; The Scarecrow Press; Metuchen, N. J.; U. S. A.; 1973; pp. 12, 78, 79, 178, 184, 185.

1468. ROLL, William G.; MORRIS, Robert L.; &MORRIS, J. D.; Editors; "Research in Parapsychology 1973"; Anthology; 250 pp.; alph.; 21.5 cm; hb.; The Scarecrow Press; Metuchen, N. J.; U. S. A.; 1974; pp. 6, 36-41, 107-120.

1469. ROLL, William G.; MORRIS, Robert L.; & WHITE, Rhea Amelia; Editors; "Research in Parapsychology 1981"; Anthology; 246 pp.; alph.; 21.5 cm; hb.; The Scarecrow Press; Metuchen, N. J.; U. S. A.; 1982; pp. 42, 73-75, 124, 190, 191.

1470. ROLL, William G.; "Studies of Communication During Out-of-Body Experiences"; *The Journal of the American Society for Psychical Research;* New York; Vol. 72; N. 1; January, 1978; bibl. 20, 21; pp. 3-21.

1471. RORIZ, Julio Cesar de Sá; "Experiências Extracorpóreas"; *Presença Espírita;* Salvador, BA; Brazil; Magazine; Monthly; Yr. IX; N. 104; October, 1982; pp. 20, 21.

1472. ROSACRUZ; Ordem; "Monografia Oficial"; Temple's Section; 8.º Grade; 8 pp.; N. 16; 25.5 cm; pb.; Ordem Rosacruz; Curitiba, PR; Brazil; no date; pp. 1, 2.

1473. ROSACRUZ; Ordem; "Monografia Oficial"; Temple's Section; 8.º Grade; 6 pp.; N. 17; 25.5 cm; pb.; Ordem Rosacruz; Curitiba, PR; Brazil; no date; pp. 1, 2.

1474. ROSE, Karen; "In the Land of the Mind"; 266 pp.; bibl. 254-260; Atheneum; New York; 1975.

1475. ROSIN, Zilda Giunchetti; "Perda de Entes Queridos"; 160 pp.; illus.; 21 cm; pb.; 8th ed.; Instituto Maria; Juiz de Fora, MG; Brazil; no date; pp. 30-32, 35, 42-44, 48, 53, 54, 76, 82, 90, 97, 101, 105, 109, 122, 123, 138, 140, 142-148.

1476. ROSSI, Hélio; "Somatorpor: Menor Resistência ao Afloramento Mediúnico"; *Correio Fraterno do ABC;* S. Bernardo do Campo, SP; Brazil; Newspaper; Monthly; Yr. XVI; N. 147; March, 1983; p. 5.

1477. ROSSI-PAGNONI, Francesco, et MORONI, Luigi; "Quelques Essais de Médiumnité Hypnotique"; transl. Francisca Vigné; 124 pp.; 22 cm; pb.; Librairie des Sciences Psychologiques; Paris; no date; pp. 115, 116.

1478. ROUHIER, Alexandre; "Le Peyotl: Des Plantes Divinatoires"; pref. Em. Perrot; XII + 376 + 34 pp.; illus.; bibl. 71, 72, 365-375; 22 cm; pb.; Guy Trédaniel; Paris; 1975; pp. 5-12, 25-28.

1479. ROURE, Lucien; "Le Merveilleux Spirite"; VIII + 398 pp.; 18 cm; hb.; 2nd ed.; Gabriel Beauchesne; Paris; 1917; pp. 104-107, 111-124.

1480. ROY, Dilip Kumar, and DEVI, Indira; "Peregrinos das Estrelas"; transl. Gilberto Bernardes de Oliveira; prol. Frederic Spielgelberg; 310 pp.; 19.5 cm; pb.; Editora Pensamento; S. Paulo; Brazil; 1976; pp. 150, 204, 219-221.

1481. RPA; Editor; "Enciclopédia de Ciências Ocultas e Parapsicologia"; transl. Clarice Tavares and J. Santos Tavares; prfr. Elizabete Reis; 4 Vol.; 1.200 pp.; illus.; 31 cm; hb.; RPA Publicações; Lisboa; Portugal; 1978; Vol. 2: pp. 7-35.

1482. RUSSELL, Edward Wriothesley C.; "Projeto para o Destino: A Revelação da Alma pela Ciência"; transl. Maio Miranda; 188 pp.; 19.5 cm; pb.; Editora Pensamento; S. Paulo; Brazil; 1983; pp. 112, 113, 135, 142, 188.

1483. RUTLEDGE, Archibald; "Things We Can't Explain"; *The Reader's Digest;* U. S. A.; Magazine; Monthly; Vol. 41; N. 247; November, 1942; pp. 30-32.

1484. RÝZL, Milan; "Der Tod und was danach Kommt"; transl. Helga Künzel; 230 pp.; 22.5 cm; hb.; dj.; Ariston Verlag; Austria; 1981; pp. 103-115; eds.: Eng., Ger.

1485. RÝZL, Milan; "Parapsicologia, Fatti e Prospettive"; transl. Jacopo Comin; pref. Ettore Mengoli; 288 pp.; glos. 273-275; alph.; 21 cm; pb.; 3rd ed.; Edizioni Mediterranee; Roma; Italy; January, 1978; pp. 91, 95, 125, 128, 137, 140-142, 235, 246, 273; eds.: Eng., It.

1486. SABOM, Michael B.; "Recollections of Death: A Medical Investigation"; 302 pp.; bibl. 287-292; alph.; 18 cm; pocket; pb.; Corgi Books; London; 1982; pp. 1-302 (Mini-library).

1487. SABOM, Michael B.; "Near-Death Experiences"; *New England Journal of Medicine;* Vol. 297; N. 19; 1977; p. 1071.

1488. SABOM, Michael B., and BLACHER, Richard S.; "The Near-Death Experiences"; *The Journal of the American Medical Association;* Vol. 244; N. 1; July 4, 1980; pp. 29, 30.

1489. SACHS, Margaret; "The Ufo Encyclopedia"; 408 pp.; illus.; bibl. 401-408; 23.5 cm; pb.; Perigee Book; New York; 1980; p. 155.

1490. SADHU, Mouni; "Samadhi: The Superconsciousness of the Future"; 182 pp.; bibl. 182; 20 cm; pb.; Unwin Paperbacks; London; 1971; pp. 171-181.

1491. SADHU, Mouni; "El Tarot"; transl. Hector Vicente Morel; 516 pp.; illus.; bibl. 513, 514; 23 cm; pb.; 3rd ed.; Editorial Kier; Buenos Aires; Argentina; 1978; pp. 330-340.

1492. SAGAN, Carl; "O Romance da Ciência"; transl. Carlos Alberto Medeiros; 346 pp.; bibl. 331-334; 21 cm; pb.; 2nd ed.; Livraria Francisco Alves Editora; Rio de Janeiro; Brazil; 1982; p. 61.

1493. SAHER, P. J.; "Zen-Yoga: A Creative Psychoterapy to Self-Integration"; XXIV + XX + 294 pp.; illus.; bibl. 240-256; alph.; 21 cm; hb.; dj.; Motilal Banarsidass; Delhi; India; 1976; pp. 26-28, 146.

1494. SAINT-JEAN, Célestin; "Guide du Magnétiseur Spirite"; 160 pp.; 17.5 cm; hb.; Librairie Spirite; Paris; 1912; pp. 130-142.

1495. SAISSET, Frédéric; "Qu'est-ce que la Métapsychique?"; 112 pp.; glos. 98-110; 18.5 cm; pb.; Éditions Niclaus; Paris; 1950; pp. 26, 98, 101-103, 109.

1496. SALLEY, Roy D.; "REM Sleep Phenomena During Out-of-Body Experiences"; *The Journal of the American Society for Psychical Research;* New York; Magazine; Monthly; Vol. 76; N. 2; April, 1982; bibl. 164, 165; pp. 157-165.

1497. SALOMON, Paule; COOPER, Charlie; et MOEBIUS (Pseud. for Jean Giraud); "La Parapsychologie et Vous"; 152 pp.; illus.; bibl. 149-151; 27 cm; cart.; Albin Michel; Paris; 1980; pp. 140-142.

1498. SALTER, William Henry; "A Further Report on Sittings with Mrs. Leonard"; *Proceedings of the Society for Psychical Research;* London; Vol. XXXII; Part. LXXXII; June, 1921; pp. 133-143.

1499. SAMDUP, Lama Kazi Dawa; "O Livro dos Mortos Tibetano" (Bardo Thödol); transl. and introd. Norberto de Paula Lima and Márcio Pugliesi; 374 pp.; illus.; glos. 367-370; bibl. 371, 372; 21 cm; pb.; Hemus Livraria Editora; S. Paulo; Brazil; 1980; pp. 201, 250.

1500. SAMUELS, Mike, and SAMUELS, Nancy; "Seeing with the Mind's Eye"; pref. Don Gerrard; XX + 332 pp.; illus.; alph.; 28 cm; cart.; Random House; New York; April, 1979; pp. 282, 283.

1501. SÁNCHEZ-PÉREZ, J. M.; "El Sexto Sentido: Bases Orgánicas de la Percepción Extrasensorial"; 160 pp.; bibl. 157, 158; 19 cm; pb.; 2nd ed.; Editorial Biblioteca Nueva; Madrid; Spain; 1977; pp. 104, 157, 158.

1502. SANDWITH, George; "Magical Mission"; 256 pp.; illus.; 21.5 cm; hb.; The Omega Press; Reigate; Surrey; Great Britain; 1954; pp. 11-17.

1503. SANGIRARDI JR.; "O Índio e as Plantas Alucinógenas"; 108 pp.; illus.; bibl. 189, 190; 21 cm; pb.; Editorial Alhambra; Rio de Janeiro; Brazil; 1983; pp. 65, 181-186.

1504. SAN MARTIN, Paulo B., and PELEGRINI, Bernardo; "A Revolução da Energia"; Brasil Reporter Dossiê 2; 34 pp.; illus.; 27.5 cm; pb.; Brasil Repórter; Londrina, PR; Brazil; no date; pp. 26, 27, 29.

1505. SANTOS, Izidoro Duarte; "Um Caso de Desdobramento"; *Estudos Psíquicos;* Lisboa; Portugal; Magazine; Monthly; 26th Yr.; N. 6; June, 1965; p. 187.

1506. SARA, Dorothy; "ESP: Fact or Fantasy?"; 192 pp.; illus.; bibl. 189-192; 18 cm; pocket; pb.; HC Publishers; New York; 1970; pp. 134-137.

1507. SARAYDARIAN, H.; "La Ciencia de la Meditacion"; transl. Hector V. Morel; 286 pp.; illus.; 23 cm; pb.; Editorial Kier; Buenos Aires; Argentina; 1979; pp. 163, 164, 178.

1508. SARGANT, William; "A Possessão da Mente"; transl. Klaus Scheel; 244 pp.; illus.; 21 cm; pb.; Imago Editora; Rio de Janeiro; Brazil; 1975; pp. 60, 61, 199-202.

1509. SATPREM (Pseud.); "Le Mental des Cellules"; 216 pp.; Éditions Robert Laffont; Paris.

1510. SATPREM (Pseud.); "El Yoga Integral de Sri Aurobindo"; 412 pp.; illus.; 20 cm; pb.; Ediciones El Caballito; Mexico, D. F.; 1970; pp. 213-221.

1511. SATURNO, Editorial; Editor; "El Libro Infernal: Tratado Completo de las Ciencias Ocultas"; 432 pp.; illus.; 19.5 cm; pb.; Editorial Saturno; Mexico, D. F.; no date; pp. 373-375.

1512. SAVA, George; "A Surgeon Remembers"; Faber and Faber; London; 1953.

1513. SCHAPIRO, S. A.; "A Classification Scheme for Out-of-Body Phenomena"; *The Journal of Altered States of Consciousness;* Vol. 2; 1976; pp. 259-265.

1514. SCHATZ, Oskar; "Manual de Parapsicologia"; transl. Claudio Gancho; 376 pp.; bibl. 248-255, 345-351; alph.; 22 cm; pb.; Editorial Herder; Barcelona; Spain; 1980; pp. 46, 181-185, 326, 339, 340.

1515. SCHIFF, Jean-Marie; "L'Espace Interieur"; 256 pp.; illus.; bibl. 254, 255; 22 cm; hb.; dj.; Celt; Paris; 1977; pp. 82, 96, 97, 109-121, 225.

1516. SCHLEICH, Carl Ludwig; "Die Wunder der Seele"; introd. Carl Gustav Jung; 522 pp.; 19.5 cm; hb.; 5th ed.; S. Fischer Verlag; Berlin; Germany; 1934; pp. 50-52, 59.

1517. SCHMEIDLER, Gertrude R.; "Interpreting Report of Out-of-Body Experiences"; *Journal of the Society for Psychical Research;* London; Magazine; Monthly; Vol. 52; N. 794; June, 1983; pp. 102-104.

1518. SCHMIDT, K. O.; "Erfahrungen bei Jenseits-Wanderungen"; *Esotera;* Freiburg; West Germany; Magazine; Monthly; Yr. 24; N. 4; April, 1973; pp. 313-315.

1519. SCHNAPER, Nathan; "Comments Germane to the Paper Intitled "The Reality of Death Experiencies" (Ernst Rodin); *The Journal of Nervous and Mental Disease;* Baltimore; Maryland; U. S. A.; Vol. 168; N. 5; 1980; bibl. 270; pp. 268-270.

1520. SCHOPFIELD, Alfred T.; "Modern Spiritism its Science and Religion"; introd. Newell Dwight Hills; XII + 260 pp.; alph.; 18.5 cm; hb.; P. Blakiston's Son & Co.; Philadelphia; Pennsylvania; U. S. A.; 1920; pp. 38, 147, 148.

1521. SCHUBERT, Suely Caldas; "Obsessão / Desobsessão"; pres. Francisco Thiesen; 192 pp.; 18 cm; pb.; Federação Espírita Brasileira; Rio de Janeiro; Brazil; 1981; pp. 35, 133.

1522. SCHUL, Bill; "The Psychic Frontiers of Medicine"; 256 pp.; bibl. 248-250; alph.; 18 cm; pocket; pb.; Fawcett Publications; Greenwich; Con.; U. S. A.; 1977; pp. 141, 216-219.

1523. SCHUL, Bill, and PETTIT, Ed.; "O Poder Secreto das Pirâmides"; transl. Miécio Araújo Jorge Honkis; 204 pp.; illus.; bibl. 201-204; 21 cm; pb.; 7th ed.; Editora Record; Rio de Janeiro; Brazil; 1981; pp. 45, 153, 154, 156.

1524. SCHUL, Bill, and PETTIT, Ed.; "The Psychic Power of Pyramids"; pref. Hugh R. Riordan; 256 pp.; illus.; bibl. 250-252; alph.; 18 cm; pb.; Fawcett Gold Medal; New York; 1976; pp. 83-87; eds.: Eng., Port.

1525. SCHUTEL, Cairbar de Souza; "A Vida no Outro Mundo"; 128 pp.; 18.5 cm; pb.; 5th ed.; Casa Editora O Clarim; Matão, SP; Brazil; 1978; pp. 21-36.

1526. SCHWARTZ, Emanuel K.; "The Phenomena of Astral Projection" (Muldoon and Carrington); Books Reviews; *The Journal of the American Society for Psychical Research;* New York; Vol. XLVI; N. 4; October, 1952; pp. 161-163.

1527. SCHWARTZ, Stephan A.; "The Secret Vaults of Time"; XIV + 370 pp.; illus.; bibl. 353-366; alph.; 23 cm; hb.; dj.; Grosset & Dunlap; New York; 1978; p. 67.

1528. SCOTT, Cyril; "An Outline of Modern Occultism"; VI + 226 pp.; bibl. 225, 226; 18.5 cm; hb.; dj.; Routledge & Kegan Paul; London; 1974; pp. 57-67.

1529. SCOTT, Mary; "Kundalini in the Physical World"; 276 pp.; illus.; glos. 253-258; bibl. 259-263; alph.; 21.5 cm; pb.; Routledge & Kegan Paul; London; 1983; pp. 28, 62-66, 72-74, 129, 220-222, 248.

1530. SCOTT, Mary; "Science & Subtle Bodies: Towards a Clarification of Issues"; Thesis; 50 pp.; bibl.; College of Psychic Studies; London; 1975.

1531. SCULTHORP, Frederick C.; "Excursions to the Spirit World"; introd. Karl E. Müller; 158 pp.; 18.5 cm; hb.; dj.; The Greater World Association; London; 1973; pp. 1-158; eds.: Eng., Ger. (Mini-library).

1532. SCULTHORP, Frederick C.; "More About the Spirit World"; introd. A. H. Hillyard; XII + 70 pp.; 18.5 cm; pb.; The Greater World Association Trust; London; 1982; pp. 1-43, 66.

1533. SEABRA, Alberto; "A Alma e o Subconsciente"; 240 pp.; 18 cm; pb.; 2nd ed.; Editora O Pensamento; S. Paulo; Brazil; 1927; pp. 50-52.

1534. SEABRA, Alberto; "Fenômenos Psíquicos"; 204 pp.; 18 cm; hb.; 2nd ed.; Editora O Pensamento; S. Paulo; Brazil; 1927; pp. 85-127.

1535. SEABRA, Alberto; "O Problema do Além e do Destino"; 320 pp.; 15.5 cm; hb.; Monteiro Lobato & Cia. Editores; S. Paulo; Brazil; 1922; pp. 57-76, 86, 98-105, 132-134.

1536. SECH, Alexandre; Co-Authors: Deolindo Amorim, Jorge Andréa, and Altivo Ferreira; "Encontro com a Cultura Espírita"; pref. José de Freitas Nobre; 206 pp.; 18.5 cm; pb.; Casa Editora O Clarim; Matão, SP; Brazil; September, 1981; pp. 161-162, 167.

1537. SEGURA, José A.; "O Campo Biopsíquico"; 260 pp.; bibl. 256-259; 21 cm; pb.; Editora do Escritor; S. Paulo; Brazil; 1980; pp. 177, 178.

1538. SEKANEK, Rudolf; "Mutter Silbert, Ein Opfergang"; introd. Gustl Silbert; 294 pp.; illus.; bibl. 281-287; 23 cm; hb.; dj.; Otto Reichl Verlag Remagen; Bietigheim; Württemberg; West Germany; 1959; pp. 77-79, 247, 272.

1539. SELDEN, Lois Ann; "Dreams: Secret Messages From Your Mind"; 128 pp.; illus.; bibl. 127, 128; 21 cm; cart.; Dream Research; Tacoma, WA; U. S. A.; September, 1981; p. 126.

1540. SENILLOSA, Felipe; "Évolution de l'Ame et de la Societé"; transl. and pref. Alfred Ebelot; 272 pp.; 17.5 cm; hb.; Chamuel, Éditeur; Paris; 1899; pp. 172, 177-190.

1541. SEPHARIAL (Pseud. for Walter Gorn Old); "A Manual of Occultism"; XII + 356 pp.; illus.; 20 cm; pb.; 3rd print.; Rider and Co.; London; 1975; pp. 326-330; eds.: Eng., Port.

1542. SERRANO, Miguel; "El Circulo Hermetico: De Hermann Hesse a C. G. Jung"; 188 pp.; illus.; 19.5 cm; pb.; 2nd ed.; Editorial Kier; Buenos Aires; Argentina; 1978; pp. 147, 148, 160.

1543. SHADOWITZ, Albert, and WALSH, Peter; "The Dark Side of Knowledge"; XII + 306 pp.; illus.; bibl. 289-296; alph.; 23.5 cm; pb.; Addison-Wesley Publishing Co.; Menlo Park; Cal.; U. S. A.; 1976; pp. 156-158.

1544. SHAPIN, Betty, and COLY, Lisette; Editors; "Parapsychology's Second Century"; Anthology; 14 + 156 pp.; illus.; 23 cm; hb.; Parapsychology Foundation; New York; 1983; pp. 77-98, 153-156.

1545. SHATTOCK, E. H.; "Power Thinking: How to Develop the Energy Potential of Your Mind"; 160 pp.; alph.; 21 cm; pb.; Turnstone Press; Wellingborough; Northamptonshire; Great Britain; 1983; pp. 138.

1546. SHAY, Joseph M.; "Out of Body Consciousness"; introd. Paul Twitchell; 108 pp.; 14 cm; pb.; Lumen Press; St. Louis; Missouri; U. S. A.; 1972; pp. 1-108 (Mini-library).

1547. SHIELS, Dean; "A Cross-Cultural Study of Beliefs in Out-of-the-Body Experiences"; *Journal of the Society for Psychical Research;* London; Vol. 49; N. 779; 1978; illus.; pp. 697-741.

1548. SHEPARD, Leslie A.; Editor; "Encyclopedia of Occultism & Parapsychology"; 2 Vol.; 1.084 pp.; 28 cm; pb.; Avon Books; New York; March, 1980; p. 60.

1549. SHEPHERD, A. P.; "A Scientist of the Invisible" (Rudolf Steiner); Biography; 222 pp.; illus.; alph.; 19 cm; hb.; dj.; 6th print.; Hodder and Stoughton; London; 1969; pp. 92, 93, 189, 190.

1550. SHERMAN, Harold; "A Vida Não Termina com a Morte"; transl. Almira Botelho Guimarães; 212 pp.; 21 cm; pb.; Editora Record; Rio de Janeiro; Brazil; 1981; pp. 68-88; eds.: Eng., It., Port.

1551. SHERMAN, Harold; "Your Mysterious Powers of ESP"; 240 pp.; 18 cm; pocket; pb.; New American Library; New York; December, 1969; pp. 180-199.

1552. SHERMAN, Loren Albert; "Science of the Soul"; XVIII + 414 pp.; illus.; 20 cm; hb.; The Sherman Co.; Port Huron; Mich.; U. S. A.; 1895.

1553. SHIRLEY, Ralph; "The Mystery of the Human Double"; 190 pp.; 18.5 cm; hb.; Rider & Co.; London; 1938; pp. 1-190.

1554. SHIRLEY, Ralph; "Occultists & Mystics of All Ages"; pref. Leslie Shepard; X + 176 pp.; illus.; 20 cm; pb.; The Citadel Press; Secaucus; New Jersey; U. S. A.; 1974; pp. IV, 106, 107.

1555. SIBLEY, Mulford Quickert; "Life After Death?"; 160 pp.; bibl. 154-157; Dillon Press; Minneapolis; Minnesota; U. S. A.; 1975.

1556. SIDGWICK, Eleanor Mildred; and GURNEY, Edmund; MYERS, Frederic W. H.; and PODMORE, Frank; "Phantasms of the Living"; 2 Vol. in one; 1.018 pp.; 24 cm; hb.; University Books; New York; 1962; pp. 151-354.

1557. SIDGWICK, Henry; JOHNSON, Alice; MYERS, Frederic W. H.; PODMORE, Frank; and SIDGWICK, Eleanor Mildred; "Report on the Census of Hallucinations"; *Proceedings of the Society for Psychical Research;* London; 464 pp.; 21 cm; hb.; 1894; pp. 207-263, 278-293.

1558. SIEVERS, Bernhard; "Die Probleme des Okkultismus und anderer Grenzgebiete"; 188 pp.; illus.; 19.5 cm; pb.; Author's Edition; Buenos Aires; Argentina; 1944; pp. 100-105, 112.

1559. SILVA, Aloysio Alfredo; "Gênios ou Ingênuos?"; 164 pp.; 21 cm; pb.; Shogun Editora e Arte; Rio de Janeiro; Brazil; 1983; pp. 23, 29, 48, 49, 53-55, 64, 97, 112.

1560. SILVA, Eponina M. Pereira da; "Corpo Astral, Exteriorização e Bilocação"; *Folha Espírita;* S. Paulo; Brazil; Newspaper; Monthly; Yr. X; N. 116; November, 1983; illus.; pp. 1, 4.

1561. SILVA, F. L. de Azevedo; "Fundamentos Científicos do Espiritismo"; Thesis; 128 pp.; 18 cm; pb.; Edição do 1.º Congresso Brasileiro de Jornalistas Espíritas; Rio de Janeiro; Brazil; 1941; pp. 106-111.

1562. SILVA, Woodrow Wilson da Matta and (Yapacani); "Umbanda e o Poder da Mediunidade"; 158 pp.; illus.; 23 cm; pb.; 2nd ed. rev.; Livraria Freitas Bastos; Rio de Janeiro; Brazil; 1978; pp. 120-126.

1563. SIMON, V.; "Desdobramento"; *Estudos Psíquicos;* Lisboa; Portugal; Magazine; Monthly; 25th Yr.; N. 9; September, 1964; pp. 280-282.

1564. SINCLAIR, Upton; "Radar der Psyche"; transl. Rosemarie Dopner; pref. Albert Einstein; introd. William Mc Dougall; 292 pp.; illus.; 21.5 cm; hb.; dj.; Scherz Verlag; Bern; Switzerland; 1973; pp. 73-78; eds.: Eng., Ger.

1565. SINNETT, Alfred Percy; "O Mundo Oculto"; transl. Mário de Alemquer; 286 pp.; 19 cm; pb.; 2nd ed.; Livraria Clássica Editora; Lisboa; Portugal; 1922; pp. 80-107.

1566. SLATER, Philip; "The Wayward Gate: Science and the Supernatural"; XVIII + 238 pp.; bibl. 235-238; 20.5 cm; hb.; dj.; Beacon Press; Boston; Massachusetts; U. S. A.; 1977; pp. 126-128.

1567. SMITH, Adam (Pseud. for George Jerome Waldo Goodman); "Powers of Mind"; VIII + 420 pp.; illus.; bibl. 403-419; 18 cm; pocket; pb.; Ballantine Books; New York; 1978; pp. 347-350.

1568. SMITH, Alson J.; "Immortality: The Scientific Evidence"; 174 pp.; illus.; 18 cm; pocket; pb.; Signet Mystic Book; New York; 1967; pp. 155, 158.

1569. SMITH, Enid S.; "Interessantes Viagens Astrais"; *Estudos Psíquicos;* Lisboa; Portugal; Magazine; Monthly; 25th Yr.; N. 1; January, 1964; pp. 10-12.

1570. SMITH, Paula, and IRWIN, Harvey; "Out-of-Body Experiences, Needs, and the Experimental Approach: A Laboratory Study"; *Parapsychology Review;* New York; Vol. 12; N. 3; May-June, 1981; bibl. 4; pp. 1-4.

1571. SMITH, Susy; "A Busca da Imortalidade: Você e a Reencarnação"; transl. Affonso Blacheyre; 174 pp.; 21 cm; pb.; Distribuidora Record; Rio de Janeiro; Brazil; no date; pp. 93-112.

1572. SMITH, Susy; "The Enigma of Out-of-Body Travel"; 190 pp.; bibl. 179-184; alph.; 21 cm; hb.; Garrett Publications; New York; 1965; pp. 1-190 (Mini-library).

1573. SMITH, Susy; "More ESP for the Millions"; 156 pp.; 21 cm; pb.; Sherbourne Press; Los Angeles; Cal.; U. S. A.; 1969; pp. 135-142.

1574. SMITH, Susy; "Out-of-Body Experiences for the Millions"; 160 pp.; 21 cm; cart.; Sherbourne Press; Los Angeles; Cal.; U. S. A.; 1968; pp. 1-160.

1575. SMITH, Susy; "O Que é ESP"; transl. Charles Marie Antoine Bovéry; 116 pp.; bibl. 115; 21 cm; pb.; Edições MM; Rio de Janeiro; Brazil; 1973; pp. 87-100.

1576. SMITH, W. S. Montgomery; "Life and Work in the Spiritual Body"; Hillside Press; London; pp. 14, 64, 87.

1577. SMITH, W. Whately; "A Theory of the Mechanism of Survival: The Fourth Dimension and its Applications"; 12 + 196 pp.; illus.; alph.; 18.5 cm; hb.; Kegan Paul, Trench, Trübner & Co.; London; 1920; pp. 149-158.

1578. SMYTHE, F. S.; "The Spirit of the Hills"; Hodder and Stoughton; London; 1937; pp. 277, 278.

1579. SNELL, Joy; "The Ministry of Angels"; 190 pp.; 23.5 cm; hb.; The Citadel Press; New York; April, 1959; pp. 91-101.

1580. SOBRINHO, J. Dias; "Forças Ocultas, Luz e Caridade"; 182 pp.; bibl. 175; 18.5 cm; hb.; 2nd ed.; Gráfica Editora Aurora; Rio de Janeiro; Brazil; 1951; p. 102.

1581. SOLLIER, Paul; "Les Phénomènes d'Autoscopie"; 176 pp.; illus.; 18 cm; hb.; Félix Alcan, Éditeur; Paris; 1903; pp. 140-147.

1582. SOMERLOTT, Robert; "Modern Occultism"; 312 pp.; illus.; bibl. 295-301; alph.; 21.5 cm; hb.; dj.; Robert Hale & Co.; London; 1972; pp. 110, 111.

1583. SOTTO, Alain, and OBERTO, Varinia; "A Vida Depois da Morte"; transl. Torquato Fernandes; 198 pp.; illus.; bibl. 196-198; 21 cm; pb.; Publicações Europa-América; Mira-Sintra; Portugal; 1978; pp. 80-96.

1584. SOUZA, Denizard; "Contribuição Cultural ao Estudo das Alucinações"; 12 pp.; Offprint; XII Congresso Latino-Americano de Psiquiatria; Porto Alegre, RS; Brazil; November, 1983; bibl. 12; pp. 11-12.

1585. SOUZA, Leal de; "No Mundo dos Espíritos: Inquérito de "A Noite""; pref. Horacio Cartier; 426 pp.; illus.; 23 cm; pb.; A Noite; Rio de Janeiro; Brazil; 1925; pp. 122-125, 376, 377, 424.

1586. SPALDING, Baird T.; "Life and Teaching of the Masters of the Far East"; 5 Vol.; 846 pp.; 21 cm; pb.; De Vorss & Co., Publishers; Marina Del Rey; Cal.; U. S. A.; 1964; Vol. I: pp. 36-40, 48-50; eds.: Eng., Port.

1587. SPARROW, Gregory Scott; "Lucid Dreaming Dawning of the Clear Light"; 70 pp.; illus.; bibl. 69; 21.5 cm; pb.; ed. rev.; Association for Research and Enlightenment Press; Virginia Beach; Virginia; U. S. A.; 1982; pp. 1, 2, 20, 21, 60, 68.

1588. SPENCE, Lewis; "An Encyclopaedia of Occultism"; XXIV + 440 pp.; illus.; 25 cm; pb.; The Citadel Press; New Jersey; U. S. A.; 1977; pp. 41, 42.

1589. SPRAGGETT, Allen; "The Case for Immortality"; 154 pp.; alph.; 21 cm; hb.; dj.; New American Library; New York; 1974; pp. 68-93.

1590. SPRAGGETT, Allen; "New Worlds of the Unexplained"; XIV + 192 pp.; 18 cm; pocket; pb.; New American Library; New York; February, 1976; pp. 86-88.

1591. SPRAGGETT, Allen; "Probing the Unexplained"; 184 pp.; alph.; 18 cm; pocket; pb.; Signet Book; New York; 1973; p. 162.

1592. SPRAGGETT, Allen; "The Unexplained"; pref. James A. Pike; X + 230 pp.; bibl. 230; 21 cm; hb.; dj.; New American Library; New York; 1967; pp. 183-195.

1593. ST. CLAIR, David; "Lessons in Instant ESP"; 200 pp.; illus.; alph.; 18 cm; pocket; pb.; New American Library; New York; September, 1979; pp. 9, 147-156.

1594. STAFF, V. S.; "Intimations of Immortality" (Robert Crookall); Books Reviews; *Journal of the Society for Psychical Research;* London; Vol. 44; N. 738; December, 1968; pp. 412-414.

1595. STANKÉ, Alain; "Lobsang Rampa: O Enigma"; transl. M. de Campos; 178 pp.; illus.; 21 cm; pb.; Publicações Europa-América; Mira-Sintra; Portugal; no date; pp. 36, 37, 55-61, 67, 68, 110, 112, 162, 171, 174-176.

1596. STARKE, D.; "Le Spiritisme"; 116 pp.; 21.5 cm; hb.; Éditions Nilsson; Paris; no date; pp. 73-84.

1597. STEAD, Estelle W.; "My Father: Personal and Spiritual Reminiscences"; Biography; 378 pp.; 18 cm; hb.; Thomas Nelson and Sons; London; no date; pp. 183, 242-248.

1598. STEAD, William Thomas; "Bordeland: A Casebook of True Supernatural Stories"; introd. Leslie Shepard; XXIV + 344 pp.; alph.; 21 cm; hb.; dj.; University Books; New York; 1970; pp. 24-51, 95-107, 132-135, 330-332.

1599. STEAD, William Thomas; "Life Eternal"; pref. Stanley de Brath; 286 pp.; 18.5 cm; hb.; Wright & Brown; London; 1933; pp. 232-235.

1600. STEBBING, Lionel; "A Dictionary of the Occult Sciences"; 8 + 252 pp.; 22 cm; pb.; Emerson Press; London; no date; pp. 14, 15, 158.

1601. STEIGER, Brad (Pseud. for Eugene E. Olson); "Astral Projection"; 234 pp.; alph.; 23.5 cm; pb.; Para Research; Rockport; Massachusetts; U. S. A.; 1982; pp. 1-234 (Mini-library).

1602. STEIGER, Brad (Pseud. for Eugene E. Olson); "Las Experiencias Psíquicas de Olof Jonsson"; transl. Antonio Ribera; introd. David Techter; 298 pp.; illus.; 21.5 cm; pb.; Ediciones Martínez Roca; Barcelona; Spain; 1974; pp. 151-158.

1603. STEIGER, Brad (Pseud. for Eugene E. Olson); "Kahuna Magic"; 128 pp.; bibl. 123; alph.; 23.5 cm; pb.; Para Research; Rockport; Massachusetts; U. S. A.; 1981; pp. 47-51.

1604. STEIGER, Brad (Pseud. for Eugene E. Olson); "The Mind Travellers"; Award Books; New York; 1969.

1605. STEIGER, Brad (Pseud. for Eugene E. Olson), and WILLIANS, Loring; "Minds Through Space and Time"; 156 pp.; Award Books; New York; 1971.

1606. STEIGER, Brad (Pseud. for Eugene E. Olson); "In My Soul I Am Free"; Biography; 208 pp.; alph.; 17.5 cm; pb.; Illuminated Way Press; Menlo Park; Cal.; U. S. A.; no date; pp. 32, 37, 38, 81-105, 134, 135, 146, 181-184.

1607. STEIGER, Brad (Pseud. for Eugene E. Olson); "Mysteries of Time and Space"; 284 pp.; illus.; alph.; 18 cm; pocket; pb.; Dell Publishing Co.; New York; March, 1976; pp. 236, 237, 245-247.

1608. STEIGER, Brad (Pseud. for Eugene E. Olson); "Sex and Supernatural"; 192 pp.; Lancer Books; New York; 1968.

1609. STEIGER, Brad (Pseud. for Eugene E. Olson); & STEIGER, Francie; "The Star People"; 202 pp.; alph.; 17.5 cm; pocket; pb.; 3rd print.; Berkley Books; New York; December, 1981; pp. 65, 66, 73, 74, 104-109.

1610. STEINER, Rudolf; "An Outline of Occult Science"; transl. Maud Monges and Henry B. Monges; prfr. Lisa D. Monges; XXXVI + 388 pp.; 18.5 cm; pb.; 2nd print.; Anthroposophic Press; Spring Valley, N. Y.; U. S. A.; 1974; pp. 47-60; eds.: Eng., Port.

1611. STEINER, Rudolf; "Come se Adquiere el Conocimiento de los Mundos Superiores?"; transl. Juan Berlin y Melchor de la Garza and Francisco Schneider; 172 pp.; 20 cm; pb.; 3rd ed.; Editorial Dedalo; Buenos Aires; 1978; pp. 129-145.

1612. STEINOUR, Harold; "Exploring the Unseen World"; 258 pp.; bibl. 244-250; alph.; 20.5 cm; hb.; dj.; The Citadel Press; New York; 1959; pp. 18, 107-109, 119, 142, 206-209, 235, 237, 240, 241.

1613. STELTER, Alfred; "Curacion Psi"; 318 pp.; bibl. 299-310; alph.; 21.5 cm; hb.; dj.; Plaza & Janes; Barcelona; Spain; 1976; pp. 78-81, 134, 135, 139, 140.

1614. STEVENS, E. W.; "The Watseka Wonder"; 32 pp.; illus.; Chicago; Ill.; U. S. A.; 1878.

1615. STEVENS, William Oliver; "The Mystery of Dreams"; VIII + 280 pp.; alph.; 20.5 cm; hb.; dj.; Dodd, Mead & Co.; New York; 1949; pp. 232-240.

1616. STEVENS, William Oliver; "Psychics and Common Sense"; 256 pp.; bibl. 244-249; alph.; 20.5 cm; hb.; dj.; E. P. Dutton & Co.; New York; 1953; pp. 112-166.

1617. STEVENS, William Oliver; "Unbidden Guests"; XVI + 322 pp.; alph.; 21.5 cm; hb.; George Allen & Unwin; London; 1951; pp. 232-240.

1618. STEVENSON, Ian; "Cases of the Reincarnation Type"; 4 Vol.; 1.492 pp.; glos. 375-377; bibl. 370-372; alph.; 25 cm; hb.; dj.; University Press of Virginia; Charlottesville; Virginia; U. S. A.; 1980/1983; Vol. III: pp. 12, 15.

1619. STEVENSON, Ian; "Research into the Evidence of Man's Survival After Death"; *The Journal of Nervous and Mental Disease;* Baltimore; Maryland; U. S. A.; Vol. 165; N. 3; 1977; pp. 152-170.

1620. STEVENSON, Ian; "Vinte Casos Sugestivos de Reencarnação"; transl. Agenor Pegado and Sylvia Pereira da Silva; supervisor Hernani Guimarães Andrade; 520 pp.; 21 cm; pb.; Editora Difusão Cultural; S. Paulo; Brazil; 1970; pp. 7, 456.

1621. STEVENSON, Ian, and GREYSON, Bruce; "Near-Death Experiences"; *The Journal of the American Medical Association;* Vol. 242; N. 3; July 20, 1979; bibl. 267; pp. 265-267.

1622. STILL, Alfred; "Nas Fronteiras da Ciência e da Parapsicologia"; transl. Leonidas Gontijo de Carvalho; 298 pp.; 20.5 cm; pb.; Ibrasa; S. Paulo; Brazil; 1965; pp. 222, 223, 236-238, 249.

1623. STOBART, Mrs. St. Clair; "Torchbearers of Spiritualism"; 232 pp.; illus.; bibl. 230, 231; 21.5 cm; hb.; George Allen & Unwin; London; 1925; pp. 192-198.

1624. STOKES, Douglas M.; "Mind Reach: Scientists Look at Psychic Ability"; *The Journal of the American Society for Psychical Research;* New York; Vol. 71; N. 4; October; 1977; pp. 437-442.

1625. STOKES, Douglas M.; "Out-of-Body Experience: A Handbook"; Books Reviews; *Parapsychology Review;* New York; Vol. 13; N. 3; September-October, 1982; pp. 22-24.

1626. STRAITH-MILLER, Elizabeth; "Huna: An Introduction to its Teachings"; 48 pp.; glos. 47, 48; 23 cm; hb.; Church of St. Michael; U. S. A.; 1966; p. 45.

1627. STRATTON, Frederick John Marrian; "An Out-of-the Body Experience Combined with ESP"; *Journal of the Society for Psychical Research;* London; Vol. 39; N. 692; June, 1957; pp. 92-97.

1628. STRINGFIELD, Leonard H.; "Situação Alerta: O Novo Cerco dos Ovnis"; pref. Donald E. Keyhoe; transl. Wilma Freitas Ronald de Carvalho; 248 pp.; illus.; 21 cm; pb.; Editorial Nórdica; Rio de Janeiro; Brazil; 1981; pp. 63, 64.

1629. SUDRE, René; "Les Nouvelles Énigmes de L'Univers"; 398 pp.; 23 cm; pb.; 2nd ed.; Payot; Paris; 1951; pp. 322, 377, 378; eds.: Fr., Sp.

1630. SUDRE, René; "Tratado de Parapsicologia"; transl. Constantino Paleólogo; 458 pp.; 21 cm; pb.; Zahar Editores; Rio de Janeiro; Brazil; 1966; pp. 31, 62, 212, 213, 281, 338, 348-450, 355-358, 362-366, 371, 375, 381.

1631. SUZUKI, Daisetz Teitaro; "Introduccion al Budismo Zen"; introd. Carl Gustav Jung; transl. Hector V. Morel; 182 pp.; 19 cm; pb.; 3rd ed.; Editorial Kier; Buenos Aires; Argentina; 1979; pp. 117-124.

1632. SWANN, Ingo; "To Kiss Earth Good-bye"; pref. Gertrude Schmeidler; XX + 218 pp.; illus.; alph.; 24 cm; hb.; dj.; Hawthorn Books; New York; 1975; pp. 65-127 (Mini-library).

1633. SWEDENBORG, Emanuel; "L'Amour Vraiment Conjugal"; without translator; 504 pp.; alph.; 21 cm; pb.; Cercle Swedenborg; Meudon; France; 1974; pp. 354, 355; eds.: Lat., Fr., Port.

1634. SWEDENBORG, Emanuel; "Arcana Coelestia: The Heavenly Arcana"; without translator; pref. John Faulkner Potts; 12 Vol.; 7.158 pp.; 20.5 cm; hb.; 37th print.; Swedenborg Foundation; New York; 1963; Vol. I: p, 2, 3; Vol. II: pp. 420, 476-484; eds.: Lat., etc.

1635. SWEDENBORG, Emanuel; "O Céu e o Inferno"; transl. and introd. Levindo Castro de La Fayette; 472 pp.; alph.; 23 cm; pb.; Oficinas Gráficas da Casa Cruz; Rio de Janeiro; Brazil; 1920; pp. 33, 34, 46, 47, 49, 94, 97, 102, 105; eds.: Lat., Eng., Fr., Port.

1636. SWEDENBORG, Emanuel; "Divina Providência"; transl. latim-francês J. F. E. Le Boys des Guays; transl. Fr.-Port. João de Mendonça Lima; 384 pp.; alph.; 23 cm; pb.; Livraria Freitas Bastos; Rio de Janeiro; Brazil; 1969; pp. 36, 271.

1637. SWEDENBORG, Emanuel; "A Nova Jerusalem e a Sua Doutrina Celeste"; transl. and pref. João de Mendonça Lima; 352 pp.; alph.; 19 cm; pb.; Translator's Edition; Rio de Janeiro; Brazil; 1945; pp. 59, 277, 341.

1638. SWEDENBORG, Emanuel; "La Sagesse des Anges"; without translator; 284 pp.; alph.; 21 cm; pb.; Cercle Swedenborg; Meudon; France; 1976; pp. 220, 221; eds.: Lat., Fr., Port.

1639. SWEDENBORG, Emanuel; "The Spiritual Diary" ("Diarii Spiritualis"); transl. George Bush, John J. Smithson, and James F. Buss; 5 Vol.; 2.350 pp.; illus.; alph.; 21 cm; hb.; Swedenborg Foundation; New York; 1971; Vol. I: pp. 1, 42, 48, 55, 69, 75, 115, 131, 133, 196, 295; eds.: Lat., Eng.

1640. SWEDENBORG, Emanuel; "A Verdadeira Religião Cristã"; transl. latin-french J. F. E. le Boys des Guays; transl. french-port. João de Mendonça Lima; 2 Vol.; 976 pp.; alph.; 23 cm; pb.; Livraria Freitas Bastos; Rio de Janeiro; Brazil; 1964; Vol. I: pp. 85, 99, 104, 172, 201, 234, 308, 311, 315, 317, 490; Vol. II: pp. 280, 284, 333, 334.

1641. TALAMONTI, Leo; "Universo Proibido"; transl. Affonso Blacheyre; 308 pp.; illus.; bibl. 302-307; 21 cm; pb.; Distribuidora Record; Rio de Janeiro; Brazil; no date; pp. 47, 129-143, 168-174, 277; eds.: It., Sp., Port.

1642. TALBOT, Michael; "Mysticism and the New Physics"; 210 pp.; illus.; glos. 185-190; bibl. 191-204; alph.; 21.5 cm; pb.; Routledge & Kegan Paul; London; 1981; pp. 162-168.

1643. TAMASSIA, Mário Boari; "Os Mortos Acordam os Vivos"; 120 pp.; 18.5 cm; pb.; 2nd ed.; Edição Círculo de Claus; Campinas, SP; Brazil; 1975; pp. 3, 19-28, 47, 50-52.

1644. TAMASSIA, Mário Boari; "Para que Serve Sonhar?"; *Jornal Espírita;* S. Paulo; Brazil; Monthly; Yr. II; N. 21; March, 1977; illus.; p. 11.

1645. TAMBASCIO, Luz, and CANEDO, Guillermo; "Cuarta Dimension"; 90 pp.; 21.5 cm; pb.; Altalena Editores; Madrid; Spain; March, 1981; pp. 71, 77-89.

1646. TANIBUR; "L'Extériorisation"; *Le Voile D'Isis;* Paris; Magazine; Monthly; Treizième Année; N. 50; Décembre, 1909; pp. 167, 168.

1647. TANOUS, Alexander, with ARDMAN, Harvey; "Beyond Coincidence"; XIV + 196 pp.; 21 cm; hb.; dj.; Doubleday & Co.; New York; 1976; pp. 113-122; eds.: Eng., Fr. (Mini-library).

1648. TANSLEY, David V.; "Le Corps Subtil: Essence et Ombre"; 96 pp.; illus.; bibl. 96; 28 cm; pb.; Éditions du Seuil; Paris; 1977; pp. 1-96; eds.: Eng., Fr.

1649. TANSLEY, David V.; "Mensajeros de la Luz"; transl. Elisa M. Ferreira; 310 pp.; illus.; bibl. 309; 20.5 cm; pb.; Edaf, Ediciones-Distribuciones; Madrid; Spain; 1979; pp. 301-308.

1650. TARG, Russel; COLE, Phyllis; and PUTHOFF, Harold; "Development of Techniques to Enhance Man/Machine Communication: A Final Report"; 100 pp.; illus.; Stanford Research Institute; Menlo Park; Cal.; U. S. A.; June, 1974.

1651. TARG, Russel; & HARARY, Stuart Keith; "The Mind Race: Understanding and Using Psychic Abilities"; introd. Willis Harman; epil. Larissa Vilenskaya; XX + 294 pp.; illus.; bibl. 265-269; 23.5 cm; hb.; dj.; Villard Books; New York; 1984; pp. 153, 154, 222-224, 232, 233.

1652. TARG, Russel; & PUTHOFF, Harold E.; "Mind-Reach: Scientists Look at Psychic Ability"; introd. Margareth Mead; pref. Richard Bach; XXVI + 230 pp.; illus.; 20.5 cm; alph.; Dell Publishing Co.; New York; November, 1978; pp. 189-212.

1653. TART, Charles Theodore; Editor; "Altered States of Consciousness"; Anthology; X + 590 pp.; bibl. 530-570; alph.; 21 cm; pb.; Doubleday & Co.; New York; 1972; pp. 153-160, 498.

1654. TART, Charles Theodore; "A Further Psychophysiological Study of Out-of-the Body Experiences in a Gifted Subject"; *Proceedings of the Parapsychological Association;* Vol. 6; 1969; pp. 43, 44.

1655. TART, Charles Theodore; "The Enigma of Out-of-Body Travel" (Susy Smith); Books Reviews; *Theta;* Durham; North Carolina; U. S. A.; Magazine; N. 13; Spring, 1966; pp. 2, 3.

1656. TART, Charles Theodore; "Journeys Out of the Body" (Robert A. Monroe); Books Reviews; The Last Whole Earth Catalog; Random House; New York; 1971; p. 415.

1657. TART, Charles Theodore; "Lucid Dreams and Out-of-the-Body Experiences" (Celia E. Green); Books Reviews; *The Journal of the American Society for Psychical Research;* New York; Vol. 64; N. 2; April, 1970; pp. 219-226.

1658. TART, Charles Theodore; "On Being Stoned: A Psychological Study of Marijuana Intoxication"; introd. Walter N. Pahnke; 334 pp.; bibl.; Science and Behavior Books; Palo Alto; Cal.; U. S. A.; 1971.

1659. TART, Charles Theodore; "Out-of-the-Body Experiences" (Celia E. Green); Books Reviews; *Theta;* Durham; North Carolina; U. S. A.; N. 25; Spring, 1969; pp. 3, 4.

1660. TART, Charles Theodore; "Psi: Scientific Studies of the Psychic Realm"; XIV + 242 pp.; illus.; bibl. 223-234; alph.; 21 cm; pb.; E. P. Dutton; New York; 1977; pp. 177-198.

1661. TART, Charles Theodore; "A Psychophysiological Study of Out-of-the-Body Experiences in a Selected Subject"; *The Journal of the American Society for Psychical Research;* New York; Vol. 62; N. 1; January, 1968; bibl. 23-27; pp. 3-27.

1662. TART, Charles Theodore; "A Second Psychophysiological Study of Out-of-the-Body Experiences in a Gifted Subject"; *International Journal of Parapsychology;* U. S. A.; 1967; pp. 251-258.

1663. TART, Charles Theodore; "States of Consciousness"; XII + 306 pp.; illus.; bibl. 287-295; alph.; 21 cm; pb.; E. P. Dutton; New York; 1975; pp. 239, 284, 285.

1664. TART, Charles Theodore; "Transpersonal Psychologies"; 502 pp.; illus.; bibl. 475-485; alph.; 23.5 cm; hb.; dj.; Harper & Row, Publishers; New York; 1975; pp. 79, 148-151, 331.

1665. TART, Charles Theodore; PUTHOFF, Harold; and TARG, Russel; Editors; "Mind at Large"; Anthology; XX + 268 pp.; illus.; 23.5 cm; hb.; dj.; Praeger Special Studies; New York; 1979; pp. 14, 15.

1666. TAYLOR, John; "Science and the Supernatural"; XII + 180 pp.; bibl. 171-174; alph.; 21 cm; hb.; dj.; E. P. Dutton; New York; 1980; pp. 152-154.

1667. TAYLOR, John; "Superminds"; 270 pp.; illus.; bibl. 255-258; alph.; 18 cm; pocket; pb.; Warner Books; New York; 1975; pp. 215, 217.

1668. TCHOU, Claude; Éditeur; "Les Corps a Prodiges"; Anthology; introd. Marcel Martiny; 320 pp.; illus.; 24 cm; pb.; Claude Tchou, Éditeur; Paris; 1977; pp. 203-208.

1669. TCHOU, Claude; Éditeur; "Les Extra-Sensoriels"; Anthology; introd. Aimé Michel; 328 pp.; illus.; bibl. 321-325; 24 cm; pb.; Tchou-Laffont; Paris; 1976; pp. 254, 279-302.

1670. TECHTER, David; "Astral Projection"; *Fate*; Evanston; Ill.; U. S. A.; Magazine; 1961; p. 85.

1671. TEIXEIRA, Cícero Marcos; "Anatomia do Desencarne"; *Desobsessão;* Porto Alegre, RS; Brazil; Newspaper; Monthly; Yr. XXXI; N. 383; January, 1980; pp. 5-8.

1672. TEIXEIRA, Cícero Marcos; "Comunicação de Um Vivo Encarnado"; *Desobsessão;* Porto Alegre, Brazil; RS; Magazine; Monthly; Yr. XXXVI; N. 431; April, 1984; pp. 2, 3.

1673. TEIXEIRA, Cícero Marcos; "O Fenômeno da Materialização"; *Desobsessão;* Porto Alegre, RS; Brazil; Newspaper; Monthly; Yr. XXXIII; N. 397; March, 1981; pp. 6, 7, 10, 12.

1674. TEUNISSEN, J.; "Zinneschok en Zweefervaring"; ("Sensory Shock and the Experience of Floating"); *Tijdschrift voor Parapsychologie;* Netherlands; N. 38; 1970; pp. 61-63.

1675. THALBOURNE, Michael A.; "A Glossary of Terms Used in Parapsychology"; introd. John Beloff; XVI + 92 pp.; bibl. 89, 90; 21.5 cm; hb.; dj.; William Heinemann; London; 1982; pp. 4-6, 25, 48, 49, 51.

1676. THIAGO, Arnaldo S.; "Dante Alighieri: O Último Iniciado"; 320 pp.; illus.; bibl. 311, 312; 23.5 cm; pb.; Gráfica Tupy Editora; Rio de Janeiro; Brazil; 1952; pp. 33-36.

1677. THIEBAULT, Jules; "L'Ani Disparu"; 188 pp.; illus.; glos. 177-187; 17 cm; hb.; Imprimerie Berger-Levrault; Nancy; France; 1917; pp. 12, 13, 179, 180.

1678. THISELTON-DYER, Thomas Firminger; "The Ghost World"; 448 pp.; Ward & Downey; London; 1898.

1679. THOMAS, Charles Drayton; "Life Beyond Death with Evidence"; 296 pp.; 19 cm; hb.; 5th print.; W. Collins Sons & Co.; London; October, 1937; pp. 260-278.

1680. THOMAS, Charles Drayton; "The Mental Phenomena of Spiritualism"; L. S. A. Publications; 1930.

1681. THOMAS, Henry, and THOMAS, Dana Lee; "Vidas de Grandes Capitães da Fé"; transl. Lino Vallandro; 208 pp.; 22 cm; illus.; hb.; 3rd print.; Editora Globo; Porto Alegre, RS; Brazil; 1958; pp. 159-167.

1682. THOULESS, Robert Henry; "From Anecdote to Experiment in Psychical Research"; X + 198 pp.; illus.; alph.; 21.5 cm; hb.; dj.; Routledge & Kegan Paul; London; 1972; pp. 155, 164; eds.: Eng., Sp.

1683. THOULESS, Robert Henry; "The Mystical Life" (J. H. Michael Whiteman); Books Reviews; *Journal of the Society for Psychical Research;* London; Vol. 42; N. 715; March, 1963; pp. 25, 26.

1684. THURSTON, Mark A.; "How to Interpret Your Dreams: Practical Techniques Based on the Edgar Cayce Readings"; XIII + 192 pp.; illus.; 22 cm; pb.; A. R. E. Press; Virginia Beach; Virginia; U. S. A.; 1978; pp. 178, 179.

1685. TINOCO, Carlos Alberto; "Fenómenos de Psicocinesia Espontânea"; 198 pp.; illus.; bibl. 191-197; 21 cm; pb.; 2nd ed.; Alfaómega Portugal; Lisboa; no date; pp. 90, 91, 94.

1686. TIRET, Colette, et TIRET, Georges; "Le Monde Invisible vous Parle"; 208 pp.; illus.; 21 cm; pb.; Vigot Frères, Éditeurs; Paris; 1954; pp. 130, 131.

1687. TISCHNER, Rudolf; "Introduction a la Parapsychologie"; transl. and pref. L. Lamorlette; 206 pp.; bibl. 197-202; alph.; 24 cm; pb.; Payot; Paris; 1973; pp. 29, 122, 126, 136, 156, 157; eds.: Fr., Sp.

1688. TOBEN, Bob, and WOLF, Fred Alan; "Space-Time and Beyond"; 176 pp.; illus.; bibl. 163-174; 28 cm; pb.; E. P. Dutton; New York; 1982; pp. 72, 73, 148, 150.

1689. TODD, John, and DEWHURST, Kenneth; "The Double: its Psycho-Pathology and Psycho-Physiology"; *The Journal of Nervous and Mental Disease;* New York; Vol. 122; N. 1; Serial N. 883; July, 1955; bibl. 55; pp. 47-55.

1690. TONDRIAU, Julien; "O Ocultismo"; transl. Maria Luísa Trigueiros; 310 pp.; illus.; glos. 183-296; bibl. 301-304; 18 cm; pb.; Difusão Européia do Livro; S. Paulo; Brazil; no date; p. 218.

1691. TORTEROLI, Angeli; "O Spiritismo no Brasil e em Portugal"; 190 pp.; glos. 57, 58; 17.5 cm; hb.; Livraria Spírita da Sociedade Acadêmica Deus, Cristo, Caridade; Rio de Janeiro; Brazil; 1896; pp. 56, 57.

1692. TOURINHO, Nazareno; "Curiosidades de Uma Pesquisa Espírita"; pref. Aparecido O. Belvedere; 188 pp.; illus.; 18 cm; pb.; Casa Editora O Clarim; Matão, SP; Brazil; January, 1983; pp. 13-17, 43-53, 55, 62, 63, 69, 81-84, 106, 108, 129, 139, 144, 151, 165, 180.

1693. TOURINHO, Nazareno; "Surpresas de Uma Pesquisa Mediúnica"; 118 pp.; 18 cm; pb.; Editora O Clarim; Matão, SP; Brazil; May, 1981; pp. 34-36, 41, 47-51, 56, 59, 60, 67, 70, 83.

1694. TOYNBEE, Arnold Joseph; KOESTLER, Arthur, y otros; "La Vida Despues de la Muerte"; transl. Carlos Gardini; 324 pp.; 20 cm; pb.; 2nd ed.; Editorial Sudamericana; Buenos Aires; Argentina; Julio, 1977; p. 269.

1695. TREBILCOCK, Edward O.; "No Earthly Reason"; 158 pp.; bibl. 157; 18.5 cm; hb.; dj.; Regency Press; London; 1968; pp. 90-94.

1696. TRESPIOLI, Gino; "Spiritismo Moderno"; 354 pp.; illus.; 18.5 cm; pb.; Editore Ulrico Hoepli; Milano; Italy; 1931; pp. 111, 354; eds.: It., Sp.

1697. TRESPIOLI, Gino; "Spiritismo Moderno: I Fenomeni"; 464 pp.; illus.; bibl. 451-464; 18 cm; hb.; Editore Ulrico Hoepli; Milano; Italy; 1934; p. 44.

1698. TRINE, Rodolfo Waldo; "En Harmonia con el Infinito"; transl. and introd. Federico Climent Terrer; 188 pp. 18.5 cm; pb.; Editorial Orion; Mexico, D. F.; 1981; pp. 103-111; eds.: Eng., Sp., Port.

1699. TRINTZIUS, René; "Au Seuil du Monde Invisible"; 448 pp.; illus.; bibl. 429, 430; 18 cm; pb.; Omnium Littéraire; Paris; 1951; pp. 363-371.

1700. THURSTON, Herbert; "Los Fenomenos Fisicos de Misticismo"; transl. Gabriel de Manterola; prol. Pedro Meseguer; pref. J. H. Crehan; 606 pp.; index of names; 19 cm; pb.; Ediciones Dinor; San Sebastian; Spain; 1953; pp. 285, 478, 479.

1701. TUBBY, Gertrude Ogden; "Psychics and Mediums: A Manual and Bibliography for Students"; 192 pp.; bibl. 177-188; alph.; 18.5 cm; hb.; Rider and Co.; London; no date; pp. 31, 46-48.

1702. TUCKER, Prentiss; "En la Tierra de los Muertos que Vivem"; without translator; 156 pp.; 17.5 cm; pb.; Editorial Kier; Buenos Aires; Argentina; 1976; pp. 44-52.

1703. TUCKETT, Ivor Ll.; "The Evidence for the Supernatural"; 410 pp.; alph.; 22.5 cm; hb.; Kegan Paul, Trench, Trübner & Co.; London; 1911; pp. 289-295.

1704. TUMMOLO, Vincenzo; "Sulle Basi Positive Dello Spiritualismo"; 710 pp.; illus.; 23 cm; hb.; Tip. Soc. Donati e C.; Viterbo; Italy; 1905; pp. 97-105.

1705. TURI, Anna Maria; "A Levitação"; transl. Maria da Graça Tavares; 190 pp.; bibl. 183-188; 21.5 cm; pb.; Edições 70; Lisboa; Portugal; September, 1979; pp. 72-74.

1706. TURNER, Gordon; "Drug-taking Causes Astral Projections"; *Psychic News;* London; Newspaper; Weekly; N. 1987; July 4, 1970; p. 7.

1707. TURVEY, Vincent Newton; "The Beginnings of Seership"; pref. William Thomas Stead; 190 pp.; 18 cm; hb.; Psychic Book Club; London; 1954; pp. 1-190 (Mini-library).

1708. TUTTLE, Hudson; "Arcana of Nature"; introd. Emmet Densmore; 472 pp.; illus.; alph.; 20.5 cm; hb.; Stillman Publishing Co.; New York; 1908; pp. 12-16.

1709. TWEEDALE, Charles L.; "Man's Survival After Death"; 2 Vol.; 536 pp.; 18 cm; hb.; 5th ed.; The Psychic Book Club; London; 1947; pp. 192-226.

1710. TWEMLOW, Stuart; GABBARD, Glen O.; and JONES, Fowler C.; "The Out-of-Body Experiences: A Phenomenological Typology Based on Questionnaire Responses"; *American Journal of Psychiatry;* Vol. 139; April, 1982; bibl. 455; pp. 450-455.

1711. TWIGG, Ena, with BROD, Ruth Hagy; "Ena Twigg: Medium"; introd. Mervym Stockwood; 318 pp.; alph.; 21 cm; hb.; dj.; Hawthorn Books; New York; 1972; pp. 56-58.

1712. TWITCHELL, Paul; "Eckankar: La Clave de los Mundos Secretos"; without translator; prol. Brad Steiger; 318 pp.; illus.; glos. 279-317; 18 cm; pocket; pb.; Illuminated Way Press; Menlo Park; Cal.; U. S. A.; 1977; pp. 1-318 (Mini-library).

1713. TWITCHELL, Paul; "Eckankar: Compiled Writings"; Vol. I; 196 pp.; 21 cm; hb.; Illuminated Way Press; San Diego; Cal.; U. S. A.; 1975; pp. 43-46, 75-81.

1714. TWITCHELL, Paul; "The Spiritual Notebook"; 220 pp.; alph.; 18 cm; pb.; 5th print.; Illuminated Way Press; Menlo Park; Cal.; U. S. A.; 1977; pp. 16, 58, 68, 86.

1715. TWITCHELL, Paul; "The Tiger's Fang"; pref. Brad Steiger; 176 pp.; 18 cm; pocket; pb.; 6th print.; Illuminated Way Press; Menlo Park; Cal.; U. S. A.; 1977; pp. 3, 4, 68, 69.

1716. TWITCHELL, Paul; "Un Entendimiento de Eckankar"; transl. Amador Botello e Sergio Aragon; 16 pp.; 21 cm; pb.; Eckankar; Menlo Park; Cal.; U. S. A.; 1976; pp. 5-13.

1717. TYRRELL, George Nuglut Merle; "Apparitions"; pref. H. H. Price; 192 pp.; alph.; 18 cm; pocket; pb.; ed. rev.; Collier Books; New York; 1970; pp. 165-171; eds.: Eng., Fr., Port.

1718. TYRRELL, George Nuglut Merle; "Au-Delà du Conscient"; transl. and pref. René Sudre; 282 pp.; 18 cm; pocket; pb.; Petite Bibliothèque Payot; Paris; 1970; pp. 8, 191-202.

1719. UCHÔA, Alfredo Moacyr de Mendonça; "O Espiritismo Científico Face às Dimensões Superiores da Realidade"; *Jornal Espírita;* S. Paulo; Brazil; Monthly; Yr. II; N. 19; January, 1977; p. 8.

1720. UCHÔA, Alfredo Moacyr de Mendonça; "Muito Além do Espaço e do Tempo"; pref. M.; 300 pp.; illus.; bibl. 283-300; 21 cm; pb.; Thesaurus Editora; Brasília; Brazil; 1983; pp. 90, 138, 167.

1721. UNDERWOOD, Peter; "Dictionary of the Occult & Supernatural"; 390 pp.; illus.; 20 cm; pb.; Fontana / Collins; London; 1979; pp. 36, 37, 111, 118, 123, 124, 206, 249, 265, 360.

1722. UPHOFF, Walter, and UPHOFF, Mary; "New Psychic Frontiers"; pref. Harold Sherman; XVIII + 278 pp.; alph.; 21.5 cm; hb.; dj.; Colin Smythe – Gerrards Cross; London; 1975; pp. 79-88; eds.: Eng., Sp.

1723. USAMI, Herick Athayde; "As Dimensões e os Extraterrestres"; 102 pp.; illus.; 21 cm; pb.; 2nd ed.; Gráfica Valci Editora; Brasília; Brazil; August, 1984; pp. 39, 93.

1724. VACHELL, Horace Anneley; "When Sorrows Come"; Cassell and Co., London; 1935; p. 278.

1725. VALÉRIO, Cícero (Pseud. for Sebastião Ladeira Marques); "Fenômenos Parapsicológicos e Espíritas"; 166 pp.; illus.; 21.5 cm; pb.; Editora Piratininga; S. Paulo; Brazil; no date; pp. 74-79.

1726. VALLE, Sérgio; "Silva Mello e os Seus Mistérios"; 414 pp.; illus.; 21 cm; pb.; 2nd ed.; Editora Lake; S. Paulo; Brazil; 1959; pp. 199, 268, 342, 346-348, 392.

1727. VALLEE, Jacques; "Messengers of Deception: Ufo Contacts and Cults"; XII + 274 pp.; illus.; bibl. 265-268; alph.; 18 cm; pocket; pb.; Bantam Books; New York; December, 1980; pp. 62, 63.

1728. VANGUARDA; Editorial; "Um Curioso Fenômeno de Desdobramento"; Section "Nas Fronteiras do Outro Mundo"; Rio de Janeiro; Brazil; Newspaper; Daily; Yr. X; N. 6.539; 21, October, 1932; p. 2.

1729. VARENNE, Jean; "El Yoga y la Tradicion Hindu"; transl. Adolfo Martin; 298 pp.; illus.; glos. 285-294; bibl. 279-281; 18 cm; pb.; Plaza & Janes, Editors; Barcelona; Spain; Deciembre, 1978; p. 182.

1730. VASCONCELLOS, Marilusa Moreira; "Confidências de Um Inconfidente"; pres. Ruy Cintra Paiva; Novel; 380 pp.; 21 cm; pb.; 4th ed.; Edicel; S. Paulo; Brazil; June, 1982; pp. 164, 245, 267, 298-300.

1731. VASCONCELLOS, Marilusa Moreira; "A Moça da Ilha"; Novel; 272 pp.; 21 cm; pb.; Editora Cultura Espírita; S. Paulo; Brazil; October, 1983; pp. 9, 18, 19, 52, 57, 74, 154-157, 161.

1732. VASILIEV, Leonid Leonidovich; "Os Misteriosos Fenômenos da Psique Humana"; transl. José Paulo do Rio Branco; 154 pp.; 21 cm; pb.; Editora Paz e Terra; Rio de Janeiro; Brazil; 1970; pp. 32, 33, 94, 95; eds.: Rus., Sp., Eng., Port.

1733. VEJA; Editorial; "Vida Após a Morte"; Section "Medicina"; Magazine; Weekly; S. Paulo; Brazil; 21, July, 1976; illus.; pp. 52, 54.

1734. VELHO, A. A. Martins; "O Espiritismo Contemporâneo"; 324 pp.; 18 cm; hb.; 2nd ed.; Livraria Clássica Editora; Lisboa; Portugal; 1926; pp. 44-56.

1735. VERNEUIL, Philippe; "Manuel de Développement et d'Utilisation des Pouvoirs Paranormaux"; 204 pp.; illus.; 20.5 cm; pb.; Guy Le Prat, Éditeur; Paris; 1984; pp. 55, 78, 79, 95, 99, 189-199.

1736. VESME, Cesare Baudi Conte di; "Storia Dello Spiritismo"; 2 Vol.; 954 pp.; 20 cm; hb.; Roux Frassati e Co. Editori; Torino; Italy; 1896; 2nd Vol.; pp. 436-441.

1737. VESME, Cesare Baudi Conte di; "L'Uomo Primitivo: Storia Dello Spiritualismo Sperimentale"; 248 pp.; 23 cm; hb.; Spartaco Giovene; Milano; Italy; Marzo, 1945; pp. 91-93.

1738. VETT, Carl; Editor; "Le Compte Rendu Officiel du Premier Congrès International des Recherches Psychiques"; 554 pp.; illus.; 22.5 cm; hb.; K. P. I. F.; Copenhague; Dinamarca; 1922; pp. 124-138, 379-395.

1739. VIEIRA, Anníbal J.; "Especulações no Abstrato"; 286 pp.; 18 cm; pb.; Editora Espiritualista; Rio de Janeiro; Brazil; 1973; pp. 158-161.

1740. VIEIRA, Waldo; "Acoplamentos Áuricos"; *Aurora;* Duque de Caxias, RJ; Brazil; Magazine; Monthly; Yr. IV; N. 9; August, 1982; illus.; p. 31.

1741. VIEIRA, Waldo; "Animais: Detectores da Consciência Projetada"; *Aurora;* Duque de Caxias, RJ; Brazil; Magazine; Monthly; Yr. V; N. 13; September, 1983; illus.; bibl.; p. 20.

1742. VIEIRA, Waldo; "Autoconsciência Extrafísica"; *Jornal Espírita;* S. Paulo; Brazil; Monthly; Yr. IX; N. 108; June, 1984; p. 5.

1743. VIEIRA, Waldo; "Bilocações de Natuzza Evolo"; *Jornal Espírita;* S. Paulo; Brazil; Monthly; Yr. IX; N. 112; October, 1984; p. 6.

1744. VIEIRA, Waldo; "Carta Aberta aos Espíritas"; *Folha Espírita;* S. Paulo; Brazil; Newspaper; Monthly; Yr. XI; N. 113; August, 1983; p. 6.

1745. VIEIRA, Waldo; "Catalepsia Projetiva"; *Jornal Espírita*; S. Paulo; Brazil; Monthly; Yr. IX; N. 107; May, 1984; p. 4.

1746. VIEIRA, Waldo; "Coração e Projeção Consciente"; *Folha Espírita;* S. Paulo; Brazil; Newspaper; Monthly; Yr. IX; N. 99; June, 1982; illus.; bibl.; p. 6.

1747. VIEIRA, Waldo; "Cristo Espera Por Ti"; Novel; 332 pp.; illus.; 21.5 cm; pb.; Edição Cec; Uberaba, MG; Brazil; 1965; pp. 31, 32, 68, 170.

1748. VIEIRA, Waldo; "Experimento do Vôo pela Vontade"; *Folha Espírita;* S. Paulo; Brazil; Newspaper; Monthly; Yr. IX; N. 106; January, 1983; illus.; bibl.; p. 5.

1749. VIEIRA, Waldo; "O Fenômeno da Autobilocação"; *Aurora*; Duque de Caxias, RJ; Brazil; Magazine; Monthly; Yr. IV; N. 10; November, 1982; illus.; bibl.; p. 16.

1750. VIEIRA, Waldo; "O Fenômeno da Bilocação Física"; *Folha Espírita;* S. Paulo; Brazil; Newspaper; Monthly; Yr. IX; N. 101; August, 1982; p. 3.

1751. VIEIRA, Waldo; "Hipnagogia"; *Jornal Espírita;* S. Paulo; Brazil; Monthly; Yr. IX; N. 109; July, 1984; p. 5.

1752. VIEIRA, Waldo; "Maturidade Extrafísica"; *Jornal Espírita;* S. Paulo; Brazil; Monthly; Yr. IX; N. 105; March, 1984; p. 4.

1753. VIEIRA, Waldo; "Mini-library"; Boletim de Projeciologia 4; *in Jornal Espírita;* S. Paulo; Brazil; Monthly; Yr. IX; N. 99; September, 1983; p. 7.

1754. VIEIRA, Waldo; "Muletas Psicofísicas Projetivas"; *Jornal Espírita;* S. Paulo; Brazil; Monthly; Yr. IX; N. 103; January, 1984; p. 4.

1755. VIEIRA, Waldo; "Pesquisas Estatísticas Sobre a Projeção Consciente"; *Folha Espírita;* S. Paulo; Brazil; Newspaper; Monthly; Yr. IX; N. 102; September, 1982; bibl.; p. 5.

1756. VIEIRA, Waldo; "A Projeção Consciente e a Pessoa Mutilada"; *Folha Espírita;* S. Paulo; Brazil; Newspaper; Monthly; Yr. IX; N. 105; December, 1982; bibl.; p. 5.

1757. VIEIRA, Waldo; "Projeção Consciente e Corpo Humano"; *Folha Espírita;* S. Paulo; Brazil; Newspaper; Monthly; Yr. IX; N. 107; February; 1983; bibl.; p. 3.

1758. VIEIRA, Waldo; "Projeção Consciente e Formas-Pensamentos"; *Folha Espírita;* S. Paulo; Brazil; Newspaper; Monthly; Yr. IX; N. 104; November, 1982; bibl.; p. 3.

1759. VIEIRA, Waldo; "Projeção Consciente Humana"; *Jornal Espírita;* S. Paulo; Brazil; Monthly; Yr. IX; N. 110; August, 1984; p. 6.

1760. VIEIRA, Waldo; "Projeção Desobsessiva"; *Jornal Espírita;* S. Paulo; Brazil; Monthly; Yr. IX; N. 111; September, 1984; p. 6.

1761. VIEIRA, Waldo; "A Projeção do Inconsciente"; *Aurora;* Duque de Caxias, RJ; Brazil; Magazine; Monthly; Yr. V; N. 12; May, 1983; illus.; bibl.; p. 22.

1762. VIEIRA, Waldo; "Projeções da Consciência: Diário de Experiências Fora do Corpo Físico"; 232 pp.; glos. 14-16; alph.; 21 cm; pb.; 2nd ed.; Livraria Allan Kardec Editora; S. Paulo; Brazil; 1982; pp. 1-232.

1763. VIEIRA, Waldo; "O Projetor e os Desencarnantes"; *Folha Espírita;* S. Paulo; Brazil; Newspaper; Monthly; Yr. IX; N. 100; July, 1982; illus.; bibl.; p. 5.

1764. VIEIRA, Waldo; "O Recesso nas Projeções Conscientes"; *Folha Espírita;* S. Paulo; Brazil; Newspaper; Monthly; Yr. IX; N. 108; March, 1983; bibl.; p. 6.

1765. VIEIRA, Waldo; "Soma e Psicossoma"; *Folha Espírita;* S. Paulo; Brazil; Newspaper; Monthly; Yr. IX; N. 103; October, 1982; bibl.; p. 5.

1766. VIEIRA, Waldo; "Sonho e Projeção Consciente"; *Folha Espírita;* S. Paulo; Brazil; Newspaper; Monthly; Yr. VIII; N. 96; March, 1982; bibl.; p. 5.

1767. VIEIRA, Waldo; "Técnica da Auto-hipnose Projetiva"; *Jornal Espírita;* S. Paulo; Brazil; Monthly; Yr. IX; N. 115; January, 1985; p. 2.

1768. VIEIRA, Waldo; "Técnica da Hetero-hipnose Projetiva"; *Jornal Espírita;* S. Paulo; Brazil; Monthly; Yr. IX; N. 114; December, 1984; p. 8.

1769. VIEIRA, Waldo; "Técnica da Projeção Consciente Assistida"; *Folha Espírita;* S. Paulo; Brazil; Newspaper; Monthly; Yr. IX; N. 97; April, 1982; bibl.; p. 5.

1770. VIEIRA, Waldo; "Técnica da Projeção Consciente Através do Sonho"; *Folha Espírita;* S. Paulo; Brazil; Newspaper; Monthly; Yr. IX; N. 98; May, 1982; p. 3.

1771. VIEIRA, Waldo; "Técnica da Projeção Consciente pelo Corpo Mental"; *Aurora;* Duque de Caxias, RJ; Brazil; Magazine; Monthly; Yr. IV; N. 8; April, 1982; bibl.; p. 13.

1772. VIEIRA, Waldo; "Técnica da Projeção Consciente pelo Dióxido de Carbono"; *Jornal Espírita;* S. Paulo; Brazil; Monthly; Yr. IX; N. 113; November, 1984; p. 8.

1773. VIEIRA, Waldo; "Utilidades da Projeção Consciente"; *Folha Espírita;* S. Paulo; Brazil; Newspaper; Monthly; Yr. VIII; N. 95; February, 1981; p. 5.

1774. VIETEN, Günter C.; "Sie standen an der Schwelle der Ewigkeit"; *Die Andere Welt;* Freiburg; West Germany; Magazine; Monthly; Yr. 19; N. 10; October, 1968; pp. 946, 947.

1775. VIOLETA-ODETE; "Guia da Mediunidade"; 192 pp.; 18.5 cm; pb.; 4th ed.; Empresa Editora O Pensamento; S. Paulo; Brazil; 1945; pp. 111-115.

1776. VISHNUDEVANANDA; "El Libro de Yoga"; transl. Sivayiotir Mayananda; introd. Marcus Bach; 440 pp.; illus.; glos.; 429-435; 18 cm; pocket; pb.; 5th ed.; Alianza Editorial; Madrid; Spain; 1981; pp. 29, 300-302.

1777. VIVANTE, Leone; "Studi Sulle Precognizioni"; 220 pp.; bibl. 9-17; 19 cm; pb.; Vallecchi Editore; Firenze; Italy; 1937; p. 122.

1778. VOLTERRI, Roberto; "Psicotrónica"; transl. Juan Giner; 218 pp.; illus.; glos. 201-213; bibl. 215-217; 21.5 cm; pb.; Ediciones Martínez Roca; Barcelona; Spain; 1981; pp. 13, 91, 98, 216, 217.

1779. VYVYAN, John; "The Case Against Jones: A Study of Psychical Phenomena"; 220 pp.; James Clarke; London; 1966.

1780. WACHTMEISTER, Constance, and others; "Reminiscências de H. P. Blavatsky e de "A Doutrina Secreta"; Biography; transl. Edilson Alkmim Cunha; 140 pp.; illus.; 19.5 cm; pb.; Editora Pensamento; S. Paulo; Brazil; 1980; pp. 105-107.

1781. WALKER, Benjamin; "Beyond the Body: The Human Double and the Astral Planes"; VIII + 224 pp.; bibl. 195-206; alph.; 21.5 cm; hb.; dj.; Routledge & Kegan Paul; London; 1977; pp. 1-224 (Mini-library).

1782. WALKER, Benjamin; "Body Magic"; 480 pp.; alph.; 20 cm; pb.; Granada Publishing; London; 1979; pp. 26-30.

1783. WALKER, Benjamin; "Encyclopedia of Esoteric Man"; X + 344 pp.; 23.5 cm; hb.; dj.; Routledge & Kegan Paul; London; 1977; p. 11.

1784. WALKER, Benjamin; "Encyclopedia of Metaphysical Medicine"; X + 324 pp.; 23.5 cm; hb.; dj.; Routledge & Kegan Paul; London; 1978; pp. 41, 96.

1785. WALKER, Benjamin; "The Encyclopedia of the Occult, the Esoteric, and the Supernatural"; XII + 344 pp.; bibl. 13, 14; 23.5 cm; pb.; Stein and Pay; New York; 1980; pp. 11-14.

1786. WALKER, Benjamin; "Masks of the Soul: The Facts Behind Reincarnation"; 160 pp.; bibl. 145-156; alph.; 22 cm; pb.; The Aquarian Press; London; 1981; pp. 32, 52, 90, 91, 108.

1787. WALLACE, Abraham; "Astral Travelling from New Zealand Resulting in Telekinetic Phenomena in London"; *Light;* London; Magazine; Vol. XLIV; 1924; p. 697.

1788. WALLACE, Alfred Russel; "Les Miracles et le Moderne Spiritualisme"; transl. M. Mangin; VIII + 382 pp.; illus.; 21.5 cm; hb.; Librairie des Sciences Psychologiques; Paris; no date; pp. 102, 326, 329, 348.

1789. WALLACE, Amy, and HENKIN, Bill; "The Psychic Healing Book"; XVI + 206 pp.; bibl. 203-205; 21.5 cm; pb.; Turnstone Press; Great Britain; 1981; pp. 198, 199.

1790. WALLACE, Mary Bruce; "The Coming Light"; Watkins; London; 1924; p. 19.

1791. WALLIS, Claudia; "Eles Voltaram da Morte e Contam o que Viram"; *Manchete;* Rio de Janeiro; Brazil; Magazine; Weekly; Yr. 30; N. 1.557; 20, February, 1982; illus.; pp. 20-22.

1792. WAMBACH, Helen; "Life Before Life"; 214 pp.; 18 cm; pocket; pb.; Bantam Books; New York; March, 1979; pp. 15, 16; eds.: Eng., Fr.

1793. WAMBACH, Helen; "Recordando Vidas Passadas: Depoimentos de Pessoas Hipnotizadas"; transl. Octavio Mendes Cajado; 168 pp.; illus.; 20 cm; pb.; Editora Pensamento; S. Paulo; Brazil; 1981; pp. 46-49, 118, 133.

1794. WANG, Solon; "The Multiple Planes of the Cosmos and Life"; Treatise; transl. T. M. Yang, and K. H. Liu; XIV + 938 pp.; illus.; 21 cm; hb.; dj.; The Society for Psychic Studies; Taipei; Taiwan; 1979; pp. 55, 56, 156-159, 165-179, 193-195, 198, 210-214, 241, 559-561; eds.: Ch., Eng.

1795. WANTUIL, Zêus; "Licantropia"; *Reformador;* Rio de Janeiro; Brazil; Magazine; Monthly; Yr. 96; January-March, 1978; N. 1.786: pp. 34, 35, 37; N. 1.787: pp. 51, 52; N. 1.788: pp. 103, 104.

1796. WARCOLLIER, René; "La Télépathie: Recherches Expérimentales"; pref. Charles Robert Richet; 364 pp.; illus.; 22 cm; hb.; Librairie Félix Alcan; Paris; 1921; pp. 79, 96-99.

1797. WARD, Brian; "El Sexto Sentido"; without translator; 96 pp.; illus.; glos. 90-92; bibl. 89, 90; alph.; 20 cm; cart.; Instituto Parramón Ediciones; Barcelona; Spain; 1978; pp. 34-36, 92.

1798. WARD, J. S. M.; "A Subaltern in Spirit Land"; 2 Vol.; 164 pp.; illus.; 18 cm; hb.; Psychic Book Club; London; no date; pp. 9, 10, 20.

1799. WATKINS, Susan K.; "Conversations with Seth"; Vol. One; introd. Jane Roberts; 290 pp.; illus.; alph.; 23 cm; hb.; dj.; Prentice-Hall; Englewood Cliffs; New Jersey; U. S. A.; 1980; pp. 17-19, 41, 51, 52.

1800. WATSON, Lyall; "The Romeo Error: A Meditation on Life and Death"; 256 pp.; bibl. 224-240; alph.; 18 cm; pocket; pb.; Dell Publishing Co.; New York; May, 1976; pp. 129-145, 153, 159, 177, 178, 219.

1801. WATSON, Lyall; "Supernature: A Natural History of the Supernatural"; 348 pp.; bibl. 317-335; alph.; 18 cm; pocket; pb.; Coronet Books; London; 1974; pp. 305-307; eds.: Eng., It., Port.

1802. WATTS, Alan W.; "The Joyous Cosmology"; introd. Timothy Leary & Richard Alpert; XX + 104 pp.; illus.; 20 cm; pb.; Vintage Books; New York; 1965; pp. 17, 83, 84, 100.

1803. WAUTHY, Léon; "Science et Spiritisme"; 398 pp.; illus.; 23 cm; pb.; Librairie des Sciences Psychiques; Paris; 1923; 162-188.

1804. WEBB, James; "The Occult Underground"; 388 pp.; illus.; alph.; 20.5 cm; hb.; Open Court Publishing; La Salle; Ill.; U. S. A.; 1974; pp. 40, 99, 174, 188.

1805. WEBB, James; "There Came Back"; 188 pp.; bibl. 181; Hawthorn Books; New York; 1974.

1806. WEBB, Richard; "Voices from Another World"; X + 278 pp.; 18 cm; pocket; pb.; Manor Books; New York; 1972; pp. 77-85.

1807. WEDECK, Harry E., and BASKIN, Wade; "Dictionary of Spiritualism"; VIII + 390 pp.; 21 cm; hb.; dj.; Peter Owen; London; 1971; p. 35.

1808. WEED, Joseph J.; "Psychic Energy"; 216 pp.; 21 cm; pb.; Parker Publishing Co.; West Nyack, N. Y.; U. S. A.; June, 1978; pp. 195-210.

1809. WEIL, Pierre; "Fronteiras da Evolução e da Morte"; 132 pp.; illus.; bibl. 129-131; 21 cm; pb.; Editora Vozes; Petrópolis, RJ; Brazil; 1979; pp. 94-122.

1810. WEIL, Pierre; "A Revolução Silenciosa"; Autobiography; 234 pp.; 19.5 cm; pb.; Editora Pensamento; S. Paulo; Brazil; 1982; pp. 67, 143-152, 229, 230.

1811. WEISS, Adolfo; "Ciencias del Mañana"; 286 pp.; 20.5 cm; pb.; Editorial Kier; Buenos Aires; Argentina; 1946; pp. 82-85, 100-112.

1812. WENDT, Victor K.; "Ein Astral-Erlebnis"; *Esotera;* Freiburg; West Germany; Magazine; Monthly; Yr. 21; N. 11; November, 1970; pp. 1002, 1003.

1813. WEOR, Samael Aun (Pseud. for Kattan Umaña Tamires); "Aos Pés do Mestre"; without translator; 36 pp.; illus.; 21 cm; pb.; Editora Gnose; Porto Alegre, RS; Brazil; no date; pp. 13-18.

1814. WEOR, Samael Aun (Pseud. for Kattan Umaña Tamires); "Desfazendo Mistérios"; without translator; pref. Luis Alberto Renderos; 138 pp.; illus.; 21 cm; pb.; Editora Gnose; Porto Alegre, RS; Brazil; October, 1976; pp. 96-102.

1815. WEOR, Samael Aun (Pseud. for Kattan Umãna Tamires); "O Livro Amarelo Kundalini Yoga"; without translator; 58 pp.; 21 cm; pb.; Sol Nascente Publicações; S. Paulo; Brazil; no date; pp. 42, 43.

1816. WEOR, Samael Aun (Pseud. for Kattan Umãna Tamires); "Logos Mantran Teurgia"; without translator; introd. Virgílio Campos Novais; 86 pp.; illus.; 10.5 cm; pb.; Associação Gnóstica de Estudos Antropológicos e Ciências; Belo Horizonte, MG; Brazil; no date; pp. 39-47.

1817. WEOR, Samael Aun (Pseud. for Kattan Umaña Tamires); "O Mistério do Áureo Florescer"; transl., pref. and prfr. Pedro Carvalho Barbosa; 162 pp.; 21 cm; pb.; Rex Collectio Editores; Santos, SP; Brazil; 1981; pp. 63-66; eds.: Eng., Sp., Port.

1818. WEOR, Samael Aun (Pseud. for Kattan Umaña Tamires); "Mistérios da Vida e da Morte"; without translator; 148 pp.; 19.5 cm; pb.; Sol Nascente Publicações; S. Paulo; Brazil; 1976; pp. 105-111.

1819. WEOR, Samael Aun (Pseud. for Kattan Umaña Tamires); "Noções Fundamentais de Endocrinologia e Criminologia"; transl. Pedro Carvalho Barbosa and Romulo Caixeta Leite; 130 pp.; 21.5 cm; pb.; Rex Collectio Editores; Santos, SP; Brazil; no date; pp. 78, 79.

1820. WEOR, Samael Aun (Pseud. for Kattan Umaña Tamires); "A Noite dos Séculos" without translator; 164 pp.; 21 cm; pb.; Editora Gnose; Porto Alegre, RS; Brazil; May, 1981; pp. 130, 131.

1821. WEOR, Samael Aun (Pseud. for Kattan Umaña Tamires); "Teurgia e Magia Prática"; without translator; 180 pp.; illus.; 21 cm; pb.; Editora Gnose; Porto Alegre, RS; Brazil; November, 1978; pp. 42-47.

1822. WEREIDE, Thorstein; "Norway's Human Doubles"; *Tomorrow;* U. S. A.; Magazine; Vol. 3; N. 2; Winter, 1955; pp. 23-29.

1823. WERNER, Edward Theodore Chalmers; "The Chinese Idea of the Second Self"; 50 pp.; The Changai Times; China; 1932.

1824. WEST, D. J.; "The Double: Its Psycho-Pathology and Psycho-Physiology"; *Journal of the Society for Psychical Research;* London; Vol. 38; N. 699; June, 1956; pp. 274, 275.

1825. WHEATLEY, James M. O., and EDGE, Hoyt L.; Editors; "Philosophical Dimensions of Parapsychology"; Anthology; XXX + 484 pp.; illus.; bibl. 464-478; alph.; 23 cm; hb.; dj.; Charles C. Thomas, Publisher; Springfield; Ill; U. S. A.; 1976; p. 354.

1826. WHEELER, David R.; "Journey to the Other Side"; 184 pp.; 17.5 cm; pocket; pb.; Ace Books; New York; 1977; pp. 1-184 (Mini-library).

1827. WHITE, John Warren; Editor and introd.; "La Experiencia Mística y los Estados de Conciencia"; Anthology; transl. David Rosenbaum; 318 pp.; 20 cm; pb.; 2nd ed.; Editorial Kairós; Barcelona; Spain; June, 1982; pp. 9, 10, 28.

1828. WHITE, John Warren; Editor; "Frontiers of Consciousness"; 416 pp.; illus.; 18 cm; pb.; pocket; Avon Books; New York; July, 1975; pp. 183, 361, 374, 386-389.

1829. WHITE, John Warren, and KRIPPNER, Stanley Curtiss; Editors; "Future Science: Life Energies and the Physics of Paranormal Phenomena"; Anthology; 598 pp.; illus.; 18 cm; pocket; pb.; Doubleday & Co.; New York; 1977; pp. 124, 218, 220, 297, 301, 312, 328.

1830. WHITE, John Warren; Editor; "The Highest State of Consciousness"; Anthology; XXIV + 492 pp.; bibl. 472-480; 18 cm; pocket; pb.; Anchor Books; New York; 1972; p. 465.

1831. WHITE, John Warren; Editor; "Kundalini Evolution and Enlightenment"; Anthology; 480 pp.; illus.; bibl. 463-466; 18 cm; pocket; pb.; Anchor Books; New York; 1979; p. 369.

1832. WHITE, John Warren; "A Practical Guide to Death & Dying"; XIV + 172 pp.; illus.; 21 cm; pb.; The Theosophical Publishing House; Wheaton; Ill.; U.S.A.; 1980; pp. 10-12, 124-134, 142, 148.

1833. WHITE, Rhea Amelia; "An Analysis of ESP Phenomena in the Saints"; *Parapsychology Review;* New York; Vol. 13; N. 1; January-February, 1982; pp. 15-18.

1834. WHITE, Rhea Amelia; "Surveys in Parapsychology"; pref. Montague Ullman; XII + 484 pp.; illus.; alph.; 21.5 cm; hb.; The Scarecrow Press; Metuchen, N. J.; U. S. A.; 1976; pp. 450-452.

1835. WHITE, Rhea Amelia, and DALE, Laura A.; "Parapsychology: Sources of Information"; XII + 304 pp.; bibl.; alph.; 21.5 cm; hb.; The Scarecrow Press; Metuchen, N. J.; U. S. A.; 1973; pp. 83-86.

1836. WHITE, Ruth, and SWAINSON, Mary; "Sete Viagens Interiores"; transl. Maio Miranda; 238 pp.; illus.; 19.5 cm; pb.; Editora Pensamento; S. Paulo; Brazil; 1978; pp. 28, 30, 56.

1837. WHITEMAN, Joseph Hilary Michael; "Lucid Dreams" (Celia E. Green); Books Reviews; *Journal of the Society for Psychical Research;* London; Vol. 45; N. 739; March, 1969; pp. 21-25.

1838. WHITEMAN, Joseph Hilary Michael; "Out-of-the-Body Experiences" (Celia E. Green); Books Reviews; *Journal of the Society for Psychical Research;* London; Vol. 45; N. 742; December, 1969; pp. 172-178.

1839. WHITEMAN, Joseph Hilary Michael; "Philosophy of Space and Times and the Inner Constitution of Nature: A Phenomenological Study"; 436 pp.; illus.; 22 cm; Humanities P.; New York; 1967.

1840. WHITEMAN, Joseph Hilary Michael; "The Mystical Life"; introd. H. H. Price; XX + 250 pp.; 23 cm; hb.; Faber & Faber; London; 1961; pp. 45-82, 143-222.

1841. WHITEMAN, Joseph Hilary Michael; "Out-of-the-Body Explorations"; *Theta;* Durham; North Carolina; U.S.A.; Magazine; N. 5; Spring, 1964; p. 3.

1842. WHITEMAN, Joseph Hilary Michael; "The Process of Separation and Return in Experiences Fully "Out of the Body"; *Proceedings of the Society for Psychical Research;* London; Vol. 50; Part 185; May, 1956; pp. 240-274.

1843. WHITMORE, Clara Helen; "Jo: The Indian Friend"; 52 pp.; The Christopher Publishing House; Boston; Massachusetts; U. S. A.; 1925.

1844. WICKLAND, Carl A.; "30 Years Among the Dead"; 390 pp.; illus.; 21.5 cm; pb.; Newcastle Publishing Co.; Hollywood; Cal.; U. S. A.; March, 1974; p. 356; eds.: Eng., Sp.

1845. WILBER, Ken; "The Spectrum of Consciousness"; 376 pp.; illus.; bibl. 344-367; alph.; 21 cm; pb.; The Theosophical Publishing House; Wheaton; Ill.; U. S. A.; 1979; pp. 120, 270, 275.

1846. WILEY, Constance; "A Star of Hope"; The C. W. Daniel Co.; London; 1938; pp. 56, 75.

1847. WILFING, Jutta; "Wenn Jemand Seiner Doppelganger Sieht"; *Die Andere Welt;* Freiburg; West Germany; Magazine; Monthly; Yr. 19; N. 6; June, 1968; illus.; pp. 516-522.

1848. WILKERSON, Ralph; "Beyond and Back"; XIV + 240 pp.; 18 cm; pocket; pb.; Bantam Books; New York; February, 1978; pp. VII, 1, 39-54.

1849. WILLIAMSON, John W.; "A New Look at Astral Projection"; *Yoga Today;* Vol. 3; N. 7; September, 1978; p. 18.

1850. WILLMANN, Laerte; "Ida e Volta: Morte e Renascimento" (Robert A. Monroe); Section "Livros"; *O Globo;* Rio de Janeiro; Brazil; Newspaper; Daily; 24, June, 1979; p. 7.

1851. WILSON, Colin; Editor; "Homens de Mistério: Uma Celebração do Oculto"; Anthology; transl. Maria Amália de Sotto-Mayor; 240 pp.; illus.; bibl. 237; 21 cm; pb.; Editora Ulisseia; Lisboa; Portugal; no date; pp. 21, 113.

1852. WILSON, Colin; "Lord of the Underworld: Jung and the Twentieth Century"; Biography; 160 pp.; bibl. 157; alph.; 21.5 cm; hb.; dj.; The Aquarian Press; Wellingborough; Northamptonshire; Great Britain; 1984; pp. 7, 8, 15.

1853. WILSON, Colin; "Mysteries"; 668 pp.; bibl. 643-652; alph.; 23 cm; hb.; dj.; G. P. Putnam's Sons; New York; 1978; pp. 155-161, 218, 337, 372-379, 476, 477, 539, 611.

1854. WILSON, Colin; "The Occult"; 606 pp.; alph.; 20.5 cm; pb.; Vintage Books; New York; February, 1973; pp. 56, 217-219, 338, 452, 503, 543-548; eds.: Eng., Port.

1855. WILSON, Colin; "Poltergeist! A Study in Destructive Haunting"; 382 pp.; bibl. 365-369; alph.; 21.5 cm; pb.; Perigee Book; New York; 1983; pp. 196, 244, 246, 273, 274, 336-339, 361.

1856. WILSON, Colin; "The Psychic Detectives"; 288 pp.; index of names; bibl. 280-283; 18 cm; pocket; pb.; Pan Books; London; 1984; pp. 125, 126, 136, 137, 160, 161, 178.

1857. WILSON, Colin; "Strange Powers"; 148 pp.; illus.; 21 cm; hb.; dj.; Random House; New York; 1975; pp. 27-72.

1858. WILSON, Colin, and GRANT, John; "The Directory of Possibilities"; 256 pp.; illus.; bibl. 223-225; alph.; 23.5 cm; hb.; dj.; Webb & Bower; Exeter; England; 1981; pp. 34, 47, 50-53, 58, 98, 124, 128, 129, 139, 142-144, 153.

1859. WILSON, Robert Anton; "Cosmic Trigger the Final Secret of the Illuminati"; introd. Timothy Leary; XXX + 290 pp.; illus.; alph.; 18 cm; pocket; pb.; Pocket Books; New York; March, 1978; pp. 86, 136, 215.

1860. WINGFIELD, Kate; "Guidance From Beyond"; pref. Helen; introd. E. Marshall Hall; 192 pp.; Philip Allan & Co.; London; 1923.

1861. WINGFIELD, Kate; "More Guidance From Beyond"; Philip Allan & Co.; London; 1925; pp. 12, 13.

1862. WINNER, Anna Kennedy; "Idéias Básicas da Sabedoria Oculta"; transl. J. Martins; 138 pp.; 19.5 cm; pb.; Editora Pensamento; S. Paulo; Brazil; 1977; pp. 90, 91.

1863. WOLMAN, Benjamin B.; DALE, Laura A.; SCHMEIDLER, Gertrude R.; and ULLMAN, Montague; Editors; "Handbook of Parapsychology"; introd. Howard M. Zimmerman; XXIV + 968 pp.; illus.; bibl. 907-920; glos. 921-936; alph.; 23 cm; hb.; dj.; Van Nostrand Reinhold Co.; New York; 1977; pp. 67, 68, 418, 600, 607, 608, 616, 659, 717, 718, 749, 750, 772, 790-792, 796, 917, 918, 922, 925, 929, 936; eds.: Eng., It.

1864. WOODS, James Hanghton; "The Yoga-System of Patañjali"; XLII + 382 pp.; glos. 366-381; 24.5 cm; pb.; Motilal Banarsidass; Delhi; India; 1977; pp. 261, 266, 267; eds.: sanskrit, Eng.

1865. WORLD ALMANAC; Editor; "Weltalmanach des Übersinnlichen"; transl. Sepp Leeb; 560 pp.; illus.; index of names; 18 cm; pocket; pb.; Wilhelm Heyne Verlag; München; West Germany; 1982; pp. 359-363.

1866. WORN, Fernando; "A Quem Deus Revela"; *Desobsessão;* Porto Alegre, RS; Brazil; Magazine; Monthly; Yr. XXXIV; N. 411; May, 1982; p. 14.

1867. WUNDERLI, Erich; "Die Einzige Realität"; *Esotera;* Freiburg; West Germany; Magazine; Monthly; Yr. 24; N. 10; October, 1973; illus.; pp. 917-922.

1868. WYLD, George; "The Evidence of Anaesthetics"; *Bordeland;* London; Magazine; Monthly; Vol. I; N. III; January, 1894; pp. 256-259.

1869. XAVIER, Francisco Cândido; "Ação e Reação"; 274 pp.; 18 cm; pb.; 6th ed.; Federação Espírita Brasileira; Rio de Janeiro; Brazil; 1978; pp. 6, 17, 107, 172, 177, 178, 192, 193, 214, 225.

1870. XAVIER, Francisco Cândido; "Ave, Cristo"; Novel; 376 pp.; 18 cm; pb.; 7th ed.; Federação Espírita Brasileira; Rio de Janeiro; Brazil; 1982; pp. 90, 172.

1871. XAVIER, Francisco Cândido; "O Caminho Oculto"; 52 pp.; 22 cm; pb.; 4th ed.; Federação Espírita Brasileira; Rio de Janeiro; Brazil; 1983; pp. 15, 41.

1872. XAVIER, Francisco Cândido; "Cartas e Crônicas"; 182 pp.; 18 cm; pb.; 4th ed.; Federação Espírita Brasileira; Rio de Janeiro; Brazil; 1979; pp. 36, 38, 56, 58, 66-68, 123, 126.

1873. XAVIER, Francisco Cândido; "O Consolador"; 234 pp.; 18 cm; pb.; 8th ed.; Federação Espírita Brasileira; Rio de Janeiro; Brazil; 1980; pp. 43, 189.

1874. XAVIER, Francisco Cândido; "Entre a Terra e o Céu"; 266 pp.; 18 cm; pb.; 6th ed.; Federação Espírita Brasileira; Rio de Janeiro; Brazil; 1978; pp. 32, 33, 49, 50, 54, 76, 77, 84, 86-89, 91, 94-105, 148-159, 173-175, 220, 241-245.

1875. XAVIER, Francisco Cândido; "Instruções Psicofônicas"; pres. Arnaldo Rocha; 296 pp.; 18 cm; pb.; 3rd ed.; Federação Espírita Brasileira; Rio de Janeiro; Brazil; 1974; pp. 219-222.

1876. XAVIER, Francisco Cândido; "Libertação"; 264 pp.; 18 cm; pb.; 8th ed.; Federação Espírita Brasileira; Rio de Janeiro; Brazil; 1980; pp. 80-82, 134, 168, 169, 185, 205-207, 237.

1877. XAVIER, Francisco Cândido; "Luz Acima"; 214 pp.; 18 cm; pb.; 4th ed.; Federação Espírita Brasileira; Rio de Janeiro; Brazil; 1978; pp. 99-101, 208.

1878. XAVIER, Francisco Cândido; "Os Mensageiros"; 266 pp.; 18 cm; pb.; 11st ed.; Federação Espírita Brasileira; Rio de Janeiro; Brazil; 1978; pp. 90, 195-203, 266.

1879. XAVIER, Francisco Cândido; "Missionários da Luz"; 348 pp.; 18 cm; pb.; 12nd ed.; Federação Espírita Brasileira; Rio de Janeiro; Brazil; 1979; pp. 64, 65, 80, 81, 86, 94, 115, 118, 123, 147, 190, 191, 230, 231, 272, 291.

1880. XAVIER, Francisco Cândido; "No Mundo Maior"; 254 pp.; 18 cm; pb.; 7th ed.; Federação Espírita Brasileira; Rio de Janeiro; Brazil; 1977; pp. 18, 24, 78, 89, 114-122, 145, 184, 192-195, 200, 240.

1881. XAVIER, Francisco Cândido; "Nos Domínios da Mediunidade"; 286 pp.; 18 cm; pb.; 8th ed.; Federação Espírita Brasileira; Rio de Janeiro; Brazil; 1976; pp. 31, 97-105, 111, 192, 252, 266-269, 273.

1882. XAVIER, Francisco Cândido; "Nosso Lar"; 282 pp.; 18 cm; pb.; 20th ed.; Federação Espírita Brasileira; Rio de Janeiro; Brazil; 1978; pp. 182, 263-266.

1883. XAVIER, Francisco Cândido; "Obreiros da Vida Eterna"; 304 pp.; 18 cm; pb.; 9th ed.; Federação Espírita Brasileira; Rio de Janeiro; Brazil; 1975; pp. 19, 138, 152, 194, 209-212, 236, 253, 254, 287-290.

1884. XAVIER, Francisco Cândido; "Palavras do Coração"; pres. Ruth de Castro Mattos; 96 pp.; illus.; 21 cm; pb.; Cultura Espírita União; S. Paulo; Brazil; 1982; pp. 35, 37, 85-87.

1885. XAVIER, Francisco Cândido; "Pontos e Contos"; 266 pp.; 18 cm; pb.; 5th ed.; Federação Espírita Brasileira; Rio de Janeiro; Brazil; 1979; pp. 37, 101, 153.

1886. XAVIER, Francisco Cândido; "E A Vida Continua"; 244 pp.; 18 cm; pb.; 9th ed.; Federação Espírita Brasileira; Rio de Janeiro; Brazil; 1981; pp. 238-240.

1887. XAVIER, Francisco Cândido; "Voltei"; 176 pp.; 18 cm; hb.; dj.; Federação Espírita Brasileira; Rio de Janeiro; Brazil; 1949; pp. 20-23.

1888. XAVIER, Francisco Cândido; "Vozes do Grande Além"; introd. Arnaldo Rocha; 282 pp.; 18 cm; pb.; 2nd ed.; Federação Espírita Brasileira; Rio de Janeiro; Brazil; 1974; pp. 31-33, 192.

1889. XAVIER, Francisco Cândido, and CUNHA, Heigorina; "Cidade do Além"; 80 pp.; illus.; 18.5 cm; pb.; 3rd ed.; Instituto de Difusão Espírita; Araras, SP; Brazil; 1983; pp. 25-27, 29.

1890. XAVIER, Francisco Cândido, and VIEIRA, Waldo; "Evolução em Dois Mundos"; 220 pp.; 18 cm; pb.; 4th ed.; Federação Espírita Brasileira; Rio de Janeiro; Brazil; 1977; pp. 29, 129-134, 159, 209.

1891. XAVIER, Francisco Cândido, and VIEIRA, Waldo; "Mecanismos da Mediunidade"; 188 pp.; 18 cm; pb.; 4th ed.; Federação Espírita Brasileira; Rio de Janeiro; Brazil; 1973; pp. 13, 15, 16, 108, 123, 145, 149-155, 163, 165.

1892. XAVIER, Francisco Cândido, and VIEIRA, Waldo; "Sexo e Destino"; 358 pp.; 18 cm; pb.; 8th ed.; Federação Espírita Brasileira; Rio de Janeiro; Brazil; 1981; pp. 50, 117-119, 124-127, 168, 307-309.

1893. YETERIAN, Dixie; "Casebook of a Psychic Detective"; 198 pp.; alph.; 23 cm; hb.; dj.; Stein and Day Publishers; New York; 1982; pp. 17, 18, 45.

1894. YOGANANDA, Paramahansa (Pseud. for Mukunda Lal Ghosh); "Autobiografia de Um Iogue Contemporâneo"; transl. Adelaide Petters Lessa Pantas; 458 pp.; illus.; 21 cm; pb.; Summus Editorial; S. Paulo; Brazil; 1976; pp. 34-37, 144-146, 184, 205, 245, 263, 264, 285, 289, 305.

1895. YOUNG, Samuel H.; "Psychic Children"; 160 pp.; 18 cm; pocket; pb.; Pocket Books; New York; May, 1978; pp. 95-97.

1896. YRAM (Pseud. for Marcel Louis Fohan); "La Evolución en los Mundos Superiores"; 190 pp.; 20 cm; pb.; Editorial Kier; Buenos Aires; 1959; pp. 62-69.

1897. YRAM (Pseud. for Marcel Louis Fohan); "Practical Astral Projection"; without translator; 254 pp.; 18 cm; pocket; pb.; 4th print.; Samuel Weiser; New York; 1979; pp. 1-254; eds.: Fr., Eng., Sp. (Mini-library).

1898. ZAIN, C. C. (Pseud. for Elbert Benjamin); "The Next Life"; Serial N. 173-182; 332 pp.; illus.; 17 cm; pb.; reed.; The Church of Light; Los Angeles; Cal.; U. S. A.; April, 1964; pp. 20, 195.

1899. ZANIAH (Pseud. for José Dali Moral); "Diccionario Esoterico"; 580 pp.; 23cm; pb.; Editorial Kier; Buenos Aires; Argentina; 1979; p. 368.

1900. Z. H. Y.; "Magnetisme & Spiritisme: Concordance"; 52 pp.; illus.; 19 cm; pb.; Bibliothèque Chacornac; Paris; no date; pp. 33-35, 44.

1901. ZINGAROPOLI, Francesco; "Morte Aparente e Sobrevivência da Alma"; introd. Domenico Antonio Tieri; transl. Francisco Klörs Werneck; 60 pp.; illus.; 17.5 cm; pb.; Translator's Edition; Rio de Janeiro; Brazil; no date; pp. 32, 33, 47-56.

1902. ZOLAR (Pseud.); "Enciclopedia del Saber Antiguo y Prohibido"; transl. Francisco Torres Oliver; 464 pp.; illus.; 18 cm; pocket; pb.; 3rd ed.; Alianza Editorial; Madrid; Spain; 1982; pp. 133-140.

1903. ZOPPI, Vitório, and MAZZONI, Lutalto; "A Tremenda Renovação do Mundo"; 168 pp.; 18 cm; pb.; Authors' Edition; Indaiatuba, SP; Brazil; no date; pp. 78, 98.

1904. ZORAB, George; Compiled by; "Bibliography of Parapsychology"; 128 pp.; alph.; 19 cm; hb.; dj.; Parapsychology Fondation; New York; 1957; pp. 22, 27, 28.

1905. ZORAB, George; "Ochêma" (J. J. Poortman); Books Reviews; *Journal of the Society for Psychical Research;* London; Vol. 44; N. 737; September, 1968; pp. 352-355.

1906. ZORAB, George; "Zinneschok en Sweefervaring" (J. Teunissen); Books Reviews; *Journal of the Society for Psychical Research;* London; Vol. 46; N. 750; December, 1971; pp. 235, 236.

1907. ZYMONIDAS, Alessandro; "The Problems of Mediumship"; XXVI + 252 pp.; illus.; 18.5 cm; hb.; Kegan Paul, Trench, Trübner & Co.; London; 1920; pp. 181-188.

OTHER WORKS BY THE AUTHOR

1. **VIEIRA, Waldo;** *100 Testes da Conscienciometria (100 Conscientiometry Tests);* 232 pp.; 100 chaps.; 14 refs.; 21 x 14 cm; pb.; 1st ed.; Rio de Janeiro, RJ, Brazil; International Institute of Projectiology and Conscientiology; 1997 (ed. in Portuguese: ISBN 85.86019.26.7).

2. **IDEM;** *Conscienciograma: Técnica de Avaliação da Consciência Integral (Conscientiogram: Technique for Evaluation of the Integral Consciousness);* 344 pp.; 100 pages of evaluation; 2,000 items; 4 indexes; 11 enu.; 7 refs.; glos. 282 terms; 150 abbr.; alph.; 21 x 14 cm; pb.; 1st ed.; Rio de Janeiro, RJ, Brazil; International Institute of Projectiology; 1996 (ed. in Portuguese: ISBN 85.86019.15.1; Spanish: ISBN 85.86019.20.8).

3. **IDEM;** *200 Teáticas da Conscienciologia (200 Conscientiology Theorices);* 260 pp.; 200 chaps.; 13 refs.; alph.; 21 x 14 cm; pb.; 1st ed.; Rio de Janeiro, RJ, Brazil; International Institute of Projectiology and Conscientiology; 1997 (ed. in Portuguese: ISBN 85.86019.24.0).

4. **IDEM;** *Manual da Dupla Evolutiva (Evolutionary Duo Manual);* 208 pp.; 40 chaps.; 16 refs.; alph.; 21 x 14 cm; pb.; 1st ed.; Rio de Janeiro, RJ, Brazil; International Institute of Projectiology and Conscientiology; 1997 (ed. in Portuguese: ISBN 85.86019.27.5).

5. **IDEM;** *Manual da Proéxis: Programação Existencial (Existential Program Manual);* 164 pp.; 40 chaps.; 10 refs.; alph.; 21 x 14 cm; pb.; 2nd ed.; Rio de Janeiro, RJ, Brazil; International Institute of Projectiology and Conscientiology; 1998 (eds. in Portuguese: ISBN 85.86019.19.4; English: ISBN 85.86019.18.6; Spanish: ISBN 85.86019.54.2).

6. **IDEM;** *Manual da Tenepes: Tarefa Energética Pessoal (Penta Manual: Personal Energetic Task);* 138 pp.; 34 chaps.; 5 refs.; glos. 282 terms; 147 abbr.; alph.; 21 x 14 cm; pb.; 1st ed.; Rio de Janeiro, RJ, Brazil; International Institute of Projectiology; 1995 (eds. in Portuguese: ISBN 85.86019.07.0; Spanish: ISBN 85.86019.17.8; English: ISBN 85.86019.16.X).

7. **IDEM;** *Manual de Redação da Conscienciologia (Conscientiology Redaction Manual);* 272 pp.; 21 x 28 cm; 1st ed.; Rio de Janeiro, RJ, Brazil; International Institute of Projectiology and Conscientiology; 1997 (ed. in Portuguese: ISBN 85.86019.22.4).

8. **IDEM;** *Máximas da Conscienciologia (Maxims of Conscientiology);* 164 pp.; 150 illus.; 450 miniphrases; 10 x 15 cm; 1st ed.; Rio de Janeiro, RJ, Brazil; International Institute of Projectiology; 1996 (ed. in Portuguese: ISBN 85.86019.12.7).

9. **IDEM;** *Minidefinições Conscienciais (Consciential Minidefinitions);* 164 pp.; 150 illus.; 450 miniphrases; 10 x 15 cm; 1st ed.; Rio de Janeiro, RJ, Brazil; International Institute of Projectiology; 1996 (ed. in Portuguese: ISBN 85.86019.14.3).

10. **IDEM;** *Miniglossário da Conscienciologia (Miniglossary of Conscientiology);* 57 pp.; 17 x 11 cm; spi.; 1st ed.; Rio de Janeiro, RJ, Brazil; International Institute of Projectiology; 1992 (eds.: Portuguese, Spanish and English).

11. **IDEM;** *A Natureza Ensina (Nature Teaches);* 164 pp.; 150 illus.; 450 miniphrases; 10 x 15 cm; 1st ed.; Rio de Janeiro, RJ, Brazil; International Institute of Projectiology; 1996 (ed. in Portuguese: ISBN 85.86019.13.5).

12. **IDEM;** *Nossa Evolução (Our Evolution);* 168 pp.; 15 chaps.; 6 refs.; glos. 282 terms; 149 abbr.; alph.; 21 X 14 cm; pb.; 1st ed.; Rio de Janeiro, RJ, Brazil; International Institute of Projectiology; 1996 (eds. in Portuguese: ISBN 85.86019.08.9; Spanish: ISBN 85.86019.21.6; English: ISBN 85.86019.42.9).

13. **IDEM;** *O Que é a Conscienciologia (The Essential Conscientiology);* 180pp.; 100 chaps.; 3 refs.; glos. 280 terms; alph.; 21 x 14 cm; pb.; 1st ed.; Rio de Janeiro, RJ; International Institute of Projectiology; 1994 (ed. in Portuguese: ISBN 85.86019.03.8).

14. **IDEM;** *Projeções da Consciência: Diário de Experiências Fora do Corpo Físico (Projections of the Consciousness: A Diary of Out-of-Body Experiences);* 224 pp.; glos. 25 terms; alph.; 21 x 14 cm; pb.; 4th ed., revised; Rio de Janeiro, RJ, Brazil; International Institute of Projectiology; 1992 (eds. in Portuguese: ISBN 85.86019.04.6; Spanish: ISBN 85.86019.02.X; English: ISBN 85.86019.25.9).

15. **IDEM;** *700 Experimentos da Conscienciologia (700 Conscientiology Experiments);* 1,058 pp.; 700 chaps.; 300 tests; 8 indexes; 2 tabs.; 600 enu.; index of names; 5,116 refs.; geo.; glos. 280 terms; 147 abbr.; alph.; 28.5 x 21.5 x 7 cm; hb.; 1st ed.; Rio de Janeiro, RJ, Brazil; International Institute of Projectiology; 1994 (ed. in Portuguese: ISBN 85.86019.05.4).

16. **IDEM;** *Temas da Conscienciologia (Conscientiology Themes);* 232 pp.; 90 chaps.; 16 refs.; alph.; 21 X 14 cm; pb.; 1st ed.; Rio de Janeiro, RJ, Brazil; International Institute of Projectiology and Conscientiology; 1997 (ed. in Portuguese: ISBN 85.86019.28.3)

GLOSSARY OF PROJECTIOLOGY

Observation. The following is a listing of 303 projectiological terms, compound words, expressions and their technical equivalents.

Abdominal brain – The umbilicochakra (center of consciential energy located above the navel), when unconsciously selected by the intraphysical consciousness, who is still fairly unevolved, as the basis of his/her manifestations. The belly-brain, gut brain, abdominal brain, abdominal *pseudo*-brain, or abdominal sub-brain, is the *gray eminence* of the natural, encephalic brain (coronochakra and frontochakra); an indefensible obstacle to conscious self-evolution.

Admiration-disagreement binomial – The posture of an intraphysical consciousness who is mature in regard to consciential evolution, knows how to live in peaceful coexistence with another intraphysical consciousness who he/she loves and admires, but with whose points of view, opinions and positions he/she is not always in 100% agreement.

Advanced existential program – The existential program of the intraphysical consciousness who is an evolutionary leader, within a specific libertarian groupkarmic task that is more universalistic and polykarmic in nature. This individual acts as a lucid, *mini*cog within a *maxi*mechanism of the multidimensional team.

Altered state of consciousness – See xenophrenia.

Alternant intraphysical pre*serenissimus* – The intraphysical consciousness who is capable, from time to time, of simultaneously living consciously in the ordinary, physical waking state, as well as projected in extraphysical dimensions.

Androchakra *(andro + chakra)* – A man's sexochakra.

Androsoma *(andro + soma)* – The masculine human body, or the soma specific to a man.

Androthosene (compound word: *andro + tho + sen + e*) – The thosene specific to the primitive male intraphysical consciousness or the *macho man.*

Animism (Latin: *animus,* soul) – The set of intracorporeal and extracorporeal phenomena produced by the intraphysical consciousness without external interference. For example, the phenomenon of lucid projection induced by one's own will.

Antithosene *(anti + tho + sen + e)* – The antagonistic thosene, common in refutations, omniquestioning and productive debates.

Aphrodisiac female sexosoma – A woman's soma, considered specifically in regard to sex, when its form is capable of acting as an aphrodisiac. See *gynosoma.*

Artifacts of knowledge – Intellectual tools; resources used by the consciousness to store, retrieve or process information, such as books, computers and the internet.

Assisted lucid projection – The projection wherein the intraphysical consciousness finds him/herself to be directly assisted, during the experiment, by a helper which is almost always an expert in lucid projectability (LPB).

Assistential - Related to or denoting assistance. An assistential task is universalistic, cosmoethical, fraternal and should ideally be clarifying (clarification task) instead of consoling (consolation task).

Auric coupling – Interfusion of the holochakral energies between 2 or more consciousnesses.

Belly-brain – See abdominal brain.

Biothosene *(bio + tho + sen + e)* – The thosene specific to the human or intraphysical consciousness.

Bithanatosis – The deactivation and discarding of the holochakra after the first desoma, including removal of the remaining energetic connections of the holochakra in the psychosoma; *second death*; second desoma.

Blind guide – The amoral or inexperienced consciousness which helps another consciousness – in an anticosmoethical manner, according to its momentary egotistic interests – to the detriment of others.

Bradythosene *(brady + tho + sen + e)* – The thosene having a sluggish flow, pertaining to the bradypsychic human consciousness.

Cardiochakra *(cardio + chakra)* – The fourth basic chakra, the influential agent in the emotionality of the intraphysical consciousness which vitalizes the heart and lungs. Also known as the heart chakra.

Chakra – A nucleus or defined field of consciential energy, the totality of which basically constitutes the *holochakra* or energetic parabody inside the body. The holochakra forms a junction between the soma and the psychosoma, acting as a point of connection through which consciential energy (CE) flows from one consciential vehicle to the other. The word *chakra* is one of our *critical neologistic limits*. The author has not encountered another single international word that is more adequate, or apt, to put in its place and eliminate the *philosophical preconception* that exists with respect to this term (as well as its derivations and cognates). What is above all important, in this context, is *conceptual content* and not *linguistic form*. We live in *deficiencyland,* but consciential evolution proceeds with holo*chakro*logy.

Chirosoma *(chiro + soma)* – The soma considered specifically in terms of the use of the hands or manual labor.

Clarification task – The advanced assistential task of elucidation or clarification which can be performed individually or in group. Plural: clarification tasks.

Coincidence – The state of alignment of the vehicles (holosoma) of manifestation of the consciousness.

Communicology. The area or subdiscipline of conscientiology that studies all natures and forms of communicability of the consciousness, including interconsciential communication between consciential dimensions, considering lucid consciential projectability and the "entire" consciousness (holosoma, holobiography, holomemory).

Con – The hypothetical unit of measurement of the level of lucidity of the intraphysical or extraphysical consciousness.

Confor *(con + for)* – The interaction of content (idea, essence) with form (presentation, language) in the processes of interconsciential communication (communicology).

Conscientese – The telepathic, non-symbolic idiom that is the native language in the consciential dimensions of very evolved extraphysical societies.

Consciential amentia – The condition of the consciousness which is incapable of thinking with reasonable mental balance.

Consciential basement – The phase of infantile and adolescent manifestation of the intraphysical consciousness up to adulthood, characterized by a predominance of more primitive strong traits of the multivehicular, multiexistential and multimillenary consciousness.

Consciential bond – The cosmoethical, self-lucid, voluntary and polykarmic link between a volunteer and an institution. The consciential bond goes beyond the employment bond.

Consciential co-epicenter – The helper that works with an intraphysical consciousness who is a veteran consciential epicenter in his/her personal energetic task (penta). This helper can work as a colleague in the daily practices of penta as well as in the assistance continuously provided to extraphysical consciousnesses which are brought to the epicenter's extraphysical clinic.

Consciential concentration – The direct, unwavering, focusing of the consciousness' senses, consciential attributes, will and intention upon a singular object.

Consciential continuism – The condition of wholeness – without gaps – in the continuity of consciential life, through opportune foresight and evolutionary self-relay. In other words, the incessant linking of the experience of the present moment to immediately prior and subsequent experiences, in a cohesive and unified whole, with neither interruption in continuity nor staunched consciential experiences.

Consciential ectopia – Unsatisfactory execution of one's existential program in an eccentric, dislocated manner, outside the programming chosen for one's own intraphysical life.

Consciential energy (CE) – The immanent energy that the consciousness employs in its general manifestations; the *ene* of thosene.

Consciential epicenter – The key intraphysical consciousness of operational epicentrism who becomes a fulcrum of interdimensional lucidity, assistentiality and constructiveness through the extraphysical clinic. Directly related to *penta* or the personal energetic task.

Consciential era – That era in which average intraphysical consciousnesses find themselves sufficiently evolved, through the impacts, redefinitions and revolutions created through their experiences of lucid projectability (LPB), implanting *self-conscientiality first and foremost.*

Consciential eunuch – The intraphysical consciousness who is conscientially castrated and manipulated by sectarians, domesticators of *satisfied robots*, the modern slaves pertaining to the unthinking masses.

Consciential gestation – Useful evolutionary productivity, on the part of the human consciousness, within the framework of the personal works of his/her existential program.

Consciential hyperspaces – Extraphysical consciential dimensions.

Consciential micro-universe – The consciousness when considered as a whole, including all of its attributes, thosenes and manifestations during its evolution. The microcosm of the consciousness in relation to the macrocosm of the universe.

Consciential monoendowment – Intraphysical life under the pressure of constant intrusion by ill beings. This is experienced by mediocre intraphysical consciousnesses having few talents and no versatility.

Consciential paracoma – The state of extraphysical coma of a projected intraphysical consciousness who invariably remains unconscious, therefore having no recall of extraphysical events.

Consciential paradigm – Leading-theory of conscientiology, based upon the consciousness itself.

Consciential restriction – Restriction of the consciousness due to the process of manifestation in the physical state, in which one's natural level of awareness is reduced.

Consciential retailing – The rudimentary system of individual behavior characterized by lesser, isolated consciential actions having a minimum of productive results or great evolutionary effects.

Consciential scaffolding – Dispensable psychological or physiological *crutches* used by the consciousness.

Consciential self-bilocation (Latin: *bis,* two; and *locus,* place) – The act whereby an intraphysical projector encounters and contemplates his/her own human body (soma) face-to-face, when the consciousness is outside the soma, headquartered in another vehicle of consciential manifestation.

Consciential self-relay – The advanced condition in which the consciousness evolves by consecutively interweaving one intraphysical existence with another *(connected existential programs),* in the manner of the links of a chain (existential seriation), within one's multiexistential cycle *(holobiography).*

Consciential tri-endowment – Quality of the 3 conjugated talents most useful to a conscientiologist: intellectuality, parapsychism and communicability.

Consciential wholesaling – The behavior of an individual characterized by a tendency to approach consciential acts in a comprehensive or wholesale manner, not leaving negative evolutionary loose ends or gaps behind.

Conscientiocentric institution – The institution that centralizes its objectives on the consciousness and its evolution, as is the case with the International Institute of Projectiology and Conscientiology (IIPC); a consciential cooperative within conscientiological intraphysical society, based on employment and consciential bonds.

Conscientiocentrism – The social philosophy that concentrates its objectives on the consciousness itself and its evolution. Conscientiocentrism is a subject covered by *conscientiocentrology,* the subdiscipline of conscientiology that studies the creation and maintenance of the conscientiocentric institution based on consciential and employment bonds – like a consciential cooperative – in conscientiological intraphysical society.

Conscientiogram – The technical plan for measuring the evolutionary level of the consciousness; the consciential megatest having *Homo sapiens serenissimus* as a model – *serenissimus* being responsible for a positive egokarmic account. The conscientiogram is the basic instrument employed in conscientiometric tests.

Conscientiologist – The intraphysical consciousness who is engaged in the continued study and objective experimentation in the field of conscientiological research. The conscientiologist operates as an agent of evolutionary renovation *(retrocognitive agent)*, in the libertarian work of consciousnesses in general.

Conscientiology – The science that studies the consciousness in an integral, holosomatic, multidimensional, multimillenary, multiexistential manner and, above all, according to its reactions in regard to immanent energy (IE), consciential energy (CE) and its multiple states.

Conscientiometry – The discipline or area that studies conscientiological (of the consciousness) measurements, using the resources and methods offered by conscientiology, that are capable of establishing the possible bases for the *mathematicization of the consciousness*. Main instrument: the conscientiogram.

Conscientiotherapy – The subdiscipline that studies the treatment, relief or remission of disturbances of the consciousness, executed through the resources and techniques derived from conscientiology.

Consciousness, the – The individual essence or intelligent principle in constant evolution. In conscientiology the word consciousness (as in "the consciousness") is considered to be synonymous with mind, ego, intelligent principle, and others, and is not being used to refer to a state of consciousness. Outworn synonyms: soul, spirit.

Consolation task – Elementary, personal or group, assistential task of consolation.

Contrathosene *(contra + tho + sen + e)* – The intraconsciential thosene of the intraphysical consciousness; mute mental refutation; *mental word*; mute thosene; a type of *intrathosene*.

Co-projector – The helper who works with the intraphysical consciousness in the development of his/her lucid, assisted consciential projections.

Coronochakra *(corono + chakra)* – The chakra in the area of the sinciput, *crowning* the holochakra; crown chakra.

Cosmoconsciousness – The consciousness' inner perception of the cosmos, of life and the order of the universe, in an indescribable intellectual and cosmoethical exaltation. In this condition, the consciousness senses the living presence of the universe and becomes one with it, in an indivisible unit. Interconsciential communication occurs in this singular condition.

Cosmoethical mimicry – The productive social impulse of imitating the evolved forebears of the intraphysical consciousness.

Cosmoethicality – The cosmoethical quality of the consciousness.

Cosmoethics *(cosmo + ethics)* – The ethics or reflection upon cosmic, multidimensional morality, or the cosmic moral code, which defines holomaturity. Cosmoethics surpasses social, intraphysical morals or those morals presented within any human classification. It is a subdiscipline of conscientiology.

Cosmothosene *(cosmo + tho + sen + e)* – The thosene specific to conscientese or the state of cosmoconsciousness; the form of communication of conscientese.

Co-therapist – The helper that works together with the intraphysical consciousness conscientiotherapist during the assistential technical procedures of conscientiotherapy that are applied to his/her patients.

Co-thosene *(co + tho + sen + e)* – The specific thosene of co-option of the collective actions of a chorus, of those praying in a group and of crowds.

Counterbody – The same as the holochakra, the specific vehicle of the intraphysical consciousness' consciential energy (CE).

Daydream – The fanciful story created by the imagination during the ordinary, physical waking state of the human consciousness.

Dermatologies of the consciousness – The compound expression attributed to the conventional, physicalist sciences that are subordinated to the Newtonian-Cartesian, mechanistic paradigm and focus their research only upon the soma, because they do not avail themselves of the instrumentation necessary for direct, technical investigation of the consciousness itself; dermatologies of the intraphysical consciousness; periconscient sciences.

Desoma *(de + soma)* – Somatic deactivation, impending and inevitable for all intraphysical consciousnesses; final projection; *first death;* biological death; monothanatosis. *First* desoma, or simply desoma, is the deactivation of the human body or soma. *Second* desoma is the deactivation of the holochakra. *Third* desoma is the deactivation of the psychosoma.

Desomatics – The study of the physical context of desoma and of the psychological, social and medicolegal contexts related to deactivation of the soma. It is a subdiscipline of conscientiology.

Destructive macro-PK – Harmful PK (psychokinesis) capable of causing injuries to the intraphysical consciousness. Destructive macro-PK can even prove fatal to the soma.

Discoincidence – The state of non-alignment of the vehicles (holosoma) of manifestation of the consciousness.

Domiciliary holothosene – The holothosene specific to the intraphysical consciousness' physical base, energetically shielded bedroom and extraphysical clinic.

Dream – The natural consciential state which is intermediary between the ordinary, physical waking state and natural sleep. Dreams are characterized by a set of ideas and images that present themselves to the consciousness. The afflictive dream that has the effect of agitation, anguish and oppression is termed: *nightmare; night terror; nightmarish hallucination.*

Egokarma *(ego + karma)* – The principle of cause and effect active in the evolution of the consciousness, when centered exclusively on the ego itself. The state wherein free will is restricted by infantile egocentrism. The word *karma* is another of our *critical neologistic limits.* The author has not encountered another single, international, word that is more adequate, or appropriate, to put in its place and combat the *philosophical preconception* that exists with respect to this term (as well as its derivations and cognates). What is above all important, in this context, is *conceptual content* and not *linguistic form.* We live in *deficiencyland,* but consciential evolution proceeds with holo*karm*ology.

Egothosene *(ego + tho + sen + e)* – The same as self-thosene; the *unit of measurement* of consciential egotism according to conscientiology or, more precisely, according to conscientiometry.

Energetic dimension – The energetic dimension of consciousnesses; the holochakral dimension; the *three-and-a-half* dimension. The natural dimension of the holochakra.

Energetic maxispringtime – The condition of a maximized or prolonged energetic springtime.

Energetic minispringtime – The condition of a minimal or ephemeral energetic springtime.

Energetic springtime – The more-or-less long-lasting personal condition wherein one's consciential energies (CEs) exhibit an optimal, healthy, constructive profile.

Energetic springtime by two – The energetic springtime of the evolutionary duo, the partners of which truly love each other and control the application of healthy consciential energy with complete lucidity, building their existential programs through consciential gestations.

Energivorous – Energy consuming, energy draining; in reference to intruder(s).

Enumerology – The didactic technique of processing texts based on informative self-critiquing.

Evolutient – The consciousness that is in the process of evolution and utilizing the services of a conscientiotherapist to further this process; outworn synonym: patient.

Evolutiologist – The consciousness which assists in the intelligent coordination of the existential program, or the consciential evolution of one or more consciousnesses of the same karmic group. The evolutionary condition between the petifree consciousness and *serenissimus.* A more adequate expression than *evolutionary orienter.*

Evolutiology – The subdiscipline of conscientiology that studies the evolution of the consciousness, which is addressed in a high-quality, integral manner. This subject is specifically related to the evolutiologist or evolutionary orienter.

Evolutionary duo – Two consciousnesses that interact positively in joint evolution; the existential condition of *cooperative evolutivity* by two.

Evolutionary orienter – See *evolutiologist*.

Existential completism – The condition wherein the existential program of the human consciousness is complete.

Existential incompletism – The condition wherein the existential program of the human consciousness is incomplete.

Existential inversion – An advanced evolutionary technique consisting of inverting sociocultural values and projects in human life, according to the principles of projectiology and conscientiology. It is based upon the prioritization of and the full-time dedication to the execution of the existential program, beginning at a young age.

Existential inverter – The intraphysical consciousness who is inclined to execute existential inversion in intraphysical life.

Existential invertibility – The quality of the intraphysical execution of existential inversion.

Existential maximoratorium – The condition of the greater existential moratorium which is given to an existential *completist*. It is an addition to his/her completed existential program. It is therefore the execution of a *healthy extension* to an existential mandate that has been concluded.

Existential maxiprogram – The maximal existential program having a *wholesale approach*, or targeting the execution of tasks of applied universalism and maxifraternity with polykarmic bases.

Existential minimoratorium – The condition of the lesser existential moratorium or one which happens to the *incompletist* intraphysical consciousness in order for him/her to compensate for a *holokarmic deficit* (deficit-based) or to achieve the condition of existential completism regarding his/her existential program. It is therefore the finishing of a still incomplete existential mandate.

Existential miniprogram – The minimum, *retail-oriented,* existential program targeting the execution of a minimal, groupkarmic task.

Existential moratorium – An extension of (a complement to) intraphysical life which is provided to select intraphysical consciousnesses according to their holokarmic merit. The existential moratorium can be either deficit-based (lesser), an existential minimoratorium; or can be profit-based (greater), an existential maximoratorium, with regard to the results of the individual's existential program.

Existential moratoriumist – One who receives an existential moratorium; moratoriumist.

Existential multicompletism – Existential completism obtained through the execution of various existential programs in diverse consecutive intraphysical lives (existential seriation).

Existential program – The specific program of each intraphysical consciousness, in his/her intraphysical existence.

Existential recyclability – The quality of the intraphysical execution of existential recycling.

Existential recycler – The intraphysical consciousness who is inclined to execute existential recycling.

Existential recycling – The evolutionary technique in which the intraphysical consciousness adopts a new set of values and priorities in his/her life, enabling the execution of the existential program.

Existential robotization – The condition of a tropospheric intraphysical consciousness who is excessively enslaved by intraphysicality or four-dimensionality.

Existential self-mimicry – Imitation on the part of the intraphysical consciousness of his/her own experiences or past experiences, whether they pertain to his/her current intraphysical life or previous intraphysical lives.

Existential seriation – 1. Evolutionary existential sequencing of the consciousness; successive existences; intraphysical rebirths in series. 2. Human or intraphysical life. Synonym outworn and exhausted by excessive use: *reincarnation;* this archaic word no longer serves those more serious individuals dedicated to leading-edge consciousness research.

Extraphysical – Relative to that which is outside, or beyond, the *intra*physical or human state; the consciential state which is *less* physical than the soma.

Extraphysical agenda – A written list of high-priority extraphysical, consciential targets – beings, places or ideas – that the projected projector seeks to gradually reach, in a chronological manner, establishing intelligent plans for its own development.

Extraphysical approach – The contacting of one consciousness by another consciousness in the extraphysical dimensions.

Extraphysical catatonia – The fixed condition wherein a projected intraphysical consciousness performs repeated stereotypical acts that are generally useless or dispensable in terms of its evolution.

Extraphysical clinic – The extraphysical treatment center of the intraphysical epicenter (penta practitioner). The resources and extraphysical *installations* of the extraphysical clinic are numerous and remarkable. The extraphysical clinic is a domiciliary holothosene.

Extraphysical community – A group of extraphysical consciousnesses living together in an extraphysical dimension.

Extraphysical consciousness – The paracitizen of an extraphysical society; a consciousness which no longer has a soma. Outworn synonym: *discarnate*.

Extraphysical euphoria – The condition of euphoria experienced after somatic deactivation, generated due to the reasonably satisfactory completion of the existential program; *post-mortem* euphoria; para-euphoria; postsomatic euphoria.

Extraphysical gang raid – The action of a group of energivorous extraphysical consciousnesses, including extraphysical blind-guides, in the paratropospheric dimensions, with the objective of vampirizing the intraphysical consciousnesses in the environments of intraphysical celebrations or events which gather persons who are predisposed to the condition of collective victimization through consciential energies.

Extraphysical melancholy – The condition of extraphysical, postsomatic or *post-mortem* melancholy due to the unsatisfactory execution of the existential program; paramelancholy.

Extraphysical monitoring – The condition wherein assistance is provided by healthy extraphysical consciousnesses to a balanced intraphysical consciousness, while that intraphysical consciousness is performing balanced tasks of consolation or clarification.

Extraphysical precognition (Latin: *pre,* before; *cognoscere,* to know) – The perceptive faculty through which the consciousness, while fully projected outside the human body, becomes aware of unknown upcoming facts, as well as objects, scenes and distant forms in the future.

Extraphysical romance – The set of acts whereby an intraphysical consciousness dates or maintains a healthy or positive romantic relationship while projected outside the body.

Extraphysical society – Society of extraphysical consciousnesses.

Free consciousness (Latin: *con + scientia, with knowledge*) (**FC**) – The consciousness – or, more precisely: the extraphysical consciousness – which has definitively freed itself (deactivation) from the psychosoma or emotional parabody and the series of lifetimes. The free consciousness is situated in the *evolutionary hierarchy* above *Homo sapiens serenissimus.*

Geoenergy *(geo + energy)* – Immanent energy (IE) deriving from the soil or earth and absorbed by the intraphysical consciousness through the *pre-kundalini.* Archaic expression: *telluric energy.*

Golden cord – The alleged energetic element – similar to a remote control – that maintains the mentalsoma connected to the parabrain of the psychosoma.

Graphothosene *(grapho + tho + sen + e)* – The *thosenic signature* of the human or intraphysical consciousness.

Group of existential inverters – The intraphysical meeting and personal experience of existential inverters with the aim of attaining the experience of planned existential inversions.

Group of existential recyclers – The intraphysical meeting and personal experience of existential recyclers with the aim of attaining the experience of planned existential recyclings.

Groupality – The quality of the evolutionary group of the consciousness; the condition of evolutivity in group.

Groupkarma *(group + karma)* – The principle of cause and effect active in the evolution of the consciousness, when centered in the evolutionary group. The state of individual free will, when connected to the evolutionary group.

Groupkarmic course – The set of the consciousness' levels within the evolutionary consciential group.

Groupkarmic interprison – The condition of groupkarmic inseparability of the evolutionary consciential principle or the consciousness.

Groupthosene *(group + tho + sen + e)* – The sectarian, corporatist and antipolykarmic thosene; however, the groupthosene can also be constructive.

Gynochakra *(gyno + chakra)* – A woman's sexochakra.

Gynosoma *(gyno + soma)* – The female human body, or that which is specific to a woman, specialized in the animal reproduction of the intraphysical life of the intraphysical consciousness; the aphrodisiac body.

Gynothosene *(gyno + tho + sen + e)* –The thosene specific to feminine language and communicability.

Hallucination (Latin: *hallucinari,* to err) – The apparent perception of an external object that is not present at the moment; mental error in the perception of the senses, which is baseless in an objective reality.

Helper – The extraphysical consciousness which is auxiliary to one or more intraphysical consciousnesses; extraphysical benefactor. Archaic equivalent expressions that have been outworn through continued use: *guardian angel; angel of light; guide; mentor; spirit guide.*

Heterothosene *(hetero + tho + sen + e)* – The thosene of another in relation to ourselves.

Holobiography – The multidimensional, multiexistential personal history of the consciousness.

Holochakra *(holo + chakra)* – The energetic parabody of the human consciousness.

Holochakral existence – Intraphysical life or the lifetime of the human consciousness.

Holochakral seduction – The energetic action of one consciousness upon another (or others) with a more or less conscious intention of domination.

Holochakrality – The quality of the manifestations of the intraphysical consciousness deriving from the holochakra or energetic body.

Holokarma *(holo + karma)* – The grouping of the 3 types of consciential actions and reactions – egokarma, groupkarma and polykarma – within the principles of cause and effect, that are active in the evolution of the consciousness.

Holomaturity *(holo + maturity)* – The condition of integrated maturity – biological, psychological, holosomatic and multidimensional – of the human consciousness.

Holomemory *(holo + memory)* – The causal, compound, multimillenary, multiexistential, implacable, uninterrupted, personal memory that retains all facts relative to the consciousness; multimemory; polymemory.

Holo-orgasm *(holo + orgasm)* – Holosomatic orgasm; maximum ecstasy generated by the energies of the entire holosoma.

Holosoma *(holo + soma)* – The set of vehicles of manifestation of the intraphysical consciousness: soma, holochakra, psychosoma and mentalsoma; and of the extraphysical consciousness: psychosoma and mentalsoma.

Holosomatic homeostasis – The integrated, healthy state of the holosoma's harmony.

Holosomatic interfusion – The state of maximal sympathetic assimilation between two consciousnesses.

Holosomatics – The specific study of the holosoma. It is a subdiscipline of conscientiology.

Holotheca – Compilation of information from artifacts of knowledge.

Holothosene *(holo + tho + sen + e)* – Aggregated or consolidated thosenes.

Homo sapiens serenissimus – The consciousness which is integrally experiencing the condition of lucid serenism. Popular synonym: *serenissimus.*

Homothosene *(homo + tho + sen + e)* – The thosene of telepathic transmission and reception; the *unit of measurement* in telepathy, according to conscientiometry.

Hyperacuity – The quality of maximum lucidity of the intraphysical consciousness, achieved through the recuperation – to the maximum degree possible – of cons.

Hyperthosene *(hyper + tho + sen + e)* – Heuristic thosene; original idea of a discovery; neophilic thosene; *unit of measurement* of invention, according to conscientiometry.

Hypnagogy (Greek: *hipnos,* sleep; and *agogos,* leader, bringer) – The transitional twilight condition of the consciousness between the ordinary, physical waking state and the state of natural sleep. It is an altered state of consciousness.

Hypnopompy (Greek: *hipnos,* sleep; and *pompikós,* procession) – The transitional condition of natural sleep, introductory to physical awakening, during the semi-sleep state that precedes the act of awakening. This state is characterized by oneiric images with auditory effects and hallucinatory visions that continue after awakening. It is an altered state of consciousness.

Hypothosene *(hypo + tho + sen + e)* – The same as protothosene or phytothosene.

Immanent energy (IE) – Energy that is primary, vibratory, essential, multiform, impersonal, diffuse and dispersed in all objects or *realities* of the universe, in an omnipotent fashion. Immanent energy has still not been tamed by the human consciousness. It is too subtle to be discovered and detected by existing technological equipment.

Incomplete couple – The couple composed of a man and a woman who do *not* form an intimate couple (a couple that practices the complete sex act), but who, nevertheless, maintain strong affectionate ties.

Integrated maturity – The state of a more evolved consciential maturity, beyond biological (physical) or mental (psychological) maturity; holomaturity.

Inter vivos **apparition** – Appearance of the consciousness of the projected human projector to intraphysical consciousnesses.

Interconsciential climate – The condition of multi-understanding in an interconsciential encounter, established through similar thosenes, especially those *with an emphasis* on consciential energies (CEs). There are interconsciential climates, *mini-climates* and *maxi-climates.*

Interdimensionality – Interaction, interrelation or interconsciential communication between intraphysical and extraphysical dimensions.

Intermissibility – The quality of the period of intermission between two intraphysical lives of a consciousness.

Intermission – The extraphysical period of the consciousness between two of its physical lives; intermissive period.

Intermissive course – The set of disciplines and theoretical and practical experiences administered to an extraphysical consciousness during the period of consciential intermission. This course occurs when one has achieved a certain evolutionary level within one's cycle of personal existences. The intermissive course objectifies consciential completism (existential completism) of the upcoming intraphysical life.

Intraconsciential compensation – The conscientiometric technique based upon the greater use of a consciential attribute that is more developed (strong trait) over another, or other less developed consciential attributes (weak traits) in the micro-universe of the intraphysical consciousness.

Intraconsciential recycling – Intraphysical, existential, *intra*consciential recycling or the cerebral renovation of the intraphysical consciousness through the creation of new synapses or interneuronal connections. The newly created synapses are capable of allowing the adjustment of the existential program, execution of existential recycling, existential inversion, the acquisition of new ideas, neothosenes, hyperthosenes and other neophilic conquests of the self-motivated human consciousness.

Intraconscientiality – The quality of the manifestations specific to the intimacy of the consciousness.

Intraphysical assistant – The intraphysical guardian of the projector's inactive human body that is emptied of the consciousness during lucid projection.

Intraphysical consciousness – Human personality; citizen of intraphysical society. Outworn synonym: *incarnate.*

Intraphysical euphoria – The condition of euphoria experienced before somatic deactivation that is generated by the reasonably satisfactory completion of the existential program; *pre-mortem* euphoria. The ideal condition predisposing one to have a positive existential moratorium.

Intraphysical melancholy – The condition of intraphysical or *pre-mortem* melancholy generated by incompletion of the existential program.

Intraphysical society – The society of intraphysical consciousnesses; human society.

Intraphysicality – The condition of human, intraphysical life, or of the existence of the human consciousness.

Intrathosene *(intra + tho + sen + e)* – The *intra*consciential thosene of the human consciousness.

Intruder – The perturbed, ill, needy, anticosmoethical consciousness; especially an extraphysical consciousness when performing a thosenic intrusion upon an intraphysical consciousness.

Intrusion – Invasion of a consciousness by another; this can be through consciential energies (CEs) or the holochakra, psychosoma, holosoma, or thosenes. It can also be interconsciential or intraconsciential.

Intrusive stigma – An evolutionary failure or derailing that is always dramatic and often pathological, generally stemming from consciential self-obcecation. This process generates either intraphysical or extraphysical melancholy and often results in parapsychic accidents.

Intrusiveness – Ill, interconsciential thosenic intrusion. Archaic equivalent expression: *obsession*; many intraphysical consciousnesses are defensive regarding this word.

Joint projection – An experience outside the human body in which two or more projected intraphysical consciousnesses participate.

Locked existence – Human experience or lifetime without the production of lucid projections (LPs); tropospheric human life with only unconscious, vegetative projections that are characteristic of the state of evolutionary paracoma; locked lifetime.

Looseness of the holochakra – The condition of relative freedom of action of the energetic parabody of the intraphysical consciousness, relative to the psychosoma and soma.

Lucid projectability (LPB) – The lucid, projective paraphysiological quality of the consciousness that is capable of provoking its discoincidence or taking its vehicles of manifestation out from the alignment of its holosoma, even through the impulsion of its willpower.

Lucid projection (LP) – Projection of the intraphysical consciousness beyond the soma; extracorporeal experience; out-of-body experience (OBE).

Lucidity-recall binomial – The set of the two conditions that are indispensable to the intraphysical consciousness for his/her achievement of a fully satisfactory lucid projection (outside the soma).

Macrosoma *(macro + soma)* – The soma that is *supercustomized* for the execution of a specific existential program.

Materthosene *(mater + tho + sen + e)* – The mother-idea or matrix for the complete development of a thesis, theory or analysis, the *leitmotif*, major pillar or predominant thosene in a holothosene.

Maxifraternity – The most evolved, universalistic, interconsciential condition that is based on pure fraternity on the part of a self-unforgiving and heteroforgiving consciousness. Maxifraternity is an inevitable goal in the evolution of all consciousnesses. Synonym: megafraternity.

Maxithosene *(maxi + tho + sen + e)* – The thosene specific to FCs or free consciousnesses.

Megagoal – The consciousness' greater self-evolutionary objective.

Megapower – The evolved condition of great, cosmoethical lucidity of the consciousness.

Mega-strong-trait – The maximal strong trait of the consciousness.

Megathosene *(mega + tho + sen + e)* – The same as orthothosene.

Mega-weak-trait – The maximal weak trait of the consciousness.

Mentalsoma *(mental + soma)* – Mental body; *parabody* of discernment of the consciousness.

Mentalsomatic cycle – The evolutionary cycle or course of the consciousness that begins when it is an FC, or free consciousness, in which it definitively deactivates its psychosoma (third death), and lives only with the mentalsoma.

Metasoma *(meta + soma)* – The same as psychosoma, the extraphysical instrument of extraphysical and intraphysical consciousnesses.

Minithosene *(mini + tho + sen + e)* – The thosene specific to the child, sometimes due to his/her still developing brain.

Mnemonic intrusion – The collision of the intrusive memory of an intrusive extraphysical consciousness upon the cerebral memory or biomemory of an intraphysical consciousness who is suffering from intrusion *(para-amnesia)*.

Mnemosoma *(mnemo + soma)* – The soma, when considered specifically in relation to the consciousness' memory, in all of its forms.

Monothanatosis – Same as *desoma*; *first desoma*.

Monothosene *(mono + tho + sen + e)* – Repetitive thosene; monoideism; fixed idea; mental echo; *re*thosene.

Morphothosene *(morpho + tho + sen + e)* – A thought or a set of thoughts when gathered and expressed, in some manner, as a *form*. Archaic expression now in disuse: *thought-form*. The accumulation of morphothosenes composes the holothosene.

Multidimensional self-awareness (MS) – The condition of mature lucidity of an intraphysical consciousness in terms of consciential life in the evolved state of multidimensionality. This condition is achieved through lucid projectability (LPB).

Multi-existential cycle – The system or condition – at our current, average evolutionary level – of continuous alternation of one period of intraphysical rebirth *(lifetime)* with another extraphysical post-somatic deactivation period *(intermission)*.

Near-death experience (NDE) – Projective occurrences that are involuntary or forced due to critical human circumstances of the human consciousness, common in cases of patients with terminal illnesses and survivors of clinical death.

Neophilia – The ready adaptation of the intraphysical consciousness to new situations, things and occurrences. The opposite of neophobia.

Neothosene *(neo + tho + sen + e)* – The thosene of the intraphysical consciousness when manifesting using new synapses or interneuronal connections, capable of generating *intra*consciential recycling; *unit of measurement* of consciential renovation, according to conscientiology or, more precisely, conscientiometry.

Oneirothosene – *(oneiro + tho + sen + e)* – The same as pathothosene.

Orgastic aura (Latin: *aura,* wisp of air) – The holochakral energy of *facies sexualis* of the man or woman at the precise moment of sexual orgasm or the climax of the sex act.

Orthothosene *(ortho + tho + sen + e)* – The *correct* or cosmoethical thosene, pertaining to consciential holomaturity; the *unit of measurement* of practical cosmoethics, according to conscientiometry.

Pangraphy – Ample and sophisticated multimodal parapsychic writing.

Para – The prefix that signifies *beyond* or *beside*, as in *parabrain*. It also signifies *extraphysical*.

Parabrain – The extraphysical brain of the psychosoma of the consciousness in the extraphysical (extraphysical consciousness), intraphysical (intraphysical consciousness) and projected (when projected in the psychosoma) states.

Paragenetics – The genetics restricted to the inheritance of the consciousness, received through the psychosoma, from the previous life to the human embryo. It is a subdiscipline of conscientiology.

Paraman – The extraphysical consciousness having the appearance of a man or a projected male intraphysical consciousness. Synonymous expression outworn through use: *male spiritual entity*.

Parapathology – Pathology of the vehicles of manifestation of the consciousness, excluding the human body or soma. It is a subdiscipline of conscientiology.

Paraphysiology – Physiology of the vehicles of manifestation of the consciousness, excluding the human body or soma. It is a subdiscipline of conscientiology.

Parapsychic – That which is paranormal or multidimensional in nature.

Parapsychic accident – Physical or psychological disturbance generated by sick energetic, interconsciential influences, generally of an extraphysical or multidimensional origin.

Parapsychic signage – The existence, identification and self-aware use of the energetic, animic, parapsychic and extremely personal signs (indicators) that every intraphysical consciousness possesses.

Parapsychism – Parapsychic capacities of the consciousness.

Parapsychophysical repercussions – Reactions between 2 vehicles of consciential manifestation, when they come into contact with each other. This can occur between different vehicles of one consciousness or between similar vehicles of two or more consciousnesses. These repercussions can be intraphysical and extraphysical.

Parasanitary encapsulation – Assistential isolation and the temporary, energetic annulment of thosenic manifestations – notably energetic or intrusive ones – from one or more ill intraphysical and/or extraphysical consciousness, in the manner of sanitary isolation (quarantine) wards in hospitals for infectious and contagious illnesses with patients who present a high potential for disease, radioactive or toxic contamination.

Parathosene *(para + tho + sen + e)* – The thosene specific to the extraphysical consciousness.

Parawoman – The extraphysical consciousness having the appearance of a woman or a projected female intraphysical consciousness. Synonymous expression outworn through use: *female spiritual entity.*

Pathothosene *(patho + tho + sen + e)* – The pathological thosene or the thosene of consciential dementia; *mental peccadillo*; pathological will; sick intention; *cerebral rumination.*

Penile aura – The sexochakral energy around the penis, notably when in erection, perceivable by any motivated individual, especially by the sexually excited man.

Penta *(p + ene + ta)* – The multidimensional, daily, personal energetic task that receives continuous assistance from the helpers on a long-term basis or for the rest of one's life. Outworn expression: *passes-to-the-void.*

Personal experience (PE) – Practical, personal, direct, non-transferable experimentation of the intraphysical consciousness on his/her evolutionary way.

Personal principles – The set of guiding values and initiatives of consciential life which are chosen by the consciousness based upon holomaturity, multidimensionality and applied cosmoethics.

Petifree – The intraphysical consciousness who is permanently and totally free of intrusion, and is completely self-aware of being in this condition.

Petifreeness – The consciential quality of the petifree being.

Phenomenon concomitant with LP – That which occurs either inside or outside the time-space *continuum*, but does so simultaneously with the experience of the lucid projection, in a spontaneous and unexpected manner.

Physical base – The safe location, chosen by the intraphysical consciousness for leaving the soma stationary or resting while lucidly projecting to other, external, consciential dimensions; *duodrome.* A domiciliary projectiogenic holothosene. It is directly related to: the energetically shielded chamber; penta; consciential epicenter; extraphysical clinic; *projectarium; precognitarium;* and *retrocognitarium.*

Phytothosene *(phyto + tho + sen + e)* – The rudimentary thosene of a plant; the *lexical unit* of a plant, according to conscientiology.

Podosoma *(podo + soma)* – The soma, when considered specifically in regard to the application of the feet or work performed with the feet, as in the case of a soccer player.

Polykarma *(poly + karma)* – The principle of cause and effect, active in the evolution of the consciousness, when centered in the sense of and the experience of cosmic maxifraternity, beyond egokarma and groupkarma.

Polykarmality – The quality of the polykarmic manifestations of the consciousness.

Postsomatic intermission – The extraphysical period of the consciousness immediately following somatic deactivation.

Precognitarium – The physical base which is technically prepared for the production of precognitive LPs (lucid projections).

Pre-couple – The preliminary, initial or flirting stage of human sexuality, a practice within intraphysical society.

Pre-intraphysical mandate – The existential program for human life, planned before the intraphysical rebirth of the consciousness; existential program.

Prekundalini – The secondary plantar (sole of the foot) chakra. There are 2 plantochakras in the holosoma of the intraphysical consciousness. This is an expression pertaining to conscientiology.

Pre-*serenissimus* – The intraphysical or extraphysical consciousness that does not yet live a life of lucid serenism.

Presomatic intermission – The extraphysical period of the consciousness immediately preceding its intraphysical rebirth.

Primothosene *(primo + tho + sen + e)* – The same as the *primary cause of the universe*; the first compound thought. This term has no plural form.

Projectarium – The physical base which is technically prepared for the production of projections of the consciousness (PCs).

Projectiocritique – Critiquing performed with a projectiological perspective. It is a subdiscipline of conscientiology.

Projectiography – The technical study of projectiological registers. It is a subdiscipline of conscientiology.

Projectiology (Latin: *projectio*, projection; Greek: *logos*, treatise) – The science that studies projections of the consciousness and their effects, including projections of consciential energies (CEs) outward from the holosoma. It is a subdiscipline of conscientiology.

Projectiotherapy – The science of the prophylaxes and therapies derived from the research and techniques of projectiology.

Projective mental target – The predetermined goal that an intraphysical consciousness plans to reach using the will, intention, mental focus and decision, upon finding itself lucid outside the body.

Projective phenomenon – The specific parapsychic occurrence within the scope of projectiology research.

Projective recess – The existential phase of the intraphysical consciousness characterized by the spontaneous cessation – almost always temporary – of lucid projective experiences, within a sequence of intensive experiences.

Protothosene *(proto + tho + sen + e)* – The more rudimentary thosene; the same as phytothosene or hypothosene.

Psychosoma (Greek: *psyche*, soul; *soma*, body) – The emotional parabody of the consciousness; the *objective body* of the intraphysical consciousness. Outworn expression: astral body.

Rethosene *(re + tho + sen + e)* – The repeated thosene. The same as *mono*thosene, fixed idea, or monoideism.

Retrocognitarium – The physical base which is technically prepared for the production of retrocognitive lucid projections (LPs).

Retrocognition (Latin: *retro*, back; *cognoscere*, to know) – The perceptive faculty through which the intraphysical consciousness becomes aware of facts, scenes, forms, objects, successes and experiences that pertain to a time in the distant past. These issues are commonly related to one's holomemory.

Retrothosene *(retro + tho + sen + e)* – The thosene specific to self-retrocognitions; the same as the *engram* of mnemotechnics; the *unit of measurement* of retrocognitions, according to conscientiometry.

Self-conscientiality – The quality of the level of self-knowledge on the part of the consciousness; megaknowledge.

Self-mimeticity– The consciential quality of existential self-mimicry.

Self-projection – Departure of the intraphysical consciousness to another consciential dimension in the mentalsoma or the psychosoma, when intentional or provoked by the will.

INAMPS = Instituto Nacional de Assistência Médica e Previdência Social (Brazilian Social Security Institute).

INAN = Instituto Nacional de Alimentação e Nutrição (Brazilian Food & Nutrition Institute).

indig. = indigenous.

introd. = introduction.

IQ = intelligence quotient.

It. = Italian language.

JLP = joint lucid projection.

JLPs = joint lucid projections.

Jpn. = Japanese language.

Lat. = Latin language.

LP = lucid projection.

LPB = lucid projectability.

LPs = lucid projections.

LPU = Least Publishable Unit of a scientific work due to be published.

LSD = Lysergic Acid Diethylamide.

m = meter or meters.

mg = milligram or milligrams.

MS = multidimensional self-awareness.

N. = number or numbers.

NDE = near-death experience.

NDEs = near-death experiences.

NGOs = *N*on-*G*overnmental *O*rganizations.

NP = nonlucid projection.

NPs = nonlucid projections.

OBE = Out-of-Body Experience; extracorporeal experience.

ono. = onomastic index; index of names.

OOBE = Out-of-the-Body Experience; extracorporeal experience.

p. = page.

pp. = pages.

pb. = paperback.

PE = personal experience.

PEE = personal extraphysical experience.

PEEs	=	personal extraphysical experiences.
PEs	=	personal experiences.
PIE	=	personal intraphysical experience.
PIEs	=	personal intraphysical experiences.
PK	=	psychokinesis; parapsychic physical effect phenomena.
PMR	=	progressive muscular relaxation.
Port.	=	Portuguese language.
postf.	=	postface.
pref.	=	preface.
pres.	=	presentation.
print.	=	printing.
prol.	=	prologue.
prfr.	=	proof-reader.
pseud.	=	pseudonym.
quest.	=	questionnaire.
refs.	=	bibliographic references.
rel.	=	religious.
rep.	=	reprint.
Rus.	=	Russian language.
S.	=	São.
Sansk.	=	Sanskrit language.
sci-fi	=	science fiction.
sen	=	sentiment or emotion.
senes	=	sentiments and consciential energies (CEs).
SLP	=	semilucid projection.
SLPs	=	semilucid projections.
Sp.	=	Spanish language.
spi.	=	spiral binding.
syn.	=	synonymy.
tab.	=	table.
tabs.	=	tables.
tho	=	thought or idea.
thosens	=	thoughts and sentiments.

transl.	=	translator; translators.
TV	=	television.
U.S.A.	=	United States of America.
UFO	=	*U*nidentified *F*lying *O*bject.
UN	=	*U*nited *N*ations.
UNESCO	=	United Nations Educational Scientific and Cultural Organization.
UNICEF	=	United Nations International Children's Emergency Fund.
vol.	=	volume or volumes; tome or tomes.
volun.	=	volunteering.
VS	=	vibrational state.
VSs	=	vibrational states.
WHO	=	*W*orld *H*ealth *O*rganization.
WIA	=	wounded in action.
wod.	=	without date; without indication of a date.
wopl.	=	without indication of the place of the publisher.
wopub.	=	without publisher; without indication of a publisher.
wot.	=	without indication of the translator.

INDEX OF ILLUSTRATIONS

Observations. The following is a listing of the 43 illustrations in this volume. Nine of the illustrations are included within the text of each respective chapter and the remainder are found together on pages 1121 to 1152.

Figure - 39

Consciential Self-Bilocation, p. 123

Figure - 60

Traveling Clairvoyance, p. 166

Figure - 80

Extraphysical Telekinesis, p. 193

1124

Figure - 103

Types of Holosomatic Vehicles, p. 239

Figure - 111

Holochakra, p. 257

Figure - 116

Human Aura, p. 264

Figure - 120

Spheres of Action of the Silver Cord, p. 275

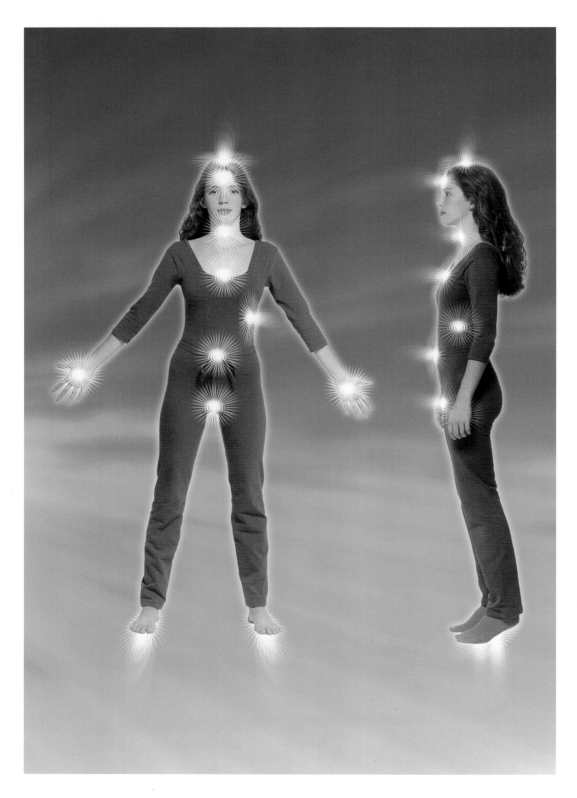

Figure - 132
Chakras, p. 299

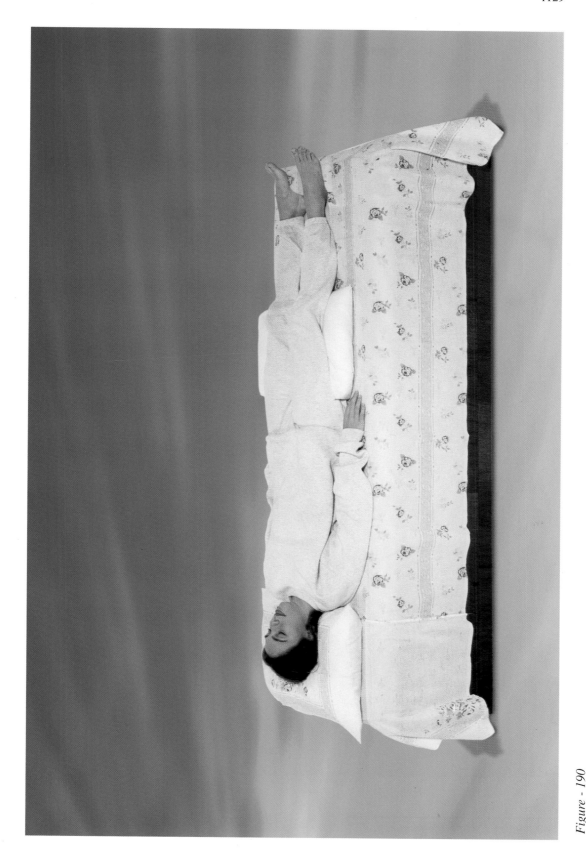

Figure - 190
Dorsal Position, p. 419

Figure - 203

Imaginative Escape Technique, p. 437

Figure - 204
Projective Visualization Technique, p. 438

1132

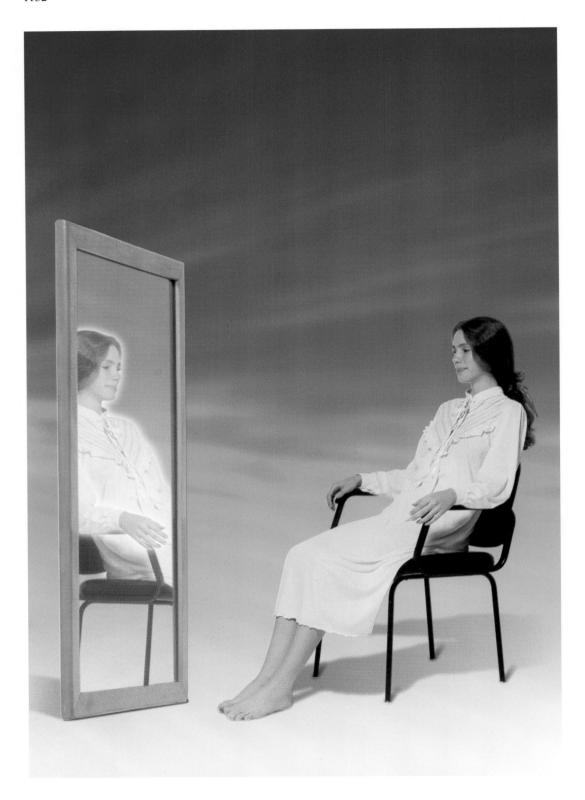

Figure - 209

Projective Self-Image Technique, p. 446

Figure - 223

Assisted Projection Technique, p. 468

1134

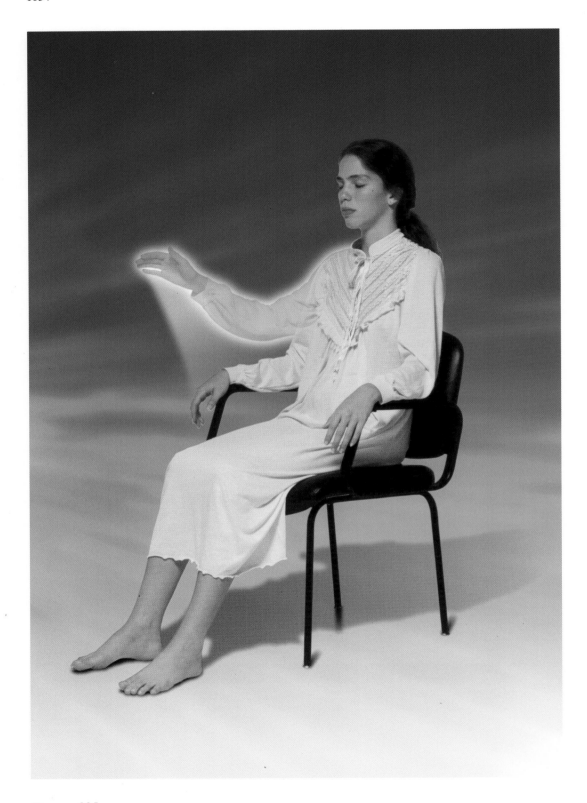

Figure - 225

Fragmented Lucid Projection Technique, p. 473

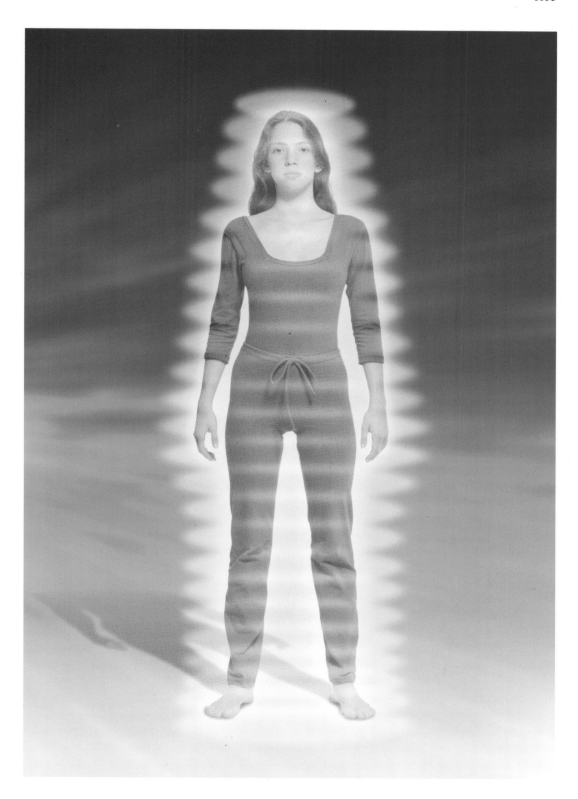

Figure - 244

Vibrational State, p. 497

1136

Figure - 252
Takeoff, p. 514

Figure - 255
Trace of Light, p. 519

Figure - 270

Tropospheric Extraphysical Dimension, p. 545

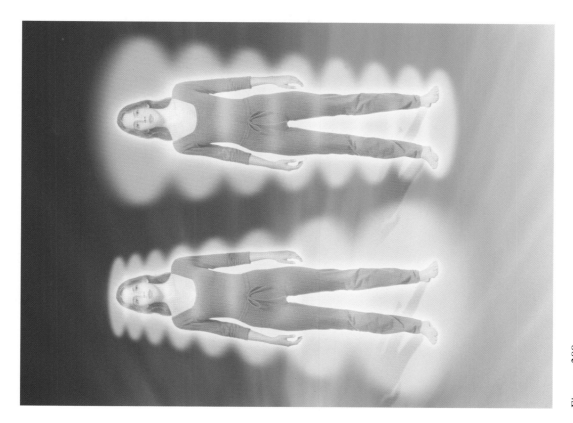

Figure - 288
Closed Circulation of Energies Technique, p. 587

Figure - 287
Mobilization of Consciential Energies, p. 584

1140

Figure - 291
Exteriorization of Consciential Energies, p. 591

Figure - 290
Absorption of Extraphysical Energies Technique, p. 590

Figure - 293

Penta Technique, p. 594

Figure - 303
Extraphysical Self-Luminosity, p. 615

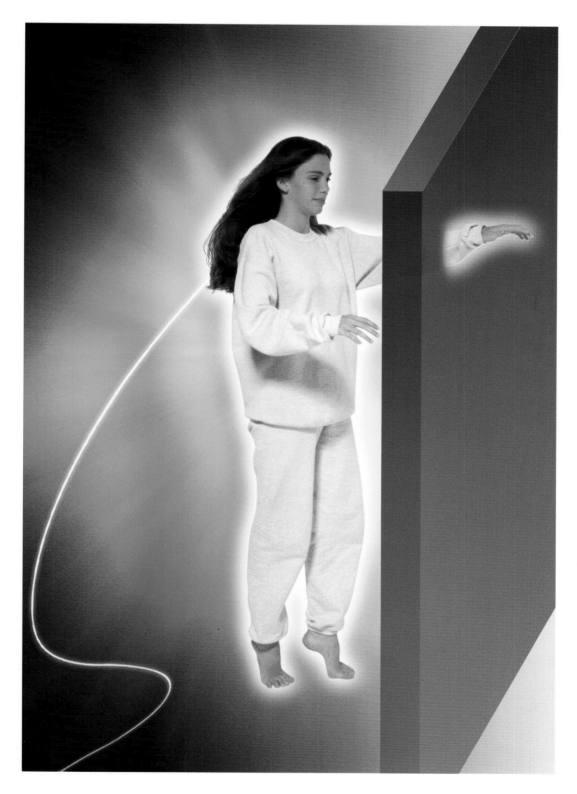

Figure - 304

Extraphysical Self-Permeability, p. 617

Figure - 305

Extraphysical Elasticity, p. 619

Figure - 323

Extraphysical Self-Transfiguration, p. 640

Figure - 347

Extraphysical Hetero-Awakening Technique, p. 677

Figure - 357

Energization by Three Technique, p. 696

1148

Figure - 367

Assistential Consciential Projection, p. 723

Figure - 420

Exoprojection, p. 808

1150

Figure - 424

Double Consciential Projection, p. 814

Figure - 436

Joint Lucid Projections, p. 830

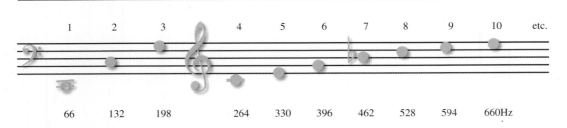

1
2
3
4
5
6
7
8
9
10
etc.
66
132
198
264
330
396
462
528
594
660Hz

Figure 1

1
2
3
4
5
6

Figure 2

(A)
(B)
(C)

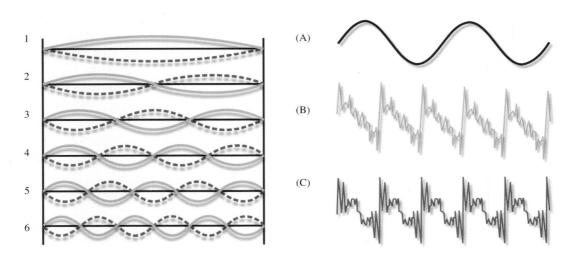

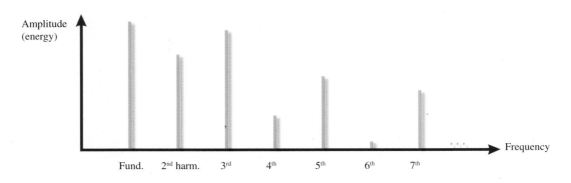

Figure 3

Amplitude
(energy)
Frequency
Fund.
2nd harm.
3rd
4th
5th
6th
7th

Figure 4

Figure - 517

Harmonic Series Model, p. 979

ONOMASTIC INDEX

Observations. The bibliographic references for each chapter were not included here. The numbers indicate pages. When there is more than one page number, the one *in italic* indicates the main reference.

GEOGRAPHICAL   INDEX

REMISSIVE INDEX

Observations. This index includes neither the bibliographic references of each chapter nor the terms of the Glossary of Projectiology. The numbers indicate pages. Where there is more than one page number, the one *in italic* indicates the main reference.

INTERNATIONAL INSTITUTE OF PROJECTIOLOGY AND CONSCIENTIOLOGY (IIPC)

Projectiology was first introduced to the public in 1981, when the physician and researcher of the consciousness Dr. Waldo Vieira published his book *Projections of the Consciousness – A Diary of Experiences Outside the Physical Body (Projeções da Consciência – Diário de Experiências Fora do Corpo Físico)*. In 1986, Dr. Vieira established the technical guidelines of this science when he published the treatise entitled *Projectiology – A Panorama of Experiences of the Consciousness Outside the Human Body (Projeciologia – Panorama das Experiências Fora do Corpo Humano)*. This work paved the way for the foundation of the International Institute of Projectiology and Conscientiology – IIPC.

Founded in 1988, IIPC is an independent, non-profit, scientific, educational and research institution designated as a federal public utility in its country of origin, namely Brazil. It is a laboratory-school for the study of the consciousness in an integral manner in its three states of manifestation: physical, extraphysical (in other dimensions) and projected (projection of the consciousness).

Since its foundation, IIPC has published many works and conducted educational activities – conferences, courses, lectures, workshops, and other scientific events – with the intention of disseminating the results of research into conscientiology and projectiology.

Study groups of various nationalities have received guidance from the interdisciplinary team of lecturers and researchers of IIPC b oth at the World Headquarters in the city of Rio de Janeiro (Brazil) and in the many offices around the world.

PORTFOLIO OF IIPC

The following institutional statistics give a clear picture of the status of IIPC in March 2002:

OFFICES:

World Headquarters: Rio de Janeiro (Brazil).

IIPC Research Complex: Brasília (Brazil).

22 offices serving 8 countries throughout the world:

- ⇨ *Argentina*: Buenos Aires.
- ⇨ *Brazil*: Belo Horizonte, Campo Grande, Curitiba, Florianópolis, Foz do Iguaçu, Manaus, Natal, Porto Alegre, Rio de Janeiro, Salvador and São Paulo.
- ⇨ *Holland*: Rotterdam.
- ⇨ *Italy*: Bergamo.
- ⇨ *Portugal*: Lisbon and Porto.
- ⇨ *Spain*: Barcelona and Madrid.
- ⇨ *UK*: London.
- ⇨ *USA*: Miami and New York.

PEOPLE:

105,860 registered people/institutions, namely: 101,879 on the national register (31,500 current and former students) and 3,981 on the international register (in 75 countries).

670 volunteers.

200 Lecturers.

51 researchers with articles published in the Journal of Conscientiology.

14 researchers with books published by IIPC's publishing arm.

IIPC PUBLICATIONS

PERIODICALS

⇨ **BIPRO – Boletim de Projeciologia,** *Porto Alegre Team, Rio Grande do Sul, Brazil.*

⇨ **Jornal da Invéxis,** *GPC-Grinvex.*

⇨ **Journal of Conscientiology,** *London Office, UK.*

⇨ **Revista Recéxis,** *GPC-Grecex.*

BOOKS

Titles in Portuguese:

⇨ **700 Experimentos da Conscienciologia,** *Waldo Vieira.*

⇨ **A Ciência Conscienciologia e as Ciências Convencionais,** *Sonia Cerato.*

⇨ **Boa Noite, Universo!,** *Ione Basílio, Luciana Ribeiro and Nivea Melo.*

⇨ **Catálogo de Pesquisas do IIPC,** *Concientiological Research Division (org.: Tânia Ferraro).*

⇨ **Conscienciograma,** *Waldo Vieira.*

⇨ **Coragem para Evoluir,** *Luciano Vicenzi.*

⇨ **Despertar para Nova Dimensão,** *Franscisco de Biaso.*

⇨ **Ensaios Extracorpóreos,** *Luiz Araujo.*

⇨ **Evolução em Cadeia,** *Cláudio Costa.*

⇨ **Hiperatividade Eficaz,** *Graça Razera.*

⇨ **Manual da Dupla Evolutiva,** *Waldo Vieira.*

⇨ **Manual da Proéxis,** *Waldo Vieira.*

⇨ **Manual da Tenepes,** *Waldo Vieira.*

⇨ **Mudar ou Mudar,** *Flavia Guzzi.*

⇨ **O que é a Conscienciologia,** *Waldo Vieira.*

⇨ **Projeciologia,** *Waldo Vieira.*

⇨ **Projeções da Consciência,** *Waldo Vieira.*

⇨ **Retrocognições,** *Wagner Alegretti.*

⇨ **Síndrome do Estrangeiro,** *Málu Balona.*

⇨ **Vivendo em Múltiplas Dimensões,** *Glória Thiago.*

Titles in English:

⇨ **Existential Program Manual,** *Waldo Vieira.*

⇨ **Our Evolution,** *Waldo Vieira.*

⇨ **Penta Manual,** *Waldo Vieira.*

⇨ **Projections of the Consciousness,** *Waldo Vieira.*

⇨ **Projectiology,** *Waldo Vieira.*

Titles in Spanish:

⇨ **Concienciograma,** *Waldo Vieira.*

⇨ **Manual de la Proexis,** *Waldo Vieira.*

⇨ **Manual de la Teneper,** *Waldo Vieira.*

⇨ **Nuestra Evolucion,** *Waldo Vieira.*

⇨ **Proyecciones de la Conciencia,** *Waldo Vieira.*

⇨ **Síndrome del Extranjero,** *Málu Balona.*

⇨ **Viviendo en Múltiples Dimensiones,** *Glória Thiago.*

ANNALS

⇨ **I International Congress on Projectiology** *(Rio de Janeiro, Brazil, 1990).*

⇨ **I National Forum on Consciential Quality** *(Curitiba, Brazil, 1995).*

⇨ **II National Forum on Consciential Quality** *(Curitiba, Brazil, 1996).*

⇨ **I National Forum on Expansion of the Consciousness** *(Blumenau, Brazil, 1996).*

⇨ **I Conscientiotherapy Symposium** *(Foz do Iguaçu, Brazil, 1996).*

⇨ **I International Congress on Existential Inversion** *(Florianópolis, Brazil, 1998).*

⇨ **I International Forum for Investigation of the Consciousness / II International Congress on Projectiology** *(Barcelona, Spain, 1999).*

RESEARCH

IIPC coordinates technical research and study activities in projectiology and conscientiology through the Conscientiological Research Division. Research is divided up into the following Consciousness Research Groups (CRGs), in accordance with the profile of the experimenter-conscientiologist:

CRG-Intraphysical Society: Research into conscientiological intraphysical society; joint intraphysical meetings and coexistence for the purpose of studying and consolidating the bases of conscientiological intraphysical society. Main subdiscipline: *Parasociology.* Keyword: *Teamwork.* Researcher Profile: *Interest in getting to know, research and experience conscientiological intraphysical society.*

CRG-Conscientiotherapy: Study and theoretical research into the subdiscipline of conscientiotherapy. Main subdiscipline: *Conscientiotherapy and its subdisciplines.* Keyword: *Sympathetic de-assimilation.* Researcher Profile: *Healthcare students and professionals with an assistential profile, namely in the areas of medicine, psychology, nursing, physiotherapy, speech therapy, nutrition.*

CRG-Information Technology Group: Intraphysical meetings and coexistence of specialists who, with their technical skills in information technology, strive to optimize all the various activities of IIPC, leading to the integration of conscientiology, projectiology and information technology. Main subdiscipline: *Infocommunicology.* Keyword: *Leading-edge Communication.* Researcher Profile: *Specialization in a specific area of information or communications technology; neophilia.*

CRG-Group of Existential Inverters: Joint, group intraphysical meetings and workshops to achieve planned existential inversion experiences. Main subdiscipline: *Existential Invertology.* Keyword: *Innovation.* Researcher Profile: *Members of CRG-Group of Existential Inverters are existential inverters.*

CRG-Group of Existential Recyclers: Joint intraphysical meetings and workshops to achieve planned existential recycling experiences. Main subdiscipline: *Existential Recyclology.* Keyword: *Renovation.* Researcher Profile: *Members of CRG-Grecex are existential recyclers.*

CRG-Penta: Penta research group; intraphysical meetings and experiences for penta practitioners. Main subdiscipline: *Assistentiology.* Keyword: *Interdimensional Assistance.* Researcher Profile: *Penta practitioners and intraphysical consciousnesses in preparation for penta practice.*

CRG-Leading-edge Research Group: Group intraphysical meetings and experiences with a view to develop study and research in any area or subdiscipline of conscientiology other than those specified above. Keyword: *Updating.* Researcher Profile: *Openness and scope.*

Individual. IIPC institutional research can also be carried out on an *individual* basis starting from any theme or line of investigation related to conscientiology and its subdisciplines.

CONSCIENTIOLOGICAL EDUCATION

Since 1988, through its Technical/Scientific Department, IIPC has been researching and conducting educational and teaching activities in several countries promoting its new approach to conscientiological education.

IIPC's course curriculum examines conscientiology and projectiology using a gradual and increasingly in-depth approach to the subject, using specific didactic techniques affording a broad and detailed vision of the study of the consciousness.

Using this pioneering educational approach, all students are constantly motivated by the lecturers to develop the key attributes for evolutionary learning: healthy multidimensional coexistence, a critical sense of assistentiality, mature questioning, the ability to conduct self-research, lucid parapsychic development and useful intellectuality.

These attributes are fostered in the regular programs and extension courses taught by IIPC using varied interactive dynamics, including group sessions, educational videos, stimulus for research and self-research, application of exercises using bioenergetic and projective techniques, an interfacing of the content studied in class with the day-to-day reality of each individual and constant incentive to achieve discernment and a critical stance.

One of the fundamental premises of conscientiological education is that all *education* is, first and foremost, *self-education*. Therefore, the main role or function of lecturers in projetiology and conscientiology is to act as retrocognitive agents both for the students and for themselves. The lecturer should assist in bringing out the students' innate ideas and, by so doing, catalyze the emergence of their own innate ideas in a process; which is essentially participative and collaborative.

As of December 2001, IIPC's teaching staff is comprised of a team of 200 professionals from different specialized backgrounds – physicians, engineers, students, businesspersons, accountants, psychologists, teachers, systems analysts, physicists and architects, among others – who dedicate a portion of their time as volunteers. The team of lecturers operates internationally in various countries on research and dissemination of the sciences of projectiology and conscientiology.

This team of lecturers is constantly trained and updated through IIPC's Professional Qualification and Training Program, which uses advanced multidimensional educational technology, in order to continually enhance the knowledge of the projectiology and conscientiology teaching staff, using a continuing education approach.

OPEN INVITATION FOR VOLUNTARY STAFF

IIPC is a third sector conscientiological organization maintained through the work of professionals from different areas, who are linked to the institution through voluntary and universal self-lucid consciential ties.

The consciential bond, as a new working relationship between the professional and the organization, is one in which each participant strives to contribute to the integral development of the individual rather than work for personal financial remuneration. The concept was created by applying conscientiology in conscienciocentric institutions, the main characteristic of which is the convergence of efforts towards consciential evolution, unlike the majority of conventional companies where profit-making is the central purpose of their existence.

Invitation. IIPC invites you to become a member of our team, thereby assisting in implementing the educational, research and practical objectives of conscientiology with ever-increasing quality and scope. Become an IIPC volunteer.

IIPC ADDRESSES

BRAZIL

WORLD HEADQUARTERS
Av. das Américas, 500, bloco 2, sala 216 e 224
Barra da Tijuca, Rio de Janeiro, RJ,
22631-000,
Tel: 55 21 3153-7575 / Fax: 55 21 3153-7941,
iipc@iipc.org.br

IIPC RESEARCH COMPLEX
SEPS 714 / 914, Ed. Porto Alegre, bloco A, sala 114 e 142,
ASA SUL, Brasília, DF,
70390-145,
Tel/Fax: 55 61 346-5573,
poloiipc@brturbo.com

BELO HORIZONTE
Av. Brasil, 283, sala 1602,
Santa Efigenia, Belo Horizonte, MG,
30140-000,
Tel/Fax: 55 31 3241-1358,
iipcbh@task.com.br

CAMPO GRANDE
R. Carandazal, 196,
Coohafama, Campo Grande, MS,
79006-020,
Tel/Fax: 55 67 721-1847,
iipccgd@ig.com.br

CURITIBA
R. Visconde Nacar, 1505, 9° andar – Ed. Gallery,
Centro, Curitiba, PR,
80410-201,
Tel/Fax: 55 41 233-5736,
iipcctb@mps.com.br

FLORIANÓPOLIS
Av. Rio Branco, 354, sala 810,
Centro, Florianópolis, SC,
88015-200,
Tel/Fax: 55 48 224-3446,
iipcfln@yatech.net

FOZ DO IGUAÇU
R Almirante Barroso, 1293, sl. 704, 7° andar, Ed. Pedro Basso,
Centro, Foz do Iguaçu, PR,
85851-020,
Tel: 55 45 523-4782 / Fax: 55 45 525-5511,
iipcfoz@ig.com.br

MANAUS
Tv. Tapajos, 664 - B,
Centro, Manaus, AM,
69025-140,
Tel/Fax: 55 93 232-4291,
iipcman@argo.com.br

NATAL
Av. Alexandrino de Alencar, 575, sala 101,
Alecrim, Natal, RN,
59020-350,
Tel: 55 84 201-3818 / Fax: 55 84 611-3413,
unipcnatal@ig.com.br

PORTO ALEGRE
R. General Andrade Neves, 159 - cj 12,
Centro, Porto Alegre, RS,
90010-210,
Tel/Fax: 55 51 3224-0707,
portoalegre@poa.iipc.org.br

RIO DE JANEIRO
Av. das Américas, 500, bloco 2, loja 114,
Barra da Tijuca, Rio de Janeiro, RJ,
22631-000,
Tel.: 55 21 3153-7574 / 55 21 3153-7590 / Fax: 55 21 3153-7941,
iipc.rj@sede.iipc.org.br

SALVADOR
Av. Tancredo Neves, 274, bloco B, sala 234, Centro Empresarial,
Iguatemi, Salvador, BA,
41820-020,
Tel/Fax: 55 71 450-0628,
iipcsdr@ufba.br

SÃO PAULO
Av. Paulista, 1159, 3° andar, bl 304,
Jardins, São Paulo, SP,
01311-200,
Tel: 55 11 287-9705 / Fax: 55 11 287-9706
cip.sp@terra.com.br

ARGENTINA   **BUENOS AIRES**
Calle Azcuenaga, 797, 2°A,
Centro, Buenos Aires, RA,
1029,
Tel: 54 11 4951-5048,
buenosaires@iipc.org

HOLLAND   **ROTTERDAM**
(contact the London Office)
netherlands@iipc.org

ITALY	**BERGAMO** (contact the Barcelona Office)
PORTUGAL	**LISBON** R. Castilho, 65, 2° dto, Lisboa, Portugal 1250-068, Tels: 351 21 386-8020, 351 21 386-8021 / Fax: 351 21 386-8022, lisboa@iipc.org
	PORTO Tel: 351 22 606-4025, unipcporto@clix.pt
SPAIN	**BARCELONA** Calle Sicilia, 236, puerta 2, Barcelona, España 8013, Tel: 34 93 232-8008, Fax: 34 93 232-8010, barcelona@iipc.org
	MADRID Calle Carretas, 12 - 2° piso 5-6, Madrid, España 28012, Tel/Fax: 34 91 701-1315 madrid@iipc.org
UNITED **KINGDOM**	**LONDON** 45 Great Cumberland Place, 3rd. floor, Marble Arch, London, UK, W1 M 7 LH, Tel: 44 20 7723-0544 / Fax: 44 20 7723-0545, london@iipc.org
USA	**MIAMI** 7800 S.W. 57 Ave. Suite 207-D, South Miami, FL, 33143, Tel: 1 305 668-4668 / Fax: 1 305 668-4663, florida@iipc.org
	NEW YORK 262 W 38 St, Suite 507, New York, NY, 10018, Tel: 1 212 869-4595 / Fax: 1 212 869-4596, newyork@iipc.org

IIPC RESEARCH COMPLEX

The *IIPC Research Complex* established in Brazil's federal capital – Brasília – is the most recent international point of reference in research into projectiology and conscientiology. As IIPC's official research headquarters, the *Complex* houses all the historical records and files of *Conscientiology* and *IIPC*.

The first segment is the *Public Library of Conscientiology,* specialized in parapsychic culture and scientific self-research, the files of which contain the entire bibliography of this *projectiology* book and will soon be open for loan of material and consultation via the *internet.*

The *Complex's* Documentation Unit is preparing the permanent exhibition of *Conscientiology* (*Holomemory*), which will be open to the public. Part of this collection is dedicated to historical research on the city of Brasília and its founder, former President Juscelino Kubitschek de Oliveira.

The *Complex* serves as a school, cultural center and Embassy of *Conscientiology* in the capital of Brazil and has a specialized bookshop, video library, event hall for activities and debates. In the near future, it will also feature a large laboratory complex destined for the dissemination of knowledge about *Conscientiology* to society at large.

In addition to *IIPC's*, educational curriculum, the *Complex* has its own original program with *day sessions, workshops, scientific and cultural sessions, study cycles, video debates and biannual research symposiums called 'meet-ins'.*

The purpose of the above activities is to acquaint the public with the sciences of *Projectiology* and *Conscientiology*, conduct in-depth studies on topics of social interest, present original practical and technical solutions for the evolutionary needs of consciousnesses, stimulate cosmoethical critique and illustrate the importance of practical self-research, in addition to uncovering innate talents.

In the research field, specific programming which is geared for *IIPC* volunteers is prepared with the intention of training lecturers, researchers and authors in *conscientiology*, promoting individual and group scientific investigation and channeling all results obtained to the needs and products of the *Complex*, namely books, exhibitions, forums and material to include in *IIPC* publications.

Brasília is a planned city located at the geographical center of the country, which brings together a wealth of Brazilian and international cultural diversity thanks to its many diplomatic missions. As a geopolitical hub in the continent, it forms a strategic base for the *extraphysical reurbanization* of Brazil and the Americas.

The **Pólo Digital** is the electronic bulletin of the Complex distributed by free subscription, which keeps hundreds of researchers informed and working in unison on the conquests, advances and results obtained by the project. Subscriptions may be sent by E-mail to: polodigi@solar.com.br

INFORMATION:

Pólo de Pesquisa IIPC / IIPC Research Complex
SEPS 714 / 914 Sul – salas 114 e 142 – CEP 70 390 - 145
Tel./Fax: 55 61 346-5573
E-mail: poloiipc@solar.com.br

INTERNATIONAL ACADEMY OF CONSCIENTIOLOGY (IAC)

Historical Background: The *International Academy of Conscientiology* is an institution dedicated to the study of the consciousness and academic research into the sciences of conscientiology, projectiology and subdisciplines thereof, as well as the *theorical* application of consciential self-experimentation.

The Academy was founded in 2000, thanks to the initiative of some of the volunteers of the International Institute of Projectiology and Conscientiology (IIPC) in Portugal, being set up as a non-profit cooperative and administered by a Board of Directors made up of IIPC volunteers.

With cosmoethical principles and assistential objectives, IAC aims to become the first European center of consciential research, providing the means and resources to assist consciousnesses in their efforts in self-research and self-awareness.

Location. IAC is situated in Evoramonte in the Alentejo region of southern Portugal, 95 mi. (150 km) from Lisbon and approximately 280 mi. (450 km) from Madrid. It is set in 120,000 sq.yd. of land and features the typical vegetation of the area, namely Hispania oak trees (the Alentejo region is considered the largest cork producing region in the world), affording plenty of shade.

Objectives:

1. To promote the scientific grouping of ideas and conduct conscientiological research into projects elaborated by Academy researchers.

2. To conduct in-depth study and broaden knowledge and techniques already existing in the sciences of conscientiology and projectiology, promoting work carried out by researchers in this and other areas.

3. To establish an ideal environment for promoting self-awareness and the application of conscientiological concepts in daily life.

4. To promote integration between consciousnesses (intraphysical and extraphysical consciousnesses) of different cultures and origins, with multidimensional lucidity.

Campus: In addition to the convention center, library, administrative areas and accommodations, the IAC campus will also have laboratories for self-experimentation of several evolutionary techniques, phenomena and themes of interest, affording ideal conditions for self-research. These laboratories will be similar to those that already exist in South America at the Center for Higher Studies of the Consciousness (CHSC) in Foz de Iguaçu, Brazil.

Among the laboratories to be built are: Cosmoconsciousness, Multidimensional Self-awareness, Retrocognition, Holokarmality, Vibrational State, Waking Physical Immobility and a *Projectarium*, which will be the first of its kind in the world.

The architectural style will attempt to merge the local Alentejo construction with modern trends such that the laboratories will be hemispheric in shape.

Work to date: Despite the fact that construction work is still in progress, IAC is fully operational, offering unprecedented activities such as workshops, seminars and debates throughout the world and conducting relevant research in line with the current state of the science.

Courses offered by IAC place great emphasis on practical experimentation by means of carefully structured and planned *workshops*. When held in Europe these courses are generally bilingual or multilingual, in order to cater to the needs of participants from various countries. The following are some of the *workshops* offered by the IAC: PROJECTIVE FIELD, OVERCOMING FEAR OF SELF-EXPOSURE, DISCOVERING THE EXISTENTIAL PROGRAM, FROM ASSISTED TO HELPER STATUS, WAKING PHYSICAL IMMOBILITY AND MENTALSOMATIC GESTATION.

In addition to the courses, various publications are to be released. The first work to be published by IAC will be *"EXTRAPHYSICAL REURBANIZATION"* by Dr. Waldo Vieira.

Similarly, the results of the first research project to be conducted under the auspices of IAC – experimental research using highly scientific criteria on out-of-body experiences – were presented at the 3rd *International Congress on Projectiology and Conscientiology,* held in New York in May 2002.

Reurbanization. The European Continent is one of the areas on this planet where human beings have lived and manifested themselves for the longest period of time.. At the present time, Europe is a grouping of several countries, cultures and traditions, which are the result of thousands of years of consciential manifestation. IAC will provide the setting for evolutionary experiences where the study and practice of projectiology and conscientiology techniques will foster the consolidation of consciential reurbanization in Europe by developing concepts of universalism and fraternity through coexistence among nations and extraphysical reurbanization.

INFORMATION:

IAC - International Academy of Conscientiology
Av. Eng. Duarte Pacheco, 19 - Sala 12
1070-1000 - Lisbon - Portugal
Tel.: 351 21 382-9770
Fax: 351 21 382-9771
Home page: www.iac.online.pt
E-mail: iac@iac.online.pt

CENTER FOR HIGHER STUDIES OF THE CONSCIOUSNESS (CHSC)

The Center for Higher Studies of the Consciousness (CHSC) – is a working project set up to conduct research into the consciousness (ego, personality, self, spirit, soul), based on conscientiology. It was established on July 15, 1995, in Iguassu Falls, State of Paraná, Brazil. It is a complex for the research, teaching and dissemination of conscientiology.

The quantity and quality of immanent energy are among the characteristics of the Iguassu region, which borders three countries (Brazil, Paraguay and Argentina) and where the city of Iguassu Falls is located. Besides the exuberant natural setting, this center features several worldwide attractions, namely the Iguassu Falls, the Guarani Aquifer and the Itaipu Binational Hydrolectric Plant.

CHSC brings together volunteers from all over Brazil and many other countries. Even while the project is still in the implementation phase, group evolutionary experiences are already underway. This situation has made it possible to set up channels of information and participation even at a distance, opening up opportunities for decentralized collaborative and administrative experiences. Suggestions and projects are often submitted from afar. The group effort concept adopted by CHSC is based on one of the most advanced forms of social organization, namely a cooperative or association of people with a common purpose and on a non-profit basis. This system was developed based on the history of trust, which marks the relations between team members and which has been gradually built up since CHSC's inception.

Through the use of its infrastructure, CHSC seeks to develop activities which contribute to further promote in-depth self-research of the consciousness. This involves courses, consciential self-research laboratory sessions, a holotheca as well as publications and projects in general which create a favorable environment for the generation of new ideas by researchers, based on multidimensional experiences and critical reflection. With these resources it is possible to broaden understanding of the experiences and the individual evolutionary context, integrating the results of the research conducted to the development of the individual's existential program.

Exhibition Hall

With a seating capacity of 600, many activities are conducted in the *Exhibition Hall*, such as technical meetings, congresses, symposiums, forums, courses, etc. Chief among these are the technical meetings or *brainstorming sessions* and in-depth debates of ideas relating to CHSC projects and to themes on conscientiology in general.

Coexistence Center

The *Coexistence Center* has a hall, reception area, restaurant, industrial kitchen and snack bar. This area permits coexistence and is a meeting place for visitors, students and researchers. As is the case with the remaining rooms, they are essentially an extension of the debating rooms, permitting a free exchange of ideas and multidimensional experiences, being thus an important research laboratory per se.

Village – Researcher's Inn

This is an inn for students participating on courses, events or laboratory experiments on consciential research. Each room accommodates up to 4 people, providing an opportunity for becoming acquainted and interacting with consciousnesses from the most far-flung cultures.

Conscientiological Condominium

This is a new working concept including accommodation and leisure in an area close to CHSC. The objective is for it to become an 'assistential factory' for other consciousness, based on the investment of the inhabitants in their multidimensional experiences.

Courses

CHSC periodically stages immersion courses in which the participants spend several days totally immersed in a study and research holothosene. The courses are an opportunity for bringing together all ideas on advanced themes of conscientiology through presentations, debates and discussions relating to experiences in conscientiological research. During the courses, the participants carry out practical experiments in CHSC's conscientiological laboratories, record them and discuss them using scientific techniques involving experimentation, refutation and elaboration of hypotheses during appraisal sessions.

Laboratories

The Consciential Self-research Laboratories are among the tools offered by CHSC for shedding light on evolution, contributing to the fact that the experimenters may draw their own conclusions based on self-research. Each environment is geared for the application of specific techniques. Although seemingly simple from an intraphysical standpoint, the laboratories are sophisticated in terms of paratechnology (extraphysical technology). Furthermore, the results of the experiments depend primarily on the will of the researchers themselves. The dynamics of the experiments works upon the interaction of the researchers and the team of technical extraphysical helpers in the subdiscipline for each laboratory. Depending on the degree of affinity established, it is possible to access pro-evolutionary ideas leading to self-knowledge and improvement of the individual level of conscientiality

There are currently 16 Consciential Self-research Laboratories at CHSC: Vibrational State (VS), Energetic Signage, Existential Programming, Penta (Personal Energetic Task), Thosenology, Self-organization, Retrocognition, Evolutiology, Mentalsomatics, Cosmoethics, Petifreeology, Waking Physical Immobility, Paragenetics, Evolutionary Duo, Projective Techniques and Cosmogram. Some of the results obtained in the laboratories are printed in CHSC publications as technical/scientific articles and reports.

Holotheca

The Holotheca (repository of collections about knowledge) represents the potentiation of self-research at CHSC. There are two environments in the Holotheca. In the first, called Holocyclo, Dr. Waldo Vieira is compiling the Encyclopedia of Conscientiology together with a team of volunteers. The fruit of this work is slated to be the most complete and definitive publication on conscientiology to date and will provide a multifaceted panorama of the consciential micro-universe. Upon entering the Holotheca, one is confronted by a passageway featuring 20 busts of renowned geniuses of humanity, which leads one to reflect upon one's personal evolution. In the second room, there is one of the largest libraries in the world specialized in out-of-body experiences, classified into over 100 topics. It also features one of the largest comic collections in Latin America, with over 20,000 comic books from 22 countries in 16 languages. The Holotheca also contains collections of shells (malacotheca), stamps (philately), coins (numismatics), books (library) and rare objects all aimed at enhancing in-depth study of the consciousness.

Theorice Cooperative

The Cooperative of Specialized Products and Services – *Theorice* (a neologism for theory + practice) was created in the context of change, maturity and a new level in the interrelations among CHSC volunteers. The objective is to provide financial support to the team of volunteers who make these projects in applied conscientiology possible, turning the CHSC experience into a company operating within intraphysical society. One of the first works involves an edition of a magazine specialized in Tourism: *Iguassu Turismo & Eventos* and Guia Iguassu – *Um Destino para o Mundo*, the purpose of which is to promote and integrate the Iguassu International Tourism Center which includes Iguassu Falls, in Brazil, and over 8 cities in Argentina and Paraguay. There are three *Theorice* cooperatives in operation in Brazil: in Iguassu Falls (state of Paraná), Venda Nova do Imigrante (state of Espirito Santo) and São Paulo (state capital).

ARACÊ ASSOCIATION

ARACÊ. The International Association for Evolution of the Consciousness seeks to provide organizational and financial viability to the objective of disseminating awareness about the evolution of the consciousness. Founded in April 2001, in line with CHSC'S expansion plans, ARACÊ will pass on information generated by the *Theorical* cooperatives to intraphysical society. Its headquarters are located in Venda Nova do Imigrantes (state of Espirito Santo, Brazil).

Purpose. One of the purposes of the Association is to administrate the founding, operation and management of companies (cooperative or otherwise) the founding principle of which involve conscientiology. It is in institution that proposes to conduct study and research into the consciousness as well as establishing the ideals of conscientiology within society by rendering consciential services. The project is being developed in a greenbelt location, with high levels of immanent energy, in the district of Aracê (state of Espirito Santo). A *Plenarium* [what be da logic behind this beastie? R.S.V.P.] was built on the site, namely an architectural complex with three separate environments in semi-spherical shape for holding technical meetings, debates, courses and apprenticeships in its workshops.

Laboratory. The project [me like, but how about 'envisions'?] future construction of another advanced laboratory for research into the consciousness, namely the Radical Heuristics Laboratory *(Serenarium)* in which researchers will be given three days to conduct their experiments in total isolation.

CHSC PUBLICATIONS

Periodicals

1. **Boletins de Conscienciologia (Conscientiology Bulletins)**
To divulge the result of research, technical information, trials and reports of experiences to the public in general, with articles written by researcher Waldo Vieira. It is published yearly in Portuguese, Spanish and English.

2. **CEAEC Newsletter (CHSC Newsletter)**
Published in Portuguese, Spanish and English, the newsletter promotes the institution, presenting the theorice of leading edge ideas in conscientiology experienced at CHSC.

3. CEAEC Serviços (CHSC Services)

Describes the philosophy, form of administration, complete infrastructure, laboratory operations, courses, events, products and services offered at CHSC. Its is published in Portuguese, Spanish and English.

4. Conscienciologia Aplicada (Applied Conscientiology)

Presents a synopsis of the main technical meetings and plenary sessions relating to projects involving the application of conscientiology in intraphysical society, in addition to updated information on ideas on applied conscientiology under study at CHSC and Aracê.

5. Conscientia

A quarterly technical/scientific publication in Portuguese, Spanish and English, providing in-depth insights into research themes in conscientiology, with technical and scientific articles of various consciousness researchers.

6. Jornal do CEAEC (CHSC Journal)

A monthly update on CHSC activities and projects including a previously unpublished article by Professor Waldo Vieira.

Books

1. A Natureza Ensina

Author: Waldo Vieira.

Prepared with phases to enrich our powers of reasoning by listening to nature both inside and outside ourselves, with regard to our evolution.

2. 100 Testes da Conscienciometria

Author: Waldo Vieira.

Comprising 100 updated conscientiometric tests with the purpose of stimulating the subjective-objective usage of mentalsomatic discernment based on analysis of somatic impulses.

3. 200 Teáticas da Conscienciologia

Author: Waldo Vieira.

This volume presents, in simple form, 200 theorices – theories (principles) and practices (techniques) of the world of conscientiology research.

4. Manual de Redação da Conscienciologia

Author: Waldo Vieira.

Aids communicability and scientific writing style, namely presentation of the results of scientific research in a manner which is logical, coherent and precise.

5. Máximas da Conscienciologia

Author: Waldo Vieira.

Contributes toward enhancing our discernment and powers of reasoning, providing phrases and maxims within the context of conscientiology.

6. Minidefinições Conscienciais

Author: Waldo Vieira.

Presents minidefinitions based on conscientiology, ranging from humor to holokarmic rigor, from straightforward reasoning to cognitive sophistication.

7. Nossa Evolução

Author: Waldo Vieira.

Answers the following questions in an objective manner: Who am I? What am I? Where am I from? What am I doing here? Where am I going? It examines the evolution of the consciousness beyond the bounds of philosophical questioning and biological development.

8. **Temas da Conscienciologia**
Author: Waldo Vieira

A technical book comprising field notes, research, diagnosis, conscientiometric tests, conscientiological techniques and aspects of the subdisciplines of conscientiology.

INFORMATION:

Centro de Altos Estudos da Consciência – CEAEC (CHSC)
Rua da Cosmoética, 11
Caixa Postal 1027 – Centro – CEP 85851-970
Foz do Iguaçu – PR – Brazil
Tel: 55-45-525-2652 / Fax: 55-45-525-5511
E-mail: ceaec@ceaec.org
Home page:www.ceaec.org

Associação Internacional para Evolução da Consciência – ARACÊ
Rua do Girassol, 269 – sala 1
Bairro Providência – CEP 29375-000
Venda Nova do Imigrante – ES – Brazil
Tel./Fax: 55-28-3546-2769
E-mail: associacao@arace.com.br
Home page:www.arace.com.br

NOTES

This work researches themes related to the field of *projectiology,* which is a subdiscipline of *conscientiology.*